📖 Let's Go writers travel on your budget.

"Guides that penetrate the veneer of the holiday brochures and mine the grit of real life."
—*The Economist*

"The writers seem to have experienced every rooster-packed bus and lunar-surfaced mattress about which they write."
—*The New York Times*

"All the dirt, dirt cheap."
—*People*

📖 Great for independent travelers.

"The guides are aimed not only at young budget travelers but at the independent traveler; a sort of streetwise cookbook for traveling alone."
—*The New York Times*

"Flush with candor and irreverence, chock full of budget travel advice."
—*The Des Moines Register*

"An indispensible resource, *Let's Go*'s practical information can be used by every traveler."
—*The Chattanooga Free Press*

📖 Let's Go is completely revised each year.

"Only *Let's Go* has the zeal to annually update every title on its list."
—*The Boston Globe*

"Unbeatable: good sightseeing advice; up-to-date info on restaurants, hotels, and inns; a commitment to money-saving travel; and a wry style that brightens nearly every page."
—*The Washington Post*

📖 All the important information you need.

"*Let's Go* authors provide a comedic element while still providing concise information and thorough coverage of the country. Anything you need to know about budget traveling is detailed in this book."
—*The Chicago Sun-Times*

"Value-packed, unbeatable, accurate, and comprehensive."
—*Los Angeles Times*

Let's Go Publications

Let's Go: Alaska & the Pacific Northwest 2001
Let's Go: Australia 2001
Let's Go: Austria & Switzerland 2001
Let's Go: Boston 2001 **New Title!**
Let's Go: Britain & Ireland 2001
Let's Go: California 2001
Let's Go: Central America 2001
Let's Go: China 2001
Let's Go: Eastern Europe 2001
Let's Go: Europe 2001
Let's Go: France 2001
Let's Go: Germany 2001
Let's Go: Greece 2001
Let's Go: India & Nepal 2001
Let's Go: Ireland 2001
Let's Go: Israel 2001
Let's Go: Italy 2001
Let's Go: London 2001
Let's Go: Mexico 2001
Let's Go: Middle East 2001
Let's Go: New York City 2001
Let's Go: New Zealand 2001
Let's Go: Paris 2001
Let's Go: Peru, Bolivia & Ecuador 2001 **New Title!**
Let's Go: Rome 2001
Let's Go: San Francisco 2001 **New Title!**
Let's Go: South Africa 2001
Let's Go: Southeast Asia 2001
Let's Go: Spain & Portugal 2001
Let's Go: Turkey 2001
Let's Go: USA 2001
Let's Go: Washington, D.C. 2001
Let's Go: Western Europe 2001 **New Title!**

Let's Go *Map Guides*

Amsterdam
Berlin
Boston
Chicago
Florence
Hong Kong
London
Los Angeles
Madrid

New Orleans
New York City
Paris
Prague
Rome
San Francisco
Seattle
Sydney
Washington, D.C.

Coming Soon: *Dublin* and *Venice*

WESTERN EUROPE

2001

Katharine Ferguson Douglas editor

Dan Barnes associate editor
Karen Kiang associate editor
Carla Mastraccio associate editor

Cristin Hodgens researcher writer

John Fiore map editor

Macmillan

HELPING LET'S GO

If you want to share your discoveries, suggestions, or corrections, please drop us a line. We read every piece of correspondence, whether a postcard, a 10-page email, or a coconut. Please note that mail received after May 2001 may be too late for the 2002 book, but will be kept for future editions. **Address mail to:**

Let's Go: Western Europe
67 Mount Auburn Street
Cambridge, MA 02138
USA

Visit Let's Go at **http://www.letsgo.com,** or send email to:

feedback@letsgo.com
Subject: "Let's Go: Western Europe"

In addition to the invaluable travel advice our readers share with us, many are kind enough to offer their services as researchers or editors. Unfortunately, our charter enables us to employ only currently enrolled Harvard students.

Published in Great Britain 2001 by Macmillan, an imprint of Macmillan Publishers Ltd, 25 Eccleston Place, London, SW1W 9NF, Basingstoke and Oxford.
Associated companies throughout the world
www.macmillan.com

Maps by David Lindroth copyright © 2001, 2000, 1999, 1998, 1997, 1996, 1995, 1994, 1993, 1992, 1991, 1990, 1989, 1988 by St. Martin's Press.

Published in the United States of America by St. Martin's Press.

ISBN: 0-333-90418-4
First edition
10 9 8 7 6 5 4 3 2 1

Let's Go: Western Europe is written by Let's Go Publications, 67 Mount Auburn Street, Cambridge, MA 02138, USA.

Let's Go® and the thumb logo are trademarks of Let's Go, Inc.
Printed in the USA on recycled paper with biodegradable soy ink.

ADVERTISING DISCLAIMER

All advertisements appearing in Let's Go publications are sold by an independent agency not affiliated with the editorial production of the guides. Advertisers are never given preferential treatment, and the guides are researched, written, and published independent of advertising. Advertisements do not imply endorsement of products or services by Let's Go, and Let's Go does not vouch for the accuracy of information provided in advertisements.
  If you are interested in purchasing advertising space in a Let's Go publication, contact: Let's Go Advertising Sales, 67 Mount Auburn St., Cambridge, MA 02138, USA.

RESEARCHER-WRITERS

Cristin Hodgens   *Belgium, Luxembourg The Netherlands*

Already a seasoned traveler, Cristin proved once again that she could handle anything. She braved the streets of Amsterdam's red-light district, charmed even the grumpiest of proprietors, and still had the energy to send Belgian chocolates back to the office. Handed the challenge of expanding the coverage of Amsterdam's infamous nightlife, Cristin's copy and new listings left us speechless—travelers in search of the perfect trip will revel in her dedication and incisive prose.

Regional Editors and Researcher-Writers

AUSTRIA AND SWITZERLAND
Nathaniel V. Popper	*Editor*
Rebecca L. Schoff	*Associate Editor*
Emily Griffin	*Lake Geneva, Lake Neuchâtel, Northeastern, Northwestern, and Central Switzerland*
Glenn Kinen	*Tyrol, Vorarlberg, Salzkammergut, Hohe Tauern, National Park, and Stryria*
Kristin E. Meyer	*The Jungfrau Region, Wallis, Italian Switzerland, Graubünden, and Appenzell*
Diana P. Moreno	*Vienna, Burgenland, Lower Austria, Linz, Salzburg, Carinthia, and Graz*

BRITAIN
Johs Pierce	*Editor*
Lisa M. Herman	*Associate Editor*
Teresa Crockett	*Midlands, Northwest England, Southern, and Central Scotland*
Emily A. Harrison	*Wales, Midlands, and Northwest England*
Winnie Li	*Edinburgh, Central Scotland, Highlands, and Islands*
Kate D. Nesin	*East Anglia, Midlands, Northeast, and Northwest England*
Jason Schwartz	*South and Southwest England*

EASTERN EUROPE
Andrea Filipí Volfová	*Editor*
Matthew DeTar Gibson, Xunhua Wong	*Associate Editors*
Nicholas Topjian	*Czech Republic*
Jessica Lucy Berenbeim	*Hungary*

EUROPE
Rebecca S. Tinio	*Editor*
Amy M. Cain, Craig Chosiad, Victoria C. Hallett	*Associate Editors*
Jamie L. Jones	*Denmark*

FRANCE
Alexander F. Mindlin	*Editor*
Jeffrey Dubner, Fiona McKinnon	*Associate Editors*
David Beecher	*The Southwest*
Sarah Dolgonos	*Berry Limousin, Poitou-Charentes, and the Loire Valley*
Chloe Taylor Evans	*Eastern Normandy and the Northeast*
Catherine Gowl	*Brittany and western Normandy*
Jérôme Luc Martin	*Provence, Lyon, Burgundy, and the Auvergne*
Matthew Sussman	*Côte d'Azur, Corsica, and the Alps*

GERMANY
Paul C. Dilley	*Editor*
Megan M. Anderson	*Associate Editor*
David A. Boyajian	*Bavaria*
Margaret Coe	*Berlin, Sachsen, and Thüringen*
Karoun Demirjian	*Niedersachsen, Nordrhein-Westfalia, and Rheinland-Pfalz*
Liz Glynn	*Berlin, Hessen, Niedersachsen, Sachsen, and Sachsen-Anhalt*
Dan Koski-Karell	*Brandenburg, Hamburg, Mecklenburg-Vorpommern, and Schleswig-Holstein*
Aram Yang	*Bavaria, Baden-Württemberg, and Hessen*

ACKNOWLEDGMENTS

WEUR THANKS: The regional editors who tolerated us, and the rws who wrote this book. You were all our favorite. Bede, for dill and wisdom; Matt D. for The Box; Melissa for her patience; John for map wonders; Andrea for fonts. Marly for Italy, Spain, Britain, Dali, and food poisoning; all those who proofed for us in the final hours; Brandon for coming through; coffee and ice for life; spreadsheeties; and Marvin Gaye.

KATHARINE THANKS: My ■lovelies: Dan, for monkeys, being my first wuv, patience, and format; Karen, for chhaaaaamany, morning coffee, and editing speed; Carla, for harvesting the crops of the Mediterranean, listening, and vibrant prose—i wuv you all. Meredith, for your friendship… may we have many more summers and trashcans to fill. Bede for belarus; Becky and the EUR ladies for bringing out the teen popstar in me; Sunny, for holding the keys to my beema'; and Matt, a friend into the next episode. Alice, for balcony talks; Olivia for Madrid and Let's Go; Nithya for understanding; and Amanda, my roomate for life. Abbey, for making me laugh out loud, and my parents for forced marches and teaching me to travel. Charlotte, this book is dedicated to you. And Western Europe, after so many late nights, can this be the end?—hold up… yeah.

DAN THANKS. Kate, Karen and Carla for being yourselves, making me laugh, giving me a Mommy, and all the wuv. Marly for proofing, traveling, climbing, introducing me to The Go, and always being there. Bede, for dinner, format, and tasty beverages. Team EUR for copy flow, dancing, and entertainment. EEUR for staying calm. Matt G. for maintaining male sanity. Marc for the possibility of falling out of a plane. My parents, Chris and Jeff for support, understanding and being all around incredible. Rosen for climbing and Vermont. Fischbach for entertaining me to no end. Cranberry for keeping me sane and giving me something to work for. Coffee and the rat for all the support. And, of course, to ■Western Europe—this is it!

KAREN THANKS. Carla, for coffee and comparison-shopping, Dan for driving and being oh-so-wuvly, and Kate, who was, throughout it all, The Mommy. Bede, for the Scandinavian dinner, EUR and EEUR for introducing me to teeny pop (and their boys, who watched the dancing and taught me all about ■mullets, Cali, and baby workouts). Marly, Melissa and Matt.D for making the 4th floor cute and WONDERFUL. The *Indy*, for all the pens, kung-fu, and late nights. Karina, Christina, Ian, Joseph, Nicky, and Dan, who make Halifax home. Kelly, Allie, Anosha, Andee, Jeannie, Jess, and Cheeks, the best roommates EVER, for the letter "e". Jason, for making the entourage come alive, his understanding, and looking both ways before we cross the street. Finally, my parents and the best big brother in the whole wide world for their love.

CARLA THANKS: karen, my one and only marmot, for serenades, and not biting (much), dan for being a paragon, and for laughing with us—not at us, Kate for coffee, copley, and dinner parties. Bede, for the soundtrack to our lets go lives and. The ladies of Eur and Eeur for dance parties and knowing all the words. Eeur for sharing the couch with me. The boys of the pod for tolerating my shopping bags. Matt G. for social criticism and hitchcock. All of WEUR for being as wonderful ly twisted as i could have asked for. Erica, spiritual president of the fashion club, Ken and Imti for dinner and cheating at ping pong., Yuan, my adopted sister- for helping me in my quest for J.F., laughing at the mess, and talks, Mish for puppies. Bec and Ves: I love you for nagging and hugging me—i'll go out on the roof with either of you anytime. Mom and Dad for the DNA and amazing love and support ; ■Joey, for letting me in the Camry.

Editor
Katharine Ferguson Douglas
Associate Editors
Dan Barnes, Karen Kiang, Carla Mastraccio
Managing Editor
Bede M. Sheppard
Map Editor
John Fiore

Western Europe

N

0 ——————— 200 miles
0 ——————— 200 kilometers

ATLANTIC
OCEAN

Orkney Islands

SCOTLAND

North Sea

NORTHERN IRELAND

• Glasgow
• Edinburgh
• Belfast

IRELAND

Dublin ✪

GREAT BRITAIN

WALES

Cardiff •

ENGLAND

London ✪

NETHERLANDS
• Amsterdam

Brussels ✪
BELGIUM
LUXEMBOURG

• Bonn

✪ Paris

• Nantes

Zurich •
SWITZERLAND ✪
Geneva • Bern

Bay of Biscay

• Bordeaux

FRANCE

Lyon •

• Santiago de Campostela

ANDORRA

Marseille •

Nice •
MONACO

Corsica (Fr.)

PORTUGAL

✪ Lisbon

Madrid ✪

SPAIN

• Seville

Granada •

• Barcelona

Valencia •

Balearic Islands (Sp.)

Sardinia (It.)

Mediterranean

Tangier •

GIBRALTAR

Rabat ✪

MOROCCO

Algiers ✪

ALGERIA

TUNISIA

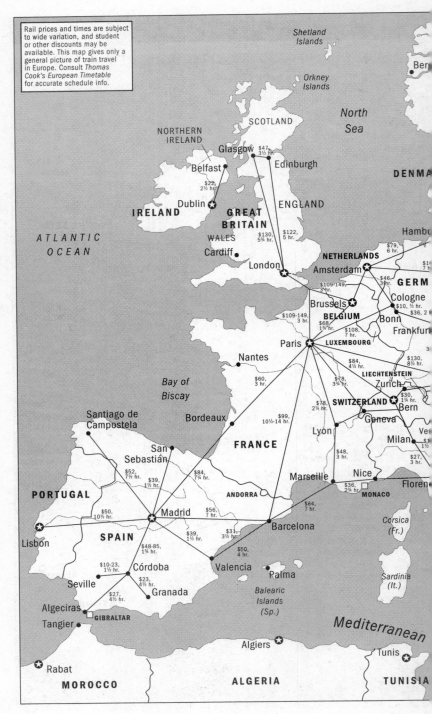

Rail prices and times are subject to wide variation, and student or other discounts may be available. This map gives only a general picture of train travel in Europe. Consult *Thomas Cook's European Timetable* for accurate schedule info.

NORWAY

SWEDEN

FINLAND

Gulf of

L. Ladoga

Helsinki

St. Petersburg

$44, 5 hr.

$18, 8 hr.

$12, 6-9 hr.

$116, 6 hr.

$6-0, 4½ hr.

Stockholm

Tallinn

$9, 5 hr.

ESTONIA

$32, 11 hr.

Moscow

Göteborg

$40, 4¼ hr.

Riga

Baltic Sea

LATVIA

$17, 7½ hr.

$32, 17 hr.

$20-30, 15-17 hr.

RUSSIA

Malmö

Copenhagen

$62, 2½ hr.

LITHUANIA

RUSSIA

Vilnius

$23, 10-14 hr.

Kharkiv

$30, 7 hr.

Gdańsk

$29, 11 hr.

$13, 5 hr.

Minsk

BELARUS

Berlin

$7-12, 3-5 hr.

$31, 3¼ hr.

Poznań

POLAND

$19, 3¼ hr.

Warsaw

$27, 12 hr.

$61, 22-24 hr.

Kiev

Wrocław

$32, 6½ hr.

$21, 5 hr.

$19, 2½ hr.

$3, 12 hr.

Prague

$59, 5¼ hr.

$47, 8½ hr.

$19, 2 hr.

$15, 10½ hr.

Kraków

Lviv

UKRAINE

Dnieper River

CZECH REPUBLIC

$45, 5 hr.

$37, 5 hr.

SLOVAKIA

Munich

$66, 5 hr.

$14, 1 hr.

Bratislava

$6, 19 hr.

Vienna

AUSTRIA

$51, 6 hr.

$34, 3½ hr.

$47, 14 hr.

MOLDOVA

Chișinău

Odessa

Sea of Azov

Ljubljana

SLOVENIA

$17, 2½ hr.

Budapest

HUNGARY

$38, 6 hr.

$86, 12 hr.

Yalta

nice

Zagreb

CROATIA

Belgrade

ROMANIA

Bucharest

Black Sea

BOSNIA-HERZEGOVINA

YUGOSLAVIA

Dubrovnik

Sarajevo

MONTENEGRO

ITALY

Rome

$21, 2 hr.

Adriatic Sea

FYR MACEDONIA

$34, 10 hr.

Sofia

BULGARIA

$42, 10 hr.

ples

$21, 5 hr.

Brindisi

Tiranë

ALBANIA

$35, 12 hr.

Istanbul

Naples

$23, 2 hr.

Thessaloniki

$6-33, 6½-9½ hr.

Ankara

henian Sea

Palermo

$22, 3½ hr.

Messina

Sicily

Ionian Sea

$49, 6 hr.

Izmir

TURKEY

Aegean Sea

Athens

GREECE

Nicosia

Sea

Sea of Crete

Crete

CONTENTS

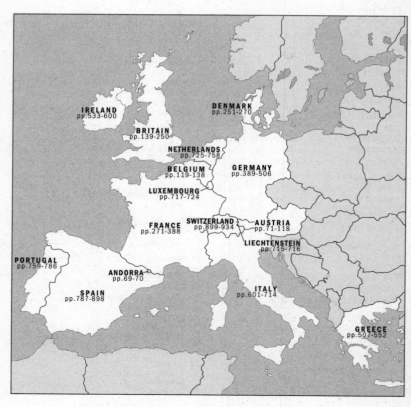

MAPS

Western Europe viii-ix
Transportation x-xi

✛ Hospital	✈ Airport	🏛 Museum	▲ Mountain
✪ Police	🚌 Bus Station	♦ Hotel/Hostel	☐ Park
✉ Post Office	🚆 Train Station	⛺ Camping	
ⓘ Tourist Office	M METRO STATION	🍴 Food & Drink	░ Beach
§ Bank	⚓ Ferry Landing	🛍 Shopping	
⚑ Embassy/Consulate	✝ Church	♪ Arts & Entertainment	▒ Water
▪ Site or Point of Interest	❋ Synagogue	🍸 Nightlife	
☎ Telephone Office	☪ Mosque	💻 Internet Café	
♥ Theater	♜ Castle	⸺ Pedestrian Zone	The Let's Go thumb always points NORTH.

HOW TO DATE THIS BOOK

Our little book, our first, is all grown up, and ready to go on her first date. We've watched in awe as the child we called *Let's Go: Western Europe 2001* slowly matured into the sophisticated individual she is today. We've seen her move from cave painting in kindergarten to the Dadaist tendencies of her more rebellious years, studied with bated breath her many accomplishments—writing sonnets, storming castles, getting her braces off. So before you take her out, as tender, loving parents we have a few simple words of advice—treat her well; we have a shotgun and a shovel.

Let's Go: Western Europe is far more than a pretty face in a cute yellow jacket. This book is a resource, one of your best friends and closest travel companions, but she isn't the jealous type. She's confident—you can leave her alone. She can tell you where to stay in Rome, and how to find the best hiking trails in Switzerland, but she's just a jumping-off point for your adventures. Don't be afraid to put her down and just go.

THE ORGANIZATION OF THIS BOOK

MEETING THE PARENTS. Straighten that tie, buy those flowers, it's time to take this book out on the town (or hiking trail, or beach, or mountain village, for that matter). Begin by getting to know a little bit of everything about Western Europe. The first chapter, **Discover Western Europe,** provides you with an overview of travel in Western Europe, including general **Suggested Itineraries** that give you an idea of what you shouldn't miss, and how long it will take to see it. For more specific itineraries, look in the individual country chapters. The chapter **Western Europe: The Grand Tour** shows you some of the highlights of the history of Western Europe, and should be used along with the cultural and historical introductions at the beginning of each chapter. The **Essentials** section outlines the practical information you will need to prepare for and execute your trip.

GOING STEADY. Well, you've gone through the ritual of the first date, and now you're ready to move on to a more, shall we say, intimate relationship with this book. Get up close and personal with the real text, countless artistic masterpieces, myriad castles, and a few pieces of dirty sculpture thrown in for kicks. Each chapter contains historical background, suggested itineraries, and a country-specific essentials section, followed by the regional coverage. *Let's Go: Western Europe 2001,* is organized alphabetically by country for quicker access. The **Heading East** chapter at the very end of the book provides information on travel to Prague and Budapest, gateway cities to Eastern Europe.

TALKING THINGS THROUGH. Communication is the key to any good relationship. The appendix contains a **phrasebook** of handy phrases in English, French, German, Italian, Spanish, Greek, Dutch, Portuguese, Czech, and Hungarian, as well as pronunciation tips. A **glossary** of foreign and technical (e.g. architectural) words is also included.

A FEW NOTES ABOUT LET'S GO FORMAT

RANKING ESTABLISHMENTS. In each section (accommodations, food, etc.), we list establishments in order from best to worst. Our absolute favorites are so denoted by the highest honor given out by *Let's Go*, the Let's Go thumb-pick (🔲).

PHONE CODES AND TELEPHONE NUMBERS. The **phone code** for each region, city, or town appears opposite the name of that region, city, or town, and is denoted by the ☎ icon. **Phone numbers** in text are also preceded by the ☎ icon.

GRAYBOXES AND WHITEBOXES. **Grayboxes** at times provide wonderful cultural insight, at times simply crude humor. In any case, they're usually amusing, so enjoy. **Whiteboxes,** on the other hand, provide important practical information, such as warnings (🔳), or helpful hints and further resources (🔳).

A NOTE TO OUR READERS The information for this book was gathered by *Let's Go* researchers from May through August of 2000. Each listing is based on one researcher's opinion, formed during his or her visit at a particular time. Those traveling at other times may have different experiences since prices, dates, hours, and conditions are always subject to change. You are urged to check the facts presented in this book beforehand to avoid inconvenience and surprises.

DISCOVER WESTERN EUROPE

If Western Europe were in high school, she'd be the girl that all the other students love to hate. She has a voice crafted by the likes of Verdi and Mozart. When she opens her mouth in class, pearls of wisdom from Dante, Sartre, and Kierkegaard drop forth. She was a classic before the word had meaning, and the rest of the school hurries to copy her style. She wore a toga in the court of Caesar, and now adorns herself in the more terrestrial chic of Chanel and Armani. She moves from sipping ambrosia to champagne with seamless grace and still has the energy to toss back a few pints of Guinness. Why waste the time envying a creation this divine when Western Europe is there for the taking, an inexhaustible supply of art, music, and natural beauty? This is one Homecoming queen who is far from unapproachable. So ask her out. Go.

FIGURES AND FACTS

POPULATION: 369,100,000.

MOUNTAIN RANGES: Sierra Nevada, Pyrenees, Alps, and Apennines.

HIGHEST POINT: Mont Blanc (4,807m).

LOWEST POINTS: Lemmefjord, DEN, and Prins Alexander Polder, NETH (7m below sea level).

FACT: In the 1960s, it was predicted that by 2000 a rocket-ship trip to Europe from the US would take under an hour.

LAND MASS: 2.5 million sq. km, almost that of the Sahara Desert

ALCOHOL: Each year, Western Europeans consume 82L of beer and 17L of wine per person.

CHEESE: The average Western European eats 40lbs. of cheese per year.

FACT: If a colony of honeybees has an average wing length of larger than 9.5mm, it is known as a European colony.

WHEN TO GO

The Renaissance masterpieces of Florence, the ruins of Greece, and England's countless medieval castles know no season—they are timeless. However, more pragmatic concerns emerge regarding the most opportune time to visit Western Europe. Summer is the high-season for travel in Western Europe. Throngs of tourists fill hostels and crowd museums, particularly during the months of July and August; you may find June or September a better time to travel. Most Western European countries, especially those along the Mediterranean, swelter in the summer; for a temperature chart, see **Essentials** (p. 17).

THINGS TO DO

Western Europe can be as overwhelming as it is exciting. In this section, and throughout the book, we humbly suggest ways approach your trip. For more specific regional attractions, see the **Suggested Itineraries** section at the beginning of each chapter. There are more **monuments, castles, beaches, museums, mountains,** and **nightclubs** than you can shake a stick at. You will stand shoulder

1

to shoulder with the greatness of the past, with the legacies of saints and conquerors (not to mention a few of their preserved body parts). Your greatest memories of the time you spend here will likely be the intangible ones, late evenings spent walking through a tiny coastal town whose name you hadn't known before you arrived. If traveling is analogous to a love affair, then Western Europe is that first, amazing fling, the one that you will never forget. Don't fight it—let the streets of Paris, the mountains of Austria and Switzerland, and the clubs of Madrid work their magic.

THE CULTURAL TAPESTRY

Western Europe has enough "culture" to keep you busy for a lifetime. But you don't have time to see every ornate church and crumbling Roman amphitheater in all of Europe—you want the highlights, the must-sees of art and architecture, and you want them now. **London** is one of Europe's finest museum cities (p. 153): peruse the Rosetta Stone, the Elgin Marbles, and other imperialist booty at the **British Museum;** saunter through the histories of art, design, and style at the **Victoria and Albert Museum;** and don't miss the spectacular collection of modern art at the **Tate Gallery. West Belfast** (p. 597) is a maze of murals and color, with political quotes and symbols adorning the street walls.

On the other side of the Channel, **Paris** contains a string of absolute gems (p. 285)—the *Venus de Milo* and *Mona Lisa* at the **Louvre** will stop you in your tracks; the **Musée d'Orsay** will impress and leave an impression with all that is Impressionist; and the pipes and modern art of the **Centre National d'Art et de Culture Georges-Pompidou** will wriggle their way into your heart. Stroll the streets of Paris, soaking in the city's various architectural styles; don't miss the breathtaking **Cathédrale de Nôtre-Dame.** Outside of Paris, the *châteaux* of the **Loire Valley** (p. 329) and Normandy's fortified abbey **Mont-St Michel** (p. 324) are also must-sees.

From France, drop down to Spain to witness **Bilbao's** shining **Museo Guggenheim** (p. 888) before continuing on to **Madrid's** museums (p. 800): the **Prado** shelters the world's largest collection of paintings; the **Museo Thyssen-Bornemizsa** surveys major artistic trends in painting from the 14th to 20th centuries; and the **Museo Nacional Centro de Arte Reina Sofía** harbors Picasso's *Guernica.* From there, head south to Muslim-infused Andalucía to witness the **mosque** in **Córdoba** (p. 839) and the **Alhambra** in **Granada** (p. 846). Before leaving Spain, delight in **Barcelona's** fanciful *Modernista* buildings and its museums devoted to Picasso and Miró (p. 856).

A quick train ride along the Riviera will bring you to Italy. First stop: **Venice** (p. 663), from the Venetian art of the **Accademia** to the modern art of the **Collezione Guggenheim.** Next up: **Florence** (p. 678), home of the Renaissance; you could lounge for an entire day at the splendid **Uffizi,** then drool for another at the image of human perfection, Michelangelo's *David,* in the **Accademia. Rome** almost invented architecture as we know it (p. 614); can we say **Pantheon, Colosseum,** and **Forum?** Michelangelo's *Pietà* in **St. Peter's Basilica,** not to mention the **Sistine Chapel** in the **Vatican Museums,** astound. Dive off the heel of the boot into Greece, where the crumbling **Acropolis,** the foundation of Western civilization, still towers above **Athens** (p. 516). After visiting one of the foremost collections of classical art at Athens' **National Archaeological Museum,** journey to the navel of the ancient world to learn your fate from the **oracle** at **Delphi** (p. 525) or visit the **temple of Apollo** on **Delos** (p. 542).

Back on the continent, **Vienna** hosts the renowned **Kunsthistoriches Museum** and the Klimt-rich **Austrian Gallery** (p. 80). Cross the German border and peruse **Munich's Neue** and **Alte Pinakothek** (p. 482) before continuing north to **Weimar,** birthplace of the **Bauhaus** architectural movement (p. 435). Continue on to **Berlin,** one of the world's great museum cities, with collections encompassing all subjects and eras (p. 404). The biggest sin you could commit in **Amsterdam** (p. 732) would be to miss the famed **Rijksmuseum, van Gogh Museum,** and the **Hash Marijuana Hemp Museum.**

LET'S GO HEDONISM

All work and no play makes Jack (or Jane) a very dull budget traveler. In the bacchanalian tradition of early pleasure-seekers such as Nero and Oscar Wilde, we are proud to present the essential stops for any debauched Grand Tour. Begin your descent into debauchery in **Spain,** on the wild isle of **Ibiza** (p. 892), where substance takes a back seat to style, style, and more style, and the outrageous clubs sport diversions ranging from foam and cream parties to live sex shows. Move on to France, where the **Cote d'Azur** (p. 351) offers sun-drenched beaches. Shed your inhibitions and your swimsuit to join the naked throngs on the shores of **Les Pissarelles** in **Cap D'Ail** (p. 363). Head to the famous **Monte Carlo Casino** (p. 363) for a game of highstakes roulette with some of the beautiful people and rid yourselves of those weighty traveler's checks while sipping champagne. If wild gyrations under the hot sun have left you drained, crawl to **The Netherlands** for a visit to that bastion of high culture, the **Sex Museum** (p. 742), in **Amsterdam,** and peruse various objects of erotic art. Walk that special someone through the city's famous **Red Light District** (p. 741), where any fantasy can become reality—for a price. No good scout can earn his hedonism merit badge without a trip to Germany for Berlin's famous **Love Parade** (p. 424), where 1.5 million participants engage in a 54 hour orgiastic parade of techno-music, ecstasy dropping, and libidinous satisfaction. On to **Italy,** to rage in the clubs of **Milan** (p. 640), and break the hearts of a few dozen supermodels. Satisfy your need for cultural enlightenment with a visit to **Amalfi** to gaze at the **Fontana di Sant'Andrea** (p. 705), a marble nude who squeezes her breasts as water pours forth from her nipples. Hedonism is a hard life (not really); finish your grand tour by pampering your deliciously debauched self with a relaxing underwater massage at the **Kurdirektion spa** in **Baden bei Wien** (p. 95), in **Austria.**

OH, WINE AND DINE ME

You can work up quite an appetite trekking through the museums, mountain ranges, and marketplaces of Western Europe. Fortunately, the region has more specialized dishes than you could safely sample. Fuel up for the big trip in **Lesvos,** Greece (p. 550) with a hearty meal of *souvlaki*—cap the meal with a taste of *ouzo,* a local licorice-flavored alcoholic treasure. After you ferry to Italy, work your way north: **Naples** (p. 698) offers *spaghetti* and *pizza,* and **Florence** (p. 678) claims to be the birthplace of the most sumptuous, creamy *gelato* on the continent. Those without a sweet tooth can find their home in the cafes that line the canals of **Venice** (p. 663), sipping a hot, strong cup of *espresso*. From northern Italy, wind your way along the Mediterranean coast, past **Provence** (quench your thirst with a glass of *pastis;* p. 346), and head into **Valencia** (p. 854) where tangy juicy oranges are grown that complement their world-famous *paella*. The center of the sherry triangle is at **Jerez de la Frontera,** (p. 838) but the port from **Porto** (p. 785) will draw you to the northwest of the Iberian peninsula, also home to *vinho verde,* a sparkling wine grown only between Porto and the Spanish border.

A trip through France, Germany, Austria, and Switzerland is no less delicious. Chug a *Maß* of beer, while tasting a *Weißwurst* in a *Biergarten* in **Munich** (p. 482). Vegetarians should keep their eyes open for *Spätzle* in **Vienna** (p. 80); meat-eaters and herbivores alike could pass up main courses for *Sacher Torte* or *Linzer Torte* at any *Konditorei* in **Salzburg** (p. 95). After stopping in **Strasbourg** (p. 379) for the wines of Alsace-Lorraine, head to **Lyon** (p. 369), one of the strongest contenders for the title of gastronomic capital of Western Europe. There you'll find *andouillettes*, sausages made of cow intestines, *cocons*, chocolates wrapped in marzipan, and even *palets d'or*, recognized as the best chocolates in France, and not just because they are dipped in gold powder. Marzipan lovers round out their European pilgrimage with visits to **Lübeck** (p. 448) and **Toledo** (p. 818).

THE GREAT OUTDOORS

Enough urban warrior—you're ready to commune with the streams, hug a few trees, and heed the call of the wild. Britain brims with national parks; our favorite is the Lake District National Park (p. 222). For starker natural beauty, head north to the Scottish Highlands; the Isle of Skye (p. 246) and the Outer Hebrides (p. 247) are particularly breathtaking. Ireland's Ring of Kerry provides wee Irish towns (p. 583), while Killarney National Park features spectacular mountains (p. 582). Back on the continent in the French Alps, Chamonix tempts skiers with some of the world's steepest slopes (p. 367), while Grenoble brims with hiking opportunities (p. 367). Spain's Parque Nacional de Ordesa is set amongst the breath-taking Pyrenees (p. 877). In Italy, gorgeous hiking on snowfields and views of the majestic Alps await in Val di Cogne while the Dolomites (p. 660) are a technicolor vision. Across the Mediterranean, the Aeolian Islands just north of Sicily boast its pristine beaches, belching volcanoes, and bubbling thermal springs (p. 712). Drop down to Greece and hike up to Mt. Olympus, where the gods used to sip ambrosia; a two-day hike will bring you to the summit (p. 535). Head to Crete, to get in touch with your inner mountain goat with a trek down the Samaria Gorge (p. 547). Austria's Kitzbühel (p. 108) and Innsbruck (p. 111) quench every hiking and skiing desire. For some fresh, Swiss Alpine air, head to the glaciers of Grindelwald (p. 929), make the pilgrimage to the Matterhorn, near Zermatt (p. 930), or dive into the adventure sports of Interlaken (p. 926). From there, disappear into Germany's buckling Bavarian Alps (p. 502) and take to the hiking trails of the Black Forest (p. 478).

OFF THE BEATEN PATH...

A Eurailpass is like French kissing: it's fun at first, but eventually leaves everyone hungry for more. As in love, getting beyond that first stage in exploring Europe takes a little savvy. Ireland's west coast is spread with a gorgeous and dense concentration of natural wonders, including the limestone moonscape of **The Burren** (p. 586), the **Cliffs of Moher** (p. 585), which soar 700 feet above the sea, and the **Inishowen Peninsula** (p. 592), an untouristed mosaic of mountains and white-sand beaches. Untouched spots still nestle in the misty forests of northwestern Spain's **Rías de Cedeira** and **Vivero** (p. 897). To the south, the cavernous gorges and white houses in **Arcos de la Frontera** arrest visitors (p. 839). Folded into the Pyrenees between Spain and France, a visit to the forgotten **Andorra** will impress all (p. 69). In France, Paris's charms distract visitors from the unblemished Alps; cobblestoned **Annency** borders Europe's purest lake (p. 369). The **Loire Valley's** (p. 329) *châteaux* and wine *caves* beckon from northwest France. A little bit out of the way, but certainly well worth it, are the gorgeous beaches of **Corsica** (p. 364) and the mountainous terrain of neighboring **Sardinia** (p. 713). In **Italy, Ravenna** hosts a stash of stunning Byzantine mosaics (p. 657). The **Aeolian Islands** (p. 712) boast some of Italy's last stretches of unspoiled beaches; **Stromboli's** active volcano belches lava and rocks nightly (p. 713). In the Greek Peloponnese lie the tiny, relaxing towns of **Dimitsana** and **Stemnitsa** (p. 527). On the mainland stands the exquisite, Byzantine **Osios Loukas,** the most beautiful of Greece's monasteries (p. 536); the mythical **Oracle of Dodoni** (p. 537) is Greece's oldest oracle.

ON THE BEACH

It would be a shame to spend your entire time in Western Europe languishing on silky beaches, but if you were to insist, you would have no problem filling your time and itinerary with sand and tanning oil. Even England hosts a tempting beach culture when it's not raining. The old artists' enclave of **St. Ives** offers sparkling beaches and blue, blue water (p. 195), while **Newquay** is a surfing capital (p. 196). **Malin Head,** at Ireland's northernmost point on the **Inishowen Peninsula,** offers a beach covered with semi-precious stones (p. 592). France packs surfers onto four kilometers of crystalline sand in **Anglet** (p. 340), while **St-Malo** combines the beauty and history of Normandy (p. 326). Skip down to Portugal, where you can party all night and sun all day along the **Algarve,** and in **Lagos** in particular (p. 779). Along Spain's **Costa del Sol, Marbella's** beaches shine with 320 days of sun per year (p. 852), while **Tossa del Mar** along the jagged **Costa Brava** is framed by red cliffs (p. 875). Spain's islands overwhelm with sunburned debauchery: the **Balearic Islands** are a must for party kids as **Ibiza** (p. 892) is manic by night. Move along to Italy and the fishing villages of **Cinque Terre,** which cling to cliffs over the bright blue sea (p. 652). Farther north in Italy, Europe's deepest lake, **Lake Como,** is peaceful perfection (p. 659). Sunbathe with the people who invented the bikini along the **Amalfi Coast** (p. 705). The **Blue Grotto** glows nearby on the island of **Capri** (p. 707). Bop down to the Greek islands: **Corfu** harbors the beautiful beach of **Agios Gordios** (p. 538); whitewashed towns balancing on plunging cliffs, burning black-sand beaches, and deeply scarred hills comprise **Santorini's** dramatic landscape (p. 545).

◪ LET'S GO PICKS

COME FOR A DAY, STAY FOR A YEAR: In the shadow of **Trujillo's** (p. 829) Moorish castle, sipping champagne in **Troyes's** (p. 386) ancient center, on the unspoiled seashores of the **Aeolian Islands** (p. 712), anywhere in **Provence's** (p. 346) carpets of lavender and olive groves.

BEST INDULGENCES: Bubbling in Baden Bei Wien's **sulfur springs** (p. 95), nibbling **gold-dusted chocolate** in Lyon (p. 369), sampling **all things herbal** in Amsterdam (p. 732), spooning **gelato** in Florence (p.), sipping **high tea** in London (p. 153), or, in the traditional sense, with a pilgrimage to **Lourdes** (p. 340).

BEST OF THE MORBID AND MACABRE: Cappuchin friars propped 8000 bodies against the walls of the **Cappuchin Catacombs** over three centuries in Palermo (p. 709); the **Basilica of the Holy Blood** in Bruges (p. 130) has a relic that allegedly holds the Christ's blood. Portugal wins the prize: under the floor of the **Igreja de São Francisco** (p. 785) in Porto, thousands of bones are stored in preparation for Judgement Day, while in Évora, the interior of the **Igreja Real de São Francisco** (p. 777) is made entirely out of human bones.

BEST PLACES TO MOOCH: Burn while sampling whiskeys at the **Old Jameson Distillery** in Dublin (p. 572), camp for free at **Odysseus's landing point** in Ithaka (p. 539), go free to the **Guinea Pig City** in the Hannover Zoo (p. 450), taste fresh brew after the tour of the **Heineken Brewery** in Amsterdam (p. 732).

BEST PLACES TO SMOOCH: In the **Trevi Fountain** in Rome (p. 614), during a picnic on the **Champ De Mars** (p. 285) near the Eiffel Tower, swooning over a gondola tour in **Venice** (p. 663), in the middle of the Via del Amore in **Cinque Terre** (p. 652), or on the desert-plateau of **Sagres** (p. 780), once thought to be the edge of the world.

BEST FESTIVALS: Bareback horse races take **Siena** by storm during **Il Palio** (July 2 and Aug. 16; p. 693) before hordes drink from winesacks and watch the bulls run for **San Fermines** in **Pamplona** (July 6-13; p. 878). "Yes" is the word during **Love Parade** in **Berlin,** (July 8-9; p. 424), the **Edinburgh International Festival** entertains with all things artsy (Aug. 18-Sept. 1; p. 232), and **Oktoberfest** revelers in **Munich** consume of 1.2 million gallons of beer (Sept. 16-Oct. 1; p. 482).

DISCOVER

SUGGESTED ITINERARIES

There is no formula for the perfect itinerary in Western Europe. Here we humbly suggest a few routes—just to give you an idea of what is possible. **The Basics** below outlines our skeletal suggestions for the best of Europe. We've also included some regional itineraries to help you plan a few extra forays. These other itineraries can be thought of as **Building Blocks** to tack onto the basic route. For more in-depth suggestions, see the **Suggested Itineraries** sections in individual country chapters.

THE BASICS

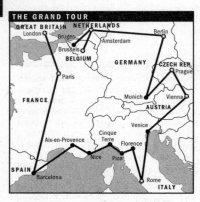

THE GRAND TOUR: BEST OF WEST-ERN EUROPE IN 1 MONTH

Start out in **London,** spinning from theater to museum to club (4 days; p. 153). Chunnel to the sights, shops, and sweetness of **Paris** (4 days; p. 285), and slip south to the daring and colorful **Barcelona** (2 days; p. 856). Return to France for a day in elegant **Aix-en-Provence** (p. 350). After an all-night party in **Nice** (1 day; p. 357); recover near the blissful mountain cliffs of **Cinque Terre** on the Italian Riviera (1 day; p. 652). Prop up the leaning tower of **Pisa** (1 day; p. 695), be enchanted by Renaissance art in **Florence** (2 days; p. 678), and pull Adam's finger in **Rome** (3 days; p. 614). Float down **Venice's** canals by gondola (2 days; p. 663) on your way to coffee in **Vienna** (2 days; p. 80). Sip absinthe in starlet **Prague** (2 days; p. 936) and sample the frothy brew in **Munich** (2 days; p. 482) before heading up to the sprawling **Berlin** (2 days; p. 404). Indulge in **Amsterdam** (2 days; p. 732), then relax with a day in Tintin's **Brussels** (p. 124) or **Bruges** (p. 130).

THE BEST OF WESTERN EUROPE IN 9 WEEKS

From **London** (4 days; p. 153), meander the halls of **Oxford** (1 day; p. 197) or **Cambridge** (1 day; p. 207), then take to the well-worn footpaths between villages in the **Cotswolds** (1 day; p. 203). Catch a play in Shakespeare's **Stratford-Upon-Avon** (1 day; p. 204), before heading to **Dublin,** home to Joyce and Guinness (2 days; p. 563). Chunnel from London to Paris, love **Paris** (4 days; p. 285) and gape at **Versailles** (1 day; p. 316). From the **Loire Valley** (1 day; p. 329), test your taste buds in the vineyards of **Bordeaux** (1 day; p. 337), proceed south to rage in **Madrid's** clubs (2 days; p. 800), and marvel at the architectural gems of **Barcelona** (3 days; p. 856). After a day each in festive **Avignon** (p. 346), **Aix-en-Provence** (p. 350), and **Nice** (p. 357), replenish in the **Cinque Terre** (2 days; p. 652), send postcards from **Pisa** (1 day; p. 695), and continue on to the orange roofs of **Florence** (2 days; p. 678). Stop at the stunning *duomo* in **Siena** (1 day; p. 693) en route to **Rome** (3 days; p. 614) before heading north to admire Giotto's frescoes in **Padua** (1 day; p. 674). Wind through **Venice's** *palazzi* (2 days; p. 663) on your way to posh **Milan** (1 day; p. 640). Grapple the **Matterhorn** from **Zermatt** (1 day;

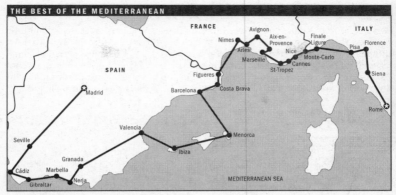

THE BEST OF THE MEDITERRANEAN

p. 930) and conquer the Swiss Alps around **Interlaken** (1 day; p. 926) before satiating your urge for *The Sound of Music* in **Salzburg** (1 day; p. 95). After **Vienna** (2 days; p. 80), soak in either the baths of **Budapest** or the bars of **Prague** (2 days; p. 936) Love your beer in **Munich,** and take a sobering daytrip to **Dachau** (3 days; p. 495). Move from the fairy-tale triumvirate of Mad King Ludwig's **Royal Castles** (1 day; p. 469) up the bucolic **Romantic Road** (2 days; p. 498), then cruise down the spectacular **Rhine River** (1 days; p. 468). From **Berlin** (2 days; p. 404) and reckless **Hamburg** (1 day; p. 439), head north to cosmopolitan **Copenhagen** (2 days; p. 256) and continue on to **Amsterdam** (3 days; p. 732). Spend a day each in **Brussels** (p. 124) and **Bruges** (p. 130) before heading home.

THE BEST OF THE MEDITERRANEAN IN SIX WEEKS From Madrid take the high-speed train to the flower filled *terrazas* of **Sevilla** (2 days; p. 830) before basking at the soft-sand beaches of **Cádiz** (2 days; p. 838). Stand on the imposing Rock of **Gibraltar** (1 day; p. 845) en route to party with the beautiful people in the Costa del Sol resort town of **Marbella** (1 day; p. 852). Skip inland to **Granada** (2 days; p. 846), and wind your way through the Albacín to the Alhambra. From **Valencia** (2 days; p. 854) island hop in the **Balearic Islands** between **Ibiza's** foam parties and **Menorca's** raw beaches (3 days; p. 893). Ferry to vibrant **Barcelona** (3 days; p. 856), before hitting the **Costa Brava** and the Dalí museum in **Figueres** (2 days; p. 875). Stretch into **France's**

provençal **Nimes** (1 day; p. 348) and follow van Gogh's traces in **Arles** (1 day; p. 349). More glory awaits in **Avignon** (1 day; p. 346), before reveling in **Aix-en-Provence** (1 day; p. 350). Taste the *bouillabaisse* in **Marseilles** (1 day; p. 351) and move on to all that glitters in Côte d'Azur. **St-Tropez** (1 day; p. 355) may be the "jewel of the Riviera," but **Cannes** (2 days; p. 356) is the flashiest diamond, and **Nice** (2 days; p. 357) wears the crown as its king. If you've any money left, hit the world-famous casino of **Monte-Carlo** (1 day; p. 363). Vacation from your vacation in **Italy's Finale Ligure** (2 days; p. 650), and snap photos in **Pisa** (1 day; p. 695) before David-hopping in **Florence's** magnificent art collection (3 days; p. 678). Check out the two-tone *duomo* of **Siena** (2 days; p. 693) and find a forum for all things ancient in **Rome** (4 days; p. 614). If you plan on traveling farther south in Italy and into Greece, add the Southern Italy and Greece building block itinerary (see below).

BUILDING BLOCKS

SOUTHERN ITALY AND GREECE IN FOUR WEEKS View the rubble of the toga-clad empire, the cathedrals of high Christianity, and the art of the Renaissance in **Rome** (5 days; p. 614). From **Naples** (2 days; p. 698), home to the world's best pizza and pickpockets, daytrip to **Pompeii** (1 day; p. 704) and check out randy Roman remains buried in AD 79. Follow in the footsteps of Roman emperors and be captivated by **Capri** (2 days; p. 707). Depending on

DISCOVER

BEST OF SOUTHERN ITALY AND GREECE

how you plan to travel to Greece, hop off the boot from **Bari** (p. 708) or **Brindisi** (p. 708), where overnight ferries go to Greece (1 day). Get off at **Corfu** (1 day; p. 538), beloved by literary luminary Oscar Wilde and partiers alike, or continue on to **Patras** (1 day; p. 526). Wrestle among the ruins in **Olympia** (1 day; p. 527) before beginning your Peloponnesian adventure with a survey of the ancient ruins in **Napflion, Mycenae,** and **Epidavros** (3 days; p. 530). Get initiated into the "mysteries of love" in equally ruinous **Corinth** (1 day; p. 531). On to chaotic **Athens,** a jumble of things ancient and modern (2 days; p. 516). Succumb to your longing Cyclades: party all night long on **Mykonos** (1 day; p. 542) and repent at the Temple of Apollo in **Delos** (1 day; p. 542) before continuing on to the earthly paradise of **Santorini** (2 days; p. 545). Catch the ferry to **Crete,** where chic **Iraklion** and **Knossos,** home to the Minotaur, await (2 days; p. 546). Base yourself in **Rethymno** or **Hania** and hike the spectacular **Samaria Gorge** (2 days; p. 547).

THE BEST OF BRITAIN AND IRELAND (3 WEEKS) From **London** (4 days; p. 153), get studious in **Oxford** (1 day; p. 197) and **Cambridge** (1 day; p. 207), then take to the **Cotswolds** (1 day; p. 203). Love all things Shakespeare in **Stratford-Upon-Avon** (1 day; p. 204), and on to **Liverpool** (2 days; p. 215), home of the Beatles. Cross the Irish Sea to **Dublin** (3 days; p. 563), the latest favorite, and daytrip to the **Wicklow Mountains** (1 day; p. 575). Run the **Ring of Kerry** (2½ days; p.

583) circuit before listening to *craic* in **Galway** (1½ days; p. 587), the culture capital. Take in the murals at **Belfast** (2 days; p. 592) and from there it's back across the Irish Sea to **Stranraer,** energetic **Glasgow** (1 day; p. 240), and nearby **Loch Lomond.** Then on to historic and exuberant **Edinburgh** (3 days; p. 232). The **Lake District** (2 days; p. 222) offers scenic diversions and historic **York** (1 day; p. 217) completes the journey. Return to London to kick back with a West End play and a glass of Tetley's bitter.

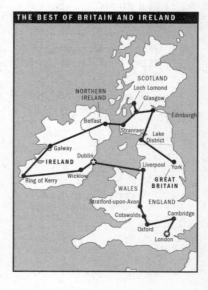

THE BEST OF BRITAIN AND IRELAND

THE BEST OF SPAIN AND PORTUGAL
(4 WEEKS) Hop off the Paris-Madrid train at gorgeous **San Sebastián** (2 days; p. 882), and check out the new Guggenheim in **Bilbao** (1 day; p. 888) before heading to **Madrid** for urban fun (4 days; p. 800). Daytrip to the austere palace of **El Escorial** (1 day; p. 817) and the medieval streets of **Toledo** (1 day; p. 818). Visit the university town of **Salamanca** (1 day; p. 825) and cross the border into **Portugal**, heading up to the unpretentious **Porto** (2 days; p. 785). Savor your port and continue down the coast to the beach resort of **Figueira da Foz** (2 days; p. 784). Marvel at the painted tiles in **Lisbon** (2 days; p. 766) with a daytrip to the town of **Sintra** (1 day; p. 774). Bake in the sun along the Algarve in **Lagos** (2 days; p. 779) where hordes of visitors dance the night away. Sleep off your hangover on the 7hr. express bus from Lagos to **Sevilla** (2 days; p. 830) and prepare for a romantic stroll along the Guadalquivir River. Delve deeper into Arab-influenced Andalucía—don't miss the Mezquita in **Córdoba** (2 days; p. 839) and love the Alhambra in **Granada** (2 days; p. 846). From Granada head up the Mediterranean Coast to stop in **Valencia** (1 day; p. 854) for the *paella* and oranges. Head to northeastern Spain to hit the sunny **Costa Brava** (2 days; p. 874), the Dalí Museum in **Figueres** (1 day; p. 875), and medieval **Girona** (1 day; p. 874). Continue with the Best of Western Europe in Nine Weeks itinerary from Barcelona (see above).

THE BEST OF FRANCE IN 3 WEEKS
You'll need at least 4 days to see the sights and shops of **Paris** (p. 285)—make time for a daytrip to **Versailles** (p. 316). Next, slip down to the Loire Valley to **Blois**

(1 day; p. 330). Travel up to the island abbey of **Mont-St-Michel** (1 day; p. 324). Next, head down to **Nantes** (1 day; p. 329) for medieval sights and modern nightlife, before soaking up the sun in beach-blessed, historical **La Rochelle** (2 days; p. 334). For a change of pace, contemplate the 17,000-year-old cave paintings of **Les-Eyzies-de-Tayac** (1 day; p. 336). Sniff, swirl, and spit in **Bordeaux** (2 days; p. 337) before zipping southwards to *basque* on the beach in **Biarritz** (1 day; p. 339). From there, follow the pilgrims to miraculous **Lourdes** (1 day; p. 340). Keep heading east to reach the stunning walls of **Carcassonne** (1 day; p. 343), guarding the town as they have done for centuries. No less formidable are the fortifications of the Palais-des-Papes in festive **Avignon** (1 day; p. 346). Students have been partying in elegant **Aix-en-Provence** (1 day; p. 350) for 600 years, but for non-stop action go to **Nice** (2 days; p. 357), undisputed capital of the Riviera. For a change of scenery, climb into the Alps to reach dynamic **Grenoble** (2 days; p. 367). **Strasbourg** (1 day; p. 379) offers a hybrid Franco-German culture. Finish off in style with a tasting at one of the many champagne *caves* in **Reims** (1 day; p. 385).

THE BEST OF GERMANY, AUSTRIAN AND SWITZERLAND IN FIVE WEEKS
Spend three nights raging in **Berlin's** chaotic nightclubs, and three days recovering in the capital's museums and cafes (p.

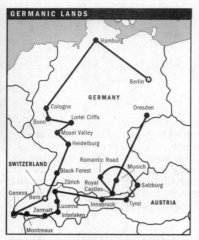

GERMANIC LANDS

the mystical **Lorlei Cliffs** (1 day; p. 469) and softly-cut **Mosel Valley** (2 days; p. 470). Brood in Germany's oldest university in **Heidelburg** (1 day; p. 472) and act out your favorite Grimms fairy tales in the **Black Forest** (p. 478). Shimmey on over to **Switzerland's Bern** via Freiberg (1 day; p. 925), play world-leader in **Geneva** (2 days; p. 907), and listen to jazz in **Montreaux** (1 day; p. 913). Oogle the **Matterhorn** from **Zermatt** (1 day; p. 930), and use **Interlaken** (2 days; p. 926) as a base for exploring the Alps. Take a train to the fairy-tale hamlet of **Lucerne** (1 day; p. 923) before satiating your thirst for culture and nightlife in **Zurich** (1day; p. 917). Skip to the snow-capped peaks of **Innsbruck** (1 day; p. 111), in the **Tyrol.** Follow Mozart's footsteps in **Salzburg** (2 days; p. 95) and spend three days along the **Romantic Road,** hitting **Mondsee, Bad Ischl, Hallstatt,** and **Gmunden** (p. 103). Back to Germany's **Munich** for boisterous beer halls (3 days; p. 482), with a daytrip to mad **King Ludwig's Castles** (1 day; p. 469). Chill out in Bavaria but save the last dance for **Dresden** (1 day; p. 426) and contemplate a trip to Prague.

404). Move north, where **Hamburg** fuses the burliness of a port town with cosmopolitan flair (2 days; p. 439), before admiring **Cologne's** cathedral, Germany's greatest (1 day; p. 453). Meander through **Bonn's** Alstadt (2 days; p. 458), and slip south to

WESTERN EUROPE
THE GRAND TOUR

Ah, Western Europe. It arrests our adjective pool—astounding, splendid, loud, and graceful. Europe has enough history and culture to keep you busy for a lifetime. As you will see, countries' political histories will reveal themselves to you in their town squares, landscapes, and canvases. Here is a primer on the intellectual and political movements that created headlines and forged Western Europe, intended to help travelers acquire a deeper understanding of what they observe on their trip. Use this abridged history in conjunction with the historical and artistic regional introductions at the beginning of each chapter, and enjoy.

IN THE BEGINNING...

—The Start of the World as We Know It, and I Feel Fine.

From the din and tundra of the Paleolithic and Neolithic periods, the **Greeks** rose as the first prosperous civilization in Western Europe. After the 16th century BC, martial mainland peoples swept down from the north and replaced the **Minoans** as the dominant civilization of the Aegean. By the 9th century BC, **city-states** had begun to expand and colonize overseas, establishing their military and cultural power throughout the Mediterranean. At the height of **Classical Greece** (500-400 BC), Athens produced art, literature, and philosophy that have been touchstones of Western culture ever since. Greek autonomy, however, was short-lived. In 146 BC the **Romans** conquered the Greeks, eventually expanding their empire over all of Western Europe. The Romans pollinated the continent with concepts of organization and government, and Greek culture. Although there were no distinct nations, cities and transportation arteries sprung up between villages and the empire kept the general peace, **pax romana** style. This led to **Diocletian's** decision in 293 to divide the empire under two leaders—splitting the empire between East and West. Between 312-337 Emperor **Constantine the Great** revoked this decision and reunited the Roman Empire, moving its capital to Byzantine (later known as Constantinople, later known as Istanbul) and declaring Christianity as the new state religion.

EARLY MIDDLE AGES (390-996)

—Where the Wild Things Were: Barbarians Grapple for Land, Meat

There's nothing like invading **Huns, Visigoths,** and **Vandals** to spoil a perfectly good empire—in 476 the last Roman emperor was removed from power. The Germanic barbarians reverted from the cities of the Roman Empire, and organized into small tribes. As life became increasingly localized, Western Europe tumbled into the poorly-lit **Dark Ages** c. 500. In 800, the pope crowned **Charlemagne** Holy Roman Emperor. Combining the power of the church and state, Charlemagne regained Spain and Italy from their respective barbarian tribes and moved the capital to **Aachen.** Following the death of Charlemagne's son, **Louis the Pious,** the Carolingian Empire was divided amongst his three sons, thus decentralizing power and leading to the rise of local lords. Europe was now divided into three parts: the **Byzantine Empire** (including the East and parts of Italy), **Islamic** (Spain), and **Latin Christendom** (which France, Belgium, Rhineland, Britain, and some of the other parts of Italy).

HIGH MIDDLE AGES(1066-1299)

—Of Monks and Meade: Feudalism Exploits Peasants, Chastity Belt Hits the
Medieval Runway, Holy Wars Rage

In the High Middle Ages, towns came out their shells and began to form leagues
for commercial and political power. Such leagues gave way to **feudalism,** a system
of local government without a state. In theory, feudalism joined people and lords
in a contract that ensured that everyone fulfilled their mutual obligations. This
hierarchy was reflected in the religious dealings of the period. The High Middle
Ages were overwrought with costly and intermittently successful attempts to
extend Christianity. Pope **Innocent III,** whose rule lasted from 1198-1216, financed
and advised regional kings to advance his goal of Christian unification to the
point that they viewed him as a feudal lord.

From 1095 to 1291, Western Europeans launched the **Holy War,** or the **Crusades,**
against Islam, although the most successful crusades attacked heathens within
Europe. In the 13th century, Christianity claimed Spain, Italy, Prussia, and the Baltic regions. Despite the questionable gains of the Crusades, the wars both strengthened and demonstrated the strength of Christian Europe.

THE RENAISSANCE (1325-1556)

—Joy at Nude Pixxx Offset by Irksome Death of Millions

In a fit of nostalgia for the Corinthian columns and toga parties of yore, 14th-cen-
tury Italy helped Classicism stage a comeback with the **Renaissance** (literally,
"rebirth"). Poets like **Dante, Petrarch,** and **Boccaccio,** and the artist **Giotto,** set the
stage during the 12th and 13th centuries with poetry and art that celebrated the
inherent dignity of humankind and the beauty of Classic virtues. In the 14th century, **Michelangelo, Da Vinci,** and **Raphael** provided the artistic apotheosis of the
Humanist philosophy, which relied on the idea that human beings were endowed
with a basic dignity, and that all the basic belief systems in circulations, could,
with effort, be synthesized into one, fundamental truth. To complicate matters, the
Black Plague swept across Europe, wiping out 25 million people from 1347 to 1352.

Centered in **Florence,** the Renaissance produced masterpieces of art and advances
in human thought that helped foster the **Age of Exploration** that began in the 1490s.
The Renaissance period was also marked by England's inaccurately named **Hundred
Years War** with France, which lasted from 1337 to 1452. Although the English won
early battles, they were eventually expelled from southwestern France. Squabbles
within the Roman Catholic Church escalated to **The Great Schism,** during which multiple popes fought for church power in Avignon from 1378 to 1417 (and when popes
get angry, bad things happen). The election of an Italian cardinal during the **Council
of Constance** ended the schism, but papal authority remained weak.

PROTESTANT REFORMATION (1517-1556)

—Luther's Bathroom Epiphany Leaves Catholicism Wrinkling its Nose

In 1517, **Martin Luther's** *95 Theses* sparked the Protestant Reformation in Germany. The shocking treatise resulted in Luther's 1521 excommunication, and
before the decade was out, the Holy Roman Empire had been divided by the issue
of reformation. **Henry VIII** divorced **Catherine of Aragon** in 1534 to wed homewrecker
Anne Boleyn, breaking with the Roman Catholic Church and causing a rift over
which heads would (literally) roll for years. With the **Act of Supremacy** in 1534,
Henry declared himself head of not only state, but of the new Protestant church as
well, instigating the **English Reformation,** which spread through Norway, Denmark,
and Scotland from 1536 to 1541.

The movement toward Reformation did not go unchecked. The **Council of Trent**
(1545-1563), the 19th ecumenical council of the Roman Catholic Church, formed
the keystone of the **Counter-reformation** argument. The council confirmed the truth

of the scripture, reaffirmed the seven sacraments and the Eucharist, and essentially defended any point that had been contested by Protestants. In 1555, however, with the **Peace of Augsburg**, **Charles V** of the Holy Roman Empire granted the princes of Germany the right to establish the religion of their own people, whether that be Catholic or Protestant.

RELIGIOUS WARS AND SCIENTIFIC REVOLUTION (1556-1688)

—Charles V Abdicates, Elizabeth Restores Church, Peace of Westphalia Resolves Thirty Year's War... Just Not Funny

Holy Roman Emperor **Charles V,** who failed in his goal to unite the empire under Christianity, abdicated the year after the Peace of Augsburg. His impotent solution to the lack of unity was to further divide power: his brother **Ferdinand I** gained control of Austrian Habsburg lands, while his son **Philip II** ruled Spain and the Netherlands. As Philip II brooded in his stone El Escorial about the necessity for Catholic reform, Spain entered its Golden Age, **siglo de oro,** and emerged as the greatest power in Europe. Spanish troops and gold supported the Catholic cause in Western Europe, aiding rebellions against the England's Protestant **Queen Elizabeth,** removing French Huguenot Protestants from power, and silencing Calvinists in the Netherlands. From 1618-1648, the **Thirty Year's War** raged as German (and Protestant) towns asserted their independence from the Roman Catholic Church and the Holy Roman Empire. The **Peace of Westphalia,** in 1648, marked the first international treaty since the Council of Constance, and reinforced the Peace of Ausburg's principal of *cuius regio eius religio* (whose the region, his the religion). Calvinism was added to the list of (barely) tolerable religions and the **staatensystem** instituted an international system of independent states. Despite initial victories, Philip's Catholic torment was embarrassingly unsuccessful. Queen Elizabeth restored the Protestant church, a Huguenot sat at the throne in France, and the Thirty Years' War ensured the safety of Calvinism in the Netherlands.

The late 17th century was a jumble of political and intellectual revolutions. England plunged into civil war, and France, under **the Sun King Louis XIV,** became the greatest power in Western Europe. The **Scientific Revolution** of the 17th century reached beyond theory and changed perceptions about the nature of religion and man. **Galileo, Descartes, Newton,** and **Hobbes** are among the familiar names of the revolution, each contributing to the belief in harmony, logic, and man's abilities. The popularization of scientific thought and method, and its increasing pertinence to everyday life, medicine, and politics formed the basis for the ideas of the Age of Enlightenment.

AGE OF ENLIGHTENMENT (1688-1789)

—Enlightenment Spreads, Proves Despots Are People, Too

During the Age of the Enlightenment, thinkers such as **Voltaire, Montesquieu, John Locke, Thomas Hobbes,** and **Jean-Jacques Rousseau** were united in their belief that the road to a better existence lay through reason. By choosing the right method of reasoning one could achieve knowledge, and thus become both free and happy. The questioning spirit of this age also affected the conception of the state—**Frederick II** of Prussia, **Catherine the Great** of Russia, and **Joseph II** of the Habsburg empire were monarchs known as the **enlightened despots,** who combined liberalizing reforms with measures to maintain control over peasants.

Intellectual and state reform didn't stop a series of land wars. In the **War of the Spanish Succession** (1701-1714), Austria and Britain went to war to keep Louis XIV's son, Philip V, from the Spanish throne. This was settled by the **Treaty of Utrecht,** which allowed Philip to take the throne but forbade him from merging the empire with France. The **Seven Years' War** (1756-1763) saw Austria and France ally to fight Prussia and Britain. War eventually spread to North America, the Caribbean, and India, hinting at the impending wave of imperialism.

FRENCH REVOLUTION AND NAPOLEON (1789-1814)

—Napoleon Invades! "Who's short now?!" yells the Frenchy.

Louis XIV's ascension to the French throne as the Sun King ushered in an era of **absolutism** and excess, perhaps best exemplified by the 14,000-room palace of **Versailles** (hey, everyone needs a little place in the country). When the populace began to grumble, Louis XIV called the first assembly of the **Estates General** in over 150 years, consisting of representatives from the three classes of the nobility, the clergy, and everyone else. From this assemblage, the **Third Estate** broke away, declaring itself the **National Assembly.** After chaos erupted across the nation, the radical Jacobin faction took control, abolished the monarchy, and declared the Republic. The Revolution entered a more radical phase, known as the **Terror,** when counter-revolutionaries were weeded out and justice dispensed by "Madame" Guillotine. The five-man **Directory,** a second try at representative government, was established in 1795. **Napoleon Bonaparte,** waging victorious military campaigns in Europe and in Egypt, deposed the Directory and declared himself Emperor and "consul for life." He abolished the Holy Roman Empire, dismembered Prussia, and captured Habsburg Vienna. The **Napoleonic Code,** the most famous legal code since the Romans and a direct result of the Age of Enlightenment ideals, defined property rights, declared all people equal before the law, and affirmed the freedoms of religion and work. After wars with Britain and Spain, Napoleon's Grand Army was disastrously defeated in Russia in 1812, after which he abdicated and was sent into exile, to chill with the turtles on Elba, and think up witty palindromes. Bourbon rule was restored in France in 1814, under Louis XVIII, but the **Treaty of France** in 1814 left France without Napoleon's land acquisitions.

INDUSTRIAL REVOLUTION (1814-1848)

—Leaves Masses Asking, "Just What *is* a Spinning Jenny?"

With the invention of the steam engine, spinning mill, and spinning jennies (cotton spinning machine) in the 18th century, the Industrial Revolution was off to a running start in Northern England. From 1800 to 1850 it spread rapidly throughout Europe, bringing with it an increase in life expectancy, population, and urbanization. The **factory** was the most visible symbol of the Industrial Age, but the time from 1830 to 1850 also saw the birth of socialist ideology and the hope for the creation of a utopian society. Heightened urbanization provided mobility for the peasant class, although work days in factories remained around 14 hours a day.

Industrial changes served as harbingers of other societal revolutions, as liberal revolts broke out in Spain, Italy, Portugal, Germany, and Poland from 1815 to 1848. The 19th century also saw new independence for several countries, as Belgium wrested autonomy from the Netherlands in 1831, and the Turks recognized Greek independence in 1832. Further change touched Britain in the form of the **Reform Act of 1832** which granted one of every five males suffrage, while later reforms abolished slavery and regulated child labor.

NATIONAL UNIFICATION (1851-1867)

—Size Does Matter: Nations Struggle for Land and Power

During the mid-19th century, European nations consolidated land and power. In Italy, the efforts of **Victor Emmanuel II, Camillo Cavour, Giuseppe Mazzini,** and General **Giuseppe Garibaldi** from 1859 to 1870, managed to unify Italy despite long-standing regional tensions. Meanwhile, back in Prussia, newly appointed Prime Minister **Otto von Bismarck** unified the new German Empire, including the new lands Prussia garnered as spoils during the **Austro-Prussian** and **Franco-Prussian Wars** (1866 and

1870-71, respectively). As it became trendy to make massive monarchal alliances, the **Dual Monarchy** of Austria-Hungary was created in 1867, the same year that the **British Reform Bill** doubled the number of English voters by granting suffrage to all heads of households.

INDUSTRIALIZATION AND IMPERIALISM (1870-1911)

—With Invention of Electricity, Sun Never Sets on Empire

The second wave of the Industrial Revolution brought rapid industrialization to Europe with inventions like the sewing machine, electricity, the telephone, and the automobile. Standards of living skyrocketed, and European powers extended their long arms to Africa and Asia, establishing dominance during the **Age of Imperialism.** Explorers and missionaries were the first to introduce Europe to Africa. **Leopold II**, King of Belgium, was especially attracted to the potential wealth of Africa, while the British and French also ventured into the "dark continent." The Dutch, British, and Russian imperialists also began to occupy parts of Asia, creating powerful empires, while suppressing the revolts of native inhabitants. Speaking of dominance, **Sigmund Freud** pioneered the theory of "blaming Mom" with the development of **psychoanalysis** in the 1890s.

WORLD WAR I (1914-1920)

—Despite International Cordiality: Skirmish

The assassination of the Austro-Hungarian **Archduke Francis Ferdinand** in 1914, was the straw that broke Europe's back. The continent had become a mess of opposing alliances: Britain and France ended centuries of conflict in 1904 by forming the **Entente Cordiale,** which Russia later joined to create the **Triple Entente.** Germany's recently unified state sought to show off its muscle by coming to Austria's defense (forming an alliance of their own, known as the **Central Powers**) after Ferdinand's assassination. Germany advanced quickly through Belgium and France before stalling at the **Battle of the Marne** in 1914 for four long years of **trench warfare.** The United States was drawn into this war when Germany's practice of **unrestricted submarine warfare** could no longer be tolerated, and the American entry quickly led the Entente forces to victory. In 1919, the **Treaty of Versailles** and the **"Big Four"** (Orlando of Italy, Lloyd George of Britain, Clemenceau of France, and Wilson of the US) assigned all of the blame for the war on Germany. The weak new **Weimar Republic** in Germany was forced to assume the financial burden of the war under the **"war guilt clause."**

INTERWAR YEARS (1920-1939)

—War and Peace...and War Again

For Germany, the Treaty of Versailles was in many ways disastrous: enormous reparations were demanded, territory was taken, and most importantly, blame for the First World War was put squarely on German shoulders. This humiliation, combined with the hyperinflation of the 1920s, set the stage for Austrian **Adolph Hitler's** rise to power. Leader of the **National Socialist German Workers' Party,** also known as the Nazis, Hitler pushed a program of Aryan supremacy (based on anti-Semitism and xenophobia), playing on the post-war insecurities of the Germans. By the 1930s, most European countries were dictatorships, most prominently Italy, under Benito Mussolini, Spain, with General Francisco Franco at the helm, and, of course, the newly-created Union of Soviet Socialist Republics. By 1933, Hitler had been appointed chancellor of Germany, banned all other parties, and created quite the totalitarian state. The **Kristallnacht** (the Night of Broken Glass), in 1938, saw the destruction of Jewish stores and homes throughout Germany, as well as attacks against and the imprisonment of thousands of Jews.

WORLD WAR II (1939-1945)

—Hitler's Desire for German Expansion and Supremacy Leads to Massive Destruction

Continuing German expansion, Hitler moved into Czechoslovakia and then on September 1, 1939, into Poland, initiating WWII. Britain and France were bound by treaty to help Poland, and declared war on Germany. As Germany overran Denmark, Norway, Luxembourg, Belgium, the Netherlands, and France, Russia, led by Joseph Stalin, stayed out of the picture because of a secret non-aggression pact signed with Hitler. This short-lived deal only lasted until the Nazis invaded the Soviet Union in 1941; however, German forces were unable to break through the Russian winter. The Allied landings at **Normandy** on June 6, 1944 (known as **D-Day**), marked the beginning of a bloody, arduous advance across Western Europe. Paris was returned to Allied forces in August, 1944, and Berlin was captured by Russia's Red Army in April 1945. Hitler's **Third Reich,** which he had boasted would last for a thousand years, was dissolved after just twelve. The **Holocaust,** with Hitler's "final solution" and the establishment of mass execution centers, concentration camps, ultimately killed at least six million Jews and five million other victims, including homosexuals, the mentally retarded, gypsies, Slavs, and other political opponents.

COLD WAR (1946-1989)

—Grown-up Game of Name-calling and Espionage

In 1945, the US, Britain, and the USSR met at **Yalta** to form the **United Nations,** plan the defeat and occupation of Nazi Germany, and determine spheres of influence in post-war Europe. **Four occupation zones** were set up in Germany, Berlin, Austria, and Vienna. Berlin and Germany became symbols of the mounting tension between the western, capital world, led by the US, and the communist sphere controlled by the USSR. East Germany, under the USSR, became known as the **German Democratic Republic.** In 1949, West Germany became the **German Federal Republic,** containing American, British, and French zones. Berlin itself was divided between the two opposing spheres, a division later marked by the construction of the **Berlin Wall** in 1961. The **North Atlantic Treaty Organization** (NATO) was also formed in 1949, with 12 nations banding together to counter Soviet aggression. While the US was stricken with McCarthyism and anti-communist fever, in western Europe, the foundations for the now vibrant **European Community** were laid. In 1967, France, Belgium, the Netherlands, Luxembourg, Italy, and West Germany created a tariff-free trading zone, to be joined in 1973 by Britain, Denmark, and Ireland, in 1981 by Greece, in 1986 by Spain and Portugal, in 1990 by Eastern Germany, and in 1995 by Austria, Sweden, and Finland.

WESTERN EUROPE TODAY: EUROPEAN UNION

—After Millennia of Discord, Nations Finally Decide to Play Nice

The fall of the Berlin Wall in November 1989 symbolized the fall of communism in Europe. With the end of the Cold War, focus turned toward the European Community and the creation of one market with no borders. At the **Treaty of Maastricht** in 1992, 12 members of the EC and sixth other European states forged an Economic Area, eliminating national barriers for the movement of goods and services, workers, and capital. As Europe unites economically, there is also a movement afoot to halt American culture from invading western Europe. A number of countries are revising dictionaries in an attempt to eradicate American phrases from the language. Currently Austria, Belgium, Denmark, Finland, France, Germany, Greece, Ireland, Italy, Luxembourg, the Netherlands, Portugal, Spain, Sweden, and the UK are all members of the **European Union,** and are in the process of preparing for mass introduction of the **EU currency,** the **Euro,** in 2002.

ESSENTIALS

Touring in Western Europe, or even just a chunk of it, can be as daunting as it is exciting. Fortunately, there are countless resources devoted to helping travelers plan a journey. All you need to do is dive in and design a trip tailored to your specific interests and needs, without losing sight of the fact that it is a vacation. Don't over plan your itinerary so that the adventure becomes one big blur; just relax and wander at your own pace.

FACTS FOR THE TRAVELER

Give careful consideration to when you travel, because the timing of your trip can end up determining its success. Summer is the high season for traveling in Western Europe. *Everything* is crowded with tourists in July and August; June or September may be a better time to go. Additionally, climate can serve as a very good guide for the best time to travel in certain areas.

SEASONAL	JANUARY			APRIL			JULY			OCTOBER		
AVG. TEMP., **RAIN**	°C	°F	in	°C	°F	in	°C	°F	in	°C	°F	in
Amsterdam	3	38	**3.1**	8	47	**1.5**	17	62	**2.9**	11	51	**4.1**
Athens	10	50	**1.9**	15	59	**0.9**	27	81	**0.2**	19	67	**2.1**
Berlin	-1	31	**1.6**	8	46	**1.6**	18	65	**2**	9	49	**1.0**
Copenhagen	1	33	**1.7**	6	43	**1.6**	17	62	**2.6**	9	49	**2.1**
Dublin	6	42	**2.5**	8	47	**1.9**	16	60	**2.6**	11	51	**2.9**
London	4	39	**3.1**	8	46	**2.1**	17	62	**1.8**	11	51	**2.9**
Madrid	6	42	**1.8**	12	53	**1.8**	24	76	**0.4**	14	58	**1.8**
Paris	4	39	**0.2**	10	50	**0.2**	19	67	**0.2**	12	53	**0.2**
Prague	-2	29	**0.8**	7	45	**1.4**	17	63	**2.6**	8	47	**1.2**
Rome	8	47	**3.2**	13	55	**2.6**	75	75	**.6**	18	64	**4.5**
Vienna	0	32	**1.5**	9	49	**2**	20	68	**2.9**	11	51	**1.9**

DOCUMENTS AND FORMALITIES

Information on European **consular services** at home, as well as foreign consular services in Europe, is located in individual country chapters.

ENTRANCE REQUIREMENTS.
Passport (p. 18). Required for all citizens visiting any Western European country.
Visa (p. 19). Most Western European countries require visas for citizens of South Africa, but not for citizens of Australia, Canada, Ireland, New Zealand, the UK or the US (for stays shorter than three months).
Inoculations (p. 27). Travelers to Western Europe are recommended to be up to date on vaccines for measles, mumps, rubella, diptheria, tetanus, pertussis, polio, haemophilus influenza B, hepatitis B, and hepatitis A.
Work Permit (p. 19). Required for all foreigners planning to work in Western Europe, except for citizens of EU member countries.
Driving Permit (p. 55). An International Driving Permit is required for all those planning to drive.

PASSPORTS

REQUIREMENTS. Citizens of Australia, Canada, Ireland, New Zealand, South Africa, the UK, and the US need valid passports to enter Western European countries and to re-enter their own countries. Most countries do not allow entrance if the holder's passport expires in under six months. Returning home with an expired passport is illegal, and may result in a fine.

PHOTOCOPIES. Be sure to photocopy the page of your passport with your photo, passport number, and other identifying information, as well as any visas, travel insurance policies, plane tickets, or traveler's check serial numbers. Carry one set of copies in a safe place, apart from the originals, and leave another set at home. Consulates also recommend that you carry an expired passport or an official copy of your birth certificate in a part of your baggage separate from other documents.

LOST PASSPORTS. If you lose your passport, immediately notify the local police and the nearest embassy or consulate of your home government. To expedite its replacement, you will need to know all information previously recorded and show ID and proof of citizenship. In some cases, a replacement may take weeks to process, and may be valid only for a limited time. Any visas stamped in your old passport will be irretrievably lost. In an emergency, ask for immediate temporary traveling papers that will permit you to re-enter your home country. Your passport is a public document belonging to your nation's government. You may have to surrender it to a foreign government official, but if you don't get it back in a reasonable amount of time (24hr.), inform your nearest embassy or consulate.

NEW PASSPORTS. File any new passport or renewal applications well in advance of your departure date. Most passport offices offer rush services for a steep fee. Citizens living abroad who need a passport or renewal should contact the nearest consular service of their home country.

Australia: (☎ 13 12 32; email passports.australia@dfat.gov.au; www.dfat.gov.au/passports.) Apply for a passport at a post office, passport office (all state capitals and Newcastle), or overseas diplomatic mission. Passports AUS$128 (32-page) or AUS$192 (64-page); valid for 10 years. Children AUS$64 (32-page) or AUS$96 (64-page); valid for 5 years.

Canada: Canadian Passport Office, Department of Foreign Affairs and International Trade, Ottawa, ON K1A OG3 (☎ (800) 567-6868 or (613) 994-3500; www.dfait-maeci.gc.ca/passport). Applications available at passport offices, Canadian missions, and post offices. Passports CDN$60; valid for 5 years.

Ireland: Pick up an application at a *Garda* station or post office, or request one from a passport office. Then apply by mail to the Department of Foreign Affairs, Passport Office, Molesworth St., Dublin 2 (☎ (01) 671 1633; fax 671 1092; www.irlgov.ie/iveagh), or the Passport Office, Irish Life Building, 1A South Mall, Cork (☎ (021) 27 25 25). Passports IR£45; valid for 10 years. Under 18 or over 65 IR£10; valid for 3 years.

New Zealand: Send applications to the Passport Office, Department of International Affairs, P.O. Box 10526, Wellington (☎ (0800) 22 50 50 or (04) 474 8100; fax (04) 474 8010; www.passports.govt.nz; email passports@dia.govt.nz). Standard processing time is 10 working days. Passports NZ$80; valid for 10 years. Children NZ$40; valid for 5 years. 3-day "urgent service" NZ$160; children NZ $120.

South Africa: Department of Home Affairs. Passports are issued only in Pretoria, but all applications must still be submitted or forwarded to the nearest South African consulate. Processing time is 3 months or more. Passports around SAR80; valid for 10 years. Under 16 around SAR60; valid for 5 years. For more information, check out http://usaembassy.southafrica.net/VisaForms/Passport/Passport2000.html.

United Kingdom: Info ☎ (0870) 521 0410; www.open.gov.uk/ukpass/ukpass.htm. Get an application from a passport office, main post office, travel agent, or online (for UK residents only) at www.ukpa.gov.uk/forms/f_app_pack.htm. Then apply by mail or in person at a passport office. Passports UK£28; valid for 10 years. Under-15 UK£14.80; valid for 5 years. The process takes about 4 weeks; faster service is an additional £12.

United States: (☎ (202) 647-0518; www.travel.state.gov/passport_services.html.) Apply at any federal or state courthouse, authorized post office, or US Passport Agency (in most major cities); see the Government, State Department section of the telephone book or a post office for addresses. Processing takes 3-4 weeks. New passports US$60; valid for 10 years. Under 16 US$40; valid for 5 years. Passports may be renewed by mail or in person for US$40. Add US$35 for 3-day expedited service.

> **ONE EUROPE.** The idea of European unity has come a long way since 1958, when the European Economic Community (EEC) was created in order to promote solidarity and cooperation between its six founding states. Since then, the EEC has become the European Union (EU), with political, legal, and economic institutions spanning 15 member states: Austria, Belgium, Denmark, Finland, France, Germany, Greece, Ireland, Italy, Luxembourg, the Netherlands, Portugal, Spain, Sweden, and the UK.
>
> What does this have to do with the average non-EU tourist? Well, 1999 established **freedom of movement** across 14 European countries— Iceland, Norway, and the entire EU minus Denmark, Ireland, and the UK. This means that border controls between participating countries have been abolished, and visa policies harmonized. While you're still required to carry a passport (or government-issued ID card for EU citizens) when crossing an internal border, once you've been admitted into one country, you're free to travel to all participating states. Britain and Ireland have also formed a **common travel area,** abolishing passport controls between the UK and the Republic of Ireland, meaning that the only times you'll see a border guard within the EU are traveling between the British Isles and the Continent—and of course, in and out of Denmark.
>
> For more important consequences of the EU for travelers, see **The Euro** (p. 21) and **European Customs** (p. 20).

VISAS AND WORK PERMITS

VISAS. Some countries require a visa—a stamp, sticker, or insert in your passport specifying the purpose of your travel and the permitted duration of your stay—in addition to a valid passport for entrance. Most standard visas cost US$10-70, are valid for one to three months, and must be validated within six months to one year from the date of issue. The countries covered by *Let's Go: Western Europe 2001* do not require visas for citizens of Australia, Canada, Ireland, New Zealand, the UK, or the US (for stays shorter than three months). All of the countries do require visas for South African citizens, except for the UK, Ireland, and Switzerland. Travelers to Andorra should contact a French or Spanish embassy for more info, while those going to Liechtenstein should contact a Swiss embassy with any inquiries.

The visa requirements above only apply to stays shorter than three months. If you plan to stay longer than 90 days, or if you plan to work or study abroad, your requirements will differ (see **Alternatives to Tourism,** p. 64). In any case, check with the nearest embassy or consulate of your desired destination for up-to-date info. US citizens can also consult www.travel.state.gov/foreignentryreqs.html

IDENTIFICATION

When you travel, always carry two or more forms of identification on your person, including at least one photo ID; a passport combined with a driver's license or birth certificate is usually adequate. Many establishments, especially banks, may require several IDs in order to cash traveler's checks. Never carry all your forms of ID together; split them up in case of theft or loss. It is useful to bring extra passport-size photos to affix to the various IDs or passes you may acquire along the way.

STUDENT AND TEACHER IDENTIFICATION. The **International Student Identity Card (ISIC),** the most widely accepted form of student ID, provides discounts on sights, accommodations, food, and transport. The ISIC is preferable to an institution-specific card (such as a university ID) because it is more likely to be recognized (and honored) abroad. All cardholders have access to a 24-hour emergency helpline for medical, legal, and financial emergencies (in North America ☎ (877) 370-ISIC, elsewhere call US collect +1 (715) 345-0505), and US cardholders are also eligible for insurance benefits (see **Insurance,** p. 31). Many student travel agencies issue ISICs, including STA Travel in Australia and New Zealand; Travel CUTS in Canada; usit in the Republic of Ireland and Northern Ireland; SASTS in South Africa; Campus Travel and STA Travel in the UK; Council Travel (www.counciltravel.com/idcards/default.asp) and STA Travel in the US (see p. 41). The fee is AUS$13, UK£5, or US$22. For more info, contact the **International Student Travel Confederation (ISTC),** Herengracht 479, 1017 BS Amsterdam, Netherlands (☎ +31 (20) 421 28 00; fax 421 28 10; email istcinfo@istc.org; www.istc.org).

YOUTH IDENTIFICATION. The **International Student Travel Confederation** issues a discount card to travelers who are 25 years old or under, but are not students. This one-year **International Youth Travel Card** (IYTC; formerly the **GO 25** Card) offers many of the benefits as the ISIC. Most organizations that sell ISIC sell the IYTC (US$22).

CUSTOMS

Upon entering a country, you must declare certain items from abroad and pay a duty on the value of those articles that exceeds that country's allowance. Note that goods and gifts purchased at **duty-free** shops abroad are not exempt from duty or sales tax at your point of return and thus must be declared as well; "duty-free" merely means that you need not pay a tax in the country of purchase. Upon returning home, you must similarly declare all articles acquired abroad and pay a duty on the value of articles in excess of your home country's allowance. In order to expedite your return, make a list of any valuables brought from home and register them with customs before traveling abroad. Also be sure to keep receipts for all goods acquired abroad.

EUROPEAN CUSTOMS. As well as moving freely within the EU (see p. 21), travelers can also move freely with goods. This means that there are no customs controls at internal EU borders (i.e., you can take the blue customs channel at the airport), and travelers are free to transport whatever legal substances they like as long as it is for their own personal (non-commercial) use—up to 800 cigarettes, 10L of spirits, 90L of wine (60L of sparkling wine), and 110L of beer. You should also be aware that **duty-free** shopping was abolished on June 30, 1999 for travel between EU member states; however, travelers between the EU and the rest of the world still get a duty-free allowance when passing through customs.

FURTHER RESOURCES

Australia: Australian Customs National Information Line (in Australia ☎ (01) 30 03 63, from elsewhere call +61 (2) 6275 6666; www.customs.gov.au).

Canada: Canadian Customs, 2265 St. Laurent Blvd., Ottawa, ON K1G 4K3 (☎ (800) 461-9999 (24hr.) or (613) 993-0534; www.revcan.ca).

Ireland: Customs Information Office, Irish Life Centre, Lower Abbey St., Dublin 1 (☎ (01) 878 8811; fax 878 0836; taxes@revenue.iol.ie; www.revenue.ie/customs.htm).

New Zealand: New Zealand Customhouse, 17-21 Whitmore St., Box 2218, Wellington (☎ (04) 473 6099; fax 473 7370; www.customs.govt.nz).

South Africa: Commissioner for Customs and Excise, Privat Bag X47, Pretoria 0001 (☎ (012) 314 9911; fax 328 6478; www.gov.za).

United Kingdom: Her Majesty's Customs and Excise, Passenger Enquiry Team, Wayfarer House, Great South West Road, Feltham, Middlesex TW14 8NP (☎ (020) 8910 3744; fax 8910 3933; www.hmce.gov.uk).

United States: US Customs Service, 1330 Pennsylvania Ave. NW, Washington, D.C. 20229 (☎ (202) 354-1000; fax 354-1010; www.customs.gov).

ESSENTIALS

MONEY

CURRENCY AND EXCHANGE

As a general rule, it's cheaper to convert money in Europe than at home. However, you should bring enough foreign currency to last for the first 24 to 72 hours of a trip to avoid being penniless should you arrive after bank hours or on a holiday. Travelers from the US can get foreign currency from the comfort of home: **International Currency Express** (☎ (888) 278-6628) delivers foreign currency or traveler's checks overnight (US$15) or on the 2nd-day (US$12) at competitive exchange rates.

When changing money abroad, try to go only to banks or bureaux de change that have at most a 5% margin between their buy and sell prices. Since you lose money with every transaction, convert large sums (unless the currency is depreciating rapidly), **but no more than you'll need.**

If you use traveler's checks or bills, carry some in small denominations (the equivalent of US$50 or less) for times when you are forced to exchange money at disadvantageous rates, but bring a range of denominations since charges may be levied per check cashed. Store your money in a variety of forms; ideally, you will at any given time be carrying some cash, some traveler's checks, and an ATM and/or credit card. All travelers should also consider carrying some US dollars or German marks (about US$50 or DM95 worth), which are often preferred by local tellers.

THE EURO. Since 1999, the official currency of 11 members of the European Union—Austria, Belgium, Finland, France, Germany, Greece, Ireland, Italy, Luxembourg, the Netherlands, Portugal, and Spain—has been the euro. But you shouldn't throw out your francs, pesetas, and Deutschmarks just yet; actual euro banknotes and coins won't be available until January 1, 2002, and the old national currencies will remain legal tender for six months after that (though July 1, 2002).

While you might not be able to pay for a coffee and get your change in euros yet, the currency has some important—and positive—consequences for travelers hitting more than one euro-zone country. For one thing, money-changers across the euro-zone are obliged to exchange money at the official, fixed rate (see below), and at no commission (though they may still charge a small service fee). So now you can change your guilders into escudos and your escudos into lire without losing fistfuls of money on every transaction. Second, euro-denominated travelers cheques allow you to pay for goods and services across the euro-zone, again at the official rate and commission-free.

The exchange rate between euro-zone currencies was permanently fixed on January 1, 1999 at 1 EUR = 40.3399 BEF (Belgian francs) = 1.95583 DEM (German marks) = 166.386 ESP (Spanish pesetas) = 6.55957 FRF (French francs) = 0.787564 IEP (Irish pounds) = 1936.27 ITL (Italian liras) = 40.3399 LUF (Luxembourg francs) = 2.20371 NLG (Dutch guilders) = 13.7603 ATS (Austrian schillings) = 200.482 PTE (Portuguese escudos) = 5.94573 FIM (Finnish markka). (Greek Drachmas had not been fixed into the euro exchange rate at the time of publication). For more info, see www.europa.eu.int.

For **currency exchange information** please see the opening page of each country chapter. Check a large newspaper or the web (e.g. finance.yahoo.com or www.bloomberg.com) for the latest exchange rates.

TRAVELER'S CHECKS

Traveler's checks (**American Express** and **Visa** are the most recognized) are one of the safest and least troublesome means of carrying funds. Several agencies and banks sell them for a small commission. Each agency provides refunds if your checks are lost or stolen, and many provide additional services, such as toll-free refund hotlines abroad, emergency message services, and stolen credit card assistance.

Money From Home In Minutes.

If you're stuck for cash on your travels, don't panic. Millions of people trust Western Union to transfer money in minutes to 176 countries and over 78,000 locations worldwide. Our record of safety and reliability is second to none. For more information, call Western Union: USA 1-800-325-6000, Canada 1-800-235-0000. Wherever you are, you're never far from home.

www.westernunion.com

WESTERN UNION | MONEY TRANSFER®

The fastest way to send money worldwide.

©2000 Western Union Holdings, Inc. All Rights Reserved.

While traveling, keep check receipts and a record of which checks you've cashed separate from the checks themselves. Also leave a list of check numbers with someone at home. Never countersign checks until you're ready to cash them, and always bring your passport with you to cash them. If your checks are lost or stolen, immediately contact a refund center (of the company that issued your checks) to be reimbursed; they may require a police report verifying the loss or theft. Less-touristed countries may not have refund centers at all, in which case you might have to wait to be reimbursed. Ask about toll-free refund hotlines and the location of refund centers when purchasing checks, and always carry emergency cash.

American Express: (in Australia ☎ (800) 251 902 ; in New Zealand (0800) 441 068; in the UK (0800) 521 313; in the US and Canada (800) 221-7282;Elsewhere call US collect +1 (801) 964-6665; www.aexp.com.) Traveler's checks are available in ten currencies at 1-4% commission at AmEx offices and banks, commission-free at AAA offices (see p. 55). *Cheques for Two* can be signed by either of 2 people traveling together.

Citicorp: (In the US and Canada ☎ (800) 645-6556; in Europe, the Middle East, or Africa call the UK +44 (020) 7508 7007; elsewhere call US collect +1 (813) 623-1709.) Call 24hr. Traveler's checks available in 7 currencies at 1-2% commission.

Thomas Cook MasterCard: (In the US and Canada ☎ (800) 223-7373; in the UK call (0800) 62 21 01; elsewhere call UK collect +44 (1733) 31 89 50.) Checks available in 13 currencies at 2% commission. Thomas Cook offices cash checks commission-free.

Visa: In the US ☎ (800) 227-6811; in the UK call (0800) 89 50 78; elsewhere call UK collect +44 (1733) 31 89 49. Call for the location of their nearest office.

CREDIT CARDS

Where they are accepted, credit cards often offer superior exchange rates—up to five percent better than the retail rate used by banks and other currency exchange establishments. Credit cards may also offer services such as insurance or emergency help, and are sometimes required to reserve hotel rooms or rental cars. **MasterCard** (a.k.a. EuroCard or Access in Europe) and Visa (a.k.a. Carte Bleue or Barclaycard) are the most welcomed; **American Express** cards work at some ATMs and at AmEx offices and major airports.

Credit cards are also useful for **cash advances,** which allow you to withdraw local currency from associated banks and ATMs throughout Western Europe instantly. However, transaction fees for all credit card advances (up to US$10 per advance, plus 2-3% extra on foreign transactions after conversion) tend to make credit cards a more costly way of withdrawing cash than ATMs or traveler's checks. In an emergency, however, the transaction fee may prove worth the cost. To be eligible for an advance, you'll need to get a **Personal Identification Number (PIN)** from your credit card company (see **Cash (ATM) Cards,** below). Be sure to check with your credit card company before you leave home, though; in certain circumstances companies have started to charge a foreign transaction fee.

CREDIT CARD COMPANIES. Visa (US ☎ (800) 336-8472) and **MasterCard** (US ☎ (800) 307-7309) are issued in cooperation with banks and other organizations. **American Express** (US ☎ (800) 843-2273) has an annual fee of up to US$55. AmEx cardholders may cash personal checks at AmEx offices abroad, access an emergency medical and legal assistance hotline (24hr.; in North America ☎ (800) 554-2639, elsewhere call US collect +1 (202) 554-2639), and enjoy American Express Travel Service benefits (including plane, hotel, and car rental reservation changes; baggage loss and flight insurance; mailgram and international cable services; and held mail). The **Discover Card** (US ☎ (800) 347-2683, elsewhere ☎ US +1 (801) 902-3100) offers small cashback bonuses, but it may not be readily accepted.

CASH (ATM) CARDS

Cash cards—popularly called ATM cards—are widespread in Western Europe. Depending on the system that your home bank uses, you can most likely access your personal bank account from abroad. ATMs get the same wholesale exchange rate as credit cards, but there is often a limit on the amount of money you can with-

ESSENTIALS

draw per day (around US$500). There is typically also a surcharge of US$1-5 per withdrawal. Be sure to memorize your PIN code in numeric form since machines elsewhere often don't have letters on their keys. Also, if your PIN is longer than four digits, ask your bank whether you need a new number. The two major international money networks are **Cirrus** (US ☎ (800) 424-7787) and **PLUS** (US ☎ (800) 843-7587). To locate ATMs in Europe, call the above numbers, or consult www.visa.com/pd/atm or www.mastercard.com/atm.

GETTING MONEY FROM HOME

Western Union: Travelers from Canada, the UK, and the US can wire money abroad through Western Union's international money transfer services. (In Canada ☎ (800) 235-0000; in the UK, (0800) 833 833; in the US, (800) 325-6000.) The rates for sending cash are generally US$10-11 cheaper than with a credit card, and the money is usually available at the place you're sending it to within an hour. Western Union maintains offices throughout Europe; to find the nearest location, consult www.westernunion.com.

US State Department (US Citizens only): In dire emergencies only, the US State Department will forward money within hours to the nearest consular office, which will then disburse it according to instructions for a US$15 fee. Contact the Overseas Citizens Service, American Citizens Services, Consular Affairs, Room 4811, US Department of State, Washington, D.C. 20520 (☎ (202) 647-5225; nights, Sundays, and holidays 647-4000; http://travel.state.gov).

COSTS

The cost of your trip will vary considerably, depending on where you go, how you travel, and where you stay. The single biggest cost of your trip will probably be your round-trip (return) **airfare** to Europe (see p. 40); a **railpass** would be another major pre-departure expense (see p. 47). Before you go, spend some time calculating a reasonable per-day **budget** that will meet your needs. To give you a general idea, a bare-bones day in Western Europe (camping or sleeping in hostels, buying food at supermarkets) would cost about US$25-35, excluding the cost of a plane ticket and railpass; a slightly more comfortable day (sleeping in hostels and the occasional budget hotel, eating one meal a day at a restaurant, going out at night) would run US$35-50; and for a luxurious day, the sky's the limit. Countries such as Britain, France, and Switzerland tend to be more costly for tourists, while Spain and Greece are relatively inexpensive alternatives. Also, don't forget to factor in emergency reserve funds (at least US$200) when planning how much money you'll need.

TIPS FOR STAYING ON A BUDGET

Considering that saving just a few dollars a day over the course of your trip might pay for days or weeks of additional travel, the art of penny-pinching is well worth learning. Learn to take advantage of freebies: for example, museums will typically be free once a week or once a month, and cities often host free open-air concerts and cultural events (especially in the summer). Bring a sleepsack (see p. 36) to save on sheet charges in European hostels, and do your laundry in the sink (unless you're explicitly prohibited from doing so). You can split accommodations costs (in hotels and some hostels) with trustworthy fellow travelers; multi-bed rooms almost always work out cheaper per person than singles. The same principle will also work for cutting down on the cost of restaurant meals. You can also buy food in supermarkets instead of eating out; you'd be surprised how tasty (and cheap) simple bread can be with cheese or spread.

With that said, don't go overboard with your budget obsession. Though staying within your budget is important, don't do so at the expense of your sanity or health. Going to Munich without hitting a beer garden or visiting London without seeing a play simply because it's "out of your budget" defeats the purpose of your visit.

TAXES

The European Union imposes a **value-added tax (VAT)** on goods and services purchased within the EU (usually included in the sticker price). Non-EU citizens may obtain a **refund** for taxes paid on retail goods, but not those on services. As the VAT in Europe ranges from 15 to 25%, you may find it worth the hassle of filing for a refund. In order to do so, you must first obtain a Tax-free Shopping Cheque, available from shops sporting the blue, white, and silver Europe Tax-free Shopping logo, and then save the receipts from all of the purchases for which you want to be refunded. Upon leaving the last EU country on your itinerary, present your (unused) goods, invoices, and Tax-free Shopping Cheque to Customs for validation, then pick up an immediate cash refund at an ETS cash refund office or file for a refund once back home. Keep in mind that goods must be taken out of the country within three months of the end of the month of purchase, and that some stores require minimum purchase amounts to become eligible for refund. For more information on tax-free shopping, visit www.globalrefund.com.

SAFETY AND SECURITY

While tourists may be more vulnerable than the average individual, a few simple precautions can help you avoid problems. There has been violence associated with the IRA and British peacekeeping efforts in Northern Ireland which has been a problem area in recent years. Be aware that certain disgruntled groups, like the skinheads in Germany and Hungary, Basque terrorists in Spain, the Mafia in Sicily, and the *Romany* (also known as Gypsies) in Paris may pose a problem. See specific country introductions for more information, as well as **Specific Concerns** (p. 60), and **Travel Advisories** (p. 26).

EXPLORING. To avoid unwanted attention, try to blend in as much as possible. Respecting local customs may placate would-be hecklers. Familiarize yourself with your surroundings before setting out, and carry yourself with confidence; if you must check a map on the street, duck into a shop. If you are traveling alone, be sure someone at home knows your itinerary, and **never admit that you're traveling alone.** When walking at night, stick to busy, well-lit streets and avoid dark alleyways. Do not attempt to cross through parks, parking lots, or other large, deserted areas. Look for children playing, women walking in the open, and other signs of an active community. If you feel uncomfortable, leave as quickly and directly as you can, but don't allow fear of the unknown to turn you into a hermit. Careful, persistent exploration will build confidence and make your stay even more rewarding.

GETTING AROUND. Trains are very safe throughout most of Western Europe, and second-class travel is more than comfortable. **Overnight trains** put you at the most risk, as your vigilance is limited while you are sleeping. For tips on protecting your valuables on overnight trains and buses, see p. 27. If you are using a **car,** learn local driving signals and wear a seatbelt. Children under 40 lbs. should ride only in a specially-designed carseat, available for a small fee from most car rental agencies. Study route maps before leaving. If your car breaks down, wait for the police to assist you. For long drives, invest in a cellular phone and a roadside assistance program (see p. 55). Be sure to park your vehicle in a garage or well-traveled area, and use a steering wheel locking device in larger cities. **Sleeping in your car** is one of the most dangerous (and often illegal) ways to get your rest. *Let's Go* does not recommend **hitchhiking** under any circumstances, particularly for women (see p. 47).

SELF DEFENSE. There is no sure-fire way to avoid all the threatening situations you might encounter when you travel, but a good self-defense course will give you concrete ways to react to unwanted advances. **Impact, Prepare,** and **Model Mugging** can refer you to local self-defense courses in the US (☎ (800) 345-5425) and Vancouver (☎ (604) 878-3838). Workshops (2-3hr.) start at US$50; full courses run US$350-500. Both women and men are welcome.

ESSENTIALS

FINANCIAL SECURITY

PROTECTING YOUR VALUABLES. There are a few steps you can take to minimize the financial risk associated with traveling. First, **bring as little with you as possible.** Leave expensive watches, jewelry, cameras, and electronic equipment (like your Discman) at home; chances are you'd break them, lose them, or get sick of lugging them around anyway. Second, buy a few combination **padlocks** to secure your belongings either in your pack—which you should **never leave unattended**—or in a hostel or train station locker. Third, **carry as little cash as possible;** instead carry traveler's checks and ATM/credit cards, keeping them in a **money belt**—not a "fanny pack"—along with your passport and ID cards. Fourth, **keep a small cash reserve separate from your primary stash.** This should entail about US$50 (US$ or German DM is best) sewn into or stored in the depths of your pack, along with your traveler's check numbers and important photocopies.

CON ARTISTS AND PICKPOCKETS. Among the more colorful aspects of large cities are con artists. They often work in groups, and children are among the most effective. They possess an innumerable range of ruses. Beware of certain classics: sob stories that require money, rolls of bills "found" on the street, mustard spilled (or saliva spit) onto your shoulder to distract you while they snatch your bag. Don't ever hand over your passport to someone whose authority you question (ask to accompany them to a police station if they insist), and don't ever let your passport out of your sight. Similarly, don't let your bag out of sight; never trust a "station-porter" who insists on carrying your bag or stowing it in the baggage compartment or a "new friend" who offers to guard your bag while you buy a train ticket or use the restroom. Beware of pickpockets in city crowds, especially on public transportation. Also, be alert in public telephone booths. If you must say your calling card number, do so very quietly; if you punch it in, make sure no one can look over your shoulder. Cities such as Rome, Amsterdam, and Barcelona are known to be particularly bad for these dangers, so be alert. Even in relatively safe areas, it is wise to be conscious to secure valuables.

ACCOMMODATIONS. Never leave your belongings unattended; crime occurs in even the most demure-looking hostel or hotel. Bring your own **padlock** for hostel lockers, and don't ever store valuables in any locker.

TRANSPORTATION. Be particularly careful on **buses** and **trains;** horror stories abound about determined thieves who wait for travelers to fall asleep. Carry your backpack in front of you where you can see it. When traveling with others, sleep in alternate shifts. When alone, use good judgement in selecting a train compartment: never stay in an empty one, and use a lock to secure your pack to the luggage rack. Try to sleep on top bunks with your luggage stored above you (if not in bed with you), and keep important documents and other valuables on your person. If traveling by **car,** don't leave valuables (such as radios or luggage) in it while you are away.

If your tape deck or radio is removable, hide it in the trunk or take it with you. If it isn't, at least conceal it. Similarly, hide baggage in the trunk—although savvy thieves can tell if a car is heavily loaded by the way it sits on its tires.

DRUGS AND ALCOHOL

Drug and alcohol laws vary widely throughout Europe: for example, in the Netherlands you can buy soft drugs on the open market. You're subject to the laws of the country in which you travel when you're abroad, so familiarize yourself with those laws before leaving. If you carry **prescription drugs,** it is vital to have both a copy of the prescriptions themselves and a note from a doctor, especially at border crossings. **Avoid public drunkenness;** it is culturally unacceptable and against the law in many countries, and can also jeopardize your safety.

TROUBLE WITH THE LAW. Travelers who run into trouble with the law, both accidentally and knowingly, do not carry over the rights of their home country; instead, they have the same rights as a citizen of the country they are in. Law mandates that police notify the embassy of a person's home country if they are arrested. Once in custody, a traveler is entitled to a visit from an abroad Consular officer. These officers can provide lists of local law firms, information on the local legal system, and can contact friends and family. They cannot, however, demand the release of citizens abroad. Being mindful of a country's laws before setting out to travel is the best way to avoid trouble with the law. US citizens should check out the Department of State's website (www.state.gov) for more information.

HEALTH AND INSURANCE

Common sense is the simplest prescription for good health while you travel. Travelers complain most often about their feet and their gut, so take precautionary measures: drink lots of fluids to prevent dehydration and constipation, wear sturdy, broken-in shoes and clean socks, and use talcum powder to keep your feet dry.

BEFORE YOU GO

Preparation can help minimize the likelihood of contracting a disease and maximize the chances of receiving effective health care in the event of an emergency. For tips on packing a basic **first-aid kit** and other health essentials, see p. 32.

In your **passport,** write the names of any people you wish to be contacted in case of a medical emergency, and also list any allergies or medical conditions of which you would want doctors to be aware. Matching a prescription to a foreign equivalent is not always easy, safe, or possible. Carry up-to-date, legible prescriptions or a statement from your doctor stating the medication's trade name, manufacturer, chemical name, and dosage. While traveling, be sure to keep all medication with you in your carry-on luggage.

IMMUNIZATIONS AND PRECAUTIONS

Travelers over two years old should be sure that the following vaccines are up to date: MMR (for measles, mumps, and rubella); DTaP or Td (for diptheria, tetanus, and pertussis), OPV (for polio), HbCV (for haemophilus influenza B), and HBV (for hepatitus B). Hepatitis A vaccine and/or immune globulin (IG) is recommended for travelers going to Eastern or Southern Europe. While yellow fever is only endemic to parts of South America and sub-Saharan Africa, many countries may deny entrance to travelers arriving from these zones without a certificate of vaccination. For more **region-specific information** on vaccinations requirements, as well as recommendations on immunizations and prophylaxis, consult the CDC (see below) in the US or the equivalent in your home country, and check with a doctor for guidance.

USEFUL ORGANIZATIONS AND PUBLICATIONS

The US **Centers for Disease Control and Prevention** (**CDC**; ☎ (877) FYI-TRIP; www.cdc.gov/travel), which is an excellent source of information for travelers, and maintains an international fax information service. The CDC's comprehensive booklet *Health Information for International Travelers*, an annual rundown of disease, immunization, and general health advice, is free on the website or US$22 via the Government Printing Office (☎ (202) 512-1800). The **US State Department** (http://travel.state.gov) compiles Consular Information Sheets on health, entry requirements, and other issues for various countries. For quick information on health and other travel warnings, call the **Overseas Citizens' Services** (☎ (202) 647-5225; after-hours 647-4000) For information on medical evacuation services and travel insurance firms, see http://travel.state.gov/medical.html. The **British Foreign and Commonwealth Office** also gives health warnings for individual countries (www.fco.gov.uk).

MEDICAL ASSISTANCE ON THE ROAD

If you are concerned about being able to access medical support while traveling, there are special support services you may employ. The *MedPass* from **Global Emergency Medical Services (GEMS)**, 2001 Westside Dr., #120, Alpharetta, GA 30004, USA (☎ (800) 860-1111; www.globalems.com), provides 24-hour international medical assistance, support, and medical evacuation resources. The **International Association for Medical Assistance to Travelers** (**IAMAT**; US ☎ (716) 754-4883, Canada ☎ (416) 652-0137, New Zealand ☎ (03) 352 2053; www.sentex.net/~iamat) has free membership, lists English-speaking doctors worldwide, and offers detailed info on immunization requirements and sanitation. If your regular **insurance** policy does not cover travel abroad, you may wish to purchase additional coverage (see p. 31).

Those with medical conditions (diabetes, allergies to antibiotics, epilepsy, heart conditions) may want to obtain a stainless-steel **Medic Alert** ID tag (first-year US$35, $15 per year thereafter), which identifies the condition and gives a 24-hour collect-call number. Contact the Medic Alert Foundation, 2323 Colorado Ave, Turlock, CA 95382, USA (☎ (800) 825-3785; www.medicalert.org). The **American Diabetes Association,** 1660 Duke St., Alexandria, VA 22314, USA (☎ (800) 232-3472), offers copies of the article "Travel and Diabetes" and a multilingual diabetic ID card.

ON THE ROAD

ENVIRONMENTAL HAZARDS

Heat exhaustion and dehydration: While trekking around Mediterranean countries such as Spain, Portugal, Greece, or Italy, where summer temperatures easily reach highs over 90°F (30°C), be aware of the possibility of heat exhaustion. Heat exhaustion is characterized by dehydration and salt deficiency, can lead to fatigue, headaches, and wooziness. Avoid it by drinking plenty of fluids, eating salty foods (e.g. crackers), and limiting dehydrating beverages (e.g. alcohol, coffee, tea, and caffeinated soda). Continuous heat stress can eventually lead to **heatstroke,** characterized by a rising temperature, severe headache, and cessation of sweating. Victims should be cooled off with wet towels and taken to a doctor.

Hypothermia and frostbite: Europe is a continent of many climates, and in the Alps, temperatures can fall to the freezing point even in the summer months. A rapid drop in body temperature is the clearest sign of overexposure to cold. Victims may also shiver, feel exhausted, have poor coordination or slurred speech, hallucinate, or suffer amnesia. **Do not let hypothermia victims fall asleep,** or their body temperature will continue to drop. To avoid hypothermia, keep dry, wear layers, and stay out of the wind. When the temperature is below freezing, watch out for **frostbite.** If skin turns white, waxy, and cold, do not rub the area. Drink warm beverages, get dry, and slowly warm the area with dry fabric or steady body contact until a doctor is found.

High altitude: Allow your body a couple of days to adjust to less oxygen before exerting yourself. Note that alcohol is more potent and UV rays are stronger at high elevations.

INSECT-BORNE DISEASES

Many diseases are transmitted by insects—mainly mosquitoes, fleas, ticks, and lice. Be aware of insects in wet or forested areas, especially while hiking and camping. **Mosquitoes** are most active from dusk to dawn. Wear long pants and long sleeves, tuck long pants into socks, and buy a mosquito net. Use insect repellents, such as DEET, and soak or spray your gear with permethrin. Consider natural repellents that make you smelly to insects, like vitamin B-12 or garlic pills. Calamine lotion or topical cortisones (like Cortaid) may stop insect bites from itching, as can a bath with a half-cup of baking soda or oatmeal. **Ticks**—responsible for Lyme and other diseases—can be particularly dangerous in rural and forested regions. Pause periodically while walking to brush off ticks using a fine-toothed comb on your neck and scalp. Do not try to remove ticks by burning them or coating them with nail polish remover or petroleum jelly.

Tick-borne encephalitis: A viral infection of the central nervous system transmitted through tick bites and the consumption of unpasteurized dairy products. Occurs chiefly in wooded areas of Central and Western Europe. Symptoms can range from nothing to headaches and flu-like symptoms, to swelling of the brain (encephalitis). A vaccine is available in Western Europe which provides protection for about three years, but the immunization schedule is impractical for most tourists.

Lyme disease: A bacterial infection carried by ticks and marked by a circular bull's-eye rash of 2 inches or more surrounding the bite. Later symptoms include fever, headache, and aches and pains. Antibiotics are effective if administered early. Left untreated, Lyme disease can cause problems in joints, the heart, and the nervous system. If you find a tick, grasp the tick's head parts with tweezers as close to your skin as possible and apply slow traction. Removing a tick within 24 hours reduces risk of infection.

Leishmaniasis: A parasite transmitted by sand flies, leishmaniasis has been reported in Switzerland, Italy, Spain, and southern France. Common symptoms are fever, weakness, and swelling of the spleen. There is a treatment, but no vaccine.

FOOD- AND WATER-BORNE DISEASES

Prevention is the best cure: be sure that everything you eat is cooked properly and that the water you drink is clean. Unpeeled fruit and vegetables and tap water should be safe throughout most of Western Europe. Nevertheless, watch out for food from markets or street vendors that may have been cooked in unhygienic conditions.

Traveler's diarrhea: Results from drinking untreated water or eating uncooked foods; a temporary (and fairly common) reaction to the bacteria in new food ingredients. Symptoms include nausea, bloating, urgency, and malaise. Try quick-energy, non-sugary foods with protein and carbohydrates to keep your strength up. Over-the-counter anti-diarrheals (e.g. Imodium) may counteract the problems, but can complicate serious infections. The most dangerous side effect is dehydration; drink 8 oz. of water with ½ tsp. of sugar or honey and a pinch of salt, try uncaffeinated soft drinks, or munch on salted crackers. If you develop a fever or your symptoms don't go away after 4-5 days, consult a doctor. Consult a doctor for treatment of diarrhea in children.

Parasites: Microbes, tapeworms, etc. that hide in unsafe water and food. **Giardiasis,** for example, is acquired by drinking untreated water from streams or lakes all over the world (including Western Europe). Symptoms include swollen glands or lymph nodes, fever, rashes or itchiness, digestive problems, eye problems, and anemia. Boil water, wear shoes, avoid bugs, and eat only cooked food.

OTHER INFECTIOUS DISEASES

Rabies: Transmitted through the saliva of infected animals; fatal if untreated. By the time symptoms appear (thirst and muscle spasms), the disease is in its terminal stage. If you are bitten, wash the wound thoroughly, seek immediate medical care, and try to have the animal located. A rabies vaccine, which consists of 3 shots given over a 21-day period, is available, but is only semi-effective.

Hepatitis B: A viral infection of the liver transmitted via bodily fluids or needle-sharing. Symptoms may not surface until years after infection. Vaccinations are recommended for health-care workers, sexually-active travelers, and anyone planning to seek medical treatment abroad. The 3-shot vaccination series must begin 6 months before traveling.

Hepatitis C: Like Hep B, but the mode of transmission differs. IV drug users, those with occupational exposure to blood, hemodialysis patients, and recipients of blood transfusions are at the highest risk, but the disease can also be spread through sexual contact or sharing items like razors and toothbrushes that may have traces of blood on them.

AIDS, HIV, STDS

The virus that leads to **Acquired Immune Deficiency Syndrome (AIDS)** is most easily transmitted through direct blood-to-blood contact with an HIV-positive person, but is most commonly transmitted by sexual intercourse. Never share intravenous drug, tattooing, or other needles, and take precautions to avoid any blood transfusions or injections while abroad. Take along a supply of latex condoms, which are often difficult to find on the road. Some countries, including Luxembourg, screen incoming travelers for HIV, primarily those planning extended visits for work or study, and deny entrance to those who test HIV-positive. For detailed information on AIDS in Europe, call the **US Centers for Disease Control's** 24-hour hotline at (800) 342-2437, or contact the **Joint United Nations Programme on HIV/AIDS (UNAIDS)**, 20 av. Appia 20, CH-1211 Geneva 27, Switzerland (☎ +41 (22) 791 36 66, fax 791 41 87). Council's brochure, *Travel Safe: AIDS and International Travel*, is available at all Council Travel offices and on their website (www.ciee.org/Isp/safety/travelsafe.htm).

Sexually transmitted diseases (STDs) such as gonorrhea, chlamydia, genital warts, syphilis, and herpes are easier to catch than HIV and can be just as deadly. **Hepatitis B** and **C** are also serious STDs (see **Other Infectious Diseases**, above). Though condoms may protect you from some STDs, oral or even tactile contact can lead to transmission. Warning signs include swelling, sores, bumps, or blisters on sex organs, the rectum, or the mouth; burning and pain during urination and bowel movements; itching around sex organs; swelling or redness of the throat; and flu-like symptoms. If these symptoms develop, see a doctor immediately.

WOMEN'S HEALTH

Women traveling in unsanitary conditions are vulnerable to **urinary tract** and **bladder infections,** common and very uncomfortable bacterial diseases that cause a burning sensation and painful (sometimes frequent) urination. To try to avoid these infections, drink plenty of vitamin-C-rich juice and clean water, and urinate frequently, especially right after intercourse.

Vaginal yeast infections may flare up in hot and humid climates. Wearing loosely fitting trousers or a skirt and cotton underwear will help, as will over-the-counter remedies like Monostat or Gynelotrimin. Bring supplies from home if you are prone to infection, as they may be difficult to find on the road. In a pinch, some travelers use a natural alternative such as a plain yogurt and lemon juice douche.

If you're on the pill or use a diaphragm, bring enough pills or contraceptive jelly, respectively, to allow for possible loss or extended stays. Condoms abroad also vary, so you might bring your favorite brand if you plan to be sexually active.

If you need an **abortion** while abroad, get in touch with the **International Planned Parenthood Federation,** European Regional Office, Regent's College Inner Circle, Regent's Park, London NW1 4NS (☎ (020) 74 87 79 00). In Germany, Pro Familia: Deutsche Gesellschaft Fur Familienplanung, Sexualpadagogik und Sexualberatung Stresemann-allee 3, D-60596 Frankfurt am Main (☎ 49 (69) 63 90 02). In France, contact the Mouvement Francais pour le Planning Familial, 4 Square Saint Irenee, F-75011, Paris (☎ 33 (1) 48 07 29 10). In Italy, go to the Unione Italiana Centri Educazione Matrimoniale e Prematrimoniale (UICEMP), Via Eugenio Chiesa 1, Milan 20122 (☎ 39 (02) 5410 2020).

INSURANCE

Travel insurance covers four basic areas: medical problems, property loss, trip cancellation/interruption, and emergency evacuation. Although your regular insurance policies may extend to travel-related accidents, you might consider travel insurance if the cost of potential trip cancellation/interruption or emergency medical evacuation is greater than you can absorb. Prices for travel insurance purchased separately generally run about US$50 per week for full coverage, while trip cancellation/interruption may be purchased separately at a rate of about US$5.50 per US$100 of coverage.

Medical insurance (especially university policies) often covers costs incurred abroad; check with your provider. **US Medicare** does not cover foreign travel. **Canadians** are protected by their home province's health insurance plan for up to 90 days after leaving the country; check with the provincial Ministry of Health or Health Plan Headquarters for details. **Australians** traveling in the UK, the Netherlands, Italy, and Malta are entitled to many of the services that they would receive at home as part of the Reciprocal Health Care Agreement. **Homeowners' insurance** (or your family's coverage) often covers theft during travel and loss of travel documents (passport, plane ticket, railpass, etc.) up to US$500. EU citizens should ask their insurer for an E111 form, which covers their emergency care in other EU countries. EU travelers to Great Britain do not need the E111 form, where the National Insurance system will provide free medical treatment.

ISIC and **ITIC** (see p. 19) provide basic insurance benefits to US citizens, including US$100 per day of in-hospital sickness for up to 60 days, US$3000 of accident-related medical reimbursement, and US$25,000 for emergency medical transport. Cardholders have access to a toll-free 24-hour helpline for medical, legal, and financial emergencies overseas (in US and Canada ☎ (877) 370-4742; elsewhere call US collect +1 (713) 342-4104). **American Express** (US ☎ (800) 528-4800) grants most cardholders automatic car rental insurance (collision and theft, but not liability) and ground travel accident coverage of US$100,000 on flight purchases made with the card.

INSURANCE PROVIDERS. Council and **STA** (see p. 41) offer a range of plans that can supplement your basic coverage. Other private insurance providers in the **US and Canada** include: **Access America** (☎ (800) 284-8300); **Berkely Group/Carefree Travel Insurance** (☎ (800) 323-3149; www.berkely.com); **Globalcare Travel Insurance** (☎ (800) 821-2488; www.globalcare-cocco.com); and **Travel Assistance International** (☎ (800) 821-2828; www.worldwide-assistance.com). Providers in the **UK** include **Campus Travel** (☎ (01865) 258 000) and **Columbus Travel Insurance** (☎ (020) 7375 0011). In **Australia,** try **CIC Insurance** (☎ 9202 8000).

PACKING

Pack light: Lay out only what you absolutely need, then take half the clothes and twice the money. The less you have, the less you have to lose (or store, or carry on your back). Any extra space left will be useful for any souvenirs or items you might pick up along the way. If you plan to do a lot of hiking, also see **Outdoors**, p. 36.

Important documents: Don't forget your **passport, traveler's checks, ATM** and/or **credit cards;** and adequate **ID** (see p. 19). Also check that you have any of the following that might apply to you: a **hosteling** membership card (see p. 33), **driver's license** (see p. 19), travel **insurance** forms, and/or **rail** or **bus pass** (see p. 47). It would be wise to make photocopies of all of these important documents to stash in a separate place, or to leave with family or friends in case of an emergency.

Luggage: If you plan to cover most of your itinerary by foot, a sturdy **frame backpack** is unbeatable. (For the basics on buying a pack, see p. 37.) Toting a **suitcase** or **trunk** is fine if you plan to live in one or two cities and explore from there, but a very bad idea if you're going to be moving around a lot. In addition to your main vessel, a **daypack** (a small backpack or courier bag) is a must.

ESSENTIALS

WALK LIKE A EUROPEAN Western Europeans have an uncanny ability to pick tourists out of a crowd. Perhaps it is because every American tourist is wearing khaki shorts, a white t-shirt, and a pair of Tevas. If you want to avoid this phenomenon, and you're ready to make the leap into Euro-chic, add this simple starter kit of must-haves to your wardrobe.

Adidas shirt: Preferably fluorescent stripes on black. Buy one that is too tight, and while you're at it get the matching windpants with chrome buttons from mid-shin down, to accommodate extremely large boots.

Asphyxiatingly tight jeans: Dark, with untapered leg. Ouch.

Really tight cargo pants: Thus negating the utility of all those pockets.

Hair gel: Men; your hair must be oiled back and appear clearly greasy.

The Cell: A mobile phone is essential. If you can't afford one, no one will stop you from pretending. Buy a fake from a wandering cigarette-lighter salesman.

The bottom line: Banish that baggy attire to the bottom of your pack and, instead, choose anything tight enough to make breathing difficult.

Clothing: No matter when you're traveling, it's always a good idea to bring a **warm jacket** or wool sweater, a **rain jacket** (Gore-Tex is both waterproof and breathable), sturdy shoes or **hiking boots,** and **thick socks.** You will be particularly grateful for warm, waterproof clothing traveling through Britain and Ireland, and northern continental Europe, where even summertime temperatures can hover around 60°F (15°C) and where rainfall is often generous. **Flip-flops** or waterproof sandals are crucial for grubby hostel showers. You may also want to add one outfit beyond the jeans and t-shirt uniform, and maybe a nicer pair of shoes if you have the room. If you plan to visit any religious or cultural sites, remember that you'll need something besides tank tops and shorts to be respectful. Some churches, especially in Italy, Greece, and Spain, will not let women enter with bare shoulders—you may want to pack a scarf for this purpose. The Western European casual style is, at least, in many cities in Spain, France, Italy, Germany, and Greece, more dressy than the North American standard.

Sleepsack: Some hostels require that you either provide your own linen or rent sheets from them. Save cash by making your own sleepsack: fold a full-size sheet in half the long way, then sew it closed along the long side and one of the short sides.

Converters and adapters: In Western Europe electricity is 220 volts AC (240V in Britain and Ireland), enough to fry any 110V North American appliance. 220/240V electrical appliances don't like 110V current, either. **Americans** and **Canadians** should buy an **adapter** (which changes the shape of the plug) and a **converter** (which changes the voltage). Don't make the mistake of using only an adapter (unless appliance instructions explicitly state otherwise). **New Zealanders** and **South Africans** (who both use 220V at home) as well as **Australians** (who use 240/250V) won't need a converter, but will need a set of adapters to use anything electrical.

Toiletries: Toothbrushes, towels, cold-water soap, talcum powder (to keep feet dry), deodorant, razors, tampons, and condoms are available in Western Europe, but if you're attached to particular brands, bring them along. **Contact lenses,** on the other hand, may be expensive and difficult to find, so bring enough extra pairs and solution for your entire trip. Bring a copy of your prescription and your glasses, in case you need emergency replacements. If you use heat-disinfection, either switch temporarily to a chemical disinfection system (check first to make sure it's safe with your brand of lenses), or buy a converter (about US$20) to 220/240V.

First-aid kit: For a basic first-aid kit, pack bandages, aspirin or other painkiller, antibiotic cream, a thermometer, a Swiss Army knife, tweezers, moleskin, decongestant, motion-sickness remedy, diarrhea or upset-stomach medication (Pepto Bismol or Imodium), an antihistamine, sunscreen, insect repellent, burn ointment, and a syringe for emergencies (get an explanatory letter from your doctor).

Film: Film and developing in Western Europe are expensive, so consider bringing enough film for your entire trip and then developing it at home. Amateur photographers may want to bring **disposable cameras** rather than an expensive permanent one. Despite disclaimers, airport security X-rays *can* fog film, so either buy a lead-lined pouch at a camera store or ask the security to hand-inspect it. Pack it in your carry-on luggage, since higher-intensity X-rays are used on checked luggage.

Other useful items: For safety purposes, you should carry a **money belt** and bring a small **padlock.** Basic **outdoors equipment** (plastic water bottle, compass, waterproof matches, pocketknife, sunglasses, hat) may also prove useful. **Quick repairs** can be done on the road with a needle and thread; also consider bringing electrical tape for patching tears. Doing your **laundry** by hand (where it is allowed) is both cheaper and more convenient than doing it at a laundromat—bring detergent, a small rubber ball to stop up the sink, and string for a makeshift clothes line. Other things you're liable to forget but shouldn't: an umbrella; sealable **plastic bags** (for damp clothes, soap, food, shampoo, and other spillables); an **alarm clock;** safety pins; rubber bands; a flashlight; earplugs; garbage bags; and a small **calculator.**

ACCOMMODATIONS

HOSTELS

Western Europe in the summer is overrun by young budget travelers. Hostels are the hub of this subculture, providing opportunities for young people from all over the world to meet, find travel partners, and learn about places to visit. At US$10-25 per night, only camping is cheaper. Guests tend to be in their teens and 20s, but most hostels welcome travelers of all ages. In northern Europe, especially in Germany and Denmark, many hostels have special family rooms. In the average hostel, however, you and anywhere from one to 50 roommates will sleep on bunk beds in a gender-segregated room, with common bathrooms and a lounge down the hall. The hostel warden may be a laid-back student, a hippie dropout, or a crotchety disciplinarian. Hostels sometimes have kitchens for your use, bike or moped rentals, storage areas, and/or laundry facilities.

Some hostels close during certain daytime lockout hours (from morning to mid-afternoon), have a curfew (a distinct cramp in your style if you plan to rage in town), don't accept reservations, or impose a maximum stay. Conditions are generally spartan and crowded, and you may run into screaming pre-teen tour groups. Quality varies dramatically: some hostels are set in gorgeous castles, others in run-down barracks. Most hostels prohibit sleeping bags: you can typically rent sheets from them, or you can avoid the charge by making a sleepsack (see p. 32).

 A HOSTELER'S BILL OF RIGHTS. Unless we state otherwise, you can assume that every hostel we list has certain standard features: no lockout, no curfew, free hot showers, secure luggage storage, and no key deposit.

HOSTELLING INTERNATIONAL

A **hostel membership** allows you to stay at hostels throughout Western Europe at unbeatable prices, and you usually need not be a youth to benefit (though some German hostels are only open to those under 26). Joining the youth hostel association in your own country (listed below) automatically grants you membership privileges in **Hostelling International (HI),** a federation of national hosteling associations. HI affiliates comply with given standards and regulations and normally display a blue triangle with the symbol of the national hostel association. *Hostelling International: Europe* (UK£7 or US$11; available from national hosteling associations) lists every HI-affiliated hostel in Europe and details the **International Booking Network (IBN),** through which you can book ahead for more than 300 hostels worldwide (US$5 per hostel; V, MC, D only; maximum of 3-7 days advance notice required). To prepay and reserve ahead from home, call ☎ (02) 92 61 11 11 in Australia; ☎ (800) 663-5777 in Canada; ☎ (1629) 58 14 18 in England and Wales; ☎ (1232) 32 47 33 in Northern Ireland; ☎ (01) 830 17 66 in the

Republic of Ireland; ☎ (09) 303 95 24 in New Zealand; ☎ (541) 55 32 55 in Scotland; or ☎ (202) 783-6161 in the US (www.hiayh.org/ushostel/reserva/ibn3.htm). If you want to make a reservation on less than three days' notice or are already in Europe, call the hostel where you want to stay directly.

Most HI hostels also honor **guest memberships**—you'll get a blank card with space for six validation stamps. Each night you'll pay a nonmember supplement (one-sixth the membership fee) and earn one guest stamp; get six stamps, and you're a member. This system works well in most of Western Europe, although in some countries you may need to remind the hostel reception. Most student travel agencies (see p. 41) sell HI cards, as do all of the national hosteling organizations listed below. For more info on hostels, see www.iyhf.org, www.hostels.com, or www.budgettravel.com/hostels.htm. All prices listed below are valid for **one-year memberships** unless otherwise noted.

Australian Youth Hostels Association (AYHA), 422 Kent St., Sydney NSW 2000 (☎ (02) 9261 1111; fax 9261 1969; www.yha.org.au). AUS$49, under 18 AUS$14.50.

Hostelling International-Canada (HI-C), 400-205 Catherine St., Ottawa, ON K2P 1C3 (☎ (800) 663-5777 or (613) 237-7884; fax 237-7868; email info@hostellingintl.ca; www.hostellingintl.ca). CDN$25, under 18 CDN$12.

An Óige (Irish Youth Hostel Association), 61 Mountjoy St., Dublin 7 (☎ (1) 830 4555; fax 830 5808; email anoige@iol.ie; www.irelandyha.org). IR£10, under 18 IR£4.

Youth Hostels Association of New Zealand (YHANZ), P.O. Box 436, 173 Cashel St., Christchurch 1 (☎ (03) 379 9970; fax 365 4476; email info@yha.org.nz; www.yha.org.nz). NZ$40, ages 15-17 NZ$12, under 15 free.

Hostels Association of South Africa, 3rd fl. 73 St. George's St. Mall, P.O. Box 4402, Cape Town 8000 (☎ (021) 424 2511; fax 424 4119; email info@hisa.org.za; www.hisa.org.za). SAR50, under 18 SAR25, lifetime SAR250.

Scottish Youth Hostels Association (SYHA), 7 Glebe Crescent, Stirling FK8 2JA (☎ (01786) 89 14 00; fax 89 13 33; www.syha.org.uk). UK£6, under 18 UK£2.50.

Youth Hostels Association (England and Wales) Ltd., Trevelyan House, 8 St. Stephen's Hill, St. Albans, Hertfordshire AL1 2DY, UK (☎ (01727) 85 52 15; fax 84 41 26; www.yha.org.uk). UK£12, under 18 UK£6; families UK£24.

Hostelling International Northern Ireland (HINI), 22-32 Donegall Rd., Belfast BT12 5JN, Northern Ireland (☎ (01232) 32 47 33; fax 43 96 99; email info@hini.org.uk; www.hini.org.uk). UK£7, under 18 UK£3.

Hostelling International-American Youth Hostels (HI-AYH), 733 15th St. NW, #840, Washington, D.C. 20005 (☎ (202) 783-6161 ext. 136; fax 783-6171; email hiayh-serv@hiayh.org; www.hiayh.org). US$25, under 18 free.

ESSENTIALS

YMCAS AND YWCAS

Young Men's Christian Association (YMCA) lodgings are usually cheaper than hotels, but more expensive than hostels. Not all YMCA locations offer lodging; those that do are often located in urban downtowns. Many YMCAs accept women and families; some will not lodge those under 18 without parental permission.

Y's Way International, 224 E. 47th St., New York, NY 10017 (☎ (212) 308-2899; fax 308-3161). For a small fee ($3 in North America, $5 elsewhere), this "booking service" makes reservations for YMCAs throughout Western Europe.

World Alliance of YMCAs, 12 Clos Belmont, 1208 Geneva, Switzerland (☎/fax +41 (22) 849 5100; email office@ymca.int; www.ymca.int).

HOTELS, GUESTHOUSES, AND PENSIONS

Hotels are quite expensive in Britain, Switzerland, Austria, and northern Europe, where rock bottom for one or two people is US$25 each. Elsewhere, couples can usually get by fairly well, as can larger groups. You'll typically share a hall bathroom; a private bathroom will cost extra, as may hot showers. In Britain and Ireland, a large breakfast is often included; elsewhere a continental breakfast of a roll, jam, coffee or tea, and maybe an egg is served. Some hotels offer "full pension" (all meals) and "half pension" (just breakfast and dinner). Smaller guesthouses and pensions are often cheaper than hotels. If you make reservations in writing, indicate your night of arrival and the number of nights you plan to stay. The hotel will send you a confirmation and may request payment for the first night. Not all hotels take reservations, and few accept checks in foreign currency. Enclosing two International Reply Coupons will ensure a prompt reply (each US$1.05; available at any post office).

BED AND BREAKFASTS (B&BS)

For a cozy alternative to impersonal hotel rooms, B&Bs (private homes with rooms available to travelers, yet more formal than the private rooms described) range from the acceptable to the sublime. Hosts will sometimes go out of their way to be accommodating by giving personalized tours or offering home-cooked meals. On the other hand, many B&Bs do not provide phones, TVs, or private baths. The British and Irish version of the B&B is extra heavy on the bacon and eggs. Hometours International, Inc., P.O. Box 11503, Knoxville, TN 37939 (US ☎ (800) 367-4668; http://thor.he.net/~hometour), offers catalogs of B&B listings in France, Italy, Portugal, Switzerland, Spain, and the UK, and also sells packets of B&B vouchers. For more info, see **Nerd World's Bed and Breakfasts by Region** (www.nerdworld.com/users/dstein/nw854), or try **Bed & Breakfast Central Information (BBCI),** P.O. Box 38279, Colorado Springs, CO 80937 (US fax (719) 471-4740; email bbci@bbonline.com; www.bbonline.com/bbci).

DORMS

Many colleges and universities open their residence halls to travelers when school is not in session—some do so even during term-time. These dorms are often close to student areas—good sources for information on things to do—and are usually very clean. Getting a room may take a couple of phone calls and require advanced planning, but rates tend to be low, and many offer free local calls. For lodgings in Paris, if you are a student or an intern, try contacting the Cite Universitaire 19 bd. Jourdan, 75014 Paris (email marie-therese.texeraud@ciup.fr). For students, single rooms range from $280-$360/month. The University of London opens its residential halls to visiting students, often giving discounts for stays over 28 days.

HOME EXCHANGES AND HOME RENTALS

Home exchange offers the traveler various types of homes (houses, apartments, condominiums, villas, even castles in some cases), plus the chance to live like a native and to cut costs. For more information and listings for, contact **HomeExchange.Com** (☎ (805) 898-9660; www.homeexchange.com/euother.html), **Intervac International Home Exchange** (www.intervac.com), or **The Invented City: International Home Exchange** (US ☎ (800) 788-CITY, elsewhere call US +1 (415) 252-1141; see www.invented-city.com). **Home rentals** are more expensive than exchanges, but they can be cheaper than comparably-serviced hotels. Both home exchanges and rentals are ideal for families with children, or travelers with special dietary needs.

CAMPING AND THE OUTDOORS

Organized campgrounds exist just outside most Western European cities, and are accessible by foot, car, and/or public transportation. Showers, bathrooms, and a small restaurant or store are common; some have more elaborate facilities. Prices are low, at US$5-15 per person, with additional charges for tents and/or cars, still making camping a much cheaper option than hosteling. **Free camping** allows you to camp in parks or public land for free. For information about camping, hiking, and biking, write or call the publishers and organizations listed below to receive a free catalog. Campers heading to Europe should consider buying an **International Camping Carnet,** which is required at a few campgrounds and provides discounts.

USEFUL PUBLICATIONS AND WEB RESOURCES

Automobile Association, A.A. Publishing. Produces the CD-ROM *AA Guide to Camping and Caravanning in Britain and Europe* (UK£20). (Order by phone: UK ☎ (0800) 389-2795; or see www.theaa.co.uk/bookshop/boocdr003.asp).

The Caravan Club, East Grinstead House, East Grinstead, West Sussex, RH19 1UA (UK ☎ (01342) 32 69 44; www.caravanclub.co.uk). Members receive a 700-page directory and handbook, discounts, and a monthly magazine (UK£27.50).

The European Federation of Campingsite Organisations, EFCO Secretariat, 6 Pullman Court, Great Western Road, Gloucester, GL1 3ND (UK ☎ 1452 526911; email efco@bhhpa.org.uk; website www.campingeurope.com). The website has a comprehensive list of links to campingsites in most of the Western European countries.

The Mountaineers Books, 1001 SW Klickitat Way #201, Seattle, WA 98134 (US ☎ (800) 553-4453 or (206) 223-6303; www.mountaineers.org).

CAMPING AND HIKING EQUIPMENT

WHAT TO BUY... Good camping equipment is both sturdy and light. It is generally more expensive in Australia, New Zealand, and the UK than in North America.

Sleeping Bag: Most sleeping bags are rated by season ("summer" means 30-40°F at night, while "four-season" or "winter" often means below 0°F). Sleeping bags are made either of **down** (warmer and lighter, but more expensive, and miserable when wet) or of synthetic material (heavier, more durable, and warmer when wet). Prices might range from US$80-210 for a summer synthetic to US$250-300 for a good down winter bag. **Sleeping bag pads** include foam pads (US$10-20), air mattresses (US$15-50), and Therm-A-Rest self-inflating pads (US$45-80). Bring a **stuff sack** to compress your bag.

Tent: The best tents are free-standing (with their own frames and suspension systems), set up quickly. Low-profile dome tents are the best all-around. Good 2-person tents start at US$90, 4-person tents at US$300. Seal the seams of your tent with waterproofer, and make sure it has a rain fly. Other tent accessories include a **battery-operated lantern**, a **plastic groundcloth**, and a **nylon tarp**.

Backpack: Internal-frame packs mold better to your back, keep a lower center of gravity, and flex adequately to allow you to hike difficult trails. **External-frame packs** are more comfortable for long hikes over even terrain, as they keep weight higher and distribute it more evenly. Whichever you choose, make sure your pack has a strong, padded hip-belt to transfer weight to your legs. Any serious backpacking requires a pack of at least 4000 in^3 (16,000cc), plus 500 in^3 for sleeping bags in internal-frame packs. Sturdy backpacks cost anywhere from US$125-420—this is one area in which it doesn't pay to economize—trust us. Fill up any pack with something heavy and walk around the store with it to get a sense of how it distributes weight before buying it. Either buy a **waterproof backpack cover,** or store all of your belongings in plastic bags inside.

Boots: Be sure to wear hiking boots with good **ankle support.** They should fit snugly and comfortably over 1-2 pairs of wool socks and thin liner socks. Break in boots over several weeks first in order to spare yourself from painful and debilitating blisters.

Other Necessities: Synthetic layers, like those made of polypropylene, and a **pile jacket** will keep you warm even when wet. A **"space blanket"** will help you to retain your body heat and doubles as a groundcloth (US$5-15). Plastic **water bottles** are virtually shatter- and leak-proof. Bring **water-purification tablets** for when you can't boil water. Since virtually every organized campground in Western Europe forbids fires or the gathering of firewood, you'll also need a **camp stove** (the classic Coleman starts at US$40) and a propane-filled **fuel bottle** to operate it. Don't forget a **first-aid kit, Swiss Army knife, insect repellent, calamine lotion**, and **waterproof matches** or a **lighter.**

...AND WHERE TO BUY IT. The mail-order/online companies listed below offer lower prices than many retail stores, but keep in mind that a visit to a local camping or outdoors store will give you a better sense of items' look and weight.

Au vieux campeur, 48-50 rue des Ecoles, Paris 75005, France (☎01 53 10 48 48). One of the largest outdoors shops in France, with 18 separate boutiques in a one-block radius; outfitting for everything from ice-climbing to beachcombing. Oodles of high-quality sleeping bags, tents, packs, boots, sporting equipment, and supplies. Open M-F 9am-6pm, Sa 9am-1pm.

Campmor, P.O. Box 700, Upper Saddle River, NJ 07458 USA (☎ (888) 226-7667; elsewhere call US +1 (201) 825-8300; www.campmor.com).

Discount Camping, 880 Main North Rd., Pooraka, South Australia 5095 (Australia ☎ (08) 8262 3399; www.discountcamping.com.au).

Eastern Mountain Sports (EMS), 327 Jaffrey Rd., Peterborough, NH 03458 (USA ☎ (888) 463-6367 or (603) 924-7231; www.shopems.com)

L.L. Bean, Freeport, ME 04033 (USA and Canada ☎ (800) 441-5713; UK ☎ (0800) 962 954; elsewhere, call US +1 (207) 552-6878; www.llbean.com).

Mountain Designs, P.O. Box 1472, Fortitude Valley, Queensland 4006 (Australia ☎ (07) 3252 8894; www.mountaindesign.com.au).

Recreational Equipment, Inc. (REI), Sumner, WA 98352, USA (☎ (800) 426-4840 or (253) 891-2500; www.rei.com).

YHA Adventure Shop, 14 Southampton St., London, WC2E 7HA, UK (☎ (020) 7836 8541). The main branch of one of Britain's largest outdoor equipment suppliers.

CAMPERS AND RVS

Renting an RV will always be more expensive than tenting or hostelling, but it's cheaper than staying in hotels and renting a car (see **Rental Cars,** p. 56), and the convenience of bringing along your own bedroom, bathroom, and kitchen makes it an attractive option, especially for older travelers and families with children.

Rates vary widely by region, season (July and August are the most expensive months), and type of RV. It always pays to contact several different companies to compare vehicles and prices.

Auto Europe (US ☎ (800) 223-5555; UK ☎ (0800) 899 893; www.autoeurope.com) rents RVs in Florence, London, Paris, Lyon, Marseilles, Hamburg, Frankfurt, Munich, Dusseldorf, Barcelona, Madrid. Weekly rates for a four-passenger RV range US$1000-1300/600-800 in high-/low-season, with rates cheaper for rentals in Germany.

FURTHER RESOURCES

Camping Your Way through Europe, Carol Mickelsen. Affordable Press (US$15).
Exploring Europe by RV, Dennis and Tina Jaffe. Globe Pequot (US$15).
Europe by Van and Motorhome, David Shore and Patty Campbell (US$14; ☎/fax (800) 659-5222; email shorecam@aol.com; http://members.aol.com/europevan).
Great Outdoor Recreation Pages, www.gorp.com.

KEEPING IN TOUCH

MAIL

SENDING MAIL TO WESTERN EUROPE

Mark envelopes "par avion" and/or "air mail."

Australia: Allow 4-7 days for regular airmail to Western Europe. Postcards cost AUS$1, letters up to 50g cost AUS$1.50; packages up to 0.5kg AUS$13, up to 2kg AUS$46. **EMS** can get a letter there in 3-5 days for AUS$32. www.auspost.com.au/pac.

Canada: Allow 4-7 days for regular airmail to Western Europe. Postcards and letters up to 20g cost CDN$0.95; packages up to 0.5kg CDN$8.50, up to 2kg CDN$28.30. www.canadapost.ca/CPC2/common/rates/ratesgen.html#international.

Ireland: Allow 2-3 days for regular airmail to the UK, 3-4 days to the continent. Postcards and letters up to 25g cost IR£0.32 (IR£0.30 to the UK). Swiftpost International speeds letter for IR£2.30 plus normal airmail cost. www.letterpost.ie.

New Zealand: Allow 6-12 days for regular airmail to Western Europe. Postcards NZ$1.10. Letters up to 20g cost NZ$1.80-6; small parcels up to 0.5kg NZ$13.20, up to 2kg NZ$41.70. www.nzpost.co.nz/nzpost/inrates.

UK: Allow 3 days for airmail to Western Europe. Letters up to 20g cost UK£0.36; packages up to 0.5kg UK£2.67, up to 2kg UK£9.42. UK Swiftair delivers letters a day faster for an extra UK£2.85 in addition to the airmail rate. www.royalmail.co.uk/calculator.

US: Allow 4-7 days for regular **airmail** to Western Europe. Postcards/aerogrammes cost US$0.55/0.60; letters under 1 oz. US$1. Packages under 1 lb. cost US$7.20; larger packages sent by parcel post cost a variable amount (around US$15). **US Express Mail** takes 2-3 days and costs US$19/23 (0.5/1 lb.). **US Global Priority Mail** delivers small/large flat-rate envelopes to Western Europe in 3-5 days for US$5/9. http://ircalc.usps.gov.

Additionally, **Federal Express** (in Australia ☎ 13 26 10; in US and Canada ☎ (800) 247-4747; in New Zealand ☎ (0800) 73 33 39; in UK ☎ (0800) 12 38 00) handles express mail services from most of the above countries to Western Europe; for example, they can get a letter from New York to Western Europe in two days for US$25.50.

RECEIVING MAIL IN WESTERN EUROPE

There are several ways to pick up letters sent to you abroad by friends and family:

General Delivery: Mail can be sent via **Poste Restante** (French for General Delivery; *Lista de Correos* in Spanish, *Fermo Posta* in Italian, and *Postlagernde Briefe* in German) to almost any city or town in Western Europe with a post office. Address mail to be held: Joaquín VEGA, *Poste Restante,* London SW1, United Kingdom. The mail will go to a special desk in the central post office, unless you specify a different post office by street address or postal code. It's best to use the largest post office in the area, since mail may be sent there regardless. It is usually safer and quicker, though more expensive, to send mail express or registered. Bring your passport (or other photo ID) for pick-up; there may rarely be a small fee. If the clerks insist that there is nothing for you, have them check under your first name as well. *Let's Go* lists post offices in the **Practical Information** section for every city and most towns.

American Express: AmEx travel offices worldwide offer a free **Client Letter Service;** they will hold mail for up to 30 days and forward upon request. Address the letter in the same manner shown above. Some offices will offer these services to non-cardholders (especially those who have purchased AmEx Traveler's Cheques), but call ahead to make sure. *Let's Go* lists AmEx office locations for most large cities in **Practical Information** sections; get a complete, free list from AmEx (US ☎ (800) 528-4800).

SENDING MAIL HOME FROM WESTERN EUROPE

Airmail from Western Europe to North America averages seven days. Times are more unpredictable from smaller towns. **Aerogrammes,** printed sheets that fold into envelopes and travel via airmail, are available at post offices. Most post offices will charge exorbitant fees or simply refuse to send aerogrammes with enclosures. In either case, it helps to write "airmail" (or *por avión, mit Luftpost, via aerea,* etc.) on the envelope, though *par avion* is generally understood. For exact postage for postcards and letters sent from Western Europe, see individual country intros.

Surface mail is by far the cheapest and slowest way to send mail. It takes one to three months to cross the Atlantic and two to four to cross the Pacific—good for items you won't need to see for a while, such as souvenirs or other articles you've acquired along the way that are weighing down your pack.

TELEPHONES

CALLING HOME FROM WESTERN EUROPE

A **calling card** is probably your cheapest bet. Calls are billed either collect or to your account. **To obtain a calling card** from your national telecommunications service before leaving home, contact one of the following:

Australia: Telstra Australia Direct (☎ 13 22 00).

Canada: Bell Canada **Canada Direct** (☎ (800) 565-4708).

Ireland: Telecom Éireann **Ireland Direct** (☎ (800) 25 02 50).

New Zealand: Telecom New Zealand (☎ (0800) 00 00 00).

South Africa: Telkom South Africa (☎ 09 03).

UK: British Telecom **BT Direct** (☎ (800) 34 51 44).

US: AT&T (☎ (888) 288-4685), **Sprint** (☎ (800) 877-4646), or **MCI** (☎ (800) 444-4141).

To **call home with a calling card,** contact the operator for your service provider in the appropriate country by dialing the toll-free access number provided in the Essentials chapter for each country under **Communications.** You can usually make **direct international calls** from pay phones, but if you aren't using a calling card, you may need to drop your coins as quickly as your words. Where available, prepaid phone cards (see below) and occasionally major credit cards can be used for direct international calls, but they are still less cost-efficient. Placing a **collect call** through an international operator is a more expensive alternative. You can typically place collect calls through the service providers listed above, even if you don't possess one of their phone cards.

LOCAL CALLS WITHIN WESTERN EUROPE

For **local calls,** the simplest way to call within a country in Western Europe may be to use a coin-operated phone. However, much of Western Europe has switched to a **prepaid phone card** system, and, in some countries, you may have a hard time finding any coin-operated phones at all. Phone cards (usually available at newspaper kiosks and tobacco stores) carry a certain amount of phone time, measured in units. Investing in a phone card usually saves time and money in the long run; just use any leftover time on a call home before leaving the country. The computerized phone will tell you how much time, in units, you have left on your card. Another kind of prepaid telephone card comes with a Personal Identification Number (PIN) and a toll-free access number. Instead of inserting the card into the phone, you call the access number and follow the directions on the card. These cards can be used to make international as well as domestic calls. **Phone rates** are highest in the morning, lower in the evening, and lowest on Sundays and late at night.

TIME DIFFERENCES

Greenwich Mean Time (GMT) is five hours ahead of New York time, eight hours ahead of Vancouver and San Francisco time, two hours behind Johannesburg time, 10 hours behind Sydney time, and 12 hours behind Auckland time. For more information on country time zones, see the inside back cover.

EMAIL AND INTERNET

Email has become the joy of backpackers worldwide, from Kathmandu to Cairo, so it's no surprise that it now a popular and easily accessible option in Western Europe as well. Though in some places it's possible to forge a remote link with your home server, in most cases this is a much slower (and thus more expensive) option than taking advantage of free **web-based email accounts** (e.g., www.hotmail.com, www.yahoo.com, www.youpy.fr, http://mail.voila.fr, http://mail.wordwalla.com). Travelers with laptops can call an internet service provider via a **modem.** Long-distance phone cards specifically intended for such calls can defray normally high phone charges; check with your long-distance phone provider to see if it offers this option. **Internet cafes** and the occasional free internet terminal at a public library or university are listed in the **Orientation and Practical Information** sections of major cities. For lists of additional cybercafes in Western Europe, check out http://cybercaptive.com or www.cyberiacafe.net/cyberia/guide/ccafe.htm.

GETTING THERE

BY PLANE

When it comes to airfare, a little effort can save you a bundle. If your plans are flexible enough to deal with complex restrictions, courier fares are the cheapest. Tickets bought from consolidators and standby tickets are also good deals, but last-minute specials, airfare wars, and charter flights often beat these fares. The key is to hunt around, to be flexible, and to ask persistently about discounts. Students, seniors, and those under 26 should never pay full price for a ticket.

DETAILS AND TIPS

Timing: Airfares to Western Europe peak between mid-June and early Sept.; mid-Dec. to early Jan. can also be expensive. The cheapest times to travel are Nov. to mid-Dec. and early Jan. to mid-Mar. Midweek (M-Th morning) round-trip flights run US$40-50 less than weekend flights, but are generally more crowded and are less likely to permit frequent flier upgrades. Traveling with an "open-return" ticket can be pricier than buying a fixed-return date ticket and paying later to change it.

Route: Round-trip flights are by far the cheapest; "open-jaw" (arriving in and departing from different cities, e.g. London-Paris and Rome-London) tickets tend to be pricier but may make sense. Patching one-way flights together is the most expensive way to travel.

Round-the-World (RTW): If Western Europe is only 1 stop on a more extensive globe-hop, consider a RTW ticket. Tickets usually include at least 5 stops and are valid for about a year; prices range US$1200-5000. Try **Northwest Airlines/KLM** (US ☎ (800) 225-2525; www.nwa.com) or **Star Alliance**, a consortium of 8 airlines including United Airlines (US ☎ (800) 241-6522; www.star-alliance.com).

Gateway Cities: Flights between capitals or regional hubs will offer the cheapest fares. The cheapest gateway cities to Western Europe are typically London, Paris, Amsterdam, and Frankfurt.

Boarding: Confirm international flights by phone within 72hr. of departure. Most airlines require that passengers arrive at the airport at least 2hr. before departure. One carry-on item and 2 checked bags is the norm for non-courier flights.

BUDGET AND STUDENT TRAVEL AGENCIES

When it comes to airfare, a litle effort can save you a bundle. If your plans are flexible enough to deal with the restrictions, courier fares are the cheapest. Tickets bought from consolidators and standby seating are also good deals, but last-minute specials, airfare wars, and charter flights often beat these fares. The key is to hunt around, to be flexible, and to ask persistently about discounts. Students, seniors, and those under 26 should never pay full price for a ticket.

usit world (www.usitworld.com). Over 50 **usit campus** branches in the UK (www.usitcampus.co.uk), including 52 Grosvenor Gardens, **London** SW1W 0AG (☎ (0870) 240 1010); **Manchester** (☎ (0161) 273 1721); and **Edinburgh** (☎ (0131) 668 3303). Nearly 20 **usit now** offices in Ireland, including 19-21 Aston Quay, O'Connell Bridge, **Dublin** 2 (☎ (01) 602 1600; www.usitnow.ie), and **Belfast** (☎ (02890) 327 111; www.usitnow.com). Offices also in Athens, Auckland, Brussels, Frankfurt, Johannesburg, Lisbon, Luxembourg, Madrid, Paris, Sofia, and Warsaw.

Council Travel (www.counciltravel.com). US offices include: Emory Village, 1561 N. Decatur Rd., **Atlanta**, GA 30307 (☎ (404) 377-9997); 273 Newbury St., **Boston**, MA 02116 (☎ (617) 266-1926); 1160 N. State St., **Chicago**, IL 60610 (☎ (312) 951-0585); 931 Westwood Blvd., Westwood, **Los Angeles**, CA 90024 (☎ (310) 208-3551); 254 Greene St., **New York**, NY 10003 (☎ (212) 254-2525); 530 Bush St., **San Francisco**, CA 94108 (☎ (415) 566-6222); 424 Broadway Ave E., **Seattle**, WA 98102 (☎ (206) 329-4567); 3301 M St. NW, **Washington, D.C.** 20007 (☎ (202) 337-6464). **For US cities not listed,** call (800) 2-COUNCIL (226-8624). In the UK, 28A Poland St. (Oxford Circus), **London**, W1V 3DB (☎ (020) 7437 7767).

CTS Travel. Budget travel services with offices in London and Paris. **London:** 44 Goodge St., W1P 2 AD (☎ (207) 391 5804554; email ctsinfo@ctstravel.com.uk); University college of London, Students' Union, 25 Gordon Street, WC 1 (☎ (207) 391 11363); University of Westminster, 35 Marylebone Road, NW 15 LS (☎ (207) 911 5836). **Paris:** Voyages 20, Rue de Carmes, 75005 (☎01 53 10 12 50 or 01 43 25 00 76).

STA Travel, 6560 Scottsdale Rd. #F100, Scottsdale, AZ 85253 (☎ (800) 777-0112; www.sta-travel.com). A student and youth travel organization with over 150 offices worldwide. Ticket booking, travel insurance, railpasses, and more. US offices include: 297 Newbury St., **Boston**, MA 02115 (☎ (617) 266-6014); 429 S. Dearborn St., **Chicago**, IL 60605 (☎ (312) 786-9050); 7202 Melrose Ave., **Los Angeles**, CA 90046 (☎ (323) 934-8722); 10 Downing St., **New York**, NY 10014 (☎ (212) 627-3111); 4341 University Way NE, **Seattle**, WA 98105 (☎ (206) 633-5000); 2401 Pennsylvania Ave., Ste. G, **Washington, D.C.** 20037 (☎ (202) 887-0912); 51 Grant Ave., **San Francisco**, CA 94108 (☎ (415) 391-8407). In New Zealand, 10 High St., **Auckland** (☎ (09) 309 0458). In Australia, 366 Lygon St., **Melbourne** Vic 3053 (☎ (03) 9349 4344).

Travel CUTS (Canadian Universities Travel Services Limited), 187 College St., **Toronto**, ON M5T 1P7 (☎ (416) 979-2406; www.travelcuts.com). 40 offices across Canada. Also in the UK, 295-A Regent St., **London** W1R 7YA (☎ (020) 7255 1944).

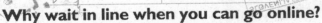

Wasteels, Platform 2, Victoria Station, **London** SW1V 1JT (☎ (020) 7834 7066; www.wasteels.dk/uk). A huge chain in Western Europe, with 203 locations. Sells the Wasteels BIJ tickets, which are discounted (30-45% off regular fare), 2nd-class international point-to-point train tickets with unlimited stopovers for those under 26 (sold only in Europe).

COMMERCIAL AIRLINES

The commercial airlines' lowest regular offer is the **APEX** (Advance Purchase Excursion) fare, which provides confirmed reservations and allows "open-jaw" tickets. Generally, reservations must be made seven to 21 days ahead of departure, with seven to 14-day minimum-stay and up to 90-day maximum-stay restrictions. These fares carry hefty cancellation and change penalties (fees rise in summer). Book peak-season APEX fares early; by May you will have a hard time getting your desired departure date. Use **Microsoft Expedia** (expedia.msn.com) or **Travelocity** (www.travelocity.com) to get an idea of the lowest published fares, then use the resources outlined here to try and beat those fares. Low-season fares should be appreciably cheaper than the high-season (mid-June to Aug.) ones listed here.

TRAVELING FROM NORTH AMERICA

Basic round-trip fares to Western Europe range from roughly US$200-750: to Frankfurt, US$300-750; London, US$200-600; Paris, US$250-700. Standard commercial carriers like **American** (☎ (800) 433-7300; www.aa.com) and **United** (☎ (800) 241-6522; www.ual.com) will probably offer the most convenient flights, but they may not be the cheapest, unless you manage to grab a special promotion.

TRAVELING FROM THE UK AND IRELAND

Because of the myriad carriers flying from the British Isles to the continent, we only include discount airlines or those with cheap specials here. The **Air Travel Advisory Bureau** in London (☎ (020) 7636 5000; www.atab.co.uk) provides referrals to travel agencies and consolidators that offer discounted airfares out of the UK.

Aer Lingus: Ireland (☎ (01) 886 88 88; www.aerlingus.ie.) Return tickets from Dublin, Cork, Galway, Kerry, and Shannon to Amsterdam, Brussels, Düsseldorf, Frankfurt, Madrid, Milan, Munich, Paris, Rennes, Rome, Stockholm, and Zürich (IR£102-244).

British Midland Airways: (UK ☎ (0870) 607 05 55; www.britishmidland.com.) Departures from throughout the UK. London to Brussels (UK£68), Madrid (UK£98), Paris (UK£71), and Frankfurt (UK£172).

buzz: UK ☎ (0870) 240 70 70; www.buzzaway.com. A subsidiary of KLM. From London to Berlin, Frankfurt, Hamburg, Milan, Paris, and Vienna (UK£50-80). Tickets can not be changed or refunded.

easyJet: (UK ☎ (0870) 600 00 00; www.easyjet.com.) London to Amsterdam, Athens, Barcelona, Geneva, Madrid, Nice, Palma, and Zurich (UK£47-136). Online tickets.

Go-Fly Limited: (UK ☎ (0845) 605 43 21, elsewhere call UK +44 (1279) 66 63 88; www.go-fly.com.) Subsidiary of British Airways. From London to Barcelona, Copenhagen, Edinburgh, Lisbon, Madrid, Naples, Prague, Rome, and Venice (return UK£53-180).

KLM: (UK ☎ (0870) 507 40 74; www.klmuk.com.) Cheap return tickets from London and elsewhere to Amsterdam, Brussels, Frankfurt, Düsseldorf, Milan, Paris, and Rome.

Ryanair: (Ireland ☎ (01) 812 12 12, UK (0870) 156 95 69; www.ryanair.ie.) From Dublin, London, and Glasgow to destinations in France, Ireland, Italy, Scandinavia, and elsewhere. Deals from as low as UK£9 on limited weekend specials.

TRAVELING FROM AUSTRALIA AND NEW ZEALAND

Air New Zealand: (New Zealand ☎ (0800) 35 22 66; www.airnz.co.nz.) Auckland to London and Frankfurt.

Qantas Air: (Australia ☎ 13 13 13, New Zealand 0800 808 767; www.qantas.com.au.) Flights from Australia and New Zealand to London for around AUS$2400.

Singapore Air: (Australia ☎ 13 10 11, New Zealand 0800 808 909; www.singaporeair.com.) Flies from Auckland, Sydney, Melbourne, and Perth to Western Europe.

Thai Airways: (Australia ☎ (1300) 65 19 60, New Zealand (09) 377 38 86; www.thaiair.com.) Auckland, Sydney, and Melbourne to Amsterdam, Frankfurt, and London.

TRAVELING FROM SOUTH AFRICA

Air France: (☎ (011) 880 80 40; www.airfrance.com.) Johannesburg to Paris; connections throughout Western Europe.

British Airways: ☎ (0860) 011 747; www.british-airways.com/regional/sa. Cape Town and Johannesburg to the UK and the rest of Western Europe from SAR3400.

Lufthansa: ☎ (011) 484 47 11; www.lufthansa.co.za. From Cape Town, Durban, and Johannesburg to Germany and elsewhere.

Virgin Atlantic (☎ (011) 340 34 00; www.virgin-atlantic.co.za) flies to London from both Cape Town and Johannesburg.

AIR COURIER FLIGHTS

Those who travel light could consider being a courier. Couriers help transport cargo on international flights by using their checked luggage space for freight. Generally, couriers must travel with carry-ons only and must deal with complex flight restrictions. Most flights are round-trip only, with short fixed-length stays (usually one week) and a limit of a one ticket per issue. Most of these flights also operate only out of major gateway cities, mostly in North America. Generally, you must be over 21 (in some cases 18), have a valid passport, and procure your own visa, if necessary. In summer, the most popular destinations usually require an advance reservation of about two weeks (you can usually book up to two months ahead). Super-discounted fares are common for "last-minute" flights (three to 14 days ahead).

TRAVELING FROM NORTH AMERICA

Round-trip courier fares from the US to Western Europe run about US$200-500. Most flights leave from New York, Los Angeles, San Francisco, or Miami in the US; and from Montreal, Toronto, or Vancouver in Canada. The first four organizations below provide their members with lists of opportunities and courier brokers worldwide for an annual fee (typically US$50-60). Alternatively, you can contact a courier broker (such as the last three listings) directly; most charge registration fees, but a few don't. Prices quoted below are **round-trip.**

Air Cargo Partners, 1983 Marcus Ave #108, Lake Success, NY 11042 (☎ (516) 358-2025 or (888) VEX-MOVE; fax (516) 358-1835). Eight US cities to Manchester and London. 90-day max. stay. Ages 19 and up. No registration fee.

Air Courier Association, 191 University Blvd #300, Denver CO 80206 (☎ (800) 282-1202; elsewhere call US +1 (303) 215-9000; www.aircourier.org). Ten departure cities throughout the US and Canada to Ireland, the UK, Copenhagen, and throughout Western Europe (high-season US$400-540). One-year US$29.

Global Delivery Systems, 147-25 176th St, Jamaica, NY 11434 (☎ (718) 995-7300). From New York to Amsterdam, Copenhagen, Rome, Milan, Paris, and Madrid (US$250-650). Ages 18 and up. No registration fee.

International Association of Air Travel Couriers (IAATC), P.O. Box 1349, Lake Worth, FL 33460 (☎ (561) 582-8320; fax 582-1581; www.courier.org). New York to 9 Western European cities. Ages 18 and up. One-year US$45-50.

Global Courier Travel, P.O. Box 3051, Nederland, CO 80466 (www.globalcouriertraveler.com). Searchable online database. Six departure points along both coasts. Some one-way flights. One-year US$40, 2 people US$55.

NOW Voyager, 74 Varick St #307, New York, NY 10013 (☎ (212) 431-1616; fax 219-1753; www.nowvoyagertravel.com). New York to London (US$516); Amsterdam, Brussels, Copenhagen, and Dublin (US$499-649); and Paris, Madrid, Rome, and Milan (US$450-749). Usually one-week max. stay. Ages 18 and up. One-year US$50.

Worldwide Courier Association (☎ (800) 780-4359, ext. 441; www.massiveweb.com). From New York, San Francisco, Los Angeles, and Chicago to Western Europe, including Milan, Madrid, and London (US$300-600). One-year US$58.

FROM THE UK, IRELAND, AUSTRALIA, AND NEW ZEALAND

Although the courier industry is most developed from North America, there are limited courier flights in other areas. The minimum age for couriers from the **UK** is usually 18. **Brave New World Enterprises,** P.O. Box 22212, London SE5 8WB (email guideinfo@nry.co.uk; www.currierflights.com) publishes a directory of all the companies offering courier flights in the UK (UK£10). The **International Association of Air Travel Couriers** (see above) often offers courier flights from London to Budapest. **Global Courier Travel** (see above) also offer flights from London and Dublin to continental Europe. **British Airways Travel Shop** (☎ (087) 06 06 11 33; www.british-airways.com/travelqa/booking/travshop/travshop.shtml) arranges return flights from London to Budapest (UK£120; specials as low as UK£60; no registration fee; ages 18 and up). From **Australia** and **New Zealand, Global Courier Travel** (see above) often has listings from Sydney and Auckland to London and occasionally Frankfurt.

ESSENTIALS

STANDBY FLIGHTS

Traveling standby requires considerable flexibility in arrival and departure dates and cities. Companies dealing in standby flights sell vouchers rather than tickets, along with the promise to get to your destination (or near your destination) within a certain window of time (typically 1-5 days). You call before your specific window of time to hear your flight options and the probability that you will be able to board a flight. You then decide which flights you want to try to make, show up at the airport at the appropriate time, present your voucher, and board if space is available. You may receive a monetary refund if every available flight within your date range is full; if you opt not to take an available (but perhaps less convenient) flight, you can only get credit toward future travel. Carefully read agreements with any company offering standby flights, as tricky fine print can leave you in a lurch. To check on a company's service record in the US, call the Better Business Bureau (☎ (212) 533-6200). One standby company in the US is **Airhitch,** 2641 Broadway, 3rd fl. #100, New York, NY 10025 (☎ (800) 326-2009; www.airhitch.org) and Los Angeles, CA (☎ (888) 247-4482), which offers one-way flights to Europe from the Northeast (US$169), the West Coast and the Northwest (US$249), the Midwest (US$219), and the Southeast (US$189). Intracontinental connecting flights within the US or Europe cost US$79-139. Airhitch's head European office is in **Paris** (☎ +33 01 47 00 16 30); there's also one in **Amsterdam** (☎ +31 (20) 626 32 20).

TICKET CONSOLIDATORS

Ticket consolidators, or **"bucket shops,"** buy unsold tickets in bulk from commercial airlines and sell them at discounted rates. The best place to look is in the Sunday travel section of any major newspaper (such as the *New York Times*), where many bucket shops place tiny ads. Call quickly, as availability is typically extremely limited. Not all bucket shops are reliable, so insist on a receipt that gives full details of restrictions, refunds, and tickets, and pay by credit card (in spite of the 2-5% fee) so you can stop payment if you never receive your tickets. For more info, see www.travel-library.com/air-travel/consolidators.html or pick up Kelly Monaghan's *Air Travel's Bargain Basement* (Intrepid Traveler, US$8).

TRAVELING FROM NORTH AMERICA

Travel Avenue (☎ (800) 333-3335; www.travelavenue.com) searches for best available published fares and then uses several consolidators to attempt to beat that fare. **NOW Voyager** (see above) arranges discounted flights, mostly from New York, to Barcelona, London, Madrid, Milan, Paris, and Rome. At 17% off published fares, they are often as cheap as courier fares, and are considerably more flexible. Other consolidators worth trying are **Interworld** (☎ (305) 443-4929; fax 443-0351); **Pennsyl-**

vania Travel (☎ (800) 331-0947); **Rebel** (☎ (800) 227-3235; email travel@rebel-tours.com; www.rebeltours.com); **Cheap Tickets** (☎ (800) 377-1000; www.cheaptickets.com); and **Travac** (☎ (800) 872-8800; www.travac.com). Yet more consolidators on the web include the **Internet Travel Network** (www.itn.com); **SurplusTravel.com** (www.surplustravel.com); **Travel Information Services** (www.tiss.com); **TravelHUB** (www.travelhub.com); and **The Travel Site** (www.the-travelsite.com). Keep in mind that these are just suggestions to get you started in your research; *Let's Go* does not endorse any of these agencies. As always, be cautious, and research companies before you hand over your credit card number.

TRAVELING FROM THE UK, AUSTRALIA, AND NEW ZEALAND

In London, the **Air Travel Advisory Bureau** (☎ (020) 76 36 50 00; www.atab.co.uk) can provide names of reliable consolidators and discount flight specialists. Also look for ads in the Sunday papers. From Australia and New Zealand, look for consolidator ads in the travel section of the *Sydney Morning Herald* and other papers.

CHARTER FLIGHTS

Charters are flights a tour operator contracts with an airline to fly extra loads of passengers during peak season. Charter flights fly less frequently than major airlines, make refunds particularly difficult, and are almost always fully booked. Schedules and itineraries may also change or be cancelled at the last moment (as late as 48 hours before the trip, and without a full refund), and check-in, boarding, and baggage claim are often much slower. However, they can also be cheaper.

Discount clubs and **fare brokers** offer members savings on last-minute charter and tour deals. Study contracts closely; you don't want to end up with an unwanted overnight layover. **Travelers Advantage,** Stamford, CT, USA specializes in European travel and tour packages.. (☎ (800) 548-1116; www.travelersadvantage.com; US$60 annual fee includes discounts, newsletters, and cheap flight directories.)

FURTHER READING: PLANE TRAVEL.
The Worldwide Guide to Cheap Airfare, Michael McColl. Insider Publications (US$15).
Discount Airfares: The Insider's Guide, George Hobart. Priceless Publications (US$14).
The Official Airline Guide, an expensive tome available at many libraries, has flight schedules, fares, and reservation numbers.

BY CHUNNEL FROM THE UK

Traversing 27 mi. under the sea, the Chunnel is undoubtedly the fastest, most convenient, and least scenic route from England to France.

BY TRAIN. Eurostar, 102-104 Victoria St., London SW1 5JL (UK ☎ (0990) 18 61 86; Belgium ☎ (02) 55 52 525; US ☎ (800) 387-6782; elsewhere call UK +44 (1233) 61 75 75; www.eurostar.com) runs a frequent train service between London and the continent. About 15 trains per day run to Paris (3hr., UK£89-145, under 26 UK£79) and Brussels (1¾hr., UK£89-125, under 26 UK£69). Both routes include stops at Ashford in England, and Calais and Lille in France. Book at major rail stations in the UK, at the office above, on the web or by phone.

BY BUS. Eurolines provides bus-ferry combinations (see p. 53).

BY CAR. If you're traveling by car, **Eurotunnel** (UK ☎ (08000) 96 99 92; www.euro-tunnel.co.uk) shuttles cars and passengers between Kent and Nord-Pas-de-Calais. Return fares for vehicle and all passengers range from UK£219-299 with car, UK£259-598 with campervan, and UK£119-299 for a trailer/caravan supplement. Same-day return costs UK£110-150, five-day return UK£139-195. Book via phone or online, which knocks £2 off all fares. Travelers with cars can also look into sea crossings by ferry (see below).

BY BOAT FROM THE UK AND IRELAND

The following fares listed are one-way for adult foot passengers unless otherwise noted. Though standard return fares are in most cases simply twice the one-way fare, fixed-period returns (usually within five days) are almost invariably cheaper. Ferries run year-round unless otherwise noted. **Bikes** are usually free, although you may have to pay up to UK£10 in high-season. For a **camper/trailer** supplement, you will have to add anywhere from UK£20-140 to the "with car" fare. A directory of ferries in this region can be found at www.seaview.co.uk/ferries.html.

P&O Stena Line: UK ☎ (087) 06 00 06 00; France ☎ 08 02 01 00 20; www.posl.com. **Dover** to **Calais** (1¼hr., every 45min.-1hr., 30 per day; UK£24 or 245F).

Hoverspeed: UK ☎ (08702) 40 80 70; France ☎ 08 20 00 35 55; www.hoverspeed.co.uk. **Dover** to **Calais** (35-50min., 12 per day, UK£24-30 or 243F) and **Ostend, Belgium** (2hr., 5 per day, UK£28 or 243F). **Folkestone** to **Boulogne, France** (55min., 4 per day, UK£24 or 243F). **Newhaven** to **Dieppe, France** (2hr., 1-3 per day, UK£28 or 280F).

SeaFrance: UK ☎ (08705) 71 17 11; France ☎ 03 21 46 80 00; www.seafrance.co.uk. **Dover** to **Calais** (1½hr., 15 per day, UK£15 or 240F, with car UK£117 or 1150-1400F).

Scandanavian Seaways: UK ☎ (0990) 44 43 33; www.scansea.com. **Harwich** to **Hamburg** (20hr., every other day) and **Esbjerg, Denmark** (22hr., every other day). **Newcastle** to **Amsterdam** (15hr., daily) and **Hamburg** (23hr.; in summer only).

P&O European Ferries: UK ☎ (0870) 242 49 99; France ☎ 01 44 51 00 51; www.poef.com. **Portsmouth** to **Le Havre** and **Cherbourg, France** (both 5½hr.; 1-7 per day; UK£20-33, with car UK£95-170) and **Bilbao, Spain** (35hr.; 2 per week; UK£55-90, with car UK£160-295). Also **Cairnryan** to **Larne** (1-2¼hr.).

Brittany Ferries: UK ☎ (0870) 901 24 00; France ☎ 08 03 82 88 28; www.brittany-ferries.com. **Plymouth** to **Roscoff, France** (6hr.; in summer 1-3 per day, off-season 1 per week; UK£25-38 or 200-330F) and **Santander, Spain** (24-30hr., 1-2 per week, return UK£80-145, 530-760). **Portsmouth** to **St-Malo** (8¾hr.; 1-2 per day; UK£26-45, 240-330F) and **Caen, France** (6hr; 1-3 per day; UK£24-40, 220-350F). **Poole** to **Cherbourg** (4¼hr.; 1-2 per day; UK£24-40, 220-300F). **Cork** to **Roscoff** (14hr. Apr.-Sept. 1 per week, 415-1510F).

P&O North Sea Ferries: UK ☎ (01482) 37 71 77; www.ponsf.com/passeng/index.htm. Daily ferries from **Hull** to **Rotterdam, Netherlands** (13½hr.) and **Zeebrugge, Belgium** (14hr.). Both UK£38-48, with car UK£161-204. Online bookings.

Irish Ferries: Ireland ☎ 189 031 31 31; UK ☎ (0807) 05 17 17 17; www.irishferries.ie. **Rosslare** to **Cherbourg** (19hr., IR£45-85); **Roscoff** (14½hr., Apr.-Sept. 1-2 per week, 315-650F); and **Pembroke, England** (3¾hr.). **Holyhead, England** to **Dublin** (2-3¼hr., return IR£35-60, students IR£28-48). **Cork** to **Roscoff** (15hr.; Apr. to mid-July 1 per week, 315-650F).

Stena Line: UK ☎ (08705) 70 70 70; elsewhere call UK +44 (1233) 64 70 22; www.stenaline.co.uk. **Harwich, England** to **Hook of Holland** (3¾hr., UK£22). **Fishguard** to **Rosslare** (1½-3½hr., UK£16-34). **Holyhead** to **Dublin** (4hr., no foot passengers, vehicles only, UK£30-35) and **Dún Laoghaire** (1½-3½hr.; £20-30, students £16-28). **Stranraer** to **Belfast** (1¾-3¼hr., Mar.-Jan., UK£20-25).

GETTING AROUND WESTERN EUROPE

Fares on all modes of transportation are either **single** (one-way) or **return** (round-trip). Unless stated otherwise, *Let's Go* always lists single fares. Round-trip fares on trains and buses in most of Western Europe are simply double the one-way fare.

BY TRAIN

In most of Western Europe, trains are the fastest and easiest way to travel. Second-class travel is pleasant, and compartments, which seat two to six, are excellent places to meet fellow travelers. Trains, however, are not always safe; for safety tips, see p. 27. For long trips make sure you are on the correct car, as trains sometimes split at crossroads. Towns listed in parentheses on Western European train schedules require a train switch at the town listed immediately before the parentheses.

You can either buy a **railpass,** which allows you unlimited travel within a particular region for a given period of time, or rely on buying individual **point-to-point** tickets as you go. Almost all countries give students or youths (usually defined as those under 26) direct discounts on regular domestic rail tickets, and many also sell a student or youth card that provides 20-50% off all fares for up to a year.

RESERVATIONS. While seat reservations are required only for selected trains (usually on major lines), you are not guaranteed a seat without one (US$10-15). Reservations are available on major trains as much as 60 days in advance (120 days for the Eurostar), and Europeans often reserve far ahead of time; you should strongly consider reserving during peak holiday and tourist seasons (at the very latest a few hours ahead). While reservations for ICE trains are highly recommended, it will be necessary to purchase a **supplement** (US$10-50) or special fare for high- speed or - quality trains such as Spain's AVE, Cisalpino, Italy's ETR500 and Pendolino, all Thalys high-speed trains, and certain French TGVs. InterRail holders must also purchase supplements (US$10-25) for trains like EuroCity, InterCity, Sweden's X2000, and many French TGVs; these supplements are unnecessary for Eurailpass and Europass holders. Reservations are included in the cost of a Eurostar ticket.

OVERNIGHT TRAINS. Night trains have their advantages: you won't waste valuable daylight hours traveling, and you will be able to forego the hassle and considerable expense of securing a night's accommodation. However, night travel has its drawbacks as well: discomfort and sleepless nights are the most obvious; the scenery probably won't look as enticing in pitch black, either. **Sleeping accommodations** on trains differ from country to country, but typically you can either sleep upright in your seat (for free) or pay for a separate space. **Couchettes** (berths) typically have 4-6 seats per compartment (about US$27-37 per person); **sleepers** (beds) in private sleeping cars offer more privacy and comfort, but are considerably more expensive (1st class US$20-210; 2nd class US$10-110). If you are using a railpass valid only for a restricted number of days, inspect train schedules to maximize the use of your pass: an overnight train or boat journey uses up only one of your travel days if it departs after 7pm (you need only write in the next day's date on your pass).

MULTINATIONAL RAILPASSES

INTERRAIL PASS. If you have lived for at least six months in one of the European countries where InterRail Passes are valid, they prove an economical option. There are eight InterRail **zones:** A (Great Britain, Northern Ireland, and the Republic of Ireland), B (Finland, Norway, and Sweden), C (Austria, Denmark, Germany, and Switzerland), D (Croatia, Czech Republic, Hungary, Poland, and Slovakia), E (Belgium, France, Luxembourg, and Netherlands), F (Morocco, Portugal, and Spain), G (Greece, Italy, Slovenia, and Turkey, including a Greece-Italy ferry), and H (Bulgaria, Macedonia, Romania, and Yugoslavia). The **Under 26 InterRail Card** allows either 22 days or one month of unlimited travel within one, two, three or all of the eight zones; the cost is determined by the number of zones the pass covers (UK£129-219). If you buy a ticket including the zone in which you have claimed residence, you must still pay 50% fare for tickets inside your own country. The **Over 26 InterRail Card** provides the same service for travelers 26 and older (UK£179-309).

Passholders receive **discounts** on rail travel, Eurostar journeys, and most ferries to Ireland and the rest of Europe. Most exclude **supplements** for high-speed trains. For info and ticket sales in Europe contact **Student Travel Center,** 24 Rupert St, 1st fl., London W1V 7FN (☎ (020) 74 34 13 06; www.student-travel-centre.com). Tickets are also available from travel agents or main train stations throughout Europe.

EURO DOMINO. Like the Interrail Pass, the Euro Domino pass is available to anyone who has lived in Europe for at least six months; it differs in that it is only valid in one country (which you designate upon buying the pass). It is available for 29 European countries as well as Morocco. Reservations must still be paid for separately.

RAIL EUROPE
RE
GROUP

BY RAIL

EUROPE

Comfort, speed
and great value

Sit back and watch the European countryside roll by. The train gives you maximum flexibility without the hassles of driving. Rail Europe offers a variety of multiple and single-country rail passes, point-to-point tickets, Eurostar – the Channel Tunnel train – and much more.

Discounts available for youth or for 2 or more traveling together.

Rail Europe is the largest distributor of European rail products in North America.

Access our website for fares, schedules and online bookings:
**go.raileurope.com
1-800-4-EURAIL**

The Euro Domino pass is available for first- and second-class travel (with a special rate for under 26ers), for three to eight days of unlimited travel within a one-month period. Euro Domino is not valid on Eurostar or Thalys trains. **Supplements** for many high-speed (e.g., French TGV and German ICE) trains are included (Spanish AVE is not), though you must still pay for **reservations** where they are compulsory (e.g., about 20F on the TGV). The pass must be bought within your country of residence (except for the Euro Domino Plus pass in the Netherlands, which also includes all bus, tram, and metro rides and can be bought in the Netherlands); each country has its own price for the pass. Inquire with your national rail company for more info.

OTHER MULTINATIONAL PASSES. If your travels will be limited to one area, regional passes are often good values. The **Benelux Tourrail Pass** for Belgium, the Netherlands, and Luxembourg is available in the UK, in the US (5 days in 1 month 2nd-class US$88, under 26 US$62), and at train stations in Belgium and Luxembourg (but not the Netherlands). The **European East Pass** covers Austria, the Czech Republic, Hungary, Poland, and Slovakia (5 days in 1 month US$205, plus US$23 per day for up to 5 additional days).

NATIONAL RAILPASSES

If you are planning to spend a significant amount of time within one country or region, a national pass—valid on all rail lines of a country's rail company—would probably be more cost-effective than a multinational pass. But consider the cons as well: many national passes are limited, and don't provide the free or discounted travel on many private railways and ferries that Eurail does. However, several national and regional passes offer companion fares, allowing two adults traveling together to save about 50% on the price of one pass. Some of these passes can be bought only in Western Europe, some only outside of Western Europe; check with a railpass agent or with national tourist offices.

The domestic analogs of the Eurailpass, national railpasses are valid either for a given number of consecutive days or for a specific number of days within a given time period. Usually, they must be purchased before you leave. Examples include

the **Britrail Pass** for England, Scotland, and Wales; **BritIreland Flexipass** covering the United Kingdom and the Republic of Ireland; **Freedom of Scotland Travelpass;** Ireland's **Emerald Card, Irish Explorer,** and **Irish Rover; France Flexipass; German Flexipass; Austrian Flexipass; Greek Flexipass; Italian Railpass** and **Flexipass; Swiss Railpass** and **Flexipass; Holland Flexipass; Iberic Flexipass; Spain Flexipass;** and **Portuguese Flexipass.** For more info, contact Rail Europe (see p. 52).

THE EURAIL AND EUROPASS

ESSENTIALS

SHOULD YOU BUY A RAILPASS? Railpasses were conceived to allow you to jump on any train in Europe, go wherever you want whenever you want, and change your plans at will. In practice, it's not so simple. You still must stand in line to validate your pass, pay for supplements, and fork over cash for seat and couchette reservations. More importantly, railpasses don't always pay off. Consult our **railplanner** (at the end of the Essentials section) to estimate the point-to-point cost of each leg of your journey; add them up and compare the total with the cost of a railpass. If you are planning to spend extensive time on trains, hopping between big cities, a railpass would probably be worth it. But in many cases, especially if you are under 26, point-to-point tickets may prove a cheaper option.

Railpasses and Europasses are designed by the EU, and can only be purchased by non-Europeans almost exclusively from non-European distributors. They must be sold at uniform prices determined by the EU. However, some travel agents tack on a US$10 handling fee, and others offer certain perks with purchase of a railpass, so shop around. You can get a replacement for a lost pass only if you have purchased insurance on it under the Pass Protection Plan (US$10).

EURAILPASS. Eurail is valid in most of Europe: Austria, Belgium, Denmark, Finland, France, Germany, Greece, Hungary, Italy, Luxembourg, the Netherlands, Norway, Portugal, the Republic of Ireland, Spain, Sweden, and Switzerland. It is **not valid** in the UK. Standard **Eurailpasses,** valid for a consecutive given number of days, are most suitable for those planning on spending extensive time on trains every few days. **Flexipasses,** valid for any 10 or 15 (not necessarily consecutive) days in a two-month period, are more cost-effective for those traveling longer distances less frequently. **Saverpasses** provide first-class travel for travelers in groups of two to five (prices are per person). **Youthpasses** and **Youth Flexipasses** provide parallel second-class perks for those under 26. Passholders often also receive reduced fares or free passage on many bus and boat lines. **Eurail freebies** (excepting surcharges such as reservation fees and port taxes) include: discounts at Hilton International and Hertz Rent-a-Car; sightseeing cruises on the Rhine (Cologne-Mainz) and Mosel (Koblenz-Cochem), as well as Europabus rides down the Romantic Road (Frankfurt-Füssen, 75% off) and Castle Road (Mannheim-Heidelberg-Nuremberg) in **Germany;** ferries between **Italy** and **Sardinia** (Civitavecchia-Golfo Aranci), **Sicily** (Villa S. Giovanni-Messina), and **Greece** (Brindisi-Patras), between **Ireland** (Rosslare/Cork) and **France** (Cherbourg/Le Havre); and boat trips between **Sweden** and **Denmark** (Helsingborg-Helsingør), **Germany** and **Denmark** (Puttgarden-Rødby), and **Germany** (Trelleborg-Sassnitz).

EURAILPASSES

	15 days	21 days	1 month	2 months	3 months
1st class Eurailpass	US$554	US$718	US$890	US$1260	US$1558
Eurail Saverpass	US$470	US$610	US$756	US$1072	US$1324
Eurail Youthpass	US$388	US$499	US$623	US$882	US$1089

EURAIL FLEXIPASSES

	10 days in 2 months	15 days in 2 months
1st class Eurail Flexipass.	US$654	US$862
Eurail Saver Flexipass	US$556	US$732
Eurail Youth Flexipass	US$458	US$599

EUROPASS. The Europass is a slimmed-down version of the Eurailpass: it allows five to 15 days of unlimited travel in any two-month period within France, Germany, Italy, Spain, and Switzerland. **First-Class Europasses** (for individuals) and **Saverpasses** (for people traveling in groups of 2-5) range from US$348/296 per person (5 days) to US$728/620 (15 days). **Second-Class Youthpasses** for those ages 12-25 cost US$233-513. For a fee, you can add **additional zones** (Austria/Hungary; Belgium/Luxembourg/Netherlands; Greece, including the ADN/HML ferry between Italy and Greece; and/or Portugal): $60 for one associated country, $100 for two. Plan your itinerary before buying a Europass: it will save you money if your travels are confined to three to five adjacent Western European countries, or if you only want to go to large cities, but would be a waste if you plan to make lots of side-trips. If you're tempted to add many rail days and associate countries, consider a Eurailpass.

BUYING YOUR PASS. Eurail passes are available through travel agents, student travel agencies like **STA** and **Council** (see p. 41), and **Rail Europe,** 500 Mamaroneck Ave, Harrison, NY 10528 (US ☎ (888) 382-7245, fax (800) 432-1329; Canada ☎ (800) 361-7245, fax (905) 602-4198; UK ☎ (0990) 84 88 48; www.raileurope.com) or **DER Travel Services,** 9501 W. Devon Ave #301, Rosemont, IL 60018 (US ☎ (888) 337-7350; fax (800) 282-7474; www.dertravel.com).

REGIONAL PASSES. Another type of regional pass covers a specific area within a country or a round-trip from any border to a destination and back; these are useful as supplements when your main pass isn't valid. The **Prague Excursion Pass** is a common purchase for Eurailers, whose passes are not valid in the Czech Republic; it covers travel from any Czech border to Prague and back out of the country (round-trip must be completed within 7 days; 2nd-class US$35, under 26 US$30). The **Copenhagen Sightseeing Pass** is valid for Europass or German railpass holders from any German or Danish border to Copenhagen and back, while the **BritRail Southeast Pass** permits unlimited travel in southeast England (3 out of 8 days US$70).

RAIL-AND-DRIVE PASSES. In addition to simple railpasses, many countries (as well as Europass and Eurail) offer rail-and-drive passes, which combine car rental with rail travel—a good option for travelers who wish both to visit cities accessible by rail and to make side trips into the surrounding areas. Rail Europe (see above) offers a EurailDrive Pass with four trains days and two rental days for between US$439 and US$529, depending on the car.

FURTHER READING AND WEBSITES: TRAIN TRAVEL.
Rail schedules: bahn.hafas.de/bin/db.w97/query.exe/en. A testament to German efficiency, with minute-by-minute itineraries and connection information.
Point-to-point fares: www.raileurope.com/us/rail/fares_schedules.index.htm. For a more convenient resource, see our **railplanner** at the front of this book.
European Railway Servers: home.wxs.nl/~grijns/timetables/time.html; mercurio.iet.unipi.it/home.html. Links to rail servers throughout Europe.
Thomas Cook European Timetable, updated monthly, covers all major and most minor train routes in Western Europe. In the US, order it from Forsyth Travel Library (☎ (800) 367-7984; www.forsyth.comUS$28). In Europe, find it at any Thomas Cook Money Exchange Center. Alternatively, buy directly from Thomas Cook (UK ☎ (8705) 66 62 22; www.thomascook.comUK£10.10).
Info on rail travel and railpasses: www.eurorail.com.
On the Rails Around Europe, Melissa Shales. Thomas Cook Ltd. (US$19).
Eurail and Train Travel Guide to Europe. Houghton Mifflin (US$15).

DISCOUNTED TICKETS

For travelers under 26, **BIJ** tickets (Billets Internationals de Jeunesse; a.k.a. **Wasteels, Eurotrain,** and **Route 26**) are a great alternative to railpasses. Available for international trips within Europe and for travel within France as well as most ferry services, they knock 20-40% off regular second-class fares. Tickets are good for two months after purchase and allow a number of stopovers along the normal direct route of the train journey. Issued for a specific international route between two points, they must be used in the direction and order of the designated route and must be bought in Europe. The equivalent for those over 26, **BIGT** tickets provide a 20-30% discount on 1st- and 2nd-class international tickets for business travelers, temporary residents of Europe, and their families. Both types of tickets are available from European travel agents, at Wasteels or Eurotrain offices (usually in or near train stations), or directly at the ticket counter in some nations. For more info, contact **Wasteels,** Victoria Station, London SW1V 1JT (☎ (020) 78 34 70 66).

BY BUS

Though Western European trains and railpasses are extremely popular, in some cases buses prove a better option. In Spain, the bus and train systems are on par; in Britain, Greece, Ireland, and Portugal, bus networks are more extensive, efficient, and often more comfortable. In the rest of Western Europe, bus travel is more of a crapshoot; scattered offerings from private companies are often cheap, but sometimes unreliable. Amsterdam, Athens, London, and Munich are centers for lines that offer long-distance rides across Europe. Often cheaper than railpasses, **interna-**

tional bus passes typically allow unlimited travel on a hop-on, hop-off basis between major Western European cities. These services in general tend to be more popular among non-American backpackers.

Eurolines, 4 Cardiff Rd., Luton, Bedfordshire L41 1PP (UK ☎ (0990) 14 32 19; fax (01582) 40 06 94); and 52 Grosvenor Gardens, London SW1W 0AU (☎ (020) 77 30 82 35; www.eurolines.co.uk or www.eurolines.com). The largest operator of Europe-wide coach services. Unlimited 30-day travel in peak/off-peak periods (UK£229/199, under 26 and over 60 UK£199/159), or 60-day (UK£279/249, under 26 and over 60 UK£249/199) travel between 48 major European cities in 21 countries.

Busabout, 258 Vauxhall Bridge Rd., London SW1V 1BS (☎ (017) 19 50 16 61; fax 19. 50 16 62; www.busabout.com). Offers 5 interconnecting bus circuits covering 17 cities and towns in Europe. Standard/student passes are valid for 15 days (US$259/229), 21 days (US$369/339), 1 month (US$489/439), 2 months (US$759/669), 3 months (US$929/839), or a season pass (US$1109/999).

BY CAR

Although travel by car may insulate you from backpacker culture, it will allow more flexibility and accessibility. While a single traveler won't save cash by renting a car, four typically will. Rail Europe and other railpass vendors offer rail-and-drive packages both for individual countries and all of Western Europe. Fly-and-drive packages are often available from travel agents or airline/rental agency partnerships. For information on preparations, see **Driving Permits and Car Insurance,** below.

Before setting off, know the laws of the countries in which you'll be driving (e.g. drive on the left in Ireland and the UK). For an informal primer on Western European road signs, conventions, and general driving guidelines, check out www.travlang.com/signs. Additionally, the **Association for Safe International Road Travel (ASIRT),** 11769 Gainsborough Rd., Potomac, MD 20854 (US ☎ (301) 983-5252; fax 983-3663; www.asirt.org; e-mail: asirt@erols.com), can provide specific information about road conditions. Western Europeans use **unleaded gas** almost exclusively.

DRIVING PERMITS AND CAR INSURANCE

INTERNATIONAL DRIVING PERMIT (IDP)

If you plan to drive a car while abroad, you must be over 18 and have an International Driving Permit (IDP), although certain countries allow travelers to drive with a valid American or Canadian license for a limited number of months. It may be a good idea to get one anyway, in case you're in a situation (e.g. if you are in an accident or stranded in a smaller town) where the police do not know English; information on the IDP is printed in 10 languages.

Your IDP, valid for one year, must be issued in your own country before you depart. You must be 18 years old and have a valid driver's license. An application for an IDP usually needs to include one or two photos, a current local license, a passport (sometimes other identification is accepted), and a fee.

Australia: Contact your local Royal Automobile Club (RAC) or the National Royal Motorist Association (NRMA; ☎ (08) 9421 4298; www.rac.com.au/travel). Permits AUS$15.

Canada: Contact any Canadian Automobile Association (CAA) branch, or write to CAA, 1145 Hunt Club Rd. #200, Ottawa, Ontario, K1V 0Y3 (☎ (613) 247-0117; fax 247-0118; www.caa.ca/CAAInternet/travelservices/frames14.htm). Permits CDN$10.

Ireland: Contact the nearest Automobile Association (AA) office or write: AA Travel, 23 Suffolk St. Dublin 2 (☎ (01) 617 9988). Permits IR£4.

New Zealand: Contact your local Automobile Association (AA), or write Auckland Central, 99 Albert St. (☎ (09) 377 46 60; fax 302 20 37; www.nzaa.co.nz.). Permits NZ$10.

South Africa: Contact your local Automobile Association of South Africa office, or write the head office at P.O. Box 596, Johannesburg 2000 (☎ (011) 799 10 00; fax 799 10 10; www.aasa.co.za). Permits SAR30.78.

UK: Visit your local AA Shop. To find the location nearest you, call ☎ (0990) 50 06 00; www.theaa.co.uk/motoringandtravel/idp/motidp002.asp. Permits UK£4.

US: Visit any American Automobile Association (AAA) office or write to AAA Florida, Travel Related Services, 1000 AAA Dr. (mail stop 100), Heathrow, FL 32746 (☎ (407) 444-4240; fax 444-7380). Permits US$10. AAA Travel Related Services (☎ (800) 222-4357) provides road maps and many travel guides free to members, and provides emergency road services and auto insurance.

CAR INSURANCE

Some credit cards cover standard insurance. If you rent, lease, or borrow a car, you will need a **green card,** or **International Insurance Certificate,** to prove that you have liability insurance. Obtain it through the car rental agency; most include coverage in their prices. If you lease a car, you can obtain a green card from the dealer. Some travel agents offer the card; it may also be available at border crossings. Verify whether your auto insurance applies abroad; even if it does, you will still need a green card to certify this to foreign officials. If you have a collision abroad, the accident will show up on your domestic records if you report it to your insurance company. Rental agencies may require you to purchase theft insurance in countries that they consider to have a high risk of auto theft (such as Italy).

ACQUIRING SOME WHEELS

RENTING A CAR. You can rent a car from a US-based firm (Alamo, Avis, Budget, or Hertz) with Western European offices, from a European-based company with local representatives (Europcar), or from a tour operator (Auto Europe or Europe By Car), which will arrange a rental for you from a European company at its own rates. Multinationals offer greater flexibility, but tour operators often strike better deals. Picking up your car in Belgium, Germany, or the Netherlands is usually cheaper than renting in Paris. Expect to pay US$80-400 per week, plus tax (5-25%), for a teensy car. Reserve ahead and pay in advance if at all possible. It is always significantly less expensive to reserve a car from the US than from Western Europe. Always check if prices quoted include tax and collision insurance; some credit card companies cover the deductible on collision insurance, allowing their customers to decline the collision damage waiver. Ask about discounts and check the terms of insurance, particularly the size of the deductible. Rates are generally lowest in Belgium, Germany, Holland, and the UK. Ask airlines about special fly-and-drive packages; you may get up to a week of free or discounted rental. Minimum age varies by country, but is usually 21 to 25. At most agencies, all that's needed to rent a car is a license from home and proof that you've had it for a year.

Car rental in Western Europe is available through the following agencies: **Auto Europe,** 39 Commercial St, P.O. Box 7006, Portland, ME 04112 (US ☎ (888) 223-5555; fax (207) 842-2222; www.autoeurope.com); **Avis** (US ☎ (800) 230-4898, Canada ☎ (800) 272-5871; UK ☎ (0870) 907 73 00; Australia ☎ (800) 22 55 33; www.avis.com); **Budget,** 4225 Naperville Rd., Lisle, IL 60532 (US ☎ (800) 527-0700; Canada ☎ (800) 268-8900; UK ☎ (0800) 18 11 81; Australia ☎ 1 300 36 28 48; www.budget.com); **Europe by Car,** One Rockefeller Plaza, New York, NY 10020 (US ☎ (800) 223-1516 or (212) 581-3040; www.europebycar.com); **Europcar,** 145 av. Malekoff, 75016 Paris (☎ (01) 55 66 84 84); US ☎ (877) 940-6900; Canada ☎ (800) 227-7368; www.europcar.com); **Hertz** 225 Brae Boulevard, Park Ridge, NJ 07656 (US ☎ (800) 654-3131; Canada ☎ (800) 263-0600; UK ☎ (0870) 844 88 44; Australia ☎ 13 30 39; www.hertz.com); and **Kemwel Holiday Autos** (US ☎ (800) 576-1590, international ☎ 914 825 31 00; www.kemwel.com).

LEASING A CAR. For longer than 17 days, leasing can be cheaper than renting; it is often the only option for those ages 18 to 21. The cheapest leases are agreements to buy the car and then sell it back to the manufacturer at a prearranged price. As far as you're concerned, though, it's a lease and doesn't entail enormous financial transactions. Leases generally include insurance coverage and are not taxed. The most affordable ones usually originate in Belgium, France, or Germany. Expect to pay around US$1100-1800 (depending on size of car) for 60 days. Contact **Auto Europe, Europe by Car,** or **Kemwel Holiday Autos** (see above) before you go.

BUYING A CAR. If you're brave and know what you're doing, buying a used car or van in Western Europe and selling it just before you leave can provide the cheapest wheels for longer trips. Check with consulates for import-export laws concerning used vehicles, registration, and safety and emission standards. Campervans and motor homes give the advantages of a car without the hassle and expense of finding lodgings. Most of these vehicles are diesel-powered and deliver roughly 24 to 30 miles per gallon of diesel fuel, which is cheaper than gas.

BY PLANE

Though flying is almost invariably more expensive than traveling by train, if you are short on time (or flush with cash) you might consider it. Student travel agencies sell cheap tickets, and budget fares are frequently available in the spring and summer on high-volume routes between northern Europe and resort areas in Italy, Greece, and Spain; consult budget travel agents and local newspapers. For info on cheap flights from Britain to the continent, see **Traveling from the UK,** p. 43.

In addition, a number of European airlines offer coupon packets that considerably discount the cost of each flight leg. Most are only available as tack-ons to their transatlantic passengers, but some are available as stand-alone offers. Most must be purchased before departure, so research in advance.

Europe by Air: (US ☎ (888) 387-2479, auto faxback (512) 404-1291; Australia ☎ (02) 92 85 68 88; New Zealand ☎ (09) 309 80 94; www.europebyair.com.) Buy passes, each good for point-to-point flights on 16 partner airlines to 130 European cities, mostly in Western Europe. Must be purchased prior to departure; available only to non-European residents (3 passes min., no max.). US$99 each, excluding airport tax.

Alitalia: (US ☎ (800) 223-5730; www.alitaliausa.com.) Program available to North Americans who fly into Milan or Rome on Alitalia allows passengers to tack on 3 coupons good for flights to 30 airports in Europe and North Africa, mostly in major cities. US$299; each additional ticket US$100; must be accompanied with a transcontinental flight on Alitalia or airline partner Continental.

Austrian Airlines: (US ☎ (800) 843-0002; www.austrianair.com/specials/visit-europe-fares.html.) "Visit Europe Fares," good to cities served by AA and partner airlines, is available in the US to Austrian Airlines transatlantic passengers (3 min., 6max.). US$100 each.

Lufthansa: US ☎ (800) 399-5838; www.lufthansa-usa.com/special_offers/discover_europe.html. "Discover Europe" is available to US travelers booked on a transatlantic Lufthansa flight or flying into Germany on a US carrier (3 coupons min.). US$170 each; up to six additional tickets.

KLM/Northwest: (US ☎ (800) 800-1504; www.nwaworldvacations.com.) "Passport to Europe," available to US transatlantic passengers on either airline, connects 90 European cities (mostly Western European, but including North African destinations; 3 min., 12 max.). US$100 each.

Iberia: (US ☎ (800) 772-4642; www.iberia.com/ibusa/special.htm#europass.) "Euro-Pass" allows North American Iberia passengers to Spain to tack on at least 2 additional destinations from the 35 they serve. Most US$125 each; some US$155 each.

BY BOAT

Most Western European ferries are quite comfortable; the cheapest ticket typically still includes a reclining chair or couchette. Fares jump sharply in July and August. Ask for discounts; ISIC holders can often get student fares, and Eurailpass holders get many reductions and free trips (for examples of popular freebies, also see p. 52). You'll occasionally have to pay a port tax (under US$10). For more info, consult the *Official Steamship Guide International* (available at travel agents), www.youra.com/ferry, or home.wxs.nl/~grijns/seatravel/ferries.html.

ENGLISH CHANNEL AND IRISH SEA FERRIES. Ferries are frequent and dependable. The main route across the **English Channel,** from England to France, is Dover-

Calais. The main ferry port on the southern coast of England is Portsmouth, with connections to France and Spain. Ferries also cross the **Irish Sea,** connecting Northern Ireland with Scotland and England, and the Republic of Ireland with Wales. For more information on sailing in this region, see **By Boat from the UK and Ireland,** p. 47.

MEDITERRANEAN AND AEGEAN FERRIES. Ferries also run across the **Aegean,** from Ancona, Italy to Patras, Greece (19hr.), and from Bari, Italy to Igoumenitsa (9hr.) and Patras (15hr.), Greece. **Eurail** is valid on certain ferries between Brindisi, Italy and Corfu (8hr.), Igoumenitsa, and Patras, Greece. Countless ferry companies operate these routes; see specific country chapters for more information. The Paleologos Travel Agency website (www.ferries.gr) contains an extensive database of Greek ferries, with connections to Italy, Cyprus, Israel, and Turkey.

BY BICYCLE

Today, biking is one of the key elements of the classic budget Eurovoyage. With the proliferation of mountain bikes, you can do some serious natural sightseeing. Many airlines will count your bike as your second free piece of luggage; a few charge extra (one-way US$60-110). Bikes must be packed in a cardboard box with the pedals and front wheel detached; many airlines sell bike boxes at the airport (US$10). Most ferries let you take your bike for free or for a nominal fee, and you can always ship your bike on trains. Renting a bike beats bringing your own if your touring will be confined to one or two regions. Some youth hostels rent bicycles for low prices. In Switzerland, train stations rent bikes and often allow you to drop them off elsewhere; check train stations throughout Europe for similar deals. In addition to **panniers** in which you can pack your luggage, you'll need a good **helmet** (US$25-50) and a good U-shaped **Citadel** or **Kryptonite lock** (from US$30). For more country-specific books on biking through France, Germany, Ireland, or the UK, or to purchase the more general *Europe by Bike,* by Karen and Terry Whitehall (US$15), try **Mountaineers Books,** 1001 S.W. Klickitat Way #201, Seattle, WA 98134 (US ☎ (800) 553-4453 or (206) 223-6303; www.mountaineersbooks.org).

If you are nervous about striking out on your own, **Blue Marble Travel** (Canada ☎ (519) 624-2494; France ☎01 42 36 02 34; US ☎ (800) 258-8689 or (973) 326-9533; www.bluemarble.org) offers bike tours for small groups for those ages 20 to 50 through the Alps, Austria, Belgium, France, Germany, Italy, Luxemburg, Portugal, Scandinavia, and Spain. **CBT Tours,** 415 W. Fullerton #1003, Chicago, IL 60614 (US ☎ (800) 736-2453) or (312) 475-0625; www.cbttours.com), offers full-package one-week biking, mountain biking, and hiking tours that are easily combined (around US$250 per day).

BY MOPED AND MOTORCYCLE

Motorized bikes don't use much gas, can be put on trains and ferries, and are a good compromise between the high cost of car travel and the limited range of bicycles. However, they're uncomfortable for long distances, dangerous in the rain, and unpredictable on rough roads and gravel. Always wear a helmet, and never ride with a backpack. If you've never been on a moped before, a twisting Alpine road is not the place to start. Expect to pay about US$20-35 per day; try auto repair shops, and remember to bargain. Motorcycles can be much more expensive and normally require a license, but are better for long distances. Before renting, ask if the quoted price includes tax and insurance, or you may be hit with an unexpected additional fee. Avoid handing your passport over as a deposit; if you have an accident or mechanical failure you may not get it back until you cover all repairs. Pay ahead of time instead. For more information, try **Europe by Motorcycle,** by Gregory Frazier (Arrowstar Publishing, US$20).

BY THUMB

Let's Go strongly urges you to consider the risks before you choose to hitch. We do not recommend hitchhiking as a safe means of transportation, and none of the information presented here is intended to do so.

No one should hitch without careful consideration of the risks involved. Hitching means entrusting your life to a random person who happens to stop beside you on the road—risking theft, assault, sexual harassment, and unsafe driving. In spite of this, there are advantages to hitching when it is safe: it allows you to meet local people and get where you're going, especially in northern Europe and Ireland, where public transportation is sketchy.

Safety-minded hitchers avoid getting in the back of a two-door car (or any car they wouldn't be able to get out of in a hurry) and never let go of their backpacks. If they ever feel threatened, they insist on being let off immediately. Acting as if you are going to open the car door or vomit on the upholstery will usually get a driver to stop. Hitch-hiking at night can be particularly dangerous; experienced hitchers stand in well-lit places, and expect drivers to be leery of nocturnal thumbers (or open-handers).

For women traveling alone, hitching is just too dangerous. A man and a woman are a safer combination, two men will have a harder time, and three will go nowhere. Where one stands is vital. Experienced hitchers pick a spot outside of built-up areas, where drivers can stop, return to the road, and have time to look over potential passengers as they approach. Hitching (or even standing) on super-highways is usually illegal: one may only thumb at rest stops or at the entrance ramps to highways. In the **Practical Information** section of many cities, *Let's Go* lists the tram or bus lines that take travelers to strategic hitching points. Finally, success will depend on appearance. Successful hitchers travel light and stack their belongings in a compact but visible cluster. Most Western Europeans signal with an open hand rather than a thumb; many write their destination on a sign in large, bold letters and draw a smiley-face under it. Drivers prefer hitchers who are neat and wholesome. No one stops for anyone wearing sunglasses.

Britain and **Ireland** are probably the easiest places in Western Europe to get a lift. Long-distance hitching in the developed countries of northwestern Europe demands close attention to expressway junctions, rest stop locations, and a destination sign. Hitching in southern Europe is generally mediocre; **France** is the worst.

Most Western European countries offer a ride service (listed in the **Practical Information** for major cities), a cross between hitchhiking and the ride boards common at many universities, which pairs drivers with riders; the fee varies according to destination. **Eurostop International** (**Verband der Deutschen Mitfahrzentralen** in Germany and **Allostop** in France) is one of the largest in Europe. Riders and drivers can enter their names on the internet through the **Taxistop** website (www.taxistop.be) or at **Hitchhikers** (www.hitchhikers.org). Not all these organizations screen drivers and riders; ask in advance.

BY FOOT

Western Europe's grandest scenery can often be seen only by foot. *Let's Go* describes many daytrips for those who want to hoof it, but native inhabitants (Europeans are fervent, almost obsessive hikers), hostel proprietors, and travelers are the best source of tips. Many Western European countries have hiking and mountaineering organizations; alpine clubs in Germany, Austria, Switzerland, and Italy provide simple accommodations in splendid settings.

SPECIFIC CONCERNS

WOMEN TRAVELERS

Women exploring on their own inevitably face some additional safety concerns, but it's easy to be adventurous without taking undue risks. If you are concerned, consider staying in hostels which offer single rooms that lock from the inside or in religious organizations with rooms for women only. Communal showers in some hostels are safer than others; check them before settling in. Stick to centrally located accommodations and avoid solitary late-night treks or metro rides.

When traveling, always carry extra money for a phone call, bus, or taxi. **Hitchhiking** is never safe for lone women, or even for two women traveling together. Choose train compartments occupied by other women or couples; ask the conductor to put together a women-only compartment if he or she doesn't offer to do so first. Look as if you know where you're going (even when you don't) and approach older women or couples for directions if you're lost or feel uncomfortable.

Generally, the less you look like a tourist, the better off you'll be. Dress conservatively, especially in rural areas. Trying to fit in can be effective, but dressing to the style of an obviously different culture may cause you to be ill at ease and an obvious target. Wearing a conspicuous **wedding band** may help prevent unwanted overtures. Some travelers report that carrying pictures of a "husband" or "children" is extremely useful to help document marriage status. Even a mention of a husband waiting back at the hotel may be enough in some places to discount your potentially vulnerable, unattached appearance.

In cities, you may be harassed no matter how you're dressed. Your best answer to verbal harassment is no answer at all; feigning deafness, sitting motionless, and staring straight ahead at nothing in particular will do a world of good that reactions usually don't achieve. The extremely persistent can sometimes be dissuaded by a firm, loud, and very public "Go away!" in the appropriate language. Don't hesitate to seek out a police officer or a passerby if you are being harassed. Memorize the emergency numbers in places you visit, and consider carrying a whistle or airhorn on your keychain. An self-defense course will not only prepare you for a potential attack, but will also raise your level of awareness of your surroundings as well as your confidence (see **Self Defense**, p. 25). Women also face some specific health concerns when traveling (see p. 30). *Journeywoman* (www.journeywoman.com) posts an online newsletter and other resources providing female-specific travel tips

FURTHER READING: WOMEN TRAVELERS.

A Journey of One's Own: Uncommon Advice for the Independent Woman Traveler (US$17) and *Adventures in Good Company: The Complete Guide to Women's Tours and Outdoor Trips* (US$7), by Thalia Zepatos. Eighth Mountain Press.

Active Women Vacation Guide, by Evelyn Kaye. Blue Panda Publications (US$18).

Safety and Security for Women who Travel, by Sheila Swan. Traveler's Tales ($13).

ESSENTIALS

TRAVELING ALONE

There are many benefits to traveling alone, among them greater independence and challenge. As a lone traveler, you have greater opportunity to interact with the residents of the region you're visiting. Without distraction, you can write a great travelogue in the grand tradition of Mark Twain, John Steinbeck, and Charles Kuralt.

On the other hand, any solo traveler is a more vulnerable target of harassment and street theft. Lone travelers need to be well-organized and look confident at all times. Try not to stand out as a tourist, and be especially careful in deserted or very crowded areas. If questioned, never admit that you are traveling alone. Maintain regular contact with someone at home who knows your itinerary.

A number of organizations also supply information for solo travelers, and others find travel companions for those who don't want to go alone. Here are a few:

The Single Traveler Newsletter, P.O. Box 682, Ross, CA 94957 (US ☎ (415) 389-0227; 6 issues US$29).

American International Homestays, P.O. Box 1754, Nederland, CO 80466 (US ☎ (800) 876-2048; www.spectravel.com/homes). Lodgings with host families in Austria, Belgium, France, and Spain.

Connecting: Solo Traveler Network, P.O. Box 29088, Delmont RPO, Vancouver, BC V6J 5C2 (Canada ☎ (604) 737-7791; www.cstn.org). Membership US$28-40.

Travel Companion Exchange, P.O. Box 833, Amityville, NY 11701 (US ☎ (800) 392-1256 or (631) 454-0880; www.whytravelalone.com). Newsletter links up travel partners (subscription US$48). Membership $159.

OLDER TRAVELERS

Senior citizens are eligible for a wide range of discounts on transportation, museums, movies, theaters, concerts, restaurants, and accommodations. If you don't see a senior citizen price listed, ask, and you may be delightfully surprised.

ElderTreks, 597 Markham St., Toronto, ON M6G 2L7 (Canada ☎ (800) 741-7956 or (416) 588-5000; email eldertreks@eldertreks.com; www.eldertreks.com).

Elderhostel, 75 Federal St., Boston, MA 02110 (US toll free ☎ (877) 426-8056, outside of the U.S. + 1 978-325-4141; www.elderhostel.org). One- to 4-week programs at universities and other institutions in Europe.

The Mature Traveler, P.O. Box 50400, Reno, NV 89513 (US ☎ (800) 460-6676 or (775) 786-7419; www.maturetraveler.com). Newsletter. Subscription US$30.

Walking the World, P.O. Box 1186, Fort Collins, CO 80522 (US ☎ (800) 340-9255 or (970) 498-0500; www.walkingtheworld.com). Trips to Britain, Ireland, France, Italy, Portugal, Norway, Greece, the Czech Republic and Switzerland.

FURTHER READING: OLDER TRAVELERS.

No Problem! Worldwise Tips for Mature Adventurers, by Janice Kenyon. Orca Book Publishers (US$16).

A Senior's Guide to Healthy Travel, by Donald Sullivan. Career Press (US$15).

Unbelievably Good Deals and Great Adventures That You Absolutely Can't Get Unless You're Over 50, by Joan Rattner Heilman. Contemporary Publishing (US$12).

ESSENTIALS

BISEXUAL, GAY, AND LESBIAN TRAVELERS

Attitudes toward bisexual, gay, and lesbian travelers are particular to each region, with acceptance generally highest in the Netherlands. Listed below are organizations and publishers which address those concerns.

Gay's the Word, 66 Marchmont St., London WC1N 1AB (☎ (020) 72 78 76 54; freespace.virgin.net/gays.theword). The largest gay and lesbian bookshop in the UK.

Giovanni's Room, 345 S. 12th St., Philadelphia, PA 19107 (US ☎ (215) 923-2960; fax 923-0813). International feminist, lesbian, and gay bookstore with mail-order service.

International Gay and Lesbian Travel Association, 4331 N. Federal Hwy. #304, Fort Lauderdale, FL 33308 (US ☎ (800) 448-8550; www.iglta.org). About 1200 companies. Call for lists of travel agents, accommodations, and events.

International Lesbian and Gay Association (ILGA), 81 rue Marché-au-Charbon, B 1000 Brussels, Belgium (☎/fax +32 (2) 502 24 71; email ilga@ilga.org; www.ilga.org). Provides political info, such as homosexuality laws of individual countries.

> **FURTHER READING: GAY AND LESBIAN TRAVELERS.**
> *Spartacus International Gay Guide,* by Bruno Gmünder Verlag. (US$40).
> *Damron Men's Guide, Damron's Accommodations, The Women's Traveller,* and travel guides including Amsterdam. Damron (US ☎ (800) 462-6654 or (415) 255-0404; www.damron.com; US$10-19).
> *Gay Travel A to Z, Men's Travel in Your Pocket, Women's Travel in Your Pocket, Inn Places,* and guides (US$14-18) including *Gay Paris.* Ferrari Guides (US ☎ (800) 962-2912; www.q-net.com).
> *The Gay Vacation Guide: The Best Trips and How to Plan Them,* by Mark Chesnut. Citadel Press (US$15).
> *Odysseus: The International Gay Travel Planner,* by Eli Angelp and Joseph H. Bain (US$29)

TRAVELERS WITH DISABILITIES

Countries vary in accessibility to travelers with disabilities. Some national and regional tourist boards provide directories on the accessibility of various accommodations and transportation services. If these services are not available, contact institutions of interest directly. Those with disabilities should inform airlines and hotels of their disabilities when making arrangements for travel; some time may be needed to prepare special accommodations. Call ahead to restaurants, hotels, parks, and other facilities to find out about the existence of ramps, the widths of doors, the dimensions of elevators, etc. **Guide dog owners** should inquire as to the specific quarantine policies of each destination country. At the very least, they will need to provide a certificate of immunization against rabies.

Rail is probably the most convenient form of travel for disabled travelers in Europe: many stations have ramps, and some trains have wheelchair lifts, special seating areas, and specially equipped toilets. Large stations in Britain are equipped with wheelchair facilities, and the French national railroad offers wheelchair compartments on all TGV (high speed) and Conrail trains. All Eurostar, some InterCity (IC) and some EuroCity (EC) trains are wheelchair-accessible and CityNightLine trains, French TGV (high speed) and Conrail trains feature special compartments. In general, the countries with the most **wheelchair-accessible rail networks** are Denmark (IC and Lyn trains), France (TGVs and other long-distance trains), Germany (ICE, EC, IC, and IR trains), Italy (all Pendolino and many EC and IC trains), the Netherlands (most trains), the Republic of Ireland (most major trains), Spain, and Switzerland (all IC, most EC, and some regional trains). Austria, Poland, and Great Britain offer accessibility on selected routes. The Czech Republic's and Hungary's rail systems have limited resources for wheelchair accessibility. Some major **car rental** agencies (Hertz, Avis, and National) may offer hand-controlled vehicles.

The following organizations either provide information or publications that might be of assistance, or arrange tours or trips for disabled travelers.

Mobility International USA (MIUSA), P.O. Box 10767, Eugene, OR 97440 (☎ (541) 343-1284 voice and TTY; fax 343-6812; www.miusa.org). Call for publications.

Moss Rehab Hospital Travel Information Service, (www.mossresourcenet.org.) An internet information resource center on international travel accessibility and other travel-related concerns for those with disabilities.

Society for the Advancement of Travel for the Handicapped (SATH), 347 Fifth Ave. #610, New York, NY 10016 (☎ (212) 447-7284; www.sath.org). Publishing the magazine *OPEN WORLD* (members free; nonmembers US$18) and info sheets on accessible destinations. Annual membership US$45, students and seniors US$30.

Directions Unlimited, 123 Green Lane, Bedford Hills, NY 10507 (☎ (800) 533-5343; fax (914) 241-0243; email cruisesusa@aol.com). Arranges individual and group vacations, tours, and cruises for the physically disabled. Group tours for blind travelers.

ESSENTIALS

MINORITY TRAVELERS

In general, minority travelers will find a high level of tolerance in large cities; the small towns and the countryside are more unpredictable. *Romany* (Gypsies) encounter the most hostility throughout Eastern Europe, and travelers with darker skin of any nationality might be mistaken for *Romany* and face unpleasant consequences. Other minority travelers, especially those of African or Asian descent, will usually meet with more curiosity than hostility; travelers of Arab ethnicity may also be treated more suspiciously. Skinheads are on the rise in Europe, and minority travelers, especially Jews and blacks, should regard them with caution. Anti-Semitism is still a problem in many countries; sad to say, it is generally best to be discreet about your religion. Still, attitudes will vary from country to country and town to town; travelers should use common sense—someone who flashes money around will become a target regardless of any racial or religious differences.

TRAVELERS WITH CHILDREN

Family vacations often require that you slow your pace, and always require that you plan ahead. When deciding where to stay, remember the special needs of young children; if you pick a B&B or a small hotel, call ahead and make sure it's child-friendly. If you rent a car, make sure the rental company provides a car seat for younger children. Be sure that your child carries some sort of ID in case of an emergency or he or she gets lost. Restaurants often have children's menus and discounts. Virtually all museums and tourist attractions also have a children's rate. Children under two generally fly for 10% of the adult airfare on international flights (this does not necessarily include a seat). International fares are usually discounted 25% for children from two to 11. Finding a private place for **breast feeding** is often a problem while traveling, so pack accordingly.

FURTHER READING: TRAVELING WITH CHILDREN.

Backpacking with Babies and Small Children, by Goldie Silverman. Wilderness Press (US$10).

Take Your Kids to Europe, by Cynthia W. Harriman. Globe Pequot (US$18).

How to take Great Trips with Your Kids, by Sanford and Jane Portnoy. Harvard Common Press (US $10).

Have Kid, Will Travel: 101 Survival Strategies for Vacationing With Babies and Young Children, by Claire and Lucille Tristram. Andrews and McMeel (US$9).

Adventuring with Children: An Inspirational Guide to World Travel and the Outdoors, by Nan Jeffrey. Avalon House (US$15).

DIETARY CONCERNS

Vegetarians should have no problem finding suitable cuisine in most of Western Europe. In city listings, *Let's Go* notes many restaurants that cater to vegetarians or that offer good vegetarian selections. Travelers who keep **kosher** should contact synagogues in larger cities for info on kosher restaurants. If you are strict in your observance, you may have to prepare your own food on the road. For more info, contact:

The Vegetarian Society of the UK (VSUK), Parkdale, Dunham Rd., Altringham, Cheshire WA14 4QG (☎ (0161) 925 20 00; fax 926 9182; www.vegsoc.org).

North American Vegetarian Society, P.O. Box 72, Dolgeville, NY 13329 (US ☎ (518) 568-7970, fax (518) 568-7979; email navs@telenet.com; www.navs-online.org).

FURTHER READING: DIETARY CONCERNS.

The Jewish Travel Guide 2001 lists synagogues and kosher restaurants in 80 countries. Ed. Michael Zaidner. Vallentine-Mitchell Publishers (US$17).

The Vegan Travel Guide: UK and Southern Ireland. Book Publishing Co. (US$15).

The Vegetarian Traveler: Where to Stay if You're Vegetarian, by Jed Civic. Larson Publishing (US$16).

Europe on 10 Salads a Day, by Mary Jane and Greg Edwards. Mustang Publishing (US$10).

ALTERNATIVES TO TOURISM

STUDYING ABROAD

The opportunities for studying in Western Europe are boundless: whether you seek a college semester abroad, a summer of foreign-language immersion, or a top-notch cooking school, you are sure to find a program tailored to your needs. Most American undergraduates enroll in programs sponsored by US universities. However, if your language skills are already decent, local universities can be much cheaper; enrolling directly in one usually involves passing a language-proficiency test.

Studying abroad in Western Europe usually requires applying for a special study **visa,** issued for a duration longer than a tourist visa. Applying for such a visa usually requires proof of admission to an appropriate university or program. In some countries, student status will affect your right to work. Information on visa and other requirements should be available from foreign embassies at home.

STUDY ABROAD ORGANIZATIONS

American Institute for Foreign Study, River Plaza, 9 West Broad St.; Stamford, CT 06902 (☎ (802) 257-7751; www.aifs.com/java/US/usprgs.htm). Organizes programs for high school and college study in universities in Austria, the Czech Republic, Britain, Ireland, France, Italy, Spain, and the Netherlands.

School for International Training, Kipling Rd., P.O. Box 676, Brattleboro, VT 05302 (☎ (802) 257-7751; fax 258-3248; www.sit.edu). Runs semester- and year-long programs in the Czech Republic, France, Germany, Greece, Spain, Ireland, the Netherlands, and Switzerland (US$12,000-13,000).

Council on International Educational Exchange (CIEE), 205 East 42nd St., New York, NY 10017 (US ☎ (800) 407-8839; fax (212) 822-2779; www.ciee.org), sponsors work, volunteer, and study abroad programs in Britain, France, Ireland, Italy, and Spain. Non-US residents should locate their country's CIEE office number on the website.

International Association for the Exchange of Students for Technical Experience (IAESTE), 10400 Little Patuxent Pkwy. #250, Columbia, MD 21044, USA (☎ (410) 997-3068; www.aipt.org). Operates 8- to 12-week programs in Eastern Europe, Austria, Switzerland, Greece, France, Germany, Ireland, Britain, Spain, and Italy for college students who have completed 2 years of technical study. US$50 application fee.

LANGUAGE SCHOOLS

Eurocentres, 101 N. Union St. #300, Alexandria, VA 22314 (☎ (703) 684-1494, fax 684-1495; www.eurocentres.com) or Head Office, Seestrasse 247, CH-8038 Zurich, Switzerland (☎ +41 (1) 485 50 40; fax 481 61 24), arranges language study and homestays in Britain, France, Germany, Italy, and Spain from 2-weeks to 36-weeks.

World Exchange, Ltd., White Birch Rd., Putnam Valley, NY 10579 (US ☎ (800) 444-3924; fax 528-9187; www.worldexchange.org), offers 1- to 4-week language-based homestay programs offered in France or Spain (up to 14 days US$850; 15-28 days US$1,150).

Languages Abroad, 502-99 Avenue Rd., Toronto, Ontario M5R-2G5 (US ☎ (800) 219-9924; (416) 925-5990; www.languagesabroad.com), organizes 2-16 week language and culture immersion programs, and arranges for homestays or apartments in Austria, France, Germany, Greece, Italy, Portugal, Spain, and Switzerland for US$545-6400. Must be 18+. Registration fee of US$100.

LanguagesPLUS, 317 Adelaide St. W., Suite 900, Toronto, Ontario M5V-1P9 (US ☎ (888) 526-4758; (416) 925-7117; www.languagesplus.com), runs 1-36 week programs in France, Spain, Italy, and Germany from US$470-5000 that include tuition, accommodations with host families or apartments, and activities. Must be 18+.

> **FURTHER READING AND RESOURCES: TRAVEL ABROAD.**
> www.studyabroad.com
> *Academic Year Abroad 2000/2001.* Institute of International Education Books (US$43)
> *Peterson's Study Abroad 2001.* Peterson's (US$30).

WORKING ABROAD

There's no better way to submerge yourself in a foreign culture than to become part of its economy. **European Union citizens** can work in any EU country; if your parents were born in an EU country, you may be able to claim dual citizenship or the right to a permit. Officially, **non-EU citizens** can hold a job in Western Europe only with a **work permit,** obtained by your employer, usually demonstrating that you have skills that locals lack.

If you are a full-time student at a US university, the simplest way to get a job abroad in Ireland, France, or Germany is through work permit programs run by **CIEE** (see p. 41). For a US$300-400 application fee, Council can procure three- to six-month work permits. European friends can expedite permits or arrange work-for-accommodations swaps. You can be an au pair or advertise to teach English. Reportedly, many permit-less agricultural workers go untroubled. Check with universities' foreign language departments for job opening connections, and contact the consulate or embassy of your destination country for more information.

interExchange, 161 Sixth Ave., New York, NY 10013 (US ☎ (212) 924-0446; fax 924-0575; www.interexchange.org), provides au pair jobs in Austria, Britain, Eastern Europe, France, Germany, Ireland, Italy, Spain, and Switzerland.

Childcare International, Ltd., Trafalgar House, Grenville Pl., London NW7 3SA (☎ +44 (0) 20 89 06 31 16; fax 89 06 34 61; www.childint.co.uk), offers au pair positions in the Czech Republic, Denmark, Hungary, Austria, Belgium, France, Germany, the Netherlands, Italy, Spain, and Switzerland.

International Schools Services, Educational Staffing Program, P.O. Box 5910, Princeton, NJ 08543 (US ☎ (609) 452-0990; fax 452-2690; www.iss.edu). Recruits teachers for American and English schools throughout Europe. Applicants must have a bachelor's degree and 2 years of relevant experience. Nonrefundable US$100 application fee.

Willing Workers on Organic Farms (WWOOF), P.O. Box 2675, Lewes, England BN7 1RB (www.phdcc.com/sites/wwoof). Membership allows you to exchange work for room and board at organic farms in Austria, Britain, Denmark, France, Germany, Hungary, Ireland, Italy, and Switzerland. Check the website for membership fees.

Archaeological Institute of America, 656 Beacon St., Boston, MA 02215 (US ☎ (617) 353-9361; fax 353-6550; www.archaeological.org). Puts out a list of field sites in Italy, France, and Greece (nonmembers US$16), available from Kendall/Hunt Publishing, 4050 Westmark Dr, Dubuque, IA 52002 (☎ (800) 228-0810).

VOLUNTEERING

Volunteer jobs are readily available almost everywhere. You may receive room and board in exchange for your labor. You can sometimes avoid the high application fees charged by placement organizations by contacting workcamps directly.

ESSENTIALS

Peace Corps, 1111 20th St. NW, Washington, DC 20526 (☎ (800) 424-8580; www.peacecorps.gov). Opportunities for US citizens only in a variety of fields in developing nations in Eastern Europe. Two-year commitment, plus three-month training. A bachelor's degree is usually required.

Service Civil International Voluntary Service (SCI-VS), 814 NE 40th St., Seattle, WA 98105 (US ☎/fax (206) 545-6585; www.sci-ivs.org). Arranges placement in workcamps in Europe for those age 18 and over. Registration fee US$125.

Volunteers for Peace, 1034 Tiffany Rd., Belmont, VT 05730 (☎ (802) 259-2759; fax 259-2922; www.vfp.org). A nonprofit organization that arranges speedy placement in 2- to 3-week, 10- to 20-person workcamps in Europe mostly during the summer. Registration fee US$195. Free newsletter. Registration fee US$200 covers room and board.

FURTHER READING: WORKING ABROAD.

International Jobs: Where they Are, How to Get Them, by Eric Koocher. Perseus Books (US$17).

How to Get a Job in Europe, by Robert Sanborn. Surrey Books (US$22).

The Alternative Travel Directory (US$20) and *Work Abroad* (US$16), by Clayton Hubbs. Transitions Abroad.

International Directory of Voluntary Work, by Victoria Pybus. Vacation Work Publications (US$16).

Teaching English Abroad, by Susan Griffin. Vacation Work Publications (US$17).

Overseas Summer Jobs 1999, Work Your Way Around the World, and *Directory of Jobs and Careers Abroad.* Peterson's (US$17-18).

OTHER RESOURCES

Let's Go tries to cover all aspects of budget travel, but we can't put *everything* in our guides. Listed below are books, travel organizations, and websites that can serve as jumping off points for your own research.

TRAVEL PUBLISHERS & BOOKSTORES

Hippocrene Books, Inc., 171 Madison Ave., New York, NY 10016 (☎ (212) 685-4371; orders (718) 454-2366; fax 454-1391; www.hippocrenebooks.com), publishes travel guides, as well as foreign language dictionaries and learning guides.

Hunter Publishing, 821 L South King St. Leesburg, VA 20175 (☎/fax (703) 777-8907; www.hunterpublishing.com), offers an extensive catalog of travel books, guides, maps, and hotel guides for throughout Europe.

Rand McNally, 150 S. Wacker Dr., Chicago, IL 60606 (US ☎ (800) 275-7263; (312) 332-2009; fax 443-9540; email store@randmcnally.com; www.randmcnally.com), publishes a number of comprehensive road atlases (US$10).

Travel Books & Language Center, Inc., 4437 Wisconsin Ave. NW, Washington, DC 20016 (US ☎ (800) 220-2665 or (202) 237-1322; fax 237-6022; www.bookweb.org/bookstore/travelbks), sells travel aids, language cassettes, dictionaries, travel books, atlases, and maps.

Bon Voyage!, 2069 W. Bullard Ave, Fresno, CA 93711-1200 (US ☎ (800) 995-9716 or (559) 447-8441; fax 266-6460; www.bon-voyage-travel.com), sells videos, travel gear, and railpasses. Free newsletter.

THE WORLD WIDE WEB

Almost every aspect of budget travel (with the most notable exception, of course, being experience) is accessible via the web. Even if you don't have internet access at home, seeking it out at a public library or at work would be well worth it.

Listed here are some budget travel sites to start off your surfing; other relevant web sites are listed throughout the book. Because website turnover is high, use search engines (such as www.yahoo.com) to strike out on your own. But in doing so, keep in mind that most travel web sites simply exist to get your money.

LEARNING THE ART OF BUDGET TRAVEL

Backpacker's Ultimate Guide: (www.bugeurope.com.) Tips on packing, transportation, hostels, cultural events, and key desinations.

Backpack Europe: (www.backpackeurope.com.) Helpful packing list, travel tips, information on work and study abroad, a bulletin board, and useful links.

How to See the World: (www.artoftravel.com.) A comprehensive online book that advises on a range of topics such as cheap flights, travel health, and packing.

TripSpot: (www.tripspot.com/europefeature.htm.) An outline of links to help plan trips, transportation, sleeping accommodations, and packing.

Rec. Travel Library: (www.travel-library.com/europe/index.html.) A set of links for general information on accommodations and tour operators, as well as personal travelogues.

COUNTRY-SPECIFIC INFORMATION

CIA World Factbook: (www.odci.gov/cia/publications/factbook/index.html.) Tons of vital statistics on European geography, governments, economies, and politics.

Foreign Language for Travelers: (www.travlang.com.) Provides free online translating dictionaries and lists of phrases in European languages from Albanian to Yiddish.

DESTINATION GUIDES

MyTravelGuide: (www.mytravelguide.com.) Country overviews, with everything from history to transportation to local newspapers. Free travel newsletter.

Geographia: (www.geographia.com.) Describes highlights and attractions of the various European countries.

Atevo Travel: (www.atevo.com/guides/destinations.) Detailed introductions, transportation tips, and suggested itineraries. Free travel newsletter.

Columbus Travel Guides: (www.travel-guides.com/navigate/region/eur.asp.) Well-organized site with practical information on geography, government, communication, health precautions, economy, and useful addresses.

LeisurePlanet: (www.leisureplanet.com/TravelGuides.) Good country-specific background with coverage of sites and basic practical information.

CNN: (www.cnn.com/TRAVEL/CITY.GUIDES.) Detailed information about services, sites, shopping, dining, nightlife and recreation in the major cities of Europe.

LINKS TO WESTERN EUROPEAN TOURISM PAGES

TravelPage: (www.travelpage.com.) Some links to official tourist office sites throughout Western Europe.

Lycos: (http://cityguide.lycos.com/europe.) General introductions to cities and regions throughout Europe, accompanied by links to applicable histories, news, and local tourism sites.

PlanetRider: (www.planetrider.com/Europe-index.cfm.) A subjective list of links to the "best" websites covering the culture and tourist attractions of major

AND OUR PERSONAL FAVORITE...

Let's Go: (www.letsgo.com.) Our recently revamped website features photos and streaming video, info about our books, a travel forum buzzing with stories and tips, and links that will help you find everything you could ever want to know about Western Europe.

FURTHER READING: SURFING THE WEB.

How to Plan Your Dream Vacation Using the Web, by Elizabeth Dempsey. Corilis Group (US$25).

Nettravel: How Travelers Use the Internet (US$25) and *Internet Travel Planner* (US$19), by Michael Shapiro. O'Reilly & Associates and Globe Pequot Press.

Travel Planning Online for Dummies, by Noah Vadnai. IDG Books (US$25).

300 Incredible Things for Travelers on the Internet, by Ken Leebow. 300Incredible.com (US$9).

Buying Travel Services on the Internet, by Durant Imboden. McGraw-Hill (US$15).

ANDORRA

Squint carefully at a map of Western Europe, and between France and Spain you'll find Andorra (pop.65,000; 468 sq. km). This tiny nation is known primarily for its mix of stunning vistas and duty-free shopping. The neon-lit streets may seem a striking contrast to the peaceful landscapes, but then Andorra has a long-standing tradition of combining various cultures. Known formally as Principat d'Andorra (the Principality of Andorra), it is governed by two co-princes; the president of France and the Bishop of Urgell, but it is the *Consell General* who possesses the bulk of the political power and represents the seven parishes of the nation. The story goes that Charlemagne gave Andorra its freedom in AD 803, after wresting it from the Moors, as a reward for the inhabitants' aid in the battle. Over the next dozen centuries or so, Andorra played the rope in a large-scale game of tug-of-war between the Spanish Counts of Urgell, the Church of Urgell, and the French King. Only in 1990 did Andorra create a commission to draft a democratic constitution, which it then adopted on March 14, 1993. The citizenry is comfortably trilingual, but the official language of Catalan is still spoken with pride.

SUGGESTED ITINERARY

THE BEST OF (OKAY, ALL OF) ANDORRA IN 3 DAYS Three days in Andorra should be spent enjoying the outdoor activities that this tiny nation has to offer. First, spend, spend, spend in the duty-free shops of **Andorra la Vella** (see p. 70; 1 day). Then hike Andorra's mountains, including its tallest peak, **Pic Alt de la Coma Pedrosa** (2946m) in nearby (and what isn't?) **La Massana** (p. 70; 2 days). In the winter, these same mountains offer unparalleled skiing—swoosh down the slopes until you collapse in your ski boots.

Andorra has no currency of its own. All establishments are required to accept both *pesetas* and *francs*, although *pesetas* are more prevalent. In fact, currency seems to flow like water, as the absence of a sales tax (and the abundance of duty-free shops) draws consumers from all over Europe. **Phones** require an STA *teletar-jeta* (telecard) available at the tourist office, post office, or kiosk (500ptas). You cannot make collect calls, and AT&T does not have an international access code. **Directory assistance:** ☎111. **Country code:** 376.

☎ TRANSPORTATION

The only way to get to Andorra is by **car** or **bus,** as the country has no airport or train station. Visitors are required to show a valid passport or an EU identity card to enter the country. All traffic from France must enter through the town of **Pas de la Casa;** the Spanish gateway town is **La Seu d'Urgell. Andor-Inter/Samar buses** (Madrid ☎91 468 41 90; Toulouse ☎61 58 14 53; Andorra ☎82 62 89) connect Andorra la Vella to **Madrid** (9hr.; departs Tu, Th, and Su; 4900ptas), while **Alsina Graells** (☎82 65 67) and **Eurolines** run to **Barcelona** (3-4hr., 4 per day, 2850ptas). All buses arrive at and depart from **Estació d'Autobusos,** on C. Bonaventura Riberaygua. To get to the station from Pl. Princep Benlloch, follow Av. Meritxell, turn right after crossing the river, and then take the first left; take the fourth right and go straight for four to five blocks (20min.). To go anywhere else in Spain, take a **La Hispano-Andorra bus** (☎82 13 72) from Andorra la Vella to La Seu d'Urgell (30min., 5-7 per day, 340ptas) and change there for an Alsina Graells bus. Efficient **intercity buses** (100-300ptas) connect the villages: all buses stop in Andorra la Vella, so don't worry about finding the right bus—look at the direction sign in the front window.

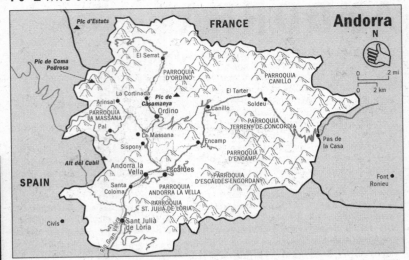

ANDORRA LA VELLA

Andorra la Vella (pop. 20,000), the country's capital, is little more than a narrow, cluttered road flanked by shop after duty-free shop. There is more to Andorra la Vella than shopping, but there isn't *much* more. The sixteenth-century **Casa de la Vall** (House of the Valleys), is the home of Andorra's pocket-sized parliament. (☎82 12 34. Open M-F 9am-1pm and 3-7pm. Guided tours only.) All buses terminate at the **Estació d'Autobusos**, on C. Bonaventura Riberaygua. To get to the **tourist office** on Av. Dr. Villanova from the bus stop on Av. Princep Benlloch, continue east just past the *plaça* on the left and take Av. Dr. Villanova down to the right. (Open July-Sept. M-Sa 9am-1pm and 3-7pm; Oct.-June M-Sa 10am-1pm and 3-7pm, Su 10am-1pm.) Send **email** from **Baviera,** opposite the tourist office. (600ptas per 30min. Open daily 8:30am-1am.) Dream of duty-free cheese at **Pensió La Rosa,** Antic C. Major 18, off Av. Princep Benlloch. (☎82 18 10. Singles 2000ptas; doubles 3500ptas.)

ELSEWHERE IN ANDORRA

"Elsewhere" is where to go in Andorra. **Ordino** (pop. 2219; 1304m), 5km northeast of La Massana, is convenient for hiking and skiing adventures. An easy four-hour hike from town tours the lakes of **Tristaina.** In Andorra, "bigger is better," unless, of course, you're talking about Ordino's mega-small **Microminiature Museum** (☎83 83 38), Edifici Coma. The **bus** from Andorra la Vella to La Massana continues on to Ordino (145ptas). The **tourist office** is on C. Nou Desvio. (☎73 70 80. Open July-Sept. Su 9am-7pm; Oct.-June M-Sa 9am-1pm and 3-7pm, Su 9am-noon.) The tiny town of **Canillo** (pop. 952; 1400-2813m), in the center of the country, suffers from the same architectural blandness as the rest of Andorra, but is surrounded by fine scenery and great **skiing. Soldeu-El Tarter** (☎85 11 51) occupies 840 hectares of skiable area between Andorra la Vella and Pas de la Casa, France; **free buses** transport skiers from hotels in Canillo. **Hotel Comerç,** on the road to Andorra La Vella, with bare rooms at bare prices, is the nearest budget place to snooze. (☎85 10 20. Singles 1500ptas; doubles 3000ptas.)

🏔 **OUTDOOR ACTIVITIES.** An extensive network of **hiking** trails traverses the country. The free and multilingual tourist office brochure *Sports Activities* includes suggested itineraries, potential routes, and bike rental locations, and is helpful for planning excursions. The *Grandes-Randonnées* trails #7 and 11 traverse nearly all of the country. La Massana is home to Andorra's tallest peak, **Pic Alt de la Coma Pedrosa** (2946m). Ordino is also a base for trails of varying difficulty levels. In the winter, Andorra offers **skiing** opportunities galore. The four outstanding resorts within its boundaries all rent equipment and attract the masses. **Pal** (☎73 70 00), 10km from La Massana, is a biggie. For more info inquire at **SKI Andorra** (☎86 43 89) or the tourist offices.

AUSTRIA

AUSTRIAN SHILLING

US$1 = 16.00 AS	10AS = US$0.62
CDN$1 = 10.81 AS	10AS = CDN$0.93
EURO€1 = 13.76 AS	10AS = EURO€0.73
UK£1 = 22.43 AS	10AS = UK£0.45
IR£1 = 17.47 AS	10AS = IR£0.57
AUS$1 = 8.95 AS	10AS = AUS$1.12
NZ$1 = 6.83 AS	10AS = NZ$1.46
SAR1 = 2.24 AS	10AS = SAR4.46

PHONE CODE | Country Code: 43. **International dialing prefix:** 00 (900 in Vienna)

The mighty Austro-Hungarian Empire may have crumbled after World War I, but Austria remains a complex, multi-ethnic country with a fascinating history. Drawing on centuries of Habsburg political maneuvering, Austria has become a skillful mediator between Eastern and Western Europe. But Austria is renowned not so much for its strategic political situation as for its brilliant artists, writers, and musicians. From Gustav Klimt's *Jugendstil* paintings to Arthur Schnitzler's dark insights into imperial decadence to Beethoven's thundering symphonies, Austria has had an indelible impact on Western art and literature. Austria owes its contemporary fame and fortune to the meeting of its history with the overpowering Alpine landscape that hovers over the remnants of Austria's tumultuous past. A mention of Austria evokes images of onion-domed churches set against snow-capped Alpine peaks, lush meadows of wildflowers, dark forests, and mighty castles.For extensive and entertaining information on Austria's attractions, pick up a copy of *Let's Go: Austria & Switzerland 2001.*

SUGGESTED ITINERARIES

THREE DAYS Spend all three days in **Vienna** (p. 80), the Imperial headquarters of romance. From the stately **Staatsoper** to the glittering **Musikverein,** the majestic **Hofburg** to Otto Wagner's simple **Kirche am Steinhof,** Vienna's attractions will leave you with enough sensory stimulation to last until your next vacation.

ONE WEEK Begin by spending two days in Western Austria in the mountain towns of **Innsbruck** (p. 111) and **Kitzbuhel** (p. 108) for an array of hiking and outdoor opportunities. Stop in **Salzburg** (1 day; p. 95) to see the home of the *Sound of Music* and Mozart. Move on to **Hallstatt** (p. 103) for hiking in the **Echental Valley** (p. 104) and **Dachstein Ice Caves** (p. 104), and end in **Vienna** (3 days; p. 80).

BEST OF AUSTRIA, TWO WEEKS Start in **Bregenz** for views of rolling hills (2 days; p. 115). Take the train to **Innsbruck,** to see museums and mountains (1 day; p. 111), then swing by **Kitzbuhel** for hiking and outdoors (1 day; p. 108). For more mountains, explore the Hohe Tauern National Park, and Krimml Waterfalls from **Zell am See** (2 days; p. 107). Next, tour **Hallstatt;** famous for its stunning hikes and ice caves (1 day; p. 103). To see the glory of rural Austria with no pretension, take a bus to **Grünau** (1 day; p. 104). Overdose on Maria von Trapp and Mozart in **Salzburg** (1 day; p. 95, then make your way to **Vienna** for a grand finale of romance, waltzes and Baroque architecture (4 days; p. 80).

LIFE AND TIMES

HISTORY AND POLITICS

IN THE BEGINNING (TO AD 900)

Beginning in Paleolithic times, nomadic hunter-gatherers roamed through what is now Austria for thousands of years and by 6000 BC, even the remotest areas of Austria had become part of a vigorous commercial network that linked mining centers and agricultural communities. Around 500 BC, the **Celts** established the kingdom of **Noricum.** In turn, the **Romans** conquered their Austrian neighbors to secure the Danube frontier against marauding Germanic tribes and eventually Christianity came to Austria via the Roman soldiers. Germanic raids, however, finally forced the Romans to retreat from Noricum in the 5th century. Over the next three centuries, various peoples, including the Huns, Ostrogoths, and Langobards romped through the Austrian territories. Eventually, three groups divided the region: the **Alemanni** in the south, the **Slavs** in the southwest, and the **Bavarians** in the north.

THE HOLY ROMAN EMPIRE AND THE HABSUBURGS (950-1720)

Austria had its first taste of imperialism in the mid-9th century when **Charlemagne,** founder of the Holy Roman Empire, turned his eyes east in hopes of heading off invaders on the frontiers of his empire. When he died, Charlemagne's kingdom collapsed and the eastern regions were overrun by marauding tribes. After his father drove invaders out of the area, **Holy Roman Emperor Otto II** entrusted **Margrave Liutpoldus** (a.k.a. **Leopold of Babenberg**) with the defense of the Empire's eastern territories. The Babenberg dynasty concentrated on stabilizing the frontiers but also on extending its protectorate by shrewdness and strategic marriages.

Unfortunately for the dynasty, the last Babenberg died childless, leaving the country fragmented. Through a bloody conflict, **Rudolf of Habsburg** emerged as victor of the crown and lay the foundation for six centuries of Habsburg dynastic rule in Austria. Gradually, the Habsburgs accumulated the various regions that make up modern Austria and then some. Friedrich III, for instance, strategically arranged the marriage of his son, **Maximilian I,** to the heiress of the powerful Burgundian kingdom, giving the Habsburgs control of much of western Europe, including the Netherlands. Maximilian's son Philip married into the Spanish royal house, endowing his son, Charles V, with a vast empire that encompassed Austria, The Netherlands, Castile, Spanish America, Aragon, and the Spanish possessions in Italy and the Mediterranean. As if this weren't enough, Charles was elected Holy Roman Emperor in 1519, gaining nominal control of Germany as well.

Despite their massive possessions and imperial veneer, the Habsburg ship hit rough waters in the 16th and 17th centuries as a result of Martin Luther's Protestant **Reformation** and the ensuing **Counter-Reformation.** Early victories over Protestant forces during the **Thirty Years War** (1618-1648) restored Habsburg control of Bohemia, where they promptly (and forcibly) converted most of the peasants back to Catholicism. Soon after, though, the Ottoman Turks besieged Vienna until **Prince Eugene of Savoy** drove them out. After the death of the last Spanish Habsburg,

---

A ROSE BY ANOTHER NAME? Medieval history celebrates Austria's two major ruling families: the Babenbergs (976-1246) and the Hapsburgs (1278-1918). Unfortunately for the history books, the Babenbergs were not actually named Babenberg, but rather Poppon; furthermore, their family seat was not the Castle Babenberch in Bamberg, Germany, but a nameless castle somewhere in German Swabia. The name Babenberg was an invention of the 12th-century historian Otto von Freising, himself a Poppon, who found the name of his ancestor Poppo von Grabfeld unsuitable, and so casually renamed the dynasty "Babenberg." This relatively harmless deception quickly became an integral part of Austrian history, with the result that historians today still refer to the "Babenbergs" without a second thought.

Austria (Österreich)

AUSTRIA

SLOVAKIA

CZECH REPUBLIC

HUNGARY

CROATIA

SLOVENIA

ITALY

LIECHTENSTEIN

SWITZERLAND

GERMANY

Munich

Český Krumlov

Drosendorf
Gmünd
Horn
Altenburg
Freistadt
Aigen
Passau
Schärding
Braunau am Inn
Linz
Wels
St. Martin
Lambach
Mauthausen
Königswiesen
Dürnstein
Spitz
Krems/Stein
Tulln
Melk
Amstetten
Mödling
Baden bei Wien
St. Pölten
Vienna
Donau
LOWER AUSTRIA
Rohrau
Neusiedl am See
Mörbisch
Rust
Neusiedlersee
Eisenstadt
Wiener Neustadt
Forchtenstein
BURGEN-LAND
Oberwart
Fürstenfeld
Riegersburg
Drava
Graz
Eggenberg
Stübing
Bruck a. d. Mur
Mariazell
Salza
Leoben
STYRIA
Judenberg
Murau
Friesach
St. Veit
Gurk
Mariasaal
Feldkirchen
CARINTHIA
Wörther-see
Klagenfurt
Villach
Drau
Gail
Lienz
EAST TYROL
Möll
Heiligenblut
Grossglockner
Spittal an der Drau
St. Michael in Lungau
Bad Kleinkirchheim
Badgastein
Obertauern
Radstadt
Bad Aussee
Hallstatt
Gmunden
Grünau
Spital am Pyhrn
Admont
St. Johann im Pongau
Zell am See
Krimml
SALZBURG
Hohe Tauern
Kufstein
Kitzbühel
Zell am Ziller
Mayrhofen
Fulpmes
Innsbruck
TYROL
Inn
Jenbach
Seefeld
Telfs
Zugspitze
Ehrwald
Reutte
Lermoos
Imst
Landeck
Sölden
St. Anton am Arlberg
Piz Buin
Stuben
Zürs
Lech
Schruns
Bludenz
Feldkirch
Bregenz
VORARLBERG
Bodensee
Lienz

Danube

Inn

Traun

Mondsee
St. Wolfgang
St. Gilgen
UPPER AUSTRIA
Kremsmünster
Ebensee
Bad Ischl
Hallein
Salzburg
St. Florian
Steyr

St. Wels

N

50 miles
50 kilometers

Eugene again came through when he led the Habsburg troops to victory over the French in the **War of Spanish Succession,** which ended with a treaty giving Spain to France, while the Habsburgs gained Belgium, Sardinia, and parts of Italy.

CASTLES CRUMBLE (1740-1900)
Like a house of cards, the Habsburg empire teetered as it grew. When, thanks to the **Pragmatic Sanction** passed by her father (which allowed succession through the female line), Maria Theresia ascended the throne in 1740, her neighbors were eager to see Habsburg power diminished. King **Friedrich the Great** of Prussia snatched a prosperous Habsburg province which Maria Theresia was never able to re-claim. The marriage of her daughter Marie Antoinette to the future Louis XVI was a tragic attempt to forge an alliance with France, which was quickly negated by the **French Revolution.** The Revolution showcased the military genius of **Napoleon Bonaparte,** who secured French possession of many Austrian territories. Napoleon's troops even invaded Vienna, where Napoleon took up residence in Maria Theresa's favorite palace, Schönbrunn (see p. 91), and married her granddaughter.

Napoleon's success led to the official establishment of the Austrian empire. In 1804, Franz II renounced his claim to the now-defunct Holy Roman crown and proclaimed himself Franz I, Emperor of Austria. During the Congress of Vienna, which redrew the map of Europe after Napoleon's defeat, Austrian Chancellor **Clemens Wenzel Lothar von Metternich** tried to restore the old order while orchestrating the re-consolidation of Austrian power. He managed to usher in a long peace of commerce and industry.

In the spring of 1848, the French philosophy of middle-class revolution reached Austria. Students and workers revolted and took control of the imperial palace, demanding a constitution and freedom of the press. The movement was divided though, allowing the government to suppress the rebellion. The epileptic emperor **Ferdinand I,** however, was pressured to abdicate in favor of his nephew, **Franz Josef I,** whose 68-year reign was one of the longest in history.

Austria's position in Europe continued to shift throughout Franz Josef's life. Prussia, under **Otto von Bismarck,** dominated European politics, defeating Austria in 1866 and establishing the dual **Austro-Hungarian** monarchy. By the turn of the century, Vienna was in political turmoil; the anti-Semitic Christian Socialists were on the rise. Meanwhile, burgeoning nationalist sentiments led to severe divisions within the multinational Austro-Hungarian Empire. Tired and disheartened after half a century on the throne, the suicide of his only son, and the murder of his wife, Franz Josef wanted to maintain *Ruhe und Ordnung* (peace and order), but he could not stop the tide of modernity.

CURRENTS OF MODERNITY (1914-1945)
Brimming with ethnic tension and locked into the rigid system of alliances that resulted from the 19th century wars, the Austro-Hungarian Empire was a disaster waiting to happen. The spark that set off the explosion was the journey **Franz Ferdinand,** the heir to the imperial throne, took to Sarajevo in June 1914, where he was assassinated by a young Serbian nationalist. Austria's declaration of war against Serbia set off a chain reaction that pulled most of Europe into the conflict, marking the beginning of World War I. Franz Josef died in 1916, leaving the throne to his reluctant grandnephew **Karl I** who struggled in vain to preserve the Habsburg inheritance. Despite his valiant efforts and those of the army, declarations of independence by the people ensured the demise of the monarchy. On November 11, 1918, Karl finally got the peace he had striven for, but only after the first **Republic of Austria** was established, ending the 640-year-old Habsburg dynasty.

Between 1918 and 1938, Austria had its first, bitter taste of parliamentary democracy as the shrunken state became the **First Republic.** The Republic suffered massive inflation, unemployment, and near economic collapse, but was stabilized by the mid-1920s. In 1933, the weak coalition government gave way to **Engelbert Dollfuss's** declaration of martial law in order to protect Austria from Hitler. Two years later he was assassinated by Austrian Nazis. The well-known conclusion to the tale of the First Republic is the Nazi **annexation** of Austria. On March 12, 1938, the new Nazi chancellor, who was placed in power by Hitler, invited German troops into

Austria. While WWII raged, tens of thousands of Jews, political and religious dissidents, handicapped persons, Gypsies, and homosexuals were forced to emigrate or sent to concentration·camps.

After Soviet troops brutally liberated Vienna in 1945, Austria was divided into four zones of occupation by Allied troops. As a Nazi victim, however, Austria enjoyed some political rights. During the Allied occupation of Austria, the Soviets tried to make Austria Communist, but finally settled for stripping their sector of anything that could be moved. Despite Russian plundering and severe famines in the late 1940s, the **Marshall Plan** helped to jump-start the Austrian economy, laying the foundation for Austria's present prosperity.

The State Treaty, along with the Federal Constitution, which was restored in 1945 from the First Republic, formed the basis for the nation, which is frequently referred to as the **Second Republic.** These documents provide for a president (head of state) who is elected for six-year terms, a chancellor (head of government), usually the leader of the strongest party, a bicameral parliamentary legislature, and strong provincial governments. Until very recently the government has been dominated by two parties, the Social Democratic Party (SPÖ), and the People's Party (ÖVP). The rigidness of the two party system has raised questions of corruption and paternalism, many of which came out in the recent election of the Freedom Party (see **Austria Today,** below). The two parties have, however, built up one of the world's most successful industrial economies, with enviably low unemployment and inflation rates, as well as a generous, comprehensive welfare state. Austria has emerged as a progressive, social democratic welfare state.

During the 1990s Austria has moved toward closer European integration. In 1994 **Thomas Klestil,** the current President, was elected on a platform of integration. In 1995 the country was accepted into the European Union (EU) and the people accepted membership through a national referendum. Austria also joined the Economic and Monetary Union (EMU), which inaugurated the euro, a common European currency, on January 1, 1999.

AUSTRIA TODAY

Austria has recently been plastered over front pages internationally thanks to the gains made by the far-right **Freedom Party** in last year's elections. This party is infamous primarily for its leader **Jörg Haider** who assumed the reigns of the then-powerless party in 1986. Haider entered the public eye for his anti-immigrant stance and his many remarks that have been seen as Nazi-sympathetic. In leading his party to power Haider called the Nazi camps "punishment camps" rather than concentration camps. He has called for Austrian military members who fought for the Nazis to have pride in their work. Politically he advocates a complete ban on immigration, playing off Austrian fears of the influx of immigrants from bordering Eastern Europe. In the November 1999 elections Haider's party claimed 27% of the vote, second among all parties, effectively breaking up the traditional two party lock that the Social Democratic Party and People's Party have held on the country's politics since WWII. (The Social Democratic Party came in first in these elections with 33% of the vote, but refused to form a coalition with Haider's party.)

Though Haider did not have a post in the new federal government—he remains governor of the province of Carinthia—the new government was met by fierce protests both domestically and internationally. In Vienna 100,000 protestors turned out on the day that the Freedom Party government was sworn in. At the same time the 14 other nations of the **European Union** levied unprecedented political sanctions against Austria in unison.

While Haider's rise gives reason for the traveler to pause before visiting Austria, careful consideration should be given to the actual circumstances before plans are changed. The primary reasons for the people's swing toward Haider's party are independent of Haider's racist views. Additionally, the Freedom Party's success— still only 27 percent of the vote—should not be seen as an endorsement by the Austrian people of Haider's racist comments. In fact the 1999 elections were not seen as either influential or decisive by the Austrian people; the election had the lowest voter turnout in Austria's post-war history.

AUSTRIA

THE ARTS

VISUAL ART AND ARCHITECTURE

Landlocked in the middle of Europe and rolling with cash, the Habsburgs married into power and bought into art. The emergence of art into its own right is exhibited by the works of **Gustav Klimt** (1862-1918) and his followers who founded what is known as the **Secession** movement. Secessionists sought to create space and appreciation for symbolist, naturalist, impressionist, and other new artistic styles. The effect of this freedom might be seen in Klimt's own later paintings, such as *The Kiss*, which combine naturalistic portraits with abstractly patterned backgrounds. **Oskar Kokoschka** and **Egon Schiele** revolted against "art *qua* art," seeking to present the energy formerly concealed behind the Secession's aesthetic surface. Schiele, like the young Kokoschka, painted with a feverish intensity in line and color. His paintings are controversial even today, for their depictions of tortured figures seemingly destroyed by their own bodies or by debilitating sexuality. His *Embrace* (1917) and *The Self Seer* (1911) offer examples of his emphasis on expression.

The emergence of architecture in Austria began with the extravagance of the **Baroque** style. With fluidly ornate forms orchestrated into a succession of grand entrances, dreamy vistas, and overwrought, cupid-covered facades, the Baroque invokes what was then the most popular art form in Europe, music. This style is exhibited exquisitely in the **Schönbrunn** (see p. 91) and **Hofburg** (see p. 89) palaces, as well as in the **Trinity** in Salzburg. Austria's 19th-century conservative modernism is showcased by the **Ringstraße** (see p. 88), the broad circular boulevard that demarcates Vienna and that was authorized in 1857 by Emperor Franz Josef to replace fortified medieval walls. This historicist taste was identified with Vienna and came to be known as the **Ringstraße Style.**

In 1897, the "young" artists split from the "old," as proponents of modernism took issue with the Viennese Academy's conservatism. This gave rise to the **Judendstil (a.k.a. Art Nouveau)** which aimed to formulate a new way of seeing the world. The new way turned out to be the ethic of function over form which was embraced by Vienna's artistic elite, and most notably by the guru of architectural modernism, **Otto Wagner.** These ideals later influenced the **Bauhaus** of Weimar Germany and paved the way for **Adolf Loos** who proclaimed, "Ornamentation is criminal."

In the 1920s and early 1930s, the **Social Democratic** administration built thousands of apartments in large **municipal projects,** their style reflecting the newfound assertiveness of the workers' movement and the ideals of **Urban Socialism.** The most outstanding project of the era is the **Karl-Marx-Hof** (Heiligenstädter Str. 82-92, XIX, Vienna). The huge structure, completed in 1930, extends over 1km and consists of 1,600 apartments clustered around several courtyards. **Hans Hollein** contributed to Viennese **postmodern** architecture in the **Haas House** (I, Stock-im-Eisen-Pl.).

LITERATURE

In the Roman settlement Vindobona, **Marcus Aurelius** wrote his *Meditations*, starting a long tradition of Viennese immigré (and emigré) artists. On a more epic scale, the **Nibelungenlied,** which dates from around 1200, is one of the most impressive heroic epics in German. Born in Vienna in 1801, **Johann Nestroy** wrote biting comedies and satires lampooning social follies such as *Der Talisman* and the *Tannhauser.* **Adalbert Stifter,** often called Austria's greatest novelist, wrote with classical themes and strongly metaphysical descriptions of nature. His short stories and novels, such as *Der Condor* (1840) and *Der Nachsommer* (1857), represent the height of the Austria's classical writers. A classicist with a more lyrical style, Franz Grillparzer penned pieces about the conflict between a life of thought and a life of action in such plays as *The Waves of the Sea and Love* (1831).

Around 1890, Austrian literature rapidly transformed in the heat of the "merry apocalypse" atmosphere that permeated society at the turn of the century. The literature dating from this second heyday of Austrian culture, known as **fin de siècle,** is legendary. **Sigmund Freud** diagnosed the crisis, **Karl Kraus** implacably unmasked it, **Arthur Schnitzler** dramatized it, **Hugo von Hofmannsthal** ventured a cautious eulogy, and **Georg Trakl** commented on the collapse in feverish verse. The cafe provided the backdrop for the *fin de siècle* literary landscape. **Sigmund Freud** is best known for his theories of sexual repression, which he considered particularly applicable for bourgeois society, and his theories of the unconscious.

Many of Austria's literary titans, such as **Marie von Ebner-Eschenbach** and **Franz Kafka,** lived within the Habsburg protectorate of Bohemia. Ebner-Eschenbach is often called the greatest female Austrian writer, known for her vivid individual portraits and her defense of women's rights. No one else could master the surrealism of Kafka's writing, however, as demonstrated in *The Metamorphosis*, a bizarre and disorienting tale which presents the idea of waking up one day and *really* not feeling like yourself. Austrian literature today is still affected and informed by its literary tradition, but there is plenty of innovation as well. **Ingeborg Bachman**'s stories and novels left an important legacy for Austrian feminism, while **Thomas Bernhard's** *Holzfäller* (Woodcutters) is a cogent and mature critique of Austrian society.

MUSIC

The first master musician of Viennese Classicism was **Josef Haydn,** but the work of **Wolfgang Amadeus Mozart** represents the pinnacle of the time period. He was the ideal child prodigy, playing violin and piano by age four, and produced such well-known operas as *Don Giovanni*. Mozart's work has been proclaimed to be "the culmination of all beauty in music." Only **Ludwig van Beethoven** could compete with Mozart for the devotion of the Viennese. His *Ninth Symphony* had an enormous cultural impact. **Johannes Brahms** straddled musical traditions but became the grand old man of the Viennese music scene in the Romantic Era.

Anton Bruckner is famous for his massively orchestrated symphonies and is recognized as one of the greatest symphonic masters of the 19th century. Between **Johann Strauss the Elder** (1804-1849), and his son **Johann Strauss the Younger** (1825-1899), the Strauss family kept Vienna on its toes for much of the 19th century. They created waltzes which offered a new exhilaration that broke free from older, more formal dances. Breaking into the modern era, **Arnold Schönberg** rejected tonal keys in favor of atonality which produced a highly abstracted sound from the melodic works of the classicists. **Anton von Webern** and **Alban Berg** were both students of Schönberg and both suffered under Nazi occupation for their creation of "degenerate art."

FOOD AND DRINK

Loaded with fat, salt, and cholesterol, traditional Austrian cuisine is a cardiologist's nightmare but a delight to the palate. Staple foods include *Schweinefleisch* (pork), *Kalbsfleisch* (veal), *Wurst* (sausage), *Ei* (egg), *Käse* (cheese), *Brot* (bread), and *Kartoffeln* (potatoes). Austria's best known dish, *Wienerschnitzel*, is a meat cutlet (usually veal or pork) fried in butter with bread crumbs. Vegetarians should look for *Spätzle* (noodles), *Eierschwammerl* (tiny yellow mushrooms), or anything with the word "Vegi" in it. The best discount supermarkets are **Billa** and **Hofer,** where you can buy cheap bags of *Semmeln* (rolls) and fruits and veggies. Natives nurse their sweet tooths at *Café-Konditoreien* with *Kaffee und Kuchen* (coffee and cake). Try *Sacher Torte*, a rich chocolate cake layered with marmalade; *Linzer Torte*, a light yellow cake with currant jam embedded in it; *Apfelstrudel;* or just about any pastry. Austrian beers are outstanding—try *Stiegl Bier*, a Salzburg brew, *Zipfer Bier* from upper Austria, and *Gösser Bier* from Styria.

ESSENTIALS

DOCUMENTS AND FORMALITIES

For citizens of the EU, Australia, Canada, New Zealand, and the US, visas are not necessary for stays of less than three months, just a valid passport; visas are required for working or studying in Austria. South Africans must have a visa and a valid passport for all stays. For more information, visit www.bmaa.gv.at/embassy/uk/index.html.en).

AUSTRIA

Austrian Embassies at Home: Australia, 12 Talbot St., Forrest, Canberra ACT 2603 (☎ (02) 6295 1533; email austria@dynamite.com.au); **Canada,** 445 Wilbrod St., Ottawa, ON KIN 6M7 (☎ (613) 789 1444; fax 789 3431; email embassy@austro.org; www.austro.org); **Ireland,** 115 Ailesbury Court Apts., 93 Ailesbury Rd., Dublin 4 (☎ (01) 269 45 77 or 269 14 51); **New Zealand,** Consular General, 22-4 Garrett St., Wellington (☎ (04) 801 9709; for visas or passports, contact Australian office); **UK,** 18 Belgrave Mews West, London SW1 X 8HU (☎ (0207) 235 37 31; email embassy@austria.org.uk; www.austria.org.uk); **US,** 3524 International Court NW, Washington DC 20008-3035 (☎ (202) 895 6700); **South Africa,** 1109 Duncan St., Momentum Office Park, 0011 Brooklyn, Pretoria; P.O. Box 95572, 0145 Waterkloof, Pretoria (☎ 012 462 483; email saembvie@ins.at).

Foreign Embassies in Austria: All foreign embassies are in **Vienna** (p. 80).

TRANSPORTATION

BY PLANE. The only major international airport is **Vienna's** Schwechat Flughafen. European flights also land in Salzburg, Graz, Innsbruck, and Klagenfurt. From the UK, **buzz** flies to Vienna (☎ (0870) 240 70 70; www.buzzaway.com. UK£50-80.)

BY TRAIN. The **Österreichische Bundesbahn (ÖBB),** Austria's federal railroad, operates an efficient 5760km of tracks accommodating frequent, fast, and comfortable trains. The ÖBB publishes the yearly *Fahrpläne Kursbuch Bahn-Inland*, a compilation of all transportation schedules in Austria (100AS). **Eurail, InterRail,** and **Europe East** passes are valid in Austria. The **Austrian Railpass** allows three days of travel within any 15-day period on all rail lines, including Wolfgangsee ferries and private rail lines; it also entitles holders to 50% off on bike rental at train stations and on DDSG steamers between Passau, Linz, and Vienna (2nd-class US$104, up to 5 additional days US$16 each). The one-month **Bundesnetzkarte** (National Network Pass), sold only in Austria, allows unlimited domestic train travel, including Wolfgangsee ferries and private rail lines, as well as half-price tickets for Bodensee and Danube ferries (2nd-class 4000AS, first-class 6000AS). The **Kilometer Bank,** sold only in Austria, involves pre-purchasing a given number of kilometers' worth of travel, which can be used by one to six people traveling together on trips of over 70km one-way in first or second class. For **rail info,** dial 01 717.

BY BUS, FERRY, AND CAR. The efficient Austrian bus system consists mainly of orange **BundesBuses,** which cover areas inaccessible by train. They usually cost about as much as trains, and railpasses are not valid. You can buy discounted tickets, valid for one week, for any particular route. A **Mehrfahrtenkarte** gives you six tickets for the price of five. For **bus info,** dial ☎ (0222) 71101 within Austria (from outside dial ☎ (1) 71101). Private **ferry** services are offered on most lakes, while the DDSG runs boats down the Danube between Vienna and Krems, Melk, Passau, and internationally to Bratislava and Budapest. Driving is a convenient way to see the more isolated parts of Austria. The roads are generally very good and well-marked, and Austrian drivers are quite careful. Be aware that Austrian law tolerates only a very minimal blood-alcohol level. **Drivers** must purchase a permit/sticker at Austria's border to place on the windshield (70AS per week) or face a US$130 fine. If renting a car, it is usually cheaper to do so in Germany.

BY BIKE AND BY THUMB. Bicycling is a great way to get around Austria; not only are the roads generally level and safe, but many private companies and train stations rent bikes (generally 150AS per day, 90AS with a railpass or valid train ticket from that day). If you get a bike at a train station, you can return it to any participating station. Look for the *Gepäckbeförderung* symbol (a little bicycle) on departure schedules to see if bikes are permitted in the baggage car. If your bike breaks down on the road, some auto clubs may rescue you; try the **Austrian Automobile, Motorcycle, and Touring Club (ÖAMTC)** (☎ 120) or **ARBÖ** (☎ 123).

Austria is a rough place to **hitchhike**—Austrians rarely stop, and many mountain roads are all but deserted. Generally, hitchhikers stand on highway *Knoten* (on-ramps) and wait. *Let's Go* does not recommend hitchhiking. For a more certain ride, there are ride service, or **Mitfahrzentrale,** offices in larger cities.

TOURIST SERVICES AND MONEY

EMERGENCY	Police: ☎ 133. **Ambulance:** ☎ 144. **Fire:** ☎ 122.

TOURIST OFFICES. Virtually every town in Austria has a **tourist office,** most marked by a green **"i"** sign. You may run into language difficulties in the small-town offices, but most brochures are available in English. The website for Austrian tourism is www.experienceaustria.com.

Tourist Boards at Home: Australia, 1st fl., 36 Carrington St., Sydney, NSW 2000 (☎ (02) 92 99 36 21; fax 92 99 38 08); **Canada,** 2 Bloor St. East #3330, Toronto, ON M4W 1A8 (☎ (416) 967-3381; fax 967-4101); **UK,** 14 Cork St., London W1X 1PF (☎ (020) 76 29 04 61; fax 74 99 60 38); **US,** 500 Fifth Ave, #800, P.O. Box 1142, New York, NY 10108-1142 (☎ (212) 944-6880; fax 730-4568; email antonyc@ibm.net).

CURRENCY AND EXCHANGE. The unit of currency in Austria is the **Schilling,** abbreviated as **AS, ÖS,** or, within Austria, simply **S.** Each *Schilling* is subdivided into 100 **Groschen (g).** Coins come in 2, 5, 10, and 50g, and 1, 5, 10, and 20AS denominations. Bills come in 20, 50, 100, 500, 1000, and 5000AS amounts. Currency exchange is easiest at ATMs, train stations, and post offices, where rates are the same as or close to bank rates.

Prices: Though Austria is not the cheapest destinations, there are ways to experience it on a tight budget. If you stay in hostels and prepare most of your own food, expect to spend anywhere from $25 to $50 per person per day in Austria. Accommodations start at about $15 in Austria, while a basic sit-down meal usually costs around $12.

Tipping and bargaining: In Austria, menus will say whether service is included (*Preise inclusive* or *Bedienung inclusiv*); if it is, you don't have to tip. If it's not, leave a tip up to 10%. Austrian restaurants expect you to seat yourself, and servers will not bring the bill until you ask them to do so. Don't leave tips on the table. Say *Zahlen bitte* (TSAHL-en BIT-uh) to settle your accounts. Be aware that some restaurants charge for each piece of bread that you eat during your meal. Don't expect to bargain in shops or markets in Austria, except at flea markets and the Naschmarkt in Vienna.

Taxes: Austria has a 20-34% **value-added tax** (VAT), which is applied to all purchases of books, clothing, souvenir items, art items, jewelry, perfume, alcohol, cigarettes, etc. You can get it refunded if the total is at least 1000AS (US$95) at one store.

ACCOMMODATIONS AND CAMPING

Rooms in Austria are usually spotless; even the least appealing of Austria's **youth hostels** *(Jugendherbergen)* are quite tolerable. Most hostels charge US$12-25 a night for dorms. Many hostels are somewhat cramped and offer little privacy; hordes of school kids may also try your patience. Austria has two independent organizations which run the over 80 HI hostels in the country; the ÖJHV and the ÖJHW. Non-HI members can stay in all of these hostels but are usually charged a surcharge. **Hotels** are usually quite expensive. If you're on a tight budget, look instead for *Zimmer Frei* or *Privatzimmer* signs, which advertise rooms in private houses for a more reasonable $10-25. Otherwise, smaller pensions and *Gästehäuser* are often within the budget traveler's range. **Camping** is a popular option; prices range from 50-70AS per person and 25-60AS per tent, with a tax of 8-10AS.

SKIING AND HIKING

Western Austria provides some of the world's best skiing and hiking; the areas around Innsbruck and Kitzbühel in the Tirol are particularly well saturated with lifts and runs. High-season runs from mid-December to mid-January and from February to March. With an extensive network of hiking trails and Alpine refuges, Austria's Alps are as accessible as they are gorgeous. A membership in the **Österreichischer Alpenverein (ÖAV)** grants half-off the cost of staying at a series of mountain **huts** across the Tirol and throughout Austria, all a day's hike apart from each other. For membership info, contact Österreichischer Alpenverein, Willhelm-

Greil-Str. 15, A-6010 Innsbruck (☎ (512) 58 78 28; fax 58 88 42). Membership (US$55, students under 25 US$40, plus US$10 one-time fee) also includes use of **Deutscher Alpenverein** (German Alpine Club) huts.

COMMUNICATION

MAIL. Letters take 1-2 days within Austria. **Airmail** to North America takes 5-7 days, but up to 2 weeks to Australia and New Zealand. Mark all letters and packages "mit Flugpost" or "par avion." The cheapest option is to send **aerogrammes.** *Poste Restante* letters to: Katie SCHULTZ, Postlagernde Briefe, A-1010 Vienna, Austria.

TELEPHONES. You can usually make international calls from a pay phone, but a better option is to buy **phone cards** *(Wertkarten)* at post offices, train stations, and *Tabak/Trafik* (50 or 100AS). The quickest and cheapest way to call abroad is to go to a post office and ask for *Zurückruf,* or "return call," and have your party call you back. **International direct dial** numbers include: **AT&T, ☎**022 90 30 11; **BT Direct, ☎**0800 20 02 09; **Canada Direct, ☎**0800 20 02 17; **MCI WorldPhone Direct, ☎**022 90 30 12; **Sprint Global One, ☎**0800 20 02 36; and **Telkom South Africa Direct, ☎**022 90 30 27.

INTERNET ACCESS. Most towns in Austria have internet cafes. It usually costs 50-100AS per hr.

LANGUAGE. German is the first language. English is the most common second language in Austria, but any effort to use the mother tongue will be appreciated. Outside of cities and among older residents, English is less common. *Grüss Gott* is the typical greeting. For phrases, see p. 958.

LOCAL FACTS

Time: Austria is 1hr. ahead of Greenwich Mean Time (GMT).

Hours: Most **stores** in Austria close daily noon-3pm, Sa afternoons, and all day Su. Many **museums** are closed M. **Banks** are usually open M-F 8am-12:30pm and 2-4:30pm.

Climate: Warm sweaters are the rule from Sept.-May, while summer is rainy and humid. July is usually the hottest month at up to 38°C (100°F), while February is the coldest, with temperatures down to -10°C (5°F). Mountainous areas get cooler and wetter the higher you go. Snow cover lasts from late Dec. to Mar. in the valleys.

Holidays: New Year's Day (Jan. 1-2); Epiphany (Jan. 6); Good Friday (Apr. 2); Easter Monday (Apr. 5); Labor Day (May 1); Ascension (June 1); Whitmonday (June 12); Corpus Christi (June 22); Assumption Day (Aug. 15); Austrian National Day (Oct. 26); All Saints' Day (Nov. 1); Immaculate Conception (Dec. 8); and Christmas (Dec. 25-26).

Festivals: Just about everything closes down on public holidays, so plan accordingly. Austrians celebrate **Fasching** (Carnaval) during the first 2 weeks of February. Austria's most famous summer **music festivals** are the **Wiener Festwochen** (mid-May to mid-June) and the **Salzburger Festspiele** (late-July to late-Aug.).

VIENNA (WIEN)   ☎0222

Vienna (pop. 1,500,000) overflows with culture, thanks to its inspired musical tradition (Mozart, Beethoven, Schubert, Strauss, Brahms), imperial wealth, and impeccable Baroque art and architecture. It was with reason, though, that satirist Karl Kraus once dubbed Vienna—birthplace of psychoanalysis, atonal music, functionalist architecture, Zionism, and Nazism—a "laboratory for world destruction." Vienna's *fin de siècle* heyday carried the seeds of its decay—the Viennese self-mockingly called it the "merry apocalypse" as they stared down their own dissolution over coffee. The whipped cream and smooth veneer of waltz music concealed a darker reality found in Freud's theories, Kafka's writings, and Mahler's music. The city is now reestablishing itself as the political, cultural, and economic gateway to Eastern Europe. Experimentalism again thrives in Vienna, where rules of genre, style, and structure are constantly redefined.

Vienna

▲ ACCOMMODATIONS
Believe It Or Not, 5
Gästehaus Pfeilgasse, 4
Hostel Ruthensteiner (HI), 8
Jugendg. Wien Briggitenau (HI), 3
Katholisches Studenthaus, 1
Köplingfamilie Wien-Meidling, 9
Lauria Apts./Hostel Panda, 7
Myrtheng. (HI)/Neustiftg. (HI), 6
Porzellaneum der Wiener U., 2
Rudolfinum, 10

AUSTRIA

✈ GETTING THERE AND AWAY

Flights: Wien-Schwechat Flughafen (☎ 700 722 231), 18km from Vienna's center, is the home of **Austrian Airlines** (☎ 17 89; www.aua.com; open M-F 8am-7pm, Sa-Su 8am-5pm). The S-7 connects the airport (Flughafen/Wolfsthal) to Wien Mitte/Landstr. on the U-3 or U-4 lines (every 30min.; 38AS, Eurail not valid). **Vienna Airport Lines Shuttle Buses** run from the airport to the City Air Terminal, opposite Wien Mitte/Landstr. (every 20-30min., 24hr.; 70AS).

Trains: Info ☎ 17 17 (24hr.); schedules online at www.bahn.at. Three main stations:

Westbahnhof, XV, Mariahilferstr. 132, primarily runs trains west. To: **Amsterdam** (14hr., 1 per day, 2276AS); **Berlin** (11hr., 1 per day, 1678AS); **Budapest** (3-4hr., 6 per day, 420AS); **Innsbruck** (6hr., every 2hr., 660AS); **Munich** (4½hr., 5 per day, 788AS); **Paris** (14hr., 2 per day, 2096AS); **Salzburg** (3hr., every hr., 430AS); and **Zurich** (9¼hr., 3 per day, 1122AS).

Südbahnhof, X, Wiedner Gürtel 1a, sends trains mostly south, but also east. To: **Berlin** (9¼hr., 1 per day, 1160AS); **Bratislava** (1hr., 3 per day, 166AS); **Kraków** (7-8hr., 2 per day, 496AS); **Prague** (4½hr., 3 per day, 550AS); **Rome** (13¾hr., 2 per day, 1352AS); and **Venice** (9-10hr., 3 per day, 880AS). Also to **Germany, Greece, Poland, Russia, Spain,** and **Turkey.**

Franz-Josefs Bahnhof, IX, Althamstr. 10, handles mostly commuter trains.

Ferries: Cruise the Danube with **DDSG Donaureisen** (☎ 58 88 00; www.ddsg-blue-danube.at). From 130-690AS; 20% off with Eurail or ISIC. In summer, ferries depart every Su from Reichbrücke (take U-1) hitting the cities of Melk, Spitz, and Dürnstein.

⎚ GETTING AROUND

Public Transportation: Info ☎ 580 00, ☎ 790 91 05 for point-to-point directions; www.wiennet.at/efa. Excellent **U-Bahn** (subway), **bus, Straßenbahn** (tram), and **S-Bahn** (elevated train) systems cover the city. **Single-fare** 22AS if purchased on a bus; 19AS in advance at ticket offices, *Tabak,* or U-Bahn station *Automaten.* The following **passes** are available: **24-hr.** 60AS, **3-day "rover"** 150AS, **7-day** 155AS (valid from M 9am to following M 9am). The 3-day **Vienna Card** (210AS) includes unlimited public transit as well as discounts at museums and sights. Regular trams and subways stop 12:30-5am, but **nightbuses** run every 30min. along most tram, subway, and major bus routes ("N" designates bus stops; 15AS; day transport passes not valid). **Maps** (15AS) and night bus schedules are in U-Bahn stations.

Taxis: ☎ 313 00, 401 00, 601 60, 814 00, or 910 91. Stands at Westbahnhof, Südbahnhof, and Karlspl. Base fare 27AS; 14AS per km. Surcharges: 27AS Su and late nights (11pm-6am); 13-26AS for heavy luggage or taxis called by radiophone.

Bike Rental: At **Wien Nord** and the **Westbahnhof.** 150AS per day, 90AS with train ticket from day of arrival. **Pedal Power,** II, Ausstellungsstr. 3 (☎ 729 72 34). 60AS per hr., 300AS per half-day. **Bike tours** of the city (180-280AS). Open May-Sept. 8am-8pm. Pick up *Vienna By Bike* at the tourist office for info on the bike scene.

Hitchhiking: For Salzburg, the highway leading to the *Autobahn* is 10km past U-4: Hütteldorf. Hitchers going south ride tram #67 to the end and wait at the rotary near Laaerberg. **Mitfahrzentrale Wien,** VIII, Daung. 1a (☎ 408 22 10), off Laudong., organizes ride-sharing. To **Salzburg** (210AS) and **Prague** (450AS). Open M-F 8am-noon and 2-7pm, Sa-Su 1-3pm. *Let's Go* does not endorse hitchhiking.

✦ ORIENTATION

Vienna is divided into 23 *Bezirke* (districts). The first district is the city center, *innere Stadt* or **Innenstadt** (inner city), bounded by the name-changing **Ringstraße** (once the site of the old city fortifications) and the Danube. Many of Vienna's major attractions lie along the southern section of the Ring, around the Hofburg (Imperial Palace), among them the **Kunsthistorisches Museum,** the **Rathaus,** and the **Burggarten,** and the **Staatsoper** (Opera House). The Staatsoper is at the intersection of the **Opernring, Kärntner Ring,** and **Kärntnerstraße,** with the **tourist office** behind it. Districts two through nine radiate clockwise from the center between the Ring and the larger, concentric **Gürtel** ("belt"), beyond which further districts similarly radiate clockwise. Street signs indicate the district numbers in Roman numerals. *Let's Go* includes district numbers in Roman numerals before street addresses.

> ❗ **CRIME.** Vienna is a metropolis with crime like any other. Be extra careful by the U-Bahn station in Karlspl., home to pushers and junkies. At night avoid the 5th, 10th, and 14th districts, as well as Landstraßer Hauptstr., Prater Park, and sections of the Gürtel (Vienna's red-light district).

🛈 PRACTICAL INFORMATION

TOURIST, FINANCIAL, AND LOCAL SERVICES

Tourist Office: Main Office, I, Am Albertinaplatz. 1 (www.info.wien.at), one block from the Opera House. Books 300-400AS rooms for a 40AS fee plus a deposit. Open daily 9am-7pm. **Branch** at the **Westbahnhof. Jugend-Info Wien** (Vienna Youth Information Service), in the underground Bellaria-Passage (☎ 17 99; email jiw@blackbox.at). Enter at Dr.-Karl-Renner-Ring/Bellaria (tram #1, 2, 46, 49, D, or J) or at the Volkstheater U-Bahn station. Get the indispensable *Jugend in Wien* brochure here. Open M-Sa noon-7pm.

Embassies: Australia, IV, Mattiellistr. 2-4 (☎ 51 28 58 00), behind Karlskirche. Open M-Th 9am-1pm and 2-5pm, F 9am-1pm. **Canada,** I, Laurenzerburg 2, 3rd fl. (☎ 531 38, ext. 3000). Open M-F 8:30am-12:30pm and 1:30-3:30pm. **Ireland,** III, Hilton Center, Landstraßer Hauptstr. 21, 6th fl. (☎ 71 54 24 60). Open M-F 9:30-11:30am and 1:30-4pm. **New Zealand,** XIX, Springsiedleg. 28 (☎ 318 85 05). **South Africa,** XIX, Sandg. 33 (☎ 320 64 930). Open M-F 8:30am-noon. **UK,** III, Jauresg. 12 (☎ 71 61 30), near Schloß Belvedere. Open M-F 9am-5pm. **US,** IX, Boltzmanng. 16, off Währingerstr. (☎ 313 39; staffed M-F 8:30am-noon and 1-5pm). Open M-F 8:30am-noon.

Currency Exchange: ATMs have best rates and typically accept Cirrus, Eurocard, V, and MC. **Banks** and **airport exchanges** offer official rates (commission on traveler's checks 65AS, cash 10AS). Most open M-W and F 8am-12:30pm and 1:30-3pm, Th until 5:30pm. The **main post office** has excellent rates and charges an 80AS fee.

American Express: I, Kärntnerstr. 21-23, P.O. Box 28, A-1015 (☎ 515 40), down the street from Stephanspl. Mail held for AmEx customers. Open M-F 9am-5:30pm, Sa 9am-noon. For 24hr. refund service, call ☎ (0800) 20 68 40.

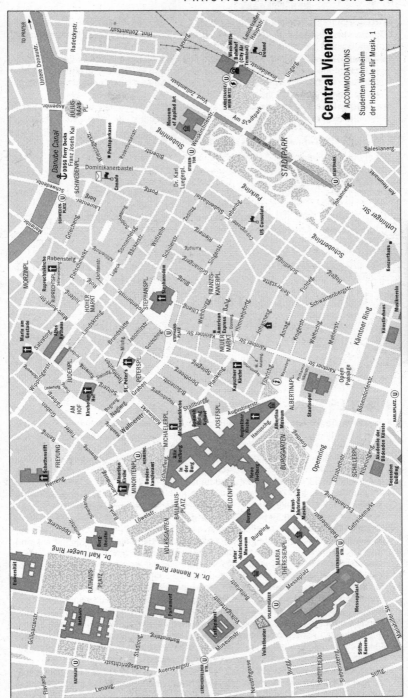

Central Vienna

▲ ACCOMMODATIONS

Studenten Wohnheim
der Hochschule für Musik, 1

AUSTRIA

Luggage Storage: Lockers at all train stations 30-50AS per 24hr.

Bookstores: Shakespeare & Company, I, Sterng. 2 (☎535 50 53). Eclectic and intelligent. Open M-F 9am-7pm, Sa 9am-5pm.

Bisexual, Gay, and Lesbian Services: Rosa Lila Villa, VI, Linke Wienzeile 102 (☎586 81 50). Open M-F 5-8pm. For gay info, pick up the monthly (German-language) magazine *Connect,* the monthly *Bussi* (free at any gay bar, cafe, or club), or the straight but hip *Falter* newspaper, which lists gay events.

Laundromat: Schnell und Sauber, VII, Westbahnhofstr. 60 (☎524 64 60). U-6: Burgg. Stadthalle. Wash 6kg for 60AS, soap included. Spin-dry 10AS. Open 24hr.

EMERGENCY AND COMMUNICATIONS

Emergencies: Police, ☎133. **Ambulance,** ☎144. **Fire,** ☎122.

Medical Assistance: Allgemeines Krankenhaus, IX, Währinger Gürtel 18-20 (☎404 00 1964). **Emergency care,** ☎141. Consulates provide lists of English-speaking physicians. **Fachärzte Lugeck** (☎512 1818) has English speaking doctors and nurses 24hr. daily. For info on **24-hour pharmacies,** ☎15 50.

Crisis Hotlines: 24hr. Rape Crisis Hotline ☎717 19. **Suicide Hotline,** ☎713 33 74.

Internet Access: Amadeus Media Café, I, Kärntnerstr. 19, on the 5th fl. of Steffl department store. Free. Open M-F 9:30am-7pm, Sa 9:30am-5pm. **Libro,** XXII, Donauzentrum (☎202 52 55). Free. Open Su-F 7am-7pm, Sa 9am-5pm.

Post Offices: Hauptpostamt, I, Fleischmarkt 19. Address mail to be held: BARNES, Chris, *Postlagernde Briefe,* Hauptpostamt, Fleischmarkt 19, **A-1010** Wien, Austria.

■ ACCOMMODATIONS

One of the few unpleasant aspects of Vienna is the hunt for rooms in high-season (June-Sept.); reserve at least five days ahead or before 9am for a shot at a same-day spot. If your choice is full, ask to be put on a waiting list, or ask for suggestions—don't waste time tramping around. University dorms convert into much-needed makeshift hostels from July to September. One-star *Pensionen* in the 7th, 8th, and 9th districts offer singles from 350AS and doubles from 500AS.

HOSTELS

■**Wombats City Hostel,** XV, Grangaße 6 (☎879 23 36; wombats@chello.at). From Westbahnhof, turn right out of the Außer Mariahilfer Straße exit, take the 6th right on Rosinagaße, and take your 2nd left. Brand new hostel with immaculate rooms, private baths, and in-the-know staff. Internet (60AS per hour). In-line skate and bike rental (both 100AS per day). Breakfast 35AS. Laundry. Dorms 175-245AS.

Hostel Ruthensteiner (HI), XV, Robert-Hamerlingg. 24 (☎893 42 02; hostel.ruthensteiner@telecom.at), 5min. from the Westbahnhof. Turn right out of the Mariahilfer Straße exit, left on Haidmannsg., and right on Robert-Hammerlingg. Dorms around a gorgeous courtyard. Internet (100AS per hour). Breakfast 29AS. 4-night max. stay. Dorms 125AS, in winter 145-169AS; doubles 235AS.

Believe It Or Not, VII, Mytheng. 10, #14 (☎526 46 58). From Westbahnhof, take U-6 (dir: Heiligenstadt) to Burgg./Stadthalle, then bus #48A (dir: Ring) to Neubaug. Backtrack a block on Burgg. and turn right on Myrtheng. (15min.). From Südbahnhof, take bus #13A (dir.: Skodag./Alerstr.) to Kellermanng. Walk left on Neustiftg. and left again on Myrtheng. Amazing caretaker gives crash-course on Vienna. Kitchen. Reception 8am-1pm. Lockout 10:30am-12:30pm. Dorms Easter-Oct. 160AS; Nov.-Easter 110AS.

Myrthengasse (HI), VII, Myrtheng. 7, opposite Believe It or Not, and **Neustiftgasse (HI),** VII, Neustiftg. 85 (☎523 63 16; email hostel@chello.at). Simple hostels 20min. from the *Innenstadt.* Breakfast included. Laundry. Reception at Myrtheng. 7am-11:30pm. Curfew 1am. Lockout 9am-2pm. Jan.-Mar.18 and Oct. 29-Dec. 23 dorms 170-200AS; rest of year dorms 185-215AS; nonmembers add 40AS.

Hostel Panda, VII, Kaiserstr. 77, 3rd fl. (☎522 53 53). From Westbahnhof, take tram #5 to Burgg. From Südbahnhof, take tram #18 to Westbahnhof first. Fun and eclectic hostel in an old-fashioned Austrian apartment building. Kitchen and TVs. Dorms Easter-Oct. 160AS; Nov.-Easter 110AS; add 50AS for one-night stay.

Hostel Zöhrer, IX, Skodagaß 26 (☎406 07 30; www.zoehrer.com). From Westbahnhof take tram #5 to Laudongaße. Turn right on Daungaße and walk a block to Skodogaße. From Südbahnhof, take bus #13a to Alserstraße, Skodagaße. Caring staff and a good location. Breakfast included. Kitchen. Lockout 11am-2pm. Dorms 170AS; doubles 460AS; triples 690AS.

Kolpingfamilie Wien-Meidling (HI), XIII, Bendlg. 10-12 (☎813 54 87). Take U-6 to Niederhofstr.; turn right on Niederhofstr. and take the 4th right onto Bendlg. Well-lit and modern in a quiet neighborhood. Breakfast 55AS. Reception 6am-midnight. Lockout midnight-4am. Dorms 150-195AS; nonmembers add 40AS.

Schloßherberge am Wilhelminenberg (HI), XVI, Savoyenstr. 2 (☎485 85 03, ext. 700; email SHB@wigast.com). U-6: Thaliastr.; tram #46 (dir. Joachimsthalerpl.) to Maroltingerg or take tram #44 from Schottentor to Wilhelminenstr. then bus #146B or #46B to Schloß Wilhelminenberg (follow signs from palace). Magnificent views and natural surroundings. Breakfast included. Keycard 25AS. Laundry. Reception 7am-11pm. Lockout 9am-2pm. Curfew midnight. Dorms 225AS.

Jugendgästehaus Wien Brigittenau (HI), XX, Friedrich-Engels-Pl. 24 (☎332 82 94), 25min. from city center. U-1 or U-4 to Schwedenpl., then tram N to Floridsdorferbrücke/Friedrich-Engels-Pl. Follow signs. Roomy. Breakfast included. Lockout 9am-1pm. Dorms 145-210AS; nonmembers add 40AS. Jan.-Mar. 13 and Nov.-Dec. 23 15AS discount.

Turmherberge Don Bosco, III, Lechnerstr. 12 (☎713 14 94), Take the U3 to Kardinal-Nagl-Pl., then go out the exit facing the park. Walk to the other side of the park and turn right on Erdbergstr. Lechnerstr. is the second left. The cheapest beds in town are here in a barren former bell tower; hot in summer. Curfew 11:45pm. Open Mar.-Nov. 80AS.

Jugendgästehaus Hütteldorf-Hacking (HI), XIII, Schloßbergg. 8 (☎877 02 63; email jgh@wigast.com). From Karlspl., take U-4 to Hütteldorf, take the Hadikg. exit, cross the footbridge, and follow signs to the hostel (10min.). Or take bus #53B from the side of the footbridge opposite the station to the hostel. A secluded hostel with sunny green grounds. Breakfast included. Keycard 25AS. Reception 7am-11:45pm. Lockout 9:30am-3:30pm. Curfew 11:45pm. Dorms 158AS-175AS; nonmembers add 40AS.

UNIVERSITY DORMS

From July through September, many university dorms become hotels, usually with singles, doubles, and a few triples and quads. These rooms don't have much in the way of character, but showers and sheets are standard, and their cleanliness and relatively low cost suffice for most budget travelers, particularly for longer stays.

Porzellaneum der Wiener Universität, IX, Porzellang. 30 (☎31 77 28 20), 10min. from the Ring. From Westbahnhof, take tram #5 to Franz-Josefs Bahnhof, then tram D (dir: Südbahnhof) to Fürsteng. From Südbahnhof, take tram D (dir. Nußdorf) to Fürsteng. Singles 190AS; doubles 380AS; quads 760AS.

Rudolfinum, IV, Mayerhofg. 3 (☎505 53 84). U-1: Taubstummeng. Large rooms in a well-managed and located facility. Breakfast included. Laundry 65AS. Reception 24hr. Singles 270AS; doubles 480AS; triples 600AS.

Gästehaus Pfeilgasse, VIII, Pfeilg. 6 (☎401 74; email acahot@academia-hotels.co.at). U-2: Lerchenfelderstr.; go right, then right on Lange Gasse, and left on Pfeilg. Breakfast included. Singles 270AS; doubles 480AS; triples 600AS.

Katholisches Studentenhaus, XIX, Peter-Jordanstr. 29 (☎ 34 74 73 12). From Westbahnhof, take U-6 (dir.: Heiligenstadt) to Nußdorferstr., then bus #35A or tram #38 to Hardtg. and turn left. From Südbahnhof, take tram D to Schottentor, then tram #38 to Hardtg. Laid-back ambience. Singles 250AS; doubles 400AS.

Studentenwohnheim der Hochschule für Musik, I, Johannesg. 8 (☎514 84 48). Walk 3 blocks down Kärnesrstr. away from the Stephansdom and turn left onto Johannesg. Fabulous location, inexpensive meals. Breakfast and shower included. Singles 430AS, with bath 490AS; doubles 760AS, 940AS; triples 840AS; quads 1000AS; quints 1250AS.

HOTELS AND PENSIONS

■ **Lauria Apartments,** VII, Kaiserstr. 77, #8 (☎522 25 55). From Südbahnhof, take tram #18 to Westbahnhof, then tram 5 to Burgg. Close to city center. TVs and kitchens. 2-night min. for reservations. Dorms 160AS; singles 480AS; doubles 530-700AS; triples 700-800AS; quads 850-940AS.

Pension Kraml, VI, Brauerg. 5 (☎587 85 88), by the city center and Naschmarkt. U-3: Zierierg.; exit onto Otto-Bauerg., take 1st left and 1st right. Take bus #13A to Esterhazyg. from Südbahnhof; walk up Brauerg. Spacious quarters. Singles 310AS; doubles 560-760AS; triples 720-930AS; apartment for 3-5 1120-1250AS.

Pension Hargita, VII, Andreasg. (☎526 1928). Take U3 to Zieglerg. then head down Mariahilferstr., away from the city center to Andreasg. This *Pension* offers comfort and a prime location. Breakfast 40AS. Reception 8am-10pm. Singles 400AS, with shower 450AS; doubles 600AS, with shower 700AS, with bath 800-900AS.

CAMPING

Wien-West, Hüttelbergstr. 80 (☎914 23 14), 8km from the center. From U-4: Hütteldorf take bus #14B or #152 (dir: Campingpl.) to Wien West. Crowded, but grassy and pleasant. Laundry, store, and cooking facilities. Reception 7:30am-9:30pm. Closed Feb. July-Aug. 75AS per person, rest of year 68AS; 40-45AS per tent. 2-person cabins 250AS; 4-person 400-440AS.

Aktiv Camping Neue Donau, XXII, Am Kleehäufel 119 (☎202 40 10) is 4km from the city center and adjacent to Neue Donau beaches. Take U-1 to Kaisermühlen, then bus #91a to Kleehäufel. Showers included. Laundry. Supermarket. Kitchen. July-Aug. 75AS, tent 45AS; May, June and Sept. 48AS, tent 40AS.

◘ FOOD

In a world full of uncertainty, the Viennese believe the least you can do is face things will a full stomach. Food in the city reflects the crazy patchwork empire of the Hapsburgs: *Knödel* (dumplings of Czech origin) and *Ungarische Gulaschsuppe* (Hungarian spicy beef stew) show Eastern European influences, and even *Wienerschnitzel* (fried and breaded veal cutlets) probably first appeared in Milan. Vienna is renowned for sublime desserts and chocolates—as high in price as in calories. But residents maintain that the sumptuous treats are worth every *Groschen*. Gorge on *Sacher Torte*, *Imperial Torte*, and *Apfelstrudel*. *Gästehäuser*, *Imbiße* (food stands), and *Beisln* (pubs) have cheap meals. Restaurants near **Kärntnerstr.** tend to be pricey—try north of the university near the Votivkirche (U-2: Schottentor), where **Universitätsstr.** and **Währingerstr.** meet, or the area around the **Rechte** and **Linke Wienzeile** near Naschmarkt (U-4: Kettenbrückeg.). The **Naschmarkt** is full of vendors selling delicacies to snack on while shopping at Vienna's premier flea market (Sa-Su only). Supermarkets **Billa, Hofer,** and **Spar** (most closed Su) provide the building blocks for cheap, basic meals.

■ **Brezelg'wölb,** I, Lederhof 9 (☎533 88 11), near Am Hof. Nestled in a tiny side street, this old-fashioned *Backstube* serves excellent, hearty Viennese cuisine. Lunch around 100AS. Open daily 11:30am-1am, hot food until midnight.

OH Pot, OH Pot, IX, Währingerstr. 22 (☎319 42 59). U-2: Schottentor. Adorable Spanish joint with amazingly good namesake "pots" (stew-like concoctions of veggie or meat varieties) 72-110AS. Open M-F 11am-midnight, Sa-Su 6pm-midnight.

Bizi Pizza, I, Rotenturmstr. 4, by Stephanspl. Italy's best for a pittance. Pizza (60-75AS) or pasta (65-75AS) whipped up before your eyes. Also at Franz-Josefs-Kai; Mariahilferstr. 22-24; and X, Favoritenstr. 105. All open daily 11am-11:30pm.

Hungerkünstler, VI, Gumpendorfstraße 48 (☎587 9210). Exceptional food with mellow atmosphere. Main dishes average 90AS. Open daily 1am-2am.

Tunnel, VIII, Florianig. 39. U-2: Rathaus; with Rathaus behind you, head right on Landesgerichtstr. and left on Florianig. Funky decor, live music, and cheap Austrian, Italian, and Middle Eastern food. Lunch *Menüs* 45AS. Beer 27AS. Open daily 10am-2am.

Rosenberger Markt, I, Mayserderg. 2 (☎512 34 58), behind the Sacher Hotel. Large and chaotic subterranean buffet with a gargantuan selection of salad (29-64AS), fruit salad, waffles (55AS), antipasti, potatoes, and pasta bars. Open daily 10:30am-11pm.

Levante, I, Wallnerstr. 2 (☎533 23 26). Walk down the Graben away from the Stephansdom, turn left on Kohlmarkt, and right on Wallnerstr. This Greek-Turkish restaurant features street-side dining and heaps of delicious dishes, including vegetarian delights. Main dishes 80-150AS. Sandwiches 40AS. Open daily 11:30am-11:30pm.

Schnitzelwirt, VII, Neubaug. 52 (☎523 37 71). Take U-2 or U-3 to Volkstheater, then bus #49 to Neubaug. You'll find every kind of *Schnitzel* imaginable here (65-125AS). Open M-Sa 10am-11pm.

Cafe Ball, I, Ballg. 5 (☎513 17 54), near Stephanspl. off Weihburgg. Listen to opera as you enjoy your lunch. Open M-Sa 11am-1am, Su noon-midnight.

◪ COFFEEHOUSES AND KONDITOREIEN

The quintessential Viennese coffee is the *Melange;* you can order every kind of coffee as a *Kleiner* (small) or *Grosser* (large), *Brauner* (brown, with a little milk) or *Schwarzer* (black). Most cafes serve hot food, but don't order it (except pastries) with coffee unless you want to be really gauche. The most serious dictate of coffeehouse etiquette is the lingering requirement. The waiter *(Herr Ober)* will serve you when you sit down, and then leave you to sip and brood. Vienna's *Konditoreien*, as traditional as its coffee shops, focus on delectable pastries rather than coffee.

■ **Café Hawelka,** I, Dorotheerg. 6 (☎512 82 30), off Grabe, three blocks from the Stephansdom. With dusty wallpaper, dark wood, and old red-striped velvet sofas, this legendary cafe is glorious. *Buchteln* (served fresh from the oven at 10pm) 35AS. *Melange* 37AS. Open M and W-Sa 8am-2am, Su 4pm-2am.

■ **Café Central,** I (☎533 37 6326), at Herreng. and Strauchg. inside Palais Ferstel. Theodor Herzl, Sigmund Freud, Vladimir Ilych Ulyanov (a.k.a. Lenin), and Leon Trotsky hung out here; many tourists have too. Piano 4-7pm. Open M-Sa 8am-8pm, Su 10am-6pm.

Demel, I, Kohlmarkt 14 (☎535 17 17), 5min. from the Stephansdom down Graben. The most luxurious *Konditorei*, Demel's was confectioner to the imperial court until the empire dissolved. Fresh chocolate made daily. Confections 40-50AS. Open 10am-7pm.

Café Sperl, VI, Gumpendorferstr. 11. U-2: Babenbergstr.; walk a block down Getreidemarkt and turn right on Gumpendorferstr. One of Vienna's oldest and most beautiful cafes. Cake 35-45AS. Open M-Sa 7am-11pm, Su 3-11pm; July-Aug. closed Su.

Cafe Griensteidl, I, Michaelerplatz 6, down the street from Café Central toward the Hofburg. Vienna's first literary cafe retains an intellectual flare. Open daily 8am-11:30pm.

Cafe Bräunerhof, I, Stallburgg. 2 (☎512 38 93), near the Hofburg. Delightfully shabby and tourist-free. Open M-F 7:30am-8:30pm, Sa 7:30am-6pm, Su 10am-6pm.

MMM...COFFEE. There is a steadfast rule for the Vienna coffeehouse— the drink matters, but the atmosphere *really* matters. Artists, writers, and thinkers fled poorly heated apartments to surround themselves with the dark wood and dusty velvet of the 19th-century coffeehouse. They ordered cups of coffee and stayed long into the night, composing operettas, writing books, and cutting into one another's work. The bourgeoisie followed suit, and the coffeehouse soon became the living room of the city—where Peter Altenberg, "the cafe writer," scribbled lines; where Kokoschka grumbled alone; where exiles Vladimir Lenin and Leon Trotsky played chess; where Theodor Herzl made plans for a Zionist Israel; where Kafka journeyed from Prague to visit the Herrenhof; and where Karl Kraus and a circle of minor writers baited Hugo von Hofmannsthal and Arthur Schnitzler. The original literary cafe, on the cusp of the "merry apocalypse" *fin de siècle* culture, was Cafe Griensteidl. After it was demolished in 1897, the torch passed first to Cafe Central and then to Cafe Herrenhof. Cafes still exist under all of these names, but only Cafe Central looks the way it originally did.

AUSTRIA

◉ SIGHTS

Viennese streets are by turns startling, scuzzy, and grandiose; the best way to see the city is simply to get lost. To wander in a more organized manner, get the brochure *Vienna from A to Z* (50AS with Vienna Card) or *Walks in Vienna*, both at the tourist office. Organized tours run 130AS; some require additional admission fees to sites. **Vienna Bike**, IX, Wasag. (☎ 319 12 58), runs **cycling tours** (2-3hr., 280AS). Another great way to see the city is to ride around the Ring on trams #1 or 2.

THE RINGSTRAße

In 1857, Emperor Franz Josef commissioned this boulevard, which defines the boundaries of the inner city, to replace the medieval city walls. Freud walked the 4km circuit of the Ring every day during his lunch break. Extending south from the Danube Canal, **Schottenring** leads past the **Borse** (Stock Exchange) to the twin spires of the **Votivkirche**, a neo-Gothic wonder surrounded by rose gardens. The next stretch, **Karl-Lueger Ring,** runs from the **Universität Wien** to the imposing **Rathaus** (town hall); look for outdoor festivals in the summer on the Rathausplatz, the inner city's largest square. Continuing around the Ring, toward the Palace, the rose-filled **Volksgarten** is on one side, and the Neoclassical, sculpture-adorned **Parlament** (Parliament) building on the other. *(Tours mid-Sept. to mid-July M-F at 11am and 3pm; mid-July to mid-Sept. M-F 9, 10, 11am, 1, 2, and 3pm.)* The **Burgring** goes between the Hofburg (Imperial Palace; see p. 89), and two of Vienna's largest museums, the **Kunsthistorisches Museum** (Museum of Art History) and the **Naturhistorisches Museum** (Museum of Natural History; see **Museums,** p. 91). On the far side of the Hofburg and its verdant Burggarten is the **Staatsoper** (State Opera). Originally completed in 1869, it was meticulously restored following heavy WWII damage. Former directors include Gustav Mahler, Richard Strauss, and Lorin Maazel. The cheapest way to partake of its fabulous gold, crystal, and red-velvet interior is to see an opera—standing room tickets are only 50AS. *(Take U-1, U-2, U-4, or tram #1, 2, J, or D to Karlsplatz and take the Staatsoper exit. Tours July-Aug. 10, 11am, 1, 2, and 3pm; May-June and Sept.-Oct. 1, 2, and 3pm; Nov.-Apr. 2 and 3pm. 60AS, students 45AS.)* **Opernring/Kärntnerring** heads to Schwarzenbergstr., marked by an equestrian statue. The Schubertring/Stubenring, which heads back to the Danube Canal, borders **Stadtpark** (City Park).

INSIDE THE RING

The **Innere Stadt** (Inner City), enclosed by the **Ringstraße** and the **Danube Canal,** is Vienna's social and geographical center. With palaces, theaters, tenements, and toilet bowls designed by master architects, it's a gallery of the history of aesthetics, from Baroque to *Jugendstil*.

NEAR STEPHANSPLATZ

This active square, the heart of Vienna, in the shadow of the city's most treasured symbol, the Gothic **Stephansdom**, whose smoothly tapered **South Tower** has become Vienna's emblem. Climb its 343 steps for a panoramic view of the city. Photographs inside chronicle the painstaking process of reconstruction following WWII damage. Downstairs in the **catacombs,** skeletons of thousands of plague victims line the walls, while another *Gruft* stores Hapsburg remains. *(U-1 or U-3: Stephansplatz. English Cathedral tours M-Sa 10:30am and 3pm, Su 3pm; 40AS. Spectacular evening tour July-Sept. Sa 7pm; 100AS. South Tower open 9am-5:30pm; 30AS. Gruft tours M-Sa 10, 11, 11:30am, 2, 2:30, 3:30, 4, and 4:30pm; Su 2, 2:30, 3:30, 4, and 4:30pm; 50AS.)* Running straight out of Stephansplatz is **Graben**, a main pedestrian street with Baroque, *Biedermeier*, *Jugendstil*, and postmodern styles, including the **Ankerhaus** (#10) and the red-marble **Grabenhof** by Otto Wagner. Heading up Seilergasse from Graben brings you to the spectacular **Neuer Markt**, where a graceful fountain and the 17th-century **Kapuzinerkirche** (Church of the Capuchin Friars) await. The church houses an imperial **Gruft** (crypt), a series of subterranean rooms whose coffins contain the remains (minus heart and entrails) of all the Hapsburg rulers since 1633. Empress Maria Theresia rests next to beloved hubby Franz Stephan in an ornate Rococo sepulcher surrounded by cherubim and a dome. *(Open 9:30am-4pm. 40AS, students 30AS.)*

FROM STEPHANSPLATZ TO JUDENPLATZ

From Stephanspl., head up Rotenturmstr. and turn left onto **Hoher Markt,** the center of town (used as a market and execution site) during the Middle Ages. The square's biggest draw is the magnificent *Jugendstil* **Ankeruhr** (clock), which features 12 historical figures (including Marcus Aurelius, Maria Theresia, and Josef Haydn) rotating past the old Viennese coat of arms; one 3m-tall figure appears every hour, but show up at noon to see all of them in succession. Peek under the bridge to see depictions of Adam, Eve, an angel, and the devil. From Hoher Markt, follow Wipplingerstr. west (right) to the impressive Baroque facade of the **Böhmische Hofkanzlei** (Bohemian Court Chancellory), the seat of Austria's Constitutional Court. The **Altes Rathaus,** directly across the street, today houses the **Austrian Resistance Museum** and various temporary exhibits. *(On Friedrich-Schmidt-Pl.* ☎ *525 50. Open M, W, and Th 9am-5pm. Tours M, W, and F 1pm. Free.)* Turn left directly after the *Hofkanzlei* to get to the **Judenplatz,** the site of the city's first Jewish ghetto. Turn left on Seitenstetteng. to reach the Jewish **Stadttempel,** the only one of Vienna's 94 synagogues to escape Nazi destruction during **Kristallnacht** (Night of Broken Glass) on November 9-10, 1938; it was only spared because it was concealed from the street. An armed guard now patrols the synagogue as a precaution against repeats of the 1983 terrorist attack that killed three people. *(Seitenstetteng. 2-4. Take your passport. Open Su-F. Free.)* Continue up Seitenstetteng. to **Judengasse** (Jew Lane), a remnant of the old Jewish ghetto.

FROM AM HOF TO MICHAELERPLATZ

On the other side of Judenpl., Drahtg. opens into the grand courtyard **Am Hof,** a medieval jousting square that now houses the **Kirche am Hof** (Church of the Nine Choirs of Angels), built from 1386-1662. Roman ruins show that Am Hof has been popular for a while. From Am Hof turn right on Bognerstr. to **Freyung,** an uneven square used for public executions in the Middle Ages. Freyung is linked to **Herrengasse,** home to Vienna's nobility during the Hapsburg era. Heading right on Herreng. brings you to the Italianate **Palais Ferstel,** home to **Café Central** (see p. 87), for "those who want to be alone in the company of others." Head left down Herreng. and turn right on Landhausg. to reach the peaceful **Minoritenplatz,** home of the 14th-century **Minoritenkirche.** The Church's tower was destroyed during the Turkish siege of Vienna in 1529. On the south side of the square stands the **Bundeskanzleramt** (Federal Chancery), where the Congress of Vienna met in 1815 and Chancellor Engelbert Dollfuss was assassinated in 1934. Follow Schauflerg. to the left and you'll run into **Michaelerplatz,** named for the unassuming **Michaelerkirche** (St. Michael's Church) on its eastern side. Leopold "the Glorious" Babenburg purportedly founded the church in gratitude for his safe return from the Crusades. *(Open May-Oct. M-Sa 10:30am-4:30pm, Su 1-5pm. 25AS.)* In the middle of Michaelerpl. are the excavated foundations of Roman Vienna, the military camp called **Vindobona** where Marcus Aurelius penned his *Meditations. (Open Sa-Su 11am-1pm. 25AS.)* A reconstructed **Café Griensteidl** is on the side of the square, inviting visitors to imagine themselves drinking coffee alongside *fin de siècle* writers Arthur Schnitzler and Hugo von Hofmannsthal. The square is dominated by the green, neo-Baroque, **Michaelertor,** the main gate of the Hofburg.

THE HOFBURG

Take tram #1 or 2 from anywhere on the Ringstr. to Heldenplatz, or enter through the Michaelertor, which is in Michaelerplatz.

The sprawling Hofburg was the Hapsburgs' winter residence until their 700-year reign ended in 1918. It experienced periods of neglect when various emperors chose to live in other palaces, such as Schönbrunn, but it remained the symbol of the family's power. Today, it houses the office of the Austrian President.

Perhaps the best way to get an overview of the Hofburg is to walk around the perimeter. The **Stallburg** (Palace Stables), accessible via Josefspl., is home to the Royal Lipizzaner stallions of the **Spanische Reitschule** (Spanish Riding School). The cheapest way to get a glimpse of the famous steeds is to watch them train. *(Mid-Feb.*

AUSTRIA

to June and Nov. to mid-Dec. Tu-F 10am-noon; early Feb. M-Sa 10am-noon, except when the horses tour. Tickets sold at the door at Josefspl., Gate 2, from about 8:30am. 100AS.) Continue down Augustinerstr. to reach the 14th-century Gothic **Augustinerkirche,** where the hearts of the Hapsburgs rest in peace in the **Herzgrüftel** (Little Heart Crypt). (Open M-Sa 10am-6pm, Su 1-6pm.) The **Albertina,** the southern wing of the Hofburg, has a film museum and the celebrated **Collection of Graphic Arts,** with an array of old political cartoons and drawings by Dürer, Michelangelo, da Vinci, Raphael, Cézanne, and Schiele. (Open Tu-Sa 10am-5pm. 70AS.)

Head up to Michaelerpl. The wooden door on the right as you enter the Hofburg via the Michaelertor leads to the **Kaiserappartements,** the former quarters of Emperor Franz Josef (1848-1916) and Empress Elisabeth (1838-1898). (Open daily 9am-4:30pm. 80AS.) As you continue through the Michaelertor, enter the courtyard **In der Burg** (within the fortress). Through the red-and-black-striped **Schweizertor** (Swiss Gate), on the left and up the stairs to the right, is the Gothic **Burgkapelle,** where the heavenly **Wiener Sängerknaben** (Vienna Boys' Choir) graces Mass-goers (see **Music,** p. 77). Below the Burgkapelle is the **Schatzkammer** (Treasury), which displays the Hapsburg jewels, the crowns of the Holy Roman and Austrian Empires, Imperial christening robes, and a tooth that reportedly belonged to John the Baptist. (Open W-M 10am-6pm. 80AS, students 50AS. One English tour per day; 30AS.) The passageway at the rear of In der Burg opens up onto **Heldenplatz** (Heroes' Square). To the left is the vast **Neue Burg** (New Fortress). The **Österreichische Nationalbibliothek** (Austrian National Library) has an outstanding museum of papyri, scriptures, and musical manuscripts. (Open May 7-Oct. 26 M-W and F-Sa 10am-4pm, Th 10am-7pm, Su 10am-1pm; Nov.-Apr. M-Sa 10am-1pm; May-Nov. 60AS, students 40AS; Nov.-Apr. 40AS.)

OUTSIDE THE RING

As the city expands beyond the Ring in all directions, the distance between notable sights also expands. What the area outside the Ring gives up in accessibility, it makes up for in the varied attractions it offers. Some of Vienna's most famous modern architecture is found outside the Ring. At the same time, this modern sprawl is also home to a number of startlingly beautiful Baroque palaces and parks that were once beyond the city limits.

KARLSPLATZ AND RESSELPARK

Karlsplatz, within the **Resselpark,** is home to Vienna's most impressive Baroque church. The **Karlskirche** (St. Charles' Church), is in the southeast corner of the park. The Karlskirche is an eclectic masterpiece, combining a Neoclassical portico with a Baroque dome and towers on both sides. The interior of the church is overwhelmingly beautiful, with colorful frescoes and a sunburst altar. In front of the church, a reflecting pool and modern sculpture designed by **Henry Moore** connect it to the 20th century. (Open M-Sa 9-11:30am and 1-5pm, Su 1-5pm. Free.) The **Historisches Museum der Stadt Wien,** to the left of the Karlskirche, stands across the square from the blocky yellow-and-blue **Kunsthalle** (see **Museums,** p. 91). **Resselpark,** the park opposite Karlskirche, is peaceful and shady, ringed by museums. On the opposite side of the square is the *Jugendstil* **Karlsplatz Stadtbahn Pavilions,** designed in 1899 by **Otto Wagner,** the architect primarily responsible for Vienna's *Jugendstil* face. Visible to the north across Lothringerstr., between Karlsplatz and the Ring, are the **Künstlerhaus,** the traditional home of Vienna's artistic community, from which the Secession artists seceded in 1897 (see **Museums,** p. 91) and the **Musikverein,** home of the **Vienna Philharmonic Orchestra** (see **Music,** p. 93). Northwest of the Resselpark across Friedrichstr. stands the nemesis of the Künstlerhaus, the **Secession Building,** whose restrained decoration and gilded dome were intended to clash with the Historicist Ringstraße. The inscription above the door reads: *Der Zeit, ihre Kunst; der Kunst, ihre Freiheit* (To the age, its art; to art, its freedom). The Secession exhibits of 1898-1903, which attracted cutting-edge artists, were led by Gustav Klimt, whose painting *Nuda Veritas* (Naked Truth) became the icon of a new aesthetic ideal. Take U-1, U-2, U-4, or any number of trams to Karlsplatz and exit toward Resselpark.

SCHLOß BELVEDERE

Take tram D to Schwarzenberg, tram #71 one stop past Schwarzenbergpl., or walk from the Südbahnhof.

The landscaped gardens of **Schloß Belvedere,** IV, originally the summer residence **Prince Eugene of Savoy,** Austria's greatest military hero, lie southeast of the center. The Belvedere palace, originally only the **Untere** (Lower) **Belvedere,** was a gift from the emperor; Eugene later added the more opulent **Obere** (Upper) **Belvedere.** The grounds of the palace, which stretch from the Schwarzenberg Palace to the Süd-bahnhof, contain spectacular sphinx-filled gardens and museums (see p. 91).

SCHLOß SCHÖNBRUNN

U-4: Schönbrunn. Apartments open daily Apr.-Oct. 8:30am-5pm; Nov.-Mar. 8:30am-4:30pm. 22-room Imperial Tour 95AS, students 85AS; more worthwhile 44-room Grand Tour 125AS, 110AS. Audio guide included. Gardens open 6am-dusk; free.

Belvedere pales in comparison to **Schloß Schönbrunn,** XIII, the former Imperial summer residence. After humble beginnings as a hunting lodge, Schönbrunn was destroyed twice before Fischer von Erlach conceived a plan for a palace to make Versailles look like a gilded outhouse. Tours of some of the palace's 1500 rooms reveal the elaborate taste of Maria Theresia's era. The frescoes lining the **Great Gallery** once witnessed the Congress of Vienna, which loved a good party after a long day of divvying up the continent. A six-year-old Mozart played in the **Hall of Mirrors.** The **Millions Room** wins the prize for excess, with Oriental miniatures covering its walls. Even more impressive than the palace are the classical **gardens** behind it, designed by Emperor Josef II, that are nearly four times the length of the palace. The gardens are an orchestration of various elements, ranging from a sprawling **zoo** to the massive stone **Neptunbrunnen** (Neptune fountain) and bogus **Roman ruins.** Edging the geometric flower beds, the trees have been carefully pruned to create the effect of a vaulted arch. Walk past the **flower sculptures** to reach Schönbrunn's labyrinths, rose gardens, and nature preserves.

ZENTRALFRIEDHOF

XI, Simmeringer Hauptstr. 234. Take tram #71 from Schwarzenbergpl. or tram #72 from Schlachthausg. The tram stops at each of the 3 main gates; Tor II is the main entrance. Or, take S-7 to "Zentralfriedhof," which stops along the southwest wall of the cemetery. Open May-Aug. 7am-7pm; Mar.-Apr. and Sept.-Oct. 7am-6pm; Nov.-Feb. 8am-5pm. 38AS.

The Viennese like to describe the Zentralfriedhof (Central Cemetery) as half the size of Geneva but twice as lively. The phrase is meant not only to poke fun at Vienna's rival but also to illustrate Vienna's healthy attitude toward death. Death doesn't get any better than at the Zentralfriedhof. Graves of the famous, infamous, and unknown spread out in a grid from the church at the center. The cemetery is the place to pay respects to your favorite Viennese decomposer: **Tor II** (the second gate) leads to Beethoven, Wolf, Strauss, Schönberg, Moser, and an honorary monument to Mozart. (His true resting place is an unmarked pauper's grave in the **Cemetery of St. Mark,** III, Leberstr. 6-8.) **Tor I** leads to the **Jewish Cemetery** and Arthur Schnitzler's burial plot. Many of the headstones are cracked, broken, lying prone, or neglected because the families of most of the dead are no longer in Austria. Various structures throughout this portion of the burial grounds memorialize the millions slaughtered in Nazi death camps.

🏛 MUSEUMS

Vienna owes its selection of masterpieces to the acquisitive Hapsburgs, as well as the city's crop of art schools and world-class artists. All city-run museums are free Friday mornings; check out the tourist office's free *Museums* brochure. The **Messepalast,** Museumspl. 1/5, originally the imperial barracks, opens this year as the **MuseumsQuartier.** (☎ 523 58 81). The modern complex houses the **Leopold Museum** (which holds one of Austria's most significant collections, including a number of valuable Schieles), a **Museum of Modern Art,** and a new **Kunsthalle.**

■ **Kunsthistorisches Museum** (Museum of Art History; ☎ 52 52 40), off the Burgring. Take U-2 or U-3 to Volkstheater. The world's 4th-largest art collection oozes with 15th- to 18th-century Venetian and Flemish paintings, including Breughels, Rembrandts, and ancient art. The Klimt mural in the lobby depicts artistic progress from the classical era to the 19th century in the Historicist style he would later attack. Open Tu-Su 10am-6pm. 120AS, students 80AS. English tours in summer 11am and 3pm; 30AS.

Österreichische Gallerie (Austrian Gallery), III, Prinz-Eugen-Str. 27 (☎ 79 55 70), in the Belvedere Palace. Walk from the Südbahnhof or take tram D, #566, 567, 666, 668, or 766 to Prinz-Eugen-Str. 19th- to 20th-century Austrian art and famous Secessionist works by Schiele, Kokoschka, and Klimt (*The Kiss*) in the **Upper Belvedere.** The **Lower Belvedere** has the **Baroque Museum** and the **Museum of Medieval Austrian Art.** Both open Tu-Su 10am-6pm. Joint ticket 60AS, students 40AS. English tour 11am.

Museum für Völkerkunde, I, in the Neue Burg on Heldenpl. U-2 or U-3: Volkstheater. Admire Benin bronzes, West African Dan heads, and Montezuma's feathered head-dress. Art and artifacts from Africa, the Americas, the Middle East, and the Far East. Open W-M 10am-4pm. 50AS, students 30AS.

Museum Moderner Kunst (Museum of Modern Art; ☎ 317 69 00; www.MMKSLW.or.at) has two locations. **Liechtenstein Palace,** IX, Fürsteng. 1, holds a few works by 20th-century masters—Magritte, Picasso, Miró, Kandinsky, Pollock, Warhol, and Klee. Take tram D (dir: Nußdorf) to Fürsteng. The **20er Haus,** III, Arsenalstr. 1, opposite the Süd-bahnhof, has influential 60s and 70s work and a great sculpture garden stocked with pieces by Giacometti, Moore, and others. Open Tu-W and F-Su 10am-6pm, Th 10am-8pm. Each museum 60AS, students 40AS; combined ticket 80AS, students 60AS.

Österreiches Museum für Angewandte Kunst (a.k.a. MAK, Austrian Museum of Applied Art; ☎ 712 80 80), Stubenring 5. Take U-3 to Stubentor. Dedicated to the beauty of design from the smooth curves of Thonet bentwood chairs to the intricate designs of Venetian glass. Design does not stop there, as each room has been fashioned by some of the brightest stars of the Viennese contemporary art scene. For Klimt aficionados, *The Embrace* is a special highlight. Open Tu-W and F-Su 10am-6pm, Th 10am-9pm. 90AS, students 45AS.

Historisches Museum der Stadt Wien (Historical Museum of the City of Vienna), IV, Karl-spl. 5 (☎ 505 87 47), to the left of the Karlskirche. Amazing collection of historical arti-facts and paintings documenting Vienna's evolution from a Roman encampment through the Turkish siege, and the subsequent 640 years of Hapsburg rule. Also holds a number of Seccecionist works by Schiele and Klimt. Open Tu-Su 9am-6pm. 50AS, stu-dents 25AS; free F 9am-noon.

Sigmund Freud Haus, IX, Bergg. 19 (☎ 319 15 96), near the Votivkirche. U-2: Schotten-tor; walk up Währingerstr. to Bergg. Freud's home from 1891 until the *Anschluß.* Lots of photos and documents, including his report cards and circumcision certificate. Open July-Sept. 9am-6pm; Oct.-June 9am-4pm. 60AS, students 40AS. Tours 75AS.

Akademie der Bildende Kunst (Academy of Fine Arts), I, Schillerpl. 3 (☎ 58 81 62 25), near Karlspl. Notorious for having rejected Hitler's application. Excellent collection, including Hieronymus Bosch's *Last Judgment* and works by Peter Paul Rubens. Open Tu-Su 10am-4pm. 50AS, students 20AS.

Secession Building, I, Friedrichstr. 12 (☎ 587 53 07), on the western side of Resselpark, across Wienzeile. Originally built to give the pioneers of modern art, including Klimt, Kokoschka, and Gauguin, space to hang artwork that didn't conform to *Künstlerhaus* standards. Substantial contemporary works are exhibited now. Klimt's 30m-long *Beethoven Frieze*—a visual interpretation of Beethoven's *Ninth Symphony*—is also dis-played. Open Tu-W and F-Su 10am-6pm, Th 10am-8pm. 60AS, students 40AS.

Künstlerhaus, Karlspl. 5 (☎ 587 96 63). Once home to the Viennese artistic establish-ment. Now it invites temporary exhibits, usually of recent, non-European art. The theater hosts **film festivals.** Open Th 10am-9pm, F-W 10am-6pm. 90AS, students 60AS.

🎵 ENTERTAINMENT

MUSIC

Vienna's musical history is full of big names: Mozart, Beethoven, and Haydn wrote their greatest masterpieces in Vienna, creating the First Viennese School. A century later, Schönberg, Webern, and Berg teamed up to form the Second Viennese School. Year round, Vienna presents performances ranging from the above-average to the sublime, with many surprisingly accessible to the budget traveler. In 1869, Emperor Franz Josef inaugurated the **Vienna Court Opera,** today's **Staatsoper** (State Opera) which remains one of the top five companies in the world and performs about 300 times from September through June. **Standing-room tickets** give you access to world-class opera for a pittance; more expensive **last-minute student tickets** go on sale 30min. before curtain. (Standing-room tickets: balcony 30AS, orchestra 50AS. Arrive 2-3hr. early in high season. The standing-room line forms inside the side door on the western side of the Opera, by Operng. Formal dress not necessary, but no shorts. Student tickets 100-150AS. Line up to the left inside the main entrance at least 1hr. before curtain; ISIC not valid, bring a university ID.) Advance tickets (120-2150AS) go on sale a month before the performance at the **Bundestheaterkasse,** I, Hanuschg. 3, around the corner from the opera. (☎514 44 29 60. Open M-F 8am-6pm, Sa-Su 9am-noon. ISIC not valid for student discounts, university ID required.) The world-famous **Wiener Philharmoniker** (Vienna Philharmonic Orchestra) has been directed by the world's finest conductors, including Gustav Mahler and Leonard Bernstein. Regular Philharmonic performances as well as other guest performances take place in the **Musikverein,** I, Bösendorferstr. 12, on the northeast side of Karlsplatz. (☎505 81 90. Box office open Sept.-June M-F 9am-7:30pm, Sa 9am-5pm. Standing-room tickets available at box office; price varies by concert.) **Wiener Symphoniker** (Vienna Symphony Orchestra), Vienna's second fiddle, is frequently on tour but plays some concerts at the grand, late-nineteenth-century **Konzerthaus,** III, Lothringerstr. 20, just around the corner and across the river Wien from the Musikverein. (☎712 1211. Open M-F 9am-7:45pm, Sa 9am-1pm; June 20-Sept. 30 9am-1pm.) The prepubescent prodigies of the famous, 500-year-old **Vienna Boys' Choir** perform Sundays at 9:15am (mid-Sept. to June only) in the **Burgkapelle** (Royal Chapel) of the Hofburg. Reserve tickets (70-380AS) at least 2 months in advance; write to Hofmusikkapelle, Hofburg, A-1010 Wien, but do not enclose money. Standing room is free, but arrive before 8am.

FESTIVALS

Vienna hosts an array of annual festivals, mostly musical; check the tourist office's monthly calendar. The **Vienna Festival** (mid-May to mid-June) has a diverse program of exhibitions, plays, and concerts. (☎589 22 22; fax 589 22 49; www.festwochen.or.at.) The Staatsoper and Volkstheater host the annual **Jazzfest Wien,** featuring famous acts (☎503 56 47; www.viennajazz.at) during the first weeks of July. While other big guns take summer siesta, Vienna has held the **Klangbogen** (☎427 17) every summer since 1952, featuring excellent concerts across Vienna, including **Wiener Kammeroper** (Chamber Opera; ☎513 0100) performances of Mozart's operas in an open-air theater, set among the ruins of Schönbrunner Schloßpark. From the end of July to the beginning of August, the **Im-Puls Dance Festival** (☎523 55 58; www.impuls-tanz.wien.at) attracts some of the world's great dance troupes and offers seminars to enthusiasts. In mid-October, the annual city-wide film festival, the **Viennale,** kicks off. In past years, the program has featured over 150 movies from 25 countries. One final free treat not to be missed is the **Rathausplatz Music Film Festival** in July and August, in the Rathauspl. at dusk, during which taped operas, ballets, and concerts enrapture audiences.

☑ NIGHTLIFE

Vienna is a great place to party, whether you're looking for a quiet evening with a glass of wine or a wild night in a disco full of black-clad Euro musclemen and drag queens. U-1 or U-4: Schwedenplatz is just blocks from the **Bermuda Dreieck** (Triangle), so dubbed both for the three-block area it covers and for the tipsy revelers who lose their way here and never make it home. If your vision isn't foggy yet, head down **Rotenturmstrasse** toward the Stephansdom, or check out the cellar bars on **Bäckerstrasse.** Just outside the Ring, the streets off **Burggasse** and **Stiftgasse** in the 7th district and the university quarter (8th and 9th districts) can be good places of refuge when the summer crowd in the Bermuda Triangle feels too pubescent or touristy. As usual, the best nights are Friday and Saturday, beginning around 1am. For the scoop on raves, concerts, and parties, grab the fliers at swanky cafes around town or pick up a copy of the indispensable *Falter* (28AS) for listings of everything from opera and theater to punk concerts to the gay and lesbian scene.

U-4, XII, Schönbrunnerstr. 222 (☎815 83 07). U-4: Meidling Hauptstr. Keeps the music fresh and the party going. Two dance areas, multiple bars, and rotating theme nights please a varied clientele. Th gay night. Cover 100AS. Open daily 11pm-5am.

Flex Halle, I, Donaulände/Augartenbrücke (☎533 7525), near the Schottenring U-Bahn station Head toward the river and down a narrow staircase. Small, dark, on-the-water club with chemically-enhanced dancing. Cover 70-150AS. Open 8pm-4am.

Cato, I, Tiefer Graben 19. U-3: Herreng.; walk down to Strauchg., turn right, and continue on to Tiefer Graben. Laid-back, super-comfortable bar—you'll be singing songs with the friendly clientele before the end of the evening. Open Su-Th 6pm-2am, F-Sa 6pm-4am.

Santo Spirito Bar, I, Kumpfg. 7 (☎512 99 98). From Stephanspl., walk down Singerstr. and turn left onto Kampfg. (5min.). Busts on the wall pay homage to famous conductors. Owner vacations in July, otherwise open daily from 6pm until people leave.

Chelsea, VIII, (☎407 93 09), Lerchenfeldergürtel, under the U-Bahn between Thaliastr. and Josefstädterstr. The best place in Vienna for underground music, featuring live bands from across Europe (except in summer). Cover 60-200AS. Open daily 7pm-4am.

Objektiv, VII, Kirchbergg. 26 (☎522 70 42). U-2 or U-3: Volkstheater; walk two blocks down Burgg. and turn right on Kirchbergg. One of the most eclectic and strangely decorated bars in Vienna. A mellow atmosphere, lively local crowd, and cheap drinks top things off. Happy Hour daily 11pm-1am. Open M-Sa 6pm-2am, Su 6pm-1am.

Blue Box, VII, Richterg. 8 (☎523 26 82). Take U3 to Neubaug., turn onto Neubaug., and take your 1st right onto Richtergasse. Clouds of smoke, blue leather couches, and a deafening bass beat. Open Tu-Th, Su 10am-2am, M 6pm-2am, F-Sa 10am-4am.

Club Berlin, I, Gonzag. 12 (☎533 04 79). Go downstairs in this house of swank to see Vienna's bold and beautiful wind their way around the partitions in this former wine cellar with great music. Open Su-Tu 6pm-2am, F-Sa 6pm-4am.

Why Not, I, Tiefer Graben 22 (☎535 11 58). Relaxed gay and lesbian bar/disco with both a chill chatting venue and a hip-hop-happening subterranean black-box dance floor. Sa drink specials 43AS. Cover 100AS. Open F-Sa 10pm-4am, Su 9pm-2am.

☑ DAYTRIPS FROM VIENNA

GRINZING

Take tram #38 from Schottentor, on the Ring, to the end of the line (40min.).

The tiny town of Grinzing certainly feels further than 40min. from Vienna, but occasional breathtaking views down into the city, from the many trails, remind of the proximity. Grinzing's main draw is its *Heurigen* (wine taverns) that it is crowded with. Created by imperial edict in the early 18th century, *Heurigen*, marked by a hanging branch of evergreen at the door, sell new wine and snacks. Good *Heuriger* wine is generally white, fruity, and full of body (try *Grüner Veltliner* or *Riesling*). Half the pleasure of visiting a *Heuriger*, however, comes not from the wine but from the atmosphere. The worn picnic benches and old shade trees provide an ideal spot to contemplate, converse, or listen to *Schrammelmusik* (sentimental, wine-lubricated folk songs). Heurigen are clustered all around the town, but there are a few that are in the vineyards themselves. To get onto a trail that goes through the vineyards and one of the Heurigen walk back along the tracks from the tram stop, cross the street you come to, and just to the right, turn left on Grinigersteige. This path leads to Wildgrubengasse. Turn left to reach ◪**Heuriger Josef Lier**, Wildgrubeng. 44 (☎320 23 19). Set right in the vineyards, *G'spritzer* are 18AS, a quarter liter of wine, 24AS. Open W-F from 3pm, Sa-Su from noon. In the town **Weingut Heuriger Reinprecht,** Cobenzlg. 22 (☎320 147 10), embodies the stereotype, with endless picnic tables under an ivy-laden trellis. Despite the many tourists here, don't be surprised to hear whole tables of nostalgic Austrians break into song on their own. Viertel 30AS. Open Mar.-Nov. daily 3:30pm-midnight.

BADEN BEI WIEN

The Badener Bahn runs from Vienna's Karlspl., beneath the Opera House, to Baden's Josefspl. (1hr., every 15min., 57AS); trains also connect Vienna's Südbahnhof and Josefspl. (57AS).

Only 26km from Vienna, Baden is a favorite weekend spot for Viennese and globe-trotters to rest their weary bones, thanks to the healing effects of its sulfur springs. Since the days of Roman rule, these naturally heated jets springing from the ground have been harnessed and used as therapeutic spas, attracting bathers from all corners of Europe. Although the waters smell like rotten eggs, they're warm, relaxing, and healthy. The **Strandbad**, Helenenstr. 19-21, lets you simmer in the sulfur thermal pool and cool off in normal chlorinated water. (☎486 70. Open M-F 8:30am-7:30pm, Sa-Su 8am-6:30pm. M-F 67AS, after 1pm 57AS; Sa-Su 79AS, 67AS.) The **Kurdirektion**, Brusattipl. 4 (☎445 31), is the center of all curative spa treatments, with an indoor thermal pool mainly for patients but also open to visitors (72AS). The spa has underwater massage therapy (295AS), sulfur mudbaths (305AS), and regular sport massages (310AS). A gigantic new complex called the **Römertherme Baden** offers even more soothing luxuries. (☎450 30. Open M noon-10pm, Tu-Su 10am-10pm.) Also be sure to smell the roses—all 20,000 of them—in Baden's **rosarium,** which extends from the center of town to the 90,000 sq. mile **Wienerwald** (Vienna Forest).

From the train station, walk toward the fountain, keep right, and follow Erzherzog-Rainer-Ring to the second left (Brusattipl.) to the **tourist office,** Brusattipl. 3 (labeled "Leopoldsbad"). In summer, the office gives free **tours** of the *Altstadt* (1½hr.; M 2pm and Th 10am) and the wine region (2hr.; W 3pm) as well as guided **hiking** and **mountain-biking** tours (except in Aug.). (☎418 33 ext. 57; fax 807 33. Open May-Oct. M-Sa 9am-6pm, Su and holidays 9am-12:30pm.) **Postal code:** A-2500.

SALZBURG ☎0662

While the *Sound of Music* has brought hordes of tourists to Salzburg's main streets, Salzburg had much to offer before it was even a glimmer in the eye of movie producers. Wedged between mountains and dotted with church spires, medieval turrets, and resplendent palaces, it offers both attractive sights and a rich musical culture. Whether it's enthusiastic tourists singing songs, street musicians playing medieval ballads, or a famed soprano bringing the house down with the *Queen of the Night* aria, Salzburg's streets are filled with music. The city's adulation for homegrown genius Wolfgang Amadeus Mozart in particular and classical music in general reaches a deafening roar every summer during the **Salzburger Festspiele** (summer music festivals).

▣ TRANSPORTATION

Trains: Hauptbahnhof, (☎017 17), Südtirolerpl. Frequent trains to: **Graz** (4½hr., 430AS); **Innsbruck** (2hr., 370AS); **Budapest** (6½hr., 750AS); **Munich** (2hr., 316AS); **Prague** (7hr., 860AS) via Linz; **Venice** (6hr., 560AS); **Vienna** (3½hr., 430AS); and **Zurich** (6hr., 888AS). Ticket office open 24hr.

AUSTRIA

Public Transportation: Lokalbahnhof (☎87 21 45), next to the train station. Tickets are cheapest from *Tabaks* (single ride 20AS, day pass 40AS); you can also purchase packs of 5 single-ride tickets from vending machines at bus stops for 75AS or buy single tickets on the bus. Punch your ticket when you board or face a 500AS fine. Buses usually make their last run from downtown to outer destinations 10:30-11:30pm.

Bike Rental: Climb every mountain and ford every stream with a bicycle from the **train station,** counter #3 (☎88 87 31 63). 150AS per day, 90AS with same-day train ticket.

Hitchhiking: Hitchers headed to Innsbruck, Munich, or most of Italy allegedly take bus #77 to the German border; for Vienna or Venice, they take bus #29 (dir: Forellenwegsiedlung) or bus #15 (dir.: Bergheim) to Autobahn entrances at Schmiedlingerstr. or Grüner Wald, respectively. *Let's Go* does not recommend hitchhiking.

✴ 🛈 ORIENTATION AND PRACTICAL INFORMATION

Just a few kilometers from the German border, Salzburg straddles the **Salzach River.** On the west bank is the **Altstadt** (old city) and the heavily touristed pedestrian district; on the east side is the **Neustadt** (new city), with the **Mirabellplatz** in the center. From the Hauptbahnhof, at the northern edge of town, head left as you exit and follow Rainerstr. all the way (under the tunnel) to Mirabellpl. (15min.).

Tourist Office: Mozartpl. 5 (☎889 87 330; fax 889 87 342; www.salzburginfo.or.at), in the *Altstadt*. From the train station, take bus #5, 6, 51, 55 to Mozartsteg. Or, on foot, turn left on Rainerstr., go to the end, cross Staatsbrücke, then continue along the river's west bank. The free hotel maps are the same as the 10AS city map. Tells travelers which hostels have available rooms. Sells the **Salzburg Card,** good for admission to all museums and sights as well as unlimited public transport (24hr. card 225AS, 48hr. 300AS, 72hr. 390AS). Open July-Aug. 8:30am-8pm; Sept.-June 9am-6pm. **Branch** at platform #2a of the train station. Open M-Sa 9:15am-9pm.

Consulates: South Africa, Buchenweg 14 (☎ 62 20 35). Open M-F 8am-1pm and 2-5pm. **UK,** Alter Markt 4 (☎84 81 33). Open M-F 9am-noon. **US,** Alter Markt 1/3 (☎84 87 76), in the Altstadt. Open M, W, and F 9am-noon.

Currency Exchange: Most banks open M-F 8am-12:30pm and 2-4:30pm. **Rieger Bank,** at Alter Markt and Getreideg. Open July-Aug. M-F 9am-7:30pm, Sa 9am-6pm, Su 10am-5pm; Sept.-June M-F 9am-6pm, Sa 9am-3pm, Su 10am-5pm.

Luggage storage: In the **train station.** Lockers 30-50AS per 2 days; luggage check 30AS per piece per day. Open daily 6am-10pm.

Gay and Lesbian Services: Frauenkulturzentrum (Women's Center), Elisabethstr. 11 (☎87 16 39). Open M 10am-12:30pm. **Homosexual Initiative of Salzburg** (HOSI), Müllner Hauptstr. 11 (☎43 59 27). Cafe-bar open F from 9pm and Sa from 8pm.

Laundromat: Norge Exquisit Textil Reinigung, Paris-Lodronstr. 16 (☎87 63 81), at Wolf-Dietrich-Str. Wash and dry 82AS, soap 28AS. Open M-F 7:30am-4pm, Sa 8-10am.

Emergencies: Police, ☎133. Headquarters at Alpenstr. 90 (☎63 83). **Ambulance,** ☎144. **Fire,** ☎122.

Pharmacies: Elisabeth-Apotheke, Elisabethstr. 1 (☎87 14 84), near the train station. Pharmacies in the city center are open M-F 8am-6pm, Sa 8am-noon. There are always 3 pharmacies open for emergencies; check the list on the door of any closed pharmacy.

Medical Assistance: When the dog bites, when the bee stings, when you're feeling sad, call the **Hospital,** Dr. Franz-Rebirl-Pl. 5 (☎658 00).

Internet Access: Cybercafé, Gstätteng. 29 (☎842 61 622). 80AS per hr. Open M-F 2-11pm, F-Su 2pm-1am.

Post Office: At the Hauptbahnhof (☎889 70). Mail your brown paper packages tied up with strings or exchange money. Address mail to be held: *Postlagernde Briefe* für Karen KIANG, Bahnhofspostamt, A-5020 Salzburg, Austria. Open 6am-11pm.

◤ ACCOMMODATIONS

Salzburg has no shortage of hostels—but then, it has no shortage of tourists either. Housing in Salzburg is even more expensive than in Vienna; most affordable options lie on the outskirts of town. Ask for the tourist office's list of **private rooms**

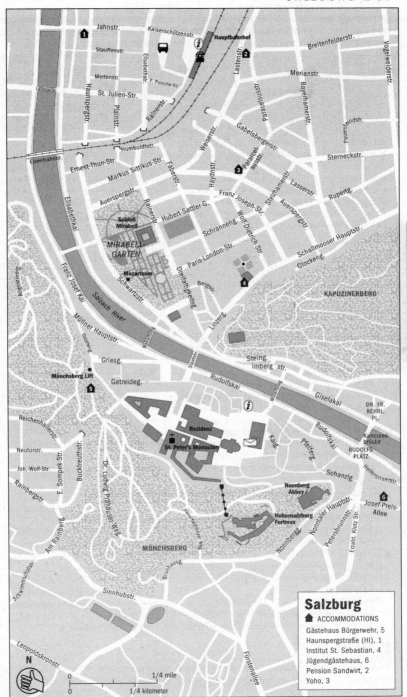

AUSTRIA

Salzburg

🔺 ACCOMMODATIONS

Gästehaus Bürgerwehr, 5
Haunspergstraße (HI), 1
Institut St. Sebastian, 4
Jügendgästehaus, 6
Pension Sandwirt, 2
Yoho, 3

or the *Hotel Plan* (which has info on hostels). From mid-May to mid-September, hostels fill by mid-afternoon—call ahead. Reserve ahead during the *Festspiele* (five weeks of summer music festivals).

HOSTELS AND DORMS

▨ **Gästehaus Bürgerwehr,** Mönchsberg 19c (☎84 17 29). Take bus #1 (dir.: Maxglan) to Mönchsberglift, walk through the stone arch on the left, and take the Mönchsberglift (elevator; runs 9am-11pm, round-trip 27AS). Turn right from the summit, climb the steps, and follow signs for "Gästehaus Naturfreundehaus," for a princely view on a pauper's budget. Breakfast 30AS. Showers 10AS for 4min. Sheets 20AS. Reception 8am-9pm. Curfew 1am. Open May to mid-Sept. Dorms 120AS.

International Youth Hotel (YoHo), Paracelsusstr. 9 (☎87 96 49; fax 87 88 10), off Franz-Josef-Str. Head left from the train station, turn left on Gabelsbergerstr. through the tunnel, and take the 2nd right on Paracelsusstr. (7min.). Daily screening of *The Sound of Music* (noon). Breakfast 30-55AS. Showers 10AS for 6min. Lockers 10AS. Reception 8am-noon. Curfew 1am. Dorms 150-200AS; doubles 400AS; quads 680AS.

Institut St. Sebastian, Linzerg. 41 (☎87 13 86). From the station, take bus #1, 5, 6, 51, or 55 to Mirabellpl. Cross the street and continue in same direction as the bus. Turn left onto Bergstr., then left again at the end on Linzerg. Hostel is through the arch on the left before the church. Breakfast included. Laundry 40AS. Reception 7:30am-noon and 1-10pm; in winter 8am-noon and 4-9pm. Dorms (Oct.-June only) 180AS, with sheets 210AS; singles 330-390AS; doubles 500-680AS; triples 870AS; quads 1000-1080AS.

Eduard-Heinrich-Haus (HI), Eduard-Heinrich-Str. 2 (☎62 59 76). Take bus #51 (dir: Salzburg-Süd) to Polizeidirektion. Cross the street and continue down Billrothstr., turn left on the Robert-Stolz-Promenade footpath, take the 1st right, and it's up the driveway on the left. Breakfast included. Laundry. Reception 7-9am and 5-11pm. Lockout 9am-5pm. Curfew 11pm-midnight; ask for a key. Dorms 186AS; nonmembers 226AS.

Haunspergstraße (HI), Haunspergstr. 27 (☎87 50 30), near the train station. Walk straight out Kaiserschützenstr., which becomes Jahnstr., and turn left on Haunspergstr. Breakfast included. Laundry 80AS. Reception 7am-2pm and 5pm-midnight. Curfew 11pm. Open July-Aug. Dorms 170AS; nonmembers add 40AS for 1st night.

HOTELS AND PENSIONS

Privitazimmer and *Pension* accommodations in the center of the city can be quite expensive, but better quality and lower prices await on the outskirts, and public transportation puts these establishments within minutes of downtown Salzburg. All northbound regional trains run to Kasern Berg (4min.; every 30min. 6:17am-11:17pm; 20AS, Eurail valid). Get off at the first stop (Salzburg-Maria Plain) and walk uphill; all the Kasern Berg *Pensionen* lie on this road.

▨ **Germana Kapeller,** Kasern Berg 64 (☎45 66 71). English-speaking hostess and traditional rooms. Breakfast included. Doubles 400AS; triples 510-600AS.

Haus Christine, Panoramaweg 3 (☎45 67 73). Spacious rooms with a country motif, on a gravel road set back 16m from the main Kasern Berg street at the top of the hill. Breakfast included. Call ahead for pick-up from the station. 180-200AS per person.

Haus Matilda Lindner, Panoramaweg 5 (☎45 66 81). Matilda (Christine's sister) offers rooms with balconies. Call for pick-up from the station. 180-200AS per person.

Haus Moser, Turnebuhel 1 (☎45 66 76), up the hidden stairs to the right of Kasern Berg road, opposite Germana Kapeller. Comfy, dark-timbered rooms. Breakfast included. Singles 170-200AS; doubles 340-400AS; triples 510-600AS; quads 700-800AS.

Haus Elisabeth, Rauchenbichlerstr. 18 (☎450 703). Take bus #51 to Itzling-Pflanzmann (last stop), walk up Rauchenbichlerstr. over the footbridge, and continue right along the gravel path. Plush rooms have TVs, balconies, and sweeping views of the city. Breakfast included. Singles 300-330AS; doubles 500-550AS; 4-person suite 1000AS.

CAMPING

Camping Stadtblick, Rauchenbichlerstr. 21 (☎45 06 52), next to Haus Elisabeth. On-site store. Laundry 70AS. Open Mar. 20-Oct. 31. 65AS per person, 20AS per tent, 4-person mobile home with fridge and stove 100AS per person.

◘ FOOD

Blessed with fantastic **beer gardens** and **Konditoreien** (pastry shops), Salzburg begs its guests to eat outdoors. The local specialty is *Salzburger Nockerl*, a large souffle of egg-whites, sugar, and raspberry filling baked into three mounds representing the three hills of Salzburg. World-famous **Mozartkugeln** ("Mozart balls") consist of hazelnut covered with marzipan and nougat and dipped in chocolate. Many supermarkets line the Mirabellpl. side of the river; look for **SPAR** (the giant **EuroSpar** sprawls next to the train station and bus terminal).

▧ **Restaurant Zur Bürgerwehr-Einkehr,** Mönchsberg 19c (☎84 17 29). Follow directions to the Gästehaus Bürgerwehr (see above). Escape the tourist throng as you enjoy the best views in town. Open April-Oct. Sa-Th 11:30am-8:45pm.

▧ **Café im Künstlerhaus,** Hellbrunnerstr. 3 (☎84 56 01). This low-key cafe is popular with students, artists, and their fans. Treat yourself to an amaretto or a shot of tequila. Local bands play Tu and Th. Sa lesbian night. Open M-Sa 11am-11pm.

Shakespeare, Hubert Sattlerg. 3 (☎87 91 06), off Mirabellpl. Culturally schizophrenic restaurant with everything from *Wienerschnitzel* to Greek salad to wonton soup (32-136AS). Doubles as a bar(d) with live music. Restaurant open M-F 11:30am-2:30pm and 6pm-midnight, Sa 6pm-midnight, Su open from 11am.

Zwettler's, Kaig. 3, in the Altstadt. Walk down Kapitelg. onto Kaig. Hearty, old-fashioned dishes. Steak and fries 180AS. Live blues every other W. Open daily 5pm-midnight.

Zum Fidelen Affen, Priesterhausg. 8, off Linzerg. Pleasant outdoor picnic tables. Drinks 30AS. Salad and main course 87-110AS. Open M-Sa 5-11pm.

◙ SIGHTS

Salzburg is a relatively small town with a disproportionate number of *Sehenswürdigkeiten* (things worth seeing). Whether you're into decadent floral gardens or stoic fortresses, Salzburg's got something for you.

THE NEUSTADT

SCHLOß MIRABELL AND MIRABELLGARTEN. Whether you walk or take the bus from the train station, you should visit Mirabellplatz, where the marvelous **Schloß Mirabell** stands. This rosy-hued wonder was built in 1606 by Archbishop Wolf Dietrich, who despite a vow of celibacy needed to house his mistress Salome Alt and their 10 children. The castle is now the seat of the city government, and some of the offices are open for public viewing. *(Mirabellpl. Open M-F 7am-4pm. Free.)* Behind the palace, the manicured **Mirabellgarten** is a maze of extravagant flower beds and groomed shrubs. Students from the nearby **Mozarteum** (Salzburg's music conservatory) often perform here. If you're struck by a feeling of *déjà vu*, it's probably because Maria von Trapp and her wards once stopped here. From one of the hedge-enclosed clearings in the Mirabellgarten, you can see a tiny wooden, moss-covered shack called the **Zauberflötenhäuschen,** allegedly where Wolfgang Amadeus composed *The Magic Flute* in just five months. It was transplanted from Vienna as a gift to Salzburg's conservatory for young musicians, the Mozarteum.

MOZARTS WOHNHAUS. Just down the street from the Mozarteum stands the house in which the composer lived from 1773 to 1780, after moving with his family at age 17 from the *Altstadt* house in which he was born. With fewer crowds than the Geburtshaus and a much more thoughtful exhibit, the Wohnhaus is the place to go. *(Makartpl. 8. ☎883 45 440. Open daily 10am-5:30pm. 65AS, students 50AS.)*

KAPUZINERKLOSTER AND SEBASTIANSKIRCHE. At the crest of the **Kapuzinerberg,** which looms to the south of the Neustadt, stands the simple **Kapuzinerkloster** (Capuchin Monastery), built by Wolf Dietrich in the late 16th century. *(From the Mirabellgarten or Mozarts Wohnhaus, follow Dreifaltigkeitsg. south to its intersection with Linzerg. head under the stone arch on the right side of Linzerg. 14 and follow the tiny stone staircase up.)*

AUSTRIA

Nearby is the 18th-century **Sebastianskirche,** with an Italian-style graveyard that contains the gaudy mausoleum of Wolf Dietrich and the tombs of Mozart's wife Constanze and father Leopold. (*Lizerg. 41. Open Apr.-Oct. 9am-7pm, Nov.-Mar. 9am-4pm.*)

THE ALTSTADT

The Alstadt lies on the other side of the Salzach River in the shadow of the hill-top fortress, where arcade passages open up into tiny courtyards filled with geraniums and creeping ivy that lead, in turn, to the tourist jammed **Getreidegasse.** This labyrinth of winding pathways and 17th- and 18th-century facades is one of the best preserved (and most visited) streets in Salzburg.

MOZARTS GEBURTSHAUS AND UNIVERSITÄTSKIRCHE. Although Mozart eventually settled in Vienna, his **birthplace** *(Geburtshaus)* holds the most impressive collection of the child genius's belongings: his first viola and violin, a pair of keyboard instruments, and a lock of hair purportedly from his noggin. (*Getreideg. 9. Open July-Aug. 9am-6:30pm; Sept.-June 9am-5:30pm. 70AS, students 55AS.*) Directly in Mozart's backyard stands the **Universitätskirche** (University Church), considered to be Fischer von Erlach's greatest masterpiece, one of the largest Baroque chapels on the continent. Its distinctive dome stands watch over Universitätspl.

TOSCANINIHOF TO THE DOM. Steps lead from **Toscaninihof,** the courtyard of **St. Peter's Monastery,** up the Mönchesberg cliffs. Adjacent to Toscaninihof, **Stiftskirche St. Peter,** within the monastery, began as a Romanesque basilica in the 1100s and still features a marble portal from 1244. In the 18th century, the building was remodeled in Rococo style. The church struggles to keep at bay the tourists who steal quick photographs of this Fabergé egg turned inside out. (*Open daily 9am-12:15pm and 2:30-6:30pm.*) Continue through the arch to the right of the church to enter the **Petersfriedhof,** one of the most peaceful places in Salzburg. This secluded spot is a popular subject for romantic painters and it served as a model for the cemetery where Rolf blew the whistle on the von Trapp family in *The Sound of Music.* (*Open Apr.-Sept. 6:30am-7pm; Oct.-Mar. 6:30am-6pm.*) Near the far end of the cemetery, against the mountains, lies the entrance to the **Katakomben** (catacombs), relatively empty, cave-like rooms where Christians worshipped in secret as early as AD 250. (*Open Tu-Su 10:30am-4pm; in winter W-Su 10:30am-3:30pm. 12AS.*) The exit at the other end of the cemetery from the Stiftskirche leads into Kapitelpl., bordered by Salzburg's immense Baroque **Dom** (cathedral), where Mozart was christened in 1756 and later worked as *Konzertmeister* and court organist. The cupola was destroyed during WWII, but was quickly repaired. (*10AS donation*).

RESIDENZ. Salzburg's ecclesiastical elite have resided in the magnificent Residenz for the last 700 years. Tours lead through stunning Baroque **Prunkräume** (state rooms), which house an astonishing three-dimensional ceiling fresco by Rottmayr, as well as false walls hiding secret doors. A **gallery** exhibits 16th- to 19th-century art. (*Residenzpl. 1. ☎ 804 22 690. Open 10am-5pm. 91AS, students 70AS; audio guide included.*)

HOHENSALZBURG FORTRESS. Built between 1077 and 1681 by the ruling archbishops, **Festung Hohensalzburg,** which looms over Salzburg from atop Mönchesberg, is the largest completely preserved castle in Europe, probably because it was never successfully attacked. (*Take the trail (20min.) or the Festungsbahn (funicular) up to the fortress from the Festungsg. Funicular runs every 10min. 9am-9pm; Oct.-Apr. 9am-5pm. Ascent 66AS; round-trip 76AS; includes entrance to fortress.*) The castle contains a "torture" chamber (though they apparently never had anyone to torture), formidable Gothic state rooms, the fortress organ (nicknamed the "Bull of Salzburg" for its off-key snorting), and an impregnable watchtower that affords an unmatched view of the city and surrounding mountains. You'll also see the archbishop's medieval indoor toilet—a technological marvel of its day. The **Burgmuseum** inside the fortress displays medieval instruments of torture. (*☎ 842 430. Fortress open July-Sept. 8:30am-7pm; Nov.-Mar. 9am-5pm; Apr.-June 9am-6pm. Entrance to fortress 42AS, allows access to the perimeter of the castle; combo ticket including fortress, castle interiors, and both museums 84AS; castle interior and both museums 42AS.*) Down the hill and to the right of the fortress, **Nonnberg Abbey** (where Maria von Trapp lived) remains a private monastic complex.

THE SOUND OF MUSIC. Three remarkably similar companies run **Sound of Music Tours;** the best choice is often the one that stops closest to your accommodation—many hostels and pensions work exclusively with one of the firms and offer discounts to guests. **Salzburg Sightseeing Tours** (☎88 16 16) and **Panorama Tours** (☎88 32 11) operate rival kiosks on Mirabellpl. *(400AS. Tours leave from Mirabellpl. daily 9:30am and 2pm.)* The renegade **Bob's Special Tours,** Kaig. 19, has no high-profile kiosk, but they do have a minibus. *(☎84 95 11. 350AS. Tours daily 9am and 2pm; in winter 10am.)* All three companies offer free pick-up from your hotel, and all tours last four hours. The tours are generally only worth it if you're a *big* fan.

MUSEUMS

Salzburg's small, specialized museums often get lost in the shadow of the *Festung*, *The Sound of Music*, and the *Festspiele*. The keywords in that sentence are "small" and "specialized." There are also small and specialized private galleries on **Sigmund-Haffnerg.** that allow budget art viewing.

ART MUSEUMS. The **Museum Carolino Augusteum,** named after Emperor Franz I's widow, Caroline Augusta, houses local Roman and Celtic artifacts on its ground floor, including mosaics and burial remains, naturally preserved thanks to the region's salt. *(Museumpl. 1. ☎841 134. Open Tu-Su 10am-6pm, Th until 8pm. 40AS, students 15AS.)* The **Barockmuseum,** in the Orangerie of the Mirabellgarten, pays elaborate tribute to the ornate aesthetic of 17th- and 18th-century Europe. *(☎877 432. Open Tu-Sa 9am-noon and 2-5pm, Su 9am-noon. 40AS, students and seniors 20AS, ages 6-14 free.)*

BEER MUSEUM. Stiegl Brauwelt (Brew World) is Salzburg's own beer museum, with three floors showcasing beer-making, the history of brewing, and modern beer culture—including "30 Ways to Open a Beer Bottle" and the wonder of the *Brauwelt*, a 2-story beer-bottle pyramid constructed of 300 Austrian beers. The tour concludes with two complimentary glasses of Stiegl beer and a souvenir beer glass. *(Take bus #1 to Brauhaus and walk up the street to the giant yellow building. Brauhausstr. 9. ☎838 71492. Open W-Su 10am-4pm. 96AS, students 60AS.)*

A U S T R I A

 ENTERTAINMENT AND NIGHTLIFE

OUTDOOR ACTIVITIES

If you're sick of the baroque ornamentation and cobblestone streets with which Salzburg assaults its visitors, or if you just want to get your blood pumping, try an adventure tour with **Crocodile Sports** (☎642 907), Gaisbergstr. 34a. Owner and operator Wolfgang will gleefully pick you up from your hotel and bring you for a day (or half a day) you'll never forget. Adventures are scheduled throughout the week (so call ahead) and include **canyoning** (590-2790AS), **canoeing** (590-2790AS), **paragliding** (1200AS), and **rafting** (550AS-840AS).

MUSIC

Max Reinhardt, Richard Strauss, and Hugo von Hofmannsthal founded the renowned **Salzburger Festspiele** (Festivals) in 1920, and ever since then operas, plays, films, concerts, and tourists have overrun every available public space from late July through the end of August. The festival prints a complete program of events one year in advance (10AS; available at any tourist office). To order tickets, contact the **Festspiele Kartenbüro,** Postfach 140, A-5010 Salzburg (☎804 55 79; fax 804 57 60; www.salzburgfestival.at), by the beginning of January. Under-26ers can try for cheap subscription tickets (2-4 tickets for 200-300AS each) by writing eight months ahead to *Direktion der Salzburger Festspiele,* attn: Ulrich Hauschild, Hofstallg. 1, A-5020 Salzburg. Those who have no luck, or can't afford what's offered, can try the **Fest zur Eröffungsfest** (Opening Day Festival), when concerts, shows, and films are either inexpensive or free. Tickets for these events are available on a first-come, first-served basis the week of the opening.

Even when the *Festspiele* are not on, many other concerts and events occur around the city. The popular **Mozarteum** (see p. 99) performs a number of concerts on a rotating schedule (available at the tourist office). For tickets, contact **Karten-büro Mozarteum,** Postfach 156, Theaterg. 2. (☎87 31 54; fax 87 29 96. Open M-Th 9am-2pm, F 9am-4pm.) For a bit more money but a lot more kitsch, you can enjoy knicker-clad musicians with powdered hair performing **Mozart Serenaden** (Mozart's Serenades) in the Gothic Hall on Burgerstpitalg, 2. (Daily in summer 8:30pm; off-season 7:30pm. 200-420AS.) For info and tickets, contact **Konzertdirektion Nerat,** A-5020 Salzburg, Lieferinger Hauptstr. 136 (☎43 68 70; fax 43 69 70). In July and August, **outdoor opera** occasionally rings out from the historical hedge-theater of Mirabellgarten (330-560AS, students 190AS). Tickets for both series are available from the **box office** in Schloß Mirabell. (☎84 85 86; fax 84 47 47. Open M-F 9am-5:30pm.) The Mirabellgarten hosts various **outdoor performances** throughout the summer, including concerts, folk-singing, and dancing. The tourist office has info, but strolling through in the evening might be just as effective.

NIGHTLIFE

Munich may be known as the world's beer capital, but a lot of that liquid gold flows south to Austria's beer gardens *(Biergärten)*. These lager oases cluster in the city center by the Salzach River. Altstadt nightclubs (especially along Gstätteng. and near Chiemseeg.) attract younger types and tourists. The other side of the river has a less juvenile atmosphere. From the Altstadt, follow the footpath from Hanuschpl. downstream, go left up the stairs past the Riverside Café, cross Müllner Hauptstr., walk uphill, and take the first left to the legendary ▓**Augustiner Bräu,** Augustinerg. 4, where great beer brewed by the Müllner Kloster is poured into massive steins from even more massive wooden kegs. (☎43 12 46. Beer 1L 68AS; tip the tap-*meister* 4AS. Open M-F 3-11pm, Sa-Su 2:30-11pm.) Settle into an armchair at **Vis à Vis,** Rudolfskai 24. (Open Su-Th 8am-4pm, F-Sa 8pm-5am.) **Zweistein,** Giselakai 9, the funkiest bar in town, rocks at night. (Open M-W 6pm-4am, Th-F 6pm-5am, Sa 2pm-5am, Su 2pm-4am.) **Pub Passage,** Rudolfskai 22-26, under the Radisson Hotel by the Mozartsteg bridge, is a promenade for youthful bar-hopping. (**Tom's Bierklinik** serves international beers; **The Black Lemon** offers Latino every W; 80s music blares from **Bräu zum Frommen Hell.**) If you get locked out of your hostel, **Schwarze Katze,** Frudi-ele, Auerspergstr. 45, opens for night owls (Tu-Sa 4am-noon).

◪ DAYTRIPS FROM SALZBURG

LUSTSCHLOSS HELLBRUNN

Take bus #55 (dir. Anif) to Hellbrunn from the train station, Mirabellpl., or the Mozartsteg, in Salzburg, or bike 40min. down Hellbrunner Allee.

Just south of Salzburg lies the unforgettable **Lustschloß Hellbrunn,** a one-time plea-sure dome for Wolf Dietrich's nephew, the Archbishop Markus Sittikus. The sprawling estate includes a large palace, fish ponds, and trimmed hedge gardens. Before entering the **Wasserspiele,** prepare yourself for wet surprises—Archbishop Markus amused himself with elaborate water-powered figurines and a booby-trapped table that could spout water on his guests. (☎820 00 30. Open July-Aug. 9am-10pm; May-June and Sept. 9am-5:30pm; Apr. and Oct. 9am-4:30pm. Compul-sory tours 40AS, students 30AS. *Wasserspiele* tour 80AS, 65AS. Joint 100AS, 80AS.)

UNTERSBERG PEAK

Bus #55 continues on from Hellbrunn to Untersberg.

The luscious **Untersberg peak** is where Charlemagne rests underground, prepared to return and reign over Europe once again when needed. Dozens of **hikes** carve through color-soaked meadows, with mountains hovering in the distance. The **Eishöhlen** (ice caves) are only a short climb from the peak (1½hr.). A **cable car** glides over Salzburg to the summit. (☎ (06246) 87 12 17. Runs July-Sept. Su-Tu and Th-Sa 8:30am-5:30pm, W 8:30am-8pm; Mar.-June and Oct. daily 9am-5pm; Dec.-Feb. daily 10am-4pm. Ascent 130AS, descent 110AS, round-trip 215AS.)

THE SALZKAMMERGUT

Every summer, bands of Austrian schoolchildren, tour groups of elderly Europeans, and tourists in-the-know come to the smooth lakes and furrowed mountains of the Salzkammergut. The region takes its name from the salt mines that, in their glory days, underwrote Salzburg's architectural treasures; today, the white gold of the Salzkammergut is no longer salt, but pure sunshine on sparkling water in summer and tons of fresh snow in winter. The **Salzkammergut Card** (65AS at local tourist offices) grants 25% off on most local sights and attractions. The area is easily navigable, with 2000km of footpaths, 12 cable cars and chairlifts, and dozens of hostels. The mountainous area is barren of rail tracks; **buses** (dial ☎ 167 from Salzburg for schedules) are the best way to travel into and throughout the lake region.

HALLSTATT   ☎ 06134

Teetering on the banks of the **Hallstättersee** lake at the southern tip of the Salzkammergut and surrounded on all sides by the sheer rocky cliffs of the Dachstein mountains is tiny Hallstatt (pop. 1400). Hallstatt is easily the most beautiful lakeside village in the Salzkammergut, if not all of Austria. In the 19th century, it was also the site of an immense, incredibly well-preserved Iron Age archaeological find; the **Prähistorisches Museum**, across from the tourist office, and the smaller **Heimatmuseum** around the corner exhibit some of the treasures. (Both open daily May-Sept. 10am-6pm; Oct. 10am-4pm. Joint ticket 50AS, students 25AS.) The fascinating charnel house next to St. Michael's Chapel at the **Pfarrkirche** is a bizarre repository for skeletons, filled with the remains of over 610 villagers dating from the 16th century on. The Celts buried their dead high in the mountains, but they soon ran out of space on their steep hillside, so the skulls and femurs of the deceased were transferred to the charnel house to make room for more corpses. (Open May-Sept. daily 10am-6pm. 10AS, students 5AS.) Tours of the 2500-year-old **Salzbergwerke**, the oldest saltworks in the world, include a zip down a wooden mining slide on a burlap sack to an eerie lake deep inside the mountain. To get there, climb up the path near the Pfarrkirche to the top (1hr.), or follow the black signs with the yellow eyes to the **Salzbergbahn** station at the south end of town. (☎ 84 00 46. Open June to mid-Sept. 9:30am-4:30pm; Apr.-May and mid-Sept. to Oct. 9:30am-3pm. Tours in English 1½hr., 140AS, students 70AS. Salzbergbahn runs daily June to mid-Sept. 9am-6pm; Apr.-May and mid-Sept. to Oct. 9am-4:30pm. 65AS, round-trip 105AS.)

Buses are the cheapest way to get to Hallstatt from Salzburg (130AS), but require layovers in both Bad Ischl and Gosaumühle. **Trains** arrive from Salzburg on the other side of the lake from downtown, but there is no staffed office to help travelers. All trains come from Attnang-Puchheim in the north or Stanach-Irnding in the south. Trains run to Attnang-Puchheim (134AS), Bad Ischl (38AS), and Salzburg via Attnang-Puchheim (210AS). **Ferries** (10min., last ferry 6:45pm; 23AS) shuttle passengers across the lake. The **tourist office**, Seestr. 169, finds rooms. (☎82 08; fax 83 52; www.discover.com/hallstatt. Open July-Aug. M-F 9am-5pm, Sa 10am-2pm; Sept.-June M-F 9am-noon and 2-5pm.) To reach **Gästehaus Zur Mühle**, Kirchenweg 36, from the tourist office, walk uphill toward the Heimatmuseum, then swing right at the end of the Platz; it's through the little tunnel on the left, by the waterfall. (☎83 18. Breakfast 40AS. Sheets 35AS. Reception 8am-2pm and 4-10pm. 110AS.) **Frühstückspension Sarstein**, Gosaumühlstr. 83, offers vistas of the lake and village. From the tourist office, turn left on Seestr. and walk for 10min.; it will be on the right. (☎82 17. Showers 10AS per 10min. Singles and doubles 270AS; triples 200AS, with bath 300AS; 20AS surcharge for 1-night stays.) **Camping Klausner-Höll**, Lahnstr. 6, is three blocks past the bus stop on Seestr. (☎83 22. Breakfast 65-110AS. Shower included. Laundry. Lock-out daily noon-2:30pm and 10pm-7am. Open mid-Apr. to mid-Oct. 65AS, 45AS per tent, 35AS per car.) **Konsum supermarket** is across from the main bus stop at the edge of town. (Open M-F 7:30am-noon and 3-6pm, Sa 7:30am-noon.) **Postal code:** A-4830.

⚡ DAYTRIPS FROM HALLSTATT

HIKING IN ECHENTAL VALLEY

To reach the valley, go toward the Salzbergwerke and continue on Malerweg or Echenweg; about 20min. later, a sign posts the area's layout. Gangstieg is about an hour up on the right side, while the glacier gardens are about 40min. up on the left.

Hallstatt offers some of the most spectacular **day hikes** in the Salzkammergut. The tourist office offers an excellent Dachstein **hiking guide** (70AS; in English) which details 38 hikes in the area, as well as a **mountain bike** trail map (35AS). The **salt mine (salzbergwerk) hike** is a simple well-paved hike leading to the salt-mine tour. To make this 45min. hike, exit the tourist office right on Seestr., turning right at the bus stop and following the Salzbegwerk signs. The **Waldbackstrub Waterfall hike** is a light, 1½hr. walk along a thundering river and up to a spellbinding waterfall. From the tourist office, turn right on Seestr. toward the bus station, and follow the brown "Malerweg" sign near the supermarket, and then continue to follow them. After about 35min. the Waldbachstrub sign appears; be sure to follow it and do not follow the Gonsteig signs unless you are accompanied by a professional guide. The waterfall is in the **Echental,** a valley carved out millennia ago by glaciers and now blazed with trails leading deep into the valley. The **Gangsteig,** a slippery, nefarious, primitive stairway, is carved into the side of a cliff, but is for experienced hikers only. Those with less gumption can visit the **Glacier Gardens** in the valley.

DACHSTEIN ICE CAVES

From Hallstatt, take the bus (10min., 8:35am-4:40pm, 25AS) from the Lahn station near the lake by turning right on Seestr. just past the tourist office and walking 6min. Get off at the Dachstein cable car station, then ride 1350m up to Schönbergalm (runs 8:40am-5:50pm; round-trip 170AS).

At the other end of the Hallstättersee in **Obertraun,** the eerily illuminated Dachstein Ice Caves give eloquent testimony to the geological hyperactivity that forged the region's natural beauty. The ice caves look like some artist's conception of another world and the eerie lighting makes the huge, strange caves even stranger. Tours are in German, but no narration is needed to wonder at the caves. (☎84 00. Open May to mid-Oct. daily 9am-5pm. Either cave 90AS, together 150AS.)

GRÜNAU

The mountain-locked town of Grünau is not really on the way to anywhere, but it is an attractive destination in its own right. Sitting in the middle of the **Totes Gebirge** (Dead Mountains) is the backpacker's dream resort, ◪**The Treehouse,** Schindlbachstr. 525. Once you've settled into your room (with private shower and goosedown blankets), you're free to take advantage of the luxurious amenities. Organized adventure tours include **paragliding** (900AS), **canyoning** (650AS), **rafting** (590AS), **bungee jumping** (990AS; Sa-Su only), and **horseback riding** (100AS per hr.). Rent a **mountain bike** (70AS per day) or ask the staff to drop you off at a nearby mountain or lake with a map so you can **hike** your way home. For winter visitors, the **ski lift** is 5min. away (lift tickets 200AS); you can borrow snow gear for free and rent skis (120AS) or a snowboard (150AS). (☎ (07616) 84 99; email treehousehotel@hotmail.com; www.hostels.com/treehouse. Breakfast included. Dorms 180AS; doubles 220AS; triple 210AS; quad 190AS.) **Regional trains** service Grünau from Wels, on the Vienna-Salzburg rail line, (1 hr., every 2hr., 80AS). Call ahead for pick-up from the station.

GMUNDEN   ☎07612

Gmunden (pop. 16,000) is the picture of a resort town. Posh boutiques and a knack for ceramic work mark the town today, but these pale in comparison to its sunny lakeside beaches and stately mountains. Enjoy the beautiful **Traunsee** lake by strolling the promenade from the town center to the Habsburg **Villa Toscana** and over the bridge to the **Seeschloß Ort** (sea castle) which sits like an imperial island. (☎77815.

Tours Th and Su 2:30pm; 40AS.) An unorthodox display of ceramics awaits at the **Klo and So Museum für Historische Sanitärobjekte,** Pepöckhaus, Traung. 4, which has a collection of 19th- and 20th-century toilets. The eccentric exhibit includes the early 19th-century chameleon chair with a removable seat, *Biedermeier* wooden boxes, gilded *Jugendstil* toilets, a *fin de siècle* circular bench draped in red robes with tassels, and international specimens including short, blue-tiled Japanese urinals. (☎794 294. Open May-Oct. Tu-Sa 10am-noon and 2-5pm, Su 10am-noon. 20AS.) With that big, beautiful **Traunsee** there, it is natural to want to play in it. For water-skiing, contact **Wasserskiclub Union Traunsee** (☎636 02). For sailing information call **Segelschule Gmunden** at ☎751 00.

Trains run frequently to Gmunden from Salzburg (1½hr., every hr. 3:20am-8:25pm, 160AS) via Attnang-Puchheim. **Buses** connect Gmunden to the rest of the region, including Grünau, and depart from the post office. To reach the town center from the station, either turn left and follow Bahnhofstr. down the hill, or hop on the tram in front of the station (18AS, day pass 22AS). From the Franz-Josef Platz terminal, continue one block and turn left to reach the **tourist office,** Am Graben 2, which provides a list of *Privatzimmern* (210-300AS) and will call to find out if rooms are available. (☎744 51. Open Oct.-Apr. M-F 8am-noon and 2-6pm; May-June and Sept. M-F 8am-6pm, Sa 9am-noon; July-Aug. M-F 8am-6pm, Sa-Su 9am-1pm and 5-7pm.) Consider heading to Grünau for the night (see above). **Postal code:** A-4810.

BAD ISCHL
☎ 06132

Bad Ischl (pop. 15,000) was a salt-mining town for centuries, until a certain Dr. Franz Wirer arrived in 1821 to study the curative properties of the heated brine baths in the area. It now serves two types of budget travelers: those who are willing to splurge and enjoy the pleasures of an affordable resort, and those who wish to simply walk around and relax in an elegant town more substantial than the tiny hamlets in the area. Other than the salt baths in the area, Bad Ischl's main attraction is the **Kaiservilla,** Emperor Franz Josef's summer palace. Inside are many interesting relics of his reign, including the desk where he signed the 1914 declaration of war against Serbia that led to WWI. (☎232 41. Open May to mid-Oct. 9-11:45am and 1-4:45pm. 130AS, with guest card 120AS, students 50AS.) Whether or not the **brine baths** really have curative powers, Bad Ischl certainly has a relaxed atmosphere. The bath facilities are mostly in the posh **Kaiser Therme,** a resort across from the tourist office on Bahnhofstr. 1. Splash around in the heated salt baths with whirlpool or consider relaxing in the spacious **sauna.** (☎233 240. Open M-Sa 9am-9pm, Su 1:30-9pm, last entrance 8pm. 111AS for 3hr., children 57AS. Sauna open Tu-Su 1:30-9pm, Th women only, Tu men only. Combined ticket with pool 153AS for 3hr., children 81AS.) Bad Ischl offers incredible hiking too; paths are shown on a map available at the tourist office (98AS).

Only one **train** comes through the station, running between Attnang-Puchheim in the north (1¼hr., 87AS) and Hallstatt (30min., 38AS) in the south. Trains go through these towns to Vienna (3¼hr., 400AS), and Zell am See (370AS). **Buses** arrive in Bad Ischl from Salzburg (1½hr., every hr., 100AS), and St. Wolfgang (35min., 60AS). The **tourist office,** Bahnhofstr. 6, can be reached from the station by turning left on Bahnhofstr. and walking for 2min. (☎277 570. Open M-F 9am-7pm, Sa 9am-3pm, Su 10am-1pm.) Every guest who stays the night in Bad Ischl must pay a *Kurtax,* which entitles you to a **guest card** (June to mid-Sept. 25-30AS per person per night; Oct.-May 13-15AS). From the tourist office, walk left on Bahnhofstr., turn right on Kaiser-Franz-Josef-Str., and keep going to find the **Jugendgästehaus (HI),** Am Rechenstag 5. (☎265 77. Breakfast included. Reception 8am-1pm and 5-7pm. Quiet after 10pm. Reservations recommended. Dorms 155AS, nonmembers 195AS.) Restaurants are tucked into every possible niche along Schulg. and the other streets of the pedestrian zone. Almost as famous as the Kaiser himself is the **Konditorei Zauner,** Pfarrg. 7 (☎235 22), famous for heavenly sweets, *tortes,* and sandwiches. The **Konsum grocery store** is conveniently located at Auböckpl. 12. (Open M-F 7:30am-6:30pm, Sa 7:30am-5pm.) **Postal code:** A-4820.

HOHE TAUERN NATIONAL PARK

The enormous Hohe Tauern National Park, the largest national park in Europe, encompasses 246 glaciers and 304 mountains over 3000m. Farmers still herd cattle over the same 2500m *Tauern* (ice-free mountain paths) once trod by Celts and Romans. The **Glocknergruppe,** in the heart of the park, has Austria's highest peak, the **Großglockner** (3798m), as well as many Alpine lakes and glaciers. The main tourist attractions are the **Krimml Waterfalls** and the spectacular high mountain road **Großglocknerstraße** (a.k.a. Bundesstr. 107).

TRANSPORTATION. Two **train** lines service towns near the park: a rail line from Zell am See runs west along the northern border of the park, terminating at Krimml (1¾hr., 100AS); another runs from Salzburg to Badgastein in the southwest corner of the park (1½hr., every 2hr., 170AS). **Buses** connect to and traverse the park, stopping in the center at Franz-Josefs-Höhe; from Zell am See, take bus #3064 (2hr., 1-3 per day, 145AS). For schedules, destinations, and maps, check the brochure *Der Bundes Bus ist Wanderfreundlich* (available at bus stations in Zell am See). The breathtaking **Großglocknerstraße,** one of the most beautiful highways in the world, winds for 50km through silent Alpine valleys, meadows of wildflowers, tumbling waterfalls, and huge glaciers between Zell am See and Lienz (about 5hr.). Many visitors traverse the Großglocknerstr. in a **tour bus** or **rental car,** but the public **bus** service is good. Heavy snow forces the Großglocknerstr. to close from October to April. For information on road conditions, call ☎ (04824) 22 12.

FRANZ-JOSEFS-HÖHE AND PASTERZE GLACIER. Großglocknerstr. buses from Zell am See, Lienz, and Heiligenblut terminate at **Franz-Josefs-Höhe,** a large observation and tourist center above the **Pasterze glacier.** Although the area is packed with visitors, they can't detract from the sight of the glacier's icy tongue extending down the valley. If the weather's right, you can glimpse the summit of the **Großglockner** (3797m). The **park office** in the parking area has a free mini-museum and organizes free daily walks around the glacier. (☎ (04824) 27 27. Open daily 10am-4pm.) The **Gletscherbahn funicular** runs from Franz-Josefs-Höhe down to the glacier, where you can walk 100m across its hard-packed surface. (Runs May 21-Oct. 10 daily 9am-2pm. Round-trip 98AS.) Take the *Panoramaweg* near the information office up the hill for a great view without a ton of tourists and walk down it to the **Swarovski Observation Center** for an even better view. Three floors of binoculars and telescopes provide excellent viewing of the surrounding terrain. Keep an eye out for marmots. (Open daily 10am-4pm. Free.)

KRIMML WATERFALLS AND TOWN. A sloping path leads from the small mountain town of **Krimml,** in the northwest corner of the park, to the extraordinary **Wasserfälle**—three roaring cascades totaling over 400m in height. A path running alongside the falls allows for unusually close and pulse-quickening views of the roaring water. The first and most spectacular cascade (150m) is visible past the entrance booth. It's about 30min. from the first falls to the second (100m) and another 30min. from there to the third (140m); the last is perhaps the most scenic and the least cluttered with gawking tourists. **Buses** from Zell am See (1½ hr., 110AS) drop you at the start of the path to the falls (get off at Maustelle Ort). The Pinzgauer Lokalbahn **train** arrives in town from Zell am See (1¾hr., 6:28am-6:49pm, 100AS; Eurail valid); catch the **bus** (20AS) across the street or walk 3km along the path to the falls. (Falls 8am-6pm 15AS, other times free.) **ÖAV/National Park Information** is next to the ticket booth. (☎ (06564) 72 12. Open May-Oct. M-Sa 11am-4pm.) The **tourist office** in Krimml Town is two minutes downhill from the Krimml Ort bus stop. (☎ (06564) 72 39; fax 75 50. Open M-F 8am-noon and 2:30-5:30pm, Sa 9-11am.) **Bauernhof Mühleg,** Krimml 24, has big rooms with mountain views. Walk five minutes past the **ADEG** supermarket, continue downhill, and it's on the right. (☎ (06564) 73 38. Doubles 220-240AS.)

HEILIGENBLUT. The cheapest, most convenient base for exploring the region is Heiligenblut, a tiny town to the south of the Großglocknerstraße. **Buses** arrive from Franz-Josefs-Höhe (30min., 9:30am-4:40pm, 47AS) and Zell am See (2½hr., 3 per day, 145AS). The **tourist office,** up the street from the bus stop and Hotel Glocknerhof, has info on park transportation. (☎ (04824) 20 01 21; fax 20 01 43. Open Sept.-June M-F 8:30am-noon and 2:30-6pm, Sa 9am-noon and 4-6pm; July-Aug. M-F 8:30am-6pm). To reach the **Jugendherberge (HI),** Hof 36, take the steep path down from the wall behind the bus stop parking lot. (☎ (04824) 22 59. Breakfast included. Reception May-Sept. 7-10am and 5-10pm. Curfew 10pm; key available. Dorms 190AS. Members only.) **Pension Bergkristall** has rooms with balconies. (☎ (04824) 20 05. Breakfast included. In summer 300AS per person; in winter 380-420AS.)

ZELL AM SEE   ☎06452

Surrounded by a ring of snow-capped mountains that slide into a broad turquoise lake, Zell am See is a year-round resort for mountain-happy European tourists. Conquer the rugged, snow-crowned peaks surrounding Zell on one of the five **cable cars.** The BundesBus (dir.: Schmittenhöhebahn/Sonnenalmbahn Talstation) goes to the **Schmittenhöhebahn,** 2km north of town on Schmittenstr. (Runs mid-July to late-Oct. daily every 30min. 8:30am-5pm. 185AS; round-trip 240AS.) The **Zeller Bergbahn** (780-1411m) is in the center of town, at Schmittenstr. and Gartenstr. (Mid-June to mid-Sept. daily 9am-5pm; 110AS, round-trip 150AS). The Schmittenhöhe lift provides brochures detailing a range of **hikes.** For more hiking info, grab a *Wanderplan* or *Three Panorama Trips of the Schmittenhohe,* available at any cable car station. The **Zell/Kaprun Ski Pass** covers Zell and nearby Kaprun (2-day 740-780AS, students 670-720AS; late-Dec. to mid-Apr. a free bus connects them every 20min). The **Kitzsteinhorn** mountain (3203m) and its glacier in Kaprun offer **year-round skiing.** (Day-pass 270AS. Full rental around 255AS per day.)

Trains (☎732 14 357) arrive at the intersection of Bahnhofstr. and Salzmannstr. from: Innsbruck (2hr., 266AS); Kitzbühel (45min., 100AS); Salzburg (1¾hr., 150AS); and Vienna (5hr., 520AS). From the station, turn right and follow the green "i" by the stairs on the left to reach the **tourist office,** at Brucker Bundesstr. 3. (☎770; http://zell.gold.at. Open July to mid-Sept. and mid-Dec. to Mar. M-F 8am-6pm, Sa 8am-noon and 4-6pm, Su 10am-noon; Apr.-June and Sept. to mid-Dec. M-F 8am-noon and 2-6pm, Sa 9am-noon.) To reach **Haus der Jugend (HI),** Seespitzstr. 13, exit the train station toward the lake (Zum See), turn right, walk 15 minutes along the footpath beside the lake, and turn left at the end on Seespitzstr. (☎571 85. Breakfast included. Key deposit 300AS or passport. Reception 7-9am and 4-10pm. Lockout noon-4pm. Curfew 10pm. Open Dec.-Oct. Reserve ahead. Dorms 165AS first night, 140AS thereafter.) **SPAR supermarket** is at Brucker Bundesstr. 4. (Open M-Th 8am-7pm, F 8am-7:30pm, Sa 7:30am-5pm.) **Postal code:** A-5700.

TYROL

Tyrol's mountains overwhelm the average mortal with their superhuman scale and beauty. Stern contours in the Kaisergebirge above St. Johann and Kufstein in the northwest soften slightly into the rounded shapes of the Kitzbühel Alps to the south, but the peaks rise again above the blue-green Zeller See, just over the border into Salzburger Land. This topography has made it impossible for Tyrol to avoid becoming one of the primary mountain playgrounds for the world. Thankfully it is an equal-opportunity play place: unsullied, crag-filled valleys like the Ötztal and Zillertal run parallel to valleys finely tuned for the resort fantasies of Royals. But Tyrol doesn't rest on its granite. The urbane capitol city of Innsbruck gives quick evidence of why it was the favorite city of so many Hapsburgs in its seamless blend between the gilded houses of the extravagant city, and the snowy mountains that are reflected in the many gold surfaces of the city.

THE ÖTZTAL

Winding its way between hundreds of sharp 3000m peaks on the Italian border, the Ötztal (Ötz valley) offers some of the wildest and most impressive scenery in the Tyrolean Alps. Tiny farms cling impossibly to the mountainside, as rivulets carve their way through rocks to feed into silt-gray rivers. The 1991 discovery of a frozen man who lived 5000 years ago, nicknamed Ötzi, proves that visitors have been enjoying the breathtaking views here for millennia. The area, known as the Ötztal Arena, is Austria's largest skiing and snowboarding center. The four main resorts in the Arena are **Sölden, Hochsölden, Vent,** and **Zwieselstein;** each one has a very distinct character. At the mouth of the valley, **Bahnhof Ötztal** sends trains to **Innsbruck** (40min., 6:08am-10:53pm, 88AS) and **St. Anton** (1hr., 5:25am-11:07pm, 108AS). **Buses** ply the 67km route up the Ötztal valley, passing through the main town of Sölden before forking into the narrow Gurgler and Venter ranges. Buses to the more remote towns run less frequently in the summer and fall.

SÖLDEN   ☎ 05254

Sitting pretty in a neck of the Ötztal valley 40km south of Bahnhof Ötztal, Sölden's prime location makes it an ideal base for exploring the surrounding villages. The high altitude of Sölden's **skiing** areas (1377-3058m) guarantees snow even in the summer. The **Gaislachkoglbahn** whisks passengers up to the top of the 3058m Gaislachkogl in a twin-cable gondola, the largest of its kind in the world. (Open mid-June to mid-Sept. and Dec.-May, round-trip 230AS). **Lift tickets** for the 32 cable cars and lifts that serve Sölden's slopes are sold at the Gaislachkoglbahn booth at the southern end of town (420-470AS). Ask at the tourist office about toboggan parties on the 5.5km long toboggan run. About 15 hikes can be taken from right next to the post office: a brown sign points the way to *Wanderwege* (1-2½hr. each way.) The **Zirmzapfen Hiking Club** (☎ 29 10), offers a wide-ranging hiking program in summer. **Cyclists** will enjoy the mountain trails around Sölden, ranging from easy 30-minute outings to the strenuous 70km Mountain Riders Trail that runs from Bahnhof Ötztal to the Karlsruher Refuge. A free mountain bike trail guide shows you where to ride, including the Stuibenfall waterfall in nearby Umhausen.

  Buses arrive in the center of town from Bahnhof Ötztal (1hr., 7:05am-7:00pm, 78AS) and Innsbruck (2hr., 5 per day, 142AS). From the bus stop, face the river, turn left and walk about 100m down the main street to the **tourist office.** (☎221 20. Open M-Sa 8am-6pm, Su 9am-noon; in summer also Su 2-6pm.) Check with the tourist office for a list of private accommodations or try **Pension Mina,** Rettenbach 90. Exit the post office facing the main road, turn left, and after crossing the small brook, go uphill a few meters. The *pension* will be on your left. (☎21 46. 260-290AS per person; in winter 460-490AS.) One of the few budget restaurants open year-round is **Café Corso,** by the river across the bridge from the tourist office. (Pizza 89-142AS, pasta 98-148AS. ☎24 98. Open Th-Tu noon-midnight.) Turn left from the post office to get to **SPAR Supermarkt.** (Open M-Sa 8am-noon and 3-6pm.) The **post office** is next to the bus stop (Open M-F 8am-noon and 2-6pm; exchange closes at 5pm.) **Postal code:** A-6450.

KITZBÜHEL   ☎ 05356

Kitzbühel welcomes tourists with glitzy casinos and countless pubs, yet few visitors remain at ground level long enough to enjoy them. The mountains surrounding the city invite wealthy vacationers and ski bums alike. The Kitzbühel **ski area,** the "Ski Circus," is one of the best in the world. A one-day **ski pass** (high-season 390-420AS) grants unlimited passage on 64 lifts and on the shuttle buses that connect them. Purchase passes at any of the lifts or at the *Kurhaus* **Aquarena,** which offers a pool, sauna, and solarium. (☎643 85. Open daily 9am-8pm. 80AS, with guest pass 70AS.) **Renting** downhill **ski equipment** from virtually any sports shop runs 170-500AS per day; **lessons** cost 500AS, **snowboards** 180-350AS. For summer visitors, more than 70 **hiking trails** snake up the mountains; some of the best views are from the **Kampenweg** and **Hochetzkogel** trails, accessible via the Bichlalm **bus** (every hr., 26AS, with guest card 20AS) or a two-hour climb.

The **Kitzbüheler Hornbahn lift** (85AS) ascends to the **Alpenblumengarten,** where more than 120 different types of flowers blossom each spring. (Open late-May to mid-Oct. 8:30am-5pm.) A three-day **summer holiday pass** is valid for all cable cars, free Bichlalm bus service, and Aquarena (450AS). Guest card holders can take advantage of the tourist office's daily three- to five-hour **mountain hikes.** (Mid-May to mid-Oct. M-F at 8:45am from the tourist office. 90AS; with guest card, free except for cable car rides.) **Mountain bike trails** abound; rent a bike from **Stanger Radsport,** Josef-Pirchlstr. 42. (☎625 49. 250AS per day. Open M-F 8am-noon and 1-6pm, Sa 9am-noon.) The **Schwarzsee** (Black Lake), 2½km northwest of Kitzbühel, is famed for its healing **mud baths.** Follow the directions above to **Camping Schwarzsee** to float in the deep blue water and gaze at the snow-capped mountains above. (☎623 81. Open 7am-8pm. 45AS, with guest card 40AS; after noon 30AS, after 4pm 15AS. Electric boats 150AS per hr., rowboats 85AS per hr.)

Trains (☎640 55 13 85) arrive frequently at the Hauptbahnhof and the Hahnenkammbahnhof from: Vienna Westbahnhof (6hr., 570AS); Innsbruck (1-1½hr., 150AS); Salzburg (1½hr., 260AS); and Zell am See (1hr., 108AS). **Buses** stop next to both train stations. To reach the Fußgängerzone (pedestrian zone) from the Hauptbahnhof, head straight down Bahnhofstr. and turn left at the main road. The **tourist office,** Hinterstadt 18, is near the Rathaus in the Fußgängerzone. (☎62 15 50; fax 623 07; www.kitzbuehel.com. Open July-Sept. and mid-Dec. to late Apr. M-F 8:30am-6:30pm, Sa 8:30am-noon and 4-6pm, Su 10am-noon and 4-6pm; Oct. to mid-Dec. and late Apr. to June M-F 8:30am-12:30pm and 2:30-6pm.) Wherever you stay, ask about the **guest card,** which provides discounts on local attractions. For **internet** access, visit **Bit and Byte,** Im Gries 1a. (50AS per 30min. Open M-F 9am-noon and 2-6pm, Sa 9am-noon.) To get to the 150-bed **Hotel Kaiser,** Bahnhofstr. 2, exit the Hauptbahnhof facing away from the tracks; the hotel will be on the left, at the end of the street. (☎647 09. In summer, doubles 400AS; more in winter.) From the Hauptbahnhof, turn left after Hotel Kaiser and look left for the inexpensive **Pension Hörl,** Josef-Pirchlstr. 60. (☎631 44. Breakfast included. In summer 190-260AS; in winter add 40AS.) If they have no vacancies, they'll try to put you up at their nearby **Gästehaus Hörl,** Bahnhofstr. 8. For **Camping Schwarzsee,** Reitherstr. 24, take the train to Schwarzsee and follow the tracks past the bathing areas around the back of the lake; it's behind the Bruggerhof Hotel (15min.). For a long walk, head right from the tourist office, go under the archway, bear right at the Wienerwald up Franz-Reischstr., and follow the Waldweg zum See signs. (☎62 80 60. Reception 8am-5pm. 95AS per person plus 7AS tax; 98AS per tent; 90-100AS per caravan.) Although many of Kitzbühel's restaurants prepare gourmet delights at astronomical prices, cheaper locales pepper the area surrounding the Fußgängerzone. The **Café-Restaurant Prima** offers a wide selection, including spaghetti and Wiener *Schnitzel.* (☎638 85. Open daily 9am-9pm.) **SPAR supermarket,** Bichlstr. 22, is at Ehrenbachg. (Open M-F 8am-7pm, Sa 7:30am-1pm.) **Postal code:** A-6370.

THE ZILLERTAL VALLEY

Wading between the Tuxer alps, the Zillertal (Ziller Valley) Alps, and the Kitzbühler alps provide spectacular, affordable, and easily accessible **hiking** and **skiing** away from crowds. The towns in the narrow valley are hugged by mountains on all sides, giving the Zillertal some of the best hiking in western Austria, with more footpaths than roads and more trail guides than police officers.

▣ TRANSPORTATION. Everyone going into the valley must go through Jenbach, at the head of the valley. **Trains** depart from the Jenbach train station for Vienna (7hr.) and Innsbruck (20min., 70AS). Traveling south down the valley, Zell am Ziller comes first. At the base of the valley, further south, is Mayrhofen. Transportation in the region is simple and convenient, thanks to the **Zillertalbahn** (better known by its nickname, the **Z-bahn**); an efficient network of private buses and trains connecting the villages (☎(05224) 46 06).

ZELL AM ZILLER. Zell am Ziller (pop. 2,000), 20km south of Jenbach, embodies many of the picture-book images of an Austrian mountain village, with clusters of wooden-shuttered alpine houses surrounded by fields of tall grass and much taller mountains. Zeller **skiing** is possible with day passes, valid on the Kreuzjoch-Rosenalm and Gerlosstein-Sonnalm slopes (1 day 370AS, children 220AS; 2 days 690AS, 420AS; 3 days 990AS, 590AS). Register in any hotel or pension to get a guest card, which snags you a **free hike** led by the tourist office (June-Sept.; register one day in advance at the office). For a down-to-earth look at Zell's history, take a tour of the nearby **gold mine.** The journey begins at a petting zoo before proceeding on a scenic 45min. hike down to the mine entrance. (☎ (05282) 230 10. 2hr. tours leave daily on the hr. 9am-4pm. Reserve in advance for English tours. 130AS, children 65AS.)

Those traveling by **ÖBB train** should get off at Jenbach and switch to the private Zillertalbahn (Z-bahn; ☎ (05282) 22 11; Jenbach to Zell am Ziller 54AS), which leaves from the front of the train station. Z-bahn trains and buses leave every hour between 6am and 8pm for Jenbach or Mayrhofen. The **tourist office** is at Dorfpl. 3a. From the train station, head right along Bahnhofstr. and turn right at the end—the office is on your left. (☎ (05282) 22 81. Open M-F 8:30am-12:30pm and 2:30-6pm, Sa 9am-noon and 4-6pm.) In an **emergency,** dial ☎ 133 for mountain rescue or police. Zell am Ziller has no shortage of lodgings. To reach **Haus Huditz,** Karl-Platzer-Weg 1, walk 10min. by crossing the rail tracks near the tourist office and continue onto Gerlosstr.; bear left onto Gaudergasse and look for Karl-Platzer-Weg on the left. (☎ (05282) 2228. Breakfast included. Shower 15AS. Singles 200AS 1st night, then 180AS; in winter 210AS, 180AS. Doubles 380AS, 340AS; in winter 400AS, 350AS.) **Camping Hofer,** Gerlosstr. 33, offers a space for your tent a few blocks from the town center. (☎ (05282) 2248. Reception 9am-noon and 3-8pm. High-season 65AS per person; off season 50-55AS; 65-80AS per campsite. Guest tax 12AS.) The local **SPAR Supermarkt** is around the corner from the tourist office. (Open M-F 7:30am-1pm and 2-6:30pm, Sa 7:30am-12:30pm and 2-5pm.) **Postal code:** A-6280.

MAYRHOFEN. At the southernmost end of the Zillertal, Mayrhofen is well-positioned for intense outdoor recreation. The town caters to the year-round sportsperson—endless **hiking** and **skiing** trails in the nearby valleys satisfy mountaineers of all skill levels. Stop by the tourist office to pick up a detailed map (80-110AS) of routes and mountain huts. The first sight that greets many visitors to Mayrhofen is the **Penkenbahn,** with its dangling gondolas passing directly above the town on their way up to the top of the 1850m Penkenberg. (☎ (05285) 622 77. May 20-Oct. 10. 9am-5pm. 165AS, 150AS with guest card, children 90AS.) The Penkenbahn leads to a variety of easy paths. Opportunities abound for **kayaking, rafting,** and **canyoning** in the white water; for rafting and canyoning, call **Action Club Zillertal,** Hauptstr. 458 (☎ (05285) 629 77; rafting from 395AS, and canyoning from 370AS). Come winter, **skiers** and **snowboarders** flock to the Ahorn, Penken, and Horberg ski areas above town, all of which are covered by the **Ski Mayrhofen pass** (1 day 370AS, youth 295AS, children 220AS; 3 days 1000AS, 800AS, 600AS).

Mayrhofen is easily accessible from **Jenbach** (50min., 26 per day, 61AS) and **Zell am Ziller** (15min., 26 per day, 23AS) by Z-bahn trains and buses. The **tourist office,** Dursterstr. 225, is located inside the massive octagonal information center. From the train station, walk along Hauptstr. in the direction of ascending street numbers and follow the green information "i" signs once you see them. The office leads free **guided tours.** (☎ (05285) 6760. Tours May-Oct. M-F; call for times. Open M-F 8am-6pm, Sa 9am-noon, Su 10am-noon; July-Aug. also Sa 2-6pm.) Finding a budget accommodation in Mayrhofen can be quite difficult, since groups tend to book up most of the available bed-and-breakfasts. Try your luck at **Haus Andreas,** Sportplatzstr. 317, about 3min. from the tourist office, which rents out well-lit, clean, comfortable singles and doubles, many with balconies. (☎ (05285) 638 45. Breakfast included. 220-270AS, in winter 230-250AS.) Touristy eateries, most of which are priced better than one might expect, crowd the center of town. **Postal code:** A-6290.

INNSBRUCK

☎ 0512

The 1964 and 1976 winter Olympics were held in Innsbruck, bringing international recognition to this beautiful mountain city. The nearby Tyrolean Alps await skiers and hikers, while back in town, the tiny Altstadt's cobblestoned streets are peppered with fancy facades and remnants of the Hapsburg Empire.

▛ TRANSPORTATION

Trains: Hauptbahnhof, (☎ 17 17), Südtirolerpl. To: **Salzburg** (3hr., 11 per day, 360AS); **Munich** (2hr., 11 per day, 350AS); **Venice** (7hr., 5 per day, 424AS); **Vienna's** Westbahnhof station (7hr., 12 per day, 660AS); and **Zurich** (4hr., 8 per day, 600AS).

Buses: Bundesbuses (☎ 503 43 82) leave from the station on Sterzingerstr., next to the Hauptbahnhof, to destinations throughout Tyrol.

Public Transportation: The main bus station is in front of the Hauptbahnhof. Buy **single-ride** (21AS), **24hr.** (35AS), or **4-ride** (61AS) tickets from any driver or *Tabak* and punch them as you board (400AS fine for riding without a validated ticket). Most buses stop running around 10:30-11:30pm, but each night the *Nachtbus* heads through Marktpl. at 11:47pm and 1:17am, via Maria-Theresien-Str.

Bike Rental: Rent bikes at the Hauptbahnhof (☎ 503 53 95). 90-200AS per day. Open Apr. to early Nov. **Sport Neuner,** Salurnerstr. 5 (☎ 561 501), near the station, rents mountain bikes for 200AS per day. Open M-F 9am-6pm, Sa 9am-noon.

▟◪▛ ORIENTATION AND PRACTICAL INFORMATION

The city center lies between the **Inn River** and the train tracks. Turn right from the Hauptbahnhof on Brunecker Str., left on Museumstr., and left on Burggraben to reach the **Altstadt** and the tourist office. **Maria-Theresien-Str.,** the city's main thoroughfare, leads south from the Altstadt; Marktgraben leads west across the river to the **University district.** Most sights are near the Altstadt.

Tourist Offices: Innsbruck Information Office, Burggraben 3, 3rd fl. (☎ 598 50; fax 598 07; www.discover.com/innsbruck). Open M-F 8am-6pm, Sa 8am-noon. **Innsbruck-Information** (email ibk.ticket@netway.at) is in the same building. Open daily 9am-6pm. The **Innsbruck Card,** sold at both, includes many sights and unlimited transportation (24hr. 230AS, 48hr. 300AS, 72hr. 370AS; children 50% discount). **Österreichischer Alpenverein,** Wilhelm-Greil-Str. 15 (☎ 595 47). Mountains of info and discounts for hikers. Membership 530AS, ages 18-25 390AS. Open M-F 9am-1pm and 2-5pm.

American Express: Brixnerstr. 3 (☎ 58 24 91). Open M-F 9am-noon and 1-5:30pm.

Laundromat: Bubblepoint Waschsalon, Andreas-Hofer-Str. 37, at the corner of Franz-Fischer-Str. 7kg wash 55AS. Open M-F 8am-10pm, Sa-Su 8am-8pm.

Bi-Gay-Lesbian Organizations: Homosexuelle Initiative Tirol, Innrain 100 (☎ 56 24 03). All meetings at 8:30pm: mixed younger crowd M, lesbian night T, gay night Th, transgender night every other F.

Emergencies: Police, ☎ 133. Headquarters at Kaiserjägerstr. 8 (☎ 590 00). **Ambulance,** ☎ 144 or 142. **Fire,** ☎ 122. **Mountain Rescue,** ☎ 140.

Medical Assistance: University Hospital, Anichstr. 35 (☎ 50 40).

Internet Access: Internet Corner, Bruneckerstr. 12 (☎ 59 42 72 61), across from the train station. 1.5AS per min. Open daily 9am-11pm.

Post Office: Maximilianstr. 2 (☎ 500 79 00), a few blocks straight from the station. Open M-F 7am-11pm, Sa 7am-9pm, Su 8am-9pm. Address mail to be held: *Postlagernde Briefe* für Linda TAYLOR, Hauptpostamt, Maximilianstr. 2, **A-6020** Innsbruck, Austria.

▛ ACCOMMODATIONS

Inexpensive accommodations are scarce in June when only two hostels are open: **Jugendherberge Innsbruck** and **Jugendherberge St. Niklaus.** The opening of student dorms to backpackers in July and August somewhat alleviates the crush. Visitors should join the free **Club Innsbruck** by registering at any Innsbruck accommodation. Membership gives discounts on skiing and ski buses (Dec. 21-Apr. 5), bike tours, and the club's fine hiking program (June-Sept.).

⊠ Haus Wolf, Dorfstr. 48 (☎54 86 73), in Mutters. Take the Stubaitalbahn tram (26AS; last tram 10:30pm) from the 3rd island in front of the Hauptbahnhof to Birchfeld, and continue in the same direction down Dorfstr. (30min.). Let proprietor Titti Wolf spoil you with attention and gigantic breakfasts. Singles 180AS; doubles 360AS; triples 540AS.

Pension Paula, Weiherburg. 15 (☎29 22 62; pensionpaula@telering.at). Take bus K to St. Nikolaus, then walk uphill. Bright rooms with antique furniture. Breakfast included. Singles 340-440AS; doubles 560-680AS; triples 750-920AS.

Hostel Fritz Prior-Schwedenhaus (HI), Rennweg 17b (☎58 58 14; fax 585 81 44; email youth.hostel@tirol.at). Follow directions to the Altstadt, but go right on Burggraben, which becomes Rennweg. Breakfast 45AS. Sheets 20AS. Reception 7-9am and 5-10:30pm. Lockout 9am-5pm. Curfew 10:30pm; ask for a key. Open July-Aug. and Dec. 27-Jan. 5. Reservations held until 6pm. Dorms 125AS; doubles 250AS; triples 495AS.

Jugendherberge Innsbruck (HI), Reichenauer Str. 147 (☎34 61 79; yhibk@tirol.com). From the train station, take bus R to König-Laurin Str., then bus O to Jugendherberge. Breakfast 85AS. Laundry 45AS. Reception Sept.-June 5-10pm, July-Aug. 3-10pm. Lockout 10am-5pm. Curfew 11pm; ask for a key. Phone reservations held until 6pm. Dorms 155-190AS first night, then 125-160AS; 2-bed rooms 220AS, 190AS. July-Aug. singles 360AS; doubles 520AS. Nonmembers add 40AS.

Haus Kaltenberger, Schulg. 15 (☎54 85 76), near Haus Wolf. Take the Stubaitalbahn to Mutters; walk toward the church, turn right on Dorfstr., and take the first left. Attractive balconies, and mountain views. Breakfast included. Singles 220AS; doubles 400AS.

Youth Hostel St. Niklaus (HI), Innstr. 95 (☎28 65 15). From the train station take bus K to Schmelzerg. and cross the street (21AS). Wooden bunkbeds and sleepover camp feel. Internet. 6-8 bed dorms 180AS first night, then 165AS; 4-bed dorms 195AS; 3-bed dorms 205AS; singles 265-365AS; doubles 215AS.

Camping Innsbruck Kranebitten, Kranebitter Allee 214 (☎28 41 80). Take bus LK from Bozner Platz (a block down Brixner Str. from the Bahnhof) to Klammstr. (20min.). At night, take bus O to Lohbachsiedlung and switch to the LK. Walk downhill to the right and follow the road. Shower included. Laundry. Reception 8am-1pm. 75AS per person, 40AS per tent, 40AS per car. Tent rental 75-110AS per person.

◖ FOOD

Gawk at overpriced delis and *Konditoreien* on Maria-Theresien-Str., then cross the river to **Innstr.** for ethnic restaurants, *Schnitzel Stuben*, and grocers. Look for **M-Preis Supermarkets** in front of the train station, on Maximilianstr. by the arch, and at Innrain 15. (Open M-Th 7:30am-6:30pm, F 7:30am-7:30pm, Sa 7:30am-5pm.)

Shere Purjab, Innstr. 19 (☎ 282 775). Serves up some of the cheapest Indian food around. Two daily *Menüs* (65-75AS). Open daily 11:30am-2:30pm and 5:50-11pm.

Salute Pizzeria, Innrain 35 (☎585 818). A popular student hangout near the university. Pizza 40-100AS; pasta 60-90AS. Open daily 11am-midnight.

Churrasco la Mamma, Innrain 2 (☎586 398). Beautiful river views by the bridge. Spaghetti 82-134AS, brick-oven pizza 74-112AS. Open daily 9am-midnight.

Gasthof Weißes Lamm, Mariahilfstr. 12 (☎283 156), on the 2nd floor. Serves up home-style Tyrolean fare with views of the river. Check out the daily *Menüs* (soup, main dish, and salad 85-115AS). Open F-W 11:30am-2pm and 6-10pm.

◉ SIGHTS

Inside the **Goldenes Dachl** (Little Golden Roof) on Herzog-Friedrich-Str., the tiny **Maximilianeum Museum** commemorates Innsbruck's favorite emperor, who ruled from 1490 to 1519 using his smarts (and well-timed marriages) to create an

ALPS   ASPEN

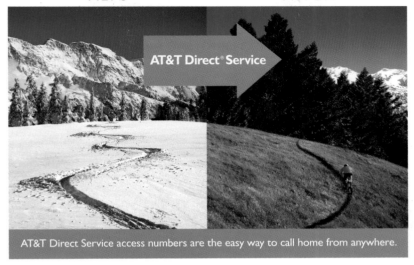

AT&T Direct® Service

AT&T Direct Service access numbers are the easy way to call home from anywhere.

The best way to keep in touch when you're traveling overseas is with **AT&T Direct®** Service. It's the easy way to call your loved ones back home from just about anywhere in the world. Just cut out the wallet guide below and use it wherever your travels take you.

For a list of AT&T Access Numbers, tear out the attached wallet guide.

AT&T

Italy ● 172-1011	Russia (Moscow) ▶▲●755-5042
Luxembourg + ..800-2-0111	(St. Petersbg.) ▶▲● ..325-5042
Macedonia ● ..99-800-4288	Slovakia ▲ ..00-42-100-101
Malta 0800-890-110	South Africa ..0800-99-0123
Monaco ● 800-90-288	Spain 900-99-00-11
Morocco 002-11-0011	Sweden 020-799-111
Netherlands ● ...0800-022-9111	Switzerland ● 0800-89-0011
Norway 800-190-11	Turkey ● 00-800-12277
Poland ▲● ..00-800-111-1111	Ukraine ▲ ....8 + 100-11
Portugal ▲ 800-800-128	U.A. Emirates ● 800-121
Romania ●......01-800-4288	U.K. 0800-89-0011

FOR EASY CALLING WORLDWIDE

1. Just dial the AT&T Access Number for the country you are calling from.
2. Dial the phone number you're calling.   *3.* Dial your card number.

For access numbers not listed ask any operator for **AT&T Direct®** Service.
In the U.S. call 1-800-331-1140 for a wallet guide listing all worldwide AT&T Access Numbers.

Visit our Web site at: **www.att.com/traveler**

Bold-faced countries permit country-to-country calling outside the U.S.

- ● Public phones require coin or card deposit to place call.
- ▲ May not be available from every phone/payphone.
- + Public phones and select hotels.
- ◆ Await second dial tone.
- ▶ Additional charges apply when calling from outside the city.
- † Outside of Cairo, dial "02" first.
- ✗ Not available from public phones or all areas.
- ✔ Use U.K. access number in N. Ireland.

When placing an international call *from* the U.S., dial 1 800 CALL ATT.

EMEA   © 8/00 AT&T

Italy ● 172-1011	Russia (Moscow) ▶▲●755-5042
Luxembourg + ..800-2-0111	(St. Petersbg.) ▶▲● ..325-5042
Macedonia ● ..99-800-4288	Slovakia ▲ ..00-42-100-101
Malta 0800-890-110	South Africa ..0800-99-0123
Monaco ● 800-90-288	Spain 900-99-00-11
Morocco 002-11-0011	Sweden 020-799-111
Netherlands ● ...0800-022-9111	Switzerland ● 0800-89-0011
Norway 800-190-11	Turkey ● 00-800-12277
Poland ▲● ..00-800-111-1111	Ukraine ▲ ....8 + 100-11
Portugal ▲ 800-800-128	U.A. Emirates ● 800-121
Romania ●......01-800-4288	U.K. 0800-89-0011

FOR EASY CALLING WORLDWIDE

1. Just dial the AT&T Access Number for the country you are calling from.
2. Dial the phone number you're calling.   *3.* Dial your card number.

For access numbers not listed ask any operator for **AT&T Direct®** Service.
In the U.S. call 1-800-331-1140 for a wallet guide listing all worldwide AT&T Access Numbers.

Visit our Web site at: **www.att.com/traveler**

Bold-faced countries permit country-to-country calling outside the U.S.

- ● Public phones require coin or card deposit to place call.
- ▲ May not be available from every phone/payphone.
- + Public phones and select hotels.
- ◆ Await second dial tone.
- ▶ Additional charges apply when calling from outside the city.
- † Outside of Cairo, dial "02" first.
- ✗ Not available from public phones or all areas.
- ✔ Use U.K. access number in N. Ireland.

When placing an international call *from* the U.S., dial 1 800 CALL ATT.

EMEA   © 8/00 AT&T

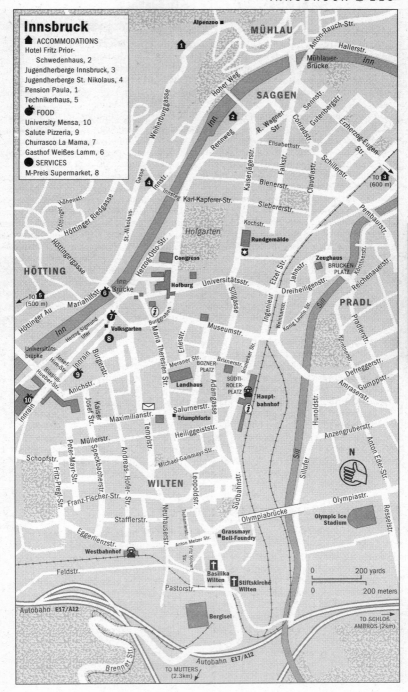

Innsbruck

🏠 ACCOMMODATIONS
Hotel Fritz Prior-
  Schwedenhaus, 2
Jugendherberge Innsbruck, 3
Jugendherberge St. Nikolaus, 4
Pension Paula, 1
Technikerhaus, 5

🍎 FOOD
University Mensa, 10
Salute Pizzeria, 9
Churrasco La Mama, 7
Gasthof Weißes Lamm, 6

⬤ SERVICES
M-Preis Supermarket, 8

AUSTRIA

Alpenzoo ■

MÜHLAU

Anton-Rauch-Str.
Hallerstr.
Mühlauer-
Brücke
Inn

SAGGEN

Weiherburggasse
Hoher Weg
Rennweg
Inn

R. Wagner-
Str.
Conradstr.
Sennstr.
Gutenbergstr.
Erzherzog-Eugen-
Str.
Schillerstr.

Elisabethstr.
Falkstr.
Claudiastr.

Kaiserjägerstr.
Bienerstr.
Siebererstr.
Kochstr.
Rundgemälde
☆

TO 3
(600 m)

Pembaurstr.

Gasse
nstr.
Innsteg
Karl-Kapferer-Str.

St.-Nikolaus-
Gasse

Höhenstr.
Höttinger Riedgasse
Höttinger Au
Höttingergasse
Mariahilfstr.

HÖTTING

TO 5
(500 m)

Inn
Herzog Sigmund Ufer
Josef-
Hirn-Str.
Blasius-
Hueber-Str.

Universitäts-
brücke

Innrain
Innrain

Hofgarten

Congress

Inn-
Brücke
Hofburg
Universitätsstr.

Sillgasse

Herzog-Otto-Str.

Zeughaus
BRÜCKEN-
PLATZ

Kapuzinergasse
Reichenauerstr.

PRADL

Pradlerstr.
Körnerstr.

Dreiheiligenstr.
Ingenieur
Jahnstr.
Etzel Str.
Weinhartstr.
König Laurin Str.

Volksgarten

Maria Theresien Str.
Burggraben
ⓘ

Meraner Str.
Erlerstr.
Museumstr.
BOZNER
PLATZ
Brixnerstr.
Bruneckerstr.

Anichstr.
Kaiser
Josef Str.
Maximilianstr.

Landhaus
Adamgasse
SÜDTI-
ROLER-
PLATZ

Haupt-
bahnhof
ⓘ

Hunoldstr.
Defreggerstr.
Amraserstr.
Gumpstr.
Anzengruberstr.
Anton Eder Str.
Resselstr.

Salurnerstr.
Triumphforte
Heiliggeiststr.

Müllerstr.
Peter-Mayr-Str.
Speckbacherstr.
Andreas-Hofer-Str.
Templstr.
Michael-Gaismayr-Str.
Leopoldstr.
Neuhauserstr.

WILTEN

N
🤙

Olympiastr.

Sillufer
Sill
Südbahnstr.

Olympic Ice
Stadium

Schopfstr.
Fritz-Pregl-Str.
Franz-Fischer-Str.
Stafflerstr.
Eggerlienzstr.

Westbahnhof

Feldstr.

Anton Metzer Str.
Anton Fritz Konzert
Str.

Grassmayr
Bell-Foundry

Olympiabrücke
Olympiabrücke

TO SCHLO.
AMBROS (2km)

Basilika
Wilten ✝
Stiftskirche
Wilten ✝

Pastorstr.

0   200 yards
0   200 meters

Autobahn E17/A12

Bergisel

Brenner Str.

Autobahn E17/A12

TO MUTTERS
(2.3km)

empire, the size of which was exceeded only by that of his nose. (Open May-Sept. 10am-6pm; Oct.-Apr. Tu-Su 10am-12:30pm and 2-5pm. 50AS, students 20AS.) Lined with pastel-colored Baroque buildings, **Maria-Theresien-Straße** begins with the **Triumphpforte** (Triumphal Arch) by the Altstadt and runs south past the **Annasäule** (Anna Column), providing a clear view of the snow-capped *Nordkette* mountains that dwarf the city. Off Maria-Theresien-Str., down Museumstr., is the **Tiroler Landesmuseum Ferdinandeum**, with a large regional collection. (Open May-Sept. M-W and F-Su 10am-5pm, Th 10am-9pm; Oct.-Apr. Tu-Su 10am-noon and 2-5pm, Su 10am-1pm. 60AS, 30AS.) A block behind the Goldenes Dachl rise the twin towers of the **Dom St. Jakob**, displaying *trompe l'oeil* ceiling murals by C.D. Asam depicting the life of St. James and an altar painting by Cranach the Elder. (Open daily Apr.-Sept. 8am-7:30pm; Oct.-Mar. 8am-6:30pm. Free.) Behind the Dom and to the right is the entrance to the grand **Hofburg** (Imperial Palace), where imposing furniture and large portraits—including one of Empress Maria Theresia's youngest daughter, Marie Antoinette (head intact)—fill sumptuously decorated rooms. (Open daily 9am-5pm. 75AS, students 45AS. Tours in German 11am and 2pm.) Across Rennweg sits the **Hofkirche** (Imperial Church), with 28 larger-than-life bronze statues of Hapsburg saints and Roman emperors, some by Dürer. An intricate sarcophagus within is decorated with scenes from Maximilian I's life, although he was buried near Vienna because the monument was not completed as he wished. The **Tiroler Volkskunstmuseum** (Tyrolean Folk Art Museum) shares the same building. (Church open daily 9am-5pm. 30AS, students 20AS. Museum open M-Sa 9am-5pm, Su 9am-noon. 60AS, students 35AS.) Up Rennweg past the *Dom*, the **Hofgarten** (Imperial Garden) is a beautifully manicured park, complete with pond, flower beds, a concert pavilion, and an outdoor chess set with three-foot tall pieces.

◪ HIKING AND SKIING

A **Club Innsbruck** membership (available at accommodations) grants access to a **hiking** program that provides guides, transportation, and equipment at no additional cost; it also grants discounts on **ski** passes and provides free rides on shuttles to suburban slopes. The **Patscherkofelbahn** in Igls takes hikers up beautiful trails to the **Alpine Garden**, Europe's highest botanical garden. (Runs daily 9am-4:30pm. 120AS, round-trip 200AS. Garden open June-Sept. 9:30am-4pm. Free.) The tourist office sells the **Innsbruck Gletscher Ski Pass**, valid for the region's 62 lifts (3-day 1260AS, Club Innsbruck members 1050AS); **rents equipment** (alpine 270AS per day, cross-country 160AS); and **glacier skiing** (1-day in summer 170-280AS, in winter 420AS; add 270AS for ski rental; 599AS package includes bus, lift, and rental).

◫ ◪ ENTERTAINMENT AND NIGHTLIFE

At a corner of the Hofgarten, the **Congress Center** and **Tiroler Landestheater** (☎52 07 44) host festivals and concerts. In August, the **Festival of Early Music** features concerts by some of the world's leading soloists on period instruments at the Schloß Ambras, Congress Center, and *Hofkirche*. (For tickets, call ☎56 15 61.) The **university quarter** is a mecca for late-night revelry. The **Viaduktbögen** contains a stretch of theme bars along Ingenieur-Etzel-Str. East meets West at ultra-hip **Jimmy's**, Wilhelm-Greilstr. 17, by Landhauspl. (Beer 35-46AS. Open M-F 11am-1am, Sa-Su 7pm-1am.) **Treibhaus**, Angerzellg. 8, is Innsbruck's favorite university-teen hangout. (Open daily 10am-1am.) Cozy **Die Alte Piccolo Bar**, Seilerg. 2, attracts a primarily gay male crowd, though women are welcome. (Open Th-Tu 10pm-4am.) The **Hofgarten Café**, accessible through the Hofgarten's back entrance, is a sprawling outdoor affair with networking twenty- and thirty-somethings. (Snacks 50-100AS. Beer 28-48AS. Open daily 10am-4am.)

🔁 DAYTRIP FROM INNSBRUCK

SCHLOß AMBRAS

The castle stands in a park to the far southeast of Innsbruck and is accessible by tram #6 (dir.: Igls) to Tummelplatz/Schloß Ambras (21AS). Follow the signs from the stop. Or, take the shuttle bus that leaves every hour from Maria-Theresien-Str. just opposite McDonalds. (Apr.-Oct every hr. from 10am-5pm; Dec.-Mar. W-M at 2, 3, and 4pm.) Walk from the city only if you have a map since, the trail is poorly marked.

One of Innsbruck's most impressive edifices and museums is **Schloß Ambras**, a Renaissance castle built by Archduke Ferdinand of Tyrol in the late 16th century. The medieval castle was once a royal hunting lodge, but Ferdinand transformed it into one of the most beautiful Renaissance castles and gardens in Austria. The museum contains an impressive exhibit of good-as-new casts of armor, swords, and lances, ceilings adorned with pagan paintings, works by Velazquez and Titian, as well as Archduke Ferdinand's personal *Wunderkammer*. The walls of the Spanish Hall, Ambras's most famous room, are covered with mythological scenes and portraits of Tyrol's princes. The castle's gardens, stocked with medicinal plants, are also pleasant for a stroll. (Schloßstr. 20. Open Su-M and W-Sa 10am-5pm. 90AS, children and students 50AS; add 30AS for tour.)

BREGENZ ☎05574

When missionaries glimpsed the gray-green waters of the Bodensee (Lake Constance), they dubbed their find "Bregenz" (Golden Bowl). The area still awes visitors, who hike the Bregenzerwald and explore the historic **Oberstadt** (Old City). The wooden **Martinturm** rules the Oberstadt with Europe's largest onion dome. Next door is the **Martinskirche,** filled with 14th-century frescoes. Hike up Schloßbergstr. to the **St. Gallus Pfarrkirche,** a white stucco sanctuary that glows under lavish gold ornaments and a detailed painted ceiling. From the tourist office, walk down the *Fußgängerzone* (pedestrian zone) to reach the avant-garde **Kunsthaus Bregenz.** (Open Tu-W and F-Su 10am-6pm, Th 10am-9pm. 60AS, students 40AS.) The **Pfänderbahn** cable car leaves from the top of Schillerstr. and sways up the Pfänder Mountain for a view spanning the Black Forest and Switzerland. (Runs daily 9am-7pm every 30min. 70AS, round-trip 125AS.) The town's main attraction is the **Bodensee,** where groomed waterfront paths surround fantastic playgrounds and paddle boat rental shops. Hop a ferry to the **Blumeninsel Mainau** (Mainau Flower Isle) to tour the island's castle, tropical palm collection, butterfly house, and gardens. (Ferries depart daily May-Sept. 9:20, 10:20, and 11:25am; return 2:50, 4:15, and 4:55pm. Round-trip 293AS. Admission 127AS.)

Trains go to: Innsbruck (2¼hr., 300AS); St. Gallen (45min., 100AS); Zurich (2¼hr., 284AS); and Lindau, Germany (10min.; see p. 482). Regional **BundesBuses** also depart from the station. For hotel reservations (30AS), head to the **tourist office,** Bahnhofstr. 14. (☎495 90; fax 49 59 59; email tourismus@bregenz.at.) Access the **internet** at **S'Logo,** Kirchstr. 47. (☎441 91. 1AS per min. Open daily 5pm-midnight.) The new **Jugendgästehaus (HI),** Mehrerauerstr. 3-5, offers clean rooms and internet access. From the train station, cross the bridge, pass the skateboard half-pipe, and look for the yellow brick building. (☎428 67. Breakfast included. Reception 7am-10pm. Dorms 237-277AS.) Two blocks behind the post office, **Pension Gunz** offers homey rooms. (☎436 57. Breakfast included. Singles 340AS; doubles 600AS. 30AS fee for 1-night stays.) **Camping Lamm** is five minutes past Jugendgästehaus at Mehrerauerstr. 50-51. (☎717 01. 50AS; children 25AS; tents 35-45AS; cars 35AS.) **Ikaros,** Deuringstr. 5, at the corner of Rathausstr. in the *Fußgängerzone* (pedestrian zone), serves up a little taste of the Mediterannean, with Greek dishes for 55-95AS. (Open M-Sa 10am-1am.) **Postal Code:** A-6900.

STYRIA

Styria, promoted by tourist offices as "the Green Heart of Austria," is Austria's second largest province (in terms of geography, not population). The province is made up primarily of mountains, which range from craggy, bare peaks in the northwest to gentle, thickly forested slopes in the southeast.

GRAZ ☎ 0316

Wonderfully under-touristed, Graz's *Altstadt* rewards the traveler with every turn of its gently winding streets, with every glance up at its graciously worn facade, and with every lick of its creamy *gelato*. This second largest of Austria's cities keeps a sweaty and energetic nightlife thanks to its 45,000 students at Karl-Franzens-Universität, where the scientist of the stars, Johannes Kepler, hit the books. When the students aren't around, its renowned music venues attract a whole slew of festivals during July and August.

⊡ TRANSPORTATION. Trains (☎ 78 48; info 17 17) run frequently from the Hauptbahnhof, Europapl. to: Vienna (3¾hr., 17 per day, 330AS); Innsbruck (6¼hr., 8 per day, 550AS); Salzburg (4¼hr., 10 per day, 410AS); Munich (6¼hr., 9 per day, 720AS); and Zurich (10hr., 4 per day, 1030AS). The **Graz-Köflach Bus** (GKB) departs from Griespl. for West Styria. For the rest of Austria, the **BundesBus** departs from Europapl. 6 (next to the train station) and from Andreas-Hofer-Pl.

⊘ PRACTICAL INFORMATION. From the train station, go down Annenstr. and cross the Hauptbrücke (bridge) to reach central Hauptpl. Turn right on Herreng. to reach the **tourist office** at #16, which lists *Privatzimmer* which generally cost 150-300AS. (☎ 807 50; fax 807 55 15; www.graztourismus.at. Open in summer M-F 9am-7pm, Sa 9am-6pm, Su 10am-3pm; off-season M-F 9am-6pm, Sa 9am-3pm, Su 10am-3pm. Tours 2½hr., June-Sept. daily 2:30pm, Oct.-May Sa only, 75AS.) For **internet** access, stop by **Cafe Zentral**, Andreas-Hofer-Pl. 9. (☎ 83 24 68. 60AS per hr. Open M-Sa 6:30-10pm.) **Postal code:** A-8010.

⊡⊡ ACCOMMODATIONS AND FOOD. Sniffing out a cheap bed in Graz may require a bit of detective work, and the ones you find are likely to be in the boondocks. Luckily, the web of local transportation provides a reliable and easy commute to and from the city center. Exit the train station, cross the street, head right on Eggenberger Gürtel, turn left at Josef-Huber-Gasse, and take the first right to reach the **Jugendgästehaus Graz (HI)**, Idlhofg. 74. (☎ 71 48 76. Internet. Breakfast included. Laundry. Reception 7am-11pm. Dorms 220AS; singles 320AS; doubles 540AS; overflow mattresses 155AS.) The **Hotel Strasser**, Eggenberger Gürtel 11, is 5min. from the station; exit the station and cross the street, then head right on Bahnhofgürtel and the hotel will be on the left. (☎ 71 39 77. Breakfast included. Singles 380-460AS; doubles 600-680AS; triples 860AS; quads 1000AS.) From the train station, take tram #3 or 6 to Jakominipl. then take bus #32 to Badstraßgang (20min.), turn right at the Billa supermarket and walk up the road to reach **Camping Central**, Martinhofstr. 3. (☎ (0676) 378 51 02. Laundry 70AS. Reception 8am-10pm. Open Apr.-Oct. 155AS includes tent site, shower and use of pool; additional adults 80AS.)

Cheap student hangouts line **Zinzendorfg.** near the university, while markets run along **Rösselmühlgass** and **Jakominstr. Kebap Haus**, Jakominstr. 16, is a Turkish restaurant with delicious pitas and Mediterranean pizza. (☎ 81 10 06. Open M-Sa 11am-midnight.) **Mangolds**, Griesgasse 11, serves fresh vegetarian dishes and desserts. (☎ 718 002. Open M-F 11am-8pm, Sa 11am-4pm.) **Da Vinci**, Jakominipl. 19, keeps the customers happy with delicious pizzas. (☎ 82 52 00. Open daily 11am-1am.)

⊞⊡ SIGHTS AND ENTERTAINMENT. Napoleon didn't manage to capture Graz's **Schloßberg** (castle hill), which had already withstood substantial battering by Ottoman Turks, until after he conquered the rest of Austria—at which point he proceded to raze it in an infantile rage in 1809. As you exit the tourist office, walk left up Herreng./Sackstr. to Schloßbergpl. and climb the **Schlo-ßstiege,** zigzagging stone steps built by Russian prisoners during WWI, to the top of the Schloßberg (today a carefully tended park) for sweeping views of the vast plain surrounding Graz. The **Landhaus,** housing the tourist office below, is a sight in itself, remodeled by architect Domenico dell'Allio in 1557 in Lombard style. The **Landeszeughaus** (Provincial Arsenal), Herreng. 16, details the history of the arsenal and the Ottoman Turk attacks and has enough spears, muskets, and armor to outfit 28,000 burly mercenaries. (Open Apr.-Oct. M-F 9am-5pm, Sa-Su 9am-1pm. 70AS, students 50AS.) The solemn 17th-century Hapsburg **Mausoleum,** on Burgg., around the corner from the cathedral, is one of the finest examples of Austrian Mannerism. The domed tomb holds the remains of Ferdinand II in the underground chamber. Master architect Fischer von Erlach designed the beautiful frescoes upstairs. (Open M-Sa 10am-noon and 1:30-3:30pm. 10AS.) Down the street, Graz's **Opernhaus,** at Opernring and Burgg., sells standing-room opera tickets an hour before curtain. (☎80 08. 130-995AS; student rush 150AS; standing-room from 45AS.)

The hub of after-hours activity is the so-called **Bermuda Triangle,** an area of the old city behind Hauptpl., bordered by Mehlpl., Färberg., and Prokopiag. The grad-student hangout **Café Harrach,** Harrachg 26, has half-liters of Gösser for 31AS. (☎32 26 71. Open July-Sept. M-F 5pm-midnight, Sa-Su 7pm-midnight; Oct.-May M-F 9am-midnight, Sa-Su 7pm-midnight.) **Tom's Bierklinik,** Färberg. 1, has the largest stock of international beers in Austria. (☎84 51 74. Open M-Sa 8pm-4am.) A young crowd demands ever louder and throbbing dance music at **Kulturhauskeller,** Elisabethstr. 30. (☎38 10 58. Open Tu-Sa 10pm-3:30am.)

CARINTHIA (KÄRNTEN)

The province of Carinthia covers the southernmost part of Austria. In the west, it juts in between East Tirol and Salzburger Land, reaching into the Hohe Tauern National Park and the Glockner mountain range. The peaks that guard the Italian and Slovenian borders in Carinthia may look severe, but they shield the province from cold northern winds. The sunny climate, Italian architecture, and laid-back atmosphere give Carinthia a Mediterranean feel. Though non-Austrians take little notice of this part of the country, natives consider Carinthia a vacation paradise, thanks to its scenic vistas and relaxing lakesides. There are nearly 200 lakes in Carinthia, including the **Wörthersee, Ossiachersee, Faakersee,** and **Millstättersee.** In summer, the warm water attracts families to the countless lake resorts, which offer an array of recreational activities. If your land-legs are surer than your sea-legs, there are rock faces to tackle all around. Abbeys and castles dot the mountainsides, mute witnesses to Carinthia's distant past. If you'll be in Carinthia for an extended period of time, consider investing in a **Kärnten Card,** good for up to 3 weeks of unlimited local transportation, free admission to most area sights and museums, and discounts on many cable cars, boat cruises, toll roads, stores, and restaurants. The card, available at area tourist offices, is a great deal at 395AS.

KLAGENFURT ☎0463

Situated on the edge of the idyllic Wörthersee, Klagenfurt (pop. 90,000) is a major summertime destination for Austrians. Klagenfurt's Wörthersee is the warmest alpine lake in Europe and serves as Europe's largest skating arena in winter. Klagenfurt and its suburbs are home to no fewer than 23 castles and mansions. Get the pamphlet, *A Walk Round Klagenfurt's Old Town,* from the tourist office to explore on your own, or participate in one of several **free guided tours.** (Tours leave from the front of the Rathaus. July-Aug. M-Sa 10am; usually in German.) At the edge of Alterpl. stands the 16th-century **Landhaus,** originally an arsenal and later the seat of the provincial diet. Inside, 665 brilliant coats of arms blanket the walls. Artist Johann Ferdinand Fromiller took nearly 20 years to complete these pieces. (Open Apr.-Sept. M-F 9am-noon and 12:30-5pm. 10AS, students 5AS.) One of Klagenfurt's largest museums is the **Landesmuseum** (Historical

Museum), Museumg. 2., which was Emperor Franz Josef's favorite. It houses the *Lindwurmschädel*, the fossilized rhinoceros skull discovered in AD 1335 that inspired the Lindwurm statue at Neuer Pl. (☎536 30 55 2. Open Tu-Sa 9am-4pm, Su 10am-1pm. 30AS, children 15AS.) On hot spring and summer days, crowds bask in the sun and loll in the clear water of the nearby Wörthersee. The two closest beaches to Klagenfurt are Strandbad Klagenfurter See and Strandbad Maiernigg. From the train station, take bus #40, 41, or 42 to Heiligengeistpl. then bus #10, 11, or 12 to Strandbad Klagenfurter See.

Trains chug to the Hauptbahnhof (☎17 17) at the intersection of Südbahngürtel and Bahnhofstr. from: Vienna's Südbahnhof station (4¼hr., 12 per day 3:42am-8:30pm, 450AS); Graz (3hr., 12 per day, 340AS) via Bruck; and Salzburg (3hr., 9 per day, 340AS). **Buses** depart from opposite the main train station and Bundes-Buses leave for **Graz** (201AS). The **tourist office** is on the 1st floor of the Rathaus in Neuer Pl. From the station, go down Bahnhofstr. and left on Paradeiserg., which opens onto Neuer Pl. (☎537 223. Open May-Sept. M-F 8am-8pm, Sa-Su 10am-5pm; Oct.-Apr. M-F 8am-5pm.) Though the summer heat dries up the pool of available rooms, Klagenfurt does find ways to compensate: two student dorms convert to youth hostels during July and August. The tourist office helps locate rooms for free. To get to **Jugendherberge Klagenfurt (HI)**, Neckheimg. 6, at Universitätstr, take bus #40, 41, or 42 from the train station to Heiligengeistpl., then bus #10 or 11 to Neckheimg. from stand #2. (☎230 020. Breakfast included. Reception 7-9am and 5-10pm. Curfew 10pm; key deposit required. Dorms 200AS; singles 300AS; doubles 250AS; non-members add 50AS.) The **Jugendgästehaus Kolping (HI)**, Enzenbergstr. 26 is a student dorm during the year. From the station, head right down Bahnhofstr., right on Viktringer Ring, left on Völkermarkter Ring, right at Feldmarschall-Conrad-Pl. (which becomes Völkermarkterstr.), and right on Enzenbergstr. (☎569 65. Breakfast included. Open early July to early Sept. Dorms 276AS; singles 356AS; 40AS extra for single-night stay; non-members add 50AS.) You don't have to walk far or look hard to find a cheap place to eat in Klagenfurt, especially in **Neuer Pl., Kardinalpl.**, and along **Burgg.** There is a **SPAR** supermarket on Hermang. just off Heiligengeistpl. (Open M-F 8am-6:30pm, Sa 8am-1pm.) **Postal Code:** A-9020.

BELGIUM
(BELGIQUE, BELGIË)

BELGIAN FRANCS

US$1 = 46.98BF	10BF = US$0.21
CDN$1 = 31.71BF	10BF = CDN$0.32
UK£1 = 66.24BF	10BF = UK£0.15
IR£1 = 51.22BF	10BF = IR£0.20
AUS$1 = 26.06BF	10BF = AUS$0.38
NZ$1 = 19.81BF	10BF = NZ$0.50
SAR1 = 6.61BF	10BF = SAR 1.51
EUR€1 = 40.34BF	10BF = EUR€0.25

PHONE CODE | **Country Code: 32. International dialing prefix:** 00.

Situated between France, Germany, and the Netherlands, Belgium rubs shoulders with some of Western Europe's most powerful cultural and intellectual traditions. Travelers too often mistake Belgium's subtlety for boredom, but its castle-dotted countryside provides a beautiful escape for hikers and bikers, and its cities offer some of Europe's finest art and architecture. Brussels, the capital and home to NATO and the European Union, buzzes with international decision-makers making news. Today, Belgium's Flemish art, French Gothic architecture, and embrace of the Euro reaffirm the border-free identity of the new Europe. Some tension persists between the Flemish-speaking Flanders and the French-speaking area of Wallonie to the south. But some things transcend politics: from the Ardennes forests to the white sands of the North Sea coast, Belgium's beauty is richer than its chocolate.

SUGGESTED ITINERARIES

THREE DAYS Jump into the heart of **Brussels** (p. 124), the **Grand-Place**, declared by Victor Hugo to be "the most beautiful square in the world." Witness Brussels's most giggled-at sight, the **Mannekin Pis,** a statue of a cherubic boy continuously urinating. Visit the **Belgian Comic Strip Centre** and pick up the requisite **Tintin** paraphernalia. Check out the **Musées Royaux des Beaux Arts** and take a trip up to the **Atomium.**

ONE WEEK After three days in **Brussels,** head to **Antwerp** and walk along the **Meir** for beer and fine chocolates (1 day; p. 134). On to **Bruges** to climb the 366 steps of the **Belfort** to see the canals slithering through rows of stone houses (2 days; p. 130). Lay out on the beaches of the **North Sea coast,** parking your pack in **Zeebrugge, Ostend,** or **Knokke** (1 day; p. 134).

BEST OF BELGIUM, TEN DAYS After your week in **Brussels** and **Bruges,** head south to explore the **Wallonie,** the castle-dotted region of the **Ardennes** (p. 136). In the cathedral of **Tournai,** gaze longingly at the treasury of medieval gold (1 day; p. 136), and nap on the train to **Namur,** where you can bike, spelunk, and kayak (2 days; p. 137).

LIFE AND TIMES

HISTORY AND POLITICS

Sandwiched between France and Germany, Belgium's strategic location has long been coveted by military leaders, including **Charlemagne** and a bevy of successive Holy Roman Emperors. Only in 1830 did Belgium gain **independence** from the **Kingdom of the Netherlands,** but assertion of its newfound sovereignty proved to be difficult—days after the first Belgian king, **Leopold I,** was crowned, the Dutch promptly invaded its new neighbor and withdrew after the intervention of the French army. Belgium then began a program of economic revival with a focus on internal investment. It was one of the first European countries to begin industrialization; coal production boosted and the first railway line in Europe (between **Brussels** and **Malines**) went into operation in 1835. Trains between **Antwerp** and **Cologne** facilitated trade between the two countries. Other major projects in the 19th century included **colonial expansion** in present-day **Congo, Rwanda,** and **Burundi.** Despite this flexing of Belgium's newfound sovereign muscle, it found itself caught in between French and German conflict. Initiatives made by kings Leopold II and Albert I to bolster the Belgian army met with disapproval from the Belgian Catholic political party, which also worked to improve the quality of life for the Flemish and rural farmers.

THE WORLD WARS (1914-1945)

In stormed the Germans during the 20th century, rumbling quickly through the nation in both the First and Second World Wars. The **Treaty of Versailles,** the settlement of WWI, gave Belgium monetary and territorial reparations. The treaty also allied Belgium with France, a break from the neutrality it had maintained since the coronation of Leopold I. In WWII, Belgium's rapid surrender infuriated and confused not only the Belgians, but the British and the French as well, as they were too suddenly faced with open space before the advancing German army. Belgium's post-war economic recovery was impressively swift, for wartime destruction was relatively limited. Of greater concern was the political instability upon the return of **King Leopold III** from Austria in 1945, where he had been sent during Nazi rule.

BELGIUM TODAY

With the exception of the brief period after the Treaty of Versailles when Belgium was allied with France, the country has maintained a neutral political stance while remaining at the forefront of international affairs, since the coronation of Leopold I. Most significantly, Belgium is the seat of the **European Union.** Belgian government in the 19th and 20th centuries was largely dominated by the minority of French speakers, concentrated in the southern region of **Wallonia,** despite cries of injustice from the **Flemish population.** To ease tensions between these two groups, the constitution was revised in 1980 to mark three distinctive linguistic and cultural communities: **Flemish** in the north, **French** in the south, and **German** in the east. The parliamentary democracy of Belgium is currently led by Prime Minister **Jean-Luc Dehaene,** of the Christian People's Party.

THE ARTS

PAINTING

Despite representing a school of painting known as the Flemish Primitives, **Jan van Eyck** (1385-1441) in fact refined techniques of oil painting, working with glazes and layers of color to produce pieces of amazing detail. His most well-known painting is the *Adoration of the Mystic Lamb*, the altarpiece of **St. Baal's Cathedral** in **Ghent** (see p. 135), controversial because of the unknown degree to which his brother **Herbert** might have participated in its creation. **Pieter**

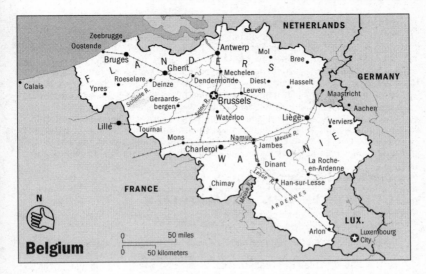

Belgium

Paul Rubens (1577-1640) was Antwerp's most famous artistic son; his paintings are distinctive for their religious symbolism, reflecting the turbulent climate of the **Counter-Reformation,** as well as for their preponderance of plump women. During the 18th and 19th centuries, with the rise of **neo-Classicism,** the general artistic trend veered towards the foreign and exotic. **Anthony van Dyck** (1599-1641) was Rubens' assistant and also an influential member of the Flemish school of painting. Van Dyck's greatest strength lay in the particular attention he paid to color and shape. In the 20th century, the leader of the **Surrealists** was **René Magritte** (1898-1967), who made memorable use of certain symbols: the torso, various household objects such as pipes, apples, chairs, and, perhaps the most famous of his icons, bowler-hatted men.

MUSIC

The star of 15th-century polyphony, music with multiple layers of voices, was **Josquin des Prez,** born in **Burgundy.** His masses, motets, and songs reflect the goal of using music to vividly express the meaning of a text. Also working in the 1400s was **Guillaume Dufay;** born in Cambrai, France, he was the chief contributor to the Flemish school of Renaissance music, composing religious motets and masses in addition to secular *chansons* (songs). **Jacques Brel** (1929-1978) was the voice of the nation—his music was adopted by the English-speaking public all over the world. Brel's most famous ballad, *Ne me quitte pas*, has been covered by, among countless other musicians, **Sting.**

COMIC-STRIPS AND MYSTERIES

In the 20th century, Belgian talent made its presence known in the world of **comic-strips** and **detective novels.** In Brussels, museums are dedicated to the history of cartooning, where tribute is paid to the work of **Georges Remi** (1907-1983), better-known as **Hergé,** creator of **Tintin** (see p. 128), and to **Peyo** (1928-1992), father of the **Smurfs.** The cunning **Commissaire Maigret** was another famous Belgian creation of the past century, conceived by **Georges Simenon** (1903-1989), who wrote the 80-book mystery series. A native of **Liège,** Simenon was sued for apparently basing his fictional characters upon his fellow townspeople. **Henri Michaux** (1899-1984) was a writer who stretched the bounds by even Surrealist standards. His poetry reflected an unusual juxtaposition between natural and fantastical worlds.

FOOD AND DRINK

Belgian cuisine can be wonderful, but a native dish may cost as much as a night in a decent hotel. **Steamed mussels** *(moules)*, a Belgian delicacy, are usually tasty and reasonably affordable (around 430BF per pot). Other specialities include *lapin* (rabbit) and *canard* (duck). Belgian beer is both a national pride and a national pastime; more varieties—over 500, ranging from the ordinary **Jupiler** to the religiously brewed **Chimay**—are produced here than in any other country. Try Leffe, Kwak, Devel, cherry-flavored *kriek*, and the wheat-based *lambric doux* before you leave. Regular or quirky blonde goes for as little as 40BF, and dark beers cost about 60-90BF. Leave room for Belgium's **waffles** *(gaufres)*—soft, warm, glazed ones on the street (50BF) and bigger, crispier ones piled high with toppings at cafes (80-200BF)—and famous Godiva and Leonidas **chocolates**.

ESSENTIALS

DOCUMENTS AND FORMALITIES

Visas are generally not required for tourist stays under three months; South African citizens are the exception.

Belgian Embassies at Home: Australia, 19 Arkana St, Yarralumba, Canberra, ACT 2600 (☎ (02) 62 73 25 01; fax 62 73 33 92); **Canada,** 80 Elgin St., Ottawa, ON K1P 1B7 (☎ (613) 236-7267; fax 236-7882; **Ireland,** 2 Shrewsbury Road, Ballsbridge, Dublin (☎ (353) 1 269 20 82, fax 1 283 84 88); **New Zealand,** 1-3 Willeston St, PB 3379, Wellington (☎ (04) 472 95 58; fax 471 27 64); **South Africa,** 625 Leyds St, Muckleneuk, Pretoria 0002 (☎ (2712) 44 32 01; fax 44 32 16); **UK,** 103-105 Eaton Sq, London SW1W 9AB (☎ (020) 74 70 37 00; fax 259 62 13; www.belgium-embassy.co.uk); **US,** 3330 Garfield St NW, Washington, DC 20008 (☎ (202) 333-6900; fax 333-3079).

Foreign Embassies in Belgium: All foreign embassies are in **Brussels** (see p. 124).

TRANSPORTATION

BY PLANE. Several major airlines fly into **Brussels** from Europe, North America, and Africa; many offer cheap deals. **Sabena Belgian World Airlines** (Belgium ☎ (02) 723 62 19; US ☎ (800) 955-2000; www.sabena.com) serves many locations, including South Africa and North America, and has cheap last-minute deals.

BY TRAIN AND BUS. The extensive and reliable **Belgian Rail** (www.sncb.be) network traverses the country in 4hr. **Eurail** is valid in Belgium (in the US, call 1-800-4EURAIL, in Canada, 1-800-361-RAIL). The **Benelux Tourrail Pass** covers five days of travel in Belgium, the Netherlands, and Luxembourg in any one-month period (6510BF, under 26 4368BF). The best deal for travelers under 26 may be the **Go Pass,** which allows 10 trips over six months in Belgium and may be used by more than one person at a time (1490BF). For travelers over 26, the **Pass 9+** allows 10 trips in Belgium after 9am (2200BF). Tourist offices sell **24-hour passes,** which cover all municipal transport in the country (150BF). Because the train network is so extensive, **buses** are used primarily for municipal transport (40-50BF).

BY FERRY. P&O European Ferries (UK ☎ (01482) 795141; Belgium ☎ (050) 54 34 30; www.ponsf.com) cross the Channel from **Zeebrugge,** north of Bruges, to **Hull, England** (14hr.; £38-48, under 26 £24-31; departures at 6:15pm). **Ostend Lines** also crosses from Ostend to **Ramsgate, England,** 2 hrs. from London's Victoria Station (☎ (059) 55 99 55; 6 per day; 1600BF return). For info on Ostend, Zeebrugge, and Knokke, see p. 134.

BY CAR, BIKE, AND THUMB. Belgium honors most foreign drivers' licenses, including those from Australia, Canada, the EU, and the US. **Speed limits** are 120km per hr. on motorways, 90km per hr. on main roads, and 50km per hr. elsewhere. **Fuel** costs about 40BF per liter. **Biking** is popular, and many roads have bike lanes (which you are required to use). **Hitchhiking** is not popular in Belgium and is not recommended as a safe means of transport, but hitchers still report a fair amount of success in some areas. *Let's Go* does not recommend hitchhiking.

TOURIST SERVICES AND MONEY

EMERGENCY	Police: ☎ 101. Ambulance: ☎ 105. Fire: ☎ 100.

TOURIST OFFICES. Bureaux de Tourisme, marked by green-and-white signs labelled "i," are supplemented by **Info-Jeunes/Info-Jeugd,** a service that helps young people secure accommodations. For info, contact the main office of the **Belgian Tourist Board,** 63 rue de Marché aux Herbes, B-1000 Brussels. (☎ (02) 504 03 90; fax 504 02 70; www.tourism-belgium.net. Open 9am-6pm.) The weekly English-language *Bulletin* (85BF at newsstands) lists everything from movies to job openings.

Tourist Offices at Home: Canada, P.O. Box 760, Succursale NDG, Montréal, Quebec H4A 3S2 (☎ (514) 484-3594; fax 489-8965). **UK,** 225 Marsh Wall, London E14 9FW (☎ (0906) 302 02 45; fax (020) 75 31 03 93). **US,** 780 Third Ave. 1501, New York, NY 10017 (☎ (212) 758-8130; fax 355-7675; www.visitbelgium.com).

CURRENCY & EXCHANGE. The unit of currency is the **Belgian franc;** bills come in 100, 200, 500, 1000, 2000, 5000 and 10,000 denominations, coins in 1, 5, 20 and 50. There are 100 centimes in one franc.

Prices: Expect to pay 750-1200BF for a room; 350-550BF for a hostel bed; 150-400BF for a cheap restaurant meal; and 100-300BF for a day's groceries. A bare-bones day in Belgium might cost US$12-25; a slightly more comfortable day might cost US$30-40.

Tipping and Bargaining: Service charges are usually included in the price in restaurants and taxis, but tip for exceptional service. Bathroom attendants usually receive 10-20BF.

Taxes: Belgium's **VAT** (generally 21%) is always included in price; refunds (usually 17% of the purchase price) are available for a minimum purchase of 5000BF per invoice.

ACCOMMODATIONS AND CAMPING

Hotels in Belgium are fairly expensive, with "trench-bottom" singles from 800BF and doubles at 1000-1100BF. Belgium's 31 **HI youth hostels,** which charge about 405BF per night, are generally modern and many boast cheap bars, but **private hostels** are often cheaper and much nicer. Pick up *Budget Holidays* or the free *Camping* at any tourist office for complete listings of hostels and campsites. **Campgrounds** charge about 130BF per night. An **international camping card** is not required.

COMMUNICATION

MAIL. A postcard or letter (up to 20g) sent to a destination within the European Union costs 30BF, and to the rest of the world costs 34BF. Most post offices open M-F 9am to 4 or 6pm (sometimes with a midday break) and sometimes Sa 9 or 10am to noon or 1pm.

TELEPHONES. Most phones require a 200BF phone card, available at PTT offices and magazine stands. Rarer coin-operated phones are more expensive and require either 5BF or 20BF coins. Calls are cheapest from 6:30pm to 8am and Sa-Su. For **operator assistance** within Benelux, dial ☎ 13 07; for **international assistance,** ☎ 13 04 (10BF). **International direct dial** numbers include: **AT&T Direct,** ☎ 0800 100 10; **Australia Direct,** ☎ 0800 100 61; **BT Direct,** ☎ 0800 100 24; **Canada Direct,** ☎ 0800 100 19; **Ireland Direct,** ☎ 0800 110 353; **MCI WorldPhone,** ☎ 0800 100 12; **New Zealand Direct,** ☎ 0800 104 23; **Sprint Access,** ☎ 0800 100 14; and **Telekom South Africa Direct,** ☎ 0800 100 27.

INTERNET ACCESS. There are cybercafes in the larger towns and cities in Belgium. For access to the web, expect to pay 100-130BF per 30min.

LANGUAGE. French (spoken in Brussels and Wallonie) and German. Most people, especially in Flanders, speak English. Flemish (a slightly different variety than is heard in the Netherlands) is also commonly heard. For the basics, see p. 958.

LOCAL FACTS

Time: Belgium is 1hr. ahead of Greenwich Mean Time (GMT).

Climate: Belgium, temperate and rainy, is best visited May to September, when temperatures average 13-21°C (54-72°F). Winter temperatures average 0-5°C (32-43°F). Bring a sweater and umbrella whenever you go.

Hours: Banks are generally open M-F 9am to 3:30pm or 4pm, sometimes with a lunch break. **Stores** are open M-Sa 10am-6pm. Most **sights** open Su but closed M except in Bruges and Tournai, where museums are closed Tu or W. Most stores close on holidays; museums stay open during all except for Christmas, New Year's, and Armistice Day.

Holidays: New Year's Day (Jan. 1); Easter (Apr. 23); Easter Monday (Apr. 24); Labor Day (May 1); Ascension Day (June 1); Whit Sunday (June 11); Whit Monday (June 12); Independence Day (July 21); Assumption Day (Aug. 15); All Saints Day (Nov. 1); Armistice Day (Nov. 11); Christmas (Dec. 25).

Festivals: Ghent hosts the **Gentse Feesten,** also know as 10 Days Off, every year in mid-July (July 14-23, 2001). Wallonie hosts a slew of quirky and creative carnival-like festivals, including the **Festival of Fairground Arts** (late May), **Les Jeux Nautiques** (early Aug.), and the **International French-language Film Festival** (early Sept.) in Namur, and the **International Bathtub Regatta** (mid-Aug.) in Dinant.

BRUSSELS (BRUXELLES, BRUSSEL) ☎02

Despite the city's instant association with NATO and the European Union, the diplomats in suits have always been outshone by the two boy heroes that Brussels loves best: Tintin, and the Mannekin Pis. In the late 1920s, cartoonist Hergé created a comic strip hero, Tintin, who, followed by his faithful white dog Snowy, righted international wrongs long before Brussels entered the diplomatic arena by becoming the capital of the EU. The cherubic Mannekin Pis perpetually pees three blocks from the Grand-Place, ruining any semblance of formality that could be caused by international politics. The museums of Brussels are rich with collections of Flemish masters, modern art, and antique sculptures, but you don't need to go inside for a visual feast—restaurants, lounges, and movie theaters that keep the town abuzz are built in the style of Art Nouveau architect Victor Horta.

▐ TRANSPORTATION

Flights: Brussels International Airport (☎090 07 00 00) has flights to major international destinations (see **Transportation,** p. 122, for Sabena Belgian World Airlines information). Trains run to the airport from Gare du Midi (25min., every 20min., 90BF); all stop at Gare Centrale and Gare du Nord.

Trains: Info ☎555 25 55. All international trains stop at **Gare du Midi/Zuid;** most also stop at **Gare Centrale** (near the Grand-Place) or **Gare du Nord** (near the Botanical Gardens). To: **Antwerp** (30min., 200BF); **Bruges** (45min., 390BF); **Paris** (1½hr., 2180BF, under 26 1000BF); **Amsterdam** (2½hr., 1310BF, under 26 640BF); **Cologne** (2¾hr., 1260BF, under 26 900BF); and **Luxembourg City** (2¾hr., 930BF). **Eurostar** goes to **London** (1¾hr., from 6200BF, under 26 2100BF).

Buses: Société des Transports Intercommunaux Bruxellois (STIB), Gare du Midi. Open M-F 7:30am-5pm, 1st and last Su of each month 8am-2pm. Also at the Porte de Namur and Rogier métro stops. Open M-F 8:30am-5:15pm. Schedule info ☎515 20 00.

Public Transportation: Runs daily 6am-midnight. 1-hour tickets (50BF) valid on **buses,** the **Métro (M),** and **trams.** Day pass 140BF. 10-trip pass 350BF.

Hitchhiking: *Let's Go* does not recommend hitchhiking. Hitchers headed to **Antwerp** and **Amsterdam** take tram #52 or 92 from Gare du Midi or Gare du Nord to Heysel; **Ghent, Bruges,** and **Oostende,** bus #85 from the Bourse to the stop before the terminus, then follow E40 signs; **Paris,** tram #52, 55, or 91 to rue de Stalle, then walk toward the E19.

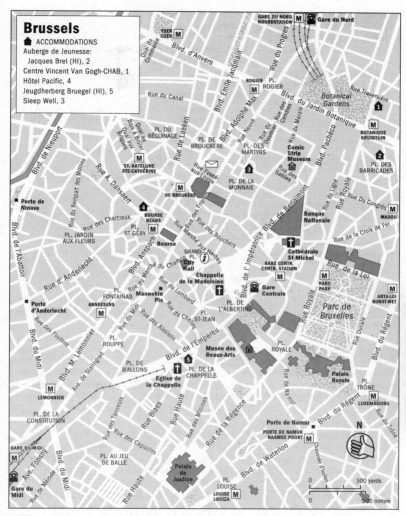

Brussels

⌂ ACCOMMODATIONS

Auberge de Jeunesse:
Jacques Brel (HI), 2
Centre Vincent Van Gogh-CHAB, 1
Hôtel Pacific, 4
Jeugdherberg Bruegel (HI), 5
Sleep Well, 3

BELGIUM

✳🛈 ORIENTATION AND PRACTICAL INFORMATION

Most major attractions are clustered around Brussels' three train stations, between the **Bourse** (Stock Market) to the west and the **Parc de Bruxelles** to the east, around the **Grand-Place.** Two **Métro** lines circle the city, and efficient trams run north to south. A **tourist passport** (300BF at the TIB and bookshops) includes two days of public transit, a map, and reduced museum prices.

> **Tourist Offices: National,** 63 rue du Marché aux Herbes (☎504 03 90; fax 504 02 70), 1 block from the Grand-Place. Books rooms all over Belgium and gives out the free weekly *What's On.* Open daily 9am-6pm. **TIB (Tourist Information Brussels;** ☎513 89 40; fax 514 45 38), on the Grand-Place, in the Town Hall, has free walking tour info. Open July-Aug. M-F 9am-6pm; May-June and Sept.-Oct. M-F 9am-6pm, Sa-Su 9am-1pm and 2-6pm; Nov.-Apr. Su only 9am-1pm.

Budget Travel: Infor-Jeunes, 9A rue du St. Catherine (☎514 41 11). Budget travel info for young travelers. Open M-F 10am-5pm.

Embassies: Australia, 6-8 rue Guimard, 1040 (☎231 05 00; fax 230 68 02); **Canada,** 2 av. Tervueren, 1040 (☎741 06 11; fax 448 00 00); **Ireland,** 89/93 rue Froissart, 1040 (☎230 53 37; fax 230 53 12); **New Zealand,** 47 bd. du Régent, 1000 (☎513 48 56); **South Africa,** 26 rue de la Loi (☎285 44 02), generally open M-F 9am-5pm; **UK,** 85 rue Arlon (☎287 62 11; fax 287 63 55); **US,** 27 bd. du Régent, 1000 (☎508 21 11; fax 511 96 52; www.usinfo.be), open M-F 9am-noon.

Currency Exchange: Many exchange booths near the Grand-Place stay open until 11pm. Most banks and booths charge 100-150BF commission to cash checks. **Goffin,** Rue du Marché aux Herbes 88 (☎502 23 82), charges 2% on travelers checks over 200BF. Open daily 9am-11pm.

Gay and Lesbian Services: Call ☎ 733 10 24 for info on local events. Staffed Tu 8-10pm, W 8-11pm, F-8-11pm.

Laundromat: Salon Lavoir, 5 rue Haute, around the corner from the Jeugdherberg Bruegel. M: Gare Centrale. Wash and dry 240BF. Open daily 7am-11pm.

Emergencies: Ambulance or **first aid,** ☎100. **Police,** ☎101.

Pharmacies: Neos-Bourse Pharmacie (☎218 06 40), bd. Anspach at rue du Marché-aux-Polets. M: Bourse. Open M-F 8:30am-6:30pm, Sa 9am-6:30pm.

Medical Assistance: Free Clinic, 154a chaussée de Wavre (☎512 13 14). Misleading name—you'll have to pay. Open M-F 9am-6pm. **Medical Services,** 24hr. ☎479 18 18.

Internet Access: Point.Net, 16 petite rue des Bouchers (☎513 14 15), off Marché-Aux-Herbes, is only one block away from the Grand Place. Students 100BF per 30min. Open M-Sa 10am-7pm, Su 10am-6pm.

Post Office: (☎226 20 17) pl. de la Monnaie, Centre Monnaie, 2nd fl. M: de Brouckère. Open M-F 8am-7pm, Sa 9:30am-3pm. Address mail to be held: Joseph ROSENBERG, Poste Restante, Pl. de la Monnaie, 1000 Bruxelles, Belgium.

▟ ACCOMMODATIONS

Accommodations in Brussels are fairly easy to find. In general, hotels and hostels are very well-kept; any and all will provide a good springboard to the city. Staffs at the five hostels will call each other if prospective guests arrive and they are booked.

Hôtel Pacific, 57 rue Antoine Dansaert (☎511 84 59). M: Bourse; cross bd. Anspach. Excellent location and basic rooms. Breakfast included. Showers 100BF. Reception 7am-midnight. Curfew midnight. Singles 1100BF; doubles 1800-2250BF.

Sleep Well, 23 rue du Damier (☎218 50 50; email info@sleepwell.be), near Gare du Nord. M: Rogier; go right on the bd. du Jardin Botanique and turn right on rue des Cendres, which turns into rue Damier. Internet. Curfew 4am. Lockout 10am-4pm. Dorms 350-510BF; singles 695BF; doubles 1140BF; triples 1500BF.

Auberge de Jeunesse "Jacques Brel" (HI), 30 rue de la Sablonnière (☎218 01 87), on pl. des Barricades. M: Botanique. From the metro stop, walk straight towards the church tower on Rue Royal and turn right onto Sablonierre. Spacious rooms. Dinner 295BF. Sheets 125BF. Reception 8am-1am. Dorms 430BF; singles 820BF; doubles 2000BF; triples 1530BF.

Centre Vincent Van Gogh-CHAB, 8 rue Traversière (☎217 01 58; email chab@ping.be). M: Botanique; exit on rue Royale, head right (as you face the Jardin Botanique), and turn right again. Lively bar and garden. Internet 50BF per 15min. Laundry 180BF. Reception 7am-2am. Dorms 340-480BF; singles 700BF; doubles 1120-1160BF.

Jeugdherberg Bruegel (HI), 2 Heilige Geeststr. (☎511 04 36). From the back exit of Gare Centrale, go right on bd. de l'Empereur and take the 2nd left after Pl. de la Justice. Sheets 130BF. Reception 7am-1am. Lockout 10am-2pm. Curfew 1am. Dorms 430BF; singles 820BF; doubles 1200BF; quads 2040BF.

Generation Europe (HI), rue de l'Elephant (☎410 38 58; www.laj.be). M: Comte de Flandre. From the metro station turn left and follow the signs. Be careful walking there at night. Reception 7am-1am. Lockout 11am-3pm. Sheets 130BF. Laundry 200BF. Dorms 430BF; singles 820BF; doubles 2000F.

FOOD

Restaurants cluster around the **Grand-Place,** but for cheap eats and small cafes, try the arcade across from the back entrance to the Central Station. Shellfish are piled on ice on **rue des Bouchers,** just north of the *place.* The small restaurants on **quai aux Briques,** in the Ste-Catherine area behind pl. St-Gery, serve cheaper seafood to a local clientele. Just south of the *place,* the **rue du Marché-aux-Fromages** is lined with Greek eateries. The abundant **Belgaufras** has hot waffles (50-80BF). Load up at **GB supermarket,** 248 rue Vierge Noire. (M: Bourse. Open M-F 9am-7pm, Sa 10am-6pm.)

Léon, rue des Bouchers 18 (☎511 14 15). You can't pass up Brussels' landmark for seafood; popular with locals and tourists alike. An order of mussels and chips (around 600F) can serve two. Open daily noon-11pm.

Arcadi Coffeeshop, rue d'Arenberg 1b. Small cafe specializing in homemade quiche (180BF) and lots of veggie options. Open M-F 7:30am-11pm, Sa-Su 10am-11pm.

Sole d'Italia, rue Grétry 67. Offers huge servings of spaghetti with bread for only 195BF. Open daily noon-late.

Zebra, St-Gèry 33-35. This chic cafe is centrally located and serves light, tasty sandwiches and pastas (around 250BF). Open daily 11:30am-2:30am.

L'Ecole Buissonnière, rue de Traversière 13, opposite the Centre Vincent Van Gogh-CHAB hostel. M: Botanique. Traditional Belgian food; 3-course menus 350BF. Open M-F noon-2:30pm and 6:30-10pm.

Hemispheres, rue de l'Ecuver 65 (☎513 93 70). Libyan, Turkish, Chinese, and Indian cuisine convene at this summit of great Eastern platters. Vegetarian meals 280-400BF. Open M-F noon-3pm and 6:30-10:30pm, Sa 6:30pm-midnight.

Maison des Crêpes, rue de Midi 13. This small restaurant down the street from the Bourse serves specialty crêpes from 80BF and waffles from 90BF. Open M-Th 11:30am-7pm, F-Sa 11:30am-10pm, Su 8am-7pm.

Ultième Hallutinatie, rue Royale 316. Bring your camera to this splendid stained glass Art Nouveau house and garden. Salads, pastas, and omelettes in the **Tavern** from 250BF. Open M-F noon-2:30pm and 6pm-midnight, Sa until 1am, Su closed.

SIGHTS

GRAND-PLACE AND ENVIRONS. One look and you'll understand why Victor Hugo called the gold-trimmed **Grand-Place** "the most beautiful square in the world" after he lived at #26 Grand Place in 1852. Built in the 15th century and ravaged by French troops in 1695, the square was restored to its original splendor in only four years. A daily flower market and feverish tourist activity add color. The best sight in town is the light show, when 800 multi-colored floodlights give the **Town Hall** on the Grand Place a manmade glow, accompanied by booming classical music. *(Apr.-Aug. and Dec. daily around 10 or 11pm.)* Three blocks behind the Town Hall on the corner of rue de l'Etuve and rue du Chêne is Brussels' most giggled-at sight, the **Mannekin Pis,** a statue of an impudent boy (with an apparently gargantuan bladder) steadily urinating. One story goes that a 17th-century mayor promised to build a statue in the position that his lost son was found; another says it commemorates a boy who ingeniously defused a bomb. Everyday, the Mannekin Pis dons a new costume; locals have created hundreds of outfits for him, competitively dressing him with the ritual coats of their organization or region, each with a little hole for his you-know-what. *(Free. He's always peeing.)*

ART MUSEUMS. The **Musées Royaux des Beaux Arts** house a huge collection of the Flemish masters, including Brueghel the Elder's *Fall of Icarus* and works by Rubens. The museum is divided into four main color-coded wings, each for a different century. Begin with the Musée d'Art Ancien wing to see Brueghel's depiction of the triumphs and tribulations of daily Flemish life in the 15th and 16th centuries; the Dutch painter Jan Steen similarly portrayed the debauchery amidst the robes and religious rites. Next is the 17th and 18th century brown tour, highlighted by **room #53,** which

BELGIUM

INTERNATIONAL MAN OF MYSTERY Tintin (pronounced "tan-tan") is the greatest comic-strip hero in the French-speaking world. From Nice to Quebec City, the journalist remains perpetually young to fans who play the hardest of hardball at auctions for Tintin memorabilia, and relish the treks he took when his creator, Georges Rémi (who took the pen-name "Hergé," his initials pronounced backwards) sent him to the Kremlin, Shanghai, Chicago, the Congo, and even into outer space. Countless dissertations and novels have been written about Tintin's possible androgyny; many also say that Indiana Jones was Tintin made into a man. Tintin stepped off comic book pages into the imaginations of many. When former French president Charles de Gaulle was asked who he feared the most, he replied, "Tintin is my only international competitor."

contains Rubens' huge, vertical sweeps of life and afterlife. The 19th century green tour features Dutch and Flemish Impressionists along with Seurat and Gauguin. No matter what your artistic tastes, the panoramic view of Brussels' cityscape from the fourth floor of the 19th century wing is worth the admission fee—you can see all the way to the Atomium and beyond. The **Musée d'Art Moderne** includes works by Miró, Picasso, and Brussels-based Magritte, as well as Jacques-Louis David's *Death of Marat*. (*Rue de la Régence 3. M: Parc or port de Namur, a block south of the Parc. Open Tu-Su 10am-5pm. 15th- to 16th- and 19th-century rooms close noon-1pm; 17th- to 18th- and 20th-century rooms close 1-2pm. 150BF, students 100BF. 1st W of each month free 1-5pm.*) The enormous **Musées Royaux d'Art et d'Histoire** cover a wide variety of periods and parts—Roman torsos without heads, Syrian heads without torsos, and Egyptian caskets with feet. (*10 parc du Cinquantenaire. M: Mérode. From the station, walk straight through the arch, turn left, go past the doors that appear to be the entrance, and turn left again for the real entrance. Open Tu-Su 10am-5pm. 150BF, students 100F.*) Early 20th-century Art Nouveau master Baron Victor Horta's graceful home, today the **Musée Horta**, is an elegant example of Brussels' architecture. (*25 rue Américaine. M: Louise; walk down Av. Louise, bear right on rue Charleroi, and turn left on rue Américaine. Open Tu-Su 2-5:30pm. 200BF.*)

BELGIAN COMIC STRIP CENTRE. This museum in the "Comic Strip Capital of the World" pays homage to *les bandes dessineés* with hundreds of Belgian comics on display. The **museum library** features a reproduction of Tintin's rocket ship and works by over 700 artists. It is located in a renovated Art Nouveau textile warehouse designed by Horta. For Tintin souvenirs, check out the museum store or the Tintin Boutique near the Grand-Place. (*20 rue des Sables. M: Rogier. ☎219 19 80. From the Gare Centrale, take bd. de l'Impératrice until it becomes bd. de Berlaimont, turn left onto rue des Sables. Open Tu-Su 10am–6pm. 200BF.*)

ATOMIUM AND BRUPARCK ENTERTAINMENT COMPLEX. The **Atomium,** a shining monument of aluminum and steel built for the 1958 World's Fair, represents a cubic iron crystal structure magnified 165 billion times to a height of 102m. It today houses a **science museum** featuring fauna and minerals from around the world. The Atomium towers over the **Bruparck entertainment complex,** home of the **Kinepolis cinema** and **IMAX,** the largest movie theater in Europe. (*M: Huysel. ☎474 89 77; www.atomium.be. Atomium open daily Apr.-Aug. 9am-7:30pm; Sept.-Mar. 10am-5:30pm. Museum 200BF. Movies from 300BF.*)

OTHER SIGHTS. Make sure to stroll through the glorious **Galerie St. Hubert,** one block behind the Grand Place, to windowshop for everything from square umbrellas to marzipan frogs. Built over the course of 6 centuries, the magnificent **Saints Michel et Gudule Cathedral** is an excellent example of the Gothic style, and mixes in a little Romanesque and modern architecture as well. (*Pl. St-Gudule, just north of Central Station. Open daily 8am-7pm. Free.*) Wander the charming hills of **Sablon,** home to antique markets, art galleries, and lazy cafes, around **le Jeu de Balles,** where you can practice the fine art of bargaining at the morning **flea market.** In the **Schuman** area, see the gleaming buildings of the **European Parliament** (called Caprice des Dieux—"Whim of the Gods"—perhaps because of their exorbitant cost). For a lazy afternoon, try the **Botanical Gardens** on rue Royale. (*Open daily 10am-10pm. Free.*)

♫ ENTERTAINMENT AND NIGHTLIFE

For info on events, snag a free copy of *What's On* from the tourist office. The flagship of Brussels' theater network is the beautiful **Théâtre Royal de la Monnaie,** on pl. de la Monnaie. (M: de Brouckère. ☎229 12 00. 300-3000BF). Renowned throughout the world for its opera and ballet, the theater had a performance of the opera *Muette de Portici* in August 1830 that inspired the audience to leave the theater early, take to the streets, and begin the revolt that led to Belgium's independence. Experience a distinctly Belgian art form at the **Theatre Toone,** 21 rue des Bouchers, a 170-year-old puppet theater that stages marionette performances. (☎511 71 37. Shows in French; in German, Flemish, or English upon request. Usually Tu-Sa 8:30pm. 400BF, students 250BF.) In summer, **concerts** are on the **Grand-Place,** the **Place de la Monnaie,** and in the **Parc de Bruxelles.**

The scene in Brussels ranges from sharing a barspace with old gents to casually glamming it up for outdoor cafes and lounges. The nightlife is crazy, but take caution if you are walking from a disco in the south back to the Gare du Nord late at night. The most stylish coffeeshops surround the **Pl. St-Gèry,** behind the Bourse. At night the **Grand-Place,** the **Bourse,** and environs come to life with street performers and live concerts. The 19th-century puppet theater **Poechenellekelder,** rue de Chêne 5, across from the Mannekin Pis, is today filled with lavishly costumed marionettes and a nice selection of Belgian beers. (Open daily noon-midnight, F-Sa until 1 or 2am. Beers from 50BF.) **La Mort Subite,** 7 rue Montagne-aux-Herbes-Potagères, across from the Arcadi Coffeeshop (open daily 10am-2am), and **La Bécasse,** rue de Tabora 11, two of Brussels' oldest and best-known cafes, specialize in *lambric,* a local wheat beer (beer 50-90BF; open daily 10am-midnight). **L'Archiduc,** 6 rue Dansaert, is a pricey but still casual Art Deco 20s lounge-turned-jazz bar. (Open daily 4pm-late.) **Le Fuse,** 208 rue Blaes, one of Belgium's trendiest clubs, pays homage to the gods of techno and rave. (Open daily 10pm-late.) Gay men socialize in a mellow atmosphere at **L'Incognito,** 36 rue des Pierres. (☎513 37 88. Open daily 4pm-dawn.)

♫ DAYTRIPS FROM BRUSSELS

WATERLOO

Bus W leaves pl. Rouppe near Brussels' Gare Midi (every 51min., 100F) and stops at Waterloo Church, across the street from Musée Wellington, at a gas station near Lion's Mound, and at the train station in Braine L'Alleud. Belgian Railways offers a B-excursion ticket, which gives round-trip transit between Brussels Midi (also available from Brussels Nord) and Braine L'Alleud, a bus pass from Braine L'Alleud to Waterloo, and entrance to all sights (710BF, students 660BF).

Napoleon was caught with both hands in his shirt at Waterloo (well, even ABBA couldn't escape if they wanted to), just south of Brussels. Modern residents are more likely to have their hands in your pockets, as history buffs and fans of the diminutive dictator shell out for a glimpse at the town's little slice of history. **The Lion's Mound,** 5km outside of town, is a huge hill overlooking the battlefield; nearby, the Visitor's Center houses a panoramic painting of the battle and a brief movie about Waterloo. A grandscale reenactment of the Battle is scheduled for June 16-17, 2001. (Open Apr.-Sept. 9:30am-6:30pm; Oct. 9:30am-5:30pm; Nov.-Feb. 10:30am-4pm; Mar. 10:30am-5pm. Lion's Mound 40BF, with movie and panorama 305BF.) In the center of Waterloo, **Musée Wellington,** Chaussée de Bruxelles 147, was Wellington's headquarters and has artifacts from the battle. (Open daily Apr.-Oct. 9:30am-6:30pm; Nov.-Mar. daily 10:30am-5pm. 100BF, students 80BF.) The **tourist office** is next to the Musée Wellington, at Chaussée de Bruxelles 149. (☎354 99 10. Open daily Apr. to mid-Nov. 9:30am-6:30pm, mid-Nov. to Mar. 10:30am-5pm.) At the Mound, eat at **R'llea,** route du Lion 56, for a touristy but relatively cheap Belgian meal. (☎384 20 03. Open daily 7:30am-10pm)

MECHELEN (MALINES)

Trains arrive from Brussels and Antwerp (both 15min., 120BF).

Historically the ecclesiastical capital of Belgium, Mechelen is best-known today for its clamorous bells and grim contribution to the Holocaust. Complete with a local institute where students still learn to play the **carillon** (a set of 49 bells); performances in **St. Rumbold's Cathedral** warrant the daytrip from Brussels (M and Sa 11:30am, Su 3pm; June 15-Sept. also M 8:30pm). Down Consciencestr. from the station, **St. Rumbold's Tower** rises 97m over **Grote Markt** and contains two carillons. You can climb the bell tower with a guide an hour before the concert. (M 2:15pm and 7:15pm. 100BF.) The Grote Markt is lined with early Renaissance buildings, including the **Stadhuis** (city hall) and the stately St. Rumbold's Cathedral. (Stadhuis open M-Sa 8:30am-5:30pm, Su 2-5:30pm.) The 18th-century military barracks used during the Holocaust as a temporary camp for Belgian and Dutch Jews en route to Auschwitz-Birkenau now houses the **Museum of Nazi Deportation and Resistance.** From the Grote Markt, head down Merodestr., left on St. Janstr. and right on Stassartstr. (Open Su-Th 10am-5pm, F 10am-1pm. Free.) The **tourist office** is in the Stadhuis and finds rooms for free. (☎ (015) 29 76 55. Open Easter-Oct. M-F 8am-6pm, Sa-Su 9:30am-12:30pm and 1:30-5pm; June-Sept. M until 7pm; Nov.-Easter reduced hours.) **Café de York Ver-O-Peso,** Wollemarkt 2, behind the cathedral, serves great pizza. (Meals 220-400BF. Open daily 10am-midnight.) **Postal Code:** 2800.

FLANDERS (VLAANDEREN)

Boogie the night away in Antwerp, breathe in beautiful Bruges, and sate your castle-cravings at Ghent's Gravensteen when in Flanders, the Flemish-speaking part of Belgium. Historically, the delta of the river Schelde at Antwerp provided the region with a major port, and the production and trade of linen, wool, and diamonds created great prosperity. Flanders' Golden Age came during the 16th century, when its commercial centers were among the largest cities in Europe and its innovative artists motivated the Northern Renaissance. Today, the well-preserved Gothic cities of Flanders, rich in art and friendly, multilingual people, hold Belgium's strongest attractions.

BRUGES (BRUGGE)   ☎ 050

The capital of Flanders is one of the most beautiful cities in Europe, and tourists know it: the home of Jan van Eyck, and famed for its lace, Bruges has become the largest tourist attraction in the country. Silver canals carve their way through rows of stone houses and lead to the breathtaking Gothic Markt. The city remains one of the best-preserved examples of Northern Renaissance architecture. Its beauty belies the destruction sustained in World War I; eight decades after the war, farmers still uncover 200 tons of artillery every year as they plough their fields.

▐ TRANSPORTATION

Trains: Depart from **Stationsplein** (☎ 38 23 82), 15min. south of the city center. To: **Brussels** (1hr., 380BF); **Antwerp** (1hr., 395BF); **Ghent** (25min., 175BF); **Ostende** (17min., 110BF); and **Zeebrugge** (10min., 80F).

Bike Rental: At the train station; 345BF per day, 500BF deposit. **'t Koffieboontje,** Hallestr. 4 (☎ 33 80 27), off the Markt by the belfry. 325BF per day, students 200BF. Open daily 9am-10pm.

Hitchhiking: Those hitching to Brussels reportedly take bus #7 to St. Michiels or pick up the highway behind the train station. *Let's Go* does not recommend hitchhiking.

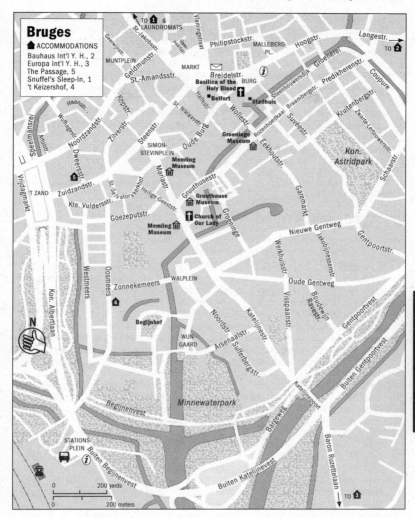

Bruges

🏠 ACCOMMODATIONS

Bauhaus Int'l Y. H., 2
Europa Int'l Y. H., 3
The Passage, 5
Snuffel's Sleep-In, 1
't Keizershof, 4

✴🛈 ORIENTATION AND PRACTICAL INFORMATION

Bruges is enclosed by a circular canal, with the train station just beyond its southern extreme. Its historic district is entirely accessible on foot, and in fact, you won't see a tram at all. The dizzying Belfort (belfry) towers high at the center of town, presiding over the handsome square of the Markt.

Tourist Offices: Burg 11 (☎ 44 86 86; email toerisme@bruges.be; www.bruges.be), behind the Markt. Head left from the station to 't Zand square, right on Zuidzandstr., and right on Breidelstr. through the Markt (15min.). Books rooms (400BF deposit) and sells maps (25BF). Open Apr.-Sept. M-F 9:30am-6:30pm, Sa-Su 10am-noon and 2-6:30pm; Oct.-Mar. M-F 9:30am-5pm, Sa-Su 9:30am-1pm and 2-5:30pm. Branch at the train station open 10:30am-1:15pm and 2-5:30pm.

Tours: Quasimodo Tours (☎37 04 70), leads excellent 30km countryside bike and bus tours to windmills, castles, and WWII bunkers. Bike tours depart mid-Mar.-Sept. daily from the tourist office at the Burg. 650BF, under 26 550BF. The Triple Treat trip stops on M, W, F at medieval castles with chocolate, waffles, and beer thrown in. 1500BF, under 26 1200BF.

Currency Exchange: Currency exchanges fill the streets around the Markt. **Goffin,** 2 Steenstr., has good rates (2% commission on traveler's checks, min. 200BF transaction). Open daily 9am-8pm.

Luggage Storage: At the train station; 80BF. **Lockers** at the tourist office; 50BF.

Laundromat: Belfort, Ezelstr. 51, next to Snuffel's Sleep-In (see p. 132). Wash 100-140BF, dry 200-300BF. Open daily 7am-10pm.

Emergencies: ☎100. **Police,** ☎101. Police station at Hauwerstr. 7 (☎44 88 44).

Internet Access: The Coffee Link, Mariastraat 38 (☎34 99 73), in the Oud Sint-Jon Historic Hospital. 60BF for 15min. Open M-Sa 10am-9:30pm, Su 1:30-6:30pm.

Post Office: Hoedenmakerstr. 2. Open M-F 9am-5pm, Tu 9am-7pm. **Poste Restante:** Ian CAINES, Poste Restante, Hoedenmakerstr. 2, Brugge 8000.

▟ ACCOMMODATIONS

Rates for accommodations become reasonable away from the Markt and 't Zand, even just a few blocks away from the center.

The Passage, Dweersstr. 26 (☎34 02 32). Take any bus from the station to St. Salvators, turn left onto Zuidzandstr. and the first right onto Dweerstr. Or walk from the station to 't Zand, go right on Zuidzandstr. and take the 1st left. Airy rooms and an ideal location. Breakfast 100BF. Reception 8:30am-midnight. Closed each Jan. for renovations. Dorms 450BF; singles 900BF; doubles 1400BF.

Bauhaus International Youth Hotel, Langestr. 133-137 (☎34 10 93; email bauhaus@bauhaus.be). Take bus #6 from the station to Kruispoort and tell the driver the destination (40BF). Internet cybercafe with lots of computers. Belgian dinners from 275BF; packed bar. Breakfast 60BF. Reception 8am-2am. Dorms 380BF; singles 550-850BF; doubles 1000-1300BF; triples 1350-1800BF.

Snuffel's Sleep-In, Ezelstr. 49 (☎33 31 33; email snuffel@flanderscoast.be). From Markt, follow Sint-Jakobstr., which becomes Ezelstr. (10min.). Breakfast 80BF. Internet. Reception 8am-2am. Snug dorms 350-390BF; quads 1960BF.

't Keizershof, Oostmeers 126 (☎33 87 28; email hotel.keizerhof@weant2move.be; http://users.skynet.be/keizerhof). From the station, walk to the traffic lights on the left, cross the street, follow signs pointing to the Memling Museum and Oud St. Jan. The hotel is 80m on your left. Pretty, comfortable rooms on a quiet street. Singles 950BF; doubles 1400BF; triples 2100BF; quads 2500BF.

Europa International Youth Hostel (HI), Baron Ruzettelaan 143 (☎35 26 79). Quiet, away from the Markt and the nightlife. Turn right from the station and follow Buiten Katelijnevest to Baron Ruzettelaan (15min.). Breakfast included. Sheets 125BF. Key deposit 100BF. Reception 7:30-10am and 1-11pm. 420BF; nonmembers 520BF.

Camping: St-Michiel, Tillegemstr. (☎38 08 19), 25min. from the Markt. Or take bus #7 from the station. 110BF per person, 130BF per tent, 130BF for a car.

◖ FOOD

Splurge on a pot of Belgium's famous *mosselen* (mussels), which at 450-500BF often includes appetizers and dessert, even in the Markt. From the Burg, cross the river and turn left to buy fresh seafood at the **Vismarkt.** For cheaper fare, head to **Nopri Supermarket,** Noordzandstr. 4, just off 't Zand. (Open M-Sa 9:30am-6:30pm.)

Ganzespel, Ganzestr. 37, serves up hearty portions of simple food. From Burg, turn up Hoogstr. and take the 2nd right after the river. Meals 245-485BF. Quiche 230BF. Open W-F noon-2pm and 6-10pm, Su noon-10pm.

The Gran Kaffee de Passage, Dweerstraat 26-28, prepares traditional Belgian cuisine. Open daily 5pm-late.

Café Craenenburg, Markt 16. Grab a quick snack on the terrace and watch the passersby. Open daily 7am-1am.

The Lotus, Wappenmakerstr. 5, has fresh veggie lunches (310-330BF). From the Markt, take the 3rd left off Philipstockstr. Open mid-Aug. to mid-July daily 11:45am-2pm.

Het Brood, Philipstockstraat 21. Organic yogurts and sandwiches. Open M and W-Sa 7am-6pm, Su 8am-6pm.

De Belegde Boterham, Kleine St. Amandstr 5, off Steenstr. Salads from 195-395BF, Sandwiches 195-295BF. Soup and quiche served in winter. Open M-Sa 12-5pm.

SIGHTS

Small enough to be thoroughly explored by short walks, and lined with gorgeous canals, Bruges is best seen on foot. The tourist office leads **walking tours** (July-Aug. daily 3pm; 150BF). **Boat tours** also ply Bruges' canals (every 30min., 190BF); ask at the tourist office or pick up tickets at the booth on the bridge between Wollestr. and Dijver. The **museum combination ticket** covers the Gruuthuse, the Groeninge Museum, the Arentshuis, and the Memling (500BF).

MARKT AND BURG. Over the **Markt** looms the 88-meter-high medieval bell tower of the **Belfort.** Climb its dizzying 366 steps during the day for a great view; return at night when the tower serves as the city's torch. *(Open daily 9:30am-5pm. Bell concerts M, W, and Sa 9pm, Su 2:15pm. 100BF, students 80BF.)* Behind the Markt, the **Burg** square is dominated by the flamboyant Gothic facade of the medieval **Stadhuis** (City Hall), filled with paintings and wood carvings. Upstairs is a gilded hall where many Bruges residents still get married. *(Open daily 9:30am-5pm. 150BF.)* Hidden in the corner of the Burg next to the Stadhuis, the **Basilica of the Holy Blood** houses a relic that allegedly holds the blood of Christ. *(Open daily Apr.-Sept. 9:30am-noon and 2-6pm; Oct.-Mar. 10am-noon and 2-4pm; closed W afternoon. 40BF.)*

MUSEUMS. From the Burg, follow Wollestr. left and head right on Dijver to reach the **Groeninge Museum,** for a comprehensive collection of Belgian and Dutch paintings from the last six centuries, featuring works by Bruges-based Jan Van Eyck, Bruges-born Hans Memling, and the master of medieval macabre himself, Hieronymous Bosch. *(Dijver 12. Open daily 9:30am-5pm. In winter closed Tu. 250BF. Last tickets sold at 4:30pm.)* Next door, the **Gruuthuse Museum,** in the lavish 15th-century home of beer magnates, houses an amazing collection of weapons, tapestries, musical instruments, and coins that date back to the 6th century. The spare room in the back is perhaps the biggest treasure in the museum, where you can sneak a peek into the **Church of Our Lady** next door. *(Dijver 17. Open Apr.-Sept. daily 9:30am-5pm; Oct.-Mar. W-M 9:30am-5pm. 130BF, students 100BF.)* Continue as Dijver becomes Gruuthusestr. and walk under the stone archway to enter the **Memling Museum,** Mariastr. 38, housed in St. John's Hospital, one of the oldest surviving medieval hospitals in Europe. The collection is scheduled to reopen in mid-2001.

OTHER SIGHTS. The 13th- to 15th-century **Church of Our Lady,** at Mariastr. and Gruuthusestr. near the Groeninge Museum, contains Michelangelo's *Madonna and Child,* one of his few works to have left Italy, as well as a number of medieval frescoed tombs and the 16th-century mausoleums of Mary of Burgundy and Charles the Bold. *(Open daily 9:30am-5pm. Church free; entrance to tombs 100BF.)* From the Church, turn left and stroll along the Mariastraat, turn right onto Stoofstr., where you will come to Walplein. Admire the geese along the canal, and cross the footbridge to enter the Beguinage, a grassy cove encircled by the residences of cloistered women in medieval times, and inhabited today by three Benedictine sisters. *(Free.)* The 230-year-old windmill **Sint-Janshuismolen,** is still used to grind flour. From the Burg, follow Hoogstr., which becomes Langestr., and turn left at the end on Kruisvest. *(Open May-Sept. daily 9:30am-12:30pm and 1:30-5pm. 40BF.)* The **Minnewater** (the Lake of Love) has a less-than-romantic history as the site of ammunition dump, but you'd never know from the picnickers lounging in the beautiful park.

🎵 ENTERTAINMENT

The best nighttime entertainment consists of wandering through the city's romantic streets and over its cobblestoned bridges, but if that isn't enough, take your pick from the 300 varieties of beer at **'t Brugs Beertje**, Kemelstr. 5, off Steenstr. (Open M-Tu and Th-Su 4pm-1am.) Next door, the **Dreipelhuisje** serves tantalizingly fruity *jenever*, a flavored Dutch gin; just beware, the flavors mask a very high alcohol content. (Open M-Tu, Th and Su 6pm-1am, W 4pm-1am, F-Sa 6pm-2am.) For fun, **Rikka Rock**, on 't Zand, is popular with local twenty-somethings. (Beers from 50BF. No cover. Open 24hr.) Continue next door to **The Break**, 't Zand 9: pulsing music and glammed up glances await. (Beer from 55BF. No cover. Open daily 1pm-late.)

🏖 DAYTRIPS FROM BRUGES

ZEEBRUGGE, OSTEND, AND KNOKKE

For info on ferries from Zeebrugge, Ostend, and Knokke, to the UK, see p. 47. Get ferry tickets from travel agents, at ports, or in the Ostend train station. Trains run to Zeebrugge (15min., 3 per hr., 150BF); Ostend (15min., 3 per hr., 110BF); and to Knokke (15min., 2 per hr., 100BF).

The towns along the North Sea coast of Belgium win fans primarily because of their **beaches.** **Zeebrugge** is little more than a port, but **Ostend** (Oostende) and **Knokke** have cute beaches and stores, just an hour-long bike ride from Bruges. To get from the Ostend train station to the **De Ploate Youth Hostel (HI)**, Langestr. 82, cross the bridge, turn right on Visserkaai, follow the Promenade for 10min., and turn left on Langestr. (☎ (059) 80 52 97. Reception 7:30am-midnight. Curfew midnight. 465BF, non-members 565BF.)

ANTWERP (ANTWERPEN, ANVERS)   ☎03

Home of the Golden Age master painter Rubens, Antwerp today is a city composed of distinct cosmopolitan layers. The Meir, Antwerp's main drag boasts an artery-clogging plethora of fine Belgian chocolate purveyors in addition to an array of department stores. At the end of the Meir, beer flows so cheaply in the cluster of bars there night after night, crowds pass another round in lieu of breakfast. Many of Antwerp's best sights are free. Walk along the **Cogels Osylei** past fanciful Art Nouveau mansions built in the wealth of the city's Golden Age. **Centraal Station** itself is beautiful, and the buildings along the **Meir** are excellent examples of Antwerp old and new. The dignified Renaissance **Stadhuis** (City Hall) is in the Grote Markt in the old city. (Call ☎203 95 33 for tour times. 30BF.) The nearby **Kathedraal van Onze-Lieve-Vrouw**, Groenpl. 21, has a showy Gothic tower and Flemish masterpieces, notably Rubens' *Descent from the Cross*. (☎213 99 40. Open M-F 10am-5pm, Sa 10am-3pm, Su 1-4pm. 70BF.) The little-known **Mayer van den Bergh Museum**, Lange Gasthuisstr. 19, showcases Brueghel's *Mad Meg*. (☎232 42 37. Open Tu-Su 10am-4:45pm. 100BF.) Antwerp's favorite son built the stunning **Rubens Huis**, Wapper 9, off Meir, and filled it with his art. (☎201 15 55. Open Tu-Su 10am-4:45pm. 100BF.) The **Royal Museum of Fine Art**, Leopold De Waelpl. 1-9, has one of the world's best collections of Old Flemish Master paintings. (Open Tu-Su 10am-5pm. 150BF, students 120BF; F free.) Pick up *Play* at the tourist office for information on Antwerp's 300 bars and nightclubs. DJs spin house music in near-rave conditions at **Café d'Anvers**, Verversrui 15. (Cover 200BF. Open Sa-Su from midnight.) The streets behind the cathedral stay crowded; **Bierland**, Korte Nieuwstr. 28, is a popular student hang-out. (☎232 92 47. Open daily 9am-late.) Next to the cathedral, over 600 Flemish religious figurines collect along with curious drinkers at **Elfde Gebod**, Torfburg 10. (☎289 34 66. Beer 70-120BF. Open daily noon-1am, weekends until 2am.) Sample local *elixir d'Anvers* at the candle-lit **Pelgrom**, Pelgrimstr. 15. (Open daily noon-late.) Gay nightlife clusters on **Van Schoonhovenstr.**, just north of Centraal Station. Closer to Grote Markt, a mixed crowd is found at gay-friendly **in de Roscam**, Vrijdagmarkt 12. (Open daily 6am-2am.)

Trains go from Centraal Station, on de Keyserlei to: Brussels (45-53min., 200BF); Amsterdam (2hr., 970BF); and Rotterdam (1½hr., 700BF). To get from the station to the **tourist office**, Grote Markt 15, turn left on De Keyserlei, which becomes Meir, curve right at Meirburg on Eiermarkt, and head straight across Groenpl. around the cathedral. (☎232 01 03; fax 231 19 37. Open M-Sa 9am-6pm, Su 9am-5pm). To get to the modern **Jeugdherberg Op-Sinjoorke (HI),** Eric Sasselaan 2, take tram #2 (dir.: Hoboken) to Bouwcentrum, walk towards the fountain, take a left followed by an immediate right after the statue of the standing man, follow the street to the end, turn left, cross the bridge, and the hostel is in front of you in the park. (☎238 02 73. Breakfast included. Sheets 125BF. Lockout 10am-3pm. Dorms 420BF, nonmembers 520BF; doubles 585BF.) **Globetrotter's Nest,** Vlagstr. 25, is small, cozy, but slightly spartan in character. (☎236 99 28. Sheets 100BF. Breakfast included. 8-bed dorms 400BF; 4-bed dorm 430BF; doubles 1200BF.) To get to **Scoutel,** Stoomstr. 3, from the station, turn left on Pelikaanstr., left on Langekievitstr., and right on Stoomstr. (☎226 46 06; email soutel@vvskm.be. Breakfast included. Reception 8am-7pm. Singles 1050F, under 26 950BF; doubles 1610BF, 1410BF; triples 1995BF, 1755BF.) Near the Jeugdherberg Op-Sinjoorke, there is **camping** at **Sted. Kamp Vogelzangan.** Follow the directions to the hotel; when you get off the tram, and are facing the Bouwventrum, turn right and walk away from the fountain, cross the street to make your first let, and the campground will be on your left after the gates. (☎238 57 17. Open Apr.1-Sept.30. 65BF per person, 35BF per car, 35BF per tent, 85BF per tent with electricity.) **Ultimatum,** on the Grote Markt at Suiker Rui, has outdoor seating and "world kitchen" dishes from Norway, Russia, and Morocco. (☎232 58 53. Open Su-F 1pm-late, Sa 10am-late. Kitchen closes at 11pm.) Middle Eastern veggies are at **Mama's Garden,** at Papenstr. and Oude Korenmarkt. (Pitas 175-295BF. Open Su-Th noon-5am, F-Sa noon-7am.) After a night of partying, head to the **Kiekenhot,** Grote Markt 35, for chicken at 4am. (☎232 15 02. Open M-Th 6pm-4am, F 6pm-6am, Su 12:30pm-4am.) **Postal Code:** 2000.

GHENT (GENT)   ☎09

Ghent is a textile town that lives and breathes industrial pride. In the city center, the castle, cathedral, and Stadhuis stand as memoirs of a grand past, while the magnificent Socialist Working-People's Building, constructed with the dues collected by textile workers at the turn of the century, is a spot that nearly every local is attached to. Everyone's mother, grandfather, or great-aunt seems to have had a stake in the workers' long, glorious struggle for freedom from the sweatshops. One major victory occurred when managers gave the workers a week of vacation in 1860—a victory still celebrated as "10 Days Off," also known as the **Gentse Feesten** (Ghent festivities; July 14-23, 2001). The streets fill with puppet shows, street performers, live music, carnival rides, and great food and beer. Lovers of fine architecture will relish a trip to Ghent's city center, where they can see the castle, cathedral, and bell tower from which was suspended the largest, world-record-breaking flower basket in 2000. The revered **Gravensteen,** the Castle of the Counts, is a sprawling medieval fortress once used as a textile factory in the 19th century. (Open Apr.-Aug. 9am-6pm. Sept.-Mar 9am-5pm. 200BF, students 100BF.) Wind your way up the towering **Belfort** to experience some classic Hitchcock vertigo. (Open mid-Mar. to mid-Nov. daily 10am-12:30pm and 2pm-5:30pm. 100BF.) The **Stadhuis** (Town Hall) is a mix of Gothic and Renaissance architecture. A block away on Limburgstr., the 14th- to 16th-century **Sint-Baafskathedraal** boasts Jan Van Eyck's *Adoration of the Mystic Lamb,* also known as the *Ghent Altarpiece.* (☎225 16 26. Cathedral open daily 8:30am-6pm. Free. Altarpiece open M-Sa 9:30am-4:30pm, Su 1-4:30pm. Entrance and audio tour 100BF.) Head to Citadel Park, near the center, for the **Museum voor Schone Kunsten's** (Museum of Fine Arts) strong Flemish collection. (☎222 17 03. Open Tu-Su 9:30am-5pm. 100BF, students 50BF.) Also located in Citadel Park is the contemporary art collection at the **SMAK,** the **Stedelijk Museum voor Actuele Kunst.** (Open Tu-Su 10am-6pm; 200BF, students 150BF). From October to July 15, young scholars cavort in the cafes and discos near the university restaurant on **Overpoortstr. Vooruit,** a huge Art Deco bar on St-Pietersnieuwstr. was once the meeting place of the Socialist Party, and later was occupied by Nazis in WWII. (☎223 82 01. Open mid-Aug. to mid-July Su-Th 11:30am-2am, F-Sa 11:30am-3am.) Beer lovers flock to **Dulle Grief**, on the Vrijdagmarkt, for the 1.2 liter "Max" for 350BF and the traditional exchange of a shoe. (☎224 24 55. Open noon-12:30am, Su noon-7pm, M 5:30pm-12:30am.) The festivities of **10 Days Off** (☎269 09 45) bring 11 nights of international DJs to a different host-nightspot each year.

   Trains run from Sint-Pietersstation (accessible by tram 1 or 12) to Brussels (40min., 245BF) and Bruges (20min., 175BF). The **tourist office** is in the crypt of the the belfry, Sint-Baafsplein 17A, right at Botermarkt. (☎266 52 32. Open daily Apr.-Oct. 9:30am-6:30pm; Nov.-Mar. 9:30am-4:30pm.) The **Hotel Flandria**, Barrestraat 3, offers big breakfasts. (☎223 06 26; www.flandria-centrum.be. Reception 7am-9pm. Doubles 1400-1800BF.) **De Draeke (HI)**, St-Widostr. 11, in the shadow of a castle, blends into downtown Ghent despite its modernity. From the station, take tram #1, 10, or 11 to Gravensteen (15min.); head left, then head right on Gewad and right again on St-Widostr. (☎233 70 50. Breakfast included. Sheets 125BF. Reception 7:30am-11pm. Dorms 510BF; singles 820BF; doubles 1200BF; nonmembers add 100BF.) To get to **Camping Blaarmeersen,** Zuiderlaan 12, take bus #9 from Sint-Pietersstation and ask the driver to connect you to bus #38 to Blaarmeersen. When you get off, take the first street on your left to the end. (☎221 53 99. Open Mar. to mid-Oct. 130BF per person, 140BF per tent, 70BF per car.) Good meals run about 200BF; try around **Korenmarkt,** in front of the post office; **Vrijdagmarkt,** a few blocks from the town hall; and **St-Pietersnieuwstr.,** down by the university. Students meet up at **Magazyne,** Bredestraat 159, for cheap, hearty fare in the historic district. (☎234 07 08. Lunch served from 12-2pm, dinner from 6-10pm.) The **Fritz Tearoom,** Korte Dagsteeg Walpoorstr., has hot sandwiches, pasta, and great waffles. (Open daily 8am-6:30pm.) **Postal Code:** 9000.

WALLONIE

Although Wallonie lacks the world-class cities of the north, the castle-dotted **Ardennes** offer a relaxing hideaway, with excellent hiking trails and cool caves for exploring. The most exceptional portion of the Belgian Ardennes lies in the southeast corner, where gorgeous trainrides sweep through peaceful farmland. Though nature lovers will probably want to spend a night in this part of the Wallonie wilderness, urban addicts pressed for time can always enjoy the scenery on their way to Brussels, Paris, or Luxembourg City.

TOURNAI   ☎069

The first city liberated by Allied forces, Tournai's medieval old town escaped major damage in WWII. Once a Roman trading post and the original capital of France, Tournai is a peaceful town less touristed than its Flemish counterparts. The city's most spectacular sight is its Romanesque and Gothic **cathedral,** with a **treasure room** that houses medieval goldware and some of St. Thomas à Becket's threads. (☎84 34 69. Open Apr.-Oct. daily 9am-noon and 2-6pm; off-season until 4pm. Treasure room 30BF.) The stunning Art Nouveau building of the **Museum of Fine Arts,** Enclos Saint-Martin, houses a fine collection of Flemish paintings. (Open daily 10am-noon and 2-5:30pm. 120BF, students 80BF.) Tournai will celebrate Charles V's 501st birthday with an **international tapestry exhibit** in the summer of 2001, with tapestries from the Netherlands displayed on the Grand Place, at the Town Hall, and at the Museum of Tapestry. (All sites open W-M 10am-6pm.)

   Trains run from the station at pl. Cromberg (☎88 62 23) to Brussels-Midi (1hr., 350BF). To get to the **tourist office,** 14 Vieux Marché Aux Poteries, exit the station, walk straight to the city center (15min.), and go around the left side of the cathedral. (☎22 20 45; fax 21 62 21; email bureau.tourisme.tournai@skynet.be; www.tournai.be. Open M-F 9am-7pm, Sa 10am-1pm and 3-6pm, Su 10am-noon and

2-6pm.) The **Auberge de Tournai,** rue St-Martin, has great tapestries. Continue straight uphill from the tourist office or take bus #7 or 88 (40BF) from the station. (☎21 61 36; email tournai@laj.be. Sheets 130BF. Reception 9am-noon and 5-10pm. Dorms 430BF, nonmembers 530BF.) Fill up at **Pita Pyramid,** 7 rue de la Tête d'Or, in the Galerie les Arcades. (Pitas 140-210BF. Open M-Th 11:30am-2pm and 5:30pm-1am, F-Su until 2am.) Party around the **Grand-Place** and the canals.

NAMUR ☎081

The quiet city of **Namur,** in the heart of Wallonie, is the last sizeable outpost before the wilderness of the Ardennes. The nearby **hiking, biking, caving,** and **kayaking** options make it the best base for exploring the Ardennes. The foreboding **citadel,** on the top of a rocky hill to the south, was built by the Spanish in the Middle Ages, expanded by the Dutch in the 19th century, the site of a bloody battle in WWI, and occupied until 1978. Climb up, or take a **mini-bus** from the tourist office at Sq. Leopold and rue de Grognon (every hr., 40BF); the bus will let you off at the Citadel, where you can pick up a **tour** of the fortress. (Open daily 11am-5pm. 210BF.)

Trains link Namur to Brussels (1hr., 245BF). Two **tourist offices,** one a few blocks left of the train station at place de la Gare, facing rue Godefroid, and the other in the **Hôtel de Ville,** help plan excursions. (Train station ☎22 28 59, Hôtel de Ville ☎24 64 44; www.ville.namur.be. Both open daily 9:30am-6pm.) To reach the friendly **Auberge Félicien Rops (HI),** 8 av. Félicien Rops, take bus #3 directly to the door, or take bus #4 and ask the driver to let you off. (☎22 36 88. Breakfast included. Sheets 100BF. Laundry 240BF. **Bikes** 500BF per day. Reception 7:30am-1am. Dorms 440BF; singles 820BF; doubles 1210BF; nonmembers add 100BF.) To **camp** at **Les Trieux,** 99 rue des Tris, 6km away in Malonne, take bus #6. (☎44 55 83. Open Apr.-Oct. 85BF per person, 85BF per tent.) If you're in the mood for Italian, step into the 15th-century cellar of **La Cava,** rue de la Monnaie 20. (Main dishes 220-380BF. Open daily noon-11pm.) Try the regional Ardennes ham (from 70F) at one of the sandwich stands throughout the city, or stop at the **Match supermarket** in the city center.

🞎 **DAYTRIP FROM NAMUR: DINANT.** Dinant is a good base for climbing and kayaking excursions. In town, the imposing **citadel** rises over the river and the small town. Explore on your own, or ride the cable car up and try to follow along with one of the French tours. (Citadel 19F. Open daily 10am-6pm.) In recent years, authorities have become more strict about access to the **caves.** Go with an experienced guide. Bring a sweater to the tour of the chilly, cascade-filled caves of **La Grotte Merveilleuse,** route de Phillippeville 142. To reach the Grotte from the citadel, cross the bridge and take the second left onto rte. de Phillippeville. (☎ (082) 22 22 10. Open daily Apr.-Oct. 10am-6pm, Mar. and Nov. 11am-5pm. 190BF.) **Dakota Raid Adventure,** rue Saint Roch 17, leads rock-climbing daytrips in the area. (☎ (082) 22 32 43. Open daily 10am-5pm.) Dinant is accessible via **train** (15min., 130BF) or **bike** from Namur; on summer weekends, take a one-way river cruise (3½hr.) on the Meuse River. The **tourist office,** Quai Cadoux 8, helps plan kayaking trips. (☎ (082) 22 28 70; www.maison-du-tourisme.net. 1-person 650BF; 2-person 800-1000BF; 3-person 1100BF). With your back to the train station, turn right, take your first left, and then your next left will land you there.

HAN-SUR-LESSE ☎084

Famous for its privately-owned caves and wilderness park, Han-sur-Lesse's lesser known treasures are its glorious, oft-unused **hiking trails.** The caves, known as **grottoes,** can be seen on the combined tram-foot-boat trip sold at the **Domain of the Grottoes** office, rue J. Lamote. (☎37 72 13; email grotte-de-han@grotte-de-han.be. Tours every 30min. July-Aug. 10am-5:30pm; May-June daily 10am-noon and 1:30-6:30pm. Adults 395BF. Small tip expected for guides given in English.) Safari-cars voyage through the **Wilderness Reserve** of a local Han estate, where you can see cross-bred version of extinct animals, once typical in the Northern Ardennes and resurrected with a little help from the international animal gene pool, producing extremely hairy mules, small horses, and lots of wild pigs. (Adults 290BF.) Buses and safari-cars pick you up outside of the Domain for the respective expeditions.

Across the street from the Domain, the offical **tourist office,** 1 Place Theo Lannoy, sells standard maps of Han's five hiking trails for 100BF. All trails are manageable for ready and able walkers, though two involve steep peaks. (☎37 75 96; email han.tourisme@euronet.be. Open daily 9:30am-4pm. Closed weekends in Jan.) Han has neither train station nor bank machine. To get to Han, take **bus** #29 from the Jemelle train station (every hr. in coordination with incoming trains from Brussels, 63BF). From the bus stop, cross the street, take your first right, walk to the end of the street, and the **Gite d'Etape Hostel,** rue du Gite d'Etape 10, will be across the street. (☎37 74 41; email g.han@skynet.be. Sheets 160BF. Laundry 150BF. Reception 8am-10pm, winter until 8pm. Quads 1580BF. Cash only.)

⚡ DAYTRIP FROM HAN: ROCHEFORT. Nestled between Jemelle and Han is the town of Rochefort, which can be reached by **bus** #29 (43BF). This town is very French, so you'll likely have to dust off that pocket dictionary of yours. The **tourist office,** at rue de Behogne 5, gives information on Rochefort's **Grote de Lorette** and impressively grand **Château Comtel** archeological site. (☎21 25 37; email rochefort.tourisme@skynet.be.) The **Grote caves** are open from April to October by appointment (☎21 20 80). Hike up to the Château for a spectacular view of the Northern Ardennes, then visit the archeological museum perched alongside. (☎21 44 09. 60BF.) Stay at the **Hotel Central,** Place Albert 1. (☎21 10 44. Breakfast included. Reception 9am-11pm. Singles 1500BF; doubles 2000F; triples 3500BF.) Try the *prix-fixe* at **Le Relais du Château,** rue Jacquet 22, for 595BF. (☎21 09 81. Open noon-3pm and 6pm-late. Closed W except in August.)

BELGIUM

BRITAIN

BRITISH POUND

US$1 = UK£0.71	UK£1 = US$1.41
CDN$1 = UK£0.48	UK£1 = CDN$2.08
IR£1 = UK£0.78	UK£1 = IR£1.28
EUR€1 = UK£0.61	UK£1 = EUR€1.63
AUS$1 = UK£0.40	UK£1 = AUS$2.52
NZ$1 = UK£0.30	UK£1 = NZ$3.30
SAR1 = UK£0.10	UK£1 = SAR10.03

PHONE CODE **Country code: 44. International dialing prefix:** 00.

The past century has not been kind to the Empire. After Britain founded modern democracy, led the Industrial Revolution, spread colonies around the globe, and helped stave off a Nazi Europe in World War II, a former colony displaced it as the world's economic power. Today, the troubles in Northern Ireland underscore the problems of union and nationalism associated with the empire. Travelers should be aware that names hold political force. "Great Britain" refers to England, Scotland, and Wales; it's neither accurate nor polite to call a Scot or Welshman "English." The political term "United Kingdom" refers to these nations as well as Northern Ireland. Because of distinctions in laws and currency, *Let's Go* uses the term "Britain" to refer to England, Scotland, and Wales. At first glance, Britain may not seem quite exotic enough for travelers aching to dive into the unknown. Look beyond London and allow time for medieval castles, rugged coasts, eerie prehistoric monuments, and wild islands that hearken back to another era. For more detailed, exhilarating coverage of Britain and London, pore over *Let's Go: Britain & Ireland 2001* or *Let's Go: London 2001*.

SUGGESTED ITINERARIES

THREE DAYS Spend it all in **London** (p. 153), visiting the city of tea, royalty, and James Bond. After a stroll through **Hyde Park,** head to **Buckingham Palace** for the changing of the guard. Experience British colonialism first hand in the **British Museum** and the **National Gallery.** Spend a night at the **Royal National Theatre** and pub in the **East End.**

ONE WEEK Begin in **Oxford** (1 day; p. 197) and then spend a day wandering the streets of the Beatles' home of **Liverpool** (p. 215). Travel north to Scotland for a day in **Glasgow** (p. 240) and two days in lively **Edinburgh** (p. 232) before chugging back to **London** (2 days; p. 153).

BEST OF BRITAIN, THREE WEEKS Start in **London** (4 days; p. 153), where you'll spin from museums to theatre to a quiet pint to a cellar club all in a day.

Move on to **Oxford** (2 days; p. 197) and tour the colleges which have housed Prime Ministers, authors, and famous scientists. Then stop by **Cheltenham** and amble through the rolling hills of the **Cotswolds** (1 day; p. 203). Then head to Shakespeare's home town of **Stratford-upon-Avon** (1 day; p. 204). On to **Conwy** and **Caernarfon** (2 days; p. 230) for their castles, then to **Liverpool** (2 days; p. 215). Afterward, head to **Manchester** for its raucous nightlife (1 day; p. 214), before moving on to **Glasgow** (1 day; p. 240) and nearby **Loch Lomond** (1 day; p. 245). Swing by the **Isle of Arran** (1 day; p. 244) for rural diversions; you'll need the rest before exuberant **Edinburgh** (3 days; p. 232). Then head to the **Lake District** (2 days; p. 222), historic **York** (1 day; p. 217), and walk the halls of **Cambridge** (1 day; p. 207).

BRITAIN

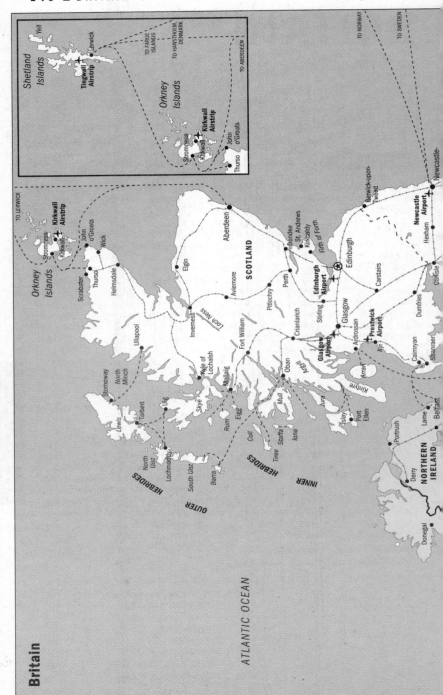

Britain

ATLANTIC OCEAN

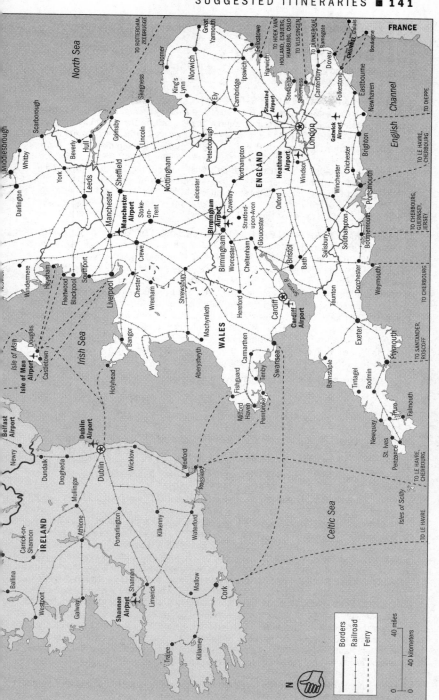

LIFE AND TIMES

HISTORY AND POLITICS

History will be kind to me, for I intend to write it.
— Winston Churchill

EARLY INVADERS (3100BC-500AD)

The stone circles at **Stonehenge** (see p. 192) and **Avebury** (see p. 192) bear mute witness to the isle's earliest inhabitants, whose peace was shattered by various Celtic and Roman invasions. The Romans under Caesar proved ultimately victorious and occupied southern Britain until AD 410, establishing **Londinium** as the Roman Empire's farthest outpost. The fierce resistance of the Pictish tribes in the north inspired the Romans to construct **Hadrian's Wall**—an edifice 112km long and 3.6m high—in an effort to limit the northern threat. The 4th century brought the decline of the Roman Empire, leaving Britain vulnerable to raids from still more foreigners. The Germanic tribes of Angles, Saxons, and Jutes established settlements and kingdoms alongside those of the resilient Celts.

CHRISTIANITY AND THE NORMANS (550-1100)

Roman Christianity officially arrived in AD 597 when eager missionary **St. Augustine** successfully converted King Æthelbert of Kent and founded England's first church, in Canterbury (see p. 188). Its spread was immortalized by the **Venerable Bede** in 731 with his *Ecclesiastical History of the English People*, in which he became the first to systematically employ the Anno Domini (AD) system of dating. Relative peace ensued until 1066, when William I (better known as **William the Conqueror**) of Normandy invaded England, winning the pivotal **Battle of Hastings,** and succeeded as King of England. William promptly set about cataloguing his new English acquisitions in the epic sheepskin **Domesday Book,** completed in 1088. This compilation of all landholders and their possessions has come to serve as the starting point of the written history of most English towns.

PLANTAGENETS AND TUDORS (1150-1530)

Henry II, a distant cousin of William I, ascended to the throne in 1154 and initiated the conquest of Ireland. His son, **Richard the Lionheart,** led the Third Crusade to Jerusalem, where he won access to the Holy Shrines. Soon after that expansion of power, noblemen, tired of royal abuses of authority, forced his brother King John to sign the **Magna Carta** in 1215 (see **Salisbury Cathedral,** p. 192). The document has been credited with laying the groundwork for modern democracy—the first **Parliament** convened 50 years later in 1265. While Britain was growing in land mass, the population suffered a serious blow under the **Black Death** which ravaged more than one third of all Britons between 1348 and 1361.

While King Richard II was on an Irish holiday in 1399, his cousin Henry Bolingbroke invaded Britain and snatched the throne. This bold move put the Lancasters in control, and gave Shakespeare something decent to write about. More Shakespearian subject matter was created when Henry V defeated the French in the **Battle of Agincourt** (1415), a victory for the British underdogs that soon became legendary. But his son Henry VI (despite being crowned King of France in 1431) blew it, lost all English land in France, was declared mad in 1453, and was eventually executed in the Tower of London. Henry VI was replaced by Richard, Duke of York, and eventually by Richard's son Edward IV, who led the Yorkists in the **Wars of the Roses** (1455-85). The boy-king Edward V ascended to the throne in 1483 at the tender age of 12, but was rapidly beheaded by his loving uncle Richard III.

After the turmoil of the Wars of the Roses, Henry VII emerged victorious and inaugurated the rule of the **House of Tudor,** a dynasty that survived until 1603. His successor, **Henry VIII,** reinforced England's imperialistic control over the Irish, proclaiming himself their king in 1542. In his infamous battle with the Pope over multiple marriages, that same Henry converted Britain from Roman Catholicism to Protestantism, establishing the Anglican Church and placing himself at its head in the **Act of Supremacy** of 1534.

REPUBLICANISM AND RESTORATION (1540-1670)

Despite Henry VIII's attempts to solidify the Protestant stronghold, his sudden death in 1547 did not really help the cause. Instead, it gave rise to the staunch Catholic **Bloody Mary**. In a nice spate of sibling rivalry, **Elizabeth I** reversed the religious convictions imposed by her sister, and cemented the success of the Reformation—under her reign the British defeated the **Spanish Armada** in 1588 to become the leading Protestant power in Europe.

Tensions erupted in the **English Civil Wars** (1642-51). The monarchy was abolished when Parliament saw to it that Charles I and his head parted ways, and the first British Commonwealth was founded in 1649. **Oliver Cromwell** emerged as a rebellious and adept military leader whose massacre of nearly half of the Irish earned him eternal bitterness from Britain's neighbor. Cromwell's son Richard succeeded him, but he lacked the leadership to retain the republic. Much to the relief of the masses, Charles II was brought back to power unconditionally in 1660. But the **Restoration** did not signal the end of the troubles: intense debate over the right of Charles II's fervently Catholic brother James II's to ascend to the throne during the **Exclusion Crisis** established two political parties, the Whigs (who were firmly Protestant) and the Tories (more Catholic).

PARLIAMENT AND THE CROWN (1680-1800)

The relatively bloodless **Glorious Revolution** erupted in 1688 to prevent James II from establishing a Catholic dynasty; Dutch Protestant William of Orange and his wife Mary were crowned when they agreed to the Bill of Rights. The ascension of **William and Mary** marked the end of a century of violent upheaval. The Bill of Rights quietly revolutionized the relationship between Crown and Parliament, bringing a triumphant Parliamentary leadership to the fore. Over the 18th century, the office of Prime Minister gradually eclipsed the monarchy as the seat of power in British government under the authority of the master negotiator **Robert Walpole** and the astute politician **William Pitt the Younger.**

EMPIRE AND INDUSTRY (EARLY 19TH-CENTURY)

During the 18th and 19th centuries, Britain came to rule more than one quarter of the world's population and two-fifths of its land, giving rise to the phrase "the sun never sets on the British Empire." To begin, the **Cape of Good Hope** was captured by the British in order to secure shipping routes to the far East. Parliament soon realized they were on to a good thing, acquiring all of Australia and New Zealand by 1840, and throwing in the Western Pacific Islands for good measure in 1877. Recognizing the wealth of India in 1857, Parliament requested that the East India Trading Company cede control of the sub-continent to the Crown, making the governmental control of the Empire complete.

The **Industrial Revolution** allowed Britain to attain the military and economic power necessary for colonization. In one of the greatest social changes in British history, massive portions of the rural populace migrated to towns, lured by growing opportunities in industrial employment. British entrepreneurs grew wealthy, as did the British government, giving both groups the means to enlarge the Empire. But world domination was not long lasting—the American colonies declared freedom in 1776, and as early as 1839 some Asian colonies began to accrue limited **self-determination.** Nationalistic movements accelerated greatly after World War I, and the majority of the British Empire was dissolved during the twentieth century. Since the 1997 turnover of **Hong Kong** to China, Britain's biggest colony is Bermuda.

THE VICTORIAN ERA (19TH-CENTURY)

The iron fist of **Queen Victoria** dominated the 19th century, in foreign and domestic politics, social changes, and even stylistic mores. She oversaw the beginnings of domestic industrial regulation, spurred by the combined force of class divisions and often frightening workplace conditions. The **Reform Act** of 1832 provided sweeping changes in working conditions while the **Chartist Movement** of the mid-19th century pressed for universal manhood suffrage. The 1840s also brought the

Irish famine, which killed over a million people and caused twice that many to emigrate. Increasing troubles with Ireland plagued the nation and Prime Minister **William Gladstone's** 1880 attempt to introduce a Home Rule Bill for Ireland splintered the Labor Party. Despite this, the government still faced the possibility of civil war in Ireland—a threat interrupted by the explosion of **World War I.**

THE WORLD WARS (1914-1945)

World War I brought British military action back to the European stage, but scarred the British spirit with the loss of a large part of a generation of young men. The technological explosion of the 19th century was evident in the new weapons and trench warfare introduced during the war. The gas attacks and the tanks caused unprecedented massive casualties on both sides. With the end of World War I, hope for a new beginning within England was generally lost even though women gained suffrage at this time. The 1930s brought depression and mass unemployment; during this period famed social economist **John Maynard Keynes** came to his fore. In December 1936, King Edward VIII shocked the world with the announcement of his abdication. Meanwhile, tensions in Europe were once again escalating with the German reoccupation of the Rhineland.

Despite attempts at **appeasement** with Hitler, peace could only last so long. In response to the German invasion of Poland, Britain declared war on Germany on September 3, 1939, thus precipitating the outbreak of **World War II.** The British were soon forced to face German air attacks as early as the summer of 1940, when the prolonged **Battle of Britain** began. London, Coventry, and other British cities were demolished by the bombings of the early 40s. The fall of France in 1940 precipitated the end of the Chamberlain government and the creation of a war cabinet led by the determined and eloquent **Winston Churchill.** American forces in Europe augmented the Allied effort in the 1944 **D-Day Invasion** of Normandy; the invasion swung the tide of the war and eventually brought peace to Europe in May 1945.

THE POST-WAR YEARS (1946-1979)

The growing affluence and diversity of the postwar era propelled Britain to the center stage of international popular culture. The extension of the welfare state with the creation of the **National Health Service** in 1946, guaranteed government-funded medical care to all Brits. **Edward Heath** finally succumbed to the pressures of the continent and Britain joined the **European Community** in 1971, a union that has received a rocky welcome from some British MPs and citizens.

Increasing economic problems in the 1970s stemmed from Britain's colonial retreat. Conservative and Labour governments alike floundered in attempts to curtail unemployment while maintaining a base level of social welfare benefits. Government after government wrangled with labor unions, culminating in a series of public-service strikes in early 1979, called the **"Winter of Discontent,"** which literally left piles of trash lying in the streets.

THE THATCHER YEARS AND BEYOND (1980-PRESENT)

It was against this backdrop that Britain grasped for change, electing the Tory **Margaret Thatcher** as Prime Minister, putting faith in her nationalism and Victorian values. Thatcher's term seemed hexed by painful economic recession, but by 1983 British victory against Argentina in the territorial dispute for the **Falkland Islands** and the embarrassing disarray in the Labour Party clinched her second term. Thatcher turned from the war in the islands to "the enemy within," referring to the labor unions, while denationalizing and dismantling the welfare state with legislation and quips like "there is no such thing as society."

Thatcher's policies brought dramatic prosperity to many, but sharpened the divide between rich and poor. Thatcher's undoing came with her refusal to let go of the unpopular **poll tax** and her resistance to the European Community. Though still divided on Europe, the Tory Party conducted a vote of no-confidence that led to Thatcher's 1990 resignation and the intra-party election of **John Major** as prime minister. In 1993, the British pound toppled out of the EC's monetary regulation system, embarrassing Major's government.

Even with these Conservative debacles, Labour failed again to shed the image of ineffectiveness gained in the 70s, and the Torries won another five years in April 1992. However, Major struggled with unpopularity and by 1995 the Conservatives began to lose parliamentary seats and to languish in the polls. The Labour Party, under the leadership of charismatic **Tony Blair,** cut ties with the labor unions, refashioned itself into the alternative for discontented voters, and finally began to rise in popularity.

BRITAIN TODAY
Despite tense relations with unions, the "new" Labour Party claimed a clear victory under Blair in the May 1997 elections, garnering the biggest Labour majority in history. In 1998, Blair nurtured closer relations with the EU, maintained a moderate economic and social position, and was named one of *People Magazine's* 50 Most Beautiful People. All in all, not a bad year for Tony. 1999 was more turbulent, with Britain's stance in the Kosovo crisis gaining Blair the title of "little Clinton" for his blind following of American foreign policy. Under Blair, Britain has held fast to its refusal to officially adopt the **euro** (a unified European currency). Both Parliament and citizens are concerned that adopting the euro will result in a decrease in economic independence and national sovereignty.

National sovereignty has become a key issue on the domestic front as well. In a September 1997 referendum, Scotland voted for **Scottish devolution,** providing the Scots with their own Parliament and the possibility of independence. Not one to be left behind for long, the **Welsh** also demanded more political autonomy while still retaining 40 MPs in Parliament. May 1999 brought a new step toward Constitutional reform when Labour removed the majority of the hereditary "peers" in the **House of Lords** in an effort to create a more democratic and representative body.

ROYALTY TODAY. It's not easy being Queen Elizabeth II. There has been no end of unabashedly publicized disaster. In 1992 over a hundred rooms in **Windsor Palace** burned, and in 1993 the Queen began to pay income tax. The sad spectacle of royal life took a tragic turn in 1997 as a car carrying **Princess Diana** fatally crashed in a tunnel in Paris. The outpouring of grief from a considerable portion of Brits has been likened to the public reaction to the death of President John F. Kennedy or Prime Minister Winston Churchill.

Most recently, royal-watchers are hoping that the marriage of the youngest royal brother, **Edward,** who tied the knot in the summer of 1999 to public relations specialist **Sophie Rhys-Jones,** will fare better than those of his three divorced siblings. However, it is clearly the young **Prince William** on whom the spotlight shines brightest.

THE ARTS

LITERATURE
From its humble roots as an obscure Germanic dialect, the English language has evolved into a collage of Saxon and Norman words, plus countless borrowings from other languages. Today it is the true lingua franca, serving as the voice of people far removed from the Isles.

OLD ENGLISH AND THE MIDDLE AGES. Perhaps the finest piece of Old English poetry for which record does exist is **Beowulf.** Dated tenuously at the first half of the 7th century, the rhythmic religious poem details the prince Beowulf's struggle against the monster Grendel. **Geoffrey Chaucer,** writing centuries later, tapped into the spirited side of Middle English; his *Canterbury Tales* (c. 1387) remain some of the funniest—and sauciest—stories in the English canon. The need to adapt religious material into a form understood by the masses led **John Wycliffe** and his followers to make the first translation of the **Bible** into English in the 1380s, an act which gave the English language credibility. In the mid-16th century King James sent 47 translators to bring forth a Word of God the Protestant King could tolerate. The resulting **King James Version,** completed in 1611, rumbles with magnificent pace and rhetoric, and remains a literary monument to this day.

SHAKESPEARE MADE EASY

To have great sex.	"Put a ducat in her clack-dish" (*Measure for Measure*)
This guy from Iceland's a moron, and I hate him.	"Pish for thee, Iceland dog! Thou prick-ear'd cur of Iceland!" (*Henry V*)
Some guy in a bar is annoying you.	"Thou art a boil, a plague-sore, or embossed carbuncle, in my corrupted blood" (*King Lear*)
You kicked his butt and want to tell your friends.	"I took by the throat the circumcised dog, and smote him, thus." (*Othello*)

THE ENGLISH RENAISSANCE. Advances in education and printing technology together allowed writers to reach a large market of readers, which caused a flourishing of English literature under Elizabeth I. **John Donne,** the pastor of London's St. Paul's Cathedral and the English language's first urban poet, wrote introspective devotional poetry and penned erotic verse on the side. The era's greatest contributions to English literature came in drama, with the appearance of the first professional playwrights. **Christopher Marlowe** guided *Tamburlaine* (c. 1587) and *Dr. Faustus* (c. 1588) into the English conscience. But the English literary figure par excellence is still **William Shakespeare,** who mixed high and low to create some of the finest comedies, histories, and tragedies ever to grace the world. An entire town bustles year-round in tribute to the man (see **Stratford-upon-Avon,** p. 204), but his plays, from *The Comedy of Errors* (1592) to *The Tempest* (1612), remain the truest monuments to his genius.

GODS AND MEN. The British Puritans of the late 16th and early 17th centuries produced a huge volume of obsessive and beautiful literature. In *Paradise Lost* (1667), the epic poem to end all epic poems, blind **John Milton** gave Satan, Adam, and Eve a complexity the Bible did not grant them. Another Puritan vision came from **John Bunyan,** whose *Pilgrim's Progress* (1678) charts the Christian's quest for redemption in a world awaiting the apocalypse. The major literary figure and critic of the late 18th century was **Samuel Johnson,** whose greatest achievement was spending nine years writing the first definitive English **dictionary.**

THE ENGLISH NOVEL COMES INTO ITS OWN. In 1719, **Daniel Defoe** inaugurated the era of the English novel with his popular island-bound *Robinson Crusoe.* **Jane Austen** brought the novel to new heights, slyly criticizing self-importance in *Pride and Prejudice* (1813) and *Emma* (1815). The harsh industrialization of the Victorian period spawned numerous classic novels: **Charles Dickens's** often biting, sometimes sentimental works, like *A Christmas Carol* (1843) draw on the bleakness of his childhood (see **Portsmouth,** p. 190). From their Haworth home, the **Brontë sisters** composed works of great intensity: Emily's *Wuthering Heights* (1847), and Charlotte's *Jane Eyre* are outstanding examples. **Thomas Hardy** brought the Victorian age to an end on a dark note in the fate-ridden Wessex landscapes of *Jude the Obscure* (1895) and *Tess of the d'Urbervilles* (1891). Like Hardy, **George Eliot's** skepticism drew her to the security of traditional village life. Her *Middlemarch* (1871) depicts the entangled lives of an entire town.

Partly in reaction to the rationalism of the preceding century, the early 19th century saw the rise of the Romantic literary movement. The beginning of Romanticism in Britain is generally considered to have come with the joint publication of *Lyrical Ballads* in 1798 by **William Wordsworth** and **Samuel Taylor Coleridge.** Their later colleagues were plagued by early deaths: **John Keats** died of tuberculosis at 26, while **Percy Bysshe Shelley** drowned off the Tuscan coast at 29. Meanwhile, the poetry of the Victorian age struggled with the impact of societal changes. **Alfred Lord Tennyson** spun gorgeous verse about faith and doubt for over a half-century, while **Matthew Arnold** rebelled against the industrialization of literature.

THE MODERN AGE. After World War I, London became the home of artistic movements like the **Bloomsbury Group,** pulling the world's intellects into its midst. **Virginia Woolf,** a key group member, explored the private yearnings of the mind in *To the Lighthouse* (1927). Sometimes associated with the group, **T.S. Eliot's** *The Waste Land* (1922), one of this century's most important poems, is a picture of a fragmented, motionless world waiting for the end. Although he spoke only a few words of English when he arrived in the country aged 21, **Joseph Conrad** proceeded to masterfully employ the language to examine evil in *Heart of Darkness* (1902).

LATE 20TH CENTURY LITERATURE. In 1949, **George Orwell's** *1984* depicted a ravenous totalitarian state striving to strip the world of memory and words of meaning. Later, the end of Empire and rising affluence splintered British literature in a thousand directions. Nostalgia pervades the poems of **Philip Larkin** and **John Betjeman,** which search for beauty amidst knowledge of mortality, in contrast to the vigorous poems of the Yorkshire-raised **Ted Hughes** and **Tony Harrison.** Postcolonial voices have also become an important literary force in an increasingly multicultural country. **Timothy Mo** examines British rule in East Asia in *An Insular Possession* (1986). **Salman Rushdie's** spellbinding *Midnight's Children* (1981) is a glorious amalgam of Indian myth and modern culture. British playwrights, as always, continue to innovate. **Tom Stoppard** challenged everything you knew about theater in grim yet hysterical plays like *Rosencrantz and Guildenstern are Dead* (1967).

FINE ARTS

British art has long been dominated by continental influences; however, in the 18th century English artists came into their own. **Sir Joshua Reynolds** (1723-92) was one of the most prominent portraitists of the 18th century and in 1768 he helped found the Royal Academy of Art, now located in Piccadilly. In the 19th century, **J.M.W. Turner** (1775-1851) glorified the English countryside with his light-filled landscape paintings. The art of illustration flourished in this period, typified by the output of mystic artist and lyric poet **William Blake** (1757-1827). The 20th century has seen revolutionary ideas shaking traditional artistic concepts. The disturbing, meat-filled portraits of **Francis Bacon** (1909-1992) have transformed British portraiture, while **Henry Moore** (1898-1986) has set major trends in 20th century sculpture.

ARCHITECTURE

British architecture has traditionally been based on the ecclesiastical model of cloisters and courtyard. Oxford's colleges (see p. 197), especially **New College** and **Balliol College,** are structured in this manner, as are the law offices and residences in London's **Inns of Court,** the **Houses of Parliament** (see p. 168), and many other official buildings and even housing around a London square. **Inigo Jones** added an Italian flare to the Covent Garden piazza (see p. 171). The 1666 **Great Fire of London** destroyed more than 13,000 houses in the center of the city and halted the use of wood and straw as building materials. The fire also gave **Christopher Wren** an opportunity to work his magic rebuilding **St. Paul's Cathedral** (see p. 172). Centuries later, the destruction of the centers of London and Coventry in World War II let British architects think outside traditional patterns. London's industrial docklands were replaced with **Canary Wharf,** one of the few skyscrapers in London, while parts of Coventry's bombed cathedral can be seen interwoven with the striking new one. Other post-war buildings include the **Barbican** Arts Complex (see p. 174), which uses modern style choices around traditional courtyards. The original square mile of Londinium has also seen some considerable renovation in recent years—**Richard Rodgers' Lloyd's Building** (see p. 173) places futuristic metal design next to Victorian spiraling chimneys. Travelers using Stansted Airport will get to see **Sir Norman Foster's** glorious use of glass and metal tree like forms.

BRITAIN

MUSIC

CLASSICAL. Britain was long called "a land without music." While this isn't entirely true, recognized British masterpieces are few and far between. The late 19th century did, however, see **Gilbert and Sullivan** produce opperettas filled with social satire, and farce, such as *The Mikado* and *H.M.S. Pinafore*. Serious music in Britain began a renaissance in the late 19th century under **Edward Elgar**, whose pomp is outweighed by circumstances of eloquence, like his "Enigma Variations."

THE BRITISH ARE COMING. Britain has continually been the source of much innovation in popular music in its various incarnations. After World War II, imported American rock and blues provided musical inspiration for the first wave of "British Invasion" rock groups. From Liverpool (see p. 215), **The Beatles** stood at the fore of every musical and cultural trend, spinning out the classic songs that became part of the international cultural vocabulary. Their Satanic Majesties **The Rolling Stones** became London's harder-edged answer to the Fab Four. **The Who** began as Kinks-like popsters, then expanded into "rock operas" like *Quadrophenia* and *Tommy*. Psychedelic drugs and high hopes spawned guitar heroes **Eric Clapton** and **Jimmy Page**, who went on to dominate mass markets in the 70s through their bands (**Cream** and **Led Zeppelin** respectively). The same period also saw the release of albums by "progressive-rock" groups like **Yes, Genesis,** and **Pink Floyd.**

ANARCHY IN THE UK. The theatrical excess of **Queen** and **Elton John** characterized mid-70s rock. "Pub rock" groups tried to return rock to the people, leading to the punk movement. The **Sex Pistols** kicked it off and indelibly marked music and culture while **The Clash** made political punk with an idealistic leftist slant. Perhaps the most popular of punk's first-wave bands among the British was **The Jam.** Long before Girl Power sloganeering, the all-female **Slits** mixed their punk with reggae. Inspired by punk's DIY ethos, but adding synthesizers, **The Cure** shook teens everywhere. From the same anti-establishment impulses as punk came the metal of **Ozzy Osbourne** and **Iron Maiden,** which was much less acclaimed but still attracted a cult following. Sheffield's **Def Leppard** took the hard-rock-big-hair ethic through the 80s.

SYNTH-POP, INDIE, AND DANCE. Alas, punk died an angry death with **Sid Vicious,** leaving the music scene increasingly receptive to the burgeoning field of electronic music. **Duran Duran** and the **Eurythmics** may have more successfully crossed the Atlantic to dominate American charts, but **Depeche Mode** and the ever-witty **The Pet Shop Boys** refined the synth-pop message and kept the home crowds dancing through the night. The producing machine of **Stock, Aitken, and Waterman** churned out a string of embarrassingly catchy hits, while **Wham!** managed to be equally embarrassing on their own. Fortunately, Manchester took on the role of center of musical development throughout the 80s. This, in turn, evolved in the mid-90s into the sounds of a diverse range of indie bands held together under the "Britpop" label, including the Beatles-esque **Oasis,** the glam **Suede,** and the wry **Blur.**

The pop charts have also been subject to the musical stylings of the **Spice Girls** and the extremely successful **Robbie Williams.** The music of other cultures, including the sitar-tinged Indian sounds of **Cornershop,** continues to influence the direction of British pop, keeping it fresh. The rave scene (and the synthetic drugs that accompanied it) exploded in Britain in the late 80s, while The Big Beat dance-rock sound of **The Chemical Brothers** and **Fatboy Slim** continue to draw the punters into the clubs. Britain in the new millenium continues to stake its long-standing claim on musical innovation with the 'in the house music' of **Basement Jaxx** and the drum 'n' bass of **Roni Size** and **Reprazent.**

FILM

The British film industry experienced its first major success with **Laurence Olivier's** glorious *Henry V* (1944). Master of suspense **Alfred Hitchcock** snared audiences with numerous films including *Dial M for Murder* (1954) and *Psycho* (1960). **David Lean** employed the brilliant **Sir Alec Guinness** as his lead in *Lawrence of Arabia* (1962) and in *Dr. Zhivago* (1965). Guinness is now famous as the original Obi-

FLAKES AND SMARTIES British food has character (of one sort or another), and the traditional menu is a mad hodgepodge of candy, crisps, yeasts, and squashes. Britain has a greater variety of **candy** for sale than most countries. Brands to watch out for include Flake by Cadbury, Crunchies (made out of honeycombed magic), and the ever-popular Smarties. Watch out for the orange ones—they're made of orange chocolate. Potato chips, or **crisps** as they are known in England, are not just salted, but come in a range of flavors, including Prawn Cocktail, Beef, Chicken, Fruit 'n' Spice, and the more traditional Salt & Vinegar. All this sugar and salt can be washed down with pineapple-and-grapefruit-flavored soda Lilt or a can of Ribena, a red currant syrup which has to be diluted with water. This latter beverage belongs to a family of drinks known as **squash,** all of which are diluted before consumption. But the food that expatriate Britons miss most is **Marmite,** a yeast extract which is spread on bread or toast. If you weren't fed Marmite as a baby, you'll never appreciate it; most babies don't either.

Wan Kenobi. The 60s phenomenon of "swingin' London" created new momentum for the British film industry and jump-started international interest in British culture. Scot **Sean Connery** drank the first of many martinis, shaken not stirred, as **James Bond** in *Dr. No* (1962). Adopted Brit **Stanley Kubrick** went beyond the infinite without leaving England in *2001: A Space Odyssey* (1968) and descended into mayhem in *A Clockwork Orange* (1971).

Elaborate costume dramas and offbeat, independent films have come to represent contemporary British film. The heroic sagas of **Hugh Hudson's** *Chariots of Fire* (1981) and **Richard Attenborough's** *Gandhi* (1982) swept the Oscars in successive years. The comedic group Monty Python created two instant cult favorites in *Monty Python and the Holy Grail* (1974) and *Monty Python's Life of Brian* (1979). The British Tourist Authority produces a "Movie Map" listing more than 200 movie locations across the country.

FOOD AND DRINK

British cuisine's deservedly lackluster reputation redeems itself in a few areas. Britain is largely a nation of carnivores; the best native dishes are the roasts—beef, lamb, and Wiltshire hams. And meat isn't just for dinner; the British like their famed breakfasts meaty and cholesterol-filled. Before you leave the country, you must try any of the sweet, glorious British puddings. The "plough man's lunch" consists of cheese, bread, and salt. Caffs are the British equivalent of US dinners. To escape English food, try Chinese, Greek or especially Indian cuisine. British **"tea"** refers both to a drink and a social ritual. Tea the drink is served strong and milky; if you want it any other way, say so in advance. Tea the social can be a meal unto itself. Afternoon high tea, served around 4pm, includes cooked meats, salad, sandwiches and pastries. Cream tea, a specialty of Cornwall and Devon, includes toast, shortbread, crumpets, scones, jam, and clotted cream.

The British pub is truly a social institution. Drinks (mostly beer) are generally served from 11am to 11pm, Sundays noon to 10:30pm. British beer is usually served room temperature. Lager (the European equivalent of American beer) is served colder though. "Real ales" are beers naturally carbonated by an ongoing fermentation process. Traditional cider, a fermented apple juice, is a potent and tasty alternative to beer. Pub grub is fast, filling, and generally cheap.

ESSENTIALS

DOCUMENTS AND FORMALITIES

EU citizens do not need a visa to enter Britain or Ireland. For visits of less than six months, citizens of Australia, Canada, New Zealand, South Africa, and the US do not need a visa to enter.

BRITAIN

British Embassies and High Comissions at Home: Australia, British High Commission, Commonwealth Ave., Yarralumla, Canberra, ACT 2600 (☎ (02) 6270 6666; fax (02) 6273 3236; www.uk.emb.gov.au); **Canada,** British High Commission, 80 Elgin St., Ottawa, K1P 5K7 (☎ (613) 237 1530; www.britain-in-canada.org); **Ireland,** British Embassy, 29 Merrion Rd., Ballsbridge, Dublin 4 (☎ (01) 205 3700; www.britishembassy.ie); **New Zealand,** British High Commission, 44 Hill St., Thorndon, Wellington 1 (☎ (04) 472 6049; www.brithighcomm.org.nz); **South Africa,** British High Commission, 91 Parliament St., Cape Town 8001 (☎ (021) 461 7220) and at 255 Hill St., Arcadia 0083, Pretoria (☎ (012) 483 1200; www.britain.org.za); **US,** British Embassy, 3100 Massachusetts Ave. NW, Washington, D.C. 20008 (☎ (202) 588-6500; www.britainusa.com/bis/embassy/embassy.stm).

Foreign Embassies in Britain: All foreign embassies are in **London** (p. 153).

TRANSPORTATION

BY PLANE. Most flights into Britain that originate outside Europe land at **London's Heathrow** and **Gatwick** airports. Flights from Europe also hit **Luton** and **Stansted,** near London, as well as **Cardiff, Liverpool, Manchester, Edinburgh,** and **Glasgow.**

BY TRAIN. There is no longer a single national rail company, although the various companies are often still referred to under the umbrella of "British Rail." Prices and schedules often change: find up-to-date information from **National Rail Inquiries** (☎ (08457) 48 49 50), or online at **Railtrack** (www.railtrack.co.uk; no price information). Despite multiple providers, rail service in Britain is extensive (and expensive). The **BritRail Pass,** available to non-British travelers outside Britain, allows unlimited travel in England, Wales, and Scotland (8-day US$265, under 26 US$215; 22-day US$505, under 26 US$355). The one-year **Young Person's Railcard,** (£18) which grants 33% off most fares in addition to discounts on some ferries, is available to those ages 16 to 25, and to full-time students at British universities over age 23, at major British Rail Travel Centres in the UK. **Eurail** is not valid in Britain.

BY BUS. Long-distance coach travel in Britain is more extensive than in most European countries, and is the cheapest option. **National Express** (☎ (08705) 80 80 80; www.nationalexpress.co.uk) is the principal operator of long-distance coach services in Britain, although **Scottish Citylink** (☎ (08705) 50 50 50) has extensive coverage in Scotland. **Discount Coachcards** are available for seniors (over 50), students, and young persons (ages 16-25) for £8 and reduce fares on National Express by about 30%. For those planning a lot of coach travel, the **Tourist Trail Pass** offers unlimited travel for a number of days within a given period (2 days out of 3 £49, students, seniors, and children £39; 5 out of 10 £85/£69; 7 out of 21 £120/£94; 14 out of 30 £187/£143).

BY FERRY. Numerous ferry lines ply the route across the English Channel; the most popular crossing is from **Dover** to **Calais, France.** Always ask about reduced fares—an HI card or ISIC with Travelsave stamps might mean a 25 to 50% discount. Book ahead June through August. Other routes between the Continent and England include Bergen, Norway to Lerwick or Newcastle; Esbjerg, Denmark to Harwich; Göteborg, Sweden to Harwich or Newcastle; Hamburg to Harwich or Newcastle; Oostende, Belgium to Ramsgate, near Dover; and Hook of Holland to Harwich. For info on boats from **Wales** to **Dublin** and **Rosslare, Ireland,** see p. 224; from **Scotland** to **Belfast,** see p. 232; and from **England** to the **Continent,** see p. 188.

BY CAR. Brits drive on the left side of the road; enter traffic circles by turning left as well. **Gas,** usually called petrol, averages about US$4 per gallon. **Roads** are generally well maintained, but parking in London is impossible and traffic is slow. In Britain, rotaries are called "roundabouts," overpasses are "flyovers," traffic jams are "tail-backs," and the breakdown lane is the "lay-by." The trunk of a car is the "boot."

BY BIKE AND BY THUMB. Much of Britain's countryside is well suited for **biking.** Many cities and villages have bike rental shops and maps of local cycle routes;

ask at the tourist office. Large-scale Ordnance Survey maps detail the extensive system of long-distance **hiking** paths. Tourist offices and National Park Information Centres can provide extra information about routes. *Let's Go* does not recommend **hitchhiking**; it is illegal on motorways (roads labeled "M") and always risky.

TOURIST SERVICES AND MONEY

EMERGENCY	Police, ambulance, fire: ☎999.

TOURIST OFFICES. The **British Tourist Authority** (BTA; www.visitbritain.com) is an umbrella organization coordinating the activities of the four separate UK tourist boards outside the UK.

Tourist Boards at Home: Australia, Level 16, Gateway, 1 Macquarie Pl., Circular Quay, Sydney NSW 2000 (☎ (02) 9377 4400; www.visitbritain.com/au); **Canada,** Air Transat Bldg., 5915 Airport Rd., Suite 120, Mississauga, Ont. L4V 1T1 (☎ (888) 847 4885 or (905) 405 1840; www.visitbritain.com/ca); **New Zealand,** 17th fl., Fay Richwhite Building, 151 Queen Street, Auckland 1 (☎ (09) 303 1446); **South Africa,** Lancaster Gate, Hyde Park Ln., Hyde Park, Sandton 2196 (☎ (011) 325 0343); **US,** 551 Fifth Ave. #701, New York, NY 10176 (☎ (800) 462-2748 or (212) 986-2200; www.travelbritain.org).

CURRENCY AND EXCHANGE. The **Pound Sterling** is the main unit of currency in the United Kingdom. It is divided into 100 pence, issued in standard denominations of 1p, 2p, 5p, 10p, 20p, 50p, and £1 in coins, and £5, £10, £20, and £50 in notes. (Scotland uses a £1 note, and you may see the discontinued £2 coin.) Scotland has its own bank notes, which can be used interchangeably with English currency, though you may have difficulty using Scottish £1 notes outside Scotland.

Prices: Britain is expensive. Expect to spend anywhere from £15-30 per person per day, depending on where you choose to visit. Accommodations start at about £6 a night for a bed in a hostel in rural areas, or £12 per night in a B&B, while a basic sit-down meal at a pub costs about £5. London in particular is a budget-buster, with £25-35 a day being the bare minimum for accommodations, food, and transport.

Tipping and bargaining: Tips in restaurants are usually included in the bill (sometimes as a "service charge") if gratuity is not included then you should tip 10-15%. Tipping the barman in pubs is not at all expected, though a waiter or waitress should be tipped. Taxi drivers should receive a 10% tip, and bellhops and chambermaids usually expect somewhere between £1 and £3. Aside from open-air markets, don't expect to barter anywhere else, including hostels, taxis, and tour guides.

Taxes: Britain has a 17.5% **Value Added Tax (VAT),** a sales tax applied to everything except food, books, medicine, and children's clothing. The tax is included within the price indicated—no extra expenses should be added at the register.

ACCOMMODATIONS AND CAMPING

Youth hostels in Britain are run by the **Youth Hostels Association (YHA) of England and Wales** and the **Scottish Youth Hostels Association (SYHA).** Unless noted as "self-catering," the YHA hostels listed in *Let's Go* (not including SYHA ones) offer cooked meals at standard rates—breakfast £3.20, small/standard packed lunch £2.80/£3.65, evening meal £4.15 (or £4.80 for a three-course meal in some hostels), and children's meals (breakfast £1.75, lunch or dinner £2.70). In Britain, a bed in a hostel will cost around £6 in rural areas, £12 in larger cities, and £13-20 in London.

For a cozier alternative to impersonal hotel rooms, **B&Bs** and guest houses (often private homes with rooms available to travelers) range from the acceptable to the sublime. **Bed and Breakfast (GB),** 94-96 Bell St., Henley-on-Thames, Oxon, England RG9 1XS (☎ (01491) 57 88 03), is a reservation service which covers England, Scotland, Wales, and Ireland. It books rooms for a minimum deposit of £30, which is not refundable, but can be deducted from the total price of your stay. **Campsites** tend to be privately owned, with basic ones costing £3 per person, and posh ones costing up to £10 per person. It is illegal to camp in national parks, since much of their land is privately owned.

COMMUNICATION

MAIL. To send a **postcard** to another European country costs UK36p; to send one to any other international destination via airmail costs UK40p. To send a **letter** within Britain costs 27p/19p (1st/2nd-class). To send one via airmail to another European country (including the Republic of Ireland) costs 36p (up to 20g), and to a non-European international destination costs 45p for letters up to 10g, and 65p for letters weighing 10-20g. Address *Poste Restante* letters to the post office, highlighting the last name (for example Virgil BARNES, *Poste Restante*, New Bond St. Post Office, Bath BA1 1A5, United Kingdom).

TELEPHONES. Public pay phones in Britain are mostly run by **British Telecom (BT).** The BT phonecard, available in denominations from £2-20, is probably a useful purchase, since BT phones tend to be omnipresent. Public phones charge a minimum of 10p for calls, and don't accept 1p, 2p, or 5p coins. For **directory inquiries,** which are free from payphones, call 192 in Britain. **International direct dial numbers** include: **AT&T,** ☎ (0800) 890011; **BT Direct,** ☎ (0800) 345144; **Canada Direct,** ☎ (0800) 890016; **MCI WorldPhone Direct,** ☎ (0800) 890222; **Sprint Global One,** ☎ (0800) 890877; and **Telkom South Africa Direct,** ☎ (0800) 890027.

INTERNET ACCESS. Britain is one of the world's most online countries, and cybercafes can usually be found in larger cities. They cost £4-6 an hour, but often you can pay only for time used, not for the whole hour. On-line guides to cybercafes in Britain and Ireland that are updated daily include **The Cybercafe Search Engine** (http://cybercaptive.com) and **Cybercafes.com** (www.cybercafes.com).

LANGUAGE. The official languages are English and Welsh. Scottish Gaelic, though unofficial, is spoken in some parts of Scotland along with English.

LOCAL FACTS

Time: Britain is often on Greenwich Mean Time (GMT), but "British Summer Time" (late-Mar. to late-Oct.) is 1hr. ahead of GMT.

Climate: In summer, temperatures average 55-70°F (12-21°C); in winter, 36-41°F (2-7°C). The mild temperatures are often accompanied by rain. Spring is a good time to visit the countryside.

Holidays in 2000: New Year's Day (Jan. 1); Good Friday (Apr. 21); Easter Sunday and Monday; May Day (May 1); Bank holiday (May 29); and Christmas (Dec. 25-26). Scotland also kicks back on Jan. 2 and Aug. 7 (both bank holidays).

Festivals: The largest festival in the world is the Edinburgh International Festival (Aug.). Manchester's Gay Village hosts Mardi Gras (late Aug.). Muddy fun abounds at the Glastonbury Festival. Highland Games offer caber-tossing goodness in Edinburgh (mid-July).

ENGLAND

A land where there is the promise of a cup of tea just beyond even the darkest moor, England, for better or worse, has determined the meaning of "civilized" for many peoples and cultures. Unfortunately coasting on its Victorian domination, English civilization began to become a bit stagnant. However, its 20th-century image as the aging seat of a dying empire has made a remarkable turn-around in recent years. England is now the heart of "Cool Britannia," a young, fashionable, hip image of a country looking forward. The avant-garde has emerged from behind the sensible plaid skirts of the mainstream and taken center stage. More than ever, England is embracing its sizable immigrant communities and allowing the venerable class boat to be rocked. But traditionalists can rest easy; for all the moving and shaking in the large metropolis, around the corner there are a handful of quaint towns, dozens of picturesque castles, and a score of comforting cups of tea.

LONDON ☎ 020

The pubs may close early, but London buzzes around-the-clock with 24-hour cafes and clubbing that runs through mid-morning. London past and present coexist seamlessly: history buffs can imagine London into centuries past, while a trip to one of Soho's futuristic boutiques will eclipse any impression, culled from bobbies and Big Ben, that London is chained to bygone days. Nightlife includes everything from jazz to dancing, the classical music is unparalleled, and the theater is perhaps the finest in the world. Fashion trends bloom and die here—see it in London and you'll see it in North America six months later. Despite the stereotypes about British food, London has steadily gained status as a culinary hotspot. Its multinational population has spiced British cuisine with an array of flavors and now, Indian food is just as common as bangers and mash. If you expected a city full of Queen-loving, tea-drinking, tweed-wearing gardeners with bad teeth, you'll be surprised at London's vibrance (and at how well Londoners care for their teeth). For an absolutely smashing little book, peruse *Let's Go: London 2001*.

■ GETTING THERE AND AWAY

Flights: Heathrow Airport (☎ 8759 4321; www.baa.co.uk) is the world's busiest airport. The **Heathrow Express** (www.heathrowexpress.com) train goes between Heathrow terminals 1-4 and Paddington Station (every 15min. 5:10am-11:40pm, £12). From **Gatwick Airport** (☎ (01293) 53 53 53), take the BR Gatwick Express train to Victoria Station (35min., every 15-30min. 24hr., £8.50). **National Express** (☎ (08705) 80 80 80) buses run from Victoria Station to Gatwick (1hr., every hr. 5:05am-8:20pm, £8.50). **Taxis** take twice as long and cost 5 times as much.

Trains: London has 8 major stations: **Charing Cross** (serves south England); **Euston** (the north and northwest); **King's Cross** (the north and northeast); **Liverpool St.** (East Anglia); **Paddington** (the west); **St. Pancras** (The Midlands); **Victoria** (the south and Gatwick Airport); and **Waterloo** (the south, southwest and the Continent). All stations are linked by Underground. Get info at station ticket offices, tourist offices, or from the **National Rail Inquires Line** (☎ (0345) 48 49 50; www.britrail.com).

Buses: Long-distance buses (known as **coaches** in the UK) arrive in London at **Victoria Coach Station**, 164 Buckingham Palace Rd. SW1 (☎ 7730 3466; Tube: Victoria). **National Express** (☎ (08705) 80 80 80; www.nationalexpress.co.uk), is the principal operator of long-distance coach services from Britain. **Eurolines** (☎ (01582) 40 45 11) runs coaches into Victoria from Europe.

⎋ GETTING AROUND

Public Transportation: London is divided into 6 concentric transport zones; fares depend on the distance and number of zones crossed. The 24hr. help line (☎ 7222 1234) helps plan subway and bus travel. The **Underground** (or **Tube**) is fast, efficient, and crowded. Open daily 6am-midnight. A single adult ticket will cost between £1.50 and £3.50, with most central London trips costing £1.50 to £1.80. Trips to, from, or within Zone 1 cost £1; any trip within outer London (not traveling in Zone 1) costs 70p. Buy your ticket before you board and pass it through automatic gates at both ends of your journey. The **Travelcard**, a must for budget travelers, is valid on the Underground, regular buses, British Rail (Network SouthEast), and the Docklands Light Railway. Available in 1-day, 1-week, and 1-month increments from any station; some restrictions apply. The **bus** network is divided into 4 zones. **Night buses** ("N") run frequently throughout London 11:30pm-6am; all pass through Trafalgar Sq. Pick up free maps and guides at **London Transport Information Centres** (look for the lower-case "i" logo on signs) at the following Tube stations: Euston, Victoria, King's Cross, Liverpool St., Oxford Circus, Piccadilly, and St. James's Park; you can also find them at Heathrow Terminals 1, 2, and 4.

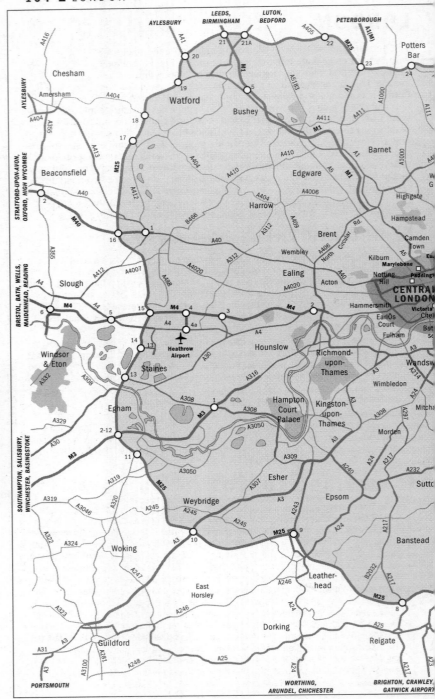

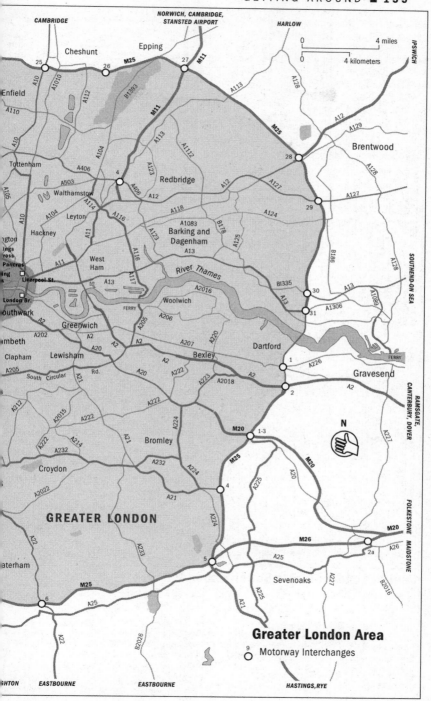

Greater London Area

○ Motorway Interchanges

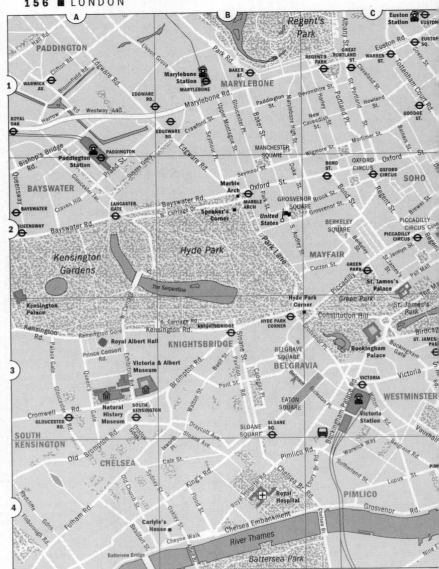

Central London: Major Street Finder

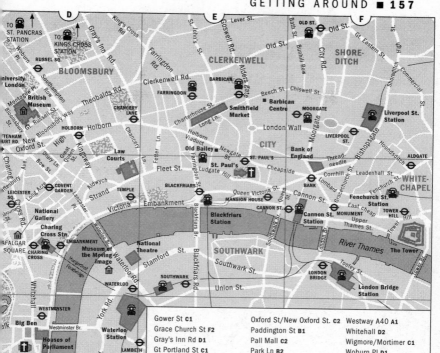

Edgware Rd **A1**
Euston Rd **C1**
Exhibition Rd **A3**
Farringdon Rd **E1**
Fenchurch/Aldgate **F2**
Fleet St **E2**
Fulham Rd **A4**
Gloucester Pl **B1**
Gloucester Rd **A3**
Goswell Rd **E1**

Gower St **C1**
Grace Church St **F2**
Gray's Inn Rd **D1**
Gt Portland St **C1**
Gt Russell St **D1**
Grosvenor Pl **C3**
Grosvenor Rd **C4**
Grosvenor St (Upr) **C2**
Haymarket **C2**
Holborn/High/Viaduct **D1**
Horseferry Rd **C3**
Jermyn St **C2**
Kensington High St/Rd **A3**
King's Cross Rd **D1**
King's Rd **B4**
Kingsway **D2**
Knightsbridge **B3**
Lambeth Palace Rd **D3**
Lisson Grove **A1**
Lombard St **F2**
London Wall **E1**
Long Acre/Grt Queen **D2**
Long Ln **E1**
Ludgate Hill **E2**
Marylebone High St **B1**
Marylebone Rd **B1**
Millbank **D4**
Montague Pl **D1**
Moorgate **F1**
New Cavendish **C1**
Newgate St **E1**
Nine Elms Ln **C4**
Oakley St **B4**
Old St **F1**
Old Brompton Rd **A4**
Onslow Sq/St **A3**

Oxford St/New Oxford St. **C2**
Paddington St **B1**
Pall Mall **C2**
Park Ln **B2**
Park Rd **B1**
Park St **B2**
Piccadilly **C2**
Pont St **B3**
Portland Pl **C1**
Queen St **E2**
Queen Victoria St **E1**
Queen's Gate **A3**
Queensway **A2**
Redcliffe Gdns **A4**
Regent St **C2**
Royal Hospital Rd **B4**
St. James's St **C2**
Seymour Pl **A1**
Seymour St **A2**
Shaftesbury Ave **C2**
Sloane/Lwr Sloane **B3**
Southampton Row **D1**
Southwark Bridge Rd **E2**
Southwark Rd **E2**
Stamford St **E2**
Strand **D2**
Sydney St **A4**
Thames St(Upr&Lwr) **F2**
The Mall **C2**
Theobald's Rd **D1**
Threadneedle St **F2**
Tottenham Ct Rd **C1**
Vauxhall Br. Rd **C4**
Victoria Embankment **D2**
Victoria St **C3**
Warwick Way **C4**
Waterloo Rd **E1**

Westway A40 **A1**
Whitehall **D2**
Wigmore/Mortimer **C1**
Woburn Pl **D1**
York Rd **D3**

RAILWAY STATIONS

Barbican **E1**
Blackfriars **E2**
Cannon St **F2**
City Thameslink **E2**
Charing Cross **D2**
Euston **C1**
Farringdon **E1**
King's Cross **D1**
Liverpool St **F1**
London Bridge **F2**
Marylebone **B1**
Moorgate **F1**
Old St. **F1**
Paddington **A2**
St Pancras **D1**
Victoria **C3**
Waterloo East **E2**
Waterloo **D3**

BRIDGES

Albert **B4**
Battersea **A4**
Blackfriars **E2**
Chelsea **C4**
Hungerford Footbridge **D2**
Lambeth **D3**
London Bridge **F2**
Southwark **E2**
Tower Bridge **F2**
Waterloo **D2**
Westminster **D3**

The Millennium Bridge will take you back into history to **St. Paul's Cathedral,** Sir Christopher Wren's famous masterwork.

Ambling around **Fleet Street and the Strand,** you'll find that London is business-as-usual. The Strand is home to the Inns of Court, where the Supreme Court of the Judicature hears important cases.

Clerkenwell

House

Doughty St.

High Holborn

Holborn

Chancery La.

Charterhouse

Beech St.

St. Bartholomew the Great

Giltspur

Holborn Viaduct

Kingsway

Inns of Court

Samuel Johnson's House

Royal Courts of Justice

Fleet St. **7**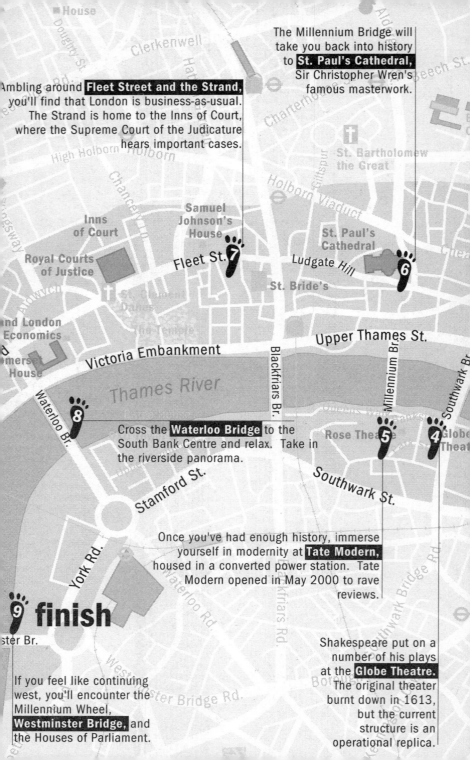

St. Paul's Cathedral

Ludgate Hill **6**

St. Bride's

Aldwych

nd London Economics

St. Clement Danes

The Temple

merset House

Victoria Embankment

Upper Thames St.

Blackfriars Br.

Millennium Br.

Southwark Br.

Thames River

Waterloo Br. **8**

Cross the **Waterloo Bridge** to the South Bank Centre and relax. Take in the riverside panorama.

Rose Theatre **5** **4** Globe Theat

Stamford St.

Southwark St.

finish **9**

ster Br.

York Rd.

Waterloo Rd.

Once you've had enough history, immerse yourself in modernity at **Tate Modern,** housed in a converted power station. Tate Modern opened in May 2000 to rave reviews.

Southwark Bridge Rd.

If you feel like continuing west, you'll encounter the Millennium Wheel, **Westminster Bridge,** and the Houses of Parliament.

Westminster Bridge Rd.

Blackfriars Rd.

Borough

Shakespeare put on a number of his plays at the **Globe Theatre.** The original theater burnt down in 1613, but the current structure is an operational replica.

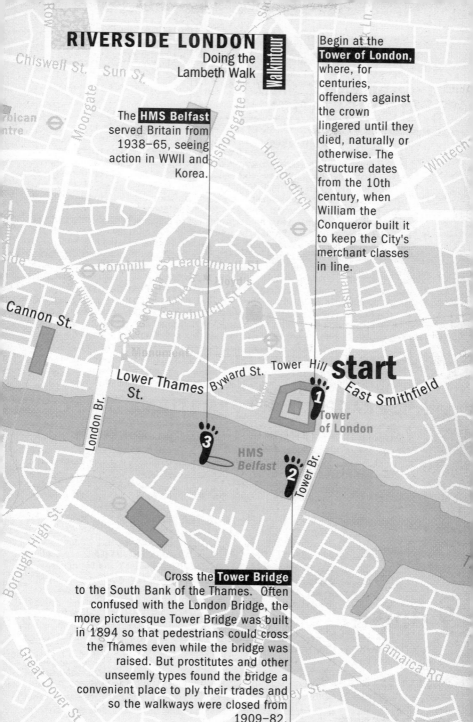

RIVERSIDE LONDON

Doing the Lambeth Walk

Walkintour

Begin at the **Tower of London,** where, for centuries, offenders against the crown lingered until they died, naturally or otherwise. The structure dates from the 10th century, when William the Conqueror built it to keep the City's merchant classes in line.

The **HMS Belfast** served Britain from 1938–65, seeing action in WWII and Korea.

start

East Smithfield

Tower Hill

Tower of London

1

3

HMS Belfast

2

Tower Br.

Cannon St.

Lower Thames St.

Byward St.

London Br.

Borough High St.

Great Dover St.

Jamaica Rd.

Chiswell St.

Sun St.

Moorgate

Bishopsgate St.

Houndsditch

Whitech

Cornhill

Leadenhall St.

Fenchurch St.

Cross the **Tower Bridge** to the South Bank of the Thames. Often confused with the London Bridge, the more picturesque Tower Bridge was built in 1894 so that pedestrians could cross the Thames even while the bridge was raised. But prostitutes and other unseemly types found the bridge a convenient place to ply their trades and so the walkways were closed from 1909–82.

Taxis: A light signifies that they're empty. Fares are steep, and 10% tip is standard. You can call a radio dispatcher for a taxi (☎7272 0272); but beware that you may be charged extra for ordering a cab by phone.

✸ ORIENTATION

Central London, on the north side of the Thames, bounded roughly by the Underground's Circle Line, contains most major sights. Within Central London, the vaguely defined **West End,** south of Oxford St., incorporates the understated elegance of **Mayfair,** the shopping streets around **Oxford Circus,** the theaters and tourist traps of **Piccadilly Circus** and **Leicester Square,** bohemian **Soho, Covent Garden,** and London's unofficial center, **Trafalgar Square.** East of the West End lies **Holborn,** center of legal activity, and **Fleet Street,** journalists' traditional haunt. North of Oxford St. are literary **Bloomsbury** and embassy-filled **Marylebone.** To the southwest are posh **Knightsbridge, Kensington,** and **Belgravia,** and to the west lie the vibrant **Notting Hill** and **Bayswater** districts. Around the southeastern corner of the Circle Line is **The City,** which refers to the ancient, and much smaller, "City of London," which covers only one of the 620 sq. mi. of today's Greater London. Today the City is the financial nerve center of London, with the Tower of London at its eastern edge and St. Paul's Cathedral nearby. Farther east is the ethnically diverse, working-class **East End.** Moving back west, along the river and the southern part of the Circle Line is the district of **Westminster,** just south of the West End, where you'll find Buckingham Palace, the **Houses of Parliament,** and Westminster Abbey. Trendy residential districts stretch to the north, including **Hampstead** and **Highgate,** with the enormous Hampstead Heath. The most useful navigational aids are street atlases, such as *London A to Z* (the "A to Zed"), *ABC Street Atlas, London Streetfinder,* or *Let's Go Map Guide: London.* London is divided into boroughs and into postal code areas, with letters standing for compass directions. The borough name and postal code appear at the bottom of most street signs; *Let's Go* lists postal codes in addresses.

🛈 PRACTICAL INFORMATION

TOURIST, FINANCIAL, AND LOCAL SERVICES

Tourist Office: British Travel Centre, 12 Regent St. (☎8846 9000). Tube: Piccadilly Circus. Ideal for travelers bound for destinations outside of London. £5 surcharge and a required deposit for accommodations booking (1 night or 15% of the total stay; does not book for hostels). Open M-F 9am-6:30pm, Sa-Su 10am-4pm. **London Tourist Board Information Centre,** Victoria Station Forecourt, SW1 (recorded message ☎(0839) 12 34 32; 39-49p per min.). Tube: Victoria. Offers information on London and England and an accommodations service (☎7932 2020, fax 7932 2021; £5 booking fee, plus 15% refundable deposit). Open Apr.-Nov. daily 8am-7pm; Dec.-Mar. M-Sa 8am-7pm, Su 8am-5pm. Additional tourist offices located at: **Heathrow Airport** (open daily Apr.-Nov. 9am-6pm; Dec.-Mar. 9am-5pm); **Liverpool St. Underground Station** (open M 8:15am-7pm, Tu-Sa 8:15am-6pm, Su 8:30am-4:45pm); and **Selfridges.**

Embassies: Australia, Australia House, The Strand, WC2 (☎7379 4334). Tube: Aldwych or Temple. Open M-F 9:30am-3:30pm. **Canada,** MacDonald House, 1 Grosvenor Sq., W1 (☎7258 6600). Tube: Bond St. or Oxford Circus. **Ireland,** 17 Grosvenor Pl, SW1 (☎7235 2171). Tube: Hyde Park Corner. Open M-F 9:30am-4:30pm. **New Zealand,** New Zealand House, 80 Haymarket, SW1 (☎7930 8422). Open M-F 10am-noon and 2-4pm. **South Africa,** South Africa House, Trafalgar Sq., WC2 (☎7451 7299). Tube: Charing Cross. Open M-F 8:45am-12:45pm. **US,** 24 Grosvenor Sq., W1 (☎7499 9000). Tube: Bond St. Phones answered 24hr.

Currency Exchange: The best rates are available walk-in at **High St.** banks, including **Barclay's, Lloyd's, National Westminster (NatWest),** and **HSBC (Midland).**

American Express: Offices throughout London; ☎ (0800) 52 13 13 for the closest one.

Gay and Lesbian Services: London Lesbian and Gay Switchboard (☎7837 7324). 24hr. advice and support service.

EMERGENCY AND COMMUNICATIONS

Emergency (Medical, Police, and Fire): Dial ☎999; no coins required.

Dental Care: Eastman Dental Hospital (☎7915 1000).

Hospitals: In an emergency, you can be treated at no charge in the Accidents and Emergencies (A&E) ward of a hospital. The following have 24hr. walk-in A&E (also known as casualty) departments: **Royal London Hospital,** Whitechapel Rd., E1 (☎7377 7000). Tube: Whitechapel. **Royal Free Hospital,** Pond St., NW3 (☎7794 0500). Tube: Belsize Park. Rail: Hampstead Heath. **Charing Cross Hospital,** Fulham Palace Rd. (entrance on St. Dunstan's Rd.), W6 (☎8846 1234). Tube: Baron's Court or Hammersmith. **St. Thomas' Hospital,** Lambeth Palace Rd., SE1 (☎7928 9292). Tube: Westminster. **University College Hospital,** Gower St. (entrance on Grafton Way), WC1 (☎7387 9300). Tube: Euston or Warren St.

Pharmacies: Every police station keeps a list of emergency doctors and chemists in its area. Listings are under "Chemists" in the Yellow Pages. **Bliss Chemists,** 5 Marble Arch, W1 (☎7723 6116), is open daily, including public holidays, 9am-midnight.

Police: Stations in every district of London. **Headquarters,** New Scotland Yard, Broadway, SW1 (☎7230 1212). Tube: St. James's Park. **West End Central,** 10 Vine St., W1 (☎7437 1212). Tube: Piccadilly Circus. For emergencies, dial ☎999.

Samaritans: 24hr. crisis hotline (☎7734 2800).

Internet Access: Cybercafes punctuate London. Get connected at ■ **easyEverything,** 9-13 Wilson Rd., W1 (☎7482 9502), directly opposite Victoria station. Tube: Victoria. This dirt-cheap (£1 per hr.) internet emporium has over 400 terminals. Open 24hr.

Post Office: Post offices are everywhere; call ☎ (0345) 22 33 44 to find the nearest one. When sending mail to the UK, be sure to write the postal district: London has seven King's Roads, eight Queen's Roads, and two Mandela Streets. The main office is the **Trafalgar Square Post Office,** 24-28 William IV St., **WC2N 4DL** (☎7484 9304; Tube: Charing Cross), which has late hours. All mail sent *Poste Restante* or general delivery to unspecified post offices ends up here. Open M-Th and Sa 8am-8pm, F 8:30am-8pm.

▐ ACCOMMODATIONS

Reserve rooms in advance for summer—landing in London without reservations is like landing on a bicycle with no seat. B&Bs are a bargain for groups of two or more, but hostels are the cheapest (and most social) option for small groups.

ACCOMMODATION DISTRICTS

What follows is a thumbnail sketch of the areas in which tourists are most likely to bunk down. Popular hotels fill up weeks in advance; call ahead.

CITY OF LONDON. Places to stay in the City are scarce, with most available space gobbled up by offices. However, many sights are nearby and the region is well served by the Tube and buses, particularly on weekdays.

WESTMINSTER. The area near Victoria Station is full of budget hotels. Play them off each other. Hotels closer to Pimlico are nicer than those around Victoria.

KENSINGTON AND KNIGHTSBRIDGE. Kensington is not the cheapest part of town; still, it's close to the stunning array of museums that line the southwest side of Hyde Park, as well as the huge department stores in Knightsbridge.

EARL'S COURT. West of Kensington, this area feeds on the budget tourist trade, spewing forth travel agencies, souvenir shops, and bureaux de change. Some streets seem solely populated by B&Bs and hostels. The area has a vibrant gay and lesbian population and is also a tremendously popular destination for Aussie travelers cooling their heels in London (in the 1970s, it gained the nickname "Kangaroo Valley"). Be careful at night. Also, beware of over-eager guides willing to lead you from the station to a hostel. Some B&Bs in the area conceal grimy rooms behind fancy lobbies and well-dressed staff; always ask to see a room.

MARYLEBONE AND BLOOMSBURY. A few hotels can be found near Marble Arch, in the sidestreets off the Edgware Road. It's convenient to Oxford St., Regent's Park, and the British Museum, and numerous night buses serve the area. The quiet residential streets are lined with B&Bs, a few halls of residence, and a few hostels. The closer the neighborhood is to the King's Cross, St. Pancras, and Euston train-station triumvirate, the dodgier it tends to be, especially after dark.

YHA HOSTELS

Staying at Youth Hostel Association hostels (YHA) is restricted to members of **Hostelling International** and its affiliated **Youth Hostel Association of England and Wales** (☎ (0870) 870 8888; www.yha.org.uk). You can join at YHA London Headquarters or at the hostels themselves for £12, under 18 £6. An **International Guest Pass** (£1.90) permits nonmembers not resident in England or Wales to stay at hostels, often at slightly higher rates. Buy six guest passes and you automatically become a full member. Hostels are not always able to accommodate every written request for reservations, much less on-the-spot inquiries, but they frequently hold a few beds available—it's always worth checking. To secure a place, show up as early as possible and expect to stand in line, or book in advance with a credit card at the number or website above; you can also write to the warden of the individual hostel.

All hostels are equipped with large **lockers** that require a padlock. Bring your own or purchase one from the hostel for £3. London hostels do not charge for a sheet or sleeping bag. Most have laundry facilities and some kitchen equipment. Theater tickets and discounted attraction tickets are available.

■ **YHA Hampstead Heath,** 4 Wellgarth Rd., NW11 (☎8458 9054; email hampstead@yha.org.uk). Tube: Golders Green, then bus #210 or 268 toward Hampstead; or on foot turn left from the station onto North End Rd., then left again onto Wellgarth Rd.; a 10min. walk. A beautiful, sprawling hostel. Laundry facilities. Restaurant. 24hr. reception. Book in advance. Dorms £19.70, under 18 £17.30; doubles £35; triples £51.95; quads £68.95; quints £85.95; 6-bed rooms £100.

■ **YHA City of London,** 36 Carter Ln., EC4 (☎ 7236 4965). Tube: St. Paul's. Sleep in quiet comfort a stone's throw from St. Paul's. Luggage storage, currency exchange, laundry, internet access (£5 per hr.), and theater box office. Reception 7am-11pm. Dorms £20.50-22.95, under 18 £18.70-24.10; singles £26.80, £23.30; doubles (some with TV) £52.10, £44.60. Private rooms £50-135, families £40-120.

YHA Holland House, Holland Walk, W8 (☎ 7937 0748; email hollandhouse@yha.org.uk). Tube: High St., Kensington, or Holland Park. Clean, spacious rooms with lockers. Full breakfast included. Laundry and kitchen facilities. Free daytime luggage storage. Dorms £19.95, under 18 £17.95.

YHA King's Cross/St. Pancras, 79-81 Euston Rd. (☎ 7388 9998). Tube: King's Cross or St. Pancras. Premium rooms include bathroom, and TV. Dinner £4. English breakfast included. Luggage storage. Laundry and internet access. Book way in advance. Dorms £23, under 18 £19.70; doubles £40; premium doubles £53; premium quads £100.

YHA Rotherhithe, 20 Salter Rd. (☎ 7232 2114). Tube: Rotherhithe or Canada Water. Bus #381 from Waterloo stops directly in front. Modern 320-bed hostel. Internet access, currency exchange, and restaurant. Breakfast included. Laundry. All rooms with bath. Book ahead. Dorms £23, under 18 £19.70; doubles £25; family bunk room (1 child under 16, at least) doubles £40, quads £80, 6 beds £120. Wheelchair accessible.

PRIVATE HOSTELS

Private hostels don't require HI/YHA membership, serve a youthful clientele, and have usually single-sex rooms. Some have kitchen facilities. Curfews are rare, and the dorms are usually cheaper. Almost all accept major credit cards.

■ **International Student House,** 229 Great Portland St., W1 (☎ 7631 8300). Tube: Great Portland St. At the foot of Regent's Park, across the street from the Tube station's rotunda. Films, concerts, discos, athletic contests, expeditions, and parties. Laundry facilities, currency exchange. Continental breakfast. Dorms £10; singles £31; doubles £22.50; triples £20; quads £17.50. With ISIC card: singles £24.50; doubles £19.50.

Ashlee House, 261-65 Gray's Inn Rd. (☎ 7833 9400). Tube: King's Cross. Clean, bright rooms within easy walking distance of King's Cross. No hot water noon-6pm. Generous breakfast included. Secure luggage room, laundry, and internet access. Reception 24hr. Check-out 10am. Dorms Apr.-Oct. £15-19, Nov.-Mar. £13-17; twins £44-48.

Central University of Iowa Hostel, 7 Bedford Pl. (☎ 7580 1121). Tube: Tottenham Court Rd. or Russell Sq. On a quiet street near the British Museum. Spartan, narrow dorm rooms with bunk beds and washbasins. Continental breakfast included. Laundry facilities, towels and sheets, TV lounge. £10 key deposit. Reception 9am-10:30pm. Open approximately May 20-Aug. 20. Dorms £20; twins £22.

Astor's Museum Inn, 27 Montague St. (☎ 7580 5360; email astorhostels@msn.com). Tube: Russell Sq. Coed dorms almost inevitable. Kitchen, cable TV. Continental breakfast included. Reception 24hr. Book a month ahead. Dorms £14-16; doubles £40; triples £51. Discounts available Oct.-Mar., including a weekly dorm rate of £70.

Tonbridge Club, 120 Cromer St. (☎ 7837 4406). Tube: King's Cross or St. Pancras. Follow Euston Rd. towards the British Library and turn left onto Judd St.; the hostel is 3 blocks down on the left. Students and foreigners only. A clean, no-frills place to sleep and shower. Men sleep in basement gym, women in karate-club hall. Blankets and pads provided. Lockout 9am-9pm; lights out 11:30pm; midnight curfew. Floor space £5.

HALLS OF RESIDENCE

London's universities rent out rooms in their **halls of residence,** which are generally the cheapest single rooms available, particularly if you have a student ID. Rooms tend to be standard, spartan student digs, but clean. The halls usually offer rooms to individuals for two or three months over the summer, and during the long Easter break in the spring. Some halls reserve a few rooms for travelers year-round. Calling ahead is advisable. The **King's Campus Vacation Bureau,** 127 Stanford St., SE1 (☎ 7928 3777), controls bookings for a number of University of London residence halls, all available from early June to mid-September.

High Holborn Residence, 178 High Holborn, WC1 (☎ 7379 5589). Tube: Holborn. A comfortable, modern, and extremely well-located place. Each room has a kitchen. Laundry facilities. English breakfast included. Open mid-June to Sept. (peak rates in July). Singles £27-34; twins £46-57, with bath £56-67; triples with bath £66-77.

Wellington Hall, 71 Vincent Sq. (☎ 7834 4740; reservations ☎ 7928 3777). Tube: Victoria. An Edwardian building on a beautiful square near Victoria Station. TV lounge, library, and bar. English breakfast included. Laundry. Rooms available around Easter and mid-June to mid-Sept. Singles £26; twins £40.

Queen Alexandra's House, Kensington Gore. (☎ 7589 1120; fax 7589 3177). Tube: South Kensington. **Women only.** Kitchen, laundry, and sitting room. Common showers and lavatories. No visitors 11pm-10am. Continental breakfast included. Min. 2-night stay. Write weeks in advance for a booking form; fax is best. Cozy singles £25.

John Adams Hall, 15-23 Endsleigh St., WC1 (☎ 7387 4086; email jah@ioe.ac.uk). Tube: Euston Sq. An elegant Georgian building with small, wrought-iron balconies. Singles are small and simple. TV lounge, pianos. Laundry facilities. English breakfast included. Open July-Sept. and Easter. Singles £24; twins £42; triples £59. Discounts for students, stays of 6 nights or more, and in the off-season.

BED AND BREAKFASTS

WESTMINSTER

■ **Luna and Simone Hotel,** 47-49 Belgrave Rd. (☎ 7834 5897; email lunasimone@talk21.com). Tube: Victoria. Stylish, fun, and immaculate; the area's best option. Luggage storage. Book a month ahead. Singles £28-34; doubles £48-60, with bath £50-75; triples £65-80, with shower £75-95. 10% discount for long-term stays.

Melbourne House, 79 Belgrave Rd. (☎ 7828 3516). Tube: Pimlico. An extraordinarily clean, well-kept establishment. Breakfast served 7:30-8:45am. Free luggage storage. Book ahead with credit card. Singles £30, with bath £50-55; doubles with bath £70-75; triples with bath £90-95; family quad with bath £100-110.

Alexander Hotel, 13 Belgrave Rd. (☎ 7834 9738). Tube: Pimlico. Sumptuously carpeted rooms are slightly cramped but attractive and sparkling clean throughout. All with private bath. Breakfast served 7:30-9am. Check-out 11am. Singles £45; doubles and twins £60-65; triples £75-80; family rooms £80-110. Winter discount.

Dover Hotel, 42/44 Belgrave Rd. (☎ 7821 9085). Tube: Pimlico. All rooms and facilities are clean and have bathrooms. Continental breakfast served 7:30-9:30am. Singles £40-55; doubles and twins £50-70; triples £60-75; quads £70-100; quints £80-110.

KENSINGTON, KNIGHTSBRIDGE, AND CHELSEA

▨ Abbey House Hotel, 11 Vicarage Gate. (☎ 7727 2594) Tube: High St. Kensington. The hotel achieves a level of comfort unrivaled at these prices. Reception 8:30am-10pm. Book far ahead. Singles £43; doubles £68; triples £85; quads £95; quints £105.

Vicarage Hotel, 10 Vicarage Gate (☎ 7229 4030). Tube: High St. Kensington. Stately foyer surpassed only by comfortable bedrooms and spotless bathrooms. Singles £45; doubles and twins £74, with bath and TV £98; triples £90; family rooms £98.

Swiss House Hotel, 171 Old Brompton Rd. (☎ 7373 2769). Tube: Gloucester Rd. A beautiful, plant-filled B&B with 16 airy, spacious rooms, most with fireplaces. Internet access. All rooms have showers. Reception M-F 7:30am-11pm, Sa-Su 8am-11pm. Singles £46, with toilet £65; doubles/twins with bath £80-90; triples with bath £104; quads with bath £118. 5% discount for cash payments.

MARYLEBONE AND BLOOMSBURY

▨ Arosfa Hotel, 83 Gower St. (☎ 7636 2115). Tube: Tottenham Court Rd. Spacious rooms, immaculate facilities, and furnishings. All rooms with TV and sink. No smoking. Singles £35; doubles £48, with bath £63; triples £65, £76; quad with bath £88.

▨ Euro Hotel, 51-53 Cartwright Gdns., WC1 (☎ 7387 4321; email reception@eurohotel.co.uk). Tube: Russell Sq. Large, high-ceilinged rooms with cable TV, radio, kettle, phone, and sink. Sparkling, spacious bathroom facilities. Free email. Singles £46, with bath £68; doubles £65, £85; triples £79, £99; quads £88, £108.

Ridgemount Hotel, 65-67 Gower St. (☎ 7636 1141). Tube: Tottenham Court Rd. Charming staff keep the loyal guests happy and the well-kept hotel radiantly clean. Snug singles with TVs. Garden in back, free tea and coffee in the TV lounge. Laundry service £3. Book ahead. Singles £32, with shower £43; doubles £48, £62; triples £63, £75; quads £72, £86; quints £78, £89.

The Langland Hotel, 29-31 Gower St. (☎ 7636 5801; email sarah@langlandhotel.freeserve.co.uk). Tube: Euston. Renovations have added bathrooms to many of the rooms and TVs to all. Cable-TV lounge with comfy blue sofas. Laundry facilities. Winter and long-term student discounts. Singles £40; doubles £50, with bath £70; triples £70; quads £90; quints £110. Rooms with bath range £60-120.

Mentone Hotel, 54-56 Cartwright Gdns. (☎ 7387 3927; email mentonehotel@compuserve.com). Tube: Russell Sq. Bright, cheery place. Airport shuttle available with advance reservation (from Heathrow £24, Gatwick £40, Luton £34, Stansted £43). Singles £42, with bath £60; doubles with bath £79; triples with bath £90; quads with bath £99. Reduced rates for longer stays Dec.-Apr.

Cosmo/Bedford House Hotel, 27 Bloomsbury Sq. (☎ 7636 4661). Tube: Holborn. Location prevails in this family-run establishment with neat, comfortable rooms that come with color TVs and sinks. Continental breakfast. Singles £36, with bath £48; doubles £58, £70; triples £75, £85; quad £85, £90.

Alhambra Hotel, 17-19 Argyle St. (☎ 7837 9575; email postmaster@alhambrahotel.demon.co.uk). Tube: King's Cross/St. Pancras. Sinks and TVs in all rooms. Singles £32, with shower £42, with bath £60; doubles £44, with shower £50, with bath £60; triples £62, with bath £77; quads with bath £92.

Jesmond Dene Hotel, 27 Argyle St. (☎ 7837 4654; email JesmondDeneHotel@msn.com). Tube: King's Cross or St. Pancras. Black-and-white rooms with sinks and large TVs are slightly worn but scrupulously clean. Reserve 2 weeks early. Singles £30; doubles £42, with shower £55; triples £60, £75; quads with bath £90; quints £95.

EARL'S COURT

▣ **Oxford Hotel,** 24 Penywern Rd. (☎ 7370 1161; email oxfordhotel@btinternet.com). Clean rooms installed with new beds and repainted every year. The stylish dining room includes a bar. Breakfast 7:30-9:30am. Luggage storage and safe. Reception 24hr. Reserve ahead. Singles with shower £34, with bath £47; doubles £53, £63; triples £63, £73; quads with shower £75, with bath £85; quints with shower £95, with bath £105. Winter and weekly rates may be 10-15% lower.

▣ **Mowbray Court Hotel,** 28-32 Penywern Rd. (☎ 7373 8285; email mowbraycrthot@hotmail.com). Staff this helpful is a rarity in London; wake-up calls, tour arrangements, taxicabs, theater bookings, and dry cleaning. Internet access. In-room safes £2 per day. Reserve ahead. Singles £45, with bath £52; doubles £56, £67; triples £69, £80; family rooms for 4 £84, £95; for 5 £100, £110; for 6 £115, £125.

Beaver Hotel, 57-59 Philbeach Gdns. (☎ 7373 4553). Warm and welcoming—plush lounge with polished wood floors and cable TV. Lift access. All rooms with desks, phones, and hair dryers. All bathrooms are a study in cleanliness. Breakfast 7:30-9:30am. Wheelchair accessible. Reserve several weeks ahead. Singles £38, with bath £55; doubles £45, £80; triples with bath £90.

Philbeach Hotel, 30-31 Philbeach Gdns. (☎ 7373 1244). The largest gay B&B in England, popular with all genders. Jimmy's Bar downstairs is residents-only. Internet access. Continental breakfast. Book 1 week ahead. Budget singles £30, else £35-50, with shower £50-60; doubles £65, with bath £85; triple £75, £90.

Half Moon Hotel, 10 Earl's Ct. Sq., SW5 (☎ 7373 9956). From Earl's Court Tube station, take a right, and Earl's Court Sq. is the second right. Looks like a two-star, charges like a budget. Continental breakfast. Singles £30, with shower £45; doubles £55, with bath £60; triples £65, £80; quads with shower £100.

⃞ FOOD

Savoring the booty of imperialism needn't be a guilty pleasure; imports from former colonies have spiced up London kitchens considerably. The city is perhaps most famous for its **Indian restaurants,** the true British food (the cheapest cluster around Westbourne Grove near Bayswater, Euston Sq., and Brick Ln. in the East End), but food from various corners of the globe can be found everywhere. The wealth of international restaurants shouldn't deter you from sampling Britain's own cuisine. As usual, **pubs** are a solid choice for meat dishes, while **fish 'n' chip shops** and **kebab shops** can be found on nearly every corner. They vary little in price but can be miles apart in quality. Look for queues out the door and hop in line. The "New British" label applies to restaurants that blend continental influences with British staples to form a tasty, if sometimes pricey, cuisine.

RESTAURANTS

THE CITY OF LONDON

▣ **Futures!,** 8 Botolph Alley (☎ 7623 4529). Tube: Monument. Off Botolph Ln. Fresh takeaway vegetarian breakfast and lunch prepared in a petite kitchen open to view. Daily main dishes, like quiche, £3.40. Spinach pizza £1.85. Open M-F 7:30-10am and 11:30am-3pm. Branch in Exchange Sq., behind Liverpool St.

The Place Below, (☎ 7329 0789) in St. Mary-le-Bow crypt, Cheapside. Tube: St. Paul's. Generous vegetarian dishes served to City executives in an impressive church crypt. Quiche and salad £6, takeaway £4.20. Takeaway discount. Open M-F 7:30am-2:30pm.

Sushi & Sozai, 51a Queen Victoria St. (☎ 7332 0108). Tube: Mansion House. A cheap sushi stand in the City. Medium sushi £4; large sushi £5. Open M-F 11am-3pm.

COVENT GARDEN AND SOHO

▣ **Belgo Centraal,** 50 Earlham St. (☎ 7813 2233). Tube: Covent Garden. Waiters in monk's cowls and great specials make this a popular restaurant. During "Beat the

Clock," (M-F 6-7:30pm) the time you order is the cost of your meal; order at 6:30, your meal costs £6.30. Open M-Sa noon-11:30pm, Su noon-10:30pm.

■ **World Food Cafe,** 14-15 Neal's Yd. (☎ 7379 0298). Tube: Covent Garden. A bit pricier than similar veggie-loving enclaves, but the quality explains it all. Features a world-wide array of *meze*, light meals, and appetizing platters (£6-8). Open M-Sa noon-5pm.

Yo! Sushi, 52 Poland St. (☎ 7287 0443). Tube: Oxford Circus. As much an eating experience as a restaurant. Diners sit at an island bar and pick and choose from dishes placed on a central conveyer belt. Plates are color-coded by price (£1.50-3.50). Great fun. Open daily noon-midnight.

PICADILLY AND MAYFAIR

Sofra, 18 Shepherd St. (☎ 7493 3320). Tube: Green Park/Hyde Park Corner. The house specialty, mixed *meze*, is £5.45, while other main courses cost £7.45-8.95. Open noon-midnight. Branches: 36 Tavistock St. (☎ 7240 3773) and Hyde Park.

WESTMINSTER

Al-Fresco (☎ 7233 8298). Tube: Victoria. Trendy variations on old standbys. Jacket potato with brie £2.75. Fresh melon juice £1.70. Panini sandwiches £2.80. Open M-F 8am-5:30pm, Sa-Su 9am-4:30pm.

Goya, 34 Lupus St. (☎ 7976 5309). Tube: Pimlico. Corner *tapas* bar popular with locals for sipping drinks and munching Spanish snacks. Outdoor tables filled on summer nights. *Tapas* £2.50-4.50. Hearty garlic chicken £4.20. Open daily noon-midnight.

KENSINGTON, KNIGHTSBRIDGE, AND CHELSEA

■ **New Culture Revolution,** 305 King's Rd. (☎ 7352 9281). Tube: Sloane Sq. Take a great leap forward and enjoy delicious north Chinese food; mostly noodles and dumplings. Open daily noon-11pm. Branches: 43 Parkway (☎ 7267 2700; Tube: Camden Town); and 42 Duncan St. (☎ 7833 9083; Tube: Angel).

Café Floris, 5 Harrington Rd. (☎ 7589 3276). Tube: High St. Kensington. A bustling cafe offering large, fresh sandwiches (£1.60-2.90) and filling breakfasts. Colossal all-day breakfast special £3.50. Min. purchase £3 noon-3pm. Open daily 6am-7pm.

Rotisserie Jules, 6-8 Bute St. (☎ 7584 0600). Tube: High St. Kensington. This lively restaurant serves free-range poultry. Dishes from £4.95. Open daily noon-11:30pm. Branches: 338 King's Rd. and 133 Notting Hill Gate.

NOTTING HILL, BAYSWATER, AND HYDE PARK

■ **The Grain Shop,** 269a Portobello Rd. (☎ 7229 5571). Tube: Ladbroke Grove. This takeaway sells a surprisingly large array of foods. Organic whole grain breads baked daily on the premises 90p-£1.90 per loaf. Main dishes from £2.40. Vegan brownies £1. Groceries also available, many organic. Open M-Sa 9:30am-6pm.

Cockney's Pie & Mash, 314 Portobello Rd. (☎ 8960 9409). Tube: Ladbroke Grove. Cheap, no-nonsense pie and mash (£1.85), with portions of eel (F-Sa only) for a mere £2.70. Open Tu-Sa 11:30am-5:30pm.

Royal China, 13 Queensway (☎ 7221 2535). Tube: Bayswater. For the full Cantonese experience, try the steamed duck's tongue (£1.80) or the marinated chicken feet (£1.80). Generous dishes £10-15. Dim sum served M-Sa noon-5pm, Su 11am-5pm. Open M-Th noon-11pm, F-Sa noon-11:30pm, Su 11am-10pm.

MARYLEBONE AND BLOOMSBURY

■ **Mandalay,** 444 Edgware Rd. (☎ 7258 3696). Tube: Edgware Rd. This Burmese restaurant is so consistently good it only needs word of mouth to attract customers. Set lunches include curry and rice £3.50; curry, rice, dessert, and coffee £5.90. Open M-Sa noon-3pm and 6-11pm; last orders 2:30pm and 10:30pm.

Wagamama, 4A Streatham St. (☎ 7323 9223). Tube: Tottenham Ct. Rd. If a restaurant could be a London must-see on the level of Buckingham Palace, this would be it. Noodles £5-7.25. Open M-Sa noon-11pm, Su 12:30-10pm.

BRITAIN

Seashell, 49-51 Lisson Grove (☎7224 9000). Tube: Marylebone. Always a contender in the eternal debate over the best fish 'n' chips in London. Cod and chips £3.25. Open M-F noon-2:30pm and 5-10:30pm, Sa noon-10:30pm.

SOUTH LONDON

■**Tas,** 33 The Cut (☎7928 2111). Tube: Waterloo. Serves gourmet quality Turkish and Mediterranean food at low prices. Starter and main for a scandalously low £6.45. Open M-Sa noon-11:30pm, Su noon-10:30pm.

EAST LONDON

Arkansas Cafe, Old Spitalfields Market. (☎7377 6999). Tube: Aldgate East. This may not give you a taste of jolly old England, but the Brits are flocking here in droves. Open M-F noon-2:30pm, Su noon-4pm.

Spitz, 109 Commercial St. (☎7247 9747). Tube: Aldgate East. Inside Spitalfields Market, this elegant bar serves delicious lunches from £5. During the weekend, there is live music upstairs, with an emphasis on folk, jazz, and klezmer. Open daily 11am-midnight.

NORTH LONDON

■**Tartuf,** 88 Upper St. (☎7288 0954). Tube: Angel. A convivial Alsatian place that serves *tartes flambées* (£4.90-6.10), like pizzas on very thin crusts, but much tastier. Open M-F noon-2:30pm and 5:45-11:30pm, Sa noon-11:30pm, Su noon-11pm.

Le Mercury, 140a Upper St. (☎7354 4088). Tube: Angel. This French restaurant feels like the quintessential Islington gourmet bistro, but with outstandingly low prices. All main courses £5.85. Reservations recommended for evening. Open daily 11am-1am.

Le Crêperie de Hampstead, 77 Hampstead High St. Tube: Hampstead. This Hampstead institution is guaranteed nirvana, serving paper-thin Brittany crepes stuffed with fillings both sweet and savory from a tiny van outside the King William IV pub. Crêpes £1.55-3.95. Open M-Th 11:45am-11pm, F-Su 11:45am-11:30pm.

TEA

Quintessentially English, the tradition of **afternoon tea** is a social ritual combining food, conversation, and of course, a pot of tea—served strong and taken with milk. Don't commit a gaffe by pouring the tea first—aficionados always pour the milk first so as not to scald it. Afternoon **high tea** includes cooked meats, salad, sandwiches, and pastries. **Cream tea,** a specialty of Cornwall and Devon, includes pastries accompanied by clotted cream (a cross between whipped cream and butter).

Claridges, Brook St. (☎7629 8860). Tube: Bond St. Old-fashioned elegance combined with comfortable sofas and armchairs encourage a long afternoon linger. Smartly dressed waiters pour your tea and present plates of sandwiches and pastries. Tea served daily 3-5:30pm; book in advance for weekends. £19; with champagne £25.

The Orangery Tea Room, Kensington Palace, Kensington Gardens (☎7376 0239). Tube: High St. Kensington. Light meals and tea served in the marvelously airy Orangery built for Queen Anne in 1705. Two scones with clotted cream and jam £4. Pot of tea £2.10, set teas from £5.25. Trundle through the gardens afterward. Open daily 10am-6pm.

◎ SIGHTS

London's landmarks annually face an onslaught of around five million visitors. Sightseers who don't qualify for student or senior discounts may want to consider the **London for Less** card, issued by Metropolis International (☎8964 4242), which grants discounts on attractions, theaters, restaurants, and hotels, and is available at all BTA offices (4-person, 8-day card £13). Many **bus tours** are "hop-on hop-off," allowing you to stop at the sights you find particularly fascinating and join later tours. Be sure to ask how often buses circle through the route. **Walking tours** can fill in the specifics that bus tours zoom past. Among the best are **The Original London Walks** (☎7624 3978) which cover a specific topic such as Legal London, Jack the Ripper, or Spies and Spycatchers. The 2hr. tours are led by well regarded guides. **Historical Tours of London** also leads popular tours. (☎8668 4019. £5, students and seniors £4.) If glancing at London from the top of a bus is unsatisfactory and hoofing it seems daunting, a tour led by **The London Bicycle Tour Company** may be the happy medium. (☎7928 6838. Tours £11.90.)

WESTMINSTER AND WHITEHALL

The city of Westminster, now a borough of London, once served as haven to a seething nest of criminals seeking sanctuary in the Abbey. For the past 100 years, Westminster has been the center of political and religious power in England.

WESTMINSTER ABBEY

Parliament Sq. Tube: Westminster or St. James's Park. ☎7222 5152. "Supertours" include admission to the Abbey and all sights inside (reservations ☎7222 7110), offered Nov.-Mar. M-Th 10, 11am, 2, and 3pm, F 10, 11am, and 2pm, Sa 10, 11am, and 12:30pm; Apr.-Oct. also M-F 10:30am and 2:30pm. Supertour £10. Audio tour £3. Open M-F 9am-4:45pm, Sa 9am-2:45pm; last admission 1hr. before closing. Abbey £5, students and UK seniors £3, ages 11-16 £2, families £10. Evensong M-Tu and Th-F 5pm, Sa-Su 3pm. Organ recitals in summer on Tu at 6:30pm. Reservations ☎7222 5152, or write to the Concert Secretary, 20 Dean's Yard, SW1P 3PA. £6, students £4.

The site of every royal coronation since 1066, Westminster Abbey's significance is secular as well as sacred. Controlled by the Crown and not the Church of England, the Abbey is the temple of England's civic religion. Only the **Pyx Chamber** and the **Norman Undercroft** (now the Westminster Abbey Undercroft Museum) survive from the original structure, which was consecrated by King Edward the Confessor on December 28, 1065. Most of the present Abbey was erected under Henry III in the 13th century, and the post-1850 North Entrance is the latest addition.

The **north transept** contains memorials to Prime Ministers Disraeli and Gladstone. Kings' tombs surround the **Shrine of St. Edward** and lead to the **Lady Chapel.** Henry VII and his wife Elizabeth lie at the end of the chapel, and nearby is the stone that once marked Cromwell's grave. Protestant Queen Elizabeth I and the Catholic cousin she ordered beheaded, Mary Queen of Scots, are buried on opposite sides of the Henry VII chapel (in the north and south aisles, respectively). At the exit of the Lady Chapel stands the **Coronation Chair,** which used to rest on the Stone of Scone.

A number of monarchs from Henry III to George II are interred in the **Chapel.** Edward I had himself placed in an unsealed crypt, in case he was needed to fight the Scots; his mummy was used as a standard by the English army in Scotland. The **Poets' Corner** begins with Geoffrey Chaucer, who was originally buried in the Abbey in 1400—the short Gothic tomb you see today in the east wall of the transept was not erected until 1556. The **south transept** is graced with the graves of Samuel Johnson and actor David Garrick, as well as busts of William Wordsworth, Samuel Taylor Coleridge, and Robert Burns. The **High Altar,** between the North and South transepts, has long been the scene of coronations, royal weddings, and funerals. The **Scientists' Corner** holds a memorial to Sir Isaac Newton, which sits next to the grave of Lord Kelvin. Past the cloisters, in the Abbey's narrow nave, the highest in England, a slab of black Belgian marble marks the **Grave of the Unknown Warrior.** Here the body of a World War I soldier is buried in soil from the battlefields of France, with an oration written in letters made from melted bullets.

THE HOUSES OF PARLIAMENT

Parliament Sq. Tube: Westminster. Public tours offered early Aug. to mid-Sept. M-Sa 9:30am-4:15pm. Tickets (£3.50) go on sale in mid-June and must be booked in advance from Ticketmaster (☎7344 9966; www.ticketmaster.co.uk). For foreign-language tours book 4 weeks ahead. At other times of the year, UK residents should contact their MP or a friendly Lord; tours normally available M-Th 9:30am-noon and F 3:30-5:30pm. Overseas visitors can request tours through the Parliamentary Education Unit, Norman Shaw Building (North), London SW1A 2TT (☎7219 3000; email edunit@parliament.uk); tours, limited to 16 people, offered only F 3:30-5:30pm, so book far ahead. Government business may lead to cancellation of tours at any time.

LIFE AFTER DEATH Oliver Cromwell's job as Lord Protectorate ended when he died of tuberculosis. His body was secretly embalmed and interred in Westminster Abbey on November 10, 1658, two weeks before his official funeral which was to cost £60,000 (an enormous sum both then and now). His eternal rest, however, did not last long. When the monarchy ousted Cromwell's son, King Charles II was unhappy with Cromwell's body lying next to the kings and queens of England. On January 30, 1661, the anniversary of the execution of Charles I, Cromwell's body was exhumed and taken to Tyburn. The procession was greeted by the "the universal outcry and curses of the people." The corpse was hanged from the gallows for a day, the body drawn and quartered, and the head taken to Westminster Hall, where it was exhibited on a pole for 25 years, until it was blown off in a storm and someone ran off with it. Never fear, though—he hasn't been forgotten. A stone in Westminster Abbey still marks his preliminary, if temporary, resting place.

For the classic view of the Houses of Parliament, as captured by Claude Monet, walk about halfway over Westminster Bridge, preferably at dusk. Like the government offices along Whitehall, the Houses of Parliament occupy the former site of a royal palace. Only **Jewel Tower** (see below) and **Westminster Hall** (to the left of St. Stephen's entrance on St. Margaret St.) survive from the original building, which was destroyed by a fire in 1834. Sir Charles Barry and A.W.N. Pugin won a competition for the design of the new houses. The immense complex blankets eight acres and includes more than 1000 rooms and 100 staircases. Space is nevertheless so scarce that Members of Parliament (MPs) have neither private offices nor staff, and the archives—the originals of every Act of Parliament passed since 1497—are stuffed into **Victoria Tower,** the large tower to the south. A flag flown from the tower indicates that Parliament is in session. **Big Ben** is not the famous northernmost clock tower but rather the 14-ton bell that tolls the hours. Ben is most likely named after the rotund Sir Benjamin Hall, who served as Commissioner of Works when the bell was cast and hung in 1858.

HOUSE OF COMMONS' GALLERY. After you sign a form promising not to read, use cameras or opera glasses, or otherwise cause disturbances, the guards will show you to the Chambers of the House of Commons. You can watch MPs at work from the House of Commons Gallery for "Distinguished and Ordinary Strangers". If you don't have an advance booking (see below), arrive early and wait at the public entrance at St. Stephen's gate; keep left (the right-hand queue is for the Lords). Weekdays after 6pm and Fridays are the least crowded; afternoon waits can be as long as two hours. Places in the gallery during Prime Minister's Question Time (W 3-3:30pm), when the Prime Minister answers questions from MPs, are particularly hard to obtain. (☎ 7219 4272. Gallery open M-W 2:30-10:30pm, Th 11:30am-7:30pm, F normally 9:30am to around 3pm. For advance tickets, UK residents should contact their MP; overseas visitors must apply for a Card of Introduction from their Embassy or High Commission in London. Book at least a month in advance. Free.)

HOUSE OF LORDS' GALLERY. To enter the Lords' Gallery, go through the Central Lobby and pass through the Peers' corridor where the MPs have bedecked the passage with scenes of Charles I's downfall. (On Parliament Sq. Tube: Westminster. ☎ 7219 4272. Gallery open M-W 2:30-10:30pm, Th 11:30am-7:30pm, F normally 9:30am to around 3pm. For advance tickets, overseas visitors must apply for a Card of Introduction from their Embassy or High Commission in London. Book at least a month in advance. House of Lords Visitors' Gallery: ☎ 7219 3107. Keep right in the queue at St. Stephen's entrance. Open M-W from 2:30pm-rise, Th from 3pm, occasionally F 11am. Free.)

OTHER SIGHTS NEAR WESTMINSTER AND WHITEHALL

10 DOWNING STREET. The Prime Minister's headquarters lies just steps up Parliament St. from the Houses of Parliament. The exterior of "Number Ten" is decidedly unimpressive, but behind the famous door spreads an extensive political network.

The Chancellor of the Exchequer forges economic policy from 11 Downing St., while the Chief Whip of the House of Commons plans Party campaigns at #12. Tony Blair's family is too big for #10, so he's moved into #11. *(Tube: Westminster.)*

THE MALL AND ST. JAMES'S
BUCKINGHAM PALACE

Buckingham Palace Rd. Tube: Victoria, Green Park, or St. James's Park. Recorded info ☎ 7799 2331, info office ☎ 7839 1377; tickets ☎ 7321 2233; www.royal.gov.uk. Open Aug.-Sept. daily 9:30am-4:30pm. £10.50, seniors £8, under 17 £5.

When a freshly-crowned Victoria moved from St. James's Palace in 1837, Buckingham Palace, built in 1825 by John Nash, had faulty drains and a host of other difficulties. Improvements were made, and now the monarch calls it home. The 20th-century facade on the Mall is only big, not beautiful—the Palace's best side, the garden front, is seldom seen by ordinary visitors as it is protected by the 40-acre spread where the Queen holds garden parties. Visitors are allowed in the **Blue Drawing Room,** the **Throne Room,** the **Picture Gallery** (filled with pictures by Rubens, Rembrandt, and Van Dyck), and the **Music Room** (where Mendelsohn played for Queen Victoria), as well as other stately rooms. In the opulent **White Room,** the large mirror fireplace conceals a door used by the Royal Family at formal dinners.

Though public support for the royal family has waned considerably in the past years, tourist enthusiasm for the fur-capped Buckingham guards has not. From April to June, the **Changing of the Guard** ceremony takes place daily; during the rest of the year, it occurs on odd-numbered dates. The "Old Guard" marches from St. James's Palace down the Mall to Buckingham Palace, leaving at approximately 11:10am. The "New Guard" begins marching as early as 10:20am. When they meet at the central gates of the palace, the officers of the regiments then touch hands, symbolically exchanging keys, *et voilà,* the guard is officially changed. The soldiers gradually split up to relieve the guards currently protecting the palace. In wet weather or on pressing state holidays, the Changing of the Guard does not occur. *(To witness the spectacle, show up well before 11:30am and stand directly in front of the palace. You can also watch along the routes of the troops prior to their arrival at the palace (10:40-11:25am) between the Victoria Memorial and St. James's Palace or along Birdcage Walk. Buckingham Palace Rd. Open daily Aug.-Sept. 9:30am-4:30pm. £10.50, seniors £8, under 17 £5. Tickets must be bought before the opening dates by calling ☎ 7321 2233.)*

OTHER SIGHTS NEAR THE MALL AND ST. JAMES'S

THE MALL. Bordered by St. James's Park and Green Park to the south and Piccadilly to the north, The Mall begins at Cockspur St., off Trafalgar Sq., and leads up to Buckingham Palace. Every Sunday it is pedestrian-only. Nearby, **St. James's Street** runs into stately **Pall Mall.** *(Tube: Charing Cross, Green Park, or St. James's Park.)*

ST. JAMES'S PALACE AND PARK. A residence of the monarchy from 1660 to 1668 and again from 1715 to 1837, **St. James's Palace** is now the home of Prince Charles, while his grandmother, the Queen Mum, bunks next door at Clarence House. The palace is closed to the public except for Inigo Jones's **Queen's Chapel,** built in 1626, open for Sunday services at 8:30 and 11am. *(Tube: Green Park. Just north of Buckingham Palace and The Mall, up Stable Yard or Marlborough Rd.)* **St. James's Park** was declared London's first royal park in 1532. Lawn chairs must be rented, but don't bother finding the attendants; sit and they'll find you (70p per 4hr.).

TRAFALGAR SQUARE AND PICCADILLY

TRAFALGAR SQUARE. Unlike many squares in London, Trafalgar Square, which slopes down from the **National Gallery** (see p. 178) into the center of a vicious traffic roundabout, has been public land ever since the razing of several hundred houses made way for its construction in the 1830s. The fluted granite pillar of **Nelson's Column** commands the square, with four majestic, beloved lions guarding the base. The monument and square commemorate Admiral Horatio Nelson, killed during his triumph over Napoleon's navy off Trafalgar—the monument's reliefs were cast from French cannons. *(Tube: Charing Cross.)*

ST. MARTIN'S-IN-THE-FIELDS. Designer James Gibbs topped the templar classicism of this 18th-century church with a Gothic steeple. The **crypt** has been cleared of all those dreary coffins to make room for a gallery, a book shop, a brass rubbing center, and a cafe. *(Trafalgar Sq. ☎ 7930 0089. Free concerts M-Tu and F 1:05pm. Reserve seats for evening concerts by phone M-F 10am-4pm ☎ 7839 8362; or in the bookstore, open M-W 10am-6pm and Th-Sa 10am-7:30pm. Cafe open M-Sa 10am-8pm, Su noon-6pm.)*

PICCADILLY CIRCUS. All of the West End's major arteries—Piccadilly, Regent St., Shaftesbury Ave., and the Haymarket—merge and swirl around Piccadilly Circus, a hub of lurid neon signs, hordes of tourists, and a fountain topped by a statue everyone calls **Eros.** Theaterland spans out from this hub. *(Tube: Piccadilly Circus.)*

BURLINGTON HOUSE. The only remnant of Piccadilly's stately past is this showy mansion, built in 1665. It was redesigned in the 18th century to house the burgeoning **Royal Academy of Arts** (see p. 177). The Academy consists of exhibition galleries and a school of art. *(Opposite 185 Piccadilly Circus. Tube: Piccadilly Circus or Green Park.)*

REGENT STREET. Running north from Piccadilly Circus are the grand facades of (Upper) Regent St., which lead to Oxford Circus. The buildings and street were built by John Nash in the early 19th century as part of a processional route. Today, the street is known for its elegant shopping. *(Tube: Piccadilly Circus or Oxford St.)*

COVENT GARDEN, SOHO, AND ENVIRONS

The cafes, pubs, upscale shops, and slick crowds animating Covent Garden today belie the square's medieval beginnings as a literal "convent garden" where monks grew vegetables. *(Tube: Covent Garden.)* For centuries, nearby Soho was London's red-light district of prostitutes and sex shows. Today Soho overflows with artists and club kids, while the gay-owned restaurants and bars of **Old Compton Street** have turned Soho into the heart of gay London. *(Tube: Tottenham Ct. Rd. or Leicester Sq.)*

CARNABY STREET. Running parallel to Regent St., this notorious hotbed of 1960s sex, fashion, and Mods is the heart of "Swingin' London." Chic boutiques and bohemian stores mix with stalls of junky souvenirs. *(Tube: Oxford Circus.)*

LEICESTER SQUARE. Just south of Shaftesbury Ave., between Piccadilly Circus and Charing Cross Rd., lies this entertainment nexus of cinemas, clubs, and street entertainers. A large queue marks the **half-price ticket booth** where same-day theater tickets are sold for a number of shows. *(Tube: Leicester Sq.)*

THEATRE ROYAL AND ROYAL OPERA HOUSE. These two venues represent a long tradition of theater in the Covent Garden area. The **Theatre Royal,** with an entrance on Catherine St., dates from 1812. The **Royal Opera House,** on Bow St., began as a theater for concerts and plays in 1732 and currently houses the Royal Opera and Royal Ballet companies. *(Tube: Covent Garden.)*

CHINATOWN. Cantonese immigrants first arrived in Britain as cooks on British ships, and then Chinatown swelled with immigrants from Hong Kong. The streets spout Chinese signs and pagoda-like phone booths. The vibrant **Chinese New Year Festival** takes place at the beginning of February. *(Tube: Leicester Sq.)*

ROYAL COURTS OF JUSTICE. The Strand and Fleet St. meet at this elaborate Gothic structure—easily mistaken for a cathedral—designed in 1874 for the Supreme Court of Judicature. At the Strand entrance, displays explain the court system. *(Tube: Temple. ☎ 7947 6000. Open M-F 9am-4:30pm.)*

THE STRAND AND FLEET STREET

Named for the one-time river (now a sewer) that flows from Hampstead to the Thames, **Fleet Street** was until recently the hub of British journalism. Nowadays, Fleet St. is just a celebrated name and a few (vacated) famous buildings. As Fleet St. runs from Holburn toward Covent Garden it changes its name to **the Strand.** As host to two major London universities, it is a center of education.

THE STRAND. Built to connect the City with Westminster Palace and Parliament, the area is now a center of education in London. The thoroughfare curves from Trafalgar Sq. past many theaters to Aldwych. *(Tube: Holborn or Charing Cross.)*

KING'S COLLEGE AND LONDON SCHOOL OF ECONOMICS. As you stroll away from the Courts of Justice on Houghton St., two of London's top educational institutions come into view. **King's College** stands opposite the prestigious **London School of Economics (LSE)**, a '60s center for student radicalism. *(Tube: Holborn.)*

SOMERSET HOUSE. A magnificent Palladian structure built by Sir William Chambers in 1776, Somerset House stands on the site of a 16th-century palace. Formerly a center of the Royal Navy, the building now houses birth records as well as the exquisite Impressionist **Courtauld Collection.** *(On the Strand. Tube: Temple.)*

ST. CLEMENT DANES. The melodious bells of this handsome church get their 15 seconds of fame in the nursery rhyme "Oranges and lemons, say the bells of St. Clement's." Designed by Christopher Wren in 1682, today it is the official church of the Royal Air Force. *(On the Strand, east of St. Mary-le-Strand's. Tube: Temple. ☎ 7242 8282. Open daily 8am-5pm. Bells ring daily 9am, noon, 3, and 6pm.)*

THE EMBANKMENT. This road runs along the Thames, parallel to the Strand. Between the Hungerford and Waterloo Bridges stands London's oldest (though not indigenous) landmark, **Cleopatra's Needle**, an Egyptian obelisk from 1450 BC, stolen by the Viceroy of Egypt in 1878. *(Tube: Charing Cross or Embankment.)*

THE CITY OF LONDON

Until the 18th century, the City of London *was* London. Today, the single-square-mile City is the financial center of Europe. When 350,000 commuters go home each weekday, they leave behind a resident population of only 6000. The City hums on weekdays, is dead on Saturdays, and seems downright ghostly on Sundays. The massive **Bank of England** controls the country's finances, and the **Stock Exchange** makes (or breaks) the nation's fortune. *(Tube: Bank.)*

ST. PAUL'S CATHEDRAL

Tube: St. Paul's. Open M-Sa 8:30am-4pm. Dome open M-Sa 9:30am-4pm. Supertours (90min.) depart at 11am, 11:30am, 1:30pm, and 2pm. £2.50, students and seniors £2, children £1. 45min. audio tours available 8:45am-3:30pm. £3.50, students and seniors £3. Admission to cathedral, galleries, and crypt £5, students and seniors £4.

St. Paul's, topped by its beautiful Neoclassical dome, is arguably the most stunning architectural sight in London, a physical and spiritual symbol of the city. Sir Christopher Wren's enormous (157m by 76m) creation dominates its surroundings. The current edifice is the 5th cathedral to stand on the site; the first was founded in AD 604 and destroyed by fire. The fourth and most massive cathedral, now referred to as "Old St. Paul's," was a medieval structure built by the Normans. This was one of the largest in Europe, topped by a spire ascending 150m, a structure taller than the current one, which tops out at 111m. Falling into almost complete neglect in the 16th-century, the cathedral became more of a marketplace than a church. Wren had already started drawing up his grand scheme in 1666 when the Great Fire demolished the cathedral, giving him the opportunity to build from scratch.

Above the marble **High Altar** looms the crowning glory, the ceiling mosaic of *Christ Seated in Majesty*. Farther into the church, the north choir aisle holds *Mother and Child*, a modern sculpture by Henry Moore. Behind the altar you'll find the **American Memorial Chapel,** dedicated to the 28,000 US soldiers based in Britain who died during World War II. Climbing to any of the three levels within the dome rewards the stout of heart, leg, and soul. Over 250 steps lead to the **Whispering Gallery,** on the inside base of the dome. It's a perfect resounding chamber: whisper into the wall, and a friend on the other side should be able to hear you. A further 119 steps up, the first external view beckons from the **Stone Gallery,** only to be eclipsed 152 steps later by the panorama from the **Golden Gallery** atop the dome. In the other vertical direction, the **crypt** (the largest in Europe) is saturated with tombs of, and monuments to, great Britons Florence Nightingale, Lawrence of Arabia, and Alexander Fleming, the discoverer of penicillin.

THE TOWER OF LONDON

Tube: Tower Hill or DLR: Tower Gateway. ☎ 7709 0765. Yeoman Warders ("Beefeaters") lead free tours every 30min. starting 9:30am M-Sa, 10am Su, plus 8 daily themed tours. Audio tours; £2. Frequent exhibitions, ceremonies, and re-enactments of historic events; call for details. For tickets to the Ceremony of the Keys, and the 700-year-old nightly ritual locking of the gates, write 6 weeks in advance to the Ceremony of the Keys, Waterloo Block, HM Tower of London, EC3N 4AB, with the full name of those attending and a choice of dates, enclosing a stamped addressed envelope or international response coupon; free. Tower open Mar.-Oct. M-Sa 9am-5pm, Su 10am-5pm; Nov.-Feb. closes 4pm. Last ticket sold at 4pm. £11, students and seniors £8.30, ages 5-15 £7.30, families £33. Avoid long queues by buying tickets in advance or from Tube stations.

The oldest continuously occupied fortress in Europe, "The Tower" was founded by William the Conqueror in 1066 to provide protection for and from his subjects. Richard the Lionheart began the construction of additional defenses around the original White Tower in 1189, and further work by Henry III and Edward I brought the Tower close to its present condition. Now 20 towers stand behind its walls, all connected by massive walls and gateways, forming fortifications disheartening to visitors even today. The whole castle used to be surrounded by a broad moat, but cholera epidemics led to its draining in 1843. The filled land became a vegetable garden during World War II but has since sprouted a tennis court for the Yeomen of the Guard Extraordinary. These "Beefeaters"—whose nickname is a reference to their daily allowance of beef in former times—still guard the fortress.

Visitors enter the Tower through the tower on the southwest of the **Outer Ward,** which sports a precariously hung portcullis. The password, required for entry here after hours, has been changed every day since 1327. German spies were executed in the Outer Ward during World War II. Along the outer wall, **St. Thomas's Tower** (named after Thomas à Becket) tops the evocative **Traitors' Gate,** through which boats once brought the condemned to the Tower.

Completed in 1097, the **White Tower** overpowers all the fortifications that were later built around it. The White Tower houses an expansive display from the **Royal Armouries** and a display of **Instruments of Torture.** The **Bell Tower** squats in the southwest corner of the **Inner Ward.** Since the 1190s, this tower has sounded the curfew bell each night. Henry III lived in the adjacent **Wakefield Tower,** the second largest in the complex. For many, a visit to the Tower climaxes with a glimpse of the **Crown Jewels.** The queue at the **Jewel House** is a miracle of crowd management. Tourists file past room after room of rope barriers while video projections on the walls show larger-than-life depictions of the jewels in action, including footage of Elizabeth II's coronation. Finally, the crowd is ushered into the vault and onto moving walkways that whisk them past the dazzling crowns and insure no awestruck gazers hold up the queue. Cromwell melted down much of the original booty; most now dates from after Charles II's restoration in 1660. The **Imperial State Crown** and the **Sceptre with the Cross** feature the Stars of Africa, cut from the Cullinan Diamond. **St. Edward's Crown,** made for Charles II in 1661, is only worn during coronation. Look for the **Queen Mother's Crown,** which contains the Koh-I-Noor diamond. Legend claims the diamond brings luck—to women only.

OTHER SIGHTS NEAR CITY OF LONDON

TOWER BRIDGE. A granite-and-steel structure reminiscent of a castle with a drawbridge, the bridge is a postcard image of the city. The **Tower Bridge Experience** explains the bridge's genesis through the eyes of its designers. *(Tube: Tower Hill; follow signs. ☎ 7403 3761. Open daily Apr.-Oct. 10am-6:30pm; Nov.-Mar. 9:30am-6pm. £6.25.)*

MONUMENT. Completed in 1677, the pillar's 202 ft. offer an expansive view of London. The monument stands mere feet from Pudding Ln., where the 1666 Great Fire broke out and then "rushed devastating through every quarter." *(☎ 7626 2717. Tube: Monument. Open Apr.-Sept. daily 10am-6pm. £1.50, child 50p.)*

LLOYD'S. This 1986 building supplies the most startling architectural clash in the City, with ducts, lifts, and chutes straight out of the 21st century; it seems not so

BRITAIN

much a building as a vertical street. The **Lutine Bell** is occasionally rung—once for bad insurance news, twice for good. *(Off Leadenhall St. Tube: Monument.)*

BARBICAN CENTRE. A 37-acre brutalist masterpiece, the Barbican is a maze of restaurants, gardens, and exhibition halls, described at its 1982 opening as "the city's gift to the nation." The Royal Shakespeare Company, the Museum of London, and the Barbican Art Gallery call this complex home, as do the many politicians and actors who reside in the Barbican's apartment buildings. *(Tube: Barbican or Moorgate. Library open M and W-F 9:30am-5:30pm, Tu 9:30am-7:30pm, Sa 9:30am-12:30pm.)*

HYDE PARK AND ENVIRONS

HYDE PARK AND KENSINGTON GARDENS. The lakes and green lawns of Hyde Park and the contiguous Kensington Gardens, the "Lungs of London," sum to the largest open area (1 sq. mi.) in the city center. *(Tube: Hyde Park Corner or Marble Arch. Park open daily 5am-midnight. Gardens open daily dawn-dusk. Free.)*

KENSINGTON PALACE. At the far west of the Gardens is Kensington, originally the residence of King William III and Queen Mary II. The birthplace of Queen Victoria, and most recently home to the late Diana, Princess of Wales, Kensington has moved in and out of vogue with the Royal Family. *(Tube: High St Kensington. ☎ 7937 9561. Tours 1¼hr., May-Sept. M-Sa every hr. 10am-5pm. £8.50, students £6.70.)*

SPEAKERS' CORNER. On summer evenings and on Sundays, proselytizers, politicos, and flat-out crazies assemble to dispense the fruits of their knowledge to whomever will bite. *(Tube: Marble Arch. In the northeastern corner of Hyde Park.)*

NOTTING HILL AND PORTOBELLO ROAD. Simultaneously shabby and extravagant, Notting Hill pulses with chaotic energy. Genteel streets with private garden squares intersect noisy avenues and the wafting incense of large West Indian and Moroccan communities (usually no Hugh Grant, though). The **Notting Hill Carnival,** Europe's biggest outdoor festival, is held the last weekend in August. *(Tube: Notting Hill Gate.)* **Portobello Rd.** is the commercial road that is the heart of Notting Hill's bustling activity. Antique stores and galleries line the southern end of Portobello near the Notting Hill Gate Tube station. Near Lancaster Rd. and the Westway (the overhead highway) vendors sell clothing, vinyl, and trinkets. *(Tube: Notting Hill Gate; turn on Pembridge Rd. from the station, and Portobello Rd. is the 3rd left.)*

NORTH LONDON

221B BAKER STREET. The area's most fondly remembered resident is Sherlock Holmes who, although fictitious, still receives 50 letters per week addressed to his residence at 221b Baker St. The **Sherlock Holmes Museum,** 239 Baker St., thrills with a re-creation of the detective's lodgings. *(Tube: Baker St.)*

REGENT'S PARK. Just to the north of Baker St. and the south of Camden Town, the 500-acre, wide-open Regent's Park is full of lakes, gardens, promenades, and Londoners. One of London's most beautiful spaces, the park contains well-kept lawns, broad walkways (including Broad Walk), playing fields, and scores of sunbathers. It also houses the **London Zoo.** *(☎ 7486 7905; constabulary ☎ 7935 1259. Tube: Regent's Park, Great Portland St., Baker St., or Camden Town. Open daily 6am-dusk.)*

CAMDEN TOWN. At the time of the canal's construction in the 19th century, Camden Town was a solid working-class district spliced with railways and covered in soot. Camden Town today is a stomping ground for trendy youth subcultures. At **Camden Market,** hundreds of merchants set up stands that draw swarms of bargain-seeking Londoners and bewildered tourists every weekend. *(Tube: Camden Town.)*

BLOOMSBURY. During the first half of the 20th century, Bloomsbury gained its reputation as an intellectual and artistic center, due largely to the presence of the famed Bloomsbury Group, which included biographer Lytton Strachey, novelist E.M. Forster, art critic Roger Fry, painter Vanessa Bell (sister of Virginia Woolf), and hovering on the fringe, T.S. Eliot, the eminent British poet from St. Louis, Missouri. Although very little of the famed intellectual gossip and high modernist argot currently emanates from 51 Gordon Sq. (Virginia Woolf's house and the center of the group), the area maintains an earnestly intellectual atmosphere. Today, the **British Museum** (p. 177), the **British Library,** and the University College London guarantee a continued concentration of cerebral, as well as tourist, activities in the area. Bloomsbury's streets are lined with B&Bs and student housing.

RUSSELL SQUARE. Directly northeast of the British Museum, Russell Square squares off as central London's second-largest, after Lincoln's Inn Fields. T.S. Eliot, the "Pope of Russell Square," hid from his emotionally ailing first wife at #24 while he worked as an editor at and later director of Faber and Faber, the famed publishing house. Also of note is the decadently Victorian **Hotel Russell** on the eastern side of the square, a confection of brick and terra-cotta. *(Tube: Russell Sq.)*

DICKENS HOUSE. Charles Dickens lived here from 1837 to 1839, scribbling parts of *Nicholas Nickleby*, *Barnaby Rudge*, and *Oliver Twist*. Now a four-floor museum and library of Dickens paraphernalia, the house holds an array of prints, photographs, manuscripts, and letters. *(48 Doughty St., east of Russell Sq. and parallel to Gray's Inn Rd. Tube: Russell Sq. or Chancery Ln. Open M-Sa 10am-5pm. £3.50, students £2.50.)*

HAMPSTEAD HEATH. The most fabulous green space in the metropolis is the perfect place to get lost in vast meadows and woodlands and forget the hustle and bustle of the city with carefree picnickers, kite-flyers, and anglers. On a hot day, take a dip in the murky waters of **Kenwood Ladies' Pond, Highgate Men's Pond,** or the **Mixed Bathing Pond.** *(Tube: Hampstead. Rail: Hampstead Heath. Pools open daily in summer 7-9:30am and 10am-7pm; off-season 7-10am. £3, students £1; free before 10am.)*

HIGHGATE. To the northeast of Hampstead lies Highgate. While not the home of glittering literati like neighboring Hampstead, it does contain one of London's most well-known cemeteries and Karl Marx's final resting place. A good way to get a feel for Highgate (and a good glimpse of London) is to climb Highgate Hill, London's highest at 424 ft. above the Thames. *(Tube: Archway (not Highgate), then Bus #210 to Highgate Village. From Hampstead, it's about a 45min. walk across the Heath, staying more or less parallel to Spaniard's Rd.)*

EAST LONDON

THE EAST END. A large working-class English population moved into the district during the Industrial Revolution, followed by a wave of Jewish immigrants fleeing persecution in Eastern Europe, who settled around **Whitechapel.** Jewish success in the rag trade drew the attention of the British Union of Fascists, who instigated anti-Semitic violence that culminated in the "Battle of Cable Street" in 1936. A mural on St. George's Town Hall at 236 Cable St. commemorates the victory won in the streets that day. In 1978, a wave of immigration brought a large Bangladeshi community to the East End. Today's East End is a conglomeration of minority groups. The most recent wave of immigrants to join the East End consists of London artists; their work occasionally hangs in the **Whitechapel Art Gallery** (see p. 180). At the heart of the Muslim Bangladeshi community is **Brick Lane,** lined with Indian and Bangladeshi restaurants and colorful textile shops. Stalls selling everything from leather jackets to salt beef sandwiches flank Brick Ln. and **Petticoat Lane.** Nearby on 82-92 Whitechapel Rd., the **East London Mosque,** London's first, testifies to the size of the Muslim community. *(Tube: Aldgate East. To reach Brick Ln., go left up Whitechapel as you exit the Tube station; turn left onto Osbourne St., which turns into Brick Ln.)*

BEVIS MARKS SYNAGOGUE. The city's oldest standing synagogue sits at Bevis Marks and Heneage Ln. The congregation traces its roots back to Spanish and Portuguese Jews who inhabited the area as early as 1657. Rabbi Menashe Ben Israel founded the synagogue in 1701, 435 years after Jews were first expelled from England. *(Tube: Aldgate. From Aldgate High St. turn right onto Houndsditch; Creechurch Ln. on the left leads to Bevis Marks. ☎ 7626 1274. Organized tours Su-W and F noon; call in advance. Open Su-M, W, and F 11:30am-1pm, Tu 10:30am-4pm. Suggested donation £1.)*

DOCKLANDS. Docklands proper covers a huge expanse (55 mi. of waterfront to be exact), from the Tower of London to Greenwich. The center of the new 8.5 sq. mi. development is on the **Isle of Dogs,** the spit of land defined by a sharp U-shaped bend in the Thames. To the east lie the **Royal Docks,** once the center of one of history's proudest trading empires. **Canary Wharf,** at a towering 800 ft., is Britain's tallest edifice and the jewel of Docklands, visible from almost anywhere in London. (*DLR: Canary Wharf.*) Getting off at Shadwell station, you'll see **St. George-in-the-East,** an old, working-class community. Drab housing, dusty streets, traditional pubs, cafes, and pie-and-mash shops stand in the throes of a major transformation brought on by an infusion of Bengali immigrants. (☎ *7481 1345. Open daily 9am-5pm.*)

THE SOUTH BANK AND LAMBETH

OXO TOWER AND GABRIEL'S WHARF. The most colorful changes in the South Bank landscape result from the unflagging efforts of a nonprofit development company, **Coin Street Community Builders (CSCB).** The nearby **Museum Of...** and the **gallery@oxo** are succeeding in their aim to provide a democratic artistic forum. (*Between Waterloo and Blackfriars Bridges on Barge House St. Tube: Blackfriars or Waterloo.*) **Gabriel's Wharf,** another CSCB project revolving around a designer crafts market, is not far from the OXO Tower on Upper Ground. In summer, there are occasional free festivals. (*Tube: Blackfriars or Waterloo. Crafts workshops Tu-Su 11am-6pm.*)

SOUTH BANK CENTRE. This massive performing-arts center occupies a series of prominent modern buildings overlooking the river. The center is comprised of the **National Film Theatre,** the **Hayward Gallery,** the **Royal Festival Hall,** and the **Royal National Theatre.** The **National Film Theatre,** tucked under Waterloo Bridge directly on the South Bank, operates a continually rotating program of British cinema, as well as classic films from other countries. The **Hayward Gallery** houses imaginative contemporary art exhibitions, and is visible for miles by the fluorescent weather sculpture that tops the building. The 3000-seat **Royal Festival Hall** is home to the London Philharmonic Orchestra, while its smaller counterparts, the **Queen Elizabeth Hall** and the **Purcell Room** host chamber concerts and smaller orchestras. There are free concerts in the Festival Hall Wednesday to Sunday lunchtimes and Friday evenings. The **Royal National Theatre** (see p. 181) contains three state-of-the-art theaters; the Olivier, the smaller Lyttleton, and the experimental Cottlesloe. (*Tube: Waterloo, then follow signs for York Rd.; or Embankment and cross the Hungerford footbridge.*)

ROSE AND GLOBE THEATRES. Southwark's greatest vice has always been theater. Shakespeare's and Marlowe's plays were performed at the Rose, which was built in 1587. Remnants of the Rose, discovered during construction in 1989, are displayed underneath a new office block at Park St. and Rose Alley. The remains of Shakespeare's **Globe Theatre** (see p. 181) were discovered just months after those of the Rose, and soon after, the late actor/director Sam Wanamaker spearheaded the reconstruction of the Globe on the riverbank. The theater held its first full season in 1997. The space itself is not only a wonderful reconstruction, but a unique experience in theater-going. (*New Globe Walk, Bankside. Tube: London Bridge.* ☎ *7902 1400. 45min. tours available May-Sept. M 9am-6pm, Tu-Su 9am-noon; Oct.-Apr. daily 10am-5pm. £6, seniors and students £5, children £4.*)

MILLENNIUM DOME. This enormous white structure cost £7 million; but Londoners still aren't sure what exactly it does. Word is Japanese investors plan to turn it into an amusement park. (*Tube: North Greenwich. There are also plans to run a link from the East India DLR station. £20, students £16.50. Reserve by calling* ☎ *(0870) 606 20 00, or online at www.dome2000.co.uk.*)

WEST LONDON

KEW GARDENS. The perfect antidote to central London, the Royal Botanic Gardens at Kew provide a breath of fresh air. Yet another example of the Empire's collecting frenzy, the 124-acre park houses the living bank of a research collection with millions of DNA and seeds and thousands of plants and flowers. The steamy, tropical **Palm House,** a masterpiece of Victorian engineering built in 1848, is replete with voluptuous fronds. But it's dwarfed by its younger Victorian sibling, the **Temperate House,** with a cooler climate that nurtures many species, arranged according to geographic origins. *(Tube: Richmond, or take a Westminster Passenger Association (☎ 7930 4721; www.wpsa.co.uk) boat from Westminster Pier (Tube: Westminster). Boat fares: £8, round-trip £12, ages 5-15 £3.50, £6; times and trip lengths depend on the tide. The tourist office here is open May-Sept. M-Sa 10am-5pm, Su 10:30am-1:30pm; Oct.-Apr. M-Sa 10am-5pm.*

HAMPTON COURT PALACE. Although a monarch hasn't lived here since George II moved out over 200 years ago, Hampton Court Palace continues to exude regal charm. Six miles down the Thames from Richmond, the brick palace housed over 1500 court members at its height. The 60 marvelous acres of the **Palace Gardens** are open and free, and contain celebrated amusements, including the **maze,** a hedgerow labyrinth first planted in 1714. *(Take the train to Hampton Court from Waterloo (32min.; every 30min.; round-trip £4, with zone 2-6 Travelcard £3.50) and walk the 2min. to the palace, or take the tube to Richmond and take the R68 bus (70p). ☎ 8781 9500; www.hrp.org.uk. Wheelchairs and electric buggies available from West Gate.)*

🏛 MUSEUMS

London's museums distinguish themselves as some of the best in the world; many are also free. The **London Go See Card** allows unlimited access to 13 participating museums for three or seven days. The card can be purchased at any of the participating museums (the V&A, the Science Museum, the Natural History Museum, the Royal Academy of Arts, the Hayward Gallery, the Design Museum, the London Transport Museum, the Museum of London, the Museum of the Moving Image, and the Courtauld Institute), but will afford you substantial discounts only if you plan to visit *many* museums, or if you plan to visit a particularly expensive museum more than once. (3-day card £16, families £32; 7-day card £26, £50.)

🏛 BRITISH MUSEUM

Great Russell St., rear entrance on Montague St. ☎ 7323 8299; www.british-museum.ac.uk. Tube: Tottenham Court Rd., Goodge St., Russell Sq., or Holborn. 1½hr. highlights tour M-Sa 10:30, 11am, 1:30pm, 2:30; Su 12:30, 1:30, 2:30, and 4pm. £7, students and under 16 £4. 1hr. focus tours depart M-Sa 1pm from upstairs, 3:30pm and Su 4:30pm downstairs; £5, £3. Visually-impaired travelers should enquire about tactile exhibits and touch-tours. Open M-Sa 10am-5pm, Su noon-6pm. Free; suggested donation £2. Special exhibits £4, students and seniors £3.

Founded in 1753, the museum began with the personal collection of Sir Hans Sloane. Robert Smirke drew up the design of the current Neoclassical building in 1824; construction took 30 years. The outstanding **Egyptian collection** contains imposing statues of Amenophis III as well as the **Rosetta Stone.** The Egyptian gallery contains papyri such as the *Book of the Dead of Ani,* a comprehensive exhibit on Egyptian funerary archaeology. The Assyrian galleries contain enormous reliefs from Nineveh (704-668 BC). The **Greek exhibits** are dominated by the **Elgin Marbles,** 5th-century BC reliefs from the Parthenon, now residing in the spacious Duveen Gallery. Other Hellenic highlights include the complete Ionic facade of the **Nereid Monument,** one of the female caryatid columns from the Acropolis. Frieze slabs and some free-standing sculpture commemorate the **Temple of Artemis,** built to replace the one buried by Herostratus in 356 BC. Among the many sculptures of the Roman antiquities, the dark blue glass of the **Portland Vase** stands out. In 1845, it was shattered by a drunken museum-goer; when it was put back together, 37 chips were left over. The **Romano-Britain section** includes the **Mindenhall Treasure,** a magnificent collection of 4th-century silver tableware. Nearby lies **Lindow Man,** an Iron Age Celt apparently sacrificed in a gruesome ritual and preserved in a peat bog.

The **Sutton Hoo Ship Burial,** an Anglo-Saxon ship buried (and subsequently dug up) in Suffolk complete with an unknown king, is the centerpiece of the **Medieval galleries.** The majority of the **Asian Collections** resides in Gallery 33. The gallery's eastern half is dedicated to the Chinese collection, renowned for its ancient **Shang** bronzes and fine porcelains, and the western half is filled by Indian and Southeast Asian exhibits. Upstairs, the collection continues with a series of three galleries displaying Japanese and Korean artifacts, paintings, and calligraphy. Downstairs by the Montague St. entrance, don't miss the **Islamic art gallery** with its tiles, ceramics and other treasures from all over the Muslim world.

▨ NATIONAL GALLERY

Trafalgar Sq. Tube: Charing Cross, Leicester Sq., or Piccadilly Circus. ☎ 7747 2885; www.nationalgallery.org.uk. Mid-May to Sept., a free Art Bus shuttles between the National Gallery, the Tate Britain, and the Tate Modern (2 per hr. 10am-6pm). Tours start from the Sainsbury Wing info desk daily at 11:30am and 2:30pm and W 6:30pm; tours for the visually impaired 3rd Sa of month 11:30am; sign-language tour 1st Sa of month 11:30am. Audioguides covering almost every work available at main entrance and Sainsbury Wing foyer. Donation requested. Orange St. and Sainsbury Wing entrances wheelchair accessible. Open Th-Tu 10am-6pm, W 10am-9pm. Free except for some exhibitions.

The National Gallery maintains one of the world's finest collections of Western art from the Middle Ages to the end of the 19th century, divided chronologically among four distinct wings. You could spend days ambling through the maze of galleries; if you're pressed for time and know what you want to see, the high-tech **Micro Gallery,** in the Sainsbury wing, will guide you through the collection on-line and print out a personalized tour of the paintings you want to see.

The **Sainsbury Wing,** the newest part of the Gallery, holds the oldest part of the collection. Botticelli's *Venus and Mars*, Raphael's *Crucifixion*, and da Vinci's *Virgin of the Rocks*, number among the more famous works, most of which are devotional works created between 1260 and 1510. Paintings from 1510 to 1600 are found in the **West Wing,** left of the Trafalgar Sq. entrance. The **North Wing** holds 17th-century Italian, Spanish, Flemish, and French paintings, including 12 Rembrandts. The **East Wing,** to the right of the main entrance, is devoted to painting from 1700 to 1900, including a strong English collection. Impressionist works include a number of Monet's near-abstract water lilies and Cézanne's *Old Woman with Roses.*

TATE MODERN

Sumner St., Bankside. Tube: Southwark. ☎ 7887 8000. Mid-May to Sept., a free Art Bus shuttles between the National Gallery, the Tate Britain, and the Tate Modern (every 30min. 10am-6pm). Daily highlights tours at 10:30, 11:30am, 2:30, 3:30pm. Free; audioguide £1. Wheelchair access; 6 wheelchairs can be reserved ☎ 7887 8888. Open Su-Th 10am-6pm, F-Sa 10pm-10pm. Free; admission charged to some exhibitions.

Some might call it instant karma. Where other millennium projects struggled to pull in the crowds, the Tate became an instant landmark and the crowning glory of the revitalized South Bank area upon its opening in May 2000. Crowds snaked around London's first large-scale museum dedicated entirely to modern art, housed in a stunning converted power station designed by Giles Gilbert Scott. The Swiss firm Herzog and de Meuron renovated the building and have turned the old turbine room into an immense top-lit cavern 155m long and 35m high while preserving the old power station's industrial feel.

Despite the fanfare that greeted its opening, Tate Modern has taken some flak for its controversial curatorial method, which groups works thematically instead of chronologically. The permanent collection is divided into four major sections ("Landscape/Matter/Environment," "Still Life/Object/Real Life," "History/Memory/Society," and "Nude/Action/Body"), spread over floors 3 and 5, with floor 4 dedicated to temporary exhibits. For instance, Cezanne's *Still Life with Water Jug* shares the room with Carl Andre's low-form sculpture *Steel Zinc Plain*. Whatever you think about the way it's arranged, there's no doubt that the Tate now has the space to put more of its collection on display. The third floor alone has Marcel Duchamps's *Fountain*, Roy Lichtenstein's *Bull Profile Series: Bull I-VI*, and Jackson Pollock's hyperactive *Summertime 9a*, while the fifth holds Andy Warhol's *Marilyn Diptych* and Picasso's *Weeping Woman*.

TATE BRITAIN

Millbank. Tube: Pimlico. ☎ 7887 8008, recorded info ☎ 7887 8000; www.tate.org.uk. Museum tour M-F 12:30pm, Sa 3pm. Turner collection tour M-F 11:30am. Audio tour £3, students and seniors £2. Touch tours for visually impaired visitors ☎ 7887 8725. Museum open daily 10am-5:50pm. Free.

With the opening of the new Tate Modern (above), the original Tate has now been renamed the Tate Britain, and holds a superb collection of British works from the 16th century to the present day. The collection starts with a room at the far end of the gallery devoted to 16th- and 17th-century painting. The **parade of Constables** includes the famous views of Salisbury Cathedral, and a number of Hampstead scenes dotted with red saddle splashes. Don't miss the visionary works of William Blake, or the haunting images of Sir John Everett Millais, a founder of the Pre-Raphaelite Brotherhood. The Tate's chronologically ordered displays have been supplemented by thematic arrangements. "Representing Britain 1500-2000" combines works to explore "Literature & Fantasy," "Public & Private," "Home & Abroad," and "Artists & Models." There are also rooms devoted to individual artists; works by Gainsborough, Hockney, Sickert, and Blake are all highlighted.

NATIONAL PORTRAIT GALLERY

St. Martin's Pl., just opposite St.-Martin's-in-the-Fields. Tube: Charing Cross or Leicester Sq. ☎ 7306 0055, recorded info ☎ 7312 2463; www.npg.org.uk. Frequent free daytime lectures. Evening lectures Th 7pm (£3, students £2); concerts F 7pm (mostly free). Audioguide available in entrance hall; suggested donation £3, ID or credit card deposit required. Orange St. entrance is wheelchair accessible. Open M-W 10am-6pm, Th-F 10am-9pm, Sa-Su 10am-6pm. Free, excluding temporary exhibits.

This unofficial Who's Who in Britain began in 1856 as "the fulfillment of a patriotic and moral ideal"—namely to showcase Britain's most officially noteworthy citizens. The museum's declared principle of looking "to the celebrity of the person represented, rather than to the merit of the artist" does not seem to have affected the quality of the works displayed. The sleek new **Ondaatje wing** opened in May 2000, providing a suite of climate-controlled top-floor rooms for the oldest paintings. The **Elizabethan portraits** hang in a room modeled after a Tudor long gallery; the dark walls and dramatic fiber-optic backlighting highlight pictures such as William Scrot's astonishing distorted-perspective portrait of Edward VI, designed to be viewed from an extreme angle. The Gallery normally commissions three new portraits a year; new backs against the wall for 2000 include stage director and physician Jonathan Miller, author Doris Lessing, and tycoon Richard Branson.

VICTORIA AND ALBERT

Cromwell Rd. Tube: South Kensington. ☎ 7942 2000; www.vam.ac.uk. Tours (1hr.) leave hourly from Cromwell St. info desk daily 12:30-3:30pm, Tu-Su also 10:30am and 11:30am. Wheelchair access at the side entrance on Exhibition Rd.; call ahead (☎ 7942 2000). Open M-Su 10am-5:45pm, W also 6:30-9:30pm. £5, seniors £3; free for students, disabled, and under 15; free for everyone daily 4:30-5:45pm. Night openings (select galleries only) £3. Season ticket for all 3 South Kensington museums (the V&A, the Science, and the Natural History) £29, two adults £49.50, students £16.

Founded in 1852 to encourage excellence in art and design, the original curators were deluged with objects from around the world. The popular **dress collection** traces clothing fashions, focusing mainly on women's wear, from the 16th-century to the present. Persian carpets and Moroccan rugs distinguish the V&A's collection of **Islamic Art,** the largest and most breathtaking piece of which is the Persian Ardabil carpet. The **Asian collections** are particularly formidable. The Gallery of Indian Art contains splendid textiles, paintings, Mughal jewelry, and decor. The elegant **Gallery of Chinese Art** divides 5000 years of Chinese art into six categories—Eating and Drinking, Living, Worship, Ruling, Collecting, and Burial. The **Japanese gallery** displays elaborate armor and intriguing contemporary sculpture, and the Korean gallery recognizes the depth and longevity of Korean culture.

BRITAIN

The **European collections** are just as impressive. The Medieval Treasury, in the center of the ground floor, features vestments, plates, stained glass, and illuminations. Among the upstairs collections you'll find the **silver, stained glass,** and the heavily-protected **jewelry** galleries. Galleries 70-74 exhibit 20th-century **design,** with some emphasis on chairs, and typefaces (including Johnston Sans Serif, the omnipresent London Transport font). The **Frank Lloyd Wright Gallery** shows designs by the architect, including the interior of the Kauffmann Office, originally commissioned for a Pittsburgh department store. On the same floor, the **Gallery of Photography** traces the history of photography and displays famous snapshots.

There are various less conventional ways to see the museum. On Sundays, the New Restaurant hosts a jazz brunch, with live music accompanying either an English breakfast or lunch. **Late View,** late night openings (most summer W and occasional F), feature lectures, live performances, guest DJs, and a bar.

OTHER MUSEUMS

■ **The Courtauld Gallery** (☎ 7848 2526), at Somerset House, on The Strand, WC2, opposite the corner of Aldwych and The Strand. Tube: Temple, Embankment, Charing Cross, or Covent Garden. Intimate 11-room gallery with world-famous masterpieces, mostly Impressionist and post-Impressionist. Open M-Sa 10am-6pm, Su 2pm-6pm. £4, students and seniors £2; M half-price.

■ **Sir John Soane's Museum,** 13 Lincoln's Inn Fields, WC2 (☎ 7405 2107). Tube: Holborn. Soane was an architect's architect, but the idiosyncratic home he designed for himself will intrigue even laypeople. Artifacts on display include Hogarth paintings and the massive sarcophagus of Seti I. Tours Sa 2:30pm. Open Tu-Sa 10am-5pm. Free.

Madame Tussaud's (☎ (0870) 400 30 00), on Marylebone Rd., NW1. Tube: Baker St. The classic waxwork museum, founded by an emigré aristocrat who made life-size models of French nobility. Beat horrific lines by going very early or very late. A green dome shelters the adjacent **Planetarium.** Both open in summer M-F 9am-5:30pm, Sa-Su 9:30am-5:30pm; rest of year opens 10am. £11.50, combined entry £13.95.

Whitechapel Art Gallery, Whitechapel High St., E1 (☎ 7377 7888). Tube: Aldgate East. Whitechapel's sunny galleries contain no permanent collection, but host some of Britain's (and the Continent's) most daring exhibitions of contemporary art. Wheelchair accessible. Gallery open Tu and Th-Su 11am-5pm, W 11am-8pm. Free.

Museum of London, 150 London Wall, EC2 (☎ 7600 3699, 24hr. info ☎ 7600 0807; email info@museum-london.org.uk). Tube: St. Paul's or Barbican. Tells London's story from its origins to the present. Wheelchair accessible. Open Tu-Sa 10am-5:50pm, Su noon-5:50pm; last admission 5:30pm. £5, students and seniors £3, under 17 free.

Science Museum (☎ (0870) 870 4868), on Exhibition Rd., SW7. Tube: South Kensington. Closet science geeks will be outed as they enter this wonderland of diagrammed motors, springs, and spaceships. Introductory exhibit romps through a "synopsis" of science since 6000 BC. Numerous exhibits geared toward the under-12 sector. Open daily 10am-6pm. £6.95, students £3.50; free for all after 4:30pm.

Wallace Collection, in Hertford House in Manchester Sq., W1. Tube: Bond St. Founded by various Marquises of Hertford and the illegitimate son of the fourth Marquis, Sir Richard Wallace, this defines the adjective "sumptuous." Also home to the largest weaponry collection outside of the Tower of London. Tours M-Tu and Th-F 1pm, W and Sa 11:30am and 1pm, Su 3pm. Open M-Sa 10am-5pm, Su 2-5pm. Free.

Royal Academy of Arts (☎ 7439 7438), on Piccadilly, W1, opposite #185. Tube: Green Park or Piccadilly Circus. Traveling exhibits of the highest order. Annual summer exhibition (June-Aug.) is a London institution—the works of established and unknown contemporary artists festoon every centimeter of wall space. Open daily M-Sa 10am-6pm, Su 10am-8:30pm. Advance tickets may be necessary. Average exhibition £6, students £4.

Design Museum, Butlers Wharf, SE1 (☎ 7403 6933; www.designmuseum.org). Tube: London Bridge. Dedicated to classics of culture and industry. Open daily 11:30am-6pm; last entry 5:30pm. £5.50, students £4.50, under 16 and over 60 £4.

London Dungeon, 28-34 Tooley St., SE1 (☎ 7403 0606). Tube: London Bridge. Plague, decomposition, and anything else remotely connected to horror and Britain thrown in for effect. Open daily Apr.-Sept. 10am-5:30pm; Nov.-Feb. 10am-5pm; last entrance 1hr. before close. £9.95; students £8.50; under 14, seniors, and disabled £6.50.

🎵 ENTERTAINMENT

On any given day or night, Londoners and visitors can choose from the widest range of entertainment options a city can offer. Suffering serious competition only from Broadway, the West End is the world's theater capital, led by a surprisingly experimental, well-financed Royal National Theatre. Music scenes range from the black ties of the Royal Opera House to Wembley mobs and nightclub raves. The work of British filmmakers like Derek Jarman, Sally Potter, and Mike Leigh is shown in cinemas all over the city. Dance, comedy, sports, and countless unclassifiable happenings can leave you in bewildered awe over the listings in *Time Out* (£1.80) and *What's On* (£1.30). **Kidsline** answers queries on children's events. (☎ 7222 8070. Open M-F 4-6pm.) **Artsline** has information about disabled access at entertainment venues across London. (☎ 7388 2227. Open M-F 9:30am-5:30pm.)

THEATER

In theaterspeak, the **West End** refers not only the part of central London where all the big theaters are, but also to all the top-class theaters. The **Fringe** is the collective name for the dozens of smaller, less commercial theaters in London: here, you'll find everything from community productions to avant-garde experiments. Fixed between those two extremes are **Off-West End** productions, which may lack West End resources but generally feature high-quality acting and intelligent writing. **Stalls** are seats nearest the stage. **Dress Circle** and **Upper Circle** refer to the balcony seats above the stalls. **Slips** are seats along the top edges of the theater, usually cheapest but with the worst views. The **interval** is the time for gin or the loo.

The **Leicester Square Half-Price Ticket Booth** sells tickets at half price (plus £1.50-2 booking fee) on the day of the performance, but carries them only for the West End, the Barbican, and the National Theatre. Tickets are sold from the top of the pile, which means you can't choose seats, and the priciest seats are sold first. Lines are particularly long on Saturdays. (Open M-Sa noon-6:30pm, Su noon-3pm. Cash only.) Your next best bet for low prices is to schlepp to a theater's box office where day seats, standbys, or student-rate tickets are often available. Major **repertory theaters** are listed below; for other venues, especially those with constant repertoires, check *Time Out*. For popular **musicals,** you should book far in advance.

Royal Shakespeare Company, Barbican Centre, Silk St. (box office ☎ 7638 8891; www.barbican.org.uk). Tube: Barbican or Moorgate. The RSC makes its London home in the two theatres of the Barbican Centre. Forward-leaning balconies in the **Barbicon Theatre** guarantee that none of the 1166 seats sit farther than 65 ft. from center stage, and every seat gives a clear view. **The Pit** provides a more intimate (200-seat) setting. Tickets for the main stage £7.50-24; weekday matinees £6-13; Saturday matinees and previews £8-18. Student and senior standby available in person or by phone from 9am on the day of performance, £8 (1 per person). Box office open daily 9am-8pm.

Royal National Theatre, South Bank Centre (☎ 7452 3400; www.nt-online.org). Tube: Waterloo. As you might expect from the "National" part of the name, the RNT's brilliant repertory company puts on a bit of everything on its three stages. All seats offer an unobstructed view of the stage. Backstage tours M-Sa £4.75, students and seniors £3.75. Book in advance; call for times. Box office open M-Sa 10am-8pm.

Olivier and **Lyttelton:** Tickets £10-32, day seats (available from 10am on day of performance) £10-14, general standby seats (available 2hr. before show) £12-16, student standby (available 45min. before show) £8-10, standing £4.50-6. Discounted admission for those in wheelchairs (all seats £15-16) and for other disabled people (£8-16). Discounted seats to matinees for under-18s (all seats £9-10) and seniors (£13-14).

Cottesloe: Tickets £10-22. Discounted admission for those in wheelchairs and the visually impaired (all seats £15) and for other disabled people (£8-15). Discounted entry to matinees for under-18s (£9) and seniors (£13).

Shakespeare's Globe Theatre, New Globe Walk, Bankside (☎ 7401 9919 or Ticketmaster ☎ 7316 4703). Tube: London Bridge. Using this reconstruction of the original Globe (where the Bard himself put on some plays) might have been nothing more than a gimmick, but the company employs the 3-tiered open-air space well. Patrons may either purchase spots on the wooden benches or stand through a performance as "groundlings." However, groundlings should prepare for the possibility of rain: umbrellas are prohibited because they impede sight lines. Shows take place May-Sept. Wheelchair access. Box office open M-Sa 10am-8pm, until 6pm by phone.

Old Vic, Waterloo Rd. (☎ 7928 7616). Tube: Waterloo. One of the most beautiful performance spaces in London. High-brow theater. £7.50-30.

FILM

The degenerate heart of the celluloid monster is **Leicester Square,** where the new releases premier a day before hitting the chains. Many cinemas reduce prices all-day Monday and for matinees Tuesday through Friday. The **Empire** (☎ (0870) 603 4567) and **Odeon Leicester Sq.** are London's biggest cinemas. Outside the main-stream, the following cinemas offer independent, foreign, and classic films.

The Prince Charles, Leicester Pl. (☎ 7734 9127; www.princecharlescinema.com). Tube: Leicester Sq. A Soho institution: 4 shows daily; generally second runs and a few classics for only £2.50-3.50 (M £1.50-2). Originator of hot trend *Sing-a-Long-a-Sound-of-Music*, where von Trappists dress as everything from nuns to "Ray, a drop of golden sun" (F 7:30pm, £12.50; Su 2pm, £10, children always £8). Catch the *Rocky Horror Picture Show,* complete with a live troupe, every F at 11:45pm for £6, students £3.

Gate Cinema, 87 Notting Hill Gate (☎ 7727 4043). Tube: Notting Hill Gate. A Victorian-interior 240-seater with an arthouse selection. £6.50, M-F first film before 3pm £3.50, M-F before 6pm and late shows F and Sa, students, and seniors £3.

National Film Theatre (NFT), South Bank Centre (☎ 7928 3232; www.bfi.org.uk). Tube: Waterloo, or Embankment and cross the Hungerford footbridge. One of the world's leading cinemas, with a mind-boggling array of films (mostly arthouse favorites and recent raves) in three auditoriums. Most screenings £6.50, students and seniors £5.

CLASSICAL MUSIC, OPERA, AND BALLET

London's unparalleled classical resources include five orchestras, two huge arts centers, and countless concert halls. Even so, its world-class orchestras provide only a fraction of the notes that fill its major music centers. Visiting orchestras continually parade through the city, and London has been the professional home of some of the greatest conductors of the century, including Sir Thomas Beecham, Otto Klemperer, and Andre Previn.

Barbican Hall, Barbican Centre, Silk St. (☎ 7638 8891; 24hr. recorded info ☎ 7382 7272; www.barbican.org.uk). Tube: Barbican or Moorgate. The venerable **London Symphony Orchestra** (www.lso.co.uk) inhabits this modern hall with superb acoustics. LSO concerts £6.50-35, under 16 £3, student and senior standby tickets sold shortly before the performance £6-8. Prices may vary for other concerts. Box office open 9am-8pm.

Royal Albert Hall, Kensington Gore (☎ 7589 8212; www.royalalberthall.com). Tube: South Kensington or Knightsbridge (buses #9, 10, and 52 go by the Hall from either station). London's premier concert hall. The **Proms** (BBC Henry Wood Promenade Concerts) never fail to enliven London summers with concerts every day for 8 weeks from mid-July to mid-Sept. £5-60. Over 1000 standing tickets available 1hr. before each concert for £3, but be ready to queue for longer. Box office open daily 9am-9pm.

Wigmore Hall, 36 Wigmore St. (☎ 7935 2141). Tube: Bond St. or Oxford Circus. Elegant venue hosts concerts and chamber music. Tickets £6-35. 1hr. standbys at lowest price. In summer, Su morning coffee concerts begin at 11:30am; £8, coffee free. Closed end of July through Aug. Box office open 10am-5pm.

Royal Opera House, at Covent Garden, Box St. (box office ☎ 7304 4000). The newly refurbished stage hosts its resident companies, the Royal Opera and the Royal Ballet. All works at the English National Opera are sung in English. It's best to call the box office, 48 Floral St. (Tube: Covent Garden) for ticket prices. Open M-Sa 10am-7pm.

London Coliseum, St. Martin's Ln. (☎ 7632 8300). Tube: Charing Cross or Leicester Sq. Seats for opera cost £6.50-55. Box office open M-Sa 10am-8pm.

Sadler's Wells, Rosebery Ave. (☎ 7863 8000). Tube: Angel. London's premier space for dance, featuring anything from ballet to contemporary dance. Free bus travel to the theatre; just show your ticket at the ticket office. Tickets £7.50-30; some student and senior tickets £5. Student and senior standbys £7.50-10, available 1hr. before performance. Box office open M-Sa 10am-8:30pm.

SPECTATOR SPORTS

FOOTBALL. London has been blessed with 13 of the 92 professional teams in England. The big three are **Arsenal,** Highbury Stadium, Avenell Rd. (☎ 7704 4000; Tube: Arsenal); **Chelsea,** Stamford Bridge, Fulham Rd. (☎ 7386 7799; Tube: Fulham Broadway); and **Tottenham Hotspur,** White Hart Lane, 748 High Rd. (☎ 8365 5000; Rail: White Hart Lane). The football (soccer) scene is very partisan and favorites vary from neighborhood to neighborhood. England plays occasional international matches at the historic but soon to be redesigned **Wembley Stadium,** usually on Wednesday evenings. (☎ 8902 8833. Tube: Wembley Park.) On a non-professional level, footy is also played in parks all over London: on Sunday morning, the massive grid of pitches on Hackney Marshes are a sight well worth beholding.

RUGBY. The most significant contests, including the springtime Six Nations championship (featuring England, Scotland, Wales, Ireland, France, and newcomer Italy) are played at **Twickenham.** (☎ 8831 6666. Rail: Twickenham.) Other venues include **Saracens,** Dale Green Rd. (☎ (01923) 496200; Tube: Oakwood), and **Rosslyn Park,** Priory Ln., Upper Richmond Rd. (☎ 8876 1879. Rail: Barnes.)

CRICKET. London's two grounds stage both county and international matches. **Lord's,** St. John's Wood Rd. (☎ 7289 1611; Tube: St. John's Wood), is the home turf of the **Marylebone Cricket Club (MCC),** the established governing body of cricket. Archaic stuffiness pervades the MCC; women have yet to see the pavilion's interior. **Foster's Oval,** Kennington Oval, home to **Surrey Cricket Club,** also fields Test Matches. (☎ 7582 7764. Tube: Oval. Tickets £7-8, internationals £21-36.)

TENNIS. Every year, for two weeks in late June and early July tennis buffs all over the world focus their attention on **Wimbledon.** If you want to get in, arrive early (6am); the gate opens at 10:30am (get off the Tube at Southfields or take buses #39, 93 or 200 from central London, which run frequently during the season). If you fail to get Centre or No. 1 Court tickets in the morning, try to find the resale booth (usually in Aorangi Park), which sells tickets handed in by those who leave early. (Info ☎ 8971 2473. Open from 2:30pm. Tickets £5 before 5pm, £3 after.)

SHOPPING

London Transport's handy *Shoppers' Bus Wheel* instructs Routemaster shoppers on the routes between shopping areas (available free from any London Transport Information Centre). Non-EU tourists who have purchased anything over £50 should ask about getting a refund on the 17.5% VAT. Each shopping area has a late night of shopping. Kings Rd. and Kensington High St., for example, stay open late on Wednesdays, while shops in the West End open their doors to the night on Thursdays. Many stores close on Sunday.

DEPARTMENT STORES

Harrods, 87-135 Brompton Rd. (☎ 7730 1234). Tube: Knightsbridge. Simply put, this is the premier store in London, perhaps in the world. The sales (July and January) get so crazy that the police bring out a whole detail to deal with the shoppers. Open M-Tu and Sa 10am-6pm, W-F 10am-7pm.

Fortnum & Mason, 181 Piccadilly (☎ 7734 8040). Tube: Green Park or Piccadilly Circus. Famed for its sumptuous food hall, with liveried clerks, chandeliers, and fountains, occupying the entire ground floor. The upper floors carry clothing, jewelry, and shoes in a posh and sophisticated setting. Open M-Sa 9:30am-6pm.

Harvey Nichols, 109-125 Knightsbridge (☎ 7235 5000). Tube: Knightsbridge. The trendiest and most expensive of London's department stores. Open M, T, and Sa 10am-7pm, W-F 10am-8pm, Su noon-6pm.

Selfridges, 400 Oxford St. (☎ 7629 1234). Tube: Bond St. There's a reason their yellow shopping bags are ubiquitous around Oxford St.: Selfridges has *everything*. The fashion departments, while not cheap, are extensive and trendy. Huge Jan. and mid-July sale. Open M-W 10am-7pm, Th-F 10am-8pm, Sa 9:30am-7pm, Su noon-6pm.

CLOTHING

■ **French Connection (fcuk),** 99-103 Long Acre (☎ 7379 6560). Tube: Covent Garden. Numerous other branches. Friendly staff and catchy slogans have let fcuk fill the gap in affordable, trendy urbanwear. Huge sales during Jan. and July. Open M-W 10:30am-7pm, Th 11am-8pm, F-Sa 10:30am-7pm, Su 11am-6pm.

■ **Top Shop/Top Man,** 214 Oxford St. (☎ 7636 7700). Tube: Oxford Circus. Many other branches. An absolute must for the club kid on a budget. This multi-story megastore offers the trendiest inexpensive fashions with something to suit everyone's flamboyant side. Open M-W and F 9am-8pm, Th and Sa 9am-9pm, Su noon-6pm.

Reiss, 78-79 New Bond St. (☎ 7493 4866) Tube: Bond St. Some branches. One of the most influential trendsetters in men's fashions, using classic fabrics and smooth lines to introduce new styles. Open M-W and F-Sa 10am-7pm, Th 10am-8pm, Su noon-6pm.

BOOKSTORES

In London, even the chain bookstores are wonders. An exhaustive selection of bookshops lines Charing Cross Rd. between Tottenham Court Rd. and Leicester Sq., and many vend secondhand paperbacks. Cecil Court, near Leicester Sq., is a treasure trove of tiny shops with specialty bookstores for seemingly any topic. Establishments along Great Russell St. stock esoteric and specialized books on any subject from Adorno to the Zohar.

■ **Maggs Brothers,** 50 Berkeley Sq. (☎ 7493 7160). Tube: Green Park. A bibliophile's paradise in an allegedly haunted 18th-century mansion. Tremendous selection of 19th-century travel narratives, and illuminated manuscripts. Open M-F 9am-5pm.

Blackwells, 100 Charing Cross Rd. (☎ 7292 5100; ; www.bookshop.blackwell.co.uk). It's academic (mostly). Go for the postmodern theory, stay for the huge selection of fiction. Open M-Sa 9:30am-8:30pm, Su noon-6pm.

The Travel Bookshop, 13-15 Blenheim Crescent (☎ 7229 5260). Yes, it's the tiny specialist bookstore featured in *Notting Hill*. No, the people behind the counter rarely look like Hugh Grant. Yes, they stock *Let's Go*. Open M-Sa 10am-6pm.

RECORD STORES

London crawls with music junkies, and fortunately, the city has a record collection to match. Don't expect any bargains, and remember that when it comes to records, "import" means "rip-off." Vinyl still remains an important part of the London music retail scene. The megastores carry vinyl versions of most major-label releases, but to get those rare promos, white labels, or collectibles, you'll probably have to go to an independent record store. In **Camden Town, Brixton,** and **Ladbroke Grove,** record stores tempt collectors and intimidate browsers with rare vinyl and memorabilia at rock star prices. The best collection of record stores, though, are probably at **Berwick Street** in Soho, and **Hanway Street,** off Tottenham Court Rd.

HMV, 150 Oxford St. (☎ 7631 3423). Tube: Oxford Circus. Jazz, classical, world music, and most everything else. Open M-F 9:30am-8pm, Sa 9am-7:30pm, Su noon-6pm.

Honest Jon's, 276-278 Portobello Rd. (☎ 8969 9822). Tube: Ladbroke Grove. Still funky after all these years. 276 holds an impressive jazz collection, 278 a wide selection of hip-hop LPs and some decent 12-inch singles, as well as soul and funk holdings. Open M-Sa 10am-6pm, Su 11am-5pm.

Rough Trade, 130 Talbot Rd. (☎ 7229 8541). Tube: Ladbroke Grove. Branch: 16 Neal's Yard (☎ 7240 0105), Tube: Covent Garden. Birthplace of the legendary independent record label. Open M-Sa 10am-6:30pm, Su 1-5pm.

SPECIALTY STORES

Dr. Marten's Dept. Store Ltd, 1-4 King St. (☎ 7497 1460). Tube: Covent Garden. Tourist-packed 5-tiered megastore; watches, sunglasses, candles, and of course the hard-as-nails shoes. Buy Docs for everyone you know, from baby to granny. Open M-W and F-Sa 10am-7pm, Th 10:30am-8pm, Su noon-6pm.

Hamley's, 188-189 Regent St. (☎ 7734 3161). Tube: Oxford Circus. Even Santa and his elves do their shopping here, in a place most kids would call heaven. London's largest toy shop spans 6 floors filled with every conceivable toy and game. Open M-W 10am-7:30pm, Th-Sa 10am-8pm, Su noon-6pm.

◪ NIGHTLIFE

PUBS AND BARS

The atmosphere and clientele of London's 7000 pubs vary considerably. Avoid pubs within a half-mile radius of a main-line train station (Paddington, Euston, King's Cross/St. Pancras, and Victoria). Some prey upon tourists by charging an extra 20-40p per pint. Stylish, lively pubs cluster around the fringes of the West End, while cheaper pubs proliferate in the East End. Many historic alehouses lend an ancient air to areas swallowed by urban sprawl, such as Hampstead. Some of the oldest pubs cluster in the City. Buy drinks at the bar; a pint should set you back £1.80-3. Just remember—don't tip the bar man!

THE CITY OF LONDON

Ye Olde Cheshire Cheese, Wine Office Ct., by 145 Fleet St. (☎ 7353 6170). Tube: Blackfriars or St. Paul's. Classic pub, dating to the 17th century, where Dr. Johnson and Dickens, as well as Americans Mark Twain and Teddy Roosevelt, hung out. Today it's hot among businesspeople and lawyers. Open M-Sa 11:30am-11pm, Su noon-3pm.

Fuego Bar y Tapas, 1 Pudding Ln. (☎ 7929 3366). Tube: Monument. This snazzy executive watering hole compensates for lack of window space and cavernous basement location with lively evening events. Spanish music M nights, Th-F disco nights. *Tapas* £2-4. Dinner main course £6.90-10. Open M-F 11:30am-2am.

HOLBORN AND THE INNS OF COURT

Black Friar, 174 Queen Victoria St. (☎ 7236 5650). Tube: Blackfriars. One of London's most exquisite pubs. The edifice's past purpose as a 12th-century Dominican friary is celebrated not only in the pub's name but in the intriguing arches, mosaics, and reliefs that line the pub's walls. Carlsberg £2.35, Tetley's £2.15. Lunch served 11:30am-2:30pm. Open M-F 11:30am-11pm, Sa noon-5pm, Su noon-4:30pm.

COVENT GARDEN AND SOHO

◪ Freud, 198 Shaftesbury Ave. (☎ 7240 9933). Tube: Covent Garden. Cheaper than an hour on the couch. Open M-Sa 11am-11pm, Su noon-10:30pm. Cash only.

Crown and Anchor, 22 Neal St. (☎ 7836 5649). Tube: Covent Garden. One of Covent Garden's most popular pubs. Open M-Sa 11am-11pm, Su noon-10:30pm.

Yo! Below, 52 Poland St. (☎ 7439 3660). Tube: Oxford Circus. Located below Yo! Sushi. Customers sit on cushions on the floor and dispense their own beer from taps at the table. Free massages and tea ceremonies, along with a karaoke-singing staff, make for a great night out. Open M-Su noon-midnight.

KENSINGTON, KNIGHTSBRIDGE, AND CHELSEA

The Social, 5 Little Portland St. (☎ 7636 4992). Tube: Oxford Circus. Raucous crowd, tiny space, great music, ear-debilitating bass. Manages to be both flashy and welcoming. Pints £2.60-2.70. Open M-Sa noon-midnight, Su 5-10:30pm.

The King's Head and Eight Bells, 50 Cheyne Walk (☎ 7352 1820). Tube: Sloane Sq. or South Kensington. Richly textured 16th-century pub close to the Thames where Thomas More would have a jar with his dangerous friend Henry VIII. Hoegaarden £3.55. Open M-Sa 11am-11pm, Su noon-10:30pm.

NOTTING HILL, BAYSWATER, AND HYDE PARK

■ **192,** 192 Kensington Park Rd. (☎ 7229 0482). Tube: Ladbroke Grove. Despite its repeated mention in the *Bridget Jones* books, this wine bar is worth a visit. Wines £2.60-6 per glass. Open M-Sa 12:30-11:30pm, Su 12:30-11pm.

The Westbourne, 101 Westbourne Park Villas (☎ 7221 1332). Tube: Westbourne Park. A fixture of the Notting Hill scene: funky inside, with a heated terrace packed to the gills outside. Open M 5-11pm, Tu-F noon-11pm, Sa 11am-11pm, Su noon-10:30pm.

SOUTH LONDON

■ **Cubana,** 48 Lower Marsh. (☎ 7928 8778). Tube: Waterloo. Staff keep people happy with spiky cocktails, live salsa music W nights, a cheap and intriguing menu (crab and papaya salad £6.95), and a wide selection of edible cigars. Open M-Sa noon-midnight.

Bread and Roses, 68 Clapham Manor St. (☎ 7498 1779). Tube: Clapham Common. With socialist roots, Bread and Roses has a history of liquoring up the people. Primarily trad pub that has great beers (Smile's Workers' Ale £2) and often hosts theater and music; call for a schedule. Open M-Sa 11am-11pm, Su noon-10:30pm.

EAST LONDON

■ **Shoreditch Electricity Showrooms,** 39a Hoxton Sq. (☎ 7739 6934). Tube: Old St. Where the super-cool go. Cocktails £6, beers from £2.30. Open Tu and W noon-11pm, Th noon-midnight, F-Sa noon-1am, Su noon-10:30pm.

Prospect of Whitby, 57 Wapping Wall (☎ 7481 1095). Tube: Wapping. Open ceilings and flagstone bar in a building dating from 1520 pale next to the glorious Thamescape. Lunch served noon-2:30pm, dinner 6-9pm daily. Open M-F 11:30am-3pm and 5:30pm-11pm, Sa 11:30am-11pm, Su noon-10:30pm.

The Vibe Bar, The Brewery, 91-95 Brick Ln., E1 (☎ 7377 2899). Tube: Aldgate East. DJs day and night. Plop on a sofa, tackle a Playstation game, or check your email for free. Pints £2.50. Open M-Sa 11am-11pm, Su noon-10:30pm.

NORTH LONDON

■ **Filthy MacNasty's Whiskey Café,** 68 Amwell St. (☎ 7837 6067). Tube: Angel. Renowned for traditional Irish music Su, and one of Shane Macgowan's favorite pubs. Live readings and music every M, and W-Th. Guinness £2.20. Open daily noon-11pm.

The Engineer, 65 Gloucester Ave. (☎ 7722 0950). Tube: Chalk Farm. A thousand miles away from boisterous Camden, join the beautiful Luvvies at this classic pub. A bright atmosphere and a sumptuous back garden makes everybody feel relaxed. Pints £2.50. Open M-Sa 9am-11pm, Su 9am-10:30pm.

CLUBS

Every major DJ in the world either lives in London or makes frequent visits there. While the US may have introduced house music to the world, the UK has taken the lead in developing and experimenting with new types of dance music. *Time Out* is the undisputed scene cop, and their starred picks of the day are usually a safe bet. Many clubs have after-hours parties called "chill outs," usually 6am-noon. The **tube** shuts down shortly after midnight and **black cabs** are especially hard to find when clubs are closing. Some late-night frolickers catch **"minicabs,"** unmarked cars that sometimes wait outside clubs; negotiate a price before you get in, and be wary of riding alone. It's advisable to arrange transportation in advance or acquaint yourself with the extensive network of **night buses** (information ☎ 72 22 12 34).

The Aquarium, 256 Old St., EC1 (☎ 7251 6136). Tube: Old Street. Ultra-trendy club comes complete with swimming pool for club kids to take a dip in. Cover £5-15. Open Th 9am-3pm, F (garage) 10pm-4am, Sa (house) 10am-5pm.

Bar Rumba, 35 Shaftesbury Ave., W1 (☎ 7287 2715). Tube: Piccadilly Circus. Brilliant nights out in a cozy underground space. Cover £4-12. Open M-Tu and Th-F 10pm-3am, W 10pm-3:30am, Sa 10pm-4am, Su 8pm-1:30am.

The Fridge, on Town Hall Parade, Brixton Hill, SW2. (☎ 7326 5100) Tube: Brixton. Out of the station, cross the street, walk left, walk up Brixton Hill Rd, and look for the long line. Converted cinema hosts some of the most popular nights in London. Cover £8-12. Open F-Sa 10pm-6am. Head next-door for the after-party at the **Fridge Bar.**

The Hanover Grand, 6 Hanover St., W1 (☎ 7499 7977). Tube: Oxford Circus. Multiple floors crammed full of well-dressed people. Getting in, however, may take ages—plan to go early, even on weekdays. Open W (hiphop and UK garage) 10:30pm-3:30am, F (garage) 10pm-4am, and Sa (house) 10:30pm-5:30am. £3-15.

Notting Hill Arts Club, 21 Notting Hill Gate, W11 (☎ 7460 4459). Tube: Notting Hill Gate. Hard beats fill the basement dance floor. Soul, Latin, jazz, house. Cover £3-5 M-Sa after 8pm, Su after 7pm. Open M-Sa 5pm-1am, Su 4pm-11pm.

Ministry of Sound, 103 Gaunt St., SE1 (☎ 7378 6528; www.ministryofsound.co.uk). Tube: Elephant and Castle. Take the exit for South Bank University. The granddaddy of all serious clubbing. Cover £10-15. Open F 10:30pm-6:30am, Sa midnight-9am.

Turnmills, 63B Clerkenwell Rd., EC1 (☎ 7250 3409). Tube: Farringdon. Walk up Turnmill St. and turn right onto Clerkenwell Rd. Gets kickin' at 3am and keeps on kickin' until noon. Get there early or late to avoid long queues, or reserve in advance. Cover £10. Open F-Sa 3am-noon.

Velvet Room, 143 Charing Cross Rd., WC2 (☎ 7439 4655). Tube: Tottenham Court Rd. A hoity-toity club-bar. Cover £4-6; student discounts. Generally open 8pm-3am.

GAY AND LESBIAN NIGHTLIFE

London has a very visible gay scene, ranging from flamboyant to mainstream. *Time Out* has a section devoted to gay listings, and gay newspapers include *Capital Gay* (free, caters to men), *Pink Paper*, and *Shebang* (for women). *Gay Times* (£3) is the British counterpart to the *Advocate; Diva* (£2) is a monthly lesbian mag. Islington, Earl's Ct, and Soho (especially **Old Compton St.**) are all gay-friendly areas. For more details about London's gay and lesbian nightlife scene, check out Boyz (www.boyz.co.uk) or QX (www.qxmag.co.uk), available free at many gay bars.

"Atelier," Thursday at The End, 18 West Central St., WC1 (☎ 7419 9199). Tube: Tottenham Court Rd. Dressing up is essential. £5, free with flyer from pre-party at **Manto,** 30 Old Compton St.

The Black Cap, 171 Camden High St., NW1 (☎ 7428 2721). Tube: Camden Town. North London's best-known drag bar. Live shows every night attract a mixed male and female crowd. When the shows aren't on, a DJ plays Top 40. M "oldies and trash" night is a favorite. Cover £2-4, free before 11pm. Open M-Th 9pm-2am, F-Sa 9pm-3am, Su noon-3pm and 7pm-midnight. Tu-Sa

The Box, Seven Dials, 32-34 Monmouth St., WC2 (☎ 7240 5828). Tube: Covent Garden or Leicester Sq. Intimate and stylish gay/mixed bar and brasserie. Menus change to match the season (main courses £6-9). Fun, hip clientele of both genders and all races. The dance floor downstairs makes this an excellent venue for a night of dancing and drinking (lager £2.50). Open M-Sa 11am-11pm, Su 7-10:30pm.

Freedom, 60-66 Wardour St., W1 (☎ 7734 0071). Tube: Piccadilly Circus. A very trendy cafe-bar that draws in a mixed crowd for cocktails. DJs and dancing space below.

▚ DAYTRIPS FROM LONDON

OXFORD. The university town bustles with activity and overflows with grandeur. Enjoy the punting and the festivals (see p. 197).

STRATFORD-UPON-AVON. Stratford offers up everything Shakespeare. Enjoy a show or explore the Bard's birthplace and various residences (see p. 204).

STONEHENGE. The incredible 22-foot high monoliths of Stonehenge, which date from 1500BC, lie near Salisbury, which is easily reached from London (see p. 192).

BRITAIN

SOUTHERN ENGLAND

Sprawling toward the continent, the landscape of southern England simultaneously asserts Britain's island heritage and reveals a continental link deeper than the Chunnel. Early Britons settled the counties of Kent, Sussex, and Hampshire from across the English Channel, and William the Conqueror left his mark upon the downsland in the form of awe-inspiring cathedrals. But Geoffrey Chaucer, Jane Austen, Charles Dickens, E.M. Forster, and Virginia Woolf—all staples of modern British culture—also all drew inspiration from these lands. To the west, the counties of Somerset, Avon, and Wiltshire boast Salisbury's medieval cathedral, the Roman Baths at Bath, and the forever-mysterious Stonehenge. Even farther west, a mist of legends shrouds the counties of Dorset, Somerset, Devon, and Cornwall in England's West Country, home to Bronze Age barrows and King Arthur.

✖ FERRIES AND TRAINS TO FRANCE, SPAIN, AND BELGIUM

Ferries run from **Dover** (see p. 189) to **Calais, France** (see p. 388) and **Ostend, Belgium** (see p. 134). Ferries also chug from **Portsmouth** (see p. 190) to **St. Malo** (see p. 326) and **Caen, France** (see p. 322); from **Plymouth** (see p. 194) to **Roscoff, France** and **Santander, Spain;** from **Folkestone** to **Boulogne, France** (see p. 388) and from **Newhaven** to **Dieppe, France** (see p. 321). Travelers with cars can head through the **Chunnel** (from Kent to Nord-Pas-de-Calais) on **Eurotunnel.** For detailed info on over- and underwater transport options to the continent, see p. 46.

CANTERBURY   ☎01227

Six hundred years ago, in his famed *Canterbury Tales*, Chaucer captured the irony of tourists in England's most famous execution site. His sometimes lewd, sometimes reverent tales speak of the pilgrims of the Middle Ages who flocked from London to the **Canterbury Cathedral.** Archbishop Thomas à Becket was beheaded there in 1170 after an irate Henry II asked, "Will no one rid me of this troublesome priest?" (☎76 28 62. Cathedral open Easter-Sept. M-Sa 9am-6:30pm, Su 12:30pm-2:30pm and 4:30-5:30pm; Oct.-Easter M-Sa 9am-5pm, Su 12:30pm-2:30pm and 4:30pm-5:30pm. Evensong services M-F 5:30pm, Sa 3:15pm, Su 6:30pm. £3, students £2. Audio tour £2.50.) **The Canterbury Tales,** on St. Margaret's St., is a museum that simulates the journey of Chaucer's pilgrims; the gap-toothed Wife of Bath and her waxen companions will entertain you with an abbreviated, Modern English version of the Tales. (☎47 92 27. Open July-Aug. daily 9am-5:30pm; Mar.-June and Sept.-Oct. 9:30am-5:30pm; Nov.-Feb. Su-F 10am-4:30pm, Sa 9:30am-5:30pm. £5.50, students and seniors £4.60.) On Stour St., the **Canterbury Heritage Museum** tells the history of Canterbury from medieval times to WWII. (☎45 27 47. Open June-Oct. M-Sa 10:30am-5pm, Su 1:30-5pm; Nov.-May closed Su. £2.40.) To see two of South England's most storied castles, head 12 mi. southeast to **Deal.** Here you will find **Deal Castle,** which was designed by Henry VIII as a coastal fortification, as well as **Walmer Castle,** which has been converted from a military bastion to an elegant country estate. **Trains** leave regularly from Canterbury (£3).

For those who can't travel to Canterbury on horseback with a group of verbally gifted pilgrims, **trains** from London's Victoria Station arrive at Canterbury's **East Station** (1½ hr., every 30 min., £15.30), while trains from London's Charing Cross and Waterloo Stations arrive at **West Station** (1½hr., every hr., £14.70). Stagecoach **buses** (☎47 20 82) leave from St. George's Ln. for London's Victoria Coach Station (1¾hr., every hr., £8). The **tourist office,** 34 St. Margaret's St., stocks free miniguides to Canterbury. (☎76 65 67; fax 45 98 40. Open daily Apr.-Aug. 9:30am-5:30pm; Sept.-Mar. 9:30am-5pm.) Check email for free at the **library,** 18 High St. (☎46 36 08). **B&Bs** cluster near both train stations; around the intersections of London Rd. and Whitstable Rd., and High St. and New Dover Rd. The **YHA youth hostel,** 54 New Dover Rd., is ¾ mi. from East Station and ½ mi. southeast of the bus station. (☎46 29 11. Lockers £1 plus deposit. Laundry. Reception 7:30-10am and 1-

11pm. Reserve ahead. Open Feb.-Dec.; call for off-season openings. Dorms £10.85.) The **Hampton House,** 40 New Dover Rd. (☎ 46 49 12), offers quiet, luxurious rooms for £20-25, while **Let's Stay,** 26 New Dover Rd (☎ 46 36 28), has beds for £10; both serve full English breakfasts. **St. Martin's Touring Caravan and Camping Site,** on Bekesbourne Ln., has good facilities. (☎ 46 32 16. £5.20 per person; £3 per tent.) **High St.** is crowded with pubs, and restaurants. For **groceries,** head to **Safeway supermarket,** on St. George's Pl. (Open M-Th and Sa 8am-8pm, F 8am-9pm, Su 10am-4pm.) **Marlowe's,** 55 St. Peter's St., prides itself on an eclectic mix of vegetarian and beefy English, American, and Mexican styles. (☎ 46 21 94. Open daily 11:30am-10:30pm.) **Patrick Casey's,** on Butchery Ln., will warm you up with traditional Irish food. **Postal code:** CT1 2BA.

DOVER   ☎ 01304

The puttering of ferries, the constant hum of hovercraft, and the chatter of French families *en vacance* coming through the Channel Tunnel drown out the roar of the English Channel at Dover. However, Dover is the most vital of Britain's ports. The view from Castle Hill Rd. toward **Dover Castle** reveals why it is famed both for its setting and its impregnability. (Buses from the town center run every hour daily Apr.-Sept., fares 45p. Castle and complex open daily Apr.-Sept. 10am-6pm; Oct. 10am-5pm; Nov.-Mar. 10am-4pm. £6.90, children £3.50, families £17.30.) **Trains** head to Dover's **Priory Station** from London's Victoria, Waterloo East, London Bridge, and Charing Cross stations (2hr., every 45min., £17.50). National Express **buses** run regularly from London's Victoria Coach Station to the bus station on Pencester Rd. and then on to the **Eastern Docks** (2¾hr., 23 per day, £9), where **P&O Stena Line** and **Hoverspeed** depart from the Prince of Wales Pier for Calais (foot passengers £25 one way). Buses also make trips to **Canterbury** (45 min., £4). The **tourist office,** on Townwall St., has lodgings info and ferry and Hovercraft tickets. (☎ (01304) 20 51 08; fax 22 54 98. Open daily 9am-6pm.) The **YHA Charlton House Youth Hostel,** 306 London Rd., is ½ mi. from the train station; turn left onto Folkestone Rd., then left again at the roundabout onto High St., which becomes London Rd. The hostel is farther from the center of Dover than the private B&Bs: expect more barren and unfriendly streets. (☎ (01304) 20 13 14; fax 20 22 36. Kitchen. Lockout 10am-1pm. Curfew 11pm. Dorms £10.15, students £9.15.) The **Gladstone Guest House,** 3 Laureston Pl., offers wonderful views and tastefully decorated rooms with hand-crafted furniture. (☎ 20 84 57; email kud3gladstone@aol.com. Dorms £25-48.) **Harthorn Farm,** at Martin Mill Station off the A258, offers **camping.** (June to mid-Sept. £3.50 per person. Two people with car and tent June to mid-Sept. £11; Mar.-May and mid-Sept.-Oct. £6.50, plus £2 extra per person.) Cheap food fries from dawn to dusk in the fish 'n' chip shops on **London Rd.** and **Biggin St.,** and a decent pub lunch can be had anywhere in the city center. **Postal code:** CT16 1PB.

BRIGHTON   ☎ 01273

According to legend, the future King George IV scuttled into Brighton (pop. 250,000) for some hanky-panky around 1784. Today, Brighton is still the unrivaled home of the "dirty weekend"—it sparkles with a tawdry luster all its own. Before indulging, check out England's long-time obsession with the Far East at the excessively ornate **Royal Pavilion,** on Pavilion Parade, next to Old Steine. (Open daily June-Sept. 10am-6pm; Oct.-May 10am-5pm. Guided tours at 11:30am and 2:30pm £1.25. Audio tour £1. £4.90, family £12.80.) Around the corner on Church St. stands the **Brighton Museum and Art Gallery,** with paintings, English pottery, and a wild Art Deco and Art Nouveau collection. Leer at Salvador Dalí's sexy red sofa, entitled *Mae West's Lips.* (Open M-Tu and Th-Sa 10am-5pm, Su 2-5pm. Free.) Before heading out to the rocky **beach,** stroll the **Lanes,** a jumble of 17th-century streets forming the heart of Old Brighton. Brighton brims with nightlife options; pick up *The Punter* or *What's On* (at music stores, news agents, and pubs) for tips. Brighton is also *the* gay nightlife spot in Britain outside London; pick up *Gay Times* (£2.50) or *Capital Gay.* Drink at **Fortune of War,** 157 King's Rd. Arches (open M-Sa 10:30am-11pm, Su 11am-10:30pm), or **The Squid,** 78 Middle St. (open M-F 5-11pm, Sa 3-11pm,

BRITAIN

Su 3-10:30pm). **Paradox** and **Event II,** on West St., are popular clubs. **The Beach,** 171-181 King's Rd. Arches, produces some of the beachfront's biggest beats, while **Casablanca,** on Middle St., plays live jazz to a mostly student crowd. The converted WWII tunnels of **Zap Club,** on King's Rd., provide space for dirty dancing. (Most clubs in Brighton are open M-Sa 10pm-2am.) **Queen's Arms,** at 8 George St (☎ 69 68 73), packs an enthusiastic gay and lesbian crowd into its Saturday night cabaret.

Trains (☎ (0345) 48 49 50) roll to London (1¼hr., 6 per hr., £9.90) and Portsmouth (1½hr., every hr., round-trip £11.50). National Express **buses** (☎ 38 37 44) head to London (2hr., 15 per day, round-trip £8). The **tourist office** is at 10 Bartholomew Sq. (☎ (09067) 11 22 55. Open M-Tu and Th-F 9am-5pm, W and Sa 10am-5pm.) The rowdy **Brighton Backpackers Hostel,** 75-76 Middle St., is the best place for meeting other backpackers. (☎ 77 77 17; fax 88 77 88; email stay@brightonbackpackers.com. **Internet** £1.50 per 30min. Dorms £10-11; doubles £25.) **Baggies Backpackers,** 33 Oriental Pl., has mellow vibes and exquisite murals. Head west of West Pier along King's Rd., and Oriental Pl. is on the right. (☎ 73 37 40; www.cisweb.co.uk/baggies. Dorms £10; doubles £25.) To get to the **YHA youth hostel,** on Patcham Pl., 4 mi. away, take Patcham Bus #5 or 5A from Old Steine in front of the Royal Pavilion to the Black Lion Hotel. (☎ 55 61 96. Curfew 11pm. Dorms £10.15, under 18 £6.85.) For cheap eats, try the fish 'n' chip shops along the beach or north of the Lanes, or head to **Safeway Supermarket,** 6 St. James's St. (☎ 57 03 63. Open M-W 8am-8pm, Th-Sa 8am-9pm, Su 10am-4pm.) **Postal code:** BN1 1BA.

CHICHESTER   ☎ 01243

The remains of Roman walls and an imposing Norman cathedral provide the backdrop for Chichester's (pop. 30,000) superb theater, arts festivals, and gallery exhibits. The **cathedral,** begun in 1091, features a glorious stained-glass window by Marc Chagall. (Open daily 7:30am-7pm; off-season 7:30am-5pm. £2 donation encouraged.) The amazingly well-preserved **Roman Palace** in nearby **Fishbourne,** dating from AD 80, is the largest Roman residence ever excavated in Britain. From the Ave de Chartres roundabout in Chichester, head west on Westgate, which becomes Fishbourne Rd. (the A259) for 1½ mi.; or take bus #11, 56, or 700 from the center of town and then walk 5min. to the palace. (Open Aug. daily 10am-6pm; Mar.-July and Sept.-Oct. daily 10am-5pm; Feb. and Nov.-Dec. daily 10am-4pm; Jan. Sa-Su 10am-4pm. £4.40, students £3.70.) Should your tastes drift to the romantic, head to the fairy-tale **castle** in nearby **Arundel** by taking a train (20min., 2 per hr., £3.40. ☎ (01903) 88 31 36. Open Apr.-Oct. Su-F noon-5pm. £7, children £4.50, family £19.)

Trains run to London's Victoria Station (1½hr., 3 per hr., £16.50); Brighton (50min., 2-3 per hr., £7.80); and Portsmouth (40min., 2-3 per hr., £4.80). **Buses** (☎ (01903) 23 76 61) depart from opposite the train station on Southgate. National Express runs to London (1 per day, round-trip £9); Coastline serves Brighton (bus #702; 3hr., 2 per hr., £4.60); and Portsmouth (bus #700 and 701; 1hr., 2 per hr., £3.90). To get to the **tourist office,** 29a South St., turn left as you exit the station onto Southgate, which becomes South St. (☎ 77 58 88; fax 53 94 49. Open M-Sa 9:15am-5:15pm; July-Aug. also Su 10am-4pm.) Expect to pay £16-20 for a bed in Chichester. **Hedgehogs,** 45 Whyke Ln., offers cozy rooms near the town center. (☎ (01243) 78 00 22. Singles and doubles £18-24 per person.) Camp at **Southern Leisure Centre,** on Vinnetrow Rd., a 15min. walk southeast of town. (☎ 78 77 15. Open Apr.-Oct. £2 per person, £8-10 per tent.) **Postal code:** PO19 1AB.

PORTSMOUTH   ☎ 023

Set Victorian prudery against prostitutes, drunkards, and a lot of bloody cursing sailors, and there you have a basic 900-year history of Portsmouth (pop. 190,500). On the **seafront,** visitors relive D-Day, explore warships, and learn of the days when Britannia ruled the seas. War buffs and historians will want to plunge head first into the unparalleled **Naval Heritage Centre,** in the Naval Base, which houses a virtual armada of Britain's most storied ships. The center includes England's first attempt at a warship, Henry VIII's Mary Rose. Although Henry was particularly fond of her, she—like many women with whom Henry associated—died before her time, sinking after setting sail from Portsmouth in July, 1545. Napoleon must be rolling in his little coffin to know that the HMS Victory, which clinched Britain's reputation as king of the waves when it defeated him at the Battle of Trafalgar in 1805, is still afloat. The five galleries of the **Royal Naval Museum** fill in the historical gaps between the three ships. Entrance is next to the tourist office on The Hard—follow the signs to Portsmouth Historic Ships. (Ships open Mar.-Oct. daily 10am-5:30pm; Nov.-Feb. 10am-5pm. £6 each sight, students £5.20.)

For information on **ferries** to France, see p. 47. **Trains** (☎ (0345) 48 49 50) run to Southsea Station, on Commercial Rd., from: London's Waterloo Station (1½hr., 3 per hr., £19); Chichester (40min., 2 per hr., £5); and Salisbury (2hr., every hr., £8.25). National Express **buses** (☎ (08705) 80 80 80) arrive from London (2½hr., 1 per hr., £10.50) and Salisbury (2hr., 1 per day, £8.25). The **tourist office** is on The Hard; there's a branch next to the train station. (☎92 82 67 22. Open daily 9:30am-5:45pm.) Moderately priced **B&Bs** (around £20) clutter **Southsea**, 1½ mi. east of The Hard along the coast. **Birchwood Guest House,** 44 Waverly Rd., offers bright, spacious ensuite rooms and an ample breakfast. (☎92 81 13 37. £16-£25 per person.) Take any Southsea bus and get off at The Strand to reach the **Portsmouth and Southsea Backpackers Lodge,** 4 Florence Rd. (☎92 83 24 95. **Internet** £2.50 per 30 min. Dorms £10; doubles £25.) Take any bus to Cosham (including #1, 3, and 40) to the police station and follow the signs to get to the **YHA youth hostel** at Wymering Manor, on Old Wymering Ln., Medina Rd., in Cosham. (☎92 37 56 61. Lockout 10am-5pm. Curfew 11pm. Open Feb.-Aug. daily; Sept.-Nov. F-Sa. Dorms £9.15, under 18 £6.20.) The **Tesco supermarket,** on Craswell St., is just off the town center. (Open M-Th 8am-8pm, F 8am-9pm, Sa 8am-7pm, Su 10am-4pm.) **Pubs** near The Hard provide weary sailors with galley fare and bottles of gin. **Postal code:** PO1 1AA.

WINCHESTER   ☎01962

The glory of Winchester (pop. 32,000) stretches back to Roman times. William the Conqueror deemed it the center of his kingdom, and Jane Austen and John Keats both lived and wrote in town. Duck under the archway, pass through the square, and behold the 900-year-old **Winchester Cathedral,** 5 The Close. Famed for its nave, the 556-foot-long cathedral is the longest medieval building in Europe; the interior holds magnificent tiles and Jane Austen's tomb. The **Norman crypt,** supposedly the oldest in England, can only be viewed in the summer by guided tour. The 12th-century Winchester Bible resides in the library. (Open daily 7:15am-5:30pm; East End closes 5pm. Tours 10am-3pm; free. Donation £3, students £2.) Fifteen miles north of Winchester is the meek village of **Chawton**, where Jane Austen lived. It was in her **cottage** that she penned *Pride and Prejudice, Emma, Northanger Abbey,* and *Persuasion,* among others. Take Hampshire **bus** #X64 (M-Sa 11 per day, round-trip £4.50), or the London and Country bus #65 on Sundays, from the bus station; ask to be let off at the Chawton roundabout and follow the brown signs. (☎ (01420) 832 62. Open Mar.-Dec. daily 11am-4:30pm; Jan.-Feb. Sa-Su 11am-4:30pm. £2.50.) **Royal Oak,** on Royal Oak Passage, next to the Godbegot House off High St., is another pub that claims to be the kingdom's oldest. (Open daily 11am-11pm.)

Trains (☎ (0345) 48 49 50) arrive at Winchester's Station Hill, at City Rd. and Sussex St., from: Chichester (50min., every hr., £9.50); London's Waterloo Station (1hr., 2 per hr., £16.60); and Portsmouth (1hr., every hr., £7). National Express **buses** (☎ (08705) 80 80 80) go to London (1½hr., 7 per day, £12); Hampshire Stagecoach (☎ (01256) 46 45 01) goes to Salisbury (#68; 1½hr., 7 per day, round-trip £4.45) and Portsmouth (#69; 1½hr., 12 per day, round-trip £4.45). The **tourist information center,** at The Guildhall, Broadway, is by the statue of Alfred the Great. (☎84 05 00; fax 85 03 48. Open June-Sept. M-Sa 10am-6pm, Su 11am-2pm; Oct.-May M-Sa 10am-5pm.) The lovely home of **Mrs. P. Patton,** 12 Christchurch Rd., between St. James Ln. and Beaufort Rd., is 5min. from the cathedral. (☎85 42 72. Singles £22-25; doubles £30-35.) Go past the Alfred statue, across the bridge, and left before Cricketers Pub to reach the **YHA youth hostel,** 1 Water Ln. (☎85 37 23. Lockout 10am-5pm. Curfew 11pm. Open July-Aug. daily; mid-Feb. to June and Sept.-Oct. Tu-Sa. £9.15.) Get **groceries** at **Sainsbury,** on Middle Brook St., off High St. (Open M-Th 8am-6:30pm, F 8am-9pm, Sa 7:30am-6pm.) **Postal code:** SO23 8WA.

SALISBURY ☎ 01722

Salisbury (pop. 36,890) revolves around **Salisbury Cathedral,** and its spire that rises an astounding 404 feet. The bases of the pillars literally bend inward under the strain of 6400 tons of limestone; if a pillar rings when you knock on it, you should probably move away. (Open daily June-Aug. M-Sa 7am-8:15pm; Su 7am-6:15pm; Sept.-May daily 7am-6:15pm. £3, students £2. Tours May-Oct. M-Sa 9:30am-4:45pm; Nov.-Feb. M-Sa 10am-4pm; May-Sept. Su 4-6:15pm; free. 90-min. roof and tower tours May-Sept. M-Sa 11am, 2, and 3pm, Su 4:30pm; £3.) One of four surviving copies of the **Magna Carta** rests in the **Chapter House.** (Open June-Aug. M-Sa 9:30am-7:45pm, Su 9:30am-5:30pm; daily Sept.-May 9:30am-5:30pm, Su 1-3:15pm. Free.)

Trains arrive on South Western Rd from London (1½hr., every hr., £22-30) and Winchester (1½hr., every hr., £10.60). National Express **buses** (☎ (08705) 80 80 80) pull into 8 Endless St. from London's Victoria Station (2¾hr., 4 per day, £11.50); Wilts & Dorset buses (☎33 68 55) arrive from Bath (#X4; 2hr., 6 per day, £3). The **tourist information center** is on Fish Row in the Guildhall, in Market Sq.; turn left on South Western Rd., bear right on Fisherton St., continue on Bridge St., cross the bridge onto High St., and walk straight on Silver St., which becomes Butcher Row and Fish Row (10-15min.). From the bus station, head left on Endless St., which (shockingly) ends and becomes Queen St., and turn right at the first old building to the right to enter Fish Row, where the **tourist office** is located. (☎33 49 56; fax 42 20 59. Open July-Aug. M-Sa 9:30am-7pm, Su 10:30am-4:30pm; June and Sept. M-Sa 9:30am-6pm, Su 10:30am-4:30pm; Oct.-May M-Sa 9:30am-5:30pm.) To get from the bus station to lodgings at **The Old Bakery,** 35 Bedwin St., head two blocks up Rollestone St., and turn left onto Bedwin St. (☎32 01 00. £15-20; with full breakfast £18-25. Backpackers' cottage £15 per person; with continental breakfast £17.) From the tourist office, head left on Fish Row, right on Queen St., left on Milford St., and straight under the overpass to find the **YHA youth hostel,** in Milford Hill House, on Milford Hill. (☎32 75 72. Lockout 10am-1pm. Curfew 11:30pm. Dorms £9.85-10.85. **Camping** £4.70 per person.) **Sainsbury's supermarket** is at The Maltings. (Open M-Th 8am-8pm, F 8am-9pm, Sa 7:30am-7pm, Su 10am-4pm.) **Postal code:** SP1 1AB.

⚟ DAYTRIPS FROM SALISBURY

STONEHENGE

*Wilts & Dorset **buses** (☎33 68 55) connect from Salisbury's center and train station (40min., round-trip £4.80).*

The 22-foot-high boulders of Stonehenge, which weigh up to 45 tons, date from about 1500 BC. Various and sundry stories attribute the monument to Druids, Phoenicians, Merlin, Mycenaean Greeks, Bjork, giants, Romans, Smurfs, Danes, and aliens. In any case, the laborers' technological capabilities were more advanced than we can imagine; their unknown methods continue to elude both archaeologists and previously fail-safe supermarket tabloids. For centuries, religious devotees have come for its mystical karmic energies, building temples and leaving us to marvel at the awe-inspiring, impressive nature of the site. You can admire Stonehenge for free from nearby Amesbury Hill, 1½ mi. up A303, or pay admission at the site. (☎ (01980) 62 53 68. Open daily June-Aug. 9am-7pm; mid-Mar.-May and Sept.-mid-Oct. 9:30am-6pm; mid-Oct. to mid-Mar. 9:30am-4pm. £4, students £3.)

AVEBURY

*Take **bus** #5 or 6 from Salisbury to Avebury (1½hr., 6 per day, £3.90).*

Avebury sprouts from within a **stone circle** that is the third-largest of its kind in Europe. Avebury's sprawling titans were constructed over 500 years before Stonehenge's. Many have studied the circle, but its meaning evades all. Just outside the circle is **Silbury Hill,** built in 2660 BC; the curious man-made mound represents another archaeological mystery. The **tourist information center** is near the car park near the stone circle. (☎ (01672) 53 94 25. Open W-Sa 10am-5pm, Su 10am-4pm.)

BRISTOL
☎ 0117

The southwest's largest city, Bristol (pop. 401,000) hums along as a working business center by day and jumps into energetic revelry by night. **John Wesley's Chapel,** the oldest Methodist building in the world, sits incongruously opposite The Galleries, Bristol's shopping shrine. (☎ 926 4740. Open M-Sa 10am-4pm. Free.) Remnants of Saxon and Norman architecture linger in **Bristol Cathedral,** proudly overlooking the College Green. (☎ 926 4879. Open daily 8am-6pm.) Elizabeth I termed the medieval church of **St. Mary Redcliffe,** 10 Redcliffe Parade West, the "fairest, goodliest, and most famous Parish Church in England." (☎ 929 1487. Open M-Sa 8am-8pm, Su 7:30am-8pm; off-season M-Sa 8am-5:30pm, Su 7:30am-8pm.) Bristol's newest attraction, **Explore@Bristol,** Explore Lane, Harbourside, educates students of all ages with interactive exhibits, live wildlife, and multimedia presentations. (☎ 915 50 00. Open daily 10am-6pm. Single sight £6.50). The **Clifton Suspension Bridge,** Brunel's architectural masterpiece spanning the Avon Gorge, is reached via a pleasant walk through Clifton. Close by on Sion Pl., the **Bridge House Visitor's Centre** documents the history of the bridge and gives a brief course in bridge engineering (☎ 974 4664. Open daily Apr.-Sept. 10am-5pm; Oct.-Mar. M-F 11am-4pm, Sa-Su 11am-5pm. £1.50.)

Trains (☎ (08457) 48 49 50) come to Bristol Temple Meads Station from: London's Paddington station (1½hr., 2per hr., £36); Bath (20min., every 15min., £4.60); and Cardiff (50min., 2 per hr., £8.90). National Express **buses** (☎ (08705) 80 80 80) trundle into the Marlborough St. Bus Station from London (2½hr.; 21 per hr.; £10, round-trip £13) and Cardiff (1¼hr.; 11 per day; £4.50, round-trip £5.50). The **tourist office,** The Annex, Wildscreen Walk, Harbourside, is adjacent to Explore@Bristol. (☎ 926 07 67. Open July-Aug. M-W and Sa-Su 10am-6pm, Th-F 10am-8pm; Sept.-June daily 10am-6pm.) **Bristol Backpackers,** 17 St. Stephen's St., a new independent hostel located in an old newspaper building, is making headlines. (☎ 925 79 00. Dorms £12.50.) The local **YHA Youth Hostel,** Hayman House, is at 14 Narrow Quay. (☎ 922 16 59. Dorms £12.15, under 18 £8.35.) **Boston Tea Party,** 75 Park St., keeps Bristol buzzing with its exquisite selection of coffees and sandwiches for £3-5. (☎ 929 86 01. Open M 7am-6pm, Tu-Sa 7am-10pm, Su 9am-7pm.)

EXETER
☎ 01392

Besieged by William the Conqueror in 1068 and flattened by German bombs in 1942, Exeter (pop. 110,000), has undergone frantic rebuilding resulting in an odd mixture of the venerable and the banal: Roman and Norman ruins poke out from parking lots, and the cash registers of a bustling department store rest on a medieval catacomb. **Exeter Cathedral** was heavily damaged in WWII but retains exquisite detail. The cathedral library's **Exeter Book** is the richest treasury of early Anglo-Saxon poetry in the world. (Cathedral open daily 7am-6:30pm; library open M-F 2-5pm. Evensong services M-F 5:30pm, Sa-Su 3pm. Free tours Apr.-Oct. M-F 11:30am and 2:30pm, Sa 11am. Donation £2.50.) Six-hundred-year-old **underground passages** are accessible from Romangate Passage next to Boots on High St. (Open July-Sept. M-Sa 10am-5:30pm; Oct.-June Tu-F 2-5pm, Sa 10am-5pm. Tours £3.50, students £2.50.)

Trains arrive in Exeter from London's Paddington Station (2½hr., 2 per hr., £39) and London's Waterloo Station (3hr., 6 per day, £38.30). National Express **buses** (☎ (08705) 80 80 80) pull into Paris St., off High St. just outside the city walls, from London's Victoria Coach Station (4hr., every 1½hr., round-trip £16) and Bath (2¾hr., 3 per day, £13); walk through the arcade to Sidwell St. and turn left to reach High St. The **tourist office,** at the Civic Centre, in the City Council Building on Paris St., is opposite the rear of the bus station. (☎ 26 57 00. Open M-Sa 9am-5pm, in summer also Su 10am-4pm.) To reach the **YHA youth hostel,** 47 Countess Wear Rd., 2 mi. from the city center off Topsham Rd., take minibus K or T from High St. to the Countess Wear Post Office (97p), then follow Exe Vale Rd. to the end and turn left. (☎ 87 33 29. Breakfast £3.10. Reception 8-10am and 5-10pm. Dorms £10.15; **camping** about half-price.) Pack a picnic at **Sainsbury's supermarket,** in the Guildhall Shopping Centre off High St. (Open M-W and F 8am-6:30pm, Th 8am-7pm, Sa 7:30am-6pm, Su 10:30am-4:30pm.) **Postal code:** EX1 1AA.

DARTMOOR NATIONAL PARK

Dartmoor is scattered with artifacts, from oddly balanced granite tors to Neolithic rock formations. Ramblers across the park will find the skeleton of a mining industry and the heavily guarded **Princetown prison.** Due to rough terrain and a harsh climate, Dartmoor has remained largely untouched except by sheep and wild ponies. Today, many spirits linger in Dartmoor's mystical bleakness, the most famous being the canine immortalized by Sir Arthur Conan Doyle's *Hound of the Baskervilles.* The last castle to be built in England isn't Norman or Tudor—it's **Castle Drogo,** built by tea baron Julius Drewe. (Open Apr.-Oct. Sa-Th 11am-5:30pm. £5.40; grounds only £2.60.) **National Park Information Centres** are found in **Ivybridge** (☎ (01752) 89 70 35; open July-Aug. M-F 9am-5pm, Sa 10am-4pm, Su 10am-2pm; Sept.-June M-Sa 9am-5pm); **Princetown** (High Moorland Visitor Centre; ☎ (01822) 89 04 14; open daily 10am-5pm; in winter 10am-4pm); and **Tavistock,** Bedford Sq. (☎ (01822) 61 29 38; open Easter-Oct. M-Sa 10am-5pm; Nov.-Easter M-Tu and F-Sa 10am-4pm). Visitors should not underestimate Dartmoor's moody weather or treacherous terrain. The Ministry of Defense uses the moor for **target practice,** and the boundaries of dangerous areas change yearly; consult your map and check weekly firing times at tourist offices. An *Ordnance Survey Outdoor Leisure 28* map (£6.50), a compass, and waterproof garb are essential. Stick to the marked paths. The *Dartmoor Visitor,* free at tourist offices, provides maps and info on accommodations and food. Tourist information centres offer detailed guides to walks, some with map supplements. The official **Dartmoor Rescue Group** (☎ (01837) 863 33) is on call through the police (**emergency** ☎ 999).

　　Buses are infrequent; plan well ahead, using the bus schedules available at every **tourist office** (TIC) in and around Dartmoor. The best day to travel to Dartmoor by bus is Sunday, when frequencies increase and the **Sunday Rover** allows unlimited bus travel (£5, students £4.50). The **Transmoor Link** (Stagecoach Devon bus #82; late May to Sept.; M-Sa 3 per day, Su 5 per day; £5) cuts through the middle of the park on its southwest-northeast route between Plymouth and Exeter. **Plymouth Buses** run to Ivybridge (#X80, 30min., 3 per hr.); Okehampton (#86; M-F 9 per day, Su 2 per day); and Tavistock (#83, 84, or 86; 1hr.; 4 per hr.). For more info, contact the **Devon County Council's Public Transportation Helpline.** (☎ (01392) 38 28 00. Open M-F 8:30am-5pm.) The invaluable *Dartmoor Public Transportation Guide,* is available in any nearby bus station or tourist office. Spend the night at **Bellever (YHA),** 1 mi. southeast of Postbridge village on bus #82 from Plymouth or Exeter to Postbridge. (☎ (01822) 88 02 27. Open July-Aug. daily; Apr.-June M-Sa; Sept.-Oct. Tu-Sa. Dorms £9.15, under 18 £6.20.) **Okehampton (YHA),** Klondyke Rd., offers occasional rock climbing outings in addition to rooms. (☎ (01837) 539 16. Open Feb.-Nov. Dorms £11, under 18 £7.50.) Although official campsites exist, many travelers **camp** on the open moor. Dartmoor land is privately owned, so ask permission before crossing or camping on land. Backpack camping is permitted on the non-enclosed moor land more than 100 yd. away from the road or out of sight of inhabited areas. Campers may only stay for one night in a single spot. Don't build fires in the moors. To camp at an official site, try **Ashburton Caravan Park,** Waterleat, Ashburton (☎ (01364) 65 25 52. July-Aug. £10 per 2-person tent; Easter-June and Sept.-Oct. £7.50), or **Higher Longford Farm,** Moorshop, Tavistock. (☎ (01822) 61 33 60. £7.50 for first adult, £2 for each additional adult.)

PLYMOUTH
☎ 01752

Plymouth is a famed port—the English fleet sailed from here to defeat the Spanish Armada in 1588, and Sir Francis Drake, Captain Cook, the Pilgrims, Lord Nelson, and millions of emigrants to the United States and New Zealand earned Plymouth a spot in the history books in their haste to escape it. Heed their age-old message. **Trains** (☎ (0345) 48 49 50) run at least every hour from Plymouth Station, on North Rd, to London's Paddington Station (4hrs., £60) and Penzance (2hrs., £10.30); take Western National bus #14, 16b, 72, 83, or 84 to the city center at Royal Parade. **Buses** leave from Bretonside Station, near St. Andrew's Cross at the eastern end of

Royal Parade; National Express (☎ (08705) 80 80 80) goes to London (4½hr., £20) and Stagecoach Devon runs to Exeter (#X38, 1¼hr., £4.15). For **ferries** (☎ (0990) 36 03 60) departing from the Millbay Docks (take bus #33 or 34 to the docks; 15min.) for France and Spain, see p. 188. The **tourist office** is in Island House, 9 The Barbican. (☎30 48 49; fax 25 79 55. Open M-Sa 9am-5pm, Su 10am-4pm.) Take bus #15 or 81 from the train station or Royal Parade to Stoke to find the **YHA youth hostel,** Belmont House, on Belmont Pl. (☎56 21 89. Lockout 10am-5pm. Curfew 11pm. Reserve ahead. Dorms £10.15.) **Plymouth Backpackers Hotel,** 172 Citadel Rd., is two blocks from the west end of the Hoe. (☎22 51 58. Laundry. Dorms £8.50; singles £10; triples £27.) **Sainsbury's,** in the Armada Shopping Centre, stocks **groceries.** (Open M-Sa 8am-8pm, Su 10am-4pm.) **Postal Code:** PL1 1AB.

CORNWALL

With Cornwall's lush vegetation stretching out into the Atlantic, a look at the terrain will alert you to the fact that you're no longer quite in England. Cornwall's isolation made it a favored place for Celtic migration in the face of Saxon conquest. While there are no longer any native speakers of the Cornish language, the area remains fiercely Cornish and only tepidly English. England's southwest tip has some of the broadest, sandiest beaches in northern Europe, and the surf is up year-round whether or not the sun decides to break through.

▇ TRANSPORTATION

By far the best base for exploring the region is Penzance, the southwestern terminus of Britain's **trains** (☎ (08457) 48 49 50). The main rail line from **Plymouth** to **Penzance** bypasses the coastal towns, but there is connecting rail service to **Newquay, Falmouth,** and **St. Ives. Rail Rover** tickets make it even easier (3 days unlimited travel within a 7-day span £24.50, 8 out of 15 days £39). The **Western National bus** network is similarly thorough, although the interior is not served as well as the coast. Buses run frequently from **Penzance** to **Land's End** and **St. Ives,** and from **St. Ives** to **Newquay,** stopping in the smaller towns along these routes. Many buses don't run on Sundays, and many run only May-Sept.; call the Camborne bus station (☎ (01209) 71 99 88) to check.

PENZANCE. Penzance is the very model of an ancient English pirate town: waterlogged, stealthy, and unabashed. A Benedictine monastery was built on the spot where St. Michael dropped by in AD 495, and today **St. Michael's Mount** sits offshore. The interior is unspectacular, but the grounds are more textured, and the 30-story views are captivating. (Open Apr.-Oct. M-F 10:30am-5:30pm; in summer usually also Sa-Su; Nov.-Mar. in nice weather. £4.40.) A causeway links the mount to the island; or take ferry bus #2 or 2A to Marazion (M-Sa 3 per hr., round-trip £0.80) and catch a ferry during high tide (round-trip £1.40). **Trains** (☎ (0345) 48 49 50) go to: London (5½hr., 1 per hr., £54); Exeter (3hr., 1 per hr., £18.60); and Plymouth (2hr., 1 per hr., £10). National Express (☎ (08705) 80 80 80) **buses** run to: London (8hr., 8 per day, £27) and Plymouth (3hr., 2 per hr., £6). Between the two stations is the **tourist office,** on Station Rd. (☎ (01736) 36 22 07. Open M-F 9am-5pm, Sa 9am-4pm, Su 10am-1pm; off-season M-F 9am-5pm, Sa 10am-1pm.) To get to the **YHA youth hostel,** Castle Horneck, walk 30min. up Market Jew and Alverton St., then take the right fork with signs for Castle Horneck. (☎ (01736) 36 26 66. Laundry. Reception 3-11pm. Lockout 10am-1pm. Dorms £10.15. **Camping** £5.) **The Turk's Head,** 49 Chapel St., is a 13th-century pub that was sacked by Spanish pirates in 1595.

ST. IVES. St. Ives perches 10 mi. north of Penzance, on a spit of land lined by pastel beaches and azure waters. Virginia Woolf was bewitched by the energy of the Atlantic at St. Ives: her masterpiece *To the Lighthouse* is thought to refer to the Godrevy Lighthouse in the distance. Whether you seek the perfect subject or the perfect strip of sand, St. Ives has it, if hidden beneath a veneer of postcards and ice cream cones. Some **trains** (☎ (0345) 48 49 50) go directly to Penzance (3-6 per day), but most connect via St. Erth (10min., 2 per hr., £3). Western National **buses** go to Penzance (3 per hr., off-season M-Sa only, £2.50) and Newquay (#57). National Express (☎ (08705) 80 80 80) stops in St. Ives between Plymouth and Penzance (6 per day). The **tourist office** is in the Guildhall on Street-an-Pol. From the stations, walk down to the foot of Tregenna Hill and turn right on Street-an-Pol. (☎ (01736) 79 62 97. Open M-Sa 9:30am-6pm, Su 10am-1pm; off-season closed Sa-Su.) **St. Ives International Backpackers,** The Stenmack, fills a renovated 19th-century Methodist church. (☎ (01736) 79 94 44. **Internet.** Dorms £8-12.) Places to camp abound in nearby **Hayle;** try **Trevalgan Camping Park** (☎ (01736) 79 64 33). **Fore St.** is packed with small bakeries. Many places also sell Cornish cream teas (a pot of tea with scones, jam, and Cornish clotted cream).

FALMOUTH. Seven rivers flow into the historic port of Falmouth (pop. 18,300), which is guarded by two spectacular castles. **Pendennis Castle,** built by Henry VIII to keep French frigates out of Falmouth, now features a walk-through diorama. (Open daily Apr.-June and Sept. 10am-6pm; July-Aug. 9am-6pm; Oct. 10am-5pm; Nov.-Mar. 10am-4pm. £3.80.) Across the channel lies another Henry VIII creation, the magnificently preserved **St. Mawes Castle.** (Open Apr.-Sept. daily 10am-6pm; Oct. daily 10am-5pm; Nov.-Mar. F-Tu 10am-1pm and 2pm-4pm. £2.50, students £2.) To get there, take the ferry from the Town Pier and The Quay (20min., 2 per hr., round-trip £3.50). To taste the surf, head to one of Falmouth's three **beaches. Trains** (☎ (0345) 48 49 50) arrive in town from: London Paddington (5½hr., 1 per hr., £64); Exeter (3½hr., 6 per day, £24); and Plymouth (2hr., 9-17 per day, £9.70). National Express (☎ (08705) 80 80 80) **buses** roll in from London (6½hr., 2 per day, £34.50). To get to the **tourist office,** 28 Killigrew St., The Moor, follow signs to Killigrew St. or Kimberley Park Rd., then go downhill toward the river. (☎ (08700) 11 00 18. Open Apr.-Sept. M-Sa 9:30am-5:30pm; July-Aug. also Su 10am-2pm; Oct.-Mar. M-F 9am-5pm.) None of the **train stations** sell tickets; get 'em at **Newell's Travel Agency,** 26 Killigrew St., The Moor, next to the tourist office. (☎ (01326) 31 50 66. Open M-F 9am-5:30pm, Sa 9am-4pm.) The **YHA youth hostel** is in Pendennis Castle, 30min. from town. (☎ (01326) 31 14 35. Reception 8:30-10am and 5-10:30pm. Curfew 11pm. Open Feb.-Sept. daily; Oct.-Nov. Tu-Sa. Reserve ahead. Dorms £9.15.) **Postal code:** TR11 3RB.

NEWQUAY. An outpost of surfer subculture, Newquay (NEW-key) lures the bald, the bleached-blond, and even the blue, to its surf and pubs. Winds descend on **Fistral Beach** with a vengeance, creating what some consider the best surfing conditions in all of Europe. The enticing **Lusty Glaze Beach** beckons from the bay side. The party beast stirs around 9pm and reigns into the wee hours. Drink up at **The Red Lion,** on North Quay Hill, at Tower Rd. and Fore St., then ride the wave down Fore St. to **Sailors.** (Cover £4-10.) Go on and shake what your momma gave you at **Bertie's,** on East St. (Open until 1am.) From the train station, just off Cliff Rd., **trains** go to Penzance (2hr., every hr., £10.30) and Plymouth (2hr., every hr., £8.10). From the **bus station,** 1 East St., Western National runs to St. Ives (2hr., June-Sept. 1 per day, £4.90). National Express (☎ (08705) 80 80 80) buses run to London (5¾hr., 3 per day, £26.50). Facing the street from the train station, go four blocks left to reach the **tourist office,** on Marcus Hill. (☎ (01637) 85 40 22. Open M-Sa 9am-6pm, Su 9am-4pm; off-season reduced hours.) **Newquay Backpackers International,** 69-73 Tower Rd., offers free shuttle service to its sister hostel in St. Ives. (☎ (01637) 87 93 66; email backpacker@dial.pipex.com. **Internet.** Dorms £10.)

EAST ANGLIA AND THE MIDLANDS

The plush green farmlands and watery fens of **East Anglia** stretch northeast from London, cloaking the counties of Cambridgeshire, Norfolk, and Suffolk. Although industry is modernizing the economies of Cambridge and Peterborough, the area in between is still characterized by its sheer flatness; much of the rustic beauty that inspired the landscape paintings of natives Constable and Gainsborough remains. To the west lie the **Midlands**—the term evokes images of industrial cities, thanks to the "dark satanic mills" foreseen by William Blake that overran the area during the Industrial Revolution. But the heart of England contains its fair share of England's must-sees; Manchester and Liverpool are home to innovative music, arts, and nightlife scenes, while Lincoln and Chester tell many of their tales in Latin.

OXFORD ☎01865

Almost a millennium of scholarship lies behind Oxford—22 British Prime Ministers were educated here, as were numerous other world leaders. Some form of teaching existed here in the 11th century, but it was in 1167 that Henry II founded the actual university, Britain's first. After his tiff with Thomas Becket, Archbishop of Canterbury, Henry ordered the return of English students studying in Paris, so that "there may never be wanting a succession of persons duly qualified for the service of God in church and state." There is no want of a succession of persons today, as trucks rumble, bus brakes screech, and bicycles crush the toes of pedestrians shoving past each other in Oxford's streets. Despite the mass of tourists, however, Oxford has an irrepressible grandeur, and there are pockets of respite to charm and edify the academic pilgrim: the basement room of Blackwell's Bookshop, the impeccable galleries of the Ashmolean, and the perfectly maintained quadrangles of Oxford's 39 colleges.

▐ TRANSPORTATION

Trains: Depart from Park End St., west of Carfax (☎ (0345) 48 49 50, recording 79 44 22). **Thames trains** run from **London's Paddington Station** (1hr., every 15-30min., round-trip £14.80). Ticket office open M-F 6am-8pm, Sa 6:45am-8pm, Su 7:45am-8pm.

Buses: Depart from Gloucester Green (follow the arrows up Cornmarket St. from Carfax). **Oxford CityLink** (☎78 54 00). Open daily 6:30am-6:30pm. Connects from: **London Victoria** (1¾hr.; 1-4 per hr.; round-trip £7.50, students £6.50); **Gatwick airport** (2hr.; every hr. daytime, every 2 hr. overnight; round-trip £19); and **Heathrow airport** (2 per hr., round-trip £12). **National Express** (☎ (08705) 80 80 80) offers national routes.

Public Transportation: The **Oxford Bus Company** (☎78 54 00) and **Stagecoach** (☎77 22 50). Most local services board on the streets around Carfax. Fares are low (usually 70p).

✳❷ ORIENTATION AND PRACTICAL INFORMATION

Queen, High, St. Aldate's, and **Cornmarket Streets** intersect at **Carfax,** the town center. The easiest way to orientate yourself in Oxford is to locate the colossal Carfax Tower. The colleges are all within 1 mi. of one another, mainly to the east of Carfax along **High St.** and **Broad St.** The **tourist office** and **bus station** lie to the northwest on Gloucester Green—from Carfax, follow Cornmarket St. to George St. and turn right onto Gloucester. Take Queen St. (which changes names to New Rd. and Park End) to get to the **train station.**

Tourist Office: The Old School (☎72 68 71; fax 24 02 61), Gloucester Green, beside the bus station. Accommodations list 60p. Map £1. Books rooms for a £2.50 fee and a 10% deposit. Two-hour **walking tours** depart 2-5 times per day (11am-2pm; £4.50, children £3). Open M-Sa 9:30am-5pm, Su 10am-3:30pm.

American Express: 4 Queen St. (☎20 71 01). Open M-Sa 9am-5:30pm, W opens at 9:30am, Sa closes at 5pm.

Luggage storage: Pensioners' Club (☎24 22 37), in Gloucester Green, by the bus station. Storage for up to a few weeks. £1-2 donation requested. Open M-Sa 9am-4:45pm.

Emergency: ☎999.

Police: ☎26 60 00. Stations on St. Aldates St. and Speedwell St.

Crisis Line: Samaritans, 123 Iffley Rd. (☎72 21 22; 24hr.); drop-in daily 8am-10pm.

Gay and Lesbian Services: Gay Switchboard, Oxford Friend (☎ 79 39 99).

Pharmacy: Boots, 6-8 Cornmarket St. (☎ 24 74 61). Open M-Sa 8:45am-6pm, Su 11am-5pm.

Internet Access: Pickwick Papers, 90 Gloucester Green (☎ 79 31 49), is conveniently located next to the bus station. £1 per 15min. Open daily 4:30am-6:30pm.

Post Office: 102/104 St. Aldates St. (☎ 20 28 63). Open M-F 9am-5:30pm, Sa 9am-6pm. Changes money. **Postal code:** OX1 1ZZ.

▌ ACCOMMODATIONS

In summer, book at least a week ahead. **B&Bs** line the main roads out of town and are accessible by Cityline buses or a 15- to 45-minute walk. More B&Bs are located in the 300s on **Banbury Rd.** (take bus 2A, 2C, or 2D); cheaper ones lie in the 200s and 300s on **Iffley Rd.** (take bus 4); between 250 and 350 on **Cowley Rd.** (take bus 51 or 52); and on **Abingdon Rd.** in South Oxford (take bus 16). Expect to pay £20-25.

Oxford Backpacker's Hotel, 9a Hythe Bridge St. (☎ 72 17 61). Great location, between the bus and train stations, a short walk away from most sights. Nonstop music enlivens the common room, hallways, and bathroom. Guests must show passport. Internet access £1.50 per 15 min. Laundry £2.50. Dorms £11-12.

YHA Youth Hostel, 32 Jack Straw's Ln. (☎ 76 29 97), Headington. Take bus #13 (4 per hr. until 11:10pm, 70p) heading away from Carfax on High St.; ask the driver to stop at Jack Straw's Ln. and walk 8min. up the hill. 105 beds. Reserve ahead in summer. Dorms £10.85, under 18 £7.45, students £1 less.

Bravalla, 242 Iffley Rd. (☎ 24 13 26; fax 25 05 11). Six sunny rooms, all with bath and TV. Reserve several weeks ahead. Singles £35; doubles £50.

Heather House, 192 Iffley Rd. (☎/fax 24 97 57). Take the bus marked "Rose Hill" from the bus station, train station, or Carfax Tower (70p). Vivian, the vibrant Australian proprietress, keeps sparkling, modern rooms. Singles £25; doubles with bath £48. Cheaper for longer stays.

Newton House, 82-84 Abingdon Rd. (☎ 24 05 61), ½ mi. from town; take any Abingdon bus across Folly Bridge. Friendly owner and TVs in all rooms. Doubles £44, with bath £58; varies with season.

Old Mitre Rooms, 4b Turl St. (☎ 27 98 21; fax 27 99 63). Lincoln College dorms. Open July to early Sept. Singles £24; doubles £44, with bath £48.50; triples £58, with bath £63.

Oxford Camping and Caravaning, 426 Abingdon Rd. (☎ 24 40 88), behind the Touchwoods camping store. 84 sites. Toilet and laundry facilities. Showers free. Max. stay for non-members is 2 nights. £4.90-6.25 per tent.

Cassington Mill Caravan Site, (☎ 88 10 81) Eynsham Rd., Cassington, about 4 mi. northwest on the A40. 87 sites. £8 for large tents, £6.50 for small tents.

◖ FOOD

Oxford students bored with cafeteria food sustain a market for budget eats in town. After hours, **kebab vans** roam around **Broad St., High St., Queen St.,** and **St. Aldates St.** If you're staying across Magdalen Bridge, try restaurants along the first four blocks of **Cowley Rd.** The **Covered Market** between Market St. and Carfax has produce, deli goods, and breads. (Open M-Sa 8am-5:30pm.) Pick up **groceries** at **J. Sainsbury,** in the Westgate Centre mall on Queen St. (Open M-F 8am-8pm, Sa 7:30am-7pm, Su 11am-5pm.) Across Magdalen Bridge is the vegetarian-friendly **Uhuru Wholefoods,** 48 Cowley Rd. (Open M-F 10am-6pm, Sa 9:30am-5:30pm.)

▨ **The Nosebag,** 6-8 St. Michael's St. (☎ 72 10 33). A different gourmet-grade menu each night, served cafeteria-style. Lunch under £6.50, dinner under £8. Open M 9:30am-5:30pm, Tu-Th until 10pm, F-Sa until 10:30pm, Su until 9pm.

Café CoCo, 23 Cowley Rd. (☎ 20 02 32). Lively atmosphere and a great Mediterranean menu. Main dishes £5.95-8.50. Open daily 10am-11pm.

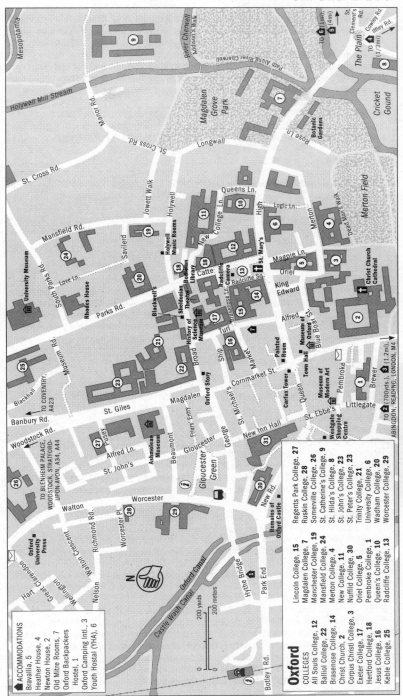

ACCOMMODATIONS
Bravallia, 5
Heather House, 4
Newton House, 2
Old Mitre Rooms, 7
Oxford Backpackers
Hostel, 1
Oxford Camping Intl., 3
Youth Hostal (YHA), 6

Oxford

COLLEGES

All Souls College, 12	Lincoln College, 15	Regents Park College, 27
Balliol College, 22	Magdalen College, 7	Ruskin College, 28
Brasenose College, 14	Manchester College, 19	Somerville College, 26
Christ Church, 2	Mansfield College, 24	St. Catherine's College, 9
Corpus Christi College, 3	Merton College, 4	St. Hilda's College, 8
Exeter College, 17	New College, 11	St. John's College, 23
Hertford College, 16	Nuffield College, 30	St. Peter's College, 23
Jesus College, 18	Oriel College, 5	Trinity College, 21
Keble College, 25	Pembroke College, 10	University College, 6
	Queen's College, 10	Wadham College, 20
	Radcliffe College, 13	Worcester College, 29

Chiang Mai, 130a High St. (☎ 20 22 33), tucked down an alley. Popular Thai restaurant with plenty of veggie options. Main dishes £5.50-9. Try the jungle curry with wild rabbit (£6.95). Reserve in advance or go for lunch to beat the crowds. Open M-Sa noon-2:30pm and 6-11pm, Su noon-3pm and 6-10pm.

Harvey's of Oxford, 58 High St. (☎ 72 31 52), near Magdalen College. Eat and run at one of Oxford's better takeaways, recognizable by the line out the door. Cherry-apple flapjacks 85p, great chunks of carrot cake £1.25, mighty sandwiches £1.60-2.90. Open M-F 8am-7pm, Sa 8am-6pm, Su 8:30am-6pm.

Heroes, 8 Ship St. (☎ 72 34 59). Filled with students feeding on sandwiches, meats and cheeses, and freshly-baked breads (£1.80-3.70). Popular for takeout, but there's also a small sit-down area. Open M-F 8am-7pm, Sa 8:30am-5pm, Su 10am-5pm.

👁 SIGHTS

King Henry II founded Britain's first university in 1167; today, Oxford's alumni register reads like a who's who of British history, literature, and philosophy. The university has traditionally been a breeding ground for the country's leaders; 22 British Prime Ministers were educated here. Oxford University's three favorite sons—Lewis Carroll, C.S. Lewis, and J.R.R. Tolkien—sat near the stone-bridged waters of the Isis (as the Thames is known here) dreaming of crossings through mirrors, through wardrobes, and through mountain passes. The tourist office's *Welcome to Oxford* guide (£2) lists the colleges' public visiting hours.

CARFAX AND SOUTH OF CARFAX. For an overview of the city, hike up the 99 spiral stairs of **Carfax Tower,** at Carfax. *(Open daily Apr.-Oct. 10am-5:30pm, Nov.-Mar. 10am-3:30pm. £1.20.)* Just down St. Aldates from Carfax, **Christ Church College** has Oxford's grandest quad and its most socially distinguished students. The **Christ Church Chapel** is also Oxford's cathedral. The Reverend Charles Dodgson (better known as Lewis Carroll) was friendly with Dean Liddell of Christ Church—and friendlier with his daughter Alice. The Cheshire Cat first grinned and vanished from the largest tree in the garden; the White Rabbit can be spotted fretting in the stained glass of the hall. *(Open M-Sa 9:30am-5:30pm, Su 1-5pm. Church services Su 8, 10, 11:15am, 6pm; weekdays 7:30am, 6pm. £2.50, students £1.50.)* The 13th-century **University College,** on High St., welcomed Bill Clinton during his Rhodes Scholar days (his rooms at 46 Leckford Rd. are an endless source of smoked-but-didn't-inhale jokes for tour guides), but expelled Percy Bysshe Shelley for writing the pamphlet *The Necessity of Atheism.* *(☎ 27 66 19. Contact the college for admission.)* The **Botanic Garden** cultivates a sumptuous array of plants that have flourished for three centuries. The path connecting the Botanic Garden to the Christ Church Meadow provides a beautiful view of the Thames as well as the cricket and tennis courts on the opposite bank. *(From Carfax, head down High St.; the Garden is on the right. Open daily Apr.-Sept. 9am-5pm; Oct.-Mar. 9am-4:30pm. Glasshouses open daily 2-4pm. Late June to early Sept. £2, children free; free the rest of the year.)*

NORTH OF CARFAX. The imposing **Ashmolean Museum** houses works by Leonardo, Monet, Manet, van Gogh, Michelangelo, Rodin, and Matisse, while the **Cast Gallery,** behind the museum, exhibits over 250 casts of Greek sculptures—the finest classical collection outside London. *(Beaumont St. From Carfax, head up Cornmarket St., which becomes Magdalen St.; Beaumont St. is on the left. Both museum and gallery open Tu-Sa 10am-5pm, Su 2-5pm. Free.)* The **Bodleian Library** is Oxford's principal reading and research library, with over five million books. As a copyright library, it receives a free copy of every book printed in Great Britain. No one has ever been permitted to take out a book, not even Cromwell. Well, especially not Cromwell. *(Catte St. Take High St. and turn left on Catte. Open M-F 9am-6pm, Sa 9am-1pm. £3.50.)* The **Sheldonian Theatre,** beside the Bodleian, is a Roman-style jewel of an auditorium, designed by Christopher Wren, where graduation ceremonies are conducted in Latin. The cupola of the theater affords an inspiring view of the spires of Oxford. *(Open M-Sa 10am-12:30pm and 2-4:30pm. £1.50, children £1.)* On Broad St. you could browse for days at **Blackwell's Bookstore,** which according to Guinness is the largest room devoted to bookselling in the world. *(Open M and W-Sa 9am-6pm, Tu 9:30am-6pm, Su 11am-5pm.)* **New College,**

named because it was founded by William of Wykeham "only" in 1379, has become one of Oxford's most prestigious colleges. A croquet garden is encircled by part of the **old city wall.** The bell tower has gargoyles representing the Seven Deadly Sins on one side, and the Seven Virtues on the other, all equally grotesque. *(New College Ln. From Carfax, head down High St. and turn onto Catte St.; New College Ln. is to the right. ☎ 27 95 55. Open daily Easter-Oct. 11am-5pm; Nov.-Easter 2-4pm, use the Holywell St. Gate. £1.50 in the summer.)* Oscar Wilde attended **Magdalen** (MAUD-lin) **College,** considered by many to be Oxford's most handsome college. *(Open July-Sept. M-F noon-6pm, Sa-Su 2pm-6pm; Oct.-June 2-5pm. Apr.-Sept. £2, students £1; Oct.-Mar. free.)*

🎵🎭 ENTERTAINMENT AND NIGHTLIFE

PUNTING

A traditional pastime in Oxford is punting on the river Thames (known in Oxford as the Isis) or on the River Cherwell (CHAR-wul). Punters receive a tall pole, a small oar, and an advisory against falling into the water before venturing out in boats that look something like shallow gondolas. Don't try swimming in any of the canals; you could wind up with a tetanus shot and stitches. Also, don't be surprised if you suddenly come across **Parson's Pleasure,** a small riverside area where men sometimes sunbathe nude. **Magdalen Bridge Boat Co.,** Magdalen Bridge, east of Carfax along High St., rents from March to November. (☎ 20 26 43. M-F £9 per hr., Sa-Su £10 per hr.; deposit £20 plus ID. Open daily 10am-9pm.)

CONCERTS AND THEATER.

Music and drama at Oxford are cherished arts. Attend a concert or Evensong service at one of the colleges (the **New College Choir** is one of the best boy choirs around) or a performance at the **Holywell Music Rooms,** the oldest in the country. The **Oxford Playhouse,** 11-12 Beaumont St, is a venue for bands, dance troupes, and the Oxford Stage Company. (☎ 79 86 00. Tickets from £6, standby tickets available for matinees for seniors and students.) During summer, college **theater groups** stage productions in local gardens and cloisters. The **City of Oxford Orchestra,** the city's professional orchestra, gives concerts once a month in the Sheldonian Theatre. (☎ 74 44 57. Tickets £10-15; 25% student discount.)

PUBS AND NIGHTLIFE

Pubs far outnumber colleges in Oxford; many even consider them the city's prime attraction. The **Turf Tavern,** on 4 Bath Pl., off Holywell St., is a sprawling 13th-century pub tucked away in an alleyway against the ruins of the city wall. (Open M-Sa 11am-11pm, Su noon-10:30pm. Kitchen open noon-8pm.) **The Eagle and Child,** 49 St. Giles, moistened the tongues of C.S. Lewis and J.R.R. Tolkien for a quarter-century; *The Chronicles of Narnia* and *The Hobbit* were first read aloud here. (Open M-Sa 11am-11pm, Su 11am-10:30pm.) **The Kings Arms,** Holywell St., draws in a huge young crowd. The coffee room at the front of the bar lets quieter folks retreat from the merry masses at the back. (Open M-Sa 10:30am-11pm, Su 10:30am-10:30pm.) **The Bear,** Alfred St., established in 1242, is covered with over 5000 ties from Oxford students and famous people. (Open M-Sa noon-11pm, Su 6-10:30pm.)

Although pubs in Oxford tend to close down by 11pm, nightlife can last until 3am; grab *This Month in Oxford* at the tourist office. For starters, check out **The Westgate Pub,** Park End St. (Dance music until 2am on F and Sa, jazz on M, comedy on Tu.) The **Zodiac,** 193 Cowley Rd., has crazy themes every night and the best bands around. (☎ 72 63 36. Cover £5.) **Walton St.** and **Cowley Rd.** host late-night clubs, as well as a jumble of ethnic restaurants, used bookstores, and alternative shops.

FESTIVALS

The university celebrates **Eights Week** at the end of May, when all the colleges enter crews in the bumping races while others nibble strawberries and sip champagne on the banks. In early September, **St. Giles Fair** invades one of Oxford's main streets with an old-fashioned carnival, complete with Victorian roundabout and whirligigs.

▶ DAYTRIP FROM OXFORD

BLENHEIM PALACE

*Stagecoach Express **buses** (☎ (01865) 77 22 50) run to Blenheim Palace from Glouces-ter Green station in Oxford (20min., round-trip £3.50); the same bus also goes to Strat-ford and Birmingham. Blenheim sprawls in Woodstock, 8 mi. north of Oxford on the A44.*

The largest private home in England and one of the loveliest, **Blenheim** (BLEN-em) **Palace** features sprawling grounds, a lake, and a fantastic garden. While attending a party here, Winston Churchill's mother gave birth to the future Prime Minister in a closet; his grave rests appropriately near in the village churchyard of **Bladon.** The palace rent is a single French franc, payable each year to the Crown—not a bad deal for a palace with 187 furnished rooms. Blenheim's full glory (and fake snow) is on display in Kenneth Branagh's 4-hour film *Hamlet.* (☎ (01993) 81 10 91. Open mid-Mar. to Oct. daily 10:30am-5:30pm; grounds open year-round 9am-9pm. £9, students £7, children £4.50.)

WINDSOR   ☎01753

The town of Windsor, and the attached village of Eton, are completely overshad-owed by their two bastions of the British class system, Windsor Castle and Eton College. Windsor itself was built up around the castle during the Middle Ages, and is now filled with specialty shops, tea houses, and pubs. Within the ancient stone walls of **Windsor Castle** lie some of the most sumptuous rooms in Europe and some of the rarest artwork in the Western world. Built by William the Conqueror as a fortress rather than as a residence, it has grown over nine centuries into the world's largest inhabited castle. Visitors can watch the **Changing of the Guard** take place in front of the Guard Room at 11am on most days. On passing through the Norman Tower and Gate (built by Edward III from 1359-60), you enter the **upper ward.** Many of its rooms are open to the public, and are richly decorated with art from the massive Royal Collection, including works by Holbein, Rubens, Rem-brandt, and Van Dyck. The **middle ward** is dominated by the **Round Tower** and its surrounding rose garden. A stroll to the lower ward brings you to **St. George's Chapel,** where ten sovereigns rest, including George V, Queen Mary, Edward IV, Charles I, and Henry VI. Henry VIII lies below a remarkably humble stone. (☎86 82 86, 24hr. info ☎83 11 18. Open daily Apr.-Oct. 10am-5:30pm, last entry 4pm; Nov.-Mar. 10am-4pm, last entry 3pm. £10, over 60 £7.50, under 17 £5, families £22.50.) **Eton College,** founded by Henry VI in 1440, is still England's preeminent public (which is to say, private) school—Prince Harry is a current student. Wan-der around the schoolyard, a central quad complete with a statue of Henry VI, where Eton boys have frolicked for centuries. (10min. down Thames St. from the town center, across the river. ☎67 11 77. Tours depart daily 2:15pm and 3:15pm; £3.60, under 16 £3. Open daily July-Aug. and late Mar. to mid-Apr. 10:30am-4:30pm; other times 2-4:30pm. £2.60, under 16 £2.)

Windsor is probably best seen as a daytrip from London. Two train stations are near Windsor Castle; follow the signs. **Trains** (☎ (08457) 484950) pull into Windsor and Eton Central from London Victoria and London Paddington via Slough (50min., 2 per hr., round-trip £5.70). Trains come in at Windsor and Eton River-side from London Waterloo (50min., 2 per hr., round-trip £5.70). Green Line (☎86 68 72 61) **buses** #700 and 702 make the trip from London, leaving from Eccleston Bridge, behind Victoria station (1-1½hr., round-trip £4.35-5.50). If you intend to spend the night, the **YHA Windsor,** Edgeworth House, Mill Ln., doesn't have a lock-out. (☎86 17 10. Dorms £10.85, under 18 £7.40.) **The Waterman's Arms** is just over the bridge into Eton and to the left at Brocas St., next to the Eton College Boat House. A traditional pub (c. 1542), it's still a local favorite with delicious cod, chips, and salad for £4.15. (☎86 10 01. Open M-Sa noon-2:30pm and 6-11pm, Su noon-3pm and 7-10pm.)

THE COTSWOLDS

Stretching across western England—bounded by Banbury in the northeast, Bradford-upon-Avon in the southwest, Cheltenham in the north, and Malmesbury in the south—the Cotswolds' verdant, vivid hills enfold tiny towns barely touched by modern life. These old Roman settlements and tiny Saxon villages, hewn from the famed Cotswold stone, demand a place on any itinerary, although their relative inaccessibility via public transportation will necessitate extra effort to get there.

TRANSPORTATION. Useful gateway cities are Cheltenham, Oxford, and Bath. **Trains** to Cheltenham arrive from: London (2½hr., every hr., £31.50); Bath (1½hr., every hr., £11.10); and Exeter (2hr., every 2hr., £28.50). National Express **buses** (☎ (08705) 80 80 80) also roll in from: London (3hr., every hr., £10.50); Exeter (3½hr., every 2hr., £18); and Stratford-upon-Avon (1hr., 2 per day, £7.50). For connections to Oxford, see p. 197; connections to Bath, see p. 206.

From Cheltenham, Oxford, and Bath, **trains** zip to: Moreton-in-Marsh (from Oxford £6.70) and Charlbury (from Oxford £3.40)—the only villages in the Cotswolds with train stations. Several **bus** companies cover the Cotswolds, but most routes are very infrequent (1-2 per week). Two unusually regular services run from Cheltenham; **Pulham's Coaches** (☎ (01451) 82 03 69) run to Moreton via Bourton-on-the-Water and Stow-on-the-Wold (50min., M-Sa 7 per day, £1.50). **Castleway's Coaches** (☎ (01242) 60 29 49) depart for Broadway via Winchcombe (50min., M-Sa 4 per day, £1.80). Snag the *Connection* timetable from any bus station or tourist office, and the Cheltenham tourist office's *Getting There from Cheltenham*.

Local roads are perfect for biking; the closely spaced villages make ideal watering holes. **Country Lanes Cycle Center** rents bikes at the Moreton-on-the-Marsh train station. (☎ (01608) 65 00 65. £14 per day. Call ahead. Open daily 9:30am-5:30pm.) Experience the Cotswolds as the English have for centuries by treading well-worn footpaths from village to village. Cotswold Way, spanning 100 mi. from Bath to Chipping Camden, gives hikers glorious vistas of hills and dales.

CHELTENHAM. The spa town of Cheltenham (pop. 107,000) is a nice break from the heavily touristed Bath and Stratford. A useful launching pad into the rest of the Cotswolds, this city also has a large student population that brings the pubs and clubs to life at night. Enjoy the diuretic and laxative effects of the waters at the **Town Hall.** Sip, don't gulp. (Open M-F 9:30am-5:30pm. Free.) Manicured gardens adorn shops and houses around town, but for a real floral fix, sunbathe at the exquisite **Imperial Gardens,** just past **The Promenade** away from the center of town. **Trains** run from the station on Queen's Rd. The **tourist office,** 77 Promenade, one block east of the bus station, posts vacancies after-hours. (☎ (01242) 52 28 78. Open M-Sa 9:30am-5:15pm.) The well-situated **YMCA,** on Vittoria Walk, accepts both men and women. At Town Hall, turn left off Promenade and walk three blocks—Vittoria Walk is on the right. (☎52 40 24. Breakfast included. Reception 24hr. Singles £15.) **Cross Ways,** 57 Bath Rd., features home-sewn bedding and curtains, TV, and a tasty breakfast with veggie options. (☎52 76 83; email crossways@btinternet.com. £20-22 per person.) **Benton's Guest House,** 71 Bath Rd., has an exuberant garden and breakfasts that barely fit on the plates. (☎51 74 12. £25-35 per person, depending on season.) Fruit stands and bakeries dot **High St.** Down the road, **Tesco** has **groceries.** (Open M-Tu and Sa 7:30am-7pm, W-F 7:30am-8pm.) **Postal code:** GL50 1AA.

STOW-ON-THE-WOLD, WINCHCOMBE, AND CIRENCESTER. Stow-on-the-Wold is a sleepy town with fine views, cold winds, and authentic stocks. The **tourist office** is in Hollis House on The Square. (☎ (01451) 83 10 82. Open Easter-Oct. M-Sa 9:30am-5:30pm, Su 10:30am-4pm; Nov.-Easter M-Sa 9:30am-4:30pm.) The **YHA youth hostel** stands just a few yards from the stocks. (☎ (01451) 83 04 97. £10.85, students £9.85. Open Apr.-Oct. daily.)

West of Stow-on-the-Wold and 6 mi. north of Cheltenham on A46, **Sudeley Castle,** once the manor of King Ethelred the Unready, enserfs the town of Winchcombe. (Open daily Apr.-Oct. 10:30am-5pm. £6.) Just 1½ mi. southwest of Sudeley Castle lies **Belas Knap,** a 4000-year-old burial mound, evidence that the area was inhabited in prehistoric times. The **tourist office** is in Town Hall, near Cheltenham. (☎ (01242) 60 29 25. Open Apr.-Oct. M-Sa 10am-5pm, Su 10am-4pm.)

Sometimes regarded as the capital of the region, Cirencester is the site of Corinium, a Roman town founded in AD 49, second in importance only to Londinium. Its **Corinium Museum,** on Park St., houses a formidable collection of Roman artifacts. (Open Apr.-Oct. M-Sa 10am-5pm, Su 2-5pm; Nov.-Mar. Tu-Sa 10am-5pm, Su 2-5pm. £2.50, students £1.) The **Cirencester Parish Church,** is Gloucestershire's largest parish church. The money to build it was endowed by wealthy local wool merchants. (Open daily 10am-5pm.) On Fridays, the town turns into a mad **antique marketplace.** The **tourist office** is in Corn Hall, on Market Pl. (☎ (01285) 65 41 80. Open Apr.-Oct. M 9:45am-5:30pm, Tu-Sa 9:30am-5:30pm; Nov.-Mar. daily 9:30am-5pm.) Your best bet is to make Cirencester and the ruins a daytrip from Cheltenham.

STRATFORD-UPON-AVON   ☎ 01789

Former native William Shakespeare is now the area's industry; you'll find the vaguest of connections to the Bard exploited here to their full potential. But at rare moments, beyond the "Will Power" t-shirts and the tour bus exhaust, the essence of Shakespeare does lurk in Stratford: in the groves of the once-Forest of Arden and in the pin-drop silence before a soliloquy in the Royal Shakespeare Theatre.

🖪 JOURNEY'S END. Thames **trains** roll in from: London's Paddington Station (2¼hr., 7-10 per day, round-trip £22.50); Birmingham (1hr., £3.60); and Warwick (25min., £2.60). National Express runs **buses** from London's Victoria Station (3hr., 12 per day, round-trip £4); Cambridge Coach connects to Cambridge (round-trip £16, students £12); and Stagecoach runs from Oxford (round-trip £5.25).

🔁 HERE CEASE MORE QUESTIONS. The **tourist office,** Bridgefoot, across Warwick Rd. at Bridge St. toward the waterside park, sells maps and has a free accommodations guide. (☎29 31 27. Open Apr.-Oct. M-Sa 9am-6pm, Su 11am-5pm; Nov.-Mar. M-Sa 9am-5pm.) Romeo and Juliet would have lived happily ever after had they had email; surf the **Internet** at **Java Café,** 28 Greenhill St. (£3 per 30min., £5 per hr.; students £2.50 per 30min., £4 per hr.) **Postal code:** CV37 6PU.

🛌 TO SLEEP, PERCHANCE TO DREAM. To B&B or not to B&B? This hamlet has tons of them (£15-26), but 'tis nobler in summer to make advance reservations. The nearest hostel is more than 2 mi. away, and the cost is comparable to many B&Bs after adding in round-trip bus fare. Keep an eye out for B&Bs on **Grove Rd., Evesham Pl.,** and **Evesham Rd. Bradbourne Guest House,** 44 Shipston Rd., is a recently redecorated Tudor-style home; an 8min. walk from the town center. (☎20 41 78. Singles £25-30; doubles £44-48.) Warm and attentive proprietors consider **The Hollies,** 16 Evesham Pl., their labor of love. (☎26 68 57. Doubles £35, with bath £45.) The **Stratford Backpackers Hotel,** 33 Greenhill St., is conveniently located just across the bridge from the train station and has clean rooms, a common room, and kitchen. (☎26 38 38. Dorms £12.) The **YHA youth hostel,** Hemmingford House, on Wellesbourne Rd., Alveston, has large, attractive grounds; take bus #X18 from Bridge St. which runs every hour for £1.70. (☎29 70 93. Breakfast included. Reception 7am-midnight. Dorms £14.05, students £13.05.) **Riverside Caravan Park,** Tiddington Rd., 1 mi. east of Stratford on B4086, provides beautiful, but sometimes crowded, sunset views on the Avon. (☎29 23 12. Open Easter-Oct. Tent and 2 people £7, each additional person £1.) Await what dreams may come.

🗂 FOOD OF LOVE. **Hussain's Indian Cuisine,** 6a Chapel St., has fantastic chicken *tikka masala;* keep an eye out for regular Ben Kingsley. (Lunch £6, main dishes from £6. Open Th-Su 12:30-2:30pm and daily 5pm-midnight.) Drink deep ere you

BRITAIN

depart at the ▨ **Dirty Duck Pub,** on Waterside, a destination of the theater crowd and the actors themselves. (Traditional pub lunch £3-9; dinner £6-18. Open M-Sa 11am-11pm, Su noon-10:30pm.) To get to the **Safeway supermarket** on Alcester Rd., take the Avon shuttle from the town center, or just cross the bridge past the rail station. (Open M-Th and Sa 8am-9pm, F 8am-10pm, Su 10am-4pm.)

■ **THE GILDED MONUMENTS.** Bardolatry peaks around 2pm, so try to hit any Will-centered sights before 11am or after 4pm. Die-hard fans can buy the **combination ticket** (£12, students £11) for admission to five official Shakespeare properties: Shakespeare's Birthplace, Anne Hathaway's cottage (1 mi. away), Mary Arden's House and Countryside Museum (4 mi. away), New Place and Nash's House, and Hall's Croft. For a little less of the Bard, buy a **Shakespeare's Town Heritage Trail ticket** (£7.50, students £6.50), which covers only the sights in town—the Birthplace, Hall's Croft, and New Place. **Shakespeare's Birthplace,** Henley St., is equal parts period recreation and Shakespeare's life-and-works exhibition. (Open Mar. 20-Oct. 19 M-Sa 9am-5pm, Su 9:30am-5pm; Oct. 20-Mar. 19 M-Sa 9:30am-4pm, Su 10am-4pm. £5.50.) **New Place,** on High St., was Stratford's hippest address when Shakespeare bought it in 1597. Only the foundation remains—it can be viewed from **Nash's House,** which belonged to the first husband of Shakespeare's granddaughter, Elizabeth. **Hall's Croft** and **Mary Arden's House** bank on their tenuous connections to Shakespeare's extended family, but provide exhibits of what life was like in Shakespeare's time. For dramatic cohesiveness, pay homage to Shakespeare's grave—his little, little grave—in the **Holy Trinity Church,** on Trinity St. (60p, students £40p.)

▨ **THE PLAY'S THE THING.** Get thee to a performance at the world-famous **Royal Shakespeare Company;** recent sons include Kenneth Branagh and Ralph Fiennes. Tickets (£5-40) for all three theaters—the Royal Shakespeare Theatre, the Swan Theatre, and The Other Place—are sold through the box office in the foyer of the Royal Shakespeare Theatre, on Waterside. (Reservations from 9am ☎40 34 03, 24hr. recording ☎40 34 04. Open M-Sa 9am-8pm; arrive at least 20min. before opening for same-day sales. Student and senior standbys for £8-12 exist in principle.)

▨ **DAYTRIP FROM STRATFORD: WARWICK CASTLE.** One of England's finest medieval castles, Warwick Castle makes an excellent daytrip from Stratford. Climb the 530 steps to the top of the towers of Warwick and see the countryside unfold like a fairy tale kingdom of hobbits and elves. The dungeons are filled with life-size wax figures of people preparing for battle, while "knights" and "craftsmen" talk about their trades. (Open daily Apr.-Oct. 10am-6pm; Nov.-Mar. 10am-5pm. Lockers £1. £11, students £8.) **Trains** arrive from Stratford (20min., round-trip £4) and Birmingham (40min., round-trip £4.70).

BIRMINGHAM   ☎0121

Birmingham, industrial heart of the Midlands, is resolutely modern in its style, packing its city center with convention-goers, cell phones, and three-piece suits. Britain's second-largest city proper is a huge transport hub. Twelve minutes south of town by rail lies ▨**Cadbury World,** an unabashed celebration of the chocolate firm. Take a train from New St. to Bournville, or buses #83, 84, or 85 from the city center. (☎451 41 80. Open daily 10am-3pm; closed certain days Nov.-Feb. £8, students and seniors £6.50, children £6. Includes about 3 free bars of chocolate.) The **Barber Institute of Fine Arts,** in the University of Birmingham on Edgbaston Park Rd., displays works by artists as diverse as Rubens, Gainsborough, and Magritte. Take bus #61, 62, or 63 from the city center. (☎414 73 33. Open M-Sa 10am-5pm, Su 2-5pm. Free.) Forget run-of-the-mill chart hits; Birmingham's club scene is on the cutting edge of dance music in Britain. Pick up a copy of the bimonthly *What's On* or the monthly *Leap* to discover the latest hotspots, or head down **Broad St. Stoodibakers,** 192 Broad St., is half club, half bar, with uplifting music that draws a lively crowd. (☎643 51 00. Cover £4 after 9:30pm F-Sa.) **Ministry of**

Sound, 55 Broad St., across from the Chamberlain Towers, offers dancing and soul. (☎632 55 01. Cover £7-12.) The **City of Birmingham Symphony Orchestra** plays in the superb acoustics of Symphony Hall at the Convention Centre on Broad St. (☎780 33 33; www.cbso.co.uk. Box office open M-F 10am-8pm, Sa 10am-10pm; Su hours dependent on showtimes. Tickets £5-32; student standbys £7.50 after 1pm on concert days.) The **Birmingham Jazz Festival** (☎454 70 20) brings over 200 jazz bands, singers, and instrumentalists to town during the first two weeks of July; book through the tourist office.

Birmingham snares a clutch of train and bus lines between London, central Wales, southwest England, and all points north. **Trains** arrive in New St. Station, (☎ (08457) 48 49 50), Britain's busiest, from: London Euston (2hr., 2 per hr., £22.50); Nottingham (1¼hr., 2-4 per hr., £8.20); Oxford (1¼hr., 1-2 per hr., £14.20); Liverpool Lime St. (1½hr., 1-2 per hr., £18.50); and Manchester Piccadilly (2½hr., 1 per hr., £14.20). Some trains pull into Moor St. and Snow Hill stations. National Express **buses** (☎ (08705) 80 80 80) arrive in Digbeth Station from: London (3¼hr., 1 per hr., round-trip £15); Cardiff (2¼hr., 4 per day, round-trip £18.75); Liverpool (2½hr., 15 per day, round-trip £11); and Manchester (2½hr., every 2hr., round-trip £12.50). The **tourist office** is at 2 City Arcade, and books rooms. (☎643 25 14. Open M-Sa 9:30am-5:30pm.) Access the **internet** at **NetAdventure Cyber Café,** 68-70 Dalton St. (☎693 66 55. £3 per hr., £1 minimum.) Despite its size, Birmingham has no hostels, and inexpensive B&Bs are rare. B&Bs line **Hagley Rd. Lyby,** 14-16 Barnsley Rd., Edgbaston, off Hagley Rd., has large rooms with TV's. To reach it, take bus #9 or 127 from Corporation St. to the Quantum pub, walk 50m back, and turn left at the New Talbot. (☎429 44 87. Singles £15; doubles £27.) Take bus #128 or 129 from Colmore Row in the city center (10min.), to reach **Woodville House,** 39 Portland Rd., which is comfortable, affordable, and well-located. (☎454 02 74. Singles £18; doubles £30, with bath £35.) Birmingham's eateries conjure up expensive delights, as well as the requisite cheap cod and kebabs (*Let's Go* does not recommend eating cod and kebabs together). **Al Frash,** 186 Ladypool Rd., has tasty, generous portions of Balti chicken for £3.90. (☎753 31 20. Open daily 5pm-1am.) **Postal code:** B2 4AA.

BATH   ☎01225

A visit to the elegant Georgian city of Bath (pop. 83,000) remains *de rigueur*, even if today it's more of a museum (or a museum gift shop) than a resort. But expensive trinkets can't conceal the fact that Bath, immortalized by Austen and Dickens, once stood second only to London as the social capital of England. Once the spot for naughty sightings, the **Roman Baths** are now a must-see for all. Most of the visible complex is not actually Roman, but rather reflects Georgian dreams of what Romans might have built. The ▧**Roman Baths Museum** underneath reveals genuine Roman Baths and highlights the complexity of Roman engineering, which included central heating and internal plumbing. Its recovered artifacts, scale models, and hot springs bring back to life the Roman spa city Aquae Salis—first unearthed in 1880 by sewer diggers. (Open daily Apr.-July and Sept. 9am-6pm; Aug. 9am-6pm and 8pm-10pm; Oct.-Mar. 9:30am-5pm; last admission 30min. before closing. £6.70.) Penny-pinchers can view one bath for free in the complex by entering through the **Pump Room** on Stall St. Next to the baths, the towering and tombstoned 15th-century **Bath Abbey** has a whimsical west facade with several angels climbing ladders up to heaven—and, curiously enough, two climbing down. (Open M-Sa 9am-4:30pm; Su 1pm-2:30pm and 4:30-5:30pm. £1.50.) Head north up Stall St., turn left on Westgate St., and turn right on Saw Close to reach Queen Sq., where Jane Austen lived at #13. Continue up Gay St. to **The Circus,** where Thomas Gainsborough, William Pitt, and David Livingstone once lived. To the left down Brock St. is the **Royal Crescent,** a half-moon of Gregorian townhouses bordering **Royal Victoria Park.** The **botanical gardens** within nurture 5000 species of plants. (Open M-Sa 9am-dusk, Su 10am-dusk. Free.) Backtrack down Brock St. and bear left at the Circus (or take a right at The Circus from Gay St.) to reach Bennett St. and the dazzling **Museum of Costume,** which will satisfy any fashion fetish. (Open daily 10am-5pm. £3.90; joint ticket with Roman Baths £8.70.) The laid-back **Paragon Wine Bar**, 1A The Paragon, is a fantastic place to kick back, while the **The Pig and Fiddle** pub, on the corner of Saracen St. and Broad St., packs in a rowdy young crowd.

   Trains head frequently to: London's Paddington Station (1½hr., 1 per hr., £34); Bristol (15min., 32 per day, £4.60); and Exeter (1¼hr., 15 per day, £21.50). National Express **buses** (☎ (08705) 80 80 80) run to London's Victoria Station (3hr., 9 per day, £11.50) and Oxford (2hr., 6 per day, £12). Both arrive near the southern end of Manvers St.; walk up Manvers to the Terrace Walk roundabout and turn left on York St. to reach the **tourist office**, in Abbey Churchyard. (☎ 47 71 01; fax 47 77 87. Open May-Sept. M-Sa 9:30am-6pm, Su 10am-4pm; Oct.-Apr M-Sa 9am-5pm, Su 10am-4pm.) **B&Bs** (from £18) cluster on **Pulteney Rd., Pulteney** and **Crescent Gardens**, and **Widcombe Hill**. The **YHA youth hostel**, on Bathwick Hill, is in a secluded mansion 20 steep minutes above the city; catch Badgerline bus #18 (dir.: University) from the bus station or the Orange Grove rotary. (☎ 46 56 74. Breakfast £3.10. Laundry. Dorms £10.15.) The **International Backpackers Hostel**, 13 Pierrepont St., is up the street from the stations and is just three blocks from the baths. (☎ 44 67 87. **Internet**. Breakfast £1.50. Laundry. Dorms £12.) To get to **Toad Hall Guest House**, 6 Lime Grove, go across Pulteney Bridge and through Pulteney Gardens. (☎ 42 32 54. £20 per person.) To reach **Newton Mill Camping**, 2½ mi. west on Newton Rd., take bus #5 from the bus station (round-trip £1.60) to Twerton and ask to be let off at the campsite. (☎ 33 39 09. Reserve ahead. 2 people, tent, and car £11.) **Guildhall Market** is between High St. and Grand Parade. (Open M-Sa 8am-5:30pm.) Try **Tilleys Bistro**, 3 North Parade Passage, for French or English fare. (Open M-Sa noon-2:30pm and 6:30-11pm, Su 6:30-10:30pm.) **The Pump Room**, in Abbey Courtyard, holds a monopoly on Bath Spa mineral water (45p). **Postal code:** BA1 1A5.

GLASTONBURY ☎ 01458

The reputed birthplace of Christianity in England and the seat of Arthurian myth, Glastonbury (pop. 6900) has evolved into an intersection of Christianity and mysticism. Present-day pagan pilgrimage site **Glastonbury Tor** is supposedly the site of the mystical Isle of Avalon, where the Messiah is slated to return. To make the trek up to the Tor, turn right at the top of High St., continue up to Chilkwell St., turn left onto Wellhouse Ln., and take the first right up the hill (buses in summer 50p). On your way down, visit the **Chalice Well**, on the corner of Welhouse Ln., the supposed resting place of the Holy Grail. (Open daily Easter-Oct. 10am-6pm; Nov.-Feb. 1-4pm. £1.50.) Back in town, the ruins of **Glastonbury Abbey**, England's oldest Christian foundation, stands behind the archway on Magdalene St. (Open daily June-Aug. 9am-6pm; Sept.-May 9:30am-6pm. £3, students £2.50.) Although no trains serve Glastonbury, Baker's Dolphin **buses** (☎ (01934) 61 60 00) run from London (3¼hr., 1 per day, round-trip £5), while Badgerline buses (☎ (01225) 46 44 46) run from Bath (round-trip £4.75; change at Wells). From the bus stop, turn right on High St. to reach the **tourist office**, The Tribunal, 9 High St. (☎ 83 29 54. Open Apr.-Sept. Su-Th 10am-5pm, F-Sa 10am-5:30pm; Oct.-Mar. daily 10am-4pm.) **Glastonbury Backpackers**, in the Crown Hotel on Market Pl., contributes its own splashes of color to the city's tie-dye. (☎ 83 33 53. **Internet**. Dorms £10; doubles £26.) Sleep in comfort at **Blake House**, 3 Bove Town. (☎ 83 16 80. £19 per person.) **Postal code:** BA6 9HG.

CAMBRIDGE ☎ 01223

The university began a mere 791 years ago when rebels defected from nearby Oxford to this settlement on the River Cam. Today, in contrast to its sister institution, Cambridge (pop. 105,000) is steadfastly determined to remain a city under its academic robes—the tourist office "manages," rather than encourages, visitors. Most colleges close to visitors during official quiet periods in May and early June, but when exams end, cobblestoned Cambridge explodes in gin-soaked glee. May Week (in mid-June, naturally) hosts a dizzying schedule of cocktail parties.

▐ TRANSPORTATION

Trains: (☎ (0345) 48 49 50), Station Rd. Tickets sold daily 5am-11pm. To: **London's King's Cross Station** and **London's Liverpool St. Station** (1¼hr., 2 per hr., £14.50).

Buses: Drummer St. **National Express** (☎ (01604) 62 00 77) arrives from **London's Victoria Station** (2hr., 17 per day, from £8). National Express and **Stagecoach Express** buses run to **Oxford** (2¾hr., £7). **Cambus** (☎42 35 54) runs regional routes (£0.65-1.60).

Bike Rental: Mike's Bikes, 28 Mill Rd. (☎31 25 91). £5 per day, £8 per week. Open M-Sa 9am-6pm, Su 10am-4pm.

✴▐ ORIENTATION AND PRACTICAL INFORMATION

Cambridge, about 60 mi. north of London, is an old city; streets twist at will. The city has two main avenues, both of which change names five times. The main shopping street starts at **Magdalene Bridge** and becomes **Bridge St., Sidney St., St. Andrew's St., Regent St.,** and finally **Hills Rd.** The other—alternately **St. John's St., Trinity St., King's Parade, Trumpington St.,** and **Trumpington Rd.**—is the academic thoroughfare, with several colleges lying between it and the River Cam. The two streets merge at **St. John's College.** From the bus station at **Drummer St.,** a quick walk down **Emmanuel St.** will land you right in the shopping district near the tourist office. To get to the heart of things from the train station on **Station Rd.,** turn right onto Hills Rd., and continue straight ahead.

Tourist Office: (☎32 26 40; fax 45 75 88; www.cambridge.gov.uk/leisure/tourism) Wheeler St., a block south of the marketplace. Books rooms for £3 fee plus a 10% deposit. Mini-guide 40p, maps 20p. Offers two-hour **walking tours** of the city and some colleges (£7). Open Apr.-Oct. M-F 10am-5:30pm, Sa 10am-5pm, Su 11am-4pm; Nov.-Mar. M-F 10am-5:30pm, Sa 10am-5pm. Info on city events is available at **Cambridge Corn Exchange** (☎35 78 51), Corn Exchange St., adjacent to the tourist office.

American Express: 25 Sidney St. (☎ (08706) 00 10 60). Open M-F 9am-5:30pm, W 9:30am-5:30pm, Sa 9am-5pm.

Laundromat: Clean Machine, 22 Burleigh St. (☎57 80 09). Open daily 7am-8:30pm.

Emergency: Dial 999; no coins required. **Police** (☎35 89 66). The central police station is on Parkside at the corner of East Rd.

Medical Assistance: Addenbrookes Hospital, (☎24 51 51) Hill Rd. Catch Cambus #95 from Emmanuel St. (95p), and get off where Hill Rd. intersects Long Rd.

Internet Access: CBI, 32 Mill Rd. (☎57 63 06), near the hostel. 10p per min. Open M-Sa 10am-8pm, Su 11am-7pm. Also at 5-7 Norfolk St. Open daily 8am-11pm.

Post Office: 9-11 St. Andrew's St. (☎32 33 25). Open M-Sa 9am-5:3-pm. Address mail to be held for Karen KIANG, *Poste Restante,* 9-11 St. Andrews St. Post Office, Cambridge, England **CB2 3AA.**

▐ ACCOMMODATIONS

This university town teaches travelers to book ahead. Many of the **B&Bs** around **Portugal St.** and **Tenison Rd.** are open only in July and August. Check the list at the tourist office, or pick up their guide to accommodations (50p).

Tenison Towers Guest House, 148 Tenison Rd. (☎56 65 11). 2 blocks from the train station. Fresh flowers grace an impeccable house. Singles £22; doubles £42.

Warkworth Guest House (☎36 36 82), Warkworth Terr. Peaceful, sunny rooms near the bus station. Packed lunch on request. Singles £25-30; twins £50-55.

Home from Home B&B, 39 Milton Rd. (☎32 35 55), 20min. from the center. Pricey, but worthwhile, thanks to the sparkling rooms and welcoming hostess. Full English breakfast included. Call ahead with a credit card. Singles £35; doubles £48.

Mrs. McCann, 40 Warkworth St. (☎31 40 98). A jolly hostess offers comfortable twin rooms with TVs near the bus station. Breakfast included. £16-18 per person.

Here's your ticket to freedom, baby!

**Wherever you want to go...
priceline.com can get you there for less.**

- Save up to 40% or more off the lowest published airfares every day!

- Major airlines serving virtually every corner of the globe.

- Special fares to Europe!

If you haven't already tried priceline.com, you're missing out on the best way to save. **Visit us online today at www.priceline.com.**

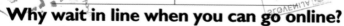

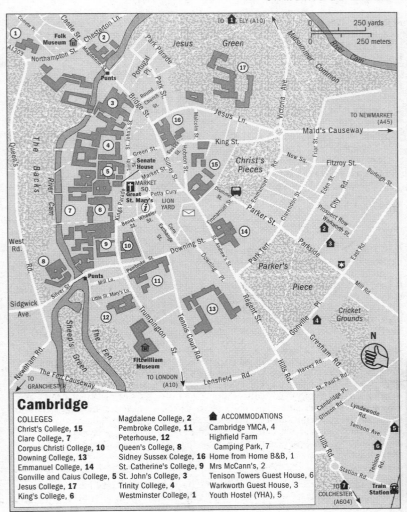

Cambridge

COLLEGES

Christ's College, **15**
Clare College, **7**
Corpus Christi College, **10**
Downing College, **13**
Emmanuel College, **14**
Gonville and Caius College, **5**
Jesus College, **17**
King's College, **6**

Magdalene College, **2**
Pembroke College, **11**
Peterhouse, **12**
Queen's College, **8**
Sidney Sussex Colege, **16**
St. Catherine's College, **9**
St. John's College, **3**
Trinity College, **4**
Westminster College, **1**

▲ ACCOMMODATIONS

Cambridge YMCA, **4**
Highfield Farm
  Camping Park, **7**
Home from Home B&B, **1**
Mrs McCann's, **2**
Tenison Towers Guest House, **6**
Warkworth Guest House, **3**
Youth Hostel (YHA), **5**

YHA Youth Hostel, 97 Tenison Rd. (☎35 46 01; fax 31 27 80). Relaxed, welcoming atmosphere. Well-equipped kitchen, laundry, TV lounge, and great cafeteria. In summer, call a week ahead with a credit card. 3- to 4-bed rooms £15.10, students £11.40.

Cambridge YMCA (☎35 69 98), Gonville Pl. Between the train station and town center. Large, clean, industrial rooms. Breakfast included. Singles £22.65; doubles £37.

Highfield Farm Camping Park, (☎26 23 08), Long Rd. Comberton. Take Cambus #118 from Drummer St. bus station. Showers, laundry. Tents £6.25-7, £7.25-8.75 with car.

🗂 FOOD

Cantabrigians are too busy learning Latin to flavor their food, so try the bright pyramids of fruit and vegetables at **Market Sq.** (Open M-Sa 9:30am-4:30pm.) Students buy their gin and cornflakes at **Sainsbury's,** 44 Sidney St., the only grocery store in the middle of town. (Open M-F 8am-9pm, Sa 7:30am-9pm, Su 11am-5pm.) The alcohol-serving curry houses on **Castle Hill** are also popular.

▧**Nadia's,** 11 St. John's St. (☎46 09 61). An uncommonly good bakery with reasonable prices. Wonderful flapjacks and quiches, 65p-£1. Open daily 8:30am-5pm.

The Little Tea Room, 1 All Saints' Passage (☎36 60 33), off Trinity St. A precious spot for traditional tea. Open M-Sa 10am-5:30pm, Su 1-5:30pm.

Clowns Coffee Bar, 54 King St. Foreigners and beautiful people meet for cappuccino and quiche at Clowns. Open daily 7:30am-midnight.

Hobbs' Pavillion, (☎36 74 80), Parker's Piece, off Park Terr. Renowned for imaginative, overpowering, rectangular pancakes. Mars Bar and cream pancake £4. Open Tu-Sa noon-2:15pm and 6-9:45pm.

Tatties, 11 Sussex St. (☎32 33 99). Cambridge is crazy for the jacket potatoes at Tatties. Fillings range from the simple (butter £1.95) to the highly imaginative (cheese and prawns in garlic tomato sauce, £5.25). Open M-Sa 8:30am-7pm, Su 10am-5pm.

Rainbow's Vegetarian Bistro, 9A King's Parade (☎32 15 51). A tiny, creative burrow featuring delicious international vegan and veggie fare. Open M-Sa 11am-11pm.

👁 SIGHTS

Cambridge is an architect's dream—it packs some of the most breathtaking examples of English architecture into less than one square mile. If you are pressed for time, visit at least one chapel (preferably King's), one garden (try Christ's), one library (Trinity's is the most interesting), and one dining hall (you'll have to adopt a convincing student disguise to get in). The familiar **Bridge of Sighs** at **St. John's College** is another particularly exquisite sight if you can squeeze it in. Cambridge is most exciting during the university's three eight-week terms: Michaelmas (Oct.-Dec.), Lent (Jan.-Mar.), and Easter (Apr.-June). Most of the colleges are open daily from 9am to 5:30pm, but hours vary often. A few are closed to sightseers during the Easter term, and virtually all are closed during exams (mid-May to mid-June).

TRINITY COLLEGE. Founded in 1546 by Henry VIII, the college is the wealthiest at Cambridge, for which it has become legendary—rumors say it was once possible to walk from Cambridge to Oxford without stepping off Trinity land. Sir Isaac Newton, who lived in E-entry for 30 years, originally measured the speed of sound by stamping his foot in the cloister along the north side of the **Great Court**—the largest courtyard in Cambridge. The college also houses the stunning **Wren Library,** which keeps such notable treasures as A.A. Milne's handwritten manuscript of *Winnie the Pooh* and less momentous achievements by Milton, Byron, Tennyson, and Thackeray, many of whom are alums of the college. *(Trinity St. ☎33 84 00. Chapel and courtyard open daily 10am-5pm. Library open M-F noon-2pm, Sa 10:30am-12:30pm. Both closed during exams. £1.75.)*

KING'S COLLEGE. E.M. Forester's alma mater dominates King's Parade St. from street level to skyline. Founded in 1441 by Henry VI, the college houses **King's College Chapel,** a spectacular Gothic monument with elaborately carved interiors. The interior of the chapel consists of one huge chamber cleft by a carved wooden choir screen. Heralding angels crown the screen and flit about against the backdrop of the world's largest fan-vaulted ceiling. Tudor roses, symbols of Henry VIII's reign, abound. Rubens' magnificent *Adoration of the Magi* hangs behind the altar. Evensong is held most evenings in the Chapel at 5:30pm and is breathtaking to behold. *(King's Parade. ☎33 11 00. College open M-F 9:30am-4:30pm, Su 9:30am-2:30pm. Tours arranged through the tourist office. £3.50, children £2.50.)*

ST. JOHN'S COLLEGE. Established in 1511 by Lady Margaret Beaufort, mother of Henry VIII, St. John's is one of seven Cambridge colleges founded by women (but *for* men). A copy of Venice's **Bridge of Sighs** connects the older part of the college to the neo-Gothic extravagance of New Court. The **School of Pythagoras,** a 12th-century pile of wood and stone, supposedly the oldest complete building in Cambridge, hides in St. John's Gardens. *(St. John's St. ☎33 86 00. Courtyard and some buildings open until 5pm. Chapel open Mar.-Oct. M-Sa 9:30am-6:30pm, Su 10:30am-6:30pm. Evensong 6:30pm most nights. Admission to the college £1.75, seniors and children £1, families £3.50.)*

QUEENS' COLLEGE. Queens has the only unaltered Tudor courtyard in Cambridge. The **Mathematical Bridge,** just past Cloister Court, was built in 1749 without a single bolt or nail, instead relying on mathematical principles. A meddling Victorian took apart the bridge to see how it worked and the inevitable occurred—he couldn't put it back together without using steel rivets every two inches. *(Silver St. ☎33 55 11. Open Mar.-Oct. daily 10am-4:30pm; closed during exams. £1.)*

CHRIST'S COLLEGE. Founded as "God's house" in 1448, Christ's has won fame for its association with John Milton and for its gorgeous gardens. Charles Darwin dilly-dallied through Christ's before dealing a blow to its religious origins. *(Off St. Andrews St., back on the other side of town near the bus station. ☎33 49 00. College open in summer 9:30am-noon; in session M-F 9:30am-4:30pm. Free.)*

FITZWILLIAM MUSEUM. A welcome break from the academia of the colleges, the Fitzwilliam Museum dwells within an immense Roman-style building. The museum stocks a hoard of Egyptian, Chinese, Japanese, and Greek treasures that only the Brits could have assembled, as well as an intimate collection of French Impressionist works. *(Trumpington St., 10min. from King's College. ☎33 29 00. Open Tu-Sa 10am-5pm, Su 2:15-5pm. Guided tours Sa 2:30pm. £3 donation requested. Tours £3.)*

KETTLE'S YARD. Created as a refuge of light and of the visual arts and music, the museum houses beautifully displayed early 20th-century artworks. *(At the corner of Castle St. and Northhampton St. ☎35 21 24. House open Apr.-Sept. Tu-Su 2-4pm; gallery open year-round Tu-Su 11:30am-5pm. Free.)*

🎵 ENTERTAINMENT

The best source of info on student activities is the student newspaper *Varsity;* the tourist office's free *Cambridge Nightlife Guide* is also helpful. **Punts** (gondola-like boats) are a favored form of entertainment in Cambridge. Beware that punt-bombing—jumping from bridges into the river alongside a punt, thereby tipping its occupants into the Cam—has evolved into an art form. **Tyrell's** (☎35 28 47), Magdalene Bridge, rents boats for £8 per hr. plus a £40 deposit. Even more traditional than punting is **pub-crawling;** Cambridge hangouts offer good pub-crawling year-round, though they lose some of their character in the summer. Live music of all kinds rollicks nightly at the **Boat Race,** 170 East Rd. **The Eagle,** Benet St., is the oldest pub in Cambridge. Nobel laureates Watson and Crick once rushed into the Eagle breathless to announce their discovery of the DNA double helix—unimpressed, the barmaid insisted they settle their four-shilling tab before she'd serve them a toast. (☎50 50 20. Open 11am-11pm, Su noon-10:30pm.) The **Free Press** (☎36 83 37), on Prospect Row behind the police station, is an off-the-beaten-path neighborhood pub. **Bar Coast,** Quayside, offers frequent dance nights, from disco to "uplifting house and garage." The gay crowd downs ale at **The Town and Gown** (☎35 37 91), on Poundhill just off Northhampton. Students drink at the **Anchor** (☎35 35 54), Silver St., and **The Mill** (☎35 70 26), on Mill Ln. off Silver St. Bridge.

🏞 DAYTRIP FROM CAMBRIDGE

GRANTCHESTER

To reach Grantchester Meadows from Cambridge, take the path that follows the River Granta (about 45 min.). Grantchester itself lies about 1 mi. from the meadows; ask the way at one of the neighborhood shops. Stagecoach Cambus #118 also runs to Grantchester (8 per day).

If you're searching for rejuvenation after the bustle of the college town, head to the idyllic setting of Grantchester, once a mecca for Cambridge literary types including Virginia Woolf, Robert Brooke, E.M. Forster, and Ludwig Wittgenstein. Today you can sip tea at **The Orchard** (☎84 57 88), Mill Way, where these same luminaries once discussed the ways of the world. The delightful walk there begins at the Silver St. Bridge in Cambridge and follows Newnham Rd. until it turns into Grantchester Meadows where it then becomes a footpath.

NORWICH ☎ 01603

One of England's largest and most populous cities before the Norman invasion, Norwich (rhymes with "porridge," pop. 120,700) today conceals its medieval heritage behind a modern facade. The 11th-century **Norwich Cathedral** and the 12th-century **Norwich Castle,** where King John signed the Magna Carta in 1215, reign over puzzling, winding streets. (Cathedral open daily mid-May to mid-Sept. 7am-7pm; mid-Sept. to mid-May 7am-6pm. Free. Castle closed for renovations until spring 2001.) **Trains** (☎ (08457) 48 49 50) arrive frequently at the corner of Riverside and Thorpe Rd. from London's Liverpool St. Station (2hr., M-Sa 30 per day, £34.50) and Cambridge (1½hr., 12 per day, £10.60). National Express **buses** (☎ (08705) 80 80 80) travel from Surrey St. to London (3hr., 7 per day, £13.80) and Cambridge (2hr., 1 per day, round-trip £10). The **tourist office,** at Guildhall, Gaol Hill, in front of city hall on the continuation of London St., has the essential map (30p). Head right from the train station, take a left on Prince of Wales Rd., and cross the bridge to the castle. From the bus station, head left on Surrey St. and then right on St. Stephen's St. to the castle. (☎ (01603) 66 60 71. Open June-Sept. M-Sa 9:30am-5pm; Oct.-May M-F 9:30am-4:30pm, Sa 9:30am-1pm and 1:30-4:30pm.) **The Earlham Guest House,** 147 Earlham Rd., offers cheerful rooms. (☎ (01603) 45 94 69. £20-22 per person.) In the heart of the city is one of England's largest and oldest open-air **markets** (open M-Sa 8:30am-4:30pm) as well as a trove of excellent restaurants. **Postal code:** NR1 3DD.

NOTTINGHAM ☎ 0115

Nottingham's (pop. 261,500) age-old tradition of taking from the rich and giving to the poor lives on as modern-day Robin Hoods lure visitors to Nottingham with a tourist industry that boasts little substance but plenty of thrill. ◪ **The Galleries of Justice,** High Pavement, is an interactive museum that puts presumably innocent tourists on trial, throws them behind bars, and lets them see the English prison system through the eyes of the convicted. (Open Tu-Su 10am-5pm. £8, students £6.) Originally constructed in 1068 by William the Conqueror, the remains of **Nottingham Castle,** atop a sandstone rise in the south of the city, now house the **Castle Museum.** (Open Mar.-Oct. daily 10am-5pm; Nov.-Feb. Sa-Th 10am-5pm. M-F free; Sa-Su £2, students £1.) From the museum entrance, enter **Mortimer's Hole,** a 100-meter-long underground passageway from the castle to the base of the cliff. (£2, students £1.) **Trains** (☎ (0345) 48 49 50) arrive frequently on Carrington St. from London (2hr., £33) and Lincoln (1hr., £5.50). National Express **buses** (☎ (08705) 80 80 80) pull in between Collin and Canal St. from London (3hr., 7 per day, £14). The **tourist office,** 1-4 Smithy Row, is just off Old Market Sq. (☎ (0115) 915 53 30. Open Apr.-Oct. M-F 9am-5:30pm, Sa 9am-5pm, Su 10am-3pm; Oct.-July closed Su.) To sleep at **Igloo,** 110 Mansfield Rd., take bus #90 from the train station to Mansfield Rd. (☎ (0115) 947 52 50. £9.50.) **Ye Olde Trip to Jerusalem,** 1 Brewhouse Yard, the "Oldest Inn in England," poured its first drink in 1189. **Postal code:** NG1 2BN.

LINCOLN ☎ 01522

Medieval streets, half-timbered Tudor houses, and a 12th-century cathedral are all relative newcomers to Lincoln (pop. 77,000), originally built as a town for retired Roman legionnaires. The king of the hill is undoubtedly the magnificent **Lincoln Cathedral.** (Open June-Aug. M-Sa 7:15am-8pm, Su 7:15am-6pm; Sept.-May M-Sa 7:15am-6pm, Su 7:15am-5pm. £3.50.) **Lincoln Castle** houses one of the four surviving copies of the Magna Carta. (Open Apr.-Oct. M-Sa 9:30am-5:30pm, Su 11am-5:30pm; Nov.-Mar. M-Sa 9:30am-4pm, Su 11am-4pm. £2.50.) The station on St. Mary's St. receives frequent **trains** from London's King's Cross Station (2½hr.; M-Sa 1 per hr., Su departs every 2hr.; £39) and Nottingham (1hr.; M-Sa 2 per hr., Su 7 per day; round-trip £5.60). Opposite the train station, National Express **buses** (☎ (08705) 80 80 80) pull in from London (5hr., £18). From either station, walk up High St., which becomes The Strait and then Steep Hill Rd., to reach the **tourist office,** 9 Castle Hill. (☎ (01522) 52 98 28. Open M-Th 9:30am-5:30pm, F 9:30am-5pm, Sa-Su 10am-5pm.)

B&Bs (£17-20) line Carline and Yarborough Rd., west of the castle. To get to the lovely **YHA youth hostel,** 77 South Park Ave., veer right from the train station, turn right on Pelham Bridge, which becomes Canwick Rd., and turn right on South Park Ave. (☎ (01522) 52 20 76. Lockout 10am-5pm. Curfew 11pm. Open Feb.-Oct. Dorms £9.80.) **Postal code:** LN5 7XX.

PEAK DISTRICT NATIONAL PARK

A green cushion between England's industrial giants of Manchester, Sheffield, and Nottingham, Britain's first national park sprawls across 555 sq. mi. of rolling hills and windswept moors, offering a playground for its 17 million urban neighbors. In the northern Dark Peak area, deep groughs (gullies) gouge the hard peat moorland against a backdrop of gloomy cliffs, and well-marked footpaths lead over mildly rocky hillsides to village clusters. Abandoned milestones, derelict lead mines, and country homes are scattered throughout the southern White Peak.

Contact **Peak District National Park Office,** Aldern House, Barlow Rd., Bakewell DE4 5AE (☎ (01629) 81 62 00), for more info. The **National Park Information Centres** at **Bakewell** (see below), **Castleton** (☎ (01433) 62 06 79), and **Edale** (☎ (01433) 67 02 07) offer walking guides; you can also ask questions at **tourist offices** in **Buxton** (☎ (01298) 251 06) and **Matlock Bath** (☎ (01629) 550 82). **YHA youth hostels** in the park cost from £7.50 to £10.15 and can be found in **Bakewell** (see below), **Buxton** (☎ (01298) 222 87), **Castleton** (see below), **Edale** (see below), and **Matlock** (☎ (01629) 58 29 83). There are 13 **YHA Camping Barns** (£3.35 per night) throughout the park; book ahead at the **Camping Barns Reservation Office,** 6 King St., Clitheroe, Lancashire BB7 2EP. (☎ (01200) 42 01 02; fax 42 01 03.) Direct all booking inquiries to the Reservation Office. The park authority operates six **Cycle Hire Centres** (£9 per day); call **Ashbourne** (☎/fax (01335) 34 31 56) or **Hayfield** (☎ (01663) 74 62 22) for info.

▐▀ TRANSPORTATION. The invaluable *Peak District Timetable* (£0.60; available in all Peak tourist offices) has transport routes and a map. Two **rail** lines originate in **Manchester** and enter the park from the west: one stops at **Buxton** near the park's edge (1hr., every hr., £5.30), and the other crosses the park via **Edale, Hope** (near Castleton), and **Hathersage** (1½hr.; 9-15 per day; Manchester to Sheffield £10.40, Manchester to Edale £6.30) on its way to **Sheffield.** From the south, a train heads from **Nottingham** to **Matlock,** on the park's southeastern edge. Trent **bus** TP (Transpeak; ☎ (01298) 230 98) serves the southern half of the park, stopping at **Buxton, Bakewell, Matlock,** and **Derby** (3hr., every 2hr.) between Manchester and Nottingham. A one-day **Wayfarer** pass (£6.60) covers unlimited train and bus travel within Greater Manchester, including most of the Peak District.

BAKEWELL, EDALE, AND CASTLETON. The Southern Peak is better served by public transportation than its northern counterpart, and is consequently more trampled. Thirty miles southeast of Manchester, **Bakewell** is the best base for exploration. Located near several scenic walks through the White Peaks, the town is known for its Bakewell pudding, created when a flustered cook inadvertently erred while making a tart. Bakewell's **National Park Information Center** (☎ (01629) 81 32 27), is at the corner of Bridge and Market St. The small and cozy **YHA youth hostel,** Fly Hill, is 5min. from the town center. (☎ (01629) 81 23 13. Open Apr.-Oct. M-Sa; Nov.-Mar. F-Sa. Dorms £7.50.) **Postal code:** DE45 1EF.

The northern Dark Peak area contains some of the wildest and most rugged hill country in England. **Edale** offers little in the way of civilization other than a church, cafe, pub, school, and nearby **YHA youth hostel.** (☎ (01433) 67 03 02. Dorms £7.50, under 18 £5.15.) Its environs, however, are arguably the most spectacular in northern England. The National Park Authority's *8 Walks Around Edale* (£1.20) details nearby **hiking** trails (1½-8½ mi.). Stay at the hostel (see above) or **camp** at **Fieldhead,** behind the tourist office. (☎ (01433) 67 03 86. £3.25 per person.) From Edale, the 3½mi. hike to **Castleton** affords a breathtaking view of the dark gritstone Edale Valley (Dark Peak) and the lighter limestone Hope Valley (White Peak) to the south. Castleton's river-carved limestone engulfs several famous caverns; **Treak Cliff Cav-**

ern holds breathtaking stalagtite chambers and massive seams of the unique Blue John Stone. (☎62 05 71. Tours 40min., every 12min. £5, students and YHA members £4, seniors £4.50, children £3.) Stay at the excellent **YHA youth hostel** (☎ (01433) 62 02 35; open Feb. to late Dec.; dorms £12.95) or **Cryer House,** across from the tourist office (☎ (01433) 62 02 44; doubles £42).

MANCHESTER   ☎0161

The Industrial Revolution transformed the once unremarkable village of Manchester into a northern hub, now Britain's second-largest urban conglomeration. With few comely corners and fewer budget accommodations in the city center, Manchester proves that you don't have to be pretty to be popular, attracting thousands with its pulsing nightlife and vibrant arts scene. The exception to Manchester's generally unremarkable buildings is the neo-Gothic **Manchester Town Hall,** on St. Peter's Sq., behind the tourist office. Nearby, the domed **Central Library** houses one of the largest municipal libraries in Europe, including the UK's second-largest Judaica collection. (☎234 19 00. Open M-Th 10am-8pm, F-Sa 10am-5pm.) In the **Museum of Science and Industry,** on Liverpool Rd. in Castlefield, working steam engines provide a dramatic vision of Britain's industrialization. (Open daily 10am-5pm. £5, students £3.) At the **Manchester United Museum and Tour Centre,** on Sir Matt Busby Way, at the Old Trafford football stadium, you can learn all about Manchester United, England's best-known football team. Follow the signs up Warwick Rd. from the Old Trafford Metrolink stop. (Open daily 9am-5pm. Tours run every 10min., 9:40am-4:30pm. Museum £4.50, seniors and children £3. Tour £3, seniors and children £2.) One of Manchester's biggest draws is its artistic community, most notably its theater and music scenes; the **Royal Exchange Theatre,** on St. Ann's Sq., regularly puts on Shakespeare and original works. (☎833 98 33. Box office open M-Sa 9:30am-7:30pm. M-Th and Sa tickets £7-23. Student discounts available.) Come nightfall, try the cafe-bar **Temple of Convenience,** 100 Great Bridgewater St., just off Oxford St. (Open daily 11am-11pm.) A player in Manchester's trendsetting club scene is **Generation X,** 11/13 New Wakefield St., off Oxford St. (Cover after 11pm £2. Open F-Sa until 2am, Su noon-10:30pm.) Northeast of Princess St., the **Gay Village** rings merrily at night; drink at bars lining **Canal St.,** the center of the village. **Manto's,** at #46, fills with all ages, genders, and orientations with its Saturday night/Sunday morning "Breakfast Club." (Cover £5. Open daily 2-6am.)

   Trains leave **Piccadilly Station,** on London Rd., and **Victoria Station,** on Victoria St., for: London Euston (2½hr., 1 per hr., £84.50); Birmingham (1¾hr., 2 per hr., £14.20); Chester (1hr., 1 per hr., £8.50); Edinburgh (4hr., 12 per day, £41.60-51.50); Glasgow (4hr.; 6 per day; £39-52); Liverpool (50min., 2 per hr., £6.95); and York (40min., 2 per hr., £15.80). **Piccadilly Bus Station** consists of about 50 bus stops around Piccadilly Gardens; pick up a free route map at the tourist office. National Express **buses** (☎ (08705) 80 80 80) go from Chorlton St., two blocks south and one east of Piccadilly, to London (4-5hr.; 7 per day; £15, round-trip £24) and Liverpool (50min.; 1 per hr.; £4, round-trip £6.50). The **Manchester Visitor Centre,** in the Town Hall Extension, is on Lloyd St., off St. Peter's Sq. (☎234 31 57; info (0891) 71 55 33. Open M-Sa 10am-5:30pm, Su 11am-4pm.) Check **email** at **interc@fe,** Piccadilly Square on the 1st floor of Debenhams. (☎832 86 66. £1.50 per 30min. Open M and W-F 9:30am-5:30pm, Tu 10am-5:30pm, Sa 9am-5:30pm, Su 11am-4:30pm.) Take bus #33 from Piccadilly Gardens toward Wigan or walk 10min. down Liverpool Rd. from the Deansgate train station to reach the swanky **YHA Manchester,** Potato Wharf, Castlefield, behind the Castlefield Hotel on Liverpool Rd. (☎839 99 60. Internet. Breakfast included. Lockers £1-2. Laundry. Reception 7am-11:30pm. Dorms £17.40, students £13.10.) To get to the friendly **Woodies Backpackers Hostel,** 19 Blossom St., Ancoats, walk 5min. up Newton St. from Piccadilly Gardens and cross Great Ancoats St.; it's just past the Duke of Edinburgh pub. (☎228 34 56. Laundry. Dorms £12 per night, £60 per week.) **Cornerhouse Café,** 70 Oxford St., is part of the trendy Cornerhouse Arts Center. (Main dishes from £3.50. Open daily 11am-8:30pm; kitchen open noon-2:30pm and 5-7pm; bar open M-Sa noon-11pm, Su noon-10:30pm.) **On the 8th Day,** 107-111 Oxford Rd., cooks eclectic and dynamic vegetarian and vegan fare. (☎273 18 50. Open M-F 9am-7pm, Sa 10am-4:30pm.) **Tesco supermarket** is on Market St. (Open M-Sa 8am-8pm, Su 11am-5pm.) **Postal code:** M2 2AA.

CHESTER   ☎01244

With fashionable shops in faux-medieval houses, tour guides in full Roman armor, a town crier in Georgian uniform, and a Barclays bank occupying a wing of its cathedral, Chester at times resembles an American theme-park collage of Ye Olde English Towne. Originally built by frontier-forging Romans and subsequently a base for Plantagenet royal campaigns against the Welsh, the crowded but lovely town now maintains a pace to match the races that circle its internationally celebrated **Roodee Race Course.** The famous **city walls** completely encircle the town. Just outside Newgate lies the unimpressive base of the largest Roman **amphitheater** in Britain. (Open daily Apr.-Sept. 10am-6pm; Oct.-Mar. 10am-1pm and 2-4pm. Free.) The lions, tigers, and playfully gladitorial orangutans have all relocated to the **Chester Zoo.** Take **bus** #8 or 8X from the bus exchange behind the town hall. (☎38 02 80. Open daily 10am to 3:30pm. £9.50, seniors £7.50, children £7.) Fight your way through the throngs for a visit to the brilliant stained-glass windows and cloisters of the awe-inspiring **cathedral.** (Open daily 7:30am-6:30pm. Suggested donation £2.) Pubs line **Lower Bridge St.** and **Watergate St.**

    Trains arrive from: London (4 hr., 7 per day, £44); Holyhead (2hr., every hr., £16.15); and Manchester (1hr., every hr., £8.50). Merseyrail arrives from Liverpool (45min., every hr., £3); take bus #20 from the train station to Foregate St. (free with rail ticket). National Express **buses** arrive on Delamere St. from London (5½hr., 5 per day, £15) and Manchester (1hr., 3 per day, £4.50). From Foregate St., enter the city walls onto Eastgate St. and turn right on Northgate St. to reach the **tourist office,** in the Town Hall, Northgate St.; from the bus station, turn left on Upper Northgate St. and head through Northgate. (☎40 21 11. Open May-Oct. M-Sa 9am-6pm, Su 10am-4pm; Nov.-Apr. M-Sa 9am-5:30pm.) **B&Bs** (from £15) cluster on Hoole Rd., 5min. from the train station; turn right from the exit, climb the steps to Hoole Rd., and turn right over the railroad tracks. To get to the **YHA youth hostel,** Hough Green House, 40 Hough Green, take bus #7 or 16 for 1½ mi. (☎68 00 56. Internet. Laundry. Reception 7am-10:30pm. Open mid-Jan. to mid-Dec. Dorms £11.) **Tesco supermarket** is at the end of an alley off Frodsham St. (Open M-F 8am-9pm, Sa 7:30am-9pm, Su 11am-5pm.)

LIVERPOOL   ☎0151

On the banks of the Mersey, much of Liverpool's (pop. 520,000) history is rooted in its docks. A transformed Albert Dock studded with restaurants and museums, two enormous cathedrals, a dynamic arts scene, wild nightlife, and (of course) the Beatles make Liverpool a great destination for travelers.

🄴 **TICKET TO RIDE. Trains** (☎ (08457) 48 49 50) connect Liverpool's Lime St. Station to: London Euston (2hr., 1 per hr., £45); Birmingham (2hr., 1 per hr., £24); Manchester (1½hr., 2 per hr., £6.50); Edinburgh (4 hr., every 2 hr., £42); and Glasgow (4½ hr., every hr., £39). National Express **buses** (☎ (08705) 80 80 80) depart from the Norton St. Coach Station for: London (4-5hr.; 6 per day; day round-trip £15, round-trip £24); Birmingham (2½hr., 6 per day, round-trip £12.50); and Manchester (1hr., 1 per hr., £4). The Isle of Man Steam Packet Company (☎ (08705) 52 35 23) runs **ferries** to the Isle of Man (2½ hr.; Apr.-Oct. 2 per day, less frequently in winter; £19-29, round-trip £36-51); Belfast (3hr., 2-3 per week, £20-50); and Dublin (2¾hr., 2-3 per week, £20-50).

🄷 **HELP!** The main **tourist office,** in the Merseyside Welcome Centre in Queen Sq., sells a map guide (£1), books beds for a 10% deposit, and organizes both bus (from £4) and walking (£1) tours of Liverpool. (☎709 36 31; fax 708 02 04. Open M-Sa 10am-5:30pm, Su 10am-4:30pm.) **Phil Hughes** runs an excellent Beatles tour in an 8-seater bus. (☎228 45 65. £9.) Get **internet** access upstairs at **Central Library,** William

Brown St. (open M-Sa 9am-5:30pm; $1 per 30min.), or at the cheerful **Planet Electra,** 36 London Rd. ($2.50 per 30 min., 20% student discount). **Postal code:** L1 1AA.

▐ HARD DAY'S NIGHT. Cheap hotels are mostly on **Lord Nelson St.,** adjacent to the train station, and **Mount Pleasant,** one block from Brownlow Hill—it's best to check all establishments at the tourist office first. ■**Embassie Youth Hostel,** 1 Falkner Sq., 15-20min. from the bus or train station at the end of Canning St., feels like a laid-back student's flat, with laundry, TV, pool table, kitchen, and all the toast and jam you can eat. (☎707 10 89. Dorms $10.50.) The **YHA youth hostel,** 24 Tabley St., The Wapping, is spanking new with an ideal location. From the train station, follow the signs to Albert Dock, turn left on Strand St., and it's on the left. (☎709 88 88; email liverpool@yha.org.uk. Laundry. Dorms $17.40.) **YWCA,** 1 Rodney St., just off Mt. Pleasant, has clean, renovated rooms in a lively neighborhood. (☎709 77 91. $12.) **Belvedere Hotel,** 83 Mount Pleasant, is one of the few family-run guest houses in the city center. (☎709 2356. Singles $18.50; doubles $37.) For camping, go to **Abbey Farm,** Dark Ln., Ormskirk, on the northern rail line from Lime St. station. (☎ (01695) 57 26 86. $4 for 1-person tent; $7 for 2-person tent.)

▐ STRAWBERRY FIELDS FOREVER. Trendy vegetarian cafes and reasonably-priced Indian restaurants line **Bold St.,** while cheap takeouts cluster on **Hardnon St.** and **Berry St.** The **Kwik Save supermarket** sits at 58 Hanover St. (Open M-Tu 8:30am-6pm, W-Sa 8:30am-6:30pm.) The **Hub Café Bar,** Berry St., dishes out veggie and vegan meals ($1.50-3) in a cafe decorated with furniture made out of bicycle parts. (Open M-Sa 10am-6pm.) Their motto "don't discriminate, integrate," the **Mets Cafe-Bar,** Rainford Gdns., off Matthew St., serves gently-priced and esoterically-designed lunch combos ($4.25) in a delightful candle-lit underground room. (Open M-Th noon-11pm, F-Sa noon-midnight, Su noon-10:30pm.) Light streams in through the windows of the two above-ground floors of **Hole in the Wall,** School Ln. The Sweets are particularly scrumptious, a deal at $2-3. (Open daily noon-6pm.)

▐ MAGICAL MYSTERY TOUR. Begun in 1904, the Anglican **Liverpool Cathedral** on Upper Duke St. boasts the highest Gothic arches ever built, the largest vault and organ, and the highest and heaviest bells in the world. Climb to the top of the 300 ft. tower for a view stretching to North Wales. (Cathedral open daily 9am-6pm. Free. Tower open daily 11am-4pm. $2.) In contrast, the **Metropolitan Cathedral of Christ the King,** Mt. Pleasant, with its gorgeous neon-blue stained glass, looks more like a rocket launcher than a house of worship. (Open daily 8am-6pm; in winter Su until 5pm. Free.) **Albert Dock,** at the western end of Hanover St., is a series of Victorian warehouses transformed into a complex of restaurants and museums; don't miss the impressive, though intimate, collection of modern art at a branch of London's **Tate Gallery.** (Open Tu-Su 10am-6pm. Free; some special exhibits $3, students $1.) Also at Albert Dock, **The Beatles Story** pays tribute to the group's work with John Lennon's white piano, a recreation of the Cavern Club, and, of course, a yellow submarine. (Open daily Apr.-Oct. 10am-6pm; Nov.-Mar. 10am-5pm; $7, students $5.) The tourist office's **Beatles Map** ($2.50) will lead you to other Beatles-themed sights, including Strawberry Fields and Penny Lane. The **Beatles Shop,** 31 Matthew St., is loaded with souvenirs and memorabilia. (Open M-Sa 9:30am-5:30pm, Su 11am-4pm.) The elegant **Walker Art Gallery,** William Brown St., houses a rich collection of art from the 1300s to the present. Most prominently displayed are the extensive archives of British pre-Raphaelite work. (Open M-Sa 10am-5pm, Su noon-5pm. $3, students $1.50.) **The Bluecoat Centre,** tucked off of School Ln. in an old tree-ringed building, is Liverpool's center for the arts, providing a terrific range of exhibition spaces, performances, workshops, a cafe, and a second-hand bookstore. (Building open M-Sa 10am-5pm; gallery open Tu-Sa 10:30am-5pm.) The **National Museums and Galleries** of Merreyside has opened its **Conservation Centre,** on Whitechapel, with an engaging interactive exhibit detailing the decisions and processes that go into the conservation and restoration of a museum's archives. (Open M-Sa 10am-5pm, Su noon-5pm. $3, students $1.50.)

PLEASE PLEASE ME. Pubs teem in almost every street in Liverpool; **Slater St.** in particular brims with £1 pints. Try *Ink*, or the *Liverpool Echo* for up-to-date arts and nightlife info. **The Jacaranda,** Slater St., site of the first paid Beatles gig, has live bands and a small dance floor. (Open M-Th 8pm-2am, F-Sa noon-2am.) John Lennon once said that the worst thing about being famous was "not being able to get a quiet pint at the Phil;" the rest of us can sip in solitude at **The Philharmonic,** 36 Hope St. (Drafts £1.60. Open M-Sa 11:30am-11pm, Su 7-10:30pm.) **Slaters Bar,** Slater St., serves cheap shots. (Open M-Sa 11am-2am, Su noon-10:30pm.) **Baa Bar,** 43-45 Fleet St., off Bold St., attracts a far-from-sheepish lesbian, gay, and trendy crowd for cappuccino during the day and cheap beer at night. (☎707 06 10. Open M-Sa 10am-2am.) **Cream,** in Wolstonholme Sq. off Parr St., is Liverpool's superclub. (Cover £11. Open Sa, plus the last F of every month.) **The Cavern Club,** 10 Mathew St., is on the site where the fab four gained prominence; today it plays regular club music (M and F-Sa 9pm-2am; free before 10pm) and showcases live music (Sa 2-6pm). At the end of August, a **Beatles Convention** draws pop fans from around the world.

NORTHERN ENGLAND

Cradled between the Pennines rising to the west and the North Sea spreading to the east, the northeastern vistas span between calm coastal corners and rich national parkland, including some of the most beautiful and desolate areas in England. Extensive path systems lace the gray and purple moors that captured the imagination of the Brontës and the emerald dales that figure so prominently in the stories of James Herriot. Northeast England continues to have a ruggedness about it—in its wilderness, in its sense of humor, and in its endurance.

YORK ☎01904

More organized than the Roman with his long spear, more aggressive than the Viking with his broad sword, more thorough than the Norman with his strong bow—she is the Tourist with her zoom camera. Unlike those before her, she invades neither for wealth nor power: she comes for the history, the medieval thoroughfares, the Georgian townhouses, and the largest Gothic cathedral in Britain.

■ TRANSPORTATION

Trains: Station Rd. Ticket office open M-Sa 5:45am-10:15pm, Su 7:30am-10:10pm. Trains (☎ (08457) 484950) from: **London King's Cross** (2hr., 2 per hr., £56); **Manchester Piccadilly** (1½hr., 2 per hr., £16.20); **Newcastle** (1hr., 2 per hr., £14.90); and **Edinburgh** (2-3hr., 2 per hr., £48).

Buses: Rougier St. **National Express** (☎ (08705) 80 80 80) arrives from: **London** (4½hr., 6 per day, £16.50); **Manchester** (3hr., 6 per day, £7.75); and **Edinburgh** (5hr., 2 per day, £21).

Public Transportation, Call Rider York (☎43 56 09) for information. Ticket office open M-Sa 9am-5pm. Yorkshire Coastliner (☎ (0113) 244 89 76 or (01653) 69 25 56) runs buses to Castle Howard (see p. 220) that board at the train station.

Bike Rental: Bob Trotter, 13 Lord Mayor's Walk (☎62 28 68). From £7.50 per day plus £50 deposit. Open M-Sa 9am-5:30pm, Su 10am-4pm.

■ ? ORIENTATION AND PRACTICAL INFORMATION

York's streets are generally winding, short, and rarely labeled, while the longer ones change names every block or so. Fortunately, most attractions lie within the city walls, so you can't get too lost, and the **Minster,** visible from seemingly every point, provides an easy marker. The **River Ouse** (OOZE) cuts through the city, curving from west to south. The city center lies between the Ouse and the Minster; **Coney St., Parliament St.,** and **Stonegate** are the main thoroughfares.

Tourist Information Centre: De Grey Rooms, Exhibition Sq. (☎62 17 56; www.york-tourism.co.uk). Follow Station Rd., which turns into Museum St. and leads over the bridge, and turn left on St. Leonards Pl. Room-booking service £3 plus a 10% deposit. The *York Visitor Guide* (50p) includes "Where to Stay" and "What to See" sections, and a detailed map. *Snickelways of York* (£5) is an off-beat self-tour guide. Open daily June-Oct. 9am-6pm; Nov.-May 9am-5pm.

American Express: 6 Stonegate (☎67 00 30). Open M-F 9am-5:30pm, Sa 9am-5pm; in summer foreign exchange also open Su 10:30am-4:30pm.

Laundromat: Haxby Road Washeteria, 124 Haxby Rd. (☎62 33 79). Open M-F 8am-6pm, Sa 8am-5:30pm, Su 8am-4:30pm. Last wash 2hr. before close.

Police: (☎63 13 21), Fulford Rd.

Medical Assistance: York District Hospital (☎63 13 13), off Wigginton Rd. Take bus #1, 2, 3, or 18 from Exhibition Sq.

Internet Access: The Gateway Internet Cafe, 26 Swinegate (☎64 64 46). Open M-Sa 10am-8pm, Su noon-4pm. 50p quick check, £1.50 per 15min., £4 per hr. 20% student discount. Branch, in the basement of City Screen on Coney St. Open daily 11am-11pm.

Post Office: 22 Lendal (☎ 617285). **Bureau de change.** Open M-Tu 8:30am-5:30pm, W-Sa 9am-5:30pm. **Postal code:** YO1 2DA.

▟ ACCOMMODATIONS

Competition for inexpensive **B&Bs** (from £16) can be fierce during the summer; try side streets along Bootham/Clifton or The Mount area (past the train station and down Blossom St.). The **tourist information centres (TICs)** can be helpful. Book weeks ahead in the summer, even for hostels and campsites.

▧ Avenue Guest House, 6 The Avenue (☎62 05 75), ¾ mi. down Bootham/Clifton. Enthusiastic hosts provide 7 immaculate rooms. Some family rooms with baths. All rooms with TVs. Singles £15-17; doubles £28-32, with bath £30-40.

Foss Bank Guest House, 16 Huntington Rd. (☎63 55 48). Follow Goodramgate/Monkgate and turn left on Huntington. Comfortable beds in clean rooms. All rooms have showers and sinks. Some with TVs. Singles £17-19; doubles £37-44.

YHA York (☎65 31 47), Water End, Clifton. From the tourist office walk ¾ mi. on Bootham St., and take a left at Water End. Excellent facilities, but pricey. Reception 7am-10:30pm. Bedroom lockout 10am-1pm. Open mid-Jan. to mid-Dec. Dorms £16, under 18 £12; singles £18.50; twins £37; family rooms £52 or £78.

York Backpackers Hostel, 88-90 Micklegate (☎62 77 20; email yorkbackpackers@cwcom.net). This hostel occupies an 18th-century urban mansion. Bar open 3 nights a week. Internet. Dorms £9-12 depending on size of room; doubles £30.

York Youth Hotel, 11-15 Bishophill Senior (☎62 59 04). A well-located hostel with excellent facilities. Breakfast £2-£3. Sheets £1. Key deposit £2. Reception 24hr. Bar open 9pm-1am. Dorms £9.50-11; singles £13-14; twins £24-33.

Queen Anne's Guest House, 24 Queen Anne's Rd. (☎62 93 89), a short walk out Bootham from Exhibition Sq. Spotless single and double rooms with TVs; some doubles with baths. Large breakfasts. Singles from £16; doubles from £32.

Cornmill Lodge, 120 Haxby Rd. (☎62 05 66; email cornmill_lodge@hotmail.com). From Exhibition Sq., go up Gillygate onto Clarence St. and then Haxby Rd. A vegetarian B&B with clean rooms, all with TV. Singles from £20; doubles from £40.

Camping: Riverside Caravan and Camping Park (☎70 58 12), York Marine Services, Ferry Ln., Bishopthorpe, 2 mi. south of York off the A64. Riverside site. Take bus #23 from the bus station, and ask the driver to let you off at the campsite (every 30min., round-trip £1.30). July-Aug. £7 for 2 people and a tent; Sept.-June £6.

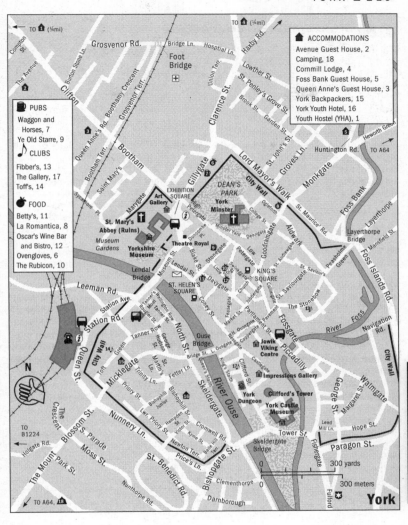

FOOD

Expensive tea rooms, medium-range bistros, fudge shops, and cheap eateries bump elbows everywhere in York. Shop for produce at the **Newgate market** between Parliament St. and the Shambles. (Open M-Sa 9am-5pm; Apr.-Dec. also Su 9am-4:30pm.) **Betty's,** 6-8 Saint Helen Sq., is the quintessential tea room experience, established in 1919 and serving the full range of teas, sweets, and main dishes for £3-8. (Open daily 9am-9pm.) **La Romantica,** 14 Goodramgate, serves delicious pastas and pizzas in candlelight. (Open daily noon-2:30pm and 5:30-11:30pm.) **Oscar's Wine Bar and Bistro,** 8 Little Stonegate, offers hearty pub fare (£5-7) in a lively setting with live jazz and blues on Monday nights. (Open daily 11am-11pm; happy hour Su-M 4pm-11pm, Tu-F 5-7pm.)

🔆 🎵 SIGHTS AND ENTERTAINMENT

The best introduction to York is the 2½ mi. walk along its **medieval walls.** Beware of the tourist stampede, which slows only in the early morning and just before the walls and gates close at dusk. At the TIC, ask for the useful *York Visitors Guide*, and then hit the cobblestone streets. Everyone and everything converges at the enormous **York Minster,** built between 1220 and 1470. Half of all the medieval stained glass in England glitters here; the **Great East Window** depicts the beginning and end of the world in over a hundred scenes. Climb 275 steps to the top of the **Central Tower** for a view over York's red roof-tops. Evensong is a particularly stunning way to experience the cathedral. (Cathedral open daily in summer 7am-8:30pm; off-season 7am-6pm; £3. Tower open daily June-Sept. 9:30am-6:30pm; Mar. and Nov. 10am-4:30pm; Apr. and Oct. 10am-5:30pm; May 10am-6pm. £2.50. Evensong M-F 5pm, Sa 4pm.) The **York Castle Museum,** in Minster Yard, by the river and Skeldergate Bridge, is housed in a former debtor's prison, and lives up to its billing as Britain's premier museum dedicated to everyday life. It contains **Kirkgate,** an intricately reconstructed Victorian shopping street complete with carriage, and **Half Moon Court,** its Edwardian counterpart. (Open daily Apr.-Oct. 9:30am-5pm; Nov.-Mar. 9:30am-4:30pm. £5.95, students £3.50.) The **Jorvik Museum Centre** (the Viking Centre), Coppergate, is one of the busiest places in York; visit early or late to avoid lines, or book at least 24hr. in advance to waltz past them altogether. Visitors wander through the York of AD 948, with authentic artifacts and painfully accurate smells, to discover Norse truths. No, the Vikings did not wear horns. (☎64 32 11; advance booking ☎54 34 03, M-F 9am-5pm. Open Apr.-Oct. daily 9am-5:30pm; Nov.-Dec. daily 10am-4:30pm; Jan.-Mar. Su-F 9am-3:30pm, Sa 9am-4:30pm. £5.50, students £4.75, children £4.) Hidden within the 10 gorgeous acres of the **Museum Gardens,** the **Yorkshire Museum** presents Roman, Anglo-Saxon, and Viking artifacts, as well as the £2.5 million **Middleham Jewel** (c. 1450). In the museum gardens, peacocks strut among the haunting ruins of **St. Mary's Abbey,** once the most influential Benedictine monastery in northern England. Visit the basement of the museum to get the lowdown on abbey life. (Enter from Museum St. or Marygate. ☎62 97 45. Open daily 10am-5pm. £3.75, families £10.50. Gardens and abbey ruins free.)

The weekly *What's On* and *Artscene* guides, available at the tourist office, have listings on live music, theater, cinema, exhibitions, and more. In **King's Square** and on **Stonegate,** barbershop quartets share the pavement with jugglers, magicians, and politicians. There are more pubs in the center of York than there are gargoyles on the east wall of the Minster. **The Gallery,** 12 Clifford St., is a glittering new nightclub, voted one of the best in Northern England that has everything from club anthems to champagne and piano bar to swing. (Open daily 9:30pm-2am.) The excellent **Toff's,** 3-5 Toft Green, plays mainly dance and house music. (☎62 02 03. No athletic shoes. Open M-Sa 9pm-2am. Cover £3.50, free F before 10:30pm.)

🏚 DAYTRIP FROM YORK

CASTLE HOWARD

Yorkshire Coastliner bus #842 runs half-day excursions to the castle (1 per day, £4).

The breathtakingly baroque Castle Howard (☎ (01653) 64 83 33) presides over 1½ sq. mi. of stunning grounds, including gardens, fountains, and lakes. The **long gallery** provides a dazzling and dwarfing promenade between enormous windows and shelves stuffed with books. Head to the **chapel** for the kaleidoscopic stained glass. Be sure to see the white-and gold-domed **Temple of the Four Winds,** with a hilltop perch that offers views of rolling hills, still waters, and lazy cows. (Castle open mid-Mar. to Oct. daily 11am-4:45pm. Grounds open mid-Mar. to Jan. daily 10am-6:30pm. Joint ticket £7, students £6.50.)

DURHAM CITY
☎ 0191

Spiralling medieval streets, footbridges, and restricted vehicle access make cliff-top Durham pedestrian-friendly. Durham's only claim to being a "city" is the magnificent **Durham Cathedral,** England's greatest Norman cathedral; it houses the tomb of the **Venerable Bede,** author of *The Ecclesiastical History of the English People.* The view from the **tower** compensates for the 325-step climb. (Cathedral open daily May-Sept. 7:30am-8pm; Oct.-Apr. 7:30am-6pm. Tower open mid-Apr. to Sept. 9:30am-4pm; Oct. to mid-Apr. M-Sa 10am-3pm. Suggested donation £2.50.) Across the cathedral green, **Durham Castle** was once a key defensive fortress. Wander along the **River Wear** for tranquil shade, ambling waters, and views of the cathedral and castle; or rent a rowboat from **Brown's Boathouse Centres,** on Elvet Bridge (£2.50 per hr.). Starting around 11pm, head to the intersection of Crossgate and North Rd., just across Framwellgate Bridge, where pubs and clubs await with open doors.

Trains (☎ 232 62 62) run to: London (3hr., every hr., £63); Newcastle (20min., 2 per hr., £3.60); and York (1hr., 2 per hr., £17). **Buses** leave North Rd. for London, Edinburgh, and Newcastle. To reach the **tourist office,** Market Pl., from the station, descend the hill on Station Approach and take the stairs to the left down to the Millburngate Bridge roundabout; cross the bridge and turn right at the first intersection into Market Pl. (☎ 384 37 20; fax 386 30 15. Open July-Aug. M-Sa 10am-5:30pm, Su 11am-4pm; June and Sept. M-Sa 10am-5:30pm; Oct.-May M-Sa 10am-5pm.) Cruise the **internet** at **Reality-X Durham,** 1 Framwellgate Bridge. (£3 per 30min. Open daily 10am-8pm.) A large supply of cheap **dormitory rooms** surrounds the cathedral. (☎ 374 34 54. Available July-Sept. and around Christmas and Easter.) **University College** in Durham Castle has rooms (☎ 374 38 63; £20.50), and **Mrs. Koltai** runs a comfy **B&B,** 10 Gilesgate (☎ 386 20 26; £16). In the **Indoor Market,** off Market Pl., you'll find produce, among butchers, and bakers. (Open M-Sa 9am-5pm.) **Postal code:** DH1 3RE.

NEWCASTLE-UPON-TYNE
☎ 0191

Hardworking Newcastle is legendary for its local pub and club scene. While you can still see straight, explore the masterful **Tyne Bridge,** neighboring **Castle Keep,** and the fine holdings of the **Laing Art Gallery.** (Castle open Apr.-Sept. Tu-Su 9:30am-5:30pm; Oct.-Mar. daily 9:30am-4:30pm. £1.50, students 50p. Museum open M-Sa 10am-5pm, Su 2-5pm. Free.) At night, the rowdy area of **Bigg Market** frowns on under-dressed student types, but milder pubs there include **Blackie Boy,** 11 Groatmarket, and **Macey's,** 31 Groatmarket. The **Quayside** (Metro: Central Station) is a slightly more relaxed, student-friendly area of town; try **The Red House,** 32 Sandhill. Revelers sway even before they've imbibed at **The Tuxedo Royale,** a boat/dance club under the Tyne Bridge. (Open M and W-Sa 7:30pm-2am.) Gays and lesbians flock to the corner of Waterloo and Sunderland St to drink at **The Village** and dance at **Powerhouse.** (Pub open daily noon-11pm. Club open M and Th 10pm-2am, Tu-W 11pm-1am, F-Sa 10pm-3am.)

Trains (☎ (08457) 48 49 50) leave for London (3hr., every hr., £72) and Edinburgh (1½hr., 16-23 per day, £31). National Express **buses** (☎ (08705) 80 80 80) leave Percy St. for London (6hr., round-trip £29.50) and Edinburgh (3hr., round-trip £18.50) as well. The **tourist office,** 132 Granger St., facing Grey's Monument, has essential maps. (☎ (0191) 277 80 00. Open M-Sa 9:30am-6pm, Th 9:30am-8pm.) To get to the crowded **YHA youth hostel,** 107 Jesmond Rd., take the metro to Jesmond and turn left on Jesmond Rd. (☎ 281 25 70. Breakfast £2.80. Lockout 10am-5pm. Curfew 11pm, or ask for the code. Open Feb.-Nov. Dorms £10.15, students £9.15.) **The Brighton Guest House,** 47-51 Brighton Grove, is cheap and cheery. Take bus #10, 34-36, or 38 from the train station, or bus #12, 39, or 40 from Blackett St. in the center of town. (☎ 273 36 00. Breakfast included. Dorms £16-22 per person.) **Don Vito's,** 82 Pilgrim St., stands out among the many Italian eateries. (Open M-F 11:45am-2pm and 5-10pm, Sa 11:45am-10:30pm.) **Postal code:** NE1 7AB.

LAKE DISTRICT NATIONAL PARK

In the Lake District, quite possibly the most beautiful place in England, dramatic mountainsides plummet down to shores gently embraced by lapping waves, and water winds its way in every direction. The area's jagged peaks and windswept fells stand in desolate splendor—except in July and August, when outdoor enthusiasts outnumber water molecules. Use **Windermere, Ambleside, Grasmere,** and **Keswick** as bases from which to ascend into the hills—the farther west you go from the **A591** connecting these towns, the more countryside you'll have to yourself.

The **National Park Visitor Centre** is in **Brockhole**, halfway between Windermere and Ambleside. (☎ (015394) 466 01. Open Easter-Oct. daily 10am-5pm, plus most weekends in winter.) **National Park Information Centres** dispense info on the camping-barn network, and book accommodations. While **B&Bs** line every street in every town (£15-20) and the region has the highest concentration of youth hostels in the world, lodgings do fill up in July and August; book ahead.

⬛ TRANSPORTATION. Two **rail** lines (☎ (08457) 48 49 50) flank the park: the south-north **Preston-Lancaster-Carlisle** line skirts the park's eastern edge, while the **Barrow-Carlisle** line serves the western coast. Oxenholme, on the southeastern edge of the Lake District, and Penrith, just to the northeast, are accessible from London's Euston Station (4-5hr., 11-16 per day, £58); Edinburgh (2½-3hr., 6 per day, £32); and Manchester's Piccadilly Station (2hr., 5-7 per day, £11.40). From Oxenholme, a short branch line covers the 10 mi. to Windermere (20min., every hr., £3.20). **National Express buses** (☎ (08705) 80 80 80) go directly to Windermere from London (7½hr., 1 per day, £24) and Manchester (3hr., 1 per day, £14), and continue north through Ambleside and Grasmere to Keswick. **Stagecoach Cumberland** buses (☎ (01946) 632 22) serve over 25 towns and villages within the district; pick up the essential *Lakeland Explorer* at any tourist office. An **Explorer** ticket offers unlimited all-day travel on all area Stagecoach buses (£5.75). The Ambleside YHA Youth Hostel offers a convenient **minibus service** (☎ (015394) 323 04; £2.50) between hostels as well as free service from the Windermere train station to the Windermere and Ambleside hostels. Potential cyclists can get **bike rental** info at tourist offices; *Ordnance Survey Cycle Tours* (£10) has route maps.

WINDERMERE AND BOWNESS. **Windermere** and sidekick **Bowness-on-Windermere** (joint pop. 8500) fill to the gills with vacationers in summer, when sailboats and waterskiers swarm over Windermere lake. **Windermere Lake Cruises** runs the **Lake Information Centre** (☎ (015394) 433 60; fax 434 68), at the north end of Bowness Pier, which provides maps, rents rowboats and motorboats, and books popular lake cruises. From Easter to October, boats sail north to Waterhead Pier in Ambleside (30min., 2 per hr., round-trip £5.70) and south to Lakeside (40min., every hr., round-trip £5.90). The **train station** sends off Lakeland Experience **buses** to Bowness (#599; 3 per hr., £1). The **tourist office** is next door. (☎ (015394) 464 99. Open daily July-Aug. 9am-7:30pm; Easter-June and Sept.-Oct. 9am-6pm; Nov.-Easter 9am-5pm.) The local **National Park Information Centre,** on Glebe Rd., is beside Bowness Pier. (☎ (015394) 428 95. Open July-Aug. daily 9:30am-6pm; Apr.-June and Sept.-Oct. daily 9am-5:30pm; Nov.-Mar. F-Su 10am-4pm.) To get to the spacious **YHA Youth Hostel,** on High Cross, Bridge Ln., Troutbeck, 1 mi. north of Windermere off the A591, take the Ambleside bus to Troutbeck Bridge and walk ¾ mi. uphill, or catch the YHA shuttle from the train station. (☎ (015394) 435 43. Bike rental. Open mid-Feb. to Oct. Dorms £9.80.) To reach the social **Lake District Backpackers Hostel,** on High St., look for the sign on the right as you descend the hill from the train station, or call for free pick-up. (☎ (015394) 463 74. Reception 9am-1pm and 5-9pm. Dorms £9.50.) Those wanting a B&B can find a room at **The Village House,** 5 Victoria St. (☎ (015394) 460 41; £16 per person). **Camp** at Limefitt Park, 4½ mi. north of Bowness Pier on A592, just below the Kirkstone path. (☎ (015394) 323 00. £3 per person; 2 people with tent and car £12.) Perhaps Windermere's most visited attraction is **The World of Beatrix Potter,** in the Old Laundry Theatre complex, Crag Bow. (☎ (015394) 884 44. Open daily April-Sept. 10am-5:30pm; Oct.-Mar. 10am-4:30pm. £3.50, children £2.)

AMBLESIDE. Just under a mile north of Windermere lake's northern tip, Ambleside has adapted to the tourist influx without selling its soul to the industry. You can't go wrong **hiking** in any direction near Ambleside; however, hidden trail markings, steep slopes, and weather-sensitive visibility all necessitate a good map and compass. Excellent warden-guided **walks** leave from National Park and tourist offices. The top of **Loughrigg,** two and a half miles from Ambleside (3½ mi. circuit descent), provides a view of higher surrounding fells. For gentler, shorter hikes, *Ambleside Walks in the Countryside* (30p) lists three easy walks from the town's center. Lakeslink **bus** #555 (☎ (015394) 322 31; every hr.) rolls into Kelsick Rd. from Windermere, Grasmere, and Keswick. The **tourist office** is on Church St. (☎ (015394) 325 82. Open daily 9am-5:30pm.) To reach the **National Park Information Centre,** Waterside, walk south on Lake or Borrans Rd. from town to the pier. (☎ (015394) 327 29. Open daily Easter-Oct. 9:30am-6pm.) Bus #555 also stops in front of the superb **Ambleside YHA Youth Hostel,** 1 mi. south of Ambleside and three miles north of Windermere, on the northern shore of Windermere Lake. (☎ (015394) 323 04; email ambleside@yha.org.uk. Bike rental. Curfew midnight. £11.15.)

GRASMERE. The peace that Wordsworth enjoyed in the village of Grasmere is still apparent during quiet mornings. The early 17th-century ◼**Dove Cottage,** 10min. from the center of town, is where Wordsworth lived from 1799 to 1808, and remains almost exactly as he left it; next door is the outstanding **Wordsworth Museum.** (Both open mid-Feb. to mid-Jan. daily 9:30am-5pm. £5, students £4.20.) The 6 mi. **Wordsworth Walk** circumnavigates the two lakes of the Rothay River, passing the poet's grave, Dove Cottage, and **Rydal Mount,** where the poet lived until his death. (Rydal Mount open Mar.-Oct. daily 9:30am-5pm; Nov.-Feb. W-M 10am-4pm. £3.75, students £3.25.) **Bus** #555 stops in Grasmere every hr. on its way south to Ambleside or north to Keswick; open-top bus #599 stops every 20min. The combined **tourist office** and **National Park Information Centre** lies in town on Redbank Rd. (☎ (015394) 352 45; fax 350 57. Open Easter-Oct. daily 9:30am-5:30pm; Nov.-Easter Sa, Su 10am-4pm.) The **Grasmere Youth Hostel (YHA)** (☎ (015394) 353 16; fax 357 98; email grasmerebh@yha.org.uk), is split into two buildings. To reach the first, **Butterlip How (YHA),** on Easedale Rd., follow the road to Easedale for 150 yards and turn right down the sign-posted drive. (Open Apr.-Oct. daily; Nov.-Jan. F-Sa; Feb.-Mar Tu-Sa. Dorms £12.) To get to **Thorney How (YHA),** follow Easedale Rd. ½ mi. out of town, turn right at the fork, and look for it a ¼ mi. down on the left. (Open Apr.-Sept. daily; mid-Feb. to Mar. and Oct.-Dec. Th-M. Dorms £10.) Sarah Nelson's famed Grasmere Gingerbread, a staple since 1854, is a steal at 22p in **Church Cottage,** outside St. Oswald's Church. (Open Easter.-Nov. M-Sa 9:15am-5:30pm, Su 12:30-5:30pm; Dec.-Easter. M-Sa 9:15am-5pm, Su 12:30-5pm.)

KESWICK. Between towering Skiddaw peak and the northern edge of Derwentwater lake, Keswick (KEZ-ick) rivals Windermere as the Lake District's tourist capital, but far surpasses it in charm. One of the best ridge hikes in the Lake District begins only a mile from Keswick; ascend the **Cat Bells** from the west shore of Derwentwater at Hawes End and stroll a gentle 3 mi. atop the ridge, passing **Maiden Moor** and **Eel Crags** on the way to **Dale Head,** one of the highest peaks in the area; then descend via the saddle-shaped Honister Pass to reach Seatoller (10-12 mi. total). The **National Park Information Centre,** in Moot Hall, is behind the clock tower in Market Sq. (☎ (017687) 726 45. Open daily Aug. 9:30am-6pm; Sept.-July 9:30am-5:30pm.) From the tourist office, bear left down Station Rd. and follow the signs to reach the stellar **Keswick YHA Youth Hostel,** on Station Rd. (☎ (017687) 724 84; email keswick@yha.org.uk. Curfew 11:30pm. Open mid-Feb. to late Dec. Dorms £10.15.) It's worth the 2 mi. ride south on B5289 (bus #79; every hr.) to Seatoller to stay at the **Derwentwater YHA Youth Hostel,** in Barrow House, Borrowdale, where you can relax by its waterfall. (☎ (017687) 772 46. Open Jan.-Oct. Dorms £10.15.) If you wish a bed and breakfast, **Century House,** 17 Church St., has bright peaches-and-cream bedrooms. (☎ (017687) 728 43. £19.50 per person.) **Camp** at **Castlerigg Hall,** southeast of Keswick on A591. (☎ (017687) 724 37. Showers £0.50. Open Apr.-Nov. £2.70-3.20 per person, £1 per car.)

BRITAIN

WALES

Wales borders England, but if many of the 2.9 million Welsh people had their way, it would be floating miles away. Since England solidified its control over the country with the murder of Prince Llywelyn ap Gruffydd in 1282, relations between the two have been marked by a powerful unease. Wales clings steadfastly to its Celtic heritage, continuing a centuries-old struggle for independence. Travelers come for the miles of sandy beaches, grassy cliffs, and dramatic mountains that typify the rich landscape of this corner of Britain, or to scan the numerous castles that dot the towns, remnants of centuries of warfare with England. Enjoy the unique landscapes and cultures, and avoid calling the Welsh "English" at all costs.

⚓ FERRIES TO IRELAND

Irish Ferries (☎ (0990) 17 17 17; www.irishferries.co.uk) runs to **Dublin, Ireland** from **Holyhead** (2hr.; round-trip £40-50, students £30-38). **Stena Line** (☎ (1233) 64 68 26; www.stenaline.co.uk), runs to **Dún Laoghaire** (near Dublin), from **Holyhead** (1½hr.; £20-35, students £16-28). **Swansea Cork Ferries** (☎ (01792) 45 61 16) run from King's Dock, **Swansea** to **Cork**, Ireland (June £27; July-Sept. £34).

CARDIFF (CAERDYDD)   ☎029

Formerly a sleepy provincial town, Cardiff (pop. 340,000) burst onto the scene in the late 19th century as the main shipping port of Welsh coal; at its height, it was the world's busiest seaport. Today, the buzzing capital of Wales brims with theaters and clubs as well as remnants of its past. Climb the Norman keep of the flamboyant **Cardiff Castle** for a sweeping view of the city and tour its mock-medieval interior, where each room is done in a different theme. (Open daily Mar.-Oct. 9:30am-6pm; Nov.-Feb. 9:30am-4:30pm. £5, children £3, family £14.) The **National Museum and Gallery of Wales,** in the Civic Centre across North Road from the castle, houses an impressive collection of Western European art and an audio-visual exhibit on the "Evolution of Wales." (☎20 39 79 51. Open Tu-Su 10am-5pm. £4.50, children free.) Renovated from the elegant old Cardiff theater, **The Prince of Wales,** at the corner of St. Mary's St. and Wood St., is a brand-new sprawling pub that puts out a fantastic performance. Grab a Guiness (£1.79) or a bap burger for £2.50. (☎20 64 44 49. Open M-Sa 11am-11pm, Su noon-10:30pm.) Cardiff's specialty, **Brains S.A.** (Special Ale), known by locals as "Brains Skull Attack," is proudly served in many local pubs. Head to the **Clwb Ifor Bach** (the Welsh Club), 11 Womanby St., for dancing and the local music scene. (Cover £2-8. Open M-Th until 2am, F-Sa until 3am.) The mighty **Zeus,** Greyfriars Rd., is a cavernous club where the party pulses to a smart, casual dress code. (☎20 37 70 14. Cover £2.50-6, free before 10:30pm with flier. Open Tu-Th 9pm-2am, F-Sa 9pm-3am.)

   Trains (☎ (08457) 48 49 50) stop in Cardiff from London's Paddington Station (2hr., 1 per hr., £37); Bath (1-1½hr., 3 per hr., £11.90); and Edinburgh (7hr., 7 per day, 100.80). National Express **buses** (☎ (08705) 80 80 80) roll to Cardiff from London's Victoria Station (3¼hr., 12 per day, £14) and Manchester (5½hr., 11 per day, £25). Schedules for **local buses** are available at the Wood St. bus station. (Open M and F 8am-5:30pm, Tu-Th and Sa 8:30am-5:30pm. Fares 55p-£1.40.) The **tourist office,** on Wood St. across from the bus station, books B&Bs and stocks maps. (☎20 22 72 81. Open Jul.-Aug. M-Sa 9am-6pm, Su 10am-4pm; Sept.-Jun. M-Sa 9am-5pm, Su 10am-4pm.) **Cardiff Internet Cafe** is located at 15-17 Wyndham Arcade off St. Mary's St. (£1.50 per 15 min. Open 24hr.) The best **B&Bs** are off Cathedral Rd. (take bus #32 or walk 15min. from the castle). To get to the colorful **Cardiff International Backpacker,** 98 Neville St., from the train station, go down Wood St., cross the river, turn right on Fitzham Embankment, and turn left at the end of the road onto Despenser St. After dark, call for pick-up from the station. (☎20 34 55 77; fax

20 23 04 04. Breakfast included. Internet. Dorms £13.50; doubles £35; triples £41.)
Anned Lon, 157-159 Cathedral Rd, has comfortably elegant interiors and all rooms
have color TV and sinks. (☎20 22 33 49; fax 206 4 08 85. £18; with bath and conti-
nental breakfast £20.) For quick food and a wide variety of options, head to the
Victorian **Central Market,** in the arcade between St. Mary St. and Trinity St. (Open
M-Sa 8am-5:30pm.) **Celtic Cauldron Wholefoods,** 47-49 Castle Arcade, serves tradi-
tional Welsh food, including rarebit and laver-bread. (Meals £3.50-9.50. Open June-
Aug. M-Sa 8:30am-9pm, Su 10am-4pm; Sept.-May M-Sa 8:30am-6pm, Su 11am-4pm.)
Postal code: CF10 2SJ.

▓ DAYTRIP FROM CARDIFF: CAERPHILLY CASTLE. Eight miles north of
Cardiff, Caerphilly Castle floats above its moats and mossy grove. Begun in 1268
by Norman warlord Gilbert de Clare, its water systems, concentric stone walls,
catapults, and pivoting drawbridges made it the most technologically advanced
fortification of its time. Today its main tower leans a precarious 10 degrees from
the vertical, and ducks and kingfishers besiege the grounds. Take the **train** (20min.,
M-Sa 2 per hr., £2.50), or hourly buses #26, 71, or 72 from Central Station stand B3.
(☎20 88 31 43. Open June-Sept. daily 9:30am-6pm; Apr.-May and Oct. daily 9:30am-
5pm; Nov.-Mar. M-Sa 9:30am-4pm, Su 11am-4pm. Admission £2.50, children £2, families £7.) Four miles west of Cardiff, the **Museum of Welsh Life** is home to 30 authentic
buildings from all corners of Wales, reassembled into an interactive telling of
Welsh history. The iron-workers' cottages, old Victorian schoolhouse, mills, sad-
dlery, and other sites arranged across the 100 green acres of St. Fagan's Park are
busily tended by traditionally-garbed craftspeople. Quieter **St. Fagan's Castle** also
marks the grounds with its gardens garnished by reflecting pools. The hourly **bus**
#32 runs to the museum from Central Station stand B1. (☎20 57 35 00, fax 20 57 34
90. Open daily June-Sept. 10am-6pm; Oct.-May 10am-5pm. £5.50, children £3.20, families £14; in winter £4.50, children £2.65, families £10.25.)

WYE VALLEY

Stitching back and forth across the southern Welsh-English border, the Wye River
has carved a valley long appreciated for its tranquility. Today visitors hike, peddle,
and paddle through green lands unsullied by tourism. With legendary castles,
abbeys, and trails tracing the Wye from its spring in central Wales to its confluence
with the Severn south of Chepstow, the valley merits inclusion in any itinerary.

▐ TRANSPORTATION. The valley is best entered from the south, at Chepstow.
Trains chug from Cardiff to: Chepstow (40min.; M-Sa 8 per day, Su 7 per day; £5.20)
and Hereford (1hr., every hr., £11.70), the nearest station to Hay-on-Wye. National
Express **buses** (☎ (08705) 80 80 80) also ride to London (2¼hr., 10 per day, £16.50)
from Cardiff and Chepstow (50min., 5 per day, £3.25). Be aware that bus service in
the region is rare on Sundays. Pick up *Discover the Wye Valley on Foot and by
Bus* in area tourist offices for schedules. Stagecoach Red and White local bus #69
loops between Chepstow, Tintern, and Monmouth (4-8 per day). One-day **Roverbus
passes** (£5) and week-long **Primerider** passes (£16), available from Stagecoach drivers, will save frequent bus travelers money.

Hiking grants the most stunning vistas of the valley. The **Wye Valley Walk** treks
north from Chepstow, passing Tintern Abbey, and the nesting peregrines on the
way to Prestatyn. **Offa's Dyke Path** clears 177 mi. of hiking and biking paths along
the length of the Welsh-English border. All trails have walks of varying length and
difficulty; consult the **Offa's Dyke Association** (☎ (01547) 52 87 53) and the Walking
Wales guide, free at tourist offices, for guidance.

CHEPSTOW AND TINTERN. Chepstow's strategic position at the mouth of the river
and the base of the English border made it an important fortification and commerce
center in Norman times. **Chepstow Castle,** Britain's oldest stone castle, grows seamlessly from the cliff it stands on, and offers awesome views of the Wye River. (Open

Apr.-May and Oct. daily 9:30am-5pm; Jun.-Sept. daily 9:30am-6pm; Nov.-Mar. M-Sa 9:30am-5pm, Su 11am-4pm. £3; students, seniors, and children £2; families £18.) **Trains** arrive on Station Rd.; **buses** stop in front of the Somerfield supermarket. Purchase tickets at **The Travel House,** 9 Moor St. (☎ (01291) 62 30 31). The **tourist office** is in the castle parking lot. (☎ (01291) 62 37 72; www.chepstow.co.uk. Open daily Apr.-Sept. 10am-5:15pm; Oct.-Mar. 10:30am-3:30pm.) For lodging, take bus #69 to the **YHA Youth Hostel** near Tintern (see below) or be welcomed at **Lower Hardwick House,** 300 yd. up Mt. Pleasant from the bus station. (☎ (01291) 62 21 62. Singles £18; doubles £30-36; camping £5 per tent.) **Postal code:** NP16 5DA.

Five miles north of Chepstow on A466, the haunting arches of **Tintern Abbey** shade crowds of tourists in the summer and "connect the landscape with the quiet of the sky"—a phrase from Wordsworth's famous poem, written just a few miles away. (☎ (01219) 68 92 51. Open June-Sept. daily 9:30am-6pm; Apr.-May and Oct. daily 9:30am-5pm; Nov.-Mar. M-Sa 9:30am-4pm, Su 11am-4pm. £2.40; students, seniors, and children £1.90; families £6.70.) Near the iron footbridge, marked paths lead to **Offa's Dyke** (45min.) and to **Devil's Pulpit** (1hr.), from which Satan is said to have tempted the monks as they worked in the fields. A mile to the north on the A466, the **tourist office** is housed in a train at the **Old Station.** (☎/fax (01291) 68 95 66. Open Apr.-Oct. daily 10:30am-5:30pm.) The **YHA Youth Hostel,** 4 mi. northeast of Tintern, occupies a 13th-century castle. From the A466 or Offa's Dyke, follow signs for 2 mi. from Bigsweir Bridge to St. Briavel's. (☎ (01594) 53 02 72. Dorms £8.75, under 18 £7.40.) Two hundred yards north of the abbey is the **Wye Barn Bed and Breakfast.** (☎ (01291) 68 94 56. Singles £22.50.) **Postal code:** NP6 6SB.

HEREFORD. Ideal for excursions into Wales, **Hereford, England** (pop. 60,000) also draws its own visitors with the 11th-century **cathedral** and the 13th-century **Mappa Mundi** within—a map of the world drawn on animal skin around 1290. (Cathedral open Th-Tu until evensong at 5:30pm; W all day. Mappa Mundi shown May-Sept. M-Sa 10am-4:15pm, Su 11am-3:15pm; Oct.-Apr. M-Sa 11am-3:15pm. £4, students £3.) The **tourist office,** 1 King St, in front of the cathedral, books beds for a 10% deposit. (☎ (01432) 26 84 30. Open May-Sept. M-Sa 9am-5pm, Su 10am-4pm; Oct.-Apr. M-Sa 9am-5pm.) The T-junction at the end of **Bodenham Rd** hosts many of the cheaper B&Bs in town (around £16 per night). Elsewhere in town, try the B&B **Holly Tree,** 19-21 Barton Rd. (☎ (01432) 35 78 45. Singles £20; doubles £40.) **Postal code:** HR4 9HQ.

HAY-ON-WYE. If not for bookseller Richard Booth, Hay-on-Wye might still be just a pretty freckle on the scenic toes of the Black Mountains. Instead, Booth transformed it into the world-renowned Town of Books, where 40 secondhand and antiquarian bookstores attract browsers from all corners of the globe to the busy stone alleyways. The ode to books climaxes every May in a literary festival where luminaries such as P.D. James and Toni Morrison give readings. The **tourist office,** on Oxford Rd., books beds for £2. (☎ (01497) 82 01 44; www.hay-on-wye.co.uk. Open daily Apr.-Oct. 10am-1pm and 2-5pm; Nov.-Mar. 11am-1pm and 2-4pm.) **The Bear,** Bear St., has traditional rooms and breakfast. (☎ (01497) 82 13 02; fax 82 05 06. Call ahead. Singles £22; doubles with bath £27.) **Postal code:** HR3 5AE.

BRECON BEACONS NATIONAL PARK

The *Parc Cenedlaethol Bannau Brycheiniog* encompasses 519 dramatic square miles of barren peaks, well-watered forests, and windswept moors. The park is divided into four regions: the rugged country around the remote western **Black Mountain; Fforest Fawr,** containing the spectacular waterfalls of Ystradfellte; the eastern **Black Mountains;** and the **Beacon** peaks, where King Arthur's mountain fortress is thought to have once stood.

▐ TRANSPORTATION. The market towns on the fringe of the park, particularly **Brecon,** on its northern edge, make pleasant touring bases. **Trains** (☎ (08457) 48 49 50) run from London's Paddington station to Abergavenny at the park's southeastern corner and to Merthyr Tydfil on the southern edge. National Express (☎ (08705) 80 80 80) **bus** #509 runs once a day to Brecon, on the northern side of the park, from London and Cardiff. Stagecoach Red and White (☎ (01633) 26 63 36) crosses the park en route to Brecon from: Cardiff via Merthyr Tydfil (#43 changing to #X4; 1½hr., M-Sa 5 per day, £5-7); Abergavenny (#20 and 21, 1hr., M-Sa 5 per day; or bus #29, Su 2 per day, £3-4.10); and Hereford and Hay-on-Wye (#39, 45min., M-Sa 5 per day; Yeomans bus #40, Su 2 per day, £3-4).

BRECON (ADERHONDDU). Just north of the mountains, Brecon is the best hiking base. **Buses** arrive at the **Bulwark,** the central square. The **tourist office** is in the parking lot; walk through Bethel Square on Lion St. (☎ (01497) 62 31 56. Open daily 10am-6pm; in winter 9:30am-5:30pm.) The **Brecon Beacons National Park Information Centre** is in the same building (☎ (01497) 62 31 56). B&Bs tile The Watton, 3min. from the town center (£17-20). The nearest hostel is the **YHA Ty'n-y-Caeau,** 3 mi. from Brecon. From the town center, walk down The Watton and continue until you reach the A40-A470 roundabout. Follow the branch leading to Abergavenny on the A40. Follow the footpath just after the roundabout on the left until you reach Groesffordd; then turn left onto the main road. Continue for 10-15min., bearing left at the fork; the hostel is the second house on the right. The Brecon-Abergavenny bus will stop at a footpath that leads to Groesffordd if you ask the driver. (☎ (01874) 66 52 70. Open July-Aug. daily; mid-Feb. to June and Sept.-Nov. M-Sa. Dorms £9, under 18 £6.20.) Camp at **Brynich Caravan Park,** 1½ mi. east of town on the A40, signposted from the A40-A470 roundabout. (☎ (01874) 62 33 25. Showers and laundry. Open Mar.-Oct. £6.50-£7.50 per person, £4 per walk-in.)

THE WATERFALL DISTRICT. Forest rivers tumble through rapids, gorges, and spectacular falls near Ystradfellte, about 7 mi. southwest of the Beacons. The **YHA Ystradfellte** is a perfect launching point. (☎ (01639) 72 03 01. Open Apr. to mid-Jul. and Sept.-Oct. F-Tu; mid-Jul. to Aug. daily. Dorms £8.10, under 18 £5.65.) Five minutes away at **Porth-yr-Ogof** the River Mellte ducks into a cliff cave and re-emerges as an icy pool. Follow marked paths from Gwann Hepste and stand on the cliff face behind the **Sgwdyr Eira** waterfall. To the west near **Abercrave,** the **Dan-yr-Ogof Show-caves** impress with enormous stalagmites. From YHA Ystradfellte, 10 mi. of trails pass **Fforest Fawr,** the headlands of the Waterfall District, on their way to the caves. (☎ (01639) 73 02 84, 24hr. information line 73 08 01. Tours every 20min. Open Apr.-Oct. 10:30am-3pm, slightly later in summer. Tours £7.50, children £4, under 3 free.) **Stagecoach Red and White** bus #63 (1½hr.; M-Sa 3 per day, Su 4 per day) pauses at the hostel, caves, and country park en route from Brecon.

THE BLACK MOUNTAINS. Located in the easternmost section of the park, the Black Mountains are a group of long, lofty ridges offering 80 square miles of solitude, linked by unsurpassed ridge-walks. Invest in the Ordnance Survey Outdoor Leisure map 13 (£6.50). Begin forays from **Crickhowell,** or travel the eastern boundary along **Offa's Dyke Path,** which is dotted with a handful of impressive ruins, notably the Llanthony Priory. There is almost no public transportation along valley routes, but Stagecoach Red and White #39 does descend the north side of the Black Mountains. The **YHA Capel-y-ffin** (kap-EL-uh-fin), along Offa's Dyke Path, is 8 mi. from Hay-on-Wye. Take Stagecoach Red and White bus #39 from Hereford to Brecon, stop before Hay, and walk uphill. (☎ (01873) 89 06 50. Lockout 10am-5pm. Open July-Sept. daily; Oct. F-Tu; Nov. and Mar.-June Sa-Su. **Camping** allowed if hostel is full. Dorms £7.35, students £6.35.)

THE BRECON BEACONS. At the center of the park, these peaks lure hikers with pastoral slopes and barren peaks. Since many paths are not marked, Landranger Ordnance Survey maps 12 and 13 (£6.50 each) are essential to navigate the park. A one-hour walk from the Mountain Center past daredevil sheep and panoramic views ends at the scant remains of an **Iron-Age fort.** The most convenient route to the top of **Pen-y-Fan** (pen-uh-van; 2907 ft.) begins at **Storey Arms,** a large parking lot and bus stop 5 mi. south of Libanus on the A470. Unfortunately, frequent use has lead to erosion of this trail. A more pleasant hiking route starts in **Llanfaes,** Brecon's western suburb, and passes **Llyn Cwm Llwch** (HLIN koom hlooch), a 2000 ft. deep glacial pool. Walk 3 mi. from Llanfaes down Ffrwdgrech Rd. to the car park (take the middle fork after the first bridge) where the trail begins.

🗒 **DAYTRIP FROM BRECON BEACONS NATIONAL PARK.** The **Big Pit Mining Museum,** amid the silent hillsides of Blaenavon, recalls the industrial age that shaped and transformed Wales. Ex-miners lead visitors down a 300 ft. shaft to a 19th-century coal mine that operated until 1980 and recount grim and humbling stories. Dress warmly. (☎ (01495) 79 03 11. Open Mar.-Nov. daily 9:30am-5pm. Last guided tour at 3:30pm. £5.75, seniors £5.50, children £3.95.) From Abergavenny, take **bus** #X4 to Bryn Mawr, then #30 to Blaenavon (Tu and F-Sa 3 per day, M and W-Th 1 per day in the morning).

ABERYSTWYTH
☎ 01970

Halfway down the sweeping Cardigan Bay coastline, the university town of Aberstwyth offers easy access to all of Wales and plenty of pubs as you wait for your connection. The **National Library of Wales,** off Penglais Rd., houses the earliest surviving manuscript of *The Canterbury Tales* and almost every book written in Welsh pertaining to Wales. (Open M-F 9:30am-6pm, Sa 9:30am-5pm. Free.) Aberystwyth's beachfront and promenade remain as they were in Victorian times. With a spare half-day, don't miss the steam engine ride on the **Vale of Rheidol Railway** through the mountains, waterfalls, and gorges of the **Devil's Bridge** area. (☎ 62 58 19. Call for schedule. Rides £10.50, accompanied child £1.) The **train station,** on Alexandria Rd., is at the receiving end of the main rail line from England into central Wales. For destinations on the scenic Cambrian Coast to the north, ride to **Machynlleth** (30min., £4.60) for connections. National Express (☎ (08705) 80 80 80) **bus** #420 runs to London (7hr., 1 per day via Birmingham, £19.25). A single TrawsCambria bus #701 runs daily from Cardiff (4hr., £10.90). **Arriva Cymru** (☎ (08706) 08 26 08) covers buses in the region; call for schedules. The **tourist office,** in Lisburne House on Terrace Rd., has information on B&Bs. (☎ 61 21 25. Open July-Aug. daily 9am-6pm; Sept.-June M-Sa 10am-5pm.) To get to the **YHA Borth,** 9 miles north in Borth, take the train to Borth Station (10min., 8-12 per day, £1.50) or take Crosville bus #511 or 512. (☎ 87 14 98. Open Apr.-Aug. daily; Sept. M-Sa; Oct. and Mar. Tu-Sa. Dorms £10, students £6.75.) In town, **Mrs. E. V. Williams,** 28 Bridge St., offers delicious cakes and comfortable beds. (☎ 61 25 50. £15 per person.) Eat and drink at **The Academy,** St. James Sq., a chapel converted into a lively student pub. (Open M-Sa 11am-11pm, Su 11am-10:30pm.) **Postal code:** SY23 1DE.

LLYN PENINSULA
☎ 01766

The Llyn has been a hotbed of tourism since the Middle Ages, when crowds of religious pilgrims tramped through on their way to Bardsey Island, just off the wild western tip of the peninsula. Now eager apostles to the cult of sun make the pilgrimage to the endless beaches that line the southern coast, putting their faith in the region's unusually good weather. **Porthmadog,** on the southeastern part of the peninsula, is its main gateway. This travel hub's principal attraction is the jolly puffing **Ffestiniog Railway,** which runs from Harbour Station on High St into the hills of Snowdonia (1hr., 2-10 per day, £13.80; runs mid-Feb. to Nov.). **Portmeirion,** 2 mi. east of Porthmadog, proves an eccentric landmark of Italy-fixation, with Mediterranean courtyards, pastel houses, palm trees, and exotic statues constituting an otherworldly diversion from the standard Welsh castles and cottages. (Open daily 9:30am-5:30pm. £4.50, students £3.60; reduced Nov.-Mar.) **Bus** #98 runs from Porthmadog to Minffordd, a scenic 1½ mi. from Portmeirion. Cambrian Coaster **trains** arrive from Aberystwyth to the south (3-5 per day, £11.80), while other trains arrive through the adjacent Snowdonia National Park. A Cambrian Coaster Day Ranger (£6.40) is a sound investment for a day's worth of train travel. The **tourist office** is at the opposite end of High St, by the harbor. (☎51 29 81. Open daily Easter-Oct. 10am-6pm; Nov.-Easter 9:30am-5pm.) Sleep comfortably in Lawrence of Arabia's first home at **Snowdon Backpackers,** 10min. from the train station down Church St., and take advantage of its TV lounge and **internet.** (☎51 53 54. £12.50 per person.)

SNOWDONIA NATIONAL PARK

Rough and handsome, misty purple and mossy green, the highest mountains of England and Wales dominate horizons across the 840 square miles from forested Machynlleth to sand-strewn Conwy. The Welsh call it *Eryri*, Place of Eagles, and Snowdonia's misty crags, lonely and barren at the peaks, are as dramatic and powerfully graceful as this most royal of Welsh symbols. Though these lands lie largely in private hands, endless public footpaths accommodate droves of visitors with untrammeled corners and quiet hikes. **Tourist Offices** and **National Park Information Centres** (☎ (01766) 77 02 74) stock walk leaflets and Ordnance Survey Maps (£5.25-6.50), and can best direct you to the nearest of the eight quality **YHAs** in the park. Check out www.gwynedd.gov.uk for information on bus schedules and tourist information for the region.

▐▀ TRANSPORTATION

Trains (☎ (08457) 48 49 50) stop at several large towns on the park's outskirts, including **Bangor** (see p. 231) and **Conwy** (see p. 231). The **Conwy Valley Line** runs through the park from **Llandudno** through **Betws-y-Coed** to **Blaenau Ffestiniog** (2-10 per day, round-trip £14.20). Buses run to the interior from these towns as well as others near the edge of the park, such as **Caernarfon** (see p. 230). At Blaneau Ffestiniog the Conwy Valley Line connects with the narrow-gauge **Ffestiniog Railway** (☎ (01766) 51 23 40), which runs through the mountains to Porthmadog, meeting the Cambrian Coaster Service to **Llanberis** and **Aberystwyth.** Consult the indispensable *Gwynedd Public Transport Maps and Timetables*, available in all regional tourist offices.

◪ HIKING

Mount Snowdon (*Yr Wyddfa*, "the burial place") is the highest peak in England and Wales, measuring 3560 ft., and the most popular destination in the park. Six principal paths of varying degrees of difficulty wind their way up Snowdon; tourist offices and National Park Information Centres provide guides on these ascents. Experienced climbers go beyond Snowdon's tended paths and pack technical climbing equipment in the **Ogwen Valley.** There, climbs to **Devil's Kitchen** *(Twll Du)*, the **Glyders** (*Glyder Fawr* and *Glyder Fach*), and **Tryfan** all begin from **Llyn Ogwen.** Those attempting the climbs should pick up both the appropriate Ordnance Survey maps and the card-sized *Walk About Guides*, which give directions, map references, and severity ratings for the climbs.

Weather on Snowdonia's exposed mountains shifts quickly and unpredictably. No matter how beautiful the weather is below, it will be cold and wet in the high mountains. Arm thyself with wet-weather gear, gloves, a hat, and wool sweater. You can peel off the layers as you descend. Pick up the Ordnance Survey Maps Landranger 115: *Snowdon and Surrounding Area* (scale 1:50,000; £5.25) and Outdoor Leisure 17: *Snowdonia, Snowdon, and Conwy Valley Areas* (scale 1:25,000; £6.50), as well as individual path guides. Maps are available at Park Information Centers and most bookstores. Contact **Mountaincall Snowdonia** (☎ (0891) 50 04 49; 36-48p per min.) for the local forecast, ground conditions, and a three- to five-day forecast. Weather forecasts are also tacked outside Park Information Centres. Park rangers lead day-walks; ask at the Centres. The land in Snowdonia is privately owned—stick to public pathways, or ask the owner's consent to hike through.

LLANBERIS ☎ 01286

Set amidst lakes deep in the mountains, Llanberis, the largest town in the park, is a great base for exploration. **Parc Padarn** holds a host of attractions, from hikes around needle-shaped **Llyn Padarn** to tours of the **Welsh Slate Museum.** (☎ 87 06 30. Museum open Easter-Oct. daily 10am-5pm; Nov.-Easter Su-F 10am-4pm. £3.50, students £2, seniors and children free.) To view the plummeting **Ceunant Mawr,** an angled waterfall, follow the well-marked ¾ mi. footpath on Victoria Terr. by the Victoria Hotel. The long and gentle Llanberis path up Snowdon commences by the **Snowdon Mountain Railway,** a good option if you don't fancy a climb. (☎ 87 02 23. Round-trip 2hr. with 30min. stop at summit. Round-trip £15.80, children £11.30.) Catch bus #88 from Caernarfon (25min.; M-Sa 2 per hr., Su 1 per hr.; £1.60) or bus #77 from Bangor (40min.; M-Sa 1 per hr., Su 5 per day; round-trip £1.55). The **tourist office,** 41a High St., doles out tips on hikes and books accommodations. (☎ (01766) 87 07 65. Open Easter-Oct. daily 10am-6pm; Nov.-Easter W and F-Su 10:30am-4:30pm.) Plenty of sheep keep hostelers company at the **YHA Llanberis.** (☎ 87 02 80. Open Apr.-Aug. daily; Sept.-Oct. and Jan.-Mar. Tu-Sa. Dorms £9.80, under 18 £6.75.)

HARLECH ☎ 01766

This tiny coastal town just south of the Llyn Peninsula commands panoramic views of sea, sand, and Snowdonian summits. Its position on the Cambrian Coaster rail line makes it easily accessible. High above the rail, sea, and brown sugar sand dunes, **Harlech Castle** crowns a 200 ft. rock and rides high on the chain of Edward I's impressive Welsh castles. (☎ 78 05 52. Open Apr.-May and Oct. daily 9:30am-5pm; June-Sept. daily 9:30am-6pm; Nov.-Mar. M-Sa 9:30am-4pm, Su 11am-4pm. £3, students £2.) The tourist office, Gwyddfor House, Stryd Fawr, doubles as a **Snowdonia National Park Information Centre.** (☎/fax 78 06 58. Open daily Apr.-Oct. 10am-1pm and 2-6pm.) The closest hostel is the **YHA Llanbedr,** 4 mi. south of town. Take the 10min. train ride to the Llanbedr. stop or ride bus #38 and ask to be let off at the hostel. (☎ (01341) 24 12 87. Open May-Aug. daily; mid-Feb. to Apr. and Sept.-Oct. Th-M; Jan. to mid-Feb. F-Su. Dorms £9, under 18 £6.20.) For great views stay at **Arundel,** Stryd Fawr. (☎ 78 06 37. £14 per person.) **Yr Ogof Bistro,** left from the castle on Stryd Fawr, offers great cuisine. (☎ 78 08 88. Open daily 10am-10:30pm.)

NORTHERN COAST

CAERNARFON ☎ 01286

Majestic and fervently Welsh, the walled city of Caernarfon (car-NAR-von) sails on the shifting tides of the Menai Strait with the mountains in its wake and a world-famous castle at the helm. Built by Edward I beginning in 1283, the ▧**Caernarfon Castle** was left unfinished when Eddie ran out of money and became distracted by unruly Scots. (☎ 67 76 17. Open June-Sept. daily 9:30am-6pm; Apr.-May and Oct. daily 9:30am-5pm; Nov.-Mar. M-Sa 9:30am-4pm. £4.20, students, seniors, and children £3.20.) Arriva Cymru (☎ (08706) 08 26 08) **bus** #5, 5a, 5b, or 5x arrives from Bangor (25min., every 10 min., £1.55) and Conwy (1hr.; M-Sa 2 per hr., Su 1 per hr.; £2.85). TrawsCambria bus #701 arrives daily from Cardiff (7½hr.) and Holyhead (1½hr.). National Express (☎ (08705) 80 80 80) bus #545 arrives daily from London via Chester (8hr., 1 per day, £21). The **tourist office,** on Castle St., is opposite the castle gate. (☎ 67 22 32. Open Apr.-Oct. daily 10am-6pm; Nov.-Mar. Th-Tu 9:30am-4:30pm.) Stay in comfortable bunks at **Totter's Hostel,** 2 High St. (☎ 67 29 63. Dorms £10.) The **Floating Restaurant,** in the waters of Slate Quay, is good for a bite. (☎ 67 28 96. Open Easter to mid-Sept. 10:30am-7:30pm.) Join the town and down a pint at **Anglesey Arms** on the Promenade just below the castle. (Open M-Sa 11am-11pm, Su noon-10:30pm.)

BANGOR
☎ 02148

This victorian port and university town is a convenient base for exploring the nearby Isle of Anglesey. The wildly opulent **Penrhyn Castle** stands testament to the staggering wealth accumulated by Welsh slate barons over a century ago. To get there, walk up High St. toward the pier, turn right on the A5122, and head 1mi. north. (Open W-M July-Aug. 11am-5pm; late Mar.-June and Sept.-Oct. noon-5pm. £5.) **Trains** arrive on Holyhead Rd., at the end of Deiniol Rd., from Chester (1¼hr., £11.90) and Holyhead (30min., £5). **Buses** roll in on Garth Rd., down the hill from the town clock; Arriva Cymru arrives from Holyhead (#4; 1¼hr.; M-Sa 2 per hr., Su 6 per day; £2.75). Arriva comes from Caernarfon (#5, 5a, 5b, 5c, and 5x; 25min.; every 10min.-1hr.; £2.35) and Conwy (#5 and 5X; 40min.; M-Sa 1-2 per hr., Su 5 per day; £2.35) TrawsCambria bus #701 follows the coast from Cardiff (7¾hr., £19.80). National Express arrives from London (7½hr., 2 per day, £21). The **tourist office,** in the Town Hall, is on Deiniol Rd. opposite Theatre Gwynedd. (☎35 27 86. Open Easter-Sept. daily 10am-1pm and 2-6pm; Oct.-Easter F-Sa 10am-1pm and 2-6pm.) To get to the **YHA Bangor,** in Tan-y-Bryn, ½ mi. from the town center, follow High St. to the water and turn right at the end on A5122 (Beach Rd.), then turn right again at the sign. (☎35 35 16. Reception 7am-11pm. Open Jan.-Nov. Dorms £9.80, under 18 £6.75.) High St. has a wide array of fruit shops and cafes, as well as a **Kwik Save** supermarket. (Open M-W and Sa 8:30am-6pm, Th-F 8:30am-7pm, Su 10am-4pm.)

CONWY. The central attraction of this modern tourist mecca is the 13th-century **Conwy Castle,** built as yet another link in Edward I's chain of impressive North Wales fortresses. (Open June-Sept. daily 9:30am-6pm; Apr.-May and Oct. daily 9:30am-5pm; Nov.-Mar. M-Sa 9:30am-4pm, Su 11am-4pm. £3.50, students £2.50.) **Arriva Cymru** (☎ (08706) 08 26 08) buses #5 and 5X frequently arrive from Caernarfon and Bangor (£2.85). **National Express** buses (☎ (08705) 80 80 80) arrive from: London (7hr., 1 per day, £19); Chester (2hr., 1 per day, £15); and Manchester (3½hr., 1 per day, £10.75). Find bus timetables at the **tourist office,** at the entrance to the castle. (☎ (01492) 59 22 48. Open daily Mar.-Oct. noon-6pm; Nov.-Mar. 10am-4pm.) To reach the **YHA Conwy,** Larkhill, Sychnant Pass Rd., head down Bangor Rd. from Lancaster Sq., turn left up Mt. Pleasant, and right at the top of the hill. (☎ (01492) 59 35 71. Open mid-Feb. to Dec. Dorms £11.90, under 18 £8.20.)

ISLE OF ANGELSEY

The ancient Isle of Anglesey, (meaning "Mona, the mother of Wales," in Welsh) attracts visitors to the prehistoric ruins and eerie Celtic burial mounds set in its flat landscape. **Bryn Celli Ddu** (bryn kay-HLEE thee), "The Mound in the Dark Grove," is a burial chamber dating from the late Neolithic period and the most famous of Anglesey's remains. Take Bangor-Holyhead bus #4 (M-Sa 9 per day) and walk 1 ++mi. from the staion, or walk there from Llanfair P.G.; ask at the tourist office. Less prehistoric is **Beaumaris Castle,** in Beaumaris, the last of Edward I's Welsh fortresses and today a World Heritage site. (Open June-Sept. daily 9:30am-6pm; Apr.-May and Oct. daily 9:30am-5pm; Nov.-Mar. M-Sa 9:30am-4pm, Su 11am-4pm. £2.20, students £1.70.) Across the Britannia Bridge from Bangor sits the longest-named village in the world, **Llanfairpwllgwyngyllgogerychwyrndrobwllllantysiliogogogoch** (Llanfair P.G.), although there's little to see apart from the sign at the train station. Llanfair P.G. holds Anglesey's sole **tourist office.** (☎ (01248) 713177; fax 715711. Open Apr.-Oct. M-Sa 9:30am-5:30pm, Su 10am-5pm; Nov.-Mar. M-F 9:30am-1pm and 1:30-5pm, Su 10am-5pm.) **Ferries** run to Dublin and Dún Laoghaire, Ireland from Holyhead. Get to Holyhead via **train** (☎ (08457) 48 49 50) from London (6hr., £57.30); Bangor (30min., £5.05); or Chester (1½hr., £16.15). Arriva Cymru **bus** #4 (☎ (01248) 75 04 44) travels from Bangor via Llanfair P.G. (1¼hr.; 2-6 per hr., £2.75).

SCOTLAND

At its best, Scotland is a world apart, a defiantly distinct nation within the United Kingdom with a culture and view all its own. Exuberant Glasgow boasts a mind-bending nightlife, Aberdeen features grand, regal architecture, and Edinburgh is the festive epicenter of Scottish culture. A little over half the land size of England but with a tenth of its population, Scotland possesses open spaces and natural splendor its southern neighbor cannot rival. The heather-covered mountains and glassy lochs of the west coast and luminescent mists of the Hebrides demand worship; the farmlands to the south and the rolling river valleys of the east coast display a gentler beauty; and the frayed northwestern coast, cut by sea lochs and girded by islands, remains the most beautiful region in Scotland and one of the last stretches of true wilderness in Western Europe.

◤ TRANSPORTATION

National Express buses (☎ (08705) 80 80 80) connecting England with **Glasgow** and **Edinburgh** (7hr., 2 per day, £22) are much cheaper than **ScotRail trains** (☎ (0141) 332 98 11 or (08547) 48 49 50; 6hr., round-trip £50). **British Airways** (☎ (08457) 773 33 77) sells a limited number of APEX return tickets from £70. **British Midland** (☎ (08706) 07 05 55) offers a Saver fare from **London** to **Glasgow** (from £70 round-trip). Reserve as far ahead as possible (at least 2 weeks) for the cheapest fare. Scotland is also linked by **ferry** to **Northern Ireland**. From **Stranraer, Stena Line** (☎ (1233) 64 68 26) ferries skim the water to **Belfast** (1¾hr.-3¼hr., 10 per day, £20-27).

Frequent trains and buses run throughout the **Lowlands** (south of Stirling and north of the Borders). In the **Highlands,** trains snake slowly on a few restricted routes, bypassing almost the entire Northwest region. Bus service reduces in the Northwest Highlands and grinds to a standstill on Sundays. In general, **buses** are more frequent and extensive than trains and are always cheaper. **Citylink** (☎ (08705) 50 50 50) operates most inter-city service buses. The **Freedom of Scotland Travelpass** (any 4 in 8 days £79, any 8 in 15 days £109) allows unlimited train travel and transportation on certain ferry lines. Purchase the pass at almost any train station or order through Rail Europe (see p. 47). **Hop-on, hop-off bus tours** are often a good way to reach more inaccessible areas: try **Haggis,** 60 High St., Edinburgh EH1 1NB (☎ (0131) 557 9393; www.radicaltravel.com; day tour £19, 3-day £79, 6-day £139; Flexitour from £69); or **MacBackpackers,** 105 High St., Edinburgh EH1 1SG (☎ (0131) 558 99 00; www.macbackpackers.com; 3-day £55, 5-day £89, 7-day £129).

EDINBURGH   ☎0131

Framed by rolling hills and the blue Firth of Forth, Edinburgh (ED-din-bur-ra; pop. 500,000) is the jewel of Scotland. The country's capital since the 12th century, seeds of Reformation were sown in the 16th century when John Knox became the minister of the High Kirk of St. Giles. An outpouring of talent later made the city a capital of the Enlightenment: the philosopher David Hume presided over a republic of letters that fostered both Adam Smith's invisible hand and the literary wanderings of Sir Walter Scott. Today, Edinburgh Castle stands watch over a litany of literary ghosts, exuberant festivals, and the omnipresent pint of dark ale.

◤ TRANSPORTATION

Flights: Edinburgh International Airport, 7 mi. west of the city center (☎333 10 00). **LRT's Airlink 100** (☎555 63 63; £3.30) and the **Edinburgh Airbus Express** (☎556 22 44; £3.60) shuttle to the airport (25min.); both depart from Waverley Bridge.

Edinburgh

ACCOMMODATIONS
- Argyle Backpackers, 6
- Brodie's, 4
- Castle Rock Hostel, 1
- Edinburgh Backpackers, 2
- High St. Hostel, 3
- Royal Mile Backpackers' Hostel, 5

200 yards
200 meters

N

Palace of Holyroodhouse

HILLSIDE
Brunswick Rd.
Montgomery St.
Hillside Cr.
London Rd.
Brunswick St.
Windsor St.
Leith Walk
GAYFIELD SQ.
Greenside Row
Greenside Ln.
Union St.
Forth St.
Broughton St.
Broughton Pl.
TO ROYAL BOTANIC GARDEN
Barony St.
Albany St.
Dublin St. Ln. S.
York Pl.
Dublin St.
Northumberland St.
Abercromby Pl.
Nelson St.
St. Andrew St.
Howe St.
Hanover St.
India St.
Gloucester Ln.
Heriot Row
Queen St.
Hill St.
Thistle St.
George St.
Rose St.
Castle St.
Frederick St.
Young St.
Charles St.
CHARLOTTE SQ.
Glenfinlas Pl.
Ainslie Pl.
Moray Pl.
Great Stuart St.
Randolph Cres.
Queensferry St.
Melville St.
Ava St.
Water of Leith
Dean Bridge

CALTON
Calton Hill
Regent Gdns.
Royal Terr.
Regent Terr.
Regent Rd.
United States
National Monument
Nelson Monument
City Observatory
Calton Rd.
Canongate
Old Tolbooth Wynd
Huntly House
St. John St.
New St.
Holyrood Rd.
Dumbiedykes Rd.
Queen's Drive
Viewcraig Gdns.
Pleasance St.
Canongate Tolbooth and People's Story Museum
Museum of Childhood
St. Mary's St.
Adam St.
Roxburgh
Richmond
Nicolson Sq.
NICOLSON ST.
St. Coll. St.
Potter Row
Lothian St.
University of Edinburgh
High St.
Blackfriars St.
Niddry St.
South Bridge
John Knox's House
E. Market St.
North Br.
Cockburn St.
Market St.
Waterloo Pl.
St. Mary's Cathedral
St. James Centre
St. Andrew's Sq.
Clyde St.
W. Register St.
Register House
St. ANDREW SQ.
Waverley Station
Waverley Br.
North Br.
High Kirk of St. Giles
Parliament House and Law Courts
Cowgate
National Library of Scotland
George IV Br.
Chambers St.
Royal Museum of Scotland
Greyfriars Kirk
Candlemaker Row
Victoria St.
Lawnmarket
Grassmarket
Scottish National Portrait Gallery and Museum of Antiquities
Portrait Gallery
St. Australia St.
David St.
Assembly Rooms
Royal Scottish Academy
Walter Scott Monument
National Gallery
The Mound
Gladstone's Land
Lady Stair's Bank House
St.
Scotch Whisky Heritage Center
Outlook Tower and Camera Obscura
Edinburgh Castle
West Princes Street Gdns.
Princes St.
Georgian House
American Express
King's Stables Rd.
Castle Terr.
Royal Lyceum Theatre
Grindlay St.
Johnston Terr.
West Port
Lawson St.
Vennel
Heriot Pl.
Keir
Lauriston Pl.
Royal Infirmary
Chalmers
High Riggs
Lauriston
Bread St.
Lothian Rd.
Earl Grey St.
TOLLCROSS
Tollcross
W. Tollcross
Lochrin Pl.
Morrison St.
Gardner's Cr.
Canning St.
Shandwick Pl.
Rutland Sq.
Canada
Moore-Geraty Pl.

To 6 (500m)
Forrest Rd.

BRITAIN

Trains: Waverley Station (☎ (0345) 48 49 50), near the center of town between North and Waverley Bridges. To: **Glasgow** (1hr., 2 per hr., £7.30); **Aberdeen** (2½hr., every hr., £32.80); and **London's** King's Cross (5hr., every 30min., £70-86).

Buses: The **south side of St. Andrew Sq.** (☎ (08705) 50 59 50) 3 blocks from the east end of Princes St., serves as the temporary **St. Andrew Sq. Bus Station** until 2002. **Scottish Citylink** buses (☎ (0990) 50 50 50) serve: **Glasgow** (2 per hr., £3); **Inverness** (every hr., £13.50); and **Aberdeen** (every hr., £14.50). **National Express** goes to **London** twice daily (£22).

Public Transportation: Although your feet will suffice, and are often faster, Edinburgh does have an efficient, comprehensive bus system. **Lothian Regional Transport (LRT)**, (☎555 63 63), with a fleet of maroon double-deckers, provides the best service. Be sure to carry coins; drivers do not carry much change for the 80p-£1 fares. You can buy a one-day **Day-Saver Ticket** (£2.40, children £1.50), and longer-term passes from any driver or from the main office, 1-4 Shrub Pl., on the Old Town side of Waverley Bridge.

Bike Rental: Edinburgh Rent-a-Bike, 29 Blackfriars St. (☎556 55 60), off High St. Bikes £5-15 per day. City tours and Highland safaris also available. Open July-Sept. 9am-9pm; Oct.-June 10am-6pm.

Hitchhiking: *Let's Go* does not recommend hitching. Those who choose to hitch to Newcastle, York, or Durham often take bus #15, 26, or 43 to get to the Musselburgh and A1 where they can be picked up; to other points south, bus #4 or 15 to Fairmilehead and A702 to Biggar. To points north, one can take bus #18 or 40 to Barnton and the Forth Rd. Bridge for better chances.

◆ 🔢 ORIENTATION AND PRACTICAL INFORMATION

Edinburgh's short distances, quiet streets, and abundance of shops make it a glorious city for walking—just remember that because it is a city on a hill, you'll be hiking up as well as down. Princes St. is the main thoroughfare in New Town, the northern section of Edinburgh. The Royal Mile (Lawnmarket, High St., and Canongate) is the major road in the Old Town—the southern half of the city—and connects Edinburgh Castle and Holyrood Palace. North Bridge, Waverley Bridge, and The Mound connect the Old and New Towns. Waverley train station lies between North Bridge and Waverley Bridge, in what used to be a loch. The St. Andrew Sq. bus station is three short blocks from the east end of Princes St.

Tourist Office: Edinburgh and Scotland Information Centre, Waverley Market, 3 Princes St. (☎473 38 00), next to Waverley Station. Books rooms for a £3 fee with a 10% deposit. Sells bus, tour, and theater tickets. Open July-Aug. M-Sa 9am-8pm, Su 10am-8pm; May-June and Sept. closes at 7pm; Oct.-Apr. closes at 6pm.

Budget Travel Services: Radical Travel Center, 60 High St. (☎557 93 93), is geared toward backpackers. Open daily 8am-7pm. **Edinburgh Travel Centre,** in Potterow Union, Bristo Sq. (☎668 22 21). Also at 92 South Clerk St. (☎667 94 88). Both open M-W and F 9am-5:30pm, Th 10am-5:30pm, Sa 10am-1pm.

American Express: 139 Princes St. (☎718 25 03), 5 long blocks west of Waverley Station. Mail held. Open M-F 9am-5:30pm, Sa 9am-4pm.

Gay and Lesbian Services: Gay and Lesbian Switchboard (☎556 40 49). Pick up *Gay Information* at the tourist office or *Gay Scotland* at bookstores.

Emergency: Dial 999; no coins required. **Police,** 5 Fettes Ave. (☎311 31 31).

Crisis Lines: Rape Crisis Center, (☎556 94 37). Staffed M-W and F 7-9pm, Th 1-3pm, Sa 9:30-11am.

Hospital: Royal Infirmary of Edinburgh, 1 Lauriston Pl. (☎536 10 00 or 536 40 40 for emergencies). From The Mound, take bus #23 or 27.

Internet Access: easyEverything, 58 Rose St. (☎220 35 77), is the undisputed champion of cheap internet access. Rates fluctuate, but £1 can often get you as many as 3hr. of emailing. Open 24hr.

Post Office: Main office at 8-10 St. James Centre (☎556 95 46). Address mail to be held: Jack Daniels, *Poste Restante,* GPO, 8-10 St. James Centre, Edinburgh **EH1 3SR,** Scotland, UK. Open M 9am-5:30pm, Tu-F 8:30am-5:30pm, Sa 8:30am-6pm.

BRITAIN

ACCOMMODATIONS

Edinburgh is packed with backpacker hostels, but in Festival season (late July-early Sept.), there are few available rooms. Book ahead. The tourist office has free hostel lists and finds rooms ($3 with 10% deposit). Most of Edinburgh's countless **B&Bs** are clustered in three areas: **Bruntsfield** to the southwest, **Newington** in the southeast, and **Leith** in the northeast.

Brodie's Backpacker Hostel, 12 High St. (☎556 67 70), at St. Mary's St. Relaxed environment. Only 50 beds, so book ahead. Laundry. Reception open 7am-midnight. Sept.-July M-Th dorms £11.90, F-Su £13.50; higher in Aug.

Edinburgh Backpackers, 65 Cockburn St. (☎220 17 17, reservations 221 00 22), just off the Royal Mile. From North Bridge, turn right on High St. and take the 1st right. Organizes legendary pub crawls most Tuesdays in summer. Pool table, TV, **internet** access (£1.50 per 15min.), and showers. Reception 24hr. Dorms £12, £14 in Aug.

Argyle Backpackers, 14 Argyle Pl. (☎667 99 91; email argylr@aol.co.uk), south of the Meadows and the Royal Mile. From the train station, take bus #40 or 41 from The Mound to Melville Dr. or walk left and turn left on Waverley Bridge; walk straight, across the Royal Mile, over the George IV Br., veering right onto Forrest Rd. and through the park. Charming rooms and lounge with TV. Reception 9am-11pm. Check-out 10:30am. Dorms £10-15; doubles and twins £15-20.

Castle Rock Hostel, 15 Johnston Terr. (☎225 96 66). Walk toward the Castle on Royal Mile, then turn left on Johnston Terr. Gigantic hostel with views of the castle. Breakfast £1.60. Laundry £2.50. **Internet** £1.80 per 30min. Dorms £10.50-12.

Royal Mile Backpackers, 105 High St. (☎557 61 20). Walk down High St. from Cockburn St.; this new hostel is directly opposite the yellow Telecom Centre. Go upstairs and veer left. Free High St. walking tours, pub crawls, and movies. Dorms £10.50-12.

High St. Hostel, 8 Blackfriars St. (☎557 39 84). Edinburgh's original hostel lacks a bit of the polish of the affiliated Royal Mile and Castle Rock hostels, but you can enjoy a pool table, TV, and movies. Dorms £10.50-12.

SYHA Eglinton, 18 Eglinton Crescent (☎337 11 20). A mile west of the town center, near Haymarket train station. Walk on Princes St. away from Calton Hill as it becomes Shandwick Pl. Turn right onto Palmerston Pl. and take the second left onto Eglinton Crescent. Or take bus #3, 4, 33 or 44 from Princes St. to Palmerston Pl. Clean and quiet. Continental breakfast included; evening meal £4.20. Reception 7am-midnight. Check-out 9:30am. Curfew 2am. Open Jan.-Nov. Dorms £11.25-13.75.

City Centre Tourist Hostel, 5 West Register St. (☎/fax 556 80 70; email ccth@hostel1.fsnet.co.uk.) Impossibly close to Waverley Station, turn right onto Princes St., take tiny West Register St. by the Burger King, across from the Balmoral Hotel. Veer left at the Guilford Pub. Immaculate and quiet. 24hr. reception. Oct.-Feb. dorms £10, 7th night free each week; March-Sept. dorms at least £12.

Camping: Edinburgh Caravans (☎312 68 74), Marine Dr., by the Forth. Take bus #28A from Frederick St. off Princes St. (90p). Toilets, showers, and a shop. Open Apr.-Oct. £4 per person, £3 per tent, £1.50 per car.

FOOD

You can get haggis cheap in many pubs. South Clerk St. and Lothian Rd. have plenty of shops offering reasonably priced Chinese or Indian takeout. For groceries, try **Sainsbury's Central** on South Saint David St., just north of the Scott monument (open M-Sa 7am-9pm, Su 9am-8pm).

The Basement, 10a-12a Broughton St (☎557 00 97). The menu changes daily, with plenty of vegetarian options and Thai and Mexican specialties. A lively mix of students and musicians in its candle-lit, cavernous environment. Kitchen open daily noon-10pm.

The Black Medicine Coffee Co., 2 Nicolson St. (☎622 72 09). Native American decor surrounds a mellow student crowd. Live music Th-Su in late afternoon. Sandwiches and pastries (£1-4). Open daily 8am-8pm.

BRITAIN

HAGGIS: WHAT'S IN THERE? Although restaurants throughout Scotland produce steamin' plates o' haggis for eager tourists, we at *Let's Go* believe all should know what's inside that strange-looking bundle before taking the plunge. An age-old recipe calls for the following ingredients: the large stomach bag of a sheep, the small (knight's hood) bag, the pluck (including lungs, liver, and heart), beef, suet, oatmeal, onions, pepper, and salt. Today's haggis is available conveniently canned and includes: lamb, lamb offal, oatmeal, wheat flour, beef, suet, onions, salt, spices, stock, and liquor (1%). Restaurants will probably serve it to you in non-traditional forms as well: unbagged (like a sloppy joe), vegetarian, and deep-fried in batter and 6 inches of grease.

The Last Drop, 72-74 Grassmarket. "Haggis, tatties, and neeps" (haggis, potatoes, and turnips) in omnivorous and veggie versions. The whole menu (save the steak) is £3 for students and hostelers until 7:30 pm. A packed pub at night. Open daily 10am-2am.

Ndebele, 57 Home St (☎221 11 41). Named after a southern African tribe, it serves copious amounts of exotic grub for under £5. Daily African specials and a huge array of African and South American coffees and juices. Open daily 10am-10pm.

Kebab Mahal, 7 Nicolson Sq (☎667 52 14). An Indian restaurant where chicken *tikka masala* is the specialty (£5.25) but the kebabs (£2.25-4.50) are good, too. Open Su-Th noon-midnight, F-Sa noon-2am; closed F for lunch.

The City Cafe, 19 Blair St. (☎220 0125). Right off the Royal Mile behind the Tron Kirk, this Edinburgh institution serves venison burgers (£4-6) and incredible shakes, immortalized in the movie *Trainspotting*. Dance club downstairs. Food served until 10pm. Open daily 11am-1am.

👁 SIGHTS

With museums, gardens and castles in abundance, Edinburgh is a marvel of sights. Experience the heritage of this Scottish capital city from the traditional to the contemporary on a tour from Edinburgh Castle to the new Scottish Parliament, with stops at the Royal Museum and Holyrood Park between.

THE OLD TOWN AND THE ROYAL MILE

The Royal Mile (Lawnmarket, High St., Canongate) defines the length of the Old Town. Defended by Edinburgh Castle at the top of the hill and the Palace of Holyroodhouse at the bottom, the Old Town once packed thousands of inhabitants into a few square miles—still visible in the narrow shop fronts and thirteen-story slum buildings—but today the street is more the domain of tourists than slum lords.

▨ EDINBURGH CASTLE. Crowning the top of the Royal Mile, the castle contains many structures that were rebuilt in recent centuries. Inside, **St. Margaret's Chapel,** a 12th-century Norman church, is believed to be the oldest structure in Edinburgh. The castle also displays the 15th-century Scottish Crown Jewels, and the legendary **Stone of Scone.** *(At the top of the Royal Mile. Open daily Apr.-Sept. 9:30am-6pm; Oct.-Mar. 9:30am-5pm. £7.)*

ALONG THE ROYAL MILE. Near the Castle, through Milne's Close, the new Scottish Parliament convenes in the temporary Debating Chamber. Watch the MPs debate. *(Sept.-June, W 2:30-5:30pm, Th 9:30am-12:30pm and 2:30-5:30pm. Free.)* You can also get reserved tickets (bookings ☎348 54 11) in the nearby Visitor Centre, at the corner of the Royal Mile and the George IV Bridge. *(☎348 50 00, www.scottish.parliament.uk. Open Sept.-June M and F 10am-5pm; Tu-Th 9am-5pm; July-Aug. M-F 10am-5pm, Sa same hours for August and early September. Last admission 15 minutes before closing. Free.)* Nearby, Lady Stair's House, a 17th-century townhouse, contains the Writer's Museum, with memorabilia and manuscripts belonging to three of Scotland's greatest literary figures: Robert Burns, Sir Walter Scott, and Robert Louis Stevenson. *(Through the passage at 477 Lawnmarket St. Open M-Sa 10am-5pm; during Festival also*

Su 2-5pm. Free.) The High Kirk of St. Giles (St. Giles Cathedral), Scotland's principal church, once stood at the center of the country's turbulent religious history. Here, John Knox delivered the fiery Presbyterian sermons that drove Mary, Queen of Scots, into exile. Now it offers free concerts year-round. *(Where Lawnmarket becomes High St., opposite Parliament. Open Easter to mid-Sept. M-F 9am-7pm, Sa 9am-5pm, Su 1-5pm; mid-Sept. to Easter M-Sa 9am-5pm, Su 1-5pm. Donation £1.)* The 17th-century chapel Canongate Kirk is the resting place of Adam Smith; royals also worship here when in residence. Canongate, the steep hill at the end of the Mile, has two museums and an excellent Scottish Poetry Library, all of them free. *(Museums open M-Sa 10am-5pm; during Festival also Su 2-5pm. Library open M-F noon-6pm, Sa noon-4pm.)*

PALACE OF HOLYROODHOUSE. Once the home of Mary, Queen of Scots, this spectacular Stewart palace, which dates from the 16th and 17th centuries, is now Queen Elizabeth II's official residence in Scotland. Behind the palace lies the 12th-century abbey ransacked during the Reformation. *(At the eastern end of the Royal Mile. Open Apr.-Oct. daily 9:30am-5:15pm; Nov.-Mar. M-Sa 9:30am-3:45pm; closed during official residences in late May and late June-early July. £6.)*

OTHER SIGHTS IN THE OLD TOWN. On Chambers St., just south of the George IV Bridge, the new **Museum of Scotland** and the connected **Royal Museum** are not to be missed. The former houses a definitive collection of Scottish artifacts in a stunning contemporary building; the latter contains a varied mix of art and natural history, plus the new **Millennium Clock** which chimes every hour. *(Open M and W-Sa 10am-5pm, Tu 10am-8pm, Su noon-5pm. Admission includes both museums; £3, students £1.50. Free Tu 4:30-8pm.)* Just across the street stands the statue of the loyal pooch Greyfriars' Bobby, marking the entrance to **Greyfriars Kirk,** built in 1620 in a beautiful and supposedly haunted churchyard. *(Gaelic services Su 12:30pm, English at 11am. Kirk visiting hours Easter-Oct. M-F 10:30am-4:30pm, Sa until 2:30pm. Free.)* Be sure to explore the nearby streets: **Candlemaker's Row, Victoria St.,** and the **Grassmarket,** where Edinburgh's criminals once hung from the gallows.

THE NEW TOWN

Edinburgh's New Town is a masterpiece of Georgian planning. James Craig, a 23-year-old architect, won the city planning contest in 1767 with the design you see today: the three main parallel streets (Queen, George, and Princes) form a rectangular, symmetrical gridiron linking two large squares (Charlotte and St. Andrew). The design was chosen to reflect the Scottish Enlightenment's belief in order. Another stop in your stroll through the New Town is the elegant **Georgian House,** a restored townhouse. *(7 Charlotte Sq. From Princes St., turn right on Charlotte St. and take your 2nd left. Open Apr.-Oct. M-Sa 10am-5pm, Su 2-5pm. £5, students £3.50.)* The **Walter Scott Monument** is a grotesque Gothic "steeple without a church" containing statues of Scott and his dog. Climb the winding 287-step staircase for an eagle's-eye view of Princes St. Gardens, the castle, and Old Town's Market St. *(On Princes St., between The Mound and Waverley Bridge. Open Apr.-Sept. M-Sa 9am-6pm; Oct.-Mar. M-Sa 9am-3pm. £2.50.)*

THE NATIONAL GALLERIES. Today, you can enlighten yourself by viewing the premier works of art in the elegant New Town buildings of the **National Galleries of Scotland.** There are four galleries, and all are free (sometimes a charge for special exhibits), top-rate, and a free shuttle bus runs between them every hour. *(All open M-Sa 10am-5pm, Su noon-5pm.)* The flagship of these four is the **National Gallery of Scotland,** on the Mound, which houses a superb collection of works by Renaissance, Romantic, and Impressionist masters and a fine spread of Scottish art. *(This gallery also open during Festival M-Sa 10am-6pm, Su 11am-6pm.)* The **Scottish National Portrait Gallery,** 1 Queen St., north of St. Andrew Sq, mounts the mugs of famous Scots. To west of town, across the street from each other, are the **Scottish National Gallery of Modern Art,** 75 Belford Rd., and the new **Dean Gallery,** 73 Belford Rd., specializing in Surrealist and Dada art. You can also take Bus #13 from Princes St. or walk (15 min.) down Queensferry Rd. and then Beford Rd. For information on Edinburgh's other (mostly free) museums, pick up the *Edinburgh Gallery Guide* at the tourist office.

GARDENS AND PARKS. You're depriving yourself of quite an experience if you don't at least try to climb **Arthur's Seat,** the extinct volcano at the east end of the city and Edinburgh's sample of the Highlands. Along with the **Salisbury Crags,** it rises from the vast **Holyrood Park,** at the east end of the Royal Mile; a relatively easy 45-min. walk up the mountain culminates with a stunning view of the city. For more great views, try the even easier **Calton Hill,** just past the east end of Princes St., which also boasts the towering **Nelson Monument** and an ersatz Parthenon. A little more manicured are the lovely **Royal Botanic Gardens,** north of the city centre. Keep walking north along Hanover St. from Princes St. or take buses #23 or 27. (☎ 552 71 71. Open daily Apr.-Aug. 9:30am-7pm; Mar. and Sept. until 6pm; Feb. and Oct. until 5pm; Nov.-Jan. until 4pm. Free.)

🎵 ENTERTAINMENT AND NIGHTLIFE

The summer season overflows with music in the gardens and a multitude of theater and film events around town. For details on pubs and clubs, pick up *The List* (£1.95). Perhaps the most omnipresent form of tourist entertainment are the countless **walking tours** available around the city. The most worthwhile is the McEwan's Edinburgh Literary Pub Tour (☎ 226 66 65), a 2hr. alcohol-friendly crash course in Scottish literature, led by professional actors. (£7, children and students £5).

HIKING. If you have limited time in Scotland, there is a thriving industry of back-packer tour companies eager to whisk you away into the Highlands. The two main companies, **MacBackpackers** (105 High St. ☎ 558 99 00; www.macbackpackers.com. Day trips £15, 3-7 day tours £39-129, Jump on-Jump off £55), and **HAGGIS** (60 High St. ☎ 557 93 93; www.radicaltravel.com. Day trips £19, 3-6 day tours £79-139, Flexi-tour from £85), both offer a number of 1-7 day tours of the Highlands which depart from Edinburgh. Especially good are their hop-on, hop-off tours which let you travel Scotland at your own pace, but with the convenience of their transportation and company. An alternative is **Celtic Connection,** which covers both Scotland and Ireland in a variety of 3-7 day tours, with one-way, round-trip, or jump on-jump off options. Book ahead whatever you decide on. Prices do not include lodging. (☎ 225 3330; www.thecelticconnection.co.uk. Tours £85-149.)

THEATER, MUSIC AND FILM. The **Festival Theatre,** 13-29 Nicholson St., stages ballet and opera, while the affiliated **King's Theatre,** 2 Leven St., promotes serious and comedic fare, musicals, and opera. Same-day seats (£5.50) for the Festival Theatre go on sale daily at 10am. (☎ 529 60 00. Box office open daily 11am-6pm.) Scottish bands and country dancing abound at the **Ross Open-Air Theatre.** (☎ 228 86 16. From 7pm). The **Filmhouse,** 88 Lothian Rd., offers quality cinema—European, art house, and Hollywood. (☎ 228 2688. Tickets £1.20-5.20.)

FESTIVALS. For a few weeks in August, Edinburgh hosts the spectacular **Edinburgh International Festival** (Aug. 12-Sept. 1 in 2001), featuring a kaleidoscopic program of music, drama, dance, and art. Tickets (£4-44) are sold beginning in April, but you can usually get tickets at the door; look for half-price tickets after 1pm on performance days. For tickets and a schedule, contact **The HUB,** Edinburgh's Festival Centre, Castlehill, Edinburgh EH1 2NE. It's the church-like structure just downhill from the Castle. (Info ☎ 473 20 01, bookings 473 20 00; www.edinburgh-festivals.co.uk). Around the festival has grown a more spontaneous **Festival Fringe** (Aug. 5-27 in 2001), which now includes over 500 amateur and professional companies presenting theater, comedy, children's shows, folk and classical music, poetry, dance, and opera events that budget travelers may find more suitable for their wallets (usually free-£5). Contact the **Fringe Festival Office,** 180 High St., Edinburgh EH1 1QS. (☎ 226 52 57, bookings 226 51 38; www.edfringe.com. Box office open July M-F 10am-6pm; daily in August.) Another August festival is the **Military Tattoo**—a spectacle of military bands, bagpipes, and drums—considered by some to be the highlight of the month. For tickets (£8-20), contact the **Tattoo Ticket Sale Office,** 33-34 Market St. (☎ 225 11 88; fax 225 86 27. Open M-F 10am-4:30pm or until the show. Shows M-Sa night.) And finally don't forget, the excellent **International Film Festival** (Aug. 12-26 in 2001 at The Filmhouse; ☎228 4051; tickets on sale at end of July). and **International Jazz and Blues Festival** (July 27-Aug. 5 in 2001; ☎467 52 00, tickets £5-30 go on sale in May).

NIGHTLIFE. If you can't find a pub in Edinburgh, you're not looking hard enough. Edinburgh claims to have the highest density of pubs anywhere in Europe, and we don't doubt it. Any news agent can provide you with an indispensable guide to the hippest of these pubs and clubs: *The List* (£1.95) is life. Pubs directly on the **Royal Mile** usually attract an older crowd, while students tend to loiter in the **Old Town** pubs clustered around the university. **The Tron,** 9 Hunter Sq., off the High St. is smashingly popular with smashingly drunk youths, who benefit from its many student/hosteler deals. There's frequent live music on its three hopping floors. (☎226 09 31. Open daily 11:30am-1am.) Just across the street is **The City Cafe,** 19 Blair St., with its smoky bar and pool tables upstairs and dance club below. More of the young and tightly-clad frequent **The Three Sisters,** 139 Cowgate, a packed indoors/ outdoors pub and meat market. (Open daily 9am-1am.) **Sheep's Heid Inn,** in the sleepy village of Duddingston, take bus #42 from The Mound, is Scotland's oldest licensed drinking establishment, with an ancient outdoor garden. (Open M-Sa 11am-11pm, Su 12:30-11pm.) The new **Espionage Bar and Club Complex,** Victoria St., has five floors of trendy partying in exotic settings. (No cover. Open daily 5pm-3am, until 4am on weekends.) Meanwhile, jazz enthusiasts crowd **The Cellar Bar,** 1 Chambers St, and **The Jazz Joint,** 8 Morrison St. **C.C. Blooms** (a raging dance club), on Leith St., and the **Blue Moon Cafe** (a mellow coffeeshop), on the corner of Broughton St. and Barony St., are especially popular.

◪ DAYTRIP FROM EDINBURGH

ST. ANDREWS
Fife Scottish buses (☎47 42 38) pull in from Edinburgh (bus X59 or X60; 2hr., every hr., £5.70, students £3.60). Trains (☎ (0345) 55 00 33) stop 5 mi. away at Leuchars (from Edinburgh 1hr., every hr., £8.10), where buses #93, 94, 95, and 96 (£1.45) depart for St. Andrews.

In St. Andrews, golf is the game; the rules of the sport were even formally established here. The **Old Course,** a frequent site of the British Open, is a golf pilgrim's Canterbury. (☎ (01334) 46 66 66 or fax 47 70 36 for reservations; or enter the on-the-spot lottery for starting times. £80 per round.) The **Balgove Course** is a much cheaper alternative offering 9 holes for £7. If you're more interested in watching than playing, the **British Golf Museum,** next to the Old Course, details the ancient origins of golf. (Open Easter-Oct. daily 9:30am-5:30pm; Nov.-Easter Th-M 11am-3pm. £3.75, students £2.75.) Despite the onslaught of pastel and polyester, one need not worship the wedge to love this city; its medieval streets and castle ruins transcend even golf. Though today it's only a shell, in the Middle Ages pilgrims journeyed to **St. Andrews Cathedral** to pray at the Saint's Shrine. Nearby, **St. Andrews Castle** maintains secret tunnels, bottle-shaped dungeons, and high stone walls to keep rebellious heretics in or out. (Cathedral and castle open daily Apr.-Sept. 9:30am-6:30pm; Oct.-Mar. 9:30am-4:30pm. Joint ticket £3.75.) Scotland's oldest (Britain's third oldest) university, **St. Andrews,** founded in the 15th century, lies just west of the castle, between North St. and The Scores.

To get to the **tourist office,** 70 Market St., from the bus station, turn right on City Rd. and take the first left. (☎ (01334) 47 20 21; fax 47 84 22; www.standrews.co.uk. Open July-Aug. M-Sa 9:30am-7pm, Su 11am-6pm; May-June and Sept. M-Sa 9:30am-6pm, Su 11am-5pm; Apr. closes daily at 5pm; Oct.-March M-Sa 9:30am-5pm.) Just across the street, hop on the **internet** at Costa Coffee, 83 Market St. (£1.50 per 15min., students 75p. Open M-Sa 8am-8pm, Su 10am-8pm.) The tourist office has **B&B** lists (many B&Bs line Murray Pl. and Murray Park near the bus station). **Brownlees,** 7 Murray Pl., offers elegant housing only a few blocks from the Old Course (☎ (01334) 47 38 68. £18-25 per person).

GLASGOW ☎ 0141

Although it has traditionally suffered a reputation for industrial lackluster, Glasgow, Scotland's largest city (pop. 675,000), thrives with a renewed energy. The millions of pounds the city has poured into the arts are reflected in its free museums, extensive galleries, and first-rate theaters; the West End oozes with trendy creativity and energy. And while it rivals Edinburgh, its sister to the east, in cultural attractions, Glasgow also remains much less touristy, infused with a flourishing economy, a passion for football, and the energy of spirited locals.

▛ TRANSPORTATION

Flights: Glasgow Airport (☎887 11 11), 10 mi. west in Abbotsinch. Citylink buses connect to **Buchanan Station** (20min., 2 per hr., £3).

Trains: Two main stations. **Central Station,** on Gordon St. U: St. Enoch. To: **London-King's Cross** (5-6hr., 5-20 per day, £50) and **Stranraer** (2½hr., 3-8 per day, £15.30). **Queen St. Station,** on George Sq. U: Buchanan St. To: **Edinburgh** (50min., 2 per hr., £7.30); **Aberdeen** (2½hr., 11-24 per day, £36.40); and **Inverness** (3¼hr., 5 per day, £29.90). Bus #398 runs between the 2 stations (4 per hr., £0.50).

Buses: Buchanan Station (☎332 71 33), on North Hanover St., 2 blocks north of the Queen St. Station. **Scottish Citylink** (☎ (08705) 50 50 50) to: **Edinburgh** (1hr., 2-4 per hr., £3); **Aberdeen** (4hr., 12-24 per day, £14.50); **Inverness** (3½-4½hr., 1 per hr., £12.80); and **Oban** (3hr., 2-4 per day, £10.70). **National Express** (☎ (08705) 80 80 80) buses arrive daily from **London** (8hr.; 1 per hr.; £22, round-trip £31).

Public Transportation: The circular **Underground (U)** subway line, a.k.a. the "Clockwork Orange" runs M-Sa 6:30am-midnight, Su 11am-6pm. Single-fare £0.80. Wave to stop **buses,** and carry exact change. Single-fare £0.45-0.95.

✴ ▟ ORIENTATION AND PRACTICAL INFORMATION

George Sq. is the physical center of town. Sections of **Sauchiehall St., Argyle St.,** and **Buchanan St.,** are pedestrian areas. **Charing Cross,** in the northwest, where Bath St. crosses M8, is used as a general landmark. The vibrant **West End** revolves around **Byres Rd.** and **Glasgow University,** 1 mi. northwest of the city center. To reach the **tourist office** from **Central Station,** exit on **Union St.,** turn left, walk two blocks, turn right on **St. Vincent St.,** and it's 3½ blocks up on your right. From **Queen St. Station,** exit onto **George St.,** and cross George Sq. From the **Buchanan Bus Station,** exit on **North Hanover St.** and follow it right to George Sq.

Tourist Office: 11 George Sq. (☎204 44 00; fax 221 35 24). U: Buchanan St. Books rooms for £2 fee plus 10% deposit. **Walking tours** depart M-Sa 6pm, Su 10:30am (1½hr.; £5, students £4). Open July-Aug. M-Sa 9am-8pm, Su 10am-6pm; June and Sept. M-Sa 9am-7pm, Su 10am-6pm; Oct.-May M-Sa 9am-6pm.

Budget Travel: STA Travel, 184 Byres Rd. (☎338 60 00). Open M-Tu and F 9:30am-5:30pm, W 10:30am-5:30pm, Th 9:30am-7pm, Sa 11am-5pm.

American Express: 115 Hope St. (☎ (08706) 00 10 60). Open July-Aug. M-F 8:30am-5:30pm, Sa 9am-5pm; Sept.-June M-F 8:30am-5:30pm, Sa 9am-noon.

Laundromat: Coin-Op Laundromat, 39/41 Bank St. (☎339 89 53). U: Kelvin Bridge. Open M-F 9am-7:30pm, Sa-Su 9am-5pm.

Emergency: ☎999; no coins required. **Police:** (☎532 30 00), on Stewart St.

Hospital: Glasgow Royal Infirmary, 84-106 Castle St. (☎211 40 00).

Internet Access: The Internet Exchange Internet Cafe, 136 Sauchiehall St. Non-members £5.50 per hr., members £1.80-4.20 per hr.; membership is free. Also, **The Internet Café,** 569 Sauchiehall St. (☎564 10 52). £3 per 30min., students £2.50. Open M-Th 9am-11pm, F-Su 9am-7pm.

Post Office: 47 St. Vincent St. Address mail to be held: Alan TAYLOR, *Poste Restante,* 47 St. Vincent St., **G2 5QX** Glasgow, UK. Open M-F 8:30am-5:45pm, Sa 9am-5:30pm.

N

500 yards
500 meters

Pinkston Rd.

Broomhill Park

M8

TO QUEEN'S CROSS

Coin St.

ST. GEORGE'S CROSS

Great Western Rd.

Dobbie's Loan

Baird St.

Lister St.

St. James's Rd.

N. Wallace St.

Kyle St.

St. Mungo Ave.

Stirling Rd.

Castle St.

John Knox St.

Royal Infirmary

St. Mungo Museum

Glasgow Cathedral

Provand's Lordship

CATHEDRAL SQUARE

TO (600 yds)

High St.

Dobbie's Loan

North Hanover St.

Killermont St.

Cathedral St.

Campus Village

Strathclyde University

George St.

TO PEOPLES' PALACE

Taylor St.

Renton

Port Dundas

Craignir Rd.

Stewart St.

Milton St.

Cowcaddens Rd.

Buchanan Bus Station

Royal Concert Hall

Parliamentary Rd.

Theatre Royal

Glasgow Film Theater

COWCADDENS

Cambridge St.

Rose St.

Bath St.

Dalhousie St.

Biccleuch St.

W. Graham St.

Scott St.

Hill St.

Garnet St.

Glasgow School of Art

McLellan Galleries

Renfrew St.

Elmbank St.

W. Regent St.

Campbell St.

Blythswood St.

Douglas St.

Holland

Bothwell St.

Pitt St.

W. George St.

St. Vincent St.

Sauchiehall St.

Wellington St.

Hope St.

Renfield St.

W. Nile St.

Nile St.

Buchanan St.

BUCHANAN ST.

NELSON MANDELA PL.

Queen St. Station

City Chambers

GEORGE SQ.

Stirling's Library

Royal Exchange Sq.

Cochrane St.

Ingram St.

Glassford St.

Hutcheson St.

Virginia St.

Wilson St.

Albion St.

Bell St.

Trongate

Tron Steeple, Tron Theatre

Osborne St.

Bridgegate

Gallowgate

City Hall/Ticket Centre

Argyle Arcade

Prince's Sq.

Queen St.

Princes Sq.

Argyle St.

ST. ENOCH SQ.

ST. ENOCH

Howard St.

Jamaica St.

Clyde St.

Union St.

Central Station

Oswald St.

Robertson St.

York St.

James Watt St.

McAlpine St.

Brown St.

Washington St.

Argyle St.

Anderston Cross Bus Station

Cadogan St.

Gordon St.

Hope St.

Broomielaw

River Clyde

BURRELL COLLECTION, GREENOCK & GLASGOW AIRPORTS

Anderston Quay

Lancefield Quay

Springfield Quay

Mavisbank Gardens

Hydepark St.

Finnieston St.

Stobcross St.

Clydeside Expwy.

TO KELVIN HALL

Newton St.

North St.

Mitchell Library

Cleveland St.

Granville St.

Beltane St.

Elderslie St.

St. Vincent St.

Berkeley St.

Kent Rd.

Claremont St.

Minerva St.

Houldsworth St.

Finnieston Pl.

Greenhill Pl.

M8

Anderson Quay

KELVINGROVE PARK

Hunterian Museum and Art Gallery

Kelvingrove Museum and Art Gallery

Glasgow University

River Kelvin

Kelvin Way

Kelvinhaugh St.

Gray St.

Derby St.

Sauchiehall St.

Kelvingrove St.

Minerva Way

Park Circus

Park Terr.

Woodlands Terr.

Royal Terr.

Park Quad

Somerset Pl.

Lynedoch Pl.

Woodside Pl.

Newton Pl.

Woodlands Rd.

Grant St.

W. Prince's

St. George's Rd.

Maryhill Rd.

TO 6 7 (½ mi.)

Claremont St.

Argyle St.

St. Vincent Crescent

TO CLYDE

BRITAIN

ACCOMMODATIONS

Reserve B&Bs and hostels in advance, especially in August. Last-minute planners may consider calling **SYHA Loch Lomond** (see p. 245). Most B&Bs cluster on **Great Western Rd.**, in the university area, or near **Westercraigs Rd.**, east of the Necropolis.

Bunkum Backpackers, 26 Hillhead St. (☎581 44 81). Though located away from the city center, Bunkum is minutes away from the West End. Spacious dorms with comfy beds. **Internet.** Lockers. Laundry (£1.50 wash). Dorms £9, £45 per week.

Glasgow Backpackers Hostel, 17 Park Terr. (☎332 90 99). U: St. George's Cross. Clean, friendly, and social hostel close to the West End party scene. **Internet.** Laundry (£2.50 for wash, dry, and fold). Open July-Sept. Dorms £10.50; twins £24.

SYHA Youth Hostel, 7-8 Park Terr. (☎332 30 04). U: St. George's Cross. From Central Station, take bus #44 from Hope St. and ask for the first stop on Woodlands Rd. then follow the signs. This hostel maintains an air of luxury. All rooms with bath. TV and game rooms. Breakfast included. Laundry. July-Aug. dorms £13.75, under 18 £12.25; Sept.-June £12.25, under 18 £11.25.

Kelvin Lodge Backpackers Hostel/B&B, 8 Park Circus, (☎331 20 00). Occupied by students term-time, the B&B rooms are only available from July-Sept.; backpackers are welcome year-round in large rooms. Laundry. B&B doubles £20, with bath £23; backpackers dorms £11, doubles £30.

Seton Guest House, 6 Seton Terr. (☎556 76 54), 20min. east of George Sq. Hop on bus #6, 6A, or 41A. Kindly hosts keep large immaculate rooms with ornate chandeliers. Out of the way, but all the quieter for it. Singles £17; twins £32.

Alamo Guest House, 46 Gray St. (☎339 23 95), opposite the Kelvingrove Museum. Gracious proprietors and spacious, quiet rooms. Singles £20-22; doubles from £34.

FOOD

The area bordered by **Otago St.** in the west, **St. George's Rd.** in the east, and along **Great Western Rd., Woodlands Rd.,** and **Eldon St.** brims with cheap kebab 'n' curry joints. **Byres Rd.** and **Ashton Ln.,** a tiny cobblestoned alley parallel to Byres Rd, thrive with cheap, trendy cafes. **Woodlands Grocers,** 110 Woodlands Rd., is open 24hr.; there's also a **Safeway** at 373 Byres Rd. (open M-Sa 8am-8pm, Su 9am-7pm).

Insomnia Café, 38/40 Woodlands Rd., near the hostels, is the hip place to gorge, day or night. Cafe and adjoining deli open 24hr.

The Bay Tree Vegetarian Café, 403 Great Western Rd., at Park Rd., also near the hostels (cut through Kelvingrove Park), offers pitas with hummus and salad for £3.50-4.50. Open M-Sa 9am-9pm, Su 9am-8pm.

The Willow Tea Room, 217 Sauchiehall St. (☎332 05 21), upstairs from Henderson the Jewellers. A Glasgow landmark. Sip one of 28 kinds of tea. £1.20-1.45 per pot. High tea £7.75. Open M-Sa 9:30am-4:30pm, Su noon-4:15pm.

SIGHTS

The red-paved **George Square** marks the busiest part of the city. The **City Chambers,** on the east side of the square, conceal an ornate marble interior in the Italian Renaissance style. (☎287 40 17. Tours M-F 10:30am and 2:30pm.) Follow George St. from the square and take a left on High St., which turns into Castle St., to reach the Gothic **Glasgow Cathedral,** the only full-scale cathedral spared the fury of the 16th-century Scottish Reformation. (Open Apr.-Sept. M-Sa 9:30am-6pm, Su 2-5pm; Oct.-Mar. M-Sa 9:30am-4pm, Su 2-4pm. Free.) On the same street is the **St. Mungo Museum of Religious Life and Art,** 2 Castle St., which surveys every religion from Hindu to Yoruba. (Open M-Sa 10am-5pm, Su 11am-5pm. Free.) Behind the cathedral is the spectacular **Necropolis,** a terrifying hilltop cemetery filled with broken tombstones. (Free.) In the West End, the large, wooded **Kelvingrove Park** lies on the banks of the River Kelvin. In the southwest corner of the park, at Argyle and Sauchiehall St., sits the magnificent, spired **Kelvingrove Art Gallery and Museum,** which shelters works by van Gogh, Monet, and Rembrandt. (U: Kelvin Hall. Open M-Th and Sa 10am-5pm; F and Su 11am-5pm. Free.) Farther west rises the Gothic central spire of the **University of Glasgow.** The main building is on University Ave., which runs into Byres Rd. While you're walking through the campus, which has churned out 57 Nobel laureates, stop by the **Hunterian Museum** or the **Hunterian Art Gallery,** across the street. (U: Hillhead. Open M-Sa 9:30am-5pm. Free.) Several buildings designed by Charles Rennie Mackintosh, Scotland's most famous architect, are open to the public; the **Glasgow School of Art,** 167 Renfrew St., south of the river, reflects a uniquely Glaswegian Modernist style. (Tours M-F 11am and 2pm, Sa 10:30am. £5, students £3.) If you tire of all that culture, shop 'til you drop at **Princes Sq.,** 48 Buchanan St., a gorgeous high-end shopping mall. If your wallet has any life left, hit **Sauchiehall St.,** which hosts shops and art galleries as well.

🎵 🎭 ENTERTAINMENT AND NIGHTLIFE

Glaswegians have a reputation for partying hard. *The List* (£1.95 from newsagents) lets you know which club is best each night. The infamous **Byers Rd.** pub crawl passes the Glasgow University area, starting at Tennant's Bar and heads toward the River Clyde. **◼Uisge Beatha,** 232 Woodlands Rd., serves over 100 kinds of malt whiskey. (£1.85-35 for each. Open M-Th 11am-11pm, F-Sa 11am-midnight, Su 12:30-11pm.) The **Cul de Sac Bar,** 46 Ashton Ln., hosts an artsy, fun crowd of pre-clubbers. (Open M-Sa 9am-midnight, Su noon-midnight.) **Russell Bar-Café,** 77 Byres Rd., is a log cabin with live DJs and meal deals. (Open Su-Th 11am-11pm, F-Sa 11am-midnight.) Fifteen bartenders staff the largest continuous bar in the UK at **Horseshoe Bar,** 17-21 Drury St. (Open M-Sa 8am-midnight, Su 12:30pm-midnight.) Look for skeletons hanging outside the second-floor windows of club **Archaos,** 25 Queen St. (Cover £3-9. Open Th-Su until 3am, Sa until 3:30am.) People of all types grind at sweating **Sub Club,** 22 Jamaica St. (Cover £3-6, Sa £8. Open Th-F and Su 11pm-3am, Sa 11pm-3:30am.)

STRANRAER
☎01776

On the westernmost peninsula of Dumfries and Galloway, Stranraer provides ferry access to Belfast in Northern Ireland. **Stena Line** (☎ (0990) 70 70 70; www.stenaline.co.uk) sails to Belfast (1¾hr.; 5 per day; £25, students and seniors £20, children £13). **Trains** (☎ (0345) 48 49 50) arrive from Glasgow (2½hr., 2-7 per day, £15.30), as do Citylink **buses** (#923; ☎ (08705) 50 50 50; 2½hr., 2 per day, £8.50). National Express buses (☎ (08705) 80 80 80) roll in from London (9hr., 2per day, £32) and Manchester (5½hr., 1 per day, £26). The **tourist office** is on Harbour St. (☎70 25 95; fax 88 91 56. Open June-Sept. M-Sa 9:30am-5:30pm, Su 10am-4:30pm; Apr.-May and Oct. M-Sa 10am-5pm; Nov.-Mar. M-Sa 11am-4pm.) If you're marooned, try the **Jan Da Mar Guest House,** 1 Ivy Pl, on London Rd. (☎70 61 94. Singles £18; twins £32.) The **Tesco supermarket** is on Charlotte St. at Port Rodie near the terminal. (Open M-F 8:30am-8pm, Sa 8am-6pm, Su 10am-5pm.)

STIRLING
☎01786

The third point of a strategic triangle completed by Glasgow and Edinburgh, Stirling has historically presided over north-south movement in the region; it was once said that he who controlled Stirling controlled Scotland. At the 1297 Battle of Stirling Bridge, **William Wallace** (of *Braveheart* fame) outwitted and overpowered the English army, enabling Robert the Bruce to finally overthrow the English in 1314 at **Bannockburn,** 2 mi. south of town, and lead Scotland to a 400-year-long stretch of independence. The ◼**Stirling Castle** possesses prim gardens and superb views of the Forth Valley that belie its militant and murderous past. (Open daily Apr.-Oct. 9:30am-6pm; Nov.-Mar. 9:30am-5pm. £6, seniors £4.50, children £1.50.) The castle also contains the fascinating **Regimental Museum of the Argyll and Sutherland Highlanders.** (Open Easter-Sept. M-Sa 10am-5:45pm, Su 11am-4:45pm; Oct.-

Easter daily 10am-4:15pm. Free.) The 19th-century **Wallace Monument Tower,** on Hillfouts Rd., 1½ mi. from town, offers incredible views from atop a set of wind-whipped stairs. (Open daily July-Aug. 9:30am-6:30pm; June and Sept. 10am-6pm; Mar.-May and Oct. 10am-5pm; Nov.-Feb. 10am-4pm. £3.30, students £3.05.)

Trains run from Goosecroft Rd. (☎ (08457) 48 49 50) to: Edinburgh (50min., 2 per hr., £5); Aberdeen (2hr.; M-Sa every hr., Su 6 per day; £30); Glasgow (30min., 1-3 per hr., £4.10); and Inverness (3hr., 4 per day, £28.90). National Express **buses** also run from Goosecroft Rd. to: Glasgow (2-3 per hr., £3.40) and Inverness (every hr., £11.20). The **Stirling Visitor Centre** is next to the castle. (☎ (01786) 46 25 17. Open daily July-Aug. 9am-6:30pm; Apr.-June and Sept.-Oct. 9:30am-6pm; Nov.-Mar. 9:30am-5pm.) In town, the **tourist office** awaits at 41 Dumbarton Rd. (☎47 50 19. Open July-Aug. M-Sa 9am-1:30pm, Su 9:30am-6:30pm; June and Sept. M-Sa 9am-6pm, Su 10am-4pm; off-season M-Sa 10am-5pm.) The **SYHA Stirling,** on St. John St., halfway up the hill to the castle, occupies the shell of the first Separatist Church in Stirling. In summer, overflow singles in the **Union St. Annexe,** known in cooler months as University of Stirling dorms, are the same prices as the hostel. (☎47 34 42. Reception 7am-11:30pm. Curfew 2am. Dorms £12.75-13.75.) The **Willy Wallace Hostel,** 77 Murray Pl., holds clean rooms in a social environment, near to both the bus and train stations. (☎44 67 73. Dorms £10; doubles £26.) **Postal code:** FK8 2BP.

ISLE OF ARRAN

With both gentle lowland hills and majestic Highland peaks, the glorious Isle of Arran (AH-ren) justifiably bills itself as "Scotland in Miniature." In the north, the gray, craggy peaks of Goatfell and the Caisteal range surge above the pine-filled foothills. Prehistoric stone circles and lone standing stones rise suddenly out of the mist in the west, while the eastern coastline winds south past meadows and white beaches. Arran is a popular destination for both hikers and bikers. Biking on the hilly island is a rewarding challenge; the full circuit takes about 9hr. Pick up a free copy of the SYHA's *Cycling on Arran.* The best walks on the island are well marked, while more demanding hikes are detailed in *Seventy Walks in Arran* (£2.50) and *My Walks of Arran* (£2.25), both available at the tourist office in Brodick. To reach Arran, take a **train** to **Ardrossan** from **Glasgow Central** (☎ (08457) 48 49 50. 45min., 4-5 per day, £4.40). From Ardrossan, the **Caledonian-MacIntyre** ferry makes the crossing to **Brodick** on Arran in sync with the train schedule (☎30 21 66; 1hr., 4-5 per day, £4.25). On the island, the best **bus** pass (☎ (01770) 30 20 00) is the **Rural Day Card** granting a full day of travel on Arran's buses (available on the bus; £3, children £1.50). The **Stagecoach Western** office is at Brodick pier. (☎30 20 00. Open daily 8am-5pm.) Its **open-top tour** passes some beautiful scenery from Brodick to Whiting Bay (45 min.; June-Sept. 6 per day; tours £3, children £2).

BRODICK   ☎01770

In addition to its major transportation connections, Arran's main town (pop. 2000) holds a glorious castle and some tasty restaurants—all against a backdrop of rugged mountains and a peaceful bay. The center of Brodick is along Shore Rd., to the right as you disembark from the ferry. Visit ■**Brodick Castle,** which surveys the harbor above fantastic wild and walled gardens; the wooded **country park** around the castle has marked trails for self-guided walks. Built on the site of an old Viking fort, the castle contains a fine porcelain collection, paintings, and scores of dead beasties. (☎30 22 02. Open Apr.-June and Oct. daily 11am-4:30pm; July-Aug. daily 11am-5pm. Castle and gardens £6; students, seniors, and children £4. Gardens only £2.50.) The **Arran Heritage Museum,** features a working forge and a cottage stuffed with 19th-century household and farming tools. (☎30 26 36. Open Apr.-Oct. daily 10:30am-4:30pm. £2.25, seniors £1.50, children £1.) The well-marked path up popular **Goatfell** (2866 ft.), Arran's highest peak, begins on the road between the Arran Heritage Museum and Brodick Castle; the hike averages 4-5hr.

Arran's only **tourist office** is located at the base of the pier. (☎30 21 40; fax 30 23 95. Open June-Sept. M-Sa 9am-7:30pm, Su 10am-5pm; Oct.-May M-F 9am-5pm, Sa

10am-5pm.) The seafront **Glenfloral B&B,** Shore Rd., has spacious rooms with TVs (☎ 30 27 07. £17 per person). To reach the rooms of **Mrs. Macmillan,** Glenard House, Manse Rd., head away from the pier on Shore Rd. and turn left just after the Heath-field Hotel; it's the fourth house on the left. (☎ 30 23 18. Open Apr.-Oct. Singles £18; doubles £36.) **Camp** at the **Glen Rosa Farm,** 2 mi. north of Brodick on the coastal road B880 to Corrie. (☎ 30 23 80. Toilets and cold water available. £2.50 per person.) Eight miles south of Brodick, the shores of Whiting Bay house a stone **SYHA Hostel** amid rolling hills. (☎ 70 03 39. Lockout 10:30am-5pm. Curfew 11:45pm. Dorms £8, under 18 £7.) You can stock up on groceries at the **Co-op,** across from the ferry terminal. (☎ 30 25 15. Open M-Sa 8am-10pm, Su 9am-7pm.)

LOCH LOMOND

With Britain's largest inland freshwater body as its base, the landscape of Loch Lomond is filled with lush bays, thickly wooded islands, and bare hills. Hikers on the northeastern edge of Loch Lomond are rewarded with stunning views, quiet splendor, and small beaches. The **West Highland Way** snakes along the entire eastern side of the Loch, stretching 95 mi. from Milngavie north to Fort William.

BALLOCH

Balloch, at the southern tip of Loch Lomond, is the major town in the area. Across the River Leven, the **Balloch Castle Country Park** provides 200 acres of gorgeous grounds, as well as a 19th-century castle housing a **Visitor's Centre.** Look for the pixies in **Fairy Glen.** (Park open daily dawn-dusk. Visitor's Centre open Easter-Oct. daily 10am-6pm.) **Sweeney's Cruises** boat tour departs from the tourist office side of the River Leven. (☎ (01389) 75 23 76; 1hr., every hr., £4.80.)

Trains arrive on Balloch Rd., opposite the tourist office, from Glasgow's Queen St. Station (45min., 2 per hr., £3.10). Citylink buses (#926, 975, and 976; ☎ (08705) 80 80 80) arrive from Glasgow (3-5 per day). First Midland (☎ (01324) 61 37 77) travels from Stirling (1½hr., 3 per day). Buses arrive a few minutes down Balloch Rd., across the bridge to the left of the **tourist office,** in Old Station Building. (Tourist office ☎ (01389) 75 35 33. Open daily July-Aug. 9:30am-7pm; June 9:30am-6pm; Sept. 9:30am-7pm; Apr.-May and Oct. 10am-5pm.) **B&Bs** congregate on **Balloch Rd. SYHA Loch Lomond,** 2 mi. north of town, is one of Scotland's largest hostels in a stunning 19th-century castle-like building. (☎ (01389) 85 02 26. Call ahead. Open early Mar. to Oct. Dorms £12.25-13.25.) To reach the **SYHA Rowardennan,** the first hostel along the West Highland Way, take the Inverberg ferry across the Loch to Rowardennan (☎ (01301) 70 23 56. May-Sept. 3 per day, £4). Huge windows at the hostel put the Loch in your lap. (☎ (01360) 87 02 59. Curfew 11:30pm. Open Mar.-Oct. Dorms £9.25.) The **Tullichewan Caravan and Camping Site,** on Old Luss Rd., is up Balloch Rd. from the tourist office. (☎ (01389) 75 94 75. Reception 8:30am-10pm. Tent and 2 people £6.50-9, with car £8.50-12.50.)

TROSSACHS

The gentle mountains and lochs of the Trossachs form the northern boundary of central Scotland. A road for walkers and cyclists traces the Loch's shoreline; tourists drop like flies after a half mile, leaving the Loch's joys to more hardy travelers. The **Steamship Sir Walter Scott** runs between Loch Katrine's Trossachs Pier and Stronachlachar. (☎ (01877) 37 63 16. Apr.-Oct. 2-3 per day, £4.60-6.) Only a few buses each day link to the area's two main towns, **Aberfoyle** and **Callander.** Citylink **bus** #974 runs through Edinburgh and Stirling to Fort William, stopping in Callander (1 per day). The Trossachs Trundler is a 1950s-style bus that creaks to Callander, Aberfoyle, and Trossachs Pier in time for the sailing of the *Sir Walter Scott* (July-Sept. Su-F 4 per day, £8). Bus #59 from Stirling connects with the Trundler in Callander. Call the **Stirling Council Public Transport Helpline** (☎ (01786) 44 27 07) for info. **Trossachs Cycle Hire,** on the pier, rents bikes. (☎ (01877) 38 26 14. Open Apr.-Oct. daily 8:30am-5:30pm. £12 per day.)

FORT WILLIAM AND BEN NEVIS

With a slew of beautiful lochs and valleys, **Fort William** makes an excellent base camp for mountain excursions to **Ben Nevis** (4406 ft.), the highest peak in Britain. To ascend the well-beaten trail from Fort William to the summit, go ½ mi. north on A82 and follow signs (5-6hr. round-trip). Buses and trains leave from the northern end of High St. **Trains** arrive in Fort William from Glasgow's Queen St. Station (2-4 per day, £20) and London's Euston Station (12hr., 3 per day, £89). Skye-Ways **buses** (☎ (01599) 53 43 28) run to Glasgow (3hr., 4 per day, £11.20); Scottish Citylink (☎ (08705) 50 50 50) goes to Edinburgh (6hr., 2 per day) and Inverness (2hr., 5-6 per day, £6.50). The nearby **tourist office** provides info on the West Highlands. (☎ (01397) 70 37 81. Open mid-June to mid-July M-Sa 9am-7pm, Su 10am-6pm; mid-July to Aug. M-Sa 9am-8:30pm, Su 9am-6pm; Sept.-Oct. M-Sa 9am-6pm, Su 10am-5:30pm; Nov.-Mar. M-Sa 9am-5pm, Su 10am-4pm; Mar.-June M-Sa 9am-6pm, Su 10am-4pm.) By far the best place to stay within striking distance of Ben Nevis is the comfy **Farr Cottage Accommodation and Activity Center** in Corpach. (☎ (01397) 77 23 15. **Internet.** Laundry. Dorms £11.) To get there, take the train two stops north of Fort William and then take the bus from High St. (10min., 1-3 per hr., £0.80). The **Fort William Backpackers Guesthouse,** on Alma Rd., is 5min. from the Fort William train station. (☎ (01397) 70 07 11. Curfew 2am. Dorms £10-11.) The **Glen Nevis Caravan & Camping Park,** is 3½ mi. east of town on Glen Nevis Rd. (☎ (01397) 70 21 91. Showers included. Open mid-Mar. to Oct. Tent and 2 people £8.70, with car £11.20.)

THE INNER HEBRIDES

ISLE OF SKYE

Often described as the shining jewel in the Hebridean crown, Skye radiates unparalleled splendor from the serrated peaks of the Cuillin Hills to the rugged northern tip of the Trotternish Peninsula. Touring Skye takes effort; pick up *Public Transport Guide to Skye and the Western Isles* (£1) at a tourist office. **Buses** on the island are infrequent; **biking** and **hiking** are better options. **MacBackpackers** in Kyleakin (☎ (01599) 534510) offer **minibus day tours** (£15) and a fantastic **Skye Trekker Tour,** an outdoors experience, with camping equipment provided (2 days £30).

KYLE OF LOCHALSH AND KYLEAKIN. The **Skye Bridge** links Kyle of Lochalsh, the last stop on the mainland before the Isle, with Kyleakin, on Skye's southeastern tail. On the mainland side perches the made-for-postcard **Eilean Donan Castle,** which struck a pose for the movie *Highlander.* (Open daily Apr.-Oct. M-Sa 9am-5:30pm; July-Sept. also Su 10am-4pm. £3.75, students £3.) To get there, take the bus from Kyle of Lochalsh (dir.: Inverness; £2.50). **Trains** (☎ (08457) 48 49 50) arrive from Inverness (2½hr., 2-4 per day; £15). The train station (☎ (01599) 53 42 05) is near the pier and the **tourist office.** (☎ (01599) 53 42 76. Open Apr.-Oct. M-Sa 9am-5:30pm; July-Sept. also Su 10am-4pm.) Scottish Citylink **buses** (☎ (01599) 53 43 28) run daily through Kyle of Lochalsh on their way to Kyleakin from: Fort William (2hr., 3 per day, £10.70); Glasgow (5½hr., 3 per day, £17.50); and Inverness (2½hr., 2 per day, £9.80). **Cuchulainn's Backpackers Hostel,** in Kyle of Lochalsh, is newly renovated. (☎ (01599) 53 44 92. Sheets £0.50. Dorms £9.)

When you're ready to skip the mainland and dive into Skye, traverse the 1½ mi. footpath or take the **shuttle bus** (2 per hr., £0.65) across the Skye Bridge. Over the bridge, quiet Kyleakin harbor is resplendent at sunset. A slippery scramble leads to the small ruins of **Castle Moil;** cross the bridge behind the SYHA hostel, turn left, follow the road to the pier, and take the gravel path. Lodgings cluster alongside the park a few hundred yards from the pier; to the right is the comfy **Skye Backpackers.** (☎ (01599) 53 45 10. Laundry. Curfew 2am. Dorms £10-11; doubles £25.)

SLIGACHAN. West of Kyleakin, the smooth, conical Red Cuillin and the rough, craggy Black Cuillin Hills meet in Sligachan, where paths wind their way up the mountains. If you plan to scale some peaks, stay at the **SYHA Glenbrittle** in Glenbrittle near the southwest coast, where expert mountaineers can give you advice on exploring the area. (☎ (01478) 64 02 78. Open Apr.-Sept. Dorms £8.50.) For camping, head to **Glenbrittle Campsite.** (☎ (01478) 64 04 04. Open Mar.-Oct. £3.50 per person.) Take bus #360 from Portree and Sligachan to Glenbrittle (M-Sa 2 per day).

PORTREE. In northern Skye is the island's capital, **Portree** (pop. 2500), with its busy shops and attractive harbor. Buses run from Portree to **Dunvegan Castle,** the seat of the clan MacLeod. The castle holds the **Fairy Flag,** more than 1300 years old and swathed in clan legend, although looking rather tattered of late. (Open daily late-Mar. to Oct. 10am-5:30pm; Nov.-Mar. 11am-4pm. £5.20, students £4.60.) **Buses** stop at Somerled Sq. The busy **tourist office** is on Bayfield Rd., a block from the harbor. (☎ (01478) 61 21 37. Open July-Aug. M-Sa 9am-8pm, Su 10am-5pm; Sept.-June M-Sa 9am-5pm.) The **Portree Independent Hostel** is right off Somerled Sq. (☎ (01478) 61 37 37. Dorms £8.50-9.50; twins £21.)

THE OUTER HEBRIDES (WESTERN ISLES)

The magical Outer Hebridean archipelago is not just extraordinarily beautiful, but also, astoundingly ancient. Much of its exposed rock has existed for about three billion years, more than half as long as the planet, and inhabitants of the island in the distant past have left behind a rich sediment of tombs, standing stones (including the remarkable stone circle at Callanish on Lewis), and Neolithic antiquities. The vehemently Calvinist islands of Lewis and Harris observe the Sabbath strictly: all shops, restaurants, and public transportation **close on Sundays.** Television and tourism are diluting some local customs, but the islands are remote enough to retain much of their charm, and Gaelic is still heard on the streets.

TRANSPORTATION. Four major **Caledonian MacBrayne** ferries (☎ (01475) 65 01 00) serve the Western Isles from **Oban** to **Barra** and **South Uist,** from **Mallaig** to **South Uist,** from **Skye** to **Harris,** and from **Ullapool** to **Lewis.** Ferries and infrequent **buses** connect the islands, and **hitchers** and **cyclists** enjoy success except during frequent rain storms (*Let's Go* does not recommend hitchhiking). Except in bilingual Stornoway and Benbecula, all road signs are in Gaelic only. Tourist offices often carry translation keys, and *Let's Go* lists Gaelic equivalents after English place names where necessary. For up-to-date transport information, consult the *Skye and Western Isles Public Transport Travel Guide* (£1 at tourist offices).

LEWIS AND HARRIS. The island of **Lewis** (Leodhas) is famous for its atmosphere: pure light and drifting mists off the Atlantic Ocean shroud the untouched miles of moorland and small *lochs* in quiet luminescence. The unearthly setting is ideal for exploring the island's many archaeological sites, most notably the **Callanish Stones,** an extraordinary (and isolated) Bronze Age circle. Buses on the W2 route from Stornoway run past the stones at Calanais (M-Sa 5 per day). Caledonian MacBrayne **ferries** from Ullapool on the mainland serve **Stornoway** (Steornobhaigh; pop. 8000), the largest town in northwestern Scotland (M-Sa 2-3 per day, £12.70, round-trip £21.75). To get from the ferry terminal to the **tourist office,** 26 Cromwell St., turn left from the pier, then hang a right on Cromwell St. (☎ (01851) 70 30 88. Open Apr.-Sept. M-Sa 9am-6pm and for late ferry arrivals; Oct.-Mar. M-Sa 9am-5pm.) For a place to lay your head and wax your surf board, head to the new **Fair Haven Hostel,** at the intersection of Francis and Keith St. (☎ (01851) 70 58 62. Dorms £10.)

Although **Harris** (Na Hearadh) is technically part of the same island as Lewis, it is an entirely different world. Lewis is mainly flat and watery, while Harris, formed by volcanic gneiss, has the ruggedness more characteristic of Scotland. Toward

BRITAIN

the west coast, the barricade of the **Forest of Harris** (ironically enough, a treeless mountain range) descends to brilliant crescents of yellow beaches bordered by indigo waters and *machair*—sea meadows of soft green grass and summertime flowers. **Ferries** serve **Tarbert** (An Tairbeart), the biggest town on Harris, from Uig on Skye (M-Sa 1-2 per day; £8.30, round-trip £14.20). Pick up essential *Ordnance Survey* hiking maps at the **tourist office,** on Pier Rd. (☎ (01859) 50 20 11. Open early Apr. to mid-Oct. M-Sa 9am-5pm and for late ferry arrivals.) Walk up the hill behind the tourist office and turn left at the grocery store to reach the comfy **Rockview Bunkhouse,** Main St. (☎ (01859) 50 22 11. Dorms £9.)

BARRA. Little Barra, the southern outpost of the Outer Isles, is an unspeakably beautiful composite of moor, *machair,* and beach. On sunny days, the island's colors are unforgettable: white sand dunes crown turquoise waters against a backdrop of green mountain slopes. **Kisimul Castle,** bastion of the old Clan Mac-Neil, inhabits Castlebay Harbor (inquire at the tourist office for details). The west coast is flanked on one side by idyllic **beaches** like **Halaman Bay,** and on the other by misty mountains speckled with **standing stones and ruins.** Caledonian MacBrayne **ferries** stop at **Castlebay** (Bagh A Chaisteil) in Barra on their way from Oban on the mainland (☎ (01475) 65 01 00. 5hr., M, W-Th, and Sa 1 per day, £18.25). You can see almost all of Barra in a day; inquire at the tourist office about the **postbus,** or rent a bike from **Castlebay Cycle Hire** (☎ (01871) 81 02 84; £11) and follow A888, which makes a 14 mi. circle around the island. The Castlebay **tourist office,** around the bend to the right from the pier, books B&Bs. (☎ (01871) 81 03 36. Open mid-Mar. to mid-Oct. M-Sa 9am-5pm, Su 10-11am, and for late ferry arrivals.) **Mrs. Clellan's,** 47 Glen, is the cheapest B&B near Castlebay. (☎ (01871) 81 04 38. £17 per person.)

ABERDEEN ☎01224

The din of students partying, the hum of a vibrant arts community, and the swish of Britain's North Sea oil industry offset the perennial grayness of Aberdeen's skies. **Old Aberdeen** and **Aberdeen University** are a short bus ride (#1-4 or 15), or a long walk along King St., from the city center. The **King's College Visitor Centre,** just off High St., greets you at the other end with an exhibit on how students used to live. (☎27 37 02. Open M-Sa 10am-5pm, Su noon-5pm. Free.) Peaceful **King's College Chapel** dates from the 16th century. (Open daily 9am-4:30pm. Tours July-Aug. Su 2-5pm.) The twin-spired **St. Machar's Cathedral,** with a heraldic ceiling and stained glass, was built in the 14th century. (Open daily 9am-5pm; Su services 11am and 6pm.) The **Lemon Tree Café and Theatre,** 5 West North St. (☎64 22 30), near Queen St., presents folk, jazz, rock, drama, and dance. Excellent and free museums abound, including the **Aberdeen Art Gallery,** on Schoolhill (☎52 37 00; open M-Sa 10am-5pm, Su 2-5pm), the **Aberdeen Maritime Museum,** Shiprow (☎33 77 00; open M-Sa 10am-5pm, Su noon-3pm) and the Gothic **Marischal Museum** (☎27 43 01; open M-F 10am-5pm, Su 2-5pm).

Trains and **buses** arrive on Guild St. Scotrail (☎ (0345) 55 00 33) from Edinburgh (2½hr., 17 per day, £28.90); Glasgow (1½hr., 16 per day, £36.40); and Inverness (2hr., 10 per day, £17.80). Scottish Citylink buses (☎ (08705) 50 50 50) roll in from Edinburgh (4hr., every hr., £14.50) and Glasgow (3½ hr., every hr., £14.50); and Citylink and Bluebird buses (☎21 22 66) come from Inverness (3½hr., every hr., £9). Turn right on Guild St., left on Market St., right on Union St., and left on Broad St. to get to the **tourist office,** in St. Nicholas House on Broad St. (☎63 27 27; fax 62 04 15. Open July-Aug. M-F 9am-7pm, Sa 9am-5pm, Su 10am-4pm; Sept.-June M-Sa 9am-5pm, Su 10am-2pm.) Take bus #14 or 15 from Union St to Queen's Rd to reach the **SYHA King George VI Memorial Hostel,** 8 Queen's Rd. (☎64 69 88. Breakfast included. Laundry. Check-out 9:30am. Lockout 9:30am-1:30pm. Curfew 2am. Dorms £10.25-13.25.) Tesco **supermarket** is in front of the St. Nicholas Centre on Union St. (Open M-W and Sa 7:30am-7pm, Th 7:30am-8:30pm, F 7:30am-7:30pm, Su 10am-5pm.)

INVERNESS AND LOCH NESS   ☎ 01463

The charms of Inverness, like the Loch Ness monster herself, are somewhat elusive, but you won't be disappointed. Disillusionment awaits those who remember Inverness as the home of Shakespeare's *Macbeth*. Nothing of the "Auld Castlehill" remains; the present reconstructed **castle** looks like it was made out of pink Legos this very morning (tours Easter-Nov. M-Sa 10:30am-5:30pm; £3). The **Tourist Trail Day Rover bus** (summer only; £6, students £4) allows unlimited travel to most sights near Inverness. In 1746 the Jacobite cause died on **Culloden Battlefield,** east of Inverness; take **Highland county bus** #12 from the post office at Queensgate (£2). One and a half miles south of Culloden, the stone circles and chambered cairns (mounds of rough stones) of the **Cairns of Clava** recall civilizations of the Bronze Age. Bus #12 will also take you to the **Cawdor Castle;** the home of the Cawdors since the 15th century; don't miss the maze. (Open May to mid-Oct. daily 10am-5:30pm. £5.50, students £4.50. Bus roundtrip £4.50.) And, of course, no trip to Inverness would be complete without taking in the deep and mysterious **Loch Ness,** which guards its secrets five miles south of Inverness. In AD 565, St. Columba repelled a savage sea beast as it attacked a monk; whether a prehistoric leftover, giant seasnake, or cosmic wanderer, the monster has captivated the imagination of the world ever since. **Ken White's Tours** and other tour agencies are the most convenient ways to see the loch. (☎ 22 31 68. £12, students £10.) Even if you don't see the real monster, vendors are all too happy to sell you a cute stuffed one.

Trains (☎ (08457) 48 49 50) run from Academy St., in Station Sq., to Edinburgh (3½-4hr., 1-2 per hr., £29.90-42.60); Aberdeen, (2¼hr., 7-10 per day, £17.80); Glasgow (3½hr., 5-7 per day, £29.90-42.60); and London (8hr., 1 per day, £81). Scottish Citylink **buses** (☎ (08705) 50 50 50) run from Farraline Park, off Academy St, to Edinburgh (4½hr., 8-10 per day, £13.40) and Glasgow (4½hr., 10-12 per day, £12.80). To reach the tourist office from the stations, turn left on Academy St., right on Union St., and left on Church St.; the **tourist office,** Castle Wynd, is visible from the end. (☎ 23 43 53; fax 71 06 09. Open mid-June to Aug. M-Sa 9am-7pm, Su 10am-6pm; Sept. to mid-June M-Sa 9am-5pm, Su 10am-4pm.) Facing the tourist office, go left on Bridge St. and right on Castle St., which leads to Culduthel Rd. and the **Inverness Student Hotel,** at #8 (☎ 23 65 56. Reception 6:30am-2:30am. Check-out 10:30am. Dorms July-Sept. £11, Oct.-June £10.) The **Bazpackers Backpackers Hotel** is farther down at #4 Culdethel Rd. (☎ 71 76 63. Reception 7:30am-midnight; check-out 10:30am. Mid-June to Sept. dorms £10, doubles £14; Oct. to mid-June £8.50, £12.)

GLEN COE   ☎ 01855

Stunning in any weather, Glen Coe is perhaps best seen in the rain, when a slowly drifting web of mist over the valley laces the innumerable rifts and crags of the steep slopes, and silvery waterfalls cascade into the River Coe. Glen Coe is infamous as the site of the 1692 **Massacre of Glencoe,** when the Clan MacDonald unkowingly welcomed a company of Campbell soldiers, henchmen of William III, into their chieftain's home and were promptly murdered. Glen Coe provides a range of opportunities to its visitors. Walkers stroll the floor of the cup-shaped valley, rockclimbers head for the cliffs, and winter ice-climbers hack their way up frozen waterfalls. Well-equipped and sure-footed hikers can scramble up the 3766ft. **Bidean nam Bian** or try the 4mi. traverse of the **Aonach Eagach** ridge on the north side of the glen. Saner walkers can find the **Hidden Valley,** where the MacDonalds once hid their pilfered cattle. The trail follows the stream on the south side of the glen, just west of the Coe Gorge (3hr. round-trip). Or avoid the 1000ft. climb by taking the **Glen Coe Ski Centre Chairlift,** located off the A82 in the middle of Glen Coe. (☎ 85 12 26. Open June-Aug. daily 9:30am-4:30pm; £4.) On a rainy day, head for the thatched-roof **Glencoe Folk Museum** in Glencoe village. (☎ 81 16 64. Open Easter-Oct. M-Sa 10am-5:30pm. £1.)

BRITAIN

Glencoe Village, essentially one street, rests at the edge of Loch Leven, at the mouth of the River Coe and the western end of Glen Coe. The A82 runs the length of the valley. Scottish Citylink (☎ (08705) 50 50 50) **buses** arrive in Glencoe village from Glasgow (4 per day, £9.80) and Edinburgh (2 per day, £13.40.) Post buses putter daily but at irregular times around the area; get the schedule from the tourist office. The **Glencoe Visitors Centre,** is 3 mi. southeast of Glencoe Village on the A82. (☎ 81 13 07. Open daily mid-May to Aug. 9:30am-5:30pm; Apr. to mid-May and Sept.-Oct. 10am-5pm.) The **tourist office,** is in Ballachulish, 1 mi. west of the village. (☎ 81 12 96. Open Apr.-June M-Sa 10am-5pm; July-Aug. M-Sa 9am-6:30pm, Su 10am-6pm; Sept.-Oct. M-Sa 9am-5pm.) For bike rental, try **Mountain Bike Hire,** at the Clachaig Inn, across the river from the visitors center (☎ 81 12 52. £12 per day). The **SYHA Glencoe** is 2 mi. southeast of Glencoe Village. (☎ 81 12 19. **Internet.** Reception 7am-midnight. Curfew midnight. Dorms £9.25) The **Leacantium Farm Bunkhouse** is 500 yd. away from the hostel and has three bunkhouses (☎ 81 12 56. £7.50). The farm's **Red Squirrel Camp Site** pitches tents next door (£4.50 per person; showers 50p).

DENMARK (DANMARK)

DANISH KRONER

US$1 = 8.69KR	10KR = US$1.15
CDN$1 = 5.87KR	10KR = CDN$1.70
UK£1 = 12.22KR	10KR = UK£0.82
IR£1 = 9.49KR	10KR = IR£1.05
AUS$1 = 4.88KR	10KR = AUS$2.05
NZ$1 = 3.74KR	10KR = NZ$2.67
SAR1 = 1.22KR	10KR = SAR8.19
EUR€1 = 7.47KR	10KR = EUR€1.34

PHONE CODE   **Country code: 45. International dialing prefix: 00.**

Like Thumbelina, the heroine of native son Hans Christian Andersen's fairy tales, Denmark has a tremendous personality crammed into a tiny body. Danes delight in their eccentric traditions, such as burning witches in effigy on Midsummer's Eve, and eating pickled herring on New Year's Day. Although the Danes are justifiably proud of their fertile farmlands, beech forests, chalk cliffs, and sand dunes, their sense of self-criticism is reflected in the Danish literary canon: the more famous voices are Søren Kierkegaard, Hans Christian Andersen, and Isak Dinesen. Wedged between Sweden and Germany, the country is the cultural and geographic bridge between Scandinavia and continental Europe. With its Viking past centuries behind it, Denmark now has one of the most comprehensive social welfare structures in the world, and liberal immigration policies have diversified the erstwhile homogeneous population. Today, Denmark has a progressive youth culture that beckons travelers to the pristine beaches of Funen and the hip pub scene in Copenhagen. Contrary to the suggestion of a certain English playwright, very little seems to be rotten in the state of Denmark.

SUGGESTED ITINERARY

BEST OF DENMARK, ONE WEEK Begin to explore Denmark in chic and progressive **Copenhagen**, where you can muse about Kierkegaardian philosophy over coffee (2 days; see p. 256). For the best beaches in Denmark, take a ferry to the island of **Bornholm** (1 day; see p. 264). Shoot south to **Roskilde** and the fascinating **Viking Ship Museum;** if you time it right, you'll hit the massive **Roskilde Festival,** when rock takes over the city (1 day; p. 263). Move west over the new bridge, Storebæltsbro, to the island of Funen and **Odense** (1 day; p. 265), the hometown of Hans Christian Andersen. Then head to the southern end of Funen, hop on a ferry to the idyllic island of **Ærø** (1 day; see p. 266), a throwback to the Denmark of several centuries ago. Cross the Lillebælt to Jutland, where laid-back **Århus** delights with students and culture, then lets them play with blocks at nearby **Legoland** (1 day; see p. 267). On your way back down south, stop in Ribe, a magnificently-preserved medieval town (1 day; see p. 270).

LIFE AND TIMES

HISTORY AND POLITICS

The former home base of raiding Norsemen and Vikings, the tiny country of Denmark (43,094 sq. km; pop. 5.3 million) has done its share of pillaging. Danes evolved from nomadic hunters to farmers, and then from the 9th to 11th centuries AD proceeded to sack and rob the English coast as Vikings. Denmark, then called **Jutland,** was Christianized in the 10th century through the work of **Saint Ansgar** and **Harald the Bluetooth,** whose conversion seems to have been more for pragmatic purposes than spiritual ones—he quickly became the first Christian king of Denmark. Under the rule of Harald's descendents, Denmark controlled England, Norway, and part of Sweden. Various disputes plagued the Danish throne, and power was ultimately divided between the monarch and a **Council of Nobles.** Under the rule of **Valdemar II** in the 14th century, Denmark strengthened its power. After his death, his daughter **Margaret** ruled as regent for her five year old son **Olaf.** She secured the crown of Sweden, but her son's death at the age of 12 left him unable to enjoy the spoils of victory. Margaret and her heirs continued to rule, but in the 15th century Sweden was granted autonomy.

The Prussians declared war on the Danes in 1864, in order to ensure the safety of the newly unified Germany. Denmark's neutrality during World War I proved financially beneficial, as Denmark profited by trade with the warring nations. World War II saw the country occupied by Nazis, but Denmark refused to comply with pressure to persecute Jewish citizens, making it the only German-occupied nation to save all of its Jews. The 20th century witnessed drastic changes in the territories, as Denmark lost Iceland in 1944 and gained Greenland in 1953.

DENMARK TODAY. Following World War II, Denmark has been plagued by periodic economic setbacks, and a high budget deficit. Skyrocketing oil prices in the 1970s saw record levels of unemployment, which were helped in part by economic reforms in the 1980s, but never completely alleviated.

THE ARTS

The relatively small population of Denmark has scarcely precluded the development of a rich cultural life. On the literary front, the fairy tales of **Hans Christian Anderson** (1805-75) have been fodder for the bedtime stories of generations of children. Although significantly more somber in content, the philosopher **Kierkegaard** (1813-55) developed the "leap of faith," the idea that true faith is equivalent to a jump into darkness. **Karen Blixen** (1885-1962) gained fame writing under the name **Isak Dinesen,** detailing her life experiences in the book *Out of Africa.*

FOOD AND DRINK

A "Danish" in Denmark is a *wienerbrød* ("Viennese bread"), found in bakeries alongside other flaky treats. For more substantial fare, Danes favor small, open-faced sandwiches called *smørrebrød.* For cheap eats, look for lunch specials *(dagens ret)* and all-you-can-eat buffets *(spis alt du kan or tag selv buffet).* Beer *(Øl)* is usually served as a *lille* or *stor fadøl* (0.25L or 0.5L draft), but bottled beer tends to be cheaper. National brews are Carlsberg and Tuborg. The drinking age in bars in Denmark is 18, but many clubs have higher age limits; you must be 15 to buy beer and wine in stores. Many **vegetarian** *(vegetarret)* options are the result of Indian and Mediterranean influences, but salads and veggies *(grøntsaker)* can be found on most menus. For more on being veggie in Denmark, contact **Dansk Vegetarforening,** Borups Allé 131, 2000 Frederiksberg (☎38 34 24 48).

ESSENTIALS

DOCUMENTS AND FORMALITIES

South Africans need a **visa** to enter Denmark for tourist visits; nationals of Australia, Canada, New Zealand, UK, and the US do not, for visits less than three months.

Danish Embassies at Home: Australia, 15 Hunter St., Yarralumla, ACT 2600 (☎ (02) 62 73 21 95; fax 62 73 38 64); **Canada,** 47 Clarence St., #450, Ottawa, ON K1N 9K1 (☎ (613) 562-1811; fax 562-1812); **Ireland,** 121 St. Stephen's Green, Dublin 2 (☎ (01) 475 64 04; fax 478 45 36); **New Zealand,** 273 Bleakhouse Rd., Howick, P.O. Box 619, Auckland 1 (☎ (09) 537 30 99; fax 537 30 67); **South Africa,** 8th fl., Sanlam Centre, corner of Pretorius and Andries St., P.O. Box 2942, Pretoria 0001 (☎ (012) 322 05 95; fax 322 05 96); **UK,** 55 Sloane St., London SW1X 9SR (☎ (020) 73 33 02 00; fax 73 33 02 70; www.denmark.org.uk); **US,** 3200 Whitehaven St. NW, Washington, DC 20008 (☎ (202) 234-4300; fax 328-1470; www.denmarkemb.org).

Foreign Embassies in Denmark: All foreign embassies are in **Copenhagen** (see p. 256).

TRANSPORTATION

BY PLANE. The airport in **Copenhagen** handles international flights from cities around the world, mostly by SAS, Delta, United, British Airways, Air France, KLM, Lufthansa, and Swissair. **Billund Airport** in Jutland handles flights to other European cities. SAS (Scandinavian Airlines; US ☎ (800) 437-5804), the national airline company, offers youth, spouse, and senior discounts to some destinations.

BY TRAIN AND BY BUS. **Eurail** is valid on all state-run **DSB** routes. The *buy-in-Scandinavia* **Scanrail Pass** allows five days within 15 (1390kr, under 26 1040kr) or 21 consecutive days (2110kr, under 26 1585kr) of unlimited rail travel through Denmark, Norway, Sweden, and Finland, as well as many free or 20-50% discounted ferry rides. This differs from the *buy-outside-Scandinavia* **Scanrail Pass.** For domestic info, call ☎ 70 13 14 15; for international info, ☎ 70 13 14 16. Remote towns are typically served by **buses** from the nearest train station. The national **bus** network is also very reliable and fairly cheap. You can take buses or trains over the new Østersund bridge from Copenhagen to Malmö, Sweden.

BY FERRY. **Railpasses** earn discounts or free rides on many Scandinavian ferries. The free *Vi Rejser* newspaper, at tourist offices, can help you sort out the dozens of smaller ferries that serve Denmark's outlying islands. For info on ferries from **Copenhagen** to **Norway, Sweden, Poland,** and **Bornholm,** see p. 256. For more on connections from **Jutland** to **England, Sweden,** and **Norway,** see p. 267.

BY CAR. Roads are **toll-free,** except for the **Storebæltsbro** (Great Belt Bridge; 210kr) and the **Øresund bridge** (around 300kr). **Car rental** is generally around US$75 per day, plus insurance and a per-kilometer fee; to rent a car, you must be at least 20 years old (in some cases even 25). Speed limits are 50km per hr. (30mph) in urban areas, 80km per hr. (50mph) on highways, and 110km per hr. (68mph) on motorways. **Service centers** for motorists, called Info-terias, are spaced along Danish highways. **Gas** averages 6.50kr per liter. Watch out for bikes, which have the right-of-way. For more info on driving in Denmark, contact the **Forenede Danske Motorejere (FDM),** Firskovvej 32, Box 500, DK-2800 Lyngby (☎ 45 27 07 07; www.fdm.dk).

BY BIKE AND BY THUMB. Flat terrain, well-marked bike routes, bike paths in the countryside, and bike lanes in towns and cities make Denmark a cyclist's dream. You can **rent bikes** (40-55kr per day) from some tourist offices, rental shops, and a few train stations. The **Dansk Cyklist Førbund** (Danish Cycle Federation), Rømersg. 7, 1362 Copenhagen K (☎ 33 32 31 21; fax 33 32 76 83; www.dcf.dk), can hook you up with longer-term rentals. For info on bringing your bike on a train (which costs 50kr or less), pick up *Bikes and Trains* at any train station. **Hitchhiking** is legal in Denmark, but *Let's Go* does not recommend hitchhiking.

TOURIST SERVICES AND MONEY

EMERGENCY | Police: ☎ 112. Ambulance: ☎ 112. Fire: ☎ 112.

TOURIST OFFICES. Contact the main tourist board in Denmark at Vesterbrogade 6D, 1620 Copenhagen V (☎ 33 11 14 15; fax 33 93 14 16; email dt@dt.dk). **Use It** in Copenhagen offers many excellent services for budget travelers (see p. 256).

Tourist Boards at Home: UK, 55 Sloane St., London SW1X 9SY (☎ (020) 72 59 59 59; fax 72 59 59 55); **US,** 655 Third Ave, New York, NY 10017 (☎ (212) 885-9700; fax 885-9710).

CURRENCY AND EXCHANGE. The Danish unit of currency is the **kroner** (kr), divided into 100 *øre*. The easiest way to get cash is from **ATMs: Cirrus** and **PLUS** cash cards are widely accepted, and many machines give advances on credit cards.

Prices: Denmark has a high cost of living; expect to spend from US$30 (hostels and supermarkets) to US$60 (cheap hotels and restaurants) per day.

Tipping: There are no hard and fast rules, but it's always polite to round up to the nearest 10kr in restaurants and for taxis. In general, service at restaurants is included in the bill. Tipping up to 15% is becoming common in Copenhagen.

Taxes: Denmark has one of the highest Value Added Taxes in Europe, a flat 25% on just about everything except food. You can get a VAT refund upon leaving the country if you have spent at least US$95 in one store.

ACCOMMODATIONS AND CAMPING

While Denmark's **hotels** are generally expensive (250-850kr per night), the country's 101 **HI youth hostels** *(vandrerhjem)* are cheap (less than 100kr per night; nonmembers add 25kr), well-run, and have no age limit. The one- to five-star rating system doesn't take lovely settings, friendly owners, or serendipitous encounters into account, but higher-rated hostels may have in-room bathrooms and longer opening hours. Sheets cost about 40kr. Breakfasts usually run 40kr. Reception desks normally break between noon and 4pm and close for the day between 9 and 11pm. Reservations are required in winter and highly recommended in summer, especially near beaches. For more info, contact the **Danish Youth Hostel Association** (☎31 31 36 12; fax 31 31 36 26; email ldv@danhostel.dk; www.danhostel.dk). Many tourist offices book rooms in private homes (125-175kr), which are often in suburbs.

Denmark's 525 official **campgrounds** (about 60kr per person) rank from one-star (toilets and drinking water) to three-star (showers and laundry) to five-star (swimming, restaurants, and stoves). You'll either need a **Danish camping pass**, available at all campgrounds and valid for one year (45kr, families 75kr, groups 120kr), or an **international camping card**. The **Danish Camping Council** *(Campingradet;* ☎39 27 80 44) sells the campground handbook, *Camping Denmark*, and passes. Sleeping in train stations, in parks, and on public property is illegal.

COMMUNICATION

MAIL. Mailing a postcard/letter to Australia, Canada, New Zealand, the US, or South Africa costs 5.50kr; to elsewhere in Europe, 4.50kr. Domestic mail costs 4kr.

TELEPHONES. There are no separate city codes; include all digits for local *and* international calls. Buy phone cards at post offices or kiosks (30 units 30kr; 53 units 50kr; 110 units 100kr). For **domestic directory info,** call ☎118; **international info,** ☎113; collect calls, ☎141. International direct dial numbers include: **AT&T,** ☎80 01 00 10; **Australia Direct,** ☎80 01 00 61; **BT Direct,** ☎80 01 02 90; **Canada Direct,** ☎80 01 00 11; **Ireland Direct,** ☎80 01 03 53; **MCI WorldPhone Direct,** ☎80 01 00 22; **Sprint,** ☎80 01 08 77; **Telecom New Zealand,** ☎80 01 00 64; and **Telkom South Africa,** ☎80 01 00 27.

LANGUAGE. Danish. The Danish add æ *(*like the "e" in "egg"*),* ø (like the "i" in "first"), and a (sometimes written as *aa;* like the "o" in "lord") to the end of the alphabet; thus Århus would follow Viborg in an alphabetical listing of cities. Knowing *ikke* ("not") will help you figure out such signs as "No smoking" *(ikke-ryger);* *aben/lukket* (O-ben/loock-eh) means open/closed. Nearly all Danes speak flawless English, but a few Danish words might help break the ice: try *skal* (skoal), or "cheers." Danish has a distinctive glottal stop known as a *stød.*

LOCAL FACTS

Time: Denmark is 1hr. ahead of Greenwich Mean Time (GMT).

Climate: Denmark's climate is more solar than polar, and more dry than wet. The four seasons are distinct and winters relatively mild.

Hours: Shop hours are normally M-Th from about 9 or 10am to 6pm, and F until 7 or 8pm; they are also usually open Sa mornings (Copenhagen shops stay open all day Sa). Regular banking hours are M-W and F 9:30am-4pm, Th 9:30am-6pm.

Holidays in 2001: Easter (Apr. 5); Common Prayer Day (Apr. 30); Ascension Day (May 9); Whit Sunday and Monday (May 23-24); Constitution Day (June 5); Midsummer (June 23-24); Christmas (Dec. 24-26); and New Year's Eve (Dec. 31).

Festivals: Danes celebrate **Fastelavn** (Carneval) in Feb. and Mar. In May, the **Copenhagen Jazz Festival** does a week of concerts, many free. The **Roskilde Festival** is an immense open-air music festival held in Roskilde in June.

DENMARK

COPENHAGEN (KØBENHAVN)

Despite the swan ponds and cobblestone clichés that Hans Christian Andersen's fairy-tale imagery brings to mind, Denmark's capital is a fast-paced modern city that offers cafes, nightlife, and style to rival those of the great European cities—all at half the cost of Oslo or Stockholm. But if you are still craving Andersen's Copenhagen, the *Lille Havfrue* (Little Mermaid), Tivoli, and Nyhavn's Hanseatic gingerbread houses are also yours to discover.

◪ TRANSPORTATION

Flights: Kastrup Airport (☎32 47 47 47). S-trains connect the airport to Central Station (12min., every 20min., 18kr).

Trains: Trains stop at **Hovedbanegården.** Domestic travel ☎70 13 14 15; international ☎70 13 14 16. To: **Berlin** (9hr.; 1 per day; 895kr, under 26 580kr); **Hamburg** (4hr.; 5 per day; 425kr; under 26 320kr); **Oslo** (9hr.; 3 per day; 740kr; 530kr); and **Stockholm** (9hr.; 4-5 per day; 700kr; 540kr). **Reservations mandatory** (20kr). For cheaper travel to **Gothenburg, Stockholm, Oslo,** and **Östersund, Sweden,** buy a **Scanrabat** ticket a week ahead; you must reserve.

Ferries: Scandinavian Seaways (☎33 42 33 42) departs daily at 5pm for **Oslo** (16hr.; 480-735kr; under 26 315-570kr; Eurail and Scanrail 50% off). Trains to **Sweden** cross over on the **Helsingør-Helsingborg** ferry at no extra charge. Hourly **hydrofoils** (☎33 12 80 88) to **Malmö** go from Havnegade, at the end of Nyhavn (40min., 19-49kr). Both **Flyvbådene** and **Pilen** run hourly hydrofoils to Malmö from 9am-11pm (45min., 50kr). **Polferries** (☎33 11 46 45) set out Su, M, and W 8am, and Th and F 7:30pm from Nordre Toldbod, 12A (off Esplanaden) to **Świnoujście, Poland** (10hr., 340kr, with ISIC 285kr). **Bornholmstrafikken** (☎33 13 18 66; fax 33 93 18 66) goes to **Bornholm** (7hr., 1-2 per day, 189kr).

Public Transportation: Bus info ☎36 13 14 15 (daily 7am-9:30pm); **train** info ☎33 14 17 01 (daily 7am-9pm). **Buses** and **S-trains** (subways and suburban trains; run M-Sa 5am-12:30am, Su 6am-12:30am) operate on a zone system; 2-zone **tickets** run 12kr; add 6kr per additional zone. The cheaper **rabatkort** (rebate card), available from kiosks and bus drivers, gets you 10 "clips," each good for one journey within a specified number of zones. The blue 2-zone *rabatkort* (80kr) can be clipped more than once for longer trips. Tickets and clips allow 1hr. of transfers. The **24hr. pass** grants unlimited bus and train transport in greater Copenhagen (70kr); buy at the Tivoli tourist office or any train station. **Railpasses,** including **Eurail,** are good on S-trains but not buses. **Night buses** run on different routes during the remaining hours and charge double fare. The **Copenhagen Card,** sold in hotels, tourist offices, and train stations, grants unlimited travel in North Zealand, discounts on ferries to Sweden, and admission to most sights (24hr. 155kr, 48hr. 255kr, 72hr. 320kr), but isn't always worth it unless you plan to ride the bus religiously and see several museums in one day.

Taxis: ☎35 35 35 35, ☎38 77 77 77, or ☎38 10 10 10. Base fare 22kr; add 8kr per km 7am-4pm, 10kr per km 4pm-7am. From Central Station to airport costs 150kr.

Bike Rental: City Bike lends bikes for free. Deposit 20kr at any of 150 bike racks citywide and retrieve the coin upon return at any rack. **Københavns Cykler,** Reventlowsgade 11 (☎33 33 86 13), rents for 50kr per day, 225kr per week; 300kr deposit. Open July-Aug. M-F 8am-6pm, Sa 9am-1pm, Su 10am-1pm; Sept.-June closed Su.

Hitchhiking: Use It has ride boards (see **Tourist Office,** below). *Let's Go* does not recommend hitchhiking.

✴ ORIENTATION AND PRACTICAL INFORMATION

Copenhagen lies on the east coast of the island of **Zealand** (Sjælland), across the sound (Øresund) from Malmö, Sweden. The new 17-mile **Øresund bridge and tunnel,** opened July 1, 2000, established the first "fixed link" between the two countries. Copenhagen's **Hovedbanegården** (Central Station) lies near the city's heart. North of

DENMARK

Copenhagen
ACCOMMODATIONS
City Public Hostel, 3
Hotel Jørgensen, 4
Mike's Guest House, 1
Sleep-In Green, 6
Sleep-In Heaven, 5
Sleep-In, 7
Vesterbros Inter Point, 2

The Little Mermaid
Poland Ferries
Christiania
Kastellet
Oslo / Bornholm Ferries
Amalienborg Palace
Sweden Ferries
Frelsers Kirke
CHRISTIANSHAVN
Frihedsmuseet
Esplanaden
Amaliegade
Marmorkirken
Bredgade
Toldbodgade
Nyhavn
Skt. Anne Plads
Torvegade
Store Kongensgade
Borgergade
Kronprinsessegade
Peder Skrams Gade
KONGENS NYTORV
Royal Theater
Kanal
Christianshavn
Strandgade
Amagerbrogade
Amager Fælled Vej
Vermlandsgade
Amagerbrogade
Øster Voldgade
Statens Museum for Kunst
Rigensgade
Rosenborg Castle
Rosenborg Park
Gothersg.
Rudeløm
Pilestræde
Christiansborg Palace
Christians Brygge
Borsgade
Vester Voldgade
National Museum
Stockholmsgade
Botanical Gardens
Arbejdermuseet
Frederiksborg
Nørreg.
STRØGET
Use It
Rådhuststræde
RÅDHUS PLADSEN
Ny Carlsberg Glyptotek
Sydhavnen
Øster Søgade
Sølvgade
Ø. Farimagsgade
Fiolstræde
Nørre Voldgade
Nansensgade
Kalvebod Brygge
Øster Søgade
Fredensgade
Blegdamsvej
Gothersg.
Frederiksborg
Farimagsgade
N. Farimagsgade
Tivoli
H.C. Andersens Boulevard
Vesterfarimagsgade
Bernstorffsgade
Colbjørnsenst.
Nørre Allé
Guldbergs Gade
Nørrebrogade
Ravnsborg
Nørre Søgade
Gyldenløvesg.
Vester Søgade
Vesterbrogade
Istedgade
Reverdilsgade
Helgolandsgade
NØRREBRO
Baggesensgade
Korsgade
Peblinge Dossering
Vodroffsvej
Absalonsgade
Skelbækgade
Sønder Boulevard
Dybbølsgade
VESTERBRO
Assistens Cemetery
Jægvej
H. Tavsensgade
Struensegade
Rantzausgade
Sankt Hansgade
Aboulevard
Rosenørn's Allé
Danasvej
Skt. Knuds Vej
Saxog. Oehlen-Schlægersgade
Valdemarsgade
Vesterbrogade
Stengade
Ågade
Due Vej
Nordre Fasanvej
Kong Georgs Vej
Holger Danskes Vej
Godthåbsvej
Rolighedsvej
Thorvaldsensvej
Bülows Vej
Gammel Kongevej
Frederiksberg Allé
Enghavevej
Vesterfælled Vej
Vesterbrogade
Carlsberg Brewery
Valby Langg.
Ny Carlsberg Vej
Gl. Carlsberg Vej
Falkoner Allé
Grundtvigsvej
Smallegade
Nyelands Vej
Frederiksberg Park
Pile Allé
Allégade
Roskildevej
Bakkes Allé
Sønder Fasanvej
Valby Langgade
Magnoliavej
Guldborg

500 yards
500 meters

N

the station, **Vesterbrogade** passes **Tivoli** and **Rådhuspladsen** (the central square and terminus of most bus lines), then cuts through the city center as **Strøget** (STROY-yet), the world's longest pedestrian thoroughfare.

TOURIST, FINANCIAL, AND LOCAL SERVICES

Tourist Office: Use It, Rådhusstr. 13 (☎33 73 06 20; www.useit.dk). From the station, follow Vesterbrog., cross Rådhuspladsen onto Frederiksbergg., and turn right on Rådhusstr. Indispensable and geared toward budget travelers. Pick up a copy of *Play Time*, a comprehensive guide to the city geared specifically to young budget travelers. Daytime luggage storage, finds lodgings, holds mail. Open mid-June to mid-Sept. daily 9am-7pm; mid-Sept. to mid-June M-W 11am-4pm, Th 11am-6pm, F 11am-2pm.

Budget Travel: Wasteels Rejser, Skoubog. 6 (☎33 14 46 33). Open M-F 9am-7pm, Sa 10am-3pm. **Kilroy Travels,** Skinderg. 28 (☎33 11 00 44). Open M-F 10am-5:30pm, Sa 10am-2pm.

Embassies: Australia, (consulate), Strand Boulevarden 122, 5th fl. (☎39 29 20 77; fax 39 29 60 77). **Canada,** Kristen Bernikowsg. 1 (☎33 48 32 00; fax 33 48 32 21). **Ireland,** Østerbaneg. 21 (☎35 42 32 33; fax 35 43 18 58). New Zealanders should contact the **New Zealand** embassy in Brussels (see p. 124). **South Africa,** Gammel Vartovvej 8 (☎39 18 01 55; fax 39 18 40 06). **UK,** Kastelsvej 36-40 (☎35 44 52 00; fax 35 44 52 93). **US,** Dag Hammarskjölds Allé 24 (☎35 55 31 44; fax 35 43 02 23).

Currency Exchange: Forex, in Central Station. 25kr commission on cash, 15kr per traveler's check. Open daily 8am-9pm.

Luggage Storage: Free at **Use It** tourist office and most hostels. At **Central Station,** 20-35kr per 24hr. Open M-Sa 5:30am-1am and Su 6am-1am.

Laundromats: Look for **Vascomat** and **Møntvask** chains. At Borgerg. 2, Nansensg. 39, and Istedg. 45. Wash and dry 40-50kr. Most open daily 7am-9pm.

Gay and Lesbian Services: National Association for Gay Men and Women, Teglgaardsstr. 13 (☎33 13 19 48). Open M-F 5-7pm. The monthly *PAN Homoguide* lists clubs, cafes, and organizations, and is available at **PAN** (see p. 262). Also check out www.copenhagen-gay-life.dk and www.gayonline.dk.

EMERGENCY AND COMMUNICATIONS

Emergencies: ☎112. **Police** (☎33 14 14 48) headquarters are at Polititorvet.

Pharmacy: Steno Apotek, Vesterbrog. 6c (☎33 14 82 66). Open 24hr.; ring the bell.

Medical Assistance: Doctors on Call (☎33 93 63 00). Open M-F 8am-4pm; after hours, call ☎38 88 60 41. Visits 120-350kr. **Emergency rooms** at **Sundby Hospital,** Kastrup 63 (☎32 34 32 34), and **Bispebjerg Hospital,** Bispebjerg Bakke 23 (☎35 31 35 31).

Internet Access: Free at **Use It** and at **Copenhagen Hovedbibliotek** (Central Library), Krystalg. 15 (open M-F 10am-7pm, Sa 10am-2pm).

Post Office: Tietgensg. 35-39, **1500** København V, behind Central Station. Open M-F 11am-6pm, Sa 10am-1pm. **Branch office** in Central Station. Address mail to be held: Adam KATZ, *Poste Restante*, Main Post Office, Tietgensgade 35-39, **1500** Kobenhavn V, DENMARK. Mail also held at **Use It**; address mail to: Adam KATZ, *Poste Restante*, Use It, 13 Rådhusstræde, **1466** Copenhagen K.

⌐, ACCOMMODATIONS

København means "merchant's port" in Danish, but the lodgings that once housed merchants disappeared ages ago, leaving in their wake lovely hostels and campgrounds, but few budget hotels. During holidays (such as the national vacation in early August) and the largest festivals, especially Karneval (mid-May), Roskilde (late June), and Copenhagen Jazz (late July), reserve rooms well in advance.

Sleep-In Heaven, Struenseeg. 7 (☎35 35 46 48; email sleepinheaven@get2net.dk), in Nørrebro. Take bus #8 (dir.: Tingbjerg) 5 stops to Rantzausg.; continue in the same direction as the bus, then turn right on Kapelvej, left on Tavsensg., and left on (poorly marked) Struenseeg. Lively courtyard and lounge. Close to hip Skt. Hans Torv nightlife. Internet 20kr per 30min. Reception 24hr. Dorms 100kr; doubles 400kr.

Hotel Jørgensen, Rømersg. 11 (☎33 13 81 86), 25min. from Central Station, 5min. from Strøget, on a quiet street. S-train: Nørreport; walk along Frederiksborgg. and turn left on Rømersg. Cramped no-frills dorms, but central and friendly. Breakfast included. Sheets 30kr. Reception 24hr. Lockout 11am-3pm. No dorm reservations. July-Sept. dorms 115kr. Oct.-June dorms 100kr; singles 400kr; doubles from 500kr; quads 560kr.

City Public Hostel, Absalonsg. 8 (☎31 31 20 70), in the Vesterbro Youth Center. From the station, walk away from the Rådhuspladsen on Vesterbrog. and turn left on Absalonsg. Happening lounge and BBQ. Sheets 30kr. Kitchen. Reception 24hr. Open early May-late Aug. Dorms 110kr; with breakfast 130kr.

Sleep-In Green, Ravnsborgg. 18, Baghuset (☎35 37 77 77). Take bus #16 from the station to Nørrebrog. Cozy, eco-friendly dorms outside the city center. Organic breakfast 30kr. Sheets 30kr. Reception 24hr. Check-out noon. Open late May-Sept. 85kr.

Mike's Guest House, Kirkevænget 13 (☎36 45 65 40). 10min. by bus or train from Central Station; always call ahead. Clean, spacious rooms—some with private balconies—in a quiet neighborhood. Singles 200kr; doubles 290kr; triples 400kr.

Vesterbros Inter Point, Vesterbros KFUM (YMCA), Valdemarsg. 15 (☎33 31 15 74). From Central Station, walk east on Vesterbrog. and turn left. Super-friendly staff; homey atmosphere. Breakfast 25kr. Sheets 20kr. Kitchen. Reception 8:30-11:30am, 3:30-5:30pm, and 8pm-12:30am. Curfew 12:30am. Open late June-early Aug. 75kr.

Sleep-In, Blegdamsvej 132 (☎35 26 50 59). Bus #6: Triangeln or S-train: Østerport; walk 10min. up Hammerskjölds (across the square from the 7-11). Near the city center and Østerbro nightlife. Quantity over privacy at this popular (and noisy) warehouse of a hostel. Sheets 30kr. Kitchen. Reception 24hr. Lockout noon-4pm. Open July-Aug. 80kr.

Ajax, Bavnehøj Allé 30 (☎33 21 24 56). S-train A: Sydhavn; walk north on Enghavevej, turn left on Bavnehøj Allé, and look for signs on the right. Sheets 20kr. Kitchen. TV. Open July-Aug. Dorms 60kr; hostel tent 50kr; camp in your own tent 45kr.

København Vandrerhjem Bellahøj (HI), Herbergvejen 8 (☎38 28 97 15; email bellahoj@danhostel.dk), in Bellahøj. Take bus #11 from the station to Primulavej. Large, modern hostel far from the city center. Breakfast 40kr. Sheets 30kr. Laundry 26kr. Reception 24hr. Open Mar. to mid-Jan. Dorms 90kr; doubles 240kr.

København Vandrerhjem Amager (HI), Vejlandsallé 200 (☎32 52 29 08). Take bus #46 (M-F 6am-5pm; at night, bus #96N) from Central Station or the S-train to Valby, then take bus #37. Far from the city center in a huge nature reserve. Laundry 25kr. Kitchen. Sheets 30kr. Safe. Reception 24hr. Check-in 1-5pm. Open mid-Jan. to Nov. Dorms 90kr; nonmembers 110kr.

Bellahøj Camping, Hvidkildevej 66 (☎38 10 11 50), 5km from the city center. Take bus #11 to Bellahøj. Shower included. Kitchen. Cafe and market. Reception 24hr. Open June-Aug. 57kr per person.

Absalon Camping, Korsdalsvej 132, Rødovre (☎36 41 06 00), 9km from the city center. From Central Station, take bus #5505. Kitchen, laundry, and store. 55kr per person, 8kr per tent; cabins 195kr plus 54kr per person.

◑ FOOD

The Vikings once slobbered down mutton and salted fish in Copenhagen; today you can seek out more refined offerings. Around **Kongens Nytorv,** elegant cafes serve sandwiches (*smørrebrød*) for around 35kr. All-you-can-eat buffets (40-70kr) are popular, especially at Turkish, Indian, and Italian restaurants. **Fakta** and **Netto** super-markets are budget fantasies; one is at Fiolstr. 7, north of Strøget (open M-F 9am-7pm, Sa 8am-5pm). Open-air **markets** provide fresh fruits and veggies; try the one at **Israels Plads** near Nørreport Station (open M-Th 9am-5:30pm, F 9am-6:30pm, Sa 9am-3pm). **Fruit stalls** line Strøget and the side streets to the north.

Nyhavns Færgekro, Nyhavn 5. Upscale fisherman's cottage atmosphere along the canal. Lunch on 10 varieties of all-you-can-eat herring (78kr). Open daily 11:30am-11:30pm.

Den Grønne Kælder, Pilestr. 48. Popular, classy vegetarian and vegan dining. Hummus 18-35kr. Veggie burgers 30kr. Open M-Sa 11am-10pm.

Café Klimt, Frederiksborgg. 29. From Strøget, turn on Købmagerg. and exit the pedestrian zone, crossing Nørre Voldg. The street becomes Frederiksborgg. The food and the atmosphere are both as pleasant and imaginative as the cafe's namesake. Excellent brunch (11am-4pm). Main dishes 60-90kr. Open daily 11am-midnight.

Kafe Kys, Læderstr. 7, on a quiet street running south of and parallel to Strøget. Sandwiches 40-60kr. Beer 35kr. Open M-Th 11am-1am, F-Sa 11am-2am, Su noon-10pm.

Café Norden, Østerg. 61, on Strøget and Nicolaj Plads, in sight of the fountain. A French-style cafe with the best vantage point on Strøget. Crepes 59-62kr; sandwiches 16-58kr; pastries 15-40kr. Open daily 9am-midnight.

Café Europa, Amagertorv, on Nicolaj Plads opposite Café Norden. If Norden is the place to see, trendy Europa is the place to be seen. Sandwiches 23-44kr. Beer 45kr per pint. Great coffee. Open M-W 9am-midnight, Th-Sa 9am-1am.

◉ SIGHTS

Compact Copenhagen is best seen by foot or bike; pick up a free **city bike** (see p. 256) to survey its stunning architecture. Various **tours** are detailed in Use It's *Playtime* and tourist office brochures. The squares along the lively pedestrian **Strøget**, which divides the city center, are **Nytorv, Nicolaj Plads,** and **Kungens Nytorv.** Opposite Kungens Nytorv is **Nyhavn,** the "new port" where Hans Christian Andersen wrote his first fairy tale, lined with Hanseatic houses and sailing boats. There are several canal tours, but **Netto boats** offers the best value (late Apr. to mid-Sept. every 20min. 10am-5pm; 20kr). **Bus #6** travels through Vesterbro, Rådhuspladsen, alongside Strøget, and on to Østerbro, acting as a sight-seeing guide to the city.

CITY CENTER. The first sight you'll see as you exit the train station is **Tivoli,** the famed 19th-century amusement park, which delights with botanical gardens, marching toy soldiers, and rides. Wednesday and weekend nights culminate with music and fireworks. An increasingly popular Christmas market is open at Tivoli mid-November through mid-December. *(Vesterbrog. 3. Open late Apr. to mid-Sept. Su-Th 11am-midnight, F-Sa 11am-1am. Children's rides open 11:30am, others 12:30pm. 45kr; before 1pm 35kr. Single-ride tickets 10-20kr. Ride pass 168kr.)* From Central Station, turn right on Bernstorffsg. and left on Tietgensg. to partake of the ancient and Impressionist art and sculpture at the beautiful **Ny Carlsberg Glyptoket.** *(Dantes Plads 7. Open Tu-Su 10am-4pm. 30kr; free W and Su or with ISIC.)* Continue along Tietgensg., which becomes Stormg., to dive into Denmark's Viking treasures and other tidbits of its cultural history at the **National Museum.** *(Ny Vestergade 10. Open Tu-Su 10am-5pm. 40kr, students 30kr; W free.)* **Christiansborg Castle,** Prins Jørgens Gård, features subterranean ruins, royal reception rooms, and the *Folketing* (Parliament) chambers. To get there, continue down Tietgensg. from the city center until you cross the canal. *(Tours May-Sept. daily 11am and 3pm; June-Aug. 11am, 1, and 3pm; Oct.-Apr. Tu-Th and Sa-Su 11am and 3pm; 40kr. Ruins 20kr. Ask about the free Parliament tours.)*

CHRISTIANSHAVN. In the southern section of Christianshavn, the "free city" of **Christiania,** founded in 1971 by youthful squatters in abandoned military barracks, is inhabited by a thriving group of artists and alterna-thinkers carrying '70s activism and free love into the new millennium. Come Christmas, there is a fabulous market with curiosities from all over the world. Exercise caution in the **Pusher St.** area, aptly named as the site of *many* hash and marijuana sales. Possession of even small amounts can get you arrested. Always ask before taking pictures, **never** take pictures on Pusher St. itself, and exercise caution in the area at night. *(From Central Station, turn right on Bernstorffs, left on Tietgensg.; continue as it changes names and bear right along the water. After crossing the water, turn left on Prinsesseg.)* Climb the golden spire of **Vor Frelsers Kirke** (Our Savior's Church) for a great view. *(Sankt Annæg. 29. Turn left off Prinsesseg. Church open daily Mar.-Nov. 9am-4:30pm, Dec.-Feb. 10am-2pm; free. Tower open Mar.-Nov. 9am-4:30pm; 20kr.)*

FREDERIKSTADEN. Edvard Eriksen's **den Lille Havfrue** (The Little Mermaid) tiny but touristed statue at the opening of the harbor honors favorite son Hans Christian

Andersen. *(S-train: Østerport; turn left out of the station, left on Folke Bernadottes Allé, right after passing a canal, and follow it to the ocean. Open daily 6am-dusk.)* Retrace your steps and turn left to cross the moat to **Kastellet**, a 17th-century fortress-turned-park. Cross through Kastellet to the **Frihedsmuseet** (Resistance Museum), which chronicles the Nazi occupation from 1940 to 1945. The fascinating museum documents Denmark's efforts to rescue its Jews and its period of acceptance of German "protection," when the Danish government arrested anti-Nazi saboteurs. *(At Churchillparken. Open May to early Sept. Tu-Sa 10am-4pm, Su 10am-5pm; mid-Sept. to Apr. Tu-Sa 11am-3pm, Su 11am-4pm. Free.)* From the museum, walk south down Amalieng. to reach the lovely **Amalienborg Palace**, residence of Queen Margarethe II and the royal family; most of the interior is closed to the public, but you can see the apartments of Christian VII. The changing of the palace guard takes place at noon on the brick plaza. *(Open daily June-Aug. 10am-4pm; May and Sept.-Oct. 11am-4pm; Jan.-Apr. Tu-Su 11am-4pm. 35kr.)* The 19th-century **Marmorkirken** (Marble Church), opposite the palace, features an ornate interior and Europe's third-largest dome. *(Church open M-Tu and Th-Sa 10:30am-4:30pm, W 10:30am-6:30pm, Su noon-4:30pm; free. Dome 20kr.)*

A few blocks north, **Statens Museum for Kunst** (State Museum of Fine Arts) displays an eclectic collection in a beautifully designed building. From the church, head away from Amalienborg, go left on Store Kongensg., turn right on Dronningens Tværg., and take an immediate right and then left onto Sølvg. *(Sølvg. 48-50. Open Tu-Su 10am-5pm. 40kr.)* Opposite the museum, **Rosenborg Slot** (Rosenborg Palace and Gardens) hoards royal treasures, including the crown jewels. *(Øster Volg. 4A. Open daily May-Sept. 10am-4pm; Oct. 11am-3pm; Nov.-Apr. Tu-Su 11am-2pm. 45kr.)*

OTHER SIGHTS. For legalized substance abuse, a trip to the **Carlsberg Brewery** will reward you with a wealth of knowledge and, more importantly, free samples. *(Ny Carlsbergvej 140. Take bus #6 west from Rådhuspladsen to Valby Langg. Open M-F 10am-3pm. Free.)* If the breweries haven't confused your senses enough, play with science at the hands-on **Experimentarium**. *(Tuborg Havnevej 7. Take bus #6 north from Rådhuspladsen. Open late June to mid-Aug. daily 10am-5pm; late Aug. to early June M and W-F 9am-5pm, Tu 9am-9pm, Sa-Su 11am-5pm. 79kr, students 61kr.)*

♫ ENTERTAINMENT

For events, consult *Copenhagen This Week* (free at hostels and tourist offices), or pick up *Use It News* from Use It. The **Royal Theater** is home to the world-famous Royal Danish Ballet. For same-day half-price tickets, head to the **Tivoli ticket office**, Vesterbrog. 3. (☎33 15 10 12. Open daily mid-Apr. to mid-Sept. 9am-9pm; mid-Sept. to mid-Apr. 9am-7pm. Royal theater tickets available at 4 or 5pm, others at noon.) Call **Arte**, Hvidkildevej 64 (☎38 88 22 22), to ask about student discounts. The relaxed **Kul-Kaféen**, Teglgårdsstr. 5, is a great place to see live performers and get info on music, dance, and theater. (Open M-Sa 11am-midnight.) During the world-class **Copenhagen Jazz Festival** (mid-July; ☎33 93 20 13; www.cjf.dk), the city teems with free outdoor concerts complementing the more refined venues. In anticipation of the summer blowout, the **Swingin' Copenhagen** festival sets the city grooving to traditional jazz (www.swingin-copenhagen.dk), and **Copenhagen Autumn Jazz** in early November keeps the city bopping long after summer is gone.

♫ NIGHTLIFE

Copenhagen's weekends often begin on Wednesday, and nights rock until 5am; "morning pubs" that open when the clubs close let you party around the clock. On Thursday, most bars and clubs have reduced covers and cheap drinks. The central pedestrian district reverberates with crowded bars and discos; **Kongens Nytorv** has fancier joints. Many buy beer at a supermarket and head to the boats and cafes of **Nyhavn** for its salty charisma. The **Scala** complex, opposite Tivoli, has many bars and restaurants; students enliven the cheaper bars in the **Nørrebro** area. Copenhagen's gay and lesbian scene is one of Europe's best.

DENMARK

Rust, Guldbergsg. 8, in the Nørrebro. Twenty-somethings pack this disco with an underground feel. Long lines by 1am. Cover 50kr; free before 11pm. Open Tu-Su 10pm-5am.

Café Pavillionen, on Borgmester Jensens Allé, in Fælleaparken. This summer-only outdoor cafe has local bands 8-10pm, plus a disco W-Sa 10pm-5am. On Mondays, enjoy a concert 2:30-5pm, then tango lessons and dancing until midnight.

Park, Østerbrog. 79, in Østerbro. Lose your inhibitions and your friends in this enormous club with 2 packed dance floors, live music hall, and rooftop patio. Pints 40kr. No tennis shoes. Cover F-Sa 50kr. Open Su-W 10am-2am, Th 10am-4am, F-Sa 10am-5am.

Enzo, Nørreg. 41. Doll yourself up and dance with a young stylish crowd. Dress code. 21+. Cover 60kr. Open F-Sa 10:30pm-5:30am.

IN Bar, Nørreg. 1. Drink *cheap* and then dance on the speakers! F-Sa cover 150kr, includes open bar. Th-Sa 20+. Open Su-Th 10pm-5am, F-Sa 10pm-10am.

JazzHouse, Niels Hemmingsens G. 10 (www.jazzhouse.dk). Turn left off Strøget from Gammeltorv (closer to Råhuspladsen) and Nytorv. Copenhagen's premier jazz venue makes for a sophisticated and potentially expensive evening. Check the calendar for prices. Concerts Su-Th 8:30pm, F-Sa 9:30pm. Club open midnight-5am.

PAN Club and Café, Knabrostr. 3. Gay cafe, bar, and disco. Publishes the *Homoguide*. Cover Th 20kr; F-Sa 50kr. Cafe opens daily 8pm, disco 11pm. Both stay open late.

Sebastian Bar and Café, 10 Hyskenstr., off Strøget. The city's best-known gay and lesbian bar. *Homoguide* available. Happy Hour 5-9pm. Open daily noon-2am.

▶️ DAYTRIPS FROM COPENHAGEN

Stunning castles, white sand beaches, and a world-class museum hide in North, Central, and South Zealand, all within easy reach of Copenhagen by train. A northern train route (every 20min.) offers easy access to many attractive daytrips that lie within an hour of Copenhagen in North Zealand.

RUNGSTED AND HUMLEBÆK

Rungsted (30min., 40kr or 4 clips on the blue rabatkort). Humlebæk (45min., 38.50kr or 4 clips).

In North Zealand, the quiet harbor town of **Rungsted,** where Karen Blixen (pseudonym Isak Dinesen) wrote *Out of Africa,* houses the author's abode, personal effects, and grave at the **Karen Blixen Museum,** Rungsted Strandvej 111. From the station, turn left on Stationsvej, right on Rungstedsvej, and left on Rungsted Strandvej. (Open May-Sept. daily 10am-5pm; Oct.-Apr. W-F 1-4pm, Sa-Su 11am-4pm. 30kr.) **Humlebæk,** farther up the coast, distinguishes itself with the spectacular **Louisiana Museum of Modern Art,** named for the three wives (all named Louisa) of the estate's original owner. The museum contains works by Picasso, Warhol, Lichtenstein, Calder, and other 20th-century masters; the building and its sculpture-studded grounds overlooking the sea are themselves worth the trip. Follow signs 1½km north from the Humlebæk station or snag bus #388. (Open Th-M 10am-5pm, W 10am-10pm. 60kr, students 50kr.)

HELSINGØR AND HORNBÆK

Helsingør is at the end of the northern line (1hr.). Bus #340 and the train outside the station run from Helsingør to Hornbæk (20min., 20kr).

Helsingør is evidence of the Danish monarchy's fondness for lavish architecture. In a region famous for castles, the most famous is the 15th-century **Kronborg Slot** in Helsingør, also known as **Elsinore,** the setting for Shakespeare's *Hamlet* (although neither the historical "Amled" nor the Bard ever visited Kronborg). Viking chief Holger Danske is buried in the castle's spooky dungeon; legend has it that he still rises to face any threat to Denmark's safety. The castle also houses the **Danish Maritime Museum,** which contains the world's oldest sea biscuit, from 1853. From the train station, turn left and follow the signs on the waterfront to the castle. (Open May-Sept. daily 10:30am-5pm; Apr. and Oct. Tu-Su 11am-4pm; Nov.-Mar. Tu-Su 11am-3pm. 45kr.) The **tourist office,** inside **Kulturhuset,** books rooms (25kr fee). The large grey building across the street from the station is the Kulturhuset; the entrance is around the corner. (☎49 21 13 33. Open mid-June to Aug. M-Th 9am-5pm, F-Sa 10am-6pm, Su 10am-3pm; Sept. to mid-June M-F 9am-4pm, Sa 10am-1pm.) **Hornbæk** offers beautiful beaches where you can see Danes at their most beautiful. There's a wild **harbor festival** on the fourth weekend in July.

HILLERØD AND FREDENSBORG

Hillerød is at the end of S-train lines A and E via Lyngby (40min., 42kr).

Another northern route brings you to **Hillerød,** home of the moated **Frederiksborg Slot,** arguably the most impressive of North Zealand's castles, with exquisite gardens and brick ramparts. Free concerts are given Thursdays at 1:30pm on the famous 1610 **Esaias Compenius organ** in the chapel. To get there from the station, cross the street onto Vibekeg. and follow the signs. (Open daily Apr.-Oct. 10am-5pm; Nov.-Mar. 11am-3pm. 40kr, students 10kr.) A final stop on the northern castle tour is **Fredensborg Castle,** on the Lille Nord rail line connecting Hillerød and Helsingør, at the Fredensborg stop. Built in 1722, the castle still serves as the spring and fall royal residence. (Castle open daily July 1-5pm; 10kr. Park open year-round; free.) Sleep with (well, near) the royals and enjoy a fantastic palace garden view at **Fredensborg Youth Hostel (HI),** Østrupvej 3, 1km from the train station. (☎48 48 03 15. Sheets 45kr. Reception 7am-9pm. Dorms 100kr; nonmembers 120kr.)

ROSKILDE

Accessible by train (25-30min., 38.50kr or 4 clips).

In Central Zealand, Roskilde served as Denmark's first capital when King Harald Bluetooth built the country's first Christian church here in 980. Several Danish monarchs repose in the ornate sarcophagi of **Roskilde Domkirke.** (Open Apr.-Sept. M-F 9am-4:45pm, Sa 9am-noon, Su 12:30-4:45pm; Oct.-Mar. M-F 9am-4:45pm, Sa 12:30-3:45pm. Concerts June-Aug. Th 8pm. 12kr, students 6kr.) The **Viking Ship Museum,** on Strandengen along the harbor, houses remnants of five trade ships and warships sunk circa 1060 and salvaged in the late 1960s. From the tourist office, walk to the cathedral and downhill through the park. (Open daily May-Sept. 9am-5pm; Oct.-Apr. 10am-4pm. May-Sept. 50kr; Oct.-Apr. 50kr. Boat trip 40kr; book ahead.) In summer, book a ride on a Viking longboat, but be prepared to take an oar—Viking conquest is no spectator sport! Roskilde hosts one of Europe's largest **music festivals** (June 28-30, 2001; ☎46 36 66 13; www.roskilde-festival.dk), drawing over 90,000 fans with bands such as REM, U2, Radiohead, Smashing Pumpkins, and Metallica. The **tourist office,** Gullandsstr. 15, sells festival tickets and books rooms for a 25kr fee. From the train station, turn left on Jernbaneg., right on Allehelgansg., left again on Barchog., and look to the left. (☎46 35 27 00. Open Apr.-June M-F 9am-5pm, Sa 10am-1pm; July-Aug. M-F 9am-6pm, Sa 9am-3pm, Su 10am-2pm; Sept.-Mar. M-Th 9am-5pm, F 9am-4pm, Sa 10am-1pm.) The **HI youth hostel,** Hørhusene 61, is on the harbor next to the Viking museum shipyard. The gorgeous, modern facility is always booked during the festival. (☎46 35 21 84. Reception 9am-noon and 4-8pm. Open Feb.-Dec. Dorms 90kr; nonmembers 115kr.) To camp by the beach at **Roskilde Camping,** Baunehøjvej 7, 4km north of town, take bus #603 towards Veddelev. (☎46 75 79 96. Reception 8am-10pm. Open Apr. to mid-Sept. 50kr per person.)

KLAMPENBORG AND CHARLOTTENLUND

Both are at the end of S-train line C.

Klampenborg and Charlottenlund, on the coastal line, feature **topless beaches.** Though less ornate than Tivoli, **Bakken** in Dyrehaven, Klampenborg, the world's oldest amusement park, delivers more thrills. From the Klampenborg train station, turn left, cross the overpass, and head through the park. (Open daily Mar. 25-Aug. 11am-midnight. Rides start at 2pm; 10-25kr each.) Bakken borders the **Jægersborg Deer Park,** the royal family's former hunting grounds, still home to their **Eremitage** summer chateau, miles of wooded paths, and over 2000 red deer.

MØN

Take the train from Copenhagen to Vordingborg, then bus #62 or 64 to Stege. Once on the island, you can take bus #54 to Møn Klint. Plan carefully: only three buses go to the island and back each day, and the last often leaves Møn before 4pm.

To see what Andersen called one of the most beautiful spots in Denmark, head south of Copenhagen to the isle of Møn's white cliffs. Locals travel to Møn to spend quiet days shopping in the villages and exploring the gorgeous chalk cliffs and the cottage-strewn pastoral landscape. For more info, contact the **Møns Turistbureau,** Storeg. 2, in Stege. (☎55 81 44 11. Open June 15-Aug. M-F 10am-6pm, Sa 9am-6pm, Su 10am-noon; Sept.-June 14 M-F 10am-5pm, Sa 9am-noon.)

BORNHOLM

Gorgeous Bornholm island gets the most sun and the least rain in Denmark, luring vacationers to its beaches and pleasant fishing villages. Ideal for avid bikers and nature-lovers, its red-roofed cliffside villas may seem southern European, but the flowers and half-timbered houses are undeniably Danish. Bornholm's unique **round churches** were both places of worship and fortresses for waiting out pirate attacks. The sandiest and longest **beaches** are at **Dueodde**, on the island's southern tip. Of the four towns, **Østerlars** is the largest, and **Nylors** the best-preserved.

E TRANSPORTATION. Ferries arrive in **Rønne,** Bornholm's capital, from Denmark, Sweden, Germany, and Poland. **Bornholmstrafikken** (Rønne ☎56 95 18 66; Copenhagen ☎33 13 18 66; Ystad ☎+46 (411) 180 65; Sassnitz ☎+49 (38392) 352 26; Rønne fax 56 91 07 66; www.bornholmferries.dk) offers combo bus/ferry routes from **Copenhagen** (6hr., 1-2 per day, 208kr); ferries from **Ystad, Sweden,** 1hr. southeast of Malmö (standard ferry 1½-2½hr., 1 per day, 98-150kr; with Scanrail 50% off); and ferries from **Sassnitz-Mukran** in **Germany** (2hr., 1 per day, 50-100kr). In July and August, **Polferries** sails between Rønne and **Świnoujście, Poland.** (☎56 95 10 69; fax 56 95 89 10. Departs Rønne W, departs Świnoujście Sa. 6hr., 180kr.) Bornholm has an efficient local BAT bus service. (35kr to Gudhjem or Sandvig-Allinge, 40kr to Svaneke; 24hr. pass 90kr). There are numerous cycling paths; pick up a guide at the tourist office in Rønne. Reserve rooms well in advance.

RØNNE. Amid cafes and cobblestoned streets, tiny Rønne, on the southwest coast, is Bornholm's principal port of entry. When you walk through, it's hard to imagine the devastation wrought by relentless bombing in WWII. Rent a **bike** from **Bornholms Cykeludlejning,** Ndr. Kystvej 5. (55kr per day. Open May-Sept. daily 7am-4pm and 8:30-9pm.) The **tourist office,** Nordre Kystvej 3, a mirrored-glass building behind the gas station by the Bornholmstrafikken terminal, books private rooms (140kr fee). (☎56 95 95 00. Open mid-June to mid-Aug. M-Sa 9:30am-6pm, Su 10am-4pm; mid-Aug. to mid-June M-F 9am-4pm, Sa 10am-1pm.) The **HI youth hostel,** Arsenalvej 12, is in a quiet, wooded area. From the ferry terminal, walk along Munch Petersens Vej, left on Skansevej, left on Zahrtmannsvej, right at the boulevard onto Søndre Allé, right on Arsenalvej; then follow the signs. (☎56 95 13 40. Dorms 100kr.) **Galløkken Camping** is at Strandvejen 4. (☎56 95 23 20. Open mid-May to Aug. 52kr per person.) Get **groceries** at **Kvickly,** in the Snellemark Centret opposite the tourist office (open M-Th 9:30am-6pm, F 9:30am-7pm, Sa 9:30am-2pm), or visit the 2nd-floor cafeteria (open M-F 9am-7pm, Sa 9am-4pm). **Postal code:** 3700.

SANDVIG-ALLINGE. On the tip of the spectacular northern coast, this smaller town's white-sand beaches attract bikers and bathers. A few kilometers from town down Hammershusvej, **Hammershus** is northern Europe's largest castle ruin. The **Nordbornholms Turistbureau,** Kirkeg. 4, is in Allinge. (☎56 48 00 01; fax 56 48 02 26. Open June-Aug. M-F 9am-5pm, Sa 10am-3pm; Sept.-May closes Sa noon.) Just outside Sandvig is the **Sandvig Vandrerhjem (HI),** Hammershusvej 94. (☎56 48 03 62. Reception 9:30-11am and 4:30-5:15pm. Members only; sells HI cards. Open Apr.-Oct.

110kr.) **Sandvig Familie Camping,** Sandlinien 5, has sites on the sea. (☎56 48 04 47. Reception 8am-10pm. Open Apr.-Oct. 45kr per person, 10kr per tent.) Near Sandvig in the village **Østerlars** is a popular fortified round church. Take bus #3 or 9 to Østerlars to reach **Østerlars Rundkirke** (open Apr.-Aug. M-Sa 9am-5pm).

FUNEN (FYN)

Situated between Zealand to the east and the Jutland Peninsula to the west, the island of Funen is Denmark's garden. This remote breadbasket is no longer isolated from the rest of Denmark—a bridge and tunnel now connect it to Zealand. Pick up maps of the **bike paths** covering the island at Funen tourist offices (75kr).

ODENSE

Visiting this hometown of Hans Christian Andersen, who once said, "To travel is to live!", may reveal the roots of his belief. Odense (OH-n-sa), Denmark's 3rd-largest city, warrants only a short visit. At **H.C. Andersens Hus,** Hans Jensens Stræde 37-45, you can learn about the author's eccentricities and see free performances of his work. From the **tourist office,** walk right on Vesterg. to Torveg., turn left, and turn right on Hans Jensens Str. (Performances June 19-July 30 11am, 1, and 3pm. Museum open mid-June to Aug. daily 9am-7pm; Sept. to mid-June Tu-Su 10am-4pm. 30kr.) A few scraps of Andersen's own ugly-duckling childhood are on display at **H.C. Andersens Barndomshjem** (Childhood Home), Munkemøllestr. 3-5. (Open mid-June to Aug. daily 10am-4pm; Sept. to mid-June Tu-Su 11am-3pm. 10kr.) Next to the main H. C. Andersens Hus, don headphones and listen to the work of another Great Dane at the **Carl Nielsen Museum,** Claus Bergs G. 11. (Open June-Aug. Tu-Su 10am-4pm; off-season reduced hours. 15kr.) Walk back to the tourist office and all the way down Vesterg., the main pedestrian drag, to the outstanding **Brandts Klædefabrik,** Brandts Passage 37 and 43. This former factory houses a modern art gallery, the **Museum of Photographic Art,** and the **Danish Press/Graphic Arts Museum.** (All open June-Aug. daily 10am-5pm; Sept.-May closed M. 30kr, 25kr, and 25kr, respectively; joint ticket 50kr.) The **Fyns Kunstmuseum,** Jernbaneg. 13, features Danish art. (Open Tu-Su 10am-4pm. 25kr.) **Ringe,** 30km away, hosts the rock-and-folk-music **Midtfyns Festival** (early July), which has featured the Eurythmics, Macy Gray, Moby, and the Counting Crows. (☎62 62 58 24; www.mf.dk.)

   Buses depart behind the train station (11kr). Ask the driver for an *omstigning,* a ticket valid for 1hr. The **tourist office,** on Rådhuspladsen, books rooms (125-175kr per person) for a 25kr fee and sells the **Odense Adventure Pass,** good for museum admission, discounts on plays, and unlimited public transport (24hr. 85kr, 48hr. 125kr). From the train station, take Nørreg., which becomes Asylg., turn left at the end on Vesterg., and it'll be on your right. (☎66 12 75 20. Open June 15-Aug. M-Sa 9am-7pm, Su 10am-5pm; Sept.-June 14 M-F 9:30am-4:30pm, Sa 10am-1pm.) The **library** in the station has free **internet.** (Open May-Sept. M-Th 10am-7pm, F 10am-4pm, Sa 10am-2pm; Oct.-Apr. M-Th 10am-7pm, F-Su 10am-4pm.) The brand-new **Danhostel Odense City (HI)** is attached to the station. (☎63 11 04 25. Reception open 8am-noon; 4-8pm. Call ahead. Dorms 140kr; singles 330kr; doubles 400kr; triples 480kr.) To camp next to the Fruens Boge park at **DCU Camping,** Odensevej 102, take bus #41 or 81. (☎66 11 47 02. Reception 7am-10pm. Open late Mar.-Sept. 50kr per person.) Get **groceries** at **Aktiv Super,** at Nørreg. and Skulkenborgg. (Open M-F 9am-7pm, Sa 8:30am-4pm, Su noon-4pm.) **Postal code:** 5000.

🖸 DAYTRIP FROM ODENSE: EGESKOV SLOT. About 30min. south of Odense on the Svendborg rail line is the town of **Kværndup** and its **🖸Egeskov Slot,** a stunning 16th-century castle that appears to float on the surrounding lake (it's actually supported by 12,000 oak piles). Spend at least two hours in the magnificently preserved Renaissance interior and the equally splendid grounds, which include a large bamboo labyrinth. On summer Sundays at 5pm, classical concerts resound in the **Knight Hall.** (Open daily May-June and Aug.-Sept. 10am-5pm; July 10am-6pm. 50kr.

Grounds open daily May and Sept. 10am-5pm; June and Aug. 10am-6pm; July 10am-8pm. 60kr.) To get to Egeskov, exit the Svendborg-bound train at Kværndrup; go right from the station until you reach Bøjdenvej, the main road. Wait for bus #920 (every hr., 11kr), or turn right and walk 2km through wheat fields to the castle.

SVENDBORG

On Funen's south coast, an hour from Odense by train, **Svendborg** is a beautiful harbor town and a departure point for ferries to the south Funen islands. Near Svendborg on an adjacent island, the regal 17th-century estate of **Valdemars Slot,** built by Christian IV for his son, holds a new **yachting museum** and a **beach.** (Open May-Sept. daily 10am-5pm; Apr. and early Oct. Sa-Su 10am-5pm. Castle 50kr; museum 25kr; joint ticket 65kr.) Cruise there on the antique passenger steamer **M/S Helge,** which leaves from Jensens Mole, behind the train station (1hr., 4 per day, round-trip 55kr).

Ferries to Ærø (see below) leave behind the train station. The **tourist office,** on the Centrum Pladsen, books ferries and accommodations. From the train station, turn left on Toldbodvej and right on Brogade, which turns into Gerritsg. The office is at the top. (☎62 21 09 80. Open late June-Aug. M-F 9am-7pm, Sa 9am-3pm; Sept. to mid-June M-F 9:30am-5:30pm, Sa 9:30am-1pm.) To get from the station to the five-star, family-oriented **HI youth hostel,** Vesterg. 45, turn left on Jernbaneg. and again on Valdemarsg., which becomes Vesterg. (☎62 21 66 99. Breakfast, sheets, and laundry 40kr each. Bikes 50kr per day. Reception 8am-8pm. Check-out 9:30am. Dorms 100kr; overflow mattresses on the floor 50kr.) **Carlsberg Camping,** Sundbrovej 19, is across the sound on Tåsinge. (☎62 22 53 84. Reception 8am-10pm. Open May-Oct. Dorms 51kr.) **Jette's Diner,** at Kullingg. 1 between the train station and the docks, puts a Danish spin on diner fare. (Open daily noon-midnight.) **Postal code:** 5700.

ÆRØ

The wheat fields, harbors, and cobblestone hamlets of Ærø (EH-ruh), a small island off the south coast of Funen, quietly preserve an earlier era in Danish history. Here, cows, rather than real estate developers, lay claim to the beautiful land.

TRANSPORTATION. Several **trains** from Odense to **Svendborg** are timed to meet the **ferry** (☎62 52 40 00) from Svendborg to **Ærøskøbing** (1¼hr.; 6 per day; 75kr, round-trip 115kr; buy tickets on board). From **Mommark,** on Jutland, **Ærø-Als** (☎62 58 17 17) sails to **Søby** (1hr.; Apr.-Sept. 2-5 per day, Oct.-Mar. Sa-Su only; 60kr), on Ærø's northwestern shore. **Bus** #990 travels between Ærøskøbing, Marstal, and Søby (16kr), but Ærø is best seen by **bike.**

ÆRØSKØBING. Thanks to economic stagnation followed by conservation efforts, the town of Ærøskøbing appears today almost as it did 200 years ago. Rosebushes and half-timbered houses attract tourist yachts from Sweden and Germany as well as vacationing Danes, but you don't have to get too far out of town to find your own serene spot. The **tourist office,** opposite the ferry landing, arranges rooms (170kr) in private homes. (☎62 52 13 00. Open June 15-Aug. M-F 9am-5pm, Sa 9am-2pm, Su 9am-noon; Sept. 14 M-F 9am-4pm, Sa 8:45-11:45am.) To get from the landing to the **HI youth hostel,** Smedevejen 15, walk left on Smedeg., which becomes Nørreg., Østerg., and finally Smedevejen. (☎62 52 10 44. Breakfast 40kr. Sheets 35kr. Reception 8am-noon and 4-8pm. Check-in by 5pm or call ahead. Reserve far in advance. Open Apr. to mid-Oct. Dorms 90kr; nonmembers 115kr.) **Ærøskøbing Camping,** Sygehusvejen 40b, is 10min. to the right as you leave the ferry. (☎62 52 18 54. Reception 8am-1pm and 3-9pm. Open May-Sept. 46kr per person.) **Emerko supermarket** is at Statene 3; walking uphill from the ferry on Vesterg., turn right on Sluttergyden, which becomes Statene. (Open M-Th 9am-5pm, F 9am-6pm, Sa 9am-4pm, Su 10am-4pm.) Rent a **bike** at the hostel or campground (40-50kr per day) to explore the towns of **Marstal** and **Søby,** on the more remote shores of the island.

JUTLAND (JYLLAND)

Homeland of the Jutes who joined the Anglos and Saxons in the conquest of England, the Jutland peninsula is Denmark's largest landmass. Beaches and camp-grounds mark the peninsula as prime summer vacation territory, while rolling hills, marshland, and sparse forests add color and variety. Jutland may be a bit out of the way, but you can take a weekend beach fling there without denting your budget.

☀ FERRIES TO ENGLAND, NORWAY, AND SWEDEN

From **Esbjerg**, on Jutland's west coast, **DFDF** sails to Harwich, England (18hr., 3-4 per week). If you need to stay, try the **HI youth hostel,** Gammel Vade Vej 80. (☎75 12 42 58; fax 75 13 68 33. Reception 8am-noon and 4-7pm. Open Feb.-Dec. 85kr; non-members 110kr.) From **Frederikshavn** (see p. 269), on the northern tip of Jutland, **Stena Line** ferries (☎96 20 02 00; in Sweden ☎ (0340) 690 900) leave for Gothenburg, Sweden (2-3¼hr.; 110-150kr, round-trip 200-230kr; 50% off with Scanrail) and Oslo (10hr.; 350kr, round-trip 400kr; 50% off with Scanrail). **SeaCat** (☎96 20 32 00) offers cheaper service to Gothenburg (2hr., 3 per day, 110-130kr). **Color Line** (☎99 56 20 00) sails to Oslo (316-352kr; 50% off with Scanrail). Boats also go from Hirtshals, on the northern tip of Jutland, to Oslo (12½hr., from 160kr) and Kristiansand, Norway (2½-4½hr., in summer from 200kr); and from Hanstholm, on the northwestern coast of Jutland, to Bergen, Norway (15½hr.; 300-680kr, round-trip 10% off).

ÅRHUS

Århus (ORE-hoos), Denmark's second-largest city and a Danish favorite, bills itself as "the world's smallest big city." Studded with impressive museums and architec-tural gems from prehistoric times through the 21st century, the city is a visual treat. Many travelers to this manageably sized and laid-back student and cultural center find themselves agreeing that size doesn't matter.

⊏ TRANSPORTATION. You can reach Århus by **train** from Aalborg (2hr.) and Copenhagen (3hr.). Most public buses leave from the train station or outside the tourist office. Tourist passes (see below) include unlimited bus transportation.

⚠ PRACTICAL INFORMATION. The **tourist office,** in the town hall, books **pri-vate rooms** (125-175kr; no fee) and sells the **Århus Passport,** which includes unlim-ited public transit and admission to most museums and sights (1 day 88kr, 2 day 110kr). If you're only interested in one or two museums, consider the **Tourist Punch Ticket** (45kr), which provides unlimited bus transportation (24hr.). To find the office, turn left as you exit the train station, and take the first right. (☎89 40 67 00; www.aarhus-tourist.dk. Open late June-early Sept. M-F 9:30am-6pm, Sa 9:30am-5pm, Su 9:30am-1pm; early Sept.-Apr. M-F 9:30am-4:30pm, Sa 10am-1pm; May to mid-June M-F 9:30am-5pm, Sa 10am-1pm.) The main **library,** at Mølleparken, has free **internet** access. (Open May-Aug. M-Th 10am-7pm, F 10am-6pm, Sa 10am-2pm; Sept.-Apr. M 10am-10pm, Tu-Th 10am-8pm, F 10am-6pm, Sa 10am-2pm.) **Postal Code:** 8100.

⌂⌂ ACCOMMODATIONS AND FOOD. The hip backpacker hang-out, **Århus City Sleep-In,** Havneg. 20, is 10min. from the train station, in the middle of the city's nightlife. Walk out of the train station and follow Ryesg., which becomes Sønderg., all the way to the canal. Take the steps or elevator down to Aboule-varden, turn right, walk to the end, and turn left on Havneg. (☎86 19 20 55; email sleep-in@mail1.stofanet.dk. Breakfast 30kr. Sheets 30kr; deposit 30kr. Kitchen. Laundry 25kr. Key deposit 50kr. Bikes 50kr per day; deposit 200kr. Reception 24hr. Check-out noon. Dorms 85kr; doubles 240-280kr.) **Pavillonen (HI),** Marien-lundsvej 10, is in the Risskov forest, 3km from the city center and 5min. from the beach. Take bus #1, 6, 9, 16, or 56 to Marienlund, then walk 300m into the park.

(☎ 86 16 72 98. Breakfast 40kr. Sheets 30kr. Laundry. Reception 7:30-10am and 4-11pm. Dorms 85kr, nonmembers 110kr; doubles 240-280kr.) **Blommehavenn Camping Århus**, Ørneredevej 35, in the Marselisborg forest, is by a beach and the royal family's summer residence. In summer, take bus #19 from the station to the grounds; in winter, take bus #6 to Hørhavevej. (☎ 86 27 02 07. Reception Apr.-early Sept. 7am-10pm; mid-Sept. to Mar. 8am-8pm. In summer 50kr per person, 15kr per tent.) **Den Grønne Hjørne**, Frederiksg. 60, has an all-you-can-eat Danish buffet (59-79kr). From the tourist office, turn left on Radhuspl., and then an immediate right. (Open M-Sa 11:30am-10pm, Su 5-10pm.) Get **groceries** at **Fakta**, Østerg. 8-12. (Open M-F 9am-7pm, Sa 9am-4pm.)

■ ■ **SIGHTS AND ENTERTAINMENT.** In the town center, the 13th-century **Århus Domkirke** (cathedral) dominates Bispetorv and the pedestrian streets that fan out around its Gothic walls. (Open May-Sept. M-Sa 9:30am-4pm; Oct.-Apr. 10am-3pm. Free.) Next door, reclaim herstory at the **Women's Museum,** Domkirkeplads 5, where provocative exhibits chronicle women throughout time. (Open June-Aug. daily 10am-5pm; Sept.-May Tu-Su 10am-4pm. 20kr.) Just west of the town center lies **Den Gamle By,** an open-air museum displaying a collection of Danish buildings from the Renaissance through the 20th century. (Open June-Aug. 9am-6pm; Apr.-May and Sept.-Oct. 10am-5pm; Nov.-Dec. 10am-4pm; Jan.-Mar. 11am-3pm. 55kr. Free after hours.) **Åboulevarden,** lined with trendy cafes, makes a perfect mid-afternoon stop for beer and sunshine. The **Århus Kunstmuseum,** on Vennelystparken, has a fine collection of Danish Golden Age paintings. (Open Tu-Su 10am-5pm. 30kr.)

Just outside town lies the spectacular **Moesgård Museum of Prehistory,** which chronicles Århus's history from 4000 BC through the Viking age. Two millennia ago, the casualties of infighting were entombed in a nearby bog and mummified by its antiseptic acidity. Today you can visit the **Grauballe Man,** the only perfectly preserved **bog person.** Take bus #6 from the train station to the end. (Open Mar.-Sept. daily 10am-5pm; Oct.-Feb. Tu-Su 10am-4pm. 35kr.) Save time for the **Prehistoric Trail,** which leads from behind the museum to a sandy **beach** (3km). In summer, bus #19 (last bus 10:18pm) returns from the beach to the Århus station. The exquisite rose garden of **Marselisborg Castle,** Queen Margarethe II's summer getaway, is open to the public. From the train station, take bus #1, 18, or 19. (Palace closed in July and whenever else the Queen is in residence.)

Århus hosts an acclaimed jazz festival in late July (☎ 89 31 82 10; www.jazzfest.dk). The **Århus Festuge** (☎ 89 31 82 70; www.aarhusfestuge.dk) is a rollicking celebration of theater, dance, and music. You can visit a smaller version of Tivoli, the **Tivoli Friheden,** at Skovbrynet. Take bus #1, 4, 6, 8, 18, or 19. (Open daily June 19-Aug. 8 1-11pm; Apr. 19-June 18 and Aug. 9-15 2-10pm. 35kr.) At night, chill at the jazz club **Bent J,** Nørre Allé 66, which jams Monday evenings and occasionally on other weekdays as well. **Valdemar,** Store Torv 4, is a popular disco in the city center. (No cover. 23+. Open Th 11pm-5am, F-Sa 10pm-5am.) The **Pan Club**, Jægergårdsg. 42, has a cafe, bar, and largely gay and lesbian dance club. (Cafe open M-Th 6pm-midnight, F-Su 8pm-5am. Club cover F-Sa 45kr; open W-Sa 11pm-4am.) **Åboulevarden** rocks at night, too; many bars offer live music and drink specials.

▣ **DAYTRIP FROM ÅRHUS: LEGOLAND.** **Billund** is renowned as the home of Legoland, an amusement park built of 40 million Lego pieces. More than just baby-babble, "Lego" is an abbreviation of *leg godt* (have fun playing). Don't skip the impressive indoor exhibitions. Unfortunately, private buses make Legoland a bit expensive. To get there, take the train from Århus to **Vejle** (45min., every hr.), then bus #912 or 44 (dir.: Legoland). A joint ticket for the bus and park (including rides) costs 165kr. (☎ 76 50 00 55; www.legoland.dk. Open daily late June-Aug. 10am-9pm; Apr. to mid-June and Sept.-Oct. 10am-8pm; rides close 2hr. earlier.)

AALBORG

The site of the earliest known Viking settlement, Aalborg (OLE-borg) is Denmark's 4th-largest city. Aalborg's spotless streets and white church garnered the title of "Europe's Tidiest City" in 1990 and brought it even farther from its unkempt Viking origins. Check out these rowdy precursors at **Lindholm Høje,** Vendilavej 11, which has 700 graves and a museum of Viking life. To reach the site, take bus #6 (13kr) from outside the tourist office. (Site open daily dawn-dusk. Museum open Apr. to mid-Oct. daily 10am-5pm; late Oct. to mid-Mar. Tu-Su 10am-4pm. 20kr.) The frescoed 15th-century **Monastery of the Holy Ghost,** on C.W. Obelsplads, is Denmark's oldest welfare institution. From the tourist office, cross the street and head down Adelg. The monastery is on the right. (English tours late June to mid-Aug. Tu and Th 1:30pm. 25kr.) The **Budolfi Church,** on Algade, has a brilliantly colored interior with ringing carillon. From the tourist office, turn left onto Østerågade and right on Algade. (Open M-F 9am-4pm, Sa 9am-2pm.) For serious rollercoasters, visit **Tivoliland,** on Karolinelundsvej. From the tourist office, turn left on Østerågade, turn right on Nytorv, and follow it until you see the rides. (Open May-Sept. daily noon to 8pm. 40kr; full-day 160kr.) From the station, cross J.F.K. Plads, then turn left on Boulevarden, which becomes Østerågade, to find the **tourist office,** Østerågade 8. (☎98 12 60 22. Open mid-June to mid-Aug. M-F 9am-6pm, Sa 10am-5pm; mid-Aug. to mid-June M-F 9am-4:30pm, Sa 9am-1pm.) **Aalborg Vandrerhjem and Camping (HI),** Skydebanevej 50, has cabins with modern facilities next to a beautiful fjord. Take bus #2, 8, or 9 (dir.: Fjordparken) to the end. (☎98 11 60 44. Laundry. Reception late-June to mid-Aug. 7:30am-11pm; late-Jan. to mid-June and early-Aug. to mid-Dec. 8am-noon and 4-9pm. Dorms 75kr; nonmembers 100kr; camping 49kr.) Bars and restaurants line **Jomfru Ane Gade;** from the tourist office, turn right on Østerågade and left onto Bispensg. Jomfru Ane Gade will be on your right. **Postal code:** 9000.

FREDERIKSHAVN

Despite noble efforts to showcase its endearing streets and hospitality, Frederik-shavn is best known and used for its **ferry** links (see p. 267). The **tourist office,** Brotorvet 1, inside the Stena Line terminal south of the rail station, reserves rooms for a 25kr fee. (☎98 42 32 66; fax 98 42 12 99. Open mid-June to mid-Aug. M-Sa 8:15am-7pm, Su 11am-7pm; mid-Aug. to mid-June M-Sa 9am-4pm.) From the tourist office, walk left 10min. to reach the bus and train stations. From the bus or train stations, walk right, then follow the signs to the **HI youth hostel,** Buhlsvej 6. (15min. ☎98 42 14 75. Reception in summer 7am-noon and 4-9pm. Always call ahead. Open Feb.-Dec. Dorms 60kr, nonmembers 85kr.) **Nordstrand Camping** is at Apholmenvej 40. (☎98 42 93 50. Open Apr.-Sept. 15. 52kr per person, 30kr per tent.) **Postal code:** 9900.

SKAGEN

Perched on Denmark's northernmost tip, sunny Skagen (SKAY-en) is a beautiful summer retreat amid long stretches of sea and white-sand dunes. The powerful currents of the North and Baltic Seas collide at **Grenen.** Don't try to swim in these dangerous waters; every year some hapless soul is carried out to sea. To get to Grenen, take bus #99 or 79 from the Skagen station to **Gammel** (11kr) or walk 3km down Fyrvej; turn left out of the train station and bear left when the road forks. In summer, you can climb the lighthouse tower for an amazing view of Grenen (5kr). The spectacular **Råberg Mile** sand dunes, formed by a 16th-century storm, migrate 15m east each year. From here, you can swim along 60km of **beaches,** where the endless summer light attracted Denmark's most famous late-19th-century painters. Their works are displayed in the wonderful **Skagen Museum,** Brøndumsvej 4. (Open June-Aug. daily 10am-6pm; off season reduced hrs. 40kr.) You can also tour the artists' homes at **Michael og Anna Archers Hus,** Markvej 2-4, and **Holger Drachmanns Hus,** Hans Baghsvej 21. Skagen has a large annual **Dixieland music festival** in late June (free-150kr); contact the tourist office for more info.

Nordjyllands Trafikselskab (☎98 44 21 33) runs **buses** and **trains** from Frederikshavn to Skagen (1hr.; 33kr, with Scanrail 50% off). The **tourist office** is in the train station. (☎98 44 13 77; fax 98 45 02 94. Open June-Aug. M-Sa 9am-7pm, Su 10am-2pm; Sept.-May reduced hrs.) The **Skagen Ny Vandrerhjem,** Roligheds- vej. 2, is wildly popular among vacationing Danish families. From the station, turn right on Chr. X's Vej, which turns into Frederikshshavnvej, and left on Rolighedsvej (☎98 44 22 00. Reception 9am-noon and 4-6pm. Open Mar.-Nov. 75-85kr, nonmembers 100-110kr.) Most **campgrounds** are open late-April to mid-September (55kr per person); try **Grenen** (☎98 44 25 46) or **Østerklit** (☎98 44 31 23), near the city center.

RIBE

Well aware of their town's historic value, the town government of Ribe forged preservation laws forcing residents to maintain the character of their houses and to live in them year-round. The result is a magnificently preserved medieval town, situated beautifully on the salt plains near Jutland's west coast. Ribe is particularly proud of the arrival of migratory storks who always roost on the roof of the town hall. For a great view of the birds and the surrounding land-scape, climb the 248 steps through the clockwork and huge bells of the 12th-cen-tury **cathedral** tower. (Open June-Aug. M-Sa 10am-6pm, Su noon-6pm; May and Sept. M-Sa 10am-5pm, Su noon-6pm; Apr. and Oct. daily 11am-4pm; Nov.-Mar. M-Su 11am-3pm. 10kr.) Next to the **Rådhus** (Old Town Hall), Van Støckens Plads, a former debtor's prison, houses a small museum on medieval torture. (Open June-Aug. daily 1-3pm; May and Sept. M-F 1-3pm. 15kr.) Follow the **night watch-man** on his rounds for an English or Danish tour of town beginning in Torvet, the main square. (35min. June-Aug. 8 and 10pm; May and Sept. 10pm. Free.) Ribe's **Vikinger,** Udin Plads 1, houses artifacts recovered from an excavation of the town, once an important Viking trading post. To get the full story on the Vikings, sit through the hourly film, in English, Danish, and German. (Open Apr.-June and Sept.-Oct. daily 10am-4pm; July-Aug. daily 10am-6pm; Nov.-Mar. Tu-Su 10am-4pm. 45kr.) South of town, the open-air **Ribe Vikingcenter,** Lustrupvej 4, re-cre-ates a Viking town. (Open July-Aug. daily 11am-4pm, May-June and Sept. M-F 11am-4pm. 45kr.) The **Vadehavscentret** (Wadden Sea Center), Okholmvej 5, Vest-ervedsted, does tours of the local marshes. Take bus #711. (☎75 44 61 61. Open daily Apr.-Oct. 10am-5pm; Feb.-Mar. and Nov. 10am-3pm. 35kr.)

   Trains to Ribe run from nearby Bramming (25min., 4-5 per day, 25kr). The **tourist office,** Torvet 3, has free maps and arranges accommodations for a 20kr fee. From the train station, walk down Dagmarsg., to the left of the Viking museum, and it'll be on your right in the main square. (☎75 42 15 00. Open July-Aug. M-F 9:30am-5:30pm, Sa 10am-5pm, Su 10am-2pm; Apr.-June and Sept.-Oct. M-F 9am-5pm, Sa 10am-2pm; Nov.-Mar. M-F 9am-4:30pm, Sa 10am-1pm.) The central **Ribe Van-drerhjem (HI),** Sct. Pedersg. 16, offers bike rental (50kr per day) and a gorgeous view of the flatlands. From the station, cross the Viking Museum parking lot, bear right, walk down Sct. Nicolaj G. to the end, turn right on Saltg., and immediately left on Sct. Peters G. (☎75 42 06 20. Breakfast 40kr. Sheets 36kr. Reception 8am-noon and 4-8pm; longer hours May-Sept. Open Feb.-Nov. 100kr, nonmembers 125kr.) **Ribe Camping,** Farupvej 2, is 1½km from the town center. (☎75 41 07 77. 50kr per person; 2-person cabins 175kr.) **Supermarkets** are around Seminarievej, near the hostel; most are open M-F 10am-6pm, Sa 10am-4pm.

FRANCE

FRENCH FRANCS

US$1 = 7.27F	1F = US$0.15
CDN$1 = 4.92F	1F = CDN$0.20
EURO€1 = 6.60F	1F = EURO€0.15
UK£1 = 10.83F	1F = UK£0.09
IR£1 = 8.33F	1F = IR£0.12
AUS$1 = 4.28F	1F = AUS$0.23
NZ$1 = 3.27F	1F = NZ$0.31
SAR1 = 1.04F	1F = SAR0.96

PHONE CODE | **Country Code: 33. International dialing prefix:** 00. France has no city codes.

The French celebrate the senses like no one else. Conventional preconceptions of France are steeped in pleasures: the vineyards of Bordeaux and Burgundy, the elaborate dishes of Dijon, the sandy expanses of the Riviera, and the crisp Alpine air. Superimposed on these notions is the rationalism that has dominated French intellectual life for over 400 years, from the philosophy of Descartes to Poincaré's mathematics. Sensuality and reason still meet in neighborhood brasseries and cafes, where lively conversation is enjoyed no less than wine or the *plat du jour*. While France no longer single-handedly controls the course of world events, it has secured a spot as one of the most influential forces in the course of Western history. As Napoleon once quipped, "'Impossible?' The word is not French." If you too are smitten by France, pick up a copy of *Let's Go: France 2001* or *Let's Go: Paris 2001* for more fact- and flavor-filled coverage.

SUGGESTED ITINERARIES

THREE DAYS Don't even think of leaving the **City of Light**—**Paris** (p. 285). Wander through the shops of the **Latin Quarter,** then cross the **Seine** to reach **Ile de la Cité** to admire **Sainte Chapelle.** Grab some ice-cream on **Ile-St-Louis** before heading over to the **Marais.** Visit the **Musée Picasso,** and then rest your tired feet in the **place des Vosges.** The next day, stroll down the **Champs-Elysées,** starting at the **Arc de Triomphe,** meander through the **Jardin des Tuileries,** and over the Seine to the **Musée d'Orsay.** Peruse part of the **Louvre** the next morning, then head out for an afternoon at **Versailles.**

ONE WEEK After three days in **Paris,** gape at the cathedral in **Chartres** (p. 318), then move down to **Rennes** where the nightlife will exhaust you (1 day; p. 325). Chug to **Tours** (p. 331) and explore the **castles** of the **Loire Valley** (p. 329). Bike or bus to **Chenonceau** (p. 332), **Chambord** (p. 330), and **Blois,** (2 days; p. 330) before heading to **Orléans** (p. 329) and **Fontainebleau** (p. 318).

BEST OF FRANCE, THREE WEEKS Whirl through the **Loire Valley,** and take the train to **Marseilles** (2 days; p. 351) before moving on to sunny **Provence** (p. 346). Dance through **Avignon** (1 day; p. 346) and **Aix-en-Provence** (1 day; p. 350). Go crazy in Van Gogh's **Arles** (1 day; p. 349) and Hedonism's **Nice** (2 days; p. 357). Show off your tan in the **Alps** (p. 367); scale the peaks near **Chamonix** (p. 367) and **Annecy** (2 days; p. 369); party in **Lyon** (2 days; p. 369); and eat in **Dijon** (1 day; p. 376). Return to Paris via the **Champagne** region (p. 385), visiting the caves of **Reims** (p. 385) and **Troyes** (2 days; p. 386).

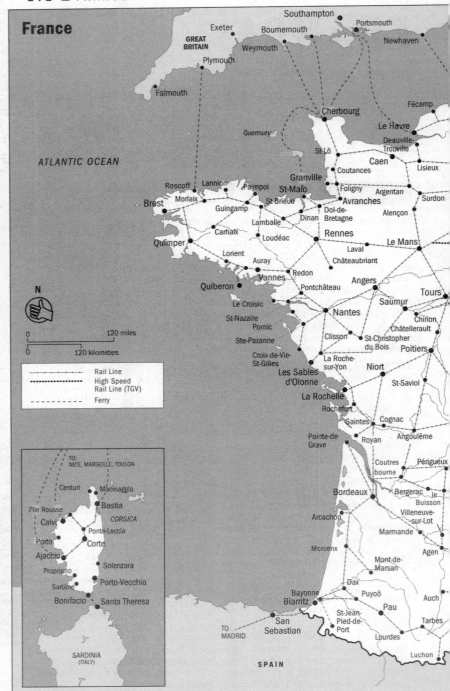

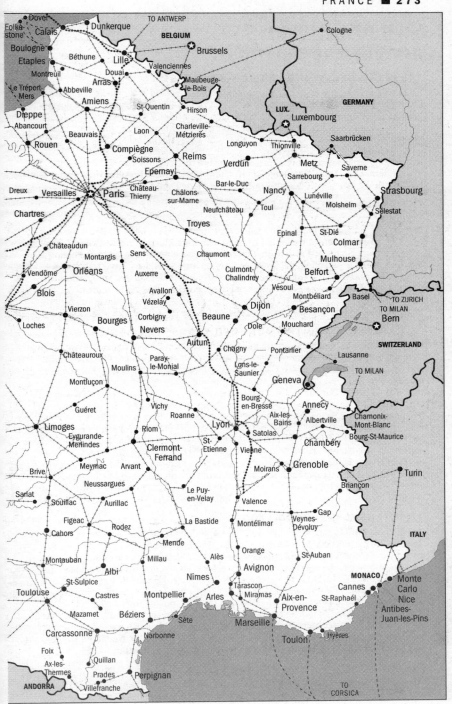

LIFE AND TIMES

HISTORY AND POLITICS

FROM THE BEGINNING: 27,000 BC-125 BC

France's fertile countryside has supported humans for tens of thousands of years—the rock shelter of **Cro-Magnon man,** at Les Eyzies in the Dordogne Valley, discovered in 1868, houses skulls dating from approximately 27,000 years ago. By 4500 BC, Neolithic peoples were carving out their place in history with giant stone monuments. These mysterious creations awed the celtic **Gauls,** who arrived from the east around 600 BC. Centuries later, in 125 BC, the **Romans** quickly established control of southern France; their legacy ranges from the well-preserved monuments of Provence to the French language itself. Under the Roman Empire, Gaul had suffered periodic Germany invasions until falling to the **Franks** in AD 260-276.

THE EARLY MIDDLE AGES: AD 400-900

During the Early Middle Ages (AD 400-900), the power of government fell increasingly to the "mayor of the palace," the king's steward. This allowed **Pepin the Elder** (d. 639) to found the **Carolingian** dynasty. **Charles Martel** crushed the Muslim advance from Spain at Poitiers in 732, leaving the kingdom to his son **Pepin the Short.** By 800, the Carolingians presided over an area stretching from the Pyrenees to the Elbe, and from the Atlantic to Austria. On Christmas Day that year, their most famous son, **Charlemagne** (742-814), was crowned Holy Roman Emperor by Pope Leo III. Charlemagne expanded his territory, renewing interest in the art and literature of the ancients, initiating what is now known as the Carolingian Renaissance.

OF CAPETIANS AND THE HUNDRED YEARS WAR 900-1500

When the last Carolingian died in 987, the nobles elected **Hugh Capet** as king, who took advantage of the insecurity of powerful vassals to maintain power over Paris and the tiny Ile-de-France. The Capetians faced the wrath of William, Duke of Normandy, who invaded England in 1066, beginning centuries of Anglo-French warfare. The French throne was thrown into question in 1328 on the death of **Charles IV,** last of the Capetians. Charles had only daughters, and since French law prohibited a woman from inheriting the throne, the nobles gave the throne to **Philippe de Valois.** But when he encroached upon English Aquitaine, in the southwestern corner of today's France, Charles IV's nephew, **Edward III** of England, claimed the throne, starting the **Hundred Years' War.** Salvation for the French came in 1429, when 17-year old **Joan of Arc** claimed divine inspiration and led the French army to a string of victories before her betrayal and capture by Burgundians, allied to the English. She was convicted of witchcraft and burnt at the stake in Rouen in 1430. But the tide of war had turned—by 1453 only Calais was left in English hands.

RELIGIOUS WARS: 1500-1600

Catherine de Medici, regent for her son **Charles IX,** king of France, tried to reconcile the Huguenots (French Protestants) with the Catholics. Nevertheless, civil war followed the **St. Bartholemew's Day Massacre** in 1572, initiated by the Duc de Guise, who accepted nothing less than papal supremacy. Over three thousand Huguenots who had gathered in Paris to celebrate the wedding of **Henri III's** sister to their leader, Henri of Navarre were killed. After he king's son died, leaving Protestant Henri heir to the throne, de Guise planned to seize power for himself. Henri III retaliated, ordering the duke's murder in 1588, but was assassinated himself a year later. Ascending the throne, **Henri IV** declared "Paris is well worth a mass," referring to his recent conversion to Catholicism. He did not abandon his Huguenot friends, and in 1598 the **Edict of Nantes** guaranteed their religious and political rights.

THE KINGDOM OF THE SUN: 1643-1715

First of the Bourbon line, Henri IV succumbed to an assassin's dagger in 1610 and was succeeded by **Louis XIII.** Louis' capable and ruthless minister, **Cardinal Richelieu,** consolidated political power for the monarchy, creating a centralized, bureaucratic administration. They were succeeded by another king-and-cardinal combo, **Louis XIV** and **Cardinal Mazarin.** Mazarin took charge until 1661, when Louis turned 24. Not known for his modesty, Louis adopted the motif of the Sun King and took the motto *"l'état, c'est moi"* ("I am the state"). He brought a personal touch to national affairs, moving the government to his new 14,000-room palace of **Versailles** (p. 316), revoking the Edict of Nantes in 1685 at the behest of his mistress, and initiating the ruinous **War of the Spanish Succession** (1701-1713).

BOURBON ON THE ROCKS: 1789

While peasants blamed the soon-to-be-*ancien* regime for their mounting debts, Louis XVI called a meeting of the **Estates General.** This assembly of delegates from the three classes of society—aristocrats, clergy, and well, everyone else—had not met since 1614, and much wrangling, the bourgeois-dominated Third Estate broke away and declared itself to be the National Assembly. The Parisian mob stormed the **Bastille** on July 14th, and a destructive orgy exploded across the nation as peasants burnt the records of their debts and obligations. The Assembly responded in August with the abolishment of feudal privileges and the **Declaration of the Rights of Man.** When the petrified king, by now under virtual house arrest, tried to flee the country in 1791, he was arrested and imprisoned. As the Revolutionary armies miraculously defeated the invaders, the radical **Jacobin** faction took control of the Assembly, abolished the monarchy, and declared a **Republic.** In January 1793, the king was guillotined; the *ancien régime* was over.

FROM GUILLOTINE TO EMPIRE: 1789-1821

When the Church refused to be subjugated to the National Assembly, it was abolished and replaced by the oxymoronic **Cult of Reason.** As the counter-revolutionary paranoia of the **Terror** set in, power lay with the "incorruptible" **Robespierre** and his Committee of Public Safety. The least suspicion of royalist sympathy led to the chopping block, and even Dr. Guillotine himself did not escape the vengeance of his fearful invention. Robespierre ordered the execution of his revolutionary rivals, before his own denunciation and death in 1794. The **Terror** was over, and power was entrusted to a five-man **Directory.** Meanwhile, a young Corsican general swept through northern Italy and forced the Austrians to capitulate. Fearful of his rising popularity, the Directory jumped at **Napoleon Bonaparte's** idea of invading Egypt to threaten the British colonies in India. Though successful on land, the destruction of his fleet at the Battle of the Nile left his disease-ridden army marooned in Cairo. Ever pragmatic, Napoleon responded by abandoning it, and hurried back to France to salvage his political career. Napoleon deposed the despised Directory, declaring himself First Consul in 1799, Consul for Life in 1802, and ultimately **Emperor** in 1804. Napoleon crafted an autocratic **legal code** which would be his most lasting achievement; elements of it are still incorporated into French law. After crushing the Austrians, the Prussians, and the Russians, only Britain remained undefeated, safe in her island refuge following **Nelson's** destruction of the French fleet at Trafalgar in 1805. Napoleon's military demise came during the Russian campaign of 1812. The Russians withdrew before the advancing *Grande Armée*, ravaging their own land to deny the enemy food and shelter. In return for abdicating in 1814, he was given the Mediterranean island of Elba, and the monarchy was reinstated under **Louis XVIII,** younger brother of his headless predecessor. In what became known as the **Hundred Days,** Napoleon, leaving Elba and landing near Cannes on March 26, 1815, marched northwards to a rapturous reception as the king fled back to England. His adventure ended three months later with the triumph of the Duke of Wellington on the field of Waterloo in Flanders (see p. 129). Napoleon was banished once again, this time to remote St. Helena in the south Atlantic, where he died in 1821. Popularly regarded as a hero in France, thousands still flock to pay their respects at his tomb at Les Invalides, Paris (see p. 306).

FRANCE

REVOLUTION AND EMPIRE, PART TWO: 1850-1904

In 1850, playing on the strength of his name, the former emperor's nephew **Louis Napoleon** was elected president. Since the constitution barred him from seeking a second term despite his immense popularity, he seized power in a coup in 1851, followed a year later by a referendum which declared him **Emperor Napoleon III.** During his 18-year reign, France's prestige was restored; **Baron Haussmann** rebuilt Paris, knocking down the medieval street plan, and replacing it with grand boulevards along which troops could be deployed. Across the Rhine, where **Bismarck** had almost completed the unification of Germany, France was surprised and swiftly overrun; the emperor was captured and as German armies advanced, the **Third Republic** was declared in 1871. Paris held out for four months, with the residents reduced to eating rats and communicating with the outside world by hot-air balloon. When the government admitted defeat, the Parisian mob revolted and declared the **Commune,** crushed only after 4000 *communards* died in street battles, and 25,000 more Parisians were summarily executed in the name of order.

The Third Republic was further undermined by the **Dreyfus affair.** In 1894, Jewish army captain **Alfred Dreyfus** was convicted and exiled on trumped-up charges of treason. When the army did not reconsider even after proof of Dreyfus's innocence was uncovered, France became polarized between the Dreyfusards, who argued for his release, and the reactionary right-wing Anti-Dreyfusards, to whom Dreyfus was an traitor regardless of the evidence. After **Emile Zola** condemned the army, government, and society for its anti-Semitic prejudice in his dramatic diatribe *J'accuse*, the momentum became unstoppable. Dreyfus was finally pardoned in 1904.

WAR AND PEACE: 1914-1944

The 1871 unification of Germany had fundamentally changed the balance of power in Europe. After centuries of conflict, the **Entente Cordiale** brought the British and the French into cooperation in 1904. With czarist Russia the three nations of the **Triple Entente** faced the **Central Powers** of Germany and the Austro-Hungarian Empire. When **World War I** erupted in 1914, German armies rapidly advanced into France, but a stalemate soon emerged as the opposing armies dug into trenches along the length of the country. The withdrawal of newly revolutionary Russia in 1917 was balanced by the entry of the USA, and victory for the West came in 1918. It is still possible to visit the fields where a generation laid down their lives (see **Memorials near Verdun**, p. 384, for details). Devastated by four years of fighting, and with 1.3 million dead, France pushed for crippling reparations from Germany; these and accompanying humiliations were often invoked by **Hitler** in his rise to power.

During the **Great Depression** of the 1930s, France was politically paralyzed and incapable of dealing with the rising threat of Nazi Germany. **World War II** began with the German invasion of Poland in 1939. France declared war on Germany in response, and in May, 1940, the Germans swept through Belgium, bypassing the **Maginot Line,** a string of fortresses along the German border which formed France's main defensive position. Allied defenses collapsed, and France capitulated in June. The country was partitioned, with the north under German occupation, and a puppet state in the south ruled from **Vichy** by WWI hero **Maréchal Pétain.** Though evidence indicates that many French people willingly collaborated with the Germans, today France prefers to commemorate the brave men and women of the **Resistance;** their headquarters in Lyon have now been made into a museum (p. 369). Under the leadership of **Charles de Gaulle,** head of the French government-in-exile, French troops liberated Paris on August 25th, 1944.

AFTER THE WAR, A NEW HOPE FOR EUROPE: 1944-1962

The Fourth Republic, proclaimed in 1944, lacked a strong executive to keep the country running when the legislature stalemated, and over the next 14 years France saw 25 governments. Despite these problems, the economy was still resurgent, and when the constitution was reformed in 1958, the **Fifth Republic,** under the renewed leadership of the still-revered de Gaulle, inherited a sound industrial base. Fiercely nationalist, his foreign policy delicately played the USA against the USSR to

France's advantage, but his domestic conservatism was problematic. In **May 1968,** what started as a student protest against the university system rapidly grew into a full-scale revolt as workers striked in support of social reform. The aging General had lost his magic touch, and he resigned after a referendum defeat in 1969. During his reign, France's international relations changed significantly. Defeat in Indochina (now Vietnam) in 1954, and Algerian independence in 1962 following eight years of civil war in between native Arabs and French settlers, ended France's role as a colonial power. France joined the new era of European cooperation, designed to put an end to the disastrous cycle of war which had devastated the continent.

FRANCE TODAY

After de Gaulle resigned in 1969, the tone of the Fifth Republic changed fundamentally. His successor, the *Gaulliste* **Georges Pompidou,** combined a laissez-faire position toward business with less assertive foreign policy. While **François Mitterrand** began his term in 1981 with widespread nationalization and expanded benefits, the international climate could not support this socialist economy. By 1986, the right had control of parliament, and Mitterrand had to appoint the ruthless conservative **Jacques Chirac** as Prime Minister. The **far right** also flourished under the leadership of **Jean-Marie Le Pen,** who formed the **Front National** upon an anti-immigration platform. The healthy post-war economy had led to the development of a new working class from North Africa, and Le Pen was able to capitalize on racism against these immigrants. Meanwhile, Chirac privatized many industries, but a transport strike and widespread terrorism damaged the right, allowing Mitterrand to win a second term in 1988. The French were more concerned with scandals involving Mitterrand's ministers than his grandiose architectural projects, and the left suffered crushing parliamentary defeats in the early 90s. Mitterrand further lost prestige when the 1991 referendum on the **Maastricht Treaty,** which would transform the European Community into the more closely integrated **European Union** (EU), scraped through with just 51% approval despite massive government support.

In the mid-90s, Mitterrand made two startling confessions. The first was that he had collaborated with the Vichy government before joining the Resistance in 1943. The second, more shocking, revelation was that he was seriously ill with cancer; his death in January 1996 came shortly after the presidency had been won by his archrival Chirac. The ascendancy of the right was short-lived; in 1997, elections returned a socialist parliament, and Chirac was forced to accept his one-time presidential rival **Lionel Jospin** as prime minister. Though Chirac's term does not expire until 2002, the left appears firmly in control of France.

THE ARTS

VISUAL ARTS AND ARCHITECTURE

EARLY DAYS: FROM PREHISTORY TO AD 1300. Protected from 17,000 years of history deep within the caves of the Perigord region, the paintings of the **caves of Lascaux** (see p. 336) and **Les Eyzies de Tayac** (see p. 336) remained hidden until the 19th century. A little later, under Charlemagne, French architects combined Classical elements with northern-Barbarian tradition to create the **Romanesque** artform. This style was characterized by round arches and barrel-vaulting, projecting a simple grandeur exemplified by churches including the Basilique St-Sernin in Toulouse and the church of the **Madeleine** at **Vézelay** (p. 378). Gothic architecture evolved at the end of the 12th century, using a system of arches and flying buttresses, with thin walls and jewel-like stained glass. This ideal is embodied by the cathedral at **Chartres** (see p. 318), and of course, by **Notre-Dame de Paris** (p. 305).

RENAISSANCE: 1300-1600. Exposed to the Renaissance during his Italian campaigns, François I invited the greatest living artists to work in France, including **Leonardo da Vinci** and **Il Rosso.** The artistic result was one of subtle eroticism, focusing on scenes of court life and classical mythology. Gunpowder moved war to the battlefield, once-fearsome chateaux were transformed into stately pleasure domes.

GOING FOR BAROQUE: 1600-1700. **Baroque** architecture reached its peak with the chateau of **Vaux-le-Vicomte** (1657), bringing architect Louis **Le Vau,** artist Charles **Le Brun,** and landscaper Louis **Le Nôtre** together for the first time. Louis XIV was so impressed with their work that he commissioned them to build him a new palace at Versailles (p. 316), which included such samples of Baroque sculpture as **Giradon's** outdoor *Apollo Tended by the Nymphs* (1666) and Antoine **Coysevox's** busts reflected in the Hall of Mirrors. Baroque painting was led by the genius of **Nicolas Poussin.** Poussin is also credited with developing the **Academic** style, espoused by the *Académie Royale* after its foundation in 1648. The **Rococo** style developed in the early 18th century, and was defined by elaborate, decadent ornamentation.

TRULY ROMANTIC: 1800-1830. The most famous work from the 19th century is **Jacques-Louis David**'s *Coronation* (1807), depicting the moment Napoleon crowned himself Emperor. In the decorative arts, the **Empire style** supplemented Roman models with a Pharaonic frenzy inspired by Napoleon's Egyptian exploits. The Neoclassical agenda was best fulfilled in the two architectural monuments dedicated to the glory of the Grande Armée: the Église de la Madeleine (see p. 308), and the Arc de Triomphe (see p. 308), both in Paris. While the Romantic movement scarcely affected French architecture, its influence in the visual arts was immense. Even though **Jean-Auguste-Dominique Ingres** took up the neo-classical mantle of David, his interest in medieval and religious themes betrayed the Romantic taste for all things Gothic. His most celebrated work, the sensuous reclining nude of *La Grande Odalisque* (1814; now in the Louvre, p. 309), prefigures the oriental fascination of his younger contemporary **Eugène Delacroix.** Delacroix's dramatic shading and masterly use of color contrasts sharply with Ingres' restrained, academic painting. The bold brushwork seen in *Liberty leading the people* (1830; also in the Louvre) would prepare the way for Impressionism.

POSITIVELY REALIST: 1830-1860. In the 1830s a group of painters settled near Fontainebleau to paint nature as they saw it. Led by **Théodore Rousseau** and **Jean-François Millet,** the artists of the **Ecole de Barbizon** celebrated the land and the humble life of those who worked it. In the 1850s, this grew into the **Realist** movement under **Gustave Courbet,** whose treatment of everyday subjects on a grand scale shocked the public. In architecture, Neoclassicism continued to reign throughout the 19th century, advocated by the dominant Ecole des Beaux Arts; the ultimate expression is found in **Charles Garnier's** Paris opera house (1862-1875; p. 307).

IMPRESSIONS OF THE LATE 19TH CENTURY. In the 1860s, the young **Edouard Manet** moved away from Realism as he found the handling of his subject more interesting than the fidelity of its reproduction. The small group of artists who clustered around him were united more by this emphasis on visual effect than any particular style or technique, and for this reason they became known as **Impressionists.** The sunny landscapes of **Claude Monet,** the rosy-cheeked faces of **Auguste Renoir,** and the working scenes of **Camille Pissarro** all combine prosaic, contemporary subjects with a sense of immediacy and freshness. But every movement inspires its reaction, and in the 1880s and 1890s the **Post-impressionists** concentrated their technical explorations in search of solidity and permanence. **Georges Seurat** developed **Pointillism,** the use of small dots of colors placed scientifically to build up a final image, and in *Une Baignade, L'Asnières* (1884), and *La Grande Jatte* (1885), millions of such points bathe his picture in a light unattainable by conventional means. In Aix-en-Provence, **Paul Cézanne** created solidity and mass using geometric forms and a limited palette. Also drawn to Provence was the Dutch painter **Vincent van Gogh,** who developed an expressive personal style of swirling brush strokes and intense colors. After a brief, tempestuous stay with van Gogh in Arles (p. 349), the ex-stockbroker **Paul Gauguin** settled in Tahiti. Here, influenced by folk art, he developed a style involving broad expanses of color to create a flat, spiritual effect.

EIFFEL AND HIS TOWER: 1876-1889. Architecture finally reawoke as engineers took matters into their own hands. In 1876, **Gustave Eiffel,** together with architect **Louis-Auguste Boileau,** designed a new building for *Le Bon Marché,* creating large skylit interior spaces in which to display merchandise. Nicknamed the "magician of iron," Eiffel is most famous for the tower that bears his name (p. 306), the star exhibit of the Universal Exhibition of 1889. A century later, of course, it stands as the best-loved landmark in France. Truly a monumental figure, Eiffel also designed the internal structure of the Statue of Liberty.

WHEN ANIMALS ATTACK: 1877-1932. Auguste Rodin only achieved recognition at the age of 35, when critics found his nude *The Age of Bronze* (1877) to be so real that they accused him of casting it from life. However, his greatest influence on sculpture was his ultimate move away from realism. In the towering *Balzac* (1898), the coarse modelling of Rodin's broodily draped figure paves the way for abstraction. The Spaniard **Pablo Picasso,** the most prolific artist of the 20th century, developed a bewildering number of styles during his 80-year career, almost all of it spent in France. He shot to notoriety in 1907 with *Les demoiselles d'Avignon*, shocking both for its illicit subject and for the angular treatment of the figures. This style presaged **Cubism,** a continuation of Cézanne's geometric approach—which presented the subject from many different angles at once to capture the three-dimensional object on a flat plane. Struggling with Pointillism during a trip to Collioure in the Languedoc, **Matisse** abandoned it and started squeezing paint from the tube directly onto the canvas. Shocked Parisian critics called the artists associated with the expressive new style *Fauves* (wild animals), and the name stuck. While **Fauvism** made only a brief splash on the canvas of time, Matisse's art remained a vibrant celebration of life; in mature works such as *The Dance* (1931-32; now in the Musée d'Art Moderne de la Ville de Paris, see p. 311) his mastery of line and color create a sense of movement and joy.

DADAISM AND SURREALISM: 1914-1939. After the First World War, a generation of young artists turned their backs on a world descending into chaos and formed a nihilistic anti-art movement known as **Dada.** Already in 1913 **Marcel Duchamp** had exhibited *Bicycle Wheel* (now lost), a bicycle wheel on a stool. This was the first of his "ready mades," and by exhibiting such commonplace, mass-produced objects Duchamp started off the whole "but is it art?" question. In 1924, André Breton published the *Surrealist Manifesto*, preaching the artistic supremacy of the subconscious. Surrealism rejected all traditional notions of art, but was fundamentally a constructive movement, plumbing the creative depths of the mind.

LITERATURE

EARLY READINGS. Epic poetry was represented by the *chansons de geste*, of which the most famous is the *Chanson de Roland* (ca. 1000), the story of Charlemagne's nephew and his doomed struggle against the Moors. The publication of **Francois Rabelais'** novel *Pantagruel* in 1532 delighted many with its unusual combination of bodily functions and progressive ideas on education. **Michel de Montaigne,** prompted by the wars of religion, created a new literary genre with his *Essays* (1580), a collection of musings on the frailty of truth. His successor in the realm of philosophy was **Rene Descartes,** who proved his own existence with the irrefutable deduction "I think, therefore I am." Also influential was the equally diverse genius of **Blaise Pascal.** After a youth misspent inventing the mechanical calculator and the science of probabilities, he became a devotee of **Jansenism,** an influential Catholic reform movement which sought salvation through inner peace and contemplation. Retiring from public life, Pascal expounded the virtues of solitude in his best-known work, the *Pensées* (1658). Another important Jansenist was the classically-oriented tragedian **Jean Racine,** whose *Phèdre* (1677) is considered by many to be the greatest play in the French literary canon. His comic counterpart, **Molière,** satirized the social pretensions of his age by combining classical structures with hilarious farce. He and his actors formed the **Comédie Française,** now the world's oldest national theater company, which still produces the definitive versions of French classics at its theatre in Paris (p. 312). Molière died in 1673, ironically during a performance of his satire on hypochondria, *The Imaginary Invalid*.

THE ENLIGHTENMENT. Social tensions created under Louis XIV prompted a period of intense philosophical activity in the years leading up to the Revolution. This **Enlightenment** was dominated by three intellectuals: **Charles-Louis de Montesquieu, Voltaire** (pseudonym of François-Marie Arouet), and **Jean-Jacques Rousseau.** Voltaire illuminated the entire century with his insistence on liberty and tolerance. His reputation as a writer rests on his short stories, such as *Candide* (1758), a comic refutation of the optimistic philosophy that "all is for the best in this best of all possible worlds." While Voltaire and Montesquieu proposed progressive reforms, Rousseau thought that society needed to be entirely reshaped. In his *Social Contract* (1762), the statement that "man was born free, but he is everywhere in chains," introduced his utopian vision. Voltaire and Rousseau were both members of the *philosophes* ("philosophers"), a diverse group of thinkers bent upon social reform. They were led by **Denis Diderot,** who directed the landmark *Encyclopédie*, aimed to encompass the entire body of human knowledge.

THE EARLY 19TH CENTURY: INCURABLE ROMANTICS. The expressive ideals of **Romanticism** first appeared in Britain and Germany rather than analytically-minded France. One of the first French Romantic works was **François-René de Chateaubriand's** novel *Atala* (1801), inspired by the time he spent waiting out the excesses of the Revolution with native Americans around Niagara Falls. Under such great writers as **Stendhal** and **Balzac**, the novel became the most influential literary medium. **Victor Hugo** dominated the Romantic age, with his novels *The Hunchback of Notre-Dame* (1831) and *Les Misérables* (1862) reaching near-mythical status. Aurore Dudevant, who took the pen-name **Georges Sand** and started a successful career as a novelist, condemned the social conventions which bound women into unhappy marriages in books such as *Valentine* (1832).

MODERN LITERATURE. The decadence and social snobbery of the turn of the century was captured by **Marcel Proust** in the seven-volume *Remembrance of Things Past* (1913-1927). Revolutionary in technique, this autobiographical portrait of upper-class society during the *Belle Époque* inspires a fanaticism which puts Star Wars to shame. The rising threat of Nazi Germany also spurred a call to arms by writers, led by the indomitable **André Malraux.** Active in the Chinese and Spanish civil wars, the former supplied the subject for his masterpiece, *The Human Condition* (1933). Another adventurer, **Antoine de Saint-Exupéry,** used his experiences as an early aviation pioneer to create the well-loved *The Little Prince* (1943). The post-war period was intellectually dominated by **existentialism,** which held that life, in itself, was meaningless; only by choosing and then committing yourself to a cause could existence take on a purpose. An era of theater of the absurd followed: in **Jean-Paul Sartre's** *No Exit* (1946), four people in a small room discover they are there for eternity; as they find out: "hell is other people." Sartre's companion, **Simone de Beauvoir,** concentrated on writing novels, but is best known for the seminal *The Second Sex* (1949), an essay attacking the myth of femininity. Though **Albert Camus** is often classed with Sartre, he could hardly be more different. He achieved fame with his debut novel *The Outsider* (1942), which tells the story of a dispassionate social misfit condemned to death for an unrepented murder.

CONTEMPORARY CINEMA

New Wave directors dominated French cinema though the 1970s. Nevertheless, the biggest-grossing film of the decade was a middle-brow comedy, **Gérard Oury's** *Les Adventures de Rabbi Jacob* (1973). In the past few decades the *Three Colors* trilogy, *Manon des Sources*, and *Au Revoir les Enfants* have moved movie-goers around the world. Actor **Gérard Depardieu** (*Cyrano de Bergerac, My Father the Hero*) is renowned for roles both serious and comic, but **Jean Reno** has had more luck making the transition into Hollywood following the success of **Luc Besson's** *The Professional* (1994), *Fifth Element* (1997), and *Taxi* (1998). Very different from the *Belle de jour* fare beloved of "Foreign Film" rentals is the recent spate of **cinéma beur,** made by second-generation North Africans coming to terms with life in the HLMs (municipal housing) of suburban Paris. These inexpensive, grafitti-decor films, such as **Mathieu Kassovitz's** *La Haine* (1995), confront the traumas of urban racism. Facing up to a history of colonialism is a preoccupation in **Claire Denis's** *Chocolat* (1988). Art cinema continues to prosper under **Marcel Hanoun** *(Bruit d'Amour et de Guerre*, 1997) and **Jacques Doillon** *(Ponette*, 1997), while the French flock to hilarious low-budget comedies like **Jean-Marie Poiré's** *Les Visiteurs* (1992).

FOOD AND DRINK

French chefs cook for the most finicky clients in the world—Charles de Gaulle once griped that no nation with 400 types of cheese could ever be united. The French breakfast **(le petit déjeuner)** is usually light, consisting of bread *(le pain)* or sometimes croissants or *brioches* (pastry-like buttery breads) and espresso with hot milk *(café au lait)*. A full French dinner includes an *apéritif*, an *entrée* (appetizer), *plat* (main course), salad, cheese, dessert, fruit, coffee, and a *digestif* (after-dinner drink). Most restaurants offer *un menu à prix fixe* (fixed-price meal) that costs less than ordering *à la carte*. The **menu** may include an *entrée* (appetizer), a main course *(plat)*, cheese *(fromage)*, and dessert, and start at around 60F. Odd-hour cravings can be satisfied at **brasseries,** the middle ground between cafes and the restaurants. The French take wine with virtually every meal. Heed the tale of the famous director who dared to order a Coke with his 1500F meal; he was promptly kicked out of the restaurant. Of him it was said, *"Il manque de savoir vivre"*—he doesn't know how to live. A warning to **vegetarians:** trust no one. The concept of meatless life is foreign to most waiters and chefs; even a salad may have ham. You'll probably have luck at *crêperies*, ethnic restaurants, and places catering to a younger crowd. The words *service compris* (service included) mean the **tip** is included. Otherwise, tip 15%.

Cafes in France, haunts of intellectuals from Hemingway to Sartre, figure pleasantly in the daily routine. Prices are cheaper at the counter *(comptoir)* than in the seating area *(salle)*; outdoor seating *(la terrasse)* may be even more expensive. Coffee, beer, and (in the south) the anise-flavored *pastis* are staple cafe drinks. If you order *café*, you'll get espresso; for coffee with milk, ask for a *café crème*. *Bière à la pression*, or draught beer, is 660ml of either pale *(blonde)* or dark *(brune)* lager. A glass of red is the cheapest wine in a cafe (starting at 4-6F).

ESSENTIALS

DOCUMENTS AND FORMALITIES

For stays shorter than 90 days, citizens of Australia, Canada, the EU, New Zealand, and the US don't require visas; South Africans do (30-day visas 165F; 90-day 195-230F). For stays longer than 90 days, all non-EU citizens require long-stay visas (650F). Non-EU nationals cannot work in France without a **work permit,** which requires a contract of employment; nor can they **study** without a **student visa,** which requires proofs of admission to a French university, financial independence, and medical insurance. For **au pair** and **teaching assistant** jobs, special rules apply; check with your local consulate.

French Embassies at Home: Australia, Consulate General, Level 26, St. Martins Tower, 31 Market St., Sydney NSW 2000 (☎ (02) 926 157 79). **Canada,** Consulate General, 130 Bloor St W., #401, Toronto, ON M5S 1N5 (☎ (416) 925-8233; web.idirect.com/~fs1tto/index.htm); Consulate General, 1100-1130 West Pender St, Vancouver, BC V6E 4A4 (☎ (604) 681-4345; www.consulfrancevancouver.org). **Ireland,** Consulate Section, 36 Ailesbury Rd, Ballsbridge, Dublin 4 (☎ (01) 260 16 66; www.ambafrance.ie). **New Zealand,** 34-42 Manners St., P.O. Box 11-343, Wellington (☎ (04) 802 77 93; www.ambafrance.net.nz). **South Africa,** 807 George Ave, Arcadia, Pretoria 0083 (☎ (12) 429 70 30; www.france.co.za). **UK,** Consulate General, 21 Cromwell Rd, London SW7 2EN (☎ (020) 78 38 20 00; www.ambafrance.org.uk). **US,** Consulate General, 4101 Reservoir Rd NW, Washington, DC 20007 (☎ (202) 944-

6000; www.france-consulat.org/dc/dc.html); Consulate General, 934 Fifth Ave, New York, NY 10021 (☎ (212) 606-3600).

Foreign Embassies in France: All embassies are in **Paris** (see p. 293). There are **UK** consulates in Bordeaux, Lille, and Marseilles, and **US** consulates in Strasbourg and Marseilles.

TRANSPORTATION

BY PLANE. The two major international airports in Paris are **Charles de Gaulle** and **Orly.** For info on cheap flights from the UK, see p. 43.

BY TRAIN. The **SNCF** (*Société Nationale de Chemins de Fer;* ☎ 08 36 35 35 35; www.sncf.fr) manages one of Europe's most efficient rail networks. Timetables are complicated but well-organized, with color-designated periods: low-traffic periods are blue (*période bleue*), while peak times are white (*période blanche*) or red (*période rouge*). Traveling in blue periods makes you eligible for reductions called **tarifs Découvertes,** often up to 25%; the *Découverte 12-25* discount is available to those ages 12-25 for any blue-period travel. Tickets must be validated in the orange machine at the entrance to the platforms at the *gare* (train station). Seat **reservations,** recommended for international trips, are mandatory on EuroCity (EC), InterCity (IC), and TGV (*train à grande vitesse*) trains. All three require a ticket supplement (US$3-18; railpass-holders exempt) and reservation fee (US$2-3). **TGV** trains, the fastest in the world, run from Paris to major cities in France, as well as to Geneva and Lausanne, Switzerland. **Rapide** trains are slower, and local **Express** trains are, oddly, the slowest option. The **Eurostar** provides rapid connections to London and Brussels (see p. 46).

Eurail is valid in France. The SNCF's **France Railpass** grants three days of unlimited rail travel in France during any 30-day period (US$175; companion travelers $140 each; up to 6 extra days $30 each); the parallel **Youthpass** provides those under 26 with four days of unlimited travel within a two-month period ($158; up to 6 extra days $26 each). The **France Rail 'n' Drive pass** combines three days of rail travel with two days of car rental (US$255; companion travelers $187 each; extra rail days $30 each, extra car days $50).

BY BUS. Within France, long-distance buses are a secondary transportation choice; service is rare and infrequent relative to that in most other European countries. However, in some regions buses can be indispensable for reaching out-of-the-way towns. Bus services operated by the SNCF accept railpasses. *Gare routière* is French for "bus station."

BY FERRY. Ferries across the English Channel (*la Manche*) link France to England and Ireland. The most common route is that from **Dover** (see p. 189) to **Calais** (see p. 388), run by **P&O Stena Line, SeaFrance,** and **Hoverspeed** (☎ 03 21 46 14 54). Other ferries go from **Boulogne-sur-Mer** (see p. 388) to **Folkestone, England** on **Hoverspeed** (☎ 03 21 30 80 40); from **Cherbourg** (see p. 324) to **Rosslare, Ireland** (see p. 576) on **Irish Ferries, Portsmouth** (see p. 190) on **P&O European Ferries,** and **Poole** on **Brittany Ferries;** from **Dieppe** (see p. 321) to **Newhaven, England** on **P&O Stena Line;** from **Le Havre** (see p. 322) to **Portsmouth** (see p. 190) on **P&O European Ferries** (☎ 02 35 19 78 50); and from **Roscoff** to **Plymouth** and **Cork** (see p. 578) on **Brittany Ferries,** and **Rosslare** and **Cork** on **Irish Ferries** (☎ 02 98 61 17 17). **Eurail** is valid on boats to Ireland (excluding 30F port tax). Students usually receive a 10% discount. For **schedules** and **prices** on English Channel ferries, see p. 47. For info on ferries from **Nice** and **Marseilles** to **Corsica,** see p. 364.

BY CHANNEL TUNNEL. Though still dogged by huge debts, the Channel Tunnel is increasing in popularity every year as people overcome their fear of traveling 27mi. under the sea. Undoubtedly the fastest and most convenient route from England to France, the Chunnel offers two types of passenger service. **Eurostar** is the high-speed train which links London to Paris and Brussels, with stops at Ashford in England and Calais and Lille in France. (Reservations in UK ☎ 01233 61 75 75; in France ☎ 01 49 70 01 75 (France); www.eurostar.co.uk. Eurostar tickets can also be bought at most major travel agents.) *Le Shuttle* is a drive-on train service which ferries cars and coaches between Folkestone and Calais (in UK ☎ (0800) 096 9992; in France ☎ 03 21 00 61 00; www.eurotunnel.co.uk).

BY CAR. Thanks to high *autoroute* tolls, France maintains its roads well, but the landscape itself often makes the roads a menace, especially in twisting Corsica. The numerous and pricy tolls (from Paris to Marseilles, for instance, costs 267F) combine with expensive **gasoline** (*essence sans plomb*, or unleaded, at about 6F per liter) to make driving a very expensive mode of transportation.

BY BIKE AND BY THUMB. Of all Europeans, the French may be alone in loving cycling more than football. French drivers usually accommodate bikers on the wide country roads, and many cities banish cars from select streets each Sunday. Renting a bike beats bringing your own if your touring will be confined to one or two regions (50-120F per day).

Many consider France the hardest country in Europe to get a lift. *Let's Go* does not recommend hitchhiking. In major cities there are ride-sharing organizations that pair drivers and riders. Contact **Eurostop International** (**Allostop** in France; www.ecritel.fr/allostop/). Not all of these organizations screen drivers and riders.

TOURIST SERVICES AND MONEY

EMERGENCY	Police: ☎ 122. Ambulance: ☎ 123. Fire: ☎ 124.

TOURIST OFFICES. The extensive French tourism support network revolves around **syndicats d'initiative** and **offices de tourisme** (in the smallest towns, the **Mairie**, the mayor's office, deals with tourist concerns), all of which *Let's Go* labels "tourist office." All three distribute maps and pamphlets, help you find accommodations, and suggest excursions to the countryside. For up-to-date events and regional info, try www.francetourism.com.

CURRENCY & EXCHANGE. The national currency of France is the **franc français** or French Franc (abbreviated to FF or F). Each franc is divided into 100 **centimes.** The franc is available in brightly colored 20F, 50F, 100F, 200F, and 500F notes, smart two-tone 10F and 20F coins, and silvery coins 1F, 2F, 5F and pale copper 5, 10, 20, and 50 *centime*s pieces.

Prices: If you stay in hostels and prepare your own food, expect to spend about 100-140F per person per day. A double room in a hostel starts at about 130F, and a decent sit-down meal with wine starts at about 65F.

Tipping and bargaining: By law, service must be included at all restaurants, bars, and cafes in France. It is not unheard of to leave extra *monnaie* (change) at a cafe or bar, maybe a franc or two per drink; exceptionally good service may be rewarded with a 5-10% tip. Otherwise, tipping is only expected for taxis and hairdressers; 10-15% is the norm. **Bargaining** is appropriate at flea markets *(marchés aux puces)*.

Taxes: Most purchases in France include a 20.6% value-added tax (TVA is the French acronym, VAT the English). Non-EU residents (including EU citizens who reside outside the EU) who are in France for less than six months can reclaim 17.1% of the purchase price on goods over 1200F bought in one store. Only certain stores participate in this **vente en détaxe** refund process; ask before you buy.

ACCOMMODATIONS AND CAMPING

Hostels generally offer dormitory accommodations in large single-sex rooms with 6-10 beds, though some have as many as 60. In France, a bed in a hostel will average around 60-90F. If you plan on doing a lot of hostelling, it is definitely worth joining **Hostelling International (HI)** before you leave home; to do so, contact one of the national organizations listed below. Many hostels in France are HI affiliates;

FRANCE

members get lower rates and can reserve in advance, often through the **International Booking Network.** Two or more people traveling together will often save money by staying in cheap **hotels** rather than hostels. The French government employs a hotel ratings system which runs from zero to four stars. Most hotels listed by *Let's Go* have zero stars or one, with a smattering of two stars.

After three thousand years of settled history, true wilderness in France is hard to find. It's **illegal to camp** in most public spaces, including and especially national parks. Instead, look forward to organized *campings* (campsites), where you'll share your splendid isolation with vacationing families and all manner of programmed fun. Most campsites have toilets, showers, and electrical outlets, though you may have to pay extra for such luxuries (10-40F); you'll often need to pay a supplement for your car, too (20-50F). Otherwise, expect to pay 50-90F per site.

COMMUNICATION

MAIL. Airmail letters under 1 oz. between the US and France take four to seven days and cost US$1.00. Letters from Canada cost CDN$0.95 for 20g. Allow at least 5 working days from Australia (postage AUS$1.00 for up to 20g) and 3 days from Britain (postage UK$0.30 for up to 20g). Envelopes should be marked *"par avion"* (airmail) to avoid having letters sent by sea. Mail can be held for pick-up through **Poste Restante** (French for General Delivery) to almost any city or town with a post office. Address letters to: LEVESQUE, Elisabeth; Poste Restante: Recette Principale; [5-digit postal code] TOWN; FRANCE; mark the envelope HOLD.

TELEPHONES. All French telephone numbers are ten digits in length; there are no city codes. When calling from abroad, drop the leading zero of the local number. To operate payphones, buy a *télécarte* (telephone card), available in denominations of 41F and 98F at train stations, post offices, and *tabacs.* Phone numbers starting with 0800 are toll-free; those starting with just 08 charge high rates. To call collect, tell the operator *"en PCV"* (ahn-pay-say-VAY). **Operator, ☎10. Directory assistance, ☎12. International operator, ☎00 33 11. International direct dial** numbers include: **AT&T, ☎888 288 4685; BT Direct, ☎800 34 51 44; Canada Direct, ☎800 565 4708; MCI ☎800 444 4141; Sprint ☎800 877 4646; Telecom Éireann Ireland Direct, ☎800 25 02 50; Telecom New Zealand, ☎0800 00 00 00; Telkom South Africa, ☎09 03;** and **Telstra Australia Direct, ☎13 22 00.**

INTERNET ACCESS. Most large towns in France have a cybercafe. Rates and speed of connection vary widely; occasionally there are free terminals in technologically-oriented museums or exhibition spaces. **Cybercafé Guide** (www.cyberiacafe.net/cyberia/guide/ccafe.htm#working_france) lists cybercafes in France.

LANGUAGE. Contrary to popular opinion, even flailing efforts to speak French will be appreciated, especially in the countryside. Be lavish with your *Monsieurs, Madames,* and *Mademoiselles,* and greet people with a friendly *bonjour* (*bonsoir* after 6pm). For basic French vocabulary and pronunciation, see p. 958.

LOCAL FACTS

Time: France is 1hr. ahead of Greenwich Mean Time (GMT).

Climate: In summer, the temperature in Paris ranges 13-24°C (55-75°F); it's cooler in the North and Alps, while southern France has scorching temperatures. Winters are generally mild near the coasts, although it rains frequently; the Alps and central France experience snow and occasional frost.

Hours: Just about everything opens at 9am, snoozes noon-2pm, and is closed Su; many provincial areas also shut down M. **Banks** tend to close around 4pm. Most **shops** generally stay open until 6:30pm. **Museums** close at least one day a week, usually M or Tu. Sights run by the local government tend to close M.

Holidays: Le Jour de l'an (also called St-Sébastien): New Year (Jan. 1); **Le lundi de Pâques:** Easter Monday (April 5); **La Fête du travail:** Labor Day (May 1); **L'Anniver-**

saire de la Liberation celebrates the Liberation in 1944 (May 8); **L'Ascension:** Ascension day (June 1); **Le lundi de Pentecôte:** Whitmonday (June 12); **La Fête Nationale:** Bastille Day (July 14); **L'Assomption:** Feast of the Assumption (Aug. 15); **La Toussaint:** All Saints' Day (Nov. 1); **L'Armistice 1918:** Armistice Day (Nov. 11); and **Le Noël:** Christmas (Dec. 25).

Festivals: Most festivals, like **fête du cinema** and **fête de la musique** (late June, when musicians rule the streets), are in summer. The **Cannes Film Festival** (May; www.festival-cannes.com) is mostly for directors and stars, but provides good people-watching. The **Festival d'Avignon** (July-Aug.; www.festival-avignon.com/gbindex3.html is famous for its theater. **Bastille Day** (July 14) is marked by military parades, *bals des pompiers* (firemen's dances) and fireworks nationwide. Although you may not be competing in the **Tour de France** (3rd or 4th Su in July; www.letour.fr), you'll enjoy all the hype. A **Vineyard Festival** (Sept., in Nice; www.nice-coteazur.org/americain/tourisme/vigne/index.html) celebrates the grape harvest with music, parades, and wine tastings. Nice and Nantes celebrate **Carnaval** in the last week or two before Ash Wednesday (culminating with Mardi Gras celebrations).

PARIS

Forget Paris? Never. *Forget France.* This is where it's at. City of light, site of majestic panoramas and showy store windows—Paris is as much the iron finger of the Eiffel Tower bronzing in the midday sun as it is the miles of electrical wiring that course beneath the Champs de Mars to feed the tower's millennial light system. Paris is an ancient, infamous, and lovely tourist trap of catacombs, palaces, cemeteries, museums, and cabarets. It is a living city full of beautiful people, art, and excellent clothes. It is open air markets; it is manicured parks; and, most of all, it is sitting for hours outside at a cafe. From the world's best bistros to the highest of *haute couture*, from the old stone of Notre-Dame to the futuristic motions of the Parc de la Villette, from the relics of the first millennium to the continual celebration of the second, Paris presents itself as both a harbor of tradition on the Seine and a place of impulse. You can't conquer Paris, old or new, in one week or in 30 years, but here are some ways to get acquainted.

✈ GETTING THERE AND AWAY

Flights: Most transatlantic flights land at **Aéroport Roissy-Charles de Gaulle,** 23km northeast of Paris. In general, Terminal 2 services Air France and its affiliates; for flight info, call the 24-hour English-speaking information center (☎01 48 62 22 80) or check www.parisairports.com. The cheapest and fastest ways to get into the city from Roissy are by **RER** or bus. To take the RER train, take the free shuttle bus from Terminal 1, gate 28, Terminal 2A gate 5, Terminal 2B gate 6, or Terminal 2D gate 6 to the Roissy train station. From there, the RER B3 will take you to central Paris. To transfer to the Métro, get off at Gare du Nord, Châtelet-Les-Halles, or St-Michel, which are both RER and Métro stops. To go to Roissy from Paris, take the RER B3, any train with a name starting with the letter E to Roissy, which is the end of the line. Then change to the free shuttle bus (RER departs every 20min.; 5am-12:30am; duration 30-35min., bus every 10min., 48F). The **Roissybus** is a shuttle that runs from in front of the American Express office on rue Scribe, near M: Opéra, to gate 10 of Terminal 2A (which also serves terminal 2C), to gate 12 of Terminal 2D (which also serves Terminal 2B), and to gate 30 of Terminal 1, arrivals level (departs every 1min. to airport 5:45am-11pm, from airport 6am-11pm, 45min., 45F). Air France Buses also run to Roissy, servicing two areas of the city. (Recorded info ☎01 41 56 89 00. 60-70F, roundtrip 105-120F.) 18km south of the city, the **Aéroport d'Orly** is used by charters and many continental flights. From Orly Sud gate H or I, platform 1, or Orly Ouest arrival level gate F, take the shuttle bus known as Orly-Rail (every 15min., 5:40am-11:15pm) to the Pont de Rungis/Aéroport d'Orly. From there, you can take the RER C2 to travel into Paris. (For info in English, call ☎08

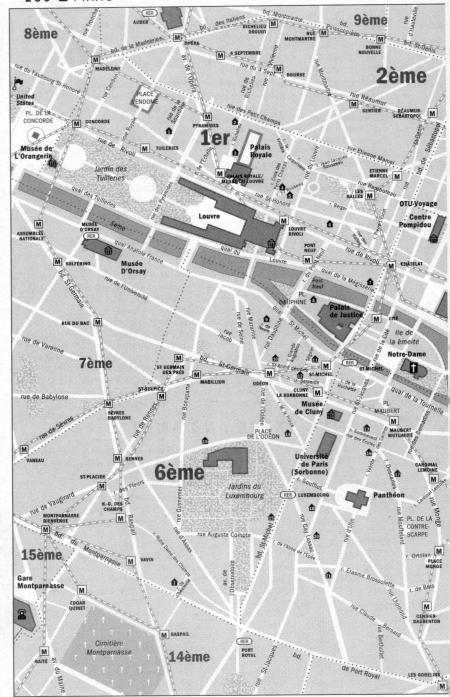

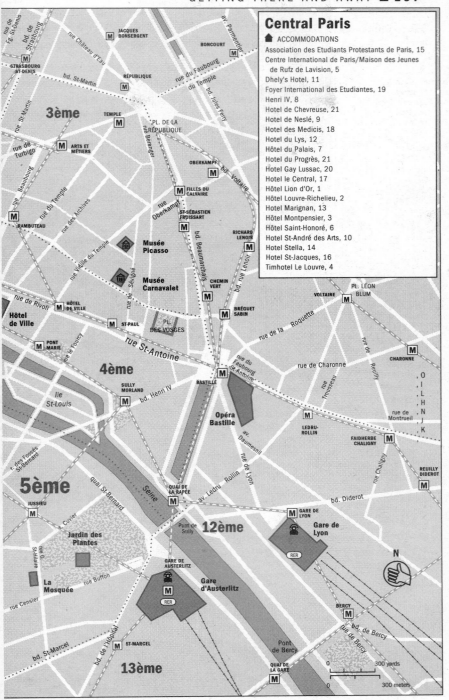

Central Paris

🏠 ACCOMMODATIONS

Association des Etudiants Protestants de Paris, 15
Centre International de Paris/Maison des Jeunes
   de Rufz de Lavision, 5
Dhely's Hotel, 11
Foyer International des Etudiantes, 19
Henri IV, 8
Hotel de Chevreuse, 21
Hotel de Neslé, 9
Hotel des Medicis, 18
Hotel du Lys, 12
Hôtel du Palais, 7
Hotel du Progrès, 21
Hôtel Gay Lussac, 20
Hotel le Central, 17
Hôtel Lion d'Or, 1
Hôtel Louvre-Richelieu, 2
Hotel Marignan, 13
Hôtel Montpensier, 3
Hôtel Saint-Honoré, 6
Hotel St-André des Arts, 10
Hotel Stella, 14
Hotel St-Jacques, 16
Timhotel Le Louvre, 4

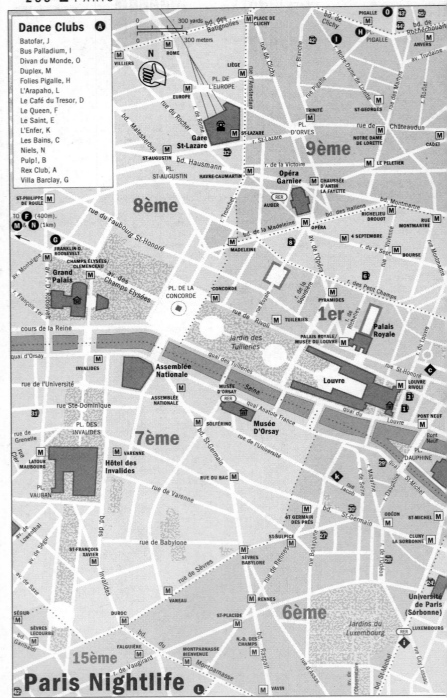

Dance Clubs Ⓐ

Batofar, J
Bus Palladium, I
Divan du Monde, O
Duplex, M
Folies Pigalle, H
L'Arapaho, L
Le Café du Tresor, D
Le Queen, F
Le Saint, E
L'Enfer, K
Les Bains, C
Niels, N
Pulp!, B
Rex Club, A
Villa Barclay, G

Paris Nightlife

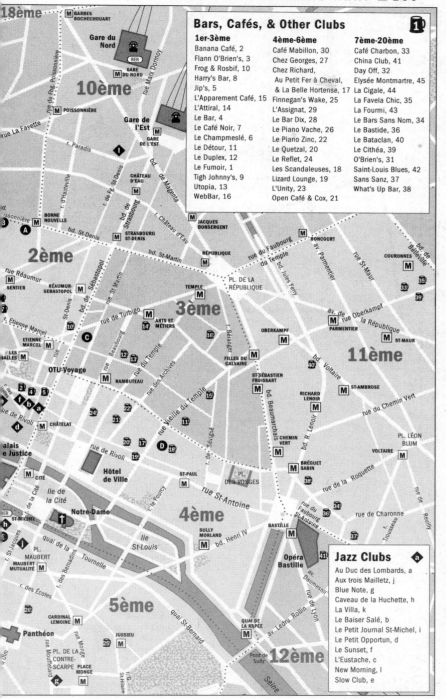

Bars, Cafés, & Other Clubs

1er–3ème
Banana Café, 2
Flann O'Brien's, 3
Frog & Rosbif, 10
Harry's Bar, 8
Jip's, 5
L'Apparement Café, 15
L'Attiral, 14
Le Bar, 4
Le Café Noir, 7
Le Champmeslé, 6
Le Détour, 11
Le Duplex, 12
Le Fumoir, 1
Tigh Johnny's, 9
Utopia, 13
WebBar, 16

4ème–6ème
Café Mabillon, 30
Chez Georges, 27
Chez Richard,
Au Petit Fer à Cheval,
& La Belle Hortense, 17
Finnegan's Wake, 25
L'Assignat, 29
Le Bar Dix, 28
Le Piano Vache, 26
Le Piano Zinc, 22
Le Quetzal, 20
Le Reflet, 24
Les Scandaleuses, 18
Lizard Lounge, 19
L'Unity, 23
Open Café & Cox, 21

7ème–20ème
Café Charbon, 33
China Club, 41
Day Off, 32
Elysée Montmartre, 45
La Cigale, 44
La Favela Chic, 35
La Fourmi, 43
Le Bars Sans Nom, 34
Le Bastide, 36
Le Bataclan, 40
Le Cithéa, 39
O'Brien's, 31
Saint-Louis Blues, 42
Sans Sanz, 37
What's Up Bar, 38

Jazz Clubs ♦

Au Duc des Lombards, a
Aux trois Mailletz, j
Blue Note, g
Caveau de la Huchette, h
La Villa, k
Le Baiser Salé, b
Le Petit Journal St-Michel, i
Le Petit Opportun, d
Le Sunset, f
L'Eustache, c
New Morning, l
Slow Club, e

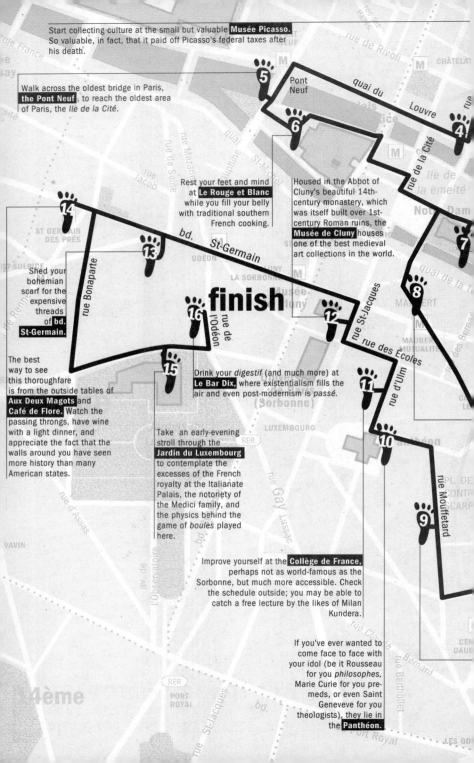

Start collecting culture at the small but valuable **Musée Picasso**. So valuable, in fact, that it paid off Picasso's federal taxes after his death.

5

Pont Neuf

quai du Louvre

CHÂTELA

M

M

rue de Rivoli

Walk across the oldest bridge in Paris, **the Pont Neuf**, to reach the oldest area of Paris, the *Ile de la Cité*.

6

4

rue de la Cité

Île de la émelité

Notre Dam

7

Rest your feet and mind at **Le Rouge et Blanc** while you fill your belly with traditional southern French cooking.

Housed in the Abbot of Cluny's beautiful 14th-century monastery, which was itself built over 1st-century Roman ruins, the **Musée de Cluny** houses one of the best medieval art collections in the world.

14

ST GERMAIN DES PRÉS

13

bd. St-Germain

ODÉON

LA SORBONN

ST-SULPICE

rue Bonaparte

Musée Cluny

M

quai de la T

8

MAR
MUBERT

Shed your bohemian scarf for the expensive threads of **bd. St-Germain**.

finish

rue de l'Odéon

16

rue St-Jacques

12

rue des Ecoles

rue d'Ulm

MAUBER
MUTUALITÉ

des Bernar

The best way to see this thoroughfare is from the outside tables of **Aux Deux Magots** and **Café de Flore**. Watch the passing throngs, have wine with a light dinner, and appreciate the fact that the walls around you have seen more history than many American states.

15

Drink your *digestif* (and much more) at **Le Bar Dix**, where existentialism fills the air and even post-modernism is *passé*.

11

(Sorbonne)

LUXEMBOURG

RER

10

Panthéon

rue Mouffetard

Take an early-evening stroll through the **Jardin du Luxembourg** to contemplate the excesses of the French royalty at the Italianate Palais, the notoriety of the Medici family, and the physics behind the game of *boules* played here.

rue Gay Lussac

9

RPL DE
CONTR
SCARP

Improve yourself at the **Collège de France**, perhaps not as world-famous as the Sorbonne, but much more accessible. Check the schedule outside; you may be able to catch a free lecture by the likes of Milan Kundera.

rue Chie

rue Berthollet

CEN
DAUB

If you've ever wanted to come face to face with your idol (be it Rousseau for you *philosophes*, Marie Curie for you pre-meds, or even Saint Geneveve for you theologists), they lie in the **Panthéon**.

VAVIN

rue d'Assas

bd.

de l'Observatoire

RER

PORT
ROYAL

4ème

rue St-Jacques

bd.

PORT Royal

LES GO

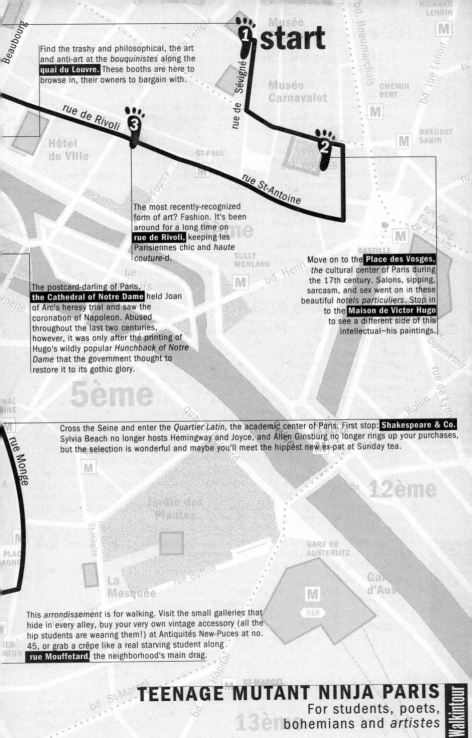

start

1. Find the trashy and philosophical, the art and anti-art at the *bouquinistes* along the **quai du Louvre.** These booths are here to browse in, their owners to bargain with.

3. The most recently-recognized form of art? Fashion. It's been around for a long time on **rue de Rivoli,** keeping *les Parisiennes* chic and *haute couture*-d.

2. Move on to the **Place des Vosges,** *the* cultural center of Paris during the 17th century. Salons, sipping, sarcasm, and sex went on in these beautiful *hotels particuliers*. Stop in to the **Maison de Victor Hugo** to see a different side of this intellectual—his paintings.

The postcard-darling of Paris, **the Cathedral of Notre Dame** held Joan of Arc's heresy trial and saw the coronation of Napoleon. Abused throughout the last two centuries, however, it was only after the printing of Hugo's wildly popular *Hunchback of Notre Dame* that the government thought to restore it to its gothic glory.

Cross the Seine and enter the *Quartier Latin*, the academic center of Paris. First stop: **Shakespeare & Co.** Sylvia Beach no longer hosts Hemingway and Joyce, and Allen Ginsburg no longer rings up your purchases, but the selection is wonderful and maybe you'll meet the hippest new ex-pat at Sunday tea.

This *arrondissement* is for walking. Visit the small galleries that hide in every alley, buy your very own vintage accessory (all the hip students are wearing them!) at Antiquités New-Puces at no. 45, or grab a crêpe like a real starving student along **rue Mouffetard,** the neighborhood's main drag.

TEENAGE MUTANT NINJA PARIS
For students, poets, bohemians and *artistes*

Walkintour

36 68 41 14; every 15min., 6am-11pm; 25min.; 35F.) The **Orlybus** runs to the airport from M: Denfert-Rochereau.

Trains: There are 6 train stations in Paris; each part of the Métro system and servicing a different geographic region.

Gare du Nord: M: Gare du Nord. Serves northern France, Belgium, the Netherlands, Britain, northern Germany. To: **Brussels** (2hr., 287F); **Amsterdam** (5hr., 378F); **Cologne/Köln** (5-6hr., 364F); and **Copenhagen** (16hr., 1265F). The **Eurostar** (☎01 49 70 01 75; see p. 46) departs here for **London** (3hr., 360-740F).

Gare de l'Est: M: Gare de l'Est. To eastern France, Austria, Luxembourg, southern Germany, and northern Switzerland. To: **Munich** (8hr., 685F) and **Vienna** (14hr., 970F).

Gare de Lyon: M: Gare de Lyon. Handles trains to southeastern France, parts of Switzerland, Italy, and Greece. To: **Geneva** (3½hr., 508F) and **Rome** (12hr., 630F).

Gare d'Austerlitz: M: Gare d'Austerlitz. Serves the Loire Valley, southwestern France, Spain, and Portugal. To: **Barcelona** (9hr., 500-800F) and **Madrid** (12-13hr., 530-850F).

Gare St-Lazare: M: Gare St-Lazare. Serves Normandy. To: **Rouen** (1hr., 103F).

Gare de Montparnasse: M: Montparnasse-Bienvenüe. Serves Brittany; also the point of departure for southbound **TGV** high-speed trains.

Buses: Gare Routière Internationale de Paris, 28 av. du Général de Gaulle (☎01 49 72 51 51; M: Gallieni) has buses running to more than 1500 towns in Europe. Also at 55 rue St-Jacques (☎01 43 54 11 99; M: St-Jacques). For more info, see www.eurolines.fr.

⌐ GETTING AROUND

Public Transportation: The efficient **Métropolitain,** or **Métro (M),** runs 5:30am-12:30am. Lines are numbered but are generally referred to by their number and final destinations; connections are called *correspondences.* **Single-fare tickets** within the city 8F; **carnet** (packet) of ten 52F. Buy extras for times when ticket booths are closed (after 10pm) and hold on to your ticket until you exit. The **RER** (Réseau Express Régional), the commuter train to the suburbs, serves as an express subway within central Paris; changing to and getting off the RER requires sticking your validated ticket into a turnstile. Watch the signboards next to the RER tracks and check that your stop is lit up before riding. **Buses** use the same 8F tickets (bought on the bus; validate in the machine by the driver), but transfer requires a new ticket. Buses run 7am-8:30pm, *Autobus du Soir* until 1am, and *Noctambus* (3-4 tickets) every hr. 1:30-5:30am at stops marked with the bug-eyed moon between the Châtelet stop and the *portes* (city exits). The **Paris Visite** pass grants unlimited travel on the Métro, RER, and buses along with other discounts (2-day 70F). The **Mobilis** pass covers the Métro, RER, and buses only (1-day 32F). To qualify for a weekly *(hebdomadaire)* **Coupon Vert,** valid from M (75F), bring a photo ID to the ticket counter to get the necessary **Carte Orange.** Refer to this book's **color maps** of Paris's transit network.

Taxis: (☎01 47 39 47 39). Cab stands are near train stations and major bus stops. 3-person max. Taxis are pricey (13F plus 4-8F per km), and even pricier if you don't speak French. The meter starts running when you phone.

Car Rental: Rent-a-Car, 79 rue de Bercy, 12ème (☎01 43 45 98 99). Open M-Sa 8:30am-7pm.

Bike Rental: Paris à vélo, c'est sympa! 37 bd. Bourdon, 4ème (☎01 48 87 60 01). M: Bastille. Rentals available with a 2500F (or credit card) deposit. 24hr. rental 150F; 9am-7pm 80F. half-day (9am-2pm or 2-7pm) 60F.

Hitchhiking: *Let's Go* does not recommend hitchhiking. Don't waste time at the portes of the city, as traffic there is too heavy for cars to stop. **Allostop-Provoya,** 8 rue Rochambeau, 9ème (☎01 53 20 42 42), matches drivers and riders. M: Cadet. To: **Frankfurt** (about 197F) and **Geneva** (188F). Open M-F 9am-7:30pm, Sa 9am-1pm and 2-6pm.

✴ ORIENTATION

The **Ile de la Cité** and **Ile St-Louis** sit at the geographical center of the city, while the **Seine,** flowing east to west, splits Paris into two large expanses: the **Rive Gauche**

(Left Bank) to the south and the **Rive Droite** (Right Bank) to the north. The Left Bank, with its older architecture and narrow streets, has traditionally been considered bohemian and intellectual, while the Right Bank, with its grand avenues and designer shops, is more chi-chi. Administratively, Paris is divided into 20 **arrondissements** (districts; e.g. 1er, 6ème) that spiral clockwise around the Louvre. Areas of interest are compact and central, and sketchier neighborhoods tend to lie on the outskirts of town. Refer also to this book's **color maps** of the city.

RIVE GAUCHE (LEFT BANK). The **Latin Quarter,** encompassing the 5ème and parts of the 6ème around the **Sorbonne** and the **Ecole des Beaux-Arts** (School of Fine Arts), has been home to students for centuries; the animated **bd. St-Michel** is the boundary between the two *arrondissements*. The area around east-west **bd. St-Germain,** which crosses bd. St-Michel just south of pl. St-Michel in the 6ème, is known as **St-Germain des Prés.** To the west, the gold-domed **Invalides** and the stern Neoclassical **Ecole Militaire,** which faces the **Eiffel Tower** across the **Champ-de-Mars,** recall the military past of the 7ème and northern 15ème, now full of traveling businesspeople. South of the Latin Quarter, **Montparnasse,** in the 14ème, eastern 15ème, and southwestern 6ème, lolls in the shadow of its tower. The glamorous **bd. du Montparnasse** belies the more residential districts around it. The eastern Left Bank, comprising the 13ème, is the city's newest up-and-coming hotspot, centered on the **pl. d'Italie.**

RIVE DROITE (RIGHT BANK). The **Louvre** and **rue de Rivoli** occupy the sight- and tourist-packed 1er and the more business-oriented 2ème. The crooked streets of **Marais,** in the 3ème and 4ème, escaped Baron Haussmann's redesign of ancient Paris and now support many diverse communities. From **pl. de la Concorde,** at the western end of the 1er, **av. des Champs-Elysées** bisects the 8ème as it sweeps up toward the **Arc de Triomphe** at **Charles de Gaulle-Etoile.** South of the Etoile, money old and new chinks in the exclusive 16ème, bordered to the west by the **Bois de Boulogne** park and to the east by the Seine and the **Trocadéro,** which faces the Eiffel Tower across the river. Back toward central Paris, the 9ème, just north of the 2ème, is defined by the sumptuous **Opéra.** East of the 9ème, the 10ème hosts cheap lodgings and the **Gare du Nord** and the **Gare de l'Est.** The 10ème, 3ème, and the happening 11ème (which peaks with the nightlife of **Bastille**) meet at **pl. de la République.** South of Bastille, the 12ème surrounds the **Gare de Lyon,** petering out at the **Bois de Vincennes.** East of Bastille, the party atmosphere gives way to the quieter, more residential 20ème and 19ème, while the 18ème is home to **Montmartre,** capped by the **Sacré-Cœur.** To the east, the 17ème starts in the red-light district of **Pigalle** and bd. de Clichy, growing more elegant toward the Etoile, the **Opéra Garnier,** and the 16ème. Continuing west along the *grande axe* defined by the Champs-Elysées, the skyscrapers of **La Défense,** Paris's newest quarter, are across the Seine from the Bois de Boulogne.

⁊ PRACTICAL INFORMATION

TOURIST, FINANCIAL, AND LOCAL SERVICES

Tourist Offices: Bureau d'Accueil Central, 127 av. des Champs-Elysées, 8ème (☎08 36 68 31 12; 23F per min.). M: Charles-de-Gaulle-Etoile. English-speaking and mobbed. Open daily 9am-8pm. **Branches** at Gare de Lyon (open M-Sa 8am-8pm) and the Orly (open daily 6am-11:30pm) and Charles de Gaulle (open daily 7am-10pm) airports.

Budget Travel: Office de Tourisme Universitaire (OTU), 119 rue St-Martin, 4ème (☎01 40 29 12 12), opposite the Centre Pompidou. M: Rambuteau. Sells ISICs and discounted student plane, train, and bus tickets; books hostel and hotel rooms for a 10F fee. Open M-F 10am-6:30pm, Sa 10am-5pm. Also at 139 bd. St-Michel, 5ème (☎01 44 41 74 74). M: Port-Royal. Open M-F 10am-6:30pm. **Council Travel,** 1 pl. Odéon, 6ème (☎01 44 41 89 80). M: Odéon. Sells ISICs, plane tickets, and train tickets (including BIJ/Eurotrain). Open M-F 9:30am-6:30pm, Sa 10am-5pm.

Embassies: Australia, 4 rue Jean-Rey, 15ème (☎01 40 59 33 00; www.austgov.fr). M: Bir-Hakeim. Open M-F 9:15am-noon and 2-4:30pm. **Canada,** 35 av. Montaigne, 8ème (☎01 44 43 29 00). M: Franklin-Roosevelt or Alma-Marceau. Open M-F 9am-noon and

2-5pm. **Ireland,** 12 av. Foch, 16ème (☎01 44 17 67 48). M: Argentine. Open M-F 9:30am-noon. **New Zealand,** 7ter rue Léonard de Vinci, 16ème (☎01 45 00 24 11). M: Victor-Hugo. Open M-F 9am-1pm and 2-5:30pm. **South Africa,** 59 quai d'Orsay, 7ème (☎01 53 59 23 23). M: Invalides. Open M-F 9am-noon. **UK,** 35 rue du Faubourg-St-Honoré, 8ème (☎01 44 51 31 00). M: Concorde. Open M-F 9:30am-12:30pm and 2:30-5pm. Consulate Section, 18bis rue d'Anjou, 8ème (☎01 44 51 31 02; www.amb-grandebretagne.fr). Open M-F 9:30am-12:30pm and 2:30-5pm. **US,** 2 av. Gabriel, 8ème (☎01 43 12 22 22). M: Concorde. Open M-F 9am-6pm. Consulate General, 2 rue St-Florentin, 8ème (☎01 43 12 22 22). Open M-F 9am-3pm.

Currency Exchange: Hotels, train stations, and airports offer poor rates but have extended hours; Gare de Lyon, Gare du Nord, and both airports have booths open 6:30am-10:30pm. Most **ATMs** accept **Visa** ("CB/VISA") and **MasterCard** ("EC"). Crédit Lyonnais ATMs take **AmEx;** Crédit Mutuel and Crédit Agricole ATMs are on the **Cirrus** network; and most Visa ATMs accept **PLUS**-network cards.

American Express: 11 rue Scribe, 9ème (☎01 47 77 79 33), opposite the rear of the Opéra. M: Opéra. Poor rates; long lines. Mail held for cardholders and AmEx Travelers Cheques holders; otherwise 5F per inquiry. Open M-F 9am-6:30pm, Sa 10am-5:30pm.

Bookstores: Shakespeare and Co., 37 rue de la Bûcherie, 5ème, across the Seine from Notre-Dame. M: St-Michel. Quirky, wide-ranging selection of new and used books. Open daily noon-midnight. **Gibert Jeune,** 5 pl. St-Michel, 5ème. M: St-Michel. The best bookstore in town, with several departments along bd. St-Michel. Books in all languages for all tastes. Open M-Sa 9:30am-7:30pm.

Gay and Lesbian Services: Centre Gai et Lesbien, 3 rue Keller, 11ème (☎01 43 57 21 47). M: Ledru Rollin. Info hub of all gay services and associations in Paris. English spoken. Open M-Sa 2-8pm, Su 7pm.

Laundromats: Most *laveries* charge about 5F for 8-12min. in the dryer (*séchoir*) and 2-5F for detergent. **LaveauClaire,** 119 rue Charenton, 11ème. Wash 18F per 6kg. Open daily 7am-9pm. **Lavage,** 69 rue de Bac, 6ème. Wash 25F per 6kg. Open daily 7:30am-9pm. **Laverie Primus,** 87 rue Didot, 14ème. Wash 25F per 7kg.

EMERGENCY AND COMMUNICATIONS

Emergencies: Ambulance, ☎15. **Fire,** ☎18. **Police,** ☎17. For non-emergencies, head to the local *gendarmerie* (police force) in each *arrondissement*.

Crisis Lines: Rape, SOS Viol (☎ (0800) 05 95 95). Call free anywhere in France for counseling (medical and legal). Open M-F 10am-7pm. **SOS Friendship** (☎01 47 23 80 80). For depressed, lonely English-speakers. Open daily 3-11pm.

Pharmacies: Pharmacie Dhéry, 84 av. des Champs-Elysées, 8ème (☎01 45 62 02 41). M: George V. **Grande Pharmacie Daumesnil,** 6 pl. Félix-Eboué, 12ème (☎01 43 43 19 03). M: Daumesnil; visible as you exit the Métro. Both open 24hr.

Medical Assistance: Hôpital Americain, 63 bd. Victor Hugo (☎01 46 41 25 25), in the suburb of Neuilly. M: Porte Maillot; then take bus #82 to the end of the line. English-speaking, but much pricier than French hospitals. The full gamut of specialists, including state-of-the-art facilities and dental services.

Telephones: To use the phones, you'll need to buy a **phone card** *(télécarte), available* at post offices, Métro stations, and *tabacs.* For **directory info,** call ☎12.

Internet Access: WebBar, 23 rue de Picardie, 3ème. M: République. 40F per hr., 300F per 10hr. Open M-F 8:30am-2am, Sa-Su 11am-2am. **Cyber Cube,** 5 rue Mignon, 6ème. 1F per min. Students 200F per 5hr., 300F per 10hr. Open M-Sa 10am-10pm. Also 12 rue Daval, 11ème. M: Bastille. **Luxembourg Micro,** 83 bd. St-Michel, 5ème. RER: Luxembourg. 0.75F per min., 23F per 30min., 45F per hr. Open M-Sa 9am-9pm.

Post Office: 52 rue du Louvre, 1er. M: Châtelet-les-Halles. Open almost 24hr. (daily 7am-6:20am). For postal info, call 01 40 28 20 40. Address mail to be held: Christina DEEGAN, *Poste Restante,* 52 rue du Louvre, 75001 Paris, France. **Postal Code:** 750xx, where "xx" is the *arrondissement* (e.g., 75003 for any address in the 3ème).

▚ ACCOMMODATIONS

Paris's hostels skip many standard restrictions—sleep sheets, curfews, and the like—but they do tend to have (flexible) maximum stays. The six HI hostels within the city are for members only. The rest of Paris's dorm-style beds are either private hostels or *foyers*, often quieter and more private than regular hostels. Hotels may be the most practical accommodations for the majority of travelers. Groups of two to four may also find hotels more economical than hostels. Expect to pay at least 160F for a single, 200-400F for a double *in the cheapest, luckiest of circumstances*. In cheaper hotels, few rooms have private baths; hall showers can cost 15-25F per use. Rooms fill quickly after morning check-out (generally 10am-noon), so arrive early or reserve ahead. Most hotels accept reservations with a one-night credit card deposit. High season in Paris fall around Easter and from May to October, peaking in July and August. Most hostels and *foyers* (student dorms) include the **taxe de séjour** (1-5F per person per day) in listed prices, but many hotels do not. If you haven't made a reservation in advance, tourist offices (see p. 293) and some organizations, listed below, can help find and book rooms.

ACCOMMODATIONS SERVICES

La Centrale de Réservations (FUAJ-HI), 4 bd. Jules Ferry, 11*ème* (☎01 43 57 02 60). M: République; follow rue du Fbg. du Temple away from pl. de la République, cross the park that divides bd. Jules Ferry, and it's a half-block up on your left. Offers same-day reservations in affiliated hostels (115F) and budget hotels. Show up early. Also arranges excursions and sells plane/bus tickets. Open 24hr.

OTU-Voyage, 119 rue St-Martin, 4*ème* (☎01 40 29 12 12), across the pedestrian mall from the Pompidou. Guarantees same-day "decent and low-cost lodging" (10F fee). Full price due with reservation. English spoken. Open Sa 10am-5pm. Also at 2 rue Malus, **5***ème* (☎01 44 41 74 74). M: Place Monge. Open M-F 10am-6:30pm.

1ER AND 2ÈME: LOUVRE-PALAIS ROYAL

Central to the **Louvre,** the **Tuileries,** the **Seine,** and the ritzy **pl. Vendôme,** this area still has a few budget hotels. Avoid rue St-Denis.

▨ **Hôtel Montpensier,** 12 rue de Richelieu (☎01 42 96 28 50). M: Palais-Royal. Lofty elegance welcomes the clientele. Shower 25F. Reserve 4 weeks in advance in high season. Singles with toilet 295F; doubles with toilet 305F; rooms with bath 435F; rooms with toilet, bathtub, and sink 515F. Extra bed 80F.

Hôtel du Palais, 2 quai de la Mégisserie (☎01 42 36 98 25). M: Châtelet. All rooms (except on the top floor) have views of the Seine and Left Bank. Reserve 3 weeks in advance. Singles 283-353F; doubles 326-386F; triples 429F; large quads 462F; quint with 2-sink bathroom and huge windows 535F. Extra bed 70F.

Hôtel Lion d'Or, 5 rue de la Sourdière (☎01 42 60 79 04; www.123france.com). M: Tuileries or Pyramides. You'll hear the bells toll from nearby Eglise St-Roch but little else. Phone and TV. Reserve 1 month in advance. 5% discount for stays of more than 3 nights. Singles 380-480F; doubles with shower 480-560F; triples with shower 560F, with bath and toilet 680F. Extra bed 60F.

Hôtel Saint-Honoré, 85 rue St-Honoré (☎01 42 36 20 38; fax 42 21 44 08). M: Louvre, Châtelet, or Les Halles. Recently renovated. All rooms with full bath and TV. Breakfast 29F. Reserve by fax or phone and confirm the night before. Singles 290F; doubles 410-450F; triples and quads 490F.

Timhotel Le Louvre, 4 rue Croix des Petits-Champs (☎01 42 60 34 86). M: Palais-Royal. From the Métro, cross rue de Rivoli to rue St-Honoré; take a left onto rue Croix des Petits-Champs. Has the only wheelchair-accessible rooms at reasonable prices in the 1*er*. Breakfast 50F. Singles 800F; doubles 800F; triple 1000F.

Centre International de Paris (BVJ)/Paris Louvre, 20 rue J.-J. Rousseau (☎01 53 00 90 90). M: Louvre or Palais-Royal. Bright, dorm-style rooms with 2-10 beds per room. Internet 1F per min. Breakfast and showers included. Reservations up to 1 week in advance; reserve by phone. Rooms held only 10min. after your expected check-in time; call if you'll be late. 130F per person.

Maisons des Jeunes de Rufz de Lavison, 18 rue J.-J. Rousseau (☎01 45 08 02 10). M: Louvre or Palais-Royal. Next door to BVJ Louvre. Quiet, spacious rooms for 50 students. Min. stay 5 nights. Reception 9am-7pm. Reservations necessary in summer; 1 night's payment required. Singles 165F; doubles 290F.

Hôtel Favart, 5 rue Marivaux (☎01 42 97 59 83). M: Richelieu Drouot. Once the home of Spanish painter Goya. Rooms have cable TV, phone, shower, toilet, and hair dryer. One wheelchair accessible room on first floor. Listed are *Let's Go* prices at substantial discounts. Singles 540F; doubles 685F; extra bed 100F.

Hôtel Vivienne, 40 rue Vivienne (☎01 42 33 13 26). M: Montmartre. Refined budget digs. Singles with shower 390F; doubles with bath 490F.

Hôtel La Marmotte, 6 rue Léopold Bellan (☎01 40 26 26 51). M: Sentier. Quiet rooms with TVs, phones, and free safe-boxes. Breakfast 25F. Shower 15F. Reserve a month in advance. Singles and doubles 180-220F, with shower 270-310F; extra bed 80F.

Hôtel des Boulevards, 10 rue de la Ville Neuve (☎01 42 36 02 29). M: Bonne Nouvelle. Quiet rooms. The higher the room, the brighter. Reserve 2 weeks ahead and confirm with credit card deposit. Singles and doubles 240F, with shower 305F, with bath 330-340F; 3rd person 60F.

3ÈME AND 4ÈME: THE MARAIS

The Marais' 17th-century mansions now house budget hotels close to the **Centre Pompidou,** the **Ile St-Louis,** and bars. Convenient for sampling nightlife further afield, as Paris's night buses converge in the 4eme at M: Châtelet.

Hôtel du Séjour, 36 rue du Grenier St-Lazare (☎01 48 87 40 36). M: Etienne-Marcel or Rambuteau. Clean, bright rooms and a warm welcome. Showers 20F. Reception 7am-10:30pm. Singles 180F-200F; doubles 280F, with bath 340F; third person 150F extra.

Hôtel de Roubaix, 6 rue Greneta (☎01 42 72 89 91). M: Réaumur-Sébastopol or Arts-et-Métiers. Advice-dispensing staff, clean rooms, and new bathrooms. All rooms with bath, telephone, locker, and TV. Some with balconies. Breakfast included. Singles 310-330F; doubles 380-410F; triples 430-490F; quads 520F; quints 550F.

Hôtel Picard, 26 rue de Picardie (☎01 48 87 53 82). M: Temple. Simple pastel rooms. Breakfast 30F. Hall showers 20F. Apr.-Sept. reserve 1 week ahead. Tax 5F. Singles 210F, with bath 260F; doubles 250-270F; triples 520F.

Hôtel Paris France, 72 rue de Turbigo (☎01 42 78 00 04, reservations ☎01 42 78 64 92). M: République or Temple. Rooms on the top floor renovated and bright, with balconies and super views. Singles 250-405F; doubles 320-560F; triples 445-615F.

Hôtel Bellevue et du Chariot d'Or, 39 rue de Turbigo (☎01 48 87 45 60). M: Etienne-Marcel. Belle Epoque lobby, with bar. Clean and modern. Rooms with baths, phones, TVs, and toilets. Singles 315F; doubles 350F; triples 425F; quads 460F.

Grand Hôtel Jeanne d'Arc, 3 rue de Jarente (☎01 48 87 62 11; www.hoteljeannedarc.com). M: St-Paul or Bastille. Rooms with bath and TVs. Reserve 2 months in advance. Singles 325F; doubles 330-660F; triples 600F; quads 660F.

Castex Hôtel, 5 rue Castex (☎01 42 72 31 52; fax 01 42 72 57 91). M: Bastille or Sully-Morland. Modern stucco decor and kind rooms. TV room. Check-in 1pm. All rooms with telephone and sink. Reserve by sending a fax with a credit card number 1 month in advance. Singles 240-320F; doubles 320-360F; triples 460F. Extra bed 70F.

Hôtel de Nice, 42bis rue de Rivoli (☎01 42 78 55 29; fax 01 42 78 36 07). M: Hôtel-de-Ville. Nice, nice rooms feature vintage catalogue illustrations, TVs, toilets, showers, and phones. A few have balconies with great views. Rooms ready at 2pm, but leave your bags earlier. Check-out 11am. Reserve by fax or phone with 1 night's deposit 1 month ahead for summer. Singles 380F; doubles 550F; triples 680F. Extra bed 130F.

Hôtel Practic, 9 rue d'Ormesson (☎48 87 80 47; fax 48 87 40 04). M: St-Paul. A clean hotel on a cobblestone square in the heart of the Marais. Rooms are modest, but all have TVs and hairdryers. Reserve by fax 2-4 weeks in advance. Singles 250F; doubles 305-450F. Extra bed 80F. Tax 3F.

Hôtel des Jeunes (MIJE) (☎42 74 23 45; www.mije.com) books beds in Le Fourcy, Le Fauconnier, and Maubuisson (see below), 3 small hostels located on cobblestone streets in old Marais residences. No smoking. Ages 18-30 only. Max. stay 7 days. Reception 7am-1am. Lockout noon-3pm. Curfew 1am. Breakfast included. Arrive before noon (call if you'll be late). Reception M-F 11:30am-1:30pm and 6:30-8:30pm. Reserve 1 month in advance. Dorms 140F; singles 240F; doubles 350F; triples 465F.

> **Le Fourcy,** 6 rue de Fourcy. M: St-Paul or Pont Marie. From M: St-Paul, walk opposite the traffic for a few meters down rue François-Miron and turn left on rue de Fourcy. Light sleepers should avoid rooms on the social courtyard. Internet 1F per min.

> **Le Fauconnier,** 11 rue du Fauconnier. M: St-Paul or Pont Marie. From M: St-Paul, take rue du Pre-vôt, turn left on rue Charlemagne, and turn right on rue du Fauconnier. Ivy-covered building steps away from the Seine and Île St-Louis. Spacious 4-bed rooms, some doubles, some singles.

> **Maubuisson,** 12 rue des Barres. M: Hôtel-de-Ville or Pont Marie. From M: Pont Marie, walk opposite traffic on rue de l'Hôtel de Ville and turn right on rue des Barres. A half-timbered former girls' convent. Smaller 2- to 7-bed rooms with nice views.

5ÈME AND 6ÈME: THE LATIN QUARTER AND ST-GERMAIN-DES-PRÉS

The lively *quartier latin* and St-Germain-des-Prés offer proximity to the **Notre-Dame,** the **Panthéon,** the **Jardin du Luxembourg,** and the bustling student cafe-culture.

Hôtel St-Jacques, 35 rue des Ecoles (☎01 44 07 45 45). M: Maubert-Mutualité. Elegant rooms at reasonable rates, with balconies and TVs. Singles 260F, with shower and toilet 480F; doubles 420-610; triples 680F.

Hôtel d'Esmeralda, 4 rue St-Julien-le-Pauvre (☎01 43 54 19 20). M: St-Michel. Walk along the Seine on quai St-Michel toward Nôtre-Dame, then turn right at parc Viviani. Breakfast 40F. Singles 160F, with bath 320F; doubles 420-490F; triples 550F.

Hôtel du Progrès, 50 rue Gay-Lussac (☎01 43 54 53 18). M: Luxembourg. From the Métro, walk away from Jardin du Luxembourg on rue Guy-Lussac. Clean, airy rooms. Breakfast included. Reserve 2-3 weeks in advance. Cash or traveler's checks only. Singles 170-190F; doubles 260F, with shower 350F; triples 290-360F.

Hôtel le Central, 6 rue Descartes (☎01 46 33 57 93). M: Maubert-Mutualité. Great location near rue Mouffetard and the Panthéon. Bright, newly painted rooms. All rooms have showers. Singles 163-188F; doubles and triples 236-266F. Cash only.

Hôtel Gay-Lussac, 29 rue Gay-Lussac (☎01 43 54 23 96). M: Luxembourg. Stately old rooms, some with fireplaces. Breakfast included. Singles 200F; doubles 400F; triples 500F; quads 600F.

Hôtel des Médicis, 214 rue St-Jacques (☎01 43 54 14 66). M: Luxembourg. Old place shuns right-angle geometry; perhaps that's why Jim Morrison slummed here (room #4). Reception 9am-11pm. Singles and doubles 180-200F.

Hôtel des Argonauts, 12 rue de la Huchette (☎01 43 54 09 82). M: St-Michel. Clean, modern rooms with new linoleum floors and photos of Greek islands. Reserve 3-4 weeks in advance. Singles with shower 285F; doubles with shower 410F, with bath 460F.

Young and Happy (Y&H) Hostel, 80 rue Mouffetard (☎01 45 35 09 53; email smile@youngandhappy.fr). M: Monge. In the heart of the student quarter. Basic but cheerful. Sheets 15F. Towels 5F. Commission-free currency exchange. Laundry nearby. Lockout 11am-5pm. Curfew 2am. Dorms 127F, off-season 107F; doubles 127F.

Centre International de Paris (BVJ): Paris Quartier Latin, 44 rue des Bernardins (☎01 43 29 34 80). M: Maubert-Mutualité. Immense, ultra-modern hostel with a shiny cafeteria. Showers in rooms. Lockers 10F. Check-in before 2:30pm. Reserve well in advance, or arrive at 9am to check for often available rooms. 138 beds. 5- and 6-person dorms 130F; singles 160F; doubles 280F.

FRANCE

Hôtel de Neslé, 7 rue du Neslé (☎01 43 54 62 41). M: Odéon. Fantastical and absolutely sparkling. For a treat, book the double room with Turkish *hammam* steam bath (600F). Singles 300-378F; doubles 400-600F; triples 478-675F.

Dhely's Hotel, 22 rue de l'Hirondelle (☎01 43 26 58 25). M: St-Michel. Wood paneling, flower boxes, modern facilities, and quiet location. Hall showers 25F. Reserve well in advance. Singles 258-338F, with shower 428F; doubles 376F, 466F; triples 516F, 606F; extra bed 100F.

Hôtel St-André des Arts, 66 rue St-André-des-Arts (☎01 43 26 96 16; email hsaintand@minitel.net). M: Odéon. Not particularly elegant, but all the bathrooms are new. Rooms all with bath. Breakfast included. Singles 337-387F; doubles 484-524F; triples 591F; quads 658F.

Hôtel de Chevreuse, 3 rue de Chevreuse (☎01 43 20 93 16; fax 01 43 21 43 72). M: Vavin. Small, clean, quiet rooms with TV and Ikea furniture. Reserve one week in advance and confirm by fax. Singles 235F; doubles 295F, with shower, TV, and toilet 375F, with full bath 415F; triples with full bath and TV 535F.

Hotel Stella, 41 rue Monsieur-le-Prince (☎01 40 51 00 25). M: Odéon. This hotel takes the exposed beam look to a whole new level. All rooms have shower and toilet. Singles 250F; doubles 300F; triples 450F; quads 500F. Cash only.

Foyer International des Etudiantes, 93 bd. St-Michel (☎01 43 54 49 63). RER: Luxembourg. Everything elegant. Breakfast included. July-Sept. hotel is coed; Oct.-June women only. Reserve in writing 2 months in advance, and as early as January for the coed summer months. 200F deposit. Check-out 10am. Call ahead or arrive at 10am for no-shows. singles 170F, 2990F per month; doubles 120F, 2030F.

Association des Etudiants Protestants de Paris, 46 rue de Vaugirard (☎01 43 54 31 49; email aepp.resa@worldnet.fr; http://home.worldnet.fr/aepp). M: Odéon; RER: Luxembourg. Simple rooms for people aged 18-26. Part summer hostel, part university residence, the building includes a kitchen, lounge, and washing machines. Breakfast included. Reserve 2 weeks in advance for stays longer than 7 days. 10F membership fee, plus 100F key deposit. Long-term applications due before May 30. Dorms 82F; singles 100-120F; doubles 190-200F. Monthly 2100F.

7ÈME: EIFFEL TOWER AND LES INVALIDES

■ **Hôtel du Champs de Mars,** 7 rue du Champ de Mars (☎01 45 51 52 30; email stg@club-internet.fr; www.adx.fr/hotel-du-champ-de-mars.com). M: Ecole-Militaire. Reserve 1 month ahead. Singles with shower 390F, with large bed and bath 425F; doubles with shower 430F, with bath 460F; triples with bath 550F.

■ **Grand Hôtel Lévêque,** 29 rue Cler (☎01 47 05 49 15; email info@hotelleveque.com; www.hotel-leveque.com). M: Ecole-Militaire. 3-star quality: clean and cheery. Satellite TV, safe (20F), phone, and ceiling fan in all rooms. Reserve 1 month ahead. Singles 300F; doubles with bath 400-470F; triples with bath 580F.

■ **Hôtel Malar,** 29 rue Malar (☎01 45 51 38 46). M: Latou-Maubourg. Elegantly furnished. Each room has a matching bathroom. TV, telephones, showers, and hairdryers. Breakfast 40F. Reserve in advance. Singles 480F, with shower, 440F; Doubles 520F, with shower 480F; extra Bed 100F.

Hôtel Eiffel Rive Gauche, 6 rue du Gros Caillou (☎01 45 51 24 56; email eiffel@easynet.fr; www.france-hotel-guide.com/h75007/eifriv.htm). M: Ecole-Militaire. On a quiet street, this family-run hotel is a favorite of Anglophone travelers. Rooms have cable TV and phone; upper floors see top of Eiffel Tower. Breakfast buffet 40F. Hall showers 15F. Singles 240-435F; doubles 280-480F; triples 460-570F. Extra bed 90F.

Hôtel de la Paix, 19 rue du Gros-Caillou (☎01 45 51 86 17). M: Ecole Militaire. Across from Hôtel Eiffel Rive Gauche (above), it's the cheapest of the bunch. Reserve one week ahead. Singles 180F, with shower 280F; doubles with shower 320F, with bath 350-395F; triple 500F. Extra bed 100F. French traveler's checks or cash only.

Hotel Amelie, 5 rue Amelie (☎01 45 51 74 75; email RESA@hotel-AMELIE.com.) M: Latour-Maubourg or Invalides. Reserve 2 weeks in advance. Singles with shower 440F; double with shower 480F, with twin beds and shower 540F, with bath 540F.

8ÈME: CHAMPS-ELYSÉES

▦ **Foyer de Chaillot,** 28 av. George V (☎01 47 23 35 32). M: George V. Take the elevator to the foyer on the 3rd floor. Cheerful, well-equipped, modern rooms, in an upscale dorm-like environment for **women only.** Dinner included M-F. Doubles 7100F per month; after a stay of two months, you can request a single for 3550F per month.

Hôtel Europe-Liège 8, rue de Moscou (☎01 42 94 01 51). M: Liège. Reasonably priced hotel with newly painted rooms. 2 wheelchair accessible rooms on the ground floor. Breakfast 37F. Singles 390F; doubles 500F.

9ÈME AND 10ÈME: OPÉRA, GARE DE NORD, GARE DE L'EST

The northern part of the 9ème mixes pumping nightlife with a red-light district; avoid M: Pigalle, M: Barbès-Rochechouart, and bd. de Clichy. In the 10ème, beware the Gare du Nord, rue du Faubourg St-Denis, bd. de Magenta, and near M: Barbès. Inexpensive hotels abound in this area.

▦ **Hôtel Chopin,** 10 bd. Montmartre, or 46, passage Jouffroy (☎01 47 70 58 10). M: Grands Boulevards. Inside a spectacular old passage lined with shops. A cut above most budget hotels. TV, phone, and fans. Singles with shower 355F, with bath 405-455F; doubles with bath 450-520F; triples with bath 595F.

▦ **Hôtel Beauharnais,** 51 rue de la Victoire (☎01 48 74 71 13). M: Le Peletier. Look for flower boxes, since there is no Hôtel sign and the lobby looks like someone's sitting room. All rooms have showers. Doubles 320F; triples 490F; quads 550F; quints 640F.

Woodstock Hostel, 48 rue Rodier (☎01 48 78 87 76; email flowers@woodstock.fr; www.woodstock.fr). M: Anvers or Gare du Nord. Internet access. Reserve ahead. 4-person dorms Apr.-Oct. 117F, Sept.-May 77F; doubles 137F, 87F.

Hôtel Moderne du Temple, 3 rue d'Aix (☎01 42 08 09 04). M: Goncourt. Walk with the traffic on rue du Faubourg du Temple, then turn right onto rue d'Aix. Breakfast 23F. Singles 120-140F, with shower 170F, with bath 220F; doubles 160F, 190F, 240F; triples 180F, 280F, 320F.

11ÈME AND 12ÈME: LA BASTILLE AND RÉPUBLIQUE

Convenient to hopping nightlife, although people traveling alone should be cautious at night.

▦ **Mistral Hôtel,** 3 rue Chaligny (☎01 46 28 10 20). M: Reuilly-Diderot. One of the best deals in Paris. Each room is unique.19 rooms. Hall showers 15F. Call to reserve 2 weeks in advance. Singles 208F, with shower 253F; 1-bed doubles 216F, with shower 266F; 2-bed doubles with shower 296F; triples with bath 349F; quads with bath 412F.

▦ **Centre International du Séjour de Paris: CISP "Ravel,"** 6 av. Maurice Ravel (☎01 44 75 60 00). M: Porte de Vincennes. Large rooms (most with less than 4 beds), art exhibits, auditorium, and outdoor pool (25F). Internet. Breakfast included. Reception 6:30am-1:30am. Curfew 1:30am. Reserve ahead by phone. Dorms with shower 143F; singles with bath 196F; doubles with bath 312F.

Hotel Moderne, 121, rue de Chemin-Vert (☎01 47 00 54 05; email modern.hotel@wanadoo.fr; www.modern-hotel.fr). M: Père Lachaise. Newly renovated, with modern furnishings and spanking clean bathrooms. Reserve with credit card. Singles 250-290F; doubles 290-350F; quads 510F; extra bed 80F.

Hôtel Rhetia, 3 rue du Général Blaise (☎01 47 00 47 18). M: Voltaire or Saint-Ambroise. Aging furnishings and narrow single beds. Hall showers 10F. Reception 7:30am-10pm. Singles 180F, with shower 290F; doubles 190F, 240F; triples 240F, 290F.

Plessis Hôtel, 25 rue du Grand Prieuré (☎01 47 00 13 38). M: Oberkampf. 5 floors of clean, bright rooms. Rooms with showers have hair dryers, fans, TVs, and balconies. Lounge with TV and vending machines. "American" breakfast 38F. Open Sept-July. Singles 195-295F; doubles 215-350F.

Hôtel Notre-Dame, 51 rue de Malte (☎01 47 00 78 76; email hotelnotredame@wanadoo.fr). M: République. Eclectic decor, cheerful lounge, and elevator. Showers 20F. Breakfast 35F. Reserve 1 month ahead. Single and double 200F, with shower 245-310F, with bath 340-390F.

Auberge de Jeunesse "Jules Ferry" (HI), 8 bd. Jules Ferry (☎01 43 57 55 60; www.cisp.asso.fr). M: République. Clean rooms with 100 bunk beds and sinks; mirrors and tiled floors. Doubles with big beds. Party atmosphere. Breakfast and showers included. Lockers 10F. Sheets 5F. Laundry 20F wash, 10F dry. Max. stay 1 week. Airport shuttle 89F. Internet access in lobby 1F per min. Lockout 10am-2pm. If there are no vacancies, the hostel can book you in another nearby hostel. 4- to 6-bed dorms 120F; doubles 250F.

13ÈME: CITÉ UNIVERSITAIRE

While the $13^{\grave{e}me}$ has little in the way of established hotels, there are some hostels with extremely reasonable prices and easy access to the Métro.

CISP "Kellerman," 17 bd. Kellerman (☎01 44 16 37 38; www.cisp.asso.fr). M: Porte d'Italie. This 392-bed hostel resembles a spaceship on stilts. Impeccably clean with TV room, laundry, and cafeteria (open daily noon-1:30pm and 6:30-9:30pm). Bunk beds. Wheelchair accessible. Breakfast included. Lockout 1:30-6:30pm. Good for last-minute reservations. Dorms 101-126F; singles 146F, with bath 196F.

14ÈME AND 15ÈME: MONTPARNASSE

Just south of the Latin Quarter, Montparnasse mixes bohemian, intellectual charm with thriving commercial centers and venerable cafes.

Three Ducks Hostel, 6 pl. Etienne Pernet (☎01 48 42 04 05). M: Félix Faure. Aimed at young Anglo fun-seekers, the Three Ducks wants you to rock with them at the in-house bar until the 2am curfew. Reserve with credit card deposit, several days ahead in summer. 2- to 8-bed dorms 97F.

Hôtel de Blois, 5 rue des Plantes (☎01 45 40 99 48). M: Mouton-Duvernet. From the Métro, turn left on rue Moutron-Duvernet, then left again on rue des Plantes. Breakfast 27F. Singles 230F; doubles 240F-280F, with shower 270F, with bath 320-360F.

Ouest Hôtel, 27 rue de Gergovie (☎01 45 42 64 99). M: Pernety. Walk against traffic on rue Raymond Losserand, and turn right on rue de Gergovie. Breakfast 20F. Singles 120F-220F; doubles 220-230F.

Hôtel Printemps, 31 rue du Commerce (☎01 45 79 83 36). M: L Motte-Picquet-Grenelle. Clean and cheap in the middle of a busy, bourgeois neighborhood. Breakfast 20F. Singles or doubles 150F, with shower 190F; doubles with bath 230F.

18ÈME: MONTMARTRE

Montmartre has two types of lodging bargains. One is the dirt-cheap hotels south of rue des Abbesses and Sacré Coeur, which are clean and fairly safe. The other type, up on the hill west of Sacré Coeur, is more expensive but offers fantastic nearby cafes and beautiful views over the city. At night, avoid M: Pigalle and M: Barbès-Rochechouart, use M: Abbesses instead, and be careful on deserted side streets.

Hôtel Caulaincourt, 2 sq. Caulaincourt (☎01 46 06 42 99). M: Lamarck-Caulaincourt. Large, simple rooms with great light and wonderful views. Singles with shower 190F, with bath 240F; doubles 230F, 280F; triples 270F, 340F.

Village Hostel, 20 rue d'Orsel (☎01 42 64 22 02). M: Anvers. Go uphill on rue Steinkerque and turn right on rue d'Orsel. Curfew 2am. Lockout 11am-4pm. TV and internet access in the lounge. Dorms 120-150F; doubles 294-310F.

🗒 FOOD

For most Parisians, life is about eating. Scratch that. Life *is* eating. Establishments range from the famous repositories of *haute cuisine* to corner *brasseries*. Inexpensive bistros and *crêperies* offer the breads, cheeses, wines, pâtés, *pôtages*, and pastries central to French cuisine. *Gauche* or gourmet, French or foreign, you'll find it in Paris. **CROUS (Centre Regional des Oeuvres Universitaires et Scolaires),** 39 av. Georges Bernanos, 5ème, has info on university restaurants. (☎01 40 51 37 10. M: Port-Royal. Open M-F 9am-5pm.) To assemble a picnic, visit the specialty shops of the **Marché Montorgeuil,** 2ème, **rue Mouffetard,** 5ème, or the **Marché Bastille,** on bd. Richard-Lenoir (M: Bastille; open Th and Su 7am-1:30pm).

1ER AND 2ÈME: LOUVRE-PALAIS ROYAL

Cheap options surround **Les Halles,** 1er and 2ème. Near the **Louvre,** the small streets of the 2ème teem with traditional bistros.

■ **Jules,** 62 rue Jean-Jacques Rousseau (☎01 40 28 99 04). M: Les Halles. Subtle blend of modern and traditional French cooking; selections change by season. 4-course *menu* 120F. Open M-F noon-2:30pm and 7-10:30pm.

■ **Les Noces de Jeannette,** 14 rue Favart, and 9 rue d'Amboise (☎01 42 96 36 89). M: Richelieu Drouot. Impress your date. *Menu du Bistro* (162F). Free *kir* with meal. Open daily noon-1:30pm and 7pm-9:30pm.

■ **Le Dénicheur,** 4 rue Tiquetonne (☎01 42 21 31 01). M: Etienne-Marcel. Diner turned disco/junkyard cafe. 2-course *menu* 50-55F; 3-course 70F. Brunch 85F. Open daily noon-3:30pm, 7:30pm-1am.

La Victoire Suprême du Coeur, 41 rue des Bourdonnais (☎01 40 41 93 95). M: Châtelet. Run by the devotees of guru Sri Chinmoy. Vegetarian, and very tasty. All-day 3-course *formule* 89F. Open M-F noon-2:30pm and 6:30-10pm, Sa noon-10pm.

Le Loup Blanc, 42 rue Tiquetonne (☎01 40 13 08 35). M: Etienne-Marcel. Men who love men and meat. Mixed *grille* allows you to sample 4 kinds of meats and sides (69-85F). Does not allow you to sample men. Vegetarian *salade mosaique* 49F. Does not include side of men. Brunch 75-95F. Open M-Sa 7:30-midnight, Su 11am-1pm.

Babylone Bis, 34 rue Tiquetonne (☎01 42 33 48 35). M: Etienne-Marcel. Antillean and African specialties. *Aloko* (flambéed bananas; 35F), *beignets de banane* (banana fritters; 50F), and *poulet braisé* (chicken; 80F). Cocktails 35F. Open daily 8pm-7am.

3ÈME AND 4ÈME: THE MARAIS

The Marais offers chic bistros, kosher delis, and same-sex cafes, serving *brûnch*, a meal invented by gay men in the 7th century.

■ **Chez Omar,** 47 rue de Bretagne (☎01 42 72 36 26). M: Arts et Métiers. One of the better Middle Eastern places in town. Couscous 60F, lamb 70-98F, chicken 70F. Open M-F noon-2:45pm and 7pm-midnight, Sa 7pm-midnight.

■ **Au Petit Fer à Cheval,** 30 rue Vieille-du-Temple (☎01 42 72 47 47). M: Hôtel-de-Ville or St-Paul. An oasis of *chèvre* (goat cheese), *kir,* and *Gauloises.* Sandwiches 20-32F; desserts 25-34F. Open daily 9am-2am; food served noon-1:15am.

Le Réconfort, 37 rue de Poitou (☎01 42 76 06 36). M: St-Sébastien-Froissart. Swank French, Indian, and Middle Eastern. Lunch *menu* 69-89F. Open M-F noon-2pm and 8:15-11pm, Sa 8:15-11pm.

En Attendant Pablo, 78 rue Vieille-du-Temple (☎01 42 74 34 65). M: Hôtel de Ville. Intimate and enormous salads 58F. Lunch *menu* 65F; brunch 89-109F. Fruit juice 26-28F. Chocolate pastries 30F. Open W-Su noon-6pm.

Taxi Jaune, 13 rue Chapon (☎01 42 76 00 40). M: Arts-et-Métiers. Eclectic and taxi-themed main dishes 35F, *plats* 85F. Lunch *menu* 72F. Open M-F noon-2:30pm and 7:30pm-2am; food served until 10:15pm.

Les Philosophes, 28 rue Vieille-du-Temple (☎01 48 87 49 64). M: Hôtel-de-Ville. Veggie options 50-58F; sandwiches 20-32F. Open daily 9am-2am.

Bofinger, 5-7 rue de la Bastille (☎01 42 72 05 23). M: Bastille. Lunch *menu* at 119F is a real steal. Go for the dressed-up atmosphere as much as the heavenly eats. Open daily noon-3pm and 7pm-midnight.

5ÈME AND 6ÈME: THE LATIN QUARTER AND ST-GERMAIN-DES-PRÉS

■ **Savannah Café,** 27 rue Descartes (☎01 43 29 45 77). M: Cardinal Lemoine. Lebanese food and other "selections from around the world." Happy Hour (7-8pm) dinner *menu* 99F; regular *ménu gastronomique* 139F. Open M-Sa 7-11pm.

■ **Le Machon d'Henri,** 8 rue Guisarde (☎01 43 29 08 70). M: Mabillon. Classic Left Bank bistro has *gigot d'agneau* and *gratin dauphinois*. Appetizers 35-40F; *plats* 70-80F; dinner *menu* 160F. Open daily noon-2:30pm and 7-11:30pm.

■ **La Crêpe Rit du Clown,** 6 rue des Canettes (☎01 46 34 01 02). M: Mabillon. If you fear clowns, let tasty, inexpensive *crêpes* revive you. *Let's Go* gets you a free, clowntastic Kir Breton. *Formule* 69F; *crêpes* 35-42F; salads start at 24F. Open M-Sa noon-11:30pm.

Comptoir Méditerranée, 42 rue Cardinal Lemoine (☎01 43 25 29 08). M: Cardinal Lemoine. Lebanese specialties. Make your own plate (4 items 32F, 6 items 48F). Open M-Sa 11am-10pm.

Au Jardin des Pâtés, 4 rue Lacépède (☎01 43 31 50 71). M: Jussieu. Organic gourmet pastas with a variety of vegetables and sauces. Appetizers 19-31F; main dishes 47-77F. Open daily noon-2:30pm and 7-11pm.

La Truffière, 4 rue Blainville (☎01 46 33 29 82). M: Place Monge. One serious restaurant near the rue Mouffetard. Lunch *menus* (90 and 120F) feature southwestern French cuisine. Reservations recommended. Open Tu-Su noon-2pm and 7-10:30pm.

Guen maï, 2bis rue de l'Abbaye (☎01 43 26 03 24). M: Mabillon. Vegetarian, organic, and macrobiotic food alongside freshly squeezed juices and organic wines. *Plats* around 25F. Store open M-Sa 9am-8:30pm; restaurant M-Sa 11:45am-3:30pm.

7ÈME: EIFFEL TOWER AND LES INVALIDES

■ **Le Lotus Blanc,** 45 rue de Bourgogne (☎01 45 55 18 89). M: Varenne. Vietnamese specialties. Lunch *formule expresse* 59F. Reservations encouraged. Open M-Sa noon-2:30pm and 7-10:30pm. Closed Aug. 12-19.

Le Club des Poètes, 30 rue de Bourgogne (☎01 47 05 06 03). M: Varenne. Not cheap (dinner with wine 120-150F), but fun—poetry readings at 10pm. Lunch *menu* 77-87F. Drinks 90F, for students 45F. Open M-Sa noon-3pm and 8pm-1am.

Chez Lucie, 15 rue Augereau (☎01 45 55 08 74). M: Ecole-Militaire. Inventive cuisine from Martinique including gumbo, crab, and chicken with lime and ginger. 3-course *menu* 98 and 148F; *plats* 65-98F. Open M-Sa noon-2:30pm and 7:30-11:30pm.

8ÈME: CHAMPS-ELYSÉES

■ **Antoine's: Les Sandwiches des 5 Continents,** 31,rue de Ponthieu (☎01 42 89 44 20). M: Franklin D. Roosevelt. 41F meal (panini, yogurt, and a drink) on bread that is probably worth that amount on its own. Open M-Sa 8am-7pm.

Restaurant LaMaline, 40 rue Ponthieu (☎01 45 63 14 14). M: Franklin D. Roosevelt. A simple, incandescent restaurant named after a poem by Arthur Rimbaud. 2-course *menu* 150F. Open daily 7:30pm-11pm.

Bankok, 28 rue de Moscou (☎01 43 87 62 56). M: Rome. Talented Thai chef and a choice of meats cooked in coconut milk, curry, or satay sauce (82-128F). Plenty of vegetarian options. Open 10:30am-2am; lunch noon-3pm; dinner 7pm-midnight.

9ÈME: OPÉRA

■ **Le Bistro de Gala,** 45 rue Faubourg-Montmartre (☎01 40 22 90 55). *Menu* is a commitment at 170F, but worth it. Open M-F noon-2:30pm and 7-11:30pm, Sa 7-11:30pm.

Haynes Bar, 3 rue Clauzel (☎01 48 78 40 63). M: St-Georges. The first African-American owned restaurant in Paris (1949). Very generous portions under 100F. Open Tu-Sa 7pm-midnight. Closed Aug.

Pizzéria King Salomon, 46 rue Richer (☎01 42 46 31 22). M: Cadet or Bonne Nouvelle. A popular kosher pizzeria. Individual pizzas 42-62F. Open Su-Th 11:30am-3pm and 6:30pm-midnight, Su 6:30pm-11:30pm.

11ÈME: LA BASTILLE

■ **La Ville de Jagannath,** 101 rue St-Maur (☎01 43 55 80 81). M: St-Maur. Lunchtime means "world cuisine;" switch to platters of vegetarian Indian food for dinner. Most basic *menu* 90F; with tangy basmati, two creamy curries and crunchy balls of cheese and spinach *kofta* will suffice. Open Tu-Sa noon-2:30pm, Su-Th 7:30-11:30pm, F-Sa 7:30-12:30pm.

Chez Paul, 13 rue de Charonne (☎01 47 00 34 57). M: Bastille. From succulent salmon to peppercorn steak (78F), Paul dishes a menu to make your palate sing. Open Sept.-July daily noon-2:30pm and 7pm-2am; food served until 12:30am.

13ÈME, 14ÈME, AND 15ÈME: BUTTE AUX CAILLES AND MONTPARNASSE

■ **Café du Commerce,** 39 rue des Cinq Diamants (☎01 53 62 91 04). M: Pl. d'Italie. Funky place with a fruit-i-ful menu. Dinner *menus* (65-120F). Lunch *menu* 50F. Open daily noon-3pm (service until 2:30pm) and 7pm-2am (service until 1am).

■ **Chez Foong,** 32 rue Frémicourt (☎01 45 67 36 99). M: Cambronne. Superb Malaysian kitchen. 3-course *menus* 85F (M-F). Open M-Sa noon-2:30pm and 7-11pm.

Au P'tit Cahoua, 39 bd. St-Marcel (☎01 47 07 24 42). M: St-Marcel. Under a tent worlds away from Paris, this kitchen spins fabulous *Maghrébin* meals. The lunch *menu* (65F) offers tabouli or *briouats au thon* (tuna in a flaky pastry), chicken, olive, and lemon *tajine*, or couscous *merguez* (a spicy sausage). Open M-F and Su noon-2:30pm and 7:30-11pm, Sa 7:30-11pm.

Indochine, 41 av. de Choisy (☎01 45 85 55 00). M: Porte de Choisy. Friendly staff. Popular with local Vietnamese residents. House specialty *Bo Bún* (rice vermicelli, veggies, and beef; 38F). *Phô* soup 36-40F and desserts 17F. Open M and W-Su 11:30am-3pm and 6-11pm.

Chez Papa, 6 rue Gassendi (☎01 43 22 41 19). M: Denfert-Rochereau. The best deal is the massive *salade boyarde*. *Menu* served until 9pm Su-Th (55F). **Also in** the 8ème (29, rue de l'Arcade), 10ème (206, rue Lafayette), and 15ème (101, rue de la Croix Nivert). Open M-Sa 10am-1am.

Crêperie Josselin, 67 rue du Montparnasse (☎01 43 20 93 50). M: Edgar Quinet. On a street full of *crêperies*, this one stands out. Savory crepes 22-70F, sweet crepes 22-42F. Open Tu-Su noon-3pm and 6-11:30pm.

18ÈME: MONTMARTRE

During the siege of Paris in 1814, Russian cossacks occupied **Montmartre;** the restaurants where they grabbed quick bites between battles became known as bistros (Russian for "quick"). The Russians are gone, replaced by land-hungry tourists, particularly around **pl. du Tertre** and **pl. St-Pierre.** Be cautious in their encampments, particularly at night. Charming bistros and cafes are common between **rue des Abbesses** and **rue Lepic.**

■ **Chez Ginette,** 101 rue Caulaincourt (☎01 46 06 01 49). M: Lamarck-Caulaincourt. Upstairs from the Métro. Inventive and inexpensive French cooking, like monkfish with prawn sauce (100F). Open M-Sa noon-2:30pm and 7:30pm-2am. Closed Aug. MC, V.

■ **Le Soleil Gourmand,** 10 rue Ravignan (☎01 42 51 00 50). M: Abbesses. 5-cheese tart with salad (58F), oriental seafood salad (65F), and house-baked cakes (30-44F). Open daily 12:30-2:30pm and 8:30-11pm.

FRANCE

☕ CAFES

French cafes conjure up images of writers and long afternoons. Popular drinks include coffee, wine, *citron pressé* (fresh-squeezed lemon juice), tea, and spring, mineral, and soda water. Cafes also serve affordable light lunches and snacks. It's cheaper at the counter (*comptoir* or *zinc*) than in the seating area.

■ **Le Fumoir**, 6 rue de l'Admiral Coligny (☎01 42 92 05 05), 1er. M: Louvre. Drink in deep green leather sofas. Best brunch in Paris, 120F; coffee, 15F. Open daily 11am-2am.

■ **L'Apparement Café**, 18 rue des Coutures St-Gervais (☎01 48 87 12 22), 3ème. M: St-Paul. Next to the Picasso Museum. Coffee 12F, designer salads 45F, and Su brunch. Open M-F noon-2am, Sa 4pm-2am, Su 12:30pm-midnight.

Le Marais Plus, 20 rue des Francs-Bourgeois (☎01 48 87 01 40), 3ème. Relaxed *salon de thé* and funky gift and book shop. Open daily noon-7pm.

Les Enfants Gâtés, 43 rue des Francs-Bourgeois (☎01 42 77 07 63), 4ème. M: St-Paul. "Spoiled children" is a sexy and lovable spot to linger. Coffee 15F; brunch 95-170F. Food served all day. Open W-M 11am-8pm.

Café Beaubourg, 43 rue St-Merri (☎01 48 87 63 96), 4ème. M: Hôtel-de-Ville. Draws models, tourists, families, and comrades for people-watching across from Centre Pompidou. Coffee 16F; hot chocolate 26F; breakfast 65F; brunch 110F. Open M-Th and Su 8am-1am, F-Sa 8am-2am.

Café de la Mosquée, 39 rue Geoffrey St-Hilaire (☎01 43 31 38 20), 5ème. M: Censier Daubenton. In the Mosquée de Paris. Delicate tiles, white-marble floors, and tropical shade. Mint tea (10F) and Maghrébin pastries (10F). Open daily 10am-midnight.

Le Séléct, 99 bd. du Montparnasse (☎01 45 48 38 24), 6ème. M: Vavin. Trotsky, Satie, Breton, Cocteau, and Picasso all frequented this art deco bistro. Coffee 6.50F at the counter; café au lait 35F; tea 22-25F; hot chocolate 35F. Open daily 7am-3am.

Aux Deux Magots, 6 pl. St-Germain-des-Prés (☎01 45 48 55 25), 6ème. M: St-Germain-des-Prés. Home to literati since 1885, named after Chinese porcelain figures, not fly larva. Coffee 23F; pastries 12-24F. Open daily 7am-1:30am.

Café de Flore, 172 bd. St-Germain (☎01 45 48 55 26), 6ème. M: St-Germain-des-Prés. Sartre composed *Being and Nothingness* here; Apollinaire, Picasso, and Breton just sipped brew. Espresso 24F; *salade Flore* 68F; pastries 31-50F. Open daily 7am-2am.

Fouquet's, 99 av. des Champs-Elysées (☎01 47 23 70 60), 8ème. M: George V. Snobbery so "French" that it seems like a Disney caricature. Love that bank-breaking coffee (38F)! Open daily 8am-2am; food served noon-3pm and 7pm-midnight.

Café de l'Industrie, 16 rue St-Sabin (☎01 47 00 13 53), 11ème. M: Breguet-Sabin. Happening cafe pays tribute to the lighter side of colonialism (unpack that one, Fanon). Coffee 10F; salads 45-58F. Prices increase 4F after 10pm. Open Su-F 10-2am.

Pause Café, 41 rue de Charonne (☎01 48 06 80 33), 11ème. M: Ledru-Rollin. Once a people-drooling and name-dropping sort of joint, Pause is now cool but kinder. Salads 40-50F; beer 15F. Open M-Sa 7:45am-2am, Su 8:30am-8:30pm.

Aux Artistes, 63 rue Falguière (☎01 43 22 05 39), 15ème. M: Pasteur. Professionals, students, and artists (not to mention American tourists) mix at this lively cafe. Lunch *menu* 58F; dinner *menu* 80F. Open M-F noon-12:30am, Sa noon-2pm.

Halle St-Pierre, 2 rue Ronsard (☎01 42 58 72 89), 18ème. A quiet cafe with coffee and tea (7-20F), cookies, brownies, and cakes (15F), salads, and the major French newspapers. A very pleasant setting ignored by tourists outside. Open Tu-Su 10am-6pm.

Le Sancerre, 35 rue des Abbesses (☎01 42 58 08 20), 18ème. M: Abbesses. Classic Montmartre cafe with some interesting dishes, from chili con carne (49-80F) to hearty crêpes maison (25-35F). Hopping at night as well. Terrace. Open daily 7am-2am.

FRANCE

⚓ SIGHTS

In a few hours, you can walk from the heart of the Marais in the east to the Eiffel Tower in the west, passing most major monuments along the way. Try to reserve a day for wandering; you don't have a true sense of Paris until you know how close medieval Notre-Dame is to the modern Centre Pompidou, or the *quartier latin* of students to the Louvre of kings. After dark, spotlights illuminate everything from the Panthéon to the Eiffel Tower, Notre-Dame to the Obélisque.

ILE DE LA CITÉ AND ILE ST-LOUIS

ILE DE LA CITÉ. If any place could be called the heart of Paris, it is this island in the river. In the 3rd century BC, when it was inhabited by the *Parisii*, a Gallic tribe of hunters, sailors, and fishermen, the Ile de la Cité was all there was to Paris. Although the city has expanded in all directions, all distance-points in France are measured from *kilomètre zéro*, a sundial on the ground in front of Notre-Dame.

CATHÉDRALE DE NOTRE-DAME DE PARIS.

M: St-Michel-Notre-Dame; exit on the island side. From the Left Bank, cross the Pont au Double and turn right. Open M-F 8am-6:45pm, Sa-Su 8am-7:45pm. Towers open Apr.-Sept. 10am-6pm; Oct.-Mar. 10am-5pm; free. Treasury open M-Sa 9:30am-6pm; 15F, students 10F. Crypt open daily Apr.-Sept. 10am-6pm; Oct.-Mar. 10am-5pm; 35F, students 23F. Tours in English leave from the booth to the right of the entrance; W and Th noon, Sa 2:30pm; free.

This 12th- to 14th-century cathedral, begun under Bishop Maurice Sully, is one of the most famous and beautiful examples of medieval architecture. After the Revolution, the building fell into disrepair and was even used to shelter livestock until Victor Hugo's 1831 novel *Notre-Dame-de-Paris* (a.k.a. *The Hunchback of Notre Dame*) inspired citizens to lobby for restoration. Architect Eugène Viollet-le-Duc made subsequent modifications, including the addition of the spire and the gargoyles. The intricately carved, apocalyptic facade and soaring, apparently weightless walls (effects produced by brilliant Gothic engineering and optical illusions) are inspiring even for the most church-weary. The cathedral's biggest draws are its enormous stained-glass **rose windows** that dominate the north and south ends of the transept. At the center of the 21m north window is the Virgin, depicted as the descendant of the Old Testament kings and judges who surround her. The base of the south window shows Matthew, Mark, Luke, and John on the shoulders of Old Testament prophets, while in the central window Christ is surrounded by the 12 apostles, virgins, and saints of the New Testament. A staircase inside the towers leads to a spectacular perch from which weather-worn gargoyles survey the city.

▨ STE-CHAPELLE AND CONCIERGERIE.

Within the courtyard of the **Palais de Justice,** which has harbored Paris's district courts since the 13th century, the opulent, Gothic **Ste-Chapelle** was built by Saint Louis (Louis IX) to house his most precious possession, Christ's crown of thorns (now in Notre-Dame). No mastery of the lower Chapel's dim gilt can prepare the visitor for the **Upper Chapel,** where twin walls of stained glass glow and frescoes of saints and martyrs shine. Read from bottom to top, left to right, the windows narrate the Bible from Genesis to the Apocalypse. *(M: Cité; take rue du Lutèce away from Notre-Dame to bd. du Palais. Open daily Apr.-Sept. 9:30am-6:30pm; Oct.-Mar. 10am-5pm. 35F; joint ticket with Conciergerie 50F, under 26 23F.)* The **Conciergerie,** around the corner from Ste-Chapelle, was one of Paris's most famous prisons; Marie-Antoinette and Robespierre were imprisoned here during the Revolution. *(1 quai de l'Horloge. M: Cité. ☎01 53 73 78 50. Open daily Apr.-Sept. 9:30am-6:30pm; Oct.-Mar. 10am-5pm. 35F, students 23F. Guided tours in French 11am and 3pm; free. For tours in English, call in advance.)*

ILE ST-LOUIS. The Ile St-Louis is home to some of Paris's most privileged elite, such as the Rothschilds and Pompidou's widow, and former home to other super-famous folks, including Voltaire, Baudelaire, and Marie Curie. At night, the island glows in the light of cast-iron lamps and candlelit bistros. Look for Paris's best ice cream at Ile St-Louis' **Berthillon,** 31 rue St-Louis-en-Ile. *(Across the Pont St-Louis from Notre-Dame; also across the Pont Marie from M: Pont Marie. Berthillon open Sept.-July 14; take-out W-Su 10am-8pm; eat-in W-F 1-8pm, Sa-Su 2-8pm. Closed 2 weeks in both Feb. and Apr.)*

THE LATIN QUARTER AND ST-GERMAIN-DES-PRÉS

The autumn influx of Parisian students is the prime cultural preservative of the *quartier latin,* so named because prestigious *lycées* and universities taught in Latin until 1798. Since the violent student riots in protest of the outmoded university system in May 1968, many artists and intellectuals have migrated to the less expensive outer *arrondissements,* and the *haute bourgeoisie* have moved in. The 5ème still presents the most diverse array of bookstores, cinemas, bars, and jazz clubs in the city. Designer shops and fascinating galleries can be found around **St-Germain-des-Prés.**

CAFES. cafes along bd. St-Germain have long been gathering places for literary and artistic notables such as Hemingway and Mallarmé. **Aux Deux Magots,** 6 pl. St-Germain-des-Prés, named for two porcelain figures that adorned a store selling Chinese silk and imports on the same spot in the 19th century, quickly became a favorite hangout of Verlaine and Rimbaud, later attracting Breton, Artaud, and Picasso as well. The **Café de Flore,** 172 bd. St-Germain, established in 1890, was made famous in the 1940s and 50s by literati Sartre and Camus, who favored its wood-burning stoves over their cold apartments. *(M: St-Germain-des-Prés.)*

BOULEVARD ST-MICHEL AND ENVIRONS. At the center of the Latin Quarter, bd. St-Michel, which divides the 5ème and 6ème, is filled with cafes, restaurants, bookstores, and clothing stores. **Place St-Michel,** at its northern tip, is filled with students, often engaged in typically Parisian protests, and lots of tourists. *(M: St-Michel.)*

JARDIN DU LUXEMBOURG. South along bd. St-Michel, the formal French gardens of the Jardin du Luxembourg are fabulous for strolling, reading, and watching the famous *guignol* puppet theater. *(RER: Luxembourg; exit onto bd. St-Michel. The main entrance is on bd. St-Michel. Open daily Apr.-Oct. 7:30am-9:30pm; Nov.-Mar. 8:15am-5pm.)*

PANTHÉON. The **crypt** of the Panthéon, which occupies the highest point on the Left Bank, houses the tombs of Voltaire, Rousseau, Victor Hugo, Emile Zola, Jean Jaurès, and Louis Braille; you can spy each tomb from behind locked gates. The **dome** features uninspiring Neoclassical frescoes. *(On pl. du Panthéon, east of the Jardin du Luxembourg. M: Cardinal Lemoine; follow rue du Cardinal Lemoine uphill and turn right on rue Clovis. Or, from RER: Luxembourg, head north on bd. St-Michel and turn right on rue Soufflot. Open daily 10am-6:30pm; last admission 5:45pm. 35F, students 23F.)*

EGLISE ST-GERMAIN-DES-PRÉS. Scarred by centuries of weather, revolution, and war, the Eglise St-Germain-des-Prés, which dates from 1163, is the oldest standing church in Paris. *(3 pl. St-Germain-des-Prés. M: St-Germain-des-Prés. Open daily 8am-7:45pm.)*

JARDIN DES PLANTES. Opened in 1640 to grow medicinal plants for King Louis XIII, the garden now features natural science museums and a **zoo,** one which Parisians raided for food during the Prussian siege of 1871. *(On pl. Valhubert. M: Jussieu; follow rue Jussieu southeast along the university building.)*

MOSQUÉE DE PARIS. The cool courtyards and ornate archways of this mosque provide a soothing setting for prayer, mint tea, or an afternoon in the *hammam.* *(On pl. du Puits de l'Ermite. M: Jussieu; take rue Linné, turn right on rue Lacépède, and left on rue de Quatrefages. Open June-Aug. Sa-Th 9am-noon and 2-6pm. Tours 15F, students 10F.)*

THE EIFFEL TOWER AND INVALIDES

EIFFEL TOWER. Built in 1889 as the centerpiece of the World's Fair, the Tour Eiffel has come to symbolize the city. Despite criticism, tacky souvenirs, and Gustave Eiffel's own sentiment that "France is the only country in the world with a 300m flagpole," the tower is unfailingly elegant and commands an excellent view of the city. At night, it will impress even the most jaded tourist. *(M: Bir Hakeim; follow bd. de*

Grenelle to the Seine and turn right on quai Branly. Or, from RER: Champ de Mars-Tour Eiffel, follow quai Branly. Open daily June-Aug. 9am-midnight; Sept.-May 9:30am-11pm. Lift closes 10:30pm; to 1st fl. 21F, 2nd fl. 43F, 3rd fl. 60F. Stairs to 1st and 2nd floors 15F.)

INVALIDES. The tree-lined **Esplanade des Invalides** runs from the impressive **Pont Alexandre III** to the gold-leaf dome crowning the **Hôtel des Invalides.** The Hôtel, built for veterans under Louis XIV, now houses the **Musée de l'Armée** and **Napoleon's Tomb.** Nearby, on rue Varenne, is the **Musée Rodin,** see p. 310. *(M: Invalides, Latour Maubourg, or Varenne.)*

THE LOUVRE, OPÉRA, MARAIS, AND BASTILLE

AROUND THE LOUVRE. World-famous art museum and former residence of kings, the **Louvre** (see p. 309) occupies about one-seventh of the 1er *arrondissement.* **Le Jardin des Tuileries,** at the western foot of the Louvre, was commissioned by Catherine de Médici in 1564 and improved by André Le Notre (designer of the gardens at Versailles) in 1649. Three blocks north along rue de Castiglione, **Place Vendôme** hides 20th-century offices and luxury shops behind 17th-century facades. Look out for Napoleon on top of the column in the center of the *place*—he's the one in the toga. *(M: Tuileries or Concorde.)* The **Palais-Royal** was commissioned in 1632 by Cardinal Richelieu, who gave it to Louis XIII. In 1784, the elegant buildings enclosing the palace's formal garden became *galeries,* the prototype of a shopping mall. The revolutions of 1789, 1830, and 1848 all began with angry crowds in the same garden. *(M: Palais-Royal/Musée du Louvre or Louvre-Rivoli.)*

OPÉRA. North of the Louvre, Charles Garnier's grandiose **Opéra** was built under Napoleon III in the eclectic style of the Second Empire. Gobelin tapestries, gilded mosaics, a 1964 Marc Chagall ceiling, and a six-ton chandelier adorn the magnificent interior. *(M: Opéra. Open daily in summer 10am-6pm; off-season 10am-5pm. 30F, students 20F. Tours in English in summer daily at noon; off-season varies; 60F, students 45F.)*

▒ MARAIS. This area, made up of the 3ème and 4ème *arrondissements,* became the most chic place to live with Henri IV's construction of the elegant **place des Vosges** at the beginning of the 17th century; several remaining mansions now house museums. Today, the streets of the Marais house the city's Jewish and gay communities as well as fun, hip restaurants and shops. At the confluence of the 1er, 2ème, 3ème, and 4ème, the **Centre Pompidou** (see p. 310) looms like a colorful factory over the vast cobblestoned *place,* where artists, musicians, and pickpockets gather. Linger in the day, but be cautious at night. *(M: Rambuteau; take rue Rambuteau to Pl. Georges Pompidou. Or, from M: Chatelet-Les Halles, take rue Rambuteau or rue Aubry le Boucher.)*

BASTILLE. Further east, Charles V built the Bastille prison to guard the eastern entrance to his capital. When it became a state prison under Louis XIII, it housed religious heretics and political undesirables. On July 14, 1789, revolutionaries stormed the Bastille, searching for gunpowder and political prisoners. By 1792, nothing was left of the prison but its outline on the *place.* On July 14, 1989, François Mitterrand inaugurated the glittering **Opéra Bastille** to celebrate the destruction of Charles' fortress. *(120 rue de Lyon. M: Bastille. Tours daily 1pm. 50F, students 30F.)*

CHAMPS-ELYSÉES, BOIS DE BOULOGNE, AND LA DÉFENSE

PLACE DE LA CONCORDE. Paris's most famous public square lies at the western edge of the Tuileries. Constructed between 1757 and 1777 to hold a monument to Louis XV, the area soon became the *place de la Révolution,* site of a guillotine that severed 1343 necks. After the Reign of Terror, the square was optimistically renamed (*concorde* means "peace"). The huge, rose-granite, 13th-century BC **Obélisque de Luxor** depicts the deeds of Egyptian pharaoh Ramses II. Given to Charles X by the Viceroy of Egypt, it is Paris's oldest monument. *(M: Concorde.)*

MERDE! The French have a love affair with their dogs, and nearly 500,000 pooches call Paris home. According to official figures, the dogs of Paris leave over 11 tons of *déjections canines* on Paris's streets per day. Sidewalks are veritable minefields; experienced Parisians keep one eye on the ground. Since 1977, the Paris government has been campaigning—under the title *"La lutte contre les pollutions canines"* (The Fight Against Canine Pollution)—to encourage people to have their best friends defecate in street gutters. Inspiring slogans include "Teach him the gutter" and "If you love Paris, don't let him do that!" Clean-up efforts are now aided by a technological triumph called the *Caninette,* or more informally the *Motocrotte* (crapmobile), hybrid motorcycle/vacuum cleaners. If you have the misfortune of stepping into some *crotte de chien,* hope it's with your left foot; according to Parisian superstition, it's good luck.

CHAMPS-ELYSÉES. Stretching west, the **avenue des Champs-Elysées** is lined with luxury shops, *haute couture* boutiques, cafes, and cinemas. The avenue is the work of Baron Haussmann, who was commissioned by Napoleon III to convert Paris into a grand capital with broad avenues, wide sidewalks, new parks, elegant housing, and sanitary sewers. The avenue is anchored by the Arc de Triomphe on one end and the **place de Concorde** on the other. The latter was formerly known as the place de la Révolution, the site of the guillotine that severed 1,343 necks from their blue-blooded bodies.

ARC DE TRIOMPHE. Napoleon commissioned the **Arc de Triomphe,** at the western terminus of the Champs-Elysées, in 1806 in honor of his Grande Armée. In 1940, Parisians were brought to tears as Nazis goose-stepped through the Arc; on August 26, 1944, British, American, and French troops liberating the city from Nazi occupation marched through to the roaring cheers of thousands. The terrace at the top has a fabulous view. (*On pl. Charles de Gaulle. M: Charles-de-Gaulle-Etoile. Open daily Apr.-Sept. 9:30am-10:30pm; Oct.-Mar. 10am-6pm. 40F, under 26 25F.*) The **Tomb of the Unknown Soldier** has been under the Arc since November 11, 1920. It bears the inscription, "Here lies a French soldier who died for his country, 1914-1918," but represents the 1,500,000 men who died during WWI. (*M: Charles-de-Gaulle-Etoile.* ☎ *01 55 37 73 77. Open daily Apr.-Sept. 9:30am-11pm; Oct.-Mar. 10am-10:30pm. Last entry 30min. before closing. Admission 40F, ages 12-25 25F, under 12 free. Buy tickets in the pedestrian underpass on the right side of the Champs-Elysées, facing the monument.*)

THE MADELEINE. Mirrored by the Assemblée Nationale across the Seine, the Madeleine—formally called Église Ste-Marie-Madeleine (Mary Magdalene)—was begun in 1764 by Louis XV and modeled after a Greek temple. Construction was halted during the Revolution, when the Cult of Reason proposed transforming the building into a bank, a theater, or a courthouse. Characteristically, Napoleon decreed that it should become a temple to the greatness of his army, while Louis XVIII shouted, "It shall be a church!" Completed in 1842, the structure stands alone in the medley of Parisian churches, distinguished by four ceiling domes that light the interior, 52 exterior Corinthian columns, and a curious altarpiece. (*Pl. de la Madeleine. M: Madeleine.* ☎ *01 44 51 69 00. Open daily 7:30am-7:15pm.*)

BOIS DE BOULOGNE. Avenue Foch, one of Haussmann's finest creations, runs from the Arc de Triomphe to the Bois de Boulogne. Though popular by day for picnics, the park is a risky choice at night—until recently it was home to many drug dealers and prostitutes. (*16ème. M: Porte Maillot, Sablons, Pont de Neuilly, or Porte Dauphine.*)

LA DÉFENSE. Outside the city limits, the skyscrapers and modern architecture of La Défense make up Paris's newest (unofficial) *arrondissement,* home to the headquarters of 14 of France's top 20 corporations. The **Grande Arche,** inaugurated in 1989, completes the *axe historique* running through the Louvre, pl. de la Concorde, and the Arc de Triomphe. There's yet another stunning view from the top. Trees, shops, and sculptures by Miró and Calder line the esplanade. (*M: La Défense, zone 2; RER, zone 3. Open daily 10am-7pm; last entrance 6pm. 43F, students 33F.*)

MONTMARTRE AND PÈRE-LACHAISE

BASILIQUE DU SACRÉ-COEUR. The Basilique du Sacré-Coeur crowns the **butte Montmartre** like an enormous white meringue. Its onion dome is visible from almost anywhere in the city, and its 112m bell tower is the highest point in Paris, offering a view that stretches up to 50km. *(35 rue du Chevalier de la Barre, 18ème. M: Château-Rouge, Abbesses, or Anvers. From Anvers, take rue de Steinkerque off bd. de Rochechouart and climb the steps. Open daily 7am-11pm; free. Dome and crypt open daily 9am-6pm; each 15F, students 8F.)* Nearby, **place du Tertre** features touristy outdoor cafes and sketch artists.

CIMETIÈRE PÈRE-LACHAISE. The Cimetière Père-Lachaise holds the remains of Balzac, Colette, Seurat, Danton, David, Delacroix, La Fontaine, Haussmann, Molière, Proust, and Sarah Bernhardt within its peaceful, winding paths and elaborate sarcophagi. Foreigners buried here include Chopin, Modigliani, Gertrude Stein, and Oscar Wilde, but the most visited grave is that of Jim Morrison. French Leftists make ceremonious pilgrimage to the **Mur des Fédérés** (Wall of the Federals), where 147 revolutionary *Communards* were executed and buried. *(16 rue du Repos, 20ème. M: Père-Lachaise. Open Mar.-Oct. M-F 8am-6pm, Sa 8:30am-6pm, Su 9am-6pm; Nov.-Feb. M-F 8am-5:30pm, Sa 8:30am-5:30pm, Su 9am-5:30pm. Free.)*

🏛 MUSEUMS

For updated info, check the bimonthly *Paris Museums and Monuments*, available at the Champs-Elysées tourist office. The weekly *Pariscope* and *L'Officiel des Spectacles* list museum hours and temporary exhibits. The **Carte Musées et Monuments** grants entry to 65 Paris museums without waiting in line; it is available at major museums and Métro stations (1-day 80F, 3-day 160F, 5-day 240F).

▨ MUSÉE DU LOUVRE

☎01 40 20 51 51. M: Palais-Royal/Musée du Louvre. Open M and W 9am-9:45pm, Th-Su 9am-6pm. Before 3pm 45F, after 3pm and Su 26F; 1st Su of each month free. Tours in English M and W-Sa; 17F.

A short list of its masterpieces includes the *Code of Hammurabi*, the *Venus de Milo*, the *Winged Victory of Samothrace*, Vermeer's *Lacemaker*, and Delacroix's *Liberty Leading the People*. Oh, yeah, and there's that lady with the mysterious smile, too—the *Mona Lisa*. Enter through I.M. Pei's controversial glass **Pyramid** in the Cour Napoléon, or skip lines by entering directly from the Métro. When visiting the Louvre, strategy is everything. Think like a four-star general: the goal is to come and see without being conquered. The Louvre is organized into three different wings: Sully, Richelieu, and Denon. Each is divided into different sections according to the artwork's date, national origin, and medium. The color-coding and room numbers on the free maps correspond to the colors and numbers on the plaques at the entrances to every room within the wing.

The Italian Renaissance collection, on the first floor of the Denon wing, is rivaled only by that of the Uffizi museum in Florence. Look for Raphael's *Portrait of Balthazar Castiglione* and Titian's *Man with a Glove*. Titian's *Fête Champêtre* inspired Manet's *Déjeuner sur l'Herbe* (see Musée d'Orsay, below). Bought by François I during the artist's visit to Paris, Leonardo da Vinci's *Mona Lisa* (or *La Joconde*, the Smiling One), smiles mysteriously at millions each year. Don't overlook her remarkable neighbors—da Vinci's *Virgin of the Rocks* displays the *sfumato* (smoky) technique for which he is famous. The *Venus de Milo* and the *Winged Victory of Samothrace* are just the tip of the Greek, Etruscan, and Roman antiquities iceberg. The painting collection begins with the Middle Ages and reaches the mid-19th century. Highlights include Hieronymous Bosch's *Ship of Fools*, Jan Van Eyck's *Madonna of Chancellor Rolin*, both in the Flemish gallery. The French works stretch through all 3 wings of the museum, and include paintings from the Neoclassical, Rococo, and Romantic schools. Don't miss Jacques-Louis David's *Le serment de Horaces (The Oath of the Horatii)* and Delacroix's controversial *La Liberté guidant le peuple (Liberty Leading the People)*.

FRANCE

▨ MUSÉE D'ORSAY

62 rue de Lille, 7ème. ☎01 40 49 48 48. RER: Musée d'Orsay. Open June 20-Sept. 20 Tu-W and F-Su 9am-5:45pm, Th 9am-9:30pm; Sept. 21-June 19 opens 10am. 40F, under 26 and Su 30F.

While it's considered the premier Impressionist museum, the museum is dedicated to presenting all major artistic movements between 1848 and WWI. Highlights include Manet's *Déjeuner sur l'Herbe*, Monet's *Gare St-Lazare* and *Rouen Cathedral*, Dégas' *L'absinthe*, and Whistler's *Mother*, as well as works by Rodin, Renoir, Cézanne, van Gogh, Toulouse-Lautrec, Gaugin, and Seurat. Built for the 1900 Universal Exposition, the Gare d'Orsay's industrial function was carefully masked by architect Victor Laloux behind glass, stucco, and a 370-room luxury hotel, so as to remain faithful to the station's elegant surroundings in the prestigious 7ème. For several decades, it was the main departure point for southwestbound trains, but newer trains were too long for its platforms and it closed in 1939.

On the ground floor, works from Classicism and Proto-Impressionism are on display, and include Edouard Manet's *Olympia*, a painting that caused a scandal when it was unveiled in 1865. Inspired by Titian's *Venus of Urbino*, a standard for female nudes in Western art, Manet asked a famous courtesan to pose for the painting. The juxtaposition of a classical reference to Titian with the vulgarity of the Paris demi-monde drew great controversy. The soft, natural light of the museum is perfect for showcasing Impressionism and post-Impressionism, on the upper level. The first room of the upper level features Manet's *Déjeuner sur l'Herbe*, in which two bourgeois gentleman picnic with a nude lady. Denied entrance to the 1863 Salon, it showed the provocative nature of what was to come while paying tribute to Titian and Raphael's nudes. Monet's *La Gare St-Lazare* and Renoir's *Le bal du Moulin de la Galette* capture the iron train stations and society balls of the industrialized Paris of the 1870s. Monet's experiments with light and atmospheric effects culminated in his *Cathédral de Rouen* series. Paintings by Alfred Sisley, Camille Pissarro, and Berthe Morisot probe the allegorical beauty of the simple country life. Edgar Dégas's dancers in *La classe de danse* scratch their backs, massage their necks, and cross their arms while listening to their teacher. James Whistler, the American artist associated with French Realism, is represented by his *Portrait of the Artist's Mother*, a painting of a seated old woman in a black dress and white bonnet staring blankly, hands folded. Over a dozen diverse works by Vincent Van Gogh follow, including his tormented *Portrait de l'Artiste*. Paul Cézanne's still lifes, portraits, and landscapes experiment with the soft colors and geometric planes that led to Cubism. Once the elegant ballroom of the Hôtel d'Orsay, the neo-Rococo Salle des Fêtes, on the middle level, displays late 19th-century salon sculpture, painting, and decorative arts, including a terrace devoted to Auguste Rodin, and rooms highlighting works of Art Nouveau.

OTHER MUSEUMS

▨ **Centre National d'Art et de Culture Georges-Pompidou (Palais Beaubourg, ☎01 44 78 12 33), 4ème.** M: Rambuteau. This inside-out building has inspired debate since its inauguration in 1977. The exterior is a sight, with chaotic colored piping and ventilation ducts (blue for air, green for water, yellow for electricity, red for heating). Its exhibit halls, library, and superb museum collections (including the **Musée National d'Art Moderne**) are very fine. The wacky outside is an appropriate shell for the collection of Fauves, Cubists, and Pop and Conceptual artists. Open June 20-Sept. 20 Tu-W and F-Su 9am-6pm, Th 9am-9:30pm; Sept. 21-June 19 Tu-W and F-Su 10am-5:45pm, Th 10am-9:45pm. Last ticket sales 30min. before closing. Admission 40F, ages 18-25 and all on Su 30F, under 18 free. Tours in English Tu-Sa, 90min., 36F. Bookstore and boutique open Tu-W and F-Su 9:30am-6:30pm, Th 9:30am-9:30pm.

▨ **Musée Rodin,** 77 rue de Varenne, (☎01 44 18 61 10), 7ème. M: Varenne; take bd. des Invalides away from the Seine and turn left on rue de Varenne. The 18th-century Hôtel Biron holds hundreds of sculptures by Auguste Rodin (and his lover, Camille Claudel), including the *Gates of Hell, The Thinker, Burghers of Calais,* and *The Kiss.* Open Tu-Su Apr.-Sept. 9:30am-5:45pm; Oct.-Mar. 9:30am-4:45pm. 28F, students and Su 18F.

🏛 **La Villette,** 19ème. M: Porte de la Villette or Porte de Pantin. A vast urban renewal project that encloses a landscaped park, a huge science museum (open M-Sa 10am-6pm, Su 10am-7pm; 50F), an Omnimax cinema (57F), a conservatory, a jazz club, a concert/theater space, and a high-tech music museum (open Tu-Th noon-6pm, F-Sa noon-7:30pm, Su 10am-6pm; 35F, students 25F).

🏛 **Musée Picasso,** 5 rue de Thorigny, (☎01 42 71 63 15), 3ème. M: Chemin-Vert; from bd. Beaumarchais, take rue St-Gilles, which becomes rue du Parc Royal, then bear right at pl. de Thorigny. Catalogs Picasso's life and career from his early work in Barcelona to his Cubist and Surrealist years in Paris and his Neoclassical work on the Riviera. Open W-M Apr.-Sept. 9:30am-6pm; Oct.-Mar. 9:30am-5:30pm. 30F, under 26 and Su 20F.

Musée de Cluny, 6 pl. Paul-Painlevé, (☎01 43 25 62 00), 5ème. M: Cluny-Sorbonne; follow bd. St-Michel away from the Seine and turn left on rue P. Sarrazin. One of the world's finest collections of medieval art, housed in a medieval monastery built on top of Roman baths. Works include *La Dame et La Licorne* (The Lady and the Unicorn) is one of the most beautiful extant medieval tapestry series. Open W-M 9:15am-5:45pm. 30F, under 25 and Su 20F.

The Invalides Museums, Esplanade des Invalides, (☎01 44 42 37 72), 7ème. M: Invalides. The resting place of Napoleon also hosts the **Musée de l'Armée,** which celebrates French military history, and the **Musée de l'Ordre de la Libération** (entrance on bd. de Latour-Maubourg), which tells the story of those who fought for the liberation of France. Open daily Apr.-Sept. 10am-6pm; Oct.-Mar. 10am-5pm. 38F, students under 26 28F. In the *cour d'honneur,* the **Musée d'Histoire Contemporaine** (☎01 44 42 54 91 or 01 44 42 38 39) probes current events. 30F, students 20F.

Musée d'Art Moderne de la Ville de Paris, 11 av. du Président Wilson, in the Palais de Tokyo, (☎01 53 6740 00), 16ème. M: Iéna; from pl. d'Iéna, take av. du Président Wilson to pl. de Tokyo. Paris's second-best collection (after the Pompidou) of 20th-century art, with works by Matisse *(The Dance)* and Picasso *(The Jester);* temporary exhibits vary. Open Tu-F 10am-5:30pm, Sa-Su 10am-6:45pm. 30-45F, students 20-35F.

Institut du Monde Arabe, 23 quai St-Bernard, (☎01 40 51 38 38), 5ème. M: Jussieu; take rue Jussieu away from rue Linné and turn right on rue des Fossés St-Bernard, which leads to quai St-Bernard. Features art from the Maghreb and the Near and Middle East. The riverside facade is shaped like a boat, representing the migration of Arabs to France; the opposite side has camera-lens windows with Arabic motifs that open and close to control the amount of sunlight in the museum. Open Tu-Su 10am-6pm. 25F.

Musée Marmottan Monet, 2 rue Louis-Boilly, (☎01 44 96 50 33), 16ème. M: La Muette; follow Chaussée de la Muette (av. du Ranelagh) through the Jardin du Ranelagh, turn right on av. Raphaël, then left on rue L. Boilly. This hunting-lodge-turned-stately-mansion features an eclectic collection of Empire furniture, Impressionist Monet and Renoir canvases, and medieval illuminations. Open Tu-Su 10am-5pm. 40F, students 25F.

Musée de l'Orangerie, (☎01 42 97 8 16), 1er. M: Concorde. Houses Renoirs, Cézannes, Rousseaus, Matisses, and Picassos, but is most famous for Monet's 8 gigantic *Water Lilies.* **Closed until December 2002.** Open W-M 10am-5pm. 30F, under 25 18F.

Musée Carnavalet, 23 rue de Sévigné, (☎01 42 72 21 13) 3ème. M: Chemin-Vert; take rue St-Gilles, which becomes rue du Parc Royal, to rue de Sévigné. In a 16th-century *hôtel particulier,* Carnavalet traces Paris's history from its very origins and guards Voltaire and Rousseau's writing supplies. Open Tu-Su 10am-5:40pm. 30F, students 20F.

📋 ENTERTAINMENT

Paris's cabarets, cinemas, theaters, and concert halls can satisfy all tastes and desires. The bibles of Paris entertainment, the weekly Pariscope (3F) and the Officiel des Spectacles (2F), on sale at any kiosk or *tabac,* have every conceivable listing. Pariscope includes an English-language pull-out section. When going out, remember that some popular nightlife areas, such as Pigalle, Gare St-Lazare, and Beaubourg, are not always safe. To avoid expensive late-night taxis, keep an eye on the time and hop on the Métro before it closes at 12:30am.

CABARET

Au Lapin Agile, 22, rue des Saules, (☎01 46 06 85 87), 18ème. M: Lamarck-Coulaincourt. Turn right on rue Lamarck, then right again up rue des Saules. Picasso, Verlaine, Renoir, and Apollinaire hung out here during the heyday of Montmartre; now a mainly tourist audience crowds in for comical poems and songs. When the artist André Gill painted a rabbit on the theater's facade, it came to be known as *le lapin à Gill* (Gill's Rabbit), a name that became *Le lapin agile* (the nimble rabbit). Shows Tu-Su at 9:15pm. Admission and first drink 130F, students 90F.

Caveau de la République, 1, bd. St-Martin, (☎01 42 78 44 45), 3ème. M: République. A Parisian crowd fills the 482 seats of this 96-year-old venue for political satire. Good French skills and knowledge of French politics needed to get the gags. Tickets sold up to 6 days in advance, daily 11am-6pm. Shows mid-Sept. to June Tu-Sa 9pm, Su 3:30pm. Admission M-Th 145-180F, Tu-Th students 85F and over 60 110F.

THEATER

■ **La Comédie Française,** 2, rue de Richelieu (☎01 44 58 15 15; www.comedie-francaise.fr), 1er. M: Palais-Royal. Founded by Molière, now the granddaddy of all French theaters. Expect wildly gesticulated slapstick farce; you don't need to speak French to understand. Performances take place in the 892-seat Salle Richelieu. Expect several plays by Molière in the coming season. Box office open daily 11am-6pm. Tickets 70-190F, under 27 65F (remainders). Rush tickets (30F) available 45min. before show; line up an hour in advance.

Odéon Théâtre de l'Europe, 1, pl. Odéon, (☎01 44 41 36 36; www.theatre-odeon.fr), 6ème. M: Odéon. Programs in this elegant Neoclassical building range from classics to avant-garde, but the Odéon specializes in foreign plays in their original language. 1042 seats. Also **Petit Odéon,** an affiliate with 82 seats. In 2000-2001, the theatre will present the poetry of Robert Wilson and Lou Reed, *Medea* by Euripides, and *L'Avare* by Molière. Open Sept.-July. Box office open M-Sa 11am-6:30pm. Tickets 30-180F for most shows; student rush tickets 50F, available 90min. before performance. Petit Odéon 70F, students 50F. Call ahead for wheelchair access.

FILM

■ **Action Christine,** 4, rue Christine, (☎01 43 29 11 30), 6ème. M: Odéon. Off rue Dauphine. Eclectic, international selection of art and cult films from the 40s and 50s. Always V.O. 40F, early show (usually 6 or 7pm) 25F; M and students 30F.

Musée du Louvre, (info ☎01 40 20 51 86; schedules and reservation ☎01 40 20 52 99), 1er. M: Louvre. Art films, films on art, and silent movies. Open Sept.-June. 25-70F, students 15-50F.

Dôme IMAX, pl. de la Défense (☎08 36 67 06 06, 2.23F/min.). M: Grande Arche de la Défense. The big dome to the right with your back to the Grand Arche. IMAX cinema. Documentaries in French, but who listens to an IMAX anyway? 55F; students, seniors, and under 16 40F. For 2 shows 75F; students, seniors, and under 16 65F.

■ SHOPPING

1ER AND 2ÈME: ETIENNE-MARCEL AND LES HALLES

Sugar and spice, and all things naughty. Fabrics are a little cheaper, and the style is younger. At the **Agnès B.** empire on rue du Jour, the black classics still rule, and **Claude Pierlot** at 3, rue de Turbigo does button-up cardigans with a well-bred touch. The stores on rue Etienne Marcel and rue Tiquetonne are best for technicolor clubwear, and outrageously sexy outfits. (M: Etienne-Marcel.)

4ÈME AND THE LOWER 3ÈME: MARAIS

The Marais trades streetwise edge for a consistent line-up of affordable, trendy boutiques. Mid-priced chains, independent designer shops, and vintage stores line **rue Vieille-du-Temple, rue de Sévigné, rue Roi de Sicile** and **rue des Rosiers.** Unique shops can also be found along **rue de Bourg-Tibourg** and **rue des Francs-Bourgeois.** The best selection of affordable-chic men's wear in Paris can be found here, especially along **rue Ste-Croix-de-la-Bretonnerie.** Most stores are open on Sundays and late on weekdays. (M: St-Paul or Hôtel-de-Ville.)

6ÈME AND EASTERN BORDER OF 7ÈME: ST-GERMAIN-DES-PRÉS

Post-intellectual, materialistic St-Germain-des-Prés, particularly the triangle bordered by bd. St-Germain, rue St-Sulpice and rue des Saints-Pères, is saturated with high-budget names. But don't just settle for *lécher les vitrines* (window shopping)—rue du Four hosts fun and affordable designers such as **Paul and Joe** (no. 40; ☎01 45 44 97 70; open daily 11am-7:30pm) and **Sinéquanone** (no. 16; ☎01 56 24 27 74; open M-Sa 10am-7:30pm). (M: St Germain des Pres.) Closer to the Jardin du Luxembourg, calm rue de Fleurus has **A.P.C.** as well as the interesting designs of **t******* at no. 7. (M: St-Placide.) In the 7ème, visit rue de Pré-aux-Clercs and rue de Grenelle to witness avant-garde jewelry at **Stella Cadente,** no. 22. The 7ème is expensive, but there are more affordable little boutiques around the Bon Marché department store on rue de Sevres, and rue du Cherche Midi. (M: Vaneau, Duroc, Sèvres-Babylone, Rue du Bac.)

⬛ NIGHTLIFE

The primary leisure pastimes of Parisians, as they would have it, are fomenting revolution and burning buildings. Actually, their nighttime pleasures tend more toward drinking, relaxing, and people-watching. For those new to the town, the exclusive nightlife scene will probably feel like a tough nut to crack, but there are definitely alternatives to the mega-trendy and mega-expensive. Those looking for live music, especially jazz, are in heaven. Those on the prowl for dancing may be frustrated by Paris's rather closed (and sometimes downright nasty) club scene, but *Let's Go* tries to list places that are tolerant of non-models. If you'd rather just drink and watch the world go by, Parisian bars won't disappoint.

BARS AND CLUBS

1ER AND 2ÈME: LOUVRE-PALAIS ROYAL

▨ **Le Fumoir,** 6 rue de l'Admiral Coligny (☎01 42 92 05 05). M: Louvre. As cool by night as it is by day. Extra dry martini 58F. See **Cafes,** p. 304.

▨ **Flann O'Brien's,** 6 rue Bailleul (☎01 42 60 13 58). M: Louvre-Rivoli. From the Métro, walk away from the Seine on rue du Louvre and make the first right after crossing rue de Rivoli. Arguably the best Irish bar in Paris. Open daily 4pm-2am.

Frog & Rosbif, 116 rue St-Denis (☎01 42 36 34 73). M: Etienne Marcel. At the corner of rue St-Denis and rue Tiquetonne. As if a slice of shoppers' London has been plugged in next to the peep shows. Open daily noon-2am.

Rex Club, 5 bd. Poissonnière (☎01 42 36 10 96). M: Bonne-Nouvelle. A non-selective club which presents a most selective DJ line-up. Large dance floor and lots of seats as well. Open Tu-Sa 11:30pm-6am.

3ÈME AND 4ÈME: THE MARAIS

▨ **La Belle Hortense,** 31 rue Vieille-du-Temple (☎01 48 04 71 60). M: St-Paul. Walk in the direction of traffic along rue de Rivoli and turn right onto rue Vieille-du-Temple. Wide wine selection from 18F a glass, 90F a bottle. Walls of books (literature, art, philosophy) and (surprise!) really mellow music to go with your merlot. Frequent exhibits, readings, and discussions in the small leather-couch-filled back room. Open daily 1pm-2am.

Le Détour, 5 rue Elizéver (☎01 40 29 44 04). M: St-Paul. Swank neo-couchical lounge beats with soul, jazz, and deep house. Hookahs (strawberry, apple, or apricot tobacco) 35F. Cocktails 50F, beer 18F. Open daily 7pm-1:30am.

Utopia, 15 rue Michel Le Comte. (☎01 42 71 63 43). M: Rambuteau. Displaying the slogan *le bar des filles qui bougent* (the bar for girls who move), Utopia boasts house beats, pool, pinball, and occasional out-there dress-up parties. Beer 18F. Happy Hour M-W 5-8pm. Open M-Sa 5pm-2am.

Les Bains, 7 rue du Bourg l'Abbé (☎01 48 87 01 80). M: Réaumur-Sébastopol or Etienne-Marcel. Ultraselective, super-crowded, and expensive. Used to be a public bath, visited at least once by Marcel Proust. More recently visited by Mike Tyson, Madonna, and Jack Nicholson. Cover and 1st drink M-F 100F; Sa-Su 120F. Subsequent drinks 70F. Open daily 11:30pm-6am.

Le Café du Trésor, 5 rue du Trésor (☎01 44 78 06 60). M: St-Paul. Walk along rue de Rivoli in the direction of traffic, turn right onto rue Vieille-du-Temple and right onto the pedestrian rue du Trésor. Color, boom, style, and youth. DJs spin house, deep house, and funk. Th-Sa 8pm-1:30am. Open daily 9am-2am; food served M-F 12:30-3pm and 7:30-10:30pm, Sa-Su 12:30-10:30pm.

Chez Richard, 37 rue Vieille-du-Temple (☎01 42 74 31 65). M: Hôtel-de-Ville. Inside a courtyard off rue Vieille-du-Temple, this super-sexy bar and lounge screams drama. The secret: on a slow night (read: not the weekend) it's an ideal chill spot, with hip bartenders and nice n' smooth beats. Beer 22-40F, cocktails 50-60F. Open daily 5pm-2am.

5ÈME AND 6ÈME: THE LATIN QUARTER AND ST-GERMAIN-DES-PRÉS

■ **Le Reflet,** 6 rue Champollion (☎01 43 29 97 27). M: Cluny-La Sorbonne. Walk away from the river on bd. St-Michel, then make a left on rue des Ecoles. Take the first right. Small, low key, crowded with students and younger Parisians. Beer 11-16F, cocktails 12-32F at bar. Open M-Sa 10am-2am, Su noon-2am.

■ **Le Bar Dix,** 10 rue de l'Odéon (☎01 43 26 66 83). M: Odéon. From the Métro, walk against traffic on bd. St. Germain and make a left on rue de l'Odéon. A classic student hangout. Open daily 6pm-2am.

■ **Chez Georges,** 11 rue des Cannettes (☎01 43 26 79 15). M: Mabillon. From the Métro, walk down rue du Four and make a left on rue des Cannettes. Former cabaret. Upstairs open Tu-Sa noon-2am, cellar open 10pm-2am. Closed August.

Le Piano Vache, 8 rue Laplace (☎01 46 33 75 03). M: Cardinal Lemoine or Maubert-Mutualité. From the Métro, walk up rue de la Montagne Saint Geneviève and make a right on rue Laplace. Relaxed, student atmosphere. Beer 20-30F, cocktails 40F. Open July-Aug. daily 6pm-2am, Sa-Su 9pm-2am; Sept.-June noon-2am, Sa-Su 9pm-2am.

Finnegan's Wake, 9 rue des Boulangers (☎01 46 34 23 65). M: Cardinal Lemoine. From the Métro, walk up rue des Boulangers to this Irish pub set in a renovated ancient wine cellar with low, black-beamed ceilings. Have a pint (25-35F) with the boisterous crowd and soak up some Irish culture. Open M-F 11am-2am, Sa-Su 6pm-2am.

7ÈME: EIFFEL TOWER AND LES INVALIDES

■ **O'Brien's,** 77 rue St-Dominique (☎01 45 51 75 87). M. Latour-Maubourg. Handsome Irish pub. Open M-Th 6pm-2am, F-Su 4pm-2am.

Master's Bar, 64 av. Bosquet (☎01 45 51 08 99). M: Ecole-Militaire. Home of the Frenchman fond of Anglo-American culture. Open M-F noon-2am, Sa 7pm-2am.

8ÈME AND 9ÈME: CHAMPS-ELYSÉES AND OPÉRA

■ **Chesterfield Cafe,** 124 rue de la Boétie (☎01 42 25 18 06) M: Franklin D. Roosevelt. Walk toward the Arc on the Champs-Elysées, and rue de la Boétie will be the second street on your right. Friendly American bar with first-class live music and dancing later at night. Open daily 10am-5am.

■ **Bus Palladium,** 6 rue Fontaine (☎01 53 21 07 33). M: Pigalle. The classiest of the mainstream clubs, Le Bus fills with a young and trendy crowd who rock the party that rocks the ex-rock 'n' roll club. Cover 100F. Free for ladies Tu; free for all W. Drinks 60F. Open Tu-Sa 11pm-6am.

Le Queen, 102 av. des Champs-Elysées (☎01 53 89 08 90). Her majesty is at once one of the cheapest and one of the most fashionable clubs in town, and thus the toughest to get in to—especially for women. M disco; W "Respect"; Th house; F-Sa house; Su "Overkitsch." Cover Su-Th 50F, F-Sa 100F. All drinks 50F. Open daily midnight to dawn.

Folies Pigalle, 11 pl. Pigalle (☎01 48 78 25 56). M: Pigalle. This club is the largest in the once-sleazy Pigalle *quartier.* Former strip joint popular with gay and straight. Mostly house and techno. Open Tu-Sa 11pm-7am, Su 3-8pm. Cover 100F. Drinks 60F.

11ÈME AND 12ÈME: PLACE DE LA BASTILLE AND RÉPUBLIQUE

■ **Café Charbon,** 109 rue Oberkampf (☎01 43 57 55 13). M: Parmentier or Ménilmontant. A spacious bar that proudly wears traces of its *fin-de-siècle* dance hall days, but still manages to pack in the punters. Open 9pm-2am.

■ **Le Bar Sans Nom,** 49 rue de Lappe (☎01 48 05 59 36). M: Bastille. Dim, jazzy lounge famous for its inventive cocktails. Open M-Sa 7pm-2am.

■ **What's Up Bar,** 15 rue Daval (☎01 48 05 88 33). M: Bastille. From the Métro, walk north on bd. Richard Lenoir and make a right on rue Duval. One of those rare Paris miracles: a place that is (almost always) free and funky. Cover F-Sa 50F. Drinks 25-50F.

China Club, 50 rue de Charenton (☎01 43 43 82 02). M: Ledru-Rollin or Bastille. Swank Hong Kong club with a speakeasy-style cellar and lacquered *fumoir chinois* look. Open M-Th 7pm-2am, F-Sa 7pm-3am.

13ÈME: BUTTE AUX CAILLES

■ **Les Oiseaux de Passage,** 7 passage Barrault (☎01 45 89 72 42). M: Corvisart. From rue de la Butte aux Cailles, turn right on rue des Cinq Diamants, then left on passage Barrault. Young, hip, and laid-back. Art openings, live music, board games, and theme evenings, including "silent discussion night." Open M-F 11am-2am, Sa-Su 4pm-2am.

■ **Batofar,** facing 11 Quai François-Mauriac (☎01 56 29 10 33). M: Quai de la Gare. A club on a light-boat! Friendly industrial environment. Open in summer Tu-Su 6pm-2am.

La Folie en Tête, 33 rue de la Butte aux Cailles (☎01 45 80 65 99). M: Corvisart. 'The' artsy axis mundi of the 13*ème*. Magazines, writing workshops, and musical instruments. Crowded concerts on Saturday nights. Open M-Sa 5pm-2am.

16ÈME: CHARLES-DE-GAULLE-ETOILE

■ **L'Etoile,** 12 rue de Presbourg (☎01 45 00 78 70). M: Charles-de-Gaulle-Etoile. Just across from the entrance to Duplex on av. Foch. Vibrant techno, hip-hop, and funk from DJ Jean-Jean from St-Tropez. Cover with drink 100F. Open daily 11:30pm to dawn.

Duplex, 2bis av. Foch (☎01 45 00 93 93). M: Charles-de-Gaulle-Etoile. Walk around the Arc to this chic nightclub where young glamouratzi party to techno-fied pop, funk, and occasionally hip-hop. Club open Tu-Su midnight-dawn.

17ÈME AND 18ÈME: MONTMARTRE

■ **L'Endroit,** 67 pl. du Dr-Félix-Lobligeois (☎01 42 29 50 00). M: Rome. Follow rue Boursault to rue Legendre, and make a right. The purveyor of cool in work-a-day Batignolles. Open daily noon-2am.

Chez Camille, 8 rue Ravignan (☎01 46 06 05 78). M: Abbesses. From the Métro, walk down rue de la Veuville and make a left on rue Drevet and another left on rue Gabrielle which becomes rue Ravignan. Small and trendy bar with a pretty terrace looking down the *butte* to the Invalides dome. Open M-Sa noon-2am.

La Cigale, 120 bd. Rochechouart (☎01 49 25 89 99). M: Pigalle. The Métro puts you right on bd. Rochechouart. One of the two large rock clubs in Pigalle, seating 2000 for international indie, punk, hard-core bands. Music starts 8:30pm.

Elysée Montmartre, 72 bd. Rochechouart (☎01 44 92 45 42). M: Anvers. The Métro lets you out right on bd. Rochechouart. The biggest-name rock, reggae, and rap venue is a neighborhood fixture.

Divan du Monde, 75 rue des Martyrs (☎01 44 92 77 66). M: Pigalle. From the Métro, walk east on bd. Rochechouart and make a left on rue des Martyrs. Not quite global, but this grungy den does try with Brazilian music, live bands, English DJs, funk, and "Creative Relaxation" evenings. Open daily 7:30pm-dawn.

JAZZ

■ **Au Duc des Lombards,** 42 rue des Lombards, 1er (☎01 42 33 22 88). M: Châtelet. From rue des Halles, walk down rue de la Ferronerie and make a right on rue Saint-Denis and another right on rue des Lombards. Still the best in French jazz, with occasional American soloists, and hot items in world music. Cover 80-100F, music students 50-80F. Music starts either 8:30pm or 10pm and wails on until 3am (4am on weekends). Open daily 7:30pm-4am.

■ **Le Baiser Salé,** 58 rue des Lombards, 1er (☎01 42 33 37 71). M: Châtelet. From rue des Halles, walk down rue de la Ferronerie and make a right on rue Saint-Denis and another right on rue des Lombards. Lower-key than Lombards. Cuban, African, Antillean music featured together with modern jazz and funk. Open daily 4pm-dawn.

Le Petit Opportun, 15 rue des Lavandières-Ste-Opportune, 1er (☎01 42 36 01 36). M: Châtelet. From the Métro, walk rue des Halles and a right onto rue des Lavandières-Ste-Opportune. Some of the best modern jazz around. Cover 50-80F depending on act. Drinks 30-60F. Open Sept.-July Tu-Sa 9pm-5am; music begins at 10:30pm.

GAY AND LESBIAN NIGHTLIFE

See above for listings. Paris's gay and lesbian life centers on the **Marais** (3ème and 4ème), with most establishments clustering around **rue Vieille-du-Temple, rue Ste-Croix de la Bretonnerie,** and **rue des Archives.** For the most comprehensive listing of gay and lesbian establishments and services, consult *Guide Gai* (79F at any kiosk).

Banana Café, 13-15 rue de la Ferronerie (☎01 42 33 35 31), 1er. M: Châtelet. From the Porte du Pont Neuf of Les Halles, go straight, left on rue St. Honoré; rue de la Ferronerie is straight ahead past the Châtelet Métro stop. Most popular gay bar in the 1er. Open daily 4pm-dawn.

Le Champmeslé, 4 rue Chabanais (☎01 42 96 85 20), 2ème. M: Pyramides or Quatre Septembre. From the Métro, walk down av. de l'Opéra and make a right on rue des Petits Champs. Make another right onto rue Cabanais. This comfy lesbian bar is Paris's oldest and most famous. Open M-W 5pm-2am, Th-Sa 5pm-5am.

Le Duplex, 25 rue Michel Le Comte (☎01 42 72 80 86), 3ème. M: Rambuteau. This gay bar d'art has a funky mezzanine, yet feels small and intimate. Not an exclusively male bar, but few women hang out here. Beer 15F. Open daily 8pm-2am.

Les Scandaleuses, 8 rue des Ecouffes (☎01 48 87 39 26), 4ème. M: St-Paul. Walk along rue de Rivoli in the direction of traffic and turn right onto rue des Ecouffes. A vibrant, ultra-hip lesbian bar set to techno beats. Men welcome if accompanied by women. Beer 22F. Happy Hour 6-8pm. Open daily 6pm-2am.

Open Café, 17 rue des Archives (☎01 42 72 26 18), 4ème. M: Hôtel-de-Ville. Recently redone, the Open Café is the most popular of the Marais gay bars. Beer 18F, cocktails 35F. Open daily 11am-2am; Su brunch (70-105F). Happy Hour 6-8pm.

⊠ DAYTRIPS FROM PARIS

VERSAILLES

Take any RER C5 train beginning with a "V" from M: Invalides to the Versailles Rive Gauche station (30-40min., every 15min., round-trip 28F). Chateau open May-Sept. Tu-Su 9am-6:30pm; Oct.-Apr. 9am-5:30pm. 45F, after 3:30pm and under 26 35F (entrance A). Audio (1hr., 25F) and guided tours (1-2hr., 25-50F) available at entrances C and D, respectively. Gardens open dawn-dusk; free.

Supposedly fearing noble conspiracy after he discovered an assassin in his father's bedchamber, Louis XIV, the Sun King, moved the center of royal power out of Paris, away from potential aristocratic subordination. Louis XIV built and held court at Versailles's extraordinary palace and gardens, 12km west of Paris. In 1661, the Sun King renovated the small hunting lodge in Versailles and enlisted the help of architect Le Vau, painter Le Brun, and landscape architect Le Nôtre. The court became the nucleus of noble life, where France's aristocrats vied for the king's favor.

FRANCE

No one knows just how much it cost to build Versailles; Louis XIV burned the accounts to keep the price a mystery. However, life there was less luxurious than one might imagine: courtiers wore rented swords and urinated behind statues in the parlors, wine froze in the drafty dining rooms, and dressmakers invented the color *puce* (literally, "flea") to camouflage the insects crawling on the noble-women. Louis XIV's great-grandson and successor Louis XV commissioned the Opéra, in the North Wing, for the marriage of Marie Antoinette and the to-be Louis XVI. The newlyweds inherited the throne and Versailles when Louis XV died of smallpox at the chateau in 1774. The Dauphin and Marie Antoinette created the Queen's pretend playland, the Hameau (Hamlet).

During the 19th century, King Louis-Philippe established a museum to preserve the chateau, against the wishes of most French people, who wanted Versailles demolished just like the Bastille. The castle returned to the limelight in 1871, when Wilhelm of Prussia became Kaiser Wilhelm I of Germany in the Hall of Mirrors after the Franco-Prussian War. The tables were turned at the end of WWI, when France brought the Germans back to the Hall of Mirrors to sign the Treaty of Versailles.

THE GARDENS. Numerous artists—Le Brun, Mansart, Coysevox—executed stat-ues and fountains, but master gardener André Le Nôtre provided the overall plan for Versailles's gardens. Tours should begin, as the Sun King commanded, on the terrace. To its left, the **Parterre du Midi** graces the area in front of Mansart's **Orange-rie**, once home to 2000 orange trees; the temperature inside still never drops below 6°C (43°F). In the center of the terrace lies the **Parterre d'Eau,** while the **Bassin de Latone** fountain below features Latona, mother of Diana and Apollo, shielding her children as Jupiter turns villains into frogs.

Past the fountain and to the left is the **Rockwork Grove,** built between 1680 and 1683. The south gate of the grove leads to the magnificent **Bassin de Bacchus,** one of four seasonal fountains depicting the God of wine crowned in vine branches reclin-ing on a bunch of grapes. The **Bassin du Miroir d'Eau** spurts near the **Bassin de Sat-urne** and the peaceful **Jardin du Roi,** an English-style garden plated with exotic trees. The king used to take light meals amid the **Colonnade's** 32 violet and blue marble columns, sculptures, and white marble basins. The north gate to the Colon-nade exits onto the 1099-foot-long **Tapis Vert** (Green Carpet), the central mall link-ing the chateau to the **Char d'Apollon** (Chariot of Apollo). Pulled by four prancing horses, the Sun God rises to enlighten the world.

On the north side of the garden is Marsy's incredible **Bassin d'Encelade.** When the fountains are turned on, a 25m jet bursts from Enceladus's mouth. Flora reclines on a bed of flowers in the **Bassin de Flore,** while a gilded Ceres luxuriates in sheaves of wheat in the **Bassin de Cérès.** The **Parterre du Nord,** full of flowers, lawns, and trees, overlooks some of the garden's most spectacular fountains. The **Allée d'Eau,** a foun-tain-lined walkway, provides the best view of the **Bassin des Nymphes de Diane.** The path slopes toward the sculpted **Bassin du Dragon,** where a dying beast slain by Apollo spurts water 27m into the air. Ninety-nine jets of water attached to urns and seahorns surround Neptune in the **Bassin de Neptune,** the gardens' largest fountain.

THE TRIANONS AND MARIE-ANTOINETTE'S HAMEAU. The Trianons and Hameau provide a racier counterpoint to the chateau: it was here that kings trysted with lovers, and Marie-Antoinette lived like the peasant she wasn't. On the right down the wooded path from the chateau, is the **Petit Trianon,** built between 1762-68 for Louis XV and his mistress Madame de Pompadour. Marie-Antoinette took con-trol of the Petit Trianon in 1774, and it soon earned the nickname "Little Vienna." A path leads to the libidinous **Temple of Love,** a domed rotunda with 12 white marble columns. The Queen was perhaps at her happiest and most ludicrous when spend-ing time at the **Hameau,** her own bucolic village down the path from the Temple of Love. Inspired by Jean-Jacques Rousseau's theories on the goodness of nature, she commissioned a compound of 12 buildings (including a mill, dairy, and gardener's house, all surrounding a quaint artificial lake). The single-story, stone-and-pink-marble **Grand Trianon** was intended as a chateau-away-from-chateau for Louis XIV.

CHÂTEAU DE FONTAINEBLEAU

*From the Gare de Lyon in Paris, **trains** run to Fontainebleau (45min., every hr., roundtrip 94F). The castle is a 30min. walk or a 10-min. bus ride away. ☎01 60 71 50 70. Open July-Aug. W-M 9:30am-6pm; May-June and Sept.-Oct. W-M 9:30am-5pm; Nov.-Apr. W-M 9:30am-12:30pm and 2-5pm. 35F; students, seniors, and Sundays 23F; under 18 free.*

Easier to take in all at once than Versailles, the Château de Fontainebleau achieves nearly the same grandeur with a unique charm. François I and Napoleon stand out among the parade of post-Renaissance kings who lived here; the first was responsible for the dazzling ballrooms lined with work of Michelangelo's school, the second restored the post-Revolution dilapidation to a home befitting of an emperor. The **Grands Appartements** provide a lesson in the history of French architecture and decoration. Dubreuil's **Gallery of Plates** tells the history of Fontainebleau on a remarkable series of 128 porcelain plates, fashioned in Sèvres between 1838 and 1844. In the long **Galerie de François I,** the most famous room at Fontainebleau, muscular figures by Il Rosso (known in French as Maître Roux) tell mythological tales of heroism. Decorated under Henri IV, the **King's Cabinet** (also known as the **Louis XIII Salon** because Louis XIII was born there) was the site of *le débotter*, the king's post-hunt boot removal. Napoleon pored over the volumes of the long, lofty, sunlit library known as the **Bibliothèque Diana.** Since the 17th century, every queen and empress of France has slept in the gold and green **Queen's Bed Chamber;** the gilded wood bed was built for Marie-Antoinette. In the **Emperor's Private Room,** known today as the **Abdication Chamber,** Napoleon signed off his empire in 1814. The tour ends with the 16th-century, Italian-frescoed **Trinity Chapel.**

CHARTRES

Take a train from Paris's Gare Montparnasse (1hr., every hr, round-trip 142F, under 26 108F). From the station, walk straight ahead, turn left into the pl. de Châtelet, turn right on rue Ste-Même, then turn left on rue Jean Moulin. ☎02 37 21 75 02. Open M-Sa 7:30am-7:15pm, Su and holidays 8:30pm-7:15pm. No casual visits during mass. Masses M, W-Th, and Sa at 11:45am and 6pm; T and F at 9am, 11:45am, and 6pm; Su 9:30am (Latin), 11am, and 6pm. Treasury closed indefinitely at time of publication. Tower open May-Aug. M-Sa 9am-6pm, Su 1-6:30pm; Sept.-Oct. and Mar.-Apr. M-Sa 9:30-11:30am and 2-5pm, Su 1-2pm; Nov.-Feb. M-Sa 10-11:30am and 2-4pm, Su 1-2pm. Tours in English Apr.-Jan. M-Sa noon and 2:45pm; 1¼hr.; 30F, students 20F. 25F, ages 12-25 15F, under 12 free.

The Cathédrale de Chartres is the best-preserved medieval church in Europe, miraculously escaping major damage during the Revolution and WWII. A patchwork masterpiece of Romanesque and Gothic design, the cathedral was constructed by generations of unknown masons, architects, and artisans who labored for centuries. The year after he became emperor in 875, Charlemagne's grandson, Charles the Bald, donated to Chartres the **Sancta Camisia,** the cloth believed to be worn by the Virgin Mary when she gave birth to Christ. Although a church dedicated to Mary had existed on the site as early as the mid-700s, the emperor's bequest required a new cathedral to accommodate the growing number of pilgrims.

Most of the **stained glass** dates from the 13th century and was preserved through both World Wars by heroic town authorities, who dismantled over 2000 sq. meters and stored the windows pane by pane in Dordogne. The medieval merchants who paid for each window are shown in the lower panels, providing a record of daily life in the 13th century. The center window shows the story of Christ from the Annunciation to the ride into Jerusalem. Bring binoculars if you can (or rent them for 10F per hr. plus ID or 300F deposit). Stories should be "read" from bottom to top, left to right. The windows of Chartres often distract visitors from the treasures below their feet. A winding **labyrinth** is carved into the floor in the rear of the nave. Designed in the 13th century, the labyrinth was laid out for pilgrims as a substitute for a journey to the Holy Land. By following this symbolic journey on their hands and knees, the devout enacted a voyage to Jerusalem. The adventurous climb the cathedral's north tower, **Tour Jehan-de-Beauce** for a stellar view of the cathedral roof, the flying buttresses, and the city below. Parts of Chartres's **crypt,** such as a well down which Vikings tossed the bodies of their victims during raids, date back to the 9th century. You can enter the subterranean crypt only as part of a tour that leaves from La Crypte, the store opposite the cathedral's south entrance.

Founded as the Roman city *Autricum*, the **town of Chartres** is a medieval village at heart. Clustered around its mammoth house of God, the town's oldest streets are named for the trades once practiced there. The **Musée des Beaux-Arts,** 29 rue du Cloître Notre-Dame, resides in the former Bishop's Palace, just next to the cathedral. Built mainly in the 17th and 18th centuries (on a site occupied by bishops since the 11th century), the palace houses an eclectic collection of painting, sculpture, and furniture. (☎ 02 37 36 41 39. Open May-Oct. M and W-Sa 10am-noon and 2-6pm, Su 2-6pm, Nov.-Apr. M and W-Sa 10am-noon and 2-5pm, Su 2-5pm. 15F, students and seniors 7.50F.) A **monument** to **Jean Moulin,** the famous WWII Resistance hero who worked closely with de Gaulle, stands on rue Jean Moulin.

DISNEYLAND PARIS

From Paris, take RER A4 Marne-la-Vallée to the last stop, Marne-la-Vallée/Chessy (45min., every 30min., round-trip 76F); the last train back leaves at 12:22am but arrives after the Métro closes. Eurailers can take the TGV from Roissy/Charles de Gaulle Airport to the park in 15min. For more information, see www.disneylandparis.com. Open in summer daily 9am-11pm; in winter hours vary. Buy passeports (tickets) on Disneyland Hotel's ground floor, at the Paris tourist office, or at any major station on RER line A. Apr.-Sept. and Dec. 23-Jan. 7 220F; off-season 175F.

It's a small, small world and Disney is hell-bent on making it even smaller. When Euro-Disney opened on April 12, 1992, Mickey Mouse, Cinderella, and Snow White were met by the jeers of French intellectuals and the popular press, who called the Disney theme park a "cultural Chernobyl." Resistance seems to have subsided since Walt & Co. renamed it Disneyland Paris and started serving wine. Despite its small dimensions, this Disney park is the most technologically advanced yet, and the special effects on some rides will knock your socks off. Everything in Disneyland Paris is in English and French. The detailed guide called the *Park Guide Book* (free at Disney City Hall to the left of the entrance) has a map and info on everything from restaurants and attractions to bathrooms and first aid. The *Guests' Special Services Guide* has info on wheelchair accessibility throughout the park. In case you hadn't planned on a full day and night of magic, Disney now offers *FastPast*, a free service that rewards those motivated enough to pick up a ticket with reduced wait times at specific rides at specific times.

GIVERNY

Fondation Claude Monet, 84, rue Claude Monet. Trains (☎ 08 36 35 35 35) run erratically from Paris-St-Lazare to Vernon, the station nearest Giverny (roundtrip 132F). When you purchase your ticket from St-Lazare, check the timetables or ask for the bus schedules for travel from Vernon to Giverny. (Buses ☎ 02 32 71 06 39. 10 min.; 4-6 per day; 12F, roundtrip 20F.) Taxis in front of the train station are another option (65F, weekends 80F). ☎ 02 32 51 28 21. Open Apr.-Oct. Tu-Su 10am-6pm. 35F, students and ages 12-18 25F. Gardens only 25F.

Today, Monet's house and gardens in Giverny are maintained by the Fondation Claude Monet. From April to July, Giverny overflows with roses, hollyhocks, poppies and the heady scent of honeysuckle. The water lilies, the Japanese bridge, and the weeping willows look like, well, like Monets. In Monet's thatched-roof house, big windows, solid furniture, and pale blue walls house his collection of 18th- and 19th-century Japanese prints.

OTHER DAYTRIPS FROM PARIS

THE LOIRE VALLEY. Between Paris and Brittany stretches the Loire Valley. This most celebrated river in France is dotted with chateaux. Try Blois or, if you time it right, visit Chambord or Cheverny (see p. 329).

ROUEN. Visit the city of a hundred spires, and party with the students, in Rouen, the largest city in Normandy (see p. 320).

RENNES. If Parisian students will travel out to Rennes for the nightlife, then you should too (see p. 325).

FRANCE

NORTHWEST FRANCE

Since the beginning of history, the fate of northwestern France has been caught up with that of its neighbor across the Channel. Although Gauls, Celts, Franks, and Normans no longer battle over the region's treasures, waves of peaceful invaders continue to flock to the chateaux of the Loire Valley, the craggy cliffs of Brittany, and the D-Day beaches and incomparable Mont-St-Michel in Normandy. But beyond these must-see sights lie a wealth of small towns, rugged coastline, and idyllic islands that have yet to succumb to the lures of mass tourism.

NORMANDY (NORMANDIE)

Fertile Normandy is a land of gently undulating fields, tiny fishing villages along a jagged coastline, and soaring cathedrals. Vikings seized the region in the 9th century, and invasions have twice secured Normandy's place in military history: in 1066, when William of Normandy conquered England, and on D-Day, June 6, 1944, when Allied armies began the liberation of France here. In the intervening centuries, Normandy exchanged its warlike reputation for a quiet agricultural role, far removed from the border wars that raged between France and its neighbors.

ROUEN

Best known as the city where Joan of Arc was burned and Emma Bovary was bored, Rouen (pop. 400,000) is no hayseed town. The city enjoyed prosperity from the 10th through 12th centuries as the capital of the Norman empire, and was later immortalized in Monet's many renditions of the cathedral. Today, a hip young population has inherited the *vieille ville.* The most famous of Rouen's "hundred spires" are those of the **Cathédrale de Notre-Dame,** in pl. de la Cathédrale, with the tallest tower in France (151m). Don't miss the stained glass in its **Chapelle St-Jean de la Nef,** which depicts the beheading of St. John the Baptist. (Open M-Sa 8am-7pm, Su 8am-6pm.) Behind the cathedral, built in just 80 years, the flamboyant **Eglise St-Maclou,** in pl. Barthélémy, features an elaborately carved pipe organ. (Open M-Sa 10am-noon and 2-5:30pm, Su 3-5:30pm.) A poorly marked passageway at 186 rue de Martainville leads to the **Aitre St-Maclou,** which served as the church's charnel house and cemetery through the later Middle Ages; a 15th-century frieze depicts the plague years. Visitors gape at the cadaver of a cat entombed alive to exorcise spirits. (Open daily 8am-8pm. Free.) Head down rue du Gros Horloge with the cathedral to your left to see the charmingly inaccurate 14th-century **Gros Horloge** (Big Clock). Joan of Arc died on **place du Vieux Marché,** to the left as you exit the station on rue du Donjon. Near the unsightly **Eglise Ste-Jeanne d'Arc,** designed to resemble an overturned Viking boat, a cross marks the spot where Joan was burned (see p. 274). A block up rue Jeanne d'Arc, the **Musée des Beaux-Arts,** on the verdant sq. Verdel, houses an excellent collection of European masters from the 16th to 20th centuries, including Monet and Renoir. (Open W-M 10am-6pm. 20F, ages 18-25 13F.) If you've overdosed on Monet, be happy that you can't be treated at the **Musée Flaubert et d'Histoire de la Médecine,** 51 rue de Lecat, far west of the art museum in pl. de la Madeleine next to the Hôtel-Dieu hospital, which showcases a gruesome array of pre-anaesthesia medical instruments, including gallstone crushers and a battlefield amputation kit. Writer Gustave Flaubert's possessions are also on display. (Open Tu 10am-6pm, W-Sa 10am-noon and 2-6pm. 12F, students free.)

Trains leave from rue Jeanne d'Arc for: Paris (1½hr., every hr., 104F) and Lille (3hr., 2 per day, 161F). **Buses** travel to Dieppe (2hr., 1-2 per day, 70F) and Le Havre (3hr., 6-10 per day, 85F). Most buses depart from quai du Havre, or quai de la Bourse. From the station, walk down rue Jeanne d'Arc and turn left to reach pl. de la Cathédrale and the **tourist office,** 25 rue du Gros Horloge. (☎02 32 08 32 40; fax 02 32 08 32 44. Open May-Sept. M-Sa 9am-7pm, Su 9:30am-12:30pm and 2:30-6pm; Oct.-

FRANCE

Mar. M-Sa 9am-6pm, Su 10am-1pm.) Check your **email** at **Place Net,** 37 rue de la République, near the Eglise St-Maclou. (37F per hr. Open M 1-9pm, Tu-Sa 11am-9pm, Su 2-8pm.) Affordable lodgings lie on the side streets between the train station and the Hôtel de Ville, next to the cathedral on pl. du Général de Gaulle. To reach the **Hôtel Normandy,** 32 rue du Cordier, head straight down rue Jeanne d'Arc from the station and left on rue Donjon to rue du Cordier. (☎02 35 71 46 15. Shower 10F. Reception 8am-8pm. Singles and doubles 130-150F.) **Hôtel des Arcades,** 52 rue de Carmes, is comfy but pricier. (☎02 35 70 10 30. Reception 7am-8pm. Singles and doubles 150-245F.) **Camping Municipal de Déville,** on rue Jules Ferry in Déville-lès-Rouen, is 4km from Rouen; take bus #1 from the train station to the Hôtel de Ville in Rouen and then change to bus #2 (dir.: Déville) and get off at Mairie. (☎02 35 74 07 59. Open June-Sept. for tents, year-round for caravans. 25F per person, 9.50F per tent, 9F per car.) Cheap eateries crowd **pl. du Vieux-Marché** and the **Gros Horloge** area. **Natural Gourmand'grain,** 3 rue du Petit Salut, off pl. de la Cathédrale, has organic veggie food. (Open Tu-Sa noon-3pm.) **Monoprix supermarket** is at 73-83 rue du Gros Horloge. (Open M-Sa 8:30am-9pm.) **Postal Code:** 76000.

⛊ DAYTRIP FROM ROUEN: MONT-ST-MICHEL. Rouen is the perfect town from which you can travel out to Mont-St-Michel (see p. 324).

NORMANDY COAST

The soils of Normandy have been invaded by many, including the Vikings, King Edward III, and, more recently, by the Allied forces during WWII. Plaques and monuments commemorate the area's liberation in 1942; soaring cliffs and beautiful beaches also provide a reason to step away from Normandy's larger cities.

DIEPPE

In 1942, Allied (mostly Canadian) forces struggled to retake Dieppe's (pop. 36,000) **beach** from Nazi control; today, tourists flock to see the long pebbly stretch and to the 15th-century **chateau** that rises from the cliffs to the west. (☎02 35 84 19 76. Open June-Sept. daily 10am-noon and 2-6pm; Oct.-May W-M 10am-noon and 2-5pm.) A somber testament to World War II is the chillingly beautiful **Canadian Cemetery** in nearby Hautot-sur-Mer. To get there, take bus #2 from the tourist office. **Trains** (☎02 35 06 69 33) leave from bd. Clemenceau for: Paris (2½hr., 6-10 per day, 138F; change at Rouen); Caen (145F; change at Rouen); and Rouen (1¼hr., 10 per day, 55F). From the station, turn right and take a left on quai Duquesne to reach the **tourist office,** on pont Jehan Ango, on the waterfront in the *centre ville*. (☎02 32 84 16 92; fax 02 32 14 40 61. Open July-Aug. daily 9am-1pm and 2-8pm; May-June and Sept. M-Sa 9am-1pm and 2-7pm, Su 10am-1pm and 3-6pm; Oct.-Apr. M-Sa 9am-noon and 2-6pm.) The **Auberge de Jeunesse (HI),** 48 rue Louis Fromager, has clean, spacious rooms. Take bus #2 (dir.: Val Druel) from the Chambre du Commerce, 200m down quai Duquesne from the train station, to Château Michel, backtrack, and take the first left. (☎02 35 84 85 73. Breakfast 19F. Sheets 17F. Reception 8-10am and 5-10pm. HI members only. Bunks 48F.)

FÉCAMP

The port town of Fécamp (pop. 20,000) is one of the jewels of the High Normandy coast. The **Palais Bénédictine,** 110 rue Alexandre Le Grand, houses impressive collections of medieval and Renaissance religious artifacts and is famous for its monk-produced after-dinner liqueur. (Open July-Sept. 3 daily 9:30am-6pm; Sept. 4-Nov. 12 and Mar. 13-June 10am-noon and 2-5:30pm; Nov. 13-Dec., Feb. 5-Mar.17 10-11:15am and 2-5pm. 29F.) The 12th- to 13th-century **Abbatiale de la Trinité** houses an even rarer liquid: the relic of a fig trunk that allegedly carried a few drops of Christ's blood to the shores of Fécamp in the 6th century. **Trains** arrive from Paris (2½hr., 6 per day, 148F); Le Havre (45min., 5 per day, 43F); and Rouen (1¼hr., 6per day, 69F). The **tourist office,** 113 rue Alexandre Le Grand, books rooms for a 10F fee. From the station, head right on rue St-Etienne as it becomes rue de Mer and then left at Palais Bénédictine; it's opposite the entrance. (☎ 02 35 28 51 01; fax 02 35 27 07 77. Open July-Aug. M-F 10am-6pm; May-June, Sept. M-F 9am-12:15pm and 1:45-6pm, Sa 10am-noon, 2:30-6:30pm, Su 10am-noon and 2-6pm. Oct.-Mar. M-F 9am-12:15pm, 1:45-6:30pm, Sa 10am-noon, 2:30-6:30pm.) **Hôtel Martin,** 18 pl. St-Etienne, has cheery rooms. (☎ 02 35 28 23 82. Reception 7:30am-11pm, closed Su night and M. Singles and doubles 150-205F.) **Marché-Plus supermarket** is at 83 quai Berigny. (Open M-Sa 7am-9pm, Su 9am-1pm.)

LE HAVRE

An elegy to concrete, Le Havre (pop. 200,000) can boast of being the largest transatlantic port in France and little else. For information on **ferries** to Portsmouth, see p. 47. **Trains** leave from cours de la République (☎ 02 35 98 50 50) for Paris (2hr., 8 per day, 151F); Fécamp (via Etretat; 1hr., 9per day, 43F); and Rouen (50min., 13 per day, 72F). To reach the **tourist office,** 186 bd. Clemenceau, from the station, follow bd. de Strasbourg across town as it changes to av. Foch; turn onto bd. Clemenceau. From the ferry terminal, walk left down quai de Southampton and then turn right. (☎ 02 32 74 04 04; fax 02 35 42 38 39. Open May-Sept. M-Sa 9am-7pm, Su 10am-12:30pm and 2:30-6pm; Oct.-Apr. M-Sa 9am-6:30pm, Su 10am-12:30pm and 2:30-6:30.) **Hôtel Jeanne d'Arc,** 91 rue Emile Zola, offers homey rooms with TVs and phones. (☎ 02 35 21 67 27. Breakfast 20F. Singles 135F; doubles 150-160F.) Stock up for the ferry ride at **Monoprix,** 38-40 av. René Coty. (Open M-Sa 8:30am-8:30pm.)

CAEN

Although Allied bombing leveled three quarters of its buildings in WWII, Caen has restored its architectural treasures and revitalized its tourist industry. Its biggest draw is the powerful **Mémorial de Caen,** which includes footage of WWII, displays on pre-war Europe and the Battle of Normandy, and a short but haunting testimonial to the victims of the Holocaust. Take bus #17 to Mémorial. (Open daily July-Aug. 9am-8pm; Feb. 15-June and Sept.-Oct. 9am-7pm; Nov.-Jan. 4 and Jan. 20-Feb. 14 9am-6pm. 74F, students 65F, veterans free.) The city's twin abbeys, **Abbaye aux Hommes** and the **Abbatiale St-Etienne,** both off rue Guillaume le Conquérant, were financed by William the Conqueror as penance for marrying his distant cousin despite the Pope's interdiction. (Tours of Abbaye aux Hommes in French daily 9:30, 11am, 2:30, and 4pm. 10F, students 5F. Abbatiale St-Etienne open daily 8:15am-noon and 2-7:30pm.) Opposite the tourist office stretch the ruins of William's **chateau.** Inside, the **Musée des Beaux-Arts** contains a fine selection of 16th- and 17th-century Flemish works and Impressionist paintings. (Chateau open daily May-Sept. 6am-1am; Oct.-Apr. 6am-7:30pm. Museum open W-M 9:30am-6pm. 25F, students 15F; W free.) Caen's old streets pulsate in moonlight, especially around **rue de Bras, rue des Croisiers,** and **rue St-Pierre.**

Trains (☎ 08 36 35 35 35) leave from the Pl. de la Gare for: Paris (2½hr., 12 per day, 156F); Rennes (3hr., 3 per day, 167F); Rouen (2hr., 5 per day, 116F); and Tours (3½hr., 2 per day, 169F). The **tourist office** sells maps, books hotel rooms for 10F, and has access to the **internet.** (☎ 02 31 27 14 14; fax 02 31 27 14 18; email tourisminfo@ville-caen.fr. Internet 37F per hr. Open July-Aug. M-Sa 9:30am-7pm, Su 10am-1pm and 2-5pm; Sept.-June M-Sa 9:30am-1pm and 2-6pm, Su 10am-1pm.) For great rooms near the *centre ville,* try **Hôtel de la Paix,** 14 rue Neuve-St-Jean. (☎ 02 31 86 18 99. Breakfast 28F. Singles 140-175F; doubles 160-195F; triples 240-260F.) The **Hôtel du Château,** 5 av. du 6 Juin, has 24 rooms also in the center of the town. (☎ 02 31 86 15 37. Breakfast included. Doubles and triples 170-240F.) **Terrain Municipal,** on rte. de Louvigny, has riverside **campsites.** Take bus #13 (dir.: Louvigny) to Camping. (☎ 02 31 73 60 92. Reception 9am-noon and 5-8pm. Gates closed from 11pm-7am. Open May-Sept. 18F per person, 10F per tent, 10F per car.) Restaurants line the few remaining medieval streets in the **quartier Vaugueux** near the chateau as well as the streets between **Eglise St-Pierre** and **Eglise St-Jean.** Get your groceries at **Monoprix,** 45 bd. du Maréchal Leclerc. (Open M-Sa 8am-8:30pm.) **Postal Code:** 14000.

BAYEUX

An ideal base for exploring the D-Day beaches, beautiful Bayeux (pop. 15,000) is also renowned for its **Tapisserie de Bayeux** (Bayeux Tapestry). The 70m of embroidery depict the Norman conquest of England in 1066. The tapestry is in the **Centre Guillaume le Conquérant,** on rue de Nesmond. (☎ 02 31 51 25 50. Open daily May-Aug. 9am-7pm; Mar. 15-Apr. and Sept.-Oct. 15 9am-6:30pm; Oct. 16-Mar. 14 9:30am-12:30pm and 2-6pm. 40F, students 18F.) Nearby is the truly extraordinary **Cathédrale Notre-Dame,** begun in 1077, a fantastic pastiche of Gothic and Romanesque styles. (Open July-Aug. M-Sa 8am-7pm, Su 9am-7pm; Sept.-June M-Sa 8:30am-noon and 2:30-7pm, Su 9am-12:15pm and 2:30-7pm.) The **Musée de la Bataille de Normandie,** on bd. Fabian Ware, recounts the summer of 1944 through old newspaper clippings, photographs, films, and uniforms. (☎02 31 92 93 41. Open May-Sept. 17 9:30am-6:30pm; Sept 18-Apr. 10am-12:30pm and 2-6pm. Closed the second two weeks in January. Adults 33F, students 16F, veterans free.)

Trains (☎02 31 92 80 50) leave from pl. de la Gare for: Paris (2½hr., 13 per day, 171F); Caen (20min., 13 per day, 31F); and Cherbourg (1hr., 10 per day, 81F). To get from the station to the **tourist office,** pont St-Jean (☎02 31 51 28 28; fax 02 31 51 28 29; www.bayeux-tourism.com), turn left onto bd. Sadi-Carnot, then bear right at the roundabout, following the signs to the *centre ville.* Continue up rue Larcher until it hits rue St-Martin, Bayeux's commercial avenue. The office will be on your right, at the edge of the pedestrian zone. The **Family Home/Auberge de Jeunesse (HI),** 39 rue General de Dais is in the center of town. From the tourist office, turn right onto rue St. Martin and follow it through its name changes and then turn left onto rue General de Dais. (☎02 31 92 15 22. Breakfast included. Dorms 95F.) Follow rue Genas Duhomme and head straight on av. de la Vallée des Prés for **Camping Municipal,** on bd. d'Eindhoven. (☎02 31 92 08 43. Open Mar. 15-Nov. 15. 18F per person, 22F per tent and car.) Get **groceries** at **Proxi,** on pl. St-Patrice. (Open Tu-Sa 7:30am-12:30pm and 2:30-7:30pm, Su 9am-12:30pm.) **Postal Code:** 14400.

D-DAY BEACHES

On June 6, 1944, over a million Allied soldiers invaded the beaches of Normandy—code-named Utah and Omaha (American), Gold and Sword (British), and Juno (Canadian). Today, the record of the battle can be clearly seen in sobering gravestones, remnants of German bunkers, and the pockmarked landscape. Most of the beaches and museums can be reached from Caen and Bayeux with **Bus Verts** (☎08 01 21 42 14). It may be cheaper to buy a day pass for 100F, or a three day pass for 150F if you plan to make many stops.

UTAH BEACH. At Utah Beach, the Americans headed the western flank of the invasion. The **Musée du Débarquement** shows how 836,000 troops, 220,000 vehicles, and 725,000 tons of equipment came ashore. (☎02 33 71 53 35. Open June-Sept. daily 9:30am-6:30pm; off-season reduced hrs. 28F, students 23F.) The beach and museum are accessible only by car or by foot from **Ste-Mère-Eglise,** of prime strategic importance during D-Day. Take a **train** from Bayeux to Caretan (30min., 10 per day) and then a bus from Caretan (15 min., 1 per day leaving at 12:50pm with the return at 6:35pm) to Ste-Mère-Eglise.

POINTE DU HOC, OMAHA BEACH, AND GOLD BEACH. The most difficult landing was that of the Rangers, an American Elite Unit at Pointe du Hoc. The grassy area beyond the cliffs is still marked by deep pits. Next to Colleville-sur-Mer and east of the Pointe du Hoc is Omaha Beach, memorialized in the American movie *Saving Private Ryan,* where 9486 graves stretch over the 172-acre **American Cemetery.** (Open daily Apr.-Nov. 8am-6pm; Dec.-Mar. 9am-5pm.) Ten kilometers north of Bayeux and just east of Omaha is **Arromanches,** a small town at the center of Gold Beach, where the British built Port Winston in a single day to provide shelter while the Allies unloaded their supplies. The **Musée du Débarquement,** on the beach, houses relics and photos of the Allied landings. (☎02 31

22 34 31. Open May-Sept. 3 9am-7pm; off-season reduced hrs.; closed Jan. 35F, students 22F.) The **Arromanches 360° Cinéma** combines images of modern Normandy with those of D-Day. Turn left on rue de la Batterie from the museum and take the steps. (☎ 02 31 22 30 30. Open daily June-Aug. 9:40am-6:40pm; off-season reduced hrs. 24F.)

JUNO BEACH AND SWORD BEACH. East of Arromanches lies Juno Beach, the landing site of the Canadian forces. The **Canadian Cemetery** is at **Bény-sur-Mer-Reviers.** In **Ouistreham,** the **No. 4 Commando Museum,** on pl. Alfred Thomas, tells the story of British and French troops who participated in the attack on Sword Beach, an amazingly successful mission accomplished with the quirky "Hobart's Funnies," tanks outlandishly fitted with bridge-building, mine-sweeping, and ditch-digging apparati. (☎ 02 31 96 63 10. Museum open Apr.-Sept. 10:30am-6pm. 25F, students 15F.)

CHERBOURG

With a strategic location at the tip of the Cotentin peninsula, Cherbourg (pop. 28,000) was the "Gateway to France," the major supply port following the D-Day offensive of 1944. The town serves as a major transport link between France and Britain, and there is enough (though just barely) to keep you busy between trains or ferries. **Ferries** leave from the *gare maritime*, northeast of the *centre ville*, along bd. Maritime, to Rosslare, Portsmouth, and Poole. (See Getting There: By Boat, p. 47.) The **train station** (☎ 02 33 44 18 74), at the base of the Bassin du Commerce, has service to: Paris (3hr., 7 per day, 218F); Bayeux (1hr., 8 per day, 81F); Caen (1½hr., 10 per day, 99F); Rennes (3.5hr., change at Lison, 3 per day, 175F); and Rouen (4.5hr., 4 per day, 182F). Across from the station, Autocars STN (☎ 02 33 88 51 00) runs **buses** around the region. (Open M-F 8:15am-noon and 2-6:30pm.) To get to the **tourist office,** turn right from the terminal onto bd. Felix Amiot. At the roundabout, go straight and continue around the bend, eventually making a right across the canal. To reach the train station, go left at the roundabout onto av. A. Briand and follow it as it becomes av. Carnot; it's at the end of the canal right off of av. Carnot on av. Millet (25min.). To get from the tourist office to the new 100-bed **Auberge de Jeunesse** (HI), 55 rue de l'Abbaye, walk left on rue de Port, pass through pl. de la Mairie, continue on the pedestrian rue de la Paix, and bear left at the fork. (☎ 02 33 78 15 15. Sheets 18F. Reception 8am-noon and 6-11pm. Lockout 10am-6pm. 52F, with breakfast 69F.) Stock up at the Continent **supermarket,** quai de l'Entrepôt, next to the station. (Open M-Sa 8:30am-9:30pm.) **Postal Code:** 50100.

MONT-SAINT-MICHEL

Rising abruptly from the sea, the island of Mont-St-Michel (pop. 42), is visible for miles. The Mont is a dazzling labyrinth of stone arches, spires, and stairways that climb up to the **abbey,** balanced precariously on the jutting rock. (Guided tours 1hr., 6 per day in English, free. Abbey open daily May-Sept. 9am-5:30pm; Oct.-Apr. 9:30am-5pm. 45F, under 26 26F. Audio tour 30F. Mass daily 12:15pm, free.) **La Merveille,** an intricate 13th-century cloister, encloses a seemingly endless web of passageways and chambers. The Mont is most stunning at night, particularly from the causeway entrance, but plan carefully—there is no late-night public transport off the island. Mont-St-Michel is best visited as a daytrip via Courriers Bretons **bus** (☎ 02 33 60 11 43) from Rennes (1½hr., M-Sa 3-6 per day, 65F) or St-Malo (1½hr., 2-4 per day, 55F). SCETA buses also run from Pontorson (15min., 8 per day, 14.40F). Hotels on Mont-St-Michel start at 300F a night, so a better deal would be to stay in nearby Pontorson. The **Pontorson tourist office** helps visitors find affordable accommodations (☎ 02 33 60 20 65; fax 02 33 60 85 67). The cheapest beds are at the **Centre Dugusclin (HI),** rue Général Patton. (☎ 02 33 60 18 65. Open June-mid-Sept. 4- to 7-person room 48F.) **Postal Code:** 50116.

BRITTANY (BRETAGNE)

Lined with spectacular beaches, misty, almost apocalyptic headlands, and cliffs gnawed by the sea into long crags and inlets, the peninsula of Brittany has always tugged away from mainland France, self-consciously maintaining its Celtic traditions. Present-day Breton culture has its roots in the 5th to the 7th centuries, when Britons fled Anglo-Saxon invaders; in the centuries that followed, they fought for and retained their independence from Frankish, Norman, French, and English invaders, uniting with France only after the last Duchess ceded it to her husband in 1532. Traditions are fiercely guarded, and lilting *Brezhoneg* (Breton) is spoken energetically at pubs and ports in the western part of the province.

RENNES

Home to two major universities and 60,000 students, Rennes (pop. 203,533) combines Parisian sophistication with traditional Breton charm. In 1720, a fire destroyed much of the city, but the lovely *vieille ville* still stands, teeming with hip cafes and bars. A popular stopover between Paris and Mont-St-Michel, Rennes also makes for a packed weekend excursion of its own.

⬛ TRANSPORTATION. Trains leave from pl. de la Gare (☎ 02 99 29 11 92) for: Paris (2hr., approx. every hr., 289-349F); Bordeaux (6hr.; 30 per day; half via Paris; 290F direct, via Paris 546F); Caen (3hr., 2 per day, 167F); Marseilles (8hr., 13 per day, 560F); Nantes (1¼-2hr., 10 per day, 114F); St. Malo (1hr., 14 per day, 70F). **Buses** (☎ 02 99 30 87 80), leave from the train station for: Angers (3hr., 1-3 per day, 98F); Paimpont, location of the Broceliande Forest (1¼hr., M-Sa 5-7 per day, 17F); and Mont-St-Michel (2½hr., 1-2 per day, 64F).

🔀 PRACTICAL INFORMATION. The **tourist office,** 11 rue Pont Saint-Yves, has free maps and listings of events, hotels, and restaurants. From the station, take av. Jean Janvier, turn left on quai Chateaubriand and walk along the river, turn right on rue George Dottin, and then right on rue Saint-Yves. (☎ 02 99 67 11 11; fax 02 99 67 11 10. Open M-Sa 9am-7pm, Su 11am-6pm.) Surf the **internet at Cybernet Online,** 22 rue St. Georges. (☎ 02 99 36 37 41. 25F per 30min. Open M 2-7:30pm, Tu-Sa 10am-7:30pm, closed Aug.) **Postal Code:** 35000.

📷📙 ACCOMMODATIONS AND FOOD. To get to the **Auberge de Jeunesse (HI),** 10-12 Canal St-Martin, take bus #1 toward Centre Commercial Nord and get off at Hotel Dieu. From the bus stop, continue down the road, turn right on rue de St-Malo, and follow the street over the mini-canal to an intersection. The hostel is on the right. (☎ 02 99 33 22 33. Breakfast included. Reception 7am-11pm. Singles 130F; doubles, triples and quads 89F per person.) **Hôtel Venezia,** 27 rue Dupont des Loges, off quai Richemont, is conveniently located; take av. Jean Janvier from the train station's north entrance and turn right on rue Dupont des Loges, just before the bridge. (☎ 02 99 30 36 56. Breakfast 30F. Singles 130F, with full bathroom 185F; doubles 160-220F.) Directly off av. Jean Janvier, **Hôtel Richemont,** 8 rue Dupont des Loges, is an airy hotel with sparkling bathrooms. (☎ 02 99 30 38 21. Breakfast 30F. Reservations recommended. Singles with bath 225-260F; doubles with bath 290F. Extra bed 55F.) For camping, take bus #3 from rue Victor Hugo to **Camping Municipal des Gayeulles** in Parc les Gayeulles. (☎ 02 99 36 91 22. Open Apr.-Sept. Electricity 17F. Hot shower 5F. 14F per person. Cars 5F. Tent 12F. Cash only.) For food in Rennes, wander around **rue de St-Malo, pl. St-Michel, rue St-Georges,** or **rue Ste-Melaine,** or try the huge Saturday market in **pl. des Lices.** At **L'os Amigos,** 13 Rue St. Malo (☎ 02 99 36 86 86), there are four always-changing *plats du jour.* (Open M-Su 8pm-midnightish.)

📷📙 SIGHTS AND ENTERTAINMENT. Built between 1541 and 1705, the **Cathédrale St-Pierre,** in the *vieille ville* just off rue des Dames, is mostly made of red-tinted marble; the center of attention is its carved and gilded altarpiece depicting the life of the Virgin. (Open daily 9am-noon and 2-5pm.) Across the street from the cathedral, down rue Porte Mordelaise, stands the **Porte Mordelaise,** former entrance to the city and the last remaining piece of the city's medieval wall. Approximately 1km to the east is the lush **Jardin du Thabor,** considered by some to be one of the most beautiful gardens in France. (Open June-Sept. daily 7am-9:30pm.) Adjacent is the magnificent, though understated 11th-19th century **Eglise Notre Dame.** Step inside to gaze at the remnants of a 15th-century fresco of the Baptism of Christ in the right transept. The **Musée des Beaux-Arts,** 20 quai Emile Zola, houses a small but eclectic collection, from Picasso canvases to Egyptian pottery. (Tours July-Aug. W and F 2:30pm. Open W-M 10am-noon and 2-6pm. 20F, students 10F.)

Rennais nightlife is so hot that Parisian students are known to make weekend trips to Rennes just for the clubs. The action centers around the **pl. Ste-Anne,** the **pl. St-Michel,** and the radiating streets. **Le Cite D'Ys,** 31 Rue Vasselot, is the home of the true Breton party. (☎ 02 99 78 24 84. Open daily 9am-1am.) **L'Espace,** 45 bd. La Tour d'Auvergne (☎ 02 99 30 21 95), pounds all night with writhers of all sizes, styles, and sexual orientations (80% gay on F and Sa, mostly "student" on W and Th). Upstairs is **L'Endroit,** which tends to have an older, predominantly gay crowd (25-30 years) reclining on its wicker furniture and grooving to techno. (Both open Th-Sa 11pm-6am, Su-W midnight-6am. Cover 60F, students 40F.)

ST-MALO

The shore of St-Malo (pop. 52,000) was the departure point for navigator Jacques Cartier's voyage to Canada, and remains the ultimate oceanside getaway. Tourists converge on its miles of warm, sandy **beaches** and crystalline blue waters as well as its historic *centre ville.* The best view of St-Malo is from its **ramparts**—enter the walled city through the Porte St-Vincent and follow the stairs up on the right. **Trains** run from pl. de l'Hermine to: Paris (5hr., 3 per day, 306F); Dinan (1hr., 7 per day, 47F); and Rennes (1hr., 8-12 per day, 72F). As you exit the station, cross bd. de la République and follow Esplanade St-Vincent directly to the **tourist office,** near the entrance to the old city. (☎ 02 99 56 64 48; fax 02 99 56 67 00. Open July-Aug. M-Sa 8:30am-8pm, Su 10am-7pm; Sept.-June reduced hrs.) The 247-bed **Auberge de Jeunesse/Centre Patrick Varangot/Centre de Rencontres Internationales (HI),** 37 av. du Révérend Père Umbricht, is three blocks from the beach. Follow bd. de la République to the right from the station, turn right on av. Ernest Renan, turn left on rue Moka, turn right on av. Pasteur and keep right for a 30-minute walk. (☎ 02 99 40 29 80; fax 02 99 40 29 02. Reception closed noon-2pm. Lockout 10am-5pm. Reservations by fax or letter only. Singles with bath 119F; dorms with sink 83F.) For **Hôtel Gambetta,** 40 bd. Gambetta, head toward the hostel and look for bd. Gambetta off av. Pasteur. (☎ 02 99 56 54 70. Showers 16F. Singles 110-220F; doubles 140-260F.) **Stoc supermarket,** on av. Pasteur, is near the hostel. (Open M-F 8:30am-1pm and 3-7:30pm, Sa 8:30am-7:30pm, Su 9:30am-noon.) **Postal Code:** 35400.

DINAN

Walking through Dinan (pop. 10,000) is like entering a history book. Perhaps the best-preserved medieval town in Brittany, the cobblestoned streets of the *vieille ville* (old town) are lined with 15th-century houses inhabited by traditional artisans. Take the **Promenade des Petits-Fossés** outside of the ramparts to the 13th-century **Porte du Guichet,** the entrance to the **Château de Dinan,** also known as the **Tour de la Duchesse Anne.** Climb to the terrace to look over the town, or inspect the galleries of the **Tour de Coëtquen,** which includes a spooky subterranean room full of tomb sculptures. (Complex open June to Oct.15 daily 10am-6:30pm; mid-Oct. to May W-M reduced hrs. 25F, students 10F.) On the other side of the ramparts from the chateau is the entrance to the **Jardin du Val Cocherel,** which holds huge bird cages, a rose garden, a checkerboard for life-sized chess pieces, a small zoo, and a children's library. (Open daily 8am-7:30pm.)

Trains run from the pl. du 11 novembre to Paris (3hr., 8 per day, 316F) and Rennes (1hr., 8 per day, 73F). To get from the station to the **tourist office,** 6 rue de l'Horloge, bear left onto rue Carnot, turn right on rue Thiers, head left at the rotary (pl. Duclos). Enter the *vieille ville* via Grande Rue on the left, turn right onto rue de la Poissonerie which becomes rue de l'Horloge. (☎ 02 96 87 69 76; fax 02 96 87 69 77; email infos@dinan-tourisme.com. Walking tours July-Aug. daily 10am and 3-5pm; 25F. Open June-Sept. M-Sa 9am-7pm, Su 10am-noon and 3-5pm; Oct.-May M-Sa 8:30am-12:30pm and 2-6pm.) To walk to the **Auberge de Jeunesse (HI),** on Moulin du Méen in Vallée de la Fontaine-des-Eaux, turn left as you exit the station, head left across the tracks, turn right, and follow the tracks and signs downhill. (☎ 02 96 39 10 83. **Internet** 1F per min. Breakfast 19F. Sheets 17F. Reception 9am-11pm. Midnight curfew. 2- to 8-bed dorms 50F.) **Hôtel du Théâtre,** 2 rue Ste-Claire, is opposite the tourist office. (☎ 02 96 39 06 91. Breakfast 25F. Singles 85F; doubles 120-130F; triples with bath 210F.) Get **groceries** at **Monoprix,** on rue de la Ferronnerie. (Open M-F 9am-12:30pm and 2:30-7:30pm, Sa 9am-7pm.) Inexpensive *brasseries* lie on **rue de la Cordonnerie** and near **rue de la Ferronnerie** and **pl. des Merciers. Postal Code:** 22100.

CÔTE D'EMERAUDE AND THE CÔTE DE GRANITE ROSE

Situated between the Côte d'Emeraude and the Côte de Granite Rose, **St-Brieuc** is a perfect base for daytrips to the scenic countryside. **Trains** arrive from Dinan (1hr., 2-3 per day, 64F) and Rennes (1hr., 15 per day, 92F). From the station, on bd. Charner, walk straight down rue de la Gare and bear right at the fork to reach the pl. de la Résistance and the **tourist office,** 7 rue St-Gouéno. (☎ 02 96 33 32 50. Open July-Aug. M-Sa 9am-7pm, Su 10am-1pm; Sept.-June M-Sa 9am-noon and 1:30-6pm.) The **Auberge de Jeunesse (HI)** is in a 15th-century house outside of town; take bus #3 (dir.: le Village) and ask to be let off at the hostel. (☎ 02 96 78 70 70. 70F. Breakfast included. Sheets 17F. Dorms 72F.)

The rust-hued cliffs of **Cap Fréhel** mark this northern point of the Côte d'Emeraude. Catch a CAT **bus** from St-Brieuc (1½hr., 3-5 per day, 44F) and follow the red-and-white-striped markers along the well-marked **GR34 trail** on the edge of the peninsula. The 13th-century **Fort La Latte** boasts drawbridges and a hair-raising view of the Cap (1½hr.). To reach the **Auberge de Jeunesse Cap Fréhel (HI),** in La Ville Hadrieux in Kerivet, walk for 35min. toward Plévenon on the D16, then follow the inconspicuous signs. (May-Sept. 15 ☎ 02 96 41 48 98; Sept. 16-Apr. ☎ 02 98 78 70 70. Breakfast 19F. Sheets 17F. Lockout noon-5:30pm. Open May-Sept. Dorms 31-45F.)

Paimpol, northwest of St-Brieuc at the end of the Côte de Granite Rose, offers access to nearby islands, beaches, and hiking. **Trains** (1hr., 4-5 per day, 68F) and CAT **buses** (1¼hr., 3-7 per day, 42F) arrive at av. Général de Gaulle from St-Brieuc. From the station, go straight on rue du 18 Juin and turn right on rue de l'Oise, which becomes rue St-Vincent, to reach the **tourist office,** on pl. de la République. (☎ 02 96 20 83 16; fax 02 96 55 11 12. Open July-Aug. M-Sa 9am-7:30pm, Su 10am-1pm; Sept.-June Tu-Su 10am-12:30pm and 2:30-6pm.) To get to the **Auberge de Jeunesse/Gîte d'Etape (HI),** turn left on av. Général de Gaulle, turn right at the first light and left at the next one, follow rue Bécot, bear right on rue de Pen Ar Run, and turn left at the end. (☎ 02 96 20 83 60. Breakfast 19F. Sheets 17F. Check-in until 9pm. Dorms 48F.)

BREST

Although it is often used as a base for exploring northwest Brittany, Brest (pop. 154,091) is the lively home of boisterous sailors and students attending Brittany's second largest university. Brest's **chateau** was the only building in the town to survive WWII, and is now the world's oldest active military institution, as well as home to the **Musée de la Marine,** which highlights the local maritime history. To get there, turn left out of pl. de la Liberté onto av. de Georges Clemenceau; then right on rue de Château, and follow it to its end. (29F, students 19F. Open W-M 10am-6:30pm, Tu 2-6:30pm; Oct.-May Tu-S 10am-noon and 2-6pm.) The newly-renovated **Océanopolis Brest,** at port de Plaisance, has tropical, temperate, and polar pavilions with space-age multimedia exhibits, a 3D theater, and a glass elevator taking you within a coral reef. From the Liberty terminal, take bus #7 across from the station to Océanopolis. (☎ 02 98 34 40 40. Bus every 30min. until 7:26pm, 6.30F. Open daily June-Aug. 9am-7pm; Sept.-May 9am-6pm.)

Trains (☎ 02 98 31 51 72) arrive from Rennes (1½hr., 15 per day, 170F) and Nantes (4hr., 6 per day, 221F). From the station, av. Georges Clemenceau leads to the inter-

FRANCE

section of rue de Siam and rue Jean Jaurès, and the **tourist office,** pl. de la Liberté. (☎02 98 44 24 96; fax 02 98 44 53 73. Open mid-June to mid-Sept. M-Sa 9:30am-12:30pm and 2-6:30pm, Su 10am-noon and 2-4pm; mid-Sept. to mid-June M-Sa 10am-12:30pm and 2-6pm.) Get your **internet access** at **Les Années Bleues,** 23 rue Bréhat Bruat. (☎02 98 44 48 19. 30F per 30min., one drink included. Open Tu-Sa 10am-1am.) To get to the **Auberge de Jeunesse (HI),** on rue de Kerbriant, 4km away from the train station, take bus #7 from opposite the station to "Port de Plaisance" (6.30F; last bus M-Sa 7:26pm, Su 6pm); facing the port, take your first right, then another right, and it's on the right. (☎02 98 41 90 41. Reception M-F 7-9am and 5-8pm, Sa-Su 7-10am and 5-8pm. Curfew July-Aug. midnight; Sept.-June 11pm; ask for a key. Dorms 72F.) **L'Eurasie,** rue Lyon 48 (☎02 98 44 78 00), offers excellent Chinese and Vietnamese food at some of the lowest prices in town (3-course lunch *menu* 55F. Open 12-2pm and 7-11pm.) For **groceries,** try the **Monoprix,** on rue de Siam. (Open M-Sa 8:30am-7:30pm.) **Postal Code:** 29200.

CROZON PENINSULA

With spectacular scenery, rugged terrain, and few inhabitants, the Crozon Peninsula *(Presqu'île de Crozon)* is a hiker's paradise, and well worth the effort to get there. The peninsula's three major towns are Crozon, Morgat, and Camaret. The more than numerous *gîtes d'étapes* (rural accommodations) that pepper the peninsula make it easy for backpackers to explore—a definite highlight is the **Cap de la Chèvre,** a 14km trail that runs from the Morgat Port to Cap de la Chèvre, passing through young pine forests and overlooking the ocean. **Crozon** is a good base from which to explore the peninsula; from Brest, take a Vedettes Armoricaines combo **boat/shuttle** (☎02 98 44 44 04; 3 per day, 57F) or a Transports Salaun **bus** (☎02 98 27 02 02. 1¼hr., 2-3 per day, 58F.) Buses to Crozon stop at the **tourist office.** (☎02 98 27 07 92. Open July-Aug. M-Sa 9:15am-7pm, Su 10am-7pm; Sept.-June M-Sa 9:30am-noon and 2-7pm.) **Presqu'île Loisirs,** across the street, rents indispensable **bikes.** (☎02 98 27 00 09. 40F per half-day, 60F per day, 350F per week. Open July-Aug. M-Sa 9am-noon and 2-7pm, Su 9am-noon; Sept.-June Tu-Sa 9am-noon and 2-7pm.) **Hôtel du Clos St-Yves,** 61 rue Alsace Lorraine, has decent rooms. From the bus stop, with the tourist office behind you, cross the street and go down the unnamed street to the right of the plant store and then turn right on rue Alsace Lorraine. (☎02 98 27 00 10. Breakfast 35F. Doubles 150-320F, 80F per extra person.)

From Crozon, you can take a bus to **Camaret** (4-6 per day, 11F), the westernmost point of the peninsula. Just a few minutes on D8 from Camaret by bike or foot (look for signs to the left of the Hôtel le Styvel) stand the **Alignements de Lagatjar,** rocky monoliths believed to have been sun-worshipping sites from 2500 BC. Behind them, the ruins of **Château de St-Pol Roux** afford a magnificent view of the bay. A path winds to the **Pointe de Penhir,** 3½km away on D8. A view of the isolated rock clusters of the **Tas de Pois** rewards those who climb to the edge. On the other side of town, D355 leads to another dramatic promontory, the **Pointe des Espagnols.** The **tourist office** will be on your left on the main road into the port. (☎02 98 27 93 60, fax 02 98 27 87 22. Open July-Aug. M-Sa 9:15am-7pm, Su 10am-7pm; Sept.-June M-Sa 9:30am-noon and 2-6pm.) The friendly **Hôtel Vauban,** 4 quai du Styvel, has comfortable rooms. (☎02 98 27 91 36. Singles and doubles 160-250F.) Camaret is also the home of **Camping Municipal du Lannic,** a huge expanse of campgrounds with immaculate grass and facilities. (12.15F; tents 11.10F.)

From Crozon, **Morgat** is a 3km walk down a steep hill. Take a left onto rue St-Yves, a right on rue Alsace Lorraine, and another left on bd. de la France Libre. You'll pass splendid beaches as you walk from Crozon into the tiny *centre ville.* Along this path is the **tourist office** on the right. (☎02 98 27 29 49. Open June-Sept. Tu-Sa 10am-noon and 3-6pm.) Morgat is also home to the only public computer on the peninsula, at **Au Relais de Pecheur,** bd. de la Plage (☎02 98 27 04 02. Open daily 10am-midnight. 10F for the first 3 min, then 1F per min.) Ask at the tourist office about **tours** of Morgat's famous **marine caves** (45min., 30-45F; May-Sept.). **Camping du Bouis** is 1.5km on the way to the Cap. (☎02 98 26 12 53. Showers 5F. Reception July-Aug. 8am-noon and 2-10pm. 1 person 35F, 2 people 68F; 15F per additional person.)

NANTES

Nantes's (pop. 500,000) ideal location, year-round festivals, and vibrant nightlife make for a smart stop. In the fortified **Château des Ducs de Bretagne,** Henri IV composed the **Edict of Nantes** (see p. 274), granting considerable religious liberties to the Huguenots in 1598. Although all of the castle's museums are closed until 2008 for renovations, the **Musée du Château des Ducs de Bretagne** hosts temporary exhibits. (☎ 02 40 41 56 56. Courtyard open for free visits daily July-Aug. 10am-7pm; Sept.-June 10am-noon and 2-6pm. Museum 10F.) Go inside the **Cathédrale St-Pierre** to gape at Gothic vaults which tower 38m and the largest stained-glass window in the country. (Open daily 8:45am-7pm.) On the opposite side of town lies the **Musée Jules Verne,** 3 rue de L'Hermiage, a small museum that unloads tons of information about the fascinating *Nantais* author and scientist. (☎ 02 40 69 72 52. Open M and W-Sa 10am-noon and 2-5pm, Su 2-5pm. 8F, students 4F, Su free.) **La Cigale,** 4 pl. Graslin, is one of the most beautiful *brasseries* in France, with *art nouveau* mosaics, gold detail, and huge mirrors. Snacks are available all day for under 50F. (☎ 02 51 84 94 94. Open daily 7:30am-12:30am.)

Trains (☎ 08 36 35 35 35) run from 27 bd. de Stalingrad to Paris (2-4hr., 20 per day, 222-360F); Bordeaux (4hr., 6-8 per day, 226F); La Rochelle (2hr., 8-11 per day, 125F); Rennes (2hr., 3-10 per day, 117F); and Saumur (1¼hr., 7 per day, 98F). The **tourist office** is on pl. du Commerce in the FNAC building. (☎ 02 40 20 60 00; fax 02 40 89 11 99; www.reception.com/Nantes. Open M-Sa 10am-7pm.) Check your **email** at **Welcome Services Copy,** 70 rue Maréchal Joffre. (☎ 02 51 81 96 25. 35F per hr. Open M 2:30-7pm, Tu-F 9am-12:30pm and 2-7pm, Sa 9:30am-12:30pm and 2:30-7pm.) To get from the tourist office to the 200-bed **Foyer des Jeunes Travailleurs, Beaulieu (HI),** 9 bd. Vincent Gâche, take bus #24 (dir.: Beaulieu) to Albert. (☎ 02 40 12 24 00. Breakfast 12F. Sheets 16F. Reception 8am-midnight. 60F, nonmembers 130F.) The **Hôtel St-Daniel,** 4 rue du Bouffay, is just off pl. du Bouffay. (☎ 02 40 47 41 25. Breakfast 25F. Singles 150F; doubles 170-220F.) The biggest **market** in Nantes is at the **Marché de Talensac,** along rue de Bel-Air behind the post office. (Open Tu-Sa 9am-1pm.) **Monoprix supermarket** is at 2 rue de Calvaire, off cours de 50 Otages. (Open M-Sa 9am-9pm.) **Quartier St-Croix,** near pl. Bouffay, is the center for the funky, with inexpensive restaurants and casual bars. **Postal Code:** 44000.

LOIRE VALLEY (VAL DE LOIRE)

Between Paris and Brittany is the fertile valley of the Loire, France's longest and most celebrated river. The valley overflows with chateaux, which range from dilapidated medieval fortresses to elegant Renaissance homes. Most were built in the 16th and 17th centuries, when French monarchs left Paris for the countryside around Tours to mix business with pleasure.

▛ TRANSPORTATION

Tours is the region's best rail hub, although the chateaux Sully-sur-Loire, Chambord, and Cheverny aren't accessible by train. Infrequent public transit from larger cities can strand travelers. Train stations distribute the invaluable *Les Châteaux de la Loire en Train Eté* and *Châteaux pour Train et Vélo* with train schedules and bike and car rental info, which are the best ways to experience the region.

ORLÉANS

Orléans (pop. 200,000), with its fairy-tale castle, expansive vineyards, and rich forests, has been besieged by jealous foreigners for millennia—today, its prominence is gradually waning as nearby Tours steals the show. Come to for a better acquainted with Joan of Arc or to explore the *chateaux.* The stained-glass windows of the stunning **Cathédrale Ste-Croix,** in pl. Ste-Croix, depict Joan's dramatic story. (Open daily 9:15am-noon and 2:15-7pm; Oct.-Apr. closes 5pm. Free.) The **Musée des Beaux-Arts,** on rue Ferdinand Rabier 1, has a fine collection of Italian, Flemish, Dutch, and French works spanning the last five centuries. (☎ 02 38 79 22

30. Open Th-Sa 10am-6pm; Tu and Su 11am-6pm; W 10am-8pm. 20F, students 10F.)
The **Maison de Jeanne d'Arc,** 3 pl. de Gaulle, off pl. du Martroi, celebrates the life and
times of the town's favorite liberator. (☎ 02 38 79 21 83. Open Tu-Su 10am-noon and
2-6pm; Nov.-Apr. Tu-Su 2-6pm. 15F, students 7F.) A pleasant daytrip down the Loire
lies the region's second-oldest castle, the imposing 14th-century fortress **Sully-sur-
Loire,** accessible by bus from the bus station (1hr., 3 per day, 57F).

   Trains arrive at the Gare d' from: Paris (1¼hr., 3 per hr., 92F); Blois (30min., 12 per
day, 53-89F); and Tours (1hr., 12 per day, 178F). To get to the **tourist office,** 6 pl.
Albert 1er, from the station, ascend into the mall, turn right, and it's on the left as
you exit the mall. (☎ 02 38 24 05 05; fax 02 38 65 43 43; www.tourismloiret.com.
Open July-Aug. M-Sa 9am-7pm, Su 9:30am-12:30pm and 3-6:30pm; Apr.-June and
Sept. M-Sa 9am-7pm, Su 10am-noon; Oct.-Mar. M-Sa 9am-6:30pm, Su 10am-noon.)
To get to the **auberge de jeunesse (HI),** 1 bd. de la Motte, take bus RS (dir.: Rosette)
or SY (dir.: Concyr/La Bolière) from pl. d'Arc to Pont Bourgogne; head straight
down bd. de la Motte and it's on the right at the end. (☎ 02 38 53 60 03. 2- to 4-person
rooms 100F, under 26 70F.) For **groceries,** head to **Carrefour,** at the back of the mall
at pl. d'Arc. (Open M-Sa 8:30am-9pm.) **Postal Code:** 45000.

BLOIS

Blois (pop. 60,000) welcomes visitors to the Loire Valley with pastoral charm.
Home to monarchs Louis XII and François I, Blois' **chateau** was the Versailles of
the late 15th and early 16th centuries; today it is decorated with painted and
carved salamanders (the symbol of François I), and displays the progression of
French architecture from 13th to the 17th-century. Housed in the castle are excellent museums: the recently renovated **Musée de Beaux-Arts,** with a 16th-century
portrait gallery in the former apartments of Louis XII, the **Musée d'Archéologie,**
showcasing locally excavated glass and ceramics, and the **Musée Lapidaire,** preserving sculpted pieces from nearby chateaux. (☎ 02 54 78 06 62. Open daily July-
Aug. 9am-8pm; Mar. 15-June 30 and Sept. 9am-6:30pm; Oct. 1-Mar. 14 9am-
12:30pm and 2-5:30pm. 35F, students 20F.) At night, move from the cafes of **pl. de
la Résistance** to **Z 64,** 6 rue Maréchal de Tassigny, for cocktails, dancing, and
karaoke (open T-Su 8:30am-4am).

   Trains run from the pl. de la Gare to: Paris (1¾hr., 8 per day, 123F); (30min., 14
per day, 53F); and Tours (1hr., 10 per day, 53F); but not to most chateaux. **Point Bus,**
2 pl. Victor Hugo (☎ 02 54 78 15 66), sends buses to Chambord and Cheverny (May
15-Aug. 31. 65F, students 50F) and other *chateaux.* Or rent a **bike** from **Atelier
Cycles,** 44 Levée des Tuileries (☎ 02 54 74 30 13), and pedal for an hour to travel
down the valley. The **tourist office,** 3 av. Jean Laigret, can point the way. (☎ 02 54 90
41 41; www.loiredeschateaux.com. Open Apr. 15-Oct. 15 T-Sa 9am-7pm, Su-M and
holidays 10am-7pm; Oct. 16-Apr. 14 T-Sa 9am-12:30pm and 2-6pm, M from 10am Su
9:30am-12:30pm.) Five kilometers west is the **auberge de jeunesse (HI),** 18 rue de
l'Hôtel Pasquier. To get there from the tourist office, follow rue Porte Côté and then
rue Denis Papin to the river, and take bus #4 (dir.: Les Grouets) to the end. (☎ 02 54
78 27 21. Reception 6:45-10am and 6-10:30pm. Lockout 10am-6pm. Curfew 10:30pm.
Open Mar.-Nov. 15. Bunks 41F.) **Le Pavillon,** 2 av. Wilson, has clean, bright rooms.
(☎ 02 54 74 23 27. Breakfast 35F. Singles 110-130F; doubles 220-260F.) Sumptuous
pavé du roi (chocolate-almond cookies) and *malices du loup* (orange peels in
chocolate) entice from **rue Denis Papin. Postal Code:** 41000.

■ DAYTRIPS FROM BLOIS: CHAMBORD AND CHEVERNY. Built to satisfy
François I's egomania, **Chambord** is the largest and most extravagant of the Loire
chateau. Seven hundred of François I's trademark stone salamanders are
stamped throughout this "hunting lodge;" 440 rooms with 365 fireplaces that kept
the king and his hounds warm. A double-helix staircase dominates the center of
the castle. (☎ 02 54 50 40 00. Open daily July-Aug. 9am-6:45pm; Apr.-June and
Sept. 9:30am-6:15pm; Oct.-Mar. 9:30am-5:15pm. 42F, under 26 26F.) Take TLC **bus
#2** from Blois (45min., 20F); hop on the TLC **Chambord-Cheverny bus circuit** (65F,

students 50F, to both chateaux plus reduced admission); or **bike** from Blois (1hr.; take D956 south 2-3km, then go left on D33).

Cheverny soothes with manicured grounds and a magnificent interior: Spanish leather walls, delicate Delft vases, an action-packed Gobelin tapestry, and an elaborate royal bedchamber. Fans of Hergé's *Tintin* books may recognize Cheverny's Renaissance facade as the inspiration for the design of *Moulinsart* (Marlinspike), Captain Haddock's mansion (see p. 128). The **kennels** hold 24 mixed English Poitevin hounds who stalk stags in hunting expeditions (Oct.-Mar. Tu and Sa). The **soupe des chiens** is not a dubious regional dish but a bizarre opportunity to see these hounds gulp down bins of ground meat in less than 60 seconds. (☎ 02 54 79 96 29. Open daily June-Sept. 15 9:15am-6:45pm; off-season reduced hrs. *Soupe des chiens* Apr.-Aug. M-Sa 5pm; Sept.-Mar. M and W-F 3pm. 38F, students 27F.) Cheverny is accessible by bus (see above) or bike from Blois (take D956 south for 45min.).

AMBOISE

The battlements of the 15th-century **chateau** at Amboise (pop. 11,000), which six French kings called home, stretch protectively across the hill above Amboise. In the **Logis de Roi,** the main part of the chateau, intricately carved 16th-century Gothic chairs stand over 6 ft. high to prevent surprise attacks from behind. Today, the jewel of the grounds is the late 15th-century **Chapelle St-Hubert;** a plaque inside marks **Leonardo da Vinci's** final resting place. (Open July-Aug. daily 9am-7:30pm; Apr.-June 9am-6:30pm; Mar. 14-31 and Sept.-Oct. 9am-6pm; Feb.-Mar. 13 and Nov. 9am-noon and 2-5:30pm; Dec.-Jan. 9am-noon and 2-5pm. 40F, students 33F.) After being invited to France by François I, da Vinci spent his last four years at **Clos Lucé** manor. A collection of his inventions, built with the materials that would have been available to him, is one of the main attractions. (☎ 02 47 57 62 88. Open daily July-Aug. 9am-8pm, Apr.-June and Sept.-Oct. 9am-7pm; Nov.-Mar. 9am-6pm; Jan. 10am-5pm. 38F, students 29F.) **Trains** run to: Paris (2¼hr., 5 per day, 140F); Blois (20min., 15 per day, 34F); and Tours (20min., 14 per day, 28F). The **Centre International de Séjour (HI) Charles Péguy,** on Ile d'Or, sits on an island in the middle of the Loire. (☎ 02 47 57 06 36. Sheets 18F. Reception M-F 3-8pm. Dorms 53F.) **Postal Code:** 35400.

TOURS

Tours (pop. 250,000) is the urban centerpiece of the Loire region, and boasts fabulous nightlife, a diverse population, great food, and historical sights. Celebrated for its impressive clarity, the **Cathédrale St-Gatien,** on rue Jules Simon, has dazzling stained glass and a flamboyant Gothic cloister. (☎ 02 47 05 05 54. Cathedral open daily 9am-7pm; free. Cloister open daily Easter-Sept. 9:30am-12:30pm and 2-6pm; Oct.-Easter 9:30am-12:30pm and 2-5pm; 15F.) At the **Musée du Gemmail,** 7 rue du Murier, *gemmail*-works (in which shards of brightly colored glass and enamel are fused) by Picasso and Braque glow in rooms of dark velvet. (☎ 02 47 61 01 19. Open Easter-Oct. Tu-Su 10am-noon and 2-6:30pm; Nov. 15-Easter Tu-F 10am-noon and 2-6:30pm, Sa-Su 10am-noon and 2-6:30pm. 30F, students 20F.) From pl. Plumereau, walk along rue du Commerce and turn left on rue National to get to the **Musée de Campagnonnage,** 8 rue Nationale, which will bring you through the past-times and amusements of centuries past. (☎ 02 47 61 07 93. Open mid-June to Sept. daily 9am-6pm; Oct.-Feb. W-M 9am-noon and 2-5pm; Mar. to mid-June W-M 9am-noon and 2-6pm. 25F, students 16F, under 12 free.) Three clubs on the *place* are stacked one above the other. The **Le Pharoan** keeps sweaty kids partying to loud rock, cover-free, while an older crowd parties upstairs at **Louis XIV;** progress upward to chill in the jazzy **Duke Ellington.** (All 3 open daily until 2am; only Louis XIV open July-Aug.)

Trains leave from 3 rue Edouard Vaillant, pl du Maréchal Leclerc, for: Paris-Montparnasse (1-2¼hr., 13 per day, 160-261F); Bordeaux (2½hr., 6 per day, 226F); and Poitiers (45min., 7 per day, 87F). The **tourist office,** 78-82 rue Bernard Palissy, books rooms and leads a historical tour. (☎ 02 47 70 37 37; fax 02 47 61 14 22; www.ligeris.com. Open mid-Apr. to mid-Oct. M-Sa 8:30am-6pm, Su 10am-12:30 and 2:30-5pm; mid-Oct. to mid-Apr. M-Sa 9:30am-12:30pm and 1:30-6pm, Su 9:30am-12:30pm.) **Email** your friends and lovers from the **Cyber Gate**, 11 rue de Président Merville. (☎02 47 05 95 94. Open M 3-9pm, Tu-Sa 11am-9pm, Su 2-9pm. 10F per 30min.) **Hotel Foch**, 20 rue du Maréchal Foch, has 15 rooms in a marvelous location with a friendly proprietor. (☎02 47 05 70 59. Singles 130-220F; doubles 150-300F; triples 240-380F; quads 330-380F.) **Hotel Regina,** 2 rue Pimbert, is near the happening rue Colbert. (☎02 47 05 25 36. Breakfast 26F. Singles 110-175F; doubles 140-240F.) Stretch out in the spacious rooms of the **Foyer des Jeunes Travailleurs,** 24 rue Bernard Palissy. (☎02 47 60 51 51. Singles with bath 100F, doubles 160F.) The diversity around **Pl. Plumereau** will knock your socks off, with dozens of great restaurants, cafes, and bars offering menus around 70F. Fight to snag a table at the **Taverne de l'Homme Tranquille,** 22 rue du Grand Marché. (☎02 47 61 46 04. Open daily noon-2pm and 7-10:30pm.) Off the beaten tourist path, but part of the everyday French experience, is the **Café Flunch,** 14 pl. Jean Jaurès, which serves up good-value meats, salads, and desserts. (☎02 47 64 56 70. Open daily 7am-10pm.) **Postal Code:** 37000.

DAYTRIPS FROM TOURS

CHENONCEAU

Trains from Tours roll into the station 2km away from the castle (45min., 3 per day, 36F). Fil Vert buses also connect Tours with Chenonceau (25min., 2 per day, 25F).

Perhaps the most exquisite chateau in France, Chenonceau arches gracefully over the Cher river. A series of women created the beauty that is the chateau: first Catherine, the wife of a royal tax collector; then Diane de Poitiers, the lover of Henri II; and then his widowed wife, Catherine de Médici. The part of the chateau bridging the Cher also marked the border between annexed and Vichy France during WWII. Chenonceau's beautiful setting makes it the most touristed of all the Loire chateaux. (☎02 47 23 90 07. Open Mar. 16-Sept. 15 daily 9am-7pm; call for off-season hrs. 50F, students 40F.)

LOCHES

Buses run from the Tours train station to Loches (50min., 4 per day, 47F; pay on board); nine trains also make the trip (1hr., 47F).

Located in a citadel and a walled medieval town, the chateau of **Loches** consists of two distinct structures at opposite ends of a hill. To the south, the 11th-century **donjon** (keep) and watchtowers went from keeping enemies out to putting them up when Charles VII turned it into a state prison, complete with suspended cages. To the north, the **Logis Royal** housed French kings from the 12th to 15th centuries. (Open daily July-Sept. 15 9am-7pm; Mar.15-June and Sept. 16-30 9:30am-1pm and 2:30-7pm; Feb.-Mar.14 and Oct. 9:30am-1pm and 2:30-6pm. Logis Royal or Donjon 24F, students 17F, for both 32F, students 22F.)

SAUMUR

Saumur (pop. 35,000) is a delight to the senses—its wines and *champignons* (mushrooms) will tickle your taste buds as its enchanting old quarter captivates your eyes. The 14th-century **chateau** is best known for its cameo appearance in the famous medieval manuscript *Les très riches heures du duc de Berry;* it looms over the city and contains the **Musée des Arts Décoratifs,** with plentiful porcelain, and the **Musée du Cheval's** gear-and-tackle collection. (Open daily June-Sept. 9:30am-6pm and 8:30-10:30pm; Oct.-May M and W-Su 9:30am-noon and 2-5:30pm, closed Tu Oct.-Mar. 38F, students 27F; gardens only 17F.) **Gratien et Meyer,** on rte. de Chinon, gives tours of its wine *cave* and offers tastings. Take bus D from pl. Bilange to Beaulieu. (☎02 41 83 13 32. Open Apr.-Sept. daily 9am-6:30pm; Oct.-Mar. M-F 9am-noon and 2-6pm, Sa-Su 10am-12:30pm and 3-6pm. 15F; 1-hour *dégustation* 50F.) The **Musée de Champignon,** on rte. de Gennes, in St-Hilaire-St-Florent, is a mushroom *cave* that offers grilled hors d'oeuvres outside the exhibit. (☎02 41 50 31 55. Open Feb. 15-Nov. 15 daily 10am-7pm. 38F, students 30F.)

Trains run frequently from the station at av. David d'Angers to Paris (1¾hr., 8 per day, 238F); Angers (30min., 23 per day, 43F); and Tours (45min., 21 per day, 56F). The **tourist office,** on pl. Bilange, just off the pont Cessart (bridge), books beds (5F fee). Exit to the right of the station on av. David d'Angers, turn right onto pont des Cadets, continue straight on av. de Général de Gaulle, and it's on your left (15min.). Bus #A will also go all the way there from the train station. (☎ 02 41 40 20 60; fax 02 41 40 20 69. Open July-Aug M-Sa 9:15am-7pm, Su 10:30am-5:30pm; mid-May to mid-Oct. M-Sa 9:15am-12:30pm and 2-6pm, Su 10:30am-5:30pm; mid-Oct.-mid-May M-Sa 9:15am-12:30pm and 2-6pm, Su 10am-noon.) The modern **Centre International de Séjour,** is on bd. Verden, on Ile d'Offard. From the station, follow the directions above to pont des Cadets, and turn left after crossing the bridge. (☎ 02 41 40 30 00. Reception 8am-8pm, in summer until 9pm. 2- to 8-bed dorms 85F.) Stock up on fungi at the indoor **market** at the end of pl. St-Pierre (daily until 1pm), or more mass-produced goods at **Atac supermarket,** 6 rue Franklin D. Roosevelt, inside a shopping center. (Open M-Th 9am-7:30pm, F until 8pm, Sa until 7pm.) **Postal Code:** 49400.

⚑ DAYTRIP FROM SAUMUR: FONTEVRAUD ABBEY. Fourteen kilometers east of Saumur lies the **Abbaye de Fontevraud,** the largest existing monastic complex in Europe. The 12th-century abbey church serves as a Plantagenêt necropolis; **Eleanor of Aquitaine,** who lived out her days here after being repudiated by her second husband, **Henry II** of England, now lies next to him along with their son **Richard the Lionheart.** (☎ 02 41 51 71 41. Open daily June-Sept. 17 9am-6:30pm, Sept. 18-Oct. 9:30am-noon and 2-5:30pm; Nov.-Mar. 7 9:30am-noon and 2-5pm or dusk; Mar. 8-May 31 9:30am-noon and 2-6pm. 32F, students 21F.) **Bus** #16 makes from Saumur's train station (25min., 3 per day, 14F). The **tourist office** (☎ 02 41 51 79 45), also houses the 12th-century Gothic **Eglise St-Michel.** From the front of the Abbaye, cross the square and head towards the church. Turn right up the path behind the church and the office will be on your right. (Open April-Oct. 15 10am-noon and 2:30-6:30pm.)

ANGERS

From behind the massive stone walls of the 15th-century **Château d'Angers,** on pl. Kennedy, the Dukes of Anjou ruled the surrounding countryside and an island across the Channel (known today as Britain). The 13th-century chateau remains beautifully preserved, a haven of medieval charm in a city now dominated by students and a vibrant pedestrian sector. The 14th-century **Tapisserie de l'Apocalypse** within, the world's largest tapestry masterpiece, was commissioned by Duke Louis I, who was inspired by an illuminated manuscript of the Book of Revelations. (Open daily June-Sept. 15 9:30am-7pm; Sept. 16-Oct. 31 10am-6pm; Nov.-Mar. 15 10am-5pm; Mar. 16-May 10am-6pm. 35F, students 23F.) Angers' other woven masterpiece, the **Chant du Monde** ("Song of the World"), in the **Musée Jean Lurçat,** 4 bd. Arago, depicts a journey through human destiny. (Open mid-June to mid-Sept. daily 9am-6:30pm; mid-Sept. to mid-June Tu-Su 10am-noon and 2-6pm. 20F.)

From rue de la Gare, **trains** roll out to: Paris-Austerlitz station (4hr., 3per day, 242F); Nantes (1hr., 5 per day, 77F); (3-4hr., 6 per day, 166F). **Buses** run to Rennes (3hr., 2 per day, 97F); and Tours (1hr., 7 per day, 84F). To get from the station to the **tourist office,** on pl. Kennedy, exit straight onto rue de la Gare, turn right at pl. de la Visitation, turn left on bd. du Roi-René, and continue until you hit the plaza. (☎ 02 41 23 51 11; fax 02 41 23 51 66. Open June-Sept. M-Sa 9am-7pm, Su 10am-6pm; July-Aug. M 10am-7pm; Oct.-May M-Sa 9am-12:30pm and 2-6:30pm.) Access the **internet** at **Cyber Espace,** 25 rue de la Roe. (☎ 02 41 24 92 71. 15F per 30min. Open M-F 9:30am-7:30pm.) To get to the **Centre d'Accueil du Lac de Maine (HI),** 49 av. du Maine, take bus #6 or 16 to Accueil Lac de Maine, turn and cross the busy road that the bus just passed, and follow the signs. (☎ 02 41 22 32 10. Breakfast included. HI members only. Doubles 198F; quads 336F.) The family-run **Royal Hôtel,** on rue d'Iéna, off pl. de la Visitation, has spacious rooms. (☎ 02 41 88 30 25. Breakfast 28-32F. Singles 110-210F; doubles 150-250F.) Grab **groceries** in **Galeries Lafayette,** at the corner of rue d'Alsace and pl. du Ralliement. (Open M-Sa 9am-7pm.) **Postal Code:** 49052.

POITOU-CHARENTES

Little-known outside France, Poitou-Charentes has sun-drenched beaches, sedate canals, craggy cliffs, fertile plains, and a rich history. The Côte d'Azur may be tops in topless beaches, and the Loire Valley may be the king of chateaux but no other region of France has so impressive a collection of both. Poitou-Charentes is a brilliant collage of natural sights and coastal towns on the shore of France.

LA ROCHELLE

As one of France's best-sheltered seaports, La Rochelle (pop. 100,000) has always been important; France and England fought over it during the Hundred Years' War, and Richelieu was so upset with the city's support of England during that country's invasion of the Ile de Ré that he had the town besieged for fifteen months, during which time three quarters of its citizens starved. La Rochelle didn't really recover until the 20th century—it was Protestant, and had frequent trouble with Paris—but is now one of France's main vacation towns with beautiful beaches, refined 14th-century architecture, and popular festivals. Climb around the fortifications of **Tour St-Nicolas** and **Tour de la Chaîne**, to the left as you face the harbor. (St-Nicolas ☎ 05 46 41 74 13. Chaîne ☎ 06 46 34 11 81. Open Apr.-Sept. daily 10am-7pm; Oct.-Mar. 10am-12:30pm and 2-5:30pm. 25F, ages 18-25 15F, under 18 free.)

Trains leave from Bd. Maréchal Joffre and go to: Paris (5hr., 1 per day, 260F; 5 TGVs per day, 3hr., 320F); Bordeaux (2hr., 5 per day, 134F); Nantes (2hr., 5 per day, 125F); and Poitiers (2hr., 8 per day, 108F). The **tourist office**, on pl. de la Petite Sirène, is in the quartier du Gabut. (☎ 05 46 41 14 68; fax 05 46 41 99 85; www.VillelaRochelle.fr. Open July-Aug. M-Sa 9am-8pm, Su 11am-5pm; May-June and Sept. M-Sa 9am-7pm, Su 11am-5pm; Oct.-Apr. M-Sa 9am-noon and 2-6pm, Su 10am-noon.) Use the **internet** at **Cyber Squat**, 63 rue St-Nicolas. (☎ 05 46 34 53 67. Open M-Sa 11am-midnight. 25F per 30min.) Take bus #10 (dir.: Port des Minimes) from av. de Colmar, one block from the train station to Auberge de Jeunesse or to the **Centre international de Séjour (HI)**, on av. des Minimes. (☎ 05 46 44 43 11. Breakfast included. Lockout 10am-2pm. Reception July-Aug. 8:30am-11pm; Sept.-June 8am-12:30pm, 1:30-7:30pm and 8:30-10:30pm. Dorms 75F; singles 110F.) **Postal Code:** 17000.

POITIERS

Poitiers's (pop. 120,000) churches are a stunning reminder of Christianity's lasting influence in the region. Facades in the 12th-century Romanesque **Notre-Dame-la-Grande,** on pl. de Gaulle, off Grand Rue, display the story of Christianity, while the massive **Cathédrale St-Pierre,** in pl. de la Cathédrale, off rue de la Cathédrale, still boasts some of its original 12th-century stained-glass windows. Nearby is the 4th-century **Baptistère St-Jean,** on rue Jean Jaurès, the oldest Christian edifice in France. (Open July-Aug. daily 10am-12:30pm and 2-7pm; Apr.-June and Sept.-Nov. W-M 10:30am-12:30pm and 3-6pm; Dec.-Mar. W-M 2:30-4:30pm. 4F.)

Trains run from the station at bd. du Grand Cerf to: Paris (2½hr., 6 per day, 260-320F); Bordeaux (2hr., 8 per day, 172F); La Rochelle (1¾hr., 8 per day, 118F); and Tours (1hr., 5 per day, 92F). To get from the station to the **tourist office,** 45 place Charles de Gaulle. (☎ 05 49 41 21 24; fax 05 49 88 65 84. Open June 21-Sept. 20 M-Sa 9am-11pm, Su 10am-6pm and 7:30-11pm; Sept. 21-June 20 M-Sa 9am-noon and 1:30-6pm.) For the **auberge de jeunesse (HI)**, 1 allée Tagault, catch bus #3 (dir.: Pierre Loti) from the traffic light in front of the station to Cap Sud. (☎ 05 49 58 03 05. Breakfast 19F. Reception M-Sa 8-10am, noon-2pm, and 6pm-midnight; Su 8-10am and 7-midnight. HI members only. Dorms with bath 51F.) **Postal Code:** 86000.

ANGOULÊME

Angoulême (pop. 46,000) is now the capital of French comic strips. In the **CNBDI (Centre national de la bande dessinée et de l'image),** 121 rue de Bordeaux, the **Musée de la Bande Dessinée** explores the history of comics. (☎ 05 45 38 65 65. Open July-Aug. M-F 10am-7pm, Sa-Su 2-7pm; Sept.-June Tu-F 10am-6pm, Sa-Su 2-6pm. 30F, students 20F.) The lack of internal columns in **Cathédrale St-Pierre,** in pl. St-Pierre,

permits an unbroken view of the interior. (☎ 05 45 95 20 38. Open daily 9am-7pm.)
Amble by the waterfalls and baby goats of **Jardin Vert** and climb the town's **ramparts**
for spectacular views. **Trains** run from Pl. de la Gare to: Paris (2¾hr., 7 per day, 310-
399F); Bordeaux (1hr., 8-10 per day, 109F); and Poitiers (1hr., 5 per day, 91F). To
get from the station to the **tourist office**, 7bis rue du Chat, follow av. Gambetta uphill
to pl. G. Perrot, continue up the rampe d'Aguesseau, turn right on bd. Pasteur. (☎ 05
45 95 16 84; fax 05 45 95 91 76. Open July-Aug. M-Sa 9:30am-7pm, Su 10am-noon and
2-5pm; Sept.-June reduced hrs.) Check **email** at **Café Arobase,** 121 rue de Bordeaux.
(☎ 05 45 38 65 65. 10F per hr. Open July-Aug. M-F 10am-3pm, Sa-Su 2-6pm; Sept.-
June M-F 10am-6pm, Sa-Su 2-6pm.) To get to the **auberge de jeunesse (HI)**, on Ile de
Bourgines, turn left from the station onto av. de Lattre de Tassigny, left again on bd.
du 8 Mai 1945, left yet again on bd. Besson Bey, and cross the bridge. (☎ 05 45 92 45
80. Breakfast 19F. Sheets 17F. 2- to 6-bed dorms 51F.) Stock up at **Stoc Supermarket,**
19 rue Périgueux. (Open M-Sa 8:30am-7:15pm, Su 9am-noon.) **Postal Code:** 16000.

SOUTHWEST FRANCE

Caught between the wild Atlantic surf and the calm brilliance of
the Mediterranean, southwestern France holds a hand full of
aces beneath its demure poker face. Gastronomes will delight in
the wines of Bordeaux and the delicacies of Gascony, paleontologists will rejoice in
the prehistoric surplus of Perigord, hikers will thrill to the vistas of the Pyrénées,
and heat-seekers will find sun throughout the vast expanses of sand and surf on
both coasts. The most geographically diverse of France's four corners, the Southwest is equally diverse culturally, with Basques in the west and Catalans in the east
proudly guarding their ancient traditions.

PERIGORD AND AQUITAINE

The images presented by Périgord and Aquitaine are seductive: green countryside
splashed with yellow sunflowers, white chalk cliffs, golden white wine, plates of
black truffles, and the smell of warm walnuts. First settled 150,000 years ago, the
area around Les Eyzies-de-Tayac has turned up more stone-age artifacts—tools,
bones, weapons, cave paintings, and etchings—than any other place on earth.

PÉRIGUEUX

The **Cathédrale St-Front** dominates Périgueux from above the Isle river (pop. 37,700)
with its five massive Byzantine cupolas and towering steeple. Encircled by the
river, Périgueux arose from the 13th-century union of two rival towns: the abbey-
centered Cité de Puy-St-Font and the Gallo-Roman Vésone. The *vieille ville* sports
Renaissance architecture, and the multi-domed **Cathédrale St-Front** combines the
styles of several eras. Nearly 1500 years of construction, restoration, rethinking and
revision have produced an ungainly edifice, the largest cathedral in southwestern
France. (Open daily 8am-7:30pm.) The **Tour de Vésone** is a remarkable Roman ruin.
In its heyday, it was a *cella*, the holiest place and center of worship of a temple.
Today, what remains is a crumbling stone barrel tube. (Open daily Apr.-Sept.
7:30am-9pm; Oct.-Mar. 7:30am-6:30pm.) **Trains** arrive at rue Denis Papin from: Paris
(4-6hr., 12 per day, 278F); Bordeaux (1½hr., 7 per day, 99F); and Toulouse (4hr., 8
per day) via Brive (184F) or via Agen (177F). The **tourist office,** 26 pl. Francheville,
has free walking tour maps. From the station, turn right on rue Denis Papin, bear
left on rue des Mobiles-de-Coulmiers (which becomes rue du Président Wilson),
pass rue Guillier (which leads to the Roman ruins), take the next right, and it's on
the left. (☎ 05 53 53 10 63; fax 05 53 09 02 70. Open July-Aug. M-Sa 9am-7pm, Su
10am-6pm; Sept.-June M-Sa 9am-6pm.) To reach the **Foyer des Jeunes Travailleurs
Résidence Lakanal,** off bd. Lakanal, from the train station, turn right onto rue Denis
Papin and follow it as it becomes rue Chanzy, turn left onto av. Cavaignac. Walk

past the church, turn right onto rue mile Lafon, and at the *rond point* Ch. Durand, turn left onto bd. Bertrand de Born and walk until you reach bd. Lakanal. (☎ 05 53 06 81 40. Sa-Su closed 3-5pm. Dorms 66F, with breakfast and sheets 73F.) **Monoprix supermarket** is on pl. de la République. (Open M-Sa 8:30am-8pm.) **Postal Code:** 24070.

SARLAT

Even with the dense mobs swarming Sarlat (pop. 10,700) in summer, the town's remarkable *vieille ville* of golden sandstone merits a mosey. Sarlat's movie-set medieval perfection has attracted the gaze of more than a few cameras—scenes from *Cyrano de Bergerac* and *Manon des Sources* were filmed here. Today, its narrow 14th- and 15th-century streets fill with flea markets, dancing violinists, and purveyors of *gâteaux aux noix* (cakes with nuts) and sweet, golden Monbazillac wines. **Trains** leave from av. de la Gare for Bordeaux (2½hr., 4 per day, 119F) and Périgueux (1½hr., 1 per day, 64F). To stop by the **tourist office,** on pl. de la Liberté, follow av. de la Gare downhill to the left and turn right on av. Thiers, which becomes av. Général Leclerc. After crossing the small pl. du 14 juillet, the road becomes rue de la République, the thoroughfare bisecting the *vieille ville.* Bear right on rue Lakanal, and then left onto rue de la Liberté. (☎ 05 53 31 45 45; fax 05 53 59 19 44. Open M-Sa 9am-7pm, Su 10am-noon and 2-6pm.) Sarlat's **Auberge de Jeunesse,** 77 av. de Selves, is 30min. from the train station but only 5-10min. from the *vieille ville.* Go straight along rue de la République (which becomes av. Gambetta), bear left at the fork onto av. de Selves, and it's on your right. (☎ 05 53 59 47 59. Sheets 16F. Open mid-Mar. to Nov. Reserve ahead. 55F first night, 50F subsequent nights. **Camping** 35F.) **Champion supermarket** is near the hostel on rte. de Montignac—continue following av. de Selves away from the *centre ville.* (Open M-Sa 9am-7:30pm, Su 9am-noon.) **Postal Code:** 24200.

▓ DAYTRIPS FROM SARLAT AND PÉRIGUEUX

CAVE PAINTINGS

CFTA (☎ 05 55 86 07 07) runs buses to the caves of Lascaux, near the town of Montignac, from Périgueux (1½hr., 1 per day, 40F). Two buses also run every morning from Sarlat (30min., 1-2 per day, 27F). Les Eyzies-de-Tayac is served by trains from Périgueux (30min., 4 per day, 41F) and Sarlat (1hr., 3 per day via Le Buisson, 47F).

The most spectacular cave paintings ever discovered hide in the **caves of Lascaux,** near the town of **Montignac,** 25km north of Sarlat. Discovered in 1940 by a few teenagers and their dog, the caves were closed in 1963 after it was found that the oohs and aahs of millions of tourists had fostered algae and micro-stalactites, ravaging the paintings. **Lascaux II** duplicates every inch of the original cave, in the same pigments used 17,000 years ago. Although the reproduction may lack ancient awe and mystery, the caves—filled with paintings of five-meter-tall bulls, horses, and bisons—nevertheless manage to inspire a wonder all their own. (Caves open May-Aug. daily 9am-7pm; Apr. and Sept.-Oct. Tu-Su 9am-6pm; Jan. 26-Mar. and Nov.-Jan. 4 Tu-Su 10am-12:30pm and 2-5:30pm. 50F.) The **tourist office** (☎ 05 53 51 82 60), on pl. Bertram-de-Born, sells tickets for Lascaux II.

At the **Grotte de Font-de-Gaume,** 1km outside **Les Eyzies-de-Tayac** on D47, 15,000-year-old horses, bison, reindeer, and woolly mammoths cavort along the cave walls. (☎ 05 53 06 86 00. Open Apr.-Sept. Tu-Th 9am-noon and 2-6pm; Mar. and Oct. 9:30am-noon and 2-5:30pm; Nov.-Feb. 10am-noon and 2-5pm. Call at least two weeks in advance for tickets. 35F, under 26 23F, art students free.) The best resource for information on the prehistoric sites of the area is the **Point Accueil Préhistoire** (☎ 06 86 66 54 43), located across from the post office on the main street through town (D47). The **tourist office** is located at pl. de la Mairie (☎ 05 53 06 97 05; fax 05 53 06 90 79), before the Point Accueil.

THE DORDOGNE VALLEY

To get to and around the valley, you'll need to rent a car or be prepared for a good bike workout—the hills are steep but manageable. You can reach the chateaux by excursion buses leaving Sarlat. Hep! (☎ 05 53 28 10 04), on pl. Pasteur, and CFTA Périgord, 21 rue de Cahors (☎ 05 53 59 01 48), run convenient but expensive buses each day.

Steep, craggy cliffs and poplar tree thickets overlook the slow-moving turquoise waters of the Dordogne River, 15km south of Sarlat. Numerous chateaux keep watch over tourists in canoes, on bikes, and in cars; by avoiding the major towns, it's also possible to find solitude. Ten kilometers southwest of Sarlat, the town of **Castelnaud-La Chapelle** snoozes in the shadow of its pale-yellow-stone chateau, a fortress of the 12th to 15th centuries, and now the most visited castle in Aquitaine. (☎ 05 53 31 30 00. Open July-Aug. daily 9am-8pm; May-June and Sept. daily 10am-6pm; Nov.16-Feb. Su-F 2-5pm. 38F.) **Domme,** the best-defended of the Dordogne Valley's villages, was built by King Philippe III (Philippe the Bold) in 1280 on a high dome of solid rock. In 1307, over 70 Templar Knights were imprisoned by King Philip IV in the **Porte des Tours.** You can see and learn about the graffiti they left scrawled upon the walls with their bare hands, fingernails and teeth, in 1-hour tours offered by the tourist office (1 tour per day; 25F, children 18F). *Chambres d'hôte* provide cheap, farmhouse accommodations near the historic sites throughout the valley; ask at any tourist office for lists of *hôtes* and campgrounds.

BORDEAUX

Wrapped in emerald vineyards, Bordeaux (pop. 700,000) toasts the deep, violet wine that made it famous. A temple to wine connoisseurs, the city itself is also a trove of not-so-hidden delights. The local government does its best to keep Bordeaux's mansions and Gothic cathedrals scrubbed clean; today, the town hosts spirited nightclubs, art galleries, concerts, and some of the best food in France.

▐ TRANSPORTATION. Trains leave from the Gare St-Jean, rue Charles Domercq (☎ 05 56 33 11 83), to: Paris (3-4 hrs., 15-25 per day, 345F); Nice (9-10hrs., 5 per day, 428F); and Toulouse (2-3hrs., 11 per day, 165F).

▐ PRACTICAL INFORMATION. From the train station, take **bus** #7 or 8 (dir.: Grand Théâtre) to pl. Gambetta and walk toward the Monument des Girondins to the **tourist office,** 12 cours du 30 Juillet, which arranges winery tours (see below). (☎ 05 56 00 66 00; fax 05 56 00 66 01; www.bordeaux-tourisme.com. Open May-Sept. M-Sa 9am-8pm, Su 9am-7pm; Oct.-Apr. M-Sa 9am-7pm, Su 9:45am-6pm.) The best deal for **internet** access is at **A.E.C.,** in the Cité Mondiale near the river off the Quai des Chartrons. (☎ 05 56 01 76 76. Open M-Th 2-6pm, F 2-5pm. Free, but limited to 1 hr. per person per day.) **Postal Code:** 33065.

▐▐ ACCOMMODATIONS AND FOOD. Smack in the center of old Bordeaux is the comfortable (and air-conditioned) **Hôtel Clemenceau,** 4 cours G. Clemenceau. (☎ 05 56 52 98 98. Singles 230F, doubles 250F; Friday and Saturday 170F and 200F.) The clean, airy **Hôtel la Boétie,** 4 rue de la Boétie, between pl. Gambetta and the Musée des Beaux-Arts, has rooms with showers, toilets, TVs, and phones. (☎ 05 56 81 76 68. Breakfast 20F. Singles 120F; doubles 135F.) For the **Hôtel Boulan,** 22 rue Boulan, take bus #7 or 8 from the station to the pl. Gambetta; follow rue Bouffard out of the pl., turn right onto rue Boulan. (☎ 05 56 52 23 62. Breakfast 20F. Singles 101F, with shower 121F; doubles 112F, 142F.) **Hôtel Studio,** 26 rue Huguerie, has brightly colored rooms and all rooms have TV and full bath. (☎ 05 56 8176 78. Singles 120F; doubles 135F.) Pitch a tent at **Camping les Gravières,** 35 av. Mirieu de Labarre in Villeneuve d'Ornon. (☎ 05 56 87 00 36. Reception 8am-12:30pm and 6-8pm. 19F per person, 22F tent, 30F tent and car.)

Living in the *région de bien manger et de bien vivre* (region of fine eating and living), *Bordelais* take their food as seriously as their wine. Hunt around **rue St-Remi** and **pl. St-Pierre** for splendid regional specialties, including oysters, *foie gras,* beef braised in wine sauce, and *canelé de Bordeaux* (a cake created in 1519). Descend into the cool cellar of **Baud et Millet,** 19 rue Huguerie, off pl. Tourny, where 105F buys all the cheese you can eat. (☎ 05 56 79 05 77. Open M-Sa 9am-midnight.) Stock up at **Auchan supermarket,** at the Centre Meriadeck on rue Claude Bonnier. (☎ 05 56 99 59 00. Open M-Sa 8:30am-10pm.)

FRANCE

■ **SIGHTS AND ENTERTAINMENT.** The best way to see the sights of Bordeaux is to work your way into the center of town from the tourist office before heading down to the river. Start with the central monument of the city, the **Monument aux Girondins,** at the place de Quinconces, a few short blocks to your right as you exit the tourist office. Its tall column is capped by an exuberantly fluttering **Liberty Statue,** "breaking the chains" of absolutist monarchical oppression. Water cascades down finely carved fountains depicting sea shell chariots pulled by web-footed sea horses. **Le Triomphe de la République,** represents republican ideals and virtues, exalting Work, Security, and Strength in the figures of the blacksmith and lion. At the feet of the horses, you'll find Vice and Ignorance with donkey ears, toppling into the abyss of Falsehood. The other, less bellicose fountain, **Le Triomphe de la Concorde** is a testament to the revolutionary moderation of the Girondins and a celebration of the fruits of peace: Art, Prosperity, Fraternity all leading to Happiness, represented in the figure of the family playing with a dolphin. Retracing your steps, you can see the monumental **Grand Théâtre** on the other side of the tourist office, one of the most classically designed opera houses in the world. Conceived as a temple of the arts and light, and built out of marble by the celebrated architect, Victor Louis, the colonnaded neo-classical facade conceals an even more impressive gilded interior. (Tours 35F, students 20F.) From the theater, take the rue Sainte Catherine. turn right on the Porte Dijeaux, and left on the rue Bouffard, to reach the **Cathédrale St-André.** Nearly 900 years after its consecration by Pope Urban II, this stunning edifice remains Bordeaux's Gothic masterpiece. Its facade features statues of angels and the apostles with deformed hands and crazed eyes. The bell-tower, the **Tour Pey-Berland,** juts 50m into the sky, a height capped by the grand statue of Notre-Dame d'Aquitaine. Climb all 229 spiraling steps to the top for an impressive view of the city. From the cathedral, on the way to the quai Richelieu near the Pont de Pierre, you'll pass the 15th-century **Porte de Cailhau** on pl. de Palais, commemorating the victory of Charles VIII at Fornoue. A couple of blocks beyond is the **place de la Bourse.** The light cream-colored stone, imposing pillars and pilasters, wrought iron facades, and the fountain at the center of the square exemplifies the 18th-century grandeur of Bordeaux.

Turn left upon the cours de Medoc for the **Vinorama de Bordeaux,** at 12 cours Medoc. This wine museum, filled with elaborate dioramas representing different stages in Bordeaux's wine producing history, also gives out samples of a wine from antiquity, newly created according to surviving ancient Roman recipes, a wine from 1850, and a modern wine. (Open June-Sept. Tu-Sa 10:30am-12:30pm and 2:30pm-6:30pm, Su 2pm-6:30pm; Oct.-May Tu-F 2pm-6:30pm, Sa 10:30am-12:30pm and 2:30pm-6:30pm. 35F.) The **Maison du Vin/CIVB,** 1 cours du 30 Juillet, opposite the tourist office, offers a 2-hour "Initiation to Wine Tasting" course which allows you to sample some of the most outstanding (and expensive) wines of the region. (☎05 56 00 22 66. Course June-Aug. twice weekly, 100F. Open M-Th 8:30am-6pm, F 8:30am-5:30pm.) For a cheaper taste, head to **Vinothèque,** 8 cours du 30 Juillet, where the locals buy their wine. (☎05 56 52 32 05. Open M-Sa 9:15am-7:30pm.)

■ **DAYTRIP FROM BORDEAUX: ST-EMILION.** Just 35km northeast of Bordeaux, the viticulturists St-Emilion have been refining their techniques since Roman times. Today, they gently crush 12,850 acres of grapes to produce 23 million liters of wine annually. Vineyards aside, the village itself is a pleasure to visit, with its medieval flavor, winding narrow streets, and cafe-lined square. The **Eglise Monolithe** is a tribute to the village's most famous inhabitant, the reclusive monk and wine connoisseur Emilion. The **tourist office** is located near the church, at pl. des Créneaux. (☎05 57 55 28 28. Open July-Aug. daily 9:30am-7pm.) **Trains** run from Bordeaux to St-Emilion (30min., 2 per day, 66F; the only return train leaves at 6:30pm). The tourist office in Bordeaux offers **guided tours** to the chateaux of wine country.

THE BASQUE COUNTRY

In the southwest corner of France, bordering Spain and the Pyrénées, the Basque Country is home to the mysterious *Euzkadi*, or Basque, people. For millennia, since before the arrival the Celts in Europe, the Basques have lived in this triangle between the Pyrénées and the Atlantic, speaking a language that linguists are still at a loss to classify. Long renowned as fierce fighters, the Basques continue to struggle today, striving to win independence for their long-suffering homeland.

BAYONNE

Bayonne (pop. 43,000) is a grand port which retains small-town appeal and a Spanish flavor. Even Hemingway, characteristically terse, mused that "Bayonne is a nice town. It is like a very clean Spanish town, and it is on a big river." The 13th-century **Cathédrale Ste-Marie,** with twin steeples needling the sky, intimidates from afar and impresses up close. (Open M-Sa 7am-noon and 3-7pm, Su 3:30-10pm. Free.) Highlights of the **Musée Bonnat,** 5 rue Jacques Laffitte, in the area of Petit-Bayonne, include works by Rubens, El Greco, and Goya. (Open W-M 10am-12:30pm and 2-6pm. 20F, students 10F.) In summer, there are free traditional Basque **concerts** are at the gazebo in pl. de Gaulle (July-Aug. Th at 9:30pm).

Trains depart from the station in pl. de la République, running to Bordeaux (1½-2½hr., 9per day, 130-138F) and Toulouse (4hr., 5 per day, 190F), as well as San Sebastián, Spain (1½-2hr., with a change at Henday). Trains do run between Bayonne and Biarritz (10min., 22 per day, 12F), but the local bus network provides more comprehensive and usually cheaper regional transit. Local STAB **buses** depart from the **Hôtel de Ville,** running to Anglet and Biarritz (every 30-40min., last bus M-Sa 8pm, Su 7pm, 7.50F). The **tourist office,** on pl. des Basques, has maps and finds rooms. From the train station, take the middle fork onto pl. de la République, veer right over pont St-Esprit, pass through pl. Réduit, cross pont Mayou, turn right on rue Bernède and turn left for a 15-minute walk down pl. des Basques. (☎ 05 59 46 01 46; fax 05 59 59 37 55. Open July-Aug. M-Sa 9am-7pm, Su 10am-1pm; Sept.-June M-F 9am-6:30pm, Sa 10am-6pm.) Decent lodgings dot the area around the train station and pl. Paul Bert, but the closest **hostel** is in Anglet. The **Hôtel Paris-Madrid,** on pl. de la Gare, has cozy rooms. (☎ 05 59 55 13 98. Breakfast 25F. Reception 6am-12:30am. Singles and doubles 95-190F.) To get to **Camping de la Chêneraie,** take bus #1 from the station to the Navarre stop; the campground is a 1.5km walk along the busy shoulderless highway. (☎ 05 59 55 01 31. Reception open July-Aug. 8am-10pm; Easter-June and Sept. 8:30am-noon and 5-7:30pm. 26F per person, 58F per tent or car.) Delicious regional specialties are served at the elegant **Le Bistrot Ste-Cluque,** 9 rue Hugues, opposite the station. (*Menu* 55F. Open daily noon-2pm and 7-11pm.)

▪️ **DAYTRIP FROM BAYONNE: ST-JEAN-PIED-DE-PORT.** The Pyrenean village of St-Jean-Pied-de-Port (pop. 1600) epitomizes the spicy splendor of the Basque interior. The narrow, cobblestoned streets ascend through the *haute ville* to the dilapidated fortress; below, the calm Nive hides acrobatic trout among the rocks of its riverbed. This medieval capital of Basse-Navarre still hosts a continual procession of pilgrims on their way to Santiago de Compostela, Spain, 900km away. **Trains** arrive from Bayonne (1hr., 5per day, 47F) at the station on av. Renaud. **Rent bikes** at **Garazi Cycles,** 1 pl. St-Laurent. (☎ 05 59 37 21 79. Passport deposit. 120F per day, 150F per weekend. Open M-Sa 8:30am-noon and 3-6pm.) From the station, turn right on av. Renaud, follow it up the slope until it ends at av. de Gaulle, and turn right to reach the **tourist office,** 14 av. de Gaulle. (☎ 05 59 37 03 57; fax 05 59 37 34 91. Open July-Aug. M-Sa 9am-12:30pm and 2-7pm, Su 10:30am-12:30pm and 3-6pm; Sept.-June M-F 9am-noon and 2-7pm, Sa 9am-noon and 2-6pm.)

BIARRITZ

Biarritz (pop. 29,000) is not a budgeteer's dream, but its free **beaches** make a daytrip *de luxe*—you too can sunbathe where Napoleon III, Bismarck, and Queen Victoria summered. At the **Grande Plage,** you'll find a wealth of surfers and bathers, and just to the north at the less-crowded **plage Miramar,** bathers repose *au naturel.* A short **hike** to **Pointe St-Martin** affords a priceless view of the water. In summer, **BASC Subaquatique,** near Plateau de l'Atalaye (☎ 05 59 24 80 40), organizes **scuba** excursions in summer for 155F.

Since Biarritz's train station is now defunct, the best way to get to the town is to hop on STAB **bus** #1 or 2 to the central Hôtel de Ville (30min., 7.50F). From there, the **tourist office,** 1 sq. d'Ixelles, is a brief walk up rue J. Petit, and helps with finding accommodations. (☎ 05 59 22 37 00. Open daily June-Sept. 8am-8pm, Oct.-May 9am-6:45pm.) The **Auberge de Jeunesse (HI),** 8 rue de Chiquito de Cambo, has a friendly staff and lakefront location. From the train station, left up the hill, turn left at the rotary, and follow rue de Movettes as it parallels the train tracks, then turn down the steep hill on the right. The hostel is across the street at the bottom. (☎ 05 59 41 76 00. Sheets 25F. HI members only. Doubles 170F, triples and quads 228-304F.) **Hôtel Barnetche,** 5bis rue Charles-Floquet, is minutes away from the beach. (☎ 05 59 24 22 25. Obligatory breakfast 35F. In Aug., obligatory half-pension 100F. Reception 7:30am-11pm. Open May-Sept. 12-bed dorm 110F, doubles 270F, with shower 330F; triples 450F; quads 600F.) **Shopi supermarket,** 2 rue du Centre, just off rue Gambetta, has typical supermarket fare and selection of local wines. (Open July-Aug. M-Sa 8:45am-12:25pm and 3-7:10pm, Su 8:45am-1pm; Sept.-June closed Su.)

ANGLET

Anglet's *raisons d'être* are its beaches, ranging from the perfect waves of the **plage Les Cavaliers** to the rocky jetty of the **Chambre d'Amour.** Anglet hosts a number of professional surfing championships during the summer (free to spectators), including the **O'Neill Surf Challenge** and the **Europe Surfing Championship.** The **Rainbow Surf-shop,** 19-21 av. Chambre d'Amour, rents boards and wetsuits and arranges surfing lesson. (☎ 05 59 03 54 67. Boards half-day 40-60F; 1000-2000F deposit. Wetsuits half-day 30F; 1000F deposit. Open Apr.-Oct. daily 9:30am-7pm.) STAB **buses** connect Anglet to Bayonne and Biarritz (every 15min., 7.50F). The **tourist office,** 1 av. de Chambre d'Amour, in pl. Leclerc, has info on summer surfing contests. (☎ 05 59 03 77 01. Open July-Sept. M-Sa 10:30am-7pm; Oct.-June M-F 10am-1pm and 3-7pm, Sa 9am-12:15pm.) The carefree **Auberge de Jeunesse (HI),** 19 rte. de Vignes, is just 600m uphill from the beach. From the Hôtel de Ville in Biarritz, take bus #4 (dir.: Bayonne Sainsontain) to Auberge. From the train station in Bayonne, take bus #4 to La Barre, then bus #9 or C to Auberge. (☎ 05 59 58 70 00. Sheets 23F. Reception 8:30am-10pm, weekends closed 12:30-6pm. July-Sept. dorms 80F, Oct.-June 73F.) The centrally located **Camping Fontaine Laborde,** 17 allée Fontaine Laborde, caters to young surfers. Take bus #4 to Fontaine Laborde, just down the road from the hostel. (☎ 05 59 03 48 16. 30F per person, 25F per site, 20F per car.) The **Crêperie Bretonne: La Pointe du Raz** serves up authentic Breton crepes. (☎ 05 59 03 10 83. Open daily Tu-Sa noon-3pm and 7pm-midnight, Su noon-midnight.) **Postal Code:** 64600.

GASCONY AND THE PYRÉNÉES

South of Aquitaine, the forests recede and the mountains of Gascony begin, shielded from the Atlantic by the Basque Country. Both Gascons and Basques are descended from the people the Romans called *Vascones.* They differ in that Gascony was more amenable to outside influences, and Gascons have long considered themselves French. Today, people come to Gascony to be healed; millions of believers descend on Lourdes hoping for miracle cures while thousands of others undergo scarcely more scientific treatments in the many *thermes* of the Pyrénées.

LOURDES

In 1858, 14-year-old Bernadette Soubirous saw the first of what would total 18 visions of the Virgin Mary in the Massabielle grotto in Lourdes (pop. 16,300). "The Lady" made a healing spring appear, and today five million rosary-toting faithful make pilgrimages here annually. To get from the **tourist office** to the **Caverne des Apparitions (La Grotte)** and the two **basilicas** above, follow av. de la Gare, turn left on bd. de la Grotte, and follow it across the river (10min.). Processions depart daily from the grotto at 5pm and 8:45pm. Dress modestly. (Grotto open daily 5am-midnight. Basilicas open daily Easter-Oct. 6am-7pm; Nov.-Easter 8am-6pm.)

Trains arrive at the station, 33 av. de la Gare, from Paris: (7-9hr., 5 per day, 456F); Bayonne (2hr., 5 per day, 106F); Bordeaux (3hr., 7 per day, 182F); and Toulouse (2½hr., 8 per day, 125F). To get to the **tourist office,** on pl. Peyramale, from the station, turn right on av. de la Gare, bear left on av. Marasin, and keep an eye out to the right. (☎ 05 62 42 77 40; fax 05 62 94 60 95; email lourdes@sudfr.com. Open May-Oct. 15 M-Sa 9am-7pm, Su 10am-6pm; Oct.15-Mar.15 M-Sa 9am-noon and 2-6pm; Mar.15-Apr. M-Sa 9am-12:30pm and 1:30-7pm; Su 10am-6pm.) To find the clean and comfortable **Hôtel Saint-Sylve,** 9 rue de la Fontaine, follow ave. Herlios away from the train station as it curves down the hill and turn left onto rue du Callat. Go under the bridge, take the first left and then the second right onto rue de la Fontaine. (☎ 05 62 94 63 48. Breakfast 25F. Shower 15F. Open Apr.-Oct. Singles 75F, with shower 120F; doubles 140F, with shower 170F; triples 210F; quads 260F.) **Camping de la Poste,** 26 rue de Langelle, is just a few minutes from the center of town. (☎ 05 62 94 40 35. Open Easter-Oct. 15. Shower 8F. 15F per person, 21F per site.) Save a few francs by heading to **Prisunic supermarket,** 9 pl. du Champ-Commun. (Open M-Sa 8:30am-12:30pm and 2-7:30pm, Su 8am-noon.) **Postal Code:** 65100.

CAUTERETS

Nestled in a narrow, breathtaking valley on the edge of the **Parc National des Pyrénées Occidentales** is tiny Cauterets. Romans discovered the therapeutic effects of Cauterets' hot sulfuric *thermes,* but today more visitors come for skiing (Dec.-Apr.; passes 115-138F per day) and hiking. Head to the **tourist office,** on pl. Foch, for info on sights in town. (☎ 05 62 92 50 27; fax 05 62 92 59 12; www.cauterets.com. Open daily July-Aug. 9am-7pm; Sept.-June 9am-12:30pm and 2-6:30pm.) For more **hiking info, advice** and **maps,** head to **Parc National des Pyrénées** (see below). **Skilys,** rte. de Pierrefitte, pl. de la Gare, has guides for hire and rents **bikes, inline skates,** and **ice skates.** (☎ 05 62 92 52 10. Open daily 9am-7pm; in winter 8am-7:30pm.)

SNCF **buses** run from pl. de la Gare to Lourdes (Eurail valid, 1hr., 6 per day, 39F). The sparkling white **Gîte d'Etape UCJG,** av. du Docteur Domer (☎ 05 62 92 52 95), is just 200m from the center of town—perfect for hardcore hikers or anyone who wants a real taste of the mountains. (Open for summer accommodations June 15-Sept. 15. 12- to 14-bed dorms 40-50F; triples in a "bungalow" 55F each.) The covered **Halles market,** in the center of town on av. du Général Leclerc, has fresh produce. (Open daily 8:30am-12:30pm and 2:30-7:30pm.) **Postal Code:** 65110.

■ **DAYTRIP FROM CAUTERETS: LUZ-ST-SAUVEUR.** Luz-St-Sauveur is actually two villages: Luz caters mostly to skiers, while St-Sauveur deals in close encounters of the thermal kind. Set in the wide, grassy Vallée du Toy, Luz itself offers few challenging hikes in the immediate vicinity, but its proximity to Gavarnie and Bagnées and its accessibility via the **SNCF bus** from Cauterets (6 per day, 39F) make it an excellent launching pad into the Pyrénées. The **tourist office,** pl. du 8 Mai 45, will provide you with a rough map and a list of hotels and send you to the Maison de la Vallée for everything else. (☎ 05 62 92 30 30; fax 05 62 92 87 19. Open M-Sa 9am-noon and 2-6:30pm.) In winter, the **Bureau des Guides, l'Ecole de Ski Français,** on pl. Clemenceau (in summer ☎ 05 62 92 62 02, off-season ☎ 05 62 92 55 06), provides ski guides and assistance.

PARC NATIONAL DES PYRÉNÉES

One of France's seven national parks, the Parc National des Pyrénées cradles endangered brown bears and lynxes, 200 threatened colonies of **marmots,** 118 lakes, and 160 unique species of plants in its snow-capped mountains and lush valleys. Punctuated with sulfurous springs and unattainable peaks, the Pyrenees change dramatically with the seasons. The lush French and barren Spanish sides of the Pyrenees are strikingly different (a six- to seven-day round trip hike from Cauterets). But there are plenty more modest opportunities as well, if you're just looking to get your feet wet in the wilderness.

Touch base with the helpful park service staff at **Parc National Office,** Maison du Parc, pl. de la Gare (☎ 05 62 92 52 56; fax 05 62 92 62 23, www.parc-pyrenees.com) before braving the trails. They have loads of information about the park and 15 different trails that begin and end in Cauterets, and as well as maps, regional and for dayhikes, you could ever need (42-58F). You'll also find a small educational **museum** displaying the park's flora, fauna, and activities. (Office and museum both open June-Aug. 9:30am-noon and 3-7pm; Sept.-May M-Tu and F-Su 9:30am-12:30 and 3-6pm, and Th 3-6pm. Closed W. Free.)

LANGUEDOC-ROUSSILLON

Languedoc and Roussillon, rugged lands whose peoples' origins are as much Spanish as French, have never been comfortable with Parisian authority. Once, an immense region called Occitania (today Languedoc) stretched from the Rhine to the foothills of the Pyrénées. Its people spoke the *langue d'oc*, not the *langue d'oïl* spoken in northern France (which evolved into modern French). The region was eventually integrated into the French kingdom, and the Cathar religion, popular among Occitanians, was severely persecuted by the Crown and Church. The *langue d'oc* faded, and in 1539, the *langue d'oïl* became official. Latent nationalism lingers on, however: many speak Catalán, a relative of the *langue d'oc*, and look to Barcelona, rather than Paris, for guidance.

TOULOUSE

Just when all of France starts to look alike, Toulouse's (pop. 350,000) eclectic architecture and squares provide a breath of fresh air. Gardens and gurgling fountains abound, from the old-school grandeur of pl. du Capitole to the cafe chit-chat of the student quarter. Once a center for the bloody persecution of Protestants by the French kings—culminating in the St. Bartholomew's Day Massacre of 1572— today Toulouse is the prosperous capital of the French aerospace industry, and its economic prosperity is reflected in its clean streets and shining edifices.

▐ TRANSPORTATION. Trains zoom from Gare Matabiau, 64 bd. Pierre Sémard, to: Paris-Austerlitz (8-9hr., 4 per day, 365-498F); Bordeaux (2-3hr., 14 per day, 165F); Lyon (6½hr., 3-4 per day, 304F); and Marseilles (4½hr., 8 per day, 241F).

▐ PRACTICAL INFORMATION. To reach the **tourist office,** at Donjon du Capitôle, on rue Lafayette, in sq. Charles de Gaulle, from the station, turn left along the canal, turn right on the allée Jean Jaurès, bear right around pl. Wilson, turn right on rue Lafayette; it's in a park near rue d'Alsace-Lorraine. (☎ 05 61 11 02 22; fax 05 61 22 03 63; www.mairie-toulouse.fr. Open May-Sept. M-Sa 9am-7pm, Su 10am-1pm and 2-6:30pm; Oct.-Apr. M-F 9am-6pm, Sa 9am-12:30pm and 2-6pm, Su 10am-12:30pm and 2-5pm.) Get wired at **Blodstation,** 42 rue Pargaminières, with **internet access.** (☎ 05 34 45 09 09. 35F per hr. Open M-Sa noon-midnight, Su 2-8pm.)

▐▐ ACCOMMODATIONS AND FOOD. To reach the spacious and well-located **Hôtel des Arts,** 1 bis rue Cantegril, at rue des Arts near pl. St-Georges, take the Métro (dir.: Basso Cambo) to Pl. Esquirol; follow rue du Metz away from the river and turn left after three blocks. (☎ 05 61 23 36 21. Singles 90-140F; doubles 145-160F; triples and quads 150-180F. Breakfast 25F. Shower 15F. Reserve ahead. V, MC.) **Hôtel du Grand Balcon,** 8 rue Romiguières, in pl. du Capitole, has a prime location, and some rooms have balconies. (☎ 05 61 21 48 08. Breakfast 25F. Singles 110-150F; doubles 130-190F; triples and quads 170-180F.) **Camp** at **Pont de Rupé,** 21 chemin du Pont de Rupé, at av. des Etats-Unis. Take bus #59 (dir.: Camping) to Rupé or drive north on N20. (☎ 05 61 70 07 35. 50F per person. 60F per two people. 16F per additional person.) **Markets** line **pl. des Carmes, pl. Victor Hugo,** and **bd. de Strasbourg** (Tu-Su 6am-1pm); inexpensive eateries line **rue du Taur** and **pl. Wilson. Postal Code:** 31000.

▐▐ SIGHTS AND ENTERTAINMENT. A good place to start your tour is just outside the tourist office at the **Capitole,** the most central monument of the city, a red brick palace. The site has served as the seat of city government since the 12th century. Inside the courtyard, you can take the "grand staircase" to the upper chambers. (Open M-F 8:30am-noon and 1:30-7pm, Sa-Su 10am-noon and 2-6pm. Free.) Just up rue du Taur from pl. du Capitole is the **Eglise Notre-Dame-du-Taur,** so named because it marks the spot where the priest Saturninus died in AD 250 after being tied to the tail of a wild bull by disgruntled pagans. (Open daily July-Sept. 9am-6:30pm; Oct.-June 8am-noon and 2-6pm.) Continuing north on rue du Taur leads to the **Basilique St-Sernin,** the longest Romanesque structure in the world; its crypt houses ecclesiastical relics gathered from Charlemagne's time. (Open July-Sept. M-Sa 9am-6:30pm, Su 9am-7:30pm; Oct.-June M-Sa 8:30-11:45am and 2-5:45pm, Su 9am-12:30pm and 2-7:30pm. Free. Tours July-Aug. 2 per day; 35F. Crypt 10F.) Backtrack to the pl. du Capitole, take a right on rue Romiguières, and turn left on rue Lakanal to get to the 13th-century **Les Jacobins,** an excellent example of the southern Gothic style. The ashes of St. Thomas Aquinas take center stage in an elevated tomb with under-lighting. (Open daily 9am-7pm. Cloister 14F.) Retracing your steps back down rue de Metz will take you to the newly restored **Hôtel d'Assézat,** at pl. d'Assézat on rue de Metz. Its intricate, marble facade encloses the **Fondation Bemberg,** with an impressive collection of Bonnards, Dufys, Pisarros, and Gauguins. (☎ 05 61 12 06 89. *Fondation* ☎ 05 61 12 06 89. Open Tu and F-Su 10am-6pm, Th 10am-9pm. 30F.) Follow rue de Metz away from the river past pl. Esquirol to the **Musée des Augustins,** 21 rue de Metz, for an unsurpassed collection of Romanesque and Gothic sculptures. (☎ 05 61 22 21 82. Open Th-M 10am-6pm, W 10am-9pm. 14F, students free.) **La Cité de l'Espace** is a new park devoted to Toulouse's space programs, complete with interactive games and a planetarium. Take bus #19 to pl. de l'Indépendance and follow the signs. (☎ 05 62 71 64 80. Open June. 15-Sept. 15 Tu-Su 9:30am-7pm; Sept. 16-June 14 Tu-Su 9:30am-6pm. 69F. Planetarium 15F.)

Toulouse has something to please almost any nocturnal whim, although nightlife is liveliest when students are in town, between October and May. Numerous cafes flank **pl. St-Georges** and **pl. du Capitole,** and late-night bars line **rue St-Rome** and **rue des Filatiers.** Cafe Populaire, 9 rue de la Colombette, opens its welcoming walls and keeps itself lively by selling beers by the boxload. (☎ 05 61 63 07 00. M-F 9pm-2am, Sa 3pm-6am. 13 beers for 120F.) **La Ciguä,** 6 rue de Colombette, just off bd. Lazare Carnot, is a friendly gay bar and a great place to ask about discos. (☎ 05 61 99 61 87. Open Tu-F and Su 9pm-2am, Sa 9pm-4am.)

CARCASSONNE

Carcassonne (pop. 45,000) has had a rough go of it. Attacked at various times by Romans, Visigoths, and Moors, Europe's largest fortress has come to exemplify stalwart opposition in the face of the enemy. The backdrop for the movie *Robin Hood: Prince of Thieves* (1991), the *cité* is now bombarded by tourists. Constructed as a palace in the 12th century, the **Château Comtal** was transformed into a citadel following submission to royal control in 1226. (☎ 04 68 25 01 66. Open daily June-Sept. 9am-7:30pm; Apr.-May 9:30am-6pm; Nov.-Mar. 9:30am-5pm. 35F, under 26 23F.) At the other end of the city, the beautiful **Basilique St-Nazaire,** in pl. de l'Eglise, is the coolest place in the city on a sultry summer afternoon. (Open July-Aug. 9am-7pm; Sept.-June 9:30am-noon and 2-5:30pm.) Turned into a fortress after the Black Prince destroyed Carcassonne in 1355, the *basse ville's* Gothic **Cathédrale St-Michel,** rue Voltaire (☎ 04 68 25 14 48), still has fortifications on its southern side, facing bd. Barbès. (Open M-Sa 7am-noon and 2-7pm, Su 9:30am-noon. Although nightlife is limited, several bars and cafes along **bd. Omer Sarraut** and **pl. Verdun** offer some excitement. Locals dance all night at **La Bulle,** 115 rue Barbacane. (☎ 04 68 72 47 70. 60F cover includes a drink. Open F-Sa only until dawn.)

Trains arrive behind Jardin St-Chenier from: Marseilles (3hr., every 2hr., 201F); Nice (6hr., 5 per day, 297F); Nîmes (2½hr., 12 per day, 139F); Toulouse (50min., 24 per day, 74F). Shops, hotels, and the train station are located in the *basse ville;* walk a steep 30min. uphill or catch the *navette* in front of the station (every 20-40min., 5.60F, until 7pm) to reach the *cité.* To reach the **tourist office,** 15 bd. Camille Pelletan, pl. Gambetta, from the train station, walk over the canal on rue Clemenceau, turn left on rue de la Liberté, then right on bd. Jean Jaurès. (☎04 68 10 24 30; fax 04 68 10 24 38. Open July-Aug. daily 9am-7pm; Sept.-June 9am-12:15pm and 1:45-6:30pm.) The **auberge de jeunesse (HI),** on rue de Vicomte Trencavel, is in the middle of the *cité.* (☎04 68 25 23 16. HI members only. Breakfast included. Sheets 17F. Laundry 30F. Dorms 74F.) The **Hôtel St-Joseph,** 81 rue de la Liberté, has 37 rooms on a tranquil street in the Basse Ville, 5min. from the train station. Take av. Maréchal Joffre across the canal, across bd. Omer Sarraut, and then continue for a block on rue G. Clemenceau before turning right. (☎04 68 71 96 89. Breakfast 25F. Singles 110F, doubles 135-185.) **Camping de la Cité,** on rte. de St-Hilaire, across the Aude 2km from town, has a pool and grocery store. A shuttle can take you there from the train station. (☎04 68 25 11 77. Reception 8am-9pm. Open Apr.-Sept.June-Sept. 95F per site. 27 per extra person; cheaper in Apr.-May.) The regional speciality is *cassoulet* (a stew of white beans, herbs, and meat). On **rue du Plo,** 55-60F *menus* abound, but save room for dessert at one of the many outdoor *crêperies* in **pl. Marcou.** Eat like a king at **Les Fontaines du Soleil,** 32 rue du Plo. (☎04 68 47 87 06. Open daily 11:30am-3pm and 7pm-10:30pm.) **Postal Code:** 11000.

THE PYRÉNÉES ORIENTALES

In the area between the Ariège and Languedoc, the valleys of this immense, mountainous area occasionally expose small hamlets of beige homes with blue shutters and hundreds of pink flowers.

FOIX

Nestled in the eastern Pyrénées, 85km south of Toulouse, the **Château de Foix** remains in perfect condition, reigning above Foix's vivacious and competitive markets. (☎05 61 65 56 05. Open July-Aug. daily 9:45am-6:30pm; June and Sept. 9:45am-noon and 2-6pm; Oct.-May W-Su 10:30am-noon and 2-5:30pm. 25F.) An hour-long boat ride takes visitors through the caves on the **Labouiche,** the longest navigable underground river in Europe open to the public. (☎05 61 65 04 11. Open July-Aug. daily 9:30am-6pm; Apr. 1-May 24 M-Sa 2-6pm, Su 10am-noon and 2-6pm; May 25-June 30 and Sept. daily 10am-noon and 2-6pm; Oct. 1-Nov. 11 Su 10am-noon and 2-6pm. 44F, in the mornings students 32F.) The **Grotte de Niaux** contains 13,000-year-old paintings of leaping herds of bison, deer, and horses. (☎05 61 05 88 37. Reservations only. 20km south of Foix. Inquire at tourist office.)

The **train station,** av. Pierre Sémard, is north of the town, off the N20. (☎05 61 02 03 64. Info and reservation desk open M-Sa 8:10am-12:20pm and 1:25-8:30pm, Su 8:15am-1:55pm and 2:15-10:20pm.) **Trains** go to Toulouse (1hr., 10 per day, 69F). **Sault Autocars,** 8 allée de Villote (☎05 61 65 08 40), also runs to Toulouse (1¼hr., 2 per day, 50F). **L.C.F. Motos,** 16 rue Labistour, rents bikes. (☎05 61 05 29 98. Open M 2-7pm, Tu-Sa 9am-noon and 2-7pm. 95F per day.) To reach the **tourist office,** 45 cours G. Fauré, leave the train station and turn right; follow the street until you reach the main road (N20), continue to the second bridge, cross it, and follow cours G. Fauré. (☎05 61 65 12 12; fax 05 61 65 64 63. Open July-Aug. M-Sa 9am-7pm, Su 10am-12:30pm and 3-6:30pm; June and Sept. M-Sa 9am-noon and 2-6pm, Su 10am-12:30pm; Oct.-May M-Sa 9am-noon and 2-6pm.) (☎05 61 02 01 02. Open M-F 8am-7pm, Sa 8am-noon.) To get to the **Foyer Léo Lagrange,** 16 rue Peyrevidal, turn left out of the tourist office; follow cours G. Fauré and turn left again just before the giant steel structure. (☎05 61 65 09 04. Breakfast 25F, lunch 55F. Reception 8am-11pm. Dorms 80F.) For regular supplies, head to **Casino** supermarket, rue Laffont. (Open M-Sa 9am-7pm.) **Postal Code:** 09000.

PERPIGNAN

Comfortably sprawled between the Mediterranean and the Pyrénées, Perpignan (pop. 108,000) has bounced between French and Spanish ownership as the former capital of the counts of Roussillon and the kings of Mallorca. While the unexpected palm trees, immense Citadel, and quiet cafes of the *quai* give Perpignan a Mediterranean allure, its best advantage is its proximity to Collioure and Céret.

TRANSPORTATION. Trains trundle to the station on rue Courteline, off av. de Gaulle, from Paris (6-10hr., 4 per day, 439-505F); Carcassonne (1½hr.; 2 per day, change at Narbonne; 70-80F); Nice (6hr., 3 per day, 299F); and Toulouse (2½-3hr.; 15 per day, some change at Narbonne; 143F).

PRACTICAL INFORMATION. Most sights, restaurants, cafes, and shops lie inside a triangle formed by the regional tourist office, **pl. de la Victoire** (farther up the cana) and the **Palais des Rois de Majorque.** To get from the station to the **tourist office,** Palais de Congrès, pl. Armand Lanoux, follow av. du Galle to pl. de Catalogne, then take bd. Georges Clemenceau across the canal past Le Castillet as it becomes bd. Wilson. (☎04 68 66 30 30; fax 04 68 66 30 26. Open June-Sept. M-Sa 9am-7pm, Su 10am-noon and 2-5pm; Oct.-May M-Sa 9am-noon and 2-6pm.M-F 9am-noon and 2-6:30pm, Sa 9am-noon and 2-6pm.) The **post office** is at quai de Barcelone, and also has **currency exchange.** (☎04 68 51 99 12. Open M-Tu and Th-F 8am-7pm, W 9am-7pm, Sa 8am-noon.) **Postal Code:** 66000.

ACCOMMODATIONS AND FOOD. The **Auberge de Jeunesse La Pépinière (HI),** on rue Marc-Pierre, is on the edge of town, between the highway and police station. From the train station, turn left on rue Valette, right on av. de Grande Bretagne, left on rue Claude Marty (rue de la Rivière on some maps), and right on rue Marc Pierre (10min.). (☎04 68 34 63 32. HI members only. Breakfast included. Sheets 18F. Lockout 11am-4pm. Check-out 11am. Open Jan. 21-Dec. 19. 4- to 8-bed dorms 70F.) **Hôtel de l'Avenir,** 11 rue de l'Avenir welcomes with its cheery canary yellow exterior, 5min. from the station. (☎04 68 34 20 30. Breakfast 25F. Shower 15F. Singles 90-190F; triples and quads 220F.) Local specialities include *touron* (nougat) and *cargolade* (grilled snails in garlic sauce). **Casino supermarket,** on bd. Félix Mercader, stockpiles food. (☎04 68 34 74 42. Open M-Sa 8:30am-8pm.)

SIGHTS AND ENTERTAINMENT. A short walk from the action, the **citadelle** is both formidable and *formidable,* with beautifully intact walls rising up from the residential area below. Within the citadel lies the 13th-century **Palais des Rois de Majorque,** the city's most impressive sight, with an immense arcaded courtyard and two curiously superimposed chapels. The courtyard now serves as a concert hall, and theater. (☎04 68 34 48 29. Enter from av. Gilbert Brutus. Open daily June-Sept. 10am-6pm; Oct.-May 9am-5pm. 20F, students 10F.) The **Musée Hyacinthe Rigaud,** 16 rue de l'Ange, contains 13th-century Spanish and Catalán paintings; canvases by Rigaud, court artist to Louis XIV; and works by Ingres, Picasso, Miró, and Dalí. On the top floor is the **Collection de Maître Rey,** with walls packed with a tiny but diverse set of paintings created for local writer Rey by his artist friends, both well-known and less so. (☎04 68 35 43 40. Open W-M noon-7pm. 25F, students 10F.) If you're looking for a night on the town in the evening, prepare yourself for a calm-cafe-centric experience. Traditional Catalonian dancing in front of Le Castillet makes for a colorful scene around pl. de Verdun, especially in summer.

DAYTRIPS FROM PERPIGNAN

COLLIOURE

Trains (☎04 68 82 05 89) roll in to the station at the top of av. Aristide Maillol from Perpignan (20min., 15 per day, 28F) and Barcelona (3½hr., 5 per day, 76F).

Where the Pyrénées finally tumble into the Mediterranean, tiny Collioure (pop. 2770) captured the fancy of Greeks and Phoenicians long before enrapturing Fauvists and Surrealists such as Dalí, Picasso, and Matisse. Its stony beaches, lighthouse, and enchanting harbor continue to cast a spell over the eye. The **tourist office,** on pl. du 18 Juin, has info on **day hikes** and coastal bus routes. (☎04 68 82 15 47; fax 04 68 82 46 29. Open July-Aug. daily 9am-8pm; Sept.-June M-Sa 9am-noon and 2-6:30pm.) **Hôtel Triton,** 1 rue Jean Bart, sits on the waterfront 10min. from the *centre ville.* (☎04 68 98 39 39. Breakfast 35F. Doubles 200-320F.)

CÉRET

Car Inter 66 (☎ 04 68 39 11 96) runs buses from Perpignan (35min., 1 per hr., 34F).

Céret (pop. 8000) prides itself on its cherry trees, celebrated in a yearly spring festival, yet it is another flowering that puts this proud Catalán village on the map. Around 1910, the warm wind, the ochre sunlight, and the narrow streets of the town inspired Picasso, Chagall, Manolo, and Herbin, creating a "Cubist Mecca." The works they left to the town are housed in the **Musée d'Art Moderne**, 8 bd. Maréchal Joffre. (☎ 04 68 87 27 76. Open July-Sept. daily 10am-7pm; May-June and Oct. daily 10am-6pm; Nov.-Apr. W-M 10am-6pm. 35F, students 20F.) From the bus stop on av. George Clemenceau, the **tourist office**, 1 av. Clemenceau, is two blocks up the hill on the right. (☎ 04 68 87 00 53. Open July-Aug. M-Sa 9am-12:30pm and 2-7pm, Su 10am-12:30pm; Sept.-Oct. M-F 10am-noon and 2-5pm, Sa 10am-noon.)

SOUTHEAST FRANCE

Heavy with the fragrance of lavender and wild herbs, the air in the southeast of France brings a piercing vitality to the landscape, a sense of eternal youth that today draws aging movie stars just as once it enticed artists like van Gogh and Cézanne. Southeastern France has it all, from some of the best skiing and hiking in the world to the most glamorous beach resorts, from unspoiled villages and natural parks to astoundingly well-preserved reminders of earlier ages.

PROVENCE

At the southern end of the Rhône River, where it cascades into the Mediterranean, the Rhône Valley towns of Provence are among France's best destinations. From the Roman arena and cobblestoned grace of Arles to the formidable Palais des Papes of Avignon to the lingering footsteps of Cézanne in Aix-en-Provence, life unfolds along Provence's shaded promenades like an endless game of *pétanque* or a bottomless glass of *pastis*.

AVIGNON

The city of Avignon (pop. 100,000) has danced with cultural and artistic brilliance ever since it snatched the papacy away from Rome for almost 70 years some 700 years ago. Film festivals, street musicians, and Europe's most prestigious theatrical gathering keep this university town lively.

TRANSPORTATION. Trains (☎ 04 90 27 81 89) run from Porte de la République to: Paris (3½hrs., 21 per day, 342-426F); Arles (30min., 10 per day, 35F); Marseilles (70min., 11 per day, 91F); Nîmes (30min., 28 per day, 46F). **Buses** leave from bd. St-Roch, right next to the train station. Cartreize (☎ 04 90 82 07 35) has service to Marceille (2hr., 4 per day, 91F); Ceyte buses (☎ 04 90 93 74 90) travel to Arles (45min., 5 per day M-Sa, 43F), and Cevennes runs to Nîmes (1-1½hr., 5 per day, 42F).

PRACTICAL INFORMATION. From the train station, walk through the porte de la République to the cours Jean Jaurès to reach the **tourist office,** 41 cours Jean Jaurès (☎ 04 32 74 32 74; fax 04 90 82 95 03; www.avignon-tourisme.com. Open Apr.-Sept. M-F 9am-6pm; Sa-Su 9am-1pm and 2-5pm; Oct.-Mar. Su 10am-noon; during festivals M-Sa 10am-8pm and Su 10am-5pm.) Take an **internet** break at **Cyberdrome,** 68 rue Guillaume Puy. (☎ 04 90 16 05 15. Open M-Sa 8am-midnight, Su 2-10pm. 50F per hr.) The **post office** is on the cours Président Kennedy near the porte de la République. (☎ 04 90 27 54 00. Open M-Sa 8:30am-12:30pm and 1:30-6:30pm, Sa 8:30am-noon.) **Postal Code:** 84000.

ACCOMMODATIONS AND FOOD. Outside festival season, Avignon's hotels and *foyers* usually have room, but unreserved beds vanish once the theater troops come to town. The **Foyer YMCA/UCJG,** 7bis chemin de la Justice, is across the

Avignon

▲ ACCOMMODATIONS
Foyer YMCA/UCJG, A
Foyer Bagatelle, 3
Hôtel du Parc, 15
Hôtel Mignon, 9
Hôtel Splendid, 16
Innova Hôtel, 12
Pont d'Avignon Camping, 2

🍴 FOOD
Gambrinus, 7
Terre de Saveur, 18

🎵 ENTERTAINMENT
Koala Bar, 14

● SERVICES
Cybercafe Cyberdrome, 19
Espace Info-Jeunes, 6
Laundromat, 17
Shakespeare Bookshop & Tearoom, 5

🏛 MUSEUMS
Musée du Petit Palais, 4
Musée Calvet, 11
Musée Louis Vouland, 10
Musée Lapidaire, 13
Maison Jean Vilar, 8

N

0   200 yards
0   200 meters

VILLENEUVE

Rhône

Ile de la Barthelasse

Pont St-Bénézet

Rocher des Doms

Notre Dame des Doms

Palais des Papes

Pont Daladier

PORTE DE L'OULLE

PORTE ST-DOMINIQUE

PORTE ST-ROCH

PORTE DE LA RÉPUBLIQUE

PORTE ST-MICHEL

PORTE ST-JOSEPH

PORTE DE LA LIGNE

PORTE ST-LAZARE

Bd. St-Lazare

r. du Rempart

r. Palapharnerie

r. des Trois

r. des Infirmières

St. Symphorien

Eglise de la Visitation

r. Guillaume Puy

r. P. Sain

r. Philonarde

r. Thiers

r. des Teinturiers

r. Bon Martinet

Av. des Sources

RN 7

Av. de la Trillade

Av. de l'Arrousaire

Pont de l'Europe

FRANCE

TO 🏠 1 (1.5km),
2 (1km)

river in Villeneuve. From the station, turn left and follow the city wall, cross the second bridge (pont Daladier), and turn left on chemin de la Justice (30min.). The foyer will be up the hill across the street from a boulangerie. Or take bus #10 (dir.: Les Angles-Grand Angles) to Général Leclerc or bus #11 (dir.: Villeneuve-Grand Terme) to Pont d'Avignon. (☎04 90 25 46 20; email ymca@avignon.packwan.net. Breakfast 25F. Reception 8:30am-6pm. Singles 136-180F, doubles 176-220F.) To get to **Foyer Bagatelle**, on Ile de la Barthelasse, follow the directions above, cross pont Daladier, and it's on the right; or take bus #10 or 11 to La Barthelasse. (☎04 90 86 30 39. Breakfast 20F. Dorms 65F, doubles 140F.) The **Hôtel Splendid**, 17 rue Perdiguier, lives up to its name, and sits right off the cours Jean Jaurès, near the tourist office. (☎04 90 86 14 46. Breakfast 30F. Singles 160-220F; doubles 210-270F.) The campsite closest to Avignon is **Pont d'Avignon**, 300 Ile de la Barthelasse, a 10min. walk past Foyer Bagatelle. (☎04 90 80 63 50. Reception daily July-Aug. 8:30am-10pm; mid-Mar.-Oct. 8:30am-7pm. Closed Sept. 10-Mar. 26. 1 person with tent or car 80F, 2 people with tent or car 125F.) Crooked **rue des Teinturiers** hosts a smattering of lively restaurants. The cafes of **pl. de l'Horloge** are best suited for after-dinner drinks, when clowns, street musicians and mimes milk crowds for smile and *centimes*.

☎ 🎵 SIGHTS AND ENTERTAINMENT. Avignon has instituted a pass system for visiting multiple sights. At the first monument or museum, you pay full admission, but afterwards, only a reduced price. The pass is good for most sites and lasts for 15 days. The 14th-century **Palais des Papes** is the most stunning fortified Gothic palace still in existence. The largest in Europe, its walls are oddly cut with the tall, ecclesiastical windows of the **Grande Chapelle** and the dark cross of arrow-loops. Although revolutionary looting deprived the interior of its lavish furnishings, the giant rooms and their frescoed walls still impress. In the **Grand Tinel,** a banquet hall 45m long by 10m wide, blue canvas flecked with gold stars deck the arched ceiling. Each year, from May through September, the palace hosts an art exhibition. (Open daily Apr.-June and Oct. 9am-7pm; July-Sept. 9am-8pm; Nov.-Mar. 9:30am-5:45pm. Palace or exhibition 46F each.) Heading from the Palais des Papes towards the Rhône, you will pass the **Petit Palais.** Beautiful frescoes with delicate work involving gold leaf and oil-painting await at the **Musée du Petit Palais** inside. (☎04 90 86 44 58. Open July-Aug. W-M 10:30am-6pm; Sept.-June 9:30am-noon and 2-6pm.) Heading in the same direction, the **Pont St-Bénézet,** the bridge immortalized in the nursery rhyme as the "Pont d'Avignon," stretches (though only partway) across the Rhône. Originally, it crossed the river with over 20 arches, and today only four remain standing, thanks to the destruction of warfare. Housed on the second arch is the **St-Nicolas Chapel,** dedicated to the patron saint of mariners. You can enjoy the view of the bridge from the riverbanks; it costs 17F to dance on it.

During the **Festival d'Avignon** (also known as the **IN;** early July-early Aug.), the most prestigious theatrical gathering in Europe, Gregorian chanters rub shoulders with all-night *Odyssey*-readers and African dancers. (Call ☎04 90 14 14 14 for tickets or info. Reservations accepted from mid-June; tickets are also on sale at each venue 45min. before shows. Tickets up to 200F per event.) Nightlife in Avignon centers around the **pl. des Corps Saints**, which is dotted with a few lively bars.

🗺 DAYTRIP FROM AVIGNON: THE VAUCLUSE. The Vaucluse is what you're most likely to see on any beautiful postcard of Provence. Tiny medieval villages perch on rocky escarpments, fields of lavender stretch as far as the eye can see, and ochre hills burn in the sunset, all a backdrop to the omnipresent *vieux papies* drinking *pastis* and playing *pétanque* in the small village squares. For centuries, the area has been home and inspiration to writers from Petrarch to the Marquis de Sade to Samuel Beckett. The region is most accessible by car; **Voyages Arnaud buses** (☎04 90 38 15 58) also travel from Avignon to Vaucluse (55min., 3 per day, 26F).

NÎMES

Nîmes (pop. 135,000) is thought to be the original home of the durable textile which has infiltrated American culture in the form of blue jeans: indeed, "denim" is likely a truncated version of the French phrase "de Nîmes" (from Nîmes). The magnificent **Les Arènes** (Roman amphitheater) was built during the first century for gory gladiatorial combats; the best way to experience it is to attend a bullfight or concert held there. (☎ 04 66 76 72 77. Open daily in summer 9am-6:30pm; off-season 9am-5:30pm. 28F, students 20F.) North of the arena stands the exquisitely sculpted **Maison Carrée** (Square House), a rectangular temple built in the first century BC. (☎ 04 66 36 26 76. Open daily in summer 9am-noon and 2:30-7pm; off-season 9am-12:30pm and 2-6pm. Free.) Across the square, the ultra-modern **Carrée d'Art** houses the eclectic collection of the **Musée d'Art Contemporain.** (☎ 04 66 76 35 70. Open Tu-Su 10am-6pm. 28F, students 20F.) The **Jardins de la Fontaine** enclose the Roman ruins of the **Temple de Diane** and the **Tour Magne.** (Gardens and Temple de Diane open daily Apr. 15-Sept. 15 7:30am-10pm; Sept. 16-Mar. 7:30am-6:30pm. Free. Tour Magne open daily July-Aug. 9am-7pm; Sept.-June 9am-5pm. 15F, students 12F.)

Trains chug from the station at bd. Talabot to Arles (30min., 10 per day, 41F); Marseilles (1¼hr., 6 per day, 96F); and Toulouse (3hr., 10 per day, 184F). **Buses** (☎ 04 66 29 52 00) depart from behind the train station for Avignon (1½hr., 2-8 per day, 44F). The **tourist office** is at 6 rue Auguste, just off pl. Comédie and near the Maison Carrée. (☎ 04 66 67 29 11; fax 04 66 21 81 04. Open May-Sept. M-F 8am-7pm, Sat. 9am-7pm, Su 10am-6pm.) The newly renovated **Auberge de Jeunesse (HI),** is at 257 chemin de l'Auberge de la Jeunesse, off chemin de la Cigale, 4½km from Quai de la Fontaine. Take bus #2 (direction: Alès or Villeverte) to Stade, Route d'Alès and follow the signs uphill; after buses stop running, call for pickup. (☎ 04 66 68 03 20. Breakfast 19F. Sheets 17F; tent sites 29F. HI members only. 4- to 6- bed dorms with bath 53F.) Stock up at **Marché U supermarket,** 19 rue d'Alès, downhill from the hostel. (Open M-Sa 8am-12:45pm and 3:30-8pm.) **Postal Codes:** 30000 and 30900.

PONT DU GARD

In 19 BC, Augustus' close friend and advisor Agrippa built an aqueduct to channel more water to Nîmes from the **Eure springs** near Uzès. The covered canal carried water a winding 50km despite only a 17m total fall in altitude. This required a skillful engineering and masonry, and the entire construction was completed without the use of mortar. The masterpiece of this 15-year project remains in the Pont du Gard, which bridges the gorge of the **Gardon River,** towering over sunbathers and swimmers. A flow of tourists has replaced the millions of gallons it once carried daily. A great way to see the Pont du Gard is to start from **Collias,** 6km towards Uzès. Here **Kayak Vert** (☎ 04 66 22 84 83) rents two-person canoes (50F per hr., 145F per day), solo kayaks (35F per hr., 90F per day) and bikes (80F per half-day, 110F per day, passport deposit). If you're afraid to go in the water, **buses** run to the Pont du Gard from Nîmes (30min., 2-5 per day, 31F), and from Avignon (45min., 7 per day. 33F). **Camping le Barralet,** rue des Aires in Collias (☎ 04 66 22 84 52) offers a pool and hot showers. (1 person with car 36-45F. Open Mar.-Sept.)

ARLES

Arles (pop. 35,000) is still marked by the legacy of the Roman empire—the **arènes,** the largest surviving amphitheater in France, and the **Théâtre Antique,** an evocatively ruined theater strewn with carved stone are both still in use, the former for *corridas* (bullfights), the latter for plays. (Each 20F, students 15F.) The city's Roman past is brought back to life in the brand-new **Musée d'Arles Antique,** av. de la 1ère DFL. (☎ 04 90 18 88 88. Open daily Mar.-Oct. 9am-7pm; Nov.-Feb. 10am-5pm. 35F, students 25F, children 5F.) The calming courtyard of the **Cloître St-Trophime,** at the place de la République, is a medieval gem (20F, students 14F). Vincent van Gogh captured the sun-baked landscapes of Provence on oil and canvas. During the two years (and ear) that he spent in Arles, he painted more than 300 works; the guide *Arles et Vincent* (5F at the tourist office) explains the markers around the city at the spots where his easel once stood. The **Fondation Van Gogh,** 26 Rond-Point des Arènes, houses tributes to the master by artists, poets, and composers. (☎ 04 90 49 94 04. Open daily in summer 10am-7pm. 30F, students 20F.) During the last weekend in June and the first in July, the city celebrates the **Fête d'Arles,** when bonfires blaze in the streets and the locals wear traditional costume.

Trains roll to: Avignon (30min., 21 per day (reduced frequency on Su), 36F); Nîmes (30min., 15 per day (reduced frequency on Su), 41F); Marseilles (1hr., 8 per day (reduced frequency on Su), 71F); and Montpellier (1hr., M-Sa 15 per day, 75F). To get to the **tourist office,** on esplanade Charles de Gaulle at bd. des Lices, turn left from the station, walk to pl. Lamartine, turn left and follow bd. Emile Courbes (10min.), then cross and turn right on bd. des Lices. (☎04 90 18 41 20; fax 04 90 18 41 29. Open Apr.-Sept. daily 9am-8:45pm; Oct.-Mar. M-Sa 9am-5:45pm, Su 10am-noon.) To get from the tourist office to the **Auberge de Jeunesse (HI),** on av. Maréchal Foch, cross bd. des Lices, walk for about 20min. down av. des Alyscamps, and follow the signs. (☎04 90 96 18 25. Sheets and breakfast included. Reception 7-10am and 5pm-midnight. Lockout 10am-5pm. Curfew 11:30pm, during festivals 1-2am. First night 80F, each additional night 68F.) The **Hôtel Gauguin** is at 5 pl. Voltaire (☎04 90 96 14 35. Doubles with shower 180-210F; twins with shower and toilet 220F; triples 260F.) The warm **Hôtel Mirador,** 3 rue Voltaire, is right next door. (☎04 90 96 28 05. Singles and doubles with shower 190F.) **Monoprix supermarket** is on pl. Lamartine, near the station. (Open M-Sa 8:30am-7:30pm.) Cafes in **pl. du Forum** or **pl. Voltaire,** have rock and jazz music on summer Wednesdays. **Postal Code:** 13200.

🗓 DAYTRIP FROM ARLES: THE CAMARGUE. Between Arles and the Mediterranean coast stretches the Camargue. Pink flamingoes, black bulls, and the famous white Camargue horses roam freely across this flat expanse of protected wild marshland. Stop at the **Centre d'Information de Ginès** along D570. (☎04 90 97 86 32. Open Apr.-Sept. daily 9am-6pm; Oct.-Mar. Sa-Th 9:30am-5pm.) Next door, the **Parc Ornithologique de Pont de Gau** provides paths through the marshland and offers views of birds and grazing bulls. (☎04 90 97 82 62. Open daily Apr.-Sept. 9am-dusk; Oct.-Mar. 10am-dusk. 35F.) The best way to see the Camargue is on **horseback;** call the **Association Camarguaise de Tourisme Equestre** for more info. (☎04 90 97 86 32. 80F per hr.) **Jeep safaris** (☎04 66 53 04 99; 220F per 4hr.) and **boat trips** (☎04 90 97 84 72; 1½hr., 60F) from Port Gardian deep into the Petit Rhône are also great ways to see the birds and bulls of the area, and while many trails are only for horseback riders, **bicycle touring** is also an option. **Buses** (☎04 90 96 36 25) run from Arles to Stes-Maries-de-la-Mer, the largest town in the Camargue (1hr., 7 per day, 37F).

AIX-EN-PROVENCE

Famous for its festivals and fountains, Aix (pop. 150,000) panders to tourists without being spoiled by them. Once home to artists such as Paul Cézanne and Victor Vasarely, a large student population now keeps the city on the cutting edge. The **Chemin de Cézanne,** 9 av. Paul Cézanne, features a self-guided walking tour devoted to the artist, including his studio. (☎04 42 21 06 53. Open daily Apr.-Sept. 10am-noon and 2:30-6pm; Oct.-Mar. 10am-noon and 2-5pm. 25F, students 10F.) The **Fondation Vasarely,** on av. Marcel-Pagnol, in quartier du Jas de Bouffan, designed by artist Victor Vasarely, is a must-see for modern art fans. (Open in summer M-F 10am-1pm and 2-7pm, Sa-Su 10am-7pm; off-season 9:30am-1pm and 2-6pm. 35F, students 20F.) **Cathédrale St-Sauveur,** on rue Gaston de Saporta, is a dramatic melange of Romanesque, Gothic, and Baroque carvings and reliefs. (Open daily 8am-noon and 2-6pm.) Aix's **International Music Festival,** June through July, features operas and concerts. (☎04 42 17 34 34. Tickets 100-350F.) Aix also hosts a two-week **jazz festival** beginning in early July (tickets 80-150F) and a two-week **dance festival** (end of July to early-Aug.; tickets 80-150F, students 60-120F). The **Office des Fetes et de la Culture** (☎04 42 96 27 79), at 1 pl. John Rewald, has festival info. Bars line the **Forum des Cardeurs,** behind the Hôtel de Ville. (Bars open M-Sa 11pm.) **Le Scat,** 11 rue Verrerie, has a club with live music and a pub. (Opens M-Sa 11pm.) **Bistro Aixois,** 37 cours Sextius, off La Rotonde, packs in students. (Open daily 6:30pm-3 or 4am.)

Trains (☎08 36 35 35 35), at the end of av. Victor Hugo, run almost exclusively from Marseilles (35min., 21 per day, 38F). **Buses** (☎04 42 91 26 80), av. de l'Europe, run to Avignon (2hr., 4 per day, 80F) and Marseilles (30min., almost every 10 min., 26F). From the train station, follow av. Victor Hugo (bear left at the fork) until it feeds into La Rotonde. On the left is the **tourist office**, 2 pl. du Général de Gaulle, which books rooms for free, sells a city museum pass (40F) and stocks city maps and guides. (☎04 42 16 11 61. Open July-Aug. M-Sa 8:30am-10pm, Su 10am-1pm and 2-6pm; Sept.-June M-Sa 8:30am-7pm, Su 10am-1pm, 2-6pm.) You can surf the **internet** at **Hublot Cyber Cafe,** 17 rue Paul Bert. (☎04 42 21 37 31. 45F per hr., 25F between 7-8pm. Open M-F 9am-8pm, Sa-Su 10am-8pm.) **Hôtel des Arts,** 69 bd. Carnot, has compact modern rooms with showers, toilets, TVs, and phones. (☎04 42 38 11 70. Breakfast 25F. Singles and doubles 149-205F.) To **camp** at **Arc-en-Ciel,** on rte. de Nice, take bus #3 from La Rotonde to Trois Sautets. (☎04 42 26 14 28. Pool and hot showers. 35F per person, tent site 31F.) Restaurants abound in Aix; eating on the cours Mirabeau is more expensive than in the pl. des Cardeurs and pl. Ramus. For good value and fresh-as-can-be-food, try the **markets** on pl. de la Madeleine (open Tu, Th, and Sa 7am-1pm) and pl. Richelme (open daily, same times) to save money without skimping on taste. **Postal Code:** 13100.

FRENCH RIVIERA (CÔTE D'AZUR)

Paradises are made to be lost. Between Marseilles and the Italian border, the sun-drenched beaches and warm waters of the Mediterranean form the backdrop for this fabled playground of the rich and famous—F. Scott Fitzgerald, Cole Porter, Picasso, Renoir, and Matisse are among those who flocked to the coast in its heyday. The area today is crammed with as many low-budget tourists as high-handed millionaires, but the Riviera's seductive loveliness has been its undoing, as shrewd developers have turned the coast's beauty into big business. Many French condemn the Riviera as a mere shadow of its former self.

MARSEILLES (MARSEILLE)

France's third-largest city, Marseilles (pop. 900,000) is like the *bouillabaisse* soup for which it is famous: steaming hot and pungently spiced, with a little bit of everything mixed in. A mix of wild nightclubs, beaches, islands, gardens, and big-city adventure, Marseilles bites its thumb at the manicured nails of Monaco and struts a true, gritty urban intensity as well as a rare and astounding cultural melange.

▟ TRANSPORTATION

Flights: Aéroport Marseille-Provence (☎04 42 14 14 14), to **Paris** and **Lyon.** Shuttle buses connect the airport with Gare St-Charles (3 per hr., 5:50am-9:50pm, 47F).

Trains: Gare St-Charles (☎08 36 35 35 35), pl. Victor Hugo. To: **Paris** (4¾hr., 12 per day, 413F); **Lyon** (3½hr., 9per day, 209F); and **Nice** (2¾hr., every hr., 149F).

Buses: Gare des Autocars, pl. Victor Hugo (☎04 91 08 16 40), half a block from the train station. Open M-Sa 6:15am-6:30pm, Su 9am-noon and 2-6pm. To: **Avignon** (2hr., 5 per day, 89F, 134F round-trip); **Cannes** (2¼-3hr., 4 per day, 122F); and **Nice** (2¾hr., 4 per day, 136F).

Ferries: SNCM, 61 bd. des Dames (☎08 36 67 95 00), runs ferries to **Corsica** (640-round trip 720F, 12% student discount) and **Sardinia** (750-850F).

Taxis: (☎04 91 09 28 79). 80-130F to hostels from the Gare St. Charles.

▟ ORIENTATION AND PRACTICAL INFORMATION

Although administratively divided into 16 *arrondissements*, Marseilles is understood by locals and visitors alike by neighborhood names and major thoroughfares. **La Canebière** divides the city into north and south, funneling into the **Vieux Port** (home of upscale restaurants, shopping, and nightlife) to the east. North of the *Vieux Port,* working-class residents pile onto the hilltop neighborhood of **Le Panier,** east of which lies **Quartier Belsunce,** the hub of the city's Arab and African communities. At night, Marseilles's dirty streets are wise to avoid. Public transportation tames Marseilles's urban sprawl. The two **Métro lines** (M in text) are clean and simple. (Métro line 1 dir.: Timone will take you to the *Vieux Port* from Gare St. Charles.) **Buses** are essential to get to beaches, which stretch along the coast, southwest of the *Vieux Port*. Both the bus and train stations lie at the top of bd. Athènes.

Every woman who has traveled on the Riviera has a story to tell about men in the big beach towns. Unsolicited pick-up techniques range from subtle invitations to more, uh, bare displays of interest. Brush them off with a biting *"laissez-moi tranquille!"* ("leave me alone") or stony indifference, but don't be shy about enlisting the help of passersby or the police to fend off Mediterranean Don Juans. Don't venture far from the lively streets near the *Vieux Port* after dark. The area around the Cours Belsunce and the bd. d'Athènes are also be dangerous at night.

Tourist office: From the train station, descend the stairs and follow bd. d'Athènes, which becomes bd. Dugommier, and turn right on La Canebière to reach the tourist office, 4 La Canebière. (☎04 91 13 89 00; fax 04 91 13 89 20.) Open July-Aug. daily 9am-8pm; Oct.-June M-Sa 9am-7pm, Su 10am-5pm. The tourist office annex is at the train station. (☎04 91 50 59 18.) Open daily July-Aug. 10am-6pm; Sept.-June M-F 10am-1pm and 1:30-6pm.

Currency exchange: Comptoir Marseillais de Bourse, 22 La Canebière (☎04 91 54 93 94). Excellent rates and no commission. Open M-Sa 9am-6pm.

Emergency: Police, 2 rue du Commissaire Becker (☎04 91 39 80 00). Also in the train station on Esplanade St-Charles (☎04 91 39 80 00, ask for poste 7097).

Internet: Check email at **Le Rozo,** 28 cours Julien (☎04 91 42 70 02). 40F per hr. Open M-Sa 10am-7pm. Access also available at **Info Cafe,** 1 Quai Rive Neuve (☎04 91 33 53 05). Open M-Sat 9am-11pm, Su 2-7pm. 35F per hr.

Post Office: 1 pl. Hôtel des Postes (☎04 91 15 47 20). Follow La Canebière towards the sea and turn right onto rue Reine Elisabeth after it becomes pl. Hôtel des Postes. **Postal Code:** 13001.

ACCOMMODATIONS

Inexpensive hotels abound in Marseilles, but walking home is potentially costly. Hotels listed here prioritize safety and location. While hostels are far from the town center, there is efficient bus service.

Auberge de Jeunesse Bonneveine (HI), impasse Bonfils (☎04 91 17 63 30), off av. J. Vidal. From the station, take Métro line #2 to "Rond-Point du Prado," and transfer onto bus #44 to pl. Bonnefon. From there, walk back towards the rond point, turn left at J. Vidal. Low-slung cement-block building with bar, restaurant, internet access, travel agency, TV room and 150 beds. Breakfast included. Lockers 10F per day. Sheets 17F. Laundry 30F. Reception daily 6am-1am. Flexible 1am curfew. Closed Jan. HI members only. Dorms in summer 72F, in winter 65F, in spring 69F; doubles 93F.

Auberge de Jeunesse Chateau de Bois-Luzy (HI), allée des Primevères (☎04 91 49 06 18). By day, take bus #6 from cours J. Thierry at the top of La Canebière (away from the port) to Marius Richard. Take a right onto Blvd. de l'Amandiere and walk to the soccer fields. Follow the road down to the right and around the fields to reach the hostel. A night bus also runs from La Canebière to Marius Richard. Laundry 30F. Reception daily 7:30-noon and 5-10:30pm. Lockout noon-5pm. Strict curfew May-Oct. 11pm, Nov.-Apr. 10:30pm. 45F, with breakfast 65F. Cash only.

Hôtel du Palais, 26 rue Breteuil (☎04 91 37 78 86). Large, well-maintained rooms almost within sight of the *Vieux Port*. Air-conditioning and soundproofing. Breakfast 30F. Singles with shower 195F; doubles with shower 230-280F; triples with bath 300F.

Hôtel Béarn, 63 rue Sylvabelle (☎04 91 37 75 83), in a quiet side-street not far from the port. Breakfast (with home-made jam) 25F. Singles with shower 104F; doubles with shower 138F, with shower, toilet and TV 208F; triples with shower, toilet and TV 262F.

Marseille
▲ ACCOMMODATIONS

Hôtel Béarn, 1
Hôtel Moderne, 4
Hôtel du Palais, 2
Hôtel Le Provencal, 3

Palais Longchamp/
Musée des Beaux-Arts

CINQ AVENUES
LONGCHAMP

bd. de la Blancarde

av. Marechal

r. du Camas

r. St. Pierre

bd. Chave

r. Monte Cristo

bd. de la Libération

bd. Eugène Pierre

bd. Baille

av. Toulon

av. J. Cantini

BAILLE

TIMONE

bd. du Longchamp

bd. National

r. des Abeilles

r. St. Pierre

r. Château

r. de la Loubière

Payan

r. de Lodi

cours Lieutaud

av.du Prado

NOTRE DAME DU
MONT-COURS JULIEN

PL. JEAN
JAURÈS

crs. F. Roosevelt

r. St.-
Savournin

CANEBIÈRE
REFORMES

Gare
St-Charles

ST-CHARLES

bd. M.
Bourdet

bd. Voltaire

PL. DES
MARSEILLAISES

allées
L. Gambetta STALINGRAD

bd.
Dugommier

r. de la
Liberté

bd. d'
Athenes

La Canebière

NOAILLES

bd
Garibaldi

cours Lieutaud

rue de Rome

PL.
CASTELLANE

CASTELLANE

Dr.
Escat

r. Dr. Fiolle

r. d'Aubagne

r. St. Ferréol

PL. DE
ROME

ESTRAGIN
PRÉFECTURE

r. Paradis

r. Breteuil

bd. Vauban

r. Longue des Capucins

r. de Rome

Musée
Cantini

r. Grignan

r. du Dragon

PL. VICTOR
HUGO

r. N. Roze

r. du Bois

r. des Dominicaines

cours Belsunce

r. d'Aix

PL. DU GAL
DE GAULLE

3

2

r. Sylvabelle

1

JULES
GUESDE

Ste-Barbe

r. Barbusse

r. H.

COLBERT

PL. SADI-
CARNOT

République

pavillon

quai des
Belges

cours J. Ballard

r. Fortia

bd. Notre Dame

Basilique de
Notre Dame
de la Garde

JOLIETTE

bd. des Dames

r. de la

r. de la Joliette

r. J.F. Leca

av. R. Schumann

r. Mazenod

PL. DE LA
CORDERIE

r. Sainte

bd. André Aune

bd. de la
Corderie

bd. Tellene

ch. du Roucas Blanc

quai de la
Joliette

Cathédrale
Nouvelle
Major

r. de l'Eveché

r. du Panier

r. de la Loge
quai du Port

VIEUX PORT
HÔTEL DE VILLE

Vieux Port

quai de Rive Neuve

r. de la Tourette

PROTIS

r. Caisserie

Tunnel

Abbaye
St-Victor

bd. Charles Livon

av. Pasteur

Jardin
du Pharo

PL. DU
4 SEPTEMBRE

r. Chateaubriand

r. du Coteau

r. d'Endoume

r. des Catalans

corniche Pres. J. F. Kennedy

Mediterranean
Sea

500 yards

500 meters

N

FRANCE

FOOD

For the city's famed seafood and North African fare, poke around the *Vieux Port*, especially **pl. Thiars** and **Honoré d'Estienne d'Orves**, where one can dine *en plein air* for as little as 60F. For a more artsy crowd and cheaper fare, head up to cours Julien, northeast of the harbor. You can pick up groceries at **BAZE**, on La Canebière. (Open M-Sa 8:30am-8pm.)

> **O'Provençal Pizzeria,** 7 rue de la Palud, off rue de Rome (☎04 91 54 03 10). Perfect portions, fast service and air-conditioning on hot days make the best pizza in Marseilles better. Menu includes individual pizzas 32-45F, omelets 25F, pasta 30-55F. M-Sa 10am-3pm, 7pm-12am.
>
> **Ce Soleil Donne,** 70 cours Julien (☎04 96 12 12 22), has exotic dishes like kangaroo and pineapple for 59F. Open daily noon-2:30pm, 8pm-10:30pm.
>
> **Country Life,** 14 rue Venture (☎04 96 11 28 00), off rue Paradis. All-you-can-eat vegan (*menu* 62F) under a huge skylight and amid a forest of foliage. Health-food store downstairs. Children and students 38F. Open M-F 11:30am-2:30pm.

SIGHTS AND ENTERTAINMENT

Métro Line 1 (dir.: Timone) takes you to the **Vieux Port**, the focus of Marseilles, which bustles every morning with a **fish market** on the **Quai des Belges**. Take a boat out to the **Château D'If**, the sun-blasted dungeon immortalized in Dumas' *Count of Monte Cristo*, or explore the old quarantine island of **Frioul**. (Boats depart from quai des Belges. Round-trip 50F for each island, 80F for both. Chateau ☎04 91 59 02 30. Open daily Apr.-Sept. 9:30am-6:30pm; Oct.-Mar. Tu-Su 9:30am-5:30pm. 25F, under 25 15F.) Marseilles in all its glory can be seen from the steps of the **Basilique de Notre Dame de la Garde,** the symbol of the city with its golden statue of the "good mother." (Take bus #60 or Rue Breteuil from the *Vieux Port*, turn right on bd. Vauban, and right on rue Fort du Sanctuaire. Open 7am-8pm, off-season 7am-7pm. Free.)

On hot afternoons, the chilling catacombs of the fortified **Abbaye St-Victor,** on rue Sainte at the end of Quai de Rive Neuve, throw open the imagination as well as the tombs of 3rd century martyrs. (☎04 96 11 22 60. Open 8:30am-6:30pm. Crypts 10F.) For more lively entertainment, take bus #83 from the Vieux Port (dir.: Rond-Point du Prado) which follows the **Promenade de la Corniche** along the inlets and beaches of Marseilles. Step off at Vallon des Auffes and across the street from the war monument lies a tiny, perfect fishing harbor with its little boats moored in rows like painted fingernails. The #83 continues to Marseilles's **plage du Prado** and **plage de la Corniche,** which offer clear water and plenty of grass for impromptu soccer matches—get off after the bus rounds the statue of David.

Marseilles's museums are sometimes remarkable less for their collections than for their locations. The city's **Musée d'Histoire de Marseille,** lies on the edge of the original Greek port just to the northeast of the present-day waterfront. Next to the museum is the **Jardin des Vestiges,** the grassy quais with their well-stacked limestone and tumbled columns make a great picnic spot. (Gardens open M-Sa noon-7pm. Museum ☎04 91 90 42 22. 12F, students 6F.) Also worth a visit is **La Vieille Charité**— the old poorhouse and orphanage that now shelters Egyptian, prehistoric and classical collections. From the Quai des Belges walk up rue de la République past pl. Sadi Carnot; take a left on rue F. Moisson. (☎04 91 14 58 80. Open Tu-Su; June-Sept. 11am-6pm, Oct.-May 10am-5pm. Permanent exhibits 12F, temporary 18F.)

From mellow jazz to fast and furious clubbing, you can find it all in Marseilles's nightlife, centered around pl. Thiars and cours Julien. All of Marseilles's youth and twenty-somethings seem to flock to the outdoor **Bar du Marché,** 15 pl. Notre-Dame du Mont, (☎04 91 92 58 89; beer from 18F), or to **L'Enigme,** 22 rue Beauvau, the only gay/lesbian spot on a street packed with lively bars. (☎04 91 33 79 20. Open daily 6pm-dawn. Drinks 10F 6pm-11pm, 20F after 11pm.) For a wild time, visit **Trolleybus,** 24 quai de Rive Neuve, which has a room each for house-garage, rock, pop-rock, and soul-funk-salsa as well as a new discotheque built around two regulation-size *boule* courts. (☎04 91 54 30 45, info ☎06 16 13 13 56. Sa cover 60F, includes 1 drink. Open Wed-Sa 11pm-7am, in winter Th-Sa.)

🏴 DAYTRIPS FROM MARSEILLE

AIX-EN-PROVENCE. Just 35min. away is beautiful Aix-en-Provence, the cultural capital of Provence. Enjoy the festivals (see p. 350).

AVIGNON. The university town is dominated by the dazzling Palais des Papes. Stroll through the medieval streets and relax with a glass of *pastis* (see p. 346).

CANNES. Mug for the camera at Cannes. Or just hit one of the beaches overlooking multi-million-dollar yachts (see p. 356).

MONACO. Royal-watch and wander through the Monte-Carlo casino (see p. 363).

ST-TROPEZ

Nowhere are the glitz and glamor of the Riviera more apparent than in the former fishing hamlet of St-Tropez. While other towns along the coast cling to past glories, *St-Trop d'Aise* (St. Too-Much-Luxury) religiously devotes itself to the holy trinity of sun, sand, and big boats. For the less sedentary, the **plage l'Escalet** is worth the trek for swimming and rock-climbing. (15km, by foot or car only.) The **chemin des Graniers** curves around the **citadel,** home to the **Musée Naval** which chronicles the town's military history. The path continues on to the small, uncrowded **plage des Graniers** for the perfect picnic spot. (Museum open daily 10am-6pm; off-season 10am-noon and 1-5pm; closed Nov. 25F, students 15F.) Paths wind along the coast; choose a cove and bask *au naturel*—tanlines mean you just arrived.

Sodetrav **buses** (☎ 04 94 97 88 51) head to St-Tropez from St-Raphaël (1½-2¼hr., 8-15 per day, 51F). The fastest, nicest, and (with a Fréjus hostel voucher) cheapest way to get here is by **boat.** At the old port, Les Bateaux de St-Raphaël (☎ 04 94 95 17 46) sail in from Cannes (July-Aug. only; T, Th, Sa 1 per day; 100F) and St. Raphaël (50min.; July-Aug. 2-5 per day; 70F, round-trip 110F). While the beaches make up much of St. Tropez's appeal, transportation logistics can be frustrating. A **free shuttle,** the *navette municipale,* which leaves from the pl. des Lices, is the only source of public transportation to Les Salins and plage Tahiti (4 per day). The **tourist office,** on quai Jean Jaurès, is on the waterfront. (☎ 04 94 97 45 21; fax 04 94 97 82 66. Open June-Sept. daily 8:30am-11pm and 3:30-11pm; May-Oct. 9am-8pm.) Budget hotels do not exist in St-Tropez, and the closest youth hostel is in Fréjus. The cheapest hotel in St. Tropez is **Les Chimères,** port du Pilon, off of av. Général Leclerc. (☎ 04 94 97 02 00. June-Sept. singles 200F; Oct.-May 150F.) **Camping** is the cheapest option, but you'll need reservations; try **Les Prairies de la Mer** in Port Grimaud. (☎ 04 94 79 09 09. Open Apr.-Oct. July-Aug. one person and tent 82F; two people 84F; with car 115F.) The **vieux port** and the streets behind the waterfront are the hub of culinary activity. To do it yourself, duck into **Prisunic supermarket,** 7 av. du Général Leclerc. (Open M-Sa 8am-8pm, Su 8:30am-8pm; off-season closed Su.) The hippest bar for cosmopolitan youth is **L'Empire,** 9 rue des Remparts. (☎ 05 16 13 13 21. W ladies drink free. Open daily 6pm-3am.)

ST-RAPHAËL AND FRÉJUS

With neither the charm of the Riviera's smaller towns, nor the liveliness of its more cosmopolitan centers, the twin cities of St. Raphaël and Fréjus are of dubious appeal except as a great (read: cheap) base from which to visit **St-Tropez** (see above). There's evidence that the Romans dropped by while building their empire; an **amphitheater,** on rue Henri Vadon, in Fréjus, marks the spot. (Open daily Apr.-Sept. W-M 10am-1pm and 2:30-6:30pm; Nov.-Mar. M-F 10am-noon and 1:30-5:30pm, Sa 9:30am-12:30pm and 1:30-5:30pm. Free.) While the cities are only 5min. apart by train, it is impossible to walk from one to another. St-Raphaël sends **trains** from the pl. de la Gare to Cannes (25min., every 30min., 34F) and Nice (50min., every 30min., 56F). **Buses** leave from behind the train station in St-Raphaël for: Cannes (70min., 8 per day, 35F); Fréjus (20min., every 30min., 8.50F); and St-Tropez (1½hr., 6 per day, 51F). The **tourist office** in St-Raphaël is opposite the train station. (☎ 04 94 19 52 52. Open June-Sept. daily 9am-7pm; Oct.-May M-Sa 9am-12:30pm and 2-6:30pm.) Exit right from the station in St-Raphaël and take your third left to get to **Le Touring,** 1 quai Albert 1er. (☎ 04 94 95 01 72. Open Dec. 16-Nov.14. Singles and doubles 190F, with shower 250F, in summer 300F.) If you exit the station onto bd. Felix Martin and take the second left onto av. Paul Doumer, you will reach the **Hôtel des Pyramides,** 77 av. Paul Doumer. (Open Mar. 15-Nov.15. Singles 150F; doubles 220-345F; triples 340F.) **Postal Codes:** St-Raphaël 83700; Fréjus 83600.

CANNES

All stereotypes of the French Riviera materialize in Cannes (pop. 78,000), a favorite stopover for the international jet-set. Less exclusive than St-Tropez, Cannes still allows even the ungroomed budget traveler to tan like a star. In May, the red carpets roll out for the **Festival International du Film** which imports Hollywood's *crème de la crème*. None of the festival's 350 screenings are open to the public, but the sidewalk show is free. The best window-shopping along the Riviera lies along **rue d'Antibes** and **bd. de la Croisette.** Farther west, the **Eglise de la Castre** and its courtyard stand on the hill on which *vieux Cannes* was built. Of Cannes' three **casinos,** the most accessible is **Le Casino Croisette,** 1 jetée Albert Edouard, next to the Palais des Festivals, with slots, blackjack, and roulette. (Gambling daily 7:30pm-4am; open for slots at 10am. No shorts, jeans, or t-shirts. 18+ with ID.) You can also lose your shirt in a different locale in Palm Beach at the eastern edge of Cannes, where **Mocambo** and **Whisky à Go Go,** on av. de Lérins, rev it up by night. **Le Loft,** 13 rue du. Doc. Monod, has no cover and offers a lively dance floor.

Coastal **trains** run to: Antibes (15min., 14F); Marseilles (2hr., 133F); Monaco (60min., 46F); Nice (35min., 32F); and St-Raphaël (25min., 34F). The **tourist office,** 1 bd. de la Croisette, helps find accommodations. (☎ 04 93 39 24 53; fax 04 92 99 84 23. Open July-Aug. daily 9am-7pm; Sept.-June M-Sa 9am-6:30pm.) Access the **internet** at **Institut Riviera Langue,** 26 rue de Mimont. (35F per hr. Open M-Sa 9am-11pm, Su 2pm.) Hostels are 10-20min. farther from the beach than other lodgings, but are the cheapest options in town. Veer left after the pl. du Cdt. Maria to the **Centre International de Séjour de Cannes (HI),** 35 av. de Vallauris. (☎ 04 93 99 26 79. Reception 8am-1pm and 3-11:30pm. Curfew 2am. 70-80F.) **Hotel Mimont,** 39 rue de Mimont, is two streets behind the train station, off bd. de la République. (☎ 04 93 39 51 64. Singles 170-190F; doubles 220-230F.) **Camp** at **Le Grand Saule,** 24 bd. Jean Moulin, in nearby Ranguin; take bus #9 from pl. de l'Hôtel de Ville (dir.: Ranguin or La Boissier; 20min., 7.70F). (☎ 04 93 90 55 10. 2 people and tent 92F. Open Apr.-Oct.) Save your francs at **Monoprix supermarket,** in Champion, 6 rue Meynadier. (Open M-Sa 8:45am-7:40pm; off-season 9am-7:30pm.) Reasonably priced restaurants abound in the pedestrian zone around **rue Meynadier. Postal Code:** 06400.

ANTIBES-JUAN-LES-PINS

Although officially joined under one name, Antibes-Juan-les-Pins (pop. 70,000), Antibes and Juan-les-Pins are 3km apart, with separate train stations and tourist offices. Antibes is quiet and serene, with sandy beaches and close-by museums. The **Musée Picasso,** in the Château Grimaldi, on pl. Mariejol, displays works by the master and his contemporaries. (☎ 04 92 90 54 20. Open Tu-Su June-Sept. 10am-6pm; Oct.-May 10am-noon and 2-6pm. 30F, students 18F.) **Musée Peynet,** pl. Nationale, has over 300 humorous and colorful drawings by local artist Raymond Peynet. (☎ 04 92 90 54 30. Open daily 10am-noon and 2-6pm. 20F, students 10F.) **Trains** leave av. Robert Soleau for: Cannes (30min., every 30min., 14F); Marseilles (2½hr., 15 per day, 139F); Nice (30min., every 30min., 22F). **Buses** leave from pl. Guynemer for: Cannes (25min., every 20min., 13F) and Nice (1hr., every 20min., 25.50F). (Open M-F 8am-noon and 2-6pm, Sa 9am-12:30pm and 2-5pm.) Exit the station, turn right on av. Robert Soleau, and follow the "Maison du Tourisme" signs to the **tourist office,** 11 pl. de Gaulle. (☎ 04 92 90 53 00. Open July-Aug. daily 8:45am-7:30pm; Sept.-June M-F 9am-12:30pm and 2-6pm, Sa 9am-noon and 2-6pm.) To get to the **Hôtel Jabotte,** 13 av. Max Maurey, follow bd. Albert 1er from pl. de Gaulle to its end, turn right on Mal. Leclerc, and walk along the beach. (☎ 04 93 61 45 89. Breakfast 30F. Check-in M-Sa before 7:30pm, Su before 1pm or after 6pm. Singles and doubles 200-400F; triples 320-55-F; quads 620-820F.) **Postal Code:** 06600.

Juan-les-Pins is Antibes's younger, hipper, and more hedonistic sibling. Boutiques remain open until midnight, cafes until 2am, and nightclubs until past dawn. The streets are packed with seekers of sea, sun, and sex; nightclubs pulse with promises of decadence. *Discothèques* are generally open from 11pm to 5am (covers around 100F, includes 1 drink). **Le Village**, 1 bd. de la Pinède, is notorious for its lively dance floor. (Open daily midnight-5am. 100F, free for women on F.) Check out the psychedelic **Whiskey à Go Go**, on la Pinède, and newcomer **Vertigo**, at the intersection of av. Maupassant and bd. Wilson. **Trains** arrive from: Antibes (5min., every 20 min., 7F); Cannes (10min., every 20min., 12F); and Nice (30min., every 20min., 24F). To get from Antibes's pl. du Général de Gaulle to Juan-les-Pins on foot, follow bd. Wilson, which runs right into the center of town (about 1.5km). Rather than make the post-party trek back to Antibes, sack out at **Hôtel Trianon**, 14 av. de L'Estérel. (☎04 93 61 18 11. Breakfast 30F. Doubles 215F, with shower 225F, with bath 260F; triples 260-280F.) **Postal Code:** 06160.

NICE

Sun-drenched and spicy, Nice triumphs as the unofficial capital of the Riviera—a rite of passage for young travelers. The city's pumping nightlife, top-notch museums, and bustling beaches enhance the native *Provençal* charms: flowery, palm-lined boulevards, casual affluence, and soothing sea breezes. During its **Carnaval** (the second half of February), the visitors and *Niçois* alike ring in the spring with wild floral revelry, grotesque costumes, and raucous song and dance. Prepare to have more fun than you'll remember.

▐ TRANSPORTATION

Flights: Aéroport Nice-Côte d'Azur (☎04 93 21 30 30). Airport open daily 24hr. **Air France**, 10 av. Félix Faure (☎08 02 80 28 02), serves **Paris** (1361F, under 25 380F).

Trains: Gare SNCF Nice-Ville (☎04 92 14 81 62), on av. Thiers. Info office open M-Sa 8am-6:30pm, Su 8:30-11:15am and 2-6pm. To: **Paris** (7hr., 2-4 per day, 485F); **Antibes** (30min., every 10-30min, 22F); **Bordeaux** (10¼hr, 3 per day, 440F); **Cannes** (40min., every 15-45min., from 32F); **Lyon** (6hr., 11 per day, 304F); **Marseilles** (2¾hr., every 30-90min., 149F); and **Monaco** (25min., every 10-30min., 22F).

Buses: 5 bd. Jean Jaurès (☎04 93 85 61 81), left at the end of bd. Jean Medecin. Information open M-F 7:30am-11:30am and 2-6pm, Sa 2-6pm. To: **Cannes** (1½hr., 3 per hr., 32F) and **Monaco** (30min., 3-4 per hr., 17-20F).

Ferries: SNCM, quai du Commerce (☎04 93 13 66 66). Take bus #1 or #2 (dir.: Port) from pl. Masséna. Take bus #1 or 2 from pl. Masséna. To **Corsica** (see p. 364). Open M-F 8am-7pm, Sa 8am-noon. Reservations daily from 8am-noon and 2pm-5:45pm. Dock open M-F 6am-7pm.

Public Transportation: Sunbus, 10 av. Félix Faure (☎04 93 16 52 10), near pl. Leclerc and pl. Masséna. Long treks to museums, the beach, and hostels make the 22F day pass, 55F 10-ticket carnet, 85F 5-day pass, or 110F 7-day pass well worth it. Individual tickets 8.50F. Bus #12 links the station, pl. Masséna, and the beach every 12min.

Bike and Scooter Rental: JML Location, 34 av. Auber (☎04 93 16 07 00), opposite the train station. Bikes 70F per day, 300F per week. Scooters 220F per day; 1500F credit card deposit required. Open M-F 8am-1pm and 2-6:30pm, Sa 8am-1pm.

▐✦🛈 ORIENTATION AND PRACTICAL INFORMATION

As you exit the train station, **av. Jean-Médecin** to the left and **bd. Gambetta** to the right run directly to the beach. **Pl. Masséna** is 10min. down av. Jean-Médecin. Along the coast, **Promenade des Anglais** is a people-watching paradise. To the southeast, past av. Jean Médecin and toward the bus station, pulsates **Vieux Nice**. Women should avoid walking alone after sundown, and everyone should exercise caution at night around the train station, in *Vieux Nice*, and on the Promenade des Anglais.

Tourist Office: Av. Thiers (☎04 93 87 07 07; fax 04 93 16 85 16; email otc@nice-cote-azur.org; www.nice-coteazur.org), beside the train station. Makes same-day reservations for hotels in Nice; your chances of nabbing a room are best between 9am and 11am.

Essential city maps as well as bus maps and schedules. Open daily mid-June to mid-Sept. 7:30am-8pm; mid-Sept. to mid-June 8am-7pm.

Consulates: Canada, 10 rue Lamartine (☎04 93 92 93 22). Open M-F 9am-noon. **USA,** 31 rue Maréchal Joffre (☎04 93 88 89 55; fax 04 93 87 07 38). Open M-F 9-11:30am and 1:30-4:30pm. **UK,** 8 rue Alphonse Karr (☎04 93 82 32 04). Open M, W, F 9:30-11:30am.

Currency Exchange: Cambio, 17 av. Thiers (☎04 93 88 56 80), opposite the train station. No commission. Open daily 7am-midnight.

American Express: 11 promenade des Anglais (☎04 93 16 53 53), at rue des Congrès. **ATM** machine. Open daily 9am-9pm.

Laundromat: Laverie Niçoise, 7 rue d'Italie (☎04 93 87 56 50), beside Basilique Notre-Dame. 15kg for 50F, dryers 2F per 4min. Open M-Sa 8:30am-12:30pm, 2:30-7:30, Su 8:30am-1pm.

Police, ☎04 93 17 22 22. At the opposite end of bd. M. Foch from bd. Jean Médecin.

Pharmacy: 7 rue Masséna (☎04 93 87 78 94). Open 24hr.

Internet Access: Organic Café, 16 rue Paganini. Mention *Let's Go* and pay 10F per 15min.; 34F per hr. Open daily 9am-10pm. **Web Nice,** 25bis Promenade des Anglais. 25F per 30min., 50F per hr. Open Tu-Su 10:30am-8:30pm.

Post Office: 21 av. Thiers (☎04 93 82 65 22), near the train station. Open M-F 8am-7pm, Sa 8am-noon. 24-hour **ATM.** Address mail to be held: Rebecca SIMMONS, *Poste Restante,* Recette Principale, Nice 06000, France. **Postal Code:** 06033 Nice Cedex 1.

▄ ACCOMMODATIONS

To sleep easy, come to Nice with reservations. Affordable places surround the train station, but without reservations (made 3-5 days ahead), you'll be forced to join the legions outside the train station, which moonlights as one of the largest and most dangerous bedrooms in France.

Hôtel Les Orangiers, 10bis av. Durante (☎04 93 87 51 41). Bright rooms, all with showers and fridges. Free luggage storage. Breakfast 20F. Closed Nov. In summer, dorms 85F; singles 95-100F; doubles 210-230F; triples 270-300F; quads 360F.

Hôtel Baccarat, 39 rue d'Angleterre (☎04 93 88 35 73). Large rooms with showers. Remember your reservation code! Dorms 87F per person; singles 177F; doubles 220F.

Hôtel Belle Meunière, 21 av. Durante (☎04 93 88 66 15), on a street facing the train station. Birds chirp in the courtyard of this elegant converted mansion. Breakfast included. Luggage storage 10F. 4- to 5-bed dorms 112F per person; doubles with shower 280F; triples 246F, with shower 336F.

Hôtel des Flandres, 6 rue de Belgique (☎04 93 88 78 94). Large rooms with high ceilings and private bathrooms. Breakfast 28F. Largest rooms accommodate 5-6, 100F per person; singles 200F; doubles 280-300F; triples 360F; quads 380-420F.

Hôtel Notre Dame, 22 rue de la Russie (☎04 93 88 70 44), at the corner of rue d'Italie, 1 block west of av. Jean Médecin. Spotless, quiet rooms with phones and pleasant decor. If full, they will shuttle you to one of their other hotels nearby. Breakfast 25F. Elegant singles 200F; doubles 250F; triples 320F; quads 380F; extra bed 60F.

Hôtel Petit Trianon, 11 rue Paradis (☎04 93 87 50 46). Left off the pedestrian rue Masséna. Large, elegantly furnished 19th-century style rooms close to the beach, markets, restaurants, and *Vieux Nice.* Breakfast 25F. Showers 10F, available from 7am to 9 or 10am. Singles 100F; doubles 200F; triples 300F.

Hôtel Little Masséna, 22 rue Masséna (☎04 93 87 72 34). Small but clean, comfortable rooms with TV and kitchenette. Singles and doubles 150F, with shower 200F, with bath 250F. Extra person 30F. Prices 10-30F cheaper in off-season.

Hôtel Au Picardy, 10 bd. Jean-Jaurès (☎04 93 85 75 51), across from the bus station. Excellent proximity to *Vieux Nice.* Rooms can be noisy if on the street. Breakfast 17F. Singles 130-150F, 180F with shower; doubles 200-250F, some with shower and toilet; triples and quads 230-290F. Extra bed 45F.

Les Mimosas, 26 rue de la Buffa (☎04 93 88 05 59). Close to the beach and the lively rue Massena. Communal bathrooms. Singles 180F; doubles 210F; triples 250F.

Hôtel Meublé Drouot, 24 rue d'Angleterre (☎04 93 88 02 03). Well-run hotel. Singles 130-150F; doubles 220-240F; triples 270F; quads 350F.

Nice

ACCOMMODATIONS

Auberge de Jeunesse (HI), 11
Hôtel Au Picardy, 10
Hôtel Baccarat, 3
Hôtel Belle Meunière, 6
Hôtel des Flanders, 2
Hôtel Les Orangiers, 5
Hôtel Little Massena, 7
Hôtel Notre Dame &
Hôtel Lyonnais, 4
Hôtel Petit Trianon, 8
Hôtel St-François, 9
Relais International de la
Jeunesse "Clairvallon", 1

Baie des Anges

Port

VIEUX NICE

CHÂTEAU

FRANCE

N

TO ▮ (3km),
MUSÉE MATISSE (1.2km)

TO ▮ (2.5km)

400 yards

400 meters

🍴 FOOD

Nice offers a smorgasbord of seafood, Asian cuisine, and Italian gastronomic delights. *Vieux Nice* is crowded and touristy, but good eats are easy to find. Stock up at the **Prisunic supermarket,** 42 av. Jean Médecin (☎04 93 62 38 90. Open M-Sa 8:30am-8:30pm.)

■ Acchiardo, 38 rue Droite (☎04 93 85 51 16), in *Vieux Nice.* Surprisingly reasonable pastas from 36F are immensely popular with a loyal local clientele. Open M-F noon-1:30pm and 7-9:30pm, Sa noon-1:30am.

Lou Pilha Leva, 13 rue du Collet (☎04 93 80 29 33). Always bustling, this is where to get a lot of *niçois* food for little money. 37F *moules* (mussels) are hard to resist. Open daily 8am-11pm.

Indyana, 11 rue Gustave de Loye (☎04 93 80 67 69). Trendy dinner spot for Nice's young and hip serving classic French fare with an Asian twist. Copious salads are meals in themselves. Open M-Sa for lunch and dinner.

L'Authentic, 18 rue Biscarra (☎04 93 62 48 88). Inviting bistro in a low-key neighborhood filled with restaurants. Emphasis on "authentic" fresh ingredients, regional recipes, and grandiose portions (59F for a filling salade nicoise).

👁 SIGHTS

Many visitors to Nice head straight for the beaches and don't retreat from the sun and water until the day is done. They're missing out; contrary to popular opinion, there are things in Nice more worth doing than a long naked sunbath on a bunch of pointy pebbles. If you see nothing else, visit the Chagall and Matisse museums. Nice's **Promenade des Anglais,** named after the English expatriates who had it built, is a sight in itself. At the **Negresco,** one of many luxury hotels that line the boulevard, the staff still don top-hats and 19th-century uniforms. Whatever dreams you've had about Nice's beach, though, the hard reality is an endless stretch of rocks; bring a beach mat if you plan to soak up the sun in comfort. If you follow the Promenade east of bd. Jean Jaures, you'll stumble upon **Vieux Nice,** a medieval quartier in which labyrinthine streets and sprawling nighttime restaurant terraces draw massive crowds. *Vieux Nice* is host to a number of lively markets in the morning, including a fish frenzy at **place St-François.** The **Eglise St. Martin,** pl. Augustine, is the city's oldest church and site of Italian revolutionary Garibaldi's baptism. Stay on the Promenade to reach **Le Château,** a flower hillside park crowned with the remains of an 11th-century cathedral. (Open daily 7am-8pm.)

Even burn-hard sunbathers will have a hard time passing by Nice's first-class museums. To the northeast of the train station just off bd. Cimiez, find the moving **Musée National Marc Chagall,** the largest public collection of his works, which treat the Bible's greatest stories with fantasy and emotion. (Av. du Dr. Ménard. 15min. walk from the train station, or take bus #15, dir.: Rimiez and Les Sources. Open July-Sept. W-M 10am-5:50pm, Oct.-June. W-M 10am-4:50pm. 20-30F.) Higher up the hill, an impressive collection of Matisse's Riviera work is housed in the **■Musée Matisse,** 1634 av. des Arènes de Cimiez. The artist lived in Nice from 1917 to 1954 in appreciation of the special quality of its light. While the collections of paintings is a bit disappointing, the 3-D work is dazzling: two voluptuous bronze reliefs, some rarely-seen early realist works, and dozens of *découpages,* the brilliantly colored cut-and-paste tableaux to which the artist devoted the last years of his life. The famous "blue nude" and books illustrated by Matisse are also inside. (Take buses #15, 17, 20, or 22 to Arènes. Open W-M Apr.-Sept. 10am-6pm; Oct.-Mar. 10am-5pm. 25F, students 20F.) Matisse, along with Raoul Dufy, is buried nearby in a cemetery beside the **Monastère Cimiez,** which contains a museum devoted to Franciscan art and is surrounded by lovely gardens. (Museum open M-Sa 10am-noon and 3–6pm; cemetery open daily 8am-6pm.) Check out the onion-domed **Cathédrale Orthodoxe Russe St-Nicolas,** 17 bd. du Tzarevitch, west of bd. Gambetta near the train station, which was funded by Tsar Nicolas II. (Open June-Aug. 9am-noon and 2:30-6pm, Sept.-May 9:30am-noon and 2:30-5pm. 15F, students 12F.)

Closer to *Vieux Nice*, the **Musée d'Art Moderne et d'Art Contemporain,** on promenade des arts at the intersection of av. St-Jean Baptiste and Traverse Garibaldi, features avant-garde works by French and American provocateurs. Highlights include a tree made of discarded hygiene bottles and a giant, crushed car. (Take bus #5, dir. St-Charles, from the station to Garibaldi. 20F, students 10F. Open W-M 10am-6pm.) More traditional devotees will enjoy the **Musée de Beaux Arts,** 33 av. Baumettes, off bd. Francois Grosso on the other side of the downtown core. Here, rooms devoted to French classicism, impressionism, Van Dongen and Dufy fill an elegant 19th century villa. (Take bus #38 from the train station to Cheret or bus #12 to Grosso.)

ENTERTAINMENT AND NIGHTLIFE

Nice's **Jazz Festival,** in mid-July at the Parc et Arènes de Cimiez near the Musée Matisse, attracts world-famous jazz and non-jazz musicians. (☎ 04 93 21 68 12. Tickets 50-250F.) The **FNAC,** 24 av. Jean Médecin, in the Nice Etoile shopping center, sells tickets for performances around town. During **Carnaval,** in late February, Nice gives Rio a run for its money with two weeks of parades, outlandish costumes, fireworks, and parties. Nice guys do finish last—here the party crowd swings long after the folks in nearby St-Tropez and Antibes have called it a night. The bars and nightclubs around rue Masséna and *Vieux Nice* frolic with dance, jazz, and rock. However, the areas around *Vieux Nice* and the Promenade des Anglais, where local men have a reputation for hassling people, can be dangerous at night. The dress code at all bars and clubs is simple: look good. Most pubs will turn you away if they catch you wearing shorts, sandals, t-shirts, or a baseball cap.

BARS

De Klomp, 6 rue Mascoinat (☎ 04 93 92 42 85). 40 types of whisky (from 30F) or 18 beers on tap (pint 40F). A variety of live music from salsa to jazz every night. Gay friendly. Happy Hour M-S 5:20-9:20pm. Open M-Sa 5:30pm-2:30am.

Le Bar Des Deux Frères, 1 rue du Moulin (☎ 04 93 80 77 61). A young, funky crowd throws back tequila (20F) and beer (15F) amid lasers and grafittied walls. Open daily 9pm-2 or 3am, in winter closed Su or M.

Wayne's, 15 rue de la Préfecture (☎ 04 93 13 46 99). Frat boys and alterna-chicks dance the night away in this wild and always-packed bar. Live music every night in the summer. Ladies drink till they drop W for 10F. Open daily 2:30pm-12:30am.

McMahon's, 20 bd. Jean Jaures (☎ 04 93 71 16 23). A meeting place for expat Brits and locals alike. 100 different shots (25F each) available at the bar. Happy Hour daily 6-9pm, karaoke on Tuesday, drink promos on Thursday, and dancing with DJs F-Sa. Open daily 6pm-2am.

Tapas la Monda, 2bis rue de l'Abbaye (☎ 04 93 62 27 46). It resembles a revolutionary secret meeting spot, but the only plotting you'll do is how to get home after braving the *bar o mètre* (100F), a meter-long wooden box of shots. Sissies can take 50cm for 60F or 25cm for 40F. Tequila and Vodka 10F. Concerts (10F) feature reggae and rock, live music M-Th. Open daily 7pm-12:30am.

Nocy-Be, 4-6 rue Jules Gilly (☎ 04 93 85 52 25). Take a time-out at this mellow Indian tea-room, with low-hanging lamps and comfortable floor rugs. Dozens of teas to choose from. Open W-M 10:30am-1:30pm and 3pm-1:30am.

CLUBS

La Suite, 2 rue Brea (☎ 04 93 92 92 91). Luring a funky, well-dressed, and moneyed crowd into its chic ambiance, La Suite is Nice's coolest club. Cover 60F, Th free. Open Th-Sa 11pm-2:30am.

La Palousa, 29 rue Alphonse Karr (☎04 93 62 81 31), at the corner of rue Georges Clemenceau. A huge wooden dance floor and ample lounge space in a double-decker of a club; well-known DJs spin disco, latin, and house for a young crowd. Cover 100F, beer 50F, free for women on Friday until 1am. Open Th-Su 11-dawn, F-Sa only in winter.

Le Duke, 11 rue Alexandre Mari (☎04 93 80 40 50), near the Palais de Justice. Cushy red sofas and the scent of incense make this swanky club one of Nice's favorites when the bars let out. Cover 100F, free for women if the night is slow. Open midnight-6am Wed-Sa in July, same hours Tu-Su in Aug.

Blue Boy, 9 rue Jean-Baptiste Spinetta (☎04 93 44 68 24), in west Nice. Though far from town, Blue Boy remains Nice's most popular gay club.

🎒 DAYTRIPS FROM NICE

THE CORNICHES

*Trains and buses between Nice and Monaco serve most of the Corniche towns frequently. With a departure about every hour, **trains** from Nice to Monaco stop at: Beaulieu-sur-Mer (10min., 12F); Cap d'Ail (20min., 16F); Eze-sur-Mer (16min., 13F); and Villefranche-sur-Mer (7min., 10F). Also departing from the train station are numerous numbered **RCA buses** (☎04 93 85 64 44) which run between Nice and Monaco, making different stops along the way. Bus #111 leaves Nice, stopping in Villefranche-sur-Mer (9 per day M-Sa). Three buses continue on to St-Jean-Cap-Ferrat. Bus #117 runs between Nice and Ville-franche-sur-Mer (11 per day). Bus #112 travels from Nice to Monte-Carlo, stopping in Eze-le-Village (3-7 per day). **RCA** and **Broch buses** (☎04 93 31 10 52) run between Nice and: Beaulieu-sur-Mer (20min., every hr., 12F); Cap d'Ail (30min., every hr., 17F); Eze-le-Village (25min., every hr., 15F); Monaco-Ville (40min., every hr., 20F); Monte-Carlo (45 min., every hr., 20F); and Villefranche-sur-Mer (10min., every hr., 8.50F).*

Rocky shores, pebble beaches, and luxurious villas glow along the Corniches, the coast between hectic Nice and high-rolling Monaco. More relaxing than their glam-fab neighbors, these tiny towns are like freshwater pearls—similar in brilliance, yet gratifyingly unique, with interesting museums, architectural finds, and breathtaking countryside. The train offers a good glimpse of the coast up close, while bus rides on the high roads allow bird's-eye views of the steep cliffs and crashing sea below.

VILLEFRANCHE-SUR-MER. Narrow streets and pastel houses have enchanted Aldous Huxley, Katherine Mansfield, and a bevy of other writers. Strolling from the train station along quai Ponchardier, a sign to the *vieille ville* points toward the spooky and dungeonesque 13th-century **rue Obscure,** the oldest street in Ville-france, layered with so many homes and shops that the only light comes from iron chandeliers hanging from the street's "ceiling." At the end of the quai stands the **Chapelle St-Pierre,** decorated by Jean Cocteau, former resident, film-maker, and jack-of-all-arts. (☎04 93 76 90 70. Call ahead for hrs. 12F.) To get to the **tourist office,** on Jardin François Binon, from the train station, head inland on av. G. Clemenceau; continue straight when it becomes av. Sadi Carnot. (☎04 93 01 73 68; fax 04 93 76 63 65. Open July-Aug. daily 9am-8pm; mid-Sept. to June M-Sa 9am-noon and 2-6pm.)

ST-JEAN-CAP-FERRAT. A lovely town with an even lovelier beach, St-Jean-Cap-Ferrat is the trump card of the Riviera. The **Fondation Ephrussi di Rothschild**—a stunning Italian villa with an impressive, eclectic collection of artwork—is the town's main draw, and the best sight between Nice and Monaco. The villa houses the collections of the Baroness de Rothschild: Monet canvases, Gobelins tapestries, and Chinese vases. (Open July-Aug. daily 10am-7pm; Sept.-Oct. and Feb. 15-June daily 10am-6pm; Nov.-Feb. 14 M-F 2pm-6pm, Sa-Su 10am-6pm. 49F, students 37F.) The town's beautiful and untouristed **beaches** merit the area's nickname *Presqu'île des Rêves* (Peninsula of Dreams), and are mostly frequented by local families.

EZE. The most colorful of the towns from Nice to Monaco, this imposing three-tiered medieval town features the **Porte des Maures,** which served as a portal for a surprise attack by the Moors, and the newly renovated **Baroque Eglise Parois-sial,** decorated with a combination of Christian and Egyptian symbols. (Open daily 9am-noon and 2-6pm.) The best views are 40min. up the **Sentier Friedrich Nietzsche,** a windy trail where Nietzsche found inspiration for part of *Thus Spake Zarathustra;* the path begins in **Eze Bord-du-Mer,** 100m east of the train station and tourist office, and ends near the base of the medieval city, by the Fragonard *parfumerie.*

CAP D'AIL. With 3km of cliff-framed foamy seashore, Cap d'Ail's (pop. 5000) **Les Pissarelles** draws hundreds of nudists, while **plage Mala** is frequented by more modest folk. Free maps and lists of daytrips are available from the **tourist office,** 87bis av. de 3 Septembre. From the train station, turn right at the village, continue on av. de la Gare, and turn right on rue du 4 Septembre. (☎04 93 78 02 33; fax 04 92 10 74 36. July-Aug. Open daily 9am-12:30pm and 2-6pm; Sept.-June M-Sa 9am-12:30pm and 2-6pm.) The **Relais International de la Jeunesse,** on av. R. Gramaglia, has an amazing beachfront location. (☎04 93 78 18 58. Breakfast included. 3-night max. stay when busy. Lockout 9:30am-5pm. Curfew midnight. 70F.)

MONACO/MONTE-CARLO ☎377

Named for a temple to Hercules, Monaco has indeed become a shrine to wealth of Herculean proportions. The world's playground for the rich and famous, this resourceless principality was actually in danger of going under until 1865, when the casino was built, ensuring that Monagasques would never again need to pay taxes.

The **Monte-Carlo Casino,** at place du Casino, is ablaze with red velvet curtains, gilded ceilings, and gold-and-crystal chandeliers. If you feel lucky, the slot machines open at 2pm, while blackjack, craps, and roulette (25F minimum) open at noon. If you need your gambling fix before noon, head next door to **Café de Paris,** where admission to the main room is free, but a peek at the high-stakes *salons privés* costs 50-100F. (☎92 16 21 21. Open daily from 10am.) At all casinos you must be over 21 to gamble, and no shorts, sneakers, sandals, or jeans are permitted. After losing your shirt in Monte Carlo, walk west to Monaco where you can admire the royal robes at the **Palais Princier,** the sometime home of Prince Rainier and his family. When the flag is down, the Prince is away and visitors can tour the lavish palace. (☎93 25 18 31. Open daily June-Sept. 9:30am-6pm; Oct. 10am-5pm. 30F, students 20F before 5pm.) Next door, the stately **Cathédrale de Monaco,** 4 rue Colonel Bellando de Castro, is where former princes of Monaco are buried. Grace Kelly's tomb, behind the altar, is simply marked "Patritia Gracia." (☎93 30 87 70. Open Mar.-Oct. 7am-7pm, Nov.-Feb. 7am-6pm.) Once run by Jacques Cousteau, the stunning **Musée Océanographique,** on av. St-Martin, houses thousands of species of marine animals. (☎93 15 36 00. Open daily July-Aug. 9am-8pm; Apr.-June and Sept. 9am-7pm; Mar. and Oct. 9:30am-7pm; Nov.-Feb. 10am-6pm. Audioguides 20F. 60F, students and ages 6-18 30F.) The **Exhibition of H.S.H. the Prince of Monaco's Private Collection of Classic Cars,** on les Terraces de Fontvieille, features 105 of the sexiest and most stately cars ever made. (☎92 05 28 56. Open daily Dec.-Oct. 10am-6pm. 30F, students 15F.) For rocking nightlife, head to **La Rascasse** (☎93 25 56 90), Quai Antoine 1er, an all-night bar that delivers live rock music in a raucous atmosphere.

Trains (☎08 36 35 35 35) run to: **Antibes** (1hr., every 30min., 38F); **Cannes** (1¼hr., every 30min., 46F); and **Nice** (20min., every 30min., 20F). From the station, turn right on av. du Port and left on bd. Albert 1er, overlooking the harbor; on the right is the quartier of **Monaco-Ville,** with its *vieille ville* and the palace, and to the left rises the fabled quartier of **Monte-Carlo** and the casino. **Bus** #4 links the train station to the Casino in Monte-Carlo. (Tickets 8.50F, 20F for a carte of 4. Buy tickets on board.) The **tourist office,** 2a bd. des Moulins, near the casino, has maps and reserves rooms. (☎92 16 61 16; fax 92 16 60 00. Open M-Sa 9am-7pm, Su 10am-noon.) Access the **internet** at **Stars N' Bars,** on quai Antoine 1er. (Open daily 10am-1:30am. 40F per 30min.) To afford a room in Monaco, you'll either need to seduce royalty or win big.

Those between the ages of 16 and 31 can try the **Centre de Jeunesse Princesse Stéphanie**, 24 av. Prince Pierre, 100m uphill from the station. Excellent location, the hostel is on a coveted piece of greenspace amidst utter urbanity. (☎93 50 83 20. Breakfast included. Lockers. Laundry 30F. Check-out 9:30am. Curfew strictly enforced. Closed mid-Nov.-mid-Dec. 4-bed dorm 80F. Cash only.) One of the more affordable dining options is **L'Escale**, 17 bd. Albert 1er, where you can dine first-class but pay like coach. The menu is Italian with a cosmopolitan twist; pizzas and pastas start at 50F. (☎93 39 13 44. Open daily noon-3 pm, 6-11 pm.)

CORSICA (LA CORSE)

A story told to Corsican children goes something like this: and on the sixth day, God made Corsica. He mixed the turquoise waters of the Mediterranean, the snow-capped splendor of the Alps, and the golden sunshine of the Riviera in order to create the island the Greeks called *Kallysté* (the most beautiful).

▚ TRANSPORTATION

Air France and its subsidiary **Compagnie Corse Méditerranée (CCM)** fly to Ajaccio and Bastia from Paris (from 1065F, students 880F); Lyon (from 865F, students 680F); Marseilles (1202F, students 822F); Nice (1081F, students 781F). There's also a direct link from **Lille** to **Bastia** (without tax: from 1200F, students 1070F). **All fares listed here are round trip.** Call Air France in Marseilles (☎04 91 00 33 83) or Paris (☎08 20 82 08 20). **Air Liberté** services **Calvi** and **Porto Vecchio (Figari)** from **Nice** (920F, students 600F) and **Marseilles** (1040F, students 640F). In Ajaccio, the Air France/CCM office is at 3 bd. du Roi Jérôme (☎0 802 802 802). In Bastia, it's at 6 av. Emile Sari. **Ferry** travel between the mainland and Corsica can be a rough trip and, in some circumstances, not much cheaper than a plane. The **Société National Maritime Corse Méditerranée (SNCM)** sends ferries from Marseilles (256-292F, under 25 224-256F), Nice (213-243F, under 25 186-213F) and Toulon (305-360F, under 25 265-305F) to Ajaccio, Bastia, Calvi, and Porto Vecchio. SNCM schedules and fees are listed in a booklet widely available at travel agencies or port offices. **All tickets must be reserved at least four days in advance. SAREMARE** (☎04 95 73 00 96) and **Moby Lines** (☎04 85 73 00 29) run from **Santa Teresa** in Sardinia, to **Bonifacio** (2-4 per day, 45-56F per person and 129-183F per car one-way). **Corsica Ferries** crosses from **Livorno** and **Savona** in Italy to **Bastia** (140-220F), with offices in **Bastia**, 5bis rue Chanoine Leschi (☎04 95 32 95 95); **Nice**, Quai Amiral Infernet (☎08 03 095 095); **Lyon**, 9 pl. des Célestins (☎08 03 095 095); and **Paris**, 25 rue de l'Arbre Sec (☎08 03 09 50 95). **Train** service in Corsica is slow and limited to the half of the island north of Ajaccio; **railpasses** are not valid. **Eurocorse Voyages buses** (☎04 95 21 06 30) provide more comprehensive service. **Hiking** is the best way to explore the island's mountainous interior. The longest marked route, **GR20**, is an extremely difficult 14- to 15-day trail (200km) traversing the island. The **Parc Naturel Régional de la Corse**, 2 Sargent Casalonga, in Ajaccio (☎04 95 51 79 10), publishes maps and a guide to *gîtes d'étapes*.

AJACCIO (AIACCIU)

Ajaccio (pop. 60,000) swings like nowhere else on the island. Napoleonophiles find Ajaccio's sights better than another 100 days in power. Start at the **Musée National de la Maison Bonaparte,** on rue St-Charles, between rue Bonaparte and rue Roi-de-Rome, containing everything from Napoleon's baby pictures to his death mask. (☎04 95 21 43 89. Open Apr.-Sept. Tu-Su 9am-noon and 2-6pm, M 2-6pm; Oct.-Mar. Tu-Su 10am-noon and 2-4:45pm, M 2-4:45pm. 22F, ages 18-25 15F, under 18 free.) Napoleon's uncle Fesch piled up a stash of money as a merchant during the Revolution, before leaving commerce for the cloth. Inside the **Musée Fesch**, 50-52 rue Cardinal Fesch, you'll find a collection including works by Raphael, Botticelli, and Titian. Within the complex is the **Chapelle Impériale**, the final resting place of most of the Bonaparte family—though Napoleon himself is buried in a modest Parisian tomb. (☎04 95 21 48 17. Open July-Aug. M 1:30-6pm, Tu-F 9am-6:30pm, Sa-Su

10:30am-6pm, and F 9pm-midnight; Apr.-June and Sept. M 1-5:15pm, T-F 9:15am-12:15pm and 2:15-5:15pm; Oct.-Mar. T-Sa 9:15am-12:15pm and 2:15-5:15pm. Museum 35F, students 25F; chapel 10F, students 5F.) The vertiginous **Îles San-guinaires** bare their black cliffs to the sea, southwest of Ajaccio at the mouth of the gulf. **Promenades en Mer** (☎ 04 95 51 31 31), at a kiosk on the port, runs excursions to the largest of the islands (Apr.-Oct. 1 per day in the afternoon, 120F).

Bus #8 (☎ 04 95 51 43 23) shuttles between the **airport** and the bus station at quai l'Herminier (26F). **Trains** (☎ 04 95 23 11 03) run from rue Jean-Jérôme Levie, between cours Napoléon and bd. Sampiero, to Bastia (4hr., 4 per day, 124F) and Calvi via Ponte Leccia (4½hr., 2 per day, 145F). Eurocorse Voyages **buses** (☎ 04 95 21 06 30) go to Bastia (3hr., 2 per day, 110F) via Corte (1½hr., 65F), while Autocars SAIB (☎ 04 95 22 41 99) runs to Porto (2¾hr., 2-3 per day, 65F). Autocars Les Beaux Voyages (☎ 04 95 65 15 02) service Calvi (3½hr., M-Sa 1 per day, 135F). The **tourist office** is at 3 bd. du roi Jérôme. (☎ 04 95 51 53 03; fax 04 95 51 53 01. Open July-Sept. M-Sa 9am-8:30pm, F until midnight, Su 9am-1pm except July 7-Aug.; Nov.-Feb. M-Sa 8am-6pm, Su 9am-1pm; Mar.-June M-Sa 8am-9pm, Su 9am-1pm.) **Hôtel Kallisté,** 51 cours Napoléon, is serene. (☎ 04 95 51 34 45. Singles 240-340F; doubles 280-390F; triples 360-520F; quads 400-650F.) **Hôtel Bella Vista** is on bd. Lantivy. (☎ 04 95 21 07 97. Singles 230-270F; doubles 240-280F; triples 300-340F; quads 390F.) **Monoprix supermarket** is at 31 cours Napoléon. (Open M-Sa 8:30am-7:30pm.)

CALVI

With its sandy beaches, warm aquamarine waters, misty mountains, and nearly 2400hrs. of sunshine per year, Calvi could well be paradise—although no benevolent god would charge these rates. Visit the alluring **citadel** at the end of the day and bask in the setting sun. Gorgeous sand and water stretch as far as the eye can see; 6km of **public beaches** dotted by rocky coves wind around the coast. **Trains** (☎ 04 95 65 00 61) travel from pl. de la Gare, on av. de la République near Port de Plaisance, to Bastia (3hr., 2 per day, 95F) and Corte (2½hr., 2 per day, 79F). Eurocourse Voyages **buses** (☎ 04 95 46 06 83), on av. Wilson, run to Ajaccio (1¾hr., M-Sa 2 per day, 65F) and Bastia (1¼hr., M-Sa 2 per day, 55F). To reach the **tourist office,** at Port de Plaisance, exit from the back of the train station, turn left (facing the beach), and follow the signs. (☎ 04 95 65 16 67; fax 65 14 09. Open May M-Sa 9am-6:30pm; July to mid-Sept. daily 9am-8pm; mid-Sept. to Apr. M-F 9am-noon and 2-5:30pm, Sa 9am-noon.) To get to the isolated but beautiful **Relais International de la Jeunesse U Carabellu,** exit the station, turn left on av. de la République, turn right at rte. de Pietra-Maggiore, follow the signs 5km up the mountain. (☎ 04 95 65 14 16. Breakfast included. Sheets 20F. Open Mar.-Oct. 85F.) **BVJ Corsotel** is on av. de la République. (☎ 04 95 65 14 15. Breakfast 30F. Open Apr.-Oct. 100F.) **Camp** at **International,** on RN 197, close to the beach past Super U and Hotel L'Onda. (☎ 04 95 65 01 75. Open Apr.-Oct. 33F per person; 18F per tent; 10F per car.)

BASTIA AND CAP CORSE

Corsica's second largest city, Bastia (pop. 45,000) seems content with its role as a transport hub. The 18th-century **Eglise St-Jean Baptiste,** on pl. de l'Hôtel de Ville, is the stunning centerpiece of the photogenic port. The **citadel,** also called Terra Nova, was the spot from where the Genoese projected their power over the island. **Shuttle buses** connect to the **airport** from pl. de la Gare (30min., 50F), where **trains** (☎ 04 95 32 80 61) also depart for Ajaccio (4hr., 4 per day, 124F) and Calvi (3hr., 2 per day, 95F). Eurocorse **buses** (☎ 04 95 21 06 30) also run to Ajaccio (3hr., 2 per day, 111F). The **tourist office** is on pl. St-Nicholas. (☎ 04 95 55 96 96; fax 04 95 55 96 00. Open June-Sept. M-Sa 8am-8pm; Oct.-May daily 8am-noon, 2-6pm.) **Riviera-Hotel,** 1bis rue du Nouveau-Port, has fairly clean rooms. (☎ 04 95 31 07 16. Singles 150F, with bath 200F; doubles 200F, with bath 250F.) **Les Orangiers camping** is 4km north in Miomo. (☎ 04 95 33 24 09. Open May-Sept. 25F per person, 13F per tent.) **SPAR supermarket** is at 14 rue César Campinchini. (Open M-Sa 7:30am-1pm and 6-9pm, Su 7:30am-1pm.)

The **Cap Corse** peninsula stretches north from Bastia, a necklace of tiny fishing villages connected by a narrow road of perilous curves and breathtaking views. Mountains rise 1000m above the rocky shore. The forest and cliffs are dotted with

FRANCE

decaying Genoan towers of hilltop chapels. **Transports Micheli** (☎ 04 95 34 64 02) offers full-day tours of the Cap, departing from 1 rue de Nouveau Port in Bastia (July-Sept. 10 M-Sa 9am; 84F), but the cheapest (and more convenient) way to see Cap Corse is to take **bus** #4 from pl. St-Nicolas in Bastia; nicely ask the driver to drop you off wherever you feel the urge to explore (every 30min., 12-40F). The bus also goes to **Erbalunga** (20min., 12F), which you will never want to leave—with white pebble beaches, secluded flat rocks perfect for sunbathing, and houses so close to the sea that fishermen drop their lines out of the windows, this hamlet is picture-perfect and easily accessible from Bastia.

CORTE

"The heart of Corsica," Corte lies amid huge sheer cliffs and snow-capped peaks, appearing to be a fairy-tale illustration from a distance. Corsica's intellectual center, Corte houses the island's only university, and students (2600 of its 6000 residents) keep prices fairly low. The town's *vieille ville*, with its steep, inaccessible topography and stone citadel, has always been a bastion of fierce Corsican patriotism. At the top of the *vieille ville*, the focus of the **citadel** is the brand new **La Musée de la Corse.** The museum also provides entrance to the higher fortifications of the citadel. (☎ 04 95 45 25 45. Museum open June 20-Sept. 20 daily 10am-8pm; Sept. 21-Nov. Tu-Su 10am-6pm; Dec.-Mar. Tu-Sa 10am-6pm; Apr.-June 20 T-Su 10am-6pm. 35F, students 20F.) **Trains** (☎ 04 95 46 00 97) zoom from the station at the rotary where av. Jean Nicoli and the N193 meet, to: Ajaccio (2½hr., 4 per day, 66F); Bastia (1¾hr., 5 per day, 59F); and Calvi via Ponte-Leccia (2½hr., 2 per day, 79F). Eurocorse Voyages runs **buses** to Ajaccio (1¾hr., M-Sa 2 per day, 65F) and Bastia (1¼hr., M-Sa 2 per day, 55F). To reach the *centre ville* from the train station, turn right on D14 (alias av. Jean Nicoli), cross two bridges, and follow the road until it ends at **cours Paoli,** Corte's main drag. A left turn on the busy street leads to beautiful **pl. Paoli,** the town center; at the *place*'s top-right corner, climb the stairway of rue Scolisca to reach the citadel and the **tourist office.** (☎ 04 95 46 26 70. Open May-June M-Sa 9am-1pm and 2-7pm; July-Aug. daily 9am-1pm and 2-7pm; Sept.-Apr. M-F 9am-noon and 2-6pm.) In the summer, students can stay in university housing for 100F per night; contact **CROUS,** 7 av. Jean Nicoli, before you arrive. (☎ 04 95 45 21 00. Office open M-F 9am-noon and 2-3:30pm.) The **Gîte d'Etape: U Tavignanu,** on chemin de Balari, offers a peaceful farmhouse and shaded **campsites.** Turn left out of the station and bear right when the road forks, first following allée du 9 Septembre and then the signs at the base of the citadel. (☎ 04 95 46 16 85. 80F with breakfast. Camping 24F per person, 12F per tent.) The huge **Casino supermarket** is on allée du 9 Septembre. (Open M-Sa 8:30am-12:30pm and 3-8pm, Sa 9:30am-12:30pm.) **Postal Code:** 20250.

PORTO VECCHIO

On an island full of memorable beaches, those on the Golfe de Porto Vecchio are still something to write home about. Reaching them is no easy task, but dedicated sunseekers will not be disappointed. **Palombaggia** is about a mile long, and summer crowds thin out as you walk farther from the parking lot. Farther south, **Santa Giulia** wins both congeniality and swimsuit competitions. Beaches north of Porto Vecchio are stunning spectacles of sand and ocean. You will reach **Punta di Benedettu** first, but it's worth the trek to continue on to **San Cipriano,** which attracts anchored sailboats into its calm cove. From July to September, Trinitours **buses** (☎ 04 95 70 13 83) go to **Palombaggia** (1 per day, one-way 20F); updated schedules are posted on the tourist office wall, but are rarely convenient for beachgoers. Eurocorse **buses** (☎ 04 95 70 13 83) stop in front of Trinitours on rue Pasteur, behind the tourist office, and run to Ajaccio (3¼hr., July-Sept. 2 per day, 120F), while Autocars Rapides-Bleus (☎ 04 95 31 03 79) goes to Bastia (3hr., Oct.-June M-Sa 2 per day, 115F). The **tourist office** is around the corner from pl. de la République. (☎ 04 95 70 09 58. Open June-Sept. M-Sa 9am-8pm, Su 9am-1pm; Oct.-May M-F 9am-12:30pm and 2-6:30pm.) There are few budget hotels in town, so be sure to call ahead. **Le Modern,** 10 cours Napoleon, has minimalist rooms. (☎ 04 95 70 06 36. Closed Oct.-Mar. Doubles 250-650F.) **Postal Code:** 20137.

THE ALPS

Natural architecture is the real attraction of the Alps. The curves of the Vercors range and the Chartreuse peaks crescendo into Europe's highest peak, Mont Blanc (4807m). **Hiking trails** are clearly marked, and winter **skiers** enjoy some of the most challenging slopes in the world; make arrangements in advance. The cheapest months for skiing are January, March, and April; most resorts close in October and November. **FUAJ** (☎ 01 43 57 02 60; www.fuaj.org), the French Youth Hostel Federation, offers skiing and sports packages.

GRENOBLE

Grenoble (pop. 115,000) hosts the eccentric cafes, dusty bookshops, and shaggy radicals you'll find in any university town, but it also boasts the snow-capped peaks and sapphire-blue lakes cherished by hikers, skiers, bikers, and aesthetes alike. **Téléphériques** (lifts) depart from quai Stéphane-Jay (every 10min.; July-Aug. M 9:15am-12:30am, Tu-Su 9am-11pm; in winter shuts down earlier) for the 16th-century **Bastille,** a fort which hovers above town. Descend via the **Parc Guy Pape,** which criss-crosses through the fortress and deposits you just across the river from the train station. The **Musée Dauphinois,** 30 rue Maurice Gignoux, toward the bottom of the Bastille hill on the north bank of the Isère, has futuristic exhibits. (Open May-Oct. W-M 10am-7pm; Nov.-Apr. 10am-6pm. 20F, students 10F.) Grenoble's major attraction is its proximity to the slopes. The biggest and most developed **ski areas** lie in the **Oisans** to the east; the **Alpe d'Huez** (☎ 04 76 80 30 30) boasts 220km of trails (lift tickets 197F per day). The **Belledonne** region, northeast of Grenoble, lacks the towering heights of the Oisans but is cheaper. **Chamrousse** is its biggest and most popular ski area (lift tickets 136F per day), and has a **youth hostel** (☎ 04 76 89 91 31). Only 30min. from Grenoble by **bus** (49F), the resort makes an ideal daytrip in summer. Favored among mountain climbers are the slopes of the **Vercors.** In traditional villages with small ski resorts, such as Gresse-en-Vercors, just a quick bus ride (46F) away, vertical drops hover at 1000m. (Tourist office ☎ 04 76 34 33 40. Lift tickets 60F per day.)

Trains (☎ 08 36 35 35 35) arrive at the Gare Europole from: Paris (3¼hr., 8per day, 371-459F); Annecy (2hr., 9 per day, 89F); Lyon (1½hr., 16 per day, 97F); Marseilles (3½hr., 15 per day, 202F); and Nice (6½hr., 10 per day, 301F). **Buses** leave from the left of the station for Chamonix (3hr., 1 per day, 161F) and Geneva (3hr., 1 per day, 151F). From the station, turn right into pl. de la Gare, take the third left on av. Alsace-Lorraine, and follow the tram tracks on rue Félix Poulat and rue Blanchard to reach the **tourist office,** 14 rue de la République. (☎ 04 76 42 41 41; fax 04 76 00 18 98. Open daily 9am-7pm.) There is no shortage of **internet** access in Grenoble. **Cybernet Café,** 3 rue Bayard, also kicks it late night as a bar. (☎ 04 76 51 73 18. 25 per 30min. Bar Happy Hour 6-8:30pm; internet Happy Hour; 2min. for the price of 1. Open M-Sa 10am-1am.) To get from the station to the **Auberge de Jeunesse (HI),** 10 av. du Grésivaudan, 4km away in Echirolles, follow the tram tracks down av. Alsace-Lorraine, turn right on cours Jean Jaurès, and take bus #1 (dir.: Pont Rouge) to La Quinzaine; it's behind the Casino supermarket. (☎ 04 76 09 33 52. Breakfast included. Sheets 17F. Laundry 30F. Reception M-Sa 7:30am-11pm, Su 7:30-10am and 5:30-11pm. Singles with bath 110F, doubles 170F.) **Hôtel de L'Europe,** 22 pl. Grenette, is in the *vieille ville.* (☎ 04 76 46 16 94. Singles from 145F; doubles from 155F.) To reach **Camping Les 3 Pucelles,** in Seyssins, take tram A to Fontaine, then bus #51 (dir.: Les Nalettes) to Mas des Iles. (☎ 04 76 96 45 73. 45F per person, tent, and car.) **La Galerie Rome,** 1 rue Trois-Cloîtres, has flawless French cuisine, including Grenoble's trademark dish, *gratin dauphinois.* (Open Tu-Su for lunch and dinner.) A **Casino Cafeteria,** on rue Guetal, has cheap, fast service. (☎ 04 76 87 62 95. Open daily 11am-9:30pm.) **Prisunic,** opposite the tourist office, stocks **groceries.** (Open M-Sa 8:30am-7:30pm.) **Postal Code:** 38000.

CHAMONIX

Just west of Mont Blanc, Chamonix (pop. 20,000), the site of the first Winter Olympics (1924) has exploited its surroundings since 19th-century gentlemen-climbers scaled the peaks in crewneck sweaters. In other Alpine towns, the peaks provide harmless backdrops; in Chamonix, daggers of mammoth glaciers seem to reach down and menace the village. If you'd rather not climb the craggy cliffs, you can ski down—both will give you an exhilarating rush.

⊡ TRANSPORTATION. Trains (☎ 04 50 53 12 98) roll from av. de la Gare to: Paris (6½hr., 6 per day, 500F); Annecy (2½hr., 6 per day, 105F); Lyon (4hr., 4 per day, 185F); and Geneva (2½hr., 4 per day, 118F). Société Alpes Transports' **buses** (☎ 04 50 53 01 15) depart from the train station for: Annecy (2¼hr., 1 per day, 95F); Grenoble (3hr., 1 per day, 161F); and Geneva (1½hr., 2 per day, 170-195F). **Local buses** connect with ski slopes and hiking trails (7.50F).

⊠ PRACTICAL INFORMATION. From the station, follow av. Michel Croz, turn left on rue du Dr. Paccard, and take the first right to reach the pl. de l'Eglise and the **tourist office,** 85 pl. du Triangle de l'Amitié. (☎ 04 50 53 00 24; fax 04 50 53 58 90. Open July-Aug. and Dec.-Feb. daily 8:30am-7:30pm; Mar.-June and Sept. 9am-noon and 2-6pm.) The **Ecole du Ski,** in the **Maison de la Montagne,** is a mountain information center across from the tourist office. (☎ 04 50 53 00 88. Open Jan.-Mar. and July-Aug. daily 8:30am-noon and 3:30-7:30pm; Sept.-Dec. and Apr.-June Tu-Sa 10am-noon and 5-7pm.) **Postal Code:** 74400.

▐▐⊡ ACCOMMODATIONS AND FOOD. Chamonix's *gîtes* (mountain hostels) and dorms are a budget traveler's dream if you can get a bed; call in advance. The **auberge de jeunesse (HI),** 127 montée Jacques Balmat, in Les Pélerins at the base of the Glacier de Bossons, offers all-inclusive winter **ski packages** (2500-3500F per week). Take the bus from pl. de l'Eglise (dir.: Les Houches) to Pélerins Ecole (4F) and follow the signs uphill, or take the train to Les Pélerins and follow the signs. (☎ 04 50 53 14 52. Breakfast included. Sheets 19F. Reception 8am-noon and 5-10pm. Dorms 78F; singles 93F; doubles 108F.) The plushly furnished **Red Mountain Lodge,** 435 rue Joseph-Vallot, is friendly and cozy. (☎ 04 50 53 94 97. Breakfast included. Dorms 100F; doubles and triples 120-160F.) To reach the popular **Le Chamoniard Volant,** 45 rte. de la Frasse, from the station, turn right, go under the bridge, and turn right across the tracks, left on chemin des Cristalliers, and then right. (☎ 04 50 53 14 09. Sheets 20F one-time fee. Reception 10am-10pm. Dorms 70F.) Turn left from the base of the Aiguille du Midi *téléphérique*, continue past the main roundabout, and look right to **camp** at **L'Ile des Barrats,** on rte. des Pélerins. (☎ 04 50 53 51 44. Reception July-Aug. 8am-10:30pm; May-June and Sept. 8am-noon and 3-7pm. Closed in winter. 32F per person; 24F per tent; 13F per car.) The **Super U,** 117 rue Joseph Vallot, has groceries. (Open M-Sa 8:15am-7:30pm, Su 8:30am-noon.)

▟ HIKING AND THE GREAT OUTDOORS. Whether you've come to climb up the mountains or to ski down them, you're in for a challenge. The **Téléphérique de l'Aiguille du Midi** (☎ 04 50 53 30 80; reservations ☎ 08 36 68 00 67; runs daily July-Aug. 6am-5pm; Apr.-June and Sept. 9am-3pm) offers a pricey but knuckle-whitening ascent over forests and snow-covered cliffs to a needle-point peak at the top. The first stop isn't really worth it, but the second and last (1½hr., round-trip 180F), reveals a fantastic panorama from 3842m. In summer, you can hike 2hr. to La Mer de Glace, a glacier that slides 30m per year. Special trains (☎ 04 50 53 12 54) also run from the small station next to Chamonix's main *gare* (round-trip 79F; July-Aug. daily 8am-6pm every 20min.; May-June and Sept.1-15 daily 8:30am-5pm every 30min.; reduced service Sept.16-Apr. daily 10am-4pm). Chamonix has hundreds of kilometers of hikes through terrain ranging from forests to glaciers. The tourist office sells a hiking map (25F) that lists the degrees of difficulty and distances of all the trails. Chamonix is surrounded by skiable mountains. To the south, **Le Tour-Col. de Balme** (☎ 04 50 54 00 58), above the village of **Le Tour,** cuddles up to the Swiss border with intermediate slopes (lift tickets 148F per day). On the northern side of the valley, **Le Brevent,** a proving ground for experts, has also expanded its slopes for beginners and intermediates (lift tickets 142F per day). Wherever you go, be cautious—one person a day on average dies on these mountains.

ANNECY

With narrow, cobblestone streets, winding canals, and a turreted castle, all bordering the purest lake in Europe, Annecy is more like a fairy-tale than a modern city. The **Palais de l'Ile** is a 13th-century castle once occupied by the counts of Geneva. The castle is now partly given over to a museum covering Annecy's history, but the old prison section, where Resistance fighters were jailed, is far more interesting. (☎ 04 50 33 87 30. Open June-Sept. daily 10am-6pm; Oct.-May W-M 10am-noon and 2-6pm. 20F, students 5F.) Bordering on the Lac d'Annecy, and graced by manicured hedges, fountains, and the occasional swan, the shaded **Jardins de l'Europe** are a perfect place to stretch out. The **Pont des Amours** (Bridge of Love) connects the gardens with the grassy **Champ de Mars.** Gardens like these helped the town win the Grand Prix for Flowered Towns three times in the last decade. **Plage des Marquisats,** to the south down rue des Marquisats, is a crowded beach. A 12th-century **chateau** is a short, steep climb from the *vieille ville.* (☎ 04 50 33 87 30. Open June-Aug. daily 10am-6pm; Sept.-May W-M 10am-noon and 2-6pm. 30F, students 10F; grounds free.)

Trains arrive in Annecy at Place de la Gare from Paris (4hr., 6 per day, 363F); Chamonix (2¼hr., 7 per day, 105F); Grenoble (1½hr., 7 per day, 89F); Lyon (2hr., 6 per day, 115F); and Nice (8hr., 2 per day, 345F). Voyages Frossard **buses** (☎ 04 50 45 73 90) leave from next to the station for Geneva (1¼hr., 6 per day, 53F) and Lyon (3½ hr., 2 per day, 99F). From the train station, take the underground passage to rue Vaugelas, follow the street left for four blocks, and enter the modern Bonlieu shopping mall to reach the **tourist office,** 1 rue Jean Jaurès, in pl. de la Libération. (☎ 04 50 45 00 33; fax 04 50 51 87 20. Open July-Aug. M-Sa 9am-6:30pm, Su 9am-12:30pm and 1:45-6:30pm; Sept.-June daily 9am-12:30pm and 1:45-6pm.) Feed your **internet** cravings at **Syndrome Cyber-café,** which has fast connections and excellent rates. (Open M-Sa noon-midnight, Su 2-10pm. 10F per 15min., 30F per hr.) In summer, you can reach the **Auberge de Jeunesse "La Grande Jeanne" (HI),** on rte. de Semnoz, via The Ligne d'Eté (dir.: Semnoz) from the station (July-Aug. daily 6 per day, June and Sept.; only Sa-Su, 6 per day; 7F); otherwise, take bus #1 (dir.: Marquisats) from the station to Hôpital and follow the signs pointing to Semnoz. (☎ 04 50 45 33 19. Breakfast included. Sheets 17F. Laundry 30F. Reception 8am-10pm. Dorms 74F.) **Camp** at 8 rte. de Semnoz, near the youth hostel. (☎ 04 50 45 48 30. 17F per car. Laundry 51F. Reception Apr.-Aug. 8am-9pm, otherwise 8am-noon and 2-10pm. Open Apr. 15-Oct. 15. 65F for tent and 2 people.) A **Prisunic supermarket** fills most of pl. de Notre-Dame. (Open M-Sa 8:30am-7:30pm.) **Postal Code:** 74000.

CENTRAL FRANCE

Central France is often overlooked by tourists speeding south from Paris toward the coasts. Thanks to the benign neglect engendered by its smokestack reputation, most of the region has escaped mass tourism; with medieval abbeys, *grands vins,* outstanding cuisine, unspoiled countryside, and magnificent chateaux, this is France in all its glory.

LYON

France's second-largest city is second in little else. With industrial and culinary *savoir faire,* Lyon (pop. 1.5 million) has established itself as a cultural and economical alternative to Paris. Lyon is friendlier and more relaxed than Paris. Unlike so many other European cities, Lyon focuses on the present: its best art collections are contemporary, and the entire metropolis overflows with a dynamic creativity.

◀ TRANSPORTATION

Flights: Aéroport Lyon-Saint-Exupery (☎ 04 72 22 72 21), 25km east of Lyon. **Sato-buses** (☎ 04 72 68 72 17) shuttle to Perrache, Part-Dieu, and the Jean Mace, Grange-Blanche, and Mermoz Pinel Métro stops (every 20min. until 9pm, 49F). The Air France office is at 10 quai Jules Courmont, 2ème (☎ 08 02 80 28 02).

FRANCE

Trains: Trains passing through Lyon stop only at **Gare de la Part-Dieu,** bd. Marius Vivier-Merle (M: Part-Dieu), in the business district on the east bank of the Rhône. Trains terminating at Lyon stop also at **Gare de Perrache,** pl. Carnot (M: Perrache). TGV trains to Paris stop at both (reservations ☎08 36 35 35 35). **SNCF info and reservation desk** at Perrache open M-Sa 8am-7:30pm; at Part-Dieu open M-F 9am-7pm, Sa 9am-6:30pm. To: **Paris** (2hr., 20 TGVs per day, 312-388F); **Dijon** (2hr., 15 per day, 132F); **Grenoble** (1¼hr., 15 per day, 96F); **Marseilles** (3hr., 13 per day, 205F); **Nice** (6hr., 15 per day, 299F); **Strasbourg** (6hr., 9 per day, 256F); **Geneva** (2hr., 8 per day, 118F).

Buses: Stations on the bottom floor of the **Perrache** station, and also at **Part-Dieu** station. (For info call **Allo Transports** ☎04 72 61 72 61.) Domestic companies include **Philibert** (☎04 78 98 56 00), **Cars Faure** (☎04 78 96 11 44), and **Transport Verney** (☎04 78 70 21 01). **Eurolines** (☎04 72 56 95 30) travels out of France. Stations open M-Sa 9am-8pm.

Public Transportation: TCL (☎04 78 71 70 00), at both train stations and major Métro stops. **Single-fare tickets** good for 1hr. including transfers (8F per ticket; 10-ticket *carnet* 68F, students 58F). The full-day *Ticket Liberté* (24F), good for unlimited public transport, is sold at tourist and TCL offices. The Métro runs 5am-midnight. **Buses** run 5am-9pm (a few until midnight), later on theater performance nights.

Taxis: Taxi Radio de Lyon (☎04 72 10 86 86). Airport to either train station 200-280F.

✦⁷ ORIENTATION AND PRACTICAL INFORMATION

Lyon is divided into nine **arrondissements** (districts). The **Saône** (to the west) and the **Rhône** (to the east) rivers run north-south through the city. West of the Saône, **Fourvière Hill** and its basilica overlook *vieux Lyon* (5ème). Between the two rivers lies the *centre ville*, home to the **Perrache** train station and **pl. Bellecour** (2ème) as well as the old **Terraux** neighborhood (1er); the **Croix-Rousse** (1er and 4ème) lies farther north. East of the Rhône (3ème and 6-8ème) lies the **Part-Dieu** train station (3ème), its commercial complex, and most of the city's population. From Perrache, it's a straight shot from pl. Carnot in front of the station down rue Victor Hugo to **pl. Bellecour** (15min.); from Part-Dieu, exit by the fountains, turn right, then turn left after three blocks on cours Lafayette, cross pont Lafayette, continue as the street changes to pl. des Cordeliers, and turn left on rue de la République, which pours into pl. Bellecour (30min.). The Métro is quicker; take line A from Perrache to Bellecour, or take line B and transfer to A at Part-Dieu.

Tourist Office: In the Pavilion, at Pl. Bellecour (☎04 72 77 69 69; fax 04 78 42 04 32), 2ème. M: Bellecour. Maps with museum listings (5F), hotel reservation office, SNCF desk, and city tours (50-60F, students 25-35F). The **Lyon City Card** (90F) grants admission to 7 museums and 1 day of public transport. Open May-Oct. M-Sa 9am-7pm, Su 10am-7pm; Nov.-Apr. daily 10am-6pm.

Consulates: Canada, 21 rue Bourgelat, 2ème (☎04 72 77 64 07). M: Ampere. Open M-F 9am-midnight. **Ireland,** 58 rue Victor Lagrange, 7ème (☎04 85 23 12 03). Open M-F 9am-noon. **UK,** 24 rue Childebert, 2ème (☎04 72 77 81 70). M: Bellecour. Open M-F 9am-12:30pm and 2-5:30pm.

Emergencies: ☎17. **Police,** 47 rue de la Charité (☎04 78 42 26 56). **Medical emergency,** ☎15.

Medical Assistance: Hôpital Edouard Herriot, 5 pl. Arsonval (☎04 72 11 73 11). M: Grange Blanche. Best equipped for serious emergencies.

Internet Access: Station-Internet, 4 rue du President Carnot, 2ème. 40F per hr., students 30F per hr. Open M-Sa 10am-7pm. Also **Connectix Café,** 19 quai St-Antoine, 2ème (☎04 72 77 98 85). 60F per hr. Open M-Sa 11am-7pm.

Post Office: (☎04 72 40 65 22), on pl. Antonin Poncet, 2ème, near pl. Bellecour. **Currency exchange** and **internet.** Open July-Aug. M-Sa 8am-midnight, Su 8am-2pm; Sept.-June M-F 8am-7pm, Sa 8am-12:30pm. Address mail to be held: Luke LAWSON, *Poste Restante*, pl. Antonin Poncet, **69002** Lyon, France. **Postal Codes:** 69000-69009; last digit indicates *arrondissement*.

rue des Tables Claudiennes
rue Burdeau
M. des Carmelites
rue des Capucins
rue R. Leynaud
rue Romarin
r. Désirée
PL. LOUIS PRADEL
quai Jean Moulin
Serlin
rue Sergent Blandan
TO PARC DE LA TÊTE D'OR (1km & CITÉ INTERNATIONALE (1.5km)
rue Clivier
quai du G. Sarrail
quai du cours de la Liberté
quai Victor Augagneur
Rhône

Amphithéâtre des Trois Gaules
r. de l'Annonciade
r. du Sgt-Blandan
rue de la Martinière
quai St-Vincent
quai de Bondy
rue St-Paul

Hôtel de Ville
r. Ste-Catherine
r. Paul Chenavard
rue d'Algérie
rue de Constantine
quai de la Pêcherie
Saône

PL. DE LA COMÉDIE
Opéra
HÔTEL DE VILLE
M
l'Arbre Sec
PL. DES TERREAUX
Musée St-Pierre d'Art Contemporain
Musée des Beaux-Arts
rue du Bât
r. du Pdt. Carnot
rue Mulet
PL. DE LA BOURSE
r. de la Bourse
r. Claudia
r. A. Stilles
r. Gentil
rue Longue
rue Neuve
rue Lanterne
rue du Président Édouard Herriot
PL. D'ALBON
quai St-Antoine
CORDELIERS
M
PL. DES CORDELIERS
r. du Président Carnot

Palais de la Miniature
Gare St-Paul
r. Fr. Vernay
rue Juiverie
M. des Carmes
M. St-Barthélemy
M. Nicolas Lange
PL. DU CHANGE
Musée de la Marionette
rue du Bœuf
rue St-Jean
M. des Chazeaux
rue de la Bombarde
Palais de Justice
P. du Palais de Justice
r. Grenette
r. Mercière
rue Tupin
rue Ferrandière
rue Thomassin
rue de la Monnaie
r. de la Barre
PL. DE LA RÉPUBLIQUE
Stella
United Kingdom
Pas de l'Argue
r. de Brest
r. Palais Grillet
r. Grôlée
r. de la République
r. Childebert
r. J. de Tournes
PL. DES JACOBINS
American Express
Hôpital Hôtel Dieu
TO GARE PART-DIEU (1.5m)
r. Jussieu
quai Jules Courmont

Tour Métallique
Chemin du Rosaire
Basilique Notre-Dame de Fourvière
FOURVIÈRE
F
Musée de la Civilization Gallo-Romaine
Théâtres Romains
Parc Archéologique
rue R. Radisson
rue Cléberg
rue de l'Antiquaille
MINIMES
F
ST-JUST
F
Chemin de Choulans

P. du Palais de Justice
quai des Célestins
r. de Savoie
r. Ch. Dullin
Émile Zola
r. des Archers
Théâtre des Célestins
r. G. André
r. d'Amboise
Bellecordiere
République
r. Gasparin
BELLECOUR
M
rue de la Barre
PLACE BELLECOUR
TO INSTITUT LUMIÈRE (2.8km)

PL. ST-JEAN
Cathédrale St-Jean
ave. A. Max
VIEUX LYON
F M
Montée du Chemin Neuf
rue Tramassac
ave. du Doyenné
Pont Bonaparte
quai Fulchiron
quai du Plat
quai Tilsitt
P. St Georges
PL. DE LA COMMANDERIE
PL. ANTOINE VOLLAN
rue Ste-Hélène
rue A. Fochier
rue Fr. Dauphin
rue Roissac
rue A. Comte
rue Victor Hugo
rue Sala
rue d'Auvergne
PL. ANTONIN PONCET
rue Ch. Bienner
r. de la Charité
r. Sala
r. des Marronniers

rue des Farges
N
Saône
quai Tilsitt
rue Guynemer
rue Vaubecour
rue Jarente
r. Bourgelat
AMPÈRE VICTOR HUGO
M
PL. AMPÈRE
Musée Historique des Tissus & Musée Lyonnais des Arts Décoratifs
r. Laurencin
rue des Remparts d'Ainay
rue Franklin
r. de Castries
r. d'Enghien
r. Henri IV
rue de Condé
r. Mazard
PLACE CARNOT
r. Duhamel
Chemin de Choulans
r. G. Plessier
PERRACHE
M
Gare de Perrache
TO (1.5km)
P. Kitchener
Marchand
autoroute A7
cours de Verdun
c. de Verdun
rue du Bélier

0   200 yards
0   200 meters

Lyon

🏠 **ACCOMMODATIONS**

Auberge de Jeunesse (HI), 1
Hôtel d'Ainay, 2
Hôtel du Dauphiné, 3
Résidence B. Delessert, 4

Funicular **F**
Métro **M**

FRANCE

ACCOMMODATIONS

As a financial center, Lyon has few empty beds during the work week but openings on the weekends. Unlike the rest of France, off-season here is actually July and August, and it's easier and cheaper to find a place in the summer. Prices rise as you approach **Place Bellecour**, but inexpensive hotels cluster just east of pl. Carnot near Perrache and just north of **pl. des Terreaux.**

Auberge de Jeunesse (HI), 41-45 Montée du Chemin Neuf, 5ème (☎04 78 15 05 50). M: Vieux Lyon. Walk west from pl. Bellecour, cross pont Bonaparte, turn right at pl. St-Jean and left on rue de la Bombarde, follow the hairpin left turn on Montée du Chemin Neuf, and climb for a room with a view. Internet. Breakfast included. Bar, kitchen. Sheets 17F. HI members only. 4- to 8-bed rooms 71F.

Résidence Benjamin Delessert, 145 av. Jean Jaurès, 7ème (☎04 78 61 41 41). M: Jean Macé. From Perrache, you can also take bus #11 or 39 to J. Macé, walk under the tracks, and look left after 3 blocks. Internet 40F per hr. Singles 91F, with shower 95F.

Hôtel d'Ainay, 14 rue des Remparts d'Ainay, 2ème (☎04 78 42 43 42), near Perrache on top of pl. Ampère. M: Ampère-Victor Hugo. Breakfast 25F. Shower 15F. Reception 7am-11pm. Singles from 140F, with shower from 205F; doubles 175F, with shower 235F.

Hôtel Bellecordière, 18 rue Bellecordière, 2ème (☎04 78 42 27 78), on a quiet side-street across from the Hospital Hôtel Dieu. All rooms have shower, toilet, telelphone, and cable TV. Breakfast 34F. Singles start 280F, doubles 320F.

Hôtel du Dauphiné, 3 rue Duhamel, 2ème (☎04 78 37 24 19), to the right of pl. Carnot near Perrache. Comfortable rooms with showers. Rooms over 205F have TV. Breakfast 27F. Singles from 135F; doubles from 205F; triples from 300F; quads 320F.

Hotel St. Vincent, 9 rue Pareille, 1er (☎04 78 27 22 56), just off the Quai Saint-Vincent, north of the Passerelle St. Vincent. Breakfast 30F. Singles with shower 180F, with bath 230F; doubles 230F, with bath 270F.

Hôtel Terminus Saint Paul, 6 rue Lainerie, 5ème (☎04 78 28 13 29), in Vieux Lyon. M: Hôtel de Ville. Breakfast 40F. Singles or doubles with shower 170-200F, with bath 240F; triples with bath 345F.

Camping Dardilly (☎04 78 35 64 55), 10km from Lyon. Take bus #19 (dir.: Ecully-Dardilly) from the Hôtel de Ville to Parc d'Affaires. Reception mid-June to mid-Sept. 8am-noon and 4-8:30pm; mid-Sept. to mid-June 8am-11pm. Electricity 20F, off-season 30F. 20F per person; 40F per tent; 50F per caravan; car free.

FOOD

The galaxy of *Michelin* guide stars adorning Lyon's restaurants confirms the city's reputation as the culinary capital of Western civilization. Cozy *bouchons*, descendants of inns, serve *andouillettes* (sausages made of cow intestines) and other local treats in the **Terreaux** district, 1er, and along **rue Mercière**, 2ème. Finish off your dinner with *tarte tatin* (think upside-down apple pie) or *cocons* (chocolates wrapped in marzipan). The market at **Les Halles**, 102 cours Lafayette, 3ème, counts Paul Bocuse—the *lyonnais* culinary messiah—among its patrons. (Open Tu-Th 7am-noon and 3-7pm, F-Sa 7am-7pm, Su 7am-noon.) Ethnic restaurants cluster off **rue de la République**, 2ème. **Prisunic supermarket** is on rue de la République, in pl. des Cordeliers, 2ème. (Open M-Sa 8:30am-8:30pm.)

Chez Mounier, 3 rue des Marronniers, 2ème (☎04 78 37 79 26). This tiny place satisfies a discriminating local clientele with generous traditional specialties. 4-course *menus* 61-96F. Open Tu-Sa noon-2pm and 7-10:30pm, Su noon-2pm.

Comptoir du Bœuf, 3 pl. Neuve St-Jean, 5ème (☎04 78 92 82 35). *Lyonnais* cuisine with an unusually light, imaginative twist. Specialties include iced avocado soup with smoked salmon. *Menus* 95-125F. Open daily noon-2pm and 7pm-midnight.

PÂTISSERIE

Bernachon, 42 cours F. Roosevelt, 6ème (☎04 78 24 37 98). Lyon's largest *pâtisserie* makes chocolate entirely from scratch, starting from the very bean. Locals take pride in the *cocons*, and the showcases sparkle with the *palets d'or*, recognized as the best chocolates in France—and not just because they're made with gold dust. Open Tu-Sa 9am-7pm. Mmm.

SIGHTS

The Presqu'île, the area outlined by the Rhône and the Saône, is the center of shopping, dancing, and people-watching. But *Vieux Lyon*, nestled in the bend of the Saône, bursts with color and history; in contrast, the Part-Dieu district in modern Lyon gleams with glass and metal.

VIEUX LYON

Pressed against the Saône at the bottom of the Fourvière hill, the narrow streets of *Vieux Lyon* wind between lively cafes, tree-lined squares, and magnificent medieval and Renaissance houses. The colorful *hôtels particuliers*, with delicate carvings, shaded courtyards, and ornate turrets, arose from the great wealth Lyon gained as the center of Europe's silk and publishing industries from the 15th to 19th centuries. The regal homes around **rue St-Jean, rue du Boeuf**, and **rue Juiverie** have housed Lyon's elite for 400 years—and still do.

TRABOULES. The most distinguishing feature of *Vieux Lyon* townhouses is the *traboules*, tunnels leading from the street through a maze of courtyards, often with vaulted ceilings and statuary niches. Although their original purpose is still debated, later *traboules* were constructed to transport silk safely from looms to storage rooms. During WWII, the passageways proved invaluable for information gathering and escape routes for the Resistance. If a door is open, peek in (many are open to the public at specific hrs.); get a list of addresses from the tourist office or, better yet, take one of their tours. *(June-Sept. 2 per week. 50F, students 25F.)*

CATHÉDRALE ST-JEAN. The southern end of *Vieux Lyon* is dominated by the Cathédrale St-Jean, with soaring columns and delicate stained glass windows that look too fragile to have withstood eight centuries of religious turmoil. Paris might have been worth a mass, but Lyon got the wedding cake; it was here that Henri IV met and married Maria de Médici in 1600. Inside, every hour between noon and 4pm, automatons pop out of the 14th-century astronomical clock in a charming re-enactment of the Annunciation—the Holy Spirit literally falls through the roof. *(Cathedral open M-F 8am-noon and 2-7:30pm, Sa-Su 2-5pm.)*

OTHER SIGHTS. Down rue St-Jean, turn left at the pl. du Change for the **Hôtel de Gadagne** and its relatively minor museums. Housed in a typical 16th-century *Vieux Lyon* building, meandering exhibits focus on local history. Slightly better is the Hôtel's **Musée de la Marionette,** which displays puppets from around the world, including models of **Guignol,** the famed local cynic, and his inebriated friend, Gnaffron. *(Pl. du Petit College, 5ème. M: Vieux Lyon. ☎04 78 42 03 61. Open W-M 10:45am-6pm. 25F, students 13F. 18 and under free.)* The **Palais de la Miniature** devotes itself to microscopic art and extraordinarily complex origami. The world's smallest bear is perched atop a pearl, visible only with a magnifying glass. *(2 rue Juiverie. ☎04 72 00 24 77. Open M-Sa 10am-1pm and 2-6pm, Su 10am-7pm. 25F, students 20F.)*

FOURVIÈRE AND ROMAN LYON

From the corner of rue du Bœuf and rue de la Bombarde in *Vieux Lyon*, climb the stairs heading straight up to reach the **Fourvière Hill,** the nucleus of **Roman Lyon.** From the top of the stairs, continue up via the rose-lined **Chemin de la Rosaire,** a series of switchbacks that leads through a garden to the **Esplanade Fourvière,** where a model of the cityscape points out local landmarks. Most prefer to take the less strenuous **funicular** (known as "*la ficelle*") from the head of av. A. Max in Vieux Lyon, off pl. St-Jean, to the top of the hill. The **Tour de l'Observatoire** offers a more mind-reeling angle on the city. On a clear day, look for Mont Blanc, about 200km east. *(Chemin de la Rosaire: open daily 6:30am-9:30pm. Tower: open June-Sept. daily 10am-noon and 2-6pm; Oct.-May Sa-Su 1:30-5:30pm only. 10F, students 5F.)*

BASILIQUE NOTRE-DAME DE FOURVIÈRE. Lyon's archbishop carried out his promise to build a church if the city was spared attack during the Franco-Prussian War. The basilica's white, merengue-like exterior is delectable from a distance. The walls are decked with gigantic, gilded mosaics depicting religious scenes, Joan of Arc at Orleans, and the naval battle of Lepante. *(Behind the Esplanade. Open daily 6am-7pm; crypt open till 9:30pm.)*

MUSÉE GALLO-ROMAIN. Almost invisible from the outside, circling deep into the historic hillside of Fourvière, the five levels of this brilliant museum hold a huge collection of arms, pottery, statues, and jewelry. Highlights include a half-dozen large, luminous mosaics and a bronze tablet inscribed with a speech by Lyon's native son, the Roman Emperor Claudius. *(17 rue Cléberg, 5ème. ☎04 72 38 81 90. Open W-Su 9:30am-noon and 2-6pm. 20F, students 10F.)*

PARC ARCHÉOLOGIQUE. Just next door to the Musée Gallo-Romain, the Parc holds the almost too-well-restored 2000-year-old **Théâtre Romain** and the smaller **Odéon,** discovered when modern developers dug into the hill to build apartment buildings. *(Park open Apr. 15-Sept. 15 7am-9pm; Sept. 16-Apr. 14 7am-7pm. Free.)*

LE PRESQU'ÎLE AND LES TERREAUX

Monumental squares, statues, and fountains are the trademarks of the **Presqu'ile,** the lively area between the Rhône and the Saône. Its heart is **pl. Bellecour,** an expanse of Martian-red gravel fringed with shops and flower stalls. The pedestrian **rue Victor Hugo** runs south from Bellecour, lined with boutiques and rollerbladers. North along pedestrian **rue de la République,** or "la Ré," the movie theaters, FNAC, and rushing crowds establish the street as the urban aorta of Lyon. It runs through **pl. de la République** and terminates at **pl. Louis Pradel** in the 1er, at the tip of the Terreaux district, *the* place to be. At **pl. des Terreaux,** Bartholi's fountain of frenzied horses teems with kids splashing in the cool water. Across the square, at **pl. Louis Pradel,** is the 17th-century **Hôtel de Ville,** framed by an illuminated cement field of miniature geysers. The **Opéra,** pl. Louis Pradel, is the building that resembles an airplane hangar perched atop a 19th-century attempt at classical architecture.

MUSÉE DES BEAUX-ARTS. In France, this museum is second only to the Louvre; it includes a comprehensive archeological wing, a distinguished collection of French paintings, works by Spanish and Dutch masters, a wing devoted to the Italian Renaissance, and a lovely sculpture garden. Even the more esoteric works mixed into all-star pre-, post-, and just-plain-Impressionist collections are delightful. Be sure to visit Maillol's bronze *Venus,* whose classic composure is disrupted by a single, lightly displaced lock of hair. *(Pl. des Terreaux. ☎04 72 10 17 40. Open W-M 10:30am-noon and 2-6pm, closed Tu. 25F, students 13F.)*

LA CROIX-ROUSSE AND THE SILK INDUSTRY

Lyon is proud of its historical dominance of European silk manufacture. Born in the 15th century, Lyon's silk industry operated 28,000 looms by the 18th century, mainly in the Croix-Rousse district on a hill in the 1er. The 1801 invention of the power-loom by *lyonnais* Joseph Jacquard intensified the sweatshop conditions endured by the *canuts* (silk workers). Unrest culminated in the riot of 1834, in which hundreds were killed. Mass silk manufacturing is based elsewhere today, and Lyon's few remaining silk workers perform delicate handiwork, reconstructing and replicating rare patterns for museum and chateau displays.

MUSÉE HISTORIQUE DES TISSUS. It's not in the Croix-Rousse *quartier,* but textile and fashion fans—along with anyone else who's ever worn clothes—will have a field day here. This world-class collection includes wonderfully preserved examples of 18th-century men's wear, scraps of luxurious Byzantine textiles, sumptuous vestments, luminous silk wall-hangings that look like stained glass windows, and rotating exhibits. Included with admission is the neighboring **Musée des Arts Décoratifs,** housed in an 18th-century *hôtel,* brimming with a comprehensive collection of period porcelain, furniture, and all ornamental excesses of the past. *(34 rue de la Charité, 2ème. ☎ 04 78 38 42 00. Tissus open Tu-Su 10am-5:30pm. Arts Décoratifs. Open Tu-Su 10am-noon and 2-5:30pm.)*

LA MAISON DES CANUTS. In a tiny back-room, an assembly of old silk-looms are all that remain of the impressive weaving techniques of the *canuts*. The Maison's shop sells silk made by its own *canuts*. A scarf costs 130F and up, but you can take home a silkworm cocoon for a few francs. *(10-12 rue d'Ivry, 4ème. ☎ 04 78 28 62 04. Open M-F 8:30am-noon and 2-6:30pm, Sa 9am-noon and 2-6pm. 25F, students 15F.)*

EAST OF THE RHÔNE AND MODERN LYON

Lyon's newest train station and monstrous space-age mall form the core of the ultra-modern Part-Dieu district. Many see the place as an eyesore and consider its greatest virtue to be its shops—some of the few open between noon and 2pm. The commercial **Tour du Crédit Lyonnais,** on the other side of the mall, is known as *"Le Crayon"* (the pencil) for its resemblance to a giant pencil standing on end. Next to it, the shell-shaped **Auditorium Maurice Ravel** hosts major cultural events.

CENTRE D'HISTOIRE, DE LA RÉSISTANCE ET DE LA DÉPORTATION. The center is housed in a building in which Nazis tortured detainees during the Occupation. Here you'll find assembled documents, photos, and films of the Resistance, whose national headquarters were based in Lyon. The museum forces upon its visitors a haunting awareness of the context of genocide and resistance in France. *(14 av. Bertholet, 7ème. Take bus #11, 26, 32, or 39. ☎ 04 78 72 23 11. Open W-Su 9am-5:15pm. 25F, students 13F. Admission includes an audio-guide in French, English and German.)*

MUSÉE D'ART CONTEMPORAIN. In the futuristic **Cité International de Lyon,** a super-modern complex with offices, shops, theaters, and Interpol's world headquarters, you'll find this extensive, wholly entertaining mecca of modern art. All the museum's exhibits are temporary; the walls themselves are built anew for each installation. Expect the inscrutable "Cai Guo Qiang: Retrospective" beginning in June 2001. *(Quai Charles de Gaulle, next to Parc de la Tête d'Or, 6ème. Bus #4 from M: Foch. ☎ 04 72 69 17 18. Open W-Su noon-7pm. 25F, students 13F.)*

PARC DE LA TÊTE D'OR. The massive park, one of the biggest in Europe, owes its name to a legend that a golden head of Jesus lies buried somewhere within its grounds. The park sprawls over 259 acres, and you can rent paddle boats to explore its artificial lake and artificial island. Very real reindeer, elephants, and a thousand other animals fill the zoo; giant greenhouses encase the botanical garden. The 60,000-bush rose gardens are stunning in summer. Children play soccer on the lawns as joggers sweat out the vast perimeter around peaceful picnickers. *(☎ 04 78 89 02 03. Park open daily Apr.-Sept. 6am-11pm; Oct.-Mar. 6am-9pm.)*

🎵🎭 ENTERTAINMENT AND NIGHTLIFE

FESTIVALS

In late June, Lyon is host to the two-week **Festival du Jazz à Vienne,** which welcomes jazz masters to Vienne, a medieval town south of Lyon, accessible by bus or train. *(☎ 04 74 85 00 05. Tickets 160F, students 150F.)* Also in June is **Les Nuits de Fourvière,** a two-month summer music festival held in the ancient Théâtre Romain and Odéon. The biannual **Festival de Musique du Vieux Lyon,** 5 pl. du Petit Collège, 5ème, brings artists from around the world to perform in the churches of Vieux Lyon (☎ 04 78 42 39 04; mid-Nov. to mid-Dec.; tickets 90-230F.)

NIGHTLIFE

Nightlife in Lyon is fast and furious. Students congregate in a series of bars on **rue Ste-Catherine** (1er) until 1am before heading to the clubs. There's a whole row of semi-exclusive joints off the Saône, on **quais Romain Rolland, de Bondy,** and **Pierre Scize** in Vieux Lyon (5ème) but the city's best and most accessible late-night spots are a strip of **riverboat dance clubs** by the east bank of the Rhône.

L'Abreuvoir, 18 rue Ste-Catherine (1er). Pound 10F tequilas like everybody else at this warm, wooden, dusky bar. Open daily 6pm-1am, F-Sa until 2am.

Le Chantier, 20 rue Ste-Catherine (1er). Slip down the spiral slide to reach the dance floor downstairs. Live music for a nominal cover W-Sa. Open Tu-Sa 9pm-3am.

Le Fish, across from 21 quai Augagneur (☎04 72 87 98 98). Has theme nights with salsa, jungle, groove, hip-hop and disco. Students only. Cover 60-80F, includes 1st drink, F-Sa free before 11pm. Open W-Sa 10pm-5am.

La Marquise (☎04 78 71 78 71), is next to Le Fish. Spends less on the boat but more on drawing big-name DJs for jungle and house. Occasional 30-40F cover. Open W-Sa 10pm till dawn.

L'United Café, impasse de la Pêcherie (☎04 78 29 93 18), in an alley off of quai de la Pêcherie. Plays American and Latino dance hits and the occasional slow song for a mixed gay-lesbian crowd. With lip-shaped urinals to boot. Open daily 9:30pm-3am.

Le Village, 8 rue St. George (☎04 78 42 02 19), off pl. de la Commanderie. Lesbian *pub dansant*. Drinks 20-45F. No cover. Open W, Th, Su 9pm-1am and F-Sa 9pm-4am.

⚡ DAYTRIP FROM LYON

THE BEAUJOLAIS

(☎04 78 98 56 62. *Guided bus tours in English are available from Lyon. Apr.-Oct. Th, F, Su 1:15pm.)*

The Beaujolais lies roughly between the Loire and the Saône, with Lyon and Mâcon on either end. The region is most famous for the cool, fruity wine that it exports. The tourist offices dotting the countryside are only too happy to furnish suggested routes that wind through seemingly endless vineyards, sleepy villages, and medieval chateaux, with a few *dégustations* (tastings) thrown in for good measure.

OTHER DAYTRIPS FROM LYON

ANNECY. A 2-hour train ride will take you into the fairytale city of Annecy, nestled in the French Alps (see p. 369).

CLUNY. Spent the afternoon exploring this untouched medieval town (see p. 377).

BURGUNDY (BOURGOGNE)

Drunk on the power of their Duchy, the rulers of Burgundy were so bold as to challenge the French monarchy during the 15th century. Shifting alliances during the Hundred Years' War brought them lands as far north as the Netherlands, but Louis XI took advantage of the death of the last duke, Charles the Bold, to annex Burgundy. Today, Burgundy's fame rests on its production of some of the world's finest wines, and dishes like *coq au vin* and *bœuf bourguignon*, which have made this region a capital in the hearts of Epicureans the world over.

DIJON

Dijon (pop. 160,000) is renowned for its snobbery within France, and for its mustard everywhere else. The city is also richly endowed with late medieval and early modern architecture, myriad museums, a marvelous culinary tradition, and fine wines. The diverse **Musée des Beaux-Arts** occupies the east wing of the colossal **Palais des Ducs de Bourgogne,** in pl. de la Libération at the center of the *vieille ville.* (☎03 80 74 52 70. Open W-M 10am-6pm. 22F, students free, Su free for all.) At the **Eglise Notre-Dame** (☎03 80 74 35 76), in pl. Notre-Dame, rub the owl on the left side of the exterior for good luck. The brightly tiled **Cathédrale St-Bénigne,** in pl. St-Bénigne, has a spooky circular crypt. (☎03 80 30 14 90. Crypt 10F.) Next door, the **Musée Archéologique,** 5 rue Dr. Maret, features Gallo-Roman sculpture and neolithic housewares. (☎03 80 30 88 54. Open June-Sept. W-M 9:30am-6:30pm; Jan.-May and Oct.-Dec. W-M 9am-noon and 2-6pm. 14F, students free, Su free.) **Grey Poupon** store, 32 rue de la Liberté, where *moutarde au vin* has been made since 1777. (☎03 80 30 41 02. Open M-Sa 9am-7pm.)

FRANCE

From the train station at Cours de la Care, at the end of av. Maréchal Foch, **trains** chug to Paris (1½hr., 14 TGVs per day, 382F); Lyon (2hr., 10 per day, 140F); and Nice (7-8hr. 9 per day, 380F). The **tourist office,** on pl. Darcy, is a straight shot down av. Maréchal Foch from the station. (☎ 03 80 44 11 44. Open daily July-Aug. 9am-8pm; Sept.-June 9am-7pm.) To get to the huge **auberge de jeunesse (HI),** 1 av. Champollion, take bus #5 (bus A at night; dir.: Epirey) from Bar Bleu at pl. Grangier to Epirey. (☎ 03 80 72 95 20. Breakfast included. Dorms 72-78F; singles, doubles, and triples 155F per person.) **Hôtel Montchapet,** 26-28 rue Jacques Cellerier, north of av. Première Armée Française off Pl. Darcy, is homey and modern. (☎ 03 80 53 95 00. Breakfast 33F. Reception 7am-10:30pm. Check-out 11am. Singles 150-215F; doubles 215-245F; triples 340F; quads 370F.) **Rues Berbisey** and **Monge** host a wide variety of low- to mid-priced restaurants. Get your mustard at the **supermarket** in the **Galeries Lafayette,** 41 rue de la Liberté. (Open M-Sa 9am-7:15pm.) **Postal Code:** 21000.

◪ **DAYTRIP FROM DIJON: BEAUNE.** Wine has poured out of the well-touristed town of **Beaune,** just south of Dijon (25min., 21 per day, 38F), for centuries. Surrounded by the famous Côte de Beaune vineyards, the town itself is packed with wineries offering free *dégustations* (tastings). The largest of the cellars belongs to **Patriarche Père et Fils,** 5-7 rue du Collège; a labyrinth of 5km of corridors is packed with ten million bottles. (☎ 03 80 24 53 78. Open daily 9:30-11:30am and 2-5:30pm. 50F.) The **tourist office,** 1 rue de l'Hôtel-Dieu, lists *caves* in the region offering tours. (☎ 03 80 26 21 30; fax 03 80 26 21 39. Open mid-June to mid-Sept. M-Sa 9am-8pm, Su 9am-7pm; mid-Sept. to mid-June hrs. vary.)

CLUNY

Cluny (pop. 5000) has not grown since the abbey controlled 10,000 monks, 1200 monasteries, 11 popes, and a few kings in the Middle Ages before succumbing to the blows of the Reformation and Revolution. The **Musée d'Art et d'Archéologie** (☎ 03 85 59 12 79) houses a reconstruction of the abbey and some religious art which escaped destruction. The Romanesque abbey church, **Cluny III,** is the third church on the site and was the largest in the world until the construction of St. Peter's in Rome. (Open July-Aug. daily 9am-7pm; Sept. 9am-6pm; Oct. 9:30am-noon and 2-5pm; Nov.-Mar. 10am-noon and 3-4pm; Apr.-June 9:30am-noon and 2-6pm. Museum and abbey tour in French 32F, under 25 21F.) To get to Cluny, take the **train** to Mâcon from Dijon (1¼hr., 10 per day, 95F) or Lyon (1hr., 13 per day, 62F), and transfer to the SNCF **bus** (40min., 5 per day, 25F).

SEMUR-EN-AUXOIS

Often called the "Athens of Burgundy," the *vieille ville*'s stunning towers and ramparts crown this unspoiled regional treasure of cobblestones and archways. Deep in the medieval town, gargoyles sneer from the 15th-century facade of the **Collégiale Notre-Dame.** The church offers up a full three-course meal; gluttons can meditate in the Chapels of the Butchers and then the Bakers, donated by their respective guilds in the 15th century. (Open in summer 9am-noon and 2-6pm; off-season closes 5pm.) TRANSCO **buses** (☎ 03 80 42 11 00) go to Dijon (1½hr., 1-3 per day, 60F). The **tourist office,** on pl. Gaveau, is by the gates of the old town. (☎ 03 80 97 05 96. Open mid-June to mid-Sept. M-Sa 9am-7pm, Su 10am-noon and 3-6pm; mid-Sept. to mid-June M-Sa 8:30am-noon and 2-6:30pm.) The **Foyer des Jeunes Travailleurs,** 1 rue du Champ de Foire, is off rue de la Liberté about 300m away from the tourist office. (☎ 03 80 97 10 22. Breakfast 10F; meals 48F. Reception M-Th 9am-9pm, F 9am-8pm, Sa-Su 11am-2pm and 6-8pm. Singles 100F.) **Camping Municipal du Lac de Pont** is 3km south of Semur on a scenic lake. (☎ 03 80 97 01 26. Electricity 15F. Reception 9am-noon and 4-8pm. Open May-Sept. 15. 20F per person, 10F per site, 10F per car.) For **groceries,** head down rue de la Liberté to **Intermarché,** on av. du Général Maziller. (Open M-Th 9am-12:15pm and 2:30-7:15pm, F 9am-7:45pm, Sa 9am-7:15pm.)

BOURGES

In 1433, Jacques Coeur, financial minister to Charles VII, chose Bourges (pop. 76,000) as the site for one of his many chateaux. You'll see more of the unfurnished **Palais Jacques-Coeur** than he ever did, for he was wrongly imprisoned for the attempted poisoning of Charles' mistress years before its completion. (July-Aug. 9am-6pm; Apr.-June and Sept. 9am-noon and 2-6pm; Oct.-Mar. 9am-noon and 2-5pm. 32F, ages 18-24 21F, under 18 free.) The **Cathédrale St-Etienne**, across town near the tourist office, has stunning 13th-century handiwork in the **tower** and **crypt**, a dramatic Gothic facade, and bright stained-glass windows. (Open daily July-Aug. 8am-9pm; June and Sept. 8:30am-7:30pm; Oct.-May 8:30am-6:30pm. 30F.) As you exit the cathedral, head right on rue des 3 Maillets and turn left on rue Molière to find the intimate **promenade des Remparts,** which offers a quiet stroll past Roman ramparts and flower-filled back gardens.

Trains leave for Paris (2½hr., 4 per day, 153F) and Tours (1½hr., 10 per day, 123F) from the station at pl. Général Leclerc. Follow av. H. Laudier (which turns into av. Jean Jaurès) from the station, bear left onto rue du Commerce, and continue straight on rue Moyenne to reach the **tourist office,** 21 rue Victor Hugo. (☎02 48 23 02 60; fax 02 48 23 02 69. Open M-Sa 9am-7pm, Su 10am-7pm.) To get to the **Auberge de Jeunesse (HI)**, 22 rue Henri Sellier, follow the above directions to rue du Commerce, then bear right on rue des Arènes (which becomes rue Fernault), cross at the intersection to rue René Ménard and follow it to the right, and turn left at rue Henri Sellier. (☎02 48 24 58 09. Reception M-F 8am-noon and 2pm-1am, Sa-Su 8am-noon and 5-10pm. 3- to 8-bunk rooms 48F.) For the **Centre International de Séjour, "La Charmille,"** 17 rue Félix-Chédin, cross the footbridge from the station over the tracks. (☎02 48 23 07 40. Singles 98F; 3 or more people 73F per person.) Outdoor tables pack **pl. Gordaine** and **rue des Beaux-Arts;** sandwich shops line **rues Moyenne** and **Mirabeau.** The **Leclerc supermarket** is on rue Prado off bd. Juraville. (Open M-F 9:15am-7:20pm, Sa 8:30am-7:20pm.) **La Cantine Berrichonne,** 6bis rue Bourbonnoux, offers a 59-69F menu. (Open daily noon-2pm and 7-10:30pm.) **Postal Code:** 18000.

VEZELAY

High atop a hillside, the village of Vézelay (pop. 497) watches over dense forest and the misty gold of wheat and white flecks of cattle in distant pastures. The houses, covered with red tile roofs and wildroses, seem lost in time. Vézelay lives up to its billing as one of the most beautiful villages in France. The town has been a major pilgrimage destination since the 11th century, thanks to the relics of St. Mary Magdelene held within the Basilique Ste-Madeleine. The main attraction is the array of grotesque, lyrical carved capitols which depict testamental monsters and tales of violence. (☎03 86 33 39 50. Open daily 8am-7:30pm. 30F suggested donation.)

There is no train station in Vézelay; **trains** run from Paris via Auxerre to Sermicelles (50min., 4 per day, 40F). On Saturdays, you can wait for the bus (☎03 86 33 35 95) which runs between Vezelay and Avallon. In summer, an SNCF **bus** leaves Avallon for Vézelay at 9:20 am and returns at 5:26pm (22min., 22F). The tiny **tourist office,** rue St-Pierre, just down the street from the church, offers free maps and a *guide pratique* with accommodations listings. (☎03 86 33 23 69; fax 03 86 33 34 00. Open daily June-Oct. 10am-1pm and 2-6pm; Nov.-May closed Thursdays.) The closest bank is in Avallon, but the **post office,** rue St-Étienne (☎03 86 33 26 35), has an ATM. (Open M-F 9am-noon and 2-5pm, Sa 9am-noon.) **Postal Code:** 89450.

NORTHEASTERN FRANCE

Commonly ignored by travelers except as a rest stop between France and the rest of Europe, the "frontier regions" of the northeast represent the last outpost of French tourism. Sprawling clockwise from the Chunnel terminus to the mountainous Swiss border, the regions of Flanders, Champagne, Alsace, Lorraine, and Franche-Comté have been memorialized as battlefields since the Middle Ages, and for many travelers of interest for historical reasons. The fields and cellars of Champagne, the wine towns surrounding Strasbourg, and the splendid hiking trails in the Jura mountains provide other motives for visiting the area.

ALSACE, LORRAINE, AND FRANCHE-COMTÉ

Heavily influenced by its tumultuous history, the northeastern frontier of France has been defined by its place as the prize in the ceaseless border wars between France and Germany. The entire region maintains a fascinating blend of local dialects, cuisine, and architecture. Germanic influences are most apparent in its cuisine, which pairs baguettes and fine wine with sauerkraut and heavy German meats, bringing an element of heartiness to traditional delicacies.

STRASBOURG

Just a few kilometers from the Franco-German border, Strasbourg (pop. 260,000) has spent much of its history being annexed by one side or another. Today the city serves as a symbol of French-German *détente*—at least in culinary terms, there are as many *winstubs* lining its squares as there are *pâtisseries*. Strasbourg is also the joint center of the European Union, along with Brussels. With half-timbered houses and flower-lined canals, the city makes a fantastic stopover.

◪ TRANSPORTATION. Air France, 15 rue des Francs-Bourgeois (☎03 88 55 29 09), sends frequent **flights** to: Paris (students from 250F-665F); Lyon (students from 665F); and London (students from 1414F). Shuttle buses (☎03 88 77 70 70) run from the airport to Baggarsee and then to the tram which can be taken into town. (12min., 3-4 per hr. 5:30am-11pm, 27F). Strasbourg is a major European rail hub. **Trains** (☎03 88 22 50 50) depart from pl. de la Gare to: Paris (4hr., 16 per day, 220F); Frankfurt (3hr., 18 per day, 218F); Luxembourg City (2½hr., 14 per day, 160F); and Zurich (3hr., 3-4 per hr., 232F). Within the city, a **tram line** provides frequent service. (Tickets 7F, carnet of 5 31F, day pass 20F.)

▨ PRACTICAL INFORMATION. The *vieille ville* (old city) is an eye-shaped island in the center of the city, bounded on the north by a large canal and on the south by the river Ill. From the station, if you turn right after crossing the bridge, you'll find yourself in **La Petite France**, a neighborhood of old Alsatian houses, narrow canals, and restaurants. The **tourist office**, 17 pl. de la Cathédrale, is right next to the cathedral and sells maps (3-24F) and makes hotel reservations for 10F. (☎03 88 52 28 28. Open June-Sept. M-Sa 9am-7pm, Su 9am-6pm; Oct.-May daily 9am-6pm.) Hop on the **internet** at Le Midi-Minuit, 5 pl. de Corbeau. (30F per 30min. Open M-W 7am-7pm, Th-Sa 7am-10pm, Su 8am-7pm.) **Postal Code:** 67000.

▨▨ ACCOMMODATIONS AND FOOD. Make reservations or arrive early to find reasonable accommodations. **CIARUS (Centre International d'Accueil de Strasbourg),** 7 rue Finkmatt, has sparkling rooms and a social atmosphere. From the station, take rue du Maire-Kuss to the canal, turn left, and follow quais St-Jean, Kléber, and rue Finkmatt; turn left on rue Finkmatt, and it's on the left. (☎03 88 15 27 88. Internet access available. Breakfast 20F. Check-in 3:30pm. Curfew 1am. Dorms 92-124F; singles 206F.) **Hôtel le Grillon,** 2 rue Thiergarten, is just one block from the station towards the center of Strasbourg. (☎03 88 32 71 88. Reception 6am-2am. Breakfast 32F. Singles 180-240F; doubles 230-310F.) **Hôtel de Bruxelles,** 13 rue Kuhn, is across the canal from the *vieille ville*. (☎03 88 32 45 31. Breakfast 28F. Singles 165-260F; doubles 165-275F; triples, and quads 237-360F.) *Winstubs* are informal eateries traditionally affiliated with wineries that serve Alsatian specialties such as *choucroute garnie* (spiced sauerkraut with meats)—look in the **La Petite France** neighborhood, especially along **rue des Dentelles** and **petite rue des Dentelles**. Try **pl. de la Cathédrale, rue Mercière,** or **rue du Vieil Hôpital** for restaurants, and **pl. Marché**

FRANCE

FRANCE

Strasbourg

▲ ACCOMMODATIONS

Auberge de Jeunesse
R. Cassin (HI), **5**

CIARUS, **1**

Hostel Parc du Rhin, **7**

Hôtel de Bruxelles, **2**

Hôtel Kléber, **4**

Hôtel le Grillon, **3**

Hôtel Michelet, **6**

300 yards
300 meters

PLACE ARNOLD

Rue L'Observatoire

Av. General de Gaulle

Rue de Reims

Jardin Botanique

Rue Goethe

Parc de l'Université

Musée Zoologique

Université

PLACE D'ATHÈNES

Rue de Rome

Rue du Maréchal Juin

Rue de Jura

Av. de la Forêt Noire

Rue de l'Université

Rue General Zimmer

Rue General Zimmer

Quai Rouget de Lisle

Allée de la Robertsau

Rue de Schweighaeuser

Quai Zorn

United States

Rue du Marie Dietrich

Bd. de la Victoire

Contades Synagogue

Av. de la Paix

Rue Oberlin

Av. des Vosges

Maréchal Joffre

PLACE DE LA RÉPUBLIQUE

Av. de la Marseillaise

Rue de l'Arc en Ciel

Rue Brûlée

Rue des Frères

Rue du Dôme

Pont du Théâtre

Quai Lezay-Marnésia

Rue de la Krutenau

Rue de Zurich

Rue de Lucerne

Château des Rohan

PL. DU MARCHÉ GAYOT

Quai des Bateliers

Rue des Orphelins

PLACE D'AUSTERLITZ

TO COLMAR, E4, A5

Quai J. Sturm

Rue de la Fonderie

PLACE BROGLIE

Rue de la Nuée Bleue

Cathédrale

PL. DU CORBEAU

Musée Alsacien

PLACE DE L'HÔPITAL

Rue Finkmatt

Rue des Tieize

Rue du Fg. de Pierre

Rue des Bonnes Gens

Rue du Travail

Rue de Sébastopol

Quai Kellermann

Rue Kléber

PLACE KLÉBER

Rue aux F. Bourgeois

Gr. Arcades

PL. GUTENBERG

rue du Vieux Marché aux Poissons

Rue Div. Leclerc

St Thomas

Quai St-Nicolas

Rue de la 1ère Armée

Bd. de Président Wilson

Les Halles

Rue du Maras Vert

Quai de Paris

Rue du Vieux Marché-aux-Vins

Rue du 22 Novembre

Grand'Rue

Rue des Dentelles

PLACE ST-PIERRE LE VIEUX

LA PETITE FRANCE

Ponts Couverts

Rue Humann

L'Ill

Rue du Fg. de Savrne

Rue Kageneck

Rue Marie Kuss

Quai de Turckheim

Bd. de Metz

Rue de la Course

Rue du Fg National

Rue Ste-Marguerite

Rue de Molsheim

Rue Rosheim

TO NANCY, METZ

Bd. de Nancy

Bd. de Lyon

TO AND

Gayot, hidden off rue des Frères, for lively cafes. For **groceries,** swing by the **ATAC Supermarket,** 47 rue des Grandes Arcades, off pl. Kléber. (Open M-Sa 8:30am-8pm.)

⬛🔲 **SIGHTS AND ENTERTAINMENT.** The ornate, Gothic **Cathédrale de Strasbourg** sends its tower 142m skyward. Inside, the **Horloge Astronomique** demonstrates the wizardry of 16th-century Swiss clockmakers. While you wait for the clock to strut its stuff—apostles troop out of the clockface while a cock crows to greet St. Peter (daily at 12:30pm)—check out the **Pilier des Anges** (Angels' Pillar), a masterpiece of Gothic sculpture. You can climb the **tower** in front of the clock to follow in the footsteps of young Goethe, who scaled its 330 steps regularly to cure his fear of heights. (Cathedral open M-Sa 7-11:40am and 12:45-7pm, Su 12:45-6pm. Tower open daily 9am-6:30pm; 20F.) **Palais Rohan,** 2 pl. du Château, houses a trio of small museums: the **Musée des Beaux-Arts, Musée des Arts Décoratifs,** and **Musée Archéologique.** (Open M and W-Sa 10am-noon and 1:30-6pm, Su 10am-5pm. 20F each; combined ticket for all three 40F, students 20F.) Next door, **Maison de l'Oeuvre Notre-Dame,** 3 pl. du Château, houses some of the cathedral's statues and reconstructed stained glass. (Open Tu-Sa 10am-6pm, Su 10am-5pm. 20F, students 10F.) Across the canal from La Petite France, the spectacular collection of the new **Musée d'Art Moderne et Contemporain,** 1 pl. Hans Jean Arp, ranges from Impressionist to avant garde. (Open Tu-W and F-Su 11m-7pm, Th noon-10pm. 30F, students 20F.) Take bus #23, 30, or 72 to L'Orangerie to see **l'Orangerie,** Strasbourg's largest park, designed by Le Notre after cutting his teeth on Versailles; there are free concerts in summer (Th-Tu 8:30pm) at the Pavillion Josephine. On the northwest edge of L'Orangerie is the **Palais de l'Europe,** av. de l'Europe, where the **Council of Europe** sits; the **European Parliament** is just opposite. During Council session (one week per month Sept.-July) you may register to sit in the visitors' gallery. (☎ 03 90 21 49 40. Bring your passport. 1-hour guided tours by advance request only.) For a little more fun, check out the free tour offered by the **Kronenbourg brewery,** 68 rte. d'Oberhausbergen. (☎ 03 88 27 41 59. Open M-Sa 9-10am and 2-3pm, in summer 11am and 4-5pm also.) Not to be outdone, **Heineken,** 4-10 rue St-Charles, also offers the same, by advance reservation only. (☎ 03 88 19 59 53. Call to schedule, M-F 8am-noon, 1:30-4:30pm.) **Les 3 Brasseurs,** 22 rue des Veaux, offers more microbrewed suds if you haven't gotten enough. (Open daily 11:30am-1am.)

LA ROUTE DU VIN (WINE ROUTE)

Since the High Middle Ages, the wines of Alsace have been highly prized—and highly priced—across Europe. The Alsatian vineyards flourish along a 170km corridor known as La Route du Vin (Wine Route) that begins at **Strasbourg** and stretches south along the foothills of the Vosges, passing through (from north to south) Molsheim, Obernai, Barr, Sélestat, Kintzheim, Riquewihr, Kaysersberg, Colmar, Eguisheim, and Guebwille along the way to **Mulhouse.** Hordes of tourists are drawn each year to explore the beautifully preserved medieval villages along the route— and, of course, for the free *dégustations* (tastings) along the way. **Colmar** and **Sélestat** are excellent bases with fascinating sights of their own; but don't miss out on smaller, less-touristed villages. Great information on regional *caves* and transportation can be found in Colmar at the **Centre d'Information du Vin d'Alsace,** 12 av. de la Foire aux Vins (☎ 03 89 20 16 20), at the **Maison du Vin d'Alsace.**

SÉLESTAT

Sélestat (pop. 17,200), an imperial city of the German Empire from the year 1217 and a center of humanism in the 15th century, has avoided the touristed fate of larger towns such as Colmar and Strasbourg. According to local legend, the town was founded by a giant named Sletto, whose massive thigh bone (which disbelievers claim to be a mammoth tusk) lies in the **Bibliothèque Humaniste,** 1 rue de la Bibliothèque. Founded in 1452, it contains a fascinating collection of ancient documents, including the 16th-century *Cosmographiae Introductio,* the first book to call the New World "America." (☎ 03 88 92 03 24. Open July-Aug. M and W-F 9am-noon and 2-6pm, Sa-Su 2-5pm; Sept.-June Sa 9am-noon, closed Su. 20F.) The **tourist office,** 10 bd. Gén. Leclerc, in the Commanderie St-Jean, has free maps and rents bikes. (☎ 03 88 58 87 20; fax 03 88 92 88 63. Open May-Sept. M-F 9am-12:30pm and 1:30-7pm, Sa 9am-noon and 2-5pm, Su 9am-3pm; Oct.-Apr. M-F 8:30am-noon and 1:30-6pm, Sa same, Su closed except in Dec.) The **Hôtel de l'Ill**, 13 rue des Bateliers, is off bd. des Thiers. (☎ 03 88 92 91 09. Breakfast 30F. Reception daily 7am-3pm and 5-11pm. Singles 140-150F; doubles 180-220F; triples with bath 400F.) **Camping Les Cigognes** is outside the ramparts on the south edge of the *vieille ville*. (☎ 03 88 92 03 98. Reception 7:30am-noon and 2-10pm; off-season 2-8pm. In summer, sites 60F for 1 person, 80F for 2-3 people.) Stop at **Halte Pizzas,** 14 rue d'Iéna. (Open M-W 11am-2pm and 5-10pm, F-Sa 11am-2pm and 5-11:30pm.) **Postal Code:** 67600.

COLMAR

Colmar (pop. 65,000) derives its name from the *colombes* (doves) Charlemagne kept at his estate along the Lauch river. Despite the tourists, the town's crooked lanes and pretty pastel houses retain a measure of charm—particularly in the **quartier des Tanneurs.** The collection at the **Musée Unterlinden,** 1 rue d'Unterlinden, ranges from Romanesque to Renaissance—its crown jewel, Grünewald's *Issenheim Altarpiece*, justifies a visit in itself. (Open Apr.-Oct. daily 9am-6pm; Nov.-Mar. M and W-Su 10am-5pm. 35F, students 25F.) The **Eglise des Dominicains,** on pl. des Dominicains, houses Colmar's other major masterpiece, Schongauer's *Virgin in the Rose Bower*. (Open daily 10am-12:45pm and 3-5:45pm. Closed Jan.-Mar. 8F, students 6F.) A great selection of local wines await at **Robert Karcher et Fils,** 11 rue de l'Ours, in the *vieille ville*. (☎ 03 89 41 14 42. Wine 26F and up. Open daily 8am-noon and 2-7pm.) To get to the **tourist office,** 4 rue des Unterlinden, from the train station, turn left on av. de la République and follow it to the right as it becomes to pl. Unterlinden. (☎ 03 89 20 68 92. Open July-Aug. M-Sa 9am-7pm, Su 9:30am-2pm; Apr.-June and Sept.-Oct. M-Sa 9am-6pm, Su 10am-2pm; Nov.-Mar. M-Sa 9am-noon and 2-6pm, Su 10am-2pm.) To reach the **Auberge de Jeunesse (HI),** 2 rue Pasteur, take bus #4 (dir.: Logelbach) to Pont Rouge. (☎ 03 89 80 57 39. Breakfast included. Sheets 20F. Lockout 10am-5pm. Midnight curfew. Reception 7-10am and 5pm-midnight. Open mid-Jan. to mid-Dec. HI members only. Dorms 48F; singles and doubles 78F per person.) Take bus #1 (dir.: Horbourg-Wihr) to Plage d'Ill for **Camping de l'Ill,** overlooking the Vosges. (☎ 03 89 41 15 94. Reception July-Aug. M-F 7am-9pm, Sa-Su 8am-noon and 2-10pm; Feb.-June and Sept.-Nov. Su 8am-noon, 2-8pm. 18F; tent 10F, site 20F.) Stock up at **Monoprix supermarket,** on pl. Unterlinden. (Open M-F 8:30am-8:30pm, Sa 8am-7:55pm.) **Tropic'ice,** pl. des Dominicains, offers nothing too tropical, but does have over 100 permutations of *galettes*, *crêpes*, and *coupes glacées*. (☎ 03 89 41 31 36. Open daily 11:30am-midnight.) **Postal Code:** 68000.

MULHOUSE

If Colmar constitutes the heart of Alsace and Strasbourg serves as the mind, then prosperous Mulhouse (pop. 110,000) provides the muscle. Its historical district centers on the festive **pl. de la Réunion,** named for the dates in 1798 and 1918 when French troops "reunited" the city with distant Paris. Nearby is the **Temple de St-Etienne,** one of France's few Protestant Gothic cathedrals. (☎ 03 89 66 30 19. Open May-Sept. M and W-Su 10am-noon and 2-6pm.) The town's industrial heritage has endowed it with a host of first-rate museums, including the **Musée Français du Chemin de Fer,** 2 rue Alfred de Glehn. Take bus #17 (dir.: Musées) from Porte Jeune Place to see the stunning collection of gleaming engines and railway cars. (☎ 03 89 42 25 67. Open daily Apr.-Sept. 9am-6pm, Oct.-Mar. 9am-5pm. 46F, students 20F.) Over 500 cars in mint condition are on display at the **Musée National de l'Automobile,** 192 av. de Colmar. (☎ 03 89 33 23 23. Take bus #1, 4, 11, 13 or 17 north to Musée Auto. Open late Mar-Oct. daily 9am-6pm; Nov.-late Mar. daily 10am-6pm; July-Aug. 9am-6:30pm W-M 10am-6pm. 60F, students 46F. Combined with Musée Français du Chemin de Fer 81F.) **Trains** run from bd. Général to Paris (4½hr., 9 per day, 275F) and Strasbourg (1hr., 14 per day, 85F). The **tourist office,** 9 av. Foch, is two blocks from the train station. (☎ 03 89 35 48 48. Open July-Aug. M-Sa 9am-7pm, Su 10am-noon; Sept.-June Sa 9am-5pm, closed Su.) To get to the cheerful **Auberge de Jeunesse (HI),** 37 rue d'Ilberg, take bus #2 (bus S1 after 8:30pm; dir.: Loteaux) to Salle des

Sports. (☎ 03 89 42 63 28. HI members only. Breakfast 19F. Sheets 17F. Reception daily 8am-noon and 4pm-midnight; off-season closes 11pm. 48F.) Hunt for food along **rue de l'Arsenal**, or buy **groceries** at **Monoprix**, on the corner of rue du Sauvage and rue des Maréchaux. (Open M-F 8:15am-8pm, Sa 8:15am-7pm.) **Le Couscoussier,** 33 rue de l'Arsenal (☎ 03 89 56 65 07), serves up hearty pots of its namesake. (Open Tu-Sa noon-2:30pm and 7-11:30pm, Su-M noon-2:30pm.) **Postal Code:** 68100.

BESANÇON

Since Julius Caesar founded a military post here in 58 BC, Besançon (pop. 120,000) has intrigued military strategists because of its geographically protected location. Now a university town known for its prosperity as France's watch-making capital, the young and hip population creates an energetic abundance of nightlife. The elegant Renaissance buildings provide plenty of eye candy, but the city's true delights lie high up in the **citadel,** designed by Louis XIV's architect, Vauban. Within the citadel, the **Musée de la Résistance et de la Déportation,** at the end of rue des Fusilles de la Résistance, chronicles the Nazi rise to power and the German occupation of France; other sights include a natural history museum, a zoo, an aquarium, and a folk arts museum. (Grounds open daily July-Aug. 9am-7pm; Apr.-June and Sept.-Oct. 9am-6pm; Nov.-Mar. 10am-5pm. Museums open daily 9am-6pm, off-season 10am-5pm. 40F, students 30F.) The **Cathédrale St-Jean,** perched on the hill beneath the citadel, mixes architectural styles from the 12th- to 18th- centuries and is crowned by the intricate 19th-century **Horloge Astronomique** clock. (Open M and W-Su 9am-7pm. Free.) The **Musée des Beaux-Arts,** on pl. de la Révolution, houses an exceptional collection ranging from ancient Egyptian treasures to works by Matisse. (Open W-M 9:30am-6pm. 21F, students free; Su and holidays free.) Small bars and *brasseries* line **rues Pasteur** and **Bersot.** Local students pack the three dance floors at **Le Queen,** 8 av. de Chardonnet. (Open W-Th 10:30pm-4am, F-Sa 10:30pm-5am.) Shoot pool at the surprisingly hip **Pop Hall,** 26 rue Proudhon; even the bathroom decorations are amazing. (Open M-Th 3pm-1am, Sa 3pm-2am, Su 6pm-2am.)

    Trains pull up at the station on av. de la Paix (☎ 08 36 35 35 35), from: Paris-Gare de Lyon (2hr., 7 per day, 318F); Dijon (1hr., 6 per day, 74F); and Strasbourg (3hr., 10 per day, 163F). **Buses** run by **Monts Jura,** 9 rue Proudhon (☎ 03 81 21 22 00), go to Pontarlier (1hr., 6 per day, 45.50F). From the train station, head downhill and cross onto Av. Maréchal Foch, continue downhill on av. de l'Helvétie until you reach pl. de la Première Armée Française. The *vieille ville* is across the pont de la République; the **tourist office,** 2 pl. de la 1ère Armée Française, is in the park to the right. (☎ 03 81 80 92 55; www.besancon.com. Open April to mid-June and Sept.15-30 M 10am-7pm, Tu-Sa 9am-7pm; mid-June to mid-Sept. also open Su 10am-noon and 3-5pm; Oct.-Mar. M 10am-6pm, Tu-Sa 9am-6pm.) Surf the **internet** at **Rom Collection,** 22 rue du Lycée. (1F per min., 50F per hr.) For the traditional hostel spirit of the **Centre International de Séjour,** 48 rue des Cras, take bus #8 from the Foch stop, off av. de la Paix, near the station (dir.: Campus) to Intermarché. (☎ 03 81 50 07 54. Singles 105F, with bath 160F; doubles 264F, 368F.) An eclectic group of restaurants line **rue Claude-Pouillet.** Buy groceries at **Monoprix,** 12 Grande Rue. (Open M-Sa 8:30am-9pm.) **La Boîte à Sandwiches,** 21 rue du Lycée, off rue Pasteur, serves serious sandwiches and salads. (Open M-Sa 11:30am-2:30pm and 6:30pm-midnight.) **Postal Code:** 25000.

    ⚑ DAYTRIP FROM BESANÇON: PONTARLIER AND THE JURA. The quiet town of **Pontarlier** (840m), makes a good base from which to reach even greater heights in the Haut-Jura mountains. The Jura are best known for cross-country **skiing;** over 60km of trails wind around the city. (Day pass 30F, under 17 20F, available at the **Le Larmont** and **Le Malmaison** trails.) Le Larmont is the closest Alpine ski area (☎ 03 81 46 55 20). **Sport et Neige,** 4 rue de la République (☎ 03 81 39 04 69), rents skis (50F per day). In summer, **fishing, hiking,** and **mountain biking** are the sports of choice. Rent a **bike** from **Cycles Pernet,** 23 rue de la République. (☎ 03 81 46 48 00. 80F per day. Open Tu-Sa 9am-noon and 2-7pm.) **Monts Jura buses,** 9 rue Proudhon in Besançon (☎ 03 81 39 88 80), run to Pontarlier (55min., 6 per day, 51F). The **tourist**

office, 14bis rue de la Gare, has info on activities, and sells hiking and topographical maps. (☎03 81 46 48 33; fax 03 81 46 83 32.) **L'Auberge de Pontarlier (HI),** 2 rue Jouffroy, is clean and central. (☎03 81 38 54 54. Breakfast 19F. Sheets 17F. Reception daily 8am-noon and 5:30-10pm. Dorms 49F.) **Postal Code:** 25300.

NANCY

Nancy (pop. 100,000) is a model of 18th-century classicism, with broad plazas, wrought-iron grillwork, and cascading fountains. The city also reigns as the cultural and intellectual heart of Lorraine. The **place Stanislas** wraps Baroque gilded-iron arms around a statue of the "Good Duke" Stanislas Lesczynski, a dethroned Polish king relocated to Lorraine by his son-in-law Louis XV. Newly renovated, the **Musée des Beaux-Arts,** 3 pl. Stanislas, has an excellent collection spanning from the 14th century to the present day. (☎03 83 85 30 72. Open M and W-Su 10:30am-6pm. 30F, students 15F; W students free.) Pass through the five-arch **Arc de Triomphe** to the tree-lined pl. de la Carrière, which leads into the relaxing **Parc de la Pépinière.** The park's **Roseraie** blooms with roses from all the world. (Open May-Sept. 14 6:30am-11:30pm; May and Sept. 1-14 closes at 10pm; Mar-Apr. and Feb. closes at 8pm.)

Trains roll frequently away from the station at pl. Thiers to: Paris (3hr., 14 per day, 209F); Metz (40min., 24 per day, 51F); and Strasbourg (1hr., 19 per day, 110F). Head left from the station and right on rue Raymond Poincaré, which leads straight to pl. Stanislas and the **tourist office.** Ask for the invaluable *Le Fil d'Ariane* guide. (☎03 83 35 22 41; fax 03 83 35 90 10. Open Apr.-Sept. M-Sa 9am-7pm, Su 10am-5pm; Oct.-Mar. M-Sa 9am-6pm, Su 10am-1pm.) Access the **internet** at **Voyager** on rue St-Jean, across from the cinema. (1F per min. Open M-Sa 9am-midnight, Su 2-11pm.) **Hôtel de l'Académie,** 7 rue des Michottes, is between the station and pl. Stanislas. (☎03 83 35 52 31. Breakfast 22F. Singles and doubles 140-200F.) Restaurants cluster around **rue des Maréchaux,** spilling over onto the nearby **pl. Lafayette** and up along Grande Rue to **pl. St-Epvre.** A **SHOPI** supermarket sits at 26 rue St-Georges. (Open M-F 8:30am-7:30pm, Sa 8:30am-7pm.) **Postal Code:** 54000.

METZ

Modern Metz (pop. 200,000) maintains classic fountains, sculptured gardens, verdant canals, and golden cobblestoned streets without mobs of tourists. Few cathedrals in France have naves that soar higher than the **Cathédrale St-Etienne,** which dominates the pl. d'Armes. Marvel at its 6500m of stained-glass windows, including some by Marc Chagall. (Open M-Sa 9am-7pm, Su 10am-7pm. Free.) At the other end of the rue des Clercs from pl. d'Armes lies the **Esplanade,** a patchwork of gardens and promenades. Down the steps from the Esplanade, shady paths wind through wooded parkland along the **Lac aux Cygnes.** In summer, watch the brightly lit fountains dance to music on weekends (June 18-Sept. 5 F-Su at dusk). Afterward, teeter and sway yourself in the student-packed bars and cafes in **pl. St-Jacques.**

Trains arrive frequently at pl. du Général de Gaulle from: Paris (3hr., 10 per day, 209F); Nancy (40min., 31 per day, 59F); Strasbourg (1½hr., 7 per day, 114F); and Luxembourg City (45min., 12 per day, 84F). Head right from the station, left on rue des Augustins, straight through pl. Quartier and pl. St-Louis, left at pl. St-Simplice on the pedestrian rue de la Tête d'Or, and right on rue Fabert to reach the **tourist office,** on pl. d'Armes. (☎03 87 55 53 76. Open July-Aug. M-Sa 9am-9pm, Su 10am-1pm and 2-5pm; Sept.-June M-Sa 9am-7pm.) Surf the **internet** at **Net Café,** 1-3 Rue Paul Bezanson, near the cathedral. (Students 30F per 30min. Open M-Sa 1-6pm.) Take bus #3 (dir.: Metz-Nord) or 11 (dir.: St-Eloy) to Pontiffroy to reach the well-run **Auberge de Jeunesse (HI),** 1 allée de Metz Plage. (☎03 87 30 44 02. Breakfast 19F. Reception 7:30-10am and 5-10pm. 2- to 6-bed dorms 49F. Nonmembers 19F extra.) Cheap eateries cluster near the hostel on **rue du Pont des Morts,** in the **pedestrian district,** and toward the station on **rue Coisin.** The **ATAC supermarket** is in the Centre St-Jacques, off pl. St-Jacques. (Open M-Sa 8:30am-7:30pm.) **Postal Code:** 57000.

VERDUN

After Charlemagne divided up the Frankish empire among his grand-children in the treaty of Verdun in 843, the city became a hotspot in the Franco-German dispute which has endured for over a thousand years. Today, its war memorials testify to the horror of the battles fought in the area between France and Germany during WWI. Built in 1200, the **Porte Chaussée,** on the quai de Londres, served as a prison and guard tower over the Meuse. At one end of the rue Frères Boulhaut, Rodin's bronze Victory guards the Port St-Paul. Marking the edge of the *haute ville,* the traditionally-styled **Monument à la Victoire** rises above a flight of 72 granite steps. This tower stands atop the remains of the **Eglise de la Magdelaine,** built in 1049 and bombed beyond recognition in 1916. (Open daily 9am-noon and 2-6pm.) The **Musée de la Princerie** is devoted to archaeology, medieval art and architecture, and old *faïence* pottery. (☎ 03 29 86 10 62. Open W-M 9:30am-noon and 2-6pm. 6F.)

Trains run from the station at pl. Maurice Genovoix to Metz (1½hr., 5 per day, 70F). **Buses** run from pl. Vauban to Metz (2hr., 8 per day, 69F) and Nancy (2¾hr., 8 per day, 95F). Verdun is split in two by the Meuse, with the train station, the cathedral, and the hostel on one side, and the tourist office and war memorials on the other. To get to the **tourist office** from the train station, take av. Garibaldi until you reach the bus station, turn left onto rue Frères Boulhaut and continue until you reach the Port Chaussée. Turn left again, cross the bridge onto pl. de la Nation and the office will be on your right. (Open July-Aug. M-Sa 8:30am-7:30pm, Su 9am-5pm; May-June and Sept. 8:30am-6:30pm, Su 9am-5pm; Mar.-Apr. and Oct.-Nov. reduced hrs.) From the bright decor, you'd never guess that hotel **Le Montaulbain,** 4 rue de la Vieille Prison, used to house a prison. (☎ 03 29 86 00 47. Breakfast 25F. Reception 7:30am-10pm. Singles 130-170F; doubles 140-200F.) **Postal Code:** 55107.

CHAMPAGNE

John Maynard Keynes once remarked that his major regret in life was not having consumed enough champagne; a trip through the rolling vineyards and fertile plains of Champagne promises many opportunities to avoid his mistake. The term *champagne* is fiercely guarded; the name can only be applied to wines made from regional grapes and produced according to a rigorous, time-honored method. In Flanders, however, by the Belgian border, beer is the order of the day, to be quaffed with lots of mussels. As you flee the ferry ports, don't overlook the intriguing Flemish culture of Arras and the world-class art collections of Lille.

REIMS

Reims (pop. 185,000) delights with the bubbly champagne of its fabulous *caves* as well as the beauty of its architectural masterpieces. The famed **Cathédrale de Notre-Dame,** built with golden limestone quarried in the Champagne *caves,* features sea-blue stained-glass windows by Marc Chagall. (☎ 03 26 47 55 34. Open daily 7:30am-7:30pm. Tours July-Aug. daily 10:30am (Su 11am), 2:30, and 4:30pm; Mar.-June and Sept.-Oct. less frequently. 35F, under 26 20F.) Enter the adjacent **Palais du Tau** through the cathedral for dazzling 16th-century tapestries and reliquaries. (☎ 03 26 47 81 79. Open July-Aug. daily 9:30am-6:30pm; Sept.-Nov. 14 and Mar. 15-June 15 daily 9:30am-12:30pm and 2-6pm; Nov. 15-Mar. 15 M-F 10am-noon and 2-5pm, Sa-Su 10am-noon and 2-6pm. 32F, students 21F.) The most elegant tour of a *cave* is at **Pommery,** 5 pl. du Général Gouraud. (☎ 03 26 61 62 56. Tours Mar. 27-Oct. 27 M-F 9-11am and 2-4:30pm, Sa-Su 9-11am and 2-5pm; Dec.-Feb. closed Sa-Su. 40F, students 20F.) Order a *coupe de champagne* at any bar (25-30F) or look in wineshops (from 70F per bottle of the good stuff). **Pl. Drouet d'Erlon** is crowded with cafes and bars; try **Le Havana,** 27 rue de Vesle. (☎ 03 26 86 85 07. Happy Hour daily 6-7pm.)

Trains (☎ 03 26 78 60 60) leave bd. Joffre for Paris (1½hr., 11per day, 121F). To get to the **tourist office,** 2 rue Guillaume de Machault, from the station, follow the right-hand curve of the rotary to pl. d'Erlon, turn left on rue de Vesle, turn right on rue du Tresor, and it's on the left before the cathedral. (☎ 03 26 77 45 25; fax 03 26 77 45 27. Open Apr.17-Oct. 15 M-Sa 9am-7pm, Su 10am-5pm; Oct. 16-Apr. 16 M-Sa 9am-6pm, Su 10am-5pm.) To get to the **Auberge de Jeunesse (HI),** on chaussée Bocquaine, next to La Comédie-Espace André Malraux, from the station, cross the park, follow the right-hand side of the traffic circle, turn right on bd. Général Leclerc, cross the first bridge (pont de Vesle), and take your first left. (☎ 03 26 40 52 60. Breakfast 18F. Singles 89F, with bath 129F; doubles and triples 69F per person, with bath 119F. Nonmembers 10F extra.) **Au Bon Accueil,** 31 rue Thillois, is off pl. d'Erlon. (☎ 03 26 88 55 74. Breakfast 25F. Singles 80-150F; doubles 140-220F.) **Monoprix supermarket** is at rue de Vesle and rue de Talleyrand. (Open M-Sa 8:30am-9pm.) **Postal Code:** 51100.

🏠 **DAYTRIP FROM REIMS: EPERNAY.** Epernay (pop. 30,000) devotes itself to the production of bubbly. **Avenue de Champagne** is distinguished by its mansions, lush gardens, and monumental champagne firms. Both tours below offer a *petite dégustation* for those over 16. **Moët & Chandon,** 20 av. de Champagne, produces the king of all wines: **Dom Perignon.** (☎ 03 26 51 20 20. Open Apr. 1-Nov. 15 daily 9:30-11:30am and 2-4:30pm; Nov. 19-Mar. 14 closed Sa-Su. 1hr. tour 40F.) **Mercier,** 70 av. de Champagne, is the self-proclaimed most popular champagne in France, and gives fascinating tours in roller-coaster-like cars. (☎ 03 26 51 22 22. Open Mar.-Nov. M-F 9:30-11:30am and 2-4:30pm, Sa-Su 9:30-11:30am and 2-5pm; Dec. 1-19 and Jan. 13-Feb. Th-M only. Tours 30F.) Frequent **trains** leave cour de la Gare for Reims (25min., 14 per day, 33F). From the town center at pl. de la République, turn left on av. de Champagne to reach the **tourist office,** 7 av. de Champagne. (☎ 03 26 53 33 00; fax 03 26 51 95 22. Open Easter-Oct. 15 M-Sa 9:30am-noon and 1:30-7pm, Su 11am-4pm; Oct. 16-Easter M-Sa 9:30am-12:30pm and 1:30-5:30pm.)

TROYES

Troyes (pop. 60,000) bears little resemblance to its grape-crazy northern neighbors. Medieval and Renaissance churches comprise the premier attractions of the *vieille ville.* Troyes has also preserved whole tracts of 16th-century houses and spiced them up with cafes and collections of modern art. The **Musée de l'Art Moderne,** on pl. St-Pierre, has over 2000 modern sculptures, drawings, and paintings by French artists, including Rodin, Degas, Courbet, Seurat, and Picasso. (Open M and W-Su 11am-6pm. 30F, students 5F; W free.) Movie theaters, arcades, and pool halls rub elbows with chic boutiques on **rue Emile Zola.** On warm evenings, *Troyers* swarm the cafes and taverns of **rues Champeaux** and **Mole** near pl. Alexandre Israel.

Trains run from av. Maréchal Joffre to Paris-Est (1½hr., 10 per day, 118F) and east to Mulhouse (3hr., 6 per day, 201F). There are two outposts of the **tourist office,** one at 16 bd. Carnot (☎ 03 25 82 62 70), near the station, and the other in the *vieille ville* on rue Mignard (☎ 03 25 73 36 88), which offer free walking tour maps and help reserve rooms. (Open M-Sa 9am-12:30pm.) From rue Mignard, walk to the place Audiffred and turn right to reach **Les Comtes de Champagne,** 56 rue de la Monnaie. (☎ 03 25 73 11 70. Breakfast 30F. Reception 7am-11pm. Singles 160F, with shower from 190F; doubles 200F, 230F.) **Camping Municipal,** 2km from Troyes, has showers, laundry, and TV. Take bus #1 (dir.: "Pont St-Marie") and ask to be let off at the campground. (☎ 03 25 81 02 64. 25F per person; 30F per tent or car. Open Apr.-Oct. 15.) Restaurants and *crêperies* line **rue Champeaux** in quartier St-Jean. On the other side of the *vieille ville,* reasonably priced eateries can be found on **rue de la Cité,** near the cathedral. Try the creamy *fromage de Troyes* or the *andouillette de Troyes,* a tasty sausage. Stock up at **Prisunic supermarket,** 78 rue Emile Zola. (Open M-Sa 8:30am-8pm.) **Postal Code:** 10000.

🏠 **DAYTRIPS FROM TROYES: LES GRANDS LACS.** Troyes is approximately 30km from over 12,500 acres of freshwater lakes, of the **Forêt d'Orient.** The sunny waters of **Lake Orient** welcome sunbathers, swimmers, and windsurfers. **Lake Temple** is reserved for fishing and bird watching, and **Lake Amance** roars with speedboats (some tugging waterskiers) from **Port Dierville.** The **Comité Départemental du Tourisme de l'Aube,** 34 quai Dampierre (☎ 03 25 42 50 91; fax 03 25 42 50 88), provides info on hotels and restaurants in the area. The tourist office in Troyes has bus schedules for routes to the Grands Lacs.

LILLE

With a rich Flemish ancestry, two fine museums and exuberant nightlife, largely untouristed Lille (pop. 175,000) flaunts big-city charm without the hassle. One of France's most respected museums, the **Musée des Beaux-Arts,** on pl. de la République (M: République), boasts an encyclopedic collection of works from 15th- to 20th-century French and Flemish masters. (☎03 20 06 78 00. Open M 2-6pm, W-Th and Sa-Su 10am-6pm, F 10am-7pm. 30F, students 20F.) The **Musée d'Art Moderne,** 1 allée du Musée, showcases Cubist and postmodern art, including works by Braque, Picasso, Léger, Miró, and Modigliani. (☎03 20 19 68 18. Open W-M 10am-6pm. 43F, students 10F.) The beautiful **Vieille Bourse** (Old Stock Exchange), on pl. Général de Gaulle, epitomizes the Flemish Renaissance and today houses flower and book markets. (Markets Tu-Su 9:30am-7:30pm.) Head down rue de Paris for the 14th- to 19th-century **Eglise St-Maurice.** (Open M-F 7:15am-7pm, Sa 8am-7pm, Su 2-6pm.) After a long day, head to the pubs and bars lining **rues Solférino** and **Masséna.**

Trains leave from **Gare Lille Flandres,** on pl. de la Gare (M: Gare Lille Flandres), for Paris (1hr., 21 per day, 208-278F) and Brussels (1½hr., 20 per day, 130F). **Gare Lille Europe,** on rue le Corbusier (☎03 20 87 30 00; M: Gare Lille Europe), is a stopover point for **Eurostar** trains en route to London, Brussels, and Paris; it also sends TGVs to the south of France. From Gare Lille Flandres, walk straight down rue Faidherbe and left through pl. du Théâtre and pl. de Gaulle to reach the **tourist office,** in Palais Rihour just beyond pl. de Gaulle, which offers maps and currency exchange. (☎03 20 21 94 21; fax 03 20 21 94 20. M: Rihour. Open M-Sa 9:30am-6:30pm, Su 10am-noon and 2-5pm.) To reach the **Auberge de Jeunesse (HI),** 12 rue Malpart, from Gare Lille Flandres, head left around the station, follow rue du Molinel, turn left on rue de Paris, and take your third right. (☎03 20 57 08 94. Breakfast included. Sheets 18F. Reception 7am-noon and 2pm-1am. Check-out 10:30am. Curfew 2am. Open Feb.-Dec. 17. Dorms 73F; singles 113F; doubles 123F.) Restaurants pepper the fashionable pedestrian area around **rue de Béthune;** try the mussels, *maroilles* cheese, or *genièvre* (juniper berry liqueur). **Monoprix supermarket** is on rue du Molinel near the Gare Lille Flandres. (Open M-Sa 8:30am-8pm.) **Postal Code:** 59000.

🖪 **DAYTRIPS FROM LILLE: ARRAS AND VIMY.** The town hall of **Arras** is built over the eerie **Les Boves tunnels,** which have sheltered medieval chalk miners and British WWI soldiers alike (ask about daily tours at the tourist office; 22F, students 14F). Flanked by Flemish facades, Grand'Place, one of the town's main squares, was divided by barbed wire when French and German forces occupied opposite sides during WWI. **Trains** arrive at pl. Maréchal Foch from Lille (45 min., 21 per day, 53F); walk from the station to rue Gambetta, turn right on rue Ronville, and turn left on rue de la Housse to reach the **tourist office,** on pl. des Héros. (☎03 21 51 26 95; fax 03 21 71 07 34; www.ot.arras.fr. Open Apr. 29-Sept. 25 M-Sa 9am-6:30pm, Su 10am-1pm and 2:30-6:30pm; Sept. 26-Apr. 28 M-Sa 9am-noon and 2-6pm, Su 10am-12:30pm and 3-6:30pm.) Stay at the central **auberge de jeunesse (HI),** 59 Grand'Place. (☎03 21 22 70 02. HI members only. Breakfast 19F. Sheets 17F. Reception 7:30-noon and 5-11pm. Lockout 10am-5pm. Curfew 11pm. Open Feb.-Nov. Bunks 48F.)

The countryside surrounding Arras (the site of heavy fighting in WWI) is dotted with war cemeteries and unmarked graves. The monument of **Vimy,** 12km from Arras, honors the more than 66,000 Canadians killed in WWI. Little details in an **underground tour** of the chalk-walled tunnels evoke the realities of life on the front: the registration room, the commander's desk, and the little maple leaf chiseled in the chalk by an anonymous soldier. (Memorial open dawn-dusk. Free tours of the tunnels Apr. to mid-Nov. 10am-6pm.) **Trains** (3 per day 10am-6pm, 12F) run from Arras to Vimy. **Buses** also run from Arras to Vimy (20min., M-Sa 7 per day, 12F). From the train station, walk to the top of the road and take a right at the T-intersection; signs to your left point to a trail that travels through the forest to the memorial.

CALAIS

Ever since Richard the Lionheart and his crusaders passed through, Calais has been the continent's main portal to Britain, more so since the opening of the Channel Tunnel. Duck over to the flamboyant, faux-Gothic **Hôtel de Ville** at bd. Jacquard and rue Royale, where Rodin's famous sculpture **The Burghers of Calais** awaits, or watch the white ships glide by from one of the town's wide, gorgeous beaches. For schedules and prices to travel to Dover, England, see p. 47. During the day, free **buses** connect the hoverport, ferry terminal, and **train station**, on bd. Jacquard, where trains leave for Paris (3¼hr., 6 per day, 215-288F); Boulogne (50min., 12 per day, 41F); and Lille (1¼hr., 12 per day, 84F). To reach the **tourist office**, 12 bd. Clemenceau, cross the street from the station, turn left, and cross the bridge; it's on your right. (☎ 03 21 96 62 40; fax 03 21 96 01 92. Open M-Sa 9am-7pm, Su 10am-1pm.) The **Centre Européen de Séjour/Auberge de Jeunesse (HI)**, on av. Maréchal Delattre de Tassigny, has 84 blue doubles, just a block from the beach. From the station, turn left, follow the main road past pl. d'Armes, cross the bridge, go left at the rotary onto bd. de Gaulle, and turn right on rue Alice Marie. (☎ 03 21 34 70 20. Checkout 11am. 94F first night, 80F per extra night; non-HI-members add 10F for 1-night max. stay.) **Hotel Bristol**, 13-15 rue du Duc de Guise, is off rue Royale. (☎ 03 21 34 53 24. Breakfast 25F. Reception 7am-8pm. Singles 150-200F; doubles 160-220F.) Morning markets are held on pl. Crèvecoeur (Th, Sa) and on pl. d'Armes (W, Sa), which is also home to **Match supermarket**. (Open M-F 9am-12:30pm, Sa 9am-7:30pm, Su 9am-12:30pm.) **Postal Code:** 62100.

BOULOGNE-SUR-MER

Legend has it that a boat carrying a statue of the Virgin Mary washed onto the beach in 636, making Boulogne-sur-Mer a pilgrimage site. The huge **Château-Musée,** on rue de Bernet, houses an eclectic art collection. Among African masks and Oceanic weapons lie a bare-faced Egyptian mummy and Napoleon's second-oldest hat. (Open W-M 10am-12:30pm and 2-5pm; Su 10am-12:30pm and 2:30-5:30pm. 20F.) Just down rue de Lille, the 19th-century **Basilique de Notre-Dame** sits above 12th-century crypts, with a blue- and white-domed ceiling behind the choir, and Baroque frieze of the Ascension. (Open July-Sept. 14 9am-noon and 2-7pm; Apr.-June 9am-noon and 2-6pm; Sept. 15-Mar. 10am-noon and 2-6pm. Crypt open M-Sa 10am-noon and 2-6pm, Su 8:30am-12:30pm, 2:30-6pm. 10F.) **Trains** leave bd. Voltaire, for: Paris (2-3hr., 11 per day, 164-276F); Calais (30min., 18 per day, 41F); and Lille (2½hr., 11 per day, 106-138F). From the station, turn right on bd. Voltaire, follow bd. Danou left to pl. Angleterre, and look left for the **tourist office,** on quai de la Poste, in Forum Jean Noël. (☎ 03 21 31 68 38; fax 03 21 33 81 09. Open July-Aug. daily 9am-7pm; Sept.-June M-Sa 8:45am-12:30pm, 1:30-6:15pm, Su 10am-1pm and 2:30-5:30pm.) The fantastic **Auberge de Jeunesse (HI),** 56 pl. Rouget de Lisle, is opposite the station. (☎ 03 21 99 15 30. **Internet** 30F per 30min. Breakfast included. Reception 8am-1am. Check-in 5pm. Check-out noon. Curfew 1am. 3- to 4-bed rooms 74F; nonmembers 93F.) **STOC supermarket** is at 54 rue Daunou. (Open M-Sa 8:30am-8pm.) **Postal Code:** 62200.

GERMANY
(DEUTSCHLAND)

DEUTSCHMARK

US$1 = DM2.18	1DM = US$0.46
CDN$1 = DM1.47	1DM = CDN$0.68
EURO€1 = DM1.96	1DM = EURO€0.51
UK£1 = DM3.23	1DM = UK£0.31
IR£1 = DM2.48	1DM = IR£0.40
AUS$1 = DM1.27	1DM = AUS$0.79
NZ$1 = DM0.97	1DM = NZ$1.04
SAR1 = DM0.31	1DM = SAR3.20

PHONE CODE	Country code: 49. **International dialing prefix:** 00.

A decade after the fall of the Berlin Wall, Germans are still trying to fashion themselves a new identity for the 21st century. After centuries of war and fragmentation, Germany finds itself a wealthy nation at the forefront of both European and global politics. Germany has always been a wellspring of revolutionaries and innovators: Charlemagne (Karl der Große) unified post-Roman Europe under relatively enlightened rule; Martin Luther became one of the most influential figures with his *95 Theses;* Karl Marx and Friedrich Engels equipped the revolutionary groundswell of the 19th-century; and Adolf Hitler forever tainted Germany's name. In the wake of Europe's most recent revolutions, Germany's role between East and West is even more important than it was during the Cold War, yet efforts to provide leadership on the Continent have been hampered by Germany's internal identity crises. For more comprehensive coverage, treat yourself to *Let's Go: Germany 2001.*

SUGGESTED ITINERARIES

THREE DAYS Begin your three days in **Berlin** (p. 404) with a stroll **Unter den Linden** from the **Fernsehturm** on the **Alexanderplatz** to the **Reichstag.** Visit the **Kurfürstendamm** and take refuge in the **Tiergarten.** For a look at the **Berlin Wall** and its history, head to **Kreuzberg** for the **Checkpoint Charlie museum.** Chill in the cafe-culture of **Prenzlauer Berg** and the clubs on **Oranienburgerstr.**

ONE WEEK After scrambling through **Berlin,** overnight to Munich for churches, museums, and frosty *Maß* (1 day; p. 482). On to **Bonn** (1 day; p. 458), and then ferry down the **Rhine** to **Cologne** (1 day; p. 453). Chug to **Hamburg** explore the **Altstadt,** the **Alster Lakes,** and the **Fischmarkt** by day, and burn the night in **Sternschanze** (1 day; p. 439).

BEST OF GERMANY, THREE WEEKS Begin in **Hamburg,** (2 days; p. 439), zig-zag to **Lübeck** (p. 448) for marzipan, and to the North Sea coast to wade through **Watt** (1 day; p. 447). Travel to **Cologne** (p. 453) and ferry down the **Rhine,** stopping at **Bonn** (2 days; p. 458). Pass the **Lorelei Cliffs** (p. 469), continue down to **Koblenz** (p. 470), **Cochem, Beilstein** (p. 471) and **Trier** (4 days; p. 471). Stop in **Frankfurt** (1 day; p. 465) on your way to **Munich** and daytrip to **Dachau** (1 day; p. 495). Hike through in the **Allgäu** region, resting at **Ottobeuren** (p. 501) or **Oberstdorf** (p. 501), or take the **Romantic Road** past **Dinkelsbühl** (p. 500) to **Würzberg** (2 days; p. 498). End in **Dresden,** spinning between clubs, palaces, and museums (3 days; p. 426).

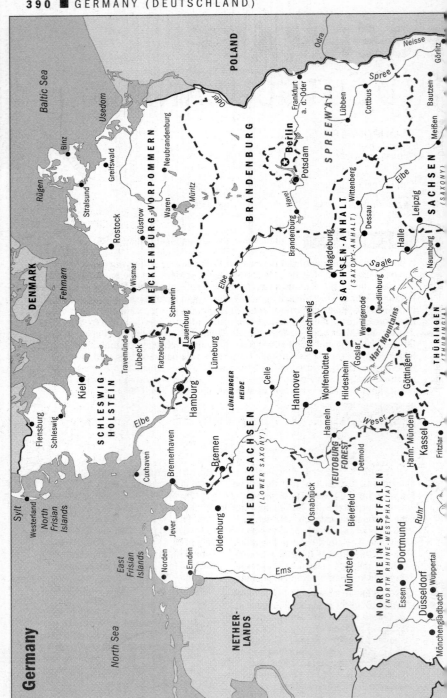

Germany

North Sea

Baltic Sea

POLAND

DENMARK

NETHER-
LANDS

SCHLESWIG-
HOLSTEIN

MECKLENBURG-VORPOMMERN

BRANDENBURG

SPREEWALD

SACHSEN-ANHALT
(SAXONY-ANHALT)

SACHSEN
(SAXONY)

THÜRINGEN
(THURINGIA)

NIEDERSACHSEN
(LOWER SAXONY)

NORDRHEIN-WESTFALEN
(NORTH RHINE-WESTPHALIA)

LÜNEBURGER
HEIDE

TEUTOBURG
FOREST

Harz Mountains

North
Frisian
Islands

East
Frisian
Islands

Rügen

Usedom

Fehmarn

Sylt
Westerland

Flensburg
Schleswig

Kiel

Binz

Greifswald

Stralsund

Rostock

Wismar

Schwerin

Güstrow

Waren

Neubrandenburg

Müritz

Travemünde
Lübeck
Ratzeburg
Lauenburg

Lüneburg

Celle

Hannover

Braunschweig

Wolfenbüttel
Hildesheim

Hameln

Detmold

Bielefeld

Osnabrück

Münster

Essen ● Dortmund
Düsseldorf
Wuppertal
Mönchengladbach

Hamburg

Bremen

Bremerhaven

Cuxhaven

Jever

Norden

Emden

Oldenburg

Berlin
Potsdam

Brandenburg

Havel

Frankfurt
a. d. Oder

Lübben

Cottbus

Bautzen

Görlitz

Meißen

Leipzig

Halle

Dessau

Wittenberg

Magdeburg

Naumburg

Quedlinburg
Wernigerode
Goslar

Göttingen

Hann. Münden

Kassel

Fritzlar

Saale

Elbe

Elbe

Elbe

Weser

Ruhr

Ems

Spree

Neisse

Oder

Odra

Havel

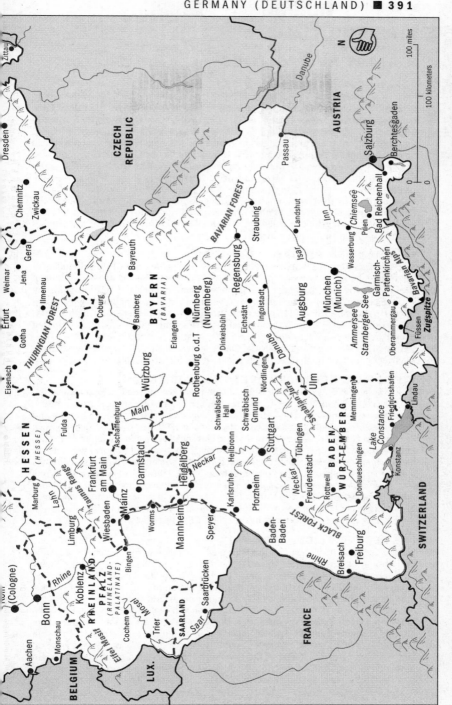

LIFE AND TIMES

HISTORY AND POLITICS

EARLY GERMAN HISTORY: 9-1517 AD

Only in a union against the Roman Empire did the clans of peoples in the region now known as Germany first become a real political entity. Under the rule of **Charlemagne** (whom Germans know as Karl der Große), nearly all of the Germanic kingdoms of Europe were united. The **Treaty of Verdun** in 843, drawn after his death, split the empire into three kingdoms, and over the next half millennium, these lands were further dismantled into a feudal society. In the 12th and 13th centuries, the kingdoms continued to expand in a fever of political competition. The grand aspirations of a succession of regional princes, prominent among whom was **Heinrich der Löwe** (Henry the Lion), maintained the state of decentralization. Under the **Habsburg** empire, the German nation began to define itself a little more clearly; the **Hanseatic League** banded a number of German merchant towns together in 1358, while outlying areas of the still-alive Holy Roman Empire, including Italy, slipped out of controlling influence entirely.

RELIGION AND REFORM: 1517-1700

On All Saints' Day 1517, **Martin Luther,** a monk and professor of Biblical studies at the University of Wittenberg (p. 437), posted his **Ninety-Five Theses** on the door of the city's castle church. Luther took issue with the Roman Catholic Church for the extravagance of the papal court in Rome and its practice of selling **indulgences**—gift certificates for the soul that promised to shorten the owner's stay in purgatory. The repercussions of the **Protestant Reformation** could not have been anticipated even by the movement's founder. Luther's greatest cultural contribution to the Reformation was a **new translation of the Bible,** which single-handedly crystallized the fragmentary German dialects into a standard, literary High German language.

RISE OF BRANDENBURG-PRUSSIA: 1700-1862

By the **Seven Years' War** in 1763, which pitted Prussia and Great Britain against the other European nations, Prussia was recognized as one of Europe's great powers. **Napoleon** conquered and disbanded what remained of the Holy Roman Empire and created a subservient **Confederation of the Rhine** in 1806. After he got bogged down in Russia, a general rebellion known as the **Wars of Liberation** ejected him from German territory. The 1815 **Congress of Vienna** partially restored the pre-war German state system by creating the Austrian-led **German Confederation.** In 1834, Prussia sponsored the **Zollverein,** a customs union that linked most German territories in a free trade zone. As revolutionary fervor spread through Europe in 1848, the **Frankfurt National Assembly** drafted a liberal constitution, and invited **Friedrich Wilhelm IV** of Prussia to serve as emperor. He spurned the offer, the assembly disbanded, and the ensuing revolt in Frankfurt was crushed by the Prussian army.

THE SECOND REICH: 1862-1914

In 1862, worldly aristocrat **Otto von Bismarck** was named chancellor. The greatest practitioner of *Realpolitik* ("the ends justify the means"), he exploited a remarkably complex series of alliances and ever-changing compromises. Blood and iron, he liked to point out, were paramount to the creation of a strong and unified German nation. Bismarck made it clear that Prussia would now dominate German affairs; in 1867, he disbanded the Confederation and replaced it with the Prussian-dominated **North German Confederation.** He suckered France into a misguided declaration of the **Franco-Prussian** war in 1870; the technologically superior Prussian army and its allies swept through France. Bismarck gleefully besieged Paris and had Wilhelm crowned **Kaiser of the German Reich** at the Palace of Versailles. He founded the German Empire in 1871 and presented German liberals with an offer they couldn't refuse: unification in exchange for an authoritarian monarchy.

WORLD WAR I: 1914-1918

On the eve of WWI, Europe was caught in a complex web of alliances in which a minor dispute could, and did, easily escalate into full-blown continental war. As Russia's rail network modernized, German generals saw their window of opportunity closing; they were strongly inclined to mobilize at the first sign of a crisis. That crisis broke out in 1914, when a Serbian nationalist assassinated the Habsburg heir to the Austrian throne, **Archduke Franz-Ferdinand,** in Sarajevo. Austria marched on Serbia; Russia came to the aid of its Slavic brethren. Almost the entire Reichstag voted to prepare for war to defend their Austrian allies, forming the **Central Powers.** When Germany entered the war on the side of Austria, France was prompted to mobilize. Germany declared war on France and demanded that Belgium allow its army to cross its frontier, but Belgium refused. Britain, which was treaty-bound to defend Belgian neutrality, declared war on Germany. Germany quickly advanced through Belgium and northern France, and suddenly virtually all of Europe was at war. Germany's policy of unrestricted submarine warfare on all ships entering European waters provoked the United States into entering on the side of France and Britain. Coupled with the industrial capacity and fresh armies of the US, a successful British naval blockade allowed the Entente, the alliance formed among Great Britain, France, and Russia, to emerge victorious.

THE WEIMAR REPUBLIC: 1918-1933

France insisted on a harsh peace in the **Treaty of Versailles,** which imposed staggering reparation payments, reduced the German army to 100,000 men, and ascribed the blame for the war to Germany. A new constitution for the German republic was drawn up in **Weimar,** chosen for its legacy as the birthplace of the German Enlightenment. Outstanding war debts and the burden of reparations produced the staggering hyperinflation of 1922-23. An Austrian corporal named **Adolf Hitler** was arrested for treason after the abortive 1923 **Beer Hall Putsch** uprising in Munich, an unsuccessful march to a patriotic monument; he served only 10 months in jail. During this time, Hitler wrote *Mein Kampf* and decided that his party, the National Socialist German Workers Party, also known as the **Nazis,** would have to seize power by constitutional means. Party membership increased to more than a million by 1930, as Europe struggled in the throes of the Great Depression. Hitler failed in a presidential bid against the nearly senile war-hero **Paul von Hindenburg** in 1932, but parliamentary elections made the Nazis the largest party in the *Reichstag.* President Hindenburg reluctantly appointed Hitler chancellor of a coalition government on January 30, 1933.

THE THIRD REICH: 1933-45

Hitler rose to power on a platform that played on a variety of German anxieties that had accumulated since 1918; his ideas drew on notions of anti-Semitism and German racial superiority. Wounded pride over WWI losses and the failing economy ensured a receptive public. Aided by **Joseph Goebbels,** his propaganda chief, Nazi rallies were masterpieces of political demagoguery, and the **swastika** embellished everything from match covers to fingernails of loyal teeny-boppers. *Heil Hitler* and the right arm salute became the legally obligatory greeting.

One of the government's first acts was to institute a boycott of Jewish businesses and to expel Jews from professions and the civil service. In 1934, after Hindenburg's death, Hitler appropriated the presidential powers for himself. The following year, the first of the anti-Semitic **Racial Purity Laws** deprived Jews of German citizenship. After a respite during the 1936 Berlin Olympics, an ironically international gesture, on November 9, 1938, known as **Kristallnacht** (Night of Broken Glass), Nazis destroyed thousands of Jewish businesses, burned synagogues, killed nearly 100 Jews, and sent at least 20,000 to concentration camps.

A massive program of industrialization restored full employment, though this productivity was hardly innocent: German business was mounting a war effort. Hitler abrogated the Versailles Treaty, thus freeing Germany from reparations payments and instigating rearmament. Next, he annexed Austria in the infamous **Anschluß** and then demanded territorial concessions from Czechoslovakia, on the grounds that it served as a home to thousands of ethnic Germans. Hitler's foreign policy was dominated by one of the fundamental tenets of Nazi ideology: the necessity of acquiring **Lebensraum** (living space) from the "inferior" Slavs in the East as a first step toward his messianic goal of expansion.

WORLD WAR II: 1939-1945

On September 1, 1939, German tanks rolled across the eastern border into Poland. Britain and France, bound by treaty to defend Poland, immediately declared war on Germany but did not attack. Having secretly divided up Eastern Europe between themselves and the Germans under the **Molotov-Ribbentrop pact,** the Soviet Union did not respond to the German invasion. Germany's new tactic of mechanized **Blitzkrieg** (literally, "lightning war") quickly crushed Poland. On April 9, 1940, Hitler overran Denmark and Norway. Luxembourg, Belgium, the Netherlands, and France were soon overwhelmed, but the Nazis failed to bomb London into submission in the aerial struggle of the **Battle of Britain.** The German **invasion of the USSR** in June 1941 ended the Hitler-Stalin pact. At the peak of his conquests in late 1941, Hitler held an empire stretching from the Arctic Circle to the Sahara Desert, from the Pyrenees to the Urals.

The Soviets suffered extremely high casualties, but the *Blitzkrieg* faltered in the Russian winter and Hitler sacrificed thousands of German soldiers in his adamant refusal to retreat. The bloody battle of **Stalingrad** was the critical turning point in the East. Hitler had already committed a fatal error when he declared war on the United States after ally Japan bombed Pearl Harbor. His attempt to save Mussolini in North Africa led to the Nazi's first battlefield defeats, and soon Germany was retreating on all fronts. The Allied landings in Normandy on **D-Day** (June 6, 1944) preceded an arduous, bloody advance across Western Europe. The Red Army overcame bitter resistance and took Berlin in April 1945. The Third Reich, which Hitler had boasted would endure for 1000 years, had lasted only 12.

THE HOLOCAUST. By the outbreak of WWII, Jews and Christians of Jewish heritage were barred from serving in any public capacity and were forced to wear the Star of David patch. Hitler made no secret of his desire to exterminate all Jews, who, associated with internationalism, communism, pacifism, and democracy, represented for him the scourge of German nationalism. The Nazis' horrific designation for the genocide of European Jewry was the **"Final Solution to the Jewish Problem."** As the war progressed, institutions of mass execution were developed for their efficiency. Seven full-fledged extermination camps, **Auschwitz, Buchenwald** (p. 435), **Chelmno, Treblinka, Majdanek, Sobibor,** and **Belzec,** plus dozens of nominal "labor" camps such as **Bergen-Belsen, Dachau** (p. 495), and **Sachsenhausen** were operating before war's end. Nearly six million Jews, two-thirds of Europe's Jewish population, were gassed, shot, starved, worked to death, or killed by exposure. Five million other victims—prisoners of war, Slavs, *Romany*, homosexuals, the mentally retarded, and political opponents—also died in Nazi camps.

OCCUPATION AND DIVISION: 1945-1949

Germans call their defeat in the Second World War *Nullstunde*—"Zero Hour"— the moment at which everything began again. In July 1945 the United States, Great Britain, and the Soviet Union met at **Potsdam** to partition Germany into zones of occupation. The east was under Soviet control, the west under British and American influence; Berlin was similarly partitioned. All German territory east of the Oder and Neisse rivers—a quarter of the nation's land—was confiscated and placed under Soviet and Polish administration, while coal-rich Saarland was put under French control. The Allied program for the **Occupation**— demilitarization, democratization, and de-Nazification—proceeded apace, but growing animosity between the Soviets and the Western Allies made joint control of Germany increasingly difficult. In 1947, the Allies merged their occupation zones into a single economic unit known as **Bizonia** (later Trizonia, after a French occupation zone was carved out of the British and American zones) and began to rebuild along the lines of a market economy with the aid of huge cash infusions from the American **Marshall Plan.** The Western Allies effectively severed the East's economy from the West's by introducing a new hard currency to Bizonia, the **Deutschmark.** Although the imposition of the new Mark seemed draconian at the time, most historians agree that it was the single greatest cause of the stabilization of West Germany.

THE FEDERAL REPUBLIC OF GERMANY

The Federal Republic of Germany (FRG; *Bundesrepublik Deutschland*, BRD) was established as the provisional government of Western Germany on May 24, 1949. A **Basic Law,** drawn up under the direction of the Western Allies, safeguarded individual rights and established a system of Federal States with freely elected parliamentary assemblies. One of the most visionary paragraphs established a **Right of Asylum,** guaranteeing refuge to any person fleeing persecution.

As the only party untainted by the Third Reich, the **Social Democratic Party** (*Sozialdemokratische Partei Deutschlands*—SPD) seemed poised to dominate postwar German politics. The **Christian Democratic Union** (*Christlich Demokratische Union*—CDU) managed to unite Germany's historically fragmented conservatives and centrists under a nondenominational platform. With former Cologne mayor **Konrad Adenauer** at the helm, the CDU won a small majority of *Bundestag* seats in the Federal Republic's first general election in mid-1949. Adenauer was perhaps the republic's greatest chancellor. He unflaggingly pursued the integration of Germany into a unified Europe and, at the same time, the return of German national self-determination. Under Adenauer, the FRG became one of the charter members of the European Economic Community in 1957. Rebuilding progressed rapidly; Germany achieved full employment by the late 1950s and soon began recruiting thousands of foreign **Gastarbeiter** (guest workers). Adenauer aligned Germany with NATO (North Atlantic Treaty Organization) in a common defense bloc when the Occupation Statute expired in 1955. Under the **Hallstein Doctrine** created in the 1950s, the Federal Republic cut ties to any government that recognized the German Democratic Republic, driving a wedge between West Germany and the entire Eastern Bloc. Social Democrat **Helmut Schmidt** became chancellor in 1974. Under Schmidt, West Germany racked up an economic record that was the envy of the industrialized world. Nevertheless, persistent structural problems in heavy industry contributed to **mounting unemployment** and dissatisfaction with the SPD in the late 1970s. In 1982, the Free Democratic Party (FDP) and the CDU formed a government under Christian Democrat **Helmut Kohl.** Kohl's government pursued a policy of welfare state cutbacks, tight monetary policy, and military cooperation with the US.

THE GERMAN DEMOCRATIC REPUBLIC

In spite of pledges to the contrary, the Soviets stopped holding freely contested elections in their sector and required voters instead to approve or reject a "unity list" of pre-selected candidates. On October 7, 1949, a People's Congress selected by such methods declared the establishment of the **German Democratic Republic** (*Deutsche Demokratische Republik*—GDR), with the national capital in Berlin. Constitutional promises of civil liberties and parliamentary democracy were empty. Real power lay in the hands of the *Politbüro* and the Party's secretary. In response to the FRG's normalization of relations with the West, the GDR was recognized by the USSR in 1954 and became a member of the **Warsaw Pact** in 1955. In 1961, to stop the flood of illegal emigrants to the FRG, the first barriers of the **Berlin Wall** were laid. East Germany moved to unquestioning subservience to the Soviet Union. The secret police, the **Stasi,** maintained a network of agents that strove to monitor every citizen; one in seven East Germans was a paid informant.

GERMANY

With *glasnost*-minded **Mikhail Gorbachev** at the helm of the USSR in 1985, liberalizing reform began to spread throughout the Eastern Bloc—except in the GDR. The foundation for *die Wende* (the turning or the change), as the sudden toppling of the GDR is referred to in Germany, began in May 1989 when Hungary dismantled the barbed-wire border with Austria, giving some 55,000 East Germans an indirect route to the West. East Germans demanded free elections, freedom of press, and freedom of travel. Meanwhile, tens of thousands of GDR citizens—largely young professionals—continued to flee via Czechoslovakia, which completely opened its border with West Germany. The entire GDR *Politbüro* resigned on November 8, and a day later, a Central Committee spokesperson announced the **opening of all borders to the West,** including the Berlin Wall.

GERMANY TODAY

The opening of the Wall was the most symbolically significant turning point for Germans since the end of WWII. In the East, a broad coalition government of non-Communist parties authorized **economic and social union** with the Federal Republic. On the day of the *Währungsunion*, July 1, 1990, GDR citizens exchanged their worthless Ostmarks for mighty Deutschmarks. The signing of the **Four-Plus-Two Treaty** by the two Germanies and the four occupying powers on September 12, 1990, signaled the **end of a divided Germany.** Despite the designation *Wiedervereinigung* (reunification), East and West Germany did not unify on an equal basis to create a new nation-state. Rather, East Germany was absorbed into the institutions and structures of the Federal Republic, leading some to call the union *der Anschluß* (annexation). On **October 3, 1990,** the Allies forfeited their occupation rights, the GDR ceased to exist, and Germany became one united, sovereign nation for the first time in 45 years.

The collapse of East Germany's inefficient industries and institutions led to massive unemployment and the Federal Republic's worst-ever recession. Many Westerners resented the inflation and taxes brought on by the cost of rebuilding the new federal states, while Easterners had to give up the generous social benefits communism afforded them. A rightward-moving political climate in the West pulled the East with it, restricting social programs not only in welfare but also in areas such as abortion. Economic frustrations led to the scapegoating of foreigners, especially asylum-seekers from Eastern Europe and the *Gastarbeiter*, many of whom had been living in Germany for decades. The violent attacks on foreigners reached horrible proportions in 1992 and 1993, when wide-scale assaults were launched against immigrants in Mölln and Rostock.

After the dramatic fall of the Berlin Wall in 1989, Kohl and his CDU seemed insurmountable. Carrying their momentum into the first all-German elections, the CDU scored a stunning victory. After that, however, Kohl's popularity plummeted to the point where, during one visit, Eastern voters pelted him with rotten vegetables, and his party failed to carry his own state in state elections. The CDU bounced back in 1994, only to be resoundingly ousted in 1998 by **Gerhard Schröder,** who led the SPD to victory as the largest party in the Bundestag. Schröder had to form a coalition with the Green party in order to attain a majority in parliament. The environmentalist **Joschka Fischer** became the new secretary of state. Under this left-wing leadership, plans were made to shut down all of Germany's remaining nuclear reactors, and debate was opened over Germany's citizenship laws.

Germany's new place within Europe remains the big political question. The burden of the past makes everyone, including Germans themselves, nervous about Germany's participation in international military operations, highlighted most recently by the **Kosovo** crisis, in which Germany played a pivotal role in negotiating a peace accord. A persistent feeling among Germans now is that they should stay out of foreign policy, acting instead as a large, benign economic machine at the heart of the European Union. Most questions surrounding Germany's larger role in world affairs remained unanswered at the close of the 20th century.

THE ARTS

VISUAL ARTS AND ARCHITECTURE

It was the late 8th- and 9th-century Frankish emperor **Charlemagne** who first marshaled Germanic drawing boards in a big way, commissioning Romanesque churches and illuminated manuscripts by the dozen. In the Renaissance, the master of the woodcut was **Albrecht Dürer.** His *Adam and Eve* still peppers advertisements today and his *Self-Portrait at 20*, one of the first self portraits in Europe, painted in 1500, famously resembles a humanist messiah. Outstanding Romanesque cathedrals can be found along the Rhine at Speyer, Trier, Mainz, and Worms, and often feature a clover-leaf floor plan, numerous towers, and sometimes a mitre-like steeple. The **Gothic** style, with its pointed rib vaulting, gradually replaced the Romanesque form between 1300 and 1500. Stained glass windows fill otherwise gloomy interiors with artificially divine light, evoking a sense of otherworldly salvation. The **cathedral** at **Cologne** is one of the most famous structures of this style in Germany (see p. 453). Secular architecture at the end of the Middle Ages is best remembered through the **Fachwerk** (half-timbered) houses that still dominate the *Altstädte* of many German cities. By 1550, Lutheran reforms had put a damper on the unrestrained extravagance of cathedrals in the north, while the Counter-Reformation in the Catholic south spurred a splendid new **Baroque** style. Based on an Italianate idiom, it sought to achieve an impression of fluidity and contrast, achieved through complex forms and sinuous contours. The **Zwinger** in Dresden is a magnificent example (see p. 426). Baroque eventually achieved a fanciful extreme with **Rococo,** as exemplified by **Schloß Sanssouci** at Potsdam (p. 425). The **Brandenburger Tor** and the buildings along **Unter den Linden** in Berlin (p. 413) were products of the new, simpler period of neo-Classicism.

German art exploded in the 20th century. **German Expressionism** recalled the symbolist tendencies of Viennese **Jugendstil** (Art Nouveau) and French Fauvism (see **Schleswig,** p. 448). Its deliberately anti-realist aesthetics intensified colors and the representation of objects to project deeply personal emotions. A 1911 exhibition in Munich entitled **Der Blaue Reiter** (The Blue Rider), led by Russian emigré **Wassily Kandinsky,** marked the rise of a second expressionist school. Kandinsky's contribution was a series called *Improvisations*. Painted in 1910-11, they are considered the some of the first totally **non-representational** paintings in Western art. **World War I** and its aftermath interrupted the flow of German art movements. Artists became increasingly bold and political in reaction to the rise of Fascism. **Max Beckmann** painted severely posed figures whose gestures and symbolism expressed a tortured view of man's condition. **Max Ernst** started a **Dadaist** group expressing artistic nihilism with collage and composition in Cologne. The grotesque, satirical works of **Otto Dix** walked a tightrope between Expressionism and Dadaism before embracing the **Neue Sachlichkeit** (New Objectivity), a movement that sought to come to terms with the rapid modernization of the times through matter-of-fact representations. The rise of Nazism drove most artists and their work into exile. Themes of *Blut und Boden* (Blood and Soil) dominated Nazi visual arts, depicting the mythical union of folkish blood and German soil through idealized images of workers, farmers, and soldiers of the "master race." In 1937, the Nazi's famous **Entartete Kunst** (Degenerate Art) exhibit placed pieces by Kandinsky, Kirchner, and other masters—which Goebbels had stolen from museums—next to paintings by psychotics, sending a clear message to all artists in Germany.

LITERATURE

The first significant German novel, **Hans J. C. von Grimmelshausen's** roguish epic *Adventurous Simplicissimus* was written during the chaos of the Thirty Years' War, a period which saw little literary development due to political turmoil. In the mid-18th century, a sentimental, unusually personalized poetry arose, best represented by the literary giant **Johann Wolfgang von Goethe.** His novel *The Sorrows of Young Werther* eschewed formula and drew the attention of Europe to the budding **Sturm und Drang** (Storm and Stress) movement, which would influence early

Romantic literature. Goethe later turned to the *Bildungsroman* (novel of educational development) and themes of Classicism and Orientalism. His masterpieces are numerous; his retelling of the **Faust** legend is often considered the pinnacle of German literature. In the early 19th century, **Romanticism** began to flower, with **Novalis** as its great poet. The movement continued to mature with the 1805 publication of *The Boy's Magic Horn*, an influential collection of popular folk tales collected by **Clemens Brentano** and **Achim von Arnim**, the more celebrated collection by the **Brothers Grimm**, *Grimms' Fairy Tales*, followed in 1812. The **novella**, usually a story based on a reported event, served as a primary vehicle for new tales; **Heinrich von Kleist** and **Ludwig Tieck** were its chief practitioners. A rush of realistic political literature exploded around the time of the revolutions of 1848. **Heinrich Heine** was the finest of the **Junges Deutschland** (Young Germany) movement and also one of the first German Jews to achieve literary prominence. From self-exile in France, he wrote telling satires as well as romantic poems like *Die Lorelei*, while **Georg Büchner** wrote several strikingly modern plays, *Woyzeck* among them, which was later prized by both Expressionists and Marxists.

Opposite this *fin-de-siècle* realism, the **Symbolist** movement of the early 20th century concentrated on fleeting, sonorous image-poems; the **George-Kreis** (George Circle), led by critic and poet **Stefan George,** combined passions for literature and stylishness. The spirituality of **Hermann Hesse** showed an Eastern flair; his 1922 quasi-Buddhist novel *Siddhartha* became a paperback sensation in the 1960s. **Thomas Mann** carried the modern novel to a high point with *Der Zauberberg* (The Magic Mountain) and *Doktor Faustus*, two allegorical recountings of Germany's fateful history. Also vital to this period were German-language writers living in Austria-Hungary, among them **Rainer Maria Rilke** and **Franz Kafka**.

The **Weimar era** was filled with surprisingly lively artistic production. Its most famous novel was **Erich Maria Remarque's** *Im Westen nichts Neues* (All Quiet on the Western Front), a blunt, uncompromising account of war's horrors which became embroiled in the political turmoil of the era. **Bertolt Brecht's** dramas and poems present humankind in all its grotesque absurdity; his *Dreigroschenoper* (Three-Penny Opera) was set to music by **Kurt Weill.** The Nazi years were more about burning books than publishing them; as Goebbels summed up, "Whenever I hear the word 'culture,' I reach for my gun."

To nurse German literature back to health, several writers joined to form **Gruppe 47,** named after the year of its founding. The group included many who would become world-class writers: **Günter Grass** and (more peripherally) the poet **Paul Celan.** Much of the ensuing literature dealt with the problem of Germany's Nazi past; the novels of Grass and **Heinrich Böll** and the poetry of **Hans Magnus Enzensberger** turned a critical eye to post-war West Germany's repressive tendencies.

Germany's philosophical tradition—one of the most respected in the world—is often very difficult reading. In 1517, **Martin Luther** defied the Catholic church, arguing against papal infallibility by claiming that only scripture was holy and that the individual should have a direct relationship with God. **Gottfried Wilhelm Leibniz** thought of God as a metaphysical watchmaker who set the individual's body and soul in motion like two synchronized clocks. **Immanuel Kant,** the foremost thinker of the **German Enlightenment,** argued that ethics can be rationally deduced. **Georg W. F. Hegel** added a dialectical twist to idealism, proposing that world history as well as the development of the individual consciousness could be understood through discerning conflicts of thesis and antithesis that would lead to a new synthesis. **Karl Marx** turned Hegel's dialectic around, asserting that class conflict was the stage on which world history was made—and the rest is history. Similarly controversial, **Friedrich Nietzsche** scorned the mediocrity of the hypocritical Christian masses. He propagated the idea of the *Übermensch*, a super-man.

Max Weber argued that modern capitalist society enchained rather than liberated society. **Martin Heidegger,** Husserl's successor at Freiburg and sometime Nazi, went his own way with *Being and Time*. This confusing, cumbersome book details the importance for man to understand what it means to question the meaning of life in a world of existential alienation.

MUSIC

Because Germany traces its origins to the Holy Roman Empire, the earliest forms of music that appeared in German lands were religious. A tradition of secular music began in the 12th century with the **Minnesänger**, German performers whose technique of singing poetry passed gradually to the **Meistersänger** of the 14th and 15th centuries. **Polyphony**, the musical phenomenon in which more than one melodic and rhythmic line operates simultaneously within a piece, developed during this period. **Johann Sebastian Bach** was the stand-out in a long line of musically successful Bachs. In mid-career he produced more secular works; the *Brandenburg Concerti* are famous for their imaginative exploration of the contrast between solo instruments and the chamber orchestra in the Baroque concerto. Bach and his contemporary **Georg Friedrich Händel** composed during the Baroque period of the 17th century, which was known for its extravagant decoration and popularized the theme-and-variation idiom. Händel is the man behind every ad campaign that uses the Hallelujah Chorus; his 1742 work **The Messiah** has made its way to more audiences than the composer could have imagined.

The 19th century was an era of German musical hegemony. **Ludwig van Beethoven's** symphonies and piano sonatas bridged Classicism and Romanticism. He pushed classical forms to their limits as he focused on rhythmic drives, extremes of musical elements, and intense emotional expressionism. His monumental *Ninth Symphony* and late string quartets were written in the 1820s after he was completely deaf. The ethereal work of **Felix Mendelssohn-Bartholdy** is well represented by his overture to *A Midsummer Night's Dream*. Immigrant **Franz Liszt** pushed piano music and the symphonic form into still further reaches of unorthodox harmony and arrangement. The second generation of Romantic composers included **Johannes Brahms,** who imbued Classical forms with Romantic emotion. **Richard Wagner,** composer of many of the world's best-known operas, *Tannhäuser, Die Meistersinger, Der Ring des Nibelungen*, attempted to revolutionize opera. His vision of **Gesamtkunstwerk** (total work of art) unified music and text, poetry and philosophy. His works were highly nationalistic in their celebration of Germanic legend, and were exploited by German-Aryan supremacists.

FOOD AND DRINK

Maybe not as compelling as other European cuisines, *Deutsche Küche* has a robust charm, especially satisfying for meat-and-potato lovers. German delights include *Schnitzel* (a lightly fried veal cutlet), *Spätzle* (a southern noodle), and *Kartoffeln* (potatoes). The typical German **Frühstück** (breakfast) consists of coffee or tea with *Brötchen* (rolls), bread, *Wurst* (cold sausage), and cheese. The main meal of the day, **Mittagessen** (lunch), includes soup, broiled sausage or roasted meat, potatoes or dumplings, and a salad or *Gemüsebeilage* (vegetable side dish). **Abendessen** or **Abendbrot** (dinner) is a reprise of breakfast, only beer replaces coffee and the selection of meats and cheese is wider. Many older Germans indulge in a daily ritual of **Kaffee und Kuchen** (coffee and cakes) at 3 or 4pm.

With few exceptions, restaurants expect you to seat yourself. In traditional restaurants, address waiters as *Herr Ober* and waitresses as *Fräulein*; in an informal setting, just say *hallo*. Ask for the **check** by saying *Zahlen, bitte*. **Tax** and **tip** are included, but it is customary to leave a little something extra. To eat on the cheap, stick to the daily Tagesmenü, buy food in supermarkets, or, if you have a student ID, head to a university **Mensa** (cafeteria). Fast-food *Imbiß* stands also provide cheap fare; try the delicious Turkish *Döner*, something like a gyro.

The average German beer is maltier and more "bread-like" than Czech, Dutch, or American beers. Among the exceptions is **Pils**, or *Pilsner*, popular in the north, whose clarity and bitter taste come from extra hops. from the south comes **Weißbier,** a smooth refreshing wheat beer. *Hefeweizen* is wheat beer with a layer of yeast in the bottom. Also try the largely overlooked German **wines,** particularly the sweet (*lieblich* or *süß*) whites of the Rhine and Mosel Valleys.

ESSENTIALS

DOCUMENTS AND FORMALITIES

Germany requires visas of South Africans, but not of nationals of Australia, Canada, the EU, New Zealand, or the US, for stays of shorter than three months.

German Embassies at Home: Australia: 119 Empire Circuit, Yarralumla, Canberra, ACT 2600 (☎ (02) 6270 1911; fax 6270 1951); **Canada:** 1 Waverly St., Ottawa, ON K2P OT8 (☎613-232-1101; fax 594-9330; email 100566.2620@compuserve.com). **Ireland:** 31 Trimleston Ave., Booterstown, Blackrock, Co. Dublin (☎ (012) 69 30 11; fax 269 39 46). **New Zealand:** 90-92 Hobson St., Thorndon, Wellington (☎ (04) 473 6063; fax 473 6069). **South Africa:** 180 Blackwood St., Arcadia, Pretoria, 0083 (☎ (012) 427 8900; fax 343 9401). **UK:** 23 Belgrave Sq., London SW1X 8PZ (☎ (020) 78 24 13 00; fax 78 24 14 35). **US:** 4645 Reservoir Rd. NW, Washington, D.C. 20007-1998 (☎202-298-4000; fax 298 4249; www.germany-info.org).

Foreign Embassies in Germany: All embassies moved back to Berlin in summer 1999. For the latest information, call the **Auswärtiges Amt,** in Berlin at ☎ (030) 20 18 60.

TRANSPORTATION

BY PLANE. Most flights to Germany land in Frankfurt, though Berlin, Munich, and Hamburg also have major international airports. **Lufthansa,** Germany's national airline, has the most flights in and out of the country, though they're not always the cheapest option. For cheap fares, look into **Icelandair** flights to neighboring Luxembourg; from there, it's only 3hr. by train to Cologne and 4hr. to Frankfurt. Flying within Germany is usually more expensive and less convenient than taking the train.

BY TRAIN. "In Germany, the trains run on time." It may be said jokingly, and it's not infallibly true, but it brings up an important truth about getting around in Germany. Averaging 120km per hr., the **Deutsche Bahn (DB)** network is Europe's best, and also one of the most expensive. Check out **schedules** and **prices** at http://bahn.hafas.de. **RE** (RegionalExpress) and slightly slower **RB** (Regionalbahn) trains include rail networks between neighboring cities. **IR** (InterRegio) trains cover larger networks between cities. **D** trains are foreign trains serving international routes. **EC** (EuroCity) and **IC** (InterCity) trains zoom along between major cities every hr. 6am-10pm. The futuristic **ICE** (InterCityExpress) trains run at speeds up to 280km per hr. You must purchase a **Zuschlag** (supplement) to ride an ICE, IC, or EC train (DM7 from the station, DM9 on the train). For basic train **lingo,** see p. 959.

DB offers numerous railpass deals. Designed for tourists, the **German Railpass** allows unlimited travel for four to 10 days within a four-week period. Non-Europeans can purchase German Railpasses in their home countries and—with a passport—in major German train stations. A second-class Railpass costs US$196 for 5 days of unlimited travel and $306 for 10. The **German Rail Youth Pass,** for tourists under 26, is US$156 for 5 days and $198 for 9. The second-class **Twin Pass,** for two adults traveling together, is US$294 for 5 days and $459 for 10. Contact DB through their web page (www.bahn.de), or, once in Germany, by calling their toll-free hotline (☎ (0180) 599 66 33). Travelers under 26 can purchase **TwenTickets,** which knock 20-60% off fares over DM10; be sure to let your ticket agent know your age. A **Schönes-Wochenende-Ticket** offers a fantastic deal for weekend trips. For a single price of DM35, up to five people receive unlimited travel on any of the slower trains (*not* ICE, IC, EC, D, or IR) from 12:01am Saturday until 2am on Monday. Single travelers often find larger groups who are amenable to sharing their ticket, either free or for a fraction of the purchase cost. The **Guten-Abend-Ticket** provides an excellent deal for long-distance night travel and entitles its holders to travel anywhere (*not* on InterCityNight or CityNightLines) in Germany between 7pm and 2am. Second-class tickets are DM59, with ICE surcharge DM69; first-class DM99, with ICE surcharge DM109; Friday and Sunday DM15 extra.

A great option for those making frequent and extensive use of German trains for more than one month, the **Bahncard** is valid one year and entitles you to a 50% discount on all trains. Passes are available at major train stations and require a passport-sized photo. A **second-class** pass is DM260; a pass for those aged 17-22 or over 60, or any student under 27, is DM130; students under 17 pay DM65.

Eurail is valid in Germany and provides free passage on S-Bahns in cities and DB bus lines but not on the U-Bahn. Urban **public transit** is excellent throughout Germany. You'll see four types: the **Straßenbahn** (streetcar), **S-Bahn** (commuter rail; abbreviated S1, S2, etc.), **U-Bahn** (subway; abbreviated U1, U2, etc.), and regular **buses.** Consider a day card *(Tageskarte)* or multiple-ride ticket *(Mehrfahrkarte)*, which usually pay for themselves by the third ride.

BY BUS. Bus service between cities and to outlying areas run from the local **Zentralomnibusbahnhof (ZOB),** which is usually close to the main train station. Buses are often slightly more expensive than the train for comparable distances. Railpasses are not valid on any buses other than a few run by Deutsche Bahn.

BY FERRY. Ferries in the **North** and **Baltic Seas** are reliable and go everywhere. Ferries run from Hamburg, Kiel, Travemünde, Rostock, and Saßnitz to England, Scandinavia, Poland, the Baltic States, and Russia. See **Hamburg** (p. 439) and **Rostock** (p. 438) for detailed information.

BY CAR. With the exception of a few secondary roads in the former GDR that have yet to be renovated, German road conditions are generally excellent. Yes, it's true, there is no set speed limit on the **Autobahn,** or German highway; only a recommendation of 130km per hr. (81mph) exists. Germans drive *fast.* Make a point to learn local driving signals and signs, and watch for signs indicating right-of-way (usually designated by a yellow triangle). The Autobahn is indicated by an intuitive "A" on signs; secondary highways, where the speed limit is usually 100km per hr., are accompanied by signs bearing a "B." Germans drive on the right side of the road, and it is illegal to pass on the right, even on superhighways. In cities and towns, speeds hover around 30-60kph (31mph). Germans use unleaded gas almost exclusively; prices run around DM7 per gallon, or about DM1.80 per liter.

BY BIKE AND BY THUMB. Bikes are sight-seeing power tools; Germany makes it easy with its wealth of trails and bike tours. Cities and towns usually have designated bike lanes. For information about bike routes, regulations, and maps, contact **Allgemeiner Deutscher Fahrrad-Club,** Postfach 10 77 47, 28077 Bremen. A bike tour guidebook, including extensive maps, is available from **Deutsches Jugendherbergswerk (DJH)** (☎ (05231) 740 10).

Although *Let's Go* does not recommend **hitchhiking** as a safe means of transportation, it is permitted and quite common on the Autobahn. Hitchers may stand only at rest stops, gas stations, and in front of the Autobahn signs at on-ramps. **Mitfahrzentralen** pair up drivers and riders, who pay the agency a fee for the match and then negotiate the payment agreement with their driver.

TOURIST SERVICES AND MONEY

EMERGENCY	Police: ☎ 110. Ambulance and fire: ☎ 112.

TOURIST OFFICES. Every city in Germany has a **tourist office,** usually located near the main train station *(Hauptbahnhof)* or central market square *(Marktplatz)*. All are marked by a thick lowercase **"i"** sign. The offices provide maps and information on cycling routes and often book rooms for a small fee.

CURRENCY AND EXCHANGE. The **deutsche Mark** or **Deutschmark** (abbreviated DM) is the unit of currency in Germany. It is one of the most stable and respected currencies in the world; indeed, in most markets in Eastern Europe, "hard currency" means US dollars and Deutschmarks exclusively. One DM equals 100 Pfennig (Pf). Coins come in 1, 2, 5, 10, and 50Pf, and DM1, 2, and 5 amounts. Bills come in DM5, 10, 20, 50, 100, 200, 500, and 1000 denominations.

Prices: If you stay in hostels and prepare your own food, expect to spend anywhere from US$25-50 per person per day when traveling in Germany. Hotels start at about $25 per night; a basic sit-down meal costs at least $6. Transportation and alcohol will increase these figures. If you plan to travel for more than a couple of days, you will need to keep handy a larger amount of cash than usual. Carrying money around, even in a money belt, is risky but necessary. Personal checks from home probably won't be accepted in Germany no matter how many forms of identification you have, and even traveler's checks may not be acceptable in some locations. Members can cash personal checks at AmEx offices throughout Germany.

Tipping and bargaining: Germans generally round up DM1-2 when tipping. However, tipping is not practiced as liberally as it is elsewhere—most Germans only tip in restaurants and bars, or when they receive a service, such as a taxi ride. Note that tips in Germany are not left on the table, but handed directly to the server when you pay. If you don't want any change, say *Das stimmt so* (DAHS SHTIMT ZO). Germans rarely bargain except at flea markets.

Taxes: Most goods and services bought in Germany will automatically include a Value Added Tax (**VAT**) of 15%. In German, this is called the *Mehrwertsteuer* (MwSt). Non-EU citizens can get the VAT refunded for large purchases of goods. At the point of purchase, ask for a Tax-Free Shopping Cheque, then have it stamped at customs upon leaving the country or at a customs authority. (You will have to present the goods, receipt, and cheque.) The goods you have purchased must remain unused until you leave the country.

ACCOMMODATIONS AND CAMPING

Germany currently has about **600 hostels**—more than any other nation on Earth. Hostelling in Germany is overseen by **Deutsches Jugendherbergswerk (DJH);** Postfach 1462, 32704 Detmold, Germany (☎ (05231) 740 10; fax 74 01 84). DJH has recently initiated a growing number of **Jugendgästehäuser,** youth guest-houses that are generally more expensive, have more facilities, and attract slightly older guests. DJH publishes *Jugendherbergen in Deutschland* (DM14.80), a guide to all federated German hostels, available at German bookstores and major train station newsstands, or by writing to DJH. The cheapest accommodations are places with **Pension, Gasthof, Gästehaus,** or **Hotel-Garni** in the name. Breakfast *(Frühstück)* is almost always included.

The best bet for a cheap bed is often a **private room** *(Privatzimmer)* in a home. Private rooms are much, much quieter than hostels, and will bring you in direct contact with the local population. Costs generally run DM20-50 per person, and usually include warm and personal service. Rooms are reserved through the local tourist office or through a private **Zimmervermittlung** (room-booking office), either for free or for a DM2-8 fee. This option works best if you have a rudimentary knowledge of German, since homeowners prefer to lay down a few household rules before handing over keys for the night. Travelers over 26 who would otherwise pay senior prices at youth hostels will find these rooms within budget range.

Germans love the outdoors, and their enthusiasm is evidenced by the 2,600 **campsites** that dot the outskirts of even the most major cities. Camping costs DM3-10 per person with additional charge for tents and vehicles. Blue signs with a black tent on a white background indicate official sites. **Deutscher Camping-Club (DCC),** Mandlstr. 28, 80802 München (☎ (089) 380 14 20) has specific information on campgrounds, and the National Tourist Office distributes a free map, *Camping in Germany*, with a list of campgrounds.

COMMUNICATION

MAIL. The main post office in a town generally has the longest hours. Mail can be sent to Germany through **Poste Restante** (the international phrase for General Delivery; **Postlagernde Briefe** in German) to almost any city or town with a post office. Address *Poste Restante* letters to: Postlagernde Briefe, für Adam HACHIKIAN, Hauptpostamt, D-70001 Stuttgart, Germany. The mail will go to a special desk in the central post office unless you specify a post office by street address or postal code.

TELEPHONES. Most public phones only accept telephone cards, though restaurants and bars sometimes have coin-operated phones. Telephones in transport hubs and near major attractions sometimes give you the option of paying by **credit card.** You can pick up a **Telefonkarte** (phone card) in post offices, at a *Kiosk* (newsstand), or at selected Deutsche Bahn counters in major train stations. The cards come in DM12, DM24, and DM50 denominations. To place **intercity calls,** dial the **Vorwahl** (area code), including the first zero that appears in the code, followed by the **Rufnummer** (telephone number). There is no standard length for telephone numbers. The smaller the city, the more digits in the city code, while telephone numbers tend to have three to ten digits. The **national information number** is ☎ 118 33. For **international information,** call ☎ 118 34. **Phone rates** tend to be highest in the morning and afternoon, lower in the evening, and lowest after 9 p.m. and on Sundays and holidays. **AT&T:** ☎ (0800) 2255 288. **Sprint:** ☎ (0800) 8880 013. **MCI WorldPhone Direct:** ☎ (0800) 888 8000. **Canada Direct:** ☎ (0800) 888 0014. **BT Direct:** ☎ (0130) 80 0144. **Ireland Direct:** ☎ (0800) 180 0027. **Australia Direct:** ☎ (0130) 80 0061. **Telecom New Zealand Direct:** ☎ (0130) 80 0064. **Telkom South Africa Direct:** ☎ (0800) 180 0027. In an **emergency,** call the police at ☎ 110; fire or ambulance at ☎ 112.

INTERNET ACCESS. While Germany lagged behind the US and UK for many years in the internet arena, German citizens and companies are coming to rely on email and the Web as a means of communication. Most German cities as well as a surprising number of smaller towns have at least one **internet cafe,** where patrons can check email, surf the web, and sip cappuccinos to the tune of DM3-7 per 30min. In addition, some German universities have banks of computers hooked up to the internet in their libraries, though ostensibly for student use.

LANGUAGE. English language ability is common in Western Germany, but less so in the East. The letter ß is equivalent to a double *s*. For German tips, see p. 958.

LOCAL FACTS

Time: Germany is 1hr. ahead of Greenwich Mean Time (GMT); see back cover.

Climate and When to Go: Germany's climate is temperate, with rain year-round (especially in summer). Temperatures range between -1-2°C (30-36°F) in deep winter to 12-25°C (55-77°F) in July and Aug. The cloudy, temperate months of May, June, and Sept. are the best time to go, as there are fewer tourists and the weather is pleasant. Germans head to vacation spots *en masse* with the onset of school vacations in early July. Winter sports gear up Nov.-Apr.; high-season for skiing is mid-Dec. to Mar.

Hours: Bank hours are often quite bizarre; a typical work week might be M-W and F 9am-12:30pm and 2:30-4pm, Th 9am-12:30pm and 2:30-5pm. **Store hours** are usually M-F 9am-6:30pm, Sa 9am-2pm. Some stores remain open until 8:30pm on Th and until 4pm on the 1st Sa of each month. In larger cities, shops inside train stations are open longer. Many smaller shops take a midday break from noon to 2pm.

Holidays: Epiphany (Jan. 6), Ash Wednesday (Mar. 8), Good Friday (Apr. 21), Easter Sunday and Monday (Apr. 23-24), Labor Day (May 1), Ascension Day (June 1), Whit Sunday and Monday (June 11-12), Corpus Christi (June 22), Assumption Day (Aug. 15), Day of German Unity (Oct. 3), Reformation Day (Nov. 1), All Saint's Day (Nov. 1), and Christmas (Dec. 25-26). Expect reduced hrs. in establishments.

Festivals: Fasching in Munich (Jan. 7-Mar.7), **Berlinale Film Festival** (Feb. 9-20), **Karneval** in Cologne (Mar. 2-7), **Hafensgeburtstag** in Hamburg (May 5-7), **International Film Festival** in Munich (late June), **Christopher St Day** in Berlin and other major cities (late June to early July), **Love Parade** in Berlin (early July), **Bach Festival** in Leipzig (July 21-30), **Wagner Festspiele** in Bayreuth (July 25-Aug. 28), **Wine Festival** in Stuttgart (Aug. 24-Sept. 3), **Oktoberfest** in Munich (Sept. 16-Oct. 1), and **Christmas Market** in Nuremberg (Dec. 24-27).

BERLIN

☎ 030

Now is the time to see Berlin. Projects are underway to transform it from the Allied-bombed and Allied-occupied city of the post-WWII years into a sparklingly whole metropolis which will once again serve as Germany's capital, irreversibly changing the city's identity. Berlin has always been dynamic; never in its history has it seemed a "completed" city, nor has it remained in any one pattern for a long period of time. The question remains whether or not the brilliantly colored, magnificently varied neighborhoods that contain Berlin's true vitality will be affected by the presence of a complete and usable city center, or whether they will somehow maintain the individuality that has grown out of the consistent lack of a true nexus over the past 50 years. Berliners live like there is no tomorrow, and this penchant for shortsighted excess continues to manifest itself in all aspects of the city's existence, from its ridiculously grandiose building endeavors to the party-until-dawn atmosphere that remains in its smoky nightclubs.

> **❗ SAFETY PRECAUTION!** With thriving minority communities, of all shapes and colors, Berlin is the most tolerant city in Germany. The media has sensationalized the new wave of Nazi extremism perhaps more than necessary; among major cities, Berlin in fact has the fewest hate crimes per capita. There are only an estimated 750 neo-Nazi skinheads in Berlin. However, there are still a few areas in which people of color as well as gays or lesbians should take precautions—the outlying areas in the eastern suburbs, particularly Bahnhof Lichtenberg, are best avoided late at night. If you see dark-colored combat boots with white laces, exercise caution, but do not panic.

✈ GETTING THERE AND AWAY

Flights: For information on the 3 airports serving Berlin, call ☎ (0180) 500 01 86. **Flughafen Tegel** is Western Berlin's main airport. Take bus #X9 from Bahnhof Zoo, bus #109 from Jakob-Kaiser-Platz on U7, or bus #128 from Kurt-Schumacher-Platz on U6. **Flughafen Tempelhof** is used for intra-German travel and flights within Europe. U6 to Platz der Luftbrücke. **Flughafen Schönefeld,** southeast of Berlin, has international flights. S45 or S9 to Flughafen Berlin Schönefeld or bus #171 from Rudow on U7.

Trains: For Deutsche Bahn Information, call ☎ (0180) 599 66 33. While construction continues on the *Megabahnhof* of the future at Lehrter Stadtbahnhof, trains to and from Berlin are serviced by **Zoologischer Garten** (almost always called **Bahnhof Zoo**) in the West, off Hardenbergstr. in Charlottenberg, and **Ostbahnhof** (formerly the Hauptbahnhof) in the East, off Str. der Pariser Kommune. Trains also connect to **Schönefeld** airport and stop at **Oranienburg, Spandau,** and **Potsdam** before entering the city. Every hr. to: **Dresden** (2hr., DM59); **Frankfurt** (4hr., DM207); **Hamburg** (2½hr., DM81); **Cologne** (4¼hr., DM190); **Leipzig** (2hr., DM58); **Munich** (7½hr., DM249); and **Rostock** (2¾hr., DM65); **Amsterdam** (6½hr., DM203); **Brussels** (7½hr., DM217); **Budapest** (12hr.); **Copenhagen** (7½hr., DM188); **Paris** (9hr., DM287); **Prague** (5hr., DM127); **Rome** (21hr.); **Vienna** (11½hr.); and **Zurich** (9hr.).

Buses: ZOB, the central bus station (☎ 301 80 28), is by the *Funkturm* near Kaiserdamm. U2 to Kaiserdamm or S4, S45, or S46 to Witzleben. Check *Zitty* and *Tip* for deals on long-distance buses, or call **Gulliver's** travel agency (☎ 78 10 21). To **Paris** (10hr., DM109) and **Vienna** (10½hr., DM79).

⬛ GETTING AROUND

Public Transportation: It is impossible to tour Berlin on foot—fortunately, the extensive **bus, Straßenbahn** (streetcar), **U-Bahn** (subway), and **S-Bahn** (surface rail) systems of Berlin will get you to your destination safely and relatively quickly. Berlin is divided into 3 transit zones. **Zone A** encompasses downtown Berlin, including Tempelhof airport.

Almost everything else falls into **Zone B,** while **Zone C** contains the outlying areas, including Potsdam and Oranienburg. An **AB ticket** is the best deal, as you can buy regional Bahn tickets for the outlying areas. A single ticket for the combined network (*Langstrecke* AB or BC, DM3.90; or *Ganzstrecke* ABC, DM4.20) is good for 2hr. after validation. Within the validation period, the ticket may be used on any S-Bahn, U-Bahn, bus or streetcar. All tickets must be canceled in the validation box marked "hier entwerten" before boarding.

Special Passes: With the high cost of single tickets, it almost always makes sense to buy a transit pass. A **Tageskarte** (AB DM7.80, ABC DM8.50) is valid from the time of cancellation until 3am the next day. A **Gruppentageskarte** (AB DM20, ABC DM22.50) allows up to 5 people to travel together on the same ticket. The **WelcomeCard** (DM32) is valid on all lines for 72hr. The **7-Tage-Karte** (AB DM40, ABC DM48) is good for 7 days of travel. For longer stays, an **Umweltkarte Standard** (AB DM99, ABC DM120) is valid for one calendar month. **Bikes** require an additional reduced fare ticket and are permitted on the U-Bahn and S-Bahn but not on buses and streetcars.

Night Transport: U- and S-Bahn lines generally do not run from 1-4am, although most S-Bahn lines run once an hr. during weekend nights. The **U9** and **U12** run all night Friday and Saturday. An extensive system of **night buses** (numbers preceded by the letter N) centered on Bahnhof Zoo runs about every 20-30min.; pick up the free *Nachtliniennetz* map at the BVG pavilion.

Taxis: ☎26 10 26. Women may request a female driver. Trips in the city can cost DM40.

Car Rental: The **Mietwagenservice,** counter 21 in Bahnhof Zoo's *Reisezentrum,* represents Avis, Hertz, Europacar and Sixt. Open daily 4:45am-11pm.

Bike Rental: Hackescher Markt Fahrradstation, downstairs at the Hackescher Markt S-Bahn stop. Also try the red trailer off the **Lustgarten,** which rents bikes for DM5 per day. S3, S5, S7, S75, or S9 to Hackescher Markt for both locations. The government's **bikecity** program rents bikes for DM5 or 10 (depending on the bike) per day. The main rental station is at **Waldenserstr. 2-4,** U9 to Turmstr. Call there (☎39 73 91 45) for info during their open hours, M-Th 7:30am-4pm, F 7:30am-2:30pm.

Hitchhiking: *Let's Go* does not recommend hitchhiking as a safe mode of transportation. It is illegal to hitch at rest stops or anywhere along the highway. Those heading west and south (Hannover, Munich, Weimar, Leipzig) take S1 or S7 to Wannsee, then bus #211 to the Autobahn entrance ramp. Those heading north (Hamburg, Rostock) ride S25 to Hennigsdorf, then walk 50m to the bridge on the right, or ask anyone in the area for the location of the *Trampenplatz.*

✥ ORIENTATION

Berlin is an *immense* conglomeration of what were once two separate and unique cities: the former East, which contains the lion's share of Berlin's landmarks and historic sites, as well as an unfortunate number of pre-fab concrete socialist architectural experiments, and the former West, which functioned for decades as a small, isolated, Allied-occupied state and is still the commercial heart of united Berlin. The situation is rapidly changing, however, as businesses and embassies move their headquarters to Potsdamer Platz and Mitte.

The commercial district of western Berlin lies at one end of the huge **Tiergarten** park and is centered on **Bahnhof Zoo** and **Kurfürstendamm** (Ku'damm for short). It is marked by the bombed-out **Kaiser-Wilhelm-Gedächtniskirche,** adjacent to the boxy tower of the **Europa-Center,** one of the few "skyscrapers" in western Berlin. A star of streets radiates from Breitscheidplatz; toward the west run **Hardenbergstr., Kantstr.,** and the great commercial boulevard of modern Berlin, the renowned and reviled Kurfürstendamm. About a kilometer down Kantstr. lies **Savignyplatz,** one of many pleasant squares in **Charlottenburg** home to cafes, restaurants, and *Pensionen.* Southeast of the Ku'damm, **Schöneberg** is a pleasant residential neighborhood renowned for its cafe culture and as the traditional nexus of the city's gay and lesbian community. Farther south, **Dahlem** houses western Berlin's largest university and museum complex.

GERMANY

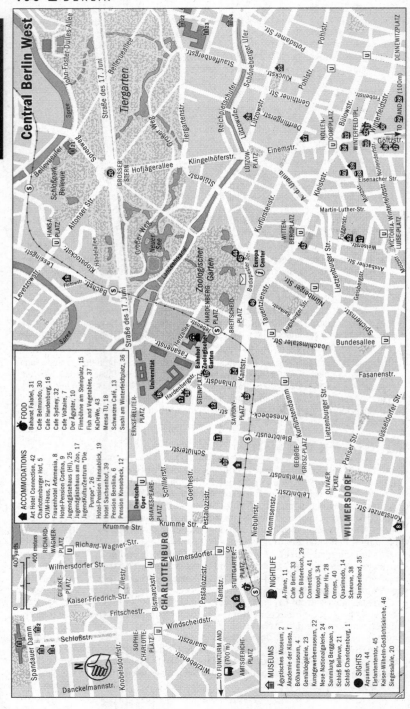

Central Berlin West

ACCOMMODATIONS
Art Hotel Connection, 42
Charlottenburger Hof, 5
CVJM-Haus, 27
Frauenhotel Artemesia, 8
Jugendgästehaus am Zoo, 17
Jugendgästehaus (HI), 25
JugendKulturZentrum "Die Pumpe", 26
Hotel Pension Cortina, 9
Hotel-Pension Hansablick, 19
Hotel Sachsenhof, 39
Pension Berolina, 6
Pension Knesebeck, 12

FOOD
Baharat Falafel, 31
Cafe Belmundo, 30
Cafe Hardenburg, 16
Cafe Sydney, 32
Cafe Voltaire, 7
Der Ägypter, 10
Filmbühne am Steinplatz, 15
Fish and Vegetables, 37
KaDeWe, 43
Mensa TU, 18
Schwarzes Café, 13
Sushi am Winterfeldtplatz, 36

NIGHTLIFE
A-Trane, 11
Cafe Berio, 33
Cafe Bilderbuch, 29
Connection, 41
Metropol, 34
Mister Hu, 28
Ohmes, 40
Quasimodo, 14
Scheune, 38
Slumberland, 35

MUSEUMS
Ägyptisches Museum, 2
Akademie der Künste, 1
Bröhanmuseum, 4
Gemäldegalerie, 23
Kunstgewerbemuseum, 22
Neue Nationalgalerie, 24
Sammlung Berggruen, 3
Schloß Bellevue, 21
Schloß Charlottenburg, 1

SIGHTS
Aquarium, 44
Elefantentor, 45
Kaiser-Wilhelm-Gedächtskirche, 46
Siegessäule, 20

GERMANY

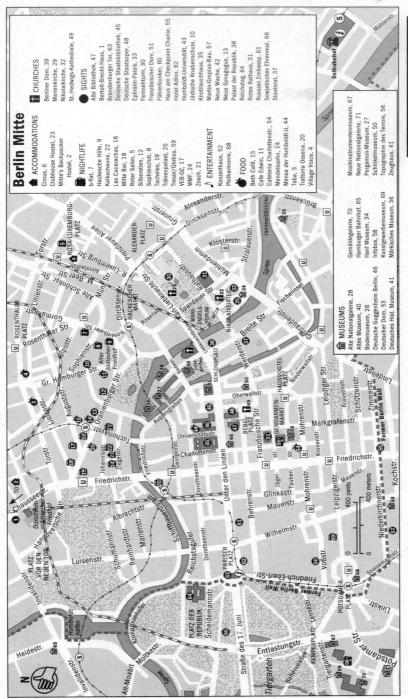

Berlin Mitte

▲ ACCOMMODATIONS
Circus, 6
Clubhouse Hostel, 23
Mitte's Backpacker
Hostel, 2

♪ NIGHTLIFE
b-flat, 7
Hackesche Höfe, 9
Kalkscheune, 22
Las Cucarachas, 16
Mitte Bar, 18
Roter Salon, 5
Silbernclub, 12
Sophienclub, 8
Tacheles, 19
Tränenpalast, 25
Tresor/Globus, 59
VEB-OZ, 17
WMF, 24
Zosch, 21

📋 CHURCHES
Berliner Dom, 39
Marienkirche, 29
Nikolaikirche, 32
St-Hedwigs-Kathedrale, 49

● SIGHTS
Alte Bibliothek, 47
Bertolt-Brecht-Haus, 1
Brandenburger Tor, 63
Deutsche Staatsbibliothek, 45
Deutsche Staatsoper, 48
Ephraim-Palais, 33
Fernsehturm, 30
Französischer Dom, 51
Führerbunker, 60
Haus am Checkpoint Charlie, 55
Hotel Adlon, 62
Humboldt-Universität, 43
Jüdische Knabenschule, 10
Knoblauchhaus, 35
Martin-Gropius-Bau, 57
Neue Wache, 42
Neue Synagogue, 13
Palast der Republik, 38
Reichstag, 64
Rotes Rathaus, 31
Russian Embassy, 61
Sowjetisches Ehrenmal, 66
Staatsrat, 37

♪ ENTERTAINMENT
Konzerthaus, 52
Philharmonie, 68

🍴 FOOD
Beth Café, 15
Café Edwin, 11
Cafeteria Charlottenstr., 54
Mendelssohn, 14
Mensa der Humboldt-U, 44
Taba, 3
Trattoria Ossena, 20
Village Voice, 4

🏛 MUSEUMS
Alte Nationalgalerie, 28
Altes Museum, 40
Bodemuseum, 26
Deutscher Dom, 53
Deutsches Hist. Museum, 41
Gemäldegalerie, 70
Hamburger Bahnhof, 65
Hanf Museum, 34
Infobox, 58
Deutsche Guggenheim Berlin, 46
Kunstgewerbemuseum, 69
Märkisches Museum, 36
Musikinstrumentenmuseum, 67
Neue Nationalgalerie, 71
Pergamon-Museum, 27
Schinkelmuseum, 50
Topographie des Terrors, 56
Zeughaus, 41

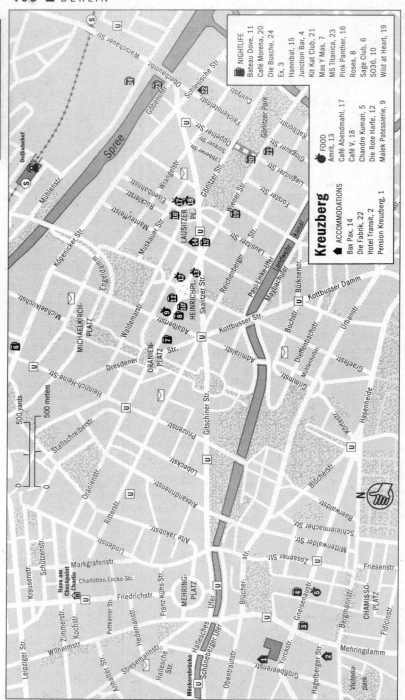

Kreuzberg

▲ ACCOMMODATIONS
Bax Pax, 14
Die Fabrik, 22
Hotel Transit, 2
Pension Kreuzberg, 1

● FOOD
Amrit, 13
Café Abendmahl, 17
Café V, 18
Chandre Kumari, 5
Die Rote Harfe, 12
Malek Patessierie, 9

▬ NIGHTLIFE
Bateau Dove, 11
Café Morena, 20
Die Busche, 24
Ex, 3
Hannibal, 15
Junction Bar, 21
Kit Kat Club, 21
Mas Y Mas, 7
MS Titanica, 23
Pink Panther, 16
Roses, 8
Sage Club, 6
SO36, 10
Wild at Heart, 19

The grand, tree-lined **Str. des 17. Juni** runs west-east through the Tiergarten to end at the triumphant **Brandenburg Gate,** which opens out onto **Pariser Platz.** Heading south from the Brandenburg Gate and the nearby **Reichstag,** Ebertstr. runs haphazardly through the construction sites to **Potsdamer Platz.** Toward the east, the gate opens onto **Unter den Linden,** Berlin's most famous boulevard and the site of many historic buildings. The broad, tree-lined *Linden* empties into socialist-realist **Alexanderplatz,** the center of the east's growing commercial district and the home of Berlin's most visible landmark, the **Fernsehturm,** a TV tower reaching a height of 365m. Southeast of Mitte lies **Kreuzberg,** a district home to an incongruous mix of radical leftists, Turks, punks, and homosexuals. Once on West Berlin's outer limits, Kreuzberg today finds itself bordering reunited Berlin's city center.

The **Spree River** snakes its way from west to east through the center of Berlin; it forms the northern border of the Tiergarten and splits just east of Unter den Linden to close off the **Museuminsel** (Museum Island). The windswept waters of the **Wannsee, Tegeler See,** and **Heiligensee** lap against the city's west side and are connected by narrow canals.

▐ PRACTICAL INFORMATION

TOURIST, FINANCIAL, AND SERVICES

Tourist Office: Tourist offices sell a useful, clearly marked **city map** (DM1). The **Liniennetz map** of public transportation can also be picked up for free. They book same-day **hotel rooms** for a DM5 fee—though room prices start at DM50 and rise to stratospheric heights. For comprehensive information on the **internet,** check out www.berlin.de. **EurAide,** in Bahnhof Zoo, doles out comprehensive info in English, French, and Spanish. Facing the Reisezentrum, go left and down the passage on your right. Open daily 8am-noon and 1-6pm. **Berlin Tourismus** (☎25 00 25; fax 25 00 24 24) reserves **rooms.** Write to: Berlin Tourismus Marketing GmbH, Am Karlsbad 11, 10785 Berlin.

Budget Travel: STA, Goethestr. 73 (☎311 09 50). U2 to Ernst-Reuter-Platz. Open M-W and F 10am-6pm, Th 10am-8pm.

Embassies and Consulates: As Berlin's construction plans include a new complex to house foreign dignitaries, the locations of the embassies and consulates remain in a state of flux. For the latest information, call the **Auswärtiges Amt Dienststelle Berlin** at ☎20 18 60 or visit their office on the Werderscher Markt. (U2 to Hausvogteiplatz.) **Australian Embassy,** Friedrichstr. 200 (☎880 08 80). U2 or U6 to Stadtmitte. Also try Uhlandstr. 181-183 (☎880 08 80; fax 88 00 88 99). U15 to Uhlandstr. Open M-F 9am-noon. **Canadian Embassy,** Friedrichstr. 95 (☎20 31 20; fax 20 31 25 90), on the 12th floor of the International Trade Center. S1, S2, S25, S3, S5, S7, S75 or S9 or U6 to Friedrichstr. Open M-F 9am-noon, appointments at 2pm. **Irish Embassy,** Friedrichstr. 200 (☎22 07 20). Open M-F 9:30am-noon, 2:30-4:45pm. **New Zealand Embassy,** Friedrichstr. 60. U6 to Oranienburger Tor. **UK Embassy,** Unter den Linden 32-34 (☎20 18 40; fax 20 18 41 58). S1, S2, S25, S3, S5, S7, S75 or S9 or U6 to Friedrichstr. Open M-F 9am-4pm. **US Citizens Service,** Clayallee 170 (☎832 92 33; fax 831 49 26). U1 to Oskar-Helene-Heim. Open M-F 8:30am-noon. Telephone advice available M-F 2-4pm; after hours, call ☎830 50 for emergency advice. **US Embassy,** Neustädtische Kirchstr. 4-5 (☎238 51 74; fax 238 62 90). S1, S2, S25, S3, S5, S7, S75 or S9 or U6 to Friedrichstr. Open 8:30am-5:30pm by appointment only.

Currency Exchange: The **Wechselstube** at Joachimstalerstr. 1-3 (☎882 10 86), near Bahnhof Zoo, has good rates and no commission. Open M-F 8am-8pm, Sa 9am-3pm. **ReiseBank,** at Bahnhof Zoo (☎881 71 17; open daily 7am-10pm) and Ostbahnhof (☎296 43 93; open M-F 7am-10pm, Sa 7am-6pm, Su 8am-4pm), is conveniently located in both major train stations, but has poorer rates.

American Express: Main Office, Bayreutherstr. 23 (☎21 49 83 63). U1, U15, or U2 to Wittenbergplatz. Mail held, banking services rendered. Open M-F 9am-6pm, Sa 10am-1pm. **Branch office,** Friedrichstr. 172 (☎20 17 40 12). U6 to Französischestr. Open M-F 9am-5:30pm, Sa 10am-1pm.

Luggage Storage: In **Bahnhof Zoo.** Lockers DM2 per day, larger lockers DM4. 72hr. max. Also at **Ostbahnhof** (lockers DM2 per day, larger DM4, 72hr. max.), **Bahnhof Lichtenberg,** and **Alexanderplatz** (lockers DM2 per day, 24hr. max.).

Bi-Gay-Lesbian Organizations: Schwules Überfall, ☎216 33 36, is a hotline and offers legal help for victims of gay-bashing. Open daily 6-9pm. **Schwulenberatung** (gay men's counseling), ☎194 46. **Lesbenberatung** (lesbian counseling), ☎215 20 00.

Laundromat: Wasch Centers at various locations: **Schöneberg,** U9 to Bundesplatz. Bergmannstr. 109; **Kreuzberg,** U7 to Gneisenaustr. Behmstr. 12; **Mitte,** S1, S2, or S25 or U8 to Gesundbrunnen. Jablonskistr. 21. Wash DM6 per 6kg. Open daily 6am-11pm.

EMERGENCY AND COMMUNICATIONS

Emergency: Police, Platz der Luftbrücke 6 (☎110). U6 to Platz der Luftbrücke. **Ambulance and Fire,** ☎112.

Crisis Lines: American Hotline ☎ (0177) 814 15 10. Crisis and referral service. **Sexual Assault Hotline,** ☎251 28 28. Open Tu and Th 6-9pm, Su noon-2pm. **Drug Crisis,** ☎192 37. Open M-F 8:30am-10pm, Sa-Su 2-9:30pm.

Pharmacies: Europa-Apotheke, Tauentzienstr. 9-12 (☎261 41 42), near the Europa Center and Bahnhof Zoo. Open M-F 9am-8pm, Sa 9am-4pm. Closed pharmacies post signs directing you to the nearest open one. For **late-night pharmacies,** call ☎011 89.

Medical Assistance: The American and British embassies have a list of English-speaking doctors. **Emergency Doctor** (☎31 00 31) available 24hr.

Internet Access: Cyberb@r, Joachimstalerstr. 5-6, near Bahnhof Zoo. On the second floor of the Karstadt Sport department store. DM5 per 30min. **Webtimes,** Chausseestr. 8 (☎280 49 890), in Mitte. U6 to Oranienburger Tor. DM7 per hr. Open M-F 9am-midnight, Sa and Su 10am-midnight. **Website,** Joachimstalerstr. 41 (☎88 67 96 30), is Berlin's trendiest cybercafe. Open daily 10am-late.

Post Offices: Budapesterstr. 42, opposite the Europa-Center near Bahnhof Zoo. **Poste Restante:** Abigail DOUGLAS, Postlagernd, Postamt in der Budapesterstr. 42, 10787 Berlin. Open M-Sa 8am-midnight, Su 10am-midnight. Branch office at **Tegel Airport** (☎417 84 90). Open daily 6:30am-9pm. **Postamt Friedrichshain,** Str. der Pariser Kommune 8-10, 10243 Berlin, near Ostbahnhof. Open M-F 7am-9pm, Sa 8am-8pm.

▟ ACCOMMODATIONS

Hostels in Berlin fall into three categories: HI-affiliated, state-owned *Jugendherbergen* and *Jugendgästehäuser,* large, privately-owned hostels, and smaller, more off-beat private hostels, respectively. **HI hostels** can be a great, cheap sleep, but they fill quickly with German school groups—**calling ahead is a must.** If you're looking for a more party-ready crew, shack up at one of the large, well-equipped **private hostels,** which have a mostly non-German clientele. If you plan to visit during the **Love Parade,** call at least two months early. Some hostels will increase prices by up to DM20 at this time. For a DM5 fee, **tourist offices** will find you a room in a hostel, *Pension,* or hotel. Be prepared to pay at least DM70 for a single and DM100 for a double. There are also over 4000 **private rooms** available in the city; the overwhelming majority are controlled by the tourist offices. Expect to pay DM80 for singles, DM100 for doubles, plus a single-night surcharge of DM5. For longer visits (more than 4 days), the various **Mitwohnzentralen** can arrange for you to housesit or sublet an apartment. For more information, contact **Home Company Mitwohnzentrale,** Joachimstalerstr. 17. (☎194 45. U9 or u15 to Kurfürstendamm. Open M-F 9am-6pm, Sa 11am-2pm.)

MITTE

▨ **Circus,** Rosa-Luxemburg-Str. 39-41 (☎28 39 14 33; email circus@mind.de). U2 to Rosa-Luxemburg-Platz. Circus makes a heroic effort at hostel hipness, with cheap internet access and a disco ball in the lobby. Sheets DM4. **Bike rental** DM12 per day. Reservations in summer are a must and should be confirmed a day before arrival. 5-6 bed dorms DM25; singles DM45; doubles DM 80; triples DM105; quads DM160.

Clubhouse Hostel, Kalkscheunenstr. 2 (☎28 09 79 79). S1, S2, or S25 to Oranienburgerstr. or U6 to Oranienburger Tor. Enter the courtyard from Johannisstr. 2 or Kalkscheunestr. Breakfast buffet DM7, served 8-11am. Internet access DM1 per 5min. Call at least 2-3 days ahead. 8-10 bed dorms DM25; 5-7 bed dorms DM30; singles DM50; doubles DM80.

Mitte's Backpacker Hostel, Chausseestr. 102 (☎262 51 40; email backpacker@snafu.de). U6 to Zinnowitzerstr. Internet access. Sheets DM5. Laundry DM5 per load. Bikes DM10-12 per day. Reception 7am-9:30pm. 5- to 6-bed room DM25; doubles DM38; triples DM30; quads DM28.

SCHÖNEBERG, TIERGARTEN, WILMERSDORF

Jugendgästehaus (HI), Kluckstr. 3 (☎261 10 97). From Bahnhof Zoo, take bus #129 (dir.: Hermannplatz) to Gedenkstätte, or U1 to Kurfürstenstr., then walk up Potsdamerstr., go left on Pohlstr., and right on Kluckstr. Offers an internet cafe, laundry facilities, and bike rentals. Breakfast included. Curfew midnight; stragglers admitted every 30min. 12:30-6am. Lockout 9am-1pm. 4- to 10-bed dorm rooms DM34, over 26 DM43.

Studentenhotel Meininger 10, Meiningerstr. 10 (☎78 71 74 14; email info@studentenhotel.de). U4, bus #146 or N46 to Rathaus Schöneberg. Walk toward the Rathaus on Freiherr-vom-Stein-Str., turn left onto Martin-Luther-Str. and then right on Meiningerstr. Breakfast included. DM10 deposit for locker keys. Dorms DM25; singles DM66; doubles DM44; 3- to 6-bed rooms DM40.

Jugendgästehaus Feurigstraße, Feurigstr. 63 (☎781 52 11). U7 to Kleistpark, or bus #204 or 348 to Kaiser-Wilhelm-Platz. Walk down Hauptstr., turn left onto Kollonenstr., and after a right onto Feurigstr. it will be on the left. Relatively close to the Schöneberg bar scene. Breakfast included. Sheets DM5 if stay less than 3 nights, otherwise free. Dorms DM40 (DM27 after August); singles DM55; doubles DM50.

Hotel-Pension München, Güntzelstr. 62 (☎857 91 20). U9 to Güntzelstr. Clean, white-walled rooms with cable-TVs and phones. Breakfast DM10. Checkout 11am. Written reservations. Singles DM66-70, with shower DM95-110; doubles DM80-90, with bath DM115-130.

Hotel Sachsenhof, Motzstr. 7 (☎216 20 74). U1, U2, U4, or U15 to Nollendorfplatz. The hotel is in a lovely old house surrounded by Nollendorfplatz's myriad cafes and gay nightlife scene. Breakfast DM10. Call for reservations between 7am and 11pm. Singles DM57, with shower DM65; doubles DM99-146, with shower DM126-156.

Jugendgästehaus am Zoo, Hardenbergstr. 9a (☎312 94 10), opposite the Technical University Mensa. Bus #145 to Steinplatz, or take the short walk from the back exit of Bahnhof Zoo straight down Hardenbergstr. Reception 9am-midnight. Check-in 10am. Check-out 9am. Lockout 10am-2pm. Small 4- to 8-bed dorms DM35, over 26 DM40; singles DM52, under 26 DM47; doubles DM95, under 26 DM85.

CHARLOTTENBURG

Pension Berolina, Stuttgarter Pl. 17 (☎32 70 90 72). S3, S5, S7, S75, or S9 to Charlottenburg or U7 to Wilmersdorferstr. Spartan rooms located near S-Bahn station. Singles DM60; doubles DM80; triples DM90; quads DM100; quints DM110.

Charlottenburger Hof, Stuttgarter Pl. 14 (☎32 90 70). S3, S5, S7, S75, or S9 to Charlottenburg (across the street) or U7 to Wilmersdorferstr. The modern art-themed decor of this hotel could pass for a gallery. Laundry DM5. All rooms have phones and TVs; the pricier doubles come with balconies and whirlpools. Singles DM80-120; doubles DM110-160; quads DM160-220.

KREUZBERG

Die Fabrik, Schlesischestr. 18 (☎611 71 16; email info@diefabrik.com). U1 or U15 to Schlesisches Tor or night bus #N65 to Taborstr. Within walking distance of Kreuzberg's nightlife. Breakfast DM10. Bike rental DM20 per day. Reserve or call ahead. Dorms for DM30; singles DM66; doubles DM94; triples DM120; quads DM144.

Bax Pax, Skalitzerstr. 104 (☎69 51 83 22; email info@baxpax.de). U1 or U15 to Görlitzer Bahnhof, right across the street. Fuzzy blue carpets, sparkling bathrooms, and an ultra-friendly staff. Sheets DM5. Reception 7am-10pm. DM25-30.

Pension Kreuzberg, Großbeerenstr. 64 (☎251 13 62). U6 or U7 or night bus #N19 to Mehringdamm. Breakfast included. Reception 8am-10pm. Singles DM75; doubles DM98; extra bed DM44 per person.

Hotel Transit, Hagelbergerstr. 53-54 (☎789 04 70). U6 or U7 or night bus #N19 to Mehringdamm. Party hard and crash in this stylin' *Pension.* Breakfast included. Singles DM90; doubles DM105; triples DM140; quads DM180; extra bed DM33.

FRIEDRICHSHAIN AND PRENZLAUER BERG

Odyssee, Grünbergerstr. 23 (☎29 00 00 81; www.hostel-berlin.de). U5 to Frankfurter Tor or S3, S5, S6, S7, S75, or S9 or U1 or U15 to Warschauerstr. Lounge with bar, colorful bedrooms, and quite possibly the slickest bathrooms of all the hostels of Germany. Bar open until dawn. Internet access DM3 per 15min. Breakfast DM5. Always reserve ahead. Dorms DM24-26; quads DM32; doubles DM36.

Lette'm Sleep Hostel, Lettestr. 7 (☎44 73 36 23). U2 to Eberswalderstr. The first hostel to open up in Prenzlauer Berg, a few blocks from Kollwitzplatz. Internet access DM1 per 5min. 3-6 bed dorms DM26-35.

TEGEL

Jugendherberge Ernst Reuter (HI), Hermsdorfer Damm 48-50 (☎404 16 10). S25 to Tegel or U6 to Alt-Tegel, then bus #125 or night bus #N25 (dir.: Frohnau/ Invalidensiedlung) to Jugendherberge. Breakfast included. Lockers. Laundry DM8. Key deposit DM20. Closed Dec. 6-bed rooms DM28; over 26 and non-members DM35.

Jugendgästehaus Tegel, Ziekowstr. 161 (☎433 30 46; email JGH-Tegel@t-online.de). S25 to Tegel or U6 to Alt-Tegel, then bus #222 or night bus #N22 (dir.: Alt-Lübars) to Titusweg. Old brick outside, new and bright inside. Breakfast included. Reception 7:30am-11pm. 3-8 bed dorms DM37.50.

CAMPING

Deutscher Camping-Club runs the Dreilinden and Kladow campgrounds in Berlin; both are adjacent to the line tracing the site of the Berlin Wall. **Written reservations** can be made by writing the Deutscher Camping-Club Berlin, Geisbergstr. 11, 10777 Berlin. Otherwise, call in advance (☎218 60 71). Both sites charge DM9.70 per person, DM4.60 per child, DM7.20 per tent, and DM12.70 for trailers.

Dreilinden (☎805 12 01). S7 to Griebnitzsee, walk back between the station and lake. A city campsite, surrounded on 3 sides by the vestiges of the Berlin Wall. Open March-Oct.

Kladow, Krampnitzer Weg 111-117 (☎365 27 97). U7 to Rathaus Spandau, then bus #135 (dir.: Alt-Kladow) to the end. Switch to bus #234 to Krampnitzer Weg/ Selbitzerstr., then follow Krampnitzer Weg 200m. Open year-round.

Backpacker's Paradise, Ziekowstr. 161 (☎433 86 40). S25 to Tegel or U6 to Alt-Tegel, then bus #222 or night bus #N22 to Titusweg. Next to the Jugendgästehaus Tegel. Breakfast buffet DM3. Lockers DM1. Open late June-Aug. DM10 for a blanket and thermal pad under a tent; add DM3 for a summer camp-like cot.

🍴 FOOD

Food in Berlin is a tasty surprise; Berlin's Turkish, Indian, Thai, and Italian immigrants bring a wide variety of quality ethnic food to restaurants and stands throughout the city. Berlin's most notable home-grown option is the sweet **Berliner Weiße mit Schuß,** a concoction of wheat beer with a shot of syrup. A lot of typical Berlin street food is Turkish, and almost every street has its own Turkish *Imbiß* or restaurant. **Aldi, Plus, Edeka,** and **Penny Markt** are the cheapest supermarket chains, and are usually open Monday to Friday 9am-6pm and Saturday 9am-4pm. At Bahnhof Zoo, **Ullrich am Zoo,** below the S-Bahn tracks, and **Nimm's Mit,** near the Reisezentrum, have longer hrs. (Open daily 6am-10pm.) The best **open-air market** fires up Saturday mornings on Winterfeldtplatz.

Taba, Torstr. 164 (☎282 67 95). U8 to Rosenthaler Platz. A lively, happening place and good Brazilian eats. Meals DM10-17; cigars for DM5. Live music F, Sa, and Su, disco every Saturday from midnight-4am. Open W-Su from 7pm.

KaDeWe, Tauentzienstr. 21-24 (☎212 10). U1, U2, or U15 to Wittenbergplatz. Satiate every desire in the 6th-floor food emporium of this tremendous department store. Open M-F 9:30am-8pm, Sa 9am-4pm.

Schwarzes Café, Kantstr. 148 (☎313 80 38). S3, S5, S7, S75, or S9 to Savignypl. In a district full of posh business-suit restaurants, this cafe caters to a pleasantly young crowd. Prices are a bit high (a milkshake is DM7), but breakfast is served around the clock. *Always* open, except from 3am-11am each Tuesday.

Amrit, Oranienstr. 202-203 (☎612 55 50). U1 or U15 to Görlitzer Bahnhof. Perhaps the best Indian food in Berlin, served under desert colored walls with just a touch of Kreuzberg flair. Fabulous vegetarian dishes like *Alu Saag* (DM12.50) as well as delectably spicy meat entrees. Open M-Th and Su noon-1am, F-Sa noon-2am.

Café V, Lausitzer Pl. 12 (☎612 45 05). U1 or U15 to Görlitzer Bahnhof. Berlin's oldest vegetarian restaurant has a dimly-lit yellow interior with cool paintings. Some vegan-friendly or fish meals available. Open daily 10am-2am.

Sprelacarte, Kollwitzplatz 18. This cafe serves a variety of breakfast combos, like the Käsefrühstück (DM11), and daily dinner specials from DM9. No one else has glowing fluorescent cows crawling up the side of a six-story building! Open daily 10am-1am.

◉ SIGHTS

Berlin's sights are spread out over an area eight times the size of Paris. Below, the sights are organized by *Bezirk* (district), beginning with Mitte and spiralling outward. Areas farther from the center are grouped together in **Outer Districts.** Many of central Berlin's major sights lie along the route of **bus #100,** which travels from Bahnhof Zoo to Prenzlauer Berg, passing the Siegessäule, Brandenburg Gate, Unter den Linden, the Berliner Dom, and Alexanderplatz along the way.

MITTE

Formerly the heart of Imperial Berlin, Mitte contains some of Berlin's most magnificent sights and museums. Much of the neighborhood languished in disuse and disrepair during GDR days, but now that the government is back in town, the district is once again living up to its name ("Mitte" means center), as embassies and national institutes pour back into the area's rapidly-renovating streets.

UNTER DEN LINDEN

The area between the Brandenburg Gate and Alexanderplatz is best reached by taking S1, S2, or S25 to Unter den Linden and heading east; alternatively, bus #100 runs the length of the boulevard every 4-6min. Beyond Friedrichstr., impressive university buildings and museums join with two squares just south of the boulevard to form one of the largest collections of notable buildings in Berlin.

BRANDENBURGER TOR AND PARISER PLATZ. For decades a barricaded gateway to nowhere, today the Brandenburg Gate is the most powerful emblem of reunited Berlin. Standing directly in the center of the city, it was within the no-man's land during the time of the Wall. It opens east onto Pariser Platz and Unter den Linden and west onto the Tiergarten and Straße des 17. Juni. All but a few of the venerable buildings near the gate have been destroyed, including the *Stadtpalais,* which stood from 1848 until its destruction in WWII. A massive reconstruction effort centered around the gate has already revived such pre-war staples as the **Hotel Adlon,** once the premier address for all visiting dignitaries and celebrities.

RUSSIAN EMBASSY. Rebuilding the edifices of the rich and famous wasn't a huge priority in the workers' state; one exception, however, is the imposing Palais at Unter den Linden 7. The building is massive, taking up nearly an entire block on the wide street. With the end of the Cold War, the *palais* has reverted to being just another embassy, and the huge bust of Lenin that once graced its red star-shaped topiary was quietly removed in 1994.

DEUTSCHE STAATSBIBLIOTHEK. The state library's shady, ivy-covered court-yard and cafe provide a pleasant respite from the surrounding landscape. *(Unter den Linden 8. ☎ 26 60. Library open M-F 9am-9pm, Sa 9am-5pm. DM1 for a day's admission. Cafe open M-F 9am-6pm, Sa 10am-4pm.)*

HUMBOLDT-UNIVERSITÄT. Just beyond the Deutsche Staatsbibliothek is the H-shaped main building of the Humboldt-Universität, the hallowed halls of which have been filled by the likes of Hegel, Einstein, the Brothers Grimm, and Karl Marx. *(Unter den Linden 6. ☎ 209 30.)*

NEUE WACHE. The new guard house was designed by Prussian architect Karl Friedrich Schinkel in the unrepentant Neoclassical style. During the GDR era, it was known as the "Monument to the Victims of Fascism and Militarism," and, iron-ically, was guarded by East German soldiers. After reunification, the building was reopened in 1993 as a war memorial. The remains of an unknown soldier and an unknown concentration camp victim are buried inside with earth from the Nazi concentration camps, as well as from the battlefields of Stalingrad, El Alamein, and Normandy. *(Unter den Linden 4. Open daily 10am-6pm.)*

BEBELPLATZ. It was here on May 10, 1933 that Nazi students burned nearly 20,000 books by "subversive" authors such as Heinrich Heine and Sigmund Freud—both Jews. A plaque in the center of the square is engraved with Heine's eerily prescient 1820 quote: "Wherever books are burned, ultimately people are burned as well." The building with the curved facade is the **Alte Bibliothek**. Once the royal library, it is now home to the Humboldt's law fac-ulty. On the other side of the square is the handsome **Deutsche Staatsoper**, fully rebuilt after the war from original sketches by Knobelsdorff. The distinctive blue dome at the end of the square belongs to the **St.-Hedwigs-Kathedrale**. Built in 1773 as the first Catholic church erected in Berlin after the Reformation, it was burnt to a crisp by American bombers in 1943. Designed after the Roman Pantheon, the church was rebuilt in the 1950s in high atheist style, such that the interior resembles a socialist nightclub instead of a house of worship. *(Cathedral open M-F 10am-5pm, Sa 10am-4:30pm, Su 1-5pm. Free.)* Next to the cathedral, the **Bundeshauptstadt Berlin** has an interactive exhibit of the new buildings being con-structed for the various governmental offices, and of the controversial plan to rebuild Berlin's own *Schloß*. *(Behrenstr. 39. ☎ 20 08 32 34. Open daily 9am-5:30pm. Free.)*

ALEXANDERPLATZ AND NIKOLAIVIERTEL

On the other side of Museuminsel, Unter den Linden becomes Karl-Liebknecht-Str., and leads into the monolithic **Alexanderpl.** Take S3, S5, S7, S9, or S75 or U2, U5, or U8 to Alexanderpl.

ALEXANDERPLATZ. Formerly the frantic heart of Weimar Berlin, the plaza was transformed in East German times into an urban wasteland of fountains and pre-fab office buildings, including some concrete-block classics. In the 1970s, the grey drear was interrupted by enormous neon signs with declarations like "Medical Instruments of the GDR—Distributed in All the World!" in order to satisfy the peo-ple's need for bright lights. Today the signs have vanished, allowing chain stores like **Kaufhof** to pop up, and relying on the punks who spend their time in the plaza to fulfill the lust for color.

FERNSEHTURM. The TV tower, the tallest structure in Berlin at 365m, is a truly awkward piece of design intended to show off the new heights achieved through five-year plans; in fact, it looks more like something from the *Jetsons*. The project proved to be somewhat of a flop when it was discovered that the sun's reflection on the tower's amber-tinted windows creates a shadow that looks very much like a crucifix, known as the *Papsts Rache*—the Pope's revenge. *(☎ 242 33 33. Open daily Mar.-Oct. 9am-1am; Nov.-Feb. 10am-midnight. DM10, under 16 DM5.)*

GENDARMENMARKT AND POTSDAMER PLATZ

Berlin's most impressive ensemble of 19th-century buildings is a few blocks south of Unter den Linden on the **Gendarmenmarkt,** also known as the French Quarter after it became the main settlement for Protestant Huguenots in the 18th century. *(Take U2 to Französischestr. or U2 or U6 to Stadtmitte.)*

DEUTSCHER DOM. Gracing the southern end of the square, the Dom is not used as a church but instead houses **Fragen zur deutschen Geschichte,** a Bundestag-sponsored exhibition that traces German political history from despotism to fascism to democracy. *(Gendarmenmarkt 5. ☎ 22 73 21 41. Open Tu-Su 10am-7pm. Free.)*

FRANZÖSISCHER DOM. At the opposite end of the square from the Deutscher Dom. Built in the early 18th century by French Huguenots, the Dom is now home to a restaurant and a small museum chronicling the Huguenot diaspora. The tower offers an interesting panorama of the surrounding construction sites. *(Gendarmenmarkt 5. ☎ 229 17 60. Museum open Tu-Sa noon-5pm. DM3, students DM2. Restaurant open daily noon-1am. Tower open daily 9am-7pm.)*

KONZERTHAUS AM GENDARMENMARKT. Located between the two churches. Designed by Karl Friedrich Schinkel in 1819, the Konzerthaus was badly damaged in air attacks toward the end of WWII. It reopened in 1984 as the most elegant concert venue in Berlin. *(Gendarmenmarkt 2. ☎ 203 09 21 01.)*

POTSDAMER PLATZ. Potsdamer Platz was built under Friedrich Wilhelm I in an approximation of Parisian boulevards with the primary purpose of moving troops quickly. After reunification, the square was chosen to become the new commercial center of Berlin. The half-finished buildings, sand lots, and newly-constructed facades of glass and steel create a landscape which is both a product and symbol of the master plans for a new Berlin; the completion date has been pushed back to 2004. *(S1, S2, or S25 or U2 to Potsdamer Platz.)*

FÜHRERBUNKER. Near Potsdamer Platz, unmarked and inconspicuous, lies the site of the bunker where Hitler married Eva Braun and then ended his life. In macabre irony, the actual bunker site is now a playground (behind the record store at Wilhelmstr. 92); tourists looking for it often mistakenly head for the visible bunker at the southern edge of Potsdamer Platz.

SCHEUNENVIERTEL

Northwest of Alexanderplatz lies the **Scheunenviertel,** once the center of Berlin's Orthodox Jewish community. Take S1, S2, or S25 to Oranienburgerstr. or U-Bahn #6 to Oranienburger Tor. Today the Scheunenviertel is better known for its teeming masses of outdoor cafes than for its historical significance as Berlin's Jewish center, but the past few years have seen the opening of several Judaica-oriented bookstores and kosher restaurants.

NEUE SYNAGOGE. This huge, oriental-style building was designed by Berlin architect Eduard Knoblauch. The synagogue, which seated 3,200, was used for worship until 1940, when the Nazis occupied it and used it for storage. Amazingly, the building survived *Kristallnacht,* when Nazis destroyed thousands of Jewish businesses, burned synagogues, killed nearly 100 Jews, and sent at least 20,000 to concentration camps. The synagogue was destroyed by bombing, but its beautiful, gold-laced domes were rebuilt and opened to the public in 1995, though it is no longer used for services. The interior houses an exhibit chronicling the synagogue's history in addition to temporary exhibits on the history of Berlin's Jews. *(Oranienburgerstr. 30. ☎ 28 40 13 16. Open M-Th and Su 10am-6pm, F 10am-2pm. Museum DM5, students DM3. Dome DM3, students DM2.)*

OTHER SIGHTS IN MITTE

BERTOLT-BRECHT-HAUS. If any single man personifies the maelstrom of political and aesthetic contradictions that is Berlin, it is **Bertolt Brecht,** who called the city home. Brecht lived and worked in the house near the intersection with Schlegelstr. from 1953 to 1956. If you understand German, take the guided tour, given in flamboyant Brechtian style. The **Brechtforum** on the second floor sponsors exhibits and lectures on artistic and metropolitan subjects; pick up a schedule. *(Chausseestr. 125. U6 to Zinnowitzerstr. Entrance only with a tour. ☎283 05 70 44. Tours every 30min. Tu-W and F 10-11:30am, Th 10-11:30am and 5-6:30pm and Sa 9:30am-1:30pm. Tours every hr. Su 11am-6pm. DM4, students DM2.)*

DOROTHEENSTÄDTISCHER FRIEDHOF. Attached to Brecht's house is the cemetery where he and his wife, Helene Weigel, are buried. Also at rest there are Karl Friedrich Schinkel, Heinrich Mann, and Hegel and Fichte, who lie side by side in the middle of the yard. A map near the entrance points out their locations. *(Open May-Aug. daily 8am-8pm; Feb.-April and Sept.-Nov. 8am-6pm; Dec.-Jan. 8am-4pm.)*

TIERGARTEN

In the center of Berlin, the lush **Tiergarten** is a relief from the neon lights of the Ku'damm to the west and the din and dust of construction work to the east. Stretching from Bahnhof Zoo to the Brandenburg Gate, the vast landscaped park was formerly used by Prussian monarchs as a hunting and parade ground. Today the Tiergarten is filled with strolling families by day and cruising gay men at night. **Straße des 17. Juni** bisects the park from west to east, connecting Ernst-Reuter-Platz to the Brandenburg Gate.

SIEGESSÄULE. In the heart of the Tiergarten, the slender 70-meter-high victory column, topped by a gilded statue of winged Victoria, commemorates Prussia's humiliating defeat of France in 1870. In 1938, the Nazis moved the monument from its former spot in front of the Reichstag to increase its height and make it more impressive. Climb the monument's 285 steps to the top for a panorama of the city. *(Großer Stern. Take bus #100, 187, to Großer Stern. ☎391 29 61. Open April-Nov. M 1-6pm, Tu-Su 9am-6pm. DM2, students DM1.)*

THE REICHSTAG. Just to the north of the Brandenburg Gate sits the imposing, stone-gray Reichstag building, former seat of the parliaments of the German Empire and the Weimar Republic, and current home of Germany's governing body, the Bundestag. In the summer of 1995, the Reichstag metamorphosed into an artsy parcel, when husband-and-wife team **Christo** and **Jeanne-Claude** wrapped the dignified building in 120,000 yards of shimmery metallic fabric. After the wrapping was torn down, a giant glass dome was constructed around an upside-down solar cone that powers the building. Most recently, the long-awaited move of Germany's parliament from Bonn to Berlin was executed in several stages throughout the summer and fall of 1999. A walkway spirals up the inside of the dome, leading visitors to a panoramic view from the top of the cone. *(☎22 62 99 33. Open daily 8am-midnight; last entrance at 10pm. Free.)*

CHARLOTTENBURG

The borough of Charlottenburg, one of the wealthiest areas in Berlin, includes the area between the Ku'damm and the Spree river.

BAHNHOF ZOO. During the city's division, West Berlin centered around Bahnhof Zoo, the station which inspired U2's "Zoo TV" tour (the U-Bahn line with the same name as the band runs through the station). The area surrounding the station is a spectacular wasteland of department stores and peepshows intermingled with souvenir shops and G-rated attractions. Across Bahnhof Zoo and through the corral of bus depots, the renowned **Zoologischer Garten** is one of the best zoos in the world, with many animals displayed in open-air habitats instead of cages. The second entrance across from Europa-Center is the famous **Elefantentor,** Budapester-str. 34, a delightfully decorated pagoda of pachyderms. *(Open May-Sept. daily 9am-6:30pm; Oct.-Feb. 9am-5pm; March-April 9am-5:30pm. DM13, students DM11.)* Next door is the excellent **Aquarium,** which houses broad collections of insects and reptiles as well as endless tanks of wide-eyed, rainbow-colored fish. Its pride and joy is its 450kg **Komodo dragon,** the world's largest reptile, a gift to Germany from Indonesia. *(Budapesterstr. 32. Open daily 9am-6pm. Aquarium DM12, students DM10. Combination ticket to the zoo and aquarium DM21, students DM17.)*

KAISER-WILHELM-GEDÄCHTNISKIRCHE. Nicknamed "the rotten tooth" by Berliners, the shattered church, with jagged edges jutting out into an otherwise smooth skyline, stands in striking contrast to the surrounding fast-food chains and department stores as a quiet reminder of the destruction caused during WWII. Built in 1852 in a Romanesque-Byzantine style, the church has an equally striking interior, with colorful mosaics covering the ceiling, floors, and walls, all bathed in a dim blue glow from stained-glass blocks. *(☎218 50 23. Exhibit open M-Sa 10am-4pm. Church open daily 9am-7pm.)*

SCHLOß CHARLOTTENBURG

Take bus #145 from Bahnhof Zoo to Luisenpl./Schloß Charlottenburg or U7 to Richard-Wagner-Platz. and walk about 15min. down Otto-Suhr-Allee. ☎32 09 11. Altes Schloß open Tu-F 9am-5pm, Sa-Su 10am-5pm. DM8, students DM4. Schinkel-Pavilion open Tu-Su 10am-5pm. DM3, students DM2. Belvedere open April-Oct. Tu-Su 10am-5pm; Nov.-March Tu-F noon-4pm and Sa-Su noon-5pm. DM3, students DM2. Mausoleum open April-Oct. Tu-Su 10am-noon and 1-5pm. DM3, students DM2. Schloßgarten open Tu-Su 6am-9pm. Free. Ticket to entire complex DM15, students DM10, under 14 free. Family card DM25.

The broad, bright Baroque palace commissioned by Friedrich I for his second wife, Sophie-Charlotte, drapes its yellow walls over a carefully landscaped park on the northern edge of Charlottenburg. The sprawling complex provides the ideal relief from the bustle of downtown, with its lazy lawns and numerous buildings. The Schloß's many buildings include the **Neringbau** (or **Altes Schloß**), the palace proper, which contains many rooms filled with historical furnishings and gratuitous use of gilding; the **Schinkel-Pavilion,** a museum dedicated to Prussian architect Karl Friedrich Schinkel; **Belvedere,** a small building housing the royal family's porcelain collection; and the **Mausoleum,** the final resting spot for most of the family. The **Galerie der Romantik,** a state museum housing Berlin's first-rate collection of German Romantic paintings, is located in a side wing (see **Museums,** p. 420). Seek out the **Schloßgarten** behind the main buildings, an elysium of small lakes, footbridges, fountains, and carefully planted rows of trees.

OTHER SIGHTS IN CHARLOTTENBURG

OLYMPIA-STADION. At the western edge of Charlottenburg, the Olympic stadium is one of the most prominent legacies of the Nazi architectural aesthetic. It was erected for the 1936 Olympic Games, in which Jesse Owens, an African-American, triumphed over the Nazis' racial theories by winning four gold medals. *(U2 to Olympia-Stadion (Ost) or S5 or S75 to Olympiastadion. Open daily in summer 8am-8pm, off-season 8am-3pm. DM2.)*

FUNKTURM. Erected in 1926 to herald the radio age, the Funkturm is the Fernsehturm's marginally less impressive twin. The tower has a stunning view of the city from its 200m observation deck. Inside, the **Deutsches Rundfunkmuseum** chronicles the history of German broadcasting, with an exhibit dedicated to the world's first TV transmission, made here in 1931. *(Take S45 or S46 to Witzleben or U2 to Kaiserdamm. ☎30 38 39 99. Panorama deck and museum open daily 10am-11pm. DM5.)*

GEDENKSTÄTTE PLÖTZENSEE. Housed in the terrifyingly well-preserved former execution chambers of the Third Reich, the memorial exhibits document death sentences of "enemies of the people," including the officers who attempted to assassinate Hitler in 1944. More than 2,500 people were murdered within this small, stark red brick complex. Still visible are the hooks from which victims were hanged. *(Hüttigpfad. Off the main road where the bus stops, down Emmy-Zehden-Weg on Hüttigpfad. Take U9 to Turmstr., then bus #123 (dir.: Saatwinkler Damm) to Gedenkstätte Plötzensee. ☎344 32 26. Open daily Mar.-Oct. 9am-5pm; Nov.-Feb. 9am-4pm. Free.)*

SCHÖNEBERG AND WILMERSDORF

South of the Ku'damm, Schöneberg and Wilmersdorf are pleasant, middle-class residential districts noted for their shopping streets, lively cafes, and good restaurants. The birthplace of Marlene Dietrich, Schöneberg is also home to the more affluent segments of Berlin's gay community.

RATHAUS SCHÖNEBERG. West Berlin's city government convened here until the Wall fell in 1989. On June 26, 1963, exactly 15 years after the beginning of the Berlin Airlift, 1.5 million Berliners swarmed the streets beneath the windowless tower to hear John F. Kennedy reassure them of the Allies' commitment to the city. His speech ended with the now-famous words: "*Ich bin ein Berliner.*" Today, the fortress with the little Berlin bear on top is home to Schöneberg's municipal government as well as an exhibit on the life of former mayor and federal chancellor Willy Brandt. (*John-F.-Kennedy-Pl. U4 to Rathaus Schöneberg.* ☎ 787 60. *Rathaus open daily 9am-6pm. Exhibit open daily 9am-1pm. Tower open daily Mar. 15-Oct. 15 10am-5pm.*)

GRUNEWALD. In summer, clear your head in the Grunewald, a 745-acre birch forest. While there, visit the **Jagdschloß,** a restored royal hunting lodge housing a worthwhile collection of European paintings, including works by Rubens, van Dyck, and Cranach. The one-room hunting museum in the same building is not for those sensitive about animal cruelty. The cabinets full of knives, guns, and spears are accompanied by racks of antlers and mounted wild boars. (*Am Grunewaldsee 29. U1 or U7 to Fehrbelliner Pl., then bus #115 (dir.: Neuruppinerstr.) to Pücklerstr. Walk west 15min. along Pücklerstr. until you see the castle.* ☎ 813 35 97. *Open Tu-Su 10am-5pm. DM4, students and seniors DM2.*)

KREUZBERG

If you find Kurfürstendamm's consumerism nauseating, Kreuzberg provides the perfect dose of counter-culture relief. During President Reagan's 1985 visit to Berlin, authorities so feared protests from this quarter that they cordoned the whole Kreuzberg district off without warning—an utterly unconstitutional measure. Much of the area was occupied by *Hausbesetzer* (squatters) in the 1960s and 70s. A conservative city government decided to forcibly evict the illegal residents in the early 80s, provoking riots and throwing the city into total consternation.

HAUS AM CHECKPOINT CHARLIE. A fascinating exhibition on the site of the famous border-crossing point with an uneasy mixture of blatant Western tourist kitsch and didactic Eastern earnestness, the Haus am Checkpoint Charlie is one of Berlin's most popular tourist attractions. The ground floor holds a pricey snack bar and a ticket desk completely buried under piles of highly-marketable, Wall-related books, stickers, and postcards. The upper floors are a giant collage of artworks, newspaper clippings, and photographs mixed in with all types of devices used to get over, under, or through the Wall. (*Friedrichstr. 44. U6 or bus #129 to Kochstr.* ☎ 251 10 31. *Museum open daily 9am-10pm. DM8, students DM5. Films M-F at 5:30 and 7:30pm, Sa-Su at 4:30, 6, and 7pm.*)

ORANIENSTRAßE. The colorful mix of cafes, bars, and stores hawking records and used clothing on Oranienstraße boast a more radical edge; the May Day parades always start on Oranienplatz, and the area was the site of frequent riots in the 1980s. Anarchists and left-wing radicals share the neighborhood with traditional Turkish families as well as much of Berlin's gay and lesbian population. The result is pure eye-candy: colorful plates of food from Indian to Turkish, outfits from spikes and leather to hemp and henna, all served up among grafitti colored walls. (*U1 or U15 to Kottbusser Tor or Görlitzer Bahnhof.*)

EASTERN KREUZBERG. The **Landwehrkanal,** a channel bisecting Kreuzberg, is where Rosa Luxemburg's body was thrown after being murdered by the Freikorps in 1919. The tree-dotted strip of the canal near Kottbusser Damm, **Paul-Linke-Ufer,**

may be the most graceful street in Berlin, with its shady terraces and old facades. *(U8 to Schönleinstr.)* The east end of Kreuzberg, near the site of the Wall and the **Schlesisches Tor,** is home to Turkish and Balkan neighborhoods, with a corresponding wealth of ethnic restaurants popular with radicals, students, and shabby genteel gourmets. At the end of Kreuzberg, the **Oberbaumbrücke** spanning the Spree was once a border crossing into East Berlin; it now serves as an entrance to Friedrichshain's nightlife scene. *(U1 or U15 to Schlesisches Tor.)*

FRIEDRICHSHAIN AND LICHTENBERG

EAST SIDE GALLERY. The longest remaining portion of the Wall, the 1.3km stretch of cement and asbestos slabs is also one of the world's largest open-air art galleries. The murals by an international group of artists who gathered in 1989 to celebrate the end of the city's division. In 1999, with the wall still standing, the same artists came together again to repaint their work. *(Along Mühlenstr. Take S3, S5, S6, S7, S75, S9, U1, U15 to Warschauerstr. and walk back toward the river. Open 24hr.)*

KARL-MARX-ALLEE. The cornerstone of the East German national construction program, Karl-Marx-Allee became the socialist-realist showcase of the Communist government in the early 1950s, when it was known as Stalinallee. Billed as Germany's "first socialist road," the ludicrously broad avenue ends with the "people's palaces" at Strausberger Platz. *(U5 to Strausberger Platz.)*

FORSCHUNGS UND GEDENKSTÄTTE NORMANNENSTRAßE. In the suburb of Lichtenberg stands perhaps the most hated and feared building of the GDR regime—the headquarters of the East German secret police, the **Staatssicherheit** or **Stasi.** The building once contained six million individual dossiers on citizens of the GDR, a country of only 16 million people. Since a 1991 law returned the records to their subjects, the "Horror-Files" have rocked Germany, exposing informants—and wrecking careers, marriages, and friendships. The exhibit displays the offices of Erich Mielke (the loathed Minister for State Security from 1957-1989), a large collection of tiny microphones and hidden cameras used for surveillance by the Stasi, and a GDR Stasi shrine full of Lenin busts. *(Ruschestr. 103, Haus 1. U5 to Magdalenenstr. From the station's Ruschestr. exit, walk up Ruschestr. and take a right on Normannenstr.; it's Haus #1 in the complex of office buildings. ☎ 553 68 54. Open Tu-F 11am-6pm, Sa-Su 2-6pm. DM5, students DM3.75.)*

PRENZLAUER BERG

Northeast of Mitte lies Prenzlauer Berg, a former working-class district largely neglected by East Germany's reconstruction efforts. Many of the older buildings are crumbling at the edges, resulting in a charming state of age and graceful decay, slightly less charming for local residents with bad plumbing and no phones. The streets of Prenzlauer Berg are studded with trendy but casual cafes and bars. To reach Kollwitzplatz and Husemannstr., take U2 to Senefelderplatz, cross the street left and walk back through the park onto Kollwitzstr.

KOLLWITZPLATZ. The heart of Prenzlauer Berg's cafe scene, Kollwitzplatz offers a little triangle of greenery, centered on a statue of the square's namesake, visual artist **Käthe Kollwitz** (see **Museums,** p. 420). The monument has been painted a number of times in past years, most notably with big pink polka-dots, in acts of affectionate rather than angry vandalism.

JÜDISCHER FRIEDHOF. Berlin's Jews slowly gravitated to Prenzlauer Berg during the 19th and early 20th centuries. The Jewish cemetery on Schönhauser Allee contains the graves of composer Giacomo Meyerbeer and painter Max Liebermann. *(Open M-Th 8am-4pm, F 8am-1pm. Men must cover their heads before entering the cemetery.)* Nearby is the **Synagoge Rykestraße,** spared on *Kristallnacht* due to its inconspicuous location in a courtyard. *(Rykestr. 53.)*

🏛 MUSEUMS

Berlin is one of the world's great museum cities, with collections of art and artifacts encompassing all subjects and eras. The **Staatliche Museen Preußischer Kulturbesitz (SMPK)** runs the four major complexes—**Charlottenburg, Dahlem, Museuminsel,** and the **Kulturforum**—that form the hub of the city's museum culture. Entrance prices for these museums are standardized; a single admission costs DM4, students DM2. A *Tageskarte* (DM8, students DM4) is valid for all SMPK museums on the day of purchase; the *Wochenkarte* (DM25, students DM12.50) is valid for the whole week. The first Sunday of every month offers free admission.

▩ **Pergamon Museum** (☎ 203 55 00), Kupfergraben. One of the world's great ancient history museums from the days of the empire when Western archaeology was king and Heinrich Schliemann traversed the world, pillaging the debris of ancient civilizations and reassembling it at home. Named for Pergamon, in present-day Turkey, the city from which the enormous **Altar of Zeus** (180 BC) that fills its main exhibit hall was taken, the museum features huge pieces of ancient Mediterranean and Near Eastern history. The big blue **Ishtar Gate** of Babylon (575 BC) and the Roman **Market Gate of Miletus** are just several of the pieces that astound. Tours of Altar of Zeus daily at 11am and 3pm. SMPK Tageskarte required for entry.

Ägyptisches Museum, Schloßstr. 70 (☎ 20 90 55 55). Across Spandauer Damm from the palace. This stern Neoclassical building contains a famous collection of ancient Egyptian art—animal mummies, elaborately-painted coffins, and original papyrus scrolls encrypted with hieroglyphics—dramatically lit for full effect. The most popular item on display is the stunning 3,300-year-old bust of **Queen Nefertiti** (1350 BC), thought by many to be the most beautiful representation of a woman in the world. Open Tu-Su 10am-6pm. DM8, students DM4.

Sammlung Berggruen, Schloßstr. 1 (☎ 326 95 80). Five floors off a central spiraling staircase offer a substantial collection of Picasso's life's work, including numerous sketches, some of which were drawn when the artist was but 16. The bottom floor also exhibits works that influenced Picasso, including late French impressionist paintings and African masks; the top floor exhibits a collection of Paul Klee's paintings and Alberto Giacometti's sculptures. Open Tu-F 10am-6pm, Sa-Su 11am-6pm. DM8, students DM4.

Deutsche Guggenheim Berlin, Unter den Linden 13-15 (☎ 20 20 93 13). Located in a newly renovated building across the street from the *Deutsche Staatsbibliothek* (see p. 414), this museum is a joint venture between the Deutsche Bank and the Guggenheim Foundation in New York, featuring contemporary avant-garde art. Open daily 11am-8pm, Th-F until 10pm. DM8, students DM5; M free.

Deutsches Historisches Museum, Unter den Linden 2 (☎ 20 30 40), in the Zeughaus. S3, S5, S7, S75, or S9 to Hackescher Markt. Permanent exhibits trace German history from the Neanderthal period to the Nazis, while rotating exhibitions examine the last 50 years. Large quantities of GDR art in the "painting-of-a-happy-faced-worker" period are present. Until renovations are completed in 2002, the museum is housed in the Kronprinzenpalais across the street. Open Th-Tu 10am-6pm. Free.

Hanfmuseum, Mühlendamm 5 (☎ 24 72 02 33). U2 to Klosterstr. Did you know that hemp can serve as a convenient insulation material? Everything you wanted to know about marijuana—including medical and textile uses, and a history of the debate over the legality of non-medical use. Mull over exhibits of hemp brownies, ice cream, oils, and cosmetics. Open Tu-F 10am-8pm, Sa-Su noon-8pm. DM5.

Gemäldegalerie (☎ 20 90 55 55), in the Tiergarten-Kulturforum, on Matthäikirchplatz. One of Germany's most famous museums, it houses a stunning and enormous collection by Italian, German, Dutch, and Flemish masters, including works by Rembrandt, Bruegel, Rubens, Vermeer, Raphael, Titian, Botticelli, and Dürer. Open Tu-Su 10am-6pm, Th until 10 pm. SMPK prices: DM4, students DM2.

Neue National Gallerie, Potsdamerstr. 50 (☎ 266 26 62). Just past the Kulturforum. This sleek building, designed by Mies van der Rohe, houses interesting temporary exhibits upstairs in its huge windowed showroom, but the permanent collection downstairs is also worth a visit. Works by Warhol, Munch, Kirchner, Pechstein, Beckmann, and Ernst provide variety and provoke thought. Open Tu-F 10am-6pm and Sa-Su 11am-6pm. SMPK prices for permanent collection; DM12, students DM6 for the whole museum.

Hamburger Bahnhof Museum für Gegenwart, Invalidenstr. 50-51 (☎397 83 11). S3, S5, S7, S75, or S9 to Lehrter Stadtbahnhof or U6 to Zinnowitzerstr. Berlin's foremost collection of contemporary art features some cheerfully amusing works by Warhol, and a few neat multimedia installations including Bill Viola's "He weeps for you," in which a magnified faucet drips slowly onto an amplified drum. Open Tu-W and F 10am-6pm, Th 10am-10pm, Sa-Su 11am-6pm. DM10, students DM5; first Su of the month free.

Topographie des Terrors (☎25 48 67 03), behind the Martin-Gropius-Bau, at the corner of Niederkirchnerstr. and Wilhelmstr. S1 or S2, or U2 to Potsdamer Platz. Built on top of the ruins of a Gestapo kitchen, the area used to be the site of the notorious Gestapo headquarters at Prinz-Albrecht-Str. (now Niederkirchnerstr.). The very comprehensive exhibit of photographs, documents, and German texts displayed amidst the crumbled building details the Nazi party's rise to power and the atrocities that occurred during the war. Open Tu-Su 10am-6pm. Free.

Brücke Museum, Bussardsteig 9 (☎831 20 29). Take U1 or U7 to Fehrbelliner Pl. then bus #115 (dir.: Neuruppinerstr.) to Pücklerstr. This museum exhibits the wildly colorful works by adherents of the Expressionist Brücke school, including work by Otto Dix. The adjacent Bernard Heihger Stiftung sculpture garden is also worth a peek. Open M and W-Su 11am-5pm. DM7, students DM3.

ZuckerMuseum, Amrumerstr. 32 (☎31 42 75 74). U9 to Amrumerstr. A cultural history of sugar explores its uses, such as in sculpture, records, and alcohol. Yum. Why is all this important? "Ohne Zucker kein Alcohol," or "without sugar, no alcohol." Open M-W 9am-5pm, Th 3-8pm, Su 11am-6pm. DM4, students DM2.

🎵 ENTERTAINMENT

Berlin has one of the most vibrant cultural scenes in the world: exhibitions, concerts, plays, and dance performances abound. Despite recent cutbacks, the city still generously subsidizes the art scene. Numerous festivals celebrating everything from Chinese film to West African music spice up the regular offerings. Reservations can be made by calling the box office directly. Always ask about student discounts; most theaters and concert halls offer up to 50% off, but only if you buy at the *Abendkasse* (evening box office), which generally opens one hr. before performance. Look for theater and concert listings in the monthly pamphlets *Konzerte und Theater in Berlin und Brandenburg* (free) and *Berlin Programm* (DM2.80), as well as in the biweekly *Zitty* and *Tip.* **Hekticket,** on Hardenbergstr. next to the gigantic Zoo-Palast cineplex, sells last-minute tickets for half-price. (☎230 99 30. Open M-F 9am-8pm, Sa 10am-8pm, Su 4-8pm.) **Berliner Festspiele,** Budapesterstr. 48-50, has tickets for a variety of shows and concerts. (☎25 48 92 50; www.berliner festspiele.de. Open M-F 10am-6pm, Su 10am-2pm.)

CONCERTS AND OPERA

Berlin reaches its musical zenith during the fabulous **Berliner Festwochen,** lasting almost the entire month of September and drawing the world's best orchestras and soloists. The **Berliner Jazztage** in November also brings in the crowds. In mid-July, the **Bachtage** offer an intense week of classical music, while every Saturday night in August, the **Sommer Festspiele** turns the Ku'damm into a multi-faceted concert hall with punk, steel-drum, and folk groups competing for attention. Tickets for the *Philharmonie* and the *Oper* are often impossible to acquire through conventional channels without writing months in advance.

Berliner Philharmonisches Orchester, Matthäikirchstr. 1 (☎25 48 81 32). Take S1, S2, or S25, or U2 to Potsdamer Platz and walk up Potsdamerstr. Currently under the baton of Claudio Abbado, the *Berliner Philharmoniker* is one of the world's finest orchestras. Check an hr. before concert or write at least 8 weeks in advance. Tickets start at DM14 for standing room, DM26 for seats. Box office open M-F 3:30-6pm, Sa-Su 11am-2pm.

Konzerthaus (Schauspielhaus Gendarmenmarkt), Gendarmenmarkt 2 (☎203 09 21 01). U2 or U6 to Stadtmitte. The opulent home of Berlin's symphony orchestra. Last-minute tickets are somewhat easier to come by. Box office open M-Sa noon-6pm, Su noon-4pm. Order tickets by writing to Deutsches Kammerorchester, Suarezstr. 15, 14057 Berlin; or call ☎325 42 29; or fax 32 60 86 10.

Komische Oper, Unter den Linden 14 (☎20 26 03 60). U6 to Französischestr., or S1, S2, S25 to Unter den Linden. Tickets DM15-94. 50% student discounts almost always available 2hr. before performance. Box office open M-Sa 11am-7pm, Su 1pm until 1½hr. before performance.

Deutsche Oper Berlin, Bismarckstr. 35 (info ☎341 02 49, tickets ☎343 84 01; toll free ☎0 800 248 98 42). U2 to Deutsche Oper. Berlin's best and youngest opera. Student discounts available 1 week or less before performance. Tickets DM15-140. Box office open M-Sa 11am until 1hr. before performance, Su 10am-2pm. Evening tickets available 1hr. before performance.

Deutsche Staatsoper, Unter den Linden 7 (☎20 35 45 55). U6 to Französischestr. Eastern Berlin's leading opera company. Tickets DM18-35. 50% student discount. Box office open M-F 10am-6pm, Sa-Su 2pm-6pm, and 1hr. before performance.

THEATER

Theater listings are available in the monthly pamphlets *Kultur!news* and *Berlin Programm*, as well as in *Zitty* and *Tip*. The repertoire of the **Deutsches Theater,** Schumannstr. 13a, runs from Büchner to Mamet to Ibsen. (☎28 44 12 25. Box office open M-Sa 11am-6:30pm, Su 3-6:30pm. Tickets DM15-25.) **Hebbel-Theater,** Stresemannstr. 29, is the avant of the avant-garde theaters in Berlin. (☎25 90 04 27. Order tickets by phone M-Su 4-7pm or show up 1hr. before performance.) **Berliner Ensemble,** Bertolt-Brecht-Pl. 1, was established by Bertolt Brecht and has a hip program. (☎282 31 60. Tickets DM12-40, 50% student discount available 1hr. before performance. Box office open M-Sa 11am-6pm, Su 3-6pm.)

▣ SHOPPING

When Berlin was a lonely outpost in the Eastern Bloc consumer wilderness, Berliners had no choice but to buy native. The high temple of the consumerist religion is the seven-story **KaDeWe department store** on Wittenbergplatz at Tauentzienstr. 21-24, the largest department store in Europe. (☎212 10. Open M-F 9:30am-8pm, Sa 9am-4pm.) The **Kurfürstendamm,** near Bahnhof Zoo, has almost every kind of shop imaginable. The **Ku'damm Eck,** at the corner of Joachimstalerstr., and **Ku'damm Block,** near Uhlandstr., are the most notable areas. The newly opened **Daimler-Benz** complex on **Potsdamer Platz** offers more than 100 new shops and a multitude of restaurants, cafes, and pubs. There is a typical *Fußgängerzone* (pedestrian zone) on **Wilmersdorferstr.,** where bakeries, *Döner* joints, trendy clothing shops, and department stores abound. (U7 to Wilmersdorferstr. or S3, S5, S7, S75, or S9 to Charlottenburg.) If you're looking for that special something for the **Love Parade** (see p. 424), **Waahnsinn Berlin** (☎282 08 29), at the corner of Hackescher Markt and Neue Promenade, caters to your every pink furry desire.

▣ NIGHTLIFE

This is the section of *Let's Go: Western Europe* where we dance. Berlin's nightlife is **absolute madness,** a teeming cauldron of debauchery that runs around the clock and threatens to inflict coronaries upon the faint of heart. Bars typically open around 6pm, and pack in around 10pm, just as the clubs are opening their doors. As the bar scenes wind down around 1am, the pace picks up and the smoke machines kick in at the clubs, which groove till dawn, when a variety of after-parties and 24-hour cafes are waiting to keep up this seemingly perpetual motion. From 1am to 4am, take advantage of the **night buses** and U9 and **U12,** which run all night on Fridays and Saturdays; normal transit service resumes after 4:30am. In addition to *Tip* and *Zitty*, the free *030*, distributed in hostels, cafes and bars, is a great source of information about bands and dance venues.

Western Berlin has a rather varied combination of scenes. **Savignyplatz** offers refined, laid-back cafes in one of Berlin's oldest (and richest) neighborhoods. Gay life in Berlin centers around **Nollendorf Platz,** where the crowds are usually mixed and establishments range from the friendly to cruisy. The **Eastern Kreuzberg** scene is in the midst of a strong Turkish community, with a dizzying array of radically alternative clubs and bars centering around Oranienstr., and radiating outward several blocks, with more gay and lesbian establishments up around Muskauerstr. Berlin's best clubs are located in **Eastern Berlin,** centering around Orangienburger-str. in **Mitte** (not to be confused with Kreuzberg's Oranienstr.). It's also worth mentioning that Berlin has **de-criminalized marijuana possession** of up to eight grams. Smoking it in public, however, has not been officially accepted, though it's becoming more common in some clubs. *Let's Go* does not recommend puffing clouds of smoke into the face of police officers.

BARS AND CLUBS

SAVIGNYPLATZ

Quasimodo, Kantstr. 12a (☎312 80 86). U2 or U12 or S3, S5, S7, S75, or S9 to Zoologischer Garten. A wide variety of artists play at this basement jazz venue; T and W are always a mere DM5, so students fill the club in the middle of the week. On weekends, cover depends on performance. Concert tickets available from 5pm or at Kant-Kasse ticket service (☎313 45 54). Club open every Tu, W, F, Sa from 9pm; other days occasionally.

A-Trane, Bleibtreustr. 1 (☎313 25 50). S3, S5, S7, S75, or S9 to Savignyplatz. With a name (partially) inspired by John Coltrane, this club makes an effort to bring quality performers. Cover DM10-20 (usually about DM15 on weekends); student discount usually DM5. Club open daily 10pm; closes at 2am weekdays, later on weekends.

SCHÖNEBERG

Metropol, Nollendorfpl. 5 (☎217 36 80). U1, U15, U2, or U4 to Nollendorfplatz, or night buses #N5, N19, N26, N48, N52, or N75. 650,000 watts of light! 35,800 watts of sound! Berlin's largest disco! Lately, the Metropol hosts the events of the former *Kit Kat Club,* taking on the combined name of **Kit Kat @ Metropol.** Cover F-Sa DM15. Open M-F 11am-3pm and 3:30-6pm.

Slumberland, Winterfeldtpl. U1, U2, U4, U12, or U15 to Nollendorfplatz. This cafe/bar boasts African motifs, complete with artwork, palm trees, and the crowning glory: sand for a floor! Head on in and listen to contemporary R&B as well as Bob Marley. Open Su-F 5pm-4am, Sa 11am-4am.

Café Bilderbuch, Akazienstr. 28 (☎78 70 60 57). U7 to Eisenacherstr. Chill on the plush sofas with the sophisticated over-30 crowd while sipping a fruity *Berliner Weiße mit Schuß* DM4.50. Open M-Sa 9am-2am, Su 10am-2am.

KREUZBERG

⬛ S036, Oranienstr. 190 (☎61 40 13 06). U1, U12, or U15 to Görlitzer Bahnhof or night bus #N29 to Heinrichplatz. Berlin's *truly* mixed club, with hip heteros, gays, and lesbians grooving to a mish-mash of wild genres. Cover varies. Open daily after 11pm.

KitKat Club, Glogauerstr. 2 (☎611 38 33). U1, U12, or U15 to Görlitzer Bahnhof or night bus #N29. People with varying degrees of clothing, some copulating, some just digging the cool trance music in the jaw-dropping fluorescent interior, leave their inhibitions outside. 4 primarily gay-lesbian events, including, on Thursdays, the cross-dressed **Fuck-Naked Sex Party** (men only!). Cover DM10-20. Open W-Su after 11pm. **After-hours party** (Su 8am-7pm) is popular, free, and more fully clothed.

Ex, Mehringhof, Gneisenaustr. 2a (☎693 58 00). U6 or U7 to Mehringdamm or night bus #N4, N19, or N76. A bar, performance space, and club run by a leftist collective in a steel and concrete courtyard. Also a site for political meetings and (primarily) lesbian events, as well as an anarchist bookstore. Open Tu-F 3pm-late, Sa-Su till late.

ORANIENBURGER STRAßE-MITTE

Tresor/Globus, Leipzigerstr. 126a (☎229 06 11). U2 or S1, S2, or S25 or night bus #N5, N29 or N52 to Potsdamer Platz. Packed from wall to wall with enthusiastic ravers. Cover W DM5, F DM10, Sa DM15-20. Open W and F-Sa 11pm-6am.

Roter Salon, Rosa-Luxemburg-Pl. (☎30 87 48 02). U2 to Rosa-Luxemburg-Platz. The club is notable because it doesn't play any electronica...well, almost none. M drum 'n bass, Tu salsa, W tango, F-Sa vary, Su happy 60s tunes. Cover DM7-12.

b-flat, Rosenthalerstr. 13. (☎283 31 23). U8 to Rosenthalerplatz. Acoustic music and jazz in a relaxed atmosphere. Cover varies; frequent student discounts of DM3-5. Open daily from 8pm; Happy Hour 9-10pm, blue hour 1-2am.

Hackesche Höfe, Rosenthalerstr. 40-41. S3, S5, S7, S75, or S9 to Hackescher Markt. The Hackesche Höfe is a series of interconnected courtyards containing restaurants, cafes, clubs, galleries, shops, apartments, and a movie theater. The low-key **Oxymoron** club (☎28 39 18 85) offers daily jazz concerts to a thirtysomething crowd. Concerts DM15-20. Open M and W-Sa after 11pm, Tu after 8:30pm, Su after 10pm.

PRENZLAUER BERG AND FRIEDRICHSHAIN

KulturBrauerei, Knaackstr. 97 (☎44 05 67 56). U2 to Eberswalderstr. This small village of *kultur* houses numerous different stages and dance floors. The venues include everything from hard-core *Ostrock* and disco to techno, and reggae. Open Tu and Th-Su after 10pm. Cover DM3-5.

Knaack, Greifwalderstr. 224 (☎442 70 61). This club does billiards and beer, but that's not why it's important. One of the few places to hear indie rock in Berlin.

Euphoria, Grünbergerstr. 60 (☎29 00 46 83), on the corner of Simon-Dachstr. This bright orange hotspot serves what are perhaps the best mixed drinks in Berlin. Happy Hour 4-6pm—all drinks half price. Open Su-Th 10am-midnight, F-Sa 10am-1am.

TREPTOW

■ **Insel der Jugend,** Alt-Treptow 6 (☎53 60 80 20). S4, S6, S8, or S9 to Treptower Park, then bus #166, 167, or 265 or night bus #N65 to Alt-Treptow. *Insel der Jugend* (island of youth) is located in the Spree River. Its 3 fiercely decorated floors of dancing have the feel of a fishbowl with fluorescent silver foil and netting. Cover Th-Sa DM5-15. Open W after 7pm, Th after 9pm, F-Sa after 10pm.

THE LOVE PARADE Every year during the second weekend in July, the Love Parade brings Berlin to its knees—its trains run late, its streets fill with litter, and its otherwise patriotic populace scrambles to the countryside in the wake of a wave of West German teenagers dying their hair, dropping ecstasy, and getting down *alles zusammen* (all together). What started in 1988 as a DJ's birthday party with only 150 people has mutated into an annual techno Woodstock, the world's only 1.5 million-man rave, and a massive corporate event. A huge "parade" takes place on Saturday afternoon, involving a snail-paced procession of tractor-trailers loaded with blasting speakers and topped by gyrating bodies that slowly works it from Ernst-Reuter-Platz to the Brandenburg Gate. The city-wide party turns the Straße des 17. Juni into a riotous dance floor, and the Tiergarten into a garden of original—and sometimes quite creative—sin. To celebrate the licentious atmosphere, the BVG offers a "No-Limit-Ticket," useful for getting around from venue to venue during the weekend's **54hr. of nonstop partying** (DM10, condom included). Keep an ear out for updates on the 2001 event; although past Love Parades have been held in the Tiergarten, the authorities might move it after environmentalists raised concerns about the 750,000 liters of urine (and undetermined amounts of other bodily fluids) which the park must absorb every year. Check out the official website (www.loveparade.de) for the latest news.

GAY AND LESBIAN NIGHTLIFE

Berlin is one of the most gay-friendly cities on the continent. Traditionally, the social nexus of gay and lesbian life has centered around **Nollendorfplatz** and the surrounding **"Schwuler Kiez"** (gay neighborhood) of Schöneberg. The city's reputation for tolerance was marred by the Nazi persecutions of the 1930s and 40s, when thousands of gay and lesbian Berliners were deported to concentration camps. A marble pink triangle plaque outside the Nollendorfplatz U-Bahn station honors their memory. The gay information center **Mann-o-Meter,** Motzstr. 5, off Nollendorfplatz, gives out information on nightlife, political activism, and gay-friendly living arrangements (☎216 80 08; DM30-75 a night). For up-to-date events listings, pick up a copy of the amazingly comprehensive *Siegessäule* (free), named after one of Berlin's most prominent phallic monuments. The second half of June is the high point of the annual queer calendar of events, culminating in the ecstatic, champagne-soaked floats of the **Christopher Street Day (CSD)** parade, a six-hour long street party drawing more than 250,000 revelers.

Omnes, Motzstr. 8 (☎23 63 83 00). U1, U15, U2, or U4 to Nollendorfplatz. A mainly male gay bar, its hrs. accommodate early-morning revelers. Weekly specials DM6-20, pasta DM7-10. Open M-F from 8am, Sa and Su from 5am.

Scheune, Motzstr. 25 (☎213 85 80). U1, U15, U2, or U4 to Nollendorfplatz. Ring the bell to enter. Men only. Mostly techno. Open Su-Th 9pm-7am, F and Sa 9pm-9am.

Café Berio, Maaßenstr. 7 (☎216 19 46). U1, U15, U2, or U4 to Nollendorfplatz. Perfect for an early evening drink. Outdoor seating in summer. Open daily 8am-1am.

Rose's, Oranienstr. 187 (☎615 65 70). Mixed gay and lesbian clientele kicks it amidst flashing red lights and glitter. Lots of glitter. Open daily 10pm-6am.

Schoko-Café, Mariannenstr. 6 (☎615 15 61). Lesbian central; a cafe with a cultural center upstairs, billiards, and dancing every second Saturday of the month (10pm). Open M-Th and Su 5pm-1am year-round, plus F-Sa from noon in the summer.

⚑ DAYTRIPS FROM BERLIN

POTSDAM

S7 runs to Potsdam-Stadt (in Zone C; see Public Transportation, p. 404) from Berlin's Bahnhof Zoo (30min., DM4.20), and hourly trains arrive from Leipzig (2hr., DM46).

Visitors disappointed by Berlin's gritty, distinctly unroyal demeanor could do no better than to head to nearby Potsdam, the glittering city of Frederick II (the Great). From 1921 through WWII, Potsdam served as Germany's "Little Hollywood," and in 1945 the Allies divided up Germany at the Potsdam Conference. The 600-acre **Park Sanssouci,** with countless marble fountains, exotic pavilions, and Baroque castles, stands as a monument to Frederick the Great's (not necessarily matching) aesthetic tastes. A **day ticket** gives you access to all of the park's four castles (DM20, students DM15). At one end of the long **Hauptallee** (central path) stands the park's main attraction, the Versailles-esque **Schloß Sanssouci,** where Frederick escaped his wife and drowned his sorrows. (☎ (0331) 969 41 90. Open Apr.-Oct. Tu-Su 9am-5pm; Nov.-Mar. Tu-Su 9am-4pm. DM10, students DM5, free with day ticket.) At the opposite end of the park is the largest of the four castles, the 200-room **Neues Palais,** built by Frederick to demonstrate Prussia's power (oh, and to house his guests). Its *Grottensaal* (reception room) glitters with seashells. (☎ (0331) 969 42 55. Open Apr.-Oct. Su-Th 9am-5pm; Nov.-Mar. Su-Th 9am-4pm. DM6, students DM4.) The most exotic of the park's pavilions is the gilded **Chinesisches Teehaus,** complete with a parasol-toting Buddha on the roof (DM2). Potsdam's second park, the **Neuer Garten,** contains several former royal residences. Built in the style of an English country manor, **Schloß Cecilienhof** hosted the signatories of the 1945 Potsdam Treaty. To get there, take **bus** #694 to Cecilienhof or streetcar #92 to Alleestr. (☎ (0331)

969 42 44. Open Tu-Su 9am-noon and 12:30-5pm. DM6, with tour DM8, students DM4.) The **tourist office,** Friedrich-Ebert-Str. 5, between the Alter Markt and Pl. der Einheit streetcar stops, books rooms (DM20-40 per person) for a DM5 fee. (☎ (0331) 27 55 80e. Open Apr.-Oct. M-F 9am-6pm, Sa 10am-4pm, Su 10am-2pm; Nov.-Mar. M-F 10am-6pm, Sa-Su 10am-2pm.)

OTHER DAYTRIPS FROM BERLIN

DRESDEN. Go to see spectacular ruins, world-class museums, and gloriously reconstructed palaces and churches (see p. 426).

LEIPZIG. Two hours on a train will take you to Leipzig, where people get their groove on in the depths of medieval tunnels (see p. 432).

EASTERN GERMANY

Saxony (Sachsen) is known primarily for Dresden and Leipzig, but the entire region offers a fascinating historical and cultural diversity that reveals a great deal about life in the former East. West of Saxony, Thuringia *(Thüringen),* the "Green Heart of Germany," is a hilly and mostly pastoral land. Echoes of Thuringia are heard throughout Europe's cultural canon: Bach, Goethe, Schiller, Luther, and Wagner all left their mark on this landscape, arguably the most beautiful in Germany. North of Thuringia and Saxony, Saxony-Anhalt's *(Sachsen-Anhalt)* endless grass plains offer one of the region's more tranquil landscapes. Its high unemployment rate mirrors the economic woes of Eastern Germany as a whole, but many construction sites mushrooming across the *Land* point toward the future.

DRESDEN ☎0351

Dresden (pop. 500,000) pulses with an intensity that is both vicious and sublime. The city was one of the cultural capitals of pre-war Germany; sadly, reminders linger of the Allied bombings which claimed over 50,000 lives and destroyed 75% of the city center. Dresden today engages visitors with spectacular ruins amid world-class museums and partially reconstructed palaces and churches, a dynamic metropolis propelled by a history of cultural turbulence.

▐ TRANSPORTATION

Trains: From the **Dresden Hauptbahnhof,** on Wienerplatz (☎ (0180) 599 66 33), trains run to: **Berlin** (2hr., 15 per day, DM52); **Frankfurt** (6hr., 14 per day, DM136); **Leipzig** (1½hr., 34 per day, DM33); **Munich** (8hr., 24 per day, DM148); **Budapest** (11hr., 4 per day, DM125); and **Prague** (3hr., 12 per day, DM38). **Bahnhof Dresden Neustadt** sits across the Elbe, sending trains primarily to other cities in Eastern Germany.

Public Transportation: Dresden is sprawling—even for short visits, familiarize yourself with the transport lines. **Single-ride** DM2.90; 4 or fewer stops DM1.80. **Day pass** DM8; **weekly pass** DM25, students DM19. Most major lines run every hr. after midnight. Dresden's **S-Bahn** network reaches from Meißen (DM7.70) to Schöna by the Czech border (DM7.70). Buy tickets from *Automaten* in the *Hauptbahnhof* and validate them in the red contraptions as you board; insert the ticket and press *hard.*

Hitchhiking: *Let's Go* does not recommend hitchhiking. Hitchers stand by Autobahn signs at on-ramps. To **Berlin:** streetcar #3 or 13 to Liststr., then bus #81 to Olter. To **Prague** or **Frankfurt:** bus #72 or 88 to Luga, or bus #76, 85, or 87 to Lockwitz.

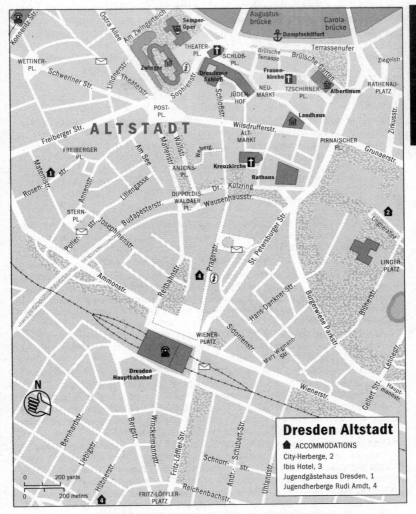

Dresden Altstadt

🏠 ACCOMMODATIONS

City-Herberge, 2
Ibis Hotel, 3
Jugendgästehaus Dresden, 1
Jugendherberge Rudi Arndt, 4

■ 🔁 ORIENTATION AND PRACTICAL INFORMATION

Dresden is bisected by the Elbe. The **Altstadt** lies on the same side as the Haupt-bahnhof; **Neustadt,** to the north, escaped most of the bombing, paradoxically making it one of the oldest parts of the city. Many of Dresden's main attractions are centered between the **Altmarkt** and the **Elbe,** 5min. from the Neustadt.

Tourist Office: Two locations: **Pragerstr.,** across from the Hauptbahnhof (☎49 19 20), and **Theaterpl.** in the Schinkelwache, in front of the Semper-Oper. Sells the **Dresden Card,** which provides 48hr. of public transit and free or reduced entry at many museums (DM26). Both open M-F 10am-6pm, Sa-Su 10am-2pm.

Currency Exchange: ReiseBank, in the train station. 2.5-4.5% commission, depending on amount; DM7.50 for traveler's checks. Open M-F 7:30am-7:30pm, Sa 8am-noon and 12:30-4pm, Su 9am-1pm. A self-service machine is open after hours.

American Express: Hoyerswerdaerstr. 20 (☎80 70 30), in the Neustadt near Rosa-Lux-emburg-Pl. Money sent and mail held. Open M-F 7:30am-6pm.

Luggage Storage: At both train stations. Lockers DM2-4. Storage DM4 per piece per 24hr. Open M-F 6am-10pm, Sa 6am-9pm.

Laundromat: Groove Station, Katharinenstr. 11-13. Wash, dry, and cup of coffee DM8; meanwhile, browse leather, tattoos, or piercings. Open Su-F 11am-2am, Sa 10am-late.

Emergency: Police, ☎ 110. Ambulance and Fire, ☎ 112.

Pharmacy: Apotheke Prager Straße, Pragerstr. 3 (☎425 08). Open M-F 8:30am-7pm, Sa 8:30am-4pm. After hours, a sign indicates the nearest open pharmacies.

Internet Access: Upd@te, Louisenstr. 30, near Die Boofe (see Accommodations, below). DM10 per hr. Open M-F noon-8pm, Sa noon-2pm.

Post Office: Hauptpostamt, Königsbrückerstr. 21/29 (☎819 13 70), in Neustadt. Open M-F 8am-7pm, Sa 8am-1pm. **Postamt 72,** St. Petersburgerstr. 26, is near the tourist office. Open M-F 8:30am-8pm, Sa 8:30am-noon. Address mail to be held: *Post-lagernde Briefe* für Katie DAVIDS, Hauptpostamt, D-01099 Dresden, Germany.

◤ ACCOMMODATIONS

New hotels and hostels are constantly being planned, built, and opened in Dresden, but come the weekend, it's hard to find anything with a good location. You can find deals at some of the hotels on Pragerstr. The tourist office can facilitate stays in private rooms and provide information on other accommodation options.

Mondpalast Backpacker, Katharinenstr. 11-13 (☎804 60 61). From Bahnhof Neustadt, walk down Antonstr. and turn left onto Königsbrückerstr.; cross the street and turn right on Katharinenstr. (10min.). By backpackers for backpackers, it's the hippest place in town. Internet DM12 per hr. Breakfast DM8. Sheets DM5. Call ahead. Dorms DM25-DM27; doubles DM62.

Hostel Die Boofe, Louisenstr. 20 (☎801 33 61). This new hostel offers immaculate rooms and cushy beds. Bike rental DM10. Breakfast DM8. Sheets DM5. Reserve ahead. Dorms DM27; doubles DM79 with sheets and breakfast.

Jugendherberge Dresden Rudi Arndt (HI), Hübnerstr. 11 (☎471 06 67). Streetcar #5 (dir.: Südvorstadt) or #3 (dir.: Plauen) to Nürnberger Platz. Continue down Nürnbergerstr. and turn right onto Hübnerstr.; the hostel is on the right. Or, from Haupt-bahnhof, walk down Fritz-Löffler-Str., bear right onto Münchenerstr., turn right on Eisenstuckstr. and walk two blocks. Sheets DM5. Check-in 3pm-1am. Curfew 1am. Reservations recommended. DM30, under 27 DM25. HI members only.

Jugendgästehaus Dresden (HI), Maternistr. 22 (☎ 49 26 20). Exit the Hauptbahnhof at Pragerstr. and turn left, following Ammonstr. to Freibergerstr.; turn right and right again onto Maternistr. Breakfast and sheets included. Check-in after 4pm. Check-out 9:30am. Rooms with sinks DM38 per person, with shower DM45; singles DM15 extra.

Ibis Hotel (☎48 56 66 61), Pragerstr. Three hotel skyscrapers on Pragerstr., across the street from the Hauptbahnhof, offer summer same-day specials good for people traveling in pairs. Doubles May-June and Sept.-Oct. DM130; DM110 at all other times.

Campingplatz Altfranken, Otto-Harzer-Str. 2 (☎410 24 00). From the Hauptbahnhof, take streetcar #17 to Tharandterstr., then bus #90 to Altfranken. DM10 per tent.

◖ FOOD

Unfortunately, the surge in Dresden tourism has raised food prices, particularly in the *Altstadt*. The cheapest eats are at **supermarkets** or **Imbiß stands** along **Pragerstr.** Most restaurants in the *Altstadt* cater almost exclusively to tourists; those in search of authenticity will probably prefer something outside the city center. The **Neustadt,** between Albertpl. and Alaunpl., spawns a new bar every few weeks and rules the roost of quirky ethnic and student-friendly restaurants.

El Perro Borracho, Alaunstr. 70 (☎803 67 23). A tiny sparkle of Spain. All main courses DM12. Open M-F 11:30am-1am, Sa-Su 10am-1am.

Blumenau, Louisenstr. 67 (☎802 65 02). One of the most popular restaurants in the Neustadt, this place offers a friendly environment perfect for Milchkaffee (milk coffee) in the mornings, and a nice spot for an evening drink. One of the cheapest restaurants in Dresden. Open daily 10am-3am.

Raskolnikoff, Böhmischestr. 34 (☎804 57 06), serves up savory Russian and Afghan fare to a local crowd in a cozy dining room. Open daily 10am-2am.

Café Aha, Kreuzstr. 7 (☎492 33 79), is across the street from the Kreuzkirche. The restuarant celebrates healthy food. Open daily 10am-midnight.

☉ SIGHTS

Consider buying the **Tageskarte** (DM12, students and seniors DM7), which covers one-day admission to the Albertinum museums, the Schloß, most of the Zwinger, and a number of other sights. The **Dresden Card** also includes free or reduced entrance to many of the major museums and is sold at the tourist office (see p. 427).

ZWINGER. The extravagant collection of Friedrich August I (the Strong), Prince Elector of Saxony and King of Poland, is housed in the magnificent **Zwinger** palace, designed by August's senior architect, Matthäus Daniel Pöppelmann, and championed as a triumph of Baroque design. The palace narrowly escaped destruction in the 1945 bombings; workers are busy restoring it to aesthetic perfection. In the Semper wing is the **Gemäldegalerie Alte Meister,** a world-class collection of paintings from 1400-1800. *(Open Tu-Su 10am-6pm. DM7, students DM4. Tours F and Su at 4pm. DM1.)* Across from the gallery is the **Rüstkammer,** a collection of courtly toys. *(Same hours as Gemäldegalerie. DM3, students DM2; covered by admission to Gemäldegalerie.)*

SEMPER-OPER. This famed opera house reverberates with the same glorious luxury as the northern wing of the Zwinger. A painstaking restoration has made this one of Dresden's major attractions. *(Theaterplatz 2. DM9, students DM6. Almost daily tours; check times at the main entrance.)*

DRESDENER SCHLOß. Across from the Zwinger, the residence of Sachsen's Electors and emperors is nearly restored from the 1945 bombings. The 100-meter-tall **Hausmannsturm** exhibits photographs and texts (available in English) discussing the bombings; the top floor offers a 360° view of the city. *(Open Apr.-Oct. Tu-Su 10am-6pm. DM5, students and seniors DM3.)* The **Katholische Hofkirche** (Catholic royal church) used to be connected to the Schloß. The back right corner shelters an altar dedicated to bombing victims. *(Open M-Th 9am-5pm, F 1-5pm, Sa 10:30am-4pm, Su noon-4pm. Free.)* If you've been mistaking Friedrich the Earnest for Friedrich the Pugnacious, stop by the **Fürstenzug** (Procession of Electors) along Augustusstr., a mural (102m) made of 24,000 Meißen china tiles, depicting the Saxon rulers from 1123 to 1904. On the Elbe, the **Brühlsche Terrasse** offers prime photo opportunities.

KREUZKIRCHE. After being destroyed four times, the Kreuzkirche's interior remains in a damaged state, with rough plaster columns and half-headed cherubs serving as powerful reminders of the war's destruction. The tower offers a bird's eye view of downtown Dresden. *(An der Kreuzkirche 6. Open in summer M-Tu and Th-F 10am-5:30pm, W and Sa 10am-4:30pm, Su noon-4:30pm; in winter M-F 10am-4:30pm, Sa 10am-3:30pm, Su noon-4:30pm. Free. Tower closes 30min. earlier. DM2, children DM1.)*

NEUSTADT. Across the magnificent **Augustusbrücke,** Hauptstr. is home to the **Goldener Reiter,** a gold-plated statue of August the Strong atop a steed in pompous glory. August's nickname was reputedly a homage to his remarkable virility; legend has it he fathered 365 kids, though the official tally is 15. At the other end of Hauptstr., **Albertplatz** is the gateway to the Neustadt scene.

SCHLACHTHOFRINGE. The **Schlachthofringe** (Slaughterhouse Circle) is a 1910 housing complex in a more dismal part of Dresden, used during WWII as a P.O.W. camp. Neglected by the tourist industry, the buildings have been left to waste away. Novelist Kurt Vonnegut was imprisoned here during the bombing of Dresden, inspiring his masterpiece *Slaughterhouse Five.* *(Take bus #82 to Ostragehege.)*

ALBERTINUM. The Albertinum holds the ▨**Gemäldegalerie der Neuen Meister,** which combines an ensemble of German and French Impressionists with a collection of Expressionists and *Neue Sachlichkeit* modernist works, including Otto Dix's renowned "War" triptych. *(Open Su-W and F-Sa 10am-6pm. DM7, students and seniors DM4; includes entrance to Grünes Gewölbe, an assemblage of Saxon trifles, upstairs.)*

STADTMUSEUM. In the 18th-century **Landhaus,** the museum tells the story of the city since the 13th century. A colorful collection of 20th-century memorabilia completes the tale, from 1945 bomb shells to a collection of protest signs from the 1989 demonstrations. *(Wilsdrufferstr. 2, near Pirnaischer Platz. Open May-Sept. M-Tu, Th, and Sa-Su 10am-6pm, W 10am-8pm; Oct.-Apr. Sa-Th 10am-6pm. DM4, students DM2.)*

DEUTSCHES HYGIENEMUSEUM. This museum long celebrated the health and cleanliness of GDR citizens. Now that that Party's over, the rather bizarre collection ranges from an examination of the culture surrounding hair, a fetus in a glass block, and plenty of glass people with colorful innards. *(Lingnerpl. 1. ☎ 484 60. Open Tu and Th-F 9am-5pm, students and seniors DM3.)*

♫▨ ENTERTAINMENT AND NIGHTLIFE

For centuries, Dresden has been a focal point for theater, opera, and music. The superb **Semper-Oper** (☎ 491 17 30) premiered many of Strauss and Wagner's greatest, but tickets are hard to come by. Dresden's nightlife scene is young and dynamic; the **Neustadt,** roughly bounded by Königsbrückerstr., Bischofsweg, Kamenzerstr., and Albertpl., is its thudding heart. At last count over 50 bars packed the area; *Kneipen Surfer* lists all of them.

Scheune, Alaunstr. 36-40, is the granddaddy of the Neustadt scene; its eclectic dance floor specializes in world music. Cover varies. Club opens at 8pm. Bar open M-F 11am-2am, Sa-Su 10am-2am.

DownTown, Katharinenstr. 11-13, below the Mondpalast hostel, keeps the beat going, fast and furious, as Dresden's young and energetic scene grooves to techno. Cover DM7, students DM5. Open 10pm-5am.

Mona Lisa, Louisenstr., on the corner of Kamenzerstr., chills nightly to techno. Happy Hour 7-9pm. Open daily from 7pm.

AZ Conni, Rudolf-Leonhard-Str. 39 (☎804 58 58). From Albertpl. follow Königsbrückerstr. until the second set of traffic lights; turn left, walk under the first railway bridge, and take a quick right. Noisy bar and dance floor; also one of the main venues in Dresden for punk and hardcore. Cover varies. Open daily 9pm until late.

▧ DAYTRIP FROM DRESDEN

MEIßEN   ☎ 03521

Reach Meißen from Dresden by train (45min., DM7.70).

Meißen, 30km from Dresden, is another testament to the frivolity of August the Strong (see Neustadt, p. 429). In 1710, the Saxon elector contracted severe *Porzellankrankheit* (the porcelain "bug," still afflicting tourists today) and turned the city's defunct castle into a porcelain-manufacturing base. The factory was once more tightly guarded than KGB headquarters to prevent competitors from learning its techniques; today anyone can tour the **Staatliche Porzellan-Manufaktur,** Talstr. 9. Peruse finished products in the **Schauhalle** (DM9, students DM7); the real fun lies in the high-tech tour of the *Schauwerkstatt* (show workshop), which demonstrates the manufacturing process. (Open daily 9am-6pm. DM5. English tapes available.) Narrow, romantic alleyways climb to the **Albrechtsburg** castle and cathedral. (Open daily Mar.-Oct. 10am-6pm, Nov.-Feb. 10am-5pm. Last entry 30min. before closing. DM6, students DM43.) From the station, walk to Bahnhofstr., follow the Elbe to the Elbbrücke, cross it, continue to the Markt, and turn right onto Burgstr.; at the end, stairs lead to the right up to Albrechtsburg. Next door looms the **Meißener Dom,** a Gothic cathedral which satisfies visitors with four 13th-century statues by the Naumburg Master, a triptych by Cranach the Elder, and the metal grave coverings of the Wettins. (Open daily Apr.-Oct. 9am-6pm, Nov.-Mar. 10am-4pm. DM3.50, students DM2.50.) The **tourist office,** Markt 3, is across from the church, and finds private rooms (DM25-55) for a DM4 fee. (☎419 40. Open Apr.-Oct. M-F 10am-6:30pm, Sa-Su 10am-3pm; Nov.-Mar. M-F 10am-6pm, Sa 10am-3pm.) **Postal Code:** 01662.

SAXON SWITZERLAND

Formerly one of East Germany's most beloved holiday destinations, Saxon Switzerland *(Sächsische Schweiz)*—so dubbed because of its stunning, Swiss-like landscape—is now one of unified Germany's favorite national parks. Perched right on the Berlin-Dresden-Prague rail line, its sandstone cliffs, sumptuous summits, and breathtaking hikes (literally) should be reason enough to lure any lover of the outdoors off the tracks and into the hills for a few days.

▮ TRANSPORTATION. Dresden's S-Bahn (line 1, dir.: Schöna) runs from inside Dresden's Hauptbahnhof east along the Elbe River, stopping at Pirna, Wehlen, Rathen, Königstein, and Bad Schandau. **Wanderwege** (footpaths) wind up into the hills, connecting all the towns in a spidery web. The S-Bahn stops just across the river from **Wehlen** (hop on a short ferry to get to town; DM1.30), the point of origin of two hiking trails to **Rathen.** The first climbs up onto the most famous cliffs of the area, the Bastei, and was a favorite of August the Strong; the other is shorter and easier but much less impressive (45min.). To get to **Hohnstein,** either hike from Rathen (see below) or hop off the S-Bahn at Pirna and catch bus 236 or 237 from the Bahnhof to Hohnstein Markt (DM5.20). From **Bad Schandau** at the end of the line, cross the river by ferry (DM1.30) and hop on the S-Bahn back to **Dresden** (50min., every 30min., DM7.70) or continue by train to **Prague** (2hr., DM30.60).

RATHEN. Wehlen is the closest town to Dresden, but its best assets are really its trails to Rathen. One of the paths climbs up the cliffs of the Bastei while the other (shorter and easier) winds along the Elbe (45min.). **Rathen,** on the edge of **Sächsische Schweiz National Park,** hosts hiking trails of all lengths and difficulties. It's also home to the **Felsenbühne,** one of Europe's most beautiful open-air theaters, with stone pillars looming over the stage and 2000 seats carved into a cliff. Follow the signs from town; on the way you'll pass the **Theaterkasse,** where you can buy tickets. (☎ (035024) 77 70. DM6-39.) A **tourist office** upstairs in the *Gästeamt,* 10min. from the ferry, has hiking info. (☎/fax (035024) 704 22. Open in summer M-F 9am-noon and 2-6pm, Sa 9am-2pm; in winter closed Sa.) Sleep in a castle above the town at **Gästehaus Burg Altrathen.** (☎ (035024) 700 37. Singles DM40-45; doubles DM70-90.)

HOHNSTEIN. The small village of **Hohnstein** ("high stone" in old Sachsen), with grand forest vistas on all sides, is linked to Rathen by two hikes through one of the National Park's most stunning valleys, flanked by large sandstone boulders and magnificent rock formations. To get here from Rathen, facing the Gästeamt, take a left through the parking lot and follow the shorter (2hr.), more challenging path of the red stripe, or the longer (3hr.) path of the green stripe. On your way, be sure to stop at the Hockstein, an isolated outcropping of land which provides a spectacular view of the valley below. The town encircles the **Naturfreundehaus Burg Hohnstein,** Am Markt 1, a fortress which holds a history and nature museum, *Aussichtsturm* (lookout tower), and **hostel.** (☎ (035975) 812 02. Reception 7am-8pm. DM26-29, nonmembers DM33-37; add DM2 for stays shorter than 3 days.) Also housed in the Naturfreundehaus is the **Museum der Geschichte des Burg Hohnstein,** which covers the history of the Burg with exhibits of medieval armor, weapons, and anti-fascist resistance in Dresden and in Saxon Switzerland. (☎ (035975) 809 87. Open daily Apr.-Oct. 9am-5pm. DM2.) The **tourist office,** Rathausstr. 10, in the Rathaus, finds rooms for free and doles out info on trails and the Burg. (☎ (035975) 194 33; fax 868 10. Open M and W-F 9am-noon and 12:30-5pm, Tu 9am-noon and 12:30-6pm.)

KÖNIGSTEIN. Above the town of Königstein looms the fortress **Festung Königstein,** with huge walls built right into the same stone spires that made Saxon Switzerland famous. The unobstructed view from the fortress is worth sweating for—it's a 45min. struggle up from town. Replete with drawbridges and impenetrable stone walls, the fortress was later converted into a feared state prison. (Open daily Apr.-Sept. 9am-8pm; Oct. 9am-6pm; Nov.-Mar. 9am-5pm. DM7, students DM5.) The cheesy **Festungs Express** is another option for those tourists too tired to make the trek. (Every 30min., DM4.) The **tourist office,** Schreiberberg 2, two blocks uphill from the Festungs Express stop, books rooms and is host to the **post office.** (☎ (035021) 682 61; fax 688 87. Open Apr.-Oct. M-F 9am-noon and 2-6pm, Sa 9am-noon; Nov.-Mar. M-F 9am-noon and 3-5pm, Sa 9-10:30am.) Königstein's **Naturfreundehaus,** Halbestadt 13, is nicer and pricier than most hostels. (☎ (035022) 424 32. Reception 6am-10pm. DM40-70.) A cheaper but less convenient option is the hostel in the **Parkhotel Albrechtshof,** Papstdorferstr. 131, in the neary town of Gohrisch. (☎ (035021) 684 74. From Reißigerplatz take a 10min. ride on bus #244 to Parkplatz (every 30min., DM1.80.) Keep walking in the same direction and take the right fork when the road splits. (Dorms DM29.) The **campground,** in the shadow of the fortress, is on the banks of the Elbe 10min. upstream from the station. (☎ (035021) 682 24. DM7.30 per person, DM6 per tent.) **Schräger's Gasthaus,** on Kirchgasse, has antlers on the wall and hearty plates (DM8-10) on the table. If quenching your thirst is the priority, check out **Bogart's,** frequented by locals and vacationers alike for *fußball* and beer, down the street from Reißigerplatz on Beilatalstr.

BAD SCHANDAU. The largest town in Saxon Switzerland, Bad Schandau serves as the region's transportation hub. The solar-powered **Kirnitzschtalbahn train** (May-Oct., every 30min., DM6, roundtrip DM8) runs to the **Lichtenhain Waterfall,** not that impressive in itself, but a starting point for 3- to 4-hour hikes to the spectacular **Schrammsteine** mountains. Backpackers can also take advantage of the town's prime location, sandwiched between the two halves of the national park, for the myriad of hiking opportunities it offers. The **tourist office,** Markt 12, finds rooms. (Open M-F 9am-6:30pm, Sa 9am-4pm.) Bad Schandau is more of a family vacation spot than any other town in the area, and for this reason its hotels fill up quickly when the weather is good. The **Jugendherberge Bad Schandau** is a 30-min. walk down Rudolf-Sendigstr. along the Elbe and then to the left into the mountains along the difficult Wlfsgraben path. It is far from the center of town, but convenient to several trailheads and a good starting point for day-hikes. (HI members only. DM24.)

LEIPZIG
☎0341

Leipzig jumps out from the calm East German landscape in a fiery blaze of nowNowNOW. The *Uni-*culture, spawned by more than 20,000 students, creates an aura of youthful vitality as it did when Goethe, Nietzsche, and Leibniz stalked these ivory towers. This boom town just bursts with style as it charges through the transformations of the *neue Bundesländer,* resolutely resisting any threats made to the student-hipster vibe by self-serving capitalists and speculators.

⌐ TRANSPORTATION. Leipzig lies on the Berlin-Munich line, with InterCity service to Frankfurt. **Trains** zoom to Berlin (2-3hr., every hr., DM46); Dresden (1½hr., every hr., DM26); Frankfurt (5hr., every 2 hr., DM90); and Munich (7hr., every hr., DM113). It's a 10-minute walk from the train station at the north of the Innenstadt to **Augustusplatz,** the **Gewandhaus,** the university, and the main post office.

⚐ PRACTICAL INFORMATION. Much of what Leipzig offers to its guests is located in the ringed **Innenstadt,** but you'll have to leave the comforting sight of the huge, metal university tower for nightlife and any untouristed underground scenes. Walk across Willy-Brandt-Platz in front of the station and turn left at Richard-Wagner-Str. to reach the **tourist office,** Richard-Wagner-Str. 1. They book **private rooms** and rooms in *Pensionen* for free, and sell tickets. (☎710 42 60; fax 710 42 71; email lipsia@aol.com. Open M-F 8am-8pm, Sa 8am-4pm.) Among the gorgeous brochures, there's a useful free map of the center and suburbs with a street name index. Spin **laundry** at **Maga Pon,** Gottschedstr. 11—it doubles as a bar and restaurant. (☎960 79 22. Wash DM6, dry DM1. Open daily 9am-late.) Check **email** at **Café le bit,** Kohlgartenstr. 2, right off Friedrich-List-Platz. (☎998 20 00. First 30min. free; DM2 each additional 15min. Open M-F 8:30am-3am, Sa 10am-late, Su 10am-1am. The **post office** is located at Hauptpostamt 1, across from Augustuspl. (☎212 25 88. Open M-F 8am-8pm, Sa 9am-4pm.)

ACCOMMODATIONS AND FOOD. The development and renovation of the Innenstadt has provided a great new hangout, but it has also chased accommodations cheaper than DM100 a night out into the suburbs. The best alternative to the overcrowded hostel is a private room (from DM40 for a single and DM70 for a double) or a cheap *Pension*. Ask for help at the tourist office, or consult **Leipziger Allerlei,** a listing of all of the accommodations in town. The **Jugendherberge Leipzig Centrum (HI),** Volksgartenstr. 24, has 2- to 6-bed rooms in a six-floor building. Take streetcar 17, 37, or 57 (dir.: Thekla or Schönefeld) to Löbauerstr. Walk past the supermarket along Löbauerstr. and take a right onto Volksgartenstr. (☎245 70 11.

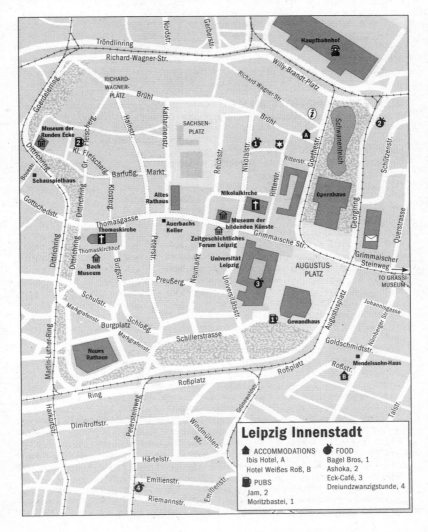

Leipzig Innenstadt

🏠 ACCOMMODATIONS
Ibis Hotel, A
Hotel Weißes Roß, B

🍴 FOOD
Bagel Bros, 1
Ashoka, 2
Eck-Café, 3
Dreiundzwanzigstunde, 4

🍺 PUBS
Jam, 2
Moritzbastei, 1

Breakfast included. Sheets DM6. Reception 2:30-11pm. Curfew 1am. DM24, over 26 DM29.) **Hotel Weißes Roß,** Roßstr. 20, is convenient. Take the streetcar to Augustusplatz, and walk down Roßpl. until it curves to the left. Go through the portal to the left; the hotel is 100m straight ahead. Reception M-F 2-8pm. Singles DM55-70; doubles DM95-110.) Rooms at **ETAP Hotel Leipzig,** Föpplstr. 7, are equipped with showers and TV. Take streetcar #17, 37, or 57 (dir.: Schönefeld or Thekla) to Löbauerstr., then bus 55 or 84 (dir.: Mockau-West) to Braunstr. (☎245 84 01. Breakfast DM8.90. Reception 6:30-10am and 5-8pm. Singles and doubles both DM54.) **Camping** at **Campingplatz Am Auensee,** Gustav-Esche-Str. 5, is an inexpensive solution to Leipzig's pricey accommodations. From the station, take streetcar #11 or 28 (dir.: Wahren) to Rathaus Wahren. Turn left at the Rathaus, and follow the twisting main road for 10min. (☎465 16 00. Reception M-Sa 6am-9:30pm, Su 6am-8:30pm. DM8 per person, DM5 per car, DM12 for caravans. Small tent-huts function as 2-bed bungalows. Small hut DM30, large hut with shower DM60.)

Budget meals are not as difficult to find in Leipzig as budget rooms. The Innenstadt is well-supplied with *Imbiß* stands, bistros, and restaurants for consumption on the go. **Ashoka,** Georgiring 8-9, to the right of the Hauptbahnhof, serves up excellent Indian food. (☎961 48 19. Lunch buffet DM14.90. Open M-F noon-3pm and 5pm-midnight, Sa-Su noon-midnight.) **Dreiundzwanzigstunden,** on corner of Emilienstr. and Petersteinweg, is a self-service restaurant that heaps on the German food at great prices. (Open daily 6am-5am.) A **Kaiser's supermarket** pops up on the Brühl, near Sachsenplatz. (Open M-F 7am-8pm, Sa 7am-4pm.)

⛨🎭 SIGHTS AND ENTERTAINMENT. Leipzig's historic **Innenstadt** suffered from both WWII bombings and from the poorly planned architectural creations of the post-war era. The heart of the city beats on at the **Marktplatz,** a colorful, cobblestoned square guarded by the slanted 16th-century **Altes Rathaus,** with its elegant **clock tower** showing four bright-blue faces. Inside, a grand festival hall runs above the **Stadtgeschichtliches Museum Leipzig,** which offers a straightforward look at Leipzig's history. (☎96 51 30. Open Tu 2-8pm, W-Su 10am-6pm. DM5, students DM2.50.) Just behind the Altes Rathaus at Grimmaischestr. 1-7 is the temporary home of the **Museum der Bildenden Künste Leipzig** (Museum of Fine Arts), which chronicles German art from the 18th century to the present. (Open Tu and Th-Su 10am-6pm, W 1-9:30pm. DM5, students DM2.50.) Head up Nikolaistr. to see the 800-year-old **Nikolaikirche,** which witnessed the birth of Bach's *Johannes Passion* as well as the GDR's peaceful revolution. (Open M-Sa 10am-6pm, Su after services. Free.) Backtrack down Nikolaistr. and turn right on Grimmaischestr., which turns into Thomasg., until you come upon the **Thomaskirche,** where Bach spent the last 27 years of his career. The **Thomascor,** one of Europe's most prestigious boys' choirs, performs here. (Open daily in summer 9am-6pm; off-season 9am-5pm. Performances F 6pm, Sa 3pm, and Su during services.) Just behind the Thomaskirche lies the **Johann-Sebastian-Bach-Museum,** Thomaskirchhof 16, which chronicles Bach's life in Leipzig from 1723-50. (Open daily 10am-5pm. DM4, students DM2.50.) Head back to Thomasg., turn left, then turn right on Dittrichring to reach Leipzig's most fascinating museum, the **Museum der "Runden Ecke,"** Dittrichring 24. Once the headquarters of the feared East German Ministry for State Security, the museum has a stunningly blunt exhibit on the history, doctrine, and tools of the secret police. On December 4, 1989, the people of Leipzig took over the *Stasi* building; inside, they found 50,000 letters seized over the last 40 years and entire floors devoted to documentation of the actions of suspected resistors. (Open W-Su 2-6pm. Free.)

Free magazines *Fritz* and *Blitz* fill you in on nightlife. **Barfußgäschen,** a street just off the Markt, serves as the see-and-be-seen bar venue for everyone from students to *schicki-micki*s (yuppies). **Markt Neun, Steel, Gohglmohsch** (whose cobblestones are covered in summer with outdoor seating from all sides), and **Spizz** fill up between 8 and 10pm and stay packed into the wee hours. Leipzig university students spent eight years excavating this series of medieval tunnels so they could get their groove on in **Moritzbastei,** Universitätsstr. 9. (☎702 59 13. Cover DM4-7 for discos. Open M-F after 10am, Sa after 2pm.) **Jam,** Große Fleischerg. 12, occupies the former *Stasi* headquarters. (☎961 74 32. Cover DM12-14.)

WEIMAR

☎ 03643

Little Weimar was declared Europe's cultural capital in 1999, and so in the months leading up to its big celebration the entire city was cleaned up. Its manicured surface still gleams, and Weimar remains one of the most completely renovated cities in East Germany; intellectual energy resonates through the former home of Goethe, Schiller, and Herder. While countless towns leap at any excuse to build a memorial to Goethe (Goethe slept here, Goethe went to school here, Goethe once asked for directions here), Weimar's **Goethehaus,** Frauenplan 1, is the real deal, where he entertained, wrote, studied, and died after 50 years in Weimar. (Open mid-Mar. to mid-Oct. Tu-Su 9am-7pm; mid-Oct. to mid-Mar. Tu-Su 9am-4pm. DM8, students DM5.) In February 2000, the opening of the new collection of the **Neues Museum Weimar** created a unique place to see modern art in Weimar. Upstairs, a serious exhibit of art from the GDR is offset by a comical set of faucets supposedly taken from great thinkers' sinks—Nietzche's faucets are marked "good" and "evil," instead of "hot" and "cold." (Open Tu-Su 10am-6pm. DM6, students DM3.) Between the Frauenplan and the Marktpl. is the beginning of **Schillerstraße,** a lively shop-lined pedestrian zone. **Schillers Wohnhaus** at #12, where the dramatist lived for the last three years of his life, today houses original drafts and chronicles his life. (Open mid-Mar. to mid-Oct. W-M 9am-7pm; mid-Oct. to mid-Mar. W-M 9am-4pm. DM5, students DM3.) A block down Hummelstr., Schiller and Goethe are joined in bronze before the **Deutsches Nationaltheater,** Am Palais, which first breathed life into their stage works and from which the Weimar Constitution also emerged in 1919. Opposite the theater is the **Bauhaus-Museum,** featuring works produced by the *Bauhaus* school of design and architecture, which originated in Weimar in 1919 before being ousted to Dessau (see p. 437). (Open Apr.-Oct. Tu-Su 10am-6pm; Nov.-Mar. 10am-4:30pm. DM5, students DM3.) The **Nietzsche-Archiv,** Humboldtstr. 36, is where the philosopher spent 1897-1900, the last three wacky years of his life. (Open mid-Mar. to mid-Oct. Tu-Su 1-6pm; mid-Oct. to mid-Mar. 1-4pm. DM4, students DM3.) On the far slopes of the Goethe-landscaped **Park an der Ilm,** on Corona-Schöfer-Str., is the poet's **Gartenhaus.** (Open mid-Mar. to mid-Oct. W-M 9am-7pm; mid-Oct. to mid-Mar. 9am-4pm. DM5, students DM2.50.)

Trains run to: Dresden (3hr., every hr., DM65); Eisenach (1hr., 3 per hr., DM19.40); Erfurt (15min., 4 per hr., DM7.60); Frankfurt (3hr., every hr., DM78); and Leipzig (1½hr., every 2hr., DM24.40). To reach Goethepl. from the station, head down Carl-August-Allee to Karl-Liebknecht-Str. (15min.); take a left down side streets for the Markt and Herderpl. The efficient **tourist office,** Marktstr. 10, in view of the Rathaus, books rooms for a DM5 fee and runs walking tours. (☎240 00; fax 24 00 40. Open Apr.-Oct. M-F 9:30am-7pm, Sa 9:30am-5pm, Su 9:30am-4pm; Nov.-Mar. M-F 10am-6pm, Sa-Su 10am-2pm. Tours daily 11am and 2pm. DM12, students DM8.) To get from Goethepl. to the student-run **Jugendhotel Hababusch,** Geleitstr. 4, follow Geleit-str. around the sharp right to the entrance tucked in behind the statue on your left. (☎85 07 37; email yh@uni-weimar.de. Key deposit DM20. Shared bedroom DM15; doubles DM40.) The **Jugendherberge Germania (HI),** Carl-August-Allee 13, is 2min. straight downhill from the station. (☎85 04 90. Sheets DM7. Lockout 10am-2pm. DM30, under 27 DM25.) For a nice dinner, look around the **Theaterpl.** Forage for food at **Rewe supermarket,** on Theaterpl., in the basement of the *Handelhaus zu Weimar.* (Open M-F 7am-8pm, Sa 7am-4pm.) **Postal Code:** 99423.

🔁 DAYTRIP FROM WEIMAR: BUCHENWALD. Two hundred fifty thousand Jews, Gypsies, homosexuals, Communists, and political prisoners were imprisoned and murdered by the Nazis at the labor camp of Buchenwald during WWII, now the **Nationale Mahnmal und Gedenkstätte Buchenwald** memorial. Many Jews were sent here, but after 1942, most were deported to Auschwitz; the camp mostly served to detain and murder political enemies of Nazism and prisoners of war. After "liberation," Soviet authorities then used the site from 1945 to 1950 as an internment camp for more than 28,000 Germans, mostly Nazi war criminals and opponents of the Communist regime; an exhibit detailing the Soviet abuses opened in 1997. A museum at the **KZ-Lager,** the remnants of the camp, documents the history of

Buchenwald (1937-45) and the general history of Nazism. On the other side of the hilltop from the KZ-Lager are the GDR-designed **Mahnmal** (memorial) and **Glocken-turm** (bell tower). A path leads through the woods, emerging at a two-way fork in the road. Head right, past the parking lot and bus stop, and continue as the street curves left (20min.). Catch **bus** #6 from Weimar's train station or Goethepl.—check the schedule carefully, as some #6 buses go to Ettersburg instead. (M-F every hr., Sa-Su every 2hr.). On your way back to Weimar, catch the bus by the parking lot near the Glockenturm. There is an **information center** near the bus stop at Buchen-wald. (Open May-Sept. Tu-Su 9:45am-5:15pm; Oct.-Apr. 8:45am-4:15pm.)

ERFURT   ☎ 0361

The capital of Thüringen, Erfurt has been renovated more thoroughly and inge-niously than most towns and cities of the former East Germany. The mammoth Gothic **Mariendom,** up on **Domhügel** hill, dominates the view from the marketplace. Martin Luther was invested as a priest here and interrupted his first mass by hurling his Bible across the altar, claiming his target was the Devil himself, which impressed his audience if not the Bishop. (Open May-Oct. M-F 9-11:30am and 12:30-5pm, Sa 9-11:30am and 12:30-4:30pm, Su 2-4pm; Nov.-Apr. M-F 10-11:30am and 12:30-4pm, Su 2-4pm. Free.) From the Dompl., Marktstr. leads down to the **Fis-chmarkt,** bordered by restored guild houses sporting wildly decorated facades. The collection of myth-depicting paintings in the neo-Gothic **Rathaus,** Fischmarkt 1, out-does those of most museums. (Open M and W-Th 7:30am-4pm, Tu 7:30am-6pm, F 7:30am-2pm, Sa-Su 10am-5pm. Free.) Farther down Markstr., the Gera River is spanned by the **Krämerbrücke,** a medieval bridge covered by small shops. From the far side of the bridge, follow Gotthardtstr. and cut left through Kircheng. to the **Augustinerkloster,** where Martin Luther spent 10 years as a Catholic priest and Augustine monk. He ultimately had the last laugh—it now functions as a Protestant college. (Tours Apr.-Oct. Tu-Sa every hr. 10am-noon and 2-4pm, Su from 11am; Nov.-Mar. Tu-Sa 10am, noon, and 2pm. DM5.50, students DM4.)

Trains chug to Dresden (3hr., every 2hr., DM64); Frankfurt (2½hr., every hr., DM72); Leipzig (2hr., 13 per day, DM32); and Weimar (15min., 4 per hr., DM7.60). Head straight down Bahnhofstr., where the train station is located, to reach the **Anger,** a wide pedestrian promenade, and then the Altstadt; cross the river on Schlößerstr. to get to the **tourist office,** Benediktspl. 1, which books rooms (DM25-50) for a DM5 fee. (☎ 664 00; fax 664 02 90. Open M-F 10am-7pm, Sa-Su 10am-4pm.) To get from the station to the **Jugendherberge Erfurt (HI),** Hochheimerstr. 12, take streetcar #5 (dir.: Steigerstr.) to the last stop, backtrack a little, turn left on Hochhe-imerstr.—the hostel is on the left corner at the first intersection. (☎ 562 67 05. Breakfast included. Sheets DM7. Reception 6-9am and 3-10pm. Curfew midnight. DM30, under 27 DM25.) **Rewe supermarket** is to the right as you exit the train station. (Open M-W 6am-7pm, Th-F 6am-8pm, Sa 7am-1pm.) **Postal Code:** 99084.

EISENACH   ☎ 03691

Birthplace of Johann Sebastian Bach and home-in-exile to Martin Luther, Eisenach boasts impressive humanist credentials. High above its half-timbered houses, the **Wartburg fortress** sheltered the excommunicated Luther (disguised as a noble named Junker Jörg) in 1521 while he worked on his landmark German translation of the Bible. (☎ 770 73. Open daily Mar.-Oct. 8:30am-5pm; Nov.-Feb. 9am-3:30pm. Mandatory tour DM11, students DM6.) By Luther's account, it took only the toss of an ink pot to ward off a visit from the Devil (amazing how often the two crossed paths; see Erfurt, p. 436). The **Bachhaus,** Frauenplan 21, is where Johann Sebastian stormed into the world in 1685. (☎ 793 40. Open Apr.-Sept. M noon-5:45pm, Tu-Su 9am-5:45pm; Oct.-Mar. M 1-4:45pm, Tu-Su 9am-4:45pm. DM5, students DM4.) The latticed **Lutherhaus,** Lutherpl. 8., is where young Martin lived. (☎ 298 30. Open daily Apr.-Oct. 9am-5pm; Nov.-Mar. 10am-5pm. DM5, students DM2.)

Frequent **trains** run to Erfurt (1hr., 3 per hr., DM14.80); Göttingen (2hr., every hr., DM35); Kassel (1½hr., every hr., DM27); and Weimar (1hr., 3 per hr., DM19.50). The **tourist office,** Markt 2, offers city tours (daily 2pm; DM5), and books rooms

(DM30-40) for free. From the station, walk on Bahnhofstr. through the tunnel, and bear left until you turn right on the pedestrian Karlstr. (☎67 02 60. Open M 10am-6pm, Sa-Su 10am-2pm.) Rest up at the **Jugendherberge Artur Becker (HI),** Mariental 24; from the station, take Bahnhofstr. to Wartburger Allee, which runs into Mariental, continue past the pond, and it will be on your right (35min.). Or take bus #3 (dir.: Mariental) to Lilienstr. (☎74 32 59. Breakfast included. Sheets DM7. Reception 4-9pm. Curfew 10pm. DM30, under 27 DM25.) **Gasthof Storchenturm,** Georgenstr. 43, fills a secluded courtyard next to a park with a restaurant, *Biergarten,* and several quiet rooms. (☎21 52 50. Breakfast DM7.50. Singles DM45; doubles DM70.) **Café Moritz,** Bahnhofstr. 7, fulfills your daily caloric intake with Thüinger specialities. (☎74 65 75. Open May-Oct. M-F 8am-9pm, Sa-Su 10am-9pm; Nov.-Apr. M-F 8am-7pm, Sa-Su 10am-7pm. Snacks from DM8.) For **groceries,** head to the **Edeka** on Johannispl. (Open M-F 7am-7pm, Sa 7am-2pm.) **Postal Code:** 99817.

WITTENBERG   ☎03491

The Protestant Reformation, which initiated centuries of religious conflict, began quietly in Wittenberg on October 13, 1517, when local professor and priest **Martin Luther** nailed his *95 Thesen* to the door of the Schloßkirche (see p. 392). All the major sights lie along **Collegienstr.** The **Lutherhalle** at #54 was Luther's home from 1508, and today houses a museum chronicling the history of the Reformation. (☎40 26 71. Open daily 9am-6pm. DM7, students DM4.) Turn right from the Lutherhalle and stroll down to Lutherstr. to behold the oak tree under which Luther defiantly burned a papal bull (a decree of excommunication, not a Catholic beast). Down the street is the **Schloßkirche,** crowned by a sumptuous Baroque cupola, which holds a copy of Luther's complaints. (Open May-Oct. M 2-5pm, Tu-Sa 10am-5pm, Su 11:30am-3:30pm; Nov.-Apr. M 2-4pm, Tu-Sa 10am-4pm, Su 11:30am-4pm. Free.) **Trains** arrive from Berlin (1½hr., every 2hr., DM39) and Leipzig (1hr., every 2hr., DM16). To get to the main pedestrian zone from the Hauptbahnhof, go straight out of the main building, or left from the bus stop, walk down the street and follow the curve to the right. Follow Collegienstr.; at the other end of the pedestrian zone is the **tourist office,** Schloßpl. 2, which provides maps and books rooms (DM25-75) for a DM3 fee. (☎49 86 10; fax 49 86 11. Open M-F 9:30am-5:30pm, Sa 10am-3pm, Su 11am-4pm.) Cross the street from the tourist office and walk straight into the castle's enclosure, then trek up the spiraling stairs to the right to reach the **Jugendherberge (HI),** housed in the castle. (☎40 32 55. Breakfast included. Sheets DM6. Reception 5-10pm. Reserve ahead. DM26, under 27 DM21.) **City-Kauf supermarket** is close to the tourist office. (Open M-F 7am-6:30pm, Sa 8am-12:30pm.) **Bosphorus,** Collegienstr. 64 (☎41 15 60), cooks up all the Turkish delights you could ever want. (Open M-Sa 9am-10pm, Su. 11am-10pm.) **Postal Code:** 06886.

DESSAU   ☎0340

Dessau, 30km west of Wittenberg, is worth a daytrip for those interested in the Bauhaus art school or in native son and musician Kurt Weill. After originating in Weimar in 1919, the Bauhaus school was based in Dessau from 1925 to 1932, when it moved to Berlin (and was soon after exiled by the Nazis in 1933). American skyscrapers were the high point of *Bauhaus,* the teachers of which were intrigued by the possibilities of glass and steel. Since 1977, the **Bauhaus,** Gropiusallee 38, has housed a design school for international architecture, and features works by *Bauhausmeisters* Gropius, Klee, and Kandinsky. From the station, turn left, go up the steps, head left over the tracks, then veer left on Kleiststr. and right on Bauhausstr. (☎650 82 51. Building open 24hr. Exhibition open Tu-Su 10am-5pm. Guided tours M-F 11am and 3pm; Sa and Su 11 am and 2pm. DM8, students DM6.) **Trains** arrive from: Berlin (2hr., every hr., DM33); Leipzig (1hr., every 2hr., DM15); and Wittenberg (35min., every 2hr., DM10). To reach the **tourist office,** Zerbsterstr. 2c, take streetcar #1 or 2 from the station to Hauptpost, walk behind the building with the huge Rathaus-Center signs, veer left on Ratsg., and take the 1st right. (☎204 14 42; fax 204 11 42. Open M-F 9am-7pm, Sa 9am-1pm. Nov.-Mar. M-F 9am-6pm, Sa 10am-1pm.) Dessau offers the unique opportunity to spend a night in the famous **Bauhaus school building.** (☎ 650 83 18. Singles DM30, doubles DM50.) The **Jugendherberge (HI),** Waldkaterweg 11, is a 25min. walk from the train station through suburban Dessau. Exit through the Westausgang of the station through the underground tunnel, and make a left onto Rathenaustr. At the end, follow Kühnauerstr. until you cross Kiefernweg. (☎ 61 94 52. Breakfast included. Sheets DM6. Reception M-F 8am-4pm, 7:30-9:30pm, Sa-Su 6-9pm. DM27, under 27 DM22.) The hip ▓**Klub im Bauhaus,** in the Bauhaus school basement, is a delightful place to indulge in angsty pretense over a light meal. (Open M-F 8am-midnight, Sa 10am-midnight, Su 10am-6pm.) **Postal Code:** 06844.

NORTHERN GERMANY

Although once a favored vacation spot for East Germans, Mecklenburg-Vorpommern, the northeasternmost portion of Germany, has unfortunately suffered in recent years from economic depression. Restoration work continues to reveal dramatic Hanseatic architecture throughout the *Land.* Just to the west, Schleswig-Holstein, which borders Denmark, has always been driven by its port towns. The region became a Prussian province in 1867 in the first step of Bismarck's unification, and chose after WWI to remain part of Germany, but the *Land* retains close cultural and commercial ties with Scandinavia. To the west, Bremen (along with Bremerhaven) constitutes Germany's smallest *Land.*

ROSTOCK   ☎ 0381

Construction workers are carefully removing the scaffolding that has covered the town of Rostock in recent years, revealing a new look that complements its economic rebirth. The 13th-century brick **Marienkirche** overlooks the renewal. (Open M-Sa 10am-5pm, Su 11am-noon. DM2 donation requested.) Wander along **Kröpeliner Straße,** Rostock's main pedestrian mall, and admire the restored buildings that reflect the city's past as a center of Hanseatic trade. **Trains** (☎ 493 44 54) connect several times a day to Berlin (2½hr., DM65); Dresden (7hr., DM118); Hamburg (3hr., DM76.20); Schwerin (1hr., every hr., DM22.20). **Ferries** leave for Scandinavia from the Überseehafen docks (TT-Linie and Scandlines Europa GT Links) and Warnemünde (DFO) docks. To get from the station to the **tourist office,** Neuer Markt 3, take streetcar #11 or 12 to Steintor; the office is in the same building as the post office. (☎ 194 33; fax 381 26 01. Open May-Sept. M-F 10am-7pm, Sa-Su 10am-4pm; Oct.-Apr. closes 5pm.) Explore the **internet** at **Surfing 'inn,** on the 3rd floor of the Galleria Kauphof on Langestr. (Open M-F 9am-8pm, Sa 9am-6pm. DM3 per 30min.) Both of Rostock's hostels are far from town and in somewhat dangerous neighborhoods, but the tourist office arranges private rooms (DM30-40) for free. To the boat-hostel **Jugendgästeschiff Rostock-Schmarl,** take the S-Bahn (dir.: Warnemünde) to Lütten Klein, then bus #35 (dir.: Schmarl Fähre; last bus 8pm) to the end of the line; follow the street to the end and board the *Traditionsschiff.* Past travelers have complained of harassment by aggressive hooligans on the way, but once inside the staff will make you feel at home. (☎ 71 62 24. DM34, under 27 DM27.50.) There's a **market** on Seinstr. (Open M-F 8am-5pm, Sa 8am-1pm.) The bakeries on **Kröpelinerstr.** sell sandwiches. **Postal Code:** 18055.

SCHWERIN   ☎ 0385

Schwerin is the grandfather of Mecklenburg-Vorpommern's cities, and with reunification, the city regained its status as capital of the *Land.* The Altstadt brims with well-preserved townhouses and remnants of its past life as an elegant spa town. A plethora of galleries and performance spaces host dozens of art festivals and concerts each year, but *haute couture* isn't all the city has to offer; it's not impossible to take in an opera and a rave in the same night. The **Schloß** is a ridiculous amalgamation of architectural styles on an island just south of the city center. Its gilded

Baroque cupolas runneth over with luxury. (Open Tu-Su 10am-6pm. DM8, students DM5.) Across from the Schloß, the **Alter Garten** was the site of mass demonstrations preceding the downfall of Communist East Germany in 1989. Atop the stairs on the right sits the **Staatliches Museum,** which houses a solid collection of 15th- to 19th-century Dutch and German works, including a few by Rembrandt, Cranach the Elder, and Rubens. (Open Tu 10am-8pm, W-Su 10am-6pm. DM7, students DM4.) Live bands keep the party going into the early morning at **Louis,** Wittenburgerstr. 50. (Open Th-Sa from 9pm.)

Trains run to: Lübeck (1½hr., every hr., DM20) and Rostock (1¼hr., every hr., DM22). To get from the station to the **tourist office,** Am Markt 1, go right on Grundthalpl., continue as it becomes Wismarschestr., then turn left on Arsenal, right on Mecklenburgstr., and left on Schmiedestr. (☎592 52 12; fax 55 50 94. Open M-F 10am-6pm, Sa-Su 10am-2pm.) To get to the **Jugendherberge (HI),** Waldschulweg 3, take bus #14 (dir.: Jugendherberge) to the end of the line and walk toward the zoo; it's on the left. (☎326 00 06. Sheets DM6. Reception 4-10pm. Curfew 10pm. DM30, under 27 DM25.) Satisfy your grocery needs at the **Edeka supermarket,** just off the Markt on Schmiedestr. (Open M-F 8am-8pm, Sa 8am-4pm.) **Postal Code:** 19053.

HAMBURG ☎040

With a fiercely activist population and a licentious, reckless sex industry, modern Hamburg is a crazy coupling of the progressive and the perverse. A proud tradition of autonomy dates back to 1618, when Hamburg gained the status of Free Imperial City, and the city today remains a politically autonomous *Land.* Restoration and riots determined the post-WWII landscape, but recently Hamburg, the largest port town in Germany, has become a harbor for lonesome sailors, contemporary artists, and revelling party-goers who absorb Germany's self-declared "capital of lust."

▐ TRANSPORTATION

Flights: Lufthansa (☎35 92 55) and **Air France** (☎50 75 24 59) fly to Hamburg. **Jasper shuttles** (☎227 10 60) make the trip from the Kirchenallee exit of the Hauptbahnhof to **Fuhlsbüttel Airport** (☎507 50; 25min., every 20min. daily 5am-9:20pm, DM8.50). Or take U1 or S1 to Ohlsdorf, then take an **express bus** to the airport (every 10min. daily 5:30am-11pm, DM3.90).

Trains: The **Hauptbahnhof,** on Glockengießerwall, handles connections to: **Berlin** (2¾hr., every hr., DM93); **Frankfurt** (3¾hr., every hr., DM191); **Hannover** (1½hr., 3 per hour, DM70); **Munich** (6hr., every hr., DM260); **Amsterdam** (5½hr., 3 per day, DM105); and **Copenhagen** (6hr., 3 per day, DM102). Open daily 5:30am-11pm. Most trains to and from **Schleswig-Holstein** stop only at **Altona** station, in the west of the city.

Buses: The **ZOB,** located across Steintorpl. from the Hauptbahnhof, runs buses to: **Berlin** (2½hrs., 8 per day, DM41); **Copenhagen** (6hr., 2 per day, DM63); and **Paris** (15hr., 1 per day, DM115). **Polenreisen** has good deals to **Poland.** Open M-F 9am-8pm, Sa 9:30am-1:30pm and 4-8pm, Su 4-8pm.

Ferries: DFDS Seaways, Van-der-Smissen-Str. 4 (☎389 03 71), about 1km west of the Fischmarkt (S1 or s3 to Königstr.), sets sail to **England** and **Ireland.** Overnight ferries run to **Harwich, England** (20hr.; every other day; DM208, in winter DM106, students 25% discount). Other destinations include **Copenhagen** and **Amsterdam.** Open M-F 10am-4:30pm; phone reservations M-F 9am-6pm, Sa 9am-2pm. Numerous companies offer harbor cruises, including **Käpitan Prüsse.** (☎31 31 30. Every 30 min., DM15.) **HADAG** offers more elaborate cruises of outlying areas from Pier 2. (☎311 70 70. Every 30 min. 9:30am-6pm.)

Public Transportation: HVV operates an efficient U-Bahn, S-Bahn, and bus network. Single tickets within the downtown area cost DM1.80. There are also 1- and 3-day tickets (DM9.50 and 23.30); consider buying a **Hamburg Card** instead (see p. 442). All tickets can be bought at orange *Automaten.*

Taxis: Taxiruf, ☎194 10.

Car Rental: Hertz has an office in the Hauptbahnhof's ReiseBank (see **Currency Exchange,** p. 442; ☎33 54 70). Rates start at DM400 per week.

Hamburg

■ ACCOMMODATIONS
Hotel Alt-Nürnberg, 23
Hotel Annerhof, 21
Hotel Terminus Garni, 22
Hotel Florida, 15
Instant Sleep, 5
Jugendherberge, 19
Schanzenstern Übernachtungs-
  und Gasthaus, 7

■ FOOD
Asia Imbiß Bok, 6
Falafel König, 4
Geo Pizza, 1
Machwitz, 3
Noodles, 9

■ NIGHTLIFE
Absolut, 14
Cave, 16
Cotton Club, 20
Frauenkneipe, 10
Große Freiheit 36/ Kaiser
  Keller, 12
Indra, 11
La Cage, 13
Logo, 2
Mojo Club, 18
Molotow, 17
Rote Flora, 8

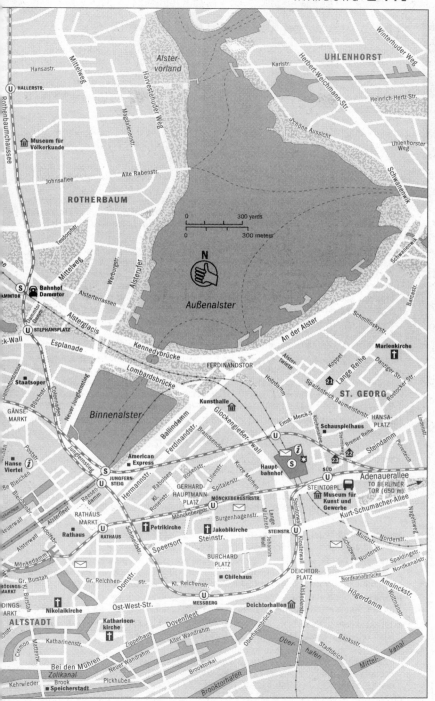

Hansastr.

Mittelweg

U HALLERSTR.

Rothenbaumchaussee

Museum für
Völkerkunde

Johnsallee

Alte Rabenstr.

ROTHERBAUM

Testorpfst.

Mittelweg

Warburgstr.

Alsterufer

Alsterterrassen

S Bahnhof
Dammtor

AMMTOR

Dammtor
Dammtor

U STEPHANSPLATZ

ck-Wall

Esplanade

Alsterglacis

Kennedybrücke

*Alster-
vorland*

Harvestehuder Weg

Magdalenenstr.

Karlstr.

UHLENHORST

Winterhuder Weg

Herbert-Weichmann-Str.

Heinrich-Hertz-Str.

Schöne Aussicht

Uhlenhorster
Weg

Schwanenwik

0   300 yards

0   300 meters

N

Außenalster

Schwanenwik

Barcastr.

Schmilinskystr.

An der Alster

*Alster-
twiete*

FERDINANDSTOR

Lombardsbrücke

Marienkirche

Koppel

Lange Reihe

Danziger Str.

ST. GEORG

Rostocker Str.

Spadenteich Baumeisterstr.

HANSA-
PLATZ

Lindenstr.

Staatsoper

ammorstrasse

Büschstr.

Colonaden

GÄNSE-
MARKT

Binnenalster

Neuer Jungfernstieg

Ballindamm

Ferdinandstr.

Brandstwiete

Glockengießer-Wall

Kunsthalle

Holzdamm

Ernst-Merck-S.

Kirchenallee

Schauspielhaus

Steinstr.

Bremer Reihe

Steindamm

Pulverteich

Hanse
Viertel

i

e Bleichen

Bleichen

Poststr.

Jungfernstieg

S JUNGFERN-
STIEG

Reesen-
damm

Hermannstr.

Rosenstr.

Kt.
Rosenstr.

Rabolsen

Lilienstr.

Kurze Mühren

Spitalerstr.

American
Express

Hauptbahnhof

S

i

SÜD
U

STEINTORPL.

Adenaueralle

TO BERLINER
TOR (650 m)

Kurt-Schumacher-Allee

Nagelswe.

Neuerwall

Alsterfleet

RATHAUS-
MARKT

Rathaus

RATHAUS

U

Schmalst.

GERHARD-
HAUPTMANN-
PLATZ

MÖNCKEBERGSTR.

Mönckebergstr.

U

Petrikirche

Jakobikirche

Burgenhagenstr.

Steinstr.

Lange Mühren

Johannis
Wall

STEINSTR.

Klosterwall

Museum für
Kunst und
Gewerbe

Steinweg

Spaldingstr.

Norderstr.

Nordkanalstr.

Mönckedamm

Gr. Burstah

Gr. Reichen- str.

Kt. Reichenstr.

Speersort

BURCHARD
PLATZ

Chilehaus

DEICHTOR-
PLATZ

Altländstr.

Nordkanalbrücke

Amsinckstr.

Högerdamm

Woltmannstr.

RÖDINGS-
ARKT

DINGS-
ARKT

ALTSTADT

Nikolaikirche

Ost-West-Str.

U

MESSBERG

Katharinen-
kirche

Deichtorhallen

Banksstr.

Cremon

Mattentwi.

Katharinenstr.

Zippelhaus

Dovenfleet

Alter Wandrahm

*Ober-
hafen*

Stadtdeich

Mittel

kanal

Bei den Mühren

Zollkanal

Brook

Neuer Wandrahm

Pickhuben

Brooktorkai

Obeibaumbrücke

Kehrwieder

Speicherstadt

Brooktorhafen

✦ 🛈 ORIENTATION AND PRACTICAL INFORMATION

Hamburg's fame as a North Sea port relies upon its huge harbor 100km inland, on the north bank of the **Elbe**. The city center, the **Altstadt**, sits between the river and the two city lakes, **Außenalster** and **Binnenalster**, formed by the confluence of the Alster and Bille with the Elbe. Most major sights lie between the **St. Pauli Landungs-brücken** port area in the west and the Hauptbahnhof in the east. Both the **Nordbahn-nhof** and **Südbahnhof** U-Bahn stations exit onto the Hauptbahnhof.

The **Hanseviertel** is a neighborhood thick with banks, shops, art galleries, and auction houses; window-shopping is an aesthetic pleasure, while the nearby shipping canals give the quarter a pseudo-Venetian charm. North of the downtown, the **university** community dominates the **Dammtor** area. To the west of the university, the **Sternschanze** neighborhood is a politically active community home to artists, squatters, and a sizeable Turkish population. The **Altona** district, with its own major train station, was once an independent city ruled by Denmark; as Hamburg grew, the Danes were ousted. At the south end of town, an entirely different atmosphere reigns in **St. Pauli,** where the raucous **Fischmarkt** (fish market) mingles with the wild (and no less smelly) **Reeperbahn,** home to Hamburg's infamous sex trade.

Tourist Offices: Hamburg's two main tourist offices supply free maps and pamphlets. The **Hauptbahnhof office** (☎30 05 12 00; fax 30 05 13 33; email info@hamburg-tourism.de; www.hamburg-tourism.de), near the Kirchenallee exit, books rooms for DM6. Open M-F 6am-10pm, Sa and Su 7am-10pm. The less-crowded **St. Pauli Landungs-brücken office** (☎30 05 12 00) is located between piers 4 and 5 (take U3 to Landungsbrücke). Open daily 10am-7pm. The offices all sell the **Hamburg Card,** which provides unlimited access to public transportation, admission to most museums, and discounts on bus and boat tours: 1 day DM12.50; 3 days DM26. A better deal is the **Group Card,** which provides the same for up to 5 people (1 day DM24; 3 days DM42).

Consulates: Canada, ABCStr. 45 (☎35 55 62 95). U2 to Gänsemarkt. **Ireland,** Feldbrun-nenstr. 43 (☎44 18 62 13). U1 to Hallerstr. Open M-F 9am-1pm. **New Zealand,** Heimhuderstr. 56 (☎442 55 50). Open M-Th 9am-5:30pm, F 9am-4:30pm. **UK,** Harvestehuder Weg 8a (☎448 03 20). U1 to Hallerstr. Open M-F 9am-noon and 2-4pm. **US,** Alsterufer 27 (☎41 17 10), on the Außenalster's west side. Open M-F 9am-noon.

Currency Exchange: ReiseBank, on the 2nd floor of the Hauptbahnhof near the Kirche-nallee exit, arranges money transfers for Western Union, cashes traveler's checks, and exchanges money for a DM5 fee. Open daily 7:30am-10pm.

American Express: Ballindamm 39, 20095 Hamburg (☎30 39 38 11 12; fax 30 39 38 12). Mail held for cardmembers up to 4 weeks; all banking services. Open M-F 9am-6pm, Sa 10am-1pm.

Gay and Lesbian Resources: Hein und Fiete, Pulverteich 21 (☎24 03 33). Open M-F 4-9pm, Sa 4-7pm. **Magnus-Hirschfeld-Centrum,** Borgweg 8 (☎279 00 69). U3 or bus #108 to Borgweg. Center open M and F 2-6pm, Tu-W 7-10pm.

Laundromat: Schnell und Sauber, Grindelallee 158, in the university district. S21 or S31 to Dammtor. Wash DM6. Dry DM1. Open daily 7am-10pm.

Emergency: Police, ☎110. From the Kirchenallee exit of the Hauptbahnhof, turn left and follow the signs for "BGS/Bahnpolizei." Another police station on the **Reeperbahn** at the corner of Davidstr. and Spielbudenplatz. **Fire** and **Ambulance,** ☎112.

Pharmacy: Senator-Apotheke (☎32 75 27), Hachmannplatz 14. Exit the Hauptbahnhof on Kirchenallee and turn right. English spoken. Open M-F 7am-8pm, Sa 8am-6pm.

Internet Access: Cyberb@r, 3rd floor of the gigantic **Karstadt** department store on Mönckebergstr. DM5 per 30min. Open M-F 9am-8pm, Sa 9am-4pm.

Post Office: At the Kirchenallee exit of the Hauptbahnhof, 20097 Hamburg. Open M-F 8am-8pm, Sa 9am-6pm, Su 10am-4pm. **Poste Restante:** Address mail to be held: Postlagernde Briefe für Daniel PETRIE, Hauptpostamt, 20099 Hamburg, Germany. The main branch is on Großer Burstah 3. Open M-F 8am-6pm, Sa 8am-noon.

GERMANY

ACCOMMODATIONS

Hamburg's single rooms, from DM60, reflect the price of the city's accommodations. Many establishments are tawdry with few comforts. A slew of small, relatively cheap *Pensionen* line Steindamm, Steintorweg, Bremer Weg, and Bremer Reihe, around the **Hauptbahnhof.** The tourist office's free *Hotelführer* aids in navigating past the filth.

Schanzenstern Übernachtungs-und Gasthaus, Bartelsstr. 12 (☎439 84 41; www.schanzenstern.de). S21 or S31, or U3 to Sternschanze. Left onto Schanzenstr., right on Susannenstr., and left to Bartelsstr. The 50-room hostel is managed by a politically progressive cooperative. Reserve ahead in summer and New Year's. Dorms DM33; singles DM60; doubles DM90.

Instant Sleep, Max-Brauer-Allee 277 (☎43 18 23 10; www.instantsleep.de). S21 or S31, or U3 to Sternschanze. From the station go straight on Schanzenstr., turn left on Altonaerstr. and follow it until it becomes Max-Brauer-Allee. Internet available (15min DM2.50), as well as a communal kitchen and laundry room. Sheets DM5. Reception 9am-2pm. Dorms DM27; singles DM35; doubles DM80.

Jugendherberge auf dem Stintfang (HI), Alfred-Wegener-Weg 5 (☎31 34 88; www.schoelzel.com/jh-hamburg/index.shtml). S1-S3 or U3 to Landungsbrücke. A convenient location near the Reeperbahn and a beautiful view of the harbor compensate for the regimental rules. Reception 12:30pm-1am. Lockout 9:30-11:30am. Curfew 1am. Call ahead. Dorms DM34.50; singles DM60. Non-members pay a DM6 surcharge.

Hotel Florida, Spielbudenpl. 22 (☎31 43 94). U3 to St.Pauli, or S1 or S3 to Reeperbahn. Hotel Florida offers small but clean rooms adjacent to Hamburg's biggest clubs. Breakfast included. Singles DM60; doubles DM95; triples DM135.

Hotel Terminus Garni, Steindamm 5 (☎280 31 44; fax 24 15 18). From the Hauptbahnhof's Kirchenalle exit, turn right. Breakfast included. 24hr. reception. Doubles DM45, with shower DM60; triples with bath DM165.

Camping: Campingplatz Rosemarie Buchholz, Kielerstr. 374 (☎540 45 32). From Altona train station, take bus #182 or #183 to Basselweg (10 min.), then walk 100m in the same direction as traffic. Showers DM1.50. Reception 8am-noon and 2pm-10pm. Check-out noon. DM7 per person. Tents DM12.50 per night.

FOOD

The most interesting part of town from a culinary standpoint is **Sternschanze,** where Turkish fruit stands, Asian *Imbiße*, and avant-garde cafes entice the hungry passersby with good food and atmosphere. **Schulterblatt, Susannenstr, and Schanzenstr.** are host to funky cafes and restaurants. Slightly cheaper establishments abound in the university area, especially along **Rentzelstr., Grindelhof, and Grindelallee.** In **Altona,** the pedestrian zone leading up to the train station is packed with ethnic food stands and produce shops. Check out the market inside Altona's massive Mercado mall, which includes everything from sushi bars to Portuguese fast-food.

Noodles, Schanzenstr. 2-4 (☎439 28 40). Along with innovative pasta creations, Noodles serves up veggie main courses. Breakfast from DM7.50. Beer DM5. Open M-Th and Su 10am-1am, F-Sa 10am-3am.

Machwitz, Schanzenstr. 121 (☎43 81 77). Join the hip student crowd in the funky angular interior. Mains DM12-17. Open Su-Th 10am-4am, F-Sa 10am-8am. Kitchen closes at midnight during the week and at 2am F-Sa.

Falafel-König, Schanzenstr. 113. An excellent option for vegetarians. Basic falafel DM5, with one of half a dozen toppings DM6. Open M-Th and Su 11:30am-midnight, F-Sa 11:30am-3am.

Indian Tandoori, Ottenser Hauptstr. 20, in the pedestrian zone near Altona train station. If you're in a hurry, grab an order of samosas (DM6); otherwise, feast on their namesake tandoori chicken (DM12). Also vegetarian-friendly. Open daily noon-11pm.

SIGHTS

Historical sites and modern commercialism abound in Hamburg's Altstadt. Within walking distance of each other are imposing churches, government buildings, and winding roads with boutiques to sate the casual browser and the serious shopper.

ALTSTADT

GROßE MICHAELSKIRCHE. The gargantuan 18th-century Michaelskirche is the grand-daddy of all Hamburg churches, affectionately referred to as *"der Michael."* While the exterior is a bit imposing—the statue of St. Michael above the doorway mischievously grins at the passing tourists—with its scalloped walls, the inside looks like a concert hall. *Der Michael's* bulbous Baroque tower is the official emblem of Hamburg; it's also the only one of the city's six spires that can be ascended by foot or by elevator. On weekends, the tower is used to project a multimedia presentation about Hamburg's millennial existence onto a five-meter-high screen. (☎ 37 67 81 00. *Open April-Sept. M-Sa 9am-6pm, Su 11:30am-5:30pm; Oct.-March M-Sa 10am-4:30pm, Su 11:30am-4:30pm. DM1. Screenings Th-Su hourly 12:30-3:30pm. DM5, students, children, and Hamburg Card holders DM2.50. Organ music April-Aug. daily at noon and 5pm. Tower DM5, students and children DM2.50. Crypt DM2.50 for the living.*)

RATHAUS. The copper spires of the town hall, a richly ornamented, neo-Renaissance monstrosity that serves as the political center of Hamburg, rises above the city center. The Rathausmarkt in front of it is the place for constant festivities, ranging from demonstrations to medieval fairs. (☎ 428 31 20 64. *Tours of the Rathaus in German every 30min. M-Th 10am-3pm, F-Su 10am-1pm. Tours in English and French every hour M-Th 10:15am-3:15pm, F-Su 10:15am-1:15pm.*)

NIKOLAIKIRCHE. In the city center rest the somber ruins of the old Nikolaikirche, a reminder of Hamburg's time as an Allied bombing target. A 1943 air raid flattened this example of early neo-Gothic architecture. In front of its bombed-out hull lies the **Hopfenmarkt,** home to a motley melange of *Imbiße,* book, and clothing stands. (*Just south of the Rathaus, off Ost-West-Str.*) Behind the church ruins is a maze of canals and bridges centered on the **Alte Börse** (old stock market). The buildings along nearby **Trostbrücke** sport huge copper models of clipper ships on their spires—a reminder of sea-trade's role in Hamburg's wealth.

KONTORHAUSVIERTEL. At the corner of Burchardstr. and Pumpen, the **Chilehaus** showcases architecture of a different generation. Designed to look like the sails of a ship when viewed from the plaza to the east, this 1922 *trompe-l'oeil* office building is the work of Expressionist architect Fritz Höger, who also designed the **Sprinkenhof** building across the street.

MÖNKEBERGSTRAßE. The pedestrian shopping zone, which stretches from the Rathaus to the Hauptbahnhof along Mönckebergstr., is punctuated by two spires. The first belongs to the **St. Petrikirche,** site of the oldest church in Hamburg. Free concerts resonate through its Gothic arches every Wednesday evening at 5:15pm. (*Open M-Tu and F 10am-6:30pm, W-Th 10am-7pm, Sa 10am-5pm, Su 9am-6pm.*) The second is part of the **St. Jakobikirche,** known for its 14th-century Arp-Schnittger organ. (☎ 32 77 49. *Open F-Sa 10am-5pm.*)

BEYOND THE ALTSTADT

ST. PAULI LANDUNGSBRÜCKEN. Hamburg's harbor, the largest port in Germany with more than 100,000 dockers and sailors, lights up at night with ships from all over the world. Numerous companies offer harbor cruises: **Kapitän Prüsse** departs every 30min. from Pier 3. (☎ 31 31 30. *DM15, children DM7.50.*) **HADAG** offers more elaborate cruises of outlying areas from Pier 2. (☎ 311 70 70. *Every 30min. 9:30am-6pm. DM15, children DM7.50.*) After sailing the East Indies, the 19th-century **Windjammer Rickmer Rickmers** was docked at Pier 1 and restored as a museum ship. Old navigation equipment, all brass and polish, is juxtaposed with modern nautical technology. (☎ *35 69 31 19. Open daily 10am-6pm. DM6, students DM5, children under 12 DM4.)* The elevator to the **old Elbe tunnel,** built in 1907 and running 1200m under the Elbe, protrudes through the floor of the building behind Pier 6. With all of its machinery exposed, the building looks like an exercise machine built for the gods.

PLANTEN UN BLOMEN. To the west of the Alster near the university area, this park features dozens of obsessively well-planned flower beds surrounding two lakes and a handful of outdoor cafes. *(Open daily 7am-11pm.)* From May to September, daily performances ranging from Irish step-dancing to Hamburg's police orchestra shake the outdoor **Musikpavillon;** there are also nightly **Wasserlichtkonzerte,** lighted fountain arrangements set to music. *(May-Aug. 10pm, Sept. 9pm.)*

ALSTER LAKES. To the north of the city center, the two Alster lakes, bordered by tree-lined paths and parks, provide refuge from crowded Hamburg. Elegant promenades and commercial facades surround **Binnenalster,** while windsurfers, sailboats, and paddleboats dominate the larger **Außenalster.** Ferries, more personal than the bigger Hamburg boats, depart here.

FISHMARKT. Anarchy reigns as charismatic vendors haul in and hawk huge amounts of fish, produce, and other goods. Heads up—to grab attention, the fruit vendors toss free pineapples into the crowd. *(U- or S-Bahn to Landungsbrücken or S-Bahn to Königstr. Market open Su 6-10am, off-season 7-10am.)*

BEYOND THE CENTER

Though not in the city center, still accessible by public transport are two very different testaments to the atrocities of the Nazi regime.

GEDENKSTÄTTE JANUSZ-KORCZAK-SCHULE. In the midst of warehouses, the school serves as a memorial to 20 Jewish children brought here from Auschwitz for "testing" and murdered by the S.S. only hours before Allied troops arrived. Visitors can plant a rose for the children in the flower garden behind the school, where plaques with the children's photographs line the fence. *(Bullenhuser Damm 92. S21 to Rothenburgsort. Follow the signs to Bullenhuser Damm along Ausschläger Bildeich and across a bridge.* ☎ *428 96 03. Open Su 10am-7pm and Th 2pm-8pm. Free.)*

KZ NEUENGAMME. An idyllic agricultural village east of Hamburg provided the backdrop for the Neuengamme **concentration camp,** where the Nazis killed 55,000 prisoners. After a period serving as a prison, the site was converted in 1989 to a more appropriate Holocaust memorial. Banners inscribed with the names and death-dates of the victims, along with four 500-page books listing their names, hang in the **Haus des Gedenkens.** *(Jean-Doldier-Weg. Take S21 to Bergedorf, then bus #227, which runs every hr., 40 min. past the hour. About 1hr. from Hamburg to Jean-Doldier-Weg.* ☎ *723 10 31. Open Tu-Su May-Oct. 10am-6pm, Sept.-April 10am-5pm.)*

MUSEUMS

The one- or three-day **Hamburg Card** (see p. 442) provides access to most of these museums, with the exception of the Deichtorhallen and the Erotic Art Museum.

Hamburger Kunsthalle, Glockengießerwall 1 (☎ 428 54 26 12). This sprawling first-rate art museum is three-pronged: the first part of the collection contains superb German and Dutch art from the medieval era through the 19th century. The next contains works by 19th-century French painters such as Millet, Courbet, Manet, and Monet. The newly built **Galerie der Gegenwart** displays works by Warhol and Picasso, and there is also a pair of Levi's nailed to the wall. Open Tu-W and F-Su 10am-6pm, Th 10am-9pm. DM15, students DM10.)

Deichtorhallen Hamburg, Deichtorstr. 1-2 (☎ 32 10 30). Follow signs from the subway station; look for two entwined iron circles. Hamburg's contemporary art scene resides here in two buildings that were former fruit market halls. New exhibits each season showcase up-and-coming artists. Outstanding, but expensive. Open Tu-Su 11am-6pm, Sa-Su 10am-6pm. Each building DM10, students DM8.

🖼 **Erotic Art Museum,** Nobistor 12 and Bernhard-Nocht-Str. 69 (☎31 78 41 26). S1 or S3 to Reeperbahn. Follow the silver sperm painted on the floor as they lead you through four floors of tactful iniquity. The first two floors examine postcard-sized sketches of assorted aristocrats and their voluptuous maids, while the top two levels focus on the art of bondage. The Reeperbahn location is home to the permanent collection, while the building at Bernhard-Nocht-Str. entertains exhibits that are just passing through. The museum is in surprisingly good taste, as evidenced by the Haring originals on the fourth floor and the sonorous classical music. Open Tu-Su 10am-midnight. DM15, groups DM10.

Hamburgisches Museum für Völkerkunde, Rothenbaumchaussee 64 (☎428 48 25 24). U1 to Hallerstr. With two floors of glass cases brimming with weapons, clothing, and cooking utensils, the exhibits are treasure troves of imperial plunder from Indonesia to the Caribbean, and everywhere in between. Open Tu-W and F-Su 10am-6pm, Th 10am-9pm. DM7, students and seniors DM3.50, under 16 DM2. Half-price on F.

🎵🖼 ENTERTAINMENT AND NIGHTLIFE

MUSIC AND FESTIVALS

As the cultural capital of the North, Hamburg patronizes the arts with money and attention, resulting in significantly lower ticket prices and an abundance of choice. The **Staatsoper,** Dammtorstr. 28, houses one of the best opera companies in Germany, tending toward the modern, but also playing a steady stream of Bizet and Puccini. (☎35 17 21. Take U1 to Stephansplatz. Open M-F 10am-6:30pm, Sa 10am-2pm. Tickets start at DM7.) **Orchestras** abound—the Philharmonie, the Norddeutscher Rundfunk Symphony, and Hamburg Symphonia (the big three) all perform at the **Musikhalle** on Johannes-Brahms-Platz. (☎34 69 20. Take U2 to Gänsemarkt or Messehallen.) The **West Port** jazz festival, Germany's largest, runs in mid-July. (Ticket info ☎44 64 21.) The most anticipated festival, however, is the "Love Parade of the North." The **G-Move** (www.g-move.com) grooves into town early in June, but unlike its techno brother in Berlin, it only draws crowds in the high-thousands. The **Hafengeburtstag** (harbor birthday) is the city's biggest bash. Hamburg owes its prosperity to May 7, 1189, when Friedrich Barbarossa granted the town the right to open a port. The city still celebrates the anniversary for a weekend in early May, featuring music and other events. During April, August, and November, the **Heiligengeistfeld** north of the Reeperbahn metamorphoses into the **Dom,** a titanic amusement park with fun-booths, kiosks, and merry-go-rounds.

NIGHTLIFE

Sternschanze, St. Pauli, and Altona areas monopolize Hamburg's crazy nightlife scene. The infamous **Reeperbahn,** a long boulevard which makes Las Vegas look like church on a Sunday, is the spinal cord of St. Pauli; sex shops, strip joints, and peep shows compete for space along the sidewalks. Though the Reeperbahn is reasonably safe, it is not recommended for women to venture to the adjacent streets. **Herbertstr.,** Hamburg's only remaining legalized prostitution strip, runs parallel to the Reeperbahn, and is open only to men over 18. Despite the sex shops and prostitutes that make St. Pauli famous, in general, Hamburg's best bars and clubs fill with a young crowd that leaves debauchery and degradation outside. Students trying to avoid the hypersexed Reeperbahn head north to the spiffy streets of **Sternschanze,** a neighborhood that hums with creative energy and creatively-dressed people. Much of Hamburg's **gay scene** is located in the **St. Georg** area of the city, near Berliner Tor. *Szene*, available at newsstands (DM5), lists events and parties.

STERNSCHANZE

🖼 **Rote Flora,** Schulterblatt 71 (☎439 54 13). Held together both figuratively and literally by the spray paint and posters that cover all its vertical surfaces, this graffiti-covered mansion serves as the nucleus of the Sternschanze scene. Weekend cover DM8 or more. Cafe open M-F 6-10pm, bar opening times vary.

Logo, Grindelallee 5 (☎410 56 58). Nightly live music at this club near the university gives locals a chance to be rock stars. Jeans and t-shirt. Open nightly from 9:30pm.

Frauenkneipe, Stresemannstr. 60 (☎43 63 77), S21 or S3 to Holstenstr. A bar and meeting place for women. Visitors who are disconcerted by the Reeperbahn and drunken-sailor scene will find another Hamburg here. For women only, gay or straight. Open M-F from 8pm, Sa from 9pm, Su from 6pm.

ST. PAULI

🔳**Mojo Club,** Reeperbahn 1 (☎43 52 32), has more attitude than it knows what to do with and a dance floor filled with all kinds of smoke. Called the best club in Germany by MTV. The attached **Jazz Café** attracts the trendy and features acid jazz. DM12 cover on weekends. Usually open 11pm-4am.

La Cage, Reeperbahn 136. Glitz drips from cascades of hanging beads and two big silver cages dominate the dance floor. The club sends out special invitations to modeling agencies in order to fill the floor with faces whose perfection matches the decor. Cover DM15-25. Open F-Sa 11pm.

Indra, Große Freiheit 64 (☎31 79 63 08), is a haven of calm live jazz just off the adrenaline-powered Reeperbahn. Cool cats talk quietly in low light over a million cigarettes. Open W-Su from 9pm; music starts around 11pm.

Große Freiheit 36/Kaiser Keller, Große Freiheit 36 (☎31 77 780). The Beatles played on the small stage downstairs during their early years. Today, everyone from Ziggy Marley to Matchbox Twenty stomps about on the big stage upstairs. The basement dance floor opens at 10pm; students admitted to the downstairs for free on Tuesdays. Call for show times and ticket prices (DM5-30) for the upstairs stage. Große Freiheit 36 opening hours vary. Kaiser Keller open from 10pm.

Cotton Club, Alter Steinweg 10 (☎34 38 78); U3 to Rödingsmarkt. Smoky atmosphere, great jazz. Cover around DM12. Open M-Sa 8pm-midnight. Shows start at 8:30pm.

⚑ DAYTRIPS FROM HAMBURG

LÜNEBURGER HEIDE (LÜNEBURG HEATH)

To see the Heide, a bike is your best bet. Extensive and detailed maps outline the major bike tours in the area; the most popular is an 80-kilometer tour leaving from Luneburg, taking you along main roads and through the endless woods and pastures of the suburbs and countryside of Luneburg and neighboring Hamburg.

Between the Elbe and Aller rivers stretches the shrub-covered Lüneburger Heide. The undulating countryside is home to farm and forest; green gives way to purple from July to September, when the bushes flower. All of Germany comes here to bike, hike, motor, and generally frolic in the late summer. The most important regional towns are **Lüneburg** and **Celle**. In Lüneburg, the **Fremdenverkehrsverband Lüneburger Heide,** Barckhausenstr. 35, finds rooms in remote hamlets barely on the map, and also provides information on the Heide's *Heu-Hotels* (hay hotels), functioning barns with rooms that farmers rent out to travelers for around DM20. (☎ (04131) 737 30.) The **Jugendherberge Lüneburg (HI)** is both cheap and charming, but like all good deals, fills up fast. To get there, take bus #11 (dir.: Rettmer/Hecklingen) from the train station to the hostel, get off at Scharnhostrstr./DJH. Otherwise, take bus #7 from Auf dem Klosterhof behind the Rathaus to Ginsterweg and walk 200m farther along Soltauerstr. (Breakfast included. Sheets DM5.70. Laundry DM5. Reception until 10pm. Curfew 10pm. DM27, under 27 DM22.)

NORTH SEA COAST

Norden is the transportation hub for excursions around the North Sea Coast. By train, it connects to Emden and Norddeich (1 per hr., DM3-5), and as the anchor of the Bäderbus, it provides easy access to every other port town. Pick up a bus schedule ahead of time; service is not always convenient to trains and ferries. Call or visit the tourist office, next to the Rathaus, for specific transportation information or to book rooms (from DM25) for free. (☎ (04931) 98 62 01; fax 98 62 90. Open M-F 9am-1pm and 2-5pm, Sa 9am-4pm.)

The low tide retreats several kilometers from the coast of East Frisia, revealing the moist brownish-blue mud of the sea floor. Visitors can tread upon this squishy plain, called the Watt, out to the middle of the sea. Towns near the coast include Norddeich, Norden, Esens, and Jever.

OTHER DAYTRIPS FROM HAMBURG

LÜBECK. For sweet marzipan and sweeter memories of the Hanseatic League, take the train to Lübeck (see below).

BREMEN. Hamburg's Hanseatic sister city to the north, Bremen has replaced its once famed medieval ambience with a thriving cosmopolitan swirl (see p. 449).

LÜBECK   ☎0451

With a skyline of Neoclassical townhouses punctuated by 13th-century copper spires, Lübeck, former capital of the Hanseatic League, is easily Schleswig-Holstein's most beautiful city. Between the Altstadt and the train station is the massive **Holstentor,** the symbol of the city and one of Lübeck's four 15th-century gates. The centerpiece of the Altstadt is the **Rathaus,** a 13th-century structure of glazed red and black bricks. (Open M-F 9:30am-6pm, Sa-Su 10am-2pm. Tours M-F 11am and noon. DM4, students DM2.) The **Marienkirche,** begun in the Romanesque style around 1200 but finished as a Gothic cathedral in 1350, houses the largest mechanical organ in the world. (Open daily in summer 10am-6pm; off-season closes 4pm. Free.) Opposite the Marienkirche is the **Buddenbrookhaus,** Mengstr. 4, the childhood home of literary giants Heinrich and Thomas Mann—today, a museum dedicated to their lives and work. (☎122 41 92. Open daily 10am-5pm. DM8, students DM5.) At the **Behnhaus** and **Drägerhaus** museums, Königstr. 11, modern art clashes with the Neoclassical architecture of an 18th-century townhouse. (Open Apr.-Sept. Tu-Su 10am-5pm; Oct.-May closes 4pm. DM5, students DM3; free 1st F of each month.)

Frequent **trains** arrive from Berlin (3¼hr., every hr., DM97); Hamburg (45min., 2 per hr., DM17); Rostock (1¾hr., every hr., DM37); and Schwerin (1¼hr., every hr., DM21). Skip absurdly expensive at the **tourist office** in the train station and instead try the one in the Altstadt, Breitestr. 62 (☎122 54 13; fax 122 54 19. Open M-F 9:30am-7pm, Sa-Su 10am-3pm). From the station, walk past the Holstentor, left on An der Untertrave, and right on Beckergrube to reach the **Rucksack Hotel,** Kanalstr. 70. (☎70 68 92. Breakfast DM8. Sheets DM6. Reception 9am-1pm and 4-10pm. Dorms DM24-26; doubles with bath DM80; quads DM112-136.) Cross the river, make a left on An der Untertrave, and turn right on Mengstr. to reach the conveniently located **Jugendgästehaus Lübeck (HI),** Mengstr. 33. (☎702 03 99. HI members only. Reception 7:30am-noon, 1:15-6pm, and 7:15pm-midnight. Lockout midnight, but guests over 18 can get a key. Doubles DM84, under 26 DM66; triples and quads DM86-158.) **Lübecker marzipan** is a delectable candy made with sugar and almonds. The confectionery **I.G. Niederegger,** Breitestr. 89 (☎530 11 26), across from the Rathaus, is the place to purchase exquisite marzipan candy in the shape of pigs, jellyfish, and even the town gate. (Open M-F 9am-7pm, Sa 9am-6pm, Su 10am-4pm.) The hip waitstaff at **Tipasa,** Schlumacherstr. 12-14, serves pizza and pasta. (Open Su-Th noon-1am, F-Sa noon-2am.) A **Co-op supermarket** is at the corner of Sandstr. and Schmiedstr. (Open M-F 8:30am-7pm, Sa 9am-4pm.) **Postal Code:** 23552.

SCHLESWIG   ☎24837

Schleswig, at the southern end of the **Schlei inlet,** has picture-perfect fishing settlements, a 16th-century castle, and extensive museum collections. Towering over the meandering streets of the Altstadt is the 12th-century **St. Petri-Dom,** famous for its intricately carved wooden altarpiece. (Open May-Sept. M-Th and Sa 9am-5pm, F 9am-3pm; Oct.-Apr. M-Th and Sa 10am-4pm, F 10am-3pm, Su 1-4pm.) By the harbor, the 16th-century **Schloß Gottorf** houses the **Landesmuseen,** a treasure trove of Dutch, Danish, and Art Deco pieces. On the other side of the castle, the **Kreuzstall** houses the **Museum des 20. Jahrhunderts,** devoted to artists of the Brücke school. The surrounding park holds an **outdoor sculpture museum.** (All open daily Mar.-Oct. 9am-5pm; Nov.-Feb. 9:30am-4pm. DM7, students DM3.) Schleswig's **train station** is 20min. south of the city center; take bus #1, 2, 4, or 5 from the stop outside the **bus terminal** (ZOB), close to the Altstadt (15min., DM1.90). **Trains** go hourly to Kiel and Hamburg (via Neumünster). The **tourist office,** Plessenstr. 7, is up the street from the harbor; from the ZOB, walk down Plessenstr. toward the water. (☎248 78; fax 207 03. Open May-Sept. M-F 9am-12:30pm and 1:30-5pm, Sa 9am-noon; Oct.-Apr. M-

Th 9am-12:30pm and 1:30-5pm, F 9am-12:30pm.) The **Jugendherberge (HI),** Spielkoppel 1, is near the center of town. With your back to the ZOB, walk right along Königstr., turn right onto Poststr. (which turns into Moltkestr.), turn left on Bellmannstr., and follow it to Spielkoppel on your left. (☎238 93. Breakfast included. Sheets DM7. Reception 7am-1pm and 5-11pm. Curfew 11pm. DM26, under 26 DM21.) Try the fresh and cheap seafood at the *Imbiße* by the **Stadthafen.**

BREMEN   ☎0421

Bremen's cultural flair, liberal politics, and strong desire to remain an independent *Land* have caused Germans to coin the adjective *bremisch,* which simply means "something unusual." The Altstadt revolves around the ornate **Rathaus,** which was spared during WWII by a bomber pilot who deliberately missed the target because he couldn't bear to bomb it. (Open for guided tours M-Sa 11am, noon, 3, and 4pm, Su 11am and noon. DM6, children DM3.) Just to the left of the Rathaus is a sculpture of the Brothers Grimm's *Die Bremer Stadtmusikanten* (The Musicians of Bremen)— a donkey, dog, cat, and rooster who terrified a band of robbers with their off-key singing en route to Bremen. Also next to the Rathaus is **St. Petri Dom,** Sandstr. 10-12, with a mosaic exterior and frescoed ceilings; its first stone was laid by Charlemagne in AD 798. Once you've seen the inside, climb the tower to gaze down upon the hubbub of the market square below. (Cathedral open M-F 10am-5pm, Sa 10am-1:45pm, Su 2-5pm. Free. Tower open May-Oct. M-F 10am-4:30pm, Sa 10am-1:45pm, Su 2-5pm. DM1.) The **Neues Museum Weserberg Bremen,** Teerhofstr. 20, off the Bürgermeister-Schmidt Brücke on the island between the Klein Weser and the Weser, houses beautiful installations by modern international artists. (☎59 83 90. Open Tu-F 10am-6pm, Sa-Su 11am-6pm. DM8, students DM5.) The **Übersee Museum,** Bahnhofsplatz 13, promises "a trip around the world in a matter of minutes," and delivers just that. Exhibits ranging from a Shinto garden to a South Sea fishing village depict the world beyond German borders. (☎361 91 76. Open Tu-Su 10am-6pm. DM10, students DM5.) The **Kunsthalle,** Am Wall 207, holds Bremen's main art collection, including Impressionist, Expressionist, and contemporary works. (☎32 90 80. Open Tu 10am-9pm, W-Su 10am-5pm. DM8, students DM4.) For the yeasty smell of brewing beer, head across the Weser to **Beck's Brewery,** Am Deich 18/19. (☎50 94 55 55. Tours with tastetests, every hr. Tu-Sa 10am-5pm, Su 10am-3pm. Tours in English at noon. DM5.)

Trains run from the Bahnhofplatz to Hamburg (1½hr., 2 per hr., DM33) and Hannover (1¼hr., 2 per hr., DM34). The best deal for local transportation, by far, is the **Bremer Kärtchen,** with unlimited rides for 2 adults for 1 calendar day (DM8). Bremen lies south of the mouth of the Weser River, and has four distinct neighborhoods: the tourist-filled **Altstadt,** where most of the sights and the oldest architecture are, the **Alte Neustadt,** a residential neighborhood south of the river, the **Schnoor,** an old area turned shopping district, and the **Viertel,** a student quarter filled with hip kids, clubs, and cheap food. The **tourist office,** in front of the train station, has museum and theater guides, as well as the **Tourist Card Bremen,** which provides free transportation and 20-50% discounts on shows and museums. (☎308 00 51; fax 308 00 30. Open June-Oct. daily 9:30am-10pm; Nov.-May M-W 9:30am-6:30pm, Th-F 9:30am-8pm, Sa 9:30am-4pm. Tourist Card 2-days, 1 adult and 1 child, DM19.50.) To reach the sleek **Jugendgästehaus Bremen (HI),** Kalkstr. 6, from the station, take Bahnhofstr. to Herdentorsteinweg, go right at Am Wall, then left on Bürgermeister-Smidt-Str. and right along the water to the 162-bed hostel. (☎17 13 69. Breakfast included. 2-day card, 1 adult and 1 child DM19.50.) **Hotel-Pension Garni Weidmann,** Am Schwarzen Meer 35, has plush comforters and cavernous rooms, equipped with coffeemakers, fit for royalty. Walk down Ostertorsteinweg, which becomes Am Schwarzen Meer. (☎498 44 55. Singles from DM40; doubles from DM80.) To get to the local **campsite,** Am Stadtwaldsee 1, take streetcar #5 or 8 to Külen Campf, and then bus #28 to the door. (☎21 20 02. Laundry DM8. DM7.50-11 per tent.) Bremen's renowned **Ratskeller** in the *Rathaus* is one of the oldest wine bars in Germany. (DM7-8 per glass; meals DM40. Open daily 11am-midnight; kitchen open noon-2:30pm and 6-11pm.) By the Weser, **Moto** offers cheap pan-Asian food including many vegetarian options. (Open daily noon-midnight.) **Postal Code:** 28195.

CENTRAL GERMANY

Stretching from the North Sea to the hills of central Germany, Lower-Saxony has two distinct flavors: along the coast, descendants of the Frisians run their fishing boats by the foggy marshland, while the majority of the *Land* is a broad, agricultural plain. Along the Dutch and Belgian borders, North Rhine-Westphalia, with 17 million inhabitants and the mighty Ruhr Valley, is the most heavily populated and economically powerful area in Germany. While the region's squalor may have inspired the philosophy of Karl Marx and Friedrich Engels, the area's natural beauty and intellectual energy of Cologne and Düsseldorf inspired the muses of Goethe, Heine, and Böll. The region of Hesse, mainly known before the 20th century as a source for mercenary soldiers (many hired by King George III to put down an unruly gang of colonials in 1776), is today the busiest commercial center in Germany, led by the banking metropolis of Frankfurt. The medieval delights and Baroque elegance outside the city remain blessedly off the beaten path.

HANNOVER (HANOVER)   ☎ 0511

⊡ TRANSPORTATION. Trains arrive frequently from: Berlin (2½hr., DM78.60); Cologne (2hr., DM93); Frankfurt (3hr., DM157); and Hamburg (1½hr., DM50).

⚠ PRACTICAL INFORMATION. As you exit the station, turn right (as you face the large rear of the king's splendid steed) to reach the **tourist office,** Ernst-August-Pl. 2. (☎ 116 84 97 10. Open M-F 9am-7pm, Sa 9:30am-3pm.) For **currency exchange,** the **ReiseBank,** right inside the main exit of the train station, has long hours and decent commissions. (Open M-Sa 7am-10pm, Su 9am-10pm.) **American Express,** Georgstr. 54, is across from the opera house. (☎ 368 10 03. Open M-F 9am-noon and 1-6pm, Sa 10am-1pm.) Surf the **internet** at **Daily Planet,** Ägidientorpl. 1. (☎ 32 30 02. Open M-Sa 11:30am-11pm.) The **post office** is in the same building as the tourist office. (Open M-F 9am-8pm, Sa 9am-4pm.) **Postal Code:** 30159.

⛉ ACCOMMODATIONS AND FOOD. To reach **Jugendherberge Hannover (HI),** Ferdinand-Wilhelm-Fricke-Weg 1, take U3 or U7 (dir.: Wettbergen) to Fischerhof/Fachhochschule; cross the tracks, walk through the parking lot, follow the path as it curves, cross the street, go over the enormous red footbridge, and walk right for 50m. (☎ 131 76 74. Reception 7:30am-11:30pm. Curfew 11:30pm; afterwards doors open every hour, on the hour. Dorms DM32-34, under 27 DM27-29.) To reach **Naturfreundehaus Stadtheim,** Hermann-Bahlsen-Allee 8, take U3 (dir.: Lahe) or U7 (dir.: Fasanenkrug) to Spannhagengarten; backtrack to the intersection, take Hermann-Bahlsen-Allee left, and follow the sign to your right down the paved road. (☎ 69 14 93. Reception 8am-noon and 3-10pm. DM49.) For the **Naturfreundehaus Misburg,** Am Fahrhorstfelde 50, take the U3 to the end, transfer to bus #124 to Misburg Garten, then switch to bus #631 to Waldfriedhof. The hostel lies at the end of Am Fahrhorstfelde, 10m off the trail. (☎ 58 05 37. Sheets DM7.50. 4- to 6-bed rooms DM39.50.) Note that the hostel and *Naturfreundehäuser* are situated in parks and woods on the outskirts of town, where walkways are deserted and poorly lit after dark; use caution late at night.

Kröpke, the once-renowned food court-cafe at the center of the pedestrian zone, is where you can find small snacks (from DM2.50) or nice sit-down meals (from DM13.50). **Uwe's Hannenfaß Hannover,** Knochenhauerstr. 36, in the center of the Altstadt, serves steaming *Niedersachsenschmaus* (potato casserole; DM8.90) and house-brewed *Hannen Alt.* (Open M-Sa noon-2am, Su 3pm-2am.) **Jalda,** Limmerstr. 97, serves a delightful combination of Italian, Greek, and Arabic dishes. For DM10-13, sample the lunch specials. (Open M-Th and Su 11:30-midnight, F-Sa noon-1am.) **Spar supermarkets** sit by the Lister Meile and Kröpcke U-Bahn stops. (Both open M-F 7am-7pm, Sa 8am-2pm.)

🖼🗾 SIGHTS AND ENTERTAINMENT. Despite its relatively small size, Hannover puts on a magical display of cultural and cosmopolitan charm. With great economic vigor, a wealth of museums, and a tradition of festivals, the city reigns as the political and cultural capital of Lower Saxony. To fully experience Hannover, follow the **Red Thread,** a walking tour (4km) guided by a red line connecting all the major sights; an accompanying guide in English (DM3) is available at the tourist office. Painstakingly recreated after World War II, the modern **Neues Rathaus** features models of Hannover's past; climb the tower for a great view of the present version. (Open Apr.-Oct. M-F 9:30am-5:30pm, Sa-Su 10am-5pm. Tower DM3, students DM2.) The **Kestner-Museum,** Trammpl. 3, next to the Neues Rathaus, exhibits the decorative arts of medieval and Renaissance Europe as well as ancient Egypt, Greece, and Rome. (Open Tu and Th-Su 11am-6pm, W 11am-8pm. DM5, students DM3; F free.) The **Herrenhausen Gardens** contain exotic vegetation, Europe's highest garden fountain (80m), and the 18th-century **Herrenhausen Palace.** Take U4 (dir.: Garbsen) or U5 (dir.: Stöcken) to Herrenhäusen Gärten. (Gardens open Apr.-Oct. M-Tu 8am-8pm, W-Su 8am-10pm; Nov.-Mar. daily 8am-dusk. DM3. Fountains open M-F 11am-noon and 3-5pm, Sa-Su 11am-noon and 2-5pm. DM3.) The **🖼Sprengel Museum,** on Kurt-Schwitters-Pl., is a modern-art-lover's dream, with works by Henry Moore, Dalí, Picasso, and Magritte. (Open Tu 10am-8pm, W-Su 10am-6pm. DM7, students DM 3.50; special exhibits DM12, students DM8.) A collection of cartoons sits in the **Wilhelm-Busch-Museum,** Georgengarten 1. (Open Tu-Sa 10am-5pm, Su 10am-6pm. DM8, students DM4.) For more animation, visit the Hannover **zoo,** on Fritz-Behrens Allee, a 40-minute walk down Schiffstr. (Open M-Sa 9am-7pm. DM24.50, children DM19.50. Guinea-pig city by the entrance free.)

When the sun goes down, the university crowds flock to the Linden-Nord area, between Goertheplatz and Leinaustr. The student- and smoke-filled **The Loft,** Georgstr. 50b, is near Kröpcke. (Open Su-Th 9pm-2am, F-Sa 9pm-5am, Su 8pm-2am.) **Finnegan's Wake,** Theaterstr. 6, heats up early even on weeknights. (Open M-F 4pm-2am, Sa-Su noon-2am.) For a faster tempo, try the dance floors of **The Capitol,** Schwarzer Bär 2 (cover DM8; open F-Sa 10pm), or the **Osho Disco,** Raschpl. 7L (cover DM5-8; open M-F 4pm-2am). There are also more than 20 theaters in Hannover—for the scoop on ballet, opera, plays, or musicals, check out the free *Hannover Live,* or the monthly *Hannover Vorschau* (DM3).

HARZ MOUNTAINS   ☎ 05322

The Harz mountains have a long and mysterious history; it was said that in the 1300s witches danced on these mist-shrouded hills. This fantastical image has remained virtually unscathed by post-WWII development. The range stretches from the northwestern **Oberharz** to the **Ostharz** in the east. The Harz are an outdoor sports utopia; summer hikers trample through the woods over extensive networks of trails, while in the winter skiers take over the slopes. The range is dotted with small villages and abandoned castles. The highest peak in the Harz is **Brocken,** at 1124m, which houses the **Brocken Museum,** a former East German electronic warfare post turned hikers' guide. Neighboring **Braunlage** is the most convenient base from where to explore Brocken and the surrounding trails—year-round ice skating and spas are a nice revival from a hard day on the mountain. **Trains** head to Hannover (2 per day, DM27), and **buses** connect Bad Harzburg to Wernigerode and Braunlage. The **tourist office** (☎ 75330; fax 75329; email info@bad-harzburg.de, www.bad-harzburg.de), is located in the **Kurzentrum** at Herzog-Wilhelmstr. 86, down the street from the train station. **Haus Königsmark** (☎ 502 06) provides pastoral bliss; from the train station, turn right and follow Dr. Heinrich Jasperstr. and then turn left on Am Schloß. (Singles and doubles from DM30 per person.)

BRAUNLAGE   ☎ 05520

The ideal stop for hikers working the trails around the Brocken, Braunlage provides a needed change from all of the other Harz villages. The town compensates for its lack of architectural flair with kilometers of excellent trails and the luxury of spas at backpacker prices. The **Kurmittelhaus,** Ramsenweg 2 (☎ 22 41), and the adjacent **Hallen- und Freizeitbad** (☎ 27 88) soak, steam, massage, and mudpack the weary into clean, relaxed, well-adjusted personalities. (Open M-F 7:30am-noon and 2-5pm. Sauna DM15, pool DM9.) The **Wurmbergseilbahn chair lift** is an exhilarating way to approach the hiking paths around Braunlage. Take the lift to the top (17min.) to access the hiking trail to the Brocken (3hr.). Alternatively, disembark at the Mittelstation to trek to the Schierke (2½hr.). **Buses** cruise from Bad Harzburg (40min., DM67) and from Torfhaus (20min., DM4). Disembark at the Von-Langen-Str. stop in the center of town. To get to the **tourist office**, Elbingeröderstr. 17 (☎ 194 33; fax 93 07 20), backtrack on Herzog-Wilhelmstr. and make a right onto Elbingeröderstr. The **Jugendherberge (HI)**, Von-Langen-Str. 28, is ideally located 15min. uphill from the bus stop. (☎ 22 38. Sheets DM5.70. Reception 1-10pm. DM27, under 27 DM22.)

WERNIGERODE ☎ 03943

Wernigerode was one of Goethe's secret spots in the hills, but with its central location between the Western and Eastern Harz, this secret was too hard to keep. Wernigerode's **Altstadt** seems untouched by time, with a mystical **Schloß,** a plush and pompous monument to the Second Reich, towering overhead. Though the castle was maintained by the GDR as a museum of feudalism, its guiding spirit was much more recent. Kaiser Wilhelm stayed here for his extravagant hunting expeditions, in the perfectly preserved **Königszimmer** guest suite, which oozes luxury down to its green and gold brocaded wallpaper. (☎ 55 30 30. Open May-Oct. daily 10am-6pm; Nov.-April Tu-F 10am-4pm, Sa-Su 10am-6pm. Last entry 30min. before closing. DM8, students DM7; tours DM1.) The **Rathaus** looms over the marketplace with sharp slopes and petite wooden figures accenting its facade. A stroll around the Altstadt will satisfy your gingerbread house appetite, with intricate brickwork and half-timbered delights that look good enough to eat—the **Krummelsche Haus,** Breitestr. 72, is one such house completely covered with ornate wood carvings.

Trains run from Halle (2hr., every 2 hrs., DM31), and **buses** travel from Bad Harzburg. The **tourist office**, Nicolaipl. 1 (☎ 63 30 35; fax 63 20 40; www.harztourist.de) sells a small town guide with an excellent map (DM3). The office will be to your right on Nicolaipl., around the corner from the Rathaus. (Open May-Oct. M-F 9am-7pm, Sa 10am-4pm, Su 10am-3pm; Oct.-Apr. M-F 9am-6pm, Sa-Su 9am-3pm.) For the **Jugendgästehaus,** turn right on Unter den Zindeln and right again on Friedrichstr. (☎ 63 20 61. Breakfast included. Sheets DM6. Reception noon-9pm. DM27, under 27 DM21.) **Café Casa Nova,** Breitestr. 89, serves delicious pizzas. (☎ 63 30 60. Open daily 11am-8pm.)

GÖTTINGEN ☎ 0551

Home of Europe's first free university, Göttingen remains a college town to the core. Forty-two Nobel laureates have been students or faculty members at **Georg-August-Universität,** including Max Planck (the father of quantum mechanics). The renowned campus fills an area bounded by Weender Landstr. and Nikolausberger Weg. In the courtyard of the **Altes Rathaus** (Old Town Hall) serves as the meeting place for the whole town. Centuries of graduates have lined up to plant a kiss on the innocent little **Gänseliesel** (goose-girl) on the fountain. The **Städtisches Museum,** Ritterplan 7, examines the city with the help of jewelry from the bronze age, Hitler youth paraphernalia, and graduation robes. (☎ 400 28 43. Open Tu-Su 10am-5pm. DM3, students DM1.) The renowned ▨**Deutsches Theater,** Theaterpl. 11, puts on the classics with tickets from DM11. (☎ 49 69 11. Box office open M-F 10am-1:30pm and 5-7pm, Sa 10am-noon, and 1hr. before performances.) The **Junges Theater,** Hospitalstr. 6, presents an edgier perspective on both the classic and the innovative. (☎ 49 50 15. Tickets DM19, students DM12.) Göttingen's nightlife centers on the *Altstadt;* **Blue Note,** Wilhelmspl. 3, is *the* place for music and to hang with students. (Cover for weekly concerts DM8-30. Open daily from 8pm.)

Trains arrive at the station on Berlinerstr. from: Berlin (2½hr., every hr., DM100); Frankfurt (2hr., every hr., DM66); Hamburg (2hr., 2 per hr., DM80); and Hannover (1hr., 2 per hr., DM30). From the station, cross Berlinerstr., follow Goetheallee (which becomes Prinzenstr.), and turn right on Weenderstr. to reach the **tourist**

office, Markt 9, in the Altes Rathaus. (☎540 00; fax 400 29 98; email tourismus@goettingen.de. Open Apr.-Oct. M-F 9:30am-5pm, Sa-Su 10am-4pm; Nov.-Mar. M-F 9:30am-1pm and 2-6pm, Sa 10am-1pm.) The helpful staff and abundant singles (for an extra DM5) make the **Jugendherberge (HI),** Habichtsweg 2, a first choice for many. Take buses #8, 10, 11, 15, or 18 to Kornmarkt, then bus #6 (dir.: Klausberg) to Jugendherberge. (☎576 22. Breakfast included. Reception 6:30am-11:30pm. DM32, under 27 DM27.) For food, try **Shucan,** Weenderstr. 11, which offers sun and people-watching in the Marktpl. (Open Su-Th 9am-2pm, F-Sa 10am-3am.) **Groceries** can be found at **Plus,** Prinzenstr. 13, opposite the library. (Open M-F 8am-7:30pm, Sa 8am-4pm.) **Postal Code:** 37073.

COLOGNE (KÖLN)   ☎0221

Founded as a Roman colony (*colonia*, the root of the word "Köln") in AD 48, Cologne gained fame and fortune in the Middle Ages as an elite university town and an important trade hub. While most of the inner city was destroyed in WWII, the magnificent Gothic cathedral survived no fewer than 14 bombings and remains Cologne's main attraction. Today, tourists come to see this symbol of Cologne's rebirth, participate in bacchanalian celebrations, and immerse themselves in the burgeoning fine arts scene.

▛ TRANSPORTATION

Flights: From Köln-Bonn Flughafen; shuttles fly to **Berlin** (☎ (01803) 80 38 03; 24 per day). Bus #170 leaves for the airport from stop #3 at the train station (20min.; daily at 5:30, 6, and 6:30am; every 15min. 7am-8pm, every 30min. 8-11pm; DM8.70).

Trains: From the Hauptbahnhof to: **Berlin** (6½hr.; every 2hr.; DM172, students DM138); **Dresden** (7 hr.; 2 per hr.; DM191, students DM153); **Düsseldorf** (1hr.; 5per hr.; DM12.60, students DM10); **Frankfurt** (2hr.; 3-4 per hr.; DM61, students DM49); **Hamburg** (5hr.; 3 per hr.; DM123, students DM98); **Munich** (6hr.; 5 per hr.; DM173, students DM138); **Amsterdam** (2½hr., every hr., DM79); **Brussels** (2½hr., every 2hr., DM54.80); and **Paris** (4hr., every 2hr., DM190.80).

Ferries: Köln-Düsseldorfer (☎208 83 18) begins its ever-popular Rhine cruises here in Cologne. Sail upstream to **Koblenz** (DM59.80, round-trip DM66.40) or take the Rhein-Jet instead of a train to **Bonn** (DM11.20, round-trip DM17.80). Students 50% off; most trips (excluding hydrofoils) covered by Eurail.

Public Transportation: VRS (Verkehrsverbund Rhein-Sieg) offices have free maps of the S- and U-Bahn, bus, and streetcar lines; one is downstairs in the train station near the U-Bahn. Single-fare tickets DM2.20-14.50; day pass DM9.50.

▟ ORIENTATION AND PRACTICAL INFORMATION

Eight bridges carry Cologne across the Rhine, but nearly all sights and the city center can be found on the western side. The train station is in the northern part of the **Innenstadt** ("town center"). The Altstadt is split into **Altstadt-Nord,** near the **Hauptbahnhof,** and **Altstadt-Süd,** south of the **Severinsbrücke.**

Tourist Office: Verkehrsamt, Unter Fettenhennen 19 (☎221 33 45; fax 22 12 33 20; www.koeln.de), opposite the Dom. Free maps; books rooms (DM6 fee). Open May-Oct. M-Sa 8am-10:30pm, Su 9am-10:30pm; Nov.-Apr. M-Sa 8am-9pm, Su 9:30am-7pm.

Currency Exchange: An office at the train station is open daily 7am-9pm, but the service charges are lower at the post office (see below).

Gay and Lesbian Services: Schulz Schwulen- und Lesbenzentrum, Kartäuserwall 18 (☎93 18 80 80), near Chlodwigpl. Info, movies, youth activities, library, and popular cafe. The tourist office also offers a "Gay City Map" with listings and locations of gay-friendly hotels, bars, and clubs.

Laundry: Eco-Express, on Richard-Wagner-Str. Wash DM6; soap included. Dry DM1 per 10min. Open M-Sa 6am-11pm.

GERMANY

Emergency: Police, ☎110. **Fire** and **ambulance,** ☎112.

Pharmacy: Dom-Apotheke, Komödienstr. 5 (☎257 67 54), near the station, posts a list of after-hours pharmacies. English spoken. Open M-F 8am-6:30pm, Sa 9am-1pm.

Internet access: In **FuturePoint** (see **Food**) and in the **Station Hostel for Backpackers** (see **Accommodations**)

Post Office: Hauptpostamt, at the corner of Breitestr. and Auf der Ruhr. **Poste restante:** Postlagernde Briefe für Kelly MAUCERI, Hauptpostamt, 50667 Köln, Germany. Open M-F 8am-8pm, Sa 8am-4pm.

▌ ACCOMMODATIONS

Most hotels fill up in spring and fall when conventions come to town, and the two hostels are nearly always booked from June to September. The main hotel haven centers around **Brandenburgerstr.**, on the less interesting side of the train station. The **Mitwohnzentrale,** An der Bottmühle 16 (☎194 45), finds apartments for longer stays. (Open M-F 9am-1pm and 2-4pm.) Call ahead.

Station Hostel and Bar, Rheingasse 34-36 (☎23 02 47; email station@t-online.de). The new addition to the Station hostel family, providing larger and cleaner rooms for just a few marks more. Reception all day except between 1pm-5pm. Singles DM50; doubles DM80; triples DM108; quads DM132.

Station Hostel for Backpackers, Marzellenstr. 44-48 (☎912 53 01; email station@t-online.de). From the station, walk 1 block along Dompropst-Ketzer-Str. and turn right on Marzellenstr. Independent hostel with impeccable rooms and a relaxed atmosphere. Sheets DM3. Laundry DM6. Internet DM1 for 30min., then 10 pfennigs per min. Reception 24hr. Dorms DM27; singles DM40; doubles DM70.

Jansen Pension, Richard-Wagner-Str. 18 (☎25 18 75). U1, U6-7, U15, U17, or U19: Rudolfplatz; then take Richard-Wagner-Str. to just before Brüsselerstr. Charming rooms in a Victorian townhouse. Breakfast included. Singles DM55-DM70; doubles DM110.

Das Kleine Stapelhäuschen, Fischmarkt 1-3 (☎257 78 62). Cross the Altenmarkt from the back of the Rathaus and take Lintgasse to the Fischmarkt. A perfectly elegant Rheinische inn replete with oak furnishings and a stunning circular staircase. Breakfast included. Singles DM75-87, with shower and TV DM98-125, with bath and TV DM125-135; doubles DM125-135, DM170-185, DM195-235.

Hotel Heinzelmännchen, Hohe Pforte 5-7 (☎21 12 17). Take bus #132 (dir.: Frankenstr.) to Waidmarkt, or walk down the Hohestr. shopping zone until it becomes Hohe Pforte. Breakfast included. Reception 6am-11pm. Singles DM65-72; doubles DM115; triples from DM125.

Jugendherberge Köln-Deutz (HI), Siegesstr. 5a (☎81 47 11), over the Hohenzollernbrücke. S6, S11, or S12: Köln-Deutz; from the main exit, go down Neuhöfferstr. and take the first right. Small but clean rooms. Breakfast included. Laundry free; soap DM1. Reception 11am-1am. Curfew 1am. DM37, under 27 DM33.

Jugendgästehaus Köln-Riehl (HI), An der Schanz 14 (☎76 70 81). U6 (dir.: Ebertplatz/Mülheim) to Boltensternstr. Or walk north along the Rhine on Konrad-Adenauer-Ufer until it becomes An der Schanz (40min.). Breakfast included. Reception 24hr. Call ahead. Dorms DM38.50; singles DM63.50.

Campingplatz Poll, Weidenweg 2 (☎83 19 66), on the Rhine, southeast of the Altstadt. U16: Marienburg; then cross the Rodenkirchener Brücke. Reception 8am-noon and 5-8pm. Open Apr.-Oct. DM8 per person, DM4 per tent, DM4 per car.

▌ FOOD

Cologne cuisine includes scrumptious *Rievekoochen* (potato pancakes), slabs of fried potato dunked in *Apfelmus* (applesauce), as well as smooth **Kölsch** beer. Small cafes and cheap restaurants line **Zülpicherstr.** (U7 or U9: Zülpicher Platz). Mid-priced ethnic restaurants lie around the perimeter of the Altstadt, particularly from **Hohenzollernring** to **Hohenstaufenring;** the city's best cheap eats are in the Turkish district on **Weideng.** Pick up groceries at **Mini-Mal,** Hohenstaufenring 30. (Open M-F 8am-8pm, Sa 8am-4pm.)

GERMANY

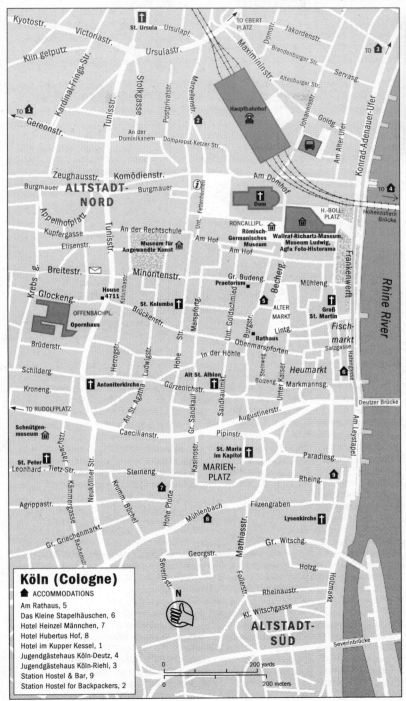

Köln (Cologne)

🏠 ACCOMMODATIONS

Am Rathaus, 5
Das Kleine Stapelhäuschen, 6
Hotel Heinzel Männchen, 7
Hotel Hubertus Hof, 8
Hotel im Kupper Kessel, 1
Jugendgästehaus Köln-Deutz, 4
Jugendgästehaus Köln-Riehl, 3
Station Hostel & Bar, 9
Station Hostel for Backpackers, 2

0   200 yards
0   200 meters

■ **Brauhaus Früh am Dom,** Am Hof 12-14 (☎258 03 97). Offers the best Kölsch in town. Patrons enjoy a number of Kölner and German specialties in the outdoor Biergarten. Meals DM9-30. Open daily 8am-midnight, menu until 11:45pm.

Café Waschsalon, Ehrenstr. 77 (☎13 33 78). Filled with decorative washing machines; turn on the spin in your head with their fine drink assortment. Breakfast served until 4pm from DM5.50. Open M-Th 8am-1am, F 8am-3am, Sa 10am-3am, Su 10am-1am.

Café Magnus, Zülpicherstr. 48 (☎24 16 14 69), is popular with the university crowd. Pizzas and salads from DM6; pasta from DM10. Open daily 9am-3pm.

Päffgen-Brauerei, Friesenstr. 64-66 (☎13 54 61). A local favorite since 1883. Room to seat 600 in this mecca of breweries. Quench more than your thirst and sample a hearty meal for DM3-DM30. Open daily 10am-midnight. Kitchen open 11am-11pm.

Sushi Nara, Friesenstr. 70, has excellent sushi at unbeatable prices. Meals from DM10. Open M-F noon-3:30pm and 5:30pm-midnight, Sa noon-midnight, Su 6-11pm.

Sasmus Island, Heinsberg 11a (☎23 34 98), at the corner of Heinsberg and Zülpicherstr. Spanish, Creole, Cajun, and South American dishes (from DM10); equally exotic drinks to match. Open daily 8am-1am, breakfast M-Sa served until 1pm, Su until 3pm.

👁 SIGHTS

INNENSTADT

In the shadow of the cathedral, the Hohenzollernbrücke crosses the Rhine at one edge of the pedestrian-friendly Innenstadt. The majestic bridge empties out onto a promenade guarded by equestrian statues of the imperial family. A monumental flight of stairs leads to **Heinrich-Böll-Platz** and its cultural center, a complex of modern architecture that succeeds in complementing the **Dom.** Further on, the squares and crooked streets of the **Altstadt** and old **Fischmarkt** district open onto paths along the river; the cafe terraces overlook an expanse of grass along the river, perfect for a picnic serenaded by musicians.

■ DOM

Directly across from the train station. ☎*52 19 77. Open daily 6am-7pm. Tower open May-Sept. 9am-6pm; Mar., Apr., and Oct. 9am-5pm; Nov.-Feb. 9am-4pm. Domschatzkammer open Apr.-Oct. M-Sa 9am-5pm, Su 1-4pm; Nov.-Mar. M-Sa 9am-4pm, Su 1-4pm. DM3, students DM1.50. Tours in German M-Sa 11am, 12:30, 2, and 3:30pm, Su 2 and 3:30pm; DM6, students DM3. Tours in English M-Sa 10:30am and 2:30pm, Su 2:30pm; DM7, students DM4. Cathedral free. Tower DM3, students DM1.50.*

Visitors exiting Cologne's train station are immediately treated to the beauty, power, and sorrow emanating from Germany's greatest cathedral. Six centuries in the making, the cathedral was finally completed in 1880 in High Gothic style, and is the largest of its kind in the world. The stunning stained-glass windows cast a harlequin display of colored light over the interior. To the right of the center altar is the **Dombild triptych,** a masterful 15th-century painting and gilded altarpiece. Look behind the altar for the brightly shining **Shrine of the Magi,** a reliquary of the Three Kings in blinding gold brought to the city in 1164. In the fenced-off area to the left of the center altar behind the floor mosaics stand the 976 **Gero crucifix,** the oldest intact sculpture of *Christus patiens* (depicting a crucified Christ with eyes shut), and Rubens' **Crucifixion of St. Peter.** In one corner of the cathedral is the **Domschatzkammer,** which holds the requisite clerical artwork and reliquaries, including thorn, cross, bits of nail, and pieces of 18 saints.

A mere 509 steps lead to the top of the **Südturm** (south tower); catch your breath 400 steps up at the **Glockenstube,** where the 24-ton **Der große Peter,** the world's heaviest swinging bell, roosts. From the top of the tower, you can peer down at the Rhine river and the city at your feet. The allure of the cathedral when it is illuminated from dusk to midnight is irresistible, drawing natives and tourists alike to the expansive **Domvorplatz** for a daily carnival of relaxation, art, and activism. Since time and acid rain have slowly eroded most of the Dom's detail, every piece is gradually being reproduced and replaced with new, treated stone. Help and play the "Dom lottery" at posts around the Domvorplatz and save a statue's fingernail.

INSULTS FOR SALE Free speech in Germany does not imply *cost-free* speech—dropping insults will unload your wallet in no time. Public humiliation in Germany carries such destructive force that officials have created an insult price list; offended or drunk budget travelers should beware. The heaviest fines are incurred by mouth-flappers who put down a police officer's respectability: belting out *Trottel in Uniform* (fool in uniform) costs DM3000, while the lesser insult *Dumme Kuh* (dumb cow) requires a mere DM1200 payoff. Call any uniformed official *Idiot* and you'll be out a whopping DM3000. The budget traveler's insult, *Holzkopf* (wood-headed), goes for DM1500. Equivalent insults in English are not exempt; stories abound of policemen who've doled out thousands of *Marks* in fines to tourists who think that Germans don't understand what "asshole" means. We tell you this merely as a warning—and prices, of course, are subject to change, you idiot.

GROß ST MARTIN. Along with the cathedral, **Groß St. Martin** defines the legendary Rhine panorama of Cologne. The renovated church was reopened in 1985 after near-destruction in WWII. The crypts house an esoteric collection of stones and diagrams. *(At Groß St. Martin 9, south of the cathedral near the Fischmarkt. ☎257 79 24. Open M-F 10:15am-6pm, Sa 10am-12:30pm and 1:30-6pm, Su 2-4pm. Church free. Crypt DM1.)*

HOUSE #4711. The magic water **Eau de Cologne,** once prescribed as a drinkable curative, made the town a household name. If you're after the real thing, be sure your bottle says *Echt kölnisch Wasser* ("real Cologne water"), or look for the "4711" label. Its name comes from the Mühlens family home, labeled House #4711 by the Napoleonic system that abolished street names. The house today is a boutique, with a small fountain continually dispensing the famous scented water. Visit the upstairs museum gallery for a full history of the famous fragrance; come on the hour to hear the **Glockenspiel,** which plays a pre-programmed selection. *(Glockeng, at the intersection with Tunisstr. From Hohestr., turn right on Brückenstr., which becomes Glockeng. Open M-F 9:30am-8pm, Sa 9:30am-4pm.)*

RÖMISCHES PRAETORIUM UND KANAL. Classical historians will be impressed by the excavated ruins of the former Roman military headquarters. Resembling the abandoned set of an epic movie, the underground museum displays remains of Roman gods and a befuddling array of rocks left by the city's early inhabitants. *(From the Rathaus, take a right toward the swarm of hotels and then a left onto Kleine Budengasse. Open Tu-F 10am-4pm, Sa-Su 11am-4pm. DM3, students DM1.50.)*

RATHAUS. Bombed in WWII, Cologne's city hall has been reconstructed in its original style. The Gothic tower stands guard over Baroque cherubs flying around an ornate 1570 Renaissance arcade called the *loggia,* the only section to survive the war. The tower is adorned with a diverse array of historical and cultural figures; Marx and Rubens loom above rows of popes and emperors. A Glockenspiel offers a titillating tintinnabulary experience daily at noon and 5pm. *(Open M-Th 7:30am-5pm, F 7:30am-2pm. Tours W at 3 pm. Free.)*

MUSEUMS. Cologne's cultural, religious, and economic significance in Europe stocks the city's museums with a vast and impressive array of holdings. The major museums are free with the **Köln Tourismus Card.** (Sold in many high-end hotels in the Innenstadt, entitles bearer to a city tour, discounts on Rhine cruises, a three-day pass to all city museums, and use of the public transportation system, DM30.) Between the cathedral and the Hohenzollernbrücke, the cultural center on Heinrich-Böll-Platz houses three complementary collections. The **Wallraf-Richartz Museum** features masterpieces from the Italian Renaissance to the French Impressionists; the **Museum Ludwig** spans Impressionism, Picasso, Dalí, Liechtenstein, Warhol, and art so new the glue has yet to dry; and the **Agfa Foto-Historama** includes a rotating display of Man Ray's works. *(Bischofsgartenstr. 1. Behind the Römisches-Germanisches Museum. ☎22 12 23 82. Open Tu 10am-8pm, W-F 10am-6pm, Sa-Su 11am-6pm. Tours Tu 6pm, W 4:30pm, Sa-Su 11:30am. DM10, students DM5.)* Next door, right off the Heinrich-Böll-Platz, the **Römisch-Germanisches Museum,** built on the ruins of a Roman villa, displays the world-famous Dionysus mosaic, the tomb of Publicus, an intimidating six-breasted sphinx, and some naughty candle-holders. *(Roncallipl. 4, between the Dom and Diözeansmusem. ☎22 12 44 28. Open Tu-Su 10am-5pm, W 10am-7pm. DM10, students DM5.)* Better than Willy Wonka's Chocolate Factory, the **Schokoladenmuseum** allows you to salivate at every step of the chocolate production process. Resist the urge to drool and wait for the free, but small, samples. *(Rheinauhafen 1a, near the Severinsbrücke. From the station, walk right along the Rhine, head under the Deutzer Brücke, and take the 1st footbridge. Open M-F 10am-6pm, Sa-Su 11am-7pm. Tours Sa 2 and 4pm, Su 11:30am, 2 and 4pm; DM3. DM10, students DM5.)* **NS-Dokumentations-Zentrum** portrays Cologne as it was during the Nazi regime and displays the 1,200 wall inscriptions made by political prisoners kept in the building. See the actual prison cells in the basement. All informational plaques and film clips in German. *(Am Appellhofpl. 23-25 at the corner of Elisenstr. ☎22 12 63 31. Open Tu-F 10am-4pm, Sa-Su 11am-4pm. Tours first Sa of the month at 2pm. DM5, students DM2.)*

🎵🎭 ENTERTAINMENT AND NIGHTLIFE

Celebrating lavishly has long been a tradition in Cologne. Roman mosaics dating back to AD 3 record the wild excesses of the city's early residents. Instead of grape-feeding and fig-wearing, modern life in Cologne now focuses on house music and a more sophisticated bump-and-grind. The city becomes a living spectacle during **Karneval,** a week-long pre-Lent festival celebrated in the hedonistic spirit of the city's Roman past. The weekend builds up to a bacchanalian parade on Rosenmontag, the last Monday before Lent (Feb. 26, 2001), when everyone is in costume and gives and receives dozens of *Bützchen* (kisses on a stranger's cheek). Pick up the *Karneval* booklet at the tourist office.

Students congregate in the *Bermuda-Dreieck* (triangle), bounded by **Zülpicherstr., Zülpicherpl., Roonstr.,** and **Luxemburgstr.** Gay nightlife runs up **Matthiasstr.** to **Mühlenbach, Hohe Pforte, Marienpl.,** and up to **Heumarkt** by the Deutzer Brücke. The tradition of Bacchus is still highly practiced in Cologne. At the **Brauhaüser,** waiters will greet you with a friendly "Kölsch?" and then proceed to bring drink after drink until you fall under the table unless you place your coaster over your glass.

Das Ding, Hohenstaufenring (☎24 63 48). Popular and smoky, with techno and other flavors. Cover DM8. Open M and W 9pm-2am, Tu and Th 9pm-3am.

Papa Joe's Jazzlokal, Buttermarkt 37 (☎257 79 31). Features high-caliber live jazz and oodles of New Orleans atmosphere. No cover. Open M-Sa 7pm-2am, Su 3:30pm-11pm.

Taco Loco, Zülpicherstr. 4a (☎240 41 88). With Happy "Hour" daily 6-8pm and tasty margaritas. Open M-Th and Su 10am-2am, F-Sa 10am-3am.

MTC, Zülpicherstr. 10 (☎240 15 16). From grunge to live concerts to recorded tunes. Cover DM6; includes 1 drink. Open M, W, and Su 9pm-2am, Tu and Th-Sa 9pm-3am.

The Corkonian, Alter Markt 51 (☎257 69 31). For a change of pace, this authentic Irish corner is pure pub. Throw out your lager for a dark beer topped with a clover. Open M-Th noon-1am, F-Sa noon-3am, and Su 11am-1am. After 8pm 20+.

GAY AND LESBIAN VENUES

Vampire, Rathenaupl. 5 (☎240 12 11). A laid-back atmosphere with a dark, soothing interior. Happy hour 8-9pm. Open Tu-Th and Su 8pm-1am; F-Sa 8pm-3am. No garlic.

Gloria, Apostelnstr. 11 (☎258 36 56). Crowded, popular, and plastered with cellophane wall-coverings, the cafe and occasional club is at the nexus of Cologne's trendy gay and lesbian scene. Cover around DM15. Open M-Th 9am-1am, Su 10am-1am.

BONN ☎0228

Derisively called the *Hauptdorf* (capital village), Bonn has been Germany's whipping boy for 50 years just because it's not Berlin. Bonn made it big by chance, being named the capital of West Germany simply because postwar chancellor Konrad Adenauer had a house in its suburbs. The Bundestag packed up and moved back to

Berlin in 1999, but Bonn remains a worthy destination with several museums, a bustling Altstadt, and a respected university.

🚆 **TRANSPORTATION. Trains** run to Cologne (30min., 6 per hr., DM10); Koblenz (1hr., 3 per hr., DM14.80); and Frankfurt (1½hr., every hr., DM59). Bonn is linked to Cologne and other riverside cities by the massive **VRS** (Verkehrsverbund Rhein-Sieg) S-Bahn and U-Bahn network. Areas are divided into Tarifzonen; the further you go, the more you pay. **Single tickets** (DM2.20-14.20), **4-ride tickets** (DM8-12.80), and **day tickets** (DM9.50-35) are available at Automaten and vending stations.

🛈 **PRACTICAL INFORMATION.** The **tourist office** is on Windeckstr. 2, am Münsterplatz, near the big Münster cathedral, in a passageway. (☎ 77 50 00; fax 77 50 77. Open M-F 9am-6:30pm, Sa 9am-4pm, Su 10am-2pm.) The **post office** is at Münsterplatz 17, down Poststr. from the train station. (Open M-F 8am-8pm, Sa 8am-4pm.) **Internet access** can be found at **Surf Inn** on the second floor of the SportArena, Remgiusstr. 6-8. (☎ 516 513. DM3 for 30min.) **Postal Code:** 53111.

🍴 **ACCOMMODATIONS AND FOOD.** Take bus #621 (dir.: Ippendorf Alten) to Jugendgästehaus to get to the **Jugendgästehaus Bonn-Venusberg (HI),** Haager Weg 42. (☎ 28 99 70. Breakfast included. Laundry DM10. Reception 9am-1am. Curfew 1am. DM39.) For a fabulous splurge, try **Hotel Hofgarten,** Fritz-Tillman-Str. 7. From the station turn right onto Maximilianstr., continue on Kaiserstr., and then turn left on Fritz-Tillman-Str. Live like an ambassador in this stately hotel. (☎ 22 34 82. Breakfast included. Call ahead. Singles DM75DM60-140; doubles DM125-185.) To reach **Campingplatz Genienaue,** Im Frankenkeller 49, take U16 or U63 to Rheinallee, then bus 613 (dir.: Giselherstr.) to Guntherstr.—turn left on Guntherstr. and right on Frankenkeller. (☎ 34 49 49. DM8 per person, DM5-8 per tent. Reception 9am-noon and 3-10pm.) **Cafe-Bistro Bonngoût,** Remigiusplatz 2-4, serves generous meals. (☎ 65 89 88. Open M-Sa 9am-1am, Su 10am-1am. Huge breakfasts for DM8-18 served M-F until noon, Sa until 1pm, Su until 3pm.)

🎭 **SIGHTS AND ENTERTAINMENT.** Bonn's old town center winds into a lively pedestrian zone littered with historic niches. The **Beethoven Geburtshaus** (birthplace), Bonng. 20, hosts a fantastic collection of his personal effects, from his primitive hearing aids to his first violin. (Open Apr.-Sept. M-Sa 10am-6pm, Su 11am-4pm; Oct.-Mar. M-Sa 10am-5pm, Su 11am-4pm. DM8, students DM6.) In its governmental heyday, the vaguely Bauhaus **Bundestag** earned the title of "least prepossessing parliament building" in the world; take U16, U63, or U66 to Heussallee/Bundeshaus, or bus #610 to Bundeshaus. Bonn's castles, palaces, and most museums lie just outside the inner city. Forty thousand students study within the **Kurfürstliches Schloß,** a huge 18th-century palace now serving as the center of Bonn's university. Down the Poppelsdorfer Allee promenade, the 18th-century **Poppelsdorfer Schloß** sports a French facade, an Italian courtyard, and manicured **botanical gardens.** (Gardens open May-Sept. M-F 9am-6pm, Su 9am-1pm; Oct.-Apr. M-F 9am-4pm, Su 9am-1pm. M-F free, Su DM1.) The **Bonncard** (DM24 per day from the tourist office) provides public transport and admission to most museums of the **Museum Mile** (U16, U63, or U66: Heussallee or Museum Koenig). The **Kunstmuseum Bonn,** Friedrich-Ebert Allee 2, has superb Expressionist and contemporary German art (open Tu and Th-Su 10am-6pm, W 10am-7pm; DM5, students DM3), while the art in the **Kunst- und Ausstellungshalle der BRD,** Friedrich-Ebert-Allee 4, is so new that you can smell the paint (open Tu-W 10am-9pm, Th-Su 10am-7pm; DM10, students DM5). The futuristic **Haus der Geschichte,** Adenauerallee 250, one block from the Kunstmuseum Bonn, offers an interactive look at German history. (Open Tu-Su 9am-7pm. Free.) For cultural and entertainment listings, check out the monthly *Schnüss,* or hang at **Café Göttlich,** on Franziskanerstr. near the university. (Open M-Sa 9am-4am, Su noon-2am.) The **Jazz Galerie,** Oxfordstr. 24, is a jumping bar and disco, as well as a hub for jazz and rock concerts. (Cover for concerts DM10-20, discos DM13, with 2 free drinks. Open M-Th and Su 9pm-3am, F-Sa 9pm-4am.)

AACHEN
☎0241

Charlemagne sang the mantra of multiculturalism when he made this the capital of his Frankish empire in the 8th century, and today international students and travelers continue to renew Aachen's vibrant atmosphere. The world-famous neo-Byzantine **Dom** is in the center of the city; beneath the chancel lie Charlemagne's bones. (☎470 91 27; www.aachendom.de. Open daily 7am-7pm. Tours M 11am and noon; Tu-F 11am, noon, 1, 2:30, and 3:30pm; Sa-Su 12:30, 1:30, 2:30, and 3:30pm. DM3.) The **Schatzkammer,** a treasury with the most famous likeness of Charlemagne, a gold-plated solid silver bust, is just around the corner to the right from the Dom, tucked into the Klostergasse. (Open M 10am-1pm, Tu-W and F-Su 10am-6pm, Th 10am-9pm. DM5, students DM3.) The 14th-century **Rathaus** looms over the wide Marktpl. and the cathedral. (Open daily 10am-6pm, Th until 9pm. DM3, students DM1.50.) You'll be greeted by a large clown in drag if you visit the ⧉**Ludwigforum für Internationales Kunst,** Jülicherstr. 97-109, in a converted Bauhaus umbrella factory, an art museum that showcases current greats (Jeff Koons's gigantic sex dolls) and soon-to-be-greats such as a 3 ft. Marge Simpson stone fertility doll. (Open Tu and Th 10am-5pm, W and F 10am-8pm, Sa-Su 11am-5pm. DM6, students DM3.)

Trains chug to: Cologne (1hr., 2-3 per hr., DM20); Amsterdam (4hr., 1-2 per hr., DM102); and Brussels (2hr., every hr., DM51). To get from the station to the **tourist office,** on Friedrich-Wilhelm-Pl. in the Atrium Elisenbrunnen, head up Bahnhofstr., turn left on Theaterstr., then right onto Kapuzinergraben. (☎180 29 60; fax 180 29 31. Open M-F 9am-6pm, Sa 9am-2pm.) **Internet access** is available at the city library, **Öffentliche Bibliothek,** Couverstr. 15. (Open Tu-W and F 11am-5:45pm, Th 1:15-8pm, Sa 10am-1pm. DM6 per hr.) The ⧉**Euroregionales Jugendgästehaus (HI),** Maria-Theresia-Allee 260, feels more like a hotel than a hostel. From the station, walk left on Lagerhausstr. until it intersects Karmeliterstr. and Mozartstr., then take bus #2 (dir.: Preusswald) to Ronheide or bus #12 (dir.: Diepenbendem) to Colynshof. (☎711 10 11. Breakfast included. Curfew 1am. DM38.50.) Take bus #5 from the bus station to Strangenhäuschen to reach **ETAP-Hotel,** Strangenhäuschen 15. (☎91 19 29. Breakfast DM8.90. Reception 6:30-10am and 5-11pm. Singles DM64; doubles DM76; F-Su all rooms DM64.) **Plus,** Marienbongard 27, off Pontstr., stocks **groceries.** (Open M-F 8am-8pm, Sa 8am-4pm.) **Pera,** Marienbongard 2, serves up generous portions of Mediterranean dishes. (☎409 37 80. Open daily 11am-1am.) **Postal Code:** 52064.

DÜSSELDORF
☎0211

The capital of North Rhine-Westphalia and the headquarters of Germany's largest corporations and fashion industry, Düsseldorf is a stately, modern metropolis, pulsing with an energy unlike anything in most other German cities. The city has rebounded from wartime destruction with resilience and fierce pride. By day, crowds line the Königsallee (a.k.a. the "Kö"), a one-kilometer-long fashion runway that sweeps down either side of the old town moat. At night, propriety (and sobriety) are cast aside as thousands of Düsseldorfers flock to the 500 pubs of the Altstadt, trading monocles and Rolexes for beer goggles and a good time.

▐ TRANSPORTATION

Trains: From the **Hauptbahnhof** to: **Berlin** (4hr.; 1-2 per hr.; DM170, student DM137); **Frankfurt** (3hr.; 3 per hr.; DM79, student DM65); **Hamburg** (3½hr.; 2 per hr.; DM116, student DM93); **Munich** (6hr.; 2-3 per hr.; DM184, student DM147); and **Amsterdam** (3hr.; every hr.; DM55); **Brussels** (3¼hr.; every hr.; DM59); **Paris** (4½hr.; 7 per day; DM140). To **Aachen** or **Cologne,** the S-Bahn is cheaper.

Public Transportation: The **Rheinbahn** includes the U-Bahn, S-Bahn, streetcars, and buses. **Single-fare tickets** DM2.10-12. The **Tagesticket** (from DM11) buys 24hr. of unlimited transport for up to 5 people. Vending machines sell tickets; pick up the *Fahrausweis* brochure in the tourist office for instructions. For **schedule info,** call ☎582 28.

■✦ 🛈 ORIENTATION AND PRACTICAL INFORMATION

The city of Düsseldorf is framed on the west by the Rhine river, and on the east by the Hofgarten, Germany's largest public park. The Altstadt is dotted with churches, museums, and plaques and signs bearing the name of Heinrich Heine, the town's favorite son.

Tourist Office: (☎17 20 20; fax 35 04 04; www.duesseldorf.de) Konrad-Adenauer-Pl. Walk up and to the right from the Hauptbahnhof. Open M-F 8:30am-6pm, Sa 9am-12:30pm; books rooms (from DM55) for a DM5 fee.

Currency Exchange: Deutsche Verkehrsbank, in the train station and the airport. Open M-Sa 7am-9pm, Su 8am-9pm.

Laundromat: Wasch Center, Friedrichstr. 92, down the street from the Kirchpl. S-Bahn. Wash DM6; soap included. Dry DM1 per 15min. Open M-Sa 6am-11pm.

Internet Access: Convenient to the train station is **Telenet-Center,** Fritz -Vomfeldestr. 34. DM3 for 30min. Open daily 9am-11pm. For food as accompaniment to web-surfing, **g@rden,** Rathansufer 8, is a futuristic option. DM10 per hour. Open daily 11am-1am.

Post Office: Hauptpostamt, Konrad-Adenauer-Pl. Address mail to be held: *Postlagernde Briefe* für Karina ISSEKUTZ, Hauptpostamt, Konrad-Adenauer-Pl., 40210 Düsseldorf, Germany. Open M-F 8am-6pm, Sa 9am-2pm. **Postal Code:** 40210.

▛ ACCOMMODATIONS

Corporate convention crowds make rooms scarce and costly; call at least a month ahead if possible. Most rooms go for at least DM50 per person even in off-season. Cheap hotels populate the seedy neighborhood around the train station.

Jugendgästehaus Düsseldorf (HI), Düsseldorferstr. 1 (☎55 73 10; email jgh-duesseldorf@t-online.de), just over the Rheinkniebrücke from the Altstadt. Take U70 or U74-77 to Luegplatz; then walk 500m down Kaiser-Wilhelm-Ring. Unbeatable location. Reception 7am-1pm. Curfew 1am, but doors open every hr. 2-6am. DM42, under 27 DM38.

Hotel Schaum, Gustav-Poengsenstr. 63. (☎311 65 10). From the main train station, exit going left along Graf-Adolfstr. Take your first left and follow it along the tracks to Gustav-Poengsenstr. Singles DM60, with bath DM80; doubles DM100-120.

Hotel Bristol, Aderstr. 8 (☎37 07 50), 1 block south of Graf-Adolfstr. Large rooms in this newly-renovated hotel. Singles DM75-95; doubles DM120-140.

Hotel Manhattan, Graf-Adolfstr. 39 (☎37 02 44), 2 blocks from the station. Here lies the ghost of mid-1980s consumer America—including neon signs and countless Coca-Cola posters. Singles DM68-105; doubles DM100-150.

Hotel Diana, Jahnstr. 31 (☎37 50 71), 5 blocks from the station. Head left down Graf-Adolfstr., left on Hüttenstr., and right on Jahnstr. Ugly tile, but it's clean. Breakfast included. Reception 24hr. Singles DM65; doubles DM95, with bath DM135.

Camping: Kleiner Torfbruch (☎899 20 38). S-Bahn to Düsseldorf Geresheim, then bus #735 (dir.: Stamesberg) to Seeweb. DM7.50 per person, DM10 per tent.

🍴 FOOD

Rows of pizzerias, *Döner* stands, and Chinese eateries reach from **Heinrich-Heine-Allee** to the banks of the Rhine in the Altstadt. **Olto Mess supermarket** in on Karlspl. in the Altstadt. (Open M-F 8am-8pm, Sa 8am-4pm.)

La Copa, Bergerstr. 4 (☎323 88 58). Offers Spanish flair with 50 tasty tapas dishes (DM8-15). Open daily noon-midnight.

Marché, Königsallee 60 (☎32 06 81), in the Kö-Galerie mall. If you must dine on the Kö, this is a classy cafeteria-style restaurant where you won't spend a whole week's budget on a meal. Main dishes from DM7. Open M-Th and Su 9am-9pm, F-Sa 9am-10pm.

Galerie Burghof, Burgallee 1-3 (☎40 14 23), next to Friedrich's Rhine ruins. U79 to Klemensplatz. Walk down Kaiserwerther Markt, turn left on the Rhine promenade. Among its decorations: a 1932 Rolls Royce filled with stuffed chickens. Open daily 11am-1am, pancakes served M-F 6-10:45pm, Sa 2-10:45pm, Su 2-11pm.

Zum Uerige, Bergerstr. 1 (☎86 69 90). Serves up heavy, traditional German fare of Blutwust (blood sausages, DM4) and Mainz cheese (DM4). Open daily 10am-midnight. Kitchen open M-F 6-9pm, Sa 1am-4pm.

👁 SIGHTS

ALTSTADT AND ENVIRONS

KÖNIGSALLEE. The glitzy Königsallee, just outside the Altstadt, embodies the vitality and glamor of Düsseldorf. What it doesn't have in fashion-center prestige à la Milan or New York, it more than makes up for in pretension. Midway up is the awesome **Kö-Galerie,** a gaudy marble-and-copper complex of one haughty store after another—even the mannequins have attitude.

KUNSTSAMMLUNG NORDRHEIN-WESTFALEN. This art museum is in the black, reflecting glass edifice west of the Hofgarten. Skylights lavish sunshine on the exhibits of works by Matisse, Picasso, Surrealists, and Expressionists. The collection of works by Paul Klee is one of the most extensive in the world. *(Grabbepl. 5. U70, U75-76, or U78-79: Heinrich-Heine-Allee; walk north 2 blocks. ☎838 10. Open Tu-Th and Sa-Su 10am-6pm, F 10am-8pm. Tours Su 11am, W 3:30pm, and F 6pm. DM5, students DM3. Special exhibits DM12, students DM8.)*

HOFGARTEN AND GOETHEMUSEUM. At the upper end of the Kö, the Hofgarten park is an oasis of green, inside urban Düsseldorf. The 18th-century Schloß Jägerhof houses the Goethemuseum behind its pink facade. *(Jakobistr. 2. In Schloß Jägerhof, at the east end of the garden. Streetcar #707 or bus #752 to Schloß Jägerhof. ☎899 62 62. Open Tu-F and Su 11am-5pm, Sa 1-5pm. DM4, students DM2.)* The Neoclassical **Ratinger Tor** gate, halfway down the length of the park, opens onto Heinrich-Heine-Allee.

KUNSTHALLE. Across the square from the Kunstsammlung Nordrhein-Westfalen is the Kunsthalle—not a museum, mind you, but a forum for modern exhibits of every shape and size. The stove-pipe on the museum is an art piece by Joseph Beuys intended to symbolize the link between art and the real world. *(Grabbepl. 4. ☎32 70 23. Open Tu-Su 11am-6pm. DM10, students DM7.)*

ELSEWHERE IN DÜSSELDORF

SCHLOß BENRATH. The Schloß (castle) sits in the suburbs of Düsseldorf, a monument to the inferiority complexes of the aristocracy. The architect used strategically placed mirrors and false exterior windows to make the squat, pink castle appear larger than it is, but the enormous, neurotically geometrical garden tempers the effect. It was originally built 200 years ago as a pleasure palace and hunting grounds for Elector Karl Theodor. *(S6 (dir.: Köln) to Benrath. Open Tu-Su 10am-5pm. DM7, students DM3.50.)*

KUNSTMUSEUM DÜSSELDORF. At the far end of the Hofgarten, where the park meets the Rhine, the **Kunstmuseum Düsseldorf** balances Baroque and Romantic art with a 20th-century collection. The **Kunstpalast** is an extension of the Kunstmuseum devoted to rotating contemporary exhibits. *(Ehrenhof 5. ☎899 62 40. Open Tu-Su 11am-6pm. DM5, students DM2.50.)*

KAISERWERTH. North on the Rhine, but still within Düsseldorf, dwell the ruins of Emperor Friedrich's palace in the tiny town of Kaiserwerth. Built in 1184, the palace was destroyed in 1702 in the War of Spanish Succession, but the gloomy Kaiserpfalz frame remains. *(Take U79 to Klemensplatz, then follow Kaiserwerther Markt to the Rhine and walk another 150m.)*

GERMANY

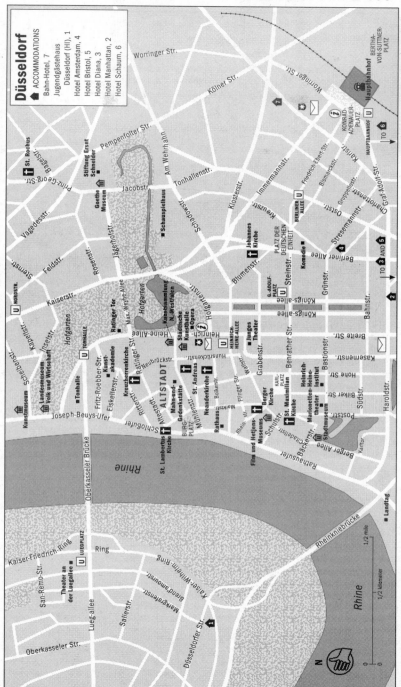

Düsseldorf

▲ ACCOMMODATIONS
Bahn-Hotel, 7
Jugendgästehaus
Düsseldorf (HI), 1
Hotel Amsterdam, 4
Hotel Bristol, 5
Hotel Diana, 3
Hotel Manhattan, 2
Hotel Schaum, 6

Frankfurt

🏠 ACCOMMODATIONS

Jugendherberge,
Pension Brüns, &
Pension Backer, A
Pension Gölz, B

EKO-HOUSE. Düsseldorf has the largest Japanese population of any European city. The EKO-House, across the Rhine from the Altstadt, is a beautiful garden and cultural center with frequent tea ceremonies and readings from Buddhist texts. *(Brüggener Weg 6. Take U70 or U74-77 to Belsenplatz. Follow Quirinstr. to Comeniusplatz and turn left again on Niederkasselerstr. ☎ 57 40 71. Open Tu-Su 1-5pm. DM5, students DM3.)*

🎵 ENTERTAINMENT

Folklore holds that Düsseldorf's 500 pubs make up *die längste Theke der Welt* ("the longest bar in the world"). Whether or not that's true, pubs in the Altstadt are standing-room-only by 6pm, and it's nearly impossible to see where one pub ends and the next begins. **Bolkerstr.** is jam-packed nightly with street performers of the musical and party-scene varieties.

Pam-Pam, Bolkerstr. 34 (☎ 854 93 93). This downstairs discotheque is overflowing by midnight. Dance the night away to house, rock, pop, and plenty of American music. Open F-Sa 10pm-dawn.

La Rocca, Grünstr. 8 (☎ 880 04 41). Just off the Kö, this posh club serves as a showcase for fashion purchases made during the day. Cover DM8. Open Th-Sa 10pm-5am.

Zum Uel, Ratingerstr. 16 (☎ 32 53 69). The quintessential German *Kneip*. The locals pack this pub, giving it a true beer-hall flavor. Stop here for a glass of Schlösser Alt (DM2.80 for 0.2L). Open M-Tu, Th, and Su 10am-1am, W and F 10am-3am.

Oberbayern, Bolerstr. 37. Come and join in the hearty singing while you take a swig from another liter. Open F-Sa 3pm-5am, Su 3pm-2am.

WORLDWIDE CALLING MADE EASY

The MCI WorldCom Card, designed specifically to keep you in touch with the people that matter the most to you.

MCI WORLDCOM   *WORLDPHONE.*

1·800·888·8000

J. L. SMITH

www.wcom.com/worldphone

HOW TO MAKE CALLS USING YOUR MCI WORLDCOM CARD

> **When calling from the U.S., Puerto Rico, the U.S. Virgin Islands or Canada** to virtually anywhere in the world:

1. Dial 1-800-888-8000
2. Enter your card number + PIN, listen for the dial tone
3. Dial the number you are calling :
   Domestic Calls: Area Code + Phone number
   International Calls:
   011+ Country Code + City Code + Phone Number

> **When calling from outside the U.S.,** use WorldPhone from over 125 countries and places worldwide:

1. Dial the WorldPhone toll-free access number of the country you are calling from.
2. Follow the voice instructions or hold for a WorldPhone operator to complete the call.

> **For calls from your hotel:**

1. Obtain an outside line.
2. Follow the instructions above on how to place a call.
   Note: If your hotel blocks the use of your MCI WorldCom Card, you may have to use an alternative location to place your call.

RECEIVING INTERNATIONAL COLLECT CALLS*

Have family and friends call you collect at home using WorldPhone Service and pay the same low rate as if you called them.

1. Provide them with the WorldPhone access number for the country they are calling from (In the U.S., 1-800-888-8000; for international access numbers see reverse side).
2. Have them dial that access number, wait for an operator, and ask to call you collect at your home number.

* For U.S. based customers only.

START USING YOUR MCI WORLDCOM CARD TODAY. MCI WORLDCOM STEPSAVERS℠

Get the same low rate per country as on calls from home, when you:

1. **Receive international collect calls to your home** using WorldPhone access numbers

2. **Make international calls with your MCI WorldCom Card** from the U.S.*

3. **Call back to anywhere in the U.S. from Abroad** using your MCI WorldCom Card and WorldPhone access numbers.

* An additional charge applies to calls from U.S. pay phones.

WorldPhone Overseas Laptop Connection Tips —
Visit our website, www.wcom.com/worldphone, to learn how to access the Internet and email via your laptop when traveling abroad using the MCI WorldCom Card and WorldPhone access numbers.

Travelers Assist® — When you are overseas, get emergency interpretation assistance and local medical, legal, and entertainment referrals. Simply dial the country's toll-free access number.

Planning a Trip?—Call the WorldPhone customer service hotline at 1-800-736-1828 for new and updated country access availability or visit our website:

www.wcom.com/worldphone

MCI WorldCom Worldphone Access Numbers

Easy Worldwide Calling

MCI WORLDCOM.

The MCI WorldCom Card.
The easy way to call when traveling worldwide.

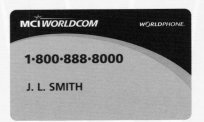

MCI **WORLDCOM**   WORLDPHONE.

1·800·888·8000

J. L. SMITH

The MCI WorldCom Card gives you…

- Access to the US and other countries worldwide.
- Customer Service 24 hours a day
- Operators who speak your language
- Great MCI WorldCom rates and no sign-up fees

For more information or to apply for a Card call:

1-800-955-0925

Outside the U.S., call MCI WorldCom collect (reverse charge) at:

1-712-943-6839

COUNTRY	WORLDPHONE TOLL-FREE ACCESS #
Argentina (CC)	
Using Telefonica	0800-222-6249
Using Telecom	0800-555-1002
Australia (CC) ♦	
Using OPTUS	1-800-551-111
Using TELSTRA	1-800-881-100
Austria (CC) ♦	0800-200-235
Bahamas (CC) +	1-800-888-8000
Belgium (CC) ♦	0800-10012
Bermuda (CC) +	1-800-888-8000
Bolivia (CC) ♦	0-800-2222
Brazil (CC)	000-8012
British Virgin Islands +	1-800-888-8000
Canada (CC)	1-800-888-8000
Cayman Islands +	1-800-888-8000
Chile (CC)	
Using CTC	800-207-300
Using ENTEL	800-360-180
China ♦	108-12
Mandarin Speaking Operator	108-17
Colombia (CC) ♦	980-9-16-0001
Collect Access in Spanish	980-9-16-1111
Costa Rica ♦	0800-012-2222
Czech Republic (CC) ♦	00-42-000112
Denmark (CC) ♦	8001-0022
Dominica+	1-800-888-8000
Dominican Republic (CC) +	
Collect Access	1-800-888-8000
Collect Access in Spanish	1121

COUNTRY	ACCESS #
Ecuador (CC) +	999-170
El Salvador (CC)	800-1767
Finland (CC) ♦	08001-102-80
France (CC) ♦	0-800-99-0019
French Guiana (CC)	0-800-99-0019
Germany (CC)	0800-888-8000
Greece (CC) ♦	00-800-1211
Guam (CC)	1-800-888-8000
Guatemala (CC) ♦	99-99-189
Haiti +	
Collect Access	193
Collect access in Creole	190
Honduras +	8000-122
Hong Kong (CC)	800-96-1121
Hungary (CC) ♦	06*-800-01411
India (CC)	000-127
Collect access	000-126
Ireland (CC)	1-800-55-1001
Israel (CC) ♦	1-800-920-2727
Italy (CC) ♦	172-1022
Jamaica +	
Collect Access	1-800-888-8000
From pay phones	#2
Japan (CC) ♦	
Using KDD	00539-121 ▶
Using IDC	0066-55-121
Using JT	0044-11-121

COUNTRY	ACCESS #
Korea (CC)	
To call using KT	00729-14
Using DACOM	00309-12
Phone Booths +	
Press red button ,03, then*	
Military Bases	550-2255
Luxembourg (CC)	8002-0112
Malaysia (CC) ♦	1-800-80-0012
Mexico (CC)	01-800-021-8000
Monaco (CC) ♦	800-90-019
Netherlands (CC) ♦	0800-022-91-22
New Zealand (CC)	000-912
Nicaragua (CC)	166
Norway (CC) ♦	800-19912
Panama	00800-001-0108
Philippines (CC) ♦	
Using PLDT	105-14
Filipino speaking operator	105-15
Using Bayantel	1237-14
Using Bayantel (Filipino)	1237-77
Using ETPI (English)	1066-14
Poland (CC) +	800-111-21-22
Portugal (CC) ♦	800-800-123
Romania (CC) +	01-800-1800
Russia (CC) ♦	
Russian speaking operator	
	747-3320
Using Rostelcom	747-3322
Using Sovintel	960-2222
Saudi Arabia (CC)	1-800-11

COUNTRY	WORLDPHONE TOLL-FREE ACCESS #
Singapore (CC)	8000-112-112
Slovak Republic (CC)	08000-00112
South Africa (CC)	0800-99-0011
Spain (CC)	900-99-0014
St. Lucia +	1-800-888-8000
Sweden (CC) ♦	020-795-922
Switzerland (CC) ♦	0800-89-0222
Taiwan (CC) ♦	0080-13-4567
Thailand (CC)	001-999-1-2001
Turkey (CC) ♦	00-8001-1177
United Kingdom (CC)	
Using BT	0800-89-0222
Using C& W	0500-89-0222
Venezuela (CC) + ♦	800-1114-0
Vietnam +	1201-1022

KEY

Note: Automation available from most locations. Countries where automation is not yet available are shown in *Italic*

(CC) Country-to-country calling available.

+   Limited availability.

✱   Not available from public pay phones.

♦   Public phones may require deposit of coin or phone card for dial tone.

●   Local service fee in U.S. currency required to complete call.

▶   Regulation does not permit Intra-Japan Calls.

✱   Wait for second dial tone.

■   Local surcharge may apply.

Hint: For Puerto Rico and Caribbean Islands not listed above, you can use 1-800-888-8000 as the WorldPhone access number.

FRANKFURT AM MAIN ☎ 069

Known to some as "Bankfurt" or "Mainhattan," Frankfurt is a thriving financial and commercial center. Although it perhaps lacks the architectural beauty common to more traditional German cities, its integral economic role as home to the central bank of the European Union lends it a glitzy vitality—international offices, skyscrapers, and expensive cars lie at every intersection—Natives Anne Frank and Goethe, as well as the social theorists of the Frankfurt School, have enriched the city's cultural treasury, and the city government spends more on cultural attractions and tourism than any other German city. If all this isn't enough to make you visit, the likelihood of your passing through Frankfurt's highly trafficked train station or airport probably is.

▢ TRANSPORTATION

Flights: Flughafen Rhein-Main (for info call ☎ 69 01). S14 and S15 connects to the Hauptbahnhof every 15min. Buy tickets (DM6.10) from the green *Automaten* (vending machines) marked *Fahrkarten*.

Trains: Info and reservations, ☎ (0180) 599 66 33. To: **Berlin** (5-6hr.; 2 per hr.; DM207, under 26 DM166); **Cologne** (2½hr.; 2 per hr.; DM70, under 26 DM61); **Hamburg** (6hr.; 2 per hr.; DM191, under 26 DM153); **Munich** (3½-4½hr.; 2 per hr.; DM212, under 26 DM118); **Paris** (6-8hr.; every 2hr.; DM140, under 26 DM115); and **Rome** (15hr.; every hr.; DM279, under 26 DM228).

Public Transportation: Runs until about 1am. Refer to the color **subway** map in the front of this guide. **Tageskarte** passes provide unlimited transportation on the U-Bahn, S-Bahn, streetcars, and buses (valid until midnight on the day of purchase); buy from any *Automat* (DM8.50). **Single-ride** tickets are valid for 1hr. in one direction, including transfers (rush-hour DM2.90, off-peak DM2.10). **Eurail** valid on the S-Bahn.

✴▢ ORIENTATION AND PRACTICAL INFORMATION

The **Hauptbahnhof** (main train station) lies at the end of Frankfurt's red-light district; walk 20min. down Kaiserstr. or Münchenerstr. to reach the **Altstadt** (old city) and the **Römerberg** (U4: Römer). To the north, the commercial **Zeil** stretches from **Hauptwache** (S1-6 or S8: Hauptwache) to **Konstablerwache** (1 stop farther). Students and cafes cluster in **Bockenheim** (U6-7: Bockenheimer Warte). South of the Main River, **Sachsenhausen** (U1-3: Schweizer Pl.) draws pub-crawlers and museum-goers.

Tourist Office: In the Hauptbahnhof (☎21 23 88 00; www.frankfurt-tourismus.de). Sells maps (DM1-2) and books rooms (DM5 fee). Also sells the **Frankfurt Card** (1-day DM12, 2-day DM19), which grants unlimited travel on all trains and buses and 50% off admission to 15 museums and other attractions. Open M-F 8am-9pm, Sa-Su 9am-6pm.

American Express: Kaiserstr. 8 (☎21 93 88 66; fax 21 93 88 66; 24-hour hotline 97 97 10 00). Open M-F 9:30am-6pm, Sa 9:30am-12:30pm.

English Bookstores: Süssman's Presse und Buch, Zeil 127 (☎131 07 51). Open M-W and F 9am-7pm, Th 9am-8pm, Sa 9am-4pm.

Laundromat: Schnell & Sauber, Wallstr. 8, near the hostel in Sachsenhausen. DM6. Open daily 6am-11pm. **Miele Washworld,** Moselstr. 17. DM7. Open daily 8am-11pm.

Emergency: Police, ☎110. **Fire** and **ambulance,** ☎112.

Pharmacy: Downstairs in the Einskaufs passage of the Hauptbahnhof (☎23 30 47). Open M-F 6:30am-9pm, Sa 8am-9pm, Su 9am-8pm. Emergencies, ☎192 92.

Internet Access: Telemark, Elisabethanstr. 45-47. DM6 per 30min. Open daily 10am-10pm. **CybeRyder Internet Café,** Töngesgasse 31 (☎92 08 40 10). DM6 per 30min. Open M-Th 9am-11pm, Fr-Sa 9am-1am, Su 2pm-11pm.

Post Office: Zeil 90 (☎13 81 26 21), inside the Hertie department store. U- or S-Bahn: Hauptwache. **Poste Restante:** Postlagernde Briefe für Katharina BARNES, Hauptpostamt, 60313 Frankfurt, Germany. Open M-F 9:30am-8pm, Sa 9am-4pm.

GERMANY

ACCOMMODATIONS

"Show me the money," is the new motto for the hotel industry in Frankfurt. However, there are a few reasonable options in the Westend/University area. If all else fails, the hostel in Mainz is less than 45min. away (take S14; see p. 469).

Pension Backer, Mendelssohnstr. 92 (☎74 79 92), past Pension Bruns (see above). U6 (dir.: Heerstr.) or 7 (dir.: Hausen) to Westend. The best value in town. Breakfast included. Showers DM3. Singles DM25-50; doubles DM60; triples DM78.

Jugendherberge (HI), Deutschherrnufer 12 (☎610 01 50). Take bus #46 from the Hauptbahnhof to Frankensteiner Pl. Turn left at the river and it's at the end of the block. After 7:30pm M-F, 5:45pm Sa, and 5pm Su, take S2-S6 to Lokalbahnhof; go down Darmstädter Landstr. with your back to the train bridge, bear right onto Dreieichstr., and turn left along the river. In the midst of the Sachsenhausen pub and museum district; loud and lively with locals. Breakfast included. Check-in after noon. Check-out 9:30am. Curfew 2am. Dorms DM33, under 27 DM27.

Pension Bruns, Mendelssohnstr. 42. (☎74 88 96). From the Hauptbahnhof, head left on Düsseldorferstr., right on Beethovenstr., and right again at the circle on Mendelssohnstr. (10-15min.). Spacious rooms with phone and TV. Breakfast included. Showers DM2. Call ahead. Doubles DM79; triples DM105; quads DM140.

Hotel-Pension Gölz, Beethovenstr. 44 (☎74 67 35). From the Hauptbahnhof, head left on Düsseldorferstr. and then turn right on Beethovenstr. U6 or U7 to Westend. Quiet, beautiful apartment-style rooms. Reservations recommended. Singles DM69-85, with shower DM85-98; doubles with shower DM135-178.

Pension Sattler, Beethovenstr. 46 (☎74 60 91), next to Pension Gölz. Basement singles without showers DM70.

FOOD

Regional specialties include *Handkäse mit Musik* (cheese curd with raw onions—Goethe's favorite), *grüne Sosse* (green sauce with various herbs, served over boiled eggs or potatoes), and *Ebbelwein* (apple wine; called *Äpfelwein* in the north). The cheapest grub surrounds the university in **Bockenheim** and nearby parts of **Westend** (U6-7: Bockenheimer Warte), and many pubs in **Sachsenhausen** (U1-3: Schweizer Pl.) serve food at a decent price. For **supermarket** grub, **HL Markt,** Dreieichstr. 56, is near the Jugendherberge (open M-F 8am-8pm, Sa 8am-4pm).

Mensa, U6 (dir.: Heerstr.) or 7 (dir.: Hausen) to Bockenheimer Warte, then follow the Mensa signs to Building 133 of Goethe U. Your best bet for a filling, hot meal (DM5) with some collegiate attitude. Open M-F 11am-3pm.

Adolf Wagner, Schweizerstr. 71 (☎61 25 65). Sauce-soaked German dishes (DM5-27) and mugs of *Äpfelwein* (DM2.70 per 0.3L) keep the patrons of this famous corner of old-world Frankfurt jolly, rowdy, and coming back for years. Open daily 10am-1am.

SIGHTS

Much of Frankfurt's historic splendor lives on only in memories and in reconstructed monuments nostalgic for the time before the 1944 bombing. At the center of the Altstadt is **Römerberg** square (U-Bahn: Römer), which has reconstructed architecture and a medieval fountain. At the west end of the Römerberg, the gables of **Römer** have marked the site of Frankfurt's city hall since 1405. Upstairs, the **Kaisersaal,** a former imperial banquet hall, is adorned with portraits of the 52 German emperors from Charlemagne to Franz II. (Open daily 10am-1pm and 2-5pm. DM3, students DM1.) Next to the Römerberg, on Domstr. stands the only building in the city that survived the bombings: the red sandstone Gothic **Dom** (cathedral), the site of coronation ceremonies from 1562 to 1792. The **museum** within contains intricate chalices and the venerated robes of the imperial electors. (Cathedral open daily 9am-noon and 2-6pm. Museum open Tu-F 10am-5pm, Sa-Su 11am-5pm. DM3, students DM1.) On the other side of the Römerberg, the **Alte Nikolaikirche** raises its considerably more modest, pinkish spires. (Open daily Apr.-Sept. 10am-8pm; Oct.-Mar. 10am-6pm. Free.) Just a few blocks up Domstr., before the street name changes to Haseng., is the **Museum für Moderne Kunst,** Domstr. 10. The museum houses a stunning modern art collection, including works by Claes Oldenburg, Roy Liechtenstein, and Jasper Johns. (Open Tu and Th-Su 10am-5pm, W 10am-8pm. DM10, students DM5; W free.) From the museum, head down Berlinerstr. past Liebfrauenstr. to find **Paulskirche** on the left. Rebuilt after the war with an elegance testament to its former glory, the church now serves as a political monument and a conference venue. The **Museumsufer,** on the Schaumainkai along the south bank of the Main between the Eiserner Steg and the Friedensbrücke, hosts an eclectic collection of museums, including the **Deutsches Filmmuseum,** Schaumainkai 41, which presents an interactive history of filmmaking. (Open Tu, Th-F, and Su 10am-5pm, W 10am-8pm, Sa 2-8pm. Tours Su 3pm. DM5, students DM2.50; W free. Films DM8, students DM6.) For a break from Frankfurt's busy streets, stroll in the **Palmengarten** (U6 or U7 to Bockenheimer Warte. Open daily Mar.-Oct, 9am-6pm; Nov.-Jan. 9am-4pm; Feb. 9am-5pm. DM10, students DM4.50.)

🎭 ENTERTAINMENT

Frankfurt excels in the realms of entertainment and nightlife. Shows and schedules of the city's stages are detailed in several publications, including *Fritz* and *Strandgut* (free at the tourist office) and the *Journal Frankfurt* (DM3.30 at newsstands). The **Alte Oper,** Opernpl. (☎134 04 00), offers a full range of classical music while the **Städtische Bühne,** Untermainanlage 11 (☎21 23 71 33; U1, U2, U3, U4 to Willy-Brandt-Pl.), mounts ballets and operas. The jazz clubs that reinvigorated the city post-WWII by drawing such legends as Duke Ellington and Ella Fitzgerald can be found on Kleine Bockenheimerstr., also known as the **Jazzgasse** (Jazz Alley). **Der Jazzkeller,** at Kleine Bockenheimerstr. 18a, is a Frankfurt institution. (Live music Th and Sa. Cover around DM8. Open Tu-Su 9pm-3am.) For a night out drinking, head to the **Alt-Sachsenhausen** district between Brückenstr. and Dreieichstr., home to a huge number of rowdy pubs and taverns specializing in *Ebbelwein.* The narrow, cobblestoned streets around **Grosse** and **Kleine Rittergasse** teem with canopied cafes, bars, and gregarious Irish pubs. Frankfurt has a number of thriving discos and prominent techno DJs, mostly in between Zeil and Bleichstr. Wear your best dancing clothes—even the hippest jeans won't make it past most bouncers. **U60311,** Roßmarkt, on the corner of Goetheplatz, is a popular hangout for the young and trendy. (Open M-F 10pm-10am, Sa-Su 10pm-6am. Cover DM15-30.) **Blue Angel,** Brönnerstr. 17, is one of the liveliest gay men's clubs in the city. (Cover DM11, including drinks F and Sa. Open daily 11pm-4am.) **Das Opium,** Brönnerstr. 7, houses an enormous disco ball that lights up a spacious, flashy dance floor. (Cover DM12-20. Open Th-Sa 10pm-4am.)

KASSEL   ☎0561

When Napoleon III was captured by Prussian troops and brought to the Schloß Wilhelmshöhe prison in 1870, *Aacheners* jeered *"Ab nach Kassel"* ("off to Kassel"). Today, hordes answer the call to see this ultra-sophisticated city. From the train station Bahnhof Wilhelmshöhe, take streetcar #1 to the last stop to reach **Wilhelmshöhe,** a hillside park with one giant Greek hero, two castles, three museums, and five waterfalls. **Schloß Löwenburg** is an amazing piece of architectural fantasy, built with stones deliberately missing to make it look like a crumbling medieval castle; **Schloß Wilhelmshöhe** was the mammoth home of Kassel's rulers. (Both open Tu-Su Mar.-Oct. 10am-5pm; Nov.-Feb. 10am-4pm. DM7, students DM5.) All of the park's paths lead up to the large **Riesenschloß,** topped by the figure of **Herkules,** the emblem of Kassel. Art-lovers descend on Kassel every 5 years to take part in **documenta,** the world's preeminent contemporary art exhibition, next scheduled for 2002. The **Museum Friedricianum,** Friedrichspl. 18, houses most *documenta*-related exhibitions. (Open W and F-Su 10am-6pm, Th 10am-8pm. DM12, students DM8.) Even the **Hauptbahnhof,** renamed **Kulturbahnhof,** gets a piece of the eclectic museum action—check out the **caricatura,** the self-proclaimed "museum of bizarre art." (Open Tu-F 2-8pm, Sa-Su noon-8pm.) The **Brüder-Grimm-Museum,** Schöne Aussicht 2, in Palais Bellevue near the Orangerie, exhibits the brothers' handwritten copy of *Kinder- und Hausmärchen,* their dark collection of fairy tales. (Open daily 10am-5pm. DM3, students DM2.) ◪**Lohmann Biergarten,** Königstor 8, is one of Kassel's oldest and largest beer gardens. (Open daily noon-2am.)

The **Wilhelmshöhe station** is the point of entry to Kassel's ancient castles and immense parks on the west side; the older **Hauptbahnhof** is the gateway to the tightly packed and entirely modernized Altstadt. Most **trains** only stop at Wilhelmshöhe, with service to: Düsseldorf (3½hr., every hr., DM145); Frankfurt (2½hr., 2 per hr., DM54); and Hamburg (2½hr., 2 per hr., DM99). The **tourist office,** which sells maps for DM1.50, is in the Bahnhof Wilhelmshöhe. (☎340 54; fax 31 52 16. Open M-F 9am-1pm and 2-6pm, Sa 9am-1pm.) To reach **Jugendherberge am Tannenwäldchen (HI),** Schenkendorfstr. 18, take streetcar #4 or 6 from the Rathaus or Bahnhof Wilhelmshöhe (dir.: Ottostr. or Lindenberg) to Annastr., continue walking up Friedrich-Ebert-Str., and make a right on Schenkendorfstr.; or, from the Hauptbahnhof, walk out the *Südausgang* (south exit), turn right on Kölnischestr., and turn right again onto Schenkendorfstr. (☎77 64 55. Sheets DM6. Breakfast included. Reception 9am-11:30pm. HI members only. DM29.50, 26 and under DM24.50.) To get to **Hotel Kö78,** Kölnischestr. 78, follow the directions to the Jugendherberge, walk up Annastr. from the stop, and turn right on Kölnischestr.; from the Hauptbahnhof, exit through the *Südausgang,* and follow Kölnischestr. uphill and to the right. (☎716 14. Breakfast included. Reception M-F 6am-10pm, Sa-Su 8am-10pm. Singles from DM59; doubles from DM93.) **E Activ** sells **groceries** on Friedrich-Ebert-Str. near Bismarkstr. (Open M-F 7am-7pm; Sa 7-4pm). **Postal Code:** 34041.

SOUTHWEST GERMANY

A trip to the Rhineland-Palatinate (Rheinland-Pfalz) to see the castles and wine towns along the Rhine is an obligatory tourist tromp. The region is a visual feast—the Mosel River curls downstream to the Rhine Gorge, a soft shore of castle-backed hills. But it also provides a literal feast; a rich agricultural tradition keeps fresh fruits and vegetables in abundance, and the vineyards of the Rhine and Mosel Valleys produce sweet, delicious wines. Just to the south, the bucolic, traditional hinterlands of the Black Forest contrast with the region's modern, industrial cities.

RHINE VALLEY (RHEINTAL)

The Rhine River may run from Switzerland to the North Sea, but in the popular imagination it exists only in the 80km of the Rhine Gorge stretching from Bonn to north of Mainz. This is the Rhine of legends: sailors' nightmares, poets' dreams, and often the center of rhetorical storms of nationalism.

◨ TRANSPORTATION. The Rhine Valley runs north from **Mainz,** easily accessible from Frankfurt, to **Bonn** (see p. 458), just south of **Cologne** via (from south to north) **Bacharach, St. Goarshausen** and **St. Goar,** and **Koblenz.** Two different **train** lines (one on each bank) traverse this fabled stretch; the line on the west bank stays closer to the water and provides superior views. **Eurail** is valid on trips between Cologne and Mainz. If you're willing to put up with lots of tourists, **boats** are probably the best way to see the sights. **Köln-Düsseldorfer (KD) Line** (see p. 453) covers the Mainz-Koblenz stretch three times per day in summer.

MAINZ   ☎06131

Much of Mainz has metamorphosed into a modern metropolis, but the colossal sandstone **Martinsdom** and the maze of streets in the Altstadt remain the heart and embody the character of the city. The Martinsdom is the resting place for the arch-bishops of Mainz, whose extravagant tombstones line the walls of the cathedral and whose faces are captured in a timeline of stained glass dating back to AD 975. (☎25 31 76. Open Apr.-Sept. M-F 9am-6:30pm, Sa 9am-4pm, Su 12:45-3pm and 4-6:30pm; Oct.-Mar. M-F 9am-5pm, Sa 9am-4pm, Su 12:45-3pm and 4-5pm. Free.) The adjacent **Diözesanmuseum** houses different exhibitions throughout the year. (Open Tu-Sa 9am-5pm, Su 11am-6pm. DM6, students DM3.) **Johannes Gutenberg,** the father of movable type, is immortalized at the **Gutenberg Museum,** Liebfrauenpl. 5, across from the Dom. The museum contains several Gutenberg Bibles, a working replica of his original press, an impressive collection of text art, and early Asian calligra-phy. (☎12 26 40. Open Tu-Su, 10am-5pm, DM6, students DM3.) On a hill several blocks south stands the Gothic **Stephanskirche,** most notable for its stunning stained-glass windows created by Russian artist-in-exile Marc Chagall. From the Dom, take Ludwigstr. until it ends at Schillerpl. and follow Gaustr. up the hill to the church. (Open daily 10am-noon and 2-5pm. Free.)

Köln-Düsseldorf **ferries** (☎23 28 00) depart from the wharfs on the other side of the Rathaus. The **tourist office** doles out free maps and finds rooms (from DM50) for a DM5 fee. (☎28 62 10; fax 286 21 55. www.info-mainz.de. Open M-F 9am-6pm, Sa 9am-1pm.) The **Jugendgästehaus (HI),** Otto-Brunfels-Schneise 4 (☎853 32), is in Weisenau in a corner of the Volkspark. Take **buses** #22, 62, 63, or 92 to Am Viktorstift/Jugendherberge and follow signs. (Reception 7am-midnight. Wheelchair accessible. Breakfast included. Doubles DM78.80.) Near the Dom, the **Central Café,** on the corner of Rheinstr. and Heugasse, cooks up traditional German fare for under DM15. (☎22 56 66. Open Su-Th 10am-1am, F-Sa 10am-2am.) **Postal Code:** 55001.

BACHARACH   ☎06743

On the west bank of the Rhine, the gorgeous yet hidden town of Bacharach brims with **Weinkeller** and **Weinstuben** (wine cellars and pubs) that do justice to its name—"altar to Bacchus." Find such sweet love at **Die Weinstube,** Oberstr. 63 (☎12 08), behind the stunning **Altes Haus** in the center of town. Also off Oberstr. is the 14th-century **Wernerkapelle,** ghost-like remains of a red sandstone chapel that took 140 years (1294-1434) to build, but only a few hours to destroy in the Palatinate War of Succession in 1689. The **tourist office,** Oberstr. 45, in the post office, is 5min. from the station on the right. (☎91 93 03; fax 91 93 04. Open Apr.-Oct. M-F 9am-5pm, Sa 10am-4pm; Nov.-Mar. M-F 9am-1pm and 1:30-5pm, Sa 10am-1pm.) Hostels get no better than the unbelievable **Jugendherberge Stahleck (HI),** a 12th-century castle with an unbeatable panoramic view of the Rhine Valley. The steep 20min. hike to the hostel is worth every step. (☎12 66. Breakfast included. Curfew 10pm, bar open until midnight. DM25.90, DM31.90 for double rooms.) **Postal Code:** 55422.

LORELEI CLIFFS AND CASTLES

The section of the Rhine just north of Bacharach was so difficult to navigate that a sailors' song developed about the siren Lorelei, who seduced sailors with her intox-icating song and drew them into the rocks; the song was eventually immortalized by poet Heinrich Heine. Most visitors today avoid such grim fates as they visit **St. Goarshausen** and **St. Goar,** on either side of the Rhine. These two towns host the spectacular **Rhein in Flammen** firework-filled celebration at the end of summer (Sep-tember 15, 2001). St. Goarshausen, on the east bank, provides access by foot to the statue and the infamous cliffs. Directly above St. Goarshausen, the fierce **Burg Katz** (Cat Castle) eternally stalks its prey, the smaller **Burg Maus** (Mouse Castle). Call ☎ 76 69 for information about the Burg Maus, or visit St. Goarshausen's **tourist office,** Bahnhofstr. 8. (☎ (06771) 91 00; fax 910 15; email loreley-tourist-info@t-online.de. Open M-F 9am-1pm and 2-5:30pm, Sa 9:30am-noon.) The "Lorelei V" **ferry** crosses the river to and from St. Goar, making the town a convenient base for Lorelei explorations. (Every 5-10min. nonstop; last ferry 11pm, DM1.50, round-trip DM2.50.) The view from the cliffs on the eastern side is spectacular, and **Burg Rheinfels** (☎ (06741) 383) is dazzling. (Open daily 9am-6pm; last entrance 5pm. DM6, students and children DM4.) St. Goar's **tourist office,** Heerstr. 6 (☎ (06741) 383; fax 72 09; www.talderloreley.de; email TalderLoreley@t-online.de), is right in the middle of the pedestrian zone. (Open M-F 8am-12:30pm and 2-5pm, Sa 10am-noon.) For convenient lodgings, the **Hotel Hauser,** Heerstr. 77, offers spotless, relaxing rooms with balconies in the middle of town. (☎ (06741) 333. Breakfast included. Singles DM46-95, with bath DM55-75; doubles DM98-140.) St. Goar's **postal code** is 56329.

KOBLENZ ☎ 0261

Koblenz's strategic position at the confluence of the Rhine and the Mosel, has attracted Roman, French, Prussian, and German conquerors for the past 2000 years. Before reunification, the city served as a large munitions dump, but now the only pyrotechnics are when the **Rhein in Flammen** fireworks festival hits the town (Aug. 11, 2001). The city's center is the **Deutsches Eck** (German Corner), a peninsula at the rivers' meeting point. The tremendous **Mahnmal der Deutschen Einheit** (Monument to German Unity) was erected in 1897 in honor of Kaiser Wilhelm I's forced reconciliation of the German Empire. Behind the Mahnmal, the **Museum Ludwig im Deutschherrenhaus,** Danziger Freiheit 1, features contemporary French art. (DM5, students DM3. Open Tu-Sa 10:30am-5pm, Su 11am-6pm.) The 12th-century **Florinskirche** was used as an encampment by Napoleon (open daily 11am-5pm), while nearby, the **Liebfrauenkirche** showcases oval Baroque towers, emerald- and sapphire-colored stained glass, and intricate ceiling latticework (open M-Sa 8am-6pm, Su 9am-12:30pm and 6-8pm; in summer Su 9am-8pm). Head across the river to the **Festung Ehrenbreitstein,** a fortress at the highest point in the city. The Prussians used it to accommodate French troops in past centuries; today, the German state uses it to accommodate you—the fortress is now a youth hostel. (Tours DM6; non-hostel guests DM2, students DM1.)

Trains go to: Cologne (1hr., 3-4 per hr., DM25); Frankfurt (2hr., 2 per hr., DM36); Mainz (1hr., 3 per hr., DM25); and Trier (2hr., every hr., DM30). Take a sharp left from the station for the **tourist office,** Löhrstr. 141. (☎ 313 04; fax 100 43 88; www.koblenz.de. Open M-F 9am-8pm, Sa-Su 10am-8pm.) The **Jugendherberge Koblenz (HI),** in the Festung, yields a spectacular view of Koblenz and the Rhine and Mosel Valleys. Take bus #9 or 10 from the stop of Lohrstr. to Charlottenstr. and continue along the Rhine side of the mountain following the "DJH" signs. Or take the chairlift (open daily Mar.-Sept., 9am-5:50pm. DM4, round-trip DM6, DM9 for non-hostel guests), a block away in the same direction. (☎ 97 28 70. Breakfast included. Reception 7:30am-11:30pm. Curfew 11:30pm. DM25.90, doubles DM31.90.) **Ferries** (DM0.60) cross the Mosel to **Campingplatz Rhein-Mosel,** Am Neuendorfer Eck. (☎ 827 19. Reception 8am-noon and 2-8pm. Open Apr.-Oct. 15. DM6.50 per person, DM5 per tent.) **Marktstübchen,** Am Markt 220, serves real German food at real budget prices. (Open M-Tu, Th, and Sa-Su 11am-midnight, W 11am-2pm, F 4pm-1am.) **Plus supermarket** is at Roonstr. 49-51. (Open M-F 8:30am-7pm and Sa 8am-2pm.) **Postal Code:** 65068.

MOSEL VALLEY (MOSELTAL)

As if trying to avoid its inevitable surrender to the Rhine at Koblenz, the Mosel meanders slowly past the sun-drenched hills, pretty towns, and ancient castles of the softly cut Mosel Valley. The valley's slopes aren't as steep as the Rhine's narrow gorge, but the arresting landscape, castles, and vineyards easily compensate.

▛ TRANSPORTATION

The Mosel Valley runs northeast from **Trier,** just 45min. from **Luxembourg City** by train (see p. 720), to **Koblenz,** where it bisects the Rhine Valley (see p. 470), passing **Beilstein** and **Cochem** en route. The best way to see the scenery is by **boat, bus,** or **bicycle;** the **train** line between Koblenz and Trier strays frequently from the river, cutting through the unremarkable countryside. Although **passenger boats** no longer make the complete Koblenz-Trier run, several companies run daily trips along shorter stretches in summer.

COCHEM AND BEILSTEIN

The wine-making village of Cochem has become a repository of German nostalgia, its quintessential quaintness devoured by busloads of city-dwellers. Yet the impressive vineyard-covered hills and majestic **Reichsburg castle,** perched high on a hill above town, simply can't be cheapened. The 11th-century castle was destroyed in 1689 by French troops led by Louis XIV, but was rebuilt in 1868. (☎ (02671) 255. Open mid-Mar. to Oct. daily 9am-5pm. Closed rest of the year. DM7, students DM6.) **Trains** run from the Bahnhofsplatz to Koblenz (1hr., 2-3 per hr., DM12) and Trier (1hr., 2 per hr., DM17). From the train station, go to the river and turn right to reach the **tourist office,** Endertpl. 1. (☎ (02671) 600 40; fax 60 04 44; www.cochem.de. Open Apr.-Oct. M-Th and Sa 9am-5pm, F 9am-6pm, Su 10am-noon; Nov.-Mar. M-F 9am-1pm and 2-5pm.) For the best hotel deals, head away from the river. **Hotel Holl,** Endertstr. 54 (☎ (02671) 43 23; www.hotel-holl.de) combines large, bright rooms with good food. (Breakfast included. Single, doubles, and apartments, all with baths, DM40-70 per person per night.) For camping, try the **Campingplatz am Freizeitzentrum,** on Stadionstr. (☎ (02671) 44 09. Reception 8am-10pm. Open Easter-Oct. DM6.50 per person, DM6-12 per tent.) **Postal Code:** 56812.

Ten kilometers upstream from Cochem lies the tiny hamlet of **Beilstein,** filled with half-timbered houses and crooked cobblestoned streets. The ruins of **Burg Metternich,** another casualty of French troops in 1689, offer a sweeping view of the valley. (☎ (02673) 936 39. Open daily Apr.-Oct. 9am-6pm. DM3, students DM2.) The Baroque **Karmelitenkirche** contains an intricately carved wooden altar and the famous 16th-century *Schwarze Madonna von Beilstein* sculpture. (Open daily 9am-8pm.) **Bus** #8060 runs to Beilstein from both Cochem's Endertpl. and train station (15min.; M-F 14 per day, Sa 7 per day, Su 3 per day; DM4.90). Beilstein's **tourist office** (☎ (02673) 90 01 91) is in Café Klapperburg, a block uphill on the left from the bus stop. The **passenger boats** of Personnen-schiffahrt Kolb (☎ (02673) 15 15) also travel between the two towns (1hr., May-Oct. 4 per day, DM18 round-trip).

TRIER ☎ 0651

The oldest town in Germany, Trier was founded by the Romans during the reign of Augustus, and reached its heyday in the 4th century as the capital of the Western Roman Empire and residence of Emperor Constantine. The city's most impressive Roman remnant is the massive 2nd-century **Porta Nigra** (Black Gate), named for the centuries of grime that have turned its originally light yellow sandstone face gray. (Open daily Palm Sunday-Sept. 9am-6pm; Oct.-Nov. and Jan.-Palm Sunday 9am-5pm; Dec. 10am-4pm. DM4, students DM2.) From there, a stroll down Simeonstr. leads to the **Hauptmarkt,** off of which the 11th-century **Dom** shelters archbishops' tombs. The reputed **Tunica Christi** (Holy Robe of Christ), brought from Jerusalem to Trier around 300 by St. Helena, mother of Emperor Constantine, is also kept in the Dom. (Open daily Apr.-Oct. 6:30am-6pm; Nov.-Mar. 6:30am-5:30pm. Free.) To get to the **Basilika,** originally the location of Emperor Constantine's throne room, take Liebfrauenstr. past Konstantinstr. and then turn left. (Open M-Sa 9am-6pm, Su 11:30am-6pm. Free.) Make a pilgrimage to the **Karl-Marx-Haus,** Brückenstr. 10, where young Karl first walked, talked, and dreamed of labor alienation. (☎430 11. Open Apr.-Oct. M 1-6pm, Tu-Su 10am-6pm; Nov.-Mar. M 2-5pm, Tu-Su 10am-1pm and 2-

5pm. DM3, students DM2.) Down Am Palastgarten from the Basilika lie the ruins of the **Kaiserthermen,** the Roman baths where Constantine once scrubbed himself. Head left on Olewigerstr. to reach the 2nd-century **amphitheater,** which once hosted demonstrations of the most spectacular and gruesome ways to inflict pain (and death) on humans and animals. (Kaiserthermen and amphitheater both same hrs. and admission as Porta Nigra; amphitheater closed Dec.)

Trains go to Koblenz (1¾hr., 2 per hr., DM30) and Luxembourg City (45min., every hr., DM15). From the station, walk down Theodor-Heuss-Allee or Christophstr. to reach the **tourist office,** which hands out maps and books rooms for free, under the shadow of the Porta Nigra. (☎97 80 80; fax 447 59; email info@tit.de. Open Apr.-Oct. M-Sa 9am-6:30pm, Su 9am-3:30pm; Nov.-Dec. M-Sa 9am-6pm, Su 9am-3:30pm; Jan.-Feb. M-F 10am-5pm, Sa 9am-1pm; Mar. M-Sa 9am-6pm, Su 9am-1pm.) Get info on **wine tasting** in the region at **Vinothek,** Margaritengässchen 2a, near the Porta Nigra. (☎994 05 40. Open daily 10am-7pm.) The **Jugendhotel/ Jugendgästehaus Kolpinghaus,** Dietrichstr. 42, is one block off the Hauptmarkt. (☎97 52 50. Reception 8am-11pm. Dorms DM27; singles DM39; doubles DM78.) To get from the station to the **Jugendgästehaus (HI),** An der Jugendherberge 4, follow Theodor-Heuss-Allee as it becomes Nordallee and bear right onto Lindenstr. to the bank of the Mosel. (☎14 66 20. Reception 7am-midnight. Singles DM54; doubles DM78.80; quads DM119.60.) **Plus supermarket** is near the Hauptmarkt, Brotstr. 54. (Open M-F 8:30am-7pm, Sa 8:30am-4pm.) **Postal Code:** 54292.

HEIDELBERG   ☎06221

Believe the tourist propaganda—Heidelberg truly shines. In 1386, the sages of Heidelberg turned from illuminating manuscripts to illuminating young German minds when they founded Germany's first and greatest university. Set against wooded hills along the Neckar River, the town and its crumbling *Schloß* have exerted a magnetic pull over numerous writers and artists, including Mark Twain, Goethe, and Hugo, and today draw thousands of shutter-clicking tourists daily.

▉ TRANSPORTATION

Trains: To: **Frankfurt** (40min., 2 per hr., DM23.40); **Mannheim** (10min., 5 per hr., DM7.80); and **Stuttgart** (40min., every hr., DM31).

Ferries: Rhein-Neckar-Fahrgastschiffahrt (☎201 81), in front of the Kongresshaus, provides round-trip Neckar cruises to (1½hr., Easter-late Oct. 9:30am-3:30pm, DM12.50).

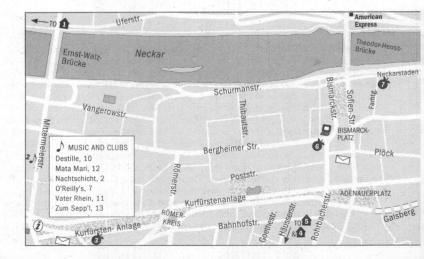

Public Transportation: Single-ride tickets DM3.30. **Day passes** are valid for 24 hrs. from the time of purchase for up to 5 people on all streetcars and buses (DM10.50); buy them at the tourist office or at ticket machines.

Bike Rental: Per Bike, Bergheimerstr. 125 (☎ 16 11 48). Half-day DM15, full day DM25. Weekend special DM55. DM50 deposit or ID required. Open M-F 9am-6pm; Apr.-Oct. also open Sa 9am-1pm.

Hitchhiking: *Let's Go* does not recommend hitchhiking. Hitchers are said to wait at the western end of Bergheimerstr. **Mitfahrzentrale,** Bergheimerstr. 125 (☎246 46), organizes ride-sharing. To: **Cologne** DM28; **Hamburg** DM54; **Paris** DM51. Open Apr.-Oct. M-F 9am-5pm and Sa 9am-noon; Nov.-Mar. closed Sa.

ORIENTATION AND PRACTICAL INFORMATION

Most of Heidelberg's attractions are clustered in the eastern part of the city, along the south bank of the Neckar. From the train station, take any bus or streetcar to Bismarckpl., then walk east down **Hauptstraße,** known as the longest pedestrian street in Germany and the city's spine, to the **Altstadt.** The two-day **Heidelberg Card** includes unlimited use of public transit as well as admission to most sights (DM19.80 from the tourist office).

Tourist Office: Tourist Information (☎ 138 81 21; fax 881 11; www.cvb.heidelberg.de), in front of the station. Books rooms for a DM5 fee and an 8% deposit. Pick up *Meier* (DM2) or *Heidelberg Aktuell* (DM1) for events info. Open Mar.-Dec. M-Sa 9am-7pm, Su 10am-6pm; Jan.-Feb. closed Su. Additional offices at the Schloß (☎211 44; open in summer daily 9am-5pm) and at Neckarmünzpl. (open in summer daily 9am-6:30pm, closed Sept. 30-May 31).

Currency Exchange: Change cash at the **Sparkassen** on Universitätspl. and Bismarckpl. Open M-Sa 7am-8:30pm, Su 9am-1pm.

American Express: Brückenkopfstr. 1 (☎45 05 17; fax 45 55 84), at the northern end of Theodor-Heuss-Brücke. Mail held. Open M-F 10am-6pm, Sa 10am-1pm.

Emergency: ☎110. **Police,** Römerstr. 2-4 (☎990). **Fire** and **ambulance,** ☎112.

Internet Access: Café Gecko, Bergheimerstr. 8 (☎60 45 20). Order a drink for access. DM4 per 30min. Open Su-Th 9am-1am, F 9am-2am, Sa 9am-3am. **La Tapa,** Steing. 16 (☎ 18 35 11). DM1.50 per 10 min. Open M, Tu, Th-Sa 11am-8pm, Su noon-5pm.

Post Office: Sofienstr. 8-10 (☎91 24 10). Address mail to be held: *Postlagernde Briefe* für Erika EHSES, Sofienstr. 8-10, 69115 Heidelberg, Germany. Open daily 9am-6:30pm. **Postal Code:** 69115.

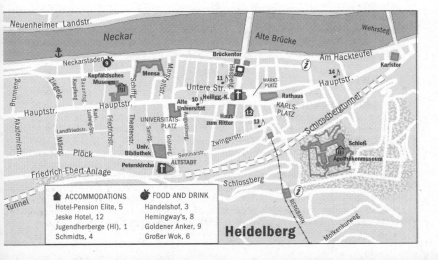

Heidelberg

ACCOMMODATIONS
Hotel-Pension Elite, 5
Jeske Hotel, 12
Jugendherberge (HI), 1
Schmidts, 4

FOOD AND DRINK
Handelshof, 3
Hemingway's, 8
Goldener Anker, 9
Großer Wok, 6

⚑ ACCOMMODATIONS

In summer, reserve ahead or arrive early in the day. If you get stuck, try the youth hostels in nearby Neckargemünd (10min.; ☎ (06223) 21 33; DM27, under 27 DM22); Eberbach (25min.; ☎ (06271) 25 93; DM27, under 27 DM22); and Zwingenberg (35min.; ☎ (06251) 759 38; DM23, under 27 DM18).

Jeske Hotel, Mittelbadg. 2 (☎237 33). From the station, take bus #33 (dir.: Ziegelhausen) or #11 (dir.: Karlstor) to Rathaus/Kornmarkt; Mittelbadg. is the 2nd left off the square. The best value in Heidelberg in an unbeatable location. Call ahead to check if open. Doubles DM52.

Jugendherberge (HI), Tiergartenstr. 5 (☎41 20 66; fax 40 25 59). From Bismarckpl. or the station, take bus 33 (dir.: Zoo-Sportzentrum) to Jugendherberge. Fax your reservation. HI members only. Sheets DM5.50. Reception until 11pm. Lockout 9am-1pm. Curfew 11:30pm. Dorms DM28, under 27 DM24.

Hotel-Pension Elite, Bunsenstr. 15 (☎257 33). From Bismarckpl., follow Rohrbacherstr. away from the river, turn right on Bunsenstr., and it's on the left. Nice rooms with high ceilings, bath, and TV. Breakfast included. DM5 credit card surcharge. Singles DM75; doubles DM100; DM20 extra per person.

Schmidts, Blumenstr. 54 (☎272 96). From Bismarckpl., follow Rohrbacherstr. away from the river. Relatively cheap rooms. Singles DM70, with shower DM120.

Camping Haide (☎ (06223) 21 11), between Ziegelhausen and Neckargemünd. Take bus #35 to Orthopädisches Klinik, cross the river, turn right, and it's on the right. DM14.50-20 per person, DM6-12 per tent, DM2 per car. Cabins DM14.50-20. Reception 8am-noon and 4:30-7:30pm. Open Apr.-Oct.

◖ FOOD

Eating out tends to be depressingly expensive in Heidelberg; most of the restaurants on and around Hauptstr. are exorbitantly priced. Get cheap grub at **Handelshof supermarket,** Kurfürsten-Anlage 60, 200m straight down from the station on the right. (Open M-F 7:30am-8pm, Sa 7:30am-4pm.) There is a **fruit market** on Marktpl. on Wednesdays and Saturdays.

Mensa, in the *Marstall* on Marstallstr. Bus #35 to Marstallstr. Or, from the Alte Brücke, with your back to the old city, take a left along the river; it's the red fortress on the left. Spend DM3-7 on lunch or dinner. Lunch M-F 11:30am-2pm. Dinner M-Sa 5pm-10pm.

Großer Wok, Bergheimerstr. 1a (☎60 25 28), near Bismarckpl. Appetizing aromas whet your taste buds for Chinese specialties (DM4-13) served quickly to go or to eat atop bar stools. Open M-Th and Su 11am-11pm, F-Sa 11am-midnight.

Thanner, Bergheimerstr. 71 (☎252 34), is a swank cafe with an eclectic international menu, original artwork on the walls, and the only *Biergarten* in Heidelberg allowed to play music. Entrees DM7-29. Open M-Th and Su 9am-1am, F-Sa 9am-2am.

◉ SIGHTS

HEIDELBERGER SCHLOß. The ramparts of Heidelberg's aging castle, the jewel in the crown of an already striking city, preside over the Altstadt. After 1329, it served as the home of the prince electors, and was thrice destroyed—twice by war (1622 and 1693) and once by lightning (1764). Over a period of almost 400 years, the castle's dwellers commissioned their distinctive additions; the conglomeration of styles ranges from Gothic to High Renaissance. While walking around the castle grounds, visitors can cool off in the musty wine cellar: its *Großer Faß* is the largest wine barrel ever made, holding 221,726L. Local lore tells of a court jester and *Faß* guardian who drank nearly 18 bottles a day and finally perished after accidentally drinking a glass of water. The castle's regal state of disrepair is best viewed from the **Philosophenweg** across the Neckar. *(Walk uphill from the base of the castle, or take the Berg-*

bahn cable car from the Bergbahn/Rathaus bus stop (round-trip DM4.70). ☎ 53 84 14. Mandatory tour inside the castle DM4, students DM2. Grounds open daily 8am-dusk; DM3, students DM1.50. Free after 5:30pm.)

MARKTPLATZ. The Altstadt centers on the cobblestoned **Marktplatz**, where accused witches and heretics were burned at the stake in the 15th century; today, tourists recline on legions of plastic chairs and admire **Hercules' Fountain.** The two oldest structures in Heidelberg line the square: the 14th-century **Heiliggeistkirche** (Church of the Holy Spirit), where residents hid during Louis XIV's invasion, and **Haus Zum Ritter,** opposite the church. *(Church open M-Sa 11am-5pm, Su 1-5pm. Free.)*

UNIVERSITÄT. Heidelberg is home to Germany's oldest and perhaps most prestigious university, established in 1368. It was at Heidelberg that Clemens Brentano compiled *Des Knaben Wunderhorn,* a collection of folk poetry that led to the Brothers Grimm's own prose compilation. It was also here that sociology became a legitimate academic subject under the leadership of Max Weber. The oldest remaining buildings border the stone-lion fountain of the Universitätsplatz. Before 1914, in the aristocratic tradition, students were exempt from prosecution by civil authorities; instead, the crimes of naughty youths were tried and punished by the university faculty. Guilty students were jailed in the **Studentenkarzer.** The walls are covered with graffiti—nothing can snuff the creativity of an incarcerated college student. *(Augustinergasse 2. ☎ 54 23 34. Open April-Oct. M-F 10am-4pm; Nov.-Mar. Tu-F 10am-4pm. DM5, students DM4.)* After some time in jail, test your literacy skills in the **Bibliothek,** with its collection of precious (though almost illegible) medieval manuscripts. *(Plöck 107-109. ☎ 54 23 80. Open M-Sa 10am-7pm. Free.)*

KURPFÄLZISCHES MUSEUM. This museum is crammed with artifacts such as the jawbone of an unfortunate *homo Heidelbergensis,* a.k.a. "Heidelberg man," one of the earliest humans ever discovered. Elsewhere in the museum are displayed well-preserved works of art by Dürer and a spectacular archaeology exhibit. *(Hauptstr. 97. Open Tu and Th-Su 10am-5pm, W 10am-9pm. DM5, students DM3; Su DM3, students DM2.)*

PHILOSOPHENWEG. A stroll across the elegant **Karl-Theodor-Brücke** to the northern bank of the Neckar, opposite the Altstadt, finds a statue of the Prince-Elector (commissioned by Theodor as a symbol of his modesty). From the far end of the bridge, clamber up the **Schlangenweg,** a winding stone stairway, to the **Philosophenweg** ("philosopher's path"), where Hegel and Max Weber indulged in afternoon walks.

ST. MICHAEL BASILIKA. Atop the **Heiligenberg** (mountain) lie the ruins of the 9th-century St. Michael Basilika, the 13th-century **Stefanskloster,** and an **amphitheater,** built under Hitler in 1934 on the site of an ancient Celtic gathering place. *(Take streetcar #1 or 3 to Tiefburg, a castle in neighboring Handschuhsheim, and hike upward. Or use the footpath next to the Karl-Theodor-Brücke.)*

🎵🏛 ENTERTAINMENT AND NIGHTLIFE

The first Saturdays in June and September, and the second in July, draw giant crowds to fireworks and pageants using the *Schloß* as a backdrop. The **Faschingsparade** (Carnival) struts through the city on Shrove Tuesday. The **Hand-Schuhsheim Fest** lures revelers across the river on the third weekend in June, while the **Schloßfestspiele Heidelberg** features a series of concerts and plays at the castle in the month of August. (Ticket info ☎ 583 52.) On September 30th, the **Heidelberger Herbst** brings a medieval market to the Altstadt. For more info on Heidelberg events, try the InfoLife (☎ 60 45 20). The **Marktplatz** is the heart of the city's action; most popular nightspots fan out from here. **Unter Straße,** on the Neckar side of the Heiliggeistkirche, boasts the most prolific and congested conglomeration of bars in the city. During fair weather, revelers fill the narrow way until 1 or 2am.

Nachtschicht (☎ 16 98 32), in Landfried-Komplex. From the Hauptbahnhof, take Mittermaierstr. past the metal dinosaur; take first left onto Alte Eppenheimerstr, and enter the parking lot. Cover DM6. W and F students half-price. Open W-Sa 10pm-4am.

VaterRhein, Untere Neckarstr. 20-22 (☎213 71), close to the river near the *Stadthalle*. College students converge to unwind among the vintage 1950s ads that decorate the wood-paneled walls. Cheap food and drinks. *Pilsner* DM4.50. Open daily 8pm-3am.

O'Reilly's (☎41 01 40), on the corner of Brückenkopfstr. and Uferstr. Cross Theodor-Heuss-Brücke, turn right, and follow the noise to Guinness's "Best Irish Pub in Germany 1999," where a young crowd drinks Guinness by the liter (DM7.50). Open M-F 5pm-1am, Sa-Su 1pm-3am.

Cave 54, Krämergasse 2 (☎278 40), keeps a somewhat older crowd jumping with live jazz (call for schedule). Other nights reggae, funk, and soul. Beer DM5. Cover DM5. Open daily 10pm-3am.

Mata Hari (☎18 18 08), on Zwingerstr. near Oberbadgasse. Cramped, subdued gay and lesbian bar. Tu men only. Beer DM5. Open Tu-Su 10pm-3am.

⚡ DAYTRIP FROM HEIDELBERG

THE NECKAR VALLEY

Trains connecting Heidelberg to Heilbronn stop at many of the small towns in the valley, including Bad Wimpfen. Local bus service between the towns is often more convenient. Castles are accessible via the Burgenweg (castle path); from the train station (15min. from Heidelberg), turn right on Bahnhofstr., turn left on Hauptstr., follow the bend in the road, then the brick Schloßsteige (castle steps) that lead up to the right.

The Neckar Valley (Neckartal), a scenic stretch of narrow, thickly wooded ridges along the Neckar River, encompasses several medieval **castles** and small, untouristed towns. At the northern end of the valley, 14km upstream from Heidelberg, is renowned for its four 12th- and 13th-century medieval castles, all within 3km of one another along the northern bank of the Neckar River. The two westernmost castles stand in ruins, while the two to the east stand in splendor. The **tourist office,** Hauptstr. 7 (☎ (07063) 920 00; fax 318), inside the Rathaus, is on the way to the *Schloßsteige*. (Open M-W 8am-noon and 1:30-3:30pm, Th 8am-noon and 1:30-5pm, F 8am-noon.)

OTHER DAYTRIPS FROM HEIDELBERG

STUTTGART. Travel to fast-paced Stuttgart, whirl through the Mercedes-Benz museum, or escape it all in one of the famed mineral baths (see p. 476).

FRANKFURT. Experience the glitz and glamour of financial Frankfurt, if you didn't pass through it already on your way into Germany (see p. 465). Nice cars.

BAD WIMPFEN   ☎07063

Until the recent influx of tour buses, Bad Wimpfen, just downstream from Heilbronn, was one of the best-kept secrets in southwest Germany. Set against the ruins of a Roman imperial **castle,** easily accessible points on the ancient battlements along the northern side of the old castle walls offer incredible views of the valley. Bad Wimpfen is home to the world's only **Pig Museum,** Kronengäßchen 2, off Hauptstr., which details the history of swine, considered a good luck symbol in Germany. Live pig on premises. (☎66 89. Open daily 10am-5pm. DM5, students DM2.50.) The **tourist office** is in the train station, off of Carl-Ulrich-Str. (☎972 00. Open M-F 9am-1pm and 2-5pm, Sa-Su 10am-noon and 2-4pm.) From the station, follow Karl-Ulrich-Str. to reach the immaculately preserved **Altstadt** (10min.).

STUTTGART   ☎0711

Leave your *Lederhosen* at home; corporate thoroughbreds Porsche and Daimler-Chrysler have made that stereotype an image of the past. Unceremoniously destroyed in WWII, Stuttgart was rebuilt in a thoroughly modern, functional and supremely uninspiring style, but the forested hills that accompanies the Neckar river add a welcome tranquility to the busy capital of Baden-Württemberg.

⊏ TRANSPORTATION. Stuttgart is the transportation hub of southwest Germany. **Trains** (☎ (0180) 599 66 33) run from the station off Cannstatterstr. to: Berlin (5½hr., every 2hr., DM256); Frankfurt (1½hr., every hr., DM88); Munich (2½hr., every hr., DM73); and Paris (6hr., 3 per day, DM136). **Single-ride tickets** for public transportation (U-Bahn, S-Bahn, streetcars, and buses) run DM3.20-9.60; a **3-day tourist pass** is valid on the U-Bahn (DM13) or the entire transit system (DM20).

⚠ PRACTICAL INFORMATION. Buy transportation passes and maps at the **tourist office, I-Punkt,** Königstr. 1, in front of the escalator down to the Klett-Passage. (☎222 80; fax 222 82 53; email info@stuttgart.tourist.de. Open May-Oct. M-F 9:30am-8:30pm, Sa 9:30am-6pm, Su 11am-6pm; Nov.-Apr. opens Su 1pm.) For info on youth travel, head to **tips 'n' trips,** Rotebühlpl. 26, in the U-Bahn passage at Theodor-Heuss-Str. and Fritz-Elsas-Str. (☎222 27 30; www.tips-n-trips.de. **Internet** DM5 per hr. Open M-F noon-7pm, Sa 10am-2pm.) Surf the web on the top floor of the **Kaufhof** department store, near the train station. (DM3 per 30min. Open M-F 9:30am-9pm, Sa 9am-4pm.) The **post office** is at the Hauptbahnhof. (Open M-F 8am-7pm, Sa 8am-noon.) **Postal Code:** 70001.

⌐⌐ ACCOMMODATIONS AND FOOD. To reach the spotless **Jugendgästehaus Stuttgart,** Richard-Wagner-Str. 2, take streetcar #15 (dir.: Ruhbank) to Bubenbad, continue in the same direction on the right side of the street, veer immediately around the corner to the right, and it's on the right. (☎24 11 32. Key deposit DM20. Reception M-F 9am-8pm, Sa-Su 11am-8pm. Singles DM40, with bath DM50.) To get to the **Jugendherberge Stuttgart (HI),** Haußmannstr. 27, take the "ZOB" exit from the Klett-Passage, continue through the Schloßgarten, cross Willy-Brandtstr., continue past the police station and climb the staircase on the other side of Schnützerstr. (☎24 15 83. Sheets DM5.50. Reception 7-9am and noon-11:30pm. Lockout 9am-noon. Curfew 11:30pm. DM29, under 27 DM24.) Take the S1, S2, or S3 to Bad Cannstatt. Exit through the back of the station and follow the signs for "Wasen." (☎55 66 96. Reception 7am-noon and 2-10pm. DM9. Campsite DM6-8.) Stop at **Weinhaus Stetter,** Rosenstr. 32, where you can choose from an incredible wine selection (DM5-7) to wash down Swabian specialties (DM7-9). Take the U-Bahn to Charlottenplatz, walk down Esslingerstr., and take a left onto Rosenstr. (Open M-F 3-11pm, Sa 10am-3am.) It's a vegetarian's dream at **Iden,** Eberhardstr. 1. (Open M-F 11am-9pm, Sa 10:30am-5pm.) For **groceries,** head to the **Kaufhof,** near the end of Königstr. on Eberhardstr. (Open M-F 9am-8pm, Sa 9am-4pm.)

▣⎍ SIGHTS AND ENTERTAINMENT. At Stuttgart's center lies an enormous pedestrian zone, centered on **Königstr.** and **Calwerstr.,** lined with shops and restaurants. The main municipal park, the tranquil **Schloßgarten,** runs south from the station to the elegant Baroque **Neues Schloß.** The north end of the park contains the **Rosensteinpark** and **Wilhelma,** Stuttgart's famous zoo and botanical garden. (Open daily Mar.-Oct. 8:15am-5pm; Nov.-Feb. 8:15am-4pm. DM14, students DM7.) Behind the Schloßgarten is the superb **▨Staatsgalerie Stuttgart,** Konrad-Adenauer-Str. 30-32, containing works by Picasso, Kandinsky, Beckmann, and Dalí. Take U1, U4, U9, or U11 to Staatsgalerie. (Open W and F-Su 10am-6pm, Tu and Th 10am-8pm. DM5, students DM3.) The **Mercedes-Benz Museum** covers the history of the luxury automobile from its creation to modern experimental models. Take S1 to Daimlerstadion, go left under the bridge, and follow the signs. (Open Tu-Su 9am-5pm. Free.) The **Porsche Museum** tells a similar story with curvier cars. Take S6 (dir.: Weil-der-Stadt) to Neuwirtshaus. (Open M-F 9am-4pm, Sa-Su 9am-5pm. Free.) The soothing waters of Stuttgart's **mineral baths** are an ideal remedy for budget travel exhaustion. The **Mineralbad Leuze,** Am Leuzebad 2-6, has spectacular facilities. (☎216 42 10. Open daily 6am-9pm. Day card DM25, students DM16.) Once refreshed, join the noisy crowd for drinks at **Palast der Republik,** Friedrichstr. 27. (Drinks DM4-12. Open M-W 11am-2am, Th-Sa 11am-3am, Su 3pm-2am; off-season Su-W 11am-1am, Th-Sa 11am-2am.) Or, check out the music and foosball at **Oblomow**, Torstr. 20. (Open daily 4pm-5am.) The dance crowd heads to **Zap**, Hauptstätterstr. 40, in Josef-Hirn-Platz, for hip-hop, house, and soul. (Cover DM8-15. Tu 9pm-3am, W-Su 10pm-4am.)

BADEN-BADEN   ☎07221

Anyone who ever wanted to lead the life of a pampered Old World aristocrat will have a ball in Baden-Baden. Although the spa town has declined somewhat since its 19th-century heyday, it remains a playground for minor royalty and the well-to-do, bathe in the curative mineral spas and drop fat sums of money in the casino. Backpackers may feel a bit out of place, but the haughtiness can be worth tolerating, if only to experience the incredible baths. Baden-Baden's history as a resort goes back nearly two millennia, when the Romans started soaking themselves in the town's first **thermal baths**. The **Friedrichsbad**, Römerpl. 1, is a beautiful 19th-century bathing palace where visitors are parched, steamed, soaked, scrubbed, doused, and pummeled by trained professionals for three hours. (Open M-Sa 9am-10pm, Su noon-8pm; last entry 3hr. before closing. Baths are co-ed Tu and F 4-10pm and all day W and Sa-Su. Standard Roman-Irish bath DM36, with soap and brush massage DM48.) The more modest or budget-minded can head next door to the beautiful **Caracalla-Thermen**, Römerpl. 11, which offers placid soaking—in bathing suits. (Open daily 8am-10pm. DM19 for 2hr.) To lose your shirt all over again, head to the **casino**, where Marlene Dietrich and Fyodor Dostoevsky once tried their luck. To gamble, you must be 21 and wear semi-formal attire. (Open Su-Th 2pm-2am, F-Sa 2pm-3am. DM5 min. Tours Apr.-Sept. 9:30am-11:45am. DM6.) When you've had enough, take **bus** #204 or 205 from Leopoldpl. to Merkurwald and ride the Bergbahn to the top, where trails plunge into the Black Forest (see p. 478).

The **train station** is 7km out of town; take **bus** #204, 205, 216 (dir.: Stadtmitte) or 201 (dir.: Oberbeuren) to Hindenburgpl. to reach the **tourist office**, Kaiserallee, in the Trinkhalle. (☎27 52 00; fax 27 52 02; www.baden-baden.de. Open May-Oct. M-F 9am-5:30pm, Sa 9am-3pm; Nov.-Apr. closes M-F 5pm.) Gloat about your pampering over **email** at **Café Contact**, Eichstr. 5, near Augustapl. (Open daily 11am-2am.) The **Werner-Dietz-Jugendherberge (HI)**, Hardbergstr. 34, is halfway between the station and the center; take bus #201, 205, or 216 to Große-Dollen-Str. (6th stop) and follow the signs uphill. (☎522 23. DM30, under 27 DM25; members only. Sheets DM6. Reception 5-11pm. Curfew 11:30pm.) Most rooms in the center are ritzy and expensive, but the **Hotel am Markt**, Marktpl. 18, has reasonable prices and a great location. (☎270 40. Singles DM56-90; doubles DM115-150; *Kurtaxe* DM5. Breakfast included. Reception 7am-10pm.) Slurp pasta (DM10-15) at the **Pizzeria Roma**, Gernsbacherstr. 14, or stock up at the **Pennymarkt** at the Große-Dollenstr. bus stop near the hostel. (Open M-W 8:30am-6:30pm, Th-F 8:30am-7pm, Sa 8:30am-2pm.)

BLACK FOREST (SCHWARZWALD)

The German cultural consciousness has always dreamt of the dark, from the fairy tales of the Brothers Grimm to the absurdities of Bertolt Brecht. Nowhere are such nightmarish thoughts more legitimated than in the Black Forest, a tangled expanse in southwestern Baden-Württemberg that owes its name to the eerie gloom that prevails under its evergreen canopy. One-time inspiration for the tale of Hansel and Gretel, the region now attracts hikers and skiers with more than just bread crumbs.

▐ TRANSPORTATION

The main entry points to the Black Forest are **Freiburg** (see p. 480); **Baden-Baden** (see p. 478); **Stuttgart** (see p. 476); and **Basel, Switzerland** (see p. 915). Only one **train** penetrates the interior; **bus** service is more thorough, albeit slow and less frequent. Visit the **Freiburg tourist office** for information about the Black Forest (see p. 480).

TITISEE AND SCHLUCHSEE

The more touristed **Titisee** (TEE-tee-zay) is only 30min. by train (dir.: Seebrugg) from Freiburg via the scenic **Höllental** (Hell's Valley). The **tourist office,** Strandbadstr. 4, dispenses maps detailing 130km of hiking trails nearby (DM1-15). From the station, turn left on Parkstr., turn left again at the intersection, and make a quick right following the road. (☎ (07651) 980 40; fax 98 04 40. Open July-Sept. M-F 8am-6pm, Sa 9am-noon and 3-5pm, Su 10am-noon; Oct.-June M-F 9am-noon and 1:30-5:30pm.) **Hiking trails** begin in front of the office; try the **Seerundweg,** or continue along Strandbadstr. and turn right on Alte Poststr. for more challenging routes. **Schluchsee,** to the south, has a slew of first-rate **hiking trails.** The **Seerundweg** circumvents the lake (18km, about 4hr.); more difficult trails depart from the **Sportplatz** parking lot, 15min. up Dresselbacherstr. **Trains** run from the Titisee station, on Parkstr., to Schluchsee (30min., every hr.). From the Schluchsee station, Bahnhofstr., turn right, walk through the underpass, and turn left on Kirchsteige to reach the **tourist office,** at the corner of Fischbacherstr. and Lindenstr. (☎ (07656) 77 32; fax 77 59. Open May-Sept. M-F 8am-6pm, Sa-Su 10am-noon; Oct.-Apr. M-F 8am-noon, 2-6pm.) The **Jugendherberge Schluchsee-Wolfsgrund (HI),** Im Wolfsgrund 28, has stunning lake views. From the station, cross the tracks, hop the fence, and follow the path over the bridge. (☎ (07656) 329. Reception closed 2-5pm. Curfew 11pm. Open May-Oct. DM30, under 27 DM25. *Kurtaxe* DM2-3.) Walk left up Bahnhofstr., continue on Freiburgerstr., turn left on Sägackerweg, go past Am Waldrain, and take another left to reach **Campingplatz Wolfsgrund.** (☎ (07656) 573. DM9.50 per person, DM10 per campsite.) Get **groceries** at **Schmidt's Markt,** Im Rappennest 2. (Open M-F 7:30am-8pm, Sa 7:30am-4pm.)

ST. PETER AND ST. MÄRGEN

North of Titisee and 17km east of Freiburg, twin villages St. Peter and St. Märgen lie between cow-speckled hills in the High Black Forest. **Bus** #7216 runs from Freiburg to St. Märgen via St. Peter; you can also take any train on the Freiburg-Neustadt line to Kirchzarten (3rd stop) and then take bus #7216 to St. Peter (only half continue to St. Märgen; check with the driver). An easy, very scenic 8km path leads from St. Peter to St. Märgen; follow the blue diamonds of the Panoramaweg. From the front of the St. Peter's Klosterkirche, make a sharp right (don't cross the stream and the main road), head for Jägerhaus, and cross the highway. The **tourist office,** in the Klosterhof, lists rooms from DM25. Get off the bus at Zähringer Eck; the office is in front of the church. (☎ (07660) 91 02 24; fax 91 02 44. Open June-Oct. M-F 8am-noon and 2-5pm, Sa 11am-1pm; Nov.-May closed Sa.) With links to all major Black Forest trails and a number of gorgeous day hikes, **St. Märgen** rightfully calls itself a *Wanderparadies* (hiking paradise). One of the more challenging trails leads to the **Zweibach waterfall;** follow the yellow signs with a black dot (16km, 4hr.). To reach the trail, walk downhill along Feldbergstr., turn left on Landfeldweg, and follow signs for Rankmühle. The **tourist office,** in the Rathaus, has good hiking and biking maps (DM5), and finds rooms for free. (☎ (07669) 91 18 17; fax 91 18 40. Open M-F 8am-noon and 2-5pm; June-Aug. also Sa 10am-noon; Nov.-Dec. closed M-F 2-5pm.)

TRIBERG ☎07722

The residents of touristy **Triberg** brag about the **Gutacher Wasserfall,** the highest **waterfall** in Germany, a series of bright cascades tumbling 163m down moss-covered rocks. The idyllic hike through the lush pine trees makes up for the unimpressive trickle. In the park you can also follow signs for the Kulturweg to the **Wallfahrtskirche,** continue on Kroneckweg, and follow the Panoramaweg signs for an excellent view of the Black Forest valley. (DM2.50, students DM2.) **Trains** chug to Triberg from Freiburg (1¾hr., every hr., DM32). To get from the station to the **tourist office,** in the Kurhaus, cross the bridge, go under it, head up steep Féjusstr., which turns into Hauptstr., pass the Marktpl., and turn left at the Hotel Pfaff. (☎ 95 32 30; fax 95 32 36. Open May-Sept. M-F 9am-5pm, Sa 10am-noon; Oct.-Apr. closed Sa.) The town's sparkling **Jugendherberge (HI),** Rohrbacherstr. 35, requires a 30-minute climb up Friedrichstr. (which becomes Rohrbacherstr.) from the tourist office.

(☎41 10. Sheets DM5.50. Reception 5-7pm and at 9:45pm. Call ahead. Dorms DM30, under 27 DM25.) The **Hotel Zum Bären,** Hauptstr. 10, is closer to the park's waterfall entrance. (☎44 93. Breakfast included. Singles DM37-45; doubles DM66-84.)

FREIBURG IM BREISGAU   ☎0761

Freiburg may be the metropolis of the Schwarzwald, but it has yet to succumb to the hectic rhythms of city life. Its relaxed atmosphere results not only from persistent French influence and the hordes of students (who flout the dour German stereotype), but also from the surrounding hills, which overflow with greenery and fantastic hiking trails. Freiburg's pride and joy is the majestic 13th- to 16th-century **Münster,** a stone **cathedral** with a 116m spire and a **tower** with the oldest bell in Germany. (Cathedral open M-Sa 10am-6pm, Su 1-6pm. Tower open May-Oct. M-F 9:30am-5pm, Su 1-5pm; Nov.-Apr. Tu-Sa 9:30am-5pm, Su 1-5pm. DM2.50, students DM1.50.) Two medieval gates—the **Schwabentor** and the **Martinstor**—stand within a few blocks of one another in the southeast corner of the Altstadt. From the Schwabentor, the pedestrian overpass across the Schloßbergring leads towards the path up the **Schloßberg,** which provides an excellent view of the city. The **Museum für Neue Kunst** (Museum of Modern Art), Marienstr. 10a, near the Schwabentor, displays the work of 20th-century German artists such as Otto Dix. (Open Tu-Su 10am-5pm. Free.) Freiburg's nightlife revolves around the **Martinstor.** Despite its name, at **Exit,** Kaiser-Josef-Str. 248, people do just the opposite. (Cover DM6. Open M and W-Th 10pm-3am, F-Sa 10pm-4am; Th and Sa students free.) **Jazzhaus,** Schnewlingstr. 1, features live music almost every night (cover from DM10).

Trains arrive from Stuttgart (1½hr., every hr., DM61); Basel, Switzerland (45min., 1-2 per hr., DM17); and Strasbourg, France (1¾hr., every hr., DM27). The **tourist office,** Rotteckring 14, is two blocks down Eisenbahnstr. from the station. (☎388 18 82; fax 388 18 87. Open June-Sept. M-F 9:30am-8pm, Sa 9:30am-5pm, Su 10am-noon; Oct.-May same hrs. except Sa 9:30am-2pm.) Check your **email** at the **Internet-Café** in the Kaufhof department store on Schusterstr. and Dreherstr. (Open M-F 9:30am-8pm, Sa 9am-4pm. DM3 per 30min.) To reach the **Jugendherberge (HI),** Kartäuserstr. 151, take streetcar #1 (dir.: Littenweiler) to Römerhof, cross the tracks, backtrack 20m, walk 10min. down Fritz-Geiges-Str., cross the stream, and follow the footpath right. (☎676 56. Reception 7am-9am and 1-10pm. Curfew 1am. DM33, under 27 DM28. HI members only.) **Hotel Zum Löwen,** Breisgauerstr. 62, doesn't feel like a budget hotel. Take streetcar #1 to Padua-Allee, backtrack 30m along the tracks, and walk 5min. down Breigauerstr. (☎809 72 20. Breakfast included. Singles DM50-70; doubles DM90-130.) **Camping Hirzberg,** Kartäuserstr. 99, provides the most economical way to stay near the city if you have a warm sleeping bag. Take streetcar #1 (dir.: Lassbergstr.) to Stadthalle, go left via the underpass, walk straight on Hirzbergstr., cross Max-Miller-Steg bridge, and take a left at the street. (☎350 54. DM9 per person, DM6-8 per tent.) Grab a meal at **Brennessel,** Eschholzstr. 17, a plucky student tavern with funk, jazz, and cheap chow. (Open M-Sa 6pm-1am, Su 5pm-1am.) Or load up at **Edeka ActivMarkt,** Eisenbahnstr. 39. (Open M-F 8am-8pm, Sa 8am-2pm.) **Postal Code:** 79098.

TÜBINGEN   ☎07071

Tübingen is a bookish city, and proud of it; nearly half of its residents are affiliated with the 500-year-old university. In addition to being populated by students, the **Altstadt** is surprisingly devoid of tourists, allowing independent travelers a chance for solo exploration. The chancel of the 15th-century **Stiftskirche,** the focal point of the Altstadt's winding alleys and gabled houses, contains the tombs of 14 members of the former House of Württemberg. (Church open daily 9am-5pm. Chancel and tower open daily Aug.-Sept. 10:30am-5pm; Apr.-July and Oct. F-Su 10:30am-5pm. Joint ticket DM2, students DM1.) Head down Kirchg. to the old market square to see the ornate painted facade of the **Rathaus.** Nearby stands the **Tübingen Evangelisches Stift,** which was built as an Augustinian monastery but later became a seminary that housed such academic luminaries as Kepler, Hegel, Schelling, and Mörike. Down Bursag. is the **Burse,** where roommates Hegel and Schelling dozed through dull theology lectures. Their third roommate, the great Friedrich Hölderlin, lived the last 36 years of his life in the nearby **Hölderlinturm** in a state of insanity. (Open Tu-F 10am-noon and 3-5pm, Sa-Su 2-5pm. DM3, students DM2.) On top of the hill in the center of town is the **Schloß Hohentübingen,** which dates from 1078 and commands the best views; inside, an ethnographic **museum** has supposedly the oldest surviving example of handiwork, a 35,000-year-old sculpted ivory horse. (Open W-Su May-Sept. 10am-6pm; Oct.-Apr. 10am-5pm. DM4, students DM2.) **Platanenallee** offers an up-close view of the Neckar.

    Trains run to Stuttgart (1hr., 2 per hr., DM17); the station is on the other side of the Neckar River from the Altstadt. Turn right from the station and left on Karlstr. to reach the **tourist office** on the Neckarbrücke, which books rooms for free. (☎913 60; fax 350 70. Open M-F 9am-7pm, Sa 9am-5pm, Su 2-5pm; Oct.-Easter closed Su.) To get from the tourist office to the **Jugendherberge (HI),** Gartenstr. 22/2, cross the Neckarbrücke and make a right. (☎230 02. Breakfast included. Reception 5-8pm and 10-11pm. Curfew midnight. DM33, under 27 DM28. HI members only.) To **camp** at **Rappernberghalde,** on the river, head upstream from the Altstadt, or turn left from the station, cross the Alleenbrücke, turn left, and follow the blue signs. (☎431 45. Reception 8am-12:30pm and 2:30-10pm. Open Mar. to mid-Oct. DM9.50 per person, DM7 per campsite.) **Tübingen Ratskeller,** Haagg. 4, with an entrance on Rathausg., serves up Swabian specialties and veggie platters. (Open M-Sa 6-11:30pm, Su 6-11pm.) Buy **groceries** at **HL Markt,** Europapl. 5, across from the post office. (Open M-F 7am-8pm, Sa 7am-4pm.) **Postal Code:** 72072.

LAKE CONSTANCE (BODENSEE)

Germany has long suffered from a Mediterranean complex, and the single strip of land along the Bodensee in southern Baden-Württemberg provides an opportunity for Italian fantasies to be enacted and Grecian longings to be satisfied with a thoroughly un-German casualness. With the snow-capped Swiss and Austrian Alps in the background, the Bodensee is one of Germany's most stunning destinations.

KONSTANZ (CONSTANCE)   ☎07531

The narrow streets of the elegant university city of Konstanz, among the few German cities to have escaped Allied bombing in WWII, wind around the beautifully painted Baroque and Renaissance facades in the town center. The **Münster** has a 76-meter soaring Gothic spire and a display of ancient religious objects, although the tower is unfortunately being renovated through 2003. (Open M-Sa 10am-6pm, Su noon-6:30pm. Free.) Wander down **Seestraße,** near the yacht harbor on the lake, or down **Rheinsteig,** along the Rhine, for picturesque promenades, or rent a **paddleboat** or **rowboat** at Am Gondelhafen. (Open Apr.-Oct. daily 10am-dusk. DM12-16 per hr.) Take bus #5 to reach **Strandbad Horn,** Konstanz's most popular public beach, with a nude sunbathing section modestly enclosed by hedges.

    Trains arrive from Freiburg (2½hr., DM43); Stuttgart (3hr., DM56); Zürich (1¼hr.). The **tourist office,** Bahnhofspl. 13, is to the right of the train station. Ask about the **Gästekarte** (DM1.50 per day), which provides unlimited bus transit in Konstanz and reduced admission to some sights for those overnighting two nights or more. (☎13 30 30; fax 13 30 60. Open Apr.-Oct. M-F 9am-6:30pm, Sa 9am-1pm; Nov.-Mar. M-F 9am-noon and 2-5pm.) Reserve ahead for the marvelous **Jugendherberge Kreuzlingen (HI),** Promenadenstr. 7, which is actually in Switzerland but is closer to downtown Konstanz than the other hostel. From the station, turn left, cross the metal bridge over the tracks, turn right, go through the parking lot to checkpoint Klein Venedig, bear left along Seestr., continue straight on the path, then head right through the castle parking lot and up the hill. (From Germany ☎ (00 41 71) 688 26 63. From Switzerland ☎ (071) 688 26 63. Breakfast included. Reception 8-9:30am and 5-9pm. Curfew 11pm. Open Mar.-Nov. Dorms DM28.) **Jugendherberge "Otto-Moericke-Turm" (HI),** Zur Allmannshöhe 18, is less luxurious, but has a great view. Take **bus** #4 from the station to Jugendherberge (7th stop), backtrack, and head straight up the hill. (☎322 60. HI members only. Breakfast and dinner included. Sheets DM6. Reception Apr.-Oct. 3-10pm; Nov.-Mar. 5-10pm. Lockout 9:30am-noon. Curfew 10pm. DM42, under 27 DM37.) Get **groceries** at **Edeka**, at Münzg. near Fischmarkt. (Open M-F 8am-8pm, Sa 8am-4pm.) **Postal Code:** 78462.

LINDAU IM BODENSEE   ☎ 08382

Tourists come to soak in Lindau's balmy climate and wander among the 14th-century gabled houses along **Maximilianstr.** The **Cavazzen-Haus** in the Marktpl. houses the **Stadtmuseum.** (☎ 94 40 73. Open Apr.-Oct. Tu-Su 10am-noon and 2-5pm. DM5, students DM3.) Roulette wheels spin at the **Spielbank** (casino) by the Seebrücke. (☎ 50 51. No jeans, tie required after 5pm. 21+. DM5 and a passport. Open daily 3pm-3am.) Lindau's biggest **beach** is **Eichwald**, a 30min. walk with your back to the island along Uferweg. (☎ 55 39. Open M-F 9:30am-7:30pm, Sa-Su 9am-8pm. DM5.) To reach the quieter **Lindenhofbad**, take bus #1 or 2 to Anheggerstr. and then bus #4 to Alwind. (☎ 66 37. Open daily 10am-8pm. DM4, students DM3.)

   Trains run to Konstanz (2hr., DM28), as do **ferries** (3½hr., 3-6 per day. DM18.80). You can rent a **boat** on the left of the casino, next to the bridge. (Open mid.-Mar. to mid.-Sept. daily 9am-9pm. Rowboats DM12; paddleboats DM14-18 per hr; motorboat DM45.) The **tourist office**, Ludwigstr. 68, is across from the train station. (☎ 26 00 30; fax 26 00 55; www.lindau-tourismus.de. Open mid-June to early Sept. M-Sa 9am-1pm and 2-7pm; May to mid-June and Sept. M-F 9am-1pm and 2-6pm, Sa 9am-1pm; Apr. and Oct. M-F 9am-1pm and 2-5pm, Sa 9am-1pm; Nov.-Mar. M-F 9am-noon and 2-5pm.) The **Jugendherberge (HI)**, Herbergsweg 11, lies across the Seebrücke off Bregenzerstr. (☎ 967 10. Breakfast included. Reception 7am-midnight. Curfew midnight. Under 27 and families with young children only. Dorms DM29.) **Park-Camping Lindau Am See**, Frauenhoferstr. 20, is 3km east of the island on the mainland; take bus #1 or 2 to Anheggerstr., then bus #3 (dir.: Zech) to the end of the line. (☎ 722 36. DM9.50 per person, DM4 per tent. *Kurtaxe* DM1.50.) Find **groceries** at **Plus**, in the basement of the department store at the corner of In der Grub and Cramerg. (Open M-F 8:30am-6:30pm, Sa 8am-1pm.) **Postal Code:** 88131

BAVARIA (BAYERN)

Bavaria is the Germany of Teutonic myth, Wagnerian opera, and fairy tales. From the Baroque cities along the Danube to Mad King Ludwig's castles perched high in the Alps, the region beckons to more tourists than any other part of the country. Indeed, when most foreigners conjure up images of Germany, they imagine Bavaria, land of beer gardens, oom-pah-pah bands, and *Lederhosen*. This largest of Germany's federal states, mostly rural, Catholic, and conservative, contrasts greatly with the rest of the country, and its unique traditions and dialect are insistently preserved: residents have always been Bavarians first and Germans second.

> ❗ **REMINDER.** HI-affiliated hostels in Bavaria generally do not admit guests over age 26, although families and groups of adults with young children are usually allowed even if the adults are over 26.

MUNICH (MÜNCHEN)   ☎ 089

The capital and cultural center of Bavaria, Munich is a sprawling, relatively liberal metropolis in the midst of solidly conservative southern Germany. The two cities of Munich and Berlin are emblematic of the two poles of German character: Munich's sensual air of merriment—most obvious during the wild *Fasching* (Germany's equivalent of Mardi Gras, Jan. 7-Feb. 27, 2001) and the legendary

Oktoberfest (Sept. 22-Oct. 7, 2001)—contrasts with Berlin's dizzying reconstruction and sense of fragmented avant-garde. Since falling from the Bavarian Golden Age of the 18th and 19th centuries and being shattered in WWII (when less than 3% of the city was left intact), Munich has proved resilient, and today basks unabashedly in West German postwar economic glory: world-class museums, handsome parks and architecture, and a rambunctious arts scene collide to create a city of astonishing vitality.

⌐ TRANSPORTATION

Flights: Flughafen München (☎97 52 13 13). S8 connects the airport and the Hauptbahnhof (every 20min. DM15.20 or 8 stripes on the *Streifenkarte*). A **Lufthansa shuttle bus** also makes the same route (45min.), with a pickup at the Nordfriedhof U-Bahn stop in Schwabing. Buses leave from Arnulfstr., on the northern side of the train station (every 20min. 6:50am-7:50pm) and return from Terminal A (*Zentralbereich*) and Terminal D (every 20min. 7:55am-8:55pm). One-way DM16, round-trip DM26.

Trains: Munich's **Hauptbahnhof** (☎22 33 12 56) is the transportation hub of southern Germany, with connections to: **Berlin** (7½hr.; 2 per hr.; DM277, youth DM222); **Cologne** (6hr.; 2 per hr.; DM173, youth DM138); **Frankfurt** (3½hr.; 3 per hr.; DM147, youth DM118); **Hamburg** (6hr.; 2 per hr.; DM268, youth DM214); **Amsterdam** (9hr.; every hr.; DM248, youth DM198); **Innsbruck** (2hr.; every hr.; DM48, youth DM37); **Paris** (10hr.; DM194, youth DM156); **Prague** (8½hr.; 6 per day; DM113, youth DM85); **Salzburg** (1¾hr.; every hr.; DM41, youth DM30); **Vienna** (5hr.; every hr.; DM106, youth DM82); and **Zürich** (5hr.; every 2 hr.; DM110, youth DM85). For schedules, fare information, and reservations call ☎ (0180) 599 66 33. Station open daily 6am-10:30pm.

Public Transportation: MVV, Munich's public transport system, runs Su-Th 5am-12:30am, F-Sa 5am-2am. Eurail, InterRail, and German railpasses are valid on the S-Bahn but *not* on the U-Bahn, streetcars, or buses. Buy tickets at the blue *MVV-Fahrausweise* vending machines and **validate them** in the boxes marked with an "E" before entering the platform. Single ride tickets DM3.80 (valid for 3hr.). **Kurzstrecke** (short trip) tickets can be used for 2 stops on the U-Bahn or S-Bahn, or for 4 stops on a streetcar or bus (DM1.90). A **Streifenkarte** (11-strip ticket; DM16) can be used by more than 1 person. Cancel 2 strips per person for a normal ride, or 1 strip per person for a *Kurzstrecke*. Beyond the city center, cancel 2 strips per additional zone. A **Single-Tageskarte** (single-day ticket) is valid for 1 day of unlimited travel until 6am the next day (DM9). A **Partner-Tageskarte** (DM14) can be used by 2 adults, 4 children under 18, and a dog. The **3-Day Pass** (DM22) is also a great deal. The best public transportation deal is the **München Welcome Card,** available at the tourist office and in many hotels, valid for 3 days of public transportation for DM29; a group ticket for up to 5 people runs DM42. The card includes a 50% discount on many of Munich's museums and on Radius bike rental (see below). Buy passes at the MVV office behind tracks 31-32 in the Hauptbahnhof.

Taxis: Taxi-Zentrale (☎216 11 or 194 10) has large stands in front of the train station and every 5-10 blocks in the central city.

Car Rental: Swing, Schellingstr. 139 (☎523 20 05), rents from DM45 per day. **Avis** (☎550 12 12), **Europcar/National** (☎550 13 41), **Hertz** (☎550 22 56), and **Sixt Budget** (☎550 24 47) have offices upstairs in the Hauptbahnhof. Prices start from DM130 per day.

Bike Rental: Radius Bikes (☎59 61 13), at the far end of the Hauptbahnhof, behind the lockers opposite tracks 30-31. From DM5 per hr., DM25 per day, DM75 per week. Deposit DM100, passport, or credit card. Students and Eurailpass holders receive a 10% discount. Open May-mid-Oct. daily 10am-6pm. **Activ-Rad,** Hans-Sachsstr. 7 (☎26 65 06), rents bikes for DM18 per day. Take U1 or U2 to Fraunhoferstr. Open M-F 9am-1pm, 2-6:30pm, Sa 9am-1pm.

GERMANY

ORIENTATION AND PRACTICAL INFORMATION

A map of Munich's center looks like a squished circle quartered by one horizontal and one vertical line. The circle is the main traffic **Ring**, which changes its name frequently along its length. The east-west and north-south thoroughfares cross at Munich's epicenter, the **Marienplatz** (home to the **Neues Rathaus**), and meet the traffic rings at **Karlsplatz** (called **Stachus** by locals) in the west, **Isartorplatz** in the east, **Odeonsplatz** in the north, and **Sendlinger Tor** in the south. The **Hauptbahnhof** is just beyond Karlsplatz outside the Ring in the west. In the east beyond the Isartor, the **Isar** flows by the city center, south to north. To get to Marienplatz from the station, go straight on Bayerstr. to the yellow buildings of Karlsplatz. Continue straight through Karlstor to Neuhauserstr., which becomes Kaufingerstr. before it reaches Marienplatz (15-20min.). Or take S1-S8 (two stops from the Hauptbahnhof, dir.: Ostbahnhof) to Marienplatz.

To the north, at Odeonsplatz, the giant **Residenz** palace sprawls over a hefty piece of downtown land; **Ludwigstraße** stretches north from there toward the university district. **Leopoldstraße,** the continuation of Ludwigstr., reaches further toward **Schwabing.** This district, also known as "Schwabylon," is student country; it lies to the west of the maddeningly mobbed Leopoldstr. **Türkenstr., Amalienstr., Schellingstr.,** and **Barerstr.** meander through the funk. To the east of Schwabing sprawls the **Englischer Garten;** to the west is the **Olympiazentrum,** the complex constructed for the 1972 games, surrounded by the verdant **Olympiapark.** Farther west sits the posh **Nymphenburg,** built around the **Schloß Nymphenburg.** Southwest of Marienplatz, **Sendlingerstr.** leads past shops to the Sendlinger Tor. From there, Lindwurmstr. proceeds to Goetheplatz, from which Mozartstr. leads to **Theresienwiese,** the site of Oktoberfest.

TOURIST, FINANCIAL, AND LOCAL SERVICES

Tourist Office: Main Office, Fremdenverkehrsamt (☎23 33 02 57; fax 23 33 02 33; email Munich_Tourist_Office@compuserve.com; www.munich-tourist.de), located on the front (east) side of the train station, next to ABR Travel on Bahnhofpl. Books **rooms** for free with a 10-15% deposit and sells excellent English city maps (DM0.50). Buy the **München Welcome Card** here, which offers free public transportation and reduced prices for 35 different sights and services (single-day ticket DM12, 3-days DM29).

EurAide in English (☎59 38 89; fax 550 39 65; email euraide@compuserve.com; www.euraide.de), along track 11 (room 3) of the Hauptbahnhof, near the Bayerstr. exit. Delve into the intricacies of Munich with one sound byte from EurAide's Alan R. Wissenberg, savior of frazzled English-speaking tourists. Open June-Oktoberfest daily 7:45am-noon and 1-6pm; Oct.-April M-F 8am-noon and 1-4pm, Sa 8am-noon; May daily 7:45am-noon and 1-4:30pm.

Consulates: Canada, Tal 29 (☎219 95 70). S-Bahn to Isartor. Open M-Th 9am-noon and 2-5pm, F 9am-noon and 2-3:30pm. **Ireland,** Mauerkircherstr. 1a (☎98 57 23). Streetcar #20 or bus #54 or 87. Open M-F 9am-noon. **South Africa,** Sendlinger-Tor-Pl. 5 (☎231 16 30). U1, U2, U3 or U6 to Sendlinger Tor. Open M-F 9am-noon. **UK,** Bürkleinstr. 10 (☎21 10 90), 4th floor. U4 or U5 to Lehel. Open M-F 8:30am-noon and 1-5pm (F to 3:30pm). **US,** Königinstr. 5 (☎288 80), beside the Englischer Garten. Open M-F 8-11am.

Currency Exchange: ReiseBank (☎551 08 37). 2 locations: one in front of the main entrance to the train station on Bahnhofplatz (open daily 6am-11pm); and the other around the corner from EurAide at track 11 (open M-Sa 7:30am-7:15pm, Su 9:30am-12:30pm and 1-4:45pm). Western Union services available.

American Express: Promenadeplatz 6 (☎29 09 00; 24hr. hotline ☎(0130) 85 31 00), in the Hotel Bayerischer Hof. Holds mail and cashes traveler's checks. Open M-F 9am-5:30pm, Sa 9:30am-12:30pm. **Branch** office at Kaufingerstr. 24 (☎22 80 13 87), by the Frauenkirche. Open M-F 9am-6pm, Sa 10am-2pm.

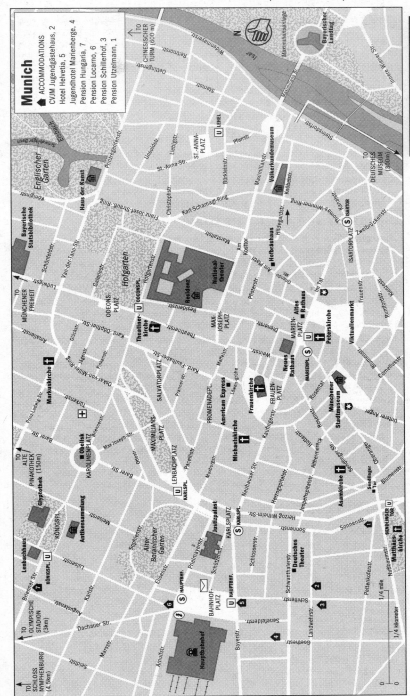

Munich

▲ ACCOMMODATIONS
CVJM Jugendgästehaus, 2
Hotel Helvetia, 5
Jugendhotel Marienberge, 4
Pension Hungaria, 7
Pension Locarno, 6
Pension Schillerhof, 3
Pension Utzelmann, 1

GERMANY

Budget Travel: Council Travel, Adalbertstr. 32 (☎38 83 89 70), near the university, sells ISICs for DM18. Open M-F 10am-1pm and 2-6:30pm, Sa 10am-3pm. **DER Reisebüro** (☎55 14 02 00; www.der.de) is in the main hall of the train station and sells train tickets and railpasses. Open M-F 9:30am-6pm and Sa 10am-1pm.

Luggage Storage: At the **train station** (☎13 08 50 47) and **airport** (☎97 52 13 75). Staffed storage room *(Gepäckaufbewahrung)* in the main hall of the train station. Open M-F 6:30am-11pm, Sa-Su 7:30am-10pm. DM4 per piece per day. Lockers in main hall and opposite tracks # 16, 24, and 28-36. DM2-4 per 24hr.

Gay and Lesbian Resources: Gay services information (☎260 30 56). **Lesbian information** and the **LeTra Lesbentraum** (Angertorstr. 3, ☎725 42 72). Telephone times M, W 2:30-5pm; Tu 10:30am-1pm; Th 7-9pm. See also **Gay and Lesbian Munich,** p. 494.

Ticket Agencies: To order almost all **tickets by phone** call **München Ticket** (☎54 81 81 81; fax. 54 81 81 54; www.muenchenticket.de).

Laundromat: City SB-Waschcenter, Paul-Heyse-Str. 21, near the train station. Right on Bayerstr., then left on Paul-Heyse-Str. Open daily 7am-11pm. **Münz Waschsalon,** Amalienstr. 61, near the university. Open M-F 8am-6:30pm, Sa 8am-1pm.

EMERGENCY AND COMMUNICATIONS

Emergency: Police, ☎110. **Ambulance** and **Fire,** ☎112.

Pharmacy: Bahnhof-Apotheke, Bahnhofpl. 2 (☎59 41 19), on the corner outside the train station. Open M-F 8am-6:30pm, Sa 8am-2pm. 24hr. service rotates among the city's pharmacies—call ☎59 44 75 for recorded information (German only).

Medical Assistance: Klinikum Rechts der Isar, across the river on Ismaningerstr. U4 or U5 to Max-Weber-Platz. STD tests are free and anonymous at the **Gesundheitshaus,** Dachauerstr. 90 (☎520 71). Open M-Th 8-11am and 1-2pm, F 8-11am. UK and US consulates carry lists of English-speaking doctors.

Internet Access: Times Square Internet Café, Bayerstr. 10a, located on the south side of the train station. DM4.50 per 15min. **Internet-Café,** Nymphenburgerstr. 145 (☎129 11 20), on the corner of Landshuter Allee. U1 to Rotkreuzplatz. Unlimited free Internet access as long as you order pasta (DM5.30-7.50) or pizza (DM5.50-8.50); otherwise, the cost is DM5 per 30min. Open daily 11am-4am. Another location, Altheimer Eck 12 (☎260 78 15), is between Marienplatz and Karlsplatz in the pedestrian zone Arcade-Passage. Open daily 11am-1am.

Post Office: Bahnhofplatz, 80335 Munich (☎59 90 87 16). Walk out of the main train station exit and it's the large yellow building directly across the street. Open M-F 7am-8pm, Sa 8am-4pm, Su 9am-3pm. **Poste Restante:** Anosha SIRIPALA, Postlagernd Brief, Bahnhofplatz, 80335 MÜNCHEN. Postamt 31 (☎552 26 20), up the escalator in the train station, sells stamps and phone cards, but doesn't mail packages or exchange money. Open M-F 7am-8pm, Sa 8am-4pm, Su 9am-3pm. **Postal Code:** 80335.

▐ ACCOMMODATIONS

Munich's accommodations usually fall into one of three categories: seedy, expensive, or booked solid. During times like Oktoberfest, only the last category exists. In summer, the best strategy is to start calling before noon or to book a few weeks in advance. Most singles (without private bath) run DM55-85, doubles DM80-120. If you're planning an extended stay in Munich, call the *Mitwohnzentrale* (☎286 60 66) or try bargaining with a *Pension* owner. Remember: Bavarian HI hostels do not accept guests over age 26. The enforcement of this rule varies. At most of Munich's hostels you can check in all day, but start your search well before 5pm.

HOSTELS

▨ **Euro Youth Hotel,** Senefelderstr. 5 (☎59 90 88 11; email info@euro-youth-hotel.de). From the Bahnhofsplatz exit of the Hauptbahnhof, make a right on Bayerstr. and a left on Senefelderstr.; the hotel will be on the left. Sleek bar open daily 8pm-2am (Maß DM3.50); Happy Hour 8-9pm. All-you-can-eat breakfast buffet DM7.90. Laundry DM6.

Doubles DM42, with private shower, and breakfast DM60; triples and quads DM36; dorm beds DM29 per night.

Jugendherberge Pullach Burg Schwaneck (HI), Burgweg 4-6 (☎793 06 43), in a castle 12km outside the city center. S7 (dir.: Wolfratshausen) to Pullach (20min.). Exit the station from the side toward Munich and walk in the direction of the huge soccerfield down Margarethenstr. and follow the signs (8min.). Breakfast included. Dinner DM8. Reception 4-11pm. Curfew 11:30pm. 6- to 8-bed dorms DM23; singles DM37.50; doubles DM35.50; quads DM26.

Jugendherberge München (HI), Wendl-Dietrich-Str. 20. (☎13 11 56; email jhmuenchen@djh-bayern.de). U1 (dir.: Westfriedhof) to Rotkreuzplatz. Go down Wendl-Dietrich-Str; to the left of the *Schwestern Schule* building; the entrance is ahead on the right. The most "central" of the HI hostels (3km from the city center). Bike rental DM24. Breakfast included. Key deposit DM20. Check-in starts at 11am, but lines form before 9am. Big dorm (37 beds) for men only DM25; 4- to 6-bed coed rooms DM30.

4 you München, Hirtenstr. 18 (☎552 16 60; www.the4you.de), 200m from the Hauptbahnhof. Exit at Arnulfstr., go left, quickly turn right onto Pfefferstr., then hang a left onto Hirtenstr. Breakfast buffet DM8. Sheets DM5. Key deposit DM20. Singles DM56; doubles DM40; 4- to 12-bed dorms DM26-32. Over 27 15% surcharge. In **adjoining hotel,** singles with bath DM79; doubles with bath DM129; extra bed DM49.

Jugendgästehaus Thalkirchen (HI), Miesingstr. 4 (☎723 65 50). U1 or U2 to Sendlinger Tor, then U3 (dir.: Fürstenrieder West) to Thalkirchen. Take the Thalkirchner Platz exit and follow Schäftlarnstr. toward Innsbruck and bear right around the curve, then follow Frauenbergstr. and head left on Münchnerstr. Although distant, the Jugendgästehaus can be reached by a 15min. subway ride from the city center. TV room, billiards, and a washer/dryer (wash and dry DM5 each). Sheets and breakfast included. Reception 7am-1am. Check-in 2pm-6pm. Curfew 1am. Singles DM42.50; 2- to 15-bed rooms DM37.50.

Jugendlager Kapuzinerhölzl ("The Tent"), In den Kirschen 30 (☎141 43 00; www.the-tent.de). Streetcar #17 from the Hauptbahnhof (dir.: Amalienburgstr.) to Botanischer Garten (15min.). Go straight on Franz-Schrank-Str. and left at In den Kirschen; The Tent is on the right. Night streetcars run at least once an hour all night. Sleep with 250 fellow "campers" under a big circus tent on a wooden floor. Laundry DM4. Internet access DM2 per 15min. Passport required as deposit. Open mid-June to Aug. DM15 gets you a foam pad, multiple wool blankets, bathrooms, a shower, and a rudimentary breakfast. Actual "beds" DM19. **Camping:** DM8 per person, DM8 per campsite.

CVJM Jugendgästehaus, Landwehrstr. 13 (☎552 14 10; fax 550 42 82; email info@cvjm-muenchen.org; www.cvjm-muenchen.org). Take the Bayerstr. exit from the train station, head straight down Goethestr. or Schillerstr., and take the 2nd left onto Landwehrstr.; it's on the right. Central location with modern rooms and showers in the hall, and a nifty 70s-decorated restaurant. Co-ed rooms for married couples only. Breakfast included. Reception 8am-12:30am. Curfew 12:30am-7am. Reservations by mail, phone, fax, or email must arrive before 4pm and can be made up to a year in advance. Hostel closed during Easter and Dec. 20-Jan. 7. Singles DM53; doubles DM45; triples DM42. Reduced rates between Dec. and Feb., increased rates during the Oktoberfest. Over 26 16% surcharge.

Jump In, Hochstr. 51 (☎48 95 34 37; www.jump-in.net). S1-S8 to Rosenheimer Platz, then take the Gasteig exit to the left and walk left on Hochstr. (10min.). Or streetcar #27 or bus #51 to Ostfriedhof. Sinks in every room, showers and toilet off the hallway. Sheets DM5. Wash DM5. Reception 10am-noon and 5-10pm. Mattresses on the floor DM29, real beds DM35; doubles DM39.

Haus International, Elisabethstr. 87 (☎12 00 60). U2 (dir.: Feldmoching) to Hohenzollernplatz, then streetcar #12 (dir.: Romanplatz) or bus #33 (dir.: Aidenbachstr.) to Barbarastr. It's the 5-story beige building behind the BP gas station. Cafeteria-style lunch and dinner available (DM12-14). Free indoor pool (score!), small beer garden, TV room, and groovy disco with bar. Singles DM55, with bath DM85; doubles DM49, with shower DM69; triples DM48; quads DM45; quints DM42.

Jugendhotel Marienberge, Goethestr. 9 (☎55 58 05), less than a block from the train station. Take the Bayerstr. exit and walk down Goethestr. Open **only to women** under 26. Breakfast included. Wash DM2, dry DM2. Reception 8am-midnight. Curfew midnight. Singles DM40; doubles DM35; triples DM35; 6-bed dorms DM30.

HOTELS AND PENSIONEN

While Munich—reputedly a city of 80,000 guest beds—has a surplus of dirt-cheap (and often dirty) accommodations, it is often a better idea to crash in a hostel. A clean room in a safe area costs at least DM55-65 for a single and DM80-100 for a double. **Always call ahead.** Call a few months in advance for Oktoberfest rooms, as some hotels are booked for the entire two weeks by early summer.

■ **Hotel Helvetia,** Schillerstr. 6 (☎590 68 50), at the corner of Bahnhofsplatz, next to the Vereinsbank, to the right as you exit the station. Friendliest hotel in all of Munich. Breakfast included. Singles DM55-65; doubles DM72-95, with shower DM99-115; triples DM105-126.

Hotel Kurpfalz, Schwanthalerstr. 121 (☎540 98 60; www.munich-hotels.com). Exit on Bayerstr. from the station, turn right and walk 5-6 blocks down Bayerstr., veer left onto Holzapfelstr., and make a right onto Schwanthalerstr. (10min.). Or streetcar #18 or 19 to Holzapfelstr. (3 stops) and walk from there. Satellite TVs, phones, private baths, and hardwood furniture in all rooms. Internet access. Breakfast buffet included. Singles from DM89, doubles from DM109, triples (doubles with cots) DM165.

Hotel-Pension Utzelmann, Pettenkoferstr. 6 (☎59 48 89). From the train station walk 4 blocks down Schillerstr. and go left on Pettenkofer; it's at the end on the left (10min.). Breakfast included. Reception 7am-10pm. Singles DM55, with shower DM95, with bath DM130; doubles DM98, with shower DM115, with bath DM150; triples DM140, with shower DM160, with bath DM180; quads DM170, with shower DM190.

Pension Locarno, Bahnhofsplatz 5 (☎55 51 64). From the train station's main entrance walk left across Bahnhofsplatz and look for the building with the "Pension" sign. Reception Su-M 7:30am-midnight, Tu-Sa 7:30am-5am. Singles DM55-75; doubles DM85; triples DM125; quads DM140.

Pension Schillerhof, Schillerstr. 21 (☎59 42 70; www.hotel-schillerhof.de). Exit onto Bahnhofsplatz from the train station, turn right, and walk 2 blocks down Schillerstr. Breakfast included. Reception 6am-10pm. Reservations can be made online. Singles DM60-80; doubles DM90-120. Extra bed DM20. Oktoberfest surcharge DM25-40.

Pension Central, Bayerstr. 55 (☎543 98 46). Hang a right out of the Bayerstr. exit of the train station and walk 5min. up Bayerstr.; pension is on the left. Singles DM65, with bath DM75; doubles DM95, with bath DM110-120; triples DM120; quads DM160-180; quints DM200-220.

Pension Frank, Schellingstr. 24 (☎28 14 51). U3 or U6 to Universität. Take the Schellingstr. exit, then the first right onto Schellingstr.; it's 2 blocks down on the right. Fabulous location for cafe and bookstore aficionados. Breakfast included. Reception 7:30am-10pm. Check-out at 11am. 3- to 6-bed rooms DM40 per person, singles DM55-65, doubles DM95.

Pension am Kaiserplatz, Kaiserplatz 12 (☎34 91 90). Located a few blocks from nightlife central. U3 or U6 to Münchener Freiheit. Take the escalator to Herzogstr., then left. Take a left at Viktoriastr. and it's at the end of the street on the right (10min.). Breakfast included. Reception 7am-9pm. Singles DM59; doubles DM89, with shower DM99-105; 6-bed rooms DM240; each additional person DM40.

Pension Geiger, Steinheilstr. 1 (☎52 15 56). U2 to Theresienstr. Take the Augustenstr. S.O. exit, and walk straight down Theresienstr. towards Kopierladen München. Take a right on Enhuberstr. and a left on Steinheilstr.; enter through the double doors on the right (5min.). Family-run *Pension* located in a quiet neighborhood. Hall showers DM2. Reception (2 floors up) 8am-9pm. Arrive by 6pm or call. Closed Dec. 24-Jan. 31. Singles DM55-DM80; doubles DM98-DM108.

Pension Theresia, Luisenstr. 51 (☎52 12 50; fax 542 06 33). U2 to Theresienstr. and take the Augustenstr. S.O. exit, head straight down Theresienstr., and take the second right onto Luisenstr.; the entrance is in the passageway left of the Dahlke store. Breakfast included. Reception (2nd floor) 7am-10pm. Reservations by phone or fax. Singles DM52-68; doubles DM89-99, with shower DM95-145 DM30 per extra person; triples and quads available.

Hotel-Pension am Markt, Heiliggeiststr. 6 (☎22 50 14), smack dab in the city center. S1-S8 to Marienplatz, then walk past the Altes Rathaus and go right down the alley behind the green church. Breakfast included. Singles DM62-64, with shower DM110; doubles DM110-116, with shower DM150-160; triples DM165, with shower DM205.

CAMPING

Munich's campgrounds are open from mid-March to late October.

Campingplatz Thalkirchen, Zentralländstr. 49 (☎723 17 07). U1 or U2 to Sendlinger Tor, then #3 to Thalkirchen, and change to bus #57 (20min.). From the bus stop, cross the busy street on the left and take a right onto the path next to the road. Well-run, crowded grounds with jogging and bike paths. Car DM8.50. Showers DM2. Curfew 11pm. DM8.40 per person, DM2.50 per child under 14; DM5.50-7 per tent.

Campingplatz Obermenzing, Lochhausenerstr. 59 (☎811 22 35). S3, S4, S5, S6, or S8 to Pasing then exit toward track 8 and take bus #76 to Lochhausenerstr. Head up Lochhausenerstr. from the bus stop; it's on the left (10min.). Showers DM2. Reception 7:30am-noon and 3-8pm. DM7.80 per person, DM4 per child under 14. Tent DM7.50. Car DM6. Oktoberfest surcharge DM2.50.

🍴 FOOD

The vibrant **Viktualienmarkt,** 2min. south of Marienplatz, is Munich's gastronomic center, offering both basic and exotic foods and ingredients. It's fun to browse, but don't plan to do any budget grocery shopping here. (Open M-F 10am-8pm, Sa 8am-4pm.) Located on every corner, the ubiquitous **beer gardens** (see **Beer, Beer, and More Beer,** p. 493) serve savory snacks along with booze. To stick your fangs into an authentic Bavarian lunch, grab a *Brez'n* (pretzel) and spread it with *Leberwurst* or cheese (DM5-6). *Weißwürste* (white veal sausages) are another native bargain, served in a pot of hot water with sweet mustard and a soft pretzel on the side. *Leberkäs,* also a Münchener lunch, is a slice of a pinkish, meatloaf-like compound of ground beef and bacon which, despite its name and dubious appearance, contains neither liver nor cheese. *Leberknödel* are liver dumplings, usually served in soup or with *Kraut. Kartoffelknödel* (potato dumplings) and *Semmelknödel* (made from white bread, egg, and parsley) are eaten along with a hearty chunk of German meat.

The large **A&P Tengelmann,** in the Karlsplatz subway station is convenient for **grocery** needs. (From the Hauptbahnhof, walk east on Bayerstr., make a right onto Sonnenstr. and enter the U-Bahn after Schlosserstr. Open M-F 8:30am-8pm, Sa 8am-4pm.) Another branch with the same hours is located at Rotkreuzplatz. (Nymphenburgerstr. 170; take U1 to Rotkreuzpl.) *Munich Found* (DM4) lists a few restaurants, while Prinz (DM5) offers a fairly complete listing of restaurants, cafes, and bars. Fruit and vegetable **markets** are held throughout the city, with many on Bayerstr. The university district off **Ludwigstraße** is Munich's best source of filling meals in an unpretentiously hip atmosphere. Many reasonably-priced restaurants and cafes cluster on **Schellingstr., Amalienstr.,** and **Türkenstr.** Ride U3 or U6 to Universität. **Plus supermarket,** Schellingstr. 38, provides **groceries.** (Open M-F 8:30am-7pm, Sa 8am-3pm.)

News Bar, Amalienstr. 55 (☎28 17 87), at the corner of Schellingstr. Trendy cafe serving large portions at reasonable prices. For lunch or dinner, choose from a wide assortment of salads (DM8.50-17.50), sandwiches (DM8.50-13.50), or pasta (DM12.90-17.90). Crepes DM12-14. Open daily 7:30am-2am.

Türkenhof, Türkenstr. 78 (☎280 02 35), offers a wide selection of global cuisine. Immensely popular with the low-key student population. Smokey and buzzing from noon 'til night. Variable daily menu with numerous veggie options; main dishes DM10.80-15.80. Open M-Th and Su 11am-1am, F-Sa 11am-2am.

Schelling Salon, Schellingstr. 54 (☎272 07 88). Bavarian *Knödel* and billiard balls. Founded in 1872, this pool joint has racked the balls of Lenin, Rilke, and Hitler. Breakfast DM5.50-9.50, *Wurst* DM6-7. A free billiard museum displays a 200-year-old Polish noble's table and the history of pool back to the Pharaohs. Restaurant open Th-M 6:30am-1am; Museum open at night, Sa-Su.

Weißes Bräuhaus, Tal 7 (☎29 98 75), across from the McDonald's at the end of Marienplatz. This traditional Bavarian restaurant is brimming with affordable and delectable dishes. Open daily 7:30am-midnight.

◉ SIGHTS

The Munich cityscape is marked by its Catholic history, in the Mariensäule and the Frauenkirche, as well as by the unmistakable signs of modernity of the BMW-Museum or the Staatsgalerie-Moderne-Kunst. Munich has reminders of every aspect of German history: from imperial to Nazi to our wacky modern times.

MARIENPLATZ. Numerous sacred stone edifices prickle the area around Marienplatz, a major S-Bahn and U-Bahn junction as well as the social nexus of the city. An ornate 17th-century monument dedicated to the Virgin Mary, the **Mariensäule** was built to commemorate the fact that the powerful Swedes did not destroy the city during the Thirty Years War. At the neo-Gothic **Neues Rathaus,** the Glockenspiel chimes with a display of jousting knights and dancing coopers. *(Daily 11am, noon, and 5pm.)* At 9pm, a mechanical watchman marches out and the Guardian Angel escorts the *Münchner Kindl* (Munich Child, the town's symbol) to bed. Don't miss the rooster perched above the knights; he crows three times after the bells stop tolling. *(Tower open M-F 9am-7pm, Sa, Su 10am-7pm. DM3, under 18 DM1.50, under 6 free.)* On the face of the **Altes Rathaus** tower, to the right of the Neues Rathaus, are all of Munich's coats of arms since its inception as a city—with one noble gap. When the tower was rebuilt after its destruction in WWII, the local government refused to include the swastika-bearing coat of arms from the Nazi era.

FRAUENPLATZ. Munich's Catholic past has left many marks on the city's architecture. From the Marienplatz, walk one block towards the Hauptbahnhof on Kaufingerstr. to find the onion-domed towers of the 15th-century Frauenkirche—one (well, maybe two) of Munich's most notable landmarks. Inside, see the final resting place of Kaiser Ludwig der Bayer. *(Towers open April-Oct. M-Sa 10am-5pm. DM4, students DM2. Free tour in German 2pm.)*

ASAMKIRCHE. A Rococo masterpiece, the Asamkirche is named after its creators, the Asam brothers, who promised God that they would build a church if they survived the wreckage of their ship. Rocks at the bottom of the facade represent rapids, the church's literal and metaphorical foundation. Inside, red and gray marble columns spiral heavenward among gold and silver adornments. *(Sendlingerstr. 32; four blocks down Sendlingerstr. from the Marienplatz. Two priests give a tour of the church June-Sept. Sa noon; DM5.)*

PETERSKIRCHE. The 11th-century Peterskirche, the city's oldest parish church, represents Munich's ritual past; its golden interior was turned Baroque in the 18th century. More than 300 steps scale the tower, christened *Alter Peter* by locals; a spectacular view of Munich and (on a very clear day) the Alps awaits at the top. *(Rindermarkt and Petersplatz, across Marienplatz from the Neues Rathaus. Open M-Sa 9am- 5pm, Su 10am-7pm. DM2.50, students DM1.50.)*

RESIDENZ. Down the pedestrian zone from Odeonsplatz, the richly decorated rooms of the Residenz (Palace), built from the 14th to 19th centuries, form the material vestiges of the Wittelsbach dynasty. The grounds now house several museums. The beautifully landscaped **Hofgarten** behind the Residenz shelters the lovely temple of Diana. The **Schatzkammer** (treasury) contains jeweled baubles, crowns, swords, china, ivorywork, and other trinkets from the 10th century on. *(Open Apr. to mid.-Oct. F-W 9am-6pm, Th. 9am-8pm. In winter daily 10am-4pm. Last admission 1 hr. before closing time. DM8; students with ID, seniors, and group members DM6; children under 15 free.)* The **Residenzmuseum** comprises the former Wittelsbach apartments and State Rooms, a collection of European porcelain, and a 17th-century court chapel. German tours of the Residenzmuseum meet just outside the museum entrance. The walls of the **Ahnengalerie,** hung with 120 "family portraits," trace the royal lineage in an unusual manner. *(Max-Joseph-Platz 3. Take U3-U6 to Odeonsplatz. ☎ 29 06 71. Open same hrs. as Schatzkammr. DM8, students and children DM6. Residenzmuseum tours Su and W 11am, Tu and Sa 2pm. DM8, Su DM10. Combination ticket to Schatzkammer and Residenzmuseum DM14, students and seniors DM11.)*

ENGLISCHER GARTEN. Extending from the city center to the *studentenheim* is the vast Englischer Garten, one of Europe's oldest landscaped public parks. Beer gardens, a Japanese tea house, Chinese pagoda, and a Greek temple share the grounds. Nude sunbathing areas are designated FKK on signs and park maps. *Müncheners* surf the white-water rapids of the Eisbach, which flows artificially through the park. The stone bridge on Prinzregentenstr., close to the Staatsgalerie Moderner Kunst, is a great vantage point for these marine stunts.

SCHLOß NYMPHENBURG. After 10 years of trying for an heir, Ludwig I celebrated the birth of his son Maximilian in 1662 by erecting an elaborate summer playground. Schloß Nymphenburg, in the northwest of town, is a handsome architectural symptom of Ludwig's desire to copy King Louis XIV of France. Ludwig's Baroque palace hides a number of treasures, including a two-story granite marble hall seasoned with stucco and frescoes. Check out King Ludwig's "Gallery of Beauties"—whenever a woman caught his fancy, he would have her portrait painted (a scandalous hobby, considering that many of the women were commoners; as well as an ironic one, given that Ludwig grappled with an affection for men throughout his life). Caution: do not confuse the "Gallery of Beauties" with the "Gallery of Horses" housed in the **Marstallmuseum** (carriage museum). Needless to say, Ludwig was a man of many fetishes. A few lakes and four manors also inhabit the palace grounds: **Amalienburg, Badenburg, Pagodenburg,** and **Magdalen hermitage.** *(Streetcar #17 (dir.: Amalienburgstr.) to Schloß Nymphenburg. All attractions open April-mid-Oct. daily 9am-6pm, Th. 9am-8pm; late Oct. to Mar. 10am-4pm daily. DM6, students DM4. Museum open Tu-Su 9am-noon and 1-5pm. Badenburg, Pagodenburg, and Magdalenen hermitage closed in winter. Schloß or Marstall museum DM7, students DM5. Each burg DM5, students DM4. Entire complex DM15; students DM12. Grounds open until 9:30pm. Free.)*

BOTANISCHER GARTEN. Next door to Schloß Nymphenburg, the greenhouses of the immense Botanischer Garten shelter rare and wonderful growths from around the world. Check out the Indian and Bolivian water lily room, the eight-foot tall, 100-year-old cycadee, and the prickly cactus alcove. *(Streetcar #17 (dir.: Amalienburgstr.) to Botanischer Garten. ☎ 17 86 13 10. Open daily 9am-8pm. Open 9-11:45am and 1-7:30pm. DM4, students DM2.)*

▥ MUSEUMS

Munich is a supreme museum city, and many of the city's offerings would require days for exhaustive perusal. The *Münchner Volksschule* offers tours of many city museums for DM8. A day pass for entry to all of Munich's museums is sold at the tourist office and at many larger museums (DM30).

Deutsches Museum, Museuminsel 1 (☎ 217 91). S1-S8 to Isartor., or street car #18 to Deutsches Museum. One of the world's largest and best museums of science and technology. Exhibits of original models include the first telephone and the work bench upon which Otto Hahn split his first atom. Don't miss the mining exhibit, which winds through a labyrinth of subterranean tunnels. Open daily 9am-5pm. DM12, students DM5.

Alte Pinakothek, Barerstr. 27 (☎23 80 52 16). U2 to Königsplatz. Commissioned in 1826 by King Ludwig I, the last of the passionate Wittelsbacher art collectors, this world-renowned hall houses works by Titian, da Vinci, Raphael, Dürer, Rembrandt, and Rubens. Open Tu-Su 10am-5pm and Th until 8pm. DM7, students DM4; a combination ticket for the Alte and the Neue Pinakotheken DM12, students DM6.

Neue Pinakothek, Barerstr. 29 (☎23 80 51 95). Sleek space for paintings and sculptures of the 18th to 20th centuries, including ones by Van Gogh, Klimt, Cézanne, Manet. Open W-M 10am-5pm and Th until 8pm. Same prices as Alte Pinakothek.

Glyptothek, Königsplatz 3 (☎28 61 00). Around the corner from the Lenbachhaus. U2 to Königsplatz. Assembled by Ludwig I in 1825 in pursuit of his Greek dream to turn Munich into a "cultural work of such sheer perfection as only few Germans have experienced." Features 2,400-year-old pediment figures from the Temple of Aphaea as well as Etruscan and Roman sculptures. Open Tu-Su 10am-5pm and Th until 8pm. DM6, students DM3.50; free tour Thursdays at 6pm. Combination ticket for the Glyptothek and the Antikensammlung available for DM 10, students DM5.

BMW-Museum, Petuelring 130 (☎38 22 33 07). U3 to Olympiazentrum. The ultimate driving museum features a display of past, present, and future products of Bavaria's second-favorite export. Open daily 9am-5pm. Last entry 4pm. DM5.50, students DM4.

Zentrum für Aussergewöhnliche Museen, Westenriederstr. 41 (☎290 41 21). Munich's Center for Unusual Museums, a brilliant place that brazenly corrals under one roof the Padlock Museum, the Museum of Easter Rabbits, and the Chamberpot Museum. Fan of Empress Elizabeth of Austria? Sass on over to the Sisi Museum. S1-S8 to Isartor or streetcar #17 or 18. Open daily 10am-6pm. DM8, students and children DM5.

Staatsgalerie moderner Kunst, Prinzregentenstr. 1. U4 or U5 to Lehel, then streetcar #17. ☎21 12 71 37. The **Haus der Kunst,** at the southern tip of the Englischer Garten, celebrates the vitality of 20th-century art, from the colorful palettes of the Expressionists to the bare canvases of the Minimalists. Showcases Beckmann, Kandinsky, Klee, Picasso, and Dalí. Constructed by the Nazis as the Museum of German Art, it opened with the famous Entartete Kunst (degenerate art) exhibit that included works of the Expressionists and Dadaists. The collection will soon be relocated to the new **Pinakotheck der Moderne Kunst,** which is expected to be completed in 2001. Open Tu-Su 10am-10pm. DM6, students DM3.50.

🎵 ENTERTAINMENT

Munich's cultural cachet rivals the world's best. Sixty theaters of various sizes are scattered throughout the city. Styles range from dramatic classics at the **Residenztheater** and **Volkstheater** to comic opera at the **Staatstheater am Gärtnerplatz** to experimental works at the **Theater im Marstall** in Nymphenburg. Standing tickets run around DM10. Munich's **opera festival** (in July) is held in the Bayerische Staatsoper and is accompanied by a concert series in the Nymphenburg and Schleißheim palaces. The *Monatsprogramm* (DM2.50) lists schedules for all of Munich's stages, museums, and festivals. Buy tickets to ballets and operas behind the national theater, **Bayerische Staatsoper,** at Maximilianstr. 11, behind the opera house, or 1hr. before performance at the side entrance on Maximilianstr. (☎26 46 20. Box office open M-F 10am-6pm, Sa 10am-1pm.)

🌙 NIGHTLIFE

Munich's nightlife is a curious collision of Bavarian *Gemütlichkeit* and trendy cliquishness. Representatives of the latter trait are often referred to as *Schicki-Mickis*, club-going German yuppies. The locals tend to tackle their nightlife as an epic voyage. The odyssey begins at one of Munich's beer gardens or beer halls; the alcohol keeps flowing at cafes and bars, which, except for Friday and Saturday nights, shut off their taps at 1am. Then the discos and dance clubs, sedate before midnight, suddenly spark and throb relentlessly until 4am. The trendy bars, cafes,

BEER GARDEN HISTORY 101 The official coat-of-arms of Munich depicts a monk holding a Bible in his right hand. Unofficially, the monk's left hand firmly clenches a large, frothy beer, raising it high and, with a twinkle in the eye, saying *"Prost."* Sacrilege? Not at all. In 1328, the Augustiner monks introduced *Bier* to unsuspecting Müncheners, who have since continued the 600-year-old trend. Bavaria proudly holds the title as the largest producer *and* consumer of beer in Germany—in a mighty big way. Local breweries produce 123 million gallons of "liquid bread" per year, 150,000 seats in Munich beer gardens beckon the thirsty, and every year, the average local imbibes more than 220 liters of the amber dew, more than twice the average drunk in the rest of Germany (though the figure does include the mighty Oktoberfest, during which locals and visitors together swig 6 million liters). The tradition of beer gardens in Bavaria is said to have begun with King Ludwig I, who allowed brewers to sell beer, but not food, in an outdoor restaurant setting. All citizens could afford to indulge in this yummy beverage by bringing their own meals to the gardens.

cabarets, and discos plugged into **Leopoldstr.** in **Schwabing** attract tourists from all over Europe. **Münchener Freiheit** is the most famous (and most touristy) bar/cafe district. The southwestern section of Schwabing, directly behind the university on Amalienstr. and Türkenstr is more low-key.

BEER, BEER, AND MORE BEER

The six great Munich labels are *Augustiner, Hacker-Pschorr, Hofbräu, Löwenbräu, Paulaner,* and *Spaten-Franziskaner,* yet most restaurants and *Gaststätte* will pick a side by only serving one brewery's beer. There are four main types of beer served in Munich: **Helles** and **Dunkles,** standard but delicious light and dark beers; **Weißbier,** a cloudy blond beer made from wheat instead of barley; and **Radler** (literally "cyclist's brew"), which is half beer and half lemon soda. Munich's beer typically has an alcohol content of 3.5%, though in *Starkbierzeit* (which runs two weeks, beginning with Lent), Müncheners traditionally drink *Salvator,* a strong, dark beer that is 5.5% alcohol. *Frühschoppen* is a morning beer-and-sausage ritual. *"Ein Bier, bitte"* will get you a liter, known as a *Maß* (DM8-11). If you want less, a *halb-Maß* (DM4-6), you must specify.

The longest beer festival in the world, Munich's **Oktoberfest** runs the last two weeks in September (Sept. 22-Oct. 7, 2001). The site of this uncontrolled revelry is the **Theresienwiese** or *"Wies'n"*—shortened perhaps after one *Maß* too many. (U4 or U5 to Theresienwiese.) Oktoberfest kicks off with speeches, a parade of horse-drawn beer wagons, and the tapping of the ceremonial first *Faß* (barrel).

Hirschgarten, Hirschgarten 1 (☎ 17 25 91). U1 to Rotkreuzplatz, then streetcar #12 to Romanplatz. The largest beer garden in Europe (seating 9000 people) is boisterous and pleasant, but somewhat remote near Schloß Nymphenburg. *Maß* DM9.30. Open daily 9am-midnight, kitchen open until 10pm.

Augustinerkeller, Arnulfstr. 52 (☎ 59 43 93), at Zirkus-Krone-Str. S1-S8 to Hackerbrücke. Founded in 1824, Augustiner is viewed by most Müncheners as the finest beer garden in town. *Maß* DM10.50. Open daily 10:30am-midnight or 1am.

Hofbräuhaus, Am Platzl 9 (☎ 22 16 76), 2 blocks from Marienplatz. In 1589, Bavarian Duke Wilhelm the Pious earned his epithet by founding the Münchener Hofbräuhaus for the worship of Germany's most revered beverages. 15,000-30,000L of beer are sold per day. *Maß* DM11.40. Open daily 9:00am-midnight with live *Blasmusik* every day.

Taxisgarten, Taxisstr. 12 (☎ 15 68 27). U1 to Rotkreuzplatz, then bus #83 or 177 to Klugstr./Gern, then walk one block east on Tizianstr. Almost always full. One of few places that serves a green variety of the normally orange Bavarian specialty *Obazer* (a mix of cheeses, DM3.80). *Maß* DM10.20. Open daily 11am-11pm.

Paulanerkeller, Hochstr. 77 (☎ 459 91 30). U2 or U7 to Silberhornstr., then bus #15 or 25, (dir.: Max-Weber-Platz), to Ostfriedhof. Walk west down St. Bonifatiusstr. over the bridge and to the right. It's big, old, and well-known among locals for its year-round sale of strong, dark beer called Salvator. *Maß* of original Münchener Helles DM9.90. Open daily 10am-11pm.

Löwenbräukeller, Nymphenburgerstr. 2 (☎52 60 21). U1 or U7 to Stiglmaierplatz. Come here to taste the real Löwenbräu, if you dare: the bitter and somewhat watery taste has a loyal core of local followers, despite general disapproval—it's considered by some to be the Budweiser of Munich beers. The *Speisenzeytung* (menu) is written in Bavarian dialect with German translations (traditional mains DM8.90-28.90). 0.5L beer DM4.40. Kitchen open 11am-midnight. Open daily 8am-1am.

BARS

Many of the city's charming cafes double as hip nightly haunts. A few stalwarts only open the doors for drink after 5pm, and by 1am many squeeze revelers out into more late-night joints.

Master's Home, Frauenstr. 11 (☎21 69 09). U3 or U6 or S-Bahn #1-8 to Marienplatz. A tremendous stuffed peacock greets visitors as they descend the gold painted staircase to the subterranean bar and faux private home. Mixed drinks DM11.50, other drinks similarly high-brow in price. Open daily 6:30pm-3am.

Lux, Reichenbachstr. 37 (☎20 23 83 93). U-Bahn to Frauenhofer. Large pastel asterisks decorate the walls of this popular hang-out. Sit at the bar or at one of the black lacquer tables. Drinks DM8-20. Open M-Th 6pm-1am, F-Sa 8pm-2am.

Treznjewski, Theresienstr. 72 (☎22 23 49). U2 to Theresienstr. Handsome bar with dark wood and stylish frescoes. Good cocktails and chatty crowds. Main dishes DM15-30. Beer DM5. Open daily 8pm-3am.

DANCE CLUBS

Kunstpark Ost, Grafingerstr. 6 (☎49 00 29 28). U5 or S1-S8 to Ostbahnhof; follow signs for the Kunstpark Ost exit, turn right onto Friedenstr. and then left onto Grafinger Str; the Park is half a block down on the right. This huge complex with 40 different venues swarms with young people dancing the night away. Try the psychedelic-trance **Natraj Temple** (☎49 00 18 95; open F-Sa), the alternative cocktail and disco joint **K41** (☎49 04 21 60; open nightly), the very chill cigars and drinks mecca **Cohibar** (☎49 00 33 12; open W-Sa), or the risque South American rock bar **Titty Twister** (☎49 04 21 10; open W-Sa).

Nachtwerk and Club, Landesbergerstr. 185 (☎578 38 00). Streetcar #18 or 19 or bus #83 to Lautensackstr. The older, larger **Nachtwerk** spins mainstream dance tunes for sweaty mainstream crowds in a packed warehouse. Its little sister **Club** offers a 2-level dance floor. Mixtures of rock, trip-hop, house, acid jazz, and rare grooves. Beer DM4.50 at both places. Cover DM10 for both. Open daily 10pm-4am.

Reactor, Domagkstr. 33 (☎324 44 23), in the Alabamahalle. U6 to Alte Heide. Situated along with three other discos on a former military base in Schwabing. Techno, house, and German oldies. Open F-Sa 9pm-4am. Try **Millennium Club** for techno highlights (Th-Su 9pm-6am; cover DM10-15), **Alabama** for German oldies (F-Sa 9pm-4am; drinks free until 1am), or **Schwabinger Ballhouse** for international jams (F-Sa 10pm-4am; cover DM15, all drinks DM1).

GAY AND LESBIAN NIGHTLIFE

The center of Munich's homosexual scene lies within the **"Golden Triangle"** stretching from the area south of the Sendlinger Tor through the Viktualienmarkt/Gärtnerplatz area to the Isartor. Pick up the free, extensive booklet *Rosa Seiten* at **Max&Milian Bookstore,** Ickstattstr. 2 (☎260 33 20; open M-F 10:30am-2pm and 3:30-8pm, Sa 11am-4pm), or at any other gay locale for extensive listings of gay nightlife hotspots and services.

Soul City, Maximiliansplatz 5 (☎59 52 72), at the intersection with Max-Joseph-Str. Purportedly the biggest gay disco in Bayern; music ranges from 70's disco to Latin to techno. Beer DM7.50 (0.3L). Open W-Sa, 10pm-late. Cover DM10-25.

Morizz, Klenzestr. 43 (☎201 67 76). U1 or U2 to Fraunhoferstr. Settle into the low red sofa chairs and enjoy a cocktail (DM12-16). European and Thai dishes available until 12:30am (main dishes DM18-26). Open Su-Th 7pm-2am, F-Sa 7pm-3am.

Bei Carla, Buttermelcherstr. 9 (☎22 79 01). S1-S8 to Isartor. Charming lesbian cafe and bar is one of Munich's best-kept secrets. Open M-Sa 4pm-1am, Su 6pm-1am.

Inge's Karotte, Baaderstr. 13 (☎201 06 69). S1-S8 to Isartor, then walk south on Baaderstr. for 2 blocks. The oldest lesbian bar in Munich, Inge's Karotte attracts an older crowd (mostly women in their 30s and 40s). Open M-F 4pm-1am, Sa 6pm-1am.

🗓 DAYTRIPS FROM MUNICH

DACHAU

Take S2 (dir.: Petershausen) to Dachau (20min., DM7.60, or 4 stripes on the Streifen-karte), then bus #724 (dir.: Kraütgarten) or 726 (dir.: Kopernikusstr.) from in front of the station to KZ-Gedenkstätte (10min., DM1.90 or one stripe on the Streifenkarte).

"Once they burn books, they will end up burning people," wrote German poet Heinrich Heine in 1820. His warning is posted at the Dachau concentration camp, next to a photograph of a Nazi book-burning. The walls, gates, gas chamber, and crematorium have been restored since 1962 in a chillingly sparse memorial to the victims of Dachau, the first German concentration camp and the model for the network of 3,000 work and concentration camps erected in Nazi-occupied Europe. Once tightly-packed barracks are now, for the most part, only foundation. However, survivors ensured that at least two barracks would be reconstructed to teach future generations about the 206,000 prisoners who were interned here from 1933 to 1945. Residents of the city of Dachau—it is important to remember that there *is* a town here, which lives in the shadow of the camp every day—watch visitors with uncertainty, and even insecurity. While the concentration camp is treated as a tourist attraction by many, it is first and foremost a memorial.

The wrought-iron gate at the **Jourhaus** reads "Arbeit Macht Frei" (Work Sets One Free); it was the first sight as prisoners entered the camp. There is also a Jewish memorial, a Protestant commemorative chapel, and the Catholic **Todesangst Christi-Kapelle** (Christ in Agony Church) on the grounds. (For more on the issues surrounding concentration camps, see **The Holocaust,** p. 394.) The museum, located in the former administrative buildings, examines pre-1930 anti-Semitism, the rise of Nazism, the establishment of the concentration camp system, and the lives of prisoners through photographs, documents, and artifacts. The thick guide (DM25, available in English) translates the propaganda posters, SS files, documents, and letters. Also on display are texts of the letters from prisoners to their families as well as internal SS memos. A short film (22min.) is screened in English at noon, 2pm, and 3:30pm; wait at the door to the theater at least 10min. in advance to ensure a seat. A new display in the **Bunker,** the concentration camp's prison and tourture chamber, chronicles the lives and experiences of the camp's special prisoners and the barbarism of SS guards. The camp is open Tu-Su 9am-5pm. Informative but lengthy two-hour **tours** of the camp in English leave from the museum (July daily 12:30pm, Aug.-June Sa-Su, and holidays at 12:30pm; DM5 donation requested). Call ☎17 41 for more information.

Dachau's tiny **tourist office,** Konrad-Adenauer-Str. 1 (☎ (08131) 845 66; fax 845 29), has information on the city and sells maps for DM1. From the train station, follow Langhammerstr. to Münchnerstr., make a right and keep going straight when Münchnerstr. becomes Karlsberg. (Open M-F 9am-6pm, Sa 9am-noon.) A 16th-century castle and a parish church built in 920 tops the Altstadt. Tours in German of the castle and the church leave from in front of the modern Rathaus, across the street from the tourist office. (Tours May-Oct. Sa-Su 3pm; DM6, children and students DM3. Castle open Tu-Su 10am-5:45pm. DM3, children DM1.50.)

OTHER DAYTRIPS FROM MUNICH

THE ROMANTIC ROAD. From Munich, any town along the Romantic Road is but a quick train ride away, including Würzberg (see p. 498), Rothenburg ob der Tauber (see p. 499), Dinkelsbühl and Nordlingen (see p. 500), and Augsburg (see p. 500).

ALLGAU ALPS. Take advantage of the less-touristed Allgau Alps and wander through the towns of Ottobeuren or Oberstdorf (see p. 501).

BAVARIAN ALPS. The towns along the bases of the Bavarian peaks are all convenient for daytripping, including Füssen, Neuschwanstein and Hohenschwangau, Linderhof, Garmisch-Partenkirchen. Take a cable-car to the top of a mountain for a spectacular view (see p. 502).

NUREMBERG (NÜRNBERG)   ☎0911

Nuremberg is a city inextricably bound to a darker past. The city served as site of the massive annual Nazi party rallies (1933-38) and lent its name to the 1935 Racial Purity Laws; Allies later chose it as the site of the post-WWII war crimes trials in order to foster a sense of justice. Although 90% of the city was reduced to rubble in 1945, today it is known as much for its toy fair and Christmas market, sausages and gingerbread, and association with Albrecht Dürer, as for its ties to Nazism.

⌐ TRANSPORTATION. Trains chug to: Berlin (6hr., 2 per hr., DM142); Frankfurt (3hr., every hr., DM73-80); Munich (2½hr., 2-3 per hr., DM54-74); Regensburg (1hr., every 2hr., DM27-34); Stuttgart (2¾hr., 6 per day, DM54); Würzburg (1hr., 2 per hr., DM28-42); and Prague (5hr., 2 per day, DM73).

⚠ PRACTICAL INFORMATION. The **tourist office** is in the train station. (☎233 61 31; fax 233 61 66; www.nuernberg.de. Open May-Sept. M-Sa 9am-6pm, Su 10am-1pm and 2-4pm; Oct.-Apr. M-Sa 9am-6pm.) Check **email** at **Internetcafé M@x,** Färberstr. 11, 4th fl. (☎23 23 84. Before 3pm DM5 per hr.; after 3pm DM9 per hr. Open M-Sa noon-1am, Su 4pm-midnight.)

▐▗▛ ACCOMMODATIONS AND FOOD. Inexpensive *Pensionen* and hostels aren't hard to find in Nuremberg, but it's always best to call ahead, especially in the summer. The friendly **Jugendgästehaus (HI),** Burg 2, is in a castle above the city. From the station, cross Frauentorgraben, turn right, walk along the outside of the city walls to Königstor, head through Lorenzerpl. over the bridge to the Hauptmarkt, bear right on Burgstr., and huff and puff up the hill. (☎230 93 60. Reception 7am-1am. Curfew 1am. 4- to 6-bed dorms DM30; singles DM60; doubles DM144.) From the station, take the underground passage to Königstr. and take an immediate left on Frauentormauerstr., follow the town wall and then turn right for **Gasthof Schwänlein,** Hintere Sterngasse 11. (☎22 51 62; fax 241 90 08. Reservations by fax or mail only. Singles DM40, with shower DM50, with bath DM60; doubles DM75, DM80, DM90.) For **Campingpark Nürnberg,** Hans-Kalb-Str. 56, behind the soccer stadium in Volkspark Dutzenteich, take S2 (dir.: Freucht/Altdorf) to Frankenstadion. (☎981 27 17. Reception 2-10pm. Closed Nov. DM8.75 per person, DM5-10 per tent, DM12.50 per car.) Nuremberg is famous for its *Rostbratwurst* (sausage); try some at the **Bratwursthäusle,** Rathauspl. 1, next to the Sebalduskirche. (Open M-Sa 10am-10:30pm.) **Edeka,** Hauptmarkt 12, near the Frauenkirche, sells **groceries.** (Open M-F 8:30am-7pm, Sa 8am-3pm.) **Postal Code:** 90402.

▣ ▙ SIGHTS AND ENTERTAINMENT. Allied bombing left little of Nuremberg for posterity; its churches, castle, and other buildings have all been reconstructed since the war. The closest part of the Altstadt to the train station is the walled-in **Handwerkerhof,** a cottage- and shop-filled tourist trap masquerading as a historical attraction; head up **Königstraße** for the real sights. The Gothic **Lorenzkirche** on Lorenzpl. features a 20m tabernacle with delicate stone tendrils that curl up into the roof vaulting. (Open M-Sa 9am-5pm, Su 1-4pm. Free tours in summer in German M-F 11am and 2pm; in winter M-F 2pm, call ahead for English.) Across the river on **Hauptmarktpl.** are the **Frauenkirche** (open M-Sa 9am-6pm, Su 12:30-6pm) and the **Schöner Brunnen** (Beautiful Fountain), with 40 imaginatively carved figures. Walk uphill from the fountain to the **Rathaus,** begun in 1340 but built mostly in early Baroque style. The **Lochgefängnisse** (dungeons) beneath contain medieval torture instruments. (☎231 26 90. Open Tu-Su 10am-4:30pm. Tour every 30min.; English translation available. DM4, students DM2.) Across from the Rathaus is the Protestant **Sebalduskirche,** which houses the remains of St. Sebaldus for 364 days a year; on the 365th, they're paraded around town. (☎22 45 72. Open daily June-Aug. 9:30am-8pm; Mar.-May and Sept.-Dec. 9:30am-6pm; Jan.-Feb. 9:30am-4pm.) Atop the hill, the **Kaiserburg** (Emperor's fortress), Nuremberg's symbol, offers the best vantage point of the city. Every Holy Roman Emperor after Konrad III spent at least his first day in office here. (☎22 57 26. Burg open daily Apr.-Sept. 9am-6pm; Oct.-Mar. 10am-4pm. Tours every 30min. DM10, students DM8.)

The ruins of **Dutzendteich Park,** site of the Nazi Party Congress rallies of 1934 and 1935, remind visitors of Germany's darker history. The **Zeppelinwiese,** a field on the far side of the lake, is near the **Tribüne,** the massive marble platform from which Hitler addressed throngs. The exhibit "Fascination and Terror", in the **Golden Hall** at the rear of the Tribüne, covers the rise of the Third Reich and the war crimes trials. (Open mid-May to Oct. Tu-Su 10am-6pm. DM5, students DM4.) To reach the park, take S2 (dir.: Freucht/Altdorf) to Dutzendteich, take the middle exit, head down the stairs, turn left, turn after Strandcafe Wanner and follow the path. On the other side of town, Nazi leaders faced Allied judges during the infamous **Nürnberg war** crimes trials held in room 600 of the Justizgebäude. To get there, take U-Bahn #1 (dir.: Stadthalle) to Bärenschanze and continue on Furtherstr.

Nuremberg's nightspots run the gamut from ultra-traditional to hyper-modern. The Altstadt is packed with bars and clubs, the best of which reside in the west, near the river. **Cine Città,** Gewerbemuseumspl. 3, packs 7 cafes, 12 cinemas, and a disco into a multimedia megaplex. (☎20 66 60. Open M-Th and Su until 3am, F-Sa until 4am.) **Café Treibhaus,** Karl-Grillenberger-Str. 28, in the west part of the Altstadt, south of Westtor, draws an older crowd with its killer cocktails and soothing cups of hot coffee. (Open M-W 8am-1am, Th-F 8am-2am, Sa 9am-2am, Su 9:30am-1am.)

BAMBERG   ☎0951

This little city on the Regnitz River boasts one of the most beautiful Altstadts in Bavaria. The residents of Bamberg are proud of their picturesque home, and they celebrate by drinking an astounding amount of beer—330L per capita annually, the highest consumption rate in the world. The 15th-century **Altes Rathaus** guards the middle of the river like an anchored ship. (☎87 18 71. Gallery open Tu-Su 9:30am-4:30pm. DM6, students DM4.) Across the river and up the hill, the 11th-century **Dom** contains the 13th-century statue of the **Bamberger Reiter** (Bamberg Knight), which embodies the chivalric ideal of the medieval warrior-king. (Dom ☎50 23 30. Open Apr.-Oct. daily 8am-6pm; Nov.-Mar. 8am-5pm. Museum ☎50 23 25. DM4, students DM2.) Opposite the Dom, the **Neue Residenz** brims with lavish furnishings. (Open Apr.-Sept. Tu-Su 9am-6pm; Oct.-Mar. Tu-Su 10am-4pm. DM6, students DM4.)

Trains arrive from: Munich (2½-4hr., 1-2 per hr., DM71-88); Nuremberg (1hr., 3 per hr., DM17); and Würzburg (1¼hr., 2 per hr., DM27). To reach the Altstadt from the station, walk down Luitpoldstr., cross the canal, walk straight on Willy-Lessing-Str., turn right at Schönleinspl. onto Langestr., then turn left on Obere Brückestr., which leads through the archway of the Rathaus and across the Regnitz (25-30min.). Once through the Rathaus, take a left, and then another, and recross the Regnitz on the wooden footbridge; the **tourist office,** Geyerswörthstr. 3, is on the right under the arches. (☎87 11 61; fax 87 19 60. Open Apr.-Oct. M-F 9am-6pm, Sa 9am-3pm, Su 10am-2pm; Nov.-Mar. closed Su.) To reach the **Jugendherberge Wolfsschlucht (HI),** Oberer Leinritt 70, take bus #18 (dir.: Bug) to Rodelbahn. (☎560 02. Breakfast included. Sheets DM5.50. Reception 7am-1pm and 5-10pm. Curfew 10pm. Open Feb. to mid-Dec. 4- to 6-bed dorms DM21.) Pick up **groceries** at **Edeka,** Langestr. 14. (Open M-F 8:30am-7pm, Sa 7:30am-4pm.) **Postal Code:** 96052.

BAYREUTH   ☎ 0921

There will be little doubt that you're in Bayreuth (Buy-ROIT), the adopted home of **Richard Wagner,** after you pass Tristanstr., Isoldenstr., and the Walküreg. Every summer from July 25 to August 28, thousands pour in for the **Bayreuth Festspiele,** a vast and bombastic—in a word, Wagnerian—celebration of the artist himself. Tickets go on sale three years in advance and sell out almost immediately (DM80-300; write to Bayreuther Festspiele, 95402 Bayreuth). The avid fan can tour Wagner's house (Haus Wahnfried), now the **Richard Wagner Museum,** Richard-Wagner-Str. 48, where Wagner, his wife Cosima, and his big black dog Russ are buried. (☎ 757 28 16. Open daily Apr.-Oct. 9am-5pm, Tu and Th until 8pm; Nov.-Mar. 10am-5pm. DM4, students DM2.) Bayreuth is an easy daytrip by **train** from Nuremberg (see p. 496; 1hr., every hr., change at Lichtenfels, DM24.60). The **tourist office,** Luitpoldpl. 9, provides maps and hotel listings. (☎ 885 88; fax 885 55. Open M-F 9am-6pm, Sa 9:30am-1pm.) To reach the friendly but regimented **Jugendherberge (HI),** Universitätsstr. 28, past the Hofgarten, from the city center, walk down Ludwigstr., turn left on Friedrichstr., and veer left on Jean-Paul-Str. (☎ 76 43 80. Breakfast included. Sheets DM5.50. Reception 7am-noon and 5-9:30pm. Lockout 9:30-11am. Curfew 10pm. Open Mar. to mid-Dec. Dorms DM21.) **Postal Code:** 95444.

ROMANTIC ROAD (ROMANTISCHE STRAßE)

Between Würzburg and Füssen lies a beautiful countryside of colorful castles, walled cities, elaborate churches, and dense forest. In 1950, sensing opportunity, the German tourist industry christened these bucolic backwaters the Romantic Road, and the region has since become the most visited in Germany.

▟ TRANSPORTATION

Although Deutsche Bahn's **Europabus** is the most popular way to see the Romantic Road, it's also one of the most inflexible—there is only one bus in each direction per day. There are two Europabus routes: the **Frankfurt-Munich** route runs via (from north to south) Würzburg, Rothenburg ob der Tauber, Dinkelsbühl, Nördlingen, and Augsburg; the **Dinkelsbühl-Füssen** route picks up from Dinkelsbühl and makes stops en route at (from north to south) Augsburg, Wieskirche (northbound only), Hohenschwangau, and Neuschwanstein. The Europabus is relatively expensive (Frankfurt to Munich DM121; Dinkelsbühl to Hohenschwangau or Füssen DM61), but students and those under 26 get 10% off, while Eurailers get 75% off. A more economical way to travel the Road is by the faster and much more frequent **trains,** which run to every town except Dinkelsbühl. The route is also excellent on **bike,** with campgrounds located 10-20km apart; tourist offices will have cycling maps and campground info.

WÜRZBURG   ☎ 0931

Surrounded by vineyard slopes and bisected by the Main River, Würzburg is a famous university town, the bustling center of the Franconian wine region, and a scenic portal to the Romantic Road. The striking 12th-century **Marienburg Fortress,** the symbol of the city, keeps vigil high on a hillside across the Main. Inside stand the 11th-century **Marienkirche;** the 40m **Bergfried** watchtower, under which lies the **Hole of Fear** (dungeon); the **Fürstengarten** (built to resemble a ship); and the deep **Brunnentempel,** which supplied the castle with water. Artifacts from the lives of the prince-bishops and a display on the destruction of Würzburg at the end of WWII fill the **Fürstenbau Museum.** Outside the walls of the main fortress is the Baroque castle arsenal, which now houses the **Mainfränkishes Museum,** with statues by Tilman Riemenschneider, the Master of Würzburg. Climb the footpath to the fortress, which starts a short distance from the statue-lined **Alte Mainbrücke,** or take bus #9 from the train station. (Tours depart from the main courtyard Tu-F 11am, 2, and 3pm,

Sa-Su every hr. 10am-4pm; DM4, students DM3. Fürstenbau Museum open April to mid-Oct. Tu-Su 9am-6pm; mid-Oct. to March Tu-Su 10am-4pm; last entry 30min. before closing. DM5, students DM4. Mainfränkisches Museum open Tu-Su 10am-6pm; Nov.-March closes 4pm. DM5, students DM2.50, children under 14 free. Pass to both museums DM8.) The **Residenz** palace on Residenzpl. is a Baroque master-piece housing the largest ceiling fresco in the world. Within, the **Residenzhofkirche** is simply astounding: the gilded moldings and pink marble place the church at the apex of Baroque fantasy. (Palace and church open daily April to mid-Oct. 9am-6pm; mid-Oct.-March 10am-4pm. DM8, students and seniors DM6; church free).

Trains roll in from: Frankfurt (2hr., 2 per hr., DM38); Munich (2½hr., every hr., DM76); and Rothenburg (1hr., every hr., DM17). **Europabuses** also go to Rothen-burg (DM29) and Munich (DM89). To get to the city's center at the Markt, follow Kaiserstr. straight from the station for two blocks, take a right on Juliusprome-nade and hang a left on Schönbornstr., the main pedestrian and streetcar road. The **tourist office** is in the Haus zum Falken, a yellow Baroque mansion on the Marktplatz. (☎37 23 98. Open M-F 10am-6pm, Sa 10am-2pm; Apr.-Oct. Su 10am-2pm.) Access the **internet** at H@ckmac2, Sanderstr. 5. (☎528 45. DM4 per 30min. Open M-F 9am-1am, Sa 10am-1am, Su 11am-1m.) The **Jugendgästehaus (HI)**, Burkarderstr. 44, is across the river from downtown; take streetcar #3 (dir.: Heid-ingsfeld) or 5 (dir.: Heuchelhof-Rottenbauer) to Löwenbrücke, backtrack, go down the stairs with the *Jugendherberge/Kapelle* sign, turn right, go through the tunnel, and it's on the left. (☎425 90. Breakfast included. Check-in 5-10pm. DM33.) **Gasthof Goldener Hahn**, Marktg. 7, is right off the Markt. (☎519 41. Singles DM50-85; doubles DM150.) For **groceries**, hit **Kupsch**, Kaiserstr. 5 near Barbarossa-platz. (Open M-F 8am-8pm, Sa 8am-4pm.) Or, try the food at the classiest, jazziest place in town, **Meyers Café & Piano Bar**, Bronnbacherg. 43. (☎173 00. Open daily 10am-1pm.) **Postal Code:** 97070.

ROTHENBURG OB DER TAUBER   ☎09861

Rothenburg ob der Tauber is probably your only chance to see a walled medieval city without a single modern building, thanks to strict preservation laws. On the Marktpl. stands the Renaissance **Rathaus**, with a 60m tower that affords a nice panorama of the town. (Rathaus open daily 8am-6pm; free. Tower open Apr.-Oct. daily 9:30am-12:30pm and 1-5pm; Nov.-Mar. M-F 9:30am-12:30pm, Sa-Su noon-3pm; DM2.) The **Jakobskirche**, Klosterg. 15, is famed for its *Altar of the Holy Blood* by Tilman Riemenschneider, its 5500-pipe organ, and its 14th-century stained-glass windows. (☎70 06 20. Open Apr.-Oct. M-Sa 9am-5:30pm, Su 10:30am-5:30pm; Dec. daily 10am-5pm. DM2.50, students DM1.) The **Medieval Crime Museum**, Burgg. 3, exhibits torture instruments and "eye for an eye" jurisprudence. (Open daily Apr.-Oct. 9:30am-6pm; Nov. and Jan.-Mar. 2-4pm; Dec. 10am-4pm. DM5, students DM4.) Head to **Christkindlmarkt** (Christ Child Market), Herrng. 2, and **Weihnachtsdorf** (Christmas Village), Herrng. 1, to explore the town's obsession with Christmas. (Open M-F 9am-6:30pm, Sa 9am-4pm; mid-May to Dec. also Su 11am-6pm.)

Trains arrive at Steinach from Munich (3hr., every hr., DM60); change there for Rothenburg (15min., every hr., DM3.30). To reach the **tourist office**, Marktpl. 2, go left from the train station and bear right on Ansbacherstr. (☎404 92; fax 868 07. Open May-Oct. M-F 9am-12:30pm and 1-6pm, Sa-Su 10am-3pm; Nov.-Apr. M-F 9am-12:30pm and 1-5pm, Sa 10am-1pm.) Surf the web at **Planet Internet**, Paradeisg. 5, to the right off Röder. (☎93 44 15. Open Su-Th noon-midnight, F-Sa noon-1am. DM6 per 30min.) To get from the tourist office to the fantastic **Jugendherberge Rossmühle (HI)**, Mühlacker 1, go left down Obere Schmiedg. and look for the small, white *Jugendherberge* sign to the right. (☎941 60. Breakfast included. Reception 7am-midnight. Check-in until 10pm. DM28.) You're obligated to try Rothenburg's *Schneeballen* (snowballs), large balls of sweet dough fried and then dipped in chocolate, nuts, and powdered sugar, with sweet marzipan or amaretto centers. Wash them down with milk from **Kupsch supermarket**, on Röderg., inside the city wall as you enter town. (Open M-F 8am-7pm, Sa 8am-2pm.) **Postal Code:** 91541.

GERMANY

DINKELSBÜHL AND NORDLINGEN

Forty-five kilometers south of Rothenburg, the historic town of **Dinkelsbühl** lays claim to medieval half-timbered houses, a climbable 16th-century church tower, and a town wall with gateways, towers, and moats. The late-Gothic **St. Georg-skirche,** which dominates the **Weinmarkt** at the center of town, sprouts a Romanesque tower and striking fan vaulting. Regional **buses** go from the town's main stop, Bahnhof, to Nördlingen (M-F 7 per day, Sa-Su 4-5 per day) and Rothenburg (transfer at Dombühl or Feuchtwangen; M-F 9 per day, Sa-Su 2 per day; DM11.40). Walk to the Marktplatz to reach the **tourist office.** (☎ (09851) 902 40; fax 902 79; email touristik.service@dinkelsbuehl.de. Open Apr.-Nov. 7 M-F 9am-noon and 2-6pm, Sa 10am-1pm and 2-6pm, Su 10am-1pm; Nov. 8-Mar. M-F 9am-noon and 2-5pm, Sa 10am-1pm.) From there, head down Segringerstr., take a right on Bauhofstr. after the Rathaus. Turn left on Koppeng. to snooze at the **Jugendherberge (HI),** Koppeng. 10. (☎ (09851) 95 09. Breakfast included. Sheets DM5.50. Reception 5-7pm. Curfew 11pm. Open Mar.-Oct. 2- to 8-bed rooms DM20-24.)

The only town in Germany with original walls that are complete, **Nördlingen** is built on the spot where a meteorite crashed some 15 million years ago. Climb up the 90m Gothic bell tower **Daniel** for a bird's-eye view of the town. (Open daily Apr.-Oct. 9am-8pm; Nov.-Mar. 9am-5:30pm. DM3.) There is even a museum dedicated to the medieval town wall in Nördlingen's **Stadtmauermuseum,** inside Löpsinger Tor. (☎91 80. Open Apr.-Oct. daily 10am-4:30pm. DM2.) **Trains** arrive from Augsburg (1hr., every hr., DM20) and Nuremberg (2hr., every other hr., DM35); change at Donauwörth for both. **Buses** also run from Dinkelsbühl (45min., 8 per day, DM7.50). The **tourist office,** Marktplatz 2, finds rooms for free. (☎ (09081) 43 80; fax 841 13; www.noerdlingen.de. Open M-Th 9am-6pm, F 9am-4:30pm, Sa 9:30am-1pm; Nov.-Easter M-Th 9am-5pm, F 9am-3:30pm.) The **Jugendherberge,** Kaiserwiese 1, is just outside the city walls on the north side of town. From the Marktplatz, follow Baldingerstr. out of the city; the hostel is on your right one street beyond the walls. (☎ (09081) 27 18 16. Reception 4:30-6pm. Curfew 10pm. DM18.)

AUGSBURG ☎0821

Founded by Caesar Augustus in 15 BC, Augsburg was the financial center of the Holy Roman Empire and a major commercial city by the end of the 15th century. The town owed its success mainly to the Fuggers, an Augsburg banking family; Jakob Fugger "the Rich," personal financier to the Habsburg Emperors, founded the **Fuggerei** quarter, the first welfare housing project in the world, in 1519; elderly residents today still only pay a "Rhine Guilder" (DM1.72) in rent annually. To reach the Fuggerei from the Rathaus, walk behind the Perlachturm tower on Perlachberg, and turn right under the archway. Luther stayed in the **St. Anna Kirche,** on Annastr. near Königspl. (Open Tu-Su 10am-12:30pm and 3-6pm.) Down Hoher Weg sits the **Hoher Dom,** the regional bishop's seat. (Open M-Sa 6am-5pm.) **Bertolt Brecht's** birthplace was renovated in 1998, on the 100th anniversary of his birth; the **museum** within chronicles his life. From the station, head up Prinzregentenstr. and turn right on Schmiedg. (Open daily 10am-4pm. DM2.50, students DM1.50.)

Trains arrive from: Munich (45min., 4-5 per hr., DM17-30); Nuremberg (2hr., 2 per hr., DM45); Stuttgart (1¾hr., 2 per hr., DM66); and Würzburg (2hr., every hr., DM76). The **tourist office,** Bahnhofstr. 7, books rooms (DM30-40) for a DM3 fee. (☎50 20 70; fax 502 07 45; www.regio-augsburg.de. Open M-F 9am-6pm.) On weekends, head to the **branch** on Rathauspl.; from the station, walk to the end of Bahnhofstr., turn left at Königspl. on Annastr., and take the third right. (☎502 07 24. Open Apr.-Sept. M-F 9am-6pm, Sa 10am-4pm, Su 10am-1pm; Oct.-Mar. M-F 9am-6pm, Sa 10am-1pm.) To get from the station to the **Jugendherberge (HI),** Beim Pfaffenkeller 3, walk up Prinzregentenstr. as it curves to the right, turn left at Karolinenstr., turn right at the cathedral on Innere Pfaffeng., and bear left on Beim Pfaffenkeller. (☎339 03. Reception 7-9am and 5-10pm. Curfew 1am. Open Feb.-Dec. DM25, under 27 DM21.) Stock up on **groceries** at **Penny Markt,** Maximilianstr. 71, to the left of the Rathaus. (Open M-F 8:30am-7pm, Sa 8am-2pm.) **Postal Code:** 86150.

ALLGAU ALPS

Stretching from the balmy shores of the Bodensee (Lake Constance) to the snow-capped peaks along the Austrian border, the Allgäu region boasts inimitably charming villages, while the surrounding alpine landscape offers some of the most beautiful hiking trails in the world. The Allgäu Alps provide Germans with an exquisite haven in which to ski, hike, and relive the last scene from *The Sound of Music.*

OTTOBEUREN ☎ 08332

The prime attraction of the Allgäu, Ottobeuren is renowned for its towering **basilica** and **Benedictine Abbey**, considered the architectural height of the German Baroque period. In this immense, detailed, and overwhelming bazaar of Catholic glory, a small, easily missed 12th-century statue of Christ on the first altar is the most venerated piece of art; its bent head and body position gave rise to the current layout of the abbey. The 25 monks who still roam the abbey's halls brag about living in the most open and accessible monastery north of the Alps. Visitors are allowed to see the grandiose library, and the impressive Emperor's Hall, adorned with statues of the Kaisers. (Church always open. Free. Abbey open Apr.-Oct. daily 10am-noon and 2-5pm; Nov.-Mar. M-F 10am-noon and 2-4pm, Sa-Su 10am-noon and 2-5pm.) **Bus** #955 runs from Memmingen to Ottobeuren (20min., M-F every hr., Sa-Su every 2hr. DM4.30). To reach Memmingen, take the **train** from Obertsdorf (1½hr., every hr., DM20). The **tourist office,** Marktpl. 14 (☎ 92 19 50; fax 92 19 92; www.ottobeuren.de) hands out a phenomenal town brochure. (Open M-Th 9am-noon and 2-5pm, F 9am-noon and 2-4pm.) Facing the church, walk down Sebastian-Kneippstr. for 15min. and turn left onto Beethovenstr. for Ottobeuren's 102-bed **Jugendherberge (HI)**, Faichtmayrstr. 38. (☎368. 3- to 14-bed dorms DM17.50.) **Primrose Café**, Luitpoldstr. 6 (☎93 73 90), serves cheap and filling eats. **Postal Code:** 87724.

OBERSTDORF ☎ 08322

Obertsdorf is heaven for hardcore hikers. Surrounded by the snow-layered Allgäu Alps, this mecca of outdoorsiness combines solitary forest paths with a refreshing sense of nature-oriented tourism. The town remains a health resort populated by Germans seeking to enjoy their native landscape. Three **Bergbahnen** (cable cars) whisk hikers to the heady heights of the Alps. The closest one to the town delivers acrophiliacs to the top of **Nebelhorn** which, at 2224m, is the highest accessible mountain in the Allgäu Alps. (☎96 00 96. Open mid-May to Oct. daily 8:20am-4:50pm.) The **Fellhornbahn** climbs 2037m for an equally thrilling view. (☎30 35. Mid-May to Oct. daily 8:20am-4:40pm. DM43 to the top of Nebelhorn; DM16 to the lowest station.) The **Söllreckbahn** carries hikers up 1358m to several mountain-traversing hiking paths (☎57 57. DM14.) To reach the Nebelhornbahn train station, walk down Nebelhornstr. from Hauptstr.; to reach the Fellhornbahn station, ride the Fellhorn **bus** from the train station. Söllereck is accessible by bus #1.

Trains link Oberstdorf to Immenstadt (30min., 2 per hr., DM8). Rent a bike at **Zweirad Center,** Hauptstr. 7. (☎44 67. Open M-F 9am-noon and 2:30-6pm, Sa 9am-noon. DM15 per day.) The Oberstdorf **tourist office,** is across from the train station at Bahnhofpl. 3. (☎70 00; fax 70 02 36; email info@oberstdorf.de; www.oberstdorf.de. Open M-F 8:30am-noon and 2-6pm, Sa 9am-noon, 2-6pm.) Close to Oberstdorf, Kornau is home to the excellent **Jugendherberge Oberstdorf (HI),** Kornau Haus 8. Take the bus from Oberstdorf to Reute, continue in the direction of the bus, and take the first right—if you miss the last bus leaving town at 9pm, you'll have an hour-long climb uphill in the dark. (☎22 25. Breakfast included. Reception 8am-noon, 5-8pm and 9:30-10pm. Open Jan.-Oct. DM26.) Most restaurants in the area close early and are quite expensive; try the **grocery stores** near Hauptstr. instead. **Postal Code:** 87561.

GERMANY

BAVARIAN ALPS (BAYERISCHE ALPEN)

Visible on a clear day from Munich are a series of snow-covered peaks and forested slopes spanning from southeastern Germany across Austria and into Italy. It was in this rugged and magical terrain that Ludwig II of Bavaria, the certifiably batty "Fairy Tale King," chose to build his dramatic castles; it's also here that even today people authentically, even nonchalantly, wear *Lederhosen*.

FÜSSEN   ☎ 08362

Curled up at the base of the Alpine foothills at the southern end of the Romantic Road, Füssen provides easy access to Mad King Ludwig's famed **Königsschlösser** (royal castles). The inner walls of the **Hohes Schloß** (High Castle) courtyard scream royalty with arresting *trompe-l'oeil* (deceive the eye; a realistic, ultra-detailed style) windows and towers. The **Staatsgalerie** in the castle shelters a collection of regional late Gothic and Renaissance art. (Open Tu-Su Apr.-Oct. 11am-4pm; Nov.-Mar. 2-4pm. DM5, students DM4.) Just below the castle rests the 8th-century Baroque **St. Mangkirche**, with a frescoed 10th-century subterranean crypt. (☎ 48 44. Tours July-Sept. Tu and Th 4pm, Sa 10:30am; May-June and Oct. Tu 4pm and Sa 10:30am; Jan.-Apr. Sa 10:30am.) Inside the **Annenkapelle**, of the **Stadtmuseum**, 20 macabre skeleton-decked panels depict the *Totentanz* (death dance), a public frenzy of despair that overtook Europe during the plague. (Open Apr.-Oct. Tu-Su 11am-4pm; Nov.-Mar. Tu-Su 2-4pm. DM5, students DM4.)

Trains run from Füssen to Augsburg (2hr., every 2hr., DM28) and Munich (2hr., every hr., DM36). To get from the station to the **tourist office**, Kaiser-Maximilian-Pl. 1, walk the length of Bahnhofstr. and head straight on Luitpoldstr. to the big yellow building. (☎ 938 50; fax 93 85 20; www.fuessen.de. Open Apr.-Sept. M-F 8:30am-6pm, Sa 9am-12:30pm; Oct.-Mar. M-F 9am-5pm, Sa 10am-noon.) Check email at the **internet** cafe in the Jugendhaus, Von Freyburgstr. 2½. (☎ 92 10 44. Open Tu-Th 4-8:30pm, F-Sa 3-9pm, Su 3-7pm.) The **Jugendherberge (HI)**, Mariahilferstr. 5, is blessed with a lovely location and friendly staff. Turn right from the station and follow the railroad tracks. (☎ 77 54. Sheets DM5.50. Reception 7-9am, 5-7pm, and 8-10pm. Curfew 11:30pm. Open Dec.-Oct. DM22.50.) **Pizza Blitz**, Luitpoldstr. 14, is a favorite local hangout for its gargantuan pizzas. (Open M-Th 11am-11pm, F-Sa 11am-midnight, Su noon-11pm.) **Postal Code:** 87629.

NEUSCHWANSTEIN AND HOHENSCHWANGAU   ☎ 08362

Ludwig II's desperate building spree across Bavaria peaked with the glitzy ◪**Schloß Neuschwanstein**, built from 1869 to 1886, now Germany's most cliched tourist attraction and the inspiration for Disneyland's Cinderella Castle. The young Ludwig II lived a mere 173 days within the extravagant edifice. The completed chambers (63 remain unfinished) include a Byzantine throne room, a small artificial grotto, and an immense *Sängersaal* (singer's hall) built expressly for Wagnerian opera performances. Ludwig grew up in the bright-yellow, neo-Gothic **Schloß Hohenschwangau** across the way. The castle houses Wagner's piano and a loaf of bread from the 1830s. (Both open Apr.-Sept. 9am-6pm, Oct.-Mar. 10am-4pm. DM14, students DM12.) Tickets for both castles can be purchased at the Ticket-Service Counter, Alpseestr. 12, (☎ 930 83 20; www.ticket-center-hohenschwangau.de), about 100m south of the Hohenschwangau bus stop. For the fairy godmother of all views, **hike** up path 33 from Neuschwanstein to the **Marienbrücke**, which spans the dramatic **Pöllat gorge** behind the Schloß Neuschwanstein. Continue uphill from there for a knockout overview of the castle and nearby lake (1hr.).

Bus #9713 runs to the castles (dir.: Königsschlösser) from Füssen's train station (2 per hr., DM2.50). Separate paths lead up from the drop-off point to each castle. The less-touristed route to Hohenschwangau is path 17, which starts from the left side of the information booth (☎ 81 98 40; open daily 9am-6pm) and meanders through the moss-covered forest (10min.). Path 32 from Car Park D is the shortest

HYPERTRAVEL TO THE CASTLES. Seeing all three of the Royal Castles during a daytrip from Munich requires some fancy footwork and luck with connections (and can only be done M-F). Take the 6:50am train from Munich to Buchloe, then transfer to the 7:46am to Füssen. After arriving in Füssen at 8:57am, hop on bus #9713 at 9:15am to get to the Königsschlößer. Arriving at 9:23am, you'll have almost 4hrs. to fight through the lines at Hohenschwangau and Neuschwanstein before catching bus #1084 at 1:13pm to Oberammergau (changing in Steingaden), and from Oberammergau, bus #9622 at 3:05pm to Schloß Linderhof. Until 5:35pm you can indulge in the surrounding opulence, when it'll be time to catch bus #9622 back to Oberammergau Post/Bahnhof. At 6pm, you'll arrive at the Oberammergau train station with plenty of time to catch the 6:08pm train to Murnau, where you'll change at 6:47pm; by 7:55, you'll hopefully grab a *Löwenbräu* back in Munich. Double check your schedule with a timetable before departing—these are times from summer 2000, and have most likely changed. A simpler and more advisable option, particularly if you don't have a railpass, is to sign on with EurAide for a castle tour (see p. 482).

but steepest trail up to Neuschwanstein (25min.). A *Tagesticket* (DM13) entitles castle-hoppers to unlimited bus travel on regional buses (including the ride to Linderhof); buy it from the bus driver.

LINDERHOF

East of Neuschwanstein and Hohenschwangau lies the exquisite Schloß Linderhof, Ludwig II's compact hunting palace, which (like Schloß Herrenchiemsee) reflected Ludwig's obsession with France's Louis XIV (the Sun King). Although the castle lacks Neuschwanstein's pristine exterior, it's bathed in gold. The royal bedchamber, the largest room in the castle, is unbelievably lush, with gold leaf and a colossal, 454kg crystal chandelier. Even more impressive is the surrounding **park.** Paths originating at the swan lake at the park entrance weave through the ornately landscaped grounds, which include an enormous, artificial **grotto** swathed in red and blue floodlights (good taste was perhaps not one of Ludwig's strengths) and the **Hunding-Hütte,** modeled after a scene in Wagner's *Die Walküre.* (Castle open Apr.-Sept. daily 9am-6pm; Oct.-Mar. 10am-4pm. Obligatory castle tour DM11, students DM9; Oct.-Mar. DM8, students DM6. Park free.) **Bus** #9622 connects to Linderhof from Oberammergau (20min., every hr., roundtrip DM9.20; last return bus 6:40pm). Oberammergau is accessible by **bus** #1084 from Füssen (1½hr., 8 per day, DM12.50) and by **train** from Munich (1¾hr., every hr., DM25.60; change at Murnau.)

GARMISCH-PARTENKIRCHEN   ☎ 08821

Once upon a time, the 1,100-year-old hamlets of Garmisch and Partenkirchen were beautiful, unassuming Bavarian villages, with a location at the base of the **Zugspitze,** Germany's tallest peak (2,964m), that ensured their tranquil isolation. To this day, the inhabitants of each assert their individuality. Take the **cog railway** from the Zugspitzebahnhof (50m behind the Garmisch main station), then a cable car, the **Gipfelseilbahn,** to the Zugspitzplatt (1¼hr., hourly 7:39am-2:39pm, DM79). Continue to the top with the Gletscherbahn cable car. **Option 2:** Get off the railway at Eibsee and take the **Eibseeseilbahn,** one of the steepest cable car runs in the world, all the way to the top (1¼hr., hourly 8am-4:15pm, DM79). For less expensive views, take the **Alpspitzbahn** to the **Osterfelderkopf** peak (2050m, roundtrip DM38), the **Kreuzeck** cable car to **Kreuzeck** (1650m, roundtrip DM28) or the **Wankbahn** to the top of the **Wank** (1780m, roundtrip DM29). The town can be reached by **train** from Munich (1½hr., every hr., DM27), and by **bus** from Füssen (2hr., 6-7 per day, DM13 with Tagesticket). To get to the **tourist office,** Richard-Strauss-Platz 2, where the staff distributes maps and books rooms for free, from the train station, turn left on Bahnhofstr. and turn left onto Von-Brug-Str.; the office faces the fountain on the square. (☎ 18 07 00; fax 18 07 55; www.garmisch-partenkirchen.de. Open M-Sa 8am-6pm, Su 10am-noon.) Near the train station, hop on bus #3 (dir.:Burgrain) to the end of the line in order to awake to the tolling of bells at the **Jugendherberge (HI)**, Jochstr. 10. (☎29 80. Sheets DM5.50. Reception 7-9am and 5pm-midnight. Lockout 9am-3:30pm. Curfew 11:30pm. Open Jan. to mid-Nov. Ages 18-26 only. DM21.) **Postal Code:** 82467.

BERCHTESGADEN   ☎08652

Hidden in the southeastern corner of the Bavarian Alps, Berchtesgaden's natural beauty and the sinister attraction of Hitler's mountaintop **Kehlsteinhaus**, dubbed "Eagle's Nest" by the American troops who occupied it after WWII, draw world travelers to the town. Although there's little more than a restaurant up top, on a clear day, the view from the 1834m peak is spectacular. Take the Oversalzburg, Kehlstein bus #9538 (June-Oct. every 45min.; DM5.90) from the train station to Oversalzburg, Hintereck; while waiting for bus #9549 to Kehlstein Parkpl./Eagle's Nest, at Hintereck, buy your combined ticket for the second leg of the bus ride and the elevator ride up at the other end (every 30min. 9:30am-4pm, DM22). Reserve your spot for the return bus when you get off. In the Altstadt, the Berchtesgaden **Schloß**, a monastic priory until Bavarian rulers appropriated the property, now houses a mixture of art and weaponry. (Open Easter-Sept. Su-F 10am-1pm and 2-5pm; Oct.-Easter same hrs., closed Su. DM7, students DM3.50.)

Hourly **trains** (☎50 74) run to Salzburg (1hr., DM12.20) and Munich (2½hr., DM48). The **tourist office**, Königsseerstr. 2, opposite the station, has tips on trails in the Berchtesgaden National Park. (☎96 71 50; fax 96 74 00. Open M-F 8am-6pm, Sa 9am-3pm.) To get from the station to the **Jugendherberge (HI)**, Gebirgsjägerstr. 52, take bus #9539 (dir.: Strub Kaserne) to Jugendherberge. Or head right from the station, left on Ramsauerstr., right on Gmündbrücke, and left up the steep gravel path. (☎943 70. Breakfast included. Sheets DM5.50. Reception 8am-noon and 5-7pm. Check-in until 10pm. Curfew midnight. Closed Nov.-Dec. 26. Dorm DM23.) Perhaps the cheapest meal in town is at the **Express-Grill Hendl**, Maximilianstr. 8, which serves up traditional Bavarian dishes. (Open 11am-8pm.) **Postal Code:** 83471.

⚡ HIKING NEAR BERCHTESGADEN. From Berchtesgaden, the 5.5km path to the **Königssee**—which winds through fields of flowers, across bubbling brooks, and past several beer gardens—affords a heart-stopping view of the Alps. From the Berchtesgaden train station, walk across the street, take a right and then a quick left over the bridge, and turn left at the stone wall. Bus #9541 also runs from near the train station to Königssee (round-trip DM7.20). Once you arrive, walk down Seestr. and look for the **Nationalpark Informationstelle** to your left, which has hiking info. From **Ramsau**, 20km southwest of Berchtesgaden, a network of well-marked hiking trails radiates throughout the surrounding Alpine landscape and into the **Berchtesgaden National Park**. The **tourist office**, Im Tal 2, has trail maps and hiking info. (☎ (08657) 275. Open M-F 8am-12:30pm and 2:30-6:30pm, Sa 8am-12:30pm.) From Berchtesgaden, **bus** #9546 (15 min., DM3.80) runs hourly to Ramsau.

THE CHIEMSEE

For almost 2000 years, artists and musicians have marveled at the picturesque islands, mountains, and forests of the Chiemsee region. **Herreninsel** and **Fraueninsel** are the two inhabited islands on Lake Chiem; the former is home to **Königsschloß Herrenchiemsee**, the third and last of Mad King Ludwig's "fairy-tale castles."

PRIEN AM CHIEMSEE. Prien, on the northwestern corner of the Chiemsee, serves as a good base from which to take the ferries to the islands. **Trains** arrive at the station, a few blocks from the city center (☎ (08051) 28 74) from Salzburg (40min., every hr., DM34) and Munich (1hr., every hr., DM36). The **tourist office**,

Alte Rathausstr. 11, finds private rooms (DM30-45) for free. (☎ (08051) 690 50; fax 69 05 40. Open M-F 8:30am-6pm, Sa 9am-noon.) The **Jugendherberge (HI),** Carl-Braun-Str. 66, is a 15min. walk from the station—head right on Seestr. and turn left on Staudenstr., which turns into Carl-Braun-Str. (☎ (08051) 687 70. Breakfast included. Sheets DM5.50. Reception 8-9am, 5-7pm, and 9:30-10pm. Lockout 9am-1pm. Curfew 10pm. Open early Feb.-Nov. Dorms DM25.) For **Campingplatz Hofbauer,** Bernauerstr. 110, turn left on Seestr. from the station, turn left at the next intersection, and walk for 30min. along Bernauerstr., heading out of town. (☎ (08051) 41 36. Open Apr.-Oct. DM10.50 per person, DM10 per tent and car.) Grab **groceries** at **HL Markt,** Seestr. 11. (Open M-F 8am-8pm, Sa 8am-4pm.)

HERRENINSEL AND FRAUENINSEL. On **Herreninsel** (Gentlemen's Island), the **Königsschloß Herrenchiemsee** is fabulously overwrought as only King Ludwig II could manage. Ludwig bankrupted Bavaria building this place—a shameless attempt to be bigger, better, and more extravagant than Versailles. A few stark, barren rooms (abandoned after the cash ran out) contrast greatly with the excessively ornate completed portion of the castle. (Open daily Apr.-Sept. 9am-6pm; Oct.-Mar. 10am-4pm. Obligatory tour DM11, students DM9. German tours every 10min.; tours in English 10:30, 11:30am, 1, 2, 3, and 4pm.) **Fraueninsel** (Ladies' Island), home to the extant nunnery that complemented the former monastery on Herreninsel, offers subtler pleasures. The 8th-century Merovingian **Cross of Bischofhofen** is on display in Michaelskapelle above the **Torhalle** (Gate), the oldest surviving part of the cloister. (Open June-Sept. Torhalle DM8, Michaelskapelle DM2.) **Ferries** run from Prien to Herreninsel and Fraueninsel (every hr., DM10-12.50). To get to the ferry port, turn right from the main entrance of the Prien train station and follow Seestr. for 20min., or hop on the green *Chiemseebahn* steam train from the station (9:40am-6:15pm, round-trip including ship passage DM16.50).

REGENSBURG   ☎ 0941

The first capital of Bavaria, the administrative seat of the Holy Roman Empire, and eventually the site of the first German parliament, Regensburg is packed with history. The impotent (Holy Roman) Imperial Parliament, lives on in the **Reichstagsmuseum** within the Gothic **Altes Rathaus.** (DM5, students DM2.50.) The high-Gothic **Dom St. Peter,** a few blocks away on Dompl., dazzles with richly colored stained glass. Inside the cathedral, the **Domschatz** contains a priceless collection of gold and jewels purchased by the Regensburg bishops. (Cathedral open daily Apr.-Oct. 6:30am-6pm; Nov.-Mar. 6:30am-5pm. Free. Nov.-Apr. M-Sa 11am, Su noon. DM4, students DM2. Domschatz open Apr.-Nov. Tu-Sa 10am-5pm, Su noon-5pm; Dec.-Mar. F-Sa 10am-4pm, Su noon-4pm; DM3, students DM1.50.) **Trains** head to: Munich (1½hr., every hr., DM38); Nuremburg (1-1½hr., 1-2 per hr., DM27); and Passau (1-1½hr., every hr., DM32). To get from the station to the **tourist office,** in the Altes Rathaus on Rathauspl., walk down Maximilianstr., turn left on Grasg., turn right at the end on Obere Bachg., and continue on Untere Bachg. (☎507 44 10; fax 507 44 19; www.regensburg.de. Open M-F 8:30am-6pm, Sa 9am-4pm, Su 9:30am-2:30pm; Apr.-Oct. open Su until 4pm.) To get from the station to the **Jugendherberge (HI),** Wöhrdstr. 60, walk to the end of Maximilianstr., turn right at the *Apotheke* on Pflugg., turn immediately left at the *Optik* sign on tiny Erhardig., walk left over the bridge, then veer right onto Wührdstr. on the other side; the hostel will be on the right. (☎574 02. Breakfast included. Reception 6am-1am. DM28.) **Historische Wurstküche,** Thundorferstr., next to the Steinerne Brücke, is a great beer garden. (Open daily 8am-7pm; Nov.-Mar. Su 8am-3pm.) **Postal Code:** 93047.

PASSAU   ☎ 0851

At the confluence of the Danube, Inn, and Ilz Rivers, this beautiful Baroque *Dreiflüssestadt* (three-river city) embodies the ideal Old World European city. Its Baroque architecture peaks in the sublime **Stephansdom** (St. Stephen's Cathedral), where hundreds of cherubs sprawl across the ceiling and the

GERMANY

world's largest **church organ** (17,774 pipes) looms above the choir. (Open M-Sa 7:30-10:45am and 12:30-6pm. Free. Organ concerts May-Oct. M-Sa noon; DM4, students DM2. Also Th 7:30pm; DM10, students DM5.) Behind the cathedral, the **Domschatz** (cathedral treasury) of the **Residenz** houses an extravagant collection of gold and tapestries. (Open Easter-Oct. M-Sa 10am-4pm. DM2, students DM1.) The 13th-century Gothic **Rathaus** contains a stunning *Prunksaal* (Great Hall), decorated with rich, wooden paneling and dark marble. (Open Apr.-Oct. and at Christmastime 10am-4pm. DM2, students DM1.) Over the Luitpoldbrücke (bridge) is the former palace of the Bishopric, the **Veste Oberhaus,** now home to the **Cultural History Museum.** (Open Apr.-Oct. M-F 9am-5pm, Sa-Su 10am-6pm; Nov.-Mar. Tu-Su 9am-5pm. DM7, students DM4.)

Trains (☎ (0180) 599 66 33) arrive from: Frankfurt (4½hr., every 2hr., DM74-131); Munich (2hr., every hr., DM52); Nuremberg (2hr., every 2hr., DM60); Regensburg (1-2hr., every hr., DM32); and Vienna (3½hr., 1-2 per hr.). To get to the **tourist office,** Rathauspl. 3, walk down Bahnhofstr. to the right, downhill across Ludwigspl. to Ludwigstr., which becomes Rindermarkt, Steinweg, and finally Große Messerg.; continue straight on Schusterg. and turn left on Schrottg. (☎ 95 59 80. Open Easter-Oct. M-F 8:30am-6pm, Sa-Su 9:30am-3pm; Nov.-Easter M-Th 8:30am-5pm, F 8:30am-4pm.) The **Jugendherberge (HI),** Veste Oberhaus 125, is in a medieval castle perched high above the Danube. Cross the suspension bridge just downstream of the Rathaus, *ignore* the sign pointing up the steps and instead continue right along the curve through the lefthand tunnel (skeptics will spend an extra 20min. in steep hell for their disbelief), head up the cobble-stoned driveway to your left, through the yellow house, and take a right to the hostel. (☎ 413 51. Breakfast included. Sheets DM5.50. Reception 7-11:30am. Check-in 4-11:30pm. Curfew 11:30pm. Dorms DM22.) Grab cheap grub at **Edeka supermarket,** on Ludwigstr. at Grabeng. (Open M-F 8am-8pm, Sa 7:30am-4pm.) **Cafe Kowalski,** Oberer Sand 1, makes the largest schnitzel in Passau. (Open Su-Th 10am-11pm, F-Sa 10am-3am.) **Postal Code:** 94032.

GREECE (ΕΛΛΑΣ)

GREEK DRACHMAS

US$1 = 369DR	100DR = US$0.29
CDN$1 = 239DR	100DR = CDN$0.42
EURO€1 = 336DR	100DR = EURO€0.30
UK£1 = 529DR	100DR = UK£0.19
IR£1 = 427DR	100DR = IR£0.23
AUS$1 = 209DR	100DR = AUS$0.48
NZ$1 = 166DR	100DR = NZ$0.60
SAR1 = 50DR	100DR = SAR2.01

GREECE

PHONE CODE | Country code: 30. **International dialing prefix:** 00.

Over the centuries, Greece has occupied a unique position at the crossroads of Europe and Asia. The relics of Crete's Minoan civilization betray the influence of flowering contemporary cultures in Egypt and Babylon. The Byzantine era saw the preservation of the mores of an Eastern empire. Four centuries under the Ottoman Turks left a certain spice in Greek food, an Oriental flair in the strains of its *bouzouki* music, and minaret tips in its skylines. Greece emerged independent in 1821 under the dual veneer of Classical Athens and Imperial Byzantium, but Ottoman ways persist. The memory of Dionysus, god of the vine, fuels the island circuit—a blur of sun, sand, and sex. In Greece's austere hills, monks and hermits lurk in structures that have aged a millennium. As the country moves toward the European Monetary Union and overhauls its infrastructure for the 2004 Summer Olympics in Athens, development has accelerated at a blistering pace. Still, when you climb above the concrete resorts and whirring tour buses—when you hear the wind's lonely, persistent whistle—you'll know that Greece remains oracles' ground. For coverage of Greece rivaling that of Pausanias, see *Let's Go: Greece 2001*.

SUGGESTED ITINERARIES

THREE DAYS To **Athens** (see p. 516). Luxuriate in the **Acropolis,** gaze at the treasures of the **National Archaeological Museum,** and pay homage in the fabulous **Parthenon.** Visit the **Ancient Athenian Agora,** and the **Panathenaic Olympic Stadium** to run a lap.

ONE WEEK Begin your week in Greece with a sojourn in **Athens** (3 days; p. 516). Move on to **Corinth** to wander through **Ancient Corinth** and the 6th-century **Temple of Apollo** (1 day; p. 531). Go to **Olympia** for ruins, ruins, and some more ruins—check out the immense **Temple of Zeus** (1 day; p. 527). Take the ferry to **Corfu** (1 day; p. 538) and then soak up some culture in **Thessaloniki** (1 day; p. 532). Ask the **Oracle at Delphi** how to top your week (1 day; p. 525).

BEST OF GREECE, THREE WEEKS Explore **Athens** (4 days) before strolling among the mansions of **Nafplion** (1 day; p. 530). Race west to **Olympia** (1 day) and ferry Patras to **Corfu** (2 days). Head to **Thessaloniki** (2 days). Move across the Halkidiki peninsula to **Mount Athos** (1 day), climb the cliffside monasteries of the **Meteora** (1 day; p. 536), and talk to the gods of **Mt. Olympus** (1 day; p. 535). Find your fate at the **Oracle of Delphi** (1 day), and ferry from Athens to **Crete,** (3 days; p. 546), home of Europe's largest gorge. Head to the **Cyclades** for a respite on **Santorini** (1 day; p. 545), debauchery on **Ios** (1 day; p. 544), the beaches of **Mykonos** (1 day; p. 542), and repenting your sins at the Temple of Apollo on **Delos** (1 day; p. 542).

LIFE AND TIMES

HISTORY AND POLITICS

STONE AND BRONZE AGE CIVILIZATIONS (13,000-1100 BC)

By about 13,000-11,000 BC, during the **Paleolithic** (Old Stone Age) period, indigenous populations began to develop stone tools and engage in basic agrarian activities. During the **Neolithic** (New Stone Age) period, shelters progressed from circular hut dwellings to compartmentalized walled towns built on high—the acropolis in its infancy. The arrival of metalworking from the east catalyzed Greek civilization. The use of bronze in toolmaking and weaponry inaugurated a period of advancement known as the **Bronze Age** and gave rise to three great Aegean civilizations: the **Helladic**—later Mycenaean—on the mainland, the **Minoan** on Crete, and the **Cycladic** on the other islands.

DORIAN INVASION AND RISE OF CITY-STATE (1100-500 BC)

Historians believe that the Aegean civilizations of the Bronze Age met an abrupt end in the 12th century BC, with the invasion of Greek-speaking **Dorians**. Their tribal leanings meant that industry, agriculture, and trade passed into the hands of hundreds of smaller, politically autonomous villages peopled by economically self-sufficient farmers. These villages and the Dorian destruction of "high" civilization in Greece paved the path to Classical splendour.

In the aftermath of the Dorian invasion the *polis*, or **city-state,** became the predominant form of political organization. A typical *polis* consisted of: an **acropolis,** first a fortified citadel and later a religious center bedecked with **temples** to the people's patron deities; an **agora** (marketplace), the center of commercial and social life; **stoas** (colonnaded porticos), where thinkers waxed philosophical and traders hawked their wares; and, outside the city center, various trappings of the frequent public spectacles and athletic contests—**amphitheaters, stadia,** and **gymnasia.** By the 9th century BC, many city-states began to expand and even colonize overseas, and began to form economic, religious, and military ties. During religious and athletic festivals such as the **Olympic Games,** athletic fields, arenas, and racetracks housed heated contests between states. In the early 5th century BC, the Hellenes, as the Greeks began to refer to themselves, faced threats on two fronts, from the **Persians** under **King Xerxes** to the east and the empire of **Carthage** to the west. The Greeks decisively defeated the Persians, and were able to repel the Carthaginians from North Africa.

CLASSICAL GREECE (500-400 BC)

The end of the Persian Wars marked the rise of the greatest *polis,* **Athens.** Athens established itself as the head of the powerful **Delian League.** From the 6th to the 5th centuries BC, Athens produced major innovations in art, literature, philosophy, and politics. In the early 6th century the law giver **Solon** ended slavery in Athens, establishing equality for all citizens before the law. **Pericles,** who came into power in 461 BC, established democracy in Athens, allowing every male citizen to participate in government. Athens' rival, **Sparta** headed the **Peloponnesian League.** Spartan males spent the first 60 years of their lives in military preparation, conquest, and defense. The culture clash exploded in the late 5th century into the **Peloponnesian War** (431-404 BC), which ended in a nominal defeat for Athens.

MACEDONIAN AND ROMAN INVASION (400 BC-AD 300)

After the Peloponnesian War, the Macedonions gained strength when **King Philip II** led them in conquering a number of Greek city-states. In 338 BC, Philip crushed the Athenian resistance and then united the various Greek cities under his control. Philip's son **Alexander the Great,** a student of famous Greek philosopher **Aristotle,** ruled Greece with an iron fist. After consolidating military control of Greece, Alexander turned his ambitions east, and by the time of his sudden death at the age of 33, he controlled Egypt and the whole of the Persian empire. However, the Mace-

Greece

donian empire quickly fell to pieces following Alexander's death. In the 3rd century BC the Romans began to fill the power void left by Alexander's death. Greek cities began to support their former enemies against Rome, and the Achaean Confederacy even started a rebellion in 146 BC, resulting in the destruction of Corinth and the beginning of a number of oppressive restrictions. When the cities were organized by Augustus into the Roman province of Achea in 27 BC, any notion that Greece was free was dispelled. As Roman legions took hold of Greek lands, Hellenic culture took hold of Roman society. Adopting what they saw as the best aspects of Greece's culture, the Romans created a very influential hybrid culture.

CONVERSION AND WAR (300-1400)

The decentralization of the Roman Empire, as a result of expansion into the Near East, led to the division of the empire and a scramble for power—won by **Constantine** in 312. He founded **Constantinople** (modern Istanbul) in 324, over the ancient Greek *polis* of Byzantium, giving the Roman Empire a new seat. Constantine died in 338 after converting to Christianity due to a battlefield vision of a flaming cross. His empire did not convert overnight, but with state support a nascent Christian culture began to emerge. During the 6th century, **Emperor Justinian's** battles against the Sassanians of Persia in the east and the Vandals in the west, led to an overextension of imperial resources, which left the empire vulnerable to the Slavs, Mongols, and Avars. As the borders of the empire contracted, an increasing number of Christians once united under a single ruler and capital were subjected to new, non-Christian rulers. This estrangement continued with the crowning of Charlemagne as Holy Roman Emperor in 800 and culminated in the **Great Schism,** or mutual excommunication, between the Greek Orthodox and Roman Catholic Churches in 1054. Despite a strong line of emperors, Byzantium contracted, until alliance through marriage with Latin, Slavic, and Turkish rulers was its only recourse. Holding only Constantinople and its environs, the Byzantines were finally overrun with the seizure of Constantinople by the **Ottoman Turks** in 1453.

OTTOMAN RULE AND THE RISE OF NATIONALISM (1400-1900)

Renamed **Istanbul**—a Turkish adaptation of the Greek *"steen Poli"* (to the City)—in 1453, Byzantium became the cornerstone of a new great empire. However, nationalist fervor began to spread. By the 19th century, movements for independence by minorities within the empire were in full swing. In the era of European revolutions, the Greek cause won mingled interest, sympathy, and distaste from foreigners all over the continent. Hundreds of "philhellenes," distinguished European fellows seeking to restore Greece to the Classical tradition they idolized, came to fight and die for Greece—drawing attention and respect to the cause, especially after the 1824 death (by pneumonia) of British poet **Lord Byron.** In 1827, Russia, Britain, and France began to pressure the Turkish Sultan to relent. The devastation of the Turkish fleet at the battle of Navarino pushed the hesitant Russian Tsar to declare war, which ended in 1829, giving Greece autonomy.

In their anxiety to limit the power of the newly assembled state, Russia, Britain, and France were hardly generous with the borders of the new Greece—it included only a fraction of the six million Greeks living under Ottoman rule. For the next century, the driving force behind Greek politics was the desire to regain the boundaries of the Byzantine era and unify the Greek population. This vision came to be called the **Megali Idhea** (Great Idea). After the 1831 assasination of the first Greek president by his citizens, Greece was declared a monarchy under German **Prince Otho.** Otho was exiled in 1862, and Danish George I installed as king.

RECENT HISTORY (1900-PRESENT)

In 1920 Cretan Prime Minister Eleftherios Venizelos attempted to use the Balkan Wars and World War I as opportunities to realize the Megali Idhea. Venizelos set up an allied revolutionary government in Thessaloniki and invaded the city of Smyrna in war-weakened Turkey. When his advances were rebuffed, Venizelos was voted out of office. In the treaty that followed, the Greeks traded 400,000 Turkish Muslims for one million Orthodox Greeks. This "resettlement" saw the end of the Megali Idhea, but spawned a new set of economic difficulties for the fledgling Greek economy. The next decade was filled with domestic strife. George II was overthrown by a series of coups that instituted a brief democracy. Greece suffered under Nazi occupation from 1941 to 1945. With its (in)visible hand in Greek politics, the red-scared US helped stave off Communist rule, but after the election of a left-wing leader, the army staged a **coup** on April 21, 1967, beginning seven years of junta rule. It ultimately fell in 1973 and the former president returned. A new constitution was drawn up in 1975, calling for a parliamentary government with a ceremonial president appointed by the legislature—a system still in use today.

THE ARTS

VISUAL ARTS

CYCLADIC AND MINOAN PERIODS (3000-1100 BC). The Cycladic civilizations of the Aegean Bronze Age made their greatest artistic contribution in the form of minimalist sculpture. Cycladic sculptures were usually small marble statuettes, marked by graceful simplification of the human form. On Crete, the Minoans also churned out miniature votive statuettes, but it was architecture, however, that brought the Minoans glory. The Minoan palaces' massive pillars, ceremonial stairways, and decorative stucco are testament to the spread of Near Eastern aesthetic and technical ideas, which came to the Minoans through commercial contact with Egypt and Mesopotamia. Minoan artists delighted in the challenge of wet plaster, portraying bull-leaping ceremonies and magical gardens in vivid frescoes. The

Minoans were also renowned throughout the Aegean for their **Kamares style pottery,** which consisted of red and white ornamentation on a dark ground.

MYCENAEAN PERIOD (1600-1100BC). The architecture of the mainland Mycenaean culture developed against the background of the Minoan civilization it began to supersede in 1500BC. The palaces at **Mycenae, Tiryns,** and **Pylos** (see p. 528) modified the layout of their Cretan prototypes to create a more symmetrical design, centered around the Near Eastern-inspired **megaron,** or reception room. The frescoes decorating the palace adapted the fanciful Minoan model to the more martial tastes of the Mycenaeans. The Mycenaeans were the first Europeans to produce monumental sculpture, best exemplified by the relief work of the triangular **Lion's Gate** at Mycenae (13th century BC) and the royal Mycenaean **tombs.** By 1500 BC, the graves of Mycenaean royalty had evolved from these tombs into stone **tholos,** beehive-shaped structures cloaked in packed earth.

GEOMETRIC AND ARCHAIC PERIODS (1100-480 BC). Out of the Dark Ages that followed the collapse of Mycenaean civilization emerged a new artistic style, with ceramics as its primary medium and Athens as its major cultural center. Athenian pottery of the **Proto-Geometric Period** (1100-900 BC) was decorated with Mycenaean-inspired spirals, arcs, wavy lines, and concentric circles. These patterns became more expressive in the **Geometric Period,** when artists decorated clay figurines and pottery with geometrical motifs reminiscent of basket-weaving patterns. Architects of the Geometric Period focused on the development of one-room temples with columned porches. This period of plenty saw the innovation of the Doric and Ionic architectural orders, whose columns have become staples of art history curricula. Around the 6th century BC, the Greek colonies along the Aegean coast of Asia Minor produced the exotic **Ionic order,** whose columns were distinguished from their more austere Doric predecessors by their twin **volute** (scrolled spiral) capitals, and their slender, fluted shafts. Temples of the Ionic order, ornate and fussy, boasted forests of columns: The highlight of early Archaic sculpture was the development of large-scale figures called **kouroi,** which stood in sanctuaries as votive offerings to deities or as memorials to fallen warriors. Athenian vase painters were exploring the human form through the **black figure technique,** featuring black silhouettes with incised features.

CLASSICAL AND HELLENISTIC PERIODS (480-46BC). The arts flourished during the Classical period, as Athens reached the pinnacle of its political and economic power under Pericles and his successors. Classical temples were more spacious and fluid than the stocky temples of the Archaic period. The peerless architectural complex of the Athenian **Acropolis** built during this period, defined "classic" for the Classical world, and its star attraction, the **Parthenon,** bears elegant testimony to the obsession with proportion that dominated the Classical Greek aesthetic. During this period, sculptors mastered the natural representation of the human form. By the middle of the 5th century BC, sculptors were using the **Severe Style** to elevate the human form to a plane of universal physical perfection.

The Hellenistic kingdoms turned ornate with flower-topped **Corinthian columns**. Hellenistic architects worked on a monumental scale, building massive complexes of temples, *stoas* (colonnaded walkways), and palaces, and enormous amphitheaters. The acoustics in these theaters are so precise that now, 2000 years after their construction, a coin dropped on the stage can still be heard from the theater's last row. Hellenistic sculpture displayed all the technical mastery and twice the emotion of its Classical predecessor. Artists even sculpted the grotesque: figures like **Laocoon** writhe and twist. The appointment of **Lysippus** as court sculptor to Alexander the Great began the Greek foray into portraiture. With the advent of the **Roman empire,** the Hellenistic style was modified to suit Roman tastes.

THE BYZANTINE ERA. The most eminent example of Byzantine architecture is Constantinople's (Istanbul's) Agia Sofia, built during the Justinian era over the remains of a church from Constantine's time. Byzantine art ranged from illuminated manuscripts to carved ivory panels. The mosaics and icons decorating Byzantine churches are at the pinnacle of the Byzantine artistic achievements. Byzantine icons were made of enamel, ivory, gold, wood, and mosaic. Mosaics were made of tesserae, small cubes of stone or ceramic covered in glass or metallic foil. The unique shimmering effect of Byzantine mosaics was achieved by setting gold and silver tesserae at sharp angles to enhance the reflection of light.

MODERN ART. After Greek independence, nationalist sentiment led the government subsidized art. Young artists were urged to study in Munich, and the work of the first wave of post-independence Greek painters, reflected their German training. However, the sculptors of this period were largely faithful to their Classical roots. For the most part, Greek art of the 20th century has followed the major European trends. The eccentric folk artist Theophilos Chatzimichael (1873-1934), known simply as **Theophilos** to modern Greek admirers but relatively unknown in his own lifetime, has been called the Greek Van Gogh. The paintings of **Yiannis Psychopedis** (b. 1945) combine social and aesthetic criticism, while the work of painter **Opy Zouni** has won her international renown for her geometric art.

LITERATURE

ANCIENT GREECE. The earliest examples of written language in Greece are tablets found among Minoan palace ruins. Somewhat uninspiring in content, these palace treasury records were inscribed on tablets in duo-syllabic scripts called **Linear A** and **B** near the end of the Bronze Age (roughly 1100 BC). The first written Greek did not appear until the middle of the 8th century BC, but the Greek literary tradition may have begun as much as 150 years earlier, with the epic "songs" of **Homer.** Homer may have recorded or dictated the *Iliad* and *Odyssey* in his own lifetime, but most scholars believe that he simply began the faithful oral tradition.

Hesiod composed the *Theogony*, the first Greek account of the creation of the world and the exploits of the gods. During the 7th century BC, **Archilochus** of Paros made the first certain contributions to written poetry in the form of anti-heroic, anti-Homeric elegies. On the island of Lesvos, during the 5th century, the gifted lyric poet **Sappho** sang of love, sex, and the beauty of nature. **Herodotus,** the so-called "Father of History," captured the monumental battles and personalities of the Greco-Persian conflict in the *Persian Wars*, while **Thucydides** immortalized the Athenian conflict with Sparta in his chronicle of the Peloponnesian Wars.

BYZANTINE LITERATURE. Since the Hellenistic Era, Greeks had been developing the pseudo-historical romance, including personal love poems and **Plutarch's** *Life of Alexander*, written in the first century AD. In the same century, Greece produced one of its better known works of literature—the original **New Testament** of the Christian Bible. In the 6th century **Procopius**, one of emperor Justinian's generals, wrote two conventional tracts for publication, *On the Wars* and *On the Buildings*, and left behind a *Secret History*—an insider's account of the debauchery that was common in the court of Justinian and his wife Theodora.

MODERN LITERATURE. Greek independence in 1821 gave rise to the **Ionian School** of modern literature, whose most distinguished writers were **Andreas Kalvos** (1796-1869) and **Dionysios Solomos** (1798-1857). Solomos, whose *Hymn to Liberty* became the Greek national anthem, is called the "national poet of Greece." A truly remarkable group of modern writers has emerged from 20th-century Greece, including **George Seferis** (1900-63), **Yiannis Ritsos** (1909-90), and **Odysseas Elytis** (1911-96). **Ikos Kazantzakis** (1883-1957) may be the best known modern Greek author. His novels include *Zorba the Greek* (1946), and *The Last Temptation of Christ* (1951) which have been made into successful films.

CINEMA

After suffering under the colonels' *junta*, the Greek film industry rebuilt itself throughout the 1980s and has recently emerged as a distinguished and prolific presence in the international arena. The 1982 reestablishment of the **Greek Film Center,** a state-supported institute, has aided this revitalization by involving itself in many of the most highly regarded modern Greek films, including works by Nikos Perakis, Pantelis Vougaris, and Nikos Panayotopoulos, Greece's most acclaimed filmmaker and winner of the 1998 Cannes Palme d'Or. The most important event in the film world is the **Thessaloniki Film Festival** every November.

FOOD AND DRINK

Recent medical studies have highlighted the Greek diet as a model for **healthy** eating; its reliance on unsaturated olive oil and vegetables prevents high rates of heart disease despite the fairly sedentary lifestyle of the populace. Penny-pinching carnivores will thank Zeus for lamb, chicken, or beef **souvlaki** and hot-off-the-spit **gyros** stuffed into a pita. Vegetarians can also eat their fill for cheap: try the feta-piled **horiatiki** (a.k.a. Greek salad), savory pastries **tiropita** (spinach pie), and the fresh fruits and vegetables found at markets in most cities. Greek-style liquid relaxation involves a few basic options: the old standbys are **ouzo** (a Greek spirit that will earn your respect) and the hard core sludge that is **Greek coffee.** In the summer, people chill out with frothy, iced coffee *frappés*. **Breakfast,** served only in the early morning, is generally very simple: a piece of toast with *marmelada* or a pastry suffices. **Lunch,** a hearty and leisurely meal, can begin as early as noon, but is more likely eaten sometime between 2 and 5pm. **Dinner** is a drawn-out, relaxed affair served late—eat with the Greeks sometime between 10pm and midnight—then party all night or head home for another nap. A Greek restaurant is known as a **taverna** or **estiatorio;** a grill is a **psistaria.** Don't be suspicious of restaurants without menus; this is common. Service is always included in the check, but it is customary to leave a few drachmas as an extra tip.

ESSENTIALS

DOCUMENTS AND FORMALITIES

Citizens of Australia, Canada, New Zealand, the EU, and the US do not require visas for stays of fewer than three months. South Africans need a visa. Apply to stay longer at least 20 days prior to the three-month expiration date at the **Aliens Bureau,** 175 Alexandras Ave., Athens 11522 (☎ (011) 30 642 30 94), or check with a Greek embassy or consulate.

  Greek Embassies at Home: Australia, 9 Turrana St., Yarralumla, Canberra, ACT 26000 (☎ (02) 6273 3011); **Canada,** 76-80 MacLaren St., Ottawa, ON K2P 0K6 (☎ (613) 238-6271); **Ireland,** 1 Upper Pembroke St., Dublin 2 (☎ (01) 6767 2545); **South Africa,** 995 Pretorius St., Arcadia, 0083, Pretoria (☎ (012) 437 35 13); **UK,** 1a Holland Park, London W113TP (☎ (0171) 229 38 50); **US,** 2221 Massachusetts Ave., N.W., **Washington, D.C.** 20008 (☎ (202) 939-5800; email greece@greekembassy.org).

  Foreign Embassies in Greece: All embassies are located in **Athens** (see p. 520).

TRANSPORTATION

BY PLANE. Flying from northern European cities is a popular way of getting to Greece. From North America, an indirect flight through **Brussels** or **Luxembourg** may cost less than a flight going directly to **Athens. Olympic Airways,** 96-100 Singrou St., 11741 Athens (☎ (01) 926 72 21), serves many large cities and islands within Greece. Olympic Airways also operates efficient and reasonably priced flights between many islands. Note that these flights are often booked weeks in advance in summer. Coverage to remote areas is spotty.

BY TRAIN. Greece is served by a number of relatively cheap (and slow) international train routes that connect Athens, Thessaloniki, and Larissa to most European cities, but count on at least a three-day journey from **Trieste** or **Vienna** to **Athens.** Train service in Greece is limited and sometimes uncomfortable, and no lines go to the western coast. The more extensive and reliable bus system is a better way to get around the country, but if you must travel by rail the new, express, air-conditioned intercity trains, though slightly more expensive and rare, are worth the price. **Eurail** passes are valid on Greek trains. **Hellenic Railways Organization (OSE)** connects Athens to other major Greek cities. In Greece, call 145 or 147 for schedules and prices.

BY BUS. Buses are cheaper than trains, but it's a real marathon to get to Greece from the rest of Europe. **Eurolines**, 4 Cardiff Rd., Luton LU1 1PP, UK (☎ (01582) 40 45 11), is Europe's largest operator of Europe-wide coach services. Most are run through **KTEL**. Smaller towns may use cafes as bus stops; ask for a schedule. **Confirm your destination** with the driver; signs may be wrong. Along the road, little blue signs marked with white buses or the word "ΣΤΑΣΗ" indicate stops, but drivers usually stop anywhere if you flag them down. Let the driver know ahead of time where you want to get off; if your stop is passed, yell *"Stasi!"*

BY FERRY. The most popular way of getting to Greece is by **ferry** from Italy. Boats travel primarily from **Italy** (Ancona and Brindisi) to **Corfu** (10hr.), **Igoumenitsa** (12hr.), and **Patras** (20hr.). Seats run L50,000-105,000 (in low season L22,000-45,000). **Rhodes** is connected by ferry to **Marmaris,** Turkey; **Limassol,** Cyprus (18,500-22,000dr); and **Haifa,** Israel (28,500-33,000dr in low season). If you plan to travel from Brindisi, Italy, in the summer, make reservations and arrive at the port well before your departure time. ISIC holders can often get student fares, and Eurail pass holders get many reductions and free trips. Everyone pays the port tax (L10,000 in Brindisi) and, in high season, a supplementary fee of L19,000.

There is frequent **ferry** service to the Greek islands, but schedules are irregular and exasperating; misinformation is common. Your best bet is to arrive early to your ferry to avoid literally missing the boat. To avoid hassles, go to **limenarheio** (port police)—every port has one, and they all carry ferry schedules. **Flying dolphins** (hydrofoils) are a speedier but more expensive alternative to ferry transport.

BY CAR. Cars are a luxury in Greece, a country where public transportation is nonexistent after 7pm. Ferries will take you island-hopping if you pay a transport fee for the car. Rental agencies may quote low daily rates that exclude the 20% tax and **Collision Damage Waiver (CDW)** insurance (2500dr per day). Foreign drivers are required to have an **International Driving Permit** and an **International Insurance Certificate** to drive in Greece. The **Automobile and Touring Club of Greece (ELPA),** Messogion 395, Athens 11527 (☎ 606 88 00), provides assistance and offers reciprocal membership to foreign auto club members. They also have 24-hour emergency road assistance (☎ 104) and an information line (in Athens ☎ 174, elsewhere ☎ 01 60 68 838; open M-F 7am-3pm).

BY BIKE AND BY THUMB. The mountainous terrain and unpaved roads make **cycling** in Greece difficult. **Mopeds** can be great for exploring, but they also make you extremely vulnerable to the carelessness of other drivers; *always* wear a helmet. The majority of tourist-related accidents each year occur on mopeds. Greeks are not eager to pick up foreigners. Sparsely populated areas have little or no traffic. Visitors who choose to **hitchhike** write their destination on a sign in both Greek and English, and hitch from turn-offs rather than along long stretches of straight road. Women should *never* hitch alone. *Let's Go* does not recommend hitchhiking.

TOURIST SERVICES AND MONEY

EMERGENCY	Police: ☎ 100. Hospital: ☎ 106. Emergency ☎ 166.

TOURIST OFFICES. Tourism in Greece is overseen by two national organizations: the **Greek National Tourist Organization (GNTO)** and the **tourist police** *(touristiki astinomia)*. The **GNTO,** known as **EOT** in Greek, can supply general information about sights and accommodations throughout the country. The main office is at 2 Amerikis St., Athens (☎ (01) 322 41 28). The **tourist police** (Athens ☎ 171, elsewhere 922 77 77) deals with more local and immediate problems: bus schedules, accommodations, lost passports, etc. They are open long hours and are willing to help, although their English is often limited.

GNTO Offices: Australia, 3rd fl., 51 Pitt St., Sydney, NSW 2000 (☎ (02) 92 41 16 63). **Canada,** 1300 Bay St., Toronto, ON M5R 3K8 (☎ (416) 968-2220; www.aei.ca/gntomtl); 1170 Place du Frére André, Suite 300, Montréal, PQ H3B 3C6 (☎ (514) 871-1535). **UK,** 4 Conduit St., London W1R DOJ (☎ (020) 77 34 59 97; www.antor.com). **US,** Olympic Tower, 645 Fifth Ave., 5th fl., New York, NY 10022 (☎ (212) 421-5777).

CURRENCY & EXCHANGE. Greek *drachmas* (abbreviated "dr") are issued in both paper notes (100, 200, 500, 1000, 5000, and 10,000dr) and coins (5, 10, 20, 50, and 100dr). If you're carrying more than US$1000 in cash when you enter Greece, you must declare it upon entry. This rule does not apply to traveler's checks. You can bring up to US$445 worth of *drachmas* into Greece. No more than 20,000dr can be taken out of the country when you leave.

Prices: To give you a general idea, a bare-bones day in Greece, staying at hostels, campgrounds, or *domatia* (rooms to let), and buying food at supermarkets or at outdoor food stands, costs about US$30-40. A day with more creature comforts, with accommodations in a more expensive *domatia* or budget hotel, eating one meal a day in a restaurant, and going out at night, runs US$50.

Tipping and bargaining: When **tipping,** you should offer enough to show respect, for the goods, but not so much to seem like a show-off. At all but the ritziest restaurants, service is included in the bill. Several hundred drachmas for a several thousand drachma meal is usually sufficient. **Bargaining** skills are essential in Greece, but you must know when to bargain. Paying the asked price for street wares will have the seller marveling at a tourist's naiveté, while bargaining at the shop of a master craftsman whose crafts are worth the stated tag will be seen as rude and disrespectful.

Taxes: The European Union imposes a **value added tax (VAT)** on goods and services purchased within the EU, which is included in the marked price. Non-EU citizens may obtain a **refund** for taxes paid on retail goods (but not services). You must spend over 40,000dr to receive a refund. The percentage will vary from **11.5% to 15.3%.**

ACCOMMODATIONS AND CAMPING

Lodgings in Greece are a bargain. **Hostels** that are not currently endorsed by HI are in most cases still safe and reputable. **Curfews** in hostels are strict, and they may leave you on the street. **Hotel** prices are regulated, but proprietors may try to push you to take the most expensive room. Check your bill carefully, and threaten to contact the tourist police if you think you are being cheated. **GNTO** offices usually have a list of inexpensive accommodations, with prices. In many areas, **domatia** (rooms to let) are an attractive and perfectly dependable option. Often you'll be approached by locals as you enter town or disembark from your boat; Greek tourist officials consider this illegal. Greece hosts plenty of official **campgrounds,** and discreet freelance camping—though illegal—is common in July and August, but may not be the safest way to spend the night. Some campgrounds offer showers and breakfast and they are certainly the cheapest way to spend a night in Greece.

COMMUNICATION

MAIL. Letters within Europe cost 200dr (up to 50g); anywhere else in the world costs 240dr (up to 150g). Mail sent to Greece from Europe generally takes at least 3 days to arrive; from the US, South Africa, and Australia airmail will take 7-10 days. Letters can be sent general delivery to almost any city or town in Greece with a post office. Address Poste Restante (the international phrase for General Delivery) letters to: Max DICKSTEIN, Poste Restante, Greece. The mail will go to a special desk in the central post office, unless you specify differently.

TELEPHONES. The **only way** to use the phone in Greece is with a **prepaid phone card.** You can buy the cards at streetside kiosks and *peripteros.* The card usually has a toll-free access telephone number and a **personal identification number (PIN).** To

GREECE

make a phone call, you dial the access number, enter your PIN, and at the voice prompt, enter the phone number of the party you're trying to reach. Wherever possible, use a calling card for **international** phone calls, as the long-distance rates for national phone services are often exorbitant. Using a calling card, simply contact your service provider's Greek operator: **AT&T:** ☎00 800 13 11; **BT Direct:** ☎00 800 44 11; **Canada Direct:** ☎00 800 16 11; **Ireland Direct:** ☎155 11 74; **MCI WorldPhone Direct:** ☎00 800 12 11; **Sprint:** ☎00 900 14 11.

INTERNET ACCESS. The availability of the internet in Greece is rapidly expanding. In most big cities and on most of the touristed islands, you will able to find internet access. Expect to pay between 500-1500dr per hour. **Cybercafe Guide** (www.cyberia-cafe.net/cyberia/guide/ccafe.htm) can help you find cybercafes in Greece.

LANGUAGE. Although many Greeks in Athens and other heavily touristed areas speak English, off the beaten path you'll probably have to stumble around a bit in Greek. To avoid misunderstandings, it is also important to know Greek body language: to say no, Greeks lift their heads back abruptly while raising their eyebrows; to indicate yes, they emphatically nod once. A hand waving up and down that seems to say "stay there" actually means "come." For help deciphering and transliterating the Greek alphabet, as well as basic phrases in Modern Greek, see p. 957. Keep in mind there are exceptions—for instance, Φ and φ are often spelled *ph*.

LOCAL FACTS

Time: Greece is 2hr. ahead of Greenwich Mean Time (GMT).

Climate: The islands are a bit milder than the mainland, and northern Greece's high altitude areas are cooler. Summer is sunny and sticky—it's almost impossible to escape the heat and humidity without A/C or a beach. Winter temperatures hover around 50°F; Oct.-Mar. is the rainy season.

Hours: Normal **business hours** in Greece include a break from about 2pm until 6pm or so. Hours vary from place to place. **Banks** are normally open M-F 8am-1:30pm, and also 3:30-6pm in some larger cities.

Holidays: Feast of St. Basil/New Year's Day (Jan. 1); **Epiphany** (Jan. 6); First Sunday in **Lent** (Mar. 18); **Greek Independence Day** (Mar. 25); **Good Friday** (Apr. 13); **St. George's Day** (Apr. 23); **Easter** (Apr. 25); **Labor Day** (May 1); **Ascension** (May 25); **Pentecost** (June 4); **Feast of the Assumption of the Virgin Mary** (Aug. 15); The **Virgin Mary's Birthday** (Sept. 8); **Feast of St. Demetrius** (Oct. 26); National Anniversary of Greek Independence (Oct. 28); Commemoration of an uprising of Greek university students (Nov. 17); **Christmas** (Dec. 25).

Festivals: Greeks take a good 3 weeks to get ready for the Lent Fast, feasting and dancing throughout Carnival (Jan. 31-Feb. 22); Patras and Cephalonia celebrate with particular zest. Apr. 23 is **St. George's Day,** when Greece—especially Limnos and Hania—honor the dragon-slaying knight with horse races, wrestling matches, and dances. The **Feast of St. Demetrius** (Oct. 26), is celebrated with particular enthusiasm in Thessaloniki, coinciding with the opening of new wine.

ATHENS (Αθηνα) ☎01

One minute dodging the packs of mopeds in Pl. Syndagma will convince you that Athens refuses to become a museum. Athens's historical skeletons aren't bottled in the closet, though: they jut up through the modern city in glowing white marble. The Acropolis looms larger than life over the city, a perpetual reminder of ancient glory. Byzantine churches recall an era of foreign invaders, when Athens was ruled from Macedonia, Rome, and Byzantium. The reborn democracy has revived the city in a wave of madcap construction: the conflicted, oddly adolescent metropolis gutted its crumbling medieval mansions to become a dense concrete jungle.

⌐ TRANSPORTATION

Flights: The **East Air Terminal** handles international and charter flights by international carriers; the **West Air Terminal** is only for domestic and international Olympic Airways flights (☎ 936 3363; 144 for a timetable recording). The **New Charter Terminal** is only for charter flights.

Trains: (☎ 145 or 147 for timetables.) Contact the railway offices to confirm schedules before your trip. **Larissis Train Station** (☎ 529 8837) serves northern Greece and Europe. Open 24hr. Take trolley #1 from Panepistimiou in Syndagma (every 10min. 5am-midnight, 120dr). Trains depart for: **Thessaloniki** (7¼hr., 10 per day, 4100-5850dr) and **Prague, Czech Republic** (35,000dr). **Peloponnese Train Station** (☎ 513 1601) is open 24hr, and serves **Patras** (1580dr) and major towns in the Peloponnese. For more info, try the office of **Hellenic Railways (OSE)**, Sina 6 (☎ 362 4402).

Buses: Terminal A: Kifissou 100 (☎ 512 4910). Take blue bus #051 there; catch it at the corner of Zinonos and Menandrou near Pl. Omonia (every 15min., 120dr). Buses depart for: **Corfu** (10hr., 4 per day, 8150dr); **Corinth** (1½hr., 1 per hr., 1750dr); **Patras** (3hr., 20 per day, 3650dr); and **Thessaloniki** (7½hr., 6 per day, 8700dr) via Larissa. **Terminal B:** Liossion 260 (☎ 831 7153, M-F). Take blue bus #024 there; catch it on Amalias street outside the National Gardens on Panepistimiou, and allow 45min. for the trip (every 20min. 5am-11pm, 120dr). Buses depart for **Delphi** (3hr., 6 per day 7:30am-8pm, 2900dr).

Ferries: Check schedules at the tourist office, in the *Athens News,* with the Port Authority of Piraeus (☎ 422 6000), or at travel agencies. Most ferries dock at **Piraeus;** some nearby **Rafina.** Those headed for the Sporades leave from **Ag. Konstantinos** or **Volos.**

Public Transportation: KTEL (ΚΤΕΛ) **buses** are punctual, so be on time. Buses around Athens and its suburbs are blue and designated by 3-digit numbers. Buy blue bus/trolley **tickets** at any street **kiosk.** Hold on to your ticket: you can be fined 1500dr by police. **Trolleys** are yellow and crowded, sporting 1- or 2-digit numbers, trolleys are distinguished from buses by their electrical antennae. Trolleys don't accept money; buy a trolley/bus **ticket** ahead of time at a **kiosk** (120dr). **Subway:** The Athens **Metro** is under construction, creating branches from the current single line from Piraeus to Kifisia in northern Athens. Trains depart from either end of the line every 5min. 5am-midnight. Buy **tickets** (120dr) at booths or at automatic machines in the station.

Car Rental: Try the many places on **Singrou.** All charge 10,000-15,000dr for a small car with 100km mileage included (prices include tax and insurance). International Driver's License not needed.

Taxis: Meter **rates** start at 250dr, with an additional 66dr per km within city limits, 130dr per km in the suburbs, 33dr per stationary min. Rates double between midnight and 5am. There's a 300dr surcharge for trips from the airport and a 150dr surcharge for trips from ports and bus and railway terminals; plus 50dr for each piece of luggage.

PIRAEUS PORT: FERRIES FROM ATHENS

Piraus is the port town for Athens, although it is a separate town, the majority of ferries from Athens leave from Piraeus Port. Ferries leave **Piraeus** for: **Chios** (9-11hr., 1 per day, 5400dr); **Hania,** Crete (10hr., 8:30pm, 5400dr); **Hydra** (1-4hr., 2 per day, 1900-3100dr); **Ios** (7½hr., 5090dr); **Iraklion,** Crete (10hr.; 7:30am, 8pm; 6400dr); **Lesvos** (9-11hr., 1 per day, 5400dr); **Milos** (3-5½hr., 1 per day, 3900-4800dr); **Mykonos** (6hr., 2 per day, 4800dr); **Naxos** (6hr., 3 per day, 4800dr); **Paros** (6hr., 3 per day, 4800dr); **Poros** (1-4hr., 2 per day, 1900-3100dr); **Rethymno,** Crete (10hr., 7:30pm, 6500dr); **Rhodes** (16hr.; 2pm, 4pm; 8600dr); **Santorini** (9hr., 5630dr); **Serifos** (3-5½hr., 1 per day, 3900-4800dr); **Sifnos** (3-5½hr., 1 per day, 3900-4800dr); and **Spetses** (1-4hr., 2 per day, 1900-3100dr). From Athens, take the **metro** to the last southbound stop (20min.). Small **ferries** depart from Akti Poseidonos; larger ferries dock at Akti Miaouli; and international ferries are at the end of Akti Miaouli toward the Customs House.

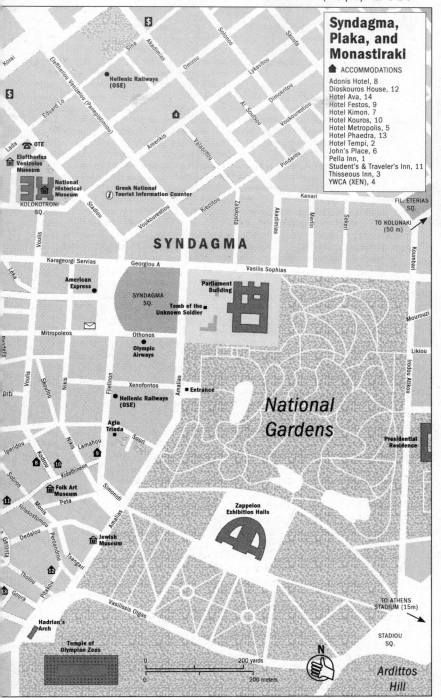

Syndagma, Plaka, and Monastiraki

🏠 ACCOMMODATIONS

Adonis Hotel, 8
Dioskouros House, 12
Hotel Ava, 14
Hotel Festos, 9
Hotel Kimon. 7
Hotel Kouros, 10
Hotel Metropolis, 5
Hotel Phaedra, 13
Hotel Tempi, 2
John's Place, 6
Pella Inn, 1
Student's & Traveler's Inn, 11
Thisseous Inn, 3
YWCA (XEN), 4

■✦ ❼ ORIENTATION AND PRACTICAL INFORMATION

GREECE

Athenian geography mystifies newcomers and natives alike. If you lose your bearings, ask for directions back to well-lit **Syndagma** or look for a cab; the **Acropolis** serves as a reference point, as does **Mt. Lycavittos.** Athenian streets often have multiple spellings or names, so check the map again before you panic. Listings and ferry information appears in the daily *Athens News* (300dr). Covering southwest **Attica,** near the coast, Athens and its suburbs occupy seven hills. Syndagma, the central *plateia* containing the Parliament building, is encircled by the other major neighborhoods. Clockwise, they are **Plaka, Monastiraki, Omonia, Exarhia, Kolonaki,** and **Pangrati.** Plaka, the center of the old city, and temporary home of most visitors to Athens, is bounded by the city's two largest ancient monuments—the **Temple of Olympian Zeus** and the **Acropolis.** Monastiraki's frenetic **flea market** is home to vendors who sell rugs, furniture, leather, *bouzoukis,* and all varieties of souvenirs. Omonia is the site of the city's **central subway station.** Two parallel avenues, **Panepistimiou** and **Stadiou,** connect Syndagma to Omonia. Omonia's neighbor to the east, progressive Exarhia sports some of Athens's most bumpin' nightlife, while nearby Kolonaki, on the foothills of Mt. Lycavittos, has plenty of glitz and swanky shops. Pangrati, southeast of Kolonak is marked by several Byzantine churches, a park, the **Olympic Stadium,** and the **National Cemetery.** A 30min. ride south takes you to the seaside suburb of **Glyfada,** where Bacchanites head to party.

Tourist Office: The **central office** and **information booth** are at Amerikis 2 (☎331 0561; fax 325 2815; www.areianet.gr/infoxenios/GNTO), near Pl. Syndagma. Bus, train, and ferry schedules, and an indispensable **map** of Athens available. Open M-F 9am-9pm, Sa-Su 10am-9pm. There's a branch of the national **tourist office** (☎961 2722; fax 964 1627) in the airport's East Terminal. Open M-F 9am-9pm, Sa-Su 10am-9pm.

Banks: National Bank of Greece, Karageorgi Servias 2 (☎334 0015), in Pl. Syndagma. Open M-Th 8am-2pm, F 8am-1:30pm; open for currency exchange only M-Th 3:30-6:30pm, F 3-6:30pm, Sa 9am-3pm, Su 9am-1pm. Currency exchange available 24hr. at the **airport,** but exchange rates and commissions may be exorbitantly high.

American Express: Ermou 2, P.O. Box 3325 (☎324 4975), above McDonald's in Pl. Syndagma. Cashes traveler's checks commission-free, holds mail for a month, and provides travel services for cardholders. Open M-F 8:30am-4pm, Sa 8:30am-1:30pm (only travel and mail services Sa).

Bookstores: Eleftheroudakis Book Store, Panepistimiou 17 (☎331 4180) and Nikis 4 (☎322 9388). A browser's delight, with Greek, English, French, and German books. Open M, W 9am-4pm; Tu, Th-F 9am-8:30pm; Sa 9am-3pm.

Laundromats: Most *plinitirios* have signs reading "Laundry." A kind Greek grandmother will wash, dry, and fold your laundry for 2000dr at **Angelou Geront 10** in Plaka. Open M-Sa 8am-8pm, Su 9am-2pm. Launder one load for 2700dr near the train stations, at **Psaron 9** (☎522 2856). Open M-F 8am-9pm, Sa 8am-5pm, Su 8am-2pm.

Emergencies: Police ☎100. **Doctors** ☎105 from Athens, 101 elsewhere; line open 2pm-7am. **Ambulance** ☎166. *Athens News* lists emergency hospitals. Free emergency health care for tourists.

Tourist Police: Dimitrakopoulou 77 (☎171). English spoken. Open 24hr.

Pharmacies: Identified by a red or green cross hanging over the street. Check *Athens News* for the day's emergency pharmacies, or look at the chart in pharmacy windows.

Hospitals: Geniko Kratiko Nosokomio (Public State Hospital), Mesogion 154 (☎777 8901). Near Kolonaki is a **public hospital,** Evangelismou 45-47 (☎722 0101). Hospital is *nosokomio* in Greek; call an operator at 131.

Internet Access: Deligrece Internet Cafe, Akadimias 87 (☎330 2929) has big-screen MTV broadcasts and espresso (650dr). 1000dr per hr. Open daily 7:30am-midnight.

Post Office: (☎322 6253) Pl. Syndagma, on the corner of Mitropolis. Address mail to be held: Becca MASSANARI, Pl. Syndagma Post Office, Athens, Greece **10300.** Open M-F 7:30am-8pm, Sa 7:30am-2pm, Su 9am-1:30pm.

ACCOMMODATIONS

The **Greek Youth Hostel Association,** Dragatsaniou 4, 7th floor, lists hostels in Greece. Go up Stadiou and then left on Dragatsaniou, then take the elevators on the right as you enter the arcade. (☎323 4107; fax 323 7590. Open M-F 9am-3pm.) The **Hellenic Chamber of Hotels,** Karageorgi Servias 2, inside the National Bank of Greece, provides info and reservations for hotels throughout Greece. Reservations require a cash deposit, length of stay, and number of people; you must call, fax, or email one month in advance. (☎323 7193; fax 322 5449; www.users.otenet.gr/ ~grhotels/index.htm. Open M-F 8:30am-2pm, Sa 9am-12:30pm.)

Hotel Dryades, Dryadon 4 (☎382 7116). Elegant Dryades offers some of Athens's nicest accommodations, with large rooms and private baths. Full kitchen and TV lounge. Breakfast 1500dr. Singles 10,000dr; doubles 14,000dr; triples 17,000dr.

George's International Students Inn, Nikis 46 (☎322 6474). Cross 2 streets with your back to the Parliament building and turn left onto Nikis. Most rooms have huge windows and open-air balconies. Curfew 1:30am (though you can try ringing the bell after hours). Closed Jan.-Feb. Dorms 3000dr; singles 5000dr; doubles 7000dr; triples 9000dr.

Hotel Festos, Filellinon 18 (☎323 2455). This backpacker-friendly hostel charges rock-bottom prices. Breakfast 500dr, dinner 1000dr. Dorms 2000-3500dr; singles 5000-7000dr; doubles 6000-8000dr; triples 12,000dr; quads 14,000dr. Monthly rates for students: singles 80,000dr; doubles 100,000dr.

YWCA (XEN), Amerikis 11 (☎362 4291), up the street from the tourist office. For women only. Spacious building has hand-wash laundry facilities, refrigerators on each floor, and a mini-cafeteria. 600dr membership fee or valid YWCA membership required. Singles 6000dr, with bath 7500dr; doubles 9000dr-9500dr; triples 12,000dr.

Thisseos Inn, Thisseos 10 (☎324 5960). Take Karageorgi Servias, which becomes Perikleous, and Thisseos is on the right. Close to Syndagma's sights but far from its noise. TV in reception area, full kitchen. Dorms 3500dr; singles 5000dr; doubles 7000dr; covered roof available in July for 2000dr (bring your own sleeping bag).

Student's and Traveler's Inn, Kidathineon 16 (☎324 4808). Superb location with inviting rooms, large courtyard, travel services, and internet access. Breakfast 6-11am (1000-1500dr). Singles 8-9000dr; doubles 10-11,000dr; triples 12,000-13,500dr; quads 14-16,000dr.

Hotel Metropolis, Mitropoleos 46 (☎321 7871), opposite Mitropoli Cathedral. Caters to privacy-oriented travelers. Private baths available. Singles 8000dr; doubles 12,000dr.

Pella Inn, Karaiskaki 1 (☎325 0598). Walk 10min. down Ermou from Pl. Syndagma; it's 2 blocks from the Monastiraki subway station. Near the hip hangouts of Monastiraki. Free luggage storage. Breakfast 800dr. Dorms 3000dr; singles 6000-8000dr; doubles 6000-9000dr, with bath 8-11,000dr; triples 9000dr; quads 10,000.

Athens International Hostel (HI), Victor Hugo 16 (☎523 4170). Walk down Tritis Septembriou from Pl. Omnia, and take a left on Veranzerou, which becomes Victor Hugo after crossing Marni. The only HI-affiliated youth hostel in Greece. HI membership (4200dr) required. Hot water 6-10am and 6-10pm. Full kitchen. Dorms 1720dr.

Hotel Orion, Em. Benaki 105 (☎382 7362). From Pl. Omonia, walk up Em. Benaki or take bus #230 from Pl. Syndagma. Orion rents small rooms with shared baths. Breakfast 1500dr. Singles 7000dr; doubles 9000dr; triples 11,000dr.

Youth Hostel #5 Pangrati, Damareos 75 (☎751 9530). From Pl. Syndagma take trolley #2 or 11 to Filolaou, or walk through the National Garden, 3 blocks down Eratosthenous Efthidiou to Damareos. There's no sign for this cheery hostel—just the number 75 and a green door. TV lounge, full kitchen facilities. Hot showers 50dr for 20min. Sheets and pillowcases 100dr each. Laundry 800dr. Quiet hours 2pm-5pm and 11pm-7am. Dorms 2000dr; roof beds 1500dr (bring a sleeping bag).

ⓕ FOOD

Athens offers a melange of stands, open-air cafes, side-street *tavernas*, and intriguing restaurants. Cheap fast food abounds in Syndagma and Omonia—try *souvlaki* (250-400dr), served either on a *kalamaki* (skewer) or wrapped in *pita; tost* (a grilled sandwich of variable ingredients, usually ham and cheese, 300-600dr); *tiropita* (hot cheese pie, 300dr); or *spanakopita* (hot spinach pie, 300dr). A *koulouri* (doughnut-shaped, sesame-coated roll; 50-100dr) makes for a quick breakfast. Pick up basic **groceries** at the minimarket on **Nikis.**

⬛ Eden Vegetarian Restaurant, Lissiou 12 (☎324 8858). Take Kidathineon to Tripidon, then left on to Lysiou; on the first corner. Greece's first vegetarian restaurant has dishes like eggplant salad (900dr) and hummus (900dr). Open W-M noon-midnight.

Kentrikon, Kolokotroni 3 (☎323 2482), near Stadiou, next to the National Historical Museum. Traditional (and lovely) Greek lunches cost around 2500dr. Vegetarian options. Open M-F noon-6pm.

O Platanos, Diogenous 4 (☎322 0666), on a street parallel to Adrianou. This restaurant takes its name from the *platanos* tree towering over the table-filled courtyard. Veal with potatoes, rice, or *fricasse* 1800dr. Open M-Sa noon-4:30pm and 8pm-midnight.

Oineas, Aisopou 9 (☎321 5614), off Karaisaki by the Pella Inn. The best food in Monastiraki: pink beet *tzatziki* (800dr), sausage in orange sauce (1400dr), veal filet in wine sauce (5000dr), pastas (2000dr), and salads (200-2500dr). Open Tu-Su 11am-2am.

Savas, Mitropoleos 86 (☎324 5048), tucked in a corner off Ermou. This grill is a budget eater's dream, with heavenly gyros (350dr). Don't sit down—prices skyrocket 1500dr extra. Open 8am-3am.

Revekka, Miaouli 22 (☎321 1174). At this authentic, menu-less eatery outside the touristy square, you'll get a plate of Greek delicacies the owner prepared that day (2000dr).

O Barba Giannis, Em. Benaki 94 (☎330 0185). From Syndagma, walk up Stadiou and make a right on Em. Benaki. Athenian students, execs, and artists all agree that "Uncle John's" is the place for cheap, delicious food and outstanding service. Lots of fish (from 950dr) and cheap wine (700dr); ask about today's choices. Open M-Su 9am-1am; closed Su in summer.

ⓢ SIGHTS

ACROPOLIS

Reach the entrance on the west side of the Acropolis either from Areopagitou to the south, by following the signs from Plaka, or by exiting the Agora to the south, following the path uphill, and turning right. ☎321 0219. Open daily 8am-6:30pm; in winter 8am-2pm. Site and Acropolis Museum 2000dr; students and EU seniors 1000dr; under 18 free.

Perched on a rocky plateau above the city, the Acropolis has crowned Athens since the 5th century BC. The brilliant Parthenon at its center towers over the Aegean and the plains of Attica, the greatest achievement of Athens's Classical glory and the era's most enduring architectural contribution. When you enter the Acropolis, the reconstructed **Temple of Athena Nike** lies before you. Though the Classical-era ramp that led to the Acropolis no longer exists, today's visitors still make an awe-inspiring climb. The path leads through the crumbling Roman **Beulé Gate,** named for the French archaeologist who unearthed it. It continues through the **Propylaea,** the incomplete entrance famous for its ambitious multi-level design begun by Mnesikles in the 5th century BC. Looming over the hillside, the **Temple of Athena Parthenos** (Athena the virgin), commonly known as the **Parthenon,** keeps vigil over Athens and the modern world. Iktinos designed the Parthenon to be the crowning glory of the Periclean project; he added two columns to the usual six in the front of the temple. Ancient Athenians saw their city as the capital of civilization, and the **metopes** (scenes in the open spaces above the columns) on the sides of the Parthenon celebrate Athens's rise. On the far right of the south side—the only side that has not been defaced—the Lapiths battle the Centaurs, on the east side, the Olympian gods defeat giants, while the north depicts the victory of the Greeks over the Trojans, and the west revels in their triumph against the Amazons.

The tiny cliff-side **Temple of Athena Nike** was raised during the Peace of Nikias, a respite from the Peloponnesian War. The temple, known as the "jewel of Greek architecture," is ringed by eight miniature Ionic columns and once housed a statue of the winged goddess Nike. One day, in a paranoid frenzy, the Athenians were seized by a fear that Nike would flee the city and take peace with her, so they clipped the statue's wings. The remains of the five-meter-thick **Cyclopean wall,** which predates the Classical Period, lie below the temple. The **Erechtheion,** to the left of the Parthenon, was completed in 406 BC, just before Sparta defeated Athens in the Peloponnesian War. The building housed many gods in its time, taking its name from the snake-bodied hero Erechtheus. Poseidon struck a truce with Athena, allowing them to share the temple—the east is devoted to the goddess of wisdom and the west to the god of the sea. The Erechtheion's south side is supported by six women frozen in stone, the Caryatids. They're actually copies—the originals are safe in the **Acropolis Museum,** which neighbors the Parthenon. It houses a superb collection of sculptures, including five of the original Caryatids of the Erechtheion. The statues seem to be replicas of one another, but a close look at the folds of their drapery reveals delicately individualized detail. Compare the stylized, entranced faces and frozen poses of the Archaic Period *Moschophoros* (calf-bearer) sculpture to the more idealized, more human Classical Period **Kritias** boy for a trip through developing Greek sculpture. *(Open M noon-6:30pm, Tu-Su 8am-6:30pm; in winter M 11am-2pm, Tu-Su 8am-2pm.)* The southwest corner of the Acropolis looks over the reconstructed **Odeon of Herodes Atticus,** a functional theater dating from the Roman Period (AD 160). See the *Athens News* for a schedule of concerts and plays there. You'll also see nearby ruins of the Classical **Theater of Dionysus,** the **Asclepion,** and the **Stoa of Eumenes II.** *(Enter on Dionissiou Areopagitou street. ☎ 322 4625. Open Tu-Su 8:30am-2:30pm. 500dr, students 250dr, children under 18 free.)*

AGORA. The Agora is Athens's heart; it served as the city's marketplace, administrative center, and center of daily life from the 6th century BC to AD 500. The debates of Athenian democracy were argued in the Agora; Socrates, Aristotle, Demosthenes, Xenophon, and St. Paul all preached here. Inhabited since 3000 BC, the Agora still stands at the center of Athens. Today, visitors have free reign over the 30-acre archaeological site it has become. *(Enter the Agora in one of three ways: off Pl. Thission, off Adrianou, or as you descend from the Acropolis. ☎ 321 0185. Open Tu-Su 8:30am-3pm. 1200dr, students and EU seniors 600dr, EU students and under 18 free.)* The **⬛Hephaesteion,** on a hill in the northwest corner of the Agora, is the best-preserved classical temple in Greece. The 415 BC temple still flaunts cool **friezes,** which depict Hercules's labors and Theseus's adventures. The **Odeon of Agrippa,** a concert hall built for Roman Emperor Augustus's son-in-law and right-hand man, now stands in ruins on the left of the Agora as you walk from the museum to the Hephaesteion. The elongated **Stoa of Attalos** was a multi-purpose building filled with shops and home to informal philosophers' gatherings. Attalos II, King of Pergamon, built the Stoa in the 2nd century BC as a 3D thank-you note to Athens for the education he had gotten there. Reconstructed between 1953 and 1956, it now houses the **Agora Museum,** which contains relics from the site. According to Plato Socrates' first trial was held at the recently excavated **Royal Promenade** of the Agora, the **Stoa Basileios.** *(Cross the subway tracks at the Adrianou exit and turn the left.)*

KERAMEIKOS. The Kerameikos's rigidly geometric design becomes clearly visible from above, before you enter the grounds; the site includes a large-scale cemetery and a 40m-wide boulevard that ran from through the Agora and the Diplyon Gate and ended at the sanctuary of **Akademos** (where Plato founded his academy). The **Oberlaender Museum** displays finds from the burial sites; its excellent collection of highly detailed pottery and sculpture is a highlight. *(Ermou 48, northwest of the Agora. From Syndagma, walk toward Monastiraki on Ermou for 25min. ☎346 3552. Open Tu-Su 8am-2:30pm. 500dr, students and EU seniors 300dr, EU students and under 18 free.)*

TEMPLE OF OLYMPIAN ZEUS AND HADRIAN'S ARCH. In the middle of downtown Athens, you'll spot the final trace of the largest temple ever built in Greece. The 15 majestic Corinthian columns of the Temple of Olympian Zeus mark where the temple once stood. Started in the 6th century BC, it was completed 600 years later by Roman emperor Hadrian, who attached his name to the centuries-long effort by adding his arch to mark the boundary between the ancient city of Theseus and Hadrian's own new city. (*Vas. Olgas at Amalias. Next to the National Garden. ☎ 922 6330. Open Tu-Su 8:30am-3pm. Temple 500dr, students and EU seniors 300dr, EU students and under 18 free. Arch free.*)

OLYMPIC STADIUM. The Panathenaic Olympic Stadium is wedged between National Gardens and Pangrati, carved into a hill. The site of the first modern Olympic Games in 1896, the city is ecstatic about hosting the **2004 Summer Olympics** at the new Irini Stadium. (*On Vas. Konstandinou. From Syndagma, walk up Amalias for 15min. to Vas Olgas, and follow it to the left. Or take trolley #2, 4, or 11 from Syndagma. Open daily 8am-8:30pm. Free.*)

AROUND SYNDAGMA. Don't miss the changing of the guard in front of the **Parliament** building. Every hour on the hour, two sets of *evzones* (guards) wind up like toy soldiers, kick their tassled heels in unison, and fall backward into symmetrical little guardhouses on either side of the **Tomb of the Unknown Warrior.** Athens's endangered species, greenery and shade, are preserved in the **National Gardens,** their natural environment. Women shouldn't stroll here alone.

MT. LYCAVITTOS. Of Athens's seven hills, Lycavittos is the largest and most central. Try ascending at sunset, when you can catch a last glimpse of Athens's densely packed continuous rooftops in daylight, and watch the city light at night. At the top you'll see the **Chapel of St. George,** where you might spy a couple tying the knot A leisurely stroll around the church will delight you with a truly incredible panorama of Athens. (*Open 8:45am-12:15am, Th 10:30am-12:15am.*)

NATIONAL ARCHAEOLOGICAL MUSEUM. The jaw-dropping collection in the National Archaeological Museum deserves a spot on even the most rushed itinerary. The museum begins with prehistoric pieces, including Heinrich Schliemann's **Mycenae** excavations. At first glance you may think the German archaeologist had the Midas touch—it is a world of gold, including the ⬛**Mask of Agamemnon,** the death mask of a king who lived at least three centuries earlier than Agamemnon himself. (*Patission 44. A 20min. walk from Pl. Syndagma down Stadiou until Aiolou and right onto Patission. ☎ 821 7717. Open Apr.-Oct. M 12:30-7pm, Tu-Su 8am-5pm; Nov.-Mar. 8am-5pm. 2000dr, seniors 1500dr, students and EU seniors 1000dr; free Su and holidays.*)

BYZANTINE MUSEUM. In an elegant Neoclassical building, the Byzantine Museum's excellent collection of Christian art spans the 4th through 19th centuries. A new wing is scheduled to open in 2001. (*Vas. Sofias 22. ☎ 723 1570. Open Tu-Su 8:30am-2:30pm. 500dr; students 300d; EU students, under 18 free. Guidebooks 2500dr.*)

NATIONAL GALLERY. The National Gallery (a.k.a. Alexander Soutzos Museum) exhibits the work of Greek artists, with periodic international displays. The permanent collection includes outstanding work by El Greco, as well as drawings, photographs, and sculpture gardens. (*Konstandinou 50. Set back from Vas. Sofias, next to the Hilton. Vas. ☎ 721 1010. Open M and W-Sa 9am-3pm, Su 10am-2pm. 1500d, students and seniors 500dr, under 12 free.*)

🎵 🎭 ENTERTAINMENT AND NIGHTLIFE

That uniquely Greek hybrid, the cafe/bar, flourishes throughout Athens. You can start your night early with a coffee and move on to a boozy binge at the same place. If you like the nightlife, you might warm up after a long meal at the cafe/bars in the city, then head out to the summer wonderland of **Glyfada** later. **Kolonaki** is brimming with cafes/bars. Try Millioni street by **Jackson Hall** or Haritos street by Plut. Summertime performances are staged in Lycavittos Theater as part of the **Athens Festi-**

val, which has included acts from the Greek Orchestra to Pavarotti to the Talking Heads. The **Festival Office,** Stadiou 4, sells student tickets. (☎322 1459. Open M-F 9:30am-4pm, Sa-Su 9:30am-2pm. Tickets 3000-5000dr.) The **Athens Flea Market,** adjacent to Pl. Monastiraki, is a potpourri of second-hand junk and high-rent antiques. (Open M, W, Sa, and Su 8am-3pm; Tu, Th, F 8am-8pm.)

Cine Paris, Kidatheneon 22 (☎322 2071). Enjoy your own *cinema paradiso* in the Athenian night breeze. Check *Athens News* for showtimes of the twice-nightly second run English-language films. Tickets 2000dr.

Bee, at the corner of Miaoli and Themidos, off Ermou; a few blocks from the heart of Psiri. DJs spin upstairs in this 3-floor, patio-equipped Athenian artistic hub. Drinks 1000-2500dr. Open 8pm to 3 or 4am.

Jazz in Jazz, Dinokratous 4. Endless old jazz records on the box draw Athens's faithfuls. Cover 1500dr; includes one drink. Open noon-3am.

Moc@fe Internet Cafe, Marnis 49 and Venanzerou (☎522 7717). This hip cafe jacks you in to a fast connection and cheap drinks. Coffees 500dr, beers 700-1000dr. 500dr for the first 20min., 1500dr per hour. Open 9am-midnight, depending on business.

The Daily, Xenokratous 47 (☎722 3430). A cafe/bar hybrid where chic foreign student populations converge to imbibe, enjoy Latin music and reggae, and watch soccer on TV. Fabulous open-air bar. Pints of Heineken 1000dr. Open 9am-2am.

Cafe 48, Karneadou 48 (☎725 2434), 2 blocks up the hill from Vas. Sofias. Expat classicists hang here, as do student travelers. With your student ID, beer costs 800dr and punch 1000dr. Open M-Sa 9am-2am, Su 4pm-2am.

DAYTRIPS FROM ATHENS

TEMPLE OF POSEIDON

Two bus routes run to Cape Sounion from Athens; the shorter and more scenic route leaves from the Mavromateon 14 stop near Areos Park in Athens (2hr., every hr. 6:30am-6:30pm, 1200dr).

Gracing the highest point on the Cape, the Temple of Posiedon has been a dazzling white landmark for sailors at sea for millennia. The original temple was constructed around 600 BC, destroyed by the Persians in 480 BC, and rebuilt by Pericles in 440 BC. The 16 remaining Doric columns sit on a promontory at **Cape Sounion,** 65km from Athens. (☎39 363. Open daily 10am-dusk. 800dr, students 400dr, EU students free.)

MARATHON

The bus from the Mavromateon 29 station in Athens heads to Marathon (1½hr., every hr. 5:30am-10:30pm, 700dr); sit in the front to keep reminding the driver of your destination, and flag the bus down on the way back.

In 490 BC, when the Athenians defeated the Persians at the bloody battle of Marathon, the messenger Pheidippides ran 42km to announce the victory and then collapsed dead from exhaustion. Although modern marathoners repeat this feat (*sans* fatal collapse), twice annually on Pheidippides' very route, others choose to reach Marathon by less strenuous means via the bus from Mavromateon 29. Although the town itself isn't that inspiring, the five rooms of the **Archaeological Museum of Marathonas** are packed with exciting archaeological finds. Ask the driver to let you off at the sign ("Mouseion and Marathonas"), then follow the signs 2km through farmlands (bear right at the one unlabeled fork in the road) to the end of the paved road, 114 Plateion. (☎55 155. Open Tu-Su 8am-3pm. 1000dr; students 500dr; EU students, children under 18, and classics or archaeology students free.)

DELPHI

Buses leave Athens for Delphi from the station at Liossion 260 (3hr., 6 per day, 2900dr). Railpass holders can take the train to Livadia and catch the bus (7 per day, 800dr). Continue east down Pavlou to reach the Oracle site.

As any Delphinian will proudly attest, this town of 2500 marks the belly button (omphalos) of the earth. According to the ancients, Zeus discovered this fact by simultaneously releasing two eagles, one toward the east and one toward the west. They collided, impaling each other with their beaks, directly over Delphi. Troubled denizens of the ancient world journeyed to the Oracle of Apollo at Delphi, where the priestess of Apollo related the god's profound, if cryptic, advice. Modern Delphi is packed with tourists—visit early in the morning. Despite tourists, truly fascinating ruins make Delphi a rewarding daytrip. From the bus station, at the western end of Delphi, walk east on Pavlou toward Athens (with the mountain edge on your right) to reach the **tourist office,** Friderikis 12, in the town hall. (☎ 82 900. Open M-F 7:30am-10:30pm.) If transportation leaves you stranded in Delphi over night, you can stay at **Hotel Sibylla,** Pavlou 9, which has wonderful views and private baths at the best prices in town. (☎ 82 335. Singles 4000dr; doubles 6000dr; triples 8000dr.)

OTHER DAYTRIPS FROM ATHENS

CORINTH. Find love among the ruins in the ancient city at Corinth (see p. 531).

PATRAS. Greek's third-largest city has the largest Orthodox cathedral in Greece, and a restored Roman theater (see p. 526).

THE PELOPONNESE (Πελοποννεσος)

Connected to the mainland by the narrow isthmus of Corinth, the Peloponnese contains the majority of Greece's most stunningly well-preserved archaeological sites, including Olympia, Mycenae, Messene, Corinth, Mystra, and Epidavros; it has some of the country's most incredible landscapes, ranging from the barren crags of the Mani to the forested peaks of Arcadia. The starkly beautiful and sparsely populated Peloponnese remains a bastion of the rapidly disappearing Greek village life.

✂ FERRIES TO ITALY AND CRETE

Boats go from **Patras** to **Brindisi** (20hr.; 6-8000dr, plus 2200dr port tax), **Trieste, Bari, Ancona,** and **Venice, Italy.** Ferries also sail from **Gython** to **Crete** (7hr., 4900dr). The trip to or from Brindisi is free for **Eurail** holders on certain ferry lines. Check the travel offices on Iroon Polytechniou and Othonas Amplias in Patras for info about tickets, and ask about discounts for those under 25.

PATRAS (Πατρας)   ☎ 061

Sprawling Patras, Greece's third-largest city, serves primarily as a transport hub, but at **Carnival** (mid-Jan. to Ash Wednesday) the port becomes one big dance floor. During the rest of the year, spend your layover heading inland from town on Ag. Nikolaou and climbing the steps to the 13th-century Venetian **castle.** (Open daily 8am-7pm. Free). Then continue to the **Ancient Odeum,** a restored Roman theater. (Open Tu-Su 8:30am-3pm. Free.) Follow the water to the west end of town to reach **Agios Andreas,** the largest Orthodox cathedral in Greece, which holds magnificent frescoes and an unusual relic—the head of St. Andrew. (Open daily 9am-dusk. Dress modestly.) Sweet black grapes are transformed into *Mavrodaphne* wine at the **Achaïa Clauss winery,** where tourists can enjoy free samples of the most famous wine in the country. Check with tourist office for a schedule of daily tours, then take bus #7 from the intersection of Kolokotroni and Kanakari.

   Trains (☎ 73 694) also go from Othonos Amalias to: Athens (8 per day, 5hr., 1600dr-3000dr); Kalamata (4½hr., 2 per day, 1500dr); and Olympia (2hr., 8 per day, 820-1220dr) via Pyrgos. KTEL **buses** (☎ 62 38 86) go from Othonos Amalias, between Aratou and Zaïmi, to: Athens (3hr., 28 per day, 3800dr); Ioannina (4 per day, 4 per day, 4550dr); Kalamata (4½hr., 2 per day, 4350dr); Thessaloniki (9½hr., 3 per day,

8800dr); and Tripoli (4hr., 2 per day, 3250dr). Daily **ferries** go to Corfu (night ferry 6-8hr., 5800dr) as well as Ithaka via Cephalonia. From the docks, turn right after leaving customs and follow Iroon Polytechniou, which becomes Othonos Amalias, to reach the center of town. If you have a **Eurail** pass, head to **HML** (☎45 25 21), on Iroon Polytechniou near Customs, for your ferry ticket. The **tourist office** is on the waterfront at the Customs entrance. (☎430 195. Open M-F 7am-9pm.) Hotels are scattered on Ag. Andreas, one block up from the waterfront. The **Youth Hostel,** Iroon Polytechniou 68, occupies a slightly creaky old mansion. (☎427 278. Dorms 2000dr.) Patras's myriad pubs and cafes are generally indistinguishable and overpriced, you can self-cater from **Dia Discount Supermarket,** on Ag. Andreas near Kolokotroni. (Open Tu-Sa 9am-5pm.) **Postal Code:** 26001.

OLYMPIA (Ολυμπια)   ☎0264

Set among meadows and shaded by cypress and olive trees, modern Olympia is a friendly and attractive town that draws tourists with its mega-attraction—the ancient **Olympic arena.** Today, the remains of a gymnasium, palaestra, stadium, and several temples and treasures are scattered around **Ancient Olympia,** although they are not labeled or particularly well-preserved. Follow the main road 5min. out of town to reach the ruins and museum. Dominating the site is the gigantic **Temple of Zeus,** which once held a statue of the god by Phidias so beautiful that it was considered one of the **seven wonders of the ancient world.** On the north edge of the Altis lie the remains of the 7th-century BC **Temple of Hera,** the ruins' best-preserved structure and the site of the quadrennial lighting of the **Olympic flame.** Across from the site, the **New Museum** houses an array of sculpture, that includes the **Nike of Paionios,** the **Hermes of Praxiteles,** the pedimental sculptures from the **Temple of Zeus,** and of course, a jumble of fun military spoils. (Site open daily 8am-7pm. Museum open M noon-7pm, Tu-Su 8am-7pm. 1200dr each, students 600dr; joint ticket 2000dr; EU students and children under 18 free.)

In New Olympia, **buses** run from opposite the tourist info booth to Tripoli (4hr., 3 per day, 2500dr). The **tourist office,** on Kondili, is on the east side of town toward the ruins. (☎231 00. Open M-F 8am-9pm, Sa 10am-5pm, closed Su.) The conveniently located **youth hostel** is at Kondili 18. (☎255 80. 1700dr. Breakfast 600dr. Check-out 10:30am. Dorms 1700dr.) **Camping Diana** is farther uphill on Kondili from Pension Poseidon. (☎22 745. 1600dr per person, 1000dr per car, 1200-16000dr per tent, adult with sleeping bag 1800dr.) **Minimarkets** along Kondili sell picnic fixings. Most eateries on Kondili are cramped and overpriced, but a walk toward the railroad station or up the hill reveals charming, inexpensive tavernas. **Postal Code:** 27065.

TRIPOLI (Τριπολη)   ☎071

Although you may have to dodge wild motorists while crossing the perilous streets of Urban Tripoli, the transport hub of Arcadia, the town offers pleasant squares and cafés to those awaiting the next bus out. The **Archaeological Museum** on Evangelistrias, in a yellow flower-bedecked building has an especially large prehistoric collection, including pottery, jewelry, and weaponry from the Neolithic to the Mycenaean periods. Four **trains** per day go to: Athens (4hr., 1500dr); Corinth (2½hr., 900dr); and Kalamata (2½hr., 840dr). **Buses** arrive at Pl. Kolokotronis, east of the center. From the station, follow Georgiou to Pl. Ag. Vasiliou; as you face the Church of Agios Vasiliou, take a left and head north on Ethnikis Antistasis to reach Pl. Petrinou. Buses go to: Athens (3hr., 14 per day, 3200dr); Kalamata (2hr., 12 per day, 1550dr); and Sparta (1hr., 10 per day, 1000dr). Crash at **Hotel Alex,** Vas. Georgios 26, between Pl. Kolokotronis and Pl. Agios Vasiliou. (☎22 34 65. Singles 7000dr; doubles 10,000dr, with bath 13,500.) **Postal Code:** 22100.

🖪 DAYTRIPS FROM TRIPOLI: DIMITSANA AND STEMNITSA. West of Tripoli, the enticing villages of Dimitsana and Stemnitsa are excellent bases for **hiking** excursions into the idyllic, rugged countryside. The quintessential Arcadian village of **Dimitsana,** clinging to a steep, rocky mountainside covered with pines, is nearly untouched by modern life or tourists. **Buses** run to Dimitsana from Tripoli (1½hr.,

1-3 per day, 1200dr). Buses to Tripoli and Olympia make frequent stops in **Karkalou,** a 20min. taxi ride (1000dr). Widespread domatia are really the only option, but fortunately, most establishments are beautifully furnished. The home of **Basilis Tsiapa** is set back from the road, through the *plateia*, before the road bends left (you'll see the Rooms to Let signs), and has gorgeous rooms with double beds. (☎31 583. Singles 9000dr; doubles 10,000dr.) A charming 11km stroll (or a 1000dr a taxi ride) along the road from Dimitsana will bring you to **Stemnitsa,** with narrow, irregular cobblestoned streets that betray its medieval roots. Many consider the town the most beautiful in Greece. The splendid **Hotel Triokolonion,** the only one in town, is on the left side of the main road from Dimitsana. (☎0795 81 297. Breakfast included. Reserve ahead. Singles 7800dr; doubles 10,600dr.)

KALAMATA (Καλαματα)   ☎0721

Kalamata, the second largest Peloponnesian city, flourishes as a port and beach resort. The survivor of a violent history, the **Castle of the Villehardouins** crowns a hill above the old city. The castle encircles an open-air theater, which hosts "Cultural Summer of Kalamata" in July and August, featuring jazz, rock, and classical Greek drama. Take the bus from Kalamata (1hr., M-Sa 2 per day, 500dr) to the well-preserved ruins of **Ancient Messene** in nearby **Mavromati,** which constitute one of Greece's most impressive archaeological sites. While the remains of a theater, stadium, gymnasium, public baths, and nine different temples have been uncovered, it is the city's **defensive walls** that usually receive the most attention. The 3m-thick walls circle a 9km perimeter, and represent the massive heft of 3rd- and 4th-century BC military architecture. A **museum** at the site houses statues and other objects. (Open daily 8:30am-3pm. 500dr, students 300dr, EU students free.) **Trains** run from Sideromikou Stathmou to: Athens (7hr., 4 per day, 2160dr); Corinth (5¼hr., 1640dr); Olympia (3hr., 900dr); Patras (5½hr., 1500dr); and Tripoli (2½hr., 840dr). **Buses** arrive in Kalamata from: Athens (4hr., 11 per day, 4400dr); Corinth (3hr., 3000dr); Patras (4hr., 2 per day, 4150dr); Sparta (2hr., 2 per day, 1150dr); and Tripoli (2hr., 1550dr). Turn right on Frantzi at the end of Pl. Georgiou and walk a few blocks to reach the town center. **Tourist information** is available at **D.E.T.A.K.,** Polivou 6, just off Aristomenous near the Old Town. Rooms to let and budget accommodations are uncommon in Kalamata. To get to **Hotel Nevada,** Santa Rosa 9, take bus #1 and get off as soon as it turns left along the water. (☎824 29. Singles 5000dr; doubles 7000dr; triples 8000dr.) **Pension Avra,** Santa Rosa 10, has sunny rooms with shared baths. (☎82 759. Singles 6000dr; doubles 7000dr.) Before leaving town, sample the famous Kalamata **olives** and figs. The immense **New Market,** across the bridge from the bus station, has an assortment of meat, cheese, and fruit shops, as well as a daily farmer's market. **Postal Code:** 24100.

PYLOS AND METHONI

With its delightful beaches, Ottoman fortress, museum, and splendid views of Navarino, the Peloponnese's largest natural bay, the town of Pylos is wonderfully and mystifyingly untouristed. Just 15min. from Pylos by bus, With hibiscus-lined streets and a relaxed atmosphere, Methoni's hibiscus-lined streets and relaxed atmosphere serve as a reprieve from the bustle of Kalamata. Known as the "Camelot of Greece," Methoni was once used as bait by Agamemnon to lure the sulking Achilles back to war.

▐ **TRANSPORTATION. Buses** (☎22 230) go to: **Kalamata** (1½hr., 9 per day, 1000dr); **Athens** (6½hr., 2 per day, 2300dr); and **Finikoundas** (1hr., 4 per day, 450dr) via **Methoni** (15min., 6 per day, 250dr). No buses travel directly to **Koroni,** but you can go through Finikoundas and take a bus to **Horokorio,** the stop nearest Koroni. Buses leave for **Kyparissia** (1½hr., 5 per day, 1200dr), stopping at **Nestor's Palace** (30min., 400dr) and **Hora** (45min., 500dr); service is reduced on weekends. Buses go to **Pylos** (15min., 7 per day, 250dr) and **Finikoundas** (30min., 4 per day, 300dr), with a reduced schedule Saturday and Sunday.

⚠ PRACTICAL INFORMATION. The **tourist police** are in the same building as the **police,** on the left side of the waterfront, going uphill. (☎23 733. Open 8am-2pm.) The **post office** is on Nileos, uphill to the left from the bus station. (☎22 247. Open M-F 7:30am-2pm.) **Postal Code:** 24001.

⌂⌂ ACCOMMODATIONS AND FOOD. There are several **Rooms to Let** signs as the bus descends into Pylos from Kalamata. Expect to pay 4-6000dr for singles, 6-10,000dr for doubles, and 8-12,000dr for triples. Perhaps the cheapest accommodations in town are found at the **Pension,** just before the OTE, with high-ceilings, private baths and A/C. (☎22 748. Singles 5000dr; doubles 7000dr; triples 9000dr.) **Hotel Nilefs,** Rene Pyot 4, has balconies with charming sea-views. (☎22 518. Singles 9000dr; doubles 10,000-12,000dr; triples 13,000dr.) **Navarino Beach Camping** is 6km north at **Yialova Beach.** (☎22 761. Electricity 800dr. 1400dr per person; 1000dr per small tent; 1300dr per large tent.) **Seaside Camping Methoni** is a 5min. walk down the beach to the right of the *plateia.* (☎31 228. 1100dr per person; 610dr per car; 700dr per small tent; 810dr per large tent; prices lower May-June and Sept.-Oct.) Pylos's waterfront restaurants cook up taverna staples accompanied by sunset views of the sea. In the waterfront *plateia,* **Meltemi** serves excellent traditional entrees. (Feta with olive oil 700dr, *moussaka* 1400dr.)

⊡⊡ SIGHTS AND ENTERTAINMENT. Historic fortresses guard both sides of Navarino Bay. **Neocastro,** to the south, is easily accessible from Pylos; walk up the road to Methoni and turn right. The well-preserved walls enclose a fast-decaying church, along with a citadel and a collection of engravings. (☎22 448. Open Tu-Su 8:30am-3pm. 800dr, seniors and students 400dr, EU students free.) A few small **beaches** surround the town. Although the sand is devoured by the ocean when the tide is in, the clear, choppy waters can still be fun for active beach-goers. The strikingly lovely, long, and wider **Yialova Beach** is 6km north of town; ask the bus driver to let you off there. To see the island of **Sfakteria** up close, you can take a **boat tour** that stops at various monuments to the **Battle of Navarino** and a sunken Ottoman ship. Inquire at the small booth on the waterfront or at the coffee bar under the police station. (1½hr. 10,000dr for 4 people. July-Aug. only.) No visitor to the southwest Peloponnese should miss Methoni's **Venetian fortress,** a 13th-century mini-city. A narrow bridge connects an islet and its fortified tower to the main structure with a whimsical touch of medieval defensive architecture. (Open M-Sa 8am-8pm, Su 9am-8pm. Free.)

SPARTA AND MYSTRA (Σπαρτη, Μυστρας)

Citizens of today's Sparta make olive oil, not war. Built directly on top of the ancient warrior city, quiet, modern Sparta has meager ruins with which to occupy its tourists. Its pleasant public gardens and broad, palm-lined boulevards make it hospitable, and it is by far the best base for exploring the more impressive ruins of Byzantine Mystras, 6km away. **Buses** arrive in Sparta from: Athens (3½hr., 9 per day, 3800dr); Areopolis (1hr., 4 per day, 1300dr); Corinth (2hr., 2400dr); Gythion (1hr., 5 per day, 800dr); Monemvassia (2hr., 3 per day, 1800dr); and Tripoli (1hr., 1100dr). To reach the town center from the bus station, walk 10 blocks west on Lykourgou; the **tourist office** is to the left of the town hall in the *plateia.* (☎ (0731) 24 852. Open daily 8am-2pm.) The **Hotel Laconia,** on Pelagou, rents slightly dim rooms. (☎ (0731) 28 952. Singles 8000dr; doubles 12,000dr.)

Mystras was once the religious center of all Byzantium, and the locus of Constantinople's rule over the Peloponnese. Its extraordinary ruins comprise a city of Byzantine churches, chapels, and monasteries. Don't miss the beautiful **Metropolis of St. Demetrios** on the lower tier, with its detailed frescoes, flowery courtyard, and museum of architectural fragments. At the extreme left of the lower tier, every inch of the **Church of Peribleptos** is bathed in exquisitely detailed religious painting; despite Ottoman vandalization, these paintings remain Mystra's most stunning relics. Dress modestly while exploring the ruins. (Open daily 8am-7pm; in winter 8:30am-3pm. 1200dr, students 600dr, EU students free.) **Buses** from Sparta to Mystra stop at the corner of Lykourgou and Kythonigou (20min., 9 per day, 220dr), two blocks past the town *plateia* away from the main bus station.

GYTHION AND AREOPOLIS (Γυθειο, Αρεοπολη)

Formerly plagued by violent family feuds and savage piracy, the sparsely settled **Mani** (Μανη) province's name comes from the word *manis*, Greek for wrath or fury, and history has affirmed its etymological roots many times. Today, the fire behind Maniot fury has been cooled by a coastal breeze, and the Maniots play excellent hosts to the visitors who stay in their traditional gray-stone tower houses, seeking beautiful beaches and views. **Gythion,** the "Gateway to the Mani," is the liveliest town in the region, near sand and stone beaches. A tiny causeway connects it to the island of **Marathonisi,** where Paris and Helen once consummated their ill-fated love; to reach the mythic love nest, follow the harbor road to the right. **Buses** arrive in Gythion at the north end of the waterfront from: Athens (4hr., 6 per day, 4700dr); Corinth (3hr., 3350dr); Kalamata (2 per day, 2050dr); Sparta (1hr., 850dr); and Tripoli (2hr., 1850dr). To explore the hard-to-reach parts of Mani, try **Moto Makis Rent-A-Moped,** on the waterfront near the causeway. (5000dr per day. Open daily 8:30am-8:30pm.) **Xenia Karlaftis Rooms,** on the water 20m from the causeway, rents spacious rooms with private baths. (☎22 719. Singles 5000dr; doubles 6000dr; triples 7000dr.) **Meltemi Camping,** is 4km toward Areopolis. (☎22 833. 1500dr per person, 1200dr per tent, 850dr per car, 1300 per tent.) **Postal Code:** 23200.

Though **Areopolis** neighbors the sea, its buildings dominate the scenery: stone tower houses and cobbled streets are framed by the dramatic purple peaks of the Taygetus. Just 4km from Areopolis, part of a subterranean river, the unusual **Vlihada Cave** (Spilia Dirou or Pyrgos Dirou) is cool, quiet, and strung with tiny crystalline, vermilion stalagmites. Discovered at the end of the 19th century, it was opened to the public in 1971; it has yet to be fully explored. (Open daily June-Sept. 8am-5pm; Oct.-May 8am-5:30pm. 3500dr.) A bus running into the Mani takes you to the **Vlihada Lake Caves** (11am, returns 12:45pm; 250dr). **Buses** stop in Areopolis' main *plateia* and go to: Athens (6hr., 5000dr); Gythion (30min., 4 per day, 500dr); Kalamata (2½hr., 2 per day, 1400dr); and Sparta (1½hr., 4 per day, 1250dr). To stay at **Tsimova,** turn left at the end of Kapetan Matapan. (☎51 301. Singles 6000dr; doubles 8000dr; triples 12,000dr; quads 14,000dr.) **Postal Code:** 23062.

GEFYRA AND MONEMVASSIA (Μονεμβασια)

The island of Monemvassia, one of the major tourist sights on the Peloponnese, has an other-worldly quality. No cars or bikes are allowed on the island; pack horses bear groceries into the city, and narrow streets hide stairways, child-sized doorways, and flowered courtyards. From Monemvassia gate, a cobblestoned main street winds up past tourist shops and restaurants to the town square. At the edge of the cliffs perches the oft-photographed 12th-century **Agia Sofia;** to get there, navigate through the maze of streets to the edge of town farthest from the sea, where a path climbs the side of the cliff to the tip of the rock. Stay in more modern and less expensive **Gefyra;** from there, it's a 20 min. walk down 23 Iouliou along the waterfront to the causeway. From there an **orange bus** runs between the causeway and Monemvasia gate all day long (every 10min. 8am-midnight, 100dr). Three buses per day leave to: Athens (6hr., 5800dr) via Molai (20min., 500dr); Corinth (5hr., 4450dr); Sparta (2½hr., 1900dr); and Tripoli (4hr., 2950dr). **Hotel Sophos** has recently renovated rooms for decent prices. (☎61 360. Singles 8000dr; doubles 10,000dr.) **Camping Paradise,** 3.5km along the water on the mainland, is more affordable. (☎61 123. 1400dr per person, 950dr per car, 900dr per small tent, 1200dr per large tent.) **To Limanaki,** offering lots of waterside seating on the mainland beside the harbor, serves exceptional Greek food, including excellent *pastitsio* (1300dr) and stuffed tomatoes (1100dr).

NAFPLION (Ναυπλιο)   ☎0752

Beautiful old Nafplion glories in its Venetian architecture, fortresses, pebble beach, and hillside stairways. The town's crown jewel is the 18th-century **Palamidi Fortress,** with its spectacular views of the town. To get there, walk the 3km road; or take a grueling 999 steps up from Arvanitias, across the park from the bus station. (Open M-F 8am-6pm, Sa-Su 8:30am-3pm; off-season daily 8:30am-3pm. 800dr, students 400dr, EU students free.) **Arvanitia,** Nafplion's small, pebbly beach, is along the road that curves around the left-hand side of Palamidi. **Buses** arrive on Singrou, off Pl. Kapodistrias, from Athens (3hr., every hr., 2650dr) and Corinth (2hr., 1100dr). To reach **Bouboulinas,** the waterfront promenade, from the bus station, go left as you exit and follow Singrou to the harbor—the **Old Town** is on your left. The **tourist office** is on 25 Martiou. (☎24 444. Open daily 9am-1pm and 4-8pm.) For the rooftop views of **Dimitris Bekas' Domatia** in the old town, turn up the stairs on Kokinou, and follow the sign for rooms off Staikopoulou; climb to the top, turn left, and go up another 50 steps. (☎24 594. Singles 5000dr; doubles 7000dr.) In the new town, try **Hotel Artemis** on Argos. (☎27 862. Singles 6000dr; doubles 6000dr.) **Taverna O Vasiles,** on Staikopoulou, serves rabbit (1650dr) that will delight even the most avid Beatrix Potter fans. **Postal Code:** 21100.

▨ DAYTRIPS FROM NAFPLION: MYCENAE AND EPIDAVROS. Excavations of ancient Mycenae have continued for 126 years, since Heinrich Schliemann first turned a spade here. Now Ancient Mycenae is one of the most visited sites in Greece, and mobs stampede to the famed Lion's Gate and Tomb of Agamemnon. (Open daily Apr.-Sept. 8am-7pm; Oct.-Mar. 8am-5pm. 1500dr, students 800dr, EU students free. Keep your ticket or pay again at Agamemnon's tomb.) Join the illustrious ranks of Heinrich Schliemann, Virginia Woolf, Claude Debussy, William Faulkner, Agatha Christie, and Allen Ginsberg, who have all stayed at **Belle Helene Hotel;** it also serves as a bus stop on the main road. (☎ (0751) 762 25. Singles 7000dr; doubles 10,000dr; triples 12,000dr.) The only direct **buses** to Mycenae are from Nafplion (30min., 4 per day, 600dr) via Argos (15min., 300dr). A bus from Athens (2½hr., 15 per day, 1800dr) stops at Fihtia, 1.5km away. From Fihtia, take the Corinth-Argos road and follow the sign to Mycenae to reach the site.

The grandest structure at the ancient site of **Epidavros** is the **theater,** built in the early 2nd century BC, with a capacity of 14,000 at its height. Henry Miller wrote that he heard "the great heart of the world" beat here; the incredible acoustics allow you to stand at the top row of seats and hear a *drachma* drop on stage. Near the theater and ruins of the sanctuary is Epidavros' **museum.** (Museum open daily 7:30am-7pm. 1500dr, students 800dr, EU students free.) From late June to mid-August, the **Epidavros Theater Festival** brings performances of classical Greek plays (in modern Greek, but it'll all be Greek to you) on Friday or Saturday nights. Shows are at 9pm; purchase tickets at the site or in advance in Athens, at the Athens Festival Box Office (☎ (01) 322 14 59), or at Nafplion's bus station (tickets 4000-6000dr, students 2000dr). **Buses** arrive in Epidavros from Nafplion (1hr., 5 per day, 600dr).

CORINTH (Κόρινθος) ☎0741

Most visitors to the Peloponnese make their first stop at New Corinth to gaze on the ruins of **Ancient Corinth,** at the base of the **Acrocorinth.** Columns, metopes, and pediments lie around the courtyard of the excellent **archaeological museum** in a tableau of fascinating chaos. As you exit the museum, the 6th-century BC **Temple of Apollo** is down the stairs to the left. The **fortress** at the top of Acrocorinth is a tough 1½hr. walk, but the struggle to the summit is rewarded with the opportunity to explore the surprisingly intact remains of the **Temple to Aphrodite,** where disciples were initiated into the "mysteries of love." (☎31 207. Open 8am-7pm, winter 8am-5pm. Admission to museum and site 1200dr, students 600dr.)

Buses leave **Ermou** and **Koliatsou Station** (☎24 481) for Athens (1½ hr., 32 per day, 1750dr). Buses leave the **Argolis Station** (☎24 403) for: Mycenae (750dr); Argos (900dr); and Nafplion (1200dr) every hour. **Trains** go from the station on Demokratias to: Athens (2hr., 14 per day, 900dr) via Isthmia and Patras (2½hr., 8 per day, 1000dr). The **Tourist Police,** Ermou 51, housed in the same building as the actual police, are near the bus station, and provide tourists with maps, brochures, and other general assistance. (☎23 282. Open M-Sa 8am-2pm and 5-8pm.) In New Corinth, **Hotel Akti,** Eth. Antistasis 3, is the best bet for inexpensive accommodations, with simple, utilitarian bedrooms and a convenient location. (☎23 337. Singles 5000dr; doubles 8000dr.) When mealtime comes, **AXINOS,** Damaskinou 41, offers cheery *al fresco* dining by the waterfront. (☎28 889. Pastitsio 1400dr, Greek salad 1200dr.)

GREECE

NORTHERN AND CENTRAL GREECE

A bastion of Greek culture under 19th-century Ottoman rule, the provinces of Thessaly, Epirus, Macedonia, and Thrace are oft-forgotten regions threaded with mountain paths that lead to some of Greece's clearest springs, most glorious vistas, and precious Byzantine treasures. Following these forgotten trails will lead you into a varied landscape of silvery olive groves, fruit-laden trees, and patchwork farmland.

THESSALONIKI (SALONICA; Θεσσαλονικη)

Thessaloniki fans out from its hilltop Byzantine-Turkish fortress to the Thermaic Gulf, a jumble of ancient, Byzantine, European, Turkish, Balkan, and contemporary Greek cultural and historical debris. At its peak, the fortress oversees the Old Town's placid streets and long, tree-lined avenues. Golden mosaics and frescoes, gleam in the Byzantine churches hidden on the industrial city's side-streets. Most travelers spend a few days in Thessaloniki clubbing and enjoying the sights, and then head out for countryside hikes or more sight seeing, or ship out to islands.

☞ TRANSPORTATION

Trains: Main Terminal (☎517 517), on Monastiriou in the western part of the city. Take any bus down Egnatia (100dr). To: **Athens** (6-8hr., 9 per day, 4250dr). **OSE** (☎51 81 13), at Aristotelous and Ermou, has tickets and schedules. Open M-Sa 8am-2:30pm.

Buses: Most **KTEL** buses depart from between the port and railway station or from north of the railway. To: **Athens** (6hr., 20 per day, 9000dr), from along Monastiriou; **Corinth** (7½hr., 10:30am, 9200dr), via Monastiriou 69 (☎527 265); and **Patras** (8hr., 2 per day, 8250dr).

Ferries and Hydrofoils: Buy tickets at **Karacharisis Travel and Shipping Agency**, Koundouriotou 8 (☎524 5 44). Open M-F 9am-9pm, Sa 9am-3pm. To: **Hios** (21hr.; Tu, F, Su midnight; 8300dr); **Lesvos** (9hr., W and Su 1am, 8300dr); **Limnos** (7hr.; Tu 6pm and midnight, W, F, Sa midnight; 5300dr); **Mykonos** (16hr.; M 2pm, Tu 3pm, and F 7:30pm; 9200dr); and **Samos** (14hr., W 1pm, 9500dr). **Flying Dolphins:** Buy tickets at **Crete Air Travel**, Dragoumi 1 (☎547 407), across from the main port. Open M-F 8:30am-9pm, Sa 8:30am-3pm, Su 9am-3pm. June-Sept., every day at 8am and Th-M in the afternoon (usually 4:30pm) to: **Alonnisos** (5hr., 9300dr); **Skiathos** (3¾hr., 8500dr); and **Skopelos** (4½hr., 9300dr).

Public Transportation: Extensive **buses** (100dr) traverse the city. Buses #8, 10, 11, and 31 run up and down Egnatia. Buy tickets at kiosks or ticket booths at major stations.

ⓘ ORIENTATION AND PRACTICAL INFORMATION

Running from the shore inland, the main streets are **Nikis, Mitropoleos, Tsimiski, Ermou, Egnatia,** and **Agios Dimitriou.** Intersecting these streets and running from the water into town are (west to east) **Dragoumi, El. Venizelou, Aristotelous, Agios Sophias,** and **Eth. Aminis.** Tsimiski, Mitropoleos, Ag. Sophias, and smaller streets between Aristotelous and Ipodromiou are the main shopping streets. The roads north of Ag. Dimitriou get smaller and steeper and lead up into the **old town.** Facing inland, go left on Mitropoleos to reach the **Ladadika** district.

Tourist Office: EOT, Pl. Aristotelous (☎27 18 88; fax 26 55 04), 1 block from the water. Open M-F 9am-5pm.

Consulates: United Kingdom, Venizelou 8 (☎278 006). Open M-F 8am-1pm and **U.S.,** Tsimiski 43 (☎242 900). Open M, W and F 9am-noon.

American Express: Memphis Travel, Aristotelous 3, 1st floor (☎282 351). Cashes **traveler's checks** (no commission) and exchanges currency (500dr flat commission). Open M-F 9:30am-3:30pm and Sa 9am-2pm.

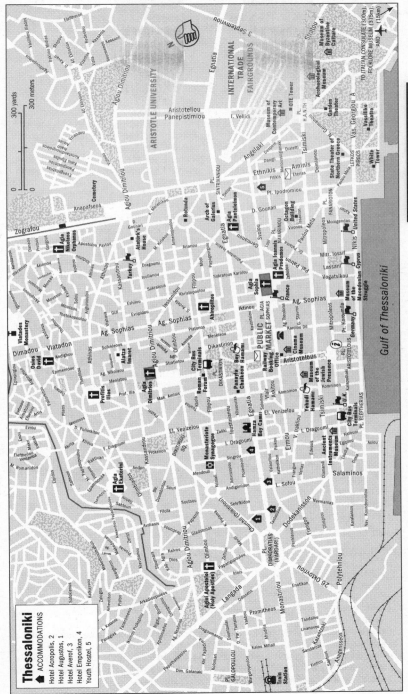

GREECE

Thessaloniki

▲ ACCOMMODATIONS

Hotel Acropolis, 2
Hotel Augustos, 1
Hotel Averof, 3
Hotel Emporikon, 4
Youth Hostel, 5

Laundromat: Bianca, L. Antoniadou 3 (☎209 602), behind the church to your right as you face the Arch of Galerius. 1800dr for wash, dry, and soap. Open M-Sa 8am-3pm.

Tourist Police: Dodekanissou 4, 5th floor (☎554 870). Free **maps** and brochures. English spoken. Open 24hr. For the general police, call ☎553 800, or 100. There are also police and tourist police booths at the train station.

Hospital: At **Ippokration Public Hospital,** A. Papanastasiou 49 (☎837 920), some doctors speak English. **Ahepa Hospital,** Kiriakidi 1 (☎993 111), is a private alternative. **Red Cross First Aid Hospital,** Koundouriotou 6 (☎530 530), offers free minor medical care at the entrance to the port. The **ETO** can help you find an English-speaking doctor.

Internet Access: Pl@net, 53 Alex. Svolu, across from the hostel, is the best in town. 600dr per hour from 10am-6pm, 800dr per hour 6pm-3am. The **British Council,** Eth. Aminis 9 (☎235 236), has free access. Open M-F 9am-1pm.

Post Office: On Aristotelous, just before Egnatia. Open M-F 7:30am-8pm, Sa 7:30am-2pm, Su 9am-1:30pm. A **branch** office, on Eth. Aminis near the White Tower (☎227 640), is open M-F 7am-8pm. **Postal Code:** 54101.

▞ ACCOMMODATIONS

Most of Thessaloniki's less expensive hotels are clustered along the western end of **Egnatia,** between Pl. Dimokratias (500m east of the train station) and Pl. Dikastiriou. Most are a bit gritty, ranging from ramshackle to merely cheerless. Egnatia is loud at all hours, but rooms on the street have balconies (read: air circulation). Women alone should be wary of the English-speaking "tourist information" people at the train station: they are often impersonators.

Hotel Augustos, Elenis Svoronou 4 (☎522 500). Walking down Egnatia, turn north at the Argo Hotel and Augustos is straight ahead. The best budget deal in Thessaloniki. Triples and doubles with bath have A/C and TVs; all rooms have phones. Singles 5000dr, with bath 8000dr; doubles 7000dr, with bath 11,00dr; triples with bath 13,000dr.

Youth Hostel, Alex. Svolou 44 (☎225 946). Take bus #8, 10, 11, or 31 west down Egnatia and get off at the Arch of Galerius (the Kamara stop); or walk toward the water and turn left after 2 blocks. Hot showers from 7am-11pm, in a cavelike basement. Reception 9am-11am and 7-11pm. Lockout 11am-6:30pm. Loosely enforced 1:30am curfew. Open Mar. 1-Nov. 30. Dorms 2500dr.

Hotel Acropolis, Tantalidou 4 (☎536 170). Tantalidou is the second right off Egnatia after Dodekanissou, coming from Pl. Dimokratias. Very quiet hotel with shared baths. Singles 5500dr; doubles 6500dr; triples 7500dr.

Hotel Averof, L. Sofou 24 (☎538 840), at Egnatia. Rooms are a bit bare and stuffy. Singles 6000dr, with bath 9000dr; doubles 8000dr, with bath 12,000dr.

Hotel Emporikon, Singrou 14 (☎525 560), at Egnatia. Quieter than most other hotels on Egnatia. All rooms share toilets. Singles 5000dr; doubles 8000dr, with shower 10,000dr; triples 12,000dr.

Hotel Tourist, Mitropoleos 21 (☎276 335), one block from Pl. Aristotelous. Centrally located hotel with rooms with bath, A/C, TV, and phone, some with balcony. Breakfast included. Singles 13,000dr; doubles 16,000dr; triples 21,000dr.

◖ FOOD

Pocketed on tiny sidestreets all over the city, Thessaloniki's **ouzeri** tables are veritable shrines to appetizer *mezedes,* upon which are heaped offerings to the gods of budget dining. The highest *ouzeri*-per-square-meter ratio can be found in the tiny streets on both sides of **Aristotelous,** while the innovative establishments a block down from Egnatia between **Dragoumi** and **El. Venizelou** cater to a younger clientele. The **open-air markets** of Vati Kioutou, just off Aristotelous to the east and west between Irakliou and Egnatia, are ideal for stocking up on fruits, veggies, bread, olives, cheese, candy, and fresh meats. The **Aretsou** area, along the bay about four kilometers toward the airport, has excellent seafood. The **Old Town** and the **Ladadika** district brim with inexpensive, family tavernas.

Ouzeri Melathron, on an alleyway between El. Venizelou and Dragoumi. From Egnatia, walk past the Ottoman Bedesten on El. Venizelou and make a right into the passageway between storefronts. Witty, 4ft. long menu features a spicy meat dish called "Lonely Nights" ("No nookie with this on your breath") and snails ("for friends of the hermaphrodite"). Main meals 1150-3600dr.

Ta Adelphi (☎266 432), in laid-back Pl. Navarino. Carnivorous meals at good prices. Popular, delicious, and very busy. Try the special chicken: it's stuffed with cheese and wrapped in bacon. Main meals 980-2750dr. Open daily noon-midnight.e

🔦 🎵 SIGHTS AND ENTERTAINMENT

The streets of modern Thessaloniki are littered with the remnants of its significance during both the Byzantine and Ottoman empires. There are ample churches to keep devout old women crossing themselves at a truly aerobic rate on the buses down Egnatia alone, not to mention those converted into mosques or squeezed in the tiny streets of the Old Town. **Agios Dimitrios,** on Ag. Dimitriou north of Aristotelous, is the city's oldest and most famous church. Although most of its interior was gutted in the 1917 fire, some lovely mosaics remain. (Open daily 8am-8pm.) South of Egnatia on the square that bares its name, **Agia Sophia** served as Thessaloniki's cathedral from the 8th century until 1523, when it was converted into a mosque. Originally part of a palatial complex designed to honor the Roman Emperor, the **Rotunda** became a church under the Byzantines. Its walls, though now under renovation, are plastered with some of city's most brilliant mosaics. (Open daily 7am-2:30pm.) A colonnaded processional once led south from the Rotunda to the **Arch of Galerius,** on the eastern end of Egnatia, which was built in the 4th century AD by Emperor Galerius to commemorate his victory over the Persians. Returning west down Egnatia, don't miss the **Bey Hamami,** which served as the bath house for the Ottoman governor and his retinue, or the **Hamza Bey Camii,** across from Venezeliou. The Camii was built in the 15th century and served as one of Thessaloniki's most prominent mosques until being converted into a movie theater in the 20th century.

Thessaloniki's **Archaeological Museum** is full of discoveries gleaned from Neolithic tombs, as well as mosaics from Roman houses, and a dazzling display of Macedonian gold. Check out the gold death masks and weapons found in the graves of Sindos. Take bus #10 down Egnatia to Pl. Hanth. (Open M 12:30-7pm, Tu-Su 8am-7pm; reduced in winter. 1500dr, students and seniors 800dr, EU students and under 18 free.) Just across the street on 3 Septembriou, the **Museum of Byzantine Culture** has three huge rooms detailing the lives of ancient Thessalonians, from church mosaics and elaborate tombs all the way to 1500 year-old personal effects like mirrors, combs, and wine jugs. (Open M 12:30-8pm, Tu-Su 8am-7pm; reduced hours in winter. 1000dr, students and seniors 500dr, EU students and under 18 free.) All that remains of a 15th-century Venetian seawall, the **White Tower** presides over the eastern edge of the waterfront like an overgrown chess piece. Once a site of bloody executions by the Ottoman Janissary corps, the Tower now fills a somewhat less belligerent role, housing a collection of early Christian art. (Open Tu-Su 8am-3pm. Free.) Right in the middle of the marketplace west of Aristoteliou, on the first floor of Irakliou 26, is the **Museum of the Jewish Presence,** which details the long history of Thessaloniki's Sephardic Jewish population. (On the first floor of an office building; ring the bell if door is closed. Open M-F 10am-1:30pm. Free.)

MOUNT OLYMPUS (Ολιμποσ)   ☎0352

Emerging from the Thermaic Gulf, the impressive height (nearly 3000m) and formidable slopes of Mt. Olympus once so awed the ancients that they proclaimed it the divine dwelling place of their gods. A network of well-maintained **hiking** trails now makes the summit accessible to just about anyone with sturdy legs and a taste for adventure, although at times you may yearn for a pair of Hermes' winged sandals. Two approaches to the peaks begin near **Litohoro** (280m), one at **Prionia** (1100m), 18km from the village, and one at **Diastavrosi** (also called **Gortsia;** 1300m), 14 km away. There is no bus to the trailheads from Litohoro, so you'll have to walk, hitch, or drive on the asphalt road. A **taxi** will cost you about 6000dr to Prionia or 1500dr to Diastavrosi. Unless you're handy with a crampon (and if you have to ask what that is, you're probably not) and an ice axe, you'll want to make your ascent between May and October. **Mytikas**, the tallest peak, is inaccessible without special equipment before June. There are three **refuges** near the summits where you can find lodgings. The EOS-run **Spilos Agapitos** ("Refuge A"; 2100m) is about 800 meters below **Skala** and Mytikas peaks. The English-speaking staff happily dispenses hiking info over the phone to prospective hikers, and can also help you reserve nights in other EOS refuges. (☎81 800. Meals served 6am-9pm. Lights out at 10pm. Open mid-May to late-Oct. 2500dr per bed, 2000dr for members of any mountain club; 500dr to tent nearby and use their facilities.)

Trains (☎22 522) run from Athens (7hr., 3 per day, 3500dr) and Thessaloniki (1½hr., 5 per day, 850dr) to the Litohoro station; from there walk 1km to the **bus stop** to catch a quick ride into town (20min., 13 per day, 250dr). A **taxi** from the train station should cost around 2000dr. Or take a direct KTEL **bus** (☎81 271) from Athens (6hr., 3 per day, 7400dr) or Thessaloniki (1½hr., 16 per day, 1750dr); they'll arrive at the station opposite the church in Litohoro's main *plateia*. Opposite the bus stop is the town's **tourist office.** (☎83 100. Open daily 8:15am-9:45pm.) The most affordable rooms are found at the **Hotel Park,** Ag. Nikolaou 23, about 10m from the *plateia*. (☎812 52. Singles 6500dr; doubles 8000dr; triples 9000dr.) **Camp at Olympus Zeus** (☎22 115) or **Olympus Beach** (☎22 112), on the beach about 5km from town.

METEORA (Μετεωρα)   ☎0432

The stunning beauty of the iron-gray pinnacles of the Meteora rock formations will take your breath away. They rise from the Thessalian plains and offer astonishing views of fields, forests, mountains, and monolithic stone. These wonders of nature are bedecked by 24 exquisite, gravity-defying Byzantine monasteries. Dress modestly; women must wear skirts. (Open Apr.-Sept. Sa-Su and W 9am-12:30pm and 3:20-6pm; staggered schedules during the rest of the week. 500dr per monastery.) The **Grand Meteoron Monastery** is the oldest, largest, and most touristed of the monasteries, with brilliant frescoes of the Roman persecution of Christians. The chapel of **Varlaam Monastery** contains 16th-century frescoes that include a particularly disturbing rendition of the Apocalypse. The most popular base for exploring Meteora is the town of **Kalambaka**. There will be **no train service** to Kalambaka due to construction of new rail lines, but **buses** arrive from: Athens (5hr., 8 per day, 5500dr); Ioannina (3hr., 2 per day, 2550dr); Patras (6hr., 2 per week, 5800dr); and Thessaloniki (3hr., 6 per day, 3700dr). From the bus station, walk uphill to reach the town's small central square. Local buses depart from Kalambaka for Meteora (20min., 9am and 1:20pm, 250dr); a **taxi** to Meteora from Kalambaka will cost about 1500dr. Most people walk the 6km downhill back to town, visiting the monasteries along the way. **Koka Roka,** in Kalambaka, offers an awe-inspiring view of the Meteora. From the central square, follow Vlachara uphill until it ends, then bear left and follow the signs to Kanari (15min.). (☎ (0432) 245 54. 3500dr per person; singles 6000dr w/ bath; doubles 8000dr w/bath; triples 10,000dr w/bath.) **Postal Code:** 42200.

OSIOS LOUKAS (Οσιος Λουκας)   ☎0267

Osios Loukas delights the eye with its mountain vistas and stunning Byzantine architecture. The exquisite monastery, built in the 10th and 11th centuries and still in use today, overlooks Boeotia and Phokis from the green slopes of Mt. Elikon more than 1700m above sea level. Gold-laden mosaics, vibrant frescoes, and intricate brick- and stonework adorn Osios Loukas, the most famous and perhaps the most gorgeous monastery in Greece. Dress modestly (long skirts for women, long pants for men, no bare shoulders). Two churches are at the site: the **katholikon,** on the right after the museum, built in AD 1011 and dedicated to the monastery's founding saint, Osios Loukas, is the most impressive of the monastery's jewels; the smaller **Church of Panagia** holds the dried body of the saint himself in a glass coffin, as well as a **crypt** with stunning frescoes that are not to be missed. (☎22 797. Open daily May 3-Sept. 15 8am-2pm and 4-7pm; Sept. 16-May 2. 8am-5pm. 800dr, seniors

400dr, under 18 and students.) Without a car or a lot of faith in the *very* sporadic traffic to the monastery (*Let's Go* does not recommend hitchhiking), you must hire a **taxi** (☎22 322; 5000-6000dr one-way) or walk along the hilly, narrow road from the town of Distomo, 9km west.

IOANNINA (Ιωαννινα)   ☎0651

On the shores of Lake Pamvotis lies Ioannina, the capital of and largest city in Epirus. The city has not yet escaped the intriguing, half-legendary historical presence of Ali Pasha, who was the Ottoman governor of Epirus before the Greek War of Independence and rebuilt the Byzantine walls of his dreamed-of capital. The walled **Frourio** (also known as the Castro), which juts regally over the lake, contains the old city. Enter on Karamanli; just inside the facing wall is a **synagogue,** Ioustinianon 16. Follow signs to the **Its Kale** (Inner Acropolis), which encloses the 18th-century **Fethiye Camii** (Victory Mosque), the **Byzantine Museum,** and the **tomb of Ali Pasha.** (☎27 761. Open M 12:30-7pm and Tu-Su 8:30am-5pm; Nov.-June Tu-Su 8am-2:30pm. 500dr; students free.) The smaller of the Frourio's walled inner areas is a little farther to the left of its Kale—follow signs through the crooked streets to the museum in the lovely **Aslan Pasha Camii.** (☎26 356. Open Oct.-May 8am-8pm. 700dr, students 300dr.) Off Averof near the city center, the **Archaeological Museum** has tablets on which puzzled ancients wrote their angsty queries to that divine Dear Abby, the oracle to Zeus, in nearby Dodoni. (Open Tu-Su 8am-2pm. 500dr, students free.) Catch a frequent **boat** (10min., 150dr) across the lake to the cleverly named **To Nisi** (The Island) to explore **Byzantine monasteries** and the **Ali Pasha Museum.** Follow the signs to Averof's end at the waterfront, and go left at the walls on Karamanli to the dock.

Buses run regularly from Zossimadon 4 to: Athens (7hr., 9 per day, 7250dr); Igoumenitsa (2hr., 10 per day, 1800dr); and Thessaloniki (7hr., 6 per day, 6200dr). The **tourist office** (☎46 662), about 500 meters down Leoforis Dodoni on the left, has maps and a guide to Ioannina, including a list of rooms available to rent. (Open in summer M-F 7:30am-2:30pm and 5:30-8pm; in winter 9am-2:30pm and Sa 9:30am-1pm.) To check your email head to **Web@r,** Stoa Sarka 31-32. Go right after the Wendy's; it's tucked off Nap. Zerva. (600dr per hr. Open daily 11am-4am.) To get to **Hotel Paris,** Tsirigoti 6, walk uphill from the station and look left at the bank. (☎205 41. Singles 6-8000dr; doubles 9-10,000dr.) **Hotel Metropolis,** Kristali 2, is on the corner of Averof toward the waterfront. (☎262 07. Singles 5-6000dr; doubles 8-10,000dr.) Dine on delicious seafood near the waterfront. **Postal Code:** 45221.

🎇 DAYTRIP FROM IOANNINA: DODONI. Ancient Dodoni (Δωδωνη), the site of mainland Greece's oldest oracle, is at the base of a mountain 22km southeast of Ioannina. According to mythology, Zeus resided in Dodoni as the roots of a giant oak while courting a nearby cypress tree (don't ask). Years later, a dove perched on the tree and told Dodoni's inhabitants that there should be an oracle to Zeus on the spot. Although the oracle no longer exists, the well-preserved **amphitheater,** as well as the impressive oak, remains. (Open daily in summer 8am-7pm; in winter 8am-5pm. 500dr, students free.) Dodoni is difficult to visit; your best bet is the 2pm bus to Melig (M, Th, F; 30min.; 450dr) from Ioannina's smaller station—ask to be let off at the theater. A return bus leaves at 5:15pm. Otherwise, take a taxi from Ioannina (at least 5000dr roundtrip).

IONIAN ISLANDS (Νησια Του Ιονιου) Just off

the western coast of Greece, the Ionian Islands are renowned for their medley of rugged mountains, farmland, shimmering olive groves, and pristine beaches, all surrounded by a seemingly endless expanse of clear, blue water with a sheer beauty that will stun even the most world-weary of world travelers.

🎇 FERRIES TO ITALY

If you want to catch a ferry to **Italy,** buy your ticket at least a day ahead in high-season; be sure to find out if the port tax (1500-2200dr) is included. Ferries go from

Corfu to: **Ancona** (21hr., 1 per day, 15,800-22,200dr); **Bari** (10hr., 3-4 per week, 9000dr); **Brindisi** (8hr., 4 per day, 7500-19,500dr); **Trieste** (24hr., 2 per week, 14,500-19,400dr); and **Venice** (26hr., 1 per day, 15,800-22,200dr). **Catamarans** also go to **Brindisi** from **Corfu** (3¼hr.; 9am; 17,800-27,000dr, under 28 5-10,000dr less). In summer, ferries connect **Cephalonia** to **Brindisi, Venice,** and **Ancona.**

CORFU (KERKYRA; Κερκυρα)   ☎0661

In the time since Odysseus washed ashore and praised its lush beauty, the seas have brought crusaders, conquerors, and colonists to verdant Corfu. Sadly, its enchanting beauty has often captivated too many, leading to the destruction of many of its beaches. Even the transportation hub, **Corfu Town,** exudes a Venetian charm, and excursions off the beaten path are richly rewarded. **Paleokastritsa beach,** where Odysseus supposedly landed, lies west of Corfu Town; take a KTEL **bus** to Paleokastritsa (45min., 7 per day, 500dr). A 90min. walk from there will bring you to the white mountaintop monastery **Panagia Theotokos** and the fort of **Angelokastro** (Castle of the Holy Angels), which jut out over the sea. South of Paleokastritsa is **Pelekas Town;** walk 30min. downhill to reach **Pelekas beach. Glyfada beach,** 5km from Pelekas Town, is accessible by free **shuttles** from Pelekas (10min., 6 per day) and by KTEL **buses** from Pl. Sanrocco in Corfu Town (8 per day, 400dr). Glyfada is one of Corfu's most popular beaches, and offers a vast expanse of shore as well as parasailing and watersailing opportunities. North of Glyfada, accessible via dirt path off the main Pelekas road, lie the isolated beaches of **Moni Myrtidon** and **Myrtiotissa** (the unofficial nude beach). **Agios Gordios,** 10km south of Pelekas, offers impressive rock formations, a beach, and the immensely popular **Pink Palace Hotel.** On weekends, toga-wearing partyers have been known to do shots of ouzo as they break plates on each other's heads, all in a spirit of revelry that would make Dionysus proud. The **Palace** has an impressive list of amenities that helps keep it a self-contained party resort: jacuzzi, basketball, volleyball, and tennis courts, on-site nightclub, clothing-optional cliff-diving (3000dr), boat daytrips, various watersports, as well as internet access and laundry service. (☎530 24. Breakfast, dinner, ferry pick-up, and drop-off included. A-class rooms 9000dr.; B-class dorms 7000dr.) Blue **buses** run to Agios Gordios from Pl. Sanrocco (45min., 7 per day, 300dr).

Ferries run from Corfu Town to Italy; Cephalonia (5hr., Sa 11am, 5200dr); and Patras (9hr., 1-2 per day, 5800dr). KTEL runs **bus/ferry** combos daily to Athens (9hr., 3 per day, 8650dr) and Thessaloniki (9hr., 2 per day, 8350dr). KTEL inter-city **green buses** depart from just off I. Theotaki; **blue buses** (municipal buses) leave from Pl. Sanrocco. From the customs house at the new port, cross the intersection and walk uphill on Avramiou, which becomes I. Theotoki, to reach Pl. Sanrocco (1km). The **National Tourist Office** is at the corner of Rizospaston Voulefton and Iak. Folila. (☎375 20. Open M-F 8am-2pm.) **The Association of Owners of Private Rooms and Apartments in Corfu,** Polila 24 (☎26 133), has a complete list of rooms for all of Corfu and can give you numbers to call for your price range. **Tourist agencies** along Arseniou and Stratigou, can help to find rooms as well. To get to **Hotel Europa,** Giantsilio 10, from the customs house, cross the main street and make a right; Giantsilio is a tiny road on your left just after the road turns and becomes Napoleonta. (☎393 04. Singles 4-5000dr; doubles 6-7000dr; triples 8000dr.) **Hotel Ionian,** Xen. Sratigou 46, is at the new port. (☎399 15. Singles 7-8000dr; doubles 9-11,000dr; triples 12-16,000dr.) A daily open-air **market** sells inexpensive food, including blissfully fresh fruit, on Dessala, off G. Theotoki below the new fortress. (Open 6am-2pm.) **Postal Code:** 49100.

CEPHALONIA (Κεφαλονια)   ☎0671

Dubbed "The Island of Peculiarities" for its disparate but beautiful beaches, subterranean caves, rugged mountains, and shady forests, Cephalonia is ideal for a long stay. **Argostoli,** the capital and transport hub of Cephalonia and Ithaka, is a busy, noisy city with palm-lined, traffic-filled streets. A small, picturesque town on a harbor surrounded by steep, lush hills, **Sami,** 24km from Argostoli, offers white-pebble beaches, proximity to underground **Melissani Lake** and **Drogati Cave,** a cavern filled with stunning stalactites and stalagmites. **Buses** arrive from Argostoli (1 per day, 500dr). **Hotel Kyma,** in the main *plateia,* has spectacular views. (☎ (0674) 220 64. Singles 6000dr; doubles 10,000dr.)

Ferries sail to Ithaka (1hr., 3 per day, 480dr) and Patras (3hr., 1 per day, 3200dr). **Buses** (☎222 81) leave from the station at the southern end of the waterfront. The **tourist office** is beside the port authority. (☎222 48. Open M-Sa 8am-2:30pm and 5-9pm; in winter M-F 7:30am-2pm.) To get from the waterfront to the main *plateia,* follow 21 Maiou (to the right of the station as you face inland) up two blocks. To reach **Villa Aspasia Rooms To Let** from the waterfront, follow the left edge of the *plateia* up the hill on Lassi, turn right past the garden, and it'll be on your left. (☎235 11. July-Aug. doubles 9000dr; Sept.-June 6000dr.)

ITHAKA (ITHAKI; Ιθάκη)   ☎0674

The least-touristed and perhaps the loveliest of the Ionian Islands, Ithaka is all too often passed over for the tourist havens of Lefkada and Cephalonia. Those who do come discover the island's pebbled, rocky hillsides and terraced olive groves. According to Homer's epic poem, Ithaka was the kingdom where **Odysseus** left his wife, Penelope, behind for two decades while he played with various sirens and monsters. Ithaka's largest town and capital, **Vathy,** wraps around a circular bay skirted by steep, green hills. Relax on one of the seductive beaches or sip a *frappè* in the serenity of an outdoor cafe. **Dexa** is the closest beach to Vathy, a 15min. walk from town. From Vathy, follow the main road out of town with the water on your right. According to legend, this is where Odysseus landed when he returned to Ithaka. Those with a poetic bent and sturdy footwear can climb up to the **Cave of the Nymphs,** where Odysseus supposedly hid his treasure. (Bring a flashlight. Open July-Aug. 200dr.) North from Vathy are the scenic villages of Lefki, Stavros, Platrithiai, Frikes, and Kioni. **Stavros** is high in the mountains on the way to Frikes, which can be reached by bus (1hr., 350dr). Kioni and was allegedly once home to **Odysseus' Palace;** the site is now a small museum filled with excavated items from the site. (Open July-Aug. Tu-Su 8am-2:30pm. Small donation expected.)

Ferries connect Vathy to Sami on Cephalonia (3hr., 1040dr) and Astakos on the mainland (4hr., 1910dr). Boats also depart from Piso Aetos (10min. taxi ride) on the southern side of Ithaka, to Sami on Cephalonia (1hr., 620dr). The island's one **bus** runs north from Vathy, passing through the villages of Lefki, Stavros, Platrithiai, Frikes, and Kioni. Schedules are erratic; check in town, but in the high season, the bus usually runs three times per day (1hr., 350dr to Frikes). For help in finding a room check with **Delas Tours** (☎321 04; open daily 9am-2pm and 4-10pm) or **Polyctor Tours** (☎331 20; open daily 9am-1:30pm and 5-9pm), both in the main square right off the water. Private *domatia* (6-8000dr in summer) are your best option for affordable accommodations. **Camping** at **Dexa Beach,** Odysseus' mythological landing point, is free. **Taverna To Trexantiri** (☎33 066), is the hands-down favorite eatery among locals. (Salads 500-900dr; main dishes under 1300dr.) **Postal Code:** 28300.

THE SPORADES (Σποραδες)

Viewed from the chaos of modern Athens, the Sporades and Evia circle like a family of enchanted sea-maidens. The matriarch is Evia, Greece's largest island after Crete. The Northern Sporades are her three daughters: quietly sophisticated Skopelos is the eldest, home to jazz-filled harbors and a population of artists. Skiathos is the middle child, in a hurry to grow up, with the best party scene for miles. Innocent Alonnisos, the youngest, is a pristine wilderness crossed by hiking trails; Skyros, in the east, is the grandmother, the purple-hilled keeper of the old ways.

▐ TRANSPORTATION

To get to most of the Sporades from Athens, take the daily bus from the station at Liossion 260 to Agios Konstantinos (2½hr., 16 per day, 2650dr), where **Nomikos/**

Goutos Lines ferries run to Skiathos (3½hr, 1-2 per day, 3300dr); Skopelos (4hr., 2 per day, 4100dr); and Alonissos (5½hr., 3 per day, 4400dr). To reach Skyros, take a bus from Athens to Kimi (3½hr., 2 per day, 2600dr), then take a ferry (1¾hr., 2 per day, 2300dr). Nomikos/Goutos runs ferries from Thessaloniki to Skopelos (6hr., 3 per week, 4800dr); as well as from Skiathos to Skopelos (1-1½hr., 3-4 per day, 1400dr) and Alonissos (2hr., 2-3 per day, 1900dr); and Skopelos to Alonissos (30min., 2 per day, 1100dr). **Flying Dolphins hydrofoils** follow the same routes, at twice the cost and double the speed. Ferries and hydrofoils also connect the various islands.

SKIATHOS (Σκιαθος)   ☎0427

Welcome to the party hub of the Sporades. Tourism is a recent phenomenon here, as little Skiathos has grown up almost overnight into a glamorous dancing queen. Package tourists pack the streets of **Skiathos Town,** while budding writers follow Papadiamantis to the beautiful beaches and nature preserves. Buses leave the port in Skiathos Town for the southern **beaches** (3 per hr., 320dr), including **Megali Ammos, Nostros, Platanias,** and **Vromolimnos.** The road and bus route end in **Koukounaries,** where the more secluded beaches begin, including the lovely, pine-wooded **Biotrope of Koukounaries;** the yellow, curved **Banana Beach;** and the nude, gay-friendly **Little Banana Beach.** When night falls, indulge yourself at the countless bars in **Pl. Papadiamantis** or along **Polytechniou** and **Evangelista,** then dance all night long at the clubs on the far right side of the coast. **Private rooms** abound, particularly on Evangelista, but in a pinch head to the **Rooms to Let Office,** in the wooden kiosk by the port. (☎22 990. Open daily 8:30am-midnight.) **Pension Danaos,** in an alley off Papadiamantis opposite the OTE, packs in a young backpacker crowd. (☎22 834. Open May 1-Sept. 30. Singles 10,000dr; doubles 8-15,000dr.) **Camping Koukounaries** is on the bus route to Koukouniares between stops 20 and 21. (☎49 250. 1800dr per person, 1000dr per tent.) Follow Papadiamantis to the kiosk and turn right to reach **Chris, Jan & Deborah's Daskalio Pub. Postal Code:** 37002.

SKOPELOS (Σκοπελος)   ☎0424

Relaxed Skopelos sits between the whirlwind of Skiathos and the largely untouched wilderness of Alonnisos. By day, the pious head to the hills, where the island's monasteries and shrines hide in woods still heady with the fading sounds of *rembetika* (folk songs). At night, the streets of Skopelos Town fill with voices, and light drips down from cafes and onto the Aegean. About eight **buses** per day leave from the stop left of the waterfront (as you face inland) for **beaches** near **Stafylos, Agnondas, Milia,** and **Loutraki. Hiking trails** wind through the terrain to monasteries and beaches. The Thalpo **tourist agency,** on the 2nd fl. behind Restaurant Akteon, is up on everything from Flying Dolphins tickets to catching octopi. (☎22 947. Open May-Oct. daily 10am-9pm.) Decent prices for rooms are found near the dock; try the **Rooms and Apartments Association of Skopelos.** (☎245 67. Open daily 10am-2pm and 6-10pm.) **Pension Sotos,** 10m to the left of Thalpos Travel, is a gem, for its setting, and its diamond-in-the-rough price. (☎22 549. Doubles 6500-12,000dr; triples 9000-16,000dr.) Endless 350dr gyros and 600dr pizzas fill **Pl. Platanos.** If you want something less greasy, try **Greca's Creperie,** 20m right of the Folk Art Museum. (Open daily 10am-3pm and 7pm-12:30am.) **Postal Code:** 37003.

ALONISSOS (Αλοννησος)   ☎0424

Of the twenty-odd islands within Greece's new National Marine Park, only Alonissos is inhabited. Most of the small, remaining islets can be visited only by organized tour boats in summer; trips are advertised and sold along the harbor (usually 1-2 days; 10-12,000dr in high-season). Alonissos' unexplored northern coast forms a boundary of clear white-sanded against the sea, and its **hiking trails** trace the high heartland; check the kiosk next to the ferry dock in **Patitiri,** for an overview of walking routes. Hikers and beachgoers may find the beautiful **Old Town** (Hora) ideal. The island's only **bus** runs between Hora and Patitiri (10min., ever hr., 300dr). A multitude of trails leads down the mountainside from the Old Town to pebbly, cliff-protected beaches. Among them, **Megalos Martias** is the largest and most established; nearby **Mikros Martias** is a contender for Ideal Greek Beach, with its rocks perfectly molded for semi-nude sunbathing sitting in the crystal water. **Alonissos Travel,** in the center of the waterfront, **exchanges currency,** finds rooms, books excursions, and sells ferry tickets. (☎65 511. Open daily 9am-10:30pm.) The **Rooms to Let Office** next to Ikos Travel can lend a hand to travelers looking for a place to stay. (☎66 188. Open daily May-Oct. 9am-4pm.) **Panorama,** down the first alley on the left from Ikion Dolophon, rents bright rooms and studios with private baths. (☎65 240. Doubles 6000-10,000dr.) Locals adore the little *ouzeri* **To Kamaki,** on the left side of Ikion Dolophon past the National Bank. Try the delectable warm octopus salad. (Open daily noon-2:30pm and 7pm-late.) **Postal Code:** 37005.

SKYROS (Σκυρος) ☎0222

From the sea, Skyros's cliffs and hills spread out in greens and yellows under an infinitely blue sky. The hilly terrain once fortified the island against marauding pirates and is now trying to fight off modern culture. The island's capital, **Skyros Town,** as well as its northern and southern wilds, remain traditional and distinctly separate from modern Greece, the last stand of ghosts, poets, and pirate kings. Above Skyros Town, the 1000-year-old **Monastery of St. George** and the **Castle of Licomidus** command magnificent views of Skyrian sunsets. (Open daily Mar.-Aug. 7am-10pm, Sept.-Feb. 7:30am-6pm. Free.) The superb **Faltaits Museum,** up the stairs from Pl. Rupert Brooke in Skyros Town, called "a place where the nine muses meet" by its staff, boasts an incredible folk art collection. (☎91 232. Open daily 10am-1pm and 5:30-8pm. 500dr.) The best way to get to Skyros is to take the **bus** from **Athens** to **Kimi** on Evia (3½hr., 2 per day, 2600dr), then the **ferry** to Skyros from Kimi (2 per day, 2300dr). Boats to Skyros arrive in **Linaria,** the tiny western port; a **local bus** takes tourists from the port to Skyros Town (20min., 4 per day, 250dr). **Skyros Travel,** past the central *plateia* on Agoras, sells Flying Dolphins and Olympic Airways tickets; it's also a de facto **tourist office,** organizing bus and boat excursions and helping visitors find lodging. (☎91 123. Open 9:15am-2pm, 7-10pm.) For the full Skyrian experience, bargain to stay in a traditional private home; the thick-walled treasure troves are brimming with Delft ceramics and Italian linens, purchased long-ago from pirates who looted much of the known world. You'll be met at the bus stop by old women offering domatia. **Camping Skyros** offers the amenities of a restaurant and a mini-market, along with the opportunity to get back to nature with some horses and an old car in the same field. (☎92 458. 1500dr per person with tent). The incredible **O Pappas Kai Ego** ("Grandpa and me") serves brilliant Skyrian specialties (main dishes 850-2200dr). **Postal Code:** 34007.

THE CYCLADES (Κυκλαδες)

When people speak longingly of the Greek islands, they are quite likely speaking of the Cyclades. Whatever your idea of the Aegean—peaceful cobblestone streets and whitewashed houses, breathtaking sunsets, sunny hikes, Bacchanalian revelry—you can find it here. Each island has quiet villages and untouched spots, but in summer most are mobbed by backpackers convening for the post-Eurail party.

▐ TRANSPORTATION

Ferries from **Athens** head to: **Ios** (7½hr., 5090dr); **Mykonos** (6hr., 2-3 per day, 5100dr); **Naxos** (3hr., 1-2 per day, 1900dr); and **Santorini** (9hr., 5630dr). Ferries from **Crete** connect to: **Mykonos** (8½hr., 5 per week, 6000dr); **Naxos** (7hr., 3 per week, 5200dr); **Paros** (9hr., 7 per week, 5200dr); and **Santorini** (4hr., 2 per day, 3700dr). Ferries also run to **Paros** from **Samos** (6hr., 6 per week, 4050dr) and **Rhodes** (16hr., 1 per week, 6950dr). Faster but more expensive Flying Dolphin **hydrofoils** ply the same routes.

MYKONOS   ☎0289

Coveted by pirates in the 18th century for its blond beaches, Mykonos is still lusted after by those seeking revelry and excess amidst a rich history. Today, the island is the expensive playground of the sleek and chic sophisticates the Greeks call *kosmopolitikos*. Lose yourself in the colorful alleyways and sunny beaches of **Mykonos Town.** All of Mykonos' beaches are technically nudist, but the degree of bareness varies; the most daring are **Plati Yialos, Paradise Beach, Super Paradise Beach,** and **Elia. Buses** run from South Station to Plati Yialos (2 per hr., 250dr), where you can catch *kaïkia* to the other three (around 400dr); direct buses also run to Paradise from South Station (2 per hr., 250dr) and to Elia from North Station (8 per day, 330dr). At night, **Caprice Bar,** on the water in Little Venice, is popular, crowded, and fruit-filled. (Open Su-Th 6:30pm-3:30am, F-Sa 6:30pm-4:30am.) Step into a Toulouse-Lautrec painting at **Montparnasse Piano Bar,** Agion Anargyron 24, in Little Venice. (Wine around 1000dr, cocktails around 3000dr. Open daily 7pm-3am.) On Matogianni, **Pierro's,** with wild dancing and irresistible hedonism, was the first gay bar in Greece (beer 1500dr, cocktails 2500dr).

Ferries run to: Naxos (3hr., 1-2 per day, 1900dr); Santorini (6hr., 3 per week, 3500dr); and Tinos (45min., 3 per day, 1200dr). Flying Dolphins sends **boats** to Paros (1 per day, 3400dr) and Ios (4hr., 1 per day, 6350dr). The helpful **tourist police** await at the ferry landing. (☎22 482. Open daily 8am-11pm.) Most budget travelers find their niche in Mykonos's several festive campsites, which offer a myriad of sleeping options beyond the standard plot of grass. The information offices on the dock are numbered according to accommodation type: one for **hotels** (☎24 540; open 9am-midnight), two for **rooms to let** (☎24 860; open 9am-11pm). **Hotel Apollon,** on the waterfront, is an antique-laden house with a view of the harbour. (☎22 223. Singles 9-14,000dr; doubles 11,500-16,000dr; triples 15-19,000dr.) **Zoris Hotel,** N. Kalogera 30, has showers and a rooftop ideal for serious sunbathing. (☎22 167. Doubles 18-25,000dr.) **Paradise Beach Camping** is 6km from the village, directly on the beach; take the **bus** (round-trip 380dr) or the free shuttle from the port. (☎22 852. 1300-2000dr per person, 900-1500dr per tent. 2-person cabin 3-6000dr; singles 4000dr.) You'll have to wait at the **Dynasty Thai Chinese Restaurant,** on Pl. Lymni, by the cinema on Meletopoulou, but it's worth it. (Main dishes 1650-2500dr. Open daily 6:30pm-12:45am.) **Kalamataria,** on Florou Zouganeli, serves Greek cuisine at fair prices. (☎24 051. Open 9am-1am.) **Postal Code:** 84600.

🚶 **DAYTRIP FROM MYKONOS: DELOS.** Delos, the sacred center of the Cycladic maelstrom, is not to be missed. Delos claims the most famous sanctuary in the Cyclades, *the* **Temple of Apollo,** built to commemorate the birthplace of the god and his twin sister, Artemis. After several centuries of inhabitation, Delos went native by the end of the 2nd century AD, taken over by legions of leaping lizards, huge spiderwebs, and members of the French School of Archaeology (well, the last just since 1873). The **archaeological site,** which occupies much of the small island, takes several days to explore completely, but the highlights can be seen in under three hours. From the dock, head straight to the **Agora of the Competaliasts;** continue in the same direction and go left onto the wide **Sacred Road** to reach the **Sanctuary of Apollo,** a collection of temples built in the god's honor from Mycenaean times to the 4th century BC. The famous **Great Temple of Apollo,** or Temple of the Delians, was completed in the 4th century BC. Continue 50m past the end of the **Sacred Road** to the beautiful **Terrace of the Lions.** The **museum,** next to the cafeteria, contains an assortment of archaeological finds. A path leads to the summit of **Mt. Kythnos,** from which Zeus watched Apollo's birth. (Open daily Tu-Su 8:30am-3pm. 1200dr, students and EU seniors 600dr, EU students free.) Excursion boats leave the dock near **Mykonos Town** for Delos (35min., Tu-Su every 30-45min., roundtrip 1900dr).

TINOS (Τηνος)   ☎0283

In southern Tinos, tree-dotted hills gently cascade into the clear sea; wildflowers line the road with brilliant color; and a bit of searching rewards the careful explorer with quiet, secluded beaches. The island is a popular destination for Greek travelers, but remains virtually undiscovered by others. In **Tinos Town (Hora),** the most visited part of the island, the **Panayia Evangelistira Church** houses the miraculous **Icon of the Annunciation,** one of the most sacred relics of the Greek Orthodox Church. (Dress modestly when visiting the church. Open daily 7am-8pm. Free.) **Beaches** surround Tinos Town; **Tinos** and **Stavros** are popular options, just a short drive from town, while **Agios Fokas,** is a brief walk east of town. To reach the stunning beach at **Porto,** take the KTEL bus (3-5 per day, 230dr). For the spectacular **Kardianis,** hop on the Pyrgos bus to Kardiani and travel down the winding street from the main road to the bay. Many hikes lead up **Mt. Exobourgo,** 14km north of Tinos Town, the site of the Venetian fortress **Xombourgo.**

Ferries arrive at the main dock next to the bus depot. Ferries travel from Tinos to Mykonos (30min., 4-5 per day, 1100dr) and Paros (2 per week, 1700dr). A **catamaran** (**Minoan**) sails daily to: Mykonos (30min., 2275dr); Paros (1¼hr., 3385dr); and Naxos (1¾hr., 3750dr). **Buses** (☎22 440), depart across the street from the National Bank for Pyrgos (3-5 times per day, 750dr) and Porto (3-5 times per day, 230dr). Check the schedule in the KTEL ticket agency opposite the bus depot. **Jason's,** on the waterfront just before Alavanou, rents **cars** and **mopeds.** (☎22 583. Cars 6-15,000dr; mopeds 2-3000dr. Open 8am-10pm.) **Yanni's,** at the far right end of the waterfront, has airy rooms in a 75-year-old blue-shuttered home. (☎250 89. Singles 5000dr; doubles 8000dr; triples 12-16,000dr.) **Tinos Camping** is 10min. from the waterfront to the right (follow the signs). (☎22 344. 1500dr per person, 900-1100dr per tent.) An abundance of *tavernas* tempt tourists to stop for a bite to eat. **Caffé Italia,** Akti Nazou 10 (☎25 756), is one of Tinos' best-kept culinary secrets. (Open 10am-3pm, 6pm-1am.) For simpler fare, there's a **supermarket** two doors to the left of the post office. (Open M-Sa 8am-9:30pm, Su 9am-1:30pm.) **Postal Code:** 84200.

PAROS (Πάρος)   ☎0284

Paros was famous in the ancient world for its slabs of pure white marble, which were shaped into the Venus de Milo, the Nike of Samothrace, and parts of Napoleon's mausoleum in Paris. Today Paros remains a favorite for its golden beaches and tangle of whitewashed villages. The island strikes a careful balance between New-World nightlife and Old-World dignity. Behind the commercial surface of **Paroikia,** Paros' port and largest city, flower-filled streets wind through archways, past windmills. Byzantine architecture buffs will be enraptured by the **Panagia Ekatontapiliani** (Church of Our Lady of 100 Gates), which looms over Paroikia's *plateia* and houses three separate churches, cloisters, and a peaceful courtyard. Tradition holds that only 99 of the church's 100 doors can be counted—when the 100th appears, Constantinople will again belong to the Greeks. (Dress modestly. Open 8am-8:30pm.) Just 10km south of town is the cool, spring-fed **Valley of the Butterflies,** or **Petaloudes,** where the rare (and tongue-twisting) *Panaxiaquadripunctaria* moth congregates in massive numbers during its mating season, from June to late September, cloaking the foliage. At nighttime, find **Pirate Blues and Jazz,** tucked away in the old town half a block from Apollon Garden Restaurant, which has an eclectic assortment of musical offerings. (Beer 800dr. Open daily 7pm-3am.)

Ferries sail to Ios (2½hr., 7-9 per day, 2450dr) and Santorini (3½hr., 6-9 per day, 3080dr). The **tourist police** are behind the OTE, across the *plateia*. (☎21 673. Open daily 9am-3:30pm.) Turn left from the dock and take a right after the ancient cemetery ruins to get to **Rena Rooms.** (☎22 220. Doubles 6-13,000dr; triples 9-14,000dr.) Shuttles run from the port to **Parasporos Camping,** 1.5km south of town. (☎22 268. 1500dr per person; 600dr per tent, tent rental 1000dr.) The Psychedelic **Happy Green Cow,** just a block inland off the *plateia* behind the National Bank, serves tasty veggie fare. (Open daily 7pm-midnight.) **Postal Code:** 84400.

NAXOS (Νάξος)   ☎0285

Mythology relates the desertion of Cretan princess Ariadne on the shores of Naxos by her ungrateful lover, Theseus, and her subsequent marriage to the god Dionysus (hey, a girl could do worse!). Today, Naxos has a great deal more than history in its favor. Old **Naxos Town** lies behind waterfront shops, on the hill leading up to the **Cas-**

tro, an old Venetian castle, which looms over town. At the top of the hill sits the **Archaeological Museum,** in the former Collège Français where Nikos Kazantzakis author of *The Last Temptation of Christ* and *Zorba the Greek*, studied. (Open Tu-Su 8am-2:30pm. 500dr, students 300dr; Su and holidays free.) The new **Mitropolis Museum** shouldn't be missed. An architectural achievement itself, it is built around an excavated site of a 13th-century BC civilization. (☎24 151. Open Tu-Su 8am-2:30pm. Free.) The marble, 6th-century BC **Portara** archway, visible from the waterfront, is one of the few archaeological sites in Greece where you can actually climb all over the ruins—with no admission, and no guards, open 24 hours, it's recommended for romantic sunsets or midnight star-watching. A **bus** goes from the port to the **beaches** of **Agia Georgios, Ag. Prokopios, Ag. Anna,** and **Plaka** every half-hour (300dr). Of the group, Plaka is the hands-down favorite for nude frolicking. seen. To properly experience the island, tourists must explore its stunning interior; **buses** run from Naxos Town to the small fishing village of **Apollonas,** on the northern tip, via a gorgeous coastal road (2hr., 3 per day, 1100dr). Some of the most exhilarating aspects of the interior, such as the **Tragea** highland valley (a vast green olive grove), however, are not serviced by buses; ask for **hiking** info at the tourist office. Pump up **The Jam,** behind the OTE, with every style of rock music imaginable. (Open daily 7pm-3:30am.)

Ferries go to: Ios (1½hr., 6 per day, 2200dr); Mykonos (2hr., 5 per week, 1740dr); Paros (1hr., 6-8 per day, 1400dr); and Santorini (3hr., 6 per day, 2900dr). The **tourist office** is 300m up from the waterfront by the bus station. (☎24 358; fax 252 00; email chateau-zeugoli@forthnet.gr. Open daily 8am-midnight.) **Pension Irene** in newer Naxos, 300m from Ag. Georgios Beach, has A/C, TV, and a shuttle to pick you up at the dock. (☎23 169. Doubles 10,000dr; triples 12,000dr; quads 15,000dr.) **Dionysus,** in Old Naxos (follow the red hand signs), is spartan, but cheap. (☎25 201. Reception 10am-6pm and 10pm-midnight. Dorms 2000dr; singles 4-5000dr; doubles and triples 5-6000dr.) **Maragas Camping** runs a shuttle bus from the dock and frequent buses to Agios Anna beach (every 30min.; 300dr); it's the furthest campground, but virtually on the beach. (☎42 552. 900-1200dr per person; 300dr tent rental. Studios 8-12,000dr; doubles with bath 6-8000dr.) **Postal Code:** 84300.

IOS ☎0286

If you're not drunk when you arrive, you will be when you leave. On Ios, the beers go down and the clothes come off faster than you can say *"Opa!"* It has everything your mother warned you about—people swimming less than 30min. after they've eaten, wine being swilled from the bottle at 3pm, drinking games all day long, men and women dancing madly in the streets, and oh-so-much more. The **port** (Yialos) is at one end of the island's paved road; the **village** (Hora) sits above it on a hill, but the **beaches** are the place to be. Most spend their days at **Mylopotas Beach,** a 20min. walk downhill from Ios town, or a bus ride from the port or village (every 10-20min., 8am-midnight, 230dr). Head just uphill from the *plateia* to reach **The Slammer Bar,** where you can **get drunk** on "tequila slammers" (900dr). Move on to packed **Blue Note,** where you can **get drunk**—down seven shots and earn a free t-shirt. Continue your pub crawl by **getting drunk** on whipped cream hands-free "blowjobs" (1500dr) at **Lemon Club,** by the *plateia*, then migrate with the masses to **Red Bull,** to **get drunk** on the Red Bull and vodka "energy special" (1700dr). Afterwards find techno techno a go-go at **Scorpion Disco,** on the way to the beach (1000dr cover after 1am). Wind up your evening at **Sweet Irish Dream,** near the "donkey steps," and for a change of pace, **get drunk** and dance on tables after 2am (no cover before 1am). Take some aspirin in the morning and head down to the beach, where three **Mylopotas Water Sports Center** shacks along the beach offer free **windsurfing, water-skiing,** and **snorkelling lessons** with rental. (1500-5000dr per hr. Open Apr.-Oct. daily.)

Ferries go to: Crete (5hr., 1 per week, 4300dr); Mykonos (4-5hr., 1 per day, 3300dr); Naxos (1½hr., 6-8 per day, 2100dr); Paros (2½hr., 5-6 per day, 2600dr); and Santorini (1¼hr., 4-6 per day, 1700dr). The **Tourist Information Center** is next to the bus stop. (☎91 135. Open daily 8am-midnight.) In the village, take the uphill steps to the left (with your back to the bank) in the *plateia* and take the first left to reach

Francesco's for spectacular harbor views and a terrace bar. (☎912 23. Dorms 3000dr; doubles 6-8000dr; triples 9-12,000dr.) Walk from the bus stop and take the right past the supermarket to reach **Pension Markos,** which has weekly barbecues and a pool. (☎91 059. Doubles 10,000dr; triples 18,000dr.) On the end of Mylopotas Beach, **Far Out Camping** has a pool, plenty of tents, parties, and parties. Did we mention parties? (☎92 301. Open Apr.-Sept. 1200dr per person; tent rental 300dr, cabins 1500-2000dr; bungalows 2000-3000dr.) For non-fermented refreshment, there's **Ios Market** (☎91 035), across from the bus stop in Hora, and the **supermarket** in the main *plateia*. **Waves Indian Restaurant and International Cuisine** serves up divine curry. (☎92 145. Opens 10am for breakfast.) **Postal Code:** 84001.

FOLEGANDROS (Φολεγανδρος)   ☎0286

The island of Folegandros is a blissfully peaceful alternative to the more hectic Cyclades. The dry, rocky, steep hills are terraced with low, snaking stone walls worn by centuries of fierce wind. Don't miss the view from the **Church of Panagia,** above the town on Paliokastro hill, at sunset; take the path from the right of the bus stop. **Agali beach,** accessible by foot (1hr.), is lined with several *tavernas;* climb up past the first one on the right and continue on the rocky trail to reach **Agios Nikolaos beach** (30min.), or continue along the main road to get to the tiny old settlement of **Ano Maria,** where you can examine Ottoman artifacts at the superb **Folklore Museum.** (Open June-Aug. daily 5-8pm. Guidebook 2000dr.) **Ferries** usually connect to: Ios (5 per week, 1500dr); Milos (3 per week); Naxos (2 per week, 2300dr); Paros (2 per week, 1900dr); and Santorini (5 per week, 1700dr). You can board the **bus** from the port **Kararostassi** to the main town of Folegandros, Hora (every 2hr., 220dr). Near the bus stop is the **Sottovento tourist office.** (☎41 444; fax 414 30. Open daily 10am-2pm and 5:30pm-midnight.) Down toward the port about 300m from the post office are **Pavlo's Rooms.** (☎41 232. Breakfast 500-1000dr. Laundry 1200dr per load. Dorms 4000dr per person; doubles 12,000dr, with bath 15,000dr.) In Hora, there are many places with Room to Let signs. Most run about 12,000-14,000dr per night for a double in high season. **Maria's Rooms** have a lovely view of the island and sea. (☎41 265. Doubles 12,000dr; triples with kitchen 18,000dr.) **Postal Code:** 84011.

SANTORINI (Σαντορινη)   ☎0286

Whitewashed towns balanced on plunging cliffs, burning black-sand beaches, and deeply scarred hills make Santorini's landscape nearly as dramatic as the volcanic explosion that created it. Despite all the kitsch in touristy **Fira,** the island's capital, nothing can destroy the pleasure of wandering its narrow, cobblestoned streets, inspecting its craft shops, and taking in the stunning sunset from its western edge. On the southwestern part of the island, the fascinating excavations at **Akrotiri,** a late Minoan city, are preserved virtually intact under layers of volcanic rock. (Open Tu-Su 8am-7pm. 1200dr, students 600dr.) **Buses** run to Akrotiri from Fira (30min., 16 per day, 400dr). Frequent buses also leave Fira for the black-sand **beaches** of **Perissa** (15min., 30 per day, 400dr) and **Kamari** (20min., 62 per day, 270dr) to the southeast. The route stops along the way in **Pyrgos** (15 min., 30 per day, 400dr); from there, you can hike to the **Profitias Ilias Monastery** (40min.) and continue to the ruins of **ancient Thira** (an additional 2hr.), near Kamari. The theater, church, and forum of Thira, the island's old capital, remain visible. (Open Tu-Su 8am-2pm.) **Ferries** run to Ios (1½hr., 4-8 per day, 1700dr); Iraklion (4hr., 1 per day, 3700dr); Naxos (4hr., 4-8 per day, 3000dr); Mykonos (7hr., 2 per week, 3600dr); and Paros (4½hr.,3-5 per day, 3200dr). Most land at **Athinios** harbor; frequent **buses** (30min., 370dr) connect to Fira. Share homemade meals with Petros at the **Pension Petros;** follow the signs for Santorini Camping one block east from Fira's main *plateia*, or catch the free shuttle from the port. (☎22 573. Doubles 7-16,000dr; triples 9-19,000dr.) Head 300m north from the *plateia* for the **Thira Youth Hostel.** (☎22 387. Sheets 300dr. Open Apr.-Oct. Dorms 1800-4000dr; doubles 5-10,000dr.) Or, follow the blue signs east from it for **Santorini Camping.** (☎229 44. Open Apr.-Oct. 1500dr per person, 800dr per tent, 1200-2000dr per tent rental, 700dr per car.) If you plan to spend substantial time baking on the black sand, take the bus from Fira to Perissa and stay at the **Youth Hostel Perissa-Anna,** 500m on the road out of town. (☎82 182. Hot showers 9am-9pm. Sheets 300dr for 3 days. Dorms 1200-1600dr; private rooms 2-4000dr.) Head north on the road to Oia for a stop at **Mama's Cyclades Cafe** (☎24 211) where Mama serves up a must-be-seen-to-be-believed breakfast special. **Postal Code:** 84700.

CRETE (Κρητη)

Greece's largest island embraces an infinite store of mosques, monasteries, mountain villages, gorges, grottoes, and beaches. Since 3000 BC, Crete has maintained an identity distinct from the rest of Greece, first expressed in the language, script, and architecture of the ancient Minoans. While the resort towns of eastern Crete my be the products of British booking agents, the riveting mountains that wind from Malia to Agios Nikolaos seem the brainchild of something slightly more divine.

▛ TRANSPORTATION

Olympic Airways and **Air Greece** connect Athens to: Sitia (2-3 per week, 23,200dr) in the east; Iraklion (45min., 13-15 per day, 19,300-21,300dr) in the center; and Hania (4 per day, 18,000dr plus 3300dr tax) in the west. **Boats** run to: Athens (14hr., 3 per day, 7000dr); Mykonos (8½hr., 5 per week, 6000dr); Naxos (7hr., 3 per week, 5200dr); Paros (9hr., 7 per week, 5200dr); and Santorini (4hr., 2 per day, 3700dr). **Hydrofoils** service most destinations in half the time, but at double the price.

    Buses run from **Rethymno, Hania,** and **Iraklion** south to the **Samaria Gorge** (from Hania 4 per day, round-trip 2800dr). Buses also go east from **Iraklion** to **Malia** (1hr., every 30min., 800dr) and **Agios Nikolaos** (1½hr., 20 per day, 1450dr). Buses from **Agios Nikolaos** continue east to **Sitia** (1½hr., 3-5 per day, 1550dr).

IRAKLION (Ηρακλιον) ☎081

The fifth-largest city in Greece, Iraklion is Crete's capital and primary port. The chic native population lives life in the fast lane, which translates into an urban brusqueness unique among the cities of Crete, and the most diverse nightlife on the island. Iraklion's main attraction, after **Knossos** (see below), is the superb **Archaeological Museum.** By appropriating major finds from all regions of the island, the Iraklion Museum has amassed a comprehensive record of the Neolithic and Minoan stages of the island's history, with a polite nod to the Hellenistic and Roman periods. (Open M 12:30pm-7pm and Tu-Su 8am-7pm. 1500dr, students and EU seniors 800dr; fine arts students, under 18, and EU students free.)

    KTEL **Terminal A,** between the old city walls and the harbor near the waterfront, sends **buses** to Agios Nikolaos (1½hr., 20 per day, 1450dr) and Malia (1hr., 2 per hr., 800dr); to reach the **Hania-Rethymno terminal,** walk down 25 Augustou to the waterfront, turn right, and walk about 500m. The **tourist office,** Xanthoudidou 1 (☎228 203), has maps and museum info. (Open M-F 8am-2:30pm.) The **tourist police** is at 10 Dikeosinis. (☎283 190. Open daily 7am-11pm.) Check your **email** at **Gallery Games Net,** Korai 14. (☎282 804. 500dr per 30min.) **Rent a Room Hellas,** Handakos 24, is two blocks from El Greco Park. (☎288 851. Dorms 2200dr; doubles 4500-6000dr; triples 6-8000dr.) To get from the bus station to the **youth hostel,** Vyronos 5, take a left (with the water on your right) on 25 Augustou and a right on Vyronos. (☎286 281. Check-out 10am. Curfew midnight. Dorms 2000dr; singles 3-4000dr; doubles 5500-6000dr; triples 7-8000dr.) The best show in town is the **open-air market** that starts near Pl. Venizelou. Stalls piled high with sweets, spices, fruits, vegetables, cheeses, meat, and Cretan muscle shirts line both sides of the narrow street. (Open M-Sa 8am-2pm, Tu and Th-F 5-9pm.) Around 11pm, the young and the restless of all nationalities overflow the small streets off **Pl. Venizelou.** A walk down D. Beaufort takes you to **Privilege Club** and **Yacht** next door. **Postal Code:** 71001.

◪ DAYTRIPS FROM IRAKLION: KNOSSOS AND MALIA. At Knossos, the most famous archaeological site in Crete, excavations have revealed the remains of the largest and most complicated of Crete's **Minoan palaces.** Sir Arthur Evans, who financed and supervised the excavations, eventually restored large parts of the palace in Knossos; his work often crossed the line from preservation to artistic interpretation, but the site is nonetheless impressive. (Open daily 8am-7pm; in winter 8am-5pm. 1500dr, students and seniors 800dr, EU students free; in winter Su free.) To reach Knossos from Iraklion, take **bus** #2 from 25 Augustou or Pl. Eleftherias.

Nearby Malia is overrun by young nightlife-seeking Brits, but the palatial Minoan site at Malia also merits a visit. The **Minoan Palace,** one of the three great cities of Minoan Crete, lacks the architectural complexity and magnificent interior of Knossos and Phaistos, but it's still imposing. Follow the road east to Agios Nikolaos for 3km and turn left toward the sea. (Open Tu-Su 8am-3pm. 800dr, students and seniors 400dr, EU students free.) **Altino Travel Service** (☎33 658; fax 29 620), across from the old church on the way to the beach, has maps, travel advice, and a rental service for **cars** (13,000-15,000dr) and **motorbikes** (5000-6000dr per day).Walking from the bus drop-off towards Agios Nikolaos, make a right onto 25 Martiou and then a left on Konstantinou to reach **Pension Aspasia.** (☎31 290. Singles 3000dr; doubles and triples 6000dr.) **Pension Menios** is one door past Aspasia. (☎313 61. Singles 4000dr; doubles 5000dr; triples 7000-7500dr.) **Postal Code:** 70007.

RETHYMNO AND HANIA (Ρεθυμνο, Χανια)   ☎0831

Nowhere in Western Crete are the manifestations of the island's turbulent occupations as mingled or as magical as in **Rethymno's** old city. Arabic inscriptions adorn the walls of the narrow streets, minarets highlight the skyline, and the 16th-century **Venetian Fortezza** stands watch over the scenic harbor and plays host to a lively **Renaissance Festival.** (Open Tu-Su 8am-7pm. 900dr, children 700dr.) The **Rethymno-Hania bus station** (☎22 212) is south of the fortress on the water. Climb the stairs behind the bus station, turn left on Igoum Gavril, which becomes Kountouriotou, and turn left on Varda Kallergi to reach the waterfront and the **tourist office,** on El. Venizelou. (☎291 48. Open M-F 8am-2:30pm.) Check your **email** at **Café Galero** at Rimondi Fountain. (☎25 750. 1400dr per hr. Open daily 7am-3am.) To get from the station to the cheerful **youth hostel,** Tombazi 41-45, walk down Igoum Gavril, take a left at the park traffic light, walk through the gate, and take your second right. (☎228 48. Breakfast 4-500dr. Sheets 150dr. Reception 8am-noon and 5-9pm. Dorms 1800dr.) **Olga's Pension,** Souliou 57, is off Antistassios. (☎532 06. Singles 5-7000dr; doubles 7-9000dr; triples 10-11,000dr.) Head to **Elizabeth Camping,** three kilometers east of town. (☎286 94. Open mid-Apr. to Oct. 1650dr per person, 1100-1500dr per tent, singles person and tent 2200dr.) **Postal Code:** 74100.

An oddly rickety tower of stone, the **Venetian lighthouse** guards the entrance to Hania's stunning architectural relic, the **Venetian Inner Harbor.** The inlet has retained its original breakwater and Venetian arsenal. (Open daily Apr.-Oct. 10am-4pm, Nov.-Mar. 10am-2pm; 600dr, students 350dr.) Narrow Venetian buildings and Ottoman domes mingle in the lively waterfront town of Hania. In the evening, head to the **harbor** for late night fun. **Ferries** arrive in the nearby port of **Souda** from Peiraias/Athens (9½hr., 1 per night, 5900-8600dr); buses connect to Hania's Municipal Market (15min., 260dr). **Buses** leave at the station (☎933 06) on the corner of Kidonias and Kelaidi for Rethymno (17 per day, 1600dr). Walk right on Kidonias and turn left on Pl. 1866 to reach the **tourist office,** Kriairi 40, just off Pl. 1866. (☎92 624. Open M-F 7:30am-2:00pm.) To get to **Hotel Fidias,** Sarpaki 6, walk toward the harbor on Halidon and turn right at the far end of the cathedral. (☎524 94. Singles 2-4000dr; doubles 3000-4500dr; triples 4500-6500dr.) **Postal Code:** 73100.

⚄ HIKING NEAR RETHYMNO AND HANIA: SAMARIA GORGE. The most popular excursion from Hania, Rethymno, and Iraklion is the 5- to 6-hour hike down the 16 kilometer Samaria Gorge, a spectacular ravine extending through the White Mountains, sculpted by the tender ministrations of rainwater over 14 million years. The gorge retains its allure despite having been trampled by thousands of visitors: rare, endemic plants peek out from sheer rock walls, wild Cretan goats climb the hills, and endangered griffin vultures and golden eagles circle overhead. (Open daily May-Oct. 15 6am-4pm. 1200dr, children under 15 and organized student groups free.) For more info about your friendly, neighborhood gorge, call **Hania Forest Service** (☎92 287). The trail starts at **Xyloskalo**; take the 6:15am or 8:30am **bus** from Hania to Xyloskalo (1½hr., 1300-1400dr), the 1:45pm bus from Hania to Omalos (just north of Xyloskalo, 2550dr), or the 5:30am bus from Iraklion to Omalos (3850dr). The trail ends in **Agia Roumeli**, on the southern coast, where you can hop on a **boat** to **Hora Sfakion** (1¼hr.; 4 per day, last ferry 6pm; 1500dr), and catch a waiting bus back to Hania (2hr., 1500dr); Iraklion (3000dr) or Rethymnon (1500dr).

AGIOS NIKOLAOS   ☎0841

Occupying a small peninsula on the northeast edge of Crete, Agios Nikolaos is a chic resort town where posh vacationers huff and puff their way up steep, boutiqued streets, then stop in at a harborside cafe to catch their breath at great leisure. **Boats** (5000dr) depart from the tourist office for the small but striking **Spinalonga island**, formerly a leper colony. From Agios Nikolaos, **ferries** go to: Athens/Peiraias (12hr., 5 per week, 7500dr); Karpathos (7hr., 3 per week, 4100dr); Rhodes (12hr., 3 per week, 6300dr); and Sitia (1hr., 5 per week, 1600dr). **Buses** (☎22 234) depart from Pl. Atlantidos, on the opposite side of town from the harbor. Head right from the station, and make your first right; follow Venizelou and then R. Koundourou to the harbor, then head to the left and across the bridge to reach the **tourist office**, S. Koundourou 21A. (☎22 357; fax 825 34. Open daily Apr.-June and Sept.-Nov. 8am-9:30pm; July-Aug. 8am-10pm.) To get to **Christodoulakis Pension**, Stratigou Koraka 7, turn right and go past the taxi station, then turn left. (☎22 525. Singles 4-5000dr; doubles 5-6000dr; triples 7500-8500dr.) For nocturnal fun, stroll around the harbor on **I. Koundourou** or walk up **25 Martiou**. **Postal Code:** 72100.

A FAMILIAR TALE The story of **King Minos**, one of the most complex and resonant myths in all Greek mythology, begins with a simple crime of ingratitude. When Minos withheld the sacrifice of a white bull that Poseidon had granted him for that purpose, Aphrodite was dispatched to exact a twisted retribution, and the tricky goddess gave Minos' queen **Pasiphaë** a burning lust for the bull. To woo the bull, Pasiphaë hired master engineer **Daedalus** to build a sexy cow costume that might rouse the bull's affections. After a roll in the hay (so to speak), Pasiphaë gave birth to the **Minotaur,** a fearsome beast with the head of a bull, the body of a man, and a taste for human flesh. The Minotaur was kept in an inescapable **labyrinth** designed by Daedalus and, to feed his queen's child, Minos imposed an annual tax of seven maidens and seven youths upon mainland Greece. A dashing Athenian prince named **Theseus** put a stop to this when he volunteered for the sacrifice and, once inside the labyrinth, slew the Minotaur. With a ball of string he'd gotten from Minos's daughter **Ariadne,** who had conspired with Daedalus to save her Athenian main squeeze, Theseus retraced his path and escaped by ship. He took Ariadne with him, promising marriage, but later he forgot and left her on the beach of Naxos to be swept off by Dionysus. Meanwhile, Minos imprisoned Daedalus and his son **Icarus** for their role in the whole mess. Resourceful Daedalus made himself and his son wings of wax, with which they went for the ultimate jailbreak. With freedom in sight, hubristic Icarus soared too close to the sun: his wings melted, and he plummeted to his death.

SITIA
☎ 0843

A winding drive on coastal and mountain roads from Agios Nikolaos leads to the fishing and port town of Sitia, where the wave of tourism slows to a trickle and pelicans walk the streets at dawn. Sitia makes a great base for exploration of Crete's east coast. The town's **beach** extends 3km to the east, while the hilltop **fortress** provides views of the town and bay. (Open Tu-Su 8:30am-3pm. Free.) **Ferries** leave Sitia for: Athens (16-17hr., 5 per week, 7600dr) via Agios Nikolaos (1½hr., 5 per week, 1600dr); Karpathos (5hr., 3 per week, 3400dr); Milos (9hr., 5 per week, 5200dr); and Rhodes (12hr., 3 per week, 6000dr). Turn right from the **bus station,** take your first right and then your first left, and follow Venizelou to the waterfront to the **tourist office.** (☎ 28 300. Open M-F 9am-9pm, Sa-Su 10am-9pm.) To get to the **youth hostel** at Therissou 4, walk right from the bus station, go right and then take the first left, turn left at the first big street, and bear left onto Therissou; or call for a ride from the station. (☎ 22 693. Sheets 100dr. Reception 9am-noon and 6-9pm. Dorms 1600dr; singles 2500dr; doubles 3500-4000dr; triples 4500-5000dr. **Camping** on lawn 1200 per person.) **Venus Rooms to Let** is at Kondilaki 60; walk up on Kapetan Sifi from the main square and go right after the telephone office. (☎ 24 307. Doubles 4000-8000dr, depending on season; 20% higher for triples.) **Cretan House,** K. Karamanli 10, off the *plateia,* serves Cretan classics for 700-1400dr. (Open daily 9am-1:30am.) Head to **Hot Summer** after midnight, down the road to Palaikastro by the beach, where a pool supplants the more traditional dance floor. (Cover 1000dr.) **Postal Code:** 72300.

EASTERN AEGEAN ISLANDS

The intricate, rocky coastlines and unassuming port towns of the **Northeastern Aegean Islands** enclose thickly wooded mountains that give way to unspoiled villages and beaches. Just miles from the Turkish coast, the islands have a sizable military presence, but nonetheless provide a rare taste of undiluted Greek culture.

SAMOS (Σαμος)
☎ 0273

Although it is perhaps the most beautiful and definitely the most touristed island in the northeast Aegean, Samos manages to remain less frenetic than some of its Cycladic and Dodecanesian siblings by accommodating a more scholarly, mature crowd. Many visitors simply stop here en route to Kuşadası and the ruins of **Ephesus** on the Turkish coast. With its quiet inland streets, palm trees, red-roof-covered hillside, and engaging archaeological museum, **Samos Town** (Vathy) is among the Northeast Aegean's most attractive port cities. The phenomenal **Archaeological Museum** is behind the municipal gardens. (☎ 27 469. Open Tu-Su 8:30am-3pm. 800dr, seniors and students 400dr, EU students free.) The ancient city of **Pythagorion,** once the island's capital, is 14km south of Samos Town. Near the town are the magnificent remains of Polykrates's 6th-century BC engineering projects: the **Tunnel of Eupalinos,** which diverted water from a natural spring to the city, a 40-meter-deep **harbor mole** (rock pier), and the **Temple of Hera.** (Tunnel open Tu-Su 8:45am-2:45pm. 500dr, students 300dr, EU students free.) Hourly **buses** arrive in Pythagorion from Samos Town (20min., 280dr). The temple is a 10min. **bus** ride (3 per day, 250dr) from Pythagorion, in nearby Heraion. (Open Tu-Su 8:30am-3pm. 800dr, students 400dr.)

Ferries arrive in Samos Town from: Athens/Peiraias (12hr., 2-3 per day, 6700dr) via Ikaria (2100dr); Lesvos (8hr., 1 per week, 4090dr); Mykonos (6hr., 4 per week, 5100dr); and Naxos (6hr., 4-7 per week, 4900dr) via Paros (4370dr). The **tourist office** is on a side street one block from Pl. Pythagoras. (☎ 28 530. Open July-Aug. M-Sa 8:30am-2pm.) Turn right at the end of the ferry dock onto E. Stamatiadou, before the Hotel Aiolis, then take the second left and head uphill to reach the **Pension Trova,** Kalomiris 26, featuring traditionally furnished rooms, some with bath and balcony. (☎ 27 759. Singles 4-6000dr; doubles with bath 5500-8000dr.) Or follow the same directions, taking the second right rather than the second left to get to **Pension Avli,** Areos 2. (☎ 22 939. Open in summer only. Doubles 6-7000dr.) **Postal Code:** 83100.

CHIOS (Χιος)   ☎0271

Chios is where the wild things *were:* Orion hunted every last beast down, leaving the island's mountainsides to pine, cypress, and mastic trees. With increasing accessibility to its striking volcanic beaches and medieval villages, Chios is rising to a new fame. **Pyrgi**, high in the hills 25km from Hios Town, is one of Greece's most striking villages, with fantastic black-and-white geometrical designs covering its buildings; take a **bus** from Hios Town (8 per day, 620dr). Farther south lies **Emborio beach,** where beige volcanic cliffs contrast with the black stones and deep-blue water below; **buses** run from Hios Town (4 per week, 720dr). **Ferries** go to: Athens/Piraeias (overnight, 1 per day, 5800dr); Kos (1 per week, 5000dr); Lesvos (3hr., 1 per week, 3400dr); Rhodes (1 per week, 7100dr); and Samos (4hr., 3 per week, 3120dr). To reach Hios Town's **tourist office,** Kanari 11, turn off the waterfront onto Kanari, walk toward the *plateia*, and look for the i sign. (☎44 344 or 44 389. Open Apr.-Oct. M-F 7am-2:30pm and 7-10pm, Sa 10am-1pm, Su 7pm-10pm; Nov.-Mar. M-F 7am-2:30pm. In a yellow building at the far right end of the waterfront, the uncommonly hospitable owners at **Chios Rooms,** Leofores 114, offer bright and breezy rooms with polished hard-wood floors, most with a sea view and some with bath. (☎20 198. Singles 4-5000dr; doubles 5-8000dr; triples 9-10,000dr.) **Postal Code:** 82100.

LESVOS   ☎0251

Once home to the sensual poet Sappho, Lesvos is still something of a mecca for lesbians paying homage to their legendary etymological roots. Lesvos's cosmopolitan, off-beat culture incorporates horse breeding, ouzo, and leftist politics with equal zeal. Huge, geographically diverse, and far from the mainland, the island attracts visitors who spend weeks exploring its therapeutic hot springs, monasteries, petrified forest, sandy beaches, mountain villages, seaside cliffs, and art colonies. Day-trippers may be overwhelmed; you'll need four or five days to get far beyond the main harbor. Most travelers pass through the modern **Mytilini,** the capital and central port city. Tucked away in a pine forest above town, the **Gattelusi Castle** stands resolute guard. (Open Tu-Su 8:30am-3pm. 500dr., students 300dr.) The enormous **Church of St. Therapon** presides over the fish market, while the **Archaeological Museum,** Argiri Eftalioti 7, houses an impressive collection of the island's archaeological finds. (Open Tu-Su 8:30am-3pm. 500dr.)

Ferries go to Hios (3hr., 1 per week, 3400dr); Limnos (5hr., 4 per week, 4400dr); Peiraias (12hr., 1-3 per day, 7200dr); and Thessaloniki (12hr., 2 per week, 8400dr). Book ferries at **NEL Lines,** Pavlou Koudoutrioti 67 (☎22 220), along the waterfront. The **tourist police,** in the corner of the ferry dock, offer maps and advice. (☎22 776. Open daily 7:15am-2:15pm and 5-8pm.) The **Rooms to Let** office is one block inland from the center of the waterfront. (Singles 5-6000dr; doubles 6-8000dr. Open M-Sa 9am-1pm.) Take an intercity **bus** from the station behind Agios Irinis Park, southwest of the harbor, to the artist colonies of **Petras** and **Molyvos** (1½hr., 4 per day, 1400dr) and their popular beaches, on the northern coast. The **Petra Women's Coop-erative,** in the main square, or the **Molyvos tourist office** just up from the bus stop, respectively, can help you find a room. (Tourist office. ☎71 347; email mithimna@aigaio.gr. Open April-Oct. 7:30am-4pm.) The monastery of **Agios Rafael** in the hills of **Thermi,** remains a major pilgrimage site; travelers can stay two nights for free. Take the bus from Mytilini (45min., 1 per hr., 300dr). **Postal Code:** 81100.

RHODES (Ροδος)

Although Rhodes is the undisputed tourism capital of the Dodecanese, the sandy beaches along its east coast, the jagged cliffs skirting its west coast, and the green mountains dotted with villages in the interior have retained a core of serenity. The island's most famous sight is one that doesn't exist, one that perhaps never existed; the **Colossus of Rhodes,** a 35-meters tall bronze statue of Helios and one of the seven wonders of the ancient world, which supposedly straddled the island's harbor but was allegedly destroyed by an earthquake in 237 BC. The beautiful, extant **City of Rhodes** has been the island's capital for over 2000 years. The **Old Town,** surrounded by remnants of the 14th-century occupation (by the Knights of St. John), lends the city a medieval flair. Begin exploring the Old Town at the top of the hill, where a tall, square tower marks the entrance to the pride of the city, the **Palace of the Grand Master**, with 300 rooms, moats, drawbridges, and battlements. (☎27 674. Open Tu-Su 8:30am-2:30pm. 800dr; students and seniors 400dr; free for EU students.) Dominating one side of the **Plateia Argykastrou**, at the base of the waterfront, with its beautiful halls and courtyards, the former **Hospital of the Knights** is now the **Archaeological Museum.** Its treasures include the small but exquisite *Aphrodite Bathing* from the 1st-century BC and the 4th-century *Apollo*. (☎27 674. Open Tu-Su 8:30am-2:30pm. 800dr; students and seniors 400dr.) The New Town is a mecca for nightlife; **Orfanidou** is popularly known as **Bar Street.** Daytrips to **Faliraki**, which is south of the City of Rhodes and known for its rowdy drinkers, leave on **excursion boats.** They stop along the way in the town **Lindos**, which is perhaps the island's most picturesque town, with vine-lined streets, courtyards covered in pebble mosaics, and whitewashed houses beneath a castle-capped acropolis. See schedules and prices on the dock along the lower end of the Mandraki (from 3500dr). **Buses** also run to Faliraki (20 per day, 450dr) and Lindos (13 per day, 1000dr).

Ferries arrive in the City of Rhodes from Hios (7000dr); Iraklion, Crete (1 per week, 6200dr); Karpathos (3 per week, 4400dr); Kos (2-3 per day, 4000dr); Mykonos (1 per week, 6800dr); Paros (1 per week, 6900dr); Patmos (1-2 per day, 5400dr); Peiraias/Athens (14hr., 1-4 per day, 9000dr); Samos (2 per week, 6500dr); and Santorini (1 per week, 5100dr). The **Greek National Tourist Office (EOT)** is up Papgou, a few blocks from Pl. Rimini, at Makariou. (☎ (0241) 232 55. Open M-F 7:30am-3pm.) Off of Sokratous, lies **Mama's Pension**, 28 Menecleous Str. (☎ (0241) 25 359. Dorms 2500dr; doubles 6000dr.) **Pension Stathis**, Omirou 60 has quiet, spacious rooms around a courtyard. (☎ (0241) 24 357. Laundry 1200dr. Checkout noon. Dorms 2500dr; singles 6000dr; doubles 6-8000dr.) Or snooze in the New Town at the **New Village Inn**, Konstantopedos 10. (☎ (0241) 34 937. Singles 5000dr; doubles 8000dr.) **Yiannis**, Apellou 41, just off Sokratous away from the New Town, serves exquisite, traditional Greek dishes. (*Elliniko* plate for 3, 2800dr. Open 10am-noon.)

KARPATHOS (Καρπαθος)

Midway between Rhodes and Crete, windy Karpathos often receives no more than a passing glance from the deck of an overnight ferry, but the charming port town and its gorgeous surroundings are well worth a stop. Words can't convey the isolation of the town of **Olympus**, where preservation of centuries-old customs makes the town itself Olympus's greatest sight. Other points of interest include the three 13th- and 14th-century churches, the oldest on Karpathos, located conveniently near the bus stop. **Buses** from **Chrisovalandu Lines** and **Karpathos 1** run daily excursions to **Olympus** (depart 8:30am, return 6pm; 5000dr); find them near the ferry docks, or make reservations through Karpathos or Possi Travel. **Ferries** arrive in Pigadia (Karpathos Town) from Rhodes (5hr., 2 per week, 5025dr); Iraklion (6hr., 2 per week, 3500dr); and Santorini (12hr., 2 per week, 4860dr). Walk from the bus station, past the supermarket, to reach **Ellas Rooms for Rent**, where rooms are both quiet and centrally located. (☎ (0245) 22 226. Singles 4-5000dr; doubles 5-6000dr.)

KOS (Κως)   ☎0242

Although it rivals Rhodes in sheer numbers, Kos tends to draw a younger, louder, and more intoxicated crowd. Don't be dismayed by the raucous bars and mammoth hotels lining the golden beaches—perseverance rewards those who take the time to explore Kos's quiet nooks and scattered ruins. In **Kos Town**, minarets of Ottoman mosques rise among grand Italian mansions. The ancient sanctuary of **Asclepion**, 4km west of Kos Town, is dedicated to the god of healing. In the 5th century BC, Hippocrates opened the world's first medical school here to foster the development of medical science. Most ruins at the Asclepion actually date from the 3rd century BC. From the lowest *andiron* (level), steps lead to the 2nd-century AD **Temple of Apollo** and 4th-century BC **Minor Temple of Asclepios**. Sixty steps lead to the third *andiron*, with the forested remains of the **Main Temple of Asclepios** and a spectacular view of the ruins, Kos Town, and the Turkish coast. The site is also easily reached by **bus** (15min., 16 per day, 150-250dr). The island's best **beaches** stretch along Southern Kos up to Kardamene; the **bus** will let you off at any of them.

Ferries run to Patmos (4hr., 1-2 per day, 2800dr); Rhodes (4hr., 2 per day, 3400dr); and the Cyclades. A **Greek National Tourist Office,** on Akti Miaouli provides visitors with maps, brochures, and schedules. (Open M-F 8am-8:30pm, Sat 8am-3pm.) Take the first right off Megalou Alexandrou, on the back left corner of the first intersection, to get to **Pension Alexis,** Herodotou 9. (☎287 98. Doubles 5500-7000dr; triples 7500dr). **Hotel Afendoulis,** Evrilpilou 1, is down Vas. Georgiou near the beach. (☎253 21. Doubles 7500-9000dr.) Most bars are located either in **Exarhia,** also known as the area's **bar street,** between Akti Koundouriotou and the more subdued **Porfiriou,** in the north near the beach. **Fashion Club,** Kanari 2, is the hottest spot in town. (Cover 2500dr; includes 1 drink.) The **Haman Club** (☎28 323), near the *agora,* is a former bathhouse turned hopping dance club. **Heaven,** on Zouroudi along the waterfront, is loud and divinely popular. (Cover 2000dr, includes 1 drink.) **Postal Code:** 85300.

PATMOS (Πατμος)   ☎0247

In ancient times, Patmians worshipped Artemis, the huntress said to have raised the island from the sea. With the arrival of St. John, exiled from Ephesus, Patmos became a center of fledgling Christianity. Declared the "Holy Island" by ministerial decree, Patmos makes its historical and religious significance as plain as day—portside signs warn that nudity and other indecent behaviors will not be tolerated here. The white houses of **Hora** and the majestic walls of the sprawling **Monastery of St. John the Theologian** above are visible from all over the island. (Monastery and treasure museum open M and Th-Su 8am-1:30pm, Tu and W 8am-1:30pm and 4-6pm, Su 8am-noon and 4-6pm. Treasury 1000dr; monastery free.) Hora is 4km from the colorful port town of **Skala;** take a **bus** (10min., 11 per day, 250dr) or **taxi** (1000dr) from Skala (walk left and follow the signs from the bus/taxi station) or tackle the steep hike. Between Skala and the Monastery of St. John in Hora, the **Apocalypsis monastery** is built on the site where St. John stayed while on Patmos. It houses the natural **Sacred Grotto of the Revelation,** where St. John dictated the last book of the New Testament, the *Book of Revelation.* (☎31 234. Open M, W, and F 8am-1:30pm, Tu, Th, and Su 8am-1:30pm and 4-6pm. Free. Dress modestly.) **Ferries** arrive in Skala from: Athens/Peiraias (10hr., 6500dr); Kos (4hr., 2700dr); Rhodes (10hr., 5600dr); Samos (4 per week, 1700dr). The **tourist office** is opposite the dock. (☎316 66. Open M-F 9am-3:30pm and 4-10:30pm, Sa 11am-1:30pm and 6:30-8pm.) A battalion of locals greets the plethora of early morning boats each day, offering domatia (singles 5-7000dr; doubles 7-10,000dr). To get to **Flower Stefanos Camping at Meloi,** walk right along the waterfront (facing inland) and follow the signs for 2km, or catch the free shuttle from the port. (☎31 821. Open mid-May to mid-Oct. 1500dr per person, 750dr per tent; 750dr for tent rental.)

REPUBLIC OF IRELAND

AND NORTHERN IRELAND

IRISH PUNT OR POUND

US$1 = IR£0.87	IR£1 = US$1.15
CDN$1 = IR£0.58	IR£1 = CDN$1.71
UK£1 = IR£1.31	IR£1 = UK£0.76
EUR€1 = IR£0.79	IR£1 = EUR€1.27
AUS$1 = IR£0.51	IR£1 = AUS$1.96
NZ$1 = IR£0.40	IR£1 = NZ$2.53
SAR1 = IR£0.12	IR£1 = SAR8.04

PHONE CODE — **Country codes:** 353 (Republic); 44 (Northern Ireland; dial 048 from the Republic). **International dialing prefixes:** 00

This largely agricultural island has retained its natural charm over thousands of centuries. Windswept scenery curls around the coast, and mountains punctuate interior expanses of bogland. Dublin and Belfast, meanwhile, have flowered into cosmopolitan cities, suffused with sophistication. But, like its natural beauty, centuries-old disputes refuse to die. The English suppressed the Catholic population after the Reformation and fighting eventually degenerated into civil war. In 1949, the Free State proclaimed itself the independent Republic of Ireland (Éire), while the British kept control of Northern Ireland. In 1998, the countries adopted a peace accord by popular vote. 1999 and 2000 have seen the accord's fate fall into uncertainty, but negotiations continue in hopes of a lasting peace.

Although the **Republic of Ireland** and **Northern Ireland** are grouped together in this chapter for geographical reasons, no political statement is intended. For info on Northern Ireland's currency exchange rates and the like, see Britain, p. 139. For more detailed coverage of Ireland, snag a copy of *Let's Go: Ireland 2001*.

SUGGESTED ITINERARIES

THREE DAYS Ah, Dublin (3 days; p. 563). Head to the gates of **Trinity College**, admire the **Book of Kells,** then chat up folks at the **Guinness Hopstore** or the **Old Jameson Distillery.** Spend a day at the **National Museums** and galleries, stopping to relax in **St. Stephen's Green.** Fulfill your pubbing potential in **Temple Bar** and **Grafton St.**

ONE WEEK From **Dublin** (2 days; p. 563) head to complex **Belfast** (1 days; p. 592). Catch the bus to **Giant's Causeway** (1 day; p. 600) and head to **Galway** (1 day; p. 587), an artsy student town. Catch up on sleep on the ride to the **Ring of Kerry** (1 day; p. 583) and return to civilization in **Cork** (1 day; p. 578).

BEST OF IRELAND, THREE WEEKS Land in **Dublin** (4 days; p. 563) before taking the train up to **Belfast** (3 days; p. 592). Catch the bus to **Giant's Causeway** (1 day; p. 600), and stop in at **Derry** (2 days; p. 598). From **Donegal Town** (1 day; p. 591), climb **Slieve League** (1 day; p. 591), the tallest seacliffs in Europe. Use **Sligo** (3 days; p. 590) as a nighttime hub and daytrip to Co. Sligo's lakes and mountains. From there, head to **Galway** (2 days; p. 587), the **Ring of Kerry** (2 days; p. 583), **Killarney National Park** (1 day; p. 582), and **Cork** (2 days; p. 578). On your way back to Dublin, take a detour to medieval **Kilkenny** (1 day; p. 576).

LIFE AND TIMES

HISTORY AND POLITICS

PRE-CHRISTIAN IRELAND (TO 450)

What little knowledge historians have of ancient Irish culture they have ascertained from the fragile and spotty remains of its stone structures, landscaping, and metalware. Ireland's first settlers came from Britain in about 7000 BC. They left behind various structures that may be identified today on the Irish landscape. **Dolmens,** arrangements of enormous stones to create table-like form, were probably created as shrines. **Passage graves** are ornamented, underground stone hallways and chambers containing corpses and cinerary urns.

In the first two centuries of the **Bronze Age** (900-700 BC), known as the Irish Golden Age, Irish culture flowered, due in part to the central position held by warrior nobles in Atlantic trade routes between Gibraltar and Sweden. The **Celts** began migrating to Ireland from central Europe around 600 BC, and kept coming for the next 600 years. The **Uliad of Ulster,** chariot warriors and the most famous chieftains, dominated the La Tene culture from their capital near Armagh.

EARLY CHRISTIANS AND VIKINGS (450-1200)

Ireland was Christianized in a piecemeal fashion by a series of hopeful missionaries starting with **St. Patrick** in the 5th century. According to legend, St. Patrick was born in England and kidnapped as a boy into Irish slavery, from which he escaped to return to England; he later returned to Ireland at the command of a prophetic vision. As barbarians overran the continent, monks began arriving in Ireland. The enormous **monastic cities** of the 6th to 8th centuries earned Ireland its reputation as the "land of saints and scholars." From their bases in Armagh, Glendalough (p. 575), Derry (p. 598), Kells, Clonmacnoise, and elsewhere, the monastics of the Early Irish Church recorded the old epics, wrote long religious and legal poems in Old Irish and Latin, and illuminated gospels. The 7th century **Book of Durrow,** the earliest surviving illuminated manuscript, and the early 9th century **Book of Kells,** are now exhibited at Trinity College, Dublin (see p. 570).

In the first decade of the new millennium, strife broke out amongst the chieftains: High King **Brian Boru** and his warlike **Dal Cais** clan of Clare, challenged the Ui Neill clan for control of Ireland with the capture of Armagh in 1002. In the following years, the clans fought ferociously amongst themselves. The Dal Cais won a pyrrhic victory in the epic **Battle of Clontarf,** fought near Dublin in 1014, in which Brian Boru was lost. Ireland was then divided between chieftains **Rory O'Connor** and **Dermot MacMurrough,** who continued fighting for the crown of High King. Dermot made the mistake of seeking the assistance of English Norman nobles in reconquering Leinster. Richard de Clare, known popularly as **Strongbow,** was all too willing to help. Strongbow and his Anglo-Normans arrived in 1169 and cut a bloody swath through south Leinster. Strongbow married Dermot's daughter **Aoife** after Dermot's death in 1171, and seemed ready to proclaim an independent Norman kingdom in Ireland. Instead, he affirmed his loyalty to King Henry II and generously offered to govern Leinster on England's behalf.

FEUDALISM (1200-1607)

Thus began English hold over Irish land. The following feudal period saw constant power struggles between Gaelic and Norman-descended English lords. Over in England, the Crown fretted over this cultural cross-pollination, and in 1366 it sponsored the notorious **Statutes of Kilkenny.** These decrees banned English colonists from speaking Irish, wearing Irish styles of dress, or marrying native Irish, and forbade the Irish from entering walled cities.

The English Crown increased its control over Ireland throughout the next century. When Henry VIII broke with the Catholic Church to create the Church of England, a newly convened Dublin Parliament passed the 1537 **Irish Supremacy Act,**

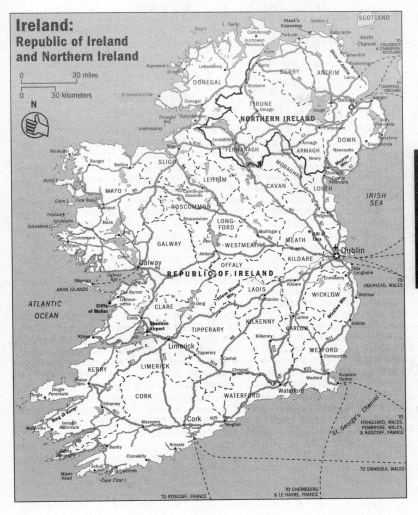

Ireland:
Republic of Ireland
and Northern Ireland

which declared Henry head of the Protestant **Church of Ireland,** and effectively made the island property of the Crown. In defiance of the Crown, **Hugh O'Neill,** an Ulster earl, raised an army of thousands in open rebellion in the late 1590s. Gaelic lords supported him, but the Old English lords were divided. O'Neill and the rest of the major Gaelic lords soared out of Ireland in 1607 in what came to be known as the **Flight of the Earls.** They promised to return with assistance from the forces of Catholic rulers on the continent, but never achieved this aim. The English took control of the land, and parceled it out to Protestants.

PLANTATION AND CROMWELL (1607-1688)

The English project of dispossessing Catholics of their land and "planting" Ireland with Protestants was most successful in Ulster. The project in the north became known as the **Ulster Plantation.** The now landless Irish revolted in Ulster in 1641 under a loose group of Gaelic-Irish leaders. **Owen Roe O'Neill,** of the next O'Neill generation, returned from the Continent to lead the insurrection, and the uprising even received the backing of the Catholic Church. The rebels advanced south, and in 1642 formed the **Confederation of Kilkenny,** an uneasy alliance of the Church and Irish and Old English lords. Negotiations between the Confederation and King Charles ended with **Oliver Cromwell's** victory in England and his arrival in Ireland.

Cromwell's army destroyed anything they did not occupy, and then some. The native Irish landowners had the options of going "to hell or to Connacht," the desolate and infertile region in Ireland's west. By 1660, the vast majority of Irish land was owned, maintained, and policed by Protestant immigrants.

THE PROTESTANT ASCENDANCY (1688-1801)

Thirty years after the English Civil War, English political disruption again resulted in Irish bloodshed. Catholic **James II,** driven from England by the "Glorious Revolution" of 1688, came to Ireland with his army, intending to gather military support to reclaim his throne. A war between William (the new Protestant king) and James ended on July 12, 1690 at the **Battle of the Boyne,** with James's defeat and exile. The war's end delivered the **Treaty of Limerick** that ambiguously promised Catholics undelivered civil rights. Instead, the **Penal Laws,** enacted at the turn of the 18th century, further limited Catholics, and banned the public practice of their religion at a time when Catholics comprised 90 percent of the island's population.

The newly secure Anglo-Irish elite built their own culture in Dublin and the Pale with garden parties, gossip, and architecture second only to London. The term **"Ascendancy"** was coined to describe a social elite whose distinction depended upon Anglicanism. Within this exclusive social structure, such thinkers as **Bishop George Berkeley** and **Edmund Burke** rose to prominence. **Trinity College** (see p. 570) flourished as the quintessential institution of the Ascendancy.

REBELLION, UNION, REACTION (1775-1848)

The American and French Revolutions inspired notions of independence in small political organizations such as the **United Irishmen.** Their Protestant leader, **Theobald Wolfe Tone,** hoped that a general uprising would create an independent, non-sectarian Ireland. A bloody uprising of peasants and priests erupted in May 1798. The rebels made their last stand at **Vinegar Hill,** near Enniscorthy in Co. Wexford; they fell in the thousands. The 1801 **Act of Union** dissolved the Dublin Parliament and created "The United Kingdom of Great Britain and Ireland;" the Church of Ireland was subsumed by the "United Church of England and Ireland."

THE FAMINE (1845-1870)

In the first half of the 19th century, the potato was the only crop capable of providing enough nutrients per acre to support the Irish population. The **Great Famine** lasted roughly from 1847-1851. In that short period of time, an estimated two to three million people died. While the Irish were eating grass, the British shipped thousands of pounds of grain from the island. British authorities often forcibly exchanged what few decent potatoes peasants could find with inedible grain. This injustice fueled the formation of more angry, young nationalist groups. In 1858, James Stephens founded the Irish Republican Brotherhood (IRB), commonly known as the **Fenians,** a secret society aimed at the violent removal of the British.

PARNELL'S CULTURAL NATIONALISM (1870-1914)

In 1870, Isaac Butt founded the **Irish Home Rule Party.** Home Ruler **Charles Stewart Parnell** was a charismatic Protestant aristocrat with an American mother and a hatred for everything English. Backed by Parnell's invigorated Irish party, William Gladstone introduced a **Home Rule Bill,** which was defeated. Meanwhile, various groups tried to revive what they took to be essential "Gaelic" culture, unpolluted by foreign influence. As the Home Rule movement grew, so did resistance to it. Between 1910 and 1913, thousands of Northern Protestants opposing Home Rule joined mass rallies, signed a covenant, and organized into a quasi-militia named the **Ulster Volunteer Force (UVF).** Nationalists led by **Eoin MacNeill** in Dublin responded in 1913 by creating the **Irish Volunteers.**

THE EASTER RISING (1914-1918)

In the summer of 1914, Irish Home Rule seemed imminent and Ulster ready to go up in flames, but neither happened—World War I did. British Prime Minister Henry Asquith passed a **Home Rule Bill** on the condition that the Irish Volunteer and Home Rule parties would recruit Irishmen for the British army. An 11,000-member armed guard, the remnants of the Volunteers, remained in Ireland. They were officially led by MacNeill, who knew nothing of the revolt that the Fenians were planning. If an architect can be ascribed to the ensuing mayhem, it was **Padraig Pearse,** who won his co-conspirators over to an ideology of "blood sacrifice."

Fenian leaders were planning to receive a shipment of German arms for use in a nationwide revolt on **Easter Sunday, 1916**. The arms arrived a day too early and were never picked up. The British captured and hanged **Roger Casement,** the man who was to meet the shipment. Fenian leaders, however, continued planning their rebellion, and mustering support from the Volunteers. On Monday, April 24, in Dublin, Pearse, James Connolly, and about one thousand others seized the **General Post Office** on O'Connell St. (see p. 572), read aloud a "Proclamation of the Republic of Ireland," and held out through five days of fighting in downtown Dublin.

The harsh reaction of the British martial-law administration to Easter Sunday turned popular opinion on its head; over ten days in May, fifteen "ringleaders" received the death sentence. In 1917, the Volunteers reorganized under master spy and Fenian bigwig **Michael Collins.** The Sinn Féin party, falsely associated with the Rising, became the political voice of military Nationalism. Collins brought the Volunteers to Sinn Féin, and Éamon de Valera became the party president.

INDEPENDENCE AND CIVIL WAR (1919-1922)

Extremist Irish Volunteers became known as the **Irish Republican Army (IRA),** which functioned as the military arm of the Sinn Féin government. The new government fought the **War of Independence** against the British. Hurried negotiations produced the **Anglo-Irish Treaty,** which created a 26-county Irish Free State while recognizing British rule over the northern counties. Lloyd George pushed the treaty forward by threatening war if it was rejected. Sinn Féin, the IRA, and the population each split on whether to accept the treaty. Collins said yes; de Valera said no. When the representative parliament voted yes, de Valera resigned from the presidency and Arthur Griffith assumed the position. The capable Collins government began the business of setting up a nation, with treasury, tax collection, a foreign ministry, and an unarmed police force. A portion of the IRA, led by **General Rory O'Connor,** opposed the treaty. O'Connor's Republicans occupied the Four Courts in Dublin, took a pro-treaty Army general hostage, and were attacked by the forces of Collins's government. Two years of **civil war** followed, tearing up the countryside and dividing the population. The pro-treaty government won, but Griffith died suddenly from the strain of the struggle and Collins was assassinated before the end of 1922. The dwindling minority of anti-treaty IRA officers went into hiding.

THE DE VALERA ERA (1922-1960)

The new 26-county Irish Free State emerged from civil war having lost its most prominent leaders, and needing to protect those ministers who remained. The Anglo-Irish Treaty required the newly elected Dáil to frame a constitution by December 6, 1922. Under the guidance of **Éamon de Valera,** the government ended armed resistance by May 1923, imprisoned Republican insurgents, and executed 77 of them. Then in 1927 de Valera broke with Sinn Féin and the IRA and founded his own political party, **Fianna Fáil,** in order to participate in government and oppose the treaty nonviolently. Fianna Fáil won the 1932 election, and de Valera held power for much of the next 20 years. "In the name of the most Holy Trinity," de Valera and the voters approved the permanent Irish Constitution in 1937. It declares the state's name to be Éire, and establishes the country's legislative structure, which consists of two chambers, both with five-year terms. The constitution originally contained a "special position" clause concerning the **Catholic Church** in Ireland, but the clause was deleted by a constitutional amendment in 1972.

IRELAND

Ireland maintained neutrality during WWII, despite German Air raids on Dublin and pressure from US President Franklin Roosevelt. A Fine Gael government under **John Costello** in 1948 had the honor of officially proclaiming "the Republic of Ireland," and ending supposed British Commonwealth membership. Britain recognized the Republic in 1949 but declared that the UK would maintain control over Ulster until the Parliament of Northern Ireland consented to join the Republic.

RECENT HISTORY (1960-1998)

By reaching out, Ireland has kept its young people in. In the 1960s, increased contact with the rest of the world slowed emigration and accelerated economic growth. In 1967, the government introduced free secondary education, including state grants for privately owned schools; in 1968, it introduced free university education for those below a certain income level. Ireland entered the European Economic Community, now the **European Union** (EU), in 1973. In 1990 the Republic broke progressive social and political ground when it elected its first female president, **Mary Robinson.** Social reform made further gains when the small, leftist **Labor Party** enjoyed enormous and unexpected success in the 1992 elections. In September of 1993, a coalition between the Labor Party and Fianna Fáil was elected. The new Taoiseach, **Albert Reynolds,** declared that his top priority was to stop violence in Northern Ireland. In August 1994 he announced the nearly miraculous cease-fire agreement with Sinn Féin and the IRA.

In June 1997, Fianna Fáil won the general election, making **Bertie Ahern,** the 45-year-old party leader, the youngest Taoiseach in the history of the state. Ahern joined the peace talks that produced the **Northern Ireland Peace Agreement** in April of 1998. On May 22, 1998, in the first island-wide election since 1918, an overwhelming 94% of voters in the Republic voted for the enactment of the Agreement.

IRELAND TODAY

As Ireland becomes more active in the global economy, the nation struggles to balance its traditionally conservative values with increasingly liberal international standards. Ireland's economy is booming, in large part due to increased foreign investment over the past decade. Relatively few regulations and huge incentives have drawn foreign investors, strengthening the currency and boosting Ireland's economy at one of Europe's fastest rates. There is some concern about economic overheating, and the effects of converting to the **euro** (see p. 23), the new EU currency that came into non-cash existence in 1999. As more young Irish spend time abroad and more international travelers spend time in Ireland, the culture's conservatism slowly cracks. While the Irish are eager to dispel the picturesque stereotype of the "land of saints and scholars" (and poverty and drunkenness), they hope to retain the safety afforded by their religious and family-oriented past.

THE ARTS

LITERATURE

1600-1880. In long-colonized Dublin, **Jonathan Swift** (1667-1745) wrote some of the most sophisticated, misanthropic, and marvelous satire in the English language. Besides his masterpiece *Gulliver's Travels*, Swift wrote political essays decrying English cruelty to the native Irish. **Oscar Wilde** (1856-1900) moved to London and set up as an aesthete to write one novel and many witty plays, including *The Importance of Being Earnest* (1895). Prolific playwright **George Bernard Shaw** (1856-1950) was also born in Dublin but moved to London in 1876, where he became an active socialist. Shaw won the Nobel Prize for Literature in 1925.

THE IRISH LITERARY REVIVAL. Members of this movement turned to Irish culture, from its ancient mythology to contemporary folktales, for inspiration. The early poems of **William Butler Yeats** (1865-1939) create a rural Ireland of loss and legend. His early work, from *Crossways* (1889) to *In the Seven Woods* (1904), won Yeats worldwide fame thanks to the appeal of his mystic vision of picturesque

Ireland. "Easter 1916" described the sudden transformation that the Easter rebels brought to the Irish national self-image: "All changed, changed utterly / A terrible beauty is born." In 1923, he became the first Irishman to win the Nobel Prize.

MODERNISM. The most famous of Ireland's expatriates is **James Joyce** (1882-1941); his novels are recognized as some of the seminal works of Modernism. His first novel, *A Portrait of the Artist as a Young Man* (1914), uses the protagonist Stephen Daedalus to describe Joyce's own youth in Dublin. Stephen Daedalus reappears in *Ulysses*, Joyce's revolutionary novel of 1922. *Ulysses* chronicles one day in the life of the antihero, Leopold Bloom, a middle-class Jewish man living his life in a stagnating Dublin. **Samuel Beckett's** (1906-89) three novels (*Molloy, Malone Dies,* and *The Unnameable*), world-famous plays *(Waiting for Godot* and *Endgame;* all written 1946-1950), and bleak prose poems convey a deathly pessimism about language, society, and life. Beckett won the Nobel Prize in 1969, but did not accept it on the grounds that Joyce had never received it.

MODERN WRITERS IN NORTHERN IRELAND. The literature of Northern Ireland describes two culturally divided groups, Catholics and Protestants. Many Northern writers attempt to create works of relevance to members of both communities. Born in rural County Derry, **Seamus Heaney** won the Nobel Prize for Literature in 1995, and is the most prominent living Irish poet. His subject matter ranges from bogs to bombings to archeological remains. While his tone is often highly lyrical, Heaney writes in an anti-pastoral mode.

FOOD AND DRINK

Food in Ireland is expensive. The basics are simple and filling. "Take-away" (takeout) **fish and chips** shops are quick, greasy, and very popular. Many pubs serve food as well as drink; typical pub grub includes **Irish stew,** burgers, soup, and sandwiches. Soda bread is delicious and keeps well, and Irish dairy products are addictive. Pubs in Ireland are the forum for banter, singing, and *craic* (a good time). In the evenings, many pubs play impromptu or organized traditional music, known as *trad.* **Guinness,** a rich, dark stout, is the most revered brew in Ireland. **Irish whiskey,** which Queen Elizabeth once claimed was her only true Irish friend, is sweeter than its Scotch counterpart. Irish monks invented whiskey, calling it *uisce beatha,* meaning "water of life." **Pubs** are usually open Monday to Saturday 10:30am to 11 or 11:30pm, Sunday 12:30 to 2pm and 4 to 11pm.

ESSENTIALS

DOCUMENTS AND FORMALITIES

Citizens of Australia, Canada, European Union countries, New Zealand, South Africa, the United Kingdom, and the United States, do not need **visas** to visit Ireland for stays shorter than three months.

Irish Embassies at Home: Australia, 20 Arkana St., Yarralumla ACT 2600 (☎ (02) 62 73 30 22); **Canada,** 130 Albert St., #1105, Ottawa, ON K1P 5G4 (☎ (613) 233 62 81); **South Africa,** Tubach Centre, 1234 Church St., 0083 Colbyn, Pretoria (☎ (012) 342 50 62); **UK,** 17 Grosvenor Pl., London SW1X 7HR (☎ (020) 72 35 21 71); **US,** 2234 Massachusetts Ave, NW, Washington, DC 20008 (☎ (202) 462-3939; www.ireland-emb.org/contact.html). **New Zealanders** should contact the embassy in Australia.

Foreign Embassies in Ireland: All embassies for the Republic of Ireland are in **Dublin** (see p. 563). The US has a consulate in **Belfast** (see Belfast, p. 592).

TRANSPORTATION

BY PLANE. Flying to London and connecting to Ireland is often easier and cheaper. Aer Lingus and several other carriers offer service on these routes. **British**

Midland Airways (in UK ☎ (0870) 607 05 55; in Republic ☎ (01) 283 0700); www.britishmidland.com) flies about seven times per day to London Heathrow. **British Airways** (in the UK ☎ (0345) 22 21 11; in the Republic ☎ (800) 62 67 47; in the US ☎ (800) 247 9297; www.british-airways.com), flies about five times per day Monday through Friday, Saturday and Sunday six per day. Prices range from UK£70-150 return but can drop from time to time. **Ryanair** (in UK ☎ (0870) 333 12 50; in Republic ☎ (01) 609 78 00) connects Kerry, Cork, and Knock to London and nine other destinations in England and Scotland. The **Air Travel Advisory Bureau,** 28 Charles Sq., London N16HT, England (☎ (0171) 636 50 00; www.atab.co.uk) will put you in touch with the cheapest carriers out of London for free.

BY TRAIN. Iarnród Éireann (Irish Rail) is useful only for travel to urban areas. While the **Eurailpass** is not accepted in Northern Ireland, it *is* accepted on trains (but not buses) in The Republic. The BritRail pass does not cover travel in Northern Ireland, but the month-long **BritRail+Ireland** works in both the North and the Republic with rail options and round-trip ferry service between Britain and Ireland (US$408-770). **Northern Ireland Railways** (☎ (01232) 89 94 11; www.nirailways.co.uk) is not extensive but covers the northeastern coastal region well. The major line connects Dublin to Belfast. A valid **Northern Ireland Travelsave** stamp (UK£6, affixed to back of ISIC) will get you 50% off all trains and 15% discounts on bus fares over UK£1 within Northern Ireland. The **Freedom of Northern Ireland** ticket allows unlimited travel by train and Ulsterbus, and can be purchased for seven consecutive days (UK£38), three consecutive days (£25), or a single day (£10).

BY BUS. Bus Éireann (the Irish national bus company) reaches Britain and even the continent by working in conjunction with ferry services and the bus company **Eurolines** (UK ☎ (01582) 404 511; www.eurolines.com). To get to Ireland from Britain, there are connecting services from Bristol and London to Cork, Waterford, Tralee, Killarney, Ennis, and Limerick, and from Cardiff and Birmingham to Cork, Waterford, Ennis, and Limerick. Prices range from IR£10 to £25. Tickets can be booked through usit, any Bus Éireann office, Irish Ferries, Stena Line, or any Eurolines (or National Express office in Britain (in UK ☎ (0990) 808 080). The immense Eurolines network connects with many European destinations. London to Dublin UK£18, return £34 (for first ferry in the morning; more expensive for later ferries and after July 1; more expensive for travelers over 26). Contact the Bus Éireann General Inquiries desk in Dublin (☎ (01) 836 61 11) or a travel agent.

Return (or round-trip) tickets are always a great value, as is purchasing a **Travel Save Stamp** (£8) if you are a student. A combined **Irish Explorer Rail/Bus** ticket allows unlimited travel eight out of 15 consecutive days on rail and bus lines (£100; children £50). Purchase these tickets from Bus Éireann at their main bus stations in transportation hubs. **Ulsterbus,** Laganside, Belfast (☎ (01232) 33 30 00; www.ulsterbus.co.uk), runs extensive and reliable routes throughout Northern Ireland, where there are no private bus services. The bus discount passes won't save you much money: a **Freedom of Northern Ireland** bus and rail pass offers unlimited travel for one day (UK£10), or several consecutive days (7-day pass £38). The **Irish Rover** pass covers both Bus Éireann and Ulsterbus services (unlimited travel for 3 out of 8 days £36, £18 child; for 8 out of 15 days £85, children £43; for 15 out of 30 £130, children £65). The **Emerald Card** offers unlimited travel on Ulsterbus; Northern Ireland Railways; Bus Éireann Expressway, Local, and City services in Dublin, Cork, Limerick, Galway, and Waterford; and intercity, DART, and suburban rail Iarnród Éireann services. The card works for eight out of 15 consecutive days (£115, children £58) or 15 out of 30 consecutive days (£200, children £100).

BY FERRY. Ferries (more economical than air travel) journey between Britain and Ireland several times per day; tickets usually range IR£20-35. Traveling mid-week at night promises the cheapest fares. **An Óige (HI) members** receive up to a 20% discount on fares from Irish Ferries and Stena Sealink. Almost all sailings in June, July, and August are "controlled sailings," which means that you must book the crossing ahead of time (a few days in advance is usually sufficient). **ISIC cardholders** with the **Travel Stamp** (see above) receive a 15% discount from Irish Ferries and an average 17% discount (variable among four routes) on StenaLine ferries. Ferries run from Cork to South Wales and Roscoff, France (see p. 578) and from Rosslare Harbour to Pembroke, Wales and Roscoff and Cherbourg, France (see p. 324).

BY CAR. Drivers in Ireland use the left side of the road, and place their steering-wheel on the right side of the car. Gas prices are high. Be particularly cautious at roundabouts (rotary interchanges)—give way to traffic from the right. Irish law requires drivers and passengers to wear seat belts—these laws are enforced. The general speed limit in the Republic is 90km per hr. (55 mph) on the open road and either 50km per hr. (30 mph) or 65km per hr. (40 mph) in town. The North's speed limits are 97km per hr. (60 mph) on single carriageways (non-divided highways), 113km per hr. (70 mph) on motorways (highways) and dual carriageways (divided highways), and usually 48km per hr. (30 mph) in urban areas. People under 21 cannot rent cars, and those under 23 often encounter difficulties. Prices range from IR£100-300 (plus VAT) per week with insurance and unlimited mileage.

BY BIKE, FOOT, AND THUMB. Much of Ireland's countryside is well-suited for cycling. Single-digit N roads in the Republic, and M roads in the North, are more busily trafficked; try to avoid them. Ireland's mountains, fields, and heather-covered hills make **walking and hiking** a joy. The **Wicklow Way** has hostels designed for hikers within a day's walk of each other. The **Ulster Way** encircles Northern Ireland with 560 mi. of marked trails. **Hitching** in Ireland has a good reputation, but there has been a recent backlash; the percentage of travelers hitching has declined. Locals in Northern Ireland do not recommend hitching there. *Let's Go* does not recommend hitchhiking.

TOURIST SERVICES & MONEY

EMERGENCY Police, Ambulance, and Fire: ☎999.

TOURIST OFFICES. Bord Fáilte (the **Irish Tourist Board**) operates a nationwide network of offices. Most tourist offices book rooms for a small fee (IR£1-3) and a 10% deposit, but many fine hostels and B&Bs are not "approved," so the tourist office can't tell you about them. Bord Fáilte's central office is at Baggot St. Bridge, **Dublin** 2, in Ireland ☎ (1850) 230 330; in UK ☎ (020) 74 93 32 01; elsewhere ☎ (353) (01) 666 1258; www.ireland.travel.ie.

> **Irish Tourist Boards at Home: Australia,** 36 Carrington St., 5th level, Sydney, NSW 2000 (☎ (02) 9299 6177); **Canada,** 2 Bloor St. W, Toronto, ON M4W 3E2 (☎ (416) 925-6368); **UK,** 150 New Bond St., London W1Y 0AQ (☎ (020) 7493 3201); **US,** 345 Park Ave., New York, NY 10154 (☎ (212) 418-0800 or 1 (800) 223 6470).

The **Northern Ireland Tourist Board** offers similar services at locations all over the North. The head office 59 North St., **Belfast**, BT1 1NB, Northern Ireland (☎ (01232) 246609; fax 240960; www.ni-tourism.com). **Dublin**, 16 Nassau St., Dublin 2 (☎ (01) 679 1977; CallSave (1850) 230230.

> **Northern Ireland Tourist Boards at Home: Canada,** 2 Bloor St. W., Toronto ON M4W3E2 (☎ (416) 925 6368); **US,** 551 Fifth Ave., Room #701, New York, NY 10176 (☎ (800) 326-0036); **UK,** British Travel Centre, 12 Lower Regent St., London SW1Y 4PQ (☎ (020) 7839 8417).

CURRENCY AND EXCHANGE. Legal tender in the Republic of Ireland is the **Irish pound** (or "**punt**"), denoted £. It comes in the same denominations as the **British pound** (which is called "**sterling**" in Ireland). Legal tender in Northern Ireland is the British pound. A good rule of thumb is only to go to banks or bureaux de change that have at most a 5% margin between their buy and sell prices. The majority of Irish towns have 24-hr. **ATMs**.

Prices: If you stay in hostels and prepare your own food, expect to spend anywhere from US$18-30 per person per day. Accommodations start at about £8-10 per night for a single bed while the cost for a basic sit-down meal begins around £6.

Tipping and bargaining: Some restaurants in Ireland figure a service charge into the bill; some even calculate it into the cost of the dishes themselves. The menu often indicates whether or not service is included (ask if you're not sure). For those restaurants that do not include a tip in the bill, more common in cities, customers should leave 10-15%. Porters, parking-lot attendants, waitstaff, and hairdressers are usually tipped. Cab drivers are usually tipped 10%. Above all, **never tip the barman**.

Taxes: Both Ireland and Northern Ireland charge Value Added Tax (VAT), a national sales tax on most goods and some services. In Ireland, the VAT ranges from 0% on food and children's clothing to 17% in restaurants to 21% on other items, such as jewelry and clothing; the VAT is usually included in listed prices. The British rate, applicable to Northern Ireland, is 17.5% on many services (such as hairdressers, hotels, restaurants, and car rental agencies) and on all goods (except books, medicine, and food). Prices stated in *Let's Go* include VAT. VAT Refunds are available for non-EU citizens and for goods taken out of the country, but not for services.

ACCOMMODATIONS AND CAMPING

HOSTELS. Hosteling is the way to go; dorm beds usually cost between £7-10, and breakfast is often included or can be tacked on for £1-3. **An Óige,** the Irish Hosteling International affiliate, runs 34 hostels that are often relatively bare and somewhat out of the way. The North's HI affiliate is **HINI** (Hostelling International Northern Ireland; formerly **YHANI**), which operates eight nicer hostels. The *An Óige Handbook* lists and details all An Óige and HINI hostels; its standard pricing system isn't always followed by every hostel listed. A number of hostels in Ireland belong to the **Independent Holiday Hostels (IHH);** they have no lockout or curfew (with a few exceptions), accept all ages, don't require membership, and are all Bord Fáilte-approved. Copious **B&Bs** (in virtually every Irish town) can provide a luxurious break from hosteling; expect to pay IR£15-25 for singles and IR£20-36 for doubles. "Full Irish breakfasts" are often filling enough to get you through to dinner. **Camping** in Irish State Forests and National Parks is not allowed; camping on public land is permissible only if there is no official campsite nearby. Most caravan and camping parks are open April through October. Pick up the *Caravan and Camping Ireland* guide from any Bord Fáilte office for info on camping in the Republic.

COMMUNICATION

MAIL. To send a **postcard** or a **letter** (up to 25g) to an international destination within Europe costs 32p; to any other international destination, 45p. Domestic postcards and letters require 30p. Address *Poste Restante* letters to (for example): "Amanda HILLMAN, Poste Restante, Enniscorthy, Co. Wexford, Ireland." Airmail letters take about 6-9 days between Ireland and North America.

TELEPHONES. Both the Irish Republic and Northern Ireland have public phones that accept **coins** (20p for about 4min.) and **pre-paid phone-cards**. For an **international operator,** dial 114 in the Republic or 155 in Northern Ireland; **operator,** 10 and 100; **directory,** 1190 and 192. **International direct dial** numbers include: **AT&T** ☎ (1800) 550000 in the Republic and ☎ (0800) 890 011 in Northern Ireland; **Australia Direct** ☎ (1800) 550 06 and ☎ (0800) 890 061; **British Telecom** ☎ (1800) 550 144 and ☎ (0800) 890353; **Canada Direct** ☎ (1800) 555 001 and ☎ (0800) 890 016; **MCI World Ring** ☎ (1800) 551 001 and ☎ (0800) 890 222; **Telecom New Zealand** ☎ (1800) 550 064 and ☎ (0800) 890 064; **Telekom South Africa** ☎ (1800) 550 027 and ☎ (0800) 890 027.

INTERNET ACCESS. Internet access is generally available in Irish cities and larger towns in privately owned cafes and occasional libraries. Thirty min. cost £2-5.

LOCAL FACTS

Time: Ireland is even with Greenwich Mean Time (GMT).

Hours: Most **banks** are open M-F 9am-4:30pm, sometimes later on Th. In big cities, **shop** hours are much longer.

Climate: Weather in Ireland is temperate (summer averages 15-18°C, or 60-65°F) yet temperamental. Keep a poncho or umbrella handy and carry a sweater.

Holidays: Much of Southern Ireland closes for holidays on January 1, St. Patrick's Day (Mar. 17), Good Friday, Easter (Apr. 13-16), and Christmas (Dec. 25-26). Northern Ireland adds on May Day (May 1), Spring or Whitsun Holiday (May 28), Orange Day (June 12), and August 27.

Festivals: All of Ireland goes green for **St. Patrick's Day** (Mar. 17th). On **Bloomsday,** Dublin (June 16) traipses about revering James Joyce.

DUBLIN ☎01

In a country known for its relaxed pace and rural sanctity, Dublin stands out for its international style and boundless energy. Although the Irish worry that it has taken on the negative characteristics of a big city, it's still as friendly a major city as you'll find. The city and its suburbs, home to one-third of Ireland's population, are at the vanguard of the country's rapid social change; countercultures flourish here in a way the rest of the Emerald Isle would summarily reject, and cutting-edge, world-renowned music bursts from the city's pub doors. It's no cultural wallflower either: the ghosts of Swift, Joyce, Beckett, Behan, and others pepper Dublin's neighborhoods with literary attractions. Dublin is a capital with a devotion to history and an appreciation of culture. The best trips to Dublin combine its duality and soak up as many of the sights and sips and sounds that the banks of the Liffey can offer.

⌐ TRANSPORTATION

Airport: Dublin Airport (☎844 4900). **Dublin buses** #41, 41B, and 41C run to Eden Quay in the city center with stops along the way (every 20min., IR£1.20). The **Airlink shuttle** runs non-stop directly to Busáras Central Bus Station and O'Connell St. (30-40min., every 10-15min., IR£3) and on to Heuston Station (50min., IR£3.50). **Airport Express buses** (☎844 4265) go to Busáras and O'Connell St. (30min.; departs every 15-30min.; M-Sa 6:30am-10:50pm, Su 7:10am-11pm; IR£2.50). A **taxi** from the airport to the city center costs roughly IR£12-15.

Trains: Irish Rail, Iarnród Éireann (EER-ann-road AIR-ann) has a travel center at 35 Lower Abbey St. (☎836 6222). Open M-F 9am-5pm, Sa 9am-1pm. **Connolly Station,** Amiens St. (☎836 3333), is north of the Liffey and close to Busáras Bus Station. Buses #20, 20A, and 90 at the station head south of the river, and the DART runs to Tara on the south quay, but it's faster to walk. Trains to: **Belfast** (2¼hr., 5-8 per day, IR£18); **Sligo** (3½hr., 3-4 per day, IR£14.50); and **Wexford** (3hr., 2-3 per day, IR£11) via Rosslare. **Heuston Station** (☎703 2132) is south of Victoria Quay, well west of the city center, a 25min. walk from Trinity College. Buses #26, 51, and 79 go from Heuston to the city center. Trains to: **Cork** (3½hr., 6-11 per day, IR£3.50); **Galway** (2½hr., 4-5 per day, IR£13-22); **Limerick** (2¼hr., 9 per day, IR£16-25); **Tralee** (4½hr., 4-7 per day, IR£34); and **Waterford** (2½hr., 3-4 per day, IR£13).

Buses: Info available at the **Dublin Bus Office,** 59 O'Connell St. (☎873 4222); the Bus Éireann window is open M-F 9am-5pm, Sa 9am-1pm. Inter-city buses to Dublin arrive at **Busáras Central Bus Station,** Store St. (☎836 6111), directly behind the Customs House and next to Connolly Station. Bus Éireann runs to: **Belfast** (3hr.; 4-7 per day, IR£10.50); **Derry** (4¼hr., 4-5 per day, IR£10.50); **Donegal Town** (4¼hr., 3-6 per day, IR£10); **Galway** (4hr., 4-14 per day, IR£9); **Limerick** (3¼hr., 7-13 per day, IR£10); **Rosslare Harbour** (3hr., 7-10 per day, IR£10); **Sligo** (4hr., 3 per day, IR£9); **Waterford** (2¾hr., 5-7 per day, IR£7); and **Wexford** (2¾hr., 7-10 per day, IR£8).

Ferries: Irish Ferries (☎661 0511) has an office off St. Stephen's Green on Merrion Row. Open M-F 9am-5pm, Sa 9:15am-12:45pm. **Stena Line** ferries arrive from **Holyhead, UK** at the **Dún Laoghaire** (see p. 575) ferry terminal (☎204 7777). **Irish Ferries** (24hr. ☎ (1890) 313 131; www.irishferries.ie) arrive from Holyhead at the **Dublin Port** (☎ 607 5665), from where buses #53 and 53A run every hr. to Busáras (80p); to get to the ferryport, **Dublin Bus** also runs connection buses timed to fit the ferry schedule (IR£2-2.50). **Merchant Ferries** also docks at the Dublin ferryport and runs a route to **Liverpool, UK** (8hr., 2 per day, IR£40, car IR£150-170); booking for Merchant is only available from **Gerry Feeney,** 19 Eden Quay (☎819 2999).

Public Transportation: Dublin Bus, 59 O'Connell St. (☎873 4222). Open M 8:30am-5:30pm, Tu-F 9am-5:30pm, Sa 9am-1pm. The Dublin buses run fairly regularly within the city, especially the smaller **City Imp** buses (every 8-15min.). Dublin Bus runs the **NiteLink** service to the suburbs (Th-Sa nights at 12:30am, 1:30am, 2:30am, and 3:30am; £3). **Travel Wide** passes offer unlimited rides for a day or a week. (Day £3.50; week £13, students with TravelSave stamp £10.) **DART** trains run up and down the coast and serve the suburbs (every 10-15min., 6:30am-11:30pm, IR£0.55-1.10).

Taxis: National Radio Cabs, 40 James St. (☎677 2222). All 24hr. IR£2.20 plus 90p per mi.; 80p call-in charge.

Car Rental: Budget, 151 Lower Drumcondra Rd. (☎837 9611), and at the airport. In summer from IR£35 per day, IR£165 per week; in winter IR£30, IR£140. Min. age 23.

Bike Rental: MacDonald Cycles, 38 Wexford St. (☎475 2586), and **Cycle Ways,** 185-6 Parnell St. (☎ 873 4748). **Dublin Bike Tours** (☎679 0889), behind the Kinlay House hostel on Lord Edward St., also rents and provides advice on route planning. IR£10 per day, IR£40 per week; students IR£8, IR£35; ID deposit.

✦🎔 ORIENTATION AND PRACTICAL INFORMATION

The **River Liffey** is the natural divide between Dublin's North and South Sides. The more famous sights, posh stores, excellent restaurants, and Heuston Station are on the **South Side.** The majority of hostels, the bus station, and Connolly Station sprout up on the **North Side.** The streets running alongside the Liffey are called **quays;** their names change every block. Each bridge over the river also has its own name, and streets change names as they cross. If a street is split into "Upper" and "Lower," then the "Lower" is always the part of the street closer to the mouth of the Liffey. **O'Connell St.,** three blocks west of the Busáras Central Bus Station, is the primary link between north and south Dublin. One block south of the Liffey, **Fleet St.** becomes **Temple Bar. Dame St.** runs parallel to Temple Bar with Trinity College as its terminus, and defines the southern edge of the district. **Trinity College** functions as the nerve center of Dublin's cultural activity, drawing legions of bookshops and student-oriented pubs into its orbit. The North Side bustles with urban grit and hawks merchandise generally cheaper than in the more touristed South Side. **Henry St.** and **Mary St.** comprise a pedestrian shopping zone that intersects with O'Connell after the **General Post Office (GPO),** two blocks from the Liffey. The North Side has the reputation of being a rougher area, especially after sunset.

TOURIST, FINANCIAL, AND LOCAL SERVICES

Tourist Information: Main Office, Dublin Tourist Centre, Suffolk St. (☎ (1850) 230 330; email information@dublintoursim.ie; www.visitdublin.com). From Connolly Train Station, walk left down Amiens St., take a right onto Lower Abbey St., pass Busáras, and continue until you come to O'Connell St. Turn left, cross the bridge, and walk past Trinity College; Suffolk St. will be on your right. Accommodation service with IR£1 booking fee and 10% non-refundable deposit; IR£2 charge to book outside Dublin.

Northern Ireland Tourist Board: 16 Nassau St. (☎679 1977 or (1850) 230 230). Books accommodations in the North. Open M-F 9am-5:30pm, Sa 10am-5pm.

Embassies: Australia, 2nd fl., Fitzwilton House, Wilton Terr. (☎676 1517; fax 678 5185). Open M-Th 8:30am-12:30pm and 1:30-4:30pm, F 9am-noon. **Canada,** 65 St. Stephen's Green South (☎478 1988). Open M-F 9am-1pm and 2-4:30pm. **New Zealand** embassy in London. **South Africa,** 2nd fl., Alexandra House, Earlsfort Centre

(☎661 5553). Open M-F 8:30am-5pm. **UK,** 29 Merrion Rd. (☎269 5211). Open M-F 9am-5pm. **US,** 42 Elgin Rd., Ballsbridge (☎668 8777). Open M-F 8:30am-5pm.

Banks: Bank of Ireland, AIB and **TSB** branches with bureaux de change and **24hr. ATMs** cluster on Lower O'Connell St., Grafton St., and in the Suffolk and Dame St. areas. Most bank branches are open M-F 10am-4pm.

American Express: 43 Nassau St. (☎679 9000). Traveler's cheque refunds. Currency exchange; no commission for AmEx Traveler's Checks. Mail held. Open M-F 9am-5pm.

Luggage Storage: Connolly Station. IR£2 per item. Open M-Sa 7:40am-9:20pm, Su 9:10am-9:45pm. **Heuston Station.** IR£1.50, IR£2.50, or IR£3.50 per item, depending on size. Open daily 6:30am-10:30pm.

Laundry: The Laundry Shop, 191 Parnell St. (☎872 3541). Closest to Busáras and the North Side hostels. Wash and dry IR£4.20-5. Open M-F 8am-7pm, Sa 9am-6pm.

EMERGENCY AND COMMUNICATIONS

Emergency: Dial ☎999; no coins required.

Police (*Garda*): Dublin Metro Headquarters, Harcourt Sq. (☎478 5295), Store St. Station (☎855 7761), Fitzgibbon St. Station (☎836 3113).

Pharmacy: O'Connell's, 35 Lower O'Connell St. (☎873 0427). Convenient to city bus routes. Open M-Sa 8:30am-10pm, Su 10am-10pm. Other branches are scattered around the city center, including Grafton St.

Hospital: St. James's Hospital, James St. (☎453 7941). Served by bus #123. **Mater Misericordiae Hospital,** Eccles St. (☎830 1122 or 830 8788), off Lower Dorset St. Served by buses #10, 11, 13, 16, 121, and 122.

Internet Access: Several chains abound, the best being **The Internet Exchange,** with branches at 146 Parnell St., the Suffolk St. tourist office, and in the Granary at Temple Bar South, in addition to two others in Temple Bar. (Open daily 9am-11pm, except Tourist Office branch, open daily 9am-5pm.)

Post Office: General Post Office (GPO), O'Connell St. (☎705 7000). Dublin is the only city in Ireland with postal codes. Even-numbered postal codes are for areas south of the Liffey, odd-numbered are for the north. *Poste Restante* pick-up at the bureau de change window. Open M-Sa 8am-8pm, Su 10am-6:30pm. **Postal code:** Dublin 1.

◤ ACCOMMODATIONS

Dublin's accommodations overflow, especially during Easter, holidays, and summer—reserve ahead. Dorms range from IR£7-15 per night. Quality **B&Bs** blanket Dublin and the surrounding suburbs, although prices have risen with housing costs (most charge IR£16-30 per person); many cluster along **Upper and Lower Gardiner St.,** on **Sherriff St.,** and near **Parnell Sq.**

HOSTELS

To deal with the large crowds, Dublin's hostels lean toward the institutional, especially in comparison to their more personable country cousins. The beds south of the river fill up fastest, as they are closest to the city's sights and nightlife.

🖾 **Barnacle's Temple Bar House,** 19 Temple Ln. (☎671 6277; email templeba@barnacles.iol.ie). All rooms with bath and excellent security. Breakfast included. June-Sept. 10-bed dorms IR£11; 6-bed dorms IR£13; 4-bed dorms IR£15; doubles and twins IR£40. Mar.-May and Oct. about IR£1 cheaper. Nov.-Feb. about IR£2-3 cheaper.

The Brewery Hostel, 22-23 Thomas St. (☎453 8600; email breweryh@indigo.ie). Follow Dame St. past Christ Church, or take bus #123. Next to Guinness and a 20min. walk to Temple Bar. All rooms with bath. Breakfast included. Laundry IR£3.50. 8- to 10-bed dorms IR£10-12; 4-bed dorms IR£15 per person; singles IR£28; doubles IR£44.

Avalon House (IHH), 55 Aungier St. (☎475 0001; email info@avalon.ie; www.avalon-house.ie). Turn off Dame St. onto Great Georges St.; the hostel is a 10min. walk down on your right. Temple Bar is within stumbling distance. Breakfast included. Towels IR£1 with IR£5 deposit. June-Sept. large dorms IR£12.50; 4-bed dorms with bath IR£16.50; doubles IR£36, with bath IR£40. Mar.-May and Oct. IR£9.50, IR£14, IR£36. Nov.-Feb. IR£8, IR£11.50, IR£28.

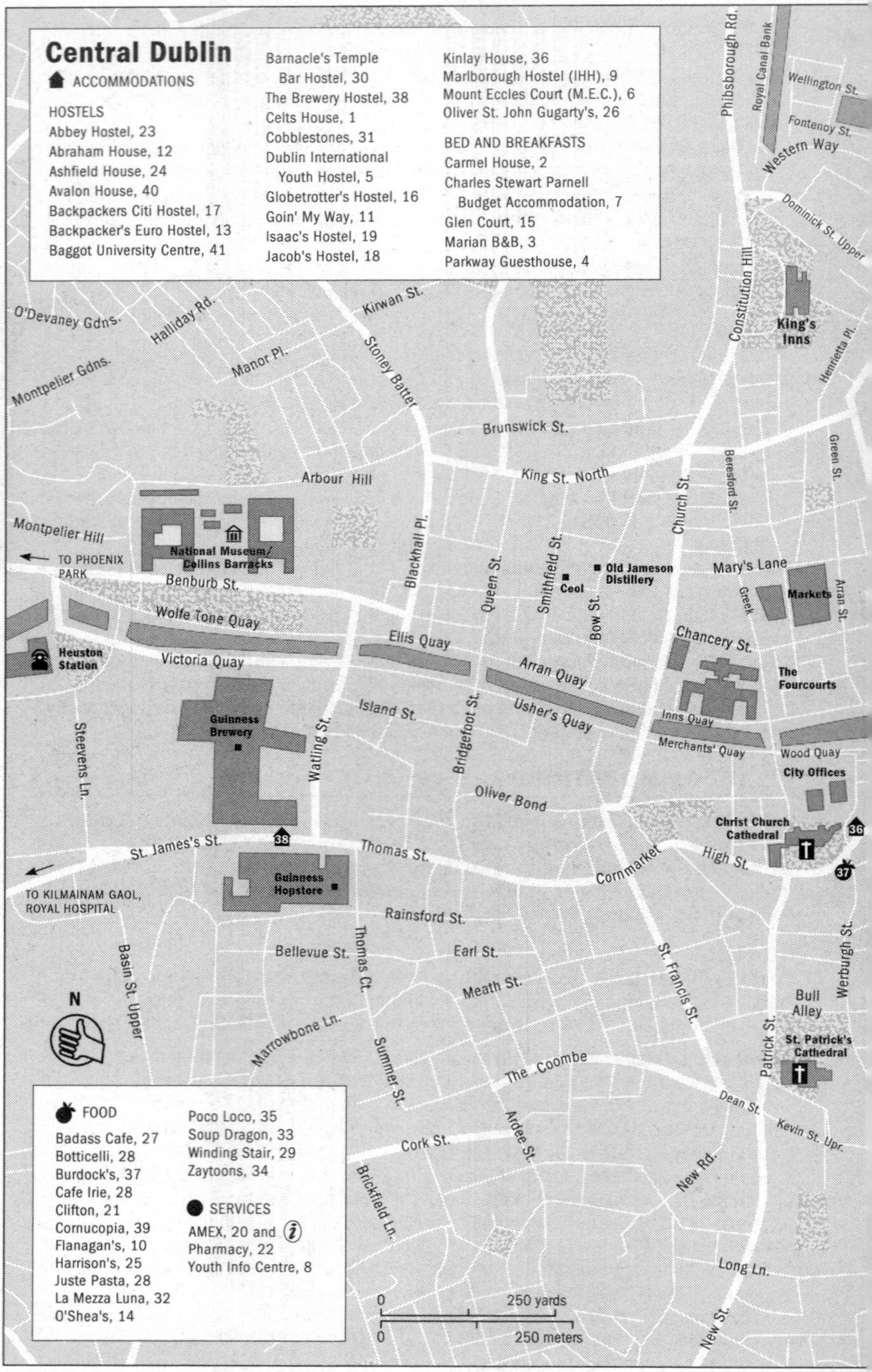

Central Dublin

♠ ACCOMMODATIONS

HOSTELS
Abbey Hostel, 23
Abraham House, 12
Ashfield House, 24
Avalon House, 40
Backpackers Citi Hostel, 17
Backpacker's Euro Hostel, 13
Baggot University Centre, 41

Barnacle's Temple
  Bar Hostel, 30
The Brewery Hostel, 38
Celts House, 1
Cobblestones, 31
Dublin International
  Youth Hostel, 5
Globetrotter's Hostel, 16
Goin' My Way, 11
Isaac's Hostel, 19
Jacob's Hostel, 18

Kinlay House, 36
Marlborough Hostel (IHH), 9
Mount Eccles Court (M.E.C.), 6
Oliver St. John Gugarty's, 26

BED AND BREAKFASTS
Carmel House, 2
Charles Stewart Parnell
  Budget Accommodation, 7
Glen Court, 15
Marian B&B, 3
Parkway Guesthouse, 4

Map labels (clockwise/by area):

Philbsborough Rd.
Royal Canal Bank
Wellington St.
Fontenoy St.
Western Way
Dominick St. Upper
Constitution Hill
King's Inns
Henrietta Pl.
Green St.

O'Devaney Gdns.
Halliday Rd.
Kirwan St.
Manor Pl.
Stoney Batter
Brunswick St.
King St. North
Church St.
Beresford St.
Montpelier Gdns.
Arbour Hill
Blackhall Pl.
Mary's Lane
Markets
Arran St.
Queen St.
Smithfield St.
Bow St.
Ceol
Old Jameson Distillery
Greek
Chancery St.

Montpelier Hill
TO PHOENIX PARK
National Museum/
Collins Barracks
Benburb St.
Wolfe Tone Quay
Ellis Quay
Arran Quay
Usher's Quay
Inns Quay
The Fourcourts
Merchants' Quay
Wood Quay

Heuston Station
Victoria Quay
Island St.
Bridgefoot St.
Oliver Bond
City Offices
Steevens Ln.
Guinness Brewery
Watling St.

Christ Church Cathedral
36

St. James's St.
Thomas St.
Cornmarket
High St.
37
Werburgh St.

TO KILMAINAM GAOL,
ROYAL HOSPITAL
Guinness Hopstore
38
Rainsford St.

Basin St. Upper
Bellevue St.
Thomas Ct.
Earl St.
Meath St.
St. Francis St.
Patrick St.
Bull Alley
St. Patrick's Cathedral
Werburgh St.

N

Marrowbone Ln.
Summer St.
The Coombe
Dean St.
Kevin St. Upr.

Cork St.
Ardee St.
New Rd.
Brickfield Ln.
Long Ln.
New St.

🍎 FOOD
Badass Cafe, 27
Botticelli, 28
Burdock's, 37
Cafe Irie, 28
Clifton, 21
Cornucopia, 39
Flanagan's, 10
Harrison's, 25
Juste Pasta, 28
La Mezza Luna, 32
O'Shea's, 14

Poco Loco, 35
Soup Dragon, 33
Winding Stair, 29
Zaytoons, 34

● SERVICES
AMEX, 20 and ⓘ
Pharmacy, 22
Youth Info Centre, 8

0   250 yards
0   250 meters

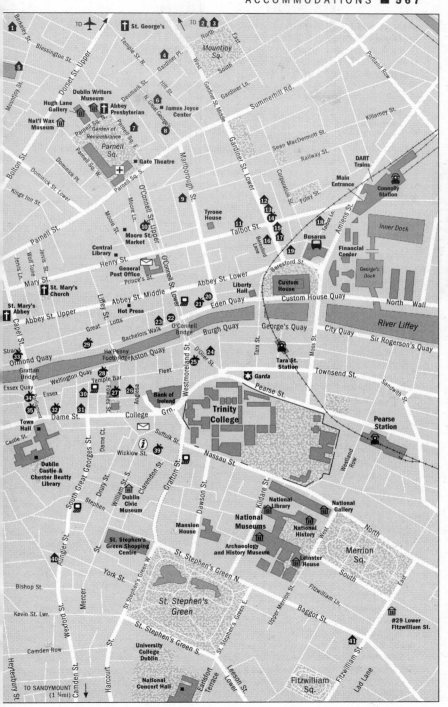

Abbey Hostel, 29 Bachelor's Walk (☎878 0700; email info@abbey-court.com). From O'Connell Bridge, turn left. A little pricey, but it's comfy. Internet access IR£1 per 7min. Breakfast included. June-Sept. dorms IR£15; 6-bed dorms IR£16, with bath IR£17; 4-bed dorms IR£18; Oct. and Mar.-May IR£11, IR£14, IR£15. Doubles IR£40-60.

Abraham House, 82-3 Gardiner St. Lower (☎855 0600; email stay@abraham-house.ie). Respectable, tidy rooms. Internet access. Light breakfast and towels included. Laundry IR£4. June-Sept. 12-bed dorms IR£9, 4-bed dorms IR£15, doubles IR£40.

Globetrotter's Tourist Hostel (IHH), 46-7 Lower Gardiner St. (☎873 5893; email gtrotter@indigo.ie). A dose of luxury for the weary backpacker. Internet access. Breakfast included. Towels 50p. July to mid-Sept. dorms IR£15; mid-Sept. to June IR£12.

Jacobs Inn, 21-28 Talbot Pl. (☎855 5660; email jacobs@isaacs.ie). Two blocks north of the Customs House, Talbot Pl. stretches from the back of the bus station up to Talbot St. Rooms, all with bath, are spacious, clean to the point of sterility, and cheery. Towels IR£1. Laundry IR£5. Lockout 11am-3pm. Apr.-Oct. dorms IR£11.25, 3-bed dorms IR£17.50, doubles IR£43; Nov.-Mar. IR£2 cheaper per person.

Dublin International Youth Hostel (An Óige/HI), 61 Mountjoy St. (☎830 4555; email anoige@iol.ie; www.irelandyha.org). O'Connell St. changes names 3 times before reaching the left turn onto Mountjoy St. Under a new captain, this 365-bed convent-turned-hostel has made giant improvements. A keycard system and lockers beef up security. Cafe has cheap meals (IR£3.50) and packed lunches (IR£2). Shuttles to Temple Bar. Breakfast included. Luggage storage IR£1. Towels IR£1. Self-service laundry IR£4. June dorms IR£11, 6- to 8-bed IR£12, 4-bed IR£13.50, doubles IR£29; July-Aug. IR£13, IR£13.50, IR£14, IR£30; Oct.-May IR£1-2 cheaper.

Celts House, 32 Blessington St. (☎830 0657; email res@celtshouse.iol.ie). 38 comfy, solid wooden bunk beds in a brightly-painted atmosphere. **Internet access.** Key deposit IR£5. May-Sept. 8-bed dorms IR£10.50, 6-bed IR£12, 4-bed IR£12.50, doubles IR£36; Sept.-May 8-bed dorms IR£9.

Mount Eccles Court (M.E.C.), 42 North Great Georges St. (☎878 0071; email meccles@iol.ie). Walk up O'Connell to Parnell St., turn right, then take the first left. A former convent. Breakfast included. Towels IR£1. Apr.-Sept. dorms IR£8.50-13.50, doubles IR£36; Oct.-Mar. dorms IR£8-12.50, doubles IR£28.

Cobblestones, 29 Eustace St. (☎677 5614). In the middle of Temple Bar action. Small breakfast included. Dorms IR£14-16; doubles IR£37.

Kinlay House (IHH), 2-12 Lord Edward St. (☎679 6644; email kindub@usit.ie). Internet access. Breakfast included. Lockers 50p. Laundry IR£5. Dorms IR£10.50-16; singles IR£22; doubles IR£34, with bath IR£36. Oct.-June prices IR£1-2.50 less.

Oliver St. John Gogarty's Temple Bar Hostel, 18-21 Anglesea St. (☎671 1822). James Joyce once roomed here with the poetic doctor Gogarty. Internet access. Laundry IR£2. June-Sept. dorms IR£16, twins IR£42 per person; triples IR£51; Mar.-May and Oct. IR£14, IR£36, IR£48; Nov.-Feb. IR£12-13, IR£32, IR£42.

BED AND BREAKFASTS

B&Bs with a green shamrock sign out front are registered, occasionally checked, and approved by Bord Fáilte. On the North Side, B&Bs cluster along **Upper** and **Lower Gardiner St.,** on **Sheriff St.,** and near **Parnell Sq.**

Parkway Guest House, 5 Gardiner Pl. (☎874 0469). Rooms are plain but high-ceilinged and immaculate, and the location just off Gardiner St. is excellent. Singles IR£23; doubles IR£36-40, with shower IR£44-48.

Marian B&B, 21 Upper Gardiner St. (☎874 4129). Brendan and Cathrine McElroy provide lovely rooms at a better price than comparable neighborhood accommodations. Singles IR£20; doubles IR£38.

Mona B&B, 148 Clonliffe Rd. (☎837 6723). Firm beds in rooms kept tidy by a proprietress who offers tea and cakes. Open May-Oct. Singles IR£17; doubles IR£36.

St. Aidan's B&B, 150 Clonliffe Rd. (☎837 6750). Good beds, non-smoking rooms, and a friendly proprietor create a relaxing atmosphere. Open Apr.-Sept. Singles IR£17; doubles IR£34, with bath IR£40.

Rita and Jim Casey, Villa Jude, 2 Church Ave. (☎668 4982), off Beach Rd. Bus #3 to the first stop on Tritonville Rd. Call for directions from the Lansdowne Rd. DART stop. Clean rooms and big breakfasts. Singles IR£16; doubles IR£32.

Mrs. Dolores Abbot-Murphy, 14 Castle Park (☎269 8413). Ask the #3 bus driver to drop you at Sandymount Green; continue past Browne's Deli and take the first left. At the end of the road, look right. A 5min. walk from Sandymount DART stop. Singles IR£23; doubles IR£38, with bath IR£44.

Mrs. Bermingham, 8 Dromard Terr. (☎668 3861), on Dromard Ave. Take the #3 bus. Disembark at the Tesco supermarket and make the next left. Down the street, the road forks. The left fork in the road is Dromard Terrace. Most rooms without bath. Open Feb.-Nov. Singles IR£18; doubles IR£34.

Bayview, 98 Clontarf Rd. (☎833 3950). The Barry family provides fresh, airy rooms, with every sort of wallpaper imaginable. Singles IR£25; doubles IR£45, with bath IR£50.·

Mrs. Geary, 69 Hampton Ct. (☎833 1199). Take bus #130 from Lower Abbey St., and up Vernon Ave. in Clontarf. Ask the bus driver to drop you at Hampton Court. Spacious and relaxing. Open Apr.-Sept. Singles IR£25; doubles IR£38, with bath IR£43.

CAMPING

Most campsites are far from the city center, but camping equipment is available in the heart of the city. **The Great Outdoors,** Chatham St., off the top of Grafton St., has an excellent selection of tents, backpacks, and cookware. (☎679 4293. 10% discount for An Óige/HI members. Open M-W and F-Sa 9:30am-5:30pm, Th 9:30am-8pm.) **Phoenix Park** is not safe for camping.

Camac Valley Tourist Caravan & Camping Park, Naas Rd., Clondalkin (☎ 464 0644; email camacmorriscastle@tinet.ie), near Corkagh Park. Accessible by bus #69 (35min. from city center, IR£1.10). Laundry IR£3.50. Showers 50p. Two people with tent and car June-Aug. IR£10; Sept.-May IR£9. Hikers/cyclists June-Aug. IR£5; IR£4.

North Beach Caravan and Camping Park (☎843 7131), in Rush. Bus #33 from Eden Quay (1hr., 23 per day) and the suburban train come here. Showers 50p. Open Mar.-Oct. IR£4 per person, children IR£2.

☕ FOOD

Dublin's **open-air markets** sell fresh and cheap fixings. On Saturdays, a gourmet open-air market takes place in **Temple Bar** in Meeting House Square. The cheapest **supermarkets** around Dublin are the **Dunnes Stores** chain, with branches at St. Stephen's Green (☎478 0188; open M-W, F-Sa 8:30am-7pm; Th 8:30am-9pm; Su 12-6pm), the ILAC Centre off Henry St., and on North Earl St. **Temple Bar** is ready to implode from the proliferation of creative eateries catering to every budget.

Cafe Irie, 11 Fownes St. (☎672 5090), above Sé Sí Progressive. Lip-smackingly good sandwiches under IR£3. Vegan-friendly. Open M-Sa 9am-8pm, Su noon-5:30pm.

La Mezza Luna, 1 Temple Ln. (☎671 2840), corner of Dame St. Celestial food. Daily lunch specials IR£5; served noon-5pm. Delicious desserts IR£3.50. Open M-Th noon-11pm, F-Sa noon-11:30pm, Su noon-10:30pm.

Zaytoons, 14-15 Parliament St. (☎ 677 3595). Persian food served on big platters of warm bread in large portions. Chicken kebab IR£3.50. Open M-W noon-3am, Th-Sa noon-4am, Su 2pm-3am.

Cornucopia, 19 Wicklow St. (☎677 7583). This vegetarian horn of plenty loads huge portions onto your plate. If you can find a seat, sit down for a rich meal (about IR£5) or just a snack (about IR£1.50). Open M-W and F-Sa 9am-8pm, Th 9am-9pm.

◉ SIGHTS

Dublin is a walkable city; most of the sights lie less than a mile from O'Connell Bridge. The **Historical Walking Tour** provides a 2 hr. crash course in Dublin's history and Irish history, stopping at a variety of Dublin sights. (Meet at Trinity's front gate. ☎878 0227; email tours@historicalinsights.ie. May-Sept. M-F 11am and 3pm, Sa-Su 11am, noon, 3pm; Oct.-Apr. F-Su noon. IR£6, students IR£5.)

TRINITY COLLEGE AND NEARBY

TRINITY COLLEGE. Ancient walls contain Trinity's sprawling expanse of stone buildings, cobblestone walks, and green grounds. The British built Trinity in 1592 as a Protestant religious seminary that would "civilize the Irish and cure them of Popery." The college became part of the accepted path that members of the Anglo-Irish elite tread on their way to high government and social positions. The Catholic Jacobites who briefly held Dublin in 1689 used the campus as a barracks and prison. Jonathan Swift, Robert Emmett, Thomas Moore, Edmund Burke, Oscar Wilde, and Samuel Beckett are just a few of the famous Irishmen who studied here. Bullet holes from the Easter 1916 uprising scar the stone entrance. Until the 1960s, the Catholic church deemed it a cardinal sin to attend Trinity; once the church lifted the ban, the size of the student body more than tripled. *(Between West-moreland and Grafton St. in the very center of Dublin, the main entrance fronts the block-long traffic circle now called College Green. Pearse St. runs along the north edge of the college, Nassau St. to its south. ☎ 608 1000. Grounds always open. Free.)*

THE OLD LIBRARY. This 1712 chamber holds an invaluable collection of ancient manuscripts, including the magnificent ▧**Book of Kells.** Around AD 800, four Irish monks squeezed multicolored ink from bugs and plants to illuminate this four-volume edition of the Gospels. Each page holds a dizzyingly intricate latticework of Celtic designs, into which images of animals and Latin text are interwoven. *(From the main gate of the Trinity, go straight; the library is on the southern side of Library Square. Open June-Sept. M-Sa 9:30am-5pm, Su noon-4:30pm; Oct.-May M-Sa 9:30am-5pm, Su noon-4:30pm. IR£4.50, students and seniors IR£4.)*

GRAFTON STREET. The few blocks South of College Green are off-limits to cars and ground zero for shopping tourists and residents alike. Grafton Street's **street performers** range from string octets to jive limboists. Upstairs at the Grafton St. branch of Bewley's is the **Bewley's Museum,** located inside the coffee chain's former chocolate factory. Tea-tasting machines and a display on Bewley's Quaker heritage are among the curiosities. *(Open daily 7:30am-11pm. Free.)*

KILDARE STREET AND NATIONAL MUSEUMS

The **Museum Link** bus runs from the adjacent Natural History and Archeology museums to Collins Barracks roughly once an hour. An all-day pass costs IR£2, while one way is 85p. *(General Information Line for all three museums, ☎ 677 7444. All open Tu-Sa 10am-5pm, Su 2-5pm and closed on Mondays. Free.)*

The largest of Dublin's museums, the **National Museum of Archaeology and History,** contains a number of beautiful artifacts spanning the last two millennia. One room gleams with the **Tara Brooch, Ardagh Hoard** (including the great chalice), and other Celtic gold work. Another section is devoted to the Republic's founding years, and shows off the bloody vest of nationalist hero **James Connolly.** *(Kildare St., adjacent to Leinster House.)* The **Natural History Museum** is a museum within a museum, with a creepily fascinating collection not so much of the natural world, as how museums used to interpret their role in it. *(Merrion Square West. Free.)* The **National Museum of Decorative Arts and History, Collins Barracks,** gleams with exhibits that range from the traditional to the multi-disciplinary. *(Benburb St., off of Wolfe Tone Quay. Take the Museum Link, or bus 10 from O'Connell. Bus 90 to Heuston Station stops across the street.)* The **National Gallery** has a collection of over 2400 canvases includes paintings by Brueghel, Goya, Caravaggio, Vermeer, Rembrandt, and El Greco. *(Merrion Square West.)* The **National Library** chronicles Irish history and exhibits literary objects in its entrance room. A genealogical research room can help one trace the thinnest tendrils of their Irish family tree. *(Kildare St, adjacent to Leinster House. ☎ 661 2523. Open M-W 10am-9pm, Th-F 10am-5pm, Sa 10am-1pm. Free.)*

ST. STEPHEN'S GREEN AND MERRION SQUARE

ST. STEPHEN'S GREEN. The 22-acre park was a private estate until the Guinness clan bequeathed it to the city. Today, the park is a hotbed of activity—during the summer, all enjoy the outdoor music and theater near the old bandstand. *(Kildare, Dawson, and Grafton St. all lead to it. Open M-Sa 8am-dusk, Su 10am-dusk.)*

MERRION SQUARE. The square and adjacent **Fitzwilliam Street** visually stimulate with Georgian buildings fronted by elaborate doorways. Farther south on **Harcourt St.,** playwright George Bernard Shaw and Dracula's creator, Bram Stoker, were once neighbors at #61 and #16, respectively. The Electricity Supply Board tore down a row of the Georgian townhouses to build a monstrous new office. Dubliners had a row over this, so to compensate the ESB funds **#29 Lower Fitzwilliam Street,** a completely restored Georgian townhouse-turned-living museum that demonstrates the lifestyle of the 18th-century Anglo-Irish elite. (☎ *702 6165. Open Tu-Sa 10am-5pm, Su 2-5pm. A short audio-visual show leads to a 25min. tour of the house. IR£2.50, students and seniors IR£1.)*

TEMPLE BAR

West of Trinity between Dame St. and the Liffey, the Temple Bar neighborhood wriggles with activity. Saved from becoming a transportation center in the mid-80s, Temple Bar has since grown at lightning speed into one of the hottest spots for nightlife in Europe. The government-sponsored Temple Bar Properties has also spent over IR$30 million to build a flock of arts-related tourist attractions. Among Temple Bar's most inviting are: **The Irish Film Centre,** featuring specialty and art house film *(6 Eustace St.;* ☎ *679 3477; emailfii@ifc.ie; www.fii.ie);* Ireland's only **Gallery of Photography** *(Meeting House Sq.;* ☎ *671 4654; email gallery@irish-photography.com);* and the sizeable **Temple Bar Gallery & Studios** *(5-9 Temple Bar;* ☎ *671 0073; email tbgs@indigo.ie; www.paddynet.ie/tbgs).*

DAME STREET AND THE CATHEDRALS

DUBLIN CASTLE. Norman King John built the castle in 1204 on top of the first Viking settlement of Dubh Linn. For 700 years after its construction, Dublin Castle was the seat of British rule in Ireland. Fifty insurgents died at the castle's walls on Easter Monday, 1916 (see **Easter Rising,** p. 557). Since 1938, the presidents of Ireland have been inaugurated here. *(Dame St., at the intersection of Parliament and Castle St.* ☎ *677 7129. IR£3, students and seniors IR£2. Grounds free.)*

CHESTER BEATTY LIBRARY. Honorary Irish citizen Alfred Chester Beatty was an American rags-to-riches mining engineer who amassed an incredible collection of Asian art, sacred scriptures, and illustrated texts. An illustrated book by Matisse and a collection of Chinese snuff bottles are two of the highlights. *(Behind Dublin Castle.* ☎ *407 0750; www.cbl.ie. Open Tu-F 10am-5pm, Sa 11am-5pm, Su 1pm-5pm. Free.)*

ST. PATRICK'S CATHEDRAL. The body of the church dates to the 12th century, although Sir Benjamin Guinness remodeled much of it in 1864. Measuring 300 ft. from stem to stern, it is Ireland's largest cathedral. St. Patrick allegedly baptized converts in the park next door. Jonathan Swift spent his last years as Dean of St. Patrick's; his crypt rises above the south nave. *(From Christ Church, Nicholas St. runs south and downhill, becoming Patrick St. Take bus #49, 49A, 50, 54A, 56A, 65, 65B, 77, or 77A from Eden Quay.* ☎ *475 4817. Open Apr.-Sept. M-F 9am-6pm; Oct.-Mar. Sa 9am-5pm. Su closed 11am-12:45pm and 3-4pm. IR£2.)* Beside the cathedral, **Marsh's Library** is Ireland's oldest public library. *(St. Patrick's Close.* ☎ *454 3511. Open M and W-F 10am-12:45pm and 2-5pm, Sa 10:30am-12:45pm. £2, students and seniors £1.)*

GUINNESS BREWERY AND KILMAINHAM

GUINNESS HOPSTORE. Guinness brews its black magic on Crane St. off James St., and perpetuates the legend of the world's best stout at its Hopstore. Farsighted Arthur Guinness signed a 9000-year lease at the original 1759 brewery nearby. Appreciate the exhibit on Guinness's infamously clever advertising, and then drink, silly tourist, drink. *(St. James's Gate. From Christ Church Cathedral, follow High St. west through its name changes—Cornmarket, Thomas, and James. Take bus #51B or 78A from Aston Quay or bus #123 from O'Connell St.* ☎ *408 4800; www.guinness.ie. Open Apr.-Sept. M-Sa 9:30am-5pm, Su 10:30am-4:30pm; Oct.-Mar. M-Sa 9:30am-4pm, Su noon-4pm. IR£5, students and seniors IR£4, under 12 IR£1.)*

KILMAINHAM GAOL. A place of bondage that is also a symbol of freedom. Almost all of the rebels who fought in Ireland's struggle for independence from 1792 to 1921 spent time here. "The cause for which I die has been rebaptized during this

DUBLINESE Mastering the Dublin dialect has been a persistent challenge to writers and thespians of the 20th century. The following is a short introduction to Dubliners' favorite phrases. **In Times of Difficulty:** Dublinese is expeditious in keeping others in line. Idiots are rebuked as "eejits;" in dire situations, they are called "head-the-ball." Total exasperation calls for "shite and onions." When all is restored to order, it's said that "the job's oxo and the ship's name is murphy." **Affectionate Nicknames for Civic Landmarks:** Over the past couple decades, the government has graced the city with several public art works that personify the Irish spirit in the female form. Dubliners have responded with poetic rhetoric. Off Grafton St., the statue of the fetching fishmongress Molly Malone is referred to as "the tart with the cart." The goddess of the River Liffy sits in a fountain on O'Connell St. and is popularly heralded as the "floozy in the jacuzzi" and even "the whore in the sewer" (pronounced WHEW-er).

past week by the blood of as good men as ever trod God's earth," wrote Sean Mac-Diarmada in a letter from Kilmainham to his family while he awaited execution for participation in the 1916 Easter Rising (see p. 557). Tours wind through the chilly limestone corridors of the prison and end in the haunting atmosphere of Kilmainham's execution yard. *(Inchicore Road. Take bus #51 from Aston Quay, #51A from Lower Abbey St., or #79 from Aston Quay. ☎ 453 5984. Open Apr.-Sept. daily 9:30am-5pm; Oct.-Mar. M-F 9:30am-4pm, Su 10am-5pm. IR£3.50, seniors IR£2.50, students and children IR£1.50.)*

IRISH MUSEUM OF MODERN ART. Built in 1679 as a hospice for retired or disabled soldiers. Today, the compound houses the **Irish Museum of Modern Art.** The facade and courtyard copy those of Les Invalides in Paris; the baroque chapel is quite a sight, too. *(Military Road. Bus #90 and 91 from Heuston Station, #78A and 79 from the City Center. ☎ 612 9900. Museum and building open Tu-Sa 10am-5:30pm, Su noon-5:30pm. Free. Guided tours W and F 2:30pm, Su 12:15pm.)*

O'CONNELL ST. AND PARNELL SQUARE

HUGH LANE MUNICIPAL GALLERY OF MODERN ART. When American painter Lane offered to donate his collection of French Impressionist paintings to the city, he did so on the condition that the people of Dublin contribute to the gallery's construction. Dubliners, however, refused to lend their support; Yeats lamented their provincial attitudes in a string of poems. *(Parnell Sq. North. Buses #3, 10, 11, 13, 16, and 19 all stop near Parnell Sq. ☎ 874 1903; www.hughlane.ie. Open Tu-Th 9:30am-6pm, F-Sa 9:30am-5pm, Su 11am-5pm. Free.)*

THE DUBLIN WRITERS' MUSEUM. Read your way through placards and placards describing the city's rich literary heritage. Rare editions, manuscripts, and memorabilia of Swift, Shaw, Wilde, Yeats, Beckett, Brendan Behan, Patrick Kavanagh, and Sean O'Casey. *(18 Parnell Sq. North. ☎ 872 2077. Open June-Aug. M-F 10am-6pm, Sa 10am-5pm, Su 11am-5pm; Sept.-May M-Sa 10am-5pm. IR£3.10, students and seniors IR£2.55 2.89. Combined ticket with either Shaw birthplace or James Joyce Centre IR£4.60.)*

JAMES JOYCE CENTER. This new museum features Joyceana—feel free to mull over Joyce's works in the library or the tearoom. Call for info on lectures, walking tours, and Bloomsday events. *(35 North Great Georges St. Up Marlborough St., and past Parnell St. ☎ 873 1984. Open M-Sa 9:30am-5pm, Su 12:30-5pm; Jul.-Aug. extra Su hours 11am-5pm. IR£3, students and seniors IR£2.)*

SMITHFIELD

OLD JAMESON DISTILLERY. Learn how science, grain, and tradition come together to create the golden fluid called **whiskey.** More entertaining and less commercial than the Guinness Brewery tour, the experience ends with a glass of the Irish whiskey of your choice; be quick to volunteer in the beginning and you'll get to sample a whole tray of different whiskeys. Feel the burn. *(Bow St. From O'Connell St., turn onto Henry St. and continue straight as the street dwindles to Mary St., then Mary Ln., then May Ln.; the warehouse is on a cobblestone street on the left. ☎ 807 2355. Tours daily 9:30am-5:30pm. IR£3.95, students and seniors IR£3.)*

ELSEWHERE

PHOENIX PARK. Europe's largest enclosed public park is most famous for the "Phoenix Park murders" of 1882. The Invincibles, a tiny nationalist splinter group, stabbed the Chief Secretary of Ireland, Lord Cavendish, and his Under-Secretary 200 yd. from the Phoenix Column. The **Phoenix Column**, a Corinthian column capped with a phoenix rising from flames, is something of a pun—the park's name actually comes from the Irish term *Fionn Uísce*, meaning "clean water." The 1760-acre park incorporates the President's residence *(Áras an Uachtaraín)*, the US Ambassador's residence, cricket pitches, polo grounds, cattle, and grazing deer. *(Take bus #10 from O'Connell St. or #25 or 26 from Middle Abbey St. west along the river. Free.)* **Dublin Zoo,** one of the world's oldest zoos and Europe's largest, is in the park. It contains 700 animals and the world's biggest egg. *(Bus #10 from O'Connell St. passes the zoo. ☎677 1425. Open M-Sa 9:30am-6pm, Su 10:30am-6pm. Closes at sunset in winter. IR£6.30, students IR£4.80, seniors IR£3.70, families IR£18.50-22.)*

🎵🎭 ENTERTAINMENT AND NIGHTLIFE

Be it poetry or punk you fancy, Dublin is equipped to entertain you. The *Event Guide* (free) is available at the tourist office, Temple Bar restaurants, and the Temple Bar Info center. Traditional music *(trad)* is an important element of the Irish culture and the Dublin music scene—some pubs in the city center have sessions nightly, others almost every night. **Whelan's** (see **Publin,** below) is one of the hottest spots in Dublin. Big bands frequent the **Baggot Inn,** 143 Baggot St. (☎676 1430). Part of the National Theater, the **Abbey Theatre,** 26 Lower Abbey St., was founded in 1904 by Yeats and Lady Gregory to promote Irish culture and modernist theater. (☎878 7222. Box office open M-Sa 10:30am-7pm. Tickets IR£10-17.50; student rate M-Th and Sa matinee IR£8.) Dublin pretty much owns two days of the year. **St. Patrick's Day** (Mar. 17) and the half-week leading up to it host a carnival of concerts, fireworks, street theater, and intoxicated madness. The city returns to 1904 on **Bloomsday** (June 16), the day on which the action of Joyce's *Ulysses* takes place. The **James Joyce Cultural Center** (☎873 1984) sponsors a reenactment of the funeral and wake, a lunch at Davy Byrne's, and a breakfast with Guinness.

James Joyce once proposed that a "good puzzle would be to cross Dublin without passing a pub." A local radio station once offered IR£100 to the first person to solve the puzzle. The winner explained that you could take any route—you'd just have to visit them all on the way. The **Dublin Literary Pub Crawl** traces Dublin's liquid history in reference to its literary history. *(Meet at The Duke, 2 Duke St. ☎670 5602; email colm@dublinpubcrawl.com. Easter-Oct. M-Sa 7:30pm, Su noon and 7:30pm; Nov.-Easter Th-Sa 7:30pm, Su noon and 7:30pm. IR£6.50, students IR£5.50.) Let's Go* recommends beginning your personal journey at the gates of Trinity College, moving onto Grafton St., stumbling onto Camden St., teetering down South Great Georges St., and crawling (triumphantly if soused) into the Temple Bar area.

PUBLIN

Sinnott's, South King St. (☎478 4698). Portrays itself as a pub for readers and writers, but let's be honest, it's for drinkers. Chart music packs the dance floor until 2am.

The Odeon, the Old Harcourt Train Station (☎478 2088). The Odeon has a columned facade, and the second longest bar in Ireland (after the one at the Galway races). Everything here is gargantuan. The upstairs is cozier (i.e. still huge). DJ on Sa. Late bar Th-Sa.

The Stag's Head, 1 Dame Ct. (☎679 3701). The subtle and ancient entrance has a mosaic of a stag's head on the sidewalk. The crowd dons anything from T-shirts to tuxes and spills out into the alleys. Main dishes around IR£5-7; served M-F 12:30-3:30pm and 5:30-7:30pm, Sa 12:30-2:30pm. Late bar Th-F till 12:30am. Closed Su.

Whelan's, 25 Wexford St. (☎478 0766). Continue down South Great Georges St. The stage venue in back hosts big-name *trad* and rock groups. Cover IR£5-8. Gigs followed Th-Su by pop and dance music. Open Th-Su until 1:30am.

The Palace, 21 Fleet St. (☎677 9290), behind Aston Quay. This classic, neighborly Dublin pub has old-fashioned wood paneling and close quarters; head for the comfy seats in the back room. The favorite of many a Dubliner.

The Porter House, 16-18 Parliament St. (☎ 679 8847). The largest selection of world beers in the country, and 8 self-brewed kinds of porter, stout, and ale. Their excellent sampler tray includes a sip of ale brewed with oysters and other oddities (IR£6). Late bar Th-F to 1:30am, Sa to midnight.

CLUBLIN

The Kitchen, the Clarence Hotel (☎ 677 6635), Wellington Quay, Temple Bar. The entrance is behind the hotel on Essex St. With 2 bars and a dance floor, this U2-owned club is exceptionally well designed and the coolest spot in town. Dress as a rocker or a model. Cover IR£8-10, Tu students IR£3-4.

PoD, 35 Harcourt St. (☎ 478 0225). Spanish-style decor meets hardcore dance music. As trendy as the Kitchen. The truly brave venture upstairs to **The Red Box** (☎ 478 0225), a separate, more intense club with a warehouse atmosphere. Often hosts the big name DJs—cover charges skyrocket. Cover IR£8-10; Th ladies free before midnight; Th and Sa IR£5 with ISIC card.

Club M, Blooms Hotel, Anglesea St. (☎ 671 5622), Temple Bar. One of Dublin's largest clubs. If at first you don't succeed, grind, grind again. Cover around IR£6.

The George, 89 South Great Georges St. (☎ 478 2983). This throbbing man o' war is Dublin's first and most prominent gay bar. The attached nightclub opens W-Su. Su night cover £5-7 after 10pm. Look spiffy—no effort, no entry. Frequent theme nights.

The Front Lounge, Parliament St. (☎ 670-4112). The velvet seats of this gay-friendly bar are popular with a very mixed, trendy crowd.

▶ DAYTRIPS FROM DUBLIN

HOWTH

To get to Howth, take a northbound DART train to the end (30min., 6 per hr., IR£1.15).

The peninsula of Howth (rhymes with "both") dangles from the mainland in Edenic isolation, less than 10 mi. from Dublin. A 3hr. **cliff walk** rings the peninsula, passing heather and thousands of seabird nests. The best section of the walk is a 1 hr. hike between the harbor and the lighthouse at the southeast tip of the peninsula. To get to the trailhead from town, turn left at the DART station and follow Harbour Rd. around the coast (20min.); or hike downhill from the lighthouse. In town, the ruins of the 14th-century **St. Mary's Abbey** stand peacefully in a cemetery at the bend in Church St. To reach the private **Howth Castle,** an awkwardly charming patchwork of styles, turn right as you exit the DART station and then left after a quarter-mile, at the entrance to the Deer Park Hotel. Farther up the hill, a vague path goes around the right side of the Deer Park Hotel to the fabulous **Rhododendron Gardens.** At the top, you emerge into an astounding floral view overlooking Howth and Dublin. Turn left out of the station to get to the **tourist office,** in the Old Courthouse on Harbour Rd. (☎ 832 0405. Open May-Aug. M-F 11am-1pm and 1:30-5pm.) **Gleann na Smól** is on the left at the end of Nashville Rd, off Thormanby Rd, which forks off upper Main St. (☎ 832 29 36. Singles IR£25; doubles IR£38-42.) Bus 31B runs to **Hazelwood** at the end of the cul-de-sac in the Thormanby Woods estate, 1 mi. up Thormanby Rd. (☎ 839 13 91. Singles IR£30; doubles IR£42.)

BOYNE VALLEY

Bus Éireann shuttles to the Visitor Centre (1½hr., 4-5 per day, round-trip IR£6.70).

The thinly populated Boyne Valley safeguards Ireland's greatest archaeological treasures. Along the curves of the river between Slane and Drogheda lie no fewer than 40 mind-boggling passage-tombs constructed by the Neolithics around the 4th millenium BC, including **Newgrange, Dowth,** and **Knowth.** The first, built over 5000 years ago using stones believed to have been carted from Wicklow 40 mi. away, is the most spectacular, covered with elaborate patterns and symbols that continue to mystify archaeologists. You can only enter Newgrange through the **Brú na Bóinne Visitor Centre,** near Donore on the south side of the River Boyne, across from the tombs. (☎ (041) 988 03 00. Open Mar.-Apr. 9:30am-5:30pm; May 9am-6:30pm; June to mid-Sept. 9am-7pm; late Sept. 9am-6:30pm; Oct. 9:30am-5:30pm; Nov.-Feb. 9:30am-5pm. Center and 1hr. tour IR£4, students IR£2.) The **Hill of Tara** was the spiritual and political center of Ireland from prehistoric times until the arrival of Christianity in the 4th century BC. Take any local (not express) bus from Dublin to **Navan** (1hr., 7-15 per day, IR£6) and ask the driver to let you off at the turn-off; the site is 1 mi. straight uphill. A flock of enormous, well-preserved Norman castles, including **Trim Castle,** which Mel Gibson sacked 800 years later for a scene in *Braveheart,* overlook **Trim** on the River Boyne. (Open May-Oct. 10am-6pm. Tours every 45min. and limited to 15 people; sign up upon arrival in Trim. No tour required to wander the grounds. Tour and grounds IR£2.50, students IR£1.) The **tourist office** is on Mill St. (☎ (046) 371 11. Open daily 10am-1pm and 2-5pm.)

DÚN LAOGHAIRE
Reach Dún Laoghaire by DART from Dublin (IR£1.10).

As Dublin's major out-of-city ferry port, Dún Laoghaire (dun-LEER-ee) is the first peek at Ireland for many tourists. Fortunately, it makes a good spot to begin a ramble along the coast south of Dublin. The **harbor** itself is a sight, filled with yachts, boat tours, car ferries, and fishermen—frequent summer evening boat races draw much of the town. ▨**James Joyce Tower,** in the Martello tower in Sandycove, is a fascinating retreat. From the Sandycove DART station, go left at Eagle House down to the coast, turn right and continue to the Martello tower; or take bus #8 from Burgh Quay in Dublin to Sandycove Ave. James Joyce stayed in the tower for a tense six days in August 1904 as a guest of Oliver St. John Gogarty, who appeared in Chapter One of *Ulysses.* The novel is partially set around the tower, with Gogarty transformed into Buck Mulligan, another guest into Haines, and Joyce into Stephen Daedalus, who meditates on the "snot-green" sea. The two-room museum contains Joyce's death mask, a page of the original manuscript of *Finnegan's Wake,* and editions of *Ulysses,* including one illustrated by Henri Matisse. (☎872 2077. Open Apr.-Oct. M-Sa 10am-1pm and 2-5pm, Su 2-6pm; Nov.-Mar. by appointment. IR£2.70, students and seniors IR£2.20.) The **tourist office,** in the ferry terminal, is equipped with copious maps and pamphlets on the area. (Open M-Sa 10am-5:30pm.) The **Belgrave Hall,** 34 Belgrave Sq., hostel has high ceilings and marble floors. (☎284 2106. Breakfast included. Laundry IR£3-6. **Bike rental** IR£10 per day. **Internet.** Summer F-Sa 10-bed dorm IR£15, Su-Th all rooms IR£ 13.)

SOUTHEAST IRELAND

Historically the power base of the Vikings and then the Normans, the influence of the Celts is faintest in southeast Ireland. Beaches are the most fruitful of the Southeast's tourist attractions, drawing mostly native Irish admirers to the coastline that runs from Kilmore Quay to tidy Ardmore. Waterford has the resources, nightlife, and grit of a real city, while Cashel boasts a superbly preserved cathedral complex. Continue your hunt for raging nightlife south from Dublin through Carlow, Kilkenny, and Waterford; alternatively, the daylight hours are most enjoyably spent exploring the pretty paths through the Wicklow Mountains and Wexford.

◪ FERRIES TO FRANCE AND BRITAIN

Irish Ferries sails from Rosslare Harbour to: **Pembroke, Wales** (4hr.); **Roscoff, France** (14½hr.); and **Cherbourg, France** (17½hr.). Ferries depart daily for Wales and every other day to France. For **24hr information** dial ☎01 661 07 15 or call the desk at Rosslare Harbour (☎331 58; fax 33544; www.irishferries.com. Fares to Britain Jan.-May, Oct.-Dec. IR£16; July-Aug. IR£20. Fares to France vary. Roughly IR£40 economy in winter; July-Aug. IRIR£80, students IR£66. 50% discount on ferries to France with Eurorail pass). **Stena Line** runs from Rosslare to Fishguard. (☎053 339 97. May-Sept. 3-4 per day; IR£29, students from IR£23.)

THE WICKLOW MOUNTAINS

Over 2000 ft. high, covered by heather, and pleated by rivers, the Wicklow summits are home to grazing sheep and a few villagers. Smooth glacial valleys embrace the two lakes and the monastic ruins. Public transportation is severely limited, so driving is the easiest way to connect the scattered sights and towns. The lush, blessed valley of **Glendalough** draws a steady summertime stream of coach tours filled with hikers and ruin-oglers. For more affordable food, B&Bs, and groceries, head to **Laragh** (LAR-a), 1 mi. up the road (10min. from the Wicklow Way). St. Kevin's **Bus Service** (☎ (01) 281 81 19) runs from Dublin's St. Stephen's Green West (2 per day; IR£6, return IR£10) and returns from the glen in the evening (2-3 per day). The **tourist office** is across from the Glendalough Hotel. (☎ (0404) 456 88. Open mid-June to Sept. Tu 11am-1pm and 2-6pm, W-Su 10am-1pm and 2-6pm.) The **National Park Information Office,** between the two lakes, is the best source for hiking advice. (☎ (0404) 454 25. Open May-Aug. daily 10am-6pm; Apr. and Sept. Sa-Su 10am-6pm.) The **Glendaloch Hostel (An Óige/HI)** is 5 min. past the Glendalough tourist office. (☎ (0404) 453 42. **Internet.** Bike rental IR£10 per day. Laundry IR£4. Dorms IR£11; doubles IR£30; off-season IRIR£1-2 less.) Laragh has tons of **B&Bs**, as well as the **Wicklow Bay Hostel.** (☎ (0404) 453 98. Dorms IR£8.50-9; private persons IR£10 per person.)

ROSSLARE HARBOUR   ☎ 053

Although Rosslare offers little in the way of Irish charm, it serves as an important transportation link to Wales, France, and the Irish coast. **Trains** run from the ferry port to Dublin (3hr., 3 per day, IR£11) and Limerick (2½hr., 1-2 per day, IR£12.50), via Waterford (1¼hr., IR£6). **Buses** run twice per day via Waterford (IR£9.20) to: Dublin (3hr., 7-10 per day, IR£10); Cork (M-Sa 4 per day, IR£13.50); Galway (IR£17); Killarney (IR£16); Limerick (2-3 per day, IR£13.50); and Tralee (IR£17). The Rosslare-Kilrane **tourist office** is 1 mi. from the harbor on Wexford Rd in Kilrane. (☎336 22. Open daily 10:30am-8pm.) If you must stay overnight before catching a ferry, try the **Rosslare Harbour Youth Hostel (An Óige/HI),** Goulding St. Take a right at the top of the cliff, head left around the corner, and it's past the **supermarket,** on the left. (☎333 99. Sheets IR£1.50. Curfew midnight. Members only; buy a membership card for IR£1. Dorms IR£8; in season quads IR£10, Sept.-Apr. IR£9. Supermarket open M-F 8am-7pm, Sa 8am-6pm, Su 9am-1pm.)

KILKENNY   ☎ 056

The best-preserved medieval town in Ireland, Kilkenny also offers rocking nightlife—nine churches share the streets with 80 pubs. Thirteenth-century **Kilkenny Castle** housed the Earls of Ormonde from the 1300s until 1932. The basement houses the **Butler Gallery,** which hangs modern art exhibitions. (Open June-Sept. daily 10am-7pm; Apr.-May daily 10:30am-5:30pm; Oct.-Mar. Tu-Sa 10:30am-12:45pm and 2-5pm, Su 11am-12:45pm and 2-5pm. Mandatory tour IR£3.50, students IR£1.50.) Climb up the thin, 100-ft. tower of **St. Canice's Cathedral,** up the hill off Dean St., for a panoramic view of the town and its surroundings. (Open Easter-Sept. M-Sa 9am-1pm and 2-6pm, Su 2-6pm. IR£1.) **Trains** (☎ 220 24) and **buses** (☎ 649 33) stop at Kilkenny Station on Dublin Rd.; buses also stop on Patrick St. in the city center. Trains go to Dublin (2hr., IR£11) and Waterford (45min., IR£5). Buses go to: Dublin (2hr., 4-5 per day, IR£7); Cork (3hr., 3 per day, IR£10); Galway (5hr., 3-5 per day, IR£17); Rosslare Harbour (2hr., 3-6 per day, IR£7); and Waterford (1½hr., 1 per day, IR£5). From Kilkenny Station, turn left on John St. to reach the Parade, dominated by the castle to your left. The **tourist office,** Rose Inn St., has free maps and info on B&Bs. (☎515 00; fax 639 55. Open July-Aug. M-Sa 9am-8pm, Su 11am-1pm and 2-5pm; May-June and Sept. M-Sa 9am-6pm, Su 11am-1pm and 2-5pm; Apr. M-Sa 9am-6pm; Oct.-Mar. M-Sa 9am-5pm.) Check your **email** at **Compustore,** in the Market Cross shopping center off High St. (IR£5 per hr. Open M-W and Sa 10am-6pm, Th-F 10am-8pm.) Waterford Rd. and more remote Castlecomer Rd. have the highest concentration of beds. **Kilkenny Tourist Hostel (IHH),** 35 Parliament St., is always brimming with activity. (☎635 41; email kilkennyhostel@tiniet.ie. Laundry IR£3. Dorms IR£7; doubles IR£20.) The biggest **grocery** in town is **Superquinn,** also in the Market Cross shopping center. (Open M-Tu and Sa 9am-7pm, W-F 9am-9pm.) **Maggie's,** St. Kieran St., is a superb wine cellar (hosts *trad* Tu-Th).

WATERFORD   ☎ 051

Behind an industrial facade of metal silos and cranes, Waterford charms with winding, narrow streets filled with pubs and shops. The town highlight is the **Waterford Crystal Factory,** 1 mi. away on the N25 (Cork Rd). One-hour tours allow you to witness the transformation of molten glass into polished crystal. Admire the finished products—and their outrageous prices—in the gallery. Catch the **City Imp** (a red-and-yellow minibus) along Parnell St. and request a stop at the factory (10-15min., runs every 15-20min., 70p) or take city bus #1 (dir: Kilbarry-Ballybeg; 2 per hr., 75p), across from the Clock Tower. (☎37 33 11. Showroom open daily Apr.-Oct. 8:30am-6pm, tours every 15min. until 4pm; Nov.-Mar. 9am-5pm, tours every 15min. until 3:15pm; Jan.-Feb. showroom only 9am-5pm. IR£3.50, students IR£2.) **Reginald's Tower,** at the end of the Quay, has guarded the entrance to the city since the 12th century. (☎30 42 20. Open daily June-Aug. 9:30am-6:30pm; Sept.-May 9:30am-6pm. IR£1.50, students 60p.) **Pubs** cluster on the Quays and on John St. The Quays are loaded with pubs; even more reside on the corner of John and Parnell St. **T&H Doolan's,** George's St. (☎841 504), has been serving crowds for 300 years.

  Trains (☎87 62 43) leave from across the bridge from the Quay; the bus station (☎87 90 00) is on the Quay by the bridge. Trains run to: Dublin (2½hr., 3-5 per day, IR£13-15); Kilkenny (40min., 3-5 per day, IR£5); Limerick (2¼hr., M-Sa 2 per day, IR£10); and Rosslare Harbour (1hr., M-Sa 2 per day, IR£6). **Buses** depart for: Dublin (2¾hr., 4-7 per day, IR£7); Cork (2½hr., 5-8 per day, IR£10); Galway (4¾hr., 5-8 per day, IR£13.50); Kilkenny (1hr., 1-2 per day, IR£5); Limerick (2½hr., 4-5 per day, IR£10.50); and Rosslare Harbour (1¼hr., 3-4 per day, IR£9.20). The **tourist office,** in the Granary at the intersection of the Quay and Hanover St., has maps. (☎87 58 23. Open Apr.-Oct. M-Sa 9am-6pm, July-Aug. also Su 11am-5pm; Nov.-Mar. M-Sa 9am-5pm.) Check your **email** at **Voyager Internet Café,** in the mall where John and Parnell St. meet. (Open M-W 8:30am-12:15am, Th-Su 8:30am-3:30am. IR£1.50 per 15min.) A friendly staff awaits at **Barnacle's Viking House (IHH),** Coffee House Ln., Greyfriars, the Quay. Follow the Quay east past the Clock Tower and a block past the post office. (☎85 38 27. Dorms IR£7.50-9; doubles IR£28-30.) Get **groceries** at **Treacy's,** on the Quay near the Granville Hotel. (Open daily 9am-11pm.)

CASHEL   ☎062

Cashel sprawls at the foot of the commanding 300 foot **Rock of Cashel** (a.k.a. **St. Patrick's Rock**), a huge limestone outcropping topped by medieval buildings. (Open daily mid-June to mid-Sept. 9am-7:30pm; mid-Sept. to mid-Mar. 9:30am-4:30pm; mid-Mar. to mid-June 9:30am-5:30pm. IR£3.50, students IR£1.50.) The two-towered **Cormac's Chapel,** consecrated in 1134, holds semi-restored Romanesque paintings. Down the cow path from the Rock lie the ruins of **Hore Abbey,** built by Cistercian monks who were fond of arches; the abbey is presently inhabited by nonchalant sheep. **Bus Éireann** (☎621 21) leaves from Bianconi's Bistro, on Main St., for: Dublin (3hr., 4 per day, IR£9); Cork (1½hr., 2-3 per day, IR£8); and Limerick (1 hr., 4 per day, IR£8.80). The **tourist office** is in the City Hall on Main St. (☎613 33. Open July-Aug. M-Sa 9:15am-6pm, Su 11am-5pm; Apr.-June and Sept. M-Sa 9:15am-6pm.) Just down Dundrum Rd. from town lies the stunning **O'Brien's Farmhouse Hostel.** (☎610 03. Dorms IR£9-10; doubles IR30; **camping** IR£4.50-5.) **Cashel Holiday Hostel (IHH),** 6 John St., is just off Main St. (☎623 30. **Internet.** Laundry IR£3.50. Key deposit IR£3. Dorms IR£8.50-10; private rooms IR£14.) **Centra Supermarket** is on Friar St. (Open daily 7am-11pm.) *Craic* is performed nightly at **Feehan's,** on Main St.

SOUTHWEST IRELAND

With a contradictory and dramatic landscape that ranges from lush lakes and mountains to stark, ocean-battered cliffs, it's no wonder Southwest Ireland has produced some of the country's greatest storytellers. Outlaws and rebels once lurked in hidden coves and glens now frequented by visitors and ruled over by publicans. If the tourist mayhem is too much for you, it's easy to retreat to the more quiet stretches along the Dingle Peninsula and southern coast.

⚓ FERRIES TO FRANCE AND BRITAIN

Cork-Swansea Ferries sails between **Cork** and **Swansea, South Wales** (10hr., 1 per day, IR£44-64, with car IR£170-358). Contact them at 52 South Mall, Cork (☎ (021) 27 11 66; fax 27 50 61). **Brittany Ferries** sails from **Cork** to **Roscoff, France** (13½hr.)

IRELAND

CORK
☎ **021**

As Ireland's second-largest city, Cork (pop. 150,000) is the center of the southwest's sports, music, and arts. Strolls along the pub-lined streets and river quays reveal grand architecture, as well as more recent commercial and industrial development—evidence of Cork's history of ruin and reconstruction. Wise visitors will more politely exploit the city's resources and use Cork as a place to eat, drink, shop, and sleep while exploring the exquisite scenery of the surrounding countryside. Within the city limits, time is best filled by taking in the vibrant street scene or meandering across the pastoral campus of the University College of Cork.

⌐ TRANSPORTATION

Trains: Kent Station (☎ 506 766; www.irishrail.ie), Lower Glanmire Rd, across the river from the city center in the northeast of town. Open M-Sa 7am-8:30pm, Su 7am-8pm. Connections to: **Dublin** (3hr.; M-Sa 7 per day, Su 5 per day; IR£33.50); **Killarney** (2hr.; M-Sa 7per day, Su 4 per day; IR£14); **Limerick** (1½hr.; M-Sa 7 per day, Su 4 per day; IR£14); and **Tralee** (2½hr.; M-Sa 3 per day, Su 3 per day; IR£18).

Buses: (☎ 508 188), Parnell Pl. Two blocks east of Patrick's Bridge on **Merchants' Quay.** Inquiries desk open daily 9am-5pm. To: **Dublin** (4½hr., 4 per day, IR£13); **Galway** (4hr., 5 per day, IR£12.50); **Killarney** (2hr.; M-Sa 8 per day, Su 6 per day; IR£9.40); **Limerick** (2hr.; M-Sa 6 per day, Su 5 per day; IR£9.60); **Rosslare Harbour** (4hr., 2 per day, IR£13.50); **Sligo** (7hr., 3 per day, IR£17); **Tralee** (2½hr.; M-Sa 8 per day, Su 6 per day; IR£10); **Waterford** (2¼hr.; M-Sa 8 per day, Sun 6 per day; IR£10); and **Belfast** (7½hr.; M-Sa 4 per day, Su 2 per day; IR£20). City buses criss-cross the city and its suburbs. From downtown, catch the buses (and their schedules) at the bus station on Merchant's Quay or on St. Patrick St., across from the Father Matthew statue.

Ferries: To: **Swansen, England** daily (IR£44-64, prices increase June-Aug.). Contact **Irish Ferries** (☎ (1890) 31 31 31 or 551 995) at the corner of MacCurtain St. and St. Patrick's bridge. For 24hr. ferry information, call ☎ (01) 661 0715.)

◢◣ 🛈 ORIENTATION AND PRACTICAL INFORMATION

Downtown Cork is the tip of an arrow-shaped island in the **River Lee.** The north side is dominated by the sight-filled **Shandon** district. The downtown action is concentrated on **Oliver Plunkett St., Saint Patrick St., Paul St.,** and the north-south streets that connect them. Heading west from the Grand Parade, **Washington St.** becomes **Western Rd.;** to the north of the Lee, **McCurtain St.** flows east into **Lower Glanmire Rd.** Cork is compact and pedestrian-friendly.

Tourist Office: Grand Parade (☎ 273 251), near the corner of South Mall and Grand Parade downtown across from the National Monument. Open M-Sa 9:15am-5:30pm.

Banks: TSB, 4-5 Princes St. (☎ 275 221). Open M-W and F 9:30am-5pm, Th 9:30am-7pm. **Bank of Ireland,** 70 Patrick St. (☎ 277 177). Open M 10am-5pm, Tu-F 10am-4pm. Most banks in Cork have 24hr. **ATMs.**

Emergency: ☎ 999. **Police, Garda** (☎ 522 000), Anglesea St.

Pharmacies: Regional Late Night Pharmacy, (☎ 344 575) Wilton Rd., opposite the Regional Hospital on bus #8. Open M-F 9am-10pm, Sa-Su 10am-10pm. **Phelan's Late Night,** 9 Patrick St. (☎ 272 511). Open M-Sa 9am-10pm, Su 10am-10pm.

Hospital: Mercy Hospital, (☎ 271 971) Grenville Pl. IR£20 fee for access to emergency room. **Cork Regional Hospital,** Wilton St. (☎ 546 400), on bus #8.

Internet Access: Favourite, 122 Patrick St. (☎ 272 646), at the top of Patrick St. near Merchant Quay. IR£1 per 10min. Open daily 9am-10:30pm.

Post Office: (☎ 272 000), Oliver Plunkett St. at the corner of Pembrooke St. Open M-Sa 9am-5:30pm.

▜ ACCOMMODATIONS

Cork's hostels range from drearily adequate to wonderfully welcoming. **B&Bs** are clustered along Western Rd. near University College. The other concentration of

IRELAND

Cork

ACCOMMODATIONS

Accommodation Centre (IHH), 7
Aaron House Hostel, 8
Campus House (IHH), 1
Cork International Hostel (HI), 2
Gamish House, 3
Kelly's Hostel, 10
Kinlay House Hostel, 4
Independent Hostel, 9
Isaac's Hostel, 6
Roman House, 5
Sheila's Budget

Military Rd.

TO 9

Kent

Summer Hill

Lower Glanmire Rd.

Railway St.

Victoria Quay

Victoria Rd.

Youghal Old Rd.

Belgrave Pl.

Sidney Park

Wellington Rd.

7

Penrose's Quay

Albert Quay

Albert Rd.

Gas Works Rd.

South City Link Rd.

Anderson's Quay

Albert

Angelsea

Infirmary Rd.

Audley Pl.

St. Patrick's Hill

Richmond Hill

MacCurtain St.

St. Patrick's Quay

Merchant's Quay

Parnel Pl.

Merchant

Lapp's Quay

Copley

South Terr.

Sawmill

Rutland

6

Leitrim

John

Upper John

5

Coburg

Camden Pl.

Lavitt's Quay

Opera House

Emmet Pl.

Drawbridge

Winthrop

Pembroke

Morrison's Quay

Union Quay

George's Quay

Douglas

Shandon Church

4

Roman

John Redmond

Dominick

Pope's Quay

Kyrl's Quay

Academy

Paul

St. Paul's Ave.

Crawford Art Gallery

St. Patrick's

Oliver Plunkett

Morgan

Cook

Marlborough

Prince's

South Mall

Mary St.

Dinan

Abbey

Evergreen

Tower

Cathedral Walk

Cathedral Rd.

Shandon

Old Market Pl.

Glen Ryan Rd.

North Mall

Bachelor's Quay

Castle

North Main

Grattan

Liberty

Sheares

Henry

Washington

Hanover

Grand Parade

Christchurch

Castle

South Main

Sullivan's Quay

Cove

French Quay

Elizabethan Fort

Industry

Barrack

Mount Carmel

Presentation Pl.

St. Anne's

Mart Akenhead Pl.

Gurranaher Ave.

Boyce's

Blarney

Sunday's Well Rd.

Grenville Pl.

Wandesford Quay

St. Finbarre's Cathedral

Bishop

Dean

Mary St.

Gould's

Orery Rd.

Cathedral Rd.

Mount Nebo Ave.

Gurranbraher Rd.

220 yards

200 meters

N

Dyke Parade

Lancaster Quay

Sharman Crawford

Gill Abbey

College Rd.

Connaught Ave.

Bandon Rd.

Hartland's Rd.

FITZGERALD PARK

Cork Museum

Mardyke Walk

Western Road

3

Donovan's Rd.

University College

Magazine Rd.

Desmond Sq.

2

River Lee (North Channel)

R. Lee (So. Channel)

Gaol Walk

Highfield Ave.

Glasheen Rd.

Coolgarten Park

1

accommodations is in the slightly more central area along McCurtain St. and Lower Glanmire Rd., near the bus and train stations.

Sheila's Budget Accommodation Centre (IHH), 4 Belgrave Pl. (☎450 5562), by the intersection of Wellington Rd. and York St. Bike rental IR£6. Internet access. Sheets 50p. Key deposit IR£5. Check-out 10:30am. Dorms IRIR£7-8.50; doubles IR£21.

Cork International Hostel (An Óige/HI), 1-2 Redclyffe, Western Rd. (☎454 3289), a 15min. walk from the Grand Parade. Bus #8 stops across the street—ask for the stop. Immaculate and spacious bunk rooms. All rooms with bath. Bike rental IR£5 per day. Breakfast IR£2. Check-in 8am-midnight. Dorms IR£8-14.50. Cheaper off-season.

Kinlay House (IHH Bob and Joan Walk ☎450 6927; email kincork@usit.ie), down the alley to the right of Shandon Church, in Shandon. Each room has a locker and sink. Continental breakfast included. Laundry IR£3.60. 50p key deposit. Internet access IR£1.50 per 15min. Dorms IR£8; doubles IR£25; singles IR£15. ISIC discount 10%.

Isaac's (IHH), 48 McCurtain St. (☎450 8388; www.ibi.ie/isaacs). From the bus stop, cross the nearby bridge and take the second left onto McCurtain St. Conveniently located near the bus and train stations. Cafe open for breakfast and lunch. Continental breakfast IR£2.25, Irish IR£3.25. 24hr. reception. Dorms IR£7.95-9.25.

Garnish House (☎427 5111), Western Rd. Prepare to be pampered at this B&B. All rooms come with telephone, color TV, and full bath. Laundry free. Singles from IR£25; doubles from IR£40, with jacuzzi from IR£50. Family room available.

🍴 FOOD

Don't explore Cork's city center on an empty stomach; delicious restaurants and cafes abound. Particularly appealing are the lanes connecting Patrick St., Paul St., and Oliver Plunkett St. **Tesco** (☎270 791), on Paul St. is the biggest grocery store in town. (Open M-W and Sa 8:30am-8pm, Th-F 8:30am-10pm.)

Scoozi (☎275 077), in the alley just off Winthrop Ave. Follow the tomato signs to this expansive, brick-and-wood-lined establishment. Pesto chicken breast on a bun with fries and coleslaw IR£6.85. Open M-Sa 9am-11pm, Su noon-10pm.

The Gingerbread House (☎296 411), Paul St. Huge windows, cool jazz, and heavenly breads, pastries, and quiche made fresh on the premises. Open M-W, Sa 8:15am-7pm, Th-F 8:15am-9pm, Su 8:15am-6pm.

🎵 SIGHTS AND ENTERTAINMENT

Cork's sights are loosely divided into several districts, but all can be reached by foot. Pick up the *Cork Area City Guide* at the tourist office (IR£1.50). Downtown Cork is located on the tip of an arrow-shaped island in the River Lee; bridges link the island to Cork's residential south side and less affluent north side. Across the river to the north, walk up Shandon St. and take a right down unmarked Church St. to reach Cork's most famous landmark, **St. Ann's Church.** The church earned the nickname of "the four-faced liar" because the four tower clocks are notoriously out of sync with one another. (☎450 59 06. Open M-Sa 9:30am-5:30pm. £5, students and seniors £4.) Housed within an elegant 18th-century customs house, the **Crawford Municipal Art Gallery** specializes in the paintings of Irish masters like James Barry and Jack Yeats, along with contemporary work. Adjacent is the monstrous, cement **Opera House.** (Emmet Place. Over the hill from Shandon Church, across the north fork of the Lee. ☎273 377. Gallery open M-Sa 10am-5pm. Free.) Do not pass go before heading to the **Cork City Gaol,** where multimedia tours of the former prison and a walk through Cork's social history await; cross the bridge at the western end of Fitzgerald Park, turn right on Sunday's Well Rd., and follow the signs. (☎430 50 22. Open daily Mar.-Oct. 9:30am-6pm; Nov.-Feb. 10am-5pm. £4.50, students £3. Admission includes audio-tape tour.) After visiting the jail, taste liberty by wandering the grounds of the nearby **University College Cork,** on the riverbank along Western Rd. Three festivals come to Cork every October.

The always lively streets of Cork make finding entertainment easy. Cork's pubs have all the variety of music and atmosphere you'd expect to find in Ireland's

KNOW YOUR WHISKEY Anyone who drinks his whiskey as it's meant to be drunk—"neat," or straight—can tell you that there's a huge difference between Irish whiskeys (Bushmills, Jameson, Power and Son, and the like), Scotch whiskys (spelled without an e), and American whiskeys. But what makes an Irish whiskey *Irish*? The basic ingredients in whiskey—water, barley (which becomes malt once processed), and heat from a fuel source—are always the same. It's the quality of these ingredients, the way in which they're combined, and the manner in which the combination is stored that gives each product its distinct flavor. The different types of whiskey derive from slight differences in this production process. American whiskey is distilled once and is often stored in oak, bourbon is made only in Kentucky, scotch uses peat-smoked barley, and Irish whiskey is triple distilled. The best way to understand the distinctions between brands is to taste the various labels in close succession to one another. Line up those shot glasses, sniff and then taste each one (roll the whiskey in your mouth like a real pro), and have a sip of water between each brand.

second-largest city. Along Oliver Plunkett St., Union Quay, and South Main St., there are more pubs than you can shake a stick at. To keep on top of the scene, check out *List Cork*, a free schedule of music available at local stores. **The Lobby,** 1 Union Quay, arguably the most famous venue in Cork, gave some of Ireland's biggest folk acts their big breaks; it features live music nightly with a view of the river. (☎319 307. Occasional cover IR£4.) **An Spailpín Fanac,** 28 South Main St. (☎277 949), is one of Cork's more popular pubs and is about as old as they get—it opened in 1790. Live *trad* complements the decor most nights. **Gallaghers,** MacCurtain St., is a traditional pub conveniently located to welcome tourists, especially on "Backpacker Nights" (M-Tu), when a three-pint pitcher sells for IR£6. **Gorbys,** Oliver Plunkett St., features young groovers grinding. (☎270 074. Cover IR£2-5.) Arguably the most popular dance club in Cork, **Sir Henry's,** South Main St., is also the most intense. Prepare to wedge yourself between sweaty, semi-conscious bodies on the three dance floors. (☎274 391. Cover IR£2-11.) Restaurant by day, nightclub by night, **The Yumi Yuki Club,** Tobin St., is a Pan-Asian themed club offering an alternative to the raucous parties nearby. (☎275 777. Open 10am-1am, food is served 12pm-12am; occasional cover IR£3.)

▌ DAYTRIPS FROM CORK

BLARNEY (AN BHLARNA)

Buses run from Cork to Blarney (10-15 per day, IR£3.00 roundtrip). ☎385 252. Open daily June-Aug. 9am-7pm, Su 9:30am-5:30pm; Sept. M-Sa 9am-6:30pm, Su 9:30am-sundown; Oct.-Apr. M-Sa 9am-6pm, Su 9:30am-sundown; May M-Sa 9am-6:30pm, Su 9:30am-5:30pm. IR£3.50, seniors and students IR£2.50, children IR£1.

Whether you're in the mood to admire the idyllic Irish countryside or simply dying to stand in a damp castle passageway, **Blarney Castle,** with its **Blarney Stone,** is the quintessential tourist spot. The prevailing myth of the stone's origin holds that it is a chip of the Scottish Stone of Scone that was presented to the King of Munster in gratitude for support during a rebellion in 1314. With everyone else doing it, you might just find yourself bending over backwards to kiss the stone in hopes of acquiring the legendary eloquence bestowed on those who smooch it. The term "blarney" refers to the Irish talent of stretching, or even obstructing, the truth.

MIDLETON

Buses run from Cork (30min., M-Sa 13-18 per day, IR£3.80). ☎613 594. Open Mar.-Oct. daily 10am-6pm. IR£3.95, students and seniors IR£3.50, children IR£1.50. Tours every 45min.

Midleton beckons pilgrims to the **Jameson Heritage Centre** with the water of life (Irish for whiskey). The center rolls visitors through a 1-hr. tour detailing the craft and history of whiskey production and includes a glass of the potent stuff. After all, "the story of whiskey is the story of Ireland."

KINSALE

☎ **21**

Each summer, affluent tourists come to swim, fish, and eat at Kinsale's famed and pricey twelve restaurants known as the "Good Food Circle;" but luckily, the town's best attractions are cheap. The star-shaped, 17th-century **Charles Fort** offers spectacular views of the town and its watery surroundings; follow the coastal **Scilly Walk** from the end of Pearse St. (30min. Open mid-June to mid-Sept. daily 9am-6pm; mid-Apr. to mid-June and mid-Sept. to mid-Oct. M-Sa 9am-5pm, Su 9:30am-5:30pm. IR£2, students IR£1.) Across the harbor, the grass-covered ruins of **James Fort** delight with panoramic views. (Open 24hr. Free.) **Buses** arrive at the Esso station on the pier from Cork (40min., M-F 3-10 per day, IR£3.80 roundtrip). The **tourist office,** Emmet Pl., is on the waterfront. (☎77 22 34. Open Mar.-Nov. daily 9am-6pm.) To get to the **Castlepark Marina Centre (IHH),** across the harbor, walk along the pier away from town for 10min., turn left to cross Duggan Bridge, take a left just past the bridge, and follow the road back toward the harbor. (☎77 49 59. Dorms IR£8-9; doubles IR£20. Open mid-Mar. to Dec.) **Dempsey's Hostel (IHH),** Cork Rd., is 2min. from town. (☎77 21 24. Dorms IR£6; doubles IR£16.)

SCHULL AND THE MIZEN HEAD PENINSULA

☎ **28**

The seaside hamlet of **Schull** is an ideal base for exploring the craggy, windswept, and beach-laden southwest tip of Ireland. In summer, it's also a jumping-off point to the striking island of **Cape Clear** (Jun.-Sept. 1-3 ferries per day, return IR£9; call ☎391 35 for ferry info). A calm harbor and numerous shipwrecks make a **diver's** paradise; the **Watersports Centre** rents gear. (Open M-Sa 9:30am-8:30pm.) Pick up the prosaic and lengthy *Schull Guide* from any store in town (IR£1.50). The Mizen becomes more scenic and less populated the farther west you go from Schull. **Betty's Bus Hire** offers tours of the Mizen via the scenic coast road. (☎284 10. IR£5. Departs Schull June-Aug. Tu and Th 11am.) **Buses** arrive in Schull from Cork (1-3 per day, IR£13 return) and Killarney (June-Sept. 1 per day). Once you've reached Schull, there's no further public transportation on the peninsula besides a Bus Éireann bus to Goleen (2 per day). Those who choose to accept the risks of **hitching** often avoid poor public transportation by waiting at the crossroads on Goleen Rd. outside of town. *Let's Go* does not recommend hitchhiking. Confident **cyclists** can daytrip to Mizen Head (18 mi. from Schull). The immaculate **Schull Backpackers' Lodge (IHH),** Colla Rd, has **hiking** and **biking** maps and info. (☎286 81. Dorms IR£8; doubles IR£24-26.) **Spar Market** is on Main St. (Open M-Sa 7am-9pm, Su 8am-8pm.)

KILLARNEY AND KILLARNEY NATIONAL PARK

☎ **064**

The town of Killarney is just minutes from some of Ireland's most glorious natural scenery. The 37 sq. mi. **national park** outside town blends forested mountains with the famous Lakes of Killarney. **Muckross House,** 3 mi. south of Killarney on Kenmare Rd., is a massive 19th-century manor with a garden that blooms brilliantly each year. A path leads to the 60-ft. **Torc Waterfall.** (House open daily July-Aug. 9am-7pm; Sept.-June 9am-6pm. £3.80, students £1.60.) Walk or drive to the 14th-century **Ross Castle** by taking a right on Ross Rd. off Muckross Rd., 2 mi. from Killarney; the numerous footpaths from Knockreer (out of town on New St.) are more scenic. (Open daily June-Aug. 9am-6:30pm; May-Sept. 10am-6pm; mid-Mar. to Apr. and Oct. 9am-5pm. Obligatory tour £3, students £1.25.) Bike around the **Gap of Dunlow,** which borders **Macgillycuddy's Reeks,** Ireland's highest mountain range. Hop on a **boat** from Ross Castle to the head of the Gap (£7; book at the tourist office). Head left over the stone bridge from Lord Brandon's Cottage, continue 2 mi. to the church, follow the hairpin turn, and huff the 1½ mi. to the top; your reward is a 7-mi. coast downhill through the park's most breathtaking scenery. The 8-mi. ride to Killarney (bear right after Kate Kearney's Cottage, turn left on the road to Fossa, and turn right on Killorglin Rd.) passes the ruins of **Dunloe Castle,** demolished by Cromwell's armies.

Trains arrive at the station (☎310 67) off East Avenue Rd., near Park Rd., from: Cork (2hr., 5 per day, roundtrip £9.50); Limerick (3hr., 3-4 per day, £15); and Dublin (3½hr., 4 per day, £33.50). **Buses** (☎300 11) rumble from Park Rd. to Cork (2hr., 3-7 per day, £9.40). **Bike rental** places abound. The **tourist office** is on Beech St., off New St. (☎316 33. Open July-Aug. M-Sa 9am-8pm, Su 10am-1pm and 2:15-6pm; June and

Sept. M-Sa 9am-6pm, Su 10am-1pm and 2:15-6pm; Oct.-May M-Sa 9:15am-5:30pm.) From either station, turn left on College St. and take a right past the courthouse to reach **The Súgán (IHH),** Lewis Rd., where exuberant management compensates for cramped quarters. (☎ 331 04. £9.) The immense **Neptune's (IHH),** Bishop's Ln., is up the 1st walkway off New St. on the right. (☎ 352 55. Dorms £7.50-9.50; doubles £20.) Call for a ride from either station to the **Aghadoe Hostel (An Óige/HI),** on Killorglin Rd. (☎ 312 40. Dorms £7.50-9.50; singles £10-12.) Pick up **groceries** at **Tesco,** in an arcade off New St. (Open M-W and Sa 8am-8pm, Th-F 8am-10pm, Su 10am-6pm.) **O'Conner's Traditional Pub,** 7 High St., mixes locals and tourists (trad M and Th).

RING OF KERRY

The Southwest's most celebrated peninsula holds wee villages, fabled ancient forts, and rugged mountains—the romantic scenery most visitors come to Ireland seeking. Although noxious, air-conditioned tour buses often hog the roads, greater rewards await those who take the time to explore the landscape on foot or by bike.

F TRANSPORTATION. The term "Ring of Kerry" is usually used to describe the entire **Iveragh Peninsula,** though it more technically refers to the ring of roads circumnavigating it. Hop on the no-frills circuit run by **Bus Éireann,** which stops at the major towns on the Ring (June-Sept. 2 per day): **Cahersiveen** (from Killorglin 50min., IR£5); **Caherdaniel** (from Cahersiveen 1½hr., IR£3.10); and **Killarney** (from Caherdaniel 1½hr., IR£7.30; from Cahersiveen 2½hr., IR£9).

CAHERSIVEEN. Cahersiveen (car-si-VEEN) is best known in Ireland as the birthplace of patriot Daniel "The Liberator" O'Connell, who won Catholic representation in Parliament in 1829. Its two hostels are excellent bases for exploring the nearby beach and historical sites, or for longer excursions to Valentia Island or the Skelligs. Two miles northwest of town across the bridge are the ruins of the **Ballycarbery Castle,** once held by O'Connell's ancestors. Two hundred yards past the castle turnoff, you can walk along the 10-ft.-thick walls of **Cahergall Fort** or visit the small stone dwellings of **Leacanabuaile Fort.** The **tourist office** is in a former barracks on the road to the castle. (☎ (066) 947 25 89. Open May to mid-Sept. M-Sa 10am-1pm and 2:15-6pm.) The friendly **Sive Hostel (IHH)** is at 15 East End, Main St. (☎ (066) 947 27 17. Dorms IR£8; doubles IR£20-25; **camping** IR£5 per person.) Equally fabulous is **Mortimer's Hostel,** Main St. (☎ (066) 947 23 38. Dorms IR£7.) Cahersiveen's 30 **original pubs** may seem like a lot, but residents wistfully recollect when there were 52.

A fantastic daytrip is the quiet ■**Valentia Island,** where shady country roads link a handful of beehive huts, *ogham* stones, and small ruins. The views in between, across to the mountainous mainland, and out over Dingle Bay, would be reason enough to come to Ireland. You can **bike** to the island, connected by bridges on either end to the mainland, or take a comically short **ferry** (3min., every 10min. Apr.-Sept. 8:15am-7:30pm, pedestrians IR£3) from **Reenard Point,** three points west of Cahersiveen; a taxi to the ferry dock from Cahersiveen runs IR£4. Another great daytrip is to the **Skellig Rocks,** a stunning mass of natural rubble about 8 mi. off the shore of the Iveragh Peninsula. From your boat, **Little Skellig** will at first appear snow-capped, but it's actually just covered with 22,000 crooning birds. Climb the vertigo-inducing 650 steps past puffins, kittiwakes, gannets, and petrels (birds to you) to reach a **monastery** built by 6th-century Christian monks, whose beehive-like dwellings are still intact. The hostels and campground in Cahersiveen will all arrange the **ferry** ride (45-90min.) for IR£20, including a ride to the dock.

CAHERDANIEL. There's little in the village of **Caherdaniel** to attract the Ring's droves of buses, but nearby **Derrynane Strand,** 1½ mi. away in Derrynane National Park, delights with 2 mi. of gorgeous beach ringed by picture perfect dunes. **Derrynane House,** signposted just up from the beach, was the cherished residence of Irish patriot Daniel O'Connell. (Open May-Sept. M-Sa 9am-6pm, Su 11am-7pm; Apr. and Oct. Tu-Su 1-5pm; Nov.-Mar. Sa-Su 1-5pm. IR£2, students IR£1.) Guests have the run of the house at **The Travellers' Rest Hostel.** (☎ (066) 947 51 75. Breakfast IR£3. Dorms IR£8.50; singles IR£9-9.50; doubles IR£20.)

IRELAND

DINGLE PENINSULA

For decades the Ring of Kerry's undertouristed counterpart, the gorgeous Dingle Peninsula remains more congested with ancient sites than tour buses. The Ring's tourist blitz has only just begun to encroach upon the spectacular cliffs and sweeping beaches of the Irish-speaking peninsula. A *gaeltacht* to the west of Dingle Town preserves centuries-old Irish heritage.

▛ TRANSPORTATION. The best base for exploring the peninsula, which lies just across the Dingle Bay from the Ring of Kerry to the south, is Dingle Town, most easily reached from Tralee (1¼hr., 4-6 per day, IR£5.90). From Dingle Town, **Bus Éireann** runs west to Ballydavid (20min., Tu and F 3 per day, return IR£3.15) as well as Dunquin and Ballyferriter (20-30min., in summer 1-4 per day, IR£2.30). In summer, additional buses also tour the south of the peninsula from Dingle (June-Sept. M-Sa 2 per day). If you only have time for a daytrip, a prepackaged Dingle/Slea Head tour runs from Killarney (M-Sa 2 per day, IR£9.70).

DINGLE TOWN. Lively Dingle Town, adopted home of **Fungi the Dolphin** (now a major focus of the tourist industry), serves as a good regional base. **Sciúird Archaeology tours** take you from the pier on a 3-hr. whirlwind bus tour of the area's ancient spots (☎ (066) 915 16 06. 2 per day, IR£8; book ahead). **Morans** runs great tours to Slea Head that stop by historical sites, film sets, and majestic views. (☎ (066) 91 51 55. IR£8.) The **tourist office** is on the corner of Main and Dykegate St. (☎ (066) 915 11 88. Open June-Aug. M-Sa 9am-6pm, Su 10am-6pm; Sept.-Oct. and mid-Mar. to May M-Sa 9am-5pm.) **Ballintaggart Hostel (IHH),** 25min. east on Tralee Rd. in a stone mansion, is supposedly haunted by the wife of the Earl of Cork, whom he strangled here. (☎ (066) 915 14 54. Free shuttle to town. Breakfast IR£2-4. Dorms IR£8-10; twins and doubles IR£30; off-season IR£1-2 less; **camping** IR£3.50.) The laid-back **Grapevine Hostel** is on Dykegate St., off Main St. (☎ (066) 915 14 34. Dorms IR£8.50-10.50.) From Dingle Town, a winding cliff-side road runs north by the 1500-foot **Connor Pass.** As the road twists downhill, a waterfall marks the base of **Pedlars Lake.**

SLEA HEAD AND DUNQUIN. Glorious Slea Head impresses with its jagged cliffs and crashing waves. Green hills, interrupted by rough stone walls and occasional sheep, suddenly break off into the foam-flecked sea. *Ryan's Daughter* and parts of *Far and Away* were filmed in this appropriately melodramatic scenery. By far the best way to see Slea Head and Dunquin in a day or less is to bike along the predominantly flat **Slea Head Drive.** Past Dingle Town toward Slea Head sits the village of **Ventry** (Ceann Trá), home to a sandy beach and the brand-new **Ballybeag Hostel;** a regular shuttle runs to Dingle Town. (☎915 98 76; email balybeag@iol.ie. **Bike rental** IR£2.50-5. Laundry IR£4. Dorms IR£7.50-9.) The **▐Celtic and Prehistoric Museum,** farther down the road, is a must-see—tour the astounding collection, ranging from 300-million-year-old sea worm fossils, to Iron Age tools and jewelry, to an electric sheep. Their newest exhibit is a 50,000-year old woolly mammoth found off the coast of Holland in 1999. (☎915 99 41; www.kerryweb.ie. Open daily April-Oct. 10am-5pm, other times call ahead. IR£3.) North of Slea Head, the scattered settlement of **Dunquin** (Dún Chaoin) boasts **Kruger's,** purportedly the westernmost pub in Western Europe. (☎915 61 27. Main dishes IR£6-8.) Its adjacent **B&B** has comfortable rooms (IR£17). Just outside of Dunquin on the road to Ballyferriter, **Blasket Center** has outstanding exhibits about the isolated Blasket Islands. (Open daily July-Aug. 10am-7pm; Easter-June and Sept.-Nov. 10am-6pm. IR£2.50, students IR£1.)

TRALEE. While tourists see Killarney as the core of County Kerry, residents are proud to identify Tralee (pop. 20,000) as its economic center. Tourists often use Tralee's abundance of quality hostels and pubs as a base to see the ring of Kerry. Ireland's second-largest museum, **Kerry the Kingdom,** Ashe Memorial Hall, Denny St., showcases a high-tech history of Ireland from 8000 BC to the present. (☎ (066) 712 7777. Open daily Mar.-Oct. 10am-6pm; Nov.-Dec. noon-4:30pm. IR£5.50, students IR£4.75.) During the last week of August, the nationally-known **Rose of Tralee Festival** brings a maelstrom of entertainment to town as lovely Irish lasses compete for the title "Rose of Tralee." **Trains** go to: Cork (2½hr., 3-5 per day, IR£17); Galway (3 per day, IR£33.50); and Killarney (40min., 4-5 per day, IR£5.50). **Buses** rumble to: Cork (2½hr., 3-6 per day, IR£9.70); Galway (4-6 per day, IR£13); Killarney (40min., June-Sept. 5-14 per day, IR£4.40); and Limerick (2¼hr., 7 per day, IR£9). To get to the **tourist office,** Ashe Memorial Hall, from either station, head to town on Edward St., turn right on Castle St. and left on Denny St. (☎ (066) 712 12 88. Open July-Aug. M-Sa 9am-7pm, Su 9am-6pm; May-June and Oct. M-Sa 9am-6pm; Oct.-Apr. M-F 9am-5pm.) The well-located **Finnegan's Hostel (IHH),** 17 Denny St., is in a 19th-century townhouse containing part of the old town castle. (☎ (066) 712 76 10. Dorms IR£10; doubles IR£25.) Call for pick-up to the **Collis-Sandes House (IHH).** (☎ (066) 712 86 58; www.colsands.com. Dorms IR£9; doubles from IR£24; **camping** IR£4.)

WESTERN IRELAND

Even Dubliners will tell you that the west is the "most Irish" part of Ireland. Yeats agreed: "For me," he said, "Ireland is Connacht." For less privileged Irish in recent centuries, Connacht mostly meant poor soil and emigration. When Cromwell uprooted the native Irish landowners in Leinster and Munster and resettled them west of the Shannon, the popular phraseology for their plight became "To hell or to Connacht." The potato famine (see p. 556) that plagued the island was most devastating in the west—entire villages emigrated or died. Today, it has less than half of its 1841 population. Though miserable for farming, the land from Connemara north to Ballina is a boon for hikers, cyclists, and hitchhikers, as they enjoy the isolation of boggy, rocky, or brilliantly mountainous landscapes.

LIMERICK CITY   ☎061

Although Limerick's 18th-century Georgian streets and parks remain regal and elegant, later industrial developments and hard economic times give the city a duller, urban feel. To reach the requisite local castle, **King John's Castle,** on Nicholas St., walk across the Abbey River and turn after St. Mary's Cathedral. (Open Mar.-Dec. daily 9:30am-6pm. IR£4.20, students IR£3.30.) **Trains** (☎315 555) leave Parnell St. for: Dublin (2hr., 8-9 per day, IR£27); Cork (2½hr., 5-6 per day, IR£14); and Waterford (2hr., M-Sa 1-2, IR£13.50). **Buses** (☎313 333) leave the train station for: Dublin (3hr., 13 per day, IR£10); Cork (2hr., 14 per day, IR£9); Galway (2hr., 14 per day, IR£9); Tralee (2hr., 10 per day, IR£10); and Waterford (2½hr., 5-6 per day, IR£9.70). The **tourist office** is on Arthurs Quay, in the space-age glass building. From the station, walk straight down Davis St., right on O'Connell St., and left just before Arthurs Quay Mall. (☎317 522. Open July-Aug. M-F 9am-7pm, Sa-Su 9am-6pm; May-June and Sept.-Oct. M-Sa 9:30am-5:30pm; Nov.-Apr. M-F 9:30am-5:30pm, Sa 9:30am-1pm.) **Finnegan's (IHH),** 6 Pery Sq., has common rooms and a convenient location. (☎310 308. Laundry IR£3-4. Dorms IR£8-12; private rooms IR£12.) Or snooze at **An Óige Hostel (HI),** 1 Pery Sq., around the corner from Finnegan's. (☎314 672. Sheets £1. Continental breakfast £2. Lockout 10am-2pm. Curfew midnight. June-Sept. 14-bed dorms £8.50; Oct.-May £7.50; £1 less for HI members.) Get **groceries** at **Tesco** in Arthurs Quay Mall. (Open M-W and Sa 8:30am-8pm, Th-F 8:30am-10pm.) Limerick's immense student population adds spice to the pub scene—**Dolan's,** (☎314 483) Dock Rd., hosts nightly *trad* and rambunctious local patrons.

CLARE COAST

Europe's best traditional Irish music, highest cliffs, and strangest landscapes are to be found on the superlative coast of County Clare. **Ennis** is the main rail hub in the region. **Bus Éireann** (☎(065) 682 41 77) runs south-north from Kilkee to Galway; a West Clare line goes from Kilkee to Doolin. **Kilkee** features the spectacular **Westend Cliff Walk** and a famously fun pub crawl. The cliff walk begins at the end of the road to the left of the seacoast and makes a gentle climb up to the top of the cliffs. **Four Pollock Holes** have natural rock pools for swimming. The **Kilkee Hostel (IHH),** among the pubs on O'Curry St., makes friends of strangers. (☎(065) 562 09. Sheets IR50p. Laundry IR£2. Dorms IR£8.) Just 20 mi. north of Kilkee and 2 mi.

inland from Spanish Point beach is **Milltown Malbay,** the best place to be for Irish music. During **Willie Week,** thousands of musicians, instrument-makers, tourists, and *craic* addicts converge in Milltown for a week of recitals, lectures, and non-stop sessions. The **Station House,** at the old railway station, has huge beds. (☎ (065) 708 40 08. Singles IR£20, doubles IR£35.) Just north of Milltown, the tiny seaside resort of **Lahinch** sits on smooth sand in a crook of the bay and is the surfing capital of Ireland. The comfortable **Lahinch Hostel (IHH),** on Church St, has a central, waterfront location. (☎ (065) 708 10 40. Bikes IR£7 per day. Laundry IR£2. Dorms IR£8-9; doubles IR£24.) A 20-min. bus ride continues around the coast to the extraordinary ◨**Cliffs of Moher,** justifiably one of Ireland's most famous sights. Standing 700 ft. above the Atlantic spray, you can see gulls circling limestone spires below you. On a clear day, the majestic cliffs afford views of **Loop Head,** the **Kerry Mountains,** the **Twelve Pins of Connemara,** and the **Aran Islands.** Eight miles north up the coast, **Doolin** is a rural backpackers' mecca. Its lower village is a handful of buildings near the sea; the tiny upper village is 1 mi. up the road. Fifteen years ago, Doolin was the trade capital, and its three legendary pubs—**McDermott's** and **McGann's** in Upper Village and **O'Connor's** in the Lower—still have fantastic sessions and tasty food. By the river between the two villages is the **Aille River Hostel (IHH),** a small cottage with a groovy ambience. (☎ (065) 707 42 60. Dorms July-Aug. £7.50-8, Sept.-May £7.50; tent sites IR£3.50. Open mid-Mar. to mid-Nov.) An 8 mi. paved and bicycle-friendly segment of the **Burren Way** links Doolin to the Cliffs of Moher; the **Doolin Bike Store** rents bikes (☎ (065) 707 42 82. IR£7 per day. Open daily 9am-8pm.)

THE BURREN

If there were wild orchids, cantankerous cows, and B&Bs on the moon, it would probably look a lot like the Burren. Its land comprises nearly 100 sq. mi. and almost one-third of Co. Clare's coastline. The lunar beauty of the Burren sees jagged gray hills resembling skyscrapers turned to rubble, hidden depressions that open up into a labyrinth of caves, ruined churches and castles, thousands of miles of stone walls, ancient megaliths, and indigenous wildflowers. The best way to see the Burren is to walk or cycle it, but it's notoriously difficult to get around. Yellow arrows mark a 26-mi. **hiking trail** from Liscannor to Ballyvaughan; Doolin and Kinvara are the best bases for biking tours. All of the surrounding tourist offices (at Ennis, the Cliffs of Moher, and Kinvara) have good maps of the region and other info. **Bus Éireann** (☎ 682 41 77) connects Galway to towns in and near the Burren a few times a day during summer but infrequently during winter. Although cars plow through town on their way from Galway to the Burren, **Kinvara** (pop. 2300) is a fairly well-kept secret with a well-preserved **medieval castle,** a vibrant artistic community, and pubs with character. **Johnston's Hostel (IHH),** on Main St., uphill from the Quay area, is a relaxing haven. (☎ (091) 371 64. Showers 50p. Sheets IR£1. Curfew 12:30am. Open June-Sept. Dorms IR£7.50; camping IR£4.50.)

◨ DAYTRIP FROM THE BURREN: COOLE PARK AND THOORE BALLYLEE.

W. B. Yeats eulogized his two retreats that lie about 20 mi. south of Galway near **Gort,** where N18 meets N66. One is now a ruin and national park; the other has been restored to appear as it did when Yeats lived there. Neither is accessible by bus; biking from Kinvara is the best option but the retreats are well-worth the transportation inconvenience. The **Coole Park** nature reserve was once the estate of Lady Augusta Gregory, a friend and collaborator of Yeats. To Yeats, the estate represented the aristocratic order that crass industrialists and wars of the 1920s were destroying. In the picnic area, the famous "autograph tree," a great copper beach, bears the initials of some important Irish figures: George Bernard Shaw, Sean O'Casey, Douglas Hyde (first president of Ireland), and Yeats himself. The **Coole Park Visitors Centre** eschews talk of Yeats in favor of local rocks, trees, and wildlife. (☎ (091) 631 804. Open mid-Apr.-mid-June Tu-Su 10am-5pm; mid-June-Aug. daily 9:30am-6:30pm; Sept. daily 10am-5pm. Last admission 45min. before closing. £2, students £1.) A mile from the garden, **Coole Lake** is where Yeats watched "nine-and-fifty swans... all suddenly mount/ And scatter wheeling in great broken rings/ Upon their clamorous wings." Swans still gather here in winter.

Three miles north of Coole Park, a road turns off Galway Rd. and runs to **Thoor Ballylee,** a tower built in the 13th and 14th centuries. In 1916, Yeats bought it for £35, renovated it, and lived here with his family off and on from 1922 to 1928. A film on Yeats's life plays at the **Visitors Centre**. (☎ (091) 631 436. Open Easter-Sept. daily 10am-6pm. £3, students £2.50.)

GALWAY CITY   ☎ 091

In the past few years, Galway's reputation as Ireland's cultural capital, with a mix of over 13,000 university students, a transient population of twenty-something Europeans, and waves of international backpackers, has developed one happening college town (pop. 60,000). The town's main attractions are its nightlife and setting—it's a convenient starting point for trips to the Clare coast or the Connemara. You can rent a **rowboat** from **Frank Dolan's,** 13 Riverside, Woodquay, and row/drift down the Corrib for great views of the city, the countryside, and nearby castles (IR£3 per hr.). In mid-July, the **Galway Arts Festival** (☎ 58 38 00), Ireland's largest arts festival, rolls into town with *trad* musicians, rock groups, theater troupes, and filmmakers. Choosing from Galway's endless list of fantastic pubs is a difficult challenge even for residents. Generally speaking, the beautiful pubs along **Quay St.** cater to tourists and students; try **Seaghan Ua Neachtain** (called **Knockton's**), one of the oldest and most genuine pubs in the county, which hosts nightly *trad.* **Buskar Browne's/The Slate House,** between Cross St. and Kirwin's Ln., was a nunnery for 300 years before turning to the Dark Side. Pubs along **Dominick St.** (across the river from the Quay) are popular with locals; **The Hole in the Wall** in **Eyre Sq.**

Direct **trains** (☎ 56 14 44) run to Dublin (3hr., 4-5 per day, IR£15-21); transfer at Athlone (IR£7.50-13.50) for all other cities. **Bus Éireann** (☎ 56 20 00) leaves for: Dub-

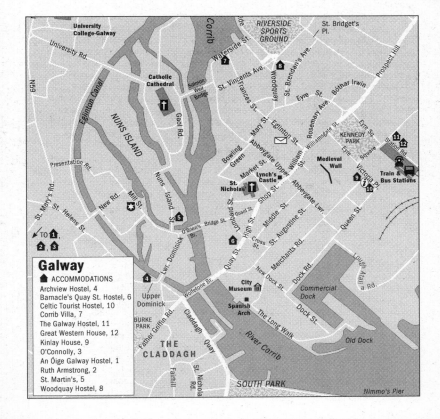

Galway

⌂ ACCOMMODATIONS
Archview Hostel, 4
Barnacle's Quay St. Hostel, 6
Celtic Tourist Hostel, 10
Corrib Villa, 7
The Galway Hostel, 11
Great Western House, 12
Kinlay House, 9
O'Connolly, 3
An Óige Galway Hostel, 1
Ruth Armstrong, 2
St. Martin's, 5
Woodquay Hostel, 8

lin (7-9 per day, IR£8); Cork (5 per day, IR£12); and Belfast (1-3 per day, IR£17). The main **tourist office,** Victoria Pl., is a block away from the bus and train stations at Eyre Sq. (☎56 30 81. Open daily July-Aug. 8:30am-7:45pm; May-June and Sept. 8:30am-5:45pm; Oct.-Apr. Su-F 9am-5:45pm, Sa 9am-12:45pm.) Check **email** at **Cyberzone,** The Old Malte Arcade, High St. (☎56 97 72. IR£5 per hr., students IR£4.) The **Salmon Weir Hostel,** on St. Vincent's Ave., provides a friendly atmosphere that allows for group pub-hopping excursions. (☎56 11 33. Laundry £4. Curfew 3am. Dorms £8.50-10.50; doubles £25.) **Great Western House (IHH),** Eyre Sq., across from the station, approaches hostel heaven with its sauna and pool room. (☎56 11 50. Laundry £5. Reception 24hr. July-Aug. dorms IR£10-12.50; singles IR£18, doubles IR£32; off-season IR£1.50-3 less.) **Kinlay House (IHH),** Merchant's Rd., across from the tourist office, is modern, big, spotless, and secure. (☎56 52 44. Internet. Breakfast included. Laundry IR£3.50. July-Sept. dorms IR£10-12.50; singles IR£20; doubles IR£29, with bath IR£33; Oct.-June dorms 50p-IR£1 less, private rooms IR£2 less. 10% ISIC discount.) For cheap food, head to the east bank; try Abbeygate St. and the short blocks around **Quay, High,** and **Shop St.** On Saturday mornings, an **open market** sets up in front of St. Nicholas Church on Market St. with seafood, pastries, and fresh fruit (open 8am-1pm). Pick up groceries at **Supervalu,** in the Eyre Sq. mall (open M-W and Sa 9am-6:30pm, Th-F 9am-9pm).

⚡ DAYTRIP FROM GALWAY CITY: DOORUS PENINSULA. Beside Kinvara, the Doorus Peninsula reaches out into Galway Bay. For those not enamored of nature, it's probably best to stay in Kinvara, but for families with cars, hikers, and bikers, Doorus is a dream come true. Three castles, several holy wells, a handful of ring forts, a cave, winged critters, panoramic views, and boggy islands await the rambler; most are detailed in *Kinvara: A Rambler's Map and Guide,* available in town for IR£2. A 10-mi. round trip west from the hostel to the **Aughinish Peninsula** offers views of the Burren across the bay. The more convenient blue-flag **Traught Strand** is just a 5min. walk from the hostel. The **Galway-Doolin bus** does not pass through Doorus but will stop upon request at the turnoff on Ballyvaughan Rd. (June-Sept. 2-4 per day; Oct.-May M-Sa 1 per day). **Campers** can pitch a tent in the field nearby and wake to the slosh of surf. The house that Yeats and Lady Augusta Gregory inhabited while planning the Abbey Theatre and collaborating on plays is now the isolated **Doorus House Hostel (An Óige/HI).** Originally the country seat of an expatriate French aristocrat, this well-appointed hostel sits gracefully among old oak trees and peers out on the great expanse of a tidal estuary. (☎63 75 12. Sheets £1. Reception 5-10:30pm. June-Sept. dorms IR£7.50; Oct.-May IR£5.50.)

ARAN ISLANDS (OILEÁIN ÁRANN)

The harsh limestone landscapes of the Aran Islands guard the entrance to Galway Bay. Awesome Iron Age forts sit atop the stark cliffs while mazes of stone walls divide deserted fields. Throngs of visitors discover the islands each summer, but islanders still maintain the lifestyle they've had for centuries by fishing, speaking Irish, and producing traditional sweaters and *curraghs* (tar-bottomed boats). Of the dozens of ruins, forts, churches, and holy wells that rise from the stony terrain of **Inishmore** (Inis Mór; pop. 900), the most amazing is the **Dún Aengus** ring fort, where a small semicircular wall surrounds a sheer 300-ft. drop.

· **Island Ferries** (☎ (091) 56 17 67, after hours 722 73) leaves from **Rossaveal** (return £15; return bus from Galway £4) and **O'Brien Shipping/Doolin Ferries** (☎ (091) 56 72 83 in Galway, in Doolin ☎ (065) 744 55) leaves from the Galway pier (return IR£12, students IR£9) and Doolin (return IR£15-20). Both have booths in the Galway tourist office. Ferries land at **Kilronan,** where the **tourist office** holds bags (75p) and changes money. (☎ (099) 612 63. Open Feb.-Nov. daily 10am-6:15pm.) Beds at **Kilronan Hostel,** near the pier, come with ocean views, spotless kitchen, and a TV lounge. A free hostel minibus meets the ferries. (☎ (099) 612 55. IR£8-9.) The **Spar Market,** past the hostel, seems to be the island's social center. (☎612 03. Open M-Sa 9am-8pm, Su 10am-6pm.) Windswept **Inishmaan** (Inis Meáin; pop. 300) elevates solitude to its greatest form. **Inisheer** (Inis Oírr; pop. 300), the smallest island, is least rugged and most budget-friendly. The **Brú Hostel**

(IHH), visible from the pier, has great views. (☎ (099) 750 24. Laundry £4. Dorms £8; singles and doubles £11 per person.) A list of Inisheer's 19 B&Bs hangs in the window of the tourist office.

CONNEMARA

Connemara, a largely Irish-speaking region, is comprised of a lacy net of inlets and islands, a rough gang of mountains, and some bogs in between. This thinly populated western arm of County Galway harbors some of Ireland's most desolate yet breathtaking scenery. The jagged southern coastline teems with sinuous estuaries, safe beaches for camping, and tidal causeways connecting to rocky islands.

CLIFDEN (AN CLOCHÁN)   ☎095

Busy, English-speaking Clifden has more amenities and modernities than its old-world, Irish-speaking neighbors. Clifden's proximity to the scenic bogs and mountains of the region attracts crowds of tourists, who enjoy the frenzied pub scene, shop in its ubiquitous arts and crafts studios, and use it as a base for exploring the region. The **Connemara Walking Center,** on Market St., runs tours of the bogs. (☎213 79. Open Mar.-Oct. M-Sa 10am-6pm. Easter-Oct. 1-2 tours per day. IR£15-25.) **Bus Éireann** goes from the library on Market St to Galway via Oughterard (2hr., 1-5 per day, IR£6.50) and Westport via Leenane (1½hr., late-June to Aug. 1-2 per day). Michael Nee runs a bus from the courthouse to Galway (June-Sept. 3 per day, IR£5). Rent a **bike** at **Mannion's,** Bridge St. (☎211 60. IR£7 per day, IR£40 per week; deposit IR£10. Open M-Sa 9:30am-6:30pm, Su 10am-1pm and 5-7pm.) The **tourist office** is on Market St. (☎211 63. Open July-Aug. M-Sa 9:45am-5:45pm and Su noon-4pm; May-June and Sept. M-Sa 9:30am-5:30pm.) Check **email** at **Two Dog Cafe,** Church Hill (☎221 86. Open M-Sa 10:30am-7pm and Su 1-5pm.). **B&Bs** litter the streets (IR£18-20). The excellent **Clifden Town Hostel (IHH)** is on Market St. (☎210 76. Dorms IR£8; doubles IR£24; triples IR£30; quads IR£36; off-season IR£1-2 less.) Head straight past the bottom of Market St. to find **Brookside Hostel,** Hulk St. (☎218 12. Laundry IR£4. Dorms IR£8; private rooms IR£8-9; doubles IR£18.) Tranquil **Shanaheever Campsite** is a little over 1 mi. outside Clifden on Westport Rd. (☎210 18. IR£8 for 2 people and tent; IR£3 per additional person.) The **O'Connor's SuperValu supermarket** is on Market St. (Open M-F 8:30am-8pm, Su 9am-7pm.) Shake your booty and down a few pints along **Market St,** in **The Square,** and on **Church Hill.**

CONNEMARA NATIONAL PARK

Connemara National Park occupies 7¾ sq. mi. of mountainous countryside that thousands of birds call home. The far-from-solid terrain of the park comprises bogs thinly covered by a screen of grass and flowers—be prepared to get muddy. The **Snuffaunboy Nature Trail** and the **Ellis Wood Trail** are easy 20-min. hikes. For the slightly more adventurous, trails lead from the back of the Ellis Wood Trail and 10min. along the Bog Road onto **Diamond Hill,** a 2hr. hike rewarding climbers with views of bog, harbor, and forest. More experienced hikers often head for the **Twelve Bens** (Na Benna Beola, a.k.a. the Twelve Pins), a rugged range that reaches 2400ft. heights (not recommended for single or beginning hikers.) A guidebook mapping out 30min. walks (50p) is available at the visitor's center, where the staff helps plan longer hikes. A tour of all 12 Bens takes experienced walkers about 10hr. Biking the 40-mi. circle through Clifden, Letterfrack, and the Inagh Valley is breathtaking, but only appropriate for fit bikers.

Tiny **Letterfrack** is the gateway to the park. The Galway-Clifden **bus** (M-Sa mid-June to Aug. 11 per week, Sept. to mid-June 4 per week) and the summertime Clifden-Westport bus (1-2 per day) stops at Letterfrack. The **Visitor's Centre** explains the fascinating differences between blanket bogs, raised bogs, turf, and heathland. Guides lead free 2-hr. **walks** over the hills and through the bogs. (☎410 54. Open daily July-Aug. 9:30am-6:30pm; June 10am-6:30pm; May and Sept. 10am-5:30pm. IR£2, students IR£1. Tours July-Aug. M, W, and F 10:30am.) Uphill from the intersection in Letterfrack, the **Old Monastery Hostel** is one of Ireland's finest. (☎411 32. Bike IR£7 per day. **Internet.** Dorms IR£8-10.) The turn-off to the **Ben Lettery Hostel (An Óige/HI),** in Ballinafad, is 8 mi. east of Clifden. (☎511 36. IR£5.50-6.)

WESTPORT ☎ 098

One of the few planned towns in the country, Westport (pop. 4300) still looks marvelous in its Georgian-period costume. Tourists savor its thriving pub life, drink tea at dapper cafes, and shop for snow-globes. The conical **Croagh Patrick** rises 2510 ft. over Clew Bay. The summit has been revered as a holy site for thousands of years. St. Patrick worked here in AD 441, praying and fasting for 40 days and nights, arguing with angels, and banishing snakes from Ireland. Climbers start their excursion from the 15th-century **Murrisk Abbey**, several miles west of Westport on R395 toward Louisburgh (4hr. round-trip). **Buses** go to Murrisk (2-3 per day), but **cabs** (☎271 71) for several people are cheaper and more convenient. Pilgrims and hikers also set out for Croagh Patrick along the Tóchar Phádraiga path from **Ballintubber Abbey** (☎ (094) 307 09), several miles south of Castlebar and 22 mi. from Croagh Patrick. Founded in 1216 by King of Connacht, the abbey still functions as a religious center. In late September, Westport celebrates its annual **Westport Arts Festival** (☎ (094) 288 33) with a week of free concerts, poetry readings, and plays.

Trains arrive at the Altamont St. Station (☎252 53), 5min. up North Mall, from Dublin via Athlone (2-3 per day, IR£15). **Buses** leave from the Octagon on Mill St. for Galway (2hr., M-F 6 per day, IR£8.80). **Breheny & Sons**, on Castlebar St., rents **bikes.** (☎250 20. IR£5-7 per day, IR£35 per week; IR£30 deposit.) The **tourist office** is at North Mall. (☎257 11. Open Apr.-Oct. M-Sa 9am-12:45pm and 2-5:45pm; July-Aug. also Su 10am-6pm.) **B&Bs** are on the Castlebar and Altamont Rd. off North Mall. **The Granary Hostel**, on Louisburgh Rd., is near the entrance to Westport House on Westport Quay. (☎259 03. Open Jan.-Nov. Dorms IR£6.) **Old Mill Holiday Hostel (IHH)**, James St., is between the Octagon and the tourist office. (☎270 45. Bike rental IR£7 per day. Sheets IR£1. Laundry IR£3. Dorms S8.) **SuperValu supermarket** is on Shop St. (Open M-W and Sa 8:30am-7:30pm, Th-F 8:30am-9pm, Su 10am-6pm.)

NORTHWEST IRELAND

The farmland of the upper Shannon spans northward into Co. Sligo's mountains, lakes, and ancient monuments. A mere sliver of land connects Co. Sligo to Co. Donegal, the second-largest and most remote of the Republic's counties. Donegal's *gaeltacht* is a storehouse of genuine, unadulterated Irish tradition.

SLIGO ☎ 071

Since the beginning of the 20th century, Sligo has been a literary pilgrimage for William Butler Yeats fanatics; the poet spent summers in town as a child, and set many of his poems around Sligo Bay. The county remains as beautiful today as it was when Yeats wrote his odes. **Sligo Town,** the commercial center of the county, does business by day but goes wild at night with one of Ireland's most colorful pub scenes, and is an excellent base from which to explore Yeats' haunts. In town, the 13th-century **Sligo Abbey**, on Abbey St., is well-preserved. (Open in summer daily 9:30am-6:30pm. IR£1.50, students IR£0.60.) **The Niland Gallery**, Stephen St., houses one of the finest collections of modern Irish art and some first editions of Yeats' works. (Open Tu-Sa 10am-noon and 2-5pm. Free.) Yeats is buried per his instructions in **Drumcliffe churchyard**, on the N15, 4 mi. northwest of Sligo. His grave is to the left of the church door. **Buses** from Sligo to Derry stop at Drumcliff (10min.; in summer 1-3 per day, off-season M-Sa 3 per day; return IR£2.60). Over 70 pubs crowd Sligo's main streets. The *International Pub Guide* ranks ▩**McLynn's**, Old Market St. (☎607 43), as the best pub for music in Sligo; locals confirm that opinion.

Trains (☎698 88) go from Lord Edward St. to Dublin via Carrick-on-Shannon and Mullingar (3 per day; IR£13.50). From the same station, **buses** (☎600 66) fan out to: Dublin (4hr., 3 per day, IR£9); Derry (3hr., 3-6 per day, IR£10); Galway (2½hr., 3-4 per day, IR£11); Westport (2½hr., 1-3 per day, IR£9.70); and Belfast (4hr., 1-3 per day, IR£12.40). Turn left on Lord Edward St., then follow the signs right on Adelaid St. and around the corner to Temple St. to find the **tourist office**, at Charles St. (☎612 01. Open M-Tu 10am-7pm, W-F 10am-9pm, Sa 10am-6pm.) **B&Bs** cluster on

Pearse Rd., on the south side of town. **Harbour House,** Finisklin Rd., is 10min. from the station. (☎715 47. Bikes IR£7. Dorms IR£10; private rooms IR£10.50.) Follow signs from the station to **Railway Hostel,** 1 Union St. (☎445 30. Dorms IR£6.50; private rooms IR£8 per person.) "Faery vats/ Full of berries/ And reddest stolen cherries" are not to be found in Sligo today; but **Quinnsworth Supermarket,** O'Connell St., sells packaged berries. (Open M-Tu 9am-7pm, W-F 9am-9pm, Sa 9am-6pm.)

DONEGAL COAST AND SLIEVE LEAGUE   ☎073

Tourists are likely to feel a bit out of place in this most remote and least Anglicized of Ireland's "scenic" provinces. Donegal escaped the widespread deforestation of Ireland; vast wooded areas engulf many of Donegal's mountain chains, while the coastline alternates beaches with cliffs. Travelers use **Donegal Town** as the gateway to the county. **Bus Éireann** (☎211 01) runs to: Dublin (4hr., 5 per day, IR£12); Galway (4hr., 3-5 per day, IR£10); and Sligo (1hr.; M-Sa 7 per day, Su 3 per day). Buses stop outside the Abbey Hotel on the Diamond; turn right with your back to the hotel to reach the **tourist office,** on Quay St., on Sligo Rd. (☎211 48; www.donegaltown.ie. Open July-Aug. M-Sa 9am-8pm, Su 10am-4pm; Sept.-Nov. and Easter-June M-F 9am-5pm, Sa 10am-2pm.) **Donegal Town Hostel (IHH)** is on Killybegs Rd. (☎228 05. Reserve ahead. Laundry IR£4. Dorms IR£7.50; doubles IR£17-18; **camping** IR£4 per person.)

To the west of Donegal Town lies the **Slieve League Peninsula,** with some of the most stunning scenery in Ireland and the highest sea cliffs in Europe. The sheer face of its 2000-ft. drop into the Atlantic is spectacular, and its rugged, wild appearance shows little evidence of human habitation. **Bus Éireann** runs from Donegal Town to Glencolmcille and Dungloe, stopping in tiny **Kilcar** (2-3 per day), the gateway to Donegal's *gaeltacht* and a commercial base for many Donegal tweed weavers. Most Slieve League hikers stay in Kilcar, from where they can comfortably drive, bike, or walk (about 6hr. round-trip) to the mountain. Nearly 2 mi. out on the coast road from Kilcar to Carrick is the fabulous **Derrylahan Hostel (IHH);** call for pick-up. (☎380 79. Laundry IR£5. Dorms IR£7; private rooms IR£10; **camping** IR£4.) On the western top of the Slieve League peninsula, **Glencolmcille** (glen-kaul-um-KEEL) is renowned for its rolling hills, sandy coves between huge seacliffs, and handmade sweaters. On sunny days, trips to the **Silver Strand** reward with stunning views of the gorgeous beach and surrounding rocky cliffs; from here, you colan start the trek along the Slieve League. McGeehan's **buses** leave from Biddy's Bar for Kilcar and Letterkenny (1-2 per day). **Bus Éireann** has services to **Donegal Town** via Kilcar (3 per day). Snooze at the just peachy **Dooey Hostel (IHO).** (☎301 30. Dorms IR£7; doubles IR£14; **camping** IR4.)

DERRYVEAGH MOUNTAINS

Here, the Donegal *gaeltacht*—Irish language, music, and dance—is lived, not practiced. Expansive, sandy beaches are isolated by the eerie stillness of the **Derryveagh Mountains.** On the eastern side of the mountains, **Glenveagh National Park** is 37 sq. mi. of forest glens, bogs, and mountains. The coastal road N56 twists and bends along the jagged edges where Donegal meets the sea, leading through spectacular scenery to **Crolly.** From Crolly, Feda O'Donnell (☎ (075) 481 14) has a daily **bus** to Galway and Donegal Town via Letterkenny; John McGinley Coaches (☎ (074) 352 01) go to Dublin; and O'Donnell Trans-Ulster Express (☎ (075) 483 56) goes to Belfast. In Croll, just past Paddy Oig's pub, a sign will point you toward **Screagan an Iolair Hill Hostel,** 4 mi. up a mountain road at **Tor** in the national park; turn left off the coastal road at the sign and follow Tor Rd. there. (SCRAG an UH-ler. ☎ (075) 485 93. Call ahead Nov.-Feb. Laundry IR£3. Dorms IR£7.50; private rooms IR£9.) Trails wind from the hostel up into the heath lands of the **Derryveagh Mountains.**

LETTERKENNY   ☎074

Letterkenny is the center of action in Donegal, but that's not saying much. Nonetheless, it's a lively place to make bus connections to the rest of Donegal, the Republic, and Northern Ireland. **Buses** leave from the junction of Port and Derry Rd. in front of the Quinnsworth Supermarket. Bus Éireann (☎213 09) runs to:

Derry (40min., 3-10 per day, IR£5); Donegal Town (50min., IR£5.50); and Sligo (2hr., 3 per day, IR£9.50). Feda O'Donnell Coaches (☎ (075) 481 14 or (091) 761 656) drive to Galway (IR£10) via Donegal Town (2-3 per day, IR£5). Lough Swilly Buses (☎228 63) head north toward the Fanad Peninsula (M-Sa 2 per day, IR£6) and to Derry (M-Sa 9 per day, IR£5). McGeehan's Bus (☎461 01) goes twice a day to Glencolmcille (IR£10). The **Chamber of Commerce Visitors Information Centre** is at 40 Port Rd. (☎248 66. Open M-F 9am-5pm.) The **Arch Hostel (IHO),** Upper Corkey is located 6 mi. out of town in Pluck; call from town for pick-up. (☎572 55. Open May-Oct. IR£7.50.)

INISHOWEN PENINSULA AND MALIN HEAD ☎077

It would be a shame to leave Ireland without seeing the Inishowen Peninsula, an untouristed mosaic of pristine mountains, forests, meadows, and white-sand beaches that reaches farther north than "the North." Inishowen's unusual inland landscape is outdone only by its striking northern and western shores. The clearly posted **Inish Eoghin 100** road navigates the peninsula's perimeter, exactly 100 mi. The peninsula's most popular attraction is **Malin Head,** remarkable for its rocky, wave-tattered coast and sky-high sand dunes, reputedly the highest in Europe (up to 100 ft.). The scattered town of Malin Head includes **Bamba's Crown,** the northernmost tip of Ireland, a tooth of dark rock rising up from the ocean spray. The raised beaches around Malin Head are covered with semi-precious stones; walkers sifting through the sands may find jasper, quartz, small opals, or amethysts. Lough Swilly **buses** (☎613 40; 1½hr.; M, W, and F 2 per day, Sa 3 per day) and Northwest Buses (☎826 19; M-Sa 2 per day) run from Derry, the nearest city to Inishowen, to points on the peninsula including Malin Head. To reach the **Sandrock Holiday Hostel (IHO),** Port Ronan Pier, take the left fork off the Inish Eoghin 100, just before the Crossroads Inn. (☎702 89. Bikes IR£6 per day. Laundry IR£3. Sheets IR£1. Dorms IR£7.)

NORTHERN IRELAND

The predominantly calm tenor of life in the North has been overshadowed overseas by media headlines concerning politics and bombs. Northern Ireland's natural beauty includes the Glens of Antrim's pockets of green and Giant's Causeway, one of the world's strangest geological sights. The ceasefires of recent years have allowed Belfast and Derry to develop into hip, pub-loving cities. Pub culture, urban neighborhoods, and tiny villages show everyday life in a divided but mostly peaceful society. The support of the 1998 Peace Agreement raises hopes for a resolution to the struggles that have divided the island for centuries, but the events of 1999 show that the success of the agreement is not yet secure.

The currency in Northern Ireland is the British pound. Northern Ireland has its own bank notes, equal in value to English and Scottish notes of the same denominations. Although this currency is *not* accepted outside Northern Ireland, both English and Scottish notes are accepted in the North; currency from the Republic of Ireland is generally not accepted in the North, with the exception of some border towns. It's best to avoid traveling in Northern Ireland during Marching Season (July 4-12), although vacation areas are less affected by the parades. Overall, Northern Ireland has one of the lowest tourist-related crime rates in the world. Border checkpoints have been removed, and armed soldiers and vehicles are less visible in Belfast and Derry. Do not take photographs of soldiers, military installations, or vehicles. Unattended luggage is always considered suspicious and worthy of confiscation. It is still generally unsafe to hitch in Northern Ireland.

BELFAST

The second-largest city on the island, Belfast (pop. 330,000) is the center of the North's cultural, commercial, and political activity. Acclaimed writers and the annual arts festival in November maintain Belfast's reputation as a thriving artistic center. West Belfast's famous sectarian murals are perhaps the most informative source on the effects of the Troubles (sectarian strife) on the city. The bar scene, a mix of Irish and British pub culture, entertains locals, foreigners, and students alike. Despite Belfast's reputation as a terrorist-riddled metropolis, the city feels more neighborly than most international—and even Irish—visitors expect.

TRANSPORTATION

Flights: Belfast International Airport (☎9442 2888) in Aldergrove. **Airbus** (☎9033 3000) runs to the Europa (Glengall St.) and Laganside (Queen's Square, off Donegall Quay) bus stations (M-Sa every 30min., Su about every hr.; UK£5). **Trains** connect the **Belfast City Airport** (**Sydenham Halt**), at the Harbour, to Central Station (UK£1).

Trains: Central Station, East Bridge St. (☎9089 9400). To **Derry** (2½hr., 3-7 per day, UK£6.70) and **Dublin** (2hr., 5-8 per day, UK£17). The **Centrelink** buses run to the city center, free with rail tickets.

Buses: Europa Station, Glengall St. (☎9032 0011) serves the west, north coast, and the Republic. To: **Derry** (1hr.40min., 6-19 per day, UK£6.50) and **Dublin** (3hr., 4-7 per day, UK£10.50). **Laganside Station,** (☎9033 3000) Donegall Quay, serves Northern Ireland's east coast. The **Centrelink** bus connects both stations with the city center.

Ferries: SeaCat (☎ (08705) 523 523; www.seacat.co.uk) leaves for: **Troon, Scotland** (2½hr.); **Heysham, England** (3¾hr.); and the **Isle of Man** from the terminal off Donegall Quay. Fares UK£10-30.

Local Transportation: The red **Citybus Network** (info ☎9024 6485), is supplemented by **Ulsterbus's** "blue buses" to the suburbs. Single-fare within the city center UK£0.50. The **Centrelink** buses traverse the city (every 12min.; M-F 7:25am-9:15pm, Sa 8:35am-9:15pm; UK£0.50, free with bus or rail ticket). Late **Nightlink** buses run to small towns outside of Belfast at 1am and 2:30am F and Sa (UK£3, available on board).

Taxis: Value Cabs (☎9023 0000). Residents of West and North Belfast use the huge **black cabs;** some are metered, and some follow set routes (under UK£1 charge).

IRELAND

ORIENTATION AND PRACTICAL INFORMATION

Buses arrive at the Europa bus station on **Great Victoria St.** To the northeast is the City Hall in **Donegall Sq.** South of the bus station, Great Victoria St meets **Dublin Rd.** at **Shaftesbury Sq.;** this stretch of Great Victoria St. between the bus station and Shaftesbury Sq. is known as the **Golden Mile. Botanic Ave.** and **Bradbury Pl.** (which becomes University Rd.) extend south from Shaftesbury Sq. into the **Queen's University area,** where cafes, pubs, and budget lodgings await. To get to Donegall Sq. from Central Station, turn left, walk down East Bridge St., turn right on Victoria St., and turn left after two blocks on May St., which runs into Donegall Sq. South. Or, take the Centrelink bus service (free with rail ticket). Divided from the rest of Belfast by the Westlink Motorway, the working-class **West Belfast** area is more politically volatile. The city center, Golden Mile, and the university area are relatively safe.

Tourist Office: 59 North St., St. Anne's Court (☎9024 6609). Supplies a great booklet on Belfast, the usual info on the surrounding areas, and an excellent map of the city with bus schedules (free). Open July-Aug. M-F 9am-7pm, Sa 9am-5:15pm, Su noon-4pm; Sept.-June M 9:30am-5:15pm, Tu-Sa 9am-5:15pm.

Banks: Banks and **ATMs** are virtually on every corner. **Bank of Ireland** is located at 54 Donegal Pl. (☎9023 4334. Open 9am-4:30pm.)

Currency Exchange: Thomas Cook, 22-24 Lombard St. (☎9088 3800). Cashes Thomas Cook traveler's checks with no commission, others with 2% commission. Open May-Oct. M-Tu and Th 5:30am-10pm, W 5:30am-11pm, F-Su 5:30am-midnight; Nov.-Apr. daily 5:45am-8pm.

Luggage Storage: For security reasons there is no luggage storage at airports, bus stations, or train stations. All four **hostels** will hold bags during the day for guests.

Laundry: The Laundry Room (Duds 'n Suds), (☎9024 3956) Botanic Ave. TV for the wait. Wash UK£1.95, dry UK£1.95; UK£1.80 each for students and seniors. Open M-F 8am-9pm, Sa 8am-6pm, Su noon-6pm.

Pharmacy: Boot's, 35-47 Donegall Pl. (☎9024 2332), next to the Europa Bus Station. Open M-W and F-Sa 8:30am-6pm, Th 8:30am-9pm, Su 1-5pm.

Emergency: ☎999; no coins required. **Police,** 65 Knock Rd. (☎9065 0222).

Hospitals: Belfast City Hospital, 9 Lisburn Rd. (☎9032 9241). From Shaftesbury Sq. follow Bradbury Pl. and take a right at the fork. **Royal Victoria Hospital,** 12 Grosvenor Rd. (☎ 9024 0503). From Donegall Sq., take Howard St. west to Grosvenor Rd.

Internet Access: Belfast Central Library, 122 Royal Ave. (☎9024 3233). 30min. of free email per day; UK£2 per hr. for web access. Open M and Th 9:30am-8pm, Tu-W and F 9:30am-5:30pm, Sa 9:30am-1pm.

Post Office: Central Post Office, 25 Castle Pl. (☎9032 3740). Open M-Sa 9am-5:30pm. *Poste Restante* mail comes here. **Postal code:** BT1 1NB. Two **branch offices** are: **Botanic Garden,** 95 University Rd. (☎ 9038 1309), across from the university (**postal code:** BT7 1NG), and **Shaftesbury Square,** 7-9 Shaftesbury Sq. (☎ 9032 6177; **postal code:** BT2 7DA). Both open M-F 8:45am-5:30pm, Sa 10am-12:30pm.

PHONE CODE	Northern Ireland is reached by using the UK **country code** **44**; from the Republic dial **048**. The **phone code** for every town in the North is **028**.

ACCOMMODATIONS

Despite a competitive hostel market, Belfast's rapidly growing tourism and rising rents have shrunk the number of available cheap digs. Nearly all are located near Queen's University, south of the city center; convenient to pubs and restaurants, this area is by far the best place to stay in the city. If you have a lot of baggage you may want to catch a **Centrelink** bus to Shaftesbury Sq., or **Citybus** #59, 69, 70, 71, 84, or 85 from Donegall Sq. East to areas in the south. A walk to these accommodations takes 10 to 20min. from the bus or train station. Hostels and B&Bs are busy in the summer; reservations are recommended.

HOSTELS AND UNIVERSITY HOUSING

The Ark (IHH), 18 University St. (☎9032 9626). A 10min. walk from Europa bus station on Great Victoria St. Take a right and head away from the Europa Hotel; at Shaftesbury Sq., take the right fork on Bradbury Pl. then fork left onto University Rd. University St. is the fourth left off University Rd. Weekend luggage storage. Internet access UK£2 per 30min. Laundry UK£4. Curfew 2am. 4- to 6-bed dorms UK£6.50-7.50; doubles UK£28.

Arnie's Backpackers (IHH), 63 Fitzwilliam St. (☎9024 2867). From the Ark (see above), Fitzwilliam St. is on your right across from the university. Key deposit UK£2. Luggage storage during the day. 4- to 6-bed dorms UK£7.50.

Belfast Hostel (HINI), 22 Donegall Rd. (☎9031 5435; www.hini.org.uk), off Shaftesbury Sq. Clean, modern rooms with 2 to 6 beds, some with bath. Breakfast UK£2. Laundry UK£3. Reception 24hr. Dorms UK£8-10.

The Linen House Youth Hostel (IHH), 18-20 Kent St. (☎9058 6400; email info@belfasthostel.com; www.belfasthostel.com) in West Belfast. From Europa Bus Station turn left on Great Victoria St. for two blocks, then right onto Howard St. for two more. Across from the main entrance to City Hall, turn left onto Donegall Place, which becomes Royal Ave. This converted 19th-century linen factory now houses scores of weary travelers (about 160 beds total). 24hr. secure parking. Internet access UK£3 per hr. Laundry UK£3. 18-bed dorms UK£6.50; 6- to 10-bed dorms UK£7.50; 8-bed dorms with bathroom UK£8.50; singles UK£12; doubles UK£28.

Queen's University Accommodations, 78 Malone Rd. (☎9038 1608). Bus #71 from Donegall Sq. East or a 25min. walk from Europa. University Rd. runs into Malone Rd.; the residence halls are on your left. Open mid-June to mid-Sept. and Christmas and Easter vacations. Singles and doubles UK£8 per person for UK students, UK£9.40 for international students, UK£11.75 for non-students.

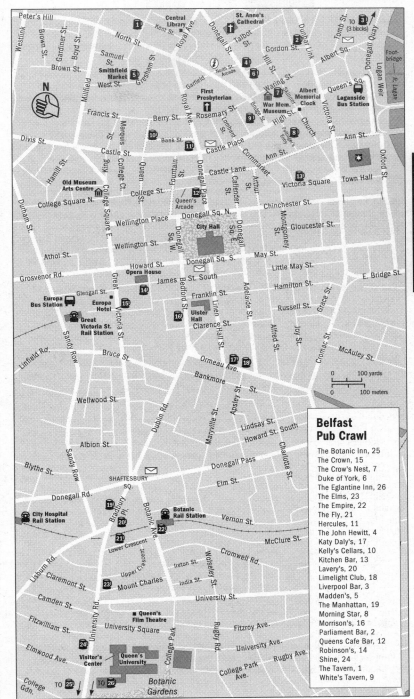

IRELAND

Belfast Pub Crawl

The Botanic Inn, 25
The Crown, 15
The Crow's Nest, 7
Duke of York, 6
The Eglantine Inn, 26
The Elms, 23
The Empire, 22
The Fly, 21
Hercules, 11
The John Hewitt, 4
Katy Daly's, 17
Kelly's Cellars, 10
Kitchen Bar, 13
Lavery's, 20
Limelight Club, 18
Liverpool Bar, 3
Madden's, 5
The Manhattan, 19
Morning Star, 8
Morrison's, 16
Parliament Bar, 2
Queens Cafe Bar, 12
Robinson's, 14
Shine, 24
The Tavern, 1
White's Tavern, 9

BED AND BREAKFASTS

B&Bs occupy every other house between **Malone** and **Lisburn Rd.,** just south of Queen's University. Calling ahead is generally a good idea; most owners, however, will refer you to other accommodations if necessary.

Marine House, 30 Eglantine Ave. (☎9066 2828). Housekeeping standards as high as the ceilings. Singles UK£22; doubles UK£40, with bath UK£45; triples UK£57.

The George, 9 Eglantine Ave. (☎9068 3212). Immaculately clean rooms, all with shower and TV. Singles UK£22; doubles UK£44. Cash only.

Botanic Lodge, 87 Botanic Ave. (☎9032 7682), on the corner of Mt. Charles Ave. B&B comfort with only a short a walk to the city center. Singles UK£22; doubles UK£40.

Liserin Guest House, 17 Eglantine Ave. (☎9066 0769). Comfy beds and a huge velvet-covered lounge. Singles UK£22; doubles UK£40; triples UK£60.

🍴 FOOD

Belfast's eateries assume a cosmopolitan character, with flavors from around the globe. **Dublin Rd., Botanic Rd.,** and the **Golden Mile** have the highest concentration of restaurants. For fruits and vegetables, plunder the lively **St. George's Market,** East Bridge St., in the enormous warehouse between May and Oxford St. (Open Tu and F 6am-3pm.). Try **Canterbury Dyke's,** 66-68 Botanic Ave. for healthy foods or more fruit and veggies. (Open M-F 7:30am-7pm, Sa-Su 8am-6:30pm.)**Lower Lisburn Rd.,** which runs parallel to University Rd., has a selection of bakeries and fruit stands.

The Other Place, 79 Botanic Ave. (☎9020 7200), 133 Stranmillis Rd. (☎9020 7100), and 537 Lisburn Rd. (☎ 9029 7300). Stomping grounds of the backpacker's unicorn, the mythic 99p breakfast. Features an array of ethnic foods. Open daily 8am-11pm.

Bookfinders, 47 University Rd. (☎9032 8269). Smoky bookstore/cafe with mismatched dishes and retro counter-culture paraphernalia. Art gallery upstairs. Soup and bread UK£1.75. Sandwiches UK£2.20-2.50. Open M-Sa 10am-5:30pm.

Feasts, 39 Dublin Rd. (☎9033 2787). Pleasant street side cafe, serving Irish and international farmhouse cheeses in sandwiches (UK£3) and other dishes. Makes its own pasta on the premises (UK£5). Open M-F 9am-7pm, Sa 10am-6pm.

🏛 SIGHTS

More than any city on your itinerary, Belfast's sights reveal its living history, the glitz and grit that evoke its political situation. If you do only one thing in this city, take a taxi tour of West Belfast (**Black Taxi Tours;** ☎9064 2264; £7.50 per person).

DONEGALL SQUARE. After Queen Victoria made Belfast a city in 1888, **Belfast City Hall** was built on the site of demolished linen warehouses. Neoclassical marble columns and arches figure prominently in A. Brunwell Thomas's 1906 design. The **City Council's** oak-paneled chambers, used only once a month, are deceptively austere considering the Council's reputation for rowdy meetings that sometimes devolve into fist fights. Directly in front of the main entrance, an enormous marble **Queen Victoria statue** stares down at visitors with a formidable grimace, as bronze figures representing shipbuilding and spinning writhe at her feet. The interior of City Hall is accessible only by guided tour. (☎9032 0202. Tours June-Sept. M-F 10:30am, 11:30am, and 2:30pm; Sa 2:30pm. Oct.-May M-Sa 2:30pm. Free.) One of Belfast's oldest establishments is the **Linen Hall Library.** The red hand of Ulster decorates the top of its street entrance. The library contains a famous collection of political documents relating to the Troubles and Northern Ireland. (17 Donegall Sq. North. ☎9032 1707. Open M-F 9:30am-5:30pm, Sa 9:30am-4pm.)

CORNMARKET AND ST. ANNE'S CATHEDRAL. Just north of the city center, a shopping district envelops eight blocks around Castle St. and Royal Ave. This area, known as Cornmarket after one of its original commodities, has been a market-place since Belfast's early days. Wander the **entries,** or tiny alleys, around the area, relics of old Belfast. Belfast's newspapers all set up shop around St. Anne's, also known as the **Belfast Cathedral.** Each of the cathedral's 10 interior pillars name Belfast's 10 fields of professionalism: Science, Industry, Healing, Agriculture, Music, Theology, Shipbuilding, Freemasonry, Art, and Womanhood. *(Donegall St., located near the tourist office. Su services: communion 10am, Eucharist 11am, evensong 3:30pm.)*

THE GOLDEN MILE. "The Golden Mile" refers to a strip along Great Victoria St. containing many of the jewels in the crown of Belfast's establishment. Belfast's pride and joy, the **Grand Opera House,** was bombed by the IRA, restored to its original splendor at enormous cost, and then bombed again. *(☎ 9024 0411. Booking office open M-Sa 9:45am-5:30pm.)* **The Grand Opera House Ticket Shop** sells tickets for performances including musicals, operas, ballets, and concerts. *(2-4 Great Victoria St. ☎ 9024 1919, 24hr. info line ☎ 9024 9129. Open M-W 8:30am-8pm, Th 8:30am-9pm, F 8:30am-6:30pm, Sa 8:30am-5:30pm.)* The National Trust has restored the highly frequented **Crown Liquor Saloon,** 46 Great Victoria St, to a showcase of carved wood, gilded ceilings, and stained-glass. Damaged by 32 bombs in its history, the **Europa Hotel** has the dubious distinction of being "Europe's most bombed hotel."

QUEEN'S UNIVERSITY AREA. Charles Lanyon designed the Tudor-revival brick campus of **Queen's University** in 1849, modeling it after Magdalen College, Oxford. The **Visitors Centre,** in the Lanyon Room to the left of the main entrance, offers Queen's-related exhibits and merchandise. *(University Road. Visitors Center ☎ 9033 5252. Open May.-Sept. M-Sa 10am-4pm, Oct.-Mar. M-F 10am-4pm.)* Bask in Belfast's occasional sun behind the university in the **Botanic Gardens.** Meticulously groomed, the gardens are a welcome respite from the traffic-laden city streets. Inside the gardens lie two 19th-century greenhouses, the toasty **Tropical Ravine House** and the more temperate Lanyon-designed **Palm House.** Stop and smell the rose gardens, featuring Europe's most fragrant blooms. *(☎ 9032 4902. Open daily 8am-dusk. Tropical House and Palm House open Apr.-Sept. M-F 10am-noon and 1-5pm, Sa-Su 2-5pm; Oct.-Mar. M-F 10am-noon and 1-4pm, Sa-Su 2-4pm. Free.)* The **Ulster Museum,** within the gardens, contains a lovely hodge-podge. *(Off Stranmillis Rd. Open M-F 10am-5pm, Sa 1-5pm, Su 2-5pm. Free.)*

NORTH BELFAST. In 1934, the Earl of Shaftesbury presented the **Belfast Castle** to the city. The ancient King Matudan had his McArt's Fort here, where the more modern United Irishmen plotted rebellion in 1795. The summit is nicknamed "Napoleon's Nose." Marked trails lead north from the fort to five caves in the area; only the lowest is accessible. *(Open M-Sa 9am-10:30pm, Su 9am-6pm. Free.)*

WEST BELFAST AND THE MURALS

Separated from the rest of the city by the Westlink motorway, the neighborhoods of West Belfast have historically been at the heart of the political tensions in the North. The Catholic area (centered on **Falls Rd.**) and the Protestant neighborhood (centered on the **Shankill**) are grimly separated by the **peace line,** a gray and seemingly impenetrable wall. West Belfast is not a center of consumer tourism or a "sight" in the traditional sense. The streets display political murals, which you will soon come across as you wander among the houses. **Be discreet when photographing murals.** The Protestant Orangemen's marching season, around July 12, is a risky time to visit the area, since the parades are underscored by mutual antagonism and can lead to political violence.

THE FALLS. On **Divis St.,** a high-rise apartment building marks the site of the **Divis Tower,** an ill-fated housing development built by optimistic social planners in the 1960s. This project soon became an IRA stronghold and saw some of the worst of Belfast's Troubles in the 1970s. The British army still occupies the top three floors, and Shankill residents refer to it as "Little Beirut." Continuing west, Divis St. turns into the **Falls Rd.** The **Sinn Fein** office is easily spotted: one side of it is covered with an enormous portrait of Bobby Sands and an advertisement for the Sinn Fein newspaper, *An Phoblacht.* Continuing down the Falls you will see a number of murals. One particularly moving mural, on the corner of the Falls and RPG Ave., shows the 10 hunger strikers who died in 1981-82 above a quote from Bobby Sands: "Our revenge will be the laughter of our children."

SHANKILL. North St., to the left of the tourist office, turns into **Shankill Rd.** as it crosses the **Westlink** and then arrives in Protestant Shankill, once a thriving shopping district. Turning left (coming from the direction of North St.) onto most side roads leads to the **peace line.** At Canmore St., a mural depicts the Apprentice Boys "Shutting the Gates of Derry—1688" as the Catholic invaders try to get through. The densely decorated **Orange Hall,** which sits at Brookmount St., was formerly Fizzel's Fish Shop and where 10 people died in an October 1993 bomb attack. The side streets on the right guide you to the **Shankill Estate,** more murals, and through the estate; **Crumlin Road** is the site of the oldest Loyalist murals.

🎵🎭 ENTERTAINMENT AND NIGHTLIFE

Belfast's many cultural events and performances are covered in the monthly *Arts Council Artslink*, which is free at the tourist office. Daily listings appear in the *Belfast Telegraph* (which also has a Friday arts supplement) as well as in Thursday's issue of the *Irish News.* For more extensive information on pub entertainment, pick up the free, biweekly, two-page news bulletin *The List,* available at the tourist office, hostels, and many pubs. Belfast reigns supreme in the art world for three weeks each November during the annual **Queen's University Belfast festival.** Over 300 separate performances of opera, ballet, film, and comedy invade venues across the city, drawing groups of international acclaim.

White's Tavern, 2-4 Winecellar Entry (☎9024 3080), off Lombard and Bridge St. Belfast's oldest tavern, serving drinks since 1630. An excellent stop for an afternoon pint. W is gay night. Open daily noon-1am, W until 2:30am.

The Manhattan, 23-31 Bradbury Pl. (☎ 9023 3131). Huge 3-story dance club that's packed with a younger crowd clad in Brit-pop fashions. Dress to impress. Events are sporadic, but F is often 70s night. No cover for first-floor bar; nightclub cover UK£4-6.

The Eglantine Inn (the "Egg"), 32 Malone Rd. (☎9038 1994). Almost an official extra-curricular activity, this pub keeps students from their studies. Satisfies their munchies, too; main dishes UK£2-6, served noon-8pm. Live music M-Tu, shake your bootie W-Sa, both free. Open until 1am.

The Kremlin, 96 Donegall St. (☎ 9080 9700). Look for the imposing statue of Stalin above the entrance. Belfast's newest and hottest gay nightspot with foam parties and internationally-renowned drag queens. Mixed crowd, but mostly men. Theme night F; "Kink" night once a month. Cover varies, but free Su, M, W, and before 9pm. Open M-Sa 7:30pm-late, Su 5pm-late.

📷 DAYTRIP FROM BELFAST

ULSTER FOLK AND TRANSPORT MUSEUM

☎904 284 28. Open July-Aug. M-Sa 10:30am-6pm, Su noon-6pm; Apr.-June and Sept. M-F 9:30am-5pm, Sa 10:30am-6pm, Su noon-6pm; Oct.-Mar. M-F 9:30am-4pm, Sa-Su 12:30-4:30pm. UK£4, students UK£2.50. Frequent buses (45min.) and trains (30min.) stop here on their way to Bangor.

In **Holywood,** the **Ulster Folk Museum** and **Transport Museum** stretches over 176 acres. Established by an Act of Parliament in the 1950s, the ▣**Folk Museum,** which aims to preserve the way of life of Ulster's farmers, weavers, and craftspeople, contains over 30 buildings from the past three centuries. The **Transport Museum** and the **Railway Museum** are across the road. Inside the **Transport Museum** is a *Titanic* exhibit that includes original blueprints and traces the Belfast-built ship and its fate. The **Railway Museum** is stuffed with 25 old railway engines, including the largest locomotive built in Ireland.

DERRY (LONDONDERRY)

Modern Derry's determined effort to cast off the legacy of the Troubles has been largely successful. Although the Derry landscape was once razed by years of bombings and violence still erupts occasionally during the Marching Season (July 4-12), recent years have been relatively peaceful and today's rebuilt city looks sparklingly new. Derry's **city walls,** 18-ft. high and 20-ft. thick, erected between 1614 and 1619, have never been breached, hence Derry's nickname "the Maiden City." The stone tower along the southeast wall past New Gate was built to protect **St. Columb's Cathedral,** off Bishop St., the symbolic focus of the city's Protestant defenders. (Open M-Sa Apr.-Oct. 9am-5pm; Nov.-Mar. 9am-4pm. Donation UK£1; chapterhouse UK50p.) At Union Hall Place, just inside Magazine Gate, the **Tower Museum's** engaging exhibits relay Derry's long history. (Open July-Aug. M-Sa 10am-5pm, Su 2-5pm; Sept.-June Tu-Sa 10am-5pm. UK£3.75, students UK£1.25.) West of the city walls, Derry's residential neighborhoods, both the Catholic **Bogside** as well as the Protestant **Waterside** and **Fountain Estate,** display brilliant murals. After dark, roll by **Peadar O'Donnell's,** 53 Waterloo St., and the **Gweedore Bar,** 59-61 Waterloo St., which have been connected since Famine times.

Trains (☎71 34 22 28) arrive on Duke St., Waterside, on the east bank, from Belfast (2½hr., 4-7 per day, UK£7). A free **Rail-Link bus** connect the train station and the **bus station,** on Foyle St., between the walled city and the river. **Ulsterbus** (☎71 26 22 61) goes to Belfast (1½-3hr., 8-15 per day, UK£7.50) and Dublin (3-5 per day, UK£11). The **tourist office** is at 44 Foyle St. (☎71 26 72 84. Open July-Sept. M-F 9am-7pm, Sa 10am-6pm, Su 10am-5pm; Oct.-Easter M-Th 9am-5:15pm, F 9am-5pm; Easter-June M-Th 9am-5:15pm, F 9am-5pm, Sa 10am-5pm.) Go down Strand Rd. and turn left on Asylum Rd. just before the RUC station to reach the **Steve's Backpackers,** 4 Asylum Rd. (☎71 37 79 89. **Internet** UK£3 per hr. Laundry UK£3. Key deposit UK£2. Dorms UK£7.50.) **Derry City Youth Hostel (YHANI/HI)** is on Magazine St. (☎71 28 41 00. Laundry UK£3.50. Check-out 10am. Dorms UK£7.50-8.50; B&B with bath UK£15.) **Tesco supermarket** is on Strand Rd., in the Quayside Shopping Center. (Open M-Sa 8:30am-9pm, Su 1-6pm.) **Postal code:** BT48.

GLENS OF ANTRIM

Nine lush green valleys, or "glens," slither from the hills and high moors of Co. Antrim down to the seashore. The villages along the coast provide beds and basic sustenance for glen-wanderers, as well as a glimpse into the cultural traditions of rural Northern Ireland.

⊡ TRANSPORTATION. Ulsterbus (Belfast ☎90 32 00 11, Larne ☎28 27 23 45) #162 runs from Belfast through Glenarm, Waterfoot, Cushendall, and Cushendun (3-5 per day). Bus #150 runs between Glenariff (M-Sa 4 per day) then Waterfoot, Cushendall, and Cushendun (M-F 5 per day, Sa 3 per day). #150 also connects to Belfast via Cushendun, Cushendall, Waterfoot, and Glenariff (M-Sa 3 per day). You can also bike along the shore.

GLENARIFF. Antrim's broadest (and arguably loveliest) glen, Glenariff, lies 4 mi. south of Waterfoot along Glenariff Rd. in the large **Glenariff Forest Park.** Bus #150 between Cushendun and Ballymena stops at the official park entrance (M-Sa 3-5 per day), but if you're walking from Waterfoot, you can enter the park 1½ mi. downhill of the official entrance by taking the road that branches left toward the Manor Lodge Restaurant. The stunning **Waterfall Trail** follows the cascading, fern-lined Glenariff River from the park entrance to the Manor Lodge. (☎21 75 87 69. Park open daily 10am-8pm. UK£3 per car or UK£1.50 per pedestrian.)

CUSHENDALL. Cushendall is the best place to base yourself in the Glens. **Ulsterbus** (☎90 33 30 00) #150 runs to Belfast via Waterfoot and Glenariff (M-Sa 3-5 per day). The **Antrim Coasters** (#252) run through Cushendall toward Portrush and Belfast (2 per day). The **tourist office,** 25 Mill St., is near the bus stop at the Cushendun end of town. (☎21 77 11 80. Open July-Sept. M-F 10am-1pm and 2-5:30pm, Sa 10am-1pm; Oct. to mid.-Dec. and Feb.-June Tu-Sa 10am-1pm.) **Cushendall Youth Hostel (YHANI/HI),** 42 Layde Rd., is ½ mi. from town. Layde Rd. is the left-hand (uphill) fork from Shore Rd. (☎21 77 13 44. Curfew 11:30pm. Dorms UK£8.50.) **Glendale,** 46 Coast Rd., has warm rooms. (☎21 77 14 95. UK£16.)

CUSHENDUN. This miniscule, picturesque seaside village is 5 mi. (an easy bike ride) north of Cushendall on A2. This white-washed and black-shuttered set of buildings lies by a beach with wonderful, dark **caves** carved within red sea cliffs. **Mary McBride's,** 2 Main St., used to be the *Guinness Book of World Records'* "smallest bar in Europe" until it expanded. (☎21 76 15 11. Steak and Guinness pie UK£5; food served daily noon-9pm.) **Buses** stop in Cushendun en route to Waterfoot via Cushendall (June-Sept. 3-9 per day; Oct.-May 1-7 per day).

CAUSEWAY COAST

Past Cushendun, the northern coast shifts from lyrical to dramatic mode. Six-hundred-foot sea-battered cliffs tower over white wave-lapped beaches and then give way to spectacular **Giant's Causeway,** for which the region is named. Thousands of visitors swarm the site today, but few venture beyond the Visitors Centre to the miles of stunning coastline.

TRANSPORTATION. In good summer weather, **Bushmills Bus** (Coleraine ☎ (01265) 70 43 33 34) outlines the coast between Coleraine, 5 mi. south of Portrush, and Giant's Causeway (July-Aug. 5 per day). In the summer, the Antrim Coaster bus #252 (Belfast ☎90 33 30 00) runs up the coast from Belfast to Portstewart via towns listed here (late-June to early-July M-Sa 2 per day; early-July to late-Sept. 2 per day).

BALLYCASTLE AND ENVIRONS. The Causeway Coast leaves the sleepy glens behind when it hits this bubbly seaside town, popular with Giant's Causeway-bound tourists. **Ulsterbus** rides to Cushendall via Cushendun (#172; 50min., M-F 1 per day) and Belfast (#252; 3hr., 2 per day). The **tourist office** is in Sheskburn House, 7 Mary St. (☎20 76 20 24. Open July-Aug. M-F 9:30am-7pm, Sa 10am-6pm, Su 2-6pm; Sept.-June M-F 9:30am-5pm.) Snooze at **Castle Hostel (IHH),** 62 Quay Rd (☎20 76 23 37), or **Ballycastle Backpackers Hostel,** 4 North St (☎70 26 36 12), next to the Marine Hotel. (Dorms UK£7-7.50; private rooms UK£8.50 per person.)

Just off the coast at Ballycastle, beautiful, bumpy, boomerang-shaped **Rathlin Island** ("Fort of the Sea") is the ultimate in escapism for 20,000 puffins, the odd golden eagle, and 100 human beings. Caledonian MacBrayne **ferries** (☎20 76 92 99) run to the island from the pier at Ballycastle, up the hill from Quay Rd on North St. (45min., 2-4 per day, return UK£8); pick up schedules from the Ballycastle tourist office. A **minibus** service (☎20 76 39 09) drives to the **Kebble Bird Sanctuary** at the western tip of the island, 4½ mi. from the harbor. (20min., every 45min., UK£2.)

Five miles west of Ballycastle, the modest village of **Ballintoy** attracts the crowds on their way to itsy-bisty teeny-tiny **Carrick-a-rede Island.** Cross the shaky, 4-inch-wide, 67-ft. fishermen's rope bridge over the dizzying 100-ft. drop to rocks and sea below; **be extremely careful in windy weather.** A sign marks the turn-off from the coastal road east of Ballintoy. The aptly titled **Sheep Island View Hostel (IHH),** 42A Main St., has beds and camping facilities. (☎20 76 93 91. Dorms UK£9.)

GIANT'S CAUSEWAY. Advertised as the eighth natural wonder of the world, Giant's Causeway is Northern Ireland's most famous sight. A spillage of 40,000 hexagonal columns of basalt form a 60-million-year-old honeycomb path from the foot of the cliffs far into the sea. The **Giant's Causeway Visitors Centre,** which sits at the entrance to the Causeway from the car park, runs a bus (every 15min.; 60p; round-trip UK£1) to the columns. (☎20 73 18 55. Open daily June 10am-6pm; July-Aug. 10am-7pm; Mar.-May and Sept. 10am-5pm; Nov.-Feb. 10am-4:30pm.)

ITALY

LIRE

US$1 = L1936	L100 = US$0.49
CDN$1 = L2029	L1000 = CDN$0.73
EURO€1 = L1375	L1000 = EUR€0.52
UK£1 = L3103	L1000 = UK£0.32
IR£1 = L2451	L1000 = IR£0.41
AUS$1 = L1194	L1000 = AUS$0.84
NZ$1 = L958	L1000 = NZ$1.04
SAR1 = L292	L1000 = SAR3.41

PHONE CODES	**Country Code:** 39. **International dialing prefix:** 00.

At the crossroads of the Mediterranean, Italy has served as the home of powerful empires, diverse communities, and some pretty crazy individuals. Over the past 2000 years, this tiny boot has been foothold of the Roman Empire, birthplace of the Renaissance, the epicenter of the Christian Church, and the motherland of pizza. However you slice it, Italian history is a full five course meal: long, messy, yet oh-so-satisfying. In the Board Meeting of the World, Italy may be viewed as the jaded senior member: "Been there, done that," he says, slumping on the couch of the Mediterranean, "let's break for lunch." Through its history, Italy has learned to enjoy the finer things in life. From the meats of the Veneto to the cheeses of Sardinia and from perfect pasta to the creation pizza, Italy has found that the best way to a country's happiness is through its stomach. But when Italy isn't eating, it's loving. The Italian language has been the trademark of romance—its mellifluous syllables inspiring passionate lovers to proclaim their *amore* from the rooftops of the world. Consume a heaping plate of tasty tips from *Let's Go: Italy 2001*.

SUGGESTED ITINERARIES

THREE DAYS Spend it all in the Eternal City, **Rome** (p. 614). Indulge in your gladiator fantasies in the marble **Colosseum,** visit the famous **Arco di Constantin,** and stand in the perfect half-sphere of the **Pantheon.** Gaze at the ceiling of the **Sistine Chapel** and the fine art in the **Capitoline Museum** and the **Galleria Borghese,** then satiate your other senses in a disco. Purify after a long night at mass at **St. Peter's Cathedral.**

ONE WEEK See the sights in **Rome** and flick a coin in the Trevi fountain (3 days). Head north to **Florence** (2 days; p. 678) and revel in the amazing Renaissance art of the Uffizi Gallery. Move to **Venice** (2 days; p. 663) to float through the canals, feed pigeons in the Piazza San Marco, and stroll over the Rialto Bridge.

BEST OF ITALY IN 3 WEEKS Begin in **Rome** (4 days; p. 614), then move to **Florence** (3 days; p. 678). Go to **Siena** (1 day; p. 693) and jaunt to the isle of **Elba** (1 day; p. 695). Move along the coast for a relaxing day in **Finale Ligure** (1 day; p. 650), and visit the gorgeous fishing villages of **Cinque Terre** (2 days; p. 652). Move on to the cosmopolitan wilds of **Milan** (1 day; p. 640) and visit the **Lake Como** for a bonanza of hiking and tanning (2 days; p. 658). Spend some time in **Venice** (3 days; p. 663) before going south to the **Bay of Naples Islands** to gaze at the Grotto Azzurra on the island of **Capri** (1 day; p. 707). Scare yourself in the Cappuchin Catacombs in **Palermo** (1 day; p. 709), and finish up with a visit to **Stromboli's** live volcano (1 day; p. 713).

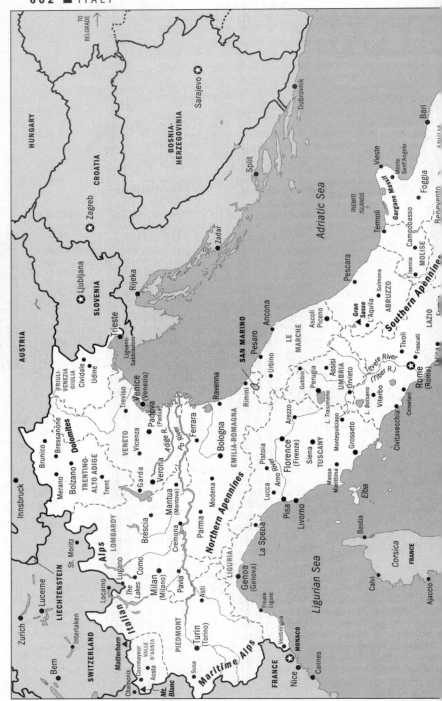

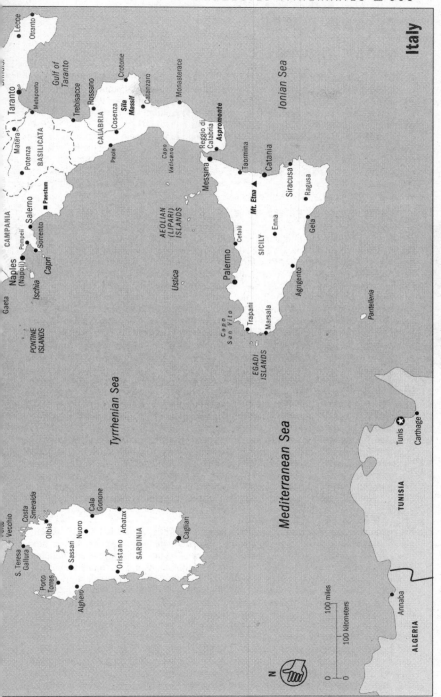

Italy

Lecce
Otranto
Gulf of
Taranto
Taranto
Metaponto
Crotone
Rossano
Trebisacce
Sila
Massif
Cosenza
CALABRIA
Paola
Capo
Vaticano
Reggio di
Calabria
Aspromonte
Taormina
Catania
Ionian Sea
Monasterace
Catanzaro
Messina
Mt. Etna ▲
Cefalù
SICILY
Enna
Siracusa
Ragusa
Gela
Agrigento
Palermo
Trapani
Marsala
Capo
San Vito
EGADI
ISLANDS
Ustica
AEOLIAN
(LIPARI)
ISLANDS
Matéra
Potenza
BASILICATA
CAMPANIA
Salerno
Sorrento
Capri
Pompeii
Ischia
Naples
(Napoli)
Gaeta
PONTINE
ISLANDS
■ Paestum
Tyrrhenian Sea
Pantelleria
Mediterranean Sea
Tunis ✪
Carthage
TUNISIA
Annaba
ALGERIA
S. Teresa
Gallura
Costa
Smeralda
Vecchio
Olbia
Cala
Gonone
Arbatax
Porto
Torres
Sassari
Nuoro
Oristano
Alghero
SARDINIA
Cagliari

100 miles
100 kilometers
0
0

N

LIFE AND TIMES

HISTORY AND POLITICS

ITALY BEFORE ROME (UNTIL 753 BC)

Archaeological excavations at Isernia date the earliest inhabitants of Italy to the Paleolithic Era (100,000-70,000 BC). More sophisticated settlements, however, did not appear until the Bronze Age, when tribes, known as the *Italics*, settled the peninsula. By the 7th century BC, the **Etruscans** eclipsed the power of the Italics. Growing **Greek** influence along the Mediterranean coast checked the rise of Etruscan power, and in the 8th century BC, Greek city-states began colonizing Italy. Greek city-states, known as **Magna Graecia**, such as Cumae, near Naples, and Syracuse, in Sicily, rose to prominence, achieving naval supremacy over their rival Etruscans. In the 3rd century BC, however, both the Greek colonies and the Etruscan city-states began to decline in the face of the rising power of Rome.

ANCIENT ROME (753 BC-AD 476)

By 616 BC, the Etruscan Tarquin family established its dominance. The Tarquins outraged the Roman public. After the king's son, Sextus Tarquinius, raped Lucretia, a virtuous noblewoman, his deed was seen as symbolic of royal tyranny. Led by Lucius Brutus, the Romans overthrew the Tarquins and established the Republic in 509 BC. Roman military campaigns culminated in 396 BC with the defeat of the Etruscans at the city of Veii. A Gallic invasion destroyed much of Rome six years later, but the Republic rebounded, setting its sights on controlling the Mediterranean. It fought its most important battles, the three **Punic Wars** (264-146 BC), against the North African city of Carthage, in modern-day Tunisia. Victory in the Punic Wars vaulted Rome into the position of world dominator. Tensions between Rome and its Italian allies fueled the **Social War,** which erupted in 91 BC. The patrician general **Sulla** marched into Rome in 82 BC, ended the war, and quickly reorganized the constitution, instituting social reforms.

In 73 BC, in the wake of this upheaval, **Spartacus,** an escaped gladiatorial slave, led an army of 70,000 slaves and farmers on a two-year rampage down the peninsula. **Marcus Crassus** and **Pompey the Great** finally quelled the uprising and took effective control of the city. Although they joined forces with **Julius Caesar,** the charismatic conqueror of Gaul, this association fell apart. By 45 BC, Caesar had defeated his "allies" and emerged as the leader of the Republic, touting himself Dictator for Life. Fearful of Caesar's growing power, a small faction of (literal) back-stabbers assassinated the leader on the Ides (15th) of March, 44 BC. Power eluded several would-be successors, among them Brutus, Marc Antony, and Caesar's adopted son, Octavian. But after defeating Antony in 31 BC, Octavian ultimately emerged victorious, and by 27 BC, assumed the title of **Augustus.**

THE EMPIRE: 27 BC-AD 476

Augustus was the first of the Empire's **Julio-Claudian** rulers (27 BC-AD 68). Maintaining Republican traditions, he governed as *princeps* (first citizen). His principate (27 BC-AD 14), considered the Golden Age of Rome, initiated the **Pax Romana** (200 years of peace). With the aid of a professional army and an imperial bureaucracy, Augustus maintained the Empire and extended Roman law and civic culture. Augustus' shoes were hard to fill: **Caligula** (AD 37-41) and **Nero** (54-68) did such a poor job that they were crossed off official Roman records. The **Flavian** dynasty (69-96), however, ushered in a period of relative prosperity, extending to new heights under **Trajan** (98-117). After Trajan's death, his adopted successor **Hadrian** established the **Antonine** dynasty (117-193). The Antonines, particularly the philosopher-emperor **Marcus Aurelius** (161-180), were known for their enlightened leadership. In 193, however, Rome's leadership faltered, and in the "Year of Four Emperors" four successive Antonine rulers attempted to claim the throne. The last, **Commodus,** was assassinated, and **Septimius Severus,** a general from North

Africa, overtook the principate, founding the **Severan** dynasty (193-235). With the death of the last of the Severans in 235, the era of dynastic succession came to a halt. **Diocletian** was one of few to secure control of the fragmented Empire. **Constantine,** Diocletian's successor, converted to Christianity. He claimed that before a decisive battle in 312, he had seen a cross of light in the sky, emblazoned with the fiery inscription *"in hoc signo vinces"* (by this sign you shall conquer). He converted, declaring Christianity the state religion two years later. After the reign of **Theodosius I** (379-95), the Empire split permanently, and the western half suffered constant invasions. **Alaric,** king of the Visigoths, sacked Rome in 410, and the fall came in 476, when the German chief **Odoacer** knocked off the last of the Western emperors, Romulus Augustulus, and crowned himself king of Italy.

THE DARK AND MIDDLE AGES (476-1375)

Continuous invasions were so stifling that Pope Stephen II was forced to appeal for help to **Charlemagne** and his Frankish army, which merely invited a Frankish invasion. On Christmas Day, 800, Charlemagne became Holy Roman Emperor. The 12th, 13th, and 14th centuries saw the division of power among city-states and town councils known as *comuni*. Amidst this factionalism, the Catholic Church consolidated its power. Though the **Crusades** of the 11th, 12th, and 13th centuries failed to win back the holy land, they strengthened the unity of Christendom and the authority of the papacy.

In the 14th century, when **Pope Boniface VIII** forbade the French King **Philippe IV (The Fair)** to tax his clergy, the monarch responded by insulting and assaulting the Pope, who died of shock. The pontiff's successors, persuaded by Philippe, moved the papacy to the French city of Avignon, where it remained for most of the century. Known as the **Babylonian Captivity** (1309-77), this confusion culminated in the **Great Schism** (1378-1417), during which as many as three popes reigned at the same time (one in France and two in Italy). By the end of the 14th century, years of instability and war had induced famine, blights of **Black Death,** and natural disaster, wreaking havoc upon the increasingly overcrowded cities of Italy.

THE RENAISSANCE (1375-1530)

Once the Black Death had eradicated one-third of the population, causing fear and generally wreaking havoc throughout the country, Italy began the long trek back to stability. Two ages of discovery began at the end of the 14th century: the geographical exploration of foreign lands and the intellectual exploration of Classicism. This desire to attain an ancient Greek or Roman education led to the rise of **Humanism,** a secular movement that glorified human achievement and potential. With the decline of Rome and other large cities, the recently established smaller *comuni* asserted themselves. Fueled by Humanist ideals, Italy inaugurated the greatest intellectual and artistic flowering in history, the **Rinascimento,** or **Renaissance,** which quickly spread throughout Europe.

Great ruling families—the Gonzagas in Mantua, the d'Estes in Ferrara, and, most importantly, the **Medici** in Florence—instituted commercial and legal reforms and accelerated the cultural and artistic activity of their cities. The Medici clan reached its apex with **Cosimo** and **Lorenzo (il Magnifico),** who broadened the family's activities from the traditional banking and politicking to the patronization of artists and sculptors. Under the golden hands of these two Renaissance men, Donatello, Brunelleschi, Michelangelo, and Botticelli achieved fame throughout the country and the continent. Despite Florence's rise in economic and intellectual power, not every city-state blossomed to the same degree. The power-hungry princes' quests for glory resulted in constant warfare. The weakened cities yielded to the invading Spanish armies of Charles V throughout the 16th century. By 1556, Naples and Milan had fallen to King Ferdinand of Aragon.

POST-RENAISSANCE: FOREIGN DOMINATION (1540-1815)

The open-mindedness of the Renaissance soon corroded into intolerance, catalyzed by religious turmoil. The **Counter-Reformation,** the Catholic Church's response to the Protestant Reformation, was strict and parochial. The 16th-century **Spanish Inquisition** encouraged narrow-minded religious fanaticism. Spain suppressed the Protestant Reformation in Italy, politically dominating the peninsula for over a century. Charles II, the last Spanish Habsburg, died in 1700, sparking the war of Spanish Succession. In the course of **Napoleon's** 19th-century march through Europe, the diminutive French Emperor united much of northern Italy into the Italian Republic, conquered Naples, and fostered the concept of national sovereignty. In 1804, Napoleon declared the newly united nation the Kingdom of Italy, with himself as monarch. After Napoleon's fall in 1815, the **Congress of Vienna** carved up Italy, granting considerable control to Austria.

THE ITALIAN NATION (1815-PRESENT)

A long-standing grudge against foreign rule prompted nationalist resurgence, the **Risorgimento,** which culminated in national unification in 1860. The success of the Risorgimento is attributed primarily to three Italian heroes: **Giuseppe Mazzini,** the movement's suave intellectual leader; **Giuseppe Garibaldi,** the charismatic military head; and **Camillo Cavour,** the political and diplomatic mastermind. **Vittorio Emanuele II,** crowned as the first ruler of the Kingdom of Italy, expanded the nation by annexing northern and central regions. France relinquished Rome on September 20, 1870, *the* pivotal date in modern Italian history.

The chaotic aftermath of WWI paved the way for the rise of Fascism, under the control of "Il Duce," **Benito Mussolini.** Mussolini established the world's first Fascist regime in 1924 and expelled all opposition parties. In 1940, Italy entered **World War II** on the side of its Axis ally, Germany. Success came quickly but was short-lived: the Allies landed in Sicily in 1943, prompting Mussolini's fall from power. As a final indignity, Mussolini and his mistress, Claretta Petacci, were captured and executed by infuriated citizens. By the end of 1943, the new government had withdrawn its support from Germany, which promptly invaded and occupied its former ally. In 1945, Italy was freed from German domination, and the country was divided between those supporting the monarchy and those favoring Fascism.

MODERN PROBLEMS: POST-WAR POLITICS (1945-92)

The **Italian Constitution,** adopted in 1948, established the **Republic,** with a president, a bicameral parliament, and an independent judiciary. Italy has seen over 50 governments since WWII, none of which has lasted longer than four years. While the postwar era was plagued with instability, the Italian economy somehow sped through industrialization at an unprecedented rate, and many regions, especially in the North, recovered economically by the 50s. Economic success gave way to violence in the late 60s. The *autunno caldo* (hot autumn) of 1969, a season of strikes, demonstrations, and riots foreshadowed the violence of the 70s. Perhaps the most shocking episode was the 1978 kidnapping and murder of ex-Prime Minister **Aldo Moro** by a group of left-wing militant terrorists, the *Brigate Rosse* (Red Brigade). The events of the 1970s had challenged the conservative Social Democrats, and in 1983, **Bettino Craxi** became Italy's first Socialist premier.

ITALY TODAY

In 1992, **Oscar Luigi Scalfaro** was elected Italy's new president. During his turbulent seven-year term, he initiated electoral reforms, hoping to make the Italian government more productive. These reforms and their accompanying judicial investigations uncovered the **"Tangentopoli"** (Kickback City) scandal. This unprecedented political crisis implicated over 2600 politicians in corruption charges. Reaction to the continued investigation has included such acts of violence as the May 1993 bombing of the Uffizi, Florence's premier art museum, the "suicides" of 10 indicted officials, and the murders of anti-Mafia judges and investigators. The elections of 1996 brought the center-left coalition, the **Olive Tree** (l'Ulivo), to power, with **Romano Prodi** as Prime Minister. Prodi, as head of Italy's second-longest lasting government since World War II, helped stabilize Italian politics. Despite the hope surrounding Prodi's government, his coalition lost a vote of confidence in October

1998. By the end of the month, his government collapsed, and former Communist **Massimo D'Alema** was sworn in as the new prime minister. D'Alema and his respected treasurer Carlo Ciampi (now Italy's president) created fiscal reforms and pushed through a 1999 budget that qualified Italy for January 1999 entrance into the European Monetary Union.

THE ARTS

VISUAL ARTS

In Rome, the Colosseum hovers above a city bus stop; in Florence, young men and women meet in front of the *duomo* to flirt and gossip; in Sicily, remnants from Greek columns are used as dining tables. Italy is a country in which daily life and artistic masterpieces are woven inextricably together. The artistic tradition is prolific and varied—to visit only the most famous pieces would be to misunderstand the pervasive presence of art in everyday Italian settings.

ETRUSCAN. Italian art history begins in the 8th century BC with the **Etruscans.** Culturally and artistically, the Etruscans are strongly linked with Asia Minor and the ancient Near East. Their sculptures and wall paintings are characterized by large eyes, enigmatic smiles, and stingy attention to anatomic detail. Etruscans used bright colors and fluid lines in necropoli, tomb paintings, and funerary statues.

GREEK AND ROMAN. The Greeks peppered southern Italy with a large number of **temples** and **theaters.** In fact, the best-preserved Greek temples in the world today are found not in Greece, but in Sicily. Stretching roughly from 200 BC to AD 350, Roman art falls mainly into two large categories—art in service of the state and private household art. Most Roman houses incorporated **frescoes,** Greek-influenced paintings daubed onto wet plaster so that both plaster and paint would dry together, forming a time-resistant compound. **Mosaic** was another popular medium from the Hellenistic period onward. Public art in Rome usually reflected the tastes of whomever was in power at the time. Romans soon began to use the column as a purely decorative device, relying on the **arch** instead of the column for support. The arch, along with the **invention of concrete,** revolutionized the Roman conceptions of architecture and made possible such monuments as the Colosseum, the Pantheon, aqueducts, amphitheaters, basilicas, and thermal baths.

EARLY CHRISTIAN AND BYZANTINE. For fear of persecution, early Christians fled underground to worship; their **catacombs** are now among the most haunting and intriguing of Italian monuments, scattered throughout Rome, Naples, and Syracuse. Inexpressive, two-dimensional human figures on flat blue or gold backgrounds were all the rage, and **mosaics** were especially suited for this style. The **Basilica of San Vitale** is remarkable both in its octagonal plan and its dazzling mosaics. It is also one of the first churches with a freestanding **campanile** or belltower, a feature peculiar to Italian churches.

ROMANESQUE AND GOTHIC. From 1000 to 1200, **Romanesque** churches sprung up throughout Europe. Characterized by **rounded arches,** heavy columns, strict geometry, thick and relatively unadorned walls, and small windows, these basilicas are not as flamboyantly ornate as the later Gothic churches. The Gothic style of the 12th to 14th centuries spread southward from France and combined the pointed arch and the flying buttress, which together supported the weight of the roof and allowed the heavy Romanesque wall to be replaced by the glorious Gothic window. Slowly but surely, Italians became bored with expressionless, flat characters, and **Giotto di Bondone** (c. 1266-1337) began to explore perspective, naturalism, and personal expression.

EARLY RENAISSANCE. The first artists to expand upon the lessons of Giotto were Filippo Brunelleschi (1377-1446), Donatello (1386-1466), and Masaccio, who succeeded in revolutionizing architecture, sculpture, and painting respectively. **Brunelleschi's** mathematical studies of ancient Roman architecture became the cornerstone of all later Renaissance building. In sculpture, **Donatello** built upon the central achieve-

ITALY

ment of classical antiquity: the realistic articulation of the human body in motion. Depicting movement and a more Northern sensibility, **Fra Filippo Lippi** (c. 1406-69) and **Fra Angelico** (c. 1400-55) followed hot on Masaccio's footsteps. Trained under Filippo Lippi, **Sandro Botticelli** (1444-1510) was a favorite painter of the Medici.

HIGH RENAISSANCE. The torch was passed at the start of the **High Renaissance** (1450-1520) to three exceptional men: Leonardo da Vinci (1452-1519), Michelangelo Buonarroti (1475-1564), and Raphael Santi (1483-1520). **Leonardo** was not only an artist but a scientist, architect, engineer, musician, and weapon designer. **Michelangelo** painted, sculpted, and designed buildings with as much skill as his contemporary but at a prolific pace. The ceiling of the **Sistine Chapel** (p. 634), on which Michelangelo created the illusion of vaults on a flat surface, remains his greatest surviving achievement in painting. Sculpture, however, was his favorite mode of expression. Classic examples are the highly polished, tranquil *Pietà* in St. Peter's, the virile, pensive *David*, and the unfinished *Slaves* in Florence's Accademia. **Raphael** created technically perfect figures. The Venetian school produced the elusive **Giorgione** (1478-1510) and **Titian** (1488-1576), whose works share the nostalgia and poetry of Giorgione but are alive with energetic movement.

MANNERISM. The emerging spirit of creative experimentation led to Mannerism, a short-lived link between the Renaissance and Baroque periods. Mannerist artists idealized the human to the point of abstraction; figures produced in this style may be oddly elongated, flattened, or colored in unusual schemes. **Parmigianino** (1503-1540) was the most famous Mannerist, and his controversial *Madonna of the Long Neck* in the Uffizi is the period's most famous work.

BAROQUE AND ROCOCO. Born of the Counter-Reformation and of absolute monarchy, the grandiose, vivid, and dynamic Baroque art and architecture were intended to inspire faith in God, and respect for the Catholic Church. Painters of this era favored Naturalism—a commitment to portraying nature in all its intensity, whether ugly or beautiful. **Caravaggio** (1573-1610) created mysterious works, incorporating often unsavory characters into religious scenes. **Gianlorenzo Bernini** (1598-1680), a High Baroque sculptor and architect, designed the colonnaded *piazza* of St. Peter's as well as the *baldacchino* over its crossing. **Giovanni Battista Tiepolo** (1696-1770), with his light-colored palate and vibrant frescoes, was a remarkablE Venetian painter of allegories and the premier exemplar of the **Rococo** style—his paintings fill museums and noble residences across the continent.

19TH AND 20TH CENTURY ART. The Italians started to lose their dexterity with the paintbrush, and chisel proficiency in the 18th and 19th centuries. **Antonio Canova** (1757-1822) explored the formal **Neoclassical** style, which professed a return to the rules of classical antiquity. The **Macchiaioli** group, spearheaded by **Giovanni Fattori** (1825-1908), revolted against the strict academic Neoclassical style with a unique technique of "blotting." The Italian **Futurist** artists of the 1910s, who sought to transfer the aesthetics and movements of machines into art, brought Italy back to the cutting edge of artistry. **Amadeo Modigliani** (1884-1920) crafted figures most famous for their long oval faces.

LITERATURE

OH GODS, YOU DEVILS. It is primarily through **Ovid's** various works that we learn the gory details of Roman mythology, a soap-opera theology that developed from and added to the Greek family of deities. Usually disguised as animals or humans, these gods and goddesses often descended to earth to intervene romantically or combatively in human affairs.

LATIN LOVERS (300 BC-200 AD). In the wake of Greek civilization, the Romans were faced with the challenge of inventing a literature that could match the majesty and scope of their burgeoning rule. The early **Plautus** (c. 259-184 BC) wrote popular comedic plays, including *Pseudolus*, which has since been adapted as the Broadway musical *A Funny Thing Happened on the Way to the Forum*. The lyric poetry of **Catullus** (84-54 BC) set a high standard for passion, and **Cicero** (106-43 BC) penned several orations while **Julius Caesar** himself (100-44 BC) gave a first-hand account of the final dissolution of the Republic in the Gallic wars.

Augustan Rome produced some of the greatest Latin authors. **Virgil** (70-19 BC) wrote the epic *Aeneid* about the godly origins of Rome. **Horace's** (65-8 BC) verse derived from his personal experiences, which can be seen in his *Odes*, *Epodes*, *Satires*, and *Epistles*. **Ovid** (43 BC-AD 17) wrote poems, among them the *Amores* (perhaps more accurately titled the "Lusts"), the mythological *Metamorphoses*, and the *Ars Amatoria*.

INTO THE LIGHT (1250-1375). The tumult of medieval life discouraged most literary musings, but three Tuscan writers reasserted the art in the late 13th century. **Dante Alighieri** (1265-1321) was one of the first Italian poets to write in the *volgare* (common Italian) instead of Latin. In his epic poem *La Divina Commedia (The Divine Comedy)*, Dante roams all levels of the afterlife with famous historical figures and his true love Beatrice. **Petrarch** (1304-74) restored the popularity of ancient Roman writers by writing love sonnets to a married woman named Laura, compiled in *Il Canzoniere*. **Giovanni Boccaccio,** a close friend of Petrarch's, composed a collection of 100 bawdy stories in *The Decameron*.

RENAISSANCE AND BEYOND (1375-1800). Fifteenth and 16th-century Italian authors branched out from the genres of their predecessors. **Alberti** and **Palladio** wrote treatises on architecture and art theory. **Baldassare Castiglione's** *The Courtier* instructed the inquiring Renaissance man on deportment, etiquette, and other fine points of behavior. One of the most lasting works of the Renaissance, **Niccolò Machiavelli's** *Il Principe (The Prince)* is a sophisticated assessment of what it takes to gain political power. As Italy's political power waned, literary production also declined, but some stars remained. The 18th-century dramatist **Carlo Goldoni** (1707-1793) replaced the stock characters of the traditional *commedia dell'arte* with unpredictable figures in his *Il Ventaglio*.

MODERN TO POSTMODERN (1800-2000). With the 19th century came the unification of Italy and the necessity for a unified language. The 1800s were an era primarily of *racconti* (short stories) and poetry. On a popular front, **Pellegrino Artusi's** 1891 cookbook *La Scienza in Cucina e L'Arte di Mangiar Bene* was the first attempt to assemble recipes from regional traditions into a unified Italian cuisine. The 20th century saw a new tradition in Italian literature as Nobel Prize-winning author and playwright **Luigi Pirandello** explored the relativity of truth in works like *Six Characters in Search of an Author*. Literary production slowed in the years preceding WWII, but the conclusion of the war ignited an explosion in antifascist fiction. **Primo Levi** wrote *Se Questo È Un Uomo (If This is a Man)* about his experiences in Auschwitz. Mid-twentieth century poets include Nobel Prize winners **Salvatore Quasimodo** and **Eugenio Montale** who founded the "hermetic movement," characterized by an intimate poetic vision and allusive imagery. More recently, **Umberto Eco's** *The Name of the Rose*, an intricate mystery set in a 14th-century monastery, draws heavily on the history of medieval Catholicism.

MUSIC

CHURCH TUNES AND MEDIEVAL JAMS. An Italian monk, **Guido d'Arezzo** (995-1050), is regarded as the originator of musical notation. Generally accepted as the home of church music, Italy's monasteries reveled in tunes through the Middle Ages and Renaissance. By the 14th century, Italian secular composers undertook the art of **madrigals,** transposing poems in vocal settings.

THE FAT LADY SINGS. The 16th century also ushered in a new form of musical extravaganza that would amass global popularity: **opera.** Italy's most cherished art form was born in Florence, nurtured in Venice, and revered in Milan. Conceived by the **Camerata,** a circle of Florentine writers, noblemen, and musicians, opera originated as an attempt to recreate the dramas of ancient Greece by setting lengthy poems to music. **Jacobo Peri** composed *Dafne*, the world's first complete opera, in 1597. The first successful opera composer, **Claudio Monteverdi** (1567-1643), drew freely from history, juxtaposing high drama, love scenes, and bawdy humor.

IF IT AIN'T BAROQUE, DON'T FIX IT. Baroque music, known for its exaggerated movements and ornamentation, took the seventeenth and eighteenth centuries by storm. During this period, two main instruments saw their popularity mushroom: the violin, the shape of which was perfected by Cremona families, including the **Stradivari,** and the piano, created in about 1709 by members of the Florentine **Cristofori** family. **Antonio Vivaldi** (1675-1741), who composed over 400 concertos, triumphed with *The Four Seasons*.

BYE BYE VERDI. With convoluted plots and strong, dramatic music, 19th-century Italian opera continues to dominate modern stages. Late in the 19th-century, **Giacomo Puccini** (1858-1924) created *Madame Butterfly*, *La Bohème*, and *Tosca*. **Gioacchino Rossini** (1792-1868) was the master of the *bel canto* ("beautiful song")— long, fluid, melodic lines. **Giuseppe Verdi** (1813-1901) remains the transcendent musical and operatic figure of 19th-century Italy. Verdi produced the touching, personal dramas and memorable melodies of *Rigoletto, La Traviata*, and *Il Trovatore* and the grand and heroic conflicts of *Aida*. Classical music *all'italiana* continued to grow in the 20th-century. **Ottorino Respighi** experimented with rapidly shifting orchestral textures. And that *pagliaccio* **Luciano Pavarotti** remains universally adored, as he tours with fellow tenors Placido Domingo and José Carreras, singing long into the night.

FILM

Through the early twentieth century, Italy's films were mostly prominent historical dramas; but by the mid-twentieth century, Italy had fallen to the back of the cinema pack. Mussolini created the *Centro Sperimentale della Cinematografia*, a national film school, nationalizing the industry for the good of the state, but avoiding aesthetic development. The fall of Fascism brought the explosion of **Neorealist cinema** (1943-50) which rejected contrived sets and professional actors, emphasizing location shooting and authentic drama. **Vittorio De Sica's** 1945 film *Ladri di Biciclette* (*The Bicycle Thief*) was perhaps the most famous and successful Neorealist film. By the mid 1950s, Italy had begun to prosper and the humble, honest ambition of *Neorealismo* gave way to the birth of a more light-hearted genre, **La Commedia all'Italiana.** In the 1960s, post-neorealist directors like **Federico Fellini** rejected plots and characters for a visual and symbolic world. Fellini's *La Dolce Vita* (1960), banned by the Pope, but regarded as the most representative Italian film, scrutinizes 1950s Rome. Recently, Oscar-winners **Giuseppe Tornatore** *(Il Nuovo Cinema Paradiso)* and **Gabriele Salvatore** have garnered the attention of US audiences. Enthusiastic sparkplug **Roberto Benigni** has become one of the leading cinematic personalities. His *La Vita e Bella* (Life is Beautiful) has gained international respect and glory, receiving Best Actor and Best Foreign Film Oscars and a Best Picture nomination at the 1999 Academy Awards.

FOOD AND DRINK

Eating for Italians is an art, a way of life, and one of its greatest joy. Italians love to eat, and they love to eat well. Italian cuisine differs radically by region. Dishes in the North are often rich, with creamy and meaty sauces, egg noodles, and more butter than olive oil. Northerners eat less pasta than they do rice *(riso)*, *risotto*, and polenta; if you want a pizza you'd do best to head farther south. **Piedmont** is known for its heavy sauces and delectable truffles, a proven aphrodisiac. **Lombardy** specializes in cheeses, *risotti*, and stewed meats like *ossobuco*. The coastal region of **Liguria** is noted for its seafood, pesto, and olive oil, while German and Austrian influences in **Trentino-Alto Adige** have popularized *gnocchi*, dumplings made of potatoes and flour. **Friuli-Venezia Giulia** offers heavy cuisine with a Middle-European flair, spiced with cumin, horseradish, and paprika. The **Veneto** is rich in artichokes, rice, and various game. **Emilia-Romagna** is Italy's gastronomic heart, the birthplace of parmesan cheese, balsamic vinegar, and parma ham *(prosciutto di Parma)*. **Tuscany** draws justifiable acclaim for its simple, hearty food: expensive olive oil, bready soups, and bean dishes are prevalent. **Umbria** grows black truffles to match Piedmont's white, but its unspiced cuisine is anything but rich. The food of the South is spicier, based more on garlic, tomatoes, and olive oil. Tomato sauces and mozzarella are popular in **Campania,** home to the authentic pizza. **Basilicata** and **Calabria** specialize in spicy cuisine. In Sicily, pasta is still eaten by the truckload, served with tomatoes and fresh vegetables. **Sardinia** has more sheep than people, and their odiferous cheese is made into pies and topped with honey, the perfect finish to a meal of veggie soup and roast game.

Italy's rocky soil, warm climate, and hilly landscape are ideal for growing grapes, and the country produces more **wine** than any other. Sicily alone boasts 200 million gallons annually. Piedmont is Italy's preeminent wine region, producing the touted *Barolo.* Tuscany is famed for its tannic *chianti* and similar reds. When in Rome, you know the drill—drink *Frascati,* a clean white wine, served cold, with an almond aftertaste. After grapes are pressed for wine, the remaining pomace is used to produce *grappa,* the national blue-collar favorite. This illegitimate cousin of wine, oft-maligned as tourist firewater, flows throughout Italy.

ESSENTIALS

DOCUMENTS AND FORMALITIES

Those wishing to stay in Italy for more than three months must apply for a *permesso di soggiorno* (residence permit) at a police station *(questura).* For more info, contact the Italian embassy in your country.

Italian Embassies at Home: Australia, 12 Grey St, Deakin, A.C.T. 2601; P.O. Box 360, Canberra City A.C.T. 2601 (☎ (02) 62 73 33 33); **Canada,** 275 Slater St., 21st fl., Ottawa, ON K1P 5H9 (☎ (613) 232 2401; www.trytel.com/~italy); **Ireland,** 63/65 Northumberland Rd, Dublin 4 (☎ (3531) 660 17 44; fax 668 27 59; email italianembassy@tinet.ie); **New Zealand,** 34-38 Grant Rd, Thorndon, Wellington (☎ (04) 473 53 39; email ambwell@xtra.co.nz); **South Africa,** 796 George Ave., Arcadia 0083, Pretoria (☎ (012) 43 55 41; fax 43 55 47; www.smartnet.co.za/ambital); **UK,** 14 Three Kings Yard, London W1Y 2EH (☎ (020) 73 12 22 00; www.embitaly.org.uk); **US,** 1601 Fuller St. NW, Washington, DC 20009 (☎ (202) 328 5500; www.italyemb.org).

Foreign Embassies in Italy: All embassies are in **Rome** (see p. 614).

TRANSPORTATION

BY PLANE. Rome's international airport (known as both Fiumicino and Leonardo da Vinci) is served by most major airlines, as is **Milan's** Malpensa or Linate airports and **Florence's** international airport. **Alitalia** (☎ 800 223 5730; www.alitalia.it/eng) is Italy's national airline and may offer off-season youth fares.

BY TRAIN. The Italian State Railway, **Ferrovie dello Stato** or **FS** (national info line ☎ 147 88 80 88; www.fs-on-line.com), offers inexpensive and efficient service, although it is commonly plagued by strikes. Several types of trains ride the Italian rails: the *locale* stops at every station along a particular line, the *diretto* goes faster but makes fewer stops than the *locale;* and the *espresso* just stops at major stations. The air-conditioned, more expensive **rapido,** an **InterCity (IC)** train, travels only to the largest cities. Tickets for the fast, pricey **Eurostar** trains (a first- and second-class train) require reservations. **Eurail** passes are valid without a supplement on all trains except **Eurostar.** If you're under 26 and plan to travel extensively in Italy, the **Cartaverde** should be your *first* purchase upon arrival. Cartaverde are available to people aged 12 to 26. The card (L40,000) is valid for one year, and entitles you to a 20% discount on any state train fare.

BY BUS. Intercity buses are often more convenient for shorter trips to destinations not served by major rail lines, though they tend to be more expensive. For **city buses,** buy tickets in *tabacchi* or kiosks, and validate them on board.

BY FERRY. The islands of Sicily, Sardinia, and Corsica, as well as the smaller islands along the coasts, are connected to the mainland by ferries *(traghetti)* and hydrofoils *(aliscafi)*. Italy's largest private ferry service is **Tirrenia;** for info, contact the Rome office at V. Bissolati, 41 (☎06 474 20 41). Ferry services in the port towns of **Bari** (p. 698), **Brindisi** (p. 708), and **Ancona** (p. 698) connect Italy to **Greece.** Unless you have a Eurailpass (honored only at Brindisi), the ferries from Bari and Ancona are preferable—they're cheaper and less crowded. Boats from **Trieste** (see p. 676) serve the Istrian Peninsula as far south as **Croatia's** Dalmatian Coast. Ferries also connect Italy's islands to the mainland. For **Sardinia,** catch a boat in **Genoa** (p. 649), **La Spezia** (p. 652), or **Naples** (p. 698). **Sicily**-bound travelers should take the ferry from **Naples** or **Reggio di Calabria.**

BY CAR. An *Autostrada* (super-highway) is a worthy successor to the Appian Way, but tolls are prohibitive, and Italian driving is frightening. Driving can be particularly challenging in Rome, Milan, and Naples; congested traffic is more common in cities and in the north. There is an extensive network of smaller highways: *strade statali* (national), *provinciali* (provincial), and *communali* (municipal). On three lane roads, be aware that the center lane is for passing. Helpful words include: *benzina* (gasoline), *entrata* (entrance), *uscita* (exit), *senso unico* (one-way) and *vietato parcheggiare* ('no parking'). Gas is about US$4 per gallon. **Mopeds** (L40-60,000 per day) can be a great way to see the islands and the more scenic areas of Italy, but can be disastrous in the rain and on rough roads.

The **Automobile Club Italiano (ACI)** is the automobile savior of Italy. The main office is located at Via Marsala 8, 00185 Roma (☎06 49 981; fax 06 499 82 34). In case of **breakdown** on any Italian road, dial **116** at the nearest telephone. The nearest ACI office will be advised to come to your assistance. On superhighways, use the emergency telephones placed every 2 kilometers. Gas costs US$4-5 per liter. Taxis are common in major cities.

BY BIKE AND BY THUMB. Bicycling is a popular national sport, but bike trails are rare, drivers often reckless, and, except in the Po Valley, the terrain challenging. *Let's Go* strongly urges you to consider the risks before you choose to hitchhike. Hitchhiking in Italy, especially in areas south of Rome or Naples, can be unsafe.

TOURIST SERVICES AND MONEY

EMERGENCY	Police: ☎112. Ambulance: ☎118. Fire: ☎115.

TOURIST OFFICES. In provincial capitals, look for the Ente Provinciale per il Turismo (EPT) or Azienda di Promozione Turistica (APT) for info on the entire province and the town. Local tourist offices, Informazione e Assistenza ai Turisti (IAT) and Azienda Autonoma di Soggiorno e Turismo (AAST), are generally the most useful. Also keep an eye out for Pro Loco, Centro Turistico Studentesco e Giovanile (CTS), and Compagnia Italiana Turismo (CIT).

Italian Government Tourist Boards (ENIT) at home: Australia, Level 26, 44 Market St, Sydney NSW 2000 (☎ (02) 92 62 16 66; fax (02) 9262 57 45); **Canada,** 1 pl. Ville Marie #1914, Montréal, Québec H3B 2C3 (☎ (514) 866 7668; fax 392 1429; email initaly@ican.net); **UK,** 1 Princess St., London WIR 9AY (☎ (020) 74 08 12 54; fax 74 93 66 95; email Enitlond@globalnet.co.uk); **US,** 630 Fifth Ave #1565, New York, NY 10111 (☎ (212) 245 5618; fax 586 9249; www.italiantourism.com).

CURRENCY & EXCHANGE. The Italian currency unit is the *lira* (plural: *lire*). Coins are minted in L50, L100, L200, and L500 denominations, and the most common bills are L1000, L2000, L5000, L10,000, L50,000, and L100,000. When changing money in Italy, try to use only banks or *bureaux de change/casas de cambio.* that have at most a 5% margin between their buy and sell prices. The most favorable rates are available through one of many ATMs in Italy, where your home bank account should be accessible.

Prices: A thrifty traveler staying in a hostel, preparing meals from supermarket supplies, and visiting few sights can get by on L55-60,000 a day. Travelers who indulge, staying in more luxurious spots, could make it on L100,000 a day.

Tipping and bargaining: Italian tipping customs are complicated and vary by region. In touristed areas, a service charge will probably be added to restaurant and hotel bills; leave an additional 5-10%. In cafes, leave L500 if you sat at a table, and L100-200 if you stood at the counter. Maids, bellhops, and valets get L1-2000 tip per day. Give taxi drivers 10%. Tour guides get L2000 tip for a half-day tour.

Taxes: The value-added tax in Italy (known as IVA) ranges from 12-35%. Upon departure from the EU, non-EU citizens can get a refund of the IVA for purchases over L300,000.

ACCOMMODATIONS AND CAMPING

Associazione Italiana Alberghi per la Gioventù (AIG), the Italian **hostel** federation and an affiliate of Hostelling International (HI), operates dozens of youth hostels *(ostelli per la gioventù)* across the country, especially in the north. A complete list is available from most **EPT** and **CTS** offices and from many hostels. Prices average about L50-55,000 per night, including breakfast. Hostels are the best option for solo travelers (single rooms are relatively scarce in hotels), but curfews, lockouts, out-of-the-way locations, and less than perfect security detract from their appeal. For more information on hostels in Italy, contact the Rome **AIG office**, V. Cavour, 44 (☎06 487 11 52). Italian **hotel** rates are set not by private owners but by the state; hotel owners will need your passport to register you—don't be afraid to hand it over for a while (usually overnight), but ask for it as soon as you think you will need it. One-star *pensioni* are the best options. Prices fluctuate by region, but singles usually start around L50,000, doubles L70,000, though these prices can skyrocket in major cities during the summer. By law, the price must be posted in each room; if it isn't, get it in writing. A room with a private bath *(con bagno)* usually costs 30-50% more. **Camping** sites tend to be loud and modern and cost around L9000 per person (or tent) plus L8000 per car, much more near big cities.

COMMUNICATION

MAIL. Sending a postcard to an international destination within Western Europe costs L1200; any other international destination via airmail costs L1500. Domestically, postcards require L1200. Sending a letter (up to 20g) to another country in Europe costs L1200; anywhere else via airmail costs L1500. Mail can be sent via *Poste Restante* (General Delivery; *Fermo Posta*) to almost any city or town in Italy with a post office. Address *Poste Restante* letters as in the following example: Annie NICHOLS, *Fermo Posta*, Ufficio Postale Centrale di Piazza Cordusio 4, Milano 20100, Italia. The mail will go to the central post office, unless you specify a post office by street address or postal code.

TELEPHONES. The most common type of phone accepts phone cards (L5000, L10,000, or L15,000 from *tabacchi*, newsstands, bars, post offices, and the occasional machine). Italian phone cards are a little tricky to maneuver; rip off the marked corner, and then insert it into the appropriate section of the pay phone. The phone card's time is measured in L200 talk units (e.g. one unit=one local minute). International calls start at L1000, and vary depending on where you are calling. A collect call is a *contassa a carico del destinatario* or *chiamata collect*. **International direct dial numbers** include: **AT&T**, ☎172 10 11; **Australia Direct**, ☎172 10 61; **BT Direct**, ☎172 00 44; **Canada Direct**, ☎172 10 01; **Ireland Direct**, ☎172 03 53; **MCI WorldPhone Direct**, ☎172 10 22; **Sprint**, ☎172 18 77; **Telecom New Zealand Direct**, ☎172 10 64; and **Telkom South Africa Direct**, ☎172 10 27.

INTERNET ACCESS. Though Italy initially lagged behind on the information superhighway, it's now playing catch-up like a pro. New internet cafes, internet bars, and even internet laundromats are popping up every day throughout the country. Access costs L10,000-20,000 per hour.

LANGUAGE. Any knowledge of Spanish, French, Portuguese, or Latin will help you understand Italian. The tourist office staff usually speaks some English. For a traveler's survival kit of basic Italian, see p. 957.

LOCAL FACTS

Time: Italy is 1hr. ahead of Greenwich Mean Time (GMT).

Climate: Summers are humid and hot in the north, drier and hotter in the south. Winters are ferocious in the Alps and cold and damp in Venice and Florence, but Sicilian waters are swimmable year-round. Mid-Apr. to mid-June or mid-Sept. to Oct. may be the best times to visit, when temperatures are moderate and the crowds are not at their peak.

Hours: Nearly everything closes from around 1 to 3 or 4pm for siesta. Most museums are open 9am-1pm and 3-6pm; some are open through lunch, however. Monday is often their *giorno di chiusura* (day of closure). Food shops have a different *giorno di chiusura* from province to province.

Holidays: Italy closes on the following holidays: New Year's Day (Jan. 1); Epiphany (Jan. 6); Easter Sunday and Monday (Apr. 23-24); Liberation Day (Apr. 25); Labor Day (May 1); Assumption of the Virgin (Aug. 15); All Saints' Day (Nov. 1); Immaculate Conception (Dec. 8); Christmas Day (Dec. 25); and Santo Stefano (Dec. 26). **August brings Ferragosto, a vacation month for all Italians; the cities shut down and empty out.** Plan your trip accordingly, as businesses close and locals leave.

Festivals: The most common excuse for a local festival is the celebration of a religious event—a patron saint's day or the commemoration of a miracle. Most of these festivals include parades, music, wine, obscene amounts of food, and general boisterousness. **Carnevale,** held in February during the 10 days before Lent, energizes Italian towns. During **Scoppio del Carro,** held in Florence's P. del Duomo on Easter Sunday, Florentines set off a cart of explosives, following a tradition dating back to medieval times. On July 2 and Aug. 16, the **Palio** hits Siena, which celebrates the event with a horse race around the central *piazza*. The entire month of August, residents of Cortona celebrate the tremendous taste of the truffle during the **Festa dei Porcini.**

ROME (ROMA)

Italy's massive capital is an eruption of marble domes, noseless statues, and motorcycle dust. Rome is a sensory overload, rushing down the hills of Lazio to knock you flat on your back, leaving you gasping for air, and dying for more. The city and those it controlled were responsible for the development of over 2000 years of world history, art, architecture, politics, and literature. Rome has been the capital of kingdoms and republics; from this city, the Roman Empire defined the western world, and from here, the Catholic Church spread its influence worldwide. For the traveler, there is so much to see, hear, eat, smell, and absorb that the city is both exhilarating and overwhelming, as if it's impossible to experience everything, or even anything. Never fear, however, because in *bella Roma*, everything is beautiful and everything tastes good. Liberate your senses from the pollution eroding the monuments and from the maniacal crush of motorcyclists, and enjoy the dizzying paradox that is the *Caput Mundi*, the Eternal City, Rome.

✈ GETTING THERE AND AWAY

Flights: da Vinci International Airport (☎06 65951), known as **Fiumicino,** handles most flights. The Termini train runs nonstop to **Stazione Termini** (30 min.; twice hourly 12 and 37min. past the hour 7:37am-10:37pm, extra trains 7:37am, 6:37, and 8:37pm; L16,000, L40,000 on board). After hours, take the blue COTRAL bus to Tiburtina (1:15,

2:15, 3:30, and 5am; L8000, pay on board). From Tiburtina, take bus 40N to Termini. Most charter flights arrive at Ciampino (☎06 794941). To get to Rome, take COTRAL (every 30min. or so, 6:10am-11pm, L2000) to Anagnina station on Metro Line A .

Trains: The main station is **Stazione Termini.** To: **Naples** (2-2½hr., L18,600); **Florence** (2-3hr., L40,900); **Venice** (5hr., L66,000); and **Milan** (4½-8hr., L50,500). Trains arriving midnight-5am may arrive at Tiburtina or Ostiense; take buses 40N or 20N-21N to Stazione Termini.

☐ GETTING AROUND

Public Transportation: The 2 **Metropolitana** subway lines meet at Termini and run 5:30am-11:30pm. **Buses** run 6am-midnight (there are limited late night routes); board at the front or back and validate your ticket in the machine. Buy **tickets** (L1500) at *tabacchi*, newsstands, and station machines; they're valid for 1 Metro ride or unlimited bus travel within 1¼hr. of validation. **B.I.G. daily tickets** (L8000) and **C.I.S. weekly tickets** (L32,000) allow unlimited bus or train travel everywhere in Rome, including Ostia but not Fiumicino. **Pickpockets are rampant on buses and trains.**

Taxis: Radiotaxi (☎06 3570), **Prontotaxi** (☎06 6645). From the city center to the airport L70,000. Base fare L4500. Surcharges: night L5000; Su L2000; luggage L2000.

Car Rental: Avis (☎06 41998; www.avis.com), **Europcar** (☎06 4882854; www.europcar.it), **Maggiore** (☎06 2291530; www.maggiore.it).

Bike and Moped Rental: Scooters for Rent, V. della Purificazione, 84 (☎06 4885485). Off P. Barberini, has bikes (L20,000 per day, L100,000 weekly) and mopeds (L50,000 per day, L250,000 weekly). Open daily in summer 9am-7pm.

☀ ORIENTATION

The train station **Stazione Termini** is the arrival point for most visitors to Rome. **Via Nazionale** is the central artery connecting **Piazza della Repubblica** with **Piazza Venezia,** home to the immense wedding-cake-like **Vittorio Emanuele II monument.** West of P. Venezia, **Largo Argentina** marks the start of **C. Vittorio Emanuele,** which leads into Centro Storico, the medieval and Renaissance tangle of sights around the **Pantheon, Piazza Navona, Campo dei Fiori,** and **Piazza Farnese.** From P. Venezia, V. dei Fori Imperiale leads southeast to the **Forum** and **Colosseum,** south of which are the ruins of the **Baths of Caracalla** and the **Appian Way,** and the neighborhoods of southern Rome, the Aventine, Testaccio, Ostiense, and EUR. **Via del Corso** stretches from P. Venezia north to **Piazza del Popolo.** East of the Corso, fashionable streets border the **Piazza di Spagna** and, to the northeast, the **Villa Borghese.** South and east are the **Fontana di Trevi, Piazza Barberini,** and the **Quirinal Hill.** Across the Tiber to the north are **Vatican City,** and, to the south, **Trastevere,** the best neighborhood for wandering.

Some people might say that it's impossible to navigate Rome without a map. These people would, in fact, be correct. Using the free, omnipresent, **McDonald's** map will get you lost, though you will likely stumble upon some of Rome's 33 McDonald's locations. Instead, pick up a free map from a tourist office or *Let's Go's* 30-page **map guide.** The invaluable **Roma Metro-Bus map** (L8000) is available at newsstands.

⑦ PRACTICAL INFORMATION

TOURIST, FINANCIAL, AND LOCAL SERVICES

Tourist Agency: Enjoy Rome, V. Marghera, 8a (☎06 4456890; fax 06 4450734; www.enjoyrome.com). From the middle concourse of Termini (between the trains and the ticket booths), exit right, with the trains behind you. Cross V. Marsala. The office is on the 3rd block down V. Marghera. Owners Fulvia and Pierluigi answer questions and offer useful tidbits about the city free of charge and in perfect English. Enjoy Rome arranges hotel accommodations (as well as short-term apartments), Internet access and a full-service travel agency, booking transportation worldwide and lodgings throughout Italy. Enjoy Rome also runs offers four three-hour English tours (all L25,000 for those under 26; L30,000 for those 26 and over), including a superlative stroll through

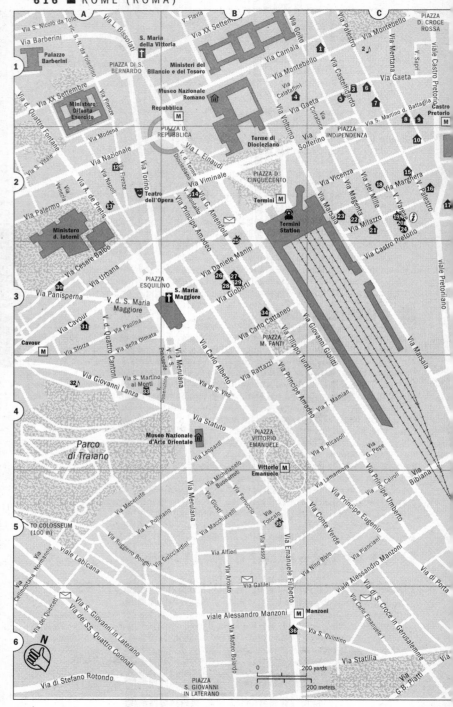

Rome: Termini & San Lorenzo

🏨 ACCOMMODATIONS

Hotel Adventure, 16	C2
Hotel Canada, 10	C2
Hotel Castelfidardo and Hotel Lazzari, 1	C1
Hotel Cervia, 15	C2
Hotel Des Artistes, 9	C1
Hotel Dolomiti and Hotel Lachea, 8	C1
Hotel Fenicia, 21	C2
Hotel Galli, 21	C2
Hotel Giu' Giu', 14	B2
Hotel Il Castello, 36	B6
Hotel Kennedy, 34	B3
Hotel Magic, 21	C2
Hotel Marini, 7	C1
Hotel Orlanda, 28	B3
Hotel Pensione Stella, 6	C1
Hotel Roxena, 23	C2
Hotel San Paolo, 30	A3
Hotel Selene, 14	B2
Hotel Serena and Pensione delle Rose, 27	B3
Hotel Sweet Home, 26	B3
Hotel Teti, 28	B3
Hotel Ventura, 16	C2
Pensione Cortorillo, 29	B3
Pensione di Rienzo, 26	B3
Pensione Ester, 17	C2
Pensione Fawlty Towers, 22	C2
Pensione Katty, 7	C1
Pensione Papa Germano, 4	B1
Pensione Sandy, 6	C1

🛍 SHOPPING

Disfunzioni Musicali, 37, 57	D3, D4
Economy Book and Video Center, 12	A2

🔴 SERVICES

Enjoy Rome, 18, 24	C2

🍅 FOOD

Africa, 5	C1
Arancia Blu, 50	D5
Armando, 39	D4
Gold Bar, 13	A2
Hostaria Il Varesino, 19	C2
Il Capellaio Matto, 46	D5
Il Pulcino Ballerino, 47	D5
La Pantera Rosa, 38	E4
Osteria da Luciano, 25	B2
Pizzeria Il Maratoneta, 52	D4
Pizzeria l'Economica, 55	D4
Pizzeria la Pappardella, 44	D5
Ristorante da Lisa, 35	B5
Trattoria Colli Emiliani, 56	D4
Trattoria da Bruno, 20	C2

🍺 PUBS

Dalhu' Pub, 43	D5
Down Town, 45	D5
Drome, 58	D4
Druid's Den, 33	A4
Julius Caesar, 3	C1
Lancelot, 53	E4
Legend Pub, 58	D4
Lupo Alberto, 41	D4
Nirvana, 48	D5
Pigmalione, 42	D5
Pub Hallo'Ween, 40	D4
Skyline Club, 51	D5

♪ CLUBS

Hangar, 32	A4
Club 52, 2	C1
Il Giardini di Adone, 54	E4

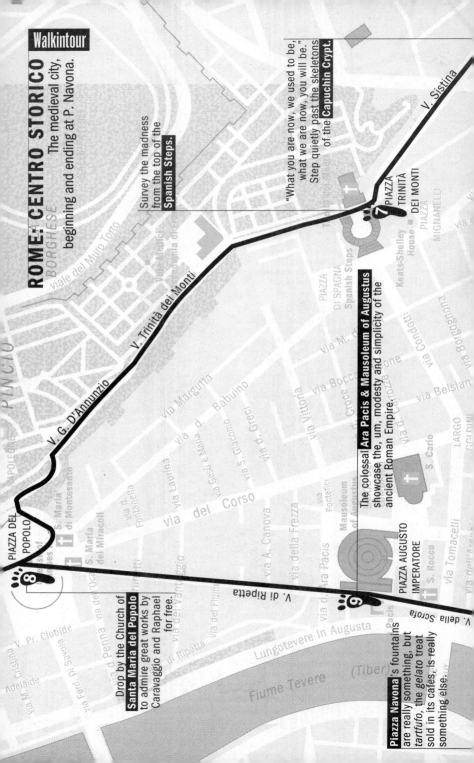

ROME: CENTRO STORICO

BORGHESE The medieval city, beginning and ending at P. Navona.

Walkintour

Survey the madness from the top of the **Spanish Steps**.

"What you are now, we used to be, what we are now, you will be." Step quietly past the skeletons of the **Capuchin Crypt.**

The colossal **Ara Pacis & Mausoleum of Augustus** showcase the, um, modesty and simplicity of the ancient Roman Empire.

Drop by the Church of **Santa Maria del Popolo** to admire great works by Caravaggio and Raphael for free.

Piazza Navona's fountains are really something, but *tartufo*, the gelato treat sold in its cafes, is really something else.

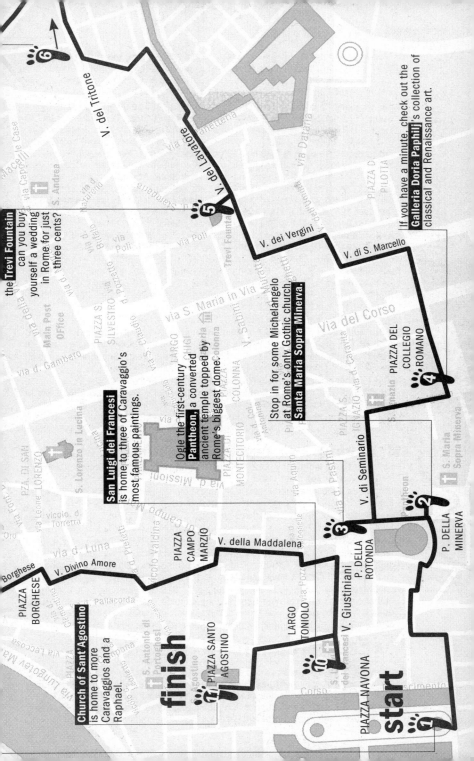

start ①

finish

the Trevi Fountain can you buy yourself a wedding in Rome for just three cents?

San Luigi dei Francesi is home to three of Caravaggio's most famous paintings.

Church of Sant'Agostino is home to more Caravaggios and a Raphael.

Ogle the first-century **Pantheon,** a converted ancient temple topped by Rome's biggest dome.

Stop in for some Michelangelo at Rome's only Gothic church, **Santa Maria Sopra Minerva.**

If you have a minute, check out the **Galleria Doria Paphili**'s collection of classical and Renaissance art.

② ③ ④ ⑤ ⑥ ⑦

PIAZZA NAVONA

PIAZZA BORGHESE

Borghese

V. Divino Amore

V. della Maddalena

V. Giustiniani

PIAZZA SANTO AGOSTINO

LARGO TONIOLO

P. DELLA ROTONDA

P. DELLA MINERVA

S. Maria Sopra Minerva

V. di Seminario

PIAZZA DEL COLLEGIO ROMANO

Via del Corso

V. di S. Marcello

V. dei Vergini

V. del Lavatore

V. del Tritone

Trevi Fountain

S. Andrea

Main Post Office

PIAZZA S. SILVESTRO

V. della Mercede

via d. Gambaro

S. Lorenzo in Lucina

PZA DI SAN LORENZO

vicolo d. Torretta

via d. Luna

PIAZZA CAMPO MARZIO

PIAZZA MONTECITORIO

PIAZZA COLONNA

S. Maria in Via

PIAZZA DI PILOTTA

PIAZZA DELLA PILOTTA

Trastevere and the Jewish Ghetto; and a comprehensive **bike tour** (L35,000); a bus tour (with film clips) of Rome's famous cinematic areas (L50,000); and Pompeii bus trips (L70,000). Branch office at V. Varese, 39 (walk down V. Marghera another block and turn right). Open M-F 8:30am-2pm and 3:30-6:30pm, Sa 8:30am-2pm.

Embassies and Consulates: Australia, V. Alessandria, 215 (☎06 852721, emergency 800 877790). Open M-Th 9am-5pm, F 9am-12:30pm. **Canada,** Consulate, V. Zara, 30 (☎06 44598421). Passport services open M-F 10am-noon and 2-4pm. Embassy, V. G. B. De Rossi, 27 (☎06 445981). **Ireland,** Consulate, P. Campitelli, 3 (☎06 6979121). Passport services open M-F 10am-12:30pm and 3-4:30pm. **New Zealand,** V. Zara, 28 (☎06 4417171). Consular and passport services open M-F 9:30am-noon. Embassy services M-F 8:30am-12:45pm and 1:45-5pm. **South Africa,** V. Tanaro, 14 (☎06 852541). Open M-F 9am-noon. **UK,** V. XX Settembre, 80a (☎06 4825441; consulate 06 42202600). Consular and passport services open M-F 9:15am-1:30pm. **US,** V. Veneto, 119a (☎06 46741). Passport and consular services open M-F 8:30-noon and 1:30-3:30pm. Visas M-F 8:30-10:30am. Closed US and Italian holidays.

American Express, P. di Spagna, 38 (☎06 67641; lost or stolen cards and/or checks ☎06 72281; fax 06 67642499). Open Sept.-July M-F 9am-7:30pm, Sa 9am-3pm. Aug. open M-F 9am-6pm, Sa 9am-12:30pm. Mail: P. di Spagna, 38; 00187 Roma.

Thomas Cook, P. Barberini, 21a (☎06 4828082). Open M-Sa 9am-8pm, Su 9:30am-5pm. Other branches: V. della Conciliazione, 23-25 (☎06 68300435; open M-Sa 8:30am-6pm, Su 9am-5pm); P. della Repubblica, 65 (☎06 486495; Open M-F 9am-5pm with 1hr. lunch break, Sa 9am-1pm).

Luggage Storage: In Termini, at track 22.

English Bookstores: ▧ **Libreria Feltrinelli International,** V. V. E. Orlando, 84-86 (☎06 482 78 78). Near P. della Repubblica. Open daily 9am-7:30pm. ▧ **Anglo-American Bookshop,** V. della Vite, 102 (☎06 679 52 22; www.aab.it). South of the Spanish Steps. Open M-F 9am-1pm and 4-8pm, Sa 9am-1pm.

Bi-Gay-Lesbian Services: ARCI-GAY, V. Orvinio, 2 (☎06 86385112) and V. Lariana, 8. (☎06 8555522). **Circolo di Cultura Omosessuale Mario Mieli, V. Corinto,** 5. (☎06 5413985; www.mariomieli.it. Open M-F 9am-1pm and 2-6pm; closed Aug.)

Laundromat: OndaBlu, OndaBlu, V. La Mora, 7 (☎800 861346). Many locations. Wash L6000 per 6½kg load; dry L6000 per 6½kg load; soap L1500. Open daily 8am-10pm.

EMERGENCY AND COMMUNICATIONS

Police: ☎113. **Carabinieri:** ☎112. **Ufficio Stranieri (Foreigners' Office):** V. Genova 2 (☎06 46 86 28 76). Open 24hr.

Pharmacies: Farmacia Internazionale, P. Barberini, 49 (☎06 487 11 95). **Farmacia Piram,** V. Nazionale 228 (☎06 488 07 54). Both open 24hr.

Hospital: First Aid, ☎118. **Policlinico Umberto I,** V.le di Policlinico, 155 (emergency ☎06 49971). M:B-Policlinico. Free first aid. Open 24hr.

Internet Access: ▧ **Marco's Bar,** V. Varese, 54 (☎06 44703591). Three blocks north of Termini, across the street from Enjoy Rome. Cool, laid-back atmosphere, with music, and a well-stocked bar. L8000 per hr. Open daily 5:30am-2am. Other internet cafes and kiosks litter the city; this is the cheapest and friendliest.

Post Office: Main Office, P. S. Silvestro 19, (☎06 679 8495). South of P. di Spagna. Address mail to be held: Ken Herrera, Palazzo delle Poste, *In Fermo Posta,* Roma **00186,** Italy. **Branch,** V. delle Terme di Diocleziano, 30 (☎06 4745602). Next to Termini. Both Open M-F 9am-6pm, Sa 9am-2pm. **Postal Codes:** 00100 to 00200.

▙ ACCOMMODATIONS

Rome swells with tourists around Easter, from May to July, and in September. Prices vary widely with the time of year, and a proprietor's willingness to negotiate increases in proportion to length of stay, number of vacancies, and group size. Termini is swarming with hotel scouts trying to bring you to their establishments. Watch out for sneaky imposters with fake badges, especially late at night.

CENTRO STORICO

If being a bit closer to the sights is important to you, then choosing Rome's medieval center over the area near Termini may be worth the higher prices.

Albergo Pomezia, V. dei Chiavari, 12 (☎/fax 06 6861 371). Behind S. Andrea della Valle. Rooms with phones and breakfast. Singles L70-100,000, with bath L100-170,000; doubles L100-170,000, L130-220,000; extra bed 35% surcharge.

Albergo della Lunetta, P. del Paradiso, 68 (☎06 6861 080). First right off V. dei Chiavari. Singles L90,000, with bath L110,000; doubles L140,000, L190,000; triples L190,000, L240,000; quads L240,000, 300,000.

Albergo Abruzzi, P. della Rotonda, 69 (☎06 6792 021). 200ft. from the Pantheon. Old-fashioned and clean. Singles L75-105,000; doubles L120-150,000; triples L200,000.

Hotel Piccolo, V. dei Chiavari, 32 (☎06 6892 330). Rooms with fans and phones. Breakfast L7000. Curfew 1am. Singles L100,000, with bath L120,000; doubles L120-160,000; triples with bath L170,000; quads with bath L180,000.

Hotel Navona, V. dei Sediari, 8, first Fl. (☎06 6864 203). V. dei Canestrari from P. Navona. This 16th-century Borromini building has been a *pensione* for 150 years. Breakfast included. Checkout 10am. Singles L140,000; doubles with bath L190,000, with A/C L220,000; triples with bath L260,000.

Albergo del Sole, V. del Biscione, 76 (☎06 68806873). Off Campo dei Fiori. Allegedly the oldest *pensione* in Rome. Parking garage (L30-40,000). Singles L110,000, with bath L130-160,000; doubles L150-170,000, L190-230,000.

Hotel Mimosa, V. Santa Chiara, 61, 2nd Fl. (☎06 68 80 17 53). Off P. della Minerva. Curfew 1am, but keys are available. Singles L110,000; doubles L150,000, with bath L170,000; extra bed L70,000. 10% less in winter.

NEAR PIAZZA DI SPAGNA

Can you really put a price tag on living a few steps from Prada? John Keats couldn't.

⊠ Pensione Panda, V. della Croce, 35 (☎06 6780 179) Enjoy the painted vaulted bathroom ceilings. Checkout 11am. In high season, singles L70,000, with bath L100,000; doubles L120-180,000; triples L180-210,000; quads L240-320,000.

Pensione Jonella, V. della Croce, 41 (☎06 6797 966). Quiet, roomy, and cool even in summer. No reception: call ahead to arrange for someone to meet you when you arrive. Singles L100,000; doubles L120,000. Cash only.

Hotel Pensione Suisse S.A.S., V. Gregoriana, 54 (☎06 6783 649). Breakfast included. Curfew 2am. Singles L135,000, with bath L155,000; doubles L165-225,000; triples L285,000; quads L340,000.

Hotel Boccaccio, V. del Boccaccio, 25 (☎06 4885 962). M:A-Barberini. Wood floors welcome you to an elegant decor and friendly staff. Singles L80,000; doubles L110,000, with bath L150,000; triples L140-180,000.

BORGO AND PRATI (NEAR VATICAN CITY)

Home to lots of priests and nuns, the Vatican and environs are pretty quiet at night.

⊠ Colors, V. Boezio, 31 (☎06 6874 030). M:A-Ottaviano. Take V. Cola di Rienzo to V. Terenzio. Sporting lots of amenities and a cool English-speaking staff, Internet, satellite TV, laundry. Terrace open until 11:30pm. Dorm beds L30,000; doubles L110-140,000; triples L130-170,000. Reserve with credit card; payment in cash only.

Pensione Ottaviano, V. Ottaviano, 6 (☎06 39 73 72 53). Satellite TV, individual lockers, fridges, a microwave, hot showers, free linens, and free email access for guests. Lockout 11am-2pm. Dorm-style rooms L30,000, L25,000 in the winter; doubles L90-60,000; triples L120,000.

Hotel Pensione Joli, V. Cola di Rienzo, 243, 6th fl. (☎06 3241 854). Winding, blue-striped walls. All rooms with bath and telephone. Breakfast included. Singles L110,000; doubles L160,000; triples L215,000; quads L270,000.

Hotel Florida, V. Cola di Rienzo, 243 (☎06 3241 872). Floral carpets, floral bedspreads, floral wall decorations. Rooms with fans, TVs, phones, and hair dryers. Singles with sink L120,000; with bath L140,000; doubles with bath L180,000; triples with bath L240,000; quads with bath L280,000.

Hotel Lady, V. Germanico, 198, 4th Fl. (☎06 3242 112). A boisterous Roman couple has been running this small *pensione* for 30 years. Phones in rooms. Singles L120,000; doubles L160,000, with bath L180,000.

TRASTEVERE

The streets of this artsy neighborhood come alive at night, and by day are filled with markets and working-class Romans going about their business.

Hotel Trastevere, V. Luciano Manara, 25 (☎06 5814 713). Take a right off V. di Trastevere onto V. delle Fratte di Trastevere. Nine quiet rooms with graceful furniture, bath, TV, phone. Breakfast L10,000. Singles L120,000; doubles L150,000; triples L180,000; quads L200,000.

Hotel Carmel, V. G. Mameli, 11 (☎06 5809 921; email hotelcarmel@hotmail.com). Take a right on V. E. Morosini off V. di Trastevere. All rooms with bath. Breakfast included. Singles L100,000; doubles L150,000; triples L190,000; quads L220,000.

TERMINI AND SAN LORENZO

Welcome to budget traveler central. The area south of Termini is sketchy at night.

NORTH OF TERMINI

■ **Pensione Fawlty Towers,** V. Magenta, 39 (☎06 4450 374; www.enjoyrome.it/ftytwhtl.htm). From Termini, cross V. Marsala onto V. Marghera, and turn right onto V. Magenta. Common room with TV, library, refrigerator, microwave, and free Internet. Check-out 9am for dorm rooms and 10am for private rooms. Dorm-style quads L30-35,000 per person (no children); singles L70-85,000; doubles L100,000, with shower L110,000, with bath L130,000; triples with shower L140,000, with bath L155,000.

Hotel Des Artistes, V. Villafranca, 20 (☎06 4454 365; www.hoteldesartistes.com). From Termini, turn left on V. Marsala, right on V. Vicenza, and then take the 5th left. Rooms for any budget, with bathrooms, safes, refrigerators, and TVs. 24hr. reception. Check-out 11am. Singles L70,000; doubles L110-170,000; triples L130-210,000; dorms (4-6 beds) L35,000. Winter 20-30% off.

Pensione Papa Germano, V. Calatafimi, 14a (☎06 48 69 19; www.hotelpapagermano.it). From Termini, turn left onto V. Marsala. Rooms with TV and phone. Internet access. Check-out 11am. Singles L45-60,000; doubles L70-100,000, with bath L90-130,000; triples with bath L100-150,000.

Hotel Dolomiti and **Hotel Lachea,** V. S. Martino della Battaglia, 11 (☎06 4957 256; www.hotel-dolomiti.it). From Termini, turn left on V. Marsala then right on V. Solferino (V. S. Martino della Battaglia). Breakfast L10,000. A/C L20,000 per night. Check-out 11am. Singles L75-120,000; doubles L85-180,000; triples 110-210,000; quads L140-230,000. Five-person rooms available at negotiable price.

Pensione Tizi, V. Collina, 48 (☎06 4820 128). From V. XX Settembre, take V. Piave, then go left on V. Flavia. Breakfast L9000. Check-out 11am. Singles L70,000, with bath L90,000; doubles L90-110,000; triples L120-148,000; quads L160-180,000.

Hotel Castelfidardo and **Hotel Lazzari,** V. Castelfidardo, 31 (☎06 4464 638). Off V. XX Settembre. Check-out 11am. Singles L70,000; doubles L95,000, with bath L120,000; triples L120-150,000; quads available.

Hotel Pensione Catharine, V. Volturno, 27 (☎06 48 36 34). From Termini, turn left onto V. Marsala (V. Volturno). Breakfast L10,000. Singles L75,000, with bath L100,000; doubles L100-120,000; triples with bath L160,000.

Hotel Adventure, V. Palestro, 88 (☎06 4469 026; www.hoteladventure.com). Off V. Marghera. Rooms with bath, satellite TV, phones, safes, and breakfast. Doubles L140,000; triples L200,000. Extra bed L35,000.

Hotel Bolognese, V. Palestro, 15 (☎06 49 00 45). The artist-owner provides extra amenities here and there. Check-out 11am. Curfew 2am. Singles L50,000, with bath L70-L80,000; doubles L80-120,000; triples L120-150,000.

Hotel Magic, V. Milazzo, 20 (☎06 4959 880). Most with bath, TV, and safe. Singles L90,000; doubles L130,000; triples L180,000; quads L200-220,000. A/C L20,000.

Hotel Baltic, V. XX Settembre, 89 (☎06 4814 775). Just past V. Palestro. Rooms with bath, TV, and phone. Breakfast L8000. Check-out 11am. Singles 90,000; doubles L120,000; triples L150,000; quads L195,000.

Pensione Monaco, V. Flavia, 84 (☎06 42 01 41 80). From V. XX Settembre, left on V. Quinto Sellia and right on V. Flavia. Check-out 9am. Student prices: singles L55,000, with bath L70,000; doubles L80-100,000; triples and quads L40,000 per person.

Pensione Piave, V. Piave, 14 (☎06 4743 447). Off V. XX Settembre. Very cozy bathrooms. Singles L65,000, with bath L95,000; doubles with bath L120,000; triples with bath L150,000; quads with bath L160-180,000.

Hotel Galli, V. Milazzo, 20 (☎06 4456 859). Rooms with bath, TV, mini-bar, safe, and breakfast. Singles L100,000; doubles L130,000; triples L180,000; quads L210,000. 10-15% lower in winter.

Hotel Fenicia, V. Milazzo, 20 (☎06 49 03 42; www.fenicia-web-page.net). Rooms with bath and TV. Singles L85,000; doubles L130,000. Extra beds L45,000. A/C L20,000.

Pensione Ester, V. del Castro Pretorio, 25 (☎06 4957 123). From Termini, turn right onto V. Marsala and left onto V. del Castro Pretorio. Airy rooms overlooking a lovely courtyard. Check-out 9am. Curfew 1am. Max. stay 10 days. Doubles L100,000; triples L135,000.

Hotel Cervia, V. Palestro, 55 (☎06 49 10 57; email hotelcervia@wnt.it). Rooms with bath include breakfast (L5000 otherwise). Check-out noon. Singles L70,000; doubles L90,000, with bath L140,000; triples L135-210,000.

Hotel Marini, V. Palestro, 35 (☎06 4440 058). This *pensione* glows with the proprietress's hospitality. All rooms have showers. Check-out 10am. Doubles L80-90,000.

Pensione Katty, V. Palestro, 35 (☎06 4441 216). Plain, large rooms. Check-out 11am. L2000 key deposit. Singles L75,000, with bath L90,000; doubles L90-130,000; triples L120-150,000; quads L140-160,000.

Hotel Ventura, V. Palestro, 88 (☎06 4451 951). Rooms with TVs and phones. Breakfast L10,000. Doubles L70,000, with bath L80,000; triples L90-105,000.

Hotel Pensione Stella, V. Castelfidardo, 51 (☎06 4441 078). Rooms with TVs, phones, luxurious baths, and teak furniture. Breakfast L10,000. Check-out 11am. Singles with bath L90,000; doubles L140,000; triples L170,000.

Hotel Roxena, V. Marghera, 13 (☎06 4456 823). A little drab, but trip out of Termini and you're here. Breakfast L10,000. Curfew 1am. 12 rooms. doubles L80,000, with bath L110,000; triples L105-130,000; quads L140,000.

SOUTH OF TERMINI (ESQUILINO)

Pensione di Rienzo, V. Principe Amedeo, 79a (☎06 4467 131). Plain, cheap, and good rooms. Breakfast L15,000. Check-out 10am. Singles L35-80,000, with bath up to L90,000; doubles L40-90,000, with bath up to L110,000.

Pensione Cortorillo, V. Principe Amedeo, 79a, 5th fl. (☎06 4466 934). TV and full bath in all rooms. Breakfast included. Check-out 10am. Singles L100,000; doubles L70-100,000; triples 210,000; quads L280,000.

Hotel Kennedy, V. F. Turati, 62-64 (☎06 4465 373; fax 06 446 54 17; email hotelkennedy@micanet.it). Private baths, satellite TV, phone, and A/C. Breakfast included. Check-out 11am. Reservations by fax only. Singles L105,000; doubles L169-179,000; triples L299,000.

Hotel Il Castello, V. V. Amedeo II, 9 (☎06 77 20 40 36; www.ilcastello.com). M:A-Manzoni. Take the first left off V. S. Quintino. A castle with small white rooms. Continental breakfast L5000. Check-out 10:30am. Dorm beds L30,000; singles L50-60,000; doubles L70-80,000, with bath L120-130,000; triples L105,000.

Hotel Orlanda, V. Principe Amedeo, 76, 3rd Fl. (☎06 4880 124). At V. Gioberti. Breakfast included. 24hr. reception. Check-out 10am. Singles L45-80,000, with bath L50-120,000; doubles L70-120,000, L90-180,000; triples L90-150,000, L120-220,000; quads L120-180,000, L160-280,000.

Hotel Giu' Giu', V. del Viminale, 8 (☎06 4827 734). In an elegant but fading *palazzo*. Breakfast L10,000. Check-out 10am. Singles L65,000; doubles L100,000, with bath L110,000; triples with bath L150,000; quads with bath L195,000.

Hotel Selene, V. del Viminale, 8 (☎06 4824 460). Rooms with bath, TV, phone, and breakfast. Singles L90,000; doubles L140,000; triples L190,000.

Hotel Sweet Home, V. Principe Amedeo, 47 (☎06 4880 954). At V. D. Manin. Checkout 11am. Singles L80-100,000, with bath L100-120,000; doubles L120-150,000/L150-180,000; triples 120-150,000/L180-210,000.

WEST OF TERMINI

Hotel San Paolo, V. Panisperna, 95 (☎06 4745 213; email hsanpaolo@tin.it). From Termini, take V. Cavour, then take a right onto V. di S. Maria Maggiore (V. Panisperna). Breakfast L10,000. Check-out 10:30am. Singles L75,000; doubles L100,000, with bath L140,000; triples L135,000; 6-10 person suite L50,000 per person.

Pensione Sandy, V. Cavour, 136 (☎06 4884 585; www.sandyhostel.com). Past Santa Maria Maggiore. No sign; look for the Hotel Valle next door. 4th floor, no elevator. Free Internet access. Individual lockers in each room. Mostly 2- to 4- person dorm rooms; L30,000, L25,000 in the winter.

CAMPING

Camping on beaches, roads, and inconspicuous plots is illegal.

Seven Hills Village, V. Cassia, 1216 (☎06 303310826). 8km north of Rome. Take bus #907 from the Cipro-Musei Vaticani Metro(A), or bus #201 from P. Mancini. Ask where to get off—it's 3-4km past the GRA (the big highway that circles the city). From the stop, follow the country road about 1km until you see the sign. Bar, market, restaurant, *pizzeria*, disco, pool. Daily Vatican shuttles leave at 8 and 9:30am, round-trip L6000. Check-in 7am-11pm. L15,000 per person, L9000 per tent, L9000 per car. Camper L16,000. Bungalow L90-150,000. Open late Mar. to late Oct.

⑤ FOOD

Ancient Roman dinners were lavish, festive affairs lasting as long as 10 hours. Peacocks and flamingos were served with their full plumage, while acrobats and fire-eaters distracted guests between their courses of camels' feet and goats' ears. Food orgies went on *ad nauseam*, literally—after gorging themselves, guests would retreat to a special room called the *vomitorium*, throw it all up, and return to the party. Meals in Rome are still lengthy affairs, although they generally involve less vomiting. Restaurants tend to close between 3 and 7pm, so plan accordingly.

RESTAURANTS

ANCIENT CITY

Despite its past glory, this area has yet to discover the noble concept of "affordable food." But along **V. dei Fori Imperiali,** several restaurants offer decent prices.

Taverna dei Quaranta, V. Claudia, 24 (☎06 7000 550), off P. del Colosseo. Outdoor dining at this *taverna* is a must. ½L of house wine L5000. Cover L3000. Open daily noon-3:30pm and 7:45pm-midnight.

I Buoni Amici, V. Aleardo Aleardi, 4 (☎06 70 49 19 93). From the Colosseum, take V. Labicana, turn right on V. Merulana, then left. *Linguine* with crayfish sauce L10,000. Cover L2500. Open M-Sa noon-3pm and 7-11:30pm.

CENTRO STORICO

The twisting streets of Rome's historic center offer many hidden gems, especially just off the main *piazzas*. No matter where you eat, you can expect to be subjected to numerous street performances, especially near P. Navona.

Pizzeria Baffetto, V. del Governo Vecchio, 114 (☎06 6861 617). At V. Sora. Once a meeting place for 60s radicals, Baffetto now overflows with Romans of the hungry persuasion. Always crowded. *Pizze* L8-14,000. Cover L1000. Open M-F noon-3pm and 7:30pm-1am, Sa-Su noon-3pm and 7:30pm-2am.

Pizzeria Pentola, V. Metastasio, 21 (☎06 68 80 26 07). Off P. di Campo Marzio. Ignore the menu: the delicious *pizze* (L8-16,000) are where it's at. Open daily noon-11pm.

Piedra del Sol, V. Rosini, 6 (☎06 6873 641). Off V. di Campo Marzio. Del Sol offers an Italian take on Mexican cooking. Try *Chimichangas del Sol* (L12,000). Margaritas L35,000 per liter. Open daily 12:30-3pm and 7:30pm-2am. Closed Aug.

CAMPO DEI FIORI AND THE JEWISH GHETTO

▓**Trattoria da Sergio,** V. delle Grotte, 27 (☎06 6546 669). Take V. dei Giubbonari and take your 1st right. Sergio offers honest-to-God Roman ambience and hearty portions of great food. Open M-Sa 12:30-3pm and 7pm-12:30am.

Ristorante da Giggetto, V. del Portico d'Ottavio, 21-22 (☎06 6861 105). Rightfully famous but increasingly pricey, Giggetto has some of the finest Roman cooking known to man. Cover L3000. Open Tu-Su 12:30-3pm and 7:30-11pm.

Al 16, V. del Portico d'Ottavio, 16 (☎06 6874 722). Near the Teatro di Marcello. Be fearless and try the *Coda alla Vaccinara* (oxtail stew; L16,000). Cover L2500. Open W-M 12:30-3pm and 7:30-11pm.

L'Insalata Ricca, Largo di Chiavari, 85 (☎06 68 80 36 56). Off C. V. Emanuele II. What kind of salad would you like? They have *all* of them (L10-16,000). Other locations: P. Pasquino, 72; V. del Gazometro, 62; P. Albania, 3; V. Polesine, 16; P. Risorgimento, 5; and V. F. Grinaldi, 52. Open daily 12:30-3:15pm and 6:45-11:15pm.

PIAZZA DI SPAGNA

Though the Spanish Steps area may seem very different from the less affluent environs of Termini, there is one big similarity—lots of bad food. The irony of it is that that the same awful food here will be twice as much. Here are some exceptions:

▓**Osteria dell'Ingegno,** P. di Pietra (☎06 6780 662), between the Trevi Fountain and the Pantheon. A modern take on Italian cuisine in an upscale setting. You also won't regret the daring cold eggplant soup with mint and yogurt (L16,000). *Secondi* (L20-30,000). Open M-Sa noon-3pm and 7:30pm-midnight.

Centro Macrobiotico Italiano-Naturist Club, V. della Vite, 14, 4th fl. (☎06 6792 509). Just off V. del Corso. The Naturist Club offers up extremely fresh, well-seasoned macrobiotic and vegetarian fare at low prices in its breezy attic restaurant. *Primi* L10-12,000; *secondi* L12-18,000. Open M-F noon-3:30pm and 7:30-11pm.

BORGO & PRATI (NEAR VATICAN CITY)

Establishments near the Vatican serve mediocre sandwiches at hiked-up prices. Just a few blocks northeast is far better and much cheaper food.

Franchi, V. Cola di Rienzo, 200-204 (☎06 6874 651). Franchi ("Frankie") has been serving the happy folks of Prati superb sandwiches and other luxurious picnic supplies for nearly 50 years, and not an unsatisfied customer yet. Open M-Sa 8:15am-9pm.

Pizza Re, V. Oslavia, 39 (☎06 3721 173). Called by many the best pizza in Rome, this chain serves Neopolitan (thick crust) pizzas with every topping imaginable. Lunch specials (pizza and drink) L11-13,000. Open M-Sa noon-3:30pm, daily 7:30-11pm.

ITALY

TRASTEVERE

By day, Trastevere's cobblestone streets rumble only with the sounds of children and Vespas, but when night falls, P. di Santa Maria di Trastevere is packed with expatriate hippies and their dogs, howling along with out-of-tune guitars.

Pizzeria San Calisto, P. S. Calisto, 9a (☎06 5818 256). Off P. S. Maria in Trastevere. The *bruschetta* (L3-4000) alone is worth a postcard home. Open Tu-Su 7pm-midnight.

Augusto, P. de' Rienzi, 15 (☎06 5803 798). North of P. S. Maria in Trastevere. Enjoy the daily pasta specials at lunch (around L8000). The homemade desserts are out of this world. Open M-F 12:30-3pm and 8-11pm, Sa 12:30-3pm. Closed Aug.

Ristorante al Fontanone, P. Trilussa, 46 (☎06 5817 312). North of P. S. Maria in Trastevere. Small restaurant with traditional Roman food, including *rigatoni con pajata* (L13,000). Open W-Su noon-2pm and 7-11pm. Closed mid-Aug. to early Sept.

TERMINI

You're near the train station, hungry, and in a hurry. This is no reason to subject yourself to the nightmare of a shady tourist trap offering a L10,000 "quick lunch."

▨ La Cantinola da Livio, V. Calabria, 26 (☎06 4282 0519). From V. XX Settembre, turn left on V. Piave, and then take the 4th left onto V. Calabria. The *spaghetti* with seafood, caviar, tomato, and cream (L12,000) is transcendent. Lobster L120,000. Cover L1500. Open M-Sa 12:30-3pm and 7:20-11:30pm. Closed first 3 weeks of Aug.

Africa, V. Gaeta, 26-28 (☎06 4941 077). Near P. Independenza. Excellent Ethiopian food. *Zighini beghi* (roasted lamb in spicy sauce; L12,000) and the *misto vegetariano* (mixed veggie dishes; L11,000) are fantastic. Cover L1500. Open M-Sa 8pm-midnight.

Gold Bar, P. del Viminale, 1 (☎06 4819 227). Off V. A. Depretis. Excellent fare at reasonable prices. Main dishes L4-5000. Open M-F noon-3pm.

Ristorante da Lisa, V. Foscolo, 16-18 (☎06 73 00 27). South of P. V. Emanuele II. A homey kosher restaurant. Try *burik con patate* (potatoes, cinnamon, and parsley wrapped in a crepe, L3000) or *kuskus bianco* (L5000). Open Su-F 1-3pm and 7-11pm.

SAN LORENZO

Rome's funky university district, San Lorenzo offers many good, cheap eateries. From Termini, walk south on V. Pretoriano to P. Tiburtino, or take bus #492. Women may find the walk a little uncomfortable at night.

Il Pulcino Ballerino, V. degli Equi, 66-68 (☎06 4941 255). Off V. Tiburtina. An artsy scene with cuisine to match. Prepare your own meal on a heated stone. Cover L1000. Open M-Sa 1-3:30pm and 8pm-midnight. Closed first week of Aug.

Arancia Blu, V. dei Latini, 65 (☎06 4454 105). Off V. Tiburtina. An elegant little vegetarian restaurant with elaborate dishes like *tonnarelli* with sheep cheese and truffles (L12,000). Extensive wine list. Open M-F noon-3pm and 7-11pm, Sa-Su 7-11pm.

Il Capellaio Matto, V. dei Marsi, 25. From V. Tiburtina, take the 4th right off V. degli Equi. Vegetarians, rejoice! This offbeat place offers imaginative salads, and a variety of crepes (L7-9000). Plenty of meat dishes, too. Cover L1500. Open W-M 8pm-midnight.

TESTACCIO

Once home to a giant slaughterhouse, this working-class southern neighborhood is the center of Roman nightlife. True to their roots, Testaccio eateries offer food made of just about every animal part imaginable.

Pizzeria Ficini, V. Luca della Robbia, 23 (☎06 5743 017). Take V. Luigi Vanvitelli off V. Marmorata, then the first left. A no-frills pizzeria befitting this working-class community. *Pizzas* (L6-8000). *Calzone* L8000. 1L wine L6000. Open Sept.-July Tu-Su 6-11:30pm.

Luna Piena, V. Luca della Robbia, 15-17 (☎06 5750 279). Savor the stupendous *carpaccio di salmone* appetizer (L10,000) or the excellent *rigatoni con pagliata* (L10,000). Open Th-Tu noon-3pm and 7:30-11:30pm.

DESSERTS

Cheap *gelato* is as plentiful on Roman streets as pairs of leather pants. Look for *gelato* with very muted (hence natural) colors, or try some of our favorite *gelaterie* and other sweet-shops.

San Crispino, V. della Panetteria, 42 (☎06 6793 924). Near P. di Trevi. Positively the world's best *gelato*. Don't miss the meringue, armagnac, and grapefruit flavors. Cups L3-10,000. Open M and W-Th noon-12:30am, F-Sa noon-1:30am, Su noon-midnight.

Tre Scalini, P. Navona, 30 (☎06 6880 1996). This chic, old-fashioned spot is famous for its *tartufo,* a hunk of truffled chocolate ice cream rolled in chocolate shavings (L5000 at the bar, L11,000 sitting). Bar open Th-Tu 9am-1:30am.

Forno del Ghetto, V. Portico d'Ottavia, 1 (☎06 6878637). This unmarked pastry bakery deep in the Jewish Ghetto serves fabulous blueberry pies, buttery cookies, chocolate, and pudding concoctions at excellent prices. Take-out only. Open Su-Th 8am-8pm, F 8am-5:30pm. Closed Jewish holidays.

ENOTECHE (WINE BARS)

Roman wine bars range from laid-back and local to chic and international.

Trimani Wine Bar, V. Cernaia, 37b (☎06 4469630). Near Termini, perpendicular to V. Volturno (V. Marsala). Pastas (L12,000), filling quiches (try the spiny lobster and leek quiche; L9000), smoked fish, impressive cheese board, and desserts. Wines from L3500 a glass. Open M-Sa 11am-3:30pm and 6pm-12:30am.

La Bottega del Vino da Anacleto Bleve, V. S. Maria del Pianto, 9a-11 (☎06 6865970). Wonderful light meals of pasta (L9-12,000) and a range of French and Italian cheeses, smoked fish, cured meats, and creative salads. Superlative wine list. Glasses begin at L4000. Open Tu and Sa 12:45-3pm, W-F 12:45-3pm and 8-10pm.

Bar Da Benito, V. dei Falegnami, 14 (☎06 6861508). Off P. Mattei in the Jewish Ghetto. You can't get more authentic than this: a tiny shop lined with bottles and hordes of hungry workmen. One hot pasta is prepared each day (L6000), along with delicious *secondi.* Open M-Sa 6am-8pm; lunch noon-3:30pm. Closed Aug.

◾ SIGHTS

Rome wasn't built in a day, and it's not likely that you'll see any substantial portion of it in 24 hours, either. Ancient temples and forums, Renaissance basilicas, 280 fountains, and 981 churches cluster together in a city bursting with masterpieces from every era of Western civilization. From Etruscan busts to modern canvases, there is more than enough in Rome to captivate visitors for years on end. A **six-day ticket book** is good for the three Musei Nazionali Romani (see p. 636), the Colosseum, and the Palatine Hill (L30,000).

ANCIENT CITY

ROMAN FORUM

Main entrance: V. dei Fori Imperiali (between P. Venezia and the Colosseum). Other entrances are opposite the Colosseum (from here, you can reach the Palatine Hill, too) and at the Clivus Capitolinus, near P. del Campidoglio. M:B-Colosseo, or bus to P. Venezia. Open M-Sa 9am-7pm, Su 9am-1pm; in winter M-Sa 9am-1hr. before sunset, Su 9am-1hr. before sunset; sometimes closes M-F by 3pm, Su and holidays by noon. Free. Guided tour with archaeologist L6000; audioguide tour for Forum L7000.

Here the people who would be known as the Romans founded a thatched-hut shantytown in 753 BC, when Romulus and Sabine leader Titus Tatius met to end the war triggered by the famous rape of the Sabine women. The entrance ramp leads to **Via Sacra,** Rome's oldest street, near the area once known as the **Civic Forum,** where the **Basilica Aemilia,** built in 179 BC, housed the guild of the *argentarii* (money changers). Next to the Basilica Aemilia stands the **Curia,** or Senate House, one of the oldest buildings in the Forum. It was converted to a church in 630 and restored by Mussolini. The broad space in front of the Curia was the **Comitium,** where male

CIAO MEOW Thanks to a bizarre 1988 law, Rome's stray cats have the right to live where they're born. Today, there are 10,000 colonies, hundreds of which are fed by the city. Look for the felines among the ruins, especially near Largo Argentina. These *colonie* of feral cats have a long history with the Eternal City—supposedly it stretches back to the 17th century. Rome's famous ruins were largely undisturbed, and grass had begun to overrun the meadows between different parishes. Shephards from Campagna would come to let there flocks graze and trim the grass, with them they brought pet cats, who ran away to breed prolifically in the tunnels of the ruins. The result? A trip to the Colosseum may end up reminding tourists of a certain Andrew Lloyd Webber musical that shall remain nameless... Ahh, memories..

citizens came to vote and representatives of the people gathered for public discussion. Bordering the Comitium is the large brick **Rostrum,** or speaker's platform, erected by Julius Caesar in 44 BC, just before his death. The hefty **Arch of Septimius Severus,** to the right of the Rostrum, was dedicated in 203 to celebrate that emperor's victories in the Middle East. The **market square** holds a number of shrines and sacred precincts, including the **Lapis Niger** (Black Stone), where Romulus was supposedly murdered by Republican senators, which once graced the square in front of the Curia. Below the Lapis Niger rest the underground ruins of a 6th-century BC altar, along with a pyramidal pillar where the oldest known Latin inscription in Rome warns against defiling the shrine. In the square the **Three Sacred Trees** of Rome—olive, fig, and grape—have been replanted by the Italian state. The newest part of the Forum is the **Column of Phocas,** erected in 608 for the visiting Byzantine emperor, Phocas. The three great temples of the **Lower Forum** have been closed off for excavations and restoration; however, the eight columns of the early 5th-century BC **Temple of Saturn,** next to the Rostrum, have at last shed their cloak of scaffolding. Around the corner, rows of column bases are all that remain of the **Basilica Julia,** a courthouse built by Julius Caesar in 54 BC. At the far end, three white marble columns and a shred of architrave mark the massive podium of the recently restored **Temple of Castor and Pollux,** built to celebrate the Roman defeat of the Etruscans. The circular building next to it is the **Temple of Vesta,** which dates back to the time of the Etruscans. In this temple, the Vestal Virgins tended the city's eternal, sacred fire, keeping it lit for more than a thousand years.

In the **Upper Forum** lies the **House of the Vestal Virgins,** which, shaded by the Palatine Hill, occupied the sprawling complex of rooms and courtyards behind the Temple of Vesta. For 30 years, the six virgins who officiated over Vesta's rites lived in seclusion here, starting at the ripe old age of seven. As long as they kept their vows of chastity, they remained among the most respected people in ancient Rome. This esteem, however, had its price; a virgin who strayed was buried alive with a loaf of bread and a candle, which would allow her to survive long enough to contemplate her sins. Near here, V. Sacra runs over the **Cloaca Maxima,** the ancient sewer that still drains water from the otherwise marsh-like valley. V. Sacra continues out of the Forum proper to the **Velia,** where the gargantuan **Basilica of Maxentius** (also known as the Basilica of Constantine) is found. The middle apse of the basilica once contained a gigantic statue of Constantine—the body was bronze, the head, legs, and arms marble. The uncovered remains, including a two-meter-long foot, are on exhibit at the **Palazzo dei Conservatori** on the Capitoline Hill (see p. 630). V. Sacra leads to an exit on the other side of the hill to the Colosseum; the path that crosses before the **Arch of Titus** heads to the Palatine Hill.

THE PALATINE HILL

Open M-Sa 9:30am-7:15pm, Su 9am-1pm; in winter M-Sa 9:30am-1hr. before sunset, Su 9am-1pm; sometimes closes M-F by 3pm, Su and holidays by noon. Last entrance 45min. before closing. L12,000, EU citizens between 18 and 24 L6000, EU citizens under 18 and over 60 free. A six-day ticket book is good for the three Musei Nazionali Romani (see p. 636), the Colosseum, and the Palatine Hill (L30,000).

The best way to attack the Palatine is from the stairs near the Forum's **Arch of Titus.** The hill, actually a plateau between the Tiber and the Forum, was home to the she-wolf that suckled Romulus and Remus. Throughout the garden complex, terraces provide breathtaking views. Lower down, excavations continue on the 9th-century BC village, the **Casa di Romulo.** To the right of the village is the podium of the 191 BC **Temple of Cybele.** The stairs to the left lead to the **House of Livia,** which is connected to the **House of Augustus** next door. Around the corner, the long, spooky **Cryptoporticus** connected Tiberius' palace with the buildings nearby. The short end of the tunnel, the path around the House of Augustus, leads to the vast ruins of a giant palace built by **Domitian** (81-96) and is divided into two wings. The solemn **Domus Augustana** was the private space for the emperors. Adjacent to the Domus Augustana lies the other wing of the palace and the sprawling **Domus Flavia,** site of a gigantic octagonal fountain that occupied almost the entire courtyard. Between the Domus Augustana and the Domus Flavia stands the **Palatine Antiquarium,** the museum that houses the major artifacts found during the excavations of the Palatine Hill. *(30 people admitted every 20min. starting at 9:10am. Free.)* Outside on the right, the palace's east wing contains the curious **Stadium of Domitian,** or *Hippodrome,* a sunken oval space once surrounded by a colonnade, but now decorated with fragments of porticoes, statues, and fountains.

FORI IMPERIALI. Across the street from the Ancient Forum are the Fori Imperiali, a conglomeration of temples, basilicas, and public squares constructed in the 1st and 2nd centuries. Built between 107 and 113 to celebrate the emperor's Dacian campaign (in modern-day Romania), the **Forum of Trajan** included a colossal equestrian statue of Trajan and an immense triumphal arch. At one end of the now decimated forum 2500 legionnaires march their way up the almost perfectly preserved spiral of ◼**Trajan's Column,** one of the greatest extant specimens of Roman relief-sculpture. The crowing statue is St. Peter, who replaced Trajan in 1588. Across V. dei Fori Imperiali, in the shade of the Vittorio Emanuele II monument, lie the paltry remains of the **Forum of Caesar,** including the ruins of Julius Caesar's **Temple to Venus Genetrix** (Mother Venus, from whom he claimed descent). Nearby, the gray tufa wall of the **Forum of Augustus** commemorates Augustus's victory over Caesar's murderers at the Battle of Philippi in 42 BC. The aptly named **Forum Transitorium** (also called the **Forum of Nerva**) was a narrow, rectangular space connecting the Forum of Augustus with the Republican Roman Forum. The only remnant of **Vespatian's Forum** is the mosaic-filled **Church of Santi Cosma e Damiano** across V. Cavour, near the Roman Forum. *(Open daily 9am-1pm and 3-7pm.)*

◼**THE COLOSSEUM.** The enduring symbol of the Eternal City—a hollowed-out ghost of travertine marble that dwarfs every other ruin in Rome; it once held as many as 50,000 crazed spectators. Within 100 days of its AD 80 opening, some 5000 wild beasts perished in the bloody arena (from the Latin word for sand, *harena,* which was put on the floor to absorb blood), and the slaughter went on for three more centuries. The floor (now partially restored and open for various concerts and Italian variety TV shows) covers a labyrinth of brick cells, ramps, and elevators used to transport wild animals from cages up to arena level. *(M:B-Colosseo. Open daily 9am-6:30pm; in winter daily 9am-1hr. before sunset. L10,000, EU citizens under 18 and over 60 free, EU citizens 18-24 L5000. Tours with archaeologist L6000; audioguide L7000.)*

ARCO DI CONSTANTINO. Between the Colosseum and the Palatine lies the **Arch of Constantine,** one of the latest and best-preserved imperial monuments to grace the area. Constantine built it to commemorate his victory over Maxentius at the Battle of the Milvian Bridge in 312. He used fragments from earlier monuments of Trajan, Hadrian, and Marcus Aurelius to create the harmonious triple arch.

THE DOMUS AUREA. This park houses just a portion of Nero's "Golden House," which once covered a huge chunk of Rome. Having decided that he was a god, Nero had the architects Severus and Celer make a house worthy of his divinity. The Forum was reduced to a vestibule of the palace; Nero crowned it with a colossal statue of himself as the sun. Standing 35m tall, the *Colossus* was the largest bronze statue ever made; it's where the Flavian Amphitheater got its nickname. The party didn't last long, however. Nero committed suicide only five years after building his gargantuan pleasure garden. Later Flavian emperors tore down his house and replaced all traces of the palace with monuments built for the public good. *(On the Oppian Hill, below Trajan's baths. From the Colosseum, walk through the gates up V. della Domus Aurea and make the first right. ☎06 39749907. Open Tu-Su 9am-8pm. Groups of 30 admitted every 15min. L10,000. Reservations recommended for all visits. L2000, L3000 for guided tour.)*

THE VELABRUM. The Velabrum is a flat flood plain south of the Jewish Ghetto. At the bend of V. del Portico d'Ottavia, a shattered pediment and a few ivy-covered columns are all that remain of the once magnificent **Portico d'Ottavia.** The stocky, gray **Teatro di Marcello** next door bears the name of Augustus's unfortunate nephew, whose early and sudden death remains a mystery. Farther down V. di Teatro di Marcello, **Chiesa di San Nicola in Carcere** incorporates three Roman temples originally dedicated to Juno, Janus, and Spes. *(☎06 6869 972; call to visit the interior. Open Sept.-July M-Sa 7:30am-noon and 4-7pm.)* Across the street, the **Chiesa di Santa Maria in Cosmedin** harbors some of Rome's most beautiful medieval decoration. The 12th-century porch and tower welcome bus loads of tourists on their way to see the portico's relief, the ▧**Bocca della Verità,** made famous by the Audrey Hepburn film, *Roman Holiday.* According to legend, the hoary face will chomp on the hand of a liar. *(Portico open daily 9am-7pm. Church open daily 10am-1pm and 3-7pm.)*

THE CAPITOLINE HILL. Home to the original capitol, the **Monte Capitolino** still serves as the seat of the city government. Michelangelo designed its crowning **Piazza di Campidoglio,** now home to the **Capitoline Museums** (see p. 636). Stairs lead up to the rear of the 7th-century **Chiesa di Santa Maria in Aracoeli.** The gloomy **Mamertine Prison,** consecrated the **Church of San Pietro in Carcere,** lies down the hill from the back stairs of the Aracoeli. Peter, imprisoned here, baptized his captors with the waters that flooded his cell. *(☎06 6792 902. Open daily 9am-noon and 2:30-6pm. Donation requested.)* At the far end of the *piazza,* opposite the stairs, lies the turreted **Palazzo dei Senatori,** which houses Rome's mayor. When Paul III remodeled the top of the hill for Charles V's visit, he not only had Michelangelo fashion the imposing statues of the twin warriors Castor and Pollux, but he also had the famous equestrian **statue of Marcus Aurelius** brought here from the Lateran Palace. *(To get to the Campidoglio, take any bus that goes to P. Venezia. From P. Venezia, face the Vittorio Emanuele II monument, walk around to the right to P. d'Aracoeli, and take the stairs up the hill.)*

CIRCUS MAXIMUS AND BATHS OF CARACALLA. Boxed in the valley between the Palatine and Aventine Hills, today's **Circus Maximus** is just a grassy shadow of its former glory. After its construction in about 600 BC, the circus drew more than 300,000 Romans, who gathered here to watch chariots careen around the quarter-mile track. The remains of the **Baths of Caracalla** are the largest and best-preserved baths in the city. *(M:B-Circo Massimo, or walk down V. di San Gregorio from the Colosseum. Circus is always open. To get to the baths, take V. delle Terme di Caracalla from the eastern end of the Circus. ☎06 575 86 26. Open daily 9am-6pm; in winter 9am-1hr. before sunset. L8000.)*

CENTRO STORICO

PIAZZA VENEZIA AND VIA DEL CORSO. Following the line of the ancient V. Lata, the **Via del Corso** takes its name from its days as Rome's premier racecourse. It runs nearly a mile between P. del Popolo and the rumbling P. Venezia (not much more than a glorified traffic circle dominated by the **Vittorio Emanuele II monument**). The crumbling **Palazzo Venezia,** right of the *piazza* as you face the monument, was one of the first Renaissance *palazzi* built in the city. Mussolini used it as an office and delivered his famous orations from its balcony. Off V. del Corso, the picturesque **Piazza Colonna** was named for the colossal **Colonna di Marco Aurelio,** designed in imitation of the emperor Trajan's earlier triumphant column. The northwest corner of the *piazza* flows into **Piazza di Montecitorio.** Bernini's **Palazzo Montecitorio,** now the seat of the Chamber of Deputies, dominates P. di Montecitorio.

THE PANTHEON. With its granite columns and pediment, bronze doors, and soaring domed interior, this famous temple has stood remarkably the same since the day it was built nearly 2000 years ago. Architects still puzzle over how it was erected—its dome, a perfect half-sphere constructed from poured concrete without the support of vaults, arches, or ribs, is the largest of its kind. The light that enters the roof was used as a sundial to indicate the passing of the hours and the dates of equinoxes and solstices. In 606, it was consecrated as the **Church of Santa Maria ad Martyres,** its official name to this day. *(Open June M-Sa 9am-7pm, Su 9am-1pm; July-Aug. M-Sa 9am-7:30pm, Su 9am-1pm; Oct.-May M-Sa 9am-4pm, Su 9am-1pm. Free.)*

PIAZZA NAVONA. Originally a stadium built by Domitian in 86, the area once saw wrestling matches and track and field events. It even hosted mock naval battles, for which the stadium was flooded and filled with fleets skippered by convicts. Bernini's **Fountain of the Four Rivers** commands the posh P. Navona. Each of the river god statues represents one of the four continents of the globe (as they were thought of then): the Ganges for Asia, the Danube for Europe, the Nile for Africa (veiled, since the source of the river was unknown), and the Rio de la Plata for the Americas. At the ends of the *piazza* are the **Fontana del Moro** and the **Fontana di Nettuno,** designed by Giacomo della Porta in the 16th century and renovated by Bernini in 1653. With a (relatively) new Borromini-designed exterior, the **Church of Sant'Agnese** dominates the *piazza*'s western side. *(Open Tu-Sa 4:30-7pm, Su 10am-1pm.)* On nearby C. del Rinascimento, the **Chiesa di Sant'Ivo**'s corkscrew cupola hovers over the **Palazzo della Sapienza,** original home of the University of Rome.

OTHER SIGHTS. In front of the temple, the *piazza* centers on Giacomo della Porta's late-Renaissance fountain, which supports an Egyptian **obelisk** added in the 18th century. Around the left side of the Pantheon, another obelisk, supported by Bernini's curious elephant statue, marks the center of tiny **Piazza Minerva.** Behind the obelisk, the **Chiesa di Santa Maria Sopra Minerva** hides some Renaissance masterpieces, including Michelangelo's *Christ Bearing the Cross, Annunciation* by Antoniazzo Romano, and a statue of St. Sebastian recently attributed to Michelangelo. The south transept houses the famous **Cappella Carafa,** home to a brilliant fresco cycle by Filippino Lippi. *(Open M-Sa 7am-7pm, Su 7am-1pm and 3:30-7pm.)* From the upper left-hand corner of P. della Rotonda, V. Giustiniani goes north to intersect V. della Scrofa and V. della Dogana Vecchia. Here stands **Chiesa di San Luigi dei Francesi,** the French National Church, home to three of Caravaggio's most famous paintings: *The Calling of St. Matthew, St. Matthew and the Angel,* and *Crucifixion.* *(Open F-W 7:30am-12:30pm and 3:30-7pm, Th 7:30am-12:30pm.)*

CAMPO DEI FIORI

Campo dei Fiori lies across C. V. Emanuele II from P. Navona. During papal rule, the area was the site of countless executions. In the middle of the Campo, a statue marks the spot of the death of **Giordano Bruno** (1548-1600). Now the only carcasses that litter the *piazza* are of the cod in the colorful produce, fish, and flower **market** that springs up every day except Sunday from 6am to 2pm. The huge, stately **Palazzo Farnese** dominates P. Farnese, south of the Campo. Alessandro Farnese, the first Counter-Reformation pope (1534-1549), built this, the greatest of Rome's Renaissance *palazzi*. To the east of the *palazzo* is the Baroque facade of the **Palazzo Spada** and the collection of the **Galleria Spada** (see p. 591).

THE JEWISH GHETTO. The Jewish community in Rome is the oldest in Europe—Israelites came in 161 BC as ambassadors from Judas Maccabei, asking for Imperial help against invaders. The Ghetto, the tiny area to which Pope Paul IV confined the Jews in 1555, was closed in 1870, but is still the center of Rome's vibrant Jewish population of 16,000. **Piazza Mattei,** in the center of the ghetto, is home to the 16th-century **Fontana delle Tartarughe.** Nearby is the **Church of Sant'Angelo in Pescheria,** installed inside the Portico d'Ottavia in 755 and named after the fish market that once flourished here. Jews were forced to attend mass here every Sunday; they quietly resisted by stuffing their ears with wax. *(Take bus #64. Open for prayer meetings W 5:30pm* *and Sa 5pm.)* Built between 1874 and 1904 on the Tiber near the Theater of Marcellus, the **Sinagoga Ashkenazita** was bombed in 1982; guards now search and question all visitors. The temple houses a **museum** with Holocaust and religious artifacts. *(☎06 6875 051. Open for services or tour through the museum.)*

PIAZZA DI SPAGNA AND ENVIRONS

■ **THE SPANISH STEPS.** Designed by an Italian, funded by the French, named for the Spaniards, occupied by the British, and under the sway of American ambassador-at-large Ronald McDonald, the **Scalinata di Spagna** exude an international air. When the steps were built in 1725, hopeful artists' models flocked here dressed as the Madonna and Julius Caesar. The pink house to the right of the Steps was the site of John Keats's 1821 death; it's now the **Keats-Shelley Memorial Museum.**

■ **FONTANA DI TREVI.** Nicolo Salvi's (1697-1751) extravagant **Fontana di Trevi** emerges from the back wall of **Palazzo Poli**, dwarfing the narrow *piazza*. The bodacious Anita Ekberg took a dip in the fountain in Fellini's *La Dolce Vita*. Legend has it that a traveler who throws a coin into the fountain is ensured a speedy return to Rome; a traveler who tosses two will fall in love in Rome. The reality is that these coins damage the travertine marble: go figure. Opposite the fountain is the Baroque **Chiesa dei Santi Vincenzo e Anastasio,** rebuilt in 1630. The crypt preserves the hearts and lungs of popes from 1590-1903.

MAUSOLEUM OF AUGUSTUS AND ARA PACIS. The circular brick mound of the **Masoleo d'Agosto** once housed the funerary urns of the Imperial family. West of the mausoleum, the glass-encased **Ara Pacis** (Altar of Augustan Peace), is propaganda completed in 9 BC to celebrate Augustus's success. *(In P. Augusto Imperatore. From P. del Popolo, take V. di Ripetta toward the Tiber. Ara Pacis Tu-Sa 9am-7pm, Su 9am-1pm. L3750.)*

PIAZZA DEL POPOLO. P. del Popolo, once a favorite venue for public executions of heretics, is now the lively "people's square." In the center is the 3200-year-old **Obelisk of Pharaoh Ramses II,** which Augustus brought back as a souvenir from Egypt in the first century BC. Behind a simple early Renaissance shell, the **Chiesa di Santa Maria del Popolo** contains several Renaissance and Baroque masterpieces. *(☎06 3610 487. Open daily 7am-noon and 4-7pm.)* The **Cappella della Rovere** holds Pinturicchio's *Adoration*, and two exquisite Caravaggios, *The Conversion of St. Paul* and *Crucifixion of St. Peter*, are in the **Cappella Cerasi.** Raphael designed the **Cappella Chigi** for the wealthy Sienese banker Agostino Chigi. At the southern end of the *piazza* are the 17th-century **twin churches** of Santa Maria di Montesano, on the left, with a facade by Bernini, and Santa Maria dei Miracoli.

VILLA BORGHESE. In celebration of becoming a cardinal, Scipione Borghese built the **Villa Borghese** north of P. di Spagna and V. V. Veneto. Its huge park is home to three notable art museums: the world-renowned **Galleria Borghese** (see p. 636), the stark **Galleria Nazionale d'Arte Moderna** (see p. 636), and the intriguing **Museo Nazionale Etrusco di Villa Giulia** (see p. 636). North of the Borghese are the **Santa Priscilla catacombs.** *(V. Salaria, 430, just before V. Antica crosses V. Ardeatina. Take bus #57 or #219 from Termini or bus #56 from V. del Tritone to P. Vescovio; walk down V. di Tor Fiorenza to P. di Priscilla. (☎06 86 20 62 72. Open Tu-Su 8:30am-noon and 2:30-5pm. L10,000.)*

TRASTEVERE

Some residents of this proud, independent neighborhood south of the Vatican boast of never crossing the river. Right off the Ponte Garibaldi stands the statue of the famous dialect poet, G. G. Belli, in the middle of his own *piazza*, which borders the busy P. Sonnino and marks the beginning of V. di Trastevere. On the left is the **Casa di Dante,** where readings of the *Divine Comedy* occur every Sunday from November to March. On V. di Santa Cecilia, behind the cars, through the gate, and beyond the courtyard full of roses, is the **Basilica di Santa Cecilia in Trastevere,** where Stefano Maderno's famous **statue of Santa Cecilia** lies under the altar. *(Open daily 8am-12:30pm and 2:30-7pm. Cloister open Tu and Th 10-11:30am, Su 11:3am-noon, donation requested. Crypt L4000.)* From P. Sonnino, V. della Lungaretta leads west to P. di S. Maria in

Trastevere, home to numerous stray dogs and expatriates, as well as the **Chiesa di Santa Maria in Trastevere,** built in the 4th century by Pope Julius II. *(Open daily 7:30am-7pm.)* North of the *piazza* are the Rococo **Galleria Corsini,** V. della Lungara, 10, (see **Museo Nazionale dell'Arte Antica, p. 697)** and, across the street, the **Villa Farnesina,** the jewel of Trastevere. Atop the Gianicolo hill rests the **Chiesa di San Pietro in Montorio,** built on the spot once believed to be the site of St. Peter's upside-down crucifixion. *(To reach the summit, take bus #41 from the Vatican, or ascend via the medieval V. Garibaldi from V. della Scala in Trastevere.)* Next door in a small courtyard is Bramante's tiny ▊**Tempietto,** constructed to commemorate the site of Peter's martyrdom. *(Church and Tempietto open daily 9:30am-12:30pm and 4-6:30pm.)*

NEAR TERMINI

The sights in the very urban part of town are concentrated northwest of the station and to the south, near P. Vittorio Emanuele II, where an **outdoor market** is held daily.

BATHS OF DIOCLETIAN. From 298 to 306, 40,000 Christian slaves were kept busy building these public baths, which could serve 3000 people at once. They contained a heated marble public toilet with seats for thirty, pools of various temperatures, gymnasiums, art galleries, gardens, libraries, and concert halls. In 1561, Michelangelo undertook his last architectural work and converted the ruins into a church, the **Chiesa di Santa Maria degli Angeli.** In the floor leading from the east transept to the altar, a sundial has provided the standard time for Roman clocks for hundreds of years. *(Church open daily 7:30am-12:30pm and 4-6:30pm. Rotonda and baths open M-F 9am-2pm, Sa-Su 9am-1pm. Free.)*

PIAZZA DEL QUIRINALE. At the southeast end of V. del Quirinale, this *piazza* occupies the summit of the tallest of Rome's seven hills. The President of the Republic officially resides in the imposing **Palazzo del Quirinale,** a Baroque collaboration by Bernini, Maderno, and Fontana. Down V. del Quirinale, V. Ferrara on the right leads down the steps to V. Milano. At the corner of V. Milano and V. Nazionale towers the **Palazzo delle Espozioni,** home to temporary art exhibitions. Farther along lies the marvelous facade of Borromini's **Chiesa di San Carlo alle Quattro Fontane.**

BASILICA DI SANTA MARIA MAGGIORE. As one of the five churches in Rome granted extraterritoriality, this basilica, which crowns the Esquiline Hill, is officially part of Vatican City. To the right of the altar, a marble slab marks the **tomb of Bernini.** The 14th-century mosaics in the **loggia** recount the story of the August snowfall that showed the pope where to build the church. *(Four blocks down V. Cavour from Termini. Open daily 7am-7pm. Loggia open daily 9:30am-noon and 2-5:30pm, L5000.)*

CHURCH OF SAN PIETRO IN VINCOLO. Dating from the 4th century, this church is named after the sacred chains with which Peter was supposedly bound after imprisonment on the Capitoline. Michelangelo's imposing ▊**statue of Moses** presides regally over the church. *(M:B-Cavour. Walk southwest on V. Cavour, down toward the Forum. Take the stairs on your left. Open daily 7am-12:30pm and 3:30-7pm.)*

TOO MUCH CAPPUCCINO WILL DO THE SAME TO YOU

The bones of 4000 Capuchin friars (for whom cappuccino is named) decorate the four rooms of the Church of L'Immacolata Concezione's Capuchin Crypt, one of the most bizarre and elaborately macabre settings in Rome. A French monk inaugurated the crypt in 1528, but never saw his brilliant concept brought to its completion because the crypt was not finished until 1870. Angels deck the halls, with hip bones serving as wings. The bodies of more recently dead friars stand, robed and hooded, beneath bone arches. Even the hanging lights are made of bones. Dirt was shipped in especially from Jerusalem to line the floors. The last chapel displays two severed arms with mummy-like skin hanging on the back wall. Also featured in this chapel is a child's skeleton plastered to the ceiling, holding a scale and a reaper, and accompanied by the uplifting inscription: "What you are now we used to be, what we are now you will be."

SOUTHERN ROME

The area south of the center is a great mix of wealthy and working class neighborhoods, and is home to the city's best nightlife and some of its grandest churches.

CAELIAN HILL. Southeast of the Colosseum, the Caelian, along with the Esquiline, is the biggest of Rome's seven original hills and home to some of the city's greatest chaos. Split into three levels, each from a different era, the **Church of San Clemente** is one of Rome's most intriguing churches. A fresco cycle by Masolino (possibly executed with help from his pupil Masaccio) dating from the 1420s graces the **Chapel of Santa Caterina.** *(M:B-Colosseo. Turn left out of the station and walk east on V. Fori Imperiali. ☎06 70451018. Open M-Sa 9am-12:30pm and 3-6pm, Su and holidays 10am-12:30pm and 3-6pm. L5000.)* The immense **Chiesa di San Giovanni in Laterano** of the diocese of Rome was the seat of the pope until the 14th century. Founded by Constantine in 314, it's Rome's oldest Christian basilica. The Gothic *baldacchino* over the altar houses two golden reliquaries, home to the heads of **St. Peter and St. Paul.** Across the street is the **Scala Santa,** which houses the so-called *acheropite* image, a depiction of Christ supposedly not created by human hand, and what are believed to be the 28 marble steps used by Jesus outside Pontius Pilate's house in Jerusalem. *(M:A-San Giovanni or bus #16 from Termini. Church open daily 7am-7:30pm. Cloister open daily 9am-6pm. L4000. Scala Santa open Apr.-Sept. 6:15am-7:30pm, Oct.-Mar. 6:15am-6:30pm.)*

THE APPIAN WAY. Since burial inside the city walls was forbidden during ancient times, fashionable Romans made their final resting places along the Appian Way. At the same time, early Christians secretly dug maze-like **catacombs** under the ashes of their persecutors. *(M:A-San Giovanni. Take bus #218 from P. di S. Giovanni to the intersection of V. Ardeatina and V. delle Sette Chiese. Open daily in summer 8:30am-5:30pm, in winter 8:30am-5pm. L8000.)* **San Callisto** is the largest catacomb in Rome, with nearly 22km of subterranean paths. Its four levels once held 16 popes, seven bishops, St. Cecilia, and 500,000 other Christians. *(V. Appia Antica, 110. Take the private road that runs northeast to the entrance to the catacombs. ☎06 5130151. Open M-Tu and Th-Su, in winter Th-Su only; closed Feb.)* **Santa Domitilla** enjoys acclaim for its paintings—it houses an intact 3rd-century portrait of Christ and the Apostles. *(Facing V. Ardeatina from the exit of S. Callisto, cross the street and walk up V. delle Sette Chiese. ☎06 5110342. Open W-M; closed Jan.)* **San Sebastiano** has a claim to fame for being the temporary home for the bodies of Peter and Paul. *(V. Appia Antica, 136. ☎06 7850350. Open M-Sa; closed Nov.)*

EUR. South of the city stands a monument to an empire that never was. EUR (AY-oor), is an Italian acronym for the 1942 Universal Exposition of Rome that Mussolini intended as a showcase of Fascist achievement. Apparently, the new, modern Rome was to shock and impress the world with its ability to build lots of identical square buildings. The center of the area is P. Guglielmo Marconi and its 1959 modernist **obelisk,** around which the EUR Museums are splayed (see p. 634). According to legend, when St. Paul was beheaded at the **Abbazia delle Tre Fontane (Abbey of the Three Fountains),** his head bounced three times, creating a fountain at each bounce. The Trappist monks who live here today sell their own potent eucalyptus liquor. *(M:B-Laurentina. Walk ½ mi. north on V. Laurentina and turn right on V. di Acque Salve. The abbey is at the bottom of the hill. Alternatively, take bus #761 north from the Laurentina stop; ask to get at V. di Acque Salve. Open M-Sa 11am-5pm, Su noon-5pm.)*

VATICAN CITY

M: A-Ottaviano or A-Cipro/Musei Vaticani. Alternatively, take bus #64 or #492 from Termini or Largo Argentina, #62 from P. Barberini, or #23 from Testaccio. The **Pilgrim Tourist Information Office,** *P. San Pietro, is to the left as you face the basilica. (☎06 69 88 44 66. Open M-Sa 8:30am-7pm.)* **Papal Audiences** *are held every W, usually at 10am behind the colonnade left of the basilica. For free tickets, stop by the Prefettura della Casa Pontificia the day before. (☎06 69 88 32 73. Open M-Sa 9am-1pm.)*

Occupying 108.5 independent acres entirely within the boundaries of Rome, Vatican City, the last foothold of the Catholic Church, once wheeled and dealed as the mightiest power in Europe. The nation preserves its independence by minting coins (in Italian *lire* but with the Pope's face), running a separate postal system, and maintaining an army of Swiss Guards.

BASILICA DI SAN PIETRO (ST. PETER'S). As you enter **Piazza San Pietro,** Bernini's colonnade draws you toward the church. Mussolini's broad V. della Conciliazione, built in the 1930s to connect the Vatican to the rest of the city, opened a wider view of St. Peter's than Bernini had ever intended. The **obelisk** in the center is framed by two fountains; round porphyry disks set in the pavement between each fountain and the obelisk mark the spots where you should stand so that the quadruple rows of Bernini's colonnades visually resolve into one perfectly aligned row. One hundred and forty statues perch above on the colonnade. Those on the basilica represent Christ (at center), John the Baptist, and the Apostles (except for Peter). The pope opens the **Porta Sancta** (Holy Door), every 25 years by knocking in the bricks with a silver hammer. The last opening was in 2000. The basilica itself rests on the reputed site of St. Peter's tomb. To the right, Michelangelo's *Pietà* has been protected by bullet-proof glass since 1972, when an axewielding fiend smashed Christ's nose and broke Mary's hand.

Inside, the crossing under the dome is anchored by four niches with statues of saints—Bernini's **San Longinus** is at the northeast. In the center of the crossing, Bernini's bronze **baldacchino** rises on spiral columns over the marble altar. Below the statue of St. Longinus, steps lead down to the **Vatican Grottoes,** the final resting place of innumerable popes and saints. The entrance to the **cupola** is near the exit from the grottoes. The ledge offers an excellent view of the basilica's roof, the *piazza*, the Vatican Gardens, and the hazy Roman skyline. *(Dress modestly Cover your knees and shoulders. Open daily Apr.-Sept. 7am-7pm, Oct.-Mar. 7am-6pm. Mass M-Sa at 9, 10, and 11am, noon, and 5pm; Su 9, 10:30, and 11:30am, and 12:10, 1, 4, and 5:45pm. Multilingual confession available. Cupola closes 75min. earlier than the Basilica, and when the Pope is inside; by foot L7000, by elevator L8000.)*

VATICAN MUSEUMS. The Vatican Museums constitute one of the world's greatest collections of art, a vast storehouse of ancient, Renaissance, and modern statuary, painting, and sundry papal odds and ends. A good place to start your tour is the stellar **Museo Pio-Clementino,** the world's greatest collection of antique sculpture. Two slobbering Molossian hounds guard the entrance to the **Stanza degli Animali,** a marble menagerie that reveals a lot about the importance of brutality in Roman pastimes. Among other gems, it features the ▩**Apollo Belvedere** and the unhappy **Laocoön** family. The Simonetti Stairway climbs to the **Museo Etrusco,** filled with artifacts from Tuscany and northern Lazio. From the Room of the Immaculate Conception, a door leads into the first of the four ▩**Stanze di Rafaele,** the apartments built for Pope Julius II in the 1510s. Raphael painted the astonishing **School of Athens** as a trial piece for Julius, who was so impressed that he fired his other painters, had their frescoes destroyed and commissioned Raphael to decorate the entire suite. The **Stanza della Segnatura** features the *School of Athens*, considered Raphael's masterpiece. From here, there are two paths: a staircase leads to the brilliantly frescoed **Borgia Apartments** and the **Museum of Modern Religious Art** and another route goes to the Sistine Chapel. *(About 10 blocks north of the right-hand side of P. San Pietro along the Vatican wall. ☎06 69883333. Open Nov.-Mar.15 M-Sa 8:45am-1:45pm; Mar. 16-Oct. 30 M-F 8:45am-4:30pm, Sa 8:45am-1:45pm. L18,000, with ISIC card L12,000; free last Su of the month 8:45am-1:45pm.)*

▩ **SISTINE CHAPEL.** Ever since its completion in the 16th century, the Sistine Chapel (named for its founder, Pope Sixtus IV) has served as the chamber in which the College of Cardinals elects new popes. The ceiling, which is flat but appears vaulted, gleams with the results of its recent restoration. The frescoes on the side walls predate Michelangelo's ceiling. On the right, scenes from the life of Moses complement parallel scenes of Christ's life on the left. The cycle was completed between 1481 and 1483 under the direction of Perugino by a team of artists including Botticelli, Ghirlandaio, Roselli, Pinturicchio, Signorelli, and della Gatta. The simple compositions and vibrant colors of Michelangelo's unquestioned masterpiece hover above, each section depicting a story from Genesis. The scenes are framed by the famous *ignudi*, young nude males. Michelangelo painted not flat on his back, but standing up and craning backwards, and he never recovered from the strain to his neck and eyes. Michelangelo's *The Last Judgement* fills the altar wall. The figure of Christ as judge hovers in the upper center, surrounded by his saintly entourage and the supplicant Mary.

CASTEL SANT'ANGELO. Built by **Hadrian** (AD 117-138) as a mausoleum for himself and his family, this hulking mass of brick and stone has served the popes as a fortress, prison, and palace. When the city was wracked with plague in 590, Pope Gregory the Great saw an angel sheathing his sword at the top of the complex; the plague abated soon after, and the edifice was rededicated to the angel. It now contains a **museum of arms and artillery** and offers an incomparable view of Rome and the Vatican. *(To enter, walk along the river with St. Peter's behind you, and the towering castle to your left; signs will point you to the entrance. ☎06 6875036. Open Tu-F and Su 9am-8pm, Sa 9am-midnight; in winter daily 9am-2pm. Admission L10,000, EU citizens under 18 or over 60 free. Audio guide L7000.)*

🏛 MUSEUMS

Etruscans, emperors, popes, and *condottiere* have been busily stuffing Rome's belly full with artwork for several millennia, leaving behind a city teeming with galleries. Museums are generally closed holidays, Sunday afternoons, and all day Monday.

- **Capitoline Museums,** (☎06 39746221) atop the Capitoline Hill (behind the Vittorio Emanuele II monument). The collections of ancient sculpture in the Capitoline Museums are among the largest in the world and the frescoes are breathtaking. The Palazzo Nuovo contains the original statue of **Marcus Aurelius** that once stood in the center of the *piazza*. See the fragments of the **Colossus of Constantine** and the famous **Capitoline Wolf,** an Etruscan statue that has symbolized the city of Rome since ancient times. At the top of the stairs, the **pinacoteca** houses 16th- and 17th-century Italian paintings. Open Tu-Su 10am-8pm, holidays 9am-1:30pm. L15,000, with ISIC L11,000.
- **Galleria Borghese,** P. Scipione Borghese, 5 (☎06 8548577). M:A-Spagna. Alternatively, take bus #910 from Termini to V. Pinciana. Bernini's most magnificent works, including his *David* and *Apollo and Daphne*. Canvases by Caravaggio, Raphael, Rubens, and Titian. Open Tu-F 9am-7:30pm, Sa 9am-11pm, Su and holidays 9am-8pm; entrance only on the hr., visits limited to 2hr.; last entrance 30min. before closing. L14,000.
- **Villa Farnesina,** V. della Lungara, 230 (☎06 68 80 17 67). Just across from Palazzo Corsini off Lungotevere Farnesina. Bus #23. Thought to be the wealthiest man in Europe, Agostino "il Magnifico" Chigi lived sumptuously and eccentrically in the villa. To the right of the entrance lies the breathtaking **Sala of Galatea.** The masterpiece of the room is Raphael's *Triumph of Galatea*. Open M-Sa 9am-1pm. L8000, under 18 L6000.
- **Galleria Nazionale d'Arte Moderna,** V. delle Belle Arti, 131 (☎06 322981). M:A-Flaminio; enter the park and walk up V. George Washington, following the signs. Skip to the 20th-century wing to see pieces by Klimt, Modigliani, Giacometti, Mondrian, Braque, Duchamp, and de Chirico. Open Tu-Sa 9am-7pm, Su 9am-8pm. L12,000.
- **Galleria Spada,** P. Capo di Ferro, 13 (☎06 328101), in the elaborate Palazzo Spada. South of Campo dei Fiori. Bus #64. 17th-century Cardinal Bernardino Spada bought a grandiose assortment of paintings and sculpture, that includes works by Tintoretto and Titian, and a frieze by Vaga, originally intended to be placed in the Sistine Chapel. Open Tu-Sa 9am-7pm, Su 9am-12:30pm. L10,000, EU citizens under 18 and over 60 free.
- **Museo Nazionale Etrusco di Villa Giulia,** P. Villa Giulia, 9 (☎06 3201951) in Villa Borghese. M:A-Flaminio or bus #19 from P. Risorgimento or #52 from P. San Silvestro. Built under Pope Julius III, who reigned from 1550 to 1555. Highlights include a graceful sarcophagus of a man and wife in Room 9 and an Etruscan chariot, or *biga*, and the petrified skeletons of two horses found beside it in Room 18. Upstairs, archaeologists have put together the fragments of an Etruscan temple facade. Open Tu-F, Su, and holidays 8:30am-7:30pm, Sa 9am-8pm; extended hours June-Sept. Sa 9am-11pm. L8000.

Museo Nazionale d'Arte Antica, V. delle Quattro Fontane, 13 (☎06 4814 591), near P. Barberini. This collection of 12th- through 18th-century art is split between Palazzo Barberini and Palazzo Corsini. **Palazzo Barberini** contains paintings from the medieval through Baroque periods. Open Tu-Sa 9am-7pm, Su 9am-8pm. L12000, EU citizens 18-25 L7000.)

Galleria Corsini, V. della Lungara, 10 (☎06 68 80 23 23), opposite Villa Farnesina in Trastevere, holds a fine collection of 17th- and 18th-century paintings. Open Tu-Su 9am-6pm. L8000, EU students L2000.

Museo Nazionale Romano Palazzo Massimo, Largo di Via Peretti, 1 (☎06 4815 576) in the left-hand corner of P. dei Cinquecento as you stand with your back to Termini. Devoted to the history of Roman art during the Empire, and includes the Lancellotti Discus Thrower, a rare mosaic of Nero's, and ancient coins and jewelry. (Open Tu-Su 9am-7pm. L12,000, EU citizens 18-24 L6000, EU citizens under 18 and over 60 free.)

Museo Nazionale Romano Palazzo Altemps, P. S. Apollinaire, 44 (☎06 39 08 71) just north of P. Navona. Ancient Roman sculpture, including the 5th-century *Ludovisi Throne*. Open Tu-Su, 9am-7pm. L10,000, EU citizens 18-24 L5000, EU citizens under 18 and over 60 free.

Museo Preistorico ed Etnografico Luigi Pigorini, P. G. Marconi, 14 (☎06 549521). An impressive collection of ethnographic artifacts, including the skull of the famous Neanderthal Guattari Man, discovered near Circeo. Often hosts visiting exhibitions. Open daily 9am-2pm. L8000, under 18 and over 65 free.

🔄 ENTERTAINMENT

Unfortunately, Roman entertainment just isn't what it used to be. Back in the day, you could swing by the Colosseum to watch a man mauled by a bear. Today, Romans seeking diversion are more likely to go to a Testaccio nightclub than fight another man to the death. Check out *Roma C'è* (which has an English-language section) or *Time Out*, available at newstands, for club, movie, and events listings.

LIVE MUSIC

The classical scene in Rome goes wild during the summer. Small festivals that run from mid-May to August are just part of the larger **Roma Estate** (www.romaestate.com). It all starts with the **Festa Europea della Musica** at the end of June. In July, the **Accademia Nazionale di Santa Cecilia** (☎06 3611 064 or 06 361 1833, credit card reservations ☎06 68 80 10 44) holds concerts in the **Villa Giulia**, in Villa Borghese. The **Theater of Marcellus**, near P. Venezia, hosts summer evening concerts organized by the **Associazione Il Tempietto**. (☎06 481 4800. L30,000.) Live Brazilian music is followed by a raging Latin disco at **Berimbau**, V. dei Fienaroli, 30b. (☎06 5813 249. Cover L10-25,000, includes a drink. Open W-Su 10:30pm-3:30am.) **Testaccio Village**, V. di Monte Testaccio, 16, features live, mostly local rock and pop. (☎06 57 28 76 61. Open Mid-June to mid-Sept. nightly around 9pm.)

THEATER

Rome's most important theatre, **Teatro Argentina**, V. di Torre Argentina, 52, runs drama and music festivals throughout the year. (☎06 68 80 46 01. Box office open M-F 10am-2pm and 3-7pm, Sa 10am-2pm.) For information on English theater, check the tourist office or the English section of *Roma C'è*.

🔲 NIGHTLIFE

CLUBS

Although Italian discos can be a flashy, sweaty good time, travelers must overcome some obstacles before donning their dancing shoes. First, you won't meet many non-Italians (could be nice for a change). Second, the scene changes as often as Roman phone numbers, and many clubs flee beachward for the steaming summer to **Fregene, Ostia**, or **San Felice Circeo**. Check *Roma C'è* or *Time Out*.

▨ **Qube,** V. Portonaccio, 212 (☎06 4381 005). From P. di Porta Maggiore, take V. Prenestina east; turn left on V. Portonaccio. Seedy neighborhood; plan to take a cab home. A warehouse-style disco, and one of Rome's biggest. "Transmania," on Su, is one of Rome's most popular gay nights. Cover L10-20,000. Open Th-Su 11pm-4am.

Radio Londra Caffè, V. di Monte Testaccio, 65b (☎06 5750 444). Packed with an energetic, good-looking crowd. Pint of Carlsberg L7000. Open Su-F 9pm-3am, Sa 9pm-4am.

C.S.I.O.A. Villaggio Globale, Lungotevere Testaccio (☎06 57 30 03 29). Take bus #27 from Termini, get off before it crosses the river, and turn left. Women may not want to walk alone here at night. Housed in a huge Testaccio slaughterhouse, it hosts all things countercultural: live music, films, art exhibits, and more. Hours and cover vary.

Alien, V. Velletri, 13-19 (☎06 8412 212). North of Termini. One of the biggest discos in Rome attracts a well-dressed crowd and plays the house you know and love. Cover L10-30,000 (includes a drink). Open Tu-Sa 11pm-4am. Moves to Fregene in summer.

Alpheus, V. del Commercio, 36 (☎06 5747 826). Off V. Ostiense. Rome's most popular gay night, "Mucassassina," (literally, cow killer) F. Other nights find live jazz, rock, folk, cabaret and comedy. Cover L10-L20,000. Students free Th. Open Tu-Su 10pm-4:30am.

Dub Club, V. dei Funari, 21a (☎06 68 80 50 24). In the Jewish Ghetto. A blue-lit underground, circular disco. Techno, funk, acid jazz, and exotica. Cover L10-20,000. Open Tu-F 11pm-4am, Sa-Su 11pm-6am. Things get rolling at 2am. Closed most of summer.

PUBS

If you're longing for the days of the organized, indoor drunkenness of your native land, your only recourse might be Rome's countless pubs, many of which have some sort of Irish theme. Drink prices often increase after 9pm.

Jonathan's Angels, V. della Fossa, 16 (☎06 6893 426). West of P. Navona. Take V. del Governo Vecchio from Campo dei Fiori, turn left onto V. Parione, and then a left toward the lights. Michelangelo's accomplishments pale before the ▨ bathroom at Jonathan's. Beer on tap L10,000, cocktails L15,000. Open daily 4pm-2am.

Trinity College, V. del Collegio Romano, 6 (☎06 6786 472). Off V. del Corso near P. Venezia. Offers degrees in such curricula as Guinness, Harp, and Heineken. Tuition L6-9000. Classes held every day noon-3am.

Pub Hallo'Ween, P. Tiburtino, 31 (☎06 4440 705). In San Lorenzo, at the corner of V. Tiburtina and V. Marsala. Plastic skulls and fake spiderwebs abound. Draft beer L6-8000, bottles L7-10,000. Cocktails L8-9000. Happy hour (free appetizers) 8:30-10pm. Open daily 8:30pm-2:30am. Closed Aug.

Abbey Theatre, V. del Governo Vecchio, 51-53 (☎06 6861 341). Have your 10am Guinness (L10,000) here. Happy hour daily 3-7pm. Open M-Th 10am-2am, F-Sa 10am-3am, Su 2:30pm-2am.

The Drunken Ship, Campo dei Fiori, 20-21 (☎06 68 30 05 35). Because you're tired of meeting Italians. Because you have an earnest desire to commune with others in the hosteling set. Because you're proud to be an American, dammit. Happy hour daily 5-9pm, all night Tu. W 9-10pm is power hour—all the beer you can drink (L10,000). Ask about the student discount on Heineken. Open daily 5pm-2am.

Caipirinha Pub-Café, V. del Gallo, 10 (☎06 6892 561). Off Campo dei Fiori. This fun Brazilian bar serves up tropical drinks and lots of Latin dancing. Cocktails around L10,000. Bud L4000, Guinness L6000, Panini L4000. Open daily 7pm-2am.

Julius Caesar, V. Castelfidardo, 49 (☎06 4461 565). Just north of Termini. Always packed with backpackers and locals. Live music. Happy Hour (beer and sandwich L10,000) 9-10pm. Beer on tap (L6-8000). Open daily 8:30pm-2am.

GAY AND LESBIAN NIGHTLIFE

Rome has fewer gay establishments than most cities its size, but those it has are solid and keep late hours. Many of the following establishments require an **ARCI-GAY pass** (L10,000 yearly), available from **Circolo di Cultura Omosessuale Mario Mieli** (☎06 5413 985). Of the above clubs, **Alpheus** and **Qube** host gay nights.

Hangar, V. in Selci, 69 (☎06 4881 397). M:B-Cavour. Near Termini; off V. Cavour. Friendly John from Philadelphia runs this small bar, once the home of Nero's wife. Hangar is considered the hotspot for gay nightlifers in Rome, attracting mostly 20-something men. Crowded, cool, and neon blue. M dirty movie night. Drinks, L3-10,000. ARCI-GAY pass required. Open W-M 10:30pm-2am. Closed three weeks in Aug.

L'Alibi, V. Monte di Testaccio, 39-44 (☎06 5743 448). In Testaccio. Bus #30N. Large, elegant, and diverse, with an expansive rooftop terrace. Especially in summer, this is *the* gay club in Rome. Underground, house, and retro. Mostly gay, though lesbians and straights are welcome. Open W-Su 11pm-4:30am. Cover L15-20,000; Th and Su free.

New Joli Coeur, V. Sirte, 5 (☎06 86 21 58 27). Off V. Eritrea. Rome's primary lesbian club is far from the center, east of Villa Ada. Seedy neighborhood; take a cab. Retro music, with the occasional live cabaret show or girl group. Women only. One-drink minimum (L15-20,000). Open Sa 11pm-3am, may be open Su.

▐ DAYTRIPS FROM ROME

TIVOLI

M:B to Rebibbia, then COTRAL bus to Tivoli (25min.; 3-5 per hour; L3000). On the street leading away from P. Garibaldi, a big "I" on a round shack marks the tourist office. (☎ (0774) 311249. Open M-Sa 9:45am-3pm.)

From P. Garibaldi, sneak your way through the gauntlet of souvenir stands through P. Trento down the path to the ▓**Villa d'Este,** the castle-garden property on your left. Villa d'Este was laid out by Cardinal Ercole d'Este (the son of Lucrezia Borgia) and his architect Piero Ligorio in 1550 with the idea of recreating the feel of the ancient Roman *nymphaea* and pleasure palaces. (☎ (0774) 31 20 70. Open daily May-Aug. 9am-6:45pm; Sept.-Apr. 9am-1hr. before sunset. Sa closes 1½hr. earlier. L8000, EU citizens under 18 and over 60 free.) Follow V. di Sibilla across town to reach the **Villa Gregoriana**—a park with paths that descend past temples and scattered grottoes carved out by rushing water. (Open June-Aug. Tu-Su 9:30am-7:30pm; Sept.-May Tu-Su 9:30am-1hr. before sunset. L3500, under 12 L1000.) From the Tivoli, it's 5km to the vast remains of the **Villa Adriana.** From the P. Garibaldi newsstand, take the orange #4x bus (L1400; buy a return ticket). The villa is the largest and most expensive ever built in the Roman Empire. Emperor Hadrian designed its buildings in the 2nd century in the styles of monuments that he had seen in his travels. (☎ (0774) 53 02 03. Open daily 9am-1½hr. before sunset. L8000.)

TARQUINIA

Trains leave from Termini (1hr., 11 per day; last train leaves Tarquinia at 10:12pm, L10,200). For bus schedules and info on southern Etruria, try the tourist office in P. Cavour, near the medieval walls. (☎ (0766) 856384. Open M-Sa 8am-2pm and 4-7pm.)

When Rome was but a few mud huts on the Palatine, Tarquin kings commanded this fledgling metropolis. Although little remains of the city, a subterranean **necropolis** lined with vibrant frescoes illustrates Tarquinia's history. In P. Cavour stands the majestic **Museo Nazionale,** one of the best collections of Etruscan art outside Rome. (☎ (0766) 85 60 36. Open Tu-Su 9am-7pm. L12000.) The ticket from the museum will admit you to the necropolis. To get there, take the bus marked Cimitero from Barriera S. Giusto or walk (15min.) from the museum. Head up C. V. Emanuele from P. Cavour and turn right on V. Porta Tarquinia. (☎ (0766) 856308. Open 9am-1hr. before sunset.)

LAKE BRACCIANO

By train, Anguillara and Bracciano are accessible by the Rome-Viterbo line (every hr.; from Rome's San Pietro station 5:35am-9:45pm, last train to Rome 10:14pm; L5300).

Bracciano provides Rome with its nearest freshwater beach, an hour away by bus. Fresh air, cool water, and a lush and hilly surrounding landscape compensate for the gravelly, volcanic sand that might hurt your rear. The impressive 15th-century **Orsini-Odescalchi Castle** dominates town and offers stunning frescoes and stuffed wild boars. Down at the beach, a ferry ride across the lake to nearby Anguillara or Trevignano offers more spectacular scenery. See *Roma C'è* for listings of classical concerts often held here in the summer.

OTHER DAYTRIPS FROM ROME

SIENA. This lovely medieval city has a Gothic *duomo* with carvings by Ghiberti and Donatello, and annual horse races that create a local fervor (see p. 693).

PISA. There's more to Pisa than its famous tilted tower—visit the dazzling *duomo* and lovely baptistery (see p. 695).

NORTHWEST ITALY

Northwest Italy's offerings are far from limited—they range from the urban chic of Milan's catwalks and industrial center to the hedonistic, sunswept shores of the Italian Riviera. And when you manage to pull your tired self away from the dizzying clubs and the scorching sands, ample food for your seemingly satiated senses awaits in the region of Piedmont, the regional center for fine and finer wines.

LOMBARDY (LOMBARDIA)

Over the centuries, Roman generals, German emperors, and French kings have vied for control of Lombardy's fertile soil. In the recent past, increases in employment and developments in industry have made Lombardy an even more vital cornerstone of the Italian economy. Cosmopolitan Milan may drive the mighty engine of progress, but don't let its exhaust fumes blind you to the beauty of Bergamo, Mantua, and the glorious foothills of the Alps.

MILAN (MILANO)

Milan's ancient history as the one-time capital of the Roman Empire is belied by its modern appearance. The pace of life in Milan is dizzying, and a stream of well-dressed Italians blurs the panorama of tree-lined boulevards and graceful architecture in this oh-so-cosmopolitan Italian city. A regional expression sums up the nature of this fashionable beast succinctly: *"Milano l'e Milano"* (Milan is just Milan). There is little time for the Milanese to stop and savor *il dolce far niente* (the sweetness of doing nothing); maintaining its balance of cutting-edge glamour and modern success is surely hard work.

▐◘ TRANSPORTATION

Flights: Malpensa Airport, 60km away, handles intercontinental flights. **Malpensa Express** leaves twice an hour from the Cardona metro station to the airport (45min., 6:50am-8:20pm, L15-20,000). **Linate Airport,** 7km away, covers domestic and European flights. Take bus #73 from MM1: P. San Babila (L1500).

Trains: Stazione Centrale, P. Duca d'Aosta (☎01 47 88 80 88), on MM2. To: **Rome** (4½hr., every hr., L71,000); **Florence** (2½hr., every hr., L40,000); **Genoa** (1½hr., every hr., L24,000); **Turin** (2hr., every hr., L24,500); and **Venice** (3hr., 21 per day, L36,000). Info office open daily 7am-9:30pm. **Luggage storage** L500 per 12hr.

Buses: Stazione Centrale, intercity buses tend to be less convenient and more expensive than trains. **SAL, SIA, Autostradale,** and other carriers leave from P. Castello and nearby (MM1: Cairoli) for Turin, Lake Country, and Bergamo.

Public Transportation: The **subway** (Metropolitana Milanese, or **MM**) runs 6am-midnight. **ATM** (toll-free ☎167 01 68 57), in the MM1,3: Duomo station, handles local transportation. Single-fare tickets (L1500) are good for 75min. of surface transportation. (Day passes L5000, 2-day L9000. Info and ticket booths open M-Sa 7:15am-7:15pm.)

✹ 🔋 ORIENTATION AND PRACTICAL INFORMATION

The layout of the city resembles a giant target, encircled by a series of ancient concentric city walls. In the outer rings lie suburbs built during the 1950s and 60s to house southern immigrants. Within the inner circle are four central squares: **Piazza Duomo,** at the end of V. Mercanti, **Piazza Cairoli,** near the Castello Sforzesco, **Piazza Cordusio,** connected to Largo Cairoli by V. Dante, and **Piazza San Babila,** the business and fashion district along C. Vittorio Emanuele. The **duomo** and **Galleria Vittorio Emanuele II** comprise the bull's-eye, roughly at the center of the downtown circle. Radiating from the center lie two large parks, the Giardini Pubblici and the Parco Sempione. Farther northeast is the colossal Stazione Centrale train station. From the station, a scenic ride on bus #60 takes you to the downtown hub, as does the more efficient commute on subway line #3. **Via Vito Pisani,** which leads to the mammoth **Piazza della Repubblica,** connects the station to the downtown area.

TOURIST, FINANCIAL, AND LOCAL SERVICES

Tourist Office: APT, V. Marconi, 1 (☎02 72 52 43 00; fax 02 72 52 43 50), in the "Palazzo di Turismo" in P. del Duomo, to the right as you face the *duomo*. Pick up the comprehensive *Milano: Where, When, How* as well as *Milano Mese* for info on activities and clubs. Open M-F 8:30am-8pm, Sa 9am-1pm and 2-7pm, Su 9am-1pm and 2-5pm. **Branch office** (☎02 72 52 43 70), at Stazione Centrale, set back off the main hall on the 2nd fl. Open M-Sa 9am-6pm, Su 9am-12:30pm and 1:30-6pm.

Budget Travel: CIT, Galleria Vittorio Emanuele (☎02 86 37 01). Also changes money. Open M-F 9am-7pm, Sa 9am-1pm and 2-6pm. **CTS,** V. S. Antonio, 2 (☎02 58 30 41 21). Open M-F 9:30am-12:45pm and 2-6pm, Sa 9:30am-12:45pm.

Currency Exchange: All **Banca d'America e d'Italia** and **Banca Nazionale del Lavoro** branches eagerly await your Visa card. Bank hours in Milan are usually M-F 8:30am-1:30pm and 2:30-4:30pm. **ATMs** abound.

American Express: V. Brera, 3 (☎02 72 00 36 93), on the corner of V. dell'Orso. Walk through the Galleria, across P. Scala, and up V. Verdi. Holds mail free for members for 1 month, otherwise US$5 per inquiry. Sends/receives wired money for AmEx card-holders; fee of L2500 per month on transactions over L150,0000. Also **exchanges currency.** Open M-Th 9am-5:30pm, F 9am-5pm.

Laundromat: Vicolo Lavandai, V.le Monte Grappa, 2 (☎02 498 39 02). MM2: Garibaldi. Wash 7kg for L6000, dry for L6000. Open daily 8am-9pm.

EMERGENCY AND COMMUNICATIONS

Emergencies: ☎118. **First Aid:** Pronto Soccorso (☎02 38 83), Red Cross (☎02 34 56 7. **Hospital: Ospedale Maggiore di Milano,** V. Francesco Sforza, 35 (☎02 550 31), 5min. from the *duomo* on the inner ring road. **Police:** ☎113 or 02 772 71. **Carabinieri:** 112. **Toll-free Operator:** 12. **International Dialing Information:** 176.

Late-Night Pharmacy: The one in the *galeria* of the Stazione Centrale never closes (☎02 669 07 35 or 02 669 09 35).

Internet Access: Mannhatten Lab, in the Università Statale, in what used to be the Ospedale Maggiore on V. Festa del Perdono. Use the entrance opposite V. Bergamini. Take the stairs on the right to the third floor. Turn left, and walk to the end of the corridor. Take two lefts; it's the third door on your left. Microsoft workstations are open to Easmus students only, but at the far end of the room are computers for the public. Free. Open M-F 8:15am-6pm.

Post Office: V. Cordusio, 4 (☎02 72 48 22 23), near P. del Duomo towards the castle. Address mail to be held: Erica CHIU, *In Fermo Posta,* Ufficio Postale Centrale di Piazza Cordusio 4, Milano 20100, Italia. Open M-F 8:30am-7:30pm, Sa 8:30am-1pm.

⚑ ACCOMMODATIONS

Every season in Milan is high season, except August, when bugs outnumber humans. A single room in a decent establishment for under L65,000 is a real find. For the best deals, try the city's southern periphery or areas south and east of the train station. When possible, make reservations well ahead of time.

Hotel Ca' Grande, V. Porpora, 87 (☎02 26 14 40 01). Take tram #33 from Stazione Centrale to avoid sore feet; it runs along V. Porpora and stops at V. Ampere, near the front door. Twenty spotless rooms with phones, TV, and use of a beautiful garden. Internet available. Breakfast included. Reception 24hr. Singles L70,000, with bath L90,000; doubles L110,000, with bath L130,000.

Hotel Ambra, V. Caccinino, 10 (☎02 26 65 465). MM1/2: Loreto. Walk 10 blocks down V. Porpora (5-10min.) and take a right on V. Cacianino. Rooms are spotless, all with bath, TV, telephone and balconies. Inquire about student discounts. Breakfast L5,000. Singles L70,000; doubles L100,000; triples L140,000.

Hotel Sara, V. Sacchini, 17 (☎02 20 17 73). MM1/2: Loreto. From Loreto take V. Porpora. The third street on the right is V. Sacchini. The hotel has been recently renovated and the street is peaceful. Single L55,000; double L80,000, with bath L100,000; triple with bath L120,000.

Hotel San Tomaso, V. Tunisia, 6, 3rd fl. (☎02 29 51 47 47). MM1: Porta Venezia. Take the C. Buenos Aires metro exit; go left at the McDonald's on V. Tunisia. Clean, renovated rooms, some overlooking a courtyard. Phones, TVs. Ask for keys if going out at night. Three singles, around L60,000; four doubles with shower L100,000, with bath L120,000; triples and quads L135-200,000.

Hotel Aurora, C. Buenos Aires, 18 (☎02 204 79 60; fax 204 92 85). MM1: Porta Venezia; exit onto C. Buenos Aires; it's on the right. Spotless rooms with phone and TV. Reception 24hr. Singles L70-90,000; doubles L120-130,000; triples L170,000.

Ostello Piero Rotta (HI), V. Salmoiraghi, 1 (☎02 39 26 70 95). MM1: QT8. Breakfast, sheets, and lockers included. 3-day max. stay. Reception 7-9:30am and 3:30pm-midnight. Daytime lockout. Lights out 11:20pm. Curfew 11:30pm. HI membership required, available at the hostel (L30,000). Mostly six-bed rooms, but some family rooms available. Closed Dec. 20-Jan 10. 350 Dorms L26,000.

Hotel Kennedy, V. Tunisia, 6, 6th fl. (☎02 29 40 09 34). MM1: Porta Venezia. Three floors above Hotel San Tomaso. Sixteen clean rooms with lovely views of Milan. Breakfast L4000. Singles with bath L60,000-70,000; doubles 100,000, with bath L100-130,000; triples L150,000; quads L160,000; quints L200,000.

Hotel Rallye, V. B. Marcello, 59 (☎02 29 53 12 09). MM1: Lima. Walk along V. Vitruvio two blocks to V. Marcello and take a left. New, simple, quiet rooms with phone and TV. Singles L65,000; doubles with bath L110,000; triples L120,000.

Camping di Monza (☎039 38 77 71), in the park of the Villa Reale in Monza straight to Viassono. Take a train or bus from Stazione Centrale to Monza, then a city bus to the campground. Restaurant and bar nearby. Hot showers L500. Open Apr.-Aug. L8,000 per person and per tent, L15,000 for caravan.

◖ FOOD

Like its fine *couture*, Milanese cuisine is sophisticated and sometimes overpriced. Specialties include *risotto giallo* (rice with saffron), *cotoletta alla milanese* (breaded veal cutlet with lemon), and *cazzouela* (a mixture of pork and cabbage). *Pasticcerie* and *gelaterie* crowd every block. Bakeries specialize in the Milanese sweet bread *panettone*, an Italian fruitcake. The newspaper *Il Giornale Nuovo* lists all restaurants and shops open in the city, and the brochure *Milano Where, When, How*, available at the tourist office, has a detailed list of foreign restaurants.

Brek, V. Lepetit, 20 (☎02 670 51 49), near the Stazione Centrale. Elegant and very popular self-service restaurant. *Primi* around L5000, *secondi* L7500. Open M-Sa 11:30am-

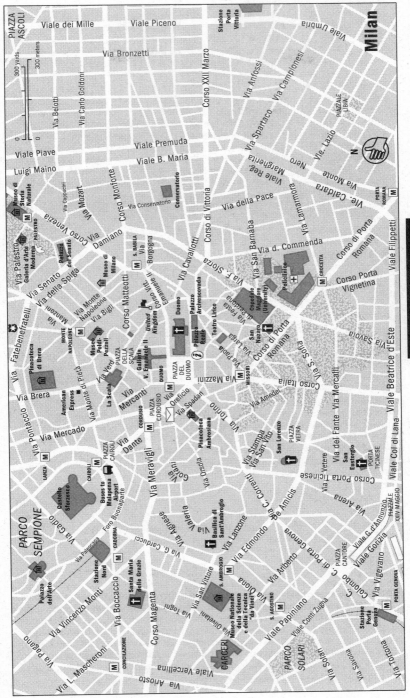

Milan

PIAZZA ASCOLI

Viale dei Mille

Viale Piceno

Stazione Porta Vittoria

Viale Umbria

Via Bronzetti

Corso XXII Marzo

Via Antossi

Via Campionesi

Via Belotti

Via Carlo Goldoni

N

PIAZZALE LIBIA

Vie. Lazio

Via Spartaco

Viale Premuda

Viale Piave

Viale B. Maria

M
PORTA ROMANA

Luigi Maino

Via Monte Nero

Viale Reg. Margherita

Vie. Caldara

Via Cappuccini

Via Mozart

Corso Monforte

Via Conservatorio

Conservatorio

Via della Pace

Corso di Vittoria

Museo di Storia Naturale

M PALESTRO

Galleria d'Arte Moderna

Palazzo del Senato

Via Palestro

Corso Venezia

Via Damiano

Museo di Milano

S. BABILA M

Via Borgogna

Via Cavallotti

Corso di F. Sforza

Via San Barnaba

Via d. Commenda

Corso di Porta Romana

M CROCETTA

Corso Porta Vignetina

Via della Spiga

Via Manzoni

Corso Vitt. Emanuele II

Via Fatebenefratelli

MONTE NAPOLEONE M

Via Monte Napoleone

Via Bigli

Duomo

Palazzo Arcivescovado

Ospedale Maggiore (University)

Policlinico

Via Lamarmora

Pinacoteca di Brera

Museo Poldi-Pezzoli

PIAZZA DELLA SCALA

United Kingdom
🇬🇧

Teatro Lirico

San Nazaro

Corso di Porta Romana

Via Savoia

Via Senato

Via Monte di Pietà

Galleria V. Emanuele II

Palazzo Reale

Via Festa del Perdono

Via Brera

La Scala

DUOMO

PIAZZA DEL DUOMO

i

Via Laghetto

Via Pace

Viale Beatrice d'Este

Via Pontaccio

American Express

Via Verdi

Via Mercanti

Oreficio

Via Spadari

Via Mazzini

MISSORI

Corso Italia

Via S. Sofia

Via Mercado

CORDUSIO M

PIAZZA CORDUSIO

Via Dante

Pinacoteca Ambrosiana

Via Torino

Via Amedei

Viale Col di Lana

PIAZZA CAIROLI

Via Meravigli

Via Orsola

Via Stampa

PIAZZA VETRA

San Lorenzo

San Eustorgio

PORTA TICINESE

Via S. Vito

M LANZA

CAIROLI

Buses to Malapensa Airport

Via Agnese

Via Valeria

C. Correnti

De Amicis

Corso Porta Ticinese

Castello Sforzesco

Foro Buonaparte

CADORNA M

Basilica di Sant'Ambrogio

Via Lanzone

Via Arena

Via S.S. Sofia

PARCO SEMPIONE

Via Gadio

Via Paleocapa

Via G. Carducci

Santa Maria delle Grazie

Stazione Nord

S. AMBROGIO M

Via San Vittore

Via Edmondo

C. di Porta Genova

PIAZZA CANTORE

Viale Gorizia

Palazzo dell'arte

Via Boccaccio

Via Vincenzo Monti

Corso Magenta

Via Togni

Museo Nationale della Scienza e della Tecnica "da Vinci"

Via Olivetani

Via Diona

S. AGOSTINO

Viale Papiniano

C. Colombo

Via G. d'Annunzio

XXIV MAGGIO

PIAZZALE XXIV MAGGIO

Via G. Alberto

Via Vigevano

PORTA GENOVA

Via Pagano

Via L. Mascheroni

CONCILIAZIONE M

Via Vincenzo Monti

CARCERI

PARCO SOLARI

Viale Conti Zugna

Stazione Porta Gengra

Via Ariosto

Viale Vercellina

Viale Gorizia

Via Solari

Via Savona

Via Tortona

PIAZZALE GENOVA

300 yards
300 meters
0

AMERICAN EXPRESS

3pm and 6:30-10:30pm. Other locations on P. Cavour (☎02 65 36 19; off V. Manzoni, MM3: M. Napoleone) and Porta Giordano (☎02 76 02 33 79; MM1: S. Babila).

Peck, V. Cantù, 3 (☎02 869 30 17), off V. Orefici, two blocks from P. del Duomo. Milan has had *Peck,* its premier *rosticceria*, since 1883. L7,500 will buy a large slice of pastry or pizza. Open Tu-F 8:45am-2:30pm and 4-7:30pm, Sa 8:30am-1:45pm and 3:45-7:30pm, Su 8am-1pm.

Tarantella, V.le Abruzzi, 35 (☎02 29 40 02 18), just north of V. Plinio. MM1: Lima. Lively sidewalk dining. Don't leave without trying the *pasta fresca* for L12,000 or one of the *pizze* (L10-20,000). Specialty salads L13-28,000. *Primi* L10-15,000, *secondi* from L125,000. Open Sept.-July M-F noon-2:30pm and 7-11:30pm, Su 7-11:30pm.

Ristorante El Recreo, V. Scarlatti, 7 (☎02 29 51 33 21). MM1: Lima. Walk up C. Buenos Aires and take a left of V. Scarlatti; it's two blocks down on the left. Home-made Italian cuisine. Pasta L13-16,000, pizza L7,500-13,000, fruit and desserts L3-8000. Open Tu-Su 12pm-2:30pm, and 7pm-11:30pm.

Il Fondaco dei Mori, V. Solferino, 33 (☎02 65 37 11). From MM2: Moscova, walk north to P. XXV Aprile and turn right onto Porta Nuova. Take the second right onto V. Solferino. No sign; ring the bell. One of the first Arab restaurants in Italy; a Milan must. Vegetarian lunch *menù* L14,000. Delicious dinner buffet L20,000. Kebabs L18-20,000. Cover L3000. Open daily Tu-Su 12:30-3pm and 7:30pm-midnight.

👁 SIGHTS

DUOMO. The looming gothic cathedral is the geographical and spiritual center of Milan and makes a good starting point for a walking tour of the city. The *duomo* is the third-largest church in the world, after St. Peter's in the Vatican and the Seville Cathedral. Gian Galeazzo Visconti founded the cathedral in 1386, hoping to flatter the Virgin into granting him a male heir. Construction proceeded sporadically over the next four centuries and was finally completed at Napoleon's command in 1809. The imposing 16th-century marble tomb of Giacomo de Medici, in the south transept of the cathedral, was inspired by the work of Michelangelo. *(MM1: Duomo. Modest dress strictly enforced. Cathedral open daily Nov.-Feb. 9am-4:15pm; Mar-Oct 9am-5:45pm. June-Sept. 7am-5pm; Oct.-May 9am-4pm. Roof open daily 7am-7pm; in winter 9am-4:30pm. L6000, with elevator L8-9000.)* Recently renovated, the **Museo del Duomo** displays treasures from the cathedral as well as a plethora of historical documents about the duomo. It is to the right as you face the *duomo,* across the piazza in the Palazzo Reale at P. del Duomo, 14. *(☎02 86 03 58. Open Tu-Su 9:30am-12:30pm and 3-6pm. L8000.)* Also in the Palazzo Reale, the **Museo d'Arte Contemporanea** holds a fine permanent collection of 20th-century Italian art, interspersed with a few Picassos. *(☎02 62 08 32 19. Open Tu-Su 9:30am-5:30pm. Free.)*

▧ TEATRO ALLA SCALA. Known simply as La Scala, this is the world's most renowned opera house. Opened in 1778, it rests on the site of the Chiesa di S. Maria alla Scala, from which it took its name. Singer Maria Callas became a legend in this Neoclassical building. To see the lavish, red, multi-tiered hall, enter through the **Museo Teatrale alla Scala.** A series of petite rooms display opera memorabilia. Don't be too shocked when you see Verdi's hair or the casts of the hands of famous conductors. *(P. della Scala. At the opposite end of the Galleria Vittorio Emanuele from the duomo. ☎02 805 34 18. Museum open daily 9am-noon and 2-5:30pm. L6000.)*

PINACOTECA DI BRERA. The Brera Art Gallery presents one of the most impressive collections of paintings in Italy, with works that range from the 14th to the 20th century, with an emphasis on the Lombard School. Works include Bellini's *Pietà,* Andrea Mantegna's brilliantly foreshortened *Dead Christ,* Raphael's *Marriage of the Virgin,* Caravaggio's *Supper at Emmaus,* and Piero della Francesca's 15th-century *Sacra Conversazione.* A limited collection of works by modern masters includes pieces by Modigliani and Carlo Carrà. *(V. Brera, 28, MM2: Lanza. ☎02 72 26 31. Open Tu-Sa 9am-7pm, Su 8:30am-11pm. L8000.)*

GALLERIA VITTORIO EMANUELE II. This monumental glass barrel vault with a beautiful glass *cupola* (48m), to the left as you face the *duomo*, is five-stories of overpriced cafes and shops. Mosaics representing different continents sieged by the Romans adorn the floors and the central octagon's upper walls. Once considered the drawing room of Milan, the Galleria is now home to the Mediastore, the largest music store in Italy. (☎06 46 02 72. Open M-Sa 10am-11pm, Su 10am-8pm.)

MUSEO POLDI PEZZOLI. The museum contains an outstanding private art collection bequeathed to the city by Poldi Pezzoli in 1879. Famous paintings include Bellini's *Ecce Homo*, and the museum's signature piece, Antonio Pollaiuolo's *Portrait of a Young Woman*. (A few minutes from La Scala on the right at V. Manzoni, 12. ☎02 79 48 89. Open 10am-6pm daily. L10,000, seniors L5,000, students L2,500 .)

CASTELLO SFORZESCO. Restored after heavy bomb damage in 1943, the Castello Sforzesco is one of Milan's best-known monuments and a great place for a picnic. The Castello houses the **Musei Civici,** which includes the **Musical Instruments Museum** and the **Applied Arts Museum.** The ground floor contains a sculpture collection most renowned for Michelangelo's unfinished *Pietà Rondanini*, his last work. (Located at MM1: Cairoli. ☎02 62 36 39 47. Open Tu-Su 9:30am-5:15pm. Free.)

CHIESA DI SANTA MARIA DELLE GRAZIE. A 15th-century convent, the church's Gothic nave is dark and elaborately patterned with frescoes. Next to the church entrance, in what was once the dining hall, is the **Cenacolo Vinciano (Vinciano Refectory),** one of Milan's most famous sites, and home to one of the most important pieces of art in the world: **Leonardo da Vinci's Last Supper.** (Church is at P. di S. Maria delle Grazie, 2, on C. Magenta, off V. Carducci below MM1: Cadorna Cairoli. ☎028 942 11 46. Open Tu-F and Su 8:15am-6:45pm, Sa 8:15am-10:15pm. L12,000, under 18 and over 65 free. Wheelchair accessible.)

STADIO GIUSEPPE MEAZZA. The true *duomo* of the Milanese youth, the *Stadio* is one of the most famous football arenas on the planet. The tour of the stadium includes visits to the locker rooms and a museum dedicated to the two local teams. (V. Piccolomini, 5; MM2: Lotto. Walk along V. Fed. Caprilli and you can't miss it. Tours M-Sa 10am-5pm. L18,000, L12,000 for under 18 or over 65.)

MUSEO NAZIONALE DELLA SCIENZA E DELLA TECNICA "LEONARDO DA VINCI. To further your study of da Vinci, explore this interesting museum, dominated by applied physics and wooden models of Leonardo's visionary inventions. (V. San Vittore, 21, off V. Carducci, at MM2: San Ambrogio. ☎02 48 55 51. Open Tu-F 9:30am-4:50pm, Sa-Su 9:30am-6:20pm. L12,000, children and seniors over 60 L8000.)

BASILICA DI SANT'AMBROGIO. A prototype for Lombard-Romanesque churches throughout Italy, the *basilica* is the most influential medieval building in Milan. The tiny 4th-century **Cappella di San Vittore,** with exquisite 5th-century mosaics adorning its cupola, lies through the seventh chapel on the right. (MM1: Sant'Ambrogio. Open M-Sa 7:30am-noon and 2:30pm-7pm, Su 3pm-7pm. Free. Audiogiudes in the back of the church for L1000.)

NAVIGLI DISTRICT. The Venice of Lombardy, the Navigli district comes alive at night. Complete with canals, small footbridges, open-air markets, cafes, alleys, and trolleys, this area constitutes part of a medieval canal system with original locks that were designed by Leonardo da Vinci. (Outside the MM2: Porta Genova station, through the Arco di Porta Ticinese.)

CHIESA DI SAN LORENZO MAGGIORE. This 4th-century church is the oldest in Milan. To its right sits the 14th-century **Cappella di Sant'Aquilino.** Inside is a 5th-century mosaic of a beardless Christ among his apostles. A staircase behind the altar leads to an early Roman amphitheater's remains. (On C. Ticinese. MM2: Porta Genova, then tram #3 from V. Torino. Open daily 7:30am-6:45pm. L2000.)

BASILICA DI SANT'EUSTORGIO. Founded in the 4th century to house the bones of the Magi, the church lost its original function when the dead wise men were spirited off to Cologne in 1164. The triumph of this church, and one of the great masterpieces of early Renaissance art, is the **Portinari Chapel,** attributed to the Florentine Michelozzo. *(P. S. Eustorgio, 3. Farther down C. Ticinese from San Lorenzo Maggiore. Tram #3. Open W-M 9:30am-noon, and 3:30pm-6pm.)*

PINACOTECA AMBROSIANA. Tiny but lovely, the Ambrosiana's 23 rooms display exquisite works from the 14th through 19th centuries, including works by Botticelli, Leonardo, Raphael, Caravaggio, Tizian and Breughel. *(P. Pio XI, 2. Follow V. Spadari off V. Torino and make a left onto V. Cantù. ☎02 86 46 29 81. Open Tu-Su 10am-5:30pm. L12,000, under 18 or over 65 L6000.)*

🎵 🎬 ENTERTAINMENT AND NIGHTLIFE

La Scala, Milan's world-famous theater, traditionally opens its opera season on December 7 (although there are other productions year-round). Ask for a *Calendario della Stagione*. Gallery seats may cost as little as L20,000, but good tickets are usually sold long in advance. (☎02 72 00 37 44. Box office open daily noon-6pm.) Forty-five minutes before the show, 200 gallery standing-room tickets are sold at the entrance of the *museo* for L10,000 each.

If Milan's status as a world-famous fashion capital has lured you here for (window) shopping, the city's most elegant boutiques are found between the *duomo* and P. Babila. Many shops in Milan are closed on Monday mornings. If you can tolerate the stigma of being an entire season behind, purchase your famous designer duds from *blochisti* (wholesale clothing outlets). Hard-core window shoppers should head to the world-famous ■**fashion district** between **Corso Vittorio Emanuele** near the *duomo* and **Via Monte Napoleone** off P. San Babila. This area gives Milan its ultra-hip reputation. Take your credit card at your own risk. The dresses come straight from the designers and the selection is more up-to-date than anywhere else in the world, including New York or Tokyo. Expect to find high-class places to buy perfume, glasses, leather goods, shoes, and jewelry. **Via Sat'Andrea** between V. Montenapoleone and V. della Spiga, among the most elite neighborhoods in the city, has similarly upscale goods.

The nocturnal scene varies with the hour and the locale. A chic, very touristed district lies by **Via Brera,** northwest of the *duomo* and east of MM1: Cairoli, where you'll find art galleries, small clubs, restaurants, and an upscale thirtysomething crowd. Younger Milanese migrate to the areas around **C. Porta Ticinese** and **P. Vetra** (near Chiesa S. Lorenzo) to sip beer at one of the many *birrerie* (pubs). The highest concentration of bars and youth can be found into the wee hours of the morning in the **Navigli district.** (MM2: Porta Genova; walk along V. Vigevano until it ends and then veer right onto V. Naviglio Pavese.)

Grand Café Fashion (☎02 89 40 07 09), on C. Porta Ticinese near V. Vetere. Stunningly beautiful crowd, often selected by a bouncer. Mandatory first drink L15,000. Happy Hour 8pm-2:30am. Open daily noon-3pm and 8pm-3:30am.

Le Trottoir, From MM2: Lanza, take V. Tivoli to the C. Garibaldi intersection. Maybe the best bar in Milan. Don't think about leaving without giving a shout out to Rich, the self-styled "Australian ambassador of good will" who runs the bar. Open daily 7pm-2:30am.

Yguana Cafe Restaurant, V. P. Gregorio XIV, 16 (☎0338 10 93 097). Go down C. Porta Ticinese, and take a left at P. Vetra. Gorgeous, but relatively down-to-earth natives sip cocktails next to their scooters. Happy Hour daily 5:30pm-9pm. Sunday brunch 12:30pm-4pm. Open daily 5:30pm-1am.

Blue Kleim, V. Vigevano, 9. Walk 3 blocks down V. Vigevano from the MM2:Porta Genova and go left. Dedicated to the author Irwin Kleim. You can't miss it; the blue lights, yellow chairs, and loud house and R&B music scream *"balliamo!"* Open Tu-Su 5pm-3am.

Fontanelle, on V. Navigli Pavese, serves beer in creative ways. Drink up, or risk spillage. Always crowded with a mix of locals and foreigners. Open daily 8pm-2am.

Totem Pub (☎02 837 50 98), at V. Naviglio Pavese and V. E. Gola, caters to a more head-banging sort of clientele. Be prepared to hear anything from Metallica to reggae. Serves beer in immeasurably large mugs for L15,000. Open daily 8:30pm-2:30am.

Rock: Hollywood, C. Como, 15 (☎02 659 89 96). One of the only discos in the city to select from the crowd at the door. Caters to bigwigs in the fashion industry and the übermodels who love them. Mmm.... models. Cover L25-30,000. Open Tu-Su 10:030pm-4am.

Lollapaloosa, C. Como, 15 (☎02 655 56 93). Next door to Rock, this Wild West bar is owned by the captain of the Italian football team. The energetic crowd will have you tipsy and dancing on the tables in no time. Cover L15,000, including a drink. Open daily 7pm-2am, F, Sa 7pm-5:30am.

Bar Magenta, V. Carducci, 13 (☎02 805 38 08). MM1/2: Cardona. Traditional, well-crafted, wood-paneled Guinness bar. Hard to get in, harder to get out—the crowd often spills onto the sidewalk. Open Tu-Su 9am-3am, sometimes until 5am.

Cafe Capoverde, V. Leoncavallo, 16 (☎02 26 82 04 30). From MM1/2: Loreto, walk on V. Costa p to this heavenly, unique cafe. Cocktails dominate, but decent food is available. *Primi* from L11,000, pizza around L12,000. Open 12-3pm and 8pm-midnight.

Artdecothe, V. Lombro, 7 (☎02 39 52 47 60) From MM1: Porta Venezia, walk three blocks up C. Buenos Aires and take a right on V. Melzi. The bar is three blocks down on the left, across from Le Lephante. Modern, and very, very cool. Each table is decorated in a different style. Happy Hour daily 6-9pm. Open daily 7am-2am.

GAY BARS AND CLUBS

Le Lephante, V. Melzi, 22 (☎02 29 51 87 68). From MM2: Porta Venezia, walk up C. B. Aires three blocks and turn right on V. Melzi. Mixed gay and straight crowd. Across from the Artdeco Cafe. Open Tu-Su 6:30pm-2am.

Cicip e Ciciap, V. Gorani, 9 (☎02 87 75 55). From MM1: Cairoli, take V. S. Giov. sul Muro which turns into V Brisa. V. Gorani is the second left. Attracts a women-only crowd. Open only Sa 8:30pm-3am.

One Way Club, V. Cavallotti, 204 (☎02 242 13 41). MM2: Sesto FS. Disco and leather. Membership card required. Open F and Sa 10:30pm-3:30am, Su 3:30-7pm.

⌘ DAYTRIPS FROM MILAN

GENOA. Stroll by gorgeous *palazzia* on Via Garibaldi, and gaze at the fishies in the fabulous aquarium (see p. 649).

TURIN. Pay a visit to the home of both the Fiat auto-company, and one of Christianity's most famous relics, the Shroud of Turin (see p. 677).

MANTUA (MANTOVA)

Mantua owes its literary fame to its most famous son, the poet Virgil. The driving force that built the city's *centro storico*, however, was not the lyric poet but the Gonzaga family. After ascending to power in 1328, the family persistently altered Mantua's small-town image by importing well-known artists and cultivating local talent. Lined with grand *palazzi* and graceful churches, Mantua also provides easy passage to the surrounding lakes. The cobblestoned **Piazza Sordello** marks the center of a vast complex built by the Gonzaga family. The huge ✎**Palazzo Ducale,** which towers over the *piazza*, gradually absorbed the Gothic **Magna Domus** (*duomo*) and **Palazzo del Capitano.** Inside, check out frescoes, tapestries, gardens, you name it. Outside the *palazzo*, signs mark the formidable **Castello di San Giorgio** (1390-1406), once a fortress before being absorbed by the *palazzo*, of which it is now a wing. (*Palazzo* open Tu-Su 8:45am-6:30pm. L12,000.) At the far south of the city, down V. P. Amedeo through P. Veneto and down Largo Parri, lies the opulent **Palazzo del Te,** built by Giulio Romano in 1534 as a suburban retreat for Francesco II Gonzaga. It is widely considered the finest building in the Mannerist style.

(☎0376 32 32 66. Open Tu-Su 9am-6pm, M 1-6pm. L12,000, students and ages 12-18 L8000, groups L7000 per person, under 11 free.) Opposite **Piazza delle Erbe,** the 11th-century Romanesque structure, just south of P. Sordello, is Alberti's **Chiesa di Sant'Andrea,** Mantua's greatest contribution to the Italian Renaissance. (Piazza open daily 10am-12:30pm and 2:30-6:30pm. Free. Chiesa open daily 8am-noon and 3-6:30pm. Free.) The **Teatro Scientifico (Bibiena)** can be reached by walking from P. dell'Erbe to P. Broletto and taking V. Accademia till the end. This acoustically marvelous theater seems to have come from a fairy-tale, with charming statues and a maroon and gray decor. (Open Tu-Su 9:30am-12:30pm and 3-6:30pm. Free.)

Trains (☎0376 32 16 47) go from P. Don Leoni to Verona (40min., every hr., L4100) and Milan (2hr., 9 per day, L16,000). From the station, head left on V. Solferino, through P. S. Francesco d'Assisi to V. Fratelli Bandiera, and right on V. Verdi to find the **tourist office,** P. Mantegna, 6, next to Sant'Andrea's church. (☎0376 32 82 53; fax 0376 36 32 92. Open M-Sa 8:30am-12:30pm and 3-6pm.) Charming **Hotel ABC,** P. Don Leoni, 25, is opposite the station. (☎0376 32 33 47. Breakfast included. Singles from L50,000; doubles L90,000; triples L140,000.) **Antica Osteria ai Ranari,** V. Trieste, 11, down V. Pomponazzo near Porta Catena, specializes in regional dishes. (☎0376 32 84 31. *Primi* L8-10,000, *secondi* L10-15,000. Cover L2000. Closed for 3 weeks late-July to early-Aug. Open Tu-Su noon-2:30pm and 7:00-11:00pm.) **Postal Code:** 46100.

BERGAMO

A medieval city awaits over the hills above Bergamo, a collection of treasure-filled art galleries and glorious churches. **Via Pignolo,** in the *città bassa* (lower city), winds past a succession of handsome 16th- to 18th-century palaces. Turning left onto V. S. Tomaso and then right brings you to the astounding **Galleria dell'Accademia Carrara,** which holds works by Titian, Rubens, Breughel, and van Dyck. (Open W-M 9:30am-12:30pm and 2:30-5:30pm. L5000; Su free.) From there, the terraced **Via Noca** ascends to the *città alta* (upper city) through Porta Sant'Agostino. Immediately left of the Cappella Colleoni is the ▓**Basilica di Santa Maria Maggiore,** a 12th-century basilica with an ornate Baroque interior and tapestries depicting biblical scenes. (Open May-Sept. 9am-noon and 3-6pm, Sa-Su 8-10:30am and 3-6pm; Oct.-Apr. 9am-noon and 3-4:30pm, Sa-Su 8-10:30am and 3-6pm. Free.) Head through the archway flanking P. Vecchia to P. del Duomo, and see the chapel **Cappella Colleoni.** (Open Tu-Su Mar.-Oct. 9am-12:30pm and 2-6:30pm; Nov.-Feb. 9am-12:30pm and 2:30-4:30pm. Free.) Stroll down V. Porta Dipinta to V. Gambito, which ends in **Piazza Vecchia,** an ensemble of medieval and Renaissance buildings flanked by restaurants and cafes at the heart of the *città alta.* Climb the **Torre Civica** (L2000) for a marvelous view of Bergamo and the hills.

The train and bus stations and many budget hotels are in the *città bassa.* **Trains** (1hr., L7200) and **buses** (L7500) pull into P. Marconi from Milan. To get to the **tourist office,** Vco. Aquila Nera, 2, in the *città alta,* take bus #1 or 1a to the funicular, then follow V. Gambito to P. Vecchia and turn right. (☎035 23 27 30; fax 24 29 94. Open daily 9am-12:30pm and 2-5:30pm.) Take bus #14 from Porto Nuova to Leonardo da Vinci and walk uphill to reach the **Ostello della Gioventù di Bergamo (HI),** V. G. Ferraris, 1. (☎035 34 30 38. Breakfast included. Members only. Dorms L25,000; singles L35,000; doubles L60,000.) **Locanda Caironi,** V. Torretta, 6B, off V. Gorgo Palazzo, is in a quiet residential neighborhood. Take bus #5 or 7 from V. Angelo Maj. (☎24 30 83. Singles L30,000; doubles L55,000.) In the *città bassa,* **Capolinea,** V. Giacomo Quarenghi, 29, right off V. Zambonate, provides full meals from L15,000. (Open Tu-Sa 6:30pm-3am, Su 7pm-3am. Kitchen closes at midnight.) In the *città alta,* the prison-turned-communist-café **Circolino Cooperativa Città Alta,** V. S. Agata, 19, features *bocce* and a view, as well as sandwiches, pizza, and salads for under L8000. (Open Th-Tu 8:30am-3am). **Postal Code:** 24122.

ITALIAN RIVIERA (LIGURIA)

The Italian Riviera stretches 350 kilometers along the Mediterranean between France and Tuscany, forming the most famous and touristed area of the Italian coastline. Genoa divides the crescent-shaped strip into the more dramatic Riviera di Levante ("rising sun") to the east and the Riviera di Ponente ("setting sun") to the west. The elegant coast beckons with lemon trees, almond blossoms, and turquoise sea. Especially lovely is the **Cinque Terre** area, just to the west of La Spezia.

▐ TRANSPORTATION

All the coastal towns are linked by the main **rail** line, which runs west from Genoa to Ventimiglia (near the French border) and east to La Spezia (near Tuscany), but slow local trains can make short distances take hours. Frequent intercity **buses** pass through all major towns, and local buses run to inland hill-towns. **Boats** connect most resort towns. **Ferries** go from Genoa to Olbia, Sardinia and Palermo, Sicily.

GENOA (GENOVA)

Urban, gritty Genoa has little in common with its resort neighbors. Flourishing trade in the 13th century allowed for the construction of parks and lavish palaces in this port town. Its financial glory was soon matched by the repute of its citizens, including Chistopher Columbus and Giuseppe Mazzini. Since falling into decline in the 18th century, modern Genoa has turned its attention away from industry to the restoration of its bygone grandeur.

▐ **TRANSPORTATION.** Most visitors arrive at one of Genoa's two train stations: **Stazione Principe**, in P. Acquaverde, or **Stazione Brignole**, in P. Verdi. From Stazione Principe take bus #19, 20, 30, 32, 35, or 41 and from Stazione Brignole take bus #19 or 40 to Piazza de Ferrari in the center of town.

▐ PRACTICAL INFORMATION. Trains go to Turin (2hr., 19 per day, L14,500-23,200) and Rome (5hr., 14 per day, L43,300-62,000). **Ferries** (see above) depart from the Ponte Assereto arm of the port; buy tickets from the Stazione Marittima. If walking from Stazione Principe, take Via Balbi to Via Cairoli, and turn right on Via XXV Aprile at P. delle Fontane Marose; from Stazione Brignole, turn right to Via Fiume, and right onto Via XX Settembre. Pick up a map (L7000) at any newsstand. The **APT tourist office** is at Porto Antico, in P. Santa Maria. From the aquarium, walk toward the complex of buildings to the left. (☎248 71. Open daily 9am-6:30pm.) Log on at **Internet Village**, at V. Brigata Bisagno and C. Buenos Aires, across from P. Vittoria. (L15,000 per hr. Open 9am-1pm and 3-7pm.) **Postal Code:** 16100.

▐░ ACCOMMODATIONS AND FOOD. Genoa may have more one-star hotels per capita than any other city in Italy. **Ostello per la Gioventù (HI)**, V. Costanzi, 120, has a cafeteria, TV, and a view of the city far below. From Stazione Principe, walk down V. Balbi to P. Delba Nunziata and catch bus #40 (every 15min.), and tell the driver your destination. (☎242 24 57. Breakfast included. Laundry L12,000 for 5kg. Reception 7-9am and 3:30pm-12:30am. Curfew midnight. Dorms L23,000. HI Members only; HI card available.) **Albergo Carola**, V. Gropallo, 4/12, has elegant rooms overlooking a garden. From Stazzione Brignole, turn right on V. de Amicis, turn right when facing Albergo Astoria, and walk 20m. (☎839 13 40. Singles L45,000; doubles L65,000, with shower L75,000.) **Albergo Balbi**, V. Balbi, 21/3, offers large, ornate rooms. (Breakfast L7000. Singles L35,0000, with bath L45,000; doubles L75,000, with bath L90,000; triples and quads add 30% per person.) **Camping** is popular; turn to the tourist office for info, as many campgrounds are booked solid. To reach **Villa Doria**, V. al Campeggio Villa Doria, 15, take the train or bus #1-3 from P. Caricamento to Pegli, then walk or transfer to bus #93 up V. Vespucci. (☎696 96 00. L9000 per person, L10-13,000 per tent.) Genoa is famous for its *pesto* and *focaccia*. **Trattoria da Maria**, V. Testa d'Oro, 14r, off V. XXV Aprile, has a new menu every day with dishes for L13,000. (Open Su-F noon-2:30pm and 7-9:30pm.)

📷 🔲 **SIGHTS AND ENTERTAINMENT.** The palaces that line Genoa's streets are its most impressive aspect, as well as the fine 16th- and 17th-century Flemish and Italian art acquired in its days of commercial power. V. Balbi, in the heart of the university quarter, contains lavish *palazzi*. The 18th-century **Palazzo Reale,** V. Balbi, 10, near Stazione Principe, is filled with Rococo rooms bathed in gold and upholstered in red velvet. (Open M-Th 9:15am-1:45pm, F-Su 8:15am-7:15pm. L8000, under 18 and seniors free.) Follow V. Balbi through P. della Nunziata and continue to L. Zecca, where V. Cairoli leads to **V. Garibaldi,** the most impressive street in Genoa, bedecked with elegant *palazzi* that once earned it the names "Golden Street" and "Street of Kings." The **Galleria di Palazzo Bianco,** V. Garibaldi, 11, exhibits Ligurian, Dutch, and Flemish paintings. Across the street, the 17th-century **Galleria Palazzo Rosso,** V. Garibaldi, 18, has magnificent furnishings in a lavishly frescoed interior. (Both open Tu and Th-F 9am-1pm, W and Sa 9am-7pm, Su 10am-6pm. L6000 each, L10,000 together. Su free.) The Villetta Di Negro, on the hill further down V. Garibaldi, contains waterfalls, grottos, and terraced gardens. Take V. M. Plaggio to P. Corvetto, then V. Roma to P. Ferrarri, where V. Boetto leads to P. Matteotti and the Palazzo Ducale, where the city's rulers once lived. On the opposite corner stands the ornate Chiesa del Gesù. (Open daily 7:30am-noon and 4-6:30pm. Free.) Head past the Chiesa del Gesù down V. di Porta Soprana to V. Ravecca to reach the medieval twin-towered Porta Soprana, the supposed boyhood home of **Christopher Columbus.** Continue further down V. Ravecca to reach the **Museo dell'Architettura e Scultura Ligure,** which features surviving art pieces from Genoa's history. (Open Tu-Sa 9am-7pm, Su 9am-12:30pm. L6000.) Off V. San Lorenzo, lies the **San Lorenzo Duomo,** a church in existence since the 9th century, which boasts a striped Gothic facade with a copiously decorated main entrance and 9th-century carved lions. (Open M-Sa 8am-7pm, Su 7am-7pm. Free.) The *duomo* lies on the southern edge of the centro storico (the historical center of town), a tangled web of alleys bordered by the port to the east, V. Garibaldi to the north, and P. Ferrari to the southeast. The region is home to some of Genoa's most memorable monuments. Once you're back on P. Matteotti, go down V. San Lorenzo toward the water, turn left on V. Chiabrera and left on V. Di Mascherona to reach the Chiesa S. Maria di Castello, a labyrinth of chapels, courtyards, cloisters, and cruxifices. (Open daily 9am-noon and 3:30-6:30pm.) Kids and ocean-lovers will adore the massive aquarium, on Porto Antico to the right of the APT tourist office. (Open M-F 9:30am-7pm, Sa-Su 9:30am-8pm; in summer Th until 11pm. L19,000.)

FINALE LIGURE

A beachside plaque proclaims the town of Finale Ligure the place for "*Il riposo del popolo,*" (the people's rest). Whether one's idea of *riposo* involves bodysurfing in the choppy waves near Torrente Porra, browsing through the chic boutiques that fill Finalmarina, or free-climbing past Finalborgo's looming 15th century Castello di San Giovanni, the *popolo* have many options. The city is divided into three sections: **Finalpia** to the east, **Finalmarina** in the center, and **Finalborgo** (the old city) further inland. In the town center, skip the narrow strip of beach across from Hotel Boncardo; instead, walk along V. Aurelia through the first tunnel and turn right to a less populated **free beach,** where you can soak in the sun in (relative) solitude and gaze at the overhanging craggy cliffs. For a more up-close and personal view of said cliffs, tourists can try climbing the tough trail to the ruins of **Castle Giovane** for a spectacular glimpse of both the 13th-century castle and the town below. Enclosed within ancient walls, Finalborgo, the historic quarter of Finale Ligure proper, is a 1km walk or short bus ride up V. Bruneghi from the station. Past the **Porto Reale,** Chiostro di Santa Caterina, a 14th-century edifice houses the **Museo Civico del Finale,** dedicated to Ligurian history. (☎ 019 69 02 20. Open Tu-Sa 10am-noon and 3-6pm, Su 9am-noon. Free.) **Pilade,** a popular bar in the historic quarter has live music nightly, with offerings that range from blues to jazz. (V. Garibladi, 67. ☎ 019 69 22 20. 10am-2am, closed Th in winter.) The numerous beachside towns near Finale Ligure are also worth the trip, especially **Borgo Verezzi,** which can be reached by the **SAR buses** that run from the train station (L1800), and offers peaceful streets and caves for tourists to explore.

Trains head to Genoa from P. Vittorio Veneto (1 hr., every hr., L6900). The IAT **tourist office,** V.S. Pietro 14, gives out free maps. (☎019 68 10 19; fax 019 68 18 04. Open M-Sa 9am-12:30pm and 3:30-7pm, Su 9am-noon.) **Castello Wuillerman (HI),** on V. Generale Caviglia, is well worth the tough hike. From the station, take a left onto V. Mazzini (which becomes V. Torino), turn left on V. degli Ulivi, and trudge up the daunting steps. (☎019 69 05 15. Breakfast and sheets included. Reception 7-10am and 5-10pm. Curfew 11:30pm. No phone reservations. Open Mar.15-Oct.15. L20,000.) **Pensione Enzo** on Gradinata delle Rose, provides double rooms at seasonal rates. (☎019 69 13 83. Open Easter-end of Sep. Doubles L60-92,000 depending on time of week/year.) To get to the convenient **Albergo Oasi,** at V. San Cagna 25, veer left on V. Brunenghi from the station, walk through the underpass on your right to Via Silla, walk up the hill, and turn left at the intersection. (☎019 69 17 17. Open Easter-Sept. Singles L45,000, doubles L90,000, extra beds L45,000.) **Albergo Carla,** V. Colombo, 44, offers a floor with 19 rooms with private bathrooms, a bar, and a restaurant. (☎019 69 22 85. Open year round. Singles L45,000; doubles L75,000 but July-Sept. prices increase with required pension L50,000 for half, up to L82, 000 for full.) The **Albergo Marita** is set back on the street leading from the station, with clean rooms and balconies. (V. Saccone, 17. ☎019 69 29 04. Breakfast L8000. 3-day min. stay. Summer reservations required. Singles L35-40,000; doubles with bath L50-80,000. Full-pension L75,000. P

rices rise July-Aug.) To access **Camping Tahiti,** on V. Varese, take the bus from P. Vittorio Veneto (dir: Calvisio) to Bar Paradiso, cross the small bridge at Via Rossini, turn left, and walk along the river to V. Vanese. (☎019 60 06 00. Offices open Easter-Oct.15, 8am-8pm. L11,000 per person, L10,000 per tent; off-season reduced.) Cheap restaurants lie inland along **V. Rossi** and **V. Roma. Spaghetteria Il Posto,** V. Porro, 21, offers mountains of well-priced pasta. (☎019 60 00 95. Cover L1500. Open Tu-Su 7-10:30pm, closed the first 2 weeks of March.) **Simpatia Crai supermarket** is at V. Bruneghi, 2a. (Open M-Sa 8am-12:30pm and 4-6:30pm.)

CAMOGLI

Picture-perfect Camogli is a cascade of color. Peach houses crowd the hilltop, red-and-turquoise boats bob in the water, and bright umbrellas dot the dark stone beaches. To reach the **beach,** turn left down the steep stairs 100m away from the station, then turn right off V. Garibaldi into the alley. If you tire of the beach and boardwalk, ferry or snorkeling trips also make interesting (but more costly) diversions. **BandB Diving Center,** V. S. Fortunato, 11/13, off P. Colombo offers ten-person boat capacities, 18 immersion spots along the coast, and three excursions daily for scuba diving and snorkeling. (☎0185 77 27 51. Scuba L65-100,000, snorkeling L20,000. Open daily 9am-7pm.) **Trains** run on the Genoa-La Spezia line to Genoa (20min., 32 per day, L2700); La Spezia (1½hr., 21per day, L6400); and Santa Margherita (10min., 24 per day, L1900). Golfo Paradiso **ferries,** V. Scalo 3 (☎0185 77 20 91), near P. Colombo, go to Portofino (Sa-Su only, L14,000, round-trip L20,000) and Cinque Terre (L20,000); buy tickets at the dock. Go right from the station to the **tourist office,** V. XX Settembre, 33, for help finding rooms. (☎0185 77 10 66. Open June-Sept. daily 8:30am-12:30pm and 3-7pm; Oct.-May M-Sa 9am-noon and 3:30-6:30pm, Su 9am-1pm.) Exit the station, walk down the stairs to the right to reach the **Albergo La Camogliese,** V. Garibaldi, 55. (☎0185 77 14 02; fax 01 85 77 40 24. Breakfast L10,000. Reserve ahead. Singles L70-90,000; doubles L90-110,000.)

SANTA MARGHERITA LIGURE

Santa Margherita Ligure led a calm existence as a fishing village until the mid-20th century, when it fell into favor with Hollywood stars. Today, the shores sparkle with glamour and glitz, Art-Deco lighting illuminates pastel walls, and palm trees line the harbor. Still, the serenity of the town's early days lingers; Santa Margherita Ligure offers leisure time and tranquility. If lapping ocean waves don't invigorate your spirit, try the holy water in the seashell basins at the **Basilica di Santa Margherita,** at P. Caprera. **Trains** along the Pisa-Genoa line go from P. Federico Raoul Nobili, at the top of V. Roma, to Genoa (40min., 2-3 per hr., L3600) and La Spezia (2 per hr., L6900) via Cinque Terre (1.5hr., L5300). **Tigullio buses** (☎0185 28 88 34) go from P. Vittorio Veneto to Portofino (20min., 3 per hr., L1600) and Camogli (30min., every hr., L2000). **Tigullio ferries**, V. Palestro, 8/1b (☎0185 28 15 98), have tour trips to Portofino (every hr., L6000, round-trip L10,000) and Cinque Terre (1 per day, L25-30,000, round-trip L35-40,000). Turn right from the train station on V. Roma, turn left on C. Rainusso, and take a hard right onto V. XXV Aprile to find the **tourist office**, V. XXV Aprile 2b. (☎0185 28 74 85. Open M-Sa 9am-12:30pm and 3-6pm, Su 9:30am-12:30pm.) **Hotel Riviera**, V. Belvedere, 10, has spacious rooms. (☎/fax 0185 28 74 03. Breakfast included. Singles L85-105,000; doubles L120-160,000; triples L165-210,000.) **Pensione Azalea**, V. Roma 60/V. Gramsci, 89, is right of the train station. (☎0185 28 61 60. Breakfast included. Doubles with bath L95,000.) **La Piadineria and Creperia**, V. Giuncheto, 5, off P. Martiri della Libertà, serves huge sandwiches (L7-10,000) and more. (Open Easter-Oct. Tu-Sa 5:30pm-3am; July-Sept. also open M 5:30pm-3am and Su 12:30pm-3am.)

PORTOFINO

Secluded and exclusive, tiny Portofino—a great daytrip from Santa Margherita—has long been a playground for the financially advantaged. Yachts may fill the harbor and chic boutiques line its streets, but both princes and paupers can enjoy the shore's curves and tiny bay. A one-hour walk along the ocean road offers the chance to scout out small rocky **beaches.** The shore at **Paraggi** (where the bus stops) is the area's only sandy beach. In town, follow the signs uphill from the bay to escape to the cool interior of the **Chiesa di San Giorgio.** A few minutes up the road toward the **castle** is a serene garden with sea views. (Open daily in summer 10am-6pm; off-season 10am-5pm. L3000.) To get to town, take the bus to Portofino Mare. From P. Martiri della Libertà, **Tigullio buses** go to Santa Margherita (3 per hr., L1600); buy tickets at the green kiosk in P. Martiri della Libertà. **Ferries** also go from Portofino to Santa Margherita (every hr. 9am-7pm, L6000) and Camogli (2 per day, L13,000). The **tourist office**, V. Roma, 35, is en route to the waterfront from the bus stop. (☎0185 26 90 24. Open in summer daily 9:30am-1:30pm and 2-7pm; off-season 9:30am-12:30pm and 2:30-5:30pm.)

TO CORSICA: LA SPEZIA

A departure point for Corsica (see p. 364) and an unavoidable transport hub for Cinque Terre, La Spezia is quite likely Italy's loveliest port in its own right, with regal palms lining its promenade and parks laden with citrus trees. La Spezia lies on the Genoa-Pisa **train** line. **Happy Lines,** with a ticket kiosk on V. Italia, sends ferries to Corsica (round-trip L124,000, off-season L84,000). **Navigazione Golfo dei Poeti,** v. Mazzini 21, has ferries that stop in each village of Cinque Terre and Portovenereo (4 per day; one-way L20,000; round-trip L33,000); Capraia (5hr., round-trip L80,000); and Elba (3½hr., round-trip L80,000.) The **tourist office** (☎0187 77 09 00) is at the port at V. Mazzini 45. To reach **Albergo Terminus**, V. Paleocapa 21, turn left out of the train station. (☎0187 77 09 34 36. Singles L40,000, with bath L55,000; doubles L65,000, with bath L90,000; triples L70,000.)

CINQUE TERRE

The five bright fishing villages of Cinque Terre cling to a stretch of terraced hillsides and steep crumbling cliffs, while a dazzling turquoise sea laps against their shores. You can hike through all five—Monterosso, Vernazza, Corniglia, Manarola, and Riomaggiore—in a few hours.

⌐ TRANSPORTATION

Trains: The towns lie on the Genoa-La Spezia (Pisa) line. From the station on V. Fegina, in **Monterosso**, trains run to: **Rome** (7hr., every 2hr., L51,500); **Florence** (3½hr., every hr., L14,500), via Pisa; **Genoa** (1½hr., every hr., L7000); **Pisa** (2½hr., every hr., L8500) and **La Spezia** (20min., every 30min., L2300). Frequent trains connect the five towns (5-20min., every 50min., L1700-2300). Schedules available at the tourist office. The 24hr. **Cinque Terre Tourist Ticket** (L5500), for unlimited trips between towns, is available at the 5 train stations—ask at the ticket window.

Ferries: Navigazione Golfo dei Poet (☎0187 96 76 76), in front of the **IAT** office at the port (on the old part of town) goes to: **Manarola** and **Riomaggiore** (6 per day, round-trip L15,000); **Portovenere** (1hr., L18,000, round-trip L30,000); and **Vernazza** (5 per day, L5000, round-trip L8000).

Taxis: ☎0335 61 65 842 and 0335 616 58 45.

✳🛈 ORIENTATION AND PRACTICAL INFORMATION

From **Monterosso,** the most central of the villages, the four others are easily accessible by train as well as by foot, ferry, and kayak, depending on your inclination and stamina. **Listings are for Monterosso unless otherwise indicated.**

Tourist Office: Pro Loco, V. Fegina, 38 (☎0187 81 75 06), below the train station. Open Apr.-Oct. M-Sa 9:30am-noon and 3:30-5:30pm, Su 10am-noon. Closed in winter. In Riomaggiore, an office in the train station (☎0187 92 06 33) provides info on trails, hotels, and excursions. Open daily June-Sept. 10am-6pm.)

Currency Exchange: At the post office. For traveler's checks transactions, head to **Banca Carige,** V. Roma, 69.

Boat Rental: Pedal boats L15-17,000 per hr., kayaks L10-15,000 per hr., L50,000 per day. Motorboats L30-45,000 per hr., L150-220,000 per day.

Emergency: ☎113. **Medical Emergency:** ☎118. **First Aid: Guardia Medica** in Monterosso ☎033 885 309 49 and ☎0187 81 76 87; ☎0187 80 09 73, in Riomaggiore; ☎0187 92 07 66, Manarola; ☎0187 82 10 84, Vernazza. **Police: Carabinieri** ☎112, in Monterosso 0187 81 75 24; in Riomaggiore ☎0187 92 01 12.

Pharmacy: V. Fegina, 14, under the train station in Monterosso. Open M-Sa 9am-12:30pm and 4-8pm, Su 9:30am-12:30pm and 4-7:30pm.

Post Office: V. Loreto, 73 (☎0187 81 83 94) in Monterosso. Open M-Sa 8am-1:30pm. Fermo posta, telephone cards. **Postal Code:** 19016.

▐ ACCOMMODATIONS

No matter the length of your visit, reserve at least several weeks in advance. Manarola's hostel, one of Italy's best, recommends reservations a month in advance. If you're still looking for a room when you arrive, gamble on the cheaper and more plentiful rooms in Riomaggiore, Monterosso, or Vernazza.

Albergo Della Gioventù-Ostello "Cinque Terre," V. B. Riccobaldi, 21 (☎0187 92 02 15), in Manarola. Go right from the train station and up the hill. Sheets and 5min. shower included. Laundry L7000 wash, L5000 dry. Reception daily Sept.16-May 31 7am-10am and 4pm-midnight; June-Sept. 15 7am-10am and 5pm-1am. Dorms L25-30,000; quads with bath L100,000.

Meublè Agavi, Lungomare Fegina, 30 (☎0187 81 71 71), in Monterosso. Go left from the station onto the boardwalk. Rooms with bath, phone, and fridge. Singles L80,000; doubles L145,000.

Hotel Souvenir, V. Gioberti, 24 (☎0187 81 75 95), in Monterosso. Breakfast L10,000. All rooms with bath. Dorms L50,000.

Albergo Punta Mesco, V. Molinelli, 35 (☎0187 81 74 95). Cramped rooms, but convenient location. Breakfast included. Open Apr.-Oct. Singles L75,000; doubles L120,000; triples L162,000; quads L190,000.

Il Villaggio Marino "Europa," (☎0187 81 22 79), in Corniglia. Go right from the station. Laundry. June-Sept. by the week only. Nov.-Mar. L800,000 per week for 4 people; Apr.-Oct. L150,000 per day for 4 people; L500,000 per 4 days; L600,000 per week.

🍴 FOOD

If you're on a tight budget in Cinque Terre, consider romantic picnics: wash your beach- or cliff-side meal down with the locally made, sweet and delicious *sciacchetrà* wine. (Open June-Sept. M-Sa 8am-1pm and 5-7:30pm, Su 8am-1pm. Closed W in winter.) Pick up some of the basics for your picnic lunch at **Superconad Margherita**, at P. Matteotti, 9, in Monterosso.

FAST, V. Roma, 13 (☎0187 81 71 64), in Monterosso, known as *La Casa dei Panini Cantanti* (The House of the Singing Sandwiches), where Fabio and Stefano speedily whip you up a fresh sandwich. Sandwiches start at L6000. Open daily 10am-2am; in winter Tu-Su 10am-2am.

Focacceria Il Frantoio, V. Gioberti, 1 (☎0187 81 83 33), in Monterosso, has a wood-burning oven that bakes every kind of *focaccia* imaginable, stuffed with olives, onions, herbs, or other fillings. Slices L2-3500. Open F-W 9am-2pm and 4-8pm.

👁🎵 SIGHTS AND ENTERTAINMENT

Private beaches dominate the coastline of Cinque Terre. However, pebbly public beaches line the shores of Monterosso. Use of most of the beach here will cost you L3000-L5000 just to enter. The largest free beach lies directly below the train station; get there early to stake your claim. For the best of both worlds, make a trek to **Guvano Beach** in Corniglia. A 15min. walk through a dark and spooky tunnel (don't walk it alone) and a L5000 toll are rewarded by a less populated beach. The more historical offerings of Cinque Terre include the **Convento dei Cappuccini** (built 1618-1622) which lies on a hill in the center of Monterosso and contains an impressive crucifixion by Flemish master Anthony van Dyck, who sojourned here during his most productive years. (Open daily 9am-noon and 4-7pm.) In Vernazza, walk up the staircase to the left of Pza. Marconi, to reach the **Castello Doria**, the remains of an 11th-century castle, which possesses a spectacular view. (Open daily 10am-6:30pm. L2000.) **Hikes** between the five towns are a superb way to explore and acquaint oneself with Cinque Terre. The distance between Monterosso and Riomaggiore can be covered in about five hours. The most challenging hike is from Monterosso to Vernazza (1½hr.), while the trail between Vernazza and Corniglia (2hr.) passes through some of the area's most spectacular scenery. To avoid scaling rocks, start at Riomaggiore and end with Vernazza or Monterosso. Walk the leisurely **Via dell'Amore** (20min.) to the #2 hike at Manarola's Punta Bonfiglio; follow it to the end or turn onto #7 from Manarola to Corniglia, uphill to the highway. The highway rejoins the trail into Vernazza. If you ever tire, just hop in the train and return to your base town.

EMILIA-ROMAGNA

Go to Florence, Venice, and Rome to sightsee, come to Emilia-Romagna to eat. Italy's wealthiest wheat- and dairy-producing region covers the fertile plains of the Po River Valley, celebrating the finest culinary traditions on the Italian Peninsula. Gorge on Parmesan cheese and *prosciutto*, fresh Bolognese pasta and *mortadella*, and Ferrarese *salama* and *grana* cheese.

BOLOGNA

With just one forkful of Bologna's *tortellini*, it becomes clear that the city appreciates the better things in life. Bright facades lean on 700-year-old porticos and cobblestoned roads twist by churches, but the city's appeal extends far beyond aesthetics. Blessed with prosperity and Europe's oldest university, Bologna has developed an open-minded character; minority and gay political activism is strong. Apart from a formidable list of its university's graduates—including Dante, Petrarch, and Copernicus—the city prides itself on its great culinary heritage.

EAT YOUR HEART OUT, CHEF BOYARDEE in

Italy, the desecration of pasta is a mortal sin. Pasta must be chosen correctly and cooked *al dente* (firm, literally "to the tooth"). To avoid embarrassment, get to know the basics. The *spaghetti* family includes all variations that require twirling, from hollow cousins *bucatini* and *maccheroni* to the more delicate *capellini*. Flat *spaghetti* include *fettuccini*, *taglierini*, and *tagliatelle*. Short pasta tubes can be *penne* (cut diagonally and occasionally *rigate*, or ribbed), *sedani* (curved), *rigatoni* (wider), or *cannelloni* (usually stuffed). *Fusilli* (corkscrews), *farfalle* (butterflies or bow-ties), and *ruote* (wheels) are fun as well as functional. Don't be alarmed if you see pastry displays labeled "pasta"; the Italian word refers to anything made of dough.

TRANSPORTATION. Bologna is a rail hub for all major Italian cities and the Adriatic coast; **trains** go to: Rome (4hr., 1-2 per hr., L35,000); Florence (1½hr., every 2hr., L8200-13,500); Milan (3hr., 2-3 per hr., L18,000); and Venice (2hr., every hr., L14,000). Arrive during the day, as the area near the station is not the safest.

PRACTICAL INFORMATION. Buses #25 and 30 run between the station and the historic center at P. Maggiore (L1800). The **tourist office**, P. Maggiore 6, is next to the **Palazzo Comunale**. (☎051 23 96 60; fax 051 23 14 54; www.comune.bologna.it. Open M-Sa 9am-7pm, Su 9am-2pm.) Check **email** at **Crazy Bull Café**, V. Montegrappa 11/e, off V. dell'Indipendenza near P. Maggiore. (L9000 per hr. Open Sept.-July Tu-Sa 10am-2am, Su 7:30pm-2am.)

ACCOMMODATIONS AND FOOD. Ostello due Torre San Sisto (HI), V. Viadagola, 5, is off V. San Donato, in the Località di San Sisto, 6km from the center of town. Walk down V. dell'Indipendenza from the station, turn right on V. della Mille, and take bus #93 to the San Sisto stop. (☎051 50 18 10. Breakfast included. Reception 7am-midnight. Lockout 10am-3:30pm. Curfew midnight. Dorms L21,000; nonmembers L5000 extra. Family rooms L22-24,000.) **Albergo Panorama,** V. Livraghi, 1, has a prime location and is sparklingly clean. (☎051 22 18 02. Singles L75,000; doubles L100,000; triples L125,000, with bath L145,000; quads L160,000.) **Hotel San Vitale,** at V. S. Vitale, 94, has simple, clean rooms with TV and phone. (☎051 22 59 66. Singles L90,000; doubles L110,000; triples L165,000.)

Don't leave without sampling Bologna's signature *spaghetti alla bolognese.* Scout **V. Augusto Righi, V. Piella,** and **V. Saragozza** for traditional *trattorie.* A **supermarket, PAM,** V. Marconi, 26, is by the intersection of V. Riva di Reno. (Open M-W and F-Sa 7:45am-7:45pm, Th 7:45am-1pm.) Locals chat over regional dishes like *tagliatelle* at **Trattoria Da Maro,** V. Broccaindosso, 71d, off Strada Maggiore. (Lunch *primi* L8000, *secondi* L9000; dinner L10-12,000. Cover L3000. Open M 8-10:15pm, Tu-Sa noon-2:30pm and 8-10:15pm.) **Nuova Pizzeria Gianna,** V. S. Stefano, 76/a, is known to loyal fans as "Mamma's." Chat with Gianna as she crafts incomparable pizza before your very eyes. (☎051 22 25 16. Pizza from L5000. Closed Aug. Open M-Sa for lunch and dinner.) Show the cashier your student ID for an amazingly inexpensive and tasty meal at **Mensa Universitaria Irnerio,** V. Zamboni, 47, at V. delle Belle Arti. (Closed in summer. Open M-F noon-2:30pm and 7-9pm, Sa-Su 12:30-2pm.) **Il Gelatauro,** V. S. Vitale 82/b, will answer my scream, your scream, our collective scream for ice cream. (From L3000. Open June-Aug. daily 11am-midnight, Sept.-May Tu-Su 11am-midnight.)

SIGHTS AND ENTERTAINMENT. Twenty-five miles of porticoed buildings line the streets of Bologna. In the 14th century, porticoes offered a solution to the housing crisis of a growing city; buildings expanded into the street but left room for mounted riders below. Tranquil **Piazza Maggiore** flaunts both Bologna's historical and modern wealth. The **Basilica di San Petronio,** the city's *duomo,* designed by Antonio da Vincenzo in 1390, was meant to be larger than Rome's St. Peter's, but the jealous Church ordered that the funds be instead used to build the nearby **Palazzo Archiginnasio.** The *duomo*'s cavernous Gothic interior played host to both the Council of Trent (when it was not meeting in Trent) and the 1530 ceremony in which Pope Clement VII gave Italy to the German king Charles V. The pomp and pageantry of the exercises at the church allegedly inspired a disgusted Martin Luther to reform religion in Germany. (Open M-Sa 7:15am-1pm and 2-6pm, Su 7:30am-1pm and 2-6:30pm. Sacristy open daily 8am-noon and 4-6pm.) The **Palazzo Archiginnasio**, behind the church, was once a university building; the upstairs theater was built in 1637 to teach anatomy to students. (Open M-F 9am-7pm, Sa 9am-2pm. Theater open M-Sa 9am-1pm. Both closed 2 weeks in Aug. Free.) **Pinacoteca Nazionale,** V. delle Belle Arti, 56, off V. Zamboni, traces the progress of Bolognese artists. (Open Tu-Sa 9am-1:50pm, Su 9am-12:50pm. L8000.) On the northern side of P. Maggiore is the **Palazzo de Podestà**, remodeled by Fioravanti's son Aristotle, who later designed Moscow's Kremlin. Next to P. Maggiore, **Piazza del Nettuno** contains Giambologna's famous 16th-century fountain, **Neptune and Attendants.** From P. Nettuno, go down V. Rizzoli to **Piazza Porta Ravegana**, where seven streets converge to form Bologna's medieval quarter. Two towers that constitute the city's emblem rise magnificently from the piazza; you can climb the **Torre degli Asinelli.** (Open daily May-Aug. 9am-6pm; Sept.-Apr. 9am-5pm. L5000.) Follow V. S. Stefano from V. Rizzoli to **P. Santo Stefano**, where four of the original seven churches of the Romanesque **Piazza Santo Stefano Church Complex** remain. Bologna's patron saint, San Petronio, lies buried under the pulpit of the **Chiesa di San Sepolcro** in the center. (Open daily 9am-noon and 3:30-6pm.) Take Strada Maggiore to P. Aldrovandi to reach the remarkably intact **Chiesa di Santa Mari dei Seru**, whose columns support an unusual combination of arches and ribbed vaulting.

Bologna's hip student population ensures raucous nighttime fun. Call ahead for hours and covers. **Cluricaune,** V. Zamboni, 18/b, is packed with students who flock to its faux-rustic interior, pool table, and dart boards. (☎ 051 26 34 19. Pints L6000. Happy Hour 5-8:30pm. Open M-Th 4pm-2am, F-Sa 4pm-2:30am, Su 11:30pm-2am.)

PARMA

Parma cultivates a mannered elegance that recalls its 16th-century artistic eminence, 19th-century refinement, and the continued perfection of its culinary palate, while at the same time vibrating with youthful energy from the nearby university. The *Parmigiani* craft silky-smooth *prosciutto crudo*, sharp and crumbly *parmigiano* cheese, and sweet, sparkling white Malvasia wine. From P. Garibaldi, follow Strada Cavour toward the train station and take the third right on Strada al Duomo to reach the 11th-century Romanesque **duomo**, in P. del Duomo, one of the country's most vibrant, filled with masterpieces. Most spectacular is the **dome**, where Correggio's *Virgin* ascends to a golden heaven in a spiral of white robes, pink *putti*, and blue sky. The pink-and-white marble **baptistery** was built between the Romanesque and Gothic periods. (*Duomo* open daily 9am-noon and 3-7pm. Baptistery open daily 9am-12:30pm and 3-7pm. L5000, students L3000.) Behind the *duomo* is the frescoed dome of the **Chiesa di San Giovanni Evangelista,** designed by Correggio. (Open daily 6:30am-noon and 3:30-8pm.) From P. del Duomo, follow Strada al Duomo across Strada Cavour, continue one block down Strada Piscane, and cross P. della Pace to reach the monolithic **Palazzo della Pilotta**, Parma's artistic treasure chest, constructed in 1602, which today houses the excellent **Galleria Nazionale.** (Open daily 9am-1:45pm. L8000.)

Parma is on the Bologna-Milan rail line. **Trains** go from P. Carlo Alberto della Chiesa to: Bologna (1hr., 2 per hr., L7400); Florence (3hr., 7 per day, L25,500); and Milan (1½hr., every hr., L12,100). Walk left from the station, right on V. Garibaldi, and left on V. Melloni to reach the **tourist office,** V. Melloni 1b. (☎ 05 21 23 47 35. Open M-Sa 9am-7pm, Su 9am-1pm.) From the station, take bus 9 (L1300) and get off when the bus turns left on V. Martiri della Libertà (10min.) to get to the **Ostello Cittadella (HI),** on V. Passo Buole, in a corner of a 15th-century fortress. (☎ 05 21 96 14 34. 3-night max. stay. Lockout 9:30am-5pm. Curfew 11pm. Dorms L16,000; members only. **Camping** open Apr.-Oct. L11,000 per person, L18,000 per site.) **Locanda Lazzaro,** Borgo XX Marzo, 14, is off V. della Repubblica, upstairs from the restaurant of the same name. (☎ 05 21 20 89 44. Singles L55-65,000; doubles L90,000. Reserve ahead.) Native *parmigiano* cheese, *prosciutto*, and sausages fill the windows of the *salumerie* along **V. Garibaldi. Le Sorelle Picchi**, Strada Farini, 27, near P. Garibaldi, is one of the best *trattorie* in town. (*Primi* L10-11,000, *secondi* L12-14,000. Cover L3000. *Trattoria* open M-Sa noon-3pm.) **K2,** at Borgo Cairoli and Borgo Coreggio, next to the Chiesa di San Giovanni Evangelista, has great *gelato.* (L2500. Open Th-Tu 11am-midnight.) **Supermarket 2B** is at V. XXII Luglio, 27c. (Open M-W and F-Sa 8:30am-1pm and 4:30-8pm, Th 8:30am-1pm.) **Postal Code:** 43100.

RAVENNA

Tired of fresco cycles? Come to Ravenna to get byzy...uh, Byzantine, and enter a world of golden mosaics. Ravenna's 15 minutes of historical superstardom came and went 14 centuries ago, when Justinian and Theodora, rulers of the Byzantine Empire, headquartered their campaign to restore order in the anarchic west here. Take V. Argentario from V. Cavour to reach the 6th-century ■**Basilica di San Vitale,** V. S. Vitale, 17. An open courtyard overgrown with greenery leads to the brilliant, glowing mosaics inside; those of the Emperor and Empress adorn the lower left and right panels of the apse. Behind S. Vitale, the city's oldest and most intriguing mosaics cover the glittering interior of the **Mausoleo di Galla Placidia.** (Both open daily Apr.-Sept. 9am-7pm; Oct.-Mar. 9:30am-4:30pm. Joint ticket L6000.) Take bus #4 or 44 from opposite the train station (L1300) to Classe, south of the city, to see the astounding mosaics at the ■**Chiesa di Sant'Apollinare in Classe.** (Open daily 9am-7pm. L4000.) Much to Florence's dismay, Ravenna is also home to the **Tomb of Dante Alighieri,** its most popular sight. In the adjoining **Dante Museum,** his heaven and hell come alive in etchings, paintings, and sculptures. From P. del Popolo, cut through P. Garibaldi to V. Alighieri. (Tomb open daily 9am-7pm. Free. Museum open Tu-Su Apr.-Sept. 9am-noon and 3:30-6pm; Oct.-Mar. 9am-noon. L3000.) One ticket (L10,000, students L8,000 at participating sight) is valid at multiple sights including the S. Vitale, S. Appolinare, and the Mausoleo. After looking at mosaics all day, buy some tiles from ■**Colori-Belle Arti,** P. Mameli 16 (☎ 05 44 37 387), off Vle. Farini, and try your own hand at it.

Trains (☎ 0544 21 78 84) connect through Bologna to: Ferrara (1hr., every 2hr., L6700) and Venice (1hr., every 1-2hr., L7400). The train station is in P. Farini. Follow Vle. Farini from the station to V. Diaz, which runs to the central P. del Popolo and the **tourist office,** V. Salara, 8. (☎ 0544 354 04; fax 0544 48 26 70. Open daily 8:30am-7pm; in winter 8:30am-6pm.) Walk down V. Farini, and go right at P. Mameli for **Albergo Al Giaciglio,** V. Rocca Brancaleone, 42. (☎ 0544 394 03. Breakfast L5000. Closed 2 weeks in Dec. or Jan. Singles L35-45,000; doubles L50-65,000; triples L80-90,000.) Take bus #1 or 70 from V. Pallavicini at the station (30min., L1300) to reach **Ostello Dante (HI),** V. Nicolodi 12. (☎ 0544 42 11 64. Breakfast included. **Internet**. Reception 2-11pm. Lockout noon-3:30pm. Curfew 11:30pm. Dorms L22,000.)

FERRARA

Rome has its mopeds, Venice its boats, and Ferrara its bicycles. Old folks, young folks, and babies perched precariously on handlebars whirl through Ferrara's jumble of major thoroughfares and twisting medieval roads inaccessible to automobiles. Grab a bike yourself and enjoy the pink church or occasional giant castle.

⌐ TRANSPORTATION. Ferrara is on the Bologna-Venice rail line; **trains** go to: Rome (3-4hr., 7 per day, L57,200); Bologna (30min., 1-2 per hr., L4900); Padua (1hr., every hr., L7600); Ravenna (1hr., 1-3 per hr., L6700); and Venice (2hr., 1-2 per hr., L10,800). ACFT (☎ 0532 59 94 92) and GGFP **buses** go from V. Rampari S. Paolo (most also leave from the train station) to Ferrara's beaches (1hr., 12 per day, L7600-8400) and Bologna (1½hr., 3-15 per day, L6000).

∄ PRACTICAL INFORMATION. To get to the center of town, turn left out of the train station and then veer right on **Viale Costituzione.** This road becomes Viale Cavour and runs to the Castello Estense at the center of town (1km). Or, take bus #2 to the Castello stop or bus #1 or 9 to the post office. (Buses run every 15-20min., 7am-8:20pm, L1400). The **tourist office** is in Castello Estense. (☎ 0532 20 93 70; www.comune.fe.it. Open daily 9am-1pm and 2-6pm.) Rent cheap bikes at **P. Stazione.** (☎ 0532 77 21 90. L12,000 per day. Open M-F 5:30am-8pm, Sa 6am-2pm; in winter M-F 5:30am-8pm, Sa 6am-6pm.) **Postal Code:** 44100.

▐▐▐ ACCOMMODATIONS AND FOOD. Walk down C. Ercole 1 d'Este from the *castello*, or take bus #4c from the station, and ask for the *castello* stop. **Ostello della Gioventu Estense (HI)**, C. B. Rossetti, 24, provides simple rooms with bunk beds, only a short walk from the town center. (☎0532 20 42 27. Reception 7-10am and 3:30-11:30pm. Lockout 10am-3:30pm. Curfew 11:40pm. Dorms L23,000; family rooms L23,000.) **Casa degli Artisti**, V. Vittoria, 66, near P. Lampronti, is in the historic center of Ferrara. (☎0532 76 10 38. Singles L34,000; doubles L60,000, with bath L85,000.) **Albergo Nazionale**, C. Porta Reno, 32, is on a busy street near the *duomo*. (☎0532 20 96 04. Curfew 12:30am. Reserve 4 days in advance July-Sept. Singles L65,000, with bath L80,000; doubles with bath L120,000; triples L145,000.) When it's time to relax, try the slightly sparkling *Uva D'Oro* (Golden Grape) wine, compliments of the slightly insane Renata Di Francia, who brought the grapes from France for her 16th-century marriage to Duca D'Ercole II D'Este. Note that all food stores in Ferrara are closed on Thursday afternoons. Try delicious *panini* (L5000) with one of 600 varieties of wine at the oldest *osteria* in Italy, **Osteria Al Brindisi**, V. G. degli Adelardi, 9b. (☎0532 20 91 42. Open Tu-Su 8:30am-1am.) For picnic supplies, stop by the **Mercato Comunale**, on V. Mercato, off V. Garibaldi and next to the *duomo*. (Open M-W 7am-1:30pm and 4:30-7:30pm, Th and Sa 7am-1:30pm, F 4:30-7:30pm.)

▐▐▐ SIGHTS AND ENTERTAINMENT. Bike the tranquil, wooded concourse along the city's nine kilometer, well-preserved **medieval wall**, which begins at the far end of C. Giovecca. Towered, turreted, and moated, **Castello Estense** stands in the center of town. C. della Giovecca lies along the former route of the moat's feeder canal, separating the medieval section from the part planned by the d'Este's architect. (☎0532 29 92 33. Open Tu-Su 9:30am-5pm. L8000, students L6000.) From the *castello*, take C. Martiri della Libertà to P. Cattedrale and the **duomo**, which contains the **Museo della Cattedrale**. (Cathedral open M-Sa 7:30am-noon and 3-6:30pm, Su 7:30am-12:30pm and 4-7:30pm. Museum ☎0532 20 74 49. Open Tu-Sa 10am-noon and 3-5pm, Su 10am-noon and 4-6pm.) From Castello Estense, cross Largo Castello to C. Ercole I d'Este and walk to the corner of C. Rossetti to reach the **Palazzo Diamanti**, built in 1493, which outshines all other ducal residences. Inside, the **Pinacoteca Nazionale** holds many of the best works of the Ferrarese school. (Open Tu-W and F-Sa 9am-2pm, Th 9am-7pm, Su and holidays 9am-1pm. L8000, reduced L4000.) Follow C. Ercole I d'Este behind the *castello* and go right on C. Porta Mare to find the **Palazzo Massari**, C. Porta Mare, 9, which houses both the **Museo d'Arte Moderna e Contemporanea "Filippo de Pisis,"** and, upstairs, the spectacular **Museo Ferrarese dell'Ottocentro/Museo Giovanni Boldini**. (Both open daily 9am-1pm and 3-6pm. Joint ticket L10,000.) From the *castello*, head down C. Giovecca, turn left on V. Montebello, and continue to V. Vigne to the **Cimitero Ebraico** (Jewish Cemetery), where a monument commemorates Ferrarese Jews murdered at Auschwitz. (☎0532 75 13 37. Open Su-F Apr.-Sept. 9am-6pm; Oct.-Mar. 9am-4:30pm.)

THE LAKES AND THE DOLOMITES

When Italy's seemingly endless parade of monuments and museums begins to blur together, it's time to escape to the natural beauty of the country's lakes and mountains. The Dolomites dominate the landscape in the province of Trentino-Alto Adige, rising from valley communities to lofty peaks ideal for skiing and hiking.

LAKE COMO (LAGO DI COMO)

Although an unworldly magnificence lingers over the northern reaches of Europe's deepest lake (410m), peaceful Lake Como is more than a figment of your imagination. *Bougainvillea* and lavish villas adorn the lake's craggy backdrop, warmed by the sun and cooled by lakeside breezes. Bellaggio, on the southern shore of the Centro Lago, is the favorite lake town of upper-crust Milanese society; steep streets lead to sidewalk cafes, silk shops, and the villas of Lombard aristocrats. Varenna, on the eastern shore, is far more peaceful and scenic.

TRANSPORTATION. The only town on the lake accessible by train is its largest urban outpost, Como, on the southwestern tip. **Trains** roll in from Milan (1hr., every hr., L9000) and Venice (4hr., 1 every hr., L39,700), while **buses** make their way from Bergamo (2hr., every 2hr., L8300). From Como, take the **C-10 bus** near Ferrovia Nord to Tremezzo or Menaggio (1hr., L4700, last bus at 10:15pm). Hourly buses also serve Varenna and Bellagio (1hr., L5000). Spend the day zipping between stores, gardens, villas, and wineries of the remaining towns on the lake by **ferry.**

COMO. Situated on the southwest tip of the lake, at the receiving end of the Milan rail line, Como is the lake's token semi-industrial town. For excellent **hiking** and stunning views, head from the far end of **Lungo Lario Trento** up to **Brunate.** To get from the station to the **tourist office,** P. Cavour, 16, walk down the steps to V. Gallio, which becomes V. Garibaldi and leads to P. Cavour via P. Volta. (☎031 26 97 12. Open M-Sa 9am-1pm and 2:30-6pm.) **Ostello Villa Olmo (HI),** V. Bellinzona, 2, offers clean rooms, great food, and discounts on various sights in Como. From the station, walk 20 minutes left down V. Borgovico, which becomes V. Bellinzona. (☎031 57 38 00. Breakfast included. Reception 7-10am and 4-11:30pm. Strict curfew 11:30pm. Lockout after 10am. Open Mar.-Nov. Dorms L20,000.) Picnickers will appreciate the **G.S. supermarket,** on the corner of V. Recchi and V. Fratelli Roselli. (Open M 2-8pm, Tu-Sa 8am-8pm, Su 10am-6pm). **Postal Code:** 22100.

The breezes in the tiny town of **Domaso** on the North Lake create perfect **windsurfing.** Surfers flock to the relaxing **Ostello della Gioventù (HI),** V. Case Sparse, 12, on the water. The modern hostel lies 2 hours from Como by bus and is also accessible by boat. (☎034 49 74 49. **Internet.** Breakfast included. Curfew midnight. Open Mar.-Oct. Dorms L20,000.)

MENAGGIO. Menaggio is home to beautiful hotels, historic streets, and unbelievable scenery. You can explore Lake Como while staying in Menaggio's youth hostel for a fraction of the cost (and double the character) of any other establishment on the lake. A one- to two-hour hike will reward you with the spectacular **Sass Corbee waterfalls;** inquire at the tourist office for directions. To get to the resort-like **Ostello La Prinula (HI),** V. IV Novembre, 86, from the bus stop or ferry port, face the water, turn right, and walk along the shore to the main thoroughfare; just past the gas station, walk up the incline to the right. (☎0344 323 56. **Internet** L4000 per 15min. Breakfast included. Bike and kayak rental L17,000 per day. Lockout 10am-5pm. Curfew 11:30pm. Open mid-Mar. to early Nov. Dorms L20,000.)

LAKE MAGGIORE (LAGO MAGGIORE)

Lacking only the frenzy of its eastern neighbors, Lake Maggiore cradles the same temperate mountain waters and idyllic shores. The charming resort town of **Stresa,** only an hour from Milan by **train** (every hr., L8200, IC supplement L6000), is the most convenient base for exploring. To get to Lake Maggiore from Lake Como, take a train from Como to Laveno (L4800; change at Saronno), on the east shore of Lake Maggiore, then take a ferry to elsewhere on the lake. To reach the **tourist office,** V. Principe Tommaso, 70-72, from the train station, turn right and go down the hill on V. Carducci, which becomes V. Gignous; V. Tommaso is on the left. (☎0323 301 50. Open M-F 8:30am-12:30pm and 3-6:15pm.) To get to **Orsola Meublé,** V. Duchessa di Genova, 45, turn right from the station, walk downhill, and go left at the intersection. (☎0323 310 87. Breakfast included. Singles L50-70,000; doubles L80-100,000.)

Alternatively, to get to the new and much cheaper **Ostello Verbania Internazionale** from Stresa, take a ferry across the lake to **Pallanza.** After disembarking the ferry, walk to the right along the water to V. Vittorio Veneto, turn left on V. Panoramica, and walk up the hill, around the bend, and take your last right; the hostel is on the left. (Breakfast included. Reception 8-11am, 4-5:30pm, 10-11pm. Dorms L23,000.) The **tourist office,** on V. Zanitello, is located between the port and the hostel.

◪ DAYTRIP FROM LAKE MAGGIORE: BORROMEAN ISLANDS. Charming

Stresa and Pallanza are perfect stepping stones to the lovely **Borromean Islands.** Daily excursion tickets (L14,800; L17,400 including travel to Laveno's train station) allow you to hop back and forth between either Stresa and Pallanza and the three islands (**Isola Bella, Isola Superiore dei Pescatori,** and **Isola Madre**). The islands boast manicured botanical gardens, elegant villas, and an opulent Baroque palace.

LAKE GARDA (LAGO DI GARDA)

Garda—the ultimate resort destination for many German families—has staggering mountains and breezy summers. **Desenzano,** the lake's southern transport hub, lies on the Milan-Venice line, 1 hour from Milan, 2 hours from Venice, and 30min. from Verona. From Desenzano, the other lake towns are easily accessible by bus and boat. The towns of Sirmione and Gardone Riviera are best explored as daytrips from Brescia, as accommodations are scant and pricey.

SIRMIONE. Sirmione is a bit like Disneyland—flashy, expensive, and quickly exhausted. Its beautifully situated medieval castle and extensive Roman ruins make for a leisurely day or a busy afternoon. **Buses** run every hour from Brescia (1hr., L5800); Desenzano (20min., L2500) and Verona (1hr., L5000). *Battelli* (water steamers) run to Desenzano (20min., L4500); Gardone (1¼hr., L10,000); and Riva (4hr., L14,100). The family-run **Albergo Grifone,** V. Bisse, 5, has a prime location by the castle. (☎030 91 60 14. Reservations necessary. Singles with bath L50,000; doubles with bath L88,000. Extra bed L27,000.)

GARDONE RIVIERA. Formerly the playground of the rich and famous, this town now prides itself on the home of famous author, and latter-day Casanova, Gabriele D'Annunzio. His quirky mansion, **Il Vittoriale,** sprawls above Gardone, off V. Roma and V. dei Colli. (Villa open Apr.-Sept. Tu-Su 8:30am-8pm. Gardens open Oct.-Mar. Tu-Su 9am-5pm.) **Buses** (☎0365 210 61) run to Desenzano (30min., 6 per day, L4100) and Milan (3hr., 2 per day, L15,500). The **APT tourist office,** V. Repubblica, 39, is in the center of Gardone Sotto. (☎0365 203 47. Open July-Aug. daily 9am-1pm and 4-10pm; Nov.-Mar. M-W and F 9am-12:30pm and 3-6pm, Th 9am-12:30pm.)

RIVA DEL GARDA. Riva has few sights, but the town is livelier, the crowd younger, and the prices lower than other places on the lake; it's a great base for exploring other lake towns. Travelers **swim, windsurf, hike,** and **climb** near the most stunning portion of the lake, where cliffs crash into the water. Riva is accessible by **bus** (☎0464 55 23 23) from Trent (1¼hr., 6 per day, L6000) and Verona (2hr., 11 per day, L9300). **Ferries** (☎030 914 95 11), on P. Matteoti, head to Gardone (L12,200). The **tourist office,** Giardini di Porta Orientale, 8, is near the water. (☎0464 55 44 44; fax 0464 52 03 08. Open M-Sa 9am-noon and 3-6pm.) Snooze at fabulous **Ostello Benacus (HI),** P. Cavour, 9, in the town center; from the bus station, walk down V. Trento, take V. Roma, and turn left under the arch. (☎0464 55 49 11. Breakfast, sheets and shower included. Reception 7-9am and 3pm-midnight. Dorms L22,000.)

THE DOLOMITES

Limestone spires shoot skyward from the pine forests of the Dolomites. These amazing peaks—fantastic for hiking, skiing, and rock climbing—start west of Trent and extend to the north and east into Austria. With their sunny skies and light, powdery snow, the mountains offer popular year-round downhill skiing.

TRENT. When you arrive in Trent, you'll find a harmonious mix of Germanic and Mediterranean flavors. The **Piazza del Duomo,** Trent's center and social heart, contains the city's best sights. The **Fontana del Nettuno** stands, trident in hand, in the center of the *piazza.* Nearby is the **Cattedrale di San Vigilio,** named for the patron saint of Trent. (Open daily 6:40am-12:15pm and 2:30-7:30pm.) Walk down V. Belenzani and go right on V. Roma to reach the well-preserved **Castello del Buonconsiglio.** (☎0461 23 37 70. Open Apr.-Sept. Tu-Su 9am-noon and 2-5:30pm; Oct.-Mar. Tu-Su 9am-noon and 2-5pm. L9000; students, those under 18, and seniors L5000.) **Monte Bondone** rises majestically over Trent, making an excellent daytrip or overnight excursion. Catch the **cable car** (every 30min., ticket L4000) from Ponte di S. Lorenzo, between the train tracks and the river, to **Sardagna,** a great picnic spot.

Trains (☎0461 82 10 00) go to Bologna (2½-3hr., 8 per day, L18,600); Bolzano (50min., every hr., L9400); Venice (2½hr., L29,400); and Verona (1hr., every hr., L14,200). **Buses** (☎0461 82 10 00) go from V. Pozzo, next to the train station, to Riva del Garda (1hr., every hr., L5500). Go right on V. Pozzo, and left on V. Torre Vanga to the **tourist office**, V. Alfieri, 4. (☎0461 98 38 80; www.apt.trento.it. Open daily 9am-7pm.) **Hotel Venezia** is at P. Duomo, 45. (☎0461 23 41 14. Breakfast L12,000. Singles L55-65,000; doubles with bath L95,000.) **Ostello Giovane Europa (HI),** V. Manzoni, 17 is by the tourist office. (☎0461 23 45. Breakfast included. Reception 3:30-11pm. Check-out 9:30am. Curfew 11:30pm. Reservations required. Dorms L22,000.)

BOLZANO. In the tug-of-war between Austrian and Italian cultural influences, Bolzano has been pulled to the Austrian side of the rope. The town's hybrid culture and prime location beneath vineyard-covered mountains make it a splendid stop-over en route to the Dolomites. With its prickly spined tower and a diamond-pat-terned roof, the Gothic **duomo,** on P. Walther, is a dark and awesome sight. (Open M-F 9:45am-noon and 2-5pm, Sa 9:45am-noon. Free.) Aside from that, the best "sights" in town are found by exploring the winding streets and admiring the facades. Pay a visit to the **South Tyrol Museum of Archaeology** to check out the actual **Ice Man**—discovered by a vacationing German couple. (☎0471 98 06 48. Open Tu-W and F-Su 10am-6pm, Th 10am-8pm. L13,000, students L7000.) **Trains** (☎0471 97 42 92) go to Milan (3½hr., 3 per day, L23,500); Trent (1-2hr., 1-2 per hr., L5300); and Verona (2hr., 1-2 per hr., L12,500). Walk up V. Stazione from the train station, or V. Alto Adige from the bus stop, to reach the **tourist office,** P. Walther, 8. (☎0471 30 70 00; fax 0471 98 01 28. Open M-F 9am-6:30pm, Sa 9am-12:30pm.) **Croce Bianca,** P. del Grano (Kornpl.) 3, is around the corner from P. Walther. (☎0471 97 75 52. Breakfast L8000. Singles L40,000; doubles L60-78,000; triples L90,000.) **Hopfen & Co.,** V. Argen-tieri, 36 (☎0471 30 07 88), offers a smorgasbord of regional specialties., more akin to traditional Austrian fare than Italian cuisine.

ASTI

Asti sparkles, just like its intoxicating progeny, the famous *Asti Spumante* wine. More than a hundred 13th-century edifices have survived the city's tumultuous his-tory, lending it a medieval air. The **Cattedrale d'Asti,** is one of Piedmont's most note-worthy Gothic cathedrals. (In P. Cattedrale. Walk down C. Alfieri and turn right on V. Mazzini. Open daily 7am-12:30pm and 3-7pm.) From the last week of June through the first week of July, **Asti Teatro,** the oldest Italian theatrical festival, commands Asti's complete attention. Asti Teatro puts on outdoor and indoor performances of theatrics, music, and dance. Call the **Teatro Alfieri,** V. al Teatro, 1, for more information. (☎0141 39 93 41). Beginning on the second Friday in Septem-ber, agricultural Asti revels in the **Douja d'Or,** a week-long exposition of local wines. **Trains** head to Milan (2hr., 1 per day, L12,500) and Turin (1hr., 2 per hr., L6000) from the station at P. Marconi, just a few blocks south of P. Alfieri. The **tourist office,** P. ALfieri, 34, helps find accommodations. (☎0141 53 03 57. Open M-Sa 9am-7pm, Su 10am-1pm.) **Hotel Cavour,** P. Marconi, 3, is across from the train station, and has immaculate rooms with TVs and phones. (☎0141 53 02 22. Reception 6am-1am. Closed in Aug. Singles L55-70,000; doubles L85-105,000.) When mealtime arrives, *Astigiano* cuisine is truly a treat, famous for its simplicity, using only a few crucial ingredients and pungent cheeses to create culinary masterpieces. The extensive fruit and vegetable **markets** in P. Alfieri and Campo del Palio provide great snacks. (Open W and Sa 7:30am-1pm.) **Postal Code:** 14100.

AOSTA

Aosta is the geographical and financial center of a region increasingly dependent upon tourism for economic livelihood. Aosta makes a good base for explorations in the area, but be aware that daytrips to the valleys often require tricky train and bus connections—if you hope to return before nightfall, arm yourself with schedules and plan ahead. Oh, that Roman Empire—they didn't even bother to clean up their messy remains. Ruins dating from the age of Augustus fill the town. Down V. Porta

Pretoria looms the massive stone archway of the **Porta Pretoria.** To the left is the entrance to the sprawling remains of the massive **Roman Theater.** (Open daily in summer 9:30am-noon and 2:30-6:30pm; in winter 9:30am-noon and 2-4:30pm. Free.)A valley with more medieval towers than tourists, Valle del Gran San Bernardo links Aosta to Switzerland via the Great St. Bernard Pass, which incorporates a 5854m tunnel through the mountains. Napoleon trekked through the pass with 40,000 soldiers in 1800. The area is better known for the 1505 **Hospice of St. Bernard,** home to the patron saint of man's best friend. The highest mountain in Switzerland, **The Matterhorn (Il Cervino)** looms majestically over the less-wonderful town of **Breuil-Cervinia** in Valtournenche. In spite of the cost, many fresh-air fiends consider these man-made deterrents a small price for the opportunity to climb up and glide down one of the world's most famous mountains. A cable car provides year-round service to **Plateau Rosà** (round-trip L42,000), where summer skiers tackle the slopes in lighter gear. Hikers can forgo the lift tickets and attempt the three-hour ascent to **Colle Superiore delle Cime Bianche** (2982m), with tremendous views of Val d'Ayas to the east. A shorter trek (1½hr.) on the same trail leads to the emerald waters of **Lake Goillet.** The **Società Guide** (☎0166 94 81 69) arranges group outings. Don't forget your **passport;** a number of trails cross into Switzerland.

Trains leave for **Turin** (2hr., every hr. 5:15am-8:40pm, L10,500) and **Milan** (4hr., 12 per day 6:12am-8:40pm, L18,600). To reach the **tourist office,** P. Chanoux, 8 (☎0165 23 66 27), go straight down Av. du Conseil des Commis from the train station. (Open M-Sa 9am-1pm and 3-8pm, Su 9am-1pm.) **La Belle Epoque,** is on V. d'Avise, 18. From the train station, take Av. du Conseil des Commis to P. Chanoux, and turn left on V. Aubert. (☎0165 26 22 76. Singles L45,000, with bath L55,000; doubles with bath L90,000; triples with bath L120,000.) Try the *salsiccette in umido* (local sausages braised in tomato sauce), at **Trattoria Praetoria,** V. Sant'Anselmo, 9, just past the Porta Praetoria. (☎0165 443 56. *Primi* L8-10,000, *secondi* L12,000. Cover L3000. Open daily in summer 12:15-2:30pm and 7:15-9:30pm; in winter F-W 12:15-2:30pm and 7:15-9:30pm.)

VAL D'AYAS

Budget-minded sports enthusiasts should consider bypassing the pleasure grounds to the west and stopping here instead. Val d'Ayas has the same outdoor activities as its flashy neighbors—skiing, hiking, and rafting—without the hype. **Trains** run to **Verrès** from Aosta (40min., 17 per day 6:35am-8:40pm, L4800) and Turin (1½hr.). **Buses** run from the train station at Verrès daily to Champoluc (1hr., 4 per day 11:30am-6pm, L4000). The **tourist office** in **Brusson** (☎0125 30 02 40; fax 0125 30 06 91) has branches in **Champoluc,** V. Varase, 16 (☎0125 30 71 13; fax 0125 30 77 85) and **Antagnod** (☎0125 30 63 35). They speak English and provide trail maps and hotel information. (All branches open daily 9am-12:30pm and 3-6pm.)

NORTHEAST ITALY

Gaze at the serene canals of Venice; enjoy the exquisite red wines of Piedmont, and the famous cuisine of Emilia-Romagna, or lounge on some of the cheapest Italian beach resorts in Friuli-Venezia Giulia—Northeast Italy has ample attractions to satisfy the most jaded palate, experienced eye, or tired tourist.

THE VENETO

From the rocky foothills of the Dolomites to the fertile valleys of the Po River, the Veneto region has a geography as diverse as its historical influences. Once loosely linked under the Venetian Empire, these towns retained their cultural independence, and visitors are more likely to hear regional dialects than standard Italian when neighbors gossip across their geranium-bedecked windows. The sense of local culture and custom that remains strong within each town may surprise visitors lured to the area by Venice, the *bella* of the north.

VENICE (VENEZIA)

It is with good reason that Venetians call their city *La Serenissima* (the most serene); they awake each morning to a refreshing absence of cars and mopeds, instead making their way on foot or by boat through an ancient maze of narrow streets and winding canals. The serenity is broken only by tourists, who swarm in Venice's *campi* (squares) and thoroughfares, searching out the city's wealth of museums and landmarks. Venice, resting on a fragile sinking network of wood, now struggles with a rapidly declining population and few economic prospects. Venetians have watched their most serene city become inundated with foreigners, its quiet canals shaking beneath heavy barges. Still, the serenity of Venice has proven stubborn, and it persists beyond the summer crowds and polluted waters, united by intertwining canals and the architectural gems of the past.

▛ TRANSPORTATION

The **train station** is on the northwest edge of the city; be sure to get off at Santa Lucia and *not* Mestre (on the mainland). **Buses** and **boats** arrive at Ple. Roma, just across the Grand Canal from the train station. To get from either station to **Piazza San Marco** or the **Rialto Bridge**, take *vaporetto* #82 or follow the signs (and the crowds) for the 40min. walk (exit left from the train station onto Lista di Spagna).

Flights: Aeroporto Marco Polo (☎041 260 61 11), 5 mi. north of the city. Ticket office open Su-Th 5:30am-9:45pm, F-Sa 5:30am-9pm. Take the **ATVO shuttle** (☎041 541 51 80; 30min., every 45min. 5:30am-8:40pm, L5000). An **AVA** office (☎041 541 50 17) makes hotel reservations. Open daily 9am-10pm.

Trains: Stazione Venezia Santa Lucia, open daily 3:45am-12:30am. **Info office** at the left as you exit the platforms. To: **Bologna** (2hr., 2 per hr., 6:10am-11:32pm,L15-20,000); **Florence** (3hr., every 2hr., L40,000); **Milan** (4hr., 1-2 per hr., 5:52am-9:18pm, L40,000); **Rome** (4-5hr., 5 per day, L64-75,000). **Lockers:** by platform 1. L3-4,000 per 6hr. **Store luggage:** by platform 14. L5000 per 12hr.

Buses: ACTV (☎041 528 78 86; fax 041 272 25 88), on P. Roma, is the local line for buses and boats. **ACTV long distance carrier** buses run to nearby cities. Ticket office open daily 6:30am-midnight.

Public Transportation: The **Grand Canal** can be crossed on foot only at the *ponti* (bridges) of Scalzi, Rialto, and Accademia. Most **vaporetti** (water buses) run 24hr. (less frequently after 11pm). **Single-ride** L6000; **round-trip** L10,000; **24-hour** *biglietto turistico* pass L18,000; **3-day** *biglietto turistico* L35,000 (L25,000 with **Rolling Venice Card;** see **Tourist Offices,** below). Buy tickets from booths in front of *vaporetto* stops, automated machines at the ACTV office in Ple. Roma or at the Rialto stop, or from the conductor; pick up some extra *non timbrati* (non-validated) tickets so you don't get stuck when the booths aren't open (validate them yourself before you board). **Lines 82** (faster) and **1** (slower) run from the station down the Grand and Giudecca Canals; **line 52** goes from the station through the Giudecca Canal to Lido and along the city's northern edge, and back to the station; and **line 12** runs from Fondamente Nuove to Murano, Burano, and Torcello.

⊕ ❼ ORIENTATION AND PRACTICAL INFORMATION

Venice spans 118 bodies of land in a lagoon and is connected to the mainland by a thin causeway. Venice is a veritable labyrinth and can even confuse its natives, most of whom simply set off in a general direction and then patiently weave their way through the city. A few tips will help you to orient yourself. Locate the following sights on a map—the **Rialto Bridge** (in the center), **Piazza San Marco** (central south), the **Accademia bridge** (southwest), **Ferrovia** (the train station, northwest), and **Piazzale Roma** (directly south of the station). The Grand Canal snakes through the city, creating six *sestieri* (sections): **Cannaregio, Castello, Santa Croce, San Polo, San Marco,** and **Dorsoduro.** Within each *sestieri,* there are no street numbers—door numbers in a section form one long, haphazard set, consisting of around 6000 numbers. While these boundaries are nebulous, they can give you a general sense of location. **Cannaregio** includes the train station, Jewish Ghetto, and Cà d'Oro; **Castello** extends east toward the Arsenal; **San Marco** fills in the area between P. S. Marco and the Accademia bridge; **Dorsoduro,** across the bridge from S. Marco, swinging from the Salute church out to Giudecca and up to Cà Rezzonico; **San Polo** runs north from Dorsoduro to the Rialto Bridge; and **Santa Croce** lies between S. Polo to the east and the train station to the west. If *sestiere* boundaries prove too vague, Venice's **parrochie** (parishes) provide a more defined idea of where you are, and *parrochia* signs, like *sestiere* signs, are painted on the sides of buildings. Venice is notoriously impossible to navigate; unglue your eyes from your map and go with the flow—it's only by getting lost that you'll discover some of the unexpected surprises that make Venice spectacular.

TOURIST, FINANCIAL, AND LOCAL SERVICES

Tourist Offices and Tours: APT, P. S. Marco 71/f (☎041 520 89 64; ☎/fax 041 529 87 40), directly opposite the Basilica. Open M-Sa 9:30am-3:30pm. The office at the **train station** (☎041 71 90 78) is usually mobbed; prepare to wait in line. Open M-Sa 8am-7pm, Su 9:30am-3:30pm. **AVA** (☎041 171 52 88), in the train station, to the right of the tourist office, makes reservations for L1000. Open in summer daily 9am-10pm. Call 041 522 22 64 or 800 843 006 for reservations. **Rolling Venice,** S. Marco 1529 (☎041 274 76 50 or 041 274 76 51; fax 041 274 76 42), on Corte Contarina. Exit P. S. Marco opposite the Basilica, turn right, follow the road left, continue through the building, look for the yellow "Comune di Venezia" signs, take a left, turn right, and go into the courtyard. Sells the **Youth Discount Card** (L5000), which provides discounts at hotels, restaurants, and museums, as well as the 3-day **Rolling Venice vaporetto pass** (L25,000). Open M, W, and F 9am-1pm, Tu and Th 10am-1pm and 3-5pm. **Branch** (☎041 524 28 52) at the train station. Open July-Sept. 8am-8pm. Rolling Venice cards also available at **Transalpino** (see below).

Budget Travel: CTS, Dorsoduro, 3252 (☎041 520 56 60; fax 041 523 69 46; www.cts.it). From Campo S. Barnaba, cross the bridge nearest the church, then turn right at the dead end, left through the *piazza*, and left through the little *piazza*. Open M-F 9:30am-1:30pm and 3-7pm. **Transalpino** (☎/fax 041 71 66 00), to the right as you exit the train station, sells discounted international train tickets. Open M-F 8:30am-12:30pm and 3-7pm, Sa 8:30am-12:30pm.

Currency Exchange: Banks and 24hr. **ATMs** line **Calle Larga XXII Marzo** (between P. S. Marco and the Accademia) and **Campo San Bartomoleo** (near the Rialto bridge). Many 24hr. automatic change machines offer low commissions and decent rates, and can be found outside banks and next to ATMs.

American Express: Sal. S. Moise, S. Marco, 1471 (☎800 87 20 00 or 041 520 08 44). Exit P. S. Marco away from the basilica, to the left. No commission; average rates. Mail held for members and traveler's check customers. Open M-Sa 9am-8pm, Su 9am-6pm. Cardmember services M-F 9am-1pm and 2-5pm, Sa 9pm-12:30am.

Bookstore: Libreria Studium, S. Marco 337 (☎041 522 23 82). From P. S. Marco, head left along the basilica; it's the last shop on the right. Open M-Sa 9am-7:30pm.

EMERGENCY AND COMMUNICATIONS

Emergency: ☎113. **First Aid:** ☎118. **Hospital: Ospedale Civile** (☎041 529 41 11), Campo SS Giovanni e Paolo.

Police: Carabinieri, Castello 4693/a (emergency ☎112 or 041 520 47 77), in Campo S. Zaccaria. **Questura,** V. Nicoladi, 24, Marghera (☎041 271 55 11). Contact the Questura if you have a serious complaint about your hotel.

Pharmacy: Farmacia Italo Inglese, S. Marco, 3717 (☎041 522 48 37), on Calle della Mandola off Campo Manin. Open M-F 9am-12:30pm and 4:45-7:30pm, Sa 9am-12:30pm. Check the door of any pharmacy or the brochure *A Guest in Venice* (available at any tourist office) for night and weekend pharmacies.

Internet Access: Omniservice, Fond. d. Tolentini, S. Croce, 220 (☎041 71 04 70; email omniservice@hotbot.com). From the station, cross the Scalzi bridge, take a right, and turn left on Fond. d. Tolentini. L3000 per 15min. Open M-F 9am-1pm and 3-7pm, Sa 9:30am-12:30pm.

Post Office: S. Marco, 5554 (☎041 271 71 11), on Salizzada Fontego dei Tedeschi, to the east of the Rialto Bridge and off Campo San Bartolomeo. Housed in an old palace, the building itself merits a visit. *Fermo Posta* at window #40. Open M-Sa 8:15am-7pm. Address mail to be held: Vanessa NASON, *In Fermo Posta*, Fontego dei Tedeschi, S. Marco 5554, **30124** Venezia, Italia. Open M-Sa 8:15am-7pm.

ACCOMMODATIONS

Plan to spend slightly more for a room in Venice than you would elsewhere in Italy. In *pensioni*, watch out for L12,000 breakfasts and other rip-offs. Always agree on what you will pay before you take a room. Dormitory-style arrangements are sometimes available in Venice without reservations, even during August and September; but single rooms vanish in the summer. The AVA hotel service will book rooms, but proprietors are more willing to bargain in person. Because of *acqua alta* flooding and renovation restrictions, few hotels are wheelchair accessible.

HOSTELS AND DORMITORIES

Ostello Venezia (HI), Fondamenta Giudecca Zitelle, 86 (☎041 523 82 11). *Vaporetto* 82 or 52: Zitelle. Institutional but friendly. Members only; HI cards sold. Breakfast and sheets included. Dinner L14,000. Reception 7-9:30am and 1-11:30pm. Lockout 9:30am-1:30pm. Curfew 11:30pm. Dorms L27,000.

Foresteria Valdese, Castello, 5170 (☎041 528 67 97). From the Rialto Bridge, head to Campo S. Bartolomeo, left to Salizzada S. Lio, and left on Calle Mondo Novo; enter Campo S. Maria Formosa and take Calle Lunga S. Maria Formosa over the 1st bridge. Amiable management and dazzling frescoed ceilings. Private rooms with TV. Breakfast included. Reception 9am-1pm and 6-8pm, Su 9am-1pm. Lockout 10am-1pm. Closed 3 weeks in Nov. Dorms L33,000 for one night, L32,000 for multiple nights; doubles L90-130,000; quads L164,000.

Domus Civica (ACISJF), S. Polo, 3082 (☎041 72 11 03), between the Frari and Ple. Roma. From the station, cross the Scalzi bridge, turn right, go left on Fond. dei Tolentini, head left through the courtyard on Corte Amai, and it's a few blocks down on the right. Church-affiliated student housing that offers rooms to tourists from mid-June to Sept. Ping-pong, TV, and piano. Check-in 7:30am-11:30pm. Curfew 11:30pm. Singles L47,000; doubles L84,000.

Suore Cannosiano, Fondamenta del Ponte Piccolo, Giudecca, 428 (☎041 522 21 57). *Vaporetto* #82: Giudecca/Palanca; walk left over the bridge. Get thee to this friendly nunnery before noon or after 3pm if you want to leave bags. Check-out 7:30-8:30am. Lockout noon-3pm. Strict curfew 10:30pm, winter 10pm. Dorms L23,000.

CANNAREGIO AND SANTA CROCE

The area around the station on Lista di Spagna offers budget accommodations and a festive atmosphere. The streets bustle at night, primarily with young travelers, even though the area is a 20- to 30-minute *vaporetto* ride from most major sights. If you prefer quiet, ask for a room away from the street.

Casa Gerotto/Hotel Calderan, Campo S. Geremia, 283 (☎041 71 55 62). Turn left from the station (2min.). Wonderful owners are justly proud of their 34 huge, bright rooms, some with TV. Internet access L6000 per 30min. Curfew 12:30am for dorms; 1am for private rooms. Dorms L30,000; singles L50-60,000; doubles L80-130,000; triples L90-160,000; quads L135-200,000.

Hotel Bernardi-Semimonthly, Campo SS. Apostoli, Cannaregio, 4366 (☎041 522 72 57). *Vaporetto* #1: Cà d'Oro, turn right on Strada Nuova, left onto Calle del Duca, and right on Calle di Loca. Gorgeous, luxurious budget digs. Breakfast included. Check-out 10:30am. Flexible curfew 1am. Singles L60-75,000; doubles L85-110,000; triples L130-150,000; quads L150-170,000.

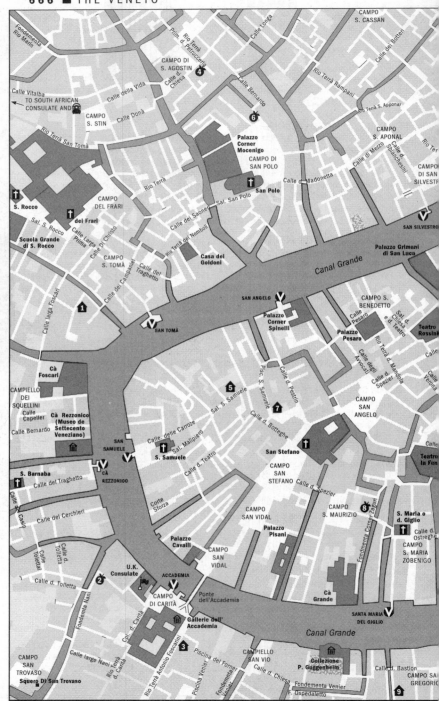

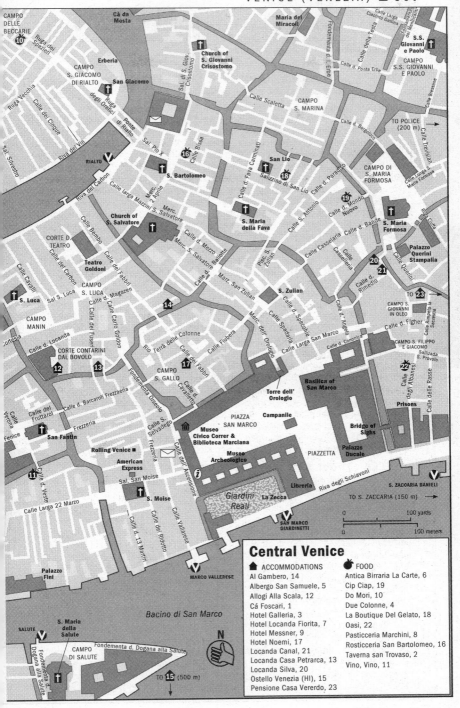

Central Venice

🏠 ACCOMMODATIONS
Al Gambero, 14
Albergo San Samuele, 5
Allogi Alla Scala, 12
Cá Foscari, 1
Hotel Galleria, 3
Hotel Locanda Fiorita, 7
Hotel Messner, 9
Hotel Noemi, 17
Locanda Canal, 21
Locanda Casa Petrarca, 13
Locanda Silva, 20
Ostello Venezia (HI), 15
Pensione Casa Vererdo, 23

🍎 FOOD
Antica Birraria La Carte, 6
Cip Ciap, 19
Do Mori, 10
Due Colonne, 4
La Boutique Del Gelato, 18
Oasi, 22
Pasticceria Marchini, 8
Rosticceria San Bartolomeo, 16
Taverna san Trovaso, 2
Vino, Vino, 11

Albergo Adua, Lista di Spagna, Cannaregio, 233a (☎041 71 61 84). Clean pastel rooms, all with phones and A/C. Breakfast L10,000. Midnight curfew. Singles L80-150,000; doubles L150-210,000.

SAN MARCO

Surrounded by exclusive shops and Venice's main sights, these accommodations are prime choices (if you can get a reservation).

Albergo San Samuele, S. Marco, 3358 (☎041 522 80 45). Follow Calle delle Botteghe from Campo S. Stefano (near the Accademia) and turn left on Salizzada S. Samuele. 10 colorful rooms with tapestry wallpaper, Italian art, and sparkling bathrooms. Reserve 1-2 months ahead with 1 night's deposit. Singles L80,000; doubles L130-190,000. Triples available with advance notice.

Hotel Noemi, Calle dei Fabbri, S. Marco, 909 (☎041 523 81 44). Exit P. S. Marco through the second *sottoporico* from the basilica, and follow Calle dei Fabbri as it turns left. Just 1min. from the *piazza*. All rooms with TV and phone. Singles L120,000; doubles L150-200,000; triples L185-280,0000; quads L225-300,000.

Al Gambero, Calle dei Fabbri, S. Marco, 4687 (☎041 522 43 84). Past Hotel Noemi (see above; 2min. from P. S. Marco). Breakfast included. Singles L90-170,000; doubles L150-230,000; triples L200-300,000.

Hotel Locanda Fiorita, Campiello Novo, S. Marco, 3457 (☎041 523 47 54). From Campo S. Stefano, take Calle de Pestrin and then climb onto the raised *piazza*. All rooms with phones and A/C. Nearby annex with rooms that also include satellite TV. Singles L140-170,000; doubles L180-250,000. Extra bed 30% more.

DORSODURO

Near the university and the Accademia, hotels in Dorsoduro are in the center of a lively, albeit less touristed area between the museum and the Frari church.

Hotel Galleria, Rio Terra A. Foscarini, Dorsoduro, 878/A (☎041 523 24 89), on the left as you face the Accademia. Outstanding views, oriental rugs, and tasteful prints lend the Galleria a certain elegance. All rooms with phone. Breakfast included. Singles L95,000; doubles L135-195,000. Extra bed 30% more.

Cà Foscari, Calle della Frescada, Dorsoduro, 3887b (☎041 71 04 01), in a quiet neighborhood near the ferry. Take *vaporetto* #1 or 82 to S. Tomà. Turn left at the dead end, cross the bridge, turn right, and then take a left onto the little alleyway. Murano glass chandeliers and Venetian Carnival masks adorn the 11 rooms. Breakfast included. 1am curfew. Rooms held until 2pm. Open Feb.-Nov. Singles with bath L95,000; doubles L110-150,000; triples L141-186,000; quads L174-224,000.

CASTELLO (FROM SAN MARCO TO SANT'ELENA)

Castello provides lodgings near the Rialto, close to the center of town, a bit removed from the throng of tourists.

Pensione Casa Verardo, Castello, 4765 (☎041 528 61 27). *Vaporetto:* S. Zaccaria; take Calle degli Albanese to Campo SS. Filippo e Giacomo, cross the campo, and continue down Rimpetto la Sacrestia. Luxurious rooms in a traditional building. Breakfast included. Singles L150,000; doubles L250,000; triples L250,000; quads L400,000.

Locanda Canal, Fondamenta del Remedio, Castello, 4422c (☎041 523 45 38). From S. Marco, walk under the clock tower, right on C. Larga S. Marco, left on Ramo dell'Anzolo, over the bridge, and left on Fondamenta del Remedio. Large rooms in a converted *palazzo*. Breakfast included. Shower L4000. Doubles L145-195,000; triples L175-235,000; quads L205-275,000.

Locanda Silva, Fondamenta del Remedio, Castello, 4423 (☎041 522 76 43), next to the Locanda Canal (above). Breakfast included. Open Feb. to mid-Nov. Singles L75,000; doubles L120-175,000; triples L225,000; quads L260,000.

Locanda Corona, Calle Corona, Castello, 4464 (☎041 522 91 74). *Vaporetto:* S. Zaccharia; take Calle degli Albanese to Campo SS. Filippo e Giacomo, continue on Rimpetto la Sacrestia, take the 1st right, and turn left onto Calle Corona. One of the few wheelchair-accessible hotels in Venice. Closed Jan. Singles L59,000; doubles L85,000; triples L106,000.

CAMPING

The **Litorale del Cavallino,** on the Lido's Adriatic side, has countless beach campsites.

Camping Miramare, Punta Sabbioni (☎041 96 61 50). Take *vaporetto* #14 from P. S. Marco to Punta Sabbioni (40min.) Min. stay 3-night in high season. Open Apr. to mid-Nov. L9600 per person, L20,500 per tent; 4-5 person bungalows L60-95,000.

Campeggio Fusina, V. Moranzani, 79 (☎ 041 547 00 55), in Malcontenta. From Mestre, take bus #1. L11,000 per person, L7000 per tent, L25,000 per tent and car.

◢ FOOD

In Venice, dining well on a budget requires exploration. The best and most affordable restaurants are hidden in the less-traveled alleyways. Venetian cuisine, with seafood as its staple, is distinct from other Italian fare. *Spaghetti al vongole* (pasta with fresh clams and spicy vegetables) is served on nearly every menu. For an inexpensive and informal option, visit any *osteria* or *bacario* in town for the chance to create a meal from the vast array of meat- and cheese-filled pastries, tidbits of seafood, rice, meat, and *tramezzini* (triangular slices of soft white bread with any imaginable filling). These tasty treats are known as *cicchetti*. **STANDA Supermarket,** Strada Nuova, Cannaregio, 3650, near Campo S. Felice, has a large grocery store in the back, behind the clothing. (Open M-Sa 8:30am-7:20pm, Su 9am-7:20pm.)

SAN MARCO

Oasi, Calle degli Albanesi, S. Marco, 4263/a (☎041 528 99 37), between the Prisons and the Danieli Hotel. A break from the rigors of the city, Oasi serves some of the city's freshest fruits and vegetables in its *frulatti* (fruit shakes, L7000) and enormous salads. L8-17,000, *panini* L4-6000. Open Feb. to mid-Dec. M-Sa noon-3pm.

Vino, Vino, Ponte delle Veste, S. Marco, 2007a (☎041 24 17 688). From Calle Larga XXII Marzo, turn onto Calle delle Veste. Wine bar with delicious, aromatic food. *Primi* L8000, *secondi* L15,000. Cover L1000. 10% off food with Rolling Venice card. Open W-F, Su-M 10:30am-midnight, Sa 10:30am-1am.

Bacaro Jazz, S. Marco, 5546 (☎041 52 85 249), across from the Post Office, near the Rialto bridge. At this chic restaurant, patrons share huge plates of *cicchetti* and relax to soothing jazz. Medium plate of *cicchetti* L10,000, *sangria* L4000. Happy Hour 2-7pm. Open Tu-Th11am-2am.

Rosticceria San Bartomoleo, Calle della Bissa, S. Marco, 5424/A (☎041 522 35 69). Follow the neon sign under the last archway on the left from Campo S. Bartolomeo. Full-service restaurant upstairs. Pasta L6500-9000, main dishes L12-23,000. Cover L2500. Open Tu-Su 9:30am-9:30pm.

Harry's Bar, Calle Vellaresso (☎041 528 57 77), across from the tourist office. For a taste of history, swagger over to this favored hangout of "Ernesto" Hemingway and other "real men." Service 15%. Open daily 10:30am-10:55pm.

SAN POLO AND SANTA CROCE

Due Colonne, Campo S. Agostin, S. Polo, 2343 (☎041 524 06 85). Cross the bridge away from the Frari, turn left and cross into Campo S. Stin, turn right on Calle Danà, and cross the bridge. The best pizza in Venice (L6-13,000). Cover L1500. Service 10%. Closed Aug. Open M-Sa 8am-3pm and 7-11pm, kitchen closes 1hr. earlier.

Antica Birraria La Carte, Campo S. Polo, S. Polo, 2168 (☎041 275 05 70). Housed in a former brewery, the Birraria stays true to its roots with an extensive selection of beers as well as several pizza options (L8-14,000). Open Tu-Su noon-2:30pm and 7-10:30pm, Sa noon-2:30pm and 7-11pm.

Do Mori, Calle dei Do Mori, S. Polo, 429 (☎041 522 54 01), near the Rialto markets. Venice's oldest wine bar and an elegant place to grab a few *cicchetti* (from L2000) or a glass of local wine. Standing room only. Open M-Sa 9am-9pm.

ITALY

DORSODURO

Taverna San Trovaso, Fondamenta Nani, Dorsoduro, 1016 (☎041 520 37 03). Young, enthusiastic staff serves great pastas and pizzas at affordable prices. *Primi* L10-15,000, *secondi* L15-27,000, pizzas L8-14,000. Cover L3000. Open Tu-Su noon-2:30pm and 7-9:45pm.

Pizza al Volo, Campo S. Margherita, Dorsoduro, 2944 (☎041 522 54 30). One of the few pizza-by-the-slice places that's open late in Venice. Take-out only. Slices L2500-3000, full pizzas L6-20,000. Open daily noon-4pm and 5pm-midnight.

CANNAREGIO

Ristorante da Poggi, Campo della Maddalena, Cannaregio, 2103 (☎041 72 11 99). Left from the station and cross 2 bridges. Traditional restaurant with delicious, fresh seafood. *Primi* and *secondi* L16-30,000. Open Tu-Su noon-3pm and 6:30pm-midnight.

CASTELLO

Cip Ciap, Calle Mondo Nuovo, 5799a (☎041 523 66 21), between Salizzada S. Lio and Campo S. Maria Formosa. Grab cheap pizza (from L4000) and enjoy in a nearby *campi*. The *disco volante* (literally flying saucer), stuffed with mushrooms, eggplant, ham, and salami, is out of this world (L11,500). Call ahead for *volante*. Open W-M 9am-9pm.

GELATERIE

 La Boutique del Gelato, Salizzada S. Lio, Castello, 5727 (☎041 522 32 83). Go. Go NOW. Enormous cones from L1500. Open daily Feb.-Nov. 10am-8:30pm.

Gelati Nico, Zattere, Dorsoduro, 922 (☎041 522 52 93). Try *gianduiotto* (hazelnut ice cream dunked in whipped cream, L4000). Cones L2-4000. Open F-W 6:45am-11pm.

◉ SIGHTS

> **❗ MINI-SKIRTS, MINI-PASSES, AND MINI-DISCOUNTS.** Many Venetian churches enforce a strict dress code—shoulders and knees must be covered. The Associazione Chiese di Venezia sells a three-day mini-pass for visits to S. Maria dei Miracoli, S. Maria Gloriosa dei Frari, S. Polo, Madonna dell'Orto, Il Redentore, S. Sebastiano, and the Tesoro of S. Marco. The L15,000 pass, available at participating churches, allows visits to any six of these churches. For information on the pass or any of these churches, call 041 275 04 62. Many sights have student, senior, and group discounts; "reduced" prices generally apply to EU visitors under 18 or over 60. Children under 12 are often admitted for free.

AROUND THE RIALTO BRIDGE

THE GRAND CANAL. The Grand Canal loops through Venice, and the splendid facades of the *palazzi* that crown its banks testify to the city's history of immense wealth. Although their external decorations vary, the palaces share the same basic structure. A nighttime tour reveals the startling beauty of the *palazzi*. *(Ride vaporetto #82 or the slower #1 from the train station to P. S. Marco.)*

THE RIALTO BRIDGE. The Rialto Bridge (1588-91) arches over the Grand Canal and symbolizes Venice's commercial past. Appropriately named, Antonio da Ponte created this image that graces postcards throughout the city. *(Vaporetto: Rialto.)*

CHIESA DI SAN GIACOMO DI RIALTO. Between the Rialto Bridge and the markets stands Venice's first church, diminutively called "San Giacometto." The statue was once a podium from where officials made announcements, at whose feet convicted thieves, forced to run naked from P. S. Marco and lashed all the way by bystanders, could finally collapse. *(Vaporetto: Rialto. Cross the bridge and head right. Open daily 10am-5pm. Free.)*

AROUND PIAZZA SAN MARCO

■ **BASILICA DI SAN MARCO.** The interior of this glittering church sparkles with both 13th-century Byzantine and 16th-century Renaissance mosaics. Behind the altar screen, is the **Pala D'Oro**, a gem-encrusted relief covering the tomb of St. Mark. To the right of the altar is the **tesoro (treasury)**, a hoard of gold and relics from the Fourth Crusade. Steep stairs in the atrium lead to the **Galleria della Basilica**, which offers a staggering perspective on the interior mosaics, a tranquil vista of the exterior *piazza*, and an intimate view of the original bronze *Horses of St. Mark*. *(Basilica open M-Sa 9am-5pm, Su 1-5pm. Basilica illuminated 11:30am-12:30pm. Free. Dress code enforced; shoulders and knees must be covered. Pala D'Oro open M-Sa 9:45am-5pm, Su 2-4:30pm. L3000, reduced L1500. Treasury open M-Sa 9:45am-5pm, Su 2-4:30pm. L4000, reduced L2000. Galleria open daily 9:45am-5pm. L3000, reduced L1500. Free guided tours in English Apr.-Oct. W-F 11am.)*

■ **PALAZZO DUCALE (DOGE'S PALACE).** Once the home of Venice's mayor, or doge, the Palazzo Ducale now houses one of Venice's best museums—its collection combines historical artifacts with spectacular artwork. Within the palace lie the Doge's private apartments and the magnificent state rooms of the Republic. Climb the richly decorated **Scala d'Oro** (Golden Staircase) to reach the Sala del Maggior Consiglio (Great Council Room), dominated by Tintoretto's *Paradise*, the largest oil painting in the world. Passages lead through the courtrooms of the much-feared Council of Ten and the even-more-feared Council of Three, crossing the Ponte dei Sospiri (Bridge of Sighs) and continuing into the prisons. *(☎041 522 49 51. Open daily Apr.-Oct. 9am-7pm; Nov.-Mar. 9am-5pm. Ticket office closes 1½hr. before closing. L18,000, students L10,000, children ages 6-14 L6000. Includes entrance to Museo Correr, Biblioteca Nazionale Marciana, Museo Archeologico, Museo di Palazzo Mocenigo, Museo del Vetro di Murano, and Museo del Merletto di Burano. Audioguides L7000.)*

■ **PIAZZA SAN MARCO.** In contrast to the narrow, labyrinthine streets that wind through most of Venice, P. San Marco (Venice's only official *piazza*) is a magnificent expanse of light and space. Enclosing the *piazza* are the unadorned 16th-century Renaissance **Procuratie Vecchie (Old Treasury Offices)**, the more ornate 17th-century Baroque **Procuratie Nuove (New Treasury Offices)**, and the smaller Neoclassical **Ala Napoleonica**, sometimes called the Procuratie Nuovissime (Really New Treasury Offices), which Napoleon constructed when he took the city in 1797. The brick **campanile** (bell tower; 96m) across the *piazza* stands on Roman foundations. *(Campanile open daily 9am-7pm. L10,000.)*

CHIESA DI SAN ZACCARIA. Dedicated to the father of John the Baptist and designed by (among others) Coducci in the late 1400s, this Gothic-Renaissance church holds one of the masterpieces of Venetian Renaissance painting, Giovanni Bellini's *Virgin and Child Enthroned with Four Saints*. *(Vaporetto: S. Zaccaria. Or from P. S. Marco, turn left along the water, cross the bridge, and turn left under the sottoportico. ☎041 522 12 57. Open daily 10am-noon and 4-7pm.)*

SAN POLO

BASILICA DI SANTA MARIA GLORIOSA DEI FRARI (I FRARI). Within the cavernous brick walls of this church rest not only two outstanding paintings by Titian but also the Renaissance master himself. His *Assumption* (1516-18) on the high altar marks the height of the Venetian Renaissance. In the Florentine chapel to the right, is Donatello's *St. John the Baptist* (1438), a wooden Renaissance sculpture. *(Vaporetto: S. Tomà. Follow signs to Campo dei Frari. Open M-Sa 9am-6pm, Su 1-6pm. L3000.)*

SCUOLA GRANDE DI SAN ROCCO. Venice's most illustrious *scuola*, or guildhall, stands as a monument to Jacopo Tintoretto. The *scuola* commissioned Tintoretto to complete all of the building's paintings, a task that took 23 years. *(Behind the Basilica dei Frari in Campo S. Rocco. ☎041 523 48 64. Open daily Apr.-Oct. 9am-5:30pm; Nov.-March 10am-4pm. Ticket office closes 30min. earlier. L9000, students L6000. Audioguides free.)*

DORSODURO

■ **GALLERIE DELL'ACCADEMIA.** The Accademia houses the most extensive collection of Venetian art in the world. At the top of the double staircase, **Room I,** topped by a ceiling full of cherubim, houses Venetian Gothic art, with a luxurious use of color that influenced Venetian painting for centuries. Among the enormous altarpieces in **Room II,** Giovanni Bellini's *Madonna Enthroned with Child, Saints, and Angels* stands out for its lush serenity. **Rooms IV** and **V** display more Bellinis, and **Giorgione's** enigmatic *La Tempesta.* On the opposite wall is Titian's last painting, a brooding *Pietà.* In **Room XX** works by Gentile Bellini and Carpaccio display Venetian processions and cityscapes so accurately that scholars use them as "photos" of Venice's past. *(Vaporetto: Accademia. ☎041 522 22 47. Open daily 9am-7pm; ticket office closes ½hr. earlier. L12,000. Guided tours L12,000.)*

■ **COLLEZIONE PEGGY GUGGENHEIM.** Ms. Guggenheim's Palazzo Venier dei Leoni now displays works by Brancusi, Marini, Kandinsky, Picasso, Magritte, Rothko, Ernst, Pollock, and Dalí. The Marini sculpture *Angel in the City,* in front of the *palazzo,* was designed with a detachable penis. Ms. Guggenheim occasionally modified this sculpture so as not to offend her more prudish guests. *(Calle S. Cristoforo, Dorsoduro, 701. Vaporetto: Accademia. Turn left and then follow the yellow signs. ☎041 240 54 11. Open M, W-F 10am-6pm, Sa 10am-10pm. L10,000, students with ISIC or Rolling Venice L8000, under 10 free. Audioguides L8000.)*

CHIESA DI SANTA MARIA DELLA SALUTE. The theatrical Salute, poised at the tip of Dorsoduro, is a prime example of the Venetian Baroque. Next to the Salute stands the Dogana, the old customs house, where ships sailing into Venice were required to stop and pay appropriate duties, and which possesses a marvelous view of the city. *(Vaporetto: Salute. ☎041 522 55 58. Open daily 9am-noon and 3-5:30pm. Free. Entrance to sacristy with donation. The Dogana is closed to the public.)*

CHIESA DI SAN SEBASTIANO. The painter Veronese took refuge here when he fled Verona in 1555 after reputedly killing a man, filling the church with some of his finest works. His breathtaking *Stories of Queen Esther* covers the ceiling. *(Vaporetto: S. Basilio. Continue straight ahead. Open M-Sa 10am-5pm, Su 3-5pm. L3000.)*

CASTELLO

CHIESA DI SANTISSIMI GIOVANNI E PAOLO (SAN ZANIPOLO). After their deaths 25 doges were brought to this Gothic church, the largest in the city. Monuments to them and other honored citizens line the walls. Outside the church stands the bronze equestrian **statue of Bartolomeo Colleoni,** a mercenary who left his inheritance to the city on the condition that a monument to him be erected in front of San Marco. The city, unwilling to honor him in such a grand space, decided to pull a fast one and place the statue in front of the *Scuola* di San Marco. *(Vaporetto: Fond. Nuove. Turn left and then right onto Fond. dei Mendicanti. ☎041 523 59 13. Open M-Sa 7:30am-12:30pm and 3:30-7pm, Su 3-6pm.)*

CHIESA DI SANTA MARIA DEI MIRACOLI. The Lombardis designed this Renaissance jewel in the late 1400s and it's still one of the prettiest churches in Venice. *(From S.S. Giovanni e Paolo, cross Ponte Rosse. Open M-Sa 10am-5pm, Su 1-5pm. L3000.)*

SCUOLA DALMATA SAN GIORGIO DEGLI SCHIAVONI. Between 1502 and 1511, Carpaccio decorated the ground floor with some of his finest paintings, depicting episodes from the lives of St. George, Jerome, and Tryfon. *(Castello, 3259/A. Vaporetto: S. Zaccaria. Turn right off the boat, then turn left on Calle d. Pietà, right on Sal. dei Greci, and left on Fond. d. Furlani. ☎041 522 88 28. Shoulders and knees must be covered. Open Apr.-Oct. Tu-Sa 9:30am-12:30pm and 3:30-6:30pm, Su 9:30am-12:30pm; Nov.-March Tu-Sa 10am-12:30pm and 3-6pm, Su 10am-12:30pm. L5000, Rolling Venice L3000.)*

GIARDINI PUBLICI AND SANT'ELENA. Longing for trees and grass? Stroll through the Public Gardens, installed by Napoleon, or bring a picnic lunch to the shady lawns of Sant'Elena. *(Vaporetto: Giardini or S. Elena. Free.)*

CANNAREGIO

JEWISH GHETTO. In 1516 the Doge forced Venice's Jewish population into the old cannon-foundry area, creating the first Jewish ghetto in Europe; the word "ghetto" is the Venetian word for "foundry." The oldest synagogue shares a building with the **Museo Comunità Ebraica (Jewish Museum)** in the Campo del Ghetto Nuovo. *(Cannaregio, 2899/B. Vaporetto: S. Marcuola. Follow the signs straight ahead and then turn left into Campo del Ghetto Nuovo. ☎ 041 71 53 59. Open June-Sept. Su-F 10am-7pm; Oct.-May Su-F 10am-4:30pm. Ticket office closes 30min. earlier. L5000. Entrance to synagogues by guided tour only (40min). English tours leave every hour on the half-hour. Museum and tour L9000.)*

CÀ D'ORO AND GALLERIA GIORGIO FRANCHETTI. The most spectacular facade on the Grand Canal and the premiere example of Venetian Gothic, the Cà d'Oro, built between 1425 and 1440, now houses the Giorgio Franchetti collection. For the best view of the palace, take the *traghetto* across the canal to the Rialto Markets. *(Vaporetto: Cà d'Oro. ☎ 041 522 23 49. Open daily 8:15am-2pm. L6000.)*

GIUDECCA AND SAN GIORGIO MAGGIORE

CHIESA DI SAN GIORGIO MAGGIORE. Standing on its own monastic island, S. Giorgio Maggiore contrasts sharply with most other Venetian churches. Palladio ignored the Venetian fondness for color and decorative excess and constructed an austere church of simple dignity. *(Vaporetto: S. Giorgio Maggiore. ☎ 041 522 78 27. Open M-Sa 10am-12:30pm and 2:30-4:30. Campanile L3000 when elevator is in service.)*

ISLANDS OF THE LAGOON

BURANO. In this traditional fishing village, fishermen haul in their catch every morning as their wives, black-clad, sit in the doorways of the fantastically colored houses, creating unique knots of Venetian lace. See their handiwork in the small **Scuola di Merletti di Burano (Lace Museum).** *(Vaporetto #12: Burano from S. Zaccaria or Fond. Nuove. Museum in P. Galuppi. ☎ 041 73 00 34. Open W-M 10am-5pm. L8000. Included on combined Palazzo Ducale ticket.)*

MURANO. Famous for its glass since 1292, the island of Murano affords visitors the opportunity to witness the glass-blowing process. The **Museo Vetrario (Glass Museum)** houses a splendid collection that includes pieces from Roman times. Farther down the street is the exceptional 12th-century **Basilica di Santa Maria e San Donato.** *(Vaporetto #12 or 52: Faro from S. Zaccaria or Fond. Nuove. Museo Vetrario, Fond. Giustian, 8. ☎ 041 73 95 86. Open Th-Tu 10am-5pm; in winter Th-Tu 10am-4pm. L8000. Included on combined Palazzo Ducale ticket. Basilica ☎ 041 73 90 56. Open daily 9:15am-noon and 4-7pm.)*

TORCELLO. Torcello boasts a lovely cathedral, **Santa Maria Assunta,** which contains 11th- and 12th-century mosaics of the Last Judgment and the Virgin Mary. *(Vaporetto #12: Torcello from S. Zaccaria or Fond. Nuove. Cathedral ☎ 041 73 00 84. Open daily 10:30am-12:30pm and 2-6:30pm. L4000.)*

LIDO. The Lido is now mostly a summer beach town, complete with cars, blaring radios, and beach bums. Head for the **public beach,** the southern end of which features an impressive shipwreck. *(Vaporetto: Lido.)*

ISOLA DI SAN MICHELE. Venice's cemetery island, marked by the first Renaissance church in Venice, is the resting place of poet Ezra Pound, composer Igor Stravinsky; and Russian choreographer Sergei Diaghilev. *(Vaporetto: Cimitero.)*

🎵 🎭 ENTERTAINMENT AND NIGHTLIFE

ENTERTAINMENT

The weekly booklet, *A Guest in Venice,* free at hotels and tourist offices, lists current festivals, concerts, and gallery shows; **Venice, 2001 Events,** also available at the tourist office, lists concerts and shows for the entire year. The famed **Biennale di Venezia,** a world-wide contemporary art exhibition, drowns the Public Gardens and the Arsenal every odd-numbered year in provocative international art. (☎ 041 241 10 58). Venice's famous **Carnevale** draws masked figures and camera-happy tourists during the 10 days before Ash Wednesday, doubling the city's population by Mardi Gras. Mark Twain may have derided the **gondola** as "an inky, rusty canoe," but it's a canoe only the gentry can afford. The minimum authorized rate, which increases after sunset, starts at L120,000 for 45 minutes. For a quick and affordable taste of a gondola ride, try one of the city's *traghetti*, ferry gondolas that cross the Grand Canal at six points for a mere L700.

NIGHTLIFE

Venetian nightlife is much more relaxed and quiet than that of other major cities. Most locals looking for nighttime action flee to the mainland after the working day is over, and those who remain generally spend their evenings sipping wine or beer rather than gyrating in a disco. The most distinct nightlife option remains a moon-lit ride on the old #82 reminiscing about the glory days. The major areas of student nightlife are **Campo Santa Margherita** in Dorsoduro, and the areas around **Fondamenta della Misericordia** in Cannaregio.

Inishark Irish Pub, Calle Mondo Novo, Castello, 5787 (☎041 523 53 00), between Campo S. Maria Formosa and Salizzada S. Lio. The most creative and elegant Irish pub in Venice. Rubber sharks, wooden mantelpieces, and other assorted junk line the walls and ceilings. Open Tu-Su 6pm-2am.

Bar Salus, Campo S. Margherita, Dorsoduro, 3112 (☎041 528 52 79). Large, comfortable booths, a roomy bar, and tons of outdoor seating make Bar Salus an extremely popular hangout for both Venetian and international students. *Fragolino* L2000.

Casanova, Lista di Spagna, Cannaregio, 158/A (☎041 275 01 99; www.casanova.it). If you're starved for a *discoteca,* join the slinkily dressed crowd and let modern-day Latin lovers show you their moves. Themes and cover charge change nightly, from alternative to latin to house music. Happy Hours 6-10pm. Open daily 10pm-4am.

⨖ DAYTRIPS FROM VENICE

FLORENCE. This Renaissance center offers tourists incredible collections of art, lovely gardens, and the best *gelati* around (see p. 678*).*

PADUA (PADOVA)

Brimming with art and student life, Padua blends university culture with high culture—book-toting students walk through sculpture-lined *piazze*, cultivating an air of liberal individualism. The one-year **Biglietto Unico** is valid at most of Padua's museums. (Buy at the tourist office and participating sights. L15,000, students L10,000.) The ⨖**Cappella degli Scrovegni** (Arena Chapel) contains Giotto's breathtaking floor-to-ceiling fresco cycle, illustrating the lives of Mary, Jesus, and Mary's parents. Buy tickets at the adjoining **Musei Civici Eremitani,** which features a restored Giotto crucifix. (☎049 820 45 50. Open Feb.-Oct. Tu-Su 9am-7pm, Nov.-Jan. Tu-Su 9am-6pm. Chapel open daily Feb.-Dec. 9am-7pm. L10,000, students L7000*.)* Thousands of pilgrims are drawn to St. Anthony's jawbone and well-preserved tongue at the **Basilica di Sant'Antonio,** in P. del Santo, a medieval conglomeration of eight domes filled with beautiful frescoes. (Open daily Apr.-Sept. 6:20am-7pm; Nov.-Mar. daily 6:30am-7pm. L3000.) In the center of P. del Santo stands Donatello's bronze equestrian **Gattamelata** statue of Erasmo da Narni (a.k.a. Gattamelata or Calico Cat), a general known for his agility and ferocity. Next to the *duomo,* in P. Duomo, lies the 12th-century **Battistero,** perhaps the most visually stunning of Padua's structures. (Open M-Sa 7:30am-noon and 3:45-7:45pm, Su 7:45am-1pm and 3:45-8:30pm. Free.) The fascinatingly bizarre **Palazzo della Ragione** (Law Courts), built in 1218, retains most of its original shape. Astrological signs line the walls, and to the right of the entrance sits the Stone of Shame, on which debtors were forced to repeat *"Cedo bonis"* (I renounce my property) while partially clad. (Open Tu-Su Jan.-Oct. 9am-7pm; Nov.-Dec. 9am-6pm. L10,000, students L6000.) Ancient university buildings are scattered throughout the city, centered in **Palazzo Bó.** For nighttime entertainment, **Lucifer Young,** V. Altinate, 89, near the university, is a hip, young bar. (☎049 66 55 31. Drinks from L6000. Open Su-Tu and Th 7pm-2am, F-Sa 7pm-4am.)

Trains depart from P. Stazione for Bologna (1½hr., 1-2 per hr., L21,000); Milan (2½hr., 1-2 per hr., L20-31,500); Venice (30min., 3-4 per hr., L4100); and Verona (1hr., 1-2 per hr., L7900). **Buses** (☎049 820 68 11), leave from P. Boschetti for Venice (45min., 2 per hr., L5300). The **tourist office** is in the train station and provides maps, pamphlets, and other info. (☎049 875 20 77; fax 049 875 50 88. Open M-Sa 9am-6pm, Su 9:30am-12:30pm.) The **post office**, is on C. Garibaldi, 33. (☎049 820 85 11. Open M-Sa 8:10am-7pm.) Take bus #3 from the station to Prato della Valle; walk away from the park, and turn left on V. Memmo, then turn right on V. Aleardi to reach **Ostello Città di Padova (HI)**, V. Aleardi, 30. (☎049 875 22 19. Breakfast, sheets, and shower included. Reception 7-9:30am and 2:30-11pm. Curfew 11pm. Reserve 1 week in advance. Dorms L21-24,000.) **Hotel Al Santo**, V. del Santo, 147, near the basilica, rents airy, well-kept rooms with phones and showers. (☎049 875 21 31. Breakfast L8000. Open Feb. to mid-Dec. Singles L50,000; doubles L85,000; triples L115,000.) Women under 30 can stay in the modern, tidy rooms at **Opera Casa Famiglia (ACISJF)**, V. Nino Bixio, 4, off P. Stazione. (☎049 875 15 54. Curfew 10:30pm. L30,000 per bed.) Join a rollicking crowd for late-night dinner on the terrace at **Pizzeria Al Borgo**, V. L. Belludi, 56, near the Basilica di S. Antonio. (Cover L2500. Open W-Su noon-3pm and 7-11:30pm.) Or, try **Alexander Bar**, V. S. Francesco, 38, near the university, for an immense range of sandwiches. (*Panini* L6-10,000. Open M-Sa 8:30am-2am.) **Postal Code:** 35100.

VERONA

After traversing the old Roman Ponte Pietra on a summer evening, with the rushing of the Adige River below and the illuminated towers of churches and castles glowing above, you'll understand why Shakespeare set *Romeo and Juliet* in Verona. Its monumental city gates and ancient amphitheater memorialize the city's Roman past, while the Scaligeri bridge and tombs harken back to Verona's Gothic glory.

▐ TRANSPORTATION. Trains go to: Rome (5hr., 5 per day, L63,100-72,700); Bologna (2hr., every 2hr., L10,500); Cinque Terre (4½hr., L33,000); Milan (2hr., every hr., L12,500); Naples (8hr., L60,000); Trent (1hr., every 2hr., L9200); and Venice (1¾hr., every hr., L10,800-17,000). **Buses** (☎045 800 41 29), on P. XXV Aprile, leave the gray building in front of the train station for: Brescia (2hr., every hr., L10,300); Riva Del Garda (2hr., 12 per day, L9300); and Sirmione (1hr., 13 per day, L5000).

▐ PRACTICAL INFORMATION. The **tourist office** is off of P. Brà, take V. Mazzini to V. Cappello, and turn left, then right. (☎045 806 86 80; fax 045 800 36 38; email tourism@verona.it. Open M-Sa 9am-6pm.) Check email at the **Internet Train**, V. Roma, 17/a, past P. Brà; go right before the arch. (☎045 803 41 00. L10,000 per hr. Open M-Sa 8:10am-7pm.) To reach the **post office**, follow V. Cairoli from P. delle Erbe. (☎045 800 39 38. Open M-Sa 8:10am-7pm.) **Postal Code:** 37122.

▐ ▢ ACCOMMODATIONS AND FOOD. Reserve lodgings ahead, especially during **opera season** (June 30-Sept. 3). The **Ostello della Gioventù (HI)**, **"Villa Francescatti,"** Salita Fontana del Ferro, 15, is in a renovated 16th-century villa with gorgeous gardens. From the station, take bus #73 or night bus #90 to P. Isolo, turn right, and follow the yellow signs uphill. (☎045 59 03 60. Breakfast, showers, and, sheets included. Max. stay 5-nights. Check-in 5pm. Check-out 7-9am. Lockout 9am-5pm. Curfew 11pm; flexible for opera-goers. No reservations. Dorms L22,000.) Women can also try the lovely **Casa della Giovane (ACISJF)**, V. Pigna, 7, 3rd fl., in the historic center of town. (☎045 59 68 80. Reception 9am-11pm. Curfew 11pm; flexible for opera-goers. Dorms L22,000; singles L32,000; doubles L50,000.) To get to **Locanda Catullo**, Vco. Catullo, 1, walk to V. Mazzini, turn onto V. Catullo, and go left. (☎045 800 27 86. July-Sept. 3-night min. stay. Reserve ahead. Singles L60,000; doubles L90-110,000; triples L135-165,000; quads L165-175,000.)

Verona is famous for its wines—its dry white *soave* and red *valpolicella, bardolino,* and *recioto.* Wine prices in **P. Isolo** are cheaper than in **P. delle Erbe.** For a large sampling, try **Oreste dal Zovo**, Vco. S. Marco in Foro, 7/5, off C. Porta Borsari. This *enoteca* has shelves of every Italian wine imaginable (from L9000), as well as *grappa* and well-known international liquors and drinks. **Cantore**, V. A. Mario, 2, a block from the Arena near V. Mazzini, serves up Verona's best pizza-ambience combo. (☎045 803 43 69. Pizza from L7000; *primi* L11-18,000; *secondi* L12-25,00. Open Th-Tu noon-3pm and 6pm-midnight.) **METÁ supermarket,** V. XX Settembre, 81, carries essentials at reasonable prices. Take bus #11, 12, 13, 14, or 51. (Open M-Tu and Th-Sa 8:30am-12:45pm and 3:45-7:30pm, W 8:30am-12:45pm.)

🎭 📍 **SIGHTS AND ENTERTAINMENT.** Serving today as Verona's modern **opera house,** the pink-marble **Arena** in P. Brà was constructed as a Roman amphitheater during the first century, and now serves as the centerpiece of the city. (☎045 800 32 04. Open Tu-Su 9am-7pm; in opera season 9am-3pm. L6000, students L4000.) From P. Brà, V. Mazzini leads to the markets and stunning medieval architecture of **Piazza delle Erbe,** once a Roman forum. The 83m **Torre dei Lambertini,** down V. Capello from P. Erbe, offers a stunning view of Verona. (☎045 803 27 26. Open Tu-Su 9:30am-6pm. Elevator L4000, students L3000; stairs L3000, students L2000.) The **Giardino Giusti,** V. Giardino Giusti, 2, is a magnificent 16th-century garden with mythological statues. (☎045 803 40 29. Open daily Apr.-Sept. 9am-8pm; Oct.-Mar. 9am-dusk. L7000; students L3000.) The della Scala fortress, the **Castelvecchio,** down V. Roma from P. Brà, is filled with walkways, parapets, and an extensive art collection that includes Pisanello's *Madonna and Child.* (☎045 50 47 34. Open Tu-Su 9am-7pm. L6000, students L4000; 1st Su of each month free.) From late June to early September Verona tourists and singers from around the world descend on the Arena for the city's annual **Opera Festival.** (For tickets, call ☎045 800 51 51. General admission seating on the steps Su-Th L38,000; F-Sa L42,000.)

FRIULI-VENEZIA GIULIA

Friuli-Venezia Giulia traditionally receives less than its fair share of recognition, but this region has served as inspiration to a number of prominent literary figures. James Joyce lived in Trieste for 12 years, during which he wrote most of *Ulysses*; Ernest Hemingway drew part of the plot for *A Farewell to Arms* from the region's role in WWI; and Freud and Rilke both worked and wrote here. The city of Trieste attracts large numbers of tourists to the cheapest beach resorts on the Adriatic.

TRIESTE (TRIEST)

Austrians took advantage of the post-Napoleonic real estate market to snatch up Trieste, the city that was once Venice's chief rival along the Adriatic. After a few more games of international ping-pong, the city became part of Italy in 1954, but echoes of its Slavic past still linger in the Neoclassical architecture, nuances of the local cuisine, and the Slovenian that is still spoken in the streets of Trieste. The **Città Nuova,** a grid-like pattern of streets lined with crumbling Neoclassical palaces centers around the **Canale Grande.** Facing the canal from the south is the striking Serbian Orthodox **Chiesa di San Spiridione.** The ornate **Municipio** complements the **Piazza dell'Unità d'Italia,** the largest *piazza* in Italy. Trieste's Neoclassical architecture contrasts with its narrow, twisting alleys, reminiscent of its medieval and Roman history. Take bus #24 to the last stop (L1400) to reach the 15th-century Venetian **Castello di San Giusto,** which presides over **Capitoline Hill,** south of P. Unità, the city's historical center. (☎040 31 36 36. Castle open daily 9am-sunset. L2000.) Hilltop **Piazza della Cattedrale** overlooks the sea and downtown Trieste; from P. Goldoni, you can ascend the hill by the daunting 265 **Scala dei Giganti** (Steps of the Giants). The archaeological **Museo di Storia e d'Arte,** V. Cattedrale, 15, is down the other side of the hill past the *duomo.* (☎040 37 05 00. Open Tu-Su 9am-1pm. L3000.)

Trains (☎040 441 14) go from **P. della Libertà,** 8, down C. Cavour from the quays, to: Milan (5hr., 1 per hr., L34,500-50,000); Venice (2hr., 2 per hr., L14,500); and Budapest (11hr., 2 per day, L120,000). The **tourist office,** is on Riva III Novembre, 9; near the Piazza della Unita. (☎040 347 83 12; fax 040 347 83 20. Open M-Sa 9am-7pm, Su 10:30am-1pm and 4-7pm.) To get from the station to **Ostello Tegeste (HI),** V. Miramare 331, take bus #36 (L1400) and ask for the *ostello.* From the stop, walk back down the road toward Trieste and take the seaside fork toward the castle.

(☎040 22 41 04. Breakfast included. Reception 8am-11pm. Check-out 10am. Lock-out 10am-1pm. Curfew midnight. Members only. Dorms L20,000.) **Hotel Alabarda,** Via Valdirivo, 22, is near the city center. From P. Oberdan, head down V. XXX Ottobre, and turn right onto V. Valdirivo. (☎040 63 02 69. Singles L50,000; doubles L80-105,000; triples L94,000; quads L120,000.) Trieste has a **covered market** with fruit, vegetables, meat, and cheese vendors at V. Carducci, 36d, on the corner of V. della Majolica. (Open M 8am-2pm, Tu-Sa 8am-7pm.) **Pizzeria Barattolo,** P. S. Antonio, 2, is along the canal and serves a fresh *Insalata Barattolo* for L10,000. (☎040 63 14 80. Pizza L7-15,000. *Primi* L8-9000, *secondi* L10-20,000. Cover L2000. Service 15%. Open daily 8:30am-midnight.) **Postal Code:** 34100.

PIEDMONT (PIEMONTE)

Piedmont has been a politically influential region for centuries, as well as a fountainhead of fine food, wine, and nobility. After native-born Vittorio Emanuele II and Camillo Cavour united Italy, Turin served as the capital from 1861 to 1865.

TURIN (TORINO)

Turin, which will host the **Winter Olympics** in 2006, is today primarily known for housing the **Fiat Auto Company** as well as one of the stranger relics of Christianity. The **Cattedrale di San Giovanni,** behind the **Palazzo Reale,** houses the **Holy Shroud of Turin** (see below). The chapel is closed due to damage following an enormous fire in 1997. While it is now hidden from sight, contained in a silver vessel behind bars, a life-size canvas copy of the relic is on display. (☎011 436 15 40. Open daily 7am-12:30pm and 3-7pm. Free. Original shroud can be viewed every year Aug. 10-Oct. 22 free of charge. Mandatory reservation at ☎800 329 329.) The **Museo Egizio,** in the **Palazzo dell'Accademia delle Scienze,** V. dell'Accademia delle Scienze, 6, boasts a collection of Egyptian artifacts second only to the British Museum, including several copies of the Egyptian Book of the Dead. (☎011 561 77 76. Open Tu-F, Su 8:30am-7:30pm and Sa 8:30am-11pm. L12,000, ages 18-25 L6000, under 18 and seniors free.) One of Guarini's great Baroque palaces, the **Palazzo Carignano,** V. dell'Accademia delle Scienze, 5, houses the **Museo Nazionale del Risorgimento Italiano,** which details the unification of Italy, from 1800 to the early 20th century. (☎011 562 37 19. Open Tu-Su 9am-7pm. L8000, students L5000, under 10 and seniors free.)

Trains roll to: Rome (4½hr., 5 per day, L54,600); Genoa (2hr., every hr., L14,500); Milan (2hr., every hr., L21,600); and Venice (4½hr., 2 per day, L51,500). **Buses** leave Turin for Aosta (3½hr., 6 per day, L14,000) and Milan (2hr., every hr., L18,000). The **tourist office,** P. Castello, 165, has free maps. (☎011 53 51 81. Open M-Sa 9:30am-7:30pm, Su 9:30am-3pm.) To get to the clean, comfortable, and distinctly orange **Ostello Torino (HI),** V. Alby, 1, take bus #52 (bus #64 on Su) from Stazione Porto Nuova to the third stop after crossing the river. Go back up V. Thoveu, bear left onto V. Curreno, and turn left onto V. Gatti, which branches off onto V. Alby. (☎011 660 29 39. Reception 7-10am and 3:30-11pm. Curfew 11:30pm; ask for a key

---

HOLY SHROUD, BATMAN!

Called a hoax by some and a miracle by others, the holy shroud of Turin (a 1m by 4.5m piece of linen) was supposedly wrapped around Jesus' body in preparation for burial after his crucifixion. Visible on the cloth are outflows of blood: around the head (supposedly from the Crown of Thorns), all over the body (from scourging), and most importantly, from the wrists and feet (where the body was nailed to the cross). Although radiocarbon dating places the piece in the 12th century AD, the shroud's uncanny resemblance to that of Christ precludes its immediate dismissal. Scientists agree that the shroud was wrapped around the body of a 5'7" man who died by crucifixion, but whether it was the body of Jesus remains a mystery. For Christian believers, however, the importance of this relic is best described by Pope Paul VI's words: "The Shroud is a document of Christ's love written in characters of blood."

for later hours. Closed Dec. 20-Feb. 1. Dorms L22,000; doubles L48,000.) To **camp** at **Campeggio Villa Rey,** Strada Superiore Val S. Martino, 27, take bus #61 north from the right side of the Porta Nuova across the Emanuele bridge. Get off at the Porta Margherita bridge, then take bus #54 or walk up C. Gabetti away from the river to the right and follow the signs. (☎011 819 01 17. Shower L1000. L7000 per person; tents L4000 for 1, L7000 for 2, and L9000 for up to 5 persons.) The cheapest fruit, cheese, and bread shops are on V. Mazzini. For basics try the supermarket, **Di Per Di,** V. Carlo Alberto, 15E, at the corner of V. Maria Vittoria. (Open M-Tu and Th-Sa 8:30am-1:30pm and 3:30-7:30pm, W 8:30am-1:30pm.) **Postal Code:** 10100.

CENTRAL ITALY

If Umbria is the "Green Heart of Italy," then Tuscany is surely its rich, red soul. The regions that comprise the central portion of Italy share a profound artistic legacy, clear in Urbino's fairytale skyline and Florence's amazing collections of Renaissance art. The green foothills of the Marches separate the gray shores of the Adriatic from the Apennines, and traditional hill-towns from umbrella-laden beaches.

TUSCANY (TOSCANA)

The vision that is Tuscany has inspired countless artists, poets, and hordes of tourists alike. Its rolling hills, prodigious olive groves, and cobblestone streets beg visitors to slow their frenetic pace, sip some wine, and relax in fields of brilliant sunflowers. Tuscany fostered some of Italy's (and the world's) greatest cultural achievements under the tender care (and devious machinations) of the powerful Medici family, gaining eternal eminence in the arts for its staggering accomplishments during a scant half-century. Although modern times have seen Tuscany's political influence disappear, tourists flock to Tuscany to witness the glory that was, and the wonder that still is, *Toscana.*

FLORENCE (FIRENZE)

If you ever find yourself disappointed by Florence, make your way to the Boboli Gardens or one of the other venues for a panorama of the city. As you gaze at soaring domes and towers, mazes of burnt-orange roofs, framed by the surrounding hills, you'll see the Florence of fairy tales. Innumerable visitors walked the city's cobblestone streets and fell under its spell. Cosmopolitan Henry James, lonely Albert Camus, romantic E. M. Forster, and cranky Mark Twain were all conquered by the city's beauty. Today, students quote Marx and Malcolm X in street graffiti, businessmen whiz by on Vespas, and children play soccer against the *duomo.*

▛ TRANSPORTATION

Flights: Amerigo Vespucci Airport (☎055 306 17 00), in the Florentine suburb of Peretola. Mostly domestic and charter flights. Orange ATAF **bus** #62 connects to the train station (L1500). **SITA,** V. S. Caterina da Siena, 157 (☎800 37 37 60 46 or 055 28 46 61) also runs regular buses to the airport from the station (L6000). Ask for info at the "air terminal" (☎055 21 60 73) at platform #5 in station, where you can check in, get an embarkation card, and register baggage (L5000). Open daily 7am-5pm.

Trains: Santa Maria Novella Station (☎147 880 88), across from S. Maria Novella. Info open daily 7am-9pm. Trains depart every hour to: **Rome** (2½hr., L35-40,000); **Bologna** (1hr., L14,200); **Milan** (3½hr., L39,700); and **Venice** (3hr., L35,100).

Buses: LAZZI, P. Adua, 1-4r (☎055 21 51 55). To **Pisa** (in summer departs every hr.; in winter 6 per day, L11,200). **SITA,** V. S. Caterina da Siena, 15r (☎800 37 60 46 or 055 28 46 61). To **Siena** (1¼-2hr., L11,000).

Public Transportation: ATAF, outside the train station, runs orange city buses 6am-1am. One-hour tickets L1500, packet of 4 L5800; 3-hour L2500; 24-hour L6000; and 3-day L11,000. Buy tickets at any newsstand, *tabacchi*, or automated ticket dispenser before boarding. Validate your ticket using the orange machine on board or risk a L75,000 fine. One-hour tickets are sold on the bus from 9pm-6am for L3000.

Taxis: (☎ 055 43 90, 055 47 98, or 055 42 42), outside the train station.

Bike and Moped Rental: Alinari Noleggi, Via Guelfa, 85r (☎ 055 28 05 00). Rents mopeds for L35-45,000 per day, bikes for L20-40,000 per day.

Hitchhiking: Hitchers take the A-1 north to Bologna and Milan or the A-11 northwest to the Riviera and Genoa. Buses #29, 30, or 35 run from the station to the feeder near Peretola. For the A-1 south to Rome and the extension to Siena, they take bus #31 or 32 from the station to Exit 23. *Let's Go* does not recommend hitchhiking.

⚡🛈 ORIENTATION AND PRACTICAL INFORMATION

From the train station, a short walk on V. de' Panzani and a left on V. de' Cerretani leads to the center of Florence. Major arteries radiate from the **duomo** and its two *piazze*. A lively walkway, **Via dei Calzaiuoli,** runs from the *duomo* to the Piazza della Signoria and the Arno. Parallel to Via dei Calzaiuoli, Via Roma leads from P.S. Giovanni through **Piazza della Repubblica** to the **Ponte Vecchio,** which spans the Arno to the Oltrarno district. **Via del Proconsolo** is located east of V. Roma, and runs parallel to it, south to the **Bargello.** Sights are scattered throughout Florence, but few lie beyond walking distance. tourist, financial, and local services

 Florence's streets are numbered in red and black sequences. **Red** numbers indicate commercial establishments and black (or blue) numbers denote residential addresses (including most sights and hotels). **Black** addresses appear in *Let's Go* as a numeral only, while red addresses are indicated by a number followed by an "r." If you reach an address and it's not what you're looking for, you've probably got the wrong color—just look for the other sequence.

Tourist Offices: Consorzio ITA (☎ 055 28 28 93), in the train station by track 16. If you show up and suggest a price range, they will find you a room (although often not the best value) for L4500-L15,000 commission. Open daily 8:45am-8pm. **Informazione Turistica** (☎ 055 21 22 45), in P. della Stazione, directly across the piazza from the main exit of the station. Info on entertainment and cultural events. Open daily Apr.-Oct. 8:30am-7:30pm; Nov.-Mar. 8:15am-5:30pm. Branch offices, Via Cavour, 1r, (☎ 055 29 08 32); Borgo Santa Croce, 29r at the airport (☎ 055 23 40 444).

Consulates: UK, Lungarno Corsini, 2 (☎ 055 28 41 33). Open M-F 9:30am-12:30pm and 2:30-4:30pm. **US,** Lungarno Vespucci, 38 (☎ 055 239 82 76), at V. Palestro, near the station. Open M-F 9am-12:30pm and 2-4pm.

Currency Exchange: Local banks offer the best rates. Most are open M-F 8:20am-1:20pm and 2:45-3:45pm. **ATMs** abound.

American Express: V. Dante Alighieri, 20-22r (☎ 055 509 81). From the *duomo,* walk down V. dei Calzaiuoli and turn left on V. dei Tavolini, and continue to the small piazza. Cashes personal checks for cardholders. Mail held; free for card- and traveler's checkholders, otherwise L3000 per inquiry. L300 to leave messages. Money wiring available. Open M-F 9am-5:30pm, Sa 9am-12:30pm.

Bookstores: Feltrinelli International, V. Cavour, 12r (☎ 055 29 21 96). Multilingual selection with English books. Open M-Sa 9am-7:30pm.

Laundromat: Launderette, V. Guelfa, 55r. Wash and dry L12,000. Open daily 8am-10pm.

Emergencies: ☎ 113. **Medical Emergency,** ☎ 118. **Fire,** ☎ 115. **Road Assistance (ACI),** ☎ 116. **Police,** ☎ 112.

24-Hour Pharmacies: Farmacia Comunale (☎ 055 28 94 35), at the train station by track 16. **Molteni,** V. dei Calzaiuoli, 7r (☎ 055 28 94 90).

Internet Access: Your **Virtual Office,** V. Faenza, 49 (☎ 055 267 00 05), has a number of terminals and offers other services such as international phone calls. Internet L6000

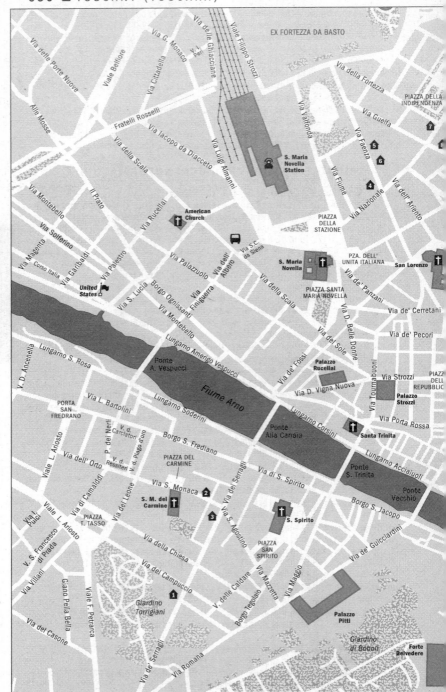

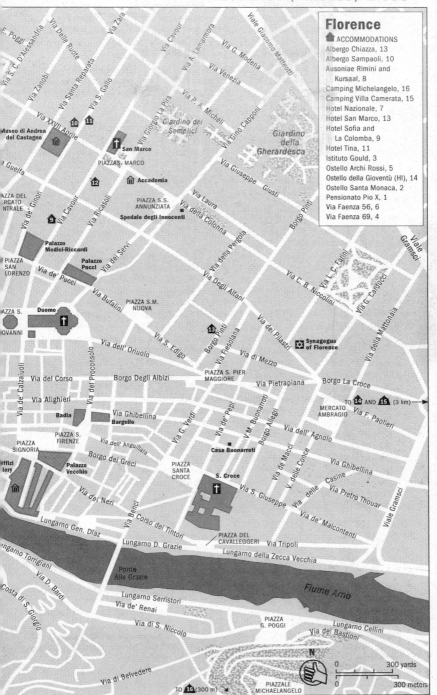

Florence
🏠 ACCOMMODATIONS
Albergo Chiazza, 13
Albergo Sampaoli, 10
Ausoniae Rimini and
  Kursaal, 8
Camping Michelangelo, 16
Camping Villa Camerata, 15
Hotel Nazionale, 7
Hotel San Marco, 13
Hotel Sofia and
  La Colomba, 9
Hotel Tina, 11
Istituto Gould, 3
Ostello Archi Rossi, 5
Ostello della Gioventù (HI), 14
Ostello Santa Monaca, 2
Pensionato Pio X, 1
Via Faenza 56, 6
Via Faenza 69, 4

per 30min., students L5000. Get on the **Internet Train** at V. Guelfa, 24a (☎055 21 47 94); V. dell'Orivolo, 25r (☎055 263 89 68); and Borgo S. Jacopo (☎055 265 79 35),. L12,000 per hr., students L10,000 per hr. With membership (free after 2hr. purchase) L2000 less per hr. Open M-F 10am-11pm, Sa 12:30-7:30pm, Su 3-7pm.

Post Office: V. Pellicceria (☎055 21 61 22). Send packages from V. dei Sassetti, 4. Address mail to be held: Yuan WANG, *In Fermo Posta*, L'Ufficio Postale, V. Pellicceria, Firenze, **50100** Italy. Open M-F 8:15am-7pm, Sa 8:15am-12:30pm. **Postal Code:** 50100.

■ ACCOMMODATIONS

Florence abounds with one-star *pensione* and private *affitta camere*. However, there is a constant stream of tourists in Florence, so make reservations *(prenotazioni)* at least 10 days in advance if you plan to visit during Easter or summer.

YOUTH HOSTELS

Ostello Archi Rossi, V. Faenza, 94r (☎055 29 08 04). Exit left from the station on V. Nazionale and turn left on V. Faenza. TV and patio brimming with young travelers. Breakfast L3-5000. Laundry L10,000. In summer, arrive before 11am. Lockout from room 9:30am, from hostel 11am. Curfew 12:30am. No phone or fax reservations. Dorms L23-28,000, with bath L25-40,000.

Istituto Gould, V. dei Serragli, 49 (☎055 21 25 76), in the Oltrarno. Exit the station by track 16, head right to P. della Stazione, walk along the left side of the church, and continue straight through the P. S. Maria Novella and down V. dei Fossi, which turns into V. dei Serragli after the bridge (15min.). Sunny, spotless rooms in a *palazzo* with courtyard. Reception M-F 9am-1pm and 3-7pm, Sa 9am-1pm. Sa afternoons or Su. Singles L48-55,000; doubles L72-78,000; triples L78-105,000; quads with bath L132,000.

Ostello Santa Monaca, V. S. Monaca, 6 (☎055 26 83 38), off V. dei Serragli in the Oltrarno. Laundry L12,000 per 5kg. Reception 6am-1pm and 2pm-1am. Curfew 1am. Reserve in writing, 3 days in advance. High-ceilinged dorms L25,000.

Pensionato Pio X, V. dei Serragli, 106 (☎/fax 055 22 50 44), past the Istituto Gould in Oltrarno. Quiet, clean rooms and comfortable lounges. Min. stay 2 nights. Arrive before 9am. Check-out 9am. Curfew midnight. No reservations. Dorms L25-30,000.

Ostello della Gioventù Europa Villa Camerata (HI), V. Augusto Righi, 2-4 (☎055 60 14 51). Take bus #17 from P. dell'Unità near the train station (25min.) Tidy and popular, a gorgeous villa with *loggia* and gardens. Breakfast and sheets included. Laundry L10,000. Reception 1-11pm. Strict midnight curfew. If they're full, sleep on a cot in their outdoor tent for L17,500. L25,000; nonmembers L30,000. Cash only.

Pensionato Pio X, V. dei Serragli, 106 (☎055 22 50 44). Follow the directions to the Istituto Gould, and walk a few blocks farther. Usually full in summer. Quiet, with 3-5 beds per room. Clean rooms and bathrooms. 4 comfortable lounges. Min. stay 2-nights. Arrive before 9am. Check out 9am. Curfew midnight. No reservations. Dorms with shower L25,000, with bath L30,000.

OLD CITY (NEAR THE DUOMO)

Though flooded by tourists, this area has a surprising array of budget accommodations. Many provide great views of Florence's monuments, while others lie hidden in Renaissance *palazzi*. Follow V. de' Panzani from the train station and take a left on V. de' Cerretani to reach the *duomo*.

Locanda Orchidea, Borgo degli Albizia,11 (☎055 248 03 46). Go left off V. Proconsolo from the southeast corner of P. del Duomo. Dante's wife was born in this 12th-century *palazzo*. Some of the rooms open onto a garden. Reservations recommended. Singles L70,000; doubles L105,000; triples L150,000.

Albergo Brunetta, Borgo Pinti, 5 (☎055 247 81 34). Excellent value with a central location. Rooftop terrace with superb view of the city. All rooms without bath, but showers are free. Singles L65,000; doubles L85,000; triples L120,000.

Hotel Il Perseo, V. de Cerretani, 1 (☎055 21 25 04), en route to the *duomo* from the station, opposite the Feltrinelli bookstore. Bright, immaculate rooms with fans. Bar and

TV lounge. Internet access available at L5000 for 30min. Breakfast included. Singles L85,000; doubles L135-155,000; triples L175-210,000.

Soggiorno Brunori, V. del Proconsolo, 5 (☎055 28 96 48), off P. del Duomo. English-speaking staff. Curfew 12:30am. Singles L60,000, with bath L80,000 (available in winter only); doubles L96-124,000; triples L130-168,000; quads 164-212,000.

Albergo Firenze, P. dei Donati, 4 (☎055 21 42 03). From the *duomo*, walk down V. del Proconsolo and head right on V. del Corso to the *piazza*. Central and tranquil, located in a lovely *palazzo*. Modern rooms with TVs and bath. Breakfast included. Singles L100,000; doubles L140,000; triples L190,000; quads L240,000.

AROUND PIAZZA SANTA MARIA NOVELLA

The budget accommodations that cluster around this attractive *piazza* in front of the train station offer a prime location near the *duomo* and the *centro*.

Hotel Giappone, V. de Banchi, 1 (☎055 26 86 75). Clean, comfortable rooms combine with central location for one of the best values in Florence. Singles L80,000, with bath L90,000; doubles L110,000, with bath L130,000, triples and quads L45,000.

Tourist House, V. della Scala, 1 (☎055 26 86 75). All rooms with bath, TV, terrace and breakfast. Singles L100,000; doubles 160,000.

Albergo Montreal, V. della Scala, 43 (☎055 238 23 31). Exit left from the train station, as you face the tracks, walk down V. degli Orti Oricellari, and turn left on V. della Scala. Cozy TV lounge. Curfew 1:30am. Singles L70,000; doubles L95-110,000; triples L150,000; quads L185,000.

Hotel Visconti, P. Ottaviani, 1 (☎/fax 055 21 38 77). From P. S. Maria Novella, follow V. de' Fossi 1 block. Neoclassical decor with huge Grecian nudes. Bar and TV lounge. Delicious breakfast in roof garden included. Singles L65,000, with bath L90,000; doubles L98,000, with bath L140,000.

Hotel Elite, V. della Scala, 12 (☎055 21 53 95; fax 055 21 38 32) past the Albergo Montreal (see above). Bubbly reception gives advice on sightseeing, eating, and playing in Florence. Breakfast L10,000. Singles L80-110,000; doubles L100-120,000.

Albergo Margaret, V. della Scala, 25 (☎055 21 01 38) past the Albergo Montreal (see above). Serene decor, kind staff, and beautiful rooms. Curfew midnight. Lower prices Sept.-May and for longer stays. Singles L80-100,000; doubles L100-120,000.

Soggiorno Abaco, V. dei Banchi, 1 (☎055 238 19 19). From the station walk straight into P. S. Maria Novella. With the church on the right, V. dei Banchi runs to the left. 7 All rooms have fan, phone, and TV. Laundry L7000. Singles L100,000, with bath L120,000; doubles L130,000, with bath L140,000.

AROUND PIAZZA SAN MARCO

This area is considerably calmer and less tourist-ridden than its proximity to the center might suggest. Turn right from the station and left on V. Nazionale. Take a right on V. Guelfa, which intersects V. S. Gallo and V. Cavour.

Hotel Tina, V. S. Gallo, 31 (☎055 48 35 19). From P. S. Marco, follow V. XXII Aprile and turn right on V. S. Gallo. Small *pensione* with high ceilings and new furniture. Singles L80,000; doubles L100,000, with bath L130,000; triples with bath L140,000; quads with bath L160,000.

La Colomba, V. Cavour, 21 (☎055 28 91 39) right off P. S. Marco. Clean rooms each with phone, TV, fridge and A/C. Big continental breakfast included. Singles L110-150,000; doubles L185-230,000.

Albergo Sampaoli, V. S. Gallo, 14 (☎055 28 48 34) before the Hotel Tina (see above). This *pensione* is a backpacker's "home away from home." Singles L90-100,000; doubles L110-160,000; extra bed L56,000.

Hotel San Marco, V. Cavour, 50 (☎055 28 42 35), right off P. S. Marco. Modern, airy rooms. Breakfast included. Curfew 1:30am. Key available by request. Singles L80-100,000; doubles L110-140,000; triples with bath L200,000.

ITALY

VIA NAZIONALE AND ENVIRONS

From P. della Stazione, V. Nazionale leads to budget hotels that are a short walk from the center, perfect for those who have an early train. The buildings on V. Nazionale, V. Faenza, V. Fiume, and V. Guelfa are filled with inexpensive establishments, but rooms facing the street may be noisy.

Hotel Nazionale, V. Nazionale, 22 (☎055 238 22 03), near P. della Indipendenza. Sunny room with comfy beds. Breakfast included. Door locks at midnight; social butterflies can request a key. Singles L90,000, with bath L100,000; doubles L130,000, with bath L150,000; triples L170,000, with bath L200,000.

Ausonia e Rimini, V. Nazionale, 24 (☎055 49 65 47). Breakfast included. Laundry L12,000; ironing L2000 per item. No curfew. Singles L90,000; doubles with bath L145,000; triples L165,000, with bath L220,000; quad with bath L280,000. V, MC.

VIA FAENZA, 56. This address houses 6 separate *pensione* that number among the best budget lodgings in the city. Take V. Nazionale from P. della Stazione and V. Faenza is the first intersecting street. The Azzi, Anna, and Paola share uniform management and prices, listed only in the description of the Azzi.

Pensione Azzi (☎055 21 38 06). Styles itself as a *locanda degli artisti* (an artists' inn), but all travelers enjoy the large, immaculate rooms and relaxing terrace. Breakfast included. No curfew. Singles L70,000; doubles L100-130,000.

Albergo Anna (☎055 239 83 22). Lovely rooms: frescoes for the aesthetes and fans to satisfy your more pragmatic needs. Singles and doubles available.

Locanda Paola (☎055 21 36 82). Minimalist, but clean double rooms, some with views of Fiesole and the surrounding hills. Curfew 2am; key available upon request.

Albergo Merlini (☎055 21 28 48). Murals and red geraniums adorn the lounge/solarium. Some rooms views of the *duomo*. Breakfast L10,000. Curfew 1:30am. Singles L70,000; doubles L100-120,000.

Albergo Marini (☎055 28 48 24). Polished wood hallway leads to inviting, spotless rooms. Breakfast L8,000. Flexible 1am curfew. Singles L80-90,000; doubles L110-130,000; triples L130-150,000; quads L140-170,000. Cash only.

Albergo Armonia (☎055 21 11 46). Clean rooms bedecked with American film posters. Singles L70,000; doubles L110,000; triples L135,000; quads L160,000. Prices lower in off season.

VIA FAENZA, 69. This building houses four accommodations under one roof.

Locanda Giovanna, 4th fl. (☎055 238 13 53). Well-kept rooms, some with garden views. Singles L50,000; doubles L75,000.

Locanda Pina and **Albergo Nella,** 1st and 2nd fl. (☎055 265 43 46). Basic rooms and friendly proprietors. Free kitchen use. Singles L60,000; doubles L90-110,000.

IN THE OLTRARNO

Only a 10-minute walk across the Arno from the *duomo*, this area and its *pensione* offer a respite from Florence's bustling hubs.

Hotel La Scaletta, V. Guicciardini, 13b (☎055 28 30 28). Turn right onto V. Roma from the *duomo*. Cross the Ponte Vecchio and continue onto V. Guicciardini. Beautiful rooms with antique furniture and rooftop terraces offer spectacular views of the Boboli gardens. Breakfast included. Singles L80-160,000; doubles L160-220,000; triples with bath L250,000; quads with bath L260-280,000.

Pensione Sorelle Bandini, P.S. Spirito, 9 (☎055 21 53 08; fax 055 28 27 61). From the train station walk down V. de' Panzani and take a right on V. Rondinelli, which becomes V. de' Tornabuoni. Cross Ponte S. Trinita to the other side of the Arno and take the third right onto V.Sant'Agostino; P.S. Spirito lies to the left. Half-a-millennium old *palazzo* with lovely views of the Boboli Gardens and *duomo*. Breakfast included. Doubles L140-172,000; triples L188-230,000; quads L240,000.

CAMPING

Campeggio Michelangelo, V. Michelangelo, 80 (☎055 681 19 77). Beneath Ple. Michelangelo. Take bus #13 from the station (15min.; last bus 11:25pm). Extremely crowded, but offers a spectacular panorama of Florence and a chance to doze under olive trees. Well-stocked food store and bar. Reception daily 6am-midnight. Open Apr.-Nov. L10,000 per person, L9000 per tent, L7000 per car, L6000 per motorcycle.

Villa Camerata, V. A. Righi, 2-4 (☎055 60 03 15), take bus #17 from the train station. Breakfast at hostel L2500. 7-night max. stay. Reception daily 1pm-midnight; if office is closed, stake your site and return before midnight to register and pay. Checkout 7-10am. L8000 per person, L6800 with camping card; L8000 per small tent, L16,000 per large tent.

☐ FOOD

Florence's hearty cuisine originated in the peasant fare of the surrounding countryside. Specialties include the Tuscan classics *minestra di fagioli* (a delicious white bean and garlic soup), *ribollita* (a hearty bean, bread, and black cabbage stew), and *bistecca alla Fiorentina* (thick sirloin steak). Wine is a Florentine staple, and genuine *chianti classico* commands a premium price; a liter of house wine costs L7-10,000 in Florence's *trattorie,* while stores sell bottles for as little as L5000. For lunch, visit a *rosticceria gastronomia,* peruse the city's pushcarts, or pick up fresh produce and meat at the **Mercato Centrale,** between V. Nazionale and S. Lorenzo. (Open June-Sept. M-Sa 7:30am-2pm; Oct.-May Sa 7am-2pm and 4-8pm.) **Vegetarians** will find several health-food markets in the city. They stock vitamins, algae, homemade takeout vegetable tarts, and organic vegetables, all with an Italian touch. One of the best is **Sugar Blues,** a five-minute walk from the *duomo* at V. XXVII Aprile, 46r. (☎055 48 36 66. Open M-F 9am-1:30pm and 4-7:30pm, Sa 9am-1pm.) For staples try **STANDA supermarket,** V. Pietrapiana 1r; take a right on V. del Proconsolo, then the first left on Borgo degli Albizi. Go straight through P.G. Salvemini, and it's on the left. (☎055 22 34 785 69. Open Tu-Su 8:30am-9pm.)

OLD CITY (THE CENTER)

Acqua al Due, V. Vigna Vecchia, 40r (☎055 28 41 70), behind the Bargello. Florentine specialties in a cozy place popular with young Italians. Their *assaggio,* with 5 types of pasta, demands a taste (L13,500). *Primi* L11,500-13,000; *secondi* from L12,000. Cover L2000. Open June-Sept. daily 7:30pm-1am; Oct.-May Tu-Su 8pm-1am.

Le Colonnine, V. dei Benci, 6r (☎055 23 46 47), above the Ponte alle Grazie. Delicious traditional fare (pizza from L8000, pasta L10,000; *secondi* from L13,000). Famous *paella* could feed a small army (L30,000). Open Tu-Su noon-2pm and 7pm-1am.

Il Latini, V. Palchetti, 6r. From the Ponte alla Carraia, walk up V.del Moro; V. Palchetti is on the right. Serves delicious Tuscan classics like *ribollita* (L8000) beneath dangling hams. *Primi* L10-12,000, *secondi* L15-25,000. Cover L3000. Open Tu-Su noon-2:30pm and 7-10pm.

Trattoria Anita, V. del Parlasco, 2r (☎055 23 46 47), just behind the Bargello. Enjoy your candlelit table as you dine on Florentine specialties like *panna e pomodore* (bread and tomato soup) and hearty pastas. Lunch menu includes *primo, secondo,* and *contorno* for L10,000. Open M-Sa for lunch and dinner.

PIAZZE SANTA MARIA NOVELLA AND ENVIRONS

Trattoria Contadino, V. Palazzuolo, 71r (☎055 238 26 73). Home-style meals. Lunch *menù* L16,000; dinner *menù* L20,000. Open M-Sa noon-3:30pm and 6–12:30am.

Trattoria da Giorgio, V. Palazzuolo, 100r. (☎055 28 43 02). Generous portions and a daily *menù* (L16,000). Expect a wait. Open M-Sa noon-2:30pm and 7-9:30pm.

Rose's Cafe, V. del Parione, 26r (☎055 28 70 90). This hip new restaurant prides itself on its New York atmosphere. Great Tuscan pasta (L15,000) and sushi bar. Open M-Sa 8am-1:30am, Su 5pm-1:30am. Sushi bar open Tu-Su 7-11pm. Closed Aug.

THE STATION AND UNIVERSITY QUARTER

Trattoria da Zà-Zà, P. del Mercato Centrale, 26r (☎055 21 54 11). Food Gabor—er, galore—in a hopping *trattoria;* try the *tris* (veggie soup; L9000) or the *tagliatelle al tartufo* (L11,000). Cover L2000 for meals outside menu. Complete dinner *menù* for L20,000. Open M-Sa noon-3pm and 7-11pm.

Trattoria da Garibaldi, P. del Mercato Centrale, 38r (☎055 21 22 67). Full of locals enjoying tasty, inexpensive food. Daily *menù* L16,000. Cover L2000 for meals outside the *menù.* Open daily June-Aug. noon-11pm; Sept.-May M-Sa noon-3pm and 7-11pm.

THE OLTRARNO

Il Borgo Antico, P. S. Spirito, 6r (☎055 21 04 37). An array of creative, tasty, and filling dishes. *Primi* L10,000; *secondi* L15-25,000. Cover L3000. Open daily 1-4pm and 6:30pm-1:30am. Reservations recommended.

Oltrarno Trattoria Casalinga, V. Michelozzi, 9r (☎055 21 86 24), near P. S. Spirito. Delicious Tuscan specialties like *pasta al pastore* (L10,000) with *famiglia*. *Primi* L6-10,500; *secondi* L8-18,000. Menu changes daily. Cover L3000. Open M-Sa noon-2:30pm and 7-9:30pm.

Osteria Santo Spirito, P. S. Spirito, 16r (☎055 238 23 83). Outdoor tables under the stars. Live music at night in the *piazza*. Rustic, tasty *casalinga* (homemade) dishes and good wine. Open daily noon-2:30pm and 8-11:30pm.

GELATERIE

Gelato is said to have been invented by Florence's own Buontalenti family; as a tourist, it's your duty to sample this creamy manifestation of the city's culture.

Vivoli, V. della Stinche, 7 (☎055 29 23 34), behind the Bargello. The most renowned Florentine *gelateria*, with the self-proclaimed "best ice cream in the world." Huge selection. Cups from L3000. Open daily 7am-1am

Perchè No?, V. Tavolini, 19r (☎055 239 89 69), off V. dei Calzaiuoli. Florence's oldest *gelateria* serves heavenly pistachio, mouth-watering chocolate and chunky *nocciolosa*. Cones from L3000. Open W-M 10am-1am; in winter W-M 10am-8pm.

Gelateria Dei Neri, V. dei Neri, 20-22r (☎055 21 00 34). A popular upstart with lip-smacking gelato. Soy-milk gelato available. Try the *semi-freddo*, a rich, creamy confection akin to mousse. Cones from L3000. Open daily Apr.-Sept. noon-midnight; Oct.-Mar. same hours, but closed W.

👁 SIGHTS

Florence's museums have recently doubled their prices (now L6-12,000 per venue) and no longer offer student discounts. In summer, watch for **Sere al Museo,** evenings when certain museums are free from 8:30 to 11pm. Additionally, don't miss Florence's churches, many of which are free treasuries of great art.

PIAZZA DEL DUOMO

DUOMO (CATTEDRALE DI SANTA MARIA DEL FIORE). In 1296 the city fathers commissioned Arnolfo di Cambio to erect a cathedral "with the most high and sumptuous magnificence" so that it would be "impossible to make it either better or more beautiful with the power and industry of man." Arnolfo and a succession of architects triumphed, completing the massive nave by 1418. One problem remained—no one had the necessary engineering skills to build the dome of the Cathedral. Finally, Filippo Brunelleschi dreamt up an ingenious technique. He used his knowledge of long-neglected classical methods to develop the revolutionary idea of using interlocking bricks that supported themselves, making a double-shelled construction. Alberti described the dome as "large enough to shelter all of Tuscany within its shadow…and of a construction that perhaps not even the ancients knew or understood"—the ultimate compliment in that classically influenced period. Today, the *duomo* claims the world's third-longest nave, after St. Peter's in Rome and St. Paul's in London. *(Open M-Sa 10am-5pm, Su 1:30-5pm; first Sa of every month 10am-3:30pm. Mass daily 7am-12:30pm and 5-7pm.)* Climb the 463 steps inside the dome to reach Michelangelo's lantern, or cupola, for an unparalleled view of the city from the 100 meter-high external gallery. *(☎055 230 28 85. Open M-Sa 8:30am-7pm. L10,000.)*

BATTISTERO. The **battistero** (baptistery) next to the *duomo*, built between the 5th and 9th centuries, was the site of Dante's christening; years later, its Byzantine mosaics inspired the details of the author's *Inferno*. Florentine artists competed fiercely for the commission to execute the baptistry's famous **bronze doors.** When Ghiberti completed the project in 1425, his work was so admired that he was immediately commissioned to forge the last set of doors, which he finished in 1452. The products—the ◪**Gates of Paradise,** as Michelangelo reportedly dubbed them—were nothing like his two earlier portals; they abandoned his earlier 28-panel design for 10 large, gilded squares, each of which employed mathematical perspective to create the illusion of deep space. They have been under restoration since a 1966 flood and will soon be housed in the Museo dell'Opera del Duomo. *(Opposite the duomo. Open M-Sa noon-6:30pm, Su 9am-1:30pm. Mass daily 10:30 and 11:30am. L5000.)*

CAMPANILE. Next to the *duomo* rises the 82 meter-high **campanile,** or the "lily of Florence blossoming in stone," with a pink, green, and white marble exterior that matches the *duomo* and *battistero*. Giotto designed and laid the foundation in 1334, but died soon after construction began. Andrea Pisano added two stories to the tower, and Francesco Talenti completed it in 1359 after doubling the thickness of the walls to support the weight. The original exterior decoration is now in the Museo dell'Opera del Duomo. The 414 steps to the top lead to beautiful views. *(Open daily Apr.-Sept. 8:30am-6:50pm; Oct. 9am-5:20pm; Nov.-Mar. 9am-4:20pm. L10,000.)*

MUSEO DELL' OPERA DEL DUOMO. Most of the art of the *duomo* resides in this museum. Up the first flight of stairs is a late *Pietà* by Michelangelo, who according to legend destroyed Christ's left arm with a hammer in a fit of frustration; soon after, a diligent pupil touched up the work, but leaving visible scars on a portion of Mary Magdalene's head. In the museum are Donatello's wooden *St. Mary Magdalene* (1555), Donatello and Luca della Robbia's *cantorie* (choir balconies with bas-reliefs of cavorting children), and four frames from the baptistery's *Gates of Paradise*. The museum also houses the sculptures that once covered the campanile's exterior. *(P. del Duomo 9. ☎ 055 230 28 85. Open M-Sa 9:30am-6:30pm. Tours in English in summer W-Th 4pm. L10,000.)*

PIAZZA DELLA SIGNORIA AND ENVIRONS

From P. del Duomo, **V. dei Calzaiuoli,** one of the city's oldest streets, leads to P. della Signoria. Built by the Romans, V. dei Calzaiuoli now bustles with crowds, chic shops, *gelaterie*, and vendors.

PIAZZA DELLA SIGNORIA. This 13th-century *piazza* became immensely popular when the homes of powerful Ghibelline families were destroyed. The square became Florence's civic and political center. In 1497, the religious zealot and social critic Girolamo Savonarola convinced Florentines to light the **Bonfire of the Vanities** in the *piazza*, a grand roast that consumed some of Florence's best art, including, according to legend, all of Botticelli's secular works that had not been sold to private collectors. A year later, disillusioned citizens sent Savonarola up in smoke on the same spot, marked today by a commemorative granite disc. Monumental sculptures cluster around the *Palazzo Vecchio*, including Donatello's *Judith and Holofernes*, a copy of Michelangelo's *David*, Giambologna's equestrian *Cosimo I*, and Bandinelli's *Hercules*. The awkward *Neptune* to the left of the *palazzo* so revolted Michelangelo that he insulted the artist: "Oh Ammannato, Ammannato, what lovely marble you have ruined!" Most Florentines share his opinion. Called *"Il Biancone"* ("the big white one") in derision, *Neptune* is continually subject to attacks of vandalism by angry aesthetes. The graceful 14th-century **Loggia dei Lanzi,** built as a stage for civic orators, is one of the best places in Florence to see world-class sculpture free of charge. It includes mostly classical Roman works, but its highlights are Renaissance pieces like Giambologna's famous *Rape of the Sabines*.

PALAZZO VECCHIO. Arnolfo del Cambio designed this fortress-like *palazzo* (1299-1304) as the seat of the *comune*'s government. Its apartments served as living quarters for the *signoria* (the city council) members during their two-month terms. The building became the family home of the Medici, and in 1470 Michelozzo decorated the now world-famous **courtyard** in the Renaissance style. The building contains minor works by Michelangelo and Leonardo and important pieces by Bronzino. *(9am-2pm; Sept.-May M-W, F-Sa 9am-7pm, Th 9am-2pm; Su year-round 9am-2pm. L10,000.)*

▨ THE UFFIZI

☎ *055 21 83 41. Open Tu-Sa 8:30am-6:50pm, Su 8:30am-1:50pm. L12,000. For an extra L2000, save yourself hours of waiting by purchasing advance tickets: call ☎ 050 47 19 60. Credit card number requested.*

Vasari designed this palace in 1554 for the offices (*uffizi*) of the administration of Duke Cosimo; today, it houses more first-class art per square inch than any other museum in the world. The museum displays an unparalleled collection of Renaissance art. Botticelli, da Vinci, Michelangelo, Raphael, Titian, Giotto, Fra Angelico, Caravaggio, Bronzino, Cimabue, della Francesca, Bellini, even Dürer, Rubens, and Rembrandt—you name it, they have it.

As you ascend the second floor of the museum, you will see a long corridor that wraps around the building and holds an impressive collection of Hellenistic and Roman marbles, the inspiration for many Renaissance pieces. Follow the hordes and begin a main visit in **Room 2,** which features three 13th- and 14th-century *Madonne* of the great forefathers of the Renaissance: Cimabue, Duccio di Buoninsegna, and Giotto. Their naturalistic figures rebelled against the prevalent Gothic style, and are far more impressive in person than in reproductions. **Room 3** features works from 14th-century Siena (including paintings by the Lorenzetti brothers and Simone Martini's dazzling *Annunciation*). One of the most awe-inspiring rooms in the museum, **Room 7,** houses two Fra Angelico paintings and a Madonna and Child by Masaccio. Domenico Veneziano's *Madonna with Child and Saints (Sacra Conversazione)* is one of the first paintings to incorporate Mary and the saints into a unified space. Piero della Francesca's double portrait of Duke Federico and his wife Battista Sforza stands out for its translucent color and intricate detail. In **Room 8,** Filippo Lippi's *Madonna and Child with Two Angels* pulls at the heart strings. **Rooms 10-14** are a shrine to Florence's cherished Botticelli—the resplendent *Primavera*, *Birth of Venus*, *Madonna della Melagrana*, and *Pallas and the Centaur* glow from their recent restoration. **Room 15** moves into the High Renaissance with Da Vinci's brilliant *Annunciation* and his even more remarkable, albeit unfinished, *Adoration of the Magi*. **Rooms 20** and **22** detour into the art of Northern Europe, showcasing Dürer's realistic *Adam and Eve* and Cranach the Elder's haunting treatment of the same subject. **Room 21** contains 15th-century Venetian artwork. View Bellini's moving *Sacred Allegory* before examining Mantegna's *Adoration of the Magi* in **Room 23.** The south corridor's windows offer a breathtaking view of Florence. **Rooms 25-27** display Florentine works, including Michelangelo's only oil painting, *Doni Tondo*, a string of Raphaels, and Pontormo's *Supper at Emmaus*. **Room 28** displays Titian's beautiful *Venus of Urbino*.

PONTE VECCHIO. From the Uffizi, turn left onto V. Georgofili, then right when you reach the river. The nearby **Ponte Vecchio** (literally old bridge), is indeed the oldest bridge in Florence, built in 1345 to replace an even older Roman version. In the 1500s butchers and tanners lined the bridge and dumped pigs' blood and intestines in the river, creating an odor that offended the noses of powerful bankers who crossed the Arno on the way to their *uffizi* (offices). In an effort to improve the area, the Medici kicked out the lower-class shopkeepers, allowing the more decorous goldsmiths and diamond-carvers to move in; their descendants now line the bridge with glittering boutiques.

THE BARGELLO AND ENVIRONS

BARGELLO. In the heart of medieval Florence, this 13th-century fortress was once the residence of Florence's chief magistrate. It later became a brutal prison that held public executions in the courtyard. In the 19th century, the Bargello was restored to its former elegance, and now houses the **Museo Nazionale,** a treasury of Florentine sculpture. Upstairs to the right, in the Salone del Consiglio Generale, Donatello's bronze *David*, the first free-standing nude since antiquity can be found. The artist's marble *David*, completed 30 years prior, stands near the left wall. The *loggia* on the first floor displays a collection of bronze animals that Giambologna created for a Medici garden grotto. Michelangelo's early works, including a debauched *Bacchus*, a handsome *Brutus*, an unfinished *Apollo*, and a *Madonna and Child*, dominate the ground floor. *(V. del Proconsolo, 4, between the duomo and P. della Signoria.* ☎238 86 06. *Open daily 8:30am-1:50pm; closed on the 1st, 3rd, and 5th Sunday and the 2nd and 4th Monday of every month. L8000.)*

BADIA. The Badia was the site of medieval Florence's richest monastery. Filippo Lippi's stunning *Apparition of the Virgin to St. Bernard*, one of the most famous paintings of the late 15th-century, hangs to the left of the entrance. *(Across V. del Proconsolo from the Bargello. Open daily 7:30am-12:30pm and 1-6pm.)*

PIAZZA DELLA REPUBBLICA. In 1890, this *piazza* replaced the Mercato Vecchio as the site of the town market. The inscription *"Antico centro della città, da secolare squalore, a vita nuova restituito"* ("The ancient center of the city, squalid for centuries, restored to new life"), epitomizes the progressive mood at the turn of the century. Elegant buildings and two of the city's most popular cafes flank the *piazza*. The pricey, decadent **Gilli**, Florence's most famous coffeehouse, was established in 1733. The nearby **Giubbe Rosse** was once the haunt of artists, Futurist writers, and Italian communists. *(From the Ponte Vecchio, walk straight up V. Por S. Maria, which turns into V. Calimala and pours into the piazza.)*

CHIESA DI SANTA MARIA NOVELLA. Built between 1279 and 1360, the *chiesa* boasts a green and white Romanesque-Gothic lower facade. Masaccio's powerful fresco *Trinity*, the first painting to use geometric perspective, on the left side of the nave, creates the illusion of a tabernacle, pulling the viewer into the scene. The **Capella di Filippo Strozzi**, to the right of the altar, contains frescoes by Fillipo Lippi. *(☎ 055 21 59 18. Open M-F 7am-noon and 3:30-6pm, Sa 7am-noon and 3:30-6:30pm.)*

SAN LORENZO AND FARTHER NORTH

BASILICA DI SAN LORENZO. In 1419, Brunelleschi designed this spacious basilica. Because the Medici lent the city the funds to build the church, they kept artistic control over its construction. Their coat of arms, featuring six red balls, appears all over the nave, and their tombs fill the two sacristies and the Cappella dei Principi behind the altar. The family cunningly placed Cosimo dei Medici's grave in front of the high altar, making the entire church his personal mausoleum. *(☎055 21 66 34. Open daily 7am-noon and 3:30-6:30pm.)* To reach the **Cappelle dei Medici** (Medici Chapels), walk around to the back entrance on P. Madonna degli Aldobrandini. Intended as a grand mausoleum, Matteo Nigetti's **Capella dei Principi** (Princes' Chapel) emulates the baptistry in P. del Duomo. Michelangelo's simple architectural design of the **Sacrestia Nuova** (New Sacristy, 1524) reveals the master's study of Brunelleschi. Michelangelo sculpted two impressive tombs for Medici dukes, Lorenzo and Giuliano, which depict day and night, dawn and dusk, life and death. Restoration is underway in both chapels, but does not significantly distract from either. *(☎055 238 86 02. Open M-Sa 8:30am-5pm, Su 8:30am-1:30pm; closed the 2nd and 4th Sunday and the 1st, 3rd, and 5th Monday of every month. L10,000.)*

MUSEO DELLA CHIESA DI SAN MARCO. Remarkable works by Fra Angelico adorn this museum, one of the most peaceful and spiritual places in Florence, with an especially lovely courtyard. A large room to the right of the entrance contains some of the painter's major works, including the church's altarpiece. Climb the stairs to see his famous *Annunciation*. Every cell in the convent contains its own Fra Angelico fresco, painted in flat colors, with sparse detail to facilitate the monks' meditation. *(Enter at 3 P. di San Marco.* ☎ 055 238 86 08 or 055 238 87 04. *Open daily 8:30am-1:30pm, Sa-Su 8:30am-6:50pm; closed the 1st, 3rd, and 5th Sunday, and the 2nd and 4th M of each month. L8000; EU Citizens 18-25 L4000; free over 65 and under 18.)*

■**ACCADEMIA.** Michelangelo's triumphant *David* stands in self-assured perfection in a rotunda designed just for him. He was moved here from P. della Signoria in 1873 after a stone hurled during a riot broke his left wrist in two places. In the hallway leading up to the *David* are Michelangelo's four *Slaves*. The master left these intriguing statues unfinished; remaining true to his theories of living stone, he chipped away only enough to liberate the slaves. *(V. Ricasoli, 60, between the churches of San Marco and S.S. Annunziata.* ☎055 238 86 09. *Open June.-Aug. Tu-F 8:30am-9pm, Sa 8:30am-midnight, Su 8:30am-8pm; Sept.-May Tu-Su 8:30am-6:50pm. L15,000.)*

PIAZZA SANTA CROCE. Follow V. Ghibellina east from the Bargello and turn right on V. Giuseppe Verdi to reach the P. Santa Croce, home to the Franciscan **Chiesa di Santa Croce.** Despite the stark asceticism of the Franciscans, it's quite possibly the most splendid church in the city, with some impressive Giotto frescoes. Among the all-star Florentines buried here are Michelangelo, Machiavelli, and Galileo. (☎ *055 29 08 32. Open M-Sa 9:30am-5:30pm, Su and holidays 3-5:30pm.*) Cool *pietra serena* pilasters and statues of the evangelists by Donatello grace Brunelleschi's small **Cappella Pazzi,** at the end of the cloister next to the church. (*Enter through Museo dell'Opera. Open Th-Tu 10am-7pm. L5000.*)

NORTH OF THE DUOMO

■ **PALAZZO PITTI.** Luca Pitti, a nouveau-riche banker of the 15th century, built his *palazzo* east of S. Spirito against the Boboli hill. The Medici acquired the *palazzo* and the hill in 1550 and enlarged everything possible. During Italy's brief experiment with monarchy, the structure served as a royal residence. Today, the Palazzo Pitti houses five museums, including the Galleria Palatina, one of only a few public galleries when it opened in 1833. Today it houses Florence's second most important collection (behind the Uffizi). It includes a number of works by Raphael, Titian, Andrea del Sarto, Rosso, Caravaggio, and Rubens. Flemish works dominate the Neoclassical Music Room and the Pitti Room. As you peruse the collection, don't forget to look up from time to time at the frescoes on the ceilings—these help make the museum all the more visually stunning. The same palace holds other museums dealing with subjects from modern art to antique porcelain. (*Palazzo* ☎ *055 21 34 40. Galleria Palatina* ☎ *055 21 03 23 open Su-F 8:30am-9pm, Sa 8:30am-midnight. L12,000. All other museums open 8:30am-1:50pm; closed on the 1st, 3rd, and 5th Monday, and the 2nd and 4th Sunday of each month. L4000.*)

■ **BOBOLI GARDENS.** This elaborately landscaped park is an exquisite example of a stylized Renaissance garden. Consisting of formal, geometrically sculpted hedges and groves of holly and gentle cypress trees, the garden fancifully interweaves artifice and nature. It extends gloriously from behind the palace, leading the eager meanderer down avenues of cypress trees to bubbling fountains with impressive nude sculptures and picturesque picnic areas. (☎ *055 21 87 41. Open daily June-Aug. 8:15am-7:30pm; Sept.-Oct. and Apr.-May 9am-6:30pm; Nov.-Feb. 9am-5pm; Mar. 9am-6pm. Closed first and last M of each month. L4000, EU citizens, L2000.*)

CHIESA DI SANTA MARIA DEL CARMINE. Inside this church, the ■ **Brancacci Chapel** holds, in glorious restored form, Masaccio's stunning and influential 15th-century frescoes, declared masterpieces even in their own time. Masaccio began these frescoes in 1424, imbuing his figures with solidity and dignity. Fifty years later a respectful Filippo Lippi completed the cycle. Masolino's *Adam and Eve* and Masaccio's *Expulsion from the Garden* stand face to face, their un-idealized human forms illustrating the young artist's innovative steps in depicting psychological drama. With such monumental works as the *Tribute Money*, this chapel became a school for many famous artists, including Michelangelo. (☎ *055 238 21 95. Open M and W-Sa 10am-5pm, Su 1-5pm. L6000.*)

PIAZZALE MICHELANGELO. Laid out in 1860, Piazzale Michelangelo offers a spectacular panorama of Florence. Sunset provides the most spectacular lighting of the city. The *piazzale* is filled with marble copies of Michelangelo's most famous statues. (*Cross Ponte Vecchio and turn left, walk through the piazza, and turn right up V. de' Bardi. Follow uphill as it becomes V. del Monte alle Croci.*)

SAN MINIATO AL MONTE. Climb the stairs from Ple. Michelangelo to this chapel for a glorious survey of the city. The inlaid marble facade and 13th-century mosaics hint at the incredible della Robbia *terra-cottas* inside the Chapel of the Cardinal of Portugal. (☎ *055 234 27 31. Take bus #13 from the station, or climb stairs from Ple. Michelangelo. Ask the sacristan for admission to the chapel. Church open daily 8am-noon; Jun.-Aug. 2-7pm; Sept.-May 2:30-6pm.*)

🎵 🎭 ENTERTAINMENT AND NIGHTLIFE

A typical nighttime *passeggiata* in Florence begins along **V. dei Calzaiuoli** and ends with coffee or *gelato* in a ritzy cafe on **P. della Repubblica,** where singers prance about the stage in front of Bar Concerto. In the **Oltrarno,** P. S. Spirito has plenty of bars and restaurants, and regular live music in summer. For info on what's hot and what's not in the nightlife scene, consult the monthly *Firenze Spettacolo* (L3000). Some of Florence's clubs require **AiCS** membership. Cards can be obtained at various clubs for L15,000 and will get you into over 20 establishments in Florence, as well as discounts at a number of local events.

During the summer and early fall a number of holidays and festivals further enliven Florence. The **Festival of San Giovanni Battista** (June 24) features a tremendous fireworks display in P. Michelangelo (easily visible from the Arno) that starts around 10pm. Late April sees the start of the summer music festivals with the classical **Maggio Musicale.** The **Estate Fiesolana** (June-Aug.) fills the Roman theater in nearby Fiesole with concerts, opera, theater, ballet, and film. September brings the **Festa dell'Unità,** a concert series at Campi Bisenzia (take bus #30). On the **Festa del Grillo** (Festival of the Cricket), the 1st Sunday after Ascension Day, crickets in tiny wooden cages are hawked in the Cascine park to be released into the grass.

BARS

Amadeus, V. dei Pescioni, 5r (☎055 239 82 29), take V. dei Pesconi from P. del Duomo, walk 2 blocks, and look left. With the "best German beer at the best price in town," this place serves a relaxed mix of Italians and visitors. Open daily 4pm-1am.

Dolce Vita, in P. del Carmine (☎055 28 45 95). Open-air bar with tables on the beautiful *piazza.* Hip local *giovani* come for occasional live music. Open M-Sa 10pm-1:30am, Su and holidays 5pm-1:30am.

The William, V. Magliabechi 7/9/11r. New, trendy pub for Italians and tourists in the know. Rowdy and packed on weekends; mellower on weeknights. Open daily 6pm-2am.

Cabiria, (☎055 21 57 32), P. S. Spirito. A regular cafe during the day, Cabiria becomes one of the happening nightspots on the P. S. Spirito by night. Open daily 5pm-late.

Angie's Pub, V. dei Neri 35r. Very Italian (despite the name) pub catering mostly to students. Imported beer and cider from L5000. Open M-Sa noon-3pm and 7pm-1am.

The Red Garter, V. dei Benci, 33r (☎055 234 49 04). A raucous mix of international students and the Italian youth who pursue them. Live music and dancing every night. Open daily 8:30pm-1am.

Monte Carla, V. dei Bardi, 2 (☎055 234 02 59), in the Oltrarno, off P. de' Mozzi. A 3-tiered wonderland of cougar print upholstery with a plastic flower motif. This plush club is mellow in the summer, and packed in the winter. Open daily 11pm-3am.

Eskimo, V. dei Canacci, 12r, near S. Maria Novella. Live music and occasional alternative theater. Club invites its *sangría*-sipping crowd to improvise on instruments. Open daily 9:30pm-3:30am.

BeBop, V. dei Servi, 76r (☎055 28 91 12). A live jazz club that mixes in a bit of blues. Open daily 9pm-1am.

The Fiddler's Elbow, P. S. Maria Novella, 74r (☎055 21 59 56). An authentic Irish pub that serves cider, Guinness, and various other draught beers to a crowd of foreign tourists. Open daily 1pm-2am.

The Checkers Pub, V. della Scala, 7/9r (☎055 28 75 88). This bar attracts a large and lively Italian crowd with its range of beers and typical pub grub. Daily Happy Hour 6:30-8pm. Open Su-Th 6pm-midnight, F-Sa 6pm-2am.

NIGHTCLUBS

Meccanò, V. degli Olmi, 1 (☎055 33 13 71), near Parco delle Cascinè. The most popular of Florence's discos among locals and tourists alike. Cover L25,000; includes 1 drink. Subsequent drinks L10,000. Open Tu-Sa 11pm-4am.

Central Park, in Parco delle Cascinè. Open-air dance floor pulses with hip-hop, jungle, reggae, and something Italians call "dance rock." Open 9pm until late.

Andromeda, V. Cimatori, 13 (☎055 29 20 02). From P. della Signoria, take V. dei Calzaiuoli toward P. del Duomo and take the 2nd right on V. Cimatori. This centrally located disco is packed with both Italians and tourists anytime after midnight, while the mirrored dance floor thumps with British, American, and Italian pop. Cover L10,000. Open M-Sa 10:30pm-4am.

Blob, V. Vinegia, 21r (☎055 21 12 09), behind the Palazzo Vecchio. With mellow evenings, wild nights, and early mornings, this little club offers DJs, movies, foosball, and an evening bar buffet. Live Cuban guitar Su nights. Requires AiCS membership. Open daily 6pm-late.

Teatro Club, Via delle Seggiole, 8r (☎055 234 52 77), near Piazza della Signoria. A young, diverse crowd. AiCS required. Happy hour 7:30-11:30pm. Open daily 7:30am-6am.

Tabasco Gay Club, P.S. Cecilia, 3r (☎055 21 30 00). In a tiny alleyway across P. della Signoria from the Palazzo Vecchio. Florence's popular gay disco caters primarily to men. 18+. Cover L15-25,000. Open Tu-Su 10pm4am.

▐ DAYTRIPS FROM FLORENCE

FIESOLE

No trains run to Fiesole, but the town is a 20-minute bus ride away; catch the ATAF city bus #7 from the train station near track #16, P. del Duomo, or P. S. Marco. It runs throughout the day (less frequently at night) and drops passengers at P. Mino da Fiesole in the town center.

Older than Florence itself, Fiesole is the site of the original Etruscan settlement that farmed the rich flood plain below. Florence was actually colonized and settled as an off-shoot of this Etruscan town. Fiesole has long been a welcome escape from the sweltering summer heat of the Arno Valley and a source of inspiration for numerous famous figures—among them Alexander Dumas, Anatole France, Marcel Proust, Gertrude Stein, Frank Lloyd Wright, and Paul Klee. Leonardo da Vinci even used the town as a testing ground for his famed flying machine. Fiesole's location provides incomparable views of both Florence and the rolling countryside to the north—it's a perfect place for a picnic or a day-long *passeggiata*. Outside the bus station, up the hill on your left, you will find the **Missionario Francesco,** the public gardens, and spectacular views of the Florentine sprawl. The **Museo Archeologico,** off P. Mino da Fiesole, has a wonderful Etruscan art collection as well as the ruins of an Etruscan temple, thermal bath, and altar bases. (Open daily 9:30am-7pm; in winter 9:30am-5pm. Tickets L12,000, students and over 65 L8000.) A **Roman amphitheater** has incredible views of Florence and the countryside.

The **tourist office,** P. Mino da Fiesole, 37, is nearby. (☎055 59 87 20; fax 055 59 88 22. Open M-Sa 8:30am-1:30pm and 3-6pm.) Accommodations in Fiesole are prohibitively expensive compared to the profusion of budget options in nearby Florence, but the town is a great place to sit down for a leisurely afternoon lunch. The **Pizzeria Etrusca** in P. S. Marco has beautiful outdoor seating and reasonable prices. (☎055 59 94 84. Open daily noon-3pm, and 7pm-1am. Pizza L8000-12,000, *primi* from L8000, *secondi* from L14,000.)

AREZZO

Trains arrive from Florence (1½hr., 2 per hr., L8000) and Rome (2hr., 1-2 per hr., L20,600). Buses pull in from Siena (1½hr., 7 per day, L8000.)

The likes of Petrarch, Michelangelo (born in the surrounding countryside), and, most recently, Roberto Benigni have found inspiration in the streets of Arezzo. The town's most famous treasure is **Piero della Francesca's** magnificent fresco cycle *Leggenda della Vera Croce* (Legend of the True Cross), which portrays the story of the wood used for Christ's cross. It is housed in the spiritual and physical center of Arezzo, the 14th-century **Basilica di San Francesco,** P. S. Francesco, up V. G. Monaco from the train station. (Open daily 8:30am-noon and 2:30-6:30pm. L10,000, EU citizens 18-25 L6000, art students L2000.) Seven 20-foot-high circular stained-glass windows let light into the massive **duomo**, in P. del Duomo. (Open daily 7am-12:30pm and 3-6:30pm.) The **Piazza Grande** showcases Arezzo's most impressive examples of architecture, including the spectacular **Chiesa di Santa Maria della Pieve.** (Open M-Sa 8am-noon and 3-7pm, Su 8:30am-noon and 4-7pm.) The **tourist office**, P. della Repubblica, 22, is to the right as you exit the train station. (☎0575 37 76 78; fax 0575 208 39. Open Apr.-Sept. M-Sa 9am-1pm and 3-7pm, Su 9am-1pm; Oct.-Mar. M-Sa 9am-1pm and 3-6:30pm.) **Ostello Villa Severi,** V. Redi, 13, is a hike from town, but well worth the effort. Take **bus** #4 (L1200) from P. G. Monaco and get off two stops after the Ospedale Vecchio. (☎0575 29 90 47. Breakfast L3000. Lunch or dinner L20,000. Reception 9am-1pm and 6-11:30pm. Dorms L25,000.)

ANOTHER DAYTRIP FROM FLORENCE

BOLOGNA. Europe's oldest student city has a vibrant nightlife, beautiful *duomo*, and a tranquil *piazza* (see p. 654).

SIENA

Many travelers rush from Rome to Florence, ignoring gorgeous, medieval Siena, but Siena is more than a poor cousin of these lauded cities. The Sienese have a rich history in arts, politics, and trade. One of their proudest celebrations is the semiannual **Palio,** a wild horse race between the city's 17 competing *contrade* (districts).

TRANSPORTATION. From P. Rosselli, **trains** (☎05 77 28 01 15) go to Rome via Chiosi (2½hr., every hr., L31,400) and Florence (1½hr., every hr., L8800) and Express **TRA-IN/SITA buses** (☎05 77 20 42 45) link P. S. Domenico 1, near the heart of the city, to Florence (every hr., L12,000) and San Gimignano (every hr., L8600).

PRACTICAL INFORMATION. Take **TRA-IN/SITA buses** #4, 7-10, 14, 17, or 77 across the street from the station to the central P. del Campo (L1400). The central **APT tourist office** is at Il Campo, 56. (☎05 77 28 05 51; fax 05 77 27 06 76. Open Apr.-Oct. M-Sa 9am-8pm; Nov.-Mar. M-Sa 9am-7pm.) **Prenotazioni Alberghiere,** in P. S. Domenico, finds rooms for L3000. (☎05 77 28 80 84. Open Apr.-Oct. M-Sa 9am-8pm; Nov.-Mar. M-Sa 9am-7pm.) Check email at **Internet Train,** V. Pantaneto, 54. (Open M-F 10am-11pm, Su 4-9pm.) **Postal Code:** 53100.

ACCOMMODATIONS AND FOOD. Finding a room in Siena can be difficult from Easter to October. Book months ahead if coming during *Palio.* The tasteful **Albergo Tre Donzelle,** is at V. Donzelle, 5. (☎05 77 28 03 58. Flexible curfew 1am. Singles L50,000; doubles L80-100,000.) Take bus #15, 35, or 36 from P. Gramsci, opposite the station, to reach the **Ostello della Gioventù "Guidoriccio" (HI),** V. Fiorentina, 89, in Località Lo Stellino, 20 minutes from *centro.* (☎0577 522 12. Breakfast included. Curfew 11:30pm. Dorms L24,000.) **Piccolo Hotel Etruria,** V. Donzelle, 3, has immaculate, modern rooms equipped with phones, TVs, and hair dryers. (☎0577 28 80 88. Breakfast L7000. Curfew 12:30am. Singles L65-75,000; doubles with bath L112,000; triples with bath L156,000; quads L192,000.) To camp at **Colleverde,** Strada di Scacciapensieri, 47, take bus #3 or 8 from P. Gramsci. (☎05 77 28 00 44. Pool L3000; children L2000. Open mid-Mar. to mid-Nov. L15,000 per adult, including tent; L8000 per child of 3-11.)

Siena specializes in rich pastries, of which the most famous is *panforte,* a confection of honey, almonds, and citron; indulge in this serious pastry at **Bar/Pasticceria Nannini,** V. Banchi di Sopra, 22-24, the oldest *pasticceria* in Siena. From P. del Duomo, take V. del Capitano to P. della Postierla and turn left to reach **Osteria il Tamburino,** V. di Stalloreggi for at #11. (Cover L1000. *Primi* L8-15,000; *secondi* L10-25,000. Open M-Sa noon-2:30pm and 7-9:30pm.) **Consortio Agrario supermarket,** V. Pianigiani 5, is off P. Salimberi. (Open M-F 7:45am-1pm and 4:30-8pm, Sa 7:45am-1pm.)

⊚⊡ SIGHTS AND ENTERTAINMENT. Siena offers a *biglietto cumulativo*, allowing entry into the **baptistery, Piccolomini library, Museo dell'Opera Metropolitana,** and the **Oratory of St. Bernadino,** valid for three days (L9500; in winter L8500). The salmon-colored **Piazza del Campo** (Il Campo), a shell-shaped brick square designed for civic events, is the focus of Sienese life. At the highest point of the square's sloping plane is the **Fonte Gaia,** still fed by the same aqueduct used in the 1300s. At the bottom, the **Torre del Mangia** clock tower looms over the graceful Gothic **Palazzo Pubblico.** (Palazzo and Tower open July-Aug. daily 10am-11pm; Mar.-June and Sept.-Oct. M-Sa 9am-6pm, Su 9am-1:30pm; Nov.-Feb. daily 10am-6pm. L10,000. Tower L10,000.) Inside, the **Museo Civico** contains excellent Gothic and early Renaissance paintings; the **Sala del Mappamondo** and the **Sala della Pace** contain stellar works. (Same hours as the *palazzo.* L12,000, students L7000; combined ticket with Tower L18,000.) Siena's Gothic **duomo** is on the edge of a hill; the apse would have been left-hanging in mid-air save for the construction of the lavishly decorated **baptistery** below. (Open daily Jan.-Mar. 14 and Nov.-Dec. 7:30am-1:30pm and 2:30-5pm; mid-Mar. to Oct. 7:30am-7:30pm. Free; when floor is uncovered L5-6000. Baptistery open daily mid-Mar. to Nov. 9am-7:30pm.; Nov. to mid-Mar. 10am-1pm and 2:30-5pm. L3000.) The **Libreria Piccolomini,** off the left aisle, holds frescoes and 15th-century musical scores. (Open mid-Mar. to Oct. 9am-7:30pm; Nov. to mid-Mar. 10am-1pm and 2:30-5pm. L2000.) To reach the *duomo,* face the palazzo Pubblico and take the stairs nearest the palazzo on the right and cross V. di Città. The **Museo dell'Opera della Metropolitana,** next to the cathedral, houses its overflow art. (Open daily mid-Mar. to Sept. 9am-7:30pm; Oct. 9am-6pm.; Nov. to mid-Mar. 9am-1:30pm. L6000.)

The central event of the **Palio di Siena** (July 2 and Aug. 16) is a traditional bareback horse race around the packed P. del Campo. Get there three days early to watch the rambunctious horse selection in the *campo* (10am) and to pick a *contrada* (neighborhood) for which to root. For tickets and a list of rooms, write the tourist office by March; arrive without a reservation and you'll be on the streets.

⊡ DAYTRIP FROM SIENA: SAN GIMIGNANO. The hilltop village of San Gimignano looks like an illumination from a medieval manuscript. The city's famous 14 towers, which are all that survive of its original 72, earned San Gimignano its nickname as the *Città delle Belle Torri* (City of Beautiful Towers). Scale the **Torre Grossa,** the tallest remaining tower, attached to **Palazzo del Popolo,** for a panorama of Tuscany. (Torre open Mar.-Oct. daily 9:30am-7:20pm; Nov.-Feb. Sa-Th 10:30am-4:20pm. L8000, reduced L6000. Palazzo open Tu-Su 9am-7:30pm.) In the shadow of the Torre Grossa, the **Museo Civico** houses an amazing collection of Sienese and Florentine artwork. (Same hours as Torre. L7000, reduced L5000. Combined with tower L12,000; reduced L9000.)

San Gimignano is easily accessible by **bus** from Siena (1hr., every hr., L8800). From the bus station, pass through the *porta,* climb the hill, and follow V. San Giovanni to the central P. della Cisterna and P. del Duomo. Accommodations are pricey in San Gimignano—*affitte camere* are around L75,000 and a good alternative. Get a list from the **tourist office,** P. del Duomo, 1. (☎05 88 94 00 08. Open daily Mar.-Oct. 9am-1pm and 3-7pm; Nov.-Feb. 9am-1pm, and 2-6pm.) The **Associazione Strutture Extralberghiere,** P. della Cisterna, 6, also finds private rooms. (☎05 77 94 31 90. Open Mar.-Nov. daily 9:30am-7:30pm.) For the **Ostello di San Gimignano,** V. delle Fonti, 1, turn off V. S. Matteo onto V. XX Settembre and follow the signs. (☎05 77 94 19 91. Breakfast and sheets included. Reception daily 7-9am and 5-11:30pm. Curfew 11:30pm. Open Mar.-Oct. Dorms L26,000. Cash only.) **Camp** at **Il Boschetto,** at Santa Lucia, a 3km bus ride (L1500) from Porta S. Giovanni. (☎05 77 94 03 52. Hot showers included. Open Apr.-Oct. 15. Reception daily 8am-1pm, 3-8pm, and 9-11pm. L8500 per person; L8500 per tent.) A small **market** sells cheap, filling sandwiches, takeout pasta, salads, and drinks at V. S. Matteo, 19. (☎05 77 94 19 52. Open Mar.-Oct. daily 9am-8pm; Nov-Feb. M-W and F-Sa 9am-8pm, Th 9am-1pm.)

ELBA

According to legend, the enchanting island of Elba grew from a precious stone that slipped from Venus' neck into the azure waters of the Tyrrhenian Sea. Napoleon, spent his exile here, coining the famous palindrome "Able was I ere I saw Elba." **Ferries** go from **Piombino Marittima** (a.k.a. Piombino Porto) to **Portoferraio**, Elba's largest city. **Portoferraio** is a strange chimera—part unattractive, modern port town and part charming Tuscan village, but if you have time to spare, stroll along the cobblestoned streets and browse the assorted Napoleon sights. Although **trains** on the Genoa-Rome line travel to **Piombino Marittima**, most stop at **Campiglia Marittima** (from Florence, change at Pisa), where a *pullman* (intercity bus; 30min., L2400) meets trains and connects to ferries in Piombino Marittima. Both Toremar (☎05 65 311 00; 30min.-1hr., 16 per day, L12-24,000; summer only) and Moby Lines (1hr., 16 per day, L12,000) run to Elba. The **tourist office, APT**, Calata Italia, 26, 1st fl., across from the Toremar boat landing, helps with rooms and transport. (☎05 65 91 46 71. Open daily 9am-1pm and 2:30-7:30pm; off-season 9am-1pm and 3-7pm.) **Ape Elbana,** Salita Cosimo de' Medici, 2, overlooks the main *piazza* of the *centro storico*. (☎05 65 91 42 45. Singles L90,000; doubles L120-130,000; Aug. half-pension required L110,000.) **Marina di Campo's** lovely white sand beaches wind their way for miles along the coast and can be reached via bus from Portoferraio. Smart kiddies head onto the strip of pebbles that borders **Marciana Marina's** waterfront; take the **bus** from Portoferraio (50min., L3500). The **tourist office,** V. Scali Mazzini, 13, finds **rooms** for free. (☎05 65 90 99 061. Open Tu-Th 8am-8pm, reduced off-season hours.) In Marciana Marina, **Albergo Imperia,** V. Amedeo, 12, offers comfortable rooms, all with TV and refrigerator. (☎05 65 990 82. Mid-Sept.-June singles L50-60,000; doubles L70-145,000; prices 20-30% higher July to mid.-Sept.)

PISA

Tourism hasn't always been Pisa's prime industry: during the Middle Ages, the city was a major port with an empire extending to Corsica, Sardinia, and the Balearics. But when the Arno River silted up and the tower started leaning, the city's power and wealth declined accordingly. Today the city seems resigned to welcoming tourists and myriad t-shirt and ice cream vendors to the **Piazza del Duomo,** also known as the **Campo dei Miracoli** (Field of Miracles), a grassy expanse enclosing the tower, *duomo*, baptistery, and Camposanto, Museo delle Sinopie, and Museo del Duomo. An **all-inclusive ticket** to the Campo's sights costs L18,000. To reach the Campo from the train station, take bus #1 (L1500); or walk straight up V. Gramsci, through P. Vittorio Emanuele, and down C. Italia across the Arno, continue on V. Borgo Stretto, turn left on any street branching west, and continue through the old town. Begun in 1173, the famous **Leaning Tower** began to tilt when the soil beneath suddenly shifted; the tower continues to slip 1-2mm every year. Visitors are no longer allowed to enter the tower. The dazzling **duomo**, also on the Campo, is a treasury of fine art, and believed to be one of the finest Romanesque cathedrals in the world. (Open late April-late Sept. daily 8am-7:45pm. Reduced hours in off-season. L3000. Free for Su mass.) Next door is the **baptistery,** with precise acoustics that allow an unamplified choir to be heard 2km away. (Open daily late Apr. to late Sept. 8am-7:45pm; off-season 9am-4:40pm.) The adjoining **Camposanto,** a cloistered cemetery, has Roman sarcophagi and a series of haunting frescoes by an unidentified 14th-century artist known only as the "Master of the Triumph of Death." (Same hours as baptistery.) The **Museo delle Sinopie,** across the *piazza* from the Camposanto, displays preliminary fresco sketches discovered during post-WWII restoration. Behind the tower is the **Museo dell'Opera del Duomo.** (Both open daily late Apr. to Sept. 8am-7:45pm; off-season 9am-4:40pm. Joint ticket L10,000, EU citizens free.) From the Campo, walk down V. S. Maria and over the bridge to the Gothic **Chiesa di Santa Maria della Spina** whose tower that allegedly holds a thorn from Christ's crown.

Trains (☎147 808 88) go from **P. della Stazione,** in the southern part of town, to Florence (1hr., every hr., L8-10,000). The main coastal line serves Rome (3hr., L42,300) and Genoa (2½hr., L23,200). The **tourist office** is to the left as you exit the station. (☎05 04 22 91; www.turismo.toscana.it. Open May-Oct. daily 8am-8pm; Nov.-Apr.

9am-7pm.) The **Centro Turistico Madonna dell'Acqua hostel,** V. Pietrasantina, 15, is 1km from the Tower. Take bus #3 from the station (4 per hr.) and ask for the *ostello.* (☎050 89 06 22. Sheets L5000. Reception 6-11pm. Check-out 9am. Dorms L23,000; doubles L60,000; triples L90,000; quads L108,000.) The **Albergo Gronchi,** P. Archivescovado, 1, just off P. del Duomo, has frescoed ceilings. (☎050 56 18 23. Curfew midnight. Singles L35,000; doubles L58,000; triples L78,000; quads L98,000.) The **Albergo Helvetia,** V. Don G. Boschi, 31, sports pristine, spacious rooms, all with TV. (☎050 55 30 84. Breakfast L7500. Singles L55,000; doubles L75-100,000; triples L125,000; quads L165,000.) **Marcovaldo,** V. S. Martino, 47, has superb food but no table service. (Sandwiches L4000. *Primi* L7000, *secondi* L10,000. Open M-Sa noon-10pm.) **Trattoria da Matteo,** V. l'Aroncio, 46 (☎050 410 57), has fresh, authentic cuisine and 40 different types of pizza. (Pizza L6500-95000. Menù L22,000. Cover L2000. Open Su-F noon-3:30pm and 7-10:30pm.) Get **groceries** at **Superal,** V. Pascoli 6, just off C. Italia. (Open M-Sa 8am-8pm.) **Postal Code:** 56100.

UMBRIA

Umbria is a land rich in natural beauty, encompassing wild woods and fertile plains, craggy gorges and tiny cobblestoned villages. This irresistible, landlocked region wedged between the Adriatic and Tyrrhenian coasts has long been a cherished and greatly contested prize. One conqueror, Christianity, transformed Umbria's architecture and regional identity, turning it into a breeding ground for saints and religious movements; it was here St. Francis of Assisi shamed the extravagant church with his humility.

PERUGIA

The extremely polite residents of Perugia may be trying to make up for two millennia of excessive nastiness, during which their ancestors regularly stoned each other and even threw tree-hugging St. Francis of Assisi into a dungeon. The city earns more dubious fame as the birthplace of the Flagellants, who wandered Europe whipping themselves, and as the site of two popes' deaths by poisoning. But Perugia now lures visitors with steep medieval streets and a mellow university atmosphere. The city's most visited sights frame **Piazza IV Novembre.** The facade of Perugia's austere Gothic **duomo,** on the *piazza,* was left unfinished when the Perugini were forced to return the marble they had stolen to build it. The *duomo* houses the Virgin Mary's purported wedding ring. The **Fontana Maggiore** in the center is adorned with sculptures and bas-reliefs by Nicolà and Giovanni Pisano. The 13th-century **Palazzo dei Priori** presides over the *piazza* with the immense collection of the **Galleria Nazionale dell'Umbria,** C. Vannucci 19. (Open M-F 9am-7pm, Sa 9am-7pm and 9pm-midnight, Su 9am-8pm; closed 1st M of each month. L8000.) The ▓**Basilica di San Pietro,** on C. Cavour, at the end of town past the Porta S. Pietro, maintains its original 10th-century basilica layout; at its far end is an exquisitely manicured garden with incredible views. (Open daily 8am-noon and 3:30pm-dusk.)

The **FS train station,** P. V. Veneto, serves: Rome (2½hr., L26,000); Assisi (25min., every hr., L3500); Florence (2½hr., every hr., L24,900); and Siena (every hr., L14,000). From the station, take bus #6, 7, or 9 to the central P. Italia (L1200), then take C. Vannucci to P. IV Novembre and the **tourist office,** in P. IV Novembre. (☎07 55 72 33 27. Open M-Sa 8:30am-1:30pm and 3:30-6:30pm, Su 9am-1pm.) To get from there to **Ostello della Gioventù/Centro Internazionale di Accoglienza per la Gioventù,** V. Bontempi, 13, pass the *duomo* and P. Dante, take the farthest street right through P. Piccinino, and turn right on V. Bontempi. (☎075 572 28 80; Sheets L2000. Kitchen. Lockout 9:30am-4pm. Curfew midnight. Open mid-Jan. to mid-Dec. Dorms L16,000.) **Albergo Anna,** V. dei Priori, 48, off C. Vannucci, has clean, 17th-century rooms with great views. (☎075 573 63 04. Singles L45-60,000; doubles L70-90,000; triples L95-120,000.) To **camp** at **Paradis d'Eté,** in Colle della Trinità, take bus# 36 from the station. (☎075 517 21 17. L7000 per person, L6000 per tent, L3000 per car.) **Trattoria Dal Mi Cocco,** C. Garibaldi, 12, up from the University for Foreigners, offers an extremely generous L25,000 *menù.* (Open Tu-Su 1-2:30pm and 8:15-10:30pm.) The **COOP,** P. Matteoti, 15, has **groceries.** (Open M-Sa 9am-8pm.) **Postal Code:** 06100.

ASSISI

Assisi's serenity originates with the legacy of monk St. Francis, who preached poverty, obedience, and love eight centuries ago. After his death in 1226, Florentine and Sienese painters decorated the **Basilica di San Francesco** with spectacular frescoes illustrating his life. From P. del Commune, take V. Portica. The dress code is strictly enforced; nothing that reveals the knee or shoulders. (☎075 81 22 38. Upper church open daily dawn-dusk; may be closed for restorations. Lower level open M-Sa 9am-12:30pm, and 3-6pm, Su 3-6pm. L3000.) The dramatic fortress **Rocca Maggiore** towers above town, offering a shady perch and tremendous views. From P. S. Rufino, go left of the *duomo* up the cobblestoned street. (Open daily 10am-sunset, July-Aug. 9am-sunset. L5000, students L3500.) Take C. Mazzini from P. del Commune to reach the **Basilica di Santa Chiara,** where St. Francis attended school and St. Clare now rests. (Open daily 7am-noon and 2-7pm.) Many of Assisi's sights were badly damaged in the 1997 earthquake and may be temporarily closed.

From the station near the Basilica Santa Maria degli Angeli, **trains** go to Rome (1 per day, from L16,500); Ancona (L20,200); Florence (2 per day, L16,5000); and Perugia (13 per day, L3200). ASP **buses** run from P. Matteoti to: Rome (3hr., 1 per day); Florence (2½hr., 1 per day, L25,000); and Perugia (1½hr., 7 per day, L5000). From the station follow V. del Torrione, bear left in P. S. Rufino, and take V. S. Rufino to the town center. The **tourist office,** P. del Comune 12, is down V. Mazzini. (☎075 81 25 34; fax 075 81 37 27. Open M-F 8am-2pm and 3:30-6:30pm, Sa 9am-1pm and 3:30-6:30pm, Su and holidays 9am-1pm.) For **Ostello della Pace (HI)**, V. di Valecchi, 177, turn right out of the station, then left onto V. di Valecchi. (☎075 81 67 67. Breakfast included. Reception 7-9:15am and 3:30-11:30pm. Check-out 9:30am. Dorms L22,-27,000.) Peaceful **Camere Annalisa Martini,** V. S. Gregorio, 6, is in the medieval core of Assisi. (☎075 81 35 36. Singles L38-40,000; doubles L60-65,000; triples L90-100,000.) **Pasticceria Santa Monica,** V. Portica, 4, sells a sinful array of nut breads, sweets, and *bricciata umbria*, a strudel-like pastry with a hint of cherries. **Postal Code:** 06081.

THE MARCHES (LE MARCHE)

In the Marches, green foothills separate the gray shores of the Adriatic from the Apennine mountains, and the traditional hill-towns from the umbrella-laden beaches. Inland towns, easily accessible by train, rely on agriculture, and preserve the region's historical legacy in the architectural remains of Gauls and Romans.

URBINO

Urbino's fairy-tale skyline, scattered with humble stone dwellings and an immense turreted palace, has changed little over the past 500 years. The city's most remarkable monument is the looming Renaissance **Palazzo Ducale** (Ducal Palace), in P. Rinascimento, though its facade is more thrilling than its interior. The enclosed **courtyard** is the essence of Renaissance balance and proportion; to the left, stairs lead to the former private apartments of the Duke, which now house the packed **National Gallery of the Marches.** Check out the underground baths, kitchen, and washroom, as well as the Duke's study, where inlaid panels give the illusion of real books. (☎07 22 27 60. Open M 8:30am-2pm, Tu-F 8:30am-7pm, Sa 8:30am-7pm and 8-11pm, Su 9am-8pm. L8000, children and seniors free.) Raphael's birthplace, **Casa di Rafaele,** V. Raffaello, 57, is now a vast and delightful museum; his earliest work, a fresco, *Madonna e Bambino*, hangs in the *sala*. (Open M-Sa 9am-1pm and 3-7pm, Su 10am-1pm. L5000.)

Bucci **buses** (☎0721 324 01) go from Borgo Mercatale to Rome (5hr., 4pm, L30,000). SAPUM **buses** runs along the Bologna-Lecce **rail** line along the Adriatic coast. From there, a short walk uphill on V. G. Mazzini leads to **P. della Repubblica,** the city center. The **tourist office,** P. Rinascimento 1, is opposite the palace. (☎07 22 26 13; fax 07 22 24 41. Open in summer M-Sa 9am-1pm and 4-7pm, Su 9am-1pm; off-season M-Sa 9am-1pm and 3-6pm.) Reserve ahead to get a room. **Pensione Fosca,** V. Raffaello 67, top floor, has charming, high-ceilinged rooms. (☎07 22 32 96 22. Singles L50,000; doubles L60,000.) The **Hotel San Giovanni,** V. Barocci 13, has a restaurant downstairs. (☎07 22 28 27. Open Aug.-June. Singles L35-53,000; doubles L50-80,000.) **Camping Pineta**, on V. San Donato, is 2km away in Cesane; take bus #4 or 7 from Borgo Mercatale and ask to get off at "camping." (☎07 22 47 10. L10,000 per person, L20,000 per tent. Reception 9-11am and 3-10pm. Open Apr. to mid-Sept.) Many *paninoteche*, *gelaterie*, and burger joints are in or near **P. della Repubblica. Margherita supermarket** is at V. Raffaello 37. (Open M-Sa 7:30am-2pm and 4:30-8pm.) At night, **The Bosom Pub**, on V. Budassi, is stacked with fun.

ANCONA

Ancona is the center point of Italy's Adriatic Coast—a major port in a small, whimsical, and largely unexplored city. **Piazza Roma** is dotted with yellow and pink buildings, and **Piazza Cavour** is the heart of the town. ANEK (☎071 207 32 22) and **Strintzis ferries** (☎071 207 10 68) go to Greece (from L62-82,000); and Strintzis also sends ferries to Venice. Ferry schedules and tickets are available at the Stazione Marittima; reserve ahead in July or August. **Trains** arrive at P. Rosselli from Rome (3-4hr., 9 per day, L23,500-40,000); Bologna (2½hr., 1-2 per hr., L18,000); Milan (5hr., 24 per day, L18,000); and Venice (5hr., 3 per day, L31,000). Take bus #1 or 1/4 to the **tourist office**, V. Thaon de Revel, 4. (☎071 35 89 91. Open M-Sa 8am-8pm, Su 8am-2pm.) **Pensione Euro**, C. Mazzini 142, 2nd fl., has airy rooms. (☎071 207 22 76. Singles L30-40,000; doubles L60-70,000; triples L75,000.) **SIDIS supermarket** is at V. Matteotti, 115. (Open M-W and F-Sa 8:15am-12:45pm and 5-7:30pm, Th 8:15am-12:45pm.)

SOUTHERN ITALY

South of Rome, the sun gets brighter, the meals longer, and the passions more heated. The introduction to the *mezzogiorno* (Italian South) begins in Campania, the fertile crescent that cradles the Bay of Naples and the Gulf of Salerno. In the shadow of Mount Vesuvius lie the famous Roman ruins of Pompeii, frozen in time by a bed of molten lava. In the Bay of Naples, Capri is Italy's answer to Fantasy Island, while the Amalfi Coast cuts a dramatic course down the lush Tyrrhenian shore. Though long subject to the negative stereotypes and prejudices of the more industrialized North, the region remains justly proud of its open-hearted populace, strong traditions, secluded beaches, and classical ruins.

NAPLES (NAPOLI)

Italy's third-largest city is arguably its most colorful, and undoubtedly its most chaotic. Below the watchful glare of Vesuvius, the streets of Naples teem with activity, a constant stream of life, love, and gossip. The amazing architectural monuments in Naples serve as the backdrop for daily life, rather than being surrounded by tour groups. The treasure trove of churches and *palazzi* are a testament to the once abundant agricultural wealth of the city. These wonders provide a glaring contrast to the ever present unemployment and poverty that plague Naples, but an increased police presence has helped to decrease crime and draw more tourists to the area.

▬ TRANSPORTATION

Flights: Aeroporto Capodichino, V. Umberto Maddalena (☎081 789 61 11), northwest of the city. Connections to all major Italian and European cities. A CLP bus (☎081 531 16 46) leaves from P. Municipio (20min., every 50min., L3000). The #14 bus runs from P. Garibaldi to the airport (L1500). **Alitalia**, V. Medina, 41/42 (☎081 542 51 11), off P. Municipio. Open M-F 9am-4:30pm. **TWA**, V. Cervantes, 55 (☎081 551 30 63). Open M-F 9am-5:30pm. British Airways (☎081 780 81 30 87), in the airport. Open M-F 8am-8pm, Sa 9am-5pm.

Trains: The **Ferrovie dello Stato** train company sends trains from **Stazione Centrale** to: **Rome** (2hr., 38 per day, L18,600); **Brindisi** (5hr., 5 per day, L35,600); and **Milan**

(8hr., 13 per day, L96,000). **Circumvesuviana** (☎081 772 24 44) also leaves Stazione Centrale for **Pompeii** (L3200) and **Herculaneum** (L2300).

Ferries: Depart from **Molo Angioino** and **Molo Beverello,** at the base of P. Municipio. From P. Garibaldi, take tram #1; from P. Municipio, take the R2 bus. **Caremar,** Molo Beverello (☎08 15 51 38 82), goes frequently to **Capri** (1-1½hr., 11 per day, L9800-L18,000) and **Ischia** (1-1½hr., 14 per day, L9800-18,000). **Tirrenia Lines,** Molo Angioino (☎08 17 20 11 11), goes to **Palermo, Sicily** (11hr., 8pm, L85,000). Schedules and prices change constantly; try *Qui Napoli* (free at the tourist office).

Public Transportation: *Giranapoli* tickets (1½hr; L1500; full-day L4500) are transportation passes valid on **buses, Metropolitana** (subway), **trams,** and **funiculars** and can be purchased at *tabacchi.* Buses run the short distances from the city center to various internal locations. The Metro covers longer distances in the city; trams move along the coast, and funiculars connect the lower city and the hilltop Vomero. Everything stops running around midnight, with the exception of the unreliable *notturno* (night) buses.

Taxis: Cotana (☎081 570 70 70), **Napoli** (☎081 556 44 44), or **Partenope** (☎081 556 02 02). Only take metered taxis.

✳🛈 ORIENTATION AND PRACTICAL INFORMATION

The central train station and major city bus terminal are both in the immense **Piazza Garibaldi,** a crumbling area on the east side of Naples. The broad, commercial Corso Umberto I leads from P. Garibaldi to **Piazza Bovio.** From here **Via de Pretis** branches to the left toward **Piazza Municipio,** the financial and administrative center of Naples, and to nearby **Piazza Trieste e Trento** and **Piazza Plebiscito. Molo Beverello** and the **Stazione Marittima** are at the foot of P. Municipio, by the waterfront, near the point of departure for the ferries. **Spaccanapoli,** the historical district, can be reached by taking a right from P. Trieste e Trento, going up **Via Toledo,** and taking a right at **Piazza Dante.** If you plan to be in town for a few days, either invest in a detailed city map from a *tabacchi* (L9000) or pick one up at the tourist office.

Tourist Offices: EPT (☎081 26 87 79; fax 081 20 66 66), at Stazione Centrale. Helpful with hotels and ferries. Grab a map and *Qui Napoli.* Open M-Sa 9am-8pm. **Main office** at P. dei Martiri, 58 (☎081 40 53 11). Open M-Sa 8:30am-3pm. **OTC** (☎081 580 82 16; fax 081 41 03 59), at Palazzo Reale in P. Plebiscito, has a staff all too eager to provide assistance. Open M-Sa 9am-6:30pm.

Consulates: South Africa, C. Umberto I (☎081 551 75 19). **UK,** V. Crispi 122 (☎081 66 35 11). Metro: P. Amedeo. Open July-Aug. M-F 8am-1:30pm; Sept.-June M-F 9am-12:30pm and 2:30-4pm. **US,** in P. della Repubblica (☎081 583 81 11; in emergency 03 37 94 50 83), at the west end of Villa Comunale. Open M-F 8am-5pm.

Currency Exchange: Thomas Cook, P. Municipio, 70 (☎081 551 83 99) and at the airport offers decent rates. Open M-F 9:30am-1pm and 3-6:30pm.

Emergencies: ☎113. **Police:** ☎113 and 081 794 11 11. **Carabinieri:** ☎112. English spoken. **Ambulance:** ☎081 752 06 96. **Hospital: Cardarelli** (☎081 747 11 11), north of town on the R4 bus line.

Internet Access: Internetbar, P. Bellini, 74. (☎081 29 52 37). Chic location to swill expensive drinks while you get your email fix. L5,000 per 30min. Open M-F 9am-3am, Sa-Su 9pm-3am.

Post Office: P. Matteotti, V. Diaz (R2 line). Address mail to be held: Jason FIELDING, *In Fermo Posta,* P. Matteotti, Naples **80100,** Italy. Open M-F 8:15am-6pm, Sa 8:15am-noon.

 DON'T TAKE CANDY FROM STRANGERS AND OTHER GOOD ADVICE. Though personal violence is rare in Naples, theft is still relatively common. Don't carry your money in wallets or purses—keep it inaccessible to pickpockets. Young women, whether alone or in groups will likely be harassed, and should travel in mixed company whenever possible. Ignore street merchants who may call to you in English; they will make it difficult for you to disentangle yourself from conversation.

ACCOMMODATIONS

Budget accommodations in Naples are generally centralized around the P. Garibaldi, while affordable rooms are scarce in the historic district. Safety is always an important consideration in Naples—check for night attendants at hotel entrances and double-locked doors to gauge how secure your lodgings are. The **ACISJF/Centro D'Ascolto**, at Stazione Centrale, helps women find safe and inexpensive rooms (☎081 28 19 93. Open M, Tu, and Th 3:30-6:30pm.) In all instances, make sure to agree on a price *before* unpacking, and don't give up your passport until you've actually seen the room. For **camping,** try **Pompei** (see p. 704) and the other small towns in the bay of Naples.

MERGELLINA

This waterfront neighborhood is accessible by metro, and offers a large youth hostel in an area packed with authentic, Neopolitan *trattorie.*

Ostello Mergellina (HI), V. Salita della Grotta, 23 (☎081 761 23 46; fax 081 761 23 91). Metro: Mergellina. From the metro station, make two rights onto V. Piedigrotta, a left onto V. Salita della Grotta, and a right on the driveway after the overpass (before the tunnel). This hostel has 200 rooms and outstanding views of Capri and Vesuvius. Breakfast, sheets, and shower included. Laundry L10,000. Lockout 9am-3pm. Curfew 12:30am. Reservations strongly advised July-Aug. Dorms L24,000; doubles L60,000.

PIAZZA GARIBALDI

Piazza Garibaldi is packed with hotels, and has several options for affordable accommodations that are both comfortable and safe (although none of them are especially quiet). Avoid the hotel solicitors who meet tourists at the station. In most cases, they will redirect you to their "hotel" which, while probably safe, may simply be an old *palazzo* divided into rooms with hastily erected partitions.

Casanova Hotel, V. Venezia, 2 (☎081 26 82 87). From piazza Garibaldi, take V. Milano and turn left at its end. The hotel is to the right. Ivied front, clean, airy rooms, and a rooftop terrace with bar. Breakfast L8000. Reserve ahead. Singles L25,000; doubles L50-80,000; triples L100,000; quads L110,000.

Hotel Eden, C. Novara, 9 (☎081 28 53 44). From the train station, turn right and continue down the street; it's on the left. Family atmosphere belies its large size (44 rooms). Breakfast L5000. Bath included. Free storage. Singles L42,000; doubles L65-75,000; triples L90,000; quads L108,000.

Pensione Mancini, P. Mancini, 33 (☎081 553 67 31), off the far end of P. Garibaldi from the station. Small, safe *pensione.* Breakfast included. Dorms L28,00; singles L40,000; doubles L65-85,000; triples L90,000; quads L110,000.

Hotel San Pietro, V.S. Pietro ad Aram, 18 (☎081 28 60 40). Exit P. Garibaldi on C. Umberto I, turn right on V. Ranieri, and then make a final right. More professional than most of its neighbors. Breakfast included. Singles L50-80,000; doubles L80-130,000.

HISTORICAL DISTRICT

Rooms are generally scarce in the historic district between P. Dante and the *duomo.* Tourist-ridden and expensive restaurants dominate the area nearby, but high-quality, low-cost meals hide on the side streets just off the *piazza*

Soggiorno Imperia, P. Miraglia, 386 (☎081 45 93 47). Take the R2 from the train station, walk up V. Mezzocannone through P. S. Domenico Maggiore, and enter the 1st set of green doors to the left on P. Miraglia. Bright, clean rooms in a refurbished 16th-century *palazzo.* Singles L30,000; doubles L55-65,000; triples L80,000.

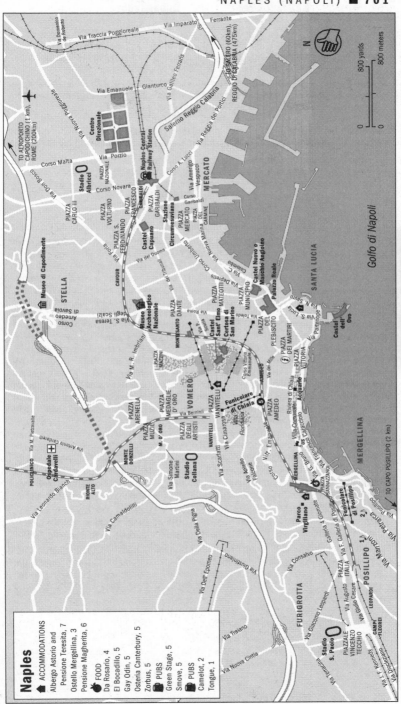

ITALY

Naples

▲ ACCOMMODATIONS
Albergo Astorio and
  Pensione Teresita, 7
Ostello Mergellina, 3
Pensione Magherita, 6

◆ FOOD
Da Rosario, 4
El Bocadillo, 5
Gay Odin, 5
Osteria Canterbury, 5
Zorbus, 5

🍺 PUBS
Green Stage, 5
Smove, 5

🍺 PUBS
Camelot, 2
Tongue, 1

Golfo di Napoli

SANTA LUCIA

Albergo Teresita, V.S. Lucia, 90 (☎081 764 01 05). Bus R3 or C25. Cozy hostel, decorated with plaster statuary and heavy yellow drapes. Sixteen large rooms with TV, fridge, and phone. Hall baths. Singles L50,000; doubles L75,000; triples L90,000.

Albergo Astoria, V. S. Lucia, 90 (☎081 764 99 033). Bus R3 or C25. What? This place looks just like Albergo Teresita! Twenty-three rooms with TV and fridge. Hall showers. Singles L45,000; doubles L75,000; triples L90,000.

VOMERO

This residential neighborhood is quite posh; cheap rooms are few and far between.

Pensione Margherita, V. Cimarosa, 29, 5th fl. (☎081 556 70 44), in the same building as the Centrale funicular station (go outside and around the corner to the right; buzz to get in). Fifteen spacious, well-appointed rooms, some with terraces. Bring an L50 coin for the elevator or take the stairs. Curfew midnight. Singles L53,000; doubles L95,000; triples L135,000.

◖ FOOD

Neopolitans invented **pizza**, and a visit to Naples will blow away any stereotypes that you may hold about this world-famous staple. It's hard to go wrong choosing a pizzeria, since natural selection, and the discriminating palates of locals have driven out underachieving establishments. Neopolitans have a long-standing relationship with **seafood**, and they prepare it with a great deal of tender loving care. Naples' many culinary offerings include fresh *cozze* (mussels) in soup or with lemon, as well as oysters, sweet crayfish, and *polipo* (octopus). **Spaghetti**, that Italian trademark, was reputedly first boiled in the kitchens of Naples. Neopolitan *spaghetti al vongole* (with clams) is a famous dish. The historic district and the area around P. Garibaldi offer delightful dining options in the form of abundant *trattorie* and *pizzerie*. Cheap, authentic fare can be found along V. dei Tribunali in Speccanapoli. Expensive, tourist-filled restaurants dominate the P. Garibaldi, but higher quality, less expensive meals can be found on the side streets off the *piazza*. To find your own fresh produce and seafood, explore the Neopolitan **markets**. Try the one on V. Soprammuro, off P. Garibaldi (open M-Sa 8am-1:30pm).

PIZZERIAS

Antica Pizzeria da Michele, V. Cesare Sersale, 1-3 (☎081 553 92 04). From P. Garibaldi, walk up C. Umberto and take the first right. Michele makes only two types of pizza, and he gets both the *marinara* (tomato, garlic, oregano, and oil; L6000) and *margherita* (tomato, mozzarella, and basil; L6000) sublimely right. Open M-Sa 8am-11pm.

Pizzeria Di Matteo, V. Tribunali, 94 (☎081 45 52 62), near V. Duomo. Students and pizza connoisseurs crowd this small eatery that President Clinton favored while attending the G-7 Conference in 1994. *Margherita* pizza L4000. Open M-Sa 9am-midnight.

Pizzeria Trianon da Ciro, V. Pietro Colletta, 42-46 (☎081 553 94 26), one block off C. Umberto I. A 1997 *New York Times* article pronounced this the best pizza in Naples. The house specialty is the pizza *Gran Trianon* (L12,000), a smorgasbord of 8 differently flavored sections. Pizzas L5500-12,500. Service 15%. Open daily 10am-4:30pm and 6:30pm-midnight.

Da Rosario, P. Sannazzaro, 72 (☎081 570 31 03), in Mergellina, has delicious *frittura* (platters of fried miscellany) for only L5000, wines from L5000, and, of course, *zuppa di cozze* (mussel soup) for L8000. Service 10%. Open Th-Tu 10am-3am.

Trattoria da Maria, V. Genova, 115 (☎081 28 27 11). From the train station, take a right on C. Novara and then a second right on V. Genova. The Riccio family keeps their small *trattoria* in true Neapolitan style. A favorite is *penne "sciuè sciuè"* (with mozzarella, tomato, and basil) for L6000. Pasta L5-6000, *secondi* from L6000. Local wines L6-8000. Cover L1000. Open M-Sa noon-3:30pm and 6:30-11pm.

👁 SIGHTS

MUSEO ARCHEOLOGICO NAZIONALE. Situated within a 16th-century *palazzo* and former barracks, one of the world's most important archeological museums houses exquisite treasures from Pompeii and Herculaneum. Highlights include the massive Farnese Hercules, showing the exhausted hero after his last labor, and the **Farnese Bull,** the largest known ancient sculpture. Carved out of a single piece of marble, the bull was touched up by Michelangelo. The **"Secret Collection,"** containing erotic paintings and objects from Pompeii, has recently opened. Ranging from images of the loves of the gods to phallic good luck charms, the collection shows another side of the ancient world. *(From M: P. Cavour, turn right and walk 2 blocks. ☎ 081 44 01 66. Open M and W-F 9am-7:30pm, Sa-Su 9am-8pm. L12,000.)*

MUSEO AND GALLERIE DI CAPODIMONTE. This museum, in a royal *palazzo*, is surrounded by a pastoral park. You can inspect the plush royal apartments, but the true gem is the **Farnese Collection,** with works by Bellini and Caravaggio. *(Take bus #110 from P. Garibaldi to Parco Capodimonte. Enter by Portas Piccola or Grande. ☎ 081 749 91 11. Open Tu-F 10am-7pm, Sa 10am-midnight, Su 9am-8pm. L14,000.)*

PALAZZO REALE. The 17th-century Palazzo Reale contains the **Museo di Palazzo Reale,** opulent royal apartments, and a fantastic view from the **Royal Chapel.** The **Biblioteca Nazionale** has 1.5 million volumes, including the scrolls from the Villa dei Papiri in Herculaneum. The **Teatro San Carlo** is reputed to have better acoustics than La Scala in Milan. *(Take the R2 bus from P. Garibaldi to P. Trieste e Trento and go around to the P. Plebiscito entrance. ☎ 081 580 81 11. Open M-F 9am-8pm, closed W. L8000.)*

CASTEL NUOVO. It's impossible to miss the five-turreted Castel Nuovo, built in 1286 by Charles II of Anjou. The double-arched entrance commemorates the arrival of Alphonse I of Aragon in Naples. Inside, admire the Museo Civico. *(From P. Trieste e Trento, walk up V. Vittorio Emanuele; take R2 bus from P. Garibaldi. ☎ 081 795 20 03. Open M-Sa 9am-7pm. L10,000.)*

DUOMO. The main attraction of the 14th-century *duomo* is the **Capella del Tesoro di San Gennaro** on the right. A beautiful 17th-century bronze grille protects the high altar, which holds a gruesome reliquary with the saint's head and two vials of his coagulated blood. Supposedly, disaster strikes if the blood doesn't liquefy on the biannual celebration of his *festa*; miraculously, it always does. *(3 blocks up V. Duomo from C. Umberto I or take #42 bus from P. Garibaldi. ☎ 081 44 90 97. Open M-F 9am-noon and 4:30-7pm, Sa-Su 9am-noon. L5000.)*

SPACCANAPOLI. This renowned east-west neighborhood "splits" the city in two (reflected in its name), is replete with gorgeous architecture, and merits at least a 30-minute stroll. To get to the neighborhood from P. Dante, walk through **Porta Alba** and **P. Bellini** before turning down **V. dei Tribunali,** which follows the location and direction of an old Roman road, and now contains some of the city's best **pizzerie.** You'll see the churches of **San Lorenzo Maggiore** and **San Paolo Maggiore.** Take a right on V. Duomo and another on V. San Biago into the heart of the area; you'll meander past the **University of Naples** and the **Chiesa di San Domenico Maggiore,** where a painting once spoke to St. Thomas Aquinas. *(In P. S. Domenico Maggiore. Open daily 7:15am-12:15pm and 4:15-7:15pm.)*

🎵 🎭 ENTERTAINMENT AND NIGHTLIFE

Neopolitan nightlife varies widely by season. While content in clubs and discos during the winter, Neopolitans take to the streets in warmer weather. People relx in the numerous *piazze*, and the outdoor bars and cafes, especially in P. Bellini.

Green Stage, P. S. Pasquale, 15 (☎ 081 245 10 55). Take V. Vittorio Colonna out of P. Amedeo, then turn right on V. S. Pasquale. An extremely popular pub. Crowds often spill out onto the *piazza* on summer nights. Open Tu-Th 7:30pm-3am, F-Su 7:30pm-4am.

1799, P. Bellini, 70 (☎ 081 29 25 37), appeals to your darker side by opting for simple, black decor and dim lighting. The eerie trance music prevents you from noticing how much you paid for that last cocktail. Beer L5000, mixed drinks L9000 and up. Open Tu-Su 10am-1am, F-Su 10am-3am.

Tongue, V. Manzoni, 207 (☎081 769 08 00), in Posillipo. Take the erratic 404d *notturno* bus from P. Garibaldi. This large discotheque and music hall frequently features visiting DJs. Cover L25,000. Open Oct.-May, F-Sa 11pm-4am.

Camelot, V. Petrarca, 101 (☎081 769 25 23), in Posillipo. No round table here. Except for the occasional live performances, they don't stray very far from pop, house, and dance. Cover L25,000. Open Oct.-May F-Sa midnight-4am.

Madison Street, V. Sgambati, 47 (☎081 546 65 66), in Vomero, features a large dance floor for weekend revelry. Cover L25,000. Open Sept.-May F-Su 10pm-4am.

■ DAYTRIPS FROM NAPLES

POMPEII

The quickest way to Pompeii (25km south of Naples) is the Circumvesuvia train (☎081 772 21 11) from Stazione Centrale (dir: Sorrento; 2 per hour., L3200). Pompeii open 9am to 1hr. before sunset: in summer around 7pm; in winter around 3pm. L16,000.

On August 24, AD 79, life in the prosperous Roman city of Pompeii suddenly halted. A fit of towering flames, suffocating black clouds, and seething lava from Mt. Vesuvius buried the city—temples, villas, theaters, and all—under more than 7m of volcanic ash. Excavations, which began in 1748, have unearthed a stunningly well-preserved picture of Roman daily life. The site hasn't changed much since then, and neither have the victims, whose ghastly remains were partially preserved by plaster casts in the hardened ash. Walk down V. D. Marina to reach the **Forum,** surrounded by a colonnade and once the commercial, civic, and religious center of the city. Exit the Forum through the upper end, by the cafeteria, and head right on V. della Fortuna to reach the **House of the Faun,** where a bronze dancing faun and the spectacular Alexander Mosaic (today in the Museo Archeologico Nazionale) were found. Continue on V. della Fortuna and turn left on V. dei Vettii to reach the **House of the Vettii,** and the most vivid frescoes in Pompeii. Cross V. della Fortuna to V. Storto, turn left on V. degli Augustali, and take a quick right to visit a small **brothel** (the Lupenar). After 2000 years, it's still the most popular place in town; you may have to wait in line. V. dei Teatri, across the street, leads to oldest-standing **amphitheater** in the world (80 BC), which held up to 12,000 spectators. To get to the **Villa of the Mysteries,** the complex's best-preserved villa, go all the way west on V. della Fortuna, right on V. Consolare, and all the way up Porta Ercolano. To get to the **tourist office,** V. Sacra, 1 (☎081 850 72 55), take a right out of the station and continue to the bottom of the hill. (Both offices open M-F 8am-3:30pm, Sa 8am-2pm.)

HERCULANEUM

Go 500m downhill from the Ercolano stop on the Circumvesuviana Line train from Naples (20min., L2200). Archaeological site open daily 9am to 1hr. before sunset. L16,000.

Herculaneum does not evoke the tragedy of Pompeii—all but a handful of its inhabitants escaped the ravages of Vesuvius. Between 15 and 20 houses are open to the public. One of the more alluring is the **House of Deer** (named for the statues of deer in the courtyard), which displays the statue of a *Satyr with a Wineskin* and one of Hercules trying to relieve himself while in a drunken stupor. Stop at the **tourist office,** V. IV Novembre, 84, to pick up a free **map.** (☎081 788 12 43. Open M, W-F 9am-1pm, Tu 4-6:30pm.)

MT. VESUVIUS

Trasporti Vesuviani buses run from Ercolano outside the Ercolano Circumvesuviana station to the crater of Vesuvius. (Buy tickets on the bus, L6000 roundtrip). From the bus stop it's a 20-30min. walk to the top.

Peer into the only active volcano on mainland Europe. Make the half-hour climb from the bus stop to the top of Mt. Vesuvius, but bring plenty of water and wear sturdy shoes. Vesuvius hasn't erupted since March 31, 1944, but although scientists say volcanoes should erupt every 30 years, experts still deem the trip safe.

AMALFI COAST

The beauty of the Amalfi coast is one of extremes. Rugged cliffs plunge downwards into calm azure waters, as coastal towns cling to the sides of narrow ravines. Visitors are drawn to the natural splendor and the unique character of each town.

◰ TRANSPORTATION

The coast is accessible from Naples, Sorrento, Salerno, and the islands by **ferry** and the blue SITA **bus** that runs along the Amalfi coast. **Trains** run directly to Salerno from Rome (2½-3hr., 18 per day, L22-45,000); Florence (5½-6½hr., 7 per day, L49-79,000); Naples (45min., 32 per day, L5100-17,100); and Venice (9hr., 1am, L64,000). Trains also run to Sorrento from Naples (1hr., L4700). SITA **buses** run from Positano to Amalfi (L2100) and Sorrento (L2300), and from Amalfi to Salerno (1¼hr., 25 per day, L3200). Buses also link Paestum and Salerno (40min., 9 per day., L4700). From Salerno, **Travelmar** (☎ 089 87 31 90) runs **ferries** to Amalfi (1hr., 3 per day, L9000) via Positano (40min., L7000). From Sorrento, **Linee Marittime Partenopee** (☎ 081 878 14 30) ferries run to Amalfi (45min., 2 per day, L16,000) via Positano (30min., 7 per day, L13,000) and Capri (50min., 3 per day, L9000); from Amalfi they service Salerno (30min., 9 per day, L16,000).

AMALFI AND ATRANI

The narrow streets and historic monuments of Amalfi nestle in incomparable natural beauty. Although there is a small beach in Amalfi itself, a 5- to 10-minute trip around the bend will bring you to a much better (and free) beach in **Atrani**. The 9th-century **Duomo di Sant'Andrea** imparts a dignified charm to the **P. del Duomo**. The *piazza* may need it; the nearby **Fontana di Sant'Andrea** features a marble female nude squeezing her breasts as water spews from her nipples. Trek up from Amalfi into the imposing **Monti Lattari**, to the **Valley of the Dragons**, named for the torrent of water and mist (like smoke from a dragon) exploding out to sea every winter. **A'Scalinatella**, P. Umberto, 12, lets hostel beds and regular rooms all over Atrani and Amalfi. (☎089 87 19 30. Dorms L20-35,000; doubles L50-120,000; **camping** L15,000 per person.) **Hotel Lidomare** (☎ 089 87 19 30), is through the alley across from the *duomo*. (Breakfast included. Singles L70-75,000; doubles L125-160,000.)

RAVELLO

Ravello and its lush villas perch 330m atop the cliffs, gazing down on a patchwork of villages and ravines extending to the sea. The Moorish cloister and meandering gardens of **Villa Rufolo**, off P. Duomo, inspired Boccaccio's *Decameron* and Wagner's *Parsifal*. (☎ 089 85 76 57. Open daily 9am-sunset. L5000.) On the small road to the right, signs lead to the impressive **Villa Cimbrone**, where floral walkways and gardens hide temples and statued grottoes. (Open daily 9am-7:30pm. L6000.) Frequent **classical music concerts** enliven Ravello's tranquility, especially in summer. The best rooms in town are found at **Hotel Villa Amore** V. dei Fusco, 5, en route to Villa Cimbrone. (☎089 85 71 35. Breakfast included. Singles L80,000; doubles L120,000; off-season L10,000 less.)

POSITANO

Positano's most frequent visitors may be the wealthy who enjoy its beachfront ballet and can afford the French chefs in its four-star hotels, but there is no denying, that Positano has its charms, and most who come here linger. As Steinbeck rightly observed, "Positano bites deep." Cliffside homes and idiosyncratic locals began luring writers, artists, and actors to Positano in the early 1900s. Not surprisingly, the invention of the bikini here in 1959 heralded a marked increase in tourism. Soon afterwards, its artsy cachet and skimpy swimwear made it a popular destination for high-rollers. To see the large *pertusione* (hole) in **Montepertuso**, one of three perforated mountains in the world (the other two are in India), hike the 45min. trail up the hillside or take the bus (every hr., L1500) from P. dei Mulini, near the port or from any other bus stop. Positano's **beaches** are also popular, and although boutiques may be a bit pricey, no one charges for window shopping. The **tourist office,** V. del Saraceno, 4 , is below the *duomo*, near the beach. (☎089 87 50 67. Open daily 8:30am-2pm and 3:30-8pm; in winter M-F 8:30am-2pm, Sa 8:30am-noon.) **Ostello Brikette,** V. G. Marconi, 358, 100m up the main coastal road to Sorrento from Vle. Pasitea, has incredible views. (☎089 87 58 57. Breakfast, shower, and sheets included. Lockout 11:30am-5pm. Midnight curfew. Dorms L35,000; doubles L100,000.) **Pensione Maria Luisa,** V. Fornillio, 42, has seaside terraces. (☎089 87 50 23. Breakfast included. Singles L60,000; doubles L100-120,000.) Prices in the local restaurants reflect the high quality of the food. Thrifty travelers head toward Fornillo. **Il Saraceno D'Oro,** Vle. Pasitea, 254 , on the road to Fornillo, has delicious pizza to go (evenings only) from L6000, and incredible *gnocchi alla Sorrentina*. (☎089 81 20 50. *Gnocchi* L12,000. Cover L2000. Open daily 1-3pm and 7pm-midnight; in winter Th-Tu 1-3pm and 7pm-midnight.)

SORRENTO

The largest, most heavily touristed town on the peninsula, lively and charming Sorrento, makes a convenient base for daytrips around the Bay of Naples. Visit **Marina Grande,** a traditional fishing harbour or go to **Punto del Capo,** a 10min. bus ride away, to see the remains of the ancient Roman **Villa di Pollio.** Caremar **ferries** (☎08 18 07 30 77) go to Capri (50min., 3 per day, L9000), while a local **bus** (L1700) shuttles between P. Tasso and the port. Halfway to the **free beach** at Punta del Capo on bus A, **Hotel Elios,** V. Capo, 33, has comfy rooms. (☎081 878 18 12. Breakfast L10,000. Singles L45,000; doubles L80,000; groups of 3 or 4 L45,000 per person.) Turn left on C. Italia from the station to reach **Hotel City,** C. Italia, 221, which provides guests with currency exchange, local bus tickets, and maps. (☎081 877 22 10. Breakfast included. Singles L75,000; doubles L120,000.) It's easy to find food that is both delicious and affordable in Sorrento. At **Ristorante e Pizzeria Giardiniello,** V. Accademia, 7, off V. Giuliani, eat Mamma Luisa's *gnocchi* (L7000) in a peaceful garden. (Cover L1500. Open June-Sept. daily 11am-2am; Oct.-May F-W 11am-2am.) **Davide,** V. Giuliani, 39, off C. Italia two blocks from P. Tasso, has divine gelato and masterful mousse. (L3500 for 2 scoops. Open daily 10am-midnight.) **Gatto Nero,** V. Correale, 21 (☎081 877 36 86) is the most stylish bar in Sorrento, with plenty of jazz, and an interior decorated in the style of modernist painters.

SALERNO AND PAESTUM

Although industrial **Salerno** is best used as a base for daytrips to nearby **Paestum,** there is a sprinkling of intriguing sights in the city's old quarter; **V. dei Mercanti** and its tiny side streets afford a taste of life in the Middle Ages. Paestum is the site of three spectacularly preserved **Doric buildings,** including the **Temple of Ceres,** the **Temple of Poseidon,** and the **basilica.** (Temples open daily 9am-1hr. before sunset. Closed 1st and 3rd Monday of each month. Last admittance 2hr. before sunset. L8000, EU citizens over 60 and under 18 free.) **Trains** head south from the **P. Veneto Station** in Salerno to Paestum (40min., 9 per day, L4700). Stay in Salerno at the cheerful **Ostello della Gioventù "Irno" (HI),** V. Luigi Guercio, 112; go left from the station on V. Torrione, then left under the bridge on V. Mobilio. (☎089 79 02 51. Breakfast included. Lockout 10:30am-3:30pm. Curfew 2am. Dorms L17,500.)

BAY OF NAPLES ISLANDS

Off the shores of the Bay of Naples, the pleasure islands **Capri,** and **Ischia** beckon weary travelers with promises of breathtaking natural sights, comfortable accommodations, and gorgeous beaches. The islands can be reached by ferries *(traghetti)* or the faster, more expensive hydrofoils *(aliscafi).* For trips to Capri, Sorrento is the closest starting point. The most frequented route to Capri and Ischia is through Naples's Mergellina and Molo Beverello ports. To reach Molo Beverello from Naples's Stazione Centrale, take tram #1 from P. Garibaldi to P. Municipio on the waterfront. Ferries and hydrofoils also run between the islands.

CAPRI

The sheer bluffs, divine landscapes, and azure waters of **Capri** have beckoned wayfarers from the mainland since Roman times. **Capri town** is above the ports, while **Anacapri** sits higher up the mountain. From P. Umberto in Capri Town, V. Roma leads up to Anacapri; buses also make the trip (every 15 min., L1800). The **Grotta Azzurra** (Blue Grotto) is a must-see—light enters the cavern through a hole in the rock under the water, creating a fantastic neon-blue glow. Take the bus from V. Roma in Capri to Anacapri (every 15min.) and a second bus to the Grotto, or go by boat (L8000) from Marina Grande. (All buses L1800. Grotto usually open daily 9am-6pm. Closed Nov.-Mar. and in inclement weather. L8000, rowboat inside L8500.) Upstairs from P. Vittoria in Anacapri, the **Villa San Michele,** for which even author Henry James could not find sufficient superlatives, has gardens, ancient sculptures, and a remarkable view of the island. (Open daily 9:30am-1hr. before dusk. L8000.) To appreciate Capri's Mediterranean beauty from higher ground, take the **chairlift** up **Monte Solaro** from P. Vittoria. (Open daily 9:30am-1hr. before dusk. Round-trip L7000.) From P. Umberto in Capri take V. Longano, which becomes V. Tiberio, to **Villa Jovis** (1hr.), the most magnificent of the 12 villas that the emperor Tiberius scattered throughout Capri. (Open daily 9am-1hr. before dusk. L4000.)

Caremar **ferries** (☎081 837 07 00) run from Marina Grande to Naples (1hr., 6 per day, L9800) and Sorrento (45min., 3 per day, L10,000). Linee Lauro sends **hydrofoils** to Ischia (40min., 1per day, L20,000) and Sorrento (20min., 12 per day, L14,000); LineaJet hydrofoils go to Naples (40min., 11 per day L16,000). The Capri AAST **tourist office** (☎081 837 06 34) is at the end of Marina Grande; in Anacapri, at V. Orlandi, 59 (☎081 837 15 24), to the right from the P. Vittoria bus stop. (Both open June-Sept. M-Sa 8:30am-8:30pm and Oct.-May 9am-1:30pm and 3:30-6:45pm.) In Anacapri, beautiful **Villa Eva**, V. La Fabbrica, 8, will pick you up from P. Vittoria. (☎081 837 15 49. Breakfast included. Singles L50,000; doubles from L80,000; triples from L105,000; quads from L140,000.) From the last bus stop, follow the signs up the stairs to **Il Girasole**, V. Linciano, 47. (☎081 837 23 51. Internet access L10,000 per hour. Doubles from L105,000; triples L135-180,000.) In Capri, **Pensione Stella Maris,** V. Roma, 27, is opposite the bus stop. (☎081 837 04 52. All rooms with bath and TV. Singles L100,000; doubles L120,000.) Get **groceries** at **STANDA** in Capri; head right at the fork at the end of V. Roma. (Open M-Sa 8:30am-1:30pm and 5-9pm, Su 9am-noon.) At night, dressed-to-kill Italians come out for *passegiatte;* bars in the streets around **P. Umberto** keep the music pumping late.

ISCHIA

Across the bay from overrun Capri, larger, less glamorous, Ischia offers luscious beaches, natural hot springs, ruins, forests, vineyards, and lemon groves. Follow the coast in a circular route from **Ischia Porto,** a port formed by the crater of an extinct volcano to **Casamicciola Terme,** with its crowded beach and legendary thermal waters; **Tacco Ameno,** the oldest Greek settlement in the western Mediterranean; and well-touristed **Forio,** whose streets house popular bars. **Buses** #1, CD, and CS (every 20min., L1700, day-pass L5200) go to these sights from Porto. Take bus #5 from Porto to the beautiful beach at **Maronti. Castello Aragonese,** a 15th-century fortress, is located on its own, tiny island off the coast of Ischia. (Take bus#7 or 8 from the port to Ischia Ponte. L15,000.)

Caremar **ferries** arrive from Naples. (☎081 98 48 18. 1-1½hr., 14 per day, L9800.) **Linee Marittime Partenopee** (☎081 99 18 88) runs hydrofoils to Sorrento (45min., 5 per day, L18,000). SEPSA **buses** come from P. Trieste (one-way L1700, full-day L5000). Stay in Ischia Porto only if you want to be close to the ferries—most *pensioni* are in Forio. In Forio, the floral **Pensione Di Lustro**, V. Filippo di Lustro, 9, where Truman Capote once stayed, is near the beach. (☎081 99 71 63. Breakfast included. July-Aug. doubles L120,000; June L100,000; Oct.-Mar. L90,000.) The **Ostello "Il Gabbiano" (HI),** Strada Statale Forio-Panza, 162, between Forio and Panza, is accessible by bus #1, CS, or CD, and also has beach access. (☎081 90 94 22. Breakfast included. Lockout 10am-1pm. Curfew 12:30am. Open Apr.-Sept. Dorms

L30,000; doubles L60,000.) **Camping Internazionale** is at V. Foschini, 22, 15min. from the port. Take V. Alfredo de Luca from V. del Porto; bear right on V. Michele Mazzella at P. degi Eroi. (☎081 99 14 49. L16,000 per person, L10,000 per tent; 2-person bungalows with bath L80,000, L20,000 per additional person. Open Apr. 15-Oct. 15.) While Ischian food, especially seafood and fruit, is a treat, it is almost impossible to find a restaurant that is not oriented towards the tourists who flood the island. Explore side streets for less-expensive, more authentic culinary options.

BARI

Most tourists only stay in Bari long enough to buy a ferry ticket to Greece, but Apulia's capital is a vibrant city, with a university, historical sights, and the world's most organized backpacker-welcoming committee. **Stop-Over in Bari,** V. Nicolai, 47 (☎080 621 45 38), continues to lure backpackers with irresistible amounts of **free stuff,** including campsites with tents and showers, bike rentals, excursions—including daytrips to the stunning, octagonal **Castel del Monte,** "big-name" Eastern European speed-metal concerts, and **internet.** Near Bari, on the Ferrovie del Sud Est **train** line, **Alberobello's** famous *trulli* (mortarless conical roofs; 1½hr.) and the spectacular **Castellana Grotte** (Grotte di Castellana Grotte stop; 1hr.) are worth a daytrip.

    Trains go to: Rome (5-7hr., 6 per day, L47-65,500); Brindisi (1-1¾hr., 27 per day, L10,100-25,100); and Naples (4½hr., 1 per day, L25,500). **Eurail** holders get **no discounts** on **ferries** from Bari (see **Brindisi,** below), but some ferries have student rates. **Poseidon Lines,** C. de Tullio 36/40 (☎080 521 00 22; window 11 at the port) goes to Turkey and Israel; **Ventouris Ferries,** V. Piccinni, 133 (☎080 521 76 99; windows 7-10) goes to: Cephalonia (15hr., July 26-Aug. 21 every other day, L63-83,000, students L57-77,000); Corfu (11hr., June 27-Sept. 29 1 per day, L53-73,000, students L47-67,000); Igoumenitsa (13hr., in summer 1 per day, L53-73,000, students L47-67,000); and Patras (18hr., 1 per day, L63-83,000, students L57-77,000); and **Marlines** (☎080 523 18 24) goes to Igoumenitsa (13hr., 2-4 per week, L50-70,000). The area around the port can be intimidating; take a bus rather than walking through the old city. **Pensione Romeo,** V. Crisanzio, 12 (☎080 521 63 52; singles L65,000; doubles L95,000), offers cheaper rooms than its star-crossed love upstairs in **Pensione Giulia** (☎080 521 66 30; singles L70-80,000; doubles L90-120,000; off-season L15-20,000 less).

BRINDISI

Every year, about a million Eurailers and InterRailers get off the train at Brindisi, walk to the port, pay a port tax, and get on a boat to Greece. If you're one of them, arrive in the afternoon, as ferries leave in the evening. In August, consider arriving early or departing from Ancona or Bari instead. **Trains** arrive from: Rome (6-9hr., 4 per day, L49-79,500); Naples (7hr., 5 per day, L31,000); and Venice (11hr., 7:50pm, L67,500). **Ferries** leave for: Corfu (8hr.); Igoumenitsa (10hr.); Cephalonia (16½hr.); and Patras (17hr.). **Adriatica,** C. Garibaldi 85/87 (☎08 31 52 38 25) and **Hellenic Mediterranean Lines,** C. Garibaldi 8 (☎08 31 52 85 31), **the only two ferry lines on which InterRail and Eurail are valid,** offer free deck passage on a space-available basis (a seat inside costs L29,000 extra), not including port tax (Adriatica L10,000, HML L12,000; June 10-Sept. Eurailers add L19,000 fee). Those without railpasses will have to shop for cheap fares—tickets are usually L30-60,000. Contrary to what you might see, Brindisi has no official Eurail or InterRail offices. Three of the more reliable companies are **Strintzis Lines,** C. Garibaldi 65 (☎08 31 56 22 00), **Fragline,** C. Garibaldi 88 (☎0831 59 01 96), and **Med Link Lines,** C. Garibaldi 49 (☎08 31 52 76 67). Board the ferry two hours in advance, and bring warm clothes or a sleeping bag.

    Corso Umberto, a jumble of ferry offices and restaurants, runs 1km from the station to the port, becoming **Corso Garibaldi** halfway down. The *stazione marittima* is on the right at the end of V. Regina Margherita. (☎08 31 52 30 72. Open in summer M-Sa 8am-7pm; off-season M-F 9am-1pm and 4-6pm.) ■**Ostello della Gioventù,** 2km from the train station, in the Casale area, rents beds for a day (L9000). After they've picked you up, do laundry while you nap before being driven back to the port. (☎08 31 41 31 23. Stay the night for L18,000. Breakfast included.) In town, try **Hotel Altair,** V. Giudea 4. (☎0831 56 22 89. Singles L25-60,000.) Stock up for the ferry ride at **Maxis Sidis supermarket,** C. Garibaldi 106, near the port.

SICILY (SICILIA)

With a history so steeped in chaos, catastrophe, and conquest, it's no wonder that the island of Sicily possesses a reputation for passionate volatility. Greek, Roman, Arab, Norman, and Aragonese conquerors each took their turn transforming Sicily's landscape, but none managed to thwart its independent spirit. Today, Sicilians speed unchecked toward the future, installing condom vending machines in front of medieval cathedrals and demonstrating against their own well-known Mafia. The tempestuousness of Sicilian history and political life is matched only by the island's dramatic landscapes, dominated by craggy slopes. Entire cities have been destroyed in seismic and volcanic catastrophes, but those that have survived have only grown stronger; Sicilian pride is a testament to resilience during centuries of occupation and destruction.

▛ TRANSPORTATION

Tirrenia ferries (☎091 33 33 00) offers the most extensive and reliable service. From southern Italy, take a **train** to Reggio di Calabria, then the NGI or Meridiano **ferry** (40min., 12 per day, L1000) or Ferrovie Statale **hydrofoil** (☎0965 86 35 40; 25min., 6-16 per day, L5000) to Messina, Sicily's transport hub. Ferries also go to Palermo from: Cagliari, Sardinia (14hr., L38-66,500); Genoa (20hr., 6 per week, L123-181,000); and Naples (11hr., 1 per day, L55-90,500). **SAIS Trasporti** (☎091 617 11 41) and **SAIS** (☎091 616 60 28) buses serve destinations throughout the island, including Corleone (perhaps you've seen *The Godfather*?). **Trains** also chug to Rome (9hr., 4 per day, L53,000) and Messina directly from Naples (4 per day, L38,500). Trains continue west to Palermo (3½hr., 16 per day, L19,500) via Milazzo (L4500); and south to Syracuse (3hr., 12 per day, L16,000) via Taormina (45min., L5500).

PALERMO

As Sicily's capital, Palermo is notorious as the cradle of Italian organized crime. The city has recently begun cleaning up its politics and revitalizing its historic district, much of which was destroyed in WWII. Palermo sports the attractions of a modern metropolis—its fast-paced streets present an amalgamation of the old and the new as horse-drawn carriages compete for road-space with Fiats. To get to the huge **Teatro Massimo,** where the climactic opera scene of *The Godfather Part III* was filmed, walk up V. Maqueda past the intersection of Quattro Canti and C. Vittorio Emanuele. (Open Tu-Su 10am-4pm for 20min. tours.) Up C. Vittorio Emanuele, the **Palazzo dei Normanni** contains the **Cappella Palatina,** which has a carved wooden stalactite ceiling, and an incredible cycle of golden Byzantine mosaics. (Open M-Sa 9-11:45am and 3-4:45pm.) The intensely morbid **Cappuchin Catacombs,** in P. Cappuccini, are only for the strong of stomach. This potentially disturbing sight showcases 8000 corpses in moth-eaten clothing that line the underground labyrinth, including a preserved baby girl and a separate room for virgins. To get there, take bus #109 or 318 from the central station to P. Indipendenza and then hop on #327. (Open M-Su 9am-noon and 3-5:30pm. L2500.)

Direct **trains** run from P. Giulio Cesare, at V. Roma and V. Maqueda, to Rome (11½hr., 4 per day, L67,000) and Milan (17½hr., 3 per day, L91,600). SAIS Trasporti **buses** have four lines, all located on V. Balsamo, next to the train station. After purchasing tickets, ask exactly where your bus will arrive and for its logo. Ask one of the mini-offices for a combined metro and bus map. The **tourist office,** P. Castelnuovo, 34, is opposite Teatro Politeama; from the train station, take any bus showing "Politeama" on its overhead screen to Piazza Politeama, at the end of V. Maqueda. (☎605 83 51. Open M-F 8:30am-6pm, Sa 9am-2pm and 4-7pm, Su 9am-1pm.) Homey **Hotel Regina,** C. Vittorio Emanuele, 316, is near V. Maqueda. (☎611 42 16. Kitchen. Singles L30-45,000; doubles L55-

LA FAMIGLIA Pin-striped suits, machine guns, horse heads, and the Godfather are a far cry from the reality of the Sicilian Mafia. The system has its roots in the *latifondi* (agricultural estates) of rural Sicily, where land managers and salaried militiamen (a.k.a. landlords and bouncers) protected their turf and people. Powerful because people owed them favors, strong because they supported one another, and feared because they did not hesitate to kill offenders, they founded a tradition that has dominated Sicilian life since the late 19th century. Since the mid-80s, the Italian government has worked to curtail Mafia influence, with visible results. Today Sicilians shy away from any Mafia discussion, referring to the system as *Cosa Nostra* (our thing). Unfortunately, "their thing" expanded to include a rigid structure of national politics, drug-smuggling, and assassination. But hey, *Ch' t' le dich'à fa'.*

80,000.) To reach the **Petit Hotel,** V. Principe di Belmonte, 84, take V. Roma from the train station, walk six blocks (past V. Cavour), and turn left. (☎ 32 36 16. Single L35,000; doubles L65,000; triples L90,000.) Take bus #101 from the station to P. de Gasperi, then take bus #628 to V. Sferracavallo; walk one block down, turn right on V. dei Manderini after the post office, and **Campeggio dell'Ulivi,** V. Pegaso, 25, is on the right, 35 minutes from the train station. (☎ 53 30 21. One person and tent L9000.) Palermo's specialty is *rigatoni alla palermitana* (with a sauce of meat and peas); indulge at **Lo Sparviero,** V. Sperlinga, 23, a block from the Teatro Massimo. (*Secondi* from L10,000. Open M-W and F-Su 11am-2pm and 7:30pm-midnight.) **STANDA supermarket** is at V. Roma, 59. (Open M 4-8pm, Tu and Th-Su 9am-1pm and 4-8pm, W 9am-1pm.) **Postal Code:** 90100.

■ DAYTRIPS FROM PALERMO

MONREALE

Bus #389 leaves Palermo's P. Indipendenza (15min., 3 per hr., L1500). Open daily 8am-noon and 3:30-6pm; free. Cloister open M-Sa 9am-1pm and 3pm-6:30pm, Su 9am-12:30pm. L4000. Roof L3000. Treasury L4000.

Ten kilometers southwest, Monreale's magnificent Norman-Saracen cathedral **Santa Maria la Nuova** has 6430 square meters of mosaics and 130 panels of gold and colored glass tiles. The church features incredible mosaics and arches; the **cloister** next door houses a renowned Sicilian sculpture collection.

CEFALÙ

Take the train from Palermo (1hr., 32 per day, L7000. ☎ 42 10 50; fax 42 23 86. Open M-F 8am-2:30pm and 3:30-7pm, Sa 9am-1pm.)

Cefalù guards a cache of Arab, Norman, and medieval architecture. In P. Duomo, off C. Ruggero, lies its 11th-century Norman **duomo.** Byzantine and Roman columns support superb capitals, while elegant horseshoe arches and a huge mosaic dazzle the eye. (Open 8:30am-noon and 3:30-6:30pm. Dress modestly.) For city views, walk up the **Rocca** by way of the Salita Saraceni; from near P. Garibaldi, off C. Ruggero, follow the signs for *"pedonale Rocca"* (30min.). On the mountain, ancient walls and crumbling cisterns lead to the 9th-century BC **Tempio di Diana.** From the station, V. Moro leads to the old town and the **tourist office,** C. Ruggero, 77.

AGRIGENTRO

Take bus #1 or 2 from the train station (L1500).

Among Sicily's classical remains, the **Valle dei Tempii** at Agrigento shares top honors with those at Syracuse. The **Tempio della Concordia,** one of the world's best-preserved Greek temples, owes its survival to consecration by St. Gregory of the Turnips. One kilometer uphill from the ruins, the **Museo Nazionale Archeologico di San Nicola** houses Greek odds and ends, even a huge *telamones,* a statue that supported the temple's weight. (Open M-Sa 8am-12:30pm. L8000.) Revisit modern fashion and convenience at the **centro storico,** a cobblestoned web of shops and eateries.

Trains arrive from Palermo (2hr., 10 per day, L12,500). The **tourist office**, V. Battista, 13, is the first left off V. Atenea. (Open in summer M-F 9am-2pm and 4:30-7pm, Sa 9am-2pm.) **Trattoria Atenea**, V. Ficani, 32, the fourth right off V. Atenea from P. Moro, has a quiet courtyard and extensive seafood offerings. (*Pasta con melanzane* L8000. Open M-Sa noon-3pm and 7pm-midnight.)

SYRACUSE (SIRACUSA)

Founded in 734 BC by Greeks, ancient Syracuse cultivated such luminaries as Pindar, Archimedes, and Theocritus. The city hasn't been the same since the Romans sacked it in 211 BC, but ancient monuments remain. Cross the bridge on C. Umberto to the island of **Ortigia**, to pay homage to the **Temples of Apollo and Athena**. The latter, now part of the city's cathedral, has an embellished facade added over several centuries. From P. Duomo, a trip down V. Picherale leads to the spring-fed **Fonte Aretusa** (pond). Syracuse's larger monuments are in or near the **Archaeological Park**, on the north side of town, which contains an enormous ancient **Greek theater** where Aeschylus faced opening-night jitters at the premiere of his *Persians*. The amazing acoustics of the **Orecchio di Dionigi** (Ear of Dionysius) spawned the legend that the tyrant Dionysius put prisoners here to eavesdrop on them. To see the 2nd-century **Roman amphitheater**, once the home of Roman gladiators and the wild animals who loved them, follow C. Gelone until it meets V. Teocrito, then walk left down V. Augusto. (Open daily 9am-2hr. before dusk. L4000.) Near the tourist office is the **Catacombe di San Giovanni.** (Open daily Mar. 15-Nov. 14 9am-12:30pm and 2-5pm; Nov. 15-Mar. 14 9am-1pm. L4000.) Those who prefer tans to temples should bus 18km to **Fontane Bianche** (bus #21, 22, or 24; L600), which is a silken beach, home to outdoor nightclubs.

Trains go to Rome (11hr., 2 per day, L67,500) and Messina (3hr., 3 per day, L16,000), and **buses** leave for Palermo (3¼hr., 7 per day, L21,500) and Taormina (2hr., 1 per day, L12,500). Solo travelers should beware the train station area at night. To get from the train station to the **tourist office**, V. S. Sebastiano, 43, turn right at the end of C. Gelone on V. Teocrito and left at the sanctuary. (☎093 16 77 10. Open M-Sa 8:30am-1:45pm and 3:30-6:30pm, Su 9am-1pm; off-season M-Sa 8:30am-2pm and 3:30-6:30pm, Su 8:30am-2pm.) From the station, follow signs from C. Gelone to find the **Pensione Bel Sit**, V. Oglio, 5. (☎093 16 02 45. Singles L40,000; doubles L50-65,000.) **Albergo Aretusa**, V. Francesco Crispi, 73, also near the train station, has marble-tiled rooms in an old *palazzo*. (☎093 12 42 11. Breakfast L5000. Reserve ahead for Aug. Singles L35-45,000; doubles L60-75,000; triples L80-100,000.) **Spaghetteria do Scugghiu**, V. D. Sciná, 11, off P. Archimede, on Ortigia, serves 18 delicious types of spaghetti. (Spaghetti L7000. Open Tu-Su noon-3pm and 5pm-midnight.) For budget eats, try **Ortigia** or **FAMILA supermarket**, V. Teracati 34. (Open M-Tu and Th-Sa 8:30am-1:45pm and 4:30-8:15pm, W 8:30am-1:45pm.)

TAORMINA

Clifftop mansions and local flora punctuate the hazy blue coastline of Taormina, a city of unsurpassed beauty. The 3rd-century **Greek theater**, at cliff's edge, is one of the most dramatic spots in Italy. To get there, walk up V. Teatro Greco, off C. Umberto I at P. Vittorio Emanuele. (Open daily 9am-dusk. L4000.) Opposite the Greek theater, the **Church of S. Caterina** hides the small **Roman Odeon** theater. Descend V. di Giovanni and follow the signs to the sculpted English garden of the **Villa Comunale**. A short trip away is **Gole Alcantara**, a haven comprised of stunning gorges, freezing waterfalls, and crystal rapids. (Six **buses** run daily, but the only return bus is at 2pm; round-trip L8500. Entrance L4000. Wetsuit L13,000.)

Reach Taormina from Messina by **bus** (L5-6000), or take the more frequent **train** (L4700) to its less central station. The **tourist office**, in P. S. Caterina, is at P. V. Emanuele in P. Corvaia off C. Umberto. (☎0942 232 43; fax 0942 249 41. Open M-F 8am-2pm and 4-7pm, Sa 9am-1pm and 4-7pm, Su 9am-1pm.) **Pensione Svizzera**, V. Pirandello, 26, has gorgeous coastal views and clean rooms. (☎0942 237 90. Open Feb.-Nov. Reserve ahead. Singles L80,000; doubles 130,000; triples 175,000.) Nearby **Inn Piero**, V. Pirandello, 20, has small, colorful rooms that overlook the sea. (☎0942 231 39. Singles L84,000; doubles L120,000. Half-pension L93,000; required in high-season. Reserve ahead.) Dining can be expensive; stock up at **STANDA supermarket,** V. Apollo Arcageta, 49, at the end of C. Umberto. (Open M-Sa 8:30am-1pm and 5-9pm.) **Bella Blu,** V. Pirandello, 28, has serves portions and a stupendous view. (L20,000 tourist *menù*. *Primi* from L6000, *secondi* from L10,000. Cover L2000. Open daily 10am-3:30pm and 6pm until the last person leaves.)

AEOLIAN ISLANDS (ISOLE EOLIE)

Home of the wind god Aeolus and the Sirens, the Aeolian (or Lipari) Islands, with their long, rocky beaches, boast some of Italy's last few stretches of unspoiled seashore. The placid island seascapes are enlivened by volcanoes belching fire and smoke, which are often an easy hike from sea level.

▐ TRANSPORTATION

The archipelago lies off the Sicilian coast, north of Milazzo, the principal and least expensive departure point. Hop off a **train** from **Messina** (40min.; L4500;) or Palermo (3hr., L15,500) and onto an orange AST **bus** for the port (10min., every hr., L1500). Siremar (☎ 090 928 32 42) and Navigazione Generale Italiana (NGI; ☎090 928 40 91) **ferries** depart for Lipari (2hr., L10,500-12,500); Vulcano (L10-12,000); and Stromboli (5hr., L16,500-18,500). Siremar and SNAV (☎090 928 45 09) **hydrofoils** (*aliscafi*) make the trip in half the time but cost twice as much. All three have ticket offices on V. Dei Mille facing the port in Milazzo. **Ferries** leave for the islands less frequently from **Naples'** Molo Beverello port. Ferries between Lipari and Vulcano cost L4500; between Lipari and Stromboli, L25,500.

LIPARI

Lipari, the largest and most developed of the islands, is renowned for its amazing beaches and stunning hillside views. To reach the popular beaches of **Spiaggia Bianca** and **Porticello,** take the Lipari-Cavedi bus a few kilometers north to Canneto, where Spiaggia Bianca is *the* spot for topless (and sometimes bottomless) sunbathing. Lipari's other offerings include a splendidly rebuilt medieval **castello,** the site of an ancient Greek acropolis. The fortress shares its hill with an **archaeological park,** the **San Bartolo church,** and the superb **Museo Archeologico Eoliano.** The **Museo,** up the right steps from the V. Garibaldi, is a dizzying parade of artifacts from prehistoric Lipari. (☎090 988 01 74. Open May-Oct. M-Su 9am-1:30pm and 4-7pm; Nov.-Apr. M-Su 9am-1:30pm and 3-6pm. L8000.)

The **AAST delle Isole Eolie tourist office,** C. Vittorio Emanuele, 202, is up the street from the ferry dock. (☎090 988 00 95; fax 090 981 11 90; email infocast@netnet.it; www.net-net.it/aasteolie. Open July-Aug. M-Sa 8am-2pm and 4-10pm, Su 8am-2pm; Sept.-June M-F 8am-2pm and 4:30-7:30pm, Sa 8am-2pm.) **Casa Vittorio,** Vico Sparviero, 15, is on a quiet side street in the center of town. Its rooms range from well-furnished singles to a five-person penthouse. (☎/fax 090 891 15 23. May-July singles L30-40,000, doubles L60-80,000.) **Pensione Enso il Negro,** V. Garibaldi is 20m up V. Garibladi and up three flights of stone stairs, and has a lovely view of Lipari. (☎090 981 31 63. Nov.-Mar. L40,000 per person; June L60,000; July L75,000; Aug. L100,000.) **Hotel Europeo,** C. Vittorio Emanuele, 98, has bright, bare rooms in a great location. (☎090 981 15 89. Singles L40-55,000; doubles L80-110,000.) **Camp** at **Baia Unci,** V. Marina Garibaldi 2, 2km from Lipari at the entrance to the hamlet of Canneto. (☎090 981 19 09; fax 090 981 17 15. Reserve in Aug. Open Mar.15-Oct. 15. L15-19,000 per person.) Stock up at **UPIM supermarket,** C. Vittorio Emanuele, 212. (Open M-Sa 8am-3:20pm and 4-11pm.) **Da Gilberto,** V. Garibaldi 22-24, is famous for what may be Italy's best sandwiches. (☎090 981 27 56. Sandwiches start at L5000. Open 7pm-2am, 7am-10pm in low season.) Lamp-lit pirate ships leave the Lipari docks for Vulcano's **Freeway Disco,** a nearby Euro-disco club. **Postal Code:** 98055.

VULCANO

This island makes an intriguing daytrip for its thermal springs, black beaches, and bubbling mudbaths; the pervading smell of sulphur makes it less attractive for longer stays. A steep one-hour **hike** to the inactive **Gran Cratere** (Grand Crater) snakes between the volcano's smoke-belching fumaroles. On a clear day, you can see all the other islands from the top. The allegedly therapeutic **Laghetto di Fanghi** (Mud Pool) is just up V. Provinciale to the right from the port. If you would prefer not to bathe in dirt, you can step gingerly into the scalding waters of the **acquacalda**, where underwater volcanic outlets make the sea percolate like a jacuzzi, or visit the black sands and clear waters of **Sabbie Nere**, just down the road from the *acquacalda*. Follow the signs off V. Ponente. To get to Vulcano, take the 30min. ferry from the port at nearby Lipari (3-4 daily; L4500). For more info, the **tourist office** is at V. Provinciale 41. (☎ 090 985 20 28. Open July-Aug. daily 8am-1:30pm and 3-5pm.) For information on **rented rooms** *(affittacamere)*, call ☎ 090 985 21 42.

STROMBOLI

If you find luscious beaches and hot springs a bit tame, a visit to Stromboli's active **volcano**, which spews orange cascades of lava and molten rock each night (roughly every 10min.), could quench your thirst for adventure. A guided hike to the crater rewards diligent climbers with a view of the nightly eruptions. **Hiking** the *vulcano* on your own is **illegal** and **dangerous**, but **Guide Alpine Autorizzate** offers tours. (☎ 090 98 62 11. Tours depart from P. Vincenzo M, W, and Sa-Su 5:30pm; return midnight. L35,000.) Bring sturdy shoes, a flashlight, snacks, water, and warm clothes. When hiking down the volcano at night, always use the same path you took up; the professional guides' shortcuts are tempting but infinitely easier to get lost on. Siremar (☎ 090 928 32 42) runs a 1½hr. ferry from Milazzo to Stromboli (Off season 3 weekly; L16,500; high season 1-2 daily except W and Su; L20,000). From July to September, however, forget finding a room unless you have a reservation; your best bet may be one of the unreservable *affittacamere*. Expect to pay between L30,000 and L50,000 for a room. Try **Casa del Sole**, on Via Giuseppe Cincotta for the best value in accommodations on Stromboli, with a communal kitchen and amazing ocean view. (Apr. 1-May and Oct. L25,000; June and Sept. L30-35,000; July-Aug. L35-40,000.)

SARDINIA (SARDEGNA)

According to Sardinian legend, when God finished making the world, he tossed a handful of leftover earth into the Mediterranean and stepped on it, forming Sardinia. The contours of that divine foot formed spectacular landscapes; the savage coastline, lush green valleys, and pink and yellow mountains inspired D.H. Lawrence to declare that the island had "escaped the net of European civilization." Its most fascinating archaeological finds are its more than 7000 *nuraghe*, cone-shaped fortified tower-houses 3500 years old, made without any mortar.

▬ TRANSPORTATION

Tirrenia **ferries** (☎ 1678 240 79) run from **Civitavecchia** (3½-7½hr., 1-4 per day, L18-110,000), just north of Rome, and **Genoa** (6-13½hr., 1-2 per day, L34-171,000) to **Olbia** on the northern tip of Sardinia. They also chug from Civitavecchia (15½hr., 1 per day, L31-70,000); Naples (15½hr., Jan.-Sept. 1 per week, L28-71,000); Palermo (13½hr., 1 per week, L30-66,500); and to **Cagliari** on the southern tip. **Trains** run from Cagliari to Olbia (4hr., L23,500) via Oristano (1½hr., L8200), branching off between Oristano and Olbia for **Alghero** (from Cagliari 1hr., L8200; from Olbia 4hr., L16,000). PANI **buses** connect major cities (Cagliari to Oristano 1½hr., 11,300).

CAGLIARI

Sardinia's capital peeks out from the southern coast of the island as a polished gem in a land of raw earth. Cagliari gracefully combines the vigor of a bustling city with the rich history of a medieval town. Its Roman ruins, Carthaginian forti-

ITALY

fications, and *nuraghe* fortress-cities contrast with tree-lined streets and flamingo-populated beaches. Climb Largo Carlo Felice to the cramped medieval quarter to reach the city's impressive **duomo**, with dazzling gold mosaics topping each of its entryways. (☎070 66 38 37. Open daily 8am-12:30pm and 4-8pm.) Sardinia's most significant Roman ruin, a 2nd-century BC **Roman ampitheater** comes alive with concerts, operas, and classic plays during the summer **arts festival**. If you prefer to worship the sun, take city **bus** P, PQ, or PF to **Il Poetto beach** (20min., L1500), with pure white sand and turquoise water. The **tourist office** is on P. Matteotti. (☎070 66 92 55. Open in summer M-Sa 8am-8pm; in winter 8am-1:30pm.) The elegant family-run **Pensione Vittoria** is at V. Roma, 75. (☎070 65 79 70. Singles L55-70,000; doubles L85-108,000.)

ALGHERO

Cool breezes blow over sandy beaches in the charming seaside town of Alghero. A leisurely walk through the *centro storico* of Alghero reveals tiny alleyways, half-hidden churches, and ancient town walls. The nearby **Grotte di Nettuno**, an eerie stalactite-filled 60-70 million-year-old cavern complex, can be reached by **bus** (1hr., 3 per day, round-trip L2400). Visitors descend 654 memorable steps between massive white cliffs to reach the ancient cave. (Open daily Apr.-Sept. 9am-7pm; Oct. 10am-5pm; Nov.-Mar. 9am-2pm. L15,000.) The **tourist office**, P. Porta Terra, 9, is to the right from the bus stop and park. (☎079 97 90 54. Open May-Sept. M-Sa 8am-8pm, Su 9am-1pm; Oct.-Apr. M-Sa 8am-2pm.) To get to the **Ostello dei Giuliani (HI)**, V. Zara, 3, 7km away in **Fertilia** but near the beach, take the orange AF city bus from V. La Marmora next to the train station (25min., every 40min., L1100); from the stop, follow the street left as you face the church and turn right on V. Zara. (☎079 93 03 53. Breakfast L2500. Showers L2000. Curfew 11:30pm. Dorms L14,000.)

ORISTANO

The town of Oristano serves as an excellent base for excursions to nearby **beaches** and **archaeological sites.** From the train station, follow V. Vittorio Veneto straight to P. Mariano, then take V. Mazzini to P. Roma to reach the town center (25min.). Explore the stark white cliffs, deep blue water, and ancient ruins at the mystical **Sinis Peninsula.** At the tip, 17 kilometers west of Oristano, lie the ruins of the ancient Phoenician port of **Tharros.** Take the ARST bus to San Giovanni di Sinis (40min., 4 per day, L2800). Gracing the coast slightly to the north off the road to Cuglieri is **S'Archittu,** where glistening youths hurl themselves from a 15m high natural limestone arch into the fabulous waters of a beautiful, rocky inlet. ARST **buses** go to S'Archittu (1hr., 6 per day, L2800). Hop back on the bus and continue to the end of the line to reach the white-quartz sands of **Is Arutas.** The **tourist office**, Pro Loco, V. Vittorio Emanuele, 8, provides maps and local information. (☎0783 706 21. Open M-Sa 9am-12:30pm and 5-8:30pm.) Get some rest at **Piccolo Hotel,** V. Martignano, 19. (☎0783 715 00. Singles L50,000; doubles L100,000.)

LIECHTENSTEIN

PHONE CODE — Liechtenstein uses the Swiss **country code** (41) and international dialing prefix (00). The **city code** is 075 country-wide.

Famous chiefly for its wines, royal family, and yes, postage stamps, Liechtenstein's minute size (160 sq. km) and population (31,320) have not prevented it from having a long and storied history. Ancient history saw an invasion by the Romans in 15 BC, but with the coming of Christianity in the 4th-century, the Germanic Tribes pushed the Romans back out. With this turn of events, the area came under the control of the German Dukedom, creating the two domains of Vaduz and Schellenberg. With the purchase of these two counties by Prince Johann Adam of Liechtenstein in 1712 came the creation of the Principality of Liechtenstein in 1719. The year 1806, however, brought the Principality under the control of Napoleon and the Rhine Confederacy only for it to become part of the German Confederacy in 1815. Continuing its volatile history, Liechtenstein separated from Germany for a final time in 1866 with the dissolution of the German Confederation. Under the rule of Johann II, Liechtenstein was granted a constitution in 1862 and the current constitution in 1921. In 1938, Prince Franz Josef ascended the throne and continued the transformation of Liechtenstein from an impoverished nation into one of the wealthiest in Europe. Continuing in the Swiss tradition, Liechtenstein established itself as an extremely desirable tax haven for international companies and individuals with its strict banking secrecy policies, adding to its incredible wealth. In 1990 Liechtenstein joined the United Nations and in 1995 it joined the European Economic Area.

A recent tourist brochure for Liechtenstein (pop. 31,000) amusingly mislabeled the already tiny 160km² country as an even tinier 160m²; that's just about how much most tourists see of the world's only German-speaking monarchy, pausing only long enough to record the visit in a passport and buy some postage stamps. But the cliff-hanging roads dotted with luxury cars are gateways to unspoiled mountains. **Biking** is a dream in flatter areas, and cheap, efficient **postal buses** link all 11 villages (most trips 2.40SFr; 1-week pass 10SFr, students 5SFr; Swisspass valid). To enter the principality, catch a bus from Sargans or Buchs in Switzerland, or from Feldkirch just across the Austrian border (20min., 3.60SFr). German is the official **language,** but many residents also speak English, French, and an Alemannic dialect. The **currency** is the Swiss franc (SFr). For the **police,** call ☎117, and for **medical emergencies,** call ☎144. **Postal code:** FL-9490.

SUGGESTED ITINERARY

BEST OF LIECHTENSTEIN, TWO (SHORT) DAYS. Spy on some of the Prince's impressive private art collection at the Staatliche Kunstmuseum, and compare stamps in the Briefmarkenmuseum in **Vaduz** (1 day, p. 715), then scan the Swiss and Austrian Alps from the Pfälzerhütte, an isolated mountain hut on the sharp ridge above tiny **Malbun** (1 day, p. 716).

VADUZ   ☎075

More a hamlet than a national capital, Vaduz is not a budget-friendly place. Tourists travel in packs, scrambling furiously to find something worthy of a photo op. Campers and bikers, however, are surrounded by an inviting countryside. The 12th-century **Schloß Vaduz,** the regal home of Hans Adam II, Prince of Liechtenstein, presides above the town. T Housed in the same building as the tourist office, the **Liechtenstein**

Staatliche Kunstmuseum, Städtle 37, houses an impressive collection, including works by Reubens, van Dyck, and Rembrandt. (☎ 232 23 41. Open daily Apr.-Oct. 10am-noon and 1:30-5:30pm; Nov.-Mar. 10am-noon and 1:30-5pm. 5SFr, students 3SFr.) Philatelists (that's stamp collectors to you) flock to the **Briefmarkenmuseum (Stamp Museum),** Städtle 37, near the tourist office. (☎ 232 61 05. Open daily Apr.-Oct. 10am-noon and 1:30-5:30pm; Nov.-Mar. 10am-noon and 1:30-5pm. Free.)

Liechtenstein has an efficient and cheap **Post Bus** system that links all 11 villages (short trips 2.40SFr; long trips 3.60SFr; SwissPass valid). A one-week bus ticket (10SFr, students 5SFr) covers all of Liechtenstein as well as buses to Swiss and Austrian border towns. Liechtenstein's **national tourist office,** Städtle 37, one block up the hill from the Vaduz Post Bus stop, stamps passports (2SFr) and gives advice on hiking, cycling, and skiing. (☎ 232 14 43; email touristinfo@lie-net.li. Open M-F 8am-noon and 1:30-5:30pm; Apr.-Oct. also Sa 10am-noon and 1-4pm, May-Sept. also Su 10am-noon and 1-4pm.) Take bus #1 (dir.: Schaan) to get to the budget-friendly **Hotel Post** in nearby **Schaan,** behind the post office. (☎ 232 17 18. Breakfast included. Reception 8am-11pm. Singles 40SFr, with shower 50SFr; doubles 80SFr, 100SFr.) Liechtenstein's lone **Jugendherberge (HI),** Untere Rütig. 6, is also in Schaan. Take bus #1 to Mühleholz; then turn left down Marianumstr. (☎ 232 50 22. Breakfast included. Dinner 12SFr. Laundry 8SFr. Reception 7-9:30am and 5-10pm. Lockout 9:30am-5pm. Curfew 10pm, key available. Open Feb.-Oct. Dorms 27SFr; doubles 65SFr; quads 113SFr.) **Camping Mittagspitze,** between Triesen and Balzers on the road to Sargans, is easily accessible by post bus. (☎ 373 1211. Reception 8-10am and 4-8pm. 7SFr, tents 4SFr, cars 4SFr.) Buy **groceries** at **Migros,** Aulestr. 20, across from the tour bus parking lot. (Open M-F 8am-1pm and 1:30-6:30pm, Sa 8am-4pm, Su 9am-6pm.) The main **post office** is near the tourist office and has an amazing selection of…postage stamps. (☎ 232 21 55. Open M-F 8am-6pm, Sa 8-11am.) **Postal code:** FL-9490.

UPPER LIECHTENSTEIN

With gorgeous views and great hiking, the villages in the upper country are far more rewarding for visitors than Vaduz. **Triesenberg** (take bus #10), the principal town, was founded in the 13th century by the Walsers, who were fleeing overpopulation, religious intolerance, and natural disaster—the usual. The **tourist office** is in the same building as the **Walser Heimatmuseum,** which chronicles the Walser's religious customs, and crafts. (☎ 262 19 26. Open Tu-F 1:30-5:30pm, Sa 1:30-5pm, Su 2-5pm; Sept.-May closed Su. 2SFr.) For a spectacular Alpine **hike** with views of the Rhine, take bus #30 (dir.: Gaflei). From the bus stop, cross the street to the gravel road and the trail is on the left; follow signs to Silum and then to Ob Tunnel, Steg. On the other side of the mountain, secluded **Malbun** is the hippest place in the principality, harboring approachable people, affordable ski slopes, and plenty of hiking. Contact the **tourist office** for info. (☎ 263 65 77. Open May-Oct. and Dec.-Apr. M-F 9am-noon and 1:30-5pm, Sa 9am-noon and 1-4pm.) Sleep in the chalets, **Hotel Alpen** and **Hotel Galina;** reception for both is at the former. (☎ 263 11 81. Open mid-May-Oct. and mid-Dec. to Apr. Reception from 7:30am-10pm. Summer singles 40SFr, with shower 70SFr, doubles 50-90SFr; in winter singles 70-90SFr, doubles 140-180SFr.)

Liechtenstein

LUXEMBOURG

FRANCS

US$1 = 42.25LUF	10LUF = US$0.24
CDN $1 = 28.59LUF	10LUF = CDN$0.35
UK£1 = 63.94LUF	10LUF = UK£0.16
IR£1 = 51.22LUF	10LUF = IR£0.20
AUS$1 = 24.91LUF	10LUF = AUS$0.40
NZ$1 = 19.83LUF	10LUF = NZ$0.50
SAR1 = 11.26LUF	10LUF = SAR0.89
EUR = 40.34LUF	10LUF = EUR0.25

PHONE CODE	Country Code: 352. International dialing prefix: 00.

Too often overlooked by budget travelers, the tiny (2586 sq. km) Grand Duchy of Luxembourg possesses impressive fortresses and castles, as well as miles of beautiful hiking trails. Founded in AD 963, the Duchy was first named *Luclinburhuc*, or "little castle." By the time successive waves of Burgundians, Spaniards, French, Austrians, and Germans had receded, the little castle had become a bristling armored mountain, and the countryside was saturated with fortresses. Only after the the the Treaty of London restored its neutrality did Luxembourg begin to cultivate its current image of peacefulness. Today the wealthy little nation, with 420,000 residents, is an independent constitutional monarchy, a member of the European Union, and a tax haven for investors worldwide. From the hilly Ardennes in the north to the fertile vineyards of the Moselle Valley in the south, the country's rural landscapes provide a sharp contrast to the high-powered banking in the capital city.

SUGGESTED ITINERARIES

THREE DAYS Be charmed by the capital, **Luxembourg City** (p. 720), gallivanting through the countryside, enjoying the looming spectre of the 10th-century **Boch Casemates** fortress, and visiting the palatial **Grand Ducal Palace.**

BEST OF LUXEMBOURG, ONE WEEK Luxembourg is a charming stopover between France or Belgium and Germany. The surprisingly striking **Luxembourg City,** though a rare stop on most travelers' grand tours, is arguably one of Europe's most beautiful capitals (2 days; p. 720). Your next stop should be **Vianden,** where gorgeous chateaux and outdoors activities make it well worth an overnight stay (1 day). If you have extra time, consider daytripping to **Diekirch** (1 day; p. 723), then hike or bike around **Echternach** and **Grevenmacher** (2 days; p. 724).

LIFE AND TIMES

HISTORY AND POLITICS

The tiny Grand Duchy of Luxembourg (2,586 km, pop. 429,000) has a long history of occupation and domination by its larger European neighbors. Ancient history saw Luxembourg controlled by Belgic tribes, conquered by Romans, and dominated by Franks at the beginning of the Middle Ages. The tiny nation was annexed by the Franks as part of Austrasia, only to become part of the **Holy Roman Empire.** Luxembourg became an independent region in AD 963, under the control of Sieg-

Luxembourg
↑ TO LIÈGE
BELGIUM
Troisvierges
Our R.
Clervaux
Cliert R.
GERMANY
Esch-sur-Sûre
Sûre R.
Vianden
Ettelbrück
Sûre R.
Diekirch
Beaufort
Echternach
Berdorf
TO TRIER →
Sûre R.
Hollenfells
Alzette R.
Bourglinster
Grevenmacher
Arlon
Mosel R.
Luxembourg City
Remich
Longwy
FRANCE
0   10 miles
0   10 kilometers
TO METZ ↓

fried, Count de Ardennes. Siegfried's descendents ruled Luxembourg, eventually taking the title of Count of Luxembourg. The region became a duchy in 1354 by edict of Emperor Charles IV, but in 1443, the Duchess of Luxembourg was forced to hand over the title to Philip III the Good. Luxembourg passed into the hands of the Habsburgs in the late 15th century, only to be controlled by France after the **Thirty Years' War** (1618-1648). During the 17th and 18th centuries Luxembourg was tossed between France and Spain, made a grand duchy and given to **William I,** King of the Netherlands, after the fall of **Napoleon** at Waterloo in 1814. After the 1830 Belgian revolt against William, part of Luxembourg was given to Belgium. A forced economic union with Prussia industrialized the previously agrarian country. The 20th century saw Luxembourg occupied by Germany during both world wars. After being freed by the Allied powers in 1944, Luxembourg became a founding member of the **Benelux Economic Union** with the Netherlands and Belgium.

LUXEMBOURG TODAY

Today Luxembourg enjoys an economic stability that is evidenced by a per capita income and standard of living that is surpassed only by that of Switzerland. The nation is governed by a constitutional monarchy, in which the bulk of the executive power lies on the shoulders of a Prime Minister selected by the Grand Duke, who in turn retains only nominal political power.

ESSENTIALS

DOCUMENTS AND FORMALITIES

The **Luxembourg Card,** available from Easter to October at tourist offices, hostels, and many hotels and public transportation offices, provides unlimited transportation on national trains and buses, and includes admission to 32 tourist sites (1-day 350LF, 2-day 600LF, 3-day 850LF). For more info, contact the **Luxembourg National Tourist Office,** P.O. Box 1001, 1010 Luxembourg (☎ (352) 42 82 82 20; fax 42 82 82 30; email tourism@ont.smtp.etat.lu; www.etat.lu/tourism).

> **Luxembourg Embassies at Home: Australia** (consulate), Level 12, 400 George St., Sydney NSW 2000 (☎ (02) 93 20 02 55; fax 92 62 40 80); **Canada** (consulate), 3877 Draper Ave, Montreal, PQ H4A 2N9 (☎ (514) 849-2101); **South Africa** (consulate), P.O. Box 782922, Sandton 2146 (☎ (011) 463 17 44; 463 32 69); **UK,** 27 Wilton Crescent, London SW1X 8SD (☎ (020) 72 35 69 61); **US,** 2200 Massachusetts Ave. NW, Washington, DC 20008 (☎ (202) 265 4171; fax 328-8270).

LUXEMBOURG

TRANSPORTATION

The Luxembourg City airport is serviced by Luxair (☎ 479 81, reservations ☎ 0800 20 00) and with flights from the UK and throughout the continent. Cheap last-minute flights on Luxair are available at www.luxair.lu. A **Benelux Tourrail Pass** allows five days of unlimited **train** travel in a one-month period in Belgium, the Netherlands, and Luxembourg (6400LUF, under 26 4400LF). The **Billet Réseau** (160LF), a network ticket, is good for one day of unlimited bus and train travel; even better is the **Luxembourg Card** (350 LUF), which covers unlimited transportation and most entrance fees. International gateways to Luxembourg include Liège (2½hr.) and Brussels (see p. 124), Belgium; Metz, France (see p. 384); and Koblenz (2¼hr.; see p. 470) and Trier (see p. 471), Germany. **Hiking** and **biking trails** run between Luxembourg City and Echternach, from Diekirch to Echternach and Vianden, and elsewhere. **Bikes** aren't permitted on buses, but are allowed on many trains for 40LF. **Ettelbrück** (30min.) and **Clervaux** (1hr.) lie on the Luxembourg City-Liège-Belgium rail line; to get to **Vianden**, take a bus from Ettelbrück.

TOURIST SERVICES AND MONEY

TOURIST OFFICES. The **Luxembourg Card**, available from Easter to October at tourist offices, hostels, and many hotels and public transportation offices, provides unlimited transportation on national trains and buses and includes admission to 32 tourist sites (1-day 350LF, 2-day 600LF, 3-day 850LF). For more info, contact the **Luxembourg National Tourist Office**, P.O. Box 1001, 1010 Luxembourg (☎ (352) 42 82 82 210; fax 42 82 82 38; email tourism@ont.smtp.etat.lu; www.etat.lu/tourism).

Tourist Boards at Home: UK, 122 Regent St., London W1R 5FE (☎ (020) 74 34 28 00; fax 77 34 12 05; www.luxembourg.co.uk); **US,** 17 Beekman Pl., New York, NY 10022 (☎ (212) 935-8888; fax 935-5896; www.visitluxembourg.com).

CURRENCY & EXCHANGE. The currency is the Luxembourg **franc**. Luxembourg *francs* are worth the same as Belgian *francs;* you can use Belgian money in Luxembourg, but not vice versa. Expect to pay 1200-1500LF for a hotel room, 435-650LF for a hostel bed, and 280-400LF for a restaurant meal. **Service** (15-20%) is included in the price; tip taxi drivers 10%. The **value-added tax** is already included in most prices. Luxembourg's **VAT refund threshold** (US$85) is lower than most other EU countries; refunds are usually 13% of the purchase price.

ACCOMMODATIONS AND CAMPING

Luxembourg's 12 **HI youth hostels** *(Auberges de Jeunesse)* are generally not filled in summer; hostels are busiest in late spring and early fall with school groups. Prices range from 435-650LF, under 27 355-650LF; nonmembers pay about 110LF extra. Breakfast is included, a packed lunch costs 125LF, and dinner 260LF. Sheets are 125LF. Half of the hostels close from mid-November to mid-December, and the other half close from mid-January to mid-February. Contact **Centrale des Auberges de Jeunesse Luxembourgeoises** (☎ 22 55 88, fax 46 39 87, email information@youth-hostels.lu) for information. **Hotels** advertise 800-1500LF per night but may try to persuade tourists to take more expensive rooms. **Campgrounds** abound. Two people with a tent will typically pay 200-360LF per night.

COMMUNICATION

MAIL. Mailing a postcard or a letter (up to 20g) from Luxembourg costs 21LF to the UK and Europe and 30LF anywhere else.

TELEPHONES. There are no city codes; just dial 352 plus the local number. International direct dial numbers include: **AT&T Direct,** ☎ 0800 01 11; **Australia Direct,** ☎ 0800 00 61; **BT Direct,** ☎ 0800 00 44; **Canada Direct,** 0800 01 19; **Ireland Direct,** ☎ 0800 89 35 30; **MCI WorldPhone,** ☎ 0800 01 12; **NZ Direct,** ☎ 0800 57 84; **Sprint Access,** 0800 01 15.

LANGUAGES. French, German, and, since a referendum in 1984, *Letzebuergesch*, a mixture of the other two that sounds a bit like Dutch. French is most common in the city, where most people also speak English. For basic phrases, see p. 895.

LOCAL FACTS

Time: Luxembourg is 1hr. ahead of Greenwich Mean Time (GMT).

Climate: Luxembourg enjoys a temperate climate with less moisture than Belgium. Anytime between May and mid-Oct. is a good time to visit.

Hours: Most **banks** are open M-F 8:30am-4:30pm; most **shops** are open M 2-6pm and Tu-Sa 9:30am-6pm, though many close at noon for 2hr., especially in the countryside.

Holidays: New Year's Day (Jan. 1); Carnival (Feb. 26); Shrove Monday (Mar. 6); Easter (Apr. 15); Easter Monday (Apr. 16); May Day (May 1); Ascension Day (June 1); Whit Sunday and Monday (June 3-4); National Holiday (June 23); Assumption Day (Aug. 15); All Saints Holiday (Nov. 1); Christmas (Dec. 25); and Boxing Day (Dec. 26).

LUXEMBOURG CITY (VILLE DE LUXEMBOURG)

With its medieval fortress and view of two lush river valleys, the 1000-year-old Luxembourg City (pop. 80,000) is one of the most attractive and dramatic capitals in Europe. Though it is home to thousands of foreign business executives due to its status as an international banking capital, most visitors find it surprisingly relaxed.

▐ TRANSPORTATION

Flights: Findel International Airport, 6km from the city. **Bus #9** (40LF) is cheaper than the Luxair bus (150LF) and runs the same route more frequently (every 20min.).

Trains: Info ☎49 90 49 90 (toll-free); see schedules at www.cfl.lu. **Gare CFL,** av. de la Gare, near the foot of av. de la Liberté, 10min. south of the city center. To: **Amsterdam** (5¾hr.;1680LF, under 26 1360LF); **Brussels** (2¾hr.; 940LF, under 26 520LF); **Frankfurt** (5hr.; 1720LF, under 26 1530 LF); and **Paris** (3½-4hr., 1560LF).

Buses: Buy a **billet courte distance** (short-distance ticket) from the driver (single-fare 40LF, full-day 160LF), or pick up a package of 10 (320LF) at the train station.

Taxis: ☎48 22 33. 32LF per km. 10% premium 10pm-6am; 25% premium on Su. 700-800LF from the city center to the airport.

Bikes: Rent from **Velo en Ville,** 8 rue Bisserwé (☎47 96 23). Open M-F 1-8pm, Sa-Su 9am-noon and 1-8pm. 250LF per half-day, 400LF per day. 20% discount if under 26.

✳ ❷ ORIENTATION AND PRACTICAL INFORMATION

Ten minutes by bus and 20min. by foot from the train station, Luxembourg City's historic center revolves around the **Place d'Armes**. Facing the **tourist office,** located in the commemorative Town Hall, turn right down Rue Chimay to reach **Bvd. Roosevelt.** To reach the museums, Grand Ducal Palace, and Bock Casemates, from the info office, walk straight ahead and onto **Rue Sigeroi.**

Tourist Offices: Grand Duchy National Tourist Office, in the train station, has tons of info and lacks the long lines of the office in town. (☎42 82 82 20; fax 42 82 82 30; www.etat.lu/tourism). Open July-Sept. 9am-7pm, Oct.-June 9:15am-12:30pm and 1:45-6pm. **Municipal Tourist Office,** pl. d'Armes (☎22 28 09; fax 46 70 70). Open Apr.-Sept. M-Sa 9am-7pm, Su 10am-6pm; Oct.-Mar. M-F 9am-6pm, Su 10am-6pm.

Budget Travel: SOTOUR, 15 pl. du Théâtre (☎46 15 14). Sells BIJ and other discount tickets for international flights; makes train reservations that begin or end in Luxembourg. Open M-F 9am-6pm, Sa 9am-noon.

Embassies: Ireland, 28 rue d'Arlon (☎45 06 10; fax 45 88 20). Open M-F 10am-12:30pm and 2:30-5pm. **UK,** 14 bd. Roosevelt (☎22 98 64; fax 22 98 67). Open M-F 9am-12:30pm. **US,** 22 bd. E. Servais (☎46 01 23; fax 46 14 01). Open M-F 8:30am-

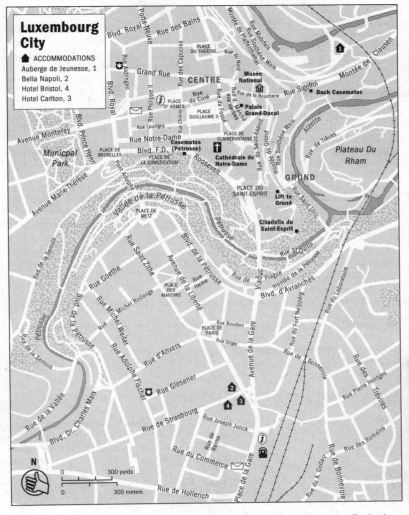

Luxembourg City

♠ ACCOMMODATIONS
Auberge de Jeunesse, 1
Bella Napoli, 2
Hotel Bristol, 4
Hotel Carlton, 3

LUXEMBOURG

12:30pm; visas M-Tu and Th-F 3:30-4:30pm. Australians, Canadians, New Zealanders, and South Africans should contact embassies in France or Belgium.

Luggage Storage: In **train station** 100LF per day (1-month max.); 2-day **lockers** 100LF.

Laundromat: Quick Wash, 31 rue de Strasbourg, near the station. Wash and dry 390F. Open M-Sa 8:30am-6:30pm. Doing your laundry is cheaper at the HI hostel (350F).

Emergencies: Police, ☎ 113. **Ambulance,** ☎ 112.

Pharmacy: Pharmacie Goedert, 5 pl. d'Armes (☎ 2 23 99-1). Open M 1-6:15pm, Tu-F 8am-6:15pm, Sa 8am-12:30pm. Check any pharmacy window for night pharmacy info.

Telephones: Outside post offices and at the train station. Coin-operated phones are rare; buy a 50-unit **phone card** at either place (each good for 50 local calls; 250LF).

Internet Access: Sparky's, 11a Ave Monterey (☎ 6 201 223), at the Pl. d'Armes. One hour 300LF. The only Internet cafe in town. Open daily 8am-8pm.

Post Office: on Rue Phillipine at Pl. D'Armes and 38 pl. de la Gare, across the street, left of the train station. Open M-F 6am-7pm, Sa 6am-noon. Address mail to be held: Imtiyaz DELAWALA, *Poste Restante,* Recette Principale, L-1009 Luxembourg City, Luxembourg.

⚑📷 ACCOMMODATIONS AND FOOD

Luxembourg City does not have bed and breakfasts, which leaves budget travelers with two basic options—the comparatively inexpensive accommodations near the train station, the unofficial red light district of the city, at prices that creep up each year, and the city's hostel, Luxembourg's overnight saviour; see below.

Auberge de Jeunesse (HI), 2 rue du Fort Olisy (☎22 19 20). Take bus #9 and ask to get off at the hostel stop; head under the bridge and turn right down the steep path. Make reservations. Breakfast included. Sheets 125LF. Laundry 300LF. Reception 7am-2am. Curfew 2am. Max 5 night stay in season. Dorms 520-580F, under 26 435-485LF; doubles 1340LF, under 26 1140LF; nonmembers add 110LF.

Bella Napoli, 4 rue de Strasbourg (☎48 46 29), opposite Hotel Carlton. Simple rooms with hardwood floors, all with bathrooms and showers. Breakfast included. Reception 7am-1am. Singles 1500LF; doubles 1800LF; triples 2400LF.

Hotel Bristol, 11 rue de Strasbourg, next to the Hotel Carlton. Comfortable rooms. Remember to clarify what price you will be paying. Breakfast included. Singles 1500-2300LF; doubles 1900-2600LF.

Camping: Kockelscheuer (☎47 18 15). Take bus #2 to Cloche d'Or/Kockelscheuer from the station. Showers included. Open Easter-Oct. 120LF per person, 140LF per tent.

The area around **Pl. d'Armes,** teems with touristy fast-food options and pricey restaurants. Stock up at **Nobilis supermarket,** 47 av. de la Gare. (Open M-F 9am-7:30pm, Sa 8:30am-6pm, Su 9am-1pm.)

Restaurant Bacchus, 32 rue Marché-aux-Herbes (☎47 13 97), down the street from the Grand Ducal palace. Excellent pizza and pasta for 290-440LF. Reservations recommended between 7-10pm. Open Tu-Su noon-10pm.

Le Beaujolais, 2a rue des Capucins (☎47 45 12), next to the Municipal tourist office. Tasty pastas and pizzas at reasonable prices (290-410LF). Sit in velvet booths, or people watch on the Pl. d'Armes. Open daily 11:30am-11:30pm.

Caffe-Veneziano, 16 rue Philippe II (☎22 08 58), serves crepes (80-150LF) and oustanding ice cream sundaes (160-350LF). Open daily 7am-11pm

👁♫ SIGHTS AND ENTERTAINMENT

FORTRESSES AND THE OLD CITY. The 10th-century **Boch Casemates** fortress, part of Luxembourg's original castle, looms over the Alzette River Valley and offers a fantastic view of the Grund and the Clausen. The strategic stronghold was closed in 1867, but was used during WWII to shelter 35,000 people while the rest of the city was ravaged. (*Entrance on rue Sigefroi just past the bridge leading to the hostel. Open Mar.-Oct. daily 10am-5pm. 70LF.*) The **Pétrusse Casemates** were built by the Spanish in the 1600s and later improved by the Austrians. (*On pl. de la Constitution. Open July-Sept. 70LF, children 40LF. Tours every hr. 11am-4pm.*) The guided **Wenzel Walk** leads through 1000 years of history, winding around the old city and down into the casemates. The view from the nearby **Pl. de la Constitution** is always incredible.

MUSEUMS. The **Luxembourg Card** (see p. 719) covers entrance to all museums in the city. The **All-in-One Ticket** covers five museums in two days (350LF at the Municipal Tourist Office). The eclectic collection at the **Musée National d'Histoire et d'Art** chronicles the influences of the various European empires that controlled Luxembourg. (*Marché-aux-Poissons, at rues Boucherie and Sigefroi. Open Tu-Su 10am-5pm. 100LF. Will partially close for renovations in 2001.*) The **Musée d'Histoire de la Ville de Luxembourg** features exhibits that allow you to view the history of the city through photographs, films, and music clips. (*14 rue du St-Esprit.* ☎22 90 50. *Open Tu-Su 10am-6pm, Th til 8pm. 200LF, students 150LF.*)

OTHER SIGHTS. Built as the city hall in 1574, the Renaissance **Grand Ducal Palace** became the official city residence of the Grand Duke in 1890. (*Tours mid-July to Sept 2 M-Sa; tickets sold at the Municipal Tourist Office. Reservations* ☎22 28 09; *specify if you want an*

English language tour. 200LF.) Nearby, the 7th-century **Notre Dame Cathedral,** which incorporates features of the Dutch Renaissance and early Baroque styles, houses the tombs of John the Blind, the 14th-century King of Bohemia and Count of Luxembourg. *(Entrance at bd. Roosevelt. Open Easter-Oct. M-F 10am-5pm, Sa 8am-6pm, Su 10am-6pm; Nov.-Easter M-F 10-11:30am and 2-5pm, Sa 8-11:30am and 2-5pm, Su 10am-5pm. Free.)*

At night, the best tickets in town are free: anyone can watch the sunset from the **Place de la Constitution** on Blvd. Roosevelt, and hear free concerts and stand-up comedy in the Pl. d'Armes. Pick up *La Semaine à Luxembourg* at the tourist office for a list of events. On the Grand Duke's birthday (June 23), the city shuts down to host a large military and religious procession. Nightlife centers on the valley in the **Grund** (by the elevator lift on Pl. du St-Esprit). Check the monthly *Nightlife.lu*, available at most cafés and newsstands. Warm up in the Grund at the candle-lit piano bar **Café des Artistes,** 22 montée du Grund, with biere for 100LF. (☎52 34 46. Open daily 2:30pm-2am, piano W-Sa nights 10:30pm-2am.)

THE ARDENNES

In 1944 the Battle of the Bulge mashed Luxembourg into slime and mud. Now, almost six decades years later, the forest is verdant again, and its quiet towns, looming castles, and sobering WWII monuments are powerful draws.

VIANDEN

Hidden in the dense Ardennes woods, the village of Vianden, home to one of the most impressive castles in Western Europe, is not to be missed. While wealthy Europeans on weekend getaways whiz down Vianden's curvy streets in antique sportscars, backpackers **hike** and **kayak** along the Sûre River, or **bike** to Diekirch (15-20min.) and Echternach (30min.). The **chateau,** a mix of Carolingian, Gothic, and Renaissance architecture, is now filled with medieval armor, 16th-century furniture, 17th-century tapestries, and 20th century photos of official state visitors. From April to September, and March through October, the chateau hosts classical weekend concerts. (☎83 41 08. Open daily Apr.-Sept. 10am-6pm.; Mar. and Oct. 10am-5pm; Nov.-Feb. 10am-4pm. 180LF. Concerts 300-500LF.) For a stellar view of the château, ride the **télésiège** (chairlift), 39 rue de Sanatorium, down the hill and across the river from the chateau. From the **tourist office,** cross the river, go left on rue Victor Hugo, then left again on rue de Sanitorium. (Open Easter-Oct. daily 10am-5pm; July and Aug until 6pm. 90LF; round-trip 160LF.)

Buses arrive from Echternach and Ettelbrück via Diekirch roughly every hour. The **tourist office,** 1 rue du Vieux Marché, next to the main bus stop, has info on kayaking and private rooms (☎83 42 57; fax 84 90 81. Open M-F 9:30am-noon and 2-6pm; high season daily from 9:30am-noon and 1-6pm.) Rent **bikes** at **Beltendorf René.** (☎84 92 22. 550LF per day.) To reach the **HI youth hostel,** 3 montée du Château, from the bus stop or tourist office, follow the Grande Rue away from the river and head up the hill; branch off onto montée du Château and follow the signs. (☎83 41 77. Sheets 125LF. Reception 5-9pm. Lockout 10am-5pm. Curfew 11pm. Open mid-Mar. to mid-Nov. Dorms 455LF, under 26 375LF.) **Camp op dem Deich,** 5min. downstream from the tourist office, is in the shadow of the *château.* (☎83 43 75. Open Easter-Oct. 150LF per person, 150LF per tent.)

DIEKIRCH

Between Vianden and Echternach lies Diekirch. Its **National Museum of Military History,** 10 Bamertal, presents a comprehensive exhibition of relics from WWII's Battle of the Bulge. Highlights include pictures taken by a German propaganda unit at the Battle of the Bulge, showing captured US Infantrymen. (☎80 89 08. Open daily Apr.-Nov. 10am-6pm; Dec.-Mar. 2-6pm. 200LF, students 120LF.) Around the corner from the military museum, the **Municipal Museum,** on pl. Guillaume, houses three Roman mosaics. (Open Easter-Oct. F-W 10am-noon and 2-6pm. 50LF.) Turn right onto Esplenade and then onto Zone Pietone to find the 15th-century **Egise Saint-Laurent.** (Open Tu-Su Easter-Oct. 10am-noon and 2-6pm.) Trains arrive from Ettlebruck at the train station hourly; from the station take the bus to Vianden (25min.). Buses stop for Vianden in the center of Diekirch at end of the Zone Pietone, in front of the nursing home. Buses roll in from Echternach hourly, and drop you off on the Esplanade in front of the Municipal Museum. To get to the **tourist information**, 3 Pl. de la Liberation, take the underground stairs to Rue St. Antione, walk to the end, and its directly across the Place. (☎80 30 23. Open daily 9am-5:30pm.) Stay across from the bus stop, at **Au Beau-Sejour**, 12 Esplanade. (☎80 34 03. Reception 8am-midnight. Singles 1500LF; doubles 2500LF.)

CLERVAUX

Northwest of Vianden and Diekirch lies tiny Clervaux, whose **chateau** houses the striking **Family of Man** exhibition, which contains 500 pictures from 68 countries depicts every facet of human life, and was compiled in 1955 by Luxembourgian photographer Edward Steichen for at the Museum of Modern Art in New York. The exhibit was displayed worldwide before being permanently installed in Clervaux. (☎92 96 57. Open Mar.-Dec. Tu-Su 10am-noon and 1-6pm. 150LF, students 80LF.) To get to the chateau and the **Benedictine Abbey** lying in Cleavaux, turn left from to the train station and walk straight. The **tourist information office,** in the castle, books private rooms at Clervaux's bed and breakfasts. (☎92 00 72. Open daily Apr.-June 30 2-5pm; July-Oct 9:45am-11:45am and 2-6pm; closed Su Sept and Oct.)

THE MOSELLE VALLEY (LA MOSELLE)

The **Moselle Valley,** with its sunny weather and fertile land, was discovered by French winemakers as a suitable substitute for the Champagne region. Today the valley is famous for its sparkling wines (often marked *méthode traditionelle*), but also for still wines such as *Riesling* and *Pinot Gris*.

GREVENMACHER

The town of Gravenmacher is at the heart of Moselle's wine culture and makes for a leisurely afternoon visit. Begin with a tour of the **Bernard-Massard winery,** rue du Pont, to learn about the Champagne method and enjoy a glass of sparkling wine. From the tourist office, turn right on rte. du Vin, then enter the *cave* through the gate. (☎75 05 45. Open daily Apr.-Oct. 9:30am-6pm. 100LF.) A small but spectacular **Jardin des Papillons** (Butterfly Garden) lies 10min. down rte. du Vin from the information office. (☎75 85 39. Opendaily Apr. to mid-Oct. 9:30am-5pm. 180LF.) To get to Gravenmacher from Luxembourg City, take the **train** to Wasserbillig (40 min.) and the **bus** to Gravenmacher. From the bus stop, turn left on rue de Treves, left on rue de la Moselle, and stop by the **tourist information office,** 10 rte. du Vin. (☎75 82 75. Open M-F 8am-noon and 2pm-5pm.) Stay in an old farmhouse behind a hill at **Scher Paul (HI),** Fruewereck 15, reached by turning left on Rte. de Treves from the bus station, right on R.P. D'Osbourg, and left onto Grou Wenreck. (☎75 02 22. Sheets 125BF. Reception 8am-noon and 5-8pm. Dorms 455LF, under 26 375LF.)

LITTLE SWITZERLAND (LE MULLERTHAL)
ECHTERNACH

A favorite vacation spot of European families, the Lower-Sûre village of **Echternach** is famous for its millenial rock formations and 7th-century monastic center. In the Middle Ages, the monastic center was known for its illuminated manuscripts; several are at the 18th-century Benedictine **Abbaye.** From the bus station, go left at the marketplace on rue. de la Gare, take the last left, and walk past the basilica. (Open July-Aug. 10am-6pm; June and Sept. 10am-noon and 2-6pm; Oct.-May 10am-noon and 2-5pm. 80LF.) Echternach is accessible by **bus** from the Ardennes towns and Luxembourg City. The **tourist office** is on Porte St-Willibrord next to the abbey. (☎72 02 30. Open M-F 9am-noon and 2-5pm; in high season open weekends.) To get from the bus station to the **youth hostel (HI),** 9 rue. André Drechscher, turn left on av. de la Gare, and make your last right. (☎72 01 58. Sheets 125LF. Reception 5-11pm. Lockout 10am-5pm. Closes one month in winter. 455LF, under 26 375LF.)

THE NETHERLANDS
(NEDERLAND)

GUILDERS

US$1 = F2.56	F1 = US$0.39
CDN$1 = F1.73	F1 = CDN$0.58
UK£1 = F3.61	F1 = UK£0.28
IR£1 = F2.80	F1 = IR£0.36
AUS$1 = F1.44	F1 = AUS$0.69
NZ$1 = F1.10	F1 = NZ$0.91
SAR1 = F0.36	F1 = SAR2.78
EUR€1 = F2.20	F1 = EUR€0.45

PHONE CODE	Country code: 31. International dialing prefix: 00.

The Dutch say that although God created the rest of the world, they created the Netherlands. The country is a masterful feat of engineering; since most of it is below sea level, vigorous pumping and a series of dikes were used to create thousands of square miles of land known as *polders*. What was once the domain of seaweed and cod is now packed with windmills, bicycles, tulips, cheese, Vermeers, van Goghs, and the occasional wooden shoe. Although devastated by two world wars, the Dutch have rebuilt their cities under the stark, modernist influence of Mondrian's de Stijl school and the architecture of Mies van der Rohe. The Netherlands' wealth of art, its canal-lined towns, and the (ahem) uniqueness of Amsterdam's perpetual party are reflected in the hordes of travelers that double the country's population every summer.

SUGGESTED ITINERARIES

THREE DAYS Soak in the blend of substances and culture in **Amsterdam** (p. 732). Stroll along cobblestoned streets and visit the impressive **Rijksmuseum** (p. 740), **Van Gogh Museum** (p. 740), and **Ann Frank House** (p. 742). But get lost in in the **Red Light District** (p. 741).

ONE WEEK Begin with two days in **Amsterdam** (p. 732), then take the train to **Haarlem** (1 day; p. 748). Stop by nearby **Aalsmeer** (1 day; p. 748) for the world's largest flower auction or tan yourself on the nude beaches in **Zandvoort** (1 day; p. 748). From **The Hague** (1 day; p. 750), make your way to **Utrecht** (p. 753) before heading back to **Amsterdam**.

BEST OF THE NETHERLANDS, TWO WEEKS Chill in **Amsterdam** (3 days, p. 732), with daytrips to **Edam** or **Hoorn** (1 day; p. 747). Then take the train to **Haarlem** (1 day; p. 748) before heading on to **Aalsmeer** (1 day; p. 748). Catch some rays in **Zandvoort** (1 day; p. 748), and make your way to **The Hague** (1 day; p. 750). Swing by **Rotterdam** (1 day; p. 752), then head to **Utrecht** for a return to European charm (2 days; p. 753). Take the train to **Maastricht** (1 day; p. 755) and head north to hike in the **Hoge Veluwe National Park,** using **Arnhem** as your base (2 days; p. 754), before trekking to **Groningen** (1 day; p. 756).

LIFE AND TIMES

HISTORY AND POLITICS

FROM ROMANS TO HABSBURGS (100 BC TO 1550AD)

Julius Caesar invaded the region in the 1st century BC and established Roman control through the 4th century. With the fall of Rome, the **Franks** merely took the place of the Romans until the 8th century. This period experienced the rise of towns as centers of power which were only loosely connected to each other. This quickly changed though in the 14th century when the **House of Burgundy** infiltrated these towns to establish a more centralized monarchy. By 1482, the Austrian **Habsburgs** had managed to marry into the throne. This move began the long and volatile history of the Netherlands; the area quickly came under Spanish control when **Philip I** of Habsburg inherited the Spanish crown in 1493.

UTRECHT AND THE WAR WITH SPAIN (1579-1648)

The Netherlands was officially founded in 1579 with the **Union of Utrecht,** which aimed at forming an independent group of provinces and cities which would be led by the **States-General.** Under the leadership of **Prince William of Orange,** the Dutch declared independence from King Philip II of Spain in 1580. The result was a prolonged struggle and series of invasions by Spain. The conflict was settled in 1609 with the drafting of the **Twelve Years' Truce,** which included Spanish recognition of the individual sovereignty of the Netherlands. Unfortunately, this peace was short-lived; Spain resumed the war in 1621. Frederick Henry of the House of Orange led the Dutch to stunning victories, while the Dutch navy thwarted the Spanish in battles off Cuba as well as the English coast. The Spanish quickly reacted by offering the **Peace of Westfalia** which not only acknowledged Dutch independence, but also pushed for friendship in order to hedge the growing power of France.

During the Age of Exploration which spanned the 17th century, Dutch conquerors fanned out over the globe and gained control of all the major trade routes across Europe. This created incredible wealth for the Dutch, the majority of which was generated by the **Dutch East India Company.** The company ventured to the Far East for spices, while also colonizing the Cape of Good Hope and other strategic posts for protecting their trade routes. Meanwhile, the **Dutch West India Company** was exploring the New World, creating new colonies such as New Amsterdam (which later became New York). All of this activity created unprecedented growth in Amsterdam which served as the chief port for the Netherlands.

WAR GAMES AND POWER STRUGGLES (1650-1795)

The success and power of the Netherlands became a major target of its neighboring European powers. The year 1651 ushered in an almost constant period of war and changing alliances for the Netherlands. England began by passing the **Navigation Act,** limiting Dutch involvement in English trade and then by launching a military attack on the Dutch navy. Peace was made soon after, however, and councillor Johan de Witt managed to rebuild the Netherlands. Unfortunately the restored King **Charles II** of England decided to re-start the war. The Dutch instantly negotiated an alliance with the French and sabotaged the English fleet.

Immediately after, in 1667, the French invaded the Netherlands threatening both England and the Dutch, pushing them to make peace and become allies. This infuriated King **Louis XIV** of France, leading him to believe the Dutch had betrayed him, so he offered the English a highly subsidized alliance in return. In 1672, the Netherlands found itself in a full-scale war with the two countries, but under the renewed leadership of **William III** managed to repeatedly defeat the allied fleets. This brought Spain and Germany into the war in support of the Dutch, forcing both France and England to retreat. Ironically, William was crowned king of England in 1688, only 14 years after defeating it in battle. With this turn of events, however, the Netherlands found itself subordinated to English will. The Dutch then saw their grip on

The Netherlands

international trade quickly erode with the expansion of French and English competition throughout the 18th century. Despite this, the nation experienced a relatively peaceful time in its history.

FRENCH RULE AND INDEPENDENCE (1795-1900)

In 1795, however, **Napoleon Bonaparte** invaded Holland and established French rule. The occupation came to an end with Napoleon's defeat at Waterloo, and the **Treaty of Vienna** (1815) established the Kingdom of the Netherlands, which also included Belgium and Luxembourg. Dutch King **William I of Orange** was placed as ruler and managed to rebuild the economy and trade routes. Soon after, the Belgians decided that they could not live under Dutch rule, so after a revolt and international intervention, Belgium gained independence in 1839. Luxembourg soon followed their lead. Under the rule of **William III** (1849-1890), the Dutch created a constitution which established the Netherlands as a constitutional monarchy where the parliament held the majority of power. It was during this time that the formation of modern political parties began. William's death in 1890 lead to the end of male succession for the throne and paved the way for **Wilhelmina** to become queen.

THE WORLD WARS (1914-1945)

The outbreak of **World War I** posed a serious threat to the Netherlands, but it managed to remain neutral while focusing its attention on maintaining its trade and economy. After the war, the Netherlands strictly reaffirmed its neutrality despite Belgian attempts to cede Dutch lands (the issue was settled by the **Treaty of Versailles**). The Dutch did not fare as well in **World War II**. Without warning, the Nazis invaded in May 1940 and occupied the nation for just under five years. Queen Wilhelmina and the government fled to England to try to run the country in exile. The Dutch suffered horribly—all acts of resistance were severely punished, the majority of Dutch Jews were sent to concentration camps, and the general population was in near-famine conditions.

THE POSTWAR ERA (1946-1990)

Returning from exile after the war, Wilhelmina proceeded to participate in sweeping democratic changes for the nation. Universal suffrage was granted as well as proportional representation. The nation also abandoned its policy of neutrality in favor of joining NATO as well as a "closer union" with Belgium and Luxembourg. The government also managed to provide a strong economic policy which focused on industrial and commercial expansion to pull it out of the destruction of the war.

While the nation experienced relative peace through the 1950s, the 60s ushered in the rioting of students and workers which was seen around the world. In the 1980s, Dutch politics saw the disintegration of parties as well as old alliances. The recent rise of the **Christian Democratic Appeal** (CDA) has provided a new outlet for the major Christian factions. While the **Labour party** (PvdA) has managed to avoid extremist groups, it had to form a coalition government in 1989 with the CDA.

THE NETHERLANDS TODAY

Most recently, Dutch politics has seen the resurgence of the Labour party with increased support for the Green Left Party, which focuses on environmental issues. **Wim Kok** (a member of the Labour party) was re-elected as Prime Minister in 1998. The government continues as a constitutional monarchy with the legislative power residing in the Parliament, while the Monarchy retains a symbolic role. The Netherlands continue to be integral in the continual evolution of the European Union (EU) and the administration of the euro which was adopted in 1999.

THE ARTS

VISUAL ARTS

The Netherlands have been the home for trendsetters in the world of painting. A founding member of the group eventually known as the **Flemish Primitives, Jan van Eyck** refined techniques of oil painting, working with glazes and layers of color to produce pieces of amazing detail. His most well-known painting is the *Adoration of the Mystic Lamb*, the altarpiece of **St. Baal's Cathedral** in **Ghent,** controversial because of the unknown degree to which his brother **Herbert** might have participated in its creation. In the 16th century, **Pieter Bruegel the Elder** mastered the balance between form and space which Italian art at that time had seemed to perfect. Bruegel's pieces were notable for their innovative religious interpretations. His *Landscape with the Fall of Icarus* and the *Triumph of Death* share a particular monumentality despite being very different in tone. A few centuries later, **Vincent van Gogh** was responsible for creating a collection of paintings of an intensely personal style. His work is characterized by bright, often harshly contrasting colors, painted on in thick brush strokes; as witnessed in his *Self-Portrait* and *Starry Night* (both from 1889). Van Gogh settled in Arles, France in the last years of his life; he captured the dry, sunny landscape in works such as *The Harvest* (1888). The mental illness which led him to cut off his own ear is perhaps one of the most famous examples of psychosis, and ultimately resulted in his suicide in 1890.

LITERATURE

Dutch literature can be traced back to the 10th century when the Old Dutch *Wachtendonck Psalm Fragments* were written. The most influential works, however, didn't come until the Dutch **Golden Age** in early 17th century. The primary author of the time was **Henric Laurenszoon Spieghel,** whose *Hertspieghel* (1614) presented the first philosophical work written in Dutch. Further legitimizing the Dutch language, the Reformed Church commissioned the first translation of the Bible into Dutch which resulted in the *States Bible* (1620). **Joost van den Vondel** completed the ascendancy of the Dutch with his dramatic tragedies and satirical treatment of the church and government. His *Lucifer* (1654) is still a masterpiece today chronicling the conflict between the angels and God. Dutch literature, unfortunately, declined throughout the 18th century as a result of the explosion in financial wealth and trade associated with Dutch imperialism. **Nicolaas Beets** led the recovery in 1839 with the publication of *Camera Obscura* which drew on the humor of Charles Dickens and Laurence Sterne. With the terror of **World War I** and **World War II** came a new focus in Dutch literature which concerned itself with social and philosophical questions. **Willem Frederik Hermans** provides a gripping treatment of the hostile environment in *De donkere kamer van Damocles* (1958).

FOOD AND DRINK

Dutch food is hearty and simple. Pancakes, salted herring, and pea soup are national specialties. Dutch cheeses transcend Gouda and Edam; try Leiden, the mild Belegen, and the creamy Kernhem too. A typical breakfast consists of meat and cheese on bread and a soft boiled egg. For a hearty brunch, try *uitsmijter*, which packs in salad, ham, cheese, and fried eggs. At dinner, reap the benefits of Dutch imperialism: *rijsttafel* is an Indonesian specialty comprising up to 25 different dishes, including curried chicken or lamb with pineapple. *Pannenkoeken* is the traditional Dutch lunch of buttery, sugary, golden brown pancakes, topped with everything from ham and cheese to strawberries and whipped cream. Wash it all down with a small, foamy glass of hometown **beer** Heineken or Amstel.

ESSENTIALS

DOCUMENTS AND FORMALITIES

Citizens of Australia, Canada, the EU, New Zealand, and the US do not need visas for stays shorter than 3 months. South Africans need visas for visits of any duration.

Netherlands Embassies at Home: Australia, 120 Empire Circuit, Yarralumba ACT 2600 (☎ (02) 62 73 31 11; fax 62 73 32 06); **Canada,** 350 Albert St., Suite 2020, Ottawa, ON K1R 1A4 (☎ (613) 237-5030; fax 237-6471); **Ireland,** 160 Merrion Rd., Dublin 4 (☎ (01) 269 34 44; fax 283 96 90); **New Zealand,** P.O. Box 840, Wellington (☎ (04) 471 63 90; fax 471 29 23); **South Africa,** P.O. Box 346, Cape Town 8000 (☎ (021) 421 56 60; fax 418 26 90); **UK,** 38 Hyde Park Gate, London SW7 5DP (☎ (020) 75 90 32 00; fax 75 81 34 58); **US,** 4200 Linnean Ave. NW, Washington, DC 20008 (☎ (202) 244-5300; fax 362-3430; www.netherlands-embassy.org).

Foreign Embassies and Consulates in the Netherlands: All embassies and most consulates are located in **The Hague** (see p. 750). The **UK** and the **US** also have consulates in **Amsterdam** (see p. 732).

TRANSPORTATION

BY PLANE. KLM Royal Dutch Airlines, Martinair, Continental, Delta, Northwest, United, and Singapore Airlines serve **Amsterdam's** Schiphol Airport. Amsterdam is a major hub for cheap transatlantic flights (see p. 732).

BY TRAIN. The national rail company is the efficient **Nederlandse Spoorwegen** (NS; Netherlands Railways; info ☎ (09) 00 92 92; www.ns.nl). Train service tends to be faster than bus service. *Sneltreins* are the fastest; *stoptreins* make the most stops. One-way tickets are called *enkele reis;* normal round-trip tickets, *retour;* and day return tickets (valid only on day of purchase, but cheaper than normal round-trip tickets), *dagretour.* **Day Trip (Rail Idee)** programs, available at train stations, have reduced-price combo transportation/entrance fees. **Eurail** and **InterRail** (see p. 48) are valid in the Netherlands. The **Holland Railpass** (US$52-98) is good for three or five travel days in any one-month period. Although available in the US, the Holland Railpass is cheaper in the Netherlands at DER Travel Service or RailEurope. The **Euro Domino Holland** card similarly allows three (f130, under 26 f100), five (f200, f150), or 10 days (f350, f275) of unlimited rail travel in any one-month period, but is only available to those who have lived in Europe for at least six months and cannot be bought in the Netherlands. **One-day train passes** cost f45.25-75.50. The **Meerman's Kaart** grants one day of unlimited travel for two to six people (f114-192).

BY BUS. A nationalized fare system covers city buses, trams, and long-distance buses. The country is divided into zones; the number of strips on a **strippenkaart** (strip card) required depends on the number of zones through which you travel. The base charge within a city is two strips, and travel between towns costs from five to 20 strips. On buses, tell the driver your destination and he or she will cancel the correct number of strips; on trams and subways, stamp your own *strippenkaart* in either a yellow box at the back of the tram or in the subway station. Bus and tram drivers sell two- (f3.50), three- (f4.75), and eight-strip tickets (f12), but they're *much* cheaper in bulk, available at public transit counters, tourist offices, post offices, and some tobacco shops and newsstands (15-strip f11.50, 45-strip f33.75). **Dagkaarten** (day tickets) are available for one to nine days (one-day f11). Riding without a ticket can result in a f60 fine plus the original cost of the ticket.

BY FERRY. Ferries traverse the North Sea, connecting **England** to the Netherlands. Boats arrive in **Hook of Holland** (3¾-8½hr.), near Delft and The Hague, from **Harwich**, northeast of London; in **Rotterdam** from **Hull** (13½hr.), near York (p. 217); and in **Amsterdam** from **Newcastle-upon-Tyne** (14hr.; p. 221). For more info, see p. 47.

BY CAR. The Netherlands has well-maintained roadways. North Americans and Australians need an International Driver's License; if your insurance doesn't cover you abroad, you'll also need a green insurance card. On maps, a green "E" indicates international highways; a red "A," national highways; and small yellow signposts and "N," other main roads. Speed limits are 50km per hr. in towns, 80km outside, and 120km on highways. Fuel prices per liter average about f2.30. The **Royal Dutch Touring Association** (ANWB) offers roadside assistance to members (☎ (06) 08 88). For more info, contact the ANWB at Wassenaarseweg 220, 2596 EC The Hague (☎ (070) 314 71 47), or Museumsplein 5, 1071 DJ Amsterdam (☎ (020) 673 08 44).

BY BIKE AND BY THUMB. Cycling is the way to go in the Netherlands—distances between cities are short, the countryside is absolutely flat, and most streets have separate bike lanes. Bikes run about f8 per day or f35 per week plus a f50-200 deposit (railpasses will often earn you a discount). Call the station a day ahead to reserve; phone numbers are listed in the free *Fiets en Trein*. For info try www.visitholland.com. Hitchhiking is somewhat effective, but on the roads out of Amsterdam there is cutthroat competition. For more info about hitching, visit www.hitchhikers.org. *Let's Go* does not recommend hitchhiking.

TOURIST SERVICES AND MONEY

EMERGENCY	Police, Ambulance, and Fire: ☎ 112

TOURIST OFFICES. VVV (vay-vay-vay) tourist offices are marked by triangular blue signs. They also have info on the **Museumjaarkaart** passes that cover admission to most of the 800 museums in the Netherlands. Contact **Museumjaarkaart Stichting** for more info. (☎ (020) 670 11 11. f55, under 25 f25; bring a passport-size photo).

Tourist Offices at Home: Canada, 25 Adelaide St. E #710, Toronto ON H5C 1Y2 (☎ (416) 363-1577; fax 363-1470). **South Africa,** P.O. Box 781738, Sandton 2146 (☎ (11) 884 81 41; fax 883 55 73). **UK** and **Ireland,** P.O. Box 523, London SW1E 6NT (☎ (020) 79 31 06 61; fax 78 28 79 41). **US,** 355 Lexington Ave., New York, NY 10017 (☎ (888) 464-6552; fax (212) 370-9507; www.goholland.com).

CURRENCY AND EXCHANGE. The Dutch currency is the **guilder** (f, a.k.a. florin), made up of 100 cents. Coins include the *stuiver* (5¢), *dubbeltje* (10¢), *kwartje* (25¢), and *rijksdaalder* (f2.50). Post offices offer reasonable **currency exchange**

rates; **GWK** often has the best rates and doesn't charge ISIC holders commission. Otherwise, expect a flat fee of about f5 and a 2.25% commission.

Prices: A bare-bones day traveling in the Netherlands will cost US$15-25; a slightly more comfortable day will run US$30-40.

Tipping and Bargaining: A 5-10% gratuity will generally be added to your hotel, restaurant and taxi bills. An additional 5% is common for superior service.

Taxes: VAT refunds in the Netherlands are usually 13.5%, and are available on purchases of more than f300 made during a single visit to a store.

ACCOMMODATIONS AND CAMPING

VVV offices supply accommodations lists and can nearly always reserve rooms in both local and other areas (fee around f4). **Private rooms** cost about two-thirds as much as hotels, but they are hard to find; check with the VVV. During July and August, many cities add approximately f2.50 tourist tax to the price of all rooms. The country's best values are the 35 **HI youth hostels,** run by the **NJHC (Dutch Youth Hostel Federation);** hostels are divided into four price categories based on quality. Most are exceedingly clean and modern and cost f28-34 for bed and breakfast, plus high-season or prime-location supplements (f1-3). The VVV has a hostel list, and the useful *Jeugdherbergen* brochure describes each one (both free). For more info, contact the NJHC at Prof. Tulpstraat 2, Amsterdam (☎ (020) 551 31 33; fax 623 49 86). Pick up a membership card at hostels (f30); nonmembers are charged an additional f5. **Camping** is available country-wide, but many sites are crowded and trailer-ridden in summer. An **international camping card** is not required.

COMMUNICATION

MAIL. Post offices are generally open M-F 9am-5pm, and some are also open Sat. 9am-12noon. Mailing a postcard or letter to the UK costs f1; to destinations outside Europe, postcards cost f1, letters (up to 20g) f1.60. Mail takes 2-3 days to the UK, 4-6 to North America, 6-8 to Australia and New Zealand, and 8-10 to South Africa.

TELEPHONES. When making international calls from pay phones, phone cards (in denominations of f10; available at post offices and train stations) are the most economical option. For directory assistance, dial 0900 8008 within the Netherlands or 06 04 18 from outside the country; for collect calls, dial 06 04 10. International dial direct numbers include: **AT&T,** 0800 022 91 11; **Sprint,** 0800 022 91 19; **Australia Direct,** 0800 022 20 61; **BT Direct,** 0800 022 00 44; **Canada Direct,** 0800 022 91 16; **Ireland Direct,** 0800 02 20 353; **MCI WorldPhone Direct,** 0800 022 91 22; **NZ Direct,** 0800 022 44 64; **Telekom South Africa Direct,** 0800 022 02 27.

INTERNET ACCESS. Email is easily accessible within the Netherlands. Cybercafes are listed in most towns and all cities. In small towns, if internet access is not listed, try the library or even your hostel. Internet access generally runs f10 per hour, except in libraries where it's often free.

LANGUAGE. Dutch is the official language of The Netherlands, however most natives speak English fluently. Knowing a few words of Dutch can't hurt though. Fill up on *dagschotel* (dinner special), *broodje* (bread or sandwich), *bier* (beer), and *kaas* (cheese). Dutch uses a gutteral "g" sound for both "g" and "ch." "J" is usually pronounced as "y"; e.g., *hofje* is "hof-YUH." "Ui" is pronounced "ow," and the dipthong "ij" is best approximated in English as "ah" followed by a long "e." For more basic lingo, see p. 959.

LOCAL FACTS

Time: The Netherlands is 1hr. ahead of Greenwich Mean Time (GMT).

Climate: Mid-May to early October is the ideal time to visit, when the day temperatures are generally 20-31°C (70-80°F), with nights around 10-20°C (50-60°F). However, it can be quite rainy; bring an umbrella. The tulip season runs from Apr. to mid May.

Hours: Banks open M-F 10am-4pm, occasionally also Th 6-8pm or 7-9pm. **Stores** are generally open M 1-6pm, Tu-F 9am-6pm, and Sa 9am-5pm. Some stay open later Th-F.

Holidays: The major holidays in The Netherlands are: New Year's Day (Jan. 1); Good Friday (Apr. 13); Easter Monday (Apr. 16); Queen's Birthday (Apr. 29); Liberation Day (May 5); Ascension Day (June 1); Whit Monday (June 4); Christmas Day (Dec. 25); and Boxing Day (Dec. 26).

Festivals: Koninginnedag (Queen's Day; Apr. 30) features huge parties. The Hague hosts the huge North Sea Jazz Festival (July 13-15, 2001). The Holland Festival (in June) celebrates the nation's cultural diversity. Bloemen Corso (Flower Parade; first Sa in Sept.) runs from Aalsmeer to Amsterdam. Many historical canal houses and windmills open to the public for National Monument Day (2nd Sa in Sept.).

AMSTERDAM ☎ 020

Some people say that the best vacation to Amsterdam is the one you can't remember. True, the city lives up to its reputation as a never-never land of bacchanalian excess: the aroma of cannabis wafts from coffeeshops, and the city's infamous sex scene swathes itself in red lights. Despite how blasé most revelers try to seem amidst the many varieties of debauchery, Amsterdam will challenge you, stoned or not, by giving you the choice of exactly how you want to trip, turn, or twist through reality. But one need not be naughty to enjoy Amsterdam. Art enthusiasts will delight in the troves of Rembrandts, Vermeers, and van Goghs, and romantics can stroll along endless cobblestoned streets and canals sparkling with reflected lights.

✈ GETTING THERE AND AWAY

Flights: Schiphol Airport (SKIP-pull; ☎ (0900) 01 41, f1 per min.). **Trains** connect the airport to Centraal Station (20min., every 10min., f6.50).

Trains: Centraal Station, Stationspl. 1, at the end of the Damrak (for international info ☎ (0900) 92 96, domestic info (0900) 92 92, f0.50 per min.; schedules at www.ns.nl/reisplan2a.asp). To: **Berlin** (8hr.); **Brussels** (3-4hr.); **Frankfurt** (5¼-6hr.); **Hamburg** (5hr.); and **Paris** (8hr.). For international info and reservations, take a number and wait (up to 1hr. in summer). Info desk open 24hr.; International reservations made daily 6:30am-11:30pm. **Lockers** f4-6.

⊟ GETTING AROUND

Buses: Trains are quicker, but the **GVB** (public transportation authority) will direct you to a bus stop for destinations not on a rail line. **Muiderpoort** (2 blocks east of Oosterpark) sends buses east; **Marnixstation** (at the corner of Marnixstr. and Kinkerstr.) west; and the **Stationsplein depot** north and south.

Public Transportation: GVB (☎ (06) 92 92), Stationspl; in front of Centraal Station. Open daily M-F 7am-9pm, Sa-Su 8am-9pm. Tram, metro, and bus lines radiate from Centraal Station. Trams are most convenient for inner-city travel; the metro leads to farther-out neighborhoods. The last trams leave Centraal Station M-F at midnight; Sa-Su 12:25am. Pick up a *nachtbussen* (night bus) schedule from the GVB office. The GVB sells offers day tickets for visitors to Amsterdam for f11 for 1 day, f17 for 2 days, and f22 for 3 days. Don't buy *dagkaart* (day passes; f12) on the bus; you'll pay dearly. The 45-strip *strippenkaart* (f35.25) is the best deal; it can be used on trams and buses throughout Holland and is available at the VVV, the GVB, and many hostels.

Taxis: (☎ 677 77 77.) Fares from f4.80 plus f2.80 per km or min. (more at night). Stands at the Dam, Spui, Nieuw Markt, Rembrantspl., Leidsepl., and Centraal Station.

Bike Rental: Beware of rampant bike theft. All train stations rent plain ol' bikes for f9.50 per day, f30 per week with a train ticket. **Damstraat Rent-a-Bike,** Pieter Jacobstr. 11 (☎ 625 50 29), is just off Damstr. near the Dam. Rentals f15 per day, f67 per week (plus a credit card slip); used bikes sold for f200 and up. Open daily 9am-6pm.

Amsterdam

⌂ ACCOMMODATIONS

Budget Hotel, 7
Casa Cara, 11
Euphemia Budget
  Hotel, 6
Hans Brinker, 5
Hotel Arrivé, 1
Hotel Bema, 10
Hotel Hortus, 14
Hotel Museumzicht, 2

Hotel van Onna
  International, 4
Lillane's Home, 12
NJHC City Hostel
  Vondelpark, 8
The Arena, 13
The Flying Pig:
  Vondelpark, 9
The Shelter: Jordaan, 3

Hitchhiking: Hitching is becoming less common in the Netherlands, but can still be done. *Let's Go* does not recommend hitchhiking. Hitchhiking is not allowed on Dutch highways. Those heading to **Utrecht,** central and southern Germany, and Belgium take tram #25 to the end and start at the bridge; **Groningen** and northern Germany, take bus #56 to Prins Bernhardpl., or the metro to Amstel, and start along Gooiseweg; **The Hague,** hop on tram #16 or 24 to Stadionpl. and start on the other side of the canal on Amstelveenseweg; **Haarlem** and **Noord Holland,** take bus #22 to Haarlemmerweg and start from Westerpark.

✸ ORIENTATION

A series of roughly concentric canals ripple out around the **Centrum** (city center), resembling a giant horseshoe with its opening to the northeast. Emerging from Centraal Station, at the top of the horseshoe, you'll hit **Damrak,** a key thoroughfare leading to the **Dam,** the main square. Just east of Damrak in the Centrum is Amsterdam's famed **red-light district,** bounded by Warmoestr., Gelderskade, and Oude Doelenstr. Don't head into the area until you've locked up your bags, either at the train station or at a hostel or hotel. South of the red-light district but still within the horseshoe lies the **Rembrandtsplein.** The canals radiating around the Centrum (lined by streets of the same names) are **Singel, Herengracht, Keizergracht,** and **Prinsengracht.** West of the Centrum, beyond Prinsengracht, lies the **Jordaan,** an attractive residential neighborhood. Moving counterclockwise around Prinsengracht you'll hit the **Leidseplein,** which lies just across the canal from the **Museum District** and **Vondelpark.** Street names change capriciously; buy a good **map** of the city (f2.75-4) at the VVV tourist office or from a magazine stand. *Use It* (f4) includes a map, info on cheap lodgings, an index of youth agencies, and city news.

PRACTICAL INFORMATION

TOURIST, FINANCIAL, AND LOCAL SERVICES

Tourist Office: VVV Stationspl. 10 (☎ (0900) 400 40 40; fax 625 28 69), to the left and in front of Centraal Station. Hefty f4.50-6 fee for room booking. Pick up *Day by Day* (f2), a fabulous listing of events. **Branches** at Centraal Station, platform 2, Leidsepl. 1, van Tuyll van Serooskerenweg (near Stadioplein) and the airport are open daily.

Budget Travel: NBBS, Rokin 38 (☎624 09 89). Open mid-May to mid-Aug. M-F 9:30am-5:30pm, Sa 10am-4pm; mid-Aug. to mid-May closes Sa at 3pm. **Budget Bus/Eurolines,** Rokin 10 (☎560 87 88). Open M-F 9:30am-5:30pm, Sa 10am-4pm.

Consulates: All **embassies** and most consulates are in **The Hague** (see p. 750). Consulates: **UK,** Koningslaan 44 (☎676 43 43). Open M-F 9am-noon and 2-3:30pm. **US,** Museumpl. 19 (☎664 56 61). Open M-F 8:30am-noon and 1:30-4:30pm.

Currency Exchange: Best rates at **American Express** (see below). The **GWK** offices at Centraal Station and Schiphol have good rates, and charge students no commission for traveler's checks. Open daily 7am-11:30pm. **Change Express,** Kalverstr. 150 (☎627 80 87; open M-Sa 8:30am-8pm and Su 10:30am-6pm), or Leidestr. 106 (☎622 14 25; open daily 8am-11pm), has good rates and a 2.25% commission plus f7.50 fee.

American Express: Damrak 66 (☎520 77 77; fax 504 87 07). Excellent rates and no commission on traveler's checks. Mail held. Open M-F 9am-5pm, Sa 9am-noon.

English Bookstores: Spui, near the Amsterdam University, is lined with bookstores and holds an open-air *Boekemarkt* F 10am-6pm.

Gay and Lesbian Services: COC, Rozenstr. 14 (☎626 30 87), is the main source of info. Open M 11am-6pm, Tu-W and F-Sa 10am-6pm, Th 11am-9pm. **Gay and Lesbian Switchboard** (☎623 65 65) daily 10am-10pm.

Laundry: Look for a *Wasserette* sign. **The Clean Brothers,** Kerkstr. 56 (☎622 02 73). Wash f8, dry f1 per 20min. Open daily 7am-9pm.

Condoms: Condomerie, Warmoesstr. 141 (☎627 41 74), next to the red-light district. Open M-Sa 11am-6pm.

EMERGENCY AND COMMUNICATIONS

Emergencies: ☎112 (police, ambulance, and fire brigade).

Police: Headquarters, Elandsgracht 117 (☎559 91 11). Police department has a department for rape crisis.

Crisis Lines: General counseling at **Telephone Helpline** (☎675 75 75). Open 24hr. **Rape crisis hotline** (☎613 02 45); staffed M-F 10:30am-11pm, Sa-Su 3:30pm-11pm. **Drug counseling,** Jellinek clinic (☎570 23 55). Open M-F 9am-5pm.

Medical Assistance: Tourist Medical Service (☎592 33 55). Open 24hr. For hospital care, call **Academisch Medisch Centrum,** Meibergdreef 9 (☎566 91 11), near the Holendrecht Metro stop. For free emergency medical care, visit the **Kruispost,** Oudezijds Voorburgwal 129 (☎624 90 31). Open M-F 9:30am-12:30pm and 7pm-9:30pm. **STD Line,** (☎555 58 22). Hotline and free clinic at Groenburgwal 44 with testing open M-F 8-10:30am and 1:30pm-3:30pm.

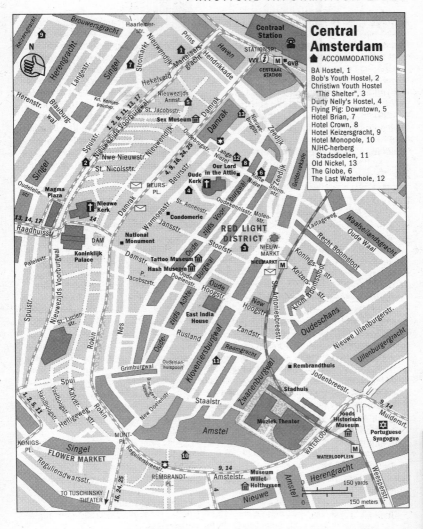

Central Amsterdam

ACCOMMODATIONS

BA Hostel, 1
Bob's Youth Hostel, 2
Christiwn Youth Hostel
  "The Shelter", 3
Durty Nelly's Hostel, 4
Flying Pig: Downtown, 5
Hotel Brian, 7
Hotel Crown, 8
Hotel Keizersgracht, 9
Hotel Monopole, 10
NJHC-herberg
  Stadsdoelen, 11
Old Nickel, 13
The Globe, 6
The Last Waterhole, 12

Pharmacies: Most are open M-F 8:30am-5pm. When closed, each *apotheek* (pharmacy) posts a sign directing you to the nearest one open. To find out the on-call pharmacy nearest you, call ☎694 87 09 after 11pm.

Internet Access: Cybercafé, Nieuwendijk 19 (☎623 51 46). f1 per 10min, f5 per hr. Open Su-Th 10am-1am, F-Sa 10am-3am. **Café ZoëZo,** Vijzelgracht 63 (☎330 67 67). f2 per 15min, f6 per hr. Open Su-Th 11am-midnight, F-Sa 11am-1am. **Easy Everything,** Reguliersbreestraat 22, the largest internet cafe in the world, is located in Rembrandtsplain next to the Tushinki Theatre. Open 24hr.

Post Office: Singel 250-256 (☎556 33 11), at Raadhuisstr. behind the Dam. Address mail to be held: Jeff BARNES, *Poste Restante*, Singel 250-256, Amsterdam **1016 AB,** The Netherlands. Open M-W, F 9am-6pm, Th 9am-8pm, Sa 10am-1:30pm. Mail held downstairs available M-F 8am-7pm and Sa 9am-noon.

❰ ACCOMMODATIONS

Accommodations closer to the **station** often take good security measures. Hostels and hotels in **Vondelpark** and the **Jordaan** are quieter (by Amsterdam's standards) and safer. They are also near their share of bars and coffeeshops, are close to large museums and the busy Leidsepl., and are only 15min. by foot or 2min. by train from the red-light district and city center. You can book (and pay for) spaces in **HI hostels** from any other HI hostel (free within the Netherlands, f4 elsewhere). The hotels and hostels in the **Red Light District** are often bars with beds over them. Consider just how much pot, noise, and music you want to inhale before booking a bed at one of them. When you tire of Amsterdam's intensity, consider staying in nearby **Edam** for a good dose of the Dutch countryside (see p. 747). Tourist offices in every town will book accommodations and **private rooms** for around f40 including booking fee. The accommodations are listed by neighborhood, with each neighborhood divided into hostel and hotel listings.

LEIDSEPLEIN AND MUSEUMPLEIN

NJHC City Hostel Vondelpark (HI), Zandpad 5 (☎589 89 96; www.njhc.org), bordering Vondelpark. Take tram #1, 2, or 5 from the station to Leidsepl., cross the canal, turn left at the Marriott, then take your 2nd right, before the park entrance. A palatial hostel with clean, spacious rooms and full baths. Three handicapped rooms available. Avoid the park after dark. Breakfast included. Lockers f3. Bike rental f10 per day. Reception 7am-12:30am. Dorms f34-38; doubles f108-158; quads f45-51. Nonmembers add f5.

International Budget Hostel, Leidsegracht 76 (☎624 27 84). Take tram #1, 2, or 5 to Prinsengracht, head right down Prinsengracht, and turn left on Leidsegracht. Well-located with a hardworking staff and a TV lounge. Breakfast f2.50-8. Min. 2-night stay in summer. Reception 9am-11pm. Dorms f35-50; doubles f100-170.

The Flying Pig Palace, Vossiusstr. 46-47 (☎400 41 87; email palace@flyingpig.nl). Take tram #1, 2, or 5 from the station to Leidsepl., cross the canal, turn left at the Marriott, pass the Vondelpark entrance, and take the next right. This clean, vibrant hostel maintains a fun atmosphere in a beautiful location. Free internet. Breakfast included. Kitchen, bar. Key deposit f10. Reception 8am-9pm. From f35.50.

Hotel Wynnobel, Vossuisstraat 9 (☎662 22 98). Bordering the Vondel Park along the same street as the Flying Pig Palace, the Hotel Wynnoble (pronounced "Y-Noble") is a beautiful old bed and breakfast. Reception 7am-12pm. f60-75 per person.

Hotel Museumzicht, Luykenstr. 22 (☎671 29 54). Take tram #2 or 5 from the station to Hobbemastr. Unbelievable view of the Rijksmuseum. Breakfast included. Reception 8am-11pm. Singles f65-85; doubles f130-175; triples f180. Off-Season 10% cheaper.

Hans Brinker, Kerkstr. 136 (☎622 06 87; www.hansbrinker.com). Take tram #1, 2, or 5 from the station, get off at Kerkstr., and it's 1 block down on the left. Clean, gigantic, and comparatively safe, with a bar and disco (guests only). Breakfast included. Key deposit f10. Reception 24hr. Dorms f42.50; singles f111; doubles f120-146; triples f186; quads/quints f150-200. Add f2.50 for 1-night stay.

Hotel Bellington, P.C Hoftstraat 78-80 (☎671 64 78; www.hotel-beliington.com). Follow directions to Hotel Museumzicht. Hoftstraat is behind Lukenstr., towards the Leideplainl. A well groomed hotel on one of Amsterdam's ritziest streets. Breakfast included. Reception 8am-5pm and 8-10pm. Doubles f130-200; triples f210-250.

Hotel Bema, Concertgebouw. 19b (☎679 13 96; email postbus@hotel-bema.demon.nl), across from the Concertgebouw. Take tram #16 from the station to Museumplein; it's a block up on the left. Breakfast included. Reception 8am-midnight. Singles f75-95; doubles f110-165; triples f150-200; quads f225.

The Golden Bear, Kerkstraat 37 (☎624 47 85; email hotel@goldenbear.nl). Take tram #1, 2 or 5 to Prinsengracht, walk back to Kerkstraat and turn left. Opened in 1948, the Golden Bear is thought to be the oldest openly gay hotel in the world. Mainly male couples though lesbians are welcome as well. Breakfast included. Reception 8pm-11pm. Standard doubles f140; triples f225.

Casa Cara, Emmastr. 24 (☎ 662 31 35; www.com-all.nl/hotels/casa-cara), 10min. beyond the Rijksmuseum. Take tram #2 or 16 from the station to Emmastr. Simple rooms in a quiet area. Breakfast included in summer. Credit card required for reservations. Min. 3-night stay in high season. Reception 7:30am-10:30pm. No drugs. Singles f80-90; doubles f100-155; triples f155-200.

Euphemia Budget Hotel, Fokke Simonszstr. 1-9 (☎ 622 90 45; email euphemia-hotel@budgethotel.a2000.nl), 10min. from Leidsepl. Take tram #16, 24, or 25 to Wetering Circuit, backtrack on Vijzelstr., cross the canal, and turn right on Fokke Simonszstr. Gay friendly. Discounts for email reservations. Breakfast f8.50. Reception until 11pm. Doubles f100-250; triples f120-240; quads f140-300.

RED-LIGHT DISTRICT AND REMBRANDTSPLEIN

NJHC-Herberg Stadsdoelen (HI), Kloveniersburgwal 97 (☎ 624 68 32), between Nieuwmarkt and Rembrandtspl. Take tram #4, 9, 16, 24, or 25 to Muntpl., walk down Amstel, cross the green bridge, and it's 1 block up on the right. Large dorms, lively lounge, and casual atmosphere. Internet. Breakfast included. Laundry f11. Bike rental f12.50. Reception 7am-12:30am. Flexible curfew 2am. Dorms f33.50; nonmembers add f5.

Flying Pig: Downtown, Nieuwendijk 100 (☎ 420 68 22), just off Damrak. Dedicated to sculpting a safe party atmosphere the Pig is what Amsterdam myths are made of. Swap books or joints, party in the bar or snuggle up in the lounge. Free internet. Women-only dorm rooms available. Breakfast included. Key deposit f10. Reception 24hr. Reserve at least a week ahead. Dorms f35.50-46.50; doubles f65; quads f49.50.

The Globe, Oudezijds Voorburgwal 3 (☎ 421 74 24). From the station, head toward Damrak, take the 2nd left on Nieuwezijds Brugsteeg and the 2nd right on Oudezijds Voorburgwal. The hostel is across the 1st bridge on your left. Lively pub (24hr. for guests) with live music F-Sa. Breakfast f7.50-15. Reception 24hr. Dorms f40, weekends f45; doubles f120-130; triples f100-110.

The Greenhouse Effect, Warmoesstr. 55 (☎ 624 49 74; www.the-greenhouse-effect.com). A bar, coffeeshop, and hotel all wrapped in one. Reception and breakfast in the bar downstairs, open 9am-1:00am, until 3:00am on F and Sa. Key deposit f50 or passport. Dorms f55; doubles from f160; triples start at f190.

Hotel Brian, Singel 69 (☎ 624 46 61; email hotelbrian@hotmail.com). From Centraal Station turn right at the Victoria Hotel, proceed until turning right onto Singel. Small rooms in a friendly atmosphere. Breakfast included. Key deposit f25. Reception 8am-10:30pm. Dorms f40-50, off-season f30-40.

Durty Nelly's Hostel, Warmoesstr. 115/117 (☎ 638 01 25; email nellys@xs4all.nl). From the station, walk 2 blocks left of the Damrak. Small hostel above an Irish pub. Breakfast included. Padlock deposit f15. Reception 24hr. No reservations. Dorms f35-40.

BA Hotel, Martelaarsgracht 18 (☎ 638 71 19; email india@cistron.nl). From the station, cross the bridge to Damrak, take a right on Prins Henrikkade, and the first left on Martelaarsgracht. Well-located, with a friendly staff and bar. Breakfast and map included. Key deposit f25. Reception 8am-midnight. On high season weekends, two night minimum stay. 8-12 bed dorms f25-45.

Hotel Centrum, Warmoesstr. 15 (☎ 420 16 66). Follow directions to The Old Quarter. Keep the groove on in the downstairs bar; then head upstairs to a thirty-roomed hotel. Reception 8am-1am. Singles f75; doubles f105; triples f150; and quads f200.

Hotel Crown, Oudezijds Voorburgwal 21 (☎ 626 96 64; www.web2day.com). Handsome accommodations. Dorms f65-90.

Old Nickel, Nieuwebrugsteeg 11 (☎ 624 19 12). Quiet hotel in a central location 2min. from the train station; turn left on Nieuw Brugstreet, the Old Nickel is on the corner at Warmoesstr. Breakfast included. Reception 8am-midnight. Singles f65; doubles f90-125; quads f160-200.

Hotel Hortus, Plantage Parklaan 8 (☎ 625 99 96). From the station, take tram #9 to Artis, backtrack on Plantage Middenlaan, and go left on Parklaan. Internet. Breakfast included. Key deposit f25. Reception 8am-11pm. Dorms f40-50, off-season f30-40.

Old Quarter, Warmoesstr. 20-22. (☎626 64 29) Turn right onto Warmoesstr from Old Nickel. The Old Nickel's larger, more-modern brother. Very clean accomodations. Reception 24hr. Doubles f125.

Christian Youth Hostel "The Shelter," Barndesteeg 21-25 (☎625 32 30), off the Nieuwmarkt (metro: Nieuwmarkt). Virtue amid the red lights. Cozy courtyard and religious slogans. Breakfast included. Key deposit f10. Lockers f10. Curfew Su-Th midnight, F-Sa 1am. Reception 24hr. Dorms f28; off-season f25.

Hotel International, Warmoesstr. 1-3. (☎624 55 20). Across the street from the Old Nickel. Breakfast included. Reception 8am-1am. Doubles f110-150; triples f150-225. Prices lower in off-season.

THE JORDAAN

Hotel van Onna, Bloemgracht 104 (☎626 58 01). Take tram #13 or 17 from the station 3 stops to Westmarkt. Charming hotel, with simple, quiet rooms and immaculate bathrooms. Breakfast included. Reception 8am-11pm. f80 per person.

Anna's Youth Hostel, Spuistraat 6 (☎620 11 55). From Centraal Station turn left onto Spuistraat. Min. 2-night stay. with Saturday check in. No drugs. Reception 8am-1pm and 5pm-3am. Off-season f25 weekdays, f30 weekends; high season f35.

The Shelter: Jordaan, Bloemstr. 179 (☎624 47 17). One street from Rozengracht in the Jordaan (tram #13 or 17: Marnixstr.). A cheap and well-located Christian hostel. Internet free. Nightly Bible study. Age limit 15-35. Breakfast included. Reception 7:30am-2am. Curfew 2am. Single sex dorms f28.

Ramenas Hotel, Haarlemerdijk 61 (☎624 69 30). Take tram #22 (dir.: Nieuwe Westerdokstraat) and stop at corner of Buiten Oranjesteeg. Turn right onto Haarlemerdijk. Clean rooms on a quiet side street, with cafe below. Breakfast included. Doubles start at f100; triples f130-190.

CAMPING

Camping Zeeburg, Zuider-Ijdijk 20 (☎694 44 30), next to the Amsterdam Rijncanal. Take bus #22, tram 14, or night bus 79 (15min.) and walk 3min. Backpacker-oriented. Live music regularly. Showers f1.50. Reception July 8am-11pm; Apr.-June and Aug.-Mar. 9-11am and 5-9pm. f7.50 per person, f5 per tent.

Gaaspercamping, Loosdrechtdreef 7 (☎696 73 26), in Gaasper Park. Take the metro (dir.: Gaasperplas) to the end; or night bus #75. Showers f1.50. Laundry f13. Reception 9am-9pm. Open mid-Mar. to Dec. f6.75 per person, f15 per tent.

◙ FOOD

Dutch food ranges from the hopelessly bland to the oddly tasty. Dutch *pannen-koeken* (pancakes), best described as thick, unrolled crepes, are prepared as both main courses and sweet desserts. In bars and beer cafes, the most popular hors d'oeuvres (or "starters") are *bitterballen*, ping-pong sized fried balls filled with a mixture of meat and cheese, then served with mustard. If you're feeling adventurous, stop by a fish stall in summer to try herring—raw, salted, with a squeeze of lemon, and best when swallowed whole in one mouthful. But Dutch food extends to Surinamese, Indonesian, Chinese, and Indian food establishments which are an upside to colonization and some of the best dining to be had in the city. Many cheap restaurants cluster around **Leidsepl., Rembrandtspl.,** and the **Spui.** Cafes, especially in the Jordaan, serve inexpensive sandwiches (f4-9) and good meat-and-potatoes fare for f12-20. Bakeries line **Utrechtsestr.,** south of Prinsengracht. Fruit, cheese, flowers, and occasionally even live chickens populate the **markets** on **Albert Cuypstr.,** behind the Heineken brewery. (Open M-Sa 10am-4:30pm.) The cheapest **groceries** are found at **Aldi Supermarket,** Nieuwe Weteringstr., off of Vijzelgracht, near the brewery. (Open M 11am-6pm, Tu-F 9am-6pm, Sa 8:30am-4pm.)

LEIDSEPLEIN AND THE JORDAAN

Balraj, Binnen Oranjestraat 1 (☎625 14 28). This cozy Indian restaurant in the Joordan serves remarkably tender chicken dishes. Dinner from f17. Open daily 5pm-10pm.

Restaurant Semhar, 259 Marnixstraat (☎638 16 34), in the Jordaan. From Leidesplain take tram #1 to Bloemgracht. Eritrean-Ethiopian food fills two for f27 each, in quiet corner restaurant. Vegetarian options. Open daily 1:00pm-11:00pm.

Bolhoed, 60-62 Prinsengracht, across the canal from the Anne Frank House. Delicious vegan options. Salads and quiche f12-19. Open daily noon-10pm.

Esoterica, Overtoom 409 (☎689 72 26). Incredible homemade vegetarian food by the Vondelpark. Indonesian specialities. Salads f5-9, meals f15-17. Open W-Su 2-10pm.

Harlem Drinks and Soul Food, Haarlemmerstraat, 7 (☎330 14 98). Easygoing staff will serve chef's daily fruitions with spunk. Jamaican, and Surinamian, food from the diaspora, plus salads for f12. Breakfast served from 8:30-11:30am. Open Su-Th 8:30am-1:00am, F-Sa 8:30am-3:00am.

Bojo, 51 Lange Leidsedwar. Delicious, heaping portions of Indonesian food at reasonable prices. Meals f13-21. Open M-Th 4pm-2am, F 4pm-4am, Sa noon-4am, Su noon-2am.

Dionysos, Overtoom 176 (☎689 44 41). From Leidsepl., walk right on Stadhouderskade and Overtoom is on the left. Greek dishes start at f12. Served daily from 5pm-11pm.

New Deli, Harlemmerstr. 73 (☎626 27 55). 10min. from Centraal Station. Salads (f6-15) and sandwiches (f5.25-18) in a slick, minimalist cafe. Lunch daily 10am-10pm.

A La Plancha, 1e Looiersdwarsstr. 15 (☎420 36 33). Bring your Spanish skills to this authentic Tapas bar near the Prinsengracht. *Grande ensalada* for f5.50; *pollo tapas* f5.50. Open Su-Th 2pm-1am, F-Sa 2pm-3am.

RED-LIGHT DISTRICT AND REMBRANDTSPLEIN

Café Restaurant Turquoise, Wolvenstr. 30 (☎624 20 26). Between Keizersgracht and Hernegracht near the Spui. Turkish cuisine in a classy atmosphere at unbeatable prices. Most meals f19-26. Vegetarian options. Open daily 5pm-12am.

Café de Jaren, Nieuwe Doelenstr. 20-22 (☎625 57 71). Borrow a magazine/newspaper and chill in the large reading room, or sit outside and savor the view. Gourmet meals f18.50-28. Open Su-Th 10am-1am, F-Sa 10am-2am; kitchen closes 10:30pm.

Pannenkoekenhuis Upstairs, Grimburgwal 2 (☎626 56 03). From Muntpl. tram stop, cross the bridge, walk along the Singel and turn right on Grimburgwal. A tiny nook with some of the best pancakes in the city. Pancakes f7.50-17.50. Open M-F noon-7pm, Sa noon-6pm, Su noon-5pm.

Downtown, Reguliersdwarsstr. 31 (☎622 99 58). Small coffeeshop minus the pot. Cappuccino f3.75, homemade quiche f7.75. Open daily 10am-7pm.

Keuhen Van 1870, Spuistr. 4 (☎624 89 65). Serves traditional Dutch food at the cheapest prices around. *Prix fix* f12.50. Open M-F 12:30-8pm, Sa-Su 4-9pm.

◉ SIGHTS

Amsterdam is fairly compact, so tourists can easily explore the area from the Rijksmuseum to the red-light district on foot. **Circle Tram 20,** geared toward tourists, stops at 30 attractions throughout the city (every 10min. 9am-6pm, one-day pass f11; buy on the tram or at VVV offices). The more peaceful **Museumboot Canal Cruise** allows you to hop on and hop off along their loop from the VVV to the Anne Frank House, the Rijksmuseum, the Bloemenmarkt, Waterlooplein, and the old shipyard—buy tickets at any stop. (☎623 98 86. Departs every 30min. 10am-5pm, f25; pass also yields 10-50% off at all museums and is valid 'till noon the next day.) Rent a **canal bike** to power your own way through the canals (☎626 55 74. 2 people f25 per hr., 4 people f40, f50 deposit; pick up and drop-off points at Westerkerk in the Jordaan, Weteringschans 24 at the Rijksmuseum, and at Leidse Bosje at the Vondelpark. Open daily 10am-7:30pm; July-Aug. until 10pm.) **Mike's Bike Tours** provide an entertaining introduction to the city's sites and the surrounding countryside. (☎622 79 70. Reserve by phone. Tours start from the entrance of the Rijksmuseum. f37, children 4-12 f25; groups f30 per person.) The economical **Museumkaart** grants year-long discounts or admission to museums and transportation throughout the country (f55, under 25 f25; buy at museums throughout The Netherlands). The **Amsterdam Leisure Pass** includes a canal trip and admission to the Rijksmuseum, the Stedelijk Museum, and the Amsterdam Historical Museum (f41.50; buy at the VVV).

MUSEUM DISTRICT

VAN GOGH MUSEUM. This architecturally breathtaking museum houses the largest collection of van Goghs in the world (mostly from his family's private collection) and a diverse group of 19th-century paintings by artists who influenced or were contemporaries of the master. The Japanese impact on Van Gogh is demonstrated by a sushi bar in the middle of the museum. Pick up the audio tour to learn about the artist, his dependency on his benefactor brother Theo, and the fact that his name is pronounced "Van Choch," not "Van Go." (*Paulus Potterstr. 2. Take tram #2 or 5 from the station.* ☎ *570 52 52. Open daily 10am-6pm. f12.50. Audio tour f8.50.*)

STEDELIJK MUSEUM OF MODERN ART. Impressionist painters Picasso, Pollock, de Kooning, Newman, Stella, and Ryman are all members of the Stedelijk's outstanding permanent collection. So too is Piet Mondrian; despite the modern master's later move to New York City, the Stedelijk chronicles his Dutch days. The museum also houses Chagall's works depicting lovers floating as well as some of his lesser-known works of pigs drinking. Rare portrait work by Malevich also beefs up his celebrated Woodcutters and wacko Suprematist experiments. Exciting up-and-coming contempory work also often shown. (*Paulus Potterstr. 13, next to the Van Gogh Museum.* ☎ *573 29 11; www.stedelijk.nl. Open daily 11am-5pm. f10.*)

RIJKSMUSEUM (NATIONAL MUSEUM). If you've made it to Amsterdam, it would be sinful to leave without seeing the Rijksmuseum's impressive collection of works by Rembrandt, Vermeer, Frans Hals, and Jan Steen. With thousands of Dutch Old Master paintings, it can be an overwhelming place—a good approach is to follow the crowds to Rembrandt's famed militia portrait **The Night Watch,** in the Gallery of Honor, and then proceed into Aria, the interactive computer room. Aria, which provides historical information on specific works, can create a personalized map of the museum to help you navigate through its enormous collection. Don't miss the doll house exhibits, chronicling the boredom of rich married women in 18th-century Holland. (*On Stadhouderskade. Take tram #2 or 5 from the station.* ☎ *674 70 47 for 24 hr. information. Open daily 10am-5pm. f12.50 for permanent collection, f25 for additional exhibits.*)

HEINEKEN MUSEUM. Call it cerveaza. birra, or beiere: in the Netherlands they call it Heineken. It's a name many Netherlanders revere more than the Royal Oranje family, who have done their own fair share of deigning to this king company of Dutch revelry; the Queen and Alfred Heineken have cultivated a famous friendship in recent years. Your introduction to the world of beer will be in an entirely refurbished museum, scheduled to reopen in April 2001. Admission gets your free beer; the money goes to charities like the Red Cross and World Wildlife Fund--so drink up. Tickets bought on sight for the self-guided tour. (*Stadhouderskade 78, off Ferdinand Bolstr. and just down Stadhouderskade from the Rijksmuseum.* ☎ *523 96 66; call for opening times. f10. Must be 18 or older or under parental guidance.*)

REMBRANDTSPLEIN AND ENVIRONS

VERZETSMUSEUM. The Dutch Resistance Museum chronicles how the Dutch had to overcome the decimation of their Jewish population from 140,000 to 40,000 during the Holocaust. Interactive exhibits challenge viewers to decide what they would have done at the time of the Nazi invasion. Located in the heart of the Amsterdam's historically Jewish neighborhood, the museum brings the struggles and strategies of the Dutch Resistance Movement down to the local level; notes thrown to loved ones on trains to Aushwitz convey the extensive effort to keep networks alive, and a neighborhood tour that tells how 150 Jewish people were successfully hidden in the lion cage in the Artis Zoo, located across the street. A 2001 exhibit will chronicle the experience of post-war return for Dutch Jews from concentration camps, and gentry from Indonesia, who were similarly held hostage by Japanese forces. *(Plantage Kerklaan 61. Take tram #7, 9, or 14 to "Artis." Or, from the Synagogue, walk down Muiderstr., which turns into Plantage Middenlaan, and turn right on Plantage Kerklaan. ☎ 620 25 35. Open Tu-F 10am-5pm, Sa-Su noon-5pm. f9, students f4.)*

TUSCHINSKI THEATER. This fabulously ornate movie theater is one of Europe's first experiments in Art Deco. Although a group of drunk Nazis once got out of hand and started a fire in its cabaret, the theater miraculously survived WWII and has remained in operation for over 75 years. A ticket to a screening of one of their Hollywood features allows you to explore on your own; theater 1 is the main stage and has private boxes. *(Reguliersbreesstr., between Rembrandtspl. and Muntpl. ☎ 0900 202 53 50 for movie listings. Tours in summer Su-M 10:30am; f10. Performances f14-38.)*

JOODS-PORTUGUESE SYNAGOGUE AND JOODS HISTORISCH MUSEUM. Having been expelled from their country in the 15th century, a sizable number of Spanish and Portuguese Jews established a community in Amsterdam and in 1675 built the handsome **Joods-Portuguese Synagogue.** The Dutch government protected the building from the Nazis' torches by declaring it a national historic site. Across the street, the **Joods Historisch Museum (Jewish Historical Museum),** housed in three connected former synagogues, traces the history of Dutch Jews. *(Jonas Daniel Meijerpl., at Waterloopl. Take tram #9 or 14. ☎ 626 99 45; www.jhm.nl. Synagogue open daily 10am-4pm. f7.50. Museum open daily 11am-5pm and resource center open daily 1pm-5pm. f8, students f4.)*

OTHER SIGHTS. Thanks to the Dutch East India company, the **Museum of the Tropics (Verzetmuseum)** multimedia presentation of artifacts from Asia, Africa, and Latin America has especially fine Indonesian art in addition to an engaging children's wing. *(Linnaeusstr. 2. Take tram #9 to Artis, east of Waterloopl. ☎ 568 82 15. Open M-F 10am-5pm, Sa-Su noon-5pm. f15, students f10.)* Stroll along the stately Herengracht on your way to the **Museum Willet-Holthuysen.** It is a 17th-century canal house, richly decorated in 19th-century furnishings and with a peaceful, pristine garden. *(Herengracht 605, between Reguliersgracht and Vijzelstr., 3min. from Rembrandtspl. ☎ 521 18 22. Open M-F 10am-5pm, Sa-Su 11am-5pm. f8. Borrow an English-language guide from the cashier.)* Recently restored in 17th-century fashion, the **Rembrandthuis** was the home of the master Rembrandt until the city confiscated the house for taxes. It holds 250 of Rembrandt's etchings and dry points, as well as many of his tools and plates. *(Jodenbreestr. 4-6, at the corner of the Oudeschans Canal. Take tram #9 or 14. ☎ 520 04 00. Open M-Sa 10am-5pm, Su 1-5pm. f12.50.)*

RED-LIGHT DISTRICT

The red-light district is surprisingly liveable. For every thrill to be bought, no matter how extreme, there is an equal number of folks there who have nothing to do with the debauchery, or are fiddling with their maps to find out where Dam Square is (at the end of Warmoestr., in the low numbers). But woe to the uninformed: pushers, porn shops, and live sex theaters do a brisk business, though in many ways you may find it less outrageous and seedy than you might have expected. **Sex shows** (f10-50) consist of costumed, disaffected couples repeatedly acting out your "wildest" (i.e., choreographed) dreams. Red neon marks houses of legalized ill repute, where prostitutes display themselves in windows. During the day, the red-light district is comparatively flaccid, with tourists milling about and consulting their maps. As the sun goes down, people get braver, and the area pulses. Cops from the police station on Warmoestr. patrol the district until midnight. Women may feel uncomfortable walking through this area, and all tourists are prime targets for pickpockets.

OUR LORD IN THE ATTIC. A secret enclave of virtue and piety hides in a 17th-century house, today known as the **Museum Amstelkring, Ons' Lieve Heer op Solder** ("Our Lord in the Attic"), where a Catholic priest, forbidden to practice his faith in public during the Reformation, established a surprisingly grand chapel in the attic. *(Oudezijds Voorburgwal 40, at the corner of Oudez. Armstr., 5min. from the station. ☎ 624 66 04. Open Tu-F 10am-5pm, Sa-Su 1-5pm. f10; students f6.)*

THE VICES. For a historical, chemical, and agricultural breakdown of the all the wacky tobacky you've been smelling, drop by the informative **Hash Marijuana Hemp Museum.** Though the museum collection is roughly 50% pro-pot pamphlets, posters, and propaganda for cannabis reform in the United States, the grow-room in back reminds you that you are still in Amsterdam. (☎62 35 91. Open daily 11am-10pm. f12.50. Seeds f20-275.) **The Tattoo Museum**—the name says it all—displays designs, and tattoo-making tools from all over the world, plus a 2000-year-old mummified and tattooed arm found in Peru. (Oudezijds Achterburgwal 130, next to the Hash Marijuana Hemp Museum. ☎625 15 65. Open M-W noon-6pm, Th-Su 1-7pm. f7.50, students f5.) See sex in every way you dreamed possible (and many you didn't) at the **Amsterdam Sex Museum,** which showcases an "only in Amsterdam" collection of erotic art and hard-core porn through the ages. But we all know that its not only in Amsterdam: see images of a female masturbation machine from 18th century France, along with copies of the Kama Sutra, and an exhibit on Oscar Wilde. (Damrak 18, near the station. Open daily 10am-11:30pm. f6; under 17 not admitted.)

OTHER SIGHTS. The area in and around the red-light district (the oldest part of the city) contains some of Amsterdam's most interesting buildings. Amsterdam's former town hall, **Koninklijk Palace** (Dam 1. ☎620 40 60, call for exact opening hours), may be a symbol of 17th-century commercialism, but its majesty is topped by the stunning **Magna Plaza Mall** next door, the 20th-century's monument to commercialism. (Open Su-M 11am-7pm, Tu-Sa 9:30am-9pm.)

THE JORDAAN

When you're through with the museums, lose the hordes in the narrow streets of the Jordaan, built as an artisan district in the Golden Age. Bounded roughly by Prinsengracht, Brouwersgracht, Marnixstr., and Lauriersgracht, and teeming with small cafes, galleries, and chocolate shops, the area is possibly the prettiest and most peaceful in the city. You can also take refuge from Amsterdam's mobbed sights and seamy streets in **Begijnhof,** a beautifully maintained grassy courtyard surrounded by 18th-century buildings that runs between Kalverstr. and the Spui. (Open daily 10am-5pm. Free.) For a bigger dose of nature, birdwatching, pick-up soccer, llama-grazing, and better people-watching, relax in the sprawling **Vondelpark.**

ANNE FRANK HUIS. The tiny space where the young journal-keeper hid with her family from the Nazis until their capture in 1944 now has video interviews with Otto Frank, Anne's father, and Miep Gies, the woman who hid with the Franks. Childhood friends chronicle her life before and during the Holocaust. An interactive, CD-Rom exhibit provides extensive information about the Franks and their life in the Annex, and relates the Holocaust to current human rights issues. (Prinsengracht 263, next to the Westerkerk. Take tram #13, 14, or 17 to Westermarkt. ☎556 71 00. Open daily Apr.-Aug. 9am-9pm; Sept.-Mar. 9am-7pm. f12.50.) While you're there, check out the **Homomonument,** in front of the Westerkerk at the banks of the canal, a memorial to those persecuted through history for their sexual orientation.

ELSEWHERE IN AMSTERDAM

GRAFFITI ART. Some of the most exciting art in Amsterdam is free—painted on doors, walls, and trams. The **Vrankrijk** building, Spuistr. 216, and the area around **Mr. Visserplein,** near Waterloopl. and the Hortus Botannicus, give evidence that graffiti is more than names and vulgar phrases. Continue the psychedelic survey at the **3D Hologram Store.** (Grimburgwal 2, near Muntpl. Open Su-M 1-5:30pm, Tu-F noon-6pm, Sa noon-5:30pm.)

MARKETS. An open-air art market takes place every Sunday in the **Spui,** where local and international artists regularly present their oils, etchings, sculptures, and jewelry, and a book market occasionally yields rare editions and 17th-century Dutch romances. (Art market open Mar.-Dec. daily 10am-6pm. Book market open F 10am-6pm.) Pick up bulbs at the flower market, **Bloemenmarkt.** (Open daily 8am-8pm.) Mill with the masses at the famous flea market on **Waterlooplein,** where you can try your hand at bargaining for antiques, birds, or farm tools. (Open M-Sa 9am-5pm.)

🎵 ENTERTAINMENT

Pick up the monthly *Day by Day* (f4) from the tourist office for comprehensive cultural listings. The mini-magazine *Boom!*, free at restaurants and cafes around the city, is chock full of tourist info; also try the free monthly *UITKRANT*. The **Amsterdam Uit Buro** (AUB), Leidsepl. 26, has fliers and other info and makes reservations for any cultural event. (☎0900 01 91. Open daily 10am-6pm.) Also check www.aub.nl for "Culture in Amsterdam." The monthly *Culture and Camp* (f5) provides info on gay venues and events. The fortnightly *Queer Fish* (f2.50) catalogues less mainstream concerts and parties.

CONCERTS

In the summer, there are free performances Wednesday through Sunday at the **Vondelpark Openluchttheater** (☎673 14 99). The **Royal Concertgebouw Orchestra** at the Concertgebouw on Van Baerlestr. is one of the world's finest. (Take tram #316 to Museumplain ☎671 83 45. Box office around the back of the building open daily 10am-7pm. Tickets from f35.) Sunday morning concerts with guided tours before the performance are a cheaper option. (Tour starts at 10:15am, f5; concerts start at 11am, f25.) Concerts also happen at **Nieuwe Kerk,** on the Dam (f5-12.50).

FILM AND THEATER

Check out the free movieguide.nl in pure pulp or on the web for movie listings. When you're in the Vondelpark, head left from the main entrance on Stadhouderskade to see what's on at the stately **Filmmuseum** independent movie theater. (☎589 14 00; email fillmuseum@nhm.nl. Info open Tu-F 10am-5pm, Sa 11am-5pm.) Frequent English-language performances and cabarets are given at the theater/cafe **Suikerhof,** Prinsengracht 381. (☎22 75 71. Open M-Sa from 5pm, Su from 2pm.) Make reservations for any cultural event at the **AUB** or at the VVV's theater desk, Stationspl. 10 (open M-Sa 10am-5pm). The **Muziektheater,** in the Stadhuis (City Center) at Watterploo. hosts the **Netherlands Opera** and the **National Ballet.** (☎625 54 55. Box office open daily 1-6pm and Su 11:30am-6pm. Opera tickets start at f50; student discounts. Ballet tickets from f25.)

FESTIVALS

The **Queen's Day** (April 30) turns the city into a huge carnival. On the same day is the year's largest flea market, when parrots, skulls, and glue sticks are bought and sold. The **Holland Festival** in June, with dance, drama, and music, is closely followed by the **Summer Festival** of small theater companies in July. (Tickets f10-15. Call the Balie Theatre at 623 29 04 for info.) On the first weekend in August, gay pride comes out in street parties along Warmoesstr., Amstel, Kerkstr., and Reguliersdwarsstr., and in the outrageously fun **Gay Pride Parade** (☎625 83 75), when floats, boats, queens, and queers take over the Prinsengracht. During **Uitmarket** weekend at the end of August, free concerts surround the Dam Square.

🎵 COFFEESHOPS AND SMART SHOPS

COFFEESHOPS

Yes, the rumors are true: marijuana and hashish have been decriminalized in the Netherlands. Coffeeshops don't just sell coffee (unless one counts the green, leafy "mother's milk" and "super skunk" varieties) but, like bars, come in a variety of styles and offer a range of atmospheres. Places calling themselves coffeeshops sell pot or hash or will let you buy a drink and smoke your own stuff. Look for the green and white 'Coffeeshop BCD' sticker that certifies a coffeeshop's credibility and means that the shop is reputable. Although Amsterdam is known as the hash capital of the world, **marijuana** is increasingly popular. You can legally possess up to 5g of marijuana or hash (the previous 30g limit was reduced in response to foreign criticism). The farther you travel from the touristed spots, the better and cheaper the establishments. Pick up a free copy of the *BCD Official Coffeeshop Guide* for the pot-smoker's map of Amsterdam. For info on the legal ins and outs, call the **Jellinek clinic** at ☎570 23 55. **Never buy drugs from street dealers.** Don't get too caught up in Amsterdam's narcotic quirk; use common sense, and remember that any experimentation with drugs can be dangerous. However, if you choose to indulge, you will find that coffeeshops carry a range of products which are described below. Dealers commonly don't get tipped. Those who prepare your drink (coffee, beer, etc.) are generally tipped f2 or a f2.50 coin. When you move from one coffeeshop to another, it is courteous to buy a drink in the next coffeeshop even if you already have weed in your pouch. Never smoke pot on the street, it's offensive to the Dutch.

SPACECAKES, SPACESHAKES, AND SPACE SWEETS. Cakes and sweets made with hash or weed. The butter used in the cake is hash or weed based. Hash chocolate, popsicles, and bon bons are also available. Because they need to go to your blood, and be digested, they take longer to affect a person, and longer to rinse out. They produce a body stone that can take up to an hour to start.

HASH. Hash comes in two varieties, black (like Afghani and Nepali; f10-24 per gram) and blonde (like Moroccan); black tends to be heavier and hits harder. It's grown at high elevations in the mountains, including by some Nepalese monks. The higher the elevation the better the hash, because the plants have to struggle to stay strong, and are that much more potent once they have been fielded.

MARIJUANA. A dried, cured plant. Different weeds come in and out of favor much like different beers. Any weed with white in its name is guaranteed to be strong, such as white widow, white butterfly, and white ice. Pot in the Netherlands is incredibly strong. As with alcohol, take it easy so you don't pass out. The Dutch tend to mix tobacco with their pot as well, so joints are harsher on your lungs. Ask the dealer at coffeeshops if pre-rolled joints available are rolled with tobacco or are pure cannabis. Dutch marijuana is the most common and costs f12-15 per gram, f25-30 for a bag. The smaller the quantity, the smoother and more potent. Staff at coffeeshops are used to explaining the different kinds of pot on the menu to tourists. It is recommended that you buy a gram at a time. Most places will supply rolling papers and filter tips. Almost no one smokes out of pipes, and while some places provide bongs, usually only tourists use them.

SMART SHOPS

Also legal are **smart shops,** which peddle a variety of **"herbal enhancers"** and **hallucinogens** that walk the line between soft and hard drugs. Some shops are alcohol-free and all have a strict no-hard-drugs policy. All **hard drugs** are illegal and possession is treated as a serious crime.

MAGIC MUSHROOMS. These start to work after 30-60min. They act on your system for 4-6hr. Never look for mushrooms outside and never buy from a street dealer; it's extremely difficult to tell the difference between poison mushrooms and hallucinogenic mushrooms. The effect mushrooms have on you will depend on your mood and environment when you take it. Overall, the effect is that you will see reality differently. Colors, forms, shapes, time and experience seem longer or shorter. A bad trip will most likely come about if you mix hallucinogens, such as 'shrooms, with alcohol. If you have been drinking before taking shrooms, drink a Coke because you will need sugar. Often people become panicky and have a faster heartbeat with 'shrooms. It will take 8hr. maximum for the effects to go away. Often people take too many 'shrooms because they don't realize that it takes half an hour for them to kick in. If a friend is tripping, it is important to never leave their side. **Call ☎122** if they need to go to the hospital, although the hospital really can't do anything either. If you are having a bad trip, don't be ashamed to tell someone, because you won't be arrested in Amsterdam for using. It is not a crime here, and they've seen it all before.

WHERE TO GO...

Barney's Coffeeshop, Haarlemmerstr. 102 (☎625 97 61). Friendly staff and amazing food. Pot choices start with Thai for beginners (f5) and graduate at the killer Sweet Tooth (f17.50). Rolled joints also available (f6). Open daily 7am-8pm.

Baba, Warmoesstr. 64 (☎624 14 09). Head straight from Centraal station, turn on Oude-brugs, continue straight to corner of Warmoesstr. Feel the riptides of a good time done on hash brownies, spaceshakes, and grass muffins (f7.50). Open Su-Th 8:30am-1:00am, F-Sa 8:00am-1:00am.

De Rokerij, Amstelstr. 8, in the Muntplein. A dark, untouristed coffeeshop with wrought-iron candlesticks and a blue-and-gold Neoclassical ceiling and walls. Strong pre-rolled joints for f6. Open daily noon-11pm. Also at Lange Leidsestr. 41 and Singel 8.

The Greenhouse Effect, Warmoesstr. 53. A relaxed atmosphere with a friendly, knowl-edgeable staff. Spaceshake for f10. Open Su-Th 9am-1am, F-Sa 9am-3am.

Tweedy, Vondelstr. 104 (☎618 03 44), next to Cafe Vertigo at Vondelpark. Watch the game and smoke with locals after hanging out in the park. Open daily noon-midnight.

Conscious Dreams Kokopelli, Warmoestraat 12. (☎421 70 00) This smart shop is a good place to begin your psychadellic survey. Books, lava lamps, and a knowledgeable staff coat your trip: magic 'shrooms, oxygen, vitamins, and herbs. f25 for happy/funny effect, f35 for real trippy. All drugs sold for 2 people. Open daily 11am-10pm.

Homegrown Fantasy, Nieuwezijds Voorburgwal 87a (☎627 56 83). A smokeshop gallery specializing in weed. Free cookies. Not a place for novices. Bags f10-25, rolled joints f5, pure cannabis joints f7.50. Spacecakes f10, space bon bons f7.50. Open daily Su-Th 9am-midnight, F-Sa 9am-1am.

Dutch Flowers, Singel 387 (☎624 76 24), near the Spui. Huge menu. Winner of the cov-eted "Highlife" cup. Outside seating on the canal. Loose weed from f10. Open M-F 10am-1am, Sa-Su 10am-2am.

The Noon, Zieseniskade 22, 10min. from Leidsepl. Owned by Americans, this small shop is one of the few to sell cannabis-only joints (f8.50). Open daily 11am-10pm.

La Tertulia, Prinsengracht 312. Defies any coffeeshop preconceptions: country music, flowers, and bookshelves full of board games surround an indoor waterfall. Rolled joints f5. Brownies f8.50. Open Tu-Sa 11am-7pm.

Global Chillage, Kerkstr. 51 (☎639 11 54). Trance music provides a chilled alternative to the Hendrix and Marley excess at the other coffeeshops. Open M-Sa noon-11pm.

◪ NIGHTLIFE

CAFES AND BARS

Amsterdam's finest cafes are the old, dark, wood-paneled *bruine kroegen* (brown cafes) of the **Jordaan,** many of which have outdoor seating lining the canal on **Prin-sengracht. Leidseplein** is the liveliest nightspot, with loud coffeeshops, loud bars, and tacky clubs galore. Dutch soap stars frequent Palladium and Raffles, also in Leidesplain, where many a beautiful person comes to be seen and drink up for sur-prisingly reasonable prices. **Rembrandtsplein** is the place to watch soccer and sing with drunk revelers. Gay bars line **Reguliersdwarsstr.,** which connects Muntpl. and Rembrandtspl., and **Kerkstr.,** five blocks north of Leidsepl.

Café 't Smalle, at the corner of Prinsengracht and Egelandiersgracht. Intimate, tiny bar founded in 1780. Famous pea soup served in winter for f8.50. Open Su-Th noon-12:15am, F-Sa noon-2am.

Café de Tuin, Tweede Tuindwarsstr. 13 (☎624 45 59). Attracts names from Dutch TV, radio, and film, but without any finger pointing. Relaxed setting to read a newspaper or start conversation. Beer starting at f3.25. Open daily noon-2am.

Absinthe, Nieuwezijds Voorburgwal 171 (☎320 67 80). Young and trendy, Absinthe sus-tains crowds all night with excellent DJ's and a conversant, quiet space in back. Shots of its namesake f7.50. Open Su-Th 8pm-3am, F-Sa until 4am.

De Prins, Prinsengracht 124 (☎ 624 93 82). Have a sip in this classic student bar in the Jordaan. Bathed in old, dark wood—no pot, no frills, but cool. Famous for its cheese fondue (f24). Open M-Th 10am-1am, F-Sa until 2am.

NL Lounge, NZ Voorburgwal 169. Too cool for an outside sign, the trendy NL is the unmarked destination where slick, chic, sophisticated Amsterdam insiders come to mingle. Mixed drinks f12. Open Su-Th 8pm-3am, F-Sa 8pm-4am.

W.F. Fockink, 31 Pijlsteeg, in Dam Square (☎ 639 26 95). Largely untouristed sight where they've been brewing famed *fockink* liqueurs for 400 years. Try a glass for f4, or a bottle for f35. Open daily 3pm-9pm.

Havana, Reguliersdwarsstr. 17-19 (☎ 620 67 88). Glam it up in plush red velvet booths in this popular gay bar. Mainly men, but fun for women too. DJ's upstairs on weekends. Open Su-Th 4pm-1am, F-Sa 4pm-3am.

Vive La Vie, Amstelstr. 7, at the corner of Rembrandtsplein. Mixed gay bar especially for women; small, lively and extremely popular. Open Su-Th 3pm-1am, F-Sa 3pm-3am.

Getto, Warmoestr. 51 (☎ 421 51 51). A gay cafe in the heart of the red light district featuring folk, alternative, house, club and two step. Wine f4.50, mixed drink f11. f5 cover. Open daily 7pm-1am. Sunday night is women only.

LIVE MUSIC

In Amsterdam you will find the lines blurred between club life and live music; two top venues, the **Mily Way** and **Paradiso,** hold club discos after performances and on non-concert nights. The **Jazzlijn** (☎ 626 77 64) provides info on local concerts. The **AUB** has the "Pop & Jazz Uitlijst" and fliers for other free concerts.

Paradiso, Weteringschans 6-8 (☎ 626 45 21). Some of the foremost punk, new-wave, and reggae bands play in this former church. Where Lenny Kravitz got his big break, and the Stones taped their latest live album. Tickets range from f10-50.

Melkweg, Lijnbaansgracht 234a (☎ 624 17 77), in a warehouse off Leidsepl. Legendary nightspot has a cutting-edge aura with crowds. Live bands, theater, films, dance shows, and an art gallery (free W-Su 2-8pm) make for sensory overload. For concerts f5 club fee; tickets range from f20-60. Club nights F-Sa 1-5am (cover f10). Box office open M-F 1-5pm, Sa-Su 4-6pm, and until 7:30pm on show days.

The Bimhuis, Oude Schans 73-77 (☎ 623 33 73), near Waterloopl. The hub of Dutch jazz. W-Sa concerts at 9pm. Ticket prices range from f15-25. Students f7.50. Su-Tu free jam sessions. Box office opens at 8pm.

Maloe, Lijnbaansgracht 163 (☎ 420 45 92). Vibrant crowds writhe to rock and blues. Cover f5 on live music nights, f2.50 on DJ Fridays, periodic jam sessions. Open Su-Th 8pm-3am, F-Sa until 4am (music starts at 9pm).

Korsakoff, Lynbaansgr. 161 (☎ 625 78 54). The leftovers of punk culture convene from Maloe. Alternative guitar and cheap beer by the bottle (f3.50) thrill in a three storied hall. Ring the bell, tip when you leave. (Open Su and Th 10pm-3am, F-Sa 10pm-4am.)

Bourbon Street Jazz & Blues Club, Leidsekruisstr. 6-8 (☎ 623 34 40). Blues, soul, funk, and rock bands keep the crowds stocked every night. The Stones have played this joint; so did BB King and Sting. Cover f5. Open Su-Th 10pm-4am, F-Sa 10pm-5am.

CLUBS AND DISCOS

Many clubs charge a membership fee in addition to normal cover, so the tab can be harsh. Be prepared for cocky doormen who live to turn away tourists; show up early or hope the bouncer thinks you're cute. A promised tip of f10-20 (left on your way out) may help you prove your worth. There are pricey discos aplenty on **Prinsengracht,** near **Leidsestr.,** and on **Lange Leidsedwarsstr.** Gay discos line **Amstelstr.** and **Reguliersdwarsstr.** and cater almost exclusively to men. Pick up a wallet-sized *Clu* guide, free at cafes and coffeeshops, for a club map of the city, and *Gay and Night*, a free monthly magazine, for info on the tons of gay parties.

Escape, Rembrandtspl. 11. Typical Euro disco plays House, trance, disco, dance classics. Pricey cover (f25) gets you into what is perhaps the most popular club in Amsterdam. Beer f4.50, mixed drinks f13. Open W-Su 11pm-4am, F-Sa 11pm-5am.

Time, Nieuwezijds Voorburgwal 163-165. Young, trendy, and tourist oriented, Time runs free shuttles to hostels. Chill dance floor topped by an upstairs lounge. Tu reggae night, W drum and base, Th House, F Progressive and trance, Sa House and funky techno. Cover f10-20. Open Su-Th 11pm-4am, F-Sa 11pm-5am.

MAZZO, Rozengracht 114 (☎ 626 75 00), in the Jordaan. Artsy, experimental disco with red Victorian couches and lamp shades. Mixed drink f10. Cover f10-12.50, Sa f15-20 depending on the DJ. Open Su-Th 11pm-4am, F-Sa 11pm-5am.

The iT, Amstelstraat 24 (☎ 625 01 11). Leather, dry ice, and S&M make the iT Amsterdam's premier hard-core discotech, specializing in house and trance. Innocence lost at rapid rates. Cover f15-25. Open Th and Su 11pm-4am, F-Sa 11pm-5am.

Exit, Reguliersdwarsstr. 42 (☎ 625 87 88). One of the most popular gay discos in Holland. Mostly men. Open Su-Th midnight-4am, F-Sa midnight-5am. Cover f10-12.50.

You II, Amstel 178 (☎ 421 09 00). Near Rembrandtslain. Popular lesbian club has circular bar in front opening into dance floor in back. Men allowed. Sunday often karaoke night. Cover f10. Drinks f4-12. Open Th and Su 10pm-4am, F-Sa til 5am.

The Arena, Gravesandestr. 51-53 (☎ 694 74 44). Take any metro to third stop, night bus #76 or 77, or tram 9 to Tropenmuseum; turn right on Mauritskade and then left on 's-Gravesandestr. Former chapel throws great parties. Cover f15. 80s, 90s dance F from 11pm; f12.50. 60s, 70s dance Sa from 10pm.

🛃 DAYTRIPS FROM AMSTERDAM

EDAM

Edam is just outside Amsterdam; take bus #114 from Centraal Station (30min., 7 strips).

When you tire of free-living Amsterdam, discover quaint cottages, peaceful parks, and lots of cheese and clogs in **Edam.** The 15th-century **Grote Kerk,** or St. Nicholaaskerk, is the largest three-ridged church in Europe and has exquisite stained-glass windows. (☎ (0299) 37 16 87. Open May-Sept. daily 2-4:30pm. Free.) Farmers still bring their famed cheese to **market** by horse and boat. (July-Aug. W 10am-12:30pm.) Rent a bike at **Ronald Schot,** Grote Kerkstraat 7/9, and head to the source yourself (☎ (0299) 37 21 55. f10 per day). At **Alida Hoeve,** Zeddewed 1, Edam cheese is still made by hand and samples are free. (Open daily 9am-6pm.) If going by bike, leave Edam, and follow the bikepath in the direction of Olendam and Amsterdam. There are a total of four cheese farms near Alida Hoeve. Farther down the path from Alida Hoeve stands a towering **windmill.** For f1, you can climb the ladder to the top while it's turning. (Open Apr.-Oct. daily 9:30am-4:30pm.) The VVV **tourist office,** Kaizergracht 1, in the old town hall, can help find a room (f35). To get to the VVV take a left at the black bridge when you get off the bus, cross the bridge, turn right, follow Lingerzijde past the church, and you're in the center of town. (☎ (0299) 31 51 25; fax 37 42 36; email info@vvv-edam.nl. Open M-Sat 10am-5pm, July and Aug. also open Su 1pm-5pm.) For reasonable, cozy meals, eat at **De Prinsen Bar,** Prinsenstraat 8. Meet the locals and have a f5 croquette. (Open daily 10:30am-1am.)

HOORN

A little farther from Amsterdam, Hoorn awaits on the edge of the **Ijsselmeer,** an inlet of the Atlantic that the ever-enterprising Dutch diked off in 1932 to form a freshwater sea. The town itself is charming, with frequent open-air markets and a picturesque harbor. If the weather cooperates, **swimming** and **sailing** in the Ijsselmeer can be the perfect tranquilizer after the frenzy of Amsterdam. The **tourist office,** Veemarkt 4, organizes walking tours. From the train station, turn left on Veermarkt. (☎ (0229) 21 83 44. Open M-F 9-11:30am and 12:30-4pm.) **De Toorts (HI)** has rooms right on the water. To get there take bus #133, 137, or 147 to Julianaplaen. (☎ (0229) 21 42 56. Open July-Aug. f28, nonmembers f33.)

OTHER DAYTRIPS FROM AMSTERDAM

HAARLEM. Easily accessible by bus, Haarlem offers a glimpse into 17th- and 18th-century culture (see below).

UTRECHT. Just 25min. from Amsterdam by train, Utrecht is a popular daytrip; Its canals and prestigious university may coerce you into a longer stay (see p. 753).

HAARLEM   ☎023

Surrounded by fields of tulips and daffodils and punctuated with Renaissance facades and placid canals, it's easy to see why Haarlem served as inspiration for native artist Frans Hals and his Golden Age contemporaries. Its city center (the **Grote Markt**) pulsates with charming cafes, and its narrow cobblestoned streets are filled with exquisite shops. The local 17th- and 18th-century *hofjes* (almshouses for elderly women), now private residences, feature elegant brickwork and idyllic courtyards. On your way to the Grote Markt, walk along the Kruisweg, the street on your right-hand when you exit the Central Station; as you continue straight onto the Kruisstraat, glance into the noteworthy **Hofje van Oirschot**, where Kruisstr. becomes Barteljorisstr. (Open 10am-5pm daily.) Along Kruisweg in the Grote Markt is the glorious medieval **Stadhuis** (Town Hall), originally the hunting lodge of the Count of Holland. The **Grote Kerk**, at the opposite end of the Grote Markt, houses the mammoth, floor-to-ceiling Müller organ at which an 11-year-old Mozart once played. (☎532 43 99. Open M-Sa 10am-4pm. f2.75.) From the church, turn left onto Damstraat, and follow it until Spaarne where you will find the **Teyler's Museum**, Spaarne 16, the Netherlands' oldest museum, which possesses an eclectic assortment of scientific instruments, fossils, paintings, and drawings, including works by Raphael, Michelangelo, and Rembrandt. (☎531 90 10. Open Tu-Sa 10am-5pm, Su noon-5pm. f10, f5 for students with ID.) The **Frans Hals Museum**, Groot Heiligland 62, is another former almshouse put to a new use; turn right when leaving the Teyler's, walk along the Zuider Buitenspaarne canal, turn right onto Kampverst and then left onto Groot Heiligland. The museum contains work by the portraitist as well as a collection of modern art. (☎511 57 75. Open M-Sa 11am-5pm, Su 12-5pm. f10, seniors f7.50, under 19 free.)

Reach Haarlem from Amsterdam both by **train** (15min., f6.50) from Centraal Station and by **bus** #80 from Marnixstr., near Leidsepl. (2 per hr., 2 strips). **Night buses** cruise from Leidsepl. to Haarlem's city center (#286; every 40min. until 5:00am F- Sa). The VVV **tourist office**, Stationspl. 1, sells maps (f4-8) and finds private rooms (from f38) for a f10 fee. (☎(0900) 616 16 00; www.vvvzk.nl; email: info@vvvzk.nl. Open M-F 9am-5:30pm, Sa 10am-2pm.) The lively **NJHC-herberg Jan Gijzen (HI)**, Jan Gijzenpad 3, is 3km from the station on the banks of a canal. Take bus #2 (dir.: Haarlem-Nord) and tell the driver your destination. (☎537 37 93. Breakfast included and dinner available for f18. Key deposit f25 or passport. Nonmembers of NJHC organization f42-46.) **Hotel Carillon**, Grote Markt 27, is ideally located, if not ideally priced. (☎531 05 91. Breakfast included. Reception and bar 7:30am-1am. Singles f60-110, doubles f110-142.) To **camp** at **De Liede**, Lie Over 68, take bus #2 (dir.: Zuiderpolder) and walk 10min. (☎533 23 60. f6 per person, f5.50 per tent; in summer add f2.50 tax.) Try cafes in the Grote Markt for cheap meals. For inexpensive and excellent sandwiches try the **Den Gevulde Broodmand** tea salon, on the corner at Kleine Houtstraat 66, near the Frans Hals Museum. (☎532 34 61, sandwiches f6.) **Grill-Pannekoekhuis De Smikkel**, Kruisweg 57, serves plump, buttery pancakes (f12-20) and steaks starting at f30. (Open M-Sa noon-10pm, Su 4-10pm.)

⚡ DAYTRIPS FROM HAARLEM: ZANDVOORT, AALSMEER, AND LISSE.

Near Haarlem, the seaside town of **Zandvoort** boasts two **nude beaches** south of town, along with more modest sands for the bashful and family-oriented (walk left when you hit the beach, 30min. from the main beach). The city also holds one of the **Holland Casinos.** A half hour walk to the right of Zandfoort Beach will bring you to the hip, jet-setty beach of **Blomendaal,** where the beach clubs **The NL Republic, Zomers,** and **Woodstock** are quite popular. The VVV **tourist office,** Schoolpl. 1, in the center, 8min. from the beach and the station, sells a lodgings guide for f2; follow signs from the station. (☎ (023) 571 79 47; fax 571 70 03. Hours vary, generally open M-Sa 9am-5pm.) The **Hotel-Pension Noordzee,** Hogeweg 15, is 100m from the beach. (☎ (023) 571 31 27. Breakfast included. Singles f55; doubles f90.) **Guest House Corper,** Koninginneweg 21, 10min. from the beach, is on a quiet street. (☎/fax (023) 571 34 49. Breakfast included. Singles f50-60; doubles f100-120; triples f150-180.) **Trains** arrive in Zandvoort from Haarlem (10min.; round-trip f6). Walk the Boulevard to get to Blomendaal's beach.

In nearby **Aalsmeer,** ninety million flowers are auctioned to brokers everyday at the **Bloemenveiling Aalsmeer,** the world's largest flower auction. Self-guided tours spring you over to the auction's gargantuan flower warehouse, and onto the auction rooms. Arrive early to see the action. (☎ 297 39 21 85, fax 297 39 00 62. Open M-F 7:30-11:00am.) From Haarlem, take **bus** #140 (45min., every 30min.) from the train station. The auction is also accessible from Amsterdam's Central Station; buses #77 and 172 (dir.: Naar Kudelstaart) stop at the industrial site every half hour. The **Frans Roozen Gardens** bloom with 500 different types of flowers; summer flower shows are free. Bus #90 from Haarlem (dir.: Den Haag, 20-25min., every 30min.) stops in front of the gardens. (☎ (023) 584 72 45. Open Mar.-early Dec. M-F 9am-5pm; tulip shows Apr.-May daily 8am-6pm.)

In the town of **Lisse** in late spring, the **Keukenhof** gardens become a kaleidoscope of color as over five million bulbs explode into life. (☎ (0252) 46 55 64; email info@keukenhof.nl. Open late-Mar. to mid-May and Aug. 3-Sept. 17 daily 8am-7:30pm; last entry 6pm. f19.) The **Zwarte Tulip Museum** details the history and science of tulip raising. (☎ (0252) 41 79 00. Open Tu-Su 1-5pm. f4.) Look for petals in motion at the **April flower parade** (on April 21, 2001). Take **bus** #50 or 51 toward Lisse from the Haarlem train station; combo bus/museum tickets are available at the station (f21). The VVV **tourist office** is at Grachtweg 53. (☎ (0252) 41 42 62. Open M noon-5pm, Tu-F 9am-5pm, Sa 9am-4pm.)

LEIDEN   ☎ 071

Home to one of the oldest and most prestigious universities in Europe, Leiden brims with bookstores, bicycles, museums, gated gardens, and hidden walkways. Rembrandt's birthplace and the site of the first **tulips,** Leiden offers visitors a picture-perfect gateway to flower country. Sharing a main gate with the Academy building is the university's 400-year-old garden, the **Hortus Botanicus,** Rapenburg 73, where the first Dutch tulips were grown. Its grassy knolls alongside the **Witte Singel** canal make it an ideal picnic spot. (Open Mar.-Nov. daily 10am-6pm, Nov.-Feb. Su-F 10am-4pm. f8.) Across the footbridge from the main gate to the Hortus, the **Rijksmuseum van Oudheden** (National Antiquities Museum), Rapenburg 28, harbors the restored Egyptian Temple of Taffeh, a gift removed from the reservoir basin of the Aswan Dam. (☎ 516 31 63. Open Tu-F 10am-5pm, Sa-Su noon-5pm. f7, free with Museumkaart.) **Rijksmuseum voor Volkenkunde** (National Museum of Ethnology), Steenstr. 1, is one of the world's oldest anthropological museums, with fantastic artifacts from the Dutch East Indies. (☎ 516 88 00. Open Tu-F, Su 10am-5pm, Sa noon-5pm. f10, students f7.50.) Inspect the innards of a functioning windmill at the **Molenmuseum "De Valk,"** 2e Binnenvestgracht 1. (Open Tu-Sa 10am-5pm, Su 1pm-5pm. f5; included in Museumkaart.) The **Museum De Lakenhal,** Oude Singel 32, exhibits works by Rembrandt and Jan Steen. (☎ 516 53 60. Open Tu-Sa 10am-5pm, Su noon-5pm. f8, included in Museumkaart.)

Leiden is easily accessed by **train** from The Hague (20min., f5) or Amsterdam (30min., f12). The VVV **tourist office,** Stationsweg 2d, sells maps (f2.50), and walking tour brochures (f1-4), and finds **private rooms** (fee f4.50). Head straight from the station and it'll be on your right after 3min. (☎ (0900) 222 23 33, fax

THE NETHERLANDS

(071) 516 12 27; www.leiden.nl. Open M-F 10am-6:30pm, Sa 10am-4:30pm; Apr., May, July, Aug. also open Su 11am-3pm.) The **Hotel Pension Witte Singel,** Witte Singel 80, 5min. from Hortus Botanicus, has immaculate rooms overlooking gardens and canals. Take bus #43 to Merenwijk and tell the driver your destination. (☎512 45 92, fax 514 78 90; email wvanvriel@pensione-ws.demon.nl. Singles f60, doubles f93-120.) The Greek restaurant **Rhodos,** Turfmarkt 5, serves Greek salads for f6-14. (☎514 23 00. Open daily 3pm-midnight.) Just off the Rapenburg, across from the Hortus, try escargot for f10 at the French inspired **M'n Broer,** Kloksteeg 7. (☎512 50 24. Open daily 5pm-midnight.) The **VIV supermarket** is opposite the train station. (Open M-F 7am-9pm, Sa 9am-8pm, Su noon-7pm.)

Ⓕ DAYTRIP FROM LEIDEN: NOORDWIJK. Beautiful white-sand beaches are 18km away from Leiden in the town of **Noordwijk.** The **NJHC-herberg De Duinark (HI),** Langevelderlaan 45, is 5min. from the beaches. Take bus #57 and walk 30min. following the signs to Sancta Maria. (☎(0252) 37 29 20. Sheets f7. Check in before 6pm. Reception 8am-midnight. f31; nonmembers f35.) A bit closer to civilization than the NJHC is the **Flying Pig Beach Hostel,** Parallel Buolevard 208, located in the center of town. Take bus #40 or 42 for 20min. to Lighthouse stop, the Pig will be in front of you. (☎ (071) 362 25 33; fax 362 25 53; www.flyingpig.nl. Internet. Reception 11am-midnight. Dorms f28-31.)

THE HAGUE (DEN HAAG)   ☎070

William II moved the royal residence to The Hague in 1248, spawning the requisite parliament buildings, museums, and sprawling parks. During the **North Sea Jazz Festival,** the city draws in world-class musicians and 50,000 swinging fans. For the rest of the year, The Hague is a hushed city where museum-gazing and embassy-sleuthing will likely be the quieter pleasures that define a stay in the central city. For snippets of Dutch politics, visit the **Binnenhof,** The Hague's Parliament complex. Guided tours leave from Binnenhof 8a and visit the 13th-century **Ridderzaal** (Hall of Knights) as well as the chambers of the States General. (Open M-Sa 10:15am-4pm. f8.) Just outside the north entrance of the Binnenhof, the 17th-century **Mauritshuis** features an impressive collection of Dutch paintings, including works by Rembrandt and Vermeer. (☎302 34 35. Open Tu-Sa 10am-5pm, Su 11am-5pm. f12.50.) The impressive modern art collection at the **Gemeentmuseum** proudly displays Piet Mondrian's famous *Victory Boogie Woogie,* and a contemporary fashion exhibit. Take tram #7 towards Staten Kwartier. (☎338 11 11. Open daily 10am-5pm. f12.50.) The **Peace Palace,** the opulent home of the International Court of Justice at Carnegiepl., 10min. from the Binnenhof, was donated by Andrew Carnegie during a bout of robber baron guilt. (☎302 41 37; email carnegie-foundation-peacepalace@wxs.nl. Tours M-F 10, 11am, 2, 3, and 4pm. Book in advance through the tourist office. f5.)

Trains (☎(0900) 92 92) serve Amsterdam (50min., f17) and Rotterdam (25min., f7.50) from Holland Spoor station (HS); trains to HS usually continue onto the Hague's second, larger Centraal Station. *Stoptrein* and trams #1, 9, and 12 connect the two stations. The VVV **tourist office,** Kon. Julianapl. 30, in front of Centraal Station next to the Hotel Sofitel books rooms for a f4 fee. (☎(0900) 340 35 05. Open M-F 9:00am-5:30pm, Sa 10am-5pm; July-Aug. also Su 11am-3pm.) To get from Centraal Station to the **NJHC City Hostel,** Scheepmakerstr. 27, take tram 1 (dir.: Delft), 9 (dir.: Vrederust), or 12 (dir.: Duindrop) to Rijswijkseplein (2 strips); cross to the left in front of the tram, cross the big intersection, and Scheepmakerstr. is straight ahead. From Holland Spoor, turn right, follow the tram tracks, turn right at the big intersection, and Scheepmakerstr. is 3min. later, on your right. (☎315 78 78; email denhaag@njhc.org. Breakfast included. Dorms f35-40; doubles f80; nonmembers add f5.) For a drink, sit outside the Binnenhof at the **Havana** bar and restaurant. (☎356 29 00. Beer f3.50 and steak f17. Open daily 10:30am-1:00am.) For more vibrant nightlife go to bars along the Boulevard in **Schevingenen,** 20min. away from the Hague Centraal station. In addition to the North Sea Jazz Festival, The Hague also hosts **Parkpop,** the largest free mainstream rock concert in Europe.

Most foreign **embassies** are located in The Hague: **Australia,** Carnegielaan 4, 2517 KH (☎310 82 00; open M-F 8:45am-12:30pm); **Canada,** Sophialaan 7, 2514 JP (☎311 16 00; open M-F 9am-1pm and 2-5:30pm); **Ireland,** 9 Dr. Kuyperstr., 2514 BA (☎363 09 93; open M-F 10am-12:30pm and 2:30-5:00pm); **New Zealand** (consulate), Carnegielaan 10 (☎346 93 24; open M-F 9am-12:30pm and 1:30-5:30pm); **South Africa** (consulate), Wassenaarseweg 40, 2596 CJ (☎392 45 01; open daily 9am-noon); **UK,** Lange Voorhout 10, 2514 ED (☎427 04 27; open M-F 9am-1pm and 2:15-5:30pm); and the **US,** Lange Voorhout 102, 2514 EJ (☎310 92 09; open M-F 8:15am-5pm).

For the pleasant 5km bike ride from The Hague to **Scheveningen** (SCHAYVE-uhning-un; so difficult to say that it was used as a code word by the Dutch in WWII), rent a **bike** from Holland Spoor or Centraal Station (both f8 per day). The VVV sells cycling maps (f8), but routes and nearby towns are clearly marked along paths. The Scheveningen **branch** of the VVV, Gevers Deynootweg 1134, has info on rooms. (☎ (0900) 340 35 05; f0.75 per min. Open July-Aug. M 1-5pm and Tu-Su 9:30am-7:30pm; Sept.-June M 2-6pm and Tu-Sa 9:30am-5:00pm.) **Hotel Scheveningen,** Gevers Deynootweg 2, has rooms with shower and TV. (☎ (06) 354 70 03. Breakfast included. Singles f50; larger rooms f40 per person.) Three blocks down the Boulevard is **Hotel De Stern,** Gevers Deynootweg 68. Rooms are more modern than Hotel Scheveningen, but also more pricy (☎(070) 350 48 00; fax 70 355 20 72. Reception 7am-midnight. Singles f64-74; doubles f117-142. Cash only.) To reach **Camping Duinhorst,** Buurtweg 135, take bus #43 from Centraal Station. (☎ (070) 324 22 70. Open Apr.-Oct. f8.80 per person, f4.50 per tent.)

DELFT ☎015

To gaze out over Delft's lilied canals from one of its stone footbridges is to behold the very images that local master Jan Vermeer immortalized on canvas over 300 years ago. Thursdays and Saturdays, when townspeople flood to the bustling marketplace, are the best days to visit. Delft is renowned for its **Delftware,** the blue-on-white china developed in the 16th century to compete with the newly imported Chinese porcelain. To gawk at precious platters in the 17th-century factory **De Porceleyne Fles,** Rotterdamseweg 196, in southern Delft take bus #63, 121, or 129 from the station to Jaffalaan. A true-to-scale rendition of Rembrandt's *Nightwatch* awaits amidst the factory's working gallery, and makes for a good first stop in the city as a whole. Walk to the end of Jaffalaan, bear left, and the factory is across the intersection. (☎251 20 30. Open Apr.-Oct. M-Sa 9am-5pm, Su 9:30am-5pm; Nov.-Apr. closed Sundays. Demonstrations every hr. f5.) Built in 1381, the **Nieuwe Kerk** on the central Markt hosts the mausoleum of Dutch liberator William the Silent. The mausoleum, flanked by a statue of his dog, was repaired in 2000 for the benefit of all. Ascend the tower, as caretakers of the 48-bell carillon have for six centuries, for a view of old Delft. (☎212 30 25. Church open Apr.-Oct. M-Sa 9am-6pm; Nov.-Mar. M-F 11am-4pm, Sa 11am-5pm. f3. Tower closes 1hr. earlier. f3.) Built as a 15th-century nun's cloister, **Het Prinsenhof,** Sint Agathapl. 1, off Oude Singel, was William's abode until a fanatic French Catholic hired by Spain's Phillip II assassinated him in 1584; today it houses paintings, tapestries, and pottery. (☎260 23 58. Open Tu-Sa 10am-5pm, Su 1-5pm. f5.) **Rondvaart Delft,** Koormkt. 113, offers canal rides. (☎212 63 85. Apr.-Oct. 10am-6pm. f8.75.) The cafe **Verderop,** Westvest 9, near the station, stirs f5 martinis and occasional live music, including Dixieland every Thursday. (Open M-Sa 10am-1am; July-Aug. opens daily at 3pm.)

Trains arrive from: Amsterdam (1hr.); The Hague (15min., f4); and Leiden (30min., f6.50). For train or **bus** info, call (0900) 92 92. The VVV **tourist office,** Markt 85, has hiking and cycling maps and books rooms (f3.50 fee plus 10% deposit). From the station, cross the bridge, turn left, turn right at the first light, and follow signs to the Markt. (☎213 01 00; www.vvvdelft.nl. Open M-Sa 9am-5:30pm; Apr.-Sept. also open Su 11am-3pm.) To reach the unmarked **Van Leeuwen**, Achterom 143, walk out straight from the station, cross four canals, and turn right on Achterom. (☎212 37 16. Singles f35; doubles f70.) Additional, affordable hotels are around the Markt, including the **Pension Van Domburg**, run by an older husband and wife above their cigar shop, at Voldersgracht 24. (☎212 30 29. Doubles f75.) To **camp** on Korftlaan in the Delftse Hout recreation area, take bus #64 from the station to Aan't Korft. (☎213 00 40. Laundry. Reception May to mid-Sept. 9am-10pm; mid-Sept. to Apr. 9am-6pm. f25 per tent.) Restaurants line **Volderstr.** and **Oude Delft. Kleyweg's Stads-Koffyhuis**, Oude Delft 133-135, with a terrace on the canal, serves sandwiches (f4-8) that were voted the best *broodje* in the Netherlands. (☎212 46 25. Omelettes and salads from f8.25. Open M-F 9am-7pm, Sa 9am-8pm.) Down the street, **Stads Pan**, Oude Delft 113-115, has savory pancakes for f5-17. (☎213 01 93. Open Tu-Su 11am-9pm.)

ROTTERDAM ☎010

After Rotterdam was bombed in 1940, experimental architects replaced the rubble with striking (some say strikingly ugly) buildings, creating an urban, industrial conglomerate. Artsy and innovative, yet desolate and almost decrepit in its hyper modernity, it's like the movie *Blade Runner* come alive. For a dramatic example of Rotterdam's eccentric designs (heavily influenced by the de Stijl school), check out the DNA-like **Kijks-Kubus** (cube houses) by Piet Blom; bus #70 offers tours so you can see what its like to live inside a rubix cube. Take the metro to Blaak, turn left, and look up. (☎414 22 85. Open Mar.-Dec. daily 11am-5pm; Jan.-Feb. open Sa-Su 11am-5pm. f3.50.) Try to decipher the architectural madness at the **Netherlands Architecture Institute**, Museumpark 25 (open Tu 10am-9pm, W-Sa 10am-5pm, Su 11am-5pm; f7.50), then refresh yourself with Rubens, van Gogh, Rembrandt, Rubinstein, Lichtenstein, Rothko, and Magritte across the street at the **Museum Boijmans van Beuningen**, Museumpark 18-20. (☎441 94 71. Metro: Eendractspl., or take tram #4 or 5. Open Tu-Sa 10am-5pm, Su 11am-5pm. f10.) The stately **Schielandshuis** (Historical Museum), Korte Hoogstr. 31, recounts the history of the city. (☎433 41 88. Open Tu-F 10am-5pm, Sa-Su 11am-5pm. f6.) Opposite the plaza lies the powerful Zadkine, or the **Monument for the Destroyed City**, a statue of an anguished man with a hole in his heart memorializes the 1940 bombing raid. The **Oude Haven** and **Oostplein** brim with cafes and students. Mellow coffee shops line **Oude Binnenweg** and **Nieuwe Binnenweg**, including the hip **Wester Paviljoen**, Mathenesserlaan 155, around the corner from the NJHC City Hostel. A good place for a bite, a drink, or a game of cards. (☎436 26 45. Salads f13, glass of wine f6.50. Open Su-Th 7pm-1am, F-Sa 8:30pm-2am.) Avoid the area west of **Dijkzigt.** For less talk and more sweat, dance the night away at **Night Town**, West Kruiskade 28. (Cover f10-25 plus f5 membership fee. Open F-Sa 11pm-late.)

Trains run to: Amsterdam (1hr., f23); The Hague (20min., f7.50); and Utrecht (45min., f15). For info on **ferries** to Hull, England, see p. 730. The VVV **tourist office**, Coolsingel 67, opposite the *Stadhuis*, books rooms for a f2.50-3.50 fee. (☎414 40 65. f0.50 per min. Open M-Th 9:30am-6pm, F 9:30am-9pm, Sa 9:30am-5pm, Su noon-5pm.) To reach the comfy **NJHC City-Hostel Rotterdam (HI)**, Rochussenstr. 107-109, take the metro to Dijkzigt; at the top of the metro escalator, exit onto Rochussentr and turn left. (☎436 57 63. Breakfast included. Sheets f7. Reception 7am-midnight. Dorms f29-37.50; doubles f80-100; nonmembers add f5.) To get from the station to the **Hotel Bienvenue**, Spoorsingel 24, exit through the back, walk straight along the canal for 5min., and it's on the right. Clean, comfortable rooms with TV in a safe area. (☎466 93 94. Reception M-F 7:30am-9pm, Sa-Su 8am-9pm. Singles f86; doubles f105-135; triples f165-185; quads f20.) Eat around **Nieuwe Binnenweg** or in the **Oude Haven. De Consul**, Westeringracht 28, draws a student crowd. (☎436 33 23. Dinner f17.50. Open Su-Tu 3pm-2am, W-Sa 3pm-4am; kitchen open daily 5:30-10pm.) Buy **groceries** at **Albert Heyn**, Lijn-

Hmm, call home or eat lunch?
With YOU^{SM}
you can do both.

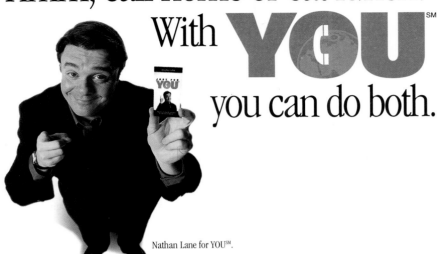

Nathan Lane for YOU^{SM}.

No doubt, traveling on a budget is tough. So tear out this wallet guide and keep it with you during your travels. With YOU, calling home from overseas is affordable and easy.

If the wallet guide is missing, call collect 913-624-5336 or visit www.youcallhome.com for YOU country numbers.

Dialing instructions:
Need help with access numbers while overseas? Call collect, 913-624-5336.

Dial the access number for the country you're in.
Dial 04 or follow the English prompts.
Enter your credit card information to place your call.

Country	Access Number	Country	Access Number	Country	Access Number
Australia **v**	1-800-551-110	Israel **v**	1-800-949-4102	Spain **v**	900-99-0013
Bahamas **+**	1-800-389-2111	Italy **+ v**	172-1877	Switzerland **v**	0800-899-777
Brazil **v**	000-8016	Japan **+ v**	00539-131	Taiwan **v**	0080-14-0877
China **+ ▲ v**	108-13	Mexico **u v**	001-800-877-8000	United Kingdom **v**	0800-890-877
France **v**	0800-99-0087	Netherlands **+ v**	0800-022-9119		
Germany **+ v**	0800-888-0013	New Zealand **▲ v**	000-999		
Hong Kong **v**	800-96-1877	Philippines **T v**	105-16		
India **v**	000-137	Singapore **v**	8000-177-177		
Ireland **v**	1-800-552-001	South Korea **+ v**	00729-16		

YOU^{SM}
Service provided by Sprint

---

v Call answered by automated Voice Response Unit.   **+** Public phones may require coin or card.
▲ May not be available from all payphones.   **u** Use phones marked with "LADATEL" and no coin or card is required.
T If talk button is available, push it before talking.

Pack the Wallet Guide
and save 25% or more* on calls home to the U.S.

It's lightweight and carries heavy savings of 25% or more*
over AT&T USA Direct and MCI WorldPhone rates. So take this
YOU wallet guide and carry it wherever you go.

To save with YOU:
- Dial the access number of the country you're in (see reverse)
- Dial 04 or follow the English voice prompts
- Enter your credit card info for easy billing

Service provided by Sprint

baanplein. From the VVV take two lefts; it's toward the end of the Lijnbaan shopping plaza. (☎413 71 33. Open M-Th 8am-8pm, F 8am-9pm, Sa 8am-7pm, Su 1-6pm.) **Postal code:** 3016 CM.

DAYTRIP FROM ROTTERDAM: GOUDA. Gouda (HOW-da) is the quintessential Dutch town, with canals, a windmill, and well-known cheese. A regional **cheese market** is held weekly in summer (Th 10am-12:30pm). The gargantuan, late Gothic **St. John's Church** has managed to maintain its collection of 16th-century stained-glass windows despite attacks by both lightning and Reformation iconoclasts. (Open Apr.-Oct. M-Sa 9am-5pm; Nov.-Mar. M-Sa 10am-4pm. f3.50, students f2.50.) The **Goudse Pottenbakkerij,** Peperstr. 76, has produced the famous Gouda clay pipes since the 17th century. (☎ (0182) 01 28 42. Open M-F 9am-5pm, Sa 11am-5pm. Free.) Around the corner on Oosthaven, the **Museum Catherine Gasthuis** houses Flemish art and early surgical instruments in its former chapel and adjoining torture chamber. (☎ (0182) 58 84 40. Open daily 8am-5pm. f5.) **Trains** roll into town from Rotterdam (15min., round-trip f12.50). From the station, cross the bridge, walk straight on Kleiweg, which turns into Hoogstr. and leads to the Markt and the VVV **tourist office.** (☎ (0182) 51 36 66. Open M-F 9am-5:30pm, Sa 9am-5pm.)

UTRECHT   ☎030

With pretty canals, a Gothic cathedral, and a prestigious university, Utrecht (pop. 233,000) is a popular daytrip from Amsterdam, but it warrants an overnight stay. Its 52,000 students produce a dynamic pulse in this seemingly quiet, picturesque old city—only in Utrecht would a traditional monument of a 17th-century Dutch hero don a hot-pink scarf. Small enough to get from central Station to the Gracht in a 10min. walk, coast through Utrecht on your own intuition. At the center of the old town stands the awe-inspiring Gothic **Domkerk,** begun in 1254 and finished 250 years later. Initially a Roman Catholic cathedral, its statues were defaced in the early 16th century by Calvinists. (Open May-Sept. M-F 10am-5pm, Sa 10am-3:30pm, Su 2-4pm; Oct.-Apr. M-F 11am-4pm, Sa 11am-3:30pm, Su 2-4pm. Free.) Originally attached to the cathedral but freestanding since a medieval tornado blew away the nave, the **Domtoren** is the highest tower in the Netherlands. (Open M-Sa 10am-5pm, Su noon-5pm. f7.50.) The **Nationaal Museum Van Speelklok tot Pierement,** Buurkerkhof 10, traces the history of mechanical musical instruments. (Open Tu-Sa 10am-5pm, Su noon-5pm. Tours depart on the hr. f9.) Take bus #4 from Centraal Station to the **Rietveld Schroder House;** unveiled in 1924, it's designed like a Mondrian painting sprung to life. (Open W-Sa 11am-5pm, Su 12:30pm-5pm. Guided tours on request. f15.) Pick up a copy of *UiLoper* at bars or restaurants to scout the bar and cultural scene. **De Winkel van Sinkel,** Oude Gracht 158, is a grand cafe with a popular bar that pulses nightly. (Cover f20. Club open F-Sa midnight-5am.) **Wolkenkrabber,** Oudegracht 43, holds gay discos Fridays and Saturdays. (☎231 97 68. Bar open daily 4pm-2am; Happy Hour Sa-Su 5:30-6:30pm; disco 11pm-4am. First F of the month women only, first Sa of the month men only.) Students party at **Woolloo Moollo** on Lucasbolwek (open Tu-Su 11pm-late; cover varies; student ID required), and **De Beurs,** Neude 35-37, in back of the post office and one black from Oude Grocht (☎233 30 07; open daily 10am-late, Th-Sa disco with pop and top 40).

Trains from Amsterdam (25min., 3-6 per hr., day return f19.75) arrive in the **Hoog Catharijne** mall; to get to the VVV **tourist office,** Vredenburg 90, exit the mall and follow the signs around the corner. (☎ (090) 04 14 14 14. Open M-F 9am-6pm, Sa 9am-5pm.) In a majestic manor house, the **Jeugdherberg Ridderhofstad (HI),** Rhijnauwenselaan 14, is one of the nicest hostels in the Netherlands. Take bus #41 from Centraal Station (12min., 3 strips) and tell the driver your destination; from the stop, cross the street, backtrack, turn right on Rhijnauwenselaan, and it's at the end of the road. (☎656 12 77. Breakfast included. Reception 8am-midnight. Summer f31.50; off-season f28.75.) **Hostel Strowis,** Boothstraat 8, is 15min. from Centraal Station. Funky vintage velvet couches in the lounge and eco bathrooms compliment well-kept wooden bunks. (☎238 02 80; email strowis@xs4all.nl. Breakfast f7.50. Reception 24hr. Check-in before 1am. Dorms f20-25; doubles f80; triples f100.) To get to **Camping De Berekuil,** Ariënslaan 5-7, take bus #57 (2 strips) from the station and tell the driver your destination. (☎271 38 70. f8 per person; f8 per tent.) Grab dinner (f10) from the ACU vegetarian **Eetcafe,** around the corner from Hostel Strowis at Voorstraat 71. DJs and live music after 10pm on alternating nights. (Cover f3. Cafe open most weekdays 6pm-8pm.) The chic **Toque Toque,** Oude Gracht 138, at Vinkenburgstr., serves up generous lunch sandwiches for f9, and pasta dishes for f22. (Open M-F 10am-midnight, Sa 9am-midnight, Su noon-midnight.) The hip relaxed **Café De Baas,** Lijnmarkt 8, near the Dom, has big dinners for f14-18. (☎231 51 85. Open W-Sa 5:30-10:30pm; kitchen closes at 8:30.)

HOGE VELUWE NATIONAL PARK

If you've made it to the Netherlands, you shouldn't miss the impressive Hoge Veluwe National Park, a 13,000-acre preserve of woods, heath, dunes, red deer, and wild boars between Arnhem and Apeldoorn that shelters a modern art museum. Tucked deep within the park, a 35min. walk from the nearest entrance, the **Rijksmuseum Kröller-Müller** has troves of van Goghs from the Kroller-Muller family's outstanding collection, as well as key works by Seurat, Mondrian, Picasso, and Brancusi. The museum's striking sculpture garden, one of the largest in Europe, has exceptional work by Rodin, Bourdelle, and Hepworth. (☎318 59 10 41. Museum open Tu-Su 10am-5pm. Sculpture garden open daily 10am-4:30pm. f8.) Take one of the free **bikes** from outside the Kroller-Muller **visitor center** to explore over 33km of paths winding through woods, alongside ponds, and amidst sand dunes. (☎055 378 81 19. Visitor Center open daily 10am-5pm. Park open Apr. daily 8am-8pm; May 8am-9pm; June and July 8am-10pm; Aug. 8am-9pm; Sept. 9am-8pm; Oct. 9am-7pm; Nov.-Mar. 9am-5:30pm. Adults f8. Children aged 6-12 f4. Children under 6 free. Cars f8.50.) The **Museonder,** at the visitor center, is an underground museum about the subterranean ecosystem. (Open daily 10am-5pm. Free.)

▣ TRANSPORTATION. Arnhem and Apeldoorn (both 15km from the park) are good bases for exploration. From March to October, bus #12 (round-trip f8) runs Tuesdays to Sundays from 10am-5pm from the **Arnhem** train station and stops at the museum and visitor center; in winter, bus #107 (dir.: Otterlo) stops in the park. After 6pm, you can take bus #2 to Schaarsbergen to pick up bikes, though you have to walk a few minutes from the bus station to the park. To reach Hoge Veluwe from **Apeldoorn,** take bus #110 from the train station (every hr. 9:40am-4:10pm, f7 or 4 strips).

ARNHEM. Arnhem itself offers little excitement, but the VVV **tourist office,** Willemspl 8, down the street and to the left of the station, has helpful park info. (☎ (090) 02 02 40 75; fax 02 64 42 26 44. www.vvvarnheim.nl. Open M 11am-5:30pm, Tu-F 9am-5:30pm, Sa 10am-4pm.) The **Jeugdherberg Alteveer (HI),** Diepenbrocklaan 27, is clean and friendly. Take bus #3 from the station (dir.: Alteveer; 10min., 3 strips) to the Rijnstate Hospital stop. A 5min. walk takes you to the hostel; turn right as you face the hospital, cross the street at the intersection and turn left on Cattepoelseweg, take the brick path leading up, and at the top of the steps turn right and you will see the hostel. (☎ (026) 351 48 92. Breakfast included. Laundry f10. Key deposit f10. Reception 8am-11pm. Curfew 12:30am. Low season dorms f36.25, high season f39.75; non-members add f5.) Take bus #2 (dir.: Haedaveld; 20min., 3 strips) to **camp** at **Kampeercentrum Arnhem,** Kemperbergerweg 771. (☎ (026) 445 61 00. Showers free. Open Apr.-Oct. f16.50 for 1 person; f21.50 for 2.)

APELDOORN. Apeldoorn is home to the exceptional **Museum Paleis Het Loo,** the magnificent 17th- and 18th-century palace of the many King Williams of Orange. The palace's pristine gardens, featuring Neoclassical sculptures, fountains, and a colonnade, have been precisely and symmetrically trimmed for over 350 years. From the station, take bus #102 or 104 (10min., 2 strips) to get to the museum. (☎ (055) 577 24 00. Open Tu-Su 10am-5pm. f12.50.) The VVV **tourist office,** Stationstr. 72, 5min. straight ahead from the station, sells bike maps for f8.95. (☎ (0900) 168 16 36; fax (055) 521 12 90. Open Apr.-Oct. M 9:30am-6pm, Tu-F 9am-6pm, Sa 9am-5pm; Nov.-Mar. M 9:30am-5:30pm, Tu-F 9am-5:30pm, Sa 9am-2pm.) To get to the lively **De Grote Beer (HI),** Asselsestr. 330, take bus #4 or 7 (dir.: Orden) from the station, get off at Chamavenlaan, cross the intersection and go right. (☎ (055) 355 31 18; fax 355 38 11. Breakfast included. **Bikes** f12.50 per day. Reception 8am-10pm. Curfew midnight. Low season dorms f36.25, high season f39.75; doubles f92.50; non-members f5 extra.)

MAASTRICHT ☎043

Situated on a narrow strip of land between Belgium and Germany, Maastricht (pop. 120,000) is one of the oldest cities in the Netherlands. Home of the prestigious **Jan van Eyck Academie of Art,** Maastricht has long been known for its abundance of art galleries and antique stores. Stitched out of cobblestoned streets dotted with elegant brick front residences, the city's charm is abundant. The new **Bonnefantenmuseum,** 250 ave. Ceramique, lies along the river and contrasts with Maastricht's traditional Dutch brickwork by using a post-modern design resembling a rocketship. The museum houses permanent collections of archaeological artifacts, medieval sculpture, Northern Renaissance painting, and a substantial collection of modern art. (☎32 901 90. Open Tu-Su 11am-5pm. f12.50.) Although the city has been a symbol of European unity since the 1991 Maastricht Treaty (establishing the European Union), it's seen its share of interstate rivalries; centuries of foreign threats culminated in an innovative subterranean defense system. The **Mount Saint Peter Caves,** with a maze-like 20,000 passages, were used as a siege shelter as late as WWII and contain inscriptions and artwork by generations of inhabitants. The **Kazematten,** 10km of underground passageways constructed between 1575 and 1825, enabled locals to detect enemies and to make surprise attacks. From Vrijtmarkt, go toward Tongersepl. and follow the signs for Waldeck Bastion. (Tours July-Aug. daily 12:30pm and 2pm; Sept.-June Su 2pm. f6.) Maastricht's above-ground marvels include the **Basilica of Saint Servatius,** Keizer Karelplein, which contains ornate ecclesiastical crafts, 11th-century crypts, and the country's largest bell, affectionately known as *Grameer* (Grandmother). With the VVV at your back, walk straight along Grote Straat to the Vrijhof area, then cross straight through the cafe action, which leads to the entrance on Kaizer Karelplein. (Open daily July-Aug. 10am-6pm; Sept.-June 10am-5pm. f4.) The **Onze Lieve Vrouwe Basiliek,** O.L. Vrouweplein, is a medieval basilica with a smaller collection of treasures. (Open Easter-Oct. M-Sa 11am-5pm, Su 1-5pm. f3.50.) The new **Natuurhistorich Museum,** De Bosuetplein 6-7, features a life size replica of a Montasaurus dinosaur found in the Maastricht area, great fish tanks, and a comprehensive collection of fossils and artifacts indigenous to southern Holland. (☎350 54 90. Open M-F 10am-5pm, Sa and Su 2-5pm. f6.)

The train station is on the eastern side of town, across the river from most of the action, but buses run frequently to the Markt. **Trains** arrive from: Amsterdam (2½hr., f51); Brussels (2hr., f30.50); and Koln (2hr., f38). The VVV **tourist office,** Kleine Staat 1, is a block from the Markt at Het Dinghuis. From the Markt bus stop, walk toward the river and turn right on Muntstr. (☎325 21 21. Open May-Oct. M-Sa 9am-6pm, Su 11am-3pm; Nov.-Apr. M-F 9am-6pm, Sa 9am-5pm.) To get from the station to **Hostel Sportel de Dousberg (HI),** Dousbergweg 4, take bus #11 on weekdays, bus #8 or 18 on Saturdays, or bus #22 on Sundays and weeknights to De Dousberg. (☎346 67 77. Breakfast included. Key deposit f10. Curfew 1am. Dorms f36-42; doubles f98.) **Maison de Chene,** Boschstraat 104-106, sports cozy rooms in a great location just off the Markt. (☎321 35 23. Breakfast included. Singles f85-125; doubles f110-125.) The **Botel Maastricht** is moored at Maasbouleverd 95, with an on-board bar, and a great view of the Bonnefanten-museum. (☎321 90 23. Breakfast included. Singles f57-67; doubles f88-93.) **De Bobbel,** Wolfstr. 32, just down the street from the tourist office, is perfect for a light meal with soups and quiche for f8. (☎217 413. Open M-Sa 11am-midnight.) On Kesselkade, **de Kadans** serves salads and pumps house in the **K-Club** downstairs. (Salads f13.50-22.50; beer f11. Brasserie open M-Th 11am-midnight, F-Sa 11am-5am, Su noon-midnight. Club open Th-Sa 11pm-5am.)

GRONINGEN   ☎050

With 35,000 students and the nightlife to prove it, the small city of Groningen (pop. 173,000) supports a surprising number of eccentric museums, quirky art galleries, and trendy cafes. The town's gem is the spectacular **Groninger Museum,** a unique pastel assemblage of squares, cylinders, and slag metal that forms a bridge between the station and the city center. The multicolored, steel-trimmed galleries create a futuristic laboratory atmosphere for their wild contemporary art exhibits including virtual-humans who spin like tops and premier Serrano photos of naked, smoking grandmothers. A more conservative assortment of 16th-century Chinese sculpture and 18th-century Dutch china is also on display. (☎366 65 55. Open Tu-Su 10am-5pm. f12.) While WWII bombing left most of the city in ruins, the 500-year-old **Martinitoren Tower** in the Grote Markt somehow weathered the German attacks. (Open Apr.-Sept. daily noon-4:30pm; Oct.-Mar. Sa-Su noon-4:30pm. f3.) Escape Groningen's gray urbanity in the serene 16th-century **Prinsenhoftuin** (Princes' Court Gardens); the entrance is on the canal behind the Martinitorin. The tiny **Theeschenkerij Tea Hut** within has 130 kinds of tea and other beverages amidst ivy-covered trellises and towering rose bushes. (Cup of tea f1.50. Open April-Sept.) Or, cool off in the **Noorderplantsoen Park,** host space to the huge **Noorderzon** (Northern Sun Festival), Groningen's annual cultural climax, which lasts 10 days each August. Groningen's nightlife jams in a corner of the **Grote Markt** and along nearby **Poelstr.** and **Peperstr.** The intimate, candle-lit **de Spieghel Jazz Café,** Peperstr. 11, has two floors of live jazz, funk, or blues every night. (☎312 63 00. Wine f4 per glass. Open daily 8pm-4am.)

To reach the **VVV tourist office,** Ged. Kattendiep 6, turn right as you exit the station, cross the first bridge to your left, head straight through the Hereplein on Herestr., turn right at Ged. Zuderdiep, and veer left onto Ged. Kattendiep. (☎ (0900) 202 30 50; fax 311 02 58. Open June-Aug. M-F 9am-6pm, Sa 10am-5pm; Sept.-May M-F 9am-5:30pm, Sa 10am-5pm.) Surrounding lakes and forests are within easy biking distance of town; rent a **bike** (f8 per day) at the station. Hang out in the snack bar at the funky **Simplon Youth Hotel,** Boterdiep 73, and admire its quirky ceiling art. Take bus #1 from the station and tell the driver your destination. (☎313 52 21. Breakfast f7.50. Sheets f4.50. Laundry. Reception 8am-12pm and 3pm-2am. Lockout noon-3pm. Dorms f21.50.) **Hotel Friesland,** Kleine Pelsterstraat 4, has well-kept rooms in the center of town. From the station, cross the museum bridge, walk straight to Gedemptezuiderdiep, take a right, then your second left onto Pelsterstraa, and the entrance is on the first street on your right. (☎312 13 07. Breakfast. Reception 7am-11pm. Singles f48; doubles f86; triples f124; quads f162.) **Het Pakhuis,** Peperstraat 8, serves daily meals from upstairs (from German to Indian) for f14-15 and mellow drinks on red velvet couches at the cafe downstairs. (☎318 06 90. Restaurant open daily 6pm-11pm. Cafe open daily 9pm-4am.) **Postal code:** 9725 BM.

WADDEN ISLANDS (WADDENEILANDEN)

Wadden means "mudflat" in Dutch, but sand is the defining characteristic of these islands: stretches of isolated beaches hide behind dune ridges with wind-blown manes of golden grass. Dutch vacationers keep these idyllic islands to themselves. Deserted, tulip-lined bike trails carve through vast, flat stretches of grazing land and lead to the serene beaches.

☐ TRANSPORTATION. The islands arch clockwise from Amsterdam around northern Holland: Texel (closest to Amsterdam), Vlieland, Terschelling, Ameland, and Schiermonnikoog. To reach **Texel**, take the train from Amsterdam to **Den Helder** (70min., f20), bus #3 from the other end to the port, and then a ferry to Texel (20min., every hr. 6am-9pm, round-trip f11). To reach **Terschelling**, take a train from Amsterdam to **Harlingen** (1¾hr., f23.25), where **ferries** (☎ (0562) 44 21 41) depart for **Terschelling** (3-5 per day, f43.50). Ferries from both Harlingen and Terschelling connect to the even tinier island of **Vlieland** (45min, f11). In summer, ferries also link the rest of the islands. **Biking** is the easiest way to get around.

TEXEL. The southernmost and largest of the Wadden Islands, Texel can be a voyeur's paradise, with two popular **nude beaches** (south of Den Hoorn and off De Cocksdorp at paal 28) and **bird watching.** You can only visit the **nature reserves** on a guided tour; book in advance at **Ecomare Museum and Aquarium,** Ruyslaan 92, in De Koog. The aquarium contains seals and exhibits on natural Texel. (☎ (0222) 31 77 41. Tours 2hr.; daily 11am. f12.50.) The island's three major villages are the central **Den Burg,** the beachfront **De Koog,** and the more isolated **De Cocksdrop** to the north. The pub **De 12 Blacken Tavern,** Weverstr. 20 in Den Burg, specializes in *'t Jutterje*, the island's popular alcohol, blended from herbs and wheat for f2.75. (Open M-Sa 10am-2am, Su noon-2am.) Pedal between them with a **bike** rented from **Verhuurbedrijf Heijne,** across from the ferry stop at 't Horntje. (f8 per day. Open daily Apr.-Oct. 9am-9pm; Nov.-Mar. 9am-6pm.) A **Texel Ticket** allows unlimited one-day travel on the island's bus system (runs mid-June to mid-Sept.; f7). The VVV **tourist office,** Emmaln 66, is in Den Burg. (☎ (0222) 31 28 47. Open M-Th 9am-6pm, F 9am-9pm, Sa 9am-5pm; July-Aug. also Su 10am-1:30pm.) Both **youth hostels (HI)** are easily accessible from the ferry; tell the bus driver your destination. Take bus #29 to **Panorama,** Schansweg 7, snuggled between sheep pastures 7km from the ferry, and 3km from Den Burg's center. (☎ (0222) 31 54 41. Bikes f8 per day. Sheets f6.50. Reception 8:30am-10:30pm. Dorms f32.50-f37.) Bus #28 goes to **De Eyercoogh,** Pontweg 106. (Open June 15-Aug. Reserve through Panorama. Dorms f30.50.) **Hotel de Merel,** Warmoestr. 22, is in the center of Den Burg. From the bus stop in Den Burg Square, turn left on Elemert and left again on Warmoerstr. (☎ (0222) 31 31 32. Breakfast included. Reception 8am-10pm. Singles from f100; doubles from f150; off-season f5-10 less.) **Campgrounds** are in De Koog (f4-7); ask at the tourist office.

JTERSCHELLING. With 80% of the island covered by a European Nature Reserve, tiny **Terschelling** (pop. 4500) offers secluded beaches that stretch around the western tip and across the northern coast of the long, narrow island. To explore the island's striking scenery, rent a **bike** from **Elslo,** Willem Baretszkade 139, on a pier 3min. from the VVV (f9 per day plus f25 deposit). The VVV **tourist office** is opposite the ferry landing. (☎ (0562) 44 30 00. Open M-Sa 9:30am-5:30pm.) One of the best dinners (f18) is at the **Terschelling Hostel (HI),** van Heusdenweg 39, just out of town. With your back to the harbor, take a right, walk along the pier, continue on the bike path to Midland, and it's straight ahead. (☎ (0562) 44 23 38. Breakfast included. Sheets f6.50. Laundry f8. Reception 9am-10pm. In summer f31.50; off-season f29.25; nonmembers add f5.) Campgrounds abound on Terschelling, including **Camping Cnossen,** 8 Hoofdweg, Terschelling West. (☎ (0562) 44 23 21. f7 per person, f5-9 per tent.) There are a few cafes in the main village, **Terschelling West,** including the cozy **Amsterdamsche Koffijuis,** Willem Barentszstraat 21, around the corner from the VVV. (☎ (0562) 44 27 00. Open daily 5pm-9:30pm.)

THE NETHERLANDS

VLIELAND. With only one village, **Vlieland** (Vlee-lond) is an easy daytrip from Terschelling. To visit the **Lighthouse** on Vlieland, turn right at the library on Dorpsstraat and walk up the hill. (☎ (0562) 45 13 26. Open April M and W 3-5pm, Sa-Su 10:30am-noon; May-June and Sept.-Oct. M-F 3-5pm, Sa 10:30am-noon; July-Aug. M-F 10:30am-noon and 3-5pm, Sa 10:30am-noon. f3.) For guided **horseback riding** adventures, **Stal Edda,** Fortweg 9, is the place to saddle up. (☎ (0562) 45 11 28. f35 per hr.) **Jan van Vlieland,** Dorpsstraat 8, next to the tourist office, has both fast and slow boat rides to see native seals in the surrounding waters. (☎ (0562) 45 15 09. Fast boat ride f17.50, slow f15. Tours daily 1pm, 1½hr.) The Vlieland VVV **tourist office,** opposite the ferry dock, can book rooms for f35. (☎ (0562) 45 11 11. Open M-Th 9am-5pm, F 9am-4:45pm, Sa-Su only open to meet arriving boats.) **Pension Duin en Dal,** Dorpsstraat 163, is one of a cluster of bed and breakfasts that line the end of Dorpstr. (☎ (0562) 45 16 84. Reception 8am-11pm. Singles f59, doubles f119, triples f177.75.)

THE NETHERLANDS

PORTUGAL

ESCUDOS

US$1 = 226.1$ (ESCUDOS)	100$ = US$0.44
CDN$1 = 153.3$	100$ = CDN$0.65
EURO€1 = 200.5$	100$ = EURO€0.50
UK£1 = 328.2$	100$ = UK£0.31
IR£1 = 254.6$	100$ = IR£0.39
AUS$1 = 130.4$	100$ = AUS$0.77
NZ$1 = 96.7$	100$ = NZ$1.04

PHONE CODE | **Country Code: 351. International dialing prefix: 00.**

During the 14th and 15th centuries, Portugal was one of the most powerful nations in the world, ruling a wealthy empire that stretched from America to Asia. Today it is often unfairly overshadowed by its larger neighbor Spain. For while it does share the beaches, nightlife, and strong architectural heritage of the Iberian Peninsula as a whole, Portugal is culturally and geographically quite unique. It contains the most pristine wilderness areas in all of Europe; some villages in the northeast have not changed in over 800 years. Thousands of visitors flock to the stunning beaches of the southern Algarve every summer, and delicious fresh seafood dominates Portuguese cuisine. Expo '98 spurred urban renewal that revived a flagging economy and rebuilt Lisbon's waterfront. Despite ongoing modernization in Lisbon and beyond, though, some of Portugal's age-old and rich traditions seem destined never to change—the wines of Porto are as fine as ever, pristine beaches still line the Atlantic seaboard, and the country's hard-earned character and loyal people continue to stand proud. *Let's Go: Spain & Portugal 2001* has more info on fabulous, vibrant Portugal.

SUGGESTED ITINERARIES

THREE DAYS Make your way through **Lisbon's** (1 day; p. 766) famous Moorish district, the **Alfama**, up to the **Castelo de São Jorge**, and to the futuristic **Parque das Nações**. By night, listen to *fado* and hit the clubs in **Barrio Alto**. Trip to **Sintra's** fairy tale castles (1 day; p. 774) before sipping sweet port in **Porto** (1 day; p. 785).

ONE WEEK From **Lisbon** (2 days; p. 766) and **Sintra** (1 day; p. 774), lounge on the beaches of **Lagos** (1 days; p. 779) and **Figueira da Foz** (1 day; p. 784), move on to the university town of **Coimbra** (1 days; p. 782), and end your week in sophisticated **Porto** (1 day; p. 785).

BEST OF PORTUGAL, TWO WEEKS After the sights, sounds, and cafes of **Lisbon** (2 days; p. 766), daytrip to **Sintra** (1 day; p. 774). Head down to the infamous beach-and-bar town **Lagos** (2 days; p. 779), where hordes of visitors dance the night away, and take an afternoon to **Sagres** (p. 780), once considered the end of the world. Check out the bone chapel in **Évora** (1 day; p. 777) and the mysterious convent in **Tomar** (1 day; p. 776). Take a break at the beach in **Figueira da Foz** (1-2 days; p. 784) and then on to **Coimbra** (2 days; p. 782). Finish your tour of Portugal in unpretentious **Porto** (2 days; p. 785).

LIFE AND TIMES

HISTORY AND POLITICS

EARLY HISTORY

Several tribes inhabited the Iberian Peninsula during the first millennium BC. The first clearly identifiable inhabitants were **Celts,** who began to settle in northern Portugal and Spanish Galicia in the 9th and 8th centuries BC. The **Greeks** and **Carthaginians** followed them, settling the coasts. After their victory over Carthage in the Second Punic War (218-201 BC) and their defeat of the Celts in 140 BC, the **Romans** gained control of central and southern Portugal. Six centuries of Roman rule, which introduced the *Pax Romana* and "latinized" Portugal's language and customs, paved the way for Christianity.

VISIGOTHS AND ARABIAN KNIGHTS (469-1139)

By AD 469, the **Visigoths,** a tribe of migrating Germanic people, had crossed the Pyrenees. Under the Visigoths, who converted to Christianity by the beginning of the 7th century, the Church became the largest landholder in Europe, and monasteries and clerical schools became centers of spiritual learning. In AD 711, however, the Muslims (also known as the **Moors**) invaded Iberia, toppling the Visigoth monarchy. Although these invaders centered their new kingdom of *al-Andalus* in Córdoba, smaller Muslim communities settled along Portugal's southern coast, an area they called the *al-Gharb*, now the Algarve.

THE RECONQUEST AND BIRTH OF PORTUGAL (1139-1415)

Though the **Reconquest** officially began in 718, it didn't pick up steam until the 11th century. When Fernando united Castilla and León in 1035, he helped the **Reconquista** by providing a strong base from which to reclaim territory. In 1139, **Afonso Henriques** (Afonso I), a noble from the frontier territory of Portucale (a region centered around Porto), declared independence from Castilla and León. By the following decade, he had named himself the first King of Portugal, though the papacy did not officially recognize the title until 1179.

The Christian kings, headlined by **Dinis I** (Dom Dinis; 1279-1325), promoted use of the Portuguese language (instead of Spanish), established Portugal's first university in 1290, and solidified its current borders 1297. With the **Treaty of Alcañices** (1297), Dinis settled border disputes with neighboring Castilla, asserting Portugal's identity as an independent nation. By the middle of the 14th century Portugal was the first unified nation-state in Europe.

THE AGE OF DISCOVERY (1415-1580)

The reign of **João I** (1385-1433), the first king of the House of Aviz, ushered in unity and prosperity never before seen in Portugal. João increased the power of the crown and in so doing established a strong base for future Portuguese expansion and economic success. To further strengthen the monarchy, João also negotiated the **Treaty of Windsor** (1386), a permanent Anglo-Portuguese alliance.

The 15th century was one of the greatest periods in the history of maritime travel and naval advances. Under the leadership of João's son, **Prince Henry the Navigator,** Portugal established itself as a world leader in maritime science and exploration. **Bartolomeu Dias** changed the world forever when he rounded Africa's Cape of Good Hope in 1488. Dias opened the route to the East and paved the way for Portuguese entrance into the spice trade. In 1498, they supported **Vasco da Gama,** who led the first European naval expedition to India. Successive expeditions added numerous East African and Indian colonies to Portugal's empire. Two years after da Gama's voyage, **Pedro Alvares Cabral** claimed Brazil for Portugal. Portugal's monarchy peaked under **Manuel I The Fortunate** (1495-1521) on the throne. Although the **Treaty of Tordesillas** (1494) with Spain limited further Portuguese colonial expansion in the Americas, Portugal still established a far-flung empire. By the beginning of the 16th century, Portuguese traders, colonists, and missionaries, often using oppressive tactics, had secured claims all around the globe.

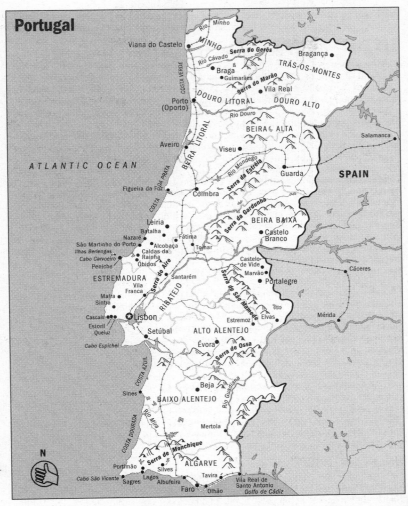

Portugal

THE HOUSES OF HABSBURG AND BRAGANÇA (1580-1807)

In 1580, Habsburg King of Spain **Felipe II** forcibly affirmed his quasi-legitimate claim to the Portuguese throne, and the Iberian Peninsula was briefly ruled by one monarch. For 60 years the Habsburg family dragged Portugal into several ill-fated wars, including the Spanish-Portuguese Armada's crushing loss to England in 1588. But by the end of Habsburg rule, Portugal had lost much of its once vast empire. In 1640, during a rebellion against King Felipe IV, the **House of Bragança** engineered a nationalist rebellion. After a brief struggle they assumed control, once again asserting Portuguese independence from Spain.

NAPOLEON'S CONQUEST AND ITS AFTERMATH (1807-1910)

Napoleon took control of France in 1801 and had grand designs on much of Europe. Napoleon's army met little resistance when it invaded Portugal in 1807. Rather than risk death, the Portuguese royal family fled to Brazil. The **Constitution of 1822,** drawn up during the royal family's absence, severely limited the power of the monarchy, and after 1826, the **War of the Two Brothers** (1826-1834) between constitutionalists (supporting Pedro, the new king of Brazil) and monarchists (supporting Miguel, Pedro's brother) reverberated through Portugal.

FROM THE "FIRST REPUBLIC" TO SALAZAR (1910-1974)

Portugal spent the first few years of the 20th century trying to recover from the political discord of the previous century. On October 5, 1910, 20-year-old King **Manuel II** fled to England. The new government, known as the **First Republic,** granted universal male suffrage and diminished the influence of the Catholic Church. Workers received the right to strike, and merit, rather than birth, became the primary qualification for civil service advancement.

But the expulsion of the Jesuits and other religious orders sparked worldwide disapproval. Portugal's decision to enter World War I (even though on the side of the victorious Allies) proved economically fatal and internally divisive. The weak republic wobbled and eventually fell in a 1926 military coup. General **António Carmona** took over as leader of the provisional military government, and in the face of financial crisis, he appointed **António de Oliveira Salazar,** a prominent economics professor, his minister of finance. In 1932 Salazar became prime minister, but he soon evolved into a dictator. His *Estado Novo* (New State) granted suffrage to women, but did little else to end the country's authoritarian tradition. A terrifying secret police (PIDE) crushed all opposition to Salazar's rule, and African rebellions were quelled in bloody battles that drained the nation's economy.

REVOLUTION AND REFORM (1974-1999)

The slightly more liberal **Marcelo Caetano** dragged on the increasingly unpopular Africa wars after Salazar's death in 1970. In the early 70s, international disapproval of Portuguese imperialism and the army's dissatisfaction with colonial entanglements had **General António de Spinola** to call for decolonization. On April 25, 1974, a left-wing military coalition calling itself the Armed Forces Movement overthrew Caetano in a quick coup. The **Revolution of the Carnations** sent Portuguese dancing into the streets; today every town in Portugal has its own Rua 25 de Abril. The Marxist-dominated armed forces established a variety of civil and political liberties and withdrew Portuguese claims on African colonies by 1975.

The landmark year 1986 brought Portugal into the European Community (now the **European Union**), ending its age-old isolation from more affluent northern Europe. During the 1990s, the Portuguese government instituted a series of economic programs (with the help of EU funds) to prepare the country for economic integration with the rest of Europe.

PORTUGAL TODAY

Despite uncertainty about Portugal's future in an integrated Europe, the nation's economy reported an astounding 3.5% growth rate by the beginning of 1999. With one of the strongest economies in the EU, Portugal was thriving on the eve of its entrance into the European Monetary Union on January 1, 1999. The "new" revitalized Portugal has entered the international arena, taking on a new role in the postcolonial era. In the past few years, Portugal has worked to help negotiate peace in Angola and East Timor, two of its former colonies.

THE ARTS

PAINTING

The Age of Discovery (1415-1580) was an era of vast cultural exchange with Renaissance Europe and beyond. King Manuel's favorite, High Renaissance artist **Jorge Afonso,** created realistic portrayals of human anatomy. Afonso's best works hang at the Convento de Cristo in Tomar and Convento da Madre de Deus in Lisbon (see p. 766). In the 20th century, Cubism, Expressionism and Futurism trickled into Portugal despite Salazar-inspired censorship. More recently, **Maria Helena Vieira da Silva** has won international recognition for her abstract works, and the master **Carlos Botelho** has become world-renowned for his wonderful vignettes of Lisbon life.

ARCHITECTURE

Portugal's signature **Manueline** style celebrates the prosperity and imperial expansion of King Manuel I's reign. Manueline works routinely merge Christian images and maritime motifs. Their rich and lavish ornaments reflect a hybrid of Northern Gothic, Spanish Plateresque, and Moorish influences. The Manueline style found its most elaborate expression in the church and tower at **Belém** (see p. 772), built to honor Vasco da Gama. Close seconds are the **Mosteiro dos Jerónimos** in Belém and the **Abadia de Santa Maria de Vitória** in Batalha (see p. 776).

LITERATURE

Portugal's literary achievements, mostly lyric poetry and realist fiction, can be traced back to the 12th century, when the lyrical aspects of Portuguese were solidified by poet-king **Dinis I. Fernando Pessoa** (1888-1935) was Portugal's most famed and creative writer of the late-19th and early-20th centuries. **José Saramago,** winner of the 1998 Nobel Prize for literature, is perhaps Portugal's most important living writer. He is best known for *Baltasar and Blimunda*, the story of lovers who escape the Inquisition in a time machine, and *The Stone Raft*, a satire about Iberia's isolation from the rest of Europe.

FOOD AND DRINK

Portugese dishes are seasoned with olive oil, garlic, herbs, and sea salt, but few spices. Portugal has a tantalizing selection of fish, such as *chocos grelhados* (grilled cuttlefish), *Linguado grelhado* (grilled sole), and *peixe espada* (swordfish). *Sopas* are **soups** and *sandes* are **sandwiches.** Vegetarians will likely eat lots of cheese sandwiches on Portugal's delectable bread. The favorite **dessert** is *pudim*, or *flan*, a caramel custard. The hearty midday meal, *almoço* (lunch), is eaten between noon and 2pm and *jantar* (dinner) between 8pm and midnight. A full meal costs 1000-2000$. **Media dose** (half-portions) cost more than half-price but are often adequate; a full portion may satisfy two. The **prato do dia** (special of the day) or **ementa** (menu) of appetizer, bread, main dish, and dessert are filling. In restaurants, expect to pay 300-500$ per person for pre-meal munchies. **Vino do porto** (port) is a dessert in itself. A six-month heating process gives **Madeira** wines a unique "cooked" flavor. Portuguese coffee are **bica** (black espresso), **galão** (coffee with milk, served in a glass), and **café com leite** (coffee with milk, served in a cup).

ESSENTIALS

DOCUMENTS AND FORMALITIES

Citizens of the US, Canada, the UK, and New Zealand can visit Portugal **visa-free** for up to 90 days. Citizens of Australia and South Africa need a visa.

Portuguese Embassies at Home: Australia, 23 Culgoa Circuit, O'Malley, ACT 2603. Mailing address P.O. Box 9092, Deakin, ACT 2600 (☎ (02) 62 90 17 33); **Canada,** 645 Island Park Dr., Ottawa, ON K1Y OB8 (☎ (613) 729-0883); **South Africa,** 599 Leyds St., Mucklenuk, Pretoria (☎ (012) 341 2340); **UK,** 11 Belgrave Sq., London SW1X 8PP (☎ (020) 72 35 53 31); **US,** 2125 Kalorama Rd. NW, Washington, D.C. 20008 (☎ (202) 328-8610). **New Zealanders** should contact the embassy in Australia.

Foreign Embassies and Consulates in Portugal: Australians can use their embassy in **France** (see p. 271); all other embassies are in **Lisbon** (see p. 766). Canada has a consulate in **Faro** and the UK's is in **Porto.**

TRANSPORTATION

BY PLANE. Portugal is easily accesible by plane from the US and Europe. Most major international airlines serve Lisbon; some serve Porto, Faro, and the Madeiras. **TAP Air Portugal** (in US and Canada ☎ (800) 221-7370; in UK ☎ (171) 828 20 92; in Lisbon ☎ (21) 841 69 90; www.tap.pt) is Portugal's national airline, serving all domestic locations and many major international cities. **Portugália** (www.pga.pt) is a smaller Portuguese airline that flies between Porto, Faro, Lisbon, all major Spanish cities, and other Western European destinations. Its offices include Lisbon (☎ (21) 842 55 00) and Manchester, UK (☎ (161) 489 50 40).

BY TRAIN. Portugal is well connected to neighboring Spain by train. Long-distance trains run from Madrid to Lisbon, and Spain's national railway is in the process of building a high-speed train from Seville to Lagos. Closer to the border, trains run from Huelva and Cáceres to Portugal. **Caminhos de Ferro Portugueses** is Portugal's national railway, but for long-distance travel outside of the Braga-Porto-Coimbra-Lisbon line, the bus is much better. The exception is around Lisbon, where local trains and commuter rails are fast and efficient. Unless you own a Eurailpass, the return on round-trip tickets must be used before 3am the following day. Anyone riding without a ticket is fined over 3500$. Children under four travel free; ages four to 11 pay half-price. **Youth discounts** are only available to Portuguese citizens. Though there is a Portugal Flexipass, it is rarely worth purchasing.

BY BUS. Buses are cheap, frequent, and connect just about every town in Portugal. **Rodoviária** (national info ☎ (21) 354 57 75), the national bus company, has recently been privatized. Each company name corresponds to a particular region of the country, such as Rodoviária Alentejo or Minho e Douro, with notable exceptions such as EVA in the Algarve. Private regional companies also operate, among them **Cabanelas, AVIC,** and **Mafrense.** Be wary of non-express buses in small regions like Estremadura and Alentejo, which stop every few minutes. Express coach service *(expressos)* between major cities is especially good; inexpensive city buses often run to nearby villages.

BY CAR. Portugal has a particularly high rate of automobile accidents. The new highway system (IP) is quite good, but off the main arteries, the narrow, twisting roads prove difficult to negotiate. The locals' testy reputation is well deserved. Speed limits are effectively ignored, recklessness common, and lighting and road surfaces often inadequate. Buses and trucks are safer options. Moreover, parking space in cities borders on nonexistent. **Gas** comes in super (97 octane), normal (92 octane), and unleaded and unusually runs 140-170$ per liter. Portugal's national automobile association, the **Automóvel Clube de Portugal (ACP),** R. Rosa Araújo, 42, 1250 Lisbon (☎ (21) 318 01 00), provides breakdown and towing service (M-F 9am-5pm) and 24-hr. first aid.

BY THUMB. In Portugal, **hitchers** are rare. Beach-bound locals occasionally hitch in summer but otherwise stick to the inexpensive bus system. Rides are easiest to come by between smaller towns. Best results are reputedly at gas stations near highways and rest stops. *Let's Go* does not recommend hitchhiking.

TOURIST SERVICES AND MONEY

EMERGENCY	Police, Medical, and Fire: ☎112.

TOURIST OFFICES. The official Portuguese tourism website is located at www.portugalinsite.pt. There are also offices in Canada, the UK and the US. When in Portugal, stop by municipal and provincial tourist offices for maps and advice.

Canada: Portuguese Trade and Tourism Commission, 60 Bloor St. West, Suite 1005, Toronto, ON M4W 3B8 (☎ (416) 921-7376; fax (416) 921-1353; email iceptor@idirect.com). **UK:** Portuguese Trade and Tourism Office, 22-25A Sackville St., 2nd-4th Floor, London W1X 2LY (☎ (20) 7474 1441; fax (20) 7494 1441; email iceplond@aol.com). **US:** Portuguese National Tourist Office, 590 Fifth Ave., 4th Fl., New York, NY 10036 (☎ (212) 354-4403; fax (212) 764-6137, www.portugal.org). Additional office in Washington D.C. (☎ (202) 331-8222).

CURRENCY & EXCHANGE. Money in Portugal comes in the form of the **escudo,** available in coins of 1, 2, 5, 10, 20, 50, 100, 200 escudos and notes of 500, 1000, 2000, 5000, and 10,000.

Prices: You can do a "bare-bones day" in Portugal (camping or sleeping in cheap hostels, buying food at supermarkets, staying in at night) for about 5000$, or US$25. A slightly more comfortable day (sleeping in nicer hostels, eating one or two meals a day in restaurants, going out at night) will probably run up to 8000$, or US$40.

Tipping and bargaining: Tipping is only customary in expensive restaurants or hotels; most cheaper restaurants include a 10% service charge. Taxi drivers do not expect a tip unless the trip was unusually long. **Bargaining** is not normal in shops, but you can give it a shot at the local market or when looking for a room.

Taxes: Taxes are included in all prices in Portugal and are not redeemable upon leaving, even for EU citizens.

ACCOMMODATIONS AND CAMPING

Movijovem, Av. Duque de Ávila, 137, 1050 Lisbon (☎ (21) 313 88 20; fax 352 14 66) looks over the country's **HI hostels.** All bookings can be made through them. A cheap bed in a *pousada da juventude* (not to be confused with plush *pousadas*) costs 1200-2900$ per night and slightly less in the off-season (breakfast and sheets included). Lunch or dinner usually costs 900$, snacks around 250$. Though often the cheapest option, hostels may lie some distance from the town center. Check-in hours are 9am to noon and 6pm to midnight. Some have lockouts 10:30am to 6pm, and early curfews might cramp club-hoppers' style. The maximum stay at one hostel is eight nights unless you get special permission. **Pensões,** also called **residencias,** are a budget traveler's mainstay. They're far cheaper than hotels and only slightly more expensive (and much more common) than crowded youth hostels. Like hostels, *pensões* generally provide sheets and towels and have commons rooms. All are rated on a five-star scale and are required to visibly post their category and legal price limits. (If you don't see this information, ask for it.) **Hotels** in Portugal tend to be pricey. Room prices typically include showers and breakfast, and most rooms without bath or shower have a sink. When business is weak, try bargaining down—the "official price" is just the maximum allowed.

In Portugal, over 150 **official campgrounds** *(parques de campismo)* feature tons of amenities and comforts. Most have a supermarket and cafes, and many are beach-accessible or near rivers or pools. Police have been cracking down on illegal camping, so don't try it—especially near official campgrounds. Tourist offices stock the free *Portugal: Camping and Caravan Sites*, a handy guide to official campgrounds. Otherwise, write to the **Federação Portuguesa de Campismo e Caravanismo,** Av. Coronal Eduardo Gallardo, 24D, 199-007 Lisbon (☎ (21) 812 69 00).

COMMUNICATION

TELEPHONES. Portugal's national telephone company is **Portugal Telecom.** Coin-operated phones are essentially non-existent in Portugal; you'll need phone cards. The country uses both the **Credifone** and **Portugal Telecom** systems. For both systems, the basic unit for all calls (and the price for local ones) is 18$. Credifone cards, with magnetic strips, are sold at drugstores, post offices, and locations posted on phone booths, and are most useful outside the two big cities. **City codes** now all begin with a 2, and local calls do not require dialing any portion of the city code. **Calling cards** remain the best method of making international calls. To call home with a calling card, contact the operator for your service provider in Portugal by dialing the appropriate **international toll-free access number: AT&T,** ☎800 800 128; **Australia Direct,** ☎800 800 610; **BT Direct,** ☎800 800 440; **Canada Direct,** ☎800 800 122; **Eircom,** ☎800 800 353; **MCI WorldPhone Direct,** ☎800 800 123; **Sprint,** ☎800 800 187; **Telecom New Zealand Direct,** ☎800 800 640; **Telkom South Africa Direct,** ☎800 800 270.

MAIL. Mail in Portugal is somewhat inefficient—**Air mail** *(via aerea)* can take from one to two weeks (or longer) to reach the US or Canada. **Surface mail** *(superficie)*, for packages only, takes up to two months. **Registered** or **blue mail** takes five to eight business days (for roughly three times the price of air mail). **EMS** or **Express Mail** will probably get there in three to four days for more than double the blue mail price. **Stamps** are available at post offices *(correios)* and automatic stamp machines outside post offices and in central locations around cities.

INTERNET ACCESS. Email is both faster and more reliable than the standard mail system. Cybercafes are common in cities and most smaller towns; when in doubt, try the library; they often have at least one computer equipped for internet access.

LANGUAGE. Portuguese is a Romance language similar to Spanish. English, Spanish, and French are fairly widely spoken. To snuggle up to Portuguese and get Romantic with other members of the family, see p. 957.

LOCAL FACTS

Time: Greenwich Mean Time.

Climate: Portugal's climate is very mild; summers are fairly hot in the south, but not too extreme and not at all humid. In winter it never gets particularly cold.

Hours: A normal workday is from about 9am-7pm with a lunch break from 1-3pm. On Saturdays most places only open in the morning; on Sundays you're on your own.

Holidays: New Year's Day (Jan. 1); Good Friday (Apr. 13); Liberty Day (Apr. 25); Labor Day (May 1); Corpus Christi (June 14); Assumption Day (Aug.15); Republic Day (Oct.5); All Saints' Day (Nov.1); Restoration of the Independence (Dec.1); Feast of the Immaculate Conception (Dec.8); Christmas Eve (Dec.24); Christmas (Dec.25).

Festivals: Just about everything closes down during public festivals, so plan accordingly. Also be prepared to be surprised by a festival, as many towns have local festivals of their own in addition to national celebrations and holidays. All of Portugal will celebrate **Carnival** in mid-March and the Holy Week in mid-April. Coimbra holds the **Burning of the Ribbons** festival in early May, and Lisbon hosts the **Feira Internacional de Lisboa** in June. Coimbra's **Feira Popular** takes place the second week of July. For more information on Portuguese festivals, see www.portugal.org.

LISBON (LISBOA)   ☎21

Over 400 years ago, Lisbon was the center of the world's richest and farthest-reaching empire. City and empire reached their apex at the end of the 15th century when Portuguese navigators pioneered explorations of Asia, Africa, and South America. Lisbon has seen more than its share of changes over the course of the 20th century. During World War II, Lisbon's neutrality and Atlantic connections made the city a rendezvous for spies on both sides. In 1974, when Mozambique and Angola won independence, hundreds of thousands of refugees converged upon the Portuguese capital. In 1998, the World Expo descended upon Lisbon, providing the impetus for massive construction projects and a citywide facelift. Since then, the revival has continued, as more tourist hot spots and sites of cultural interest emerge. Like Portugal itself, Lisbon has managed to preserve its traditions, continually renovating its historic monuments and meticulously maintaining its black and white mosaic sidewalks, pastel facades, and cobbled, medieval alleys.

▐ TRANSPORTATION

Lisbon has an efficient system of buses, subways, trams, funiculars, and trains. Use them to full advantage—no suburb takes longer than 90 min. to reach. Train service in Lisbon is potentially confusing, as there are five main stations, each serving different destinations. For further info about Portugal's railway system call **Caminhos de Ferro Portuguêses** (☎888 40 25 or 346 50 22; www.cp.pt).

Flights: Aeroporto de Lisboa (☎841 37 00). Walk out of the terminal, turn right, and follow the road around the curve to the bus stop. From there take **bus #44** or 45 (20-40min., 165$) to Pr. Restauradores; the bus stops directly in front of the tourist office. Alternatively, take the express **AeroBus** (bus #91; 15min., every 20min., 460$) to Pr. Restauradores; this bus, which leaves directly from the airport exit, is a better option during rush hour. A **taxi** to the downtown area costs about 1500$, plus a 300$ fee for luggage. Major airlines have offices at Pr. Marquês de Pombal and along Av. Liberdade.

Lisbon

ACCOMMODATIONS
- Camping Municipal, 1
- Casa de Hóspedes Globo, 5
- Pensão Beira-Mar, 7
- Pensão Campos, 4
- Pensão Moderna, 6
- Pousada da Juventude de Catalazete (HI), 8
- Pousada da Juventude de Lisboa (HI), 2
- Residencial Florescente, 3

PORTUGAL

Trains: Estação Rossio (M: Rossio or Restauradores) serves destinations west. To **Sintra** (45min., every 10min., 210$), via **Queluz** (140$). **Estação Santa Apolónia** runs the international, northern and eastern lines. To: **Coimbra** (2½hr., 7 per day, 1510-2700$); **Porto** (4½hr., 12 per day, 2080-3700$); **Madrid** (10hr., 1 per day, 8200$); and **Paris** (21hr., 1 per day, 29,000$). **Estação Cais do Sodré** (M: Cais do Sodré). To **Estoril** and **Cascais** (30min., every 20min., 210$). **Estação Barreiro**, across the Rio Tejo, serves southern destinations like the Costa Azul and the Algarve. **Ferries** leave every 30min. and take 30min.; ferry ticket included in the price of connecting train ticket (otherwise 85$, round-trip 200$). Trains to **Évora** (2½hr., 7 per day, 1200$) and **Lagos** (5½hr., 5 per day, 2800$).

Buses: Arco do Cego, Av. João Crisóstomo, around the block from the M: Saldanha. All "Saldanha" buses (#36, 44, 45) stop in the *praça* (165$). This is the terminal for virtually all buses. The terminal has fast **Rede Expressos** (☎354 54 39 or 310 31 11; www.rede-expressos.pt) to many destinations. To: **Coimbra** (2½hr., 16 per day, 1500$); **Évora** (2hr., 13 per day, 1500$); **Lagos** (5hr., 9 per day, 2500$); and **Porto** (4hr., 7per day, 2300$), via **Leiria.**

Public Transportation: CARRIS (☎361 30 00; www.carris.pt) runs the buses, trams, and funiculars in Lisbon. Fare 165$ within the city; pay on the bus. If you plan to stay for any length of time, consider investing in a *passe turístico* (tourist pass), good for unlimited travel on all CARRIS transports. 1-, 3-, 4-, and 7-day passes available (460$, 1080$, 1760$, 2490$). The **metro** (☎355 84 57; www.metrolisboa.pt) covers downtown and the modern business district in 4 color-coded lines. Individual tickets 100$; book of 10 tickets 850$. Trains run daily 6am-1am, though some stations close earlier. **Trams** offer views of the harbor and older neighborhoods (tickets 165$). Line #28 is great for sight-seeing in the Alfama and Mouraria (stop in Pr. Comércio); line #15 heads from Pr. Comércio or Pr. Figueira to Belém and the monastery complex.

Taxis: Rádio Táxis de Lisboa (☎811 90 00), **Autocoope** (☎793 27 56), and **Teletáxis** (☎811 11 00) all lie along Av. Liberdade and Rossio. Flat rate of 300$ for luggage.

Car Rental: Pick up cars at the airport or in one of several locations downtown. Contact the agencies for pickup locations. **Budget,** R. Castilho, 167B (☎386 05 16); **Hertz,** R. Castilho, 72A (☎381 24 30); **Avis,** (☎356 11 76) R. Castilho.

✦🛈 ORIENTATION AND PRACTICAL INFORMATION

According to legend, Lisbon, like Rome, was built on seven hills, though at times it might seem like many more. The city center is made up of three main *bairros* (neighborhoods): the **Baixa** (low district, resting in the valley), the **Bairro Alto** (high district), and the twisty-turny, topsy-turvy **Alfama.** The Baixa is the center of town, sandwiched between Bairro Alto and Alfama. Its grid of small, mostly pedestrian streets begins at the **Praça Dom Pedro IV** (better known as the **Rossio**) and ends at the **Praça do Comércio** on the **Rio Tejo.**

Adjacent to Rossio are two other important squares, **Praça dos Restauradores** and **Praça da Figueira,** which borders the medieval/Moorish district, **Alfama.** The lone survivor of the 1755 earthquake, Alfama is the city's oldest district, a labyrinth of narrow alleys and stairways beneath the **Castelo de São Jorge.** Across the Baixa from Alfama is Bairro Alto with its upscale shopping district, the **Chiado,** traversed by **Rua do Carmo** and **Rua Garrett,** where much of the city's nightlife is located. Stretching out along the river are some of the fastest growing parts of Lisbon. The former Expo '98 grounds, now called the **Parque das Nações** (Park of Nations), occupies Lisbon's eastern end, while the **Alcântara** and the **Docas do Santo Amaro** show off Lisbon's most happening nightlife to the west.

Tourist Office: Palácio da Foz (☎346 63 07), Pr. Restauradores, M: Restauradores. Open daily 9am-8pm. Office at the **Aeroporto de Lisboa** (☎849 43 23), just outside the baggage claim area. Open daily 6am-2am. Look for kiosks with signs that read "Ask me about Lisboa" at Santa Apolónia, Rossio, and Parque das Nações.

American Express: Top Tours, Av. Duque de Loulé, 108 (☎319 42 90). M: Marquês de Pombal. Exit the metro stop and walk up Av. Liberdade toward the Marquês de Pombal statue, then turn right; the office is 2 blocks up on the left side of the street. The often-crowded Top Tours office handles all AmEx functions. English spoken. Open M-F 9:30am-1pm and 2:30-6:30pm.

Luggage Storage: Estação Rossio. Lockers 550$ for 48hr. Open daily 8:30am-11:30pm.

Laundromat: Lavatax, R. Francisco Sanches, 65A (☎812 33 92). One block from M: Arroios. Wash, dry, and fold 1100$ per 5kg load. Open M-F 8:30am-1pm and 3-7pm, Sa 8:30am-1pm.

Emergency: ☎112. **Police,** R. Capelo, 3 (☎346 61 41). English spoken.

24-Hour Pharmacy: ☎118 (directory assistance). The name and address of the next night's open location is posted on the door of each pharmacy in town.

Medical Services: British Hospital, R. Saraiva de Carvalho, 49 (☎395 50 67). **Cruz Vermelha Portuguesa,** R. Duarte Galvão, 54 (☎771 40 00; **ambulance** ☎942 11 11).

Internet Access: Web Café, R. Diário de Notícias, 126 (☎342 11 81). 300$ for 15min., 500$ for 30min., 700$ for 45min., 800$ per hr. Open daily 4pm-2am.

Post Office: Marked by red *Correios* signs. **Main office** (☎346 32 31), Pr. Comércio. Telephone, fax, *Posta Restante,* and international express mail (EMS). Open M-F 8:30am-6:30pm. **Postal Code:** 1100.

▐▘ ACCOMMODATIONS

Most hotels are in the center of town on **Av. Liberdade,** while many convenient budget hostels are in the **Baixa** along the **Rossio** and on **R. Prata, R. Correeiros,** and **R. Ouro.** Lodgings near the **Castelo de São Jorge** or in the **Bairro Alto** are quieter and closer to the sights. If central accommodations are full, head east to the hostels along **Av. Almirante Reis.** At night, be careful in the Baixa, the Bairro Alto, and especially the Alfama; many streets are isolated and poorly lit.

BAIXA

Dozens of hostels surround the three connected *praças,* **Pr. Restauradores, Pr. Dom Pedro IV,** and **Pr. Figueira,** that form the heart of downtown Lisbon. Staying in this area is incredibly practical, as it makes a good base for visiting sights.

Residencial Estrela do Mondego, Calçada do Carmo, 25 (☎324 08 40), next to the Estação Rossio. Large, comfortable rooms, all with phones, cable TV, and A/C. English spoken. Laundry 1500$. Singles with bath 5000$; doubles 6000-6500$; triples with bath 7000$; quads with bath 8000$.

Residencial Duas Nações, R. Vitória, 41 (☎346 07 10), on the corner of R. Augusta, 2 blocks up from M: Baixa-Chiado. 69 good-sized, centrally-located rooms with phones. Breakfast included. Laundry available. Reserve ahead during the summer. Singles 3500$, with bath 6000$; double 4500$, with bath 7500$; triples with bath 9000$.

Pensão Campos, R. Jardim do Regedor, 24, 3rd fl. (☎346 28 64), between Pr. Restauradores and R. Portas de Santo Antão. M: Restauradores. Street-facing rooms can get a bit noisy at night, but back rooms provide quiet. Laundry 1500$. Singles 4000$; doubles with shower 6000-7000$; triples 7000$.

Pensão Moderna, R. Correeiros, 205, 4th fl. (☎346 08 18), 1 block from Pr. Figueira, toward the water. M: Rossio. Comfortable apartment-style rooms are filled with antiques. Singles 2500$; doubles 4000$; triples 6000$.

Pensão Prata, R. Prata, 71, 3rd fl. (☎346 89 08), 2 blocks from Pr. Comércio. M: Rossio. Clean rooms with baths. Laundry 1500$. Singles 5000$; doubles 6000-7000$.

Residência do Sul, Pr. Dom Pedro IV, 59, 2nd fl. (☎342 25 11), through the souvenir shop. M: Rossio. Somewhat dark but otherwise excellent rooms, all with TV and phone. Singles 4500-7500$; doubles 6000-8000$; triples 10000$; quads 12500$.

BAIRRO ALTO

The Bairro Alto has a communal feel that the town center lacks, but the uphill hike is inconvenient and daunting for luggage-bearers. Most of Lisbon's nightlife is in Bairro Alto, but be cautious if you're out late alone.

Residencial Camões, Tr. Poço da Cidade, 38, 1st fl. (☎347 75 10), off R. Misericórdia. From the top of Ascensor Glória, turn left onto R. S. Pedro, which becomes R. Misericórdia; Tr. Poço da Cidade is the 5th right. A pristine set of rooms in the heart of the party district. Common room with TV. Breakfast included. Reserve 1 week ahead during the summer. Singles 2500-3000$; doubles 5500-7500$, with bath 6500-8000$; triples with bath 8000-10,000$.

Pensão Londres, R. Dom Pedro V, 53, 2nd fl. (☎346 22 03; fax 346 56 82; www.desenvolve.com/plondres). Take the Ascensor Glória from Pr. Restauradores to the top. Turn right and walk up R. S. Pedro to R. Dom Pedro V. These spacious, well-lit rooms (all with phones, some with TV) overlook the old town. Breakfast included. Laundry available. Reserve a month ahead in the summer. Singles 5500-9000$; doubles 7700-12,200$; triples 12,800-15,200$; quads 17,200$.

ALFAMA

Staying in the Alfama grants flowering balconies and amazing views. It also means steep streets, a long walk to the hostel, and potential danger at night. However, rooms are cheap and surprisingly comfy, and the Alfama's narrow side streets and friendly *praças* are well worth exploring.

Pensão Ninho das Águias, R. Costa do Castelo, 74 (☎885 40 70), right behind the Castelo. From Pr. Figueira take R. Madalena to Largo Adelino Costa, then head uphill to R. Costa do Castelo. Canary-filled garden looks out over the old city. 16 cheerful rooms with phones. Reserve at least 1 month ahead during the summer. Singles 5000$; doubles 7500$, with bath 8000$; triples 10,000$.

YOUTH HOSTELS

Pousada da Juventude de Lisboa (HI), R. Andrade Corvo, 46 (☎353 26 96). M: Picoas. Exit the metro station, turn right, and walk 1 block; the hostel is on your left. Huge, ultra-clean youth haven in an inconvenient location. English spoken. Breakfast included. Lockers 300$ per day. Reception 8am-midnight. Check out 10:30am. Wheelchair accessible. HI card required. June-Sept. dorms 2900$, doubles with bath 6500$; Oct.-May dorms 2000$, doubles 5000$.

Pousada da Juventude de Parque das Nações, R. de Moscavide, lote 4-71-01 (☎892 08 90). M: Oriente. Exit the station and go left on Av. Dom João II, walking past the Parque das Nações until the street intersects with R. de Moscavide. Internet 100$ for 15min., 150$ for 30min. English spoken. Breakfast included. Lunch and dinner 950$ each. Reception 8am-midnight. Midnight curfew. Wheelchair accessible. June-Sept. dorms 2100$, doubles 5100$; Oct.-May dorms 1700$, doubles 4300$.

CAMPING

Information on campgrounds is available from the tourist office in the free booklet *Portugal: Camping and Caravan Sites.* There are 30 campgrounds within a 45-min. radius of the capital; listed below is the only one in Lisbon proper.

Parque de Campismo Municipal de Lisboa (☎760 20 61), on the road to Benfica. Take bus #43 from the Rossio to the Parque Florestal Monsanto. Municipal campground has a pool, bar, supermarket, and even an amphitheater. Reception 9am-9pm. July-Aug. 840$ per person and per tent, 540$ per car; May, June, and Sept. 760$ per person, 750$ per tent, 480$ per car; Oct.-Apr. 600$ per person and per tent, 380$ per car.

◖ FOOD

Lisbon has some of the least expensive restaurants and some of the best wine of any European capital. A full dinner costs about 2000-2200$ per person; the *prato do dia* (daily special) is often a great deal. Snack on a surprisingly filling, incredibly cheap, and sinfully delicious Portuguese pastry; *pastelarias* (pastry shops) are everywhere. Specialties include *amêjoas à bulhão pato* (steamed clams), *creme de mariscos* (seafood chowder with tomatoes), and a local classic, *bacalhau cozido com grão e batatas* (cod with chick-peas and boiled potatoes). A **supermarket, Supermercado Celeiro,** R. 1 de Dezembro, 73, is two blocks from Estação Rossio. (☎342 74 95. Open M-F 9am-8pm, Sa 9am-7pm.)

Hell's Kitchen, R. Atalaia, 176 (☎342 28 22). From the top of C. Glória (the steep hill from Pr. Restauradores), walk a few blocks into Bairro Alto and turn right on R. Atalaia. Small, but with an extensive selection of delicious main dishes (1100-1650$), including vegetarian options. Open Tu-Su 8pm-12:30am.

Casa da Té, R. D. Pedro V, 63 (☎347 62 58), just past Parque de São Pedro de Alcântara in the Bairro Alto, near the corner of R. da Rosa. So small the entire menu changes daily. Takeout also available, making it the natural choice for a picnic in the park. Main dishes 750-900$. Open daily 8am-8pm.

Restaurante Calcuta, R. do Norte, 17 (☎342 82 95), near Lg. Camões in the Bairro Alto. Fancy yet inexpensive Indian restaurant with a wide selection of vegetarian meals (900-1000$). Meat dishes 1200-1600$. Open daily noon-3pm and 6:30-11pm.

Restaurante Bonjardim, Tr. Santo Antão, 11 (☎342 43 89), off Pr. Restauradores. The self-proclaimed *rei dos frangos* (king of chicken) legitimately rules the roost with its delicious roast chicken (1400$). Main dishes 980-2900$. Open daily noon-11:30pm.

👁 SIGHTS

BAIXA

Although the Baixa features few historic sights, a lively atmosphere surrounding the neighborhood's three main *praças* makes it a monument in its own right.

AROUND THE ROSSIO. The best place to embark upon your tour of Lisbon's Enlightenment-era center is from its heart—the **Rossio.** The city's main square, also known as the **Praça Dom Pedro IV,** was once a cattle market and home to a public execution stage, bullfighting arena, and carnival ground. Adjoining the Rossio is the elegant **Praça Figueira,** which lies on the border of the Alfama district.

AROUND PRAÇA DOS RESTAURADORES. Just past the Rossio train station, an obelisk and a sculpture of the "Spirit of Independence" commemorate Portugal's independence from Spain in 1640. Pr. Restauradores is also the start of **Avenida da Liberdade,** Lisbon's most imposing yet elegant promenades. Modeled after the wide boulevards of 19th-century Paris, this mile-long thoroughfare ends at **Praça do Marquês do Pombal;** from there an 18th-century statue of the Marquês, who oversaw the the city's reconstruction after the 1755 earthquake, overlooks the city.

BAIRRO ALTO

In the Bairro, pretentious intellectuals mix with insecure teens and idealistic university students. It's the only place in Lisbon that never sleeps; here, there is as much to do at night as there is to see during the day.

AROUND THE ASCENSOR DE SANTA JUSTA. Although it's just as easy to get from the Baixa to the Bairro Alto by walking, the Ascensor de Santa Justa, a historic elevator built in 1902 inside a Gothic wrought-iron tower, transports sightseers. From the upper terrace, a narrow walkway leads to the 14th-century **Igreja do Carmo.** The 1755 earthquake left the church roofless but its dramatic Gothic arches remain. *(Elevator runs M-F 7am-11pm, Sa-Su 9am-11pm. One-way 165$.)*

MUSEU NACIONAL DE ARTE ANTIGA. This museum hosts an interesting survey of European painting dating back as far as the 12th century and ranging from Gothic primitives to 18th-century French masterpieces. *(R. das Janelas Verdes, Jardim 9 Abril. 30min down Av. Infante Santo from the Ascensor de Santa Justa. Buses #40 and 60 stop to the right of the museum exit and head back to the Baixa. ☎391 28 00. Open Tu 2-6pm, W-Su 10am-6pm. 600$, students 300$. Free Su before 2pm.)*

PARQUE DE SÃO PEDRO DE ALCÂNTARA. For a perfect picnic, head to this mercifully shaded park. The Castelo de São Jorge in the Alfama stares back from the cliff opposite the park. A mosaic points out the landmarks included in this vista. *(On the right off R. São Pedro de Alcântara—the continuation of R. Misericórdia. Walk up R. Misericórdia from Pr. Camões; the park is right next to C. Glória.)*

BASÍLICA DA ESTRÊLA. Half-mad Maria I, desiring a male heir, made fervent religious vows promising God everything if she were granted a son. When a baby boy was finally born, she built this church. *(On Pr. Estrêla. Accessible by tram #28 from Pr. Comércio (165$). ☎ 21 396 09 15. Open daily 8am-12:30pm and 3-7:30pm. Free.)*

ALFAMA

The Alfama, Lisbon's medieval quarter, was the lone neighborhood to survive the 1755 earthquake. The neighborhood slopes in tiers from the Castelo de São Jorge facing the Rio Tejo. Between the Alfama and the Baixa is the Mouraria (Moorish quarter), established after the Moors were expelled in 1147.

THE LOWER ALFAMA. While any of the small uphill streets a few blocks east of the Baixa lead to the Alfama's streets, the least confusing way to see the neighborhood is by climbing up R. Madalena, which begins two blocks away from Pr. Comércio (take R. Alfandega from the *praça*). Turn right when you see the Igreja da Madalena in the Largo Madalena on the right. Take R. Santo António da Sé and follow the tram tracks to the cleverly designed and ornamented **Igreja de Santo António da Sé.** The construction was funded with money collected by the city's children, who fashioned miniature altars bearing images of the saint to place on doorsteps. The custom is re-enacted annually on June 13, the saint's feast day and Lisbon's largest holiday. *(☎ 886 91 45. Open daily 8am-7pm. Mass daily 11am, 5, and 7pm.)*

CASTELO DE SÃO JORGE. Near the top of the Alfama lies the must-see Castelo de São Jorge, which offers spectacular views of Lisbon and the ocean. Built in the 5th century by the Visigoths and enlarged by 9th-century Moors, this castle was a playgound for the royal family between the 14th and 16th centuries. Now, anyone can wander around the ruins, soak in the view of the cityscape below, explore the ponds, or gawk at the exotic bird population of the castle gardens. *(From the cathedral, follow the yellow signs for the castle on a winding uphill walk. Castle open daily Apr.-Sept. 9am-9pm; Oct.-Mar. 9am-7pm. Free.)*

ALONG TR. SÃO VICENTE. On the far side of the castle, follow the main tram tracks along Tr. São Tomé (which becomes R. São Vicente as it winds uphill) to Largo São Vicente and the **Igreja de São Vicente de Fora,** built between 1582 and 1629 and dedicated to Lisbon's patron saint. At the **Feira da Ladra** (flea market) that takes place in the church's backyard, the din of a lively social scene drowns out cries of merchants hawking used goods. *(From the bottom of R. Correeiros in the Baixa, take bus #12 or tram #28 (165$). Church open Tu-Sa 9am-6pm, Su 9am-12:30pm and 3-5pm. Free. Flea market open Tu and Sa 6am-5pm.)* The **Igreja de Santa Engrácia (National Pantheon)** is farther down toward the coast. This church, with its impressive dome, took almost 300 years to complete (1682-1966), giving rise to the famous Portuguese expression, "Endless like the building of Santa Engrácia." *(Walk along R. São Vicente and keep left as the road branches. Open Tu-Su 10am-5pm.)*

SALDANHA

Amid Lisbon's business affairs, this modern district has two excellent museums, both owned by the Fundação Gulbenkian. The **Museu Calouste Gulbenkian** houses oil tycoon Calouste Gubenkian's extensive art collection. The collection is divided into two sections: ancient art—Egyptian, Greek, Roman, Islamic, and Oriental—and European pieces from the 15th to 20th centuries. *(Av. Berna, 45. M: Palhavã or S. Sebastião. Bus # 16, 31, 46. ☎ 782 30 00. Open Tu-Su 10am-5pm. 500$, free Su mornings for students and seniors.)* The adjacent **Museu do Centro de Arte Moderna** is home to an extensive collection of modern art as well as beautiful gardens. *(R. Dr. Nicolau Bettencourt. M: S. Sebastião. Bus #16, 31, 46. ☎ 795 02 41. Open Tu-Su 10am-5pm. 500$, free Su mornings for students and seniors.)*

BELÉM

A number of well-maintained museums and historical sites showcase the opulence and extravagance of the Portuguese empire. To get to Belém, take tram #15 from Pr. Comércio (20min., 165$), bus #28 or 43 from Pr. Figueira (20min., 165$), or the train from Estação Cais do Sodré (10min., every 15min., 140$). From the train station, cross over the tracks, then cross the street and go left. From the bus station, follow the avenue straight ahead.

MOSTEIRO DOS JERÓNIMOS. The Mosteiro dos Jerónimos rises from the banks of the Tejo behind a lush public garden. Established by King Dom Manuel I in 1502 to give thanks for the success of Vasco da Gama's voyage to India, this monastery showcases Portugal's native Manueline style, combining Gothic forms with early Renaissance details. Inside, the symbolic tombs of Luís de Camões and navigator Vasco da Gama lie in two opposing transepts. *(☎362 00 34. Open Tu-Su 10am-5pm. 600$, students 300$. Cloisters open Tu-Su 10am-5pm. Free.)*

TORRE DE BELÉM. The Torre de Belém rises from the north bank of the Tejo and is surrounded by the ocean on three sides due to the receding shoreline. Today, it is only accessible by a small bridge, offering spectacular panoramic views of Belém, the Tejo, and the Atlantic beyond. *(A 10min. walk along the water from the monastery. Take the underpass by the gardens to cross the highway. ☎362 00 34. Open Tu-Su 10am-6pm. 600$, students and seniors 300$.)*

PARQUE DAS NAÇÕES. The Parque das Nações (Park of Nations), the former Expo '98 grounds is the newest addition to Lisbon's growing list of sights. After Expo '98 flopped, the government took a risk, pumping millions of dollars into the land and converting it into the Parque das Nações. *(M: Oriente. ☎891 93 33; www.parquedasnacoes.pt.)* The biggest attraction is the **Pavilhão dos Oceanos**, the largest oceanarium in Europe, which showcases the four major oceans (right down to the sounds, smells, and climates). All of these connect to the main tank, which houses fish, sharks, and other sea creatures. *(Open daily Apr.-Sept. 10am-7pm; Oct.-Mar. 10am-6pm. 1700$, under 18 and seniors 900$).* In addition to various museums, gardens, and pavilions scattered throughout the park, there is the 145m **Torre Vasco de Gama**. An elevator ascends to the observation tower, which offers spectacular views of the city. *(Open daily 10am-8pm. 500$, under 18 or over 65 250$.)* For those who don't want to walk between attractions, a **teleférico** (gondola) connects one end of the park to the other. *(Runs M-F 11am-8pm, Sa-Su 10am-9pm. 500$, under 18 and seniors 250$.)*

🎵🎭 ENTERTAINMENT AND NIGHTLIFE

Agenda Cultural and *Follow Me Lisboa*, free at kiosks in the Rossio, on R. Portas de Santo Antão, and at the tourist office, contain information on concerts, movies, plays, and bullfights.

BARS AND CLUBS

Lisbon's nightlife is centered in the **Bairro Alto,** where a plethora of small bars and clubs invite exploring the side streets. In particular, **R. Norte, R. Diário Notícias,** and **R. Atalaia** have many small clubs packed into three short blocks, making club-hopping as easy as crossing the street. Most gay and lesbian clubs are found in the Rato area near the edge of Bairro Alto. The newest hot spot is the revamped **Docas de Santo Amaro,** a strip of waterfront bars, clubs, and restaurants. On the way to the Docas, look for additional party places along Av. 24 de Julho. A cab from Rossio (the only real choice for transportation to these locations) costs 800-1200$. There's no reason to arrive before midnight; crowds flow in around 2am.

Cosmos, Armazem 243 (☎397 27 47). Torches welcome the crowd of trendy twenty-somethings out on the patio. Cover 2000$, includes 4 beers or 2 mixed drinks. Restaurant open daily 11am-midnight; disco open midnight-6am.

Salsa Latina (☎395 05 55). Gare Marítima de Alcântara. Sophisticated crowds come for the live salsa (on the weekends after midnight). Minimum consumption 2000$. Beer 500$, mixed drinks 1000$. Open M-Th 8-11pm, F-Sa 8pm-1:30am.

Memorial, R. Gustavo de Matos Sequeira, 42A (☎396 88 91), 1 block from R. Escola Politécnica in the Bairro Alto. Women and men, gay and straight, and young and old alike let loose to Euro-pop. The 1000$ cover charge includes 2 beers or 1 mixed drink. Open Tu-Su 11pm-4am.

Divina Comida, Largo Santa Martinho, 6-7 (☎887 55 99), in the Alfama. The food is pricey, but the bar is divine. Try the killer Brazilian *caipirinha* (sugarcane alcohol; 1000$). Open M-Th 12:30pm-2am, F-Sa 12:30pm-3am.

Trumps, R. Imprensa Nacional, 104B (☎397 10 59). Lisbon's biggest gay club features several bars in addition to a massive dance floor. Cover 1000$ (includes 1 drink), with minimum consumption of 2000$. Open Tu-Su 11:30pm-6am.

CAFES

Relaxing in cafes during the day and late into the night is a popular pastime in Lisbon. The famous 19th-century **A Brasileira,** R. Garrett, 120-122, in the Chiado neighborhood is considered by many to be "the best cafe in Portugal." (☎360 95 41. Coffee 80-300$. Mixed drinks 650-900$. Open daily 8pm-2am.) **Costa do Castelo,** Calçada Marquês de Tancos, 1-1B, just behind the Castelo in Alfama, is a small, self-consciously trendy bar-cafe with outdoor patio. (☎888 46 36. Sandwiches 250$. Tapas 400-500$. Mixed drinks 300-700$. Open Tu-Su 12:30pm-2am.)

FADO

Lisbon's trademark is the heart-wrenching *fado*, an expressive art that combines elements of singing and narrative poetry. *Fadistas*, cloaked in black dresses and shawls, perform emotional tales of lost loves and faded glory. The Bairro Alto has many *fado* joints off R. Misericórdia and on side streets radiating from the Museu de São Roque; prices alone may turn a knife in your heart. To avoid these, try exploring nearby streets; various bars and other small venues often offer free performances. **Adega Machado,** R. Norte, 91, draws as many locals as it does tourists. (☎322 46 40. Minimum consumption 2900$. Open Tu-Su 8pm-3am.)

⚑ DAYTRIPS FROM LISBON

SINTRA

Trains (☎21 923 26 05) arrive on Av. Dr. Miguel Bombarda from Lisbon's Estação Rossio (45min., every 15min., 200$). Stagecoach buses leave from outside the train station for Cascais (#417; 40min., every hr., 520$) and Estoril (#418; 40min., every hr., 440$). Mafrense buses (down the street) go to Mafra (50min., every hr., 410$).

In the epic poem *Childe Harold*, British Romantic poet Lord Byron described Sintra as a "glorious Eden." His adulation made Sintra (pop. 20,000) a chic destination for 19th-century European aristocrats. These days, Sintra is a favorite among foreign tour groups and backpackers alike, all drooling over its fairy-tale castles and mountain vistas. The **Palácio Nacional de Sintra** sits at the center of it all in Pr. República and was once the summer residence of Moorish sultans and their harems. (Open Th-Tu 10am-5:30pm. 600$, students 300$.) On the mountain overlooking the old town, **Sintra-Vila,** is the **Castelo dos Mouros,** providing stunning views of the mountains and coast. (Open daily 10am-6pm. Free.) The 3km ascent (1-1½hr.) starts to the left of the tourist office; follow the blue signs up the mountain. Bus #434 also runs to the top from the tourist office (15min., 2 per hr., 600$ all-day pass). One kilometer farther uphill is the **Palácio Nacional da Pena,** built in the 1840s by Prince Ferdinand of Bavaria, the husband of Queen Maria II, is an amalgamation of German and Portugese styles. (Open July-Sept. Tu-Su 10am-6:30pm; Oct.-June Tu-Su 2-4:30pm. 600$, students 400$.)

Head left out of the train station, turn right downhill at the next intersection and left in front of the castle-like Câmara Municipal, then follow the road uphill to reach the **tourist office,** Pr. República 23. (☎21 923 11 57; fax 21 923 51 76. Open daily June-Sept. 9am-8pm; Oct.-May 9am-7pm.) To get to the **Pousada da Juventude de Sintra (HI),** on Sta. Eufémia, take bus #434 from either in front of the train station or to the left of the tourist office to the **Palácio Nacional de Pena** and walk through the palace gardens to the hostel; look for signs. (☎21 924 12 10. Reception 9am-noon and 6pm-midnight. Dorms 1500$; doubles 3500-3800$.)

QUELUZ

Take the train toward Sintra from Lisbon's Estação Rossio (M: Rossio) and get off at the Queluz-Belas stop (25min., every 15min., 140$). Exit the station through the ticket office, go left on Av. Antonio Ennes, and follow the signs to the palace (10min.).

The only reason to visit Queluz, 12km west of Lisbon, is the amazing **Palácio Nacional de Queluz,** a pink-and-white Rococo wedding cake of a palace. In the mid-18th century, Dom Pedro III turned an old hunting lodge into this summer residence—check out the **Sala dos Embaixadores,** with its gilded thrones and Chinese vases, and the *azulejo*-lined canal in the garden. (Open W-M 10am-5pm. 600$, students 300$, children under 14 free. Garden 100$.)

ESTORIL

Trains from Lisbon's Estação do Sodré (M: Cais do Sodré) stop in Estoril en route to Cascais (30min., every 20min., 300$). Bus #418 to Sintra departs from Av. Marginal, just down the street from the train station (40min., every hr., 440$).

Beautiful beaches, stately vistas, and a bustling casino give Estoril a reputation of opulence. **Praia Estoril Tamariz beach** greets visitors on arrival. **Casino Estoril,** Europe's largest casino, beckons those feeling lucky. (Open daily 3pm-3am. No jeans or shorts. Must be 18 for slots, 21 for game room. Foreigners must show passport.) From the train station, cross Av. Marginal and to the **tourist office** on Arcada do Parque. (☎21 466 38 13; fax 467 22 80. Open M-Sa 9am-7pm, Su 10am-6pm.)

CASCAIS

Trains from Lisbon's Estação do Sodré head to Cascais via Estoril (30min., every 20min., 200$). Stagecoach bus #417 leaves from the train station for Sintra (40min., every hr., 520$). Or walk 20min. along the coast or Av. Marginal from Estoril.

Once the summer vacation resort of the royal family, Cascais still caters to a well-to-do crowd. Four popular **beaches** close to the center draw throngs of locals and tourists. To get to the **tourist office,** Av. dos Combatentes 25, which books **rooms,** turn right at the fork in the promenade, follow the train tracks to the station, cross the square, and turn right at the McDonald's on Av. Valbom. (☎486 82 04. Open July-Sept. 15 M-Sa 9am-8pm, Su 10am-6pm; Sept. 16-June M-Sa 9am-7pm, Su 10am-6pm.)

MAFRA

Frequent Mafrense buses stop in front of the palace from Sintra (1hr., every hr., 380$) and Lisbon (1½hr., every hr., 540$).

Sleepy Mafra is home to one of Portugal's most impressive sights and one of Europe's largest historical buildings, the Palácio Nacional de Mafra. The monstrous 2000-room castle took 50,000 workers 13 years to complete. (☎26 181 75 50. Open W-M 10am-4:30pm. 600$, students 300$. Free tours daily in English at 11am and 2:30pm). To reach the **tourist office,** on Av. 25 de Abril, take a right off the main steps of the palace and bear left—look for the blue Turismo sign. (☎26 181 20 23. Open M-F 9am-7pm, Sa-Su 9:30am-1pm, 2:30-6pm.)

OTHER DAYTRIPS FROM LISBON

COIMBRA. Party or people-watch in this vibrant university town (see p. 782).

BEJA. More than just the perfect setting for romantic exploits, Beja is also a haven of traditional food, music, and handicrafts (see p. 778).

ÉVORA. Peruse the halls of the "museum city," including the cathedral—perhaps Portugal's finest—and theuniquely grotesque Capela dos Ossos (see p. 777).

CENTRAL PORTUGAL

Jagged cliffs and whitewashed fishing villages line Estremadura's Costa de Prata (Silver Coast), with beaches that rival even those in the Algarve. Nearby, the fertile region of the Ribatejo (Banks of the Tejo) is perhaps the gentlest and greenest in Portugal. In this region just north of Lisbon, relatively untouristed towns beckon travelers with historical sights and lush scenery.

TOMAR
☎ 249

For centuries, the arcane Knights Templar—made up of monks and warriors—plotted crusades from a celebrated convent-fortress high above this small town. The ⬛**Convento de Cristo** complex was the Knights' powerful and mysterious headquarters. The first structure was built in 1160, but some cloisters, convents, and buildings were added later. The **Claustro dos Felipes** is one of Europe's masterpieces of Renaissance architecture. Walk out of the tourist office, take the second right, bear left at the fork, and follow either the dirt path to the left or the cars up the road. (☎ 31 34 81. Complex open June-Aug. 9am-6:30pm; Sept.-May 9am-5pm. 600$, students 300$.) The **Museu dos Fósforos** (match museum), in the Convento de São Francisco, opposite the stations, exhibits Europe's largest matchbox collection. (Open daily 10-11am and 3-5pm. Free.) Hiking trails lead the **Parque da Mata Nacional dos Sete Montes** from opposite the tourist office. (Park open daily 10am-6pm. Free.)

Trains (☎ 31 28 15) go from Av. Combatentes da Grande Guerra, at the southern edge of town, to: Lisbon (2hr., 18 per day, 1020-2040$); Coimbra (2½hr., 6 per day, 960-1200$); Porto (4½hr., 7 per day, 1510-2210$); and Santarém (1hr., 18 per day, 520-840$). Rodoviaria Tejo **buses** (☎ 31 27 38) leave from Av. Combatentes Grande Guerra, by the train station, for: Lisbon (2hr., 4 per day, 1150$); Coimbra (2½hr., 1 per day, 1450$); Porto (4hr., 1 per day, 1900$); and Santarém (1hr., 2 per day, 1150$). From either station, go through the square onto Av. General Bernardo Raria, go left after four blocks on Av. Dr. Cândido Madureira, continue to the end of the street, and look right for the **tourist office.** (☎ 32 24 27. Open daily June-Sept. 10am-8pm; Oct.-May 10am-6pm.) **Residencial União,** R. Serpa Pinto 94, is halfway between Pr. República and the bridge. (☎ 32 31 61. Breakfast included. Singles 4000$; doubles 6500-7000$; triples 7500-8000$.) **Postal code:** 2300.

🚺 **DAYTRIP FROM TOMAR: BATALHA.** The only reason (but a good one) to visit Batalha (pop. 6000) is the gigantic, flamboyant ⬛**Mosteiro de Santa Maria da Vitória.** Built by Dom João I in 1385 to commemorate his victory over the Spanish, the complex of cloisters and chapels remains one of Portugal's greatest monuments. Through the **Claustro de Dom Afonso V,** out the door and to the right are the impressive **Capelas Imperfeitas** (Imperfect Chapels), with massive buttresses designed to support a large dome that was never actually constructed. Napoleon's troops sacrilegiously turned the nave into a brothel. To get to the monastery, enter through the church. (Open daily June-Aug. 9am-6pm; Sept.-May 9am-5pm. Monastery 600$, under 25 300$. Church free.) **Buses** run from near Pensão Vitória on Largo Misericórdia to Lisbon (2hr., 6 per day, 1200$) and Tomar (1½hr., 3 per day, 520$). The **tourist office,** on Pr. Mouzinho de Albuquerque along R. Nossa Senhora do Caminho, stands opposite the unfinished chapels of the *mosteiro.* (☎ (244) 76 51 80. Open daily May-Sept. 10am-1pm and 3-7pm; Oct.-Apr. 10am-1pm and 2-6pm.)

SANTARÉM
☎ 243

Perhaps the most charming of Ribatejo's cities, Santarém (pop. 30,000) presides from atop a rocky mound over the calm Rio Tejo and the soft green pastures. Once a flourishing medieval center, the city was the capital of the Portuguese Gothic style. Santarém's many appealing churches still exhibit a mind-boggling range of architectural styles. The austere facade of the **Igreja do Seminário dos Jesuítas** dominates **Pr. Sá da Bandeira,** Santarém's main square. (Open Tu-Su 9:30am-12:30pm and 2-5:30pm. Free.) Take R. Serpa Pinto from Pr. Sá da Bandeira to Pr. Visconde de Serra Pilar to reach the **Praça Visconde de Serra Pilar,** where Christians, Moors, and Jews gathered centuries ago. The 12th-century **Igreja de Marvilha,** off the *praça,* has a 17th-century *azulejo* interior. (Open Tu-Su 9:30am-12:30pm and 2-5:30pm. Free.) Nearby is the early Gothic **Igreja da Graça;** within the chapel lies Pedro Alvares Cabral, the explorer who discovered Brazil. (Church and chapel open Tu-Su 9:30am-12:30pm and 2-5:30pm. Free.) From there, take R. Cons. Figueiredo Leal, which becomes Av. 5 de Outubro, to the **Portas do Sol,** a paradise of flowers and fountains surrounded by old Moorish walls. (Open daily 8am-11pm. Free.)

The **train station** (☎ 32 11 99), 2km from town, serves Lisbon (1hr., 10-20 per day, 670-1050$); Coimbra (2hr., 11 per day, 1020-1400$); Porto (4hr., 4 per day, 1720-2100$); and Tomar (1hr., every hr., 520$). Buses (10min., every 1hr., 210$) connect the train station with the **bus station** (☎ 33 32 00), on Av. Brasil, near Pr. Sá da Bandeira. **Buses** serve: Lisbon (1-1½hr., 20 per day, 850-950$); Coimbra (2hr., 2 per day, 1600$); and Porto (4hr., 2 per day, 2100$). The **tourist office,** R. Capelo Ivêns 63, is nearby. (☎ 39 15 12. Open Tu-F 9am-7pm, Sa-M 10am-12:30pm and 2:30-5:30pm.) Around the corner is **Residencial Abidis,** R. Guilherme de Azevedo 4. (☎ 32 20 17. Singles 4000$, with bath 5500$; doubles 4500, with bath 7000$.) **Postal code:** 2000.

NAZARÉ ☎ 262

It's hard to tell where authenticity stops and tourism starts in Nazaré, an unabashed beachtown. Fishermen clad in traditional garb go barefoot while the day's catch dries in the hot sun. But if Nazaré is part theater, at least it puts on a good show—and everyone gets front row seats on the glorious beach. You, too, should go to the **beach.** For an evening excursion, take the **funicular** (every 15min., 105$), which runs from R. Elevador off Av. República to the **Sítio,** a clifftop area replete with uneven cobbled streets, weathered buildings, and wonderful views of the town and ocean. Around 6pm, fishing boats return to the **port** beyond the far left end (facing the ocean) of the beach; head over to watch fishermen at work and eavesdrop as local restaurateurs spiritedly bid for the most promising catches at the **fish auction** (M-F 6-10pm). **Cafes** in Pr. Souza Oliveira teem with people until about 1am. The intimate cafe-bar **Ta Bar Es** (☎ 55 33 53), on R. Mouzinho Albuquerque, hosts live music most summer nights (Beer 150-400$, mixed drinks 600$. Open daily July-Sept. noon-4am; Oct.-June 2pm-4am). **Bullfights** are popular as well; Nazaré is on the revolving schedule that brings *corridas* to a different city in the province each summer weekend (Sa 10pm; tickets start at 2500$).

Nazaré is only accessible by **bus.** Buses run to: Lisbon (2hr., 6 per day, 1250$); Coimbra (2hr., 5 per day, 1400$); Porto (3½hr., 5 per day, 1800$); and Tomar (1½hr., 3 per day, 850$). The **tourist office** is beachside on Av. República. (☎ 56 11 94. Open daily July-Aug. 10am-10pm; Sept. 10am-8pm; Oct.-March 9:30am-1pm and 2:30-6pm; Apr.-June 10am-1pm and 3-7pm.) Look along Pr. Dr. Manuel de Arriaga and Pr. Sousa Oliveira for the best deals on accommodations. **Residencal Marina,** R. Mouzinho de Albuquerque, 6A, off Pr. Sousa Oliveira, is close to the beach. (☎ 55 15 41. Reception 9am-11pm. Doubles 4000$.) For **camping,** head to **Vale Paraíso,** Estrada Nacional, 242, 2½km out of town. Take the bus to Alcobaça or Leiria (15min., 8 per day). (☎ 56 18 00. Free showers. Reception daily 8am-10pm. June-Sept. 630$ per person, 510-720$ per tent, 515$ per car; Apr.-May and Oct. 520$ per person, 435-600$ per tent, 435$ per car; Nov.-Mar. 390$ per person, 335-460$ per tent, 335$ per car.) **Supermarkets** line R. Sub-Vila, parallel to Av. República and Pr. Dr. Manuel de Arriaga. **Postal code:** 2450.

ÉVORA ☎ 266

Designated a UNESCO World Heritage site, Évora (pop. 54,000) is justly known as the "Museum City." The picture-perfect town boasts a Roman temple, an impressive cathedral, a 16th-century university, and streets that wind past Moorish arches. The city's most famous monument is the 2nd-century **Roman temple,** on Largo do Vila Flor. Only a platform and 14 Corinthian columns remain. Facing the temple is the town's best-kept secret, the **Igreja de São João Evangelista** (1485), its interior covered with dazzling *azulejos* (tiles); ask to see the church's hidden chambers. (Open Tu-Su 10am-12:30pm and 2-6pm. 500$.) From Pr. Giraldo, head up R. 5 de Outubro to the colossal 12th-century **cathedral;** the 12 apostles on the doorway are masterpieces of medieval Portuguese sculpture. The **Museu de Arte Sacra,** above the nave, has interesting religious artifacts. (Cathedral open daily 9am-12:30pm and 2-5pm. Museum open Tu-Su 9am-12:30pm and 2-5pm. Cathedral free. Cloister and museum 450$.) Attached to the pleasant **Igreja Real de São Francisco,** the bizarre **Capela dos Ossos** (Chapel of Bones), was built entirely out of the bones of 5000 people by three morbid Franciscan monks. Above the door an irreverent sign taunts visitors: *"Nós*

PORTUGAL

ossos que aqui estamos, pelos vossos esperamos" ("We bones lie here awaiting yours"). From Pr. Giraldo, follow R. República; the church is on the right and the chapel around back to the right of the main entrance. (Open M-Sa 9am-1pm and 2:30-6pm, Su 10-am-1pm and 2:30-6pm; chapel closed during mass. 100$, students 50$.) The **Feira de São João** festival keeps the town up all night with a huge country fair in the last week of June.

Trains (☎ 70 21 25) go from the end of R. Dr. Baronha to: Lisbon (3hr., 7 per day, 1380$); Faro (4hr., 4 per day, 1720$); and Porto (6½hr., 3 per week, 2650$). From the train station, flag down bus #6 (100$) from just down the tracks or hike up R. Dr. Baronha, which becomes R. República and leads to the central Pr. Giraldo (20min.). **Buses** (☎ (266) 76 94 10) go from the continuation of R. Raimundo, 15min. downhill from Pr. Giraldo, just past the gas station, to Lisbon (2½hr., 10 per day, 1550$) and Faro (5hr., 4 per day, 1900$). The **tourist office** is at Pr. Giraldo 73. (☎ 70 26 71. Open Apr.-Oct. M-F 9am-7pm, Sa-Su 9am-12:30pm and 2-5:30pm; daily Nov.-Mar. 9am-12:30pm and 2-5:30pm.) Check **email** at **Oficin@**, R. Moeda 27, off Pr. Giraldo. (500$ per hr. Open daily Sept.-June 6pm-2am; July-Aug. 8:30pm-2am.) Most *pensões* cluster on side streets around **Pr. Giraldo.** From the end of Pr. Giraldo, opposite the church, walk down R. República and bear left on R. Miguel Bombarda (a.k.a. R. São Vicente) to reach the excellent **Pousada de Juventude (HI),** R. Miguel Bombarda 40. (☎ 74 48 48. Reception 8am-midnight. Curfew midnight. Dorms 2500$; doubles 5500$.) From the tourist office, walk down the street and three blocks right to get to **Casa Palma,** R. Bernando Mato 29A. (☎ 70 35 60. Singles 2500-3000$, with bath 3500-4500$; doubles 5000-6000$, with bath 6500-7000$.) Buses from Pr. Giraldo go near **Orbitur's Parque de Campismo de Évora,** on Estrada das Alcáçovas, which branches off the bottom of R. Raimundo. (☎ 70 51 90. Reception 8am-10pm. 640$ per person, 500-640$ per tent, 550$ per car.) Many budget restaurants are near **Pr. Giraldo,** particularly along **R. Mercadores.** Grab **groceries** at **Maxigrula,** R. João de Deus 130. (Open M-Sa 9am-7pm.) **Postal code:** 7000.

BEJA

☎284

Tucked amid the vast, monotonous wheat fields of the southern Alentejo, Beja is a town of remarkable architecture and truly scorching temperatures. Its name, pronounced like the Portuguese word for "kiss" (beija), is highly appropriate. Besides being a summer-time oven and a prime getaway destination for romantic exploits, Beja is a haven of traditional Portugese food, music, and handicrafts. The **Museu Rainha Dona Leonor,** Lg. da Conceiçao, makes an excellent starting point. Built on the site of Sister Mariana Alcoforado's famed indiscretion with a French officer, the museum features a replica of the cell window through which the lovers exchanged secret passionate vows. The *azulejos* and Persian-style ceiling make the house look like a mini mosque. (Open Tu-Su 9:45am-12:30pm and 2-5:15pm. 100$, Su free.) One block downhill from the Museu Rainha Dona Leonor is the 13th-century **Igreja de Santa María da Feira,** transformed into a mosque during the Moorish invasion and back into a church when the city reverted to Portuguese control. A miniature bull on its corner column symbolizes the city's spirit. (Church open daily 10am-1pm and 3-7pm. Free.) From here, R. Aresta Branco leads past handsome old houses to the city's massive **castelo,** built around 1300 on the remnants of a Roman fortress. (Open May-Sept. Tu-Su 10am-1pm and 2-6pm; Oct.-Apr. 9am-noon and 1-4pm. Free.) The castle's **Torre de Menagem** provides an impressive view of the vast Alentejan plains (100$).

Trains run from the station (☎ 32 61 35), about 1km outside of town, to: Lisbon (2½-3hr., 4 per day, 1530$); Évora (1½hr., 3 per day, 750$); and Faro (3½hr., 2 per day, 1330$). The **bus station** (☎ 31 36 20) is on R. Cidade de São Paulo, near the corner of Av. Brasil. **Buses** motor to: Lisbon (3-3½hr., 6 per day, 1550$); Évora (1½hr., 7 per day, 1200$); and Faro (3-3½hr., 6 per day, 1550$). To get to the town center, turn right onto R. Afonso de Albuquerque and left on R. Capitão J. F. de Sousa, where the **tourist office,** R. Capitão J. F. de Sousa, 25, is located. (☎ 31 19 13. Open M-Sa May-Sept. 9am-8pm; Oct.-Apr. 10am-1pm and 2-6pm). **Residencial Bejense,** R. Capitão J. F. de Sousa, 57 (☎ 32 50 01; fax 32 50 02), is down the street from the tourist office. (Singles 5000-6000$; doubles 8000-8500$.) Beja is one of the best places to taste authentic (and affordable) Portuguese cuisine. Try **Restaurante Alentejano** (☎32 38 49), Largo dos Duques de Beja, down the steps near the museum (*pratos do dia* 850-1000$; open Sa-Th noon-3pm and 7-10pm).

ALGARVE

Behold the Algarve—a freak of nature, a desert on the sea, an inexhaustible vacationland where happy campers from all over the world bask in the sun. Nearly 3000 hours of sunshine per year have transformed this one-time fishermen's backwater into one of Europe's favorite vacation spots. In July and August, tourists mob the Algarve's resorts in search of perfect tans and wild nights in bars and discos. In the off-season, a less intense sun presides over tranquil grotto beaches at the bases of rugged cliffs. The westernmost town of Sagres offers isolated beaches and steep cliffs, while the eastern border near Tavira features floating flamingo wetlands.

LAGOS   ☎282

As the town's countless expatriates will attest, Lagos is a black hole: come for two days and you'll be tempted to stay a month. For as long as anyone in Lagos can remember, this modestly sized town (pop. 22,000) has played host to swarms of sun-worshipping foreigners. Although there isn't much more than beaches and bars, between soaking in the view from the cliffs, soaking in the sun on the beach, and soaking in drinks at the bars, you won't find anyone complaining.

▭ TRANSPORTATION

Trains: ☎76 29 87. Across the river (over the metal drawbridge) from the city center. To **Lisbon** (6½hr., 5 per day, 2110-2280$) and **Évora** (6hr., 2 per day, 1930$).

Buses: EVA bus station, off Av. Descobrimentos, just past the train station bridge (as you leave town). To **Lisbon** (5hr., 7-10 per day, 2500$) and **Seville, Spain** (6hr., 1 per day, 3000$). For more info on getting to Seville, ask at the hostel.

▰▱ ORIENTATION AND PRACTICAL INFORMATION

Avenida dos Descobrimentos, the main road, runs along the river. From the train station, exit left, go around the pinkish building, cross the river, and turn left on Av. Descobrimentos. From the bus station, turn right on the main thoroughfare as you exit and follow R. Portas de Portugal, which leads to the center of the old town at **Praça Gil Eanes.** Most everything hovers near this *praça*, the adjoining **Rua 25 de Abril,** and the parallel **Rua Cândido dos Reis.** Farther down Av. Descobrimentos, on the right, closer to the **fortaleza,** is **Praça República.**

Tourist Office: (☎76 30 31), R. Vasco de Gama, past the bus station going out of town on R. Descobrimentos. Go through the traffic circle and pass the gas station; the office is on the left. Brochures, maps, transport info, and a list of rooms. Open daily 9:30am-12:30pm and 2-5:30pm.

Emergency: ☎112. **Police** (☎76 29 30), R. General Alberto Silva.

Medical Services: Hospital (☎76 30 34), R. Castelo dos Governadores.

Internet Access: Irish Rover, R. de Ferrador, 9 (☎282 76 80 33). 300$ per 15min.; 500$ per 30min.; 900$ per 1hr. Open daily July-Sept. 2pm-2am; Oct.-June 6pm-2am.

Post Office: (☎77 02 50), R. Portas de Portugal, between Pr. Gil Eanes and the river. Open M-F 9am-6pm. For *Posta Restante,* label all letters "Estação Portas de Portugal" or they may arrive at the branch office. **Postal Code:** 8600.

▰ ACCOMMODATIONS

In the summertime, *pensões* (and the youth hostel) fill up quickly and cost a bundle. Reserve rooms over a week in advance. Rooms in *casas particulares* run around 2000-3000$ per person in summer; haggle with owners at the stations.

Pousada da Juventude de Lagos (HI), R. Lançarote de Freitas 50 (☎ 76 19 70). From Pr. República, follow the street in the back until it becomes R. Lançarote de Freitas. Central courtyard and TV room/bar. Internet access. Reception open daily 9am-1am. Check-out noon. In summer, book through the central Movijovem office (☎ 282 21 359 60 00; fax 21 359 60 01; email movijovem@mail.telepac.pt). July-Sept. dorms 2500$; doubles with bath 4300$. Oct.-June dorms 1700$; doubles with bath 3800$.

Residencial Rubi Mar, R. Barroca 70 (☎ 76 31 65; email rubimar01@hotmail.com), off Pr. Gil Eanes towards Pr. Infante Dom Henrique. July-Oct. doubles 7000$, with bath 8500$; quads 15,000$. Nov.-June doubles 5500$, with bath 6500$, quads 10,000$.

Residencial Caravela, R. 25 de Abril 8 (☎ 76 33 61), just up the street from Pr. Gil Eanes. 16 small but well-located rooms off a courtyard, some with balconies. Singles 4300$; doubles 6000$, with bath 6500$; triples 9000$.

Camping: Camping is the way most experience the Algarve; as a result, sites are crowded and expensive. **Camping Trindade** (☎ 76 38 93), is outside town. Follow Av. Descobrimentos toward Sagres. 580$ per person, 630-735$ per tent, 620$ per car.

⚫ FOOD

Tourists can peruse multilingual menus around **Pr. Gil Eanes** and **R. 25 de Abril,** but a budget Portuguese meal is hard to find. The cheapest option is the morning **market,** on Av. Descobrimentos 5min. from the town center. **Supermercado São Toque**, R. Portas de Portugal, 61, is opposite the post office. (☎ 282 76 28 55. Open July-Sept. M-F 9am-8pm, Sa 9am-7pm; Oct.-June M-F 9am-7:30pm, Sa 9am-7pm).

Casa Rosa, R. Ferrador, 22. Enjoy cheap meal deals (from 650$) with backpacker hordes. Monday is all-you-can-eat spaghetti and garlic bread day (999$). Wide-ranging menu with many vegetarian options (650-1400$). Open daily 7pm-2am.

Mullen's, R. Cândido dos Reis, 86 (☎ 76 12 81). A Lagos hotspot serves up huge portions of spicy food. Main dishes 1125-2225$. After dinner, it turns into a bar. Restaurant open daily noon-2pm and 7-10:30pm; bar open until 2am.

🎵 SIGHTS AND ENTERTAINMENT

Lagos's **beaches** are seductive any way you look at them. Flat, smooth, sunbathing sands (crowded during the summer, pristine in the off-season) line the 4km-long **Meia Praia,** across the river from town. Hop on the 30-second ferry near Pr. República (70$ each way). For beautiful cliffs that hide smaller, less-crowded beaches and caves, follow Av. Descobrimentos toward Sagres to **Praia de Pinhão** (20 min.). Five minutes farther lies **Praia Dona Ana,** with sculpted cliffs and grottoes.

Although sunbathing and non-stop debauchery have long erased memories of Lagos's rugged, sea-faring past, most of the city is still surrounded by a nearly intact 16th-century wall. The **Fortaleza da Ponta da Bandeira,** a 17th-century fortress holding maritime exhibitions, overlooks the Marina. (☎ 76 14 10. Open Tu-Sa 10am-1pm and 2-6pm, Su 10am-1pm. 330$, students 170$.) Also on the waterfront is the old **Mercado de Escravos** (slave market). Legend has it that in 1441 the first sale of African slaves on Portuguese ground took place here.

You're tan, you're glam, now go find yourself a (wo)man. The streets of Lagos pick up as soon as the sun dips down, and by midnight the city's walls are shaking. The area between Pr. Gil Eanes and Pr. Luis de Camões is filled with cafes. Several areas in town are packed with bars, including **R. Cândido dos Reis, R. do Ferrador,** and the intersection of **R. 25 de Abril, R. Silva Lopes,** and **R. Soeiro da Costa.** The **Phoenix Club,** R. São Gonçalo, 29, rises for great after-hours dancing. (☎ 76 05 03. Cover 1000$, includes 2 beers or 1 mixed drink. Open nightly 1-6am.)

📷 DAYTRIPS FROM LAGOS

SAGRES

Rodoviária buses (☎ 282 76 29 44) pull in from Lagos (1hr., 8 per day, 450$).

Marooned atop a bleak desert plateau in Europe's southwesternmost corner, desolate Sagres and its cape were once considered the edge of the world. Near the town lurks the **Fortaleza,** the fortress where Prince Henry stroked his beard, decided to map the world, and founded his famous **school of navigation.** (Open daily June-Aug. 10am-8:30pm; Sept.-May 10am-6:30pm. 600$.) Six kilometers west lies the dramatic **Cabo de São Vicente,** where the second most powerful lighthouse in Europe shines over 96km out to sea. To get there, hike 1hr. or bike past the several fortresses perched atop the cliffs. (Get permission to climb up from the gatekeeper, who is there for much of the day but not noon-2pm.) The most notable **beach** in the area is **Mareta,** at the bottom of the road from the town center. Just west of town, **Praia de Martinhal** and **Praia da Baleeira** have great windsurfing. The **tourist office,** on R. Comandante Matoso, is next to the bus stop. (☎282 62 48 73. Open Tu-Sa 9:30am-12:30pm and 2-5pm, Su 9:30am-noon.)

▨ PRAIA DA ROCHA

From Lagos, take a bus to Portimão (35min., 10 per day, 360-450$), then switch at the station to the Praia da Rocha bus (10min., every 15min.)

A short jaunt from Lagos, this grand **beach** is perhaps the very best the Algarve has to offer. With vast expanses of sand, surfable waves, rocky red cliffs, and plenty of secluded coves, the beach has a well-deserved reputation. The **tourist office** is at the end of R. Tomás Cabreina. (☎282 42 22 90. Open May-Sept. daily 9:30am-8pm; Oct.-Apr. M-F 9:30am-12:30pm and 2-6pm, Sa-Su 9:30am-12:30pm.)

OTHER DAYTRIPS FROM LAGOS

ALBUFERIA. Although it's a packaged tourist town, Albuferia's spectacular slate of beaches and late-night nightlife are worth the kitsch (see p. 781).

FARO. A quiet and refreshingly local town, with a perfectly preserved old town and calm beaches (see p. 782).

ALBUFEIRA ☎289

Albufeira (pop. 22,000), the largest seaside resort in the Algarve, attracts visitors hell-bent on having a good time. Sun, surf, and booze satisfy the masses, nary a Portuguese roams its cobblestoned streets, and graceful Moorish buildings fill the town...but who are we kidding? The town's spectacular slate of **beaches** ranges from the popular **Galé** and **São Rafael** (4-8km toward Lagos) to the central **Baleira** and **Inatel** (the easiest to reach) to the chic **Falésia** (10km toward Faro). After a day at the beach, you could, nay, will go to a bar. Join the crowds at **Fastnet Bar,** R. Cândido dos Reis, 5. (Beer 500$; mixed drinks 600$. Open daily 11am-4am.) **7½ Disco** (☎51 33 06), on R. São Gonçalo de Lagos, is a popular beachside dance club. Many of the hottest new clubs are just outside of Albufeira (600-1200$ by taxi). Try **Reno's Bar, IRS Disco,** or **Kiss Disco** (open daily 2am-6am).

The **train station,** 6km inland, serves to: Lisbon (4-5½hr., 5 per day, 2030$); Faro (45min., 6 per day, 300$); Lagos (1hr., 5 per day, 520$); and Tavira (2hr., 6 per day, 780$). EVA **buses** (☎57 16 16) connect to the town center (10min., every hr., 200$). The **bus station** (☎58 97 55), on Av. Liberdade at the entrance to town, sends buses to Lisbon (3½-4hr., 12 per day, 2600-2800$); Faro (1hr., every hr., 600$); Lagos (1½hr., 7 per day, 645-870$); and Tavira (1½hr., 5 per day, 780$). From the bus station, turn right and walk downhill to Largo Eng. Duarte Pacheco, turn right out of the square, then turn left on R. 5 de Outubro to get to the **tourist office,** R. 5 de Outubro 8. (☎58 52 79. Open daily 9:30am-7pm.) Book ahead or ask for *quartos* at the tourist office or any restaurant or bar. The modern **Pensão Albufeirense,** R. Liberdade 16, is a few blocks downhill from the bus station. (☎51 20 79. Singles 4000$; doubles 6500$; triples 8600$. Open May-Sept.) Weary campers can succumb to the **Parque de Campismo de Albufeira,** a few kilometers outside town toward Ferreiras. (☎58 76 29. 850$ per person and per car, 795$ per tent.)

TAVIRA ☎281

Farmers teasing police by riding their motor scooters over the Roman pedestrian bridge may be about as eventful as Tavira gets. But for most visitors to this relaxing haven—speckled with white houses, palm trees, and Baroque churches—

that's just fine. Steps from the central Pr. República lead up to the **Igreja da Misericórdia.** (Open daily 10am-1pm and 3-6:30pm. Free.) Just beyond it, the remains of the city's **Castelo Mouro** (Moorish Castle) sit next to the **Santa Maria do Castelo.** (Castle open M-F 8am-5pm, Sa-Su 10am-7:30pm. Church open M-F 10am-1pm and 3-6pm, Sa 10am-1pm. Free.) Local beaches, including **Araial do Barril,** are accessible year-round by the bus to **Pedras D'el Rei** (10min., 8 per day, 170$). To reach the great beach on **Ilha da Tavira,** an island 2km away, take the ferry from the end of Estrada das 4 Aguas downstream (every 15min., round-trip 250$).

EVA **buses** (☎32 25 46) leave from the station upstream from Pr. República for Faro (1hr., 10 per day, 435$). **Trains** (☎32 23 54) also head to Faro (1hr., 6 per day, 300$). The **tourist office,** R. Galeria, 9, is up the stairs off Pr. República. (☎32 25 11. Open M-Sa 9:30am-12:30pm and 2-5:30pm, Su 9:30am-12:30pm.) To get from Pr. República to the riverfront **Pensão Residencial Lagôas Bica,** R. Almirante Cândido dos Reis, 24, cross the footbridge, continue down R. A. Cabreira, turn right, and go down one block. (☎32 22 52. Singles 3500$; doubles 5000$, with bath 7000$; in winter 500$ less.) **Ilha de Tavira campground** is on the Ilha da Tavira. (☎32 50 21. Follow directions above. 430$ per person, 700-800$ per tent. Reception 8am-midnight. Showers 100$. Open May-Oct. 15). Try restaurants on **Pr. República** or opposite the garden on **R. José Pires Padinha.**

FARO
☎289

Although many begin their holidays in the Algarve's capital, largest city, and transport hub (pop. 55,000), few stay long enough to see its **old town,** an untouristed, traditional medley of museums, handicrafts shops, and ornate churches. From Pr. Gomes, walk through the gardens to get to the entrance of the old town. **Trains** (☎80 17 26) run from Largo Estação to: Lisbon (5-6hr., 6 per day, 2280$); Albufeira (45min., 14 per day, 300$); Évora (5hr., 2-4 per day, 1650$); and Lagos (2hr., 7-9 per day, 750$). EVA **buses** (☎289 89 97 00) go from Av. República to Albufeira (1hr., 14 per day, 600$); Lagos (3hr., 6 per day, 720$); and Tavira (1hr., 11 per day, 435$). Renex (☎81 29 80) goes from across the street to Lisbon (4½hr., 9 per day, 2500$) and Porto (8½hr., 9 per day, 3500$); Intersul (☎89 97 70) runs to Seville (2800$). From the stations, turn right down Av. República along the harbor, then turn left past the garden to reach the **tourist office,** R. Misericórdia 8, at the entrance to the old town. (☎289 80 36 04. Open daily June-Aug. 9:30am-7pm; Sept.-May 9:30am-5:30pm.) **Pensão-Residencial Central,** Largo Terreiro Do Bispo, 12, is near the pedestrian area up R. 1 de Maio. (☎289 80 72 91. Reception 10am-1am. Curfew 3am. June-Sept. singles 5000$, doubles 7000-7500$; Oct.-May singles 5000$, doubles 6500-7000$.) Enjoy some coffee and local marzipan at one of the Algarve's best cafes, many along **R. Conselheiro Bívar,** off Pr. Gomes.

NORTHERN PORTUGAL

Although their landscapes and Celtic history invite comparison with the northwest of Spain, the Douro and Minho regions of northern Portugal are more populated, developed, and wealthy than Spanish Galicia. Hundreds of trellised vineyards for *porto* and *vinho verde* wines beckon connoisseurs, while *azulejo*-lined houses draw visitors to charming, quiet streets. The Three Beiras region offers a sample of the best of Portugal: the unspoiled Costa da Prata (Silver Coast) in the Beira Litoral (coastal region) begins with the resort town of Figueira da Foz, while Coimbra, a bustling university city, overlooks the region from high above the Rio Mondego.

COIMBRA
☎239

The country's only university city from the mid-16th to the early 20th century, Coimbra serves as a mecca for the country's youth and backpackers alike. A slew of cheap cafes and bars and the student body keep Coimbra swinging from September to May. The city's charm has long since blotted out Coimbra's infamous dual roles as center of the Portuguese Inquisition and the site of former dictator António Salazar's education.

▐ TRANSPORTATION

Trains: (☎82 46 32). Trains from other regions stop only at **Estação Coimbra-B (Velha)**, 3km northwest of town, while regional trains stop at Coimbra-B and **Estação Coimbra-A (Nova)**, 2 blocks from the lower town center. Bus 5 connects the 2 stations (5min., every 15min., 140$). Trains to: **Lisbon** (3hr., 23 per day, 1540-2700$); **Figueira da Foz** (1¼hr., 26 per day, 290$); and **Porto** (2hr., 21 per day, 1040$).

Buses: (☎82 70 81). To reach the bus station, go from Av. Fernão Magalhães, on the university side of the river 10min. from town, past Coimbra-A. Buses to: **Lisbon** (2½hr., 17 per day, 1550$); **Évora** (4hr., 2 per day, 2000$); **Faro** (8hr., 4 per day, 3000$); **Porto** (1½hr., 10 per day, 1400$).

▟▛ ORIENTATION AND PRACTICAL INFORMATION

There are three major parts of town, all on the same side of the river. The most central is the **lower town** (site of the **tourist office** and Coimbra-A **train station**), in the triangle formed by the river, **Largo da Portagem**, and **Praça 8 de Maio**. Coimbra's **university district** is atop the steep hill overlooking the lower town. On the other side of the university, **Praça da República** plays host to cafes and the youth hostel.

Tourist Office: (☎85 59 30), off Largo Portagem, in a yellow building 2 blocks up the river from Coimbra-A. From the bus station, turn right, follow the avenue to Coimbra-A, then walk to Largo Portagem (15min.). Open M-F 9am-7pm, Sa-Su 10am-1pm and 2:30-5:30pm. **University branch office** (☎83 25 91), in Pr. Dom Dinis. Open M-F 9am-6pm, Sa-Su 9-12:30pm and 2:30-5:30pm.

Emergency: ☎12. **Police, special division** for foreigners (Serviço de Estrangeiros), R. Venâncio Rodrigues, 25 (☎239 82 40 45).

Hospital: Hospital da Universidade de Coimbra (☎40 04 00). Take the #7 or 29 bus to the Hospital stop.

Internet Access: Museu Sandwich Bar, R. da Matemática, 46 (☎82 75 66), off R. São João near the university. 600$ per hr., includes a drink. Open M-F 4-7pm and 10pm-3am, Sa 10pm-3am.

Post Office: Central office (☎85 07 00), on Av. Fernão de Magalhães. Open M-F 8:30am-6:30pm. **Postal Code:** 3000.

▛ ACCOMMODATIONS

Decent hostels, most on side streets off **Av. Fernão de Magalhães**, start at 5000$ for doubles; prices drop in winter.

Pousada da Juventude de Coimbra (HI), R. Henrique Seco, 14 (☎82 29 55). From either Coimbra-A or Largo Portagem, walk 20min. uphill along R. Olímpio Nicolau Rui Fernandes to Pr. República, then up R. Lourenço Azevedo (to the left of the park). Take the 2nd right; the hostel is on the right. Alternatively, take bus #2, 7, 8, 29, or 46 to Pr. República and walk the rest of the way (5min.). Breakfast included. Reception daily 8am-noon and 6pm-midnight. June 16-Sept. 15 dorms 1900$, doubles with bath 4600$; Sept. 16-June 15 dorms 1700$, doubles with bath 4300$.

Pensão Santa Cruz, Pr. 8 de Maio, 21, 3rd floor (☎82 61 97), directly across from the Igreja da Santa Cruz. Comfortable rooms, all with cable TV, some with bath. Singles 4000$; doubles 6000$; triples 7500$.

Residência Moderna, R. Adelino Veiga, 49 (☎82 54 13). All rooms with private bath, phone, A/C, and cable TV. Breakfast included. June-Oct. singles 5000$, doubles 7500$, triples 9500$; Nov.-May singles 4000$, doubles 6000$, triples 7500$.

Camping: Municipal Campground (☎70 14 97), the entrance is at the arch off Pr. 25 de Abril; take the bus #5 or 7 from Largo Portagem outside the tourist office. Showers free. Reception May-Sept. 9am-10pm; Oct.-Apr. 9am-6pm. May-Sept. 474$ per person, 312$ per tent, 602$ per car; Oct.-Apr. 237$ per person, 156$ per tent, 301$ per car.

🍴 FOOD

The best cuisine in Coimbra lies around **R. Direita,** off Pr. 8 de Maio; on the side streets between the river and Largo Portagem; and around **Pr. República** in the university district. **Supermercado Minipreço,** R. António Granjo 6C, is in the lower town center; turn left as you exit Coimbra-A and take another left. (Open M-Sa 9am-8pm, Su 10am-1pm and 3:30-5:30pm.)

> **UC Cantina,** R. Oliveiro, the university's student cafeteria, is the cheapest food around—a mere 300$ buys an entire meal. Open M-F noon-2:15pm and 7-9:15pm.
>
> **Café Santa Cruz,** Pr. 8 de Maio, 5 (☎83 36 17), was once part of the cathedral and still has a vaulted ceiling and stained-glass windows. Sandwiches 230-400$. Open May-Sept. M-Sa 7am-2am; Oct.-Apr. M-Sa 7am-midnight.

👁 🎵 SIGHTS AND ENTERTAINMENT

Take in the old town sights by climbing from the river up the narrow stone steps to the university. Begin your ascent at the **Arco de Almedina,** a remnant of the Moorish town wall, one block uphill from Largo Portagem. At the top is the looming 12th-century Romanesque **Sé Velha** (Old Cathedral), complete with tombs, Gregorian chants, and a cloister. (Open M-Th 10am-noon and 2-7:30pm, F-Su 10am-1pm. Cloisters 150$, students 100$.) Follow signs to the late 16th-century **Sé Nova** (New Cathedral), built for the Jesuits (open Tu-Sa 9am-noon and 2-6:30pm; free), just a few blocks from the 16th-century **University of Coimbra.** The **Porta Férrea** (Iron Gate), off R. São Pedro, opens onto the old university, whose buildings were Portugal's de facto royal palace when Coimbra was the kingdom's capital. The stairs to the right lead to the **Sala dos Capelos,** which houses portraits of Portugal's kings, six Coimbra-born. (Open daily 9:30am-12:30pm and 2-5:30pm. 250$.) The **university chapel** and the mind-boggling, entirely gilded 18th-century **Biblioteca Joanina** (the university library) lie past the Baroque clock tower. Press the buzzer by the library door to enter three golden halls with 300,000 works from the 12th through 19th centuries. (Open daily 9:30am-noon and 2-4:30pm. 250$, students free. All university sights 500$; buy tickets from the office in the main quad.) The 12th-century **Igreja de Santa Cruz,** Pr. 8 de Maio, at the far end of R. Ferreira Borges in the lower town, has a splendid **sacristy.** (Open M-Sa 9am-noon and 2-5:45pm. Cloisters 200$.) Cross the bridge in front of Largo Portagem to find the 14th-century **Convento de Santa Clara-a-Velha** and the 17th-century **Convento de Santa Clara-a-Nova.**

Nightlife in Coimbra gets highest honors. After dinner, outdoor cafes around **Pr. República** are popular; try the **Café-Bar Cartola.** (Beer from 150$. Open M-Sa 8am-2am, Su 8am-1am.) **Via Latina,** R. Almeida Garrett, 1, around the corner and uphill from Pr. República, is hot in all senses of the word. (Open F-Sa midnight-8am.) **Diligência Bar,** R. Nova 30, off R. Sofia, is known for its *fado* (10pm-2am). In early May, graduates burn narrow ribbons they got as first-years and get wide ones in return during Coimbra's week-long festival, the **Queima das Fitas** (Burning of the Ribbons).

FIGUEIRA DA FOZ   ☎233

Figueira da Foz's best features are its 3 sq. km. Sahara-like beach and its partying. Pleasure-seekers who don't mind concrete buildings come here to worship the sun and the neon sign—in Figueira, entertainment is the sight, and vice versa. For those who seek a bit more relaxation, the little fishing town of **Buarcos,** on the northern end of the beach, replaces mindless entertainment with a breath of serenity. Bars and clubs line **Av. 25 de Abril,** next to and above the tourist office. Most popular of all is the **casino** complex, on R. Bernardo Lopes. (☎40 84 00. Casino open daily July-Sept. 12:30pm-6am; Oct.-June 12:30pm-3am. Free. Club cover 1000$, includes 2 beers. Open Oct.-June 11:30pm-6am.) **Trains** (☎42 83 16) leave near the bridge for: Lisbon (3½hr., 9 per day, 1510$); Coimbra (1hr., 27 per day, 290$); and Porto (2¼hr., 8 per day, 1120$). From there, walk with the river to the left on Av. Saraiva de Carvalho, which becomes R. 5 de Outubro and then curves into the central Av. 25 de Abril

(25min.). **Buses** (☎42 67 03) go to Lisbon (3hr., 4 per day, 1550$) and Faro (12hr., 2 per day, 3100$). Facing the church, turn right on R. Dr. Santos Rocha, walk 10min. toward the waterfront, and turn right on R. 5 de Outubro to reach the **tourist office**, Av. 25 de Abril. (☎40 28 27; fax 40 28 20. Open daily June-Sept. 9am-midnight; Oct.-May M-F 9am-5:30pm, Sa-Su 10am-12:30pm and 2:30-6:30pm.) Most hotels and eats line **R. Bernardo Lopes,** four blocks inland from Av. 25 de Abril. 🏨**Pensão Central,** R. Bernardo Lopes 36, is down the street from the casino. (☎42 23 08. Breakfast included. June-Sept. singles 5000$, doubles 8000$, triples 10,000$; Oct.-April singles 3000$, doubles 3000$, triples 3000$.) With the beach on the left, walk up Av. 25 de Abril, turn right at the rotary on R. Alexandre Herculano, and turn left at Parque Santa Catarina to reach the **Parque Municipal de Campismo da Figueira da Foz Municipal,** on Estrada Buarcos. (☎40 28 10. Showers 100$. Reception daily June-Sept. 8am-8pm; Oct.-May 8am-7pm. June-Sept. parties of 2 or more only. 400$ per person, 300-400$ per tent, 300$ per car.) For groceries, check out **Supermercado Ovo,** on the corner of R. Francisco António Dinis and R. Bernardo Lopes (☎42 00 52; open M-Sa 8am-8pm, Su 9am-2pm).

PORTO (OPORTO)   ☎22

Porto is famous for its namesake—sugary-strong port wine. Developed by English merchants in the early 18th century, the port industry is at the root of the city's successful economy. But there's more to Porto than just port (no, really). Situated on a gorge cut by the Douro River, Portugal's second-largest city, is punctuated with granite church towers, orange-tiled houses, and graceful bridges.

📧 **TRANSPORTATION.** All trains pass through Porto's main station, **Estação de Campanhã** (☎519 13 00), east of the center. **Trains** go to Lisbon (4½hr., 5 per day, 2080-3700$) and Coimbra (2¼hr., 12 per day, 1010-1040$). Trains connect to the **Estação de São Bento** (5min., 140$), a block from the central Pr. Liberdade. Garagem Atlântico **buses** leave from R. Alexandre Herculano 366 (☎200 69 54) for Lisbon (4hr., 12 per day, 2300$) and Coimbra (1½hr., 11 per day, 1410$). Renex goes from R. Carmelitas 34 (☎200 33 95) to Lagos (9½hr., 8 per day, 3500$). Rodoviaria Entre Douro e Minho (☎22 200 31 52), 2 blocks from Pr. República, has buses to Braga (1hr.; M-F 26 per day, Sa-Su 9-12 per day; 680$). Buy tickets for the **intracity buses** and **trams** from small kiosks around the city, or at the STCP office, Pr. Almeida Garrett, 27, half a block downhill and across the street from Estação de São Bento (prepurchased single ticket 90$; pre-purchased book of 10 tickets; single ticket 180$).

🛈 **PRACTICAL INFORMATION.** Get a map at the **tourist office,** R. Clube dos Fenianos, 25, off Pr. Liberdade. (Open July-Sept. M-F 9am-7pm; Oct.-June M-F 9am-5:30pm, Sa 9am-5:30pm.) Check **email** at **Portweb,** Pr. Gen. Humberto Delgado 291, by Pr. Liberdade. (100-240$ per hr. Open M-Sa 9am-2am, Su 3pm-2am.) The **Post Office** is located on Pr. Gen. Humberto Delgado. (☎340 02 00. Open M-F 8:30am-9pm, Sa-Su 9am-6pm.) **Postal code:** 4000.

🏠 **ACCOMMODATIONS AND FOOD.** For good deals, look west of Av. Aliados or on R. Fernandes Tomás and R. Formosa, perpendicular to Aliados Square. To get from the station to the spacious **Residencial Paris,** R. Fábrica 27-9, cross Pr. Liberdade and turn left on R. Dr. Artur de Magalhães Basto, which turns into R. Fábrica. (☎207 31 40. Breakfast included. Singles 3450$, with bath 5300$; doubles 5100$, with bath 7250$; triples 6600$, with bath 9450$.) Take bus #35 from Estação Campanha or #37 from Pr. Liberdade to **Pousada de Juventude do Porto (HI),** R. Paulo da Gama 551; be careful in this area at night. (☎617 72 47. Reception 9-11am and 6pm-midnight. June-Sept. dorms 2500$; doubles with bath 6000$; Oct.-May 2000$, 5000$.) From Av. Aliados, go two blocks up R. Elísio de Melo, and turn right on R. Almada to find the small and tidy **Pensão Porto Rico,** R. Almada 237, 2nd fl. (☎339 46 90. Breakfast included. Singles 4500$; doubles 7500$; triples 9000$.) Take bus #6 from Pr. Liberdade (bus #54 at night) to **camp** at **Prelada,** on R. Monte dos Burgos, in Quinta da Prelada, 2km from the center. (☎831 26 16. 620$ per person, 520$ per tent and per car. Reception 8am-11pm.) In pricey Porto you might want to head to **Mercado de Bolhão,** at R. Formosa and R. Sá de Bandeira. (Open M-F 8am-5pm, Sa 8am-1pm.) Doling out more *escudos* will land you some tasty dishes; look near the river in the **Ribeira** district on C. Ribeira, R. Reboleira, and R. Cima do Muro. **Churrasqueira Moura,** R. Almada, 219, on a street parallel to Av. Aliados, will satisfy even the grumpiest of stomachs and stingiest of travelers. (☎200 56 36. Half-portions 450-990$; full portions 450-1800$. Open M-Sa 9am-10pm.)

■ **SIGHTS AND ENTERTAINMENT.** Your first brush with Porto's rich stock of fine artwork may be the celebrated collection of *azulejos* (tiles) in the **Estação São Bento.** Walk past the station and uphill on Av. Afonso Henriques to reach Porto's pride and joy, the 12th- to 13th-century Romanesque **Cathedral.** (Open M-Sa 9am-12:30pm and 2:30-6pm, Su 2:30-6pm. Cloister 250$.) From the station, follow signs downhill on R. Mouzinho da Silveira to R. Ferreira Borges and the **Palácio da Bolsa** (Stock Exchange), the epitome of 19th-century elegance. The ornate **Sala Árabe** (Arabic Hall) took 18 years to decorate. (Open M-F 9am-6:40pm, Sa-Su 9am-12:30pm and 2-6:30pm. Tours every 30min. 800$; main courtyard free.) Next door, the Gothic **Igreja de São Francisco** glitters with an elaborately gilded wooden interior. Under the floor, thousands of human bones are stored in preparation for Judgment Day. (Open M-F 9am-6pm. 500$, students 250$.) From Pr. Liberdade up R. Clérigos rises the **Torre dos Clérigos** (Tower of Clerics), adjacent to the **Igreja dos Clérigos.** (Tower open daily 10am-noon and 2-5pm; 200$. Church free.) From there, head up R. Restauração, right on R. Alberto Gouveia, and left on R. Dom Manuel II to reach the **Museu Nacional Soares dos Reis,** R. Dom Manuel II, 44. This former royal residence now houses an exhaustive collection of 19th-century Portuguese painting and sculpture. (☎339 37 70. Open Tu-Su 10am-5:30pm. 350$, students and seniors 175$.) To get to Porto's rocky and polluted (but popular) **beach,** in the ritzy Foz district, take bus #7 or 78 from Pr. Liberdade.

But we digress—back to your main focus of interest. You can enjoy the warm glow of port wine by embarking on a **wine cruise** down the Douro River. Fine and bounteous port wines are available for tasting at 20-odd port wine lodges, usually *gratuito* (free). The lodges are all across the river in Vila Nova da Gaia—from the Ribeira, district cross the lower level of the large bridge. **Sandeman,** with its costumed guides (500$), is a good start; **Cálem,** next door, has a less-stilted tour and the port is almost as good. **Taylor's** wins the tasty and inebriating, but highly unscientific, *Let's Go* poll for best port lodge in Porto. (Most open daily 10am-6pm.)

◪ **DAYTRIP FROM PORTO: BRAGA.** Braga (pop. 160,000) originally served as the capital of a district founded by Celtic tribes in 300 BC. Today's residents still consider their city's beautiful gardens, plazas, museums and markets worthy of the nickname "Portuguese Rome." While the stunning cathedral and Igreja Do Bom Jesús warrant a daytrip in and of themselves, Braga is also an excellent base for **hiking** in nearby mountain towns. In Portugal's oldest **cathedral,** the treasury showcases the archdiocese's most precious paintings and relics, including a collection of *cofres cranianos* (brain boxes). (Cathedral and treasury open daily June-Aug. 8:30am-6:30pm; Sept.-May 8:30am-5:30pm. Cathedral free. Treasury 300$.) Braga's most famous landmark, **Igreja do Bom Jesús,** is actually 5km outside of town. To visit Bom Jesús, either take the 285m ride on the antique funicular (8am-8pm; 120$), or take the long walk (25-30min.) up the granite-paved pathway that forks into two zig-zagging 565-step stairways. **Trains** (☎ 253 26 21 66), on Largo Estação, run to Porto (1½hr., 10 per day, 330$). The **tourist office,** Av. Central, 1, is on the corner of Pr. República. (☎253 26 25 50; fax 253 61 33 87. Open July-Sept. M-F 9am-6pm, Sa 9am-12:30pm and 2-5pm, Su 9am-12:30pm; Oct.-June M-F 9am-7pm, Sa 9am-12:30pm and 2-5pm.) From the tourist office entrance, take a right and follow Av. Combatentes and turn left at the intersection with R. Santa Margarida to reach the **Pousada da Juventude de Braga (HI),** R. Santa Margarida, 6. (☎253 61 61 63. Breakfast included. Reception 9am-noon and 6pm-midnight. June-Sept. dorms 1700$; doubles 4000$. Oct.-May dorms 1500$; doubles 3500$.)

SPAIN (ESPAÑA)

PESETAS

US$1 = 187.4PTAS	100PTAS = US$0.53
CDN$1 = 127PTAS	= CDN$0.79
EURO€1 = 166.4PTAS	= EURO€0.60
UK£1 = 272.6PTAS	= UK£0.37
IR£1 = 211.3PTAS	= IR£0.45
AUS$1 = 108.2PTAS	= AUS$0.92
NZ$1 = 80.2PTAS	= NZ$1.25
SAR1 = 26.9PTAS	= SAR3.73

PHONE CODE | Country Code: 34. International dialing prefix: 00.

Noble flamenco dancers, graceful bullfighters, and five different spoken languages set Spain apart from the rest of Europe; and draw almost 50 million tourists annually. The landscape is a microcosm of all that Europe has to offer, with lush wilderness reserves, long sunny coastlines, snowy mountain peaks and the dry, golden plains wandered by Don Quixote. Art lovers flock to the northeast, home of the likes of Chagall, Dalí, and Gaudí. Adventure-seekers trek through the northern Pyrenees, and architecture buffs are drawn to the country's stunning Baroque, Mudejar, and Mozarabic cathedrals and palaces. From the south come flamenco, bullfighting and tapas—the passionate expressions that embody Spanish culture. The raging nightlife of Madrid, Barcelona, and the Balearic Islands has inspired the popular saying "Spain never sleeps." You can do Spain in one week, one month, or one year. But you must do it at least once. For more detailed coverage of the glories of Spain, grab the scintillating *Let's Go: Spain, Portugal, and Morocco 2001.*

SUGGESTED ITINERARIES

THREE DAYS Soak in **Madrid's** (p. 800) blend of art and cosmopolitan life. Walk through the **Retiro's** gardens, peruse the famed halls of the **Prado, Thyssen-Bornemisza,** and **Nacional Centro de Arte Reina Sofia.** By night, move from the tapas bars of **Santa Anna** to **Malasaña** and **Chueca.** Daytrip to **Segovia** (p. 822) or somber **Valle de los Caídos** (p. 817).

ONE WEEK Begin in southern Spain for two days, exploring the Alhambra's Moorish palaces in **Granada** (p. 846) and the mosque in **Cordoba** (p. 839). After two days in **Madrid** (p. 800), travel east to **Barcelona** (2 days; p. 856) and the beaches of **Costa Brava** (1 day; p. 874).

BEST OF SPAIN, THREE WEEKS Begin in **Madrid** (3 days; p. 800), with daytrips to **El Escorial** (p. 817) and **Valle de los Caídos**(1 day; p. 817). Take the high-speed train to **Córdoba** (2 days; p. 839), and on to **Sevilla** (2 days; p. 830). Catch the bus to the white town of **Arcos de la Frontera** (1 day; p. 839) before heading south to the Costa del Sol, **Marbella** (1 day; p. 852). Head inland to **Granada** (2 days; p. 846). Move along the coast to **Valencia** (1 day; p. 854) and escape to **Gandía** (1 day; p. 855). Up the coast to **Barcelona** (2 days; p. 856), where worthwhile daytrips in Cataluña include **Tossa de Mar** (1 day; p. 875), **Montserrat** (1 day; p. 873), or **Figueres** (1 day; p. 875). From Barcelona, on to the beaches and tapas of **San Sebastián** (2 days; p. 882) and **Bilbao** (1 day; p. 888), home of the Guggenheim museum.

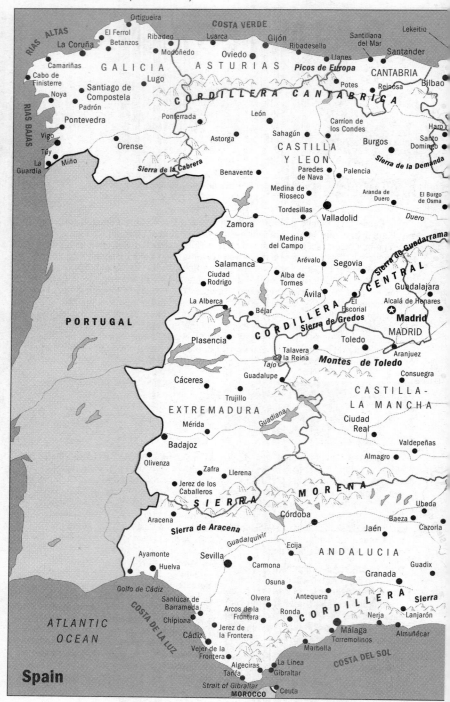

Spain

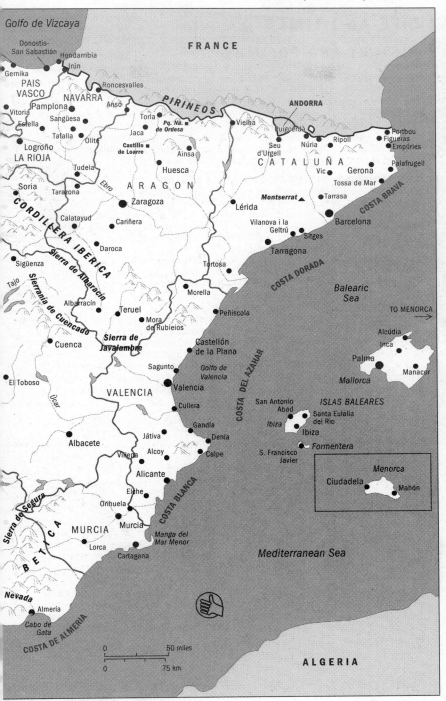

Golfe de Vizcaya

FRANCE

Donostia-San Sabastián
Hondarribia
Gernika
Irún
PAIS
VASCO
NAVARRA
Vitoria
Pamplona
Ansó
Estella
Sangüesa
Torla
Pq. Na.
de Ordesa
Vielha
ANDORRA
Tafalla
Jaca
Castillo
de Loarre
Puigcerdá
Portbou
Logroño
Olite
Ainsa
Seu
d'Urgell
Núria
Ripoll
Figueras
Empúries
LA RIOJA
Tudela
Huesca
C A T A L U Ñ A
Palafrugell
Soria
Tarazona
A R A G O N
Vic
Gerona
CORDILLERA IBERICA
Calatayud
Zaragoza
Montserrat
Tarrasa
Tossa de Mar
COSTA BRAVA
Sigüenza
Cariñena
Lérida
Barcelona
Daroca
Vilanova i la
Geltrú
Sierra de Albarracín
Albarracín
Teruel
Sitges
Tarragona
Tajo
Sierrania de Cuenca
Morella
Tortosa
COSTA DORADA
Balearic
Sea
Cuenca
Sierra de
Javalambre
Mora
de Rubieios
Peñiscola
TO MENORCA
El Toboso
Sagunto
Castellón
de la Plana
Alcúdia
Inca
Palma
Ucar
VALENCIA
Valencia
Golfo de
Valencia
COSTA DEL AZAHAR
Manacor
Culiera
Mallorca
ISLAS BALEARES
Albacete
Játiva
Gandía
Denia
San Antonio
Abad
Santa Eulalia
del Rio
Villena
Alcoy
Ibiza
Ibiza
Alicante
Calpe
Formentera
Elche
COSTA BLANCA
S. Francisco
Javier
Menorca
Orihuela
Sierra de Segura
MURCIA
Murcia
Ciudadela
Mahón
B E T I C A
Lorca
Manga del
Mar Menor
Mediterranean Sea
Nevada
Cartagena
Almería
Cabo de
Gata
COSTA DE ALMERIA
0   50 miles
0   75 km
ALGERIA

LIFE AND TIMES

HISTORY AND POLITICS

Spain was colonized and characterized by a succession of civilizations—**Basque, Tartesian, Iberian, Celtic, Greek, Phoenician,** and **Carthaginian**—before the **Romans** dropped in with a vengeance in the 3rd century BC. Over nearly seven centuries, the Romans drastically altered the face and character of Spain, introducing Rome's language, architecture, roads, irrigation techniques, and use of grapes, olives, and wheat. A slew of Germanic tribes, including the Swabians and Vandals, swept over Iberia in the early 400s AD, but the **Visigoths,** newly converted Christians, emerged above the rest. The Visigoths established their court at Barcelona in 415 and effectively ruled Spain for the next 300 years.

THE MOORISH OCCUPATION (711-1492 AD)

Following Muslim unification and a victory tour through the Middle East and North Africa, a small force of Arabs, Berbers, and Syrians invaded Spain in 711. Practically welcomed by the divided Visigoths, the Moors encountered little resistance, and the peninsula soon fell under the dominion of the caliphate of Damascus. These events precipitated the infusion of Muslim influence, which peaked in the 10th century. The Moors set up their Iberian capital in Córdoba (see p.839). During **Abderramán III's** rule (936-76), some considered Spain the wealthiest and most cultivated country in the world. Abderramán's successor, **Al Mansur** (976-1013), snuffed out all opposition within his extravagant court and undertook a series of military campaigns that climaxed with the destruction of Santiago de Compostela (see p.894), a Christian holy city, in 997.

The turning point in Muslim-Christian relations came when Al Mansur died, leaving a power vacuum in Córdoba. At this point, caliphate holdings shattered into petty states called *taifas.* With power less centralized, Christians were able to gain the upper hand. The Christian policy was official toleration of Muslims and Jews, which fostered a culture and even a style of art, **Mudéjar.** Later, though, countless Moorish structures were ruined in the Reconquest, and numerous mosques were replaced by churches (like Córdoba's Mezquita; see p.843).

THE CATHOLIC MONARCHS (1469-1516)

In 1469, the marriage of **Fernando de Aragón** and **Isabel de Castilla** joined Iberia's two mightiest Christian kingdoms. By 1492, the dynamic duo had captured Granada (see p.846), the last Moorish stronghold, and shuttled off **Columbus** to explore the New World. By the 16th century, the pair's leadership made Spain's empire the world's most powerful. The Catholic monarchs introduced the **Inquisition** in 1478, executing and burning heretics. The Spanish Inquisition's dual aims were to strengthen the authority of the Church and to unify Spain. In 50 years of rule, the Catholic monarchs heightened Spain's position as a world economic, political, and cultural power—made all the more enduring by conquests in the Americas.

LA MOVIDA After 40 years of Franco-imposed repression, Madrid was a cultural explosion waiting to happen. Franco's death in 1975 served as a catalyst for change: not a day had passed before every newspaper had printed a pornographic photo on its front page. *El Destapeo* ("the uncorking" or "uncovering" which followed Franco's regime) and *la Movida* ("the Movement," which took place a few years later) both exploded in Madrid, inspiring political diversity, apolitical revelry, and eccentricity of all kinds. Remnants of *la Movida* are still visible, however, in today's outrageous clubs, ambitious bars, and in the excitement of young *madrileños* planning to *ir de marcha* ("to party," literally "to go marching").

THE HABSBURG DYNASTY (1516-1713)

The daughter of Fernando and Isabel, **Juana la Loca** (the Mad), married **Felipe el Hermoso** (the Fair) of the powerful Habsburg dynasty. Mr. Handsome (who died playing *cesta punta*, or *jai alai*) and Mrs. Crazy (who refused to believe he had died and dragged his corpse through the streets) produced **Carlos I** (Charles V, 1516-56). Carlos I, the last official Holy Roman Emperor, reigned over an immense empire comprising modern-day Netherlands, Belgium, Austria, Spain, parts of Germany and Italy, and the American colonies. Carlos did his part: as a good Catholic, he embroiled Spain in a war with Protestant France; as an art patron of superb taste, he nabbed Titian as his court painter; as a fashion plate, he introduced Spain to the Habsburg fashion of wearing only black.

But trouble was brewing in the Protestant Netherlands, then called the Low Countries and Flanders. After Carlos I died, his son **Felipe II** (1556-98) was left holding the bag full of rebellious territories. He annexed Portugal after its ailing King Henrique died in 1580. One year later the Dutch declared their independence from Spain, and Felipe began warring with the Protestants, spurring further tensions with England. The war with the British ground to a halt when **Sir Francis Drake** and bad weather buffeted the **Invincible Armada** in 1588. His enthusiasm and much of his European empire sapped, Felipe retreated to his grim, newly built palace, **El Escorial** (see p. 817) and remained there through the last decade of his reign.

Felipe III (1598-1621), preoccupied with both religion and the finer aspects of life, allowed his favorite adviser, the **Duque de Lerma,** to pull governmental strings. In 1609, Felipe III and the Duke expelled nearly 300,000 of Spain's remaining Moors. Mustached **Felipe IV** (1621-65) painstakingly held the country together through his long, tumultuous reign. Emulating his great-grandfather Carlos I, Felipe IV patronized the arts (painter Diego Velázquez and playwrights Lope de Vega and Calderón de la Barca were in his court; see **The Arts,** p. 793) and architecture (the Buen Retiro in Madrid; see p. 812). Then the **Thirty Years' War** (1618-48) broke out over Europe, and defending Catholicism drained Spain's resources; the war ended with the marriage of Felipe IV's daughter, María Teresa, and Louis XIV of France. Felipe's successor **Carlos II** (1665-1700), the *"hechizado"* (bewitched), was epileptic and impotent, the product of inbreeding. From then on, little went right: Carlos II died, Spain fell into a depression, and cultural bankruptcy ensued.

BOURBONS, CONSTITUTIONS, AND LIBERALS (1713-1930)

The 1713 **Treaty of Utrecht** seated **Felipe V** (1713-46), a Bourbon grandson of French Louis XIV, on the Spanish throne. The king built huge, showy palaces (to mimic Versailles in France) and cultivated a flamboyant, debauched court. Despite his undisciplined example, the Bourbons who followed Felipe ably administered the Empire, at last beginning to regain control of Spanish-American trade. They also constructed scores of new canals and roads, organized settlements, and instituted agricultural reform and industrial expansion. **Carlos III** (1759-88) was probably Madrid's finest "mayor," founding academies of art and science and generally beautifying the capital. Spain's global standing recovered enough for it to team with France to help the American colonies gain independence from Britain.

In 1808, **Napoleon** invaded Spain (1808-14) in his quest for world domination. The invasion's battles were particularly bloody; painter **Francisco de Goya** captured the brutality in two brilliant works (see **The Arts,** p. 793). The French occupation ended when the Protestant Brits defeated the Corsican's troops at Waterloo (1814). This victory led to the restoration of arch-reactionary **Fernando VII** (1814-33), who sought to revoke the progressive Constitución de Cádiz of 1812. Galvanized by Fernando's ineptitude and inspired by liberal ideas in the new constitution, most of Spain's Latin American empire soon threw off its yoke. Lingering dreams of an empire were further curbed by the loss of the Philippines, Puerto Rico, and Cuba to the US in the 1898 **Spanish-American War.**

THE SECOND REPUBLIC AND THE CIVIL WAR (1931-1939)

In April 1931, **King Alfonso XIII** (1902-31), disgraced by his support for Rivera's dictatorship, shamefully fled Spain, thus giving rise to the **Second Republic** (1931-36). Republican Liberals and Socialists established safeguards for farmers and industrial workers, granted women's suffrage, assured religious tolerance, and chipped away at traditional military dominance. National euphoria, however, faded fast. The 1933 elections split the Republican-Socialist coalition, in the process increasing the power of right-wing and Catholic parties. By 1936, radicals, anarchists, Socialists, and Republicans had formed a loosely federated alliance to win the next elections. But the victory was short-lived. Once **Generalísimo Francisco Franco** snatched control of the Spanish army, militarist uprisings ensued, and the nation plunged into war. The three-year **Civil War** (1936-39) ignited worldwide ideological passions. Germany and Italy dropped troops, supplies, and munitions into Franco's lap, while the stubbornly isolationist US and liberal European states were slow to aid the Republicans. Although Franco enjoyed popular support in Andalucía, Galicia, Navarra, and parts of Castilla, the Republicans controlled the industrial centers. The Soviet Union called for a **Popular Front** of Communists, Socialists, and other leftist sympathizers to battle Franco's fascism. Soon, however, the West abandoned the coalition, and aid from the Soviet Union waned as Stalin began to see the benefits of an alliance with Hitler. Without international aid, Republican forces were cut off from supplies, and began to surrender to the Nationalists. Bombings, executions, combat, starvation, and disease took nearly 600,000 lives, and in 1939 Franco's forces marched into Madrid and ended the war.

FRANCO AND THE TRANSITION TO DEMOCRACY (1939-1999)

Brain-drain (as leading scientists, artists, and intellectuals emigrated or were assassinated en masse), worker dissatisfaction, student unrest, and international isolation characterized the first few decades of Franco's dictatorship. Several anarchist and nationalist groups, notably the Basque ETA, resisted the dictatorship throughout Franco's reign, often via terrorist acts. In his old age, Franco tried to smooth international relations by joining NATO and encouraging tourism, but the "national tragedy" (as it was later called) did not officially end until Franco's death in 1975. **King Juan Carlos I** (1975-), grandson of Alfonso XIII and a nominal Franco protégé, carefully set out to undo Franco's damage. In 1978 Spain adopted a new constitution in a national referendum that led to the restoration of parliamentary government and regional autonomy.

Charismatic **Felipe González** led the **Spanish Socialist Worker's Party** (PSOE) to victory in the 1982 elections. González opened the Spanish economy and championed consensus policies, overseeing Spain's integration into the **European Community** (EC; now the EU) in 1986. Despite his support for continued membership in NATO (he had originally promised to withdraw if he won) and unpopular economic stands, González was reelected in 1986 and continued a program of massive public investment. The years 1986 to 1990 were outstanding for Spain's economy, as the nation enjoyed an average annual growth rate of 3.8%. By the end of 1993, however, recession had set in, and González and the PSOE only barely maintained a majority in Parliament over the increasingly popular conservative **Partido Popular (PP)**. Revelations of large-scale corruption led to a resounding Socialist defeat at the hands of the PP in the 1994 European parliamentary elections.

José María Aznar led the PP into power after González's support eroded and managed to maintain his delicately balanced coalition while leading the Spanish economy to its best performance in years. Fears of a rightist reversion have faded and most Spaniards seem pleased with the process of parliamentary democracy.

SPAIN TODAY

The last two years have seen mixed progress in one of Spain's most pressing areas of concern, Basque nationalism and terrorism. On September 12, 1998, the federal government issued the **Lizarra Declaration,** which called for an open dialogue between all parties (including the militant ETA) and was endorsed by the Basque

National Party (PNV). Six days later, ETA publicly declared a truce with the national government. On December 3, 1999, however, the ETA publicly declared an end to the 14-month cease-fire due to lack of progress with negotiations. The past year has since seen a return of periodic terrorist murders of PP and PSOE members, journalists and army officers, as well as instances of arson.

On a brighter note, the Spanish economy is currently in good and improving shape. Over the past four years, unemployment has dropped from 23% to 15% with the creation of two million new jobs—half of the total for the entire European Union during that time. Aznar talks of visions of "a new Spain" and plans to reduce unemployment even further, draw more women into the workforce, and improve the faltering birthrate by restructuring family and work arrangements.

THE ARTS

PAINTING

Residents of the Iberian peninsula were creating art as early as 13,000 BC, the birthdate of the fabulous cave paintings at **Altamira.** In the 11th and 12th centuries, fresco painters and manuscript illuminators decorated churches and their libraries along the Camino de Santiago, and in León (see p. 826) and Toledo (see p. 818). **Pedro Berruguete's** (1450-1504) use of traditional gold backgrounds in his religious paintings exemplifies the Italian-influenced style of early Renaissance works. Berruguete's style is especially evident in his masterpiece, the altarpiece of San Tomás in Ávila (1499-1503; see p. 823). Not until after Spain's imperial ascendancy in the 16th century did painting reach its **Golden Age** (roughly 1492-1650). Felipe II imported foreign art and artists in order to jump-start native production and embellish his palace, El Escorial. Although he came to Spain seeking a royal commission, **El Greco** (1541-1614), was rejected by Felipe II for his shocking and intensely personal style. Confounding his contemporaries, El Greco received appreciation in the 20th century for his elongated figures and dramatic use of light and color. Setting up camp in Toledo, El Greco graced the Church of Santo Tomé with his masterpiece *The Burial of Count Orgaz* (1586-1588).

Felipe IV's foremost court painter, **Diego Velázquez** (1599-1660), is considered one of the world's greatest artists. Whether representing Felipe IV's family or lowly court jesters and dwarves, Velázquez painted with the same naturalistic precision. Nearly half of this Sevillian artist's works reside in the Prado, including his famous *Las Meninas* (1656; see **Museo del Prado,** p. 813). Other Golden Age painters of note include **José de Ribera** (1591-1652), **Francisco de Zurbarán** (1598-1664), and **Bartolomé Esteban Murillo** (1618-1682). Each treated religious subjects with a distinctive vision: Italian-born Ribera took a realistic and even crude approach, Sevillian Zurbarán painted for monastic orders in a fittingly austere style, and Murillo depicted Catholic scenes with idealism and sentimentality.

During the era of Spain's waning power, **Francisco de Goya** (1746-1828) ushered European painting into the modern age. Hailing from provincial Aragón, Goya rose to the position of official court painter under the degenerate Carlos IV. Not bothering with flattery, Goya's depictions of the royal family came closer to caricature, as Queen María Luisa's cruel jawline in the famous *The Family of Charles IV* (1800) can attest. After an earlier Neoclassical period during which Goya stuck to smiling scenes of upper class gaiety, his later paintings graphically protest the lunacy of warfare. His series of etchings *The Disasters of War* (1810-1814), which includes the landmark *El dos de mayo* and *El tres de mayo*, records the horrific Napoleonic invasion of 1808. Deaf and despondent in his later years, Goya painted nightmarish and wildly fantastic visions, inspiring Expressionist and Surrealist artists of the next century. The Prado museum houses an entire room of his chilling *Black Paintings* (1820-1823; see p. 813).

It is hard to imagine an artist who has had as profound an effect upon 20th-century painting as Andalucían-born **Pablo Picasso** (1881-1973). A child prodigy, Picasso headed for Barcelona, which was a breeding ground of Modernist architecture and political activism. Picasso's Blue Period, beginning in 1900, was characterized by somber depictions of society's outcasts. His permanent move to Paris in 1904 initiated his Rose Period, during which he probed into the curiously engrossing lives of clowns and acrobats. With his French colleague Georges Braque, he founded **Cubism,** a method of painting objects simultaneously from multiple perspectives. His gigantic 1937 mural *Guernica* portrays the bombing of that Basque city by Nazi planes during the Spanish Civil War. A vehement protest against violence and fascism, *Guernica* resides in the Centro de Arte Reina Sofia in Madrid (see p. 814).

Catalán painter and sculptor **Joan Miró** (1893-1983) created simplistic, almost child-like shapes in bright, primary colors. His haphazard, undefined creations became a statement against the authoritarian society of Fascist Spain. By contrast, fellow Catalán **Salvador Dalí** (1904-89) scandalized both high society and leftist intellectuals in France and Spain by supporting the Fascists. Dalí's name is virtually synonymous with **Surrealism.** The wildly mustached painter tapped into dreams and the unconscious for images like the melting clocks in *The Persistence of Memory* (1931). His haunting *Premonition of the Civil War* (1936), subtitled *Soft Construction with Boiled Beans*, envisioned war as a distorted monster of putrefying flesh. A shameless self-promoter (he often spoke of himself only in the third person), Dalí founded the Teatre-Museo Dalí in Figueres, which defines Surrealism in its collection, its construction, and its very existence (see p. 875).

Since Franco's death in 1975, a new generation of artists has thrived. With new museums in Madrid, Barcelona, Valencia, Sevilla, and Bilbao, Spanish painters and sculptors once again have a national forum for their work. Catalán **Antonio Tapiès** constructs collages out of unusual and unorthodox materials and is a founding member of the self-proclaimed "Abstract Generation," while **Antonio López García** has distinguished himself for his hyperrealist paintings. Upstarts include abstract artist **José María Sicilia,** sculptor **Susana Solano,** and **Miguel Barceló,** whose portraits resemble swarms of black flies.

ARCHITECTURE

Scattered **Roman ruins** testify to six centuries of colonization. Highlights include some of the finest remains in existence: the aqueduct in Segovia (see p. 822), the theater in Mérida, and the town of Tarragona.

After the invasion of 711, the **Moors** constructed mosques and palaces throughout southern Spain. Because the Koran forbade representations of humans and animals, architects lavished buildings with stylized geometric designs, red-and-white horseshoe arches, ornate tiles, courtyards, pools, and fountains. The spectacular 14th-century **Alhambra** in Granada (see p. 846) and the **Mezquita** in Córdoba, one-time capital of the Muslim empire (see p. 843), epitomize the Moorish style.

The combination of Islam and Christianity created two architectural movements unique to Spain: **Mozarabic** and **Mudéjar.** The former describes Christians under Muslim rule (Mozarabs) who adopted Arab devices like the horseshoe-shaped arch and the ribbed dome. The more common Mudéjar architecture was created by Moors in the years between Christian resurgence (11th century) and the Reconquest (1492). Extensive use of brick and elaborately carved wooden ceilings typify Mudéjar style, which reached its height in the 14th century with **alcázars** (palaces) in Sevilla and Segovia and **synagogues** in Toledo and Córdoba.

The first Gothic cathedral in Spain was built in Burgos (1221; see p. 828), followed closely by Toledo and León. The **Spanish Gothic** style, brought pointed arches, flying buttresses, slender walls, airy spaces, and stained-glass windows. Regional variations evolved: the Catalán style, for example, employed internal wall supports rather than external buttresses. Other Spanish alterations of the French original include centrally placed *coros* (choirs) and oversized *retablos* (brightly colored carved pieces placed above the high altar).

New World riches inspired the **Plateresque** ("in the manner of a silversmith") style, a flashy embellishment of Gothic that transformed wealthier parts of Spain. Intricate stonework and extravagant use of gold and silver splashed 15th- and

16th-century buildings, most notably in Salamanca, where the university practically drips with ornamentation. In the late 16th century, **Italian Renaissance** innovations in perspective and symmetry arrived in Spain to sober up the Plateresque style. **El Escorial** (1563-84), Felipe II's grand palace, was designed by **Juan de Herrera,** one of Spain's most prominent architects, and best exemplifies the unadorned Renaissance style (see p. 817).

Opulence seized center stage once again in 17th- and 18th-century **Baroque** Spain. The Churriguera brothers pioneered this style—called, appropriately, **Churrigueresque**—which is equal parts ostentatious, ornamental, and difficult to pronounce. Wildly elaborate works with extensive sculptural detail and twisted columns, like the altar of the Toledo cathedral (see p. 818), help set this period in Spanish architecture apart.

In the late 19th and early 20th centuries, Catalán's **Modernistas** burst onto the scene in Barcelona, led by the eccentric genius of **Antoni Gaudí, Luis Domènech i Montaner,** and **José Puig i Caldafach.** Modernista structures defy previous standards with their voluptuous curves and abnormal textures. The new style was inspired partly by Mudéjar relics, but far more so by organic forms and unbridled imagination. Spain's outstanding architectural tradition continues to this day with such trendsetters as **Josep María Sert, Ricardo Bofill,** and **Rafael Moneo.**

LITERATURE

Spain's literary tradition first blossomed in the late Middle Ages (1000-1500). **Fernando de Rojas's** *La Celestina* (1499), a tragicomic dialogue most noted for its folkloric witch character, helped pave the way for picaresque novels like *Lazarillo de Tormes* (1554) and *Guzmán de Alfarache* (1599), rags-to-riches stories about mischievous boys with good hearts. This literary form surfaced during Spain's **Golden Age** (1492-1681). Poetry particularly thrived in this era. Some consider the sonnets and romances of **Garcilaso de la Vega** the most perfect ever written in Castilian. **Francisco de Quevedo** also contributed to the rebirth of sonnets, treating erotic themes with a sardonic twist. This period also produced outstanding dramas, including works from **Calderón de la Barca** and **Lope de Vega,** who wrote nearly 2000 plays. Both espoused the Neoplatonic view of love, claiming that love always changes one's life dramatically and eternally. **Miguel de Cervantes'** two-part *Don Quixote de la Mancha* (1605-15) is the most famous work of Spanish literature. Cervantes relates the satiric parable of the hapless Don and his sidekick, Sancho Panza, who think themselves bold *caballeros* (knights) out to save the world.

The 19th century bred a multiplicity of styles, from the biting journalistic prose of **Mariano José de Larra** to **José Zorrilla's** romantic poem *Don Juan Tenorio* (1844) to the naturalistic novels of **Leopoldo Alas ("Clarín").** The modern literary era began with the **Generación del '98,** a group led by essayist **Miguel de Unamuno** and cultural critic **José Ortega y Gasset.** Reacting to Spain's embarrassing defeat in the Spanish-American War (1898), these nationalistic authors argued, through essays and novels, that each individual must spiritually and ideologically attain internal peace before society can do the same. These authors heavily influenced the **Generación del 1927,** a clique of experimental lyric poets who used Surrealist and vanguard poetry to express profound humanism. This group included **Jorge Guillén, Federico García Lorca** (assassinated at the start of the Civil War), **Rafael Alberti,** and **Luis Cernuda.** In the 20th century, the Nobel Committee has honored playwright and essayist **Jacinto Benavente y Martínez** (1922), poet **Vicente Aleixandre** (1977), and novelist **Camilo José Cela** (1989), author of *La Familia de Pascal Duarte* (1942). Female writers, like **Mercè Rodoreda** and **Carmen Martín Gaite,** have likewise earned critical acclaim. Since the fall of the Fascist regime in 1975, Spanish artists have again flocked to Madrid. In the 1980s, an avant-garde spirit—known as *La Movida* (see 790)—was reborn in the capital. **Ana Rossetti** and **Juana Castro** led a new generation of erotic poets into the 80s. With this newest group of poets, women are at the forefront of Spanish literature for the first time.

FILM

One of the greatest influences on Spanish film was not a filmmaker, but a politician. Franco's regime (1939-75) defined Spanish film during and after his rule. Censorship stifled most creative tendencies and left the public with nothing to watch but cheap westerns and bland spy flicks. As government supervision slacked in the early 1970s, Spanish cinema showed signs of life, led by **Carlos Saura's** subversive hits such as *El Jardin de las Delicias* (1970) and *Cría Cuervos* (1975).

In 1977, in the wake of Franco's death, domestic censorship laws were revoked, bringing artistic freedom along with financial hardship for Spanish filmmakers, who found their films shunned domestically in favor of newly permitted foreign films. Internationally, however, depictions of the exuberant excesses of liberated Spain found increasing attention. **Pedro Almodovar's** *Law of Desire* (1986), featuring **Antonio Banderas** as a homosexual, perhaps best captures the risqué themes of transgression and sexuality most often treated by contemporary Spanish cinema. His *Women on the Verge of a Nervous Breakdown* (1988) expresses post-Franco disillusion in an unrefined, fashion-conscious Madrid. Other directors to look for in Spain include **Bigas Luna,** director of the controversial *Jamón Jamón* (1992), **Fernando Trueba, Vicente Aranda, Victor Érice,** and **Pilar Micó.** Trueba's *Belle Epoque* won an Oscar in 1994, and Almodovar's *Todo Sobre Mi Madre* claimed Best Foriegn Film in 2000.

BULLFIGHTING

A visit to Spain is not complete without the experience of a bullfight. The national spectacle that is bullfighting dates, in its modern form, back to the early 1700s. A bullfight is divided into three principal stages: in the first, *picadors* (lancers on horseback) pierce the bull's neck; next, assistants on foot thrust *banderillas* (decorated darts) into the back; and finally, the matador performs the kill. If a matador has shown special skill and daring, the audience waves white handkerchiefs to implore the bullfight's president to reward the coveted ears (and, very rarely, the tail) to the matador. Although bullfighting has always had its critics—the Catholic church in the 17th century felt that the risks made it equivalent to suicide—the late 20th century has seen an especially strong attack from animal rights' activists. Whatever its faults, however, bullfighting is an essential element of the Spanish national consciousness. For an American take on the myth, meaning, and *machismo* of the bullfight, check out Ernest Hemingway's *Death in the Afternoon* (1932) and *The Sun Also Rises* (1926).

FOOD AND DRINK

Spaniards start their day with a breakfast of coffee or hot chocolate and *bollos* (rolls) or *churros* (lightly fried fritters). Lunch is served between 2 and 3pm, and is several courses. Supper at home is light—often a sandwich—and eaten around 9pm. Supper out—also a light meal—begins later, usually around 10pm. Some restaurants are "open" from 8am until 1 or 2am, but most only serve meals from 1 or 2 to 4pm and from 8pm until midnight. Prices for a full meal start at about 800ptas in the cheapest bar-restaurant. Many places offer a *plato combinado* (combination platter–main course and side dishes on a single plate, plus bread, and sometimes beverage–roughly 500-1200ptas) or a *menú del día* (two or three set dishes, bread, beverage, and dessert–roughly 800-1500ptas). Spain's **tapas** (small portions of savory meats and vegetables cooked according to local recipes) are truly tasty. *Raciones* are basically large tapas served as main dishes. **Bocadillos** are sandwiches. Spanish specialties include *tortilla de patata* (potato omelette), *jamón serrano* (smoked ham), *calamares fritos* (fried squid), *arroz* (rice), *chorizo* (spicy sausage), *gambas* (shrimp), *lomo* (pork), **paella** (steamed saffron rice with seafood, chicken, and vegetables), and *gazpacho* (cold tomato-based soup). Vegetarians should remember the phrase *"yo soy vegetariano"* (I am a vegetarian). *Vino blanco* is white wine and *tinto* is red. Beer is *cerveza;* Mahou and Cruzcampo are the most common Spanish brands. *Sangría* is made of red wine, sugar, brandy, and fruit. *Tinto de verano* is red wine with flavored seltzer.

ESSENTIALS

DOCUMENTS AND FORMALITIES

Travelers need legal passports or visas to enter and leave Spain. A passport allows Canadian, British, New Zealand, and US citizens to remain for 90 days. Citizens of South Africa and Australia need a **visa** to enter Spain. Admission as a visitor does not include the right to **work,** which is authorized only by a work permit; entering Spain to **study** requires a special visa.

Spanish Embassies at Home: Australia, 15 Arkana St., Yarralumla, ACT 2600. Mailing address: P.O. Box 9076, Deakin, ACT 2600. (☎ (02) 62 73 35 55); **Canada,** 74 Stanley Ave., Ottawa, ON K1M 1P4 (☎ (613) 747-2252); **Ireland,** 17A Merlyn Park, Ballsbridge, Dublin 4 (☎ (01) 269 1640); **South Africa,** 169 Pine St., Arcadia, P.O. Box 1633, Pretoria 0083 (☎ (012) 344 3875); **UK,** 39 Chesham Pl., London SW1X 8SB (☎ (020) 72 35 55 552); **US,** 2375 Pennsylvania Ave. NW, Washington, D.C. 20037 (☎ (202) 728-2330).

Foreign Embassies in Spain: Embassies are in Madrid (see p. 800). All countries have consulates in **Barcelona** (see p. 856). **Australia, UK,** and US consulates are in **Sevilla** (see p. 830). Another **Canadian** consulate is in Málaga; the **South African** consulate is in Bilbao; **UK** consulates are in Bilbao, Palma de Mallorca, Ibiza, Alicante, and Málaga; US consulates are in Málaga, Valencia, La Coruña, and Palma de Mallorca.

TRANSPORTATION

BY PLANE. Airports in Madrid and Barcelona handle most international flights; Sevilla also has a major international airport. **Iberia** serves all domestic locations and all major international cities. **Air Europa** (US ☎ (888) 238-7672 or (718) 244-6016; Spain ☎ 902 30 06 00; email easyspain@g-air-europa.es; www.g-aireuropa.es) flies out of New York City and most European cities to Spain and has discounts available for those under 22.

BY TRAIN. RENFE (www.renfe.es), the Spanish centralized national rail system, has clean, punctual, reasonably priced trains with various levels of service. Its network radiates from Madrid; many small towns are not served. *Alta Velocidad Española* (AVE) trains are the fastest between Madrid-Córdoba-Sevilla. *Talgos* are almost as fast; *Talgo 200s* run on *AVE* rails—there are four lines from Madrid to Málaga, Algeciras, Cádiz, and Huelva. *Intercity* is cheaper and a bit dowdier, but still fairly fast. *Estrellas* are slow night trains with bunks. *Cercanías* (commuter trains) go from cities to suburbs and nearby towns. *Tranvía, semidirecto,* and *correo* trains are slower-than-slow. Trains connect with most major European cities via France. The other train company in Spain is **FEVE,** which sluggishly but dependably runs between many northern towns not served by RENFE.

There are several **RailEurope** passes that cover travel within Spain. You must purchase railpasses at least 15 days before departure. Call 1-800-4EURAIL in the US or go to www.raileurope.com. **Spain Flexipass** offers three days of unlimited travel in a two-month period. (1st class US$200; 2nd class US$155. Each additional rail-day, up to 7, US$35 for 1st class, US$30 for 2nd class.) **Iberic Railpass** is good for three days of unlimited 1st-class travel in Spain and Portugal for US$205. Each additional rail-day (up to 7) US$45. **Spain Rail 'n' Drive Pass** is good for three days of unlimited 1st-class train travel and two days of unlimited mileage in a rental car.

BY BUS. In Spain, ignore romanticized versions of European train travel—**buses** are cheaper, run more frequently, and are sometimes faster than trains. Bus routes, far more comprehensive than the rail network, provide the only public transportation to many isolated areas and almost always cost less than trains. Spain has numerous private companies; the lack of a centralized bus company may make itinerary planning an ordeal. **ALSA** (☎ 915 28 28 03), serves Madrid, Galicia, Asturias, and Castilla y León, as well as international destinations in Portugal, Morocco, France, Italy, and Poland. **Auto-Res/Cunisa, S.A.** (☎ 915 51 72 00), serves Madrid, Castilla y León, Extremadura, Galicia, and Valencia.

BY FERRY. The main ferry company in Spain is **Transmediterranea** (☎902 45 46 45; www.transmediterranea.com). Ferries link mainland Spain to the **Balearic Islands,** the **Canary Islands,** and **Morocco.**

BY CAR. Spain has an extensive road grid covering close to 340,000km; of this total, 7,000km are highways (toll motorways, freeways, and dual-carriageways). Gas prices average 130-140ptas per liter. **Speed limits** are as follows: 50km per hr. (30 mph) in cities; 90 or 100km per hr. (56 or 62 mph) outside cities; and 120km per hr. (74 mph) on expressways. In residential areas the speed limit is 20km per hr. (12 mph); roads marked **A** for *autopista* are toll roads.

Renting a car in Spain is considerably cheaper than in many other Western European countries. International rental companies offer services throughout the country, but you may want to check with **Atesa** (www.atesa.es), Spain's largest national rental agency. The Spanish automobile association is **Real Automóbil Club de España (RACE),** C. Jose Abascal, 10, Madrid (☎914 47 32 00). **Taxis** are readily available in almost every Spanish city, and they are a much wiser form of transportation than a personal car in Madrid and Barcelona.

BY BIKE AND BY THUMB. Due to its mountainous terrain, Spain does not have as extensive of a **bike tour** industry as some other Western European countries. It is certainly explorable by bicycle, however, and it shouldn't be hard to rent a bicycle in tourist centers, especially in southern regions. **Hitchhikers** report that Castilla and Andalucía offer little more than a long, hot wait, and that hitchhiking out of Madrid is virtually impossible. The Mediterranean Coast and the islands are much more promising. *Let's Go* does not recommend hitchhiking.

TOURIST SERVICES AND MONEY

EMERGENCY	Emergency: ☎112. Local Police: ☎091. National Police: ☎092. Medical: ☎124.

TOURIST OFFICES. The Spanish Tourist Office is eager to help tourists. They operate an extensive official website (www.tourspain.es) and have 29 offices abroad. Municipal tourist offices, generally called *oficinas de turismo,* are a good first stop to make upon arrival in a Spanish town; they usually have free maps and region-specific advice for travelers.

> **Tourist offices at home: Canada,** Tourist Office of Spain, 2 Bloor St. West, Ste. 3402, Toronto, ON M4W 3E2 (☎ (416) 961-3131; fax (416) 961-1992); **UK,** Spanish National Tourist Office, 22-23 Manchester Square, London W1M 5AP (☎ (171) 486 8077; fax (171) 486 8034; email info.londres@tourspain.es); **US,** Tourist Office of Spain, 666 Fifth Ave., 35th Fl., New York, NY 10103 (☎ (212) 265-8822; fax (212) 265-8864), additional offices in Chicago, IL (☎ (312) 642-1992), Beverly Hills, CA (☎ (323) 658-7188) and Miami, FL (☎ (305) 358-1992).

CURRENCY AND EXCHANGE. Money in Spain comes in the form of the *peseta* (ptas), available in coins of 1, 5, 10, 25, 50, 100, 200 and 500ptas and notes of 1000, 2000, 50000, and 10,0000ptas. **Traveler's checks** are widely accepted and used in Spain; ATM cards are probably an even easier way to exchange money and will earn you a better rate. If you are using travelers' checks, **Banco Central Hispano** often provides good rates.

> **Prices:** You can do a "bare-bones day" in Spain (camping or sleeping in cheap hostels, buying food at supermarkets, staying in at night) for about 5000ptas, or US$30-35. A slightly more comfortable day (sleeping in nicer hostels, eating one or two meals a day in restaurants, going out at night) will probably run up to 7500ptas, or US$50.
>
> **Tipping and bargaining:** Tipping is not very common in Spain. In restaurants, all prices include service charge. Satisfied customers occasionally toss in some spare change—usually no more than 5%—but this is purely optional. Many people give train, airport and hotel porters a 100ptas coin per bag, while taxi drivers sometimes get 5-10%. Bar-

gaining is common at flea markets and with street vendors. Travelers can try bargaining for hostel prices in the off-season, especially in less-touristed areas.

Taxes: Spain has a 7% **Value Added Tax**, known as IVA, on all restaurant and accommodations. The prices listed in *Let's Go* include IVA unless otherwise mentioned. Retail goods bear a much higher 16% IVA, although listed prices are usually inclusive. Non-EU citizens who have stayed in the EU fewer than 180 days can claim back the tax paid on purchases at the airport. Ask the shop where you have made the purchase to supply you with a tax return form.

ACCOMMODATIONS AND CAMPING

Spanish accommodations have many aliases, distinguished by the different grades of rooms. The cheapest and barest options are **casas de huéspedes** and **hospedajes**, while **pensiones** and **fondas** tend to be a bit nicer. All are basically just boarding houses. Higher up the ladder, **hostales** generally have sinks in bedrooms and provide sheets and lockers, while **hostal-residencias** are similar to hotels in overall quality. The government rates *hostales* on a two-star system; even establishments receiving one star are typically quite comfortable. The system also fixes each *hostal*'s prices, posted in the lounge or main entrance. If you have any troubles (with rates or service), ask for the **libro de reclamaciones** (complaint book), which by law must be produced on demand. The argument will usually end immediately, since all complaints must be forwarded to the authorities within 48hr. In Spain, **campgrounds** are generally the cheapest choice for two or more people. Most charge separate fees per person, per tent, and per car; others charge for a *parcela*—a small plot of land—plus possible per-person fees. Tourist offices provide info on official areas, including the hefty *Guía de campings*. Reservations are usually necessary in the summer.

COMMUNICATION

MAIL. Air mail *(por avión)* takes around 6 business days to reach the US and Canada, approximately 3 days to the UK and Ireland and up to 10 days to Australia and New Zealand. Standard postage is 115ptas to North America. **Surface mail** *(por barco)*, while considerably less expensive than air mail, can take over a month, and packages will take two to three months. **Registered** or **express mail** *(registrado or certificado)*, is the most reliable way to send a letter or parcel home, and takes four to seven business days (letter postage 237ptas). **Stamps** are sold at post offices and tobacconists *(estancos or tabacos)*. To send mail *Poste Restante* to Spain, address the letter as follows: TSAO, Jennie; Lista de Correos; City Name; Postal Code; SPAIN; AIR MAIL.

TELEPHONES. The central Spanish phone company is **Telefónica**. Local calls cost 20ptas. The best way to make local calls is with a phone card, issued in denominations of 1000 and 2000ptas and available at tobacconists *(estancos or tabacos)* and most post offices. International calls can be made using phone cards, but are very expensive; the best way to call home is with an international calling card issued by your phone company. To call home with your calling card, contact the operator for your service provider in Spain by dialing the appropriate **international toll-free access number: AT&T,** ☎900 99 00 11; **Australia Direct,** ☎900 99 00 61; **BT Direct,** ☎900 99 00 44; **Canada Direct,** ☎900 99 00 15; **Eircom,** ☎900 99 03 53; **MCI WorldPhone Direct,** ☎900 99 00 14; **Sprint,** ☎900 99 00 13; **Telecom New Zealand Direct,** ☎900 99 00 64; **Telkom South Africa Direct,** ☎900 99 00 27.

INTERNET ACCESS. Email is easily accessible within Spain. An increasing number of bars offer internet access for a fee of 600-1000ptas per hour; many also offer specials with rates much cheaper than that. Cybercafes are listed in most towns and all cities. In small towns, if internet access is not listed, try the library or tourist office where travelers can sometimes get access for a small fee. The website www.tangaworld.com lists nearly 200 cybercafes across Spain.

LANGUAGE. There are 5 official languages in Spain, plus plenty of dialects. Catalán is the language of choice in Catalonia, Valencian in Valencia. The Basque (Euskera) language is spoken in north-central Spain, and Galician (Gallego, related to Portuguese) is spoken in the once-Celtic northwest. Spanish (Castilian, or *castellano*) is spoken everywhere. To partake of some *castellano*, see p. 957.

LOCAL FACTS

Time: Spain is 1hr. ahead of Greenwich Mean Time (GMT).

Climate: The northwest is rightly called "wet" Spain, with a humid, temperate climate. The interior's climate resembles that of Central Europe—long winters and, in the lowlands, hot, dry summers. The east and south coasts enjoy a Mediterranean climate. The northeast coast can be humid, but the southwest is the sweltering, especially Sevilla and Córdoba.

Hours: The day gets started around 9am, shops close down for a long lunch from 1:30 or 2pm until 4:30 or 5pm, when they reopen until 8pm. On Saturday, shops are usually open only in the morning, and Sunday is a day of rest for almost all places of business. Banking hours in Spain are M-F 9am-2pm; Oct.-May, banks are also open Sa 9am-1pm.

Holidays: New Year's Day (Jan. 1-2); Epiphany (Jan. 6); Maundy Thursday (Apr. 12); Good Friday (Apr. 13); Easter (Apr.15); Labor Day (May 1); Corpus Christi (June 22); Feast of St. James the Apostle (July 25); La Asunción (Aug. 25); National Day (Oct. 12); All Saints' Day (Nov.1); Constitution Day (Dec. 6); Feast of the Immaculate Conception (Dec.8); Christmas (Dec.25).

Festivals: Spain loves festivals—in total there are more than 3000, far too many to list here. All of Spain will celebrate **Carnaval** from Feb. 15 to 25 this year; the biggest partying goes on in Cataluña and Cádiz. Valencia will host the annual **Las Fallas** in mid-March. From April 9 to 15, the entire country will honor the Holy Week, or **Semana Santa.** Sevilla's **Feria de Abril** takes place in late April. In June and July, Granada will host the International Dance and Music Festival and Córdoba will host the International Guitar Festival. Mérida's **Festival de Teatro Clásico** will be in July and August, and Pamplona's infamous **San Fermines** (Running of the Bulls) takes place from July 6 to 14. San Sebástian's international film festival is in the last week of September. For more information on fiestas throughout Spain, see www.tourspain.es, www. SiSpain.org, or www.cyberspain.es.

MADRID

There are a few minutes, in the orange light of Madrid's early morning, when the city finally seems to sleep. Just moments later, steel shutters blink open and the streets once again fill with an unending stream of pedestrians and cars. While tourists inundate the city, spending their days absorbing its "Old World" monuments, world-renowned museums, and raging nightlife, Madrid's population of 4,500,000 roams the labyrinthine neighborhoods, living life with a simple and energetic joy. With Franco's death came an explosion known as *la Movida* ("Shift" or "Movement"). After decades of totalitarian repression, Madrid burst out laughing and crying, and life poured into the city. A 200,000-strong student population took to the streets and stayed there, shedding the decorous reserve of their predecessors. In their frenetic state, post-Franco youth seemed neither cognizant of their city's history nor preoccupied with its future; they haven't stopped moving yet.

Today the city continues to serve as the country's political, intellectual, and cultural center. It has become a city of immigrants—families hoping to find relief from Spain's high unemployment, students seeking higher education at Madrid's universities, and yet-to-be-discovered artists all flood the growing metropolis.

✈ GETTING THERE AND AWAY

Flights: All flights land at **Aeropuerto Internacional de Barajas,** 30min. northeast of Madrid. The **Barajas metro line,** inaugurated in June 1999, connects the airport to all of Madrid (130ptas). From the airport, follow signs to the metro. Another option is the green **Bus-Aeropuerto** (look for "EMT" signs just outside the doors), which leaves from the national and international terminals and runs to the city center (4:45am-6:17am, every 25min.; 6:17am-10pm, every 15min.; 10pm-1:45am, every hr.; 385ptas). The bus stops underground beneath the Jardines del Descubrimiento in **Plaza de Colón** (M: Colón). Fleets of **taxis** swarm the airport. Taxi fare to central Madrid should be around 3000ptas, including the 400ptas airport surcharge. Serving international and national destinations, **Iberia** is located at Santa Cruz de Marcenado, 2 (☎91 587 81 56). M: San Bernardo. Open M-F 9:30am-2pm and 4-7pm. Reservations and info (☎902 40 05 00) open 24hr. **Aviaco**, C. Maude, 51 (☎91 554 36 00), is a domestic affiliate.

Trains: Two *Largo Recorrido* (long distance) RENFE stations, **Madrid-Chamartín** and **Madrid-Atocha,** connect Madrid to the rest of the world. Call RENFE (☎91 328 90 20) for reservations and info. **RENFE Main Office,** C. Alcalá, 44, at Gran Vía (M: Banco de España) sells tickets.

Estación Chamartín (24hr. info for international destinations ☎93 49 01 122; domestic destinations ☎90 224 02 02, Spanish only), Agustín de Foxá. M: Chamartín. Bus #5 runs to and from Sol (45min.). Ticket windows open 8:30am-10:30pm. Chamartín services both international and domestic destinations. Most *cercanías* (local) trains leave from Chamartín; many stop at Atocha. To: **Barcelona** (7hr., 10 per day, 6,585ptas); **Lisbon** (10hr., 6,700ptas); **Nice** (22hr., 21,000ptas); and **Paris** (13hr., 19,300ptas).

Estación Atocha (☎91 328 90 20). M: Atocha. Ticket windows open 6:30am-11:30pm. Trains to: **Andalucía, Castilla-La Mancha, Extremadura, Valencia, Castilla y León, Sierra de Guadarrama, and El Escorial. AVE** service (☎91 534 05 05) to **Córdoba** (1¾hr., 16 per day, 5100-7200ptas and **Sevilla** (2½hr., 19 per day, 8400-9900ptas). **Luggage storage** (400-600ptas).

Buses: Numerous private companies, each with its own station and set of destinations, serve Madrid; many buses pass through the **Estación Sur de Autobuses.**

Estación Sur de Autobuses, C. Méndez Alvaro (☎91 468 42 00). M: Méndez Álvaro. Info booth open daily 7am-11pm. **Empressa Galiano Continental** (☎91 527 29 61) to **Toledo** (1hr., every 30min., 585ptas). **Empressa Larrea** (☎91 539 00 05) to **Avila** (2hrs., 3-8 per day, 930ptas, roundtrip 1485ptas).

Estación Auto Res: Pl. Conde de Casal, 6 (☎91 551 72 00). M: Conde de Casal. To: **Trujillo** (3¼hr., 11-12 per day, 2035ptas); **Cuenca** (2½hr., 8-10 per day, 1325ptas); **Salamanca** (3-3¼hr., 7 per day, 1480ptas); and **Valencia** (4hr., 13 per day, 2875ptas).

Estación La Sepulvedana: Po. Florida, 11 (☎91 530 48 00). M: Príncipe Pío (via extension from M: Ópera). To **Segovia** (1½hrs., every 30 min., 825ptas) and **Ávila** (1½hr., 3-8 per day, 930ptas).

◨ GETTING AROUND

Metro: Madrid's metro puts most major subway systems to shame. Green timers hanging above most platforms show the amount of time since the last train departed. An individual metro ticket costs 135ptas, but savvy riders opt for the **bonotransporte** (ticket of 10 rides for either the metro or bus system) at 705ptas. Buy both at machines in any metro stop, *estanco* (tobacco shop), or newsstand. For more details, call **Metro info** (☎91 580 19 80) or ask at any ticket booth.

Bus: The fare is 135ptas. Buses run from 6am to 11:30pm. From 11:30pm until 3am, the night bus service, *buho* (owl), travels from Pl. Cibeles to the outskirts every 30min.; from 3-6am, it runs every hour. Night buses (N1-N20) are the cheapest form of transportation for late-night revelers. For more information, call **Empresa Municipal de Transportes** (☎91 406 88 10; Spanish only).

Taxi: Call ☎91 445 90 08 or 91 447 32 32. A green *libre* sign in the window or a lit green light indicates availability. The base fare is 190ptas, plus 50-75ptas per km. Common fare supplements include: airport (400ptas); bus and train stations (125ptas); luggage charge (50ptas per bag); Sundays and holidays (6am-11pm, 125ptas); and nighttime (11pm-6am, 125ptas). To request **taxi service for the disabled,** call ☎91 547 85 00. If you leave possessions in a taxi, visit or call the **Negociado de Objetos Perdidos,** Pl. Legazpi, 7 (☎91 588 43 46). Open M-F 9am-2pm.

Car Rental: There is no reason to rent a car in Madrid. Don't drive unless you're planning to zoom out of the city, and even then bus and train fares will be cheaper. Tobacco

Central Madrid

TO GLORIETA
PUERTA DE TOLEDO

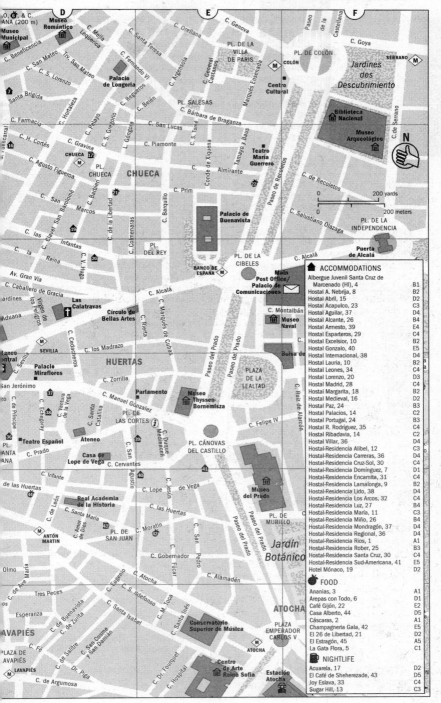

shops sell parking permits. **Europcar,** Estación de Atocha, AVE terminal (☎91 530 01 94; reservations ☎91 721 12 22; www.europcar.com). M: Atocha Renfe. Cheapest car 8200ptas per day, 49,800ptas per week. Unlimited mileage. Minimum age 21. Open 8am-midnight. **Avis,** Estación de Atocha, AVE terminal (☎91 530 01 68; fax 91 528 26 83; reservations ☎91 348 03 48). M: Atocha Renfe. Cheapest car 12,300ptas per day, 61,000ptas per week. Unlimited mileage. With more than 3 days, drop off in other cities free. Minimum age 23. Open daily 8am-midnight.

Moped Rental: Motocicletas Antonio Castro: C. Conde Duque, 13 (☎91 542 06 57). M: San Bernardo. Honda costs 4500ptas per day (8am-8pm) or 19,500ptas per week, including unlimited mileage and insurance. 40,000ptas deposit. 16% IVA not included. Renters must be at least 18. Open M-F 8am-1:30pm and 5-8pm, Sa 9-11am.

✈ ORIENTATION

Kilómetro 0 in **Puerta del Sol** ("Sol" for short) is the epicenter of the city (and the country), within walking distance of most sights. Just to the west is the **Plaza Mayor;** farther west lie the **Palacio Real** and the **Ópera** district. East of Sol lies **Huertas,** a one-time literary district and today the hub of cafe, theater, and museum life. Huertas is centered around **Plaza Santa Ana,** bordered by C. Alcalá to the north, Po. Prado to the east, Sol to the west, and C. Atocha to the south. The area north of Sol is bordered by the **Gran Vía,** which runs northwest to **Plaza de España.** North of Gran Vía are three club and bar-hopping districts linked by **Calle de Fuencarral: Malasaña, Bilbao,** and **Chueca.** Beyond Gran Vía and east of Malasaña and Chueca lies modern Madrid. East of Sol, the thoroughfare **Paseo de la Castellana-Paseo de Recoletos-Paseo del Prado** splits Madrid in two, running from **Atocha** in the south to **Plaza de Castilla** in the north, passing the Prado, the fountains of **Plaza Cibeles** and **Plaza Colón.** Northwest of Sol lies **Argüelles,** an energetic neighborhood of families and students spilling over from **Moncloa,** the student district that centers on C. Isaac Peral.

Get a map at the tourist office and refer also to this book's **color maps.** Madrid is safe compared to other European cities, but Puerta del Sol, Pl. Dos de Mayo in Malasaña, Pl. de Chueca, and Pl. España are particularly intimidating late at night.

READ THIS. The **Guía del Ocio,** available behind the counter of any news kiosk, should be your first purchase in Madrid (125ptas). It has concert, theater, sports, cinema, and TV schedules. It also lists exhibits, restaurants, bars, and clubs. Although it is in Spanish, the alphabetical listings of clubs and restaurants are invaluable even to non-speakers. For an English magazine with articles on new finds in and around the city, pick up *In Madrid,* distributed free at tourist offices and restaurants.

🛈 PRACTICAL INFORMATION

TOURIST, FINANCIAL, AND LOCAL SERVICES

Tourist Offices: Municipal, Pl. Mayor, 3 (☎91 366 54 77; fax 91 366 54 77). M: Sol. Open M-F 10am-8pm, Sa 10am-2pm and 3-8pm. **Regional/Provincial Office of the Comunidad de Madrid,** main office, Duque de Medinacelia, 2 (☎91 429 49 51). Brochures, transport info, and maps for towns in the Comunidad. Other offices at Estación Chamartín and the airport.

General Info Line: ☎010. 20ptas per min. From outside Madrid dial ☎901 300 600.

Embassies: Australia, Santa Engracia 120 (☎91 441 93 00; fax 91 442 53 62; www.embaustralia.es). **Canada,** C. Núñez de Balboa 35 (☎91 423 32 50; fax 91 423 32 51; info.ic.gc.ca/tourism). M: Velázquez. **New Zealand,** Pl. de la Lealtad 2 (☎91 523 02 26; fax 91 523 01 71). M: Banco de España. **South Africa,** Claudio Coello 91, 6th fl. (☎91 435 66 88; fax 91 577 74 14). **UK,** C. Fernando el Santo, 16 (☎91 700 82 00; fax 91 700 83 11). M: Colón. **US,** C. Serrano 75 (☎91 587 22 00; fax 91 587 22 39). M: Rubén Darío.

Budget Travel: Viajes TIVE, C. Fernando el Católico, 88 (☎91 543 74 12; fax 91 544 00 62). M: Moncloa. Exit the metro at C. Isaac Peral, walk straight down C. Arcipreste de Hita, and turn left on C. Fernando el Católico; it is on your left. ISIC 700ptas, HI card 1800ptas. Open M-F 9am-2pm, Sa 9am-noon.

Currency Exchange: Banco Central Hispano charges no commission on cash or traveler's checks. **Main branch,** Pl. Canalejas, 1 (☎91 558 11 11). M: Sol. From Sol, follow C. San Jeronimo to Pl. Canalejas. Open Apr.-Sept. M-F 8:30am-2:30pm, Sa 8:30am-1pm; Oct.-Mar. M-Th 8:30am-4:30pm, F 8:30am-2:30pm, Sa 8:30am-1pm.

American Express: Pl. Cortés, 2 (☎91 322 54 52; info ☎91 322 54 00). M:Sevilla. From the metro stop, take a right on C. Alcala, another right down C. Cedacero and a left on C. San Jerónimo; office is on the left. Open M-F 9am-5:30pm, Sa 9am-noon.

Luggage Storage: Barajas Airport. Follow the signs to *consigna.* One day 425ptas, 2-15 days 530-740ptas per day, after day 15 105-210ptas per day. **Estación Chamartín** and **Estación Atocha.** Lockers 400-600ptas per day. Open daily 6:30am-12:30am.

Gay and Lesbian Services: Colectivo de Gais y Lesbianas de Madrid (COGAM), C. Fuencarral, 37 (☎/fax 91 523 00 70). M: Gran Vía. Provides a wide range of services and activities. (☎91 522 45 17; M-F 6-10pm). Reception daily M-Sa 5-9pm. Free counseling M-Th 7-9pm.

Laundromat: Lavandería, C. Cervantes 1. M: Puerta del Sol or Banco de España. From Pl. Santa Ana follow C. Prado, turn right on C. Leon and then left onto C. Cervantes. Wash 400ptas, dry 100ptas for 9min. Open M-Sa 9am-8pm.

EMERGENCY AND COMMUNICATIONS

Emergency: ☎112. For national and local police, ☎091 or 092.

Police: C. Luna, 17 (☎91 521 12 36). M: Callao. From Gran Vía, walk down C. Arenal. Forms in English available. To report crimes committed in the **metro,** go to the office in the Sol station (☎91 521 09 11). Open daily 8am-11pm.

Crisis Lines: Rape Hotline (☎91 574 01 10). Open M-F 10am-2pm and 4-7pm.

Late-Night Pharmacy: Dial 098 to find the nearest one. One located at **C. Mayor, 59** (☎91 548 00 14), near M: Sol.

Hospitals: For non-emergency concerns, **Anglo-American Medical Unit,** Conde de Aranda, 1, 1st fl. (☎91 435 18 23) is quick and friendly. M: Serrano or Retiro. Doctors, dentists, and optometrists. Run partly by British and Americans. Initial visit 9,000ptas for students, 10,000-15,000ptas for non-students. MC, Visa, AmEx.

Emergency Clinics: In a **medical emergency,** dial 061. **Equipo Quirúrgico Municipal No. 1,** C. Montesa, 22 (☎91 588 51 00). M: Manuel Becerra. **Hospital Ramón y Cajal,** Ctra. Colmenar Viejo (☎91 336 80 00). Bus #135 from Pl. Castilla.

Internet Access: Euronet, C. Mayor, 1, 4th fl., office 11 (☎655 021 793). M: Sol. Take the elevator up and buzz the office. Absolutely unbeatable 250ptas per hr., 150ptas for 30 min. Open daily 10am-11pm. **Interpublic,** C. San Jeronimo 18, 1st fl. M: Sol. 299ptas per hr. Open daily 9:30am-midnight. **La Casa de Internet,** C. Luchana, 20. M: Bilbao. 900ptas per hr.; students 700ptas. M-Sa noon-2am, Su 4pm-2am.

Post Office: Palacio de Comunicaciones, C. Alcala, 51, on Pl. Cibeles (☎902 19 71 97). M: Banco de España. Windows open M-Sa 8:30am-9:30pm, Su 9am-2pm for stamp purchases, certified mail, telex and **fax** service. **Postal Code:** 28080.

▛ ACCOMMODATIONS

The demand for rooms is always high and increases dramatically in summer. But never fear—Madrid is rife with hostels. Prices average about 2600ptas per person for a basic room, a bit more for a two-star hostel, and slightly less for a *pensión.*

EL CENTRO: SOL, ÓPERA, AND PLAZA MAYOR

Prices and locations in the Centro are as good as they get, especially if you are planning to brave the nightlife. The following listings fall in the area between the Sol and Ópera metro stops. Buses #3, 25, 39, and 500 serve Ópera; buses #3, 5 (from Atocha), 15, 20, 50-53, and 150 serve Sol.

SPAIN

Hostal Paz, C. Flora, 4, 1st and 4th fl. (☎91 547 30 47). M: Ópera. Don't be deterred by the dark street, parallel to C. Arenal, off C. Donados or C. Hileras. Sheltered from street noise and lavished with comfort-enhancers, including hand-held climate control, satellite TV, A/C, and spotless bathrooms. Laundry 1200ptas. Singles 2500ptas; doubles 3800ptas, with shower 4300ptas; triples with shower 5700ptas.

Hostal-Residencia Luz, C. Fuentes, 10, 3rd fl. (☎91 542 07 59 or 91 559 74 18; fax 91 542 07 59), off C. Arenal. M: Ópera. 12 sunny, newly redecorated rooms ooze with comfort: hardwood floors, elegant furniture, beautiful curtains and bedspreads. Satellite TV, fax, and public phone. Laundry 1000ptas. Singles 2500ptas; doubles 3700ptas; triples 5500ptas. Discounts for longer stays.

Hostal Esparteros, C. Esparteros, 12, 4th fl. (☎/fax 91 521 09 03) Cheap, small, sparkling rooms with balcony or large windows (no fans). The best owner in Madrid speaks English and ensures a terrific stay. Laundry 1000ptas. Singles 2000ptas, with shower 2200ptas, with bath 2700ptas; doubles with shower 3200ptas, with bath 3700ptas; triples with shower 4400ptas, with bath 5500ptas. Discounts for longer stays.

Hostal-Residencia Rober, C. Arenal, 26, 5th fl. (☎91 541 91 75). M: Ópera. All 14 pristine rooms have their own tiny TVs and A/C. Singles with shower 3600ptas, with bath 4500ptas; doubles with bath 5700ptas; triples with bath 7000ptas.

Hostal Madrid, C. Esparteros, 6, 2nd fl. (☎91 522 00 60; fax 91 532 35 10). M: Sol. Off C. Mayor. Spacious rooms with shiny wood floors and large windows. All have TVs, telephones, enormous closets with safes, telephones, A/C and new bathrooms. Singles 6500ptas; doubles 9500ptas; triple with balcony 12,000ptas.

Hostal Alcante, C. Arenal, 16, 2nd fl., on the right (☎91 531 78). Rooms with TV, heat, and AC. Singles 2800ptas, with shower 3000ptas, with bath 4000ptas; doubles with shower 5500ptas, with bath 6000ptas; triples with bath 7500ptas.

Hostal-Residencia Cruz-Sol, Pl. Santa Cruz, 6, 3rd fl. (☎91 532 71 97). M: Sol. Jan. A good deal. Last year's renovations left modern rooms with parquet floors, double-paned windows, safes, heat, phones, and A/C. Laundry 1000ptas. Singles 3500ptas, with bath 4000ptas; doubles 6000-7000ptas; triples 8,500ptas; quads 9,000ptas.

Hostal-Residencia Santa Cruz, Pl. Santa Cruz, 6, 2nd fl. (☎/fax 91 522 24 41). M: Sol. Palatial lounge gives way to servant-sized rooms. Renovations, including A/C, on the way. Tiny, sinkless singles 2200ptas, with shower 3500ptas; doubles 4200ptas, with bath 5200ptas; triples 6000ptas, with bath 6200ptas.

HUERTAS

Although *madrileños* have never settled on a nickname for this neighborhood, the area between C. San Jeronimo and C. de las Huertas is generally referred to as Huertas. Once a seedy neighborhood—and a Hemingway hangout—Huertas has shaped up into a hotbed of food and drink. Sol, Pl. Mayor, *el triángulo del arte*, and the Atocha train station are all within walking distance. Sol-bound buses stop on C. Príncipe, C. Nuñez de Arce, and C. San Jerónimo; buses #14, 27, 37 and 45 run along Po. del Prado. The metro stops are Sol and Antón Martín.

Hostal Aguilar, C. San Jerónimo, 32, 2nd fl. (☎91 429 59 26 or 91 429 36 61; fax 91 429 26 61). M: Sol. More than 50 clean, modern rooms with vast bathrooms, telephones, A/C, and TVs. Singles 4000ptas; doubles 600ptas; triples 8000ptas.

Hostal-Residencia Mondragón, C. San Jerónimo, 32, 4th fl. (☎91 429 68 16). M: Sol. Communal bathrooms. Singles 2000ptas; doubles 3000ptas; triples 3900ptas.

Hostal Villar, C. Príncipe, 18, 1st-4th fl. (☎91 531 66 00; fax 91 521 50 73). M: Sol. Walk down C. San Jerónimo and turn right on C. Príncipe. TVs, phones, and A/C. Singles 2650ptas, with bath 3200ptas; doubles 3500ptas, with bath 4800ptas; triples 4900ptas, with bath 6720ptas; quads 6300ptas, with bath 8640ptas.

Hostal Gonzalo, C. Cervantes, 34, 3rd fl. (☎91 429 27 14; fax 91 420 20 07). M: Antón Martín. Off C. León, which is off C. Atocha. A budget traveler's dream: firm beds, TV, and fans in summer. Singles 4800ptas; doubles 5800ptas; triples 7500pts.

Hostal Leones, C. Nuñez de Arce, 14, 2nd fl. (☎91 531 08 89). A classic hostel with narrow hallways, spartan rooms, and spotless bathrooms. Singles 2250ptas; doubles 3900ptas, with bath 4500ptas. IVA not included.

GRAN VÍA

The neon lights of Broadway and the Champs-Élysées have met their match in Gran Vía. This is not a street you want to be returning to late at night; Centro and Huertas provide safer bargains. Buses #1, 2, 44, 46, 74, 75, 133, 146, 147, and 148 reach Callao; buses #1, 2, 3, 40, 46, 74, 146, and 149 service both Pl. España and Callao. The closest metro stops are Gran Vía and Callao.

Hostal Margarita, Gran Vía, 50, 5th fl. (☎/fax 91 547 35 49). M: Callao. Rooms tastefully sparse, with big windows, pretty bathrooms, TVs, and telephones. Huge, plush lounge and big kitchen. Laundry 1200ptas. Singles 3400ptas; doubles 5100ptas, with bath 5400ptas; triples with shower 6900ptas.

Hostal-Residencia Lamalonga, Gran Vía, 56, 2nd fl. (☎91 547 26 31 or 91 547 68 94). M: Santo Domingo. Large bathrooms and decadently wide halls compete for the sparkle award. All rooms have TVs, baths, and telephones. Singles 4500ptas; doubles 6500ptas; triples 8500ptas. 10% discount for stays over 5 days.

MALASAÑA AND CHUECA

Split down the middle by C. Fuencarral, Malasaña and Chueca are both hard-core party pits. Unless techno helps you sleep, make sure your room has sound-proof windows. Chueca is hip, fun, funky, and largely gay, but can be dangerous, especially for solo travelers. Buses #3, 40, and 149 run along C. Fuencarral and Hortaleza. Metro stops Chueca, Gran Vía, and Tribunal serve the area.

Hostal Palacios and **Hostal Ribadavia,** C. Fuencarral, 25, 1st-3rd fl. (☎91 531 10 58 or 91 531 48 47). M: Gran Vía. Both run by the same cheerful family. Palacio (1st and 2nd fl.) offers large, tiled rooms with elegant modern furniture. Ribadavia (3rd fl.) is older but still has comfortable rooms, all with new TVs. Singles 2500ptas, with bath 3500ptas; doubles with shower 4000ptas, with bath 5000ptas; triples 6000ptas, with bath 7000ptas; quads with bath 9000ptas.

Hostal Lorenzo, C. las Infantas, 26, 3rd fl. (☎91 521 30 57; fax 91 532 79 78). M: Gran Vía. Tastefully decorated rooms are pricey but have all the amenities: bathrooms, TVs, telephones, A/C, music, and chandeliers. Sound-proof windows muffle daytime traffic and the nighttime revelry below. Breakfast 350ptas. Singles 5500ptas; doubles 7500ptas; triples 9500ptas. IVA not included.

Hostal Abril, C. Fuencarral, 39, 4th fl. (☎91 531 53 38). M: Tribunal or Gran Vía. Brand new doors and granite floors; some fluorescent lighting. Singles 2000ptas, with shower 2300ptas, doubles 3500ptas, with bath 3800ptas; triples with bath 5200ptas.

ELSEWHERE AND CAMPING

Budget lodgings are rare near the **Chamartín** train station, as is the case in most of the residential districts located away from the city center. Near the **Madrid-Atocha** train station are a handful of hostels, the closest of which are down Po. Santa María de la Cabeza. The tourist office in Pl. Mayor has a full list of lodgings. Tourist offices can provide info about the 13 campsites within 50km of Madrid. Similar info is in the *Guía Oficial de Campings* (official camping guide), a big book which they gladly let you look through. For further camping info, contact the *Consejería de Educación de Juventud* (☎91 522 29 41).

Albergue Juvenil Santa Cruz de Marcenado (HI), C. Santa Cruz de Marcenado, 28 (☎91 547 45 32; fax 91 548 11 96). M: Argüelles. From the metro, walk 1 block down C. Alberto Aguilera away from C. Princesa, turn right on C. Serrano Jóve, then left on C. Santa Cruz de Marcenado. The 72 beds fill quickly, even in winter. Lockers are outside the rooms (200ptas extra). Breakfast included. Sheets (but no towels) provided. Max stay 3-day. Curfew 1:30am. Silence after midnight. Reception daily 9am-1:30pm. Reserve a space (by mail, fax, or in person only) in advance, or arrive early and pray. Closed Christmas and New Year's. An HI (YHA) card is required and can be purchased for 1800ptas. Dorms 1200ptas; over 26 yrs. 1820ptas.

Camping Osuna (☎91 741 05 10; fax 91 320 63 65), on Av. Logroño. M: Canillejas. From the metro, cross the pedestrian overpass, walk through the parking lot, and turn right along the freeway. Pass under two bridges (the first a freeway and the second an arch) and look for campground signs on the right; or bus #101 from the metro toward Barajas and ask for the campsite. 690ptas per person, per tent, and per car. 625ptas for electricity. 7% IVA not included.

◘ FOOD

In Madrid, it's not hard to fork it down without forking over too much. Most restaurants offer a *menú del día*, which includes bread, one drink, and one choice from each of the day's selections for appetizers, main courses, and desserts (1000-1500ptas). Keep in mind the following essential buzz words for quicker, cheaper *madrileño* fare: *bocadillo* (a sandwich on a long, hard roll, 350-450ptas); *sandwich* (a sandwich on sliced bread, ask for it *a la plancha* if you want it grilled, 300ptas); *ración* (a large *tapa*, served with bread 300-600ptas); and *empanada* (a puff pastry with meat fillings, 200-300ptas). Vegetarians should check out the *Guía del Ocio*, which has a complete listing of Madrid's vegetarian havens under the section "Otras Cocinas." For **groceries, %Dia** and **Simago** are the cheapest supermarket chains. More expensive are **Mantequerías Leonesas, Expreso,** and **Jumbo.**

■ **El Estragón,** Pl. de la Paja, 10 (☎91 365 89 82). M: La Latin. From the metro, follow C. Duque de Alba, turn right through to Pl. Puerta de Moros and leave the church on the right; it's on the far side of Pl. de la Paja. Perhaps the best reasonably priced restaurant—of any kind—in Madrid, with vegetarian food that could turn the most die-hard carnivores into switch-hitters. Delicious and creative *menú* (M-F 1200ptas; Sa-Su and night 2475ptas). Open daily 1-4pm and 8pm-1am.

Museo del Jamón, C. San Jerónimo, 6 (☎91 521 03 46). M: Sol. Five other much-loved locations throughout the city, including one at C. Mayor 7 (☎91 531 45 50). Head upstairs to the dining room (opens at 1pm) for a sampling of the chef's specialties (600-1160ptas). Bocadillos from 175ptas. *Menú* 1000ptas. Generous combo plates 650-950ptas. Open M-Th 9am-12:30pm, F-Sa 9am-1am, Su 10am-12:30pm.

Casa Alberto, C. Huertas, 18 (☎91 429 93 56). M: Antón Martín. Interior dining room decorated with bullfighting and Cervantine relics; Cervantes wrote the second part of "El Quixote" here. The tapas are all original house recipes. Try the *gambas al ajillo* (shrimp in garlic and hot peppers; 1600ptas). Open Tu-Sa 10am-1:30am, Su 10am-4pm.

Champagneria Gala, C. Moratin, 22 (☎91 429 25 62). Down the hill on Moratin from C. Atocha. The funky paella buck stops here. *Menú* (1750ptas per person). Open daily 1:30-5pm and 9pm-12:30am.

El Granero de Lavapiés, C. Argumosa, 10 (☎91 467 76 11), off the plaza. M: Lavapiés. For 16 years, frescoes, inventive vegetarian specials, and fresh bread have kept this hideaway packed with locals. Vegetarian *menú* M-Sa (1200ptas). Open daily 1-4pm.

El 26 de Libertad, C. Libertad, 26 (☎91 522 25 22), off C. las Infantas. M: Chueca. Innovative and exotic Spanish cuisine. Lunchtime *menú* (1300ptas) is fantastic. Open M-Th 1-4pm and 8pm-midnight; F-Sa 1-4pm and 9pm-12:30am; Su 1-4pm.

La Gata Flora, C. 2 de Mayo, 1, and across the street at C. San Vicente Ferrer, 33 (☎91 523 10 26). M: Noviciado or Tribunal. Young people and good, cheap food makes for a fun scene. *Menú* 1075ptas. Pizzas 850-1000ptas. Luscious salads 700-900ptas. *Sangría* 600-900ptas. Open daily Su-Th noon-1am, F-Sa noon-3am.

La Granja Restaurante Vegetariano, C. San Andrés, 11 (☎91 532 87 93), off Pl. 2 de Mayo. M: Tribunal. Warm atmosphere with plants and pottery. Ask the owner about smoking the hookah after your meal. Lunch *menú* 975ptas. Open W-M 1:30-4:30pm and 9pm-midnight.

Arepas con Todo, C. Hartzenbusch, 19 (☎91 448 75 45) off C. Cardenal Cisernos, which is off C. Luchana. This classic Columbian restaurant really does have *todo,* with a different *menú* (1600-2000ptas) every night of the month, and 60 fixed dishes (1800-2400ptas). Open M-W 2pm-1am.

TAPAS To the untrained reader, tapas menus are often cryptic and undecipherable—if the bar has even bothered to print any. To make sure you don't end up eating the stewed parts of the oxen you rode in on, just keep the following words in mind. Servings come in three sizes: *pincho* (normally eaten with toothpicks between sips of beer), *tapa* (small plate), or *racion* (sizable, meal portion). *Aceitunas* (olives), *albondigas* (meatballs), *anchoas* (anchovies), *callos* (tripe), *chorizo* (sausage), *croqetas* (breaded and fried combinations), *gambas* (shrimp), *jamon* (ham), *patatas alioli y bravas* (potatoes with sauces), *pimentoes* (peppers), *pulpo* (octopus), and *tortilla* (omelette) comprise any basic menu.

TAPAS AND CLASSIC CAFES

Since tapas and cafes grant Madrileños two of their favorite things—eating and being out in the streets—it's no wonder they are the bedrock institutions of Madrid's culture. Not so long ago, bartenders in Madrid used to cover *(tapar)* drinks with saucers to keep the flies out. Later, servers began putting little sandwiches on top of the saucers, and there you have it: tapas. Hopping from bar to bar gobbling tapas is an active alternative to a full sit-down meal. Even when chilling, however, Madrileños like to watch the frenzied streets. It's customary to linger for an hour or two in the atmosphere, history and image of Madrid's classic cafes. Soak up culture, rest weary legs, and check out passers-by from behind your coffee cup.

TAPAS

La Toscana, C. Manuel Fernández González, 10-12 (☎91 429 60 31), at C. Ventura de la Vega. M: Sol. Despite the antique lettering and wrought iron, as the tapas are anything but medieval. Spacious bar area jam-packed on weekends. Try the *morcilla* (200ptas), but don't ask what you're eating until you're done. Most tapas around 800ptas. Open Th-Tu noon-4pm and 8pm-midnight.

Casa Amadeo, Pl. de Cascorro, 18 (☎91 365 94 39). M: La Latina. The jovial owner of 60 years has excellent house specialty *caracoles* (snails; small plate 700ptas, big plate 1500ptas) and *chorizo* (sausage) made with snails (750ptas). *Raciones* 350-900ptas. Open M-F 10:30am-4pm and 7-10:30pm, Su 7-11pm.

La Trucha, C. Nuñez de Arce, 6 (☎91 429 58 33). M: Sol. Cramped but cheap. Their fresh vegetables and daily specials are popular with locals. Impressive selection of seasonal veggies (800-1500ptas), but don't skip the stewed bull's tail (*rabo de toro*). Main dishes 200-2500ptas. Open M-Sa 12:30-4pm and 7:30pm-midnight.

Cafetería-Restaurante El Encinar del Bierzo, C. Toledo, 82 (☎91 366 23 89). M: La Latina. A neighborhood landmark. House specialties *conejo al ajillo* (rabbit with garlic, 2000ptas) and *gambas a la plancha* (fried shrimp, 1100ptas). *Menú* 1100ptas, 1300ptas on Su. Open daily 1-4:30pm and 9pm-11:30pm.

CLASSIC CAFES

Café Gijón, Po. Recoletos, 21 (☎91 521 54 25). M: Colón. On its 100th anniversary in 1988, Gijón was designated a historic site for its intellectual significance. It has long since been a favorite of the literati. Open daily 9am-1:30am.

Café Círculo de Bellas Artes, C. Alcalá, 42 (☎91 360 54 00). M: Banco de España. Tourists rest museum-weary feet outside and enjoy a reasonably priced snack. Beer 350-500ptas. Sandwiches 400-600ptas. For a 100ptas cover, lounge on leather couches beneath high frescoed ceilings and fabulous crystal lights. Coffee or tea 200ptas. Open M-F 9am-1am, Sa-Su 9am-3am.

Café de Oriente, Pl. Oriente, 2 (☎91 547 15 64). M: Ópera. Spectacular view of the Palacio Real from the *terraza*. Specialty coffees 540-840ptas. Open Su-Th 8:30am-1:30am, F-Sa 8:30am-1:30am.

Café Comercial, Glorieta de Bilbao, 7 (☎91 531 34 52). M: Bilbao. Traditional cafe with high ceilings, cushioned chairs, and huge mirrors perfect for people-watching. The first anti-Franco protests took place here. Coffee 160ptas at the bar, 260ptas at a table. The upstairs **Cybercafe Comercial** has coin-operated computers (500ptas per hr.) Open Su-Th 8am-12:45am, F-Sa 8am-1:45am.

👁 SIGHTS

Madrid, large as it may seem, is a walker's city. Although the word *paseo* refers to a major avenue—such as *Paseo de la Castellana* or *Paseo del Prado*—it literally means "a stroll." Do just that from Sol to Cibeles and from the Plaza Mayor to the Palacio Real—sights will introduce themselves. In the following pages, sights are arranged by neighborhood, offering opportunities for extensive walking tours in each. Each section has a designated center from which all directions are given.

CENTRO

The area known as El Centro, spreading out from the Puerta del Sol ("Gate of Sun"), is the gateway to the history and spirit of Madrid. Although several rulers carved the winding streets, the Habsburg and Bourbon families left the Centro's most celebrated monuments. As a result, the Centro is divided into two major sections: Madrid de los Habsburgs and Madrid de los Borbones. All directions are given from the Puerta del Sol.

PUERTA DEL SOL. Kilómetro 0—the origin of six national highways fanning out to the rest of Spain—marks the country's physical and psychological center in the most chaotic of Madrid's plazas, Puerta del Sol. Government buildings dominate the plaza, where citizens and tourists alike converge upon *El oso y el madroño*, a bronze statue of a bear and a strawberry tree, now a symbol of Madrid.

HABSBURG MADRID

"Old Madrid," the city's central neighborhood, is the most densely packed with both monuments and tourists. In the 16th century, the Habsburgs built **Plaza Mayor** and the **Catedral de San Isidro** from scratch. When Felipe II moved the seat of Castilla from Toledo to Madrid (then only a town of 20,000) in 1561, he and his descendants commissioned the court architects (including Juan de Herrera) to update many of Madrid's buildings to the latest styles.

PLAZA MAYOR. In 1620, the plaza was completed for Felipe III; his statue, installed in 1847, still graces the plaza's center. Though designed by Juan de Herrera, the architect of the austere El Escorial, Pl. Mayor is much softer in style. Toward evening, Pl. Mayor awakens as *madrileños* resurface, tourists multiply, and cafe tables fill with lively patrons. Live performances of flamenco and music are a common treat. On Sunday mornings, the plaza marks the starting point of **El Rastro** (see p. 814). *(From Pta. Sol, walk down C. Mayor. The plaza is on the left. M: Sol.)*

CATEDRAL DE SAN ISIDRO. Designed in the Jesuit Baroque style at the beginning of the 17th century, the cathedral received San Isidro's remains in 1769. During the Civil War rioting workers burned the exterior and damaged much of the cathedral—only the primary nave and a few Baroque decorations remain from the original. *(From the Pta. Sol, take C. Mayor to Pl. Mayor, cross the plaza, and exit onto C. Toledo. M: Latina. Open for mass only.)*

PLAZA DE LA VILLA. Pl. Villa marks the heart of what was once old Madrid. Though only a handful of medieval buildings remain, the plaza still features a stunning courtyard (surrounding the statue of Don Alvara de Bazón), beautiful tilework, and eclectic architecture. Across the plaza is the 17th-century **Ayuntamiento (Casa de la Villa),** designed in 1640 by Juan Gomez de Mora as both the mayor's home and the city jail. *(From Pta. Sol, go down C. Mayor, past Pl. Mayor. M: Sol.)*

BOURBON MADRID

Weakened by plagues and political losses, the Habsburg era in Spain ended with the death of Carlos II in 1700. Felipe V, the first of Spain's Bourbon monarchs, ascended the throne in 1714 after the 12-year War of the Spanish Succession. Bankruptcy, industrial stagnation, and widespread disillusionment compelled Felipe V to embark on a crusade of urban renewal. The lavish palaces, churches, and parks that remain are the most touristed in Madrid.

PALACIO REAL. The impossibly luxurious Palacio Real lounges at the western tip of central Madrid, overlooking the Río Manzanares. Felipe V commissioned Giovanni Sachetti to replace the Alcázar, which had burned down in 1734, with a palace that would dwarf all others—he succeeded. Today, the unfinished palace is only used by King Juan Carlos and Queen Sofía on special occasions. The palace's most impressive rooms are decorated in the Rococo style. The **Salón de Gasparini**, site of the king's ceremonial dressing before the court, houses Goya's portrait of Carlos IV and a Mengs ceiling fresco. The **Salón del Trono (Throne Room)** also contains a ceiling fresco, painted by Tiepolo, outlining the qualities of the quintessential ruler. The **Biblioteca** shelves first editions of *Don Quixote*. Also open to the public is the **Real Armería (Armory)** which displays the swords of El Cid and the armor of Carlos V and Felipe II. *(From Pta. Sol, take C. Mayor and turn right on C. Bailen. M: Sol. Open Apr.-Sept. M-Sa 9am-6pm, Su 9am-3pm; Oct.-Mar. M-Sa 9:30am-5pm, Su 9am-2pm. 900ptas, with tour 1000ptas; students 400ptas, with tour 100ptas. W free for EU citizens.)*

CATHEDRAL DE LA ALMUDENA. Begun in 1879 and finished a century later, the cathedral—especially its interior—is a stark contrast to the gilded Palacio Real. The cathedral's frescoes and stained glass windows exhibit a discordant mix of traditional and abstract styles. The simplicity of the gray stone walls clashes with the ceiling panels, where brilliant colors and sharp geometric shapes bring a modern tierack to mind. *(From Pta. Sol, go down C. Mayo and turn right on C. Bailen; the cathedral is just before the Palacio Real. Closed during mass. Open M-Sa 1-7pm. Free.)*

PLAZA DE ORIENTE. A minor architectural miscalculation was responsible for this sculpture park. Most of the statues in the plaza were designed for the palace roof, but because they were too heavy, they were placed in this shady plaza instead. Elegant *terrazas* encompass the plaza, an opportunity to treat yourself to an overpriced coffee (see p. 809). The **Jardines de Sabatini,** just to the right as you are face the palace, is the romantic's park of choice. *(From Pta. Sol, take C. Arenal to the plaza.)*

HUERTAS

The area east of Sol is a wedge bounded by C. de Alcalá to the north, C. Atocha to the south, and Po. Prado to the east. Huertas's sights, from authors' houses to famous cafes, reflect its artistic focus. Home to Cervantes, Góngora, Quevedo, Calderón, and Moratín in its heyday during the "Siglo de Oro," Huertas enjoyed a fleeting return to literary prominence when Hemingway frequented the neighborhood in the 1920s. **Plaza Santa Ana** and its *terrazas* are the center of this old literary haunt. **Casa de Lope de Vega** is the home where the prolific playwright and poet spent the last 25 years of his life and wrote over two thirds of his plays. The highlights include the simple garden described in his works and the library filled with crumbling, aromatic books. Among the more interesting tidbits revealed on the mandatory tour are the tangible signs of affection Vega would leave for his young daughters. *(C. Cervantes, 11. With your back to Pl. Santa Ana, turn left on C. Prado, right on C. León, and left on C. Cervantes. ☎91 429 92 16. Open Tu-F 9:30am-2pm, Sa 10am-2pm. 200ptas, students 100ptas. W free.)*

GRAN VÍA

Urban planners paved the Gran Vía in 1910 to link C. Princesa with Pl. Cibeles. After Madrid became wealthy as a neutral supplier during World War I, the city funneled much of its earnings into making the Gran Vía into one of the world's great thoroughfares. At Gran Vía's highest elevation in **Plaza de Callao** (M: Callao), C. Postigo San Martín splits off southward, where you'll find the famed **Monasterio de las Descalzas Reales.** The **Salón de Tapices** contains 10 renowned tapestries based on cartoons by Rubens. *(Pl. Descalzas, between Pl. Callao and Pta. de Sol. ☎91 559 74 04. M: Callao or Sol. Open Tu-Th and Sa 10:30am-12:45pm and 4-5:45pm, F 10:30am-12:45pm, Su 11am-1:45pm. 700ptas, students 300ptas. W free for EU citizens.)* Westward from Pl. Callao, the Gran Vía makes its descent toward **Plaza de España** (M: Pl. España), where a statue commemorates Spain's most prized fictional duo: Cervantes' Don Quixote and Sancho Panza, riding horseback and muleback, respectively.

MALASAÑA AND CHUECA

By night, these districts bristle with Madrid's alternative scene. The area between **Calle de Fuencarral** and **Calle de San Bernardo** is home to some of Madrid's most avant-garde architecture and current art exhibitions. Though not packed with historic monuments, the labyrinthine streets provide many spontaneous undocumented "sights," from platform-shoe stores to street performers. An ultra-modern, funkdafied relief for those weary of crucifixes and brushstrokes, Chueca promises hip **boutiques** and a happening stroll.

ARGÜELLES

The area known as Argüelles and the zone surrounding **Calle San Bernardo** form a cluttered mixture of elegant middle-class houses, student apartments, and bohemian hangouts, all brimming with cultural activity. Heavily bombarded during the Civil War, Argüelles inspired Chilean poet Pablo Neruda, then a resident, to write *España en el corazón*. Directions in this section are given from M: Argüelles.

TEMPLE DE DEBOD. Built by Pharaoh Zakheramon in the 4th century BC, it's the only Egyptian temple in Spain. Grateful for Spanish archaeologists who helped rescue monuments from the Aswan dam floods, the Egyptian government shipped the temple stone by stone to Spain. The temple and two of its three original gateways stand in the **Parque de la Montaña**. *(M: Argüelles. From the metro, walk down C. Princesa and turn right on C. Ventura Rodriguez into the Parque de la Montaña. ☎91 409 61 65. Open Tu-Su 10am-1:45pm and 6-7:45pm; off-season Tu-F 10am-2pm and 4-6pm, Sa-Su 10am-2pm. 300ptas, students 150ptas. W and Su free.)*

ERMITA DE SAN ANTONIO DE LA FLORIDA. Although out of the way, the Ermita is worth the trouble. It contains Goya's pantheon—a frescoed dome arches above his buried corpse. Curiously enough, Goya's skull, apparently stolen by a phrenologist, was missing when the corpse arrived from France. *(M: Principe Pio. From the metro, go left on C. de Buen Altamirano, walk through the park, and turn left on Po. Florida. ☎91 542 07 22. Open Tu-F 10am-2pm and 4-8pm, Sa-Su 10am-2pm. Free.)*

RETIRO

Felipe IV intended the 300-acre Parque del Buen Retiro, once a hunting ground, to be a "buen retiro" (nice retreat). Today it's full of palm-readers, soccer players, and sunbathers. Avoid venturing alone into the park after dark. A rectangular lake in the middle of the park, the **Estanque Grande**, is popular among rowers; it's also the perfect way to cool off. *(Boat rentals daily 9:30am-8:30pm. Paddle boats 560ptas for 4 people, motorboats 155ptas per person.)* Built by Ricardo Velázquez to exhibit Philippine flowers, the exquisite steel-and-glass **Palactio de Cristal** hosts a variety of art shows. *(Open Tu-Sa 11am-2pm and 5-8pm, Su 10am-2pm. Admission varies.)* All artists should dream of having their art displayed in the **Palacio de Velázquez**, with its billowing ceilings, marble floors, and ideal lighting. *(Past the Estanque, turn left on Paseo del Venezuela. ☎91 575 62 45. Open M-Sa 11am-8pm, Su 11am-6pm. Free.)*

EL PARDO

Built as a hunting lodge for Carlos I in 1547, El Pardo was enlarged by generations of Habsburgs and Bourbons. El Pardo gained attention in 1940 when Franco decided to make it his home; he resided here until his death in 1975. Renowned for its collection of tapestries—several of which were designed by Goya—the palace also holds paintings by Velázquez and Ribera. *(Take bus #601 from the stop in front of the Ejército del Aire building above M: Moncloa (15min., 150ptas). Palace open Apr.-Sept. M-F 9:30am-6pm, Su 9:25am-1:40pm; Oct.-Mar. M-F 10:30am-5pm, Su 9:55am-1:40pm. Compulsory 45min. guided tour in Spanish. 650ptas, students 250ptas. W free for EU citizens.)*

🏛 MUSEUMS

Madrid's great museums need no introduction. If you plan on visiting the three famous ones, your best bet is the **Paseo del Arte** ticket (1275ptas) that grants admission to the Museo del Prado, Museo Thyssen-Bornemisza, and Centro de Arte Reina Sofía. The pass is on sale at all three museums.

🏛 MUSEO DEL PRADO

Po. Prado at Pl. Cánovas del Castillo. M: Banco de España. ☎91 420 37 68 or 91 330 28 00; www.museoprado.mcu.es Open Tu-Sa 9am-7pm, Su 9am-2pm. 500ptas, students 250ptas, Sa after 2:30 and Su free.

The Prado is Spain's pride and joy, as well as one of Europe's finest museums. Its 7000 pieces are the result of hundreds of years of Bourbon art collecting. Each room is numbered and described in the museum's free guide. On the second floor, keep an eye out for unforgiving realism and use of light in the works of **Diego Velázquez** (1599-1660), which resonate even in the 20th century. Several of his most famous paintings are here, including *Los borrachos (The Drunkards)* and *Las lanzas (The Spears* or *The Surrender of Breda)*. Velazquez's technique, called illusionism, climaxed in his magnum opus *Las meninas (The Maids of Honor)*, since dubbed an "encounter."

Follow the shift in the works of the court portraitist **Francisco de Goya y Lucientes** (1746-1828) to the stark *Dos de Mayo* and *Fusilamientas de Tres de Mayo*, which depict the terrors of the Revolution of 1808. Goya painted the *Pinturas Negras (Black Paintings)* at the end of his life, deaf and alone. *Saturno devorando a su hijo (Saturn Devouring His Son)* stands out among the *Pinturas Negras*. The Prado also displays many of **El Greco's** religious paintings. *La Trinidad (The Trinity)* and *La adoración de los pastores (The Adoration of the Shepherds)* are characterized by El Greco's luminous colors, elongated figures, and mystical subjects. On the second floor are other works by Spanish artists, including **Murillo, Ribera,** and **Zurbarán.**

The Prado also has a formidable collection of **Italian** works, including pieces by **Titian, Raphael, Tintoretto, Botticelli,** and **Rubens.** As a result of the Spanish Habsburgs' control of the Netherlands, the **Flemish** holdings are also top-notch. Works by **Van Dyck** and **Albrecht Durer** are here. Especially harrowing is **Peter Breughel the Elder's** *The Triumph of Death*, in which death drives a carriage of skulls on a decaying horse. **Hieronymus Bosch's** moralistic *The Garden of Earthly Delights* depicts hedonism and the destiny that awaits its practitioners.

🏛 MUSEO THYSSEN-BORNEMISZA

On the corner of Po. Prado and C. San Jerónimo. M: Banco de España. Bus #6, 14, 27, 37, or 45. ☎91 369 01 51. Open Tu-Su 10am-7pm. 700ptas, seniors and students with ISIC 400ptas, under 12 free.

Unlike the Prado and the Reina Sofía, the Thyssen-Bornemisza covers a wide range of periods and media, with exhibits ranging from 14th-century canvases to 20th-century sculptures. Baron Heinrich Thyssen-Bornemisza donated his collection in 1993 and today the museum, with over 775 pieces, is the world's most extensive private showcase. To view the collection in chronological order and observe the evolution of styles and themes, begin on the top floor and work your way down—the organization of the Thyssen-Bornemisza provokes natural comparisons across centuries. The top floor is dedicated to the **Old Masters** collection, which includes such notables as Hans Holbein's austere *Portrait of Henry VIII* and El Greco's *Annunciation*. In both variety and quality, the Thyssen-Bornemisza's **Baroque** collection, including pieces by Caravaggio, José de Ribera, and Claude Lorraine, outshines that of the Prado. The **Impressionist** and **Post-Impressionist** collections explode with texture and color—look for works by Renoir, Manet, Pisarro, Degas, Monet, van Gogh, Toulouse-Lautrec, Cézanne, and Matisse. Though less well-known, the **Expressionist** artists are also well-represented, with noteworthy works by Nolde, Marc, and Beckmann. The highlight of the tour is the museum's **20th-century** collection, located on the first floor. The modern artists represented include Picasso, Léger, Mondrian, Miró, Kandinsky, Gorky, Pollack, Rothko, Dalí, Hopper, Chagall, Ernst, Klee, and O'Keefe, to name a few.

MUSEO NACIONAL CENTRO DE ARTE REINA SOFÍA

C. Santa Isabel, 52, opposite Estación Atocha at the south end of Po. Prado. M: Atocha. ☎ 91 467 50 62. Open M and W-Sa 10am-9pm, Su 10am-2:30pm. 500ptas, students 250ptas. Sa after 2:30pm and Su free.

Since Juan Carlos I decreed this renovated hospital the national museum in 1988, the Reina Sofía's collection of **20th-century art** has grown steadily. Rooms dedicated to Juan Gris, Juan Miró, and Salvador Dalí display Spain's vital contributions to the Surrealist movement. Picasso's masterwork **Guernica** is the centerpiece of the Reina Sofía's permanent collection. It depicts the Basque town bombed by the Germans at Franco's request during the Spanish Civil War. Picasso denounced the bloodshed in a huge, colorless work of contorted, agonized figures. When asked by Nazi officials whether he was responsible for this work, Picasso answered, "No, you are." He gave the canvas to New York's Museum of Modern Art on the condition that they return it to Spain when democracy was restored. The subsequent move to the Reina Sofía sparked an international controversy—Picasso's other stipulation had been that the painting hang only in the Prado, to affirm his equivalent status with artists like Titian and Velázquez.

OTHER MUSEUMS

Museo de América, Av. Reyes Católicos, 6 (☎91 549 26 41), next to the Faro de Moncloa. M: Moncloa. This under-appreciated museum documents the cultures of America's pre-Columbian civilizations and the effects of the Spanish conquest. Artifacts include solid gold Columbian ornaments and Mayan treasures. Open Tu-Sa 10am-3pm, Su 10am-2:30pm. 500ptas, students 250ptas.

Museo de la Real Academia de Bellas Artes de San Fernando, Alcalá, 13. ☎91 522 14 91. M: Sol or Sevilla. A beautiful museum with a collection of Old Masters surpassed only by the Prado. Goya's La Tirana and Velázquez's portrait of Felipe IV are masterpieces; other attractions include 17th-century canvases by Ribera, Murillo, Zurbarán, and Rubens. The top floor also has Picasso sketches. Open Tu-F 9am-7pm, Sa-M 9am-2:30pm. 400ptas, students 200ptas. W free.

🎵 ENTERTAINMENT

Anyone interested in the latest on live entertainment—from music to dance to theater—should stop by the **Circulo de Bellas Artes,** C. Alcala 47 (☎91 360 54 00; fax 91 523 13 06; email presa@c-bellasartes.es). M: Sevilla or Banco de España. Their monthly magazine, *Minerva*, is indispensable.

🏛 EL RASTRO (FLEA MARKET)

For hundreds of years, El Rastro has been a Sunday morning tradition in Madrid. From Pl. Mayor and its Sunday stamp and coin market, walk down C. Toledo to Pl. Cascorro (M: La Latina), where the market begins, and follow the crowds to the end, at the bottom of C. Ribera de Curtidores. In El Rastro you can find anything, from pots to jeans to antique tools to pet birds. The flea market is a pickpocket paradise, so leave your camera in the room and turn that backpack into a front-pack. (Open Su and holidays 9am to 2pm.)

FLAMENCO

Flamenco in Madrid is tourist-oriented and expensive. A few nightlife spots are authentic (see **Cardamomo**, p. 816), but they too are pricey. **Casa Patas,** C. Cañizares, 10 is good quality, for less than usual; call for prices. (☎91 369 04 96.) At **Corral de la Morería,** C. Morería, 17, by the Viaducto on C. Bailén, shows start at 10:45pm and last until 2am. (☎91 365 84 46. M: La Latina. Cover 4000ptas.)

FÚTBOL

Spaniards obsess over *fútbol* (soccer). If either **Real Madrid** or **Atlético de Madrid** wins a match, count on streets clogged with honking cars. Every Sunday and some Saturdays between September and June, one of these teams plays at home. Real Madrid plays at **Estadio Santiago Bernebéu,** Po. Castellana, 104 (☎91 457 11 12; M: Lima). Atlético de Madrid plays at **Estadio Vicente Calderón,** C. Virgen del Puerto, 67 (☎91 366 47 07; M: Pirámides or Marqués de Vadillos). Tickets cost 3000-7000ptas.

BULLFIGHTING

Bullfighters are either loved or loathed. So too are the bullfights themselves. Nevertheless, bullfights are a Spanish tradition, and locals joke that they are the only things in Spain ever to start on time. Hemingway-toting Americans and true fans clog Pl. de Ventas for the events. From May 15 to 22 every year, the **Fiestas de San Isidro** provide a *corrida* (bulfight) every day with top *matadors* and the fiercest bulls. **Plaza de las Ventas,** C. Alcalá, 237, east of central Madrid, is the biggest ring in Spain. (☎91 356 22 00. M: Ventas.) A seat runs 450-15,200ptas, depending on whether it's in the sun (*sol*) or shade *(sombra);* shade is more expensive. **Plaza de Toros Palacio de Vista Alegre,** a new ring in town, hosts bullfights and other cultural events. (☎91 422 07 80. M: Vista Alegre. Ticket window open M-F 10am-2pm and 5-8pm.) If you're intrigued by the lore but not the gore, head to the **Museo Taurino,** C. Alcalá, 237, at Pl. Monumental de Las Ventas. The museum displays a remarkable collection of capes, bullfighter's outfits, and posters of famous *corridas.* (☎91 725 18 57. Open M-F 9:30am-2:30pm, on fight days 10am-1pm. Free.)

FESTIVALS

The brochure *Las Fiestas de España,* available at tourist offices and the bigger hotels, contains historical background and general information on Spain's festivals. Madrid's **Carnival** (February 15-25 in 2001) was inaugurated in the Middle Ages and prohibited during Franco's dictatorship. The **Fiestas de San Isidro** (see above) in honor of Madrid's patron saint, brings concerts, parades, and Spain's best bullfights. Throughout the summer, the city sponsors the **Veranos de la Villa,** an outstanding set of cultural activities. On November 1, **Todos los Santos** (All Saints' Day), an International Jazz Festival, brings great musicians to Madrid.

◪ NIGHTLIFE

Proud of their nocturnal offerings (they'll tell you straight-faced that New York and London bored them), *madrileños* party hard until they've "killed the night"—and a good part of the next day. The last thing they do is stop; an average night makes the most of countless offerings, perhaps starting in the bars of Huertas, moving to Malasaña's youthful scene, and ending at the crazed parties of Chueca or after-hours clubs of Gran Via. Most clubs and discos don't liven up until around 2am; don't be surprised if there's still a line at 5:30am. The *Guía del Ocio* features the latest hotspots and info about virtually all of Madrid's nighttime establishments.

CENTRO

In the middle of Madrid and at the heart of the action are the grandiose and flamboyant clubs of El Centro. The mainstream clubs found among these streets are often tourist hotspots; as a result, a night of fun here is the most expensive in the city. El Centro includes more territory than Madrid's other neighborhoods, so make a plan and bring a map.

   Joy Eslava, C. Arenal, 11 (☎91 366 37 33). M: Sol or Ópera. A massive, black 3-tiered disco featuring 3 bars, laser lights, and live dance shows. Best to come around 2am; dress well to secure entrance. Cover 1500-2000ptas, includes 1 drink. Open M-Th 11:30pm-5:30am, F-Su 7pm-6am.

El Barbu, C. Santiago, 3 (☎91 542 56 98), across C. Mayor from the Ayuntamiento. M: Sol or Ópera. Chill to lounge music in a brick three-room interior. Open Tu-Su 8pm-3am. Sundays bring the transformation to **"8th,"** a rave-like setting with popular local DJs Cover 1000ptas. Open 10:30pm-5:30am.

Azúcar, Po. Reina Cristina, 7 (☎91 501 61 07). M: Atocha. Sweet, sweet salsa. No sneakers. Salsa classes daily 9:30-11pm; call ahead. Cover 1200ptas, includes 1 drink; Sa 1800ptas, includes 2 drinks. Open M-Sa11:00pm-5am, Su 9pm-dawn.

Refugio, C. Dr. Cortezo, 1 (☎91 869 40 38). M: Tirso de Molina. Steel doors covered in steel vines lead to an outrageous gay scene. W nights bring *naturaleza,* when clothes are, ahem, not allowed. Cover 1000ptas, includes 1 drink. Open W-Sa 11:30pm-dawn.

◎ HUERTAS

In Huertas lies **Plaza Santa Ana,** brimming with *terrazas,* bars, and live music. Many bars convert to clubs as the night unfolds, spinning house and techno on intimate dance floors. With its variety of styles, Huertas is simply the best place to party. Be sure to check out the *discotecas* on **Calle Atocha.** Most locals begin their evenings here and emerge from Malasaña and Chueca (see p. 816) in the morning.

Kapital, C. Atocha, 125 (☎91 420 29 06), a block off Po. Prado. M: Atocha. To be safe, take the metro. One of the most extreme results of *la Movida,* this *macro-discoteca* tries even harder than its glittered 20-something clientele. From hip-hop to house, open *terraza* to cinema, 7 floors of over-stimulation necessitate a ground-floor directory. Cover 2000ptas, includes 1 drink. Open Th 12:30-6am, F-Sa 6-11pm and 12:30-6am.

Cardamomo, C. Echegaray, 15 (☎91 369 07 57). M: Sevilla. Flamenco music spins all night in this brick-walled, designer-lit bar. Open 9pm-4am.

La Comedia, C. Príncipe, 16 (☎91 521 51 64). M: Sevilla. Americans feel at home in a crowd dancing to hip-hop, R&B, and reggae. Hit up DJ Jay with requests; he spins to please. Beer 500ptas; drinks 900ptas. Open daily 9pm-4am.

El Café de Sheherezade, C. Santa María, 18, a block from C. Huertas. M: Antón Martín. Surrounded by Middle Eastern music and decor, groups cluster around *pipas* (pipes; 800-1200ptas) that filter sweet smoke through whiskey or water. Open daily 7pm-5am.

Mauna Loa, Pl. Santa Ana, 13 (☎91 429 70 62). M: Sevilla or Sol. Feels like Hawaii— birds fly freely between low chairs and the scantily clad dance to upbeat tunes. *"Fuerte volcano"* drinks 825-1650ptas. Open Su-Th 7pm-2am, F-Sa 7pm-3am.

O'Neil's, C. Principe, 12 (☎91 521 20 30). Just off Pl. Santa Ana. Irish pubs are actually a routine stop during most young Spaniards' nights, and this is one of the best. Pints 650ptas, half-pints 350ptas. Open Su-Th midnight-2am, F-Sa midnight-3am.

GRAN VÍA

Even the side streets of Gran Vía never sleep, pulsating in the early morning to the bass beats of landmark **after-hours clubs.** Subtlety has never been a strong point for this area, nor is it exactly known for its safety; a mix of sketchy tourists and sketchier locals makes the Gran Vía less than ideal for late-night wandering.

Sugar Hill, Mesonero Romanos, 13 (☎91 532 15 24). M: Gran Vía or Callao. Named after the original, this is the only real hip-hop club in town. Cover 1500ptas, includes 1 drink. Drinks 1000ptas. Open Sa only, 12:45-5:30am.

Goa After Club, C. Mesonero Romanos, 13 (☎91 531 48 27). M: Callao or Gran Vía. After-hours party features high-energy techno and even higher-energy clubbers after Sugar Hill (and sanity) departs. Cover 1000ptas, includes 1 drink. Open Sa-Su 6-10am.

MALASAÑA AND CHUECA

The dark cafes and darker clubs of Malasaña and Chueca filter jazz, techno, and foam into the night and early morning. Known for their bohemian crowds, Malasaña's hotspots radiate from **Plaza 2 de Mayo** and **Calle San Vincente Ferrer.** People are high on life, drugs, and booze; be wary at night. **Calle de Pelayo** is the main drag in flamboyant and gay Chueca. The safest walking route at night is up C. Fuencarral from Gran Vía and right on C. Augusto Figueroa.

Acuarela, C. Gravina, 8, off C. Hortaleza. M: Chueca. A welcome alternative to the club scene. Buddhas and candles surround antique furniture grouped into enclaves. Spend hours just chilling. Liquers 500ptas. Open Su-Th 3pm-2am, F-Sa 3pm-4am.

Midday, C. Amaniel, 13 (☎91 547 25 25). M: Noviciado. The **after-hours** club for Madrid's beautiful people. Techno and house. Open Su 9am-3pm.

Black & White, C. Libertad, 34 (☎91 531 11 41). M: Chueca. A lively disco/bar with room to chat, mingle, and groove on packed dance floors. 2 floors of male fun for a gay crowd. W is international exchange night. Beer 500ptas. Mixed drinks 1000ptas. Open Su-Th 9pm-5am, F-Sa 9pm-6am.

El Truco, C. Gravina, 10 (☎91 532 89 21). M: Chueca. Classy bar featuring local artists' works. Lesbian-friendly. Open Su-Th 8pm-2am, F-Sa 9pm-4am. Same owners run **Escape,** a club down the street. Open F-Sa midnight-7am.

BILBAO

In the student-filled streets radiating from **Glorieta de Bilbao,** it's easy to find a cheap drink and even easier to find someone to drink it with. Boisterous customers sip icy Mahou on **Pl. Olavide, C. Fuencarral,** and **C. Luchana.**

Vaivén, Travesía de San Mateo, 1 (☎91 523 14 87). M: Tribunal. Swivel hips with the best at this exclusive salsa club, crawling with well-dressed locals. Mid-week concerts. Beer 600ptas. Mixed drinks 1000ptas. Open daily 9pm-4am.

Big Bamboo, C. Barquillo, 42 (☎91 562 88 38). M: Alonso Martínez. Walk 3 blocks east of C. Pelayo on C. Gravina and turn left on C. Barquillo. A friendly, international club that jams to smooth reggae. Open 10:30pm-6am, F-Sa 10:30pm-7am.

◪ DAYTRIPS FROM MADRID

EL ESCORIAL

Autocares Herranz buses leave from Madrid's "Moncloa" metro station for El Escorial's Plaza Virgen de Gracia, the center of town (50min., every 15min., round-trip 805ptas). The Autocares Herranz office, C. Reina Victoria 3, and the bar/casino at C. Rey 27 sell tickets to Madrid. Complex ☎91 890 59 03. Open Apr.-Sept. Tu-Su 10am-7pm; Oct.-Mar. 10am-6pm. 900ptas, students 400ptas; W free for EU citizens. Tour 1000ptas.

The **Monasterio de San Lorenzo del Escorial** was a gift from Felipe II to God, the people, and himself, commemorating his victory over the French at the battle of San Quintín in 1557. Near the town of **San Lorenzo,** El Escorial is filled with artistic treasures, two palaces, two pantheons, a church, and a magnificent library. *Don't* come on Monday, when the complex and most of the town shut down. To avoid crowds, enter via the gate on the west side on C. Florida Blanca into a collection of Flemish tapestries and paintings. The adjacent **Museos de Arquitectura** and **Pintura** chronicle the construction of El Escorial and include masterpieces by Bosch, El Greco, Titian, Tintoretto, Velázquez, Zurbarán, and Van Dyck. The **Palacio Real,** lined with 16th-century *azulejos* (tiles), includes the **Salón del Trono** (Throne Room), Felipe II's spartan 16th-century apartments, and the luxurious 18th-century rooms of Carlos III and Carlos IV. The macabre **Panteón Real** is filled with tombs of monarchs and glitters with intricate gold-and-marble designs. The **tourist office** is located at C. Grimaldi, 2. (☎91 890 53 13. Open M-Th 11am-6pm, F-Su 10am-7pm.)

EL VALLE DE LOS CAÍDOS

El Valle de los Caídos is accessible only via El Escorial. Autocares Herranz runs one bus to the monument (15min.; leaves El Escorial Tu-Su 3:15pm, returns 5:30pm; round-trip 1030ptas includes admission but excludes funicular). Open daily in summer 9:30am-7pm; off-season 10am-6pm. Mass daily 11am. 800ptas, students 350ptas; W free for EU citizens. Funicular 350ptas.

In a valley of the Sierra de Guadarrama, 8km north of El Escorial, Franco built the overpowering monument of **Santa Cruz del Valle de los Caídos** (Valley of the Fallen) as a memorial to those who gave their lives in the Civil War. Naturally, the massive granite cross was meant to honor only those who died "serving *Dios* and *España*," i.e., the Fascist Nationalists. Non-fascist prisoners of war were forced to work building the monument, and thousands died during its construction. Although Franco lies buried beneath the high altar, there is no mention of his tomb in tourist literature—testimony to modern Spain's view of the dictator.

OTHER DAYTRIPS FROM MADRID

TOLEDO. To the architecture-loving tourist, Toledo is paradise, glorious former capital of the Holy Roman, Visigoth, and Muslim empires (see p.818).

SEGOVIA. The impressive Alcázar and hulking aqueduct merit a spot on any tour, and the town's twisted alleys, fruit stands, and *paseos* represent Castilla y León at its finest (see p. 822).

ÁVILA. Stand on Ávila's medieval walls, 2.5km of magnificently preserved 12th-century stone that encircle the old city (see p.823).

CENTRAL SPAIN

Castilla La Mancha, surrounding Madrid to the west and south, is one of Spain's least-developed regions; medieval cities and olive groves sprinkle the land. On the other sides of Madrid are Castilla y León's dramatic cathedrals; despite glorious historical architecture and history, the regions have not been as economically successful as their more high-tech neighbors. Farther west, bordering Portugal, stark Extremadura's arid plains bake under intense summer sun, relieved by scattered patches of glowing sunflowers and refreshingly few tourists.

CASTILLA LA MANCHA

Cervantes chose to set Don Quixote's adventures in La Mancha (*manxa* is Arabic for parched earth) in an effort to evoke a cultural and material backwater. No fantasy of the Knight of the Sad Countenance is needed to transform the austere beauty of this battered, windswept plateau. Its tumultuous history, gloomy medieval fortresses, and awesome crags provide enough food for the imagination.

TOLEDO

Toledo (pop. 65,000) may today be marred by armies of tourists and caravans of kitsch, but this former capital of the Holy Roman, Visigoth, and Muslim empires remains a treasure trove of Spanish culture. The city's churches, synagogues, and mosques reflect a time when Spain's three religions peacefully coexisted.

▆ TRANSPORTATION

Trains: Po. Rosa, 2 (☎925 22 30 99), in an exquisite neo-Mudéjar building opposite the Puente de Azarquiel. To **Madrid's Atocha** (1½hr., 10-20 per day, 775ptas).

Buses: (☎925 21 58 50), 5min. from the city gate. From Pl. Zocodóver, take C. Armas. Serviced by various companies. **T. Galiano Continental** (☎925 22 36 41) runs to **Madrid** (1½hr., every 30min., 585ptas). **ALSINA** (☎925 22 39 15) buses go to **Valencia** (M-F 1 per day, 2300ptas).

Public Transportation: Buses #5 and 6 stop to the right of the train station and across the street from the bus station; both head to Pl. Zocodóver (120ptas).

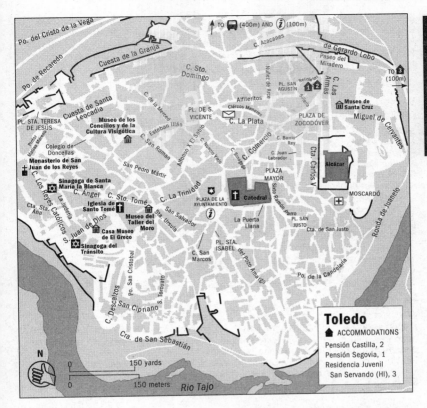

Toledo

🔺 ACCOMMODATIONS

Pensión Castilla, 2
Pensión Segovia, 1
Residencia Juvenil
San Servando (HI), 3

✦🛈 ORIENTATION AND PRACTICAL INFORMATION

Toledo is an almost unconquerable maze of narrow streets where pedestrians and cars battle for sovereignty. To get to **Plaza de Zocodóver** in the town center, take bus #5 or 6 (120ptas) from the stop on the right after you exit the train station. From the town center, take C. Armas downhill as it leads through the gates (Puerta Nueva de Bisagra), and cross the intersection to reach the tourist office (10min.).

Tourist Office: (☎25 22 08 43; fax 925 25 26 48), just outside the Puerta Nueva de Bisagra, on the north side of town. Open M-Sa 9am-7pm and Su 9am-3pm. There is a **second office** in Pl. Ayuntamiento (☎925 25 40 30), opposite the cathedral. Open Tu-Su 10:30am-2:30pm and 4:30-7pm.

Currency Exchange: Banco Central Hispano, C. Comercio, 47 (☎925 22 98 00). Open Apr.-Sept. M-F 8:30am-2:30pm; Oct.-Mar. M-F 8:30am-2:30pm, Sa 8:30am-1pm.

Luggage Storage: At the bus station (100-200ptas), open daily 8am-11:30pm. Train station (400ptas), open daily 7am-9:30pm.

Emergency: ☎091 or 092. **Police,** (☎925 21 34 00), Av. Portugal.

Pharmacy: (☎925 22 17 68), Pl. Zocodóver. List of late-night pharmacies posted.

Medical Services: Hospital Virgen de la Salud (☎925 26 92 00), Av. Barber.

Internet Access: Scorpions (☎925 21 25 56), on C. Pintor Matías Moreno. 100ptas for 5min. Open daily noon-midnight. Visa, MC, AmEx.

Post Office: C. Plata, 1 (☎925 22 36 11), off Pl. Zocodóver via C. Comercio. Lista de Correos. Open M-F 8:30am-8:30pm, Sa 9am-2pm. **Postal Code:** 45070.

▛ ACCOMMODATIONS

Toledo is chock-full of accommodations, but finding a bed during the summer can be a hassle, especially on weekends. If you run into trouble, try the tourist office.

Residencia Juvenil San Servando (HI), (☎925 22 45 54; reservations 925 26 77 29), on Castillo San Servando, uphill from the train station (10min.). Cross the street from the station, turn left and then immediately right up Callejón del Hospital; follow signs to Hospital Provincial. Closed various times throughout the year—call ahead. Laundry 500ptas. Reception open 7-9:40am, 10am-7:40pm, 8-11:50pm. Curfew 12:30am. Dorms 1200ptas, over 26 1400ptas.

Pensión Descalzos, C. Descalzos, 30 (☎925 22 28 88; email h-descalzos@jet.es), down the steps off Po. San Cristóbal. Recently refurbished, high-class hostel with some stunning views of the surrounding hills. Light modern rooms with TV, A/C, full bath and phone. Apr.-Oct. singles 3690ptas, doubles 5900ptas; Oct.-Mar. singles 3500ptas, doubles 5600ptas. 7% IVA not included.

Pensión Nuncio Viejo, C. Nuncio Viejo, 19, 3rd fl. (☎925 22 81 78), the street leading off the cathedral. The 7 rooms may be cramped but they're light and clean with rare waits for the bathroom. Singles 1900ptas; doubles 3900ptas, with bath 4400ptas.

Pensión Segovia, C. Recoletos, 2 (☎925 21 11 24). Simple rooms with decent beds. Singles 2200ptas; doubles 3000ptas; triples 4500ptas.

Camping El Greco, (☎925 22 00 90). 1.5km from town on the road away from Madrid (C-502). Bus #7 (from Pl. Zocodóver) stops at the entrance. 550ptas per person (children 450ptas), 570ptas per tent, 550ptas per car. 7% IVA not included.

▛ FOOD

Toledo grinds almonds into marzipan of every shape and size, from colorful fruity nuggets to half-moon cookies; *pastelerías* beckon on every corner. If your pocket permits, dining out in Toledo can be a pleasurable culinary experience (*menús* 1400-1600ptas). Alternatively, buy fresh fruit and the basics at **Frutería-Pan,** C. Real Arrabal 24, opposite the tourist office. (Open daily 9am-10pm.)

Restaurante El Zoco, C. Barrio Rey, 7 (☎925 22 20 51), off Pl. Zocodóver. Small, with big front window and simple green and white tablecloths. *Menús* 950 and 1500ptas. Open daily 1:30-4pm and 8-10:30pm.

Pastucci, C. Sinagoga, 10 (☎925 21 48 66). Standard and tasty pizzas and pastas (850-975ptas). Open daily 12:15pm-midnight.

Restaurante-Mesón Palacios, C. Alfonso X El Sabio, 3 (☎ 925 21 59 72), off C. Nuncio Viejo. English menu and cool, dim interior tempt weary sight-seers. Two daily *menús* (1000 or 1700ptas). Open M-Sa 1-4pm and 7-11pm, Su 1-4pm.

▛ SIGHTS AND ENTERTAINMENT

Toledo's major sights (many closed on Mondays) lie within the walls; despite well-marked streets, you'll probably get lost. Southwest of Pl. Zocodóver, Toledo's grandiose **catedral** at the Arco de Palacioz, boasts five naves, delicate stained glass, and unapologetic ostentatiousness. (Open July-Aug. M-Sa 10:30am-7pm, Su 2-6pm; Sept.-June M-Sa 10:30am-6pm, Su 2-6pm. 700ptas; tickets sold at the store opposite the entrance.) Toledo's most formidable landmark, the **Alcázar,** Cuesta Carlos V 2, uphill from Pl. Zocodóver, has been a stronghold of Romans, Visigoths, Moors, and Fascists. Today, it houses a national military museum. (Open Tu-Su 9:30am-2pm. 200ptas; W free for EU citizens.)

Greek painter Doménikos Theotokópoulos, or **El Greco,** spent most of his life in Toledo. Many of his works are displayed throughout town; on the west side of town, the **Iglesia de Santo Tomé,** on Pl. Conde, houses his famous *El entierro del Conde de Orgaz (Burial of Count Orgaz)*. (Open daily 10am-7pm. 200ptas.) Downhill and to the left lies the **Casa Museo de El Greco,** C. Samuel Levi 3, with 19 works by the master. (Open Tu-Sa 10am-2pm and 4-6pm, Su 10am-2pm. 200ptas, students free; Sa and Su afternoons free for all.) The impressive and untouristed

Museo de Santa Cruz, C. Cervantes 3, off Pl. Zocodóver, also exhibits a handful of El Greco's in its eclectic collection. (Open M 10am-2pm and 4-6:30pm, Tu-Sa 10am-6:30pm, Su 10am-2pm. 200ptas, students 100ptas.)

The simple exterior of the 14th-century **Sinagoga del Tránsito,** on C. Samuel Levi, hides an ornate interior with Mudéjar plasterwork, an intricate wooden ceiling, and Hebrew inscriptions, and now houses the **Museo Sefardí.** (Open Tu-Sa 10am-2pm and 4-6pm, Su 10am-2pm. 400ptas, students 200ptas; free Sa 4-6pm and Su.) The 12th-century **Sinagoga de Santa María la Blanca,** down the street to the right, was built as a mosque and then used as the city's main synagogue until converted to a church in 1492. (Open daily June-Aug. 10am-2pm and 3:30-7pm; Sept.-May closes 6pm. 200ptas.) At the western edge of the city, with great views is the Franciscan **Monasterio de San Juan de los Reyes,** commissioned by Isabel and Fernando. (Open June-Aug. daily 10am-2pm and 3:30-6pm; Sept.-May until 5pm. 150ptas.)

For nightlife, try **C. Santa Fe,** east of and through the arch from Pl. Zocodóver, which brims with beer and local youths. **Zaida,** in the Centro Comercial Miradero, downhill on C. Armas, is a perennial hot spot for dancing. (Open daily 9pm-5am.) Look for **Enebro,** tucked away on Pl. Santiago Caballeros off C. Cervantes. Their claim to fame is their free tapas in the evenings. (☎ 925 22 21 11. Beer 300ptas. No cover. Open until 3am.) The town goes crazy for **Corpus Christi,** celebrated the eighth Sunday after Easter.

CUENCA

Cuenca (pop. 47,000) is a vertical hilltop city surrounded by two rivers and stunning rock formations. The enchanting **old city** safeguards most of Cuenca's unique charm, including the famed *casas colgadas* (hanging houses) that dangle high above the Río Huécar, on C. Obispo Vaero off Pl. Mayor. Cross the San Pablo bridge to **Hoz del Huécar** for a spectacular view of the *casas* and cliffs. Many of the *casas* now house museums; on Pl. Ciudad de Ronda is the excellent **Museo de Arte Abstracto Español.** (Open Tu-F and holidays 11am-2pm and 4-6pm, Sa 11am-2pm and 4-8pm, Su 11am-2:30pm. 500ptas.) In the Pl. Mayor, the perfectly square **cathedral,** 25m on each side, is the only Anglo-Norman Gothic cathedral in Spain. (Open daily June-Aug. 11am-2pm and 4-6pm; Sept.-May 10:30am-2pm and 4-6pm. Free.)

Trains (☎ 902 24 02 02) leave from Po. Ferrocarril, in the new city to: Madrid (2½-3hr., 5-6 per day, 1405ptas) and Valencia (3-4hr., 4 per day, 7:40am-6:40pm, 1545ptas). **Buses** (☎ 969 22 70 87) depart from C. Fermín Caballero for Madrid (2½hr., 7 per day, 1325-1615ptas) and Toledo (3hr., M-F 1 per day, 1620ptas). From either station, go left to the first bus shelter and take bus 1 or 2 (every 30min., 1-3 per day, 85ptas) to the end to reach Pl. Mayor and the **tourist office.** (☎ 969 23 21 19. Open daily July-Aug. 10:30am-2pm and 4:30-7:30pm; Sept.-June 10am-2pm and 4-6:30pm.) To reach **Pensión Tabanqueta,** C. Trabuco 13, in the old city, head up C. San Pedro from the cathedral, which turns into C. Trabuco after Pl. Trabuco. (☎ 969 21 12 90. Singles 2000ptas; doubles 4000ptas; triples 6000ptas.) In the new city, take C. Fermín Caballero from the bus station, turn left on C. Hurtado de Mendoza and continue on Av. República Argentina to **Pensión Cuenca** at #8, 2nd fl. (☎ 969 21 25 74. Singles 1800ptas, with shower 2100ptas; doubles 2700ptas, with shower 3800ptas.) Budget eateries line **C. Cervantes** and **C. República Argentina.** Grab **groceries** at **%Día,** on Av. Castilla La Mancha at Av. República Argentina. (Open M-Th 9:30am-2pm and 5:30-8:30pm, F-Sa 9am-2:30pm and 5:30-9pm.) **Postal Code:** 16004.

CASTILLA Y LEÓN

Castilla y León's hilltop cities emerge like islands from a sea of burnt sienna. Hill-rise homesteads, long and low, from the fistful of wet rock that dripped walls between the fields, surrender to the intricate stone masterpieces above. The monuments—the majestic Gothic cathedrals of Burgos and León, the slender Romanesque belfries along León's Camino de Santiago, the intricate sandstone of Salamanca, and the proud city walls of Ávila—have emblazoned themselves as regional and national images.

SEGOVIA

Legend has it that the devil built Segovia's famed aqueduct in one night, in an effort to win the soul of a Segovian water-seller named Juanilla. When the shocked Juanilla woke up to find the aqueduct almost completed, she prayed to the Virgin Mary, who made the sun rise a bit earlier in order to foil the Devil's scheme. In the 12th and 13th centuries Segovia (pop. 55,000) had more Romanesque monuments than anywhere else in Europe. Today, its remaining cathedrals and castles represent Castilla at its finest—a labyrinthine town of twisted alleys and sharp aromas. Pleasure has its price: prices for food and accommodations are much higher than in Madrid. In the Sierra de Guadarrama, 88km northwest of Madrid, Segovia is close enough to the capital to be a daytrip but definitely warrants a longer stay.

F TRANSPORTATION. Trains arrive from Madrid (2hr., 9 per day, 775ptas) and Ávila (1hr., 16 per day, 980ptas). **Buses** go from: Madrid (1½hr., every hr., 775ptas); Ávila (1hr., 2-7 per day, 555ptas); and Salamanca (3hr., 1-3 per day, 1260ptas).

⁊ PRACTICAL INFORMATION. The city is impossible to navigate without a map. Locals describe it as the "Stone Ship." The **Alcázar** is the bow, the aqueduct the stern, and the cathedral towers the mainmast. **Trains** (☎921 42 07 74), Po. Obispo Quesada head to **Madrid** (2hr., 9 per day, 850ptas) while **buses** have more destinations: **Madrid** (1½hr., every 30min., 825ptas); **Ávila** (1hr., 2-6 per day, 555ptas); **Salamanca** (3hr., 3 per day, 1280ptas); **Valladolid** (2hr., 8-11 per day, 870ptas). To get to **Plaza Mayor,** the city's historic center and site of the **tourist office,** take any bus from the train station (100ptas). On weekdays, some buses go only as far as Po. del Salón, in which case go left up the steps of **Puerta del Sol,** turn right on C. Juderia Vieja, and make the first left onto C. Isabel La Católica up to the plaza. Your first stop should be the **Regional Tourist Office,** Pl. Mayor 10, in front of the bus stop, which has indispensable maps. (☎921 46 03 34. Open daily 10am-2pm and 5-7pm.) **Kitius,** Av. Fernández Ladreda 28, has a fast **internet** connection and AC. (Open M-Sa 9am-2pm and 5-8:30pm. 900ptas per hr.) **Postal Code:** 40001.

▰ ACCOMMODATIONS AND FOOD. In summer, finding a *hostal* room can be a nightmare; book ahead and prepare to pay at least 3000ptas for a single. The **Residencia Juvenil "Emperador Teodosio" (HI),** Av. Conde de Sepúlveda, is only open to travelers in July and August, when its hotel-like doubles and triples, all with private baths, make it extremely popular. From the train station, turn right, cross the street, and walk along Po. Obispo Quesada, which becomes Av. Conde de Sepúlveda (10min.). From the bus station, turn right on C. Ezequiel González, which becomes Av. Conde Sepúlveda (10min.). (☎921 44 11 11. 3-night max. stay. Dorms 1000ptas, with full meals 2200ptas; over 26 1450ptas, with full meals 3000ptas.) **Hostal Juan Bravo,** C. Juan Bravo 12, 2nd fl., on the main thoroughfare in the old town, has bright, newly renovated rooms. (☎921 46 34 13. Singles 4300-4700ptas; doubles 3900-4200ptas.) To get to **Hostal Don Jaime,** Ochoa Ondategui 8, face away from the aqueduct stairs and it will be on the first street to your left. (☎921 44 47 87. Breakfast 375ptas. Singles 3200ptas; doubles 4500ptas, with bath 5600ptas; triples with bath 7000ptas.) **Pensión Ferri,** C. Escuderos, 10, off Pl. Mayor, has five clean, small rooms. (☎921 46 09 57. Showers 300ptas. Singles 1600ptas; doubles 2500ptas.) **Camping Acueducto,** Ctra. Nacional 601, km 112, is 2km toward La Granja. Take the Autobus Urbano from Pl. Azoguejo to Nueva Segovia. (Bus 100ptas. ☎921 42 50 00. Open year-round. July-Aug. 575ptas per person and per tent; Sept.-June 535ptas.)

Sample Segovia's famed lamb, *croquetas,* or *sopa castellana,* but steer clear of pricey Pl. Mayor and Pl. Azoguejo. Get **groceries** at **%Día,** C. Fernández Jiménez 3. (Open M-Th 9:30am-2pm and 5:30-8:30pm, F-Sa 9am-2:30pm and 5:30-9pm.) The local color of the hidden **Bar-Mesón Cueva de San Estéban,** C. Valdeláguila 15, off Pl. San Estéban and C. Escuderos, is worth seeking out. (*Menú* 900ptas. Open daily 10am-midnight.)

SIGHTS AND ENTERTAINMENT. Segovia rewards the wanderer. Whether palace, church, house, or sidewalk, almost everything deserves close observation. Look for *esgrafía*, lacy patterns on the facades of buildings. The **cathedral,** commissioned by Carlos I in 1525, towers above Pl. Mayor. Inside, the **Sala Capitular** displays intricate tapestries; the **museum** has a series of 17th-century paintings on marble depicting the Passion of Christ. (Open daily Apr.-Oct. 9am-7pm; Nov.-Mar. 9:30am-6pm.). The **Alcázar,** a late-medieval castle and site of Isabel's coronation in 1474, dominates the northern end of the old quarter. In the **Sala de Solio** (throne room), an inscription reads: *tanto monta, monta tanto* ("she mounts, as does he"). Elevate your mind from the gutter long enough to appreciate this statement, which signified Fernando and Isabel's equal authority as sovereigns. The **Sala de Armas** holds an arsenal of medieval weaponry. From Pl. Mayor, follow C. Marques del Arco and walk through the park. (Open daily Apr.-Sept. 10am-7pm; Oct.-Mar. 10am-6pm. 400ptas.) The serpentine **roman aqueduct** commands the entrance to the old city. Constructed by the Romans around 50 BC, it is built from 20,000 blocks of granite, without any mortar holding them together. View it at its maximum height (28.9m) from Pl. del Azoguejo, or catch its profile from the steps on the left side of the plaza. This spectacular engineering feat was restored by the monarchy in the 15th century and was still in use 50 years ago. **Pl. Mayor** and its tributaries reign at night; **Pl. Azoguejo** and **C. Carmen,** down near the aqueduct, are also filled with bars. For clubs, head to **C. de Ruiz de Alda,** off Pl. Azoguejo.

DAYTRIP FROM SEGOVIA: LA GRANJA DE SAN ILDEFONSO. The royal palace and grounds of **La Granja,** 9km southeast of Segovia, were commissioned by Philip V, the first Bourbon King. Of the four royal summer retreats (the others being El Pardo, El Escorial, and Aranjuez), this "Versailles of Spain" is by far the most extravagant. Marble, lace curtains, lavish crystal chandeliers, and a world-class collection of Flemish tapestries enliven the palace. Manicured gardens and a forest surround the palace. (☎921 47 00 19. Open daily June-Sept. 10am-6pm; Oct.-Mar. Tu-Sa 10am-1:30pm and 3-5pm, Su 10am-2pm; Apr.-May Tu-F 10am-1:30pm and 3-5pm, Sa-Su 10am-6pm. 700ptas, students 300ptas, W free for EU citizens.) **Buses** run to La Granja from Segovia (20min., 10-14 per day, round-trip 210ptas).

ÁVILA

Oh, if walls had ears, what stories Ávila's medieval *murallas* could tell. The 2½km of magnificent 12th-century stone walls, are even better preserved than the various body parts of Santa Teresa that grace the city's shrines and museums. Santa Teresa would have been pleased at the peace of Ávila life. Today, the inner walls are a time warp, untouched by pollution, advertisements, or the blare of tourist traffic. Just west of Segovia and northwest of Madrid, Ávila (pop. 50,000) is a reasonable daytrip from either.

TRANSPORTATION. Trains run to Ávila from Madrid (2hr., 12 per day, 980ptas) and Valladolid (1hr., 7 per day, 1065ptas). **Buses** go from Madrid (2hr., 4 per day, 910ptas); Salamanca (1-2hr., 2-7 per day, 750ptas); and Segovia (1hr., 555ptas).

PRACTICAL INFORMATION. Trains leave the station at Av. José Antonio (☎920 25 02 02), for Villalba (transfer point for Segovia; 1hr., 16 per day, 1020ptas); Madrid (1½-2hr., 20-25 per day, 900-1550ptas); and Salamanca (1¾hr., 3 per day, 855ptas). From the train station, take Av. José Antonio, turn right on Av. del Dieciocho, turn left on Av. Madrid, and turn left again on C. Duque de Alba to reach Pl. de Santa Teresa. The **bus station,** Av. Madrid 2 (☎920 22 01 54), on the northeast side of town, serves Segovia (1hr., 2-7 per day, 555ptas); Madrid (1½hr., 5-8 per day, 930ptas); and Salamanca (1½hr., 2-4 per day, 700ptas). Cross the street and follow C. Duque de Alba to reach Pl. de Santa Teresa. To continue on to Ávila's **tourist office,** Pl. Catedral 4, walk through the main gate and turn right on C. Alemania. (☎920 21 13 87. Open daily M-F 10am-2pm and 5-7pm, Sa-Su 10am-2pm and 5-8pm.) Get on the **internet** at **Arroba@25,** C. Ferreol Hernandez 1. (400ptas per hr.) **Postal Code:** 05001.

SPAIN

ACCOMMODATIONS AND FOOD. Ávila's walls brim with comfortable and reasonable accommodations. Those near the cathedral and Pl. Santa Teresa fill up in the summer, so call a day in advance. Next to the tourist office, a winding wooden staircase leads to absolutely cavernous rooms at **Pensión Continental,** Pl. Catedral, 6. (☎920 21 15 02. 7% IVA not included. Singles 2200ptas; doubles 3700ptas, with bath 4500ptas; triples 5500ptas, with bath 6700ptas; 6-room suite 11,500ptas.) At **Hostal Casa Felipe,** Pl. Victoria, 12, near the cathedral, clean stucco-walled halls lead to well-lit rooms with TVs and sinks. (☎920 21 39 24. July-Oct. singles 2600ptas, doubles 4500ptas, with bath 5500ptas; less Nov.-June). Behind the pleasant front garden from which its name derives, **Hostal Jardin,** C. San Segundo 38, offers large rooms with TVs and phones. (July-Sept. singles 2675ptas, with bath 4280ptas, doubles 3785ptas, with bath 5350ptas; less Oct.-June.)

The city has won fame for its *ternera de Ávila* (veal) and *mollejas* (sweetbread). The *yemas de Santa Teresa* or *yemas de Ávila,* local confections made of egg yolk and honey, are delectable. **Calle San Segundo,** off Pl. Santa Teresa, is lined with budget diamonds. At **Las Leales,** C. Pl. de Italia, 4, dine quietly in style. From Pl. Teresa, take C. Estrada to Pl. de Italia. (☎920 21 13 29. Classic *menú* 1200ptas. Open W-M 1-4:30pm and 8:30-10:30pm.) **Restaurante El Grande,** Pl. Santa Teresa 8, is a festive family-style restaurant. (☎920 22 30 83. Generous *menú* 1350ptas. Open daily 1-4pm and 8-10:30pm). Find a **supermarket** at C. Juan José Martin, 6. (☎920 227 571. Heading away from Pl. Teresa, left off C. Duque de Alba just after the Monasterio de San Jose. Open M-Sa 9:45am-2pm and 5-8pm.)

SIGHTS AND ENTERTAINMENT. Ávila's **medieval walls,** the oldest and best-preserved walls in Spain, date from 1090. Eighty-eight massive towers reinforce the three-meter-thick walls—the most imposing of the towers, **Cimorro,** is also the cathedral's bold apse. To walk along the walls, start from the Puerta del Alcázar, directly before you with your back to the Pl. de la Teresa. Inside the walls, the profile of the **cathedral** looming over the watchtowers is believed to have inspired Santa Teresa's metaphor of the soul as a diamond castle. View the **Altar de La Virgen de la Caridad,** where 12-year-old Santa Teresa prostrated herself after the death of her mother. (From the Pl. de la Teresa, walk through the *puerta* and turn right on C. Cruz Vieja. ☎920 21 16 41. Open daily Apr.-Oct. 10am-1pm and 3:30-6pm; Nov.-Mar. 10am-1:30pm and 3:30-5:30pm. 300ptas.) Santa Teresa's admirers built the 17th-century **Convento de Santa Teresa** on the site of her birthplace and childhood home. (From the Pl. de Sta. Teresa, turn left on C. San Segundo, right on Po. del Rastro, and left into the Puerta de Sta. Teresa. Open daily May-Sept. 9:30am-1:30pm and 3:30-9pm; Oct.-Apr. 9:30am-1:30pm and 3:30-8:30pm.) To the right of the convent, the **Sala de Reliquias** holds Santa Teresa relics, including her right ring finger and the cord with which she flagellated herself. (Open daily 9:30am-1:30pm and 3:30-7:30pm. Free.) A short distance outside the city walls on Po. Encarnación is the **Monasterio de la Encarnación,** where Santa Teresa lived for 30 years. The mandatory 15-minute guided tour in Spanish visits Santa Teresa's tiny cell and the staircase where she had her mystical encounter with the child Jesus. (Open daily in summer 10am-1pm and 4-7pm; off-season 10am-1pm and 3:30-6pm. 150ptas.)

The best view of the walls and of Ávila itself is from the **Cuatro Postes,** a four-pillared structure past the Río Adaja on the highway to Salamanca, 1.5km northwest of the city. It was at this spot that Santa Teresa was caught by her uncle while she and her brother were trying to flee to the Islamic south. (From Pl. Santa Teresa, walk through the inner city and out the Puenta Puerta del Puente; cross the bridge and follow the road to your right for about 1km. Total walk 25min.) Fairs and parades of *gigantes y cabezudos* (giant effigies) pass through when the city gets crazy honoring Santa Teresa (the week surrounding Oct. 15th, her day). In mid-July, the **Fiestas de Verano** bring folk-singing, dancing, fireworks, and a bullfight.

SALAMANCA

For centuries, the gates of Salamanca have welcomed scholars, saints, rogues, and royals. The bustling city is famed for its warm golden sandstone architecture as well as for its university—the oldest in Spain, and once one of the "four leading lights of the world," along with the universities of Bologna, Paris, and Oxford.

▣ TRANSPORTATION. Trains chug from Po. Estación Ferrocarril (☎923 12 02 02) to: Madrid (2½hr., 4 per day, 2130ptas); Ávila (1¾hr.; 2 per day; regional 865ptas, intercity 1095ptas); and Lisbon (6hr., 1 per day, 4800ptas). **Buses** run from Av. Filiberto Villalobos 71-85 (☎923 23 67 17) to: Madrid (2½-3hr., 21 per day, 1460-1480ptas); Ávila (1½hr., 4-5 per day, 700ptas); León (2½hr., 1-3 per day, 1160ptas); and Segovia (3hr., 1-2 per day, 1280ptas). Bus #1 (100ptas) from the train station and bus #4 from the bus station head to **Gran Vía,** a block from **Pl. Mercado** (next to the town center at Pl. Mayor).

▨ PRACTICAL INFORMATION. The **tourist office** is at Pl. Mayor 14. (☎923 21 83 42. Open M-Sa 9am-2pm and 4:30-6:30pm, Su 10am-2pm and 4:30-6:30pm.) Access the **internet** at **Informática Abaco Bar,** C. Zamora 7. (Open M-F 9:30am-2am. 150ptas per 30min.) Exchange money at **Banco Central Hispano,** Rua Mayor, 35-37 (☎923 26 87 56). The **post office** sits at Gran Vía, 25-29. (☎923 27 04 11. Open M-F 8:30am-8:30pm, Sa 9:30am-2pm.) **Postal Code:** 37001.

▨▨ ACCOMMODATIONS AND FOOD. Reasonably priced *hostales* and *pensiones* cater to the floods of student visitors, especially off Pl. Mayor and C. Meléndez. **Pensión Estefanía,** C. Jesús 3-5, off Pl. Mayor, has a prime location and clean rooms. (☎923 21 73 72. Showers 150ptas. Singles 2000ptas; doubles with shower 3500ptas; triples 4800ptas.) Ideal for families and groups, **Pensión Bárez,** C. Meléndez, 19, 1st fl., has several large, simple rooms. (☎923 21 74 95. Showers 150ptas. Singles 1500ptas; doubles 3500ptas; triples 4500ptas.) **Pensión Villanueva,** C. San Justo, 8, 1st fl. (☎923 26 88 33), has soft beds and spacious rooms. Exit Pl. Mayor via Pl. Poeta Iglesias, cross the street, and take the first left. (Singles 1600ptas, with shower 1700ptas; doubles 3200ptas, with shower 3600ptas; triples 4500ptas. Extra beds available at 1500ptas per person. Cash only.) Albetur buses shuttle **campers** from Gran Vía (every 30min.) to the first class **Regio,** 4km toward Madrid on the Ctra. Salamanca. (☎923 13 88 88. 450ptas per person; 850ptas per tent; 450ptas extra per car.) **Champion,** C. Toro 64, has a downstairs supermarket. (Open M-Sa 9:30am-8:30pm.) Cafes and restaurants surround Pl. Mayor; full meals in cheaper back alley spots run around 1000ptas. **Restaurante El Bardo,** C. Compañía 8, between the Casa de Conchas and the Clerecía, is a traditional Spanish restaurant with veggie options and a lively bar downstairs. (☎923 21 90 89. Main dishes 1100-1900ptas. Open daily 1:30-4:30pm and 9:30-11:30pm., bar until 1am.)

▨▨ SIGHTS AND ENTERTAINMENT. The **Plaza Mayor,** designed by Alberto Churriguera, exemplifies the best of the city's famed architecture and has been called one of the most beautiful squares in Spain. Between its nearly 100 sandstone arches hang medallions with bas-reliefs of famous Spaniards, from El Cid to Franco. Walk down C. Rua Mayor to Pl. San Isidro to reach the 15th-century **Casa de las Conchas** (House of Shells), one of Salamanca's most famous landmarks, adorned by over 300 rows of scallop shells chiseled in sandstone. Go down Patio de las Escuelas, off C. Libreros (which leads south from Pl. San Isidro), to enter the **Universidad,** founded in 1218. The university's 16th-century **entry facade** is one of the best examples of Spanish Plateresque, named for the delicate filigree work of *plateros* (silversmiths). Hidden in the sculptural work lies a tiny frog; according to legend, those who can spot the frog without assistance will be blessed with good luck and even marriage. The **Antigua Biblioteca,** the oldest library in Europe, is the most spectacular room of all, located atop a magnificent Plateresque staircase displaying statues and historic books. Inside the Patio de Escuelas Menores, the University Museum contains the **Cielo de Salamanca,** a 15th-century fresco of the zodiac. (Open M-F 9:30am-1:30pm and 4-7:30pm, Sa 9:30am-1:30pm and 4-7pm, Su 10am-1:30pm. 300ptas, students 150ptas.)

Continue down Rua Mayor to Pl. Anaya to reach the *vieja* (old) and *nueva* (new) cathedrals. Begun in 1513 to accommodate the growing tide of Catholics, the spindly-spired late-Gothic **Catedral Nueva** wasn't finished until 1733. While several subsequent architects decided to retain the original late-Gothic style, they could not resist adding touches from later periods, most notably its Baroque tower, one of the tallest in Spain. Restorers from the 20th century succumbed to the same temptation, adding an astronaut, a bull, and even a demon eating ice cream to the side entrance's facade.The smaller Romanesque **Catedral Vieja** (1140) has a striking cupola with depictions of apocalyptic angels separating the sinners from the saved. The **museum** in the latter houses a Mudéjar Salinas organ, one of the oldest organs in Europe. (*Nueva* open daily Apr.-Sept. 9am-2pm and 4-8pm; Oct.-Mar. 9am-1pm and 4-6pm. Free. *Vieja*, cloister, and museum have the same hrs. 300ptas.) If religious zeal appeals, inquire at the tourist office about Salamanca's impressive **convents.** The **Casa Lis Museo Art Nouveau Y Art Deco,** C. Gibraltar, 14, behind the cathedrals, houses the oddities of Miguel de Lis's art nouveau and art deco collection. (Open Apr. 1-Oct. 15 Tu-F 11am-2pm and 5pm-9pm, Sa-Su 11am-9pm; Oct. 16-Mar. 31 Tu-F 11am-2pm and 4-7pm, Sa-Su 11am-8pm. 300ptas.)

Nightlife centers on **Pl. Mayor.** Also check out **C. Bordadores** and **Gran Vía. Camelot,** C. Bordadores 3, a monastery-turned-club. Swing to Top 40 songs at the popular **Café Moderno,** Gran Vía 75. For a more relaxed setting, **Birdland,** C. Azafranal 57 by Pl. España, features jazz. A mixed gay and straight clientele grooves under black lights at **Submarino,** C. San Justo 27, built to resemble an old submarine.

⊠ DAYTRIP FROM SALAMANCA: CIUDAD RODRIGO. A medieval town of fabulous masonry and honey-colored stone, Ciudad Rodrigo rises from the plains near the Portuguese border. The cathedral is the town's masterpiece; with biblical and mythological scenes in intricate stonework, the cloister alone is worth the trip. Fascinating figures festoon the columns—making love, playing peek-a-boo, or nibbling body parts. The cathedral's museum includes an ancient clavichord and Velázquez's *Llanto de Adam y Eva por Ariel muerto.* (Cathedral open daily 10am-1pm and 4-7pm, free. Cloister and museum same hrs. 200ptas.) **Buses** arrive from Salamanca (1¼hr., 5-12 per day, 735ptas).

LEÓN

Formerly the center of Christian Spain, today León is best known for its 13th-century Gothic **cathedral** on La Pulchra Leonina, arguably the most beautiful cathedral in Spain. Its spectacular blue stained-glass windows have earned the city the nickname *La Ciudad Azul* (The Blue City) and alone warrant a trip to León. The cathedral's **museo** includes gruesome wonders, including a sculpture depicting the skinning of a saint. (Cathedral open daily in summer 8:30am-1:30pm and 4-8pm; off-season closes at 7pm. Free. Museum open M-F 9:30am-2pm and 4-7pm, Sa 9:30am-12:30pm, 4pm-6:30pm. 500ptas. Claustro 100ptas.) The **Basílica de San Isidoro,** dedicated in the 11th century to San Isidoro de Sevilla, houses the corpses of countless royals in the impressive **Panteón Real.** From Pl. Santo Domingo, walk down C. Ramón y Cajal. (Open July-Aug. M-Sa 9am-8pm, Su 9am-2pm; Sept.-June M-Su 9am-1:30pm, 4-7pm, Su 9am-2pm. 400ptas.) During the "early" night, the area around **Pl. San Martín** sweats with bars, discos, and techno-pop. After 2am, the crowds stagger to **C. Lancia** and **C. Conde de Guillén,** streets filled with discos and bars.

Trains (☎987 27 02 02) run from Av. Astorga 2 to Madrid (4½hr., 8 per day, 3380ptas) and La Coruña (4½-7hr., 3 per day, 3900ptas). **Buses** (☎987 21 10 00) leave from Po. Ingeniero Saenz de Miera for Madrid (4½hr., 8-12 per day, 2665ptas). Take a right as you exit the train station (or a left from the bus station) and follow Av. de Palencia, which leads across the river to Pl. Guzmán el Bueno, turns into Av. de Ordoño II, and eventually leads to the cathedral and the adjacent **tourist office,** Pl.

Regla 3. (☎987 23 70 82; fax 987 27 33 91. Open M-F 9am-2pm and 5-7:30pm, Sa-Su 10am-2pm and 4:30-8:30pm.) **Hostal Oviedo,** Av. Roma 26, 2nd fl., off Pl. Guzmán el Bueno, offers huge rooms. (☎987 22 22 36. Singles 2000ptas; doubles 3500ptas; triples 5500ptas.) Nearby is **Hostal Orejas,** Av. Roma, 26, 2nd fl. Pricey, but includes telephones, cable TV, free internet access, and free breakfast. (☎987 25 29 09. Singles 5500ptas; doubles 6500ptas.) Pick up **groceries** at **Día Auto Servicion,** in Pl. Picara Justina (open M-Sa 9:30am-2:15pm and 5-8:15pm), or eat at **Calle Ancha,** on C. Ancha, 11, between C. General Mola and C. Conde Luna (*menús* 900-950ptas; open daily noon-4pm and 9:15pm-midnight, F-Sa until 3:30am). **Postal Code:** 24071.

🔟 **DAYTRIP FROM LEON: ASTORGA.** Upon approaching Astorga, visitors might imagine themselves facing a giant version of a child's drip-castle. And so appears Astorga's fanciful 🔳**Palacio Episcopal (Bishop Palace),** designed by **Antoni Gaudí** in the late 19th century, now houses the Museo de los Caminos. (Open daily June-Sept. 10am-2pm and 4-8pm; Oct.-May 11am-2pm and 3:30-6:30pm. 500ptas.) Opposite the palacio is Astorga's **cathedral** and **museum** with its detailed 18th-century facade. (Open daily June-Sept. 9:30-10:30am and 5-6:30pm; Oct.-May 9:30am-10:30am and 4:30-6pm. Free.) Trains run from León (45min., 8 per day, 400ptas). Buses are more frequent (40min., 16 per day, 405ptas).

VALLADOLID

When Fernando and Isabel were married here in 1469, Valladolid stood at the forefront of Spanish politics, finance, and culture, and it became the capital of Spain in the 16th century. Close to a century later, shady dealings brought the glory days to an end; in return for a whopping bribe, Lerma took Valladolid out of the running for capital of Spain. Madrid won, Valladolid lost, and history moved on. Yet today, the city makes up for its lack of national status with an impressive sculpture museum and endearing quirks. The Museo Nacional de Escultura in the **Colegio de San Gregorio** offers the thrill of 20 churches in one location, charting the region's religious art history through transplanted segments of now-destroyed monasteries and churches, including figurines, tableaux, sculpted choirs, and intricate ceilings. (☎983 25 03 75. Open Tu-Sa 10am-2pm and 4-6pm, Su 10am-2pm. 400ptas, students 200ptas; Sa afternoon and Su free.) The city's **cathedral,** C. Arribas, 1, in Pl. Universidad, was designed by Juan de Herrera, the creator of El Escorial (see p. 817). Only the gold of the *retablo* interrupts the monochromatic atmosphere. The **Museo Diocesano,** inside, is worth a visit for its original model of the basilica, its many statues of Jesus, Mary, and the saints, and its gruesome Jesus with real matted hair. (☎983 30 43 62. Both open M-F 10am-2pm and 5-8pm, Sa-Su 10am-2:30pm. Museum closed Su. Cathedral free. Museum 400ptas.)

Trains (☎983 30 35 18), C. Recondo, at the end of Campo Grande run to: Madrid (3-3¾hr., 18-21 per day, 1900ptas); Burgos (1¾-2½hr., 8-10 per day, 975-1070ptas); León (2-3hr., 8-10 per day, 1265ptas); and San Sebastián (5hr., 3060ptas). **Buses,** Puente Colgante, 2 (☎010 or 983 23 63 08), zip to: Madrid (2¼hr., 17-18 per day, 1580ptas); Burgos (1¾-2¾hr., 5-7 per day, 1045ptas); León (2hr., 8-9 per day, 1090ptas); and San Sebastián (6hr., 2840ptas). To get from the bus station to the **tourist office,** C. Santiago, 19, turn left on Paseo del Arco de Ladrillo and then veer off the busy street onto C. Laprillo. Walk through the stone archway, which cuts through the wooded park Campo Grande and ends at Pl. Zorrilla. (☎983 34 40 13. Open daily 9am-2pm and 5-7pm.) Cheap lodgings are easy to come by. The streets off Av. Acera Recoletos near the train station are packed with hostels, as are the streets near the cathedral and behind Pl. Mayor at Pl. Val. From the train station, walk up Av. Acera Recoletos and turn right on C. Perú to reach **Pensión Dos Rosas,** C. Perú, 11. (☎983 20 74 39. Singles 1650ptas; doubles 2900ptas; triples 4100ptas.) **Pensión Dani,** C. Perú, 11, 1st fl., is below Dos Rosas. (☎ 983 30 02 49. Singles 1650ptas; doubles 2900ptas; triples 4200ptas.) Eateries abound between Pl. Mayor and Pl. Val; explore the cathedral area for tapas. The **Mercado del Val,** on C. Sandoval in Pl. Val, has fresh foods. (Open M-Sa 6am-3pm.) **Postal Code:** 47001.

SPAIN

BURGOS

During its 500 years as capital of Castile, Burgos (pop. 180,000) witnessed the birth of the extraordinary cathedral and Rodrigo Díaz de Vivar, better known as El Cid Campeador, the national hero of Spain. Nine centuries after El Cid's banishment, General Franco stationed his headquarters here. Today, natives share the streets with history-seeking tourists and pilgrims completing the Camino de Santiago. The spires of Burgos's magnificent Gothic **cathedral** rise high above the city. The 13th-century Gothic north facade starkly contrasts with the intricate 15th-century towers and 16th-century stained-glass dome of the **Capilla Mayor,** where parts of El Cid's body rest. (☎947 20 47 12. Open daily 9:30am-1pm and 4-7pm. Sacristy, museum, and Capilla Mayor 400ptas, students 250ptas, children 100ptas.) Opposite the cathedral stands the **Iglesia de San Nicolás,** on Pl. Santa Maria, which contains 15th- and 16th-century Hispano-Flemish paintings and altars. (☎047 20 70 95. Open July-Sept. M-Sa 9am-2pm and 4-8pm; Oct.-Apr. Tu-F 6:30-7:30pm, Sa 9:30am-2pm and 5-7pm, Su 9am-2pm and 5-6pm. Free.) Altarpieces await up C. Pozo Seco at the **Iglesia de San Esteban/Museo del Retablo,** C. Pozo Seco. (☎947 27 37 52. Open Tu-Sa 10:30am-2pm and 4:30-7pm, Su 10:30am-2pm. 200ptas, students 100ptas.) The 200 steps behind the museum lead to an astounding view of the red roofs of Burgos from the ruins of a medieval **castle** presiding over Burgos from high above the cathedral. The **Museo-Monasterio de las Huelgas Reales,** built by King Alfonso VIII in 1188, is slightly out of the way, but certainly worth the trip. Inside the monastery, the **Museo de Telas** (Textile Museum) houses the burial wardrobe of Fernando de Cerda and family. Take the Barrio del Pilar bus (75ptas) from Pl. España to the Museo stop. (☎947 20 56 87. Open Apr.-Sept. Tu-Sa 10:30am-1:15pm and 3:30-5:45pm, Su 10:30am-2:15pm; Oct.-Mar. Tu-Sa 11am-1:15pm and 3:30-5:45pm, Su 10:30am-2:15pm. 650ptas, students and under 14 250ptas, under 5 free; W free.) By midnight, **C. Avellanos** (opposite Pl. Alonso Martínez) is at full boil. Crowds bubble over into nearby **C. Huerto del Rey,** then steam it up at *discotecas* along **C. San Juan.** Dance to pulse-pumping music all night at **Twenty,** Pl. Huerto del Rey, 20. (Open M-Sa 7pm-5am, Su 7pm-midnight.)

Trains (☎947 20 35 60) go from the end of Av. Conde de Guadalhorce, across the river from the town center (south of the river), to: Madrid (3-5½hr., 8 per day, 3060-3500ptas); Barcelona (9-13¾hr., 7 per day, 5000ptas); Bilbao (2½-4hr., 5 per day, 2000ptas); León (2-3hr., 6 per day, 2100ptas); and San Sebastián (3-3½hr., 9 per day, 2095-2500ptas). Follow Av. Conde de Guadalhorce across the river and take the first right on Av. Generalísimo Franco, which turns into Po. Espolón, to reach the town center (10min.). **Buses** (☎947 28 88 55) leave C. Miranda, 4, off Pl. Vega south of the river, for: Madrid (2¾hr., 1950ptas); Barcelona (7½hr., M-Sa 4 per day, 5085ptas); Bilbao (2-3hr., 7 per day, 1420ptas); and León (3½hr., M-Sa 10:45am, 1700ptas). To get to the **tourist office,** Pl. Alonso Martínez, 7, follow C. Madrid through Pl. Vega and across the river, then turn right on Po. Espolón, left on C. Santander, and follow the signs. (☎947 20 31 25. Open M-F 9am-2pm and 5-7pm, Sa-Su 10am-2pm and 5-8pm.) The **Café Cabaret Ciber-Café** is at C. Puebla, 21. (☎947 20 27 22. 500ptas per 30min. Open Su-Th 5pm-2am, F-Sa 4pm-4am.) Cheap hostels line the streets near Pl. Alonso Martínez, north of the river. To get from Pl. España to the family-run **Pensión Peña,** C. Puebla, 18, 2nd. fl., take C. San Lesmes and then your third right. (☎947 20 63 23. Singles 1600-1700ptas; doubles 2800-2900ptas.) From the bus station, walk toward the center and look right before C. Valladolid to reach **Pensión Dallas,** Pl. Vega 1-6. (☎947 20 54 57. Showers 300ptas. Singles 2000ptas; doubles 4000ptas.) To get to **Camping Fuentes Blancas,** take the bus from Pl. España. (dir.: Fuentes Blancas; July to mid-Sept. 4 per day, 75ptas. Open Apr.-Sept. 540ptas per person; 475ptas per tent and per car.) Pl. Alonso Martínez teems with restaurants. **La Posada,** Plaza Santo Domingo de Guzmán, 18, is a shrine to Spain's matadors. (☎947 20 45 78. Open daily 1-4pm and 9-11pm.) **Spar Supermercado,** on C. Concepción, is between C. Hospital Militar and C. San Cosme. (☎ 947 26 00 07. Open M-F 9am-2pm and 5-8pm, Sa 9am-2pm.) **Postal Code:** 09070.

EXTREMADURA

The aptly named Extremadura is a land of harsh beauty and cruel extremes. These lands hardened New World *conquistadors* such as Hernán Cortés and Francisco Pizarro, but the traveler who braves the Extremaduran plains is rewarded with stunning ruins and intimate, peaceful towns. Compared to the hectic pace of nearby Madrid, life in Extremadura is slower and less modern, as if the region's rich history dominates its character in the present.

TRUJILLO

The gem of Extremadura, hill-perched Trujillo (pop. 10,000) is an unspoiled joy. Scattered with medieval palaces, Roman ruins, Arabic fortresses, and churches of all eras, Trujillo's **old city** is a glorious hodgepodge of histories and cultures. The **Plaza Mayor** was the inspiration for the Plaza de Armas in Cuzco, Perú, which was constructed after Francisco Pizarro defeated the Incas. Festooned with stork nests, **Iglesia de San Martín** dominates the northeastern corner of the plaza. (All churches are open 9am-2pm and 4:30-7pm. 200ptas each or 800ptas for all.) Follow the road behind the plaza up to Trujillo's highest and most impressive monument: the 10th-century **Moorish castle,** commanding the top of the hill and a resplendent panorama of Extremadura.

Buses run from Madrid (2½hr., 10 per day, 3665ptas round-trip). To get to the **Plaza Mayor,** turn left as you exit the station (up C. de las Cruces), right on C. de la Encarnación, following signs to the tourist office, then left on C. Chica; turn left on C. Guia and right on C. Burgos, continuing onto the Plaza (15min.). The **tourist office** is across the plaza and posts info in its windows when closed. (☎927 32 26 77. Open daily 10am-2pm and 4-8pm.) **Pensión Boni,** C. Mingo de Ramos, 11 7, is off Pl. Mayor to the right of the church. (☎927 32 16 04. Singles 2000ptas; doubles 3000ptas, with bath 4500ptas; luxury triple with full bath and A/C 7500ptas.) The Plaza Mayor teems with tourist eateries. **Meson Alberca,** C. Victoria, 8, has a shaded interior garden and an excellent *menú* for 1650ptas. (☎927 32 22 32. Open Su-T and Th-Sa, 11am-midnight.)

SOUTHERN SPAIN (ANDALUCÍA)

Andalucía derives its spirit from an intoxicating amalgam of cultures. Under Moorish rule, which lasted from AD 711 until 1492, Sevilla and Granada reached the pinnacle of Islamic arts, and Córdoba matured into the most culturally influential Islamic city. The Moors preserved, perfected, and blended Roman architectural techniques with their own, creating a style that became distinctively and uniquely Andalucian. Intriguing patios, garden oases with fountains and fish ponds, and alternating red brick and white stone were its hallmarks.

Andalucía has been bequeathed as the convergence point of popular images of Spanish culture, sent the world over by advertising campaigns. Bullfighting, flamenco, white-washed villages, sherry *bodegas*, sandy beaches, and the blazing sun are what the region offers tourists, but beyond those outstanding elements lie vivacious and warm-hearted residents who believe their most important job is the art of living well. Despite being one of the poorest regions of Spain, Andalucians retain an unshakable faith in the good life. The never-ending *festivales, ferias,* and *carnavales* of Andalucía are world famous.

FERRIES TO MOROCCO

Ferries hop the Straits of Gibraltar from **Gibraltar** and **Algeciras.** From Gibraltar, **Tourafrica Int. Ltd.,** 2a Main St (☎776 66; fax 767 54), sails to **Tangier** (3 per week, UK£20, round-trip UK£30). From Algeciras, boats go in summer to **Ceuta** (1½hr., 24-28 per day, 2890-3095ptas) and **Tangier** (2½hr., 12 per day, 3500ptas per person, 20% off with Eurail.) Service is limited in winter and is not offered during bad weather.

SEVILLA

The 16th-century maxim *"Qui non ha visto Sevilla non ha visto maravilla"* ("he who has not seen Sevilla has not seen a marvel") remains true five centuries later. Site of a small Roman acropolis founded by Julius Caesar, capital of the Moorish empire, focal point of the Spanish Renaissance, and guardian angel of traditional Andalucian culture, this city has yet to disappoint its visitors. Santa Cruz's winding and colorful alleys, Triana's legacy as shipmen's quarters, and Macarena's streets dotted with churches are just a few of the city's distinct neighborhoods that instill pride in their residents and a love of the city. As such, Sevilla's vibrancy is infectious. During *Semana Santa* and the *Feria de Abril*, two of the most extravagant festivals in Europe, Sevilla's jasmined balconies and exotic parks spring to life, with matadors, flamenco dancers, and virgins leading the town in endless revelry. Sevilla's reputation for gaiety is rivaled only by its notoriety as *la sartenilla de España* (the frying pan of Spain)—not even the mellow Guadalquivir River can quell the blistering summer heat.

TRANSPORTATION

Flights: All flights depart and land at **Aeropuerto San Pablo** (☎954 44 90 00), 12km out of town on Ctra. Madrid. A taxi ride between the airport and the town center costs about 2000ptas. Los Amarillos (☎954 98 91 84) runs a bus from outside the Hotel Alfonso XIII at the Pta. Jerez (M-F every 30-45min., Sa-Su every hr., 350ptas).

Trains: All train services are centralized in the modern **Estación Santa Justa** (☎954 41 41 11), on Av. Kansas City. Buses C1 and C2 link Santa Justa and the Prado de San Sebastián bus station. They stop on Av. Kansas City, to the left as you exit the train station. In town, the **RENFE** office, C. Zaragoza, 29 (☎954 54 02 02), is near Pl. Nueva. Open M-F 9am-1:15pm and 4-7pm. **AVE** trains run to: **Madrid** (2½hr., 20 per day, 8400-9900ptas); **Barcelona** (12hr., 6 per day, 6400ptas); **Cádiz** (1½hr., 2 per day, 1600-2100ptas); **Córdoba** (45min., 17 per day, 2400-2800ptas). **Talgo** trains run to: **Cáceres** (5½hr., 1 per day, 3000ptas); **Granada** (3hr., 5 per day, 2660ptas); **Valencia** (8½hr., 4 per day, 5300ptas).

Buses: The old bus station at Prado de San Sebastián (☎954 41 71 11), C. Manuel Vazquez Sagastizabal, s/n, mainly serves Andalucía:

- **Transportes Alsina Graells** (☎954 41 88 11). To: **Córdoba** (2hr., 10-13 per day, 1225ptas); **Granada** (3hr., 9 per day, 2400ptas); and **Málaga** (2½hr., 10-12 per day, 1850ptas).
- **Transportes Comes** (☎954 41 68 58). To: **Cádiz** (1½hr., 12 per day, 1385ptas); **Jerez de la Frontera** (2hr., 7per day, 890ptas).
- **Los Amarillos** (☎954 98 91 84). To: **Arcos de la Frontera** (2hr., 2 per day, 940ptas); **Marbella** (3hr., 1-2 per day, 975ptas).
- **Enatcar-Bacoma** (☎902 42 22 42). To: **Barcelona** (16hr., 1 per day, 9755ptas) and **Valencia** (10hr., 2 per day, 6485ptas).
- **Plaza de Armas** (☎954 90 77 37), the newer bus station at on the river bank at the Puente del Cachorro, serves destinations beyond Andalucía, including Portugal and other European countries (open daily 5:30am-1:30am). Buses C1, C2, C3, and C4 stop nearby.
- **Socibus** (☎954 90 11 60). To: **Madrid** (6hr., 15 per day, 2745ptas) and **Lagos** (6hr., 1 per day, from 2590ptas).

Public Trasnportation: TUSSAM (☎900 71 01 71), the city bus network, is extensive and useful. Most lines run every 10min. (6am-11:15pm) and converge on Pl. Nueva, Pl. Encarnación, or in front of the cathedral on Av. Constitución. Limited night service departs from Pl. Nueva (every hr., midnight-2am; fare 125ptas, bonobús (10 rides) 650ptas). Buses C3 and C4 circle the center, and #34 hits the youth hostel, university, cathedral, and Pl. Nueva.

✳ 🔢 ORIENTATION AND PRACTICAL INFORMATION

Over the centuries, Sevilla has incorporated a number of neighboring villages, now distinct neighborhoods. The **Río Guadalquivir** flows roughly north to south through the city. Most of the touristed areas of Sevilla, including the alleyways of the old **Barrio de Santa Cruz** and **El Arenal,** are on the east bank. The historic **Barrio de Triana,** the **Barrio de Santa Cecilia,** and the fair-grounds occupy the west bank. The **cathedral,** next to Barrio de Santa Cruz, is Sevilla's centerpiece. **Avenida de la Constitución,** home of the regional tourist office, runs alongside the cathedral. **El Centro,** a busy commercial pedestrian zone, lies north of the cathedral, starting where Av. Constitución hits **Plaza Nueva,** site of the Ayuntamiento. **Calle Tetuan,** a popular shopping street, takes off from Pl. Nueva and runs northward through El Centro.

Tourist Offices: Centro de Información de Sevilla, C. Arjona, 28 (☎954 50 56 00), at the Puente Isabel II. Free maps and monthly magazine for tourists. Open M-F 9am-9pm, Sa-Su 8:30am-2:30pm. Another office at Junta de Andalucía, Av. Constitución, 21B (☎954 22 14 04; fax 954 22 97 53), 1 block from the cathedral. Open M-F 9am-7pm, Sa 10am-2pm and 3-7pm, Su 10am-2pm. Info booths in Est. Santa Justa and Pl. Nueva stock maps and bus guides.

Consulates: Australia, Federico Rubio, 14 (☎95 422 09 71; fax 95 421 11 45); **UK,** Pl. Nueva, 87 (☎22 88 74; fax 95 421 03 23); **US,** Po. Delicias, 7 (☎23 18 85; fax 23 20 40).

Currency Exchange: Banco Central Hispano, C. Sierpes, 55 (☎954 56 26 84). Open M-F 8:30am-2:30pm, Sa 8:30am-1pm.

American Express: Pl. Nueva, 7 (☎954 21 16 17). Changes cash and traveler's checks without commission, holds mail, and offers emergency services for cardholders. Open M-F 9:30am-1:30pm and 4:30-7:30pm, Sa 10am-1pm.

Luggage Storage: At Pr. San Sebastián bus station (250ptas per day), Pl. Armas bus station (300ptas per day), and Santa Justa train station (300-500ptas per day).

Gay and Lesbian Services: COLEGA (Colectiva de Lesbianas y Gays de Andalucía), Cuesta del Rosario, 8 (☎954 18 65 10). Open M-F 10am-2pm.

Laundromat: Lavandería Auto-servicio, C. Castelar, 2 (☎954 21 05 35), From the cathedral, walk 2 blocks down G. Vinuesa and turn left. Wash and dry 1000ptas. Open M-F 9:30am-1:30pm and 3-8:30pm, Sa-Su 9am-2pm.

Emergency: ☎091 or 092. **Police,** Po. Delicias, 15 (☎954 61 54 50).

24hr. Pharmacy: Check list posted at any pharmacy for those open 24hr.

Medical Assistance: Ambulatorio Esperanza Macarena (☎954 42 01 05). Hospital Universitario Virgen Macarena (☎954 24 81 81), Av. Dr. Fedriani. English spoken.

Internet Access: Sevilla Internet Center, C. Almirantazgo, 2, 2nd fl. (☎954 50 02 75), across from the Cathedral. 10ptas per min. Open M-F 9am-10pm, Sa-Su noon-10pm.

Post Office: Av. Constitución, 32 (☎954 21 64 76), opposite the cathedral. Lista de Correos and faxes. Open M-F 10am-8:30pm, Sa 9:30am-2pm. **Postal Code:** 41080.

▉ ACCOMMODATIONS

During *Semana Santa* and *Feria de Abril,* rooms vanish and prices soar. Make reservations months ahead. At other times, call a few days before arriving. The tourist office has lists of *casas particulares* that open on special occasions.

BARRIO DE SANTA CRUZ AND EL ARENAL

The narrow streets east of the cathedral around **C. Santa María la Blanca** are full of cheap hostels with virtually identical rooms. The neighborhood is overwhelmingly touristed, but its disorienting streets and shaded plazas are all within a few minutes walk of the cathedral, the Alcázar, and El Centro.

▨ **Hostal Sierpes,** C. Corral del Rey, 22 (☎954 22 49 48, fax 954 21 21 07), on the continuation of C. Argote de Molina. Simple rooms with telephones, some with A/C, the others with fans. Reservations recommended. Singles with shower 3000-4000ptas, with bath 4000-5000; doubles with shower 4000-6000ptas, with bath 5500-10,000ptas; triples with shower 5500-8000ptas, with bath 7000-14,000ptas.

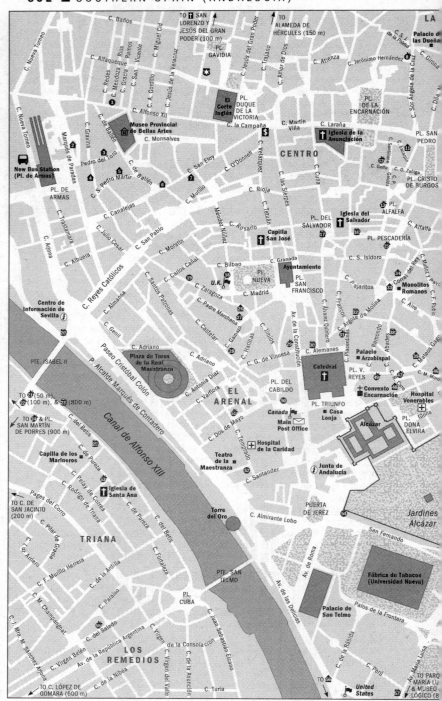

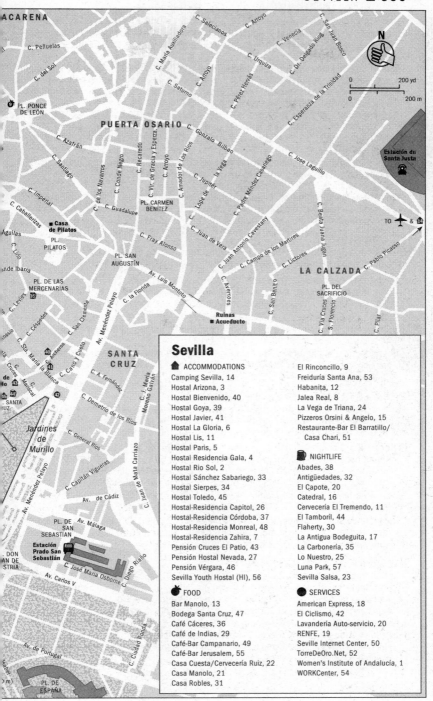

ACARENA

C. Peñuelas
C. del Sol

PL. PONCE
DE LEÓN

C. Azafrán

C. Santiago

C. Imperial

C. Caballerizas

Águilas

■ Casa
de Pilatos

PL.
PILATOS

nde Ibarra

PL. DE LAS
MERCENARIAS

C. Leves
C. Céspedes
C. Sta. María la Blanca
de
lo
SANTA
CUZ

PUERTA OSARIO

C. Saleclanos
C. Arroyo
C. Venecia
C. Dr. Delgado Ríos
C. San Juan Bosco

C. María Auxiliadora
C. Arroyo
C. Urquiza

C. Pérez Hervás
C. Saturno

C. Esperanza de la Trinidad

Estación de
Santa Justa

C. Gonzalo Bilbao

C. de los Navarros
C. Conde Negro
C. Recaredo
C. Vir. de Gracia y Esperz.
C. Amador de Los Ríos
C. Arroyo
C. Jupiter
C. la Vega
Lope de

C. Jose Laguillo

PL. CARMEN
BENÍTEZ

C. Guadalupe
C. Juan de Vera

C. Padre Méndez Casariego

C. Fray Alonso

PL. SAN
AGUSTÍN

C. Juan Antonio Cavestany

C. Campo de los Mártires

C. Beata Juana Jugan

C. Pablo Picasso

TO ✈ & 🏛

Av. Luis Montoto

Av. Menéndez Pelayo

C. la Florida

C. Averroes

C. San Benito

C. Lictores

LA CALZADA

PL. DEL
SACRIFICIO

Ruinas
■ Acueducto

C. Cano y Cueto
C. San Clemente
C. Andueza

SANTA
CRUZ

C. A. Fernández

C. Demetrio de los Ríos

C. J. María
Moreno Galván

C. Via Cruces
S. Florencio

C. Pilar

Jardines
de
Murillo

C. General Ríos

C. Capitán Vigueras

Av. Menéndez Pelayo

Av. de Cádiz

C. Juan de Mata Carriazo

. DON
AN DE
STRIA

PL. DE
SAN
SEBASTIÁN

Estación
Prado San
Sebastián

Av. Málaga

C. José María Osborne
C. Diego Riaño

C. Ciudad Ronda

Av. Carlos V

Av. de Portugal

) m)

PL. DE
ESPAÑA

Sevilla

🏠 ACCOMMODATIONS

Camping Sevilla, 14
Hostal Arizona, 3
Hostal Bienvenido, 40
Hostal Goya, 39
Hostal Javier, 41
Hostal La Gloria, 6
Hostal Lis, 11
Hostal Paris, 5
Hostal Residencia Gala, 4
Hostal Rio Sol, 2
Hostal Sánchez Sabariego, 33
Hostal Sierpes, 34
Hostal Toledo, 45
Hostal-Residencia Capitol, 26
Hostal-Residencia Córdoba, 37
Hostal-Residencia Monreal, 48
Hostal-Residencia Zahira, 7
Pensión Cruces El Patio, 43
Pensión Hostal Nevada, 27
Pensión Vérgara, 46
Sevilla Youth Hostal (HI), 56

🍎 FOOD

Bar Manolo, 13
Bodega Santa Cruz, 47
Café Cáceres, 36
Café de Indias, 29
Café-Bar Campanario, 49
Café-Bar Jerusalem, 55
Casa Cuesta/Cervecería Ruiz, 22
Casa Manolo, 21
Casa Robles, 31

El Rinconcillo, 9
Freiduría Santa Ana, 53
Habanita, 12
Jalea Real, 8
La Vega de Triana, 24
Pizzeros Orsini & Angelo, 15
Restaurante-Bar El Barratillo/
  Casa Chari, 51

🍸 NIGHTLIFE

Abades, 38
Antigüedades, 32
El Capote, 20
Catedral, 16
Cervecería El Tremendo, 11
El Tamboril, 44
Flaherty, 30
La Antigua Bodeguita, 17
La Carbonería, 35
Lo Nuestro, 25
Luna Park, 57
Sevilla Salsa, 23

⚫ SERVICES

American Express, 18
El Ciclismo, 42
Lavandería Auto-servicio, 20
RENFE, 19
Seville Internet Center, 50
TorreDeOro.Net, 52
Women's Institute of Andalucía, 1
WORKCenter, 54

0 _____ 200 yd
0 _____ 200 m

Pensión Vergara, C. Ximénez de Enciso, 11, 2nd fl. (☎954 21 56 68), at C. Mesón del Moro. Impeccably clean and spacious rooms make this newly renovated 15th-century house a bargain for the district. Bathrooms in the hallway. Up to 4 people in a room. 2500ptas per person.

Hostal Sánchez Sabariego, C. Corral del Rey, 23 (☎954 21 44 70), on the continuation of C. Argote de Molina. Friendly owner makes you feel like family. Antique furniture and painstakingly decorated rooms. A/C upstairs, fans all other rooms. Singles 4000ptas; doubles with bath 8000ptas; triples with bath 9000ptas.

Pensión Cruces El Patio, C. Cruces, 10 (☎954 22 96 33 or 954 22 60 41). Gregarious owner oversees hostel and multiple bird cages. Fans on request. Dorms 1500-2000ptas; singles 2000ptas; doubles 4000-5000ptas, with bath 5000-6000ptas.

Hostal Bienvenido, C. Archeros, 14 (☎954 41 36 55). Small singles with big windows; spacious doubles with balconies. Terrace on the roof converted to outdoor lounge. All rooms have sinks. Up to 4 people per room. Singles 2000-2500ptas; doubles 4000-4600ptas; triple 2000-2300ptas per person.

Hostal-Residencia Capitol, C. Zaragoza, 66 (☎954 21 24 41), near Pensión Hostal Nevada. Spacious rooms. Lounge with phone and TV. A/C. Singles 3210-ptas; doubles with shower 5500ptas, with bath 6420ptas.

EL CENTRO

El Centro, a mess of narrow streets radiating from **Pl. Encarnación,** is a bustling shopping district during the day but at night most streets are deserted.

Hostal Lis, C. Escarpín, 10 (☎954 21 30 88), on an alley near Pl. Encarnación. Each room decorated with its own unique Sevillian tiles. All have fans. Up to 4 in a room. Singles 3000ptas; doubles 6000ptas, with bath 7000ptas; triples with bath 9000ptas.

Hostal La Gloria, C. San Eloy, 58, 2nd fl. (☎954 22 26 73), at the end of a lively shopping street. Tiled floors and lounge with TV and sofa. Singles 2000-2500ptas; doubles 4000ptas, with bath 4500ptas; triples 6000ptas.

Hostal-Residencia Zahira, C. San Eloy, 43 (☎954 22 10 61). Hotel-sized lobby masks smaller rooms. All rooms with bath and A/C. Lounge with TV. Singles 3500-4000ptas; doubles 6000-7000ptas.

NEAR ESTACIÓN PLAZA DE ARMAS

Most hostels around the Pl. Armas bus station center around **C. Gravina,** parallel to C. Marqués de las Paradas and two blocks from the station. These are the most convenient to El Centro and the lively C. Betis on the west bank of the river.

🔳 **Hostal Rio Sol,** C. Marquéz de Parada, 25 (☎954 22 90 38), 1 block from Plaza de Armas bus station. The convenient location cannot be surpassed. Small rooms have newly renovated bathrooms. All rooms have A/C. Singles with sink 2000ptas, with bath 3000-4000ptas; doubles with bath 6500ptas; triples with bath 9000ptas.

Hostal Paris, C. San Pedro Mártir, 14 (☎954 22 98 61), off C. Gravina. All rooms with bath, A/C, phone, and TV. Singles 3500ptas; doubles 6000ptas; triples 9000ptas.

Hostal Arizona, C. Pedro del Toro, 14 (☎954 21 60 42), off C. Gravina. Clean rooms with fans and tiled floors; some have balconies. Singles 2000-2500ptas; doubles 4500ptas, with bath 4500ptas; triples 5000-6000ptas.

ELSEWHERE AND CAMPING

Sevilla Youth Hostel (HI), C. Isaac Peral, 2 (☎954 61 31 50). Take bus #34 from Pr. San Sebastián; it stops behind the hostel just after Po. Delicias. A bit out of the way. Breakfast included. Up to 4 per room. Dorms 1605ptas, over 26 2140ptas. Non-members can pay an additional 300ptas a night for 6 nights to become members.

Camping Sevilla, Ctra. Madrid-Cádiz, km 534 (☎954 51 43 79), near the airport. From Pr. San Sebastián, take bus #70, which stops 800m away at Parque Alcosa. Grassy sites, hot showers, supermarket, and pool. 475ptas per person, per car, and per tent; children 375ptas.

❐ FOOD

Sevillians offset the merciless midday sun by keeping their cuisine light. The city claims to be the birthplace of tapas; locals prepare and devour them with a vengeance. Other favorites include *caracoles* (snails), *cocido andaluz* (a thick soup of chick peas), and all manner of fresh seafood. Defying the need for hydration, locals imbibe Sevilla's Cruzcampo beer, a light, smooth pilsner. **Mercado del Arenal,** near the bullring on C. Pastor y Leandro, between C. Almansa and C. Arenal, has fresh meat and produce and screaming vendors. (Open M-Sa 9am-2pm.) For a **supermarket,** try **%Día,** C. San Juan de Ávila, near El Corte Inglés. (Open M-F 9:30am-2pm and 6:30-9pm, Sa 9am-1pm.)

BARRIO DE SANTA CRUZ AND EL ARENAL

Restaurants near the cathedral cater almost exclusively to tourists. Beware the unexceptional, omnipresent *menús* featuring *gazpacho* and *paella* for 1000ptas. Food and prices improve in the backstreet establishments between the cathedral and the river in El Arenal, and along sidestreets in the Barrio Santa Cruz.

Restaurante-Bar El Baratillo/Casa Chari, C. Pavia, 12 (☎954 22 96 51), on a tiny street off C. Dos de Mayo. Call or ask in advance for the tour-de-force: homemade *paella* with a jar of wine, beer, or *sangría* (2500ptas for 2). *Menú* 500ptas. Open M-F 9am-11pm, Sa noon-5pm.

Casa Robles, C. Placentines, 2 (☎954 21 31 62), 1 block from the Cathedral. Hidden from tourists and deemed by locals as one of the best eateries in the neighborhood, this restaurant caters to a well-dressed crowd. Tapas 250ptas, main dishes 800-2200ptas. Open daily noon-1am.

Cafe de Indias, Av. Constitución, 10 (☎954 27 47 43), across from the cathedral. This cafe's special *batidos* with liquer (350ptas) are not to be missed. Open Su-Th 7:30am-midnight, F-Sa 8:15am until the early morning.

EL CENTRO

Inexpensive tapas restaurants lurk along streets radiating out from **Plaza Alfalfa.**

Jalea Real, Sor Ángela de la Cruz, 37 (☎954 21 61 03). From Pl. Encarnación, walk 150m on C. Laraña, then turn left at Iglesia de San Pedro. Fabulous vegetarian cuisine. Fresh and tasty salads 475-800ptas, *menú* 1250ptas. Open July-Aug. M-F 1:30-5pm and 8:30-11:30pm, Sa 8:30-11:30pm; Sept.-June M-Sa 2-5pm and 8:30-11:30pm.

Bar Manolo, Pl. de Alfalfa, 3 (☎954 21 41 76). As one of the mainstays of the plaza, the outdoor seating area is always packed. The tapas here are fresh and filling. Tapas 200-425, *raciones* 1100ptas. Open daily 7am-12:30pm.

El Rinconcillo, C. Gerona, 40 or C. Alhóndiga, 2 (☎ 954 22 31 83). This *bodega,* founded in 1670, is a popular pit-stop with quite a history. Tapas 185-300ptas, *raciones* 225-1850ptas.

TRIANA AND BARRIO DE SANTA CECILIA

This old maritime neighborhood, on the far side of the river, was once a separate village. Avoid overpriced C. Betis and plunge down less expensive sidestreets, where fresh seafood and *caracoles* abound. Tapas bars cluster around Pl. San Martín and along C. San Jacinto.

▨ La Vega de Triana, C. Asturias at Pl. San Martín de Porres. A hectic atmosphere behind the bar and wine-barreled tables make for a lively meal like no other. Both the friendly service and the well-served tapas deserve acclaim. Tapas 200-300ptas, *raciones* 1100-1300ptas. Open daily 11am-midnight.

Café-Bar Jerusalem, C. Salado, 6, at C. Virgen de las Huertas. Bar with an international crowd and creative tapas. Chicken, lamb, or pork and cheese *schwarmas* called a *bocadillo hebreo* (400-625ptas). Open daily 8pm-3am.

SIGHTS

SPAIN

Sevilla is brimming with sights, from the Alcázar and cathedral to the churches, monuments, and winding streets of the *casco viejo* and Barrio de Santa Cruz.

THE CATHEDRAL. With 44 individual chapels, the cathedral is the third largest in the world, after St. Peter's Basilica in Rome and St. Paul's Cathedral in London, and is the world's biggest Gothic edifice ever constructed. Not surprisingly, it took more than a century to build. In 1401, Christians destroyed a 12th-century Almohad mosque to clear space and all that remains of the former mosque is the **Patio de Los Naranjos** and the famed minaret **La Giralda,** built in 1198. The tower and its twins in Marrakesh and Rabat, Morocco, are the oldest and largest surviving Almohad minarets. The 35 ramps inside lead to the top of the tower and offer amazing city views.

In the middle of the cathedral, the **Capilla Real** and its altar stand opposite the dark wooden **choir stalls** made of mahogany recycled from a 19th-century Austrian railway. The **retablo mayor** (altarpiece), one of the largest in the world, is a golden wall of wrought figurines depicting 36 biblical scenes. Circle the choir to see the **Sepulcro de Cristóbal Colón** (Columbus's tomb). There is mystery surrounding the actual whereabouts of Columbus's remains, since there are currently four of his tombs throughout the world. The **Sacristía Mayor** holds works by Ribera and Murillo and a glittering Corpus Christi icon, La Custodia Processional. In the corner of the cathedral are the impressive **Sala de Las Columnas** and the perfectly oval **cabildo** (chapter house). (☎ 954 21 49 71. Open M-Sa 10:30am-5pm, Su 2-6pm. Tickets sold until 1hr. before closing. 700ptas, seniors and students 200ptas, under 12 free. Su free.)

ALCÁZAR. The imposing 9th-century walls of the Alcázar which face the cathedral date from the Moorish era, as do many of the palace's interior residences. Visitors enter through the **Patio de la Montería,** directly across from which stands the intricate Almohad facade of the Moorish palace. Through the archway lies the **Patio del Yeso** and the exquisitely carved **Patio de las Muñecas** (Patio of the Dolls), named so because of its miniature proportions. Court life revolved around the **Patio de las Doncellas** (Maids' Court), encircled by archways adorned with glistening tilework. The astonishing golden-domed **Salón de los Embajadores** is allegedly the site where Fernando and Isabel welcomed Columbus back from America. Nearby, the **Corte de las Muñecas** contains the palace's private quarters, decorated with the building's most exquisite carvings. Verdant and peaceful gardens stretch from the residential quarters in all directions. (Pl. Triunfo, 7. ☎ 954 50 23 23. Open Tu-Sa 9:30am-7pm, Su 9:30am-6pm. Audio guides 400ptas. 700ptas; students, seniors, and under 16 free.)

MUSEO PROVINCIAL DE BELLAS ARTES. This museum contains Spain's finest collection of works by painters of the Sevilla school, notably Murillo, Valdés Leal, and Zurbarán, as well as El Greco and Dutch master Jan Breughel. The building itself is a work of art—take time to sit in its shady gardens. (Pl. Museo, 9, off C. Alfonso XII. ☎ 954 22 07 90. Open Tu 3-8pm, W-Sa 9am-8pm, Su 9am-3pm. 250ptas, EU citizens free.)

BARRIO DE SANTA CRUZ. King Fernando III forced Jews fleeing Toledo to live in the Barrio de Santa Cruz, now a neighborhood of winding alleys, wrought-iron gates and fountained courtyards. Beyond C. Lope de Rueda, off C. Ximénez de Enciso, is the charming and fragrant Plaza de Santa Cruz. South of the plaza are the **Jardines de Murillo,** a shady expanse of shrubbery and benches. The **Convento de San José** in Pl. Santa Cruz houses the grave of the artist Murillo, who died in what is now known as the **Casa Murillo** after falling from a scaffold. The **Iglesia de Santa María la Blanca** was built in 1391 on the foundation of a synagogue and features Murillo's Last Supper. (Open M-Sa 10-11am and 6:30-8pm, Su 9:30am-2pm and 6:30-8pm.)

SIERPES AND THE ARISTOCRATIC QUARTER. Originating from Pz. Duque de Victoria, **Calle de Sierpes,** a bustling commercial street, cuts through the Aristocratic Quarter. A plaque marks the spot where the royal prison once loomed—scholars believe Cervantes began writing *Don Quixote* there. The 15th-century **Casa de Pilatos** is a typical Andalucian palace with a mix of medieval and Renaissance artistic elements, including several courtyards and a pond. (Open daily 9am-7pm. 1000ptas.)

EL ARENAL AND PASEO ALCALDE MARQUÉS DE CONTADERO. The inviting riverside esplanade Po. Marqués de Contadero stretches along the banks of the Guadalquivir and El Arenal, once a stretch of sand by the harbour that was later exposed when the river was diverted to its present course. The tiled boardwalk leads to the **Plaza de Toros de la Real Maestranza,** a veritable temple of bullfighting. Home to one of the two great bullfighting schools (the other is in Ronda), the plaza fills to capacity for the 13 *corridas* of the *Feria de Abril* as well as weekly fights. The museum inside houses costumes, paintings, and antique posters. *(Open on non-bullfight days 9:30am-2pm and 3-7pm, on bullfight days 9:30am-3pm. Tours every 30min., 500ptas.)*

LA MACARENA. The quarter, northwest of El Centro, is named not for the popular mid-90s dance, but rather for the virgin of Sevilla. It is traversed by the *ruta de los conventos* (route of convents). The founder of **Convento de Santa Inés,** as legend has it, was pursued so insistently by King Pedro the Cruel that she disfigured her face with boiling oil so he would leave her alone. Cooking liquids are used more positively today—the cloistered nuns sell patented puff pastries and coffee cakes through the courtyard's revolving window. A stretch of **murallas** (fortress walls), created in the 12th century, runs between the Pta. Macarena and Pta. Córdoba on the Ronda de Capuchinos road. At the west end of the walls, the **Basílica Macarena** houses the venerated image of *La virgen de la macarena,* which is hauled around town during Semana Santa processions. A treasury glitters with the virgin's jewels and other finery. *(Basilica open daily 9:30am-1pm and 5-9pm. Free. Treasury open daily 9:30am-1pm and 5-8pm. 400ptas.)* Toward the river is **Iglesia de San Lorenzo y Jesús del Gran Poder,** with Montañés's remarkably lifelike sculpture *El cristo del gran poder.* Worshipers kiss Jesus' ankle through an opening in the bulletproof glass for luck. Semana Santa culminates in a procession honoring his statue. *(Open Sa-Th 8am-1:45pm and 6-9pm, F 7:30-10pm. Free.)*

OTHER SIGHTS. Lovely tropical gardens and innumerable courtyards abound in the monstrous **Parque de María Luisa,** southeast of the city center. *(Open daily 8am-10pm.)* The expansive neighboring **Plaza de Espana** boasts tiled murals. **Triana,** the neighborhood west of the cathedral and across the river, was Sevilla's chaotic 16th- and 17th- century mariners' quarters. North of Triana, visit the **Museo de Arte Contemporáneo.** *(Open Tu-Sa 10am-8pm, Su 10am-3pm. 300ptas. Guided tours at 11am, noon, 5pm, and 6pm.)*

🎵🎭 ENTERTAINMENT AND NIGHTLIFE

Sevilla's reputation for gaiety is tried and true. Popular bars can be found around **C. Mateos Gago** near the cathedral, **C. Adriano** by the bullring, and **C. Betis** across the river in Triana. Sevilla is also famous for its **botellón,** where crowds of students converge in plazas or at bars along the river to start the night. In the winter, the most popular place to botellón is at Pl. Alfalfa in El Centro and in the summer, the crowds sweep towards the river in hopes of a breeze—even on "slow" nights, *terrazas* will stay open until 4am. The tourist office and stores distribute *El Giraldillo,* a free monthly magazine with complete listings on music, art exhibits, theater, dance, fairs, and film.

- ▨ **La Carbonería,** C. Levies, 18 (☎954 21 44 60), off C. Santa María La Blanca, in Santa Cruz. Live flamenco in an intimate, cave-like space. Includes a huge outdoor patio and bar (also with live music). Beer 200-275ptas. Flamenco nightly at 10:30pm. Open M-Sa 8pm-3:30am, Su 8pm-2:30am.

- ▨ **Capote Bar,** at the Pte. Isabel II, in El Centro. Make your way through the throngs of young people who start the night at this hugely popular *terraza* bar for mixed drinks and beer. Open nightly 11pm-3am.

- **La Antigua Bodeguita,** Pl. del Salvador, 6 (☎954 56 18 33), in El Centro. The crowds just can't be contained at any hour of the day in this tiny bustling bar that claims beer as their specialty. Glass of beer 125ptas, tapas 200ptas. Open daily 12:30-4pm and 8pm-midnight.

Lunar Park, Av. de Maria Luisa at Av. del Perú, across from the Lope de Vega theater, in Santa Cruz. With an ancient-rock motif resembling Stonehenge, this half-indoor, half-outdoor club has two floors for latin and pop music, as well as a dance floor just for locals. No cover. Open Th-Su 11pm-dawn.

BULLFIGHTS AND FESTIVALS

The cheapest place to buy bullfight tickets is at the ring on Po. Marqués de Contadero. However, when there's a good *cartel* (line-up), the booths on C. Sierpes, C. Velázquez, and Pl. Toros might be the only source of advance tickets (tickets 3000-13,000ptas). Sevilla's world-famous **Semana Santa** lasts from Palm Sunday to Good Friday. In each neighborhood of Sevilla, thousands of penitents in hooded cassocks guide floats, called *tronos*, lit by hundreds of candles through the streets each day. Two or three weeks after Semana Santa, the city rewards itself for its Lenten piety with the **Feria de Abril.** A spectacular array of flowers and lanterns decorates over 1000 kiosks, tents, and pavilions, collectively called *casetas.* Each has the elements necessary for a rollicking time: small kitchen, bar, and dance floor. Locals stroll from one to the next, sharing drinks and good food amid the lively music and dance.

▶ DAYTRIPS FROM SEVILLA

CÁDIZ

RENFE trains (☎956 25 43 01) arrive at Pl. Sevilla, off Av. Puerto, from Sevilla (2hr., 12 per day, 1290ptas) and Córdoba (5hr., 10-12 per day, 3700-3900ptas). Transportes Generales Comes buses (☎956 22 78 11) arrive at Pl. Hispanidad 1 from Sevilla (2hr., 11 per day, 1385ptas).

Founded by the Phoenicians in 1100 BC, Cádiz (pop. 155,000) is considered the oldest inhabited city in Europe. **Carnaval** is perhaps Spain's most dazzling party (Mar. 2-12 in 2000), while the city attracts year-round with golden, pebble-strewn **beaches** that put those of its eastern neighbors to shame. **Playa de la Caleta** is the most convenient, but better sand awaits in the new city; take bus 1 from Pl. España (115ptas) and get off at Pl. Glorieta Ingeniero (in front of Hotel Victoria) to roast at the squeaky clean ■**Playa Victoria.** Back in town, the gold-domed, 18th-century **cathedral** is considered the last great cathedral built by colonial riches. From Pl. San Juan de Dios, follow C. Pelota. (Museum open Tu-Sa 10am-1pm and 4-7pm. 500ptas. Cathedral open M-F 5:30-8pm. Free.) From the train station, walk two blocks past the fountain, with the port on your right, and look left for **Pl. San Juan de Dios** (the old town center). From the bus station, walk 5min. down Av. Puerto with the port on your left and Pl. de San Juan de Dios will be after the park on your right, with the **tourist office** at #11. (☎ 956 24 10 01. Open M-F 9am-2pm and 5-8pm.) Most *hostales* huddle around the harbor, in Pl. San Juan de Dios, and just behind it on C. Marqués de Cádiz. **Hostal Colón** is at C. Marqués de Cádiz 6. (☎ 956 28 53 51. Singles 2000ptas; doubles 3500ptas; triples 4500ptas.)

JEREZ DE LA FRONTERA

Trains (☎956 34 23 19) arrive at Pl. Estación from Sevilla (1¼hr., 12 per day, 910ptas) and Cádiz (45min., 12 per day, 430ptas). Buses (☎956 34 52 07) Sevilla (1½hr., 7-13 per day, 700ptas); Arcos (30min., 8-17 per day, 300ptas); Cádiz (1hr., 19 per day, 360ptas); and Ronda (2¾hr., 4 per day, 1320ptas).

Although unremarkable in appearance, Jerez de la Frontera (pop. 200,000) is the cradle of three staples of Andalucian culture: flamenco, Carthusian horses, and, of course, *jerez* (sherry). Most *bodegas* (wine cellars) offer tours in English, but many are closed in August. **González Byass,** C. Manuel María González, 12 , has the tour of choice, visiting royalty and celebrities, with a motorized trolley, costumed guides and trained mice that climb miniature ladders to sip the juice. (☎956 35 70 16. English tours M-F at 10:30, 11:30am, 12:30, 1:30, 5:30, and 6:30pm. 1000ptas.) From the train station, exit right, follow C. Cartuja past the bus station, continue on C. Medina, and go left at Pl. Romero Martínez on C. Cerrón, which leads to C. Santa

María, C. Lencería, and then C. Larga, to reach the **tourist office**, C. Larga 39; from the bus station, exit left and follow the directions above. (☎956 33 11 50. Open June-Aug. M-F 9am-2pm and 5-8pm, Sa-Su 10am-2pm and 5-7pm; Sept.-May M-F 8am-3pm and 4-7pm, Sa-Su 10am-2pm and 5-7pm.) Take bus L8 from the bus station or bus L1 from Pl. Arenal (10min.) to reach the **Albergue Juvenil (HI),** Av. Carrero Blanco 30. (☎956 14 39 01. Call ahead. Dorms 1100-1800ptas, under 27 800-1300ptas; nonmembers add 300ptas.)

ARCOS DE LA FRONTERA

From C. Corregidores, Transportes Generales Comes buses (☎956 70 20 15) go to Cádiz (1½hr., 6 per day 675ptas); Ronda (1¾hr., 4 per day, 950ptas); and points on the Costa del Sol (3-4hr., 1 per day, 1535-2060ptas). Los Amarillos buses (☎956 70 02 57) go to Sevilla (2hr., 2 per day, 905ptas) and Jerez (15min., 19 per day, 300ptas).

The premier *pueblo blanco* (white village) on *la ruta de los pueblos blancos*, with Roman ruins and castles at every turn, Arcos (pop. 33,000) is in essence a historic monument. Wander the winding white alleys, ruins, and hanging flowers of the **old quarter,** and marvel at the stunning view from **Pl. Cabildo.** In the square is the **Iglesia de Santa María,** a mix of Baroque, Renaissance, and Gothic styles. To reach the old quarter from the bus station, exit left, turn left, and continue 20min. uphill on C. Muñoz Vásquez as it changes names. One block to the right is the **tourist office,** on Pl. Cabildo. (☎956 70 22 64; fax 956 70 09 00. Open June-Aug. M-F 9am-2pm and 5:30-7:30pm, Sa 9am-2pm and 5-6:30pm, Su 10:30am-12:30pm; Sept.-May M-Sa 9am-2pm and 5-7pm, Sa 10am-2pm and 5-6:30pm.) **Pensión El Patio** (a.k.a. Callejón de las Monjas), C. Dean Espinosa, 4, is in the old quarter behind Iglesia de Santa María. Roomy, with fans or A/C; all rooms have bath and TV. (☎956 70 23 02. Doubles 4000ptas, with bath 6000ptas.)

RONDA

Trains (☎95 287 16 73), Av. Alférez Provisional, near Av. Andalucía, run to Algeciras (2hr., 6 per day, 910ptas). Change at Bobadilla for Málaga (2hr., 6 per day, 1225ptas); Granada (3hr., 3 per day, 1800ptas); and Sevilla (3hr., 2 per day, 2955ptas). Buses (☎95 218 70 61) go from Pl. Concepción García Redondo, 2, near Av. Andalucía, to Marbella (1½hr., 8 per day, 605ptas); Málaga (2½hr., 8 per day, 1120ptas); Cádiz (4hr., 5 per day, 1610ptas); and Sevilla (2½hr., 5 per day, 1335ptas).

Most people's strongest impression of Ronda (pop. 38,000), the birthplace of bull fighting, is the stomach-churning ascent to get there. Divided in two by a 100m gorge, Ronda was called Arunda ("surrounded by mountains") by Pliny, Ptolemy, and pfriends, German poet Rainer Maria Rilke wrote his *Spanish Elegies* here, Orson Welles had his ashes buried on a bull farm outside of town, and Hemingway loved the bullfights. The precipitous gorge, carved by the Río Guadalevín, dips below the **Puente Nuevo,** opposite Pl. España. Bullfighting aficionados charge over to Ronda's **Plaza de Toros,** Spain's oldest bullring (est. 1785) and cradle of the modern *corrida.* The **Museo Taurino** inside is filled with interesting factoids. (Open daily June-Sept. 10am-8pm; Oct.-May 10am-6pm. 500ptas.) To reach the town center from the **train station,** turn right on Av. Andalucía and follow it through Pl. Merced past the **bus station** (it becomes C. San José) until it ends. Take a left on C. Jerez, and follow it past the lush park and Pl. Toros, to **Plaza de España** and the new bridge. The **tourist office** is at Pl. España 1. (☎95 287 12 72. Open M-F 9am-2pm and 4-7pm, Sa-Su 10am-3pm.) The **Hostal Ronda Sol,** C. Almendra, 11. (☎952 87 44 97. Singles 1700ptas; doubles 2800ptas; triples 4000ptas.) Some of the best restaurants line the streets around **Pl. España** and those near **Cra. Espinel. Postal code:** 29400.

CÓRDOBA

"Sevilla is a young girl, gay, laughing, provoking—but Córdoba...Córdoba is a dear old lady."

Nowhere else are the remnants of Spain's Islamic, Jewish, and Catholic heritages so visibly intermixed as in Córdoba (pop. 315,000). This Andalucian historical and cultural melange has left Córdoba a unique artistic and architectural legacy. The famous mosque testifies to Córdoba's political and intellectual reemergence under Islamic rule (711-1263) and the influence of the Jewish philosopher Maimonides, who spearheaded the return to centrality that helped make Córdoba the seat of the Western caliphate. Córdoba, though a small city, is not overwhelmed by its incredible history. Springtime festivals, flower-filled patios, and a busy nightlife make it one of Spain's most beloved cities. Both delicate and wise, Córdoba may be a "a dear old lady," but she is far from tired.

▬ TRANSPORTATION

Trains: (☎957 40 02 02), Plaza de las Tres Culturas, Av. América. To: **Madrid** (2-6hr., 14 per day, 3700-6000ptas); **Barcelona** (10-11hr., 7 per day, 6100-8400ptas); **Cádiz** (2¾hr., 2 per day, 3700ptas; regular 3-4hr., 5 per day, 2370-3700ptas); **Granada** (4½hr., 3 per day, 2130-2785ptas); **Málaga** (3hr., 13 per day, 1650-3000ptas); and **Sevilla** (45min., 18 per day, 2300ptas). For international tickets, contact **RENFE,** Ronda de los Tejares, 10 (☎957 49 02 02).

Buses: Estacion de Autobuses, Glorieta de las Tres Culturas, s/n (☎957 40 40 40), across from the train station.

Alsina Graells Sur (☎957 27 81 00) covers most of Andalucía. To: **Algeciras** (5hr., 2 per day, 2805ptas); **Cádiz** via Los Amarillos or Comes Sur (4-5hr., 1 per day, 2120ptas); **Granada** (3hr.; 8 per day; 1635-1810ptas, round-trip 3000ptas); **Málaga** (3-3½hr.; 5 per day; 1540ptas, round-trip 2575ptas); **Marbella** (4hr., 2 per day, 2310ptas); and **Sevilla** (2hr.; 10-13 per day; 1200ptas, round-trip 1750ptas).

Bacoma (☎957 45 65 14) to: Baeza, Ubeda, Valencia, and **Barcelona** (10hr., 1 per day, 8475ptas).

Secorbus (☎902 22 92 92) provides exceptionally cheap service to **Madrid** (4½hr.; 7 per day; 1600ptas, round-trip 2560), departing from Camino de los Sastres in front of Hotel Melia.

Transportes Ureña (☎957 40 45 58) runs to **Jaén** (2hr., 7 per day 7:30am-8pm, 990ptas).

Eurobus (☎902 11 96 99) to: **Bilbao** (10¼hr., 3 per day, 4875ptas); **San Sebastián** (12hr., 3 per day, 5560ptas); and **Sevilla** (2hr., 3 per day).

Intra-provincial buses depart from Av. República and Po. Victoria: **Autocares Priego** (☎957 40 44 79) runs anywhere in the Sierra Cordobesa; **Empresa Carrera** (☎957 40 44 14) functions in the Campiña Cordobesa; **Empresa Rafael Ramírez** (☎957 42 21 77) runs buses to nearby towns and camping sites.

Public Transportation: There are 12 bus lines (☎957 25 57 00) that run through the modern parts of the city and neighborhoods in the outskirts. Most buses run from the early morning until 11pm. Check the tourist office for a listing of urban routes and to the outskirts of town. **Bus #3** makes a loop from the bus and train stations through Pl. Tendillas, along the river, and up C. Doctor Fleming. **Bus #10** will take you from the train station to Barrio Brillante (115ptas).

Taxis: Radio Taxi (☎957 76 44 44) has stands at most busy intersections. From the Judería to the bus and train stations about 500ptas; to Barrio Brillante about 600ptas.

Car Rental: Hertz (☎957 40 20 60), in the train station. Minimum age 25. From 9200ptas per day. Open M-F 8:30am-9pm, Sa 9am-1pm and 3:30-7pm, Su 9am-1pm.

✴️⁷ ORIENTATION AND PRACTICAL INFORMATION

Córdoba is split into two parts: the **old city** and the **new city.** The modern and commercial northern half extends from the train station on **Av. América** down to **Plaza de las Tendillas,** the center of the city. The old part in the south is a medieval maze known as the **Judería** (Jewish quarter). To get to the center of the city, exit left from the station and make a right onto Av. de los Mozarabes. When you reach Gta. Sargentos Provisionales, cross the park on your left and make a right on Paseo de la Victoria. Turn left on C. Concepción and walk straight into Pl. Tendillas, or take bus #3 from the front of the bus station to Pl. Tendillas.

Tourist Offices: Oficina Municipal de Turismo y Congresos (☎957 20 05 22; fax 957 20 02 77), Pl. Judá Leví, next to the youth hostel, has maps and many free brochures about festivals and events in the Cordoba region. Open M-F 8:30am-2:30pm. **Tourist Office of Andalucía,** C. Torrijos, 10 (☎957 47 12 35; fax 957 49 17 78), in the Junta de Andalucía, across from the Mezquita. From the train station, take bus #3 (bus stops

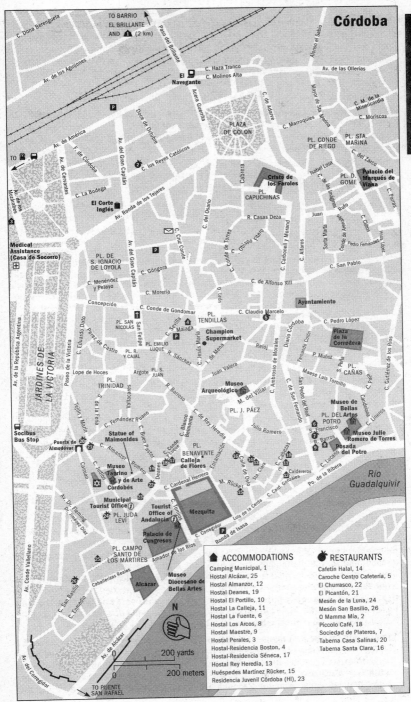

Córdoba

SPAIN

TO BARRIO
EL BRILLANTE
AND 🏕 (2 km)

C. Doña Berenguela

C. Dona Berenguela

Paso del Brillante

C. Haza Tranco

C. Molinos Alta

El Navegante

Av. de las Ollerías

Acera Guerita

C. de Adarve

C. M. de la Misericordia

C. Moriscos

Av. de los Aguijones

Doce de Octubre

C. Marroquíes

Mayor de Sta. Marina

PLAZA DE COLON

PL. CONDE DE RIEGO

PL. STA. MARINA

C. del Zarco

Av. de América

Av. F. de Córdoba

C. del Gran Capitán

C. los Reyes Católicos

Cabrera

Isabel Losa

C. de las Indignas

PL. D. GOME

Palacio del Marqués de Viana

C. Parras

TO 🚍🚌

Av. de Cervantes

C. La Bodega

Cristo de los Faroles

Juan

Rufo

Santa María

Conde de Arco

Pedro Fernández de

C. Colón

Hos. Isph

Av. de los Muzárabes

Av. de los Muzárabes

El Corte Inglés

Av. Ronda de los Tejares

PL. CAPUCHINAS

R. Casas Deza

Obispo Ftero

C. Alfaros

C. San Pablo

Medical Assistance (Casa de Socorro)

C. del Osario

C. Cruz Conde

C. de Torres

C. Conde de Torres

C. Carbonell y Morand

PL. DE S. IGNACIO DE LOYOLA

C. Menéndez y Pelayo

C. Góngora

C. Morería

C. de Alfonso XIII

Ayuntamiento

C. Pedro López

Concepción

C. del Gran Capitán

C. Conde de Gondomar

PL. TENDILLAS

C. Claudio Marcelo

Diario Córdoba

Plaza de la Corredera

PL. SAN NICOLÁS

San Felipe

C. Sevilla

C. Málaga

Jesús María

Champion Supermarket

Reloj

Fernando Colón

C. de la Feria

Paseo de la Victoria

C. Eduardo Dato

PL. R. Y CAJAL

PL. EMILIO LUQUE

R. Sánchez

I. de Mena

C. Ambrosio de Morales

C. San Pedro del Real

C. Muñoz

PL. CAÑAS

Av. de la República Argentina

JARDINES DE LA VICTORIA

Lope de Hoces

PL. S. JUAN

Argote

Juan Valera

Maese Luis Tornillo

C. Gutiérrez de los Ríos

PL. TRINIDAD

R. Barroso

Vallicanos

Museo Arqueológico

M. del Villar

PL. J. PÁEZ

C. de San Fernando

Museo de Bellas Artes

PL. DEL Artes POTRO

C. Cineros

Socibus Bus Stop

Puerta de Almodóvar

C. Fernández Pruano

Statue of Maimónides

C. Buen Pastor

C. Blanco Belmonte

C. de Rey Heredia

Julio Romero

S. Francisco

Barros

Museo Julio Romero de Torres

Posada del Potro

Av. Dr. Fleming

Tejón y Marín

C. de la Feria

Romero

C. Almanzor

Deanes

Conde

PL. BENAVENTE

Calleja de Flores

Encarnación

Calle de Osío

Sta. Ana

C. Cabezas

C. Lucano

Po. de la Ribera

Río Guadalquivir

Museo Taurino y de Arte Cordobés

Cairuán

Municipal Tourist Office ℹ

PL. JUDA LEVÍ

Tourist Office of Andalucía ℹ

C. Cardenal Herrero

M. Rücker

C. Cand. González

Calderreros

C. Corregidor

Av. Dr. Jiménez Díaz

Palacio de Congresos

Merquita

Luis de la Cerda

Ronda de Isasa

Av. Conde Vallellano

Amador de los Ríos

C. Corregidor

Caballerizas Reales

PL. CAMPO SANTO DE LOS MÁRTIRES

Alcázar

Museo Diocesano de Bellas Artes

C. San Basilio

C. Enmedio

N

Av. de Alcázar

👉

200 yards
200 meters

Av. del Corregidor

TO PUENTE SAN RAFAEL

🏠 **ACCOMMODATIONS**

Camping Municipal, 1
Hostal Alcázar, 25
Hostal Almanzor, 12
Hostal Deanes, 19
Hostal El Portillo, 10
Hostal La Calleja, 11
Hostal La Fuente, 6
Hostal Los Arcos, 8
Hostal Maestre, 9
Hostal Perales, 3
Hostal-Residencia Boston, 4
Hostal-Residencia Séneca, 17
Hostal Rey Heredia, 13
Huéspedes Martínez Rücker, 15
Residencia Juvenil Córdoba (HI), 23

🍎 **RESTAURANTS**

Cafetín Halal, 14
Caroche Centro Cafetería, 5
El Churrasco, 22
El Picantón, 21
Mesón de la Luna, 24
Mesón San Basilio, 26
O Mamma Mía, 2
Piccolo Café, 18
Sociedad de Plateros, 7
Taberna Casa Salinas, 20
Taberna Santa Clara, 16

on Av. América between the train and bus stations) along the river until the stone arch is on the right. Office is 1 block up C. Torrijos. Open May-Sept. M-F 9:30am-8pm, Sa 10am-7pm, Su 10am-2pm; Oct.-Apr. 9:30am-6pm, Su 10am-2pm.

Currency Exchange: Banco Central Hispano (☎957 47 42 67), Pl. Tendillas, charges no commission. Open June-Aug. M-F 8:30am-2:30pm; Sept.-May M-F 8:30am-2:30pm, Sa 9am-1pm. Banks and **ATMs** dot Pl. Tendillas.

Emergency: ☎091 or 092. **Police** (☎957 47 75 00), Av. Medina Azahara.

Medical Assistance: Red Cross Hospital (☎957 42 06 66; emergency ☎957 22 22 22), Po. Victoria. English spoken. **Ambulance,** ☎29 55 70.

24-Hour Pharmacy: On a rotating basis. Refer to the list posted outside the pharmacy in Pl. Tendillas or the local newspaper.

Internet Access: El Navegante Café Internet, C. Llanos del Pretorio, 1 (☎957 49 75 36), at the intersection of Av. América and Paso del Brillante. A bar with a nouveau-nautical theme. 300ptas per 30min., 500 per hr. Open daily 8am-4pm and 5pm-3am.

Post Office: C. Cruz Conde, 15 (☎902 19 71 97), 2 blocks up from Pl. Tendillas. Lista de Correos. Open M-F 8:30am-8:30pm, Sa 9:30am-2pm. **Postal Code:** 14070.

▚ ACCOMMODATIONS

Hostels in Córdoba are quite impressive: charming, well-maintained, and affordable. Córdoba is especially crowded during Semana Santa (the week before Easter) and from May through September; you may have to call two to three months in advance for reservations. The **Judería's** whitewashed walls, narrow, twisting streets, and proximity to major sights make it the nicest and most convenient area in which to stay. Take bus #3 from the train station to Pl. Tendillas and walk down C. Jesus María veering right as the streets curve. The white walls signal the Judería. However, between the Mezquita and C. de San Fernando, the quieter, more residential area of **old Córdoba** is still near the sights but a step away from the tourists. Buses stop along C. de San Fernando, the main corridor of the area.

Residencia Juvenil Córdoba (HI), Pl. Juda Leví (☎957 29 01 66), next to the municipal tourist office and a 2min. walk from the Mezquita. The place to stay in Córdoba. Huge, modern, and antiseptic, all rooms are doubles or quads with bath. A/C. Public telephones. Breakfast included, lunch and dinner 650ptas each. Towels 175ptas. Reception 24hr. Reservations recommended. 1605ptas per person; ages 26 and up 2140ptas. 300ptas extra per day for nonmembers for 6-night stay to gain membership.

Hostal Deanes, C. Deanes, 6 (☎957 29 37 44). From the top left corner of the Mezquita take C. Cardenal, then a sharp right onto C. Romero which becomes C. Deanes. The hostel will be on the left. Traditional patio is shared with a popular restaurant and bar. No reservations. Doubles 4000ptas, with bath 5000ptas.

Hostal La Fuente, C. San Fernando, 51 (☎957 48 78 27 or 957 48 14 78; fax 957 48 78 27), between C. San Francisco and C. Julio Romero. Spanish authenticity meets modern comforts. All rooms with bath, some with TV. Breakfast 275ptas. Singles 3000ptas; doubles 4000-5000ptas; 1800ptas per person for large groups.

Hostal Maestre, C. Romero Barros, 4-5 (☎957 47 53 95), off C. de San Fernando. All rooms have private bathrooms, some have TVs. English spoken. Parking 900ptas per day. Singles 2500-2850ptas; doubles 4000-5000ptas; triples 5000-6500pta; 10% discount for group rates.

Huéspedes Martínez Rücker, Martínez Rücker, 14 (☎957 47 25 62). Take a right off the right side of the Mezquita. Rooms are clean and sparse. Modern common bathrooms. All rooms have fans. 1500-2000ptas per person; up to 4 in a room.

Camping Municipal, Av. Brillante, 50 (☎957 28 21 65). From the train station, turn left on Av. América, left on Av. Brillante, and walk uphill for about 20min; or take bus #10 or 11 from Av. Cervantes near the station. Pool, currency exchange, supermarket, restaurant, free hot showers, laundry service. Camping equipment for rent. Wheelchair accessible. Individual tents 400ptas, family tents 560ptas; tax not included.

🍴 FOOD

The Mezquita area attracts nearly as many high-priced eateries as tourists to eat in them, but a five-minute walk in any direction yields local specialties at reasonable prices. In the evenings, locals converge at the outdoor terrazas between **C. Severo Ochoa** and **C. Dr. Jimenez Diaz** for drinks and tapas before dinner. Cheap eateries cluster farther away from the Judería in **Barrio Cruz Conde**, around **Av. Menéndez Pidal and Pl. Tendillas**. Regional specialties include *salmorejo* (a gazpacho-like cream soup topped with hard-boiled eggs and pieces of ham) and *rabo de toro* (bull's tail simmered in tomato sauce). **Supermarket Champion**, C. Jesús María, lies half a block from Pl. Tendillas. (Open M-Sa 9:15am-9:15pm.)

El Picantón, C. F. Ruano, 19, 1 block from the Puerta de Almodovar. From the top right corner of the Mezquita, walk up Romero and turn left. Take ordinary tapas, pour on some *salsa picante*, stick it in a roll, and voilà, you've got lunch (150-300ptas). Nothing else as cheap or as filling. Open daily 10am-3pm and 8pm-midnight.

Taberna Santa Clara, C. Osio, 2 (☎957 47 50 36). From the right side of the Mezquita, take C. Martinez Rucker and turn left. Women of Córdoba stop by in the early evening to have a glass of their very own white wine, La Peresosa. Two pages of meat-free dishes and fresh fish on F. *Menú* 1300ptas, main dishes 800-1800ptas, salads 650ptas. Open Th-Tu 12am-4pm and 7-11pm.

Mesón San Basilio, C. San Basilio, 19 (☎957 29 70 07), to the left of the Alcázar, past Campo Santo de los Martires. The locals love it, and so will you. *Menú del día* 1000ptas, *raciones* 450-2000ptas, meat and fish dishes 800-1750ptas. Open daily 1-4pm and 8pm-midnight.

👁 SIGHTS

▨ LA MEZQUITA

☎957 47 05 12. Open daily Apr.-June 10am-7:30pm; July-Oct. 10am-7pm; Nov-March 10am-6pm. 900ptas, ages 8-13 450ptas. Same ticket valid for Museo Diocesano de Bellas Artes. Last ticket sold 30min. before closing. Opens at 8:30am for Mass M-Sa 9:30am; Su 11am, noon, and 1pm.

Built in 784 on the site of a Visigoth Basilica, Córdoba's mosque is considered the most important Islamic monument in the Western world. Over the next two centuries, this architectural masterpiece was enlarged to cover an area the size of several city blocks with more than 850 columns, making it the largest mosque in the Islamic world at the time. Made of granite, jasper, and marble, the pillars are capped by brick-and-stone arches, creating the illusion of height and spaciousness. Visitors enter through the **Patio de los Naranjos,** an arcaded courtyard featuring carefully spaced orange trees, palm trees, and fountains, where the dutiful would wash before prayer. The **Torre del Alminar** encloses remains of the minaret from where the muezzin would call for prayer.

The most elaborate additions, consisting of the dazzling **mihrab** (prayer niche) and the triple **maksourah** (caliph's niche) were created in the 10th century. The mihrab, whose prayer arch faces Mecca, formerly housed a gilded copy of the Koran; pilgrims circled it seven times on their knees, as evidenced by the worn stones. The intricate gold, pink, and blue marble Byzantine mosaics shimmering across its arches were given by the Emperor Constantine VII to the Cordobés caliphs; his gift is estimated to weigh close to 35 tons.

At the far end of the Mezquita lies the **Capilla Villaviciosa,** where Caliphal vaulting, greatly influential in later Spanish architecture, appeared for the first time. It was the first Christian chapel to be built in the mosque, completed in 1371. Thus began the transition of the mosque to a place of Christian worship. The townspeople were far from pleased, and even Carlos V lamented the changes to the Mezquita, griping: "You have destroyed something unique to create something commonplace." What remains, though, is far from commonplace.

IN AND AROUND THE JUDERÍA

A combined ticket for the Alcázar, Museo Taurino y de Arte Cordobés, and Museo Julio Romero (see Outside the Judería, below) is available at all three locations. 1075ptas, students 550ptas. Individually, admission to each sight costs 450ptas. F free.

ALCÁZAR. Along the river on the left side of the Mezquita lies the Alcázar. Built in 1328 during the Reconquest, the building served as both a fortress and residence for Alfonso XI. Fernando and Isabel bade Columbus farewell here, and from 1490 to 1821 it served as a headquarters for the Inquisition. Inside, the museum displays first-century Roman mosaics and a 3rd-century Roman marble sarcophagus. (☎957 42 01 51. *Open May-Sept. Tu-Sa 10am-2pm and 6-8pm, Su 9:30am-3pm; Oct.-Apr. Tu-Sa 10am-2pm and 4:30-6:30pm, Su 9:30am-3pm. Illuminated gardens open July-Aug. 8pm-midnight. 300ptas, students 150ptas. Friday free.*)

MUSEO TAURINO Y DE ARTE CORDOBÉS. The museum is dedicated to the history and lore of the bullfight. The main exhibit includes a replica of the tomb of Spain's most famous matador, Manolete, and the hide of the bull that killed him. (*Pl. Maimonides.* ☎957 20 10 56. *Open May-Sept. Tu-Sa 10am-2pm and 6-8pm, Su 9:30am-3pm; Oct.-Apr. M-Sa 10am-2pm and 5-7pm, Su 9:30am-3pm. 450ptas, students 225ptas, seniors free. Friday free.*)

MUSEO DIOCESANO DE BELLAS ARTES. The works of 13th- to 18th-century local artists are on display in this splendid 17th-century palace. (*C. Torrijos, across from the Mezquita in the Palacio de Congresos.* ☎957 47 93 75. *Open June-Sept. M-F 9:30am-3pm, Sa 9:30am-1:30pm; Oct.-Mar. M-F 9:30am-1:30pm and 3:30-5:30pm, Sa 9:30am-1:30pm. 150ptas, under 12 free. Free with admission to Mezquita.*)

OUTSIDE THE JUDERÍA

MUSEO DE BELLAS ARTES. This museum now occupies the building that was once Fernando and Isabel's Hospital de la Caridad. Its small collection displays works by Córdoban artists. Check out the sculptures by Mateo Inurria and Juan de Mesa on the ground floor. (*Pl. Potro, 5-10 min. from the Mezquita.* ☎957 47 33 45. *Open Tu 3-8pm, W-Sa 9am-8pm, Su 9am-3pm. 250ptas; EU citizens free.*)

PALACIO DEL MARQUÉS DE VIANA. An elegant 14th-century mansion, the palace displays 12 quintessentially Córdoban patios complete with sprawling gardens and majestic fountains, as well as tapestries, furniture, and porcelain. (*Pl. Don Gome, 2. A 20min. walk from the Mezquita.* ☎957 48 01 34. *Open June 16-Sept. M-Sa 9am-2pm; Oct.-May M-Sa 10am-1pm and 4-6pm; closed June 1-15. Patio only 200ptas. Guided tours every hr. 500ptas, children 200ptas.*)

OTHER SIGHTS. Near the Palacio del Marqués de Viana, in Pl. Capuchinos (a.k.a. Pl. Dolores) and next to the monastery is the **Cristo de los Faroles** (Christ of the Lanterns). This is one of the most famous religious icons in Spain and is the site of frequent all-night vigils. The eight lanterns that are lit at night symbolize the eight provinces of Andalucía. Facing the Museo de Bellas Artes and the Museo Julio Romero de Torres is the **Posada del Potro,** a 14th-century inn mentioned in *Don Quixote.* Across the river from the Mezquita stands the **Torre de la Calahorra,** a Muslim military tower which was built in 1369 to protect the Roman bridge and now houses a museum that covers Cordoba's cultures during the Middle Ages.

🎵🖼 ENTERTAINMENT AND NIGHTLIFE

From the first weekend of June until the heat subsides, the cool **Barrio Brillante,** uphill from Av. América, is the place to be at night. Throngs of well-dressed, young Codobeses walk the streets, hopping from one packed outdoor bar to another until reaching a dance club. Bus #10 goes to Brillante from the train station until about 11pm; a taxi should cost 500-900ptas. If you're walking, head up Av. Brillante passing along the way **El Rocio, Pub BSO,** and **El Navegante** at C. Llanos de Pretorio. Once in Barrio Brillante, where C. Poeta Emilia Prados meets C. Poeta Juan Ramon Jimenez, go through **Cafeteria Terra** to discover a massive open-air patio where the backs of nearly ten bars (**Havanna, Canaveral,** and **El Puerto** to name a few) converge. Proceed down Av. Brillante toward the city center, passing the popular nightclub **El Cachao**, as well as **Pub La Mondoa, Club Pon Luis, Club Kachomba**, and **Bar Chicote** along the way. During the cooler months of winter, the nightlife centers around the pubs surrounding the Universidad de Cordoba, mostly on C. Antonio Maura and C. Camino de los Sastres. From there, the masses move to the bars lining Av. Gran Capitan, Av. Ronda de los Tejares, and C. Cruz Conde. Pick up a free copy of *La Guía de Ocio*, a monthly guide to cultural events and nightlife, at the tourist office.

The month of May is a never-ending party, beginning with the **Concurso de los Cruces** the first week in May. Organizations sponsor the decoration of crosses that go up for display around the city. During the **Festival de los Patios,** beginning the first weekend in May and lasting for two weeks, Córdoba is transformed into a lush garden, when more than 150 private patios are open to the public. The last week in May brings the riotous week-long **Feria de Nuestra Señora de la Salud** (commonly known as *La Feria*), for which thousands of Córdoban women don colorful, traditional apparel while bullfights are held daily. The **Concurso Nacional de Arte Flamenco** (National Flamenco Contest) is held every third year during May. The next one will be in 2001.

DAYTRIPS FROM CÓRDOBA

MADINAT AL-ZAHRA

*Reaching Madinat Al-Zahra takes some effort if you don't go with an organized tour. The O-1 **bus** leaves from Av. República Argentina in Córdoba for Cruce Medina Azahara; from there you can walk 45min. to the palace. (Info ☎957 25 57 00; or ask at the tourist office. Departs every hr. 115ptas.) **Medina**, ☎957 32 91 30. Open May-Sept. Tu-Sa 10am-2pm and 6-8:30pm, Su 10am-2pm; Oct.-Apr. Tu-Sa 10am-2pm and 4-6:30pm, Su 10am-2pm. Admission 250ptas, EU citizens free. Córdoba Vision offers a 2½-hour guided visit to the site in English. (☎957 23 17 34. 2500ptas.)*

Built in the Sierra Morena, Córdoba's mountain range, by Abd al-Rahman III for his favorite wife, Azahara, this 10th-century medina was considered one of the greatest palaces of its time. The site, long thought to be mythical, was discovered in the mid-19th century and excavated in the early 20th century, and today is one of Spain's most impressive archaeological finds. The Medina Azahara is divided into three terraces: one for the palace (*alcázar*), another for the servants' living quarters, and a third for an enclosed garden and almond grove. After moving from Granada, Azahara missed the Sierra Nevada. To appease her, Abderramán planted the white-blossoming almond groves as a substitute for her beloved snow. The Salón de Abd al-Rahman III, also known as the *salón rico*, on the lower terraces, is being restored to its original intricate and geometrical beauty.

OTHER DAYTRIPS FROM CÓRDOBA

CÁDIZ. This city offers a little of everything to its visitors—a metropolis trimmed by golden sand beaches (see p. 838).

MÁLAGA. Known more for its bars than its untouched sands, Málaga has the requisite beachtown monuments and a welcoming modern atmosphere (see p. 852).

GIBRALTAR

E.T. PHONE HOME Gibraltar's phone code is ☎9567 from Spain; ☎350 from Britain; and ☎350 from the US. For **BT Direct** dial ☎84 00; **USA Direct** ☎88 00.

Anglophiles and homesick Brits will get jolly well excited over Gibraltar's fish 'n' chips, while everyone else goes batty over the tax-free cigarettes. Britain and Spain have long contested the enclave, and there remains a massive British military presence. Although pesetas are accepted everywhere (except in pay phones), the **pound sterling (£)** is the preferred method of payment in Gibraltar. Despite the Rock's history and refreshingly diverse population, it's basically a tourist trap. Admire the view of Iberia and the Straits from the imposing Rock, speak some English, then scurry back to the Spanish coast. Cable cars run from the southern end of Main St. to the northern tip of the massif known as **Top of the Rock,** stopping halfway up at **Apes' Den,** home to a colony of monkeys that has inhabited the Rock since before the Moorish invasion. The ruins of a Moorish wall crumble down the road from the cable car station to the south, near the spooky chambers of **St. Michael's Cave.** (Cable car every 10min. M-Sa 9:30am-6pm. UK£3.65 with 1hr. walk down, round-trip UK£4.90; includes Apes' Den and cave.)

Buses arrive in the bordering Spanish town of **La Línea** from Madrid (7hr., 2 per day, 3280ptas); Algeciras (40min., every 30min., 235ptas); Cádiz (3hr., 5 per day, 1500ptas); Granada (5-6hr., 2 per day, 2475ptas); Málaga (3¼hr., 4 per day, 1270ptas); Marbella (1¾hr., 4 per day, 695ptas); and Sevilla (6hr., 3 per day, 2640ptas). From the bus station, walk toward the Rock; the border is 5min. away. After passing Spanish customs and Gibraltar's passport control, cross the airport tarmac and head along the highway into town (20min.) or catch bus #9 or 10 (UK40p or 100ptas). The **tourist office,** in Duke of Kent House, Cathedral Sq., is across the park from the Gibraltar Museum. (☎450 00; fax 749 43. Open M-F 9am-5:30pm.) To get to **Queen's Hotel,** 1 Boyd St., walk through Southport Gate, bear right, and enter around the back. (☎740 00. Breakfast included. Laundry. Singles UK£36; doubles UK£30-40; triples UK£60.) **Emile Youth Hostel Gibraltar,** on Line Wall Rd., is opposite the square at the beginning of Main St. (☎511 06. Breakfast included. Lockout 10:30am-4:30pm. Curfew 11:30pm. Dorms UK£12; singles UK£15; doubles UK£26.) There's a **Safeway** in the Europort commercial complex. (Open M-Sa 8am-8pm.)

ALGECIRAS

Algeciras has some pleasant older areas, but most tourists see only the dingy port, which offers easy access to Gibraltar and Morocco; Moroccan migrant workers, Spanish army recruits, and tourists traffic the area day and night. RENFE **trains** (☎902 24 02 02) run from Ctra. Cádiz, way down C. Juan de la Cierva, to: Madrid (6hr., 5 per day, 5200-9100ptas); Córdoba (5hr., 5 per day, 2575-4500ptas); Granada (4hr., 4 per day, 2415-2665ptas); and Málaga (3½hr., 2 per day, 2100ptas). Empresa Portillo **buses** (☎956 65 10 55) leave from Av. Virgen del Carmen 15 for Granada (5hr., 2 per day, 2595ptas) and the Costa del Sol. Linesur La Valenciana (☎956 66 76 49) runs from C. Juan de la Cierva 5 to Sevilla (3hr., 3 per day, 1985ptas). Transportes Generales Comes (☎956 65 34 56) goes from C. San Bernardo 1 to La Línea/Gibraltar (45min., every 30min., 235ptas). To get from the train or bus stations to the **tourist office,** on C. Juan de la Cierva, follow C. San Bernardo/C. Juan de la Cierva along the tracks toward the port, past a parking lot on the left. (☎956 57 26 36; fax 956 57 04 75. Open M-F 9am-2pm.) To get to the **ferry** port from the tourist office, continue down C. Juan de la Cierva and turn left on Av. Virgen del Carmen. Hostels cluster around **C. José Santacana,** parallel to Av. Marina one block inland. To get to **Hostal Rif,** C. Rafael de Muro 11, follow C. Santacana into the market square, bear left around the kiosk, and continue one block up C. Rafael del Muro. (☎956 65 49 53. Singles 1200-1500ptas; doubles 2400ptas; quads 4800ptas.) **Hostal Residencia Versailles,** is at C. Moutero Ríos 12, off C. Cayetano del Toro. (☎956 65 42 11. Singles 2500ptas; doubles 3300-4000ptas; triples with bath 5500ptas.)

GRANADA

"Give him alms, woman! For there is nothing crueler in life than to be blind in Granada," proclaims an inscription in the spectacular red-clay Alhambra, the palace-fortress complex in the hills of Granada. The last Muslim stronghold in Spain, Granada was lost by the ruler Boabdil to Catholic monarchs Fernando and Isabel in 1492. Although the Christians torched all the mosques and the lower city, embers of Granada's Arab essence still linger. The Albaicín, an enchanting maze of Moorish houses and twisting alleys, is Spain's best-preserved Arab settlement and the only part of the Muslim city to survive the Reconquest intact.

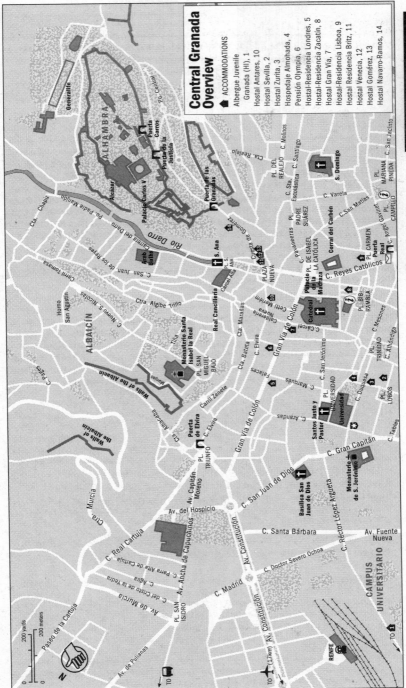

Central Granada Overview

▲ ACCOMMODATIONS

Albergue Juvenile
Granada (HI), 1
Hostal Antares, 10
Hostal Sevilla, 2
Hostal Zurita, 3
Hospedaje Almohada, 4
Pensión Olympia, 6
Hostal-Residencia Londres, 5
Hostal-Residencia Zacatín, 8
Hostal Gran Vía, 7
Hostal-Residencia Lisboa, 9
Hostal Residencia Britz, 11
Hostal Venecia, 12
Hostal Gomérez, 13
Hostal Navarro-Ramos, 14

▄ TRANSPORTATION

Flights: Airport (☎958 24 52 37), 17km west of the city. A **Salidas** bus (☎958 13 13 09) runs from Gran Vía, in front of the cathedral (M-Sa 5 per day, Su 2 per day; 425ptas). A **Taxi** to the airport costs 2000ptas.

Trains: RENFE Station (☎902 24 02 02), Av. Andaluces. To: **Madrid** (5-6hr., 2 per day, 3800ptas); **Algeciras** (5-7hr., 3 per day, 2675ptas); **Barcelona** (12-13hr., 2 per day, 6500ptas); and **Sevilla** (4-5hr., 5 per day, 2665ptas).

Buses: Station on Ctra. Madrid, near C. Arzobispo Pedro de Castro. **Alsina Graells** (☎958 18 54 80) runs to: **Córdoba** (3hr., 9 per day, 1540ptas); **Sevilla** (3hr., 9 per day, 2380ptas); **La Línea/Madrid** (5hr., 10 per day, 1980ptas); **Algeciras** (5hr., 6 per day, 2595ptas); and **Gibraltar** (4hr., 10 per day, 2445ptas). **Bacoma** (☎958 15 75 57) goes to: **Alicante** (6hr., 5 per day, 3410ptas); **Barcelona** (14hr., 3 per day, 8055ptas); and **Valencia** (8hr., 4 per day, 4995ptas).

Public Transportation: Take bus #10 from the bus station to the youth hostel, C. de Ronda, C. Recogidas, or C. Acera de Darro; or bus #3 from the bus station to Av. Constitución, Gran Vía, or Pl. Isabel la Católica. "Bus Alhambra" leaves from Pl. Nueva. All buses 120ptas, *bonobus* (15 tickets) 1000ptas. Handy free map at the tourist office.

Car Rental: Atasa, Pl. Cuchilleros, 1 (☎ 958 22 40 04; fax 958 22 77 95). Cheapest car 46,000ptas per week with unlimited mileage and insurance. Prices rise with shorter rentals. Must be at least 20 and have had a license for at least 1 year.

▄▟ ORIENTATION AND PRACTICAL INFORMATION

The geographic center of Granada is the small **Plaza de Isabel la Católica,** the intersection of the city's two main arteries, **Calle de los Reyes Católicos** and **Gran Vía de Colón.** To reach Gran Vía and the **cathedral** from the train station, walk three blocks up Av. Andaluces to take bus #3-6, 9, or 11 from Av. Constitución; from the bus station, take bus #3. Two short blocks uphill on C. Reyes Católicos sits **Plaza Nueva.** Downhill on C. Reyes Católicos lies Pl. Carmen, site of the **Ayuntamiento** and **Puerta Real.** The **Alhambra** commands the steep hill up from Pl. Nueva.

Tourist Office: Oficina Provincial, Pl. Mariana Pineda, 10 (☎958 22 66 88; fax 958 22 89 16; www.dipgra.es). From Pta. Real, turn right onto C. Angel Ganivet, then take a right 2 blocks later to reach the plaza. Open M-F 9:30am-7pm, Sa 10am-2pm.

American Express: C. Reyes Católicos, 31 (☎958 22 45 12), between Pl. Isabel la Católica and Pta. Real. Exchanges money, cashes checks, and holds mail for members. Open M-F 9am-1:30pm and 2-9pm, Sa 10am-2pm and 3-7pm.

Luggage Storage: At the train and bus stations (400ptas). Open daily 4-9pm.

Laundromat: C. La Paz, 19. From Pl. Trinidad, take C. Alhóndiga, turn right on C. La Paz, and walk 2 blocks. Wash 400ptas per load; dry 100ptas for 15min. Open M-F 9:30am-2pm and 4:30-8:30pm, Sa 9am-2pm.

Emergency: ☎091 or 092. **Police,** C. Duquesa, 21 (☎958 24 81 00). English spoken.

Pharmacy: Farmacia Gran Vía, Gran Vía, 6 (☎958 22 29 90). Open M-F 9:30am-2pm and 5-8:30pm.

Medical Assistance: Clínica de San Cecilio, C. Dr. Oloriz, 16 (☎958 28 02 00 or 958 27 20 00), on the road to Jaén. **Ambulance,** ☎958 28 44 50.

Internet Access: Net (☎958 22 69 19) has 3 locations: C. Santa Escolástica, 13, up C. Pavaneras from Pl. Isabel la Católica; Pl. de los Girones, 3, 1 block away from first locale; C. Buensucesco, 22, 1 block from Pl. Trinidad. 100ptas per hr. All open M-Sa 9am-1am, Su 3pm-1am.

Post Office: (☎958 22 48 35; fax 958 22 36 41), Pta. Real, on the corner of C. Acera de Darro and C. Angel Ganinet. Lista de Correos and **faxes.** Open M-F 8am-9pm, Sa 9:30am-2pm. Wires money M-F 8:30am-2:30pm. **Postal Code:** 18009.

ACCOMMODATIONS

Near **Pl. Nueva,** hostels line Cuesta de Gomérez, the street leading uphill to the Alhambra. The area around C. Mesones and C. Alhóndiga is close to the cathedral; hostels cluster around **Pl. Trinidad,** at the end of C. Mesones as you approach from Pta. Real. Hostels are sprinkled along **Gran Vía.** Call ahead during *Semana Santa.*

Hostal Venecia, Cuesta de Gomérez, 2, 3rd floor (☎958 22 39 87). Wake up to a soothing cup of tea, candles, and incense. Singles 1800ptas; doubles 3500ptas; triples and quads 1700ptas per person.

Hostal Residencia Britz, Cuesta de Gomérez, 1 (☎/fax 958 22 36 52), on the corner of Pl. Nueva. Laundry 600ptas. 24hr. reception. Singles 2500ptas, with bath 4000ptas; doubles 4100ptas, with bath 5700ptas.

Hospedaje Almohada, C. Postigo de Zarate, 4 (☎958 20 74 46). Walk 1 block from Pl. Trinidad along C. Duquesa; it's to the right down C. Málaga. Guests enjoy socializing in the courtyard, living room, and kitchen. Laundry 500ptas per load. Singles 2000ptas; doubles 3700ptas. Longer stays common (33,000-36,000ptas per month).

Hostal Gomérez, Cuesta de Gomérez, 10 (☎958 22 44 37). Clean rooms with firm beds. Laundry 1000ptas. Singles 1700ptas; doubles 2800ptas; triples 3800ptas.

Hostal Antares, C. Cetti Meriém, 10 (☎958 22 83 13), on the corner of C. Elvira, 1 block from Gran Vía. Spotless and cheap in a great location, 1 block from the cathedral. All rooms have balconies and sinks. Singles 2500ptas; doubles 3500ptas, with bath 5500ptas; triples 5250ptas.

Hostal Navarro-Ramos, Cuesta de Gomérez, 21 (☎958 25 05 55). Comfortable and cool in the evening. Small balconies in some rooms. Showers 150ptas. Singles 1600ptas; doubles 2600ptas, with bath 4000ptas; triples with bath 5300ptas.

Hostal-Residencia Lisboa, Pl. Carmen, 29 (☎958 22 14 13). Take C. Reyes Católicos from Pl. Isabel la Católica. Phones and fans. Singles 2700ptas, with bath 4000ptas; doubles 4000ptas, with bath 5800ptas; triples 5400ptas, with bath 7800ptas.

Hostal Zurita, Pl. Trinidad, 7 (☎958 27 50 20). Beautiful rooms, high-quality beds, remote-controlled A/C, and 24hr. hot water. Singles 2000ptas; doubles 4000ptas, with bath 5000ptas; triples 5000ptas, with bath 7000ptas.

Hostal-Residencia Zacatín, C. Ermita, 11 (☎958 22 11 55). Enter through the Alcaicería archway from C. Reyes Católicos; C. Ermita is on the left. Ideal location. Singles 1900ptas, with bath 2700ptas; doubles 3200ptas, with bath 4400ptas.

Hostal Gran Vía, Gran Vía, 17 (☎958 27 92 12), about 4 blocks from Pl. Isabel la Católica. Clean rooms all with fans. Singles with shower 4500ptas; doubles 3000ptas, with shower 3500ptas, with bath 4500ptas; triples with bath 5500ptas.

Hostal-Residencia Londres, Gran Vía, 29, 6th fl. (☎958 27 80 34). Pretty rooms and a big patio with views of the Alhambra. 1 large bathroom for every 2 bedrooms. Singles 2500ptas; doubles 3500ptas; 1500ptas per additional person.

Albergue Juvenil Granada (HI), Ramón y Cajal, 2 (☎958 00 29 00 or 958 00 29 01; fax 958 00 29 08). From the bus station take bus #10; from the train station #11; ask the driver to stop at El Estadio de la Juventud. Spacious rooms with comfortable beds. 24hr. reception. Towels 175ptas. Dorms 1800ptas, over 26 2300ptas; to join non-HI guests can pay an extra 300ptas per night for 6 nights.

Camping: Sierra Nevada, Av. Madrid, 107 (☎958 15 00 62). Take bus #3 or 10. Lots of shady trees, modern facilities, and free hot showers. 560ptas per person, per tent, and per vehicle. Children under 10 460ptas. Open Mar.-Oct.

FOOD

Granada offers a variety of ethnic restaurants to emancipate your taste buds from the fried-fish-and-pig-products doldrums. Cheap and tasty cuisine can be found in and around the **Albaicín.** Near Pl. Nueva and Pl. Trinidad, the usual *menú* fare awaits. The adventurous eat well in Granada—try *tortilla sacromonte* (omelette with calf's brains, bull testicles, ham, shrimp, and veggies), *sesos a la romana* (batter-fried calf's brains), and *rabo de toro* (bull's tail). Get groceries at **Supermercado T. Mariscal,** C. Genil (open M-F 9:30am-2pm and 5-9pm, Sa 9:30am-2pm.)

La Nueva Bodega, C. Cetti Meriém, 9 (☎958 22 59 34), out of Pl. Nueva on a small side street off C. Elvira. Popular with locals and tourists. *Menús* 1000-1100ptas. *Bocadillos* 275ptas. Open daily noon-midnight.

Naturi Albaicín, C. Calderería Nueva, 10 (☎958 22 06 27). Excellent vegetarian cuisine. *Menús* 950-1150ptas. Open Sa-Th 1-4pm and 7-11pm, F 7-11pm.

Las Cuevas, Placeta de San Gregorio, 30 (☎958 22 68 33), at the top of C. Calderería Nueva. A delightful selection of local main dishes served at outdoor tables. Main dishes 650-900ptas, *raciones* 600-1200ptas. Open daily noon-4am.

Botánico Cafe, C. Málaga, 3 (☎958 27 15 98), 2 blocks from Pl. Trinidad. Manhattan meets Spanish modernity at this student hangout. Main dishes 800-1500ptas. Open M-Th 10am-3am, Su noon-1am.

👁 SIGHTS

▨ THE ALHAMBRA

Follow C. Cuesta de Gomérez from Pl. Nueva, and be prepared to pant (20min.). Or take the Alhambra-Neptuno microbus (every 5min., 120ptas) from Pl. Isabel la Católica or Pl. Nueva. ☎958 22 15 03; fax 958 21 05 84. Open Apr.-Sept. daily 8:30am-8pm; Oct.-Mar. M-Sa 9am-5:45pm. Nighttime visits June-Sept. Tu, Th, and Sa 10-11:30pm; Oct.-May Sa 8-10pm. 1000ptas, free for the disabled and children under 8. Limited to 7700 visitors per day June-Sept., 6300 Oct.-May, so get there early to stand in line. Enter the Palace of the Nazarites (Alcázar) during the time specified on your ticket, but stay as long as desired. It is possible to reserve tickets a few days in advance at banks.

"If you have died without seeing the Alhambra, you have not lived." From the streets of Granada, the Alhambra appears simple, blocky, faded—but up close the fortress-palace reveals its astoundingly elaborate detail. The first Nazarite King Alhamar built the fortress **Alcazaba,** the section of the complex with the oldest recorded history. A dark, spiraling staircase leads to the **Torre de la Vela** (watchtower), where visitors get a great 360° view of Granada and the surrounding mountains. Follow signs to the *Palacio Nazaries* to see the stunningly ornate **Alcázar,** a royal palace built for the Moorish rulers Yusuf I (1333-1354) and Mohammed V (1354-1391), where tourists gape at dripping stalactite archways, multicolored tiles, and sculpted fountains. Fernando and Isabel restored the Alcázar after they drove the Moors from Spain. Two generations later, Emperor Carlos V demolished part of it to make way for his **Palacio de Carlos V.** Although glaringly incongruous when juxtaposed with such Moorish splendor, the palace is considered by many one of the most beautiful Renaissance buildings in Spain. Over a bridge are the blossoms, cypresses, and waterways of **El Generalife,** the sultan's vacation retreat.

THE ALBAICÍN. The Moors built their first fortress in this fascinating and gorgeous old Arab quarter. After the Reconquest, a small Arab population clung to the neighborhood on this hill until their expulsion in the 17th century. A labyrinth of steep slopes and dark narrow alleys, the Albaicín warrants caution at night. Take C. Acera de Darro from Pl. Nueva, climb the Cuesta del Chapiz on the left, then wander aimlessly through Muslim ramparts past whitewashed walls dripping with bright flowers. The terrace adjacent to **Iglesia de San Nicolás** affords the city's best view of the Alhambra, especially in winter, when snow adorns the Sierra Nevada. (*Bus #12 runs from beside the cathedral to C. Pagés, at the top of the Albaicín. Another Alhambra bus goes from Pl. Nueva to the top; from there, walk down C. Agua through Pta. Arabe.*)

OTHER SIGHTS. Downhill from the Alhambra's Arab splendor, the Capilla Real (Royal Chapel), Fernando and Isabel's private chapel, exemplifies Christian Granada. The **crypt** houses their lead caskets. The **sacristy** houses Isabel's private **art collection,** which favors 15th-century Flemish and German artists, as well as the glittering **royal jewels.** (☎958 22 92 39. Capilla Real and Sacristy both open Apr.-Sept. M-Sa

SPAIN

*10:30am-1pm and 4-7pm; Oct.-Mar. M-Sa 10:30am-1pm and 3:30-6:30pm, Su 11am-1pm.
350ptas.)* The adjacent **cathedral** was built from 1523 to 1704 by Fernando and Isabel upon the foundation of an Arab mosque. The first purely Renaissance cathedral in Spain, its Corinthian pillars support an astonishingly high (45m) vaulted nave. (☎958 22 29 59. *Open daily Apr.-Sept. 10:30am-1:30pm and 4-7pm; Oct.-Mar. M-Sa 10:30am-1:30pm and 3:30-6:30pm, Su 11am-1:30pm. 350ptas.)*

🎵 🍸 ENTERTAINMENT AND NIGHTLIFE

Entertainment listings are near the back of the daily paper, the *Ideal* (120ptas), under *Cine y Espectáculos;* the Friday supplement lists bars and special events. The *Guía del Ocio,* sold at newsstands (100ptas), lists clubs, pubs, and cafes. The tourist office also distributes a monthly guide, *Cultura en Granada.* Tourists and locals alike flock to **Los Jardines Neptuno,** on C. Arabial, near the Neptuno shopping center at the base of C. Recogidas for **flamenco.** (☎958 52 25 33. Cover 3800ptas; includes 1 drink.) A smoky, intimate setting awaits at **Eshavira** (☎958 29 08 29), on C. Postigo de la Cuna, in an alley off C. Azacayes, between C. Elvira and Gran Vía.

Perhaps the most boisterous nightspots belong to **C. Pedro Antonio de Alarcón,** running from Pl. Albert Einstein to Ancha de Gracia, while hip new bars and clubs line **C. Elvira** from Cárcel to C. Cedrán. Gay bars cluster around Carrera del Darro; a complete list of gay clubs and bars is available at the tourist office. Granada's student population swarms to the trendy new *bar musical* **Sur,** C. Reyes Católicos, 55. (Mixed drinks 400-900ptas. Open daily 10pm-6am.) Young and well-dressed bar hoppers stop at **Temple,** C. Elvira, 98, to see and be seen. (Opens daily 10pm.) **Vaticano,** Camino del Sacromonte, 33, beyond the Albaicín, offers all-night dancing in a cave bar. (Opens daily 11pm.) A young and mellow throng of vacationers lounge on the cobblestone patio of **Taberna El 22,** Pl. Santa Gregorio, 5, close to Pl. Nueva, at the top of C. Calderería Nueva. (Beer 150ptas; wine 175ptas. Open daily noon-3pm and 9pm-3am.) **Kasbah,** C. Calderería Nueva, 4, offers silky pillows, romantic nooks, and tasty Marroqua beverages. (Open daily 3pm-3am.)

🎿 DAYTRIP FROM GRANADA

THE SIERRA NEVADA
The Autocares Bonal bus (☎958 27 31 00) from Granada to Veleta is a bargain (9am, returns 4:30pm from Albergue; round-trip 800ptas). Buy tickets in the bar El Ventorrillo, next to the bus stop.

The peaks of **Mulhacén** (3481m) and **Veleta** (3470m), the highest in Spain, sparkle with snow and buzz with tourists for most of the year. **Ski** season runs from December to April. In the rest of the year, the bare mountains are arguably less attractive, as black slate slopes are dotted by patches of yellow-green moss; nevertheless, tourists **hike, parasail,** and take **jeep tours.** Before you go, check road and snow conditions (☎958 24 91 19) and hotel vacancies.

COSTA DEL SOL

The coast has sold its soul to the Devil; now he's starting to collect. Artifice covers once-natural charms, as chic promenades and swanky hotels line its shore. The Costa del Sol officially extends from Tarifa in the southwest to Cabo de Gata, east of Almería; post-industrial Málaga is right in the middle. To the northeast, rocky beaches have helped to preserve some natural beauty. To the southwest, water seems to wash up on more concrete than sand, and high season bring swarms of tourists (so reserve ahead or ask about private rooms), but nothing can detract from the coast's eight months of spring and four months of summer. June is the best time to visit, after summer has hit the beach but tourists haven't. Railpasses are not valid on the Costa del Sol, but train prices are reasonable.

MÁLAGA

In the hundred years since the Romantics discovered Málaga (pop. 531,140), the 19th-century villas have been replaced by 70s highrises and the beach has become better known for its bars than for untouched sand. The second-largest city in Andalucía and a critical transportation hub for the province, Málaga has all the requisite historical monuments—fortress, cathedral, bullring—but they are best seen in passing, en route to more enjoyable coastal stops. Guarding the east end of Po. Parque, the 11th-century **Alcazaba** structure was originally built as a fortified palace for Moorish kings. (Open W-M 9:30am-8pm. Free.) Málaga's **cathedral,** C. Molina Lario, is a pastiche of Gothic, Renaissance, and Baroque styles. (Open M-Sa 9am-6:45pm. 200ptas.) Diehard fans can visit Picasso's birthplace which now houses the **Picasso Foundation,** Pl. Merced. (Open M-Sa 10am-2pm and 6-9pm, Su 11am-2pm. Free.) In summer, folks crowd the bars in the seaside district of **El Pedregalejo** and between **C. Comedias** and **C. Granada,** which leads out of Pl. Constitución.

From **Estación de Málaga** (☎ 952 36 02 02), Explanada de la Estación, trains go to: Madrid (7hr., 8000ptas); Barcelona (13hr., 6700ptas); Córdoba (2hr., 12 per day, 2000-2800ptas); and Sevilla (3hr., 5 per day, 2130ptas). One block from the RENFE station along C. Roger de Flor, **buses,** Po. Tilos (☎ 95 235 00 61), go to Madrid (7hr., 10 per day, 2650ptas); Algeciras (3hr., 17 per day, 1390ptas); Córdoba (3hr., 5 per day, 1500ptas); Granada (2hr., 17 per day, 1205ptas); Marbella (1½hr., every hr., 615ptas); and Sevilla (3hr., 6-10 per day, 1900ptas). To reach the center from the bus station take bus #4 or 21; from the train station take bus #3 (115ptas). The **tourist office,** Av. Cervantes 1, is in a little gray house on Po. Parque. (☎ 95 260 44 10; fax 95 221 41 20. Open M-F 8:15am-2:45pm and 4:30-7pm, Sa 9:30am-1:30pm.) Most budget establishments are in the old town, between Pl. Marina and Pl. Constitución. **Hostal La Palma,** C. Martínez 7, is off C. Marqués de Larios. (☎ 95 222 67 72. Singles 2000-3000ptas; doubles 3500-5000ptas; triples 3300-4500ptas; quads 4400-6000ptas.) **Hostal Aurora,** Muro de Puerta Nueva 1, is 5min. from Pl. Constitución. (☎ 95 222 40 04. Singles 2000-3000ptas; doubles 3200-4500ptas.) Seaside Po. Marítimo stretches toward El Pedregalejo (bus #11 or 40min. on foot), where restaurants specialize in seafood. A **supermarket** is in **El Corte Inglés,** Av. Andalucía 4-6, near the post office. (Open June-Aug. M-Sa 10am-10pm; Sept.-May 10am-9:30pm.) **Postal Code:** 29080.

MARBELLA

Like your vacation spots shaken, not stirred? A host of international jet-setters choose five-star Marbella (pop. 100,000) to dock their yachts, park their weary jets, and live the glitzy, glam life. But it's still possible to steal away from the city with a budgeted good time. The city's controversial mayor has "cleaned up" the "marginal" elements (drug dealers, prostitutes, dogs, fellow politicians, etc.); catch it now before he sets his sights on backpackers. Although the beaches beckon with 320 days of sunshine per year, no visit to Marbella would be complete without a stroll through the **casco antiguo,** a maze of cobblestoned streets and ancient whitewashed facades. City buses along Av. Richard Soriano (dir.: San Pedro; 135ptas) bring you to chic and trendy **Puerto Banús.** Buffered by imposing white yachts, this is where it's at. With 22km of **beach,** Marbella offers a variety of sizzling settings, from below its chic promenade to **Playa de las Chapas,** 10km east via the Fuengirola bus. In the *casco antiguo* are mellow bars. Between the beach and the old town, C. Puerta del Mar is home to several gay bars. Later in the evening, the city's young 'uns head to the **Puerto Deportivo** ("The Port"), a world of disco-bars. Nightlife in Marbella begins and ends late. The rowdiest corner of the *casco antiguo* is where C. Mesoncillo meets C. Peral. Loud music and cheery Spaniards spill out from **El Güerto,** C. Peral, 9, and **The Tavern,** C. Peral, 7. (Both open daily at 10pm.) The **Museo del Grabado Español Contemporáneo,** on C. Hospital Bazán, is a treasure trove of engravings by Miró, Picasso, Dalí, and Goya. (Open M-F 10:15am-2pm and 5:30-8:30pm. 300ptas.)

Accessible only by bus, the new **station** (☎ 95 276 44 00), atop Av. Trapiche sends **buses** to Madrid (7½hr., 10 per day, 3085ptas); Algeciras (1½hr., 9 per day, 770ptas); Barcelona (16hr., 4 per day, 9365ptas); Granada (4hr., 4 per day, 1820ptas); Málaga (1½hr., every 30min., 610ptas); and Sevilla (4hr., 3 per day, 1975ptas). To reach the main strip, exit and walk left, make the first right on Av. Trapiche, and follow any downhill route to the perpendicular Av. Ramón y Cajal, which becomes Av. Ricardo Soriano on the way to Puerto Banús. C. Peral curves up from Av. Ramón y Cajal around the **casco antiguo**. The **tourist office** (☎95 277 14 42) is on C. Glorieta de la Fontanilla. A **branch** is in the old town (☎95 282 35 50) on Pl. Naranjos. (Both open June-Aug. M-F 9:30am-9pm; Sept.-May M-F 9:30am-8pm, Sa 10am-2pm.) The area in the *casco antiguo* around Pl. Naranjos is packed with hostels. **Hostal del Pilar**, C. Mesoncillo 4, is off either C. Peral, an extension of C. Huerta Chica; or from the bus station it is off C. San Francisco. (☎95 282 99 36; email hostal@marbellascene.com. Breakfast 700ptas. 1500-2500ptas per person.) The excellent **Albergue Juvenil (HI)**, C. Trapiche 2, downhill from the bus station, is just like a proper hotel, only you can afford to stay here. (☎95 277 14 91. Call ahead. 1100-1800ptas; under 27 800-1300ptas. **Tents** outside 700ptas per person.) On the Marbella-Fuengirola bus line; ask the bus driver to stop at **Camping Marbella Playa**. (☎95 277 83 91. 325-585ptas per person, 530-980ptas per tent.) A **24-hour minimarket** beckons from the corner of C. Pablo Casals and Av. Fontanilla. **Postal Code:** 29600.

EASTERN SPAIN

Valencia's rich soil and famous orange groves, nourished by Moor-designed irrigation systems, have earned its nickname, *Huerta de España* (Spain's Orchard). Dunes, sandbars, jagged promontories, and lagoons mark the grand coastline, and lovely fountains and pools grace carefully landscaped public gardens in Valencian cities. The famed Spanish rice dish *paella* was created somewhere in Valencia.

ALICANTE (ALACANT)

Sun-drenched Alicante (pop. 250,000) has somehow been chiseled into the most redeeming sort of resort town—dutifully entertaining, yet quietly charming. While nightlife energizes the city, Alicante's mosaic-lined waterside Explanada relaxes it at sunset. High above the rows of bronzed bodies, the ancient *castillo*, guards the wicked tangle of streets in the cobblestoned *casco antiguo*. Complete with drawbridges, dark passageways, and hidden tunnels, the Carthaginian **Castell de Santa Bárbara** keeps silent guard over Alicante's beach. A paved road from the old section of Alicante leads to the top, but most people take the **elevator** from a hidden entrance on Av. Jovellanos, across the street from Playa Postiguet. (Castle open daily Apr.-Sept. 10am-7:30pm; Oct.-Mar. 9am-6:30pm. Free. Elevator 400ptas.) A crowd of Valencian modernist art pieces roost along with works by Miró, Picasso, Kandinsky, and Calder in the **Museu de Arte del Siglo XX La Asegurada**, Pl. Santa María 3, at the east end of C. Mayor. (Open May-Sept. Tu-Sa 10:30am-1:30pm and 6-9pm, Su 10:30am-1pm; Oct.-Apr. Tu-Sa 10am-1pm and 5-8pm, Su 10am-1pm. Free.) Alicante's own **Playa de El Postiguet** attracts sun worshipers, as do nearby **Playa de San Juan** (take TAM bus #21, 22, or 31) and **Playa del Mutxavista** (take TAM bus #21; all buses depart every 15min., 105ptas). Warm weather nightlife also centers on the **Playa de San Juan**; the **Tresnochador** night train (F-Sa every hr., Su-Th 10:30pm-6am; round-trip 150-700ptas) runs from Estació Marina to "Discotecas" and other stops along the beach, where discos are packed until dawn. Try **Penélope, Pachá, KU, KM**, and **Insomnia** (cover from 1500ptas; open nightly until 9am) at the Disco Benidorm stop (round-trip 650ptas). In Alicante, the **new port** and the old section of town, **El Barne**, overflow with students and *bar-musicales*. During the hedonistic **Festival de Sant Joan** (June 20-29), *fogueres* (symbolic or satiric effigies) are paraded around the *casco antiguo* and then burned in a bonfire on the 24th.

RENFE **trains** (☎902 24 02 02) run from **Estación Término** on Av. Salamanca, at the end of Av. Estación, to Madrid (4hr., 9 per day, 4700-6900ptas); Barcelona (4½-6hr., 9 per day, 6000-9900ptas); and Valencia (1½hr., 12 per day, 2900-4700ptas). Trains from **Estació Marina**, Av. Villajoyosa 2 (☎96 526 27 31), on Explanada d'Espanya, serve the Costa Blanca. **Buses** (☎965 13 07 00) run from C. Portugal 17 to Madrid (6½hr., 7 per day, 3000ptas); Barcelona (8hr., 6 per day, 4700ptas); Valencia (1980ptas); and Granada (6hr., 5 per day, 3375ptas). From the bus station, turn left on C. d'Italia, take the third right on Av. Dr. Gadea, and turn left at the waterfront to reach the Explanada d'Espanya and the **tourist office** at #2. (☎96 520 00 00; fax 96 520 02 43. Open June-Aug. M-F 10am-8pm, Sa 10am-2pm and 3-8pm; Sept.-May M-F 10am-7pm, Sa 10am-2pm.) Log on the **internet** at **Yazzgo**, Explanada, 3. (250ptas per 30min. Open daily 8am-11:30pm.) For lodgings, stay away from most places along C. San Fernando and around the Església de Santa María, and opt instead for places in the newer section of town. The **Pensión Les Monges Palace,** C. Monjas 2, is behind the Ayuntamiento, in the center of the historic district. (☎965 21 50 46. Singles 2200-3400ptas; doubles 4000-5000ptas; triples 5300-6300ptas.) **Habitaciones México,** C. General Primo de Rivera 10, off the end of Av. Alfonso X El Sabio, wins the award for nicest hostel owner. (☎965 20 93 07; email mexrooms@lix.ctv.es. **Internet** 800ptas. per hr. Singles 1900ptas; doubles 3600-4200ptas; triples 6000ptas.) Take bus #21 to **camp** at **Playa Mutxavista.** (☎965 65 45 26. 520ptas per person and per tent.) For food, try the family-run *bar-restaurantes* in the *casco antiguo*, between the cathedral and the castle steps. Buy basics at **Supermarket Mercadona,** C. Alvarez Sereix 5, off Av. Federico Soto. (Open M-Sa 9am-9pm.) **Postal Code:** 03070.

VALENCIA

Stylish, cosmopolitan, and business-oriented, Valencia is a striking contrast to the surrounding orchards and mountain ranges. Parks and gardens soothe the city's congested environment, and nearby beaches complement the frenetic pace.

⌐ TRANSPORTATION. Trains arrive at C. Xàtiva 24 (☎96 352 02 02) from Madrid (5-7½hr., 12 per day, 2890-5600ptas); Alicante (2hr., 9 per day, 1400-3000ptas); and Barcelona (4-6hr., 11 per day, 3300-4900ptas). From the station, follow Av. Marqués de Sotelo to the central **Pl. Ayuntamiento. Buses** (☎96 349 72 22) go from Av. Menéndez Pidal 13 to: Madrid (4-5hr., 3175ptas); Alicante (2¼-3hr., 9 per day, 1980ptas); and Barcelona (4½hr., 10 per day, 2900ptas). Bus #8 (125ptas) connects to Pl. Ayuntamiento and the train station. Trasmediterránea **ferries** (☎902 45 46 45) sail to the Balearic Islands (see p. 890); take bus #4 from Pl. Ayuntamiento.

⛊ PRACTICAL INFORMATION. The main **tourist office,** C. Paz 46-48, has branches at the train station and on Pl. Ayuntamiento. (☎96 398 64 22. Open M-F 10am-6pm, Sa 10am-2pm.) **Email** your mother at **Agora Internet,** C. Paz 33. (400-500ptas per 30min.) Send postcards from the **post office,** Pl. Ayuntamiento, 24. (☎96 351 67 50. Open M-F 8:30am-8:30pm, Sa 9:30am-2pm.) **Postal Code:** 46080.

⌐⌐ ACCOMMODATIONS AND FOOD. The best lodgings are around **Pl. Ayuntamiento** and **Pl. Mercado;** avoid areas around Pl. Pilar. To get from the train station to the **Pilgrim's Youth Hostel,** Pl. Hombres del Mar 25, take the metro to "Benimaclet," switch to L4 toward Av. Dr. Lluch, and get off at "Las Arenals"; the entrance is on the other side of the building. (☎96 356 42 88; email albergue@ran.es. **Internet.** Reception 24hr. Reserve ahead. 1500-2000ptas, under 27 1000ptas.) To get from the train station to the spotless **Hostal-Residencia El Cid,** C. Cerrajeros 13, pass Pl. Ayuntamiento and take the second left off C. Vicente Mártir. (☎96 392 23 23. Singles 1700ptas; doubles 3200ptas, with bath 4500ptas.) **Hostal-Residencia Universal,** C. Barcas 5, is off Pl. Ayuntamiento. (☎96 351 53 84. Singles 2400ptas; doubles 3600-4200ptas; triples 5100ptas.) From Pl. Ayuntamiento, turn right at C. Barcas, left at C. Poeta Querol, and take the 2nd right onto C. Salvá to find **Pensión Paris,** C. Salvá, 12. (☎96 352 67 66. Singles 2500ptas; doubles 3600ptas, with shower 4200ptas, with bath 4800ptas; triples 5400ptas.) **Paella** is the most famous of Valencia's 200 rice dishes; try as many as you can before leaving. To get to **⊠Restaurante La Utielana,** Pl. Picadero dos Aguas 3, take C. Barcelonina off Pl. Ayuntamiento, turn left at the end across Pl. Rodrigo Botet, turn right on C. Procida, and go down a little alley on the left. (Seafood paella 375ptas. Open Sept.-July M-F 1:15-4pm and 9-11pm, Sa 1:15-4pm.) Get **groceries** at **El Corte Inglés,** C. Pintor Sorolla 26. (Open M-Sa 10am-9:30pm.) **Postal Code:** 46080.

SIGHTS AND ENTERTAINMENT. Most sights line the **Río Turia** or cluster near **Pl. Reina,** down C. San Vicente Mártir from Pl. Ayuntamiento. Touring Valencia on foot is complicated. Most of the sights line the Río Turia or cluster near Pl. Reina, which is linked to Pl. Ayuntamiento by C. San Vicente Mártir. EMT bus #5, dubbed the Bus Turistic (☎96 352 83 99), makes a loop around the old town sights (110ptas; 1-day pass 500ptas). The 13th-century **cathedral,** on Pl. Reina, was built on the site of an Arab mosque. In a fit of hyperbole (or vertigo), Victor Hugo counted 300 bell towers from the **Micalet** (cathedral tower); in reality, there are about 100. The **Museo de la Catedral** squeezes many treasures into very little space. (Cathedral open daily in summer 8am-2pm and 5-8pm; off-season closes earlier; free. Tower open daily 10am-1pm and 4:30-7pm; 200ptas. Museum open Mar.-Nov. M-F 10am-1pm and 4:30-7pm, Sa 10am-1pm; Dec.-Feb. M-Sa 10am-1pm. 200ptas.) Across the river, the **Museu Provincial de Belles Artes,** on C. Sant Pius V, next to the **Jardines del Reial,** displays superb 14th- to 16th-century Valencian art. (Open Tu-Su 10am-2pm and 4-7:30pm. Free.) West across the old river, the **Instituto València de Arte Moderno (IVAM),** C. Guillem de Castro 118, has works by 20th-century sculptor Julio González. (Open Tu-Su 10am-7pm. 350ptas, students 175ptas; Su free.) In an effort to aid its weak tourism industry, Valencia has recently completed what the city calls "the largest urban complex under development in Europe." Built along the dried-up bed of the Río Turia, this mini-city has already become the fourth biggest tourist destination in Spain. The complex is divided into four large attractions: **L'Hemisfèric** wows the eyes with its IMAX theater and planetarium; **L'Oceanografic** is an underground water-world and recreation of diverse aquatic environments; the beautiful **Palau de les Arts** houses stages for opera, theater and dance; and the **Museu de Les Ciencies Principe Felipe** is an interactive playground for science and technology fiends. (South along the riverbed bank off the highway to Salér. Buses #13, 14, and 15 go. General info ☎902 100 031; www.cac.es. IMAX shows 1000ptas, weekdays children and students 700ptas.) The most popular **beaches** are **Las Arenas** and **Malvarrosa;** take bus #19 from Pl. Ayuntamiento (in summer also #20, 21, and 22). To get to the more attractive **Saler,** 14km from the center of town, take an Autobuses Buñol bus (☎96 349 14 25) from Gran Vía Germanias and C. Sueca (25min., every 30 min., 160ptas).

Bars and pubs abound in the **El Carme** district. Follow Pl. Mercado and C. Bolsería (bear right at the fork) to **Pl. Tossal** to guzzle *agua de Valencia* (orange juice, champagne, and vodka) with the masses, then head to **Av. Blasco Ibañez** with your dancing shoes. Dirty dance at Valencia's best late night haunts, **El Caballito Del Mar** and **Curious,** next door on Malvarrosa beach. (Weekend cover 1000pta. Open 1am-7am.) The most famed festival in Valencia is **Las Fallas** (Mar. 12-19), which culminates with a burning of gigantic (up to 30m) satirical papier-mâché effigies.

COSTA BLANCA

This "white coast" which extends from Denía through Calpe, Alicante, and Elche, derives its name from its fine, white sands. UBESA **buses** (Valencia ☎96 340 08 55) run to Gandía (1½hr., 12 per day) and Calpe (3-3½hr., 10 per day). From Alicante buses run to Calpe (1½hr., 18 per day). **Trains** also run from Valencia to Gandía (1hr., every 30min., 495ptas). Going to **Calpe** (Calp) is like stepping into a Dalí landscape that has been mobbed by sun-seeking tourists. The town cowers beneath the **Peñó d'Ifach** (327m), a giant rock protrusion whose precipitous face drops straight to the sea. **Gandía** attracts with fine sand beaches. The **tourist office,** Marqués de Campo, is opposite the train station. (☎96 287 77 88. Open June-Aug. M-F 10am-2pm and 4:30-7:30pm, Sa 10am-1pm; Sept.-May 9:30am-1:30pm and 4-7pm, Sa 10am-1pm.) La Amistad **buses** (8 per day, 125ptas) go from outside the train station in Gandía to **Platja de Piles,** 10km south, where you'll find beach, beach, and more beach. To sleep at the fantastic **Alberg Mar i Vent (HI)** in Platja, follow the signs down C. Dr. Fleming. (☎96 283 17 48. No alcohol. Washing machine and library. 3-day max. stay, flexible if uncrowded. Sheets 300ptas for entire stay. Curfew weeknights 2am, Sa 4am. Open Feb. 15-Dec. 15. Dorms 800ptas, with breakfast 900ptas, with full board 1900ptas; over 26 300-500ptas extra.)

NORTHEAST SPAIN

Northeastern Spain encompasses the country's most avidly regionalistic areas as well as some of its best cuisine. **Cataluñans** are justly proud of their treasures, from mountains to beaches to hip Barcelona. The glorious **Pyrenees** line the French border, presenting a prickly face to the rest of the continent. Little-known **Navarra** basks in the limelight once a year when bulls race through the streets of Pamplona. Industrious **Aragón** packs in busy cities and the most dramatic parts of the Pyrenees. The **Basques** are fiercely regionalistic, but happily share their beautiful coasts and rich history. The **Balearic Islands** are always ready for the next party.

CATALUÑA

From rocky Costa Brava to the lush Pyrenees and chic Barcelona, Cataluña is a vacation in itself. Graced with the nation's richest resources, it is one of Spain's most prosperous regions. Catalán is the region's official language (though most everyone is bilingual), and local cuisine is lauded throughout Spain.

BARCELONA

Paris, London, and New York have been described as *noir* cities, best captured in black and white, but Barcelona is best seen in vivid color. The 1992 Summer Olympics consummated Barcelona's recent rise to glory and won it worldwide admiration. The late-19th century welcomed brilliantly daring *Modernista* architecture; after Franco's regime ended, the city reclaimed its role as the world's premier showcase of avant-garde architecture. Today, amidst the graceful gothic churches, a serpentine old town, wrought-iron balconies, and grand, tree-lined European avenues, Antoni Gaudí's technicolor flights of fancy battle for attention with the city's latest architectural triumphs—carefully angled and glassy-white museums and malls. An unprecedented tourist boom continues to draw in Eurail travelers; reserve early, dress well, and prepare yourself for a circus.

✈ GETTING THERE AND AWAY

Flights: All domestic and international flights land at **El Prat de Llobregat** airport (☎93 298 38 38), 12km southwest of Barcelona. The **Aerobus** conveniently links the airport to Plaça de Cataluña, the center of town (40min.; every 15min.; to Pl. Cataluña M-F 6am-midnight, Sa-Su 6:30am-midnight; to the airport M-F 5:30am-11:15pm, Sa-Su 6am-11:20pm; 500ptas). **RENFE** trains provide slightly cheaper transportation to and from the airport (20min.; every 30min.; 6:13am-10:40pm from airport, 5:40am-10:13pm from Pl. Cataluña; M-Sa 305ptas, Su 350ptas). Three **national airlines** serve domestic and major international destinations. **Iberia/Aviaco,** C. Diputació, 258 (24hr. reservation and info ☎902 40 05 00), has the most extensive coverage and usually offers student discounts. **Air Europa** (24hr. reservation and info ☎902 24 00 42) and **Spanair** (☎902 13 14 15) offer fares that are often cheaper.

Trains: Barcelona has 3 main train stations. For general info about trains and train stations, call ☎902 24 02 02. **Estació Barcelona-Sants** (☎902 24 02 02), in Pl. Països Catalans. M: Sants-Estació. Barcelona-Sants is the main terminal for domestic and international traffic. **Estació França** (☎902 24 02 02), on Av. Marqués de L'Argentera. M: Barceloneta. Services a few domestic and international destinations. **Ferrocarrils de la Generalitat de Cataluña (FFCC)** (☎93 205 15 15; www.fgc.catalunya.net), has commuter trains with main stations at Pl. Cataluña and Pl. Espanya.

RENFE: (☎902 24 02 02, international ☎93 490 11 22; www.renfe.es). RENFE has extensive service in Spain and Europe. A few of the most popular connections include: **Madrid** (7-8hr., 6 per day, 6500-8400ptas); **San Sebastián** (8hr., 3 per day, 5000-10,000ptas); **Sevilla** (12hr., 3per

SPAIN

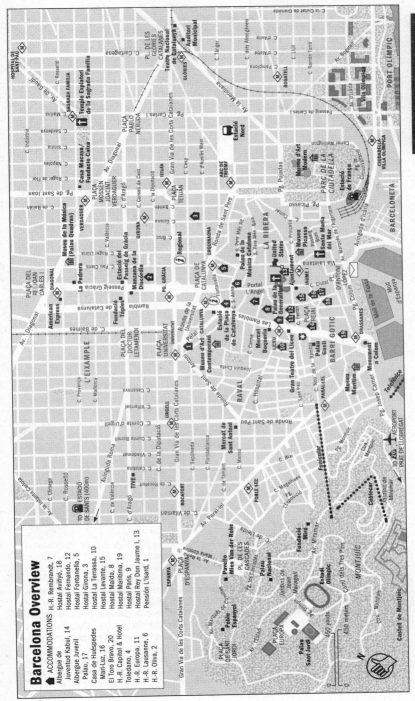

Barcelona Overview

ACCOMMODATIONS
Albergue de
  Juventut Kabul, 14
Albergue Juvenil
  Palau, 17
Casa de Huéspedes
  Mari-Luz, 16
El Toro Bravo, 20
H.-R. Capitol & Hotel
  Toledano, 4
H.-R. Europa, 11
H.-R. Lausanne, 6
H.-R. Oliva, 2
H.-R. Rembrandt, 7
Hostal Aviñyó, 18
Hostal Fernando, 12
Hostal Fontanella, 5
Hostal Girona, 3
Hostal La Terrassa, 10
Hostal Levante, 15
Hostal Malda, 8
Hostal Marítima, 19
Hostal Paris, 9
Hostal Rey Don Jaume I, 13
Pensión L'Isard, 1

day, 10,000-27,700ptas); and **Valencia** (3hr., 15 per day, 5000-7200ptas); **Milan, Italy** via Figueres or Montpelier (13hr., 1 per day, 12,608-43,800ptas); **Montpellier, France** with connections to Geneva, Paris, and the French Riviera (4½hr., 3 per day, 12,608-43,800ptas).

Trenes Euromed: A subsidiary of RENFE offering high-speed service along Spain's Mediterranean coast. Trains leave from Barcelona-Sants for **Alicante** (4¾hr., 3 per day, 6600ptas) and **Valencia** (3hr., 6 per day, 4900ptas), stopping in smaller towns along the way.

Buses: Most buses arrive at the **Estació del Nord,** C. Ali-bei, 80 (☎93 265 65 08; info office open daily 7am-9pm. M: Arc de Triomf (exit to Nàpols).

Enatcar: Estació del Nord (☎93 245 25 28 or 902 42 22 42; www.enatcar.es). Open daily 7am-1am. To: **Madrid** (8hr., 18 per day, 2690ptas); **Alicante** (9hr., 5 per day); and **Valencia** (4hr., 16 per day, 2690ptas).

Sarfa: Estació del Nord (☎93 265 65 08 or 93 265 11 58). Sarfa buses stop at many beach towns along the Costa Brava, north of Barcelona. Open daily 8am-8:30pm. To: **Cadaques** (2½hr., 2 per day) and **Tossa** (1½hr., 9 per day).

Linebús: Estació del Nord (☎93 265 07 00). Open M-F 8am-2pm and 3-8pm, Sa 8:30am-1:30pm and 4:30-8pm. Discounts for travelers under 26. To: **London** (25hr., 3 per week, 14,650-26,375ptas) and **Paris** (15hr., 6 per week, 11,200-22,900ptas). Also has daily service to southern France.

Julià Vía: Estación del Nord (☎93 232 10 92). To: **Marseille, France** (10hr., 5 per week, 7100ptas); **Paris, France** (15hr., 6 per week, 12,000ptas); and **Frankfurt, Germany** (19hr., 4 per week, 14,300ptas).

Ferries: For details on ferries to the Balearic Islands, see **Balearic Islands,** p. 890. **Transmediterránea,** Estació Marítima-Moll Barcelona (☎ 902 45 46 45; fax 93 295 91 34), Moll de Sant Bertran. M: Drassanes. From the metro, head down Las Ramblas to the Columbus monument. Columbus points straight toward the Estació Marítima. Cross Ronda Litoral and pass the Aduana building on the left. During the summer, ferries to Mallorca (3hr.) leave 3 times a day; Ibiza ferries (9hr.) depart 5 times a week; and starting in mid-June ferries leave for Menorca daily. One-way trips start at about 10,350ptas. Main office is open M-F 8am-9pm.

▣ GETTING AROUND

Metro and Bus: Barcelona's public transportation system (☎010) is quick, cheap, and extensive. The useful *Guía d'Autobusos Urbans de Barcelona,* free at tourist offices and in metro stations, maps out all of the city's bus routes and the five metro lines. If you plan to use the metro and bus systems extensively, consider buying a **T1 Pass** or a **T-DIA** Card. The T1 Pass (795ptas), valid for 10 rides on the bus, metro, and most FFCC trains, is a great deal, especially since multiple people can share one pass. The T-DIA Card entitles you to unlimited bus and metro travel for one (625ptas) or three days (1600ptas).

Metro: (☎93 486 07 52; www.tmb.net). Automatic vending machines and ticket windows sell metro passes. Riding without a ticket carries a hefty 5000ptas fine. Trains run M-Th 5am-11pm, F-Sa 5am-2am, Su 6am-midnight. 150ptas.

Buses: Go just about anywhere, usually from 5am-10pm. 150ptas.

Nitbus: (☎93 395 31 11). At night you'll have to ride the Nitbus. Run 10:30pm-4:30am. Stops in front of most of the club complexes. 160ptas.

Bus Turístic: The clearly marked Bus Turístic stops at 25 points of interest along two different routes (red for the northern; blue for the southern). The easiest place to hop on the Bus Turístic is Pl. Cataluña, in front of El Corte Inglés. Buses run Mar. 28-Jan. 6 every 10-30min., 9am-9:30pm. Purchase tickets on the bus or at the Pl. de Cataluña tourist office. Full-day pass 2000ptas; 2-day pass 2500ptas.

Taxis: A *libre* sign in the windshield or a lit green light on the roof means they are vacant; yellow means they are occupied. Cabs can be summoned by phone (☎93 330 03 00 or 93 300 11 00; for disabled travelers ☎93 358 11 11 or 93 357 77 55). The first 6min. or 1.9km cost 300ptas; each additional kilometer is 110ptas.

Car Rental: Docar, C. Montnegre, 18 (24hr. ☎93 439 81 19). Free delivery and pickup. From 4700ptas per day, 23ptas per km. Insurance included. Open M-F 8:30am-2pm and 3:30-8pm, Sa 9am-2pm. **Tot Car,** C. Berlín, 97 (☎93 430 01 98; fax 93 419 22 94). Free delivery and pickup. From 4500ptas per day, 21ptas per km. Insurance included. Open M-F 8am-2pm and 3-8pm, Sa 9am-1pm.

Bicycle and Moped Rental: Vanguard Rent a Car, C. Londres, 31 (☎93 439 38 80; fax 93 410 82 71). Mopeds Tu-Th 4740ptas per day, F-M 7280ptas per day. Insurance, helmet, and IVA included. **Biciclot,** C. Sant Joan de Malta, 1 (☎93 307 74 75). M: Clot. 10-speeds or mountain bikes 500ptas per hr., 2000ptas per day. Tandem 1000ptas per hr., 4000ptas per day. Multi-day and group rates available. Open M-F 9am-2pm and 5-8pm, Sa 10am-2pm.

☒ ORIENTATION

Barcelona slopes gently upward from the harbor to the mountains. **Passeig de Colon** runs parallel to the shore; from Pg. Colón, **Las Ramblas,** the city's main thorough-fare, runs from the harbor to **Plaça de Cataluña,** the city's center. Las Ramblas is divided into five parts: **Rambla de Santa Mónica, Rambla de Caputxins, Rambla de Sant Josep, Rambla de Estudis,** and **Rambla de Canaletas.** The **Barri Gòtic** area is enclosed by Las Ramblas to the west and **Vía Laietana** to the east and is bisected by east-west **Carrer de Ferran.** East of Vía Laietana lies the maze-like neighborhood of **La Ribera,** which borders the **Parc de la Ciutadella** and the **Estació de França train station.** Far-ther east is the **Vila Olímpica,** along with a shiny array of malls, discos, and hotels. West of Las Ramblas is **El Ravel,** including the shrinking red-light district. Farther west rises **Montjuïc,** a picturesque hill crammed with sights. South of Pg. Colon, a bridge leads from the **Port Vell** (Old Port) to the ultramodern malls in **Moll d'Espanya** and **Maremagnum.** The gridded **L'Eixample** district, created during urban expansion, fans toward the hills from Pl. Cataluña and is split by the main shopping street **Passeig de Gràcia. Avinguda Diagonal** separates L'Eixample from **Gràcia,** a residential area farther north. The peak of **Tibidabo** to the northwest is the highest point in Bar-celona. For more detail, refer to this book's **color maps** of the city and metro.

Barcelona is fairly safe, even at night, but secure your valuables while in outdoor cafes, in the Pl. Reial and Barri Gòtic, on Las Ramblas, and deep in El Ravel. Most areas with nightlife are well-policed, lit, and, for the most part, safe.

☒ PRACTICAL INFORMATION

TOURIST, FINANCIAL, AND LOCAL SERVICES

Tourist Info: (☎010; 906 30 12 82; or 93 304 34 21; www.barcelonaturisme.com). Bar-celona has 4 main tourist offices and numerous mobile information stalls.

Informacio Turistica at Plaça Cataluña, Pl. Cataluña, 17-S. M: Cataluña. The biggest, best, and busiest tourist office. Provides multilingual advice, maps, pamphlets, transportation passes, hotel information, currency exchange, telephone cards, e-mail kiosks, and souvenirs for pur-chase. Open daily 9am-9pm.

Informacio Turista at Plaça Sant Jaume, Pl. Sant Jaume, 1. M: Jaume I. Fewer services but more personal attention than its big sister in Pl. Cataluña. Open M-Sa 10am-8pm, Su 10am-2pm.

Estació Central de Barcelon-Sants, Pl. Paisos Catalans, in the Barcelona-Sants train station. M: Sants-Estació. Open June-Aug. M-F 8am-8pm; Sept.-May M-F 8am-8pm, Sa-Su 8am-2pm.

Aeroport El Prat de Llobregat (☎93 478 47 04), in the international terminal. Open M-Sa 9:30am-8:30pm, Su 9:30am-3pm.

Budget Travel Offices: Most are located near the university. **Unlimited Student Travel (USIT),** Rda. Universidad, 16 (☎90 232 52 75; www.unlimited.es), 1½ blocks from Pl. Cataluña. M: Cataluña. Also at C. Rocafort, 116-118, 2 blocks from the metro. M: Rocafort. Bring your ISIC card. Open M-F 10am-8pm, Sa 10am-1:30pm.

Consulates: Australia, Gran Vía Carlos III, 98, 9th fl. (☎93 330 94 96); **Canada,** Elisenda de Pinos, 8 (☎93 204 27 00); **New Zealand,** Traversa de Gracia, 64, 4th fl. (☎93 209 03 99); **South Africa,** Teodora Lamadrid 7-11 (☎93 418 64 45); **US,** Pg. Reina Elisenda, 23 (☎932 80 22 27).

Currency Exchange: General banking hours M-F 8:30am-2pm. **Banco de Espanya,** Pl. Cataluña, 17 (☎93 482 47 00) and the American Express office (see below) charge no commission on traveler's checks. Change US dollars at **Estació de Barcelona-Sants** (☎993 490 77 70) for no commission. Open daily 8am-10pm.

American Express: Pg. Gràcia, 101 (24hr. traveler's check information ☎90 099 44 26). M: Diagonal. The entrance is around the corner on C. Rosselló. Mail held free for cardholders. Open M-F 9:30am-6pm, Sa 10am-noon. Another office is located on Las Ramblas, 74 and is open daily 9am-midnight.

Luggage Storage: Estació del Nord. M: Arc de Triomf. Lockers 300-600ptas. Open 24hr.

El Corte Inglés: Pl. Cataluña, 14 (☎93 306 38 00), Av. Diagonal, 471-473, and Av. Diagonal, 617. Behemoth department store. Gives out a great map. Also has English books, haircutting, rooftop cafeteria, supermarket, currency exchange, and telephones. Open M-Sa 10am-9:30pm.

English Bookstores: LAIE, Av. Pau Claris, 85 (☎93 318 17 39), 1 block from the Gran Vía. M: Urquinaona or Pl. Cataluña. Open M-F 10am-9pm, Sa 10:30am-9pm.

Laundromats: Tintorería San Pablo, C. San Pau, 105 (☎93 329 42 49). M: Paralell. Wash, dry, and fold 1600ptas; do-it-yourself 1200ptas. Open M-F 9am-1:30pm and 4-8:30pm. **Tintorería Ferran,** C. Ferran, 11. M: Liceu. Ferran runs off Las Ramblas, just below Liceu. Full service 1500ptas. Open daily 8:30am-2pm and 4:30-7:30pm.

EMERGENCY AND COMMUNICATIONS

Emergency: National police ☎091; local police ☎092; medical ☎061.

Police: Las Ramblas, 43 (☎93 344 13 00 or 93 301 90 60), across from Pl. Reial and next to C. Nou de La Rambla. M: Liceu. Multilingual officers. Open daily 7am-midnight.

Late-Night Pharmacy: Pharmacies open 24hr. on a rotating basis. Check pharmacy windows for current listings.

Hospitals: Barcelona Centro Médico (BCM), Av. Diagonal, 612, 2nd fl., #14 (☎93 414 06 43), coordinates referrals, especially for foreigners. **Hospital Clínic,** Villarroel, 170 (☎93 454 60 00). M: Hospital Clínic. Main entrance at the intersection of C. Rosselló and C. Casanova.

Internet Access: Travel Bar, C/Boqueria, 27 (☎93 342 52 52). M: Liceu. This innovative joint is an everything-in-one tourist heaven: Internet access, bar, restaurant, tour information, and travel library. 450ptas per 30min. Open M-Su 9am-2am. **Net Movil,** Las Ramblas, 130, (☎93 342 42 04). M: Liceu. 50 high-speed computers. 300ptas per 15min., each additional min. 10ptas; 10hr. pass 4500ptas. **El Cafe de Internet,** Gran Vía de les Corts Catalanes, 656 (☎93 412 19 15). M: Cataluña. From the metro, walk up Pg. Gràcia and turn right onto Gran Vía. Free buffet. 500ptas per 30min., students 800ptas per hr. Open M-Sa 8am-midnight.

Post Office: (☎93 318 38 31), in Pl. Antoni López, at the end of Vía Laietana, portside. M: Jaume I or Barceloneta. Fax and Lista de Correos. Open M-F 8:30am-9:30pm. A little shop in the back of the post office building, across the street, wraps packages for mailing (about 300ptas). Open M-Sa 9am-2pm and 5-8pm. **Postal Code:** 08003.

▗ ACCOMMODATIONS

Ciutat Vella, the region of Barcelona between Pl. Cataluña and the water that consists of the **Barri Gòtic, Las Ramblas, El Raval,** and **La Ribera,** offers a wealth of budget accommodations, but visitors without reservations will still end up scrambling in summer. Signs with a large "P" or "H" mark the location of hostels. *Albergues* (youth hostels), which offer the basics at the lowest prices, are the best places to meet fellow backpackers.

LOWER BARRI GÒTIC

The following hostels are centrally located in the areas of the Barri Gòtic south of **C. Portaferrissa.** Backpackers flock here to be close to the port and hip Las Ramblas. Be careful at night, especially in the Placa Reial and on C. Escudellers.

▨ **Hostal Fernando,** C. Ferrán, 31 (☎93 301 79 93; www.barcelona-on-line.es/fernando). M: Liceu. This hostel is a backpacker's dream. One of the most social lodgings in the area. Internet 200ptas per 8min. Dorm beds 2100ptas; singles 2800ptas; doubles with bath 6500ptas; triples with bath 7500ptas.

Hostal-Residencia Rembrandt, C. Portaferrisa, 23 (☎/fax 93 318 10 11). M: Liceu. From the port, walk up Las Ramblas and turn right onto C. Portaferrisa. Common spaces with comfy couches scattered throughout. Breakfast 400ptas. Singles 3200ptas, with bath 4300ptas; doubles 5000ptas, with bath 6700ptas; triples 7000ptas.

Hostal Levante, Baixada de San Miguel, 2 (☎93 317 95 65). M: Liceu. Walk down C. Ferrán, turn right onto C. Avinyó, and take the first left onto Baixada de San Miguel. Singles 3500ptas; doubles 5500ptas, with bath 6500ptas.

Hostal Avinyó, C. Avinyó, 42 (☎93 318 79 45; www.barcelona-on-line.es/avinyo). M: Drassanes. Bedrooms boast couches, high ceilings, fans, and stained glass windows. Rooms 1700-1900ptas per person, with bath 2300-2600ptas.

Hostal Malda, C. Pí, 5 (☎93 317 30 02). M: Liceu. Turn onto C. Portaferrissa from Las Ramblas and right onto C. Pí. Clean. Nicely furnished rooms make this one of the best deals in the Barri Gòtic. Singles 1500ptas; doubles 3000ptas, with bath 3500ptas; triples 4000ptas, with bath 4500ptas.

Hotel Call, Arco San Ramón del Call, 4 (☎93 302 11 23; fax 93 301 34 86). M: Liceu. From Las Ramblas, take C. Boqueria to its end, then veer left onto C. Call. Quiet, and all rooms equipped with private phones, sparkling bathrooms, and firm beds. Singles 4500ptas; doubles 6000ptas; triples 8000ptas; quads 7500ptas. Tax not included.

Hostal Layetana, Pl. Ramón Berenguer el Gran, 2 (☎/fax 93 319 20 12). M: Jaume I. Balconies open onto the cathedral or a fashionable plaza. Showers 200ptas. Singles 2700ptas; doubles 4700ptas, with bath 5900ptas; triples 6400ptas, with bath 8000ptas. Tax not included.

Hotel Rey Don Jaume I, C. Jaume I, 11 (☎/fax 93 310 62 08; email r.d.jaime@atriumhotels.com). M: Jaume I, in the heart of chic La Ribera. Bathroom and telephone in every room. Singles 5000ptas; doubles 7400ptas; triples 10,500ptas.

Albergue Juvenil Palau (HI), C. Palau, 6 (☎93 412 50 80). M: Liceu. From Las Ramblas, take C. Ferrán to C. Enseyança, which eventually becomes C. Palau. Use the kitchen and airy common room to swap stories with fellow backpackers. 2-8 people per room; 40 beds total. Breakfast included. Showers available 8am-noon and 4-10pm. Sheets 200ptas. Reception daily 7am-3am. Curfew 3am. Dorms 1900ptas.

UPPER BARRI GÒTIC

This stunning section of the Barri Gòtic includes the area south of Pl. Cataluña, bounded by **C. Fontanella** to the north and **C. Portaferrisa** to the south. Accommodations here are a bit pricier than those in the Lower Barri Gòtic. The nearest metro stop is Pl. Cataluña, unless otherwise specified.

▧ Mare Nostrum, La Rambla, 67 (☎93 318 53 40). M: Liceu. Chill in your air-conditioned palace and gaze onto the Ramblas. Singles 5000ptas, with shower 5800ptas; doubles 7500ptas, with bath 8975ptas; triples 8975ptas, with bath 11,200ptas.

Hostal Fontanella, Vía Laietana, 71 (☎/fax 93 317 59 43). M: Urquinaona. Hotel-quality beds and baths. Singles 3000ptas, with bath 4000ptas; doubles 5000ptas, with shower 5800ptas; with bath 6900ptas.Cataluña

Hotel Toledano/Hostal Residencia Capitol, Las Ramblas, 138 (☎93 301 08 72; email toledano@idgrup.ibernet.com), just off Pl. Cataluña. A family-owned, split-level hotel/hostel. Fourth-floor hotel: singles 3900ptas, with bath 4400ptas; doubles with bath 7600ptas; triples with bath 9500ptas; quads with shower 7400ptas, with bath 10,600ptas. Fifth-floor hostel: singles 3600ptas; doubles 5100ptas, with shower 5800ptas; triples 6500ptas, with shower 7200ptas.

Hostal Residencia Opera, C. San Pablo, 20 (☎93 318 82 01). M: Liceu. All the amenities: huge bathroom, phone, TV, A/C. Singles 3000ptas, with bath 5000ptas; doubles with bath 7000ptas; triples with bath 9000ptas.

Hostal Plaza, C. Fontanella, 18 (☎93 301 01 39; email plazahostal@retemail.es). C. Fontanella stems right from Pl. Cataluña at El Corte Inglés. All the comforts of home: phone, fax (300ptas), TV, internet access (600ptas for 30min.), and a kitchen. Laundry 1500ptas for 5kg. Reception closed 2-5pm. Singles 6000ptas, with bath 7000ptas;

doubles with shower 8000ptas, with bath 9000ptas; triples 11,000ptas, with bath 12,000ptas. 1000ptas off if you pay in cash.

Pensión Dalí, C. Boqueria, 12 (☎93 318 55 90; email pensiondali@wamadoo.es). Designed as a religious house by Luis Domenech i Montaner, the architect of the Palau de la Musica Catalana, Pensión Dalí still retains the stained glass and gaudy iron doors of its early years. Internet access 100ptas for 4min. Doubles 6000ptas, with bath 7000ptas; triples 9600ptas, with bath 12,000ptas.

Hostal Palermo, C. Boqueria, 21 (☎93 302 40 02). M: Liceu. Backpacker culture is a constant party, and this hostel's big rooms hold dozens of your nearest and dearest. Singles 4800ptas, with bath 6800ptas; doubles 7000ptas, with bath 8000ptas.

Pensión Nevada, Av. Portal de L'Angel, 16 (☎93 302 31 01), just past Hostal Residencia Lausanne, under the "Raphael Roca Optico" sign. Great location. Bedrooms are just like grandma's house, complete with matching throw pillows. TV lounge. Singles 3800ptas; doubles 7000ptas.

EL RAVAL

Hostels in El Raval, the area west of Las Ramblas, are harder to come by and less-touristed; staying here will give you a better grasp of living *la vida española.*

Pensión L'Isard, C. Tallers, 82 (☎93 302 51 83), near MACBA, the new contemporary art museum. M: Universitat. Take the C. Pelai exit from the metro, turn left at the end of the block, and then left again at the pharmacy. Singles 2400ptas; doubles 4400ptas, with bath 5000ptas; triples 6000ptas.

Hostal La Terrassa, Junta de Comerç, 11 (☎93 302 51 74; fax 93 301 21 88). M: Liceu. From the metro, take C. Hospital and turn left after Teatre Romea. A hostel experience for the minimalist, with 50 small, basic, clean rooms. Singles 2400ptas, with shower 3600ptas; doubles 3800ptas, with shower 4600ptas; triples with shower 6000ptas.

L'EIXAMPLE

Barcelona's most beautiful accommodations lie along L'Eixample's wide, safe avenues—style is of the essence in this famously bourgeois neighborhood.

Hostal Residencia Windsor, Rambla Cataluña, 84 (☎93 215 11 98), near the intersection with C. Mallorca. M: Pg. Gràcia. With crimson carpets and palatial decor, this hostel lives up to its royal name. Singles 3900ptas, with bath 4900ptas; doubles 6500ptas, with bath 7900ptas. Tax not included.

Hostal Residencia Oliva, Pg. Gràcia, 32, 4th fl. (☎93 488 01 62), at the intersection with C. Diputació. M: Pg. Gràcia. Some windows overlook the *manzana de discordia,* where buildings by Puig, Domènech, and Gaudí compete for aesthetic prominence. Singles 3200ptas; doubles 6200ptas, with bath 7200ptas.

Hostal Girona, C. Girona, 24, 1st fl. (☎93 265 02 59), located between C. Casp and C. Ausias Marc. M: Urquinaona. Carpeted hallways, immense wooden doors, and TVs come at a surprisingly small price. Singles 3000ptas, with bath 4500ptas; doubles 6000ptas, with bath 7500ptas.

GRÀCIA

Locals outnumber travelers in Gràcia, a five-minute walk from M: Diagonal. Its deceptively quiet atmosphere has earned it a reputation as Barcelona's "undiscovered" quarter, but native 20-somethings have most definitely "discovered" Gracia's lively weekend nightlife.

Hostal Bonavista, C. Bonavista, 21 (☎93 237 37 57). M: Diagonal. Head toward the fountain at the end of Pg. Gràcia and take the first right; the hostel is just off the traffic circle. Well-lit, clean, cared-for rooms with sinks. Showers 300ptas. No reservations. Singles 2500ptas; doubles 3800ptas, with bath 4800ptas. Tax not included.

Pensión San Medín, C. Gran de Gràcia, 125 (☎93 217 30 68). M: Fontana. Newly renovated rooms have nice furniture and phones. Common room with TV. Singles 3000ptas, with bath 4000ptas; doubles 6000ptas, with bath 7000ptas.

ELSEWHERE

Albergue Mare de Déu de Montserrat (HI), Pg. Mare de Déu del Coll, 41-51 (☎93 210 51 51), beyond Parc Güell (way out there). Bus #28 from Pl. Cataluña and Nitbus N-4 stop across the street from the hostel. Otherwise, from M: Vallcarca, walk up Av. República Argentina and cross the bridge at C. Viaducte de Vallcarca; signs point the way up the hill. This 180-bed government-sponsored hostel is nicer than most museums. HI members only. Breakfast included. Sheets 350ptas. Max stay 3 days. Reception 8am-11pm. Lockout 10am-2pm. Midnight curfew, but doors open every 30min. midnight-3am. Dorms 1900ptas, over 25 2500ptas.

Hostal De Joves Municipal (HI), Pg. Pujades, 29 (☎93 300 31 04). M: Arc de Triomf. From the metro, exit to C. Nápols and walk toward Parc de la Ciutadela. Sixty-eight beds and 6 bathrooms. No locks on doors. Breakfast included. Showers 7-9:30am and 3-10pm. Sheets 350ptas. Laundry. Max stay 5 days. Reception 8-10am and 3pm-midnight. Curfew midnight, doors open at 1 and 2am. Dorms 1500ptas.

CAMPING

Although there are no campsites within the city, intercity buses (200ptas) run to the following locations in 20 to 45min. For more campsites, contact the **Associació de Càmpings de Barcelona,** Gran Vía Corts Catalanes, 608 (☎93 412 59 55).

El Toro Bravo (☎93 637 34 62), 11km south of Barcelona, is accessible by bus L95 from Pl. Cataluña. Laundry facilities, currency exchange, pool, and supermarket. Reception 8am-7pm. 1300ptas per person, 775ptas per tent. Tax not included.

Filipinas (☎93 658 28 95), 1km down the road from El Toro Bravo, is accessible by bus L95. The same prices and services as El Toro Bravo.

🖸 FOOD

Drawing from both Spanish and Catalan culinary traditions, Barcelona's restaurants are a mix of authentic neighborhood haunts and stylish cosmopolitan cuisine. Many of the best restaurants serve *cuisina del mercado,* menus created daily to match the market offerings. Consult the weekly *Guía del Ocio* (125ptas) for dining options. **Champion Supermarket,** Las Ramblas, 113, has plenty of essentials. (M: Liceu. ☎93 302 48 24. Open M-Sa 9am-9pm.) **Condis Supermercats,** Junta de Comercio, 19, is in El Ravel. (M: Liceu. ☎93 317 04 52.)

LOWER BARRI GÒTIC

The farther into the lower Barri Gòtic you trek, the more delicious the food. Great restaurants are scattered on **C. Escudellers** and **C. Clave.** Some of the liveliest between-meal hangouts surround Església Santa María del Pí—relax at the *terrazas* for drinks and ice cream. (From Las Ramblas, enter Llano de la Boquería, turn left at the Banco Central Hispano, and follow C. Cardenal Casanyes into Pl. Pí.)

La Fonda, C. Escudellers, 10 (☎93 301 75 15). M: Drassanes or Liceu. Off Las Ramblas, between Liceu and Drassanes. Be prepared to fight locals and tourists alike for a table. Main dishes 500-1000ptas. Open daily 1-3:30pm and 8:30-11:30pm.

Irati, C. Cardenal Casañas, 17 (☎93 302 30 84). An excellent Basque restaurant that attracts droves of hungry tapas-seekers. All tapas 140ptas (they count the toothpicks to tally). Main dishes around 2000ptas. Open Tu-Sa noon-midnight, Su noon-5pm.

Juicy Jones, Cardenal Casañas, 7 (☎93 302 43 30). M: Liceu. Head down Las Ramblas from the metro and take the first left. Some of the best vegan cuisine around. Daily *menú* 1100ptas. Open 10am-11:15pm, *menú* after 1pm.

UPPER BARRI GÒTIC

In the upper Barri Gòtic, the interiors of old buildings are continually being disemboweled to make room for classy cafes and restaurants. Thanks to free-market competition, the more cafes that pop up, the cheaper they get.

Els Quatre Gats, C. Montsió, 3 (☎93 302 41 40). M: Cataluña. From the metro, go down Av. Portal de L'Angel and take the 2nd left. Modernista hangout of Picasso's; he loved it so much he designed a personalized menu. Tapas (150-650ptas) are the best way to go. Main dishes about 2000ptas. Live music 9pm-1am. Open M-Sa 9am-2am, Su 5pm-2am. Closed Aug.

El Cervol Roig, C. Comtal, 19 (☎93 318 92 99). M: Urquinaona. A loud, animated gathering spot for locals. *La comida* is a steal at 1195ptas. Starters 700ptas. Main dishes 1300-2500ptas. Open daily 9am-9pm.

Restaurante Self Naturista, C. Santa Anna, 11-17 (☎93 318 26 84), off Las Ramblas. M: Cataluña. A self-service vegetarian cafeteria with enormous selection. Main dishes under 500ptas. Lunch menú 965ptas. Open M-Sa 11:30am-10pm.

EL RAVAL

Students and blue-collar workers congregate in typical Catalán joints west of Las Ramblas. Restaurants line the streets and are fairly inexpensive. Establishments off **C. Lluna** and **Joaquín Costa** often serve Galician fare.

Restaurante Can Lluís, C. Cera, 49 (☎93 441 11 87). M: San Antoni. From the metro, head down Ronda S. Pau and take the 2nd left on C. Cera. For over 100 years, Can Lluís has been a defining force in Catalán cuisine. The menu overflows with hard-to-pronounce delicacies you've never tried before but should, among them *cabrit* (goat) and *conill* (rabbit). Daily *menú* 950ptas. Open M-Sa 1:30-4pm and 8:30-11:30pm.

Can Maxim, C. Bonsuccés, 8 (☎93 302 02 34), off Las Ramblas (to the right as you face the port). M: Cataluña. Slabs of meat hang from the ceiling of this packed local spot. Specialties include oily *torrades* (475-700ptas). Lunch *menú* 1100ptas, tapas 350-650ptas. Open Oct.-Aug. M-Sa 1-4pm and 8pm-1am.

LA RIBERA

East of Vía Laietana, La Ribera is home to the Museu Picasso and numerous bars and small restaurants. Menus are available only in Spanish and Catalán, but if you guess right, you'll get some of the city's best bargains.

La Habana Vieja, Carrer dels Banys Vells, 2 (☎93 268 25 04). C. Baños Viejos is parallel to C. Montcada. The pulsing Cuban music will tempt you to leave your seat to dance; the delicious food will convince you to stay put. Cuban rice 600-900ptas. Meat dishes 1600-2000ptas. Open M-Sa 8pm-1am, F and Sa also 1pm-4pm.

Txirimira, C. Princesa, 11 (☎93 310 18 05). Enough tapas to fill a small village, or at least to decorate it (140ptas each). Sit at the long wooden bar and try *la gula*, a seafood and veggie specialty from northern Spain. Open Tu-Su noon-midnight.

L'EIXAMPLE

L'Eixample has its fair share of tapas bars on **Passeig de Gracia**. Small sidewalk cafes pop up everywhere.

Saler, Consejo de Ciento, 316 (☎93 488 03 95). Quiet Saler has earned local acclaim for its excellent gazpacho and delicious Galician seafood specialties. Main dishes 950-2300ptas. *Menú* 1075ptas. Open M-Sa 1-4pm, 8:30-11:30pm.

ba-ba-reeba, Pg. Gràcia, 28 (☎93 301 43 02). M: Pg. Gràcia. So many tapas, so little time (most under 500ptas). Good Catalan *pa* (bread) as well. Outdoor dining on the *passeig* recommended. Open daily 9am-2am.

GRÀCIA

You know you are in mellow Gràcia when you hear fellow diners speaking Catalán instead of Spanish, English, French, or German. The food is likewise authentic.

Restaurant Illa de Gràcia, C. Sant Domenic, 19 (☎93 238 02 29). A vegetarian refuge from the hot sun of Gràcia's many plaças. *Menú del día* 850ptas. Salads 500ptas. Open Tu-F 1-4pm and 8pm-midnight, Sa-Su 2-4pm and 8pm-midnight.

XAMPANYERIES For Barcelona natives, no dining out experience is complete without a glass of *cava*, a Spanish wine similar to white sparkling champagne. *Xampanyeries* (champagne-bars) fill the time between lengthy dinners and late-night clubbing. Most xampanyeries are chi-chi and ordering full bottles of cava can get pricey. A glass or two won't break the budget, however. Try **Xampu Xampany**, Gran Via, 702 (☎93 265 04 83; open 6pm-2:30am) or **Barcelonin de Vins i Esperits**, C. Valencia, 304 (☎93 215 70 83; open 6pm-2am).

◉ SIGHTS

Architecturally, Barcelona is defined by its unique Modernista treasures (see **Ruta del Modernisme**, below). **Las Ramblas**—a long bustling avenue smack in the city center—and the **Barri Gòtic**, Barcelona's "old city," are the traditional tourist areas. But don't neglect vibrant **La Ribera** and **El Raval**, the upscale avenues of L'Eixample, the panoramic city views from Montjuïc and Tibidabo, Gaudí's Parc Güell, and the harbor-side Port Olímpic. Many museums offer **free admission** the first Sunday of each month; almost all close on Mondays.

RUTA DEL MODERNISME

In the late-19th and early-20th centuries, Barcelona's flourishing bourgeoisie commissioned a new class of architects to build their houses, reshaping the face of L'Eixample with Modernista architecture. **Luis Domènech i Montaner** is known for his heavily decorated surfaces (see the Palau de la Musica Catalana and Casa Lleó i Morera), while **José Puig i Caldafach** developed an antiquarian style uniting local and foreign traditions. Most famous of all Modernista architects is **Antoni Gaudí**, with his serpentine rooftops, warrior-like chimneys, and fantastical facades.

   Ruta del Modernisme passes (600ptas, students 400ptas) are good for a month and give holders a 50% discount on entrance to Palau Güell, La Sagrada Familia, Casa Milà (La Pedrera), Palau de la Música, Casa-Museu Gaudí, Fundació Antoni Tápies, and the Museu d'Art Modern. Purchase passes at **Casa Lleó Morera**, on the corner of Pg. Grácia and C. Consedel (☎93 488 01 39; see p.868).

LAS RAMBLAS

Las Ramblas's pedestrian-only median strip is a veritable urban carnival, where street performers dance, fortune-tellers tell, human statues shift poses, and vendors sell birds—all, of course, for a small fee. The sights below are arranged beginning with Pl. Cataluña in the north, continuing to the port in the south.

UPPER LAS RAMBLAS. A port-ward journey begins at the **Font de Canaletes** (more a pump than a fountain), where visitors who wish to eventually return to Barcelona are supposed to sample the water. The upper part of Las Ramblas has been dubbed "Rambla de las Flores" for the numerous flower vendors that inhabit it. Halfway down Las Ramblas, **Joan Miró's** pavement mosaic brightens up the street.

GRAN TEATRE DEL LICEU. The Gran Teatre del Liceu has been Barcelona's **opera house** for over a century. It was once one of Europe's leading stages, nurturing the likes of José Carreras. Ravaged by a fire in January 1994, the Teatre reopened for performances in 1999. It is adorned with palatial ornamentation, gold facades, sculptures, and grand circular side rooms—a Spanish Hall of Mirrors. (*Las Ramblas, 61, on the corner of C. Sant Pau. Guided tours 800ptas, students 600ptas.*)

PALAU GÜELL. The interior of Antoni Gaudí's Palau Güell is a cross between Modernista apartment building and haunted house. The rooftop chimneys display Gaudí's first use of the *trencadis*, or covering surfaces with irregular shards of ceramic or glass. (*C. Nou de la Rambla, 3-5, 2 blocks from the Teatre Liceu. ☎93 317 51 98. Open M-Sa 10am-1pm and 4-7pm. 400ptas, students 200ptas.*)

MUSEU D'ART CONTEMPORANI (MACBA). This monstrosity of a building was constructed by American architect Richard Meier with the idea that sparse decor would allow the art to speak for itself. And it does—the MACBA has received world-wide acclaim for its focus on avant-guard art between the two world wars, as well as surrealism and contemporary art. *(Pl. dels Angels, 1. M: Universitat or Cataluña. ☎93 412 08 10; www.macba.es. Open M and W-F 11am-8pm, Sa 10am-8pm, Su 10am-3pm. 775ptas, students 550ptas, under 17 free. W 375ptas.)*

MONUMENT A COLOM. At the port end, off Las Ramblas, the Monument a Colom towers above the city. When Renaixença enthusiasts "rediscovered" Spain's role in the discovery of the Americas, they convinced themselves that Columbus was really Catalán. The fact that the statue proudly points toward Libya, not the Americas, is symbolic of the people's mistake; history shows that Columbus was actually Genoese. Take the elevator up to the top for a stunning view of Barcelona. *(Portal de la Pau. ☎93 39 02 52 24. June-Sept. 9am-8:30pm; Oct.-Mar. M-F 10am-1:30pm and 3:30-7:30pm, Sa-Su 10am-6:30pm; Apr.-May M-F 10am-1:30pm and 3:30-7:30pm, Sa-Su 10am-7:30pm. 250ptas, children 150ptas.)*

L'AQUÀRIUM DE BARCELONA. Barcelona's new aquarium is state of the art, featuring an 80m-long glass tunnel and a moving walkway through a tank of sharks and tropical fish. *(In Moll d'Espanya del Port Vell, next to Maremagnum and the cinema. M: Barceloneta. ☎93 221 74 74. Open July-Aug. 9:30am-11pm; Sept.-June 9:30am-9pm. Whopping 1450ptas per person, students 10% off.)*

BARRI GÒTIC

While the weathered, narrow streets of the Barri Gòthic, including **Carrer de la Pietat** and **Carrer del Paradis,** have preserved their medieval charm, the ever-growing tourist economy has infused a new, multilingual liveliness into the area.

PLAÇA DE SANT JAUME. Any tour of the "Old Quarter" should begin in the handsome Plaça de Sant Jaume, Barcelona's political center since Roman times. Two important buildings have dominated the square since 1823: the **Palau de la Generalitat,** the headquarters of Cataluña's autonomous government, and the **Ajuntament,** the Spanish government's seat of power. *(Palau de la Generalitat open the 2nd and 3rd Sunday of each month 10am-2pm. 30min. tours. Ajuntament open Sa-Su 10am-2pm. Free.)*

ESGLÉSIA CATEDRAL DE LA SANTA CREU. The jagged spires of the 14th-century Gothic Església Catedral de la Santa Creu are a sight in themselves. Barcelona's patron saint, Santa Euália, naps in the church **crypt.** The cathedral's **cloister** has magnolias growing in the middle and geese waddling around the periphery. *(In Pl. Seu, past the Generalitat and up C. Bisbe. Cathedral open daily 8am-1:30pm and 4-7pm. Cloister open 9am-1:15pm and 4-7pm. Free. Elevator to the rooftop M-F 9:30am-12:30pm and 4-6:30pm, Sa-Su 9:30am-12:30pm. 200ptas. Choral Chamber 125ptas.)*

LA RIBERA

In the 18th century, Felipe V demolished much of La Ribera to make space for the Ciutadella. The erstwhile stomping ground of Barcelona's many fishermen and local merchants, in recent years the neighborhood has evolved into Barcelona's bohemian nucleus, complete with art galleries, chic eateries, and exclusive bars.

PALAU DE LA MÚSICA CATALANA. In 1891, the growing Orfeo choir society commissioned Modernista architect Luis Domènech i Montaner to design this fabulous, must-see palace. The music hall glows with tall stained-glass windows, an ornate chandelier, marble reliefs, intricate woodwork, and mosaics. Debate continues over the political message of the inverted dome, which is painted with 40 women dressed as angels. Some believe that Montaner was implying that women "sing like angels" and should have been allowed in the choir (at that time it was exclusively male). Others think he was emphasizing woman's fickleness by painting her 40 "different faces." *(C. Sant Francesc de Paula, 2, off Vía Laietana near Pl. Urquinaona. Head up Vía Laietana to the intersection of C. lonqueres. ☎93 268 10 00. Open daily 10am-9pm. 700ptas, students 500ptas; 350ptas with Ruta del Modernisme pass. Box office open M-Sa 10am-9pm, Su from 1hr. before concert. Concert tickets 1000-26,000ptas.)*

MUSEU PICASSO. This incredible museum traces the development of Picasso as an artist, with a collection of his early works that weaves through the Gothic **Palau Berenguer Daguería,** five connected mansions once occupied by Barcelona's nobility. Although the museum offers little from Picasso's more well-known middle years, it has the world's best collection of work from his formative period in Barcelona. The collection includes lithographs, ceramics, pencil sketches by an 11-year-old Picasso, and an excellent display of the artist's Cubist interpretations of Velázquez's *Las Meninas* (which hangs in the Prado, see p.813). *(C. Montcada, 15-19. M: Jaume I. Walk down C. Princesa from the metro, and turn right on C. Montcada. ☎ 93 319 63 10. Open Tu-Sa 10am-8pm, Su 10am-3pm. 750ptas, students 400ptas, under 16 free.)*

SANTA MARIA DEL MAR. La Ribera's streets converge at the foot of the **Eglésia Santa María del Mar's** octagonal towers. Built in the 14th century in a quick 55 year timespan, this church is a fascinating example of the limits of Gothic architecture—were it two feet higher, it would collapse. *(☎ 93 310 23 90. Open M-Sa 9am-1:30pm and 4:30-8pm, Su 9am-2pm and 5-8:30pm.)*

PARC DE LA CIUTADELLA AND VILA OLÍMPICA

PARC DE LA CUITADELLA. Host of the 1888 Universal Exposition, the park harbors several museums, well-labeled horticulture, the wacky **Cascada** fountains, a **pond,** and a zoo. Buildings of note include Domènech i Montaner's Modernista **Castell dels Tres Dragons** (now **Museu de Zoología**), the **geological museum** (a few buildings down P. Picasso from M. Zoología), and Josep Amergós's **Hivernacle.** Expo '88 also inspired the small **Arc de Triomf,** just across Pg. Pujades from the park. Little Snowflake *(Copito de Nieve),* the world's only albino gorilla behind bars, vegetates in the **Parc Zoològic,** on the end of the park closer to the sea. *(☎ 93 221 25 06. Open June-Aug. Tu-W and F-Su 10am-2pm, Th 10am-6:30pm; Sept.-May 10am-5pm. 850ptas.)* In the center of the park, on Pl. Armes, is the **Museu d'Art Modern,** which houses a potpourri of works by 19th-century Catalán artists. *(M: Barceloneta or Arc de Triomf. ☎ 93 319 57 28. Open Tu-Sa 10am-7pm, Su 10am-2:30pm. 500ptas, students 350ptas.)*

VILA OLÍMPICA. The Vila Olímpica, beyond the east side of the zoo, was built (on top of what was once a working-class neighborhood) to house 15,000 athletes and entertain millions of tourists for the 1992 Summer Olympics. These days, it's home to several public parks, a shopping center, and business offices. In the area called **Barceloneta,** mediocre beaches stretch out from the port. *(From M: Ciutadella/Vila Olímpica, walk along the waterfront on Ronda Litoral toward the two towers.)*

L'EIXAMPLE

The Catalán Renaissance and the growth of Barcelona during the 19th century pushed the city past its medieval walls and into ordered modernity. Ildefons Cerdà, a Catalán architect, drew up an aerial plan for a new neighborhood that called for a geometric grid of squares. Dizzied by the utopian bug as the rest of the continent, Cerdà envisioned both an escape from the stress that had festered in the overcrowded Barri Gòtic as well as a new city where people of all social classes could live side by side. The resulting Eixample neighborhood gave rise to *passeigs* (streets) lined with high-brow shopping and some must-see designs.

LA SAGRADA FAMILIA. Only Gaudí's genius could draw thousands of tourists to a half-finished church. The architect himself estimated that the **Temple Expiadori de la Sagrada Familia** would take 200 years to complete. For 43 years, Gaudí obsessed over the building, even living there for the last 11 years of his life. Since then, construction has progressed erratically and controversially. Of the church's three proposed facades, only the first (actually one of the smaller ones), the nativity facade, was finished under Gaudí. A furor has arisen over recent additions, including sculptor Josep Subirach's Cubist Passion Facade on C. Sardenya (the facade you see as you enter), which some argue clashes with the rest of the structure. Elevators and a maze of staircases lead to the church's towers and bridges. The **museum** displays a model of the structure as it was meant to be completed. *(C. Marinara,* *between C. Mallorca and C. Provença. M: Sagrada Familia. ☎93 207 30 31. Open daily Apr.-Aug. 9am-8pm; Sept.-Oct. and Mar. 9am-7pm; Nov.-Feb. 9am-6pm. Church and museum 800ptas, students 600ptas. Elevator 200ptas.)*

MANZANA DE LA DISCÒRDIA. A short walk from Pl. Cataluña, the odd-numbered side of Pg. Gràcia between C. Aragó and Consell de Cent is popularly known as *la manzana de la discordia* (block of discord), referring to the clashing, aesthetic competition of the three buildings on the block. Regrettably, the bottom two floors of **Casa Lleó i Morera,** by Domènech i Montaner, were destroyed to make room for a fancy store. Here, you can buy the **Ruta del Modernisme pass** and take a tour of the upstairs, where sprouting flowers, stained glass, and legendary doorway sculptures adorn the interior. Puig i Cadafalch opted for a geometric, Moorish-influenced pattern on the facade of **Casa Amatller** at #41. Gaudí's balconies ripple like skulls and tiles sparkle in blue-purple glory on **Casa Batlló,** #43. Experts and tourists alike debate the meaning of Battllo's forboding facade; the most popular theory is that the rooftop represents Cataluña's patron Sant Jordi slaying a dragon (the chimney plays the lance).

CASA MILÀ (LA PEDRERA). *Modernisme* buffs argue that the spectacular Casa Milà apartment building, an undulating mass of granite popularly known as *La Pedrera* (the Stone Quarry), is Gaudí's most refined work. Note the intricate ironwork around the balconies and the irregularity of the front gate's egg-shaped window panes. The roof sprouts chimneys resembling armored soldiers, one of which is decorated with broken champagne bottles. Rooftop tours provide a closer look at the "Prussian helmets" (spiral chimneys inspired by the helmets worn in Wagner's operas). The winding brick attic (recently restored along with the rooftop in a multi-million-*peseta* project) has been transformed into the **Espai Gaudí,** a multimedia presentation of Gaudí's life and works. *(Pg. Gràcia, 92. Enter around the corner on C. Provença. ☎93 484 59 95. Open daily 10am-8pm. Tour M-F at noon and 6pm, Sa-Su 11am. 600ptas, students 350ptas.)*

MONTJUÏC. Throughout Barcelona's history, whoever controlled Montjuïc (Hill of the Jews) controlled the city. Dozens of rulers have modified the **fortress,** built atop an ancient Jewish cemetery; Franco made it one of his "interrogation" headquarters. The fort was not available for recreational use until Franco rededicated it to the city in 1960—a huge stone monument expresses Barcelona's (forced) gratitude for its return. The three statues in the monument symbolize the three seas surrounding Spain. *(To get to Parc de Montjuïc, take the metro to Pl. Espanya (M: Espanya) and catch bus #50 at Av. Reina María Cristina (every 10min.).)*

PALAU NACIONAL. The **Fonts Luminoses** (Illuminated Fountains), dominated by the huge central **Font Màgica** (Magic Fountain), are visible from Pl. Espanya up Av. Reina María Cristina. During the summer, they are employed in a weekend music and laser show that illuminates the mountainside and the **Palau Nacional,** located behind the fountains. *(Apr. 30-Oct. 3 Th-Su, every 30min., 9:30-11:30pm.)* The palace now houses the **Museu Nacional d'Art de Cataluña.** *(Pl. Pau Vila, 3. M: Barceloneta. ☎93 225 47 00. Open Tu-Th 10am-7pm, F-Sa 10am-8pm, Su 10am-2:30pm. 550ptas, students 350ptas.)*

OLYMPIC AREA. In 1929, Barcelona inaugurated the **Estadi Olímpic de Montjuïc** in its bid for the 1932 Olympic games. Over 50 years later, Catalán architects Federic Correa and Alfons Milà, who were also responsible for the overall design of the **Anella Olímpica** (Olympic Ring) esplanade, renovated the shell with the help of Italian architect Vittorio Gregotti. *(☎93 426 20 89. Open daily 10am-8pm. Free.)* Designed by Japanese architect Arata Isozaki, the **Palau d'Esports Sant Jordi** is the most technologically sophisticated of the structures. *(☎93 426 20 89. Call in advance.)* Test your swimming mettle in the **Olympic pools** or visit the **Galeria Olímpica.** *(Galeria ☎93 426 06 60. Open Apr.-Sept. Tu-Sa 10am-2pm and 4-8pm, Su 10am-2pm; Oct.-Mar. Tu-F 10am-1pm and 4-6pm, Su 10am-2pm. 390ptas, students 340ptas.)*

FUNDACIÓ JOAN MIRÓ. Skylights illuminate an extensive collection of statues, paintings, and tapestries from Miró's career. The collection includes the stunning

Barcelona Series, which depicts Miró's personal reaction to the Spanish Civil War, and several paintings from Miro's *Las Constelaciones* series, a reaction to Nazi invasion during World War II. His best-known pieces in the museum include *El Carnival de Arlequin, La Masia,* and *L'or de L'azuz.* Room 13 displays experimental work by young artists. *(In Parc de Montjuïc. On Av. Miramar, 71-75, at Pl. Neptú. M: Espanya, then bus #50 from Pl. Espanya. ☎ 93 329 19 08. Open July-Sept. Tu-W and F-Sa 10am-8pm, Th 10am-9:30pm, Su 10am-2:30pm; Oct.-June Tu-W and F-Sa 10am-7pm, Th 10am-9:30pm, Su 10am-2:30pm. 800ptas, students and seniors 450ptas.)*

CASTELL DE MONTJUÏC. At the top of Montjuïc mountain, this historically rich castle watches over the port. From the castle's exterior ramparts, gaze over the bay and the city. Inside, the **Museu Militar** has a large armaments display. From Barcelona, take the **funicular** to Av. Miramar. *(Pl. Raquel Meller. M: Parallel. ☎ 93 298 70 00. Every 10min., July 19-Sept. 23 10:45am-10pm; Sept. 24-July 18 10:45am-8pm. 225ptas, round-trip 375ptas.)* Take the **teleferic cable car** to the top *(June 19-Nov. 1 M-F 11:15am-8pm, Sa-Su 11:15am-9:30pm; Nov. 2-June 18, M-F 11:15am-6:30pm, Sa-Su 11:15am-7:30pm.)*

GRÀCIA

Just beyond L'Eixample, this neighborhood charms and confuses with its narrow alleys and numerous plazas. In August, Gracia hosts one of Barcelona's best festivals, **Fiesta Mejor.**

PARC GÜELL. The park was designed entirely by Gaudí, and—in typical Gaudí fashion—was not completed until after his death. Gaudí intended Parc Güell to be a garden city, and its multicolored dwarfish buildings and sparkling ceramic-mosaic stairways to house the city's elite. Two mosaic staircases flank the park, leading to a towering Modernista pavilion that Gaudí originally designed as an open-air market. The longest park bench in the world, a multicolored serpentine wonder made of tile shards, decorates the top of the pavilion. In the midst of the park is the **Casa-Museu Gaudí.** *(Access the park by bus #24 from Pg. Gràcia, which stops at the upper park entrance. Park ☎ 93 219 38 11. Open daily May-Aug. 10am-9pm; Apr. and Sept. 10am-8pm; Mar. and Oct. 10am-7pm; Nov.-Feb. 10am-6pm. Free.)*

CASA VICENS. *Modernisme* brushed Gràcia in one of Gaudí's youthful experiments, Casa Vicens. The *casa* illustrates the colorful influence of Arabic architecture and a rigidness of angles that is uncharacteristic of Gaudí's later works. *(C. Carolines, 24-26. The interior is currently closed to the public.)*

TIBIDABO

This area, although heavily touristed, affords incredible views of Barcelona, the Pyrenees, the Mediterranean, and even, on clear days, Mallorca. The souvenir shop and telescopes tucked away in the spires of the huge **Temple del Sagrat Cor (Church of the Sacred Heart)** make its religious function appear an afterthought *(round-trip elevator ride 75ptas)*. The adjacent **Parc d'Atraccions** is a favorite among Barcelona's youngsters. *(☎ 93 211 79 42. Open June W-F 10am-6pm, Sa-Su noon-8pm; July-Aug. M-F noon-10pm, Sa-Su noon-1am. Unlimited use of 12 rides 1900ptas, no rides 700ptas.)* Riding the elevator up the nearby **Torre de Collserola** communications tower (560m above sea level) can be almost as scary as the amusement park *(500ptas)*. The Tibibús runs from Pl. Cataluña to the Torre de Collserola. *(June 9-Sept. 9 every 30min., from 30min. before park opening until 30min. after closing, Sept. 10-June 8 Sa-Su and holidays every hr. 270ptas.)* An FFCC train from Pl. Cataluyna runs to Av. Tibidabo *(round-trip 1900ptas including funicular and entrance fee)*.

🎭 ENTERTAINMENT

ART GALLERIES

One of the capitals of cutting-edge art, Barcelona showcases many of the latest artistic trends. Many private showings display the works of both budding artists and renowned masters. Most of Barcelona's galleries are located in **La Ribera** around C. Montcada. Three of the best-known in the La Ribera area include: **Gallery Surrealista, Galeria Maeght,** and **Galeria Montcada.** For more in-depth gallery info, check the *Guía del Ocio.* The **Palau de la Virreina** also has information on cultural events. (*Las Ramblas, 99. Between La Boqueria market and C. Carme. M: Liceu.* ☎93 301 77 75. *Open M-F 10am-2pm and 4-8pm.*) **Centro de Informacion Cultural** distributes *Metropolitan,* Barcelona's only cultural magazine in English. (*Las Ramblas, 118.* ☎93 302 15 22, ext. 266. Open M-F 11am-2pm and 4-8pm, Sa 10am-2pm.)

THE SARDANA

The Sardana, Cataluña's regional dance, is one of the highlights of any stint in Barcelona. It is a communal dance in which men and women join hands in a closed circle and perform a series of kicks and short steps to upbeat music; travelers are welcome to participate, as long as they observe the dance's solemn atmosphere. Dances take place Saturdays at 6:30pm and Sundays at noon in front of the cathedral, in Pl. Sagrada Familia, or near Parc de la Ciutadella's fountains. Dances are also held in Pl. Sant Jaume on Sundays at 6:30pm, at Parc de l'Espanya Industrial on Fridays at 7:30pm, and elsewhere in the city on Tuesdays, Thursdays, and Fridays. Consult papers for current information.

FÚTBOL

For the record, the lunatics that run around the city covered head to toe in red and blue didn't just escape from a nearby asylum—they are **F.C. Barcelona** fans. Grab some face paint and head to the 110,000-seat **Nou Camp,** which has a box office on C. Aristedes Maillol, 12-18 (☎ 93 496 36 00). **R.C. Deportivo Espanyol,** a.k.a. *los periquitos* (parakeets), Barcelona's second professional soccer team, spreads its wings at **Estadi Olímpic,** Pg. Olímpic, 17-19 (☎93 405 02 97). Obtain tickets for both from Banca Catalana or by phoning TelEntrada (24hr. ☎902 10 12 12).

BULLFIGHTS

Although the best bullfighters rarely venture out of Madrid, Sevilla, and Málaga, Barcelona's **Plaça de Toros Monumental** (tickets ☎913 56 2200), on C. Castillejos, 248, is an excellent facility (M: Monumental). Bullfights usually take place during the tourist season (June-Oct. Sundays at 7pm; doors open at 5:30pm). Tickets are available at local travel agencies or ServiCaixa ("la Caixa" banks; ☎902 33 22 11; 2400-12,500ptas). The box office also sells tickets just before the start of the corrida. Seats range from 2600-15,000ptas; the cheapest are in the Andanada section.

FIESTAS

Fiestas abound in Barcelona. Before Christmas, the **Feria de Santa Llúcia** fills Pl. Catedral and the area around the Sagrada Familia with stalls and booths. City residents celebrate **Carnaval** February 7 to 13, but many head to even more raucous celebrations in Sitges and Vilanova i la Geltrù. Soon thereafter, the **Festa de Sant Jordi** (St. George), April 23, brings feasts in honor of Cataluña's patron saint. This is Barcelona's St. Valentine's Day; men give women roses, and women give men books. Barcelona erupts on June 23, the night before **Día de Sant Joan.** Bonfires roar throughout the city, and the fountains of Pl. Espanya and Palau Reial light up in anticipation of fireworks on Montjuïc. On August 15-21, city folk jam at Gràcia's **Fiesta Mayor.** Lights blaze in the plazas and streets, and rock bands play all night. On September 11, the **Fiesta Nacional de Cataluña** brings traditional costumes, dancing, and Catalán flags hanging from balconies. The **Feria de Cuina i Vins de Cataluña** draws wine and *butifarra* (sausage) producers to the Rbla. Cataluña. The beginning of November marks the **Fiesta del Sant Çito,** when locals and tourists alike roll up their sleeves and party on Las Ramblas. Finally, from October through November, the **Festival Internacional de Jazz** hits the city's streets and clubs. For information on all festivals, call ☎93 301 77 75 (open M-F 10am-2pm and 4-8pm).

☑ NIGHTLIFE

As in Madrid, nightlife here begins with a 5pm stroll and doesn't wind down until nearly14hr. later—if even then. The Barcelona evening can be divided into thirds: start at the *bar-restaurantes* or *cervecerías*, move to the *bares-musicales*, and finish up with a bang at the *discotecas*. As a general rule, the farther from Las Ramblas and the narrower the street, the less-touristed the bar. The trendiest *bares-musicales* are scattered around **Gracia**. Barcelona's clubs don't heat up until 2am, and most don't wind down until morning. If you are planning on clubbing, make sure to look your finest— many of the most popular *discotecas* expect a certain level of formality. At clubs, expect to be charged around 600ptas for a beer and 900ptas and up for mixed drinks. Keep in mind that what's popular changes on a daily basis—talk to locals for an up-to-the-minute report. Consult the *Guía del Ocio* for information on movies (*ciné* section), live concerts (*música*), bars, discos (*Tarde/Noche*), and cultural events.

BARRI GÓTIC

Here, cookie-cutter *cervecerías* and *bar-restaurantes* can be found every five steps. Nightlife in the Barri Gótic is perfect for chit-chatting your night away, sipping *sangría*, or scoping out your next dance partner.

Les Bosq des Fades (☎93 317 26 49), just off Las Ramblas near the water. M: Drassanes. A fairy-tale world, complete with gnarly trees, a small bridge, and plush side rooms. Open M-Th until 1:30am, F and Sa until 2:30am.

Schilling, C. Ferrán, 23 (☎93 317 67 87). M: Liceu. Though plush sofas and chandeliers cry out "exclusive," this chic bar is surprisingly diverse. Mixed gay and straight crowd. Mixed drinks 300ptas. Open M-F 9am-2am, Sa-Su 11am-2am. Su noon-2:30am.

Molly Malones, C. Ferran, 7 (☎93 342 40 26). Only one year old, this Irish bar is turning many a Spaniard into a Guinness lover. Guinness and Fargo beer on tap 650ptas. Open M-F 8pm-2:30am, Sa-Su 7pm-3am.

EL RAVAL

Though El Raval has traditionally been home to a local, unpretentious set of bars, this neighborhood is rapidly becoming a hotspot for new lounges.

El Cafe que pone Muebles Navarro, Riera Alta 4-6 (☎907 18 80 96). Friends get friendlier as they snuggle in this mellow lounge and drink themselves silly. Beer and wine 250ptas. Mixed drinks 500-700ptas. Open Tu-Th 5pm-1am, F-Sa 5pm-2:30am.

La Oveja Negra, C. Sitges, 5 (☎93 317 10 87). M: Cataluña. From Pl. Cataluña, go down Las Ramblas and take the first right onto C. Tallers; C. Sitges is the first left. Gossip about your European backpacking tryst over pitchers. Beer 325ptas. Open M-Th 9am-2:30am, F 9am-3:30am, Sa-Su 5pm-3am.

Casa Almirall, C. Joaquim Costa, 33. A cavernous space with a decaying ceiling and weathered couches, this is the oldest bar in Barcelona. Bartenders serve *absenta* (absinthe; 500ptas), the powerful licorice-flavored liquor banned everywhere except Spain and the Czech Republic for its eerie effects on the mind. Open daily 7pm-3am.

LA RIBERA

In La Ribera, the name of the game is tapas bars, where the young and beautiful gather and indulge.

Mudanzas, C. Vidrieria, 15. Everything is black, even the suits. The only color comes from hundreds of illuminated bottles lining the wall behind the bar. Wide selection of rum, whiskey, and wines (300ptas). Open daily 9:30am-2pm.

Cafe-Bar Vincent Van Gogh, C. Princesa, 23 (☎93 319 89 18). An international joint where young thangs play chess and pool. Van Gogh artwork stands out against all-black walls. Beer 300ptas. Cocktails 750ptas. Open M-F noon-3am, Sa-Su 10am-3am.

GRÀCIA

Nightlife in Gràcia is *la crème de la crème*, to borrow a phrase from Spain's northern neighbor. Most of Barcelona's funkiest *bares-musicales* are here.

Lizard, Platon 15 (☎93 414 00 32). With devil-red lighting, a central dance floor, and plenty of pool tables, Lizard is nothing but ultra-cool. Open Th-Sa 11:30pm-3am.

Mas i Mas, Maria Cubi, 199 (☎93 209 45 02). A small, crazy bar-musical. Spaniards cram themselves in to be part of the action. Open Th-Sa 11pm-3am.

Universal, Maria Cubi, 182 (☎93 201 35 96). Mention a stop at Universal and you have definitely risen in the popularity ranks. Open 11pm-3am.

MONTJUÏC

Lower Montjuïc is home to Barcelona's epic "disco theme park," **Poble Espanyol,** Av. Marqués de Comillas (☎93 322 03 26). M: Pl. Espanya. Take a cab from the metro and fall in lust with the craziest disco experience in all of Barcelona. Some of the most popular (and surreal) discos include **La Terrrazza** (an outdoor mad house), **Torres de Avila** (with speedy glass elevators), and **Sixty-Nine** (no description needed). Dancing starts at around 1:30am and doesn't end until 9am. Most clubs have cover discounts. Open July-Aug. nightly; Sept.-June Th-Sa.

PORT OLÍMPIC

Tracing the coast and marked by a gigantic metallic fish structure, the Olympic Village brims with glitzy restaurants and throngs of European dance fiends. Nearly 20 bars and clubs occupy the strip. Revelry begins at midnight and winds down at 6am. From the metro stop Ciutadella-Vila Olímpica (L4), walk down C. Marina toward the twin towers.

Luna Mora, C. Ramon Trias Fargas (Marina Village). Two levels, seven bars—enough said. Latin music and house are the specialties. On Friday nights, they teach salsa to locals and tourists alike. Open Th-Sa 11pm-5am, Su 7pm-1am.

Baja Beach Club, P. Maritim (Marina Village). Another disco, another crazy scene. Music is more mainstream. Open Th-Su until 5am.

El Gran Casino, C. de la Marina (Marina Village). Minimum bets for blackjack, American roulette, French roulette, craps, slots, and Punto Banco hover around 500ptas. No sneakers allowed. Passport ID required. Entrance fee 750ptas. Open daily 1pm-5am.

MAREMAGNUM

Like Dr. Jekyll and Mr. Hyde, Barcelona's biggest mall has more than one personality. At the stroke of midnight, the complex turns into an overwhelming tri-level maze of dance clubs. Each club plays its own music (expect to hear a lot of American pop) for crowds of international students, tourists, and the occasional Spaniard. (Beer 300-800ptas. Mixed drinks 1000ptas.) To get to Maremagnum, walk down Las Ramblas and cross over the wavy bridge to the mall.

ELSEWHERE

Most of the biggest and best *discotecas* are outside the tourist-heavy Ramblas area—these are where most natives do their dancing.

Otto Zutz, C. Lincoln, 15 (☎93 238 07 22), uptown near Pl. Molina, where C. Balmes intersects Vía Augusta. M: FFCC Muntaner. The hippest club around. 23 floors, 6 bars. The beautiful people don't show up until after 3am. Open W-Sa midnight-5am.

Les Carpes del Cel, Castelldefels "Canal Olímpic," on Autovia A-16, Castelldefels Platja exit. Huge outdoor disco complex with 3 tents, each pumping different types of music. 18 bars. Cover 1000ptas, includes 1 drink. Open June 19-Sept. 19 10:30pm-5am.

DAYTRIPS FROM BARCELONA

MONTSERRAT

FFCC trains (☎ 93 205 15 15) to Montserrat leave from M: Espanya in Barcelona (1hr.; every hr.; 1185ptas, round-trip 1855ptas); get off at Aeri de Montserrat, not Olesa de Montserrat. From the base of the mountain at the other end, the Aeri cable car runs up to the monastery (every 15min. 9:25am-1:45pm and 3-6:15pm; round-trip 950ptas, included in train fare). From the upper cable car station, turn left and walk to Pl. Creu, where there's an info booth. (☎ 93 877 72 01. Open July-Sept. daily 10am-7pm; Oct.-June M-F 9am-6pm, Sa-Su 10am-7pm.)

An hour northwest of Barcelona, the mountain of Montserrat is where a wandering 9th-century mountaineer had a blinding vision of the Virgin Mary. In the 11th century, a monastery was founded to worship the Virgin, and the site has since evolved into a major pilgrimage center. The **monastery's** ornate **basilica** is above Pl. Creu. Right of the main chapel is a route through the **side chapels** that leads to the 12th-century Romanesque **La Moreneta** (the black Virgin Mary), Montserrat's venerated icon. (Open daily in summer 8-10:30am, noon-6:30pm, and 7:30-8:30pm.) In Pl. Santa María, the **Museo de Montserrat** exhibits a sweeping range of art, from an Egyptian mummy to several Picassos. (Open daily in summer 9am-6pm; off-season 9:30am-6:30pm. 500ptas, students 300ptas.) The **Santa Cova funicular** descends from Pl. Creu to paths that wind along to ancient hermitages. (Every 20min. daily in summer 10am-1pm and 2-6pm; off-season Sa-Su only; round-trip 360ptas.) Take the **St. Joan funicular** up for more inspirational views. (Every 20min. spring through fall 10am-7pm. Round-trip 895ptas.) The dilapidated **St. Joan monastery** and **shrine** are only 20min. from the highest station. The real prize is **St. Jerónim** (1235m), about 2hr. from Pl. Creu (1hr. from the terminus of the St. Joan funicular); take the sharp left after 45min. at the little old chapel.

SITGES

Cercanías Trains link Sitges to Barcelona's Sants Station and M: Gràcia (40min., every 15min., 310-355ptas; last train back 11pm).

Forty kilometers south of Barcelona, the resort town of Sitges is famed for its prime tanning grounds, lively cultural festivals, international gay community, and wired nightlife. Long considered a watered-down Ibiza, Sitges has better beaches than the notorious Balearic hotspot, and on mainland Spain, you won't find much crazier beach-oriented nightlife. The **beach** is 10min. from the train station via any street. In town, **C. Parellades** is the main tourist drag. Late-night foolhardiness clusters around **C. Primer de Maig**, which runs directly from the beach, and its continuation, **C. Marques Montroig**. The wild things are at the "disco-beach" **Atlántida**, in Sector Terramar. Shuffle your feet at **Pachá**, on Pg. Sant Didac, in nearby Vallpineda. Buses run from midnight to 4am to the two discos from C. Primer de Maig. During **Carnaval**, March 2-12 in 2000, Spaniards crash the town for a frenzy of dancing, costumes, and alcohol. The **tourist office**, on Pg. Vilafranca, is near the train station. From the station, turn right on C. Artur Carbonell and go downhill. (☎ 93 894 42 51; fax 93 894 43 05. Open in summer daily 9am-9pm; in winter W-M 9am-2pm and 4-6:30pm.) If you plan to stay the night, reserve early. **Hostal Internacional** is at Sant Francesc, 52. (☎ 93 894 26 90. Doubles 5500ptas, with bath 6500ptas.)

OTHER DAYTRIPS FROM BARCELONA

GIRONA. Meander through the jumbled streets of historic, charming, and under-tourist Girona (see below).

THE COSTA BRAVA. Besides its stunning cliffs and beaches, the towns along the Costa Brava also offer a historic community (see p. 874).

GIRONA (GERONA)

A world-class city patiently waiting for the world to notice, Girona (pop. 70,500) is really two cities in one: a hushed medieval masterpiece on one riverbank, and a thriving, modern metropolis on the other. Though founded by the Romans, the city owes more to the renowned *cabalistas de Girona*, who for centuries spread the teachings of Kabbalah (mystical Judaism) in the West. Still a cultural center and university town, Girona is a magnet for artists, intellectuals, and activists. Most sights are in the old city, across the river from the train station. After crossing over the Pont de Pedra, turn left down Rambla de la Llibertat, continue on C. Argenteria, bear right across C. Cort Reial, climb the stairs, and head left to reach C. Força. **El Call,** the medieval Jewish neighborhood, begins at C. Sant Llorenç; take a right off C. Força into a narrow alleyway. A thriving community in the Middle Ages, it was virtually wiped out by the 1492 expulsion, mass emigration, conversion, and the Inquisition. The entrance to **Centre Bonastruc Ça Porta,** the site of the last synagogue in Girona (today a museum), is off C. Sant Llorenç about halfway up the hill. (☎972 21 67 61. Open June-Oct. M-Sa 10am-8pm, Su 10am-2pm; Nov.-May M-Sa 10am-6pm, Su 10am-2pm. Free.) Uphill on C. Força and around the corner to the right, the Gothic **cathedral** rises a record-breaking 90 Rococo steps from the plaza below. The **Tesoro Capitular** within contains some of Girona's most precious possessions, including the **Tapis de la Creació,** a 15th-century tapestry depicting the creation story. (Both open July-Aug. Tu-Su 10am-2pm and 4-7pm; Sept.-June Tu-Sa 10am-2pm and 4-7pm, Su 10am-2pm. 500ptas.) Bars near **Pl. Ferrán Catòlic** draw crowds, but during the summer, **Parc de la Devesa,** across the river from the old town and several blocks to the left, has all the cachet and live music. Of Girona's four discos, the most popular is **La Sala de Cel,** C. Pedret, 118, off Pl. Sant Pere, in the north quarter of the city. (☎972 21 46 64. Cover 2000ptas, includes 2 drinks. Open Sept.-July Th-Su.) Artsy folk mill around the bars and cafes in the old quarter.

Girona is the Costa Brava's transport center: all trains between Barcelona and southern France stop here, and scores of buses travel daily to the Costa Brava. **Trains** (☎972 20 70 93) depart from off C. Barcelona in the new town to Madrid (9-10½hr., 1 per day, 6000-7500ptas); Barcelona (1¼hr., 21 per day, 1265ptas); and Figueres (45min., 22 per day, 325ptas). **Buses** (☎972 21 23 19) depart from just around the corner. To get to the old city from the station, head straight through the parking lot, turn left on C. Barcelona, bear right via C. Santa Eugenia to the Gran Vía de Jaume III, continue straight across to C. Nou, and cross the Pont de Pedra. The **tourist office,** Rambla de la Llibertat 1, is directly on the other side. (☎972 22 65 75; fax 972 22 66 12. Open M-F 8am-8pm, Sa 8am-2pm and 4-8pm, Su 9am-2pm.) The ultra-modern **Alberg-Residència Cerverí de Girona (HI),** C. Ciutadans 9, is on the street to the left directly after the Pont de Pedra. (☎972 21 81 21, in Aug. ☎934 83 83 63. Sheets 350ptas. Dorms 1900ptas, over 25 2500ptas.) The **Pensió Viladomat,** C. Ciutadans 5, next to the hostel, has clean, well-furnished rooms. (☎972 20 31 76. Singles 2300ptas; doubles 4500ptas, with bath 6600ptas; triples 6500ptas.) Girona abounds with innovative Cataluñan cuisine; for inexpensive food, try restaurants along **C. Cort Reial. Café Le Bistrot,** Pujada Sant Domènec 4, packs in locals for its lunchtime *menú* (1400ptas), pizza, and crêpes. (Open M-Sa 1-5pm and 7pm-1am, M-Th until 1:30am.) Pick up **groceries** at **Supeco,** C. Sequia 10, a block from C. Nou off the Gran Vía. (Open M-Sa 9am-1:30pm and 5-8:30pm.) **Postal Code:** 17070.

THE COSTA BRAVA

The Costa Brava's jagged cliffs cut into the Mediterranean Sea from Barcelona to the French border. Though rugged by name, the Brave Coast is tamed in July and August by the planeloads of Europeans dumped onto its once tranquil beaches (you'll make the most friends if you speak German). Unlike its counterparts, Costa Blanca and Costa del Sol, Costa Brava offers more than just high-rises and touristy beaches. The rocky shores have traditionally attracted artists, like Marc Chagall and Salvador Dalí, a Costa Brava native.

TOSSA DE MAR

Far from undiscovered, pretty Tossa de Mar (pop. 3800), about 40km north of Barcelona, is packed with tourists in summer. That said, the town still stands out for its **beaches**, framed by reddened cliffs; its **calas** (small bays), accessible by foot; and its small-town sincerity, long since abandoned by larger resort towns. Inside the walled **Vila Vella** (Old Town), spiraling medieval alleys lead to a tiny plaza, where the **Museu Municipal** displays 20s and 30s art. (Open June-Sept. Tu-Su 10am-7pm; Oct.-May Tu-Su 10am-1pm and 3-6pm. 1000ptas.) Sarfa **buses** run to Pl. de les Nacions Sense Estat, at the corner of Av. de Pelegrí and Av. Ferrán Agulló, from Girona (1hr., 2 per day, 615ptas) and Barcelona (3½hr., 8-9 per day, 1070ptas). The **tourist office** shares the same building. (☎972 34 01 08; fax 972 34 07 12. Open mid-June to mid-Sept. M-Sa 9am-9pm, Su 10am-1pm; May to mid-June and mid-Sept. to Oct. M-Sa 10am-1pm and 4-8pm; Nov.-Apr. M-F 10am-1pm and 4-7pm, Sa 10am-1pm.) **Pensión Pepi**, C. Sant Miguel 10, offers cozy rooms with bath. Turn left off Av. de Pelegrí onto Maria Auxiliadora and veer right onto C. Sant Miguel. (☎972 34 05 26. Singles 2000ptas; doubles 4000ptas.) To get to **Fonda/Can Lluna,** C. Roqueta 20, turn right off Pg. Mar onto C. Peixeteras, walk through C. Estalt, turn left at the end, and head straight. (☎972 34 03 65. 1750-1900ptas per person.) **Camp** at **Can Martí,** at the end of Rambla Pau Casals, off Av. Ferrán Agulló. (☎972 34 08 51; fax 972 34 24 61. 675ptas per person, 725ptas per car.) Try the paella at **Restaurant Marina,** C. Tarull 6. (Open *Semana Santa*-Oct. daily 11am-11pm.) **Postal Code:** 17320.

FIGUERES

In 1974, Salvador Dalí chose his native, beachless Figueres (pop. 37,000), 36km north of Girona, as the site to build a museum to house his works, catapulting the city to instant fame. Despite his reputation as a self-promoting fascist, his self-monument is undeniably a masterpiece—and the second most popular museum in Spain. The ▓**Teatre-Museu Dalí,** in Pl. Gala i S. Dalí, parades the artist's erotically nightmarish landscapes, and bizarre installations. From the Rambla, take C. Girona, which becomes C. Jonquera, and climb the steps. (Open July-Sept. daily 9am-7:15pm and 10pm-12:30am; Oct.-June 6 10:30am-5:15pm and 10pm-12:30am. 1000ptas, students 800ptas.) **Trains** (☎972 20 70 93) run to Girona (30min., 21 per day, 325ptas) and Barcelona (1½hr., 21 per day, 1300ptas). **Buses** (☎972 67 33 54) truck to Girona (1hr., 4-6 per day, 475ptas); Barcelona (2¼hr., 4-6 per day, 1750ptas); and Cadaqués (1¼hr., 2-5 per day, 490ptas). The **tourist office** is on Pl. Sol. (☎972 50 31 55. Open July-Aug. M-Sa 8am-9pm, Su 9am-6pm; Easter-June and Oct. M-F 8:30am-3pm and 4:30-8pm, Sa 9:30am-1:30pm and 3:30-6:30pm; Sept. and Nov.-Easter M-F 8:30am-3pm.) Get on the **internet** at Bar-Arcadia, C. Sant Antoni, 7. (☎972 67 38 91. 500ptas per 30min. Open M-Sa 9am-10pm.) Even finding a place to sleep in Figueres can be a surreal experience, but **Alberg Tramuntana (HI),** C. Anciet de Pagès 2, behind the tourist office, is cheap and chock full o' amenities. (☎972 50 12 13; fax 972 67 38 08. Members only; sells HI cards. Breakfast included. Sheets 350ptas. Reception 8am-2pm and 4-11pm. Lockout M-F 2-4pm, Sa-Su 1-7pm. Curfew midnight; in summer open for 10min. at 1, 2, 3, and 4am. Reserve in advance through the Barcelona office (☎93 483 83 63) or call the hostel 2-3 days ahead. 1900ptas, under 27 2500ptas.) Buy groceries at **MAXOR,** Pl. Sol 5. (Open July-Sept. M-F 8am-9pm, Sa 8am-9pm; Oct.-June M-Sa 8am-8:30pm.) **Postal Code:** 17600.

CADAQUÉS

The whitewashed houses and rocky beaches of Cadaqués (pop. 1800) have attracted artists, writers, and musicians—not to mention tourists—ever since Dalí built his summer home here in the 30s. The **Centre d'Art Perrot-Moore,** C. Vigilant 1, near the town center, houses a Dalí erotic fantasy room. (Open July-Aug. daily 10:30am-1:30pm and 4:30-8:30pm; Apr.-June and Sept.-Oct. M-Sa 10:30am-1:30pm and 4:30-8pm. 800ptas, students 500ptas.) ▓**Casa-Museu Salvador Dalí,** Port Lligat, Dalí's home until 1982, is complete with a pop-art miniature Alhambra and lip-shaped sofa. Follow the signs to Port Lligat (bear right with your back to the statue of liberty) and then to the Casa de Dalí. (Open mid-June to mid-Sept. daily 10:30am-

> ## IS THAT A MELTING CANDLE IN YOUR POCKET?
>
> By age 15, Dalí already had high hopes for himself: "I'll be a genius and the world will admire me." Dalí was influenced by Sigmund Freud, and sought to connect the unconscious with the conscious in his paintings. Surrealism itself attempted to explore the language of dreams in order to tap the unconscious. Although Dalí's paintings can be confusing at first, aspects of their symbol-language are consistent enough to be translated. Here are a few examples:
>
> A rotting **donkey** or **fish** is Dalí's symbol of the bourgeoise.
> The **crutches** propping up bits of soft flesh are symbols of masturbation.
> The **grasshopper** is a symbol of terror, as Dalí had a great fear of the insect.
> **Staircases** are a Freudian image, representing the fear of intercourse.
> A **melting candle** is a symbol of impotence.
> **Lions** represent animal aggression and **knives** are meant to be phallic symbols.
> A **fish hook** (found in Dalí's head) is a symbol of his entrapment.

9pm; mid-Mar. to mid-June and mid-Sept. to Nov. Tu-Su 10:30am-6pm. 1200ptas, students 700ptas.) For a beach excursion, try the rocky **Platja Gran,** near the town center, or Sa Concha, 5min. away. **Buses** arrive from Figueres (1hr., 3-5 per day, 500ptas); Girona (2hr., 1-2 per day, 940ptas); and Barcelona (2½hr., 2-5 per day, 2045ptas). With your back to the Sarfa office at the bus stop, walk right along Av. Caritat Serinyana; the **tourist office,** C. Cotxe 2, is off Pl. Frederic Rahola opposite the *passeig*. (☎972 25 83 15; fax 15 95 42. Open July-Aug. M-Sa 10am-2pm and 4-9pm, Su 10am-1pm; Sept.-June M-Sa 10:30am-1pm and 4-8pm.) **Hostal Cristina,** C. Riera, has newly renovated, waterfront rooms. (☎972 25 81 38. Singles 3000ptas; doubles 5000-6000ptas.) **Camping Cadaqués,** Ctra. Portlligat 17, is on the left on the way to Dalí's house. (☎972 25 81 26. Open June to mid-Sept. 565ptas per person, 710ptas per tent, 565ptas per car; add 7% IVA.) Pack a picnic from **Super Auvi,** C. Riera. (Open daily mid-July to Aug. M-Sa 8am-9pm, Su 8am-2pm; Sept. to mid-July M-Sa 8am-2pm and 4-9pm, Su 8am-2pm.) **Postal Code:** 17488.

THE PYRENEES

The jagged green mountains, Romanesque churches, and tranquil towns of the Pyrenees draw hikers and high-brow skiers in search of outdoor adventures. Mist and fog obscure visibility at high altitudes, creating either a dreamy atmosphere or slightly nerve-racking driving conditions. *Ski España* lists vital statistics of all ski stations in Spain. Without a car, transport is tricky, but feasible.

VAL D'ARAN

Some of the Catalán Pyrenees' most dazzling peaks cluster around Val d'Aran, in the northwest corner of Cataluña. The Val d'Aran is best known for its chic ski resorts—the Spanish royal family's favorite slopes are those of **Baquiera-Beret.** Ladies, it's probably as good a place as any to have a chance encounter with the very eligible Prince Felipe. The **Albergue Era Garona (HI),** a few kilometers away in the town of **Salardú,** is accessible by shuttle **bus** in high-season from Vielha (see below). (☎973 64 52 71. HI members only; HI cards sold. Breakfast included. Sheets 350ptas. July-Aug. and winter weekends dorms 1900ptas, over 25 2250ptas; rest of the year dorms 1775ptas, over 25 1900ptas.) For skiing info, contact the **Oficeria de Baquiera-Beret** (☎973 64 44 55) or the tourist office in Vielha (☎973 64 01 10).

The biggest town in the valley, **Vielha** (pop. 3700) welcomes hikers and skiers to its lively streets with every sort of service the outdoorsy-type might desire. Only 12km from Bacquiera-Beret, shuttle **buses** connect the two in July and August (schedules at the tourist office). Alsina Graells **buses** (☎973 26 85 00) also run to Barcelona (5½hr., 4 per day, 3325ptas). The **tourist office,** C. Sarriulèra 6, is one block upstream from the *plaça*. (☎973 64 01 10; fax 973 64 05 37. Open daily July to mid-Sept. 9am-1pm and 4-8pm; mid-Sept. to June M-Sa 10am-1pm and 4:30-7:30pm.)

Several inexpensive *pensiones* cluster at the end of C. Reiau, off Pg. Libertat (which intersects Av. Casteiro at Pl. Sant Antoni); try **Casa Vicenta** at # 3. (☎973 64 08 19. Singles 2500-3000ptas; doubles 4000-4500ptas.)

PARQUE NACIONAL DE ORDESA

The beauty of Ordesa's Aragonese Pyrenees will reduce even the most seasoned of travelers to monosyllabic stupefaction. Well-maintained trails cut across idyllic forests, jagged rock faces, snow-covered peaks, rushing rivers, and magnificent waterfalls. The **visitor center "El Parador"** is beyond the Ordesa park entrance. (Open daily June 9am-1:30pm and 4-7pm; July-Aug. 9am-1pm and 3:30-7pm; Apr.-May 9am-2pm and 3:30-6pm.) The **Soaso Circle** is the most practical hike; frequent signposts clearly mark the 5hr. journey, which can be cut to a 2hr. loop.

It is easiest to enter the park through the village of **Torla**, where you can buy the indispensable *Editorial Alpina* guide (675ptas). **La Oscense** (☎974 35 50 60) sends a **bus** from Jaca to **Sabiñánigo** in July (30min.; M-Sa 10:15am and 6:15pm, Su 10:15am; 110ptas). Sabiñánigo is also easily accessible by **train;** all trains on the Zaragoza-Huesca-Jaca line stop here. From there **Compañia Hudebus** (☎974 21 32 77) runs to **Torla** (55min.; Sept.-June 1 per day, 11am; July-Aug. 2 per day, 11am and 6pm; 355ptas). A bus shuttles between Torla and Ordesa during July and August (every 15min., round-trip 200ptas). Off-season, you'll have to hike the 8km to the entrance or cab it. (☎974 48 62 43. 1500-2000ptas.) To leave the area, catch the bus as it passes through Torla at 3:30pm on its way back to Sabiñánigo. In the park, many **refugios** (mountain huts) allow overnight stays. The 120-bed **Refugio Góriz** is a 4hr. hike from the parking lot. (☎974 34 12 01. 1000ptas per person.) In Torla, ascend C. Francia one block to reach **Refugio L'Atalaya**, C. Francia 45 (☎974 48 60 22), and **Refugio Briet** (☎974 48 62 21), across the street. (Both 1000ptas per person.) Opposite Refugio L'Atalaya, **Compañia de Ordesa** (☎974 48 64 17) rents mountain bikes and organizes excursions. Outside Torla are **Camping Río Ara** (☎974 48 62 48) and **Camping San Anton** (☎974 48 60 63). (Both 550ptas per person, per tent, and per car. Open Apr.-Oct.) Stock up at **Supermercado Torla,** on C. Francia. (Open daily Feb.-Nov. 8am-2pm and 4-8pm; Dec.-Jan. 10am-2pm and 4-8pm.)

JACA

For centuries, pilgrims bound for Santiago would cross the Pyrenees into Spain, spend the night in Jaca (pop. 14,000), and be off by dawn. They had the right idea; use it as launching pad for the Pyrenees. RENFE **trains** (☎974 36 13 32) run from C. Estación to Madrid (7hr., 1 per day, 4200ptas) and Zaragoza (3hr., 2 per day, 1325ptas); **buses** shuttle from the station to the Ayuntamiento on the central C. Mayor. From the **bus station** on Av. Jacetania, walk through the *plaça* to C. Zocotin and go straight two blocks to reach C. Mayor. La Oscense **buses** (☎974 35 50 60) run to Pamplona (2hr., 1 per day, 860ptas) and Zaragoza (2hr., 1 per day, 1460ptas). The **tourist office,** Av. Regimiento de Galicia 2, is off C. Mayor. (☎974 36 00 98. Open July-Aug. M-F 9am-2pm and 4:30-8pm, Sa 10am-1:30pm and 5-8pm, Su 10am-1:30pm; Sept.-June M-F 9am-1:30pm and 4:30-7pm, Sa 10am-1pm and 5-7pm.) To get to the **Albergue Juvenil de Escuelas Pias (HI),** Av. Perimetral 6, from C. Mayor, turn left on C. Regimiento de Galicia, turn left on Av. Perimetral, and turn right after the bend on the dirt driveway before the sports center. (☎974 36 05 36. Curfew midnight. 2500ptas per person, over 26 3100ptas; nonmembers add 500ptas.) Or check out the decidedly hip *casa rural* **El Arco,** C. San Nicolas, 4, where each room has its own distinctive flavor. (☎974 36 44 48. 1800ptas per bunk or 1, 2 and 3-person suites available from 3000-4000ptas.)

NAVARRA

The spirit of the Navarrese emanates from the rustic Pyrenean *pueblos* on the French border to bustling Pamplona to the dusty villages in the south. Bordered by Basque Country to the west and Aragón to the east, Navarra's little-visited villages greet tourists with open arms.

PAMPLONA (IRUÑA)

Long, long ago, Pamplona's fiesta in honor of its patron saint *San Fermín* was just another religious holiday. These days *San Fermines*, July 6-14, is the most talked about holiday in Spain and on the European backpacker circuit. Ever since Nobel-prize-winning author Ernest Hemingway brought the city international attention with *The Sun Also Rises*, hordes of visitors from around the world have come to witness and experience the legendary running of the bulls. At the bullring, a statue of Hemingway welcomes fans to Europe's premier festival, an eight-day extravaganza of dancing, dashing, and of course, drinking. Though *San Fermines* may be the city's only irresistable attraction, Pamplona (pop. 150,000) is a pleasant place to visit the other 357 days of the year as well.

⎚ TRANSPORTATION

Flights: Aeropuerto de Noaín (☎948 16 87 00), 6km away, accessible only by taxi (about 1200ptas).

Trains: Estación RENFE (☎948 13 02 02), off Av. San Jorge. Take bus #9 from Po. Sarasate (20min., 95ptas). Info open daily 6am-10pm. Trains run to: **Madrid** (5hr., 8 per day, 4200ptas); **Barcelona** (6-8hr., 2-3 per day, 4100-5300ptas); **San Sebastián** (2hr., 2 per day, 1195-1500ptas); and **Zaragoza** (2hr., 6 per day, 1565-1900ptas).

Buses: Estación de Autobuses (☎948 22 38 54), at the corner of C. Conde Oliveto and C. Yanguas y Miranda leave town for **Madrid** (5hr., 4-7 per day, 3215ptas); **Barcelona** (5½hr., 3-4 per day, 2820ptas); **Bilbao** (2hr., 6-7 per day, 1520-1500ptas); **San Sebastián** (1 hr., 9 per day, 790ptas); and **Zaragoza** (2-3hr., 6-7 per day, 1655ptas).

Public Transportation: 14 buses cover the city. Bus #9 (orange line) runs from Po. Sarasate to the train station (20min., every 10-15min., 95ptas). During *San Fermines* buses run 24hrs. (150ptas).

Car Rental: Hertz (☎948 31 15 95), in Hotel Tres Reyes, on Jardines de la Taconera. Rentals start at 8000ptas per day plus taxes. Must be over 25 to rent. Open M-Sa 9am-1pm and 4-7pm.

✳❼ ORIENTATION AND PRACTICAL INFORMATION

The **casco antiguo**, in the northeast quarter of the city, houses almost everything of interest in Pamplona. **Plaza del Castillo**, marked by a bandstand, is Pamplona's center. From the **bus station**, turn left onto Av. Conde Oliveto. At the traffic circle on Pl. Príncipe de Viana, take the second left onto Av. San Ignacio, follow it to the end of the pedestrian thoroughfare Po. Sarasate, and bear right. From the **train station**, take bus #9 (95ptas); disembark at the last stop, cut across Po. Sarasate, and walk diagonally to Pl. Castillo.

Tourist Office: C. Hilarión Eslava, 1 (☎948 20 65 40; fax 948 20 70 34; www.pamplona.net). From Pl. Castillo, take C. San Nicolas, turn right on C. San Miguel, and walk straight through Pl. San Francisco. Info about currency exchange, public baths, and campsite buses is posted on a bulletin board outside. Open during *San Fermines* daily 10am-5pm; July-Aug. M-Sa 10am-2pm and 4-7pm, Su 10am-2pm; Sept.-June M-F 10am-2pm and 4-7pm, Sa 10am-2pm.

Luggage Storage: At the **bus station**. Bags 200ptas per day, large packs 300ptas per day. Open M-Sa 6:15am-9:30pm, Su 6:30am-1:30pm and 2-9:30pm. Closes for *San Fermines*, when the **Escuelas de San Francisco**, the big stone building at one end of Pl. San Francisco, opens. 300ptas each time you check on your luggage.

Emergency: ☎112. **Municipal Police,** C. Monasterio de Irache, 2 (☎092).

Medical Services: Hospital de Navarra (☎948 42 21 00), C. Irunlarrea. The **Red Cross** sets up stands in the bus station and the *corrida* during *San Fermines*.

Internet: iturNet cibercafé, C. Iturrama, 1 (☎948 25 28 20; www.iturnet.es), on the corner of C. Abejeras. Bus #2 stops on C. Iturrama. From the bus station, take a left on C. Yanguas y Miranda, then head across Pl. Fueros to C. Abejeras. 500ptas per hr. Open M-Sa 10am-2pm and 4:30-10pm; daily 9am-2pm during San Fermines.

Post Office: Po. Sarasate, 9 (☎948 21 26 00). Open M-F 8:30am-8:30pm, Sa 9:30am-2pm; *San Fermines*, closed July 7, M-Sa 8:30am-2pm. **Postal Code:** 31001.

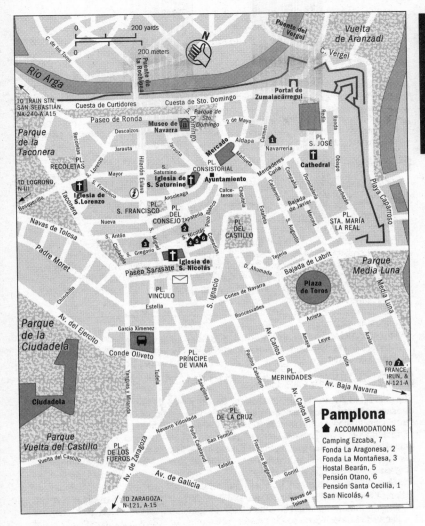

Pamplona

⌂ ACCOMMODATIONS

Camping Ezcaba, 7
Fonda La Aragonesa, 2
Fonda La Montañesa, 3
Hostal Bearán, 5
Pensión Otano, 6
Pensión Santa Cecilia, 1
San Nicolás, 4

▲ ACCOMMODATIONS

And now, kids, a lesson in supply and demand: smart *sanferministas* book their rooms up to a year (at least two months) in advance, often paying up-front rates up to four times higher than those listed here. Beware hawkers at the train and bus stations—quality and prices vary tremendously. Check the newspaper *Diario de Navarra* for **casas particulares.** Many roomless folks find themselves sleeping on the lawns of the Ciudadela or on Pl. Fueros, Pl. Castillo, or the banks of the river. Be careful—if you can't store your backpack (storage fills fast), sleep on top of it.

Pensión Santa Cecilia, C. Navarrería, 17 (☎948 22 22 30). From C. Chapitela (off Pl. Castillo), take the 1st right on C. Mercaderes, then turn left; the hostel is on the left. Laundry 500ptas. *San Fermines* 6000ptas per person. Rest of year singles 2500ptas; doubles 4000-5000ptas; triples 6000ptas.

Angeles Arrondo Lizarraga Pensión, C. Estafeta, 25, 5th fl. (☎948 22 18 16). Look for the green and white CAMAS sign. Cozy rooms with clean, colorful bathrooms. *San Fermines* 4000-6000ptas per person. Rest of year singles 1500ptas; doubles 3000ptas.

Fonda La Aragonesa, C. San Nicolás, 22 (☎948 22 34 28). For reception, cross the street to Hostal Bearán. Simple rooms, shiny hallways, and aromatic bathrooms. *San Fermines* doubles 9000ptas. July-Sept. doubles 3500ptas; rest of the year doubles 3000ptas.

Hostal Bearán, C. San Nicolás, 25 (☎948 22 34 28). Squeaky-clean salmon-colored rooms with phone, TV, bath, safebox, and a whopping pricetag. *San Fermines* singles 13,000ptas; doubles 15,000ptas. July-Sept. singles 5500ptas; doubles 6500ptas. Oct.-June singles 4500ptas; doubles 5500ptas.

Fonda La Montañesa, C. San Gregorio, 2 (☎948 22 43 80). You can't beat the price. No reservations are accepted during the fiesta, so show up early in the morning. Owner may be flexible with how many to a room. *San Fermines* single 6000ptas; doubles 12,000ptas; rest of year singles 1800ptas; doubles 3500ptas.

Pension Otano, C. San Nicolas, 5 (☎948 27 85 08). Doubles have bath, TV, winter-heating and air-conditioning. *San Fermines* doubles 16,000ptas; 5500ptas rest of year.

San Nicolás, C. San Nicolás, 13 (☎948 22 13 19). Helpful staff keeps small but pleasant rooms all with shared baths and decent beds. *San Fermines* dorms 5000ptas. Rest of year dorms 2000-2500ptas.

Camping: Camping Ezcaba (☎948 33 03 15), in Eusa, 7km outside Pamplona on the road to Irún. From Pl. Toros, La Montañesa bus runs to Eusa (4 per day, 9:10am-8:30pm) or take the city bus, line 4-1 (every 20min, 95ptas). Get off at the gasoline station, the last stop. Capacity 714 campers, although it fills fast during *San Fermines*. No reservations accepted. 540ptas per person, per tent, and per car; 1100ptas during *San Fermines*. Open June-Oct.

🍴 FOOD

While *San Fermines* draws street vendors selling everything from roast chicken to *churros*, the tiny neighborhoods of Pamplona advertise hearty *menús* throughout the year. Try the side streets in the area above Pl. San Francisco, and C. Jarauta and C. Descalzos, near Po. Ronda. Grab **groceries** at **Vendi,** on C. Hilarión Eslava and C. Mayor. (Open during *San Fermines* M-Sa 9am-2pm; otherwise M-F 9am-2pm and 5:30-7:30pm, Sa 9am-2pm.)

Restaurante Sarasate, C. San Nicolás, 19-21 (☎948 22 57 27), above the seafood store. Healthy and delicious vegetarian cuisine awaits toxin-filled *Sanferministas* in a pleasant, spotless dining room. Lunchtime *menú* 1500ptas. Open M-Th 1:15-4pm and 8:15-11pm, F-Sa 1:15-4pm and 9-11pm.

Restaurante San Fermín, C. San Nicolás, 44-46 (☎948 22 21 91). Tranquil upstairs dining room. *The* place to celebrate your brush with death. Main dishes 1800-2400ptas. Open M-F 1-3:30pm and 9-11:30pm, Sa 1-3:30pm and 8:30-11:30pm; *San Fermines* M-Sa 1-5pm and 8:30pm-12:30am, Su 1-3:30pm.

Hong Kong, C. San Gregorio, 38 (☎948 22 66 35). Come with friends and split a 2, 3, 4, or 5-person *menú* (2700-6750ptas). Noodle and fried rice dishes 600-1000ptas. Open daily noon-4pm and 8pm-midnight.

👁 🎵 SIGHTS AND ENTERTAINMENT

Pamplona's rich architectural legacy gives reason enough to visit. The recently restored late 14th-century **Gothic cathedral** is at the end of C. Navarrería. (Open M-F 10am-1:30pm and 4-7pm, Sa 10am-1:30pm. Tours at 10:30, 11:30am, 12:30, and 5pm. 500ptas.) The impressive walls of the pentagonal **Ciudadela** once humbled even Napoleon; today the Ciudadela hosts free exhibits and concerts in summer. From the old quarter, pick up C. Redín at the far end of the cathedral plaza, head left along the walls past the **Portal de Zumalacárregui** and along the Río Arga, and bear left through the **Parque de la Taconera.** (Open daily 7am-10pm; closed for *San Fermines.* Free.) Throughout the year, **Pl. de Castillo** is the social heart of the city. Hemingway's favorite haunt was the **Café-Bar Iruña,** which he immortalized in *The Sun Also Rises.* (Open daily 5pm-3am.) The young and the restless booze up at bars in the *casco antiguo,* around **Calles de Jarauta, San Nicolas,** and **San Gregorio.**

Although Pamplona is usually a very safe city, crime skyrockets during *San Fermines,* when some unfortunately come to the fiesta to take advantage of tourists—beware assaults and muggings. Do not roam alone at night, and take extreme care in the parks and shady streets of the *casco antiguo.*

LOS SAN FERMINES (JULY 6-14, 2001)

Visitors from the world overcrowd Pamplona for one week of the year in search of Europe's greatest party. Pamplona delivers, with an eight-day frenzy of parades, bullfights, parties, dancing, fireworks, concerts, and wine. Pamplonese, uniformly clad in white garb with red sashes and bandanas, literally throw themselves into the merry-making, displaying obscene levels of both physical stamina and alcohol tolerance. The "Running of the Bulls," called the *encierro,* is the focal point of *San Fermines;* the first *encierro* of the festival takes place on July 7 at 8am and is repeated at 8am every day for the following seven days. Hundreds of bleary-eyed, hung-over, hyper-adrenalized runners flee from very large bulls as bystanders cheer from barricades, windows, balconies, and doorways. Both the bulls and the mob are dangerous; terrified runners, all convinced the bull is right behind them, flee for dear life, and without concern for those around them. Hemingway had the right idea: don't run. Watch the *encierro* from the bullring instead; arrive around 6:45am. Tickets for the Grada section of the ring are available before 7am (M-F 450ptas, Sa-Su 600ptas). You can watch for free, but the free section is overcrowded, and it can be hard to see and breathe. If you want to participate in the bullring excitement, you can line up by the Pl. Toros well before 7:30am and run in *before* the bulls are even in sight. To watch one of the bullfights, wait in the line that forms at the bullring around 8pm every evening (from 2000ptas). As one bullfight ends, tickets go on sale for the next day's fight. Once the running is over, the insanity spills into the streets and gathers steam until nightfall, when it explodes with singing in the bars, dancing in the alleyways, spontaneous parades, and a no-holds-barred party in Pl. Castillo, which quickly becomes Europe's biggest open-air dance floor.

RUNNING SCARED So, you're going to run danger. No one wants to see you end up on evening news programs around the world, so here are a few words of *San Fermines* wisdom:

■ Research the *encierro* before you run. The tourist office dispenses a pamphlet that outlines the route of the three-minute run and offers tips for inexperienced runners.

■ Do not stay up all night drinking and carousing. Not surprisingly, hung-over foreigners have the highest rate of injury. Experienced runners get lots of sleep the night before. Access to the course closes at 7:30am.

■ Give up on getting near the bulls and concentrate on getting to the bullring in one piece. Although some whack the bull with rolled newspapers, runners should never distract or touch the animals; anyone who does is likely to anger the bull and locals alike.

■ Try not to cower in a doorway; people have been trapped and killed this way.

■ Be particularly wary of isolated bulls—they seek company in the crowds.

■ If you fall, **stay down.** Curl up into a fetal position, lock your hands behind your head, and **do not get up** until the clatter of hooves has passed.

ARAGÓN

A striking collage of semi-deserts and lush mountain peaks, Aragón's landscape reflects the influence of both a Mediterranean and a Continental climate. In the south, sun-baked towns give way to prosperous Zaragoza, while up north the stunning snow-capped peaks of the Pyrenees peer down on tiny medieval towns. The region's harsh terrain and climate, coupled with its strategic location, have produced a martial culture known among Spaniards for its obstinacy.

ZARAGOZA

Augustus founded Zaragoza (pop. 603,000) in 14 BC, modestly naming it Caesaraugusta after himself. The city gained everlasting fame when the Virgin Mary later dropped in for a visit; it's been a pilgrimage site ever since. The massive Baroque **Basílica de Nuestra Señora del Pilar** dominates the vast **Plaza del Pilar,** defining the skyline with brightly colored tiled domes. The interior is even more incredible, with frescoes by Goya and Velázquez. Don't leave without seeing the panoramic views from one of the towers; take the elevator in the corner, on the left as you face the **Museo del Pilar,** which exhibits the glittering *Joyero de la Virgen* (Virgin's jewels). (Basilica open daily 5:45am-9:30pm; free. Museum open daily 9am-2pm and 4-6pm; 200ptas. Elevator runs June-Aug. Sa-Th 9:30am-2pm and 4-7pm; Sept.-May Sa-Th 9:30am-2pm and 4-6pm; 200ptas.) The **Palacio de la Aljafería,** on C. Castillo, is the principle relic of Aragón's Moorish era. Head left on C. Coso from Pl. España as you face the *casco viejo,* continue on Conde Aranda, and turn right on Pl. Maria Agustín, then left on C. Aliaferia. (Open Apr. 15- Oct.15 M-W and Sa 10am-2pm and 4:30-8pm, F 4:30-8pm, Su 10am-2pm; mid-Oct. to mid-Apr. closed Sa. 300ptas, students 150ptas.) The **Museo Pablo Gargallo,** on Pl. San Felipe, houses marvelous works by one of the most innovative sculptors of the 1920s. From Pl. España, walk down C. Don Jaime I, turn left on C. Menéndez Nuñez, and walk 5min. to the plaza. (Open Tu-Sa 10am-2pm and 5-9pm, Su 10am-2pm. Free.)

Trains (☎976 21 11 66) run from Av. Anselmo Clavé to Madrid (3hr., 8 per day, 3300ptas); Barcelona (4hr., 7 per day, 3400ptas); San Sebastián (4hr., 2 per day, 2900ptas); and Valencia (6hr., 2 per day, 2525ptas). Agreda Automóvil **buses** (☎976 22 93 43) go from Po. María Agustín 7 to Madrid (3½hr., 15-18 per day, 1750ptas) and Barcelona (3½hr., 16-19 per day, 1640ptas). From the train station, cross Av. Anselmo Clavé, head down C. General Mayandía, turn right on Po. María Agustín (which becomes Po. Pamplona and leads to Pl. Paraíso), follow Po. Independencia from the plaza to Pl. de España, and continue on C. Don Jaime I (to the right) to reach Pl. Pilar; from the bus station, turn right as you exit and follow the same directions. The **tourist office** is on Pl. Pilar, in the black glass cube. (☎972 20 12 00; fax 972 20 06 35. Open daily 10am-8pm.) Take bus #22 from the train station to reach **Albergue-Residencia Juvenil Baltasar Gracián (HI),** C. Franco y Lopez, 4. (☎976 55 15 04. Curfew midnight. Dorms 1100ptas, over 25 1500ptas.) **Hostal Ambos Mundos** is on Pl. Pilar 16, at C. Don Jaime I. (☎976 29 97 04. Singles 2700ptas; doubles 5000ptas.) **Casa Pascualillo,** C. Libertad, 5, in the El Tubo district, serves cheap, wholesome food. (☎976 39 72 03. *Menú* 1000ptas. Open Tu-Sa 1-4pm and 8-11pm, Su 1-4pm.) Get **groceries** at **Galerías Primero,** C. San Jorge the continuation of C. Merdeo Nuñez. (Open M-Sa 9am-2pm and 5-8:30pm.) **Postal Code:** 50001.

BASQUE COUNTRY (PAÍS VASCO)

The varied landscape of Basque Country resembles a nation complete unto itself, combining cosmopolitan cities, verdant hills, industrial wastelands, and quaint fishing villages. Many believe that the strongly nationalistic Basques are the native people of Iberia, as their culture and language date back several millennia. Although Castilian Spanish is the predominant language, Basque *euskera* has enjoyed a resurgence of popularity. Basque cuisine is some of Iberia's finest. Tapas in País Vasco, considered regional specialties, are called *pintxos;* locals wash them down with *sidra* (cider) and the local white wine, *txakoli.*

SAN SEBASTIÁN (DONOSTIA)

Glittering on the shores of the Cantabrian Sea, San Sebastián (pop. 180,000) is a cool, elegant city. By the beginning of the 19th century the city had become one of Spain's great ports, but much of the city was destroyed during the Peninsular

War—in 1813 Anglo-Portuguese troops set fire to it after taking it from the French. The city gained international fame when Queen Isabel II made it her summer residence in 1846. Its popularity has been increasing ever since, particularly among land-locked Spaniards desperate to escape the heat of central Spain. Vacationers come for its beaches, tapas, and bars, as well as its strong sense of regional culture.

▐ TRANSPORTATION

Flights: Airport (☎943 66 85 00) in Hondarribia (Fuenterrabía), 20km east of the city. **Interurbanos** buses to Hondarribia pass by the airport (45min., every 15min., 7:45am-11pm, 200ptas). Taxi 3200ptas.

Trains: RENFE, Estación del Norte (☎943 28 30 89), on Po. Francia, on the east side of Puente María Cristina. Info open daily 7:15am-11:15pm. To: **Madrid** (8hr., 4 per day, 4600-4800ptas); **Barcelona** (9hr., 2-3 per day, 4700-4900ptas); **Burgos** (3½hr., 7-8 per day, 2400-2600ptas); **Pamplona** (2hr., 2-12 per day, 1500ptas); and **Zaragoza** (4hr., 4 per day, 2700-3900ptas).

Buses: Several private companies run from different points in the city but most set-up shop at the tiny "station," right around the corner from the main concourse at Po. Vizcaya, 16. Buses drop off on Pl. Pío XII, a block from the river and about 13 blocks south of Av. Libertad on Av. Sancho el Sabio. Public bus #28 goes to the city center from the bus station. To: **Madrid** (6hr., 9-12 per day, 3800ptas); **Barcelona** (7hr., 3-5 per day, 3350ptas); **Bilbao** (1¼hr., every 30min., 1120ptas); **Burgos** (3-3½hr., 8 per day, 1855ptas); and **Pamplona** (1hr., 9 per day, 790ptas).

Public Transportation: List of 19 routes at the tourist office, or call ☎943 28 71 00. Each trip 115ptas. Bus #16 goes from Alameda del Boulevard to campground and beaches.

Taxis: Santa Clara (☎943 31 01 11) or **Donostia** (☎943 46 46.46).

Car Rental: Europcar (☎943 32 23 04; fax 943 29 07 00), Estatión de RENFE. Must be 21 or over and have passport and driver's licence (international driver's licence not required). Open M-F 8am-1pm and 4-7:30pm, Sa 9am-1pm.

✳▐ ORIENTATION AND PRACTICAL INFORMATION

The city center and most beaches lie on a peninsula on the west side of the **Río Urumea** (river); at the tip, the **Monte Urgulla** juts out into the bay. Inland, nightlife rages and budget accommodations and restaurants cluster in the **parte vieja**. To the south, at the base of the peninsula, is the commercial area. From the bus station, head right (north) up Av. Sancho el Sabio toward the cathedral, ocean, and *parte vieja*. East of the river are the **RENFE station** and the **Playa de la Zurriola**. Head straight from the train station, cross the Puente María Cristina (bridge), head right at the fountain for four blocks, and then left on Av. Libertad to the port; the *parte vieja* will lie to your right and the **Playa de la Concha** to your left.

Tourist Office: Centro de Atracción y Turismo (☎943 48 11 66; fax 943 48 11 72), C. Reina Regente, on the corner of the plaza right next to the river. From the train station, turn right immediately after crossing Puente María Cristina. Continue until reaching Puente Zurriola; C. Reina Regente will be on the left. From the bus station, go down Av. Sancho el Sabio. At Pl. Centenario, bear right on C. Prim and follow the river, passing two bridges. At the third bridge, Puente Zurriola, look to the plaza at your left and the office is on the corner. Open June-Sept. M-Sa 8am-8pm, Su 10am-1pm; Oct.-May M-Sa 9am-2pm and 3:30-7pm, Su 10am-1pm.

Luggage Storage: Lockers at **RENFE station.** 400ptas per day. Open daily 7am-11pm. Buy tokens at ticket counter.

Laundromat: Lavomatique, C. Iñigo, 13 (☎943 42 38 71), off C. San Juan. 575ptas wash (cold water only), 400ptas dry. Soap 60ptas. Ironing 75ptas for 15min. Open M-F 10am-1pm and 4-7pm, Sa-Su 10am-2pm.

Hiking Info: Izadi, C. Usandizaga, 18 (☎943 29 35 20). Sells hiking guides and maps, some in English. Organizes tours and rents skis, wetsuits, and hiking equipment. Open M-F 10am-1pm and 4-8pm, Sa 10am-1:30pm and 4:30-8pm.

Emergency: ☎091 or 092. **Police,** Municipal (☎943 45 00 00), C. Easo.
Medical Services: Casa de Socorro, Bengoetxea, 4 (☎943 44 06 33).
Internet Access: Netline, C. Urdaneta, 8 (☎943 44 50 76). 300ptas for 30min.
Donosti-Net, C. Embletran, 2 (☎943 42 58 70; email donostinet@hotmail.com) is on the corner of C. Narrica. 350ptas per 30min. Open 9am-9pm.
Post Office: (☎943 46 34 17; fax 943 42 43 90), C. Urdaneta, the street just south of the cathedral. Open M-F 8:30am-8:30pm, Sa 9:30am-2pm. Lista de Correos at window #11. Address *Poste Restante* mail: Alexandra PRICE, Lista de Correos, C.Urdaneta, 2080 San Sebastian. **Postal Code:** 20006.

ACCOMMODATIONS

Desperate backpackers will scrounge for rooms in July and August, particularly during *San Fermines* (July 6-14) and *Semana Grande* (starts the Sunday of the week of Aug. 15); September's film festival is not much better. Budget options center in the *parte vieja* and around the cathedral. Most hostel owners know of **casas particulares**—don't be afraid to ask for help.

PARTE VIEJA
A bit of a hike from the bus and train stations, the parte vieja is brimming with reasonably priced *pensiones*. Its proximity to Playa de la Concha and the port makes this area a prime nightspot; scores of *pensiones* reside above loud tapas bars.

Pensión Amaiur, C. 31 de Agosto, 44, 2nd fl. (☎943 42 96 54). From Alameda del Boulevard, go up C. San Jerónimo to the end and turn left. *Semana Santa*-Oct. 3000-3800ptas per person; Nov.-*Semana Santa* 1900-2500ptas per person.

Pensión San Lorenzo, C. San Lorenzo, 2 (☎943 42 55 16), off C. San Juan. Cheerful doubles all have TV, radio and small fridge. Immaculate modern bathrooms. Computer in hallway for internet use (100ptas per 12min). Laundry 1000ptas. July-Sept. doubles 8000ptas, 7000ptas for foreigners; Oct.-June doubles 4000ptas.

Pensión Loinaz, C. San Lorenzo, 17 (☎943 42 67 14), off C. San Juan. Laundry 1000ptas. July-Aug. doubles 5500-6000ptas, triples 8500ptas; Apr.-June 21 doubles 4000ptas, triples 6000ptas; Sept.-Mar. doubles 3500ptas, triples 5000ptas.

Pension Urgull, Esterlines, 10, 3rd fl. (☎943 43 00 47). Attractive old rooms with tall windows, small balconies and sinks. July-Aug. singles 3000ptas, doubles 5000-6000ptas; Sept.-June singles 2500ptas, doubles 3500ptas.

Pensión Boulevard, Alameda del Boulevard, 24 (☎943 42 94 05). Beautiful, modern rooms, all with radios, some with balconies. July-Aug. doubles 6500ptas, triples 9000ptas; Sept.-June doubles 4500ptas.

Pensión Puerto, C. Puerto, 19, 2nd fl. (☎943 43 21 40), off C. Mayor. Clean rooms with big closets, good beds and some balconies. 3000-4000ptas per person.

OUTSIDE THE OLD CITY
Most of these hostels lie in the heart of the commercial zone, around the cathedral. They tend to be quieter than those elsewhere in the city, yet are still close to the port, beach, bus, and train stations, and all of the action in the *parte vieja*.

Albergue Juvenil la Sirena (HI), Po. Igueldo, 25 (☎943 31 02 68; email udala_youthhostel@donostia.org), 3 min. from the beach at the far west end of the city. Bus #24 runs from the train and bus stations to Av. Zumalacárregui (the stop in front of the San Sebastián Hotel). From Av. Zumalacárregui, take the street that angles toward the mountain (Av. Brunet) and turn left at its end. HI members and ISIC-carriers only. Breakfast included. Sheets 395ptas. Best to arrive before 11am. Lockout 10am-3pm. Curfew June-Aug. daily 2am; Sept.-May Su-Th midnight, F-Sa 2am. June-Oct.15 and *Semana Santa* 2100ptas, over 26 2555ptas; Oct.15-May 1600ptas, over 26 2000ptas.

Pensión Urkia, C. Urbieta, 12, 3rd fl. (☎943 42 44 36). C. Urbieta borders the cathedral on the west; the hostel is one block north at C. Arrasate. Rooms with lovely blue and white linens, full bathrooms, and TV. July-Sept. doubles 6000ptas, triples 9000ptas; Oct.-June singles 3000ptas, doubles 4000ptas, triples 6000ptas.

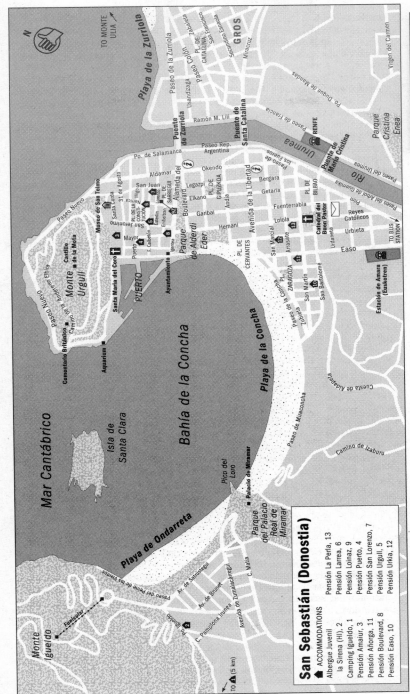

San Sebastián (Donostia)

♦ ACCOMMODATIONS

Albergue Juvenil
la Sirena (HI), 2
Camping Igueldo, 1
Pensión Amaiur, 3
Pensión Añorga, 11
Pensión Boulevard, 8
Pensión Easo, 10
Pensión La Perla, 13
Pensión Larrea, 6
Pensión Loinaz, 9
Pensión Puerto, 4
Pensión San Lorenzo, 7
Pensión Urgull, 5
Pensión Urkia, 12

Pensión La Perla, C. Loiola, 10, 2nd fl. (☎943 42 81 23), on the street directly ahead of the cathedral. Grand stairway leads to attractive rooms with polished floors. July-Sept. singles 4000ptas, doubles 6000ptas; Oct.-June singles 3500ptas, doubles 4500ptas.

Pensión Añorga, C. Easo, 12, 1st fl. (☎943 46 79 45), at C. San Martín. Shares entryway with 2 other *pensiones*. July-Aug. singles 4000ptas, doubles 5000-6500ptas; Sept.-June singles 2000ptas, doubles 3000-4000ptas.

Camping: Camping Igueldo (☎943 21 45 02), 5km west of town. Bus #16 (Barrio de Igueldo-Camping) runs between the site and Alameda del Boulevard (every 30min., 110ptas). Reception June-Aug. 8am-midnight; Sept.-May 9am-1pm and 5-9pm. *Parcela* (including tent and up to 2 people): June-Aug. and *Semana Santa* 2889ptas, extra person 425ptas; Sept.-May 1386ptas, extra person 357ptas.

◖ FOOD

Pintxos (tapas; rarely more than 175ptas each), chased down with the fizzy regional white wine *txacoli*, are a religion here; bars in the lively old city spread an array of enticing tidbits on toothpicks or bread. The entire **parte vieja** seems to exist for no other purpose than to feed. **Mercado de la Bretxa,** on Alameda del Boulevard at C. San Juan, sells fresh produce. (Both open M-F 7:30am-2pm and 5-7:30pm, Sa 7:30am-2pm.) **Super Todo Todo,** on Alameda del Boulevard, is around the corner from the tourist office. (Open M-Sa 8:30am-9pm, Su 10am-2pm.)

Bar La Cepa, C. 31 de Agosto, 7-9 (☎94 42 63 94). Locals stop in for their delicious *pintxos* 160-325ptas and cheap *bocadillos* (450-475ptas). Lunch *menú* 1700ptas. Open daily 1pm-midnight.

Bar Intza, C. Esterlines, 12 (☎943 42 48 33). An attractive bar with a distinct cosmopolitan flare and modern wall paintings. Outdoor seating and tasty *pintxos*. *Bocadillos* 400-450ptas. Open Su-Th 10am-4pm and 6:30-11:30pm, later F-Sa.

Bar Juantxo, C. Embeltrán, 6 (☎943 42 74 05). A local favorite, famous for its *bocadillos* (285-495ptas). *Pintxos* 130-200ptas. Open daily 8:30am-midnight.

Caravanseri Café, C. San Bartolomé, 1 (☎943 47 54 78), alongside the cathedral. Trendy and chic without pretentious prices. Fabulous vegetarian options including veggie burgers (400ptas). Open M-Th 8am-12am, F-Sa 8am-1am, Su 10:30am-midnight.

◉ SIGHTS

San Sebastián's most attractive sight is the city itself—green walks and parks, grandiose buildings, and hillsides encircle a placid, fan-shaped bay and the pleasant island of Santa Clara. Although the views from both of San Sebastián's mountains are spectacular, those from **Monte Igueldo** are superior. By day the countryside meets the ocean in a line of white and blue; by night Isla Santa Clara seems to float on a ring of light. The sidewalk toward the mountain ends before the base of Monte Igueldo with Eduardo Chillida's sculpture *El peine de los vientos*. (☎943 21 02 11. Open daily June-Sept. 11am-10pm. 170ptas.) Across the bay from **Monte Igueldo,** the gravel paths through the shady woods of Monte Urgull are peppered with monuments, love-struck teenagers, and stunning vistas. The overgrown **Castillo de Santa Cruz de la Mota** tops the summit with cannons and a chapel; the castle is crowned by the statue of the Sagrado Corazón de Jesús, which blesses the city. (Open daily June-Aug. 8am-8pm; Sept.-May 8am-6pm.) **El Palacio de Miramar,** between Playa de la Concha and Playa de Ondarreta, has passed through the hands of the Spanish court, Napoleon III, and Bismarck. Today anyone can stroll through the "cottage-style" grounds and contemplate the picturesque views of the bay. (Open daily June-Aug. 9am-9pm; Sept.-May 10am-5pm.) The other royal residence, **Palacio de Ayete,** is closed to the public, though the surrounding trails are not. (Head up Cuesta de Aldapeta or take Bus #19. Grounds open June-Aug. 10am-8:30pm; Sept.-May 10am-5pm.) The **Museo de San Telmo** resides in a Dominican monastery. The serene, overgrown cloister is strewn with Basque funerary relics. The main museum beyond the cloister contains a fascinating array of pre-historic Basque artifacts, some El Grecos, a couple of dinosaur skeletons, and a piece of contemporary art. (Po. Nuevo. ☎943 42 49 70. Open Tu-Sa 10:30am-1:30pm and 4-8pm, Su 10:30am-2pm. Free.) An **aquarium** lies on the edge of the port with fish and sea creatures from various aquatic habitats. (Po. Muelle, 34. ☎943 44 00 99. Open July-Aug. 10am-10pm; Sept.-June 10am-1:30pm and 3:30-7:30pm. 1100ptas, students 550ptas.) Thirty minutes from the town center, between a lush hill and a dark, gray-green bay, lies the town of **Pasajes de San Juan.** The charming fishing village's houses and small bay crowded with colorful *chalupas* (little boats) make an enchanting time warp. A Herribus bus (every 20-30min., 120ptas) goes to Pasajes de San Juan from Pl. Gipúzkoa.

🎵 ENTERTAINMENT

The gorgeous **Playa de la Concha** curves from the port to the **Pico del Loro,** the beak-shaped promontory which is home to the Palacio de Miramar. Crowds jam onto the smaller and steeper **Playa de Ondarreta,** beyond Miramar. Across the river from Mt. Urgull, surfers crowd **Playa de la Zurrida.** Picnickers can head for the alluring **Isla de Santa Clara** in the center of the bay. Frequent motorboats leave for the island (5min., June-Sept. only, round-trip 250ptas), or rent a rowboat. Check at the portside kiosk for info on both options. Several sports-related groups offer a variety of activities/lessons. For **windsurfing** and **kayaking,** call the Real Club Nautico, C. Igentea, 9 (☎943 42 35 75), classes range from 5000-8000ptas. For **parachuting,** try Urruti Sport, C. José Maria Soroa, 20 (☎943 27 81 96). **Surfers** can check out the Pukas Surf Club, C. Mayor, 5. (☎943 42 72 28; email pukas@facilnet.es. Open 10am-1pm and 4-8pm.) For info on all sports, pick up a copy of the *UDA-Actividades deportivas* brochure at the tourist office.

The *parte vieja* pulls out all the stops after dark. **C. Fermín Calbetón,** three blocks in from Alameda del Boulevard, sweats bars. Along the beach, the music starts thumping at midnight. **The World's End,** Po. de Salamanca, 14, one block outside of the *parte vieja* near the beach, is a favorite among expatriates and young travelers looking for a good pub-ambience. (☎943 42 62 53. Open Su-Th 2pm-2:30am, F-Sa 2pm-3:30am.) **Molly Malone,** C. San Martin, 55, right off the Paseo de la Concha, is a classic Irish pub. (☎943 46 98 22. Beer 400-600ptas. Open 3pm-3am.)

🏖 DAYTRIP FROM SAN SEBASTIÁN

HONDARRIBA

Interurbanos buses (☎943 64 13 02) arrive on C. Zuluaga from San Sebastián (45min., every 15 min., 210ptas).

Refreshingly simple Hondarribia (pop. 14,000) flaunts a silky-smooth **beach** as well as a gorgeous stone-and-timber *casco antiguo,* centered around Carlos V's imposing **palace** in Pl. Armas, that provides welcome relief from Coppertone fumes. Six kilometers up Av. Monte Jaizkibel, **Monte Jaizkibel,** the highest mountain on the Costa Cantábrica, guards the **Santuario de Guadalupe** and offer incredible views of the coast. **Boats** leave from the end of C. Domingo Egia, off La Marina (every 15min., reduced off-season, 200ptas), for the **beach** town of Hendaye, France, 5km away. The **tourist office,** C. Javier Ugarte 6, is in Pl. San Cristóbal. (☎943 64 54 58. Open July-Aug. M-Sa 10am-2pm and 3-8pm; Sept.-June M-F 9am-1:30pm and 4-6:30pm, Sa 10am-2pm.) To get from the bus stop to the modern **Albergue Juan Sebastián Elcano (HI),** Ctra. Faro, head down C. Itsasargi, bear left at the beach, turn left at the rotary, and follow the signs uphill. (☎943 64 15 50; fax 943 64 00 28. Members only; HI cards 1000-1500ptas. Breakfast included. Sheets 115ptas. 3-night max. stay when full. Reception 9am-noon and 4-7pm. Curfew midnight; doors open briefly at 1 and 2am. Call ahead. 1975ptas; under 31 1325ptas.) Several **markets** spill onto **C. San Pedro,** three blocks inland from the port.

SPAIN

BILBAO (BILBO)

Graced with the marvelous new Guggenheim Museum, Bilbao (pop. 1,000,000) is finally overcoming its reputation as a business-minded industrial center. Though the city may not win any beauty pageants, its medieval *casco viejo*, wide 19th-century boulevards lined by grandiose buildings, and stunning brand new subway and a stylish riverwalk project, all executed by renowned international architects, make this up-and-coming city well worth a stop. However, it is the Guggenheim that has fueled Bilbao's rise to international prominence.

■ TRANSPORTATION. RENFE **trains** (☎94 423 86 23) arrive at the **Estación de Abando,** Pl. Circular 2, from Madrid (5¾-9hr., 2 per day, 4200-4400ptas); Barcelona (9½-11hr., Su-F 2 per day, 5100ptas); and Salamanca (5½-6½hr., 2 per day, 3500ptas). From Pl. Circular, head right around the station and cross the Puente del Arenal (bridge) to reach Pl. Arriaga, the entrance to the *casco viejo*. Most **bus companies** leave from the **Termibús terminal,** C. Gurtubay 1 (☎94 439 50 77; M: San Mamés), on the west side of town, for Pamplona (2hr., 4-6 per day, 1580ptas); Salamanca (5hr.; 1-2 per day, 3200ptas); San Sebastián (1hr., 8-23 per day, 1120ptas); and Zaragoza (4hr., 9-10 per day, 2430ptas). To get there, take the metro to the Casco Viejo, exit onto Pl. Unamuno, take a right on C. Sombreria, and turn right on C. Correo. **ANSA (GETSA, VIACAR) buses** leave from C. Autonomía 17 (☎94 444 31 00) for Madrid (4-5hr., 10-17 per day, 3270ptas); Barcelona (7hr., 3-4 per day, 4900ptas); and Burgos (2hr., 4-5 per day, 1435ptas). To get there from the station, go left as you exit down C. Hurtado de Amézaga, and bear right at Pl. Zabálburu.

Bilbao recently opened a **metro.** Hang onto your ticket after entering—you'll need it again to exit. (☎94 425 40 25; www.metrobilbao.net. Travel within 1 zone 140ptas; 2 zones 165ptas; 3 zones 195ptas. 10-trip ticket within 1 zone 860ptas; 2 zones 1020ptas; 3 zones 1225ptas. Trains run Su-Th 6am-11pm, F-Sa 6am-11pm and every 30min. from 11pm-6am.) **Bilbobús** runs 23 lines across the city. (☎94 448 40 80. 6am-11:30pm; M-F 125ptas, Sa-Su 140ptas; 10-ride coupon 715ptas.)

◪ PRACTICAL INFORMATION. The city's main artery, **Gran Vía,** leads east from the oval Pl. Federico Moyúa to **Plaza Circular** (sometimes referred to by its former name, Plaza Espana), the axis for many important stops and stations. To reach the **tourist office,** on Pl. Arenal, turn left after crossing the bridge from the train station. (☎94 479 57 60; fax 94 479 57 61; www.bilbao.net. Open M-F 9am-2pm and 4-7:30pm, Sa 9am-2pm, Su 10am-2pm.) Surf the internet at **El Senor de la Red,** C. Rodriguez Arias, 69. From Gran Vía, turn left on C. Maria Diaz de Haro and take your first right. (☎944 277 773. 200ptas per 30min. Open daily 10am-10pm.) To get to the **post office,** Alameda Urquijo, 19, walk one block down Gran Vía from Pl. España and turn left after El Corte Inglés; it's on the corner of C. Bertendona. (☎94 422 05 48; fax 94 443 00 24. Open M-F 8am-8:30pm, Sa 8am-2pm.) **Postal Code:** 48005.

▛▟ ACCOMMODATIONS AND FOOD. The tourist office has a list of recommended budget hostels, most of which are in the *casco viejo*. After crossing the Puente del Arenal toward the *casco viejo* turn right on C. Ribera, then left onto C. Santa Maria and left again on C. Jardines to reach **Hostal Mardones,** C. Jardines, 4, 3rd fl. (☎94 415 31 05. Singles 4000ptas, with bath 5000ptas; doubles 5600ptas, with bath 6600ptas, triples 8500ptas, with bath 10,500ptas.) **Pensión Méndez,** C. Santa María, 13, 4th fl., is insulated from the raging nightlife below. From the bridge, turn right on C. Ribera and right on C. Santa María is on the left as the street turns. (☎94 416 03 64. Singles 3000-4000ptas, with bath 6000ptas; doubles 5000ptas, with bath 8000ptas; triples 7500ptas, with bath 10,000ptas.) Running along one side of Pl. Arriaga, C. Bidebarrieta leads to **Hostal Gurea,** C. Bidebarrieta, 14. (☎94 416 32 99. Singles 3600ptas, with bath 3900ptas; doubles 4000ptas, with bath 4800ptas. To reach **Albergue Bilbao Aterpetxea (HI),** Ctra. Basurto-Kastrexana Errep., 70, take bus #58 from Pl. Circular. Individual bathrooms available (500ptas). In addition to gardens and dining room, the hostel offers laundry, bike rental, money exchange and **internet** use. (☎94 427 00 54;

email aterpe@albergue.bilbao.net. Breakfast included. July-Sept. 2300ptas, 2500ptas for 25 and over; Oct.-June 2100ptas, 2300ptas for 25 and over.) Restaurants and bars in the *casco viejo* offer a wide selection of local dishes, plus *pintxos* and *bocadillos* aplenty. **Restaurante Peruano Ají Colorado,** C. Barrencalle, 5, combines Andean decorations and traditional Peruvian cuisine. (☎94 415 22 09. Open M-Sa 1:30-3:30pm and 9-11:30pm.) Or if you're in the neighborhood of the Guggenheim, try the classy **Aitxiar,** C. María Muñoz, 8. Try the special *merluza a la vasca* for 2200ptas, or the 1500ptas lunch *menú.* (☎94 415 09 17. Open daily 1-3:30pm and 8-11pm.) **Mercado de la Ribera,** on the the river as you head left from the tourist office, is the biggest indoor market in Spain. (Open daily 7am-noon.) Pick up **groceries** at **Simago,** Pl. Santos Juanes. (Open M-Sa 9am-9pm.)

🔳🚇 SIGHTS AND ENTERTAINMENT. Frank O. Gehry's ▨**Guggenheim Museum Bilbao** can only be described as breathtaking. Lauded in the international press with every superlative imaginable, it has catapulted Bilbao straight into cultural stardom. Visitors are greeted by Jeff Koons's "Puppy," a dog composed of 60,000 plants and standing almost as tall as the actual museum. The main attraction is constructed mainly out of titanium, limestone, and glass in a series of interconnected pieces. The amazingly light and airy interior features a towering atrium and a series of non-traditional exhibition spaces, including a gargantuan 130 meter by 30 meter hall. The museum currently hosts rotating exhibits drawn from the Guggenheim Foundation's collection, but will gradually acquire its own international sampling of 20th-century works. (Av. Abandoibarra, 2. ☎94 435 90 00; www.guggenheim.bilbao.es. Open daily July-Aug. 9am-9pm; Sept.-June Tu-Su 10am-8pm. 1200ptas, students and seniors 600ptas, under 12 free. 900ptas includes entrance to Guggenheim and Museo de Bellas Artes. Guided tours in English Tu-F 11am, 12:30, 4, and 6:30pm, Sa-Su 1 and 4pm; sign up 30min. before tour at Info Desk.) From the Guggenheim, follow the Alameda de Mazarredo to the often overshadowed **Museo de Bellas Artes,** Pl. Museo 2, which hoards aesthetic riches behind an unassuming facade. An impressive art collection ranges from the 12th to 20th century and features excellent 15th- to 17th-century Flemish paintings, as well as works by El Greco, Zurbarán, Goya, Gauguin, Francis Bacon, Velázquez, Picasso, and Mary Cassatt. (Pl. Museo, 2. ☎94 439 60 60. Open Tu-Sa 10am-8pm, Su 10am-2pm. 600ptas, seniors and students 300ptas, under 12 free; free W.) The best **view** of Bilbao's surrounding landscape and the perfect place for a picnic is from the mirador on Monte Archanda, north of the old town and equidistant from the *casco viejo* and the Guggenheim. (Funicular to the top every 15min., 110ptas.)

In the *casco viejo,* revelers spill out into the streets to sip their *txikitos* (small glasses of beer or wine characteristic of the region), especially on **C. Barrencalle** (Barrenkale). Teenagers and twentysomethings also jam at **C. Licenciado Poza** on the west side of town. For a mellower scene, people-watch at the elegant 19th-century **Café Boulevard,** C. Arenal 3. The massive blowout fiesta in honor of *Nuestra Señora de Begoña* takes place during **Semana Grande,** a nine-day party beginning the weekend after Aug. 15.

🚩 DAYTRIP FROM BILBAO: GUERNICA (GERNIKA). On April 27, 1937, the Nazi "Condor Legion" released an estimated 29,000kg of explosives on Guernica, obliterating 70% of city in 3hr. The nearly 2000 people who were killed in the bombings were immortalized in Pablo Picasso's stark masterpiece *Guernica,* now in Madrid's Reina Sofía gallery (see p. 814). The eerily modern city today offers the **Gernika Museoa,** Foru Plaza 1, which features a moving exhibition chronicling the bombardment (open July-Aug. daily 10am-7pm; Sept.-June M-Sa 10am-2pm and 4-7pm, Su 10am-2pm; 300ptas, under 16 free), and the 2000-year-old **El Arbol** (tree), the emotional focus of the city. Despite the limited sights, it's a good daytrip for those interested in learning more about this infamous event and its ramifications. **Trains** (☎94 625 11 82) roll in from Bilbao (45min., every 30 min., 315ptas).

BALEARIC ISLANDS

Every year, discos, ancient history, and beaches—especially beaches—draw nearly two million of the hippest Europeans to the *Islas Baleares*, 100km off the east coast of Spain. Mallorca, home to Palma, the islands' capital, absorbs the bulk of invaders who come to explore their limestone cliffs, orchards, and clear turquoise waters. Ibiza, a counter-culture haven since the 1960s, boasts an active gay community; its capital Eivissa offers what many consider the best nightlife in all of Europe. Wrapped in green fields and stone walls, Menorca leads a private life of empty white beaches, hidden coves, and mysterious Bronze Age megaliths.

⬛ TRANSPORTATION

Flights to the islands, fast and cheap, are the easiest way to get there. Those under 26 often get discounts from **Iberia/Aviaco Airlines** (☎902 40 05 00; www.iberia.com), which flies to Palma de Mallorca and Ibiza from Madrid (1hr., students round-trip 25-30,000ptas); Barcelona (40min., students round-trip 10-20,000ptas); and Valencia. **Air Europa** (☎902 24 00 42) and **SpanAir** (☎902 13 14 15; www.spanair.com) offer budget flights to and between the islands. Most cheap round-trip charters include a week's stay in a hotel; some companies called *mayoristas* sell "seat-only" deals. **Ferries** to the islands serve as a secondary mode of transport. **Trasmediterránea** (☎902 45 46 45; www.trasmediterranea.com) departs from Barcelona's Estació Marítima Moll and Valencia's Estació Marítima for Mallorca and Ibiza. **Buquebus** (☎902 41 42 42; email reservas@buquebus.es) goes from Barcelona to Palma (4hr., 2 per day, 8150ptas). Book airline or ferry tickets through a travel agency in Barcelona, Valencia, or on the islands.

Within the islands, **ferries** are the most cost-efficient; they run from Palma to Ibiza (2½-4½hr., 6 per week, 3330-5210ptas) and Mahón (6½hr., Su, 3045ptas). **Iberia** flies from Palma to Ibiza (35min., 4 per day, 8900ptas) and Mahón, Menorca (35min., 4 per day, 8900ptas). The major islands have good **bus** systems. A day's **car** rental costs around 4500ptas, **mopeds** 2700ptas per day, and **bikes** 1000ptas per day.

MALLORCA

Sought after since the days of the Romans, Mallorca has a long history of popularity. It has continually attracted the rich and famous, whether as the site of the scandalous honeymoon of Polish pianist Fréderic Chopin and French novelist George Sand or as the vacation spot of choice for Spain's royal family. There are reasons for such Mallorca lust. To the northwest, white sand beaches, frothy water, lemon groves, and olive trees adorn the jagged Sierra de Tramontana. To the east, expansive beaches sink into calm bays, while to the southeast, a network of caves masks underground beauty.

⬛ TRANSPORTATION.
Bus travel in Mallorca is like putting salt on an open wound— painful; though travel to and from the capital is relatively easy, travel between most other areas is indirect and will probably route you through Palma. The tourist office and the info kiosk in Palma's Pl. Espanya have a complete schedule. **Buses** from Palma to: Cap de Formentor (5 per day, 595ptas); Cuevas Drach (M-Sa 4 per day, 1100ptas); Deià (45min., 5 per day, 295ptas); Puerto de Alcúdia (1hr., 5-17 per day, 590ptas); and Puerto de Sóller via Valldemossa (2hr., 5 per day, 450ptas). To get from the airport to the center of Palma, take bus #17 to Pl. d'Espanya (15min., every 20min., 295ptas).

◪ PRACTICAL INFORMATION.
The information presented for Mallorca is in the capital city, Palma, unless otherwise indicated. The Palma branch of the **tourist office** resides at C. Sant Dominic 11; follow Pg. Marítim (a.k.a. Av. Juan Roca) to Av. Antoni Maura, follow C. Conquistador out of Pl. de la Reina, and continue on C.

Sant Dominic. (☎971 71 15 27. Open M-F 9am-8pm, Sa 9am-1:30pm.) The island tourist office, Pl. Reina 2, offers info on the other islands, a good city map, bus and train schedules, hiking info, and lists of all sporting and cultural events on Mallorca. (☎971 71 22 16. Open M-F 9am-1pm and 5-8pm, Sa 9am-1:30pm.) Check **email** at **Cyber Central,** C. Soletat, 4, Pl. Reina. (☎971 71 29 27. 1000ptas per hr. Open M-Sa 9am-10pm, Su 12pm-8pm.)

▓▓ ACCOMMODATIONS AND FOOD. Accommodations are scarce and often packed in Mallorca; your best bet is to book ahead and use Palma as a base for exploring the island. **Hostal Apuntadores,** C. Apuntadores, 8, is in the middle of the action, less than a block from Pl. Reina. (☎971 71 34 91; email apuntadores@jet.es. Dorms 1800ptas; singles 2700ptas; doubles 4500ptas, with showers 4800ptas.) From the port, go left on Av. Gabriel Roca and turn right on C. Argentina to reach **Hostal Cuba,** C. San Magí 1. (☎971 73 81 59. Singles 2000ptas; doubles 4000ptas; triples 5500ptas.) Take bus #15 from Pl. d'Espanya (every 8min., 175ptas) and ask to get off at Hotel Acapulco to reach the pristine and palatial **Alberg Platja de Palma (HI),** C. Costa Brava 13. (☎971 26 08 92. HI members only. Sheets 200ptas. Breakfast included. Reception daily 8am-3am. Curfew Su-Th midnight, F-Sa 3am. 1700ptas.) **Camp** at **Platja Blava,** 8km down the highway between Alcúdia and C'an Picafort. Take Autocares Mallorca buses from Pl. d'Espanya. (2 per day, 575ptas. ☎971 53 78 63. 600ptas per person; 1300-3000ptas per site.) **Servicio y Precios,** on C. Felip Bauzà, near Pl. Reina, has **groceries.** (Open M-F 8:30am-8:30pm, Sa 9am-2pm.)

▨▧ SIGHTS AND ENTERTAINMENT. The capital of the Balearics, **Palma** (pop. 323,000) does not shy from conspicuous consumption, but it provides plenty of old quarter charm and local flavor. The **Catedral o la Sea,** one of the world's largest cathedrals, towers over Palma and its bay. The cathedral, dedicated to Palma's patron saint San Sebastián, was begun in the 1300s, finished in 1601, and then modified by Gaudí in modernist fashion in 1909. (Off Pl. Reina. ☎971 72 31 33. Cathedral and museum open Apr.-Oct. M-F 10am-6pm, Sa 10am-2pm; Nov.-Mar. M-F 10am-3pm. 500ptas.) The tourist office distributes a list of over 40 nearby **beaches,** many a mere bus ride from Palma; one popular choice is **El Arenal** (Platja de Palma; bus #15), 11km southeast (toward the airport). After sunning, many head to the streets around **Pl. Reina** and **La Llotja** to imbibe. **ABACO,** C. Sant Joan, 1, in the Barri Gòtic near the waterfront, is the perfect place for a cocktail. (Drinks 1900-2100ptas. Open daily 9pm-2:30am.) Every Friday, the newspaper *El Día de Mundo* (125ptas) lists bars and discos. Clubbers boogie on the beaches and near **El Terreno**—a mother lode of clubs centers on **Pl. Gomila** and along **C. Joan Miró. Baccus,** around the corner on C. Lluis Fábregas, 2, draws a gay and lesbian crowds. **Tito's Palace,** Paseo Maritimo is perhaps Palma's hippest disco, in an indoor colosseum of mirrors and lights overlooking the water. (☎971 73 00 17. Cover 2000ptas. Open 11am-6am.)

The **west coast** of Mallorca is one of the most beautiful landscapes in the Mediterranean. In **Puerto de Sóller,** a pebble and sand beach lines the small bay, where windsurfers zip back and forth. **Hotel Miramar** is at C. Marina, 12. (☎971 63 13 50. Singles 4900ptas; doubles 5150ptas; triples 7600ptas.) A favorite of artists and intellectuals, **Deià** affords sensational views of miles and miles of twisted olive trees. In the town center, picturesque houses and the occasional church line lantern-lit cobblestone squares. Known for their long beaches and fine sand, the **northern gulfs** of Mallorca have become quite popular. The end of **Cap de Formentor** has the best beaches on the northern coast. **Puerto de Alcúdia** is far from undiscovered, as tourists line the packed beaches, the old Roman town and the **Parc Natural de L'Albufera.** On the **southeast coast,** scalloped fringes of bays and caves are investors' most recent discovery. The **Cuevas Drach,** near Porto Cristo, are among the most dramatic natural wonders in Mallorca. The caves amaze with their droopy, finger-like rock formations, illuminating the cave in a spectrum of red and pink color. Walk to the depths of the cave to an underground amphitheater facing an underground lake or listen to a concert of classical music from the lit rowboats gliding in the lake.

IBIZA

Perhaps nowhere on Earth does style rule over substance more than on the island of Ibiza (pop. 84,000). Ibiza's style warriors arrive in droves to showcase themselves in the island's outrageous nightlife and to debauch in a sex- and substance-driven summertime culture. A hippie enclave since the 60s, Ibiza's summer camp for disco fiends and trendsetters evokes a sense of new-age decadence. Although a thriving gay community still lends credence to its image as a "tolerant" center, the island's high price tags preclude economic diversity. As shocking as it may sound, there is more to Ibiza than just nightlife—the beaches and mountains are some of the most spectacular in the Balearics.

⌐ TRANSPORTATION. The **bus** system in Ibiza is much more organized than her Balearic sisters. The three main stops are Av. Isidor Macabich, 42, Av. Isidor Macabich, 20, and Av. España (Voramar buses). For an exact schedule, check the tourist office or *El Diario*. Intercity buses are 250ptas or less and run from Av. Isidor Macabich, 42 (☎971 31 21 17) to San Antonio (M-Sa every 15min., Su every 30min.). Buses to the beaches run frequently and cost 125ptas.

⚑ PRACTICAL INFORMATION. The local paper *Diario de Ibiza* (www.diario-deibiza.es; 125ptas) features an *Agenda* page with everything you need to know about Ibiza. The **tourist office,** C. Antoni Riquer, 2, is on the water. (☎971 30 19 00; www.ibizaonline.com. Open M-F 9:30am-1:30pm and 5-7pm, Sa 10:30am-1pm.) In between foam parties, head to **Centro Internet Eivissa,** Av. Ignacio Wallis, 39. (☎971 31 81 61. 400ptas per 30min.)

⌂⌂ ACCOMMODATIONS AND FOOD. Cheap accommodations in Eivissa are rare. The letters "CH" *(casa de huéspedes)* mark many doorways; call the owners at the phone number on the door. **Hostal Residencia Sol y Brisa** is at Av. B. V. Ramón 15, parallel to Pg. Vara de Rey. (☎971 31 08 18. Singles 3500ptas; doubles 6000ptas.) **Hostal Residencia Ripoll** is at C. Vicente Cuervo 14. (☎971 31 42 75. July-Sept. singles 3500ptas; doubles 5500ptas.) **Hostal La Marina,** Puerto de Ibiza, C. Barcelona, 7, is across from Estació Marítima but right in the middle of the raucous bar scene. (☎971 31 01 72. Singles 3250-7000ptas; doubles 5000-12,000ptas.) **Hostal Juanito** and **Hostal Las Nieves,** C. Juan de Austria 17-18 are run by the same owner and offer inexpensive housing in a central area. (☎971 19 03 19. Singles 2000ptas; doubles 4000ptas, with bath 5000ptas.) For a **supermarket,** try **Comestibles Tony,** C. d'Enmig 1. (Open daily 9am-2pm and 5-8pm.)

▣♫ SIGHTS AND ENTERTAINMENT. First, the formalities. Wrapped in 16th-century walls, **Dalt Vila** (High Town) hosts 20th-century urban bustle in the city's oldest buildings. Its twisting, sloping streets lead up to the 14th-century cathedral and superb views of the city and ocean. No beach is within quick walking distance, but **Platja de Talamanca, Platja des Duros, Platja d'en Bossa,** and **Platja Figueredes** are at most 20min. away by bike. The most stunning beach near Eivissa is **Playa de Las Salinas** where the nude sunbathers are almost as beautiful as the crystal-blue water and silk sand. Buses leave for beaches from Av. Isidor Macabich 20 for Platja d'en Bossa (every 30min., 125ptas).

Finally, the fun. **Eivissa** (Ibiza City) is the world's biggest 24-hour party; the show begins at sunset. Ibizans are full of pomp: men masquerade as women and vamps stalk the portside walkways, vying for attention and turning the sidewalks into catwalks. The island's **discos** (virtually all of which have a mixed gay-and-straight crowd) are world-famous and ever-changing. For complete listings, check out *Ministry in Ibiza* or *Party Sun*, free at many hostels, bars, and restaurants. **Calle Virgen** is the center of gay nightlife. The **Discobus** runs to and from all the major hotspots (midnight-6:30am, 250ptas). Wild, wild **Privilege** is best known for Monday night "manumission" parties. (Cover from 4000ptas, includes 1 drink. Open June-Sept. M and W-Sa midnight-7am.) At **Amnesia,** on the road to San Antonio, you can forget who you are, where you're from, and who you came with, at what may just be the craziest disco scene ever. (Cream parties Th; foam parties W and Su. Cover 4000-7000ptas. Open daily midnight-6am.) Both lie on the discobus route to San Antonio. **El Divino,** Puerto Ibiza Nueva, caters to the non-tourist, well-connected crowd. (☎971 19 01 76. Cover 5000ptas. Open mid-June to mid-Sept. daily 1-6am.) Playful **Pachá,** on Pg. Perimitral, is 20min. from the port; Thursdays bring circus night. (Cover 5000ptas; includes 1 drink. Open daily 11:15pm-7:30am.) Cap off your night with a dancing morning in **Space,** Platja d'en Bossa. (Open daily 7am-4pm.)

MENORCA

Menorca's 200-kilometer coastline of raw beaches, rustic landscape, and well-preserved ancient monuments draw ecologists, sun worshippers, and photographers alike. Unfortunately, although tourists are fewer on Menorca than on the other Balearics, the island's unique qualities has resulted in elevated prices that can be hard on the budget traveler. Perched atop a steep bluff, **Mahón** (pop. 23,300) is the main gateway to the island. From the **airport,** take a taxi (1300ptas) to downtown Mahón. From the **ferry station,** walk left (with your back to the water) for 150 meters, turn right at the steps, take Portal de Mar to Costa de Sa, which becomes C. Hannover and then C. Ses Moreres, and continue straight ahead to the **tourist office,** Pl. s'Esplanada 40. (☎971 36 37 90; fax 971 36 74 15; www.menorca.com. Open M-F 8:30am-7:30pm, Sa 9am-2pm.) To get to **Hostal La Isla,** C. Santa Catalina 4, take C. Concepció from Pl. Miranda. (☎971 36 64 92. Singles 2200ptas; doubles 5200ptas.) To reach the **Hostal Orsi,** C. Infanta 19, from Pl. s'Esplanada, take C. Ses Moreres, which becomes C. Hannover, turn right at Pl. Constitució, and follow C. Nou through Pl. Reial. (☎971 36 47 51. Breakfast included. Singles 2500ptas; doubles 4400ptas, with shower 5000ptas; add 7% IVA.) **Hostal-Residencia Jume,** C. Concepció, 6, is off Pl. Miranda. (☎971 36 32 66. Breakfast included. 2800ptas.)

The more popular **beaches** outside Mahón are accessible by bus (under 30min., 50-250ptas); many of the best beaches require a vehicle, but are worth the extra hassle. Autocares Fornells **buses** (6 per day) leave C. Vasallo in Mahón for sandy **Arenal d'en Castell,** while TMSA buses (6 per day) go to touristy **Calean Porter** and its whitewashed houses, orange stucco roofs, and red sidewalks. Take a Transportes Menorca bus from Mahón (6 per day) for the gorgeous beaches surrounding **Son Bou. Albufera Es Grau** entices visitors with lagoons, pine woods, and farmland, as well as diverse flora and fauna. Recreational activities include hiking to coves across the bay or taking a nature walk through the protected lands; take the Autocares Fornells bus (3 per day) from C. Vasallo in Mahón. At **Cala Bosch,** jagged cliffs plummet into pale-blue water; take Torres bus (18 per day) from Ciutadella.

Ciutadella (Ciudadela; pop. 21,200), the other main town on Menorca, combines colorful stucco and medieval cobblestone with a tranquility that eludes Mahón, but you'll pay for it. Transportes Menorca (TMSA) **buses** shuttle between Mahón and Ciutadella (55min., 6 per day, 550ptas). The **tourist office** is at Pl. Catedral 3. (☎971 38 26 93. Open M-F 8am-3pm and 4:30-8pm, Sa 10am-2pm.) **Hotel Geminis** is at C. Josepa Rossinyol, 4; take C. Sud off Av. Capital Negrete, as you approach from Pl. s'Esplanada, and turn left on C. Josepa Rossinyol. (☎971 38 58 96. Breakfast included. Singles 4500ptas; doubles 8000ptas.)

NORTHWESTERN SPAIN

Northwestern Spain is the least-visited part of the country; its seclusion is half its charm. Rainy **Galicia** hides mysterious Celtic ruins, left when the Celts made a pit stop on its quiet beaches along the west coast. Tiny **Asturias** is tucked on the northern coast, allowing access to its dramatic Picos de Europa.

GALICIA (GALIZA)

If, as the old Galician saying goes, "rain is art," then there is no gallery more beautiful than the misty skies of northwestern Spain. Often veiled in a silvery drizzle, it is a province of fern-laden eucalyptus woods, slate-roofed fishing villages, and seemingly endless white beaches. Galicians speak *gallego*, a linguistic missing link of sorts between Castilian and Portuguese. While newspapers and street signs alternate between languages, most conversations are conducted in Spanish.

SANTIAGO DE COMPOSTELA

Ever since the remains of the Apostle St. James were discovered here in 813, Santiago has drawn a plethora of pilgrims, many of whom have just completed the legendary Camino de Santiago. Built over the saint's alleged remains, the cathedral marks the end of the Camino, an 800-year-old, 900km pilgrimage believed to halve one's time in purgatory. Today, sunburnt pilgrims, street musicians, and hordes of tourists fill the granite streets by the cathedral. In addition to the religious monuments, visitors enjoy the modern art gallery, the state-of-the-art concert hall, and an eclectic and lively nightlife.

▐▀ TRANSPORTATION

Trains: (☎981 52 02 02) go from C. de Hórreo in the southern end of the city to: **Madrid** (8hr., 5700ptas); **Bilbao** (10¾hr., 5600ptas); **Burgos** (8hr., 4600ptas); and **León** (6½hr., 3500ptas). Schedule printed daily in *El Correo Gallego*.

Buses: Estación Central de Autobuses (☎981 58 77 00), C. San Cayetano, a 20min. walk from downtown. Bus #10 and bus C Circular leave from Pl. Galicia for the station (every 15-20min., 100ptas). **ALSA** (☎981 58 61 33) runs to: **Madrid** (8-9hr., 4 per day, 5135ptas); **Bilbao** (11¼hr., 6345ptas); and **San Sebastián** (13½hr., 7150ptas).

Public Transportation: (☎981 58 18 15). Bus #6 to the train station (daily 10am-10:30pm); #9 to the campgrounds (daily 10am-8pm), #10 to the bus station. All buses stop in Pl. Galicia—check the signs to see which side. Except for bus #6 and 9, buses run daily 7am-10:30pm (100ptas).

◤✦ 🏢 ORIENTATION AND PRACTICAL INFORMATION

Street names in Santiago can be confusing since languages do not always coordinate between street signs and maps: *calle* in Castilian becomes *rúa* in Galician, *del* becomes *do*. The **cathedral** marks the center of the old city, which is located above the new city. From the **train station** in the southern end of town, three main streets lead to the cathedral: **Rúa de Franco** (C. Franco), **Rúa de Vilar** (C. Vilar), and **Rúa Nova** (C. Nueva). From the station, cross the street, bear right at the top of the stairs, and take R. Hórreo (not Av. Lugo) to Pl. Galicia, then go one more block to C. Bautizatos, where the three cathedral-bound streets originate. From the **bus station,** take bus #10 or bus C Circular to Pl. Galicia (every 15-20min., 100ptas). On foot, exit the station onto R. Angel Castro and turn left onto R. Pastoriza; continue for 20min. through the street's name changes. Turn right onto R. Atalia, then left after one block onto Pl. Pena. Follow this road through Pl. San Mariño to the cathedral's Pl. Immaculada.

Tourist Office: (☎981 58 40 81). One **branch** on R. Vilar in the old town under the arches of a colonnade. Open M-F 10am-2pm and 4-7pm, Sa 11am-2pm and 5-7pm, Su and festivals 11am-2pm.

American Express: Ultratur Viajes, Av. Figueroa, 6 (☎981 58 70 00). Open M-F 9:30am-2pm and 4:30-7pm, Sa 10am-12:30pm.

Emergency: ☎091 or 092. **Police: Guardia Civil** (☎981 58 16 11).

Late-Night Pharmacy: Bescansa, Pl. Toural, 11 (☎981 58 59 40), 1 block toward the cathedral from Pl. Galicia.

Medical Assistance: Hospital Xeral (☎981 54 00 00), on C. Galeras.

Internet Access: Nova 50, R. Nova, 50 (☎981 56 01 00). 26 fast computers. 200ptas per hr. Open daily 9am-1am.

Post Office: (☎981 58 12 52), Travesa de Fonseca, on the corner of R. Franco. Lista de Correos (around the corner, R. Franco, 6) and **faxes.** Open M-F 8:30am-8:30pm, Sa 9:30am-2pm. **Postal Code:** 15701.

▟ ACCOMMODATIONS

Santiago's rooms are not the cheapest, but they are plentiful. Hostels and *pensiones* cluster around R. Vilar and R. Raíña (between R. Vilar and R. Franco), and hand-drawn *habitaciones* signs are just about everywhere else. Call ahead in winter when university students occupy most rooms.

▨ Hospedaje Ramos, C. Raíña, 18, 2nd fl. (☎981 58 18 59), above O Papa Una restaurant. Spacious, sparkling clean rooms. Reservations recommended. Singles 1800ptas, with bath 2000ptas; doubles 3350ptas, with bath 3650ptas. Cash only.

Hospedaje Itatti, Pl. Mazarelos, 1 (☎981 56 01 11). From Pl. Galicia, take a right onto R. Fonte San Antonio, then the 1st left. Rooms with TVs, phones, bathrooms. June-Sept. singles 3000ptas, doubles 5000ptas; Oct.-May singles 2000ptas, doubles 3500ptas.

Hospedaje Santa Cruz, R. Vilar, 42, 2nd fl. (☎981 58 28 15). Big windows in these large rooms overlook a popular street. Reserve ahead in summer. June-Sept. singles 3500ptas, doubles 4000ptas; Oct.-May singles 2000ptas, doubles 3500ptas.

Monte do Gozo (HI), Ctra. Santiago-Aeropuerto km 3 (☎981 55 89 42). Take Bus #6 2km outside of town (dir.:Lavacolla Airport). Beware the influx of pilgrims June-Aug. Reservations required. Singles under 26 with HI card 7510ptas, over 26 1000ptas.

Camping: Camping As Cancelas, R. 25 de Xullo, 35 (☎981 58 02 66), 2km from the cathedral on the northern edge of town; take bus #6 or 9. Laundry, supermarket, and pool. Electricity 450ptas extra. 575ptas per person, 615ptas per car and per tent.

▟ FOOD

Tapas-weary budget travelers will appreciate Santiago's selection of restaurants. Bars and cafeterias line the streets with a variety of remarkably inexpensive *menús;* most restaurants are on R. Vilar, R. Franco, and R. Raíña. In the new city, look near Pl. Roxa. End your meal with a *tarta de Santiago*, rich almond cake emblazoned with a sugary St. James cross. **Supermercado Lorenzo Froiz,** Pl. Toural, is one block into the old city from Pl. Galicia. (Open M-Sa 9am-3pm and 4:30-9pm, Sa 9am-3pm and 5-9pm.)

▨ O Cabaliño do Demo, R. Aller Ulloa, 7 (☎981 58 8146). Walk to A Porta Do Camino, where Rúa Cerca meets Rúa San Pedro. Chic vegetarian restaurant with creative, organic recipes and filling portions. Specialty salad 350ptas. *Menú* 1000ptas. Open daily 2-4pm and 9pm-midnight. Cafe downstairs open 8am-midnight. Cash only.

La Crepe (☎ 981 57 76 43), Pl. Quintana, in front of the cathedral. A cozy *comedor* hidden above terrace cafes. Delectable *crêpes* (600-900ptas) and main dishes (900-950ptas) and a gorgeous view of the plaza. Open daily 10am-1am.

▟ SIGHTS AND ENTERTAINMENT

Offering a cool, quiet sanctuary to priest, pilgrim, and tourist alike, Santiago's **cathedral** rises above the lively old city center. Each of its four facades is a masterpiece from a different time period, and entrances open up onto four different plazas: Platerías, Quintana, Obradoiro, and Azabaxería. The southern **Praza de Platerías** is the oldest of the four facades; the 18th-century Baroque **Obradoiro** facade encases the Maestro Mateo's **Pórtico de la Gloria,** considered the crowning achievement of Spanish Romanesque sculpture. The revered remains of **St. James** lie beneath the high altar in a silver coffer. Inside the **museum** are gorgeous 16th-century tapestries and two poignant

THESE BOOTS WERE MADE FOR WALKING

One night in AD 813, a hermit trudged through the hills on the way to his hermitage. Suddenly, miraculously, bright visions revealed the long-forgotten tomb of the Apostle James ("Santiago" in Spanish). Around this *campus stellae* (field of stars) the cathedral of Santiago de Compostela was built, and around this cathedral a world-famous pilgrimage was born. Since the 12th century, thousands of pilgrims have traveled the 900km of the Camino de Santiago. Clever Benedictine monks built monasteries to host *peregrinos* (pilgrims) along the *camino*, helping to make Santiago's cathedral the most frequented Christian shrine in the world. The scallop-edged conch shell, used for dipping in streams, has become a symbol of the Camino de Santiago; the shells, tied onto weathered backpacks, make pilgrims easy to spot, as do crook-necked walking sticks and sunburned faces. Pilgrims must cover 100km on foot or horse or 200km on bike to receive *La Compostela*, a certificate of completion issued by the cathedral. Shelters along the way offer free lodging to pilgrims and stamp "pilgrims' passports" to prove that they were there. At 30km per day, the entire *camino* takes about a month. For inspiration, keep in mind that you are joining the ranks of such illustrious pilgrims as Fernando and Isabel, Francis of Assisi, Pope John Paul II, and Shirley MacLaine. For more info, contact the Officinal de Acogida del Peregrino, C. Vilar 1 (☎981 56 24 19).

statues of the pregnant Virgin Mary. (☎981 58 35 48. Open daily 7am-9pm. Museum open June-Sept. M-Sa 10am-1:30pm and 4-7:30pm, Su and holidays 10am-1:30pm; Oct.-Feb. M-Sa 11am-1pm and 4-6pm, Su and holidays 11am-1pm; Mar.-June M-Sa 10:30am-1:30pm and 4-6:30pm, Su 10:30-1:30pm. Museum 500ptas.) Those curious about the Camino de Santiago can head to the **Museo das Peregrinacións,** Pl. San Miguel. (☎981 58 15 58. Open Tu-F 10am-8pm, Sa 10:30am-1:30pm and 5-8pm, Su 10:30am-1:30pm. 400ptas, students 200ptas.)

At night, crowds looking for post-pilgrimage consumption flood cellars throughout the city. To boogie with local students, hit the bars and clubs off **Pl. Roxa** (take C. Montevo Ríos). **Casa das Crechas,** Vía Sacra 3, just off Pl. Quintana, pumps Guinness. The **Discoteca Liberti,** Alfredo Branas, across from Casting Araguaney, plays mainstream hits. (☎981 59 91 81. Cover 500ptas. Open daily midnight-6am.)

⚡ DAYTRIP FROM SANTIAGO: O CASTRO DE BAROÑA

Hefsel buses run between Noya and Riveira, stopping (but often passing—tell the driver where you are going) in O Castro de Baroña in front of Café-Bar O Castro (30min.; M-F 14 per day 6:50am-9:30pm, Sa 7 per day 8am-9pm, Su 11 per day 8am-10pm; 205ptas). Catch the bus across the road on the way back.

Nineteen kilometers south of the town of **Noya** is a little-known treasure of historical intrigue and mesmerizing natural beauty: the seaside remains of the 5th-century Celtic fortress ▇**O Castro de Baroña.** The foundations dot the isthmus, ascending to a rocky promontory above the sea and then descending down to a crescent **beach.**

RÍAS ALTAS

If Galicia is the forgotten corner of Spain, then the small *rías* of the Costa de la Muerte are the forgotten corner of Galicia. However, the beaches here are arguably the emptiest, cleanest, and loveliest in all of Spain. This solitary coastline permits nature lovers to enjoy secluded spots, nearly empty beaches, and rustic sights without the tedium of overdeveloped, commercialized tourism.

LA CORUÑA (A CORUÑA)

While the newer parts of La Coruña are mundane, recent massive efforts have cleaned up its *ciudad vieja* (old city) and pleasant **beaches.** Hercules allegedly erected the 2nd-century **Torre de Hércules,** now the world's oldest working lighthouse, upon the remains of an unfortunate enemy; you can climb a 239-step tunnel to the pinnacle. (Take the seaside path from the Orzán and Riazor beaches, or bus #9 or 13 (115ptas). Open Apr.-Sept. 10am-7pm; Oct.-Mar 10am-6pm. 250ptas, seniors and children free.) **Trains** (☎981 15 02 02) go from Pr. San Cristóbal to Madrid (11hr., 1-3 per day, 6200-17400ptas) and Santiago de Compostela (1hr., 19 per day, 545-645ptas). **Buses** (☎981 23 96 44) go from C. Caballeros, across Av. Alcalde Molina from the train station, to Madrid (8½hr., 6 per day, 4955-6975ptas); Oviedo (5hr., 4 per day, 3175ptas); and Santiago (1½hr., 17 per day, 825ptas). From the bus station, take bus #1 or 1A (115ptas) to the **tourist office,** on Dársena de la Marina. (☎981 22 18 22. Open M-F 9am-2pm and 4:30-6:30pm, Sa 10:30am-1:30pm; weekend hours extended from July15-Sept.15 Sa 10:30am-1pm and 5pm-7pm, Su 10am-2pm and 5-7pm.) **Hospedaje María Pita,** C. Riego de Agua 38, 3rd fl., has a homey feel. (☎981 22 11 87. Doubles 2900-3500ptas.) For **groceries,** go to **Supermercados Claudio.** (Open daily 9am-3pm and 5-9pm.)

RÍAS DE CEDEIRA AND VIVERO

Tourist brochures assert that Vivero "*No es un sueño. Existe.*" ("Is not a dream. It exists.") Where the average tourist seldom treads, fern-covered rainforests give way to soft, empty beaches. Thick mists veil the valleys of these northernmost *rías.* Seaside **Vivero's** (pop. 14,000) tiny old city huddles at the forest's edge. The nearest beach is in the resort town of **Covas,** 1km across the river; **Playa de Area** suns itself 4km away. IASA **buses** (☎981 56 01 03), run to El Ferrol (2hr., 6 per day, 985ptas) and La Coruña (4hr., 5 per day, 6:30am-7:30am, 1635ptas). Vivero's **tourist office** is on Av. Ramón Canosa. (☎982 56 08 79. Open daily 11am-2pm and 5:30-8:30pm.) **Fonda Bossanova,** Av. Galicia 11, is one block from the bus station toward Covas. (☎982 56 01 50. Singles 2000ptas; doubles 2500ptas).

When cuckolding Lancelot fled England to escape the ire of King Arthur, he allegedly landed in **Cedeira** (pop. 8500), founding the town and sowing his seed. Small Cedeira offers pretty beaches and breathtaking scenery. The **Santuario de San Andrés de Teixido** (a steep 12km hike from town), which still hosts pagan cults with thriving rituals, overlooks the sea from 620m. **Bus** service is fairly sparse; RIALSA runs from Cedeira to El Ferrol (1hr., 7 per day, 420ptas), where other buses connect to La Coruña. To get to Vivero, take an IASA bus from C. Ezequiel Lopez 28 to Campo do Hospital (15min., 4 per day, 120ptas), then change to the Campo do Hospital-Vivero IASA bus line. Get off at the second bus stop in Cedeira for the **tourist office,** C. Ezequiel Lopez 22. (☎981 48 21 87. Open Apr.-Sept. M-F 10:30am-1:30pm and 5-8pm, Sa 10am-2pm, Su and holidays noon-2pm.) The rest of the year try **Casa Consistorial,** C. Real, 15 (☎981 48 00 00; fax 981 48 25 06). **Hostal Chelsea,** Pr. Sagrado Corazón 9, is around the corner from the first bus stop. (☎981 48 23 40. Doubles 4000-4500ptas.)

ASTURIAS

Seething cliffs and hell-reaching ravines lend an epic scope to the tiny land of Asturias, tucked between Basque Country and Galicia. An extensive network of tourist towns, cottages, and country inns in old *casas de indianos* (rambling Victorian mansions built by settlers) provides the residents of Asturias and Cantabria a means to get rich off Spain's vacationing elite.

PICOS DE EUROPA

God bless tectonic folding and contracting—300 million years ago, 'twas a mere flapping of Mother Nature's limestone bedsheet that erected the Picos de Europa, a mountain range of curious variation and chaotic beauty. Most of the area has been granted environmental protection as the **Picos de Europa National Park,** a rugged playpen for mountaineers, trekkers, and idle admirers. Near the **Cares Gorge** (Garganta del Cares) lie the park's popular trails and famous peaks. For a list of mountain **refugios** (typically cabins with bunks but not blankets) and general information on the park, contact the **Picos de Europa National Park Visitors Center** (☎985 84 86 14).

OVIEDO

Though Oviedo (pop. 200,000), the area's capital and transport hub, isn't necessarily the prettiest city in Spain, it provides an excellent base for exploring the mountains. Before setting out for the mountains, load up on **maps** and other info in Oviedo. **TIVE,** C. Calvo Sotelo 5, is a budget travel agency with info on hiking and excursions. (☎985 23 60 58. Open M-F 8am-3pm.) **ICONA,** C. Arquitecto Reguera 13, 2nd fl. (☎985 24 14 12), has trail and camping info. **Federación Asturiana de Montaña,** C. de Julián Clavería, organizes excursions, has good trail maps, and provides mountain guides. (☎985 25 23 62. Open M-F 6-8:30pm.) ALSA **buses** also run to several other good bases from which to explore the mountains, including **Cangas de Onís** (1¼hr., 9-10 per day, 700ptas) and **Covadonga** (1¾hr., 4-7 per day, 805ptas).

ALSA buses (☎985 28 12 00) arrive in Pl. Primo de Rivera from: Madrid (6hr., 10-15 per day, 3825-6000ptas); Burgos (4hr., 2 per day, 1540ptas); León (2hr., 7 per day, 1030ptas); and Santiago de Compostela (8hr., 3-4 per day, 3740ptas). C. Fray Ceferino leads from the other side of the plaza to C. Uría, where **RENFE trains** (☎985 24 33 64) arrive from León (2½hr., 7 per day, 945-2300ptas) and Madrid (6½-8hr., 3 per day, 4500-5900ptas). Walking down C. Uría with the station behind you, the old city is to the left; its two main plazas are **Pl. Mayor** and **Pl. de Alfonso II,** known to locals as Pl. de la Catedral and to tourists as Pl. de la **Tourist Office.** (☎985 21 33 85. Open M-F 9:30am-1:30pm and 4:30-6:30pm, Sa 9am-2pm.) To get to **Residencia Juvenil Ramón Menéndez Pidal,** C. Julián Clavería 14, just off Pl. Toros, take bus #2 from C. Uría. (☎985 23 20 54. 1000ptas, under 27 780ptas.) Near the cathedral are **Pensión Pomar,** C. Jovellanos 7 (☎985 22 27 91; singles 3000-4000ptas, doubles 4000-5000ptas, triples 4500-6000ptas), and **Pensión Martinez,** C. Jovellanos 5 (☎985 21 53 44; singles 1600ptas, doubles 3000ptas, triples 3000ptas). Feed the big, bad wolf in you at **Mesón Luferca,** a.k.a. **La Casa Real del Jamón,** C. Covadonga 20. (Open M-Sa 8:30am-midnight.) Grab **groceries** at **El Corte Inglés,** on C. General Elorza, opposite the bus station. (Open M-Sa 10am-9:30pm.)

SWITZERLAND
(SCHWEIZ, SVIZZERA, SUISSE)

SWISS FRANC

US$1 = 1.77SFR	1SFR = US$0.56
CDN$1 = 1.20SFR	1SFR = CDN$0.84
EURO€1 = 1.52SF	1SFR = EURO€0.66
UK£1 = 2.49SFR	1SFR = UK£0.40
IR£1 = 1.93SFR	1SFR = IR£0.52
AUS$1 = 1.00SFR	1SFR = AUS$1.00
NZ$1 = 0.76SFR	1SFR = NZ$1.31
SAR1 = 0.25SFR	1SFR = SAR04.02

PHONE CODE Country Code: 41. International dialing prefix: 00.

The unparalleled natural beauty of Switzerland entices hikers, skiers, bikers, paragliders, and scenery gazers from all over the globe to romp about its Alpine playground. Three-fifths of the country is dominated by mountains: the Jura cover the northwest region, bordering France, while the Alps stretch gracefully across the entire lower half of Switzerland, flirting with Italy in the southern Lepontine chain and colliding with Austria in the eastern Rhaetian Alps. The cities that lie around blue lakes make their own claim to fame as international centers of commerce and diplomacy. While the stereotypes of Switzerland as a "Big Money" banking and watch-making mecca are true (nearly 4% of the Swiss are employed in the banking industry), its energetic youth culture belies its staid reputation. Although the country is not known for being cheap, Swiss hospitality and sublime vistas are priceless. For the skinny, check out *Let's Go: Austria and Switzerland 2001.*

SUGGESTED ITINERARIES

THREE DAYS Admire the great outdoors by starting in **Interlaken** for a day (p. 926). Then head to **Lucerne** (p. 923) for the perfect combination of city culture and natural splendor before heading to the diverse city of **Geneva** (p. 907).

ONE WEEK Begin in **Geneva** (p. 907), then head to **Montreaux** for relaxation and views (p. 913). Swing by **Interlaken** (p. 926) for a day then head on to **Lucerne** (p. 923). Travel north to **Zurich**, a banker's dream (p. 917). Swoop back to reality in the capital city of **Bern** (p. 925) before finishing **Neuchâtel** (p. 914).

BEST OF SWITZERLAND, TWO WEEKS Begin in **Geneva** (1 day; p. 907), take the train to **Lausanne** (1 day; p. 913), and then jump over to **Montreaux** (1 day; p. 913). Head to **Zermatt** and admire the Matterhorn (2 days; p. 930). Take a break in the Mediterranean climate of **Locarno** (1 day; p. 934), before heading on to **Zurich** (1 day; p. 917). Nearby **Lucerne** (2 days; p. 923) and southward **Interlaken** (1 day; p. 926) serve up a raucous nightlife and hiking. Climb in the Jungfrau region from **Lauterbrunnen** (1 day; p. 929), head to **Bern** (2 days; p. 925), and end in tasty **Neuchâtel** (1 day; p. 914).

LIFE AND TIMES

HISTORY AND POLITICS

PRE-HISTORY: FROM CAVE MEN TO CELTS (UNTIL AD 500)
By 750 BC, Switzerland had become an important center of Celtic culture. The artistic and warlike **Helvetii** gained notoriety for their (largely unsuccessful) attempts to invade Roman Italy in 222 BC and again, as allies of Carthage, between 218 and 203 BC. Romanized between 47 BC and AD 15, they survived as a peaceful, urban civilization for the next two centuries. Around AD 250, the **Burgundians** settled the west of today's Switzerland, merging peacefully with the Romanized Celts. Meanwhile, the more aggressive **Alemanni** foisted their own culture on the Celts of central and northern Switzerland, eventually pushing the Burgundians west to the Sarine River, which remains the border between German and French Switzerland.

AGAINST THE EMPIRE: AN ALEMANNI LEGACY (AD 500-1500)
The feisty Alemanni, with their aversion to conformity and centralized government, set the stage for centuries of Swiss individualism. Switzerland had been loosely united since 1032 as part of the **Holy Roman Empire,** but it was not until Emperor Rudolf of Habsburg's crusade in the late 13th century that the Swiss decided to rebel. In a secret pact, three of the Alemanni communities (the "Forest Cantons") signed an **Everlasting Alliance** in 1291—an agreement that obligated the cantons to defend each other from outside attack. The Swiss consider this moment to be the beginning of the Swiss Confederation. The Everlasting Alliance also marked the beginning of 350 years of struggle against the **Habsburg Empire.** One by one, Bern, Lucerne, Zurich, Glarus, and Zug jumped on the Confederation bandwagon, but a union of such fiercely independent and culturally distinct states made for an uneasy marriage. The **Swabian War** of 1499-1500 against the Habsburgs brought virtual independence from the Holy Roman Empire, but domestic struggles continued as cultural and religious differences between the cantons festered.

REFORMATION TO REVOLUTION (1520-1800)
With no strong central government to settle quibbles between cantons of different faith, the Swiss were ill equipped to deal with the **Protestant Reformation.** As Lutheranism swept Northern Europe, radical theologian **Ulrich Zwingli** of Zurich spearheaded his own brand of reform that advocated a less literal reinterpretation of the bible. Meanwhile, in Geneva, **John Calvin** instituted puritanical reforms. While Zurich and Geneva became strongholds of the Protestant movement, the rural Forest Cantons remained loyal to the Catholic faith. Religious differences resulted in full-fledged battle, climaxing in the defeat of the Protestants at Kappel in 1531. The Confederation interceded in the mid-16th century, granting Protestants freedoms but prohibiting them from imposing their faith on certain others. Despite religious differences, the Confederation remained neutral during the **Thirty Years War,** escaping the devastation wrought on the rest of Central Europe. The 1648 **Peace of Westphalia** granted the Swiss official independence from the Austrian Habsburg Empire, ending 350 years of strife. Free from the Austrians but not the French, Swiss independence was short lived. After the success of the French Revolution, Napoleon invaded Switzerland in 1798 and established the **Helvetic Republic.** After Napoleon's defeat at Waterloo in 1815, the Congress of Vienna recognized Swiss neutrality.

NEUTRALITY AND DIPLOMACY (1815 TO THE 20TH CENTURY)
Neutrality established, Switzerland could turn its attention to domestic issues. Industrial growth brought relative material prosperity, but the era was not exactly golden. Religious differences continued to create increased tension between cantons, and in 1846 the **Sonderbund** (a separatist league of Catholic cantons) and the **Diet** (a parliamentary body of the other cantons) were created. In keeping with the fashion of the time, a civil war broke out, but it only lasted 25 days. The Protestant federalist forces were victorious, and the country wrote a new constitution in 1848,

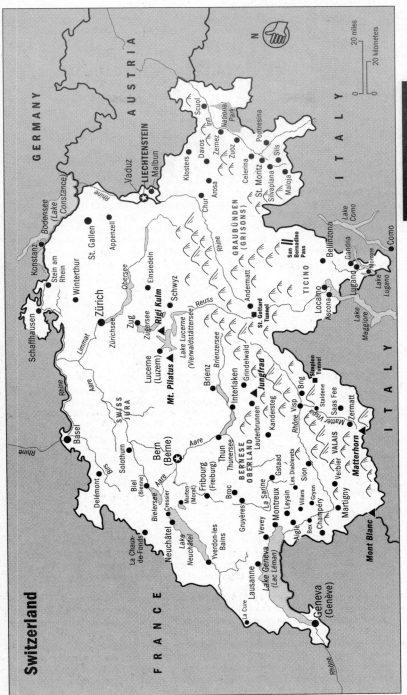

Switzerland

modeled after that of the United States. Once turmoil had given way to stability, Switzerland cultivated its reputation for resolving international conflicts. The **Geneva Convention of 1864** established international laws for conduct during war. Geneva also became the headquarters for the **International Red Cross.**

Not quite free of the tangle of alliances that characterized Europe's turn-of-the-century balance of power, Switzerland's neutrality was tested in **World War I** as French- and German-speaking Switzerland claimed different cultural loyalties. In 1920, Geneva welcomed the headquarters of the ill-fated **League of Nations,** solidifying Switzerland's reputation as the center for international diplomacy. During **World War II,** both sides found it useful to have Switzerland (and its banks) as neutral territory. While some Jews, escaping Allied prisoners, and other refugees from Nazi Germany found safe haven in Switzerland, the Swiss government, not eager to incur the wrath of the monster that surrounded it, generally impeded passage through its territory and assumed the hiding-tortoise position.

As the rest of Europe cleaned up the rubble of two world wars, Switzerland nurtured its already sturdy economy. Zurich emerged as a banking and insurance center, while Geneva invited international organizations, including the World Health Organization and the World Council of Churches. Although Geneva became the headquarters for international diplomacy, Switzerland remained isolationist in its relations with the rest of Europe, declining membership to the United Nations, NATO, and the European Economic Community.

SWITZERLAND TODAY

Switzerland has become increasingly wealthy, liberal, successful, and service-oriented since WWII, and is still fiercely independent and wary of entanglements with the rest of Europe. While conservative in some respects, the Swiss are remarkably progressive in other areas. In 1999, two women were elected to the seven-member Bundesrat (executive authority), one of whom, **Ruth Dreifuss,** will serve a one-year term as president. Switzerland also has one of the world's most stringent ecological policies to protect its fragile Alpine environment. In the past few years, Swiss banks have come under intense scrutiny for their "blind account" policy, which allowed Holocaust victims and Nazi leaders alike to deposit money during WWII.

Swiss government is based on a three-tiered system of communes, cantons, and confederation. Over 3000 communes compose the 26 cantons. The cantons are incorporated into the Confederation and its two-chamber legislature, the Federal Assembly. One chamber, the National Council, distributes its 200 seats based on population; the other, the Council of States, distributes equal seats to the cantons. The executive branch consists of a group of 7 members—the **Bundesrat (Federal Council)**—elected to 4-year terms by a joint meeting of both legislative chambers. The Bundesrat chooses a president from among its ranks. The president holds office for 1 year, and the post is more symbolic than functional. **Referenda** and **initiatives** make political decisions a part of the daily life of the Swiss people.

THE ARTS

20TH-CENTURY PAINTING AND SCULPTURE

Although Swiss artists are not as well known as their French and Italian counterparts, there are a few early greats among them, such as **Urs Graf,** a swashbuckling, soldier-artist-poet skilled in court portraiture, and **Ferdinand Hodler,** an early Symbolist painter who used Swiss landscapes to convey metaphysical messages. One of Switzerland's most famous artists is **Paul Klee,** a member of *der Blaue Reiter* (The Blue Rider) school and of the Bauhaus faculty. His delicately colored watercolors and oil paintings helped shape the beginnings of abstraction, calling dominant modes of artistic expression into question.

During the World Wars, Switzerland's art scene was energized by an influx of talented refugees, a group of whom produced the **Dada** explosion in Zurich in 1916, including **Hans Arp, Richard Hülsenbeck, Janco,** and **Hugo Ball.** Rejecting traditional ideas of the aesthetic, Dadaism aimed to force people to reconsider their social values. Marginal participants in the Zurich Dada scene later developed into artists in their own right. Between and after the wars, Switzerland still attracted liberal artistic thinkers. The **Zurich School of Concrete Art,** which operated primarily between wars, combined elements of Surrealism with ideas from Russian Constructivism in an attempt to work with objects and environments to explore interactions between humans and space. The school includes **Meret Oppenheim,** a Surrealist famous for her *Fur Cup.* The philosophy guided sculptor **Alberto Giacometti** rejected the premise of Surrealism in order to concentrate on a deep representationalism, creating small, exaggerated, slender figures like *Man Pointing.*

LITERATURE
Though Switzerland is not particularly renowned for its literary traditions, many famous and talented writers have called Switzerland home. Among them is **Jean-Jacques Rousseau,** best known for his *Social Contract* that inspired the French Revolution. He was born in 1712 and always proudly recognized his Swiss background—despite the fact that he spent most of his time outside the country and that the Swiss burned his books. A more conventional Swiss resident, **Jacob Burckhardt** promoted a new history of culture and art from his Basel home in the late 19th century. His works include *History of the Italian Renaissance* and *Cicerone: A Guide to the Enjoyment of Italian Art.*

When Romanticism caught on in Swiss literature, **J.J. Bodmer** and **J.J. Breitinger's** advocacy of literature in Swiss German brought them into conflict with many of their German contemporaries, who strove to standardize German through literature. The Swiss-born **Madame de Staël** (née Germaine Necker) was both an important writer in her own right and the driving force behind Romanticism's spread from Germany to France. **Conrad Ferdinand Meyer** was another highly influential Swiss poet, whose writings featured strongly individualistic heroes, effectively uniting characteristics of Romanticism and Realism.

It is only in the 20th century that Swiss literature has come into its own with such greats as **Hermann Hesse,** who received he Nobel Prize for literature in 1946 for his collected *oeuvre.* Hesse's works, including *The Steppenwolf* and *Narcissus and Goldmund,* deal with the crisis of existence and the power of laughter. Alongside Hesse, Switzerland has produced two widely respected modern playwrights. Critics laud **Max Frisch** for his Brechtian style and thoughtful treatment of Nazi Germany; his most widely known works are the play *Andorra* and the novel *Homo Faber,* which was made into a film in the early 1990s. **Friedrich Dürrenmatt** has written a number of cutting, funny plays, most notably *The Visit of the Old Lady* and *The Physicists.*

FOOD AND DRINK
Switzerland's hearty cooking will keep you warm through those frigid alpine winters but will skyrocket your cholesterol. Bernese *Rösti,* a plateful of hash brown potatoes skilleted and sometimes flavored with bacon or cheese is prevalent in the German regions, as is *fondue* in the French. Try Valaisian *raclette,* made by melting cheese over a fire, then scraping it onto a baked potato and garnishing with meat or vegetables. Self-serve cafeterias and supermarkets Migros and Co-op supply the most essential Swiss culinary invention, **milk chocolate** (*Lindt, Toblerone,* and *Nestlé* are native favorites), on the cheap. Each canton has its own local **beer.** Beer is relatively cheap, often less expensive than Coca-Cola. Order *ein helles* for a light beer, *ein dunkles* for a dark one.

ESSENTIALS

DOCUMENTS AND FORMALITIES
Switzerland does not require visas for nationals of Australia, Canada, the EU, New Zealand, South Africa, or the US, for stays of shorter than three months.

Swiss Embassies at Home: Australia, 7 Melbourne Ave., Forrest, **Canberra,** ACT 2603 (☎ (02) 6273 3977; email swiemcan@dynamite.com.au); **Canada,** 5 Marlborough Ave., Ottawa, Ontario KIN 8E6 (☎ (613) 235 1837); **Ireland,** 6 Ailesbury Rd., Ballsbridge, Dublin 4 (☎ (01) 218 6382; email vertretung@dub.rep.admin.ch); **New Zealand,** 22 Panama St., Wellington (☎ (04) 472 1593); **South Africa** Pretoria, 818 George Ave., Arcadia 0083, P.O. Box 2289, 0001 Pretoria (☎ (012) 43 67 07; email swiempre@cis.co.za); during the sessions of Parliament (Jan.-June), the embassy is based in Capetown, P.O. Box 1546, Capetown 8000 (☎ (021) 426 12 01/02); **UK,** 16-18 Montague Pl., London W1H 2BQ (☎ (020) 7616 60 00; email vertretung@lon.rep.admin.ch); **US,** 2900 Cathedral Ave. NW, Washington D.C. 20008-3499 (☎ (202) 745 7900; website wwww.swissemb.org).

Foreign Embassies in Switzerland: Nearly all foreign embassies are in **Bern** (p. 925). Most consulates are in **Zurich** (see p. 917).

TRANSPORTATION

BY PLANE. Major international airports for oversees connections are located in **Bern, Geneva,** and **Zurich.** From the UK **easyJet** (☎ (0870) 600 00 00; www.easyjet.com) has flights from London to Geneva, and Zurich (UK£47-136). From Ireland **Aer Lingus** (☎(01) 886 88 88; www.aerlingus.ie) has return tickets from Dublin, Cork, Galway, Kerry, and Shannon to Munich, and Zürich for IR£102-240.

BY TRAIN. Federal **(SBB, CFF)** and private railways connect most towns and villages. **Schnellzüge** (express trains) speed between metropoli, while **Regionalzüge** chug into small towns. **Eurail, Europass,** and **Interrail** passes are all valid on Switzerland's trains. For national railpasses there is the **Swiss Transfer Ticket,** which is good for a one-day trip from any entry point (airport or border crossing) to any single destination within Switzerland, and the return trip back to the border, within a period of one month (US$71). The **Swiss Card** offers the same round trip as the Swiss Transfer Ticket, plus 50% off unlimited rail and bus tickets within the period of the month between your entry and departure (US$104). The mother of all passes is the **SwissPass,** which is sold worldwide and offers unlimited rail travel for a certain number of consecutive days: choose between 4 days, 8 days, 15 days, 21 days, or 1 month, 1st or 2nd class. In addition to rail travel, it entitles you to unlimited urban transportation in 36 cities, unlimited travel on certain private railways and lake steamers, and 25% discounts on excursions to most mountaintops. One adult, second class 4 day-passes start at US$160, 8 days at $220, 15 days at $265, 21 days at $305, and 1 month at $345. The **Swiss Flexipass** entitles you to any 3-9 days of unlimited rail travel within a 1-month period, 1st or 2nd class, with the same benefits as the Swiss Pass. Second class adult passes are priced as follows: 3-day US$156; 4-day US$184; 5-day US$212; 6-day US$240; 7-day US$261; 8-day US$282; 9-day US$303. For nation **rail info,** dial ☎ (090) 030 0300.

BY BUS AND FERRY. TT **postal buses** connect rural villages and towns. Swiss-Passes are valid on many buses, Eurailpasses are not. Buy tickets in advance at the automatic machines found at most bus stops. The system works on an honor code and inspections are infrequent, but expect to be hit for 30-50SFr if you're caught riding without a valid ticket. *Tageskarten,* valid for 24 hours of free travel, run 2-7.50SFr, but most Swiss cities are small enough to cover on foot. On most lakes, notably Lake Geneva, Lake Neuchâtel, and Lake Lucerne, **ferries** run between towns. Swisspass generally grants free passage; Eurail may get you a discount.

BY CAR. Road travel (by car or bus) is relatively safe in Switzerland. With armies of mechanized road crews ready to remove snow at a moment's notice, roads at altitudes of up to 1500m generally remain open throughout winter. The **speed limit** is 50km per hr. (31mph) within cities; outside towns, the limit is 130km per hr. (81mph) on highways, 100km per hr. (62mph) on all other roads. Many small Swiss towns forbid cars to enter; some forbid only visitors' cars, require special permits, or restrict driving hours. EU citizens driving in Switzerland don't need any special documentation, just registration and a license. To rent a car, you must have had a valid driver's license for at least one year. Drivers under 25 must pay a daily "young driver" fee. Rates for all cars rented in Switzerland include an obligatory 40SFr annual **road toll,** called a *vignette.* All cars must carry a first-aid kit and a red emergency triangle. Emergency phones are located along all major highways. The **Swiss Touring Club,** rue Pierre-Fatio 9, CH-1211 Geneva 3 (☎ (022) 737 12 12) operates road patrols that assist motorists in need; dial 140 for help.

BY BIKE AND BY THUMB. Cycling, though strenuous, is a splendid way to see the country; rental at most train stations is 27SFr per day (slightly more to return to another station). The **Touring Club Suisse,** Cyclo Tourisme, chemin Riantbosson 11-13, CH-1217 Meyrin (☎ (022) 785 12 22), will send you information, maps, brochures, route descriptions, and mileage charts. In Switzerland, men and women traveling in groups might consider **hitching** (called "autostop") beyond the range of bus or train routes. *Let's Go* does not recommend hitchhiking.

TOURIST SERVICES AND MONEY

EMERGENCY	Police: ☎ 117. Ambulance: ☎ 144. Fire: ☎ 118.

TOURIST OFFICES. Tourist offices are available in nearly every small town in Switzerland; most speak English. The **Swiss National Tourist Office,** marked by a standard blue **"i"** sign, is represented in nearly every town in Switzerland, though in smaller towns the staff may not speak English. The English language website for Swiss tourism is www.myswitzerland.com.

Tourist Boards at Home: UK and **Ireland,** Swiss Centre, Swiss Centre, Swiss Court, London W1V 8EE (☎(02) 7851 1710;); **US** and **Canada,** 6608 Fifth Ave., New York, NY 10020 (☎ (212) 757 5944; email info.usa@switzerlandtourism.ch; in Canada call (800) 100 200 30 to be transferred to New York).

CURRENCY & EXCHANGE. The Swiss monetary unit is the **Swiss Franc (SFr),** which is divided into 100 *centimes* (called *Rappen* in German Switzerland). Coins are issued in 5, 10, 20, and 50 *centimes* and 1, 2, and 5SFr; bills in 10, 20, 50, 100, 500, and 1000SFr denominations. Currency exchange is easiest at ATMs, train stations, and post offices, where rates are the same as or close to bank rates.

Prices: Though Switzerland is not the cheapest destination, there are ways to experience it on a tight budget. If you stay in hostels and prepare most of your own food, expect to spend US$30-65 per person per day.

Tipping and bargaining: There is technically no need for tipping in Switzerland, as gratuities are already automatically factored into prices. However, it is considered polite in Switzerland to round up your bill to the nearest 1 or 2 Francs as a nod of approval for good service.

Taxes: There is no VAT tax in Switzerland, though there are frequently tourist taxes of a few SFr for a night at hostel.

ACCOMMODATIONS AND CAMPING

Like most things Swiss, accommodations in Switzerland are usually clean, orderly, and expensive. **Hotels** and **pensions** tend to charge at least US $35-40 for a single room while hostel beds are usually US$18 and up. There are hostels (*Jugendherbergen* in German, *Auberges de Jeunesse* in French, *Ostelli* in Italian) in all big cities, in most small towns, and in some mountain villages. In Switzerland the local **HI** organization is the *Schweizer Jugendherbergen* (SJH or Swiss Youth Hostels) which runs the 63 HI hostels in Switzerland. The SJH has a comprehensive website that contains contact information for all member hostels, and allows you to make reservations at many of them (www.youthhostel.ch). Non-HI members can stay in all of these hostels but are usually charged a US$5 surcharge. Switzerland also has the smaller, more informal **Swiss Backpackers (SB)** organization. SB is an organization of 28 hostels that appeal to the young, foreign traveler interested in socializing. **Camping sites** are not isolated areas, they are large plots with many camper vans and cars. Camping in Switzerland is less about getting out into nature and more about having a cheap place to sleep. Most sites are open in the summer only, but some sites are specifically set aside for winter camping. Prices average US$6 per person, US$6 per tent site.

SKIING AND HIKING

Switzerland's 9000km of **hiking paths** range from simple foothill excursions to ice-axe-wielding glacier expeditions. Bands of white-red-white mark trails; if there are no markings, you're on an "unofficial" trail, which is not always a problem—most are well maintained. Blue-white-blue markings indicate that a trail requires special equipment, either for difficult rock climbs or glacier climbing. **Swiss Alpine Club (SAC) huts** are modest and extremely practical for those interested in trekking in higher, more remote areas of the Alps. Bunk rooms sleep 10 to 20 side by side, with blankets (no electricity or running water) provided. One night's stay without food averages 30SFr (members 20-25SFr). Membership costs 126SFr. Contact the SAC, Sektion Zermatt, Haus Dolomite, CH-3920 Zermatt, Switzerland (☎ (028) 67 26 10). The best maps to bring are the **Freytag-Berndt** and **Kümmerly-Frey** maps (around US$10), available in Swiss bookstores.

Skiing in Switzerland is often less expensive than in North America if you avoid the pricey resorts. Passes (valid for transportation to, from, and on lifts) run 30-50SFr per day and 100-300SFr per week. A week of lift tickets, equipment rental, lessons, lodging, and *demi-pension* (half-pension—breakfast plus one other meal, usually dinner) averages 475SFr. Summer skiing is no longer as prevalent as it once was, but is still available in Zermatt.

COMMUNICATION

MAIL. **Airmail** from Switzerland averages 7-20 days to North America, although times are more unpredictable from smaller towns. Domestic letters take 1-3 days. Send *Poste Restante* letters to: Leah ROSE, *Postlagernde Briefe*, CH-1211 Geneva, Switzerland. CH is the mail code for Switzerland.

TELEPHONES. Wherever possible, use a calling card for international phone calls, as the long-distance rates for national phone services are often exorbitant. **Prepaid phone cards** and occasionally **major credit cards** can be used for direct international calls, but they are still less cost-efficient. The simplest way to call within the country is to use a pay phone. Most pay phones in Switzerland accept only **prepaid phone cards**. Phone cards are available at kiosks, post offices, or train stations. **International direct dial** numbers include: **AT&T** (☎ (022) 90 30 11); **BT Direct** (☎ (0800) 20 02 09); **Canada Direct** (☎ (0800) 20 02 17); **MCI WorldPhone Direct** (☎ (022) 90 30 12); **Sprint** (☎ (0800) 2002 36); **Telkom South Africa Direct** (☎ (022) 90 30 27).

INTERNET ACCESS. Most towns have internet cafes. The standard price is 12SFr (US$8) per hr.

LANGUAGES. German, French, Italian, and Romansch. English is the most common 2nd language in Switzerland, and most urban Swiss speak it fluently. Outside of cities and among older residents, however, you may have to rely on phrasebooks. Leap right in with our language charts on p. 958, you multilingual fool, you.

LOCAL FACTS

Time: Switzerland is 1hr. ahead of Greenwich Mean Time (GMT).

Climate: Switzerland is surprisingly mild; in July, temperatures can briefly reach temperatures 38°C (100°F), while in Feb. they get down to -10°C (5°F). Mountainous areas are cooler and wetter the higher you get; as a rule, temperatures drop about 1.7°C (3°F) with each additional 300m. Bring warm sweaters Sept.-May; add a thick coat, hat, and gloves in winter. The lake regions are very rainy.

Hours: Most stores in Switzerland close for lunch (noon-3pm), Sa afternoons, and all day Su. Many museums close M. Banks are open M-F 8am-12:30pm and 2-4:30pm.

Holidays: New Year's Day (Jan. 1-2); Good Friday (Apr. 5); Easter Monday (Apr. 5); Labor Day (May 1); Ascension Day (June 1); Whit Monday (June 11); Swiss National Day (Aug. 1); and Christmas (Dec. 25-26).

Festivals: Two raucous festivals are Basel's **Fasnacht** (Carnival) in Mar. and Geneva's **Escalade.** **"Open-Air"** music festivals occur throughout the summer. A few highlights include the **Montreux JazzFest** (July), **Bern's Gurtenfestival** (mid-July), **Paléo Festival Nyon** near Geneva (late July), and the **Open-Air St. Gallen** (late June).

WESTERN (FRENCH) SWITZERLAND

GENEVA
☎ 022

Step onto one of Geneva's lakeside quays, and you'll be confronted instantly by bankers barking into cellular phones, students strolling hand-in-hand, and families just enjoying the shore. There is no typical resident of this small (pop. 178,000) city. Geneva's long and belligerent tradition of battling for its political and religious independence is perhaps the one theme uniting the city's wildly diverse group of citizens. In 1536, Geneva welcomed a young, unknown John Calvin to its cathedral; later, aesthetes and free thinkers including Voltaire, Madame de Staël, and Rousseau lived here. Today, multinational organizations (including the Red Cross and the United Nations) continue to lend the city an international feel that contrasts strongly with the homogeneity of most Swiss towns. Indeed, many say that the only thing Geneva shares with the rest of Switzerland is its neutral foreign policy and the state religion, banking.

▆ TRANSPORTATION

Flights: Cointrin Airport (☎ 717 7111, flight information ☎ 799 31 11) is a hub for **Swissair** (☎ (0848) 800 700). **Air France** (☎ 827 87 87) and **British Airways** (☎ (0848) 801 010) are the other major airlines to service Geneva. **Bus #10** connects to the center of town (15min., every 6min., 2.20SFr), while the **train** (6min., every 10min., 4.80SFr) runs to Gare Cornavin.

Trains: Gare Cornavin, on pl. Cornavin, is the main station (www.sbb.ch). To: **Bern** (2hr., every hr., 40SFr); **Basel** (3hr., every hr., 72SFr); **Interlaken** (3hr., every hr., 65SFr); **Lyon** (2hr.; every hr.; 58SFr, under 26 48SFr); **Milan** (4-5hr.; 10 per day; 164SFr, under 26 132SFr); **Paris** (3¾hr.; every hr.; 196SFr, under 26 166SFr); and **Zurich** (3½hr., every hr., 77SFr). Reservations and info open M-F 8:30am-7pm, Sa 9am-5pm. **Gare des Eaux-Vives** (☎ 736 16 20), on the eastern edge of the city, connects to France via tram #12 (dir.: Amandoliers SNCF). To **Annecy** (1½hr., 6 per day, 14SFr) and **Chamonix** (2½hr., 4 per day, 24SFr).

Ferries: CGN (☎ 741 52 31) runs hugely popular routes to **Lausanne** and **Montreux,** that depart from quai du Mont-Blanc. Round-trip 47-57SFr.

Public Transportation: Transport Publics Genevois (☎ 308 34 34), next to the tourist office in Gare Cornavin, has free bus route maps. Open daily 6:15am-8pm. 1hr. of unlimited bus travel 2.20SFr; 3 stops or fewer 1.50SFr. **Day passes** 5SFr for 1 zone, 8.50SFr for 4. Buses run roughly 5:30am-midnight. A new Noctambus (3SFr, 1:30-4:30am) runs when the others don't. Buy multi-fare and day tickets at the train station, others at automatic vendors at every stop. Stamp multi-use tickets before boarding or risk a 60SFr fine. SwissPass valid on all buses; Eurail not valid.

Taxis: Taxi-Phone (☎331 41 33). 6.30SFr base fare, plus 2.70SFr per km. Taxi from airport to city 25-30SFr (15-20min.; 4 passengers max.).

Bike Rental: Genève Roule, pl. Montbrillant 17 (☎740 13 43), behind the station. 5 free bikes (50SFr deposit). Nicer ones from 5SFr per day. Open daily 7:30am-9:30pm.

Hitchhiking: *Let's Go* does not recommend hitchhiking. Those headed to Germany or northern Switzerland reportedly take bus #4 to Jardin Botanique. Those headed to France take bus #4 to Palettes, then line D to St. Julien.

✴ 🛈 ORIENTATION AND PRACTICAL INFORMATION

On the southwestern shore of **Lac Léman** (Lake Geneva), the labyrinthine cobblestoned streets and quiet squares of the *vieille ville* surround the **Cathédrale de St-Pierre** and the **university.** Banks, bistros, and boutiques line the **Rhône River** to the north. Farther north, the United Nations, Red Cross, and World Trade Organization overlook the city. Carry your **passport** with you at all times; the French border is close by, and regional buses and local trams (#12 and 16) often cross it. City buses provide swift service, with major hubs at the Gare Cornavin, Rd.-Pt. de Plainpalais, and pl. Bel Air (near the *ponts de l'Ile*); trips that stay within zone 10 (most of the city) officially cost 2.20SFr.

TOURIST, FINANCIAL, AND LOCAL SERVICES

Tourist Offices: The **main office,** rue du Mont-Blanc 18 (☎909 70 00; fax 909 70 11; www.geneve-tourisme.ch), 5min. from Cornavin towards the pont du Mont-Blanc in the Central Post Office Building. English-speaking staff books hotel rooms (5SFr fee) and offers walking tours. The office maintains a free direct phone line to Geneva hotels in Gare Cornavin, as well as a board listing budget accommodations. Open July-Aug. 9am-6pm; Sept.-June M-Sa 9am-6pm. During the summer, head for the magic bus, Geneva's **Centre d'Accueil et de Renseignements** (CAR; ☎731 46 47), parked in by the Metro Shopping entrance to Cornavin Station. Open June 15-Sept. 15 9am-11pm.

Consulates: Australia, chemin des Fins 2 (☎799 91 00). **Canada,** av. de l'Ariana 5 (☎919 92 00). **New Zealand,** chemin des Fins 2 (☎929 03 50). **South Africa,** rue de Rhône 65 (☎849 54 54). **UK,** rue de Vermont 37 (☎918 24 26). **US,** World Trade Center Bldg. #2 (☎798 16 05; recorded info ☎798 16 15).

Currency Exchange: ATMs have the best rates. **Gare Cornavin** offers good rates, no commission on traveler's checks, and credit card advances (200SFr min.); also arranges Western Union transfers. Open Nov.-Mar. 6:45am-8pm; Apr.-Oct. 6:45am-9:30pm. Western Union desk open daily 7am-7pm.

Gay and Lesbian Services: Dialogai, rue de la Navigation 11-13 (☎738 02 00). Mostly male resource group with programs from support groups to outdoor activities. Publishes *Dialogai,* a guide to French-speaking Switzerland's gay scene. Open M-Th 2-7pm.

Laundromat: Lavseul, rue de-Monthoux 29 (☎735 90 51 or 732 61 46). 5SFr to wash, 1SFr for 10min. to dry. Open 7am-midnight.

EMERGENCIES AND COMMUNICATIONS

Emergencies: Police, rue de Berne 6 (☎117, non-emergency ☎715 38 50), next to post office. **Fire,** ☎118. **Ambulance,** ☎144.

Medical Assistance: Hôpital Cantonal, rue Micheli-du-Crest 24 (☎372 33 11). Bus #1 or 5 or tram #12. Call the **Association des Médecins** (☎320 84 20) for walk-in clinic.

Pharmacy: Every night a changing set of 4 pharmacies stays open late (9 or 11pm). Consult *Genève Agenda* for addresses and phone numbers. The pharmacy at the train station has the longest regular hours.

Internet Access: Open Vidéo Club, rue Chantepoulet, has 12 PCs. Internet 5SFr per hr. Open M-Th 9:30-3am, F 9:30am-5am, Sa 11am-5am, Su 3pm-1am. **Point 6,** rue de Vieux-Billard 7a (☎800 26 00), off rue des Bains, rents spots at the screen for 4SFr per 30min., 6SFr per hr. Open M-Tu and Th noon-midnight, W 10am-midnight, F noon-2am, Sa 10am-2am, Su 10am-10pm.

Poste Centrale, rue de Mont-Blanc 18, a block from Gare Cornavin in the Hôtel des Postes. Open M-F 7:30am-6pm, Sa 8:30-noon. Address mail to be held: Dan BARNES, *Poste Restante,* Genève 1 Mont-Blanc, **CH-1211,** Geneva.

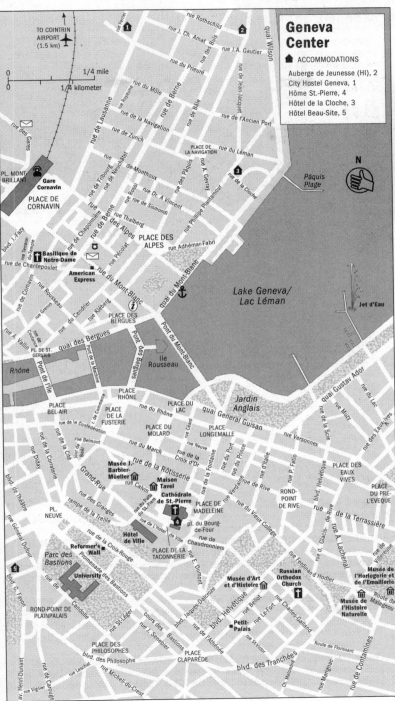

Geneva Center

🏠 ACCOMMODATIONS

Auberge de Jeunesse (HI), 2
City Hostel Geneva, 1
Hôme St.-Pierre, 4
Hôtel de la Cloche, 3
Hôtel Beau-Site, 5

ACCOMMODATIONS

You can usually find dorm beds and hostel rooms in Geneva, but hotels fill quickly, so reserve in advance. If the places listed below are booked, try one of the 50 others listed in *Info Jeunes* (free at the tourist office). We list the highlights below.

City Hostel Geneva, rue Ferrier 2 (☎901 15 00; www.cityhostel.ch). From the station, turn left on rue de Lausanne, walk 5min., turn left onto rue de Prieuré, and right onto rue Ferrier. **Internet** access (7SFr per hr.). sheets 3SFr. Reception 8-11:30am and 3-10pm. Single-sex, 4-bed dorms 24SFr; singles 50SFr; doubles 70SFr.

Auberge de Jeunesse (HI), rue Rothschild 28-30 (☎732 62 60). Walk left from the station down rue de Lausanne (10min.), turn right on rue Rothschild, and take bus #1 (dir.: Wilson) to the end. Breakfast included. Laundry. 5-night max. stay. Reception 6:30-10am and 4pm-midnight (in winter from 5pm). Lockout 10am-4pm (in winter 5pm). Curfew midnight. Dorms 24SFr; doubles 65-75SFr; quads 99SFr.

Cité Universitaire, av. Miremont 46 (☎839 22 11). Take bus #3 (dir.: Crêts-de-Champel) from the Le Popeye restaurant on pl. de 22 Cantons, on the far right as you exit the station, to the end. Institutional housing with small grocery shop. Reception M-F 8am-noon and 2-10pm, Sa 8am-noon and 6-10pm, Su 9-11am and 6-10pm. For dorms only: lockout 11am-6pm and curfew 11pm. Dorms (July-Sept. only) 17SFr; singles 38SFr; doubles 55SFr; studios with kitchenette and bathroom 68SFr.

Hôme St-Pierre, cours St-Pierre 4 (☎310 37 07), seconds from the cathedral. Cross pont du Mont-Blanc from the station, head up rampe de la Treille, and take the 3rd right (15min.). Spectacular rooftop views and a convivial atmosphere. **Women only.** Breakfast M-Sa 5SFr. Laundry 7SFr. Reception M-Sa 9am-noon and 4-8pm, Su 9am-noon. Reserve ahead. Dorms 23SFr; singles 36-45SFr; doubles 50-60SFr.

Hôtel de la Cloche, rue de la Cloche 6 (☎732 94 81), off quai du Mont-Blanc, across from the Noga Hilton. A converted mansion—each room has chandeliers, antique mirrors, balconies, and TVs. Breakfast 5SFr. Reception 8am-midnight. Reserve ahead. Singles 50SFr; doubles 80SFr; triples 95SFr; quads 130SFr. In winter 5-10SFr discount.

Centre St-Boniface, av. du Mail 14 (☎322 26 00). From the station, head right on blvd. Fazy, across pont de La Couluvrenière, and along av. du Mail (20min.). Jesuit-run with singles only. Reception M-F 9am-noon and 4-7pm. Reserve ahead. Singles 40SFr.

Hôtel Beau-Site, pl. du Cirque 3 (☎328 10 08; www.hotel-beau-site.ch). From the station, turn right on blvd. Fazy, cross the Rhône at pont de la Couluvrenière, and follow blvd. Georges-Favon to pl. du Cirque (20min.). Breakfast included. Reception 7am-11pm. Check-out 11:15am. Singles 60SFr, with shower 70SFr, with bath and toilet 85SFr; doubles 82SFr, with shower 90SFr, with bath and toilet 110SFr; triples 100SFr, with shower 110SFr; quads 110SFr, with shower 115SFr.

Camping Pointe-à-la-Bise (☎752 12 96), on chemin de la Bise. Take bus #9 to Rive, then bus E (north) to Bise (about 7km). Reception 8am-noon and 4-8pm. Open Apr.-Oct. 6SFr per person. No tents provided; beds are 18SFr each.

FOOD

You can find anything from sushi to paella in Geneva, but you may need a banker's salary to foot the bill. *Boulangeries* and *pâtisseries* offer unparalleled opportunities for gourmet food at budget prices. In the area called **Les Paquis,** almost any sort of ethnic food is available. Around **pl. du Cirque** and **plaine de Plainpalais** are a number of cheap, student-oriented "tea rooms," offering bakery and traditional fare at reasonable prices. Many supermarkets also have cafeterias with some of the best deals available, and *Info Jeunes* lists university cafeterias that won't tax your wallet. Pick up **groceries** at **Co-op,** on the corner of rue du Commerce and rue du Rhône, in the Centre Rhône Fusterie. (☎310 77 11. Open M 9am-6:45pm, Tu-W and F 8:30am-6:45pm, Th 8:30am-8pm, Sa 8:30am-5pm.)

Le Rozzel, Grand-Rue 18 (☎312 42 72). Take bus #5 to pl. Neuve, and walk up the hill past the cathedral on rue Jean-Calvin to Grand-Rue. Sit outside and enjoy Breton-style crêpes (dinner 7-17SFr, dessert 5-12SFr). Open M-F 8am-10pm, Sa 10am-10pm.

Restaurant Manora, rue de Cornavin 4 (☎909 44 10), 3min. to the right of the station in the Placette department store. Self-serve restaurant with salads (from 4.20SFr), fruit tarts (3.20SFr), and main dishes (from 11SFr). Open M-Sa 7am-9pm, Su 9am-9pm.

La Crise, rue de Chantepoulet 13 (☎738 02 64). From the station, turn right on rue de Cornavin and left on rue de Chantepoulet. Healthy portions of veggie food with slender prices. Quiche and veggies 8.50SFr, soup 3.50SFr. Open M-F 6am-8pm, Sa 6am-3pm.

Chez Ma Cousine, rue de Bourg-Four 6, in the *vieille ville*. Don't come here looking for anything but chicken. It is perfectly cooked, served with fries and salad for 12.90SFr. Open M-F 7am-midnight, Sa 11am-midnight, Su 11am-11pm.

Auberge de Saviese, rue des Pâquis 20 (☎732 83 30). From Gare Cornavin, turn left onto rue de Lausanne and right on rue de Zurich, which brings you to rue des Pâquis. Load up on traditional Swiss specialties. Excellent *fondue au cognac* (19.50SFr) and *raclette* with all the trimmings (30SFr). Open M-F 9am-10:30pm, Sa-Su 6-11pm.

◉ SIGHTS

For centuries Geneva was tightly constrained by a belt of walls and trenches. By the mid-19th century when they were finally removed, the city's most interesting historical sites were already established in a dense, easily walkable space. The tourist office offers 2hr. **walking tours** during the summer. *(June 14-Oct. 2 M-F 10am; rest of the year Sa 10am. 12SFr, students and seniors 8SFr, children 6SFr.)*

VIEILLE VILLE AND WATERFRONT. Begin exploring Geneva in the *vieille ville* where the **Cathédrale de St-Pierre** stands as testimony to Calvin's Reformation of Geneva. After visiting the austere church, climb its 157-step **north tower** for a spectacular view over the old town. *(Cathedral open June-Sept. M-Sa 9am-7pm, Su 11:30am-1pm; Oct.-May M-Sa 10am-noon and 2-5pm, Su 11am-12:30pm and 1:30-5pm. Tower open July-Aug., closes 30min. before the cathedral. 3SFr.)* The ruins of a Roman sanctuary, a 4th-century basilica, and a 6th-century church rest in an **archaeological site** below the cathedral. *(Open June-Sept. Tu-Sa 11am-5pm, Su 10am-5pm; Oct.-May Tu-Sa 2-5pm, Su 10am-noon and 2-5pm. 5SFr, students 3SFr.)* There are many quiet streets surrounding the cathedral. Near the west end of the cathedral sits the 14th-century **Maison Tavel,** Geneva's oldest civilian medieval building, a posh, fortified urban palace that today houses a historical municipal **museum.** *(Open Tu-Su 10am-5pm. Free.)* A few steps away is the 15th- to 17th-century **Hôtel de Ville** (Town Hall), where world leaders met on August 22, 1864, to sign the **Geneva Convention** that still governs conduct during war. The **Grand-Rue** leading away from the Hôtel de Ville is crammed with art galleries, medieval workshops, and 18th-century mansions; plaques along the street commemorate famous residents, including philosopher Jean-Jacques Rousseau, born at #40. Below the cathedral on rue de la Croix-Rouge, the lovely **Parc des Bastions** includes the **Mur des Réformateurs** (Reformers' Wall), a sprawling collection of bas-relief narrative panels and the towering figures of the Reformers themselves, including Knox, Calvin, and Cromwell. A beautiful stroll down its center walkway, the Promenade des Bastions, will lead you to the world-class **■Petit-Palais,** where you will find works by Picasso, Renoir, Gauguin, Cézanne, and Chagall. *(Terrasse St-Victor 2, off bd. Helvétique. Take bus #17 to Petit Palais or #1, 3, or 5 to Claparède. Open M-F 10am-6pm, Sa-Su 10am-5pm. 10SFr, students 5SFr.)* A few blocks east of the Petit-Palais lie the glittering domes of the **Russian Orthodox Church,** whose interior is filled with hauntingly lovely icons, stained glass, and a heavy aroma of incense. *(Rue Toepffer. Take me des Chaudronniers from the vieille ville.)*

As you descend toward the lake from the cathedral, you will fast-forward 600 years; medieval lanes give way to wide, flower-lined quays, chic boutiques and watch shops, revealing Geneva's cosmopolitan air. The largest fountain in the world, the **Jet d'Eau,** down quai Gustave-Ardor on the waterfront, spews a spectacular plume of water 140m into the air (about seven tons at once). In the nearby **Jardin Anglais,** a floral clock (perhaps Geneva's most overrated attraction) pays homage to Geneva's watch industry with over 6500 plants. However, the waterfront's true treasures are its quays and beaches such as **Paquis Plage,** on the left bank, which offer stunning views of the lake and surrounding mountains, as well as the ice cream stands and various shops which dot the area.

FOR ART'S SAKE In the summer of 1996 a group of artists staged a sit-in demonstration at place du Bourg-de-Four just below the Cathédrale de St-Pierre. They ripped up pavement, built bonfires, and confused the hell out of tourists for six days until the city capitulated and granted them a no-rent lease for an abandoned industrial park on the left bank, now called **Artamis** (☎ 320 39 30; www.artamis.org). You'll find it at 12 rue de Strand, accessible by bus #2 or 10 (Palladium). This 10-building complex, a former run-down factory, displays high-quality graffiti and houses a mix of thriving art workshops, theaters, and fund-raising facilities as well as some of the best deals in town: an **internet cafe** (5SFr per hr.), a movie theater (2SFr), and bars. The Database building is a recording studio where many of the top house and jungle DJs in the area come to experiment and exchange ideas. All facilities and the main phone line (with information on performances and events) are open daily 4pm to 2am.

INTERNATIONAL HILL. Spectacular views of Lac Léman with Mont-Blanc in the background await in a series of garden-parks on the northern side of Geneva, up the hill behind the train station. For even better vistas, climb higher to Geneva's international city, home to myriad embassies and multilateral organizations. The highlight is the ▧**International Red Cross Museum.** Detailing the organization's history from its founding by Henry Dunant to it advances in WWI and tragic impotence to aid civilians in WWII, the museum's images present an emotional tour-de-force. Even the most ironic and detached will find Dostoevsky's "each of us is responsible to everyone for everything" resonating a bit more clearly after a visit here. (*Av. de la Paix 17. Take bus #8, F, V, or Z to Appia or Ariana.* ☎ 748 95 25. *Open W-M 10am-5pm. 10SFr, students 5SFr. Self-guided audio tours 5SFr.*) In the Red Cross's shadow stands the European headquarters of the **United Nations,** housed in the building that once sheltered the League of Nations. The guided tour of the UN proves less interesting than the constant traffic of international diplomats often wearing handsome non-Western dress. (*Open July-Aug. daily 9am-6pm; Apr.-June and Sept.-Oct. daily 10am-noon and 2-4pm; Nov.-Mar. M-F 10am-noon and 2-4pm. 8.50SFr, students 6.50SFr.*)

♫ ▥ ENTERTAINMENT AND NIGHTLIFE

Genève Agenda, available at the tourist office, is your guide to fun, with event listings ranging from major festivals to movies (be warned—a movie runs about 16SFr). In July and August, the **Cinelac** turns Genève Plage into an open-air cinema screening mostly American films. Check listings in *Genève Agenda* for indoor cinemas ("v.o." indicates original language, with French and sometimes German subtitles; "st. ang." indicates English subtitles). There's also the biggest celebration of the **American Independence Day** outside the US (July 4), and the **Fêtes de Genève** in early August is filled with international music and fireworks. **Free jazz concerts** take place in July and August at the *Théâtre de Verdure* in Parc de la Grange.

Geneva's internationalism has had the effect of bringing an incredible diversity to its nightlife. Summer nightlife tends to center around the cafes on the lakeside quays in **Pl. du Bourg-de-Four,** below Cathédrale de St-Pierre, and the village of **Carouge** (take tram #12 to pl. du Marché), home to **Au Chat Noir,** rue Vautier 13, a popular venue for jazz, funk, rock, salsa, and sax-moaning blues, with live concerts every night. (Open M-Th 6pm-4am, F 6pm-5am, Sa 9pm-5am, Su 9pm-4am. Concerts 9:30pm; 15SFr.) Back in the *vieille ville*, consort with the artsy patrons of the famous, chic bar **La Clémence,** pl. du Bourg-de-Four 20 (open M-Th 7am-12:30am, F-Sa 7am-1:30am), or chat merrily in the friendly Irish cellar bar **Flanagan's,** rue du Cheval-Blanc 4, off Grand-Rue (Guinness 8SFr; live music Th-Sa 10pm-2am; open daily 4pm-2am). A single strand of red lights traverse the sophisticated and gay friendly **Sunset Cafe,** Rue de la Navigation. (☎ 906 40 47. Open W-Su 5pm-midnight.)

LAUSANNE   ☎021

The story of Lausanne is a tale of two cities: the *vieille ville* is cosmopolitan and businesslike, while the lakefront at Ouchy is lazy and decadent. In the *vieille ville* (M: Lausanne-Flan), follow the medieval covered stairs to the hilltop to reach the Gothic **cathédrale**, consecrated in 1275 under Holy Roman Emperor Rudolph and Pope Gregory X. Climb the 200-step **tower** for a spectacular view of the city, lake, and mountains beyond. (Cathedral open July to mid-Sept. 7am-7pm; mid-Sept. to June 7am-5pm.) While there, check out the brand new **Museum of Design and Contemporary Applied Arts** (☎315 25 30). Last year it featured an out-there display of all things inflatable. (Open Tu 11am-9pm, W-Su 11am-6pm. 6SFr, students and seniors 4SFr.) Stretch your legs on Ouchy's main promenades, the **quai de Belgique** and **pl. de la Navigation.** The **Musée Olympique,** quai d'Ouchy 1, is a high-tech temple to modern Olympians with a smaller exhibit on the ancient games. (Open May-Sept. F-W 9am-6pm, Th 9am-8pm; Oct.-Apr. Tu-W and F-Su 9am-6pm, Th 9am-8pm. 14SFr, students 9SFr; the idyllic grounds are free.) Lausanne's most enthralling cultural repository may be the ▤**Collection de l'Art Brut,** filled with disturbing and beautiful artwork by atypical artists—schizophrenics, peasants, and convicted criminals. The biographies of the artists are nearly as rich and fascinating as the art. Take bus #2 or 3 to "Jomini." (☎647 54 35. Open Tu-Su 11am-1pm and 2-5pm. 6SFr, students 4SFr.) If time permits, stroll through the 2000-year-old remains of the Roman city **Vicus de Lousanna.** Take bus #2 to Bois-de-Vaux and follow the signs.

Frequent **trains** (☎157 22 22) arrive at pl. de la Gare 9, halfway between the *vieille ville* and the lakefront, from: Basel (2½hr., 2 per hr., 62SFr); Geneva (50min., every 30min., 20SFr); Montreux (20min., every 30min., 9.40SFr); and Zurich (2½hr., 3 per hr., 67SFr). Take **Métro Ouchy** or **bus** #1, 3, or 5 to downtown. The **tourist office,** in the train station, reserves rooms. (☎613 73 73; www.lausanne.tourisme.ch. Open daily 9am-7pm.) To reach the large and gleaming **Jeunotel (HI),** chemin du Bois-de-Vaux 36, take bus #2 (dir.: Bourdonette) to "Bois-de-Vaux," cross the street, and follow the signs. (☎626 02 22; fax 626 02 26. Dorms 25-32SFr; singles 58-82SFr; doubles 88-104SFr; triples and quads 35SFr per person.) Conveniently located near the waterfront and *vielle ville,* **La Croisee,** av. Marc Dufour 15, is a 15min. walk from the train station. Take av. du Ruchonnet and continue as it turns into av. Marc Dufour. (☎321 09 09. 4- to 12- bed dorms 30-40 SFr; singles 90SFr; doubles 65SFr; triples and quads 55-65SFr.) To get to the lakeside **Camping de Vidy,** chemin du Camping 3, take bus #2 from M: Ouchy (dir.: Bourdonnette) to Bois-de-Vaux, then cross the street and go down chemin du Boix-de-Vaux past Jeunotel and under the overpass. The office is straight ahead across rte. de Vidy. (☎622 50 00; fax 622 50 01. Reception 8am-12:30pm and 5-8pm. 6.50SFr, students 6SFr; tents 7-11SFr; 1- to 2-person bungalows 54SFr; 3- to 4- person bungalows 86SFr; city tax 1.20SFr per person and 1.30SFr per car.) Restaurants, cafes, and bars cluster around **pl. St-François** and the **vieille ville. Migros supermarket,** av. de Rhodanie 2, is near the Ouchy Métro stop. (Open M 9am-9:45pm, Tu-Sa 8am-9:45pm.) **Postal code:** CH-1001.

MONTREUX   ☎021

Montreux is postcard Switzerland at its swanky, genteel best. The crystal-blue water of Lac Léman (Lake Geneva) and the snow-capped Alps are a photographer's dream. The gloomy medieval fortress, the **Château de Chillon,** on a nearby island, is one of the most visited attractions in Switzerland. It features all the comforts of home—including prison cells, a torture chamber, and a weapons room. The priest Francoic de Bonivard spent four years manacled in the dungeon for preaching Reformation doctrine and inspired Lord Byron's *The Prisoner of Chillon* as well as works by Rousseau, Hugo, and Dumas. (☎966 89 10; www.chillon.ch. Open Apr.-Sept. 9am-6pm; Mar. and Oct. 9:30am-5pm; Nov.-Feb. 10am-4pm. 7SFr, students 5.50SFr.) Take the CGN **ferry** (13SFr, under 26 5.50SFr) or bus #1 to Chillon (2.60SFr). The **Montreux Jazz Festival,** world famous for exceptional musical talent and one of the biggest parties in Europe, pushes everything aside for 15 days starting the first Friday in July. Write to the tourist office well in advance, call the **Jazz Boutique** ticket sellers (☎ 963 82 82; open mid-Mar. to summer), or check out www.montreuxjazz.com for info and tickets (39-69SFr). If you can find a room but no tickets, come anyway for the **Jazz Off,** 500 hours of free, open-air concerts by new bands and established musicians.

Trains (☎ 963 45 15) arrive frequently on av. des Alpes from: Bern (1½hr., every hr., 40SFr); Geneva (1hr., every 30min., 29SFr); and Lausanne (20min., every 5-25min., 9.40SFr). Descend the stairs opposite the station, head left on Grand Rue, and look to the right for the **tourist office,** on pl. du Débarcadère. (☎962 84 84; fax 963 78 95; www.montreux.ch. Open mid-June to mid-Sept. daily 8:30am-7pm; late Sept. to early June M-F 8:30am-5pm, Sa-Su 10am-3pm.) Cheap rooms are scarce in Montreux and almost nonexistent during the jazz festival; book ahead. To get to the modern and social **Auberge de Jeunesse Montreux (HI),** passage de l'Auberge 8, walk 20min. along the lake past the Montreux Tennis Club. (☎963 49 34. Laundry 8SFr. Reception Apr.-Sept. 7-10am and 4-11pm; Oct.-Mar. 7:30-9:30am and 5-10pm. Lock-out 10am-4pm. Curfew midnight; key available. Dorms 29SFr; doubles 38-42SFr; nonmembers add 5SFr.) To reach the **Hôtel Pension Wilhelm,** rue du Marché 13-15, from the station, take a left on av. des Alpes, walk up 3min. and take a left on rue du Marché. (☎963 14 31. Breakfast included. Reception daily 7am-midnight. Closed Oct.-Feb. unless you call ahead. Singles (off-season only) 65SFr; doubles 50-120SFr.) To **camp** at **Les Horizons Bleus,** take bus #1 to Villeneuve and follow the lake to the left for 5min. (☎960 15 47. Reception 9am-12:30pm and 4-9pm. 7SFr per person, 6-12SFr per tent.) The **Co-op,** Grand Rue 80, offers groceries. (Open M-F 8am-12:15pm and 2-6:30pm, Sa 8am-5pm.) **Postal code:** CH-1820.

▶ DAYTRIPS FROM MONTREUX: LEYSIN AND GRYON. From small (Leysin) to diminutive (Gryon), these two towns are unlikely stops on a grand tour of Europe. However, both are idyllic locations between breathtaking mountains and fantastic hostels that are ideal places to recharge. Anglophone-friendly Leysin is full of once-mobile backpackers who came, saw, and stayed, bolstering a local industry catering to skiers, snowboarders, climbers, mountain bikers, paragliders, and hikers. The **tourist office** (☎ (024) 494 22 44), in the Centre Sportif, up the road to the left from the pl. du Marché, provides **hiking maps,** while the **Swiss Climbing School** (☎ (024) 494 18 46) organizes **trekking** and all activities **alpine.** Just 50m from the start of the skiing and biking trails, the **◪Hiking Sheep Guesthouse,** in Villa La Joux, features shining facilities, breathtaking balconies, and a super-friendly manager. (☎ (024) 494 35 35. June 15-Dec. 15 dorms 26SFr, doubles 33SFr; Dec. 16-June 14 dorms 30SFr, doubles 35SFr.) To reach Leysin, take the **cog railway** from Aigle (30min., every hr., 8-10SFr), accessible by **train** from Montreux (10min., 2 per hr.) and Lausanne (30min., 2 per hr.).

Tiny Gryon has experienced a relative population explosion in recent years (now pop. 1000), but the explosion doesn't seem to have marred Gryon's untouched, tranquil setting. Its main draw is the **◪Swiss Alp Retreat,** housed in the **Chalet Martin,** a pocket of Australian and Swiss enthusiasm high in the Alps. To reach the hostel from the Gryon stop, take a right, head uphill, and follow the signs. The English-speaking staff maintains a cooperative-style establishment where bohemian backpackers taking a "vacation from their vacation" have been known to stay…and stay. The hostel rents skis and videos and has daily sign-ups for **cheese farm tours, paragliding, thermal baths,** and other daily excursions. (**Internet.** Check-in 9am-9pm. 25SFr first night, 20SFr per night for 2-night stay, 100SFr per week; 3SFr more in winter.) To reach Gryon, take the **cog railway** from Bex (30min., every hr., 5.60SFr; Swisspass and Eurail valid), one stop down from Aigle on the rail line.

NEUCHÂTEL

☎ 032

Though Alexandre Dumas was referring to the unique yellow stone common to Neuchâtel's architecture when he likened the city to a carving made of butter, his comment could easily be misinterpreted as a reference to the city's many *pâtisseries.* But aside from its gastronomic delights, Neuchâtel also glows with a remarkable medieval beauty. The *vieille ville* is centered around the **pl. des Halles;** the r. de Château leads from there up to the **Collégiale** church and the chateau for which the city is named. (Church open Apr.-Sept. 9am-8pm; Oct.-Mar. 9am-6:30pm. Free concerts last F of each month. Chateau tours Apr.-Sept. M-F every hr. 10am-noon and 2-4pm, Sa 10-11am and 2-4pm, Su 2-4pm). Downhill from the chateau on r. Jehanne-de-Hochberg, climb the **Tour des Prisons** (Prison Tower) for a stunning vista of the lake and city. (Open daily Apr.-Sept. 8am-6pm. 1SFr.) Neuchâtel has a number of museums; among them is the **Musée d'Art et d'Histoire,** Esplanade Léopold-Robert 1, in a magnificent building on the waterfront. The museum covers the city's history and a range of art; unfortunately most explanations are not offered in English. (Open Tu-Su 10am-5pm. 7SFr, students 4SFr, under 17 free; Th free.) A daytrip to nearby **Cressier** will delight with wine-tasting and vineyard strolls; **trains** run hourly to Cressier (10min., 3.60SFr).

Trains run frequently to Bern (45min., 17.20SFr); Basel (1¾hr., 37-52SFr); Geneva (1½hr., 42SFr); and Interlaken (2hr., 42SFr). From the station, take bus #6 to pl. Pury to get to the center of town. From pl. Pury, face the lake and walk to the left to reach the **tourist office,** Hôtel des Postes. (☎889 68 90; www.ne.ch/tourism. Open mid-June to mid-Sept. M-F 9am-6:30pm, Sa 9am-5pm, Su 2-5pm; late Sept. to early June M-F 9am-noon and 1:30-5:30pm, Sa 9am-noon.) The quirky **Oasis Neuchâtel,** r. du Suchiez 35, overlooks the lake. From pl. Pury, take bus #1 (dir.: Cormondrèche) to Vauseyon; walk back toward town, then take the stairs marked Escaliers de Suchiez. (☎731 31 90. Breakfast included. Reception 8-10am and 5-9pm. Dorms 24SFr; doubles 60SFr.) If it's full, ask for the *Hôtel Restaurant* guide for cheap options in nearby towns. The laid-back **Crêperie Bach et Buck,** av. du Premier-Mars 22, sells crêpes for under 10SFr. (Served M-Th 11:30am-2pm and 5:30-10pm; F-Sa 11:30am-2pm and 5:30-11:30pm; Su 6-10pm.) Dance the night away at the **Casino de la Rotonde,** fbg. du Lac 14. (Beer 3-5SFr. Cover around 10SFr. Open F-Sa 10pm-4am.) Behind the casino stands the **Bar Au 21,** Foubourg de Lac 23, which has a young and relaxed crowd. (☎725 81 98. Open M-Th 7am-1am, F 7am-2am, Sa 5pm-2am, Su 5pm-1am.) **Postal code:** CH-2001.

CENTRAL AND NORTHERN (GERMAN) SWITZERLAND

With one of the largest banking centers in Western Europe (Zurich), German Switzerland has traditionaly been thought of as a financial mecca. Gradually, the region has managed to change its image with the increasing popularity of the outdoor playground Interlaken and with the perfect combination of cosmopolitan offerings and outdoor splendor found in Lucerne.

BASEL (BÂLE)   ☎061

Perched on the Rhine, a stone's throw from France and Germany, Switzerland's third-largest city (rhymes with "nozzle," pop. 193,000) blends the two cultures into a distinct character of its own. Basel is home to a large medieval quarter and one of the oldest universities in Switzerland—graduates include Erasmus, Bernoulli, and Nietzsche. As you wander Basel's streets, you'll encounter art from Roman times to the 20th century and be serenaded by student musicians on every corner.

TRANSPORTATION. Basel has three **train stations:** the French SNCF (☎157 22 22) and Swiss SBB stations (☎157 22 22; 1.19SFr per min.) are on Centralbahnpl., near Altstadt. The German DB station (☎690 11 11) is across the Rhine down Greifgasse. Trains chug to Bern (1¼hr., every hr., 37SFr); Geneva (3hr., every hr., 72SFr); Zurich (1hr., every 15-30min., 31SFr); Paris (5-6hr.; 12 per day; 138SFr, under 26 25% off); and Munich via Zurich (5¼hr.; every hr.; 204SFr, under 26 25% off).

> **MONSTER MADNESS** In 1529, Basel's residents spiritedly joined the Reformation and ousted the bishop, keeping his *crozier* (staff) as the town's emblem. The staff shares this honor with the basilisk (Basel-isk), a creature part bat, part dragon, and part rooster, which caused what may be the world's first and only public trial and execution of a chicken. In 1474, a hen allegedly laid an egg on a dung heap under a full moon, an action sure to hatch the horrible creature. The bird was tried, found guilty, and beheaded, and the egg was ceremonially burnt.

⚐ PRACTICAL INFORMATION. To reach the **tourist office,** Schifflände 5, from the SBB station, take tram #1 to Schifflände; the office is on the river, near the Mittlere Rheinbrücke. (☎ 268 68 68; fax 268 68 70; www.baseltourismus.ch. Open M-F 8:30am-6pm.) For **internet** access swing by **Domino,** Steinenvorstadt 54. (10SFr per hr., 12 SFr per hr. after 6pm. Must be 18 years old. Open M-Th 9am-midnight, F-Sa 9am-1am, Su 1pm-midnight.) Take tram #1 or 8 to Marktpl. and walk one block away from the river to find the post office. (Open M-W and F 7:30am-6:30pm, Th 7:30am-8pm, Sa 8am-noon.) **Postal codes:** CH-4000 to CH-4059.

⚐⚐ ACCOMMODATIONS AND FOOD. Basel's biggest shortcoming is its lack of cheap lodgings. Call ahead to ensure a spot in the only hostel in town. Walk 12min. from the SBB station down Aeschengraben to St. Alban Anlage and follow the signs downhill from the tower to the **Jugendherberge (HI),** St. Alban-Kirchrain 10. (☎ 272 05 72. Breakfast included. Laundry. Reception 7-10am and 2pm-midnight. Check-out 7-10am. Dorms 29-31SFr; singles 79SFr; doubles 49SFr. Jan.-Feb. 19 and Nov.-Dec. 2.50SFr less.) The **Hotel-Pension Steinenschanze,** Steinengraben 69, is a three-star hotel. From the SBB station, turn left on Centralbahnstr., follow the signs for Heuwaage for 5min., go up the ramp under the bridge, and turn left on Steinengraben. (☎ 272 53 53. Breakfast included. Students three-night max. stay. Singles 110-180SFr, under 25 with ISIC 60SFr; doubles 160-250SFr, 100SFr.) For **Camp Waldhort,** Heideweg 16, in Reinach, take tram #11 to Landhof, backtrack 200m, cross the main street, and follow the signs. (☎ 711 64 29. Reception 7am-12:30pm and 2-10pm. Open Mar.-Oct. 7SFr per person, 10SFr per tent.)

With all the students about, cheap eateries are numerous. **Barfüsserpl., Marktpl.,** and the streets connecting them are full of restaurants. Migrate to **Migros** branches at Steinenvorstadt, and Clarapl. 17 (both open M-W and F 8am-6:30pm, Th 8am-9pm, Sa 7:30am-5pm) or Bahnhof SBB (open M-F 6am-10pm, Sa-Su 7:30am-10pm). Tasty German fare can be found at **Zum Schnabel,** Trillengässlein 2. (Bratwurst, *Rösti,* and salad 12.80SFr. Open M-Th 8am-midnight, Sa-Su 8am-1am.)

⚐⚐ SIGHTS AND ENTERTAINMENT. Most sights lie on the **Groß-Basel** (Greater Basel) side of the Rhine, on the same side as the train station. Basel's medieval heritage is presented in its **Münster** (cathedral), on the site of an ancient Celtic settlement and a Roman fort. You can visit the tombs of Erasmus and Bernoulli, or climb the tower for a spectacular view of the city, the Rhine, and the Black Forest. (Cathedral open Easter-Oct. 15 M-F 10am-5pm, Sa 10am-4pm, Su 1-5pm; Oct. 16-Easter M-Sa 11am-4pm, Su 2-4pm. Free. Tower 3SFr.) From the Münster, walk away from the river up Münsterberg and turn right on Freiestr. to reach the Marktpl. and the blinding red, green, and gold **Rathaus** (town hall). Freie Strasse's other end boasts **Theaterplatz** and the chaotic, iron-sculpted **Jean Tinguely Fountain.** Basel has an astounding 30 museums; the most interesting of which, **⚐Kunstmuseum** (Fine Arts Museum), St. Alban-Graben 16, dates from 1661, and houses an outstanding collection of works by old and new masters, including Picasso, Klee and Giacametti. (Take tram #2 to Kunstmuseum. ☎ 206 6262. Open Tu and Th-Su 10am-5pm, W 10am-7pm. 7SFr, students 5SFr; first Su of the month free.) Nearby and included in the ticket price is the **Museum für Gegenwartskunst** (Museum of Contemporary Art), St. Alban-Rheinweg 60, which houses rotating, edgy exhibits, including important pieces by Calder, Johns, Warhol, Lichtenstein, and Pollock. (Open Tu-Su 11am-5pm.) Perhaps the true star of Basel's museums is **Fondation Beyeler,** in the suburb of Riehen. Take tram #6 (dir.: Riehen Grenze) to Riehen Dorf, then walk straight for 5min. The museum is stuffed full of greats; Picasso, Matisse, Cézanne, Pollock, and Lichtenstein are just a handful. The outdoor lily-pond is only matched by a Monet version within. (Baselstr. 107. Open daily 10am-6pm, W until 8pm. 12SFr, students 9SFr.) Check out the **Museum Jean Tinguely** for the artist's bizarre fountains and other fascinating creations. (Tram #2 or 15 to Wettsteinpl. then bus #31 to Museum Tinguely. Open W-Su 11am-7pm. 7SFr, students 5SFr.)

In a year-round party town, Basel's carnival, or **Fasnacht**, still manages to distinguish itself. The festivities commence the Monday before Lent with the *Morgenstraich*, a not-to-be-missed 4am parade over 600 years in the running, and end precisely 72 hours later (Mar. 5-7, 2001). Head to **Barfüsserpl.** to begin an evening of bar-hopping. **Atlantis**, Klosterburg 10, is a multilevel, sophisticated bar that sways to reggae, jazz, and funk. (Concerts 10-23SFr. Open M-Th 11am-2am, F 11am-4am, Sa 5pm-4am.) **Brauerei Fischerstube**, Rheing. 45, is an old-school Biergarten adjacent to Basel's only brewery. (Beer 2.50-5.90SFr. Open M-Th 10am-midnight, F-Sa 10am-1am, Su 5pm-midnight.)

ZURICH (ZÜRICH)   ☎ 01

Switzerland has a bank for every 1200 people; about half of these are in Zurich (pop. 400,000), where battalions of ballyhooed and Bally-shoed executives charge daily to the world's premier gold exchange and fourth-largest stock exchange. But there's more to Zurich than money. Ulrich Zwingli led the Swiss Protestant Reformation here in the 16th century, and revolution brewed again in 1916 when James Joyce toiled away on *Ulysses* in the city, while exiled Vladimir Lenin read Marx and dreamed of revolution in another. Meanwhile, a group of raucous young artists next door, who called themselves the Dadaists, pushed the limits of the ridiculous at the Cabaret Voltaire. The counterculture spirit shared by these thinkers continues to run through the veins of the Altstadt and student quarter, only steps away from the rabid capitalism of the famous Bahnhofstraße shopping district.

▐▌ TRANSPORTATION

Flights: Kloten Airport (☎816 25 00). Zurich is **Swissair's** main hub (☎ (0848) 80 07 00). **Trains** run to the Hauptbahnhof (every 10-20min., 5.40SFr; Eurailpass and Swisspass valid).

Trains: Hauptbahnhof, on Bahnhofpl. To: **Basel** (1hr., 2-4 per hr., 31SFr); **Bern** (1¼hr., 1-2 per hr., 48SFr); **Geneva** (3hr., every hr., 77SFr); **Milan** (4½hr., every hr., 76SFr); **Munich** (4hr., 4 per day, 91SFr); **Paris** (8hr., every hr., 137SFr); **Salzburg** (6hr., 3 per day, 102SFr); **Venice** (7½hr., every hr., 99SFr); and **Vienna** (9hr., 5 per day, 131SFr).

Public Transportation: All public buses, trams, and trolleys run 5:30am-midnight. **Short rides** (fewer than 5 stops) 2.10SFr; **long rides** 3.60SFr. Buy a ticket before boarding and validate it in the machine or face a fine (from 50SFr). A **Tageskarte** is good for 1 day of unlimited public transport (7.20SFr). **Nightbuses** run F-Sa 1, 1:30, 2, and 3am.

Taxis: ☎444 44 44 or 222 22 22. 6SFr base fare and 3SFr per km.

Bike Rental: At the baggage counter *(Gepäckexpedition Fly-Gepäck)* in the station. 27SFr per day; 7SFr surcharge if you leave it at another station. Open daily 6:45am-7:45pm.

Hitchhiking: *Let's Go* does not recommend hitchhiking. Hitchers to Basel, Geneva, Paris, or Bonn often take tram #4 to Werdhölzli or bus #33 to Pfingstweidstr.; to Lucerne, Italy, and Austria, they take tram #9 or 14 to Bahnhof Wiedikon and walk down Schimmelstr. to Silhölzli; to Munich, they take tram #14 or 7 to Milchbuck and walk to Schaffhauserstr. toward St. Gallen and St. Margarethen.

✦█ ▌ ORIENTATION AND PRACTICAL INFORMATION

The **Hauptbahnhof,** on the western bank of the **Limmat River,** sits at the top of Bahnhofstr., which overflows with bankers and well-coiffed shoppers by day but falls

SWITZERLAND

dead quiet by 6pm. In contrast, the university district on the hillside of the eastern bank pulses nightly with crowded bars and hip restaurants. Sprawling along the Limmat, the Altstadt is a giant pedestrian zone. The Altstadt's **Limmatquai,** which becomes Uto-Quai and Seefeldquai across the bridge from the Hauptbahnhof, is a favorite strolling destination for many residents and tourists.

Tourist Offices: Main office (☎214 40 00; hotel reservation service ☎215 40 40; fax 215 40 44; www.zurichtourism.ch), in the Hauptbahnhof. Open Apr.-Oct. M-F 8:30am-8:30pm, Sa-Su 8:30am-6:30pm; Nov.-Mar. M-F 8:30am-7pm, Sa-Su 8:30am-6:30pm.

Consulates: UK, Minervastr. 117 (☎383 65 60). Open M-F 9am-noon. **US,** Dufourstr. 101 (☎422 25 66). Open M-F 10am-1pm. **Australian, Canadian, Irish,** and **South African** citizens should contact embassies in Bern. **New Zealand's** consulate is in Geneva.

Currency Exchange: At the Hauptbahnhof. Cash advances on V, MC, DC. Open daily 6:30am-10pm. **Credit Suisse,** Bahnhofstr. 53. 2.50SFr commission. Open M-F 9am-6pm, Th 9am-7pm, Sa 9am-4pm. **ATMs** are all over (most only accept MC).

American Express: Uraniastr. 14, CH-8023 (☎228 77 77). Mail held. **ATM.** Open M-F 8:30am-6pm.

Luggage Storage: At the Hauptbahnhof. Lockers 4-8SFr per day. Luggage storage 5SFr at the *Gepäck* counter. Open daily 6am-10:50pm.

Bi, Gay, and Lesbian Services: Homosexuelle Arbeitsgruppe Zürich (HAZ), Sihlquai 67, P.O. Box 7088, CH-8023 (☎271 22 50), offers a library, meetings, and the free newsletter *InfoSchwül.* Open Tu-F 7:30-11pm, Su noon-2pm and 6-11pm.

Laundromat: Selbstbedienung-Wäscherei (☎242 99 14), Müllerstr. Wash and dry 10.20SFr per 5kg. Open daily 6am-11pm.

Emergencies: Police, ☎117. **Fire,** ☎118. **Ambulance,** ☎144; English spoken. **Medical Emergency,** ☎269 69 69.

24-Hour Pharmacy: Theaterstr. 14 (☎252 56 00), on Bellevuepl.

Internet Access: Telefon Corner, downstairs in the train station. 5SFr per hr. with 10SFr deposit. Open M-F 7am-10:30pm, Sa-Su 9am-9pm.

Post Office: Main Office, Sihlpost, Kasernestr. 97, just behind the station. Open M-F 7:30am-8pm, Sa 8am-4pm. Address mail to be held: Sihlpost, *Postlagernde Briefe* für Bill WOOD, **CH-8021** Zürich, Switzerland.

▐ ACCOMMODATIONS

The few budget accommodations in Zurich are easily accessible via Zurich's public transportation. Reserve at least a day in advance, especially during the summer.

▓ **Justinus Heim Zürich,** Freudenbergstr. 146 (☎361 38 06). Take tram #9 or 10 to Seilbahn Rigiblick, then take the hillside tram (by the Migros) uphill to the end. Quiet, cheap, private rooms overlooking Zurich. Breakfast included. Reception 8am-noon and 5-9pm. Singles 35-60SFr; doubles 80-100SFr; triples 120-140SFr.

Martahaus, Zähringerstr. 36 (☎251 45 50). Turn left from the station, cross Bahnhofbrücke, and take the 2nd (sharp) right after Limmatquai at the Seilgraben sign. The most comfortable budget accommodations in the Altstadt. Breakfast included. Reception 24hr. Dorms 35SFr; singles 70SFr; doubles 98-108SFR; triples 120SFr.

Foyer Hottingen, Hottingenstr. 31 (☎256 19 19). Take tram #3 (dir.: Kluspl.) to Hottingerpl. to reach this impeccably clean and newly renovated house with modern facilities and a multilingual staff. Breakfast included. Reception 6am-midnight. Dorms 30SFr; singles 65-95SFr; doubles 100-140SFr; triples 130SFr; quads 160SFr; quints 200SFr.

Jugendherberge Zürich (HI), Mutschellenstr. 114 (☎482 35 44). Take tram #7 (dir.: Wollishofen) to Morgental and backtrack 5min. along Mutschellenstr. A little close and can get crowded, but offers CNN and free nightly movies. Breakfast included. Laundry. Dorms 31SFr; doubles 90SFr; nonmembers add 5SFr.

The City Backpacker-Hotel Biber, Niederdorfstr. 5 (☎251 90 15). Cross Bahnhofbrücke in front of the station and turn right on Niederdorfstr. Has a party-happy rooftop deck and a prime location. Internet 10SFr per hr. Sheets 3SFr. Laundry 9SFr. Reception 8-11am and 3-10pm. Dorms 29SFr (27SFr in winter); singles 65SFr; doubles 88SFr.

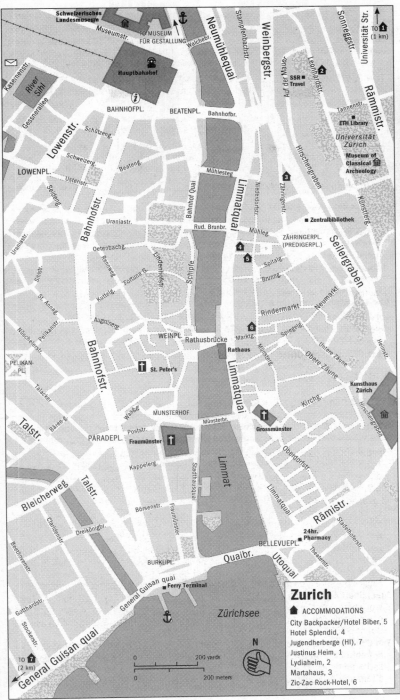

Zurich

▲ ACCOMMODATIONS

City Backpacker/Hotel Biber, 5
Hotel Splendid, 4
Jugendherberge (HI), 7
Justinus Heim, 1
Lydiaheim, 2
Martahaus, 3
Zic-Zac Rock-Hotel, 6

Zic-Zac Rock-Hotel, Marktg. 7 (☎261 21 81). Funky furniture and trendy lighting in each room. All with TV, phone, and sink. Breakfast 4.50SFr. Reception 24hr. Singles 68-88SFr; doubles 116-160SFr; triples 156-165SFr; quads 260SFr.

Camping Seebucht, Seestr. 559 (☎482 16 12). Take tram #11 to Bürklipl., then catch bus #161 or 165 to Stadtgrenze. Market and cafe. Tents and caravans available. Showers 2SFr. Reception 7:30am-noon and 3-10pm. Open May to late-Sept. 8SFr per person; 12SFr per tent; 1.50SFr per car.

◐ FOOD

The cheapest meals in Zurich are available at *Würstli* stands which sell sausage and bread for 5SFr. For heartier appetites, Zurich prides itself on its *Geschnetzeltes mit Rösti,* slivered veal in cream sauce with hash-brown potatoes. **Co-op Super Center,** straddling the Limmat River next to the train station, is indeed a super Co-op. (Open M-F 7am-8pm, Sa 7am-4pm.) **Migros,** Mutschellenstr. 189, is under the train station in *Shop-Ville.* (Open M-F 7am-8pm, Sa-Su 8am-8pm.)

▨ Bodega Española, Münsterg. 15 (☎251 23 10). Delicious Catalan delights. Egg and potato tortilla dishes 15.50SFr. Enormous salads 9.50SFr. Open daily 10am-12:30am.

Gran-Café, Limmatquai 66 (☎252 31 19). Outdoor seating and some of the cheapest meals around. Daily *menüs* (11.80SFr) are guaranteed in 7min. or they're free. Open M-F 6am-midnight, Sa-Su 7:30am-midnight.

Hiltl, Sihlstr. 28 (☎227 70 00). Trade carrot sticks with the vegetarian elite at this swank restaurant. All-day salad buffet 4.60SFr per 100g (15SFr for large salad). Indian dinner buffet 4.60SFr per 100g. Open M-Sa 7am-11pm, Su 11am-11pm.

Raclette Stube, Zähringerstr. 16 (☎251 41 30). Family-oriented restaurant that serves a high-quality Swiss fare. Fondue 23.50SFr per person. Open daily from 6pm.

Johanniter, Niederdorfstr. 70 (☎251 46 00). A favorite with locals, this Swiss restaurant along Niederdorfstr. has elegant sidewalk seating. Hearty Swiss *Rösti* and noodle dishes 15-18SFr. Open daily 10am-4am.

◉ SIGHTS

ALTSTADT. The stately, tree-lined promenade known as the **Bahnhofstraße** runs from the Hauptbahnhof to the head of the Zürichsee and hosts Cartier, Rolex, Chanel, and Armani. Half-way down Bahnhofstr. lies **Paradeplatz,** the town center, under which Zurich's banks reputedly keep their gold reserves. Directly off of Paradepl., is the 13th-century Gothic **Fraumünster.** Though it's a Protestant church, Jewish artist Marc Chagall agreed to design its stunning stained-glass windows in the 1970s. The merging of Old and New Testament stories in the five windows reveals Chagall's radical personal interpretation of the texts. *(Open daily May-Sept. 9am-noon and 2-6pm; Oct.-Feb. 10am-noon and 2-5pm, Mar.-Apr. 10am-noon and 2-6pm.)* Near the Fraumünster, **St. Peter's Church** has the largest clock face in Europe, with a second hand nearly 4m long. The **Grossmünster,** directly across the Münsterbrücke from the Fraumünster, is where Ulrich Zwingli spearheaded the Reformation in German-speaking Switzerland (one of his Bibles lies in a case near the pulpit from which he preached). The church's twin neo-Gothic towers have become a symbol of Zurich. Head up the twisting stairs to the top of one of the **towers** for a panoramic view of Zurich. *(Church open daily Mar. 15-Oct. 9am-6pm; Nov.-Mar. 14 10am-4pm. Tower open Mar.-Oct. daily 1:30-5pm; Oct.-Mar. Sa-Su 1:30-4:30pm. Tower 2SFr.)* Follow Münsterg. from the Grossmünster to **Spiegelgasse** to step on the came cobblestones as some of Zurich's most prominent ghosts; Lenin lived at #14, and Dadaism got its start at #3 with the Cabaret Voltaire and Hans Arp, Tristan Tzara, and Hugo Ball.

MUSEUMS. The incredible ▨**Kunsthaus Zürich,** on Rämistr., deserves its excellent reputation for broad coverage of Western art from the 15th century to the present with emphasis on the 20th century. Local Giacomettis and Hodlers rest alongside other European greats. *(Heimpl. 1. Take tram #3, 5, 8, or 9 to Kunsthaus.* ☎251 67 65.)

Open Tu-Th 10am-9pm, F-Su 10am-5pm. 4SFr, students 3SFr; Su free.) The **Museum Rietberg,** in two mansions in Rieter Park, presents an exquisite collection of Asian, African, and other non-European art. *(Take tram #3, 5, 8, or 9 to Kunsthaus. ☎ 251 6765. Open Tu-Th 10am-9pm, F-Su 10am-5pm. 5SFr, students 3SFr.)* The **Museum of Classical Archaeology** astounds with a basement full of replicas of nearly every great statue in the ancient world from 800 BC on, as well as Greco-Roman art on the first floor. *(Rämistr. 73. Take tram #6, 9, or 19 to ETH. ☎ 257 28 20. Open Tu-F 1-6pm, Sa-Su 11am-5pm. Free.)* The **Schweizerisches Landesmuseum** (Swiss National Museum) contains 16th-century astrological instruments, Ulrich Zwingli's weapons from the Battle of Kappel (in which he died in 1531), and a tiny bejeweled clock, with a golden skeleton morbidly indicating the time, as well as mediocre medieval artifacts. *(Museumstr. 2. ☎ 218 65 11. Open Tu-Su 10:30am-5pm. Free.)*

OTHER SIGHTS. Take tram #6, 9, or 10 to ETH uphill from the university (above the town on the Grossmünster side of the river) to reach the grave of author **James Joyce,** in the Fluntern Cemetery. Farther from town, visitors to the **Lindt and Sprüngli Chocolate Factory** are welcomed with an open box of Lindt chocolate and depart with free souvenir boxes. *(Seestr. 204. Take S-1 or S-8 to Kilchberg from the Hauptbahnhof (5.40SFr) or bus #165 to Kilchberg; turn right out of the station, turn left down the 1st street, take an immediate right, and continue for 3min. ☎ 716 22 33. Open W-F 10am-noon and 1-4pm. All exhibits in German. Free.)*

🎵🎭 ENTERTAINMENT AND NIGHTLIFE

Niederdorfstr. rocks as the epicenter of Zurich's nightlife (although women may not want to walk alone in this area at night), and Münsterg. and Limmatquai are lined with cafes and bars. Pick up *ZüriTip* or check posters around town for hotspots. On Friday and Saturday nights in summer, **Hirschenpl.** hosts sword-swallowers and other daredevil street performers. Locals and students crowd the terrace, drinking reasonably priced beer at **Double-U (W) Bar,** Niederdorfstr. 21, on the first floor of Hotel Schafli. (Open M-Th 2pm-late, F-Su 4pm-later.) **Casa Bar,** Münsterg. 30, is a tiny, crowded pub with first-rate live jazz. (☎ 262 20 02. Open daily 7pm-2am.) **Castel DADA,** Münsterg. 26, next to Casa Bar, is a lively bar and disco on the former site of the Cabaret Voltaire. (Open Su-Th 6pm-2am, F-Sa 8pm-2am; disco open until 4am.) Thornton Wilder and Vladimir Lenin used to get sloshed at the posh, artsy **Bar Odeon,** Limmatquai 2, on Bellevuepl. (Open Su-Th 7am-2am, F-Sa 7am-4am.)

🏔 DAYTRIPS FROM ZURICH

LUCERNE. A traveler's dream come true, Lucerne offers a perfect combination of cosmopolitan culture and outdoor opportunities (see p. 923).

INTERLAKEN. Go for the crystal blue Thunersee and Brienzersee lakes as well as the largest mountains in Switzerland. Stay for the outdoor activities (see p. 926).

ST. GALLEN ☎ 071

Though it lacks the medieval charm of Schaffhausen, St. Gallen's easy access to Zurich, Germany, Austria, the *Bodensee,* and small mountain villages makes it a popular stopover for people moving between these places. Book lovers gasp at the sight of St. Gallen's astounding main attraction, the **Stiftsbibliotek** (Abbey Library), a Baroque library designated a World Heritage Treasure by UNESCO. Perfectly preserved golden spines, lavishly carved and polished exotic wood bookcases, and shiny parquet enhance its collection of 140,000 volumes and 2000 manuscripts. Umberto Eco was seen sniffing around here to get inspiration for *The Name of the Rose.* (Open Apr.-Oct. M-Sa 9am-noon and 1:30-5pm, Su 10am-noon and 1:30-4pm; Nov.-Mar. M-Sa 9am-noon and 1:30-4pm. 7SFr, students 5SFr.) Also in the abbey, the **Kathedrale St. Gallen** has an unforgettable exterior and a golden gate spanning the interior of the church. (Open daily 7am-6pm except during mass.) Follow the Marktplatz away from the train station to reach **Museumstraße,** which holds four museums, the largest of which are the **Historisches** and **Ethnology Museums** at #50, while the Art and Natural History collections are housed in Musemstr. 32. (All open Tu-Sa 10am-noon and 2-5pm, Su 10am-5pm. Ticket for all four 10SFr, students 4SFr.) In late June, the **Open Air St. Gallen Music Festival** features 20 live bands; past performers include the Beastie Boys, Red Hot Chili Peppers, Cypress Hill, B. B. King, and James Brown. (☎ 222 21 21. June 29-July1, 2001. Tickets 144SFr.)

Trains roll to Bern (2½hr., 65SFr); Geneva (4½hr., 95SFr); Zurich (1hr., 29SFr); and Munich (3hr.; 4 per day; 63SFr, under 26 49SFr). To get to the **tourist office,** Bahnhofpl. 1a, from the train station, head through the bus stop and past the fountain on the left; it's on the right. (☎ 227 37 37. Tours June 12-Sept. M, W, and F 2pm; 15SFr. Open M-F 9am-noon and 1-6pm, Sa 9am-noon.) Get on the **internet** at **Media Lounge,** 10 Katerineng. (2SFr per 10min. Open M-F 9am-9pm, Sa 10am-5pm.) Perched on a hill above town, the 🏠**Jugendherberge St. Gallen (HI),** Jüchstr. 25, has a terrace, barbecue pit, and library. Take the orange train (dir.: Trogener) from the smaller Appenzeller/Trogener station to the right of the main station to Schülerhaus; walk uphill, turn left across the train tracks, and walk 2min. downhill. (☎ 245 47 77. Breakfast included. Reception daily 7-10am and 5-10:30pm. Check-out 10am. Closed Dec. 17-first week in March. Dorms 24-33SFr; singles 58SFr; doubles 66SFr; nonmembers add 5SFr.) **Hotel Elite,** Metzgerg. 9-11, is central. (☎ 222 12 36. Breakfast included. Singles 60-70SFr; doubles 110SFr.) A secluded rooftop awaits at **Pizzeria Testarossa,** Metzgerg. 20, up the street across from the Marktpl. bus stop. (Pizzas from 13SFr. Open Tu-F 10am-midnight, Sa-Su 10am-2pm and 5pm-midnight.) There is a **Migros supermarket** on St. Leonhardstr., one block behind the train station. (Open M-W and F 8am-6:30pm, Th 8am-9pm, Sa 8am-5pm.) **Postal code:** CH-9000.

🏁 **DAYTRIP FROM ST. GALLEN: APPENZELL.** St. Gallen is an ideal urban base from which to hike the pastoral hills of Appenzell. **Appenzell** offers great **hiking** without the temperature extremes of Zermatt or the Ticino region. Ask at the **tourist office,** Hauptg. 4 (☎ (071) 788 96 41; www.myappenzellerland.ch), next to the *Rathaus,* for a detailed trail map and hiking suggestions. The office also makes hotel reservations, books cable car excursions, and arranges **cheesemaking** tours. The ever-present aroma of Appenzeller cheese lingers around **Gasthaus Hof,** on Landsgemeindeplatz in the center of town, a family-run restaurant that provides guest rooms in a separate house. (☎ (071) 787 22 10. Breakfast included. Check-in 11am-midnight. Restaurant open 8am-11pm. Dorms 28SFr; singles 65SFr; with shower 95SFr; doubles with shower 130SFr.) Many hiking trails are dotted with **Gasthöfe** (guesthouses), splendid old farmhouses and restaurants for the road-weary. The rattling but prompt **Appenzellerbahn** chugs between Appenzell and St. Gallen twice an hour from 6am-midnight (1hr., 10SFr).

AROSA
☎081

The beautiful, secluded town of Arosa, in the canton of Graubünden, makes an effort to cater to budget-conscious **skiers** and **snowboarders** with affordable ski-and-stay packages. Developed ski trails dominate only one side of the valley; on the other, **hiking** trails stretch to isolated valleys. A free **shuttle bus** runs between the hottest spots in town, including the ski lifts and the **tourist office,** which arranges hiking trips and ski lessons and makes free hotel reservations. (☎378 70 20; www.arosa.ch. Open Dec. 7-Apr. 13 M-F 9am-6pm, Sa 9am-5:30pm, Su 4-6:30pm; Apr. 14-Dec. 6 M-F 8am-noon and 2-6pm, Sa 9am-1pm; June 29-Aug. 17 M-F 8am-noon and 2-6pm, Sa 9am-1pm and 2-4pm.) Two large houses rule the budget accommodations scene (☎378 84 23 for both). 🏠**Haus Florentium,** a former convent buried in the woods at the top of the town, has been converted to a 150-bed party house. From the tourist office, follow the cobblestoned path down the hill, turn right at the road at the top, left at the gravel path, and right at Pension Suveran. (Breakfast included. Dec.-Apr. 1-night stay and 2-day ski pass 150SFr; 6-night stay and 7-day ski pass 511SFr. July-Aug. 36SFr per night.) The smaller **Haus Bellaval,** above the train station, offers basic dorms. (In winter 1-night stay and 2-day ski pass 140SFr; 6-night stay and 7-day pass 423SFr. In summer 1-night stay and 2-day hiking lift pass 53SFr.) In summer, lifts are not necessary for hiking, so the better choice (and closer to more hiking trails) is the **Jugendherberge (HI)**, on Seewaldstr. Go past the tourist office, bear left down the hill, and follow the sign. (☎377 13 97. Breakfast included. Reception 7-10am and 5-10pm. Curfew 10pm; key available. Open mid-June to mid-Oct. and mid-Dec. to mid-Apr. Dorms 27SFr; doubles 64SFr.) Get groceries at the **Co-op**, before the tourist office on Poststr. (Open M-F 8am-12:30pm and 2-6:30pm, Sa 8am-4pm.) Arosa is accessible by **train** only by a scenic route via Chur from Basel (2¾hr., every hr. 4:50am-10:16pm, 62SFr); St. Gallen (1½hr., every hr. 4:50am-10:16pm, 34SFr.); or Zurich (1½hr., every hr. 4:50am-10:16pm, 38SFr). **Postal code:** CH-7050.

LUCERNE (LUZERN)   ☎041

Lucerne just may be the fondue pot at the end of the rainbow—the Swiss traveler's dream come true. The city is small but cosmopolitan, ready to satisfy sophisticated culture lovers and, at the same time, provides a plethora of outdoor opportunities for the adventurous. Sunrise over the city's most acclaimed peak, **Mount Pilatus**, has hypnotized hikers and artists, including Twain, Wagner, and Goethe, for centuries.

E TRANSPORTATION. Trains arrive at the Bahnhofpl. (☎157 2222) from Bern (1½hr., every 30min. to 3hr., 32SFr); Basel (1¼hr., 1-2 per hr., 31SFr); Geneva (3hr., every hr., 70SFr); Interlaken (2hr., every hr., 26SFr); Lausanne (2½hr., every hr., 58SFr); Lugano (2¾hr., every hr., 58SFr); Zurich (1hr., 2 per hr., 22SFr); and Zurich airport (1¼hr., every hr., 26SFr). The train station is the cheapest place to rent a **bike** (26SFr per day). **VBL buses** depart from in front of the station and provide extensive coverage of Lucerne (1 zone 1.70SFr, 2 zones 2.20SFr; Swiss Pass valid).

⑦ PRACTICAL INFORMATION. The **tourist office**, in the station, has a free city guide and free hotel reservation service. Ask about the **Visitor's Card**, which, in conjunction with a hotel or hostel stamp, gives discounts at museums, bars, car rental, and more. (☎227 17 17; fax 227 17 18. Open May-Oct. M-F 8:30am-7:30pm, Sa-Su 9am-7:30pm; Nov.-May M-F 8:30am-6pm, Sa 9am-6pm, Su 9am-1pm.) **C+A Clothing**, on Hertensteinstr. at the top of the Altstadt, has two busy terminals to satisfy your **internet** cravings. (Free. Open M-W 9am-6:30pm, Th-F 9am-9pm, Sa 8:30am-4pm.) The main branch of the **post office** is near the station on the corner of Bahnhofstr. and Bahnhorpl. Address mail to be held: Bob DYLAN, Postlagernde Briefe, Hauptpost; **CH-60000** Luzerne 1. (Open M-F 7:30am-6:30pm, Sa 8am-noon.)

▛▟ ACCOMMODATIONS AND FOOD. Relatively inexpensive beds are available only in limited numbers in Lucerne, so call ahead in order to ensure a roof over your head. To reach ◼**Backpackers**, Alpenquai 42, walk 15min. by turning right from the station onto Inseliquai and follow it until it becomes Alpenquai. (☎360 04 20; fax 360 04 42. Sheets 3SFr. Kitchen. Reception 7:30-10am and 4-11pm. Dorms 22-268SFr.) From the station, walk on Bahnhofstr., along the river at Speurbrucke and then make a left onto St. Karliquai to get to **Tourist Hotel Luzerne**, St. Karliquai 12, which offers cheap, clean rooms near the center of the Altstadt. (☎410 24 74. Internet. Breakfast. Laundry 10SFr. Dorms 30-33SFr; quads 172SFr, students 156SFr; doubles 108SFr, 98SFr. In winter rooms 10-15SFr less per person.) Take bus #18 to Jugendherberge for the **Jugendherberge (HI)**, Sedelstr. 12. After 7:30pm, take bus #19 to Rosenberg, continue in the direction of the bus, and bear right at the fork. (☎420 88 00. Breakfast included. Laundry 12SFr. Reception Apr.-Oct. 7-10am and 2pm-midnight; Nov.-Mar. 7-9:30am and 4pm-midnight. Dorms May-Oct. 31SFr, Nov.-Apr. 28SFr; doubles 38-44SFr.) Take bus #2 (dir.: Würzenbach) to Verkehrshaus to reach **Camping Lido**, Lidostr. 8 on the Lido beach. (☎370 21 46. Showers 0.50SFr per 3min. Reception 8am-6pm. Open Mar. 15-Oct. 6.50SFr, tent 3SFr, car 5SFr.) Stop by **Pourquoi Pas**, Nationalquai (in front of the Musikpavillon), along the far side of the lake from the station for a great selection of crepes for 4-7.50SFr. (Open M-F 11:45am-1:30pm and 5-8pm, Sa-Su 1pm-whenever.) Pick up groceries at **Migros**, in the station (open M-W and Sa 6:30am-8pm, Th-F 6:30am-9pm, Su 8am-8pm.) and at Herten-steinstr. 44 which also has a restaurant with the same hours (open M-W 8:30am-6:30pm, Th-F 8:30am-9pm, Sa 8am-4pm).

SIGHTS AND ENTERTAINMENT. The Altstadt, across the river over Spreuerbrücke from the station, is famous for its frescoed houses, especially those on Hirschenpl. For a taste of the middle ages, traipse along the 660-year-old **Kapell-brücke,** a famous wooden-roofed bridge that runs from left of the train station (as you exit) to the Altstadt and is ornately decorated with Swiss historical scenes. Further down the river from the Kapellbrücke lies the **Spreuerbrücke,** a bit quieter and more interesting. This bridge is decorated by Kaspar Meglinger's eerie *Totentanz* (Dance of Death) paintings. For a magnificent view of Lucerne, climb the ramparts of the medieval city *(Musegg Mauern).* Take the trail on the far side of the wall to reach stairs up to the path along the wall; several towers have stairs to the top. East of the wall, join the hordes to view the city mascot, the dying **Lion of Lucerne,** which is carved into a cliff on Denkmalstr. Mark Twain called the 9m monument, honoring the Swiss Guard who died defending Marie Antoinette in Revolutionary Paris, "the most mournful and moving piece of stone in the world."

The **Picasso Museum,** Furreng. 21, in Am Rhyn Haus, is one of Lucerne's best offerings. Two hundred charming, sad, and amusing photographs of the artist and his family, taken by his close friend David Duncan, grace this small museum. Head down Rathausquai from Schwanenpl. and bear right on Furreng. (Open daily Apr.-Oct. 10am-6pm; Nov.-Mar. 11am-1pm and 2-4pm. 6SFr, students 3SFr.) Walk 15min. along the lake to reach the **Verkehrshaus der Schweiz** (Transport Museum), Lidostr. 5, which features a planetarium, IMAX shows, and a virtual reality exhibit. (Open daily Apr.-Oct. 9am-6pm; Nov.-Mar. 10am-5pm. 18SFr, students 16SFr. IMAX 14SFr. 33% off with Eurail.) The **Richard Wagner Museum,** Wagnerweg 27, in Wagner's former lakeside home, displays the composer's original letters, scores, and instruments. Turn right from the station and walk 25min. along the lake. (Open Mar. 15-Nov. 30 Tu-Su 10am-noon and 2-5pm. 5SFr, students 4SFr.)

The Altstadt is quiet after 7pm, when the action moves to Haldenstr. and the streets near the station. **Hexenkessel,** Haldenstr. 21, going for that mock-pagan look, is a two-story cauldron of loud music and spinning DJs. (Obligatory beer 7SFr. Open daily 9pm-2:30am.) There is a movie every night from mid-July to mid-Aug. with **Open Air Kino Luzerne,** at the outdoor theater in the Seepark near Backpackers Luzern (14SFr per seat)—most movies are in English, so check the tourist office to see what's playing. Lucerne attracts big names for its summer **Blue Balls Festival** (July 21-29, 2001) and fall **Blues Festival** (Nov. 8-11, 2001).

DAYTRIPS FROM LUCERNE

MT. PILATUS AND RIGI KULM

The view of the Alps from the top of Mt. Pilatus (2132m) is absolutely phenomenal. For the most memorable trip, catch a boat from Lucerne to Alpnachstad (90min.), ascend by the world's steepest **cogwheel train** (48° gradient), descend by cable car to Krienz, and take the bus back to Lucerne (entire trip 77.60SFr; with Eurail or Swisspass 41SFr). With a little more time and exercise, cut down on the price by taking a train or boat to Hegiswil and hiking up to Fräkmüntegg (3hr.), a half-way point on the cable car (22SFr, 25% off with Eurail or Swisspass). While you miss the cog train, the hike offers constant views back to the lake and Lucerne.

Across the sea from Pilatus soars the Rigi Kilm, which has a view of the lake and its magnificent neighbor. Sunrise on the summit is a must-see for any Lucerne visitor; sunsets get good reviews, too (see Mark Twain's *A Tramp Abroad*). **Ferries** run from Lucerne to Vitznau, where you can catch a cogwheel train to the summit. You can also conquer Rigi on foot; it's 5hr. from Vitznau to the top, and anyone who tires out halfway can pick the train up at Rigi Kaltbad (3hr. up the hill) to drag them the rest of the way. To make sunrise viewing possible, stay at **Massenlager Rigi Kulm,** which is on the summit. (☎ (041) 855 03 03. Reception 8am-10pm. Dorms 25SFr.)

Afterward, return by train, take the cable car from Rigi Kaltbad to Weggis, and return to Lucerne by boat (round-trip 86SFr, with Eurail or Swisspass 42SFr).

INTERLAKEN. With nearby adventure playgrounds and the natural beauty of its surroundings, make Interlaken a favorite backpacking stop (see p. 926).

ZURICH. While primarily famous for its banks, Zurich offers impressive museums and the Lindt and Sprüngli chocolate factory (see p. 917).

BERN   ☎031

Although Bern has been Switzerland's capital since 1848, don't expect a slick political machine. Parliament is in session only four times a year, and politics is considered part-time work. You'll probably see more suitors than suits in Bern: the city is known for Toblerone, flowers, bears, and a decidedly romantic design.

▐ TRANSPORTATION. Trains (☎157 22 22; or 24hr. ☎ (0900) 300 300, 1.19SFr per min.) run to Bahnhofpl. from: Basel (1¼hr., 2 per hr., 37SFr); Geneva (2hr., 2 per hr., 50SFr); Interlaken (50min., every hr., 25SFr); Lucerne (1½hr., every hr., 32SFr); Zurich (1¼hr., 2 per hr., 48SFr); Berlin (8hr., 3 per day, 254SFr); Milan (3½hr., 13 per day, 73SFr); Munich (5½hr., 4 per day, 123SFr); Paris (4½hr., 4 per day, 109SFr); and Vienna (10½hr., 4 per day, 162SFr). Under 26ers get 25% off international fares.

▐ PRACTICAL INFORMATION. The tourist office, on the street level of the station, makes free room reservations. (☎328 12 12. Open June-Sept. daily 9am-8:30pm; Oct.-May M-Sa 9am-6:30pm, Su 10am-5pm. Tours daily in summer; 6-23SFr.) **Embassies: Canada,** Kirchenfeldstr. 88 (☎352 32 00; fax 357 32 10); **Ireland,** Kirchenfeldstr. 68 (☎352 14 42; fax 352 14 55); **South Africa,** Alpenstr. 29 (☎350 13 13); **UK,** Thunstr. 50 (☎359 77 00); and **US,** Jubiläumsstr. 93 (357 70 11; fax 351 73 44). Check **email** at the **Soundwerk Café,** Wasserwerkg. 5, by the river near the bottom of Nydeggbr. (Free. Open M-F 11am-7pm, Sa 11am-4pm.) **Postal code:** CH-3000.

▐ ACCOMMODATIONS AND FOOD. Bern's only hostel is usually reliable for a last-minute bed, but if it's full, cheap accommodations are rare. The tourist office has a list of **private rooms.** To get from the station to the **Jugendherberge (HI),** Weiherg. 4, cross the tram lines, go down Christoffelg., take the road through the gates left of the Park Café, and follow the signs down to Weiherg. (☎311 63 16; fax 312 52 40. Breakfast 6SFr. Laundry 6SFr. 3-night max. stay. Reception June-Sept. 7-9:30am and 3pm-midnight; Oct.-May 7-9:30am and 5pm-midnight. Check-out before 10am. Reserve by fax. Closed 2 weeks in Jan. Dorms 28SFr, overflow mattresses on the floor 14SFr; nonmembers add 5SFr.) **Pension Marthahaus,** Wyttenbachstr. 22a, is in a quiet suburb. From the station, turn left on Bollwerk, cross Lorrainebr., bear right onto Victoriastr., and take the first left on Wyttenbachstr. Or, take bus #20 (dir.: Wyler) to Gewerbeschule, and then the first right. (☎332 41 35. Breakfast included. Laundry 8SFr. Reception 7:30am-9pm. Reserve ahead. Singles 60-90SFr, doubles 95-120SFr, triples 120-150SFr; 5-10SFr less in winter.) To reach the **Landhaus Hotel,** Altenbergstr. 4/6, take bus #12 (dir.: Schlosshalde) to Bärengraben and walk down to the Aare on the left. (☎331 41 66. Breakfast 7SFr. Laundry 4-6SFr. Internet. Dorms 30SFr; doubles 110-140SFr.) To get to **Camping Eichholz,** Strandweg 49, take tram #9 to Wabern, backtrack 50m, and take the first right. (☎961 26 02. Showers 1SFr. Laundry 5SFr. Reserve ahead. Open May-Sept. 6.90SFr, students 5.50SFr; tents 5-8.50SFr; rooms 15-22SFr.)

   Almost every locale ending in "-platz" overflows with cafes and restaurants, though the bigger ones tend to be pricier and more tourist-infested. **Manora,** Bubenbergpl. 5a, has tasty salads, fruit, and main dishes. (Open M-Sa 6:30am-11pm, Su 8:30am-11:15pm.) The bustling **Café des Pyrénées,** Kornhauspl. 17, offers inventive sandwiches. (Open M-F 9am-12:30am, Sa 8am-5pm.) Produce **markets** sprawl over Bärenpl. (May-Oct. daily 8am-6pm) and over Bundespl (Tu and Sa). **Migros,** on Marktg., sells **groceries.** (Open M-W and F 8am-6:30pm, Th 8am-9pm, Sa 7am-4pm.)

SWITZERLAND

⊙♫ SIGHTS AND ENTERTAINMENT. Dominating the Aare is the **Bundeshaus** (Parliament), which is a good starting point for a city tour. (When Parliament is not in session, 45min. tours every hr. M-Sa 9-11am and 2-4pm, Su 10-11am and 2-3pm.) From the state house, Kockerg. and Herreng. lead to the 15th-century Protestant **Münster** (cathedral). Climb the spire—the tallest in all of Switzerland—for a fantastic view of the Aare and beyond. (Open Easter-Oct. Tu-Sa 10am-5pm, Su 11:30am-5pm; Nov.-Easter Tu-F 10am-noon and 2-4pm, Sa 10am-noon and 2-5pm, Su 11am-2pm. Tower closes 30min. earlier; 3SFr.) Head down Münsterg., take a right on Hotelg. and turn left on Kramg. to reach the 13th-century **Zytglogge** (clock tower), whose figures creak to life at 4min. before the hour with a couple of pallid rooster squawks that are less entertaining than the fervent oohs and aahs of the gathered tourists. (Tours of the interior daily June-Sept. 11:30am and 6:30pm; May and Oct. 4:30pm.) Follow Kramg., which becomes Gerechtigkeitsg., and cross the Nydegg-brücke to reach the **Bärengraben** (bear pits), which date back to the 15th century. (Open daily June-Sept. 8am-6pm, Oct.-May 8am-dusk.)

The **Kunstmuseum** (Fine Arts Museum), Hodlerstr. 8-12, focuses on 20th-century art, including the works of Kandinsky, Feininger, and the world's largest Paul Klee collection—2500 works of his geometrically dreamy art. Take a left on Bollwerk from the station, walk toward Lorrainebr., then turn right on Hodlerstr. (Open Tu 10am-9pm, W-Su 10am-5pm. 7SFr, students and seniors 5SFr, under 16 free.) Cross the Aare at Kirchenfeldebr. to get to **Helvetiapl.**, where several more museums cluster. The most interesting is the **Bernisches Historisches Museum**, Helvetiapl. 5, which is jam-packed with exhibits ranging from Münster artifacts to illuminated Islamic manuscripts. (☎ 350 77 11. Open Tu-Su 10am-5pm. 5SFr, students 3SFr; free Sa.) Much smaller is **Albert Einstein's House**, Kramg. 49, in the Altstadt between the clock tower and the cathedral, which was the scientist's residence from 1903-05. It was here that he conceived the theory of relativity; now it houses his photos and letters. (Open Feb.-Nov. Tu-F 10am-5pm, Sa 10am-4pm. 3SFr, students 2SFr.)

Berner Altstadtsommer features free dance and music concerts in the squares of the Altstadt. July's **Gurten Festival** attracts big names like Bob Dylan and Björk (www.gurtenfestival.ch). From mid-July to mid-August, **OrangeCinema** screens recent films (including many American ones; www.orangecinema.ch). At night, the fashionable folk linger in the Altstadt, while a seedier scene gathers under the Lorraine-brücke, behind and to the left of the station down Bollwerk. The popular **Le Pery Bar**, Schmiedenpl. 3, off Kornhauspl., is a bar with dancing on the first floor. (Open M-W 5pm-1:30am, Th 5pm-2:30am, F-Sa 5pm-3:30am.) The **Klötzlikeller Weine Stube**, Gerechtigkeitsg. 62, is the city's oldest wine cellar. (3.40-5.20SFr per glass. Open Tu-Th 4pm-12:30am, F-Sa 4pm-1:30am.)

INTERLAKEN ☎ 033

Interlaken lies between the crystal-blue Thunersee and Brienzersee lakes at the base of the largest mountains in Switzerland: the **Eiger, Mönch,** and **Jungfrau.** With easy access to these adventure playgrounds, Interlaken has earned its rightful place as one of Switzerland's prime tourist attractions. The tourism explosion has spurred the development of some of Switzerland's most varied and exciting accommodations. Beneath the enchanting sight of the Jungfrau rising 4158m above the gardens lining Höheweg, Interlaken spreads out around a large central green, the **Höhenmatte**, the main function of which seems to be as a landing pad for the hundreds of paragliders that drift down from the skies each day. Interlaken is one of the paragliding capitals of the world (alongside Queensland, New Zealand).

⊏ TRANSPORTATION. There are two train stations in town. The **Westbahnhof** (☎826 47 50) borders the Thunersee in the center of town; the **Ostbahnhof** (☎828 73 19) is on the Brienzersee, 10min. from the center. **Trains** arrive at both from: Bern (5:34am-10:34pm, 8.60SFr); Geneva (5:34am-9:40pm, 65SFr); Lucerne (5:34am-7:19pm, 27SFr); Lugano (5:34am-5:17pm, 72SFr); and Zurich (5:34am-10:34pm, 62SFr). **Jungfraubahnen**, Harderstr. 14 (☎828 71 11; www.jungfraubahn.ch) runs all trains to the small towns before the Jungfrau. Swisspass valid for Wengen, Grindelwald, and Mürren (25% discount at higher stops). Eurailpass provides 25% discount on the Jungfraubahnen. Trains to the **mountains** leave every 30min. from the Ostbahnhof to Grindelwald (9.40SFr), and Lauterbrunnen (6.20SFr) from June-Sept., and hourly from Sept.-May.

◪ PRACTICAL INFORMATION. To get from the Westbahnhof to the **tourist office**, Höheweg 37, in the Hotel Metropole, turn left on Bahnhofpl. and right on Bahnhofstr., which becomes Höheweg. (☎822 21 21. Open July-Aug. M-F 8am-6pm, Sa 9am-noon; Sept.-June M-F 8am-noon and 2-6pm, Sa 9am-noon.) Rent **bikes** at either train station (21SFr per half day). For **snow and weather info** in the Jungfrau, call 855 10 22. A **late-night pharmacy** is a call away; dial 111, or stop by **Grosse Apotheke**, Bahnhofstr. 5A (☎822 72 62. Open M-F 7:15am-6:30pm, Sa 7:15am-5pm.) In case of **emergency**, call the **police** (☎117), or the **hospital** (☎826 26 26). **The Wave**, Rosenstr. 13, provides late-night **Internet access**. Go right at the main circle between the station and the tourist office. (☎823 40 32. 14SFr per hr., students 11SFr. Open M-F 11am-11pm, Sa-Su 2-11pm.) To get to the **post office**, Marktg. 1, from the Westbahnhof, go left on Bahnhofpl. (☎224 89 50. Open M-F 7:45am-noon and 1:30-6:15pm, Sa 8:30am-noon.) **Postal Code:** CH-3800.

▐▞☰ ACCOMMODATIONS AND FOOD. The ▨Backpackers Villa Sonnenhof, Alpenstr. 16, diagonally across Höhenmatte from the tourist office, offers spacious, airy rooms with priceless mountain views. (☎826 71 71; fax 826 71 72; email backpackers@villa.ch. Breakfast included. Bike rental. Internet. Reception 7:45-11am and 4-9pm. Reserve ahead. Dorms 29-33SFr; doubles 37SFr per person. Add 3SFr for Jungfrau view, balcony, and bathroom.) Something like an American fraternity house, **Balmer's Herberge**, Hauptstr. 23-25, is in the village of Matten. Head left from Westbahnhof, veer right onto Bahnhofstr., turn right on Centralstr., and follow the signs. Sign in and return at 5pm, when beds are assigned. (☎ (033) 822 19 61. Internet. Bike rental. Small breakfast included. Showers 1SFr per 5min. Laundry. Reception in summer 6:30am-11pm; off-season 6:30-9am and 4:30-11pm. No reservations. 2- to 8-bed dorms 19-28SFr; doubles 56SFr. Overflow mattresses 13SFr.) **The Funny Farm**, down Hauptstr. past Balmer's in nearby Matten, is more commune than youth hostel, and offers volleyball, a pool, and an outdoor bar. (☎ (079) 652 61 27. Internet. Breakfast included. 25SFr.) **Hotel Alpina**, Hauptstr. 44 has spacious rooms equipped with sinks, TVs, towels, and fluffy, warm comforters, all cared for by the motherly keeper Dora. Reserve a spot by email a few days before arriving. (☎822 80 31; email alpina_interlaken@bluewin.ch. Reception 7am-midnight. Closed Nov. Singles and doubles 42SFr.) **Camping Sackgut** is just across the river from the Ostbahnhof. (☎ (079) 656 89 58. Reception 9-11am and 4-7pm. Open May-Oct. 14.10-22.10SFr per person.)

Many hostels serve cheap food, but you can also eat on the cheap at **Migros market**, across from Westbahnhof, or at their restaurant upstairs. (Open M-Th 8am-6:30pm, F 8am-9pm, Sa 7:30am-4pm.) **Restaurant Goldener Anker**, Marktg. 57, has traditional specialties and lowfat vegetarian dishes. (☎822 16 72. Open M-W and F-Su 10am-12:30am.) Enjoy chocolate boots for 2SFr and strawberry tarts for 4.20SFr at **Confiserie Schuh**, across from the tourist office. (☎822 94 41. Open daily 8am-11pm.)

Interlaken's adventure sports industry is thrilling and usually death-defying, but accidents do happen. Be aware that on July 27, 1999, 19 adventure-seeking tourists were killed by a sudden flash flood while canyoning on the Saxeten river.

▐▟ OUTDOORS AND HIKING. Interlaken's steep precipices, raging rivers, and open spaces are prime spots for such adrenaline-pumping activities as paragliding, whitewater rafting, bungee-jumping, and canyoning (which involves putting on a wetsuit and harness and rappeling and swimming down a waterfall). Competition has driven prices down, and most companies charge similar prices. **Alpin Raft** (AR; ☎823 41 00), the original company, has wild Australian guides. **Alpine Center** (AC;

☎823 55 23), the newest and smallest company, provides the most personal service. Both companies offer **paragliding** (AR/AC 140SFr); **canyoning** (AR 95SFr, AC 115SFr); **river rafting** (AR 95SFr, AC 90SFr); and **skydiving** (AC/AR 380SFr). Alpin Raft also offers **bungee-jumping** (155SFr) and **hang gliding** (155SFr). A number of horse and hiking tours, as well as rock-climbing lessons, are available upon request. Minutes from Interlaken on the Brienzersee, Alpin Raft's **sea kayaking** provides a strenuous day in the sun and on the water (30SFr).

Swiss Alpine Guides (☎822 60 00) leads full-day ice-climbing clinics (May-Oct., 145SFr, warm clothing rental included), as well as full-day glacier treks (in summer daily; 120SFr). Interlaken's winter activities include skiing, snowboarding, ice canyoning, snow rafting, and glacier skiing. Contact the **tourist office** (☎826 53 00), or any of the adventure companies for information. There are three **skiing** areas in the Jungfrau region (info ☎828 71 11; 1-day passes 52SFr, 2-day 105SFr).

The towns closer to the mountains are where the serious **hiking** starts, but Interlaken has a few good hikes of its own. The most worthwhile hike climbs to the **Harder Kulm.** The half-day hike reveals a striking mountainscape including the Eiger, Mönch, and Jungfrau. The easiest starting point is near the Ostbahnhof. From the Ostbahnhof, head toward town and take the first road bridge across the river; follow the yellow signs and then the white-red-white *Bergweg* blazes on the rocks. From the top, signs lead back down to the Westbahnhof. A **funicular** runs from the trailhead near the Ostbahnhof to the top. (May-Oct. 2hr. up, 1½hr. down. 12.80SFr, round-trip 20SFr; 25% off with Eurailpass or SwissPass.)

More horizontal trails lead along the lakes that flank the city. Turn left from the train station, then left before the bridge and follow the canal over to the nature reserve on the shore of the Thunersee. The trail winds up the Lombach river, then through pastures at the base of the Harder Kulm back toward town (2hr.).

🎭 **ENTERTAINMENT.** If you still have energy at the end of the day there are plenty of options. **Balmer's** (see p. 927) is always popular and busy. (Beer 4.50SFr; bar open 9pm-1am.) When the party dies down there, revelers head to the **Caverne Bar** in the basement of the Mattenhof Hotel, in front of the Funny Farm. (Beer 3.50SFr. Open W-Su 10pm-2:30am.) If you're feeling adventurous, head beyond the hostel confines to one of the local hangouts. **Buddy's,** Höheweg 33, is a small, crowded English pub. (Open Su-Th 10am-1am, F-Sa 10am-1:30am.) Drunken herds then migrate to Interlaken's oldest disco, **Johnny's Dancing Club,** Höheweg 92, downstairs in the Hotel Carlton. (Open Tu-Su 9:30pm-3am.) For smoky blues try **Brasserie,** Rosenstr. 17, where live bands play Thursdays with no cover charge. (Beer from 3SFr. Open M-Sa 8:30am-12:30am, Su 3pm-12:30am.)

🚗 **DAYTRIPS: THUNERSEE AND BRIENZERSEE.** Appreciate Bernese Oberland's calm waters and stark mountain peaks on a lake cruise on either the **Thunersee** (to the west) or the **Brienzersee** (to the east). Ferries on Thunersee are free with Eurail, Swisspass, and Bernese Oberland passes. Major towns on the Thunersee are **Thun** and **Spiez,** which each boast several castles. **Brienz** is the main town on the Brienzersee, filled with preserved traditional Swiss dwellings and wood-carvers galore. **Trains** run to Thun from Interlaken's Westbahnhof (2 per hr., 14.60SFr.) and Bern (2 per hr., 12.60SFr); and to Spiez every hr. from Interlaken's Westbahnhof (20min., 8.60SFr), Bern (30min., 17.20SFr), and Thun (10min., 6.20SFr). **Boats** also connect towns on each lake. Spiez and Thun have **tourist offices** adjacent to their respective train stations (Spiez ☎654 20 20; Thun ☎222 23 40). Perhaps the best reason to visit the Thunersee is the ◪**Swiss Adventure Hostel,** in the tiny town of Boltigen, 45min. from Spiez by train (dir.: Zweissimen). This restful, wholesome alternative to the partying adventure scene in Interlaken offers the same adventure sports opportunities as Interlaken companies, with a more personal experience. (☎773 73 73. Internet. Bike rental. All-you-can-eat breakfast 5SFr. Two free shuttles run from Interlaken each day; call for times. 19-25SFr; double 34SFr per person.)

JUNGFRAU REGION

The most famous (and most-visited) region of the Bernese Oberland, the Jungfrau area has attracted tourists for hundreds of years with glorious hiking trails and permanently snow-capped peaks. The three most famous mountains are the **Jungfrau** (Maiden), the **Eiger** (Ogre), and the **Mönch** (Monk). Locals say that the monk protects the maiden by standing between her and the ogre, but at 4158m, she could probably beat the puny Eiger (3970m) up. From Interlaken, the valley splits at the foot of the Jungfrau: the eastern valley contains Grindelwald, with easy access to two glaciers, while the western valley (the Lauterbrunnen) hosts many smaller towns, including Wengen, Gimmelwald, Murren, and Lauterbrunnen, each with unique hiking opportunities. The two valleys are divided by an easily hikeable ridge. Pick up the *Lauterbrunnen/Jungfrau Region Wanderkarte* (15SFr at any tourist office) for an overview of the hikes.

GRINDELWALD ☎ 036

Beneath the north face of the Eiger and within walking distance of the only glaciers accessible by foot in the Bernese Oberland, Grindelwald is a cold-weather paradise for hikers, climbers, and skiers. To reach the trail leading up the side of the **Upper Glacier** (Obere Grindelwaldgletscher), take the postal bus from Grindelwald (dir.: Grosse Scheidegg) to "Oberslaubkule," walk uphill, and follow the "Glecksteinhütte" signs for continuing. Access to the **Lower Glacier** (Untere Grindelwaldgletscher) is closer to town: walk up the main street away from the station, follow signs downhill to "Pfingstegg," and then follow signs up the glacial valley to "Stieregg," a hut that offers food to the weary (4hr. round-trip). This hike is moderately steep, becoming steeper the farther you go up the trail. The **Männlichen**, can be reached by the Männlichen Gondalbahn. From the station, a quick hike scales the Männlichen peak before continuing as a flat, one hour hike to Kleine Scheidegg and its intimate views of the Eiger, Mönch, and Jungfrau.

Jungfraubahn **trains** run from Interlaken's Ostabahnhof (9.40SFr). There is also a bus from Balmers (round-trip 15SFr). To reach the **tourist office,** in the Sport-Zentrum, turn right from the station. (☎854 12 12; fax 854 12 10. Open July-Aug. M-F 8am-7pm, Sa 8am-5pm, Su 9-11am and 3-5pm; Sept.-June M-F 8am-noon and 2-6pm, Sa 8am-noon and 2-5pm.) The **Jugendherberge (HI)** sits in a beautiful wooden chalet above town. Exit the train station and turn left; go straight (5-7min.), cut uphill to the right (8min.) just before Chalet Alpenblume, and follow the steep trail all the way up the hill. (☎853 10 09; fax 853 50 29. Breakfast included. Bikes 15SFr per day. Dorms 26.30-29.80SFr; doubles 48.80-51.30SFr.) The bright blue **Mountain Hostel,** at the Grund station next to the river, is equally far, but charming. Turn right out of the station, then right on the small trail toward "Grund;" go to the bottom of the valley, bearing right at the Glacier Hotel. (☎853 39 00; fax 853 47 30. Breakfast included. Dorms 32SFr; doubles 84SFr.) To **camp** at **Gletscherdorf,** turn right out of the station, take the first right after the tourist office, and then the third left. (☎853 14 29. 9.10SFr per person, 9SFr per tent.) Frugal gourmets shop at the **Co-op** across from the tourist office. (Open M-F 8am-6:30pm, Sa 8am-4pm.) A **Migros supermarket** lies farther down the main street, away from the station. (Open M-F 8am-noon and 1:30-6:30pm, Sa 8am-4pm.) **Postal code:** CH-3818.

LAUTERBRUNNEN ☎ 033

The "loud springs" that give the beautiful Lauterbrunnen valley its name are the 72 waterfalls that plummet down the sheer walls of the narrow, glacier-cut valley. **Lauterbrunnen Town,** which lies in the middle of the valley, is an ideal base for hiking and skiing. It also lies near the **Staubbach Falls** (280m). To reach the main hiking trail, follow the right branch of the main road as it leaves town, which eventually dwindles to a dirt trail. The first, most-touristed segment of the trail leads past the Staubbach, Spissbach, Agertenbach, and Mümenbach Falls to the greatest of them all, the **Trümmelbach Falls,** comprising 10 glacier-bed chutes that gush up to 20,000L of water per second, generating mighty winds and a roaring din (40min.). Explore tunnels, footbridges, and an underground elevator. (Elevator open July-Aug. 8am-6pm; Apr.-June and Sept.-Nov. 9am-5pm. 10SFr.) The trail becomes less-trafficked as it continues on to the town **Stechelberg** (1½hr. from Lauterbrunnen), where **cable cars** leave for Gimmelwald (7.40SFr), Mürren (14.40SFr), Birg (34SFr), and Schilthorn (49.60SFr), small towns throughout the Lauterbrunnen Valley. The first two are free with the Swisspass, and Eurailers get 25% off all four.

Trains connect to Lauterbrunnen Town from Interlaken's Ostbahnhof (20min., 6:05am-11:05pm, 6.20SFr). The **tourist office,** is 200m left of the station on the main street. (☎855 85 68; fax 855 85 69. Open M-F 8am-noon and 2-6pm; July-Aug. also Sa 9am-noon and 1-5pm.) **Valley Hostel** is left off the main street, down a driveway, and past the Co-op on the right. This clean hostel has comfy beds. (☎855 20 08. Reception 8am-10pm. Dorms 20SFr; double 50SFr.) To reach **Hotel Staubbach** from the station, go left on the main street toward the waterfall (400m); the hotel is on the left. The rooms, most with private bath, have unobstructed views of the Staubbach Falls. (☎855 54 54. Parking and breakfast included. Singles 50SFr, with shower 60SFr; doubles 70-120SFr; 3- to 6-bed rooms 35-40SFr per person. 5SFr extra per person in high season.) **Camping Jungfrau,** up the main street from the station toward the large waterfall, has cheap beds, kitchens, showers, lounges, and a store. (☎856 20 10. Reception in summer 8am-9pm; off-season 8am-noon and 2:30-6:30pm. Dorms 20-22SFr; camping 8-10SFr per person, 6-15SFr per tent.) Pick up groceries at the **Co-op,** near the post office on the main road. (Open M-F 8am-noon and 2-6:30pm, Sa 8am-noon and 1:30-4pm.) **Postal code:** CH-3822.

ZERMATT AND THE MATTERHORN ☎027

A trick of the valley blocks out the great Alpine summits surrounding **Zermatt,** allowing the **Matterhorn** (4478m), to rise alone above the town. The Matterhorn is the Holy Grail for serious climbers, but only those with loads of money (around 800SFr), experience, equipment, and time to train in the area. Fortunately, miles of spectacular, well-marked paths are accessible to all visitors. No visit to Zermatt is complete without struggling up to the **Hörnlihütte,** the base camp for climbs up to the Matterhorn and a strenuous four- to five-hour hike past the tiny lake **Schwarzsee;** a **cable car** also runs to the Schwarzsee (20.50SFr, round-trip 33SFr). Zermatt is one of the world's best-equipped ski centers, with 245km of challenging ski runs in winter and more summer ski trails than any other Alpine resort. **Ski and boot rental** prices are fairly standard (1-day 50SFr). A one-day **ski pass** in any one of the individual regions runs between 62SFr and 77SFr.

Cars and buses are illegal in Zermatt to preserve the Alpine air—the only way in is the hourly BVZ (Brig-Visp-Zermatt) **rail line.** Connect from Visp (from Lausanne; 35SFr) or Stalden-Saas (from Saas Fee; 1hr., 31SFr). The **tourist office,** on Bahnhofpl., in the station complex, sells hiking maps for 25SFr. (☎967 01 81; fax 967 01 85. Open mid-June to mid-Oct. M-F 8:30am-6pm, Sa 8:30am-7pm, Su 9:30am-noon and 4-7pm; mid-Oct. to mid-June M-Sa 8:30am-noon and 1:30-7pm.) The **Alpine Center,** on Bahnhofstr., to the right from the station past the post office, houses the **Bergführerbüro** (Guides Office; ☎966 24 60; fax 966 24 69) and **Skischulbüro** (Ski School Office; ☎967 24 66). **Hotel Bahnhof,** 1min. from the station (turn left down Bahnhofstr. as you exit), offers hotel housing at hostel rates. (☎967 24 06. Laundry. Reception 8am-8pm. Open mid-Dec. to mid-Oct. Dorms 30SFr; singles 52-56SFr; doubles 82-88SFr.) The **Matterhorn Hostel** is a 12min. walk from the station; turn right along Bahnhofstr., left at the church, and right after the river on Schluhmattstr. (☎968 19 19; email info@matterhornhostel.com. Laundry. **Internet.** Reception 7:30-11am and 4-10pm. Dorms 24-29SFr.) **Camping Matterhorn Zermatt,** on Bahnhofstr., is 5min. to the left of the station. (☎967 39 21. Reception May-Sept. 8:30-9:30am and 5:30-7pm. 8.50-9SFr.) **Café-Konditorei Hörnli,** is a relaxed little place. (Breakfast 6-14SFr, salads 8.50SFr. Open daily mid-Aug. to mid-July 7:30am-7pm; mid-July to mid-Aug. 7:30am-10pm.) Pick up **groceries** at **Co-op Center** opposite the station. (Open M-Sa 8:30am-12:15pm and 1:45-6:30pm.) **Postal code:** CH-3920.

SAAS FEE ☎ 027

Nicknamed "the pearl of the Alps," Saas Fee (1800m) is in a hanging valley above the Saastal, snuggled among thirteen 4000m peaks, including the **Dom** (4545m), the second-highest mountain in Switzerland. Visitors turn their attention to the mountains and the glacial glory of the **Feegletscher.** Summer **skiers** enjoy 20km of runs, and in winter an immense network of lifts opens (day-passes 58SFr). Stores in the **Swiss Rentasport System** rent several grades of equipment (skis 28-50SFr per day, snowboards 28-38SFr, boots 15-19SFr). In summer, the **Alpine Guide's office** by the church has a selection of **climbs** and **hikes** for both amateurs and experts. (☎ 957 44 64. Open M-Sa 9:30am-noon and 3-6pm.)

Post **buses** run hourly to Visp (50min., 14.60SFr), where you can connect to Lausanne, and Stalden Saas (40min., 11.80SFr), which links up with Zermatt (add 30SFr). Reserve a place on the bus at least 2hr. ahead (call ☎ 958 11 45 or stop by the station). The **tourist office,** opposite the bus station, dispenses season information and gives hiking advice. (☎ 958 18 58; fax 958 18 60. Open July to mid-Sept. and mid-Dec. to mid-Apr. M-F 8:30am-noon and 2-6:30pm, Sa 8am-7pm, Su 9am-noon and 3-6pm; mid-Sept. to mid-Dec and mid-Apr. to June M-Sa 8:30am-noon and 2-6pm, Su 10am-noon and 4-6pm.) Those willing to sacrifice comfort can find bargains in hotel basements. The cheapest is **Hotel Garni Imseng;** from the station, head down the main street, left of the tourist office, then turn left and pass the church. (☎ 958 12 58. Breakfast 15SFr. sheets 5SFr. Dorms 20SFr.) Across the street behind Hotel Feehof Garni, the subterranean dorm at the **Hotel Berghof** is a bit more spacious. (☎ 957 24 84. Breakfast 10SFr. Closed in May. Dorms 25SFr.) For groceries, the **Supermarkt** is on the main street near the tourist office. (Open M-F 8:30am-12:15pm and 2:25-6:30pm, Sa 8:30am-12:15pm and 2:15-5pm.) **Postal code:** CH-3906.

GRAUBÜNDEN

The largest, least populous, and most alpine of the Swiss cantons, Graubünden is made up of remote valleys and snow-clad peaks that are bound to bring out the wild-hearted, lusting-for-life yodeler in everyone. Deep, rugged gorges, forests of larch and fir, and eddying rivers imbue the region with a wildness seldom found in ultra-civilized Switzerland. The area is also a microcosm of Swiss cultural heterogeneity—from valley to valley the language slips from German to Romansh to Italian. There is more to Graubünden than the glamorous ski resorts of the Upper Engadine, as travelers willing to go a little farther afield discover. Visitors should plan their trips carefully, especially in ski season, when reservations are absolutely required. Beware, almost everything shuts down in May and June.

CHUR ☎ 081

Chur (pop. 32,000) is the capital of Graubünden and, at 5000 years old, probably Switzerland's oldest settlement. Its museums and hip restaurants give the town—situated in the most rural and wild canton—an unexpected cultural and artsy edge. Chur's highlight is the cavernous 12th-century Romanesque **Dom** (cathedral) at the top of the old town, which displays eight altarpieces in addition to the **Hochaltar,** a flamboyant 15th-century masterpiece of gold and wood. The crypts, where the Capuchin martyr St. Fidelis is buried, also house the **Dom-Museum,** replete with relics. (☎ 252 9250. Open Tu-Sa 10am-noon and 2-4pm.) Chur's **Bündner Kunstmuseum,** Bahnhofstr. 35, at the corner of Bahnhofstr. and Grabenstr., blazes with the art of the three Giacomettis: Giovanni, Alberto, and Augusto. Works by Swiss artists Angelika Kauffman and Ferdinand Hodler occupy the ground floor. (☎ 257 2868. Open Tu-W and F-Su 10am-noon and 2-5pm, Th 10am-noon and 2-8pm. 10SFr, students 7SFr, children under 16 free.)

Chur is the transportation hub for Graubünden. **Trains** connect Chur to Arosa (1hr., every hr., 11.80SFr); Basel (2¾hr., every hr., 62SFr); St. Gallen (1½hr., every hr., 34SFr); and Zurich (1½hr., every hr., 38SFr). To get to the **tourist office,** Grabenstr. 5, from Postpl., turn left on Grabenstr. The office finds rooms for free. (☎ 252 1818. Open M 1:30-6pm, Tu-F 8:30am-noon and 1:30-6pm, Sa 9am-noon.) No luxurious budget accommodations await in Chur; the lack of a youth hostel is sorely felt. The nearest hostel is in **Arosa** (see p. 922). Another good option is staying in nearby **Bad Ragaz,** but if you need to be in Chur, try **Hotel Schweizerhaus,** Kasernenstr. 10. From the Postpl., turn right on Grabenstr. and follow as it becomes Engadinestr. and crosses the bridge; turn right over the bridge, and the street turns into Kasernenstr. (☎ 252 1096. Breakfast included. Reception 7am-midnight. 35SFr per person.) Chur has a surprising number of trendy eating establishments. Try **Restaurante Controverse,** Steinbruchstr. 2, which has lip-smacking good food. Get there by turning left on Grabenstr. (☎ 252 9944. Open M-Sa 11am-midnight, Su 6-11pm. Closed July 15-Aug. 13.) **Postal code:** CH-7000.

LOWER ENGADINE VALLEY

The Lower Engadine valley represents Graubünden at its purest. Skiing never quite caught on here, and, unaltered by the swift torrent of change brought by the ski industry, the people maintain a strong connection to their land and culture. The Lower Engadine is a stronghold of the **Romansh language,** and nearly every sign is printed in this Latinate relic. The region may not be a skier's paradise, but **hikers** revel in the untouched alpine ecosystem of the **Swiss National Park** just south of the valley. Regional travel is easy with the **Lower Engadine Regional Pass** that covers all trains and post buses in the area (3 of 7 days, 45SFr; 7 of 14 days, 65SFr).

THE SWISS NATIONAL PARK

The Swiss National Park offers hikes with views that rival the best hiking areas elsewhere in Switzerland. But the park has one thing that no other areas have: the park's isolation from man-made constructs allows hikers to experience the undiluted wildness of the natural terrain. The Swiss National Park is one of the most strictly environmentally regulated nature preserves in the world. During June and July, the Park's alpine flora is in full bloom. A network of 20 hiking trails runs throughout the park, mostly concentrated in the center of the park. All trails are clearly marked, and it is against park rules to wander off of the designated trails. Few of the trails are level; most trails in the park involve a lot of climbing, often into areas still covered in snow. Be sure to check in at the **Parkhouse** in Zernez to see which trails are navigable. Their advice is not tempered by paranoia of liability, so when they say a trail is too dangerous, they mean it. An extremely helpful park trail map (scale: 1:45,000; 14SFr) in five languages, as well as a written guide to all twenty trails (10SFr), is available at the Parkhouse in Zernez . The Parkhouse also sells a geological map and a vegetation map of the park (scale: 1:50,000). The trails that require no mountaineering gear are marked with white-red-white blazes. The Swiss are practically mountain goats, so even some of the non-mountaineering routes can be tricky.

The towns of Scuol, Zernez, and S-chanf lie just north of the park along the same Rhätische Bahn **train line. Post buses** wind along the three major roads that skirt the park. Camping and campfires are prohibited, as is collecting flowers and plants. A team of wardens patrols the park at all times, so it's better not to test the rules. The central office of the park is in Zernez. The park is closed from Nov.-May. Spend the night at **Ova Spin,** just outside the western park boundary. With kitchen facilities next door, it will cost you much less than many of the other possibilities. (☎ 856 10 52. Dorms 15SFr, best to reserve one week in advance.) Take the bus from Zernez toward Müstair to get to the hostel. (20min., every hr. 8:55am-8:20pm, 2.20SFr). If you want to get out into the woods immediately head to one of the **mountain huts** scattered throughout the park. **Camping** is not allowed in the park, but Zernez, Scuol, and S-chanf have campsites right outside the park boundaries.

MY, WHAT BIG FEET YOU HAVE From the Chamanna Cluozza (with binoculars), you can see the tracks of the theropod, a 4 to 5m-long herbivorous dinosaur that roamed this area over 200 million years ago. The footprints measure 25-30cm across, with a stride of up to 2.2m, similar to those 70-year-old Swiss women who pass you by on the trail.

SOUTHEAST (ITALIAN) SWITZERLAND

Ever since Switzerland won the Italian-speaking canton of Ticino (Tessin in German and French) from Italy in 1512, the region has been renowned for its mix of Swiss efficiency and Italian *dolce vita*—no wonder the rest of Switzerland vacations here among jasmine-laced villas painted the bright colors of Italian *gelato*. Lush emerald lakes and shaded castles render Ticino's hilly countryside as romantic as its famed resorts, Lugano and Locarno.

LUGANO
☎ 091

Lugano, Switzerland's 3rd largest banking center, lies in the crevassed bay between San Salvatore and Monte Bré. Warmed by a Mediterranean climate, Lugano's shady streets are lined with tiles, climbing vines, and blood-red wildflowers. The leafy frescoes of the 16th-century **Cattedrale San Lorenzo,** just below the train station, are still magnificently vivid. The national monument **Basilica Sacro Cuore,** on C. Elevezia, has frescoes which feature Swiss hikers walking alongside the disciples. The most spectacular fresco in town, however, is the gargantuan *Crucifixion* which adorns the **Chiesa Santa Maria degli Angiuli,** on the waterfront to the right of the tourist office. The **Museo delle Culture Extraeuropee,** 324 V. Cortivo, on the footpath to Gandria in the Villa Heleneum, features masks, statues, and shields from New Caledonia and other distant locales. (☎ 971 73 53. Open Mar. 5-Oct. 31 W-Su 10am-5pm. 5SFr, students 3SFr.) Armed with topographic **maps** and **trail guides** (sold at the tourist office, lent at the hostel), hikers can tackle **Monte Bré** (933m) or **Monte San Salvatore** (912m). Alpine guides at the **ASBEST Adventure Company,** V. Basilea 28 (☎ 966 11 14), offer everything from **snowshoeing** and **skiing** (full-day 90SFr) to **paragliding** (165SFr) and **canyoning** (from 90SFr). The **Pave Pub,** riva Albertolli 1, is a self-proclaimed *museo di birra* (beer museum), with 50 different brands. (From 4SFr. Open daily 11am-1am.)

   Trains (☎ (0900) 30 03 00) run frequently to: Bern via Lucerne (5hr., every hr., 77SFr); Locarno via Bellinzona (1hr., 2 per hr., 16.40SFr); Zurich (3½hr., every hr., 62SFr); and Milan (1½hr., every hr., 14SFr). From the station, cross the Centro footbridge, take V. Cattedrale onto V. Pessina, go left on V. dei Pesci, then turn left again on Riva via Vela for the **tourist office.** (☎ 913 32 32. Open Apr.-Oct. M-F 9am-6:30pm, Sa 9am-12:30pm and 1:30-5pm, Su 10am-2pm; Nov.-Mar. M-F 9am-12:30pm and 1:30-5pm.) To reach the luxury-villa-turned-independent-hostel **Hotel Montarina,** V. Montarina 1, walk 200m to the right from the station and cross the tracks. (☎ 966 72 72; email info@montarina.ch. Sheets 4SFr. Reception 8am-10pm. Open Mar.-Oct. Dorms 25SFr; singles 50-65SFr; doubles 100-120SFr.) To reach the posh **Ostello della Gioventù (HI)** at #13, in Lugano-Savosa, exit left from the station, go down the 2nd ramp, cross the street, go 100m uphill, catch bus #5 to Crocifisso (6th stop), then backtrack and turn left up V. Cantonale. (☎ 966 27 28. Breakfast 7SFr. Reception daily 7am-12:30pm and 3-10pm. Curfew 10pm. Open mid-Mar. to Oct. Dorms 23SFr; singles 35SFr; doubles 56-70SFr.) To **camp** at **La Palma** (☎ 605 25 61) or **Eurocampo** (☎ 605 21 14), two of the five sites in Agno, take the Ferrovia-Lugano-Ponte-Tresa (FLP) train to Agno (4.40SFr), turn left from the stop and left again on V. Molinazzo. (Open Apr.-Oct. 7-7.50SFr per person, 6-10SFr per tent.) **La Tinèra,** V. dei Gorini 2, behind Credit Suisse in P. della Riforma, is a low-lit underground restaurant with great specials. (Open M-Sa 8:30am-3pm and 5:30-11pm.) A **Migros supermarket,** V. Pretoria 15, is two blocks left of the post office on V. Pretoria in the center of town. (Open M-F 8am-6:30pm, Sa 7:30am-5pm.) **Postal code:** CH-6900.

LOCARNO ☎ 091

On the shores of Lake Maggiore, Locarno basks in warm near-Mediterranean breezes and bright Italian sun, with luxuriant palm trees replacing the rugged Alps. During its famous **film festival** each August, 150,000 people descend to one of the most important movie premiere events in the world. Locarno's most striking church is the **Madonna del Sasso** (Madonna of the Rock), accessible by foot or **funicular** (next to the McDonald's by the station; 6SFr round trip, 4.50SFr with Swiss-Pass). The orange-yellow complex includes a densely ornate sanctuary and a museum next door. (Grounds open daily 7am-7pm. Museum open Apr.-Oct. M-F 2-5pm, Su 10am-noon and 2-5pm; 2.50SFr, students 1.50SFr.) Heed the call of Locarno's lake by renting a **paddle-** or **motorboat** along the shore, or catch a **ferry** (1¼hr., 9 per day, 20SFr) to the botanical gardens on the nearby island of **Brissago.** (Gardens open 9am-6pm; 6SFr.)

Trains (☎ 743 65 64) run from P. Stazione to Lucerne (3hr., 2 per hr., 56SFr); Lugano (45min., 2 per hr., 16.40SFr); Milan (2½hr., several per day, 63SFr); and Zurich (2¾hr., every hr., 60SFr). For Geneva (5¾hr., 91SFr); Montreux (4¾hr., 74SFr); or Zermatt (4hr., 88SFr), change in Domodossola, Italy (1¾hr., 2 per hr., 41SFr). From the station, walk diagonally to the right, cross V. della Stazione, continue through pedestrian V. alla Ramogna, and cross Largo Zorzi to the left to reach the **tourist office** on P. Grande, in the same building as the *Kursaal* (casino). (☎ 751 00 91; fax 751 90 70; www.maggiore.com. Open mid-Mar. to mid-Oct. M-F 9am-6pm, Sa 10am-4pm, Su 10am-noon and 1-3pm; mid-Oct. to mid-Mar. M-F 9am-6pm.) The **Pensione Città Vecchia**, V. Toretta 13, has the best prices and location in town. From P. Grande, turn right on V. Toretta (*not* Vigola Toretta; look for a brown sign with the *alberghi* on it) and continue to the top. (☎ 751 45 54. Breakfast 5SFr. Check-in 1-6pm; call ahead to arrive later. Open Mar.-Oct. Dorms 22-24SFr; singles 33-35SFr; doubles 64-76SFr.) From the station, turn left, follow V. alla Romogna to P. Grande, turn right on V. della Motta, bear left on V. B. Rusca past P.S. Francesco, take V. Varenna, and follow the signs to reach the **Palagiovani Youth Hostel (HI)**, 18 V. Varenna. (☎ 756 15 00. Laundry 6SFr. Reception in summer 8-10am and 3-11:30pm; in winter 8-10am and 3-10:30pm. Dorms 31-38SFr; doubles 33-43SFr. Off-season 2.50SFr less.) Dining and revelry are centered on P. Grande and the lake, both excellent areas to seek out your favorite variety of *gelato*. On the left as you exit the station, **Inova**, 1 V. della Stazione, is a huge self-serve restaurant. (Salad bar 5-10SFr. Pasta buffet 9SFr. Meaty menus 12-15SFr. Open M-Sa 7:30am-10pm, Su 8am-10pm.) For cheap **supermarket** fare, try **Aperto**, at the station (open daily 6am-10pm) or **Migros**, on P. Grande (open M-Sa 9am-7pm). **Postal code:** CH-6600.

▷ DAYTRIP FROM LOCARNO: ASCONA. In addition to enjoying Ascona's tropical sunshine and sparkling water, history buffs can trace the steps of the 19th-century leftist thinkers and bohemian artists who tried to establish Utopia on the mountain above, known as **Monte Verità**. The **tourist office** (☎ 791 00 90; email buongiorno@maggiore.ch; www.maggiore.ch) is in the Casa Serodine, behind the **Chiesa SS Pietro e Paolo**. Reach Ascona by **bus** #31 from Locarno (15min., every 15min., 2.40SFr) or by **ferry** (1hr., 6 per day, day-pass 11SFr).

HEADING EAST: PRAGUE AND BUDAPEST

During the Cold War, "Eastern Europe" was a name imposed by Westerners on the Soviet satellites east of the Berlin Wall. It has always been somewhat of a misnomer, capturing a political rather than geographical reality: Vienna lies farther east than Prague, Croatia sits on the Mediterranean, and most of Russia is, in fact, in Asia. But Eastern Europe is not merely a Western construction. The region is united by what it longs to leave behind—an arduous history of political upheaval and disillusionment—and by what it now confronts—a more optimistic but similarly uncertain future. To understand the remarkable complexity of Eastern Europe is to imagine a map of the region a little over a decade ago: in 1989, there were a total of seven countries behind the Iron Curtain; today, that same area is comprised of 19 independent states. In that time, the region has undergone an astounding political and cultural transformation. While communism has fallen throughout Europe and the Soviet Union no longer exists, Eastern Europe continues to be defined by its historical legacy.

More than a decade after the sweeping of communism from Europe, Eastern Europe has become the darling of budget travelers. Undiscovered cities, pristine national parks, open hostel beds, and ridiculously cheap beer steadily lure backpackers seeking bargains, culture, and adventure. In particular, it has been the twin stars of Prague and Budapest that have exploded from relative obscurity into tourist destinations rivalling the great capitals of Western Europe. To discover the real secrets of the east, check out *Let's Go: Eastern Europe 2001*.

ESSENTIALS

DOCUMENTS AND FORMALITIES

VISAS

Americans may visit the **Czech Republic** visa-free for up to 30 days, Irish and New Zealand citizens for up to 90 days, and Canadian and UK citizens for up to 180 days. Australians and South Africans must obtain 30-day tourist visas. Citizens of Canada, Ireland, South Africa, the UK, and the US can visit **Hungary** without visas for 90 days, provided their passport does not expire within six months of their journey's end. Australians and New Zealanders must obtain 90-day tourist visas from a Hungarian embassy or consulate. Visas can be purchased from your destination country's consulate or embassy. In most cases, you will have to send a completed visa application (obtained from the consulate), the required fee, and your passport.

EMBASSIES AND CONSULATES

Czech Embassies at Home: Australia, 38 Culgoa Circuit, O'Malley, Canberra, ACT 2606 (☎ (612) 290 13 86; fax 290 00 06; email canberra@embassy.mzv.cz). **Canada,** 541 Sussex Dr., Ottawa, ON K1N 6Z6 (☎ (613) 562-3875; fax 562-3878; email ottawa@embassy.mzv.cz). **Ireland,** 57 Northumberland Rd., Ballsbridge, Dublin 4 (☎ (3531) 668 11 35; fax 668 16 60; email dublin@embassy.mzv.cz). **New Zealand (Honorary Consul),** 48 Hair St., Wainuiomata, Wellington (☎/fax (644) 564 60 01). **South Africa,** 936 Pretorius St., Arcadia 0083, PRETORIA; P.O. Box 3326, PRETORIA 0001 (☎

(012) 342 3477; fax 430 20 33; email pretoria@embassy.mzv.cz; www.icon.co.za/Íczmzv/). **UK,** 26 Kensington Palace Gardens, London W8 4QY (☎ (020) 7243 1115; fax 7727 9654; email london@embassy.mzv.cz). **US,** 3900 Spring of Freedom St. NW, Washington, D.C. 20008 (☎ (202) 274-9100; www.czech.cz/washington).

Hungarian Embassies at Home: Australia Consulate, Suite 405, Edgecliff Centre 203-233, New South Head Rd., Edgecliff, NSW 2027 (☎ (612) 93 28 78 59; fax 93 27 18 29). **Canada,** 299 Waverley St., Ottawa, ON K2P 0V9 (☎ (613) 230-2717; fax 230-7560; email h2embott@docuweb.ca; www.docuweb.ca/Hungary). **Ireland,** 2 Fitzwilliam Pl., Dublin 2 (☎ (01) 661 29 03; fax 661 28 80). **South Africa,** 959 Arcadia St., Hatfield, Arcadia; P.O. Box 27077, Sunnyside 0132 (☎ (012) 43 30 20; fax 430 3029; email hunem@cis.co.za). **New Zealand,** 151 Orangi Kaupapa Rd., Wellington, 6005 (☎ (644) 938 04 27; fax 938 04 28; email sztmay@attglobal.net; www.geocities.com/CapitolHill/Lobby/1958/ContentsEn.htm). **UK,** 35 Eaton Pl., London SW1X 8BY (☎ (020) 7235 5218; fax 7823 1348; www.huemblon.org.uk). **US,** 3910 Shoemaker St. NW, Washington, D.C. 20008 (☎ (202) 362-6730; fax 966-8135; email office@huembwas.org; www.hungaryemb.org**)**.

PRAGUE (PRAHA) ☎ 02

KORUNA, OR CSK

US$1 = 39Kč	10Kč = US$0.25
CDN$1 = 27Kč	10Kč = CDN$0.37
UK£1 = 58Kč	10Kč = UK£0.17
IR£1 = 45Kč	10Kč = IR£0.22
AUS$1 = 23Kč	10Kč = AUS$0.44
NZ$1 = 17Kč	10Kč = NZ$0.59
SAR 1 = 5.70Kč	10Kč = SAR 0.18

PRAGUE'S PHONE SYSTEM — Prague continues to reform its phone system. Businesses often receive no more than three weeks notice before their numbers change. The four- to eight-digit numbers provided in these listings are the least likely to be obsolete by the time you read this—but things change fast.

According to legend, Countess Libuše stood above the Vltava in the 9th century and declared, "I see a city whose glory will touch the stars; it shall be called Praha (threshold)." Medieval kings, benefactors, and architects fulfilled the prophecy, building soaring cathedrals and lavish palaces that reflected Prague's status as capital of the Holy Roman Empire. Yet legends of demons, occult forces, and mazelike alleys lent this "city of dreams" a dark side that inspired Franz Kafka's tales of paranoia. Since the fall of the Iron Curtain, hordes of Euro-trotting foreigners have flooded Prague (pop. 1,500,000). In summer, tourists pack streets so tightly that crowd-surfing seems a viable way to get around. Yet walk a few blocks from any of the major sights and you'll be lost in the cobblestoned alleys, looming churches, and dark cellars; head to an outlying metro stop, and you'll find haggling *babičky*, supermodel-esque natives, and not a backpack in sight.

▌ TRANSPORTATION

Flights: Ruzyně Airport (☎20 11 11 11), 20km northwest of the city. Take bus #119 to Metro A: Dejvická (12Kč, plus 6Kč per piece of large luggage; runs daily 5am-midnight); buy tickets from kiosks or machines. Late at night, take tram #51 to Divoká Šárka, then night bus #510 to the center. **Airport buses** (☎20 11 42 96) go every 30min. from outside Metro stops at Nám. Republiky (90Kč) and Dejvická (60Kč).

Trains: ☎24 22 42 00; international ☎24 61 52 49. Prague has 4 main terminals: **Praha hlavní nádraží** (main station), ☎24 22 42 00. Metro C: Hlavní nádraží. **BIJ Wasteels** (☎24 61 74 54), 2nd fl., to the right of the stairs, sells discounted interna-

Central Prague

▲ ACCOMMODATIONS
Dům u krále Jiřího, 4
Pension Týn, 14
Traveller's Hostel Dlouhá 33, 16
Traveller's Hostel Křížovnická 7, 2
U Lilie, 3

■ PUBS, CAFES AND NIGHTLIFE
Cafe Marquis De Sade, 17
Roxy, 15
Jazz Club Železna, 12
Blatouch, 11
U Staré Paní, 8
Žïznivý Pes (Thirsty Dog), 7
Lávka, 1

◆ FOOD
Pizza Express, 13
U Špirků, 10
Country Life, 9
Klub architektů, 5
Shalom, 6

200 yards

200 meters

Havlíčkova
NÁMĚSTÍ REPUBLIKY
Masarykovo nádraží
Na Florenci
Diaždená
SENOVÁŽNÉ NÁM.
Jubilee (Jubilejní)
Jeruzalémská
Růžová
Jindřišská
St. Henry (sv. Jindřich)
Hello Travel
Hybernská
Senovážna
NÁMĚSTÍ REPUBLIKY
Nekázanka
V cipu
Mucha Museum
Kotra Department Store
Revoluční
Truhlářská -
Benediktská
Rybná -
Králodvorská
U Obecního Domu
NÁM. REPUBLIKY
Municipal House (Obecní dům)
American Express
Powder Tower (Prašná brána)
Rzbná
Templova
Jakubská
St. Jacob (sv. Jakub)
Malá Štupartská
Masná
Týnská
Štupartská
House of the Golden Ring
Celetná
Czech Museum of Fine Arts
OVOCNÝ TRH.
Na příkopě
MŮSTEK
VÁCLAVSKÉ NÁM.
Kamziková
Estates Theatre (Stavovské divadlo)
Havířská
St. Gall (sv. Havel)
Havelská tržiště
Na můstku
Přikrášná
Rytířská
Dlouhá
16
Kozí
Golz-Kinský Palace
Týn Church (Panna Marie před Týnem)
Jan Hus monument
STAROMĚSTSKÉ NÁM.
ŽELEZNÁ
Karolínum (Charles University)
STAROMĚSTSKÁ
Melantrichova
Kožná
Michalská
Hlavsova
Jilská
8
V kotcích
UHELNÝ TRH.
Škořepka
Skřepka
Dušní
Vězeňská
Spanish (Panvská)
sv. Duch
Dušní
V Kolkovně
Kostečná
St. Salvator (sv. Salvátor)
American Express
Pařížská
Kafka Museum
Cathedral of St. Nicholas (sv. Mikuláš)
Old Town Hall (Staroměstská radnice)
MALÉ NÁM.
St. Giles (sv. Jiljí)
5
Zlatá
Husova
Bethlehem Chapel (Betlémská kaple)
BETLÉMSKÉ NÁM.
El. Krásnohorské
High (Vysoká)
Jewish Town Hall (Židovská radnice)
6
Maisel (Maiselova)
Maiselova
Žatecká
Rísě Loutek Theater
Pařížská
Platnéřská
MARIÁNSKÉ NÁM.
Husova
Řetězová
Liliová
Náprstkova
Náprstek Museum
Borsov
Staroměstská
Decorative Arts Museum (Umělecko-průmyslové)
U Starého hřbitova
Ceremonial Hall
Cemetery
Klaus (Klausová)
Pinkas (Pinkasova)
Siroká
Kaprova
Valentinská
STAROMĚSTSKÁ
17. listopadu
Valentinská
Rudolfinum (Dům umělců)
NÁM. JANA PALACHA
Alšovo nab.
Veleslavínova
Klementinum and sv. Kliment (St. Clement Church)
2
Křižovnická
Anenská
ANENSKÉ NÁM.
Museum of Medieval Torture Instruments
3
Museum of Medieval Torture Instruments
Karolíny Světlé
Thomas Cook
Karlova
Karlova
Dvořákovo náb.
Mánesův most
Rudolfinum
St. Francis (sv. František)
Smetana Museum
Charles Bridge (Karlův most)
Theatre at the Balustrade (Divadlo na zábradlí)
River Vltava

N

tional tickets to those under 26 and books couchettes. Open in summer M-F 7:30am-8pm, Sa 8-11:30am and 12:30-3pm; off-season M-F 8:30am-6pm. **Holešovice, ☎ 24 61 72 65.** Metro C: Nádraží Holešovice. Services most international destinations. Buy **BIJ Wasteels** and regular train tickets from the Czech Railways Travel Agency (☎ 80 08 05). Open M-F 9am-5pm; Sa-Su 8am-4pm. To: **Berlin** (5hr., 5 per day, 1580Kč); **Budapest** (10hr., 5 per day, 1290Kč); **Munich** (6hr., 3 per day, 1450Kč); and **Vienna** (4½hr., 3 per day, 780Kč). **Masarykovo, ☎** 24 61 72 60. Metro B: Nám. Republiky. **Smíchov, ☎** 24 61 72 55. Metro B: Smíchovské nádraží. Opposite Vyšehrad.

Buses: ČSAD has several bus stations. The biggest is **Florenc,** Křižíkova 4 (☎ 24 21 49 90). Metro B, C: Florenc. Buy tickets in advance, as they often sell out. To: **Berlin** (6hr., 1 per day, 1040Kč) and **Vienna** (8½hr., 1 per day, 870Kč). Students may get 10% discount. The **Tourbus** office upstairs (☎ 24 21 02 21) sells tickets for Eurolines and airport buses. Open M-F 8am-8pm, Sa-Su 9am-8pm.

Public Transportation: Buy tickets for the **metro, tram,** or **bus** from newsstands and *tabák* kiosks, machines in stations, or **DP** (Dopravní podnik; transport authority) kiosks. The basic 8Kč ticket is good for 15min. (or 4 stops on the metro); 12Kč is valid for 1hr. (8pm-5am 1½hr.), with unlimited connections on the entire network in any one direction. Large bags and bikes require an extra 6Kč ticket. The Metro's 3 lines run daily 5am-midnight: A is green on the maps, B yellow, C red. **Night trams** #51-58 and **buses** run all night after the last Metro and can be picked up at the Charles Bridge; look for the dark-blue signs at bus stops.

Taxis: Taxi Praha (☎ 85 77 or 10 87) or **AAA** (☎ 24 32 24 32). Both open 24hr. Taxi drivers are notorious scam artists. Check that the meter is set to zero, and ask the driver to start it (*"Zapněte taximetr"*). Always ask for a receipt (*"Prosím, dejte mi paragon"*) with distance traveled and price paid. If the driver doesn't write the receipt or set the meter to zero, you aren't obligated to pay. Set rates in Prague 25Kč, plus 13Kč per km.

✳ 🔁 ORIENTATION AND PRACTICAL INFORMATION

Straddling the river **Vltava,** Prague is a gigantic mess of suburbs and labyrinthine medieval streets. Fortunately, nearly everything of interest lies within the compact downtown. The river runs through central Prague and separates the **Staré Město** (Old Town) and the **Nové Město** (New Town) from **Malá Strana** (Lesser Side). The Old Town's **Staroměstské náměstí** (Old Town Square) is the focal point of the city. From the square, the elegant **Pařížská ulice** (Paris Street) leads north into **Josefov,** the old Jewish ghetto; unfortunately, all that remains are six synagogues and the Old Jewish Cemetery. In the opposite direction from Pařížská lies **Nové Město.** It houses **Václavské** náměstí (Wenceslas Square), the administrative and commercial heart of the city. West of Staroměstské nám., **Karlův most** (Charles Bridge) traverses the Vltava and connects the Old Town with **Malostranské náměstí** (Lesser Town Square). **Pražský Hrad** (Prague Castle) sits on the **Hradčany** hilltop.

Prague's main **train station, Hlavní nádraží,** and **Florenc bus station** sit in the northeastern corner of Václavské nám. All train and bus terminals are on or near the excellent **Metro** system. To get to Staroměstské nám., take the Metro A line to Staroměstská and walk down Kaprova away from the river. *Tabák* stands and bookstores sell the indexed plán města (map); this, along with the English-language weekly *The Prague Post,* is essential for visitors.

TOURIST, FINANCIAL, AND LOCAL SERVICES

Tourist Office: Green "i"s mark tourist information. **Pražská Informační Služba** (Prague Info Service), is in the Old Town Hall (☎ 24 48 25 62; English ☎ 54 44 44). Branches at Na příkopě 20, the main train station, and in the tower on the Malá Strana side of the Charles Bridge. All open in summer M-F 9am-7pm, Sa-Su 9am-6pm; off-season M-F 9am-6pm, Sa-Su 9am-5pm.

Budget Travel: GTS, Ve smečkách 27 (☎ 54 34 55). Metro A, C: Muzeum. Offers student discounts on airfares. Open M-F 8am-6pm, Sa 9am-4pm.

Passport Office: Foreigner police, Olšanská 2 (☎683 17 39). Metro A: Flora; turn right on Jičínská with the cemetery on your right, then right on Olšanská. Or, take tram #9 from Václavské nám. toward Spojovací and get off at Olšanská. For visa extensions, get a 90Kč stamp inside. Open M-Tu and Th 7:30-11:30am and 12:30-2:30pm, W 7:30-11:30am and 12:30-5pm, F 7:30am-noon.

Embassies: Australia (☎24 31 00 71) and **New Zealand** (☎25 41 98) have consuls, but citizens should contact the UK embassy in an emergency. **Canada,** Mickiewiczova 6 (☎24 31 11 08). Metro A: Hradčanská. Open M-F 8am-noon and 2-4pm. **Hungary,** Badeniho 1 (☎36 50 41). Metro A: Hradčanská. Open M-W and F 9am-noon. **Ireland,** Tržiště 13 (☎53 09 11). Metro A: Malostranská. Open M-F 9:30am-12:30pm and 2:30-4:30pm. **South Africa,** Ruská 65 (☎67 31 11 14). Metro A: Flora. Open M-F 9am-noon. **UK,** Thunovská 14 (☎57 32 03 55). Metro A: Malostranská. Open M-F 9am-noon. **US,** Tržiště 15 (☎57 53 06 63; emergency ☎53 12 00). Metro A: Malostranská. From Malostranská nám., head down Karmelitská and take a right onto Tržiště. Open M-F 8am-1pm and 2-4:30pm.

Currency Exchange: Komerční banka, Na příkopě 33 (☎24 43 21 11), buys notes and checks for a 2% commission. Open M-F 8am-5pm.

American Express: Václavské nám. 56, 113 26 Praha 1 (☎22 80 02 37). Metro A, C: Muzeum. **ATM** outside takes AmEx cards. Cashes AmEx checks commission-free and grants V, MC cash advances for a 3% commission. Open July-Sept. M-F 9am-6pm, Sa 9am-2pm; Oct.-June M-F 9am-5pm, Sa 9am-noon. **Branches:** Mostecká 12 (near the Charles Bridge; open daily 9:30am-7:30pm), Celetná 17, and Staroměstské nám. 5.

Luggage Storage: Lockers in all train and bus stations take two 5Kč coins. If these are full, or if you need to store your cargo longer than 24hr., use the luggage offices to the left in the basement of **Hlavní nádraží** (15-30Kč per day; open 24hr.) and halfway up the stairs at **Florenc** (10-25Kč per day; open daily 5am-11pm).

Laundromat: Laundry Kings, Dejvická 16 (☎312 37 43), one block from Metro A: Hradčanská. Cross the tram and railroad tracks, then turn left on Dejvická. Wash 60Kč per 6kg; dry 15Kč per 8min. Soap 10-20Kč. Open M-F 6am-10pm, Sa-Su 8am-10pm.

EMERGENCY AND COMMUNICATIONS

Emergencies: Na Homolce (Hospital for Foreigners), Roentgenova 2 (☎52 92 21 74; after-hours ☎57 21 11 11). Open M-F 8am-4pm, but offers 24-hr. emergency service.

Pharmacy: "U Anděla," Štefánikova 6 (☎57 32 09 18). Metro B: Anděl. Open 24hr.

Internet Access: Terminal Bar, Soukenická 6 (☎21 87 19 99). Metro B: Nám. Republiky. 1.5Kč per min. Open M-Th and Su 11am-1am, F-Sa 11am-3am. **Café Electra,** Rašínovo nábřeží 62 (☎297 038). Metro B: Karlovo nám. 80Kč per hr. Open M-F 9am-midnight, Sa-Su 11am-midnight.

Post Office: Jindřišská 14. Metro A, B: Můstek (☎21 13 15 20). Get stamps at window #11; letters and small parcels at windows #12-14; *Poste Restante* at window #17. To send large boxes go to booths #3-9. Open daily 7am-8pm. Address mail to be held: Nithya RAMAN, POSTE RESTANTE, Jindřišská 14, 110 00 Praha 1, Czech Republic.

▚ ACCOMMODATIONS

The hostel market is glutted and prices have stabilized around 270-420Kč per night. Most accommodations have 24hr. reception, and require check-in after 2pm, and check-out by 10am. Tourist season is July and August.

ACCOMMODATIONS AGENCIES

The going rate for apartments hovers around 600-1200Kč, depending on proximity to the city center. Instead of haggling, try a private agency. Ask where the nearest tram, bus, or metro stop is, and get details in writing. **Hello Travel Ltd.,** Senovážné nám. 3, arranges housing. Metro B: Nám Republiky. (☎24 21 26 47. 500-1500Kč per person in summer, 400-1200Kč off-season. Open M-F 8am-7pm.) **Ave.,** Hlavní nádraží, 2nd fl. of the station, offers rooms from 800Kč and books hostels from 300Kč. (☎24 22 35 21. Open daily 6am-11pm.)

HOSTELS

If you're schlepping a backpack in Hlavní nádraží or Holešovice, you *will* be bombarded by hostel runners trying to coerce you back to their hostel, which is often a university dorm that frees up from June to August; often you'll be offered transport to the room. It's best to phone the night before you arrive or at 10am when they know who's checking out in order to snag a bed.

Hostel Boathouse, Lodnická (☎/fax 402 10 76). From Hlavní nádraží, Karlovo nám., Staré Město, or the Charles Bridge, take tram #3 south toward Sídliště and get off at Černý Kůň (20min.). From Holešovice, take tram #17. From the tram stop, follow the yellow signs down to the river. As Věra the owner says, "This isn't a hostel; it's a crazy house." Call ahead; if they're full, she might find space. Breakfast 50Kč. Laundry. Min. stay 2 night. Dorms 290Kč.

Penzion v podzámčí, V podzámčí 27 (☎/fax 41 44 46 09). From Metro C: Budějovická, take bus #192 to the 3rd stop—ask the driver to stop at Nad Rybníky. Eva and her student staff make this the homiest hostel in Prague. Kitchen. Laundry 100Kč per load. Dorms 280Kč; doubles 640Kč; triples 900Kč.

Domov Mládeže, Dykova 20 (☎/fax 22 51 25 97 or 22 51 17 77), in Vinohrady. Metro A: Jiřího z Poděbrad; follow Nitranská and turn left on Dykova; it's 2 blocks down on the right. So peaceful you might forget you're in Prague. Dorms 430Kč; lone double 650Kč. Sister hostels: **Amadeus,** Slavojova 108/8. Metro C: Vyšehrad; descend the bridge to Čiklova, turn left, and it's on the left. **Máchova,** Máchova 11. Metro A: Nám. Míru; walk down Ruská and turn right on Máchova. **Košická,** Košická 12. Metro A: Nám. Míru.

Hostel U Melounu (At the Watermelon), Ke Karlovu 7 (☎/fax 24 91 83 22), in Nové Město. Metro C: I.P. Pavlova; follow Sokolská to Na Bojišti. Breakfast included. Dorms 380Kč; singles 450Kč; doubles 840Kč. 100Kč discount with ISIC.

Traveller's Hostels, in Staré Město. At all branches, breakfast is included and internet access is available (27Kč per 15min.). **Dlouhá 33** (☎24 82 66 62; fax 24 82 66 65). Metro B: Nám Republiky. Follow Revoluční toward the river, turn left on Dlouhá, on right. Unbeatable location. Dorms 350-380Kč; doubles 1100Kč; triples 1290Kč. **Husova 3** (☎24 21 53 26). Metro B: Národní třída; turn right on Spálená (which becomes Na Perštýně after Národní), and then Husova. Dorms 400Kč. **Křížovnická 7** (☎232 09 87). Metro A: Staroměstská. Dorms 230Kč. **Střelecký ostrov** (☎24 91 01 88), on an island off Most Legií. Metro B: Národní třída. 300Kč. **Růžová 5** (☎24 21 69 71). Metro C: Hlavní nádraží. Dorms 220Kč.

Pension Týn, Týnská 19 (☎/fax 24 80 83 33; backpacker@razdva.cz), near the Old Town. Metro A: Staroměstská. From Old Town Square, head down Dlouhá, bear right at Masná, and right onto Týnská. Conveniently located in the center of the Old Town. Dorms 400Kč; singles 1000Kč; doubles 1200Kč.

Strahov Complex, Vaníčkova 5 (☎52 71 90), west of center. Metro A: Dejvická; take bus #217 or 143 to Koleje Strahov. Strahov is known as "hostel ghetto"—10 concrete blocks, open all year. Singles 300Kč; doubles 440Kč. Students 180Kč a bed.

HOTELS AND PENSIONS

Budget hotels are now scarce. Beware of those that may try to bill you for a more expensive room than the one in which you stayed; some cheap establishments require reservations up to a month in advance, but many refuse them altogether. Call first, then confirm by fax with a credit card.

B&B U Oty (Ota's House), Radlická 188 (☎/fax 57 21 53 23), west of the center. Metro B: Radlická; exit left and go right 400m up the slope. Charming, English-speaking Ota will make your stay a joy. Singles 700Kč; doubles 770Kč; triples 990Kč; quads 1250Kč. One-night surcharge 100Kč.

Pension Unitas/Cloister Inn, Bartolomějská 9 (☎24 21 10 20), in the Old Town. Metro B: Národní třída; cross Národní, head down Na Perštýnw away from Tesco, and turn left on Bartolomějská. Beethoven once performed here, and Václav Havel was once incarcerated here. Breakfast included. Singles 1020Kč; doubles 1200Kč; triples 1650Kč.

Dům U krále Jiřího, Liliová 10 (☎22 22 09 25; email kral.jiri@telecom.cz), in the Old Town. Metro A: Staroměstská; exit onto Nám. Jana Palacha, walk down Křížovnická toward the Charles Bridge, turn left onto Karlova, and Liliová is the 1st right. Gorgeous rooms with private bath. Breakfast included. Singles 1700Kč, doubles 2900Kč; off season singles 1500Kč, doubles 2700Kč.

U Lilie, Liliová 15 (☎22 22 04 32; fax 22 22 06 41), in Old Town. Metro A: Staroměstská; follow directions to U krále Jiřího (above). TV. Breakfast included. Singles 1700Kč; doubles 3400Kč, with bath 4600Kč.

CAMPING

Campsites have taken over both the outskirts and the centrally located Vltava islands. Bungalows must be reserved in advance, but tent space is generally available without prior notice. Tourist offices sell a guide to sites near the city (15Kč).

Císařská louka, on a peninsula on the Vltava. Metro B: Smíchovské nádraží; then take tram #12 (dir: Hlubočepy) to Lihovar and go toward the river. Or, take the ferry from Smíchovské nádraží. **Caravan Park** (☎54 50 64) is near the ferry. 90-140Kč per tent, plus 95Kč per person. Singles 365Kč; doubles 630Kč; triples 945Kč. **Caravan Camping** (☎/fax 54 01 29) is near the tram. 90-120Kč per tent, 110Kč per person.

Sokol Troja, Trojská 171 (☎/fax 83 85 04 86), north of the center in the Troja district. Metro C: Nádraží Holešovice; take bus #112 to Kazanka, the 4th stop. Tents 105-130Kč, plus 100Kč per person. Dorms 250Kč; bungalows 230Kč per person.

🍴 FOOD

The basic rule is that the nearer you are to the downtown the more you'll pay; away from the center, you can get traditional Czech fare such as pork, cabbage, dumplings, and a half-liter of beer for 50Kč. Check your bill carefully; you'll pay for everything the waiter brings to the table. Outlying Metro stops become markets in the summer. **Tesco,** Národní třída 26, has **groceries** next to Metro B: Národní třída. (Open M-F 7am-8pm, Sa 8am-7pm, Su 9am-7pm.) Look for the **daily market** at the intersection of Havelská and Melantrichova in Staré Město.

Universal, V jirchářích 6 (☎24 91 81 82), in Nové Město. Metro B: Národní třída; turn left onto Spálená and right on Myslíkova, then right on Křemencova. A transplanted California-style eatery with huge, fresh salads 97-143Kč. Open daily 11:30am-1am.

Velryba (The Whale), Opatovická 24 (☎24 91 23 91), in Nové Město. Metro B: Národní třída; exit to left, right onto Ostrovní. Relaxed cafe-restaurant with a chic gallery in back. International and Czech dishes (38-155Kč). Open daily 11am-2am.

Bar bar, Všehrdova 17 (☎53 29 41), in Malá Strana. Metro A: Malostranská; follow tram tracks down Letenská, Malostranské nám., and Karmelitská; turn left on Všehrdova after the museum. The eatery has a good vibe, good music, and 40 varieties of good whiskey (from 55Kč). Open daily noon-midnight.

U Špirků, Kožná ulička 12 (☎24 23 84 20), in the Old Town. Metro A: Staroměstská; with your back to astronomical clock on Staroměstské náměstí, go down Melantrichova and take first left onto Kožná. Some of the city's best and cheapest food in a spacious pub. Main dishes 89-138Kč. Open daily 11am-midnight.

Lotos, Platnéřská 13 (☎232 23 90). Metro A: Staroměstská. Exit the Metro onto the corner of Kaprova and Valentinská. Turn left down Valentinská away from the Jewish cemetery, then right onto Platnéřská. Vegetarian restaurant that deserves applause for its Czech soups (23-28Kč). 0.5L Pilsner 33Kč. Open daily 11am-10pm.

Restaurace U Pravdů, Žitná 15 (☎29 95 92). Metro B: Karlovo nám. A deservedly popular Czech lunch spot, where spillover from the dining room is seated in the beer garden. Main dishes 80-149Kč. Open M-F 10am-11pm, Sa-Su 11am-11pm.

LATE-NIGHT EATING

4:45am. Charles Bridge. Lávka's house disco beat is still pumping ferociously, but all you can hear is your stomach growling. Don't go home hungry—grab a *párek v rohlíku* (hot dog) or a *smažený sýr* (fried cheese sandwich) from a vendor on Václavské nám., or a gyros from a stand on Spálená or Vodičkova. **Radost FX,** Bělehradská 120, is a late-night veggie cafe. (☎24 25 47 76. Metro C: I.P. Pavlova. Open Su-Th 11am-late, F-Sa 11am-later.) **Iron Door,** Michalská 13., provides trendy atmosphere and an international menu. (Kitchen open daily until 3am.)

CAFES

When Prague journalists are bored, they churn out yet another "Whatever happened to cafe life?" feature. The answer: it turned into *čajovna* (teahouse) culture.

U malého Glena, Karmelitská 23 (☎535 81 15). Metro A: Malostranská; take tram #12 to Malostranské nám. With their motto "Eat, Drink, Drink Some More," they've got consumption down to a science. Killer margaritas 80Kč. Nightly jazz or blues 9pm. Cover 60-120Kč. Open daily 10am-2am; Su brunch 10am-3pm.

Dobrá Čajovna U Čajovníka (Good Tearoom), Boršov 2. Metro A: Staroměstská; follow Křížovnická past Charles Bridge, bear left onto Karoliny Světlé. Knock at the door. 90 teas from all over the world (12-150Kč). Open M-Sa 10am-midnight, Su noon-midnight.

Jazz Café 14, Opatovická 14 (☎24 92 00 39). Metro B: Národní třída. Perpetually filled with smoke and twentysomethings. No live jazz, but photos of Louis and Miles, along with recordings just as good. Snacks (30Kč) and drinks (16Kč). Open daily noon-11pm.

The Globe Coffeehouse, Pštrossova 6 (☎24 91 62 64). Tasty black coffee (20Kč), gazpacho (35Kč), and fresh fruit smoothies (60Kč), as well as plenty of English speakers trying to make a love connection. Open Su-Th 10am-midnight, F-Sa 10am-1am.

SIGHTS

The only Central European city left entirely unscathed by either natural disaster or WWII, Prague at its center is a well-preserved combination of medieval alleys and Baroque buildings. Central Prague is best explored on foot. Don't leave without wandering the back alleys of **Josefov,** exploring the hills of **Vyšehrad,** and getting lost in the maze of **Malá Strana's** streets.

NEW TOWN (NOVÉ MĚSTO)

Established in 1348 by Charles IV, Nové Město is not exactly new. Its age, however, is not readily apparent; its wide boulevards and sprawling squares seem hundreds of years ahead of their time.

WENCESLAS SQUARE (VÁCLAVSKÉ NÁMĚSTÍ). Not so much a square as a broad boulevard running through the center of Nové Město, Wenceslas Square owes its name to the Czech ruler and saint **Wenceslas** (Václav), whose statue sits in front of the **National Museum** (Národní muzeum). At the northern end of Wenceslas Square, near the Můstek Metro station, Art Nouveau design is expressed in everything from lampposts to windowsills. The glass **Radio Prague Building,** behind the National Museum, was the scene of a battle during the Prague Spring, as citizens tried to protect the radio studios from Soviet tanks with a human barricade. *(Metro A, C: Muzeum.)*

FRANCISCAN GARDENS AND VELVET REVOLUTION MEMORIAL. Perhaps if the Franciscans took a break from talking to the birds, they could divulge how they managed to preserve the serene **rose garden** (Františkánská zahrada) in the heart of Prague's bustling commercial district. *(Metro A, B: Můstek; Metro B: Národní třída. Enter through the arch at Jungmannova and Národní. Open daily mid-Apr. to mid-Sept. 7am-10pm; mid-Sept. to mid-Oct. 8am-8pm; mid-Oct. to mid-Apr. 8am-7pm. Free.)* Under the arcades halfway down Národní třída stands a memorial to the hundreds of Prague's citizens beaten on November 17, 1989 during the Velvet Revolution.

THE DANCING HOUSE. Built by American architect Frank Gehry of Guggenheim-Bilbao fame (see p. 888), the undulating building at the corner of Resslova and Rašínovo nábřeží is called Fred and Ginger by Anglophones and the Dancing House (Taneční dům) by Czechs. *(Metro B: Karlovo nám.)*

MUNICIPAL HOUSE. By far the most impressive Art Nouveau building in the city, the Municipal House (Obecní dům) captures the opulence of Prague's 19th-century cafe culture. *(Nám. Republiky 5. Metro B: Nám. Republiky. Open daily 10am-6pm.)*

OLD TOWN (STARÉ MĚSTO)

Settled in the 10th century, Staré Město remains a labyrinth of narrow roads and alleys. It's easy to get lost, but accepting the inevitable is the best way to appreciate the neighborhood's charm.

CHARLES BRIDGE (KARLŮV MOST). Thronged with tourists and the hawkers who prey on them, this bridge is easily Prague's most recognizable landmark. Five years ago, the bridge's vendors peddled Red Army gear and dodgy black market currency deals; today, it's watercolors of the bridge and other junk. The foundation stone of the bridge was laid at 5:31am on July 9, 1357, the most significant astrological point for Leo, the mascot of Bohemia.

OLD TOWN SQUARE (STAROMĚSTSKÉ NÁMĚSTÍ). The heart of Staré Město is Old Town Square, surrounded by no fewer than eight magnificent towers. Next to the grassy knoll, Old Town Hall (Staroměstská radnice) is the multi-facaded building with a bit blown off the front. The building was partially demolished by the Nazis in the final week of WWII, receiving Prague's only visible damage from the war. *(Open in summer daily 9am-5:30pm. 30Kč, students 15Kč.)* Crowds gather on the hour to watch the wonderful astronomical clock *(orloj)* chime with its procession of apostles, a skeleton, and a thwarted Turk. *(Metro A: Staroměstská; Metro A,B: Můstek. Clock animated until 9pm.)* The Czech Republic's most famous martyred theologian, Jan Hus, hovers over Old Town Square in bronze effigy. Opposite the Old Town Hall, the spires of Týn Church (Matka Boží před Týnem) rise above a mass of medieval homes. The famous astronomer Tycho de Brahe is buried inside—he overindulged at one of Emperor Rudolf's lavish dinner parties, where it was unacceptable to leave the table unless the Emperor himself did so. When poor Tycho de Brahe needed to go, he was forced to stay seated, and his bladder burst.

GOLTZ-KINSKÝ PALACE. The flowery 14th-century Goltz-Kinský Palace is the finest of Prague's Rococo buildings. It is also the official birthplace of Soviet communism in the Czech Republic: on February 21, 1948, Klement Gottwald declared communism victorious from its balcony. *(On Staroměstské nám. at the corner of Dlouhá, next to Týn Church. Open Tu-F 10am-5pm; closes early in summer for daily concerts.)*

POWDER TOWER. (Prašná brána). The gothic Powder Tower looms at the edge of Nám. Republiky as the entrance to Staré Město. Of the eight original city gates, this is the only one that remains. After its stint as royal fortification, it was used primarily for gunpowder storage. A small history exhibit is inside, but forego it for a climb to the top. *(Metro B: Nám. Republiky. Open daily Apr.-Sept. 10am-6pm.)*

JOSEFOV

Metro A: Staroměstská. ☎ 231 71 91. Synagogues and museum open Su-F 9am-6pm. Closed for Jewish holidays. All sights except New Synagogue 450Kč, students 330Kč. New Synagogue 200Kč, students 140Kč. Museum only 280Kč, students 200Kč.

Prague's historic Jewish neighborhood and the oldest Jewish settlement in Europe, Josefov lies north of Staromětstské nám., along Maiselova and several sidestreets. In 1180, Prague's citizens built a 12-foot wall around the area. The closed city bred legends, many focusing on **Rabbi Loew ben Bezalel** (1512-1609) and his legendary golem—a mud creature that supposedly came to life to protect Prague's Jews. For the next 500 years, the city's Jews were exiled to this cramped ghetto, and were deported by the Nazis to Terezín (see p. 946.)

THE SYNAGOGUES. The **Maisel Synagogue** (Maiselova synagoga) exhibits treasures from the extensive collections of the Jewish Museum. *(On Maiselova, between Široká and Jáchymova.)* Turn left down Široká to reach the 16th-century **Pinkas Synagogue** (Pinkasova synagoga), converted in 1958 into a sobering memorial to the 77,000 Czech Jews killed in the Holocaust. Backtrack up Široká and go left on Maiselova to see the oldest operating synagogue in Europe, the 700-year-old **Old-New Synagogue** (Staronová synagoga). Further up Široká on Dušní is the ornate Moorish interior of the **Spanish Synagogue** (Španělská synagoga).

OLD JEWISH CEMETERY AND CEREMONY HALL. The Old Jewish Cemetery (Starý židovský hřbitov) remains Josefov's most popular attraction. Between the 14th and 18th centuries, 20,000 graves were laid in 12 layers. Rabbi Loew is buried by the wall directly opposite the entrance. *(At the corner of Široká and Žatecká.)* Originally a ceremonial hall for the Jewish Burial Society, Ceremony Hall (Obřadní dům), it now houses the renowned exhibit, "Children's Drawings from Terezín: 1942-44;" most of the young artists died at Auschwitz. *(On Červená, just off Maiselova.)*

LESSER TOWN (MALÁ STRANA)

The seedy hangout of criminals and counter-revolutionaries for nearly a century, the cobblestone streets of Malá Strana have become the most prized real estate on either side of the Vltava. Malá Strana is centered around **Malostranské nám.** and its center-piece, the Baroque **St. Nicholas' Cathedral** (Chrám sv. Mikuláš), with a towering dome that is one of Prague's most notable landmarks. *(Metro A: Malostranská; then follow Leten-ská to Malostranské nám. Open daily 9am-4pm. 45Kč, students 15Kč.)* Along Letenská, a wooden gate opens through a 10-meter wall into the beautiful **Wallenstein Garden** (Valdštejnská zahrada), one of Prague's best-kept secrets. *(Letenská 10. Metro A: Malos-transká. Open daily May-Sept. 9am-7pm; Mar. 21-Apr. and Oct. 10am-6pm.)* Opposite the Malostranská metro station, a plaque hidden in a lawn constitutes the **Charousková Memorial,** the only monument to those slain in the 1968 Prague Spring. Unlike other churches in Prague, the modest **Church of Our Lady Victorious** (Kostel Panna Marie Vítězná) is not notable for its exterior but for the famous wax statue of the **Infant Jesus of Prague** inside, said to bestow miracles on the faithful. *(Metro A: Malostranská; then follow Letenská through Malostranské nám. and continue onto Karmelitská. Open M-F 8:30am-6:30pm, Sa 7:30am-8pm, Su 9am-9pm; off-season same but Su 9am-8pm. Free.)*

PRAGUE CASTLE (PRAŽSKÝ HRAD)

Metro A: Hradčanská. Open daily Apr.-Oct. 9am-5pm; Nov.-May 9am-4pm. Buy tickets oppo-site St. Vitus's Cathedral. Three-day ticket valid at Royal Crypt, Cathedral, and Powder Towers, Old Royal Palace, and Basilica of St. George. 120Kč, students 60Kč.

Prague Castle has been the seat of the Bohemian government since its founding 1000 years ago. From the metro station, cross the tram tracks and turn left onto Tychonova, which leads to the newly renovated **Royal Summer Palace** (Královský letohrádek). The main **castle entrance** is at the other end of the 1534 **Royal Garden** (Královská zahrada) in front of the palace, across the **Powder Bridge** (Prašný most). Before touring the castle, pass through the main gate to explore the **Šternberský Pal-ace,** home of the National Gallery's European art collection. *(Open Tu-Su 10am-6pm. 90Kč, students 40Kč.)*

ST. VITUS' CATHEDRAL (KATEDRÁLA SV. VÍTA). Inside the castle walls stands Prague Castle's centerpiece, the colossal St. Vitus' Cathedral, which may look Gothic but in fact was only finished in 1929—600 years after construction began. The cathedral's stained-glass windows were created by some of the most gifted Czech artists; Alphonse Mucha's brilliant depiction of St. Ludmila and Wenceslas is the most recognizable and haunting. To the right of the high altar stands the **tomb of sv. Jan Nepomucký,** 3m of solid, glistening silver that weighs 1800kg. In the main church, the walls of **St. Wenceslas's Chapel** (Svatováclavská kaple) are lined with precious stones and a painting cycle depicting the legendary saint. Climb the 287 steps of the **Cathedral Tower** for the best view of the city.

OLD ROYAL PALACE (STARÝ KRÁLOVSKÝ PALÁC). The Old Royal Palace, to the right of the cathedral behind the Old Provost's House and the statue of St. George, houses the lengthy expanse of the **Vladislav Hall,** which once hosted jousting com-petitions. Upstairs is the **Chancellery of Bohemia,** where on May 23, 1618, angry Protestants flung two Habsburg officials (and their secretary) through the win-dows, triggering Europe's extraordinarily bloody Thirty Years' War.

ST. GEORGE'S BASILICA (BAZILIKA SV. JIŘÍ) AND ENVIRONS. Behind the cathedral and across the courtyard from the Old Royal Palace stand the Romanesque St. George's Basilica and its adjacent convent. The convent houses the **National Gallery of Bohemian Art** (Klášter sv. Jiří), with art ranging from Gothic to Baroque. *(Open Tu-Su 10am-6pm. 90Kč, students 40Kč.)* The palace street **Jiřská** begins to the right of the basilica. Halfway down, the **Golden Lane** (Zlatá ulička) heads off to the right; alchemists once worked here, and Kafka later lived at #22.

MUSEUMS

Prague's magnificence isn't best reflected in its museums, which often have striking facades but mediocre collections. But the city has many rainy days, and it has a few public museums that shelter interesting and quirky collections. **House of the Golden Ring** (Dům u zlatého prstenu), Týnská 6, behind Týn Church, houses an astounding collection of 20th-century Czech art. (☎ 24 82 80 04. Metro A: Staroměstská. Open Tu-Su 10am-6pm. 60Kč, students 30Kč; 1st Tu of each month free.) The National Gallery (Národní galerie) is spread around nine different locations; the notable Šternberský palác and Klášter sv. Jiří are in the Prague Castle. St. Agnes' Cloister (Klášter sv. Anežky) is the other major branch of the National Gallery, well worth seeing for its collection of 19th-century Czech art. St. Agnes', however, is undergoing renovation, and its collection has been moved into the **Trade Fair Palace and the Gallery of Modern Art** (Veletržní palác a Galerie moderního umění), which generally displays 20th-century Czech art. (Dukelských hrdinů 47. Metro C: Vltavská. ☎ 24 30 11 11. Open Tu-W and F-Su 10am-6pm, Th 10am-9pm. 90Kč, students 40Kč.) The **Czech Museum of Fine Arts** (České muzeum výtvarných umění), Celetná 34, itself one of Prague's best examples of Cubist architecture, contains a collection of Czech Cubism. (☎ 24 21 17 31. Metro A: Nám. Republiky. Open Tu-Su 10am-6pm. 40Kč, students 10Kč.)

🎵 🎭 ENTERTAINMENT AND NIGHTLIFE

For concerts and performances, consult *The Prague Post*, *Threshold*, or *Do města-Downtown* (the latter two are free at many cafes and restaurants). Most performances start at 7pm and offer unsold tickets 30min. before. Between mid-May and early June, the **Prague Spring Festival** draws musicians from around the world. For tickets (400-3500Kč), try **Bohemia Ticket International**, Malé nám. 13, next to Čedok. (☎ 24 22 78 32. Open M-F 9am-5pm, Sa 9am-2pm.) The **National Theater** (Národní divadlo), Národní třída 2/4, features drama, opera, and ballet. (☎ 24 90 14 19. Metro B: Národní třída. Tickets 100-1000Kč. Box office open M-F 10am-6pm, Sa-Su 10am-12:30pm and 3-6pm, and 30min. before performances.)

NIGHTLIFE

The most authentic way to experience Prague at night is in an alcoholic fog. With some of the best beers in the world on tap, pubs and beerhalls are understandably the city's favorite form of nighttime entertainment. Prague is not a clubbing city; the city's many excellent jazz and rock clubs are more popular. Otherwise, you can always retreat to the Charles Bridge to sing along with aspiring Britpop guitarists into the wee hours. The monthly *Amigo* (39Kč) is the most thorough guide to gay life in the Czech Republic and Slovakia, with a lot in English. *Gayčko* (59Kč) is a glossier piece of work mostly in Czech.

    🏠 **U Fleků**, Křemencova 11 (☎ 24 91 51 18). Metro B: Národní třída; turn right on Spálená, away from Národní, right on Myslíkova, and right on Křemencova. The oldest brewhouse in Prague (1491). A steep 50Kč per 0.4L of beer. Open daily 9am-11pm.

ABSINTHE MAKES THE HEART GROW FONDER

Shrouded in Bohemian mystique and taboo, this translucent turquoise fire water is a force to be reckoned with. Despite being banned in all but three countries this century due to allegations of opium-lacing and fatal hallucinations, Czechs have had a long love affair with absinthe. It has been the mainstay spirit of the Prague intelligentsia since Kafka's days, and during WWII every Czech adult was rationed a half-liter of it per month. Today, backpackers (who apparently will drink anything) have discovered the liquor, which at its strongest can be 160 proof. The bravest and most seasoned ex-pats sip it on the rocks, but for the most snapshot-worthy ritual douse a spoonful of sugar in the alcohol, torch it with a match until the sugar caramelizes and the alcohol burns off, and dump the residue into your glass.

HEADING EAST

Roxy, Dlouhá 33 (cell ☎0603 35 699 27 78). Metro B: Nám. Republiky; walk up Revoluční toward the river and turn left on Dlouhá. Hip locals and in-the-know tourists come here for experimental DJs and endless dancing. Cover from 150-200Kč. Open July-Aug. daily 9pm-late; Sept.-June Tu-Su 9pm-late.

Kozička (The Little Goat), Kozí 1 (☎24 81 83 08). Metro A: Staroměstské; take Dlouhá from the square and take a left onto Kozí. This cellar bar is always packed; you'll know why after your first 25Kč 0.5L of Krušovice. Open M-F noon-4am, Sa-Su 4pm-4am.

Iron Door, Michalská 13. Metro B: Národní třída; go down Spálená, turn right onto Národní, left onto Perlová, through the intersection. A trendy nightspot that serves everything from Czech favorites to sushi. Beer 30Kč. Kitchen open daily till 3am.

Vinárna U Sudu, Vodičkova 10 (☎22 23 22 07). Metro A, B: Můstek; cross Václavské nám. to Vodičkova, follow the curve left, and it's on your left. Infinite labyrinth of cellars. Red wine 110Kč per 1L. Open M-F 11am-midnight, Sa-Su 2pm-midnight.

Újezd, Újezd 18 (☎53 83 62). Metro B: Národní třída; exit onto Národní, turn left toward the river, cross the Legií bridge, continue straight on Vítězná, turn right on Újezd. Mecca of mellowness. DJ or live acid jazz 3 times a week. Beer 22Kč. Open daily 11am-4am.

Molly Malone's, U obecního dvora 4. Metro A: Staroměstská; turn right on Kližonvická away from the Charles Bridge, turn right after Nám. Jana Palacha on Široká, which veers left and becomes Vězeňská, and turn left at the end. Staropramen 30Kč; pint of Guinness 70Kč (cheaper than in Ireland). Open Su-Th noon-1am, F-Sa noon-2am.

U střelce, Karolíny Světlé 12 (☎24 23 82 78). Metro B: Národní třída. Under the archway on the right. Gay club that pulls a diverse crowd for its F and Sa night cabarets. Cover 80Kč. Open W, F, Sa 9:30pm-5am.

Radost FX, Bělehradská 120 (☎25 69 98). Metro C: I.P. Pavlova. Heavily touristed, but still plays bad-ass techno, jungle, and house music. Hi-tech laser lights, Nintendo and twistedly creative drinks (sex with an alien 140Kč) *will* expand your clubbing horizons. Cover 80-150Kč. Open M-Sa 10pm-dawn.

🚌 DAYTRIPS FROM PRAGUE

TEREZÍN (THERESIENSTADT)

The bus from Prague's Florenc station (1hr., every 1-2hr., 59Kč) stops by the central square, where the tourist office sells a 29Kč map. (Open daily until 6pm.)

In 1941, Terezín became a concentration camp for Jews—by 1942, the entire prewar civilian population had been evacuated. Nazi propaganda films successfully touted the area as an almost idyllic spa resort where Jews were "allowed" to educate their young, partake in arts and recreation, and live a "fulfilling" life. In reality, 35,000 died here; 85,000 others were transported to other death camps, primarily Auschwitz. **The Ghetto Museum,** on Komenského in town, sets Terezín in the wider Nazi context. (☎ (0416) 78 25 77. Open daily Apr.-Sept. 9am-6pm; Oct.-Mar. 9am-5:30pm. 130Kč, students 100Kč; including Small Fortress 150Kč, 110Kč.) East of the town and across the river sits the **Small Fortress** (Malá Pevnost). (Open daily Apr.-Sept. 8am-6pm; Oct.-Mar. 8am-4:30pm.) The furnaces and autopsy lab at the Jewish cemetery and crematorium are as they were 50 years ago. Men should cover their heads. (Open Mar.-Nov. Su-F 10am-5pm.)

KUTNÁ HORA

Take a bus (1½hr., 6 per day, 46Kč) from Prague's Florenc station, then walk or take a local bus to Sedlec (2km) and follow the signs for the chapel.

East of Prague, the former mining town of Kutná Hora (Mining Mountain) has a history as morbid as the bone church that has made it famous. After 13th-century monks sprinkled soil from the Biblical Golgotha Cemetery on Kutná Hora's own cemetery, the rich and superstitious grew quite keen to be buried there, and it soon became overcrowded. In a fit of whimsy, the monk in charge began designing flowers out of pelvi and crania. František Rint eventually completed the project in 1870 with flying butt-bones, femur crosses, and a grotesque chandelier made from every bone in the human body. (Open daily Apr.-Oct. 8am-6pm; Nov.-Mar. 9am-noon and 1-4pm. 30Kč, students 15Kč.)

ČESKÝ KRUMLOV
☎ 0337

The worst part about Český Krumlov is leaving. Winding medieval streets, cobblestoned promenades, and Bohemia's second-largest castle make the gorgeous, UNESCO-protected town of Český Krumlov one of the most popular spots in Eastern Europe. The stone courtyards of the **castle,** perched high above the town, are free to the public. Two tours cover different parts of the lavish interior, including a frescoed ballroom, a splendid Baroque theater, and Renaissance-style rooms. The **galleries of the crypts** showcase local artists' sculptures and ceramics. Ascend the 162 steps of the **tower** for a fabulous view. (☎71 16 87. Castle open June-Aug. Tu-Su 9am-6pm; May and Sept. Tu-Su 9am-5pm; Apr. and Oct. Tu-Su 9am-4pm. 130Kč, students 65Kč. Tower open daily May-Sept. 9am-6pm, Oct. and Apr. 11am-3pm.; 30Kč, students 20Kč. Crypts open May-Oct. Tu-Su 10am-5pm, July-Aug. also open M 10am-5pm; 30Kč, students 20Kč.) The Austrian painter Egon Schiele (1890-1918) lived in Český Krumlov for a while—until the citizens ran him out for painting burghers' daughters in the nude. Decades later, the **Egon Schiele International Cultural Center,** Široká 70-72, displays his work along with paintings by other 20th-century Central European artists. (☎70 40 11. Open daily 10am-6pm. 120Kč, students 60Kč.) Borrow an **inner tube** from your hostel to spend a lazy day drifting down the Vltava, or hike up into the hills to go horseback riding. At night., throw 'em back with live snakes at **U Hada** (Snake Bar), Rybarška 37 (open daily 7pm-3am) or **U baby,** Rooseveltova 66 (☎712 300; open daily 6pm-late).

From the station, head to the upper street (near stops 20-25), turn right (with the station to your back), follow the small dirt path that veers left and heads uphill, turn right on Kaplická, cross the highway at the light, and head straight onto Horní, which brings you to Nám. Svornosti, where the **tourist office** in the town hall books pension rooms (from 600Kč) as well as cheaper private rooms. (☎71 16 50. Open daily 9am-6pm.) To get to the awesome **U vodníka,** Po vodě 55, or **Krumlov House,** Rooseveltova 68, follow the directions above from the station and turn left onto Rooseveltova after the light (just before the bridge). From there, follow the signs to U vodníka or continue down the street to Krumlov House. (☎71 19 35; email vodnik@ck.bohem-net.cz. Bike rental 200Kč per day. Dorms 200Kč; doubles 500Kč.) Get **groceries** at **SPAR,** Linecká 49. (Open M-Sa 7am-6pm, Su 9am-6pm.)

BUDAPEST
☎ 01

FORINTS (FT, OR HUF)

US$1 = 290 FORINTS (FT, OR HUF)	100FT = US$0.34
CDN$1 = 200FT	100FT = CDN$0.51
UK£1 = 430FT	100FT = UK£0.24
IR£1 = 330FT	100FT = IR£0.30
AUS$1 = 170FT	100FT = AUS$0.60
NZ$1 = 120FT	100FT = NZ$0.80

Budapest (pop. 1,885,000) doesn't feel very Hungarian. While the rest of the country seems to linger in a slower, friendlier state, Budapest speeds along, whirling and honking through its crowded streets and frantically hopping among hip nightclubs, towering apartment buildings, and neon-bedecked Western companies, periodically pausing in a Turkish bath for a deep breath (but not too deep–Őoh, the pollution). Cosmopolitan and confident, Budapest is reassuming its place as a major European capital; even 40 years in a communist coma couldn't kill the spirit of this stronghold of Magyar nationalism. Endowed with an architectural majesty befitting of royalty, the noble dignity of the Hungarian capital is only enhanced by the now tattered landscape. No toyland Prague, Budapest is bigger, dirtier, and more vibrant—flashing lights and legions of tourists may have added tinsel to its tenacious streets, but beneath the kitsch, the indefatigable Budapest spirit charges on.

HEADING EAST

⌐ TRANSPORTATION

Flights: Ferihegy Airport (☎296 96 96; info ☎296 715; reservations toll-free ☎ (0680) 212 121, M-F 7:30am-6pm, Sa 7:30am-2pm). The cheapest way to the center is to take the Ferihegy/red **bus #93,** followed by the M3 to Köbanya-Kispest (50min.). Or, **Centrum buses** go to Erzsébet Tér (45min., every 30min. from 5:30am to 9pm). The **Airport Minibus** (☎296 85 55) serve the entire city 24hr.; call a day in advance for service to the airport. One-way 1500Ft; round trip 2500Ft.

Trains: ☎461 54 00 (24hr.). *Pályaudvar,* often abbreviated "pu.," means train station. Those under 26 get 33% off international tickets; show your ISIC and destination and tell the clerk "*diák*" (DEE-ak; student). The 3 main stations—**Keleti pu., Nyugati pu.,** and **Déli pu.**—are also Metro stops. Most international trains arrive at Keleti pu. To: **Berlin** (12hr., 1 per day, 20,400Ft; night train 15hr., 1 per day, 35,200Ft); **Prague** (7hr., 5 *EuroCity* per day, 13,564Ft; night train 9hr., 1 per day, 12,064Ft); and **Vienna** (3hr., 17 per day, 7150Ft). The daily **Orient Express** stops on its way from Paris to **Istanbul.**

Buses: ☎ 117 29 66. Most buses to Western Europe leave from **Volánbusz main station,** V, Erzsébet tér (international ticket office ☎317 25 62; fax 266 54 19). M1, 2, or 3: Deák tér. The international cashier upstairs will help you with Eurail passes and reservations. Open June M-F 6am-6pm, Sa 6:30am-4pm. Buses to most of Eastern Europe depart from **Népstadion,** Hungária körut 48/52 (☎252 18 96). M2: Népstadion. To: **Berlin** (14½hr., 2-5 per week, 16,110Ft); **Prague** (8½hr., 1-3 per week, 9900Ft); and **Vienna** (3½hr., 5 per week, 5190Ft).

Public Transportation: The **subway, buses,** and **trams** are inexpensive, convenient, and easy to navigate—by far the best way to get around town. Pick up free **route maps** from hostels, Tourinforms, and train stations. The **Metro** has 3 lines: yellow (M1), red (M2), and blue (M3). All public transport uses the same blue **tickets** (one-way on 1 line 95Ft), sold in Metro stations, *Trafik* shops, and by some street vendors. 1-day pass 740Ft, 3-day 1500Ft, 1-week 1850Ft, 2-week 2400Ft, 1-month 3600Ft. The Metro stops around midnight but gates lock at 11:45pm. Buses and trams stop at 11pm. **Night buses** whose numbers are marked with an "É" run along major routes midnight-5am. Bus #7É and 78É run along the same route as M2, and bus #14É runs along M3.

Car Rental: There are several reliable rental agencies in Budapest, charging roughly US$38-49 per day for the cheapest cars. Few agencies rent to those under 21. **Vista** (see **Tourist Offices,** below) can help you find the most affordable option.

Taxis: Prices should be approximately the following: 6am-10pm basic fee 200Ft, 200Ft per km or 50Ft per min. waiting; 10pm-6am basic fee 280Ft, 280Ft per km or 70Ft per min. waiting. Taxis ordered by phone are cheaper than those hailed on the street. **Budataxi** (☎233 33 33) runs for 100Ft per km on the street and 90Ft by phone.

◈ 🛈 ORIENTATION AND PRACTICAL INFORMATION

The formerly separate cities of Buda (BUDDHA) and Pest (PESHT), separated by the **Danube** river, have combined to form modern Budapest. On the west bank, **Buda** inspires countless artists with its hilltop citadel, trees, and cobblestoned **Castle District,** while **Pest,** on the east bank, is the heart of the modern city. Three bridges link the two halves: **Széchenyi lánchíd;** slender, white **Erzsébet híd;** and green **Szabadság híd. Moszkva tér** (Moscow Square), just down the northern slope of the Castle District, is Budapest's bus and tram transportation hub. One metro stop away toward Örs vezér tere, **Batthyány tér,** on the west bank opposite the **Parliament** (Országház) building, is the starting point of the **HÉV commuter railway.** Budapest's three **Metro** lines (M1, M2, and M3) converge at **Deák tér,** at the core of Pest's loosely concentric boulevards, next to the main international bus terminal at **Erzsébet tér.** Two blocks west toward the river lies **Vörösmarty tér.** As you face the statue of Mihály Vörösmarty, the main pedestrian shopping zone, **Váci u.,** is to the right.

Budapest is divided into 23 **districts;** "I" indicates Central Buda, while "V" means downtown Pest. Because many streets have shed their communist labels, an up-to-date **map** is essential; pick up a free one at American Express or Tourinform, or buy the *Belváros Idegenforgalmi Térképe* at any Metro stop (199Ft).

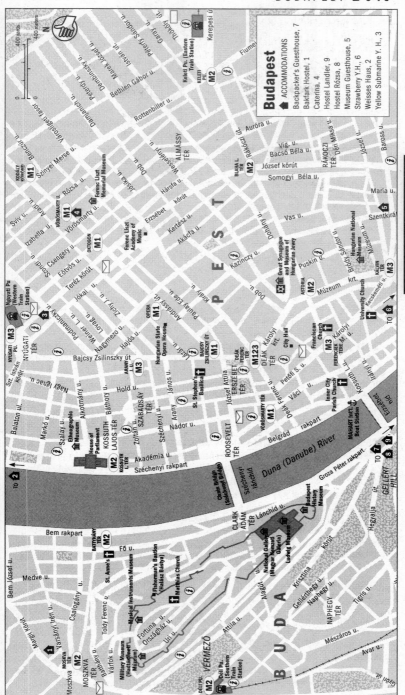

HEADING EAST

Budapest

▲ ACCOMMODATIONS
Backpacker's Guesthouse, 7
Bakfark Hostel, 1
Caterina, 4
Hostel Landler, 9
Hostel Rózsa, 8
Museum Guesthouse, 5
Strawberry Y.H., 6
Weisses Haus, 2
Yellow Submarine Y. H., 3

TOURIST, FINANCIAL, AND LOCAL SERVICES

Tourist Offices: At all tourist offices and metro stations, you can purchase the **Budapest Card** (Budapest Kártya). For 2800Ft, you get 2 days of public transportation, entrance to all museums, reduced rates on car rental and the airport minibus, and discounts at many shops and restaurants (3-day card 3400Ft). **Tourinform,** V, Sütő u. 2 (☎317 98 00; fax 317 95 78), off Deák tér behind McDonald's. M1, 2, 3: Deák tér. A veritable tourist temple and the best place for information about events, tours, and performances in Budapest. Open daily 8am-8pm. **Vista Travel Center: Visitor's Center,** Pauley Ede 7 (☎267 86 03), deals with city tourist information.

Budget Travel: Express, V, Zoltán út 10 (☎311 98 98). Offers same youth discounts as the train station. 10-30% off flights. Open M-Th 8am-4:30pm, F 8:30am-3pm.

Embassies and Consulates: Australia, XII, Királyhágó tér 8/9 (☎457 9777). M2: Déli pu., then bus #21 to Királyhágó tér. Open M-Th 9am-5pm, F 9am-2pm, Sa-Su 9am-noon. **Canada,** XII, Budakeszi út 32 (☎275 12 00). Take bus #158 from Moszkva tér to the last stop. Open M-F 9am-noon. **South Africa,** VII, Rákóczi út 1/3 (☎266 21 48). **UK,** V, Harmincad u. 6 (☎266 28 88), off the corner of Vörösmarty tér. M1: Vörösmarty tér. Open M-F 9:30am-noon and 2:30-4pm. **US,** V, Szabadság tér 12 (☎267 45 55; emergency ☎266 93 31). M2: Kossuth Lajos. Walk 2 blocks down Akademia and turn on Zoltán. Open M and W 8:30-11am, Tu and Th-F 8:30-10:30am. **New Zealand** and **Irish** nationals should contact the UK Embassy.

Currency Exchange: Magyar Külkereskedelmi Bank, V, Szent István tér 11 (☎269 09 22). M1, 2, 3: Deák tér, at the basilica's entrance. One of the few banks to give MC/Visa **cash advances** (no commission, Ft only) and cash **traveler's checks** in US$ (2% commission, US$20 minimum). Open M-Th 8am-4:30pm, F 8am-3pm.

American Express: V, Deák Ferenc u. 10 (☎235 43 30; fax 267 20 28). M1: Vörösmarty tér. Next to Hotel Kempinski. Open June-Sept. M-F 9am-6:30pm, Sa-Su 9am-5:30pm; Oct.-May M-F 9am-5:30pm, Sa 9am-2pm.

Luggage storage: At Keleti pu., 200Ft. Lockers are also available at Déli pu. and Nyugati pu. for 200Ft. Nyugati pu. has a 24hr. luggage desk in the waiting room next to the ticket windows. 140Ft per day. Open M and F-Sa 6am-8pm, Tu-Th and Su 6am-7pm.

Bi, Gay, Lesbian Services: Hotline (☎ (0630) 932 33 34; fax 351 20 15; http://ourworld.compuserve.com/homepages/budapest) is the best resource in town.

Laundromats: Irisz Szalon, V, Városház u. 3/5 (☎317 20 92). M3: Ferenciek tére. Wash 7kg 1100Ft; dry 450Ft per 15min. Open M-F 7am-7pm, Sa 7am-1pm.

EMERGENCY AND COMMUNICATIONS

Tourist Police Station: Kulföldiket Elenörzö Osztály (KEO), VI, Városligeti Fasor 46/48 (☎443 50 00). M1: Hősök tér. Walk 3 blocks up Dósza György út. Open Tu 8:30am-noon and 2-6pm, W 8:30am-1pm, Th 10am-6pm, F 8:30am-12:30pm.

24hr. Pharmacies: II, Frankel L. út 22 (☎212 44 06); III, Szentendrei út 2/A (☎388 65 28); IV, Pozsonyi u. 19 (☎389 40 79); VII, Rákóczi út 39 (☎314 36 95); IX, Boráras tér 3 (☎217 07 43); X, XII, Alkotás u. 1/B (☎355 46 91). At night, call the number on the door or ring the bell; you will be charged a slight fee for the service.

Medical Assistance: Falck Személyi Olvosi Szolgálat (SOS) KFT, II, Kapy út 49/B (☎200 01 00 and 275 15 35). English spoken. Ambulance service. First-aid is free for foreigners. Open 24hr. The US embassy has a list of English-speaking doctors.

Internet Access: Cybercafes litter the city, but computers still need to be reserved well ahead of time; 3hr. lines are not uncommon. **Telephone,** Petőfi Sandor u. 17. M1, 2, 3: Deák tér. 300Ft per 30min. Open M-F 9am-8pm, Sa 10am-3pm. **Vista Travel Center,** Panlay Ede u. 7 (☎268 0888; see **Tourist Offices,** p. 938). 11Ft. per min. Open M-F 8am-11pm, Sa-Su 10am-11pm. **Eckermann,** VI, Andrássy út 24 (☎374 40 76). M1: Opera. Free. Call 2-3 days ahead. Open M-Sa 8am-10pm, Su closed.

Post Office: V, Városház u. 18 (☎318 48 11). Pick up *Poste Restante* (Postán Mar) here. Open M-F 8am-8pm, Sa 8am-2pm. **Branches** at Nyugati pu. (☎312 12 00), VI, Teréz krt. 105/107. **Postal code:** 1052.

■ ACCOMMODATIONS

In July and August, the city fills with tourists; save yourself some blisters by phoning first or stashing your pack while you seek out a bed for the night. Travelers arriving at Keleti pu. enter a feeding frenzy as hostel solicitors elbow their way to tourists in order to hawk rooms. Be cautious, but keep an open mind—these hostels may be as good as anything else you'll find at the last minute.

ACCOMMODATION AGENCIES

Arrive early to secure the lower-priced rooms. Haggle and bring cash.

Budapest Tourist, I, Deli Pálaudrar (☎212 46 25). Well-established. Singles in Central Pest 5000-7000Ft; doubles 6000-10000Ft; triples 6000-12000Ft. Off-season prices considerably lower. Rents flats for stays longer than 1 week. 3000-7000Ft per day. Open M-F 9am-5pm.

IBUSZ, V, Ferenciek tér (☎485 27 00). M3: Ferenciek tér. Rents rooms at a base price plus 1050Ft per day. Doubles 3500Ft; triples 4500Ft; quads 5000Ft. Also rents centrally located Pest apartments with kitchen and bath. 1-bedroom doubles from 5000Ft; 2-bedroom triples and quads from 6000Ft. Open M-F 8:15am-6pm.

Non-Stop Hotel Service, V, Apáczai Csere J. u. 1 (☎318 48 48), M1: Vörösmarty tér. Tourist office and accommodation service for rooms in Pest. Singles 6000Ft; doubles from 7500Ft in summer, off-season 6000Ft; triples and quads from 8000Ft, 7000Ft. English spoken. Open 24hr.

YEAR-ROUND HOSTELS

Budapest's hostels are generally social centers, each with its own quirks. Many hostel accommodations, including university dorms, are now under the aegis of the Hungarian Youth Hostel Association, which operates from a small office in Keleti pu. Their representatives wear Hostelling International t-shirts and will—along with legions of competitors—accost you as soon as you get off the train, if not before. Theft is rampant in hostels. Always make sure that you keep your belongings in lockers when available, or take all valuables with you.

▨ Backpacker's Guesthouse, XI, Takács Menyhért u. 33 (☎/fax 385 89 46; email backpackguest@hotmail.com). From Keleti pu. or anywhere along Rákóczi út., take bus #7 or 7A toward Buda. Get off at Tétenyi u., walk back under the railway bridge, and make a sharp left. Then take the 3rd right; it's on the left. Laundry 1000Ft. Reception 24hr. Reserve 1 or 2 weeks in advance. 5- to 8-bed dorms 1600Ft; small dorm 1900Ft; doubles 2400Ft per person.

Station Guest House (HI), XIV, Mexikói út 36/B (☎221 88 64; email station@mail.matav.hu). From Keleti pu., take bus #7 1 stop to Hungária Körút, walk under the railway pass, and take a right onto Mexikói út. All rooms with private lockers. Internet access 20Ft per min. Breakfast 300Ft. Laundry 600Ft per 4kg. Reserve a day in advance. Attic 1400Ft, 1200 by 3rd night; 6- to 8-bed dorms 2000Ft, 1400Ft by 4th night; 2- to 3-bed dorms 2800Ft, 2200Ft by 4th night; 200Ft more for nonmembers.

Ananda Youth Hostel, IX, Alsoérdósor ut. 12 (☎322 0502; email anandyn@hotmail.com). Internet. Laundry. Reception 24hr. 8-bed dorms 2000Ft; doubles 3500Ft.

Yellow Submarine Youth Hostel, VI, Teréz Körút 56, 3rd fl. (☎/fax 331 98 96). Across from Nyugati pu. Bright, spacious rooms and friendly staff. Breakfast included. Laundry 500Ft wash, 500Ft dry. Check-out 9am, but luggage stored all day. 8-10-bed dorms 2200Ft; 4-bed dorms 3800Ft; doubles 7000Ft; 10% off with HI.

SUMMER HOSTELS

Many university dorms reinvent themselves as hostels in July and August. Conveniently accessible by tram, the majority are clustered around Móricz Zsigmond Körtér in district XI.

Hostel Bakfark, I, Bakfark u. 1/3 (☎343 0748). M2: Moszkva tér. From the Metro, walk along Margit krt. with Burger King to your right. Check-out 10am. Reservations recommended. Open June 15-Aug. 31. 4- to 6-bed dorms 2700Ft; 300Ft off with HI.

HEADING EAST

Hostel Landler, XI, Bartók Béla út 17 (☎463 36 21). Take bus #7 or 7A across the river and get off at Géllert. Laundry. Check-out 9am. Open July 5-Sept. 5. Singles 4800Ft; doubles 3200Ft; triples and quads 2900Ft; 10% off with HI.

Hostel Rózsa, XI, Bercsényi u. 28/30 (☎463 42 50). M2: Blaha Lujzatér. Continue on tram #4 and get off 3 stops after the river. Free transport from bus or train station. Laundry 160Ft, wash only. Open July-Sept. 5. Doubles 3200Ft. 10% off with HI.

Martos, XI, Stoczek u. 5/7 (☎463 37 76). From Keleti pu., take red bus #7 to Móricz Zsigmond Körtér and trek back 300m toward the river on Bartók Béla út. One of Buda's best deals, with cheap, clean rooms. Free internet and laundry. Check-out 9-10am. Singles 2500Ft; doubles, triples, and quads 1800Ft.

Strawberry Youth Hostels, IX, Ráday u. 43/45 (☎218 47 66), and Kinizsi u. 2/6 (☎217 30 33). M3: Kálvin tér. With Hotel Mercure to your right, walk down Vámház krt. Ráday is 1 block toward the river on the left. There's a "pub" downstairs. Free Keleti pu. pickup. Coin-operated laundry (400Ft wash). Check-out 10am. Open June 29-Sept. 1. Doubles 3200Ft; triples and quads 2900Ft. 10% off with HI.

GUEST HOUSES

Guest houses and rooms in private homes lend a personal touch for about the same price as an anonymous hostel bed. These should not be confused with pensions, or *panzió*, which are larger and rarely charge less than 4000Ft per person.

⌧ Museum Guesthouse, VIII, Mikszáth Kálmán tér 4, 1st fl. (☎318 95 08 or 318 21 95). M3: Kálvin tér. In the heart of a hopping bar scene. Internet 1000Ft per hr., free after 6pm. Laundry (1000Ft wash and dry). 500Ft locker and key deposit. Reception 24hr. Check-out 10am. Reserve the morning of your stay. All beds 1800Ft.

Caterina, VI, Andrássy út 47, 3rd fl., apt. #18, ring bell 11. (☎291 95 38; email caterina@mail.inext.hu). M1: Oktogon. Or, trams #4 and 6. TV in all rooms. Quiet hours after 10pm. Internet access 550Ft per 30min. Laundry 700Ft per 5kg. Reception 24hr. Check-out 9am. Lockout 10am-2pm. Reserve in advance by fax or email. Triple 2000Ft; 2-bed loft 2700Ft; dorm 2000Ft; 6-person room for groups US $10 per person.

CAMPING

For those undaunted by the commute, Budapest's two fully-loaded campgrounds by no means compromise comfort to the budget gods. For a full listing of Hungary's campsites, pick up the pamphlet *Camping Hungary*, available at tourist offices.

Zugligeti "Niche" Camping, XII, Zugligeti út 101 (☎/fax 200 83 46). Take bus #158 from Moszkva tér to the last stop. An easy commute to central Budapest, located right next to the János Negyi chairlift. Communal showers and a safe. 850Ft per person. Tents 500Ft; big tents 900Ft. Cars 700Ft. Electricity 500Ft.

Római Camping, III, Szentendrei út 189 (☎368 62 60). M2: Batthyány tér, then take the HÉV to Római fürdő and walk 100m toward the river. Communal showers and kitchen. Open mid-Apr. to mid-Oct. Tents 1950Ft; bungalows with cold water 1350-2000Ft. 10% of with HI.

🅒 FOOD

Even the most expensive restaurants in Budapest may fall within your budget, but eating at family joints can be tastier and more fun. A 10% tip is generally expected; another 10% if your meal is accompanied by live music. Explore the cafeterias beneath "Önkiszolgáló Étterem" signs for something greasy and cheap. For kicks, the **world's largest Burger King** is on Oktogon. The **Grand Market Hall,** IX, Fövamtér 1/3, is next to Szabadság híd (M3: Kálvin Tér).

⌧ Fatâl Restaurant, V, Váci út 67 (☎266 26 07). Packs them in for hearty Hungarian meals. Giant main dishes from 860Ft. Hugely popular with tourists, necessitating the red velvet rope and reservations-only policy. Open daily 11:30am-2am.

Marquis de Salade, VI, Hajós u. 43 (☎302 40 86). M3: Arany János. At the corner of Bajcsy-Zsilinszky út, 2 blocks from the Metro. Chic cuisine served by waiters clad in head-to-toe black. Main dishes 700-2200Ft. Open daily noon-midnight.

Marxim, II, Kisrókus u. 23 (☎316 02 31). M2: Moszkva tér. Walk along Margit krt. with your back to the castle-like building, then turn left down the industrial road. Communist-kitsch dishes served in barbed wire booths. Great pizzas 300-900Ft. Linger over your Cold War Cup ("ice-cream with frozen dreams and hopes," 300Ft) with a crowd of hip young people. Open M-F noon-1am, Sa noon-2am, Su 6pm-1am.

Gandhi, V, Vigyázó Ferenc u. 4 (☎269 16 25). A superior vegetarian restaurant, serving dishes without the fat, meat, and fried cheese of traditional Hungarian food, but also without its generous portions. Main dishes 860-1080Ft. Open M-Sa noon-10:30pm.

▐ CAFES

More than just a place to indulge in dessert and coffee, a cafe in Budapest is a living museum of a bygone era. Once the haunts of Budapest's literary, intellectual, and cultural elite as well as its political dissidents, the cafes now serve a history lesson filled with grandeur and rebellion along with its cheap and absurdly rich pastries.

▨ Művész Kávéház, VI, Andrássy út 29 (☎352 13 37). M1: Opera. Diagonally across from the Opera. The name means "artist cafe," and—unlike most remaining Golden Age coffee houses—the title fits. Enjoy a fabulous *Művész torta* (jam and hazelnut; 190Ft) and cappuccino (200Ft) on the terrace. Open daily 9am-midnight.

Cafe New York, VII, Erzsébet krt. 9-11 (☎322 38 49). M2: Blaha Lujza tér. Once the biggest swing club in Eastern Europe, this symbol of the city's *fin-de-siècle* Golden Age fell into disrepair under communism. The exterior still bears scars left by a Soviet tank. Ice cream and coffee (750-1150Ft). Pastries 300-550Ft. Open daily 10am-midnight.

◄► SIGHTS

In 1896, Hungary's 1000th birthday bash prompted the construction of what are today Budapest's most prominent sights—a testament to the optimism of a capital on the verge of its Golden Age. Among the works commissioned by the Habsburgs were **Heroes' Square** (Hősök tere), **Liberty Bridge** (Szbadság híd), and **Vajdahunyad Castle** (Vajdahunyad vár). The domes of **Parliament** (Országház) and **St. Stephen's Basilica** (Szent István Bazilika) are both 96m high—references to the historic date.

BUDA

Buda is older, more conservative, and more disjointed than its sister pest, but with the city's best parks, lush hills, and Danube islands, it is no less worth exploring. The **Castle District** lies atop **Castle Hill** and contains the bulk of Buda's sights.

CASTLE DISTRICT. Towering above the Danube, the **Castle District** has been razed three times in its 800-year history, most recently in 1945. With its winding, statue-filled streets, breathtaking views, and magnificent hodge-podge of architectural styles, the UNESCO-protected district now appears much as it did in Hapsburg times (though today it's much more touristed). Though bullet holes in the **castle** facade still recall the 1956 Uprising, the reconstructed palace today houses a number of fine museums (see **Museums**, p. 955). *(M1, 2, 3: Deák tér. From the Metro, take bus #16 across the Danube. Get off just after the river at the base of the Széchenyi Chain Bridge and take the funicular (sikló) up the hill. 300Ft up, 250Ft down. Runs daily 7:30am-10:30pm; closed 2nd and 4th Monday of the month. Or, take the Metro to M2: Moszkva tér, walk up to the hill on Várfok u., and enter the Castle at Vienna Gate, Becsi kapu.)*

MATTHIAS CHURCH AND FISHERMAN'S BASTION. The multi-colored roof of the neo-Gothic **Matthias Church** (Mátyás templom), which was converted into a mosque when Ottoman armies seized Buda in 1541 (and re-converted 145 years later when the Hapsburgs defeated the Turks), is one of the most-photographed sights in Budapest. Descend the stairway to the right of the altar to enter the **crypt** and **treasury**. *(From the cable car, turn right on Színház and veer left at Tárnok u. From Vienna Gate, walk straight down Fortuna u. High mass with full orchestra and choir Sunday 7am, 8:30am, 10am, noon, and 8:30pm; come early for a seat. Organ concerts most Fridays at 7:30pm. Treasury open daily 9:30am-5:30pm. 200Ft.)* Behind St. Matthias Church is the grand equestrian monument of King Stephen bearing his trademark double cross in front of the **Fisherman's Bastion** (Halászbástya). The view across the Danube from the squat, fairy-tale **tower** is stunning. *(M free; Tu-Su 200Ft.)*

GELLÉRT HILL. The Pope sent Bishop Gellért to the coronation of King Stephen, the first Christian Hungarian monarch, to assist in the conversion of the Magyars; those unconvinced by his message gave the hill its name (Gellért-hegy) by hurling the good bishop to his death from the top. The **Liberation Monument** (Szabadság Szobor), created to honor Soviet soldiers who died liberating Hungary, looks over Budapest from atop the hill. The view from the top of the adjoining **Citadel,** built as a symbol of Habsburg power after the foiled 1848 revolution, is especially spectacular at night. At the base of the hill sits the **Gellért Hotel and Baths** (see **Baths,** p. 955), Budapest's most famous Turkish Bath. *(To ascend the hill, take tram #18 or 19 to Hotel Gellért. Follow Szabó Verjték u. to Jubileumi Park, continuing on the marked paths to the summit. Or, take bus #27 to the top; get off at Búsuló Juhász and walk another 5min. to the peak.)*

PEST

The winding streets of Pest were constructed in the 19th century and today host European chain stores, corporations and banks, and myriad monuments. The old **Inner City** (Belváros), rooted in the pedestrian **Váci u.** and **Vörösmarty tér,** is a crowded tourist strip with street vendors hawking overpriced wares.

PARLIAMENT. Pest's riverbank sports a string of luxury hotels leading up to its magnificent Neo-Gothic **Parliament** (Országház), modeled after Britain's. The massive structure has always been too big for Hungary's government; today, the legislature uses only 12% of the building. *(M2: Kossuth Lajos tér. ☎ 268 49 04. English tours daily at 10am and M-F also 2pm. Purchase tickets at gate #10; enter at gate #12. Reservations recommended. 900Ft, students 500Ft.)*

ST. STEPHEN'S BASILICA. The city's largest church (Sz. István Bazilika) was decimated by Allied bombs in WWII. Its neo-Renaissance facade remains under reconstruction, but the ornate interior continues to attract both tourists and worshippers. The **Panorama Tower** offers an amazing 360° view, but the highlight is the **Basilica Museum,** where St. Stephen's mummified right hand, one of Hungary's most revered religious relics, sits on public display. For the devout and the macabre, a 100Ft donation dropped in the box will light up the religious relic for 2min. of closer inspection. *(M1, 2, 3: Deák tér. Basilica and museum open May-Oct. M-Sa 9am-5pm; Nov.-Apr. M-Sa 10am-4pm. Tower open daily June-Aug. 9:30am-6pm; Sept.-Oct. 10am-5:30pm; Apr.-May 10am-4:30pm. Tower 400Ft, students 300Ft.)*

SYNAGOGUE. Much of the artwork in Pest's Moorish synagogue (zsinagóga), the largest active synagogue in Europe and the second-largest in the world, is blocked from view, as it has been under renovation since 1988. In back is the **Holocaust Memorial,** a metal tree that sits above a mass grave for thousands of Jews killed near the end of WWII. *(M2: Astoria. At the corner of Dohány u. and Wesselényi u. Open May-Oct. M-Th 10am-5pm, F 10am-3pm, Su 10am-2pm; Nov.-Apr. M-F 10am-3pm, Su 10am-1pm. 500Ft.)*

ANDRÁSSY ÚT AND HEROES' SQUARE. Hungary's grandest boulevard, Andrássy út, extends from **Erzsébet tér** in downtown Pest to **Heroes' Square** (Hősök tere) to the northeast. Perhaps the most vivid reminder of Budapest's Golden Age is the **Hungarian National Opera House** (Magyar Állami Operaház), whose 24-carat gilded interior glows on performance nights. If you can't see an opera, make sure to take a tour. *(Andrássy út 22. M1: Opera. ☎ 332 81 97. English tours daily 3 and 4pm. 900Ft, students 450Ft. 20% off with Budapest card.)* At the Heroes' Square end of Andrássy út, the **Millennium Monument** (Millenniumi emlékmű) commemorates the nation's most prominent leaders. Right off Heroes' Square is the **Museum of Fine Arts** (see **Museums,** below).

CITY PARK. The **Városliget** is home to a zoo, a circus, a run-down amusement park, and the lake-side **Vajdahunyad Castle** (Vajdahunyad Vár), whose Disney-esque collage of Romanesque, Gothic, Renaissance, and Baroque styles is intended to chronicle the history of Hungarian architecture. Outside the castle broods the hooded statue of **Anonymous,** the secretive scribe to whom we owe much of our knowledge of medieval Hungary. Rent a **rowboat** or **ice skates** on the lake next to the castle, or a **bike-trolley** to navigate the paths. *(M1: Széchenyi Fürdő. Boat and bike-trolley rental open June to mid-Sept. M-F 10am-8pm, Sa-Su 9am-8pm; ice skates rented daily Nov.-Mar. 9am-1pm and 4-8pm. Boats 400Ft per 30min.; ice skates and bike-trolleys 300Ft per 30min.)*

MUSEUMS

Buda Castle, on Castle Hill, houses several museums, divided by the different wings. Wing A contains the ▨**Museum of Contemporary Art** (Kortárs Művészeti Múzeum) and the **Ludwig Museum** upstairs, devoted to Warhol, Lichtenstein, and other modern masters. Wings B-D hold the **Hungarian National Gallery** (Magyar Nemzeti Galéria), a hoard of Hungarian paintings and sculptures. Artifacts from the 1242 castle revealed by WWII bombings lie in the **Budapest History Museum** (Budapesti Történeti Múzeum) in Wing E. *(Wings A-D open Tu-Su 10am-6pm. Wing E open daily May 16-Sept. 15 10am-6pm; Sept. 16-Oct. and Mar.-May 15 M and W-Su 10am-6pm; Nov.-Feb. 28 M and W-Su 10am-4pm. Wing A 400Ft, students 200Ft. Wings B-D 400Ft together, students 200Ft.)* ▨**Museum of Fine Arts** (Szépművészeti Múzeum), XIV, Dózsa György út 41, has a simply spectacular collection of everything from Raphael to Rembrandt, Gaugin to Goya. *(☎343 97 59. M1: Hősök tere. Open 10am-5:30pm. 500Ft, students 200Ft. Tours for up to 5 people 2000Ft.)* The **Museum of Applied Arts** (Iparművészeti Múzeum), IX, Üllői út 33-37, exhibits Tiffany glass, furniture, and Fabergé eggs. *(☎217 52 22. M3: Ferenc körút. Open Mar. 15-Oct. Tu-Su 10am-6pm; Nov.-Mar. Tu-Su 10am-4pm. 300Ft, students 100Ft.)* The **Jewish Museum** (Zsidó Múzeum), VII, Dohány út 2, juxtaposes a celebration of Hungary's rich Jewish past with haunting photographs and documents from the Holocaust. *(☎342 89 49. M2: Astoria. Open M-F 10am-3pm, Su 10am-2pm. 500Ft, students 250Ft.)* The **Hungarian National Museum** (Magyar Nemzeti Múzeum), VIII, Múzeum krt. 14/16, has a myriad of exhibits, from the Hungarian Crown Jewels to Soviet propaganda guarded by a cheery Stalin. *(☎338 21 22. M3: Kálvin tér. Open Mar. 15-Oct. 15 Tu-Su 10am-6pm; Oct. 16-Mar. 14 Tu-Su 10am-5pm. 400Ft, students 150Ft. English tour 500Ft.)*

🎵🎭 ENTERTAINMENT AND NIGHTLIFE

Programme in Hungary, Budapest Panorama, and the "Style" section of the *Budapest Sun* are the best English-language guides to entertainment. All three are available at most tourist offices and hotel lobbies. Although it may take a little translating, *Pesti Est* is hands-down the best local entertainment guide.

THEATER AND MUSIC. Like any large city, Budapest hosts a world of intimate theaters, smoky club performances, and showcases of local talent, many of which merit at least as much attention as the gilt stages of Budapest's grand cultural venues. The **Central Theater Booking Office,** VI, Andrássy út 18 (☎312 00 00), next to the Opera House (open M-Th 9am-6pm, F 9am-5pm), and at Moszkva tér 3 (☎212 56 78; open M-F 10am-6pm), sells tickets to almost every performance in the city for no commission. The **State Opera House** (Magyar Állami Operaház), VI, Andrássy út 22, is one of Europe's leading performance centers. (☎332 81 97. M1: Opera. Open Tu-Sa 11am-1:45pm and 2:30-7pm, Su 10am-1pm and 4-7pm.) The **Philharmonic Orchestra,** V, Vörösmarty tér 1, has equally grand music in a slightly more modest venue. (☎317 62 22. Concerts almost every evening Sept.-June. Open M-F 10am-6pm, Sa-Su 10am-2pm. Tickets 1200-1700Ft, less on the day of the show.)

THERMAL BATHS. To soak away weeks of city grime, crowded trains, and yammering camera-clickers, sink into a thermal bath, the essential Budapest experience. The baths were first built in 1565 by Arslan, a Turkish ruler of Buda who feared that a siege of the city would prevent the population from bathing. ▨ **Gellért,** XI, Kelenhegyi út 4/6, offers a huge range of inexpensive à la carte options, including mudbaths, ultrasound, and the new "Thai massage," featuring "the world famous masseuses of the Bangkok wat po:" women trained to use their feet, elbows, and knees in an exhausting 1½hr. massage of strategic pressure points. (Bus #7 or tram #47 or 49 to Hotel Gellért, at the base of Gellért-hegy. ☎466 61 66. Call for reservations. Thermal bath 1000Ft, under 18 900Ft; with pool privileges

1600Ft. 15min. massage 1200Ft. Open May-Sept. M-F 6am-6pm, Sa-Su 6am-4pm; Oct.-Apr. M-F 6am-6pm, Sa-Su 6am-1pm. Pools open daily May-Sept. 6am-6pm; Oct.-Apr. M-F 6am-6pm, Sa-Su 6am-4pm.)

NIGHTLIFE

On any given night out in Budapest, you can experience an amazing diversity of scenes, from the lively atmosphere of all-night outdoor parties to the decadent elegance of after-hours clubs. Despite the throbbing crowds in the clubs and 4am chatter in the pubs, the streets themselves—often lit only by a single dim bulb—are surprisingly empty at night, echoing pre-capitalist times. To find out what's going on where and when, pick up a copy of *Budapest Week* (126Ft). Choose your scene carefully, but remember: you'll have a better time if you choose more than one.

Undergrass, VI, Liszt Ferenc tér 10 (☎322 08 30). M1: Oktogon. Or, tram #4 or 6. A slick underground bar and the hottest spot in Pest's trendiest area. Open daily 8pm-5am; disco starts at 10pm (Tu-Su).

Fat Mo's Speakeasy, V, Nyári Pal u. 11 (☎267 31 99). M3: Kálvin tér. Fourteen varieties of tap beer (0.5L 350-750Ft) and live jazz (Su, M, and Th 9-11pm) to make the booze flow quicker. Th-Sa DJ from 11:30pm. Open M-F noon-2am, Sa-Su 6pm-4am.

Piaf, VI, Nagymező u. 25 (☎312 38 23). A much-loved after hours place and the final destination of any decent pub crawl in Budapest. Knock on a rather inconspicuous—albeit intimidating—door. 500Ft cover includes 1 drink. Open daily 10pm-6am.

Club Seven, Akácfa u. 7 (☎478 90 30). More upscale and less of a dive than the average Budapest club, but just as crowded. Weekends men 1000Ft, women free. Coffeehouse open 9pm-4am, restaurant 6pm-midnight, dance floor 10pm-5am.

Old Man's Pub, VII, Akácfa u. 13 (☎322 76 45). M2: Blaha Lujza tér. Although the name implies otherwise, this crowd is in the larval phase of yuppie-dom. Open M-Sa 3pm-4:30am.

Morrison's Music Pub, VI, Révay u. 25 (☎269 40 60). M1: Opera. Just left of the opera. Jostling nightspot pulls in a crowd ready to party in any language. British telephone booth inside actually works but moonlights as a voyeuristic make-out spot. June-Aug. men pay 500Ft. Open M-Sa 8:30pm-4am.

Capella Cafe, V, Belgrád rakpart 23 (☎318 62 13). Popular spot draws a mixed crowd for a line-up that varies from transvestite lip-synchs to W night stripteases. Nightly shows at midnight. Cover 500Ft; 500Ft minimum. Open Tu-Su 9pm-5am.

APPENDIX

GLOSSARY

addition (F): check

aérogare (F): air terminal

affitacamere (I): room for rent

agora (Gr): a level city square; marketplace

albergue (S): youth hostel

alcázar (S): Muslim fortress-palace

Altstadt (G): old city

apse: nook beyond the altar of a church

arrondissement (F): district (of city)

auberge de jeunesse (F): youth hostel

autobus (G): bus

autoroute (F): motorway

ayuntamiento (S): city hall

Bahnhof (G): train station

barrio viejo (S): old city

billet (F): ticket

boulangerie (F): bakery

Brücke (G): bridge

caff (B): diner-style restaurant

calle (S): street

campanile (I): bell tower

campo (I): square

carabinieri (I): military police

carnet (F): packet

carrer (S): street

casco antiguo (S): old city

casco viejo (S): old city

cave (F): wine cellar

centre commercial (F): shopping plaza

centre ville (F): town center

(el) centro (S): city center

cerveza (S): beer

chambres d'hôtes (F): bed and breakfasts

charcuterie (F): shop selling cooked meats

château (F): castle

chiesa (I): church

ciudad nueva (S): new city

ciudad vieja (S): old city

cloitre (F): cloister

con bagno (I): (room) with private bath

confiserie (F): candy store

correspondance (F): connection, transfer (subway)

corso (I): principal street or avenue

craic (Ir): a good (pub) time

dégustation (F): tasting (i.e., wine tasting)

domatia (Gr): room in private home

droit(e) (F): right (i.e., right-hand side)

duomo (I): cathedral

église (F): church

entrée (F): appetizer

essence (F): gasoline

estación (S): station

fermo posta (I): *Poste Restante*

ferrovia (I): railways

formidable (F): terrific

foyer (F): student dorm

Fremdenverkehrsamt (G): tourist office

gabinetto (I): toilet, WC

gare (F): train station

gauche (F): left (i.e., left-hand side)

gîte d'étape (F): hostel

Hauptbahnhof (G): main train station

hebdomadaire (F): weekly

hospedajes (S): cheap accommodation

hostal (S): hostel

hôtel de ville (F): town hall

iglesia (S): church

Innenstadt (G): city center

Jugendherberge (G): youth hostel

Kirche (G): church

laverie (F): laundromat

leoforeo (Gr): bus

mairie (F): mayor's office

marché (F): outdoor market

marché aux puces (F): flea market

Marktplatz (G): marketplace

Mehrbettzimmer (G): dorm

Mensa (G): university cafeteria

midi (F): noon

minuit (F): midnight

monnaie (F): change

museo (S): museum

nave: central body of a church

navette (F): shuttlebus

Neustadt (G): new city

ostello (I): youth hostel

paella (S): rice dish with seafood, meat, and vegetables

palais (F): palace

panini (I): sandwiches

palazzo (I): palace

paleochora (Gr): old town

parque (S): park

paseo (S): promenade (abbreviated *po.*)

passeig (S): promenade (abbreviated *pg.*)

pâtisserie (F): pastry shop

pensione (S): room in private home

pensao (P): cheap accommodation

pietà (I): scene of the Virgin mourning the dead Christ

plaça (S): square

place (F): square

plage (F): beach

plat (F): main course

plateia (Gr): town square

Platz (G): square

playa (S): beach

plaza (S): square

pleio (Gr): ferry

piazza (I): city square

piazzale (I): large open square

pont (F): bridge

ponta (P,S): bridge

ponte (I): bridge

praça (P): square

praia (P): beach

primi (I): first course (usually pasta)

Privatzimmer (G): room in a private home

quartier (F): neighborhood

secondi (I): second course (usually meat or fish)

souvlaki (Gr): shish kebab

spiaggia (I): beach

spotted dick (B): steamed sponge pudding with raisins

stazione (I): station

Straße (G): street

Straßenbahn (G): streetcar; tram

tabac (F): all-purpose newsstand

tabbacchi (I): all-purpose newspaper

Tageskarte (G): "day card"; pass valid for one day

tapas (S): appetizers; snacks

taverna (Gr): restaurant or tavern

télécarte (F): phone card

téléphérique (F): cable car lift

terrible (F): awesome, great

torvet (D): main square

trad (Ir): traditional Irish music

train à grande vitesse or TGV (F): super-fast train

traiteur (F): delicatessen

transept: in a cruciform church, the arm of the church that intersects the nave

vendange (F): grape harvest

via (I): street

viale (I): street

vicolo (I): alley, lane

vieille ville (F): old city

vino (S): wine

Zimmer frei (G): room available

Zug (G): train

B=British, **C**=Czech, **D**=Danish, **F**=French, **G**=German, **Gr**=Greek, **I**=Italian, **Ir**=Irish, **P**=Portugese, **S**=Spanish

LANGUAGES

GERMAN

Consonants are the same as in English, except for c (pronounced k); j (pronounced y); k (pronounced, even before n); p (nearly always pronounced, even before f); qu (pronounced kv); s (pronounced z at the beginning of a word); v (pronounced f); w (pronounced v); z (pronounced ts). The ß, or ess-tsett, is a double s. Pronounce sch as sh. Vowels are pronounced as follows: a as in "father"; e as the a in "hay" or the indistinct vowel sound in "uh"; i as the ee in "cheese"; o as in "oh"; u as in "fondue"; y as the oo in "boot"; au as in "sauerkraut"; eu as the oi in "boil." With ei and ie, pronounce the last letter as a long English vowel—heiße is HIGH-ssuh, viele is FEEL-uh.

FRENCH

Don't pronounce any final consonants except l, f, or c; an e on the end of the word, however, means that you should pronounce the final consonant sound, e.g., muet is moo-AY but muette is moo-ET. Nor should you pronounce the final s in plural nouns. J is like the s in "pleasure." C sounds like a k before a, o, and u; like an s before e and i. A ç always sounds like an s. Vowels are short and precise: a as in the o in "mom"; e as in "help" (é becomes the a in "hay"); i as the ee in "creep"; o as in "oh." Ui sounds like the word "whee." U is a short, clipped oo sound; hold your lips as if you were about to say "ooh," but say ee instead. Ou is a straight OO sound. At the ends of words, -er and -et are pronounced "ay." With few exceptions, all syllables receive equal emphasis.

ITALIAN

There are seven vowel sounds in standard Italian: a as in "father," i as the ee in "cheese," u as the oo in "droop," e either as ay in "bay" or eh in "set," and o both as oh in "bone" and o as in "off." H is always silent, r always rolled. C and g are hard before a, o, or u, as in cat and goose, but they soften into ch and j sounds, respectively, when followed by i or e, as in ciao (chow; "goodbye") and gelato (jeh-LAH-toh; "ice cream"). Cc and gg are also hard. Ch and gh are pronounced like k and g before i and e, as in chianti (ky-AHN-tee) and spaghetti (spah-GEHT-tee). Pronounce gn like the ni in onion, as in bagno (BAHN-yoh; "bath"). Gli is like the lli in million, so sbagliato ("wrong") is said "zbal-YAH-toh." When followed by a, o, or u, sc is pronounced as sk, as in scusi (SKOO-zee; "excuse me"); when followed by an e or i, sh as in sciopero (SHOH-pair-oh).

SPANISH

Spanish pronunciation is very regular. Vowels are always pronounced the same way: a as in "father"; e as in escapade; i as the ee in "eat"; o as in "oat"; u as in "boot"; y, by itself, as ee. Consonants are the same as in English except for: j and soft g (before "e" or "i"), pronounced like an h; ll, like the y in "yes"; ñ, as in "cognac"; rr (trilled "r"); h is always silent; x retains its English sound; z and soft c ("th"). The stress in Spanish words falls on the last syllable, unless the word ends in a vowel, "s," or "n," or has an accent.

THE GREEK ALPHABET

GREEK	ROMAN	GREEK	ROMAN	GREEK	ROMAN	GREEK	ROMAN
Α, α	A, a	Η, η	I, i; E,e	Ν, ν	N, n	Τ, τ	T, t
Β, β	V, v	Θ, θ	Th, th	Ξ, ξ	X, x	Υ, υ	Y, y; I, i
Γ, γ	G, g; Y, y	Ι, ι	I, i	Ο, ο	O, o	Φ, φ	F, f
Δ, δ	D, d	Κ, κ	K, k	Π, π	P, p	Χ, χ	Ch, ch; H, h
Ε, ε	E, e	Λ, λ	L, l	Ρ, ρ	R, r	Ψ, ψ	Ps, ps
Ζ, ζ	Z, z	Μ, μ	M, m	Σ, σ, ς	S, s	Ω, ω	O, o

USEFUL WORDS AND PHRASES

ENGLISH	FRENCH	SPANISH	GERMAN	ITALIAN
THE BASICS				
hello	bonjour	hola	hallo	buon giorno / buona sera / buona notte
goodbye	au revoir	adios / hasta luego	Auf Wiedersehen (*f.*) Tschüs (*inf.*)	arrivederci (*f.*) ciao (*inf.*)
please	s'il vous plaît	por favor	bitte	per favore
thank you / you're welcome	merci / je vous en pris (*f.*) de rien (*inf.*)	gracias / de nada	danke / bitte	grazie / prego
yes / no / maybe	oui / non / peut-être	sí / no / tal vez	ja / nein / vielleicht	sì / no
excuse me / sorry	excusez-moi / je suis désolé(e).	perdón	Entschuldigung / Verzeihung	scusi / mi dispiace
How are you?	Comment ça va?	¿Como está?	Wie geht es Ihnen?/ Wie geht es dir?	Come sta (*f.*)/stai (*inf.*)?
Fine / well.	Ça va. / Bien.	Así así. / Bien.	Mir geht es gut.	Sto bene.
Do you speak English?	Parlez-vous anglais?	¿Habla inglés?	Sprechen Sie Englisch?	Parla inglese?
What's your name? My name is...	Comment vous appelez-vous? Je m'appelle...	¿Cómo se llama? Me llamo...	Wie heißen Sie? Ich heiße...	Come si chiama? Mi chiamo...
Sorry? / Please repeat	Pardon? / Répétez, s'il vous plaît.	¿Perdón? / ¿Puede repetir?	Wie bitte / Können Sie das wiederholen?	Prego / Potrebbe ripetere?
I don't understand	Je ne comprends pas.	No entiendo.	Ich verstehe nicht.	Non capisco.
How do you say...?	Comment dit-on ...en français?	¿Cómo se dice...en español?	Wie sagt man...auf Deutsch?	Come si dice...?
I'd like to make a call to...	J'aimerais faire un appel aux ...	Quisiera llamar a ...	Ich möchte ... anrufen	Vorrei telefonare a ...
I'm ill / hurt.	Je suis malade / blessé.	Estoy enfermo(a) / herido(a).	Ich bin krank / verletzt.	Sono amalato / Faccio male.
Help! / Stop!	Au secours! / Arrêtez!	¡Socorro! / ¡Déjame!	Hilfe! / Stop!	Aiuto! / Ferma!
post office	la poste	correos	die Post	posta
the police	la police	la policia	die Polizei	la polizia
the hospital	l'hôpital	el hospital	das Krankenhaus	l'ospedale
pharmacy	l'apothécaire	la farmacia	die Apotheke	
a doctor	un médecin	un doctór	der Arzt	dottore
telephone	téléphone	teléfono	die Telefon	telefono
bathroom	les toilettes/la salle de bain	el baño	die Toilette	il bagno
church	une église	una iglesia	die Kirche	la chiesa
grocery store	un magasin d'alimentation	el supermercado	ein Lebensmittelgeschäft	il supermercato
market	un marché	el mercado	der Markt	il mercato
DIRECTIONS				
Where is...?	Où est...?	¿Dónde está...?	Wo ist...?	Dov'è...?
straight ahead	toute droite	recto	gerade aus	sempre diritto
(to the) right / left	(à) droite / gauche	(a la) derecha / izquierda	(nach) rechts / links	(a) destra /sinistra
north/south/east/west	nord/sud/est/ouest	notre/sur/este/oeste	nord/süd/ost/west	nord/sud/est/ovest
near / far	loin / proche	cerca / lejos	nahe / weit	lontano / vicino
I'm lost.	Je me suis égaré (m.) / égarée (f.).	Estoy perdido (m.) / perdida (f.).	Ich habe mich verirrt.	Mi sono perso (m.)/ persa (f.)
town center/old city	vieille ville	el centro	die Altstadt	il centro
TRANSPORTATION				
bus station	la gare routière	la estación de autobús	Zentraler Omnibusbahnhof (ZOB)	stazione di autobus
train station	la gare	la estación de tren	der Bahnhof	stazione

ENGLISH	FRENCH	SPANISH	GERMAN	ITALIAN
arrival /departure	arrivée / départ	llegada / salida	die Ankunft / die Abfahrt	l'arrivo / la partenza
ticket / supplement	billet / supplément	billete / suplemento	die Fahrkarte / die Zuschlag	biglietto / supplemento
platform / track	la voie	anden / vía	der Bahnstein / das Gleis	binario
bus stop (tram stop)	arrêt d'autobus (arrêt de tramway)	parada de autobus	Bushaltestelle (Straßebahnbaltestelle)	fermata dell'autobus
car	voiture	coche	Auto/Wagen	macchina/automobile
taxi	taxi	taxi	Taxi	tassì
entrance / exit	entrée / sortie	entradas / salida	der Eingang / der Ausgang	l'ingresso / l'uscita
seat reservation	réservation de place	reserva	die Sitzplatzreservierung	prenotazione posti
timetable	horaire	horario	der Fahrplan	orario
berth / couchette	place couchée / couchette	cama / cabina de literas	Bettplatz / Liegeplatz	letto / cuccetta
I would like a one-way (round-trip) ticket to...	Je voudrais un billet (aller-retour) pour...	Quisiera un billete ida (de ida y vuelta) a...	Ich möchte eine einfache Fahrkarte (Rückfahrkarte) nach...	Vorrei un biglietto solo andata (andata e ritorna) per...
first / second class	première / deuxième class	primera / segunda clase	erste / zweite Klasse	prima / seconda classe
left luggage	consigne	consigna	Schliessfächer (lockers)	deposito bagagli
What time does the train / bus / ferry leave?	A quelle heure part le train / l'autobus / le bac?	¿Cuándo sale el tren / autobús / barca de pasaje?	Um wieviel Uhr fährt der Zug / der Autobus / die Fähre ab?	A che ora parte il treno / l'autobus / il traghetto?
Do you stop at...?	Vous arrêtez à...?	¿Para en/a...?	?Halten Sie an...?	Ferma a...?

ACCOMMODATIONS

hotel	l'hôtel	el hotel	Hotel	albergo
hostel	auberge de jeunesse	hostal / albergue	Jugendherberge	ostello
guesthouse	(no equivalent)	pensión	Gasthof/Gästehaus	pension
camping	camping	camping	Campingplatz	campeggio
I'd like a single /double.	Je voudrais une chambre simple / pour deux.	Quisiera un cuarto simple / un doble.	Ich möchte ein Einzelzimmer / Doppelzimmer	Vorrei una càmera sìngola / doppia.
How much is the room?	Le chambre coûte combien?	¿Cuanto cuesta el cuarto?	Wieviel kostet das Zimmer?	Quanto costa la camera?
I'd like to make a reservation.	Je voudrais faire une réservation.	Quisiera hacer una reserva.	Ich möchte eine Reservierung machen.	Vorrei fare una prenotazione.

MONEY

I am a student.	Je suis étudiant(e).	Soy estudiante.	Ich bin Student(in).	Sono studente / studentessa
Are there student discounts?	Y-a-t'il des tarifs réduits pour des étudiants?	¿Hay descuentos para los estudiantes?	Gibt es Studentenermäßigungen?	Ci sono sconti per studenti?
cheap / expensive	bon marché / cher	barato / caro	billig / teuer	economico / caro
Do you accept credit cards / travelers' checks?	Acceptez-vous des cartes de credit / chèques de voyages?	¿Aceptan tarjetas de crédito / cheques de viajero?	Nehmen Sie Kreditkarten / Reiseschecks?	Prende la carta di credito / l'assegno di viaggiatore?
reduced price	tarif réduit	precio reducido	Ermäßigung	sconto
How much does this cost?	Ça coûte combien?	¿Cuanto cuesta éste?	Wieviel kostet das?	Quanto costa?
I don't want to buy anything.	Je ne veux rien acheter.	No quiero comprar nada.	Ich will nichts einkaufen.	Non voglio comprare niente.

FOOD

breakfast / lunch / dinner / dessert	le petit déjeuner / le déjeuner / le diner / le dessert	el desayuno / el almuerzo / la cena / el postre	Frühstück / Mitagessen / Abendessen / Nachtisch	la colazione / pranzo / cena / dolce
bread	le pain	el pan	das Brot	pane

ENGLISH	FRENCH	SPANISH	GERMAN	ITALIAN
chicken / beef / fish / vegetables	du poulet / du viande / du poisson / des légumes	el pollo / la carne / el pescado / los legumbres	das Huhn / das Rind / Fisch / Gemüse	pollo / carne / pesce / verdure
Do you have food without meat?	Avez-vous des plats sans viande?	¿Tienen comida sin carne?	Gibt es etwas ohne Fleisch?	Ha cibo senza carne?
I am a vegetarian.	Je suis végétarien(ne).	Soy vegetariano(a).	Ich bin Vegetarier(in).	Sono vegetariano / vegetariana.
restaurant	un restaurant	el restaurante	das Restaurant	ristorante

TIME AND NUMBERS

yesterday	hier	ayer	gestern	ieri
today	aujourd'hui	hoy	heute	oggi
tomorrow	demain	mañana	morgen	domani
day after tomorrow	lendemain	(no equivalent)	übermorgen	dopodomani
morning	matin	mañana	Morgen	mattina
afternoon	après-midi	tarde	Nachmittag / Abend	pomeriggio
daily/weekly/monthly	quotidien / hebdomadaire / mensuel	diario / semanal / mensual	täglich / wöchentlich / monatlich	quotidiano / settimanale / mensile
when?	quand?	¿cuándo?	wann?	quando?
What time do you open / close?	A quelle heure êtes-vous ouvert / fermé?	¿A que hora abre / cierra?	Um wieviel Uhr öffnen /schließen Sie?	A che ora si apre / chiude...?
Monday, Tuesday, Wednesday, Thursday, Friday, Saturday, Sunday	lundi, mardi, mercredi, jeudi, vendredi, samedi, dimanche	lunes, martes, miércoles, jueves, viernes, sábado, domingo	Montag, Dienstag, Mittwoch, Donnerstag, Freitag, Samstag, Sonntag	lunedì, martedì, mercoledì, giovedì, venerdì, sabato, domenica
one	un	uno	eins	uno
two	deux	dos	zwei	due
three	trois	tres	drei	tre
four	quatre	cuatro	vier	quattro
five	cinq	cinco	fünf	cinque
six	six	seis	sechs	sei
seven	sept	siete	sieben	sette
eight	huit	ocho	acht	otto
nine	neuf	nueve	neun	nove
ten	dix	diez	zehn	dieci
eleven	onze	once	elf	undici
twelve	douze	doce	zwölf	dodici
twenty	vingt	veinte	zwanzig	venti
thirty	trente	treinta	dreißig	trenta
forty	quarante	cuarenta	vierzig	quaranta
fifty	cinquante	cinquenta	fünfzig	cinquanta
sixty	soixante	seseta	sechzig	sessanta
seventy	soixante-dix	setenta	siebzig	settanta
eighty	quatre-vingt	ochenta	achtzig	ottanta
ninety	quatre-vingt-dix	noventa	neunzig	novanta
one hundred	cent	cien	hundert	cento
one thousand	mille	mil	tausend	mille

ENGLISH	GREEK	PRONOUNCED
hello	Γεα σου	YAH-soo
goodbye	αντιο	an-DEE-oh
please	Παρακαλω	pah-rah-kah-LO
thank you	Ευχαριστω	ef-hah-ree-STO
yes / no	Ναι / Οχι	NEH / OH-hee
sorry / excuse me	Συγνομη	seeg-NO-mee
Do you speak English?	Μιλας αγγλικα?	mee-LAHS ahn-glee-KAH?
I don't understand.	Δεν καταλαβαινω.	dhen kah-tah-lah-VEH-no.

ENGLISH	GREEK	PRONOUNCED
Help!	βοηтнεα!	vo-EETH-ee-ah!
Where is...?	Που ειναι...?	pou EE-neh...?
left / right / straight ahead	αριστερα / δεξα /ευθεα	a-ree-stair-AH / dek-see-AH / ef-THEE-a
What time does [the train / bus /boat☎ (depart /arrive)?	Τι ωρα (φευγει/φτανει) το τρενο / το λεωφορειο / το καραβι?	tee OR-ah (feev-yee /ftah-nee) [toe TRAY-no /toe lee-oh-for-EE-oh / toe kah-RAH-vee
today / tomorrow /yesterday	σημερα/αυριο/χθες	SEE-mer-a / AV-ree-o / k-THES
I'd like a (one-way) /round-trip) ticket.	Θα ηθελα (μονο εσιτηριο / εσιτηριο με επιστροφη).	tha ETH-eh-la (mo-NO ee-see-TEE-ree-o / ee-see-TEE-ree-o me eh-pee-stro-FEE)
How much does it cost?	ποσο κανει?	PO-so KAH-nee
hostel	ξενωναζ νεοτητοζ	zee-NO-naz nee-OH-tee-toes
hotel	ξενοδοχειο	zee-no-do-HEE-oh
camping	καμπιγκ	KAHM-ping
I'd like a (single /double) room?	Θελω ενα (μονο /διπλο) δωματιο	THEL-oh EH-na (mon-OH / dee-PLO) doh-MA-tee-oh

ENGLISH	DUTCH	PRONOUNCED
hello	hallo	hallo
goodbye	tot ziens	toht-zeens
please	alstublieft	ALST-ew-bleeft
thank you	dank u wel	dahnk ew vel
yes / no	ja / nee	ya / nay
sorry / excuse me	excuseert u mij	ex-kew-ZAYRT ew my
Do you speak English?	Spreekt u engels?	sprayhkt ew ENG-els
I don't understand.	Ik begrijp u niet.	ik beh-GHRIPE ew neet
Help!	help!	help
Where is...?	Waar iz...?	var iss
left / right / straight ahead	links / rechts/rechtdoor	links / hrechts / hrecht-door
What time does [the train / bus /boat☎ (depart /arrive)?	Hoe laat (vertrekt / komt) de [trein /bus / kom☎ ?	HOO laht (ver-TRECHT / komt) der [trine / buhs / kom☎
today / tomorrow /yesterday	vandaag / morgen /gisteren	fon-DAHG / MOR-ghun / GHIST-er-un
I'd like a (one-way/round-trip) ticket.	Ik wil graag (een enkele reis / een retour).	ik vil khrahk ayn (ENG-kuh-luhrice /ayn ruh-toor)
How much is it?	Wat kost dit?	vaht kost dit
hostel	jeugdherberg	yuh-ahghd-hair-bearght
hotel	hotel	ho-TELL
camping	kamperen	kahm-PAHR-en
I'd like a (single /double) room.	Ik wil graag een (een- / twee-) persoonska-mer.	ik vil ghrahgh ayn (AYN/TVAY) per-sones-kah-mer

ENGLISH	PORTUGESE	PRONOUNCED
hello	olá	oh-LAH
goodbye	adeus	ah-DAY-oosh
please	por favor	pur fah-VOR
thank you	obrigado(-a) (m./f.)	oh-bree-GAH-doo/da
yes / no	sim/não	seeng/now
sorry / excuse me	desculpe	dish-KOOL-peh
Do you speak English?	Fala inglês?	FAH-lah een-GLAYSH?
I don't understand.	não compreendo	now kompreeAYNdoo
Help!	Socorro!	so-ko-RO!
Where is...?	Onde é que é ...?	OHN-deh eh keh eh
left / right / straight ahead	esquerda/direita/em frente	ish-CARE-da/dee-RAY-ta/ayn FRAIN-teh
What time does [the train / bus /boat] (depart /arrive)?	A que horas (parte/chega) o [combóio/ camioneta/barco☎ ?	ah keh AW-rahsh (PAR-teh/cheh-gah) oh kohn-BOY-oo/kam-yoo-NET-ah/bar-koh
today / tomorrow /yesterday	hoje/amanhã/ontem	OH-zheh/ah-ming-YAH/ohn-tane
I'd like a (one-way /round-trip) ticket.	Queria um bilhete (simples/de ida e volta)	kay-ree-ah um bee-YEH-teh (seem-plays/ deh EE-da ee VOL-ta)
How much does it cost?	Quanto custa?	KWAHN-too KOOSH-tah?
hostel	pousada de juventude	poh-ZA-da deh zhoo-vain-TOO-deh
hotel	Hotel	ot-TEL
camping	campismo	cahm-peez-mo

ENGLISH	PORTUGESE	PRONOUNCED
I'd like a (single /double) room?	Tem um quarto individual / duple?	tem om-KWAR-toe een-DE-vee-DU-ahl/DOO-play?

ENGLISH	CZECH	PRONOUNCED
hello	Dobrý den	DO-bree den
goodbye	Na shledanou	nah SLEH-dah-noh-oo
please	Prosím	PROH-seem
thank you	Děkuji	DYEH-koo-yih
yes / no	Ano/ne	AH-no/neh
sorry / excuse me	Promiňte	PROH-mihn-teh
Do you speak English?	Mluvíte anglicky?	MLOO-vit-eh ahng-GLIT-ski
I don't understand.	Nerozumím.	neh-rohz-oo-MEEM
Help!	Pomoc!	poh-MOTS
Where is...?	Kde?	k-DEH
left / right / straight ahead	vlevo/vpravo/rovně	LEH-vah/PRAH-vah
What time does [the train / bus /boat] (depart /arrive)?	Kdy (odjíždí/přijíž) [vlak/autobus/loď☎?	k-DEE (ot-yeezh-dee/pree-yeezh) [vlahk/OUT-oh-boos/loadge☎
today / tomorrow /yesterday	dnes/zítra	dness/ZEE-tra
I'd like a (one-way/round-trip) ticket.	Rád/Ráda bych (jen tam/zpáteční) jízdenku do...	rahd/rahd-ah bikh (yen tam/SPAH-tech-nyee) YEEZ-denkoo DOH...
How much is it?	Kolik stojí?	KOH-lihk STOH-yee
hostel	mládežnická noclehárna	mla-dezh-nit-ska nots-le-har-na
hotel	hotel	ho-TELL
camping	kemping	KEM-ping
I'd like a (single /double) room.	Máte volné (jednolůžkový/dvolůžkový) pokoj.	MAH-te VOL-nee (YED-no-loosh-ko-vee/DVOH-loosh-ko-vee) PO-koy

ENGLISH	HUNGARIAN	PRONOUNCED
hello	jó napot	YOH naw-pot
goodbye	szia	SEE-ya
please	kérem	KAY-rem
thank you	köszönöm	KUR-sur-num
yes / no	igen / nem	EE-gen / nem
sorry / excuse me	sajnálom	shoy-na-lawm
Do you speak English?	Beszél angolul?	BES–el AWN-gohlul
I don't understand.	Nem értem	NEM AYR-tem
Help!	Segítség!	SHEH-gheet-shayg
Where is...?	Hol van...?	hole von
left / right / straight ahead	bal / jobb / elöre	ball / yobe / eh-LEW-ray
What time does [the train / bus /boat] (depart /arrive)?	Mikor (indul /érkesik) [vonat /busz-kompa☎.	MEE-kawr (EEN-dool / AIR-keh-zik) [VO-nawt / boose /kompa☎
today / tomorrow /yesterday	ma / holnap / tegnap	ma / OLE-nap / teg-nap
I'd like a (one-way/round-trip) ticket.	Szeretnék egy (jegyet csak oda / returje-gyet).	SEH-rett-nake edge (YED-jet chok AW-daw / rih-toor-YED-jet).
How much is it?	Mennyibe kerül?	menyeebeh keh rewl
hostel	szálló	SA-lo
hotel	szálloda	SA-lo-da
camping	kemping	KEM-ping
I'd like a (single /double) room.	Szeretnék egy (egyágyas / kétágyas) szobát	SEH-rett-nake edge (EDGE-ah-dyosh /KAY-tah-dyosh) SAW-baat.

PRICES (US$), TRAVEL TIMES, AND DISTANCES (KM) BY TRAIN

	Amsterdam	Barcelona	Berlin	Brussels	Budapest	Copenhagen	Florence	Madrid	Milan	Munich	Paris	Prague	Rome	Venice	Vienna	Zürich
Amsterdam		1773	673	246	1620	807	1540	2013	1053	885	554	1044	1789	1662	1249	990
Barcelona	$204; 16½hr.[1]		2193	1679	2267	2096	1493	728	1044	1335	1219	2583	1443	1363	2000	1160
Berlin	$117; 7hr.	$314 27¼hr.[1]		836	993	841	1253	2633	1271	679	1174	408	1650	1234	772	963
Brussels	$42; 2½hr.	$182 14hr.[1]	$138; 11hr.		1191	904	1722	1771	664	877	460	1049	1848	1201	1346	613
Budapest	$248; 17½hr.[1]	$259; 26½hr.[1]	$104; 13hr.	$215; 16½hr.[1]		1260	1146	3112	1156	735	1653	621	1275	705	267	1023
Copenhagen	$166; 14hr.	n/a	$104; 7½hr.	$178; 12hr.	n/a		1890	2575	1608	1235	759	651	2106	n/a	1052	1268
Florence	$227; 18½hr.[1]	$116; 19hr.[1]	$185; 17½hr.	$181; 16hr.[1]	$123; 14½hr.[1]	$299; 19½hr.[1]		1936	316	655	1137	1094	316	257	879	1109
Madrid	$215; 17½hr.[1]	$56; 7hr.	$291; 25¼hr.[1]	$201; 15hr.[1]	$351; 31¼hr.[1]	$379; 27¾[1]	$176; 25hr.[1]		1535	2349	1459	2823	1880	1806	2849	2073
Milan	$206; 14½hr.	$107; 13hr.	$183; 17½hr.[1]	$137; 12hr.	$127; 15¾hr.[1]	$297; 22hr.	$31; 3½hr.	$170; 25¼hr.[1]		592	953	1031	632	267	889	293
Munich	$155; 9½hr.	$204; 16¾hr.[1]	$115; 10hr.	$143; 8½hr.	$93; 8hr.	$222; 10½hr.[1]	$72; 9hr.	$257; 24hr.	$68; 7½hr.		923	439	971	577	469	354
Paris	$94; 4¼hr.	$110; 12¼hr.	$197; 12hr.	$72; 1¾hr.	$218; 18hr.	$231; 15¼hr.	$133; 12½hr.	$133; 13¼hr.	$94; 7½hr.	$128; 8½hr.		1364	1585	1220	1390	614
Prague	$175; 12½hr.[1]	$280; 27¼hr.[1]	$58; 5½hr.	$159; 13½hr.[1]	$59; 7¾hr.	$161; 12¼hr.	$146; 15hr.[1]	$319; 28¼hr.[1]	$130; 13½hr.[1]	$74 6hr.	$186; 15hr.		1410	700	407	767
Rome	$272; 20hr.[1]	$143; 21¼hr.[1]	$207; 20¼hr.[1]	$174; 18¾hr.[1]	$124; 25hr.[1]	$332; 25hr.[1]	$31; 1¾hr.	$192; 30½hr.[1]	$49; 4½hr.	$92; 10¼hr.	$158; 14½hr.	$154; 16¼hr.[1]		573	1203	979
Venice	$222; 17hr.[1]	$141; 22hr.[1]	$255; 17hr.	$161; 15¼hr.[1]	$87; 13hr.	$280; 22hr	$28; 2¾hr.	$189; 30½hr.[1]	$24; 3hr.	$69; 7hr.	$137; 12½hr.	$110; 13½hr.	$46; 4¾hr.		630	614
Vienna	$196; 13hr.[1]	$221; 23hr.	$92; 10hr.	$181; 15hr.[1]	$38; 3hr.	$265; 17½hr.[1]	$85; 11½hr.	$324; 28¼hr.[1]	$89; 12¾hr.	$67; 5hr.	$191; 15hr.	$46; 5hr.	$102; 13hr.	$68; 9hr.		902
Zürich	$166; 9hr.	$128; 13hr.	$191; 8hr.[1]	$98; 8hr.	$120; 13½hr.	$277; 15hr.[1]	$83; 8hr.	$213; 21½hr.[1]	$61; 3¾hr.	$70; 4¼hr.	$80; 8¼hr.	$123; 11½hr.	$99; 8¼hr.	$81; 8hr.	$100; 9¼hr.	

1 These routes require a change of trains. Travel times do not include layover.

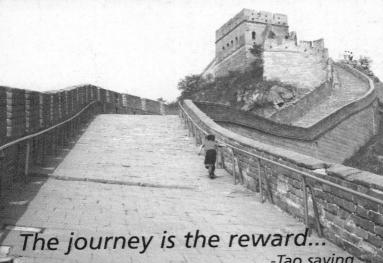
INDEX

INDEX

A

Aachen, GER 460
Aalborg, DEN 268
Aalsmeer, NETH 748
Aberdeen, BRI 248
Aberystwyth, BRI 228
abortion 30
accommodations 33
  B&Bs 35
  dorms 36
  guesthouses 35
  hostels 33
  hotels 35
  pensions 35
Acropolis, GRE 522
Aeolian Islands, ITA 712–713
Aer Lingus 43
Ærø, DEN 266
aerogrammes 39
Ærøskøbing, DEN 266
Agios Nikolaos, GRE 548
Agrigentro, ITA 710
AIDS 30
air courier flights 44
Air France 44
Air New Zealand 43
airlines 43–44
airplane travel
  charter flights 46
  fares 40
  standby 45
Aix-en-Provence, FRA 350
Ajaccio, FRA 364
Albufeira, POR 781
alcohol 27
Algarve, POR 779–782
Algeciras, SPA 846
Alghero, ITA 714
Alicante, SPA 853
Alitalia 57
Alonissos, GRE 540
Alps, FRA 367–369
Alsace, Lorraine, and Franche
  Comté, FRA 379–384
altitude, high 28
Amalfi Coast, ITA 705–708
Ambleside, BRI 223
Amboise, FRA 331
American Express 23, 24
Amsterdam, NETH 732–747
Ancona, ITA 698
Andalucía, SPA 829–851
Andorra 69–70
  Andorra la Vella 70
Andorra la Vella, AND 70
Angers, FRA 333
Anglet, FRA 340
Angoulême, FRA 334
Annecy, FRA 369
Antibes-Juan-les-Pins, FRA
  356
Antwerp, BEL 134
Aosta, ITA 649

Apeldoorn, NETH 755
Appenzell, SWI 922
Aragón, SPA 881–882
Aran Islands, IRE 588
Arcos de la Frontera, SPA 839
Ardennes, LUX 723
Areopolis, GRE 530
Arezzo, ITA 692
Argostoli, GRE 538
Århus, DEN 267
Arles, FRA 349
Arnhem, NETH 754
Arosa, SWI 922
Arras, FRA 387
Arromanches, FRA 323
Ascona, SWI 934
Assisi, ITA 697
Asti, ITA 661
Astorga, SPA 827
Athens, GRE 516–525
ATM cards 23
Atrani, ITA 705
Augsburg, GER 500
Austria 71–118
  Bad Ischl 105
  Baden Bei Wien 95
  Bregenz 115
  Carinthia 117
  Echental Valley 104
  Gmunden 104
  Graz 116
  Großglocknerstraße 106
  Grünau 104
  Hallstatt 103
  Heiligenblut 107
  Hohe Tauern National Park
    106–107
  Innsbruck 111–115
  Kitzbühel 108
  Klagenfurt 117
  Krimml Waterfalls 106
  Mayrhofen 110
  Ötztal 108
  Pasterze Glacier 106
  Salzburg 95–102
  Salzkammergut 103
  Sölden 108
  Styria 116
  Tyrol 107–115
  Vienna 80–95
  Zell Am See 107
  Zell Am Ziller 110
  Zillertal Valley 109
Austrian Airlines 57
Avignon, FRA 346
Ávila, SPA 823–824

B

B&Bs 35
Bacharach, GER 469
Bad Ischl, AUS 105
Bad Schandau, GER 432
Bad Wimpfen, GER 476
Baden Bei Wien, AUS 95

Baden-Baden, GER 478
Bakewell, BRI 213
Bakken, DEN 263
Balearic Islands, SPA 890–
  893
Ballycastle, NIRE 600
Bamberg, GER 497
Bangor, BRI 231
Bari, ITA 708
Barra, BRI 248
Basel, SWI 915–917
Basque Country, FRA 339–
  340
Bastia, FRA 365
Batalha, POR 776
Bath, BRI 206
Bavarian Alps, GER 502
Bay of Naples Islands, ITA 706
Bayeux, FRA 323
Bayonne, FRA 339
Bayreuth, GER 498
Beaune, FRA 377
Beer Garden History 101 493
Beja, POR 778
Belfast, NIRE 592–598
Belgium 119–138
  Antwerp 134
  Bruges 130
  Brussels 124–130
  Flanders 130–136
  Ghent 135
  Knokke 134
  Mechelen 130
  Namur 137
  Ostend 134
  Tournai 136
  Wallonie 136–138
  Zeebrugge 134
Ben Nevis, BRI 246
Benelux Tourrail Pass 51
Bény-sur-Mer-Reviers, FRA
  324
Berchtesgaden, GER 504
Bergamo, ITA 648
Berlin, GER 404–426
Bern, SWI 925–926
Besançon, FRA 383
Biarritz, FRA 339
bicycles
  getting around by 58
Bilbao, SPA 888–889
Billund, DEN 268
Birmingham, BRI 205
Black Forest, GER 478
Blarney (An Bhlarna), IRE 581
Blenheim Palace, BRI 202
Blois, FRA 330
boat
  getting around by 57
Bologna, ITA 654–656
Bolzano, ITA 661
Bonn, GER 458
Bordeaux, FRA 337–338
Bornholm, DEN 264

MAP INDEX

Find Yourself. Somewhere Else.

Don't just land there, do something. Away.com
is the Internet's preferred address for those
who like their travel with a little something
extra. Our team of travel enthusiasts and
experts can help you design your ultimate
adventure, nature or cultural escape. Make
Away.com your destination for extraordinary
travel. Then find yourself. Somewhere else.

away.com

1.877.769.2929

Will you have enough stories to tell your grandchildren?

Yahoo! Travel

Do You Yahoo!?